A
CONCORDANCE
TO THE
AMERICAN BOOK OF
COMMON PRAYER

Edited by

MILTON HUGGETT

Assistant Professor of English
Texas A&M University

Programmer

JAMES M. PYE

Research Associate
Office of Vice President for Reasearch
Texas A&M University

THE CHURCH HYMNAL CORPORATION

A Contributing Affiliate of
THE CHURCH PENSION FUND · 800 Second Avenue, New York, N. Y. 10017

A Concordance to the Book of Common Prayer has been greatly needed — by scholars, by clergymen in their day-to-day planning of services, by Church School teachers, and by other interested students of the Prayer Book. Concordances to the 1892 edition of the American Prayer Book and to the English Book of Common Prayer are long out of print and were only marginally useful.

The Analytical Index by G. W. Pepper (Philadelphia, John C. Winston Co., 1948) constructed on different principles, served a useful purpose, but did not fill the need for a general context-concordance.

Old methods of constructing a Concordance were laborious, time-consuming, and expensive. Now, by the use of modern data-processing technology, a Concordance is available at reasonable cost.

The Standing Liturgical Commission has been in touch with Professor Huggett throughout the preparation of the work, and has expressed its approval of the project by formal Resolutions. On behalf of the Commission, then, as well as on my own part, I welcome A Concordance to the American Book of Common Prayer and commend it to the Church.

CHARLES MORTIMER GUILBERT

Custodian of the Standard Book of Common Prayer
Secretary of the Standing Liturgical Commission

PREFACE

To the concordancer who uses the computer, liturgical literature presents problems. These difficulties stem only in part from the Prayer Book's consisting of prose instead of poetry. They derive also from the liturgy's oral character and changes of style in the liturgy during its development through the centuries. Adding to the problems are the non-liturgical portions of the Prayer Book, such as the two Prefaces and the Articles of Religion. Despite these problems, or because of them, the plan of this computerized concordance has been kept simple. That plan has been determined partly by the computer's dependence on rules and the programmer's need to avoid increasing them so much that they create other problems in place of those they solve.

The numbers opposite each context in which an index word appears refer to the page and line in the Prayer Book. Since in the Prayer Book the lines on a page are not numbered, each line of type (including every line of a title or rubric) is treated as a line assigned a number. Thus the first line of a title at the top of a page on which an office or other section of the Prayer Book begins becomes line number 1. Likewise, the shortened title at the top of all other pages is counted as line number 1. Since all copies of the Prayer Book in editions 32mo. and larger agree in paging and seldom disagree in number of lines on a page (then only by the addition of a part of a line at the bottom of a page), this reference method has been adopted as the most

exact. The letter *R* before the page number is a sign that the context is a rubric or part of one. Rubrics omitted from the Concordance after their first appearance in the Prayer Book are *Answer, Bishop, Minister, Or this, Or else this psalm, Or this psalm.*

Contexts have been made as long as the rules of the computer program permitted. One rule adopted was that no context should extend beyond a sentence. The cases in which no context appears alongside the index word are accounted for most often by their being one-word sentences. Other cases are single words bounded by a semicolon or by a colon and a semicolon. A two- or three-word context is most often a sentence (or an independent clause ending with a colon or a semicolon).

Common words omitted from the list of index words, together with the number of times each omitted word occurs in the Prayer Book, follow:

A	1250	been	91
about	104	before	265
above	88	but	781
after	225	by	668
again	144	can	54
against	177	cannot	52
all	1355	could	13
also	338	did	91
am	185	do	337
an	186	doing	15
and	8433	done	110
are	801	down	210
as	927	etc.	16
at	339	for	1945
be	1855	trom	724
because	165	he	1836

her	140	then	394
here	93	there	319
him	1406	therefor	1
his	1542	therefore	184
I	1583	these	225
if	277	they	1215
in	2989	this	674
indeed	11	those	183
into	395	thou	1137
is	1686	through	393
it	835	thy	2131
may	789	to	3147
me	1076	too	13
moreover	8	toward	26
my	1298	towards	36
nevertheless	20	until	59
not	1152	unto	1534
now	226	up	358
O	969	upon	567
of	5491	us	795
off	32	very	67
on	331	was	548
or	394	we	909
our	1096	were	326
out	351	what	197
over	91	when	481
shall	1608	where	86
she	51	which	689
should	157	while	61
so	457	who	620
than	86	whom	181
that	2775	whose	99
the	461	with	1273
thee	1063	ye	765
their	633	you	584
them	1165	your	264

Whenever a versicle or response is repeated on the same page, only its first occurrence as context is cited. These versicles and responses are the following:

Amen.
Good Lord, deliver him.
Good Lord, deliver us.
Have mercy upon him.
Have mercy upon us.
Let us pray.
Lord, have mercy.
Lord, have mercy upon us.
Lord, have mercy upon us, and incline our hearts to keep this law.
O Christ, hear us.
O Lamb of God, who takest away the sins of the world;
O Lord, have mercy upon us.
Son of God, we beseech thee to hear us.
We beseech thee to hear us, Good Lord.

Because the Lord's Prayer occurs twenty-one times in the Prayer Book, only its occurrence in Morning Prayer is concorded. Other places in the Prayer Book where the Lord's Prayer occurs are pages 24, 58, 67, 82, 280, 289, 298, 302, 306, 308, 318–319, 334, 340, 561, 571, 580, 587, 589, 592, 593. Also omitted are the titles of the Canonical Books and the Apocrypha listed in Article VI of the Articles of Religion and the dates of Holy Days for which Collects, Epistles and Gospels are assigned.

The inclusion of the Psalter warrants mention. The Prayer Book version of the psalms, except for some changes by twentieth century scholars, is the version contained in the Great Bible (1539) — not that contained in the King James Bible (1611). This concordance, therefore, will help identify Coverdale's translation of the psalms. To facilitate locating a passage on the page, the number at the beginning of a verse and the asterisk wherever it appears within a line have been retained as part of the context.

Titles, instead of being concorded, are indexed separately as an appendix. This index of titles lists not only principal titles but also subordinate titles — those for individual prayers, canticles, psalms, epistles and gospels, and other components of the services and non-liturgical portions of the Prayer Book.

A frequency count of the index words has been included as an appendix. These word counts are exact except for the words composing the few sentences listed as being repetitions of versicles and for the words in the Lord's Prayer. The number of times a word is used in the Prayer Book may have meaning for linguists and literary scholars, as well as for theologians.

This concordance resulted from an inquiry into linguistic and computer applications to literature, a project made possible

by a grant allocated to the Department of English of Texas A&M University by Dr. Frank W. R. Hubert, Dean of the College of Liberal Arts, acting for the University's Council on Organized Research. Mr. James Pye wrote the computer program in its final form and supervised its execution on the IBM Computer 360–65. Professor Robert Bower, Acting Director of the Data Processing Center, and Dr. Dan D. Drew, Assistant Director, helped expedite the project. It would never have been begun without the approval and help of Professor Robert L. Smith, at the time Director of the Data Processing Center, who welcomed the intrusion of the humanities into the brave new world of the computer. Two of his graduate students were especially helpful: Donald Moore, who wrote the first program, and Melvin Emmons, who refined and developed it. Both the publisher and the printer were consulted at several stages in preparing the program for the computer. If anything distinguishes compilation and formatting of a concordance by computer it is that the result must be seen clearly and accurately before the program is written. Understanding of this was demonstrated repeatedly by Mr. Robert A. Robinson and Mr. Edward M. Fuller of the Church Hymnal Corp. and by Mr. Charles F. Woodard, Jr., of the Plimpton Press, who cheerfully provided the information needed to devise a program that would produce a print-out conforming to their specifications. My indebtedness extends to Canon Charles M. Guilbert, Custodian of the Book of Common Prayer, and also to Dr. Massey H. Shepherd, Jr., Professor of Liturgics, the Church Divinity School of the Pacific. The interest voiced by these men and the Standing Liturgical Commission of the Episcopal Church emboldened me to confront the computer with the Prayer Book. To them and all others who helped with the project, I yield most hearty thanks.

Milton Huggett

PROGRAMMER'S PREFACE

A program is a series of instructions which direct a computer to produce a desired result (*output*). In the case of the Prayer Book, the desired result is a concordance which would be helpful to scholars, clergy, and users in general.

The foremost problem connected with prose concordance production is the selection of rules which will produce meaningful context. Poetry is comparatively easy to concord because one will generally accept a single line of verse as context; prose, however, presents a different and more difficult problem. An entire sentence would suffice to convey meaning, but the economics of publication and the practical considerations of textual bulk and ease of use rule out this approach. Rules, then, must be selected that will generate enough context to convey meaning, but not so much context as to be objectionable. The problem is to devise a series of instructions that will pick meaningful context but will operate within constraints set by the publisher and editor.

The program for this concordance was written in COBOL (Common Business Oriented Language) and implemented on an IBM System/360 Model I 65. As the editor indicates in the preface, liturgical text presents a unique challenge to the programmer because of the changing nature of the text. Because the text is generally over-punctuated to facilitate oral recitation and response, punctuation could not be used as the sole guideline for picking meaningful context. The general approach taken in the program was to scan a line of text (a line of text in the computer was composed of three lines from the Prayer Book) until either the maximum fifty-three character output line was filled or a terminal mark of punctuation (in this case a period, colon, or semicolon) was encountered. The presence of a comma was ignored until the scan approached either the beginning or the end of the fifty-three character line of context. By this technique, the program was able to include in the context an entire series whose members were separated by commas and not merely a portion because that portion was bounded by commas. The scan for context operated first from right to left of the index word, and then from left to right in order to try to include as much of the beginning of the syntactic unit as possible.

The major limitation of a computer-produced concordance is that the program logic cannot anticipate all possible situations. Invariably a line of text will occur that will present an unforeseen problem. Experience has shown that an attempt to correct isolated problems will usually result in either a loss of efficiency in the program or, even worse, the inability to adequately process the majority of the text.

The advantages of producing a concordance with aid of a computer lie in its ability to identify "trouble spots" and in its speed. When in the early stages of production the computer program iden-

tifies the problem areas, the programmer is aided in recognizing the logical conditions necessary to produce acceptable output. Thus, while testing the program, the programmer can correct the program logic and so eliminate the greater percentage of exceptions. It is, I suppose, a programmer's utopia to expect to adjust the logic to handle all exceptions and thus produce perfect output which is acceptable to every reader.

The advantage of speed is considerable. This concordance was produced in less than forty minutes. More than 19,000 lines of text were scanned; from the text 70,642 lines of context were produced and then sorted according to the index word and place of occurrence in the Prayer Book. It then took less than fifteen minutes to arrange the concordance into the format desired by the publisher and printer.

Acknowledgment is due to Donald Moore, Melvin Emmons, and John Prewitt, all graduate students at Texas A&M University, who contributed much time and effort to the early development of the program. To my colleagues at the Data Processing Center, who contributed suggestions during the development of the program, I extend my deepest appreciation.

James M. Pye

INTRODUCTION

Anyone who has moved from the house where a family has lived for many years can probably remember the fascination of reading a bundle of old letters found in a trunk in the attic. Years slip away as if by magic as one enters another time and place and overhears the conversation of family and friends, some unknown, some legendary.

The Prayer Book has been called the diary of the Christian Church. It is not unlike the faded letters in the attic in one sense but quite unlike them in others: this diary is in constant use, and it is continually being added to by younger members of the family. It is a living document.

The early Church used no books in common worship except the Scriptures. Prayers were spontaneous and in the Eucharist were freely composed by the celebrant according to his ability. Gradually collections of prayers and liturgical forms began to appear. They were called Church Orders and usually represented the usage of a certain place or were attributed to the authorship or the editing of a well known person. Later these were elaborated into collections of rites and prayers called Sacramentaries. The earliest is the Leonine Sacramentary, dating from the middle of the 6th century. Its attribution to Pope Leo I (d. 461) is arbitrary though some of the prayers may well be his compositions. The Gregorian Sacramentary was sent in 790 by Pope Hadrian I to the Emperor Charlemagne and became widely used in the Frankish Em-

pire. Almost two centuries earlier a version of the same text had been taken to England by St. Augustine of Canterbury when he came as a missionary to the English people in 597. The third of these collections, the Gelasian Sacramentary, contains the oldest known Missal with the Feasts according to the Church Year. A Missal is a book containing all that is necessary to be sung or said at the celebration of the Holy Communion throughout the year. In 1549 the various service books and all the local "uses" were put together for the first time and done into English, "the language of the people," under the direction of Thomas Cranmer, Archbishop of Canterbury. The first official Prayer Book of the American Episcopal Church was issued in 1789, the same year as the Constitutional Convention. The most recent was approved by the General Convention of 1928. The Prayer Book is at present being revised again and many of us have become familiar with some of the proposals through experimental use.

To go back to the analogy of the letters in the attic, one of the earliest diary entries is the Sanctus, the familiar "Holy, holy, holy" of the Communion Service, on p. 77. The origin of it is to be found in Isaiah's vision of God (Isa. 6:1–3). A form of it was used in the liturgy of the Jewish synagogue whence it was taken over by the Church. Another early entry is the Sursum Corda, "Lift up your hearts," p. 76. It appears in all of the historical liturgies of East and West, is mentioned by St. Cyprian as early

as 252. An example of a familiar prayer with a long history is the beautiful "Collect for Purity" which begins the Order for Holy Communion. It can be traced back to the Englishman Alcuin (d. 804), Charlemagne's prime minister and liturgical scholar. Whether it was his own composition or whether he found it in an older source is unknown to us but we do know that it has been in constant use in the Church for well over a thousand years.

As the family letters reflect the issues, feelings, and events of their times so do the prayers in the Prayer Book. The first prayer 'For Missions,' p. 38, was composed by the missionary bishop of Calcutta (d. 1866). The prayer 'For our Country,' p. 36, written by the rector of St. Michael's, Bristol, R.I., was first published in 1883. It reflects the turbulent period in our history marked by the influx of thousands of immigrants, the rapid development of the West, "big business," and the emergence of the United States as a world power.

So also the prayers 'For Christian Service,' 'For Social Justice,' 'For Every Man in his Work,' pp. 43–44, represent the godly hopes of their authors. The prayer 'For the Family of Nations,' p. 44, written by Bishop Parsons of California for the 1928 Prayer Book, is both topical and timeless. In the text of the Prayer Book now in preparation there will appear many new prayers, new forms of worship, new ways of doing old things as the family moves, changes, reflects its need to view the contemporary scene with a clear eye while at the same time holding steadily to old truths and worshiping the Lord in the beauty of holiness.

Now a word on how to use this Concordance. The Prayer Book may be used in public worship, it may be used for saying Morning and Evening Prayer when alone, it may be used as a manual for private devotion, it may be used simply as an interesting book to read. This Concordance should have a double value. For one picking up the Prayer Book as a book to read, interest will be stimulated by the references themselves. For one wishing to find a reference, a word, a phrase right at the edge of one's mind, it will be an invaluable tool.

To come back one last time to the bundle of letters, in reading them one glimpses the family through all its years being itself. So in the pages of the Prayer Book — collects, liturgy, occasional prayers, psalms, scripture, rites and ceremonies — one discovers the Church on her knees, in prayer and praise, in adoration and thanksgiving through all the centuries serving the Lord with gladness.

Robert N. Rodenmayer

A
CONCORDANCE
TO THE
AMERICAN BOOK OF
COMMON PRAYER

PAGE LN

AARON

BY THE HAND OF MOSES AND AARON 434 24
6 MOSES AND AARON AMONG HIS PRIESTS, AND SAMUEL AMONG 462 27
AND AARON WHOM HE HAD CHOSEN 471 24
AND AARON THE SAINT OF THE LORD 473 33
10 YE HOUSE OF AARON, PUT YOUR TRUST IN THE LORD 485 30
OF ISRAEL, HE SHALL BLESS THE HOUSE OF AARON 486 03
3 LET THE HOUSE OF AARON NOW CONFESS, * 488 04
PRAISE THE LORD, YE HOUSE OF AARON 511 09

AARON'S

EVEN UNTO AARON'S BEARD, AND WENT DOWN TO THE SKIRTS 509 16

ABASED

EVERY ONE THAT EXALTETH HIMSELF SHALL BE ABASED 205 33
FOR WHOSOEVER EXALTETH HIMSELF SHALL BE ABASED 214 20

ABBA

CRYING, ABBA, FATHER 005 17
CRYING, ABBA, FATHER 104 23
AND HE SAID, ABBA, FATHER, ALL THINGS ARE POSSIBLE 141 35
WHEREBY WE CRY, ABBA, FATHER 200 09
WHEREBY WE CRY, ABBA, FATHER 330 22

ABEL

BLOOD OF RIGHTEOUS ABEL UNTO THE BLOOD OF ZACHARIAS 100 24

ABHOR

ABHOR THAT WHICH IS EVIL 111 22
THE LORD WILL ABHOR BOTH THE BLOOD-THIRSTY AND 348 12
DELIGHTETH IN WICKEDNESS, DOTH HIS SOUL ABHOR 354 32
NEITHER DOTH HE ABHOR ANY THING THAT IS EVIL 384 02
AND ALL FALSE WAYS I UTTERLY ABHOR 498 26
I HATE AND ABHOR THEM 501 07

ABHORRED

DESPISED NOR ABHORRED THE LOW ESTATE OF THE POOR 367 20
MADE ME TO BE ABHORRED OF THEM 449 12
BUT THOU HAST ABHORRED AND FORSAKEN THINE ANOINTED, 452 16
THAT HE ABHORRED HIS OWN INHERITANCE 475 17
18 THEIR SOUL ABHORRED ALL MANNER OF MEAT, * 477 11

ABHORREST

14 LORD, WHY ABHORREST THOU MY SOUL, * 449 24

ABHORRETH

GOOD OF THE COVETOUS, WHOM THE LORD ABHORRETH 353 10

ABIDE

THY WORD, AND TO ABIDE IN THY LOVE 043 10
SAYING, ABIDE WITH US 168 03
THAT HE MAY ABIDE WITH YOU FOR EVER 181 10
BUT WHO MAY ABIDE THE DAY OF HIS COMING 232 07
ABIDE IN ME, AND I IN YOU 238 09
EXCEPT IT ABIDE IN THE VINE 238 11
CAN YE, EXCEPT YE ABIDE IN ME 238 12
IF A MAN ABIDE NOT IN ME, HE IS CAST FORTH AS A 238 14
IF YE ABIDE IN ME, AND MY WORDS ABIDE IN YOU, YE 238 17
AND MY WORDS ABIDE IN YOU, YE SHALL ASK WHAT YE 238 17
YE SHALL ABIDE IN MY LOVE 238 22
AND ABIDE IN HIS LOVE 238 23
WHO WEARS IT MAY ABIDE IN THY PEACE, AND CONTINUE IN 302 20
O LORD, WHO MAY ABIDE IT 328 08
IN THE LORD, AND ABIDE PATIENTLY UPON HIM 385 06
THAT PATIENTLY ABIDE THE LORD, THOSE SHALL INHERIT 385 12
THE LORD WILL ABIDE IN IT FOR EVER 420 15
I WILL PATIENTLY ABIDE ALWAY, * 426 02
SHALL ABIDE UNDER THE SHADOW OF THE ALMIGHTY 454 29
AND WOULD NOT ABIDE HIS COUNSEL 473 28
UNGODLY SHALL NOT ABIDE UPON THE LOT OF THE 504 29
O LORD, WHO MAY ABIDE IT 507 13
WHO IS ABLE TO ABIDE HIS FROST 523 30
AND AFFLICTIONS ABIDE ME 550 18

PAGE LN

ABIDE   CONTINUED

THY PEOPLE MAY ABIDE IN THY FAVOUR AND BE GUIDED IN 562 12
UNDERSTANDING ABIDE ALL THE DAYS OF HIS LIFE 598 03

ABIDETH

WHOSOEVER ABIDETH IN HIM SINNETH NOT 117 24
AND NOW ABIDETH FAITH, HOPE, CHARITY, THESE THREE 123 14
NOT HIS BROTHER ABIDETH IN DEATH 191 14
WE KNOW THAT HE ABIDETH IN US, BY THE SPIRIT WHICH HE 191 34
HE THAT ABIDETH IN ME, AND I IN HIM, THE SAME 238 13
BEING IN HONOUR ABIDETH NOT, * 400 30
LAID THE FOUNDATION OF THE EARTH, AND IT ABIDETH 496 06

ABIDING

SHEPHERDS ABIDING IN THE FIELD, KEEPING WATCH OVER 099 11
ETERNAL LIFE ABIDING IN HIM 191 16
AND GRANT HIM AN ABIDING SENSE OF THY 313 07
THE PATIENT ABIDING OF THE MEEK SHALL NOT PERISH FOR 352 29
CONSUME IN THE SEPULCHRE, AND HAVE NO ABIDING 401 04
AND THINE ABIDING PEACE BESTOW 545 07
AND THINE ABIDING PEACE BESTOW 557 13

ABILITIES

TO OUR ABILITIES AND OPPORTUNITIES 588 32

ABILITY

DO IT AS OF THE ABILITY WHICH GOD GIVETH 179 20
ACCORDING TO HIS ABILITY, DETERMINED TO SEND RELIEF 241 20
ACCORDING TO HIS ABILITY, DETERMINED TO SEND RELIEF 246 29
WHEN OF ABILITY, TO LEAVE BEQUESTS FOR RELIGIOUS R 320 23
THAT WILL AND ABILITY IS GIVEN OF GOD ALONE 540 31
GIVE ALMS TO THE POOR, ACCORDING TO HIS ABILITY 611 04

ABIRAM

AND COVERED THE CONGREGATION OF ABIRAM 474 03

ABJECTS

THE VERY ABJECTS CAME TOGETHER AGAINST ME 382 24

ABLE

NO CREATURE IS ABLE TO RESIST, TO WHOM IT BELONGETH 041 10
SHALL GIVE AS HE IS ABLE, ACCORDING TO THE BLESSING 073 16
WHICH IS ABLE TO SAVE YOUR SOULS 175 04
SUFFER YOU TO BE TEMPTED ABOVE THAT YE ARE ABLE 201 28
THAT YE MAY BE ABLE TO BEAR IT 201 29
ALSO HATH MADE US ABLE MINISTERS OF THE NEW 206 16
IN LOVE, MAY BE ABLE TO COMPREHEND WITH ALL SAINTS 212 17
UNTO HIM THAT IS ABLE TO DO EXCEEDING ABUNDANTLY 212 21
AND NO MAN WAS ABLE TO ANSWER HIM A WORD, NEITHER 215 22
THEE WE ARE NOT ABLE TO PLEASE THEE 215 27
THAT YE MAY BE ABLE TO STAND AGAINST THE WILES 219 07
THAT YE MAY BE ABLE TO WITHSTAND IN THE EVIL 219 12
YE SHALL BE ABLE TO QUENCH ALL THE FIERY DARTS OF THE 219 17
WHEREBY HE IS ABLE EVEN TO SUBJECT ALL THINGS UNTO 222 25
ARE YE ABLE TO DRINK OF THE CUP THAT I SHALL DRINK 247 12
THEY SAY UNTO HIM, WE ARE ABLE 247 14
THAT YE MAY BE ABLE AFTER MY DECEASE TO HAVE THESE 248 12
WHICH IS ABLE TO SAVE YOUR SOULS 265 28
THAT YOU ARE NOT ABLE TO DO THESE THINGS OF YOURSELF, 289 13
HE MAY BE ABLE TO GO TO THINE HOUSE, TO OFFER 315 31
SICK PERSON BE NOT ABLE TO COME TO THE CHURCH, R 321 11
OR SUCH AS ARE NOT ABLE TO ATTEND THE PUBLIC R 323 33
SHALL BE ABLE TO SEPARATE US FROM THE LOVE 331 13
WHEREBY HE IS ABLE TO SUBDUE ALL THINGS UNTO HIMSELF 333 23
WHEREBY HE IS ABLE TO SUBDUE ALL THINGS UNTO HIMSELF 337 16
SHALL NOT BE ABLE TO STAND IN THE JUDGMENT, * 345 19
THEY SHALL NOT BE ABLE TO STAND, * 362 14
AS THEY ARE NOT ABLE TO PERFORM 365 28
AND SHALL NOT BE ABLE TO STAND 384 22
BE MORE THAN I AM ABLE TO EXPRESS 390 26
THAT I AM NOT ABLE TO LOOK UP 391 11
SHALL NOT BE ABLE TO EXALT THEMSELVES 417 18
ENEMY SHALL NOT BE ABLE TO DO HIM VIOLENCE 451 19
WHO IS ABLE TO ABIDE HIS FROST 523 29
HIS GRACE, WHICH IS ABLE TO BUILD YOU UP, AND TO GIVE 551 04

ABLE   CONTINUED

    SO THAT YOU MAY BE ABLE BY THEM TO TEACH AND EXHORT   554 31
    THAT THOU ART NOT ABLE TO DO THESE THINGS OF THYSELF,   580 17

ABODE

    AND MAKE OUR ABODE WITH HIM   181 26

ABOLISH

    AND ABOLISH, CEREMONIES OR RITES OF THE   610 02

ABOMINABLE

    AND BECOME ABOMINABLE IN THEIR DOINGS   356 14
    THEY ARE ALTOGETHER BECOME ABOMINABLE   356 20
    UNTIL HIS ABOMINABLE SIN BE FOUND OUT   383 29
    AND BECOME ABOMINABLE IN THEIR WICKEDNESS   405 14
    THEY ARE ALTOGETHER BECOME ABOMINABLE   405 20

ABOUND

    AND ALL GOOD LEARNING FLOURISH AND ABOUND   042 25
    USEFUL LEARNING MAY FOR EVER FLOURISH AND ABOUND   047 37
    THAT YE MAY ABOUND IN HOPE, THROUGH THE POWER OF THE   093 02
    SO YE WOULD ABOUND MORE AND MORE   127 25
    YOUR LOVE MAY ABOUND YET MORE AND MORE IN KNOWLEDGE   221 02

ABOUNDING

    ALWAYS ABOUNDING IN THE WORK OF THE LORD, FORASMUCH   330 15

ABRAHAM

    OUR FOREFATHER ABRAHAM, *   014 19
    OUR FOREFATHERS, ABRAHAM AND HIS SEED, FOR EVER   026 27
    SIT DOWN WITH ABRAHAM, AND ISAAC, AND JACOB, IN THE   115 20
    ARE THEY THE SEED OF ABRAHAM   120 29
    IS WRITTEN, THAT ABRAHAM HAD TWO SONS, THE ONE BY A   130 30
    ABRAHAM IS DEAD, AND THE PROPHETS   133 19
    THAN OUR FATHER ABRAHAM, WHICH IS DEAD   133 22
    YOUR FATHER ABRAHAM REJOICED TO SEE MY DAY   133 28
    YET FIFTY YEARS OLD, AND HAST THOU SEEN ABRAHAM   133 31
    UNTO YOU, BEFORE ABRAHAM WAS, I AM   133 32
    THOUGH ABRAHAM BE IGNORANT OF US, AND ISRAEL   139 22
    OF THE STOCK OF ABRAHAM, AND WHOSOEVER AMONG YOU   168 24
    AND SEETH ABRAHAM AFAR OFF, AND LAZARUS IN HIS BOSOM   190 12
    AND SAID, FATHER ABRAHAM, HAVE MERCY ON ME, AND SEND   190 13
    BUT ABRAHAM SAID, SON, REMEMBER THAT THOU IN THY   190 16
    ABRAHAM SAITH UNTO HIM, THEY HAVE MOSES AND THE   190 25
    AND HE SAID, NAY, FATHER ABRAHAM   190 27
    TO ABRAHAM AND HIS SEED WERE THE PROMISES MADE   207 19
    GOD GAVE IT TO ABRAHAM BY PROMISE   207 26
    TO OUR FATHER ABRAHAM, THAT HE WOULD GRANT UNTO US,   244 06
    ARE JOINED UNTO THE PEOPLE OF THE GOD OF ABRAHAM   399 07
    6 O YE SEED OF ABRAHAM HIS SERVANT, *   470 14
    9 EVEN THE COVENANT THAT HE MADE WITH ABRAHAM   470 20
    AND ABRAHAM HIS SERVANT   472 22

ABRAHAM'S

    ANGELS INTO ABRAHAM'S BOSOM   190 10

ABRIDGED

    MAY BE ALTERED, ABRIDGED, ENLARGED, AMENDED, OR   V 07

ABROAD

    WENT THIS SAYING ABROAD AMONG THE BRETHREN, THAT THAT   102 09
    THEY MADE KNOWN ABROAD THE SAYING WHICH WAS TOLD THEM   106 13
    THIS WAS NOISED ABROAD, THE MULTITUDE CAME TOGETHER,   180 26
    FAME HEREOF WENT ABROAD INTO ALL THAT LAND   224 29
    ARE SCATTERED ABROAD, GREETING   239 07
    WERE NOISED ABROAD THROUGHOUT ALL THE HILL COUNTRY OF   243 27
    BUT SCATTER THEM ABROAD AMONG THE PEOPLE, AND PUT   411 27
    THOU HAST CAST US OUT, AND SCATTERED US ABROAD   412 13
    AND THINE ARROWS WENT ABROAD   434 17
    THINE ENEMIES ABROAD WITH THY MIGHTY ARM   450 27
    AND SHALL SPREAD ABROAD LIKE A CEDAR IN LEBANON   456 25
    HE HATH DISPERSED ABROAD, AND GIVEN TO THE POOR,   483 34
    AND SPREAD A NET ABROAD WITH CORDS   516 19
    BUT SCATTERETH ABROAD ALL THE UNGODLY   521 33
    WERE SCATTERED ABROAD AS SHEEP HAVING NO SHEPHERD   538 16
    ARE DISPERSED ABROAD, AND FOR HIS CHILDREN WHO ARE IN   540 02
    INTO HEAVEN, SENT ABROAD INTO THE WORLD HIS APOSTLES,   545 17
    READY TO SPREAD ABROAD THY GOSPEL, THE GLAD TIDINGS   557 29

ABSENCE

    IN THE ABSENCE OF A PRIEST, A DEACON MAY SAY ALL   R 084 25
    MUCH MORE IN MY ABSENCE, WORK OUT YOUR OWN SALVATION   106 03
    UNTO THEM IN THE ABSENCE OF THE MULTITUDE   148 20
    IN THE ABSENCE OF THE PRIEST TO BAPTIZE INFANTS   533 16
    THEIR NECESSARY ABSENCE, TWO MEMBERS OF THE VESTRY)   R 570 07

ABSENT

    WILL THE LORD ABSENT HIMSELF FOR EVER   311 12
    AWAKE, AND BE NOT ABSENT FROM US FOR EVER   396 07
    ART THOU ABSENT FROM US SO LONG   430 03
    7 WILL THE LORD ABSENT HIMSELF FOR EVER   433 29
    WHOM WE LOVE, NOW ABSENT FROM US   597 02

ABSOLUTION

    AND ABSOLUTION ARE OMITTED, THE MINISTER MAY, AFTER   R 003 10
    THE ABSOLUTION FROM THE ORDER FOR THE HOLY   R 007 05
    THE ABSOLUTION AND REMISSION OF THEIR SINS   007 10
    AND ABSOLUTION ARE OMITTED, THE MINISTER MAY, AFTER   R 021 07
    THE ABSOLUTION AND REMISSION OF THEIR SINS   024 12
    GRANT YOU ABSOLUTION AND REMISSION OF ALL YOUR SINS,   024 23
    TO PRONOUNCE ABSOLUTION AND BLESSING IN GOD'S NAME   294 15
    THE CONFESSION AND THE ABSOLUTION   R 323 06
    AND ABSOLUTION THE FOLLOWING MAY BE USED   R 323 10
    GRANT YOU ABSOLUTION AND REMISSION OF ALL YOUR SINS,   323 19

ABSOLVE

    WE BESEECH THEE, ABSOLVE THY PEOPLE FROM THEIR   223 15

ABSOLVED

    BY THY MERCIFUL PARDON MAY BE ABSOLVED   062 11

ABSOLVETH

    PARDONETH AND ABSOLVETH ALL THOSE WHO TRULY REPENT,   007 11
    PARDONETH AND ABSOLVETH ALL THOSE WHO TRULY REPENT,   024 13

ABSTAIN

    WHEN YE WILFULLY ABSTAIN FROM THE LORD'S TABLE, AND   089 16
    THAT YE SHOULD ABSTAIN FROM FORNICATION   127 28
    AND PILGRIMS, ABSTAIN FROM FLESHLY LUSTS, WHICH WAR   173 13
    OR TO ABSTAIN FROM MARRIAGE   609 22

ABSTINENCE

    OF FASTING OR ABSTINENCE, OR ON ANY DAY WHEN THE   R 003 05
    TO USE SUCH ABSTINENCE, THAT, OUR FLESH BEING SUBDUED 125 28

ABUNDANCE

    UPON US THE ABUNDANCE OF THY MERCY   206 07
    AND ABUNDANCE OF PEACE, SO LONG AS THE MOON   427 11
    FACE WITH THE ABUNDANCE OF THY GRACE   544 07
    FACE WITH THE ABUNDANCE OF THY GRACE   556 15
    GIVE THE ABUNDANCE OF THY GRACE   574 09

ABUNDANT

    IN LABOURS MORE ABUNDANT, IN STRIPES ABOVE MEASURE,   120 30
    TO CHILDREN AN ABUNDANT ENTRANCE INTO THY KINGDOM   340 30
    OF THINE ABUNDANT KINDNESS SHALL BE SHOWED   521 06

ABUNDANTLY

    WE MAY LABOUR ABUNDANTLY TO MAKE KNOWN TO ALL MEN THY 038 21
    AND THAT THEY MIGHT HAVE IT MORE ABUNDANTLY   186 19
    LABOURED MORE ABUNDANTLY THAN THEY ALL   205 17
    DO EXCEEDING ABUNDANTLY ABOVE ALL THAT WE ASK OR   212 22
    AND THAT THEY MIGHT HAVE IT MORE ABUNDANTLY   539 10
    HIS GIFTS ABUNDANTLY UPON MEN, MAKING SOME APOSTLES,   557 25

ACCEPT

    MERCIFULLY TO ACCEPT OUR (ALMS AND) OBLATIONS,   074 09
    MERCIFULLY TO ACCEPT THIS OUR SACRIFICE OF PRAISE AND 081 16
    BESEECH THEE TO ACCEPT THIS OUR BOUNDEN DUTY AND   081 30
    MERCIFULLY ACCEPT OUR PRAYERS   188 33
    ACCEPT OUR PRAYERS ON BEHALF OF THE SOUL OF THY   268 22
    DOST THOU ACCEPT HIM, AND DESIRE TO FOLLOW HIM AS THY 278 05
    MERCIFULLY ACCEPT OUR PRAYERS, AND GRANT TO THY   312 13
    ACCEPT, WE BESEECH THEE, MERCIFUL LORD, THE DEVOUT   313 05
    HIS CONTRITION, ACCEPT HIS TEARS, ASSUAGE HIS PAIN,   314 07
    ACCEPT OUR PRAYERS ON BEHALF OF THE SOUL OF THY   334 14
    AND ACCEPT THY BURNT-SACRIFICE   364 21
    AND ACCEPT THE PERSONS OF THE UNGODLY   443 20
    VOUCHSAFED TO ACCEPT AND TAKE THESE THY SERVANTS UNTO 534 31
    ACCEPT, O LORD, THIS SERVICE AT OUR HANDS, AND BLESS   565 11
    THAT THOU MAYEST ACCEPT THEIR BOUNDEN DUTY AND   566 20
    GRACIOUSLY ACCEPT THE DEDICATION OF THIS PLACE TO THY 567 06
    THEE TO ACCEPT THIS OUR MORNING SACRIFICE OF PRAISE   587 25
    AND ACCEPT, O LORD, OUR INTERCESSIONS FOR ALL   590 22

ACCEPTABLE

    BE ALWAYS ACCEPTABLE IN THY SIGHT, O LORD, MY   003 20
    BE ALWAY ACCEPTABLE IN THY SIGHT, O LORD, MY STRENGTH 021 22
    BE FOUND AN ACCEPTABLE PEOPLE IN THY SIGHT, WHO   093 30
    PROCLAIM THE ACCEPTABLE YEAR OF THE LORD, AND THE DAY 107 04
    ACCEPTABLE UNTO GOD, WHICH IS YOUR REASONABLE   110 05
    AND ACCEPTABLE, AND PERFECT, WILL OF GOD   110 08
    WHAT IS ACCEPTABLE UNTO THE LORD   129 15
    THIS IS ACCEPTABLE WITH GOD   172 09
    HOLY TEMPLE ACCEPTABLE UNTO THEE   254 31
    ACCEPTABLE TO GOD BY JESUS CHRIST   259 32
    TO PREACH THE ACCEPTABLE YEAR OF THE LORD   261 20
    HOLY TEMPLE ACCEPTABLE UNTO THEE   290 23
    ARE GOOD, AND ACCEPTABLE UNTO THY DIVINE MAJESTY   298 15
    MAY BE FOUND ACCEPTABLE IN THY SIGHT   335 09
    BE ALWAY ACCEPTABLE IN THY SIGHT, *   364 14
    HIS WAY ACCEPTABLE TO HIMSELF   386 09
    IN AN ACCEPTABLE TIME   422 28
    BE ALWAY ACCEPTABLE IN THY SIGHT, O LORD, OUR   572 23
    HOLY TEMPLE ACCEPTABLE UNTO THEE   574 08
    PLEASANT AND ACCEPTABLE TO GOD, WITHOUT THE GRACE OF   605 02
    PLEASING AND ACCEPTABLE TO GOD IN CHRIST, AND DO   605 13

ACCEPTABLY

AND WORSHIP HIM ACCEPTABLY   047 14

ACCEPTANCE

AS TO HIS ACCEPTANCE OF THE CHRISTIAN FAITH, AND AS   R 313 18

ACCEPTED

NOT SO EASILY ACCEPTED AND ALLOWED BEFORE GOD   088 29
THEE IN A TIME ACCEPTED, AND IN THE DAY OF SALVATION   126 05
NOW IS THE ACCEPTED TIME   126 07
IS ACCEPTED WITH HIM   166 14
IS ACCEPTED WITH HIM   184 02
AND GRACIOUSLY ACCEPTED BY OUR HEAVENLY FATHER   564 20
IN THE END BE ACCEPTED OF THEE AS THY FAITHFUL   594 26

ACCESS

HAVE BOLDNESS AND ACCESS WITH CONFIDENCE BY THE FAITH   108 27
THE PRAYER OF HUMBLE ACCESS   R 323 08

ACCIDENT

FROM BODILY ACCIDENT AND HARM THE WORKMEN AT THEIR   599 28

ACCOMMODATED

SUCH OF THE CLERGY AS CAN BE THERE ACCOMMODATED   R 564 07

ACCOMPANY

TO ACCOMPANY ME WITH A PURE HEART, AND   006 10
TO ACCOMPANY ME WITH A PURE HEART, AND   023 19
GOD TO ACCOMPANY WITH HIS BLESSING EVERY ENDEAVOUR   VI 40

ACCOMPLISH

CHEERFULLY ACCOMPLISH THOSE THINGS WHICH THOU   217 20
HE SHOULD ACCOMPLISH AT JERUSALEM   248 29
THAT HE MAY ACCOMPLISH HIS WORK WHICH HE HATH BEGUN   543 20

ACCOMPLISHED

DAYS WERE ACCOMPLISHED THAT SHE SHOULD BE DELIVERED   099 06
DAYS WERE ACCOMPLISHED FOR THE CIRCUMCISING OF THE   106 20
CONCERNING THE SON OF MAN SHALL BE ACCOMPLISHED   123 20
MUST YET BE ACCOMPLISHED IN ME, AND HE WAS RECKONED   150 09
WERE NOW ACCOMPLISHED, THAT THE SCRIPTURE MIGHT BE   160 24
ARE ACCOMPLISHED IN YOUR BRETHREN THAT ARE IN THE   193 07
MOSES WERE ACCOMPLISHED, THEY BROUGHT HIM TO   232 24
WARFARE IS ACCOMPLISHED, THAT HER INIQUITY IS   242 18

ACCOMPLISHING

HE ACCOMPLISHING IN YOU THE GOOD WORK WHICH HE   555 31

ACCORD

TIME WITH ONE ACCORD TO MAKE OUR COMMON SUPPLICATIONS   020 04
TIME WITH ONE ACCORD TO MAKE OUR COMMON SUPPLICATIONS   034 04
UPON HIM WITH ONE ACCORD, AND CAST HIM OUT OF THE   100 10
WERE ALL WITH ONE ACCORD IN ONE PLACE   180 18
WHICH OPENED TO THEM OF HIS OWN ACCORD   245 23
WERE ALL WITH ONE ACCORD IN SOLOMON'S PORCH   249 23
AND WITH ONE ACCORD MAKE OUR PRAYERS UNTO HIM, THAT   280 16

ACCORDING

OF SINS, ACCORDING TO THE RICHES OF HIS GRACE   004 34
THE PEOPLE, 'ACCORDING TO THE VARIOUS EXIGENCY OF   V 09
ACCORDING TO THE VARIOUS EXIGENCY OF TIMES AND   V 17
DO THAT WHICH, ACCORDING TO HER BEST UNDERSTANDING,   V 34
AND ALTHOUGH, ACCORDING TO HER JUDGMENT, THERE BE NOT   V 39
ACCORDING TO THY PROMISES DECLARED UNTO MANKIND IN   006 26
OF THE PSALMS, ACCORDING TO THE USE OF THIS CHURCH   R 009 22
FIRST LESSON, ACCORDING TO THE TABLE OR CALENDAR   R 009 31
NEW TESTAMENT, ACCORDING TO THE TABLE OR CALENDAR   R 014 03
HE ROSE AGAIN ACCORDING TO THE SCRIPTURES   016 10
RELIEVE THEM, ACCORDING TO THEIR SEVERAL NECESSITIES   019 08
ACCORDING TO THY PROMISES DECLARED UNTO MANKIND IN   023 33
OF THE PSALMS, ACCORDING TO THE USE OF THIS CHURCH   R 025 15
FIRST LESSON, ACCORDING TO THE TABLE OR CALENDAR   R 026 05
ACCORDING TO THY WORD   028 10
HE ROSE AGAIN ACCORDING TO THE SCRIPTURES   030 15
HONOUR THEM, ACCORDING TO THY BLESSED WORD AND   032 12
RELIEVE THEM, ACCORDING TO THEIR SEVERAL NECESSITIES   033.06
IT MAY WORK ACCORDING TO GOD'S WILL, SERVE HIM   047 13
UNITY WHICH IS ACCORDING TO THY WILL, WHO LIVEST AND   049 08
ASKED ACCORDING TO THY WILL, MAY EFFECTUALLY BE   050 11
LIVE ACCORDING TO THY WILL IN THIS LIFE, AND ALSO MAY   051 10
IN THIS WORLD ACCORDING TO THY WILL, AND ALSO MAY BE   053 16
OUR LIVES ACCORDING TO THY HOLY WORD   057 17
NOT WITH US ACCORDING TO OUR SINS   058 12
REWARD US ACCORDING TO OUR INIQUITIES   058 13
ACCORDING TO THE MULTITUDE OF THY MERCIES DO AWAY   060 11
HE ROSE AGAIN ACCORDING TO THE SCRIPTURES   071 12
EVERY MAN DO ACCORDING AS HE IS DISPOSED IN HIS   072 17
AS HE IS ABLE, ACCORDING TO THE BLESSING OF THE LORD   073 16
ACCORDING TO THE TIME, IF THERE BE ANY   R 077 02
ACCORDING TO WHOSE MOST TRUE PROMISE, THE HOLY GHOST   078 25
ACCORDING TO THE INSTITUTION OF THY DEARLY   080 37
RECEIVING THEM ACCORDING TO THY SON OUR SAVIOUR JESUS   081 11
ACCORDING TO THE FORM BEFORE PRESCRIBED   R 083 08
ACCORDING TO THE UTTERMOST OF YOUR   087 25

ACCORDING   CONTINUED

ACCORDING TO MINE OFFICE, I BID YOU IN THE   089 06
TOWARD ANOTHER ACCORDING TO CHRIST JESUS   092 19
OLD AND UNDER, ACCORDING TO THE TIME WHICH HE HAD   103 28
A MINISTER, ACCORDING TO THE GIFT OF THE GRACE OF GOD   108 16
WISDOM OF GOD, ACCORDING TO THE ETERNAL PURPOSE WHICH   108 25
THINK SOBERLY, ACCORDING AS GOD HATH DEALT TO EVERY   110 12
DIFFERING ACCORDING TO THE GRACE THAT IS GIVEN TO US,   111 15
US PROPHESY ACCORDING TO THE PROPORTION OF FAITH   111 17
OF THE LORD, ACCORDING TO ALL THAT THE LORD HATH   138 29
ON THEM ACCORDING TO HIS MERCIES, AND ACCORDING TO   138 31
AND ACCORDING TO THE MULTITUDE OF HIS   138 32
ALL THE PEOPLE ACCORDING TO THE LAW, HE TOOK THE   147 19
AND RULE US ACCORDING TO THY WILL, COMFORT US IN ALL   183 23
TO LIVE ACCORDING TO THY WILL   201 02
FOR OUR SINS ACCORDING TO THE SCRIPTURES   205 05
THE THIRD DAY ACCORDING TO THE SCRIPTURES   205 06
MANY AS WALK ACCORDING TO THIS RULE, PEACE BE ON   211 03
GRANT YOU, ACCORDING TO THE RICHES OF HIS GLORY, TO   212 14
ASK OR THINK, ACCORDING TO THE POWER THAT WORKETH IN   212 22
IS CORRUPT ACCORDING TO THE DECEITFUL LUSTS   216 13
OF HIS GLORY, ACCORDING TO THE WORKING WHEREBY HE IS   222 24
ALL MIGHT, ACCORDING TO HIS GLORIOUS POWER, UNTO ALL   224 06
PURIFICATION ACCORDING TO THE LAW OF MOSES WERE   232 23
A SACRIFICE ACCORDING TO THAT WHICH IS SAID IN THE   232 28
IN PEACE, ACCORDING TO THY WORD   233 06
ALL THINGS ACCORDING TO THE LAW OF THE LORD, THEY   233 24
BE IT UNTO ME ACCORDING TO THY WORD   236 29
IS GIVEN GRACE ACCORDING TO THE MEASURE OF THE GIFT   237 12
ACCORDING TO THE EFFECTUAL WORKING IN THE   237 31
EVERY MAN ACCORDING TO HIS ABILITY, DETERMINED TO   241 20
TRULY REPENT ACCORDING TO HIS PREACHING   242 11
EVERY MAN ACCORDING TO HIS ABILITY, DETERMINED TO   246 28
REWARD HIM ACCORDING TO HIS WORKS   254 08
IN WEDLOCK ACCORDING TO THY HOLY ORDINANCE   267 06
OF HIS LIFE ACCORDING TO THIS BEGINNING   280 18
TO LIVE ACCORDING TO THY WILL   287 29
US DO PART, ACCORDING TO GOD'S HOLY ORDINANCE   301 31
US DO PART, ACCORDING TO GOD'S HOLY ORDINANCE   302 07
AND LIVE ACCORDING TO THY LAWS   303 11
LIVE ACCORDING TO THY WILL IN THIS LIFE, AND ALSO MAY   306 30
AND THEN, ACCORDING TO HIS DISCRETION, ONE OF THE   R 308 08
WHO, ACCORDING TO THE MULTITUDE OF THY MERCIES,   313 30
ASK ANY THING ACCORDING TO HIS WILL, HE HEARETH US   322 16
SHALL PROCEED ACCORDING TO THE FORM BEFORE PRESCRIBED   R 322 30
ACCORDING TO THE MULTITUDE OF THY MERCIES, DO AWAY   323 15
ARE THE CALLED ACCORDING TO HIS PURPOSE   330 32
O LORD, ACCORDING TO THE FAVOUR WHICH THOU BEAREST   332 03
ACCORDING TO THE MIGHTY WORKING WHEREBY HE IS ABLE TO   333 22
ACCORDING TO THE MIGHTY WORKING WHEREBY HE IS ABLE TO   337 16
OF THE GOSPEL ACCORDING TO ST   R 339 20
ACCORDING TO MY RIGHTEOUSNESS, AND ACCORDING TO THE   350 07
AND ACCORDING TO THE INNOCENCY THAT IS IN ME   350 07
UNTO THE LORD, ACCORDING TO HIS RIGHTEOUSNESS   350 27
ACCORDING TO THE CLEANNESS OF MY HANDS DID HE   361 07
AND ACCORDING UNTO THE CLEANNESS OF MY HANDS IN HIS   361 16
BUT ACCORDING TO THY MERCY THINK THOU UPON ME, O   369 31
AND ACCORDING TO THE WICKEDNESS OF THEIR OWN   373 13
4 REWARD THEM ACCORDING TO THEIR DEEDS, *   373 13
O LORD MY GOD, ACCORDING TO THY RIGHTEOUSNESS   383 11
ACCORDING TO THY WORSHIP AND RENOWN   396 21
9 O GOD, ACCORDING TO THY NAME, SO IS THY PRAISE UNTO   399 29
ACCORDING TO THE MULTITUDE OF THY MERCIES DO AWAY   403 09
EVERY MAN ACCORDING TO HIS WORK   414 24
THEE UNTO ME ACCORDING TO THE MULTITUDE OF THY   423 05
THY PEOPLE ACCORDING UNTO RIGHT, *   426 33
I SHALL JUDGE ACCORDING UNTO RIGHT   432 02
ACCORDING TO THE GREATNESS OF THY POWER, PRESERVE   440 27
REWARDED US ACCORDING TO OUR WICKEDNESSES   466 26
O LORD, ACCORDING TO THE FAVOUR THAT THOU BEAREST   473 06
PITIED THEM, ACCORDING TO THE MULTITUDE OF HIS   475 28
O LORD GOD, ACCORDING UNTO THY NAME   481 12
O SAVE ME ACCORDING TO THY MERCY   481 22
THOU ME, ACCORDING TO THY WORD   491 18
THOU ME ACCORDING UNTO THY WORD   491 24
THY SALVATION, ACCORDING UNTO THY WORD   492 23
UNTO ME, ACCORDING TO THY WORD   493 27
ACCORDING UNTO THY WORD   494 12
ACCORDING TO THY WORD UNTO THY SERVANT   495 07
THIS DAY ACCORDING TO THINE ORDINANCE   496 07
O LORD, ACCORDING TO THY WORD   497 12
O STABLISH ME ACCORDING TO THY WORD, THAT I MAY LIVE   497 30
THY SERVANT ACCORDING UNTO THY LOVING MERCY, *   498 17
O LORD, ACCORDING UNTO THY LOVING-KINDNESS   500 08
QUICKEN ME, ACCORDING TO THY JUDGMENTS   500 09
QUICKEN ME ACCORDING TO THY WORD   500 20
O QUICKEN ME, ACCORDING TO THY LOVING-KINDNESS   500 30
UNDERSTANDING ACCORDING TO THY WORD   501 21
DELIVER ME ACCORDING TO THY WORD   501 23
PRAISE HIM ACCORDING TO HIS EXCELLENT GREATNESS   525 24
ACCORDING TO THE FORM HEREAFTER FOLLOWING,   529 22
TRULY CALLED, ACCORDING TO THE WILL OF OUR LORD JESUS   532 31
AND ACCORDING TO THE CANONS OF THIS CHURCH,   532 32
YOUR FAMILIES, ACCORDING TO THE DOCTRINE OF CHRIST   533 26
WHO, ACCORDING TO THE CANONS OF THE CHURCH, MAY HAVE   533 31
IS GIVEN GRACE ACCORDING TO THE MEASURE OF THE GIFT   537 32
LIETH IN YOU, ACCORDING TO YOUR BOUNDEN DUTY, TO   540 17
UNTO YOU, ACCORDING TO THE RULE OF THE SAME   541 06
TRULY CALLED, ACCORDING TO THE WILL OF OUR LORD JESUS   541 31
AND ACCORDING TO THE CANONS OF THIS CHURCH,   541 32
THE SAME, ACCORDING TO THE COMMANDMENTS OF GOD   542 14
YOUR FAMILIES, ACCORDING TO THE DOCTRINE OF CHRIST   542 33
WHO, ACCORDING TO THE CANONS OF THE CHURCH, MAY HAVE   543 12
ACCORDING TO THE WILL OF OUR LORD JESUS   554 17
TO ALL MEN, ACCORDING TO OUR ABILITIES AND   588 32

ACCORDING   CONTINUED

TO THEM ACCORDING TO THEIR SEVERAL NECESSITIES   591 03
AND ACCORDING TO THE GREATNESS OF THY POWER, PRESERVE   600 09
BE CALLED ACCORDING TO GOD'S PURPOSE BY HIS   606 11
FRAME HIS LIFE ACCORDING TO THAT LAW, AND THE LIGHT   606 34
MINISTERED ACCORDING TO CHRIST'S ORDINANCE, IN ALL   606 40
MAY BE CHANGED ACCORDING TO THE DIVERSITY OF   609 33
OR ORDERED ACCORDING TO SAID FORM, WE DECREE ALL SUCH   610 35
TO THE POOR, ACCORDING TO HIS ABILITY   611 04
SO IT BE DONE ACCORDING TO THE PROPHET'S TEACHING, IN   611 09

ACCORDINGLY

AND WE FIND ACCORDINGLY, THAT, SEEKING TO KEEP THE   V 24
THEY MAY SET IT FORTH, AND SHOW IT ACCORDINGLY   055 33
ACCORDINGLY, A COMMISSION FOR A REVIEW WAS ISSUED IN   VI 04

ACCOUNT

REMEMBERING THE ACCOUNT THEY SHALL BE CALLED UPON TO   047 19
TO GIVE AN ACCOUNT OF THE SAME TO THE ORDINARY,   R 085 18
LET A MAN SO ACCOUNT OF US, AS OF THE MINISTERS OF   094 03
WHICH WOULD TAKE ACCOUNT OF HIS SERVANTS   221 14
GIVE A STRICT ACCOUNT OF OUR THOUGHTS, WORDS,   588 22
REMEMBERING THE ACCOUNT WHICH WE MUST ONE DAY GIVE,   599 21
DO RECEIVE, AND ACCOUNT THEM CANONICAL   604 13

ACCOUNTABLE

THAT YOU ARE ACCOUNTABLE TO US HERE, AND TO THE CHIEF   569 26

ACCOUNTED

THEM SHOULD BE ACCOUNTED THE GREATEST   149 18
THEM SHOULD BE ACCOUNTED THE GREATEST   250 04
MAN SHALL BE ACCOUNTED OR TAKEN TO BE A LAWFUL   529 20
WE ARE ACCOUNTED RIGHTEOUS BEFORE GOD, ONLY FOR THE   605 06

ACCURSED

BY THE SPIRIT OF GOD CALLETH JESUS ACCURSED   203 20
ARE TO BE HAD ACCURSED THAT PRESUME TO SAY, THAT   606 32

ACCUSATION

HIS HEAD HIS ACCUSATION WRITTEN, THIS IS JESUS THE   137 02
OF HIS ACCUSATION WAS WRITTEN OVER, THE KING OF THE   146 13

ACCUSE

AND THEY BEGAN TO ACCUSE HIM, SAYING, WE FOUND THIS   152 28
THINGS WHEREOF YE ACCUSE HIM   153 25

ACCUSED

BY SIN ARE ACCUSED, BY THY MERCIFUL PARDON MAY BE   062 10
AND WHEN HE WAS ACCUSED OF THE CHIEF PRIESTS AND   135 21
CHIEF PRIESTS ACCUSED HIM OF MANY THINGS   145 08
AND VEHEMENTLY ACCUSED HIM   153 16
CAST DOWN, WHICH ACCUSED THEM BEFORE OUR GOD DAY AND   252 13
AS THE PARTY ACCUSED SHALL BE FOUND CLEAR OF THAT   R 530 27
AS THE PARTY ACCUSED SHALL BE FOUND CLEAR OF THAT   R 537 03
AND THAT THEY BE ACCUSED BY THOSE THAT HAVE KNOWLEDGE   608 20

ACCUSER

FOR THE ACCUSER OF OUR BRETHREN IS CAST DOWN, WHICH   252 12

ACCUSTOMED

AS HATH BEEN ACCUSTOMED, OR AS THE ORDINARY SHALL   R 305 05
MUST OFFER ACCUSTOMED OFFERINGS, WHICH SHALL BE   R 307 07
EXTEND THY ACCUSTOMED GOODNESS TO THIS THY SERVANT   309 28
ENJOY ALL THE ACCUSTOMED TEMPORALITIES APPERTAINING   569 30

ACELDAMA

PROPER TONGUE, ACELDAMA, THAT IS TO SAY, THE FIELD OF   234 17

ACKNOWLEDGE

TO ACKNOWLEDGE AND CONFESS OUR MANIFOLD SINS   005 30
HUMBLY TO ACKNOWLEDGE OUR SINS BEFORE GOD   006 04
WE ACKNOWLEDGE THEE TO BE THE LORD   010 08
WORLD DOTH ACKNOWLEDGE THEE   010 19
I ACKNOWLEDGE ONE BAPTISM FOR THE REMISSION OF SINS   016 19
I ACKNOWLEDGE MY TRANSGRESSIONS, AND MY SIN IS   022 04
TO ACKNOWLEDGE AND CONFESS OUR MANIFOLD SINS   023 05
HUMBLY TO ACKNOWLEDGE OUR SINS BEFORE GOD   023 12
I ACKNOWLEDGE ONE BAPTISM FOR THE REMISSION OF SINS   030 24
WE ACKNOWLEDGE IT THY GOODNESS THAT WE WERE NOT   052 11
FOR I ACKNOWLEDGE MY FAULTS, *   060 15
WHO MEEKLY ACKNOWLEDGE OUR TRANSGRESSIONS, AND TRULY   062 22
I ACKNOWLEDGE ONE BAPTISM FOR THE REMISSION OF SINS   071 21
WE ACKNOWLEDGE AND BEWAIL OUR MANIFOLD SINS AND   075 18
AND ISRAEL ACKNOWLEDGE US NOT   139 22
TO ACKNOWLEDGE THE GLORY OF THE ETERNAL   186 25
ACKNOWLEDGE, WE HUMBLY BESEECH THEE, A SHEEP OF THINE   319 28
3 FOR I ACKNOWLEDGE MY FAULTS, *   403 13
RECEIVE AND ACKNOWLEDGE YOU, THE REV   570 28

ACKNOWLEDGED

AND ALTERABLE, AND SO ACKNOWLEDGED   V 16
5 I ACKNOWLEDGED MY SIN UNTO THEE   377 30

ACKNOWLEDGED   CONTINUED

26 I HAVE ACKNOWLEDGED MY WAYS, AND THOU HEARDEST ME   491 19

ACKNOWLEDGING

SINS AND ACKNOWLEDGING OUR WRETCHEDNESS, MAY OBTAIN   124 15
AND ACKNOWLEDGING YOURSELVES BOUND TO BELIEVE AND TO   296 25
ACKNOWLEDGING OUR MANIFOLD TRANSGRESSIONS OF THY   589 30

ACQUAINTANCE

SOUGHT HIM AMONG THEIR KINSFOLK AND ACQUAINTANCE   110 25
AND ALL HIS ACQUAINTANCE, AND THE WOMEN THAT FOLLOWED   155 19
OF MINE ACQUAINTANCE WERE AFRAID OF ME   376 16
AWAY MINE ACQUAINTANCE FAR FROM ME, *   449 11
HID MINE ACQUAINTANCE OUT OF MY SIGHT   449 34

ACQUAINTED

AND ART ACQUAINTED WITH ALL MY WAYS   514 24

ACT

TO PERFORM EVERY ACT OF SACERDOTAL FUNCTION AMONG THE   569 19

ACTING

AND ACTING AGREEABLY TO THEIR OWN REASON AND   564 13

ACTION

NEITHER BEGIN AN ACTION WITHOUT A PURE INTENTION NOR   594 22

ACTIONS

AND ACTIONS TO HIM WHOM THOU HAST APPOINTED   588 23

ACTS

OF THOSE MIGHTY ACTS, WHEREBY THOU HAST GIVEN UNTO US   147 10
CHAPTER OF THE ACTS OF THE APOSTLES   296 12
12 THROUGH GOD WILL WE DO GREAT ACTS   413 04
EXPRESS THE NOBLE ACTS OF THE LORD, *   473 02
13 THROUGH GOD WE SHALL DO GREAT ACTS   479 30
SHALL SPEAK OF THE MIGHT OF THY MARVELLOUS ACTS   521 05
2 PRAISE HIM IN HIS NOBLE ACTS   525 24
OR THE PRIEST WHO ACTS AS INSTITUTOR, WHO SHALL GO   R 570 06
OR THE PRIEST WHO ACTS AS THE INSTITUTOR, SHALL SAY, R 570 10
OR THE PRIEST WHO ACTS AS THE INSTITUTOR, SHALL JUDGE R 570 21

ACTUAL

BUT ALSO FOR ACTUAL SINS OF MEN   603 16
SINS OF THE WHOLE WORLD, BOTH ORIGINAL AND ACTUAL   609 15

ADAM

FOR AS IN ADAM ALL DIE, *   163 15
FOR AS IN ADAM ALL DIE, EVEN SO IN CHRIST SHALL ALL   328 24
THE FIRST MAN ADAM WAS MADE A LIVING SOUL   329 24
THE LAST ADAM WAS MADE A QUICKENING SPIRIT   329 25
IN THE FOLLOWING OF ADAM, (AS THE PELAGIANS DO VAINLY   604 29
NATURALLY IS ENGENDERED OF THE OFFSPRING OF ADAM   604 31
AFTER THE FALL OF ADAM IS SUCH, THAT HE CANNOT TURN   604 42

ADD

THIS PRAYER, OR MAY ADD OTHERS, AS OCCASION MAY   R 047 05
OR AT HIS DISCRETION ADD OTHER PRAYERS FROM THIS   R 059 29
BY BEING ANXIOUS CAN ADD ONE CUBIT UNTO THE MEASURE   211 19
BY BEING ANXIOUS CAN ADD ONE CUBIT UNTO THE MEASURE   266 17
THE MINISTER SHALL ADD, THE ALMIGHTY GOD, THE FATHER R 281 06
SHALL THE MINISTER ADD, THE LORD BE WITH YOU   R 294 20
SHALL THE MINISTER ADD, O ETERNAL GOD, CREATOR AND   R 303 02
THE MINISTER MAY ADD ONE OR BOTH OF THE FOLLOWING   R 303 13
THE MINISTER SHALL ADD THIS BLESSING   R 304 10
OF HIS WEAKNESS MAY ADD STRENGTH TO HIS FAITH,   310 23

ADDED

IT WAS ADDED BECAUSE OF TRANSGRESSIONS, TILL THE SEED   207 27
THINGS SHALL BE ADDED UNTO YOU   211 32
MUCH PEOPLE WAS ADDED UNTO THE LORD   241 09
WERE THE MORE ADDED TO THE LORD, MULTITUDES BOTH OF   249 25
THINGS SHALL BE ADDED UNTO YOU   266 30
ANOTHER DAY IS ADDED TO OUR LIVES   588 05
HERE MAY BE ADDED ANY SPECIAL PRAYERS   R 592 26
HERE MAY BE ADDED ANY SPECIAL PRAYERS   R 593 17

ADDER

EVEN LIKE THE DEAF ADDER, THAT STOPPETH HER EARS   410 16
13 THOU SHALT GO UPON THE LION AND ADDER   455 21

ADDER'S

ADDER'S POISON IS UNDER THEIR LIPS   516 14

ADDRESS

MINISTER SHALL ADDRESS THEM ON THIS WISE, THE PERSONS R 277 18
MINISTER SHALL ADDRESS THE SICK PERSON ON THE MEANING R 313 15
MAKE TO HIM THE ADDRESS, AS PRESCRIBED IN THIS OFFICE R 574 30

ADMINISTER

IMPARTIALLY ADMINISTER THE LAW IN THE FEAR OF THEE   036 04
IMPARTIALLY ADMINISTER JUSTICE, TO THE PUNISHMENT OF   074 18
AND DULY ADMINISTER THY HOLY SACRAMENTS   074 24
TO ADMINISTER TO ALL SUCH AS SHALL BE RELIGIOUSLY AND   086 29
PRESENT MAY ADMINISTER HOLY BAPTISM, USING THE   R 281 28
AND TO ADMINISTER CONFIRMATION   294 09
AND DULY ADMINISTER THE GODLY DISCIPLINE THEREOF   549 12
FAITHFULLY ADMINISTER THY HOLY SACRAMENTS, AND BY MY   573 21
AND TO ADMINISTER THE HOLY EUCHARIST TO HIS   R 574 25
GOD OF PITY, ADMINISTER TO THEM ACCORDING TO THEIR   591 03
AND THOSE WHO ADMINISTER TO HIM OF THY HEALING GIFTS   597 16

ADMINISTERED

SHOULD BE ADMINISTERED UPON SUNDAYS AND OTHER HOLY   R 273 05
MAY BE ADMINISTERED UPON ANY OTHER DAY   R 273 06
BE PUBLICLY ADMINISTERED IN THE CHURCH   R 321 09

ADMINISTRATION

AND ADMINISTRATION IN THE SAME   039 10
NOW CALLED TO THE LIKE OFFICE AND ADMINISTRATION   531 19
APPERTAINING TO THE ECCLESIASTICAL ADMINISTRATION   R 535 23
TO THIS ADMINISTRATION, WE WILL EXAMINE YOU IN   554 12

ADMINISTRATIONS

OF ADMINISTRATIONS, BUT THE SAME LORD   182 23
OF ADMINISTRATIONS, BUT THE SAME LORD   203 23

ADMIT

THAT CASE OUGHT TO ADMIT THE PENITENT PERSON TO THE   R 085 16
OF THE CHURCH, ADMIT HIM A DEACON, IN SUCH MANNER AND   529 31
BEFORE WE ADMIT AND SEND FORTH THIS PERSON   553 11
BEFORE WE ADMIT YOU TO THIS ADMINISTRATION, WE WILL   554 12

ADMITTED

THOSE WHO ARE ADMITTED INTO THE FELLOWSHIP OF   173 07
SHALL BE ADMITTED AS SPONSORS, IF IT BE DESIRED   R 273 11
SO HE MAY BE ADMITTED TO THE HOLY COMMUNION   R 281 15
SHALL NONE BE ADMITTED TO THE HOLY COMMUNION,   R 299 08
APPROVED AND ADMITTED THEREUNTO BY LAWFUL AUTHORITY   529 17
AND ADMITTED THEREUNTO, ACCORDING TO THE   529 22
NONE SHALL BE ADMITTED A DEACON, PRIEST, OR BISHOP,   529 24
AS COME TO BE ADMITTED DEACONS   530 04
TO BE ADMITTED DEACONS   530 11
OUGHT NOT TO BE ADMITTED TO THAT OFFICE, LET HIM COME   530 24
NOW TO BE ADMITTED TO THE ORDER OF DEACONS, AND TO   531 05
IF HE BE ADMITTED THERETO BY THE BISHOP   533 17
HE MAY BE ADMITTED BY HIS DIOCESAN TO THE ORDER OF   R 535 24
AS COME TO BE ADMITTED PRIESTS   R 536 04
TO BE ADMITTED TO THE ORDER OF PRIESTHOOD   536 11
NOW TO BE ADMITTED TO THE ORDER OF PRIESTS, AND TO   537 11
NOW TO BE ADMITTED TO THE ORDER OF DEACONS (OR   560 27

ADMITTING

EASINESS IN ADMITTING VARIATIONS IN THINGS ONCE   V 25
ON HANDS, AND ADMITTING ANY PERSON TO GOVERNMENT IN   554 09

ADMONISH

SHALL OFTEN ADMONISH THE PEOPLE, THAT THEY DEFER NOT   R 273 03

ADMONISHING

TEACHING AND ADMONISHING ONE ANOTHER IN PSALMS AND   116 12

ADMONITION

FOR OUR ADMONITION, UPON WHOM THE ENDS OF THE WORLD   201 23

ADMONITIONS

WITH A GLAD MIND AND WILL THEIR GODLY ADMONITIONS   533 33
THEIR GODLY ADMONITIONS, AND SUBMITTING YOURSELVES TO   543 14

ADO

NATIONS MAKE MUCH ADO, AND THE KINGDOMS ARE MOVED   398 04

ADOPTION

THY CHILDREN BY ADOPTION AND GRACE, MAY DAILY BE   096 16
THY CHILDREN BY ADOPTION AND GRACE, MAY DAILY BE   104 08
RECEIVE THE ADOPTION OF SONS   104 22
WAITING FOR THE ADOPTION, TO WIT, THE REDEMPTION OF   194 23
THE SPIRIT OF ADOPTION, WHEREBY WE CRY, ABBA, FATHER   200 09
THE SPIRIT OF ADOPTION, WHEREBY WE CRY, ABBA, FATHER   330 22
THEY BE MADE SONS OF GOD BY ADOPTION   606 13
AND OF OUR ADOPTION TO BE THE SONS OF GOD BY THE   608 28

ADORABLE

THINE ADORABLE, TRUE, AND ONLY SON   010 22

ADORATION

AND ADORATION, AS WELL OF IMAGES AS OF RELICS,   607 15

ADORE

O COME, LET US ADORE HIM   R 008 17
O COME, LET US ADORE HIM   R 008 19
O COME, LET US ADORE HIM   R 008 22
O COME, LET US ADORE HIM   R 008 24
O COME, LET US ADORE HIM   R 008 26
O COME, LET US ADORE HIM   R 008 28
O COME, LET US ADORE HIM   R 008 30
O COME, LET US ADORE HIM   R 008 32
O COME, LET US ADORE HIM   R 008 34
ABOVE ALL, WE ADORE THY MERCY IN SENDING THY ONLY SON   591 11

ADORN

IN ALL THINGS MAY ADORN THE DOCTRINE OF GOD OUR   047 28
THY DOCTRINE, AND ADORN THEM WITH INNOCENCY OF LIFE,   531 20
THY DOCTRINE, AND ADORN THEM WITH INNOCENCY OF LIFE,   537 24
THY DOCTRINE, AND ADORN THEM WITH INNOCENCY OF LIFE,   548 03
THY DOCTRINE, AND ADORN HIM WITH INNOCENCY OF LIFE,   553 30

ADORNED

ESTATE CHRIST ADORNED AND BEAUTIFIED WITH HIS   300 13
AS A BRIDE ADORNED FOR HER HUSBAND   567 14

ADULT

THE BAPTISM OF AN ADULT, THERE SHALL BE PRESENT WITH   R 273 22
BE BAPTIZED BE AN ADULT, THE MINISTER SHALL TAKE HIM   R 279 30
THAT EVERY ADULT, THUS BAPTIZED, SHOULD BE CONFIRMED   R 281 13
IN THE CASE OF AN ADULT, THE MINISTER SHALL FIRST ASK   R 281 25

ADULTERER

HIS WORD, AN ADULTERER, OR BE IN MALICE, OR ENVY,   087 32

ADULTERERS

ADULTERERS, OR EVEN AS THIS PUBLICAN   205 26
AGAINST THE ADULTERERS, AND AGAINST FALSE SWEARERS,   232 17
AND HAST BEEN PARTAKER WITH THE ADULTERERS   402 27

ADULTERY

THOU SHALT NOT COMMIT ADULTERY   069 10
NOT COMMIT ADULTERY, THOU SHALT NOT KILL, THOU SHALT   090 25
ADULTERY, FORNICATION, UNCLEANNESS, LASCIVIOUSNESS,   209 20
THOU SHALT NOT COMMIT ADULTERY   287 09
THOU SHALT NOT COMMIT ADULTERY   579 16

ADULTS

IS USED FOR ADULTS, THE MINISTER SHALL ADDRESS THEM   R 277 18
PROVIDED IN THIS OFFICE FOR THE BAPTISM OF ADULTS   R 281 26

ADVANCEMENT

TO THE ADVANCEMENT OF THY GLORY, THE GOOD OF THY   035 12
TENDS TO THE ADVANCEMENT OF TRUE RELIGION AND USEFUL   047 36

ADVANTAGE

ENEMY HAVE NO ADVANTAGE OF HIM   308 27
AND THEREOUT SUCK THEY NO SMALL ADVANTAGE   428 29

ADVENT

OR SAID, ON THE SUNDAYS IN ADVENT   R 008 16
ON THE SUNDAYS IN ADVENT, THE LATTER PORTION THEREOF   R 014 05
FIRST SUNDAY IN ADVENT, THE FIRST SUNDAY IN LENT, AND   R 085 23
OTHER COLLECTS IN ADVENT, UNTIL CHRISTMAS DAY   R 090 20

ADVERSARIES

POWER OF ANY ADVERSARIES, THROUGH THE MIGHT OF JESUS   017 10
OUR ADVERSARIES HAVE TRODDEN DOWN THY SANCTUARY   139 28
AND SETTETH ME UP ABOVE MINE ADVERSARIES   363 03
ME NOT OVER INTO THE WILL OF MINE ADVERSARIES   372 24
MINE ADVERSARIES ARE ALL IN THY SIGHT   423 12
5 THINE ADVERSARIES ROAR IN THE MIDST OF THY   430 12
AND TURNED MY HAND AGAINST THEIR ADVERSARIES   443 09
MADE ALL HIS ADVERSARIES TO REJOICE   452 25
28 LET MINE ADVERSARIES BE CLOTHED WITH SHAME   481 29

ADVERSARY

WHO IS MINE ADVERSARY   144 20
BECAUSE YOUR ADVERSARY THE DEVIL, AS A ROARING LION,   193 04
WITH THINE ADVERSARY QUICKLY, WHILES THOU ART IN THE   198 12
ANY TIME THE ADVERSARY DELIVER THEE TO THE JUDGE, AND   198 13
WAS IT MINE ADVERSARY THAT DID MAGNIFY HIMSELF   407 13
LONG SHALL THE ADVERSARY DO THIS DISHONOUR   430 27
AND LET AN ADVERSARY STAND AT HIS RIGHT HAND   480 14
THAT THE ADVERSARY MAY BE ASHAMED, HAVING NOTHING TO   555 11

ADVERSARY'S

FROM THE ADVERSARY'S HAND, *   473 20

ADVERSITIES

TROUBLES AND ADVERSITIES, WHENSOEVER THEY OPPRESS US   058 18
FROM ALL ADVERSITIES WHICH MAY HAPPEN TO THE BODY,   127 18
US FROM ALL ADVERSITIES, WHO LIVEST AND REIGNEST, ONE   186 28

ADVERSITIES   CONTINUED

AND COMFORTED IN ALL DANGERS AND ADVERSITIES   192 27
FROM ALL ADVERSITIES, AND DEVOUTLY GIVEN TO SERVE   220 18
AND HAST KNOWN MY SOUL IN ADVERSITIES   376 05
TROUBLES AND ADVERSITIES HAST THOU SHOWED ME   426 17
DEFEND US FROM ALL DANGERS AND ADVERSITIES   589 03

ADVERSITY

OR ANY OTHER ADVERSITY   074 33
POWER WE MAY BE DEFENDED AGAINST ALL ADVERSITY   120 19
THAT ARE IN ADVERSITY, *   361 22
LOOK UPON MY ADVERSITY AND MISERY, *   370 20
15 BUT IN MINE ADVERSITY THEY REJOICED, AND GATHERED   382 23
FOR THE YEARS WHEREIN WE HAVE SUFFERED ADVERSITY   454 21
IN TIME OF ADVERSITY, *   458 12
HE SAW THEIR ADVERSITY, *   475 25
CONSIDER MINE ADVERSITY, AND DELIVER ME, *   500 17

ADVERTISE

HE SHALL ADVERTISE HIM, THAT HE PRESUME NOT TO COME   R 085 03

ADVICE

GODLY COUNSEL AND ADVICE, AS MAY TEND TO THE QUIETING   088 08
WITH THE ADVICE OF OUR PRESBYTERS, ARE TO BE   569 36

ADVISE

TIME TO TIME, TO ADVISE THE PEOPLE, WHILST THEY ARE   R 320 21

ADVISEDLY

IN THINGS ONCE ADVISEDLY ESTABLISHED, SHE HATH,   V 26
ADVISEDLY, SOBERLY, AND IN THE FEAR OF   300 18

ADVOCATE

HONOUR OF OUR ADVOCATE AND MEDIATOR, JESUS CHRIST   018 24
HONOUR OF OUR ADVOCATE AND MEDIATOR, JESUS CHRIST   032 23
MEDIATOR AND ADVOCATE, JESUS CHRIST OUR LORD   059 27
OUR MEDIATOR AND ADVOCATE   063 13
CHRIST'S SAKE, OUR ONLY MEDIATOR AND ADVOCATE   075 06
WE HAVE AN ADVOCATE WITH THE FATHER, JESUS   076 22
SUFFER FOR THEE, OUR ONLY MEDIATOR AND ADVOCATE   100 03
OUR ONLY MEDIATOR AND ADVOCATE   336 29

AFAR

PETER FOLLOWED HIM AFAR OFF, EVEN INTO THE PALACE OF   142 34
AND PETER FOLLOWED AFAR OFF   151 08
FROM GALILEE, STOOD AFAR OFF, BEHOLDING THESE THINGS   155 20
AND SEETH ABRAHAM AFAR OFF, AND LAZARUS IN HIS BOSOM   190 12
STANDING AFAR OFF, WOULD NOT LIFT UP SO   205 28
WHICH STOOD AFAR OFF   210 03
MY KINSMEN STOOD AFAR OFF   388 13
HE BEHOLDETH THEM AFAR OFF   514 09

AFFECT

AND AFFECT THEIR HEARTS WITH MORE DEVOTION   564 18

AFFECTING

MOST AFFECTING AND MAJESTIC MANNER, FOR THE   VI 42

AFFECTION

IT WITH PURE AFFECTION, AND TO BRING FORTH THE FRUITS   056 16
SET YOUR AFFECTION ON THINGS ABOVE, NOT ON THINGS ON   164 05
AFFECTION, AND DEVOTION OF MIND, THAT   566 20
IN CONSTANT AFFECTION THOSE WHO, IN HOLY WEDLOCK,   598 25
SOME THE AFFECTION, SOME THE DESIRE, OF THE FLESH,)   604 37

AFFECTIONED

BE KINDLY AFFECTIONED ONE TO ANOTHER WITH BROTHERLY   111 23
KINDLY AFFECTIONED WITH BROTHERLY LOVE   598 29

AFFECTIONS

FROM ALL INORDINATE AND SINFUL AFFECTIONS   054 27
OUR CORRUPT AFFECTIONS WE MAY BE BURIED WITH HIM   161 15
WILLS AND AFFECTIONS OF SINFUL MEN   174 19
WITH THE AFFECTIONS AND LUSTS   209 29
AND CARNAL AFFECTIONS, MAY BE EVERMORE READY TO   246 20
ALL SINFUL AFFECTIONS MAY DIE IN HIM, AND THAT ALL   278 21
WILLS AND AFFECTIONS OF SINFUL MEN   285 26
AND KINDLED AFFECTIONS, WE MAY WORSHIP THEE IN SPIRIT   594 08

AFFIRMED

CONFIDENTLY AFFIRMED, SAYING, OF A TRUTH THIS FELLOW   151 16

AFFIXED

WE HAVE HEREUNTO AFFIXED OUR EPISCOPAL SEAL AND   569 38

AFFLICT

NOT WILLINGLY AFFLICT OR GRIEVE THE CHILDREN OF MEN   045 32

AFFLICTED

THE LORD HATH AFFLICTED ME   004 32
ARE ANY WAYS AFFLICTED, OR DISTRESSED, IN MIND, BODY,   019 05
ARE ANY WAYS AFFLICTED, OR DISTRESSED, IN MIND, BODY,   033 03
THOU HAST AFFLICTED US   040 25
HE WAS AFFLICTED, AND THE ANGEL OF HIS PRESENCE SAVED   139 02
SICK AND THE AFFLICTED, AND THOSE WHO TRAVEL BY LAND   600 06

AFFLICTION

AND GIVE HIM PATIENCE UNDER HIS AFFLICTION   045 18
IN ALL THEIR AFFLICTION HE WAS AFFLICTED, AND THE   139 02
IN THEIR AFFLICTION, AND TO KEEP HIMSELF UNSPOTTED   176 17
IN THEIR AFFLICTION, AND TO KEEP HIMSELF UNSPOTTED   266 08

AFFLICTIONS

AND A HAPPY ISSUE OUT OF ALL THEIR AFFLICTIONS   019 10
AND A HAPPY ISSUE OUT OF ALL THEIR AFFLICTIONS   033 08
THE AFFLICTIONS OF THY PEOPLE   040 32
GRACIOUSLY LOOK UPON OUR AFFLICTIONS   059 10
IN AFFLICTIONS, IN NECESSITIES, IN   126 10
IN ALL OUR AFFLICTIONS, DEFEND US FROM ALL ERROR, AND   183 24
THE SAME AFFLICTIONS ARE ACCOMPLISHED IN YOUR   193 07
ENDURE AFFLICTIONS, DO THE WORK OF AN EVANGELIST,   253 23
BONDS AND AFFLICTIONS ABIDE ME   550 17
GRANT US PATIENCE UNDER OUR AFFLICTIONS   588 30

AFFORD

JUDGE WHETHER IT AFFORD JUST CAUSE TO SUSPEND THE   R 570 22

AFFORDS

OPPORTUNITY IT AFFORDS FOR SPIRITUAL PROFIT   R 313 16

AFFRIGHTED

AND THEY WERE AFFRIGHTED   165 28
AND HE SAITH UNTO THEM, BE NOT AFFRIGHTED   165 29
TERRIFIED AND AFFRIGHTED, AND SUPPOSED THAT THEY HAD   169 30

AFORE

AS I WROTE AFORE IN FEW WORDS, WHEREBY, WHEN YE   108 10
THAT HEWED TIMBER AFORE OUT OF THE THICK TREES,   430 14
WHICH WITHERETH AFORE IT BE GROWN UP   506 32

AFOREHAND

SHE IS COME AFOREHAND TO ANOINT MY BODY TO THE   140 14

AFORETIME

WERE WRITTEN AFORETIME WERE WRITTEN FOR OUR LEARNING,   092 15

AFRAID

AND THEREFORE AM AFRAID TO COME   088 30
AND THEY WERE SORE AFRAID   099 14
HE WAS AFRAID TO GO THITHER   107 19
THOU THEN NOT BE AFRAID OF THE POWER   114 17
BUT IF THOU DO THAT WHICH IS EVIL, BE AFRAID   114 19
HEARD THAT SAYING, HE WAS THE MORE AFRAID   159 11
FOR THEY WERE AFRAID   166 03
YOUR HEART BE TROUBLED, NEITHER LET IT BE AFRAID   182 02
AND BE NOT AFRAID OF THEIR TERROR, NEITHER BE   196 02
OUR CONSCIENCE IS AFRAID, AND GIVING US THOSE GOOD   206 08
LIFT IT UP, BE NOT AFRAID   243 04
AND NONE SHALL MAKE THEM AFRAID   262 17
AND ARE AFRAID AT THY WRATHFUL INDIGNATION   325 26
OF WHOM THEN SHALL I BE AFRAID   326 07
6 I WILL NOT BE AFRAID FOR TEN THOUSANDS OF THE   347 02
THE OVERFLOWINGS OF UNGODLINESS MADE ME AFRAID   359 32
OF WHOM THEN SHALL I BE AFRAID   371 26
LAID AGAINST ME, YET SHALL NOT MY HEART BE AFRAID   371 30
ACQUAINTANCE WERE AFRAID OF ME   376 17
16 BE NOT THOU AFRAID, THOUGH ONE BE MADE RICH,   401 07
6 THEY WERE AFRAID WHERE NO FEAR WAS   405 25
I AM SOMETIME AFRAID, *   408 19
I WILL NOT BE AFRAID WHAT MAN CAN DO UNTO ME   409 05
EARTH SHALL BE AFRAID AT THY TOKENS, *   416 30
THE WATERS SAW THEE, AND WERE AFRAID   434 15
AND MAKE THEM AFRAID WITH THY STORM   445 03
AND ARE AFRAID AT THY WRATHFUL INDIGNATION   453 32
THOU SHALT NOT BE AFRAID FOR ANY TERROR BY NIGHT,   455 05
THE EARTH SAW IT, AND WAS AFRAID   461 05
FOR THEY WERE AFRAID OF THEM   472 14
7 HE WILL NOT BE AFRAID OF ANY EVIL TIDINGS   483 30
REBUKE THAT I AM AFRAID OF   492 17
53 I AM HORRIBLY AFRAID, *   493 16
AND I AM AFRAID OF THY JUDGMENTS   498 09
MAY MAKE US BOTH AFRAID AND ASHAMED TO OFFEND THEE   588 20
WE MAY NEVER BE AFRAID TO DIE   591 30
HE BE SOMETIME AFRAID, HE YET MAY PUT HIS TRUST IN   597 25

AFTERWARD

HE WAS AFTERWARD AN HUNGRED   126 25
SO BAPTIZED BE AFTERWARD BROUGHT TO THE CHURCH, AT   R 281 32
AFTERWARD THEY THAT ARE CHRIST'S AT HIS COMING   328 26
AND AFTERWARD THAT WHICH IS SPIRITUAL   329 27

AGABUS

ONE OF THEM NAMED AGABUS, AND SIGNIFIED BY THE SPIRIT   241 17
ONE OF THEM NAMED AGABUS, AND SIGNIFIED BY THE SPIRIT   246 25

AGAR

WHICH GENDERETH TO BONDAGE, WHICH IS AGAR   131 05
FOR THIS AGAR IS MOUNT SINAI IN ARABIA, AND ANSWERETH   131 05

AGE

SHE WAS OF A GREAT AGE, AND HAD LIVED WITH AN HUSBAND   233 17
SHE HATH ALSO CONCEIVED A SON IN HER OLD AGE   236 26
OF THEIR TENDER AGE THEY CANNOT PERFORM THEM   292 32
COME TO A COMPETENT AGE, AND CAN SAY THE CREED,   R 295 13
SPAN LONG, AND MINE AGE IS EVEN AS NOTHING IN RESPECT   324 23
THE DAYS OF OUR AGE ARE THREESCORE YEARS AND TEN   325 32
SPAN LONG, AND MINE AGE IS EVEN AS NOTHING IN RESPECT   389 18
8 CAST ME NOT AWAY IN THE TIME OF AGE   425 23
O GOD, IN MINE OLD AGE, WHEN I AM GRAY-HEADED, *   426 10
10 THE DAYS OF OUR AGE ARE THREESCORE YEARS AND TEN   454 07
MORE FRUIT IN THEIR AGE, *   456 28
TAKE ME NOT AWAY IN THE MIDST OF MINE AGE   465 29
EXCEPT HE BE OF THE AGE WHICH THE CANON IN THAT CASE   529 25
AND PERFECTNESS OF AGE IN CHRIST, THAT THERE BE NO   540 21
OF THEIR TENDER AGE THEY CANNOT PERFORM THEM   581 32
WHEN THEY COME TO AGE, THEMSELVES ARE BOUND TO   581 34
COME TO A COMPETENT AGE, AND CAN SAY THE CREED, THE   R 582 36
AS WE GROW IN AGE, WE MAY GROW IN GRACE,   588 09

AGED

MAY BE USED WITH AGED AND BED-RIDDEN PERSONS,   R 323 32
100 I AM WISER THAN THE AGED   496 26
CARE FOR ALL AGED PERSONS, AND ALL LITTLE CHILDREN,   600 05

AGES

WHICH IN OTHER AGES WAS NOT MADE KNOWN UNTO THE SONS   108 12
THROUGHOUT ALL AGES, WORLD WITHOUT END   212 24
AND THY DOMINION ENDURETH THROUGHOUT ALL AGES   521 19
THROUGH THE AGES ALL ALONG, THIS MAY BE OUR   544 12
THROUGH THE AGES ALL ALONG, THIS MAY BE OUR   556 20

AGONY

BY THINE AGONY AND BLOODY SWEAT   055 10
AND BEING IN AN AGONY HE PRAYED MORE EARNESTLY   150 21

AGREE

THY HOLY NAME MAY AGREE IN THE TRUTH OF THY HOLY   074 14
DIDST NOT THOU AGREE WITH ME FOR A PENNY   120 08
DID THEIR WITNESS AGREE TOGETHER   143 09
AND THESE THREE AGREE IN ONE   171 03
AGREE WITH THINE ADVERSARY QUICKLY, WHILES THOU ART   198 11

AGREEABLE

THINGS AS ARE AGREEABLE TO THE SAME   173 09
WITH A LIFE AGREEABLE TO THE SAME   541 02
HOLY WORD, OR AGREEABLE TO THE SAME, AS THE MEANS OF   547 10
AS MOST AGREEABLE WITH THE INSTITUTION OF CHRIST   608 32

AGREEABLY

AND ACTING AGREEABLY TO THEIR OWN REASON AND SENSE OF   564 14

AGREED

AND WHEN HE HAD AGREED WITH THE LABOURERS FOR A PENNY   119 17
BUT THEIR WITNESS AGREED NOT TOGETHER   143 05

AGREEMENT

UNTO THAT AGREEMENT IN THE FAITH AND KNOWLEDGE OF   540 19

AGREETH

AND THY SPEECH AGREETH THERETO   143 32

AH

AND SAYING, AH, THOU THAT DESTROYEST THE   146 19

AHAZ

SPAKE AGAIN UNTO AHAZ, SAYING, ASK THEE A SIGN OF THE   235 25
BUT AHAZ SAID, I WILL NOT ASK, NEITHER WILL I TEMPT   235 27

AID

BY THY MIGHTY AID, BE DEFENDED AND COMFORTED IN   192 26
OBTAIN THY MERCIFUL AID AND PROTECTION   259 22
IMMORTAL GOD, THE AID OF ALL WHO NEED, THE HELPER OF   274 09
ALL HEALTH, AND THE AID OF THEM THAT TURN TO THEE FOR   315 14
GRACE AND HEAVENLY AID, AND FILL THE HEARTS WHICH   544 19
GRACE AND HEAVENLY AID, AND FILL THE HEARTS WHICH   556 27

AILETH

5 WHAT AILETH THEE, O THOU SEA, THAT THOU FLEDDEST   485 02

AIM

HER GENERAL AIM IN THESE DIFFERENT REVIEWS AND   V 33

AIR

ALL YE FOWLS OF THE AIR, BLESS YE THE LORD   013 14
PRAY ALSO FOR ALL WHO TRAVEL BY LAND, SEA, OR AIR   048 05
BY WATER, OR BY AIR, ALL WOMEN IN CHILD-BIRTH,   056 31
NOT AS ONE THAT BEATETH THE AIR   119 10
AND THE FOWLS OF THE AIR DEVOURED IT   121 22
BEHOLD THE FOWLS OF THE AIR   266 14
TO MEET THE LORD IN THE AIR   269 09
8 THE FOWLS OF THE AIR, AND THE FISHES OF THE SEA   351 15
OUT WATER, THE AIR THUNDERED, *   434 16
THE FOWLS OF THE AIR, *   440 02
THE FOWLS OF THE AIR HAVE THEIR HABITATION, *   468 17

AISLE

SHALL GO UP THE AISLE OF THE CHURCH, OR CHAPEL, TO   R 563 07

ALABASTER

HAVING AN ALABASTER BOX OF OINTMENT OF SPIKENARD VERY   140 04

ALBEIT

ALBEIT THAT GOOD WORKS, WHICH ARE THE FRUITS OF   605 11

ALEXANDER

THE FATHER OF ALEXANDER AND RUFUS, TO BEAR HIS CROSS   146 06
ALEXANDER THE COPPERSMITH DID ME MUCH EVIL   254 06

ALEXANDRIA

OF JERUSALEM, ALEXANDRIA, AND ANTIOCH, HAVE ERRED   606 42

ALIEN

EVEN AN ALIEN UNTO MY MOTHER'S CHILDREN   422 19

ALIENATED

BEING ALIENATED FROM THE LIFE OF GOD THROUGH THE   216 06

ALIKE

WITH A WHIRLWIND, THE GREEN AND THE BURNING ALIKE   410 28
THE DARKNESS AND LIGHT TO THEE ARE BOTH ALIKE   515 12
OUGHT TO BE MINISTERED TO ALL CHRISTIAN MEN ALIKE   609 12

ALIVE

WHILE HE WAS YET ALIVE, AFTER THREE DAYS I WILL RISE   162 18
BUT ALIVE UNTO GOD THROUGH JESUS CHRIST OUR LORD   163 09
EVEN SO IN CHRIST SHALL ALL BE MADE ALIVE   163 16
A VISION OF ANGELS, WHICH SAID THAT HE WAS ALIVE   167 26
HE SHEWED HIMSELF ALIVE AFTER HIS PASSION BY MANY   177 26
UNTO SIN, BUT ALIVE UNTO GOD THROUGH JESUS CHRIST OUR   197 25
WAS DEAD, AND IS ALIVE AGAIN   202 25
WAS DEAD, AND IS ALIVE AGAIN   203 07
THAT WE WHICH ARE ALIVE AND REMAIN UNTO THE COMING OF   269 03
THEN WE WHICH ARE ALIVE AND REMAIN SHALL BE CAUGHT UP   269 08
EVEN SO IN CHRIST SHALL ALL BE MADE ALIVE   328 24
AND KEEP HIM ALIVE, THAT HE MAY BE BLESSED UPON   391 32
LET THEM GO DOWN ALIVE INTO THE PIT   407 21
2 THEY HAD SWALLOWED US UP ALIVE   504 10
ALONE CANST KEEP ALIVE IN US THE HOLY DESIRES THOU   594 19

ALLEGED

SHALL BE ALLEGED, OR SUSPECTED, THE MINISTER SHALL   R 301 04

ALLEGORY

WHICH THINGS ARE AN ALLEGORY   131 03

ALLELUIA

ALLELUIA   R 008 18
ALLELUIA   R 008 19
ALLELUIA   R 008 23
ALLELUIA   R 008 24
ALLELUIA   R 008 25
ALLELUIA   R 008 26
ALLELUIA   R 008 27
ALLELUIA   R 008 28

ALLOW

AS GOD'S WORD DOTH ALLOW, THEIR MARRIAGE IS NOT   300 30

ALLOWED

OFFENCE BE ALLOWED, PROVIDED THE SUBSTANCE OF THE   V 04
IF ALLOWED SUCH JUST AND FAVOURABLE   V 42
OUGHT TO BE ALLOWED TO ALL HUMAN WRITINGS   YET UPON   V 43
ACCEPTED AND ALLOWED BEFORE GOD   088 29
SAME IS HEREBY ALLOWED FOR WEIGHTY CAUSE   R 336 32
STATES OF LIFE ALLOWED IN THE SCRIPTURES   607 41

ALMIGHTY

LORD GOD ALMIGHTY, WHICH WAS, AND IS, AND IS TO   005 18

ALMIGHTY   CONTINUED

THE FACE OF ALMIGHTY GOD OUR HEAVENLY FATHER   005 32
OUR SINS UNTO ALMIGHTY GOD   006 14
ALMIGHTY AND MOST MERCIFUL FATHER   006 17
ALMIGHTY GOD, THE FATHER OF OUR LORD JESUS CHRIST,   007 06
GOD THE FATHER ALMIGHTY, MAKER OF HEAVEN AND EARTH   015 19
ON THE RIGHT HAND OF GOD THE FATHER ALMIGHTY   015 26
GOD THE FATHER ALMIGHTY, MAKER OF HEAVEN AND EARTH,   015 33
ALMIGHTY AND EVERLASTING GOD, WHO HAST SAFELY   017 13
ALMIGHTY AND EVERLASTING GOD, FROM WHOM COMETH EVERY 018 18
ALMIGHTY GOD, FATHER OF ALL MERCIES, WE, THINE   019 14
ALMIGHTY GOD, WHO HAST GIVEN US GRACE AT THIS TIME   020 01
OUR SINS UNTO ALMIGHTY GOD   023 02
THE FACE OF ALMIGHTY GOD OUR HEAVENLY FATHER   023 07
ALMIGHTY AND MOST MERCIFUL FATHER   023 24
ALMIGHTY GOD, THE FATHER OF OUR LORD JESUS CHRIST,   024 08
THE ALMIGHTY AND MERCIFUL LORD GRANT YOU ABSOLUTION   024 23
HEAVENLY KING, GOD THE FATHER ALMIGHTY   025 26
GOD THE FATHER ALMIGHTY, MAKER OF HEAVEN AND EARTH   029 24
ON THE RIGHT HAND OF GOD THE FATHER ALMIGHTY   029 31
GOD THE FATHER ALMIGHTY, MAKER OF HEAVEN AND EARTH,   030 04
ALMIGHTY GOD, WHOSE KINGDOM IS EVERLASTING AND POWER 032 04
ALMIGHTY AND EVERLASTING GOD, FROM WHOM COMETH EVERY 032 17
ALMIGHTY GOD, FATHER OF ALL MERCIES, WE, THINE   033 12
ALMIGHTY GOD, WHO HAST GIVEN US GRACE AT THIS TIME   034 03
ALMIGHTY GOD, WHO SITTEST IN THE THRONE JUDGING   035 31
ALMIGHTY GOD, WHO HAST GIVEN US THIS GOOD LAND FOR   036 09
ALMIGHTY AND EVERLASTING GOD, WHO BY THY HOLY SPIRIT 036 26
ALMIGHTY GOD, WHOSE COMPASSIONS FAIL NOT, AND WHOSE   038 14
ALMIGHTY GOD, OUR HEAVENLY FATHER, WHO HAST PURCHASED 038 25
ALMIGHTY GOD, THE GIVER OF ALL GOOD GIFTS, WHO OF THY 039 07
O ALMIGHTY GOD, LOOK MERCIFULLY UPON THE WORLD WHICH 039 17
ALMIGHTY GOD, WHO HAST BLESSED THE EARTH THAT IT   039 24
ALMIGHTY AND MOST MERCIFUL FATHER, WE HUMBLY BESEECH 040 23
O ALMIGHTY GOD, THE SUPREME GOVERNOR OF ALL THINGS,   041 26
THINE ALMIGHTY ARM TO STRENGTHEN AND PROTECT   041 26
TAKE INTO THY ALMIGHTY AND MOST GRACIOUS PROTECTION   042 05
ALMIGHTY GOD, OUR HEAVENLY FATHER, IN WHOSE HANDS ARE 042 14
ALMIGHTY GOD, WE BESEECH THEE, WITH THY GRACIOUS   042 22
ALMIGHTY GOD, OUR HEAVENLY FATHER, WHO HAST COMMITTED 042 30
ALMIGHTY GOD, WHO HAST CREATED MAN IN THINE OWN   044 09
ALMIGHTY GOD, OUR HEAVENLY FATHER, WHO DECLAREST THY 044 17
ALMIGHTY GOD, OUR HEAVENLY FATHER, GUIDE, WE BESEECH 044 27
COMMEND TO THY ALMIGHTY PROTECTION, THY SERVANT,   046 10
BESEECH THEE, ALMIGHTY GOD, THAT THE WORDS WHICH WE   049 17
ALMIGHTY GOD, THE FOUNTAIN OF ALL WISDOM, WHO KNOWEST 049 29
ALMIGHTY GOD, WHO HAST PROMISED TO HEAR THE PETITIONS 050 06
THANKS TO ALMIGHTY GOD FOR HER SAFE DELIVERANCE   R 051 04
O ALMIGHTY GOD, WE GIVE THEE HUMBLE THANKS FOR THAT   051 05
O ALMIGHTY GOD, WHO ART A STRONG TOWER OF DEFENCE   052 07
ALMIGHTY GOD AND HEAVENLY FATHER, WE GIVE THEE HUMBLE 053 10
BESEECHING ALMIGHTY GOD TO ACCOMPANY WITH HIS   VI 40
ALMIGHTY GOD, UNTO WHOM ALL HEARTS ARE OPEN, ALL   067 16
MAY SAY, O ALMIGHTY LORD, AND EVERLASTING GOD,   070 06
GOD THE FATHER ALMIGHTY, MAKER OF HEAVEN AND EARTH,   071 02
ALMIGHTY AND EVERLIVING GOD, WHO BY THY HOLY APOSTLE 074 06
CONFESSION TO ALMIGHTY GOD, DEVOUTLY KNEELING   075 13
ALMIGHTY GOD, FATHER OF OUR LORD JESUS CHRIST,   075 17
SAY, ALMIGHTY GOD, OUR HEAVENLY FATHER,   076 02
HOLY FATHER, ALMIGHTY, EVERLASTING GOD   076 33
BE TO THEE, ALMIGHTY GOD, OUR HEAVENLY FATHER, FOR   080 06
OF THY ALMIGHTY GOODNESS, VOUCHSAFE TO BLESS AND   081 09
O FATHER ALMIGHTY, WORLD WITHOUT END   081 34
BE TO THEE, ALMIGHTY GOD, AND ENDING WITH THESE   R 083 09
THE PRIEST SAY, ALMIGHTY AND EVERLIVING GOD, WE MOST 083 16
HEAVENLY KING, GOD THE FATHER ALMIGHTY   084 06
BLESSING OF GOD ALMIGHTY, THE FATHER, THE SON,   084 21
THANKS TO ALMIGHTY GOD, OUR HEAVENLY FATHER, FOR THAT 086 35
YOURSELVES TO ALMIGHTY GOD, WITH FULL PURPOSE OF   087 20
PETITIONS UNTO ALMIGHTY GOD, OUR HEAVENLY FATHER   089 21
ALMIGHTY GOD, GIVE US GRACE THAT WE MAY CAST AWAY THE 090 11
ALMIGHTY GOD, WHO HAST GIVEN US THY ONLY-BEGOTTEN SON 096 13
O ALMIGHTY GOD, WHO OUT OF THE MOUTHS OF BABES AND   102 21
O ALMIGHTY GOD, WHO HAST GIVEN US THY ONLY-BEGOTTEN SON 104 05
ALMIGHTY GOD, WHO MADEST THY BLESSED SON TO BE   105 19
ALMIGHTY GOD, WHO HAST POURED UPON US THE NEW LIGHT   106 25
ALMIGHTY AND EVERLASTING GOD, WHO DOST GOVERN ALL   111 10
ALMIGHTY AND EVERLASTING GOD, MERCIFULLY LOOK UPON   112 26
ALMIGHTY AND EVERLASTING GOD, WHO HATEST NOTHING THAT 124 11
ALMIGHTY GOD, WHO SEEST THAT WE HAVE NO POWER OF   127 15
BESEECH THEE, ALMIGHTY GOD, LOOK UPON THE HEARTY   128 25
BESEECH THEE, ALMIGHTY GOD, THAT WE, WHO FOR OUR EVIL 130 24
BESEECH THEE, ALMIGHTY GOD, MERCIFULLY TO LOOK UPON   132 18
ALMIGHTY AND EVERLASTING GOD, WHO, OF THY TENDER LOVE 134 05
ALMIGHTY GOD, WHOSE MOST DEAR SON WENT NOT UP TO JOY 138 04
ALMIGHTY FATHER, WHOSE DEAR SON, ON THE NIGHT BEFORE 152 07
ALMIGHTY GOD, WE BESEECH THEE GRACIOUSLY TO BEHOLD   156 21
ALMIGHTY AND EVERLASTING GOD, BY WHOSE SPIRIT THE   156 27
ALMIGHTY GOD, WHO THROUGH THINE ONLY-BEGOTTEN SON   163 22
BESEECH THEE, ALMIGHTY GOD, THAT WE WHO CELEBRATE   168 19
ALMIGHTY FATHER, WHO HAST GIVEN THINE ONLY SON TO DIE 170 19
ALMIGHTY GOD, WHO HAST GIVEN THINE ONLY SON TO BE   171 28
ALMIGHTY GOD, WHO SHOWEST TO THEM THAT ARE IN ERROR   173 04
O ALMIGHTY GOD, WHO ALONE CANST ORDER THE UNRULY   174 18
BESEECH THEE, ALMIGHTY GOD, THAT LIKE AS WE DO   177 14
ALMIGHTY AND MOST MERCIFUL GOD, GRANT, WE BESEECH   182 15
BESEECH THEE, ALMIGHTY GOD, THY HOLY SPIRIT INTO OUR 183 22
ALMIGHTY AND EVERLASTING GOD, WHO HAST GIVEN UNTO US 186 23
LORD GOD ALMIGHTY, WHICH WAS, AND IS, AND IS TO   187 23
DECLAREST THY ALMIGHTY POWER CHIEFLY IN SHOWING MERCY 204 22
ALMIGHTY AND EVERLASTING GOD, WHO ART ALWAYS MORE   206 04
ALMIGHTY AND MERCIFUL GOD, OF WHOSE ONLY GIFT IT   207 12
ALMIGHTY AND EVERLASTING GOD, GIVE UNTO US THE   209 08
O ALMIGHTY AND MOST MERCIFUL GOD, OF THY BOUNTIFUL   217 17
ALMIGHTY GOD, WHO DIDST GIVE SUCH GRACE UNTO THY HOLY 226 18

ALMIGHTY   CONTINUED

ALMIGHTY AND EVERLIVING GOD, WHO, FOR THE GREATER   228 05
ALMIGHTY AND EVERLIVING GOD, WE HUMBLY BESEECH THY   231 28
O ALMIGHTY GOD, WHO INTO THE PLACE OF THE TRAITOR   233 31
O ALMIGHTY GOD, WHO HAST INSTRUCTED THY HOLY CHURCH   237 05
O ALMIGHTY GOD, WHOM TRULY TO KNOW IS EVERLASTING   238 29
O LORD GOD ALMIGHTY, WHO DIDST ENDUE THY HOLY APOSTLE 240 28
ALMIGHTY GOD, BY WHOSE PROVIDENCE THY SERVANT JOHN   242 07
O ALMIGHTY GOD, WHO BY THY SON JESUS CHRIST DIDST   244 22
O ALMIGHTY AND EVERLASTING GOD, WHO DIDST GIVE TO   249 14
O ALMIGHTY GOD, WHO BY THY BLESSED SON DIDST CALL   250 20
ALMIGHTY GOD, WHO DIDST INSPIRE THY SERVANT SAINT   253 16
O ALMIGHTY GOD, WHO HAST BUILT THY CHURCH UPON THE   254 27
O ALMIGHTY GOD, WHO HAST KNIT TOGETHER THINE ELECT IN 256 05
ALMIGHTY AND EVERLASTING GOD, WHO DOST ENKINDLE THE   258 04
O ALMIGHTY GOD, WHO HAST CALLED US TO FAITH IN THEE, 258 11
O ALMIGHTY GOD, WHO HAST COMMITTED TO THE HANDS OF   260 19
ALMIGHTY GOD, LORD OF HEAVEN AND EARTH   261 29
MINISTER SAY, ALMIGHTY AND IMMORTAL GOD, THE AID OF   274 09
AND SAY, ALMIGHTY AND EVERLASTING GOD, HEAVENLY   276 07
HOLY FATHER, ALMIGHTY, EVERLASTING GOD, FOR THAT THY 279 08
THANKS UNTO ALMIGHTY GOD FOR THESE BENEFITS   280 15
SHALL ADD, THE ALMIGHTY GOD, THE FATHER OF OUR LORD   281 07
GOD THE FATHER ALMIGHTY, MAKER OF HEAVEN AND EARTH   284 13
ON THE RIGHT HAND OF GOD THE FATHER ALMIGHTY   284 20
O ALMIGHTY GOD, WHO ALONE CANST ORDER THE UNRULY   285 25
O ALMIGHTY GOD, WHO HAST BUILT THY CHURCH UPON THE   290 19
ALMIGHTY AND EVERLIVING GOD, WHO HAST VOUCHSAFED TO   297 14
THE BISHOP SAY, ALMIGHTY AND EVERLIVING GOD, WHO   298 13
O ALMIGHTY LORD, AND EVERLASTING GOD, VOUCHSAFE,   298 26
BLESSING OF GOD ALMIGHTY, THE FATHER, THE SON,   299 03
O ALMIGHTY GOD, CREATOR OF MANKIND, WHO ONLY ART THE 303 14
IT HATH PLEASED ALMIGHTY GOD, OF HIS GOODNESS, TO   305 11
O ALMIGHTY GOD, WE GIVE THEE HUMBLE THANKS FOR THAT   306 24
HEAR US, ALMIGHTY AND MOST MERCIFUL GOD AND SAVIOUR   309 27
THE ALMIGHTY LORD, WHO IS A MOST STRONG TOWER TO   314 15
O ALMIGHTY GOD, WHO ART THE GIVER OF ALL HEALTH,   315 13
O ALMIGHTY GOD, WITH WHOM DO LIVE THE SPIRITS OF JUST 317 11
THE ALMIGHTY AND MERCIFUL LORD GRANT THEE PARDON AND 319 15
GOD THE FATHER ALMIGHTY WHO CREATED THEE   319 20
IT SHALL PLEASE ALMIGHTY GOD TO CALL THEM, THE   R 321 05
ALMIGHTY, EVERLIVING GOD, MAKER OF MANKIND, WHO DOST 321 18
O ALMIGHTY FATHER, LORD OF HEAVEN AND EARTH, WE   323 12
THE ALMIGHTY AND MERCIFUL LORD GRANT YOU ABSOLUTION   323 19
SHALL SAY, UNTO ALMIGHTY GOD WE COMMEND THE SOUL OF   333 14
ALMIGHTY GOD, WITH WHOM DO LIVE THE SPIRITS OF THOSE 334 19
O ALMIGHTY GOD, THE GOD OF THE SPIRITS OF ALL FLESH, 335 25
ALMIGHTY AND EVERLIVING GOD, WE YIELD UNTO THEE MOST 336 16
SHALL SAY, UNTO ALMIGHTY GOD WE COMMEND THE SOUL OF   337 09
ALMIGHTY AND MERCIFUL FATHER, WHO DOST GRANT TO   340 29
ALMIGHTY GOD, FATHER OF MERCIES AND GIVER OF ALL   342 09
MAY ALMIGHTY GOD, THE FATHER, THE SON, AND THE HOLY   342 14
14 WHEN THE ALMIGHTY SCATTERED KINGS FOR THEIR SAKE, 420 09
SHALL ABIDE UNDER THE SHADOW OF THE ALMIGHTY   454 29
A VOW UNTO THE ALMIGHTY GOD OF JACOB   508 07
ALMIGHTY GOD, WHO BY THY DIVINE PROVIDENCE HAST   531 14
ALMIGHTY GOD, GIVER OF ALL GOOD THINGS, WHO OF THY   534 30
BLESSING OF GOD ALMIGHTY, THE FATHER, THE SON,   535 16
ALMIGHTY GOD, GIVER OF ALL GOOD THINGS, WHO BY THY   537 20
THE BISHOP SAY, ALMIGHTY GOD, WHO HATH GIVEN YOU THIS 543 18
AND SAY, ALMIGHTY GOD, AND HEAVENLY FATHER,   545 12
BLESSING OF GOD ALMIGHTY, THE FATHER, THE SON,   547 17
ALMIGHTY GOD, GIVER OF ALL GOOD THINGS, WHO BY THY   547 31
ALMIGHTY GOD, WHO BY THE SON JESUS CHRIST DIDST GIVE 549 07
OUR PRAYERS TO ALMIGHTY GOD, BEFORE WE ADMIT AND SEND 553 10
ALMIGHTY GOD, GIVER OF ALL GOOD THINGS, WHO BY THY   553 26
SHALL SAY, ALMIGHTY GOD, OUR HEAVENLY FATHER, WHO   555 28
ALMIGHTY GOD, AND MOST MERCIFUL FATHER, WHO, OF THINE 557 20
BLESSING OF GOD ALMIGHTY, THE FATHER, THE SON,   559 20
BLESSING OF GOD ALMIGHTY, THE FATHER, THE SON,   568 16
UNTO THEE, O ALMIGHTY FATHER, IN HIS PREVAILING NAME 571 13
O ALMIGHTY GOD, WHO HAST BUILT THY CHURCH UPON THE   574 03
GOD THE FATHER ALMIGHTY, MAKER OF HEAVEN AND EARTH   577 28
ON THE RIGHT HAND OF GOD THE FATHER ALMIGHTY   578 04
ALMIGHTY AND EVERLASTING GOD, IN WHOM WE LIVE AND   587 19
ALMIGHTY AND EVERLASTING GOD, WHO HAST SAFELY   592 19
O ALMIGHTY GOD, WHO POUREST OUT ON ALL WHO DESIRE IT, 594 04
ALMIGHTY GOD, WHO ALONE GAVEST US THE BREATH OF LIFE, 594 18
ALMIGHTY GOD, HEAVENLY FATHER, WHO HAST BLESSED US   596 24
ALMIGHTY GOD, WE ENTRUST ALL WHO ARE DEAR TO US TO   597 09
ALMIGHTY GOD OUR HEAVENLY FATHER, WE BESEECH THEE   597 21
ALMIGHTY GOD, WE REMEMBER THIS DAY BEFORE THEE THY   598 06
ALMIGHTY GOD, OUR HEAVENLY FATHER, WHO SETTEST THE   598 19
O GOD, ALMIGHTY AND MERCIFUL, WHO HEALEST THOSE THAT 599 03
ALMIGHTY GOD, WHOSE LOVING HAND HATH GIVEN US ALL   599 19

ALMOST

AND ALMOST ALL THINGS ARE BY THE LAW PURGED WITH   147 25
SABBATH DAY CAME ALMOST THE WHOLE CITY TOGETHER TO   260 26
MY FEET WERE ALMOST GONE, *   428 12
15 YEA, AND I HAD ALMOST SAID EVEN AS THEY   429 06
87 THEY HAD ALMOST MADE AN END OF ME UPON EARTH   495 31

ALMS

SHALL RECEIVE THE ALMS FOR THE POOR, AND OTHER   R 073 28
AND WHEN THE ALMS AND OBLATIONS ARE BEING RECEIVED R 073 34
TO ACCEPT OUR (ALMS AND) OBLATIONS, AND TO RECEIVE   074 09
RELIEVED WITH THE ALMS OF THE PARISHIONERS, OR   533 20
LIBERALLY TO GIVE ALMS TO THE POOR, ACCORDING TO HIS 611 04

ALOES

SMELL OF MYRRH, ALOES, AND CASSIA   396 32

ALONE

MADE BY THE PRIEST ALONE, STANDING   R 007 03
MADE BY THE PRIEST ALONE, STANDING   R 024 07
ADMINISTER THE LAW IN THE FEAR OF THEE ALONE   036 05
LORD GOD, WHO ALONE SPREADEST OUT THE HEAVENS, AND   042 03
WHICH IT IS THINE ALONE TO GIVE   045 27
O ETERNAL GOD, WHO ALONE SPREADEST OUT THE HEAVENS,   046 08
FORASMUCH AS THOU ALONE BRINGEST LIGHT OUT OF   046 26
WHO ALONE MAKEST MEN TO BE OF ONE MIND IN A   052 17
WHEREBY ALONE WE OBTAIN REMISSION OF OUR SINS,   086 33
NOT LIVE BY BREAD ALONE, BUT BY EVERY WORD THAT   126 29
I HAVE TRODDEN THE WINEPRESS ALONE   138 17
AND JESUS SAID, LET HER ALONE   140 10
AND GAVE HIM TO DRINK, SAYING, LET ALONE   146 33
ALMIGHTY GOD, WHO ALONE CANST ORDER THE UNRULY WILLS   174 18
EVERY MAN TO HIS OWN, AND SHALL LEAVE ME ALONE   177 06
AND YET I AM NOT ALONE, BECAUSE THE FATHER IS WITH   177 07
WHEN THE VOICE WAS PAST, JESUS WAS FOUND ALONE   249 09
ALMIGHTY GOD, WHO ALONE CANST ORDER THE UNRULY WILLS   285 25
CONCLUDING PRAYER ALONE, AS IT STANDS AMONG THE   R 305 04
HE MUST LET THAT ALONE FOR EVER   400 21
THOU ART GOD ALONE   447 24
THAT SITTETH ALONE UPON THE HOUSETOP   464 24
FOR THAT WILL AND ABILITY IS GIVEN OF GOD ALONE   540 31
ALMIGHTY GOD, WHO ALONE GAVEST US THE BREATH OF LIFE,   594 18
OF LIFE, AND ALONE CANST KEEP ALIVE IN US THE HOLY   594 19
NONE OTHER SATISFACTION FOR SIN, BUT THAT ALONE   609 16

ALONG

THE AGES ALL ALONG, THIS MAY BE OUR ENDLESS SONG   544 12
THE AGES ALL ALONG, THIS MAY BE OUR ENDLESS SONG   556 20

ALOUD

TO THEE ALL ANGELS CRY ALOUD   010 11
MULTITUDE CRYING ALOUD BEGAN TO DESIRE HIM TO DO AS   145 17

ALREADY

IF IT HATH NOT ALREADY BEEN SAID, SHALL FOLLOW THE   R 016 28
IF IT HATH NOT ALREADY BEEN SAID, SHALL FOLLOW THE   R 030 33
THE PRINCIPLES ALREADY LAID DOWN, IT CANNOT BUT BE   VI 02
LITANY HATH BEEN ALREADY SAID, THE MINISTER MAY PASS   R 061 19
THAT HE WAS DEAD ALREADY, THEY BRAKE NOT HIS LEGS   161 03
NOT IS CONDEMNED ALREADY, BECAUSE HE HATH NOT   185 04
PERSON) BEEN ALREADY BAPTIZED, OR NO   273 13
IF THOU ART NOT ALREADY BAPTIZED, N   282 13
THE LORD HATH DONE GREAT THINGS FOR US ALREADY   505 13

ALTAR

WHOM YE SLEW BETWEEN THE TEMPLE AND THE ALTAR   100 25
THE PORCH AND THE ALTAR, AND LET THEM SAY, SPARE THY   125 03
THY GIFT TO THE ALTAR, AND THERE REMEMBEREST THAT THY   198 08
GIFT BEFORE THE ALTAR, AND GO THY WAY   198 10
I WILL GO UNTO THE ALTAR OF GOD   310 02
I MAY GO UNTO THE ALTAR OF GOD, EVEN UNTO THE GOD OF   310 13
AND SO WILL I GO TO THINE ALTAR   371 09
I MAY GO UNTO THE ALTAR OF GOD, EVEN UNTO THE GOD OF   394 12
SHALL THEY OFFER YOUNG BULLOCKS UPON THINE ALTAR   404 17
EVEN UNTO THE HORNS OF THE ALTAR   489 24
WHO SERVE AT THE ALTAR SHOULD LIVE OF THE THINGS   569 28
SHOULD LIVE OF THE THINGS BELONGING TO THE ALTAR   569 29
WHO SHALL GO WITHIN THE RAILS OF THE ALTAR   R 570 06
AND LEFT OF THE ALTAR, WITHOUT THE RAILS   R 570 08
THE RAILS OF THE ALTAR, AND PRESENT HIM THE BIBLE,   R 571 23
KNEEL AT THE ALTAR, TO PRESENT HIS SUPPLICATION FOR   R 573 09
IN THY HOUSE, AND TO SERVE AT THY HOLY ALTAR   573 14

ALTARS

EVEN THY ALTARS, O LORD OF HOSTS, MY KING AND MY GOD   445 18

ALTER

I NOT BREAK, NOR ALTER THE THING THAT IS GONE OUT OF   452 09

ALTERABLE

AND ALTERABLE,   V 15

ALTERATIONS

CHANGES AND ALTERATIONS SHOULD BE MADE THEREIN,   V 18
OCCASIONAL ALTERATIONS AND AMENDMENTS IN HER FORMS OF   V 23
TO MAKE SUCH ALTERATIONS IN SOME PARTICULARS, AS IN   V 29
REVIEWS AND ALTERATIONS HATH BEEN, AS SHE FURTHER   V 33
THAT FURTHER ALTERATIONS WOULD IN TIME BE FOUND   VI 03
TO THOSE ALTERATIONS IN THE LITURGY WHICH BECAME   VI 16
WHILE THESE ALTERATIONS WERE IN REVIEW BEFORE THE   VI 22
SUCH OTHER ALTERATIONS AND AMENDMENTS THEREIN AS   VI 26
DIFFERENT ALTERATIONS AND AMENDMENTS   VI 28

ALTERED

MAY BE ALTERED, ABRIDGED, ENLARGED, AMENDED, OR   V 07
COUNTENANCE WAS ALTERED, AND HIS RAIMENT WAS WHITE   248 26

ALTERNATELY

PSALM ALTERNATELY, THE BISHOP ONE VERSE AND THE   R 563 09

ALTHOUGH

AND ALTHOUGH, ACCORDING TO HER JUDGMENT, THERE BE NOT   V 39
AND ALTHOUGH WE OUGHT, AT ALL TIMES, HUMBLY TO   006 03
AND ALTHOUGH WE OUGHT, AT ALL TIMES, HUMBLY TO   023 11
AND ALTHOUGH WE ARE UNWORTHY, THROUGH OUR MANIFOLD   081 28
SAID UNTO HIM, ALTHOUGH ALL SHALL BE OFFENDED,   141 22
SOUL'S HEALTH, ALTHOUGH HE DO NOT RECEIVE THE   R 323 31
ALTHOUGH THE LAW GIVEN FROM GOD BY MOSES, AS TOUCHING   604 19
AND ALTHOUGH THERE IS NO CONDEMNATION FOR THEM THAT   604 38
WE THE REST, ALTHOUGH BAPTIZED, AND BORN AGAIN IN   605 35
ALTHOUGH THE CHURCH BE A WITNESS AND A   607 06
ALTHOUGH IN THE VISIBLE CHURCH THE EVIL BE EVER   608 08
AND PROMISE, ALTHOUGH THEY BE MINISTERED BY EVIL MEN   608 17
A LIVELY FAITH, ALTHOUGH THEY DO CARNALLY AND VISIBLY   609 04

ALTOGETHER

MAN LIVING IS ALTOGETHER VANITY   324 24
THEY ARE ALTOGETHER BECOME ABOMINABLE   356 19
OF THE LORD ARE TRUE, AND RIGHTEOUS ALTOGETHER   364 02
MAN LIVING IS ALTOGETHER VANITY   389 19
THEY ARE ALTOGETHER BECOME ABOMINABLE   405 19
THEY ARE ALTOGETHER LIGHTER THAN VANITY ITSELF   414 17
LET US MAKE HAVOC OF THEM ALTOGETHER   430 22
BUT THOU, O LORD, KNOWEST IT ALTOGETHER   514 26

ALWAY

OF MY HEART, BE ALWAY ACCEPTABLE IN THY SIGHT,   021 22
REJOICE IN THE LORD ALWAY   095 13
AS SORROWFUL, YET ALWAY REJOICING   126 19
THY CHURCH, BEING ALWAY PRESERVED FROM FALSE   234 02
GRACE TO USE THEM ALWAY TO THY HONOUR AND GLORY   240 31
I AM WITH YOU ALWAY, EVEN UNTO THE END OF THE   275 31
THE POOR SHALL NOT ALWAY BE FORGOTTEN   352 28
5 HIS WAYS ARE ALWAY GRIEVOUS   353 13
HAVE SET THE LORD ALWAY BEFORE ME   358 06
OF MY HEART, BE ALWAY ACCEPTABLE IN THY SIGHT,   364 14
I WILL ALWAY GIVE THANKS UNTO THE LORD   380 03
LET THEM SAY ALWAY, BLESSED BE THE LORD, WHO   383 20
AND THY TRUTH ALWAY PRESERVE ME   391 09
THY SALVATION, SAY ALWAY, THE LORD BE PRAISED   391 22
THAT HE SHALL LIVE ALWAY, *   400 22
THEY ARE ALWAY BEFORE ME   402 07
10 I WILL ALWAY GIVE THANKS UNTO THEE FOR THAT THOU   405 07
8 SO WILL I ALWAY SING PRAISE UNTO THY NAME, *   413 22
YOUR TRUST IN HIM ALWAY, YE PEOPLE   414 13
THY SALVATION SAY ALWAY, THE LORD BE PRAISED   424 28
WHEREUNTO I MAY ALWAY RESORT   425 08
MY PRAISE SHALL BE ALWAY OF THEE   425 18
PATIENTLY ABIDE ALWAY, *   426 02
I AM ALWAY BY THEE   429 22
AND WILL ALWAY BE SHOWING FORTH THY PRAISE FROM   440 33
THEY WILL BE ALWAY PRAISING THEE   445 20
MY SONG SHALL BE ALWAY OF THE LOVING-KINDNESS OF THE   450 04
9 HE WILL NOT ALWAY BE CHIDING   466 23
8 HE HATH BEEN ALWAY MINDFUL OF HIS COVENANT AND   470 18
ARE THEY THAT ALWAY KEEP JUDGMENT, *   473 04
14 LET THEM ALWAY BE BEFORE THE LORD, *   480 30
GIRDLE THAT HE IS ALWAY GIRDED WITHAL   481 09
THAT IT HATH ALWAY UNTO THY JUDGMENTS   491 07
44 SO SHALL I ALWAY KEEP THY LAW   492 28
109 MY SOUL IS ALWAY IN MY HAND   497 15
THY STATUTES ALWAY, *   497 21
I AM WITH YOU ALWAY, EVEN UNTO THE END OF THE   552 14
OF HIS HEART, BE ALWAY ACCEPTABLE IN THY SIGHT,   572 23

ALWAYS

OF MY HEART, BE ALWAYS ACCEPTABLE IN THY SIGHT,   003 20
THAT THEY MAY ALWAYS INCLINE TO THY WILL, AND WALK IN   017 33
THEE WE MAY ALWAYS PROVE OURSELVES A PEOPLE   036 11
AND WILL ALWAYS DECLARE THY LOVING-KINDNESS   051 26
THY PROPERTY IS ALWAYS TO HAVE MERCY   062 18
WHOSE PROPERTY IS ALWAYS TO HAVE MERCY   082 17
BE AMONGST YOU, AND REMAIN WITH YOU ALWAYS   084 23
THAT WE SHOULD ALWAYS REMEMBER THE EXCEEDING GREAT   086 12
WHICH HE SHALL ALWAYS DO UPON THE SUNDAY, OR SOME   R 086 25
AS YE HAVE ALWAYS OBEYED, NOT AS IN MY PRESENCE ONLY,   105 31
NATURE WE CANNOT ALWAYS STAND UPRIGHT   114 06
THE POOR WITH YOU ALWAYS, AND WHENSOEVER YE WILL YE   140 12
BUT ME YE HAVE NOT ALWAYS   140 13
THAT WE MAY ALWAYS SERVE THEE IN PURENESS OF LIVING   170 22
GRACE THAT WE MAY ALWAYS MOST THANKFULLY RECEIVE THAT   171 30
TO THINK AND DO ALWAYS SUCH THINGS AS ARE RIGHT   200 30
WHO ART ALWAYS MORE READY TO HEAR THAN WE TO   206 04
THY GRACE MAY ALWAYS PREVENT AND FOLLOW US, AND MAKE   213 14
I THANK MY GOD ALWAYS ON YOUR BEHALF, FOR THE GRACE   214 28
GIVING THANKS ALWAYS FOR ALL THINGS UNTO GOD AND THE   217 30
PRAYING ALWAYS WITH ALL PRAYER AND SUPPLICATION IN   219 19
OF YOU, ALWAYS IN EVERY PRAYER OF MINE FOR YOU ALL   220 23
PRAYING ALWAYS FOR YOU, SINCE WE HEARD OF   223 23
HAVE THESE THINGS ALWAYS IN REMEMBRANCE   248 13
THY HOLY ANGELS ALWAYS DO THEE SERVICE IN HEAVEN, SO,   251 29
THEIR ANGELS DO ALWAYS BEHOLD THE FACE OF MY FATHER   253 11
GIVE THANKS ALWAYS FOR ALL THINGS UNTO GOD AND THE   267 11
TO THINK AND DO ALWAYS SUCH THINGS AS ARE RIGHT   287 27
THEY MAY BE ALWAYS IN READINESS TO DIE, WHENSOEVER IT   R 321 04
ALWAYS ABOUNDING IN THE WORK OF THE LORD,   330 14
THEIR ANGELS DO ALWAYS BEHOLD THE FACE OF MY FATHER   339 31
LITTLE ONES DO ALWAYS BEHOLD IN HEAVEN   340 25
THAT THEY, HAVING ALWAYS THE TESTIMONY OF A GOOD   535 05
AND REMAIN WITH YOU ALWAYS   535 17
HAVE ALWAYS THEREFORE PRINTED IN YOUR REMEMBRANCE,   540 05
DILIGENCE ALWAYS SO TO MINISTER THE DOCTRINE AND   542 11

ALWAYS   CONTINUED

AND REMAIN WITH YOU ALWAYS   547 18
AND REMAIN WITH YOU ALWAYS   559 21
AND REMAIN WITH YOU ALWAYS   568 17
WHICH HE SHALL ALWAYS PRONOUNCE,) THE WARDENS,   R 574 27
BUT MAY ALWAYS GO TO OUR REST IN PEACE, CHARITY,   590 17
GRANT US GRACE ALWAYS TO LIVE IN SUCH A STATE THAT WE 591 29
THE FLESH LUSTETH ALWAYS CONTRARY TO THE SPIRIT   604 33

AMALEK

7 GEBAL, AND AMMON, AND AMALEK   444 18

AMAZED

AND WHEN THEY SAW HIM, THEY WERE AMAZED   110 32
BEGAN TO BE SORE AMAZED, AND TO BE VERY HEAVY   141 30
FOR THEY TREMBLED AND WERE AMAZED   166 02
AND THEY WERE ALL AMAZED AND MARVELLED, SAYING CNE TO 180 29
HEARD HIM WERE AMAZED, AND SAID   231 05

AMBASSADOR

WHICH I AM AN AMBASSADOR IN BONDS   219 24

AMEN

AND WORSHIPPED GOD, SAYING, AMEN   256 31
AMEN   257 03
AMEN   306 07
AMEN, AND AMEN   453 12
AMEN, AND AMEN   453 13
IN THE NAME OF GOD, AMEN   552 28
AMEN   558 15
THEREFORE I SAY, AMEN, SO BE IT   581 06

AMEND

THY HOLY SPIRIT TO AMEND OUR LIVES ACCORDING TO THY   057 16
AMEND YOUR LIVES, AND BE IN PERFECT CHARITY WITH ALL   086 02
WHEREFORE THEN DO YE NOT REPENT AND AMEND   088 31
HE OF THEM THE HOUR WHEN HE BEGAN TO AMEND   220 07
ARISE AGAIN, AND AMEND OUR LIVES   606 02

AMENDED

AMENDED, OR OTHERWISE DISPOSED OF, AS MAY   V 07
REPENTED AND AMENDED HIS FORMER EVIL LIFE, THAT THE R 085 05

AMENDMENT

REPENTANCE, AMENDMENT OF LIFE, AND THE GRACE AND   024 25
PURPOSE OF AMENDMENT OF LIFE   087 21
REPENTANCE, AMENDMENT OF LIFE, AND THE GRACE AND   323 21

AMENDMENTS

AND AMENDMENTS IN HER FORMS OF PUBLIC WORSHIP   V 23
AND AMENDMENTS THEREIN AS MIGHT BE DEEMED EXPEDIENT   VI 26
ALL THE DIFFERENT ALTERATIONS AND AMENDMENTS   VI 29

AMENDS

AND TO MAKE AMENDS FOR THAT WHEREIN HE HIMSELF   R 085 13
THAT HE MAKE AMENDS TO THE UTTERMOST OF HIS   R 313 23

AMERICA

UNITED STATES OF AMERICA, AND A SECURITY FOR SUCH AS   042 09
EPISCOPAL CHURCH IN THE UNITED STATES OF AMERICA   552 32

AMERICAN

THESE AMERICAN STATES BECAME INDEPENDENT WITH RESPECT VI 07

AMIABLE

O HOW AMIABLE ARE THY DWELLINGS, *   445 11

AMIDST

FAINT OF HEART AMIDST THE SORROWS AND DIFFICULTIES OF 316 19

AMISS

IN ANY THING IT IS AMISS, REFORM IT   037 19
BUT THIS MAN HATH DONE NOTHING AMISS   155 06
MARK WHAT IS DONE AMISS, *   328 08
WE HAVE DONE AMISS, AND DEALT WICKEDLY   473 12
MARK WHAT IS DONE AMISS, *   507 13
REFORM WHATEVER IS AMISS IN THE TEMPER AND   590 12

AMMON

7 GEBAL, AND AMMON, AND AMALEK   444 18

AMONGST

LATELY RAISED UP AMONGST US   052 21
HOLY GHOST, BE AMONGST YOU, AND REMAIN WITH YOU   084 22
HOLY GHOST, BE AMONGST YOU, AND REMAIN WITH YOU   535 17
HOLY GHOST, BE AMONGST YOU, AND REMAIN WITH YOU   547 18
HOLY GHOST, BE AMONGST YOU, AND REMAIN WITH YOU   559 21
HOLY GHOST, BE AMONGST YOU, AND REMAIN WITH YOU   568 17

AMORITES

11 SIHON, KING OF THE AMORITES   510 24
19 SIHON, KING OF THE AMORITES   512 20

ANABAPTISTS

AS CERTAIN ANABAPTISTS DO FALSELY BOAST   611 02

ANANIAS

WAS A CERTAIN DISCIPLE AT DAMASCUS, NAMED ANANIAS   230 14
AND TO HIM SAID THE LORD IN A VISION, ANANIAS   230 15
A MAN NAMED ANANIAS COMING IN, AND PUTTING HIS HAND   230 20
THEN ANANIAS ANSWERED, LORD, I HAVE HEARD BY MANY OF   230 21
AND ANANIAS WENT HIS WAY, AND ENTERED INTO THE HCUSE   230 29

ANCIENT

SCRIPTURE AND ANCIENT AUTHORS, THAT FROM THE   529 11
AND THE ANCIENT CANONS COMMAND, THAT WE SHOULD NCT BE 554 08

ANDREW

OF HIS DISCIPLES, ANDREW, SIMON PETER'S BROTHER,   131 32
OF HIS DISCIPLES, ANDREW, SIMON PETER'S BROTHER,   225 28
APOSTLE SAINT ANDREW, THAT HE READILY OBEYED THE   226 19
CALLED PETER, AND ANDREW HIS BROTHER, CASTING A NET   227 25

ANEW

REGENERATE AND BORN ANEW OF WATER AND OF THE HOLY   273 31

ANGEL

LO, THE ANGEL OF THE LORD CAME UPON THEM,   099 12
AND THE ANGEL SAID UNTO THEM, FEAR NOT   099 14
THERE WAS WITH THE ANGEL A MULTITUDE OF THE HEAVENLY   099 20
THE ANGEL OF THE LORD APPEARETH TO JOSEPH IN A DREAM, 103 16
BEHOLD, THE ANGEL OF THE LORD APPEARED UNTO HIM IN A   105 03
SLEEP DID AS THE ANGEL OF THE LORD HAD BIDDEN HIM,   105 13
SO NAMED OF THE ANGEL BEFORE HE WAS CONCEIVED IN THE   106 21
BEHOLD, AN ANGEL OF THE LORD APPEARETH IN A   107 12
AND THE ANGEL OF HIS PRESENCE SAVED THEM   139 02
THERE APPEARED AN ANGEL UNTO HIM FROM HEAVEN,   150 20
THE MESSAGE OF AN ANGEL, SO BY HIS CROSS AND PASSICN   235 20
SIXTH MONTH THE ANGEL GABRIEL WAS SENT FROM GOD UNTO   236 05
AND THE ANGEL CAME IN UNTO HER, AND SAID, HAIL,   236 09
AND THE ANGEL SAID UNTO HER, FEAR NOT, MARY   236 13
SAID MARY UNTO THE ANGEL, HOW SHALL THIS BE, SEEING I 236 20
AND THE ANGEL ANSWERED AND SAID UNTO HER, THE HOLY   236 21
AND THE ANGEL DEPARTED FROM HER   236 30
BEHOLD, THE ANGEL OF THE LORD CAME UPON HIM,   245 12
AND THE ANGEL SAID UNTO HIM, GIRD THYSELF, AND BIND   245 16
NOT THAT IT WAS TRUE WHICH WAS DONE BY THE ANGEL   245 20
AND FORTHWITH THE ANGEL DEPARTED FROM HIM   245 25
LORD HATH SENT HIS ANGEL, AND HATH DELIVERED ME CUT   245 27
AND I SAW ANOTHER ANGEL ASCENDING FROM THE EAST,   256 16
7 THE ANGEL OF THE LORD TARRIETH ROUND ABOUT THEM   380 15
AND THE ANGEL OF THE LORD SCATTERING THEM   381 28
AND LET THE ANGEL OF THE LORD PURSUE THEM   381 29

ANGELS

TO THEE ALL ANGELS CRY ALOUD   010 11
O YE ANGELS OF THE LORD, BLESS YE THE LORD   012 02
THE LORD, YE ANGELS OF HIS, YE THAT EXCEL IN   029 12
THEREFORE WITH ANGELS AND ARCHANGELS, AND WITH ALL   077 04
THEREFORE WITH ANGELS, ETC   077 19
THEREFORE WITH ANGELS, ETC   078 04
THEREFORE WITH ANGELS, ETC   079 04
THEREFORE WITH ANGELS AND ARCHANGELS, AND WITH ALL   079 28
BETTER THAN THE ANGELS, AS HE HATH BY INHERITANCE   096 30
UNTO WHICH OF THE ANGELS SAID HE AT ANY TIME, THCU   097 02
AND LET ALL THE ANGELS OF GOD WORSHIP HIM   097 06
WHO MAKETH HIS ANGELS SPIRITS, AND HIS MINISTERS A   097 07
AND OF THE ANGELS HE SAITH, WHO MAKETH HIS ANGELS   097 07
TO PASS, AS THE ANGELS WERE GONE AWAY FROM THEM INTO   106 07
HE SHALL SEND HIS ANGELS WITH A GREAT SOUND OF A   118 21
OF MEN AND OF ANGELS, AND HAVE NOT CHARITY, I AM   122 21
HE SHALL GIVE HIS ANGELS CHARGE CONCERNING THEE   126 33
AND, BEHOLD, ANGELS CAME AND MINISTERED UNTO   127 11
ANGELS AND AUTHORITIES AND POWERS BEING MADE SUBJECT   162 03
SEEN A VISION OF ANGELS, WHICH SAID THAT HE WAS   167 25
CARRIED BY THE ANGELS INTO ABRAHAM'S BOSOM   190 09
PRESENCE OF THE ANGELS OF GOD OVER ONE SINNER THAT   193 33
WAS ORDAINED BY ANGELS IN THE HAND OF A MEDIATOR   207 29
THE SERVICES OF ANGELS AND MEN IN A WONDERFUL   251 28
AS THY HOLY ANGELS ALWAYS DO THEE SERVICE IN   251 29
MICHAEL AND HIS ANGELS FOUGHT AGAINST THE DRAGON   252 03
FOUGHT AND HIS ANGELS, AND PREVAILED NOT   252 05
AND HIS ANGELS WERE CAST OUT WITH HIM   252 09
IN HEAVEN THEIR ANGELS DO ALWAYS BEHOLD THE FACE OF   253 11
VOICE TO THE FOUR ANGELS, TO WHOM IT WAS GIVEN TO   256 16
AND ALL THE ANGELS STOOD ROUND ABOUT THE THRONE,   256 29
AND ALL THE HOLY ANGELS WITH HIM, THEN SHALL HE SIT   258 29
THE LORD, YE ANGELS OF HIS, YE THAT EXCEL IN   312 28
NOR LIFE, NOR ANGELS, NOR PRINCIPALITIES, NOR POWERS, 331 10
IN HEAVEN THEIR ANGELS DO ALWAYS BEHOLD THE FACE OF   339 31
WHOSE FACE THE ANGELS OF THY LITTLE ONES DO ALWAYS   340 24
LOWER THAN THE ANGELS, *   351 09
GOD ARE TWENTY THOUSAND, EVEN THOUSANDS OF ANGELS   420 17
AND SENT EVIL ANGELS AMONG THEM   438 07
HE SHALL GIVE HIS ANGELS CHARGE OVER THEE, *   455 17
THE LORD, YE ANGELS OF HIS, YE THAT EXCEL IN   467 15
4 HE MAKETH HIS ANGELS WINDS, *   467 32

ANGELS   CONTINUED

ALL YE ANGELS OF HIS   524 07

ANGELS'

SO MAN DID EAT ANGELS' FOOD   436 20

ANGER

SLOW TO ANGER, AND OF GREAT KINDNESS,   004 22
BUT SO TURN THINE ANGER FROM US, WHO MEEKLY   062 22
SLOW TO ANGER, AND OF GREAT KINDNESS, AND   124 25
TREAD THEM IN MINE ANGER, AND TRAMPLE THEM IN MY   138 18
THE PEOPLE IN MINE ANGER, AND MAKE THEM DRUNK IN MY   138 26
AND WRATH, AND ANGER, AND CLAMOUR, AND EVIL SPEAKING,   216 27
NATION I WILL ANGER YOU   227 18
PUT ME NOT TO REBUKE, O LORD, IN THINE ANGER   387 21
OF HIS WRATH, ANGER, DISPLEASURE, AND TROUBLE   438 07
AND LET THINE ANGER CEASE FROM US   446 15
KEEPETH HE HIS ANGER FOR EVER   466 24
PROVOKED HIM TO ANGER WITH THEIR OWN INVENTIONS   474 27

ANGERED

16 THEY ANGERED MOSES ALSO IN THE TENTS, *   473 33
32 THEY ANGERED HIM ALSO AT THE WATERS OF STRIFE,   474 33

ANGRY

AND BE NOT ANGRY WITH US FOR EVER   054 17
OF THE HOUSE BEING ANGRY SAID TO HIS SERVANT, GO OUT   192 13
THAT WHOSOEVER IS ANGRY WITH HIS BROTHER WITHOUT A   198 04
AND HE WAS ANGRY, AND WOULD NOT GO IN   202 31
BE YE ANGRY, AND SIN NOT   216 18
FOR WHEN THOU ART ANGRY ALL OUR DAYS ARE GONE   325 30
LEST HE BE ANGRY, AND SO YE PERISH FROM THE   346 21
WHO MAY STAND IN THY SIGHT WHEN THOU ART ANGRY   433 03
HOW LONG WILT THOU BE ANGRY   440 09
LONG WILT THOU BE ANGRY WITH THY PEOPLE THAT PRAYETH   441 10
FOR WHEN THOU ART ANGRY ALL OUR DAYS ARE GONE   454 04

ANGUISH

NO MORE THE ANGUISH, FOR JOY THAT A MAN IS BORN INTO   174 12

ANIMA

ANIMA MEA, MAY BE SUNG OR SAID THE GLORIA   R 025 18

ANNA

AND THERE WAS ONE ANNA, A PROPHETESS, THE DAUGHTER OF   233 16

ANNUNCIATION

ON THE PURIFICATION, AND THE ANNUNCIATION   R 008 31
ANNUNCIATION, AND TRANSFIGURATION   R 077 28

ANOINT

THOU FASTEST, ANOINT THINE HEAD, AND WASH THY FACE   125 13
COME AFOREHAND TO ANOINT MY BODY TO THE BURYING   140 14
MIGHT COME AND ANOINT HIM   165 20
I ANOINT THEE WITH OIL (OR I LAY MY HAND UPON THEE),   320 15
ANOINT AND CHEER OUR SOILED FACE WITH THE ABUNDANCE   544 06
ANOINT AND CHEER OUR SOILED FACE WITH THE ABUNDANCE   556 14

ANOINTED

THY GOD, HATH ANOINTED THEE WITH THE OIL OF GLADNESS   097 12
THE LORD HATH ANOINTED ME TO PREACH GOOD TIDINGS UNTO   106 31
HOW GOD ANOINTED JESUS OF NAZARETH WITH THE HOLY   166 19
HOW GOD ANOINTED JESUS OF NAZARETH WITH THE HOLY   184 06
BECAUSE HE HATH ANOINTED ME TO PREACH THE GOSPEL TO   261 17
THOU HAST ANOINTED MY HEAD WITH OIL, AND MY CUP SHALL   338 27
AGAINST THE LORD, AND AGAINST HIS ANOINTED   345 29
UNTO DAVID HIS ANOINTED, AND UNTO HIS SEED FOR   363 08
HELPETH HIS ANOINTED, AND WILL HEAR HIM FROM HIS HOLY   364 26
THOU HAST ANOINTED MY HEAD WITH OIL, AND MY CUP SHALL   368 20
AND HE IS THE WHOLESOME DEFENCE OF HIS ANOINTED   373 26
THY GOD, HATH ANOINTED THEE WITH THE OIL OF GLADNESS   396 30
AND LOOK UPON THE FACE OF THINE ANOINTED   445 30
HOLY OIL HAVE I ANOINTED HIM   451 16
FORSAKEN THINE ANOINTED, *   452 16
AND SLANDERED THE FOOTSTEPS OF THINE ANOINTED   453 11
FOR I AM ANOINTED WITH FRESH OIL   456 20
TOUCH NOT MINE ANOINTED, *   471 02
TURN NOT AWAY THE FACE OF THINE ANOINTED   508 24
I HAVE ORDAINED A LANTERN FOR MINE ANOINTED   509 09

ANOINTING

THROUGH ANOINTING OR LAYING ON OF HANDS, THE MINISTER R 320 06
THOU THE ANOINTING SPIRIT ART, WHO DOST THY SEVENFOLD   543 33
THE SOUL'S ANOINTING FROM ABOVE   544 24
THOU THE ANOINTING SPIRIT ART, WHO DOST THY SEVENFOLD   556 08
THE SOUL'S ANOINTING FROM ABOVE   557 03

ANOTHER

AND IN BROTHERLY CHARITY ONE TOWARDS ANOTHER   048 04
OWE NO MAN ANY THING, BUT TO LOVE ONE ANOTHER   090 23
HE THAT LOVETH ANOTHER HATH FULFILLED THE LAW   090 24
ONE TOWARD ANOTHER ACCORDING TO CHRIST JESUS   092 19
RECEIVE YE ONE ANOTHER, AS CHRIST ALSO RECEIVED US TO   092 22

ANOTHER   CONTINUED

OR DO WE LOOK FOR ANOTHER   094 18
ONE WITH ANOTHER, AND THE BLOOD OF JESUS CHRIST HIS   101 27
SAID ONE TO ANOTHER, LET US NOW GO EVEN UNTO   106 08
OWN COUNTRY ANOTHER WAY   109 25
AND EVERY ONE MEMBERS ONE OF ANOTHER   110 16
ONE TO ANOTHER WITH BROTHERLY LOVE   111 24
IN HONOUR PREFERRING ONE ANOTHER   111 25
BE OF THE SAME MIND ONE TOWARD ANOTHER   111 31
AND TO ANOTHER, COME, AND HE COMETH   115 14
FORBEARING ONE ANOTHER, AND FORGIVING ONE ANOTHER, IF   116 05
FORGIVING ONE ANOTHER, IF ANY MAN HAVE A QUARREL   116 06
ADMONISHING ONE ANOTHER IN PSALMS AND HYMNS AND   116 12
RIGHT HAND, AND ANOTHER ON THE LEFT   137 05
AND ANOTHER SAID, IS IT I   141 04
I WILL BUILD ANOTHER MADE WITHOUT HANDS   143 08
A LITTLE WHILE ANOTHER SAW HIM, AND SAID, THOU ART   151 14
ONE HOUR AFTER ANOTHER CONFIDENTLY AFFIRMED, SAYING,   151 16
US CONSIDER ONE ANOTHER TO PROVOKE UNTO LOVE AND TO   158 24
BUT EXHORTING ONE ANOTHER   158 27
AND AGAIN ANOTHER SCRIPTURE SAITH, THEY SHALL LOOK ON   161 09
YE HAVE ONE TO ANOTHER, AS YE WALK, AND ARE SAD   167 11
THEY SAID ONE TO ANOTHER, DID NOT OUR HEART BURN   168 09
HE SAITH ALSO IN ANOTHER PSALM, THOU SHALT NOT SUFFER   169 13
ONE TO ANOTHER WITHOUT GRUDGING   179 15
THE SAME ONE TO ANOTHER, AS GOOD STEWARDS OF THE   179 17
SAYING ONE TO ANOTHER, BEHOLD, ARE NOT ALL THESE   180 29
SHALL GIVE YOU ANOTHER COMFORTER, THAT HE MAY ABIDE   181 10
TO ANOTHER THE WORD OF KNOWLEDGE BY THE SAME SPIRIT   182 28
TO ANOTHER FAITH BY THE SAME SPIRIT   182 29
TO ANOTHER THE GIFTS OF HEALING BY THE SAME SPIRIT   182 29
TO ANOTHER THE WORKING OF MIRACLES   182 30
TO ANOTHER DISCERNING OF SPIRITS   182 31
TO ANOTHER PROPHECY   182 31
TO ANOTHER DIVERS KINDS OF TONGUES   182 32
TO ANOTHER THE INTERPRETATION OF TONGUES   182 32
LET US LOVE ONE ANOTHER   189 08
WE OUGHT ALSO TO LOVE ONE ANOTHER   189 16
IF WE LOVE ONE ANOTHER, GOD DWELLETH IN US, AND HIS   189 17
AND LOVE ONE ANOTHER, AS HE GAVE US COMMANDMENT   191 31
AND ANOTHER SAID, I HAVE BOUGHT FIVE YOKE OF OXEN,   192 09
AND ANOTHER SAID, I HAVE MARRIED A WIFE, AND   192 10
SUBJECT ONE TO ANOTHER, AND BE CLOTHED WITH HUMILITY   192 30
ONE OF ANOTHER, LOVE AS BRETHREN, BE PITIFUL, BE   195 20
TO ANOTHER THE WORD OF KNOWLEDGE BY THE SAME SPIRIT   203 28
TO ANOTHER THE GIFTS OF HEALING BY THE SAME SPIRIT   203 29
TO ANOTHER FAITH BY THE SAME SPIRIT   203 29
TO ANOTHER THE WORKING OF MIRACLES   203 30
TO ANOTHER PROPHECY   203 31
TO ANOTHER DISCERNING OF SPIRITS   203 31
TO ANOTHER DIVERS KINDS OF TONGUES   203 32
TO ANOTHER THE INTERPRETATION OF TONGUES   203 32
SHALL NOT LEAVE IN THEE ONE STONE UPON ANOTHER   204 14
FORBEARING ONE ANOTHER IN LOVE   213 21
FOR WE ARE MEMBERS ONE OF ANOTHER   216 18
YE KIND ONE TO ANOTHER, TENDER-HEARTED, FORGIVING ONE   216 29
FORGIVING ONE ANOTHER, EVEN AS GOD FOR CHRIST'S SAKE   216 30
ONE TO ANOTHER IN THE FEAR OF GOD   217 32
ONE TO HIS FARM, ANOTHER TO HIS MERCHANDISE   218 11
BISHOPRICK LET ANOTHER TAKE   234 20
THAT YE LOVE ONE ANOTHER, AS I HAVE LOVED YOU   241 25
THINGS I COMMAND YOU, THAT YE LOVE ONE ANOTHER   255 12
AND I SAW ANOTHER ANGEL ASCENDING FROM THE EAST,   256 14
THEM ONE FROM ANOTHER, AS A SHEPHERD DIVIDETH HIS   258 31
ONE TO ANOTHER IN THE FEAR OF GOD   267 13
COMFORT ONE ANOTHER WITH THESE WORDS   269 11
AFTER ANOTHER HYMN, THE MINISTER SHALL PROCEED WITH   R 292 02
FROM ONE GENERATION TO ANOTHER   325 14
OF FLESH OF MEN, ANOTHER FLESH OF BEASTS, ANOTHER OF   329 12
FLESH OF BEASTS, ANOTHER OF FISHES, AND ANOTHER OF   329 13
OF FISHES, AND ANOTHER OF BIRDS   329 13
AND THE GLORY OF THE TERRESTRIAL IS ANOTHER   329 16
OF THE SUN, AND ANOTHER GLORY OF THE MOON, AND   329 16
OF THE MOON, AND ANOTHER GLORY OF THE STARS   329 17
DIFFERETH FROM ANOTHER STAR IN GLORY   329 18
THAT RUN AFTER ANOTHER GOD *   357 27
2 ONE DAY TELLETH ANOTHER   363 15
AND ONE NIGHT CERTIFIETH ANOTHER   363 16
ONE DEEP CALLETH ANOTHER, BECAUSE OF THE NOISE OF THY   393 18
TO BE REMEMBERED FROM ONE GENERATION TO ANOTHER   397 22
ONE WITH ANOTHER   400 09
SHALL ENDURE FROM ONE GENERATION TO ANOTHER   400 28
WICKEDNESS TO ANOTHER, *   423 30
FROM ONE GENERATION TO ANOTHER   427 07
HE PUTTETH DOWN ONE, AND SETTETH UP ANOTHER   432 13
OUT THY WRATH FROM ONE GENERATION TO ANOTHER   446 17
SHOWING THY TRUTH FROM ONE GENERATION TO ANOTHER   450 06
SET UP THY THRONE FROM ONE GENERATION TO ANOTHER   450 12
FROM ONE GENERATION TO ANOTHER   453 19
ONE NATION TO ANOTHER, *   470 28
ONE KINGDOM TO ANOTHER PEOPLE   470 29
AND LET ANOTHER TAKE HIS OFFICE   480 17
ALSO REMAINETH FROM ONE GENERATION TO ANOTHER   496 05
FROM ONE GENERATION TO ANOTHER   510 29
THY WORKS UNTO ANOTHER, *   520 33
AND ANOTHER BISHOP SHALL READ THE EPISTLE   R 549 16
THEN ANOTHER BISHOP SHALL READ THE GOSPEL   R 551 12
THE BISHOP ONE VERSE AND THE CLERGY ANOTHER   R 563 09
THAT ANOTHER DAY IS ADDED TO OUR LIVES   588 05
THAT IT BE REPUGNANT TO ANOTHER   607 06
OUGHT TO HAVE AMONG THEMSELVES ONE TO ANOTHER   608 35

ANOTHER'S

TO WASH ONE ANOTHER'S FEET   156 17

ANSWER

THE KING SHALL ANSWER AND SAY UNTO THEM, VERILY I SAY	073	02
WE MAY GIVE AN ANSWER TO THEM THAT SENT US	095	27
WIST THEY WHAT TO ANSWER HIM	142	09
YE WILL NOT ANSWER ME, NOR LET ME GO	151	32
BUT JESUS GAVE HIM NO ANSWER	159	13
BUT THE ANSWER OF A GOOD CONSCIENCE TOWARD	161	31
THEY COULD NOT ANSWER HIM AGAIN TO THESE THINGS	214	07
MAN WAS ABLE TO ANSWER HIM A WORD, NEITHER DURST ANY	215	22
THE RIGHTEOUS ANSWER HIM, SAYING, LORD, WHEN SAW WE	259	09
THE KING SHALL ANSWER AND SAY UNTO THEM, VERILY I SAY	259	14
FROM WITHIN SHALL ANSWER AND SAY, TROUBLE ME NOT	262	30
IF THEY ANSWER, NO	R 273	28
AND THE ANSWER THERETO), THE DECLARATION, WE RECEIVE	R 282	05
ONE SHALL AUDIBLY ANSWER, I DO	R 296	29
EVERY ONE SHALL ANSWER, I DO	R 297	05
AS YE WILL ANSWER AT THE DREADFUL DAY OF	300	24
THE MAN SHALL ANSWER, I WILL	R 301	11
THE WOMAN SHALL ANSWER, I WILL	R 301	20
THOU SHALT ANSWER FOR ME, O LORD MY GOD	388	22
THE SINGERS ALSO AND TRUMPETERS SHALL MAKE ANSWER	448	26
SO SHALL I MAKE ANSWER UNTO MY BLASPHEMERS	492	24
THE PRIEST SHALL ANSWER, I HAVE INQUIRED CONCERNING	R 530	17
THE PRIEST SHALL ANSWER, I HAVE INQUIRED CONCERNING	R 536	18
YE SHALL ANSWER PLAINLY TO THESE THINGS, WHICH WE,	541	27
SHALL ANSWER BY VERSES, AS FOLLOWETH	R 556	05
AND CAN ANSWER TO THE OTHER QUESTIONS OF THIS SHORT	R 583	02

ANSWERED

JESUS ANSWERED AND SAID UNTO THEM, GO AND SHEW JOHN	094	19
AND HE ANSWERED, NO	095	26
JOHN ANSWERED THEM, SAYING, I BAPTIZE WITH WATER	096	02
THE CENTURION ANSWERED AND SAID, LORD, I AM NOT	115	10
BUT HE ANSWERED ONE OF THEM, AND SAID, FRIEND,	120	07
BUT HE ANSWERED AND SAID, IT IS WRITTEN, MAN SHALL	126	28
BUT HE ANSWERED HER NOT A WORD	128	11
BUT HE ANSWERED AND SAID, I AM NOT SENT BUT UNTO THE	128	13
BUT HE ANSWERED AND SAID, IT IS NOT MEET TO TAKE THE	128	16
THEN JESUS ANSWERED AND SAID UNTO HER, O WOMAN, GREAT	128	19
PHILIP ANSWERED HIM, TWO HUNDRED PENNYWORTH OF BREAD	131	30
THEN ANSWERED THE JEWS, AND SAID UNTO HIM, SAY WE NOT	133	12
JESUS ANSWERED, I HAVE NOT A DEVIL	133	14
JESUS ANSWERED, IF I HONOUR MYSELF, MY HONOUR IS	133	23
AND ELDERS, HE ANSWERED NOTHING	135	22
AND HE ANSWERED HIM TO NEVER A WORD	135	24
THE GOVERNOR ANSWERED AND SAID UNTO THEM, WHETHER OF	136	02
THEN ANSWERED ALL THE PEOPLE, AND SAID, HIS BLOOD BE	136	12
AND HE ANSWERED AND SAID UNTO THEM, IT IS ONE OF THE	141	04
AND JESUS ANSWERED AND SAID UNTO THEM, ARE YE COME	142	24
HIS PEACE, AND ANSWERED NOTHING	143	12
BUT HE ANSWERED NOTHING	145	09
BUT JESUS YET ANSWERED NOTHING	145	11
BUT PILATE ANSWERED THEM, SAYING, WILL YE THAT I	145	18
AND PILATE ANSWERED AND SAID AGAIN UNTO THEM, WHAT	145	22
AND JESUS ANSWERED AND SAID, SUFFER YE THUS FAR	150	34
AND HE ANSWERED HIM AND SAID, THOU SAYEST IT	153	02
BUT HE ANSWERED NOTHING	153	14
JESUS ANSWERED AND SAID UNTO HIM, WHAT I DO THOU	156	03
JESUS ANSWERED HIM, IF I WASH THEE NOT, THOU HAST NO	156	06
THE JEWS ANSWERED HIM, WE HAVE A LAW, AND BY OUR LAW	159	08
JESUS ANSWERED, THOU COULDEST HAVE NO POWER AT ALL	159	16
CHIEF PRIESTS ANSWERED, WE HAVE NO KING BUT CAESAR	159	29
PILATE ANSWERED, WHAT I HAVE WRITTEN I HAVE WRITTEN	160	08
JESUS ANSWERED THEM, DO YE NOW BELIEVE	177	04
JESUS ANSWERED AND SAID UNTO HIM, IF A MAN LOVE ME,	181	24
THEN ANSWERED PETER, CAN ANY MAN FORBID WATER,	184	26
JESUS ANSWERED AND SAID UNTO HIM, VERILY, VERILY, I	188	04
JESUS ANSWERED, VERILY, VERILY, I SAY UNTO THEE,	188	09
NICODEMUS ANSWERED AND SAID UNTO HIM, HOW CAN THESE	188	17
JESUS ANSWERED AND SAID UNTO HIM, ART THOU A MASTER	188	18
HIS DISCIPLES ANSWERED HIM, FROM WHENCE CAN A MAN	199	14
THOU HAST ANSWERED RIGHT	208	18
AND ANSWERED THEM, SAYING, WHICH OF YOU SHALL HAVE AN	214	04
PHILIP ANSWERED HIM, TWO HUNDRED PENNYWORTH OF BREAD	225	26
AND THOMAS ANSWERED AND SAID UNTO HIM, MY LORD AND MY	229	06
THEN ANANIAS ANSWERED, LORD, I HAVE HEARD BY MANY OF	230	22
PETER ANSWERED AND SAID UNTO JESUS, BEHOLD, WE HAVE	231	12
THAT TIME JESUS ANSWERED AND SAID, I THANK THEE,	235	03
AND THE ANGEL ANSWERED AND SAID UNTO HER, THE HOLY	236	21
AND HIS MOTHER ANSWERED AND SAID, NOT SO	243	19
AND SIMON PETER ANSWERED AND SAID, THOU ART THE	246	02
AND JESUS ANSWERED AND SAID UNTO HIM, BLESSED ART	246	04
BUT JESUS ANSWERED AND SAID, YE KNOW NOT WHAT YE ASK	247	11
OF THE ELDERS ANSWERED, SAYING UNTO ME, WHAT ARE	257	04
JESUS ANSWERED AND SAID UNTO THEM, HAVE YE NOT READ,	268	05
JESUS ANSWERED AND SAID UNTO HIM, VERILY, VERILY, I	275	09
JESUS ANSWERED, VERILY, VERILY, I SAY UNTO THEE,	275	14

ANSWEREST

SAYING, ANSWEREST THOU NOTHING	143	10
SAYING, ANSWEREST THOU NOTHING	145	10

ANSWERETH

IN ARABIA, AND ANSWERETH TO JERUSALEM WHICH NOW IS,	131	06

ANSWERING

AND HE ANSWERING SAID UNTO HIM, THOU SAYEST IT	145	07
BUT THE OTHER ANSWERING REBUKED HIM, SAYING, DOST NOT	155	02
WAS CLEOPAS, ANSWERING SAID UNTO HIM, ART THOU ONLY A	167	12
AND SIMON ANSWERING SAID UNTO HIM, MASTER, WE HAVE	196	15
AND HE ANSWERING SAID TO HIS FATHER, LO, THESE MANY	202	33

ANSWERING   CONTINUED

AND HE ANSWERING SAID, THOU SHALT LOVE THE LORD THY	208	14
AND JESUS ANSWERING SAID, A CERTAIN MAN WENT DOWN	208	20
AND JESUS ANSWERING SAID, WERE THERE NOT TEN	210	10
AND JESUS ANSWERING SPAKE UNTO THE LAWYERS AND	213	31
TO BE BAPTIZED ANSWERING THE QUESTIONS FOR	R 277	19
ARE PRESENT, ANSWERING BY VERSES, AS FOLLOWETH	R 543	28

ANSWERS

WERE ASTONISHED AT HIS UNDERSTANDING AND ANSWERS	110	31
OR REPEATING THE ANSWERS AS APPOINTED	R 283	14
THE PEOPLE READING OR REPEATING THE ANSWERS	R 287	32

ANTHEM

HERE FOLLOWETH THE ANTHEM	R 031	30
HERE MAY BE SUNG A HYMN OR AN ANTHEM	R 070	21
OR AN OFFERTORY ANTHEM IN THE WORDS OF HOLY SCRIPTURE	R 073	35
HERE MAY BE SUNG A HYMN OR ANTHEM	R 331	28
HERE MAY BE SUNG A HYMN OR AN ANTHEM	R 340	02

ANTIOCH

THAT HE SHOULD GO AS FAR AS ANTIOCH	241	05
HE HAD FOUND HIM, HE BROUGHT HIM UNTO ANTIOCH	241	12
DISCIPLES WERE CALLED CHRISTIANS FIRST IN ANTIOCH	241	15
DAYS CAME PROPHETS FROM JERUSALEM UNTO ANTIOCH	241	16
DAYS CAME PROPHETS FROM JERUSALEM UNTO ANTIOCH	246	24
AND PARMENAS, AND NICOLAS A PROSELYTE OF ANTIOCH	532	18
AND ANTIOCH, HAVE ERRED	606	42

ANTIPHON

SHALL SAY THE ANTIPHON FOLLOWING, AND THEN, ACCORDING	R 308	08
WITH ANTIPHON AND COLLECT	R 309	09

ANXIETIES

AND WORLDLY ANXIETIES, AND GRANT THAT NO CLOUDS OF	596	06

ANXIOUS

UNTO YOU, BE NOT ANXIOUS FOR YOUR LIFE, WHAT YE SHALL	211	12
OF YOU BY BEING ANXIOUS CAN ADD ONE CUBIT UNTO THE	211	19
AND WHY ARE YE ANXIOUS CONCERNING RAIMENT	211	20
BE NOT THEREFORE ANXIOUS, SAYING, WHAT SHALL WE EAT	211	27
BE NOT THEREFORE ANXIOUS FOR THE MORROW	211	33
MORROW WILL BE ANXIOUS FOR ITSELF	211	34
BE NOT ANXIOUS FOR YOUR LIFE, WHAT YE SHALL	266	11
OF YOU BY BEING ANXIOUS CAN ADD ONE CUBIT UNTO THE	266	17
AND WHY ARE YE ANXIOUS FOR RAIMENT	266	18
THEREFORE BE NOT ANXIOUS, SAYING, WHAT SHALL WE EAT	266	25
BE NOT THEREFORE ANXIOUS FOR THE MORROW	266	31

ANY

OR ABSTINENCE, OR ON ANY DAY WHEN THE LITANY OR HOLY	R 003	05
ON ANY DAY, SAVE A DAY OF FASTING OR ABSTINENCE,	R 003	05
AND SEE IF THERE BE ANY SORROW LIKE UNTO MY SORROW	004	30
THERE BE NOT ANY THING IN IT CONTRARY TO THE WORD OF	V	40
BUT NOTE, THAT ON ANY DAY WHEN THE HOLY COMMUNION	R 010	03
AFTER ANY ONE OF THE FOLLOWING CANTICLES	010	04
AND ANY CHURCHES MAY, INSTEAD OF THE WORDS, HE	R 015	14
FEAR THE POWER OF ANY ADVERSARIES, THROUGH THE MIGHT	017	10
NEITHER RUN INTO ANY KIND OF DANGER	017	17
ALL THOSE WHO ARE ANY WAYS AFFLICTED, OR DISTRESSED,	019	05
MAY BE SAID WHEN ANY DESIRE THE PRAYERS OF THE	R 019	12
MAY BE SAID WHEN ANY DESIRE TO RETURN THANKS FOR	R 019	33
AND ANY CHURCHES MAY, INSTEAD OF THE WORDS, HE	R 029	21
ALL THOSE WHO ARE ANY WAYS AFFLICTED, OR DISTRESSED,	033	05
MAY BE SAID WHEN ANY DESIRE THE PRAYERS OF THE	R 033	10
MAY BE SAID WHEN ANY DESIRE TO RETURN THANKS FOR	R 033	31
THE SESSION OF ANY GENERAL OR DIOCESAN CONVENTION,	R 037	09
WHERE IN ANY THING IT IS AMISS, REFORM IT	037	18
SHALL BE ORDAINED TO ANY HOLY FUNCTION, GIVE THY	038	32
ARE TO BE CALLED TO ANY OFFICE AND ADMINISTRATION IN	039	10
MAY OMIT ANY OF THE CLAUSES IN THIS	R 047	04
TO BE SAID WHEN ANY WOMAN, BEING PRESENT IN CHURCH,	R 051	03
TO REVIVE IT BY ANY NEW COMMISSION	VI	06
AND UNRESTRAINED BY ANY WORLDLY AUTHORITY WHATSOEVER)	VI	24
CHURCH OF ENGLAND IN ANY ESSENTIAL POINT OF DOCTRINE,	VI	32
NOT MAKE TO THYSELF ANY GRAVEN IMAGE, NOR THE	068	08
NOR THE LIKENESS OF ANY THING THAT IS IN HEAVEN	068	09
NOR HIS ASS, NOR ANY THING THAT IS HIS	069	22
MAY BE USED ON ANY OTHER OCCASION OF PUBLIC WORSHIP	R 073	25
THE CONGREGATION FOR ANY WHO HAVE DESIRED THE PRAYERS	R 074	02
SICKNESS, OR ANY OTHER ADVERSITY	074	32
IF ANY MAN SIN, WE HAVE AN ADVOCATE WITH THE FATHER,	076	22
IF THERE BE ANY SPECIALLY APPOINTED	R 077	02
HOLY GHOST, WITHOUT ANY DIFFERENCE OF INEQUALITY	079	11
IN WHICH THERE IS ANY WINE TO BE CONSECRATED	R 080	34
TO OFFER UNTO THEE ANY SACRIFICE	081	29
IN LIKE MANNER, (IF ANY BE PRESENT,) AND, AFTER THAT,	R 082	27
AND IF ANY OF THE CONSECRATED BREAD AND WINE REMAIN	R 084	30
MINISTER SHALL KNOW ANY TO BE AN OPEN AND NOTORIOUS	R 084	35
OR TO HAVE DONE ANY WRONG TO HIS NEIGHBOURS BY WORD	R 085	02
SO REPELLING ANY, AS IS HEREIN SPECIFIED, SHALL BE	R 085	17
DONE BY YOU TO ANY OTHER	087	26
IF ANY OF YOU BE A BLASPHEMER OF GOD,	087	31
OR ENVY, OR IN ANY OTHER GRIEVOUS CRIME	087	33
IF THERE BE ANY OF YOU, WHO BY THIS MEANS CANNOT	088	03
ARE CALLED, WITHOUT ANY CAUSE, MOST UNTHANKFULLY	088	21
IF ANY MAN SAY, I AM A GRIEVOUS SINNER, AND THEREFORE	088	29
APPOINTED FOR ANY SUNDAY OR OTHER FEAST MAY BE USED	R 090	06

ANY   CONTINUED

OWE NO MAN ANY THING, BUT TO LOVE ONE ANOTHER   090 23
AND IF THERE BE ANY OTHER COMMANDMENT, IT IS BRIEFLY   090 27
AND IF ANY MAN SAY OUGHT UNTO YOU, YE SHALL SAY, THE   091 16
ANGELS SAID HE AT ANY TIME, THOU ART MY SON, THIS DAY   097 02
WITHOUT HIM WAS NOT ANY THING MADE THAT WAS MADE   097 23
IF IN ANY CHURCH THE HOLY COMMUNION BE TWICE   R 098 07
IF THERE BE ANY MORE DAYS BEFORE THE SUNDAY   R 103 34
ONE ANOTHER, IF ANY MAN HAVE A QUARREL AGAINST ANY   116 06
IF ANY MAN HAVE A QUARREL AGAINST ANY   116 07
THEN IF ANY MAN SHALL SAY UNTO YOU, LO, HERE IS   118 03
LEST THAT BY ANY MEANS, WHEN I HAVE PREACHED TO   119 12
PUT NOT OUR TRUST IN ANY THING THAT WE DO   120 18
WHEREINSOEVER ANY IS BOLD, (I SPEAK   120 27
GIVING NO OFFENCE IN ANY THING, THAT THE MINISTRY BE   126 08
THEE UP, LEST AT ANY TIME THOU DASH THY FOOT AGAINST   127 02
HIS BROTHER IN ANY MATTER   127 32
IS AN IDOLATER, HATH ANY INHERITANCE IN THE KINGDOM   129 08
NOT DENY THEE IN ANY WISE   141 26
WHAT NEED WE ANY FURTHER WITNESSES   143 17
UNTO YOU, I WILL NOT ANY MORE EAT THEREOF, UNTIL IT   149 04
AND SHOES, LACKED YE ANY THING   150 05
WHAT NEED WE ANY FURTHER WITNESS   152 02
IF IN ANY CHURCH THE HOLY COMMUNION BE TWICE   R 164 30
NEITHER SAID THEY ANY THING TO ANY MAN   166 03
THEY ANY THING TO ANY MAN   166 03
HAVE YE HERE ANY MEAT   170 04
FOR IF ANY BE A HEARER OF THE WORD, AND NOT A DOER,   176 06
IF ANY MAN AMONG YOU SEEM TO BE RELIGIOUS, AND   176 13
AND NEEDEST NOT THAT ANY MAN SHOULD ASK THEE   177 02
IF ANY MAN SPEAK, LET HIM SPEAK AS THE ORACLES OF   179 18
IF ANY MAN MINISTER, LET HIM DO IT AS OF THE ABILITY   179 19
IF IN ANY CHURCH THE HOLY COMMUNION BE TWICE   R 182 11
SHALL ASK BREAD OF ANY OF YOU THAT IS A FATHER,   183 14
ANSWERED PETER, CAN ANY MAN FORBID WATER, THAT THESE   184 26
BY ME IF ANY MAN ENTER IN, HE SHALL BE SAVED, AND   186 15
MAN HATH SEEN GOD AT ANY TIME   189 17
LEST AT ANY TIME THE ADVERSARY DELIVER THEE TO THE   198 12
WE, WHO CANNOT DO ANY THING THAT IS GOOD WITHOUT   200 31
TRANSGRESSED I AT ANY TIME THY COMMANDMENT   202 34
OURSELVES TO THINK ANY THING AS OF OURSELVES   206 14
AVAILETH ANY THING, NOR UNCIRCUMCISION, BUT A NEW   210 32
THOU ART BIDDEN OF ANY MAN TO A WEDDING, SIT NOT DOWN   214 11
NEITHER DURST ANY MAN FROM THAT DAY FORTH ASK   215 23
DAY FORTH ASK HIM ANY MORE QUESTIONS   215 24
CAREST THOU FOR ANY MAN   223 02
IF IN ANY YEAR THERE BE TWENTY-SIX SUNDAYS AFTER   R 224 31
BUT IF ANY MAN DRAW BACK, MY SOUL SHALL HAVE NO   228 19
THAT IF HE FOUND ANY OF THIS WAY, WHETHER THEY WERE   229 28
NEITHER KNOWETH ANY MAN THE FATHER, SAVE THE SON,   235 09
IF ANY OF YOU LACK WISDOM, LET HIM ASK OF GOD, THAT   239 11
HE SHALL RECEIVE ANY THING OF THE LORD   239 17
IF YE SHALL ASK ANY THING IN MY NAME, I WILL DO IT   240 23
NO MAN IN THOSE DAYS ANY OF THOSE THINGS WHICH THEY   249 10
THEIR PLACE FOUND ANY MORE IN HEAVEN   252 06
NEITHER THIRST ANY MORE   257 12
LIGHT ON THEM, NOR ANY HEAT   257 13
SHAME OF THE HEATHEN ANY MORE   262 19
SHALL ASK BREAD OF ANY OF YOU THAT IS A FATHER, WILL   263 07
FOR IF ANY BE A HEARER OF THE WORD, AND NOT A DOER,   265 29
IF ANY MAN AMONG YOU SEEM TO BE RELIGIOUS, AND   266 04
OR WRINKLE, OR ANY SUCH THING   267 23
BE ADMINISTERED UPON ANY OTHER DAY   R 273 02
WHEN ANY SUCH PERSONS AS ARE OF RIPER YEARS ARE TO   R 273 17
EXTREME SICKNESS, OR ANY IMMINENT PERIL, IF A   R 281 27
BE PROCURED, THEN ANY BAPTIZED PERSON PRESENT MAY   R 281 28
DOUBT WHETHER ANY PERSON WAS BAPTIZED WITH WATER,   R 282 08
NOT MAKE TO THYSELF ANY GRAVEN IMAGE, NOR THE   286 08
NOR THE LIKENESS OF ANY THING THAT IS IN HEAVEN   286 09
NOR HIS ASS, NOR ANY THING THAT IS HIS   287 22
WE, WHO CANNOT DO ANY THING THAT IS GOOD WITHOUT   287 28
THEREFORE IS NOT BY ANY TO BE ENTERED INTO   300 17
IF ANY MAN CAN SHOW JUST CAUSE, WHY THEY MAY NOT   300 20
EITHER OF YOU KNOW ANY IMPEDIMENT, WHY YE MAY NOT BE   300 26
THAT IF ANY PERSONS ARE JOINED TOGETHER   300 29
IF ANY OF   R 304 22
OR ANY PART THEREOF, MAY BE USED AT THE   R 308 03
WHEN ANY PERSON IS SICK, NOTICE SHALL BE GIVEN   R 308 05
HERE MAY BE SAID ANY ONE OR MORE OF THE PSALMS   R 309 09
ANY OF THE FOLLOWING PSALMS, 20, 27, 42, 91,   R 313 09
BE SUBSTITUTED FOR ANY OF THOSE GIVEN ABOVE   R 313 10
IF HE HATH OFFENDED ANY OTHER, TO ASK THEM   R 313 22
INJURY OR WRONG TO ANY MAN, THAT HE MAKE AMENDS TO   R 313 23
TROUBLED WITH ANY MATTER   R 313 25
THE MINISTER MAY USE ANY PART OF THE SERVICE OF THIS   R 314 23
OR ANY PART THEREOF, AT THE DISCRETION OF   R 315 03
WHEN ANY SICK PERSON SHALL IN HUMBLE FAITH DESIRE   R 320 05
THAT, IF WE ASK ANY THING ACCORDING TO HIS WILL,   322 16
IF ANY MAN EAT OF THIS BREAD, HE SHALL LIVE FOR EVER   322 26
THE MINISTER, OR BY ANY OTHER JUST IMPEDIMENT,   R 323 24
NOR DEPTH, NOR ANY OTHER CREATURE, SHALL BE ABLE TO   331 12
OUR LAST HOUR, FOR ANY PAINS OF DEATH, TO FALL FROM   332 32
MAY ALSO USE ANY OF THE FOLLOWING PRAYERS BEFORE THE   R 335 23
PROVIDED THAT IN ANY OTHER CASE THE MINISTER MAY,   R 337 03
NEITHER THIRST ANY MORE   341 23
LIGHT ON THEM, NOR ANY HEAT   341 24
WHO WILL SHOW US ANY GOOD   347 09
NEITHER SHALL ANY EVIL DWELL WITH THEE   348 08
IF I HAVE DONE ANY SUCH THING   349 27
OR IF THERE BE ANY WICKEDNESS IN MY HANDS   349 28
HIM THAT WITHOUT ANY CAUSE IS MINE ENEMY   349 30
TO SEE IF THERE WERE ANY THAT WOULD UNDERSTAND,   356 17
OR WHO HATH ANY STRENGTH, EXCEPT OUR GOD   361 31
NEITHER IS ANY MIGHTY MAN DELIVERED BY MUCH STRENGTH   379 20
SHALL HE DELIVER ANY MAN BY HIS GREAT STRENGTH   379 23

ANY   CONTINUED

DOTH HE ABHOR ANY THING THAT IS EVIL   384 02
NEITHER IS THERE ANY REST IN MY BONES, BY REASON OF   387 26
UP OUR HANDS TO ANY STRANGE GOD, *   396 02
TO SEE IF THERE WERE ANY THAT WOULD UNDERSTAND,   405 17
AGAINST ME, WITHOUT ANY OFFENCE OR FAULT OF ME, C   411 09
NEITHER FOUND I ANY TO COMFORT ME   423 15
THAT UNDERSTANDETH ANY MORE   430 26
SHALT THOU WORSHIP ANY OTHER GOD   442 32
NOT BE AFRAID FOR ANY TERROR BY NIGHT, *   455 05
NEITHER SHALL ANY PLAGUE COME NIGH THY DWELLING   455 16
20 WILT THOU HAVE ANY THING TO DO WITH THE THRONE OF   458 26
NEVER SHOULD MOVE AT ANY TIME   468 03
THROUGH ANY PLAGUE OR TROUBLE   478 25
NOT BE AFRAID OF ANY EVIL TIDINGS   483 30
THAN TO PUT ANY CONFIDENCE IN MAN   488 14
THAN TO PUT ANY CONFIDENCE IN PRINCES   488 16
OF MY HEAD TO TAKE ANY REST   508 11
NEITHER IS THERE ANY BREATH IN THEIR MOUTHS   511 05
WELL IF THERE BE ANY WAY OF WICKEDNESS IN ME   516 06
HEART BE INCLINED TO ANY EVIL THING   517 15
AS LONG AS I HAVE ANY BEING, I WILL SING PRAISES UNTO   522 04
IN PRINCES, NOR IN ANY CHILD OF MAN   522 06
DELIGHTETH HE IN ANY MAN'S LEGS   523 16
NOT DEALT SO WITH ANY NATION   524 02
PRESUME TO EXECUTE ANY OF THEM, EXCEPT HE WERE FIRST   529 15
SUFFERED TO EXECUTE ANY OF THE SAID FUNCTIONS,   529 21
ANY PERSON TO BE A MAN OF VIRTUOUS   529 27
OF YOU WHO KNOWETH ANY IMPEDIMENT, OR NOTABLE CRIME,   530 21
IF THERE BE ANY OF YOU WHO KNOWETH ANY IMPEDIMENT, OR   530 21
OR NOTABLE CRIME, IN ANY OF THESE PERSONS PRESENTED   530 22
AND IF ANY GREAT CRIME OR IMPEDIMENT BE OBJECTED,   R 530 26
OF YOU WHO KNOWETH ANY IMPEDIMENT, OR NOTABLE CRIME,   536 27
BUT YET, IF THERE BE ANY OF YOU WHO KNOWETH ANY   536 27
OR NOTABLE CRIME, IN ANY OF THEM, FOR THE WHICH HE   536 28
AND IF ANY GREAT CRIME OR IMPEDIMENT BE OBJECTED,   R 537 02
BY ME IF ANY MAN ENTER IN, HE SHALL BE SAVED, AND   539 06
THE SAME CHURCH, OR ANY MEMBER THEREOF, DO TAKE ANY   540 10
DO TAKE ANY HURT OR HINDRANCE BY REASON OF   540 11
THAT YE CANNOT BY ANY OTHER MEANS COMPASS THE DOING   540 33
AND ADMITTING ANY PERSON TO GOVERNMENT IN THE   554 09
IF THERE BE ANY, PRESENTED TO HIM   R 564 08
SHALL THERE BE ANY MORE PAIN   567 20
IN ANY DIOCESE, THE CONCLUDING PARAGRAPH IN THE   R 569 10
AS YOU SHALL AT ANY TIME RECEIVE FROM US   569 21
AND IN CASE OF ANY DIFFERENCE BETWEEN YOU AND YOUR   569 34
BUT IF ANY OF YOU CAN SHOW JUST CAUSE WHY HE MAY NOT   570 17
IF ANY OBJECTION BE OFFERED, THE BISHOP, OR THE   R 570 21
NOT MAKE TO THYSELF ANY GRAVEN IMAGE, NOR THE   578 27
NOR THE LIKENESS OF ANY THING THAT IS IN HEAVEN   578 28
NOR HIS ASS, NOR ANY THING THAT IS HIS   579 22
LET ONE OF THEM, OR ANY OTHER WHO MAY BE APPOINTED,   R 587 05
OR MISTRESS, OR ANY OTHER WHO MAY BE APPOINTED,   R 589 14
TO ALL WHO ARE IN ANY TROUBLE   591 02
NEITHER RUN INTO ANY KIND OF DANGER   592 23
HERE MAY BE ADDED ANY SPECIAL PRAYERS   R 592 26
HERE MAY BE ADDED ANY SPECIAL PRAYERS   R 593 17
TO BE REQUIRED OF ANY MAN, THAT IT SHOULD BE BELIEVED   603 31
AUTHORITY WAS NEVER ANY DOUBT IN THE CHURCH   603 34
THEM TO ESTABLISH ANY DOCTRINE   604 04
TO BE RECEIVED IN ANY COMMONWEALTH   604 21
THE CHURCH TO ORDAIN ANY THING THAT IS CONTRARY TO   607 04
OUGHT NOT TO DECREE ANY THING AGAINST THE SAME,   607 08
IT NOT TO ENFORCE ANY THING TO BE BELIEVED FOR   607 08
IT IS NOT LAWFUL FOR ANY MAN TO TAKE UPON HIM THE   607 19
THAT THEY HAVE NOT ANY VISIBLE SIGN OR CEREMONY   607 43
YOUNG CHILDREN IS IN ANY WISE TO BE RETAINED IN THE   608 31
NEITHER HATH IT ANY THING THAT, OF ITSELF, IS   610 33

ANYWHERE

CONFIDENCE ANYWHERE BUT IN THEE   046 24

APACE

LET THEM FALL AWAY LIKE WATER THAT RUNNETH APACE   410 21

APART

WHEREFORE LAY APART ALL FILTHINESS AND SUPERFLUITY OF   175 02
WHEREFORE LAY APART ALL FILTHINESS AND SUPERFLUITY OF   265 26
PURPOSE OF SETTING APART THIS PLACE IN SOLEMN MANNER,   564 23
THIS PLACE NOW SET APART TO THY SERVICE, THY HOLY   568 10

APIECE

THE JEWS, CONTAINING TWO OR THREE FIRKINS APIECE   113 20

APOSTLE

WHO BY THY HOLY APOSTLE HAST TAUGHT US TO MAKE   074 07
OF THY BLESSED APOSTLE AND EVANGELIST SAINT JOHN, MAY   101 07
TO BE CALLED AN APOSTLE, BECAUSE I PERSECUTED THE   205 14
UNTO THY HOLY APOSTLE SAINT ANDREW, THAT HE READILY   226 19
SUFFER THY HOLY APOSTLE THOMAS TO BE DOUBTFUL IN THY   228 06
OF THE BLESSED APOSTLE SAINT PAUL, HAST CAUSED THE   229 18
ENDUE THY HOLY APOSTLE BARNABAS WITH SINGULAR GIFTS   240 29
GIVE TO THY APOSTLE SAINT PETER MANY EXCELLENT GIFTS,   244 23
AS THINE HOLY APOSTLE SAINT JAMES, LEAVING HIS FATHER   246 16
GIVE TO THINE APOSTLE BARTHOLOMEW GRACE TRULY TO   249 15
CUSTOM TO BE AN APOSTLE AND EVANGELIST   250 21
BY HIS HOLY APOSTLE SAINT PAUL, NOT TO BE SORRY,   335 03
YET THE APOSTLE DOTH CONFESS, THAT CONCUPISCENCE AND   604 39
AND JAMES HIS APOSTLE, SO WE JUDGE, THAT CHRISTIAN   611 07

APOSTLES

COMPANY OF THE APOSTLES PRAISE THEE   010 16
OF THE BLESSED APOSTLES, AND HAST PROMISED, THROUGH   036 28
UNTO THINE APOSTLES, PEACE I LEAVE WITH YOU, MY PEACE   049 05
TO ALL HIS APOSTLES, AND IN THEIR SIGHT ASCENDED UP   078 18
UNTO HIS HOLY APOSTLES AND PROPHETS BY THE SPIRIT   108 13
AND THE TWELVE APOSTLES WITH HIM   148 34
UNTO THE APOSTLES WHOM HE HAD CHOSEN   177 25
WHEN THE APOSTLES WHICH WERE AT JERUSALEM HEARD THAT   185 21
THEN OF ALL THE APOSTLES   205 11
LEAST OF THE APOSTLES, THAT AM NOT MEET TO BE CALLED   205 13
TO BE OF THE NUMBER OF THE TWELVE APOSTLES   233 33
FROM FALSE APOSTLES, MAY BE ORDERED AND GUIDED BY   234 02
AND HE WAS NUMBERED WITH THE ELEVEN APOSTLES   234 33
AND HE GAVE SOME, APOSTLES   237 19
OF THY HOLY APOSTLES, SAINT PHILIP AND SAINT JAMES,   238 32
HANDS OF THE APOSTLES WERE MANY SIGNS AND WONDERS   249 21
OF THE APOSTLES AND PROPHETS, JESUS CHRIST HIMSELF   254 28
OF THE APOSTLES AND PROPHETS, JESUS CHRIST HIMSELF   255 06
OF THE APOSTLES AND PROPHETS, JESUS CHRIST HIMSELF   290 20
IN THE EIGHTH CHAPTER OF THE ACTS OF THE APOSTLES   296 12
WHEN THE APOSTLES WHICH WERE AT JERUSALEM HEARD THAT   296 13
OF THY HOLY APOSTLES, WE HAVE NOW LAID OUR HANDS, TO   298 17
INSPIRE THINE APOSTLES TO CHOOSE INTO THE ORDER OF   531 16
WHOM THEY SET BEFORE THE APOSTLES   532 19
AND HE GAVE SOME, APOSTLES   538 06
WRITINGS OF THE APOSTLES, OF WHAT DIGNITY, AND OF HOW   539 27
THE WORLD HIS APOSTLES, PROPHETS, EVANGELISTS,   545 18
TO THY HOLY APOSTLES MANY EXCELLENT GIFTS, AND DIDST   549 08
HE CHOSE AND SENT FORTH HIS TWELVE APOSTLES   553 06
THAT THE HOLY APOSTLES PRAYED BEFORE THEY ORDAINED   553 07
AND HIS APOSTLES, OFFER UP OUR PRAYERS TO   553 10
MAKING SOME APOSTLES, SOME PROPHETS, SOME   557 26
OF THE APOSTLES AND PROPHETS, JESUS CHRIST HIMSELF   574 04
OF THE APOSTLES, PARTLY ARE STATES OF LIFE ALLOWED IN   607 41

APOSTLES'

BE SAID THE APOSTLES' CREED BY THE MINISTER AND THE   R 015 15
BE SAID THE APOSTLES' CREED BY THE MINISTER AND THE   R 029 20
OR ELSE THE APOSTLES' CREED   R 070 29
IN THE APOSTLES' CREED   276 32
IN THE APOSTLES' CREED   278 09
IN THE APOSTLES' CREED   284 10
BE SAID THE APOSTLES' CREED BY THE MINISTER AND   R 284 11
IN THE APOSTLES' AND NICENE CREEDS   291 02
IN THE APOSTLES' TEACHING AND FELLOWSHIP   291 14
THAT FROM THE APOSTLES' TIME THERE HAVE BEEN THESE   529 12
CALLED THE APOSTLES' CREED, OUGHT THOROUGHLY TO BE   604 25

APOSTLESHIP

MINISTRY AND APOSTLESHIP, FROM WHICH JUDAS BY   234 29

APOSTOLIC

CATHOLIC AND APOSTOLIC CHURCH   016 19
CATHOLIC AND APOSTOLIC CHURCH   030 24
CATHOLIC AND APOSTOLIC CHURCH   071 21
THE CREEDS AS ONE, HOLY, CATHOLIC, AND APOSTOLIC   291 05
APOSTOLIC   291 14
MINISTERS OF APOSTOLIC SUCCESSION TO THE END OF THE   572 18
OF THY HOLY APOSTOLIC CHURCH, AND WITH ONE MOUTH MAY   574 11

APPAREL

GLORIOUS IN HIS APPAREL, TRAVELLING IN THE GREATNESS   138 13
RED IN THINE APPAREL, AND THY GARMENTS LIKE HIM THAT   138 15
BEHOLD, TWO MEN STOOD BY THEM IN WHITE APPAREL   178 16
AND HATH PUT ON GLORIOUS APPAREL   457 04
HATH PUT ON HIS APPAREL, AND GIRDED HIMSELF WITH   457 05
HAVE COVETED NO MAN'S SILVER, OR GOLD, OR APPAREL   551 06

APPARELLED

DECENTLY APPARELLED, AND THERE SHALL KNEEL DOWN IN   R 305 08

APPARENT

THOSE GREAT AND APPARENT DANGERS WHEREWITH WE WERE   052 10

APPEAR

NOW TO APPEAR IN THE PRESENCE OF GOD FOR US   022 24
SUCH AS MAY APPEAR IN OUR LIVES BY AN HUMBLE, HOLY,   050 26
THEY WILL APPEAR, AND IT IS TO BE HOPED, THE REASONS   VI 29
IT WILL ALSO APPEAR THAT THIS CHURCH IS FAR FROM   VI 31
YE SHALL NOT APPEAR BEFORE THE LORD EMPTY   073 15
WHEN HE SHALL APPEAR AGAIN WITH POWER AND GREAT   117 08
IT DOTH NOT YET APPEAR WHAT WE SHALL BE   117 18
WHEN HE SHALL APPEAR, WE SHALL BE LIKE HIM   117 19
AND THEN SHALL APPEAR THE SIGN OF THE SON OF MAN IN   118 17
THAT THEY MAY APPEAR UNTO MEN TO FAST   125 11
THAT THOU APPEAR NOT UNTO MEN TO FAST, BUT UNTO THY   125 13
NOW TO APPEAR IN THE PRESENCE OF GOD FOR US   147 32
FOR HIM SHALL HE APPEAR THE SECOND TIME WITHOUT SIN   148 10
OUR LIFE, SHALL APPEAR, THEN SHALL YE ALSO APPEAR   164 07
SHALL YE ALSO APPEAR WITH HIM IN GLORY   164 08
SHALL I COME TO APPEAR BEFORE THE PRESENCE OF GOD   393 02
AND WHEN HIS GLORY SHALL APPEAR   465 12
SHEPHERD SHALL APPEAR, YOU MAY RECEIVE THE   558 30

APPEARED

MANIFESTLY APPEARED TO ALL HIS APOSTLES, AND IN THEIR   078 18

APPEARED   CONTINUED

SALVATION HATH APPEARED TO ALL MEN, TEACHING US THAT,   098 18
OF THE LORD APPEARED UNTO HIM IN A DREAM, SAYING,   105 03
OF THEM DILIGENTLY WHAT TIME THE STAR APPEARED   109 12
THEN APPEARED THE TARES ALSO   116 22
HOLY CITY, AND APPEARED UNTO MANY   137 30
WORLD HATH HE APPEARED TO PUT AWAY SIN BY THE   148 06
AND THERE APPEARED AN ANGEL UNTO HIM FROM HEAVEN,   150 20
AND HATH APPEARED TO SIMON   168 14
AND THERE APPEARED UNTO THEM CLOVEN TONGUES LIKE AS   180 21
THAT APPEARED UNTO THEE IN THE WAY AS THOU   230 31
WHO APPEARED IN GLORY, AND SPAKE OF HIS DECEASE WHICH   248 28
SION HATH GOD APPEARED *   401 24

APPEARETH

OF THE LORD APPEARETH TO JOSEPH IN A DREAM, SAYING,   103 16
OF THE LORD APPEARETH IN A DREAM TO JOSEPH IN EGYPT,   107 13
AND WHO SHALL STAND WHEN HE APPEARETH   232 08
GOD OF GODS APPEARETH EVERY ONE OF THEM IN SION   445 26

APPEARING

THE GLORIOUS APPEARING OF THE GREAT GOD AND OUR   098 22
BUT UNTO ALL THEM ALSO THAT LOVE HIS APPEARING   253 30

APPEASE

PLEASED THEE TO APPEASE THE SEDITIOUS TUMULTS WHICH   052 20

APPERTAINETH

ONLY IT APPERTAINETH TO FORGIVE SINS   062 19
IT APPERTAINETH TO THE OFFICE OF A DEACON, IN THE   533 10
IT APPERTAINETH TO THE DISCIPLINE OF THE CHURCH,   608 19

APPERTAINING

THE THINGS APPERTAINING TO THE ECCLESIASTICAL   R 535 22
APPERTAINING TO YOUR CURE, UNTIL SOME URGENT REASON   569 30
ALL THINGS APPERTAINING TO THE PERFECTION OF MAN'S   603 22

APPLE

8 KEEP ME AS THE APPLE OF AN EYE   359 02

APPLIED

WHICH SHALL BE APPLIED BY THE MINISTER AND THE   R 307 08
112 I HAVE APPLIED MY HEART TO FULFIL THY STATUTES   497 21

APPLY

LIFE IS, WE MAY APPLY OUR HEARTS UNTO THAT HEAVENLY   045 08
THAT WE MAY APPLY OUR HEARTS UNTO WISDOM   326 02
THAT WE MAY APPLY OUR HEARTS UNTO WISDOM   454 13
WILL YOU APPLY ALL YOUR DILIGENCE TO FRAME   533 24
STUDY YE OUGHT TO APPLY YOURSELVES, AS WELL TO SHOW   540 26
IN YOU, YE WILL APPLY YOURSELVES WHOLLY TO THIS ONE   541 13
I WILL APPLY MYSELF THERETO, THE LORD BEING   543 04
YET DOTH IT NOT APPLY THEM TO ESTABLISH ANY DOCTRINE   604 03

APPOINT

TO APPOINT UNTO THEM THAT MOURN IN ZION, TO GIVE UNTO   107 06
AND I APPOINT UNTO YOU A KINGDOM, AS MY FATHER HATH   149 27
AND I APPOINT UNTO YOU A KINGDOM, AS MY FATHER HATH   250 13
AT SUCH OTHER TIME AS THE MINISTER SHALL APPOINT   R 273 16
WHOM WE MAY APPOINT OVER THIS BUSINESS   532 12

APPOINTED

IN THE LITANY, AS THERE APPOINTED   R 003 14
AND CEREMONIES APPOINTED TO BE USED THEREIN, BEING   V 14
DAYS FOR WHICH OTHER CANTICLES ARE APPOINTED   R 008 10
A LESSON OF THE NEW TESTAMENT, AS IT IS APPOINTED   R 028 05
HAST APPOINTED DIVERS ORDERS IN THY CHURCH   039 08
THE MINISTER APPOINTED SHALL READ THE EPISTLE, FIRST   R 070 18
THE MINISTER APPOINTED SHALL READ THE GOSPEL,   R 070 22
FIT PERSONS APPOINTED FOR THAT PURPOSE, SHALL RECEIVE R 073 27
TO THE TIME, IF THERE BE ANY SPECIALLY APPOINTED   R 077 03
THAT IS BEFORE APPOINTED UNTO THE END OF THE GOSPEL   R 084 25
ALL THAT IS APPOINTED AT THE COMMUNION, UNTO THE END   R 084 28
AND GOSPEL, APPOINTED FOR THE SUNDAY, SHALL SERVE ALL R 090 04
THE COLLECT APPOINTED FOR ANY SUNDAY OR OTHER FEAST   R 090 06
WHOM HE HATH APPOINTED HEIR OF ALL THINGS, BY WHOM   096 25
UNTIL THE TIME APPOINTED OF THE FATHER   104 17
THE COLLECT APPOINTED FOR THE DAY, UNTIL PALM SUNDAY   R 124 18
THE COLLECT APPOINTED FOR THE DAY, UNTIL GOOD FRIDAY   R 134 13
AS THE LORD APPOINTED ME   135 18
AND AS IT IS APPOINTED UNTO MEN ONCE TO DIE, BUT   148 07
MY FATHER HATH APPOINTED UNTO ME   149 28
AND THEY APPOINTED TWO, JOSEPH CALLED BARSABAS, WHO   234 25
MY FATHER HATH APPOINTED UNTO ME   250 13
THE LORD APPOINTED OTHER SEVENTY ALSO, AND SENT THEM   254 11
FORM BEFORE APPOINTED IN THIS OFFICE   R 282 11
READING OR REPEATING THE ANSWERS AS APPOINTED   R 283 14
AT THE TIME APPOINTED, TO RECEIVE INSTRUCTION BY THE   R 295 12
UPON THE DAY APPOINTED, ALL THAT ARE TO BE CONFIRMED   R 296 05
SOME MINISTER APPOINTED BY HIM, MAY SAY, HEAR THE   R 296 10
DAY AND TIME APPOINTED FOR SOLEMNIZATION OF   R 300 03
THOSE WHO ARE APPOINTED TO COMMUNICATE WITH THE SICK, R 323 02
FOR THOSE APPOINTED ABOVE   R 323 34
OF THE SERVICE APPOINTED TO BE SAID AT THE GRAVE,   R 336 31
AS SHEEP APPOINTED TO BE SLAIN   396 05

APPOINTED   CONTINUED

3 IN THE APPOINTED TIME, SAITH GOD, *   432 02
THOSE THAT ARE APPOINTED TO DIE   440 28
IN THE TIME APPOINTED, AND UPON OUR SOLEMN FEAST-DAY   442 17
THEM THAT ARE APPOINTED UNTO DEATH   465 20
THOU HAST APPOINTED FOR THEM   468 09
19 HE APPOINTED THE MOON FOR CERTAIN SEASONS,   468 32
10 AND APPOINTED THE SAME UNTO JACOB FOR A LAW,   470 22
AT THE TIMES APPOINTED, OR ELSE, ON URGENT OCCASION,   529 30
WHEN THE DAY APPOINTED BY THE BISHOP IS COME, THERE   R 530 03
OF THE LITANY APPOINTED, MAY BE SAID THE LITANY FOR   R 531 10
HAST APPOINTED DIVERS ORDERS OF MINISTERS IN THY   531 15
YOU SHALL BE APPOINTED TO SERVE   533 07
HE SHALL BE APPOINTED TO SERVE, TO ASSIST THE PRIEST   533 11
ONE OF THEM, APPOINTED BY THE BISHOP, SHALL READ THE   R 534 14
AT THE TIMES APPOINTED IN THE CANON   R 535 25
WHEN THE DAY APPOINTED BY THE BISHOP IS COME, THERE   R 536 03
OF THE LITANY APPOINTED, MAY BE SAID THE LITANY FOR   R 537 16
SPIRIT HAST APPOINTED DIVERS ORDERS OF MINISTERS IN   537 21
AND MINISTRY, APPOINTED FOR THE SALVATION OF MANKIND,   545 24
THEY SHALL BE APPOINTED THY MINISTERS, THY HOLY NAME   545 33
BE LAWFULLY APPOINTED THEREUNTO   546 27
AS IS IN THIS OFFICE BEFORE APPOINTED   R 547 28
SPIRIT HAST APPOINTED DIVERS ORDERS OF MINISTERS IN   547 32
OTHER BISHOP APPOINTED BY THE BISHOPS PRESENT,   R 549 04
TO THE BISHOP APPOINTED, SITTING IN HIS CHAIR,   R 552 19
SPIRIT HAST APPOINTED DIVERS ORDERS OF MINISTERS IN   553 27
OTHER PERSONS APPOINTED FOR THAT PURPOSE   R 563 06
BY SOME PERSON APPOINTED BY HIM, AND THEN LAID BY HIM R 566 26
THE INSTITUTOR APPOINTED BY HIM, ATTENDED BY THE NEW   R 570 03
HAST APPOINTED DIVERS ORDERS IN THY CHURCH   572 07
HIM WHO IS NOW APPOINTED TO OFFER THE SACRIFICES OF   572 20
AT THE TIME APPOINTED, AND OBEDIENTLY TO HEAR AND TO   R 582 33
THAT IS HERE APPOINTED FOR THEM TO LEARN   R 582 35
WHO MAY BE APPOINTED, SAY AS FOLLOWETH, ALL KNEELING, R 587 05
WHOM THOU HAST APPOINTED THE JUDGE OF QUICK AND DEAD,   588 23
WHO MAY BE APPOINTED, SAY AS FOLLOWETH, ALL KNEELING, R 589 14
THOSE THAT ARE APPOINTED TO DIE   600 11

APPOINTING

SERVANT WITH APPOINTING HIM TO STAND IN THY HOUSE,   573 13

APPOINTMENT

BY THY APPOINTMENT, THEY MAY SUCCOUR AND DEFEND   251 30

APPREHENDED

WHEN HE HAD APPREHENDED HIM, HE PUT HIM IN PRISON,   245 04

APPRENTICES

AND APPRENTICES, WHO HAVE NOT LEARNED THEIR   R 582 32

APPROACH

OR THE NEAR APPROACH OF DEATH, ESPECIALLY NEED OUR   048 09
NOR THE WICKED APPROACH TO HURT HIM   308 28

APPROACHING

AS YE SEE THE DAY APPROACHING   158 28

APPROPRIATE

OFFICE IS APPROPRIATE TO BE USED ONLY FOR THE   R 337 02
SERVANTS TO APPROPRIATE AND DEVOTE THIS HOUSE TO THY   566 29

APPROVE

THAT YE MAY APPROVE THINGS THAT ARE EXCELLENT   221 03
ALSO FAVOURABLY APPROVE OUR GODLY PURPOSE OF SETTING   564 22

APPROVED

OF HANDS, WERE APPROVED AND ADMITTED THEREUNTO BY   529 17
WORKS HAVE BEEN APPROVED OF AND GRACIOUSLY ACCEPTED   564 20
BE ORDAINED AND APPROVED BY COMMON AUTHORITY, OUGHT   609 38

APPROVETH

6 THE LORD APPROVETH THE RIGHTEOUS   354 30

APPROVING

IN ALL THINGS APPROVING OURSELVES AS THE MINISTERS OF   126 09

APT

PRESENT UNTO US, BE APT AND MEET, FOR THEIR LEARNING   530 14
PRESENT UNTO US, BE APT AND MEET, FOR THEIR LEARNING   536 15
TO HOSPITALITY, APT TO TEACH   549 21

ARABIA

IS MOUNT SINAI IN ARABIA, AND ANSWERETH TO JERUSALEM   171 05
THE KINGS OF ARABIA AND SABA SHALL BRING GIFTS   427 17
AND UNTO HIM SHALL BE GIVEN OF THE GOLD OF ARABIA   427 27

ARABIANS

CRETES AND ARABIANS, WE DO HEAR THEM SPEAK IN OUR   181 05

ARBITER

BE THE ULTIMATE ARBITER AND JUDGE   569 37

ARCHANGEL

VOICE OF THE ARCHANGEL, AND WITH THE TRUMP OF GOD   269 06

ARCHANGELS

ANGELS AND ARCHANGELS, AND WITH ALL THE COMPANY OF   077 04
ANGELS AND ARCHANGELS, AND WITH ALL THE COMPANY OF   079 28

ARCHELAUS

HE HEARD THAT ARCHELAUS DID REIGN IN JUDAEA IN THE   107 18

ARIGHT

ORDERETH HIS WAY ARIGHT, WILL I SHOW THE SALVATION OF   403 05
NOT THEIR HEART ARIGHT, AND WHOSE SPIRIT CLAVE NOT   435 15
OR FEARETH ARIGHT THY INDIGNATION   454 12

ARIMATHAEA

A RICH MAN OF ARIMATHAEA, NAMED JOSEPH, WHO ALSO   162 07

ARISE

I WILL ARISE AND GO TO MY FATHER, AND WILL SAY UNTO   004 26
O LORD, ARISE, HELP US, AND DELIVER US FOR THY NAME'S   058 26
O LORD, ARISE, HELP US, AND DELIVER US FOR THINE   059 03
A DREAM, SAYING, ARISE, AND TAKE THE YOUNG CHILD AND   103 17
IN EGYPT, SAYING, ARISE, AND TAKE THE YOUNG CHILD AND   107 14
FOR THERE SHALL ARISE FALSE CHRISTS, AND FALSE   118 04
THAT SLEEPEST, AND ARISE FROM THE DEAD, AND CHRIST   129 22
WHY DO THOUGHTS ARISE IN YOUR HEARTS   169 32
I WILL ARISE AND GO TO MY FATHER, AND WILL SAY UNTO   202 12
HE SAID UNTO HIM, ARISE, GO THY WAY   210 13
AND HE SAID, YOUNG MAN, I SAY UNTO THEE, ARISE   213 05
OR TO SAY, ARISE, AND WALK   217 08
OF THE PALSY,) ARISE, TAKE UP THY BED, AND GO UNTO   217 11
SAID UNTO HIM, ARISE, AND GO INTO THE CITY, AND IT   230 07
SAID UNTO HIM, ARISE, AND GO INTO THE STREET WHICH IS   230 17
HIM UP, SAYING, ARISE UP QUICKLY   245 14
ARISE UP FOR ME IN THE JUDGMENT THAT THOU HAST   350 02
13 ARISE, O LORD GOD, AND LIFT UP THINE HAND   353 32
26 ARISE, AND HELP US, *   396 12
ARISE THOU THEREFORE TO HELP ME, AND BEHOLD   411 12
LET GOD ARISE, AND LET HIS ENEMIES BE SCATTERED   419 09
23 ARISE, O GOD, MAINTAIN THINE OWN CAUSE   431 22
WOULD NOT SUFFER HIS WHOLE DISPLEASURE TO ARISE   437 17
8 ARISE, O GOD, AND JUDGE THOU THE EARTH   444 02
THOU STILLEST THE WAVES THEREOF WHEN THEY ARISE   450 25
OF THE WICKED THAT ARISE UP AGAINST ME   456 22
2 ARISE, THOU JUDGE OF THE WORLD, *   457 21
13 THOU SHALT ARISE, AND HAVE MERCY UPON SION   465 04
8 ARISE, O LORD, INTO THY RESTING-PLACE   508 19
SELVES SHALL MEN ARISE, SPEAKING PERVERSE THINGS, TO   550 32
O LORD, ARISE, HELP US   562 02
OF GOD WE MAY ARISE AGAIN, AND AMEND OUR LIVES   606 02

ARISETH

22 THE SUN ARISETH, AND THEY GET THEM AWAY TOGETHER,   469 04
THE STORMY WIND ARISETH, *   477 26
THE GODLY THERE ARISETH UP LIGHT IN THE DARKNESS   483 24

ARK

OF NOAH, WHILE THE ARK WAS A PREPARING, WHEREIN FEW,   161 28
THOU, AND THE ARK OF THY STRENGTH   508 20

ARM

HE HATH SHOWED STRENGTH WITH HIS ARM   026 20
AND WITH HIS HOLY ARM, *   027 06
THINE ALMIGHTY ARM TO STRENGTHEN AND PROTECT   041 26
THEREFORE MINE OWN ARM BROUGHT SALVATION UNTO ME   138 24
WITH HIS GLORIOUS ARM, DIVIDING THE WATER BEFORE   139 11
STRONG HAND, AND HIS ARM SHALL RULE FOR HIM   243 06
THE LAMBS WITH HIS ARM, AND CARRY THEM IN HIS BOSOM,   243 09
WAS IT THEIR OWN ARM THAT HELPED THEM   394 28
AND THINE ARM, AND THE LIGHT OF THY   394 30
THINE ENEMIES ABROAD WITH THY MIGHTY ARM   450 27
14 THOU HAST A MIGHTY ARM   450 33
AND MY ARM SHALL STRENGTHEN HIM   451 17
AND WITH HIS HOLY ARM, *   461 27
12 WITH A MIGHTY HAND AND STRETCHED-OUT ARM   512 06

ARMED

THAT WE, BEING ARMED WITH THY DEFENCE, MAY BE   041 14
WHEN A STRONG MAN ARMED KEEPETH HIS PALACE, HIS GOODS   130 05

ARMIES

HE SENT FORTH HIS ARMIES, AND DESTROYED THOSE   218 14
AND GOEST NOT FORTH WITH OUR ARMIES   395 12
KINGS WITH THEIR ARMIES DID FLEE, AND WERE   420 04

ARMOUR

PUT UPON US THE ARMOUR OF LIGHT, NOW IN THE TIME OF   090 13
LET US PUT ON THE ARMOUR OF LIGHT   091 05

ARMOUR   CONTINUED

OF GOD, BY THE ARMOUR OF RIGHTEOUSNESS ON THE RIGHT   126 15
FROM HIM ALL HIS ARMOUR WHEREIN HE TRUSTED, AND   130 07
PUT ON THE WHOLE ARMOUR OF GOD, THAT YE MAY BE ABLE   219 06
YOU THE WHOLE ARMOUR OF GOD, THAT YE MAY BE ABLE TO   219 11

ARMS

CHILDREN WITH THE ARMS OF THY MERCY, AND DOST MAKE   043 08
HE HIM UP IN HIS ARMS, AND BLESSED GOD, AND SAID,   233 04
TOOK THEM UP IN HIS ARMS, PUT HIS HANDS UPON THEM,   274 32
THE CHILD INTO HIS ARMS, AND SHALL SAY TO THE   R 279 23
HIM INTO THE ARMS OF THY MERCY, INTO THE BLESSED REST   319 31
THE LAMBS WITH HIS ARMS, AND CARRY THEM IN HIS BOSOM   338 13
CHILDREN INTO HIS ARMS AND BLESS THEM   342 04
AND MINE ARMS SHALL BEND EVEN A BOW OF STEEL   362 04
17 FOR THE ARMS OF THE UNGODLY SHALL BE BROKEN,   385 29

ARMY

THE NOBLE ARMY OF MARTYRS PRAISE THEE   010 18

AROSE

WHEN HE AROSE, HE TOOK THE YOUNG CHILD AND HIS MOTHER   103 20
AND HE AROSE, AND TOOK THE YOUNG CHILD AND HIS   107 16
SAINTS WHICH SLEPT AROSE, AND CAME OUT OF THE GRAVES   137 29
AND THERE AROSE CERTAIN, AND BARE FALSE WITNESS   143 05
MULTITUDE OF THEM AROSE, AND LED HIM UNTO PILATE   152 27
SPENT ALL, THERE AROSE A MIGHTY FAMINE IN THAT LAND   202 05
AND HE AROSE, AND CAME TO HIS FATHER   202 16
AND HE AROSE, AND DEPARTED TO HIS HOUSE   217 12
AND JESUS AROSE, AND FOLLOWED HIM, AND SO DID HIS   224 14
AND TOOK HER BY THE HAND, AND THE MAID AROSE   224 29
AND SAUL AROSE FROM THE EARTH   230 10
AND AROSE, AND WAS BAPTIZED   230 36
AND HE AROSE, AND FOLLOWED HIM   251 14
9 WHEN GOD AROSE TO JUDGMENT, *   433 06

ARRANGING

TO MAKE WILLS ARRANGING FOR THE DISPOSAL OF THEIR   R 320 22

ARRAYED

MOCKED HIM, AND ARRAYED HIM IN A GORGEOUS ROBE, AND   153 17
GLORY WAS NOT ARRAYED LIKE ONE OF THESE   211 23
THESE WHICH ARE ARRAYED IN WHITE ROBES   257 05
GLORY WAS NOT ARRAYED LIKE ONE OF THESE   266 21

ARROGANCY

FROM PRIDE AND ARROGANCY, AND FROM EVERY EVIL WAY   036 14
TAUGHT WITHOUT ARROGANCY AND IMPIETY   605 25

ARROW

THEM WITH A SWIFT ARROW, *   415 34
NOR FOR THE ARROW THAT FLIETH BY DAY   455 06

ARROWS

HE ORDAINETH HIS ARROWS AGAINST THE PERSECUTORS   350 20
MAKE READY THEIR ARROWS WITHIN THE QUIVER, *   354 22
HE SENT OUT HIS ARROWS, AND SCATTERED THEM   360 26
2 FOR THINE ARROWS STICK FAST IN ME, *   387 23
5 THY ARROWS ARE VERY SHARP IN THE HEART OF THE   396 25
ARE SPEARS AND ARROWS, AND THEIR TONGUE A SHARP   409 22
THEY SHOOT THEIR ARROWS, LET THEM BE ROOTED OUT   410 22
SHOOT OUT THEIR ARROWS, EVEN BITTER WORDS   415 24
BRAKE HE THE ARROWS OF THE BOW, *   426 26
AND THINE ARROWS WENT ABROAD   434 17
MIGHTY AND SHARP ARROWS, WITH HOT BURNING COALS   502 12
5 LIKE AS THE ARROWS IN THE HAND OF THE GIANT,   505 31
SHOOT OUT THINE ARROWS, AND CONSUME THEM   520 03

ART

OUR FATHER, WHO ART IN HEAVEN, HALLOWED BE THY NAME   007 23
THOU ART THE KING OF GLORY, O CHRIST   010 24
THOU ART THE EVERLASTING SON OF THE FATHER   010 25
BLESSED ART THOU, O LORD GOD OF OUR FATHERS   011 16
BLESSED ART THOU FOR THE NAME OF THY MAJESTY   011 18
BLESSED ART THOU IN THE TEMPLE OF THY HOLINESS   011 20
BLESSED ART THOU THAT BEHOLDEST THE DEPTHS, AND   011 22
BLESSED ART THOU ON THE GLORIOUS THRONE OF THY   011 25
BLESSED ART THOU IN THE FIRMAMENT OF HEAVEN   011 27
O GOD, WHO ART THE AUTHOR OF PEACE AND LOVER OF   017 05
FOR THOU ONLY ART HOLY   026 02
THOU ONLY ART THE LORD   026 02
WITH THE HOLY GHOST, ART MOST HIGH IN THE GLORY OF   026 03
TO GLORIFY THEE, WHO ART THE ONLY GIVER OF ALL   041 18
WHO ART EVER READY TO HEAR THE PRAYERS   041 19
LOOK UNTO THEE, WHO ART THE FOUNTAIN OF ALL WISDOM   042 27
O ALMIGHTY GOD, WHO ART A STRONG TOWER OF DEFENCE   052 07
MAY KNOW THAT THOU ART OUR SAVIOUR AND MIGHTY   052 14
O GOD, WHO ART THE GIVER OF LIFE, OF HEALTH, AND OF   052 29
GRACIOUS ART THOU, O LORD, AND FULL OF COMPASSION TO   053 03
AND CLEAR WHEN THOU ART JUDGED   060 19
O GOD, THOU THAT ART THE GOD OF MY HEALTH   061 06
FOR THOU ART A MERCIFUL GOD, FULL OF COMPASSION,   062 31
O LORD, AND THOU ART EXALTED AS HEAD ABOVE ALL   073 21
AND THE HOLY GHOST, ART ONE GOD, ONE LORD, IN TRINITY   079 08
BUT THOU ART THE SAME LORD, WHOSE PROPERTY IS ALWAYS   082 17
FOR THOU ONLY ART HOLY   084 13

ART   CONTINUED

THOU ONLY ART THE LORD   084 13
WITH THE HOLY GHOST, ART MOST HIGH IN THE GLORY OF   084 14
AND SAID UNTO HIM, ART THOU HE THAT SHOULD COME,   094 18
TO ASK HIM, WHO ART THOU   095 22
ART THOU ELIAS   095 24
ART THOU THAT PROPHET   095 25
THEY UNTO HIM, WHO ART THOU   095 26
HE AT ANY TIME, THOU ART MY SON, THIS DAY HAVE I   097 02
BUT THOU ART THE SAME, AND THY YEARS SHALL NOT FAIL   097 18
WHEREFORE THOU ART NO MORE A SERVANT, BUT A SON   104 24
IN THE LAND OF JUDA, ART NOT THE LEAST AMONG THE   109 08
SAYING, THOU ART MY BELOVED SON, IN WHOM I AM   112 23
NOT WELL THAT THOU ART A SAMARITAN, AND HAST A DEVIL   133 13
ART THOU GREATER THAN OUR FATHER ABRAHAM, WHICH IS   133 21
JEWS UNTO HIM, THOU ART NOT YET FIFTY YEARS OLD,   133 30
ASKED HIM, SAYING, ART THOU THE KING OF THE JEWS   135 19
WHEREFORE ART THOU RED IN THINE APPAREL, AND THY   138 15
DOUBTLESS THOU ART OUR FATHER, THOUGH ABRAHAM BE   139 21
THOU, O LORD, ART OUR FATHER, OUR REDEEMER   139 23
AND SAID UNTO HIM, ART THOU THE CHRIST, THE SON OF   143 13
SURELY THOU ART ONE OF THEM   143 31
FOR THOU ART A GALILAEAN, AND THY SPEECH AGREETH   143 32
PILATE ASKED HIM, ART THOU THE KING OF THE JEWS   145 06
AND WHEN THOU ART CONVERTED, STRENGTHEN THY BRETHREN   149 33
AND SAID, THOU ART ALSO OF THEM   151 14
SAYING, ART THOU THE CHRIST   151 30
THEN SAID THEY ALL, ART THOU THEN THE SON OF GOD   151 34
ASKED HIM, SAYING, ART THOU THE KING OF THE JEWS   152 31
SEEING THOU ART IN THE SAME CONDEMNATION   155 03
THEE NOT AS THOU ART REVEALED IN THE GOSPEL OF THY   157 07
UNTO JESUS, WHENCE ART THOU   159 12
THIS MAN GO, THOU ART NOT CAESAR'S FRIEND   159 20
SAID UNTO HIM, ART THOU ONLY A STRANGER IN JERUSALEM,   167 13
SECOND PSALM, THOU ART MY SON, THIS DAY HAVE I   169 09
SAYING, THOU ART WORTHY, O LORD, TO RECEIVE   187 29
WE KNOW THAT THOU ART A TEACHER COME FROM GOD   188 02
AND SAID UNTO HIM, ART THOU A MASTER OF ISRAEL,   188 19
AND THOU ART TORMENTED   190 18
WHILES THOU ART IN THE WAY WITH HIM   198 12
POWER AND MIGHT, WHO ART THE AUTHOR AND GIVER OF ALL   198 20
UNTO HIM, SON, THOU ART EVER WITH ME, AND ALL THAT I   203 05
EVERLASTING GOD, WHO ART ALWAYS MORE READY TO HEAR   206 04
THAN WE TO PRAY, AND ART WONT TO GIVE MORE THAN   206 05
UNTO THEM, WHEN THOU ART BIDDEN OF ANY MAN TO A   214 10
BUT WHEN THOU ART BIDDEN, GO AND SIT DOWN IN THE   214 15
AND STRENGTH, WHO ART THE AUTHOR OF ALL GODLINESS   222 09
WE KNOW THAT THOU ART TRUE, AND TEACHEST THE WAY OF   222 31
AND HE SAID, WHO ART THOU, LORD   230 03
THOU THAT ART HIGHLY FAVOURED, THE LORD IS WITH   236 09
BLESSED ART THOU AMONG WOMEN   236 10
SOME SAY THAT THOU ART JOHN THE BAPTIST   245 34
AND SAID, THOU ART THE CHRIST, THE SON OF THE LIVING   246 03
UNTO HIM, BLESSED ART THOU, SIMON BAR-JONA   246 04
UNTO THEE, THAT THOU ART PETER, AND UPON THIS ROCK I   246 07
WE KNOW THAT THOU ART A TEACHER COME FROM GOD   275 07
IF THOU ART NOT ALREADY BAPTIZED, N   282 13
POWER AND MIGHT, WHO ART THE AUTHOR AND GIVER OF ALL   283 08
OF MANKIND, WHO ONLY ART THE WELL-SPRING OF LIFE   303 15
BUT THOU, O LORD, ART MY DEFENDER   309 18
THOU ART MY WORSHIP, AND THE LIFTER UP OF MY HEAD   309 18
FOR THOU ART THE GOD OF MY STRENGTH   310 08
AND WHY ART THOU SO DISQUIETED WITHIN ME   310 16
WHY ART THOU SO HEAVY, O MY SOUL   310 16
WHEN THOU ART PLEASED TO TAKE HIM HENCE,   314 11
O ALMIGHTY GOD, WHO ART THE GIVER OF ALL HEALTH,   315 13
NOR FAINT WHEN THOU ART REBUKED OF HIM   321 29
THOU ART GOD FROM EVERLASTING, AND WORLD WITHOUT END   325 16
FOR WHEN THOU ART ANGRY ALL OUR DAYS ARE GONE   325 30
WHO FOR OUR SINS ART JUSTLY DISPLEASED   332 23
FOR THOU ART WITH ME   338 24
SAID UNTO ME, THOU ART MY SON, THIS DAY HAVE I   346 11
THOU ART MY WORSHIP, AND THE LIFTER UP OF MY HEAD   346 29
3 BUT THOU, O LORD, ART MY DEFENDER   346 29
4 FOR THOU ART THE GOD THAT HAST NO PLEASURE IN   348 07
IS MAN, THAT THOU ART MINDFUL OF HIM   351 07
THOU ART SET IN THE THRONE THAT JUDGEST RIGHT   351 29
FOR THOU ART THE HELPER OF THE FRIENDLESS   354 08
THOU ART MY GOD   357 23
THOU THAT ART THE SAVIOUR OF THEM WHICH PUT THEIR   358 31
AND ART SO FAR FROM MY HEALTH, AND FROM THE WORDS OF   366 05
9 BUT THOU ART HE THAT TOOK ME OUT OF MY MOTHER'S   366 20
THOU ART MY GOD EVEN FROM MY MOTHER'S WOMB   366 24
THOU ART MY SUCCOUR, HASTE THEE TO HELP ME   367 10
FOR THOU ART WITH ME   368 17
FOR THOU ART THE GOD OF MY SALVATION   369 26
4 FOR THOU ART MY STRONG ROCK, AND MY CASTLE   375 27
FOR THOU ART MY STRENGTH   375 30
I HAVE SAID, THOU ART MY GOD   376 25
8 THOU ART A PLACE TO HIDE ME IN   378 05
21 THOU ART MY HELPER AND REDEEMER   391 26
6 WHY ART THOU SO FULL OF HEAVINESS, O MY SOUL   393 11
AND WHY ART THOU SO DISQUIETED WITHIN ME   393 12
14 WHY ART THOU SO VEXED, O MY SOUL   393 31
AND WHY ART THOU SO DISQUIETED WITHIN ME   393 31
2 FOR THOU ART THE GOD OF MY STRENGTH   394 06
AND WHY ART THOU SO DISQUIETED WITHIN ME   394 15
5 WHY ART THOU SO HEAVY, O MY SOUL   394 15
5 THOU ART MY KING, O GOD   394 32
10 BUT NOW THOU ART FAR OFF, AND PUTTEST US TO   395 11
2 THOU ART FAIRER THAN THE CHILDREN OF MEN   396 18
O GOD, THOU THAT ART THE GOD OF MY HEALTH   404 05
FOR THOU ART THE GOD OF MY REFUGE   411 22
FOR THOU, O GOD, ART MY REFUGE, AND MY MERCIFUL GOD   412 10
AND THAT THOU, LORD, ART MERCIFUL   414 23

ART　　　　　CONTINUED

O GOD, THOU ART MY GOD　　　　　　　　　　　　　　　414 26
THOU, O GOD, ART PRAISED IN SION　　　　　　　　　　416 11
THOU THAT ART THE HOPE OF ALL THE ENDS OF THE EARTH,　416 22
O HOW WONDERFUL ART THOU IN THY WORKS　　　　　　　417 17
18 THOU ART GONE UP ON HIGH, THOU HAST LED CAPTIVITY　420 19
35 O GOD, WONDERFUL ART THOU IN THY HOLY PLACES　　421 27
6 THOU ART MY HELPER, AND MY REDEEMER　　　　　　　424 32
TO HELP ME, FOR THOU ART MY HOUSE OF DEFENCE, AND MY　425 09
THOU, O LORD GOD, ART THE THING THAT I LONG FOR　　425 14
THOU ART MY HOPE, EVEN FROM THY YOUTH　　　　　　　425 15
THOU ART HE THAT TOOK ME OUT OF MY MOTHER'S WOMB　　425 17
O GOD, WHEREFORE ART THOU ABSENT FROM US SO LONG　　430 03
4 THOU ART GLORIOUS IN MIGHT, *　　　　　　　　　　432 28
7 THOU, EVEN THOU ART TO BE FEARED　　　　　　　　　433 02
THY SIGHT WHEN THOU ART ANGRY　　　　　　　　　　　433 03
14 THOU ART THE GOD THAT DOEST WONDERS, *　　　　　434 10
ART ONLY THE MOST HIGHEST OVER ALL THE EARTH　　　445 09
THOU ART BECOME GRACIOUS UNTO THY LAND　　　　　　446 08
5 FOR THOU, LORD, ART GOOD AND GRACIOUS, *　　　　447 13
10 FOR THOU ART GREAT, AND DOEST WONDROUS THINGS　447 23
THOU ART GOD ALONE　　　　　　　　　　　　　　　　447 24
THOU, O LORD GOD, ART FULL OF COMPASSION AND MERCY, *　448 04
18 FOR THOU ART THE GLORY OF THEIR STRENGTH, *　　451 08
SHALL CALL ME, THOU ART MY FATHER, *　　　　　　　451 27
AND ART DISPLEASED AT HIM　　　　　　　　　　　　　452 17
THOU ART GOD FROM EVERLASTING, AND WORLD WITHOUT END　453 21
9 FOR WHEN THOU ART ANGRY ALL OUR DAYS ARE GONE　　454 04
UNTO THE LORD, THOU ART MY HOPE, AND MY STRONGHOLD　454 30
9 FOR THOU, LORD, ART MY HOPE　　　　　　　　　　　455 13
BUT THOU, LORD, ART THE MOST HIGHEST FOR EVERMORE　456 15
THOU ART FROM EVERLASTING　　　　　　　　　　　　457 10
9 FOR THOU, LORD, ART HIGHER THAN ALL THAT ARE IN THE　461 14
THOU ART EXALTED FAR ABOVE ALL GODS　　　　　　　461 15
BUT THOU ART THE SAME, AND THY YEARS SHALL NOT FAIL　466 03
THOU ART CLOTHED WITH MAJESTY AND HONOUR　　　　　467 25
O LORD MY GOD, THOU ART BECOME EXCEEDING GLORIOUS　467 25
THOU ART A PRIEST FOR EVER AFTER THE ORDER OF　　482 14
AND ART BECOME MY SALVATION　　　　　　　　　　　489 25
THOU ART MY GOD, AND I WILL PRAISE THEE　　　　　489 25
28 THOU ART MY GOD, AND I WILL THANK THEE　　　　489 25
12 BLESSED ART THOU, O LORD　　　　　　　　　　　490 22
THOU ART MY PORTION, O LORD　　　　　　　　　　　493 24
68 THOU ART GOOD AND GRACIOUS　　　　　　　　　　494 17
114 THOU ART MY DEFENCE AND SHIELD　　　　　　　　497 26
RIGHTEOUS ART THOU, O LORD　　　　　　　　　　　　499 13
QUICKEN ME, AS THOU ART WONT　　　　　　　　　　　500 24
2 THOU ART ABOUT MY PATH, AND ABOUT MY BED　　　　514 23
AND ART ACQUAINTED WITH ALL MY WAYS　　　　　　　514 24
UP INTO HEAVEN, THOU ART THERE　　　　　　　　　　515 02
DOWN TO HELL, THOU ART THERE ALSO　　　　　　　　515 03
UNTO THE LORD, THOU ART MY GOD, *　　　　　　　　516 20
THOU ART MY HOPE, AND MY PORTION IN THE LAND OF THE　518 14
FOR THOU ART MY GOD　　　　　　　　　　　　　　　519 13
THE ANOINTING SPIRIT ART, WHO DOST THY SEVENFOLD　543 33
WHERE THOU ART GUIDE, NO ILL CAN COME　　　　　　544 19
THE ANOINTING SPIRIT ART, WHO DOST THY SEVENFOLD　556 08
WHERE THOU ART GUIDE, NO ILL CAN COME　　　　　　556 17
NOT THINK THAT THOU ART BOUND TO BELIEVE, AND TO DO,　577 20
THAT THOU ART NOT ABLE TO DO THESE THINGS OF THYSELF,　580 16
MERCIFUL GOD, WHO ART OF PURER EYES THAN TO BEHOLD　589 26
AT THY HANDS, WHO ART EVER READY TO RECEIVE HUMBLE　590 05
O GOD, WHO ART THE LIFE OF MORTAL MEN, THE LIGHT OF　595 04
AND KNOW THAT THOU ART GOD　　　　　　　　　　　595 23
KNOWING THAT THOU ART DOING FOR THEM BETTER THINGS　597 11

ARTICLE

BELIEVED AS AN ARTICLE OF THE FAITH, OR BE THOUGHT　603 31
UNDER THIS ARTICLE, DOTH CONTAIN A GODLY AND　　　610 06
THIS ARTICLE IS RECEIVED IN THIS CHURCH, SO FAR AS　R 610 24

ARTICLES

LIKEWISE IN HER ARTICLES AND HOMILIES, DECLARED THE　V 22
BELIEVE ALL THE ARTICLES OF THE CHRISTIAN FAITH, AS　276 31
BELIEVE ALL THE ARTICLES OF THE CHRISTIAN FAITH, AS　278 08
BELIEVE ALL THE ARTICLES OF THE CHRISTIAN FAITH　　283 26
BELIEVE ALL THE ARTICLES OF THE CHRISTIAN FAITH　　284 08
RECITE THE ARTICLES OF THE CHRISTIAN FAITH AS　　284 09
LEARN IN THESE ARTICLES OF YOUR BELIEF　　　　　　284 27
YOU IN CERTAIN ARTICLES, TO THE END THAT THE　　　554 13
BELIEVE ALL THE ARTICLES OF THE CHRISTIAN FAITH　　577 17
REHEARSE THE ARTICLES OF THY BELIEF　　　　　　　577 27
LEARN IN THESE ARTICLES OF THY BELIEF　　　　　　578 09
OF THE FORMER ARTICLES IS OMITTED　　　　　　　　R 607 11
TO THE REMAINING PARTS OF IT, IN OTHER ARTICLES　R 607 12

ASCEND

WE MIGHT ALSO ASCEND, AND REIGN WITH HIM IN GLORY　078 21
AND MIND THITHER ASCEND, AND WITH HIM CONTINUALLY　177 17
3 WHO SHALL ASCEND INTO THE HILL OF THE LORD　　　368 32
3 WHO SHALL ASCEND INTO THE HILL OF THE LORD　　　563 15

ASCENDED

HE ASCENDED INTO HEAVEN, AND SITTETH ON THE RIGHT　015 25
AND ASCENDED INTO HEAVEN, AND SITTETH ON THE RIGHT　016 11
HE ASCENDED INTO HEAVEN, AND SITTETH ON THE RIGHT　029 30
AND ASCENDED INTO HEAVEN, AND SITTETH ON THE RIGHT　030 16
AND ASCENDED INTO HEAVEN, AND SITTETH ON THE RIGHT　071 13
IN THEIR SIGHT ASCENDED UP INTO HEAVEN, TO PREPARE A　078 19
CHRIST TO HAVE ASCENDED INTO THE HEAVENS　　　　177 16
AND NO MAN HATH ASCENDED UP TO HEAVEN, BUT HE THAT　188 24

ASCENDED　　　　　CONTINUED

WHEN HE ASCENDED UP ON HIGH, HE LED CAPTIVITY　　237 14
NOW THAT HE ASCENDED, WHAT IS IT BUT THAT HE ALSO　237 15
SAME ALSO THAT ASCENDED UP FAR ABOVE ALL HEAVENS,　237 17
HE ASCENDED INTO HEAVEN, AND SITTETH ON THE RIGHT　284 19
WHEN HE ASCENDED UP ON HIGH, HE LED CAPTIVITY　　537 34
NOW THAT HE ASCENDED, WHAT IS IT BUT THAT HE ALSO　538 02
SAME ALSO THAT ASCENDED UP FAR ABOVE ALL HEAVENS,　538 04
AND WAS ASCENDED INTO HEAVEN, SENT ABROAD INTO　545 17
AND WAS ASCENDED INTO HEAVEN, POURED DOWN HIS　557 24
HE ASCENDED INTO HEAVEN, AND SITTETH ON THE RIGHT　578 03
WHEREWITH HE ASCENDED INTO HEAVEN, AND THERE SITTETH,　603 23

ASCENDETH

THE LORD ASCENDETH INTO HEAVEN　　　　　　　　　R 008 26

ASCENDING

ANOTHER ANGEL ASCENDING FROM THE EAST, HAVING THE　256 14

ASCENSION

WEEK AND UNTIL ASCENSION DAY　　　　　　　　　　R 008 23
ON ASCENSION DAY AND UNTIL WHITSUNDAY　　　　　　R 008 25
BY THY GLORIOUS RESURRECTION AND ASCENSION　　　055 12
EASTER DAY, ASCENSION DAY, WHITSUNDAY, AND TRINITY　R 070 32
UPON ASCENSION DAY, AND SEVEN DAYS AFTER　　　　R 078 15
HIS MIGHTY RESURRECTION AND GLORIOUS ASCENSION　081 04
AND ASCENSION, AND BY THE COMING OF THE HOLY GHOST　318 07

ASCRIBE

ASCRIBE UNTO THE LORD WORSHIP AND STRENGTH　　　373 30
ASCRIBE UNTO THE LORD, O YE MIGHTY, *　　　　　　373 30
2 ASCRIBE UNTO THE LORD THE HONOUR DUE UNTO HIS NAME　373 32
STRENGTH WILL I ASCRIBE UNTO THEE　　　　　　　　411 22
34 ASCRIBE YE THE POWER TO GOD OVER ISRAEL　　　421 25
7 ASCRIBE UNTO THE LORD, O YE KINDREDS OF THE　　460 13
ASCRIBE UNTO THE LORD WORSHIP AND POWER　　　　460 13
8 ASCRIBE UNTO THE LORD THE HONOUR DUE UNTO HIS NAME　460 14

ASER

THE DAUGHTER OF PHANUEL, OF THE TRIBE OF ASER　　233 17

ASH

BUT NOTE, THAT ON ASH WEDNESDAY AND GOOD FRIDAY THE　R 008 12

ASHAMED

ARE YE NOT ASHAMED TO SAY YE WILL NOT COME　　　088 32
A FLINT, AND I KNOW THAT I SHALL NOT BE ASHAMED　144 18
THEN IN THOSE THINGS WHEREOF YE ARE NOW ASHAMED　198 32
WHOSOEVER BELIEVETH ON HIM SHALL NOT BE ASHAMED　226 31
HE SHALL NOT BE ASHAMED TO CONFESS THE　　　　　280 06
ALL THEY THAT HOPE IN THEE SHALL NOT BE ASHAMED　369 21
AND THEIR FACES WERE NOT ASHAMED　　　　　　　　380 12
17 LET THEM BE ASHAMED, AND CONFOUNDED TOGETHER,　391 16
GOD OF HOSTS, BE ASHAMED FOR MY CAUSE　　　　　422 14
2 LET THEM BE ASHAMED AND CONFOUNDED THAT SEEK AFTER　424 22
22 O LET NOT THE SIMPLE GO AWAY ASHAMED　　　　431 20
MAKE THEIR FACES ASHAMED, O LORD, *　　　　　　445 04
SEE IT, AND BE ASHAMED, *　　　　　　　　　　　448 10
AND WILL NOT BE ASHAMED　　　　　　　　　　　　492 31
THAT I BE NOT ASHAMED　　　　　　　　　　　　　495 17
SHALL NOT BE ASHAMED WHEN THEY SPEAK WITH THEIR　506 03
ADVERSARY MAY BE ASHAMED, HAVING NOTHING TO SAY　555 12
BOTH AFRAID AND ASHAMED TO OFFEND THEE　　　　　588 20

ASHES

THEM BEAUTY FOR ASHES, THE OIL OF JOY FOR MOURNING,　107 07
OF GOATS, AND THE ASHES OF AN HEIFER SPRINKLING THE　132 29
TO EARTH, ASHES TO ASHES, DUST TO DUST　　　　　333 16
EARTH TO EARTH, ASHES TO ASHES, DUST TO DUST　　333 16
9 FOR I HAVE EATEN ASHES AS IT WERE BREAD, *　　464 27
AND SCATTERETH THE HOAR-FROST LIKE ASHES　　　　523 28

ASIA

IN PONTUS, AND ASIA, PHRYGIA, AND PAMPHYLIA, IN　181 03
THAT I CAME INTO ASIA, AFTER WHAT MANNER I HAVE BEEN　550 07

ASIDE

A DREAM, HE TURNED ASIDE INTO THE PARTS OF GALILEE　107 20
AND LAID ASIDE HIS GARMENTS　　　　　　　　　　　155 31
AND HE TOOK HIM ASIDE FROM THE MULTITUDE, AND PUT HIS　206 32
AND THAT TURN ASIDE THE STRANGER FROM HIS RIGHT, AND　232 19
LET US LAY ASIDE EVERY WEIGHT, AND THE SIN WHICH DOTH　258 21
LAYING ASIDE ALL MALICE, AND ALL GUILE, AND　　259 25
STARTING ASIDE LIKE A BROKEN BOW　　　　　　　　438 27
TO FORSAKE AND SET ASIDE, AS MUCH AS YE MAY, ALL　541 07
THE SAME, LAYING ASIDE THE STUDY OF THE WORLD AND THE　542 28

ASK

HOLY WORD, AND TO ASK THOSE THINGS WHICH ARE　006 08
HOLY WORD, AND TO ASK THOSE THINGS WHICH ARE　023 17
ALL WHICH WE ASK THROUGH JESUS CHRIST OUR LORD　036 23
BEFORE WE ASK, AND OUR IGNORANCE IN ASKING　　049 30
BLINDNESS WE CANNOT ASK, VOUCHSAFE TO GIVE US, FOR　050 03
OF THOSE WHO ASK IN THY SON'S NAME　　　　　　　050 07

ASK   CONTINUED

EVERY COMMANDMENT, ASK GOD MERCY FOR THEIR   R 067 24
HERE THE PRIEST MAY ASK THE SECRET INTERCESSIONS OF   R 074 02
FROM JERUSALEM TO ASK HIM, WHO ART THOU   095 22
THAT THEY SHOULD ASK BARABBAS, AND DESTROY JESUS   135 36
AND IF I ALSO ASK YOU, YE WILL NOT ANSWER ME, NOR LET   151 31
WERE DESIROUS TO ASK HIM, AND SAID UNTO THEM,   174 04
WHATSOEVER YE SHALL ASK THE FATHER IN MY NAME,   176 21
ASK, AND YE SHALL RECEIVE, THAT YOUR JOY MAY BE FULL   176 22
AT THAT DAY YE SHALL ASK IN MY NAME   176 26
THAT ANY MAN SHOULD ASK THEE   177 02
TO HIS DISCIPLES, ASK, AND IT SHALL BE GIVEN YOU   183 10
IF A SON SHALL ASK BREAD OF ANY OF YOU THAT IS A   183 14
OR IF HE ASK A FISH, WILL HE FOR A FISH GIVE HIM A   183 15
OR IF HE SHALL ASK AN EGG, WILL HE OFFER HIM A   183 16
SPIRIT TO THEM THAT ASK HIM   183 19
AND WHATSOEVER WE ASK, WE RECEIVE OF HIM, BECAUSE WE   191 27
MAKE THEM TO ASK SUCH THINGS AS SHALL PLEASE THEE   203 13
WE ARE NOT WORTHY TO ASK, BUT THROUGH THE MERITS AND   206 09
ABOVE ALL THAT WE ASK OR THINK, ACCORDING TO THE   212 22
FROM THAT DAY FORTH ASK HIM ANY MORE QUESTIONS   215 23
THINGS WHICH WE ASK FAITHFULLY WE MAY OBTAIN   222 12
ASK IT EITHER IN THE DEPTH, OR IN THE HEIGHT ABOVE   235 26
UNTO AHAZ, SAYING, ASK THEE A SIGN OF THE LORD THY   235 26
I WILL NOT ASK, NEITHER WILL I TEMPT THE LORD   235 28
IN YOU, YE SHALL ASK WHAT YE WILL, AND IT SHALL BE   238 18
LACK WISDOM, LET HIM ASK OF GOD, THAT GIVETH TO ALL   239 12
BUT LET HIM ASK IN FAITH, NOTHING WAVERING   239 14
WHATSOEVER YE SHALL ASK IN MY NAME, THAT WILL I DO,   240 22
IF YE SHALL ASK ANY THING IN MY NAME, I WILL DO IT   240 23
WHATSOEVER YE SHALL ASK OF THE FATHER IN MY NAME,   242 03
JESUS ANSWERED AND SAID, YE KNOW NOT WHAT YE ASK   247 11
AND I SAY UNTO YOU, ASK, AND IT SHALL BE GIVEN YOU   263 03
IF A SON SHALL ASK BREAD OF ANY OF YOU THAT IS A   263 07
OR IF HE ASK A FISH, WILL HE FOR A FISH GIVE HIM A   263 09
OR IF HE SHALL ASK AN EGG, WILL HE OFFER HIM A   263 10
SPIRIT TO THEM THAT ASK HIM   263 13
SAYING, ASK, AND YE SHALL HAVE   274 15
SO GIVE NOW UNTO US WHO ASK   274 17
THE HAND, AND SHALL ASK THE WITNESSES THE NAME   R 279 31
MINISTER SHALL FIRST ASK THE QUESTIONS PROVIDED IN   R 281 25
THE MINISTER SHALL ASK THEM THE QUESTIONS WHICH   R 283 13
TO THE PEOPLE, SHALL ASK THE QUESTION FOLLOWING,   R 284 25
MINISTER SAY, LET US ASK GOD'S HELP TO KNOW AND TO   285 19
TO THEM, SHALL ASK THE QUESTIONS WHICH FOLLOW, THE   R 287 31
THE MINISTER SHALL ASK THEM THE QUESTIONS CONCERNING   R 290 26
THE MINISTER SHALL ASK THE PEOPLE THE FOLLOWING   R 294 02
ANY OTHER, TO ASK THEM FORGIVENESS   R 313 22
ALL WHICH WE ASK THROUGH JESUS CHRIST OUR LORD   317 07
IN HIM, THAT, IF WE ASK ANY THING ACCORDING TO HIS   322 16
WHATSOEVER WE ASK, WE KNOW THAT WE HAVE THE   322 18
UNTO THEE, AND TO ASK SUCH THINGS AS ARE REQUISITE   566 17
THE GRACE TO ASK WHAT THOU WOULDEST HAVE US TO DO,   595 28

ASKED

WE HAVE FAITHFULLY ASKED ACCORDING TO THY WILL, MAY   050 10
AND THEY ASKED HIM, WHAT THEN   095 24
AND THEY ASKED HIM, AND SAID UNTO HIM, WHY BAPTIZEST   095 31
AND HIS DISCIPLES ASKED HIM, SAYING, WHAT MIGHT THIS   121 28
PASS BY, HE ASKED WHAT IT MEANT   123 28
WAS COME NEAR, HE ASKED HIM, SAYING, WHAT WILT THOU   123 35
AND THE GOVERNOR ASKED HIM, SAYING, ART THOU THE KING   135 19
IN THE MIDST, AND ASKED JESUS, SAYING, ANSWEREST THOU   143 10
THE HIGH PRIEST ASKED HIM, AND SAID UNTO HIM, ART   143 13
AND PILATE ASKED HIM, ART THOU THE KING OF THE JEWS   145 07
AND PILATE ASKED HIM AGAIN, SAYING, ANSWEREST THOU   145 09
ON THE FACE, AND ASKED HIM, SAYING, PROPHESY,   151 25
AND PILATE ASKED HIM, SAYING, ART THOU THE KING OF   152 31
OF GALILEE, HE ASKED WHETHER THE MAN WERE A   153 07
HITHERTO HAVE YE ASKED NOTHING IN MY NAME   176 22
THEY ASKED OF HIM, SAYING, LORD, WILT THOU   178 05
AND HE ASKED THEM, HOW MANY LOAVES HAVE YE   199 16
THE SERVANTS, AND ASKED WHAT THESE THINGS MEANT   202 28
WAS A LAWYER, ASKED HIM A QUESTION, TEMPTING HIM, AND   215 08
JESUS ASKED THEM, SAYING, WHAT THINK YE OF   215 16
UNTO THEM THAT ASKED NOT AFTER ME   227 20
AND HE ASKED FOR A WRITING TABLE, AND WROTE, SAYING,   243 23
HE ASKED HIS DISCIPLES, SAYING, WHOM DO MEN   245 32
4 HE ASKED LIFE OF THEE   365 11

ASKETH

AND NONE OF YOU ASKETH ME, WHITHER GOEST THOU   175 07
EVERY ONE THAT ASKETH RECEIVETH   183 12
EVERY ONE THAT ASKETH RECEIVETH   263 05

ASKING

BEFORE WE ASK, AND OUR IGNORANCE IN ASKING   049 31
HEARING THEM, AND ASKING THEM QUESTIONS   110 29
IS THE FIRST (SECOND OR THIRD) TIME OF ASKING   R 304 25

ASLEEP

AND WHEN HE HAD SAID THIS, HE FELL ASLEEP   100 17
HE FOUND THEM ASLEEP AGAIN, (FOR THEIR EYES WERE   142 08
UNTO THIS PRESENT, BUT SOME ARE FALLEN ASLEEP   205 10
THEM WHICH ARE ASLEEP, THAT YE SORROW NOT, EVEN AS   268 29
THE LORD SHALL NOT PREVENT THEM WHICH ARE ASLEEP   269 05
AT LENGTH FALL ASLEEP PEACEFULLY IN THEE, AND AWAKE   336 13

ASS

NOR HIS OX, NOR HIS ASS, NOR ANY THING THAT IS HIS   069 21

ASS   CONTINUED

YE SHALL FIND AN ASS TIED, AND A COLT WITH HER   091 15
AND SITTING UPON AN ASS, AND A COLT THE FOAL OF AN   091 21
AND A COLT THE FOAL OF AN ASS   091 21
AND BROUGHT THE ASS, AND THE COLT, AND PUT ON THEM   091 23
OF YOU SHALL HAVE AN ASS OR AN OX FALLEN INTO A PIT,   214 05
NOR HIS OX, NOR HIS ASS, NOR ANY THING THAT IS HIS   287 21
NOR HIS OX, NOR HIS ASS, NOR ANY THING THAT IS HIS   579 22

ASSAULT

WHICH MAY ASSAULT AND HURT THE SOUL   127 20

ASSAULTS

SERVANTS IN ALL ASSAULTS OF OUR ENEMIES   017 08
THE CRAFTS AND ASSAULTS OF THE DEVIL   054 20

ASSEMBLE

TO DO, WHEN WE ASSEMBLE AND MEET TOGETHER TO RENDER   006 05
TO DO, WHEN WE ASSEMBLE AND MEET TOGETHER TO RENDER   023 13
OR ABOUT TO ASSEMBLE) IN THY NAME AND PRESENCE   R 037 12
ASSEMBLE THE ELDERS, GATHER THE   124 30
SERVANTS SHALL ASSEMBLE IN THY NAME, TO OFFER UP   564 32

ASSEMBLED

SENATE AND REPRESENTATIVES IN CONGRESS ASSEMBLED   035 11
CHURCH HERE ASSEMBLED IN THY NAME AND PRESENCE   036 30
HERE ASSEMBLED IN THY NAME, BEING CHANGED TO   R 037 11
CHANGED TO NOW ASSEMBLED (OR ABOUT TO ASSEMBLE) IN   R 037 12
WITH HIM WERE ASSEMBLED ALL THE CHIEF PRIESTS AND THE   142 32
DISCIPLES WERE ASSEMBLED FOR FEAR OF THE JEWS,   171 16
BEING ASSEMBLED TOGETHER WITH THEM, COMMANDED   177 29
YEAR THEY ASSEMBLED THEMSELVES WITH THE CHURCH,   241 13
THE PEOPLE ASSEMBLED IN THE CHURCH WHERE YOU SHALL BE   533 07
DISCIPLES WERE ASSEMBLED FOR FEAR OF THE JEWS,   551 29
WE HAVE ASSEMBLED FOR THE PURPOSE OF   570 12

ASSEMBLING

FORSAKING THE ASSEMBLING OF OURSELVES TOGETHER,   158 26

ASSEMBLY

SANCTIFY A FAST, CALL A SOLEMN ASSEMBLY   124 29
MIDST OF THE ASSEMBLY OF THE SAINTS UPON THE EARTH   568 08

ASSES

AND THE WILD ASSES QUENCH THEIR THIRST   468 16

ASSIST

ASSIST US MERCIFULLY, O LORD, IN THESE OUR   049 11
MERCIFULLY ASSIST OUR PRAYERS WHICH WE MAKE BEFORE   058 17
SO TO ASSIST US WITH THY GRACE, THAT WE MAY   083 26
ASSIST US MERCIFULLY WITH THY HELP, O LORD GOD OF OUR   147 08
A DEACON IS, TO ASSIST THE PRIEST IN DIVINE SERVICE,   294 17
TO SERVE, TO ASSIST THE PRIEST IN DIVINE SERVICE, AND   533 11

ASSISTANCE

THROUGH GOD'S ASSISTANCE, TO ADMINISTER TO ALL SUCH   086 29
THE HEAVENLY ASSISTANCE OF THE HOLY GHOST   541 17
THE CONSTANT ASSISTANCE OF THY HOLY SPIRIT   588 16
DIRECTION AND ASSISTANCE OF THY HOLY SPIRIT   590 11

ASSISTANCES

ASSISTANCES, AND COMFORTS OF THY HOLY   591 16

ASSUAGE

HIS TEARS, ASSUAGE HIS PAIN, AS SHALL SEEM TO THEE   314 07

ASSURANCE

IN FULL ASSURANCE OF THE GLORY THAT SHALL BE   144 09
HEART IN FULL ASSURANCE OF FAITH, HAVING OUR HEARTS   158 20

ASSURE

AND DOST ASSURE US THEREBY OF THY FAVOUR AND GOODNESS   083 20
AND SHALL ASSURE OUR HEARTS BEFORE HIM   191 23
AND A PLEDGE TO ASSURE US THEREOF   292 13
MINISTER SHALL ASSURE HIM OF GOD'S MERCY AND   R 313 26
AND I WILL ASSURE THEE, O ISRAEL, *   442 29
AND A PLEDGE TO ASSURE US THEREOF   581 15

ASSURED

FOR BE YE WELL ASSURED, THAT IF ANY PERSONS ARE   300 28

ASSYRIA

8 ASSYRIA ALSO IS JOINED WITH THEM   444 20

ASTONISHED

HIM WERE ASTONISHED AT HIS UNDERSTANDING AND ANSWERS   110 30
MADE US ASTONISHED, WHICH WERE EARLY AT THE   167 23
BELIEVED WERE ASTONISHED, AS MANY AS CAME WITH PETER,   184 22
FOR HE WAS ASTONISHED, AND ALL THAT WERE WITH HIM, AT   196 24

ASTONISHED   CONTINUED

MEASURE ASTONISHED, SAYING, HE HATH DONE ALL THINGS   207 07
TREMBLING AND ASTONISHED SAID, LORD, WHAT WILT THOU   230 05
THEY WERE ASTONISHED, AND SUDDENLY CAST DOWN   399 18

ASTRAY

ALL WE LIKE SHEEP HAVE GONE ASTRAY   022 14
FOR YE WERE AS SHEEP GOING ASTRAY   172 18
ARE BORN, THEY GO ASTRAY, AND SPEAK LIES   410 13
4 THEY WENT ASTRAY IN THE WILDERNESS OUT OF THE WAY,   476 12
176 I HAVE GONE ASTRAY LIKE A SHEEP THAT IS LOST   502 02

ASUNDER

HE BURST ASUNDER IN THE MIDST, AND ALL HIS BOWELS   234 14
GOD HATH JOINED TOGETHER, LET NOT MAN PUT ASUNDER   268 11
GOD HATH JOINED TOGETHER LET NO MAN PUT ASUNDER   303 32
THEIR BONDS ASUNDER, *   346 02
ARE SMITTEN ASUNDER AS WITH A SWORD, *   393 27

ATE

AND ATE THE OFFERINGS OF THE DEAD   474 25

ATHIRST

LET HIM THAT IS ATHIRST COME   022 30
2 MY SOUL IS ATHIRST FOR GOD, YEA, EVEN FOR THE   392 31

ATTAIN

THIS LIFE, TO ATTAIN EVERLASTING JOY AND FELICITY   018 04
IT MAY AT LENGTH ATTAIN TO LIFE EVERLASTING   101 09
FOUND WORTHY TO ATTAIN TO EVERLASTING JOYS   168 21
NOT FINALLY TO ATTAIN THY HEAVENLY PROMISES   207 16
WE, WITH THEM, ATTAIN TO THINE ETERNAL JOY   258 16
I CANNOT ATTAIN UNTO IT   514 30
GOD'S MERCY, THEY ATTAIN TO EVERLASTING FELICITY   606 15

ATTAINMENT

TOWARDS THE ATTAINMENT OF EVERLASTING SALVATION   049 13

ATTEND

ARE NOT ABLE TO ATTEND THE PUBLIC MINISTRATION IN   R 323 33

ATTENDED

BY HIM, ATTENDED BY THE NEW INCUMBENT, AND BY THE   R 570 03

ATTENDING

ATTENDING CONTINUALLY UPON THIS VERY   114 24

ATTENTION

THE ATTENTION OF THIS CHURCH WAS IN THE FIRST PLACE   VI 15

AUDIBLY

EVERY ONE SHALL AUDIBLY ANSWER, I DO   R 296 29

AUGUSTINE

AS SAINT AUGUSTINE SAITH) THE SACRAMENT OF THE BODY   609 05

AUGUSTUS

FROM CAESAR AUGUSTUS, THAT ALL THE WORLD SHOULD BE   098 29

AUTHOR

WHO ART THE AUTHOR OF PEACE AND LOVER OF   017 05
WHO ART THE AUTHOR AND GIVER OF ALL GOOD THINGS   198 20
WHO ART THE AUTHOR OF ALL GODLINESS   222 09
HIM WHO IS THE AUTHOR AND FINISHER OF OUR FAITH, THY   258 17
UNTO JESUS THE AUTHOR AND FINISHER OF OUR FAITH   258 24
WHO ART THE AUTHOR AND GIVER OF ALL GOOD THINGS   283 08
THE AUTHOR OF EVERLASTING LIFE   303 04
AND THE AUTHOR OF EVERLASTING LIFE   545 15
AND THE AUTHOR OF EVERLASTING LIFE   557 23

AUTHORITIES

ANGELS AND AUTHORITIES AND POWERS BEING MADE SUBJECT   162 03
BE PROMPTLY REPORTED TO THE PARISH AUTHORITIES   R 281 30

AUTHORITY

CONSENT AND AUTHORITY, MAY BE ALTERED, ABRIDGED,   V 07
IN PLACE OF AUTHORITY SHOULD, FROM TIME TO TIME,   V 19
AND ALL OTHERS IN AUTHORITY   017 31
AND TO ALL IN AUTHORITY, WISDOM AND STRENGTH TO KNOW   018 11
ALL OTHERS IN AUTHORITY, THAT THEY, KNOWING WHOSE   032 08
WHOSE AUTHORITY THEY BEAR, MAY FAITHFULLY AND   032 10
WE ENTRUST THE AUTHORITY OF GOVERNMENT, THAT THERE   036 18
AND FOR ALL THAT ARE IN AUTHORITY   047 17
AND THE CIVIL AUTHORITY HAS NOT SINCE THOUGHT PROPER   VI 05
BY ANY WORLDLY AUTHORITY WHATSOEVER) TO TAKE A   VI 24
AND EXHORT, AND REBUKE WITH ALL AUTHORITY   098 26
AM A MAN UNDER AUTHORITY, HAVING SOLDIERS UNDER ME   115 13
THAT EXERCISE AUTHORITY UPON THEM ARE CALLED   149 21
HERE HE HATH AUTHORITY FROM THE CHIEF PRIESTS TO BIND 230 24

AUTHORITY   CONTINUED

GREAT EXERCISE AUTHORITY UPON THEM   247 22
THAT EXERCISE AUTHORITY UPON THEM ARE CALLED   250 06
TO HONOUR AND OBEY THE CIVIL AUTHORITY   288 28
RULE AND ALL AUTHORITY AND POWER   328 29
AND ADMITTED THEREUNTO BY LAWFUL AUTHORITY   529 18
TAKE THOU AUTHORITY TO EXECUTE THE OFFICE OF A   534 05
TAKE THOU AUTHORITY TO READ THE GOSPEL IN THE CHURCH   534 11
TAKE THOU AUTHORITY TO EXECUTE THE OFFICE OF A PRIEST 546 17
TAKE THOU AUTHORITY TO PREACH THE WORD OF GOD, AND TO 546 25
AS BY THE AUTHORITY OF GOD'S WORD, AND BY THE ORDER   555 16
AND USE THE AUTHORITY GIVEN HIM, NOT TO DESTRUCTION,   558 02
LICENCE AND AUTHORITY TO PERFORM THE OFFICE OF A   569 16
TO HONOUR AND OBEY THE CIVIL AUTHORITY   580 04
BLESS ALL IN AUTHORITY OVER US   590 27
AND OF A SOUND MIND TO ALL IN PLACES OF AUTHORITY   600 03
OF WHOSE AUTHORITY WAS NEVER ANY DOUBT IN THE CHURCH   603 34
AND AUTHORITY IN CONTROVERSIES OF FAITH   607 03
HAVE PUBLIC AUTHORITY GIVEN UNTO THEM IN THE   607 23
HAVE CHIEF AUTHORITY IN THE MINISTRATION OF THE WORD   608 10
COMMISSION AND AUTHORITY, WE MAY USE THEIR MINISTRY,   608 12
THAT HATH AUTHORITY THEREUNTO   609 30
BY COMMON AUTHORITY, OUGHT TO BE REBUKED OPENLY,   609 38
HURTETH THE AUTHORITY OF THE MAGISTRATE, AND WOUNDETH 609 40
CHURCH HATH AUTHORITY TO ORDAIN, CHANGE, AND ABOLISH, 609 42
ONLY BY MAN'S AUTHORITY, SO THAT ALL THINGS BE DONE   610 02
BUT HATH NO AUTHORITY IN THINGS PURELY SPIRITUAL   610 39
TO THE CIVIL AUTHORITY, REGULARLY AND LEGITIMATELY   610 41

AUTHORIZE

SO WE AUTHORIZE YOU TO CLAIM AND ENJOY ALL THE   569 29

AUTHORIZED

OR OTHER AUTHORIZED PRAYERS AND INTERCESSIONS   R 071 30

AUTHORS

AND ANCIENT AUTHORS, THAT FROM THE APOSTLES' TIME   529 12

AVAIL

EXCUSES WILL AVAIL BEFORE GOD   089 02

AVAILETH

CIRCUMCISION AVAILETH ANY THING, NOR UNCIRCUMCISION,   210 32

AVENGE

DEARLY BELOVED, AVENGE NOT YOURSELVES, BUT RATHER   113 03
AVENGE THOU MY CAUSE, MY GOD AND MY LORD   383 09
AND AVENGE ME IN THY STRENGTH   406 03
154 AVENGE THOU MY CAUSE, AND DELIVER ME   500 19
FOR THE LORD WILL AVENGE HIS PEOPLE, *   510 30
THE LORD WILL AVENGE THE POOR, *   517 02

AVENGED

SEETH THAT I BE AVENGED, *   362 34
WILT THOU BE AVENGED OF THEM THAT PERSECUTE ME   495 26
7 TO BE AVENGED OF THE NATIONS, *   525 15

AVENGER

THE LORD IS THE AVENGER OF ALL SUCH, AS WE ALSO HAVE   127 32
THOU MIGHTEST STILL THE ENEMY AND THE AVENGER   351 03
FOR THE ENEMY AND AVENGER   395 27

AVOID

THAT THEY MAY AVOID THOSE THINGS THAT ARE CONTRARY TO 173 08

AWAKE

AWAKE, AWAKE   004 18
AWAKE, AWAKE   004 18
IT IS HIGH TIME TO AWAKE OUT OF SLEEP   090 31
HE SAITH, AWAKE THOU THAT SLEEPEST, AND ARISE FROM   129 21
AND WHEN THEY WERE AWAKE, THEY SAW HIS GLORY, AND THE 248 31
IN THEE, AND AWAKE UP AFTER THY LIKENESS   336 13
AND WHEN I AWAKE UP AFTER THY LIKENESS, I SHALL BE   359 20
23 AWAKE, AND STAND UP TO JUDGE MY QUARREL   383 09
AWAKE, AND BE NOT ABSENT FROM US FOR EVER   396 06
AWAKE, LUTE AND HARP   409 31
9 AWAKE UP, MY GLORY   409 31
I MYSELF WILL AWAKE RIGHT EARLY   409 32
2 AWAKE, THOU LUTE AND HARP   479 07
I MYSELF WILL AWAKE RIGHT EARLY   479 07

AWAKED

66 SO THE LORD AWAKED AS ONE OUT OF SLEEP, *   439 08

AWAKEN

THE INNOCENT, AWAKEN THE GUILTY   046 25

AWAKETH

EVEN LIKE AS A DREAM WHEN ONE AWAKETH   429 16

AWAY

THAT TAKEST AWAY THE SINS OF THE WORLD, HAVE	025 28
THOU THAT TAKEST AWAY THE SINS OF THE WORLD, RECEIVE	025 30
AND THE RICH HE HATH SENT EMPTY AWAY	026 25
TAKE AWAY ALL HATRED AND PREJUDICE, AND WHATSOEVER	037 28
OF THY MERCIES DO AWAY MINE OFFENCES	060 12
CAST ME NOT AWAY FROM THY PRESENCE, *	060 32
AND HATH TAKEN AWAY THE SIN OF THE WORLD	078 10
RECEIVE THE CROWN OF GLORY THAT FADETH NOT AWAY	079 27
THAT TAKEST AWAY THE SINS OF THE WORLD, HAVE	084 08
THOU THAT TAKEST AWAY THE SINS OF THE WORLD, RECEIVE	084 10
THAT WE MAY CAST AWAY THE WORKS OF DARKNESS, AND PUT	090 12
SHALL NOT PASS AWAY, TILL ALL BE FULFILLED	093 19
HEAVEN AND EARTH SHALL PASS AWAY	093 20
BUT MY WORDS SHALL NOT PASS AWAY	093 21
MINDED TO PUT HER AWAY PRIVILY	105 02
ANGELS WERE GONE AWAY FROM THEM INTO HEAVEN, THE	106 07
MANIFESTED TO TAKE AWAY OUR SINS	117 23
UP, IT WITHERED AWAY, BECAUSE IT LACKED MOISTURE	121 23
AND TAKETH AWAY THE WORD OUT OF THEIR HEARTS,	121 34
AND IN TIME OF TEMPTATION FALL AWAY	122 05
WHETHER THERE BE KNOWLEDGE, IT SHALL VANISH AWAY	123 06
THEN THAT WHICH IS IN PART SHALL BE DONE AWAY	123 09
BECAME A MAN, I PUT AWAY CHILDISH THINGS	123 11
CAME AND BESOUGHT HIM, SAYING, SEND HER AWAY	128 13
THEY LED HIM AWAY, AND DELIVERED HIM TO PONTIUS	134 33
ON HIM, AND LED HIM AWAY TO CRUCIFY HIM	136 25
TAKE AWAY THIS CUP FROM ME	142 02
AND AGAIN HE WENT AWAY, AND PRAYED, AND SPAKE THE	142 07
AND LEAD HIM AWAY SAFELY	142 19
AND THEY LED JESUS AWAY TO THE HIGH PRIEST	142 31
NEITHER TURNED AWAY BACK	144 13
AND CARRIED HIM AWAY, AND DELIVERED HIM TO PILATE	145 05
SOLDIERS LED HIM AWAY INTO THE HALL, CALLED	145 30
HE APPEARED TO PUT AWAY SIN BY THE SACRIFICE OF	148 06
AT ONCE, SAYING, AWAY WITH THIS MAN, AND RELEASE UNTO	153 30
AND AS THEY LED HIM AWAY, THEY LAID HOLD UPON CNE	154 09
GOATS SHOULD TAKE AWAY SINS	157 23
HE TAKETH AWAY THE FIRST, THAT HE MAY ESTABLISH THE	157 32
CAN NEVER TAKE AWAY SINS	158 05
BUT THEY CRIED OUT, AWAY WITH HIM, AWAY WITH HIM,	159 27
AWAY WITH HIM, AWAY WITH HIM, CRUCIFY HIM	159 27
AND THEY TOOK JESUS, AND LED HIM AWAY	159 31
AND THAT THEY MIGHT BE TAKEN AWAY	160 34
US (NOT THE PUTTING AWAY OF THE FILTH OF THE FLESH,	161 31
AND, STEAL HIM AWAY, AND SAY UNTO THE PEOPLE, HE IS	162 21
THE STONE TAKEN AWAY FROM THE SEPULCHRE	164 12
THEY HAVE TAKEN AWAY THE LORD OUT OF THE SEPULCHRE,	164 15
THE DISCIPLES WENT AWAY AGAIN UNTO THEIR OWN HOME	164 28
WHO SHALL ROLL US AWAY THE STONE FROM THE DOOR OF THE	165 23
THEY SAW THAT THE STONE WAS ROLLED AWAY	165 25
GRANT US SO TO PUT AWAY THE LEAVEN OF MALICE AND	170 21
IT IS EXPEDIENT FOR YOU THAT I GO AWAY	175 10
FOR IF I GO NOT AWAY, THE COMFORTER WILL NOT COME	175 11
SAID UNTO YOU, I GO AWAY, AND COME AGAIN UNTO YCU	182 03
AND IF I SEND THEM AWAY FASTING TO THEIR OWN HOUSES,	199 12
AND HE SENT THEM AWAY	199 25
BESEECH THEE TO PUT AWAY FROM US ALL HURTFUL THINGS,	199 30
CARRIED AWAY UNTO THESE DUMB IDOLS, EVEN AS	203 18
WHICH GLORY WAS TO BE DONE AWAY	206 22
WHEREFORE PUTTING AWAY LYING, SPEAK EVERY MAN TRUTH	216 16
BE PUT AWAY FROM YOU, WITH ALL MALICE	216 28
AND TAKE HIM AWAY, AND CAST HIM INTO OUTER	218 27
CAST NOT AWAY THEREFORE YOUR CONFIDENCE, WHICH HATH	228 14
CHILDREN CARRIED AWAY WITH EVERY BLAST OF VAIN	237 08
IN ME THAT BEARETH NOT FRUIT HE TAKETH AWAY	238 07
AS THE FLOWER OF THE GRASS HE SHALL PASS AWAY	239 20
THE RICH MAN FADE AWAY IN HIS WAYS	239 24
AND GOD SHALL WIPE AWAY ALL TEARS FROM THEIR EYES	257 16
MYSTICAL WASHING AWAY OF SIN	279 16
DOST SO PUT AWAY THE SINS OF THOSE WHO TRULY REPENT,	313 31
DRIVEST AWAY FROM MEN'S BODIES ALL SICKNESS	315 07
SINS MAY BE DONE AWAY BY THY MERCY, AND HIS PARDCN	316 14
WAS SLAIN TO TAKE AWAY THE SINS OF THE WORLD	317 18
PURGED AND DONE AWAY, IT MAY BE PRESENTED PURE AND	317 21
OF GOD, WHO TAKEST AWAY THE SINS OF THE WORLD	318 23
FROM SIN, AND DRIVE AWAY ALL PAIN OF SOUL AND BODY,	320 10
OF THY MERCIES; DO AWAY OUR OFFENCES AND CLEANSE US	323 16
THE LORD GAVE, AND THE LORD HATH TAKEN AWAY	324 15
BEAUTY TO CONSUME AWAY, LIKE AS IT WERE A MOTH	325 03
AND FADE AWAY SUDDENLY LIKE THE GRASS	325 23
FOR WE CONSUME AWAY IN THY DISPLEASURE, *	325 26
SO SOON PASSETH IT AWAY, AND WE ARE GCNE	325 35
CAST THY SERVANT AWAY IN DISPLEASURE	326 25
DEATH DIDST TAKE AWAY THE STING OF DEATH	336 11
AND GOD SHALL WIPE AWAY ALL TEARS FROM THEIR EYES	341 27
THE WIND SCATTERETH AWAY FROM THE FACE OF THE EARTH	345 17
AND CAST AWAY THEIR CORDS FROM US	346 02
AND WORN AWAY BECAUSE OF ALL MINE ENEMIES	349 12
8 AWAY FROM ME, ALL YE THAT WORK INIQUITY	349 14
HE HIDETH AWAY HIS FACE, AND HE WILL NEVER SEE IT	353 31
TO TAKE AWAY MY SOUL	359 05
CAST THY SERVANT AWAY IN DISPLEASURE	372 17
3 O PLUCK ME NOT AWAY, NEITHER DESTROY ME WITH THE	373 10
COUNSEL TO TAKE AWAY MY LIFE	376 23
MY BONES CONSUMED AWAY THROUGH MY DAILY COMPLAINING	377 27
SHALT LOOK AFTER HIS PLACE, AND HE SHALL BE AWAY	385 15
EVEN AS THE SMOKE SHALL THEY CONSUME AWAY	386 03
HE SHALL NOT BE CAST AWAY	386 10
11 TAKE THY PLAGUE AWAY FROM ME	389 29
BEAUTY TO CONSUME AWAY, LIKE AS IT WERE A MOTH	389 32
SHOWED HIS VOICE, AND THE EARTH SHALL MELT AWAY	398 06
SHALL CARRY NOTHING AWAY WITH HIM WHEN HE DIETH, *	401 09
LEST I PLUCK YOU AWAY, AND THERE BE NONE TO DELIVER	403 03
OF THY MERCIES DO AWAY MINE OFFENCES	403 10

AWAY   CONTINUED

11 CAST ME NOT AWAY FROM THY PRESENCE, *	403 31
THEN WOULD I FLEE AWAY, AND BE AT REST	406 31
THEN WOULD I GET ME AWAY FAR OFF, *	406 32
7 LET THEM FALL AWAY LIKE WATER THAT RUNNETH APACE	410 21
8 LET THEM CONSUME AWAY LIKE A SNAIL, AND BE LIKE THE	410 23
HE SHALL TAKE THEM AWAY WITH A WHIRLWIND, THE GREEN	410 27
SO SHALT THOU DRIVE THEM AWAY	419 12
8 CAST ME NOT AWAY IN THE TIME OF AGE	425 23
NOT THE SIMPLE GO AWAY ASHAMED	431 20
TURNED HE HIS WRATH AWAY, *	437 16
A WIND THAT PASSETH AWAY, AND COMETH NOT AGAIN	437 19
AND FELL AWAY LIKE THEIR FOREFATHERS	438 26
AND TOOK HIM AWAY FROM THE SHEEP-FOLDS	439 20
THOU HAST TURNED AWAY THE CAPTIVITY OF JACOB	446 09
3 THOU HAST TAKEN AWAY ALL THY DISPLEASURE, *	446 12
AND ARE CUT AWAY FROM THY HAND	449 06
7 THOU HAST PUT AWAY MINE ACQUAINTANCE FAR FROM ME,	449 11
HAST THOU PUT AWAY FROM ME, *	449 33
42 THOU HAST TAKEN AWAY THE EDGE OF HIS SWORD,	452 26
AND FADE AWAY SUDDENLY LIKE THE GRASS	453 28
7 FOR WE CONSUME AWAY IN THY DISPLEASURE, *	453 31
SO SOON PASSETH IT AWAY, AND WE ARE GONE	454 10
DAYS ARE CONSUMED AWAY LIKE SMOKE, *	464 15
MY GOD, TAKE ME NOT AWAY IN THE MIDST CF MINE AGE	465 28
AT THE VOICE OF THY THUNDER THEY HASTE AWAY	468 07
AND THEY GET THEM AWAY TOGETHER, *	469 04
WHEN THOU TAKEST AWAY THEIR BREATH, THEY DIE, AND ARE	469 19
TO TURN AWAY HIS WRATHFUL INDIGNATION, LEST HE SHCULD	474 16
THOSE THAT LED THEM AWAY CAPTIVE TO PITY THEM	475 29
THEIR SOUL MELTETH AWAY BECAUSE OF THE TROUBLE	477 29
AND LET NOT THE SIN OF HIS MOTHER BE DONE AWAY	480 29
AND AM DRIVEN AWAY AS THE GRASSHOPPER	481 17
HE SHALL GNASH WITH HIS TEETH, AND CONSUME AWAY	484 05
28 MY SOUL MELTETH AWAY FOR VERY HEAVINESS	491 23
37 O TURN AWAY MINE EYES, LEST THEY BEHOLD VANITY	492 13
39 TAKE AWAY THE REBUKE THAT I AM AFRAID OF	492 17
115 AWAY FROM ME, YE WICKED	497 28
119 THOU PUTTEST AWAY ALL THE UNGODLY OF THE EARTH	498 06
EYES ARE WASTED AWAY WITH LOOKING FOR THY HEALTH, *	498 15
TURN NOT AWAY THE FACE OF THINE ANOINTED	508 23
21 AND GAVE AWAY THEIR LAND FOR AN HERITAGE	512 24
THEY THAT LED US AWAY CAPTIVE, REQUIRED OF US THEN A	513 09
HIS TIME PASSETH AWAY LIKE A SHADOW	519 29
TO BANISH AND DRIVE AWAY FROM THE CHURCH ALL	542 20
DRIVE FAR AWAY OUR GHOSTLY FOE, AND THINE ABIDING	545 06
TO DRAW AWAY DISCIPLES AFTER THEM	550 33
TO BANISH AND DRIVE AWAY FROM THE CHURCH ALL	555 03
DRIVE FAR AWAY OUR GHOSTLY FOE, AND THINE ABIDING	557 12
AND GOD SHALL WIPE AWAY ALL TEARS FROM THEIR EYES	567 18
FOR THE FORMER THINGS ARE PASSED AWAY	567 21
CANNOT PUT AWAY OUR SINS, AND ENDURE THE SEVERITY CF	605 12
SHOULD TAKE AWAY THE SINS OF THE WORLD	605 34
ORDINANCE TAKEN AWAY BY THEIR WICKEDNESS, NOR THE	608 14

AWE

WHOLE EARTH STAND IN AWE OF HIM	009 18
WHOLE EARTH STAND IN AWE OF HIM	021 20
4 STAND IN AWE, AND SIN NOT	347 19
STAND IN AWE OF HIM, ALL YE THAT DWELL IN THE WORLD	379 02
WHOLE EARTH STAND IN AWE OF HIM	460 17
MY HEART STANDETH IN AWE OF THY WORD	501 04

AXES

WITH AXES AND HAMMERS	430 17

BAAL-PEOR

UNTO BAAL-PEOR, *	474 25

BABE

YE SHALL FIND THE BABE WRAPPED IN SWADDLING CLOTHES,	099 18
AND JOSEPH, AND THE BABE LYING IN A MANGER	106 12

BABES

OF THE MOUTHS OF BABES AND SUCKLINGS HAST ORDAINED	102 21
AND PRUDENT, AND HAST REVEALED THEM UNTO BABES	235 06
AS NEWBORN BABES, DESIRE THE SINCERE MILK OF THE	259 26
OF THE MOUTH OF BABES AND SUCKLINGS THOU HAST	260 15
THE MOUTH OF VERY BABES AND SUCKLINGS HAST THOU	350 34
LEAVE THE REST OF THEIR SUBSTANCE FOR THEIR BABES	359 18

BABYLON

OF EGYPT AND BABYLON, *	448 18
BY THE WATERS OF BABYLON WE SAT DOWN AND WEPT,	513 05
8 O DAUGHTER OF BABYLON, WASTED WITH MISERY	513 21

BACK

THEY TURNED BACK AGAIN TO JERUSALEM, SEEKING	110 26
GAVE HIS BACK TO THE SMITERS AND HID NOT HIS	144 07
I GAVE MY BACK TO THE SMITERS, AND MY CHEEKS TC THEM	144 13
I WAS NOT REBELLIOUS, NEITHER TURNED AWAY BACK	144 13
WAS HEALED, TURNED BACK, AND WITH A LOUD VOICE	210 08
BUT IF ANY MAN DRAW BACK, MY SOUL SHALL HAVE NO	228 19
OF THEM WHO DRAW BACK UNTO PERDITION	228 20
SHALL BE TURNED BACK, AND PUT TO SHAME SUDDENLY	349 19
ENEMIES ARE DRIVEN BACK, *	351 26
LET THEM BE TURNED BACK, AND BROUGHT TO CONFUSION,	381 25
13 I HAVE NOT KEPT BACK THY LOVING MERCY AND TRUTH *	391 06

BACK   CONTINUED

HEART IS NOT TURNED BACK, *   395 30
TURNED THEMSELVES BACK IN THE DAY OF BATTLE   435 18
42 THEY TURNED BACK, AND TEMPTED GOD, *   437 23
SO WILL NOT WE GO BACK FROM THEE   442 07
JORDAN WAS DRIVEN BACK   484 30
THAT THOU WAST DRIVEN BACK   485 03
AS FOR SUCH AS TURN BACK UNTO THEIR OWN WICKEDNESS,   505 02
PLOWED UPON MY BACK, *   506 25
AND HOW I KEPT BACK NOTHING THAT WAS PROFITABLE UNTO   550 10
TO BE KEPT BACK BY FRAUD   599 31

BACKS

ALSO TO TURN THEIR BACKS UPON ME, *   362 19
US TO TURN OUR BACKS UPON OUR ENEMIES, *   395 13
AND EVER BOW THOU DOWN THEIR BACKS   423 22
THEY TURNED THEIR BACKS, AND FELL AWAY LIKE THEIR   438 26

BACKWARD

THEM BE DRIVEN BACKWARD, AND PUT TO REBUKE, THAT WISH   391 17
THEM BE TURNED BACKWARD AND PUT TO CONFUSION THAT   424 23
HIS ENEMIES BACKWARD, *   439 10
AND TURNED BACKWARD, *   506 29

BAD

AS THEY FOUND, BOTH BAD AND GOOD   218 20

BADE

A GREAT SUPPER, AND BADE MANY   192 03
AND HE THAT BADE THEE AND HIM COME AND SAY TO THEE,   214 13
THAT WHEN HE THAT BADE THEE COMETH, HE MAY SAY UNTO   214 16

BADGES

BE NOT ONLY BADGES OR TOKENS OF CHRISTIAN MEN'S   607 31

BALMS

LET NOT MY HEAD REFUSE THEIR PRECIOUS BALMS   517 21

BAND

UNTO HIM THE WHOLE BAND OF SOLDIERS   136 17
AND THEY CALL TOGETHER THE WHOLE BAND   145 31

BANDS

DELIVERED FROM THE BANDS OF THOSE SINS, WHICH BY OUR   223 17
I HAVE BROKEN THE BANDS OF THEIR YOKE, AND DELIVERED   262 12

BANISH

TO BANISH AND DRIVE AWAY FROM THE CHURCH   542 20
TO BANISH AND DRIVE AWAY FROM THE CHURCH   555 03

BANISHED

WEAKNESS MAY BE BANISHED AND HIS STRENGTH RECALLED   315 09

BANNER

FIGHT UNDER HIS BANNER, AGAINST SIN, THE WORLD, AND   280 08

BANNERS

AND SET UP THEIR BANNERS FOR TOKENS   430 13

BANNS

AND OF THE BANNS OF MATRIMONY, AND OF OTHER MATTERS   R 071 27
BY PUBLISHING THE BANNS IN CHURCHES, OR BY LICENCE,   R 304 17
AND WHEN THE BANNS ARE PUBLISHED, IT SHALL BE IN   R 304 21
I PUBLISH THE BANNS OF MARRIAGE BETWEEN N   R 304 22

BANQUET

TO FEED ON THE BANQUET OF THAT MOST HEAVENLY FOOD   089 18

BAPTISM

ACKNOWLEDGE ONE BAPTISM FOR THE REMISSION OF SINS   016 20
ACKNOWLEDGE ONE BAPTISM FOR THE REMISSION OF SINS   030 25
ONE FAITH, ONE BAPTISM, ONE GOD AND FATHER OF US ALL,   037 31
BY THY BAPTISM, FASTING, AND TEMPTATION,   055 07
ACKNOWLEDGE ONE BAPTISM FOR THE REMISSION OF SINS   071 22
AND PREACH THE BAPTISM OF REPENTANCE FOR THE   112 08
EVEN BAPTISM, DOTH ALSO NOW SAVE US (NOT   161 30
AFTER THE BAPTISM WHICH JOHN PREACHED   166 18
AFTER THE BAPTISM WHICH JOHN PREACHED   184 06
WITH HIM BY BAPTISM INTO DEATH   197 12
ONE FAITH, ONE BAPTISM, ONE GOD AND FATHER OF ALL,   213 24
FROM THE BAPTISM OF JOHN, UNTO THAT SAME DAY THAT HE   251 22
WITH THE BAPTISM THAT I AM BAPTIZED WITH   247 13
WITH THE BAPTISM THAT I AM BAPTIZED WITH   247 15
DEFER NOT THE BAPTISM OF THEIR CHILDREN, AND THAT IT   R 273 04
CONVENIENT THAT BAPTISM SHOULD BE ADMINISTERED UPON   R 273 05
SO REQUIRE, BAPTISM MAY BE ADMINISTERED UPON ANY   R 273 06
THE TIME OF THE BAPTISM OF AN ADULT, THERE SHALL BE   R 273 22
TO THY HOLY BAPTISM, MAY RECEIVE REMISSION OF SIN,   274 13
HAVE COME HITHER DESIRING TO RECEIVE HOLY BAPTISM   277 21
SOON AFTER HIS BAPTISM AS CONVENIENTLY MAY BE   R 281 14

BAPTISM   CONTINUED

OFFICE FOR THE BAPTISM OF ADULTS   R 281 26
ADMINISTER HOLY BAPTISM, USING THE FOREGOING FORM   R 281 28
SUCH BAPTISM SHALL BE PROMPTLY REPORTED TO THE PARISH   R 281 29
PARTS OF BAPTISM), SUCH PERSON MAY BE BAPTIZED IN THE   R 282 10
MY SPONSORS GAVE ME THIS NAME IN BAPTISM   283 18
AND VOWS OF MY BAPTISM, AND DECLARING MY LOYALTY AND   291 25
THAT IS TO SAY, BAPTISM, AND THE SUPPER OF THE LORD   292 07
THE OUTWARD AND VISIBLE SIGN OR FORM IN BAPTISM   292 18
SIGN OR FORM IN BAPTISM IS WATER   292 19
WHAT IS THE INWARD AND SPIRITUAL GRACE IN BAPTISM   292 23
GRACE IN BAPTISM IS A DEATH UNTO SIN, AND A NEW BIRTH   292 24
VOWS OF THEIR BAPTISM, AND BE CONFIRMED BY THE   294 25
OR THAT WAS MADE IN YOUR NAME, AT YOUR BAPTISM   296 24
BE RECEIVED BY BAPTISM INTO THE CONGREGATION OF   565 20
VOWS OF THEIR BAPTISM, AND BE CONFIRMED BY THE   565 25
MY SPONSORS IN BAPTISM   577 09
THAT IS TO SAY, BAPTISM, AND THE SUPPER OF THE LORD   581 10
IS THE OUTWARD VISIBLE SIGN OR FORM IN BAPTISM   581 20
COMMITTED AFTER BAPTISM IS SIN AGAINST THE HOLY   605 39
BE DENIED TO SUCH AS FALL INTO SIN AFTER BAPTISM   605 41
THAT IS TO SAY, BAPTISM, AND THE SUPPER OF THE LORD   607 37
SACRAMENTS WITH BAPTISM, AND THE LORD'S SUPPER,   607 42
BAPTISM IS NOT ONLY A SIGN OF PROFESSION, AND MARK OF   608 24
THAT RECEIVE BAPTISM RIGHTLY ARE GRAFTED INTO THE   608 27
THE BAPTISM OF YOUNG CHILDREN IS IN ANY WISE TO BE   608 31

BAPTIST

THY SERVANT JOHN BAPTIST WAS WONDERFULLY BORN,   242 08
SOME SAY THAT THOU ART JOHN THE BAPTIST   245 34

BAPTIZE

SAYING, I BAPTIZE WITH WATER   096 02
JOHN DID BAPTIZE IN THE WILDERNESS, AND PREACH THE   112 08
BUT HE SHALL BAPTIZE YOU WITH THE HOLY GHOST   112 17
ALL NATIONS, AND BAPTIZE THEM IN THE NAME OF THE   279 13
I BAPTIZE THEE IN THE NAME OF THE FATHER, AND OF THE   279 28
I BAPTIZE THEE IN THE NAME OF THE FATHER, AND OF THE   281 21
I BAPTIZE THEE IN THE NAME OF THE FATHER, AND OF THE   282 13
TO BAPTIZE   294 14
OF THE PRIEST TO BAPTIZE INFANTS   533 16

BAPTIZED

AND WERE ALL BAPTIZED OF HIM IN THE RIVER OF JORDAN,   112 11
I INDEED HAVE BAPTIZED YOU WITH WATER   112 16
AND WAS BAPTIZED OF JOHN IN JORDAN   112 19
THAT AS WE ARE BAPTIZED INTO THE DEATH OF THY BLESSED   161 13
FOR JOHN TRULY BAPTIZED WITH WATER   178 02
BUT YE SHALL BE BAPTIZED WITH THE HOLY GHOST NOT MANY   178 03
ARE WE ALL BAPTIZED INTO ONE BODY, WHETHER WE BE JEWS   183 04
SHOULD NOT BE BAPTIZED, WHICH HAVE RECEIVED THE HOLY   184 27
THEM TO BE BAPTIZED IN THE NAME OF THE LORD   184 29
ONLY THEY WERE BAPTIZED IN THE NAME OF THE LORD   185 26
OF US AS WERE BAPTIZED INTO JESUS CHRIST WERE   197 10
CHRIST WERE BAPTIZED INTO HIS DEATH   197 11
AND WERE ALL BAPTIZED UNTO MOSES IN THE CLOUD AND IN   201 07
SIGHT FORTHWITH, AND AROSE, AND' WAS BAPTIZED   230 36
AND TO BE BAPTIZED WITH THE BAPTISM THAT I AM   247 13
THAT I AM BAPTIZED WITH   247 13
MY CUP, AND BE BAPTIZED WITH THE BAPTISM THAT I AM   247 15
THAT I AM BAPTIZED WITH   247 16
THEIR CHILDREN BAPTIZED IN THEIR HOUSES   R 273 08
TO BE BAPTIZED, WHEN THEY CAN BE HAD, TWO GODFATHERS   R 273 09
CHILDREN TO BE BAPTIZED, THE PARENTS OR SPONSORS   R 273 12
YEARS ARE TO BE BAPTIZED, TIMELY NOTICE SHALL BE   R 273 17
BEEN ALREADY BAPTIZED, OR NO   273 26
THAT HE MAY BE BAPTIZED WITH WATER AND THE HOLY   274 04
YE HAVE BROUGHT THIS CHILD HERE TO BE BAPTIZED   276 20
WILT THOU BE BAPTIZED IN THIS FAITH   277 02
PERSONS TO BE BAPTIZED ANSWERING THE QUESTIONS FOR   R 277 19
WILT THOU BE BAPTIZED IN THIS FAITH   278 11
NOW TO BE BAPTIZED THEREIN, MAY RECEIVE THE FULNESS   279 17
PERSON TO BE BAPTIZED BE AN ADULT, THE MINISTER SHALL   R 279 30
THUS BAPTIZED, SHOULD BE CONFIRMED BY THE   R 281 13
THEN ANY BAPTIZED PERSON PRESENT MAY ADMINISTER HOLY   R 281 28
OR PERSON SO BAPTIZED BE AFTERWARD BROUGHT TO THE   R 281 32
WILT THOU BE BAPTIZED IN THIS FAITH   R 282 04
ANY PERSON WAS BAPTIZED WITH WATER, IN THE NAME OF   R 282 08
PERSON MAY BE BAPTIZED IN THE FORM BEFORE APPOINTED   R 282 10
ART NOT ALREADY BAPTIZED, N   282 13
MADE A MEMBER OF THE CHURCH WHEN I WAS BAPTIZED   290 30
AND ALL BAPTIZED PEOPLE ARE THE MEMBERS   290 33
THE PERSON IS BAPTIZED, IN THE NAME OF THE FATHER,   292 20
WHAT IS REQUIRED OF PERSONS TO BE BAPTIZED   292 27
ARE INFANTS BAPTIZED, WHEN BY REASON OF THEIR TENDER   292 31
ONLY THEY WERE BAPTIZED IN THE NAME OF THE LORD   296 18
THE PERSON IS BAPTIZED, IN THE NAME OF THE FATHER,   581 21
WHAT IS REQUIRED OF PERSONS TO BE BAPTIZED   581 27
ARE INFANTS BAPTIZED, WHEN BY REASON OF THEIR TENDER   581 31
FOR THEM THAT BELIEVE AND ARE BAPTIZED   604 39
ALTHOUGH BAPTIZED, AND BORN AGAIN IN CHRIST,   605 35

BAPTIZEST

UNTO HIM, WHY BAPTIZEST THOU THEN, IF THOU BE NOT   095 32

BAPTIZING

BETHABARA BEYOND JORDAN, WHERE JOHN WAS BAPTIZING   096 07
ALL NATIONS, BAPTIZING THEM IN THE NAME OF THE   275 28
ALL NATIONS, BAPTIZING THEM IN THE NAME OF THE   552 11

BAR-JONA

BLESSED ART THOU, SIMON BAR-JONA   246 05

BARABBAS

THEY HAD THEN A NOTABLE PRISONER, CALLED BARABBAS   135 28
BARABBAS, OR JESUS WHICH IS CALLED CHRIST   135 30
THEY SHOULD ASK BARABBAS, AND DESTROY JESUS   135 36
THEY SAID, BARABBAS   136 04
RELEASED HE BARABBAS UNTO THEM   136 13
WAS ONE NAMED BARABBAS, WHICH LAY BOUND WITH THEM   145 14
RATHER RELEASE BARABBAS UNTO THEM   145 22
RELEASED BARABBAS UNTO THEM, AND DELIVERED JESUS,   145 28
AND RELEASE UNTO US BARABBAS   153 30

BARACHIAS

SON OF BARACHIAS, WHOM YE SLEW BETWEEN THE TEMPLE AND   100 24

BARE

AND THEY BARE IT   113 23
AND SPRANG UP, AND BARE FRUIT AN HUNDREDFOLD   121 26
IS THE WOMB THAT BARE THEE, AND THE PAPS WHICH THOU   130 19
AND HE BARE THEM, AND CARRIED THEM ALL THE DAYS CF   139 04
FOR MANY BARE FALSE WITNESS AGAINST HIM, BUT THEIR   143 04
AROSE CERTAIN, AND BARE FALSE WITNESS AGAINST HIM,   143 05
WOMBS THAT NEVER BARE, AND THE PAPS WHICH NEVER GAVE   154 17
AND HE THAT SAW IT BARE RECORD, AND HIS RECORD IS   161 05
WHO HIS OWN SELF BARE OUR SINS IN HIS OWN BODY CN THE   172 16
AND THEY THAT BARE HIM STOOD STILL   213 04
THAT SHALL BE, BUT BARE GRAIN, IT MAY CHANCE OF   329 09
AND STRIPPETH BARE THE FORESTS   374 15
OF WOMEN THAT BARE THE TIDINGS   420 03

BAREST

THOU NEVER BAREST RULE OVER THEM   139 29

BARLEY

WHICH HATH FIVE BARLEY LOAVES, AND TWO SMALL FISHES   131 33
OF THE FIVE BARLEY LOAVES, WHICH REMAINED CVER AND   132 10
WHICH HATH FIVE BARLEY LOAVES, AND TWO SMALL FISHES   225 30
OF THE FIVE BARLEY LOAVES, WHICH REMAINED CVER AND   226 09

BARN

BUT GATHER THE WHEAT INTO MY BARN   116 32

BARNABAS

HOLY APOSTLE BARNABAS WITH SINGULAR GIFTS CF THE HOLY   240 29
THEY SENT FORTH BARNABAS, THAT HE SHOULD GC AS FAR AS   241 05
THEN DEPARTED BARNABAS TO TARSLS, FOR TO SEEK SAUL   241 10
BY THE HANDS OF BARNABAS AND SAUL   241 22
BY THE HANDS OF BARNABAS AND SAUL   246 31
THEN PAUL AND BARNABAS WAXED BOLD, AND SAID, IT WAS   260 30

BARNS

SO SHALL THY BARNS BE FILLED WITH PLENTY, AND THY   005 22
NEITHER DO THEY REAP, NOR GATHER INTO BARNS   211 17
NEITHER DO THEY REAP, NOR GATHER INTO BARNS   266 15

BARREN

THOU BARREN THAT BEAREST NOT   131 09
BLESSED ARE THE BARREN, AND THE WOMBS THAT NEVER   154 16
THE SIXTH MONTH WITH HER, WHO WAS CALLED BARREN   236 27
IN A BARREN AND DRY LAND WHERE NO WATER IS   414 28
LAND MAKETH HE BARREN, *   478 14
8 HE MAKETH THE BARREN WOMAN TO KEEP HOUSE, *   484 23

BARS

HATH MADE FAST THE BARS OF THY GATES, *   265 02
AND SMITTEN THE BARS OF IRON IN SUNDER   477 08
HATH MADE FAST THE BARS OF THY GATES, *   523 21

BARSABAS

JOSEPH CALLED BARSABAS, WHO WAS SURNAMED JUSTUS,   234 26

BARTHOLOMEW

APOSTLE BARTHOLOMEW GRACE TRLLY TO BELIEVE AND TC   249 15

BASHAN

FAT BULLS OF BASHAN CLOSE ME IN ON EVERY SIDE   366 27
15 AS THE HILL OF BASHAN, SO IS GOD'S HILL   420 11
EVEN AN HIGH HILL, AS THE HILL OF BASHAN   420 12
WILL BRING MY PEOPLE AGAIN, AS I DID FROM BASHAN   420 31
AND OG, THE KING OF BASHAN   510 25
20 AND OG, THE KING OF BASHAN   512 22

BASIN

IN A DECENT BASIN TO BE PROVIDED BY THE PARISH   R 073 29

BASKETS

FILLED TWELVE BASKETS WITH THE FRAGMENTS CF THE FIVE   132 09
UP OF THE BROKEN MEAT THAT WAS LEFT SEVEN BASKETS   199 24

BASKETS   CONTINUED

FILLED TWELVE BASKETS WITH THE FRAGMENTS OF THE FIVE   226 08

BASON

WATER INTO A BASON, AND BEGAN TO WASH THE DISCIPLES'   155 32

BATTLE

IN THE DAY OF BATTLE, AND IN THE TIME OF PEACE KEEP   041 27
FROM BATTLE AND MURDER, AND FROM SUDDEN DEATH,   054 31
THOU HAST GIRDED ME WITH STRENGTH UNTO THE BATTLE   362 16
EVEN THE LORD MIGHTY IN BATTLE   369 12
IN PEACE FROM THE BATTLE THAT WAS AGAINST ME   407 28
THE SHIELD, THE SWORD, AND THE BATTLE   432 27
TURNED THEMSELVES BACK IN THE DAY OF BATTLE   435 19
AND GIVEST HIM NOT VICTORY IN THE BATTLE   452 27
THEY MAKE THEM READY TO BATTLE   502 20
THOU HAST COVERED MY HEAD IN THE DAY OF BATTLE   516 23
EVEN THE LORD MIGHTY IN BATTLE   563 27

BAY-TREE

AND FLOURISHING LIKE A GREEN BAY-TREE   387 05

BEAM

PERCEIVEST NOT THE BEAM THAT IS IN THINE OWN EYE   195 07
BEHOLDEST NOT THE BEAM THAT IS IN THINE CWN EYE   195 09
CAST OUT FIRST THE BEAM OUT OF THINE OWN EYE, ANC   195 11

BEAMS

TO CAST THY BRIGHT BEAMS OF LIGHT UPCN THY CHURCH,   101 06
3 WHO LAYETH THE BEAMS OF HIS CHAMBERS IN THE WATERS,   467 29

BEAR

AUTHORITY THEY BEAR, MAY FAITHFULLY AND OBEDIENTLY   032 11
THOU SHALT NOT BEAR FALSE WITNESS AGAINST THY   069 16
THOU SHALT NOT BEAR FALSE WITNESS AGAINST THY   090 26
FOR A WITNESS, TO BEAR WITNESS OF THE LIGHT, THAT ALL   097 27
BUT WAS SENT TO BEAR WITNESS OF THAT LIGHT   097 29
HAVE SEEN IT, AND BEAR WITNESS, AND SHEW UNTO YCU   101 16
DRAW OUT NOW, AND BEAR UNTO THE GOVERNOR OF THE   113 22
HANDS THEY SHALL BEAR THEE UP, LEST AT ANY TIME THOU   126 34
THEY COMPELLED TO BEAR HIS CROSS   136 27
AND RUFUS, TO BEAR HIS CROSS   146 07
WAS ONCE OFFERED TO BEAR THE SINS OF MANY   148 08
THAT HE MIGHT BEAR IT AFTER JESUS   154 11
ARE THREE THAT BEAR WITNESS, THE SPIRIT, AND THE   171 02
BUT YE CANNOT BEAR THEM NOW   175 18
AND YE ALSO SHALL BEAR WITNESS, BECAUSE YE HAVE BEEN   179 27
YE MAY BE ABLE TO BEAR IT   201 29
FOR I BEAR IN MY BODY THE MARKS OF THE LORD JESUS   211 05
VESSEL UNTO ME, TO BEAR MY NAME BEFORE THE GENTILES,   230 26
SHALL CONCEIVE, AND BEAR A SON, AND SHALL CALL HIS   235 32
THE BRANCH CANNOT BEAR FRUIT OF ITSELF, EXCEPT IT   238 10
THAT YE BEAR MUCH FRUIT   238 19
AND YE ALSO SHALL BEAR WITNESS, BECAUSE YE HAVE BEEN   255 33
THE LAND, NEITHER BEAR THE SHAME OF THE HEATHEN ANY   262 19
THOU SHALT NOT BEAR FALSE WITNESS AGAINST THY   287 15
TO BEAR NO MALICE NOR HATRED IN MY HEART   288 32
WE SHALL ALSO BEAR THE IMAGE OF THE HEAVENLY   329 32
AND THEY BEAR A TYRANNOUS HATE AGAINST ME   370 23
ARE LIKE A SORE BURDEN, TOO HEAVY FOR ME TO BEAR   387 29
HER FELLOWS SHALL BEAR HER COMPANY, AND SHALL BE   397 15
I BEAR UP THE PILLARS OF IT   432 05
AND HOW I DO BEAR IN MY BOSOM THE REBUKES OF MANY   453 08
12 THEY SHALL BEAR THEE IN THEIR HANDS, *   455 19
HAVE A TRIAL, AND BEAR WITNESS, HOW YOU ARE MINDED TC   554 14
THOU SHALT NOT BEAR FALSE WITNESS AGAINST THY   579 18
TO BEAR NO MALICE NOR HATRED IN MY HEART   580 11

BEARD

EVEN UNTO AARON'S BEARD, AND WENT DOWN TO THE SKIRTS   509 16
RAN DOWN UNTO THE BEARD, *   509 16

BEAREST

THOU BARREN THAT BEAREST NOT   131 09
WHICH THOU BEAREST UNTO THY PEOPLE, AND GRANT THAT,   332 04
FAVOUR THAT THOU BEAREST UNTO THY PEOPLE   473 07

BEARETH

FOR HE BEARETH NOT THE SWORD IN VAIN   114 20
BEARETH ALL THINGS, BELIEVETH ALL THINGS, HOPETH ALL   123 02
THE SPIRIT THAT BEARETH WITNESS, BECAUSE THE SPIRIT   170 32
SPIRIT HIMSELF BEARETH WITNESS WITH OUR SPIRIT, THAT   200 10
IN ME THAT BEARETH NOT FRUIT HE TAKETH AWAY   238 06
BRANCH THAT BEARETH FRUIT, HE PURGETH IT, THAT IT MAY   238 07
SPIRIT HIMSELF BEARETH WITNESS WITH OUR SPIRIT,   330 23
WAY WEEPING, AND BEARETH FORTH GOOD SEED, *   505 18

BEARING

MEET YOU A MAN BEARING A PITCHER OF WATER   140 27
A MAN MEET YOU, BEARING A PITCHER OF WATER   148 26
AND HE BEARING HIS CROSS WENT FORTH INTO A PLACE   159 31
AS CONTINUALLY BEARING IN MIND THAT YOU ARE   569 26

BEAST

AS A BEAST GOETH DOWN INTO THE VALLEY, THE SPIRIT OF	139 15
SET HIM ON HIS OWN BEAST, AND BROUGHT HIM TO AN INN,	208 31
NEITHER SHALL THE BEAST OF THE LAND DEVOUR THEM	262 15
SHALT SAVE BOTH MAN AND BEAST	384 08
EVEN AS IT WERE A BEAST BEFORE THEE	429 21
BOTH OF MAN AND BEAST	510 19

BEASTS

O ALL YE BEASTS AND CATTLE, BLESS YE THE LORD	013 16
CAUSE THE EVIL BEASTS TO CEASE OUT OF THE LAND	262 05
ANOTHER FLESH OF BEASTS, ANOTHER OF FISHES, AND	329 13
AND THE BEASTS OF THE FIELD	351 14
COMPARED UNTO THE BEASTS THAT PERISH	400 31
COMPARED UNTO THE BEASTS THAT PERISH	401 17
10 FOR ALL THE BEASTS OF THE FOREST ARE MINE,	402 10
AND THE WILD BEASTS OF THE FIELD ARE IN MY SIGHT	402 13
SAINTS UNTO THE BEASTS OF THE LAND	440 03
AND THE WILD BEASTS OF THE FIELD DEVOUR IT	441 29
11 ALL BEASTS OF THE FIELD DRINK THEREOF, *	468 15
WHEREIN ALL THE BEASTS OF THE FOREST DO MOVE	468 35
BOTH SMALL AND GREAT BEASTS	469 11
10 BEASTS AND ALL CATTLE	524 23

BEAT

AND FINALLY TO BEAT DOWN SATAN UNDER OUR FEET	056 24
43 I WILL BEAT THEM AS SMALL AS THE DUST BEFORE THE	362 23

BEATEN

THRICE WAS I BEATEN WITH RODS, ONCE WAS I STONED,	121 02

BEATETH

NOT AS ONE THAT BEATETH THE AIR	119 10

BEAUTIFIED

ADORNED AND BEAUTIFIED WITH HIS PRESENCE AND FIRST	300 14

BEAUTIFUL

PUT ON THY BEAUTIFUL GARMENTS, O JERUSALEM	004 19
HOW BEAUTIFUL ARE THE FEET OF THEM THAT	227 09

BEAUTY

THE LORD IN THE BEAUTY OF HOLINESS	009 17
THE LORD IN THE BEAUTY OF HOLINESS	021 19
IN TRUTH, IN BEAUTY, AND IN RIGHTEOUSNESS,	044 22
TO GIVE UNTO THEM BEAUTY FOR ASHES, THE OIL OF JOY	107 07
THE KING IN HIS BEAUTY, WHO WITH THEE, O FATHER, AND	248 04
THOU MAKEST HIS BEAUTY TO CONSUME AWAY, LIKE AS IT	325 03
BEHOLD THE FAIR BEAUTY OF THE LORD, AND TO VISIT HIS	326 10
7 MY BEAUTY IS GONE FOR VERY TROUBLE, *	349 12
BEHOLD THE FAIR BEAUTY OF THE LORD, AND TO VISIT HIS	372 02
THOU MAKEST HIS BEAUTY TO CONSUME AWAY, LIKE AS IT	389 32
11 SO SHALL THE KING HAVE PLEASURE IN THY BEAUTY	397 07
THEIR BEAUTY SHALL CONSUME IN THE SEPULCHRE, AND HAVE	401 03
IN PERFECT BEAUTY	401 24
AND THEIR BEAUTY INTO THE ENEMY'S HAND	438 35
THE LORD IN THE BEAUTY OF HOLINESS	460 16
WHO HAST FILLED THE WORLD WITH BEAUTY	596 18

BECAME

AMERICAN STATES BECAME INDEPENDENT WITH RESPECT TO	VI 08
THE LITURGY WHICH BECAME NECESSARY IN THE PRAYERS FOR	VI 16
BUT WHEN I BECAME A MAN, I PUT AWAY CHILDISH THINGS	123 11
AND BECAME OBEDIENT UNTO DEATH, EVEN THE	134 21
13 I BECAME A REPROACH AMONG ALL MINE ENEMIES,	376 15
14 I BECAME EVEN AS A MAN THAT HEARETH NOT, *	388 19
10 I BECAME DUMB, AND OPENED NOT MY MOUTH	389 27
AND BECAME AS THE DUNG OF THE EARTH	444 24
WHICH BECAME A SNARE UNTO THEM	475 09
WHO FOR OUR SAKES BECAME POOR, THY SON, OUR SAVIOUR	599 16

BECKONED

AND THEY BECKONED UNTO THEIR PARTNERS, WHICH WERE IN	196 19

BECOME

ONE FOLD, SHALL BECOME PARTAKERS OF EVERLASTING LIFE	037 06
THAT THEY MAY BECOME THE KINGDOM OF OUR LORD AND	044 30
GAVE HE POWER TO BECOME THE SONS OF GOD, EVEN TO THEM	097 34
NOT CHARITY, I AM BECOME AS SOUNDING BRASS, OR A	122 22
AND BECOME THE FIRSTFRUITS OF THEM THAT SLEPT	163 11
FROM SIN, AND BECOME SERVANTS TO GOD, YE HAVE YOUR	199 03
BE CONVERTED, AND BECOME AS LITTLE CHILDREN, YE SHALL	252 26
CHRIST'S CHURCH, BECOME THE RECIPIENTS OF HIS GRACE,	292 34
THE DEAD, AND BECOME THE FIRSTFRUITS OF THEM THAT	328 21
BE CONVERTED, AND BECOME AS LITTLE CHILDREN, YE SHALL	339 25
ARE CORRUPT, AND BECOME ABOMINABLE IN THEIR DOINGS	356 14
ARE ALTOGETHER BECOME ABOMINABLE	356 20
HEAREST NOT, I BECOME LIKE THEM THAT GO DOWN INTO THE	373 05
I AM BECOME LIKE A BROKEN VESSEL	376 20
ARE THEY, AND BECOME ABOMINABLE IN THEIR WICKEDNESS	405 14
ARE ALTOGETHER BECOME ABOMINABLE	405 20
8 I AM BECOME A STRANGER UNTO MY BRETHREN, *	422 18
6 I AM BECOME AS IT WERE A MONSTER UNTO MANY,	425 19
4 WE ARE BECOME AN OPEN SHAME TO OUR ENEMIES,	440 06
THOU ART BECOME GRACIOUS UNTO THY LAND	446 08

BECOME   CONTINUED

AND HE IS BECOME A REPROACH TO HIS NEIGHBOURS	452 22
6 I AM BECOME LIKE A PELICAN IN THE WILDERNESS,	464 21
MY GOD, THOU ART BECOME EXCEEDING GLORIOUS	467 25
24 I AM BECOME ALSO A REPROACH UNTO THEM	481 20
AND IS BECOME MY SALVATION	488 29
AND ART BECOME MY SALVATION	489 11
IS BECOME THE HEAD-STONE IN THE CORNER	489 12
83 FOR I AM BECOME LIKE A BOTTLE IN THE SMOKE	495 23

BECOMES

LIVE AS BECOMES IT	590 24

BECOMETH

AMONG YOU, AS BECOMETH SAINTS	129 04
REVERENCE WHICH BECOMETH A SERVANT OF GOD	288 31
FOR IT BECOMETH WELL THE JUST TO BE THANKFUL	378 19
HOLINESS BECOMETH THINE HOUSE FOR EVER	457 17

BED

TO HIM A MAN SICK OF THE PALSY, LYING ON A BED	217 02
ARISE, TAKE UP THY BED, AND GO UNTO THINE HOUSE	217 11
AND MY CHILDREN ARE WITH ME IN BED	262 32
NIGHT WASH I MY BED, AND WATER MY COUCH WITH MY	349 11
MISCHIEF UPON HIS BED, AND HATH SET HIMSELF IN NO	383 33
MAKE THOU ALL HIS BED IN HIS SICKNESS	392 05
LORD COMFORT HIM WHEN HE LIETH SICK UPON HIS BED	392 05
THEE IN MY BED, *	415 05
NOR CLIMB UP INTO MY BED	508 09
2 THOU ART ABOUT MY PATH, AND ABOUT MY BED	514 23

BED-RIDDEN

WITH AGED AND BED-RIDDEN PERSONS, OR SUCH AS ARE NOT	R 323 32

BED-TIME

A LITTLE BEFORE BED-TIME, LET THE MASTER OR MISTRESS,	R 589 13

BEDS

AND LAID THEM ON BEDS AND COUCHES, THAT AT THE LEAST	249 28
LET THEM REJOICE IN THEIR BEDS	525 12

BEELZEBUB

DEVILS THROUGH BEELZEBUB THE CHIEF OF THE DEVILS	129 27
YE SAY THAT I CAST OUT DEVILS THROUGH BEELZEBUB	129 33
AND IF I BY BEELZEBUB CAST OUT DEVILS, BY WHOM DO	129 34

BEES

CAME ABOUT ME LIKE BEES, AND ARE EXTINCT EVEN AS THE	488 23

BEFALL

THINGS THAT SHALL BEFALL ME THERE	550 16

BEFELL

WHICH BEFELL ME BY THE LYING IN WAIT OF THE JEWS	550 09

BEFRIEND

MIGHTILY BEFRIEND INNOCENT SUFFERERS, AND SANCTIFY TO	599 09

BEG

AND THIS WE BEG FOR JESUS CHRIST'S SAKE	019 11
AND THIS WE BEG FOR JESUS CHRIST'S SAKE	033 09
WE HUMBLY BEG IN THE NAME AND MEDIATION OF	035 20
BE VAGABONDS, AND BEG THEIR BREAD	480 19
AND DEVOUTLY BEG HIS BLESSING ON THIS OUR	564 24
ALL WHICH WE BEG FOR JESUS CHRIST'S SAKE, OUR MOST	566 23
TO US, WE HUMBLY BEG, THROUGH THE MERITS AND	589 06

BEGAN

WHICH HAVE BEEN SINCE THE WORLD BEGAN	014 13
JESUS BEGAN TO SAY UNTO THE MULTITUDES	094 25
AND THEY BEGAN TO BE SORROWFUL, AND TO SAY UNTO HIM	141 03
AND JOHN, AND BEGAN TO BE SORE AMAZED, AND TO BE VERY	141 30
AND SOME BEGAN TO SPIT ON HIM, AND TO COVER HIS FACE,	143 20
SAW HIM AGAIN, AND BEGAN TO SAY TO THEM THAT STOOD	143 29
BUT HE BEGAN TO CURSE AND TO SWEAR, SAYING, I KNOW	143 32
CRYING ALOUD BEGAN TO DESIRE HIM TO DO AS HE HAD EVER	145 17
HIS HEAD, AND BEGAN TO SALUTE HIM, HAIL, KING OF THE	145 33
AND THEY BEGAN TO ENQUIRE AMONG THEMSELVES, WHICH OF	149 16
AND THEY BEGAN TO ACCUSE HIM, SAYING, WE FOUND THIS	152 28
INTO A BASON, AND BEGAN TO WASH THE DISCIPLES' FEET,	155 33
ALL JUDAEA, AND BEGAN FROM GALILEE, AFTER THE BAPTISM	166 18
OF ALL THAT JESUS BEGAN BOTH TO DO AND TEACH, UNTIL	177 23
HOLY GHOST, AND BEGAN TO SPEAK WITH OTHER TONGUES, AS	190 33
ALL JUDAEA, AND BEGAN FROM GALILEE, AFTER THE BAPTISM	184 05
WITH ONE CONSENT BEGAN TO MAKE EXCUSE	192 06
SO THAT THEY BEGAN TO SINK	196 22
AND HE BEGAN TO BE IN WANT	202 06
AND THEY BEGAN TO BE MERRY	202 25
THE TEMPLE, AND BEGAN TO CAST OUT THEM THAT SOLD	204 16
DEAD SAT UP, AND BEGAN TO SPEAK	213 05
THE HOUR WHEN HE BEGAN TO AMEND	220 07
WHICH HAVE BEEN SINCE THE WORLD BEGAN	244 02

BEGAN   CONTINUED

AND HE BEGAN TO SAY UNTO THEM, THIS DAY IS THIS   261 24
SINCE THE WORLD BEGAN, HATH THY SEAT BEEN PREPARED   457 09

BEGAT

OF HIS OWN WILL BEGAT HE US WITH THE WORD CF TRUTH,   174 29
OF HIS OWN WILL BEGAT HE US WITH THE WORD CF TRUTH,   265 21

BEGGAR

WAS A CERTAIN BEGGAR NAMED LAZARUS, WHICH WAS LAID AT   190 05
TO PASS, THAT THE BEGGAR DIED, AND WAS CARRIED BY THE   190 09

BEGGED

TO PILATE, AND BEGGED THE BODY OF JESUS   162 08

BEGGING

A CERTAIN BLIND MAN SAT BY THE WAY-SIDE BEGGING   123 27
NOR HIS SEED BEGGING THEIR BREAD   386 13

BEGIN

THE MINISTER SHALL BEGIN THE MORNING PRAYER BY   R 003 03
THE MINISTER SHALL BEGIN THE EVENING PRAYER BY   R 021 03
HOLY TABLE, AND BEGIN THE OFFERTORY,SAYING ONE CR   R 071 32
WHEN THESE THINGS BEGIN TO COME TO PASS, THEN LCCK   093 12
THEN SHALL THEY BEGIN TO SAY TO THE MOUNTAINS,   154 18
AND THOU BEGIN WITH SHAME TO TAKE THE LOWEST PLACE   214 14
WHICH THOU DIDST BEGIN IN THEM MAY BE PERFECTED UNTO   335 29
SHALL BEGIN THE COMMUNION SERVICE, IN WHICH   R 549 05
BISHOP SHALL BEGIN, AND THE BISHOPS, AND THE CTHERS   R 556 04
INSTITUTOR SHALL BEGIN THE OFFICE   R 571 04
WILL BE PROPER TO BEGIN WITH A CHAPTER, CR PART CF A   R 592 06
WE MAY NEITHER BEGIN AN ACTION WITHOUT A PURE   594 22

BEGINNETH

HERE BEGINNETH SUCH A CHAPTER (OR VERSE OF SUCH   R 009 32

BEGINNING

IT WAS IN THE BEGINNING, IS NOW, AND EVER SHALL BE,   008 05
IT WAS IN THE BEGINNING, IS NOW, AND EVER SHALL BE,   009 29
US TO THE BEGINNING OF THIS DAY   017 14
IT WAS IN THE BEGINNING, IS NOW, AND EVER SHALL BE,   025 11
IT WAS IN THE BEGINNING, IS NOW, AND EVER SHALL BE,   059 07
IT WAS IN THE BEGINNING, IS NCW, AND EVER SHALL BE,   061 17
OF THE LAW, BEGINNING, HEAR WHAT OUR LORD JESUS   R 067 30
CHAPTER OF -, BEGINNING AT THE - VERSE   R 070 19
CHAPTER OF -, BEGINNING AT THE - VERSE   R 070 23
BEGINNING AT, ALL GLORY BE TO THEE, ALMIGHTY GOD,   R 083 09
IN THE BEGINNING HAST LAID THE FOUNDATICN CF   097 13
IN THE BEGINNING WAS THE WORD, AND THE WORD WAS WITH   097 20
WAS IN THE BEGINNING WITH GOD   097 21
WAS FROM THE BEGINNING, WHICH WE HAVE HEARD, WHICH WE   101 12
WHICH FROM THE BEGINNING OF THE WORLD HATH BEEN HID   108 22
THE BEGINNING OF THE GOSPEL OF JESUS CHRIST, THE SON   112 03
MAN AT THE BEGINNING DOTH SET FORTH GOOD WINE   113 27
THIS BEGINNING OF MIRACLES DID JESUS IN CANA OF   113 30
FOR THE DEVIL SINNETH FROM THE BEGINNING   117 29
THEIR HIRE, BEGINNING FROM THE LAST UNTO THE FIRST   119 30
ALL JEWRY, BEGINNING FROM GALILEE TO THIS PLACE   153 06
IT WAS IN THE BEGINNING, IS NOW, AND EVER SHALL EE,   163 19
AND BEGINNING AT MOSES AND ALL THE PROPHETS, HE   167 32
ALL NATIONS, BEGINNING AT JERUSALEM   170 15
BECAUSE YE HAVE BEEN WITH ME FROM THE BEGINNING   179 28
OUT AMONG US, BEGINNING FROM THE BAPTISM OF JOHN,   234 22
BECAUSE YE HAVE BEEN WITH ME FROM THE BEGINNING   255 34
IT WAS IN THE BEGINNING, IS NOW, AND EVER SHALL EE,   265 08
THEM AT THE BEGINNING MADE THEM MALE AND FEMALE, AND   268 06
THE REST OF HIS LIFE ACCORDING TO THIS BEGINNING   280 18
THIS OFFICE, BEGINNING, WE YIELD THEE HEARTY THANKS,   R 281 24
IT WAS IN THE BEGINNING, IS NOW, AND EVER SHALL EE,   285 08
IT WAS IN THE BEGINNING, IS NOW, AND EVER SHALL EE,   306 06
BEGINNING WITH THE COLLECT, EPISTLE,   R 321 15
BEGINNING AT THESE WORDS, YE WHO DO TRULY,   R 322 31
YOU FROM THE BEGINNING OF THE WORLD   335 13
IN THE HEAVENS OVER ALL, FROM THE BEGINNING   421 22
IN THE BEGINNING HAST LAID THE FOUNDATICN OF   465 31
LORD IS THE BEGINNING OF WISDOM   483 14
THE BISHOP BEGINNING, AND THE PRIESTS, AND CTHERS   R 543 28
IT WAS IN THE BEGINNING, IS NOW, AND EVER SHALL BE,   564 04
OF US FROM THE BEGINNING OF OUR LIVES TO THIS DAY   587 22
US TO THE BEGINNING OF THIS DAY   592 20

BEGOTTEN

BEGOTTEN OF HIS FATHER BEFORE ALL WORLDS, GOD OF GOD,   016 03
BEGOTTEN, NOT MADE   016 04
BEGOTTEN OF HIS FATHER BEFORE ALL WORLDS, GOD OF GOD,   030 08
BEGOTTEN, NOT MADE   030 09
BEGOTTEN OF HIS FATHER BEFORE ALL WORLDS, GCD OF GOD,   071 05
BEGOTTEN, NOT MADE   071 06
THIS DAY HAVE I BEGOTTEN THEE   097 03
AS OF THE ONLY BEGOTTEN OF THE FATHER,) FULL OF GRACE   098 06
THIS DAY HAVE I BEGOTTEN THEE   169 10
THIS DAY HAVE I BEGOTTEN THEE   346 11
OF THE FATHER, BEGOTTEN FROM EVERLASTING OF THE   603 09

BEGUN

WHICH THOU HAST BEGUN IN THEM MAY BE PERFECTED   042 19

BEGUN   CONTINUED

IN ALL OUR WORKS BEGUN, CONTINUED, AND ENDED IN THEE,   049 25
THAT HE WHICH HATH BEGUN A GOOD WORK IN YOU WILL   220 26
AND WHEN HE HAD BEGUN TO RECKON, ONE WAS BROUGHT UNTC   221 15
WORK WHICH HE HATH BEGUN IN YOU   543 21
WORK WHICH HE HATH BEGUN, YOU MAY BE FOUND PERFECT   555 32
IN ALL OUR WORKS BEGUN, CONTINUED, AND ENDED IN THEE,   571 10

BEHALF

CHILD IN WHOSE BEHALF WE BLESS AND PRAISE THY NAME,   053 13
IN GOD'S BEHALF, I BID YOU ALL WHO ARE HERE   088 14
YOU IN CHRIST'S BEHALF, I EXHORT YOU, AS YE LCVE YOUR   089 08
ALWAYS ON YOUR BEHALF, FOR THE GRACE OF GOD WHICH IS   214 28
OUR PRAYERS ON BEHALF OF THE SOUL OF THY SERVANT   268 23
CALL UPON THEE ON BEHALF OF THIS THY SERVANT   311 22
AND GOODNESS IN BEHALF OF THIS THY SERVANT, THAT HE   315 15
FOR SUCCOUR IN BEHALF OF THIS THY SERVANT, HERE LYING   316 08
OUR PRAYERS ON BEHALF OF THE SOUL OF THY SERVANT   334 15
IN THE NAME AND BEHALF OF -- PARISH (OR CHURCH) I DC   570 27

BEHAVE

UP, DOTH NOT BEHAVE ITSELF UNSEEMLY, SEEKETH NCT HER   122 31
HATH LEFT OFF TO BEHAVE HIMSELF WISELY, AND TO DC   383 31
NOR BEHAVE OURSELVES FROWARDLY IN THY COVENANT   395 29
MAY SO WELL BEHAVE THEMSELVES IN THIS INFERIOR   535 07
YOU ARE MINDED TO BEHAVE YOURSELF IN THE CHURCH CF   554 15

BEHAVED

14 I BEHAVED MYSELF AS THOUGH IT HAD BEEN MY FRIEND   382 20

BEHAVIOUR

OF GOOD BEHAVIOUR, GIVEN TO HOSPITALITY,   549 21

BEHELD

AMONG US, (AND WE BEHELD HIS GLORY, THE GLORY AS CF   098 05
A CERTAIN MAID BEHELD HIM AS HE SAT BY THE FIRE,   151 11
WHILE THEY BEHELD, HE WAS TAKEN UP   178 13
WAS COME NEAR, HE BEHELD THE CITY, AND WEPT CVER IT,   204 06
AFTER THIS I BEHELD, AND, LO, A GREAT MULTITUDE,   256 23

BEHIND

JESUS TARRIED BEHIND IN JERUSALEM   110 22
LEAVE A BLESSING BEHIND HIM   124 27
LIVING CREATURES FULL OF EYES BEFORE AND BEHIND   187 17
SO THAT YE COME BEHIND IN NO GIFT   214 32
CAME BEHIND HIM, AND TOUCHED THE HEM OF HIS   224 18
CAST MY WORDS BEHIND THEE   402 25
HAST BESET ME BEHIND AND BEFORE, *   514 27

BEHOLD

BEHOLD, I BRING YOU GOOD TIDINGS OF GREAT   004 08
BEHOLD, AND SEE IF THERE BE ANY SORROW LIKE UNTC MY   004 29
FROM THY THRONE BEHOLD ALL THE DWELLERS UPCN EARTH   017 28
THY FAVOUR TO BEHOLD AND BLESS THY SERVANT THE   017 30
BEHOLD, THE TABERNACLE OF GOD IS WITH   021 28
FOR BEHOLD, FROM HENCEFORTH *   026 14
BEHOLD, WE BESEECH THEE, THE AFFLICTIONS OF THY   040 31
FAVOUR TO BEHOLD OUR UNIVERSITIES, CCLLEGES, AND   042 23
BESEECH THEE TO BEHOLD, VISIT, AND RELIEVE THY SICK   045 13
WITH PITY BEHOLD THE SORROWS OF OUR HEARTS   059 11
BEHOLD, I WAS SHAPEN IN WICKEDNESS, *   060 20
DAUGHTER OF SION, BEHOLD, THY KING CCMETH UNTO THEE,   091 20
BEHOLD THE FIG TREE, AND ALL THE TREES   093 14
BEHOLD, THEY THAT WEAR SOFT CLOTHING ARE IN KINGS'   094 28
IT IS WRITTEN, BEHOLD, I SEND MY MESSENGER BEFCRE THY   094 31
SURE CONFIDENCE BEHOLD HIM WHEN HE SHALL COME TO BE   098 14
BEHOLD, I BRING YOU GOOD TIDINGS OF GREAT JOY,   099 14
AND BY FAITH BEHOLD THE GLORY THAT SHALL BE REVEALED   099 28
OF GOD, AND SAID, BEHOLD, I SEE THE HEAVENS OPENED,   100 07
BEHOLD, I SEND UNTO YOU PROPHETS, AND WISE MEN,   100 19
BEHOLD, YOUR HOUSE IS LEFT UNTO YOU DESOLATE   100 31
ON THESE THINGS, BEHOLD, THE ANGEL OF THE LCRD   105 02
SAYING, BEHOLD, A VIRGIN SHALL BE WITH   105 09
HEROD WAS DEAD, BEHOLD, AN ANGEL OF THE LORD   107 12
HEROD THE KING, BEHOLD, THERE CAME WISE MEN FRCM THE   108 31
BEHOLD, THY FATHER AND I HAVE SOUGHT THEE SCRRCWING   110 33
IN THE PROPHETS, BEHOLD, I SEND MY MESSENGER BEFCRE   112 04
BEHOLD, THERE CAME A LEPER AND WORSHIPPED HIM,   114 30
BEHOLD, WHAT MANNER OF LOVE THE FATHER HATH BESTCWED   117 14
BEHOLD, I HAVE TOLD YOU BEFORE   118 07
SAY UNTO YOU, BEHOLD, HE IS IN THE DESERT   118 08
BEHOLD, HE IS IN THE SECRET CHAMBERS   118 09
SAID UNTO THEM, BEHOLD, WE GO UP TO JERUSALEM,   123 18
BEHOLD, NOW IS THE ACCEPTED TIME   126 06
BEHOLD, NOW IS THE DAY OF SALVATION   126 07
AS DYING, AND BEHOLD, WE LIVE   126 18
LEAVETH HIM, AND, BEHOLD, ANGELS CAME AND MINISTERED   127 14
BEHOLD, A WOMAN OF CANAAN CAME OUT OF THE SAME   128 08
BEHOLD, THE VEIL OF THE TEMPLE WAS RENT IN TWAIN   137 25
FROM HEAVEN, AND BEHOLD FROM THE HABITATION CF THY   139 18
BEHOLD, THE SON OF MAN IS BETRAYED INTO THE HANDS OF   142 12
BEHOLD, THE LORD GOD WILL HELP ME   144 20
BEHOLD, ALL YE THAT KINDLE A FIRE, THAT COMPASS   144 26
BEHOLD HOW MANY THINGS THEY WITNESS AGAINST THEE   145 10
HEARD IT, SAID, BEHOLD, HE CALLETH ELIAS   146 31
SAID UNTO THEM, BEHOLD, WHEN YE ARE ENTERED INTC THE   148 25
BEHOLD, THE HAND OF HIM THAT BETRAYETH ME IS   149 13
SIMON, BEHOLD, SATAN HATH DESIRED TO HAVE YOU,   149 31

BEHOLD   CONTINUED

THEY SAID, LORD, BEHOLD, HERE ARE TWO SWORDS   150 12
HE YET SPAKE, BEHOLD A MULTITUDE, AND HE THAT WAS   150 27
BEHOLD, I, HAVING EXAMINED HIM BEFORE YOU, HAVE   153 23
BEHOLD, THE DAYS ARE COMING, IN THE WHICH THEY   154 15
GRACIOUSLY TO BEHOLD THIS THY FAMILY, FOR WHICH CUR   156 21
SAITH UNTO THEM, BEHOLD, I BRING HIM FORTH TO YOU,   158 34
SAITH UNTO THEM, BEHOLD THE MAN   159 05
UNTO THE JEWS, BEHOLD YOUR KING   159 26
WOMAN, BEHOLD THY SON   160 21
TO THE DISCIPLE, BEHOLD THY MOTHER   160 22
BEHOLD THE PLACE WHERE THEY LAID HIM   165 30
THAT WE MAY BEHOLD THEE IN ALL THY WORKS   166 08
BEHOLD, TWO OF HIS DISCIPLES WENT THAT SAME DAY TO A   167 03
BEHOLD, YE DESPISERS, AND WONDER, AND PERISH   169 23
BEHOLD MY HANDS AND MY FEET, THAT IT IS I MYSELF   169 32
WHICH THEY SHALL BEHOLD, GLORIFY GOD IN THE DAY CF   173 16
BEHOLD, THE HOUR COMETH, YEA, IS NOW COME, THAT YE   177 04
AS HE WENT UP, BEHOLD, TWO MEN STOOD BY THEM IN WHITE   178 15
JESUS SAID, BEHOLD, I SEND THE PROMISE OF MY FATHER   178 21
ONE TO ANOTHER, BEHOLD, ARE NOT ALL THESE WHICH SPEAK   180 30
I LOOKED, AND BEHOLD, A DOOR WAS OPENED IN HEAVEN   186 31
BEHOLD, A THRONE WAS SET IN HEAVEN, AND ONE SAT   187 04
NOT STEDFASTLY BEHOLD THE FACE OF MOSES FOR THE GLORY   206 20
BEHOLD, A CERTAIN LAWYER STOOD UP, AND TEMPTED   208 11
BEHOLD THE BIRDS OF THE HEAVEN, THAT THEY SCW NCT,   211 15
GATE OF THE CITY, BEHOLD, THERE WAS A DEAD MAN   212 30
BEHOLD, THERE WAS A CERTAIN MAN BEFORE HIM WHICH   213 30
BEHOLD, THEY BROUGHT TO HIM A MAN SICK OF THE   216 34
BEHOLD, CERTAIN OF THE SCRIBES SAID WITHIN   217 04
WHICH ARE BIDDEN, BEHOLD, I HAVE PREPARED MY DINNER   218 07
JOHN'S DISCIPLES, BEHOLD, THERE CAME A CERTAIN RULER,   224 13
BEHOLD, A WOMAN, WHICH WAS DISEASED WITH AN   224 17
BEHOLD, THE DAYS COME, SAITH THE LORD, THAT I WILL   225 09
BEHOLD, THE DAYS COME, SAITH THE LORD,   225 14
THY FINGER, AND BEHOLD MY HANDS   229 04
AND HE SAID, BEHOLD, I AM HERE, LORD   230 16
BEHOLD, HE PRAYETH, AND HATH SEEN IN A VISION A   230 19
SAID UNTO JESUS, BEHOLD, WE HAVE FORSAKEN ALL, AND   231 12
BEHOLD, I WILL SEND MY MESSENGER, AND HE SHALL   232 03
BEHOLD, HE SHALL COME, SAITH THE LORD OF HOSTS   232 06
BEHOLD, THERE WAS A MAN IN JERUSALEM, WHOSE NAME   232 29
MARY HIS MOTHER, BEHOLD, THIS CHILD IS SET FOR THE   233 11
BEHOLD, A VIRGIN SHALL CONCEIVE, AND BEAR A SCN, AND   235 31
BEHOLD, THOU SHALT CONCEIVE IN THY WOMB, AND   236 14
BEHOLD, THY COUSIN ELISABETH, SHE HATH ALSO   236 25
AND MARY SAID, BEHOLD THE HANDMAID OF THE LORD   236 28
BEHOLD, THE LORD GOD WILL COME WITH STRCNG HAND, AND   243 05
CITIES OF JUDAH, BEHOLD YOUR GOD   243 05
BEHOLD, HIS REWARD IS WITH HIM, AND HIS WORK BEFORE   243 07
BEHOLD, THE ANGEL OF THE LORD CAME UPON HIM, ANC   245 12
BE PERMITTED TO BEHOLD THE KING IN HIS BEAUTY,   248 04
BEHOLD, THERE TALKED WITH HIM TWO MEN, WHICH   248 27
IN THE HOUSE, BEHOLD, MANY PUBLICANS AND SINNERS CAME   251 16
ANGELS DO ALWAYS BEHOLD THE FACE OF MY FATHER WHICH   253 11
BEHOLD, I SEND YOU FORTH AS LAMBS AMONG WOLVES   254 16
BEHOLD THE FOWLS OF THE AIR   266 14
FAVOURABLY TO BEHOLD THESE THY SERVANTS NOW (OR ABOUT   267 05
DOWN FROM HEAVEN, BEHOLD, VISIT, AND RELIEVE THIS THY   309 04
MINE EYES SHALL BEHOLD, AND NOT AS A STRANGER   324 12
BEHOLD, THOU HAST MADE MY DAYS AS IT WERE A SPAN   324 22
OF MY LIFE, TO BEHOLD THE FAIR BEAUTY OF THE LORD,   326 10
BEHOLD, HE THAT KEEPETH ISRAEL *   327 25
BEHOLD, I SHEW YOU A MYSTERY   329 35
BEHOLD, HE THAT KEEPETH ISRAEL *   339 09
ANGELS DO ALWAYS BEHOLD THE FACE OF MY FATHER WHICH   339 31
ONES DO ALWAYS BEHOLD IN HEAVEN   340 25
15 BEHOLD, THE UNGODLY TRAVAILETH WITH INIQUITY   350 21
COUNTENANCE WILL BEHOLD THE THING THAT IS JUST   355 03
FOR ME, I SHALL BEHOLD THY PRESENCE IN RIGHTEOUSNESS   359 19
OF MY LIFE, TO BEHOLD THE FAIR BEAUTY OF THE LCRD,   372 02
17 BEHOLD, THE EYE OF THE LORD IS UPON THEM THAT FEAR   379 24
6 BEHOLD, THOU HAST MADE MY DAYS AS IT WERE A SPAN   389 17
COME HITHER, AND BEHOLD THE WORKS OF THE LCRD,   398 09
5 BEHOLD, I WAS SHAPEN IN WICKEDNESS, *   403 18
4 BEHOLD, GOD IS MY HELPER   406 10
ARISE THOU THEREFORE TO HELP ME, AND BEHOLD   411 12
7 BEHOLD, THEY SPEAK WITH THEIR MOUTH, AND SWCRCS ARE   411 18
THAT I MIGHT BEHOLD THY POWER AND GLORY   414 30
COME HITHER, AND BEHOLD THE WORKS OF GOD   417 22
HIS EYES BEHOLD THE NATIONS   417 26
BEHOLD, AND VISIT THIS THY VINE   441 31
9 BEHOLD, O GOD OUR DEFENDER, *   445 29
4 BEHOLD, PHILISTIA ALSO   448 20
EYES SHALT THOU BEHOLD, *   455 11
DID THE LORD BEHOLD THE EARTH   465 18
HIMSELF TO BEHOLD THE THINGS THAT ARE IN HEAVEN AND   484 17
14 BEHOLD, O LORD, HOW THAT I AM THY SERVANT   487 16
LEST THEY BEHOLD VANITY   492 13
40 BEHOLD, MY DELIGHT IS IN THY COMMANDMENTS   492 19
4 BEHOLD, HE THAT KEEPETH ISRAEL *   502 28
2 BEHOLD, EVEN AS THE EYES OF SERVANTS LOOK UNTC THE   503 29
BEHOLD, HOW GOOD AND JOYFUL A THING IT IS, *   509 13
BEHOLD NOW, PRAISE THE LORD, *   509 23
MERCIFULLY BEHOLD THESE THY SERVANTS NOW CALLED TO   531 18
MERCIFULLY BEHOLD THESE THY SERVANTS NOW CALLED TC   537 22
MERCIFULLY BEHOLD THESE THY SERVANTS NCW CALLED TC   547 33
AND NOW, BEHOLD, I GO BOUND IN THE SPIRIT UNTO   550 14
AND NOW, BEHOLD, I KNOW THAT YE ALL, AMONG WHOM I   550 22
MERCIFULLY BEHOLD THIS THY SERVANT, NOW CALLED TC THE   553 28
OF HEAVEN SAYING, BEHOLD, THE TABERNACLE OF GOD IS   567 15
THE THRONE SAID, BEHOLD, I MAKE ALL THINGS NEW   567 21
EYES THAN TO BEHOLD INIQUITY, AND HAST PROMISED   589 26
MIND OPENED TO BEHOLD THINGS INVISIBLE AND UNSEEN,   594 24
OUR EYES TO BEHOLD THY GRACIOUS HAND IN ALL THY   596 18

BEHOLD   CONTINUED

GRACIOUSLY TO BEHOLD AND BLESS THOSE WHOM WE LOVE,   597 02

BEHOLDEST

ART THOU THAT BEHOLDEST THE DEPTHS, AND DWELLEST   011 22
AND WHY BEHOLDEST THOU THE MOTE THAT IS IN THY   195 05
THOU THYSELF BEHOLDEST NOT THE BEAM THAT IS IN THINE   195 09
FOR THOU BEHOLDEST UNGODLINESS AND WRONG, THAT THCU   354 04

BEHOLDETH

FOR HE BEHOLDETH HIMSELF, AND GOETH HIS WAY, AND   176 08
FOR HE BEHOLDETH HIMSELF, AND GOETH HIS WAY, AND   265 31
AND BEHOLDETH ALL THE CHILDREN OF MEN   379 14
THE PROUD, HE BEHOLDETH THEM AFAR OFF   514 09

BEHOLDING

AND THE PEOPLE STOOD BEHOLDING   154 27
TO THAT SIGHT, BEHOLDING THE THINGS WHICH WERE DCNE,   155 17
AFAR OFF, BEHOLDING THESE THINGS   155 20
UNTO A MAN BEHOLDING HIS NATURAL FACE IN A GLASS   176 07
UNTO A MAN BEHOLDING HIS NATURAL FACE IN A GLASS   265 31

BEHOVED

AND THUS IT BEHOVED CHRIST TO SUFFER, AND TC RISE   170 12

BEING

BE USED THEREIN, BEING THINGS IN THEIR OWN NATURE   V 15
TO HIS PEOPLE, BEING PENITENT, THE ABSOLUTION AND   007 10
THAT WE BEING DELIVERED OUT OF THE HAND OF OUR   014 20
BEING OF ONE SUBSTANCE WITH THE FATHER   016 05
ALL OUR DOINGS, BEING ORDERED BY THY GCVERNANCE, MAY   017 17
THAT BEING GUIDED BY THY PROVIDENCE, WE MAY   018 09
TO HIS PEOPLE, BEING PENITENT, THE ABSOLUTION AND   024 12
THE LESSON READ BEING FOLLOWED BY ONE OF THE EVENING   R 026 08
BEING OF ONE SUBSTANCE WITH THE FATHER   030 10
THAT BY THEE, WE, BEING DEFENDED FROM THE FEAR CF OUR   031 22
DISPERSED SHEEP, BEING GATHERED INTO ONE FOLD, SHALL   037 06
IN THY NAME, BEING CHANGED TO NOW ASSEMBLED (OR ABCUT   R 037 11
THAT WE, BEING ARMED WITH THY DEFENCE, MAY BE   041 13
BEING MADE STRONG BY THY HOLY SPIRIT, THEY MAY   043 11
BEING INSPIRED BY THY LOVE, THEY MAY WORTHILY   044 03
WHEN ANY WOMAN, BEING PRESENT IN CHURCH, SHALL HAVE   R 051 03
WE THY SERVANTS, BEING HURT BY NO PERSECUTICNS,   058 22
IMPORTANT WORK BEING BROUGHT TO A CONCLUSION,   VI 35
BEING OF ONE SUBSTANCE WITH THE FATHER   071 07
AND OBLATIONS ARE BEING RECEIVED AND PRESENTED,   R 073 34
WHICH BEING SO DIVINE AND COMFORTABLE A THING TC THEM   087 05
BEING READY TO MAKE RESTITUTION AND SATISFACTION,   087 24
AND BEING LIKEWISE READY TO FORGIVE OTHERS WHO HAVE   087 27
TO COME THERETO, BEING SO LOVINGLY CALLED AND BIDDEN   088 16
GRANT THAT WE BEING REGENERATE, AND MADE THY CHILDREN   096 15
WHO BEING THE BRIGHTNESS OF HIS GLORY, AND THE   096 26
BEING MADE SO MUCH BETTER THAN THE ANGELS, AS HE HATH   096 30
HIS ESPOUSED WIFE, BEING GREAT WITH CHILD   099 05
AND , BEING FILLED WITH THE HOLY GHOST, MAY LEARN TC   099 29
BEING FULL OF THE HOLY GHOST, LOOKED UP   100 05
THAT IT, BEING ILLUMINED BY THE DOCTRINE OF   101 06
FROM AMONG MEN, BEING THE FIRSTFRUITS UNTO GOD AND TC   103 11
GRANT THAT WE BEING REGENERATE, AND MADE THY CHILDREN   104 07
HER HUSBAND, BEING A JUST MAN, AND NOT WILLING TC   104 30
WHICH BEING INTERPRETED IS, GOD WITH US   105 11
THEN JOSEPH BEING RAISED FROM SLEEP DID AS THE ANGEL   105 12
ALL OUR MEMBERS, BEING MORTIFIED FROM ALL WORLDLY AND   105 22
BEING WARNED OF GOD IN A DREAM,   107 20
AND BEING WARNED OF GOD IN A DREAM THAT THEY SHCULD   109 23
SO WE, BEING MANY, ARE ONE BODY IN CHRIST, AND EVERY   110 14
OUR FLESH BEING SUBDUED TO THE SPIRIT, WE MAY   125 29
CHRIST BEING COME AN HIGH PRIEST OF GOOD THINGS TO   132 23
WHO, BEING IN THE FORM OF GOD, THOUGHT IT NCT RCBBERY   134 17
AND BEING FOUND IN FASHION AS A MAN, HE HUMBLED   134 20
AND BEING IN BETHANY IN THE HOUSE OF SIMON THE LEPER,   140 02
WHICH IS, BEING INTERPRETED, THE PLACE OF A SKULL   146 08
WHICH IS, BEING INTERPRETED, MY GOD, MY GOD, WHY HAST   146 28
SURNAMED ISCARIOT, BEING OF THE NUMBER OF THE TWELVE   148 15
AND BEING IN AN AGONY HE PRAYED MORE EARNESTLY   150 21
AND SUPPER BEING ENDED, THE DEVIL HAVING NOW PUT INTC   155 27
BRING US TO GOD, BEING PUT TO DEATH IN THE FLESH,   161 24
AND POWERS BEING MADE SUBJECT UNTO HIM   162 03
CHRIST BEING RAISED FROM THE DEAD DIETH NO MORE   163 04
DAY AT EVENING, BEING THE FIRST DAY OF THE WEEK, WHEN   171 14
THE TREE, THAT WE, BEING DEAD TO SINS, SHOULD LIVE   172 16
HE BEING NOT A FORGETFUL HEARER, BUT A DOER   176 11
INFALLIBLE PROOFS, BEING SEEN OF THEM FORTY DAYS, AND   177 27
BEING ASSEMBLED TOGETHER WITH THEM, COMMANDED   177 29
I SPOKEN UNTO YOU, BEING YET PRESENT WITH YOU   181 29
OF THAT ONE BODY, BEING MANY, ARE ONE BODY   183 03
IF YE THEN, BEING EVIL, KNOW HOW TO GIVE GOOD GIFTS   183 17
THAT THY CHURCH, BEING GATHERED TOGETHER IN UNITY BY   185 15
LIFT UP HIS EYES, BEING IN TORMENTS, AND SEETH   190 11
OF THE HOUSE BEING ANGRY SAID TO HIS SERVANT.   192 13
THOU BEING OUR RULER AND GUIDE, WE MAY SO PASS   194 06
THAT CHRIST BEING RAISED FROM THE DEAD DIETH NC MORE   197 21
BUT NOW BEING MADE FREE FROM SIN, AND BECOME SERVANTS   199 02
DAYS THE MULTITUDE BEING VERY GREAT, AND HAVING   199 08
WHICH OF YOU BY BEING ANXIOUS CAN ADD ONE CUBIT UNTO   211 19
THAT YE, BEING ROOTED AND GROUNDED IN LOVE, MAY BE   212 17
BEING ALIENATED FROM THE LIFE OF GOD   216 06
WHO BEING PAST FEELING HAVE GIVEN THEMSELVES OVER   216 08
THAT WE, BEING READY BOTH IN BODY AND SOUL, MAY   217 19
BEING CONFIDENT OF THIS VERY THING, THAT HE WHICH   220 25

BEING   CONTINUED

BEING FILLED WITH THE FRUITS OF RIGHTEOUSNESS,   221 05
UNTO ALL PLEASING, BEING FRUITFUL IN EVERY GOOD WORK,   224 05
US ALL, THAT WE, BEING CALLED BY THY HOLY WORD, MAY   226 21
THE DOORS BEING SHUT, AND STOOD IN THE MIDST,   228 32
THAT THY CHURCH, BEING ALWAY PRESERVED FROM FALSE   234 02
US GRACE THAT, BEING NOT LIKE CHILDREN CARRIED AWAY   237 07
UNTO US, THAT WE BEING DELIVERED OUT OF THE HAND OF   244 07
GRANT THAT WE, BEING DELIVERED FROM THE DISQUIETUDE   248 03
CHRIST HIMSELF BEING THE HEAD CORNER-STONE   254 29
CHRIST HIMSELF BEING THE CHIEF CORNER-STONE   255 06
IF YE THEN, KNOW HOW TO GIVE GOOD GIFTS   263 11
HE BEING NOT A FORGETFUL HEARER, BUT A DOER   266 02
WHICH OF YOU BY BEING ANXIOUS CAN ADD ONE CUBIT UNTO   266 17
AND NOW, BEING PERSUADED OF THE GOOD WILL OF OUR   276 03
I WILL, GOD BEING MY HELPER   277 17
TO GRANT, THAT HE, BEING DEAD UNTO SIN, MAY LIVE UNTO   280 32
AND BEING BURIED WITH CHRIST IN HIS   280 33
CHILD (OR PERSON) BEING NAMED BY SOME ONE WHO IS   R 281 19
THE PEOPLE BEING SEATED, THE MINISTER SHALL ASK   R 283 13
THE PEOPLE BEING SEATED, THE MINISTER, TURNING   R 287 31
CHRIST HIMSELF BEING THE HEAD CORNER-STONE   290 21
THE PEOPLE BEING SEATED, THE MINISTER SHALL   R 290 25
OR BY LICENCE, BEING DIFFERENT IN THE SEVERAL STATES, R 304 18
THAT HIS HEALTH BEING THEREUPON RESTORED, HE MAY   315 10
BEING RESTORED TO HEALTH OF BODY, VIGOUR OF   315 29
WILES OF SATAN, BEING PURGED AND DONE AWAY, IT MAY BE   317 20
AND BODY, THAT BEING RESTORED TO SOUNDNESS OF HEALTH,   320 11
SICKNESS OF BODY BEING PUT TO FLIGHT, THE BLESSING OF   320 18
THINGS NECESSARY BEING PREPARED, THE MINISTER SHALL   R 321 14
CAUSE OF SICKNESS BEING REMOVED, HE MAY BE RESTORED   322 08
WHILE THE EARTH IS BEING CAST UPON THE BODY, THE   R 341 12
MAN BEING IN HONOUR ABIDETH NOT,   400 30
WHO BEING HARNESSED, AND CARRYING BOWS, TURNED   435 17
I WILL PRAISE MY GOD WHILE I HAVE MY BEING   469 28
BEING FAST BOUND IN MISERY AND IRON   476 25
MY SUBSTANCE, YET BEING IMPERFECT   515 20
LONG AS I HAVE ANY BEING, I WILL SING PRAISES UNTO MY   522 04
THE SERMON BEING ENDED, A PRIEST SHALL PRESENT UNTO   R 530 07
EACH OF THEM BEING DECENTLY HABITED, SAYING THESE   R 530 09
OF A DEACON, BEING FOUND BLAMELESS   531 31
THE PEOPLE BEING SEATED, THE BISHOP SHALL   R 532 23
SO DO, THE LORD BEING MY HELPER   533 29
SO TO DO, THE LORD BEING MY HELPER   533 34
EACH OF THEM BEING DECENTLY HABITED, AND SHALL   R 536 09
THE PEOPLE BEING SEATED, THE BISHOP SHALL SAY   R 539 22
I WILL, THE LORD BEING MY HELPER   542 25
SO TO DO, THE LORD BEING MY HELPER   542 30
THE LORD BEING MY HELPER   543 04
SO DO, THE LORD BEING MY HELPER   543 10
SO DO, THE LORD BEING MY HELPER   543 16
THE COMMUNION BEING DONE, AFTER THE LAST COLLECT,   R 547 02
NOT A NOVICE, LEST BEING LIFTED UP WITH PRIDE HE FALL   549 27
DAY AT EVENING, BEING THE FIRST DAY OF THE WEEK, WHEN   551 27
WHICH BEING ENDED, THE ELECTED BISHOP, VESTED WITH   R 552 17
THE PEOPLE BEING SEATED, THE PRESIDING BISHOP,   R 554 05
AM READY, THE LORD BEING MY HELPER   555 07
SO DO, THE LORD BEING MY HELPER   555 13
AND BEING FILLED WITH THY GRACE AND HEAVENLY   565 31
BY CANON, AND BEING SATISFIED THAT THE PERSON CHOSEN R 569 05
NO OBJECTION BEING OFFERED, OR THE INSTITUTOR   R 570 23
CHRIST HIMSELF BEING THE CHIEF CORNER-STONE   574 05
FOR BEING BY NATURE BORN IN SIN, AND THE CHILDREN OF   581 25
IN WHOM WE LIVE AND MOVE AND HAVE OUR BEING   587 20
THE FAMILY BEING TOGETHER, A LITTLE BEFORE   R 589 13
FOR OUR BEING, OUR REASON, AND ALL OTHER ENDOWMENTS   591 08
ALL OUR DOINGS, BEING ORDERED BY THY GOVERNANCE, MAY   592 23
GOD AND MAN, BEING BOTH GOD AND MAN   604 17
OF THE GOSPEL, BEING SUCH AS HAVE GROWN PARTLY OF THE   607 40
AND FINALLY, BEING FOUND GUILTY, BY JUST JUDGMENT BE   608 21

BELIEF

CHIEFLY LEARN IN THESE ARTICLES OF YOUR BELIEF   284 28
REHEARSE THE ARTICLES OF THY BELIEF   577 27
CHIEFLY LEARN IN THESE ARTICLES OF THY BELIEF   578 10

BELIEVE

AND UNFEIGNEDLY BELIEVE HIS HOLY GOSPEL   007 12
WE BELIEVE THAT THOU SHALT COME TO BE OUR JUDGE   010 32
I BELIEVE IN GOD THE FATHER ALMIGHTY, MAKER OF HEAVEN   015 19
I BELIEVE IN THE HOLY GHOST   015 28
I BELIEVE IN ONE GOD THE FATHER ALMIGHTY, MAKER OF   015 33
AND I BELIEVE IN THE HOLY GHOST, THE LORD, AND GIVER   016 15
AND I BELIEVE ONE CATHOLIC AND APOSTOLIC CHURCH   016 18
AND UNFEIGNEDLY BELIEVE HIS HOLY GOSPEL   024 14
I BELIEVE IN GOD THE FATHER ALMIGHTY, MAKER OF HEAVEN   029 24
I BELIEVE IN THE HOLY GHOST   029 33
I BELIEVE IN ONE GOD THE FATHER ALMIGHTY, MAKER OF   030 04
AND I BELIEVE IN THE HOLY GHOST, THE LORD, AND GIVER   030 20
AND I BELIEVE ONE CATHOLIC AND APOSTOLIC CHURCH   030 23
I BELIEVE IN ONE GOD THE FATHER ALMIGHTY, MAKER OF   071 02
AND I BELIEVE IN THE HOLY GHOST, THE LORD, AND GIVER   071 17
AND I BELIEVE ONE CATHOLIC AND APOSTOLIC CHURCH   071 20
HOW SHALL THEY BELIEVE IN HIM OF WHOM THEY HAVE NOT   073 07
THAT ALL THAT BELIEVE IN HIM SHOULD NOT PERISH,   076 15
THE SAME WE BELIEVE OF THE SON, AND OF THE HOLY   079 10
THAT WHICH WE BELIEVE OF THY GLORY, O FATHER, THE   079 10
THE LIGHT, THAT ALL MEN THROUGH HIM MIGHT BELIEVE   097 28
TO THEM THAT BELIEVE ON HIS NAME   098 02
BELIEVE IT NOT   118 04
BELIEVE IT NOT   118 10
LEST THEY SHOULD BELIEVE AND BE SAVED   121 35
FOR A WHILE BELIEVE, AND IN TIME OF TEMPTATION FALL   122 04

BELIEVE   CONTINUED

WHY DO YE NOT BELIEVE ME   133 10
AND WE WILL BELIEVE HIM   137 12
THAT WE MAY SEE AND BELIEVE   146 24
UNTO THEM, IF I TELL YOU, YE WILL NOT BELIEVE   151 31
KNOWETH THAT HE SAITH TRUE, THAT YE MIGHT BELIEVE   161 07
SLOW OF HEART TO BELIEVE ALL THAT THE PROPHETS HAVE   167 29
BY HIM ALL THAT BELIEVE ARE JUSTIFIED FROM ALL   169 20
SHALL IN NO WISE BELIEVE, THOUGH A MAN DECLARE IT   169 25
BECAUSE THEY BELIEVE NOT ON ME   175 14
BY THIS WE BELIEVE THAT THOU CAMEST FORTH FROM GOD   177 03
JESUS ANSWERED THEM, DO YE NOW BELIEVE   177 04
LIKE AS WE DO BELIEVE THY ONLY-BEGOTTEN SON OUR LORD   177 15
WHEN IT IS COME TO PASS, YE MIGHT BELIEVE   182 07
HOW SHALL YE BELIEVE, IF I TELL YOU OF HEAVENLY   188 23
AND YE BELIEVE NOT, HOW SHALL YE BELIEVE, IF   188 23
THAT WE SHOULD BELIEVE ON THE NAME OF HIS SON JESUS   191 30
WITH CHRIST, WE BELIEVE THAT WE SHALL ALSO LIVE WITH   197 20
JESUS CHRIST MIGHT BE GIVEN TO THEM THAT BELIEVE   208 05
YE SEE SIGNS AND WONDERS, YE WILL NOT BELIEVE   219 33
AND SHALT BELIEVE IN THINE HEART THAT GOD HATH   226 27
HOW SHALL THEY BELIEVE IN HIM OF WHOM THEY HAVE NOT   227 06
ALL DOUBT, TO BELIEVE IN THY SON JESUS CHRIST, THAT   228 08
BUT OF THEM THAT BELIEVE TO THE SAVING OF THE SOUL   228 21
THRUST MY HAND INTO HIS SIDE, I WILL NOT BELIEVE   228 30
THAT YE MIGHT BELIEVE THAT JESUS IS THE CHRIST, THE   229 11
BELIEVE IN GOD, BELIEVE ALSO IN ME   239 30
YE BELIEVE IN GOD, BELIEVE ALSO IN ME   239 30
BELIEVE ME THAT I AM IN THE FATHER, AND THE FATHER IN   240 16
OR ELSE BELIEVE ME FOR THE VERY WORKS' SAKE   240 18
GRACE TRULY TO BELIEVE AND TO PREACH THY WORD   249 15
OF THEM WHICH BELIEVE NOT, LEST THE LIGHT OF THE   251 03
ONES WHICH BELIEVE IN ME, IT WERE BETTER FOR HIM THAT   252 31
FOR IF WE BELIEVE THAT JESUS DIED AND ROSE AGAIN,   268 30
OF THOSE WHO BELIEVE, AND THE RESURRECTION OF THE   274 11
DOST THOU BELIEVE ALL THE ARTICLES OF THE CHRISTIAN   276 31
TO KNOW AND BELIEVE TO HIS SOUL'S HEALTH   277 12
DOST THOU BELIEVE IN JESUS THE CHRIST, THE SON OF THE   278 02
DOST THOU BELIEVE ALL THE ARTICLES OF THE CHRISTIAN   278 08
THAT I SHOULD BELIEVE ALL THE ARTICLES OF THE   283 26
THAT YOU SHOULD BELIEVE ALL THE ARTICLES OF THE   284 08
I BELIEVE IN GOD THE FATHER ALMIGHTY, MAKER OF HEAVEN   284 13
I BELIEVE IN THE HOLY GHOST   284 22
I LEARN TO BELIEVE IN GOD THE FATHER, WHO HATH MADE   284 29
GOD IS TO BELIEVE IN HIM, TO FEAR HIM, AND TO LOVE   288 16
THEY STEDFASTLY BELIEVE THE PROMISES OF GOD TO THEM   292 29
BOUND TO BELIEVE AND TO DO ALL THOSE THINGS WHICH YE   296 26
UNTO YOU THAT BELIEVE ON THE NAME OF THE SON OF GOD   322 12
AND THAT YE MAY BELIEVE ON THE NAME OF THE SON OF   322 14
AND STEDFASTLY BELIEVE THAT JESUS CHRIST HATH   R 323 27
BUT THAT I BELIEVE VERILY TO SEE THE GOODNESS OF THE   326 28
YE BELIEVE IN GOD, BELIEVE ALSO IN ME   331 17
BELIEVE IN GOD, BELIEVE ALSO IN ME   331 18
US STEDFASTLY TO BELIEVE THAT THIS THY CHILD HATH   340 26
BUT THAT I BELIEVE VERILY TO SEE THE GOODNESS OF THE   372 27
SUCH AS WILL NOT BELIEVE SHALL NOT BE ABLE TO EXALT   417 27
TO SUCH AS BELIEVE, A WHOLESOME EXAMPLE IN WORD,   559 10
THAT I SHOULD BELIEVE ALL THE ARTICLES OF THE   577 16
ART BOUND TO BELIEVE, AND TO DO, AS THEY HAVE   577 21
I BELIEVE IN GOD THE FATHER ALMIGHTY,   577 28
I BELIEVE IN THE HOLY GHOST   578 06
I LEARN TO BELIEVE IN GOD THE FATHER, WHO HATH MADE   578 11
GOD IS TO BELIEVE IN HIM, TO FEAR HIM, AND TO LOVE   579 27
THEY STEDFASTLY BELIEVE THE PROMISES OF GOD MADE TO   581 29
FOR THEM THAT BELIEVE AND ARE BAPTIZED   604 39

BELIEVED

THEY CALL ON HIM IN WHOM THEY HAVE NOT BELIEVED   073 07
NOW IS OUR SALVATION NEARER THAN WHEN WE BELIEVED   091 03
HIS DISCIPLES BELIEVED ON HIM   113 32
AS THOU HAST BELIEVED, SO BE IT DONE UNTO THEE   115 24
FIRST TO THE SEPULCHRE, AND HE SAW, AND BELIEVED   164 26
WHILE THEY YET BELIEVED NOT FOR JOY, AND WONDERED,   170 03
AND HAVE BELIEVED THAT I CAME OUT FROM GOD   176 29
WHICH BELIEVED WERE ASTONISHED, AS MANY AS CAME WITH   184 22
HE HATH NOT BELIEVED IN THE NAME OF THE ONLY-BEGOTTEN   185 04
HAVE KNOWN AND BELIEVED THE LOVE THAT GOD HATH TO US   189 24
UNLESS YE HAVE BELIEVED IN VAIN   205 02
WERE I OR THEY, SO WE PREACH, AND SO YE BELIEVED   205 19
AND THE MAN BELIEVED THE WORD THAT JESUS HAD SPOKEN   220 04
AND HIMSELF BELIEVED, AND HIS WHOLE HOUSE   220 11
THEY CALL ON HIM IN WHOM THEY HAVE NOT BELIEVED   227 06
WHO HATH BELIEVED OUR REPORT   227 12
BECAUSE THOU HAST SEEN ME, THOU HAST BELIEVED   229 08
THEY THAT HAVE NOT SEEN, AND YET HAVE BELIEVED   229 09
WORD WHICH HE BELIEVED, AND BOTH TO PREACH AND   249 17
AS MANY AS WERE ORDAINED TO ETERNAL LIFE BELIEVED   261 08
23 BECAUSE THEY BELIEVED NOT IN GOD, *   436 14
AND BELIEVED NOT HIS WONDROUS WORKS   437 02
12 THEN BELIEVED THEY HIS WORDS, *   473 25
10 I BELIEVED, AND THEREFORE WILL I SPEAK   487 07
FOR I HAVE BELIEVED THY COMMANDMENTS   494 14
IS IT TO BE BELIEVED, THAT HE WENT DOWN INTO HELL   603 18
IT SHOULD BE BELIEVED AS AN ARTICLE OF THE FAITH,   603 31
OUGHT THOROUGHLY TO BE RECEIVED AND BELIEVED   604 26
ANY THING TO BE BELIEVED FOR NECESSITY OF SALVATION   607 09

BELIEVERS

DIDST OPEN THE KINGDOM OF HEAVEN TO ALL BELIEVERS   010 29
AND BELIEVERS WERE THE MORE ADDED TO THE LORD,   249 25

BELIEVEST

BELIEVEST THOU NOT THAT I AM IN THE FATHER, AND THE   240 13

BELIEVETH

ALL THINGS, BELIEVETH ALL THINGS, HOPETH ALL THINGS,   123 02
NAME WHOSOEVER BELIEVETH IN HIM SHALL RECEIVE   166 31
BUT HE THAT BELIEVETH THAT JESUS IS THE SCN OF GOD   170 29
HE THAT BELIEVETH ON THE SON OF GOD HATH THE WITNESS   171 06
HE THAT BELIEVETH NOT GOD HATH MADE HIM A LIAR   171 07
BECAUSE HE BELIEVETH NOT THE RECORD THAT GOD GAVE OF   171 08
NAME WHOSOEVER BELIEVETH IN HIM SHALL RECEIVE   184 19
THAT WHOSOEVER BELIEVETH IN HIM SHOULD NOT PERISH,   184 33
HE THAT BELIEVETH ON HIM IS NOT CONDEMNED   185 02
BUT HE THAT BELIEVETH NOT IS CONDEMNED ALREADY,   185 03
THAT WHOSOEVER BELIEVETH IN HIM SHOULD NOT PERISH,   188 28
THE HEART MAN BELIEVETH UNTO RIGHTEOUSNESS   226 29
WHOSOEVER BELIEVETH ON HIM SHALL NOT BE ASHAMED   226 31
HE THAT BELIEVETH ON ME, THE WORKS THAT I DO   240 19
THE SON, AND BELIEVETH ON HIM, MAY HAVE EVERLASTING   269 20
MY WORD, AND BELIEVETH ON HIM THAT SENT ME, HATH   321 34
HE THAT BELIEVETH ON ME HATH EVERLASTING LIFE   322 21
HE THAT BELIEVETH IN ME, THOUGH HE WERE DEAD, YET   324 06
LIVETH AND BELIEVETH IN ME, SHALL NEVER DIE   324 07
WHOM WHOSOEVER BELIEVETH, SHALL LIVE, THOUGH HE DIE   334 32
AND BELIEVETH IN HIM, SHALL NOT DIE   335 02
HE THAT BELIEVETH IN ME, THOUGH HE WERE DEAD, YET   338 06
LIVETH AND BELIEVETH IN ME, SHALL NEVER DIE   338 07
AND BELIEVETH IN THE LORD   483 31

BELIEVING

AND PEACE IN BELIEVING, THAT YE MAY ABOUND IN HCPE,   093 02
AND BE NOT FAITHLESS, BUT BELIEVING   229 05
AND THAT BELIEVING YE MIGHT HAVE LIFE THROUGH HIS   229 12

BELLIES

THIS LIFE, WHOSE BELLIES THOU FILLEST WITH THY HID   359 15

BELLY

HAVE FILLED HIS BELLY WITH THE HUSKS THAT THE SWINE   202 08
WHOSE GOD IS THEIR BELLY, AND WHOSE GLORY IS IN THEIR 222 20
OUR BELLY CLEAVETH UNTO THE GROUND   396 11

BELONG

DETERMINED TO BELONG TO DOCTRINE MUST BE REFERRED TO   V 06
THE LORD OUR GOD BELONG MERCIES AND FORGIVENESSES,   022 06
THE THINGS WHICH BELONG UNTO THY PEACE   204 08

BELONGED

HE KNEW THAT HE BELONGED UNTO HEROD'S JURISDICTICN,   153 08

BELONGETH

TO WHOM IT BELONGETH JUSTLY TO PUNISH SINNERS,   041 11
SALVATION BELONGETH TO THE LORD   309 24
8 SALVATION BELONGETH UNTO THE LORD   347 07
THAT POWER BELONGETH UNTO GOD   414 22
WHOM VENGEANCE BELONGETH, *   457 19
WHOM VENGEANCE BELONGETH, SHOW THYSELF   457 20

BELONGING

ALL THINGS BELONGING TO THE SPIRIT MAY LIVE AND GROW   278 22
OF THE THINGS BELONGING TO THE ALTAR   569 29

BELOVED

DEARLY BELOVED BRETHREN, THE SCRIPTURE MOVETH   005 29
DEARLY BELOVED BRETHREN, THE SCRIPTURE MOVETH US,   023 04
THY MOST DEARLY BELOVED SON JESUS CHRIST OUR LORD   078 16
OF THY DEARLY BELOVED SON OUR SAVIOUR JESUS CHRIST,   080 38
DEARLY BELOVED IN THE LORD, YE WHO MIND TO COME TO   085 25
DEARLY BELOVED, ON -- DAY NEXT I PURPOSE, THROUGH   086 28
DEARLY BELOVED BRETHREN, ON -- INTEND, BY GOD'S   088 12
MOST DEARLY BELOVED IN CHRIST, TAKE YE GOOD HEED,   088 24
MY BELOVED, AS YE HAVE ALWAYS OBEYED, NOT   105 31
THOU ART MY BELOVED SON, IN WHOM I AM WELL PLEASED   112 23
DEARLY BELOVED, AVENGE NOT YOURSELVES, BUT RATHER   113 03
OF GOD, HOLY AND BELOVED, A HEART OF COMPASSION,   116 03
BELOVED, NOW ARE WE THE SONS OF GOD, AND IT DOTH NOT   117 17
DEARLY BELOVED, I BESEECH YOU AS STRANGERS AND   173 12
MY BELOVED BRETHREN, LET EVERY MAN BE   174 31
BELOVED, LET US LOVE ONE ANOTHER   189 08
BELOVED, IF GOD SO LOVED US, WE OUGHT ALSO TO LCVE   189 15
BELOVED, IF OUR HEART CONDEMN US NOT, THEN HAVE WE   191 25
THIS IS MY BELOVED SON, IN WHOM I AM WELL PLEASED   248 18
THIS IS MY BELOVED SON   249 07
DO NOT ERR, MY BELOVED BRETHREN   265 18
MY BELOVED BRETHREN, LET EVERY MAN BE   265 23
DEARLY BELOVED, FORASMUCH AS OUR SAVIOUR CHRIST   273 29
DEARLY BELOVED, YE HAVE BROUGHT THIS CHILD HERE TO BE 276 19
THAT THY DEARLY BELOVED SON JESUS CHRIST, FOR THE   279 09
DEARLY BELOVED BRETHREN, THAT THIS CHILD (THIS   280 13
DEARLY BELOVED, WE ARE GATHERED TOGETHER HERE IN   300 08
THY MOST DEARLY BELOVED SON, JESUS CHRIST OUR LCRD   314 13
MY BELOVED BRETHREN, BE YE STEDFAST,   330 14
WERE THY BELOVED DELIVERED   412 21
6 THAT THY BELOVED MAY BE DELIVERED   479 15
SO HE GIVETH HIS BELOVED SLEEP   505 28
AND MOST DEARLY BELOVED SON JESUS CHRIST, TO BE CUR   545 14

BELOVED   CONTINUED

ONLY AND DEARLY BELOVED SON JESUS CHRIST, TO BE CUR   557 22
DEARLY BELOVED IN THE LORD   564 10
DEARLY BELOVED IN THE LORD, WE HAVE ASSEMBLED   570 12

BEND

FOR LO, THE UNGODLY BEND THEIR BOW, AND MAKE READY   354 21
AND MINE ARMS SHALL BEND EVEN A BOW OF STEEL   362 05

BENEATH

OR IN THE EARTH BENEATH, OR IN THE WATER UNDER THE   068 10
AND AS PETER WAS BENEATH IN THE PALACE, THERE COMETH   143 23
OR IN THE EARTH BENEATH, OR IN THE WATER UNDER THE   286 10
AND DOWN TO THE VALLEYS BENEATH   468 09
AND FASHIONED BENEATH IN THE EARTH   515 19
OR IN THE EARTH BENEATH, OR IN THE WATER UNDER THE   578 29

BENEDIC

DEUS MISEREATUR, BENEDIC, ANIMA MEA, MAY BE SUNG CR R 025 18

BENEDICTION

GIVE THY GRACE AND HEAVENLY BENEDICTION   039 02
FRUITS OF THE EARTH BY THY HEAVENLY BENEDICTION   041 02
THE FINAL PRAYER OF BLESSING OF THE BENEDICTICN   R 050 16
AND HEAVENLY BENEDICTION, AND MADE ONE BODY WITH HIM, 081 27
EVERLASTING BENEDICTION OF THY HEAVENLY WASHING, AND   274 19
BE FILLED WITH THY GRACE AND HEAVENLY BENEDICTICN   295 02
SPIRITUAL BENEDICTION AND GRACE   304 14
BEFORE THE BENEDICTION, SHALL BE SAID THIS COLLECT   R 534 29
BEFORE THE BENEDICTION, SHALL BE SAID THIS COLLECT   R 547 03
BEFORE THE BENEDICTION, SHALL BE SAID THIS PRAYER   R 559 04
AND HEAVENLY BENEDICTION, MAY, TO THEIR GREAT AND   565 32
AFTER THE BENEDICTION, (WHICH HE SHALL ALWAYS   R 574 26

BENEDICTUS

THE VENITE, BENEDICTUS ES, BENEDICTUS, JUBILATE,   R 009 24
BENEDICTUS, JUBILATE, MAY BE, AND AT THE END OF   R 009 24

BENEFACTORS

AUTHORITY UPON THEM ARE CALLED BENEFACTORS   149 21
AUTHORITY UPON THEM ARE CALLED BENEFACTORS   250 07

BENEFIT

AND THE BENEFIT OF THY HOLY CHURCH   039 14
YIELD HER INCREASE FOR OUR USE AND BENEFIT   040 28
AND TO THE BENEFIT OF OUR FELLOW MEN   044 23
FOR AS THE BENEFIT IS GREAT, IF WITH A TRUE PENITENT 085 30
HIS INESTIMABLE BENEFIT, AND ALSO DAILY ENDEAVOUR   171 31
SHALL ENJOY THE BENEFIT OF THIS PIOUS WORK, MAY SHCW 566 31
AND THE BENEFIT OF THY HOLY CHURCH   572 13
SO EXCELLENT A BENEFIT OF GOD, BE CALLED ACCORDING TO 606 11

BENEFITS

FOR THE GREAT BENEFITS THAT WE HAVE RECEIVED AT HIS   006 06
FOR THE GREAT BENEFITS THAT WE HAVE RECEIVED AT HIS   023 14
AND FORGET NOT ALL HIS BENEFITS   029 07
THE INNUMERABLE BENEFITS PROCURED UNTO US BY THE   081 05
AND ALL OTHER BENEFITS OF HIS PASSION   081 20
THE INNUMERABLE BENEFITS WHICH BY HIS PRECICUS   086 14
GIVE THANKS UNTO ALMIGHTY GOD FOR THESE BENEFITS   280 16
AND OF THE BENEFITS WHICH WE RECEIVE THEREBY   293 06
WHAT ARE THE BENEFITS WHEREOF WE ARE PARTAKERS IN THE 293 17
THE BENEFITS WHEREOF WE ARE PARTAKERS IN THE   293 19
FOR ALL THE BENEFITS THAT HE HATH DONE UNTO ME   305 28
AND FORGET NOT ALL HIS BENEFITS   312 22
REMEMBERING THE BENEFITS THEY HAVE THEREBY, AND GIVING R 323 28
AND POURETH HIS BENEFITS UPON US   420 24
AND FORGET NOT ALL HIS BENEFITS   466 11
FOR ALL THE BENEFITS THAT HE HATH DONE UNTO ME   487 10
THESE SO GREAT BENEFITS OF THY ETERNAL GOODNESS, AND 545 21
UNTO THEE FOR THESE AND ALL THY OTHER BENEFITS   545 29
AND ALL OTHER BENEFITS OF HIS PASSION   565 34
THANKS FOR THE BENEFITS WHICH THEY HAVE RECEIVED AT   566 15
AND OF THE BENEFITS WHICH WE RECEIVE THEREBY   582 05
WHAT ARE THE BENEFITS WHEREOF WE ARE PARTAKERS   582 15
THE MERCIES AND BENEFITS OF THE PAST DAY   591 19

BENJAMIN

THERE IS LITTLE BENJAMIN THEIR RULER, AND THE PRINCES 421 08
BEFORE EPHRAIM, BENJAMIN, AND MANASSEH, *   441 06

BENT

HE HATH BENT HIS BOW, AND MADE IT READY   350 18
THE SWORD, AND HAVE BENT THEIR BOW, *   385 23

BEQUESTS

TO LEAVE BEQUESTS FOR RELIGIOUS AND CHARITABLE USES R 320 23

BESEECH

I PRAY AND BESEECH YOU, AS MANY AS ARE HERE PRESENT, 006 10
WHEREFORE LET US BESEECH HIM TO GRANT US TRUE   007 14
MOST HEARTILY WE BESEECH THEE, WITH THY FAVOUR TC   017 29
WE HUMBLY BESEECH THEE FOR ALL SORTS AND CONDITICNS   018 27

BESEECH CONTINUED

WE BESEECH THEE, GIVE US THAT DUE SENSE OF ALL 019 25
I PRAY AND BESEECH YOU, AS MANY AS ARE HERE PRESENT, 023 18
WHEREFORE LET US BESEECH HIM TO GRANT US TRUE 024 16
OUR DARKNESS, WE BESEECH THEE, O LORD 031 26
WE HUMBLY BESEECH THEE FOR ALL SORTS AND CONDITIONS 032 27
WE BESEECH THEE, GIVE US THAT DUE SENSE OF ALL 033 23
WE HUMBLY BESEECH THEE, AS FOR THE PEOPLE OF 035 08
WE BESEECH THEE SO TO GUIDE AND BLESS THE LEGISLATURE 035 24
WE HUMBLY BESEECH THEE TO BLESS THE COURTS OF JUSTICE 035 32
WE HUMBLY BESEECH THEE THAT WE MAY ALWAYS PROVE 036 10
WE BESEECH THEE TO BE WITH THE COUNCIL OF THY CHURCH 036 29
VOUCHSAFE, WE BESEECH THEE, SO TO DIRECT, SANCTIFY, 036 32
WE HUMBLY BESEECH THEE FOR THY HOLY CATHOLIC CHURCH 037 15
GRANT, WE BESEECH THEE, UNTO US THY SERVANTS, THAT 038 19
WE HUMBLY BESEECH THEE, TO ALL THOSE WHO ARE 039 09
WE BESEECH THEE OF THINE INFINITE GOODNESS TO HEAR 040 04
SEND US, WE BESEECH THEE, IN THIS OUR NECESSITY, 040 18
WE HUMBLY BESEECH THEE, OF THY GREAT GOODNESS, TO 040 23
BEHOLD, WE BESEECH THEE, THE AFFLICTIONS OF THY 040 32
WE HUMBLY BESEECH THEE, FROM THE HANDS OF OUR 041 12
ALMIGHTY GOD, WE BESEECH THEE, WITH THY GRACIOUS 042 22
MAKE READY, WE BESEECH THEE, THE HEARTS AND MINDS OF 043 20
WE BESEECH THEE TO BLESS ALL WHO, FOLLOWING IN HIS 043 29
DELIVER US, WE BESEECH THEE, IN OUR SEVERAL CALLINGS, 044 19
WE BESEECH THEE, THE NATIONS OF THE WORLD INTO 044 27
DELIVER US, WE BESEECH THEE, FROM OUR PERIL 045 05
WE HUMBLY BESEECH THEE TO BEHOLD, VISIT, AND RELIEVE 045 13
WITH PITY, WE BESEECH THEE, UPON THE SORROWS OF THY 046 02
GUARD HIM, WE BESEECH THEE, FROM THE DANGERS OF THE 046 11
WE HUMBLY BESEECH THEE, OF THY GOODNESS, TO COMFORT 046 19
GRANT, WE BESEECH THEE, ALMIGHTY GOD, THAT THE WORDS 049 17
WE BESEECH THEE TO HAVE COMPASSION UPON OUR 049 31
WE BESEECH THEE MERCIFULLY TO INCLINE THINE EARS TO 050 07
WE BESEECH THEE, GIVE US A JUST SENSE OF THESE 050 25
GRANT, WE BESEECH THEE, MOST MERCIFUL FATHER, THAT 051 09
GRANT, WE BESEECH THEE, O GRACIOUS FATHER, THAT HE, 053 14
WE SINNERS DO BESEECH THEE TO HEAR US, O LORD GOD 055 18
WE BESEECH THEE TO HEAR US, GOOD LORD 055 21
WE BESEECH THEE TO HEAR US, GOOD LORD 056 04
WE BESEECH THEE TO HEAR US, GOOD LORD 057 04
SON OF GOD, WE BESEECH THEE TO HEAR US 057 19
WE HUMBLY BESEECH THEE, O FATHER, ETC R 058 10
WE HUMBLY BESEECH THEE, O FATHER, MERCIFULLY TO LOOK 059 21
WE HUMBLY BESEECH THEE, O FATHER, IN THE LITANY R 060 04
O LORD, WE BESEECH THEE, MERCIFULLY HEAR OUR PRAYERS, 062 08
OUR HEARTS, WE BESEECH THEE 069 24
VOUCHSAFE, WE BESEECH THEE, TO DIRECT, SANCTIFY, 070 07
WE HUMBLY BESEECH THEE MOST MERCIFULLY TO ACCEPT OUR 074 08
WE BESEECH THEE ALSO, SO TO DIRECT AND DISPOSE THE 074 16
WE MOST HUMBLY BESEECH THEE, OF THY GOODNESS, 074 30
WE MOST HUMBLY BESEECH THEE, O MERCIFUL FATHER, TO 081 07
YET WE BESEECH THEE TO ACCEPT THIS OUR BOUNDEN DUTY 081 30
AND WE HUMBLY BESEECH THEE, O HEAVENLY FATHER, 083 26
AND BESEECH YOU, FOR THE LORD JESUS CHRIST'S SAKE, 088 14
WE BESEECH THEE TO CAST THY BRIGHT BEAMS OF 101 05
O LORD, WE BESEECH THEE MERCIFLLLY TO RECEIVE THE 109 29
I BESEECH YOU THEREFORE, BRETHREN, BY THE MERCIES OF 110 03
O LORD, WE BESEECH THEE TO KEEP THY CHURCH AND 115 28
GRANT US, WE BESEECH THEE, THAT, HAVING THIS HOPE, WE 117 06
O LORD, WE BESEECH THEE FAVOURABLY TO HEAR THE 118 28
WITH HIM, BESEECH YOU ALSO THAT YE RECEIVE NOT THE 126 03
WE BESEECH YOU, BRETHREN, AND EXHORT YOU BY THE LORD 127 23
WE BESEECH THEE, ALMIGHTY GOD, LOOK UPON THE HEARTY 128 25
GRANT, WE BESEECH THEE, ALMIGHTY GOD, THAT WE, 130 24
WE BESEECH THEE, ALMIGHTY GOD, MERCIFULLY TO LOCK 132 18
ALMIGHTY GOD, WE BESEECH THEE GRACIOUSLY TC BEHOLD 156 21
WE HUMBLY BESEECH THEE THAT, AS BY THY SPECIAL GRACE 163 24
GRANT, WE BESEECH THEE, ALMIGHTY GOD, THAT WE WHO 168 19
I BESEECH YOU AS STRANGERS AND PILGRIMS, 173 12
GRANT, WE BESEECH THEE, ALMIGHTY GOD, THAT LIKE AS WE 177 14
WE BESEECH THEE, LEAVE US NOT COMFORTLESS 179 06
GRANT, WE BESEECH THEE, THAT BY THE INDWELLING 182 15
SEND, WE BESEECH THEE, ALMIGHTY GOD, THY HOLY SPIRIT 183 22
GRANT, WE BESEECH THEE, MERCIFUL GOD, THAT THY 185 14
WE BESEECH THEE THAT THOU WOULDEST KEEP US STEDFAST 186 27
KEEP US, WE BESEECH THEE, UNDER THE PROTECTION OF THY 191 06
O LORD, WE BESEECH THEE MERCIFULLY TO HEAR US 192 24
O LORD, WE BESEECH THEE, THAT THE COURSE OF THIS 195 15
WE HUMBLY BESEECH THEE TO PUT AWAY FROM US ALL 199 29
TO US, LORD, WE BESEECH THEE, THE SPIRIT TC THINK AND 200 29
AND THEY BESEECH HIM TO PUT HIS HAND UPON HIM 206 31
GRANT, WE BESEECH THEE, THAT WE MAY SO FAITHFULLY 207 14
KEEP, WE BESEECH THEE, O LORD, THY CHURCH WITH THY 210 17
O LORD, WE BESEECH THEE, LET THY CONTINUAL PITY 212 04
OF THE LORD, BESEECH YOU THAT YE WALK WORTHY OF THE 213 18
WE BESEECH THEE, GRANT THY PEOPLE GRACE TO 214 23
KEEP US, WE BESEECH THEE, FROM ALL THINGS THAT MAY 217 18
GRANT, WE BESEECH THEE, MERCIFUL LORD, TO THY 218 32
WE BESEECH THEE TO KEEP THY HOUSEHOLD THE 220 16
BE READY, WE BESEECH THEE, TO HEAR THE DEVOUT PRAYERS 222 10
O LORD, WE BESEECH THEE, ABSOLVE THY PEOPLE FROM 223 15
STIR UP, WE BESEECH THEE, O LORD, THE WILLS OF THY 225 04
GRANT, WE BESEECH THEE, THAT WE, HAVING HIS WONDERFUL 229 19
WE HUMBLY BESEECH THY MAJESTY, THAT, AS THY 231 28
WE BESEECH THEE, O LORD, POUR THY GRACE INTO OUR 235 18
LEAVE US NOT, WE BESEECH THEE, DESTITUTE OF THY 240 30
WE BESEECH THEE, ALL BISHOPS AND PASTORS 244 25
GRANT, WE BESEECH THEE, UNTO THY CHURCH, TC LOVE THAT 249 16
HEAR, WE BESEECH THEE, THE PRAYERS OF THY PEOPLE, AND 259 20
WE HUMBLY BESEECH THEE, BY THE INSPIRATION OF THY 260 21
WE BESEECH THEE TO POUR FORTH THY BLESSING UPON THIS 261 29
GRANT, WE BESEECH THEE, THAT WE AND ALL THE PEOPLE OF 263 18
WE HUMBLY BESEECH THEE, FAVOURABLY TO BEHOLD 267 04
VOUCHSAFE, WE BESEECH THEE, TO THY WHOLE CHURCH IN 268 15

BESEECH CONTINUED

I BESEECH YOU TO CALL UPON GOD THE FATHER, THROUGH 273 32
REGARD, WE BESEECH THEE, THE SUPPLICATIONS OF THY 279 14
AND HUMBLY WE BESEECH THEE TO GRANT, THAT HE, BEING 280 32
OUR HEARTS, WE BESEECH THEE 287 24
TO US, LORD, WE BESEECH THEE, THE SPIRIT TO THINK AND 287 26
WE BESEECH THEE, O LORD, WITH THE HOLY GHOST, 297 17
WE BESEECH THEE, EVER BE OVER THEM 298 20
VOUCHSAFE, WE BESEECII THEE, TO DIRECT, SANCTIFY, 298 27
O LORD, I BESEECH THEE, DELIVER MY SOUL 305 23
GRANT, WE BESEECH THEE, MOST MERCIFUL FATHER, THAT 306 28
GRANT, WE BESEECH THEE, O HEAVENLY FATHER, 307 03
SANCTIFY, WE BESEECH THEE, O LORD, THE SICKNESS OF 310 21
HEAR, O LORD, WE BESEECH THEE, THESE OUR PRAYERS, 311 21
ACCEPT, WE BESEECH THEE, MERCIFUL LORD, THE DEVOUT 313 05
WE HUMBLY BESEECH THEE, O LORD 313 14
WE BESEECH THEE, THIS THY MERCY TOWARDS HIM 315 27
WE BESEECH THEE, SO MUCH THE MORE CONTINUALLY 316 10
COMFORT, WE BESEECH THEE, MOST GRACIOUS GOD, THIS THY 316 18
MAKE US, WE BESEECH THEE, DEEPLY SENSIBLE OF THE 316 26
WE SINNERS DO BESEECH THEE TO HEAR US, O LORD GOD 318 10
WE BESEECH THEE TO HEAR US, GOOD LORD 318 14
WE BESEECH THEE TO LOOSE THE SPIRIT OF THIS THY 319 08
WE HUMBLY BESFECH THEE, A SHEEP OF THINE OWN FOLD, A 319 29
RELIEVE, WE BESEECH THEE, BY THY INDWELLING POWER, 320 08
WE BESEECH THEE TO HAVE MERCY UPON THIS THY SERVANT 321 20
AND WE BESEECH THEE, THAT WE, WITH ALL THOSE WHO ARE 334 25
WE HUMBLY BESEECH THEE, O FATHER, TO RAISE US FROM 335 05
GRANT THIS, WE BESEECH THEE, O MERCIFUL FATHER, 335 13
WE BESEECH THEE, TO THOSE WHO REST IN 335 27
US GRACE, WE BESEECH THEE, TO ENTRUST THE SOUL OF 342 04
O LORD, I BESEECH THEE, DELIVER MY SOUL 486 26
MAKE THEM, WE BESEECH THEE, O LORD, TO BE MODEST, 535 03
AND WE HUMBLY BESEECH THEE, BY THE SAME THY BLESSED 545 26
WE BESEECH THEE TO SEND UPON THESE THY 547 04
GIVE GRACE, WE BESEECH THEE, TO ALL BISHOPS, THE 549 09
WE BESEECH THEE TO HEAR US, GOOD LORD 553 22
GRANT, WE BESEECH THEE, TO THIS THY SERVANT, SUCH 557 28
SEND DOWN, WE BESEECH THEE, UPON THIS THY SERVANT THY 559 05
TO REPROVE, BESEECH, AND REBUKE, WITH ALL PATIENCE 559 08
ONE GOD, WE BESEECH THEE TO HEAR US, GOOD LORD 560 11
WE BESEECH THEE TO HEAR US, GOOD LORD 560 14
WE BESEECH THEE TO HEAR US, GOOD LORD 561 06
GRANT, WE BESEECH THEE, BLESSED LORD, THAT WHOSOEVER 566 13
GRANT, WE BESEECH THEE, THAT IN THIS PLACE NOW SET 568 09
THY GRACE, WE BESEECH THEE, TO THY SERVANT, TO WHOM 572 09
WE HUMBLY BESEECH THEE TO HAVE COMPASSION ON OUR 588 14
WE BESEECH THEE, IN MERCY, AND FORGIVE US ALL OUR 590 02
VOUCHSAFE US, WE BESEECH THEE, THE DIRECTION AND 590 11
WE BESEECH THEE TO CONTINUE THY GRACIOUS 591 25
OUR DARKNESS, WE BESEECH THEE, O LORD 593 13
WE BESEECH THEE, FOR THY COMPASSION'S SAKE, TO 594 20
BRING US, WE BESEECH THEE, IN SAFETY TO THE MORNING 595 08
OPEN, WE BESEECH THEE, OUR EYES TO BEHOLD THY 596 18
WE HUMBLY BESEECH THEE GRACIOUSLY TO BEHOLD AND BLESS 596 31
WE BESEECH THEE GRACIOUSLY TO COMFORT THY 597 21
WE BESEECH THEE TO HAVE MERCY UPON ALL THY 598 13
FROM THEM, WE BESEECH THEE, EVERY ROOT OF BITTERNESS, 598 22

BESEECHING

BESEECHING THEE TO CONTINUE THY LOVING-KINDNESS UNTO 052 02
BESEECHING THEE STILL TO CONTINUE SUCH THY MERCIES 052 12
MOST HUMBLY BESEECHING THEE TO GRANT TO ALL OF US 052 22
AND EARNESTLY BESEECHING ALMIGHTY GOD TO ACCOMPANY VI 40
BESEECHING THEE TO INSPIRE CONTINUALLY THE UNIVERSAL 074 11
BESEECHING THEE TO GRANT THEM CONTINUAL GROWTH IN THY 074 35
MOST HUMBLY BESEECHING THEE TO GRANT THAT, BY THE 081 17
HUMBLY BESEECHING THEE, THAT WE, AND ALL OTHERS WHO 081 23
A CENTURION, BESEECHING HIM, AND SAYING, LORD, MY 115 07
BESEECHING THEE TO CONTINUE THY LOVING-KINDNESS TO 265 14
BESEECHING THEE, THAT IT MAY BE PRECIOUS IN THY 317 16
BESEECHING THE MERCY OF OUR LORD JESUS CHRIST, THAT 320 17
MOST HUMBLY BESEECHING THEE TO GIVE US GRACE SO TO 336 20
HUMBLY BESEECHING THEE TO ACCEPT THIS OUR MORNING 587 25
BESEECHING THEE TO CONTINUE THESE THY BLESSINGS TO 591 20

BESET

DOTH SO EASILY BESET US, AND LET US RUN WITH PATIENCE 258 22
4 THOU HAST BESET ME BEHIND AND BEFORE, * 514 27

BESIDE

BESIDE THOSE THINGS THAT ARE WITHOUT, THAT WHICH 121 10
AND BESIDE ALL THIS, TO-DAY IS THE THIRD DAY SINCE 167 21
AND BESIDE ALL THIS, BETWEEN US AND YOU THERE IS A 190 19
AND LEAD ME FORTH BESIDE THE WATERS OF COMFORT 338 20
AND LEAD ME FORTH BESIDE THE WATERS OF COMFORT 368 13
SHALL FALL BESIDE THEE, AND TEN THOUSAND AT THY RIGHT 455 09
12 BESIDE THEM SHALL THE FOWLS OF THE AIR HAVE THEIR 468 17

BESIDES

VOLUNTARY WORKS BESIDES, OVER AND ABOVE, GOD'S 605 24
THE SAME, SO BESIDES THE SAME OUGHT IT NOT TC ENFORCE 607 08

BESIEGED

OF HIM THAT BESIEGED THEE 405 26

BESOUGHT

CAME AND BESOUGHT HIM, SAYING, SEND HER AWAY 128 12
AN HIGH DAY,) BESOUGHT PILATE THAT THEIR LEGS MIGHT 160 32

BESOUGHT   CONTINUED

UNTO HIM, AND BESOUGHT HIM THAT HE WOULD COME DOWN,   219 30
HIS FEET, AND BESOUGHT HIM, SAYING, HAVE PATIENCE   221 27

BEST

ACCORDING TO HER BEST UNDERSTANDING, MIGHT MOST TEND   V 35
UPON THE BEST AND SUREST FOUNDATIONS, THAT PEACE AND   035 15
BRING FORTH THE BEST ROBE, AND PUT IT ON HIM   202 21
PRAISE WITH THE BEST MEMBER THAT I HAVE   479 05

BESTOW

AND THOUGH I BESTOW ALL MY GOODS TO FEED THE POOR,   122 26
BESTOW UPON THESE THY SERVANTS, IF IT BE THY WILL,   303 15
AND BESTOW UPON HIM THE HELP OF THY MERCIFUL   311 23
OUR GHOSTLY FOE, AND THINE ABIDING PEACE BESTOW   545 07
OUR GHOSTLY FOE, AND THINE ABIDING PEACE BESTOW   557 13

BESTOWED

PROVIDENCE BESTOWED UPON THIS NATION AND PEOPLE   050 24
THE FATHER HATH BESTOWED UPON US, THAT WE SHOULD BE   117 14
THE LORD HATH BESTOWED ON US, AND THE GREAT GOODNESS   138 29
WHICH HE HATH BESTOWED ON THEM ACCORDING TO HIS   138 31
GRACE WHICH WAS BESTOWED UPON ME WAS NOT IN VAIN   205 16

BETHABARA

WERE DONE IN BETHABARA BEYOND JORDAN, WHERE JOHN WAS   096 06

BETHANY

AND BEING IN BETHANY IN THE HOUSE OF SIMON THE LEPER, 140 02
OUT AS FAR AS TO BETHANY, AND HE LIFTED UP HIS HANDS, 178 24

BETHLEHEM

WHICH IS CALLED BETHLEHEM   099 03
THAT WERE IN BETHLEHEM, AND IN ALL THE COASTS   103 27
GO EVEN UNTO BETHLEHEM, AND SEE THIS THING WHICH IS   106 09
WAS BORN IN BETHLEHEM OF JUDAEA, IN THE DAYS OF HEROD 108 30
UNTO HIM, IN BETHLEHEM OF JUDAEA   109 06
AND THOU BETHLEHEM, IN THE LAND OF JUDA, ART NOT THE   109 08
SENT THEM TO BETHLEHEM, AND SAID, GO AND SEARCH   109 12

BETHPHAGE

WERE COME TO BETHPHAGE, UNTO THE MOUNT OF OLIVES,   091 12

BETIDE

PREVENTING GUIDE, NO EVIL CAN OUR STEPS BETIDE   545 09
PREVENTING GUIDE, NO EVIL CAN OUR STEPS BETIDE   557 15

BETIMES

SHALT THOU HEAR BETIMES, O LORD   348 04
PRAISE THY MERCY BETIMES IN THE MORNING   412 07
LOVING-KINDNESS BETIMES IN THE MORNING   519 07

BETRAY

CHIEF PRIESTS, TO BETRAY HIM UNTO THEM   140 19
CONVENIENTLY BETRAY HIM   140 22
WITH ME SHALL BETRAY ME   141 02
HOW HE MIGHT BETRAY HIM UNTO THEM   148 18
OPPORTUNITY TO BETRAY HIM UNTO THEM IN THE ABSENCE OF 148 20
SIMON'S SON, TO BETRAY HIM   155 28
KNEW WHO SHOULD BETRAY HIM   156 11

BETRAYED

IN WHICH HE WAS BETRAYED, (A) HE TOOK BREAD   080 17
WHICH HAD BETRAYED HIM, WHEN HE SAW THAT HE WAS   135 02
IN THAT I HAVE BETRAYED THE INNOCENT BLOOD   135 05
TO THAT MAN BY WHOM THE SON OF MAN IS BETRAYED   141 08
SON OF MAN IS BETRAYED INTO THE HANDS OF SINNERS   142 12
AND HE THAT BETRAYED HIM HAD GIVEN THEM A TOKEN,   142 17
BUT WOE UNTO THAT MAN BY WHOM HE IS BETRAYED   149 16
IN WHICH HE WAS BETRAYED TOOK BREAD   152 18
CONTENTED TO BE BETRAYED, AND GIVEN UP INTO THE HANDS 156 23

BETRAYEST

JUDAS, BETRAYEST THOU THE SON OF MAN WITH A   150 29

BETRAYETH

IS HE THAT BETRAYETH THEE   102 06
HE THAT BETRAYETH ME IS AT HAND   142 13
OF HIM THAT BETRAYETH ME IS WITH ME ON THE TABLE   149 13

BETTER

GRACE RETURN TO A BETTER MIND   089 20
MADE SO MUCH BETTER THAN THE ANGELS, AS HE HATH BY   096 30
THEMSELVES WITH BETTER SACRIFICES THAN THESE   147 29
IT IS BETTER, IF THE WILL OF GOD BE SO, THAT YE   161 21
IN ME, IT WERE BETTER FOR HIM THAT A MILLSTONE WERE   252 32
IT IS BETTER FOR THEE TO ENTER INTO LIFE HALT OR   253 04
IT IS BETTER FOR THEE TO ENTER INTO LIFE WITH ONE   253 08
ARE YE NOT MUCH BETTER THAN THEY   266 16
DAY FORWARD, FOR BETTER FOR WORSE, FOR RICHER FOR   301 29
DAY FORWARD, FOR BETTER FOR WORSE, FOR RICHER FOR   302 05

BETTER   CONTINUED

IS BETTER THAN GREAT RICHES OF THE UNGODLY   385 27
IS BETTER THAN THE LIFE ITSELF   414 31
BETTER THAN A BULLOCK THAT HATH HORNS AND HOOFS   424 06
IS BETTER THAN A THOUSAND   445 31
8 IT IS BETTER TO TRUST IN THE LORD, *   488 14
9 IT IS BETTER TO TRUST IN THE LORD, *   488 16
REPENTANCE AND BETTER MINDS   590 33
DOING FOR THEM BETTER THINGS THAN WE CAN DESIRE OR   597 11
THE SAME TO SERVE BETTER TO GODLINESS   609 24

BETTERS

MYSELF LOWLY AND REVERENTLY TO ALL MY BETTERS   580 07

BETWEEN

THE HAPPY MEAN BETWEEN TOO MUCH STIFFNESS IN   V 24
AND DWELLEST BETWEEN THE CHERUBIM   011 23
WHOM YE SLEW BETWEEN THE TEMPLE AND THE ALTAR,   100 25
THE LORD, WEEP BETWEEN THE PORCH AND THE ALTAR,   125 03
WERE AT ENMITY BETWEEN THEMSELVES   153 20
BESIDE ALL THIS, BETWEEN US AND YOU THERE IS A GREAT   190 19
IS NO DIFFERENCE BETWEEN THE JEW AND THE GREEK   227 02
WAS SLEEPING BETWEEN TWO SOLDIERS, BOUND WITH TWO   245 10
CIVIL CONTRACT BETWEEN THE PARTIES   R 304 20
OF MARRIAGE BETWEEN N   R 304 22
HE SITTETH BETWEEN THE CHERUBIM, BE THE EARTH NEVER   462 17
BETWEEN YOU AND THEM   569 33
ANY DIFFERENCE BETWEEN YOU AND YOUR CONGREGATION,   569 34
CONNECTION BETWEEN YOU AND THEM, WE, YOUR BISHOP,   569 35
ONLY MEDIATOR BETWEEN GOD AND MAN, BEING BOTH GOD AND 604 17

BETWIXT

USE WITH THOSE, BETWIXT WHOM HE PERCEIVETH MALICE AND R 085 09
UNION THAT IS BETWIXT CHRIST AND HIS CHURCH   300 12
VOW AND COVENANT BETWIXT THEM MADE, (WHEREOF THIS   303 08
AND UNITY BETWIXT CHRIST AND HIS CHURCH   303 22
VOW AND COVENANT BETWIXT THEM MADE, AND MAY REMAIN IN 566 11

BEWAIL

ACKNOWLEDGE AND BEWAIL OUR MANIFOLD SINS AND   075 19
OR DEED, THERE TO BEWAIL YOUR OWN SINFULNESS, AND TO   087 19

BEWAILED

WHICH ALSO BEWAILED AND LAMENTED HIM   154 12

BEWARE

BEWARE THEREFORE, LEST THAT COME UPON YOU, WHICH IS   169 22
BEWARE OF FALSE PROPHETS, WHICH COME TO YOU IN   200 15
AS ALSO TO BEWARE THAT NEITHER YOU YOURSELVES OFFEND, 540 28

BEYOND

DONE IN BETHABARA BEYOND JORDAN, WHERE JOHN WAS   096 06
THAT NO MAN GO BEYOND AND DEFRAUD HIS BROTHER IN ANY   127 32
AND WERE BEYOND MEASURE ASTONISHED, SAYING, HE HATH   207 07

BIBLE

THEM KNEELING, THE BIBLE INTO HIS HAND, SAYING,   R 546 23
DELIVER HIM THE BIBLE, SAYING, GIVE HEED UNTO   R 558 20
PRESENT HIM THE BIBLE, BOOK OF COMMON PRAYER,   R 571 23

BID

CHRISTIAN PEOPLE, I BID YOUR PRAYERS FOR CHRIST'S   047 06
IN GOD'S BEHALF, I BID YOU ALL WHO ARE HERE PRESENT   088 14
TO MINE OFFICE, I BID YOU IN THE NAME OF GOD, I CALL   089 07
AS YE SHALL FIND, BID TO THE MARRIAGE   218 18

BIDDEN

CALLED AND BIDDEN BY GOD HIMSELF   088 16
OF THE LORD HAD BIDDEN HIM, AND TOOK UNTO HIM HIS   105 13
TO THEM THAT WERE BIDDEN, COME   192 05
MEN WHICH WERE BIDDEN SHALL TASTE OF MY SUPPER   192 21
THOSE WHICH WERE BIDDEN, WHEN HE MARKED HOW THEY   214 09
WHEN THOU ART BIDDEN OF ANY MAN TO A WEDDING, SIT NOT 214 10
MAN THAN THOU BE BIDDEN OF HIM   214 12
BUT WHEN THOU ART BIDDEN, GO AND SIT DOWN IN THE   214 15
THEM THAT WERE BIDDEN TO THE WEDDING   218 05
THEM WHICH ARE BIDDEN, BEHOLD, I HAVE PREPARED MY   218 07
THEY WHICH WERE BIDDEN WERE NOT WORTHY   218 17

BIDDING

MAY BE SAID THE BIDDING PRAYER, OR OTHER AUTHORIZED R 071 29
AND WELCOME HIM, BIDDING HIM GOD-SPEED   R 574 28

BIER

AND HE CAME AND TOUCHED THE BIER   213 03

BIND

HE HATH SENT ME TO BIND UP THE BROKENHEARTED, TO   107 02
THE TARES, AND BIND THEM IN BUNDLES TO BURN THEM   116 30
TO THE SERVANTS, BIND HIM HAND AND FOOT, AND TAKE HIM 218 26
CHIEF PRIESTS TO BIND ALL THAT CALL ON THY NAME   230 24
GIRD THYSELF, AND BIND ON THY SANDALS   245 16

BIND   CONTINUED

THOU SHALT BIND ON EARTH SHALL BE BOUND IN HEAVEN	246 10
BIND THE SACRIFICE WITH CORDS, YEA, EVEN UNTO THE	489 22
8 TO BIND THEIR KINGS IN CHAINS, *	525 17
HEAL THE SICK, BIND UP THE BROKEN, BRING AGAIN THE	558 27
AND RITES, DO NOT BIND CHRISTIAN MEN, NOR THE CIVIL	604 20

BINDETH

NEITHER HE THAT BINDETH UP THE SHEAVES HIS BOSOM	507 03

BIRD

SHOULD FLEE AS A BIRD UNTO THE HILL	354 20
ESCAPED EVEN AS A BIRD OUT OF THE SNARE OF THE	504 18

BIRDS

BEHOLD THE BIRDS OF THE HEAVEN, THAT THEY SOW NOT,	211 16
ANOTHER OF FISHES, AND ANOTHER OF BIRDS	329 13
17 WHEREIN THE BIRDS MAKE THEIR NESTS	468 28

BIRTH

REMEMBRANCE OF THE BIRTH OF THINE ONLY SON JESUS	098 12
THE BIRTH OF JESUS CHRIST WAS ON THIS WISE	104 27
AND A NEW BIRTH UNTO RIGHTEOUSNESS	292 25
AND A NEW BIRTH UNTO RIGHTEOUSNESS	581 24

BISHOP

FOR THE BISHOP OF THIS DIOCESE), THAT THEY MAY	047 24
THE PRIEST (THE BISHOP IF HE BE PRESENT) STAND UP,	R 075 32
THE PRIEST (THE BISHOP IF HE BE PRESENT) SHALL LET	R 084 16
THE SHEPHERD AND BISHOP OF YOUR SOULS,	172 19
BE BROUGHT TO THE BISHOP TO BE CONFIRMED BY HIM	277 15
CONFIRMED BY THE BISHOP, SO SOON AFTER HIS BAPTISM AS	R 281 14
WHAT IS THE OFFICE OF A BISHOP	294 07
THE OFFICE OF A BISHOP IS, TO BE A CHIEF PASTOR IN	294 08
UNDER THE DIRECTION OF THE BISHOP	294 19
CONFIRMED BY THE BISHOP, MAY RECEIVE SUCH A MEASURE	294 21
BE BROUGHT TO THE BISHOP TO BE CONFIRMED BY HIM	295 16
ORDER BEFORE THE BISHOP, SITTING IN HIS CHAIR NEAR TO	R 296 06
THEN THE BISHOP, OR SOME MINISTER APPOINTED BY HIM,	R 296 10
THEN SHALL THE BISHOP SAY, DO YE HERE, IN THE	R 296 21
THEN SHALL THE BISHOP SAY, DO YE PROMISE TO FOLLOW	R 297 12
BEFORE THE BISHOP, HE SHALL LAY HIS HAND UPON THE	R 297 24
THEN SHALL THE BISHOP SAY, THE LORD BE WITH YOU	R 297 30
THEN SHALL THE BISHOP SAY THE LORD'S PRAYER,	R 298 03
THEN SHALL THE BISHOP SAY, ALMIGHTY AND EVERLIVING	R 298 12
THEN THE BISHOP SHALL BLESS THEM, SAYING THUS,	R 299 02
TO BE A LAWFUL BISHOP, PRIEST, OR DEACON, IN THIS	529 20
OR BISHOP, EXCEPT HE BE OF THE AGE WHICH THE	529 24
AND THE BISHOP, KNOWING EITHER BY HIMSELF, OR BY	529 26
APPOINTED BY THE BISHOP IS COME, THERE SHALL BE A	R 530 03
PRESENT UNTO THE BISHOP, SITTING IN HIS CHAIR NEAR TO	R 530 07
THEN THE BISHOP SHALL SAY UNTO THE PEOPLE, BRETHREN,	R 530 20
BE OBJECTED, THE BISHOP SHALL CEASE FROM ORDERING	R 530 26
THEN THE BISHOP (COMMENDING SUCH AS SHALL BE FOUND	R 530 29
DISCRETION OF THE BISHOP, INSTEAD OF THE LITANY	R 531 09
BEING SEATED, THE BISHOP SHALL EXAMINE EVERY ONE OF	R 532 23
IF HE BE ADMITTED THERETO BY THE BISHOP	533 17
OBEY YOUR BISHOP, AND OTHER CHIEF MINISTERS, WHO	533 30
THE BISHOP SHALL LAY HIS HANDS SEVERALLY	R 534 02
THEN SHALL THE BISHOP DELIVER TO EVERY ONE OF THEM	R 534 09
LICENSED BY THE BISHOP HIMSELF	534 13
APPOINTED BY THE BISHOP, SHALL READ THE GOSPEL	R 534 14
THEN SHALL THE BISHOP PROCEED IN THE COMMUNION	R 534 26
THE HOLY COMMUNION THE SAME DAY, WITH THE BISHOP	R 534 27
GOOD UNTO THE BISHOP,) TO THE INTENT HE MAY BE	R 535 21
APPOINTED BY THE BISHOP IS COME, THERE SHALL BE A	R 536 03
PRESENT UNTO THE BISHOP, SITTING IN HIS CHAIR NEAR TO	R 536 07
THEN THE BISHOP SHALL SAY UNTO THE PEOPLE, GOOD	R 536 21
BE OBJECTED, THE BISHOP SHALL CEASE FROM ORDERING	R 537 02
THEN THE BISHOP (COMMENDING SUCH AS SHALL BE FOUND	R 537 05
DISCRETION OF THE BISHOP, INSTEAD OF THE LITANY	R 537 15
BEING SEATED, THE BISHOP SHALL SAY UNTO THOSE WHO ARE	R 539 22
OBEY YOUR BISHOP, AND OTHER CHIEF MINISTERS, WHO,	543 11
SHALL THE BISHOP SAY, ALMIGHTY GOD, WHO HATH GIVEN	R 543 17
THE BISHOP SHALL SING OR SAY THE VENI,	R 543 27
THE BISHOP BEGINNING, AND THE PRIESTS, AND OTHERS	R 543 27
THAT DONE, THE BISHOP SHALL PRAY IN THIS WISE,	R 545 10
IS DONE, THE BISHOP WITH THE PRIESTS PRESENT,	R 546 06
AND THE BISHOP SAYING, RECEIVE THE HOLY	R 546 08
THEN THE BISHOP SHALL DELIVER TO EVERY ONE OF THEM	R 546 23
BE SAID, AND THE BISHOP SHALL GO ON IN THE SERVICE OF	R 546 28
THE PRESIDING BISHOP, OR SOME OTHER BISHOP APPOINTED	R 549 04
OR SOME OTHER BISHOP APPOINTED BY THE BISHOPS	R 549 04
AND ANOTHER BISHOP SHALL READ THE EPISTLE	R 549 16
THE OFFICE OF A BISHOP, HE DESIRETH A GOOD WORK	549 19
A BISHOP THEN MUST BE BLAMELESS, THE HUSBAND OF ONE	549 19
THEN ANOTHER BISHOP SHALL READ THE GOSPEL	R 551 12
THE ELECTED BISHOP, VESTED WITH HIS ROCHET, SHALL BE	R 552 17
THE PRESIDING BISHOP, OR TO THE BISHOP APPOINTED,	R 552 18
BISHOP, OR TO THE BISHOP APPOINTED, SITTING IN HIS	R 552 18
TO BE ORDAINED AND CONSECRATED BISHOP	552 23
THE PRESIDING BISHOP DEMAND TESTIMONIALS OF THE	R 552 24
CHOSEN BISHOP OF THE PROTESTANT EPISCOPAL CHURCH IN	552 28
THE PRESIDING BISHOP SHALL MOVE THE CONGREGATION	R 553 02
OF THE PRESIDING BISHOP, INSTEAD OF THE LITANY, MAY	R 553 23
NOW CALLED TO THE WORK AND MINISTRY OF A BISHOP	553 29
THE PRESIDING BISHOP, SITTING IN HIS CHAIR, SHALL SAY	R 554 05
THE PRESIDING BISHOP SHALL SAY, ALMIGHTY GOD, OUR	R 555 27
THEN SHALL THE BISHOP ELECT PUT ON THE REST OF THE	R 556 02
THE PRESIDING BISHOP SHALL BEGIN, AND THE BISHOPS,	R 556 04

BISHOP   CONTINUED

THE PRESIDING BISHOP SHALL SAY, LORD, HEAR OUR	R 557 16
THE PRESIDING BISHOP AND BISHOPS PRESENT SHALL LAY	R 558 09
OF THE ELECTED BISHOP, KNEELING BEFORE THEM, THE	R 558 10
THE PRESIDING BISHOP SAYING,	R 558 11
AND WORK OF A BISHOP IN THE CHURCH OF GOD, NOW	558 13
THE PRESIDING BISHOP SHALL DELIVER HIM THE BIBLE,	R 558 20
THE PRESIDING BISHOP SHALL PROCEED IN THE COMMUNION	R 559 02
NEWLY CONSECRATED BISHOP, WITH OTHERS, SHALL ALSO	R 559 03
CONSECRATION OF A BISHOP SHALL BE SAID, THAT IT MAY	R 560 32
THE BISHOP IS TO BE RECEIVED AT THE ENTRANCE OF THE	R 563 05
THE BISHOP AND THE CLERGY WHO ARE PRESENT SHALL GO UP	R 563 07
THE BISHOP ONE VERSE AND THE CLERGY	R 563 09
THE BISHOP SHALL GO WITHIN THE RAILS, WITH SUCH OF	R 564 06
THE BISHOP, SITTING IN HIS CHAIR, SHALL HAVE THE	R 564 07
THEN THE BISHOP, KNEELING, SHALL SAY THE FOLLOWING	R 564 26
AFTER THIS THE BISHOP SHALL STAND UP, AND TURNING	R 565 16
CONFIRMED BY THE BISHOP, MAY RECEIVE SUCH A MEASURE	565 25
THE BISHOP SITTING IN HIS CHAIR, THE SENTENCE	R 566 25
AFTER WHICH, THE BISHOP SHALL SAY, BLESSED BE THY	R 566 27
THE BISHOP SHALL SAY THIS PRAYER	R 568 04
THE BISHOP HAVING RECEIVED DUE NOTICE OF THE	R 569 04
AND TO THE CHIEF BISHOP AND SOVEREIGN JUDGE OF ALL,	569 27
WE, YOUR BISHOP, WITH THE ADVICE OF OUR	569 36
THE BISHOP, OR THE INSTITUTOR APPOINTED	R 570 02
EXCEPT THE BISHOP, OR THE PRIEST WHO ACTS AS	R 570 05
IN OPEN VIEW, THE BISHOP, OR THE PRIEST WHO ACTS AS	R 570 10
BE OFFERED, THE BISHOP, OR THE PRIEST WHO ACTS AS THE	R 570 21
THE GRACIOUS BISHOP AND SHEPHERD OF OUR SOULS,	574 21
WHEN THE BISHOP OF THE DIOCESE IS PRESENT AT THE	R 574 29
THEY SHALL BE BROUGHT TO THE BISHOP	R 583 04
WHENSOEVER THE BISHOP SHALL GIVE KNOWLEDGE FOR	R 583 05
PRESENTED TO THE BISHOP TO BE CONFIRMED	R 583 09

BISHOPRICK

AND HIS BISHOPRICK LET ANOTHER TAKE	234 20

BISHOPS

DOWN UPON OUR BISHOPS, AND OTHER CLERGY, AND UPON THE	018 20
DOWN UPON OUR BISHOPS, AND OTHER CLERGY, AND UPON THE	032 19
THY SERVANTS THE BISHOPS AND PASTORS OF THY FLOCK,	038 29
FOR BISHOPS (AND HEREIN MORE ESPECIALLY FOR THE	047 23
ILLUMINATE ALL BISHOPS, PRIESTS, AND DEACONS, WITH	055 30
TO ALL BISHOPS AND OTHER MINISTERS, THAT THEY	074 21
THE SAME TO THE BISHOPS, PRIESTS, AND DEACONS,	R 082 26
ALL BISHOPS AND PASTORS DILIGENTLY TO PREACH	244 05
BISHOPS, PRIESTS, AND DEACONS	294 05
-- BISHOPS, PRIESTS, AND DEACONS	529 13
ILLUMINATE ALL BISHOPS, ETC	R 531 03
ILLUMINATE ALL BISHOPS, ETC	R 537 09
APPOINTED BY THE BISHOPS PRESENT, SHALL BEGIN THE	R 549 04
TO ALL BISHOPS, THE PASTORS OF THY CHURCH, THAT	549 10
PRESENTED BY TWO BISHOPS OF THIS CHURCH UNTO THE	R 552 18
THE BISHOPS WHO PRESENT HIM SAYING,	R 552 19
ILLUMINATE ALL BISHOPS, ETC	R 553 15
AND THE BISHOPS, AND THE OTHERS THAT ARE	R 556 04
BISHOP AND BISHOPS PRESENT SHALL LAY THEIR HANDS UPON	R 558 09
TO INSPIRE ALL BISHOPS, PRIESTS, AND DEACONS, WITH	560 18
BISHOPS, PRIESTS, AND DEACONS, ARE NOT COMMANDED BY	609 21
CONSECRATION OF BISHOPS, AND ORDERING OF PRIESTS AND	610 31

BIT

MUST BE HELD WITH BIT AND BRIDLE, ELSE THEY WILL NOT	378 11

BITTER

US NOT INTO THE BITTER PAINS OF ETERNAL DEATH	332 27
EVEN BITTER WORDS	415 24

BITTERLY

AND PETER WENT OUT, AND WEPT BITTERLY	151 23

BITTERNESS

LET ALL BITTERNESS, AND WRATH, AND ANGER, AND	216 27
EVERY ROOT OF BITTERNESS, THE DESIRE OF VAIN-GLORY,	598 22

BLADE

BUT WHEN THE BLADE WAS SPRUNG UP, AND BROUGHT FORTH	116 21

BLAMED

THAT THE MINISTRY BE NOT BLAMED	126 09

BLAMELESS

THAT YE MAY BE BLAMELESS IN THE DAY OF OUR LORD JESUS	215 03
USE THE OFFICE OF A DEACON, BEING FOUND BLAMELESS	531 31
THEN MUST BE BLAMELESS, THE HUSBAND OF ONE WIFE,	549 20
PURE AND BLAMELESS, UNTO THE COMING OF OUR LORD AND	590 19

BLASPHEME

LONG WILL YE BLASPHEME MINE HONOUR, *	347 13
THE WICKED BLASPHEME GOD, *	353 34
THE ENEMY BLASPHEME THY NAME FOR EVER	430 28

BLASPHEMED

PEOPLE HATH BLASPHEMED THY NAME	431 13

BLASPHEMED   CONTINUED

HAVE BLASPHEMED THEE, *   440 30
ENEMIES HAVE BLASPHEMED THEE, *   453 10

BLASPHEMER

OF YOU BE A BLASPHEMER OF GOD, AN HINDERER OR   087 31
SLANDERER AND BLASPHEMER, *   395 26

BLASPHEMERS

42 SO SHALL I MAKE ANSWER UNTO MY BLASPHEMERS   492 24

BLASPHEMETH

SAID WITHIN THEMSELVES, THIS MAN BLASPHEMETH   217 05
FOOLISH MAN BLASPHEMETH THEE DAILY   431 23

BLASPHEMING

SPOKEN BY PAUL, CONTRADICTING AND BLASPHEMING   260 30

BLASPHEMOUS

WERE BLASPHEMOUS FABLES, AND DANGEROUS   609 19

BLASPHEMOUSLY

THINGS BLASPHEMOUSLY SPAKE THEY AGAINST HIM   151 27

BLASPHEMY

YE HAVE HEARD THE BLASPHEMY   143 18
HAVE HEARD THE BLASPHEMY OF THE MULTITUDE, AND FEAR 376 21
AND SPEAK OF WICKED BLASPHEMY   428 24
13 AND FOR THE BLASPHEMY WHEREWITH OUR NEIGHBOURS   440 29

BLAST

AWAY WITH EVERY BLAST OF VAIN DOCTRINE, WE MAY BE   237 08

BLASTING

O LORD, AT THE BLASTING OF THE BREATH OF THY   360 30

BLEMISH

BUT THAT IT SHOULD BE HOLY AND WITHOUT BLEMISH   267 24

BLESS

THY PEOPLE, AND BLESS THINE HERITAGE   011 04
WORKS OF THE LORD, BLESS YE THE LORD   011 31
OF THE LORD, BLESS YE THE LORD   012 02
O YE HEAVENS, BLESS YE THE LORD   012 04
THE FIRMAMENT, BLESS YE THE LORD   012 06
OF THE LORD, BLESS YE THE LORD   012 08
O YE SUN AND MOON, BLESS YE THE LORD   012 10
STARS OF HEAVEN, BLESS YE THE LORD   012 12
SHOWERS AND DEW, BLESS YE THE LORD   012 14
O YE WINDS OF GOD, BLESS YE THE LORD   012 16
YE FIRE AND HEAT, BLESS YE THE LORD   012 18
WINTER AND SUMMER, BLESS YE THE LORD   012 20
DEWS AND FROSTS, BLESS YE THE LORD   012 22
YE FROST AND COLD, BLESS YE THE LORD   012 24
O YE ICE AND SNOW, BLESS YE THE LORD   012 26
NIGHTS AND DAYS, BLESS YE THE LORD   012 28
AND DARKNESS, BLESS YE THE LORD   012 30
AND CLOUDS, BLESS YE THE LORD   012 32
O LET THE EARTH BLESS THE LORD   013 02
AND HILLS, BLESS YE THE LORD   013 04
UPON THE EARTH, BLESS YE THE LORD   013 06
O YE WELLS, BLESS YE THE LORD   013 08
SEAS AND FLOODS, BLESS YE THE LORD   013 10
IN THE WATERS, BLESS YE THE LORD   013 12
FOWLS OF THE AIR, BLESS YE THE LORD   013 14
BEASTS AND CATTLE, BLESS YE THE LORD   013 16
CHILDREN OF MEN, BLESS YE THE LORD   013 18
O LET ISRAEL BLESS THE LORD   013 20
OF THE LORD, BLESS YE THE LORD   013 22
OF THE LORD, BLESS YE THE LORD   013 24
OF THE RIGHTEOUS, BLESS YE THE LORD   013 26
MEN OF HEART, BLESS YE THE LORD   013 28
LET US BLESS THE FATHER, AND THE SON, AND THE HOLY   013 30
TO BEHOLD AND BLESS THY SERVANT THE PRESIDENT OF THE 017 30
WE BLESS THEE FOR OUR CREATION, PRESERVATION, AND ALL 019 20
WE PRAISE THEE, WE BLESS THEE, WE WORSHIP THEE, WE   025 23
UNTO US, AND BLESS US, *   028 17
GOD SHALL BLESS US   028 30
AND BLESS THINE INHERITANCE   031 09
WE BLESS THEE FOR OUR CREATION, PRESERVATION, AND ALL 033 18
SO TO GUIDE AND BLESS THE LEGISLATURE OF THIS STATE, 035 25
BESEECH THEE TO BLESS THE COURTS OF JUSTICE AND THE 035 32
BLESS OUR LAND WITH HONOURABLE INDUSTRY, SOUND   036 12
BLESS THE LABOURS OF THE HUSBANDMAN, AND GRANT SUCH 039 27
VOUCHSAFE TO BLESS THE LANDS AND MULTIPLY THE   040 08
BLESS ALL WHO TEACH AND ALL WHO LEARN   042 25
WE BESEECH THEE TO BLESS ALL WHO, FOLLOWING IN HIS   043 30
WE BLESS THY HOLY NAME, THAT IT HATH PLEASED THEE TO 052 19
WE BLESS THY HOLY NAME, THAT THOU HAST BEEN PLEASED TO 052 30
IN WHOSE BEHALF WE BLESS AND PRAISE THY NAME, IN THE 053 13
MAY PLEASE THEE TO BLESS AND PRESERVE ALL CHRISTIAN 055 26
MAY PLEASE THEE TO BLESS AND KEEP ALL THY PEOPLE   056 05
THE LORD BLESS US, AND KEEP US   063 15
AND WE ALSO BLESS THY HOLY NAME FOR ALL THY SERVANTS 074 34

BLESS   CONTINUED

VOUCHSAFE TO BLESS AND SANCTIFY, WITH THY WORD AND   081 09
WE PRAISE THEE, WE BLESS THEE, WE WORSHIP THEE, WE   084 03
LEARN TO LOVE AND BLESS OUR PERSECUTORS BY THE   099 30
BLESS THEM WHICH PERSECUTE YOU   111 28
BLESS, AND CURSE NOT   111 29
LOVE YOUR ENEMIES, BLESS THEM THAT CURSE YOU, DO GOOD 264 05
THE BISHOP SHALL BLESS THEM, SAYING THUS, THE   R 299 02
BLESS, O LORD, THIS RING, THAT HE WHO GIVES IT AND   302 19
WHOM WE BLESS IN THY NAME   303 06
THE HOLY GHOST, BLESS, PRESERVE, AND KEEP YOU   304 12
THE LORD BLESS THEE, AND KEEP THEE   314 27
HE MAY BLESS THY HOLY NAME   315 11
WE BLESS THY WONDERFUL GOODNESS, FOR HAVING TURNED   315 20
AND TO BLESS THY HOLY NAME FOR ALL THY   315 32
THE LORD BLESS YOU AND KEEP YOU   332 11
THE LORD BLESS HIM AND KEEP HIM, THE LORD MAKE HIS   341 15
INTO HIS ARMS AND BLESS THEM   342 04
THE HOLY GHOST, BLESS YOU AND KEEP YOU, NOW AND FOR 342 15
UNTO US, AND BLESS US, *   418 23
7 GOD SHALL BLESS US   419 04
THEY CURSE, YET BLESS THOU   481 26
AND HE SHALL BLESS US   485 34
EVEN HE SHALL BLESS THE HOUSE OF ISRAEL, HE SHALL   486 02
HE SHALL BLESS THE HOUSE OF AARON   486 02
13 HE SHALL BLESS THEM THAT FEAR THE LORD, *   486 04
OF SION SHALL SO BLESS THEE, *   506 16
16 I WILL BLESS HER VICTUALS WITH INCREASE, *   509 04
MAY PLEASE THEE TO BLESS THESE THY SERVANTS, NOW TO 531 04
MAY PLEASE THEE TO BLESS THESE THY SERVANTS, NOW TO 537 10
MAY PLEASE THEE TO BLESS THIS OUR BROTHER ELECTED,   553 17
TO SANCTIFY AND BLESS THY CHURCH THROUGHOUT THE   560 15
MAY PLEASE THEE TO BLESS THESE THY SERVANTS, NOW TO 560 26
MAY PLEASE THEE TO BLESS THIS OUR BROTHER ELECTED,   561 02
AT OUR HANDS, AND BLESS IT WITH SUCH SUCCESS AS MAY 565 12
PLEASED TO BLESS THE MINISTRY AND SERVICE OF HIM WHO 572 19
THY MERCIES, WE BLESS AND MAGNIFY THY GLORIOUS NAME 587 24
BLESS ALL IN AUTHORITY OVER US   590 27
WE BLESS THEE FOR THY PATIENCE WITH US,   591 14
THE LORD BLESS US AND KEEP US   593 18
TO BEHOLD AND BLESS THOSE WHOM WE LOVE, NOW ABSENT   597 02
BLESS, WE PRAY THEE, THY SERVANT, (N   597 15
AND TO BLESS THE MEANS MADE USE OF FOR HIS   597 23
BLESS AND GUIDE HIM WHEREVER HE MAY BE, KEEPING HIM 597 29
BLESS THE CONGREGATION OF THY POOR   599 08
BLESS ALL THOSE WHO LABOUR IN WORKS OF MERCY OR IN   600 03
BLESS, O FATHER, THY GIFTS TO OUR USE AND US TO THY 600 15

BLESSED

PART OF THAT BLESSED *LIBERTY WHEREWITH CHRIST HATH   V 02
BLESSED ART THOU, O LORD GOD OF OUR FATHERS   011 16
BLESSED ART THOU FOR THE NAME OF THY MAJESTY   011 18
BLESSED ART THOU IN THE TEMPLE OF THY HOLINESS   011 20
BLESSED ART THOU THAT BEHOLDEST THE DEPTHS, AND   011 22
BLESSED ART THOU ON THE GLORIOUS THRONE OF THY   011 25
BLESSED ART THOU IN THE FIRMAMENT OF HEAVEN   011 27
BLESSED BE THE LORD GOD OF ISRAEL   014 08
ALL GENERATIONS SHALL CALL ME BLESSED   026 15
ACCORDING TO THY BLESSED WORD AND ORDINANCE   032 12
OUR MOST BLESSED LORD AND SAVIOUR   035 21
COUNCIL OF THE BLESSED APOSTLES, AND HAST PROMISED, 036 27
DIDST SEND THY BLESSED SON TO PREACH PEACE TO THEM   038 07
TO ALL MEN THY BLESSED GIFT OF ETERNAL LIFE   038 21
WHO HAST BLESSED THE EARTH THAT IT SHOULD BE   039 24
WHOSE BLESSED SON CAME NOT TO BE MINISTERED   043 28
THE BLESSED COMPANY OF ALL FAITHFUL PEOPLE   047 07
SEASONABLE AND BLESSED CHANGE OF WEATHER   051 25
O HOLY, BLESSED, AND GLORIOUS TRINITY, ONE GOD   054 11
OUR BLESSED LORD AND SAVIOUR   VI 43
MEDIATION OF THY BLESSED SON, JESUS CHRIST OUR LORD 063 06
THE LORD BLESSED THE SEVENTH DAY, AND HALLOWED IT   068 31
IT IS MORE BLESSED TO GIVE THAN TO RECEIVE   072 03
REMEMBRANCE HIS BLESSED PASSION AND PRECIOUS DEATH, 081 02
OF HIS MOST BLESSED BODY AND BLOOD   081 14
OF HIS MOST BLESSED BODY AND BLOOD   R 083 10
WHICH IS THE BLESSED COMPANY OF ALL FAITHFUL PEOPLE 083 23
BLESSED IS HE THAT COMETH IN THE NAME OF THE LORD   091 28
BLESSED LORD, WHO HAST CAUSED ALL HOLY SCRIPTURES TO 092 07
HOLD FAST, THE BLESSED HOPE OF EVERLASTING LIFE,   092 11
AND BLESSED IS HE, WHOSOEVER SHALL NOT BE OFFENDED IN 094 23
LOOKING FOR THAT BLESSED HOPE, AND THE GLORIOUS   098 21
TO THEE, O BLESSED JESUS, WHO STANDEST AT THE RIGHT 099 32
YE SHALL SAY, BLESSED IS HE THAT COMETH IN THE NAME 100 33
DOCTRINE OF THY BLESSED APOSTLE AND EVANGELIST SAINT 101 07
WHO MADEST THY BLESSED SON TO BE CIRCUMCISED, AND   105 19
THINGS OBEY THY BLESSED WILL   105 23
O GOD, WHOSE BLESSED SON WAS MANIFESTED AT THE MIGHT 117 04
WHICH IS BLESSED FOR EVERMORE, KNOWETH THAT I   121 15
SAID UNTO HIM, BLESSED IS THE WOMB THAT BARE THEE,   130 19
YEA RATHER, BLESSED ARE THEY THAT HEAR THE WORD OF   130 20
TOOK BREAD, AND BLESSED, AND BRAKE IT, AND GAVE TO   141 10
ART THOU THE CHRIST, THE SON OF THE BLESSED   143 14
LORD GOD, WHOSE BLESSED SON, OUR SAVIOUR, GAVE HIS   144 06
THEY SHALL SAY, BLESSED ARE THE BARREN, AND THE WOMBS 154 16
FETCH THEM HOME, BLESSED LORD, TO THY FOLD, THAT THEY 157 10
THE DEATH OF THY BLESSED SON, OUR SAVIOUR JESUS   161 14
O GOD, WHOSE BLESSED SON DID MANIFEST HIMSELF TO HIS 166 06
TOOK BREAD, AND BLESSED IT, AND BRAKE, AND GAVE TO   168 06
TO FOLLOW THE BLESSED STEPS OF HIS MOST HOLY LIFE   171 32
MAN SHALL BE BLESSED IN HIS DEED   176 12
WHILE HE BLESSED THEM, HE WAS PARTED FROM THEM,   178 25
HIS HANDS, AND BLESSED THEM   178 25
AND HE BLESSED, AND COMMANDED TO SET THEM ALSO BEFORE 199 21
BLESSED ARE THE EYES WHICH SEE THE THINGS THAT YE   208 07

BLESSED   CONTINUED

OUR BLESSED LORD AND SAVIOUR   223 19
BLESSED ARE THEY THAT HAVE NOT SEEN, AND YET HAVE   229 08
PREACHING OF THE BLESSED APOSTLE SAINT PAUL, HAST   229 17
IN HIS ARMS, AND BLESSED GOD, AND SAID, LORD, NCW   233 05
AND SIMEON BLESSED THEM, AND SAID UNTO MARY HIS   233 11
BLESSED ART THOU AMONG WOMEN   236 10
BLESSED IS THE MAN THAT ENDURETH TEMPTATICN   239 24
BLESSED BE THE LORD GOD OF ISRAEL   243 32
SAID UNTO HIM, BLESSED ART THOU, SIMON BAR-JCNA   246 04
WHO BY THY BLESSED SON DIDST CALL MATTHEW FROM   250 20
SO TO FOLLOW THY BLESSED SAINTS IN ALL VIRTUOUS AND   256 08
SAYING, BLESSED ARE THE POOR IN SPIRIT   257 21
BLESSED ARE THEY THAT MOURN   257 22
BLESSED ARE THE MEEK   257 23
BLESSED ARE THEY WHICH DO HUNGER AND THIRST AFTER   257 24
BLESSED ARE THE MERCIFUL   257 25
BLESSED ARE THE PURE IN HEART   257 26
BLESSED ARE THE PEACEMAKERS   257 27
BLESSED ARE THEY WHICH ARE PERSECUTED FOR   257 28
BLESSED ARE YE, WHEN MEN SHALL REVILE YOU, AND   257 30
COME, YE BLESSED OF MY FATHER, INHERIT THE   259 04
BE DRAWN TO THY BLESSED KINGDOM   260 23
AND HATH BLESSED THY CHILDREN WITHIN THEE   265 03
WHO HAST BLESSED THE LABOURS OF THE   265 11
MAN SHALL BE BLESSED IN HIS DEED   266 04
UPON THEM, AND BLESSED THEM   274 33
THY MERCY, O BLESSED LORD GOD, WHO DOST LIVE, ANC   278 30
THE LORD BLESSED THE SEVENTH DAY, AND HALLCWED IT   286 31
WE RECEIVE THE BLESSED SACRAMENT OF THE BODY AND   294 29
BLESSED BE THE NAME OF THE LORD   297 09
HIM WITH THY BLESSED SPIRIT   314 10
BLESSED BE THY NAME THAT THOU DIDST NOT FORSAKE HIM   315 23
INTO THE BLESSED REST OF EVERLASTING PEACE,   320 02
O BLESSED REDEEMER, RELIEVE, WE BESEECH THEE,   320 08
OF HIS MOST BLESSED BODY AND BLOOD   R 323 08
BLESSED BE THE NAME OF THE LORD   324 15
FROM HENCEFORTH BLESSED ARE THE DEAD WHO DIE IN THE   333 26
COME, YE BLESSED CHILDREN OF MY FATHER,   335 11
DIDST PROCLAIM, BLESSED ARE THE DEAD WHO DIE IN THE   335 26
WITH THY BLESSED SAINTS IN GLORY EVERLASTING   336 08
COME, YE BLESSED OF MY FATHER, INHERIT THE KINGDOM   336 26
BLESSED ARE THE PURE IN HEART   340 16
BLESSED BE THE NAME OF THE LORD   340 18
BLESSED IS THE MAN THAT HATH NOT WALKED IN THE   345 07
BLESSED ARE ALL THEY THAT PUT THEIR TRUST IN HIM   346 23
AND BLESSED BE MY STRONG HELPER, *   362 32
BLESSED IS HE WHOSE UNRIGHTEOUSNESS IS FORGIVEN,   377 22
2 BLESSED IS THE MAN LNTO WHOM THE LORD IMPUTETH NO   377 24
12 BLESSED ARE THE PEOPLE WHOSE GOD IS THE LORD   379 11
AND BLESSED ARE THE FOLK THAT HE HATH CHOSEN TO HIM,   379 12
BLESSED IS THE MAN THAT TRLSTETH IN HIM   380 17
THEM SAY ALWAY, BLESSED BE THE LORD, WHC HATH   383 20
22 SUCH AS ARE BLESSED OF GOD, SHALL POSSESS THE   386 06
AND HIS SEED IS BLESSED   386 16
5 BLESSED IS THE MAN THAT HATH SET HIS HOPE IN THE   390 18
BLESSED IS HE THAT CONSIDERETH THE POOR AND NEEDY   391 30
THAT HE MAY BE BLESSED UPON EARTH   392 02
13 BLESSED BE THE LORD GOD OF ISRAEL, *   392 25
BECAUSE GOD HATH BLESSED THEE FOR EVER   396 19
4 BLESSED IS THE MAN WHOM THOU CHOOSEST, AND   416 17
BLESSED BE GOD   421 29
WHICH SHALL BE BLESSED IN HIM   427 34
18 BLESSED BE THE LORD GOD, EVEN THE GCD OF ISRAEL,   428 02
19 AND BLESSED BE THE NAME OF HIS MAJESTY FCR EVER   428 04
4 BLESSED ARE THEY THAT DWELL IN THY HOUSE   445 19
5 BLESSED IS THE MAN WHOSE STRENGTH IS IN THEE   445 21
BLESSED IS THE MAN THAT PUTTETH HIS TRUST IN THEE   446 05
16 BLESSED IS THE PEOPLE, O LORD, THAT CAN REJOICE IN   451 04
12 BLESSED IS THE MAN WHOM THOU CHASTENEST, O LCRD,   458 10
3 BLESSED ARE THEY THAT ALWAY KEEP JUDGMENT, *   473 04
46 BLESSED BE THE LORD GOD OF ISRAEL, FROM   475 33
BLESSED IS THE MAN THAT FEARETH THE LORD   483 18
THE GENERATION OF THE FAITHFUL SHALL BE BLESSED   483 21
2 BLESSED BE THE NAME OF THE LCRD *   484 10
15 YE ARE THE BLESSED OF THE LORD, *   486 08
26 BLESSED BE HE THAT COMETH IN THE NAME OF THE LORD   489 19
BLESSED ARE THOSE THAT ARE UNDEFILED IN THE WAY,   489 31
2 BLESSED ARE THEY THAT KEEP HIS TESTIMONIES,   490 02
12 BLESSED ART THOU, O LORD   490 22
BLESSED ARE ALL THEY THAT FEAR THE LORD, *   506 06
SHALL THE MAN BE BLESSED *   506 14
9 BLESSED SHALL HE BE THAT TAKETH THY CHILDREN,   513 24
BLESSED BE THE LORD MY STRENGTH, *   519 22
BLESSED ARE THE PEOPLE WHO HAVE THE LORD FOR   520 25
4 BLESSED IS HE THAT HATH THE GOD OF JACOB FCR HIS   522 10
AND HATH BLESSED THY CHILDREN WITHIN THEE   523 22
BLESSED ARE THOSE SERVANTS, WHOM THE LORD WHEN HE   534 20
FIND THEM SO, BLESSED ARE THOSE SERVANTS   534 25
THY BLESSED UNCTION FROM ABOVE, IS COMFORT, LIFE, AND   544 02
BY THE SAME THY BLESSED SON, TO GRANT UNTO ALL, WHICH   545 26
AND THY BLESSED KINGDCM ENLARGED   546 02
IT IS MORE BLESSED TO GIVE THAN TO RECEIVE   551 11
THY BLESSED UNCTION FROM ABOVE, IS COMFORT, LIFE, AND   556 10
OF THE BLESSED SPIRIT, AND ACTING AGREEABLY TO THEIR   564 13
JESUS CHRIST OUR BLESSED LORD AND SAVIOUR   565 14
THIS PLACE THE BLESSED SACRAMENT OF THE BODY AND   565 29
WE BESEECH THEE, BLESSED LORD, THAT WHOSOEVER SHALL   566 13
OUR MOST BLESSED LORD AND SAVIOUR   566 24
SHALL SAY, BLESSED BE THY NAME, O LORD, THAT IT HATH   566 28
THE GLORY OF THY BLESSED NAME   566 33
BLESSED BE THY NAME, O LORD GOD, FOR THAT IT HATH   568 06
IS GOD OVER ALL, BLESSED FOR EVERMORE   572 03
IN THE SAME, O BLESSED SPIRIT, WHOM, WITH THE FATHER   572 30
OF THE SAME THY BLESSED SON JESUS CHRIST, THE   574 20

BLESSED   CONTINUED

THE LORD BLESSED THE SEVENTH DAY, AND HALLCWED IT   579 12
AND RECEIVE THE BLESSED ENCOURAGEMENT OF THY   596 13
WHO HAST BLESSED US WITH THE JOY AND CARE OF   596 24
THE WOMB OF THE BLESSED VIRGIN, OF HER SUBSTANCE   603 11

BLESSEDNESS

PLACE OF REFRESHMENT AND EVERLASTING BLESSEDNESS   318 18

BLESSEST

THE EARTH, AND BLESSEST IT   416 32
OF RAIN, AND BLESSEST THE INCREASE OF IT   417 06

BLESSETH

38 HE BLESSETH THEM, SO THAT THEY MULTIPLY   478 22

BLESSING

POUR UPON THEM THE CONTINUAL DEW OF THY BLESSING   018 23
SHALL GIVE US HIS BLESSING   028 29
POUR UPON THEM THE CONTINUAL DEW OF THY BLESSING   032 22
OR OF BLESSING, OR BEFORE THE GRACE   R 035 04
FINAL PRAYER OF BLESSING OF THE BENEDICTION   R 050 16
WITH HIS BLESSING EVERY ENDEAVOUR FOR PROMULGATING   VI 40
TO THE BLESSING OF THE LORD THY GOD WHICH HE HATH   073 16
PRESENT) SHALL LET THEM DEPART WITH THIS BLESSING   R 084 17
AND THE BLESSING OF GOD ALMIGHTY, THE FATHER, THE   084 21
CONCLUDING WITH THE BLESSING   R 084 29
AFTER THE BLESSING, REVERENTLY EAT AND DRINK THE   R 084 32
AND LEAVE A BLESSING BEHIND HIM   124 27
PRAISING AND BLESSING GOD   178 29
BUT CONTRARIWISE BLESSING   195 23
THAT YE SHOULD INHERIT A BLESSING   195 24
BLESSING, AND GLORY, AND WISDOM, AND THANKSGIVING,   256 31
POUR FORTH THY BLESSING UPON THIS LAND, AND TO GIVE   261 30
AND THE PLACES ROUND ABOUT MY HILL A BLESSING   262 08
THERE SHALL BE SHOWERS OF BLESSING   262 09
ABSOLUTION AND BLESSING IN GOD'S NAME   294 15
THE BLESSING OF GOD ALMIGHTY, THE FATHER,   299 03
SEND THY BLESSING UPON THESE THY SERVANTS, THIS MAN   303 05
BE A HAVEN OF BLESSING AND OF PEACE   303 26
THE MINISTER SHALL ADD THIS BLESSING   R 304 10
AND THY BLESSING IS UPON THY PEOPLE   309 24
TO FLIGHT, THE BLESSING OF HEALTH MAY BE RESTORED   320 19
THE BLESSING   R 323 09
PROVIDED IN THIS BOOK, ENDING WITH THE BLESSING   R 331 31
RECEIVE THAT BLESSING, WHICH THY WELL-BELOVED SCN   335 10
THE FOLLOWING PRAYERS BEFORE THE FINAL BLESSING   R 335 24
AND THY BLESSING IS UPON THY PEOPLE   347 07
WILT GIVE THY BLESSING UNTO THE RIGHTEOUS, *   348 28
RECEIVE THE BLESSING FROM THE LORD, *   369 05
AND GIVE THY BLESSING UNTO THINE INHERITANCE   373 27
HIS PEOPLE THE BLESSING OF PEACE   374 20
SHALL GIVE US HIS BLESSING   419 03
HE LOVED NOT BLESSING, THEREFORE SHALL IT BE FAR FROM   481 03
PROMISED HIS BLESSING, *   509 20
GIVE THEE BLESSING OUT OF SION   509 30
AND THE BLESSING OF GOD ALMIGHTY, THE FATHER, THE   535 16
UPON THESE THY SERVANTS THY HEAVENLY BLESSING   547 05
AND THE BLESSING OF GOD ALMIGHTY, THE FATHER, THE   547 17
UPON THIS THY SERVANT THY HEAVENLY BLESSING   559 06
AND THE BLESSING OF GOD ALMIGHTY, THE FATHER, THE   559 20
RECEIVE THE BLESSING FROM THE LORD, *   563 20
BEG HIS BLESSING ON THIS OUR UNDERTAKING   564 25
FOR BLESSING THY PEOPLE IN THY NAME, AND FOR ALL   565 10
THE FINAL BLESSING, THE BISHOP SHALL SAY THIS PRAYER   R 568 04
AND THE BLESSING OF GOD ALMIGHTY, THE FATHER, THE   568 16
INTENTION NOR CONTINUE IT WITHOUT THY BLESSING   594 23
THIS DAY SUCH BLESSING THROUGH OUR WORSHIP CF THEE,   595 14
THE CUP OF BLESSING IS A PARTAKING OF THE BLCOD CF   608 38

BLESSINGS

AND ALL THE BLESSINGS OF THIS LIFE   019 21
AND ALL THE BLESSINGS OF THIS LIFE   033 19
ALL THE OTHER BLESSINGS OF HIS MERCIFUL PROVIDENCE   050 18
ALL THE OTHER BLESSINGS OF THY MERCIFUL PROVIDENCE   050 24
THE MANIFOLD BLESSINGS OF THY GRACE   267 08
THE MANIFOLD BLESSINGS OF THY LOVE, THAT THE GCCD   335 28
HIM WITH THE BLESSINGS OF GOODNESS, *   365 09
SEND DOWN THY BLESSINGS, TEMPORAL AND SPIRITUAL,   590 30
THESE THY BLESSINGS TO US, AND TO GIVE US GRACE TC   591 20
FOR THE TIMELY BLESSINGS OF THE DAY, AND HUMBLY   595 06

BLEST

CREATOR BLEST, VOUCHSAFE WITHIN OUR SOULS TC   544 17
CREATOR BLEST, VOUCHSAFE WITHIN OUR SOULS TO   556 25

BLINC

THE BLIND RECEIVE THEIR SIGHT, AND THE LAME WALK, THE   094 20
A CERTAIN BLIND MAN SAT BY THE WAY-SIDE   123 27
AND THE MAIMED, AND THE HALT, AND THE BLIND   192 16
UNTO THEM, CAN THE BLIND LEAD THE BLIND   195 02
A PARABLE UNTO THEM, CAN THE BLIND LEAD THE BLIND   195 03
AND THE BLIND AND THE LAME CAME TO HIM IN THE TEMPLE   260 08
OF SIGHT TO THE BLIND, TO SET AT LIBERTY THEM THAT   261 19
THE LORD GIVETH SIGHT TO THE BLIND   522 17

BLINDED

THIS WORLD HATH BLINDED THE MINDS OF THEM WHICH	251 03
THEIR EYES BE BLINDED, THAT THEY SEE NOT	423 21
DULNESS OF OUR BLINDED SIGHT	544 05
DULNESS OF OUR BLINDED SIGHT	556 13

BLINDFOLDED

THEY HAD BLINDFOLDED HIM, THEY STRUCK HIM ON THE	151 24

BLINDNESS

AND FOR OUR BLINDNESS WE CANNOT ASK, VOUCHSAFE TO	050 03
FROM ALL BLINDNESS OF HEART	054 23
BECAUSE OF THE BLINDNESS OF THEIR HEART	216 07

BLISS

CONSUMMATION AND BLISS, BOTH IN BODY AND SOUL, IN THY	334 27

BLOOD

THROUGH HIS BLOOD, THE FORGIVENESS OF SINS, ACCORDING	004 33
WHOM THOU HAST REDEEMED WITH THY PRECIOUS BLOOD	010 34
HAST MADE OF ONE BLOOD ALL NATIONS OF MEN FOR TO	038 05
BY THE PRECIOUS BLOOD OF THY DEAR SON	038 27
REDEEMED BY THE BLOOD OF THY DEAR SON, AND INCLINE	039 18
THY MOST PRECIOUS BLOOD, AND BE NOT ANGRY WITH US FOR	054 16
FOR (E) THIS IS MY BLOOD OF THE NEW TESTAMENT,	080 26
BE PARTAKERS OF HIS MOST BLESSED BODY AND BLOOD	081 14
FAITH IN HIS BLOOD, WE, AND ALL THY WHOLE CHURCH,	081 19
PRECIOUS BODY AND BLOOD OF THY SON JESUS CHRIST,	081 26
AND TO DRINK HIS BLOOD, THAT OUR SINFUL BODIES MAY BE	082 19
HIS MOST PRECIOUS BLOOD, AND THAT WE MAY EVERMORE	082 21
CUP SHALL SAY, THE BLOOD OF OUR LORD JESUS CHRIST,	083 03
THAT CHRIST'S BLOOD WAS SHED FOR THEE, AND BE	083 05
PARTAKERS OF HIS MOST BLESSED BODY AND BLOOD	R 083 10
PRECIOUS BODY AND BLOOD OF THY SON OUR SAVIOUR JESUS	083 19
OF THE BODY AND BLOOD OF OUR SAVIOUR CHRIST, MUST	085 26
OF THE BODY AND BLOOD OF CHRIST	086 31
WERE BORN, NOT OF BLOOD, NOR OF THE WILL OF THE	098 03
ALL THE RIGHTEOUS BLOOD SHED UPON THE EARTH, FROM THE	100 23
FROM THE BLOOD OF RIGHTEOUS ABEL UNTO THE	100 23
ABEL UNTO THE BLOOD OF ZACHARIAS SON OF BARACHIAS,	100 24
AND THE BLOOD OF JESUS CHRIST HIS SON	101 27
NEITHER BY THE BLOOD OF GOATS AND CALVES, BUT BY HIS	132 26
BUT BY HIS OWN BLOOD HE ENTERED IN ONCE INTO THE HOLY	132 26
FOR IF THE BLOOD OF BULLS AND OF GOATS, AND THE ASHES	132 28
MORE SHALL THE BLOOD OF CHRIST, WHO THROUGH THE	132 31
SINNED IN THAT I HAVE BETRAYED THE INNOCENT BLOOD	135 06
THE TREASURY, BECAUSE IT IS THE PRICE OF BLOOD	135 11
THE FIELD OF BLOOD, UNTO THIS DAY	135 13
AM INNOCENT OF THE BLOOD OF THIS JUST PERSON	136 11
AND SAID, HIS BLOOD BE ON US, AND ON OUR CHILDREN	136 12
AND THEIR BLOOD SHALL BE SPRINKLED UPON MY GARMENTS,	138 19
THIS IS MY BLOOD OF THE NEW TESTAMENT, WHICH IS	141 13
THE FIRST TESTAMENT WAS DEDICATED WITHOUT BLOOD	147 18
HE TOOK THE BLOOD OF CALVES AND OF GOATS,	147 20
THIS IS THE BLOOD OF THE TESTAMENT WHICH GOD HATH	147 22
HE SPRINKLED WITH BLOOD BOTH THE TABERNACLE, AND ALL	147 24
SHEDDING OF BLOOD IS NO REMISSION	147 26
ALL THINGS ARE BY THE LAW PURGED WITH BLOOD	147 26
EVERY YEAR WITH BLOOD OF OTHERS	148 03
TESTAMENT IN MY BLOOD, WHICH IS SHED FOR YOU	149 12
GREAT DROPS OF BLOOD FALLING DOWN TO THE GROUND	150 22
DID INSTITUTE THE SACRAMENT OF HIS BODY AND BLOOD	152 09
THIS CUP IS THE NEW TESTAMENT IN MY BLOOD	152 22
POSSIBLE THAT THE BLOOD OF BULLS AND OF GOATS SHOULD	157 23
THE HOLIEST BY THE BLOOD OF JESUS, BY A NEW AND	158 17
CAME THERE OUT BLOOD AND WATER	161 05
CAME BY WATER AND BLOOD, EVEN JESUS CHRIST	170 30
NOT BY WATER ONLY, BUT BY WATER AND BLOOD	170 31
THE SPIRIT, AND THE WATER, AND THE BLOOD	171 03
AGAINST FLESH AND BLOOD, BUT AGAINST PRINCIPALITIES,	219 08
WITH AN ISSUE OF BLOOD TWELVE YEARS, CAME BEHIND HIM,	224 18
THAT IS TO SAY, THE FIELD OF BLOOD	234 18
FOR FLESH AND BLOOD HATH NOT REVEALED IT UNTO THEE,	246 05
HIM BY THE BLOOD OF THE LAMB, AND BY THE WORD OF	252 14
THEM WHITE IN THE BLOOD OF THE LAMB	257 09
OF HIS MOST PRECIOUS SIDE BOTH WATER AND BLOOD	279 11
IS THE BODY AND BLOOD OF CHRIST, WHICH ARE	293 15
BY THE BODY AND BLOOD OF CHRIST, AS OUR BODIES ARE	293 21
OF THE BODY AND BLOOD OF CHRIST, COMING TO THOSE HOLY	294 30
CROSS AND PRECIOUS BLOOD HAST REDEEMED US	313 13
PRAY THEE, IN THE BLOOD OF THAT IMMACULATE LAMB,	317 17
OF THE BODY AND BLOOD OF OUR SAVIOUR CHRIST, WHEN IT	R 321 08
PARTAKERS OF HIS MOST BLESSED BODY AND BLOOD	R 323 08
CHRIST'S BODY AND BLOOD, THE MINISTER SHALL INSTRUCT	R 323 25
AND SHED HIS BLOOD FOR HIS REDEMPTION, EARNESTLY	R 323 28
DRINK THE BODY AND BLOOD OF OUR SAVIOUR CHRIST	R 323 30
THAT FLESH AND BLOOD CANNOT INHERIT THE KINGDOM OF	329 33
THROUGH THE BLOOD OF THE EVERLASTING COVENANT	335 18
INQUISITION FOR BLOOD, HE REMEMBERETH THEM, *	352 13
DRINK-OFFERINGS OF BLOOD WILL I NOT OFFER, *	357 29
IS THERE IN MY BLOOD, *	375 10
AND DRINK THE BLOOD OF GOATS	402 17
FOOTSTEPS IN THE BLOOD OF THE UNGODLY	410 30
BE DIPPED IN THE BLOOD OF THINE ENEMIES, *	420 33
DEAR SHALL THEIR BLOOD BE IN HIS SIGHT	427 25
THEIR WATERS INTO BLOOD, *	437 29
3 THEIR BLOOD HAVE THEY SHED LIKE WATER ON EVERY SIDE	440 04
OF THY SERVANTS' BLOOD THAT IS SHED, *	440 23
AND CONDEMN THE INNOCENT BLOOD	458 24
THEIR WATERS INTO BLOOD, *	471 30
AND SHED INNOCENT BLOOD, EVEN THE BLOOD OF THEIR SONS	475 11

BLOOD   CONTINUED

BLOOD, EVEN THE BLOOD OF THEIR SONS AND OF THEIR	475 11
AND THE LAND WAS DEFILED WITH BLOOD	475 13
WITH HIS DEATH, AND FOR WHOM HE SHED HIS BLOOD	540 08
I AM PURE FROM THE BLOOD OF ALL MEN	550 25
WHICH HE HATH PURCHASED WITH HIS OWN BLOOD	550 29
NO LESS PRICE THAN THE EFFUSION OF HIS OWN BLOOD	554 11
OF THE BODY AND BLOOD OF CHRIST, MAY COME TO THAT	565 29
THROUGH THE BLOOD OF THE EVERLASTING COVENANT	573 05
THE BODY AND BLOOD OF CHRIST, WHICH ARE SPIRITUALLY	582 12
BY THE BODY AND BLOOD OF CHRIST, AS OUR BODIES ARE BY	582 18
A PARTAKING OF THE BLOOD OF CHRIST	608 39
OF THE BODY AND BLOOD OF CHRIST	609 06

BLOOD-GUILTINESS

ME FROM BLOOD-GUILTINESS, O GOD, THOU THAT ART THE	061 06
ME FROM BLOOD-GUILTINESS, O GOD, THOU THAT ART THE	404 04

BLOOD-SHEDDING

PRECIOUS BLOOD-SHEDDING HE HATH OBTAINED FOR US	086 15

BLOOD-THIRSTY

BOTH THE BLOOD-THIRSTY AND DECEITFUL MAN	348 12
NOR MY LIFE WITH THE BLOOD-THIRSTY	371 15
25 THE BLOOD-THIRSTY AND DECEITFUL MEN SHALL NOT LIVE	408 08
FROM THE BLOOD-THIRSTY MEN	411 07
YE BLOOD-THIRSTY MEN	515 29

BLOODY

THINE AGONY AND BLOODY SWEAT	055 10

BLOW

BLOW THE TRUMPET IN ZION, SANCTIFY A FAST, CALL A	124 28
THE EAST-WIND TO BLOW UNDER HEAVEN	436 22
3 BLOW UP THE TRUMPET IN THE NEW MOON, *	442 16

BLOWETH

THE WIND BLOWETH WHERE IT LISTETH, AND THOU HEAREST	188 14
OF THE LORD BLOWETH UPON IT	242 30
THE WIND BLOWETH WHERE IT LISTETH, AND THOU HEAREST	275 19
HE BLOWETH WITH HIS WIND, AND THE WATERS FLOW	523 32

BOAR

13 THE WILD BOAR OUT OF THE WOOD DOTH ROOT IT UP,	441 28

BOAST

UNGODLY HATH MADE BOAST OF HIS OWN HEART'S DESIRE, *	353 08
SHALL MAKE HER BOAST IN THE LORD	380 05
THAT BOAST THEMSELVES AGAINST ME	383 18
9 WE MAKE OUR BOAST OF GOD ALL DAY LONG, *	395 09
AND BOAST THEMSELVES IN THE MULTITUDE OF THEIR	400 17
IN THY RIGHTEOUSNESS SHALL THEY MAKE THEIR BOAST	451 07
AND MAKE OUR BOAST OF THY PRAISE	475 32
AS CERTAIN ANABAPTISTS DO FALSELY BOAST	611 02

BOASTEST

WHY BOASTEST THOU THYSELF, THOU TYRANT, *	404 19

BOASTING

AND MAKE SUCH PROUD BOASTING	457 26

BODIES

OUR HEARTS AND BODIES, IN THE WAYS OF THY LAWS, AND	070 08
OUR SOULS AND BODIES, TO BE A REASONABLE, HOLY,	081 22
THAT OUR SINFUL BODIES MAY BE MADE CLEAN BY HIS BODY,	082 20
YE PRESENT YOUR BODIES A LIVING SACRIFICE, HOLY,	110 04
OUTWARDLY IN OUR BODIES, AND INWARDLY IN OUR SOULS	127 17
AND MANY BODIES OF THE SAINTS WHICH SLEPT AROSE, AND	137 28
AND OUR BODIES WASHED WITH PURE WATER	158 22
THAT THE BODIES SHOULD NOT REMAIN UPON THE CROSS ON	160 31
HEALING OF OUR BODIES AND OUR SOULS	253 19
OUGHT MEN TO LOVE THEIR WIVES AS THEIR OWN BODIES	267 25
OF CHRIST, AS OUR BODIES ARE STRENGTHENED AND	293 21
OUR HEARTS AND BODIES, IN THE WAYS OF THY LAWS, AND	298 28
AWAY FROM MEN'S BODIES ALL SICKNESS AND ALL	315 07
OUR SOULS AND BODIES ARE RENEWED	322 07
BODIES, AND BODIES TERRESTRIAL	329 14
ALSO CELESTIAL BODIES, AND BODIES TERRESTRIAL	329 14
OUR MORTAL BODIES, BY HIS SPIRIT THAT DWELLETH IN US	333 06
THE CORRUPTIBLE BODIES OF THOSE WHO SLEEP IN HIM	333 20
THE CORRUPTIBLE BODIES OF THOSE WHO SLEEP IN HIM	337 14
2 THE DEAD BODIES OF THY SERVANTS HAVE THEY GIVEN TO	439 32
WITH THE DEAD BODIES, AND SMITE IN SUNDER THE HEADS	482 19
THAT ARE NEEDFUL BOTH FOR OUR SOULS AND BODIES	588 34
OF CHRIST, AS OUR BODIES ARE BY THE BREAD AND WINE	582 18
OUR SOULS AND OUR BODIES TO THEE AND THY SERVICE,	588 06

BODILY

TO THEIR BODILY SUSTENANCE	040 17
DELIVER FROM HIS BODILY SICKNESS THIS THY SERVANT,	052 31
DELIVER FROM HIS BODILY SICKNESS THE CHILD IN WHOSE	053 12
AND RECOVER HIS BODILY HEALTH, IF IT BE THY GRACIOUS	321 23
SHIELD FROM BODILY ACCIDENT AND HARM THE WORKMEN AT	599 28

BODY

	PAGE	LN
SO AS THAT THE MAIN BODY AND ESSENTIAL PARTS OF THE	V	30
AS WELL FOR THE BODY AS THE SOUL	006	09
THE RESURRECTION OF THE BODY	015	30
IN MIND, BODY, OR ESTATE	019	06
AS WELL FOR THE BODY AS THE SOUL	023	18
THE RESURRECTION OF THE BODY	030	02
IN MIND, BODY, OR ESTATE	033	04
AS THERE IS BUT ONE BODY AND ONE SPIRIT, AND ONE HOPE	037	30
MAY BE PRESERVED IN BODY AND SOUL	070	11
(C) THIS IS MY BODY, WHICH IS GIVEN FOR YOU	080	21
OF HIS MOST BLESSED BODY AND BLOOD	081	14
THE MOST PRECIOUS BODY AND BLOOD OF THY SCN JESUS	081	25
AND MADE ONE BODY WITH HIM, THAT HE MAY DWELL IN US,	081	27
MADE CLEAN BY HIS BODY, AND OUR SOULS WASHED THRCUGH	082	20
HE SHALL SAY, THE BODY OF OUR LORD JESUS CHRIST,	082	31
PRESERVE THY BODY AND SOUL UNTO EVERLASTING	082	32
PRESERVE THY BODY AND SOUL UNTO EVERLASTING	083	04
OF HIS MOST BLESSED BODY AND BLOOD	R 083	10
THE MOST PRECIOUS BODY AND BLOOD OF THY SCN OUR	083	19
IN THE MYSTICAL BODY OF THY SON, WHICH IS THE BLESSED	083	22
COMMUNION OF THE BODY AND BLOOD OF OUR SAVICUR	085	26
SACRAMENT OF THE BODY AND BLOOD OF CHRIST	086	31
AND OF THE SAME BODY, AND PARTAKERS OF HIS PROMISE IN	108	13
MANY MEMBERS IN ONE BODY, AND ALL MEMBERS HAVE NCT	110	13
BEING MANY, ARE ONE BODY IN CHRIST, AND EVERY CNE	110	15
TO THE WHICH ALSO YE ARE CALLED IN ONE BODY	116	10
BUT I KEEP UNDER MY BODY, AND BRING IT INTO	119	11
THOUGH I GIVE MY BODY TO BE BURNED, AND HAVE NOT	122	28
MAY HAPPEN TO THE BODY, AND FRCM ALL EVIL THOUGHTS	127	19
BOTH IN BODY AND SOUL	132	20
TO ANOINT MY BODY TO THE BURYING	140	15
THIS IS MY BODY	141	11
HAVING A LINEN CLOTH CAST ABOUT HIS NAKED BODY	142	29
THIS IS MY BODY WHICH IS GIVEN FOR YOU	149	10
SACRAMENT OF HIS BODY AND BLOOD	152	09
THIS IS MY BODY, WHICH IS BROKEN FOR YOU	152	19
SPIRIT THE WHOLE BODY OF THE CHURCH IS GOVERNED AND	156	28
WOULDEST NOT, BUT A BODY HAST THOU PREPARED ME	157	25
THE OFFERING OF THE BODY OF JESUS CHRIST ONCE FCR	158	02
AND BEGGED THE BODY OF JESUS	162	08
COMMANDED THE BODY TO BE DELIVERED	162	09
HAD TAKEN THE BODY, HE WRAPPED IT IN A CLEAN LINEN	162	10
THEY FOUND NOT HIS BODY, THEY CAME, SAYING, THAT THEY	167	24
OUR SINS IN HIS OWN BODY ON THE TREE, THAT WE, BEING	172	15
FOR AS THE BODY IS ONE, AND HATH MANY MEMBERS,	183	02
MEMBERS OF THAT ONE BODY, BEING MANY, ARE ONE BCCY	183	03
BEING MANY, ARE ONE BODY	183	04
BAPTIZED INTO ONE BODY, WHETHER WE BE JEWS OR	183	05
FOR THE BODY IS NOT ONE MEMBER, BUT MANY	183	07
THE REDEMPTION OF OUR BODY	194	23
WITH HIM, THAT THE BODY OF SIN MIGHT BE DESTROYED,	197	18
THE DEEDS OF THE BODY, YE SHALL LIVE	200	06
FOR I BEAR IN MY BODY THE MARKS OF THE LORD JESUS	211	05
NOR YET FOR YOUR BODY, WHAT YE SHALL PUT ON	211	14
THE FOOD, AND THE BODY THAN THE RAIMENT	211	15
THERE IS ONE BODY, AND ONE SPIRIT, EVEN AS YE ARE	213	23
BEING READY BOTH IN BODY AND SOUL, MAY CHEERFULLY	217	19
SHALL CHANGE THE BODY OF OUR HUMILIATION THAT IT MAY	222	23
CONFORMED UNTO THE BODY OF HIS GLORY, ACCORDING TC	222	24
THE EDIFYING OF THE BODY OF CHRIST	237	22
FROM WHOM THE WHOLE BODY FITLY JOINED TOGETHER AND	237	30
INCREASE OF THE BODY UNTO THE EDIFYING OF ITSELF IN	238	02
IN THE MYSTICAL BODY OF THY SON CHRIST OUR LORD	256	07
NOR YET FOR YOUR BODY, WHAT YE SHALL PUT CN	266	12
THAN FOOD, AND THE BODY THAN RAIMENT	266	14
AND HE IS THE SAVIOUR OF THE BODY	267	17
ARE MEMBERS OF HIS BODY, OF HIS FLESH, AND CF HIS	267	28
GRAFTED INTO THE BODY OF CHRIST'S CHURCH, LET US GIVE	280	14
THE RESURRECTION OF THE BODY	284	24
TO KEEP MY BODY IN TEMPERANCE, SOBERNESS, AND	289	02
THE CHURCH IS THE BODY OF WHICH JESUS CHRIST IS THE	290	32
BECAUSE IT IS ONE BODY UNDER ONE HEAD	291	08
IS THE BODY AND BLOOD OF CHRIST, WHICH ARE	293	14
OF OUR SOULS BY THE BODY AND BLOOD OF CHRIST, AS CUR	293	21
SACRAMENT OF THE BODY AND BLOOD OF CHRIST, COMING TO	294	30
MAY BE PRESERVED IN BODY AND SOUL	298	31
SHALL COME INTO THE BODY OF THE CHURCH, OR SHALL BE	R 300	04
TO HEALTH OF BODY, VIGOUR OF MIND, AND CHEERFULNESS	315	30
HERE LYING IN GREAT WEAKNESS OF BODY	316	09
NOW DEPARTED FROM THE BODY	319	28
PAIN OF SOUL AND BODY, THAT BEING RESTORED TO	320	11
AND SICKNESS OF BODY BEING PLT TO FLIGHT, THE	320	18
COMMUNION OF THE BODY AND BLOOD OF OUR SAVICUR	R 321	08
DEPART FROM THE BODY, IT MAY BE WITHOUT SPOT	321	24
OF HIS MOST BLESSED BODY AND BLOOD	R 323	08
OF CHRIST'S BODY AND BLOOD, THE MINISTER SHALL	R 323	25
EAT AND DRINK THE BODY AND BLOOD OF OUR SAVIOUR	R 323	30
MEETING THE BODY, AND GOING BEFORE IT, EITHER INTC	R 324	03
AND THOUGH THIS BODY BE DESTROYED, YET SHALL I SEE	324	10
AND WITH WHAT BODY DO THEY COME	329	06
SOWEST NOT THAT BODY THAT SHALL BE, BUT BARE GRAIN,	329	08
BUT GOD GIVETH IT A BODY AS IT HATH PLEASED HIM, AND	329	10
AND TO EVERY SEED ITS OWN BODY	329	11
IT IS SOWN A NATURAL BODY	329	22
IT IS RAISED A SPIRITLAL BODY	329	22
THERE IS A NATURAL BODY, AND THERE IS A SPIRITUAL	329	23
AND THERE IS A SPIRITUAL BODY	329	23
WHILE THE BODY IS MADE READY TO BE LAID INTC	R 332	16
BE CAST UPON THE BODY BY SOME STANDING BY, THE	R 333	12
AND WE COMMIT HIS BODY TO THE GROUND	333	15
AND MADE LIKE UNTO HIS OWN GLORIOUS BODY	333	22
AND BLISS, BOTH IN BODY AND SOUL, IN THY ETERNAL AND	334	28
ARE OF THE MYSTICAL BODY OF THY SON, MAY BE SET CN	336	24
AND WE COMMIT HIS BODY TO THE DEEP	337	10

BODY   CONTINUED

	PAGE	LN
AND MADE LIKE UNTO HIS GLORIOUS BODY	337	16
MEETING THE BODY, AND GOING BEFORE IT, EITHER INTC	R 338	03
BEING CAST UPON THE BODY, THE MINISTER SHALL SAY,	R 341	12
WE COMMIT THE BODY OF THIS CHILD TO THE GROUND	341	15
IN THE MIDST OF MY BODY IS EVEN LIKE MELTING WAX	366	32
MY SOUL AND MY BODY	376	10
AND THERE IS NO WHOLE PART IN MY BODY	388	05
THE FOOLISH BODY HATH SAID IN HIS HEART, *	405	12
OF THE FRUIT OF THY BODY *	508	27
THE EDIFYING OF THE BODY OF CHRIST	538	09
IS HIS SPOUSE, AND HIS BODY	540	10
THE SPOUSE AND BODY OF CHRIST	540	15
SACRAMENT OF THE BODY AND BLOOD OF CHRIST, MAY CCME	565	29
AS WELL FOR THE BODY AS FOR THE SOUL, MAY DO IT WITH	566	18
I DEVOTE MYSELF, BODY, SOUL, AND SPIRIT, WITH ALL	573	15
THE RESURRECTION OF THE BODY	578	08
TO KEEP MY BODY IN TEMPERANCE, SOBERNESS, AND	580	11
DEFEND US IN ALL DANGERS BOTH OF SOUL AND BODY	581	02
THE BODY AND BLOOD OF CHRIST, WHICH ARE	582	12
OF OUR SOULS BY THE BODY AND BLOOD OF CHRIST, AS CUR	582	18
OTHER ENDOWMENTS AND FACULTIES OF SOUL AND BODY	591	09
DEFEND THEM FROM ALL DANGERS OF SOUL AND BODY	597	04
TO HEALTH OF BODY AND OF MIND	597	18
WITHOUT BODY, PARTS, OR PASSIONS	603	03
AND TOOK AGAIN HIS BODY, WITH FLESH, BONES, AND ALL	603	21
A PARTAKING OF THE BODY OF CHRIST	608	38
THE BODY OF CHRIST IS GIVEN, TAKEN, AND EATEN,	608	44
MEAN WHEREBY THE BODY OF CHRIST IS RECEIVED AND EATEN	608	45
SACRAMENT OF THE BODY AND BLOOD OF CHRIST	609	06

BOLD

	PAGE	LN
TAUGHT US, WE MAKE BOLD TO SAY,	048	25
TAUGHT US, WE ARE BOLD TO SAY,	082	03
I AM BOLD ALSO	120	27
ANY IS BOLD, (I SPEAK FOOLISHLY,) I AM BOLD ALSC	120	27
BUT ESAIAS IS VERY BOLD, AND SAITH, I WAS FOUND CF	227	19
AND BARNABAS WAXED BOLD, AND SAID, IT WAS NECESSARY	260	30

BOLDLY

	PAGE	LN
LET US COME BOLDLY UNTO THE THRONE OF GRACE,	005	08
MAY OPEN MY MOUTH BOLDLY, TO MAKE KNOWN THE MYSTERY	219	23
I MAY SPEAK BOLDLY, AS I OUGHT TO SPEAK	219	25
SPEAK THE TRUTH, BOLDLY REBUKE VICE, AND PATIENTLY	242	12

BOLDNESS

	PAGE	LN
GIVING THEM BOLDNESS WITH FERVENT ZEAL CONSTANTLY TO	078	29
IN WHOM WE HAVE BOLDNESS AND ACCESS WITH CONFIDENCE	108	27
BOLDNESS TO ENTER INTO THE HOLIEST BY THE	158	16
WE MAY HAVE BOLDNESS IN THE DAY OF JUDGMENT	189	26
ANC GREAT BOLDNESS IN THE FAITH WHICH IS IN CHRIST	532	04

BOND

	PAGE	LN
OF SPIRIT, IN THE BOND OF PEACE, AND IN RIGHTECUSNESS	019	03
OF SPIRIT, IN THE BOND OF PEACE, AND IN RIGHTECUSNESS	032	34
UNITED IN ONE HOLY BOND OF TRUTH AND PEACE, OF FAITH	037	33
WHICH IS THE BOND OF PERFECTNESS	116	08
THE VERY BOND OF PEACE AND OF ALL VIRTUES,	122	17
WHETHER WE BE BOND OR FREE	183	06
THE SPIRIT IN THE BOND OF PEACE	213	22
SERVANT FROM EVERY BOND, AND SET HIM FREE FROM ALL	319	05
AND IN THE BOND OF PEACE, THAT THEY MAY BE AN	574	07

BOND-SERVANT

	PAGE	LN
EVEN JOSEPH, WHO WAS SOLD TO BE A BOND-SERVANT	471	07

BONDAGE

	PAGE	LN
WERE IN BONDAGE UNDER THE ELEMENTS OF THE WCRLD	104	18
BRING YOU INTO BONDAGE, IF A MAN DEVOUR YOU, IF A MAN	120	23
GENDERETH TO RONDAGE, WHICH IS AGAR	131	04
ANC IS IN BONDAGE WITH HER CHILDREN	131	07
FROM THE BONDAGE OF CORRUPTION INTO THE GLORIOUS	194	18
THE SPIRIT OF BONDAGE AGAIN TO FEAR	200	08
TFE SPIRIT OF BONDAGE AGAIN TO FEAR	330	21
OUT OF THE HOUSE OF BONDAGE	578	25

BONDMAID

	PAGE	LN
THE ONE BY A RONDMAID, THE OTHER BY A FREEWOMAN	130	31

BONDS

	PAGE	LN
FOR WHICH I AM AN AMBASSADOR IN BONDS	219	25
AS BOTH IN MY BONDS, AND IN THE DEFENCE AND	220	29
LET US BREAK THEIR BONDS ASUNDER, *	346	02
AND BRAKE THEIR BONDS IN SUNDER	477	03
HAST BROKEN MY BONDS IN SUNDER	487	18
SAYING THAT BONDS AND AFFLICTIONS ABIDE ME	550	17

BONDWOMAN

	PAGE	LN
WHO WAS OF THE BONDWOMAN WAS BORN AFTER THE FLESH	130	32
CAST OUT THE BONDWOMAN AND HER SON	131	15
THE SON OF THE BONDWOMAN SHALL NOT BE HEIR WITH THE	131	16
OF TFE BONDWOMAN, BUT OF THE FREE	131	18

BONE

	PAGE	LN
BE FULFILLEC, A BONE OF HIM SHALL NCT BE BROKEN	161	08

BONES

THAT THE BONES WHICH THOU HAST BROKEN MAY REJOICE	060 27
HATH NOT FLESH AND BONES, AS YE SEE ME HAVE	169 34
OF HIS FLESH, AND OF HIS BONES	267 29
HEAL ME, FOR MY BONES ARE VEXED	349 03
AND ALL MY BONES ARE OUT OF JOINT	366 31
I MAY TELL ALL MY BONES	367 07
AND MY BONES ARE CONSUMED	376 14
MY BONES CONSUMED AWAY THROUGH MY DAILY COMPLAINING	377 26
HE KEEPETH ALL HIS BONES, *	381 08
10 ALL MY BONES SHALL SAY, LORD, WHO IS LIKE UNTO	382 09
ANY REST IN MY BONES, BY REASON OF MY SIN	387 26
12 MY BONES ARE SMITTEN ASUNDER AS WITH A SWORD,	393 27
THAT THE BONES WHICH THOU HAST BROKEN MAY REJOICE	403 26
HATH BROKEN THE BONES OF HIM THAT BESIEGED THEE	405 26
AND MY BONES ARE BURNT UP AS IT WERE A FIREBRAND	464 16
MY BONES WILL SCARCE CLEAVE TO MY FLESH	464 19
BOWELS LIKE WATER, AND LIKE OIL INTO HIS BONES	481 07
14 MY BONES ARE NOT HID FROM THEE, *	515 18
8 OUR BONES LIE SCATTERED BEFORE THE PIT, *	517 26
WITH FLESH, BONES, AND ALL THINGS APPERTAINING	603 22

BONUM

CANTATE DOMINO, BONUM EST CONFITERI, NUNC DIMITTIS,	R 025 17

BOOK

THE PREFACE OF HER BOOK OF COMMON PRAYER, LAID IT	V 13
OR VERSE OF SUCH A CHAPTER) OF SUCH A BOOK	R 009 33
TAKEN OUT OF THIS BOOK, AS HE SHALL THINK FIT,	R 017 23
TAKEN OUT OF THIS BOOK, AS HE SHALL THINK FIT	R 031 32
OF THIS WITH THE BOOK OF COMMON PRAYER OF THE CHURCH	VI 30
HIS DISCRETION ADD OTHER PRAYERS FROM THIS BOOK	R 059 30
SCRIPTURE OR OF THE BOOK OF COMMON PRAYER, UNDER THE	R 073 36
IT IS NOT IN THIS BOOK OTHERWISE ORDERED	R 090 05
SPRINKLED BOTH THE BOOK AND ALL THE PEOPLE, SAYING,	147 22
THE VOLUME OF THE BOOK IT IS WRITTEN OF ME,) TO DO	157 28
WHICH ARE NOT WRITTEN IN THIS BOOK	229 11
IS WRITTEN IN THE BOOK OF PSALMS, LET HIS HABITATION	234 18
UNTO HIM THE BOOK OF THE PROPHET ESAIAS	261 14
HE HAD OPENED THE BOOK, HE FOUND THE PLACE WHERE IT	261 15
AND HE CLOSED THE BOOK, AND HE GAVE IT AGAIN TO THE	261 21
THE SERVICE OF THIS BOOK, WHICH, IN HIS DISCRETION,	R 314 23
PROVIDED IN THIS BOOK, ENDING WITH THE BLESSING	R 331 30
OTHER PARTS OF THIS BOOK, AS MAY BE FITTING	R 337 05
OR OTHER FITTING PRAYERS FROM THIS BOOK	R 340 23
THE VOLUME OF THE BOOK IT IS WRITTEN OF ME, THAT I	390 31
ARE NOT THESE THINGS NOTED IN THY BOOK	408 31
BE WIPED OUT OF THE BOOK OF THE LIVING, *	423 32
AND IN THY BOOK WERE ALL MY MEMBERS WRITTEN	515 21
THINK UPON THE THINGS CONTAINED IN THIS BOOK	558 22
HIM THE BIBLE, BOOK OF COMMON PRAYER, AND BOOKS OF	R 571 23
THE SECOND BOOK OF HOMILIES, THE SEVERAL TITLES	610 05
AS DOTH THE FORMER BOOK OF HOMILIES, WHICH WERE SET	610 07
THE BOOK OF CONSECRATION OF BISHOPS, AND ORDERING OF	610 31

BOOKS

NOT CONTAIN THE BOOKS THAT SHOULD BE WRITTEN	102 17
WITH THEE, AND THE BOOKS, BUT ESPECIALLY THE	254 06
COMMON PRAYER, AND BOOKS OF CANONS OF THE GENERAL AND	R 571 23
RECEIVE THESE BOOKS	571 25
THOSE CANONICAL BOOKS OF THE OLD AND NEW TESTAMENT,	603 33
AND THE OTHER BOOKS (AS HIEROME SAITH) THE CHURCH	604 02
ALL THE BOOKS OF THE NEW TESTAMENT, AS THEY ARE	604 12
AS IT DECLARES THE BOOKS OF HOMILIES TO BE AN	R 610 24

BORDERS

PEACE IN THY BORDERS, *	265 04
HAST SET ALL THE BORDERS OF THE EARTH	431 10
THEM WITHIN THE BORDERS OF HIS SANCTUARY, *	438 18
PEACE IN THY BORDERS, *	523 23

BORN

FOR UNTO YOU IS BORN THIS DAY IN THE CITY OF DAVID A	004 10
UNTO US A CHILD IS BORN	R 008 19
THYSELF TO BE BORN OF A VIRGIN	010 27
BY THE HOLY GHOST, BORN OF THE VIRGIN MARY	015 22
BY THE HOLY GHOST, BORN OF THE VIRGIN MARY	029 27
ONLY SON, TO BE BORN AS AT THIS TIME FOR US	077 15
AT THIS TIME TO BE BORN OF A PURE VIRGIN	096 15
WHICH WERE BORN, NOT OF BLOOD, NOR OF THE WILL OF THE	098 02
FOR UNTO YOU IS BORN THIS DAY IN THE CITY OF DAVID A	099 16
AT THIS TIME TO BE BORN OF A PURE VIRGIN	104 07
WHEN JESUS WAS BORN IN BETHLEHEM OF JUDAEA, IN THE	108 30
WHERE IS HE THAT IS BORN KING OF THE JEWS	108 33
HE DEMANDED OF THEM WHERE CHRIST SHOULD BE BORN	109 06
THE BONDWOMAN WAS BORN AFTER THE FLESH	130 32
AS THEN HE THAT WAS BORN AFTER THE FLESH PERSECUTED	131 13
HIM THAT WAS BORN AFTER THE SPIRIT, EVEN SO IT IS	131 14
WERE IT FOR THAT MAN IF HE HAD NEVER BEEN BORN	141 09
WHATSOEVER IS BORN OF GOD OVERCOMETH THE WORLD	170 26
JOY THAT A MAN IS BORN INTO THE WORLD	174 12
EVERY MAN IN OUR OWN TONGUE, WHEREIN WE WERE BORN	180 32
EXCEPT A MAN BE BORN AGAIN, HE CANNOT SEE THE KINGDOM	188 06
HOW CAN A MAN BE BORN WHEN HE IS OLD	188 07
SECOND TIME INTO HIS MOTHER'S WOMB, AND BE BORN	188 09
EXCEPT A MAN BE BORN OF WATER AND OF THE SPIRIT, HE	188 10
AND THAT WHICH IS BORN OF THE SPIRIT IS SPIRIT	188 12
THAT WHICH IS BORN OF THE FLESH IS FLESH	188 12
YE MUST BE BORN AGAIN	188 14
EVERY ONE THAT IS BORN OF THE SPIRIT	188 17

BORN   CONTINUED

ONE THAT LOVETH IS BORN OF GOD, AND KNOWETH GOD	189 09
ME ALSO, AS OF ONE BORN OUT OF DUE TIME	205 12
WHICH SHALL BE BORN OF THEE SHALL BE CALLED THE SON	236 24
WAS WONDERFULLY BORN, AND SENT TO PREPARE THE WAY OF	242 08
BE REGENERATE AND BORN ANEW OF WATER AND OF THE HOLY	273 31
EXCEPT A MAN BE BORN AGAIN, HE CANNOT SEE THE KINGDOM	275 11
HOW CAN A MAN BE BORN WHEN HE IS OLD	275 12
SECOND TIME INTO HIS MOTHER'S WOMB, AND BE BORN	275 14
EXCEPT A MAN BE BORN OF WATER AND OF THE SPIRIT, HE	275 15
THAT WHICH IS BORN OF THE FLESH IS FLESH	275 16
AND THAT WHICH IS BORN OF THE SPIRIT IS SPIRIT	275 17
YE MUST BE BORN AGAIN	275 18
EVERY ONE THAT IS BORN OF THE SPIRIT	275 21
THAT HE MAY BE BORN AGAIN, AND BE MADE AN HEIR OF	276 12
BY THE HOLY GHOST, BORN OF THE VIRGIN MARY	284 16
MAN, THAT IS BORN OF A WOMAN, HATH BUT A SHORT	332 18
I HAVE BEEN LEFT UNTO THEE EVER SINCE I WAS BORN	366 23
THAT SHALL BE BORN, WHOM THE LORD HATH MADE	368 07
AS SOON AS THEY ARE BORN, THEY GO ASTRAY, AND SPEAK	410 13
THEE HAVE I BEEN HOLDEN UP EVER SINCE I WAS BORN	425 17
IN SION WERE THEY BORN	448 21
AND THAT ONE WERE BORN IN HER	448 23
IN SION WERE THEY BORN	448 25
WHICH SHALL BE BORN SHALL PRAISE THE LORD	465 16
BY THE HOLY GHOST, BORN OF THE VIRGIN MARY	577 31
FOR BEING BY NATURE BORN IN SIN, AND THE CHILDREN OF	581 25
IN EVERY PERSON BORN INTO THIS WORLD, IT DESERVETH	604 34
AND BORN AGAIN IN CHRIST, YET OFFEND IN	605 35

BORNE

WHICH HAVE BORNE THE BURDEN AND HEAT OF THE DAY	120 06
AND AS WE HAVE BORNE THE IMAGE OF THE EARTHY,	329 31
THEN I COULD HAVE BORNE IT	407 12

BORROWETH

21 THE UNGODLY BORROWETH, AND PAYETH NOT AGAIN	386 04

BOSOM

WAS CARRIED BY THE ANGELS INTO ABRAHAM'S BOSOM	190 10
SEETH ABRAHAM AFAR OFF, AND LAZARUS IN HIS BOSOM	190 12
SHALL MEN GIVE INTO YOUR BOSOM	194 30
CARRY THEM IN HIS BOSOM, AND SHALL GENTLY LEAD THOSE	243 10
AND CARRY THEM IN HIS BOSOM	338 13
AND MY PRAYER SHALL TURN INTO MINE OWN BOSOM	382 19
HAND OUT OF THY BOSOM TO CONSUME THE ENEMY	430 30
O LORD, SEVEN-FOLD INTO THEIR BOSOM	440 31
I DO BEAR IN MY BOSOM THE REBUKES OF MANY PEOPLE	453 08
NEITHER HE THAT BINDETH UP THE SHEAVES HIS BOSOM	507 03

BOTH

WITNESSES UNTO ME BOTH IN JERUSALEM, AND IN ALL	005 13
IT WITH HIM, BOTH HERE, AND WHERESOEVER ELSE IT IS	R 007 21
TO JUDGE BOTH THE QUICK AND THE DEAD	016 13
TO JUDGE BOTH THE QUICK AND THE DEAD	030 18
THAT BOTH BY THEIR LIFE AND DOCTRINE THEY MAY SHOW	039 02
THY HELP, MAY BOTH FAITHFULLY LIVE IN THIS WORLD	053 15
AND THAT BOTH BY THEIR PREACHING AND LIVING THEY MAY	055 32
BOTH NOW AND EVER VOUCHSAFE TO HEAR US, O CHRIST	059 15
AND GIVE US PEACE, BOTH NOW AND EVERMORE	063 18
AND GOVERN, BOTH OUR HEARTS AND BODIES, IN THE WAYS	070 07
MIGHTY PROTECTION, BOTH HERE AND EVER, WE MAY BE	070 10
TO JUDGE BOTH THE QUICK AND THE DEAD	071 15
THAT THEY MAY, BOTH BY THEIR LIFE AND DOCTRINE,	074 22
HOLY COMMUNION IN BOTH KINDS HIMSELF, AND PROCEED TO	R 082 25
OUR SAVIOUR CHRIST, BOTH GOD AND MAN	086 08
MAJESTY TO JUDGE BOTH THE QUICK AND THE DEAD, WE MAY	090 16
THE LORD COME, WHO BOTH WILL BRING TO LIGHT THE	094 11
WORKETH IN YOU BOTH TO WILL AND TO DO OF HIS GOOD	106 05
GRANT THAT THEY MAY BOTH PERCEIVE AND KNOW WHAT	109 31
OF THE DOCTORS, BOTH HEARING THEM, AND ASKING THEM	110 29
AND BOTH JESUS WAS CALLED, AND HIS DISCIPLES, TO THE	113 12
LET BOTH GROW TOGETHER UNTIL THE HARVEST	116 28
KEEP US BOTH OUTWARDLY IN OUR BODIES, AND INWARDLY IN	127 16
PRESERVED EVERMORE, BOTH IN BODY AND SOUL	132 20
GRANT, THAT WE MAY BOTH FOLLOW THE EXAMPLE OF HIS	134 09
AND SPRINKLED BOTH THE BOOK AND ALL THE PEOPLE,	147 21
WITH BLOOD BOTH THE TABERNACLE, AND ALL THE VESSELS	147 24
TO GO WITH THEE, BOTH INTO PRISON, AND TO DEATH	149 35
SO THEY RAN BOTH TOGETHER	164 18
THINGS WHICH HE DID BOTH IN THE LAND OF THE JEWS,	166 23
SON TO BE UNTO US BOTH A SACRIFICE FOR SIN, AND ALSO	171 29
THAT JESUS BEGAN BOTH TO DO AND TEACH, UNTIL THE DAY	177 23
WITNESSES UNTO ME BOTH IN JERUSALEM, AND IN ALL	178 10
THINGS WHICH HE DID BOTH IN THE LAND OF THE JEWS, AND	184 10
WE MAY PLEASE THEE, BOTH IN WILL AND DEED	189 05
SHALL THEY NOT BOTH FALL INTO THE DITCH	195 03
AND FILLED BOTH THE SHIPS, SO THAT THEY BEGAN	196 21
ORDERETH ALL THINGS BOTH IN HEAVEN AND EARTH	199 29
HE MAKETH BOTH THE DEAF TO HEAR, AND THE DUMB TO	207 08
WE, BEING READY BOTH IN BODY AND SOUL, MAY CHEERFULLY	217 19
MANY AS THEY FOUND, BOTH BAD AND GOOD	219 30
INASMUCH AS BOTH IN MY BONDS, AND IN THE DEFENCE AND	220 29
HE BELIEVED, AND BOTH TO PREACH AND RECEIVE THE SAME	249 17
MULTITUDES BOTH OF MEN AND WOMEN	249 26
BUT NOW HAVE THEY BOTH SEEN AND HATED BOTH ME AND MY	255 27
BOTH SEEN AND HATED BOTH ME AND MY FATHER	255 27
MOST PRECIOUS SIDE BOTH WATER AND BLOOD	279 11
WHO MAKEST US BOTH TO WILL AND TO DO THOSE	298 13
AND GOVERN, BOTH OUR HEARTS AND BODIES, IN THE WAYS	298 27
MIGHTY PROTECTION, BOTH HERE AND EVER, WE MAY BE	298 30

BOTH   CONTINUED

AND CHARGE YOU BOTH, AS YE WILL ANSWER AT THE   300 24
SO LONG AS YE BOTH SHALL LIVE   301 10
SO LONG AS YE BOTH SHALL LIVE   301 19
MAY ADD ONE OR BOTH OF THE FOLLOWING PRAYERS   R 303 13
SHALL BE SAID BY BOTH OF THEM THE FOLLOWING HYMN,   R 305 15
GIVE THEE PEACE, BOTH NOW AND EVERMORE   314 30
AND GIVE YOU PEACE, BOTH NOW AND EVERMORE   332 14
AND BLISS, BOTH IN BODY AND SOUL, IN THY ETERNAL AND   334 27
AND GIVE HIM PEACE, BOTH NOW AND EVERMORE   341 18
THE LORD WILL ABHOR BOTH THE BLOOD-THIRSTY AND   348 12
SHALT SAVE BOTH MAN AND BEAST   384 08
BOTH THE CHARIOT AND HORSE ARE FALLEN   432 33
BOTH SMALL AND GREAT BEASTS   469 11
BOTH SMALL AND GREAT   486 04
BOTH OF MAN AND BEAST   510 18
LIGHT TO THEE ARE BOTH ALIKE   515 12
OF LIFE, THAT, BOTH BY WORD AND GOOD EXAMPLE, THEY   531 21
AND TO MAKE BOTH YOURSELVES AND THEM, AS MUCH AS IN   533 26
OF LIFE, THAT, BOTH BY WORD AND GOOD EXAMPLE,   537 25
AS YOUR OFFICE IS BOTH OF SO GREAT EXCELLENCY,   540 24
FRAMING THE MANNERS BOTH OF YOURSELVES, AND OF THEM   541 05
AND TO USE BOTH PUBLIC AND PRIVATE MONITIONS AND   542 22
AND TO MAKE BOTH YOURSELVES AND THEM, AS MUCH AS IN   542 34
AND THEE, OF BOTH, TO BE BUT ONE   544 11
SUFFICE THAT THE LITANY BE ONCE SAID FOR BOTH   R 547 21
OF LIFE, THAT, BOTH BY WORD AND GOOD EXAMPLE, THEY   548 04
TESTIFYING BOTH TO THE JEWS, AND ALSO TO THE   550 13
OF LIFE, THAT, BOTH BY WORD AND DEED, HE MAY   553 31
AND BOTH PRIVATELY AND OPENLY TO CALL UPON AND   555 04
AND THEE, OF BOTH, TO BE BUT ONE   556 19
SO DOING THOU SHALT BOTH SAVE THYSELF AND THEM THAT   558 24
OF OUR HAPPINESS BOTH TEMPORAL AND SPIRITUAL   565 13
HEARERS THEREOF MAY BOTH PERCEIVE AND KNOW WHAT   566 05
THAT ARE NEEDFUL BOTH FOR OUR SOULS AND BODIES   580 33
US IN ALL DANGERS BOTH OF SOUL AND BODY   581 02
THEY PROMISE THEM BOTH BY THEIR SURETIES   581 33
WE HERE DEDICATE BOTH OUR SOULS AND OUR BODIES TO   588 06
AS MAY MAKE US BOTH AFRAID AND ASHAMED TO OFFEND   588 19
AND GRANT THAT BOTH THEY AND WE, DRAWING NEARER TO   597 04
OF ALL THINGS BOTH VISIBLE AND INVISIBLE   603 05
FOR BOTH IN THE OLD AND NEW TESTAMENT EVERLASTING   604 15
GOD AND MAN, BEING BOTH GOD AND MAN   604 17
WAS CLEARLY VOID, BOTH IN HIS FLESH, AND IN HIS   605 32
USE THEIR MINISTRY, BOTH IN HEARING THE WORD OF GOD,   608 13
FOR BOTH THE PARTS OF THE LORD'S SACRAMENT, BY   609 10
OF THE WHOLE WORLD, BOTH ORIGINAL AND ACTUAL   609 15

BOTTLE

PUT MY TEARS INTO THY BOTTLE   408 31
AM BECOME LIKE A BOTTLE IN THE SMOKE   495 23

BOTTOM

FORGIVE FROM THE BOTTOM OF HIS HEART ALL THAT THE   R 085 12
WAS RENT IN TWAIN FROM THE TOP TO THE BOTTOM   137 26
WAS RENT IN TWAIN FROM THE TOP TO THE BOTTOM   147 02
FROM THE BOTTOM OF HIS HEART, ALL PERSONS   R 313 21

BOUGHS

AND THE BOUGHS THEREOF WERE LIKE THE GOODLY   441 23
AND HER BOUGHS UNTO THE RIVER   441 25

BOUGHT

BECAUSE THEY HAD BOUGHT A FARM, OR WOULD TRY THEIR   089 04
THAT SOLD AND BOUGHT IN THE TEMPLE, AND OVERTHREW THE   091 34
TOOK COUNSEL, AND BOUGHT WITH THEM THE POTTER'S   135 11
AND SALOME, HAD BOUGHT SWEET SPICES, THAT THEY MIGHT   165 19
UNTO HIM, I HAVE BOUGHT A PIECE OF GROUND, AND I MUST   192 07
I HAVE BOUGHT FIVE YOKE OF OXEN, AND I GO TO   192 09
OUT THEM THAT SOLD THEREIN, AND THEM THAT BOUGHT   204 17
THAT SOLD AND BOUGHT IN THE TEMPLE, AND OVERTHREW THE   260 04
WHICH HE BOUGHT WITH HIS DEATH, AND FOR WHOM   540 07

BOUND

WE BE TIED AND BOUND WITH THE CHAIN OF OUR SINS, YET   063 11
BUT CHIEFLY ARE WE BOUND TO PRAISE THEE FOR THE   078 07
THE OPENING OF THE PRISON TO THEM THAT ARE BOUND   107 04
AND WHEN THEY HAD BOUND HIM, THEY LED HIM AWAY, AND   134 32
WHOLE COUNCIL, AND BOUND JESUS, AND CARRIED HIM AWAY,   145 05
WHICH LAY BOUND WITH THEM THAT HAD MADE INSURRECTION   145 14
WENT TO HIM, AND BOUND UP HIS WOUNDS, POURING IN OIL   208 30
MIGHT BRING THEM BOUND UNTO JERUSALEM   229 29
MIGHT BRING THEM BOUND UNTO THE CHIEF PRIESTS   231 08
TWO SOLDIERS, BOUND WITH TWO CHAINS   245 11
ON EARTH SHALL BE BOUND IN HEAVEN   246 11
THINK THAT YOU ARE BOUND SO TO DO   283 29
YOURSELVES BOUND TO BELIEVE AND TO DO ALL THOSE   296 26
BEING FAST BOUND IN MISERY AND IRON   476 25
BEHOLD, I GO BOUND IN THE SPIRIT UNTO JERUSALEM   550 15
THAT THOU ART BOUND TO BELIEVE, AND TO DO, AS THEY   577 20
THEMSELVES ARE BOUND TO PERFORM   581 35
TO THEE, MAY BE BOUND TOGETHER BY THY LOVE IN THE   597 05
MUCH AS THEY ARE BOUND TO DO, BUT THAT THEY DO MORE   605 27

BOUNDEN

AND OUR BOUNDEN DUTY, THAT WE SHOULD AT ALL   076 31
ACCEPT THIS OUR BOUNDEN DUTY AND SERVICE   081 30
AS WE ARE MOST BOUNDEN, CONTINUAL THANKS   086 20
AND OUR BOUNDEN DUTY, THAT WE SHOULD GIVE   279 07

BOUNDEN   CONTINUED

WHAT IS YOUR BOUNDEN DUTY AS A MEMBER OF THE CHURCH   291 16
MY BOUNDEN DUTY IS TO FOLLOW CHRIST,   291 18
TO YOUR BOUNDEN DUTY, TO BRING ALL SUCH AS ARE OR   540 18
ACCEPT THEIR BOUNDEN DUTY AND SERVICE, AND VOUCHSAFE   566 21
THAN OF BOUNDEN DUTY IS REQUIRED   605 28

BOUNDS

SET THEM THEIR BOUNDS, WHICH THEY SHALL NOT PASS, *   468 11

BOUNTEOUS

THAT OF HIS BOUNTEOUS MERCY HE WILL GRANT TO THIS   274 02

BOUNTIFUL

BEFORE US, THY BOUNTIFUL GRACE AND MERCY MAY SPEEDILY   095 08
OF THY BOUNTIFUL GOODNESS KEEP US, WE BESEECH   217 17
THROUGH THY BOUNTIFUL GOODNESS WE MAY ALL BE   223 16

BOUNTY

THEE HUMBLE THANKS FOR THIS THY SPECIAL BOUNTY   052 02
RECEIVING THY BOUNTY, MAY EVERMORE GIVE THANKS UNTO   261 32
THEE HUMBLE AND HEARTY THANKS FOR THIS THY BOUNTY   265 14
MAY BE FAITHFUL STEWARDS OF THY BOUNTY   599 23

BOW

THOU SHALT NOT BOW DOWN TO THEM, NOR WORSHIP THEM   068 11
EVERY KNEE SHOULD BOW, OF THINGS IN HEAVEN, AND   105 28
EVERY KNEE SHOULD BOW, OF THINGS IN HEAVEN, AND   134 25
FOR THIS CAUSE I BOW MY KNEES UNTO THE FATHER OF OUR   212 11
THOU SHALT NOT BOW DOWN TO THEM, NOR WORSHIP THEM   286 11
UNDER THE EARTH, DO BOW AND OBEY   314 17
HE HATH BENT HIS BOW, AND MADE IT READY   350 18
UNGODLY BEND THEIR BOW, AND MAKE READY THEIR ARROWS   354 21
SHALL BEND EVEN A BOW OF STEEL   362 05
THE STRINGS OF THY BOW SHALT THOU MAKE READY AGAINST   365 30
2 BOW DOWN THINE EAR TO ME   375 24
AND HAVE BENT THEIR BOW, *   385 23
AND THEIR BOW SHALL BE BROKEN   385 26
WILL NOT TRUST IN MY BOW, *   395 05
HE BREAKETH THE BOW, AND KNAPPETH THE SPEAR IN   398 12
SHALL THINE ENEMIES BOW DOWN UNTO THEE   417 19
AND EVER BOW THOU DOWN THEIR BACKS   423 22
HE THE ARROWS OF THE BOW, *   432 26
STARTING ASIDE LIKE A BROKEN BOW   438 27
BOW DOWN THINE EAR, O LORD, AND HEAR ME   447 05
5 BOW THY HEAVENS, O LORD, AND COME DOWN   519 31
THOU SHALT NOT BOW DOWN TO THEM, NOR WORSHIP THEM   578 30

BOWED

AND THEY BOWED THE KNEE BEFORE HIM, AND MOCKED HIM,   136 20
AND HE BOWED HIS HEAD, AND GAVE UP THE GHOST   160 29
10 HE BOWED THE HEAVENS ALSO, AND CAME DOWN, *   360 15

BOWELS

SOUNDING OF THY BOWELS AND OF THY MERCIES TOWARD ME   139 20
SHUTTETH UP HIS BOWELS OF COMPASSION FROM HIM,   191 20
AND ALL HIS BOWELS GUSHED OUT   234 15
COME INTO HIS BOWELS LIKE WATER, AND LIKE OIL INTO   481 06

BOWING

UPON HIM, AND BOWING THEIR KNEES WORSHIPPED HIM   146 02

BOWS

AND CARRYING BOWS, TURNED THEMSELVES BACK IN THE DAY   435 18

BOX

HAVING AN ALABASTER BOX OF OINTMENT OF SPIKENARD VERY   140 04
AND SHE BRAKE THE BOX, AND POURED IT ON HIS HEAD   140 05

BOZRAH

COMETH FROM EDOM, WITH DYED GARMENTS FROM BOZRAH   138 12

BRAKE

(B) HE BRAKE IT, AND GAVE IT TO HIS   080 19
AND SHE BRAKE THE BOX, AND POURED IT ON HIS HEAD   140 05
AND BLESSED, AND BRAKE IT, AND GAVE TO THEM, AND   141 10
GAVE THANKS, AND BRAKE IT, AND GAVE UNTO THEM,   149 09
GIVEN THANKS, HE BRAKE IT, AND SAID, TAKE, EAT   152 19
THE SOLDIERS, AND BRAKE THE LEGS OF THE FIRST, AND OF   160 34
DEAD ALREADY, THEY BRAKE NOT HIS LEGS   161 03
BLESSED IT, AND BRAKE, AND GAVE TO THEM   168 06
AND THEIR NET BRAKE   196 19
GAVE THANKS, AND BRAKE, AND GAVE TO HIS DISCIPLES TO   199 19
AND HE BRAKE HIS COVENANT   407 34
3 THERE BRAKE HE THE ARROWS OF THE BOW, *   432 26
AND BRAKE THEIR BONDS IN SUNDER   477 03

BRAKEST

THOU BRAKEST THE HEADS OF THE DRAGONS IN THE WATERS   431 03

BRANCH

FOR THAT BRANCH OF THE SAME PLANTED BY GOD IN THIS 047 11
DAVID A RIGHTEOUS BRANCH, AND A KING SHALL REIGN AND 225 10
EVERY BRANCH IN ME THAT BEARETH NOT FRUIT HE TAKETH 238 06
AND EVERY BRANCH THAT BEARETH FRUIT, HE PURGETH IT, 238 07
AS THE BRANCH CANNOT BEAR FRUIT OF ITSELF, EXCEPT IT 238 10
CAST FORTH AS A BRANCH, AND IS WITHERED 238 15
AND THE BRANCH THAT THOU MADEST SO STRONG FOR 441 33

BRANCHES

OTHERS CUT DOWN BRANCHES FROM THE TREES, AND STRAWED 091 26
I AM THE VINE, YE ARE THE BRANCHES 238 12
OUT HER BRANCHES UNTO THE SEA, * 441 24
AND SING AMONG THE BRANCHES 468 18

BRASS

BECOME AS SOUNDING BRASS, OR A TINKLING CYMBAL 122 23
THE GATES OF BRASS, * 477 07

BRAWLER

NOT A BRAWLER, NOT COVETOUS 549 23

BRAWN

70 THEIR HEART IS AS FAT AS BRAWN 494 20

BREAD

GIVE US THIS DAY OUR DAILY BREAD 007 25
US TO WORK WITH QUIETNESS, AND EAT OUR OWN BREAD 039 27
HOLY TABLE, THE BREAD AND THE WINE R 073 33
SO ORDERED THE BREAD AND WINE, THAT HE MAY WITH THE R 080 02
DECENCY BREAK THE BREAD BEFORE THE PEOPLE, AND TAKE R 080 04
NIGHT IN WHICH HE WAS BETRAYED, (A) HE TOOK BREAD 080 18
B) AND HERE TO BREAK THE BREAD R 080 31
C) AND HERE TO LAY HIS HAND UPON ALL THE BREAD R 080 32
AND CREATURES OF BREAD AND WINE 081 11
HE DELIVERETH THE BREAD, HE SHALL SAY, R 082 30
IF THE CONSECRATED BREAD OR WINE BE SPENT BEFORE ALL R 083 07
OF THE CONSECRATED BREAD AND WINE REMAIN AFTER THE R 084 30
TO EAT OF THAT BREAD, AND DRINK OF THAT CUP 085 29
COMMAND THAT THESE STONES BE MADE BREAD 126 28
SHALL NOT LIVE BY BREAD ALONE, BUT BY EVERY WORD THAT 126 29
THE CHILDREN'S BREAD, AND TO CAST IT TO DOGS 128 17
SHALL WE BUY BREAD, THAT THESE MAY EAT 131 28
PENNYWORTH OF BREAD IS NOT SUFFICIENT FOR THEM, THAT 131 30
FEAST OF THE PASSOVER, AND OF UNLEAVENED BREAD 139 33
DAY OF UNLEAVENED BREAD, WHEN THEY KILLED THE 140 22
JESUS TOOK BREAD, AND BLESSED, AND BRAKE IT, AND 141 09
OF UNLEAVENED BREAD DREW NIGH, WHICH IS CALLED THE 148 12
DAY OF UNLEAVENED BREAD, WHEN THE PASSOVER MUST BE 148 21
AND HE TOOK BREAD, AND GAVE THANKS, AND BRAKE IT, AND 149 08
SAME NIGHT IN WHICH HE WAS BETRAYED TOOK BREAD 152 18
AS YE EAT THIS BREAD, AND DRINK THIS CUP, YE DO SHEW 152 24
THE UNLEAVENED BREAD OF SINCERITY AND TRUTH 163 02
THE UNLEAVENED BREAD OF SINCERITY AND TRUTH 165 15
HIMSELF TO HIS DISCIPLES IN THE BREAKING OF BREAD 166 07
WITH THEM, HE TOOK BREAD, AND BLESSED IT, AND BRAKE, 168 06
AND HOW HE WAS KNOWN OF THEM IN BREAKING OF BREAD 168 16
IF A SON SHALL ASK BREAD OF ANY OF YOU THAT IS A 183 14
THESE MEN WITH BREAD HERE IN THE WILDERNESS 199 15
MY FATHER'S HAVE BREAD ENOUGH AND TO SPARE, AND I 202 11
PHARISEES TO EAT BREAD ON THE SABBATH DAY, THAT THEY 213 29
SHALL WE BUY BREAD, THAT THESE MAY EAT 225 25
PENNYWORTH OF BREAD IS NOT SUFFICIENT FOR THEM, 225 27
THEN WERE THE DAYS OF UNLEAVENED BREAD 245 04
IF A SON SHALL ASK BREAD OF ANY OF YOU THAT IS A 263 07
LORD'S SUPPER IS; BREAD AND WINE, WHICH THE LORD HATH 291 10
REFRESHED BY THE BREAD AND WINE 293 22
I AM THAT BREAD OF LIFE 322 22
THIS IS THE BREAD WHICH COMETH DOWN FROM HEAVEN, THAT 322 24
I AM THE LIVING BREAD WHICH CAME DOWN FROM HEAVEN 322 26
AND THE BREAD THAT I WILL GIVE IS MY FLESH, WHICH I 322 27
MAN EAT OF THIS BREAD, HE SHALL LIVE FOR EVER 322 27
PEOPLE AS IT WERE BREAD, AND CALL NOT UPON THE LORD 356 23
NOR HIS SEED BEGGING THEIR BREAD 386 14
DID ALSO EAT OF MY BREAD, HATH LAID GREAT WAIT FOR 392 18
EATING UP MY PEOPLE AS IF THEY WOULD EAT BREAD 405 23
BUT CAN HE GIVE BREAD ALSO, OR PROVIDE FLESH FOR HIS 436 10
THEM WITH THE BREAD OF TEARS, * 441 12
SO THAT I FORGET TO EAT MY BREAD 464 18
ASHES AS IT WERE BREAD, * 464 27
AND BREAD TO STRENGTHEN MAN'S HEART 468 25
AND DESTROYED ALL THE PROVISION OF BREAD 471 05
THEM WITH THE BREAD OF HEAVEN 472 18
HIS CHILDREN BE VAGABONDS, AND BEG THEIR BREAD 480 19
AND EAT THE BREAD OF CAREFULNESS 505 27
AND WILL SATISFY HER POOR WITH BREAD 509 05
BREAD AND WINE, WHICH THE LORD HATH 582 07
BODIES ARE BY THE BREAD AND WINE 582 19
THE SAME, THE BREAD WHICH WE BREAK IS A PARTAKING OF 608 37
THE SUBSTANCE OF BREAD AND WINE) IN THE SUPPER OF THE 608 40

BREADTH

WHAT IS THE BREADTH, AND LENGTH, AND DEPTH, AND 212 18

BREAK

AND WHERE THIEVES BREAK THROUGH AND STEAL 072 08
THIEVES DO NOT BREAK THROUGH NOR STEAL 072 11
AND DECENCY BREAK THE BREAD BEFORE THE PEOPLE, AND R 080 03

BREAK   CONTINUED

B) AND HERE TO BREAK THE BREAD R 080 31
AND WHERE THIEVES BREAK THROUGH AND STEAL 125 18
THIEVES DO NOT BREAK THROUGH NOR STEAL 125 20
BREAK FORTH AND CRY, THOU THAT TRAVAILEST NOT 131 09
3 LET US BREAK THEIR BONDS ASUNDER, * 346 02
AND BREAK THEM IN PIECES LIKE A POTTER'S VESSEL 346 15
17 BREAK THOU THE POWER OF THE UNGODLY AND MALICIOUS 354 09
THEREFORE SHALL HE BREAK THEM DOWN, AND NOT BUILD 373 19
6 THOU DOST BREAK THE SHIPS OF THE SEA * 399 22
6 BREAK THEIR TEETH, O GOD, IN THEIR MOUTHS 410 19
7 BUT NOW THEY BREAK DOWN ALL THE CARVED WORK THEREOF 430 16
ALSO WILL I BREAK, * 432 21
32 IF THEY BREAK MY STATUTES, AND KEEP NOT MY 452 04
WILL I NOT BREAK, NOR ALTER THE THING THAT IS GONE 452 09
THE BREAD WHICH WE BREAK IS A PARTAKING OF THE BODY 608 37
DOTH OPENLY BREAK THE TRADITIONS AND CEREMONIES OF 609 36

BREAKETH

OF THE LORD BREAKETH THE CEDAR-TREES 374 07
THE LORD BREAKETH THE CEDARS OF LEBANON 374 08
HE BREAKETH THE BOW, AND KNAPPETH THE SPEAR IN 398 11
20 MY SOUL BREAKETH OUT FOR THE VERY FERVENT DESIRE * 491 06
AS WHEN ONE BREAKETH AND HEWETH WOOD UPON THE EARTH 517 27

BREAKING

TO THE BREAKING DOWN THE KINGDOM OF SIN, 037 04
IN THE BREAKING OF BREAD 166 07
OF THEM IN BREAKING OF BREAD 168 16

BREAST

LEANED ON HIS BREAST AT SUPPER, AND SAID, LORD, 102 05
SMOTE UPON HIS BREAST, SAYING, GOD BE MERCIFUL TO ME 205 30

BREASTPLATE

ON THE BREASTPLATE OF RIGHTEOUSNESS 219 14

BREASTS

AND THOSE THAT SUCK THE BREASTS 124 31
SMOTE THEIR BREASTS, AND RETURNED 155 18
WHEN I HANGED YET UPON MY MOTHER'S BREASTS 366 22

BREATH

LET THY BREATH GO FORTH THAT IT MAY RENEW THE FACE OF 040 09
BLASTING OF THE BREATH OF THY DISPLEASURE 360 30
OF THEM BY THE BREATH OF HIS MOUTH 378 30
TAKEST AWAY THEIR BREATH, THEY DIE, AND ARE TURNED 469 19
THOU LETTEST THY BREATH GO FORTH, THEY SHALL BE MADE 469 21
131 I OPENED MY MOUTH, AND DREW IN MY BREATH 498 32
IS THERE ANY BREATH IN THEIR MOUTHS 511 05
3 FOR WHEN THE BREATH OF MAN GOETH FORTH, HE SHALL 522 08
THING THAT HATH BREATH * 525 32
GAVEST US THE BREATH OF LIFE, AND ALONE CANST KEEP 594 18

BREATHED

SAID THIS, HE BREATHED ON THEM, AND SAITH UNTO THEM, 171 22
SAID THIS, HE BREATHED ON THEM, AND SAITH UNTO THEM, 552 03

BREATHING

AND SAUL, YET BREATHING OUT THREATENINGS AND 229 25

BRETHREN

DEARLY BELOVED BRETHREN, THE SCRIPTURE MOVETH US, IN 005 29
DEARLY BELOVED BRETHREN, THE SCRIPTURE MOVETH US, 023 04
AND NOW, BRETHREN, SUMMING UP ALL OUR PETITIONS, 048 23
OF THESE MY BRETHREN, YE HAVE DONE IT UNTO ME 073 04
BRETHREN, THAT YE BE NOT JUDGED OF THE 085 33
DEARLY BELOVED BRETHREN, ON -- INTEND, BY GOD'S 088 12
FROM YOUR BRETHREN, WHO COME TO FEED ON THE BANQUET 089 17
AMONG THE BRETHREN, THAT THAT DISCIPLE SHOULD NOT 102 10
YOU THEREFORE, BRETHREN, BY THE MERCIES OF GOD, THAT 110 03
PERILS IN THE SEA, IN PERILS AMONG FALSE BRETHREN 121 08
NOW WE, BRETHREN, AS ISAAC WAS, ARE THE CHILDREN OF 131 12
SO THEN, BRETHREN, WE ARE NOT CHILDREN OF THE 131 18
WHEN THOU ART CONVERTED, STRENGTHEN THY BRETHREN 149 34
BRETHREN, BOLDNESS TO ENTER INTO THE 158 16
MEN AND BRETHREN, CHILDREN OF THE STOCK OF ABRAHAM, 168 24
MEN AND BRETHREN, THAT THROUGH THIS MAN IS PREACHED 169 18
MY BELOVED BRETHREN, LET EVERY MAN BE SWIFT TO HEAR, 174 31
FOR I HAVE FIVE BRETHREN 190 24
MARVEL NOT, MY BRETHREN, IF THE WORLD HATE YOU 191 11
BECAUSE WE LOVE THE BRETHREN 191 13
WE OUGHT TO LAY DOWN OUR LIVES FOR THE BRETHREN 191 18
IN YOUR BRETHREN THAT ARE IN THE WORLD 193 08
LOVE AS BRETHREN, BE PITIFUL, BE COURTEOUS 195 21
BRETHREN, WE ARE DEBTORS, NOT TO THE FLESH, TO LIVE 200 03
BRETHREN, I WOULD NOT THAT YE SHOULD BE IGNORANT, 201 05
BRETHREN, I WOULD NOT HAVE YOU IGNORANT 203 16
BRETHREN, I DECLARE UNTO YOU THE GOSPEL WHICH I 204 29
FIVE HUNDRED BRETHREN AT ONCE 205 08
BRETHREN, THE GRACE OF OUR LORD JESUS CHRIST BE WITH 211 06
MY BRETHREN, BE STRONG IN THE LORD, AND IN THE POWER 219 05
BRETHREN, BE FOLLOWERS TOGETHER OF ME, AND MARK THEM 222 15
SAW TWO BRETHREN, SIMON CALLED PETER, AND ANDREW HIS 227 24
SAW OTHER TWO BRETHREN, JAMES THE SON OF ZEBEDEE, AND 227 29

BRETHREN   CONTINUED

	PAGE	LN
OR BRETHREN, OR SISTERS, OR FATHER, OR	231	19
MEN AND BRETHREN, THIS SCRIPTURE MUST NEEDS HAVE BEEN	234	08
MY BRETHREN, COUNT IT ALL JOY WHEN YE FALL INTO	239	08
RELIEF UNTO THE BRETHREN WHICH DWELT IN JUDAEA	241	21
RELIEF UNTO THE BRETHREN WHICH DWELT IN JUDAEA	246	29
MOVED WITH INDIGNATION AGAINST THE TWO BRETHREN	247	20
ACCUSER OF OUR BRETHREN IS CAST DOWN, WHICH ACCUSED	252	12
OF THESE MY BRETHREN, YE HAVE DONE IT UNTO ME	259	16
YE SALUTE YOUR BRETHREN ONLY, WHAT DO YE MORE THAN	264	12
DO NOT ERR, MY BELOVED BRETHREN	265	18
MY BRETHREN, LET EVERY MAN BE SWIFT TO HEAR,	265	23
TO BE IGNORANT, BRETHREN, CONCERNING THEM WHICH ARE	268	28
DEARLY BELOVED BRETHREN, THAT THIS CHILD (THIS	280	13
NOW THIS I SAY, BRETHREN, THAT FLESH AND BLOOD CANNOT	329	33
MY BELOVED BRETHREN, BE YE STEDFAST, UNMOVEABLE,	330	14
22 I WILL DECLARE THY NAME UNTO MY BRETHREN	367	16
UNTO MY BRETHREN, *	422	18
8 FOR MY BRETHREN AND COMPANIONS' SAKES, *	503	22
FOR BRETHREN TO DWELL TOGETHER IN UNITY	509	13
THE PEOPLE, BRETHREN, IF THERE BE ANY OF YOU WHO	530	21
BRETHREN, LOOK YE OUT AMONG YOU SEVEN MEN	532	10
YE HAVE HEARD, BRETHREN, AS WELL IN YOUR PRIVATE	539	24
AND NOW, BRETHREN, I COMMEND YOU TO GOD, AND TO THE	551	02
BRETHREN, IT IS WRITTEN IN THE GOSPEL OF SAINT LUKE,	553	04
AND WOUNDETH THE CONSCIENCES OF THE WEAK BRETHREN	609	41

BRIDE

	PAGE	LN
THE SPIRIT AND THE BRIDE SAY, COME	022	29
AND THE BRIDE OUT OF HER CLOSET	124	32
PREPARED AS A BRIDE ADORNED FOR HER HUSBAND	567	13

BRIDEGROOM

	PAGE	LN
CALLED THE BRIDEGROOM, AND SAITH UNTO HIM, EVERY MAN	113	26
LET THE BRIDEGROOM GO FORTH OF HIS CHAMBER, AND THE	124	32
FORTH AS A BRIDEGROOM OUT OF HIS CHAMBER, AND	363	22

BRIDLE

	PAGE	LN
HELD WITH BIT AND BRIDLE, ELSE THEY WILL NCT OBEY	378	12
AS IT WERE WITH A BRIDLE, *	389	07

BRIDLETH

	PAGE	LN
AND BRIDLETH NOT HIS TONGUE, BUT DECEIVETH	176	14
AND BRIDLETH NOT HIS TONGUE, BLT DECEIVETH	266	05

BRIEF

	PAGE	LN
THE READING OF A BRIEF PORTION OF HOLY SCRIPTURE,	R 592	09
THE READING OF A BRIEF PORTION OF HOLY SCRIPTURE,	R 593	03

BRIEFLY

	PAGE	LN
IT IS BRIEFLY COMPREHENDED IN THIS SAYING, NAMELY,	090	28

BRIGHT

	PAGE	LN
THEE TO CAST THY BRIGHT BEAMS CF LIGHT UPON THY	101	05

BRIGHTNESS

	PAGE	LN
KINGS TO THE BRIGHTNESS OF THY RISING	022	03
WHO BEING THE BRIGHTNESS OF HIS GLORY, AND THE	096	26
13 AT THE BRIGHTNESS OF HIS PRESENCE HIS CLOUDS	360	22

BRIM

	PAGE	LN
AND THEY FILLED THEM LP TO THE BRIM	113	22

BRIMSTONE

	PAGE	LN
FIRE AND BRIMSTONE, STORM AND TEMPEST	354	33

BRING

	PAGE	LN
MAY LEAD ME, AND BRING ME UNTO THY HOLY HILL, AND TO	003	23
BEHOLD, I BRING YOU GOOD TIDINGS OF GREAT JCY,	004	08
SHALL THE EARTH BRING FORTH HER INCREASE	028	28
BRING THE NATIONS INTO THY FOLD, POUR OUT THY SPIRIT	038	09
BE FRUITFUL AND BRING FORTH WHATSOEVER IS NEEDFUL FOR	039	25
AND THE EARTH BRING FORTH HER INCREASE	040	31
THAT THEY MAY BRING FORTH IN US THE FRUIT CF GOOD	049	20
THAT IT MAY BRING FORTH FRUIT FOR THE USE OF	051	17
AND TO BRING FORTH THE FRUITS OF THE	056	16
MAY PLEASE THEE TO BRING INTO THE WAY OF TRUTH ALL	056	19
AND REVERENTLY BRING IT TO THE PRIEST, WHO SHALL	R 073	30
AND BRING YOU TO EVERLASTING LIFE	076	07
THAT HE MIGHT BRING US OUT OF DARKNESS INTO HIS CWN	077	24
LOOSE THEM, AND BRING THEM UNTC ME	091	15
WHO BOTH WILL BRING TO LIGHT THE HIDDEN THINGS OF	094	11
BEHOLD, I BRING YOU GOOD TIDINGS OF GREAT JOY,	099	15
THOU THERE UNTIL I BRING THEE WORD	103	18
AND SHE SHALL BRING FORTH A SON, AND THOU SHALT CALL	105	06
AND SHALL BRING FORTH A SON, AND THEY SHALL	105	10
YE HAVE FOUND HIM, BRING ME WORD AGAIN, THAT I MAY	109	14
UNDER MY BODY, AND BRING IT INTO SUBJECTICN	119	11
IF A MAN BRING YOU INTO BONDAGE, IF A MAN	120	23
OF THIS LIFE, AND BRING NO FRUIT TO PERFECTION	122	07
KEEP IT, AND BRING FORTH FRUIT WITH PATIENCE	122	10
AND I WILL BRING DOWN THEIR STRENGTH TO THE	138	27
AND THEY BRING HIM UNTO THE PLACE GOLGOTHA, WHICH IS,	146	07
BEHOLD, I BRING HIM FORTH TO YOU, THAT YE MAY	159	02

BRING   CONTINUED

	PAGE	LN
THAT HE MIGHT BRING US TO GOD, BEING PUT TO DEATH IN	161	23
HELP WE MAY BRING THE SAME TO GOOD EFFECT	163	27
THEM ALSO I MUST BRING, AND THEY SHALL HEAR MY VCICE	172	31
ALL THINGS, AND BRING ALL THINGS TO YOUR REMEMBRANCE,	181	32
WHOM THOU DOST BRING UP IN THY STEDFAST FEAR AND	191	05
OF THE CITY, AND BRING IN HITHER THE POOR, AND THE	192	15
THEREFORE IF THOU BRING THY GIFT TO THE ALTAR,	198	08
A GOOD TREE CANNOT BRING FORTH EVIL FRUIT, NEITHER	200	20
CAN A CORRUPT TREE BRING FORTH GOOD FRUIT	200	21
TO HIS SERVANTS, BRING FORTH THE BEST ROBE, AND PUT	202	21
AND BRING HITHER THE FATTED CALF, AND KILL IT	202	23
AND THEY BRING UNTO HIM ONE THAT WAS DEAF, AND HAD AN	206	29
OF PEACE, AND BRING GLAD TIDINGS OF GOOD THINGS	227	10
OR WOMEN, HE MIGHT BRING THEM BOUND UNTO JERUSALEM	229	29
THAT HE MIGHT BRING THEM BOUND UNTO THE CHIEF	231	08
IN THY WOMB, AND BRING FORTH A SON, AND SHALT CALL	236	15
THAT IT MAY BRING FOR TH MORE FRUIT	238	08
YE SHOULD GO AND BRING FORTH FRUIT, AND THAT YOUR	241	33
AFTER EASTER TO BRING HIM FORTH TO THE PEOPLE	245	06
TAKE MARK, AND BRING HIM WITH THEE	254	02
WHEN THOU COMEST, BRING WITH THEE, AND THE BOOKS, BUT	254	05
IN JESUS WILL GOD BRING WITH HIM	269	02
AND SPONSORS SHALL BRING THOSE, FOR WHOSE RELIGICUS	R 295	10
MAY LEAD ME, AND BRING ME UNTO THY HOLY HILL, AND TO	310	12
WE BRING OUR YEARS TO AN END, AS IT WERE A TALE THAT	325	31
AND BRING ME FORTH IN THE PATHS OF RIGHTEOUSNESS FCR	338	21
CARE AND LOVE, AND BRING US ALL TO THY HEAVENLY	342	06
THAT WILL BRING FORTH HIS FRUIT IN DUE SEASON	345	13
AND SHALT BRING DOWN THE HIGH LOOKS OF THE PROUD	361	23
AND BRING ME FORTH IN THE PATHS OF RIGHTEOUSNESS FOR	368	14
O BRING THOU ME OUT OF MY TROUBLES	370	18
THE HINDS TO BRING FORTH YOUNG, AND STRIPPETH BARE	374	14
3 BRING FORTH THE SPEAR, AND STOP THE WAY AGAINST	381	22
WHICH THEY BRING ON ME, AND MY DARLING FROM THE	382	30
AND HE SHALL BRING IT TO PASS	385	03
FOR THAT SHALL BRING A MAN PEACE AT THE LAST	387	09
AND BRING ME UNTO THY HOLY HILL, AND TO THY DWELLING	394	10
SHALL HEAR ME, AND BRING THEM DOWN	407	31
THOU, O GOD, SHALT BRING THEM INTO THE PIT OF	408	06
WHO WILL BRING ME INTO EDOM	412	30
SHALL THE EARTH BRING FORTH HER INCREASE	419	02
HATH SAID, I WILL BRING MY PEOPLE AGAIN, AS I DID	420	30
MINE OWN WILL I BRING AGAIN, AS I DID SOMETIME FROM	420	31
SO SHALL KINGS BRING PRESENTS UNTO THEE	421	14
THAT THEY HUMBLY BRING PIECES OF SILVER	421	16
ALSO SHALL BRING PEACE, *	427	02
AND SABA SHALL BRING GIFTS	427	17
WAS KNOWN TO BRING IT TO AN EXCELLENT WORK	430	15
BRING PRESENTS UNTO HIM THAT OUGHT TO BE FEARED	433	11
2 TAKE THE PSALM, BRING HITHER THE TABRET, *	442	14
WE BRING OUR YEARS TO AN END, AS IT WERE A TALE THAT	454	05
DELIVER HIM, AND BRING HIM TO HONOUR	455	27
13 THEY ALSO SHALL BRING FORTH MORE FRUIT IN THEIR	456	28
BRING PRESENTS, AND COME INTO HIS COURTS	460	15
15 THAT HE MAY BRING FOOD OUT OF THE EARTH, AND WINE	468	23
AND WHO WILL BRING ME INTO EDOM	479	25
WITH JOY, AND BRING HIS SHEAVES WITH HIM	505	20
9 BRING MY SOUL OUT OF PRISON, THAT I MAY GIVE THANKS	518	19
SAKE BRING MY SOUL OUT OF TROUBLE	519	16
THAT OUR SHEEP MAY BRING FORTH THOUSANDS, AND TEN	520	19
THEM ALSO I MUST BRING, AND THEY SHALL HEAR MY VCICE	539	20
BOUNDEN DUTY, TO BRING ALL SUCH AS ARE OR SHALL BE	540	18
UP THE BROKEN, BRING AGAIN THE OLTCASTS, SEEK THE	558	27
TO YOUR CHARGE, TO BRING ABOUT A SEPARATICN, AND	569	32
SHALL EITHER BRING, OR SEND IN WRITING, WITH HIS HAND	R 583	07
BRING US, WE RESEECH THEE, IN SAFETY TO THE MCRNING	595	08
GIFT OF FAITH WE BRING OUR PERPLEXITIES TO THE LIGHT	596	12
OF MANKIND, AND TO BRING THEM BY CHRIST TO	606	09

BRINGEST

	PAGE	LN
AS THOU ALONE BRINGEST LIGHT OUT OF DARKNESS, AND	046	26
O ZION, THAT BRINGEST GOOD TIDINGS, GET THEE UP INTO	243	02
THAT BRINGEST GOOD TIDINGS, LIFT UP THY	243	03
MIGHTY GOD, WHO BRINGEST DOWN TO THE GRAVE, AND	315	19
THE GRAVE, AND BRINGEST UP AGAIN	315	20
AND THOU BRINGEST ME INTO THE DUST OF DEATH	367	02

BRINGETH

	PAGE	LN
WHEN HE BRINGETH IN THE FIRST-BEGOTTEN INTO	097	05
OF GOD THAT BRINGETH SALVATION HATH APPEARED TO ALL	098	18
A CORRUPT TREE BRINGETH FORTH EVIL FRUIT	200	19
EVERY GOOD TREE BRINGETH FORTH GOOD FRUIT	200	19
EVERY TREE THAT BRINGETH NOT FORTH GOOD FRUIT IS HEWN	200	22
AND BRINGETH FRUIT, AS IT DOTH ALSO IN YCU,	223	28
THE SAME BRINGETH FORTH MUCH FRUIT	238	13
10 THE LORD BRINGETH THE COUNSEL OF THE HEATHEN TO	379	06
AN HOUSE, AND BRINGETH THE PRISONERS OUT OF	419	22
14 HE BRINGETH FORTH GRASS FOR THE CATTLE, *	468	21
AND SO HE BRINGETH THEM UNTO THE HAVEN WHERE THEY	478	05
OF THE LORD BRINGETH MIGHTY THINGS TO PASS	488	31
OF THE LORD BRINGETH MIGHTY THINGS TO PASS	488	31
7 HE BRINGETH FORTH THE CLOUDS FROM THE ENDS OF THE	510	15
AND BRINGETH THE UNGODLY DOWN TO THE GROUND	523	06

BRINGING

	PAGE	LN
PLENTEOUSLY BRINGING FORTH THE FRUIT OF GOOD WORKS,	225	05
UNTO JERUSALEM, BRINGING SICK FOLKS, AND THEM WHICH	249	31
WITH THE RAIN, BRINGING THE WINDS OUT OF HIS	510	16

BROAD

THAT REMAIN IN THE BROAD SEA	416 24
BUT THY COMMANDMENT IS EXCEEDING BROAD	496 18

BROILED

HIM A PIECE OF A BROILED FISH, AND OF AN HONEYCOMB	170 05

BROKEN

A BROKEN AND A CONTRITE HEART, O GOD, THOU WILT NOT	004 24
OF GOD ARE A BROKEN SPIRIT	004 24
THE DEPTHS ARE BROKEN UP, AND THE CLOUDS DROP DOWN	005 26
THE DEPTHS ARE BROKEN UP, AND THE CLOUDS DROP DOWN	050 20
WHICH THOU HAST BROKEN MAY REJOICE	060 27
A BROKEN AND CONTRITE HEART, O GOD, SHALT THOU NOT	061 13
MY BODY, WHICH IS BROKEN FOR YOU	152 20
LEGS MIGHT BE BROKEN, AND THAT THEY MIGHT BE TAKEN	160 13
A BONE OF HIM SHALL NOT BE BROKEN	161 09
TOOK UP OF THE BROKEN MEAT THAT WAS LEFT SEVEN	199 23
WHEN I HAVE BROKEN THE BANDS OF THEIR YOKE, AND	262 12
THOSE THAT ARE BROKEN IN HEART, *	264 23
THOU HAST BROKEN THE TEETH OF THE UNGODLY	347 05
AM BECOME LIKE A BROKEN VESSEL	376 20
SO THAT NOT ONE OF THEM IS BROKEN	381 09
AND THEIR BOW SHALL BE BROKEN	385 26
UNGODLY SHALL BE BROKEN, *	385 29
WHICH THOU HAST BROKEN MAY REJOICE	403 26
A BROKEN AND CONTRITE HEART, O GOD, SHALT THOU NOT	404 11
FOR GOD HATH BROKEN THE BONES OF HIM THAT BESIEGED	405 26
YE BE, AND LIKE A BROKEN HEDGE	414 03
21 REPROACH HATH BROKEN MY HEART	423 13
ASIDE LIKE A BROKEN BOW	438 27
HAST THOU THEN BROKEN DOWN HER HEDGE, *	441 26
38 THOU HAST BROKEN THE COVENANT OF THY SERVANT,	452 12
AND BROKEN DOWN HIS STRONGHOLDS	452 20
16 FOR HE HATH BROKEN THE GATES OF BRASS, *	477 07
THOU HAST BROKEN MY BONDS IN SUNDER	487 18
THE SNARE IS BROKEN, AND WE ARE DELIVERED	504 19
THOSE THAT ARE BROKEN IN HEART, *	522 32
HATH GIVEN THEM A LAW WHICH SHALL NOT BE BROKEN	524 17
BIND UP THE BROKEN, BRING AGAIN THE OUTCASTS,	558 27
THOSE THAT ARE BROKEN IN HEART, AND TURNEST THE	599 04

BROKENHEARTED

UP THE BROKENHEARTED, TO PROCLAIM LIBERTY TO THE	107 02
HEAL THE BROKENHEARTED, TO PREACH DELIVERANCE TO THE	261 18

BROOK

UNTO JABIN AT THE BROOK OF KISHON	444 23
SHALL DRINK OF THE BROOK IN THE WAY	482 21

BROTHER

AND SEETH HIS BROTHER HAVE NEED, AND SHUTTETH UP HIS	072 29
AND DEFRAUD HIS BROTHER IN ANY MATTER	127 32
SIMON PETER'S BROTHER, SAITH UNTO HIM, THERE IS A LAD	131 32
AND HATETH HIS BROTHER, HE IS A LIAR	189 31
LOVETH NOT HIS BROTHER WHOM HE HATH SEEN, HOW CAN HE	189 32
GOD LOVE HIS BROTHER ALSO	189 35
HATETH HIS BROTHER IS A MURDERER	191 14
LOVETH NOT HIS BROTHER ABIDETH IN DEATH	191 14
AND SEETH HIS BROTHER HAVE NEED, AND SHUTTETH UP HIS	191 19
TO THY BROTHER, BROTHER, LET ME PULL OUT THE MOTE	195 08
THOU SAY TO THY BROTHER, BROTHER, LET ME PULL OUT THE	195 08
ANGRY WITH HIS BROTHER WITHOUT A CAUSE SHALL BE IN	198 04
SHALL SAY TO HIS BROTHER, RACA, SHALL BE IN DANGER OF	198 05
THAT THY BROTHER HATH OUGHT AGAINST THEE	198 09
TO THY BROTHER, AND THEN COME AND OFFER THY GIFT	198 11
UNTO HIM, THY BROTHER IS COME	202 29
FOR THIS THY BROTHER WAS DEAD, AND IS ALIVE AGAIN	203 07
HOW OFT SHALL MY BROTHER SIN AGAINST ME, AND I	221 09
EVERY ONE HIS BROTHER THEIR TRESPASSES	222 06
SIMON PETER'S BROTHER, SAITH UNTO HIM, THERE IS A LAD	225 29
AND ANDREW HIS BROTHER, CASTING A NET INTO THE SEA	227 25
AND JOHN HIS BROTHER, IN A SHIP WITH ZEBEDEE THEIR	227 30
ON HIM SAID, BROTHER SAUL, THE LORD, EVEN JESUS,	230 31
LET THE BROTHER OF LOW DEGREE REJOICE IN THAT HE IS	239 18
KILLED JAMES THE BROTHER OF JOHN WITH THE SWORD	244 33
KILLED JAMES THE BROTHER OF JOHN WITH THE SWORD	247 07
THIS OUR BROTHER TO SOME DEGREE OF HIS FORMER HEALTH	315 22
OUR DEAR BROTHER, INTO THY HANDS, AS INTO THE HANDS	317 14
THE SOUL OF OUR BROTHER DEPARTED, AND WE COMMIT HIS	333 15
THE SOUL OF OUR BROTHER DEPARTED, AND WE COMMIT HIS	337 10
AS THOUGH IT HAD BEEN MY FRIEND OR MY BROTHER	382 21
MAY DELIVER HIS BROTHER, *	400 18
20 THOU SATTEST AND SPAKEST AGAINST THY BROTHER	402 30
BLESS THIS OUR BROTHER ELECTED, AND TO SEND THY GRACE	553 17
BE CONSECRATED, BROTHER, FORASMUCH AS THE HOLY	554 07
BLESS THIS OUR BROTHER ELECTED, AND TO SEND THY GRACE	561 02

BROTHER'S

THAT IS IN THY BROTHER'S EYE, BUT PERCEIVEST NOT THE	195 06
THAT IS IN THY BROTHER'S EYE	195 12

BROTHERHOOD

LOVE THE BROTHERHOOD	173 25

BROTHERLY

OF GOD, AND IN BROTHERLY CHARITY ONE TOWARDS ANOTHER	048 04

BROTHERLY   CONTINUED

ANOTHER WITH BROTHERLY LOVE	111 24
WITH BROTHERLY LOVE	598 29

BROUGHT

WHO HAST SAFELY BROUGHT US TO THE BEGINNING OF THIS	017 14
THE MULTITUDES BROUGHT HITHER OUT OF MANY KINDREDS	036 16
AND MAY BE BROUGHT TO NEWNESS OF LIFE	046 29
BE BROUGHT TO NOUGHT	058 21
WORK BEING BROUGHT TO A CONCLUSION, IT IS HOPED THE	VI 35
HERITAGE BE BROUGHT TO CONFUSION	063 04
WE HAVE BEEN BROUGHT OUT OF DARKNESS AND ERROR INTO	078 31
AND BROUGHT THE ASS, AND THE COLT, AND PUT ON	091 23
AND SHE BROUGHT FORTH HER FIRSTBORN SON, AND WRAPPED	099 07
NOT TILL SHE HAD BROUGHT FORTH HER FIRSTBORN SON	105 14
SPRUNG UP, AND BROUGHT FORTH FRUIT, THEN APPEARED THE	116 21
HIM TO BE BROUGHT UNTO HIM	123 34
ITSELF IS BROUGHT TO DESOLATION	129 30
AND BROUGHT AGAIN THE THIRTY PIECES OF	135 03
MINE OWN ARM BROUGHT SALVATION UNTO ME	138 24
WHERE IS HE THAT BROUGHT THEM UP OUT OF THE SEA WITH	139 08
AND LED HIM, AND BROUGHT HIM INTO THE HIGH PRIEST'S	151 07
YE HAVE BROUGHT THIS MAN UNTO ME, AS ONE THAT	153 22
THAT SAYING, HE BROUGHT JESUS FORTH, AND SAT DOWN IN	159 22
WHEN THEY HAD BROUGHT THEIR SHIPS TO LAND, THEY	196 29
OWN BEAST, AND BROUGHT HIM TO AN INN, AND TOOK CARE	208 31
BEHOLD, THEY BROUGHT TO HIM A MAN SICK OF THE PALSY,	216 34
ONE WAS BROUGHT UNTO HIM, WHICH OWED HIM TEN	221 15
AND THEY BROUGHT UNTO HIM A PENNY	223 07
WHICH BROUGHT UP THE CHILDREN OF ISRAEL OUT	225 16
WHICH BROUGHT UP AND WHICH LED THE SEED OF	225 18
BY THE HAND, AND BROUGHT HIM INTO DAMASCUS	230 12
THEY BROUGHT HIM TO JERUSALEM, TO PRESENT HIM TO THE	232 24
WHEN THE PARENTS BROUGHT IN THE CHILD JESUS, TO DO	233 03
WE MAY BE BROUGHT UNTO THE GLORY OF HIS RESURRECTION	235 21
FOUND HIM, HE BROUGHT HIM UNTO ANTIOCH	241 11
AND SHE BROUGHT FORTH A SON	243 14
HEROD WOULD HAVE BROUGHT HIM FORTH, THE SAME NIGHT	245 09
THAT THEY BROUGHT FORTH THE SICK INTO THE STREETS,	249 27
HE HAD BEEN BROUGHT UP	261 11
THEY BROUGHT YOUNG CHILDREN TO CHRIST, THAT HE SHOULD	274 25
THOSE THAT BROUGHT THEM	274 27
YE HAVE BROUGHT THIS CHILD HERE TO BE	276 19
BE BROUGHT TO THE BISHOP TO BE CONFIRMED	277 15
BE AFTERWARD BROUGHT TO THE CHURCH, AT WHICH TIME	R 282 02
THEY SHALL BE BROUGHT TO THE BISHOP TO BE CONFIRMED	R 295 15
THEIR CHILDREN BROUGHT UP IN THY FAITH AND FEAR, TO	303 17
WE BROUGHT NOTHING INTO THIS WORLD, AND IT IS CERTAIN	324 13
MOUNTAINS WERE BROUGHT FORTH, OR EVER THE EARTH AND	325 15
THEN SHALL BE BROUGHT TO PASS THE SAYING THAT IS	330 09
OF PEACE, WHO BROUGHT AGAIN FROM THE DEAD OUR LORD	335 16
AND BROUGHT FORTH FALSEHOOD	350 22
THERE WERE THEY BROUGHT IN GREAT FEAR, EVEN WHERE NO	356 25
20 HE BROUGHT ME FORTH ALSO INTO A PLACE OF LIBERTY	361 04
HE BROUGHT ME FORTH, EVEN BECAUSE HE HAD A FAVOUR	361 05
8 THEY ARE BROUGHT DOWN AND FALLEN	364 31
THOU, LORD, HAST BROUGHT MY SOUL OUT OF HELL	374 28
TURNED BACK, AND BROUGHT TO CONFUSION, THAT IMAGINE	381 25
6 I AM BROUGHT INTO SO GREAT TROUBLE AND MISERY,	388 02
2 HE BROUGHT ME ALSO OUT OF THE HORRIBLE PIT,	390 11
AND BROUGHT THEM FORTH INTO THE HOUSE OF	393 07
FOR OUR SOUL IS BROUGHT LOW, EVEN UNTO THE DUST	396 10
14 SHE SHALL BE BROUGHT UNTO THE KING IN RAIMENT OF	397 14
AND SHALL BE BROUGHT UNTO THEE	397 16
SHALL THEY BE BROUGHT, *	397 17
HE HATH BROUGHT UPON THE EARTH	398 10
REWARD BE SOON BROUGHT TO SHAME, *	424 25
20 THOU HAST BROUGHT ME TO GREAT HONOUR, *	426 20
CONFOUNDED AND BROUGHT UNTO SHAME THAT SEEK TO DO ME	426 28
17 HE BROUGHT WATERS OUT OF THE STONY ROCK, *	435 33
HIS POWER HE BROUGHT IN THE SOUTHWEST-WIND	436 23
54 HE BROUGHT THEM OUT SAFELY, THAT THEY SHOULD NOT	438 16
55 AND BROUGHT THEM WITHIN THE BORDERS OF HIS	438 18
8 THOU HAST BROUGHT A VINE OUR OF EGYPT	441 18
THY GOD, WHO BROUGHT THEE OUT OF THE LAND OF EGYPT	442 33
MOUNTAINS WERE BROUGHT FORTH, OR EVER THE EARTH AND	453 20
23 HE BROUGHT DOWN MY STRENGTH IN MY JOURNEY,	465 26
30 THEIR LAND BROUGHT FORTH FROGS	471 32
36 HE BROUGHT THEM FORTH ALSO WITH SILVER AND GOLD	472 11
THEIR DESIRE HE BROUGHT QUAILS	472 17
42 AND HE BROUGHT FORTH HIS PEOPLE WITH JOY, *	472 23
AND WERE BROUGHT DOWN IN THEIR WICKEDNESS	475 23
12 HE ALSO BROUGHT DOWN THEIR HEART THROUGH	476 28
14 FOR HE BROUGHT THEM OUT OF DARKNESS, AND OUT OF	477 02
ARE MINISHED AND BROUGHT LOW *	478 24
11 AND BROUGHT OUT ISRAEL FROM AMONG THEM	512 04
FOR I AM BROUGHT VERY LOW	518 16
OF PEACE, WHO BROUGHT AGAIN FROM THE DEAD OUR LORD	573 10
THY GOD, WHO BROUGHT THEE OUT OF THE LAND OF EGYPT,	578 24
THEY SHALL BE BROUGHT TO THE BISHOP	R 583 03
CHILDREN TO BE BROUGHT UNTO HIM FOR THEIR	R 583 05
WHO HAST SAFELY BROUGHT US TO THE BEGINNING OF THIS	592 20

BROUGHTEST

10 THOU BROUGHTEST US INTO THE SNARE	418 02
AND THOU BROUGHTEST US OUT INTO A WEALTHY PLACE	418 05
AND BROUGHTEST ME FROM THE DEEP OF THE EARTH	426 19
16 THOU BROUGHTEST OUT FOUNTAINS AND WATERS OUT OF	431 06

BRUISE

9 THOU SHALT BRUISE THEM WITH A ROD OF IRON, *	346 15

PAGE LN

BRUISED

THEM THAT ARE BRUISED, TO PREACH THE ACCEPTABLE YEAR   261 20

BUCKLER

MY BUCKLER, THE HORN ALSO OF MY SALVATION, AND MY   359 27
THE SHIELD AND BUCKLER, *   381 20
AND TRUTH SHALL BE THY SHIELD AND BUCKLER   455 04

BUFFET

HIS FACE, AND TO BUFFET HIM, AND TO SAY UNTO HIM,   143 21

BUFFETED

WHEN YE BE BUFFETED FOR YOUR FAULTS, YE SHALL   172 07

BUILD

THREE DAYS I WILL BUILD ANOTHER MADE WITHOUT HANDS   143 08
THIS ROCK I WILL BUILD MY CHURCH   246 07
THE LORD DOTH BUILD UP JERUSALEM, *   264 21
THEM DOWN, AND NOT BUILD THEM UP   373 19
BUILD THOU THE WALLS OF JERUSALEM   404 13
SAVE SION, AND BUILD THE CITIES OF JUDAH, *   424 14
THE LORD SHALL BUILD UP SION, *   465 11
THAT THEY MAY BUILD THEM A CITY TO DWELL IN   478 19
EXCEPT THE LORD BUILD THE HOUSE, *   505 22
IS BUT LOST THAT BUILD IT   505 23
2 THE LORD DOTH BUILD UP JERUSALEM, *   522 30
WHICH IS ABLE TO BUILD YOU UP, AND TO GIVE YOU AN   551 04

BUILDED

WHOM YE ALSO ARE BUILDED TOGETHER FOR AN HABITATION   255 09

BUILDERS

STONE WHICH THE BUILDERS REFUSED, *   489 12

BUILDEST

THE TEMPLE, AND BUILDEST IT IN THREE DAYS, SAVE   137 07
THE TEMPLE, AND BUILDEST IT IN THREE DAYS, SAVE   146 19

BUILDING

THAT IS TO SAY, NOT OF THIS BUILDING   132 25
IN WHOM ALL THE BUILDING FITLY FRAMED TOGETHER   255 07

BUILT

WHO HAST BUILT THY CHURCH UPON THE FOUNDATION OF   254 27
AND ARE BUILT UPON THE FOUNDATION OF THE APOSTLES AND   255 05
LIVELY STONES, ARE BUILT UP A SPIRITUAL HOUSE,   259 31
WHO HAST BUILT THY CHURCH UPON THE FOUNDATION OF   290 19
7O AND THERE HE BUILT HIS TEMPLE ON HIGH, *   439 16
3 JERUSALEM IS BUILT AS A CITY *   503 12
WHO HAST BUILT THY CHURCH UPON THE FOUNDATION OF   574 03

BULL

THE DRAGON AND THE BULL, WITH THE LEADERS OF THE   421 15

BULLOCK

9 I WILL TAKE NO BULLOCK OUT OF THINE HOUSE, *   402 08
BETTER THAN A BULLOCK THAT HATH HORNS AND HOOFS   424 06

BULLOCKS

OFFER YOUNG BULLOCKS UPON THINE ALTAR   404 17
I WILL OFFER BULLOCKS AND GOATS   418 11

BULLS

IF THE BLOOD OF BULLS AND OF GOATS, AND THE ASHES OF   132 28
THAT THE BLOOD OF BULLS AND OF GOATS SHOULD TAKE AWAY   157 23
FAT BULLS OF BASHAN CLOSE ME IN ON EVERY SIDE   366 27

BULLS'

THAT I WILL EAT BULLS' FLESH, *   402 16

BULWARKS

MARK WELL HER BULWARKS, CONSIDER HER PALACES,   400 02

BUNDLES

AND BIND THEM IN BUNDLES TO BURN THEM   116 31

BURDEN

WEARIED WITH THE BURDEN OF OUR SINS   062 18
THE BURDEN OF THEM IS INTOLERABLE   075 25
HAVE BORNE THE BURDEN AND HEAT OF THE DAY   120 06
IS EASY, AND MY BURDEN IS LIGHT   235 14
FROM THE BURDEN OF THE FLESH, ARE IN JOY AND   334 22
ARE LIKE A SORE BURDEN, TOO HEAVY FOR ME TO BEAR   387 29
23 O CAST THY BURDEN UPON THE LORD, AND HE SHALL   408 04
SHOULDER FROM THE BURDEN, *   442 23

PAGE LN

BURDENSOME

DIFFICULT OR BURDENSOME, AND COMFORT THEM CONCERNING   599 27

BURIAL

BY THY PRECIOUS DEATH AND BURIAL   055 11
AND PASSION, BY THY PRECIOUS DEATH AND BURIAL   318 05

BURIED

WAS CRUCIFIED, DEAD, AND BURIED   015 24
HE SUFFERED AND WAS BURIED   016 09
WAS CRUCIFIED, DEAD, AND BURIED   029 29
HE SUFFERED AND WAS BURIED   030 14
HE SUFFERED AND WAS BURIED   071 12
WE MAY BE BURIED WITH HIM   161 16
WHO DIED, AND WAS BURIED, AND ROSE AGAIN FOR US,   161 18
THE RICH MAN ALSO DIED, AND WAS BURIED   190 11
THEREFORE WE ARE BURIED WITH HIM BY BAPTISM INTO   197 12
AND THAT HE WAS BURIED, AND THAT HE ROSE AGAIN THE   205 05
AND BEING BURIED WITH CHRIST IN HIS DEATH, MAY ALSO   281 02
WAS CRUCIFIED, DEAD, AND BURIED   284 18
WAS CRUCIFIED, DEAD, AND BURIED   578 02
AND BURIED, TO RECONCILE HIS FATHER TO US, AND   603 15
AS CHRIST DIED FOR US, AND WAS BURIED   603 18

BURN

THEM IN BUNDLES TO BURN THEM   116 31
IS OFFENDED, AND I BURN NOT   121 13
DID NOT OUR HEART BURN WITHIN US, WHILE HE TALKED   168 09
THE SUN SHALL NOT BURN THEE BY DAY, *   327 29
THE SUN SHALL NOT BURN THEE BY DAY, *   339 13
SHALL THY JEALOUSY BURN LIKE FIRE FOR EVER   440 10
AND SHALL THY WRATH BURN LIKE FIRE   452 33
AND BURN UP HIS ENEMIES ON EVERY SIDE   461 02
THE SUN SHALL NOT BURN THEE BY DAY, *   503 02

BURNED

MY BODY TO BE BURNED, AND HAVE NOT CHARITY, IT   122 28
AND BURNED UP THEIR CITY   218 15
AND CAST THEM INTO THE FIRE, AND THEY ARE BURNED   238 17

BURNETH

IN SUNDER, AND BURNETH THE CHARIOTS IN THE FIRE   398 12
AS THE FIRE THAT BURNETH UP THE FOREST, *   444 32

BURNING

LAMPS OF FIRE BURNING BEFORE THE THRONE, WHICH ARE   187 13
RISEN WITH A BURNING HEAT, BUT IT WITHERETH THE   239 21
GREEN AND THE BURNING ALIKE   410 28
WITH HOT BURNING COALS   502 13
10 LET HOT BURNING COALS FALL UPON THEM   516 29
LOINS BE GIRDED ABOUT, AND YOUR LIGHTS BURNING   534 16

BURNT

THUS HAVE THEY BURNT UP ALL THE HOUSES OF GOD IN THE   430 22
16 IT IS BURNT WITH FIRE, AND CUT DOWN   442 02
AND MY BONES ARE BURNT UP AS IT WERE A FIREBRAND   464 16
THE FLAME BURNT UP THE UNGODLY   474 05

BURNT-OFFERING

9 BURNT-OFFERING AND SACRIFICE FOR SIN HAST THOU NOT   390 29

BURNT-OFFERINGS

BUT THOU DELIGHTEST NOT IN BURNT-OFFERINGS   061 12
IN BURNT-OFFERINGS AND SACRIFICES FOR SIN THOU HAST   157 26
AND BURNT-OFFERING AND OFFERING FOR SIN THOU   157 29
FOR THY BURNT-OFFERINGS, THEY ARE ALWAY BEFORE ME   402 07
BUT THOU DELIGHTEST NOT IN BURNT-OFFERINGS   404 10
WITH THE BURNT-OFFERINGS AND OBLATIONS   404 16
WITH BURNT-OFFERINGS, AND WILL PAY THEE MY VOWS, *   418 07

BURNT-SACRIFICE

AND ACCEPT THY BURNT-SACRIFICE   364 21

BURNT-SACRIFICES

FAT BURNT-SACRIFICES, WITH THE INCENSE OF RAMS   418 10

BURST

THY PRESSES SHALL BURST OUT WITH NEW WINE   005 23
HE BURST ASUNDER IN THE MIDST, AND ALL HIS   234 14

BURY

POTTER'S FIELD, TO BURY STRANGERS IN   135 12
THERE WAS NO MAN TO BURY THEM   440 05

BURYING

COME AFOREHAND TO ANOINT MY BODY TO THE BURYING   140 15

BUSINESS

I AM OTHERWISE HINDERED WITH WORLDLY BUSINESS   088 28
YE NOT THAT I MUST BE ABOUT MY FATHER'S BUSINESS   111 03

BUSINESS   CONTINUED

NOT SLOTHFUL IN BUSINESS	111 25
OCCUPY THEIR BUSINESS IN GREAT WATERS	477 23
WHOM WE MAY APPOINT OVER THIS BUSINESS	532 13

BUSY

THE FLATTERERS WERE BUSY MOCKERS, *	382 27
AND THE BUSY WORLD IS HUSHED, AND THE FEVER OF	594 31

BUTTER

BUTTER AND HONEY SHALL HE EAT, THAT HE MAY KNOW TO	236 02
WERE SOFTER THAN BUTTER, HAVING WAR IN HIS HEART	407 35

BUY

WHENCE SHALL WE BUY BREAD, THAT THESE MAY EAT	131 28
HIS GARMENT, AND BUY ONE	150 08
WHENCE SHALL WE BUY BREAD, THAT THESE MAY EAT	225 24

BY-WORD

US TO BE A BY-WORD AMONG THE NATIONS, *	395 22

CAESAR

OUT A DECREE FROM CAESAR AUGUSTUS, THAT ALL THE WORLD	098 29
GIVE TRIBUTE TO CAESAR, SAYING THAT HE HIMSELF IS	152 30
MAKETH HIMSELF A KING, SPEAKETH AGAINST CAESAR	159 22
WE HAVE NO KING BUT CAESAR	159 29
GIVE TRIBUTE UNTO CAESAR, OR NOT	223 04
THEREFORE UNTO CAESAR THE THINGS WHICH ARE CAESAR'S	223 10
WHICH CAME TO PASS IN THE DAYS OF CLAUDIUS CAESAR	241 19
WHICH CAME TO PASS IN THE DAYS OF CLAUDIUS CAESAR	246 28

CAESAR'S

THOU ART NOT CAESAR'S FRIEND	159 20
THEY SAY UNTO HIM, CAESAR'S	223 09
UNTO CAESAR THE THINGS WHICH ARE CAESAR'S	223 10

CAESAREA

THE COASTS OF CAESAREA PHILIPPI, HE ASKED HIS	245 31

CALAMITIES

SOUL FROM THE CALAMITIES WHICH THEY BRING ON ME,	382 30

CALENDAR

ACCORDING TO THE TABLE OR CALENDAR	R 009 31
ACCORDING TO THE TABLE OR CALENDAR	R 014 03
ACCORDING TO THE TABLE OR CALENDAR	R 026 05

CALF

THE SECOND LIKE A CALF, AND THE THIRD HAD A FACE AS A	187 18
HITHER THE FATTED CALF, AND KILL IT	202 23
KILLED THE FATTED CALF, BECAUSE HE HATH RECEIVED HIM	202 30
THOU HAST KILLED FOR HIM THE FATTED CALF	203 04
6 HE MAKETH THEM ALSO TO SKIP LIKE A CALF	374 09
19 THEY MADE A CALF IN HOREB, *	474 06
THE SIMILITUDE OF A CALF THAT EATETH HAY	474 09

CALL

ALL WHO PROFESS AND CALL THEMSELVES CHRISTIANS MAY BE	018 32
GENERATIONS SHALL CALL ME BLESSED	026 14
HEAR US WHEN WE CALL UPON THEE	031 15
ALL WHO PROFESS AND CALL THEMSELVES CHRISTIANS MAY BE	032 32
HEARKEN TO US WHO CALL UPON THEE, AND GRANT US THY	041 21
HOW THEN SHALL THEY CALL ON HIM IN WHOM THEY HAVE NOT	073 06
THE NAME OF GOD, I CALL YOU IN CHRIST'S BEHALF, I	089 07
AND THOU SHALT CALL HIS NAME JESUS	105 07
AND THEY SHALL CALL HIS NAME EMMANUEL, WHICH	105 11
OF THY PEOPLE WHO CALL UPON THEE	109 30
UNTO THY STEWARD, CALL THE LABOURERS, AND GIVE THEM	119 30
SANCTIFY A FAST, CALL A SOLEMN ASSEMBLY	124 29
DO UNTO HIM WHOM YE CALL THE KING OF THE JEWS	145 24
AND THEY CALL TOGETHER THE WHOLE BAND	145 31
YE CALL ME MASTER AND LORD	156 14
DAVID IN SPIRIT CALL HIM LORD, SAYING, THE LORD SAID	215 19
IF DAVID THEN CALL HIM LORD, HOW IS HE HIS SON	215 21
HIS SERVANTS TO CALL THEM THAT WERE BIDDEN TO THE	218 05
RICH UNTO ALL THAT CALL UPON HIM	227 03
FOR WHOSOEVER SHALL CALL UPON THE NAME OF THE LORD	227 04
HOW THEN SHALL THEY CALL ON HIM IN WHOM THEY HAVE NOT	227 05
TO BIND ALL THAT CALL ON THY NAME	230 25
A SON, AND SHALL CALL HIS NAME IMMANUEL	235 32
A SON, AND SHALT CALL HIS NAME JESUS	236 15
HENCEFORTH I CALL YOU NOT SERVANTS	241 29
BLESSED SON DIDST CALL MATTHEW FROM THE RECEIPT OF	250 20
I AM NOT COME TO CALL THE RIGHTEOUS, BUT SINNERS TO	251 23
YOUNG RAVENS THAT CALL UPON HIM	264 31
I BESEECH YOU TO CALL UPON GOD THE FATHER, THROUGH	273 32
WE CALL UPON THEE FOR THIS CHILD (THIS THY SERVANT),	274 12
HAST VOUCHSAFED TO CALL US TO THE KNOWLEDGE OF THY	276 09
TRUST IN THEE, TO CALL UPON HIM	288 20
SHALL PLEASE GOD TO CALL ME	289 11
AT ALL TIMES TO CALL FOR BY DILIGENT PRAYER	289 16
THEREFORE WILL I CALL UPON HIM AS LONG AS I LIVE	305 21
OF SALVATION, AND CALL UPON THE NAME OF THE LORD	305 29
I DID CALL UPON THE LORD WITH MY VOICE	309 11

CALL   CONTINUED

I DID CALL UPON THE LORD WITH MY VOICE, AND HE HEARD	309 20
I CALL TO REMEMBRANCE MY SONG, AND IN THE NIGHT I	311 10
OUR PRAYERS, AS WE CALL UPON THEE ON BEHALF OF THIS	311 22
ALMIGHTY GOD TO CALL THEM, THE MINISTERS SHALL	R 321 05
4 I DID CALL UPON THE LORD WITH MY VOICE, *	346 31
HEAR ME WHEN I CALL, O GOD OF MY RIGHTEOUSNESS	347 10
WHEN I CALL UPON THE LORD HE WILL HEAR ME	347 17
IT WERE BREAD, AND CALL NOT UPON THE LORD	356 24
3 I WILL CALL UPON THE LORD, WHICH IS WORTHY TO BE	359 29
WHEN WE CALL UPON THEE	365 03
5 CALL TO REMEMBRANCE, O LORD, THY TENDER MERCIES,	369 28
AND CALL THE LANDS AFTER THEIR OWN NAMES	400 28
4 HE SHALL CALL THE HEAVEN FROM ABOVE, *	401 28
15 AND CALL UPON ME IN THE TIME OF TROUBLE	402 20
AS FOR ME, I WILL CALL UPON GOD, *	407 23
9 WHENSOEVER I CALL UPON THEE, THEN SHALL MINE	408 32
2 I WILL CALL UNTO THE MOST HIGH GOD, *	409 15
OF THE EARTH WILL I CALL UPON THEE, *	413 08
6 I CALL TO REMEMBRANCE MY SONG, *	433 27
AND CALL TO MIND THY WONDERS OF OLD TIME	434 04
AND WE SHALL CALL UPON THY NAME	442 08
FOR I WILL CALL DAILY UPON THEE	447 09
UNTO ALL THEM THAT CALL UPON THEE	447 14
MY TROUBLE I WILL CALL UPON THEE	447 17
27 HE SHALL CALL ME, THOU ART MY FATHER, *	451 27
15 HE SHALL CALL UPON ME, AND I WILL HEAR HIM	455 26
AMONG SUCH AS CALL UPON HIS NAME	462 28
INCLINE THINE EAR UNTO ME WHEN I CALL	464 13
UNTO THE LORD, AND CALL UPON HIS NAME	470 05
THEREFORE WILL I CALL UPON HIM AS LONG AS I LIVE	486 22
AND CALL UPON THE NAME OF THE LORD	487 11
AND WILL CALL UPON THE NAME OF THE LORD	487 20
I CALL WITH MY WHOLE HEART	499 31
146 YEA, EVEN UNTO THEE DO I CALL	500 02
I CALL UPON THEE	517 08
UNTO ALL THEM THAT CALL UPON HIM	521 28
ALL SUCH AS CALL UPON HIM FAITHFULLY	521 29
YOUNG RAVENS THAT CALL UPON HIM	523 14
HATH PLEASED GOD TO CALL YOU	541 12
HAST VOUCHSAFED TO CALL THESE THY SERVANTS HERE	545 22
HERE OR ELSEWHERE CALL UPON THY HOLY NAME, THAT WE	545 27
AND CALL UPON GOD BY PRAYER FOR THE TRUE	554 30
AND OPENLY TO CALL UPON AND ENCOURAGE OTHERS TO THE	555 05
WHOM THOU DOST CALL TO THE MINISTRY OF THY CHURCH	561 08
THAT ALL WHO SHALL CALL UPON THEE HERE MAY WORSHIP	567 07
TRUST IN HIM, TO CALL UPON HIM	579 31
SHALL PLEASE GOD TO CALL ME	580 15
AT ALL TIMES TO CALL FOR BY DILIGENT PRAYER	580 19
WHICH THEY CALL WORKS OF SUPEREROGATION, CANNOT BE	605 25
TO CALL AND SEND MINISTERS INTO THE	607 23

CALLED

MORE WORTHY TO BE CALLED THY SON	004 28
SHALT BE CALLED THE PROPHET OF THE HIGHEST	014 24
CREED COMMONLY CALLED THE NICENE	R 015 32
OR SAID THE HYMN CALLED MAGNIFICAT, AS FOLLOWETH	R 026 06
OR SAID THE HYMN CALLED NUNC DIMITTIS, AS FOLLOWETH	R 028 06
CREED COMMONLY CALLED THE NICENE	R 030 03
WHO ARE TO BE CALLED TO ANY OFFICE AND ADMINISTRATION	039 10
THEY SHALL BE CALLED UPON TO GIVE AT THE LAST GREAT	047 20
CREED COMMONLY CALLED THE NICENE, OR ELSE THE	R 070 29
BEING SO LOVINGLY CALLED AND BIDDEN BY GOD HIMSELF	088 16
YET THEY WHO ARE CALLED, WITHOUT ANY CAUSE, MOST	088 20
MY HOUSE SHALL BE CALLED THE HOUSE OF PRAYER	092 03
WHICH IS CALLED BETHLEHEM	099 03
OF EGYPT HAVE I CALLED MY SON	103 24
AND HE CALLED HIS NAME JESUS	105 15
HIS NAME WAS CALLED JESUS, WHICH WAS SO NAMED OF THE	106 21
THEY MIGHT BE CALLED TREES OF RIGHTEOUSNESS, THE	107 09
DWELT IN A CITY CALLED NAZARETH	107 21
HE SHALL BE CALLED A NAZARENE	107 23
HE HAD PRIVILY CALLED THE WISE MEN, ENQUIRED OF THEM	109 11
BOTH JESUS WAS CALLED, AND HIS DISCIPLES, TO THE	113 13
OF THE FEAST CALLED THE BRIDEGROOM, AND SAITH UNTO	113 26
WHICH ALSO YE ARE CALLED IN ONE BODY	116 10
THAT WE SHOULD BE CALLED THE SONS OF GOD	117 15
FOR MANY BE CALLED, BUT FEW CHOSEN	120 13
FOR GOD HATH NOT CALLED US UNTO UNCLEANNESS, BUT UNTO	128 02
THEY WHICH ARE CALLED MIGHT RECEIVE THE PROMISE OF	133 06
THAT FIELD WAS CALLED, THE FIELD OF BLOOD, UNTO THIS	135 13
NOTABLE PRISONER, CALLED BARABBAS	135 28
OR JESUS WHICH IS CALLED CHRIST	135 31
JESUS WHICH IS CALLED CHRIST	136 05
COME UNTO A PLACE CALLED GOLGOTHA, THAT IS TO SAY,	136 28
THEY WERE NOT CALLED BY THY NAME	139 30
AND PETER CALLED TO MIND THE WORD THAT JESUS SAID	143 35
INTO THE HALL, CALLED PRAETORIUM	145 30
WHICH IS CALLED THE PASSOVER	148 13
UPON THEM ARE CALLED BENEFACTORS	149 21
AND HE THAT WAS CALLED JUDAS, ONE OF THE TWELVE, WENT	150 27
WHEN HE HAD CALLED TOGETHER THE CHIEF PRIESTS AND THE	153 21
PLACE WHICH IS CALLED CALVARY, THERE THEY CRUCIFIED	154 23
A PLACE THAT IS CALLED THE PAVEMENT, BUT IN THE	159 24
INTO A PLACE CALLED THE PLACE OF A SKULL, WHICH IS	159 33
A SKULL, WHICH IS CALLED IN THE HEBREW GOLGOTHA	159 33
DAY TO A VILLAGE CALLED EMMAUS, WHICH WAS FROM	167 04
FOR EVEN HEREUNTO WERE YE CALLED	172 10
WHO HATH CALLED US UNTO HIS ETERNAL GLORY BY	193 09
YE ARE THEREUNTO CALLED, THAT YE SHOULD INHERIT A	195 23
TO EAT, JESUS CALLED HIS DISCIPLES UNTO HIM, AND	199 09
MORE WORTHY TO BE CALLED THY SON	202 15
MORE WORTHY TO BE CALLED THY SON	202 20
AND HE CALLED ONE OF THE SERVANTS, AND ASKED WHAT	202 28

CALLED   CONTINUED

AM NOT MEET TO BE CALLED AN APOSTLE, BECAUSE I   205 13
WENT INTO A CITY CALLED NAIN   212 28
WHEREWITH YE ARE CALLED, WITH ALL LOWLINESS AND   213 20
EVEN AS YE ARE CALLED IN ONE HOPE OF YOUR CALLING   213 23
FOR MANY ARE CALLED, BUT FEW ARE CHOSEN   218 29
AFTER THAT HE HAD CALLED HIM, SAID UNTO HIM, O THOU   221 33
HE SHALL BE CALLED, THE LORD OUR RIGHTEOUSNESS   225 13
THAT WE, BEING CALLED BY THY HOLY WORD, MAY FORTHWITH   226 21
SIMON CALLED PETER, AND ANDREW HIS BROTHER,   227 25
AND HE CALLED THEM   227 31
OF THE TWELVE, CALLED DIDYMUS, WAS NOT WITH THEM WHEN   228 25
STREET WHICH IS CALLED STRAIGHT, AND ENQUIRE IN THE   230 17
OF JUDAS FOR ONE CALLED SAUL, OF TARSUS   230 18
THEM WHICH CALLED ON THIS NAME IN JERUSALEM, AND CAME   231 06
THE WOMB SHALL BE CALLED HOLY TO THE LORD   232 27
AS THAT FIELD IS CALLED IN THEIR PROPER TONGUE,   234 16
JOSEPH CALLED BARSABAS, WHO WAS SURNAMED JUSTUS,   234 25
AND SHALL BE CALLED THE SON OF THE HIGHEST   236 16
OF THEE SHALL BE CALLED THE SON OF GOD   236 24
WITH HER, WHO WAS CALLED BARREN   236 27
DISCIPLES WERE CALLED CHRISTIANS FIRST IN ANTIOCH   241 14
BUT I HAVE CALLED YOU FRIENDS   241 30
AND THEY CALLED HIM ZACHARIAS, AFTER THE NAME OF HIS   243 18
BUT HE SHALL BE CALLED JOHN   243 20
KINDRED THAT IS CALLED BY THIS NAME   243 21
HOW HE WOULD HAVE HIM CALLED   243 23
SHALT BE CALLED THE PROPHET OF THE HIGHEST   244 02
BUT JESUS CALLED THEM UNTO HIM, AND SAID, YE KNCW   247 20
UPON THEM ARE CALLED BENEFACTORS   250 07
THAT OLD SERPENT, CALLED THE DEVIL, AND SATAN,   252 07
AND JESUS CALLED A LITTLE CHILD UNTO HIM, AND SET HIM   252 24
FOR THEY SHALL BE CALLED THE CHILDREN OF GCD   257 28
WHO HAST CALLED US TO FAITH IN THEE, AND HAST   258 11
MY HOUSE SHALL BE CALLED THE HOUSE OF PRAYER   260 07
THAT HE HATH CALLED ME TO THIS STATE OF SALVATICN,   284 02
THEN CALLED I UPON THE NAME OF THE LORD   305 22
WHEN I CALLED UPON THEE, THOU HEARDEST ME   312 02
THE DEEP HAVE I CALLED UNTO THEE, O LORD   328 03
THEM WHO ARE THE CALLED ACCORDING TO HIS PURPOSE   330 32
JESUS CALLED THEM UNTO HIM AND SAID, SUFFER THE   338 09
AND JESUS CALLED A LITTLE CHILD UNTO HIM, AND SET HIM   339 23
6 I HAVE CALLED UPON THEE, O GOD, FOR THOU SHALT HEAR   358 29
6 IN MY TROUBLE I CALLED UPON THE LORD, *   360 04
5 THEY CALLED UPON THEE, AND WERE HOLPEN   366 12
BUT WHEN HE CALLED UNTO HIM HE HEARD HIM   367 22
FOR I HAVE CALLED UPON THEE   376 30
AND CALLED THE WORLD, FROM THE RISING UP OF THE SUN   401 22
THEY HAVE NOT CALLED UPON GOD   405 24
15 I CALLED UNTO HIM WITH MY MOUTH, *   418 14
THAT HAVE NOT CALLED UPON THY NAME   440 13
I HAVE CALLED DAILY UPON THEE, I HAVE STRETCHED   449 14
THESE CALLED UPON THE LORD, AND HE HEARD THEM   462 28
16 MOREOVER, HE CALLED FOR A DEARTH UPON THE LAND,   471 04
THEN CALLED I UPON THE NAME OF THE LORD   486 25
5 I CALLED UPON THE LORD IN TROUBLE   488 08
59 I CALLED MINE OWN WAYS TO REMEMBRANCE, *   493 29
WAS IN TROUBLE, I CALLED UPON THE LORD, *   502 07
THE DEEP HAVE I CALLED UNTO THEE, O LORD   507 08
3 WHEN I CALLED UPON THEE, THOU HEARDEST ME   514 02
HE WERE FIRST CALLED, TRIED, EXAMINED, AND KNOWN TO   529 15
EXCEPT HE BE CALLED, TRIED, EXAMINED, AND ADMITTEC   529 21
THY SERVANTS NOW CALLED TO THE LIKE OFFICE AND   531 18
THEN THE TWELVE CALLED THE MULTITUDE OF THE DISCIPLES   532 08
YOU ARE TRULY CALLED, ACCORDING TO THE WILL OF CUR   532 31
WORTHY TO BE CALLED UNTO THE HIGHER MINISTRIES IN THY   535 09
THEY ARE LAWFULLY CALLED TO THEIR FUNCTION AND   536 25
THY SERVANTS NOW CALLED TO THE OFFICE OF PRIESTHCOD   537 23
THIS OFFICE IS, WHEREUNTO YE ARE CALLED   539 28
TO HOW WEIGHTY AN OFFICE AND CHARGE YE ARE CALLED   539 32
YOU ARE TRULY CALLED, ACCORDING TO THE WILL OF CUR   541 30
THY SERVANTS NOW CALLED TO THE OFFICE OF DEACON AND   547 34
THY SERVANTS NOW CALLED TO THE OFFICE OF PRIEST   548 02
TO EPHESUS, AND CALLED THE ELDERS OF THE CHURCH   550 04
HOLY GHOST HATH CALLED HIM   553 13
WHEREUNTO HE IS CALLED, TO THE EDIFYING OF THY   553 19
THY SERVANT, NOW CALLED TO THE WORK AND MINISTRY CF A   553 29
YOU ARE TRULY CALLED TO THIS MINISTRATION, ACCORDING   554 16
WHEREUNTO HE IS CALLED, TO THE EDIFYING OF THY   561 04
WHICH IS CALLED BY THY NAME   572 21
THAT HE HATH CALLED ME TO THIS STATE OF SALVATICN,   577 23
MISTRESS HAVING CALLED TOGETHER AS MANY OF THE FAMILY R   587 04
WHICH ARE CALLED MORAL   604 25
WHICH IS COMMONLY CALLED THE APOSTLES' CREED, OUGHT   604 25
OF THE FLESH, CALLED IN GREEK, PHRONEMA SARKOS,   604 36
OF GOD, BE CALLED ACCORDING TO GOD'S PURPOSE BY HIS   606 11
HE BE LAWFULLY CALLED, AND SENT TO EXECUTE THE SAME   607 21
BE CHOSEN AND CALLED TO THIS WORK BY MEN WHO HAVE   607 22
TO JUDGE LAWFULLY CALLED AND SENT, WHICH BE CHOSEN   607 22
FIVE COMMONLY CALLED SACRAMENTS, THAT IS TC SAY,   607 38

CALLEDST

7 THOU CALLEDST UPON ME IN TROUBLES, AND I DELIVERED   442 25

CALLETH

WHEN GOD CALLETH YOU, ARE YE NOT ASHAMED TO SAY YE   088 32
THIS MAN CALLETH FOR ELIAS   137 20
BEHOLD, HE CALLETH ELIAS   146 31
AND HE CALLETH HIS OWN SHEEP BY NAME, AND LEADETH   186 05
COMETH HOME, HE CALLETH TOGETHER HIS FRIENDS AND   193 22
FOUND IT, SHE CALLETH HER FRIENDS AND HER NEIGHBOURS   193 30
SPIRIT OF GOD CALLETH JESUS ACCURSED   203 20
9 ONE DEEP CALLETH ANOTHER, BECAUSE OF THE NOISE OF   393 18

CALLETH   CONTINUED

AND CALLETH THEM ALL BY THEIR NAMES   523 02
AND HE CALLETH HIS OWN SHEEP BY NAME, AND LEADETH   538 28

CALLING

MINDFUL OF THEIR CALLING TO SERVE THIS PEOPLE IN THY   018 13
ONE HOPE OF OUR CALLING, ONE LORD, ONE FAITH, CNE   037 31
STONED STEPHEN, CALLING UPON GOD, AND SAYING, LCRD   100 13
EVEN AS YE ARE CALLED IN ONE HOPE OF YOUR CALLING   213 24
OBEYED THE CALLING OF THY SON JESUS CHRIST, AND   226 20
UNTO THE CALLING OF THY SON JESUS CHRIST, AND   246 18
AND WITH THINE EARS CONSIDER MY CALLING   325 07
THE VOICE OF MY CALLING, MY KING AND MY GOD   347 32
AND WITH THINE EARS CONSIDER MY CALLING   390 03
AND HE INCLINED UNTO ME, AND HEARD MY CALLING   390 10
INCLINE THINE EAR UNTO MY CALLING   448 31
TO FAITH, AND CALLING UPON GOD   604 44
THEY THROUGH GRACE OBEY THE CALLING   606 12

CALLINGS

IN OUR SEVERAL CALLINGS, FROM THE SERVICE OF MAMMON,   044 20
THEIR SEVERAL CALLINGS TO THE GLORY OF GOD, AND THE   047 18
ALL THINGS, AND DILIGENT IN OUR SEVERAL CALLINGS   588 29

CALVARY

WHICH IS CALLED CALVARY, THERE THEY CRUCIFIED HIM,   154 23

CALVES

OF GOATS AND CALVES, BUT BY HIS OWN BLOOD HE ENTERED   132 26
TOOK THE BLOOD OF CALVES AND OF GOATS, WITH WATER,   147 20

CAME

FOR OUR SALVATION CAME DOWN FROM HEAVEN, AND WAS   016 06
FOR OUR SALVATION CAME DOWN FROM HEAVEN, AND WAS   030 11
WHOSE BLESSED SON CAME NOT TO BE MINISTERED UNTO, BUT   043 28
THE SAKE OF HIM WHO CAME AMONG US AS ONE THAT   044 24
FOR OUR SALVATION CAME DOWN FROM HEAVEN, AND WAS   071 09
THAT CHRIST JESUS CAME INTO THE WORLD TO SAVE   076 19
THE HOLY GHOST CAME DOWN AS AT THIS TIME FROM HEAVEN,   078 26
SON JESUS CHRIST CAME TO VISIT US IN GREAT HUMILITY   090 14
THE SAME CAME FOR A WITNESS, TO BEAR WITNESS OF THE   097 27
HE CAME UNTO HIS OWN, AND HIS OWN RECEIVED HIM NCT   097 32
AND IT CAME TO PASS IN THOSE DAYS, THAT THERE WENT   098 28
ANGEL OF THE LORD CAME UPON THEM, AND THE GLCRY CF   099 12
BEFORE THEY CAME TOGETHER, SHE WAS FOUND WITH   104 29
AND IT CAME TO PASS, AS THE ANGELS WERE GONE AWAY   106 07
AND THEY CAME WITH HASTE, AND FOUND MARY, AND JCSEPH,   106 11
AND HIS MOTHER, AND CAME INTO THE LAND OF ISRAEL   107 17
AND HE CAME AND DWELT IN A CITY CALLED NAZARETH   107 21
BEHOLD, THERE CAME WISE MEN FROM THE EAST TO   108 31
TILL IT CAME AND STOOD OVER WHERE THE YOUNG   109 17
AND IT CAME TO PASS, THAT AFTER THREE DAYS THEY FOUND   110 27
DOWN WITH THEM, AND CAME TO NAZARETH, AND WAS SUBJECT   111 04
THAT JESUS CAME FROM NAZARETH OF GALILEE, AND   112 18
AND IT CAME TO PASS IN THOSE DAYS, THAT JESUS CAME   112 18
AND THERE CAME A VOICE FROM HEAVEN, SAYING, THOU ART   112 22
BEHOLD, THERE CAME A LEPER, AND WORSHIPPED HIM,   114 30
THERE CAME UNTO HIM A CENTURION,   115 07
HIS ENEMY CAME AND SOWED TARES AMONG THE   116 20
OF THE HOUSEHOLDER CAME AND SAID UNTO HIM, SIR,   116 23
AND WHEN THEY CAME THAT WERE HIRED ABOUT THE ELEVENTH   119 31
BUT WHEN THE FIRST CAME, THEY SUPPOSED THAT THEY   119 33
AND IT CAME TO PASS, THAT AS HE WAS COME NIGH UNTO   123 26
WHEN THE TEMPTER CAME TO HIM, HE SAID, IF THOU BE THE   126 26
BEHOLD, ANGELS CAME AND MINISTERED UNTO HIM   127 11
A WOMAN OF CANAAN CAME OUT OF THE SAME COASTS, AND   128 08
AND HIS DISCIPLES CAME AND BESOUGHT HIM, SAYING,   128 12
THEN CAME SHE AND WORSHIPPED HIM, SAYING, LCRD, HELP   128 15
AND IT CAME TO PASS, WHEN THE DEVIL WAS GONE OUT,   129 25
MY HOUSE WHENCE I CAME OUT   130 12
AND IT CAME TO PASS, AS HE SPAKE THESE THINGS,   130 17
AND AS THEY CAME OUT, THEY FOUND A MAN OF CYRENE,   136 25
SLEPT AROSE, AND CAME OUT OF THE GRAVES AFTER HIS   137 29
SAT AT MEAT, THERE CAME A WOMAN HAVING AN ALABASTER   140 03
WENT FORTH, AND CAME INTO THE CITY, AND FOUND AS HE   140 32
AND THEY CAME TO A PLACE WHICH WAS NAMED GETHSEMANE   141 27
THEN CAME THE DAY OF UNLEAVENED BREAD, WHEN THE   148 21
AND HE CAME OUT, AND WENT, AS HE WAS WONT, TO THE   150 13
AND THE SCRIBES CAME TOGETHER, AND LED HIM INTO THEIR   151 29
ALL THE PEOPLE THAT CAME TOGETHER TO THAT SIGHT,   155 11
THEN CAME JESUS FORTH, WEARING THE CROWN OF THORNS,   159 03
THEN CAME THE SOLDIERS, AND BRAKE THE LEGS OF THE   160 34
BUT WHEN THEY CAME TO JESUS, AND SAW THAT HE WAS DEAD   161 02
AND FORTHWITH CAME THERE OUT BLOOD AND WATER   161 04
WAS COME, THERE CAME A RICH MAN OF ARIMATHAEA, NAMED   162 06
AND PHARISEES CAME TOGETHER UNTO PILATE, SAYING, SIR,   162 16
BY MAN CAME ALSO THE RESURRECTION OF THE DEAD   163 13
FOR SINCE BY MAN CAME DEATH, *   163 13
OTHER DISCIPLE, AND CAME TO THE SEPULCHRE   164 17
OUTRUN PETER, AND CAME FIRST TO THE SEPULCHRE   164 19
WHICH CAME FIRST TO THE SEPULCHRE, AND HE   164 25
OF THE WEEK, THEY CAME UNTO THE SEPULCHRE AT THE   165 02
AND IT CAME TO PASS, THAT, WHILE THEY COMMUNED   167 06
NOT HIS BODY, THEY CAME, SAYING, THAT THEY HAD ALSO   167 25
AND IT CAME TO PASS, AS HE SAT AT MEAT WITH THEM, HE   168 05
DAYS OF THEM WHICH CAME UP WITH HIM FROM GALILEE NO   169 04
THIS IS HE THAT CAME BY WATER AND BLOOD, EVEN JESUS   170 30
FEAR OF THE JEWS, CAME JESUS AND STOOD IN THE MIDST,   171 16
BELIEVED THAT I CAME OUT FROM GOD   176 29
I CAME FORTH FROM THE FATHER, AND AM COME INTO THE   176 30

CAME   CONTINUED

AND IT CAME TO PASS, WHILE HE BLESSED THEM, HE WAS   178 25
AND SUDDENLY THERE CAME A SOUND FROM HEAVEN AS CF A   180 19
THE MULTITUDE CAME TOGETHER, AND WERE CONFOUNDED,   180 27
AS MANY AS CAME WITH PETER, BECAUSE THAT CN THE   184 23
ALL THAT EVER CAME BEFORE ME ARE THIEVES AND ROBBERS   186 11
THE SAME CAME TO JESUS BY NIGHT, AND SAID UNTO HIM,   187 35
BUT HE THAT CAME DOWN FROM HEAVEN, EVEN THE   188 25
MOREOVER THE DOGS CAME AND LICKED HIS SORES   190 08
AND IT CAME TO PASS, THAT THE BEGGAR DIED, AND WAS   190 08
SO THAT SERVANT CAME, AND SHEWED HIS LORD THESE   192 12
IT CAME TO PASS, THAT, AS THE PEOPLE PRESSED UPCN HIM   196 06
AND THEY CAME, AND FILLED BOTH THE SHIPS, SO THAT   196 21
FOR DIVERS OF THEM CAME FROM FAR   199 14
AND WHEN HE CAME TO HIMSELF, HE SAID, HOW MANY HIRED   202 10
AND HE AROSE, AND CAME TO HIS FATHER   202 16
AND AS HE CAME AND DREW NIGH TO THE HOUSE, HE HEARD   202 27
THEREFORE CAME HIS FATHER OUT, AND INTREATED HIM   202 32
OF TYRE AND SIDON, CAME UNTO THE SEA OF GALILEE,   206 28
AND BY CHANCE THERE CAME DOWN A CERTAIN PRIEST THAT   208 24
WAS AT THE PLACE, CAME AND LOOKED ON HIM, AND PASSED   208 27
AS HE JOURNEYED, CAME WHERE HE WAS   208 28
AND IT CAME TO PASS, AS JESUS WENT TO JERUSALEM,   209 31
AND IT CAME TO PASS, THAT, AS THEY WENT, THEY WERE   210 06
AND IT CAME TO PASS THE DAY AFTER, THAT JESUS WENT   212 27
NOW WHEN HE CAME NIGH TO THE GATE OF THE CITY,   212 29
AND HE CAME AND TOUCHED THE BIER   213 03
AND THERE CAME A FEAR ON ALL   213 07
IT CAME TO PASS, AS JESUS WENT INTO THE HOUSE OF CNE   213 28
PASSED OVER, AND CAME INTO HIS OWN CITY   216 33
AND WHEN THE KING CAME IN TO SEE THE GUESTS, HE SAW   218 22
VERY SORRY, AND CAME AND TOLD UNTO THEIR LORD ALL   221 31
BEHOLD, THERE CAME A CERTAIN RULER, AND WORSHIPPED   224 13
BLOOD TWELVE YEARS, CAME BEHIND HIM, AND TOUCHED THE   224 18
AND WHEN JESUS CAME INTO THE RULER'S HOUSE, AND SAW   224 24
CALLED DIDYMUS, WAS NOT WITH THEM WHEN JESUS CAME   228 26
THEN CAME JESUS, THE DOORS BEING SHUT, AND STOOD IN   228 32
AS HE JOURNEYED, HE CAME NEAR DAMASCUS   229 30
IN JERUSALEM, AND CAME HITHER FOR THAT INTENT,   231 07
AND HE CAME BY THE SPIRIT INTO THE TEMPLE   233 02
AND THE ANGEL CAME IN UNTO HER, AND SAID, HAIL,   236 09
OF THESE THINGS CAME UNTO THE EARS OF THE CHURCH   241 03
WHO, WHEN HE CAME, AND HAD SEEN THE GRACE OF GOD,   241 06
AND IT CAME TO PASS, THAT A WHOLE YEAR THEY ASSEMBLED   241 12
AND IN THESE DAYS CAME PROPHETS FROM JERUSALEM UNTO   241 15
WHICH CAME TO PASS IN THE DAYS OF CLAUDIUS CAESAR   241 18
FULL TIME CAME THAT SHE SHOULD BE DELIVERED   243 13
THE EIGHTH DAY THEY CAME TO CIRCUMCISE THE CHILD   243 17
AND IT CAME TO PASS, THAT ON THE EIGHTH DAY THEY CAME   243 17
AND FEAR CAME ON ALL THAT DWELT ROUND ABOUT THEM   243 26
ANGEL OF THE LORD CAME UPON HIM, AND A LIGHT SHINED   245 12
SECOND WARD, THEY CAME UNTO THE IRON GATE THAT   245 22
WHEN JESUS CAME INTO THE COASTS OF CAESAREA PHILIPPI,   245 31
IN THESE DAYS CAME PROPHETS FROM JERUSALEM UNTO   246 24
WHICH CAME TO PASS IN THE DAYS OF CLAUDIUS CAESAR   246 27
THEN CAME TO HIM THE MOTHER OF ZEBEDEE'S CHILDREN   247 06
AS THE SON OF MAN CAME NOT TO BE MINISTERED UNTC,   247 26
WHEN THERE CAME SUCH A VOICE TO HIM FROM THE   248 17
THIS VOICE WHICH CAME FROM HEAVEN WE HEARD, WHEN WE   248 20
AND IT CAME TO PASS ABOUT AN EIGHT DAYS AFTER THESE   248 23
AND IT CAME TO PASS, AS THEY DEPARTED FROM HIM, PETER   248 32
THUS SPAKE, THERE CAME A CLOUD, AND OVERSHADOWED   249 05
AND THERE CAME A VOICE OUT OF THE CLOUD, SAYING, THIS   249 06
THERE CAME ALSO A MULTITUDE OUT OF THE CITIES RCUND   249 29
AND IT CAME TO PASS, AS JESUS SAT AT MEAT IN THE   251 15
AND SINNERS CAME AND SAT DOWN WITH HIM AND HIS   251 16
AT THE SAME TIME CAME THE DISCIPLES UNTO JESUS,   252 22
AND WHENCE CAME THEY   257 06
ARE THEY WHICH CAME OLT OF GREAT TRIBULATICN,   257 07
HIS DISCIPLES CAME UNTO HIM   257 19
IN PRISON, AND YE CAME UNTO ME   259 09
OR IN PRISON, AND CAME UNTO THEE   259 13
BLIND AND THE LAME CAME TO HIM IN THE TEMPLE   260 08
NEXT SABBATH DAY CAME ALMOST THE WHOLE CITY TOGETHER   260 26
JESUS CAME TO NAZARETH, WHERE HE HAD BEEN BROUGHT UP   261 11
FOR I CAME DOWN FROM HEAVEN, NCT TO DO MINE CWN WILL,   269 15
THE SAME CAME TO JESUS BY NIGHT, AND SAID UNTO HIM,   275 06
JESUS CAME AND SPAKE LNTO THEM, SAYING, ALL POWER IS   275 26
LIVING BREAD WHICH CAME DOWN FROM HEAVEN   322 26
FOR SINCE BY MAN CAME DEATH, BY MAN CAME ALSC THE   328 22
CAME DEATH, BY MAN CAME ALSO THE RESURRECTION OF THE   328 23
AT THE SAME TIME CAME THE DISCIPLES UNTO JESUS,   339 21
5 THE PAINS OF HELL CAME ABOUT ME   360 02
AND MY COMPLAINT CAME BEFORE HIM   360 07
HEAVENS ALSO, AND CAME DOWN, *   360 15
HE CAME FLYING UPON THE WINGS OF THE WIND   360 17
19 THEY CAME UPON ME IN THE DAY OF MY TROUBLE   361 02
AND MY FOES, CAME UPON ME TO EAT UP MY FLESH, *   371 28
THE VERY ABJECTS CAME TOGETHER AGAINST ME UNAWARES,   382 24
5 FEAR CAME THERE UPON THEM   399 20
THAT WHEN THEY CAME UP, *   435 09
IN JACOB, AND THERE CAME UP HEAVY DISPLEASURE AGAINST   436 12
HEAVY WRATH OF GOD CAME UPON THEM, AND SLEW THE   436 33
WHEN HE CAME OUT OF THE LAND OF EGYPT, AND HAD HEARD   442 21
17 THEY CAME ROUND ABOUT ME DAILY LIKE WATER,   449 31
19 UNTIL THE TIME CAME THAT HIS CAUSE WAS KNCWN   471 10
23 ISRAEL ALSO CAME INTO EGYPT, *   471 18
THE WORD, AND THERE CAME ALL MANNER OF FLIES, *   471 34
THE GRASSHOPPERS CAME, AND CATERPILLARS INNUMERABLE,   472 06
14 BUT LUST CAME UPON THEM IN THE WILDERNESS,   473 29
WHEN ISRAEL CAME OUT OF EGYPT, *   484 27
12 THEY CAME ABOUT ME LIKE BEES, AND ARE EXTINCT EVEN   488 23
ALL THAT EVER CAME BEFORE ME ARE THIEVES AND ROBBERS   539 04
FIRST DAY THAT I CAME INTO ASIA, AFTER WHAT MANNER I   550 07
FEAR OF THE JEWS, CAME JESUS, AND STOOD IN THE MIDST,   551 29

CAME   CONTINUED

JESUS CAME AND SPAKE UNTO THEM, SAYING, ALL POWER IS   552 09
BUT GRACE AND TRUTH CAME BY JESUS CHRIST   572 02
HE CAME TO BE THE LAMB WITHOUT SPOT, WHO, BY   605 33

CAMEL'S

WAS CLOTHED WITH CAMEL'S HAIR, AND WITH A GIRDLE OF A   112 12

CAMEST

BELIEVE THAT THOU CAMEST FORTH FROM GOD   177 03
FRIEND, HOW CAMEST THOU IN HITHER NOT HAVING A   218 24
THE WAY AS THOU CAMEST, HATH SENT ME, THAT THOU   230 32

CANA

WAS A MARRIAGE IN CANA OF GALILEE   113 11
DID JESUS IN CANA OF GALILEE, AND MANIFESTED FORTH   113 30
THAT HE WROUGHT IN CANA OF GALILEE, AND IS COMMENDED   300 15

CANAAN

A WOMAN OF CANAAN CAME OUT OF THE SAME COASTS, AND   128 08
GIVE THE LAND OF CANAAN, *   470 24
WHOM THEY OFFERED UNTO THE IDOLS OF CANAAN   475 13
AND ALL THE KINGDOMS OF CANAAN   510 25

CANDID

WITH A MEEK, CANDID, AND CHARITABLE FRAME OF MIND   VI 37

CANDLE

DOTH NOT LIGHT A CANDLE, AND SWEEP THE HOUSE, AND   193 29
29 THOU ALSO SHALT LIGHT MY CANDLE   361 24

CANON

THE AGE WHICH THE CANON IN THAT CASE PROVIDED MAY   529 25
AT THE TIMES APPOINTED IN THE CANON   R 535 25
AS PRESCRIBED BY CANON, AND BEING SATISFIED THAT THE   R 569 05

CANONICAL

THOSE CANONICAL BOOKS OF THE OLD AND NEW TESTAMENT,   603 33
AND ACCOUNT THEM CANONICAL   604 13

CANONICALLY

AND AS A CANONICALLY INSTITUTED PRIEST INTO THE   569 23

CANONS

LEARNED AS THE CANONS REQUIRE, MAY, AT THE TIMES   529 29
ACCORDING TO THE CANONS OF THIS CHURCH, TO THE   532 33
ACCORDING TO THE CANONS OF THE CHURCH, MAY HAVE THE   533 31
ACCORDING TO THE CANONS OF THIS CHURCH, TO THE ORDER   541 32
ACCORDING TO THE CANONS OF THE CHURCH, MAY HAVE THE   543 12
AND THE ANCIENT CANONS COMMAND, THAT WE SHOULD NCT BE   554 08
THE RUBRICS AND CANONS OF THE CHURCH, AND WITH SUCH   569 20
AND BOOKS OF CANONS OF THE GENERAL AND DIOCESAN   R 571 24

CANST

IF THOU WILT, THOU CANST MAKE ME CLEAN   114 32
WHO ALONE CANST ORDER THE UNRULY WILLS AND   174 18
SOUND THEREOF, BUT CANST NOT TELL WHENCE IT COMETH,   188 15
EITHER HOW CANST THOU SAY TO THY BROTHER, BROTHER,   195 07
SOUND THEREOF, BUT CANST NOT TELL WHENCE IT COMETH,   275 20
WHO ALONE CANST ORDER THE UNRULY WILLS AND   285 25
THAT THOU CANST DO MISCHIEF   404 20
IF THOU CANST SAY THE LORD'S PRAYER   580 20
OF LIFE, AND ALONE CANST KEEP ALIVE IN US THE HOLY   594 19

CANTATE

THE MAGNIFICAT, CANTATE DOMINO, BONUM EST CONFITERI,   R 025 17

CANTICLE

THEN SHALL BE SAID OR SUNG THE FOLLOWING CANTICLE   R 008 09
OR THIS CANTICLE   R 011 14
OR THIS CANTICLE   R 011 29

CANTICLES

WHICH OTHER CANTICLES ARE APPOINTED   R 008 10
THE FOLLOWING CANTICLES OF MORNING PRAYER HAS BEEN   R 010 05
BEING FOLLOWED BY ONE OF THE EVENING CANTICLES   R 026 09

CAPERNAUM

ENTERED INTO CAPERNAUM, THERE CAME UNTO HIM A   115 06
WHOSE SON WAS SICK AT CAPERNAUM   219 29

CAPPADOCIA

AND CAPPADOCIA, IN PONTUS, AND ASIA, PHRYGIA,   181 02

CAPTAINS

PRIESTS AND CAPTAINS, HOW HE MIGHT BETRAY HIM UNTC   148 17
AND CAPTAINS OF THE TEMPLE, AND THE ELDERS,   151 02
THE POOR MAY FALL INTO THE HANDS OF HIS CAPTAINS   353 29

CAPTIVE

HE LED CAPTIVITY CAPTIVE, AND GAVE GIFTS UNTO MEN 237 14
LED CAPTIVITY CAPTIVE, AND RECEIVED GIFTS FROM MEN 420 20
LED THEM AWAY CAPTIVE TO PITY THEM 475 29
THAT LED US AWAY CAPTIVE, REQUIRED OF US THEN A SCNG, 513 09
HE LED CAPTIVITY CAPTIVE, AND GAVE GIFTS UNTO MEN 537 34

CAPTIVES

FOR ALL PRISONERS AND CAPTIVES 048 06
TO SHOW THY PITY UPON ALL PRISONERS AND CAPTIVES 056 33
LIBERTY TO THE CAPTIVES, AND THE OPENING OF THE 107 03
TO THE CAPTIVES, AND RECOVERING OF SIGHT TC THE 261 19

CAPTIVITY

HE LED CAPTIVITY CAPTIVE, AND GAVE GIFTS UNTO 237 14
TURNETH THE CAPTIVITY OF HIS PEOPLE, THEN SHALL JACOB 356 31
LORD WOULD DELIVER HIS PEOPLE OUT OF CAPTIVITY 405 30
AND BRINGETH THE PRISONERS OUT OF CAPTIVITY 419 22
THOU HAST LED CAPTIVITY CAPTIVE, AND RECEIVED GIFTS 420 19
POWER INTO CAPTIVITY, * 438 34
AWAY THE CAPTIVITY OF JACOB 446 09
SUCH AS ARE IN CAPTIVITY, * 465 20
AGAIN THE CAPTIVITY OF SION, * 505 07
5 TURN OUR CAPTIVITY, O LORD, * 505 15
LEADING INTO CAPTIVITY, AND NO COMPLAINING IN OUR 520 22
HE LED CAPTIVITY CAPTIVE, AND GAVE GIFTS UNTO 537 34

CARCASE

WHERESOEVER THE CARCASE IS, THERE WILL THE EAGLES BE 118 12

CARE

OF NURSING CARE AND PROTECTION, HATH, IN THE PREFACE V 12
TO THY MERCIFUL CARE, THAT BEING GUIDED BY THY 018 08
THY HOLY CHURCH THE CARE AND NURTURE OF THY CHILDREN 042 31
AND THE PRINCIPAL CARE HEREIN WAS TO MAKE THEM VI 17
UPON ME DAILY, THE CARE OF ALL THE CHURCHES 121 11
CASTING ALL YOUR CARE UPON HIM 193 03
TO AN INN, AND TOOK CARE OF HIM 208 32
SAID UNTO HIM, TAKE CARE OF HIM 208 34
THAT SO DUE CARE MAY BE TAKEN FOR THEIR EXAMINATION, R 273 18
TO MINISTER TO THE PEOPLE COMMITTED TO HIS CARE 294 13
THY NEVER-FAILING CARE AND LOVE, AND BRING US ALL TO 342 06
CASTING EVERY CARE ON THEE, THEY MAY KNOW THE 342 11
YOUR LABOUR, YOUR CARE AND DILIGENCE, UNTIL YE HAVE 540 16
SEE WITH HOW GREAT CARE AND STUDY YE OUGHT TO APPLY 540 26
HOW SHALL HE TAKE CARE OF THE CHURCH OF GOD 549 26
A PATTERN TO THE FLOCK COMMITTED TO THY CARE 571 29
UNDER THY FATHERLY CARE AND PRCTECTION 589 04
FOR THY CONTINUAL CARE AND WATCHFUL PROVIDENCE OVER 591 17
AND TO CAST ALL OUR CARE ON THEE, WHO CAREST FOR US 596 05
US WITH THE JOY AND CARE OF CHILDREN 596 25
WHOSE FATHERLY CARE REACHETH TO THE UTTERMCST 596 30
THY NEVER-FAILING CARE AND LOVE, FOR THIS LIFE AND 597 10
TO THY CONTINUAL CARE THE HOMES IN WHICH THY PECPLE 598 21
CARE FOR ALL AGED PERSONS, AND ALL LITTLE CHILDREN, 600 05

CARED

AND NO MAN CARED FOR MY SOUL 518 12

CAREFUL

BE CAREFUL FOR NOTHING 095 15

CAREFULNESS

AND EAT THE BREAD OF CAREFULNESS 505 27

CARES

ARE CHOKED WITH CARES AND RICHES AND PLEASURES CF 122 06
ALL WORLDLY CARES AND STUDIES 541 08
AND DRAW ALL YOUR CARES AND STUDIES THIS WAY 541 14

CAREST

IN TRUTH, NEITHER CAREST THOU FOR ANY MAN 223 02
THOU GOD CAREST NOT FCR IT 354 02
CARE ON THEE, WHO CAREST FOR US 596 05

CARETH

AN HIRELING, AND CARETH NOT FOR THE SHEEP 172 26
FOR HE CARETH FOR YOU 193 03
SO PROUD, THAT HE CARETH NOT FOR GOD, * 353 11
BUT THE LORD CARETH FOR ME 391 25
THE LORD CARETH FOR THE RIGHTEOUS 522 19
9 THE LORD CARETH FOR THE STRANGERS 522 20
AN HIRELING, AND CARETH NOT FOR THE SHEEP 539 15

CARNAL

ALL WORLDLY AND CARNAL LUSTS, WE MAY IN ALL THINGS 105 23
ALL WORLDLY AND CARNAL AFFECTIONS, MAY BE EVERMORE 246 20
OR BY HIS OWN CARNAL WILL AND FRAILNESS 314 05
FOR CURIOUS AND CARNAL PERSONS, LACKING THE SPIRIT OF 606 22

CARNALLY

THEY DO CARNALLY AND VISIBLY PRESS WITH THEIR TEETH 609 04

CARPUS

AT TROAS WITH CARPUS, WHEN THOU COMEST, BRING WITH 254 05

CARRIED

IT SHALL NOT BE CARRIED OUT OF THE CHURCH R 084 31
BARE THEM, AND CARRIED THEM ALL THE DAYS OF OLD 139 04
BOUND JESUS, AND CARRIED HIM AWAY, AND DELIVERED HIM 145 05
FROM THEM, AND CARRIED UP INTO HEAVEN 178 26
AND WAS CARRIED BY THE ANGELS INTO ABRAHAM'S 190 09
WERE GENTILES, CARRIED AWAY UNTO THESE DUMB IDOLS, 203 18
WAS A DEAD MAN CARRIED OUT, THE ONLY SON OF HIS 212 30
LIKE CHILDREN CARRIED AWAY WITH EVERY BLAST CF VAIN 237 08
TO AND FRO, AND CARRIED ABOUT WITH EVERY WIND OF 237 26
THE HILLS BE CARRIED INTO THE MIDST OF THE SEA 327 06
THE HILLS BE CARRIED INTO THE MIDST OF THE SEA 397 28
AND CARRIED THEM IN THE WILDERNESS LIKE A FLOCK 438 15
26 THEY ARE CARRIED UP TO THE HEAVEN, AND DOWN AGAIN 477 28
OR TO BE CARRIED ABOUT, BUT THAT WE SHOULD DULY 608 03
CARRIED ABOUT, LIFTED UP, OR WORSHIPPED 608 48

CARRY

ALL DANGERS, AND CARRY US THROUGH ALL TEMPTATICNS 114 08
WITH HIS ARM, AND CARRY THEM IN HIS BOSOM, AND SHALL 243 09
CARRY NEITHER PURSE, NOR SCRIP, NOR SHOES 254 17
IS CERTAIN WE CAN CARRY NOTHING OUT 324 14
WITH HIS ARMS, AND CARRY THEM IN HIS BOSCM 338 13
17 FOR HE SHALL CARRY NOTHING AWAY WITH HIM WHEN HE 401 09

CARRYING

AND CARRYING BOWS, TURNED THEMSELVES BACK 435 18

CARVED

DOWN ALL THE CARVED WORK THEREOF * 430 16
THEY THAT WORSHIP CARVED IMAGES, AND THAT DELIGHT IN 461 10

CASE

IN WHICH CASE THE LORD'S PRAYER SHALL BE SAID WITH R 003 12
IN WHICH CASE THE LORD'S PRAYER SHALL BE SAID WITH R 021 09
MINISTER IN THAT CASE OUGHT TO ADMIT THE PENITENT R 085 16
IN CASE HE SHALL SEE THE PEOPLE NEGLIGENT TO R 088 10
OF YOU IN SUCH A CASE WOULD NOT BE MOVED 088 22
YE SHALL IN NO CASE ENTER INTO THE KINGDCM OF HEAVEN 197 30
THAT IN THE CASE OF AN ADULT, THE MINISTER R 281 25
THEY MAY, IN CASE OF SUDDEN VISITATION, HAVE R 321 09
THAT IN ANY OTHER CASE THE MINISTER MAY, AT HIS R 337 03
15 HAPPY ARE THE PEOPLE THAT ARE IN SUCH A CASE 520 24
THE CANON IN THAT CASE PROVIDED MAY REQUIRE 529 25
AND IN CASE OF ANY DIFFERENCE BETWEEN YOU AND YOUR 569 34
THE WARDENS (OR, IN CASE OF THEIR NECESSARY ABSENCE, R 570 07

CASES

IN CASES OF EXTREME SICKNESS, OR ANY IMMINENT R 281 27

CASSIA

THY GARMENTS SMELL OF MYRRH, ALOES, AND CASSIA 396 32

CAST

CAST ME NOT AWAY FROM THY PRESENCE, * 060 32
GRACE THAT WE MAY CAST AWAY THE WORKS OF DARKNESS, 090 11
LET US THEREFORE CAST OFF THE WORKS OF DARKNESS, 091 04
TEMPLE OF GOD, AND CAST OUT ALL THEM THAT SOLD AND 091 33
ONE ACCORD, AND CAST HIM OUT OF THE CITY, AND STCNED 100 11
WE BESEECH THEE TO CAST THY BRIGHT BEAMS OF LIGHT 101 05
KINGDOM SHALL BE CAST OUT INTO OUTER DARKNESS 115 21
BE THE SON OF GOD, CAST THYSELF DOWN 126 32
AND TO CAST IT TO DOGS 128 17
YE SAY THAT I CAST OUT DEVILS THROUGH BEELZEBUB 129 33
IF I BY BEELZEBUB CAST OUT DEVILS, BY WHCM DC YOUR 129 34
WHOM DO YOUR SONS CAST THEM OUT 130 02
THE FINGER OF GOD CAST OUT DEVILS, NO DOUBT THE 130 03
CAST OUT THE BONDWOMAN AND HER SON 131 15
THEY UP STONES TO CAST AT HIM 133 33
AND HE CAST DOWN THE PIECES OF SILVER IN THE TEMPLE, 135 07
MY VESTURE DID THEY CAST LOTS 136 33
CRUCIFIED WITH HIM, CAST THE SAME IN HIS TEETH 137 14
A LINEN CLOTH CAST ABOUT HIS NAKED BODY 142 29
ABOUT A STONE'S CAST, AND KNEELED DOWN, AND PRAYED, 150 17
AND FOR MURDER, WAS CAST INTO PRISON 153 32
AND MURDER WAS CAST INTO PRISON, WHOM THEY HAD 154 07
HIS RAIMENT, AND CAST LOTS 154 26
US NOT REND IT, BUT CAST LOTS FOR IT, WHOSE IT SHALL 160 13
MY VESTURE THEY DID CAST LOTS 160 16
EVER AND EVER, AND CAST THEIR CROWNS BEFORE THE 187 28
THOU HYPOCRITE, CAST OUT FIRST THE BEAM OUT OF THINE 195 10
AND THOU BE CAST INTO PRISON 198 15
IS HEWN DOWN, AND CAST INTO THE FIRE 200 22
THINE ENEMIES SHALL CAST A TRENCH ABOUT THEE, AND 204 10
AND BEGAN TO CAST OUT THEM THAT SOLD THEREIN, AND 204 16
AND TO-MORROW IS CAST INTO THE OVEN, SHALL HE NCT 211 25
TAKE HIM AWAY, AND CAST HIM INTO OUTER DARKNESS 218 27
BUT WENT AND CAST HIM INTO PRISON, TILL HE SHOULD PAY 221 29
CAST NOT AWAY THEREFORE YOUR CONFIDENCE, WHICH HATH 228 14
AT HIS SAYING, AND CAST IN HER MIND WHAT MANNER CF 236 12
NOT IN ME, HE IS CAST FORTH AS A BRANCH, AND IS 238 15
GATHER THEM, AND CAST THEM INTO THE FIRE, AND THEY 238 16
HE SAITH UNTO HIM, CAST THY GARMENT ABOUT THEE, AND 245 17
GREAT DRAGON WAS CAST OUT, THAT OLD SERPENT, CALLED 252 06

CAST CONTINUED

HE WAS CAST OUT INTO THE EARTH, AND HIS ANGELS WERE 252 08
AND HIS ANGELS WERE CAST OUT WITH HIM 252 09
OF OUR BRETHREN IS CAST DOWN, WHICH ACCUSED THEM 252 12
CUT THEM OFF, AND CAST THEM FROM THEE 253 04
OR TWO FEET TO BE CAST INTO EVERLASTING FIRE 253 06
PLUCK IT OUT, AND CAST IT FROM THEE 253 07
TWO EYES TO BE CAST INTO HELL-FIRE 253 09
TEMPLE OF GOD, AND CAST OUT ALL THEM THAT SOLD AND 260 03
AND TO-MORROW IS CAST INTO THE OVEN, SHALL HE NOT 266 23
I WILL IN NO WISE CAST OUT 269 15
THIS THY SERVANT, CAST DOWN AND FAINT OF HEART AMIDST 316 19
NOR CAST THY SERVANT AWAY IN DISPLEASURE 326 24
I WILL IN NO WISE CAST OUT 333 04
THE EARTH SHALL BE CAST UPON THE BODY BY SOME R 333 12
THE EARTH IS BEING CAST UPON THE BODY, THE MINISTER R 341 12
AND CAST AWAY THEIR CORDS FROM US 346 02
CAST THEM OUT IN THE MULTITUDE OF THEIR UNGODLINESS 348 23
I SHALL NEVER BE CAST DOWN, * 353 17
FOR IF I BE CAST DOWN, THEY THAT TROUBLE ME WILL 356 05
WATCHING TO CAST US DOWN TO THE GROUND 359 09
DISAPPOINT HIM, AND CAST HIM DOWN 359 12
HE CAST FORTH LIGHTNINGS, AND DESTROYED THEM 360 26
AND WILL NOT CAST OUT HIS COMMANDMENTS FROM ME 361 12
I WILL CAST THEM OUT AS THE CLAY IN THE STREETS 362 24
AND CAST LOTS UPON MY VESTURE 367 08
NOR CAST THY SERVANT AWAY IN DISPLEASURE 372 12
I AM CAST OUT OF THE SIGHT OF THINE EYES 377 11
HAND OF THE UNGODLY CAST ME DOWN 384 07
THEY ARE CAST DOWN, AND SHALL NOT BE ABLE TO STAND 384 22
TO CAST DOWN THE POOR AND NEEDY, AND TO SLAY SUCH AS 385 23
HE SHALL NOT BE CAST AWAY 386 10
THAT TROUBLE ME CAST ME IN THE TEETH 393 28
AND SUDDENLY CAST DOWN 399 19
AND HAST CAST MY WORDS BEHIND THEE 402 24
11 CAST ME NOT AWAY FROM THY PRESENCE, * 403 31
23 O CAST THY BURDEN UPON THE LORD, AND HE SHALL 408 04
DISPLEASURE SHALT CAST THEM DOWN 408 29
O GOD, THOU HAST CAST US OUT, AND SCATTERED US 412 12
OVER EDOM WILL I CAST OUT MY SHOE 412 27
10 HAST NOT THOU CAST US OUT, O GOD 412 31
WHO HATH NOT CAST OUT MY PRAYER, * 418 20
8 CAST ME NOT AWAY IN THE TIME OF AGE 425 23
50 HE CAST UPON THEM THE FURIOUSNESS OF HIS WRATH, 438 06
56 HE CAST OUT THE HEATHEN ALSO BEFORE THEM, * 438 21
THOU HAST CAST OUT THE HEATHEN, AND PLANTED IT 441 19
5 FOR THEY HAVE CAST THEIR HEADS TOGETHER WITH ONE 444 14
4 CAST OFF AMONG THE DEAD, LIKE UNTO THEM THAT ARE 449 04
AND CAST HIS CROWN TO THE GROUND 452 19
AND CAST HIS THRONE DOWN TO THE GROUND 452 28
TAKEN ME UP, AND CAST ME DOWN 464 30
27 TO CAST OUT THEIR SEED AMONG THE NATIONS, * 474 23
OVER EDOM WILL I CAST OUT MY SHOE 479 22
LET THEM BE CAST INTO THE FIRE, AND INTO THE PIT, 516 30
O CAST NOT OUT MY SOUL 517 29
6 CAST FORTH THY LIGHTNING, AND TEAR THEM 520 02
OF THE UNGODLY TO CAST THEM DOWN 574 15
OF THEE, AND TO CAST ALL OUR CARE ON THEE, WHO CAREST 596 05
THOSE WHO ARE CAST DOWN 599 09

CASTAWAY

PREACHED TO OTHERS, I MYSELF SHOULD BE A CASTAWAY 119 13

CASTEST

AND CASTEST THEM DOWN, AND DESTROYEST THEM 429 13

CASTETH

OF THEM SAID, HE CASTETH OUT DEVILS THROUGH BEELZEBUB 129 27
BUT PERFECT LOVE CASTETH OUT FEAR 189 28
NONE EFFECT, AND CASTETH OUT THE COUNSELS OF PRINCES 379 08
17 HE CASTETH FORTH HIS ICE LIKE MORSELS 523 29

CASTING

JESUS WAS CASTING OUT A DEVIL, AND IT WAS DUMB 129 24
HIS GARMENTS, CASTING LOTS 136 31
HIS GARMENTS, CASTING LOTS UPON THEM, WHAT EVERY MAN 146 11
CASTING ALL YOUR CARE UPON HIM 193 03
HIS BROTHER, CASTING A NET INTO THE SEA 227 25
WHO MOURN, THAT, CASTING EVERY CARE ON THEE, THEY MAY 342 11

CASTLE

4 FOR THOU ART MY STRONG ROCK, AND MY CASTLE 375 27
FOR THOU ART MY HOUSE OF DEFENCE, AND MY CASTLE 425 10
MY FORTRESS, MY CASTLE AND DELIVERER, MY DEFENDER IN 519 24

CATCH

THOU SHALT CATCH MEN 196 29
HATH LAID PRIVILY CATCH HIMSELF 382 05

CATCHETH

AND THE WOLF CATCHETH THEM, AND SCATTERETH THE SHEEP 172 25
AND THE WOLF CATCHETH THEM, AND SCATTERETH THE SHEEP 539 14

CATECHISM

AND TO INSTRUCT THE YOUTH IN THE CATECHISM 533 16
IN SOME PART OF THIS CATECHISM R 582 30
LEARNED THEIR CATECHISM, TO COME TO THE CHURCH AT THE R 582 32

CATECHISM CONTINUED

OF THIS SHORT CATECHISM, THEY SHALL BE BROUGHT TO THE R 583 03

CATERPILLAR

UNTO THE CATERPILLAR, * 437 33

CATERPILLARS

AND CATERPILLARS INNUMERABLE, * 472 07

CATHOLIC

THE HOLY CATHOLIC CHURCH 015 28
I BELIEVE ONE CATHOLIC AND APOSTOLIC CHURCH 016 19
THE HOLY CATHOLIC CHURCH 029 33
I BELIEVE ONE CATHOLIC AND APOSTOLIC CHURCH 030 24
FOR THY HOLY CATHOLIC CHURCH 037 16
CHRIST'S HOLY CATHOLIC CHURCH, THE BLESSED COMPANY OF 047 07
I BELIEVE ONE CATHOLIC AND APOSTOLIC CHURCH 071 21
THE HOLY CATHOLIC CHURCH 284 22
AS ONE, HOLY, CATHOLIC, AND APOSTOLIC 291 05
CATHOLIC, 291 11
OF THE CATHOLIC CHURCH 317 04
THE HOLY CATHOLIC CHURCH 578 06

CATTLE

ALL YE BEASTS AND CATTLE, BLESS YE THE LORD 013 16
THY CATTLE, AND THE STRANGER THAT IS 068 28
FODDER UNTO THE CATTLE, * 264 30
THY CATTLE, AND THE STRANGER THAT IS 286 28
AND SO ARE THE CATTLE UPON A THOUSAND HILLS 402 11
49 HE SMOTE THEIR CATTLE ALSO WITH HAILSTONES, 438 04
GRASS FOR THE CATTLE, * 468 21
NOT THEIR CATTLE TO DECREASE 478 23
FODDER UNTO THE CATTLE, * 523 13
10 BEASTS AND ALL CATTLE 524 23
THY CATTLE, AND THE STRANGER THAT IS 579 09

CAUGHT

REMAIN SHALL BE CAUGHT UP TOGETHER WITH THEM IN THE 269 08

CAUSE

WITHOUT ANY CAUSE, MOST UNTHANKFULLY REFUSE TO COME 088 21
FOR THIS CAUSE I WILL CONFESS TO THEE AMONG 092 26
FOR THIS CAUSE I PAUL, THE PRISONER OF JESUS CHRIST 108 06
FOR FOR THIS CAUSE PAY YE TRIBUTE ALSO 114 23
AND FOR THIS CAUSE HE IS THE MEDIATOR OF THE NEW 133 03
I HAVE FOUND NO CAUSE OF DEATH IN HIM 153 35
THEY FOUND NO CAUSE OF DEATH IN HIM, YET DESIRED THEY 168 30
BROTHER WITHOUT A CAUSE SHALL BE IN DANGER OF THE 198 04
FOR THIS CAUSE I BOW MY KNEES UNTO THE FATHER OF OUR 212 11
FOR THIS CAUSE WE ALSO, SINCE THE DAY WE HEARD IT, DO 223 32
THEY HATED ME WITHOUT A CAUSE 255 29
OF PEACE, AND WILL CAUSE THE EVIL BEASTS TO CEASE OUT 262 05
AND I WILL CAUSE THE SHOWER TO COME DOWN IN HIS 262 08
FOR THIS CAUSE SHALL A MAN LEAVE HIS FATHER AND 267 29
AND SAID, FOR THIS CAUSE SHALL A MAN LEAVE FATHER AND 268 07
EXCEPT FOR URGENT CAUSE, THEY SEEK NOT TO HAVE THEIR R 273 07
MAN CAN SHOW JUST CAUSE, WHY THEY MAY NOT LAWFULLY BE 300 20
SHALL CAUSE THE MAN WITH HIS RIGHT HAND TO R 301 25
IF ANY OF YOU KNOW CAUSE, OR JUST IMPEDIMENT, WHY R 304 23
AND DEFEND MY CAUSE AGAINST THE UNGODLY PEOPLE 310 05
HAVE THE LESS CAUSE TO BE DISQUIETED FOR LACK OF THE R 321 10
EVERY CAUSE OF SICKNESS BEING REMOVED, HE MAY 322 08
THE SAME IS HEREBY ALLOWED FOR WEIGHTY CAUSE R 336 32
THAT WITHOUT ANY CAUSE IS MINE ENEMY 349 31
4 FOR THOU HAST MAINTAINED MY RIGHT AND MY CAUSE 351 28
50 FOR THIS CAUSE WILL I GIVE THANKS UNTO THEE, 363 05
WITHOUT A CAUSE SHALL BE PUT TO CONFUSION 369 22
PLEAD THOU MY CAUSE, O LORD, WITH THEM THAT STRIVE 381 17
EVEN WITHOUT A CAUSE HAVE THEY MADE A PIT FOR MY 382 02
LAID THEIR NET TO DESTROY ME WITHOUT A CAUSE 382 02
WITH THEIR EYES, THAT HATE ME WITHOUT A CAUSE 382 36
AVENGE THOU MY CAUSE, MY GOD AND MY LORD 383 10
AND DEFEND MY CAUSE AGAINST THE UNGODLY PEOPLE 394 03
SHALL PERFORM THE CAUSE WHICH I HAVE IN HAND 409 16
AND DEFENDETH THE CAUSE OF THE WIDOWS 419 20
HATE ME WITHOUT A CAUSE ARE MORE THAN THE HAIRS OF MY 422 07
O LORD GOD OF HOSTS, BE ASHAMED FOR MY CAUSE 422 14
6 AND THIS IS THE CAUSE THAT THEY ARE SO HOLDEN WITH 428 20
O GOD, MAINTAIN THINE OWN CAUSE 431 22
8 THOU DIDST CAUSE THY JUDGMENT TO BE HEARD FROM 433 04
TIME CAME THAT HIS CAUSE WAS KNOWN 471 10
OF HATRED, AND FOUGHT AGAINST ME WITHOUT A CAUSE 480 08
AND CAUSE THOU ME TO MAKE MUCH OF THY LAW 491 25
154 AVENGE THOU MY CAUSE, AND DELIVER ME 500 19
PRINCES HAVE PERSECUTED ME WITHOUT A CAUSE 501 03
AND MAINTAIN THE CAUSE OF THE HELPLESS 517 03
FOR THIS SELF-SAME CAUSE, HOW YE OUGHT TO FORSAKE AND 541 07
AND SHALL CAUSE THEM TO BE READ R 552 25
YOU CAN SHOW JUST CAUSE WHY HE MAY NOT BE INSTITUTED, 570 17
IT AFFORD JUST CAUSE TO SUSPEND THE SERVICE R 576 22
SHALL CAUSE THEIR CHILDREN, SERVANTS, AND R 582 31
IN A CAUSE OF FAITH AND CHARITY, SO IT BE 611 09

CAUSED

THOU HAST CAUSED A NEW LIGHT TO SHINE IN OUR 077 30
WHO HAST CAUSED ALL HOLY SCRIPTURES TO BE 092 07
OF THE LORD CAUSED HIM TO REST 139 16
SAINT PAUL, HAST CAUSED THE LIGHT OF THE GOSPEL TO 229 18

CAUSED   CONTINUED

27 HE CAUSED THE EAST-WIND TO BLOW UNDER HEAVEN   436 22
CAUSED THEIR LAND TO BE DIVIDED AMONG THEM FOR AN   438 21
WHEREIN THOU HAST CAUSED ME TO PUT MY TRUST   493 09
FAITHFULNESS HAST CAUSED ME TO BE TROUBLED   495 05

CAUSES

FOR REASONABLE CAUSES IT SHALL OTHERWISE SEEM GOOD   R 535 21

CAVIL

SEEK OCCASION, OF CAVIL OR QUARREL AGAINST HER   V 38

CEASE

WE SHALL NOT CEASE TO MAKE OUR HUMBLE PETITIONS UNTO   089 21
WHETHER THERE BE TONGUES, THEY SHALL CEASE   123 05
HEARD IT, DO NOT CEASE TO PRAY FOR YOU, AND TO DESIRE 223 33
THE EVIL BEASTS TO CEASE OUT OF THE LAND   262 05
HE MAKETH WARS TO CEASE IN ALL THE WORLD   398 11
LET THINE ANGER CEASE FROM US   446 15
THE STORM TO CEASE, *   478 02
THE BISHOP SHALL CEASE FROM ORDERING THAT PERSON,   R 530 26
THE BISHOP SHALL CEASE FROM ORDERING THAT PERSON,   R 537 02
SEE THAT YE NEVER CEASE YOUR LABOUR, YOUR CARE AND   540 16

CEASED

THEY NOT HAVE CEASED TO BE OFFERED   157 19
UNTO HIM, AND CEASED NOT IN THE NIGHT SEASON   311 02
MOUTHS AT ME, AND CEASED NOT   382 25
UNTO HIM, AND CEASED NOT IN THE NIGHT SEASON   433 19
AND SO THE PLAGUE CEASED   474 30
OF THREE YEARS I CEASED NOT TO WARN EVERY ONE NIGHT   550 34

CEASING

WAS MADE WITHOUT CEASING OF THE CHURCH UNTO GOD FOR   245 08
EVERY GOOD MAN SING OF THY PRAISE WITHOUT CEASING   375 19

CEDAR

ABROAD LIKE A CEDAR IN LEBANON   456 25

CEDAR-TREES

5 THE VOICE OF THE LORD BREAKETH THE CEDAR-TREES   374 07
BOUGHS THEREOF WERE LIKE THE GOODLY CEDAR-TREES   441 23

CEDARS

LORD BREAKETH THE CEDARS OF LEBANON   374 08
EVEN THE CEDARS OF LEBANON WHICH HE HATH PLANTED   468 27
FRUITFUL TREES AND ALL CEDARS   524 22

CELEBRATE

DO CELEBRATE AND MAKE HERE BEFORE THY   080 39
TO CELEBRATE THE LORD'S SUPPER   088 13
THAT WE WHO CELEBRATE WITH REVERENCE THE PASCHAL   168 20
TO CELEBRATE THE HOLY COMMUNION   294 14
SHALL THERE CELEBRATE THE HOLY COMMUNION, BEGINNING R 321 15

CELEBRATED

BE TWICE CELEBRATED ON CHRISTMAS DAY, THE FOLLOWING R 098 07
BE TWICE CELEBRATED ON EASTER DAY, THE FOLLOWING   R 164 30
BE TWICE CELEBRATED ON WHITSUNDAY, THE FOLLOWING   R 182 11

CELEBRATING

FOR CELEBRATING THY HOLY SACRAMENTS, FOR   565 08

CELEBRATION

TIME OF THE CELEBRATION OF THE COMMUNION, AFTER THE R 085 21
FOR THE CELEBRATION OF THE HOLY COMMUNION, (WHICH HE R 086 24

CELESTIAL

THERE ARE ALSO CELESTIAL BODIES, AND BODIES   329 14
GLORY OF THE CELESTIAL IS ONE, AND THE GLORY OF THE   329 15
LIGHTEN WITH CELESTIAL FIRE   543 32
LIGHTEN WITH CELESTIAL FIRE   556 07

CENTRE

OF MY WILL CENTRE IN WHAT THOU HAST COMMANDED   573 19

CENTURION

UNTO HIM A CENTURION, BESEECHING HIM, AND SAYING,   115 07
THE CENTURION ANSWERED AND SAID, LORD, I AM NOT   115 10
SAID UNTO THE CENTURION, GO THY WAY   115 23
NOW WHEN THE CENTURION, AND THEY THAT WERE WITH HIM,   137 31
AND WHEN THE CENTURION, WHICH STOOD OVER AGAINST HIM, 147 02
NOW WHEN THE CENTURION SAW WHAT WAS DONE, HE   155 15

CEPHAS

HE WAS SEEN OF CEPHAS, THEN OF THE TWELVE   205 07

CEREMONIES

THE RITES AND CEREMONIES APPOINTED TO BE USED   V 14
AS TOUCHING CEREMONIES AND RITES, DO NOT BIND   604 20
AND MANNER OF CEREMONIES, BUT ALSO IN MATTERS OF   606 44
RITES OR CEREMONIES, AND AUTHORITY IN CONTROVERSIES   607 03
AND CEREMONIES BE IN ALL PLACES ONE, OR UTTERLY LIKE   609 32
AND CEREMONIES OF THE CHURCH, WHICH BE NOT REPUGNANT   609 37
AND ABOLISH, CEREMONIES OR RITES OF THE CHURCH   610 02

CEREMONY

VISIBLE SIGN OR CEREMONY ORDAINED OF GOD   607 43

CERTAIN

UNTO JERICHO, A CERTAIN BLIND MAN SAT BY THE WAY-SIDE 123 27
THESE THINGS, A CERTAIN WOMAN OF THE COMPANY LIFTED   130 17
FOLLOWED HIM A CERTAIN YOUNG MAN, HAVING A LINEN   142 28
AND THERE AROSE CERTAIN, AND BARE FALSE WITNESS   143 05
BUT A CERTAIN MAID BEHELD HIM AS HE SAT BY THE FIRE,   151 10
WHO FOR A CERTAIN SEDITION MADE IN THE CITY, AND FOR   153 31
AND CERTAIN WOMEN ALSO OF OUR COMPANY MADE US   167 22
AND CERTAIN OF THEM WHICH WERE WITH US WENT TO THE   167 26
HIM TO TARRY CERTAIN DAYS   184 30
THERE WAS A CERTAIN RICH MAN, WHICH WAS CLOTHED IN   190 03
AND THERE WAS A CERTAIN BEGGAR NAMED LAZARUS, WHICH   190 05
A CERTAIN MAN MADE A GREAT SUPPER, AND BADE MANY   192 03
JESUS SAID, A CERTAIN MAN HAD TWO SONS   201 31
PARABLE UNTO CERTAIN WHICH TRUSTED IN THEMSELVES THAT 205 21
BEHOLD, A CERTAIN LAWYER STOOD UP, AND TEMPTED   208 11
A CERTAIN MAN WENT DOWN FROM JERUSALEM TO   208 21
CAME DOWN A CERTAIN PRIEST THAT WAY   208 24
BUT A CERTAIN SAMARITAN, AS HE JOURNEYED, CAME WHERE   208 28
ENTERED INTO A CERTAIN VILLAGE, THERE MET HIM TEN MEN 210 02
THERE WAS A CERTAIN MAN BEFORE HIM WHICH HAD THE   213 30
BEHOLD, CERTAIN OF THE SCRIBES SAID WITHIN   217 04
IS LIKE UNTO A CERTAIN KING, WHICH MADE A MARRIAGE   218 03
THERE WAS A CERTAIN NOBLEMAN, WHOSE SON WAS SICK AT   219 28
LIKENED UNTO A CERTAIN KING, WHICH WOULD TAKE ACCOUNT 221 13
THERE CAME A CERTAIN RULER, AND WORSHIPPED HIM,   224 13
AND THERE WAS A CERTAIN DISCIPLE AT DAMASCUS, NAMED   230 14
THEN WAS SAUL CERTAIN DAYS WITH THE DISCIPLES WHICH   231 02
HIS HANDS TO VEX CERTAIN OF THE CHURCH   244 32
HIS HANDS TO VEX CERTAIN OF THE CHURCH   247 02
AND DESIRING A CERTAIN THING OF HIM   247 07
CONFIDENCE OF A CERTAIN FAITH   317 05
AND IT IS CERTAIN WE CAN CARRY NOTHING OUT   324 13
IN SURE AND CERTAIN HOPE OF THE RESURRECTION UNTO   333 17
IN SURE AND CERTAIN HOPE OF THE RESURRECTION UNTO   337 11
IN SURE AND CERTAIN HOPE OF THE RESURRECTION TO   341 13
THE MOON FOR CERTAIN SEASONS, *   468 32
EXAMINE YOU IN CERTAIN ARTICLES, TO THE END THAT THE   554 13
PROVED BY MOST CERTAIN WARRANTS OF HOLY SCRIPTURE   604 27
RATHER THEY BE CERTAIN SURE WITNESSES, AND EFFECTUAL   607 32
AS CERTAIN ANABAPTISTS DO FALSELY BOAST   611 02

CERTAINLY

SAYING, CERTAINLY THIS WAS A RIGHTEOUS MAN   155 16

CERTIFIED

THAT I MAY BE CERTIFIED HOW LONG I HAVE TO LIVE   324 21
THAT I MAY BE CERTIFIED HOW LONG I HAVE TO LIVE   389 16

CERTIFIETH

AND ONE NIGHT CERTIFIETH ANOTHER   363 15

CERTIFY

OUR HANDS, TO CERTIFY THEM, BY THIS SIGN, OF THY   298 18

CHAFF

THEY ARE LIKE THE CHAFF, WHICH THE WIND SCATTERETH   345 17

CHAIN

AND BOUND WITH THE CHAIN OF OUR SINS, YET LET THE   063 11

CHAINS

SET FREE FROM THE CHAINS OF SIN, AND MAY BE BROUGHT   046 28
BETWEEN TWO SOLDIERS, BOUND WITH TWO CHAINS   245 11
AND HIS CHAINS FELL OFF FROM HIS HANDS   245 15
THEIR KINGS IN CHAINS, *   525 17

CHAIR

SITTING IN HIS CHAIR NEAR TO THE HOLY TABLE, THE   R 296 06
SITTING IN HIS CHAIR NEAR TO THE HOLY TABLE, SUCH AS R 530 08
SITTING IN HIS CHAIR NEAR TO THE HOLY TABLE, ALL   R 536 07
SITTING IN HIS CHAIR, NEAR THE HOLY TABLE   R 552 19
SITTING IN HIS CHAIR, SHALL SAY TO HIM THAT IS TO BE R 554 05
SITTING IN HIS CHAIR, SHALL HAVE THE INSTRUMENTS OF R 564 07
SITTING IN HIS CHAIR, THE SENTENCE OF CONSECRATION IS R 566 25

CHAMBER

GO FORTH OF HIS CHAMBER, AND THE BRIDE OUT OF HER   124 32
AND IN YOUR CHAMBER, AND BE STILL   347 20
OUT OF HIS CHAMBER, AND REJOICETH AS A GIANT TO RUN   363 22

CHAMBERING

NOT IN CHAMBERING AND WANTONNESS, NOT IN STRIFE AND   091 06

CHAMBERS

HE IS IN THE SECRET CHAMBERS   118 09
BEAMS OF HIS CHAMBERS IN THE WATERS, *   467 29
EVEN IN THEIR KINGS' CHAMBERS   471 33

CHANCE

AND BY CHANCE THERE CAME DOWN A CERTAIN PRIEST THAT   208 24
IT MAY CHANCE OF WHEAT, OR OF SOME OTHER   329 09

CHANCEL

THE OTHER CLERGY PRESENT, SHALL ENTER THE CHANCEL   R 570 04
STANDING IN THE CHANCEL OR CHOIR, EXCEPT THE BISHCP,   R 570 05

CHANCES

THE CHANGES AND CHANCES OF THE MORTAL LIFE, THEY MAY   049 14

CHANGE

AND BLESSED CHANGE OF WEATHER   051 25
WHO SHALL CHANGE THE BODY OF OUR HUMILIATICN THAT IT   222 23
SHALT THOU CHANGE THEM, AND THEY SHALL BE CHANGED   466 02
OR THE CHANGE OF THE SUBSTANCE OF BREAD AND WINE) IN   608 40
TO ORDAIN, CHANGE, AND ABOLISH, CEREMCNIES OR RITES   609 42

CHANGED

THY NAME, BEING CHANGED TO NOW ASSEMBLED (OR ABCUT TO   R 037 11
AND THEY SHALL BE CHANGED   097 17
WE SHALL ALL BE CHANGED, IN A MOMENT, IN THE   330 02
BE RAISED INCORRUPTIBLE, AND WE SHALL BE CHANGED   330 05
IN HIM SHALL BE CHANGED, AND MADE LIKE UNTC HIS CWN   333 21
IN HIM SHALL BE CHANGED, AND MADE LIKE UNTC HIS   337 15
SHALT THOU CHANGE THEM, AND THEY SHALL BE CHANGED   466 03
AND MAY BE CHANGED ACCORDING TO THE DIVERSITY OF   609 33

CHANGERS

AND THE CHANGERS OF MONEY SITTING   567 27

CHANGERS'

POURED OUT THE CHANGERS' MONEY, AND OVERTHREW THE   567 30

CHANGES

SUCH CHANGES AND ALTERATIONS SHOULD BE   V 18
AMONG ALL THE CHANGES AND CHANCES OF THE MCRTAL LIFE,   049 14
AND MANIFOLD CHANGES OF THE WORLD, OUR HEARTS MAY   174 22
AND MANIFOLD CHANGES CF THE WORLD, OUR HEARTS MAY   285 29

CHAPEL

OF THE CHURCH, OR CHAPEL, BY THE CHURCH-WARDENS AND   R 563 05
OF THE CHURCH, OR CHAPEL, TO THE HOLY TABLE,   R 563 08

CHAPTER

VERSE OF SUCH A CHAPTER) OF SUCH A BOOK   R 009 33
BEGINNETH SUCH A CHAPTER (OR VERSE OF SUCH A CHAPTER)   R 009 33
WRITTEN IN THE - CHAPTER OF -, BEGINNING AT THE -   R 070 19
WRITTEN IN THE - CHAPTER OF -, BEGINNING AT THE -   R 070 23
IN THE TENTH CHAPTER, AT THE THIRTEENTH VERSE   274 24
IN THE THIRD CHAPTER, AT THE FIRST VERSE   275 04
TWENTY-EIGHTH CHAPTER, AT THE EIGHTEENTH VERSE   275 24
IN THE EIGHTH CHAPTER OF THE ACTS OF THE APOSTLES   296 12
OF THE FIFTEENTH CHAPTER OF THE FIRST EPISTLE OF ST   R 328 18
THE EIGHTEENTH CHAPTER OF THE GOSPEL ACCORDING TO ST   R 339 19
IN THE TWENTIETH CHAPTER OF EXODUS, SAYING, I AM THE   578 23
TO BEGIN WITH A CHAPTER, OR PART OF A CHAPTER, FRCM   R 592 06
OR PART OF A CHAPTER, FROM THE NEW TESTAMENT   R 592 06

CHARGE

TO THEIR CHARGE, THE HEALTHFUL SPIRIT OF THY GRACE   018 21
TO THEIR CHARGE, THE HEALTHFUL SPIRIT OF THY GRACE   032 20
LORD, LAY NOT THIS SIN TO THEIR CHARGE   100 16
GIVE HIS ANGELS CHARGE CONCERNING THEE   126 34
I REQUIRE AND CHARGE YOU BOTH, AS YE WILL ANSWER AT   300 24
THEY LAID TO MY CHARGE THINGS THAT I KNEW NOT   382 11
GIVE HIS ANGELS CHARGE OVER THEE, *   455 17
MAY HAVE THE CHARGE AND GOVERNMENT OVER YOU   533 32
AN OFFICE AND CHARGE YE ARE CALLED   539 31
HOW GREAT A TREASURE IS COMMITTED TO YOUR CHARGE   540 06
COMMITTED TO YOUR CHARGE, UNTO THAT AGREEMENT IN THE   540 19
TO INSTRUCT THE PEOPLE COMMITTED TO YOUR CHARGE   542 06
TO YOUR CURE AND CHARGE WITH ALL DILIGENCE TO KEEP   542 16
THAT ARE OR SHALL BE COMMITTED TO YOUR CHARGE   543 07
MAY HAVE THE CHARGE AND GOVERNMENT OVER YOU   543 13
AND DIDST CHARGE THEM TO FEED THY FLOCK   549 09
TO INSTRUCT THE PEOPLE COMMITTED TO YOUR CHARGE   554 24
COMMITTED TO YOUR CHARGE, TO BRING ABOUT A   569 32
TO WHOM THE CHARGE OF THIS CONGREGATION IS NOW   572 09
COMMITTED TO MY CHARGE, GRANT THAT I MAY FAITHFULLY   573 21

CHARGED

AND HE CHARGED THEM THAT THEY SHOULD TELL NO MAN   207 05

CHARGED   CONTINUED

BUT THE MORE HE CHARGED THEM, SO MUCH THE MORE A   207 06
4 THOU HAST CHARGED *   490 06

CHARIOT

BOTH THE CHARIOT AND HORSE ARE FALLEN   432 33
THE CLOUDS HIS CHARIOT, AND WALKETH UPCN THE WINGS CF   467 30

CHARIOTS

THEIR TRUST IN CHARIOTS, AND SOME IN HORSES   364 29
AND BURNETH THE CHARIOTS IN THE FIRE   398 13
17 THE CHARIOTS OF GOD ARE TWENTY THOUSAND, EVEN   420 16

CHARITABLE

ANC CHARITABLE FRAME OF MIND   VI 37
RELIGIOUS AND CHARITABLE USES   R 320 23

CHARITY

OF FAITH ANC CHARITY, AND MAY WITH ONE MIND AND CNE   037 33
AND IN BROTHERLY CHARITY ONE TOWARDS ANOTHER   048 04
ARE IN LOVE AND CHARITY WITH YOUR NEIGHBOURS,   075 09
BE IN PERFECT CHARITY WITH ALL MEN   086 03
THINGS PUT ON CHARITY, WHICH IS THE BOND CF   116 08
DOINGS WITHOUT CHARITY ARE NOTHING WORTH   122 15
GIFT OF CHARITY, THE VERY BOND OF PEACE AND OF ALL   122 16
ANC HAVE NOT CHARITY, I AM BECOME AS SOUNDING BRASS,   122 22
AND HAVE NOT CHARITY, I AM NOTHING   122 26
AND HAVE NOT CHARITY, IT PROFITETH ME NOTHING   122 28
CHARITY ENVIETH NOT   122 29
CHARITY SUFFERETH LONG, AND IS KIND   122 29
CHARITY VAUNTETH NOT ITSELF, IS NOT PUFFED UP,   122 30
CHARITY NEVER FAILETH   123 03
HOPE, CHARITY, THESE THREE   123 14
BUT THE GREATEST OF THESE IS CHARITY   123 15
HAVE FERVENT CHARITY AMONG YOURSELVES   179 14
FOR CHARITY SHALL COVER THE MULTITUDE OF SINS   179 14
UNTO US THE INCREASE OF FAITH, HOPE, AND CHARITY   209 09
ANC TO BE IN CHARITY WITH ALL MEN   293 30
AND BE IN CHARITY WITH ALL THE WORLD   R 313 20
AND IN PERFECT CHARITY WITH THE WORLD   317 07
WITH FAITH, CHARITY, AND TRUE REPENTANCE   565 31
AND BE IN CHARITY WITH ALL MEN   582 26
REST IN PEACE, CHARITY, AND GOOD-WILL, WITH A   590 17
ENKINDLE FERVENT CHARITY AMONG US ALL, THAT WE BE   598 28
OF FAITH AND CHARITY, SO IT BE DONE ACCORDING TO THE   611 09

CHARM

CHARM HE NEVER SO WISELY   410 18

CHARMER

THE VOICE OF THE CHARMER, *   410 17

CHARTERS

OR CHARTERS OF THE CHURCH IN THE SAME   R 569 11

CHASTEN

REBUKES DOST CHASTEN MAN FOR SIN, THOU MAKEST HIS   325 02
NEITHER CHASTEN ME IN THY DISPLEASURE   348 34
MY REINS ALSO CHASTEN ME IN THE NIGHT SEASON   358 05
NEITHER CHASTEN ME IN THY HEAVY DISPLEASURE   387 22
REBUKES DOST CHASTEN MAN FOR SIN, THOU MAKEST HIS   389 31

CHASTENED

AS CHASTENED, AND NOT KILLED   126 19
10 I WEPT, AND CHASTENED MYSELF WITH FASTING, *   422 23
AND CHASTENED EVERY MORNING   429 04
THE LORD HATH CHASTENED AND CORRECTED ME   489 04

CHASTENEST

MAN WHOM THOU CHASTENEST, O LORD, *   458 10

CHASTENETH

LOVETH HE CHASTENETH, AND SCOURGETH EVERY SCN WHCM HE   321 30

CHASTENING

NOT THOU THE CHASTENING OF THE LORD, NCR FAINT WHEN   321 28

CHASTISE

WILL THEREFORE CHASTISE HIM, AND RELEASE HIM   153 27
WILL THEREFORE CHASTISE HIM, AND LET HIM GO   154 02
DOST LOVE, AND CHASTISE EVERY ONE WHOM THOU DOST   321 19

CHASTITY

MY BODY IN TEMPERANCE, SOBERNESS, AND CHASTITY   289 03
IN FAITH, IN CHASTITY, AND IN PURITY   559 11
MY BODY IN TEMPERANCE, SOBERNESS, AND CHASTITY   580 11

CHEEK-BONE

THOU SMITEST ALL MINE ENEMIES UPON THE CHEEK-BONE   347 05

CHEEKS

AND MY CHEEKS TO THEM THAT PLUCKED OFF THE   144 14

CHEER

BUT BE OF GOOD CHEER   177 10
BE OF GOOD CHEER   217 04
ANOINT AND CHEER OUR SOILED FACE WITH THE ABUNDANCE   544 06
ANOINT AND CHEER OUR SOILED FACE WITH THE ABUNDANCE   556 14
CHEER WITH HOPE ALL DISCOURAGED AND UNHAPPY PEOPLE,   599 10

CHEERFUL

GOD LOVETH A CHEERFUL GIVER   072 19
MAKE A CHEERFUL NOISE UNTO THE GOD OF JACOB   442 12
TO MAKE HIM A CHEERFUL COUNTENANCE, AND BREAD TO   468 25

CHEERFULLY

AND SOUL, MAY CHEERFULLY ACCOMPLISH THOSE THINGS   217 20

CHEERFULNESS

HE THAT SHEWETH MERCY, WITH CHEERFULNESS   111 21
AND CHEERFULNESS OF SPIRIT, HE MAY BE ABLE TO   315 30
WILL WITH CHEERFULNESS WHILE IT WAS DAY, WE MAY, WHEN   594 15
OF MIND AND CHEERFULNESS OF SPIRIT, AND GIVE THEM   598 15

CHERISH

TO LOVE AND TO CHERISH, TILL DEATH US DO PART,   301 31
TO LOVE AND TO CHERISH, TILL DEATH US DO PART,   302 07
AND CHERISH EACH OTHER, AND SO LIVE TOGETHER   303 24

CHERISHETH

AND CHERISHETH IT, EVEN AS THE LORD THE CHURCH   267 27

CHERUBIM

TO THEE CHERUBIM AND SERAPHIM CONTINUALLY DO CRY,   010 13
THE DEPTHS, AND DWELLEST BETWEEN THE CHERUBIM   011 23
RODE UPON THE CHERUBIM, AND DID FLY   360 17
THYSELF ALSO, THOU THAT SITTEST UPON THE CHERUBIM   441 05
BETWEEN THE CHERUBIM, BE THE EARTH NEVER SO UNQUIET   462 17

CHICKENS

GATHERETH HER CHICKENS UNDER HER WINGS, AND YE WOULD   100 30

CHIDING

AT THY CHIDING, O LORD, AT THE BLASTING OF THE BREATH   360 29
9 HE WILL NOT ALWAY BE CHIDING   466 23

CHIEF

GATHERED ALL THE CHIEF PRIESTS AND SCRIBES OF THE   109 04
BEELZEBUB THE CHIEF OF THE DEVILS   129 27
WAS COME, ALL THE CHIEF PRIESTS AND ELDERS OF THE   134 30
OF SILVER TO THE CHIEF PRIESTS AND ELDERS, SAYING, I   135 04
AND THE CHIEF PRIESTS TOOK THE SILVER PIECES, AND   135 09
WAS ACCUSED OF THE CHIEF PRIESTS AND ELDERS, HE   135 21
BUT THE CHIEF PRIESTS AND ELDERS PERSUADED THE   135 35
LIKEWISE ALSO THE CHIEF PRIESTS MOCKING HIM, WITH THE   137 09
AND THE CHIEF PRIESTS AND THE SCRIBES SOUGHT HOW THEY   139 33
WENT UNTO THE CHIEF PRIESTS, TO BETRAY HIM UNTO THEM   140 19
FROM THE CHIEF PRIESTS AND THE SCRIBES AND   142 16
ASSEMBLED ALL THE CHIEF PRIESTS AND THE ELDERS AND   142 33
AND THE CHIEF PRIESTS AND ALL THE COUNCIL SOUGHT FOR   143 02
IN THE MORNING THE CHIEF PRIESTS HELD A CONSULTATION   145 03
AND THE CHIEF PRIESTS ACCUSED HIM OF MANY THINGS   145 08
HE KNEW THAT THE CHIEF PRIESTS HAD DELIVERED HIM FOR   145 20
BUT THE CHIEF PRIESTS MOVED THE PEOPLE, THAT HE   145 21
LIKEWISE ALSO THE CHIEF PRIESTS MOCKING SAID AMONG   146 21
AND THE CHIEF PRIESTS AND SCRIBES SOUGHT HOW THEY   148 13
COMMUNED WITH THE CHIEF PRIESTS AND CAPTAINS,   148 17
AND HE THAT IS CHIEF, AS HE THAT DOTH SERVE   149 23
SAID UNTO THE CHIEF PRIESTS, AND CAPTAINS OF THE   150 35
THE PEOPLE AND THE CHIEF PRIESTS AND THE SCRIBES CAME   151 28
SAID PILATE TO THE CHIEF PRIESTS AND TO THE PEOPLE,   153 03
AND THE CHIEF PRIESTS AND SCRIBES STOOD AND   153 15
TOGETHER THE CHIEF PRIESTS AND THE RULERS AND THE   153 21
OF THEM AND OF THE CHIEF PRIESTS PREVAILED   154 04
WHEN THE CHIEF PRIESTS THEREFORE AND OFFICERS SAW   159 05
THE CHIEF PRIESTS ANSWERED, WE HAVE NO KING BUT   159 29
THEN SAID THE CHIEF PRIESTS OF THE JEWS TO PILATE,   160 06
THE CHIEF PRIESTS AND PHARISEES CAME   162 16
AND HOW THE CHIEF PRIESTS AND OUR RULERS DELIVERED   167 18
OF ONE OF THE CHIEF PHARISEES TO EAT BREAD ON THE   213 29
THEY CHOSE OUT THE CHIEF SEATS   214 10
AUTHORITY FROM THE CHIEF PRIESTS TO BIND ALL THAT   230 24
BOUND UNTO THE CHIEF PRIESTS   231 08
WHOSOEVER WILL BE CHIEF AMONG YOU, LET HIM BE YOUR   247 25
AND HE THAT IS CHIEF, AS HE THAT DOTH SERVE   250 09
HIMSELF BEING THE CHIEF CORNER-STONE   255 07
AND WHEN THE CHIEF PRIESTS AND SCRIBES SAW THE   260 09
BISHOP IS, TO BE A CHIEF PASTOR IN THE CHURCH   294 08
EVEN THE CHIEF OF ALL THEIR STRENGTH   472 10
JERUSALEM ABOVE MY CHIEF JOY   513 17
AND OTHER CHIEF MINISTERS, WHO, ACCORDING TO   533 31
AND OTHER CHIEF MINISTERS, WHO, ACCORDING TO   543 12
THAT WHEN THE CHIEF SHEPHERD SHALL APPEAR, YOU MAY   558 30
AND TO THE CHIEF BISHOP AND SOVEREIGN JUDGE OF   569 26
HIMSELF BEING THE CHIEF CORNER-STONE   574 05

CHIEF   CONTINUED

THE EVIL HAVE CHIEF AUTHORITY IN THE MINISTRATION OF   608 10

CHIEFEST

AS WELL IN THE CHIEFEST MATERIALS, AS IN THE FRAME   V 31

CHIEFLY

YET OUGHT WE CHIEFLY SO TO DO, WHEN WE ASSEMBLE AND   006 04
YET OUGHT WE CHIEFLY SO TO DO, WHEN WE ASSEMBLE AND   023 13
BUT CHIEFLY ARE WE BOUND TO PRAISE THEE FOR THE   078 07
ALMIGHTY POWER CHIEFLY IN SHOWING MERCY AND PITY   204 22
WHAT DO YOU CHIEFLY LEARN IN THESE ARTICLES OF YOUR   284 27
WHAT THEN DO YOU CHIEFLY LEARN FROM THE TEN   288 10
WHAT DOST THOU CHIEFLY LEARN IN THESE ARTICLES OF THY   578 09
WHAT DOST THOU CHIEFLY LEARN BY THESE COMMANDMENTS   579 23

CHILD

UNTO US A CHILD IS BORN   R 008 18
AND THOU, CHILD, SHALT BE CALLED THE PROPHET OF THE   014 24
OVER THE SICK CHILD FOR WHOM OUR PRAYERS ARE OFFERED,   045 25
SICKNESS THE CHILD IN WHOSE BEHALF WE BLESS AND   053 12
MARY HIS ESPOUSED WIFE, BEING GREAT WITH CHILD   099 05
AND TAKE THE YOUNG CHILD AND HIS MOTHER, AND FLEE   103 17
SEEK THE YOUNG CHILD TO DESTROY HIM   103 19
HE TOOK THE YOUNG CHILD AND HIS MOTHER BY NIGHT, AND   103 20
AS LONG AS HE IS A CHILD, DIFFERETH NOTHING FROM A   104 14
SHE WAS FOUND WITH CHILD OF THE HOLY GHOST   104 29
SHALL BE WITH CHILD, AND SHALL BRING FORTH A SON, AND   105 10
SAYING WHICH WAS TOLD THEM CONCERNING THIS CHILD   106 14
OF THE CHILD, HIS NAME WAS CALLED JESUS, WHICH WAS SO   106 20
AND TAKE THE YOUNG CHILD AND HIS MOTHER, AND GO INTO   107 14
AND TOOK THE YOUNG CHILD AND HIS MOTHER, AND CAME   107 16
GO AND SEARCH DILIGENTLY FOR THE YOUNG CHILD   109 13
WHERE THE YOUNG CHILD WAS   109 18
THEY SAW THE YOUNG CHILD WITH MARY HIS MOTHER, AND   109 20
THEY RETURNED, THE CHILD JESUS TARRIED BEHIND IN   110 22
I SPAKE AS A CHILD, I UNDERSTOOD AS A CHILD, I   123 09
WHEN I WAS A CHILD, I SPAKE AS A CHILD, I UNDERSTOOD   123 09
I UNDERSTOOD AS A CHILD, I THOUGHT AS A CHILD   123 10
I UNDERSTOOD AS A CHILD, I THOUGHT AS A CHILD   123 10
DELIVERED OF THE CHILD, SHE REMEMBERETH NO MORE THE   174 12
COME DOWN ERE MY CHILD DIE   220 02
BROUGHT IN THE CHILD JESUS, TO DO FOR HIM AFTER THE   233 03
BEHOLD, THIS CHILD IS SET FOR THE FALL AND RISING   233 12
AND THE CHILD GREW, AND WAXED STRONG IN SPIRIT,   233 26
THE EIGHTH DAY THEY CAME TO CIRCUMCISE THE CHILD   243 18
WHAT MANNER OF CHILD SHALL THIS BE   243 30
AND THOU, CHILD, SHALT BE CALLED THE PROPHET OF THE   244 10
AND THE CHILD GREW, AND WAXED STRONG IN SPIRIT,   244 17
CALLED A LITTLE CHILD UNTO HIM, AND SET HIM IN THE   252 24
AS THIS LITTLE CHILD, THE SAME IS GREATEST IN THE   252 28
ONE SUCH LITTLE CHILD IN MY NAME RECEIVETH ME   252 30
HATH THIS (PERSON) BEEN ALREADY BAPTIZED, OR   273 26
WILL GRANT TO THIS CHILD (THIS PERSON) THAT WHICH BY   274 03
UPON THEE FOR THIS CHILD (THIS THY SERVANT), THAT HE,   274 12
THAT THIS CHILD (THIS THY SERVANT) MAY ENJOY THE   274 18
OF GOD AS A LITTLE CHILD, HE SHALL NOT ENTER THEREIN   274 31
FATHER TOWARD THIS CHILD (THIS PERSON), DECLARED BY   276 04
SPIRIT TO THIS CHILD (THIS THY SERVANT), THAT HE MAY   276 12
HAVE BROUGHT THIS CHILD HERE TO BE BAPTIZED   276 19
THE NAME OF THIS CHILD, RENOUNCE THE DEVIL AND ALL   276 24
THE NAME OF THIS CHILD, MADE THESE PROMISES, WILT   277 08
HEED THAT THIS CHILD LEARN THE CREED, THE LORD'S   277 10
HEED THAT THIS CHILD, SO SOON AS SUFFICIENTLY   277 14
SO THIS CHILD (THIS THY SERVANT) MAY DIE TO   278 19
GRANT THAT THIS CHILD (THIS THY SERVANT), NOW TO BE   279 17
SHALL TAKE THE CHILD INTO HIS ARMS, AND SHALL SAY TO   R 279 23
THE GODFATHERS AND GODMOTHERS, NAME THIS CHILD   279 25
NAMING THE CHILD AFTER THEM, HE SHALL DIP HIM   R 279 26
WE RECEIVE THIS CHILD (PERSON) INTO THE CONGREGATION   280 03
THAT THIS CHILD (THIS PERSON) IS REGENERATE, AND   280 13
THAT THIS CHILD (THIS PERSON) MAY LEAD THE REST   280 17
TO REGENERATE THIS CHILD (THIS THY SERVANT) WITH THY   280 29
HIM FOR THINE OWN CHILD, AND TO INCORPORATE HIM INTO   280 31
THE CHILD (OR PERSON) BEING NAMED BY SOME ONE WHO   R 281 19
EXPEDIENT THAT A CHILD OR PERSON SO BAPTIZED BE   R 281 32
WE RECEIVE THIS CHILD (OR PERSON), ETC   R 282 06
OF CHRIST, THE CHILD OF GOD, AND AN INHERITOR OF THE   283 19
O LORD, THIS THY CHILD WITH THY HEAVENLY GRACE   297 26
THAT THE CHILD OF THIS THY SERVANT MAY DAILY   307 04
OR THIS THY CHILD)   336 06
CALLED A LITTLE CHILD UNTO HIM, AND SET HIM IN THE   339 23
AS THIS LITTLE CHILD, THE SAME IS GREATEST IN THE   339 27
ONE SUCH LITTLE CHILD IN MY NAME RECEIVETH ME   339 29
THAT THIS THY CHILD HATH BEEN TAKEN INTO THE SAFE   340 26
THE BODY OF THIS CHILD TO THE GROUND   341 15
THE SOUL OF THIS CHILD TO THY NEVER-FAILING CARE AND   342 05
IT LOW, LIKE AS A CHILD THAT IS WEANED FROM HIS   507 27
MY SOUL IS EVEN AS A WEANED CHILD   507 29
NOR IN ANY CHILD OF MAN   522 06
OF CHRIST, THE CHILD OF GOD, AND AN INHERITOR OF THE   577 10
MY GOOD CHILD, KNOW THIS   580 16
WATCH OVER THY CHILD, O LORD, AS HIS DAYS INCREASE   597 28

CHILD-BED

TO THE RELIEF OF DISTRESSED WOMEN IN CHILD-BED   R 307 09

CHILD-BIRTH

AND PERIL OF CHILD-BIRTH, THIS WOMAN, THY SERVANT,   051 07
ALL WOMEN IN CHILD-BIRTH, ALL SICK PERSONS, AND YOUNG   056 31

CHILD-BIRTH　　　CONTINUED

PRESERVE YOU IN THE GREAT DANGER OF CHILD-BIRTH　　305 13
AND PERIL OF CHILD-BIRTH, THIS WOMAN, THY SERVANT,　306 26

CHILD'S

SOUGHT THE YOUNG CHILD'S LIFE　　　　　　　　　107 16
A CROSS UPON THE CHILD'S (OR PERSON'S) FOREHEAD　R 280 11

CHILDISH

I PUT AWAY CHILDISH THINGS　　　　　　　　　　123 11

CHILDREN

O YE CHILDREN OF MEN, BLESS YE THE LORD　　　　013 18
HOLY CHURCH THE CARE AND NURTURE OF THY CHILDREN　043 02
DOST EMBRACE CHILDREN WITH THE ARMS OF THY MERCY, AND　043 07
OR GRIEVE THE CHILDREN OF MEN　　　　　　　　045 32
TO THE CHILDREN OF MEN　　　　　　　　　　　053 04
ALL SICK PERSONS, AND YOUNG CHILDREN　　　　　056 32
THE FATHERLESS CHILDREN, AND WIDOWS, AND ALL WHO ARE　057 02
UPON THE CHILDREN, UNTO THE THIRD AND FOURTH　068 13
MAKE US THE CHILDREN OF GOD, AND EXALT US TO　086 11
AND MADE THY CHILDREN BY ADOPTION AND GRACE, MAY　096 16
GATHERED THY CHILDREN TOGETHER, EVEN AS A HEN　100 29
SLEW ALL THE CHILDREN THAT WERE IN BETHLEHEM, AND IN　103 26
WEEPING FOR HER CHILDREN, AND WOULD NOT BE COMFORTED,　103 32
AND MADE THY CHILDREN BY ADOPTION AND GRACE, AND MADE　104 08
WHEN WE WERE CHILDREN, WERE IN BONDAGE UNDER THE　104 17
BUT THE CHILDREN OF THE KINGDOM SHALL BE CAST OUT　115 21
LITTLE CHILDREN, LET NO MAN DECEIVE YOU　　　117 26
GATHER THE CHILDREN, AND THOSE THAT SUCK THE BREASTS　124 31
YE THEREFORE FOLLOWERS OF GOD, AS DEAR CHILDREN　128 30
OF GOD UPON THE CHILDREN OF DISOBEDIENCE　　129 11
WALK AS CHILDREN OF LIGHT　　　　　　　　　129 13
WHICH NOW IS, AND IS IN BONDAGE WITH HER CHILDREN　131 07
HATH MANY MORE CHILDREN THAN SHE WHICH HATH AN　131 11
ARE THE CHILDREN OF PROMISE　　　　　　　　131 12
WE ARE NOT CHILDREN OF THE BONDWOMAN, BUT OF THE　131 18
THEY OF THE CHILDREN OF ISRAEL DID VALUE　　135 14
AND SAID, HIS BLOOD BE ON US, AND ON OUR CHILDREN　136 13
ARE MY PEOPLE, CHILDREN THAT WILL NOT LIE　138 33
BUT WEEP FOR YOURSELVES, AND FOR YOUR CHILDREN　154 15
SENT UNTO THE CHILDREN OF ISRAEL, PREACHING PEACE BY　166 15
AND BRETHREN, CHILDREN OF THE STOCK OF ABRAHAM,　168 24
UNTO US THEIR CHILDREN, IN THAT HE HATH RAISED UP　169 08
KNOW HOW TO GIVE GOOD GIFTS UNTO YOUR CHILDREN　183 18
MY LITTLE CHILDREN, LET US NOT LOVE IN WORD, NEITHER　191 21
LIBERTY OF THE CHILDREN OF GOD　　　　　　　194 18
AND IF CHILDREN, THEN HEIRS　　　　　　　　200 11
THAT WE ARE THE CHILDREN OF GOD　　　　　　200 11
AND THY CHILDREN WITHIN THEE　　　　　　　204 13
SO THAT THE CHILDREN OF ISRAEL COULD NOT STEDFASTLY　206 19
HIS WIFE, AND CHILDREN, AND ALL THAT HE HAD, AND　221 18
BROUGHT UP THE CHILDREN OF ISRAEL OUT OF THE LAND OF　225 16
AND THE CHILDREN OF ISRAEL　　　　　　　　230 27
OR WIFE, OR CHILDREN, OR LANDS, FOR MY NAME'S SAKE,　231 19
BEING NOT LIKE CHILDREN CARRIED AWAY WITH EVERY BLAST　237 07
BE NO MORE CHILDREN, TOSSED TO AND FRO, AND CARRIED　237 25
OF ZEBEDEE'S CHILDREN WITH HER SONS, WORSHIPPING HIM,　247 06
AS LITTLE CHILDREN, YE SHALL NOT ENTER INTO THE　252 26
TRIBES OF THE CHILDREN OF ISRAEL　　　　　256 22
BE CALLED THE CHILDREN OF GOD　　　　　　　257 28
HE DID, AND THE CHILDREN CRYING IN THE TEMPLE,　260 11
AND MY CHILDREN ARE WITH ME IN BED　　　　262 31
KNOW HOW TO GIVE GOOD GIFTS UNTO YOUR CHILDREN　263 11
YE MAY BE THE CHILDREN OF YOUR FATHER WHICH IS IN　264 08
BLESSED THY CHILDREN WITHIN THEE　　　　　265 03
OF THEIR CHILDREN, AND THAT IT IS MOST CONVENIENT　R 273 04
TO HAVE THEIR CHILDREN BAPTIZED IN THEIR HOUSES　R 273 08
WHEN THERE ARE CHILDREN TO BE BAPTIZED, THE PARENTS　R 273 12
PEOPLE WITH THE CHILDREN, MUST BE READY AT THE FONT,　R 273 14
BROUGHT YOUNG CHILDREN TO CHRIST, THAT HE SHOULD　274 25
THE LITTLE CHILDREN TO COME UNTO ME, AND FORBID THEM　274 28
IS USED FOR CHILDREN, THE MINISTER SHALL SPEAK UNTO　R 276 17
REMAIN IN THE NUMBER OF THY FAITHFUL CHILDREN　279 19
UPON THE CHILDREN, UNTO THE THIRD AND FOURTH　286 13
AND THEIR CHILDREN THY GLORY　　　　　　　290 09
WE ARE MADE THE CHILDREN OF GRACE　　　　　292 26
SO SOON AS CHILDREN ARE COME TO A COMPETENT AGE,　R 295 13
THE GIFT AND HERITAGE OF CHILDREN　　　　　303 16
MAY SEE THEIR CHILDREN BROUGHT UP IN THY FAITH AND　303 17
COME AGAIN, YE CHILDREN OF MEN　　　　　　325 19
THAT WE ARE THE CHILDREN OF GOD　　　　　　330 23
AND IF CHILDREN, THEN HEIRS　　　　　　　　330 24
YE BLESSED CHILDREN OF MY FATHER, RECEIVE THE KINGDOM　335 12
THE LITTLE CHILDREN TO COME UNTO ME, AND FORBID THEM　338 10
AS LITTLE CHILDREN, YE SHALL NOT ENTER INTO THE　339 25
DOST GRANT TO CHILDREN AN ABUNDANT ENTRANCE INTO THY　340 30
DID TAKE LITTLE CHILDREN INTO HIS ARMS AND BLESS　342 03
EYELIDS TRY THE CHILDREN OF MEN　　　　　　354 29
FROM AMONG THE CHILDREN OF MEN　　　　　　355 07
THE CHILDREN OF MEN ARE PUT TO REBUKE　　355 26
HEAVEN UPON THE CHILDREN OF MEN, *　　　　356 16
15 THEY HAVE CHILDREN AT THEIR DESIRE, *　　359 17
FROM AMONG THE CHILDREN OF MEN　　　　　　365 26
ALL THE CHILDREN OF MEN　　　　　　　　　379 15
11 COME, YE CHILDREN, AND HEARKEN UNTO ME　380 23
AND THE CHILDREN OF MEN SHALL PUT THEIR TRUST UNDER　384 09
FAIRER THAN THE CHILDREN OF MEN　　　　　　396 18
THOU SHALT HAVE CHILDREN, *　　　　　　　397 19
HEAVEN UPON THE CHILDREN OF MEN, *　　　　405 16
EVEN AMONG THE CHILDREN OF MEN, THAT ARE SET ON FIRE,　409 21

CHILDREN　　　CONTINUED

9 AS FOR THE CHILDREN OF MEN, THEY ARE BUT VANITY　414 15
THE CHILDREN OF MEN ARE DECEITFUL　　　　414 16
TOWARD THE CHILDREN OF MEN　　　　　　　417 23
EVEN AN ALIEN UNTO MY MOTHER'S CHILDREN　422 19
DEFEND THE CHILDREN OF THE POOR, AND PUNISH THE WRONG　427 05
HAVE CONDEMNED THE GENERATION OF THY CHILDREN　429 07
THEM FROM THE GENERATIONS TO COME　　　434 33
COMMANDED OUR FOREFATHERS TO TEACH THEIR CHILDREN　435 06
AND THE CHILDREN WHICH WERE YET UNBORN　435 07
SHOW THEIR CHILDREN THE SAME　　　　　　435 10
10 LIKE AS THE CHILDREN OF EPHRAIM　　　　435 17
YE ARE ALL THE CHILDREN OF THE MOST HIGHEST　443 29
HAVE HOLPEN THE CHILDREN OF LOT　　　　　444 21
31 BUT IF HIS CHILDREN FORSAKE MY LAW, *　452 02
COME AGAIN, YE CHILDREN OF MEN　　　　　　453 24
AND THEIR CHILDREN THY GLORY　　　　　　　454 22
28 THE CHILDREN OF THY SERVANTS SHALL CONTINUE,　466 05
WORKS UNTO THE CHILDREN OF ISRAEL　　　　466 20
LIKE AS A FATHER PITIETH HIS OWN CHILDREN　466 32
AND HIS RIGHTEOUSNESS UPON CHILDREN'S CHILDREN　467 10
YE CHILDREN OF JACOB HIS CHOSEN　　　　　470 14
DOETH FOR THE CHILDREN OF MEN　　　　　　476 21
DOETH FOR THE CHILDREN OF MEN　　　　　　477 06
DOETH FOR THE CHILDREN OF MEN　　　　　　477 19
DOETH FOR THE CHILDREN OF MEN　　　　　　478 09
8 LET HIS CHILDREN BE FATHERLESS, *　　　480 18
9 LET HIS CHILDREN BE VAGABONDS, AND BEG THEIR BREAD　480 19
TO HAVE COMPASSION UPON HIS FATHERLESS CHILDREN　480 24
AND TO BE A JOYFUL MOTHER OF CHILDREN　　484 24
YOU AND YOUR CHILDREN　　　　　　　　　486 07
HE GIVEN TO THE CHILDREN OF MEN　　　　　486 11
4 LO, CHILDREN, AND THE FRUIT OF THE WOMB, *　505 29
EVEN SO ARE THE YOUNG CHILDREN　　　　　505 32
4 THY CHILDREN LIKE THE OLIVE-BRANCHES *　506 12
THY CHILDREN'S CHILDREN, *　　　　　　　506 18
13 IF THY CHILDREN WILL KEEP MY COVENANT, AND MY　508 29
THEIR CHILDREN ALSO SHALL SIT UPON THY THRONE FOR　508 30
7 REMEMBER THE CHILDREN OF EDOM, O LORD, IN THE DAY　513 18
THAT TAKETH THY CHILDREN, *　　　　　　　513 24
BLESSED THY CHILDREN WITHIN THEE　　　　523 22
OLD MEN AND CHILDREN, PRAISE THE NAME OF THE LORD　524 27
EVEN THE CHILDREN OF ISRAEL, EVEN THE PEOPLE THAT　524 31
AND LET THE CHILDREN OF SION BE JOYFUL IN THEIR KING　525 06
RULING THEIR CHILDREN AND THEIR OWN HOUSES WELL　532 02
AND FOR HIS CHILDREN, WHO ARE IN THE MIDST OF THIS　540 02
TOWARDS THE CHILDREN OF GOD, TOWARDS THE SPOUSE AND　540 15
HAVING HIS CHILDREN IN SUBJECTION WITH ALL GRAVITY　549 24
UPON THE CHILDREN, UNTO THE THIRD AND FOURTH　578 32
IN SIN, AND THE CHILDREN OF WRATH, WE ARE HEREBY MADE　581 25
HEREBY MADE THE CHILDREN OF GRACE　　　　581 26
EXAMINE SO MANY CHILDREN OF HIS PARISH, SENT UNTO　R 582 29
CAUSE THEIR CHILDREN, SERVANTS, AND APPRENTICES,　R 582 32
SO SOON AS CHILDREN ARE COME TO A COMPETENT AGE,　R 582 36
KNOWLEDGE FOR CHILDREN TO BE BROUGHT UNTO HIM FOR　R 583 05
THOU UNDERSTANDEST ALL THY CHILDREN　　596 11
HAST BLESSED US WITH THE JOY AND CARE OF CHILDREN　596 25
UPON ALL THY CHILDREN WHO ARE LIVING IN MENTAL　598 14
HEART OF THE CHILDREN TO THE FATHERS　　598 27
FATHERS TO THE CHILDREN, AND THE HEART OF THE　598 27
AND ALL LITTLE CHILDREN, THE SICK AND THE AFFLICTED,　600 05
OF YOUNG CHILDREN IS IN ANY WISE TO BE RETAINED IN　608 31

CHILDREN'S

TO TAKE THE CHILDREN'S BREAD, AND TO CAST IT TO DOGS　128 17
UPON CHILDREN'S CHILDREN　　　　　　　　467 10
SHALT SEE THY CHILDREN'S CHILDREN, *　　　506 18

CHOICE

AND WISELY MAKE CHOICE OF FIT PERSONS, TO SERVE IN　038 30
WHO HAVE BEEN THE CHOICE VESSELS OF HIS GRACE AND THE　048 17
WHO HAVE BEEN THE CHOICE VESSELS OF THY GRACE,　336 19

CHOICES

FROM ALL FALSE CHOICES, AND THAT IN THY LIGHT WE MAY　595 30

CHOIR

IN THE CHANCEL OR CHOIR, EXCEPT THE BISHOP, OR THE　R 570 05

CHOKED

UP WITH IT, AND CHOKED IT　　　　　　　　121 25
GO FORTH, AND ARE CHOKED WITH CARES AND RICHES AND　122 06

CHOOSE

JUDAS DIDST CHOOSE THY FAITHFUL SERVANT MATTHIAS TO　233 32
THE EVIL, AND CHOOSE THE GOOD　　　　　　236 03
SHALL HE TEACH IN THE WAY THAT HE SHALL CHOOSE　370 09
4 HE SHALL CHOOSE OUT AN HERITAGE FOR US, *　398 27
THINE APOSTLES TO CHOOSE INTO THE ORDER OF DEACONS　531 16

CHOOSEST

MAN WHOM THOU CHOOSEST, AND RECEIVEST UNTO THEE　416 17

CHOOSING

THE INSTITUTOR CHOOSING TO GO ON WITH THE SERVICE,　R 570 23

CHOSE

HE MARKED HOW THEY CHOSE OUT THE CHIEF SEATS	214 09
AND CHOSE NOT THE TRIBE OF EPHRAIM	439 12
69 BUT CHOSE THE TRIBE OF JUDAH, *	439 14
71 HE CHOSE DAVID ALSO HIS SERVANT, *	439 19
AND THEY CHOSE STEPHEN, A MAN FULL OF FAITH AND CF	532 15
BEFORE HE CHOSE AND SENT FORTH HIS TWELVE	553 06

CHOSEN

AND MAKE THY CHOSEN PEOPLE JOYFUL	031 07
FOR MANY BE CALLED, BLT FEW CHOSEN	120 13
HE BE CHRIST, THE CHOSEN OF GOD	154 29
UNTO WITNESSES CHOSEN BEFORE OF GOD, EVEN TC US, WHC	166 26
COMMANDMENTS UNTO THE APOSTLES WHOM HE HAD CHOSEN	177 26
UNTO WITNESSES CHOSEN BEFORE OF GOD, EVEN TO US,	184 14
FOR HE IS A CHOSEN VESSEL LNTO ME, TO BEAR MY NAME	218 29
TWO THOU HAST CHOSEN, THAT HE MAY TAKE PART OF THIS	230 26
BUT I HAVE CHOSEN YOU, AND ORDAINED YOU, THAT YE	234 29
YE HAVE NOT CHOSEN ME, BUT I HAVE CHOSEN YOU, ANC	241 32
DIDST REVEAL TO CHOSEN WITNESSES THINE CNLY-BEGCTTEN	241 32
BUT I HAVE CHOSEN YOU OUT OF THE WORLD,	247 31
OF MEN, BUT CHOSEN OF GOD, AND PRECIOUS, YE ALSC, AS	255 16
THE LORD HATH CHOSEN TO HIMSELF THE MAN THAT IS	259 30
FOLK THAT HE HATH CHOSEN TO HIM, TO BE HIS	347 16
SMOTE DOWN THE CHOSEN MEN THAT WERE IN ISRAEL	379 12
3 I HAVE MADE A COVENANT WITH MY CHOSEN	436 34
HAVE EXALTED ONE CHOSEN OUT OF THE PEOPLE	450 09
YE CHILDREN OF JACOB HIS CHOSEN	451 14
AND AARON WHOM HE HAD CHOSEN	470 15
AND HIS CHOSEN WITH GLADNESS	471 25
FELICITY OF THY CHOSEN, *	472 24
HAD NOT MOSES HIS CHOSEN STOOD BEFORE HIM IN THE GAP,	473 08
30 I HAVE CHOSEN THE WAY OF TRUTH, *	474 15
FOR I HAVE CHOSEN THY COMMANDMENTS	491 27
FOR THE LORD HATH CHOSEN SION TO BE AN HABITATICN FCR	501 28
THE LORD HATH CHOSEN JACOB UNTO HIMSELF, *	508 32
CHOSEN BISHOP OF THE PROTESTANT EPISCOPAL CHURCH IN	510 09
THAT THE PERSON CHOSEN IS A QUALIFIED MINISTER CF	552 28
WHOM HE HATH CHOSEN IN CHRIST OUT OF MANKIND, ANC TC	R 569 06
WHICH BE CHOSEN AND CALLED TO THIS WORK BY MEN	606 09
	607 22

CHRIST

GOD OUR FATHER, AND FROM THE LORD JESUS CHRIST	004 03
WHICH IS CHRIST THE LORD	004 11
WHEREWITH CHRIST HATH MADE US FREE,' THAT IN HIS	V 02
UNTO MANKIND IN CHRIST JESUS OUR LORD	006 27
OF OUR LORD JESUS CHRIST, WHO DESIRETH NOT THE DEATH	007 06
THROUGH JESUS CHRIST OUR LORD	007 18
CHRIST THE LORD ASCENDETH INTO HEAVEN	R 008 25
THOU ART THE KING OF GLORY, O CHRIST	010 24
AND IN JESUS CHRIST HIS ONLY SON OUR LORD	015 21
IN ONE LORD JESUS CHRIST, THE CNLY-BEGOTTEN SON CF	016 02
MIGHT OF JESUS CHRIST OUR LORD	017 10
THROUGH JESUS CHRIST OUR LORD	017 19
THROUGH JESUS CHRIST OUR LORD	018 04
THROUGH JESUS CHRIST OUR LORD, WHO LIVETH AND	018 14
HONOUR OF OUR ADVOCATE AND MEDIATOR, JESUS CHRIST	018 24
REDEMPTION OF THE WORLD BY OUR LORD JESUS CHRIST	019 23
THROUGH JESUS CHRIST OUR LORD, TO WHOM, WITH THEE AND	019 30
OF OUR LORD JESUS CHRIST, AND THE LOVE OF GOD, ANC	020 12
US THE VICTORY THROUGH OUR LORD JESUS CHRIST	022 18
BE RISEN WITH CHRIST, SEEK THOSE THINGS WHICH ARE	022 19
ARE ABOVE, WHERE CHRIST SITTETH ON THE RIGHT HANC OF	022 20
CHRIST IS NOT ENTERED INTO THE HOLY	022 22
UNTO MANKIND IN CHRIST JESUS CUR LORD	024 02
OF OUR LORD JESUS CHRIST, WHO DESIRETH NOT THE DEATH	024 08
THROUGH JESUS CHRIST OUR LORD	024 20
THE ONLY-BEGOTTEN SON, JESLS CHRIST	025 27
THOU ONLY, O CHRIST, WITH THE HOLY GHOST, ART MOST	026 03
AND IN JESUS CHRIST HIS ONLY SON OUR LORD	029 26
IN ONE LORD JESUS CHRIST, THE CNLY-BEGCTTEN SON CF	030 07
MERITS OF JESUS CHRIST OUR SAVIOUR	031 24
LOVE OF THY ONLY SON, OUR SAVIOUR, JESUS CHRIST	031 29
THROUGH JESUS CHRIST OUR LORD, WHO WITH THEE AND THE	032 13
HONOUR OF OUR ADVOCATE AND MEDIATOR, JESUS CHRIST	032 23
REDEMPTION OF THE WORLD BY OLR LORD JESUS CHRIST	033 21
THROUGH JESUS CHRIST OUR LORD, TO WHOM, WITH THEE AND	033 28
OF OUR LORD JESUS CHRIST, AND THE LOVE OF GOD, AND	034 12
OF JESUS CHRIST, OUR MOST BLESSED LORD AND SAVICUR	035 20
THROUGH JESUS CHRIST, THY SON, OUR LORD	035 28
THY SON, OUR SAVIOUR JESUS CHRIST	036 06
ASK THROUGH JESUS CHRIST OUR LORD	036 24
THY SON JESUS CHRIST, TO BE WITH THY CHURCH TO THE	036 28
GOSPEL OF CHRIST MAY BE TRULY PREACHED, TRULY	037 03
DEATH OF JESUS CHRIST OUR SAVIOUR	037 08
FOR US, JESUS CHRIST, THY SON, OUR LORD	037 22
OF OUR LORD JESUS CHRIST, OUR ONLY SAVIOUR, THE	037 25
THROUGH JESUS CHRIST OUR LORD	038 03
THY SON JESUS CHRIST OUR LORD	038 11
THROUGH JESUS CHRIST OUR LORD	038 22
THROUGH JESUS CHRIST OUR LORD	039 04
THROUGH JESUS CHRIST OUR LORD	039 15
THY SON JESUS CHRIST OUR LORD	039 21
THROUGH JESUS CHRIST OUR LORD	039 31
THROUGH CHRIST JESUS OUR LORD	040 13
BY THY SON JESUS CHRIST HAST PROMISED TO ALL THCSE	040 15
THROUGH JESUS CHRIST OUR LORD	040 21
THROUGH JESUS CHRIST OUR LORD	040 28
THE LOVE OF JESUS CHRIST OUR LORD, TC WHOM, WITH THEE	041 05
OF THY SON, JESUS CHRIST OUR LORD	041 16
THROUGH JESUS CHRIST OUR LORD	041 22

CHRIST   CONTINUED

THROUGH JESUS CHRIST OUR LORD	041 31
THROUGH JESUS CHRIST OUR LORD	042 12
THROUGH JESUS CHRIST THY SON OUR LORD	042 19
THROUGH JESUS CHRIST OUR LORD	042 28
THROUGH JESUS CHRIST OUR LORD	043 05
O LORD JESUS CHRIST, WHO DOST EMBRACE CHILDREN WITH	043 07
OF THY SON JESUS CHRIST DIDST PREPARE THE DISCIPLES	043 19
THE SAME JESUS CHRIST OUR LORD	043 25
THE SAME THY SON, OUR SAVIOUR JESUS CHRIST	044 07
THROUGH THE SAME THY SON, OUR SAVIOUR JESUS CHRIST	044 14
THY SON JESUS CHRIST OUR LORD	044 25
THE KINGDOM OF OUR LORD AND SAVIOUR JESUS CHRIST	044 31
THROUGH JESUS CHRIST OUR LORD	045 10
THROUGH JESUS CHRIST OUR LORD	045 21
THROUGH JESUS CHRIST OUR LORD	045 27
THROUGH JESUS CHRIST OUR LORD	046 06
THROUGH JESUS CHRIST OUR LORD	046 16
THROUGH JESUS CHRIST OUR LORD	046 29
FAITHFULLY AND WISELY THE DISCIPLINE OF CHRIST	047 25
THE WORDS WHICH CHRIST HATH TAUGHT US, WE MAKE BCLD	048 24
O LORD JESUS CHRIST, WHO SAIDST UNTO THINE APOSTLES,	049 05
THROUGH JESUS CHRIST OUR LORD	049 16
THROUGH JESUS CHRIST OUR LORD	049 22
THROUGH JESUS CHRIST OUR LORD	049 27
OF THY SON JESUS CHRIST OUR LORD	050 04
THROUGH JESUS CHRIST OUR LORD	050 13
THROUGH JESUS CHRIST OUR LORD, TO WHOM, WITH THEE AND	050 28
THROUGH JESUS CHRIST OUR LORD	051 12
THROUGH JESUS CHRIST OUR LORD	051 20
THROUGH JESUS CHRIST OUR LORD	051 28
THROUGH JESUS CHRIST OUR LORD	052 05
THROUGH JESUS CHRIST OUR LORD	052 15
THROUGH JESUS CHRIST OUR LORD	052 27
THROUGH JESUS CHRIST OUR LORD	053 07
THROUGH JESUS CHRIST OUR LORD	053 18
THROUGH JESUS CHRIST OUR LORD	053 27
O CHRIST, HEAR US	057 25
CHRIST, HAVE MERCY UPON US	057 29
THROUGH JESUS CHRIST OUR LORD	058 24
FROM OUR ENEMIES DEFEND US, O CHRIST	059 09
BOTH NOW AND EVER VOUCHSAFE TO HEAR US, O CHRIST	059 15
GRACIOUSLY HEAR US, O CHRIST	059 16
GRACIOUSLY HEAR US, O LORD CHRIST	059 17
JESUS CHRIST OUR LORD	059 28
THE SAKE OF JESUS CHRIST, OUR BLESSED LORD AND	VI 42
CHRIST, HAVE MERCY UPON US	061 22
THROUGH CHRIST OUR LORD	062 11
THROUGH JESUS CHRIST OUR LORD	062 25
JESUS CHRIST OUR LORD	063 07
HONOUR OF JESUS CHRIST, OUR MEDIATOR AND ADVOCATE	063 13
THROUGH CHRIST OUR LORD	067 20
OUR LORD JESUS CHRIST SAITH	R 067 30
OUR LORD JESUS CHRIST SAITH	069 26
CHRIST, HAVE MERCY UPON US THEN THE PRIEST MAY SAY,	070 03
THROUGH OUR LORD AND SAVIOUR JESUS CHRIST	070 12
GOSPEL MAY BE SAID, PRAISE BE TO THEE, O CHRIST	070 28
IN ONE LORD JESUS CHRIST, THE ONLY-BEGOTTEN SON CF	071 04
OF OUR LORD JESUS CHRIST, MAKER OF ALL THINGS, JUDGE	075 17
THROUGH JESUS CHRIST OUR LORD	075 30
THROUGH JESUS CHRIST OUR LORD	076 07
WORDS OUR SAVIOUR CHRIST SAITH UNTO ALL WHO TRULY	076 10
BE RECEIVED, THAT CHRIST JESUS CAME INTO THE WORLD TC	076 19
THE FATHER, JESUS CHRIST THE RIGHTEOUS	076 23
DIDST GIVE JESUS CHRIST, THINE ONLY SCN, TO BE BCRN	077 14
THROUGH JESUS CHRIST OUR LORD	077 22
OF THY SON JESUS CHRIST OUR LORD	078 03
OF THY SON JESUS CHRIST OUR LORD	078 08
BELOVED SON JESUS CHRIST OUR LORD	078 17
THROUGH JESUS CHRIST OUR LORD	078 30
AND OF THY SON JESUS CHRIST	079 03
OF THY SON JESUS CHRIST OUR LORD, AND FOR THE SENDING	079 16
ONLY SON JESUS CHRIST TO SUFFER DEATH UPON THE CROSS	080 08
OUR SAVIOUR JESUS CHRIST, WE, THY HUMBLE SERVANTS, DO	080 38
OF THY SON JESUS CHRIST, AND THROUGH FAITH IN HIS	081 18
OF THY SON JESUS CHRIST, BE FILLED WITH THY GRACE AND	081 26
THROUGH JESUS CHRIST OUR LORD	081 32
AS OUR SAVIOUR CHRIST HATH TAUGHT US, WE ARE BCLD TO	082 02
DEAR SON JESUS CHRIST, AND TO DRINK HIS BLOOD,	082 19
OF OUR LORD JESUS CHRIST, WHICH WAS GIVEN FCR THEE,	082 31
REMEMBRANCE THAT CHRIST DIED FOR THEE, AND FEED CN	082 33
OF OUR LORD JESUS CHRIST, WHICH WAS SHED FOR THEE,	083 03
AND BLOOD OF THY SON OUR SAVIOUR JESUS CHRIST	083 20
THROUGH JESUS CHRIST OUR LORD, TO WHOM, WITH THEE AND	083 29
THE ONLY-BEGOTTEN SON, JESUS CHRIST	084 07
THOU ONLY, O CHRIST, WITH THE HOLY GHOST, ART MOST	084 14
OF HIS SON JESUS CHRIST OUR LORD	084 20
OF OUR SAVIOUR JESUS CHRIST, MUST CONSIDER HOW SAINT PAUL	085 27
STEDFAST FAITH IN CHRIST OUR SAVIOUR	086 02
OF OUR SAVIOUR JESUS CHRIST, BOTH GOD AND MAN	086 07
JESUS CHRIST, THUS DYING FOR US, AND THE	086 14
SACRAMENT OF THE BODY AND BLOOD OF CHRIST	086 31
OUR SAVIOUR JESUS CHRIST, NOT ONLY TO DIE FCR US,	087 03
DEARLY BELOVED IN CHRIST, TAKE YE GOOD HEED, LEST YE,	088 24
THY SON JESUS CHRIST CAME TO VISIT US IN GREAT	090 14
ON THE LORD JESUS CHRIST, AND MAKE NOT PROVISICN FOR	091 08
THOU HAST GIVEN US IN OUR SAVIOUR JESUS CHRIST	092 13
ACCORDING TO CHRIST JESUS	092 19
EVEN THE FATHER OF OUR LORD JESUS CHRIST	092 21
ONE ANOTHER, AS CHRIST ALSO RECEIVED US TO THE GLCRY	092 22
I SAY THAT JESUS CHRIST WAS A MINISTER OF THE	092 23
O LORD JESUS CHRIST, WHO AT THY FIRST CCMING DIDST	093 24
THE MINISTERS OF CHRIST, AND STEWARDS OF THE	094 04
THE WORKS OF CHRIST, HE SENT TWO OF HIS DISCIPLES,	094 17
THROUGH JESUS CHRIST OUR LORD, TO WHOM, WITH THEE AND	095 09

CHRIST   CONTINUED

AND MINDS THROUGH CHRIST JESUS   095 19
BUT CONFESSED, I AM NOT THE CHRIST   095 24
THOU BE NOT THAT CHRIST, NOR ELIAS, NEITHER THAT   095 32
OUR LORD JESUS CHRIST, WHO LIVETH AND REIGNETH WITH   096 18
OF THE BIRTH OF THINE ONLY SON JESUS CHRIST   098 12
OF THE GREAT GOD AND OUR SAVIOUR JESUS CHRIST   098 23
WHICH IS CHRIST THE LORD   099 17
THROUGH JESUS CHRIST OUR LORD   101 10
AND WITH HIS SON JESUS CHRIST   101 20
BLOOD OF JESUS CHRIST HIS SON CLEANSETH US FROM ALL   101 27
THROUGH JESUS CHRIST OUR LORD   102 27
OUR LORD JESUS CHRIST, WHO LIVETH AND REIGNETH WITH   104 10
THEN AN HEIR OF GOD THROUGH CHRIST   104 25
BIRTH OF JESUS CHRIST WAS ON THIS WISE   104 27
THY SON JESUS CHRIST OUR LORD   105 24
THAT JESUS CHRIST IS LORD, TO THE GLORY OF GOD THE   105 30
THROUGH JESUS CHRIST OUR LORD   106 28
THY SON JESUS CHRIST OUR LORD   108 03
PRISONER OF JESUS CHRIST FOR YOU GENTILES, IF YE HAVE   108 06
IN THE MYSTERY OF CHRIST) WHICH IN OTHER AGES WAS NOT   108 11
OF HIS PROMISE IN CHRIST BY THE GOSPEL   108 15
THE GENTILES THE UNSEARCHABLE RICHES OF CHRIST   108 20
IN GOD, WHO CREATED ALL THINGS BY JESUS CHRIST   108 23
HE PURPOSED IN CHRIST JESUS OUR LORD   108 26
OF THEM WHERE CHRIST SHOULD BE BORN   109 06
THROUGH JESUS CHRIST OUR LORD   109 33
ARE ONE BODY IN CHRIST, AND EVERY ONE MEMBERS ONE OF   110 15
THROUGH JESUS CHRIST OUR LORD   111 13
GOSPEL OF JESUS CHRIST, THE SON OF GOD   112 03
THROUGH JESUS CHRIST OUR LORD   112 29
THROUGH JESUS CHRIST OUR LORD   114 09
THROUGH JESUS CHRIST OUR LORD   115 32
EVEN AS CHRIST FORGAVE YOU, SO ALSO DO YE   116 07
LET THE WORD OF CHRIST DWELL IN YOU RICHLY IN ALL   116 11
LO, HERE IS CHRIST, OR THERE   118 03
THROUGH JESUS CHRIST OUR SAVIOUR, WHO LIVETH AND   118 31
THROUGH JESUS CHRIST OUR LORD   120 20
ARE THEY MINISTERS OF CHRIST   120 30
OF OUR LORD JESUS CHRIST, WHICH IS BLESSED FOR   121 15
THROUGH JESUS CHRIST OUR LORD   124 17
THROUGH JESUS CHRIST OUR LORD   127 20
THROUGH JESUS CHRIST OUR LORD   128 28
WALK IN LOVE, AS CHRIST ALSO HATH LOVED US, AND HATH   128 31
IN THE KINGDOM OF CHRIST AND OF GOD   129 08
THE DEAD, AND CHRIST SHALL GIVE THEE LIGHT   129 22
THROUGH OUR LORD AND SAVIOUR JESUS CHRIST   130 27
THROUGH JESUS CHRIST OUR LORD   132 21
CHRIST BEING COME AN HIGH PRIEST OF GOOD THINGS TO   132 23
THE BLOOD OF CHRIST, WHO THROUGH THE ETERNAL SPIRIT   132 31
OUR SAVIOUR JESUS CHRIST, TO TAKE UPON HIM OUR FLESH,   134 07
THE SAME JESUS CHRIST OUR LORD   134 11
WHICH WAS ALSO IN CHRIST JESUS   134 16
THAT JESUS CHRIST IS LORD, TO THE GLORY OF GOD THE   134 27
OR JESUS WHICH IS CALLED CHRIST   135 31
SHALL I DO THEN WITH JESUS WHICH IS CALLED CHRIST   136 05
ART THOU THE CHRIST, THE SON OF THE BLESSED   143 14
THY SON JESUS CHRIST OUR LORD   144 10
LET CHRIST THE KING OF ISRAEL DESCEND NOW FROM THE   146 23
THROUGH JESUS CHRIST OUR LORD   147 11
FOR CHRIST IS NOT ENTERED INTO THE HOLY PLACES MADE   147 30
SO CHRIST WAS ONCE OFFERED TO BEAR THE SINS OF MANY   148 08
INTO THEIR COUNCIL, SAYING, ART THOU THE CHRIST   151 30
THY SON JESUS CHRIST OUR LORD, WHO NOW LIVETH AND   152 12
HE HIMSELF IS CHRIST A KING   152 30
IF HE BE CHRIST, THE CHOSEN OF GOD   154 29
IF THOU BE CHRIST, SAVE THYSELF AND US   154 35
OUR LORD JESUS CHRIST WAS CONTENTED TO BE BETRAYED,   156 22
THROUGH OUR LORD AND SAVIOUR JESUS CHRIST   157 03
JESUS CHRIST OUR LORD, WHO LIVETH AND   157 12
THE BODY OF JESUS CHRIST ONCE FOR ALL   158 02
OUR SAVIOUR JESUS CHRIST, SO BY CONTINUAL MORTIFYING   161 14
THY SON JESUS CHRIST OUR LORD   161 19
FOR CHRIST ALSO HATH ONCE SUFFERED FOR SINS, THE JUST   161 22
BY THE RESURRECTION OF JESUS CHRIST   162 02
CHRIST OUR PASSOVER IS SACRIFICED FOR US   162 30
CHRIST BEING RAISED FROM THE DEAD DIETH NO MORE   163 04
GOD THROUGH JESUS CHRIST OUR LORD   163 09
CHRIST IS RISEN FROM THE DEAD, *   163 13
EVEN SO IN CHRIST SHALL ALL BE MADE ALIVE   163 15
SON JESUS CHRIST HAST OVERCOME DEATH, AND OPENED UNTO   163 23
THE SAME JESUS CHRIST OUR LORD, WHO LIVETH AND   163 28
BE RISEN WITH CHRIST, SEEK THOSE THINGS WHICH   164 03
ARE ABOVE, WHERE CHRIST SITTETH ON THE RIGHT HAND OF   164 04
LIFE IS HID WITH CHRIST IN GOD   164 06
WHEN CHRIST, WHO IS OUR LIFE, SHALL APPEAR, THEN   164 07
THE SAME THY SON JESUS CHRIST OUR LORD   165 08
FOR EVEN CHRIST OUR PASSOVER IS SACRIFICED FOR US   165 12
THY SON JESUS CHRIST OUR LORD   166 09
PREACHING PEACE BY JESUS CHRIST   166 16
OUGHT NOT CHRIST TO HAVE SUFFERED THESE THINGS, AND   167 30
THROUGH JESUS CHRIST OUR LORD   168 22
THUS IT BEHOVED CHRIST TO SUFFER, AND TO RISE FROM   170 13
THY SON JESUS CHRIST OUR LORD   170 24
THAT CAME BY WATER AND BLOOD, EVEN JESUS CHRIST   170 30
THY SON JESUS CHRIST OUR LORD   172 02
BECAUSE CHRIST ALSO SUFFERED FOR US, LEAVING US AN   172 10
THROUGH OUR LORD JESUS CHRIST   173 10
THROUGH JESUS CHRIST OUR LORD   174 24
THROUGH OUR LORD JESUS CHRIST   176 03
OUR LORD JESUS CHRIST TO HAVE ASCENDED INTO THE   177 16
ONLY SON JESUS CHRIST WITH GREAT TRIUMPH UNTO THY   179 05
OUR SAVIOUR CHRIST IS GONE BEFORE, WHO LIVETH AND   179 08
THROUGH JESUS CHRIST, TO WHOM BE PRAISE AND DOMINION   179 21

CHRIST   CONTINUED

THE MERITS OF CHRIST JESUS OUR SAVIOUR, WHO LIVETH   180 12
THROUGH JESUS CHRIST OUR LORD, WHO LIVETH AND   182 18
SO ALSO IS CHRIST   183 04
THROUGH JESUS CHRIST OUR LORD, WHO WITH THEE AND THE   183 26
PREACHING PEACE BY JESUS CHRIST   184 03
THROUGH JESUS CHRIST OUR LORD, WHO LIVETH AND   185 17
THROUGH JESUS CHRIST OUR LORD   189 05
THROUGH JESUS CHRIST OUR LORD   191 08
OF HIS SON JESUS CHRIST, AND LOVE ONE ANOTHER,   191 31
THROUGH JESUS CHRIST OUR LORD   192 28
ETERNAL GLORY BY CHRIST JESUS, AFTER THAT YE HAVE   193 09
THE SAKE OF JESUS CHRIST OUR LORD   194 09
THROUGH JESUS CHRIST OUR LORD   195 18
THROUGH JESUS CHRIST OUR LORD   197 08
INTO JESUS CHRIST WERE BAPTIZED INTO HIS DEATH   197 11
THAT LIKE AS CHRIST WAS RAISED UP FROM THE DEAD BY   197 13
WE BE DEAD WITH CHRIST, WE BELIEVE THAT WE SHALL ALSO   197 20
KNOWING THAT CHRIST BEING RAISED FROM THE DEAD DIETH   197 21
GOD THROUGH JESUS CHRIST OUR LORD   197 26
THROUGH JESUS CHRIST OUR LORD   198 24
THROUGH JESUS CHRIST OUR LORD   199 05
THROUGH JESUS CHRIST OUR LORD   199 32
AND JOINT-HEIRS WITH CHRIST   200 12
THROUGH JESUS CHRIST OUR LORD   201 03
AND THAT ROCK WAS CHRIST   201 11
LET US TEMPT CHRIST, AS SOME OF THEM ALSO TEMPTED,   201 19
THROUGH JESUS CHRIST OUR LORD   203 14
THROUGH JESUS CHRIST OUR LORD   204 27
HOW THAT CHRIST DIED FOR OUR SINS ACCORDING TO THE   205 04
OF JESUS CHRIST, THY SON, OUR LORD   206 10
HAVE WE THROUGH JESUS CHRIST TO GOD-WARD   206 13
MERITS OF JESUS CHRIST OUR LORD   207 17
BUT AS OF ONE, AND TO THY SEED, WHICH IS CHRIST   207 21
BEFORE OF GOD IN CHRIST, THE LAW, WHICH WAS FOUR   207 22
BY FAITH OF JESUS CHRIST MIGHT BE GIVEN TO THEM THAT   208 04
THROUGH JESUS CHRIST OUR LORD   209 11
THROUGH JESUS CHRIST OUR LORD   210 21
SHOULD SUFFER PERSECUTION FOR THE CROSS OF CHRIST   210 27
OF OUR LORD JESUS CHRIST, BY WHOM THE WORLD IS   210 30
FOR IN CHRIST JESUS NEITHER CIRCUMCISION AVAILETH ANY   210 32
OF OUR LORD JESUS CHRIST BE WITH YOUR SPIRIT   211 06
THROUGH JESUS CHRIST OUR LORD   212 07
OF OUR LORD JESUS CHRIST, OF WHOM THE WHOLE FAMILY IN   212 12
THAT CHRIST MAY DWELL IN YOUR HEARTS BY FAITH   212 16
KNOW THE LOVE OF CHRIST, WHICH PASSETH KNOWLEDGE,   212 19
IN THE CHURCH BY CHRIST JESUS THROUGHOUT ALL AGES,   212 24
THROUGH JESUS CHRIST OUR LORD   213 16
THROUGH JESUS CHRIST OUR LORD   214 26
GRACE OF GOD WHICH IS GIVEN YOU BY JESUS CHRIST   214 29
THE TESTIMONY OF CHRIST WAS CONFIRMED IN YOU   214 31
WAITING FOR THE COMING OF OUR LORD JESUS CHRIST   215 02
BE BLAMELESS IN THE DAY OF OUR LORD JESUS CHRIST   215 04
JESUS ASKED THEM, SAYING, WHAT THINK YE OF CHRIST   215 17
THROUGH JESUS CHRIST OUR LORD   215 30
BUT YE HAVE NOT SO LEARNED CHRIST   216 10
THROUGH JESUS CHRIST OUR LORD   217 21
THE FATHER IN THE NAME OF OUR LORD JESUS CHRIST   217 31
THROUGH JESUS CHRIST OUR LORD   219 03
THROUGH JESUS CHRIST OUR LORD   220 20
YOU WILL PERFORM IT UNTIL THE DAY OF JESUS CHRIST   220 27
TENDER MERCIES OF CHRIST JESUS   220 32
AND WITHOUT OFFENCE TILL THE DAY OF CHRIST   221 05
ARE BY JESUS CHRIST, UNTO THE GLORY AND PRAISE OF   221 06
THROUGH JESUS CHRIST OUR LORD   222 13
THAT THEY ARE THE ENEMIES OF THE CROSS OF CHRIST   222 19
WE LOOK FOR THE SAVIOUR, THE LORD JESUS CHRIST   222 22
THE SAKE OF JESUS CHRIST, OUR BLESSED LORD AND   223 19
OF OUR LORD JESUS CHRIST, PRAYING ALWAYS FOR YOU,   223 23
OF YOUR FAITH IN CHRIST JESUS, AND OF THE LOVE WHICH   223 24
WHO IS FOR YOU A FAITHFUL MINISTER OF CHRIST   223 31
THROUGH JESUS CHRIST OUR LORD   225 07
OF THY SON JESUS CHRIST, AND FOLLOWED HIM WITHOUT   226 20
THE SAME JESUS CHRIST OUR LORD   226 24
IN THY SON JESUS CHRIST, THAT OUR FAITH IN THY SIGHT   228 09
THE SAME JESUS CHRIST, TO WHOM, WITH THEE AND THE   228 10
THAT JESUS IS THE CHRIST, THE SON OF GOD   229 12
THROUGH JESUS CHRIST OUR LORD   229 23
HE PREACHED CHRIST IN THE SYNAGOGUES, THAT HE IS THE   231 04
PROVING THAT THIS IS VERY CHRIST   231 10
THY SON JESUS CHRIST OUR LORD   231 32
BEFORE HE HAD SEEN THE LORD'S CHRIST   232 34
THROUGH JESUS CHRIST OUR LORD   234 04
OF THY SON JESUS CHRIST BY THE MESSAGE OF AN ANGEL,   235 20
THE SAME JESUS CHRIST OUR LORD   235 22
THROUGH JESUS CHRIST OUR LORD   237 10
ACCORDING TO THE MEASURE OF THE GIFT OF CHRIST   237 13
FOR THE EDIFYING OF THE BODY OF CHRIST   237 22
MEASURE OF THE STATURE OF THE FULNESS OF CHRIST   237 25
WHICH IS THE HEAD, EVEN CHRIST   237 30
THY SON JESUS CHRIST TO BE THE WAY, THE TRUTH,   238 31
THY SON JESUS CHRIST OUR LORD   239 03
OF THE LORD JESUS CHRIST, TO THE TWELVE TRIBES WHICH   239 06
THROUGH JESUS CHRIST OUR LORD   240 32
THY SON JESUS CHRIST OUR LORD   242 14
BY THY SON JESUS CHRIST DIDST GIVE TO THY APOSTLE   244 22
THY SON JESUS CHRIST OUR LORD   244 28
THOU ART THE CHRIST, THE SON OF THE LIVING GOD   246 03
OF THY SON JESUS CHRIST, AND FOLLOWED HIM   246 19
THE SAME JESUS CHRIST OUR LORD   246 21
AS OUR LORD JESUS CHRIST HATH SHEWED ME   248 11
OF OUR LORD JESUS CHRIST, BUT WERE EYEWITNESSES OF   248 15
THROUGH JESUS CHRIST OUR LORD   249 18
THY SON JESUS CHRIST, WHO LIVETH AND REIGNETH WITH   250 24
GOSPEL OF CHRIST, WHO IS THE IMAGE OF GOD, SHOULD   251 04

CHRIST   CONTINUED

	PAGE	LN
BUT CHRIST JESUS THE LORD	251	06
OF THE GLORY OF GOD IN THE FACE OF JESUS CHRIST	251	10
THROUGH JESUS CHRIST OUR LORD	251	31
KINGDOM OF OUR GOD, AND THE POWER OF HIS CHRIST	252	12
THY SON JESUS CHRIST OUR LORD	253	20
JESUS CHRIST HIMSELF BEING THE HEAD	254	29
THE SAME JESUS CHRIST OUR LORD	254	32
JESUS CHRIST HIMSELF BEING THE CHIEF	255	06
BODY OF THY SON CHRIST OUR LORD	256	07
THY SON JESUS CHRIST OUR LORD	256	11
THROUGH JESUS CHRIST OUR LORD	258	08
THY SON JESUS CHRIST OUR LORD	258	18
THROUGH JESUS CHRIST OUR LORD	259	23
ACCEPTABLE TO GOD BY JESUS CHRIST	259	33
THROUGH JESUS CHRIST OUR LORD	260	24
THROUGH JESUS CHRIST OUR LORD	262	02
THROUGH JESUS CHRIST OUR LORD	263	21
THROUGH JESUS CHRIST OUR LORD	265	16
THROUGH JESUS CHRIST OUR LORD	267	09
THE FATHER IN THE NAME OF OUR LORD JESUS CHRIST	267	12
THE WIFE, EVEN AS CHRIST IS THE HEAD OF THE CHURCH	267	16
IS SUBJECT UNTO CHRIST, SO LET THE WIVES BE TO THEIR	267	17
EVEN AS CHRIST ALSO LOVED THE CHURCH, AND GAVE	267	19
SPEAK CONCERNING CHRIST AND THE CHURCH	267	32
THROUGH JESUS CHRIST OUR LORD	268	19
THROUGH JESUS CHRIST OUR LORD	268	26
AND THE DEAD IN CHRIST SHALL RISE FIRST	269	07
AS OUR SAVIOUR CHRIST SAITH, NONE CAN ENTER INTO THE	273	29
OUR LORD JESUS CHRIST, THAT OF HIS BOUNTEOUS MERCY HE	274	02
HAST PROMISED BY CHRIST OUR LORD	274	21
YOUNG CHILDREN TO CHRIST, THAT HE SHOULD TOUCH THEM	274	25
THIS PERSON), DECLARED BY HIS SON JESUS CHRIST	276	05
OUR LORD JESUS CHRIST, WHO LIVETH AND REIGNETH WITH	276	14
OUR LORD JESUS CHRIST WOULD VOUCHSAFE TO RECEIVE HIM,	276	21
OUR LORD JESUS CHRIST WOULD VOUCHSAFE TO RECEIVE YOU,	277	22
IN JESUS THE CHRIST, THE SON OF THE LIVING GOD	278	02
THAT LIKE AS CHRIST DIED AND ROSE AGAIN, SO THIS	278	18
BELOVED SON JESUS CHRIST, FOR THE FORGIVENESS OF OUR	279	10
THE SAME JESUS CHRIST OUR LORD, TO WHOM, WITH THEE,	279	20
THE FAITH OF CHRIST CRUCIFIED, AND MANFULLY TO	280	07
BEING BURIED WITH CHRIST IN HIS DEATH, MAY ALSO BE	281	02
THROUGH CHRIST OUR LORD	281	05
OF OUR LORD JESUS CHRIST, OF WHOM THE WHOLE FAMILY IN	281	08
CHRIST DWELLING IN YOUR HEARTS BY FAITH, YE MAY	281	10
THROUGH JESUS CHRIST OUR LORD	283	12
MADE A MEMBER OF CHRIST, THE CHILD OF GOD, AND AN	283	19
THROUGH JESUS CHRIST OUR SAVIOUR	284	03
AND IN JESUS CHRIST HIS ONLY SON OUR LORD	284	15
THROUGH JESUS CHRIST OUR LORD	285	31
THROUGH JESUS CHRIST OUR LORD	287	30
OUR LORD JESUS CHRIST TEACH US ABOUT THESE	288	02
OUR LORD JESUS CHRIST TEACHES US THAT THEY ARE SUMMED	288	04
AS OUR SAVIOUR CHRIST HATH TAUGHT US, AND SAY,	289	19
OF OUR LORD JESUS CHRIST, AND THE LOVE OF GOD, AND	289	29
JESUS CHRIST HIMSELF BEING THE HEAD	290	21
THE SAME JESUS CHRIST OUR LORD	290	24
OF WHICH JESUS CHRIST IS THE HEAD, AND ALL BAPTIZED	290	32
DUTY IS TO FOLLOW CHRIST, TO WORSHIP GOD EVERY SUNDAY	291	18
AND DEVOTION TO CHRIST AS MY MASTER, I RECEIVE THE	291	26
SACRAMENTS HATH CHRIST ORDAINED IN HIS CHURCH	292	04
CHRIST HATH ORDAINED TWO SACRAMENTS ONLY,	292	06
ORDAINED BY CHRIST HIMSELF, AS A MEANS WHEREBY WE	292	12
OF THE DEATH OF CHRIST, AND OF THE BENEFITS WHICH WE	293	06
BODY AND BLOOD OF CHRIST, WHICH ARE SPIRITUALLY TAKEN	293	15
BODY AND BLOOD OF CHRIST, AS OUR BODIES ARE	293	21
MERCY THROUGH CHRIST, WITH A THANKFUL REMEMBRANCE OF	293	29
THROUGH JESUS CHRIST OUR LORD	294	28
BODY AND BLOOD OF CHRIST, COMING TO THOSE HOLY	294	30
THROUGH JESUS CHRIST OUR LORD	295	03
OF OUR LORD JESUS CHRIST, AND THE LOVE OF GOD, AND	295	04
TO FOLLOW JESUS CHRIST AS YOUR LORD AND SAVIOUR	297	03
OUR LORD JESUS CHRIST, WHO WITH THEE AND THE SAME	298	23
THROUGH OUR LORD AND SAVIOUR JESUS CHRIST	298	32
THAT IS BETWIXT CHRIST AND HIS CHURCH	300	12
WHICH HOLY ESTATE CHRIST ADORNED AND BEAUTIFIED WITH	300	13
THROUGH JESUS CHRIST OUR LORD	302	21
THROUGH JESUS CHRIST OUR LORD	303	11
THROUGH JESUS CHRIST OUR LORD	303	19
AND UNITY BETWIXT CHRIST AND HIS CHURCH	303	22
THE SAME JESUS CHRIST OUR LORD, WHO LIVETH AND	303	27
THROUGH JESUS CHRIST OUR LORD	306	32
THROUGH JESUS CHRIST OUR LORD	307	06
CHRIST, HAVE MERCY UPON US	308	15
THROUGH JESUS CHRIST OUR LORD	309	08
THROUGH JESUS CHRIST OUR LORD	309	32
THROUGH JESUS CHRIST OUR LORD	310	25
THROUGH JESUS CHRIST OUR LORD	311	24
THROUGH JESUS CHRIST OUR LORD	312	16
THROUGH JESUS CHRIST OUR LORD	313	07
JESUS CHRIST OUR LORD	314	13
BUT ONLY THE NAME OF OUR LORD JESUS CHRIST	314	22
THROUGH JESUS CHRIST OUR LORD	315	11
THROUGH JESUS CHRIST OUR LORD	315	17
THROUGH JESUS CHRIST OUR SAVIOUR, TO WHOM, WITH THEE	316	02
THROUGH JESUS CHRIST OUR LORD	316	23
ASK THROUGH JESUS CHRIST OUR LORD	317	08
MERITS OF JESUS CHRIST THINE ONLY SON OUR LORD	317	22
CHRIST, HAVE MERCY	318	30
THROUGH JESUS CHRIST OUR LORD, WHO LIVETH AND	319	11
THE NAME OF JESUS CHRIST WHO REDEEMED THEE	319	22
OF OUR LORD JESUS CHRIST, THAT ALL THY PAIN AND	320	18
OF OUR SAVIOUR CHRIST, WHEN IT SHALL BE PUBLICLY R	321	08
THROUGH JESUS CHRIST OUR LORD	321	26
THROUGH JESUS CHRIST OUR LORD	322	10

CHRIST   CONTINUED

	PAGE	LN
THAT JESUS CHRIST HATH SUFFERED DEATH UPON THE CROSS R	323	27
OF OUR SAVIOUR CHRIST PROFITABLY TO HIS SOUL'S R	323	30
NOW IS CHRIST RISEN FROM THE DEAD, AND BECOME THE	328	21
EVEN SO IN CHRIST SHALL ALL BE MADE ALIVE	328	24
CHRIST THE FIRSTFRUITS	328	25
US THE VICTORY THROUGH OUR LORD JESUS CHRIST	330	13
HEIRS OF GOD, AND JOINT-HEIRS WITH CHRIST	330	25
IT IS CHRIST THAT DIED, YEA RATHER, THAT IS RISEN	331	04
WHO SHALL SEPARATE US FROM THE LOVE OF CHRIST	331	06
WHICH IS IN CHRIST JESUS OUR LORD	331	14
THROUGH JESUS CHRIST OUR LORD, WHO LIVETH AND	332	07
UNTO ETERNAL LIFE, THROUGH OUR LORD JESUS CHRIST	333	18
CHRIST, HAVE MERCY UPON US	334	04
THROUGH JESUS CHRIST OUR LORD	334	18
THROUGH JESUS CHRIST OUR LORD	334	29
OF OUR LORD JESUS CHRIST, WHO IS THE RESURRECTION AND	334	31
THROUGH JESUS CHRIST, OUR MEDIATOR AND REDEEMER	335	14
OUR LORD JESUS CHRIST, THE GREAT SHEPHERD OF THE	335	17
THROUGH JESUS CHRIST, TO WHOM BE GLORY FOR EVER AND	335	21
MAY BE PERFECTED UNTO THE DAY OF JESUS CHRIST	335	30
THY SON JESUS CHRIST OUR LORD	336	03
THROUGH JESUS CHRIST OUR LORD	336	09
O LORD JESUS CHRIST, WHO BY THY DEATH DIDST TAKE AWAY	336	10
THY SON JESUS CHRIST, OUR ONLY MEDIATOR AND ADVOCATE	336	29
DEPARTED IN CHRIST, PROVIDED THAT IN ANY OTHER CASE R	337	03
THROUGH OUR LORD JESUS CHRIST	337	12
CHRIST, HAVE MERCY UPON US	340	07
THROUGH JESUS CHRIST OUR LORD	340	28
THROUGH JESUS CHRIST OUR LORD	341	04
OF OUR LORD JESUS CHRIST, AND THE LOVE OF GOD, AND	341	05
OUR LORD JESUS CHRIST, WE COMMIT THE BODY OF THIS	341	14
THY SON, JESUS CHRIST OUR LORD	342	07
THROUGH JESUS CHRIST OUR LORD	342	13
IN THE CHURCH OF CHRIST, AND ALSO, HOW THE PEOPLE R	530	05
OUR SAVIOUR JESUS CHRIST, WHO LIVETH AND REIGNETH	531	24
FAITH WHICH IS IN CHRIST JESUS	532	05
OF OUR LORD JESUS CHRIST, AND ACCORDING TO THE CANONS	532	32
ETERNAL SALVATION THROUGH FAITH IN JESUS CHRIST	533	04
ACCORDING TO THE DOCTRINE OF CHRIST	533	26
WHOLESOME EXAMPLES OF THE FLOCK OF CHRIST	533	28
STRONG IN THY SON CHRIST, MAY SO WELL BEHAVE	535	07
OUR SAVIOUR JESUS CHRIST, TO WHOM BE GLORY AND	535	11
OF HIS SON JESUS CHRIST OUR LORD	535	15
IN THE CHURCH OF CHRIST, AND ALSO, HOW THE PEOPLE R	536	05
OUR SAVIOUR JESUS CHRIST, WHO LIVETH AND REIGNETH	537	28
ACCORDING TO THE MEASURE OF THE GIFT OF CHRIST	537	33
FOR THE EDIFYING OF THE BODY OF CHRIST	538	09
MEASURE OF THE STATURE OF THE FULNESS OF CHRIST	538	12
OF OUR LORD JESUS CHRIST, THAT YE HAVE IN	539	30
BE SAVED THROUGH CHRIST FOR EVER	540	04
ARE THE SHEEP OF CHRIST, WHICH HE BOUGHT WITH HIS	540	07
TOWARDS THE SPOUSE AND BODY OF CHRIST	540	16
OF AGE IN CHRIST, THAT THERE BE NO PLACE LEFT AMONG	540	21
SAVIOUR JESUS CHRIST, FOR THE HEAVENLY ASSISTANCE OF	541	17
AND DOCTRINE OF CHRIST, THAT YE MAY BE WHOLESOME AND	541	22
CONGREGATION OF CHRIST MAY ALSO UNDERSTAND YOUR MINDS	541	24
OF OUR LORD JESUS CHRIST, AND ACCORDING TO THE CANONS	541	31
ETERNAL SALVATION THROUGH FAITH IN JESUS CHRIST	542	04
THE DISCIPLINE OF CHRIST, AS THE LORD HATH COMMANDED,	542	13
ACCORDING TO THE DOCTRINE OF CHRIST	542	34
EXAMPLES AND PATTERNS TO THE FLOCK OF CHRIST	543	03
THROUGH JESUS CHRIST OUR LORD	543	21
BELOVED SON JESUS CHRIST, TO BE OUR REDEEMER, AND THE	545	14
THY SON JESUS CHRIST OUR LORD, WHO LIVETH AND	546	03
THROUGH JESUS CHRIST OUR LORD	547	13
OF HIS SON JESUS CHRIST OUR LORD	547	16
OUR SAVIOUR JESUS CHRIST, WHO LIVETH AND REIGNETH	548	07
BY THE SON JESUS CHRIST DIDST GIVE TO THY HOLY	549	07
THY SON JESUS CHRIST OUR LORD	549	15
AND FAITH TOWARD OUR LORD JESUS CHRIST	550	14
SO HELP ME GOD, THROUGH JESUS CHRIST	552	32
THAT OUR SAVIOUR CHRIST CONTINUED THE WHOLE NIGHT IN	553	05
OF OUR SAVIOUR CHRIST, AND HIS APOSTLES, OFFER UP OUR	553	09
OUR SAVIOUR JESUS CHRIST, WHO LIVETH AND REIGNETH	554	02
IN THE CHURCH OF CHRIST, WHICH HE HATH PURCHASED WITH	554	10
OF OUR LORD JESUS CHRIST, AND THE ORDER OF THIS	554	18
ETERNAL SALVATION THROUGH FAITH IN JESUS CHRIST	554	22
THROUGH JESUS CHRIST OUR LORD	555	33
BELOVED SON JESUS CHRIST, TO BE OUR REDEEMER, AND THE	557	22
THE SAME JESUS CHRIST OUR LORD, WHO, WITH THEE AND	558	06
TO THE FLOCK OF CHRIST A SHEPHERD, NOT A WOLF	558	25
THROUGH JESUS CHRIST OUR LORD	558	32
OF HIS SON JESUS CHRIST OUR LORD	559	19
CHRIST, HAVE MERCY UPON US	561	23
THE MYSTERIES OF CHRIST, THAT BY THEIR MINISTRY AND	562	11
THROUGH JESUS CHRIST OUR LORD, WHO LIVETH AND	562	13
THROUGH JESUS CHRIST OUR BLESSED LORD AND SAVIOUR	565	14
BODY AND BLOOD OF CHRIST, MAY COME TO THAT HOLY	565	30
THROUGH JESUS CHRIST OUR LORD	566	34
THROUGH JESUS CHRIST OUR LORD	567	10
THROUGH JESUS CHRIST OUR LORD	568	12
OF HIS SON JESUS CHRIST OUR LORD	568	15
WELL-BELOVED IN CHRIST, A	569	13
OF THE FLOCK OF CHRIST WHICH IS NOW INTRUSTED TO YOU	569	25
THROUGH JESUS CHRIST OUR LORD, WHO HATH TAUGHT US TO	571	12
BUT GRACE AND TRUTH CAME BY JESUS CHRIST	572	02
THROUGH JESUS CHRIST, OUR ONLY MEDIATOR AND REDEEMER	572	14
OUR LORD JESUS CHRIST, THE GREAT SHEPHERD OF THE	573	04
THROUGH JESUS CHRIST, TO WHOM BE GLORY FOR EVER AND	573	08
THE SAKE OF JESUS CHRIST THY SON OUR SAVIOUR	573	28
JESUS CHRIST HIMSELF BEING THE CHIEF	574	05
BLESSED SON JESUS CHRIST, THE GRACIOUS BISHOP AND	574	20
MADE A MEMBER OF CHRIST, THE CHILD OF GOD, AND AN	577	10
THROUGH JESUS CHRIST OUR SAVIOUR	577	24

CHRIST   CONTINUED

AND IN JESUS CHRIST HIS ONLY SON OUR LORD   577 30
MERCY AND GOODNESS, THROUGH OUR LORD JESUS CHRIST   581 06
SACRAMENTS HATH CHRIST ORDAINED IN HIS CHURCH   581 07
ORDAINED BY CHRIST HIMSELF, AS A MEANS WHEREBY WE   581 13
OF THE DEATH OF CHRIST, AND OF THE BENEFITS WHICH WE   582 05
BODY AND BLOOD OF CHRIST, WHICH ARE SPIRITUALLY TAKEN   582 12
BODY AND BLOOD OF CHRIST, AS OUR BODIES ARE BY THE   582 18
MERCY THROUGH CHRIST, WITH A THANKFUL REMEMBRANCE OF   582 25
AGAIN FOR US, THY SON OUR SAVIOUR JESUS CHRIST   587 28
KNOWLEDGE OF OUR LORD AND SAVIOUR JESUS CHRIST   588 10
THY SON JESUS CHRIST OUR LORD   588 24
OF THY SON JESUS CHRIST, OUR LORD AND SAVIOUR   589 07
OF OUR LORD JESUS CHRIST, AND THE LOVE OF GOD, AND   589 09
OF THY SON JESUS CHRIST, OUR ONLY SAVIOUR AND   590 07
THE COMING OF OUR LORD AND SAVIOUR JESUS CHRIST   590 20
THY SON OUR SAVIOUR JESUS CHRIST   591 05
THY SON OUR SAVIOUR JESUS CHRIST   591 23
OF THY SON CHRIST JESUS, IN WHOSE NAME WE OFFER UP   591 32
OF OUR LORD JESUS CHRIST, AND THE LOVE OF GOD, AND   592 02
THROUGH JESUS CHRIST OUR LORD   592 25
OF OUR LORD JESUS CHRIST, AND THE LOVE OF GOD, AND   592 27
LOVE OF THY ONLY SON, OUR SAVIOUR, JESUS CHRIST   593 16
THROUGH JESUS CHRIST OUR LORD   594 09
THROUGH JESUS CHRIST OUR LORD   594 17
THROUGH JESUS CHRIST OUR SAVIOUR   594 27
THY SON, OUR SAVIOUR JESUS CHRIST   595 10
THE SAME CHRIST OUR LORD   595 16
THROUGH JESUS CHRIST OUR LORD   595 23
THROUGH JESUS CHRIST OUR LORD   595 32
IN THY SON, JESUS CHRIST OUR LORD   596 09
THY SON, JESUS CHRIST OUR LORD   596 21
THE EXAMPLE OF THEIR SAVIOUR JESUS CHRIST   596 28
THROUGH JESUS CHRIST OUR LORD   597 07
THROUGH JESUS CHRIST OUR LORD   597 12
THROUGH JESUS CHRIST OUR LORD   597 18
THROUGH JESUS CHRIST OUR LORD   597 26
THROUGH JESUS CHRIST OUR LORD   598 04
THROUGH JESUS CHRIST OUR LORD   598 11
THROUGH JESUS CHRIST OUR LORD   598 17
THROUGH JESUS CHRIST OUR LORD   598 30
BECAME POOR, THY SON, OUR SAVIOUR JESUS CHRIST   599 17
THROUGH JESUS CHRIST OUR LORD   599 23
LOVE OF THY DEAR SON, OUR SAVIOUR JESUS CHRIST   600 13
THROUGH JESUS CHRIST OUR LORD   600 19
WHEREOF IS ONE CHRIST, VERY GOD, AND VERY MAN   603 14
AS CHRIST DIED FOR US, AND WAS BURIED   603 18
CHRIST DID TRULY RISE AGAIN FROM DEATH, AND TOOK   603 21
TO MANKIND BY CHRIST, WHO IS THE ONLY MEDIATOR   604 16
GRACE OF GOD BY CHRIST PREVENTING US, THAT WE MAY   605 02
AND SAVIOUR JESUS CHRIST BY FAITH, AND NOT FOR OUR   605 07
TO GOD IN CHRIST, AND DO SPRING OUT NECESSARILY OF A   605 13
THE GRACE OF CHRIST, AND THE INSPIRATION OF HIS   605 17
AS THEY SPRING NOT OF FAITH IN JESUS CHRIST   605 18
WHEREAS CHRIST SAITH PLAINLY, WHEN YE HAVE DONE ALL   605 28
CHRIST IN THE TRUTH OF OUR NATURE WAS MADE LIKE UNTO   605 31
AND BORN AGAIN IN CHRIST, YET OFFEND IN MANY THINGS   605 36
TO BRING THEM BY CHRIST TO EVERLASTING SALVATION, AS   606 09
HE HATH CHOSEN IN CHRIST OUT OF MANKIND, AND TO BRING   606 09
THE IMAGE OF HIS ONLY-BEGOTTEN SON JESUS CHRIST   606 14
OUR ELECTION IN CHRIST, IS FULL OF SWEET, PLEASANT,   606 16
OF THE SPIRIT OF CHRIST, MORTIFYING THE WORKS OF THE   606 18
ENJOYED THROUGH CHRIST, AS BECAUSE IT DOTH FERVENTLY   606 21
THE SPIRIT OF CHRIST, TO HAVE CONTINUALLY BEFORE   606 23
THE NAME OF JESUS CHRIST, WHEREBY MEN MUST BE SAVED   606 35
VISIBLE CHURCH OF CHRIST IS A CONGREGATION OF   606 38
ORDAINED OF CHRIST BE NOT ONLY BADGES OR TOKENS OF   607 31
ORDAINED OF CHRIST OUR LORD IN THE GOSPEL, THAT IS TO   607 36
NOT ORDAINED OF CHRIST TO BE GAZED UPON, OR TO BE   608 02
AS MOST AGREEABLE WITH THE INSTITUTION OF CHRIST   608 32
WE BREAK IS A PARTAKING OF THE BODY OF CHRIST   608 38
OF BLESSING IS A PARTAKING OF THE BLOOD OF CHRIST   608 39
THE BODY OF CHRIST IS GIVEN, TAKEN, AND EATEN   608 44
THE BODY OF CHRIST IS RECEIVED AND EATEN IN THE   608 46
THE SACRAMENT OF THE BODY AND BLOOD OF CHRIST   609 06
YET IN NO WISE ARE THEY PARTAKERS OF CHRIST   609 06
THE OFFERING OF CHRIST ONCE MADE IS THAT PERFECT   609 14
PRIEST DID OFFER CHRIST FOR THE QUICK AND THE DEAD,   609 18
BY OUR LORD JESUS CHRIST, AND JAMES HIS APOSTLE,   611 07

CHRIST'S

BEG FOR JESUS CHRIST'S SAKE   019 11
BEG FOR JESUS CHRIST'S SAKE   033 09
PRAYERS FOR CHRIST'S HOLY CATHOLIC CHURCH, THE   047 05
WHOLE STATE OF CHRIST'S CHURCH   074 05
FOR JESUS CHRIST'S SAKE, OUR ONLY MEDIATOR AND   075 05
OUR LORD JESUS CHRIST'S SAKE, FORGIVE US ALL THAT IS   075 27
SAVIOUR JESUS CHRIST'S HOLY INSTITUTION, IN   081 12
THAT CHRIST'S BLOOD WAS SHED FOR THEE, AND BE   083 05
WHOLE STATE OF CHRIST'S CHURCH, THE PRIEST MAY SAY   R 085 22
THE LORD JESUS CHRIST'S SAKE, THAT YE WILL NOT REFUSE   088 15
I CALL YOU IN CHRIST'S BEHALF, I EXHORT YOU, AS YE   089 08
ONLY SON JESUS CHRIST'S SAKE   122 19
FELLOWSHIP OF CHRIST'S RELIGION, THAT THEY MAY AVOID   173 07
THEY THAT ARE CHRIST'S HAVE CRUCIFIED THE FLESH WITH   209 28
EVEN AS GOD FOR CHRIST'S SAKE HATH FORGIVEN YOU   216 30
RECEIVED INTO CHRIST'S HOLY CHURCH, AND BE MADE A   274 05
CONGREGATION OF CHRIST'S FLOCK   280 04
AND TO CONTINUE CHRIST'S FAITHFUL SOLDIER AND SERVANT   280 09
THE BODY OF CHRIST'S CHURCH, LET US GIVE THANKS UNTO   280 15
RECEIVED INTO CHRIST'S CHURCH, BECOME THE RECIPIENTS   292 34
FOR JESUS CHRIST'S SAKE   323 17
SACRAMENT OF CHRIST'S BODY AND BLOOD, THE MINISTER   R 323 25
THEY THAT ARE CHRIST'S AT HIS COMING   328 26

CHRIST'S   CONTINUED

OF MINISTERS IN CHRIST'S CHURCH, -- BISHOPS, PRIESTS,   529 13
TO SEEK FOR CHRIST'S SHEEP THAT ARE DISPERSED ABROAD,   539 34
BE MERCIFUL FOR CHRIST'S SAKE TO POOR AND NEEDY   555 24
CONGREGATION OF CHRIST'S FLOCK, MAY BE SANCTIFIED BY   565 20
MAY CONTINUE CHRIST'S FAITHFUL SOLDIER AND SERVANT   565 21
BEG FOR JESUS CHRIST'S SAKE, OUR MOST BLESSED LORD   566 23
FOR CHRIST'S SAKE   600 16
ACCORDING TO CHRIST'S ORDINANCE, IN ALL THOSE THINGS   606 40
BUT IN CHRIST'S, AND DO MINISTER BY HIS   608 12
THE EFFECT OF CHRIST'S ORDINANCE TAKEN AWAY BY THEIR   608 14
BECAUSE OF CHRIST'S INSTITUTION AND PROMISE, ALTHOUGH   608 17
REDEMPTION BY CHRIST'S DEATH   608 36
WAS NOT BY CHRIST'S ORDINANCE RESERVED, CARRIED   608 47
BY CHRIST'S ORDINANCE AND COMMANDMENT,   609 11

CHRISTENED

THAT BE NOT CHRISTENED, BUT IT IS ALSO A SIGN OF   608 25

CHRISTIAN

GOOD CHRISTIAN PEOPLE, I BID YOUR PRAYERS FOR   047 06
PRESERVE ALL CHRISTIAN RULERS AND MAGISTRATES, GIVING   055 26
EVERY SINCERE CHRISTIAN, WITH A MEEK, CANDID,   VI 37
HEARTS OF ALL CHRISTIAN RULERS, THAT THEY MAY TRULY   074 17
OF THE CHRISTIAN RELIGION   R 273 20
OF THE CHRISTIAN FAITH, AS CONTAINED IN THE APOSTLES'   276 31
THINGS WHICH A CHRISTIAN OUGHT TO KNOW AND BELIEVE TO   277 11
OF THE CHRISTIAN FAITH, AS CONTAINED IN THE APOSTLES'   278 09
WHAT IS YOUR CHRISTIAN NAME   283 15
MY CHRISTIAN NAME IS --   283 16
OF THE CHRISTIAN FAITH   283 26
OF THE CHRISTIAN FAITH   284 08
OF THE CHRISTIAN FAITH AS CONTAINED IN THE APOSTLES'   284 09
OF THE CHRISTIAN FAITH, AND AS TO WHETHER HE REPENT   R 313 19
DEPART, O CHRISTIAN SOUL, OUT OF THIS WORLD, IN THE   319 19
AMONG ALL CHRISTIAN PEOPLE, AND ESPECIALLY AMONG THEM   543 08
OF THE CHRISTIAN FAITH   577 17
DO NOT BIND CHRISTIAN MEN, NOR THE CIVIL PRECEPTS   604 20
NO CHRISTIAN MAN WHATSOEVER IS FREE FROM THE   604 22
OR TOKENS OF CHRISTIAN MEN'S PROFESSION, BUT RATHER   607 31
WHEREBY CHRISTIAN MEN ARE DISCERNED FROM OTHERS THAT   608 25
TO ALL CHRISTIAN MEN ALIKE   609 12
FOR ALL OTHER CHRISTIAN MEN, TO MARRY AT THEIR OWN   609 23
EXPLICATION OF CHRISTIAN DOCTRINE, AND INSTRUCTIVE IN R 610 25
IS FORBIDDEN CHRISTIAN MEN BY OUR LORD JESUS CHRIST,   611 06
WE JUDGE, THAT CHRISTIAN RELIGION DOTH NOT PROHIBIT,   611 07

CHRISTIANITY

WHAT CHRISTIANITY IS, AND WHAT THE TRUTHS OF THE   VI 39

CHRISTIANS

THEMSELVES CHRISTIANS MAY BE LED INTO THE WAY OF   018 32
THEMSELVES CHRISTIANS MAY BE LED INTO THE WAY OF   032 32
OF CHRISTIANS IN THESE STATES WERE LEFT AT FULL AND   VI 10
WERE CALLED CHRISTIANS FIRST IN ANTIOCH   241 14
ALL CHRISTIANS MAY BE SO JOINED TOGETHER IN   574 06
THE LOVE THAT CHRISTIANS OUGHT TO HAVE AMONG   608 34
AND GOODS OF CHRISTIANS ARE NOT COMMON, AS TOUCHING   610 44

CHRISTMAS

ON CHRISTMAS DAY AND UNTIL THE EPIPHANY   R 008 18
BE SAID ON CHRISTMAS DAY, EASTER DAY, ASCENSION DAY,   R 070 31
UPON CHRISTMAS DAY, AND SEVEN DAYS AFTER   R 077 13
UNTIL CHRISTMAS DAY   R 090 21
CELEBRATED ON CHRISTMAS DAY, THE FOLLOWING COLLECT,   R 098 07
FOLLOWING CHRISTMAS DAY, THE FIRST EPISTLE AND GOSPEL R 103 34
AND GOSPEL FOR CHRISTMAS DAY SHALL SERVE FOR THEM   R 104 02

CHRISTS

ARISE FALSE CHRISTS, AND FALSE PROPHETS, AND SHALL   118 05

CHURCH

IN EVERY CHURCH, WHAT CANNOT BE CLEARLY   V 05
EPISCOPAL CHURCH IN THESE STATES IS INDEBTED, UNDER   V 10
THE CHURCH OF ENGLAND, TO WHICH THE PROTESTANT   V 10
THE SAME CHURCH HATH NOT ONLY IN HER PREFACE,   V 21
THE PRESERVATION OF PEACE AND UNITY IN THE CHURCH   V 36
ACCORDING TO THE USE OF THIS CHURCH   R 009 23
THE HOLY CHURCH THROUGHOUT ALL THE WORLD DOTH   010 19
THE HOLY CATHOLIC CHURCH   015 28
AND I BELIEVE ONE CATHOLIC AND APOSTOLIC CHURCH   016 19
PRAY FOR THY HOLY CHURCH UNIVERSAL   018 30
ACCORDING TO THE USE OF THIS CHURCH   R 025 16
THE HOLY CATHOLIC CHURCH   029 33
AND I BELIEVE ONE CATHOLIC AND APOSTOLIC CHURCH   030 24
PRAY FOR THY HOLY CHURCH UNIVERSAL   032 30
THE GOOD OF THY CHURCH, THE SAFETY, HONOUR, AND   035 13
AND THY WHOLE CHURCH, WE HUMBLY BEG IN THE NAME   035 19
TO BE WITH THY CHURCH TO THE END OF THE WORLD   036 29
COUNCIL OF THY CHURCH HERE ASSEMBLED IN THY NAME AND   036 30
OF THIS CHURCH, OR OF THE DIOCESE CONCERNED   R 037 10
HUMBLY BESEECH THEE FOR THY HOLY CATHOLIC CHURCH   037 16
FOR PLANTING THY CHURCH IN ALL THE EARTH   038 19
AN UNIVERSAL CHURCH BY THE PRECIOUS BLOOD OF THY DEAR   038 26
TO SERVE IN THE SACRED MINISTRY OF THY CHURCH   038 31
HAST APPOINTED DIVERS ORDERS IN THY CHURCH   039 09
AND THE BENEFIT OF THY HOLY CHURCH   039 14
THEMSELVES TO THE SACRED MINISTRY OF THY CHURCH   039 20

CHURCH   CONTINUED

TO THY HOLY CHURCH THE CARE AND NURTURE OF THY   042 31
AND DOST MAKE THEM LIVING MEMBERS OF THY CHURCH   043 09
HOLY CATHOLIC CHURCH, THE BLESSED COMPANY OF ALL   047 07
BUT THE FAITH OF THY CHURCH   049 07
BEING PRESENT IN CHURCH, SHALL HAVE DESIRED TO RETURN R   051 03
PRAYERS OF THY CHURCH, AND TURNED OUR DEARTH AND   051 31
TO RETURN HIS THANKS UNTO THEE IN THY HOLY CHURCH   053 24
GOVERN THY HOLY CHURCH UNIVERSAL IN THE RIGHT WAY   055 20
EVERMORE GIVE THANKS UNTO THEE IN THY HOLY CHURCH   058 23
ATTENTION OF THIS CHURCH WAS IN THE FIRST PLACE DRAWN   VI 15
PRAYER OF THE CHURCH OF ENGLAND   VI 31
APPEAR THAT THIS CHURCH IS FAR FROM INTENDING TO   VI 31
DEPART FROM THE CHURCH OF ENGLAND IN ANY ESSENTIAL   VI 32
MEMBER OF OUR CHURCH, AND EVERY SINCERE CHRISTIAN,   VI 37
AND I BELIEVE ONE CATHOLIC AND APOSTOLIC CHURCH   071 21
ANY WHO HAVE DESIRED THE PRAYERS OF THE CHURCH   R   074 01
US PRAY FOR THE WHOLE STATE OF CHRIST'S CHURCH   074 05
THE UNIVERSAL CHURCH WITH THE SPIRIT OF TRUTH,   074 12
AND ALL THY WHOLE CHURCH, MAY OBTAIN REMISSION OF OUR   081 19
IT SHALL NOT BE CARRIED OUT OF THE CHURCH   084 31
STATE OF CHRIST'S CHURCH, THE PRIEST MAY SAY THIS   R   085 22
IF IN ANY CHURCH THE HOLY COMMUNION BE TWICE   098 07
OF LIGHT UPON THY CHURCH, THAT IT, BEING ILLUMINED BY   101 06
BE KNOWN BY THE CHURCH THE MANIFOLD WISDOM OF GOD,   108 25
THEE TO KEEP THY CHURCH AND HOUSEHOLD CONTINUALLY IN   115 28
WHOLE BODY OF THE CHURCH IS GOVERNED AND SANCTIFIED   156 28
MEN IN THY HOLY CHURCH, THAT EVERY MEMBER OF THE   156 30
IF IN ANY CHURCH THE HOLY COMMUNION BE TWICE   R   164 30
IF IN ANY CHURCH THE HOLY COMMUNION BE TWICE   R   182 11
THAT THY CHURCH, BEING GATHERED TOGETHER IN   185 15
THAT THY CHURCH MAY JOYFULLY SERVE THEE IN ALL GODLY   195 17
I PERSECUTED THE CHURCH OF GOD   205 14
O LORD, THY CHURCH WITH THY PERPETUAL MERCY   210 17
THY CONTINUAL PITY CLEANSE AND DEFEND THY CHURCH   212 05
BE GLORY IN THE CHURCH BY CHRIST JESUS THROUGHOUT ALL   212 24
THY HOUSEHOLD THE CHURCH IN CONTINUAL GODLINESS   220 17
TO HEAR THE DEVOUT PRAYERS OF THY CHURCH   222 11
GRANT THAT THY CHURCH, BEING ALWAY PRESERVED FROM   234 02
THY HOLY CHURCH WITH THE HEAVENLY DOCTRINE OF THY   237 06
THE EARS OF THE CHURCH WHICH WAS IN JERUSALEM   241 04
WITH THE CHURCH, AND TAUGHT MUCH PEOPLE   241 13
FORTH HIS HANDS TO VEX CERTAIN OF THE CHURCH   244 32
CEASING OF THE CHURCH UNTO GOD FOR HIM   245 08
AND UPON THIS ROCK I WILL BUILD MY CHURCH   246 08
FORTH HIS HANDS TO VEX CERTAIN OF THE CHURCH   247 02
UNTO THY CHURCH, TO LOVE THAT WORD WHICH HE   249 17
MANIFEST IN THY CHURCH THE LIKE POWER AND LOVE, TO   253 18
HAST BUILT THY CHURCH UPON THE FOUNDATION OF THE   254 27
YEAR WE PRAISE FOR THE DEDICATION OF THIS CHURCH   259 20
EVERMORE GIVE THANKS UNTO THEE IN THY HOLY CHURCH   262 02
EVEN AS CHRIST IS THE HEAD OF THE CHURCH   267 16
THEREFORE AS THE CHURCH IS SUBJECT UNTO CHRIST,   267 17
ALSO LOVED THE CHURCH, AND GAVE HIMSELF FOR IT   267 20
A GLORIOUS CHURCH, NOT HAVING SPOT, OR WRINKLE, OR   267 22
EVEN AS THE LORD THE CHURCH   267 27
BUT I SPEAK CONCERNING CHRIST AND THE CHURCH   267 32
TO THY WHOLE CHURCH IN PARADISE AND ON EARTH, THY   268 15
CHRIST'S HOLY CHURCH, AND BE MADE A LIVING MEMBER OF   274 05
BODY OF CHRIST'S CHURCH, LET US GIVE THANKS UNTO   280 15
AND TO INCORPORATE HIM INTO THY HOLY CHURCH   280 32
OF THY HOLY CHURCH, HE MAY BE AN INHERITOR OF THINE   281 04
BROUGHT TO THE CHURCH, AT WHICH TIME THESE PARTS OF   R   282 02
THE HOLY CATHOLIC CHURCH   284 22
HAST BUILT THY CHURCH UPON THE FOUNDATION OF THE   290 19
CONCERNING THE CHURCH WHICH FOLLOW, THE PEOPLE   R   290 26
WHEN WERE YOU MADE A MEMBER OF THE CHURCH   290 28
A MEMBER OF THE CHURCH WHEN I WAS BAPTIZED   290 29
WHAT IS THE CHURCH   290 31
THE CHURCH IS THE BODY OF WHICH JESUS CHRIST   290 32
HOW IS THE CHURCH DESCRIBED IN THE APOSTLES' AND   291 02
THE CHURCH IS DESCRIBED IN THE CREEDS AS   291 04
WE MEAN THAT THE CHURCH IS ONE   291 07
IS YOUR BOUNDEN DUTY AS A MEMBER OF THE CHURCH   291 17
TO WORSHIP GOD EVERY SUNDAY IN HIS CHURCH   291 19
MEANS DOES THE CHURCH PROVIDE TO HELP YOU TO DO ALL   291 21
THE CHURCH PROVIDES THE LAYING ON OF HANDS,   291 23
SACRAMENTS HATH CHRIST ORDAINED IN HIS CHURCH   292 05
INTO CHRIST'S CHURCH, BECOME THE RECIPIENTS OF HIS   292 34
WHAT ORDERS OF MINISTERS ARE THERE IN THE CHURCH   294 04
HAVE BEEN IN THE CHURCH FROM THE EARLIEST TIMES   294 06
TO BE A CHIEF PASTOR IN THE CHURCH   294 09
OPENLY IN THE CHURCH, INSTRUCT OR EXAMINE THE YOUTH   R   295 08
TO THE CHURCH AT THE TIME APPOINTED, TO RECEIVE   R   295 11
THE BODY OF THE CHURCH, OR SHALL BE READY IN SOME   R   300 04
UNION THAT IS BETWIXT CHRIST AND HIS CHURCH   300 13
MARRIAGE AND UNITY BETWIXT CHRIST AND HIS CHURCH   303 22
COME INTO THE CHURCH DECENTLY APPARELLED, AND THERE   R   305 07
HE MAY GIVE THANKS UNTO THEE IN THY HOLY CHURCH   309 32
THIS SICK MEMBER IN THE UNITY OF THE CHURCH   314 06
IN THE COMMUNION OF THE CATHOLIC CHURCH   317 04
IT SHALL BE PUBLICLY ADMINISTERED IN THE CHURCH   R   321 09
TO COME TO THE CHURCH, AND YET IS DESIROUS TO RECEIVE R   321 11
MINISTRATION IN CHURCH, SUBSTITUTING THE COLLECT,   R   323 33
EITHER INTO THE CHURCH OR TOWARDS THE GRAVE, SHALL   R   324 03
ARE COME INTO THE CHURCH, SHALL BE SAID ONE OR MORE   R   324 16
SHELTER OF THE CHURCH THE WHOLE OR A PART OF THE   R   336 31
EITHER INTO THE CHURCH OR TOWARDS THE GRAVE, SHALL   R   338 03
ARE COME INTO THE CHURCH, SHALL BE SAID THE FOLLOWING R   338 14
IN CHRIST'S CHURCH, -- BISHOPS, PRIESTS, AND DEACONS   529 13
ESTEEMED IN THIS CHURCH, NO MAN SHALL BE ACCOUNTED OR   529 19
IN THIS CHURCH, OR SUFFERED TO EXECUTE ANY OF   529 21
THE FACE OF THE CHURCH, ADMIT HIM A DEACON, IN SUCH   529 31
ORDER IS IN THE CHURCH OF CHRIST, AND ALSO, HOW THE   R   530 05
AND THE EDIFYING OF HIS CHURCH   530 16

CHURCH   CONTINUED

EDIFYING OF THY CHURCH, AND THE GLORY OF THY HOLY   531 07
MINISTERS IN THY CHURCH, AND DIDST INSPIRE THINE   531 15
OF THY NAME, AND .THE EDIFICATION OF THY CHURCH   531 23
CANONS OF THIS CHURCH, TO THE MINISTRY OF THE SAME   532 33
ASSEMBLED IN THE CHURCH WHERE YOU SHALL BE APPOINTED   533 07
A DEACON, IN THE CHURCH WHERE HE SHALL BE APPOINTED   533 11
READ HOLY SCRIPTURES AND HOMILIES IN THE CHURCH   533 15
THE CANONS OF THE CHURCH, MAY HAVE THE CHARGE AND   533 32
A DEACON IN THE CHURCH OF GOD COMMITTED UNTO THEE   534 06
THE GOSPEL IN THE CHURCH OF GOD, AND TO PREACH THE   534 11
SERVANTS UNTO THE OFFICE OF DEACONS IN THY CHURCH   535 02
CALLED UNTO THE HIGHER MINISTRIES IN THY CHURCH   535 10
THE FACE OF THE CHURCH, IN SUCH MANNER AND FORM AS   R   535 26
ORDER IS IN THE CHURCH OF CHRIST, AND ALSO, HOW THE R   536 05
AND THE EDIFYING OF HIS CHURCH   536 17
EDIFYING OF THY CHURCH, AND THE GLORY OF THY HOLY   537 13
DIVERS ORDERS OF MINISTERS IN THY CHURCH   537 22
AND THE EDIFICATION OF THY CHURCH   537 27
THE CHURCH AND CONGREGATION WHOM YOU MUST SERVE, IS   540 08
THAT THE SAME CHURCH, OR ANY MEMBER THEREOF, DO TAKE   540 10
AND OF HIS CHURCH, SHALL DEMAND OF YOU TOUCHING   541 28
CANONS OF THIS CHURCH, TO THE ORDER AND MINISTRY OF   541 32
AND AS THIS CHURCH HATH RECEIVED THE SAME, ACCORDING   542 14
AWAY FROM THE CHURCH ALL ERRONEOUS AND STRANGE   542 20
THE CANONS OF THE CHURCH, MAY HAVE THE CHARGE AND   543 13
A PRIEST IN THE CHURCH OF GOD, NOW COMMITTED UNTO   546 10
A PRIEST IN THE CHURCH OF GOD, NOW COMMITTED TO THEE   546 18
DIVERS ORDERS OF MINISTERS IN THY CHURCH   547 33
OF THY NAME, AND THE EDIFICATION OF THY CHURCH   548 06
PREPARED IN THE CHURCH, AND SET IN ORDER, THE   R   549 03
PASTORS OF THY CHURCH, THAT THEY MAY DILIGENTLY   549 10
TAKE CARE OF THE CHURCH OF GOD   549 26
TO EPHESUS, AND CALLED THE ELDERS OF THE CHURCH   550 05
TO FEED THE CHURCH OF GOD, WHICH HE HATH PURCHASED   550 28
BISHOPS OF THIS CHURCH UNTO THE PRESIDING BISHOP,   R   552 18
AND WORSHIP OF THE PROTESTANT EPISCOPAL CHURCH   R   552 27
EPISCOPAL CHURCH IN N   552 29
EPISCOPAL CHURCH IN THE UNITED STATES OF AMERICA   552 31
EDIFYING OF THY CHURCH, AND TO THE HONOUR, PRAISE,   553 20
DIVERS ORDERS OF MINISTERS IN THY CHURCH   553 28
AND THE EDIFYING AND WELL-GOVERNING OF THY CHURCH   553 33
GOVERNMENT IN THE CHURCH OF CHRIST, WHICH HE HATH   554 10
YOURSELF IN THE CHURCH OF GOD   554 15
AND THE ORDER OF THIS CHURCH   554 18
AWAY FROM THE CHURCH ALL ERRONEOUS AND STRANGE   555 03
THE ORDER OF THIS CHURCH, IS COMMITTED TO YOU   555 17
TO THE EDIFYING AND MAKING PERFECT HIS CHURCH   557 28
A BISHOP IN THE CHURCH OF GOD, NOW COMMITTED UNTO   558 13
GRANT PEACE TO THE WHOLE WORLD, AND TO THY CHURCH   560 13
AND BLESS THY CHURCH THROUGHOUT THE WORLD   560 16
MINISTERS OF THY CHURCH WITH DEVOTION TO THY GLORY   560 22
EDIFYING OF THY CHURCH, AND TO THE GLORY OF THY HOLY   560 29
EDIFYING OF THY CHURCH, AND TO THE HONOUR, PRAISE,   561 05
WHOM THOU DOST CALL TO THE MINISTRY OF THY CHURCH   561 09
MINISTERS OF THY CHURCH, THAT THE GOSPEL MAY BE   561 13
THAT THY CHURCH MAY BE ONE   561 17
WHO DOST EVER HALLOW AND PROTECT THY CHURCH   562 09
ENTRANCE OF THE CHURCH, OR CHAPEL, BY THE   R   563 05
THE AISLE OF THE CHURCH, OR CHAPEL, TO THE HOLY   R   563 08
INTO A PARISH OR CHURCH, AS PRESCRIBED BY CANON,   R   569 05
MINISTER OF THIS CHURCH, MAY PROCEED TO INSTITUTE HIM R   569 06
CHARTERS OF THE CHURCH IN THE SAME   R   569 12
IN THE PARISH (OR CHURCH) OF E   569 17
SAID PARISH, (OR CHURCH,) POSSESSED OF FULL POWER TO   569 18
AND CANONS OF THE CHURCH, AND WITH SUCH LAWFUL   569 21
OF -- PARISH, (OR CHURCH,) YOU ARE FAITHFULLY TO FEED   569 24
THE KEYS OF THE CHURCH IN HIS HAND, IN OPEN VIEW,   R   570 10
THIS PARISH, (OR CHURCH,) AS PRIEST AND RECTOR OF THE   570 14
THE KEYS OF THE CHURCH TO THE NEW INCUMBENT, SAYING, R   570 26
OF -- PARISH (OR CHURCH) I DO RECEIVE AND ACKNOWLEDGE   570 27
GIVE UNTO YOUR HANDS THE KEYS OF THIS CHURCH   570 30
AND IN EXERCISING THE DISCIPLINE OF THE CHURCH   571 28
HAST APPOINTED DIVERS ORDERS IN THY CHURCH   572 08
AND THE BENEFIT OF THY HOLY CHURCH   572 14
AN UNIVERSAL CHURCH, AND HAST PROMISED TO BE WITH THE   572 17
HAST BUILT THY CHURCH UPON THE FOUNDATION OF THE   574 03
HOLY APOSTOLIC CHURCH, AND WITH ONE MOUTH MAY PROFESS   574 11
THAT THY CHURCH MAY JOYFULLY SERVE THEE IN ALL GODLY   574 17
THE HOLY CATHOLIC CHURCH   578 06
SACRAMENTS HATH CHRIST ORDAINED IN HIS CHURCH   581 08
OPENLY IN THE CHURCH, INSTRUCT OR EXAMINE SO MANY   R   582 28
TO COME TO THE CHURCH AT THE TIME APPOINTED, AND   R   582 33
BE GRACIOUS UNTO THY CHURCH   590 25
WHOSE AUTHORITY WAS NEVER ANY DOUBT IN THE CHURCH   603 34
SAITH) THE CHURCH DOTH READ FOR EXAMPLE OF LIFE AND   604 02
THE VISIBLE CHURCH OF CHRIST IS A CONGREGATION OF   606 38
AS THE CHURCH OF JERUSALEM, ALEXANDRIA, AND ANTIOCH,   606 42
SO ALSO THE CHURCH OF ROME HATH ERRED, NOT ONLY IN   606 43
THE CHURCH HATH POWER TO DECREE RITES OR CEREMONIES,   607 03
LAWFUL FOR THE CHURCH TO ORDAIN ANY THING THAT IS   607 04
ALTHOUGH THE CHURCH BE A WITNESS AND A KEEPER OF HOLY   607 07
PRAYER IN THE CHURCH, OR TO MINISTER THE SACRAMENTS,   607 28
OF THE PRIMITIVE CHURCH, TO HAVE PUBLIC PRAYER IN THE   607 28
IN THE VISIBLE CHURCH THE EVIL BE EVER MINGLED WITH   608 08
DISCIPLINE OF THE CHURCH, THAT INQUIRY BE MADE OF   608 19
BAPTISM RIGHTLY ARE GRAFTED INTO THE CHURCH   608 27
RETAINED IN THE CHURCH, AS MOST AGREEABLE WITH THE   608 32
OF THE CHURCH IS RIGHTLY CUT OFF FROM THE UNITY OF   609 26
THE UNITY OF THE CHURCH, AND EXCOMMUNICATED, OUGHT TO   609 27
RECEIVED INTO THE CHURCH BY A JUDGE THAT HATH   609 29
CEREMONIES OF THE CHURCH, WHICH BE NOT REPUGNANT TO   609 37
ORDER OF THE CHURCH, AND HURTETH THE AUTHORITY OF THE   609 40
OR NATIONAL CHURCH HATH AUTHORITY TO ORDAIN, CHANGE,   609 42
OR RITES OF THE CHURCH ORDAINED ONLY BY MAN'S   610 02

CHURCH   CONTINUED

RECEIVED IN THIS CHURCH, SO FAR AS IT DECLARES THE   R 610 24
INAPPLICABLE TO THE CIRCUMSTANCES OF THIS CHURCH   R 610 27
OF THIS CHURCH IN 1792, DOTH CONTAIN ALL THINGS   610 32

CHURCH-WARDENS

CHURCH-WARDENS, OR OTHER FIT PERSONS   R 073 27
AND THE CHURCH-WARDENS TO THE RELIEF OF DISTRESSED   R 307 08
BY THE CHURCH-WARDENS AND VESTRYMEN, OR SOME OTHER   R 563 06

CHURCHES

AND ANY CHURCHES MAY, INSTEAD OF THE WORDS, HE   R 015 16
AND ANY CHURCHES MAY, INSTEAD OF THE WORDS, HE   R 029 21
RESPECTIVE CHURCHES, AND FORMS OF WORSHIP, AND   VI 11
THE CARE OF ALL THE CHURCHES   121 11
THE BANNS IN CHURCHES, OR BY LICENCE, BEING DIFFERENT   R 304 18
TO BE READ IN CHURCHES BY THE MINISTERS, DILIGENTLY   610 09
HOMILIES IN CHURCHES, UNTIL A REVISION OF   R 610 27

CIRCUMCISE

THEY CAME TO CIRCUMCISE THE CHILD   243 17

CIRCUMCISED

SON TO BE CIRCUMCISED, AND OBEDIENT TO THE LAW FOR   105 20
THEY CONSTRAIN YOU TO BE CIRCUMCISED   210 25
WHO ARE CIRCUMCISED KEEP THE LAW   210 27
TO HAVE YOU CIRCUMCISED, THAT THEY MAY GLORY IN YOUR   210 28

CIRCUMCISING

FOR THE CIRCUMCISING OF THE CHILD, HIS NAME WAS   106 20

CIRCUMCISION

BY THY HOLY NATIVITY AND CIRCUMCISION   055 07
OF THE CIRCUMCISION FOR THE TRUTH OF GOD, TO CONFIRM   092 23
US THE TRUE CIRCUMCISION OF THE SPIRIT   105 21
THEY OF THE CIRCUMCISION WHICH BELIEVED WERE   184 22
NEITHER CIRCUMCISION AVAILETH ANY THING, NOR   210 32

CIRCUMSPECTLY

YE WALK CIRCUMSPECTLY, NOT AS FOOLS, BUT AS WISE,   217 23

CIRCUMSTANCES

THAN LOCAL CIRCUMSTANCES REQUIRE   VI 34
WHEN CIRCUMSTANCES RENDER IT EXPEDIENT TO SHORTEN   R 323 04
TO THE CIRCUMSTANCES OF THIS   R 610 26

CITIES

SAY UNTO THE CITIES OF JUDAH, BEHOLD YOUR GOD   243 05
OUT OF THE CITIES ROUND ABOUT UNTO JERUSALEM,   249 30
EVEN AS THE CITIES WHICH THOU HAST DESTROYED, WHOSE   351 33
AND BUILD THE CITIES OF JUDAH, *   424 14

CITIZEN

HIMSELF TO A CITIZEN OF THAT COUNTRY   202 07

CITIZENSHIP

FOR OUR CITIZENSHIP IS IN HEAVEN   222 21

CITY

THIS DAY IN THE CITY OF DAVID A SAVIOUR, WHICH IS   004 10
SHALL MAKE GLAD THE CITY OF GOD, THE HOLY PLACE OF   022 27
ALL THE CITY WAS MOVED, SAYING, WHO IS   091 31
ALL WENT TO BE TAXED, EVERY ONE INTO HIS OWN CITY   098 32
OUT OF THE CITY OF NAZARETH, INTO JUDAEA,   099 02
UNTO THE CITY OF DAVID, WHICH IS CALLED   099 03
THIS DAY IN THE CITY OF DAVID A SAVIOUR, WHICH IS   099 16
CAST HIM OUT OF THE CITY, AND STONED HIM   100 11
PERSECUTE THEM FROM CITY TO CITY   100 22
AND PERSECUTE THEM FROM CITY TO CITY   100 22
CAME AND DWELT IN A CITY CALLED NAZARETH   107 21
IN PERILS IN THE CITY, IN PERILS IN THE WILDERNESS,   121 06
TO HIM OUT OF EVERY CITY, HE SPAKE BY A PARABLE   121 19
UP INTO THE HOLY CITY, AND SETTETH HIM ON A PINNACLE   126 31
WENT INTO THE HOLY CITY, AND APPEARED UNTO MANY   137 30
GO YE INTO THE CITY, AND THERE SHALL MEET YOU A MAN   140 26
AND CAME INTO THE CITY, AND FOUND AS HE HAD SAID UNTO   140 33
ENTERED INTO THE CITY, THERE SHALL A MAN MEET YOU,   148 26
MADE IN THE CITY, AND FOR MURDER, WAS CAST INTO   153 31
WHERE JESUS WAS CRUCIFIED WAS NIGH TO THE CITY   160 05
BUT TARRY YE IN THE CITY OF JERUSALEM, UNTIL YE BE   178 22
AND LANES OF THE CITY, AND BRING IN HITHER THE POOR,   192 14
HE BEHELD THE CITY, AND WEPT OVER IT, SAYING,   204 06
JESUS WENT INTO A CITY CALLED NAIN   212 28
TO THE GATE OF THE CITY, BEHOLD, THERE WAS A DEAD MAN   212 30
MUCH PEOPLE OF THE CITY WAS WITH HER   212 32
AND PASSED OVER, AND CAME INTO HIS OWN CITY   216 34
THOSE MURDERERS, AND BURNED UP THEIR CITY   218 15
AND GO INTO THE CITY, AND IT SHALL BE TOLD THEE WHAT   230 07
TO THEIR OWN CITY NAZARETH   233 25
FROM GOD UNTO A CITY OF GALILEE, NAMED NAZARETH, TO A   236 06
UNTO THE IRON GATE THAT LEADETH UNTO THE CITY   245 22
HIS FACE INTO EVERY CITY AND PLACE, WHITHER HE   254 12
ALMOST THE WHOLE CITY TOGETHER TO HEAR THE WORD OF   260 26

CITY   CONTINUED

MAKE GLAD THE CITY OF GOD   327 09
ME MARVELLOUS GREAT KINDNESS IN A STRONG CITY   377 10
MAKE GLAD THE CITY OF GOD   397 33
IN THE CITY OF OUR GOD, EVEN UPON HIS HOLY HILL   399 11
SIDE LIETH THE CITY OF THE GREAT KING   399 13
HAVE WE SEEN IN THE CITY OF THE LORD OF HOSTS, IN THE   399 24
OF HOSTS, IN THE CITY OF OUR GOD   399 25
HAVE SPIED UNRIGHTEOUSNESS AND STRIFE IN THE CITY   407 05
AND RUN ABOUT THROUGH THE CITY   411 17
AND WILL GO ABOUT THE CITY   412 03
9 WHO WILL LEAD ME INTO THE STRONG CITY   412 29
AND THEY OF THE CITY SHALL FLOURISH LIKE GRASS UPON   427 31
THOU MAKE THEIR IMAGE TO VANISH OUT OF THE CITY   429 17
THOU CITY OF GOD   448 16
DOERS FROM THE CITY OF THE LORD   464 05
AND FOUND NO CITY TO DWELL IN   476 13
MIGHT GO TO THE CITY WHERE THEY DWELT   476 18
MAY BUILD THEM A CITY TO DWELL IN   478 19
10 WHO WILL LEAD ME INTO THE STRONG CITY   479 24
IS BUILT AS A CITY *   503 12
THE LORD KEEP THE CITY, *   505 24
WITNESSETH IN EVERY CITY, SAYING THAT BONDS AND   550 17
I JOHN SAW THE HOLY CITY, NEW JERUSALEM, COMING DOWN   567 12

CIVIL

AND THE CIVIL AUTHORITY HAS NOT SINCE THOUGHT PROPER   VI 05
WITH RESPECT TO CIVIL GOVERNMENT, THEIR   VI 08
PRAYERS FOR OUR CIVIL RULERS, IN CONSEQUENCE OF THE   VI 17
AND OBEY THE CIVIL AUTHORITY   288 28
THAT REGARDS THE CIVIL CONTRACT BETWEEN THE PARTIES   R 304 20
AND OBEY THE CIVIL AUTHORITY   580 04
NOR THE CIVIL PRECEPTS THEREOF OUGHT OF   604 20
OF A LOCAL AND CIVIL NATURE, AND IS PROVIDED   R 607 11
THE POWER OF THE CIVIL MAGISTRATE EXTENDETH TO ALL   610 38
OBEDIENCE TO THE CIVIL AUTHORITY, REGULARLY AND   610 41

CLAIM

AUTHORIZE YOU TO CLAIM AND ENJOY ALL THE ACCUSTOMED   569 29

CLAIMED

HAVE I CLAIMED AS MINE HERITAGE FOR EVER   497 19

CLAMOUR

AND ANGER, AND CLAMOUR, AND EVIL SPEAKING, BE PUT   216 28

CLAP

LET THE FLOODS CLAP THEIR HANDS, AND LET THE HILLS BE   027 21
O CLAP YOUR HANDS TOGETHER, ALL YE PEOPLES   398 21
9 LET THE FLOODS CLAP THEIR HANDS, AND LET THE HILLS   462 10

CLAUDIUS

IN THE DAYS OF CLAUDIUS CAESAR   241 19
IN THE DAYS OF CLAUDIUS CAESAR   246 28

CLAUSE

THE CLAUSE, HERE ASSEMBLED IN THY NAME, BEING CHANGED   R 037 11
AND THE CLAUSE, GOVERN US IN OUR WORK, TO GOVERN THEM   R 037 13

CLAUSES

OMIT ANY OF THE CLAUSES IN THIS PRAYER, OR MAY ADD   R 047 04

CLAVE

AND WHOSE SPIRIT CLAVE NOT STEDFASTLY UNTO GOD   435 15
16 HE CLAVE THE HARD ROCKS IN THE WILDERNESS,   435 30

CLAY

THEM OUT AS THE CLAY IN THE STREETS   362 24
OUT OF THE MIRE AND CLAY, *   390 12

CLEAN

O GOD, MAKE CLEAN OUR HEARTS WITHIN US   016 31
O GOD, MAKE CLEAN OUR HEARTS WITHIN US   031 13
SHALT PURGE ME WITH HYSSOP, AND I SHALL BE CLEAN   060 24
MAKE ME A CLEAN HEART, O GOD, *   060 30
OF SIN, TO MAKE US CLEAN FROM ALL SIN   077 18
BODIES MAY BE MADE CLEAN BY HIS BODY, AND OUR SOULS   082 20
MAY COME HOLY AND CLEAN TO SUCH A HEAVENLY FEAST,   087 13
IF THOU WILT, THOU CANST MAKE ME CLEAN   114 32
BE THOU CLEAN   115 02
HIS FEET, BUT IS CLEAN EVERY WHIT   156 10
AND YE ARE CLEAN, BUT NOT ALL   156 10
THEREFORE SAID HE, YE ARE NOT ALL CLEAN   156 12
HE WRAPPED IT IN A CLEAN LINEN CLOTH, AND LAID IT IN   162 11
THEE WITH PURE AND CLEAN HEARTS, BY THE SAME THY SON   231 31
NOW YE ARE CLEAN THROUGH THE WORD WHICH I HAVE SPOKEN   238 08
IS HIS MERCY CLEAN GONE FOR EVER   311 14
THOU SHALT BE CLEAN, *   361 20
27 WITH THE CLEAN THOU SHALT BE CLEAN, *   361 20
OF THE LORD IS CLEAN, AND ENDURETH FOR EVER   363 33
EVEN HE THAT HATH CLEAN HANDS, AND A PURE HEART   369 02
14 I AM CLEAN FORGOTTEN AS A DEAD MAN OUT OF MIND   376 19
UNGODLY SHALL BE CLEAN GONE   385 13
SHALT PURGE ME WITH HYSSOP, AND I SHALL BE CLEAN   403 23

CLEAN   CONTINUED

10 MAKE ME A CLEAN HEART, O GOD, *   403 29
SUCH AS ARE OF A CLEAN HEART   428 11
8 IS HIS MERCY CLEAN GONE FOR EVER   433 31
LET HIS NAME BE CLEAN PUT OUT   480 26
EVEN HE THAT HATH CLEAN HANDS, AND A PURE HEART   563 17

CLEANNESS

TO THE CLEANNESS OF MY HANDS DID HE RECOMPENSE ME   361 07
UNTO THE CLEANNESS OF MY HANDS IN HIS EYESIGHT   361 16

CLEANSE

OUR SINS, AND TO CLEANSE US FROM ALL UNRIGHTEOUSNESS   022 12
AND CLEANSE ME FROM MY SIN   060 13
CLEANSE THE THOUGHTS OF OUR HEARTS BY THE INSPIRATION   067 18
OUR SINS, AND TO CLEANSE US FROM ALL UNRIGHTEOUSNESS   101 31
CONTINUAL PITY CLEANSE AND DEFEND THY CHURCH   212 05
SANCTIFY AND CLEANSE IT WITH THE WASHING OF WATER BY   267 21
OUR OFFENCES AND CLEANSE US FROM OUR SINS   323 16
O CLEANSE THOU ME FROM MY SECRET FAULTS   364 08
AND CLEANSE ME FROM MY SIN   403 11
A YOUNG MAN CLEANSE HIS WAY   490 16

CLEANSED

THE LEPERS ARE CLEANSED, AND THE DEAF HEAR, THE DEAD   094 22
AND IMMEDIATELY HIS LEPROSY WAS CLEANSED   115 03
TO PASS, THAT, AS THEY WENT, THEY WERE CLEANSED   210 07
WERE THERE NOT TEN CLEANSED   210 11
THEY MAY BE CLEANSED FROM ALL THEIR SINS, AND SERVE   219 02
THEN HAVE I CLEANSED MY HEART IN VAIN, *   429 02

CLEANSETH

CHRIST HIS SON CLEANSETH US FROM ALL SIN   101 28

CLEAR

IN THY SAYING, AND CLEAR WHEN THOU ART JUDGED   060 19
AND ERROR INTO THE CLEAR LIGHT AND TRUE KNOWLEDGE OF   078 31
RIGHTEOUSNESS AS CLEAR AS THE LIGHT, *   385 04
IN THY SAYING, AND CLEAR WHEN THOU SHALT JUDGE   403 17
THE NIGHT IS AS CLEAR AS THE DAY   515 11
SHALL BE FOUND CLEAR OF THAT CRIME   R 530 28
SHALL BE FOUND CLEAR OF THAT CRIME   R 537 04

CLEARER

AND A CLEARER KNOWLEDGE OF THY WILL   596 14

CLEAREST

MANKIND IN THE CLEAREST, PLAINEST, MOST AFFECTING AND   VI 41

CLEARING

FOR THE CLEARING OF THEM, AS WELL FROM OBSOLETE   R 610 28

CLEARLY

WHAT CANNOT BE CLEARLY DETERMINED TO BELONG TO   V 05
SHALT THOU SEE CLEARLY TO PULL OUT THE MOTE THAT IS   195 11
AND THAT YE HAVE CLEARLY DETERMINED, BY GOD'S GRACE,   541 11
WHICH HE WAS CLEARLY VOID, BOTH IN HIS FLESH,   605 32

CLEARNESS

TO THE CLEARNESS AND EXCELLENCY OF THY HOLY WORD   573 27

CLEAVE

CLEAVE TO THAT WHICH IS GOOD   111 23
HEART THEY WOULD CLEAVE UNTO THE LORD   241 08
TO HIM SHALT THOU CLEAVE, AND SWEAR BY HIS NAME   263 30
AND SHALL CLEAVE TO HIS WIFE   268 03
SHALL NO SUCH CLEAVE UNTO ME   463 23
BONES WILL SCARCE CLEAVE TO MY FLESH   464 20
LET MY TONGUE CLEAVE TO THE ROOF OF MY MOUTH   513 15

CLEAVETH

AND MY TONGUE CLEAVETH TO MY GUMS, *   367 02
SAY THEY, CLEAVETH FAST UNTO HIM   392 15
OUR BELLY CLEAVETH UNTO THE GROUND   396 11
MY SOUL CLEAVETH TO THE DUST   491 17

CLEOPAS

WHOSE NAME WAS CLEOPAS, ANSWERING SAID UNTO HIM, ART   167 12

CLEOPHAS

THE WIFE OF CLEOPHAS, AND MARY MAGDALENE   160 18

CLERGY

AND OTHER CLERGY, AND UPON THE CONGREGATIONS   018 20
AND OTHER CLERGY, AND UPON THE CONGREGATIONS   032 19
FOR THE CLERGY HERE RESIDING), THAT THEY MAY SHINE AS   047 27
WITH THE CLERGY AND PEOPLE PRESENT, SAY THE   R 530 30
WITH THE CLERGY AND PEOPLE PRESENT, SAY THE   R 537 06
BISHOP AND THE CLERGY WHO ARE PRESENT SHALL GO UP THE   R 563 07
ONE VERSE AND THE CLERGY ANOTHER   R 563 09

CLERGY   CONTINUED

WITH SUCH OF THE CLERGY AS CAN BE THERE ACCOMMODATED   R 564 06
THEN ALL THE CLERGY PRESENT STANDING IN THE CHANCEL   R 570 04
AND BY THE OTHER CLERGY PRESENT, SHALL ENTER THE   R 570 04
ALL MEN, AS WELL CLERGY AS LAITY, IN ALL THINGS   610 38

CLIMB

NOR CLIMB UP INTO MY BED   508 09
7 IF I CLIMB UP INTO HEAVEN, THOU ART THERE   515 02

CLIMBETH

BUT CLIMBETH UP SOME OTHER WAY, THE SAME   185 31
BUT CLIMBETH UP SOME OTHER WAY, THE SAME   538 24

CLOAK

NOT DISSEMBLE NOR CLOAK THEM BEFORE THE FACE OF   005 32
NOT DISSEMBLE NOR CLOAK THEM BEFORE THE FACE OF   023 07
BE UNTO HIM AS THE CLOAK THAT HE HATH UPON HIM, *   481 08
WITH THEIR OWN CONFUSION, AS WITH A CLOAK   481 31

CLOKE

YOUR LIBERTY FOR A CLOKE OF MALICIOUSNESS, BUT AS THE   173 23
THE CLOKE THAT I LEFT AT TROAS WITH CARPUS, WHEN THOU   254 04
NOW THEY HAVE NO CLOKE FOR THEIR SIN   255 24

CLOSE

AND THEY KEPT IT CLOSE, AND TOLD NO MAN IN THOSE DAYS   249 09
BULLS OF BASHAN CLOSE ME IN ON EVERY SIDE   366 28
KEEP THEMSELVES CLOSE, *   408 26

CLOSED

AND HE CLOSED THE BOOK, AND HE GAVE IT AGAIN TO THE   261 21

CLOSET

OF HIS CHAMBER, AND THE BRIDE OUT OF HER CLOSET   125 02

CLOTH

TABLE SHALL HAVE UPON IT A FAIR WHITE LINEN CLOTH   R 067 06
COVERING THE SAME WITH A FAIR LINEN CLOTH   R 083 13
HAVING A LINEN CLOTH CAST ABOUT HIS NAKED BODY   142 29
HE LEFT THE LINEN CLOTH, AND FLED FROM THEM NAKED   142 31
IN A CLEAN LINEN CLOTH, AND LAID IT IN HIS OWN NEW   162 11

CLOTHE

IF GOD DOTH SO CLOTHE THE GRASS OF THE FIELD, WHICH   211 24
HE NOT MUCH MORE CLOTHE YOU, O YE OF LITTLE FAITH   211 26
IF GOD SO CLOTHE THE GRASS OF THE FIELD, WHICH TO-DAY   266 22
HE NOT MUCH MORE CLOTHE YOU, O YE OF LITTLE FAITH   266 24
I SHALL CLOTHE THEM WITH SHAME   509 10

CLOTHED

A MAN CLOTHED IN SOFT RAIMENT   094 28
AND JOHN WAS CLOTHED WITH CAMEL'S HAIR, AND WITH A   112 12
AND THEY CLOTHED HIM WITH PURPLE, AND PLATTED A CROWN   145 31
THE RIGHT SIDE, CLOTHED IN A LONG WHITE GARMENT   165 27
ELDERS SITTING, CLOTHED IN WHITE RAIMENT   187 10
WHICH WAS CLOTHED IN PURPLE AND FINE LINEN, AND   190 03
AND BE CLOTHED WITH HUMILITY   192 30
WHEREWITHAL SHALL WE BE CLOTHED   211 29
BEFORE THE LAMB, CLOTHED WITH WHITE ROBES, AND PALMS   256 26
AND YE CLOTHED ME   259 07
OR NAKED, AND CLOTHED THEE   259 12
WHEREWITHAL SHALL WE BE CLOTHED   266 27
LET THEM BE CLOTHED WITH REBUKE AND DISHONOUR, THAT   383 17
THOU ART CLOTHED WITH MAJESTY AND HONOUR   467 25
17 HE CLOTHED HIMSELF WITH CURSING LIKE AS WITH A   481 05
ADVERSARIES BE CLOTHED WITH SHAME   481 29
THY PRIESTS BE CLOTHED WITH RIGHTEOUSNESS   508 21
THAT THEY MAY BE CLOTHED WITH RIGHTEOUSNESS, AND THAT   547 06
THY PRIESTS BE CLOTHED WITH RIGHTEOUSNESS   562 04

CLOTHES

ON THEM THEIR CLOTHES, AND THEY SET HIM THEREON   091 24
HIM IN SWADDLING CLOTHES, AND LAID HIM IN A MANGER   098 08
IN SWADDLING CLOTHES, LYING IN A MANGER   099 19
LAID DOWN THEIR CLOTHES AT A YOUNG MAN'S FEET,   100 12
PRIEST RENT HIS CLOTHES, AND SAITH, WHAT NEED WE ANY   143 17
AND PUT HIS OWN CLOTHES ON HIM, AND LED HIM OUT TO   146 04
SAW THE LINEN CLOTHES LYING   164 20
SEETH THE LINEN CLOTHES LIE, AND THE NAPKIN, THAT WAS   164 22
WITH THE LINEN CLOTHES, BUT WRAPPED TOGETHER IN A   164 24

CLOTHING

THAT WEAR SOFT CLOTHING ARE IN KINGS' HOUSES   094 29
YOU IN SHEEP'S CLOTHING, BUT INWARDLY THEY ARE   200 16
HER CLOTHING IS OF WROUGHT GOLD   397 13
AND WENT DOWN TO THE SKIRTS OF HIS CLOTHING   509 17

CLOUD

WITH SO GREAT A CLOUD OF WITNESSES THAT WE, REJOICING   079 23
OF MAN COMING IN A CLOUD WITH POWER AND GREAT GLORY   093 11
AND A CLOUD RECEIVED HIM OUT OF THEIR SIGHT   178 13

CLOUD   CONTINUED

WERE UNDER THE CLOUD, AND ALL PASSED THROUGH THE SEA   201 06
UNTO MOSES IN THE CLOUD AND IN THE SEA   201 08
THERE CAME A CLOUD, AND OVERSHADOWED THEM   249 05
AND THEY FEARED AS THEY ENTERED INTO THE CLOUD   249 06
A VOICE OUT OF THE CLOUD, SAYING, THIS IS MY BELCVEC   249 07
WITH SO GREAT A CLOUD OF WITNESSES   258 12
WITH SO GREAT A CLOUD OF WITNESSES, LET US LAY ASIDE   258 21
HE LED THEM WITH A CLOUD, *   435 28
38 HE SPREAD OLT A CLOUD TO BE A COVERING, *   472 15

CLOUDS

UP, AND THE CLOUDS DROP DOWN THE DEW   005 26
YE LIGHTNINGS AND CLOUDS, BLESS YE THE LORD   012 32
UP, AND THE CLOUDS DROP DOWN THE DEW   050 20
MAN COMING IN THE CLOUDS OF HEAVEN WITH POWER AND   118 19
AND COMING IN THE CLOUDS OF HEAVEN   143 16
THE HEAVEN WITH CLOUDS, AND PREPARETH RAIN FOR THE   264 27
WITH THEM IN THE CLOUDS, TO MEET THE LORD IN THE AIR   269 09
AND THICK CLOUDS TO COVER HIM   360 20
HIS PRESENCE HIS CLOUDS REMOVED   360 22
AND THY FAITHFULNESS UNTO THE CLOUDS   384 05
AND THY TRUTH UNTO THE CLOUDS   410 03
AND THY CLOUDS DROP FATNESS   417 08
HIS WORSHIP AND STRENGTH IS IN THE CLOUDS   421 26
17 THE CLOUDS POURED OUT WATER, THE AIR THUNDERED,   434 16
HE COMMANDED THE CLOUDS ABOVE, *   436 16
IS HE AMONG THE CLOUDS, *   450 15
2 CLOUDS AND DARKNESS ARE ROUND ABOUT HIM   460 32
AND MAKETH THE CLOUDS HIS CHARIOT, AND WALKETH UPCN   467 30
AND THY TRUTH REACHETH UNTO THE CLOUDS   479 12
FORTH THE CLOUDS FROM THE ENDS OF THE WORLD, *   510 15
THE HEAVEN WITH CLOUDS, AND PREPARETH RAIN FOR THE   523 10
AND GRANT THAT NO CLOUDS OF THIS MORTAL LIFE MAY HIDE   596 07

CLOUDY

THEM OUT OF THE CLOUDY PILLAR   462 30

CLOVEN

UNTO THEM CLOVEN TONGLES LIKE AS OF FIRE, AND IT SAT   180 21

COALS

THOU SHALT HEAP COALS OF FIRE ON HIS HEAD   113 07
HIS MOUTH, SO THAT COALS WERE KINDLED AT IT   360 13
HAILSTONES AND COALS OF FIRE   360 20
HAILSTONES AND COALS OF FIRE   360 25
MIGHTY AND SHARP ARROWS, WITH HOT BURNING COALS   502 13
10 LET HOT BURNING COALS FALL UPON THEM   516 29

COASTS

AND IN ALL THE COASTS THEREOF, FROM TWO YEARS CLD AND   103 27
DEPARTED INTO THE COASTS OF TYRE AND SIDON   128 07
OUT OF THE SAME COASTS, AND CRIED UNTO HIM, SAYING,   128 09
FROM THE COASTS OF TYRE AND SIDON, CAME UNTO THE SEA   206 27
THE MIDST OF THE COASTS OF DECAPOLIS   206 29
CAME INTO THE COASTS CF CAESAREA PHILIPPI, HE ASKED   245 31
AND DESTROYED THE TREES THAT WERE IN THEIR COASTS   472 05

COAT

NOW THE COAT WAS WITHOUT SEAM, WOVEN FROM THE TCP   160 11
AND ALSO HIS COAT   160 11

COCK

BEFORE THE COCK CROW TWICE, THOU SHALT DENY ME   141 24
AND THE COCK CREW   143 28
THE SECOND TIME THE COCK CREW   143 34
BEFORE THE COCK CROW TWICE, THOU SHALT DENY ME   144 02
PETER, THE COCK SHALL NOT CROW THIS DAY,   150 02
HE YET SPAKE, THE COCK CREW   151 19
BEFORE THE COCK CROW, THOU SHALT DENY ME THRICE   151 22

COCK-CROWING

OR AT THE COCK-CROWING, OR IN THE MORNING   021 26

COLD

O YE FROST AND COLD, BLESS YE THE LORD   012 24
FASTINGS OFTEN, IN COLD AND NAKEDNESS   121 09

COLDNESS

TO THEE, FROM COLDNESS OF HEART AND WANDERINGS CF   594 06

COLLECT

SHALL FOLLOW THE COLLECT FOR THE DAY, EXCEPT WHEN THE   R 017 02
AND THEN THE COLLECT FOR THE DAY SHALL BE CMITTED   R 017 03
BE SAID THE COLLECT FOR THE DAY, AND AFTER THAT THE   R 031 15
AFTER THE THIRD COLLECT AT MORNING OR EVENING PRAYER,   R 034 03
PRAYER AND THE COLLECT FOLLOWING, THE PEOPLE   R 067 07
PRIEST SAY THE COLLECT OF THE DAY   R 070 17
AND AFTER THE COLLECT THE MINISTER APPOINTED SHALL   R 070 17
THE COLLECT, EPISTLE, AND GOSPEL, APPCINTED FOR THE   R 090 04
THE COLLECT APPOINTED FOR ANY SUNDAY CR OTHER FEAST   R 090 04
THIS COLLECT IS TO BE REPEATED EVERY DAY, AFTER THE   R 090 20
THIS COLLECT IS TO BE SAID DAILY THROUGHOUT THE   R 096 20
THE FOLLOWING COLLECT, EPISTLE, AND GCSPEL MAY BE   R 098 08

COLLECT   CONTINUED

THIS COLLECT IS TO BE SAID DAILY THROUGHOUT THE   R 108 04
AFTER THE COLLECT APPOINTED FOR THE DAY, UNTIL   R 124 18
THIS COLLECT IS TO BE SAID EVERY DAY IN LENT,   R 124 18
THE SAME COLLECT, EPISTLE, AND GOSPEL SHALL SERVE   R 125 23
AFTER THE COLLECT APPOINTED FOR THE DAY,   R 134 13
THIS COLLECT IS TO BE SAID EVERY DAY, AFTER THE   R 134 13
THIS COLLECT IS TO BE SAID DAILY THROUGHOUT EASTER   R 163 31
THE FOLLOWING COLLECT, EPISTLE, AND GOSPEL MAY BE   R 164 31
THIS COLLECT IS TO BE SAID DAILY THROUGHOUT THE   R 177 20
THE SAME COLLECT, EPISTLE, AND GOSPEL SHALL SERVE   R 178 30
THIS COLLECT IS TO BE SAID DAILY THROUGHOUT WHITSUN   R 180 15
THE FOLLOWING COLLECT, EPISTLE, AND GOSPEL MAY BE   R 182 12
THIS COLLECT IS TO BE SAID DAILY THROUGHOUT THE   R 256 12
THE PSALMS FOLLOWING, WITH ANTIPHON AND COLLECT   R 309 10
WITH THE COLLECT, EPISTLE, AND GOSPEL, HERE   R 321 15
OR THE FOLLOWING COLLECT, EPISTLE, AND GOSPEL   R 322 04
SUBSTITUTING THE COLLECT, EPISTLE, AND GOSPEL FCR THE   R 323 34
WITH THE COLLECT, EPISTLE, AND GOSPEL, AS FCLLCWETH   R 531 11
AFTER THE LAST COLLECT, AND IMMEDIATELY BEFCRE THE   R 534 28
BE SAID THIS COLLECT FOLLOWING   R 534 29
WITH THE COLLECT, EPISTLE, AND GOSPEL, AS FCLLOWETH   R 537 17
AFTER THE LAST COLLECT, AND IMMEDIATELY BEFCRE THE   R 547 02
SHALL BE SAID THIS COLLECT   R 547 03
THE COLLECT SHALL BE AS FOLLOWETH   R 547 28
IN WHICH THIS SHALL BE THE COLLECT   R 549 06
SHALL BE THE COLLECT, EPISTLE, AND GOSPEL   R 567 02
MAY FOLLOW THE COLLECT FOR THE DAY   R 587 16
MAY FOLLOW THE COLLECT FOR THE DAY   R 589 23

COLLECTS

AFTER THAT THE COLLECTS AND PRAYERS FOLLCWING   R 031 15
USED AFTER THE COLLECTS OF MORNING OR EVENING PRAYER,   R 049 03
AFTER THE OTHER COLLECTS IN ADVENT, UNTIL CHRISTMAS   R 090 20

COLLEGES

COLLEGES, AND SCHOOLS, THAT KNOWLEDGE   042 23
ALL SCHOOLS, COLLEGES, AND SEMINARIES OF SOUND AND   047 33

COLOURS

WROUGHT ABOUT WITH DIVERS COLOURS   397 04

COLT

AN ASS TIED, AND A COLT WITH HER   091 15
UPON AN ASS, AND A COLT THE FOAL OF AN ASS   091 21
THE ASS, AND THE COLT, AND PUT ON THEM THEIR CLCTHES,   091 23

COME

SON OF GOD, LET US COME BOLDLY UNTO THE THRCNE CF   005 08
THE HOLY GHOST IS COME UPON YOU   005 12
GOD ALMIGHTY, WHICH WAS, AND IS, AND IS TC CCME   005 19
AT THE LAST WE MAY COME TO HIS ETERNAL JOY   007 18
THY KINGDOM COME   007 24
O COME, LET US ADORE HIM   R 008 17
O COME, LET US ADORE HIM   R 008 19
O COME, LET US ADORE HIM   R 008 21
O COME, LET US ADORE HIM   R 008 24
O COME, LET US ADORE HIM   R 008 26
O COME, LET US ADORE HIM   R 008 28
O COME, LET   R 008 29
O COME, LET US ADORE HIM   R 008 32
O COME, LET US ADORE HIM   R 008 34
O COME, LET US SING UNTO THE LORD   009 03
LET US COME BEFORE HIS PRESENCE WITH THANKSGIVING   009 05
O COME, LET US WORSHIP AND FALL DOWN, *   009 13
THAT THOU SHALT COME TO BE OUR JUDGE   010 32
WITH GLADNESS, AND COME BEFORE HIS PRESENCE WITH A   015 05
THENCE HE SHALL COME TO JUDGE THE QUICK AND THE DEAD   015 27
AND HE SHALL COME AGAIN, WITH GLCRY, TO JUDGE BOTH   016 12
AND THE LIFE OF THE WORLD TO COME   016 21
AND IN THE WORLD TO COME LIFE EVERLASTING   020 10
THE GENTILES SHALL COME TO THY LIGHT, AND KINGS TC   022 02
THE SPIRIT AND THE BRIDE SAY, COME   022 29
AND LET HIM THAT HEARETH SAY, COME   022 30
AND LET HIM THAT IS ATHIRST COME   022 30
AT THE LAST WE MAY COME TO HIS ETERNAL JOY   024 20
THENCE HE SHALL COME TO JUDGE THE QUICK AND THE DEAD   029 32
AND HE SHALL COME AGAIN, WITH GLCRY, TO JUDGE BCTH   030 17
AND THE LIFE OF THE WORLD TO COME   030 26
AND IN THE WORLD TO COME LIFE EVERLASTING   034 10
HIM WHO SHALL COME TO BE OUR JUDGE, THY SON, OUR   036 06
AND DWELL WITH THEM IN THE LIFE THAT IS TO CCME   043 14
PARTAKER OF EVERLASTING GLORY IN THE LIFE TO CCME   051 12
PARTAKER OF EVERLASTING GLORY IN THE LIFE TO CCME   053 17
AND LET OUR CRY COME UNTO THEE   062 06
WE MAY EVER LIVE WITH THEE IN THE WORLD TO COME   062 25
AND GRACE TO KEEP THE LAW FOR THE TIME TO COME   067 22
AND HE SHALL COME AGAIN, WITH GLCRY, TO JUDGE BOTH   071 14
AND THE LIFE OF THE WORLD TO COME   071 23
ALL THINGS COME OF THEE, O LORD, AND OF THINE CWN   073 23
SAY TO THOSE WHO COME TO RECEIVE THE HOLY COMMUNICN,   R 075 07
COME UNTO ME; ALL YE THAT TRAVAIL AND ARE HEAVY   076 12
DO NOT PRESUME TO COME TO THIS THY TABLE, C MERCIFUL   082 13
IF AMONG THOSE WHO COME TO BE PARTAKERS OF THE HCLY   R 084 34
HE PRESUME NOT TO COME TO THE LORD'S TABLE, UNTIL HE   R 085 04
YE WHO MIND TO COME TO THE HOLY COMMUNION OF THE BODY   085 25
BUT SO THAT YE MAY COME HOLY AND CLEAN TC SUCH A   087 12
YOUR SINS, OR ELSE COME NOT TO THAT HOLY TABLE   087 34
THAT NO MAN SHOULD COME TO THE HOLY COMMUNION, BUT   087 35
OR COUNSEL, LET HIM COME TO ME, OR TO SOME OTHER   088 06

COME CONTINUED

COME CONTINUED		PAGE	LN
PEOPLE NEGLIGENT TO COME TO THE HOLY COMMUNION,	R	088	10
WILL NOT REFUSE TO COME THERETO, BEING SO LOVINGLY		088	16
MOST UNTHANKFULLY REFUSE TO COME		088	21
AND THEREFORE AM AFRAID TO COME		088	31
ARE YE NOT ASHAMED TO SAY YE WILL NOT COME		088	33
YOUR BRETHREN, WHO COME TO FEED ON THE BANQUET OF		089	17
WHEN HE SHALL COME AGAIN IN HIS GLORIOUS MAJESTY		090	15
AND WERE COME TO BETHPHAGE, UNTO THE MOUNT		091	12
AND WHEN HE WAS COME INTO JERUSALEM, ALL THE CITY WAS		091	30
THINGS BEGIN TO COME TO PASS, THEN LOOK UP, AND LIFT		093	12
YE SEE THESE THINGS COME TO PASS, KNOW YE THAT THE		093	17
UNTIL THE LORD COME, WHO BOTH WILL BRING TO LIGHT THE		094	11
THOU HE THAT SHOULD COME, OR DO WE LOOK FOR ANOTHER		094	18
THY POWER, AND COME AMONG US, AND WITH GREAT MIGHT		095	04
HIM WHEN HE SHALL COME TO BE OUR JUDGE, WHO LIVETH		098	15
THAT UPON YOU MAY COME ALL THE RIGHTEOUS BLOOD SHED		100	22
THESE THINGS SHALL COME UPON THIS GENERATION		100	26
HE TARRY TILL I COME, WHAT IS THAT TO THEE		102	08
HE TARRY TILL I COME, WHAT IS THAT TO THEE		102	12
OF THE TIME WAS COME, GOD SENT FORTH HIS SON, MADE OF		104	19
THIS THING WHICH IS COME TO PASS, WHICH THE LORD HATH		106	10
THE EAST, AND ARE COME TO WORSHIP HIM		109	02
OUT OF THEE SHALL COME A GOVERNOR, THAT SHALL RULE MY		109	09
THAT I MAY COME AND WORSHIP HIM ALSO		109	15
AND WHEN THEY WERE COME INTO THE HOUSE, THEY SAW THE		109	20
MINE HOUR IS NOT YET COME		113	16
WHEN HE WAS COME DOWN FROM THE MOUNTAIN, GREAT		114	29
UNTO HIM, I WILL COME AND HEAL HIM		115	09
THAT THOU SHOULDEST COME UNDER MY ROOF		115	11
AND TO ANOTHER, COME, AND HE COMETH		115	14
THAT MANY SHALL COME FROM THE EAST AND WEST, AND		115	19
SO WHEN EVEN WAS COME, THE LORD OF THE VINEYARD SAITH		119	29
AND WERE COME TO HIM OUT OF EVERY CITY,		121	19
WHICH IS PERFECT IS COME, THEN THAT WHICH IS IN PART		123	08
THAT AS HE WAS COME NIGH UNTO JERICHO, A CERTAIN		123	26
AND WHEN HE WAS COME NEAR, HE ASKED HIM, SAYING, WHAT		123	34
KINGDOM OF GOD IS COME UPON YOU		130	04
THAN HE SHALL COME UPON HIM, AND OVERCOME HIM, HE		130	06
SAW A GREAT COMPANY COME UNTO HIM, HE SAITH UNTO		131	27
PROPHET THAT SHOULD COME INTO THE WORLD		132	13
CHRIST BEING COME AN HIGH PRIEST OF GOOD THINGS TO		132	23
OF GOOD THINGS TO COME, BY A GREATER AND MORE PERFECT		132	24
THE MORNING WAS COME, ALL THE CHIEF PRIESTS AND		134	30
AND WHEN THEY WERE COME UNTO A PLACE CALLED GOLGOTHA,		136	27
BE THE SON OF GOD, COME DOWN FROM THE CROSS		137	08
LET HIM NOW COME DOWN FROM THE CROSS, AND WE		137	11
WHETHER ELIAS WILL COME TO SAVE HIM		137	24
AND THE YEAR OF MY REDEEMED IS COME		138	22
SHE IS COME AFOREHAND TO ANOINT MY BODY TO THE		140	14
IT IS ENOUGH, THE HOUR IS COME		142	12
AS SOON AS HE WAS COME, HE GOETH STRAIGHTWAY TO HIM,		142	20
UNTO THEM, ARE YE COME OUT, AS AGAINST A THIEF, WITH		142	24
LET HIM COME NEAR TO ME		144	20
SAVE THYSELF, AND COME DOWN FROM THE CROSS		146	20
THE SIXTH HOUR WAS COME, THERE WAS DARKNESS OVER THE		146	26
WHETHER ELIAS WILL COME TO TAKE HIM DOWN		146	33
WHEN THE HOUR WAS COME, HE SAT DOWN, AND THE TWELVE		148	34
OF THE VINE, UNTIL THE KINGDOM OF GOD SHALL COME		149	08
AND WAS COME TO HIS DISCIPLES, HE FOUND THEM		150	24
COME TO HIM, BE YE COME OUT, AS AGAINST A THIEF,		151	03
WHICH WERE COME TO HIM, BE YE COME OUT,		151	03
YE DO SHEW THE LORD'S DEATH TILL HE COME		152	25
AND WHEN THEY WERE COME TO THE PLACE WHICH IS CALLED		154	22
THAT HIS HOUR WAS COME THAT HE SHOULD DEPART OUT OF		155	24
AND THAT HE WAS COME FROM GOD, AND WENT TO GOD		155	30
OF GOOD THINGS TO COME, AND NOT THE VERY IMAGE OF THE		157	15
THEN SAID I, LO, I COME (IN THE VOLUME OF THE BOOK IT		157	27
THEN SAID HE, LO, I COME TO DO THY WILL, O GOD		157	32
WHEN THE EVEN WAS COME, THERE CAME A RICH MAN OF		162	06
LEST HIS DISCIPLES COME BY NIGHT, AND STEAL HIM AWAY,		162	20
THAT THEY MIGHT COME AND ANOINT HIM		165	20
THINGS WHICH ARE COME TO PASS THERE IN THESE DAYS		167	14
LEST THAT COME UPON YOU, WHICH IS SPOKEN OF IN THE		169	22
IN TRAVAIL HATH SORROW, BECAUSE HER HOUR IS COME		174	11
COMFORTER WILL NOT COME UNTO YOU		175	11
AND WHEN HE IS COME, HE WILL REPROVE THE WORLD OF		175	12
SPIRIT OF TRUTH, IS COME, HE WILL GUIDE YOU INTO ALL		175	19
AND HE WILL SHEW YOU THINGS TO COME		175	21
FROM WHOM ALL GOOD THINGS DO COME		175	29
THE FATHER, AND AM COME INTO THE WORLD		176	30
YEA, IS NOW COME, THAT YE SHALL BE SCATTERED,		177	05
THEY THEREFORE WERE COME TOGETHER, THEY ASKED OF HIM,		178	04
THE HOLY GHOST IS COME UPON YOU		178	09
SHALL SO COME IN LIKE MANNER AS YE HAVE SEEN		178	18
THE COMFORTER IS COME, WHOM I WILL SEND UNTO YOU FROM		179	24
WHEN THE TIME SHALL COME, YE MAY REMEMBER THAT I TOLD		180	03
PENTECOST WAS FULLY COME, THEY WERE ALL WITH ONE		180	17
I WILL COME TO YOU		181	15
AND WE WILL COME UNTO HIM, AND MAKE OUR ABODE		181	26
I GO AWAY, AND COME AGAIN UNTO YOU		182	03
TOLD YOU BEFORE IT COME TO PASS, THAT, WHEN IT IS		182	06
WHEN IT IS COME TO PASS, YE MIGHT BELIEVE		182	06
THAT LIGHT IS COME INTO THE WORLD, AND MEN LOVED		185	06
WHO, WHEN THEY WERE COME DOWN, PRAYED FOR THEM,		185	24
I AM COME THAT THEY MIGHT HAVE LIFE, AND THAT THEY		186	18
WHICH SAID, COME UP HITHER, AND I WILL SHEW THEE		187	02
WHICH WAS, AND IS, AND IS TO COME		187	24
THOU ART A TEACHER COME FROM GOD		188	03
TO US, THAT WOULD COME FROM THENCE		190	22
LEST THEY ALSO COME INTO THIS PLACE OF TORMENT		190	25
SUPPER TIME TO SAY TO THEM THAT WERE BIDDEN, COME		192	05
AND THEREFORE I CANNOT COME		192	11
AND COMPEL THEM TO COME IN, THAT MY HOUSE MAY BE		192	19
THAT THEY SHOULD COME AND HELP THEM		196	21

COME CONTINUED		PAGE	LN
AND THEN COME AND OFFER THY GIFT		198	11
SHALT BY NO MEANS COME OUT THENCE, TILL THOU HAST		198	16
WHICH COME TO YOU IN SHEEP'S CLOTHING, BUT		200	15
UPON WHOM THE ENDS OF THE WORLD ARE COME		201	24
AND HE SAID UNTO HIM, THY BROTHER IS COME		202	30
AS THIS THY SON WAS COME, WHICH HATH DEVOURED THY		203	03
AND WHEN HE WAS COME NEAR, HE BEHELD THE CITY,		204	06
FOR THE DAYS SHALL COME UPON THEE, THAT THINE ENEMIES		204	10
THE SEED SHOULD COME TO WHOM THE PROMISE WAS MADE		207	28
WHEN I COME AGAIN, I WILL REPAY THEE		208	35
BADE THEE AND HIM COME AND SAY TO THEE, GIVE THIS MAN		214	13
SO THAT YE COME BEHIND IN NO GIFT		214	32
AND THEY WOULD NOT COME		218	06
COME UNTO THE MARRIAGE		218	09
THAT JESUS WAS COME OUT OF JUDAEA INTO GALILEE, HE		219	29
HIM THAT HE WOULD COME DOWN, AND HEAL HIS SON		219	31
UNTO HIM, SIR, COME DOWN ERE MY CHILD DIE		220	02
WHEN HE WAS COME OUT OF JUDAEA INTO GALILEE		220	12
WHICH IS COME UNTO YOU, AS IT IS IN ALL THE WORLD		223	27
BUT COME AND LAY THY HAND UPON HER, AND SHE SHALL		224	15
BEHOLD, THE DAYS COME, SAITH THE LORD, THAT I WILL		225	09
BEHOLD, THE DAYS COME, SAITH THE LORD, THAT THEY		225	15
SAW A GREAT COMPANY COME UNTO HIM, HE SAITH UNTO		225	23
PROPHET THAT SHOULD COME INTO THE WORLD		226	12
SHALL COME WILL COME, AND WILL NOT TARRY		228	18
AND HE THAT SHALL COME WILL COME, AND WILL NOT TARRY		228	18
SHALL SUDDENLY COME TO HIS TEMPLE, EVEN THE MESSENGER		232	05
BEHOLD, HE SHALL COME, SAITH THE LORD OF HOSTS		232	07
AND I WILL COME NEAR TO YOU TO JUDGMENT		232	15
COME UNTO ME, ALL YE THAT LABOUR AND ARE HEAVY LADEN,		235	10
HOLY GHOST SHALL COME UPON THEE, AND THE POWER OF THE		236	22
TILL WE ALL COME IN THE UNITY OF THE FAITH, AND OF		237	22
FOR YOU, I WILL COME AGAIN, AND RECEIVE YOU UNTO		239	33
THE LORD GOD WILL COME WITH STRONG HAND, AND HIS ARM		243	06
AND WHEN PETER WAS COME TO HIMSELF, HE SAID, NOW I		245	25
FOR I AM NOT COME TO CALL THE RIGHTEOUS, BUT SINNERS		251	22
IN HEAVEN, NOW IS COME SALVATION, AND STRENGTH, AND		252	10
FOR THE DEVIL IS COME DOWN UNTO YOU, HAVING GREAT		252	18
FOR IT MUST NEEDS BE THAT OFFENCES COME		253	02
DO THY DILIGENCE TO COME SHORTLY UNTO ME		253	31
CITY AND PLACE, WHITHER HE HIMSELF WOULD COME		254	13
IF I HAD NOT COME AND SPOKEN UNTO THEM, THEY HAD NOT		255	22
THE COMFORTER IS COME, WHOM I WILL SEND UNTO YOU FROM		255	30
THAT WE MAY COME TO THOSE UNSPEAKABLE JOYS		256	09
SON OF MAN SHALL COME IN HIS GLORY, AND ALL THE HOLY		258	28
ON HIS RIGHT HAND, COME, YE BLESSED OF MY FATHER,		259	03
CAUSE THE SHOWER TO COME DOWN IN HIS SEASON		262	08
IN HIS JOURNEY IS COME TO ME, AND I HAVE NOTHING TO		262	29
GIVETH ME SHALL COME TO ME		269	14
HAVING COME TO THE FONT, WHICH IS THEN TO	R	273	24
AND MAY COME TO THE ETERNAL KINGDOM WHICH		274	20
LITTLE CHILDREN TO COME UNTO ME, AND FORBID THEM NOT		274	29
THOU ART A TEACHER COME FROM GOD		275	08
YOU HAVE COME HITHER DESIRING TO RECEIVE HOLY		277	20
THENCE HE SHALL COME TO JUDGE THE QUICK AND THE DEAD		284	21
COME YE, AND LET US WALK IN THE LIGHT OF THE LORD		290	05
AND LET OUR CRY COME UNTO THEE		290	15
OF THOSE WHO COME TO THE LORD'S SUPPER		293	23
OF THOSE WHO COME TO THE LORD'S SUPPER TO EXAMINE		293	25
AS CHILDREN ARE COME TO A COMPETENT AGE, AND CAN SAY	R	295	13
WHO, WHEN THEY WERE COME DOWN, PRAYED FOR THEM,		296	16
AND LET OUR CRY COME UNTO THEE		297	12
AND MORE, UNTIL HE COME UNTO THY EVERLASTING KINGDOM		297	28
CONFIRMED TO COME, WITHOUT DELAY, TO THE LORD'S	R	299	07
TO BE MARRIED SHALL COME INTO THE BODY OF THE CHURCH,	R	300	04
TWO PERSONS PRESENT COME NOW TO BE JOINED		300	20
IN THE WORLD TO COME YE MAY HAVE LIFE EVERLASTING		304	15
HER DELIVERY, SHALL COME INTO THE CHURCH DECENTLY	R	305	07
AND LET OUR CRY COME UNTO THEE		306	22
PARTAKER OF EVERLASTING GLORY IN THE LIFE TO COME		306	31
UNTIL HE COME TO THY ETERNAL JOY		307	05
AND LET OUR CRY COME UNTO THEE		309	02
AND IS HIS PROMISE COME UTTERLY TO AN END FOR		311	15
BE NOT ABLE TO COME TO THE CHURCH, AND YET IS	R	321	11
AND SHALL NOT COME INTO CONDEMNATION		322	02
AFTER THEY ARE COME INTO THE CHURCH, SHALL BE SAID	R	324	16
AGAIN THOU SAYEST, COME AGAIN, YE CHILDREN OF MEN		325	19
SO STRONG THAT THEY COME TO FOURSCORE YEARS, *		325	33
AND WITH WHAT BODY DO THEY COME		329	06
NOR THINGS TO COME, NOR HEIGHT, NOR DEPTH, NOR ANY		331	12
FOR YOU, I WILL COME AGAIN, AND RECEIVE YOU UNTO		331	21
WHEN THEY COME TO THE GRAVE, WHILE THE BODY IS MADE	R	332	16
GIVETH ME SHALL COME TO ME		333	03
FEAR THEE, SAYING, COME, YE BLESSED CHILDREN OF MY		335	11
COME, YE BLESSED OF MY FATHER, INHERIT THE KINGDOM		336	26
LITTLE CHILDREN TO COME UNTO ME, AND FORBID THEM NOT		338	10
WHEN THEY ARE COME INTO THE CHURCH, SHALL BE SAID	R	338	14
AND LET OUR CRY COME UNTO THEE		340	21
WHEN THEY ARE COME TO THE GRAVE SHALL BE SAID OR	R	341	08
OF THY MERCY I WILL COME INTO THINE HOUSE		348	14
OF THE PEOPLES COME ABOUT THEE		350	04
OF THE UNGODLY COME TO AN END		350	09
HIS TRAVAIL SHALL COME UPON HIS OWN HEAD, *		350	25
DESTRUCTIONS ARE COME TO A PERPETUAL END		351	32
2 LET MY SENTENCE COME FORTH FROM THY PRESENCE		358	19
AND COME TREMBLING OUT OF THEIR STRONGHOLDS		362	30
12 MANY OXEN ARE COME ABOUT ME		366	27
FOR MANY DOGS ARE COME ABOUT ME, *		367	04
32 THEY SHALL COME, AND SHALL DECLARE HIS		368	06
KING OF GLORY SHALL COME IN		369	10
KING OF GLORY SHALL COME IN		369	14
SHALL NOT COME NIGH HIM		378	04
11 COME, YE CHILDREN, AND HEARKEN UNTO ME		380	23
SUDDEN DESTRUCTION COME UPON HIM UNAWARES, AND HIS		382	04

COME   CONTINUED

	PAGE	LN
THE FOOT OF PRIDE COME AGAINST ME	384	19
THEN SAID I, LO, I COME	390	30
TROUBLES ARE COME ABOUT ME	391	10
6 AND IF HE COME TO SEE ME, HE SPEAKETH VANITY,	392	10
WHEN SHALL I COME TO APPEAR BEFORE THE PRESENCE OF	393	02
THOUGH ALL THIS BE COME UPON US, YET DO WE NOT FORGET	395	28
8 O COME HITHER, AND BEHOLD THE WORKS OF THE LORD,	398	09
MAY TELL THEM THAT COME AFTER	400	03
3 OUR GOD SHALL COME, AND SHALL NOT KEEP SILENCE	401	31
AND TREMBLING ARE COME UPON ME, *	406	28
16 LET DEATH COME HASTILY UPON THEM, AND LET THEM GO	407	20
UNTO THEE SHALL ALL FLESH COME	416	14
4 O COME HITHER, AND BEHOLD THE WORKS OF GOD	417	22
14 O COME HITHER, AND HEARKEN, ALL YE THAT FEAR GOD	418	12
SHALL THE PRINCES COME OUT OF EGYPT	421	18
FOR THE WATERS ARE COME IN, EVEN UNTO MY SOUL	421	32
I AM COME INTO DEEP WATERS, SO THAT THE FLOODS RUN	422	03
AND NOT COME INTO THY RIGHTEOUSNESS	423	31
THY POWER TO ALL THEM THAT ARE YET FOR TO COME	426	13
6 HE SHALL COME DOWN LIKE THE RAIN UPON THE MOWN	427	08
5 THEY COME IN NO MISFORTUNE LIKE OTHER FOLK	428	18
AND COME TO A FEARFUL END	429	14
AND IS HIS PROMISE COME UTTERLY TO AN END FOR	433	32
THEM FROM THE CHILDREN OF THE GENERATIONS TO COME	435	02
THE HEATHEN ARE COME INTO THINE INHERITANCE	439	29
FOR WE ARE COME TO GREAT MISERY	440	17
OF THE PRISONERS COME BEFORE THEE	440	26
THY STRENGTH, AND COME AND HELP US	441	07
4 THEY HAVE SAID, COME, AND LET US ROOT THEM OUT,	444	11
HAST MADE SHALL COME AND WORSHIP THEE, O LORD	447	21
SHALL MY PRAYER COME BEFORE THEE	449	23
AGAIN THOU SAYEST, COME AGAIN, YE CHILDREN OF MEN	453	24
SO STRONG THAT THEY COME TO FOURSCORE YEARS, *	454	08
BUT IT SHALL NOT COME NIGH THEE	455	10
SHALL ANY PLAGUE COME NIGH THY DWELLING	455	16
O COME, LET US SING UNTO THE LORD	459	05
2 LET US COME BEFORE HIS PRESENCE WITH THANKSGIVING	459	07
6 O COME, LET US WORSHIP AND FALL DOWN, *	459	15
BRING PRESENTS, AND COME INTO HIS COURTS	460	15
FOR HE IS COME TO JUDGE THE EARTH	462	11
WITH GLADNESS, AND COME BEFORE HIS PRESENCE WITH A	463	06
3 WHEN WILT THOU COME UNTO ME	463	20
AND LET MY CRYING COME UNTO THEE	464	10
THOU HAVE MERCY UPON HER, YEA, THE TIME IS COME	465	06
FOR THOSE THAT COME AFTER, *	465	15
THE UNGODLY SHALL COME TO AN END	469	32
AND IT SHALL COME INTO HIS BOWELS LIKE WATER, AND	481	06
THY YOUNG MEN COME TO THEE AS DEW FROM THE WOMB OF	482	13
THY LOVING MERCY COME ALSO UNTO ME, O LORD, *	492	22
THY LOVING MERCIES COME UNTO ME, THAT I MAY LIVE	495	09
SEE THAT ALL THINGS COME TO AN END	496	17
LET MY COMPLAINT COME BEFORE THEE, O LORD	501	20
LET MY SUPPLICATION COME BEFORE THEE	501	22
SHALL DOUBTLESS COME AGAIN WITH JOY, AND BRING HIS	505	19
3 I WILL NOT COME WITHIN THE TABERNACLE OF MINE	508	08
O LORD, AND COME DOWN	519	31
BY THE BISHOP IS COME, THERE SHALL BE A SERMON,	R 530	03
OFFICE OF SUCH AS COME TO BE ADMITTED DEACONS	R 530	04
LET HIM COME FORTH IN THE NAME OF GOD, AND	530	24
TO MEAT, AND WILL COME FORTH AND SERVE THEM	534	23
AND IF HE SHALL COME IN THE SECOND WATCH, OR COME IN	534	23
SECOND WATCH, OR COME IN THE THIRD WATCH, AND FIND	534	24
BY THE BISHOP IS COME, THERE SHALL BE A SERMON,	R 536	03
OFFICE OF SUCH AS COME TO BE ADMITTED PRIESTS	R 536	04
LET HIM COME FORTH IN THE NAME OF GOD,	536	30
TILL WE ALL COME IN THE UNITY OF THE FAITH, AND OF	538	09
I AM COME THAT THEY MIGHT HAVE LIFE, AND THAT THEY	539	08
COME, HOLY GHOST, OUR SOULS INSPIRE, AND LIGHTEN WITH	543	31
WHERE THOU ART GUIDE, NO ILL CAN COME	544	09
COME, HOLY GHOST, CREATOR BLEST, VOUCHSAFE WITHIN OUR	544	17
COME WITH THY GRACE AND HEAVENLY AID, AND FILL THE	544	19
AND WHEN THEY WERE COME TO HIM, HE SAID UNTO THEM, YE	550	05
COME, HOLY GHOST, OUR SOULS INSPIRE, AND LIGHTEN WITH	556	06
WHERE THOU ART GUIDE, NO ILL CAN COME	556	17
COME, HOLY GHOST, CREATOR BLEST, VOUCHSAFE WITHIN OUR	556	25
COME WITH THY GRACE AND HEAVENLY AID, AND FILL THE	556	27
AND LET OUR CRY COME UNTO THEE	557	18
AND LET OUR CRY COME UNTO THEE	562	07
KING OF GLORY SHALL COME IN	563	25
KING OF GLORY SHALL COME IN	563	29
OF CHRIST, MAY COME TO THAT HOLY ORDINANCE WITH	565	30
THAT THOU SHOULDEST COME UNDER MY ROOF	573	12
THE FOOT OF PRIDE COME NIGH TO HURT THEM, NOR THE	574	14
THENCE HE SHALL COME TO JUDGE THE QUICK AND THE DEAD	578	05
WHEN THEY COME TO AGE, THEMSELVES ARE BOUND	581	14
OF THOSE WHO COME TO THE LORD'S SUPPER	582	20
THEIR CATECHISM, TO COME TO THE CHURCH AT THE TIME	R 582	33
AS CHILDREN ARE COME TO A COMPETENT AGE, AND CAN SAY	R 582	36
WE COME BEFORE THEE IN AN HUMBLE SENSE OF OUR OWN	589	29
THAT THE DAYS TO COME MAY BE SPENT IN THY SERVICE	595	15
FOR THIS LIFE AND THE LIFE TO COME	597	11
OF THE PRISONERS COME BEFORE THEE	600	09

COMERS

	PAGE	LN
MAKE THE COMERS THEREUNTO PERFECT	157	18

COMES

	PAGE	LN
AND THE EVENING COMES, AND THE BUSY WORLD IS HUSHED,	594	31

COMEST

	PAGE	LN
ME WHEN THOU COMEST INTO THY KINGDOM	155	07

COMEST   CONTINUED

	PAGE	LN
WHEN THOU COMEST, BRING WITH THEE, AND THE	254	05
WHEN THOU COMEST FROM THE HILLS OF THE ROBBERS	432	28

COMETH

	PAGE	LN
THE HOUR COMETH, AND NOW IS, WHEN THE TRUE	003	30
HE COMETH, FOR HE COMETH TO JUDGE THE EARTH	009	19
FOR HE COMETH, FOR HE COMETH TO JUDGE THE EARTH	009	19
FROM WHOM COMETH EVERY GOOD AND PERFECT GIFT	018	18
OF THE HOUSE COMETH, AT EVEN, OR AT MIDNIGHT, OR AT	021	25
FOR HE COMETH TO JUDGE THE EARTH	027	22
FROM WHOM COMETH EVERY GOOD AND PERFECT GIFT	032	17
BEHOLD, THY KING COMETH UNTO THEE, MEEK, AND SITTING	091	20
IS HE THAT COMETH IN THE NAME OF THE LORD	091	29
EVERY MAN THAT COMETH INTO THE WORLD	097	30
IS HE THAT COMETH IN THE NAME OF THE LORD	100	33
THERE COMETH ONE MIGHTIER THAN I AFTER ME,	112	14
AND TO ANOTHER, COME, AND HE COMETH	115	15
AS THE LIGHTNING COMETH OUT OF THE EAST, AND SHINETH	118	10
THAT WHICH COMETH UPON ME DAILY, THE CARE OF ALL THE	121	11
THEN COMETH THE DEVIL, AND TAKETH AWAY THE WORD CUT	121	34
OF THESE THINGS COMETH THE WRATH OF GOD UPON THE	129	10
AND WHEN HE COMETH, HE FINDETH IT SWEPT AND	130	13
WHO IS THIS THAT COMETH FROM EDOM, WITH DYED GARMENTS	138	11
IN THE EVENING HE COMETH WITH THE TWELVE	140	34
AND HE COMETH, AND FINDETH THEM SLEEPING, AND SAITH	142	03
AND HE COMETH THE THIRD TIME, AND SAITH UNTO THEM,	142	10
HE YET SPAKE, COMETH JUDAS, ONE OF THE TWELVE, AND	142	14
THE PALACE, THERE COMETH ONE OF THE MAIDS OF THE HIGH	143	23
THEN COMETH HE TO SIMON PETER	155	34
WHEREFORE WHEN HE COMETH INTO THE WORLD, HE SAITH,	157	24
DAY OF THE WEEK COMETH MARY MAGDALENE EARLY, WHEN IT	164	10
SHE RUNNETH, AND COMETH TO SIMON PETER, AND TO THE	164	13
THEN COMETH SIMON PETER FOLLOWING HIM, AND WENT INTO	164	21
FROM ABOVE, AND COMETH DOWN FROM THE FATHER OF	174	27
BUT THE TIME COMETH, WHEN I SHALL NO MORE SPEAK UNTO	176	24
BEHOLD, THE HOUR COMETH, YEA, IS NOW COME, THAT YE	177	05
THE TIME COMETH, THAT WHOSOEVER KILLETH YOU WILL	179	30
OF THIS WORLD COMETH, AND HATH NOTHING IN ME	182	08
NEITHER COMETH TO THE LIGHT, LEST HIS DEEDS	185	08
THAT DOETH TRUTH COMETH TO THE LIGHT, THAT HIS DEEDS	185	10
THE THIEF COMETH NOT, BUT FOR TO STEAL, AND TO KILL,	186	17
TELL WHENCE IT COMETH, AND WHITHER IT GOETH	188	16
AND WHEN HE COMETH HOME, HE CALLETH TOGETHER HIS	193	22
ONLY GIFT IT COMETH THAT THY FAITHFUL PEOPLE DO UNTO	207	13
HE THAT BADE THEE COMETH, HE MAY SAY UNTO THEE,	214	16
SO THEN FAITH COMETH BY HEARING, AND HEARING BY THE	227	13
NO MAN COMETH UNTO THE FATHER, BUT BY ME	240	06
BUT WOE TO THAT MAN BY WHOM THE OFFENCE COMETH	253	03
BUT THIS COMETH TO PASS, THAT THE WORD MIGHT BE	255	28
FROM ABOVE, AND COMETH DOWN FROM THE FATHER OF	265	19
AND HIM THAT COMETH TO ME I WILL IN NO WISE CAST OUT	269	14
TELL WHENCE IT COMETH, AND WHITHER IT GOETH	275	20
THE WOMAN, THAT COMETH TO GIVE HER THANKS, MUST OFFER	R 307	07
THE BREAD WHICH COMETH DOWN FROM HEAVEN, THAT A MAN	322	24
FROM WHENCE COMETH MY HELP	327	20
MY HELP COMETH EVEN FROM THE LORD, *	327	21
THEN COMETH THE END, WHEN HE SHALL HAVE DELIVERED UP	328	26
NO MAN COMETH UNTO THE FATHER, BUT BY ME	331	26
HE COMETH UP, AND IS CUT DOWN, LIKE A FLOWER	332	19
AND HIM THAT COMETH TO ME I WILL IN NO WISE CAST OUT	333	04
FROM WHENCE COMETH MY HELP	339	04
MY HELP COMETH EVEN FROM THE LORD, *	339	05
11 MY HELP COMETH OF GOD, *	350	13
WHICH COMETH FORTH AS A BRIDEGROOM OUT OF HIS	363	22
A NIGHT, BUT JOY COMETH IN THE MORNING	375	03
OF THE RIGHTEOUS COMETH OF THE LORD	387	13
AND WHEN HE COMETH FORTH, HE TELLETH IT	392	12
AND THE UNGODLY COMETH ON SO FAST	406	23
FOR OF HIM COMETH MY SALVATION	413	28
THE GOD OF WHOM COMETH SALVATION	420	25
7 FOR PROMOTION COMETH NEITHER FROM THE EAST,	432	10
PASSETH AWAY, AND COMETH NOT AGAIN	437	19
13 FOR HE COMETH, FOR HE COMETH TO JUDGE THE EARTH	460	26
HE COMETH, FOR HE COMETH TO JUDGE THE EARTH	460	26
BE HE THAT COMETH IN THE NAME OF THE LORD	489	19
FROM WHENCE COMETH MY HELP	502	23
2 MY HELP COMETH EVEN FROM THE LORD, *	502	24
AND GIFT THAT COMETH OF THE LORD	505	30
THAT WHEN HE COMETH AND KNOCKETH, THEY MAY OPEN UNTO	534	19
THE LORD WHEN HE COMETH SHALL FIND WATCHING	534	21
THE THIEF COMETH NOT, BUT FOR TO STEAL, AND TO KILL,	539	07
WHEN THE NIGHT COMETH, REJOICE TO GIVE THEE THANKS	594	16

COMFORT

	PAGE	LN
PLEASE THEE TO COMFORT AND RELIEVE THEM, ACCORDING TO	019	08
PLEASE THEE TO COMFORT AND RELIEVE THEM, ACCORDING TO	033	06
THE EARTH TO OUR COMFORT, AND TO THY HONOUR	040	20
AND GOD OF ALL COMFORT, OUR ONLY HELP IN TIME OF	045	12
COMFORT HIM WITH A SENSE OF THY GOODNESS	045	16
COMFORT HIM WITH A SENSE OF THY GOODNESS	046	04
THY GOODNESS, TO COMFORT AND SUCCOUR ALL PRISONERS	046	20
TO OUR GREAT COMFORT, AND TO THE GLORY OF THY HOLY	051	19
TO THY GLORY AND OUR COMFORT	052	04
AND TO COMFORT AND HELP THE WEAK-HEARTED	056	23
AND COMFORT, ALL WHO ARE IN DANGER, NECESSITY,	056	27
O GIVE ME THE COMFORT OF THY HELP AGAIN, *	061	02
RECEIVE AND COMFORT US, WHO ARE GRIEVED AND WEARIED	062	17
O LORD, TO COMFORT AND SUCCOUR ALL THOSE WHO, IN THIS	074	31
AND TAKE THIS HOLY SACRAMENT TO YOUR COMFORT	075	12
TO OUR GREAT AND ENDLESS COMFORT	086	18
FURTHER COMFORT OR COUNSEL, LET HIM COME TO ME, OR TO	088	05
BY PATIENCE AND COMFORT OF THY HOLY WORD, WE MAY	092	10

COMFORT   CONTINUED

PATIENCE AND COMFORT OF THE SCRIPTURES MIGHT HAVE   092 17
TO COMFORT ALL THAT MOURN   107 06
BY THE COMFORT OF THY GRACE MAY MERCIFULLY   130 26
HOLY GHOST TO COMFORT US, AND EXALT US UNTO THE SAME   179 07
AND EVERMORE TO REJOICE IN HIS HOLY COMFORT   180 12
TO THY WILL, COMFORT US IN ALL OUR AFFLICTIONS,   183 24
HE SAID, DAUGHTER, BE OF GOOD COMFORT   224 22
COMFORT YE, COMFORT YE MY PEOPLE, SAITH YOUR GOD   242 16
COMFORT YE, COMFORT YE MY PEOPLE, SAITH YOUR GOD   242 16
YIELD HER INCREASE, TO THY GLORY AND OUR COMFORT   265 16
WHEREFORE COMFORT ONE ANOTHER WITH THESE WORDS   269 10
THOU LOVE HER, COMFORT HER, HONOUR, AND KEEP HER IN   301 08
THOU LOVE HIM, COMFORT HIM, HONOUR, AND KEEP HIM IN   301 16
GIVE HIM COMFORT AND SURE CONFIDENCE IN THEE,   309 06
MY SOUL REFUSED COMFORT   311 03
THE WEAK AND THE COMFORT OF SUFFERERS   312 12
AND GOD OF ALL COMFORT, OUR ONLY HELP IN TIME OF   316 06
COMFORT, WE BESEECH THEE, MOST GRACIOUS GOD, THIS THY   316 18
IN THE COMFORT OF A REASONABLE, RELIGIOUS, AND HOLY   317 05
THE GRACE AND COMFORT OF THE HOLY SPIRIT   319 16
AND HE SHALL COMFORT THINE HEART   326 31
AND LEAD ME FORTH BESIDE THE WATERS OF COMFORT   338 20
AND THY STAFF COMFORT ME   338 25
FATHER OF MERCIES AND GIVER OF ALL COMFORT   342 10
AND LEAD ME FORTH BESIDE THE WATERS OF COMFORT   368 13
AND THY STAFF COMFORT ME   368 18
AND HE SHALL COMFORT THINE HEART   372 31
3 THE LORD COMFORT HIM WHEN HE LIETH SICK UPON HIS   392 04
12 O GIVE ME THE COMFORT OF THY HELP AGAIN, *   403 33
WORD WILL I COMFORT ME   409 03
FOUND I ANY TO COMFORT ME   423 15
MY SOUL REFUSED COMFORT   433 20
4 COMFORT THE SOUL OF THY SERVANT   447 11
15 COMFORT US AGAIN NOW AFTER THE TIME THAT THOU HAST   454 19
COMFORT THOU ME ACCORDING UNTO THY WORD   491 23
THE SAME IS MY COMFORT IN MY TROUBLE   493 10
AND RECEIVED COMFORT   493 15
KINDNESS BE MY COMFORT, *   495 07
O WHEN WILT THOU COMFORT ME   495 22
FROM ABOVE, IS COMFORT, LIFE, AND FIRE OF LOVE   544 03
FROM ABOVE, IS COMFORT, LIFE, AND FIRE OF LOVE   556 11
AND ENDLESS COMFORT, OBTAIN REMISSION OF THEIR SINS,   565 33
GRACIOUSLY TO COMFORT THY SERVANT IN HIS SUFFERING,   597 22
COMFORT HIM WHEN DISCOURAGED OR SORROWFUL   597 31
AND COMFORT THEM CONCERNING THEIR TOIL   599 27
AND VERY FULL OF COMFORT, AS MORE LARGELY IS   605 09
AND UNSPEAKABLE COMFORT TO GODLY PERSONS, AND SUCH AS   606 17

COMFORTABLE

THAT THE COMFORTABLE GOSPEL OF CHRIST MAY BE TRULY   037 02
HEAR WHAT COMFORTABLE WORDS OUR SAVIOUR CHRIST SAITH   076 10
THE MOST COMFORTABLE SACRAMENT OF THE BODY AND BLOOD   086 30
DIVINE AND COMFORTABLE A THING TO THEM WHO RECEIVE IT   087 05
BECAUSE IT IS SO COMFORTABLE   406 15
FOR THY LOVING-KINDNESS IS COMFORTABLE   423 04

COMFORTABLY

SPEAK YE COMFORTABLY TO JERUSALEM, AND CRY UNTO HER,   242 17

COMFORTED

RELIEVED AND COMFORTED OUR SOULS BY THIS SEASONABLE   051 24
WOULD NOT BE COMFORTED, BECAUSE THEY ARE NOT   103 33
BUT NOW HE IS COMFORTED, AND THOU ART TORMENTED   190 18
DEFENDED AND COMFORTED IN ALL DANGERS AND   192 27
FOR THEY SHALL BE COMFORTED   257 23
AND COMFORTED ME ON EVERY SIDE   426 20
HOLPEN ME, AND COMFORTED ME   448 11

COMFORTER

ALSO THE HOLY GHOST, THE COMFORTER   010 23
THE DISCIPLES FOR THE COMING OF THE COMFORTER   043 20
SENDING TO US OF THE HOLY GHOST, THE COMFORTER   079 17
NOT AWAY, THE COMFORTER WILL NOT COME UNTO YOU   175 11
WHEN THE COMFORTER IS COME, WHOM I WILL SEND UNTO YOU   179 24
YOU ANOTHER COMFORTER, THAT HE MAY ABIDE WITH YOU FOR   181 10
BUT THE COMFORTER, WHICH IS THE HOLY GHOST, WHOM THE   181 30
BUT WHEN THE COMFORTER IS COME, WHOM I WILL SEND UNTO   255 30
THE COMFORTER, AND DAILY INCREASE IN THEM THY   297 18
TO THEE, THE COMFORTER, WE CRY   544 21
TO THEE, THE COMFORTER, WE CRY   556 29

COMFORTLESS

WE BESEECH THEE, LEAVE US NOT COMFORTLESS   179 06
I WILL NOT LEAVE YOU COMFORTLESS   181 14
FOR THE COMFORTLESS TROUBLES' SAKE OF THE NEEDY,   355 16

COMFORTS

VISIT HIM WITH COMFORTS FROM ABOVE   315 25
THY COMFORTS HAVE REFRESHED MY SOUL   458 25
ALL THE OTHER COMFORTS AND CONVENIENCES OF LIFE   591 10
AND COMFORTS OF THY HOLY SPIRIT   591 16

COMING

LEST COMING SUDDENLY HE FIND YOU SLEEPING   021 26
DISCIPLES FOR THE COMING OF THE COMFORTER   043 19
AND BY THE COMING OF THE HOLY GHOST,   055 12
UNTIL HIS COMING AGAIN   080 16

COMING   CONTINUED

THINGS WHICH ARE COMING ON THE EARTH   093 09
THE SON OF MAN COMING IN A CLOUD WITH POWER AND GREAT   093 11
WHO AT THY FIRST COMING DIDST SEND THY MESSENGER TO   093 24
AT THY SECOND COMING TO JUDGE THE WORLD WE MAY BE   093 29
HE IT IS, WHO COMING AFTER ME IS PREFERRED BEFORE ME,   096 04
AND STRAIGHTWAY COMING UP OUT OF THE WATER, HE SAW   112 20
SO SHALL ALSO THE COMING OF THE SON OF MAN BE   118 11
THE SON OF MAN COMING IN THE CLOUDS OF HEAVEN WITH   118 19
OF POWER, AND COMING IN THE CLOUDS OF HEAVEN   143 16
WHO PASSED BY, COMING OUT OF THE COUNTRY, THE FATHER   146 06
A CYRENIAN, COMING OUT OF THE COUNTRY, AND ON HIM   154 10
THE DAYS ARE COMING, IN THE WHICH THEY SHALL SAY,   154 16
ALSO MOCKED HIM, COMING TO HIM, AND OFFERING HIM   154 30
SEETH THE WOLF COMING, AND LEAVETH THE SHEEP, AND   172 24
WAITING FOR THE COMING OF OUR LORD JESUS CHRIST   215 02
MAN NAMED ANANIAS COMING IN, AND PUTTING HIS HAND ON   230 20
BUT WHO MAY ABIDE THE DAY OF HIS COMING   232 08
AND SHE COMING IN THAT INSTANT GAVE THANKS LIKEWISE   233 21
YOU THE POWER AND COMING OF OUR LORD JESUS CHRIST,   248 15
TO WHOM COMING, AS UNTO A LIVING STONE, DISALLOWED   259 29
REMAIN UNTO THE COMING OF THE LORD SHALL NOT PREVENT   269 04
THAT HE, COMING TO THY HOLY BAPTISM, MAY RECEIVE   274 13
BLOOD OF CHRIST, COMING TO THOSE HOLY MYSTERIES IN   294 30
WHO, COMING INTO THE SICK PERSON'S PRESENCE, SHALL   R 308 06
AND BY THE COMING OF THE HOLY GHOST   318 08
AND THY COMING IN, *   327 33
AFTERWARD THEY THAT ARE CHRIST'S AT HIS COMING   328 26
AT WHOSE COMING IN GLORIOUS MAJESTY TO JUDGE THE   333 18
AT WHOSE COMING IN GLORIOUS MAJESTY TO JUDGE THE   337 12
AND THY COMING IN, *   339 17
FOR HE HATH SEEN THAT HIS DAY IS COMING   385 21
AND THY COMING IN, *   503 06
SEETH THE WOLF COMING, AND LEAVETH THE SHEEP, AND   539 13
THAT THE INCREASE COMING THEREBY MAY BE MANIFEST UNTO   558 23
NEW JERUSALEM, COMING DOWN FROM GOD OUT OF HEAVEN,   567 12
UNTO THE COMING OF OUR LORD AND SAVIOUR JESUS CHRIST   590 20
THE DUTIES OF THE COMING DAY   591 29

COMMAND

HIS HOLY GOSPEL COMMAND US TO CONTINUE, A PERPETUAL   080 14
THE SON OF GOD, COMMAND THAT THESE STONES BE MADE   126 27
COMMAND THEREFORE THAT THE SEPULCHRE BE MADE SURE   162 19
MAKE US TO LOVE THAT WHICH THOU DOST COMMAND   209 11
DO WHATSOEVER I COMMAND YOU   241 28
THESE THINGS I COMMAND YOU, THAT YE LOVE ONE ANOTHER   255 12
THE MIGHT OF THY COMMAND, DRIVEST AWAY FROM MEN'S   315 07
ANCIENT CANONS COMMAND, THAT WE SHOULD NOT BE HASTY   554 08
BY THE EXPRESS COMMAND OF GOD, OR BY THE SECRET   564 12

COMMANDED

AND HAST COMMANDED US TO WORK WITH QUIETNESS,   039 26
THY SON HATH COMMANDED US TO MAKE   080 41
AS HE HIMSELF HATH COMMANDED   089 13
DID AS JESUS COMMANDED THEM, AND BROUGHT THE ASS, AND   091 22
THAT MOSES COMMANDED, FOR A TESTIMONY UNTO THEM   115 05
AND COMMANDED HIM TO BE BROUGHT UNTO HIM   123 33
THEN PILATE COMMANDED THE BODY TO BE DELIVERED   162 09
AND HE COMMANDED US TO PREACH UNTO THE PEOPLE,   166 28
WITH THEM, COMMANDED THEM THAT THEY SHOULD NOT DEPART   177 30
AND HE COMMANDED US TO PREACH UNTO THE PEOPLE, AND TO   184 15
AND HE COMMANDED THEM TO BE BAPTIZED IN THE NAME OF   184 28
AS THOU HAST COMMANDED, AND YET THERE IS ROOM   192 17
AND HE COMMANDED THE PEOPLE TO SIT DOWN ON THE   199 17
AND COMMANDED TO SET THEM ALSO BEFORE THEM   199 21
HIS LORD COMMANDED HIM TO BE SOLD, AND HIS WIFE,   221 17
FOR GOD, WHO COMMANDED THE LIGHT TO SHINE OUT OF   251 07
HATH THE LORD COMMANDED US, SAYING, I HAVE SET THEE   261 03
I HAVE COMMANDED YOU   275 31
THE LORD HATH COMMANDED TO BE RECEIVED   293 11
FOR ME IN THE JUDGMENT THAT THOU HAST COMMANDED   350 03
HE COMMANDED, AND IT STOOD FAST   379 04
WHICH HE COMMANDED OUR FOREFATHERS TO TEACH THEIR   435 05
24 SO HE COMMANDED THE CLOUDS ABOVE, *   436 16
AS THE LORD COMMANDED THEM   475 05
HE HATH COMMANDED HIS COVENANT FOR EVER   483 11
THAT THOU HAST COMMANDED *   499 15
HE COMMANDED, AND THEY WERE CREATED   524 14
THE LORD HATH COMMANDED, AND AS THIS CHURCH HATH   542 13
I HAVE COMMANDED YOU   552 13
OF MY WILL CENTRE IN WHAT THOU HAST COMMANDED   573 19
THE LORD HATH COMMANDED TO BE RECEIVED   582 09
WILLED AND COMMANDED THEM TO BE DONE, WE DOUBT NOT   605 21
ALL THAT ARE COMMANDED TO YOU, SAY, WE ARE   605 29
ARE NOT COMMANDED BY GOD'S LAW, EITHER TO VOW THE   609 21

COMMANDEDST

AND COMMANDEDST HIM EARNESTLY TO FEED THY   244 24

COMMANDEST

WHICH THOU COMMANDEST, AND DESIRE THAT WHICH THOU   174 20
ACCOMPLISH THOSE THINGS WHICH THOU COMMANDEST   217 21
WHICH THOU COMMANDEST, AND DESIRE THAT WHICH THOU   285 28

COMMANDMENT

AND COMMANDMENT, TO HIS MINISTERS, TO DECLARE   007 09
AND COMMANDMENT, TO HIS MINISTERS, TO DECLARE   024 11
FULFIL HIS COMMANDMENT, AND HEARKEN UNTO THE VOICE OF   029 13
THY WORD AND COMMANDMENT, GOOD LORD, DELIVER US   055 04
AFTER EVERY COMMANDMENT, ASK GOD MERCY FOR THEIR   R 067 23

COMMANDMENT   CONTINUED

PART OF THE COMMANDMENT WHICH IS INSET   R 067 27
THIS IS THE FIRST AND GREAT COMMANDMENT   069 29
BE ANY OTHER COMMANDMENT, IT IS BRIEFLY COMPREHENDED   090 27
GAVE ME COMMANDMENT, EVEN SO I DO   182 10
AND THIS COMMANDMENT HAVE WE FROM HIM, THAT HE WHO   189 34
THIS IS HIS COMMANDMENT, THAT WE SHOULD BELIEVE ON   191 29
AS HE GAVE US COMMANDMENT   191 31
TRANSGRESSED I AT ANY TIME THY COMMANDMENT   202 35
IS THE GREAT COMMANDMENT IN THE LAW   215 10
THIS IS THE FIRST AND GREAT COMMANDMENT   215 12
THIS IS MY COMMANDMENT, THAT YE LOVE ONE ANOTHER,   241 25
AND GAVE COMMANDMENT TO HIS DISCIPLES, THAT THEY   279 12
AFTER EVERY COMMANDMENT THE PEOPLE SHALL SAY THE   R 285 34
PART OF THE COMMANDMENT WHICH IS INSET MAY BE   R 286 04
THIS IS THE FIRST AND GREAT COMMANDMENT   288 08
FULFIL HIS COMMANDMENT, AND HEARKEN UNTO THE VOICE OF   312 29
THE COMMANDMENT OF THE LORD IS PURE, AND GIVETH LIGHT   363 31
FULFIL HIS COMMANDMENT, AND HEARKEN UNTO THE VOICE OF   467 16
BUT THY COMMANDMENT IS EXCEEDING BROAD   496 17
FORTH HIS COMMANDMENT UPON EARTH, *   523 25
AND COMMANDMENT, OUGHT TO BE MINISTERED TO ALL   609 11

COMMANDMENTS

TO OBEY THY COMMANDMENTS, AND ALSO THAT BY THEE, WE,   031 21
OBEDIENTLY WALK IN THY HOLY COMMANDMENTS   052 24
AND DILIGENTLY TO LIVE AFTER THY COMMANDMENTS   056 12
REHEARSE DISTINCTLY THE TEN COMMANDMENTS   R 067 23
THE TEN COMMANDMENTS, THE PRIEST MAY OMIT THAT PART   R 067 26
IN THEM THAT LOVE ME AND KEEP MY COMMANDMENTS   068 15
THESE TWO COMMANDMENTS HANG ALL THE LAW AND THE   069 31
OF THY LAWS, AND IN THE WORKS OF THY COMMANDMENTS   070 09
THE COMMANDMENTS OF GOD, AND WALKING FROM HENCEFORTH   075 10
CONVERSATIONS BY THE RULE OF GOD'S COMMANDMENTS   087 17
KNOW WHAT COMMANDMENTS WE GAVE YOU BY THE LORD JESUS   127 26
HAD GIVEN COMMANDMENTS UNTO THE APOSTLES WHOM HE HAD   177 25
IF YE LOVE ME, KEEP MY COMMANDMENTS   181 09
HATH MY COMMANDMENTS, AND KEEPETH THEM, HE IT IS THAT   181 18
KEEPING THY COMMANDMENTS WE MAY PLEASE THEE, BOTH IN   189 04
WE KEEP HIS COMMANDMENTS, AND DO THOSE THINGS THAT   191 28
KEEPETH HIS COMMANDMENTS DWELLETH IN HIM, AND HE IN   191 32
WAY OF THY COMMANDMENTS, MAY OBTAIN THY GRACIOUS   204 25
THESE TWO COMMANDMENTS HANG ALL THE LAW AND THE   215 14
OBEDIENTLY TO FULFIL THY HOLY COMMANDMENTS   226 23
YE KEEP MY COMMANDMENTS, YE SHALL ABIDE IN MY LOVE   238 22
MY FATHER'S COMMANDMENTS, AND ABIDE IN HIS LOVE   238 23
BE EVERMORE READY TO FOLLOW THY HOLY COMMANDMENTS   246 21
WILL AND COMMANDMENTS, AND WALK IN THE SAME ALL THE   277 05
AND THE TEN COMMANDMENTS, AND ALL OTHER THINGS WHICH   277 11
WILL AND COMMANDMENTS, AND WALK IN THE SAME ALL THE   278 14
WILL AND COMMANDMENTS, AND WALK IN THE SAME ALL THE   283 27
YOU SHOULD KEEP GOD'S HOLY WILL AND COMMANDMENTS   285 14
ME HOW MANY COMMANDMENTS THERE ARE   285 15
ARE TEN COMMANDMENTS, GIVEN IN OLD TIME BY GOD TO THE   285 16
THE TEN COMMANDMENTS, AND AFTER EVERY COMMANDMENT THE   R 285 33
REPEAT THE COMMANDMENTS, THE MINISTER SAYING THE   R 286 02
IN THEM THAT LOVE ME AND KEEP MY COMMANDMENTS   286 15
JESUS CHRIST TEACH US ABOUT THESE COMMANDMENTS   288 03
THAT THEY ARE SUMMED UP IN THESE TWO COMMANDMENTS   288 05
DO YOU CHIEFLY LEARN FROM THE TEN COMMANDMENTS   288 11
I LEARN TWO THINGS FROM THESE COMMANDMENTS   288 12
WALK IN THE COMMANDMENTS OF GOD, AND TO SERVE HIM,   289 14
AND THE TEN COMMANDMENTS, AND ARE SUFFICIENTLY   R 295 14
OF THY LAWS, AND IN THE WORKS OF THY COMMANDMENTS   298 29
TO THY HOLY COMMANDMENTS, THAT AT THE DAY OF THE   336 22
OUT HIS COMMANDMENTS FROM ME   361 12
BUT TO KEEP HIS COMMANDMENTS   435 12
AND KEEP NOT MY COMMANDMENTS   452 04
UPON HIS COMMANDMENTS TO DO THEM   467 12
ALL HIS COMMANDMENTS ARE TRUE   483 08
HE HATH GREAT DELIGHT IN HIS COMMANDMENTS   483 19
THAT WE SHALL DILIGENTLY KEEP THY COMMANDMENTS   490 07
WHILE I HAVE RESPECT UNTO ALL THY COMMANDMENTS   490 11
O LET ME NOT GO WRONG OUT OF THY COMMANDMENTS   490 19
TALK OF THY COMMANDMENTS, *   490 27
NOT THY COMMANDMENTS FROM ME   491 04
CURSED ARE THEY THAT DO ERR FROM THY COMMANDMENTS   491 09
MAKE ME TO UNDERSTAND THE WAY OF THY COMMANDMENTS   491 21
WAY OF THY COMMANDMENTS, *   491 31
35 MAKE ME TO GO IN THE PATH OF THY COMMANDMENTS   492 09
MY DELIGHT IS IN THY COMMANDMENTS   492 19
FOR I SEEK THY COMMANDMENTS   492 29
BE IN THY COMMANDMENTS,*   493 02
UP UNTO THY COMMANDMENTS, WHICH I HAVE LOVED   493 04
BECAUSE I KEPT THY COMMANDMENTS   493 22
TO KEEP THY COMMANDMENTS   493 32
AND KEEP THY COMMANDMENTS   494 07
FOR I HAVE BELIEVED THY COMMANDMENTS   494 14
KEEP THY COMMANDMENTS WITH MY WHOLE HEART   494 19
THAT I MAY LEARN THY COMMANDMENTS   494 29
BUT I WILL BE OCCUPIED IN THY COMMANDMENTS   495 12
86 ALL THY COMMANDMENTS ARE TRUE   495 29
BUT I FORSOOK NOT THY COMMANDMENTS   495 32
93 I WILL NEVER FORGET THY COMMANDMENTS   496 11
FOR I HAVE SOUGHT THY COMMANDMENTS   496 14
THROUGH THY COMMANDMENTS, HAST MADE ME WISER THAN   496 22
BECAUSE I KEEP THY COMMANDMENTS   496 27
THROUGH THY COMMANDMENTS I GET UNDERSTANDING   497 02
BUT YET I SWERVED NOT FROM THY COMMANDMENTS   497 18
KEEP THY COMMANDMENTS OF MY GOD   497 28
I LOVE THY COMMANDMENTS *   498 23
THEREFORE HOLD I STRAIGHT ALL THY COMMANDMENTS   498 25
FOR MY DELIGHT WAS IN THY COMMANDMENTS   498 33
AND SO SHALL I KEEP THY COMMANDMENTS   499 07

COMMANDMENTS   CONTINUED

YET DO I NOT FORGET THY COMMANDMENTS   499 22
YET IS MY DELIGHT IN THY COMMANDMENTS   499 26
FOR ALL THY COMMANDMENTS ARE TRUE   500 12
HOW I LOVE THY COMMANDMENTS   500 29
AND DONE AFTER THY COMMANDMENTS   501 14
KEPT THY COMMANDMENTS AND TESTIMONIES   501 17
FOR ALL THY COMMANDMENTS ARE RIGHTEOUS   501 27
FOR I HAVE CHOSEN THY COMMANDMENTS   501 29
FOR I DO NOT FORGET THY COMMANDMENTS   502 03
TO THE COMMANDMENTS OF GOD   542 14
WILL AND COMMANDMENTS, AND WALK IN THE SAME ALL THE   577 18
THAT YOU SHOULD KEEP GOD'S COMMANDMENTS   578 18
IN THEM THAT LOVE ME AND KEEP MY COMMANDMENTS   578 34
DOST THOU CHIEFLY LEARN BY THESE COMMANDMENTS   579 23
WALK IN THE COMMANDMENTS OF GOD, AND TO SERVE HIM,   580 17
AND THE TEN COMMANDMENTS, AND CAN ANSWER TO THE OTHER   R 583 02
OF THE COMMANDMENTS WHICH ARE CALLED MORAL   604 23
GOD'S COMMANDMENTS, WHICH THEY CALL WORKS OF   605 24

COMMEND

WE COMMEND THIS NATION TO THY MERCIFUL CARE, THAT   018 08
WE COMMEND TO THY FATHERLY GOODNESS ALL   019 03
WE COMMEND TO THY FATHERLY GOODNESS ALL   032 34
WE COMMEND TO THY ALMIGHTY PROTECTION, THY SERVANT,   046 09
INTO THY HANDS I COMMEND MY SPIRIT   155 13
WE HUMBLY COMMEND THE SOUL OF THIS THY SERVANT, OUR   317 13
WE COMMEND THE SOUL OF THY SERVANT, NOW   319 27
ALMIGHTY GOD WE COMMEND THE SOUL OF OUR BROTHER   333 14
ALMIGHTY GOD WE COMMEND THE SOUL OF OUR BROTHER   337 09
INTO THY HANDS I COMMEND MY SPIRIT   375 31
BRETHREN, I COMMEND YOU TO GOD, AND TO THE WORD   551 02
WE COMMEND TO THY CONTINUAL CARE THE HOMES IN WHICH   598 20

COMMENDED

AND IS COMMENDED OF SAINT PAUL TO BE HONOURABLE AMONG   300 15
THEY ALSO THAT SWEAR BY HIM SHALL BE COMMENDED   415 16

COMMENDING

OF THE TRUTH COMMENDING OURSELVES TO EVERY MAN'S   250 31
THE BISHOP (COMMENDING SUCH AS SHALL BE FOUND MEET TO   R 530 29
THE BISHOP (COMMENDING SUCH AS SHALL BE FOUND MEET TO   R 537 05

COMMISSION

A COMMISSION FOR A REVIEW WAS ISSUED IN THE YEAR   VI 04
THOUGHT PROPER TO REVIVE IT BY ANY NEW COMMISSION   VI 06
BY HIS COMMISSION AND AUTHORITY, WE MAY USE THEIR   608 12

COMMIT

THOU SHALT NOT COMMIT ADULTERY   069 10
THOU SHALT NOT COMMIT ADULTERY, THOU SHALT NOT KILL,   090 25
NEITHER LET US COMMIT FORNICATION, AS SOME OF THEM   201 17
THOU SHALT NOT COMMIT ADULTERY   287 09
AND PROTECTION WE COMMIT THEE   314 26
AND PROTECTION WE COMMIT YOU   332 10
AND WE COMMIT HIS BODY TO THE GROUND   333 15
AND WE COMMIT HIS BODY TO THE DEEP   337 10
JESUS CHRIST, WE COMMIT THE BODY OF THIS CHILD TO THE   341 14
5 COMMIT THY WAY UNTO THE LORD, AND PUT THY TRUST IN   385 02
THOU SHALT NOT COMMIT ADULTERY   579 16

COMMITTAL

SENTENCE OF COMMITTAL, THE MINISTER SHALL SAY,   R 337 07

COMMITTED

CONGREGATIONS COMMITTED TO THEIR CHARGE, THE   018 21
CONGREGATIONS COMMITTED TO THEIR CHARGE, THE   032 20
WHO HAST COMMITTED TO THY HOLY CHURCH THE CARE AND   042 30
HAVE COMMITTED, BY THOUGHT, WORD, AND DEED, AGAINST   075 20
WHO HAD COMMITTED MURDER IN THE INSURRECTION   145 15
BUT COMMITTED HIMSELF TO HIM THAT JUDGETH   172 14
SOME OF THEM COMMITTED, AND FELL IN ONE DAY THREE AND   201 17
WHICH BY OUR FRAILTY WE HAVE COMMITTED   223 18
WHO HAST COMMITTED TO THE HANDS OF MEN THE   260 19
TO THE PEOPLE COMMITTED TO HIS CARE   294 13
CHURCH OF GOD COMMITTED UNTO THEE   534 06
A TREASURE IS COMMITTED TO YOUR CHARGE   540 06
OR SHALL BE COMMITTED TO YOUR CHARGE, UNTO THAT   540 19
THE PEOPLE COMMITTED TO YOUR CHARGE   542 06
THE PEOPLE COMMITTED TO YOUR CURE AND CHARGE WITH ALL   542 16
OR SHALL BE COMMITTED TO YOUR CHARGE   543 09
OF GOD, NOW COMMITTED UNTO THEE BY THE IMPOSITION OF   546 10
OF GOD, NOW COMMITTED TO THEE BY THE IMPOSITION OF   546 18
THE PEOPLE COMMITTED TO YOUR CHARGE   554 23
IS COMMITTED TO YOU   555 17
OF GOD, NOW COMMITTED UNTO THEE BY THE IMPOSITION OF   558 13
CONGREGATION COMMITTED TO YOUR CHARGE, TO BRING ABOUT   569 32
TO THE FLOCK COMMITTED TO THY CARE   571 29
THE CHARGE OF THIS CONGREGATION IS NOW COMMITTED   572 10
THE PEOPLE NOW COMMITTED TO MY CHARGE, GRANT THAT I   573 21
SIN WILLINGLY COMMITTED AFTER BAPTISM IS SIN AGAINST   605 39

COMMITTETH

WHOSOEVER COMMITTETH SIN TRANSGRESSETH ALSO THE LAW   117 21
HE THAT COMMITTETH SIN IS OF THE DEVIL   117 28
16 THE POOR COMMITTETH HIMSELF UNTO THEE   354 07

COMMON

AND THEREFORE, BY COMMON CONSENT AND AUTHORITY, MAY	V 06
OF HER BOOK OF COMMON PRAYER, LAID IT DOWN AS A RULE,	V 13
AS IN COMMON EQUITY OUGHT TO BE ALLOWED TO ALL HUMAN	V 43
TO MAKE OUR COMMON SUPPLICATIONS UNTO THEE	020 04
TO MAKE OUR COMMON SUPPLICATIONS UNTO THEE	034 04
WITH THE BOOK OF COMMON PRAYER OF THE CHURCH OF	VI 30
OR OF THE BOOK OF COMMON PRAYER, UNDER THE DIRECTION	R 073 36
JESUS INTO THE COMMON HALL, AND GATHERED UNTO HIM THE	136 16
BUT SUCH AS IS COMMON TO MAN	201 26
AND COMMON USES, IN ORDER TO FILL MEN'S	564 17
AND COMMON USES	565 06
BOOK OF COMMON PRAYER, AND BOOKS OF CANONS OF	R 571 23
AND APPROVED BY COMMON AUTHORITY, OUGHT TO BE REBUKED	609 38
AGAINST THE COMMON ORDER OF THE CHURCH, AND HURTETH	609 39
ARE NOT COMMON, AS TOUCHING THE RIGHT, TITLE, AND	610 44

COMMONLY

OR THE CREED COMMONLY CALLED THE NICENE	R 015 32
OR THE CREED COMMONLY CALLED THE NICENE	R 030 03
SAID THE CREED COMMONLY CALLED THE NICENE, OR ELSE	R 070 29
AS THEY ARE COMMONLY RECEIVED, WE DO RECEIVE, AND	604 12
THAT WHICH IS COMMONLY CALLED THE APOSTLES' CREED,	604 25
THOSE FIVE COMMONLY CALLED SACRAMENTS, THAT IS TO	607 38
WHICH IT WAS COMMONLY SAID, THAT THE PRIEST DID OFFER	609 17

COMMONWEALTH

OF NECESSITY TO BE RECEIVED IN ANY COMMONWEALTH	604 21

COMMUNE

IN THE NIGHT I COMMUNE WITH MINE OWN HEART, AND	311 10
COMMUNE WITH YOUR OWN HEART, AND IN YOUR CHAMBER, AND	347 19
AND COMMUNE AMONG THEMSELVES, HOW THEY MAY LAY	415 27
IN THE NIGHT I COMMUNE WITH MINE OWN HEART, AND	433 28

COMMUNED

HIS WAY, AND COMMUNED WITH THE CHIEF PRIESTS AND	148 17
WHILE THEY COMMUNED TOGETHER AND REASONED, JESUS	167 07

COMMUNICANTS

AND OTHER COMMUNICANTS	R 084 31

COMMUNICATE

SHALL BE GIVEN TO THOSE PRESENT TO COMMUNICATE	R 082 29
I WILL NOT COMMUNICATE, BECAUSE I AM OTHERWISE	088 27
THERE ARE TO COMMUNICATE WITH HIM	R 321 13
APPOINTED TO COMMUNICATE WITH THE SICK, AND LAST OF	R 323 02
WITH OTHERS, SHALL ALSO COMMUNICATE	R 559 03

COMMUNICATED

ALL HAVE COMMUNICATED, THE PRIEST IS TO CONSECRATE	R 083 07
ALL HAVE COMMUNICATED, THE PRIEST SHALL RETURN TO THE	R 083 11

COMMUNICATION

NO CORRUPT COMMUNICATION PROCEED OUT OF YOUR MOUTH,	216 23

COMMUNICATIONS

MANNER OF COMMUNICATIONS ARE THESE THAT YE HAVE ONE	167 10

COMMUNING

THEIR COMMUNING IS NOT FOR PEACE	383 02

COMMUNION

LITANY OR HOLY COMMUNION IS IMMEDIATELY TO FOLLOW,	R 003 06
ABSOLUTION FROM THE ORDER FOR THE HOLY COMMUNION	R 007 05
WHEN THE HOLY COMMUNION IS IMMEDIATELY TO FOLLOW, THE	R 010 03
AT ONCE TO THE COMMUNION SERVICE	R 010 06
THE COMMUNION OF SAINTS	015 29
WHEN THE COMMUNION SERVICE IS READ	R 017 02
WHEN THE HOLY COMMUNION IS TO FOLLOW	R 017 21
THE COMMUNION OF SAINTS	029 34
OR COMMUNION, AT THE DISCRETION OF THE	R 049 03
OR BEFORE THE HOLY COMMUNION	R 054 04
GIVEN OF THE COMMUNION, AND OF THE BANNS OF	R 071 27
THERE IS A COMMUNION, SHALL RETURN TO THE HOLY TABLE,	R 071 31
THE HOLY COMMUNION, YE WHO DO TRULY AND EARNESTLY	R 075 07
THE HOLY COMMUNION, HUMBLY KNEELING	R 075 16
OF THIS HOLY COMMUNION, MAY WORTHILY RECEIVE THE MOST	081 24
RECEIVE THE COMMUNION, THIS PRAYER FOLLOWING	R 082 12
THE HOLY COMMUNION IN BOTH KINDS HIMSELF, AND PROCEED	R 082 25
AT THE COMMUNION, UNTO THE END OF THE GOSPEL,	R 084 28
NO SERMON OR COMMUNION,) MAY BE SAID ALL THAT IS	R 084 28
AFTER THE COMMUNION, IT SHALL NOT BE CARRIED OUT OF	R 084 30
OF THE HOLY COMMUNION, THE MINISTER SHALL KNOW ANY TO	R 084 34
TO THE HOLY COMMUNION, AND NOT HIM THAT IS OBSTINATE	R 085 16
OF THE COMMUNION, AFTER THE PRAYER FOR THE WHOLE	R 085 21
TO THE HOLY COMMUNION OF THE BODY AND BLOOD OF OUR	085 26
OF THE HOLY COMMUNION, (WHICH HE SHALL ALWAYS DO UPON	R 086 24
OF THE HOLY COMMUNION DOTH NOTHING ELSE BUT INCREASE	087 29
TO THE HOLY COMMUNION, BUT WITH A FULL TRUST IN GOD'S	088 02
TO THE HOLY COMMUNION, INSTEAD OF THE FORMER, HE MAY	R 088 10
THAT YE WILL BE PARTAKERS OF THIS HOLY COMMUNION	089 09
TO RECEIVE THE COMMUNION IN REMEMBRANCE OF THE	089 12
THE HOLY COMMUNION BE TWICE CELEBRATED ON CHRISTMAS	R 098 07

COMMUNION   CONTINUED

AND GOSPEL MAY BE USED AT THE FIRST COMMUNION	R 098 09
THE HOLY COMMUNION BE TWICE CELEBRATED ON EASTER DAY,	R 164 30
AND GOSPEL MAY BE USED AT THE FIRST COMMUNION	R 164 32
THE HOLY COMMUNION BE TWICE CELEBRATED ON WHITSUNDAY,	R 182 11
AND GOSPEL MAY BE USED AT THE FIRST COMMUNION	R 182 12
ELECT IN ONE COMMUNION AND FELLOWSHIP, IN THE	256 06
THAT SO HE MAY BE ADMITTED TO THE HOLY COMMUNION	R 281 15
THE COMMUNION OF SAINTS	284 23
OR HOLY COMMUNION, FOR THE CONTINUAL STRENGTHENING	291 31
TO CELEBRATE THE HOLY COMMUNION	294 14
TO THE HOLY COMMUNION, UNTIL SUCH TIME AS HE BE	R 299 08
IF THERE BE A COMMUNION, IT IS CONVENIENT THAT SHE	R 307 09
IS CONVENIENT THAT SHE RECEIVE THE HOLY COMMUNION	R 307 10
IN THE COMMUNION OF THE CATHOLIC CHURCH	317 03
OF THE HOLY COMMUNION OF THE BODY AND BLOOD OF OUR	R 321 07
TO RECEIVE THE COMMUNION IN HIS HOUSE	R 321 12
THE HOLY COMMUNION, BEGINNING WITH THE COLLECT,	R 321 15
FOR THE HOLY COMMUNION, BEGINNING AT THESE WORDS, YE	R 322 31
RECEIVE THE COMMUNION HIMSELF, AND AFTER MINISTER	R 322 34
THE COMMUNION	R 323 09
FOR THE COMMUNION, WITH THE COLLECT, EPISTLE,	R 531 11
THE HOLY COMMUNION, AND TO HELP HIM IN THE	533 13
THEN SHALL THE BISHOP PROCEED IN THE COMMUNION	R 534 26
THE HOLY COMMUNION THE SAME DAY, WITH THE BISHOP	R 534 27
THE COMMUNION ENDED, AFTER THE LAST COLLECT,	R 534 28
FOR THE COMMUNION, WITH THE COLLECT, EPISTLE,	R 537 17
SERVICE OF THE COMMUNION, WHICH ALL THEY WHO RECEIVE	R 546 29
SUCH TIME AS THEY HAVE RECEIVED THE COMMUNION	R 546 31
THE COMMUNION BEING DONE, AFTER THE LAST COLLECT,	R 547 02
BEGIN THE COMMUNION SERVICE, IN WHICH THIS SHALL BE	R 549 05
PROCEED IN THE COMMUNION SERVICE	R 559 02
FOR THE HOLY COMMUNION, OR AT MORNING PRAYER OR	R 563 03
HIM UPON THE COMMUNION TABLE	R 566 27
THERE IS A COMMUNION, THE FOLLOWING SHALL BE THE	R 567 02
FOR THE HOLY COMMUNION, OR AT MORNING PRAYER OR	R 569 08
CONTINUING IN COMMUNION WITH US, AND COMPLYING WITH	569 20
IF THERE BE A COMMUNION, THE INSTITUTED MINISTER	R 574 24
THE COMMUNION OF SAINTS	578 07
LOVE IN THE COMMUNION OF THY HOLY SPIRIT, AND IN THE	597 05

COMMUNION-TIME

AT THE COMMUNION-TIME THE HOLY TABLE SHALL HAVE	R 067 05

COMPACTED

TOGETHER AND COMPACTED BY THAT WHICH EVERY JOINT	237 31

COMPANIED

MEN WHICH HAVE COMPANIED WITH US ALL THE TIME THAT	234 21

COMPANION

EVEN THOU, MY COMPANION, *	407 16
63 I AM A COMPANION OF ALL THEM THAT FEAR THEE,	494 06

COMPANIONS'

BRETHREN AND COMPANIONS' SAKES, *	503 22

COMPANY

THE GLORIOUS COMPANY OF THE APOSTLES PRAISE THEE	010 16
THE BLESSED COMPANY OF ALL FAITHFUL PEOPLE	047 07
AND WITH ALL THE COMPANY OF HEAVEN, WE LAUD AND	077 05
AND WITH ALL THE COMPANY OF HEAVEN, WE LAUD AND	079 29
IS THE BLESSED COMPANY OF ALL FAITHFUL PEOPLE	083 23
HAVE BEEN IN THE COMPANY, WENT A DAY'S JOURNEY	110 24
WOMAN OF THE COMPANY LIFTED UP HER VOICE, AND SAID	130 18
AND SAW A GREAT COMPANY COME UNTO HIM, HE SAITH UNTO	131 27
HIM A GREAT COMPANY OF PEOPLE, AND OF WOMEN, WHICH	154 12
ALSO OF OUR COMPANY MADE US ASTONISHED, WHICH WERE	167 23
AND SAW A GREAT COMPANY COME UNTO HIM, HE SAITH UNTO	225 23
THE FACE OF THIS COMPANY, TO JOIN TOGETHER THIS MAN	300 09
THEN SHALL THE MINISTER SPEAK UNTO THE COMPANY	R 304 02
GOD AND THIS COMPANY, AND THERETO HAVE GIVEN AND	304 05
THE GLORIOUS COMPANY OF THE SAINTS IN LIGHT	320 03
SHALL BEAR HER COMPANY, AND SHALL BE BROUGHT UNTO	397 16
GREAT WAS THE COMPANY OF WOMEN THAT BARE THE TIDINGS	420 02
18 AND THE FIRE WAS KINDLED IN THEIR COMPANY	474 04
THEN SHALL THE RIGHTEOUS RESORT UNTO MY COMPANY	518 21
AND A GREAT COMPANY OF THE PRIESTS WERE OBEDIENT TO	532 22

COMPARED

WORTHY TO BE COMPARED WITH THE GLORY WHICH SHALL BE	194 12
WORTHY TO BE COMPARED WITH THE GLORY WHICH SHALL BE	330 27
HE MAY BE COMPARED UNTO THE BEASTS THAT PERISH	400 31
IS COMPARED UNTO THE BEASTS THAT PERISH	401 17
THAT SHALL BE COMPARED UNTO THE LORD	450 15

COMPARISON

UPON A COMPARISON OF THIS WITH THE BOOK OF	VI 30
I DESIRE IN COMPARISON OF THEE	429 27
HEAVEN IS IN COMPARISON OF THE EARTH	466 27

COMPASS

A FIRE, THAT COMPASS YOURSELVES ABOUT WITH SPARKS	144 26
ABOUT THEE, AND COMPASS THEE ROUND, AND KEEP THEE IN	204 11
MINE ENEMIES COMPASS ME ROUND ABOUT, TO TAKE AWAY MY	359 05
THE COMPASS OF THE WORLD, AND THEY THAT DWELL	368 29

COMPASS   CONTINUED

	PAGE	LN
THOU SHALT COMPASS ME ABOUT WITH SONGS OF	378	06
THAT COMPASS ME ABOUT	516	28
ANY OTHER MEANS COMPASS THE DOING OF SO WEIGHTY A	540	34
THE COMPASS OF THE WORLD, AND THEY THAT DWELL	563	12

COMPASSED

AND APPARENT DANGERS WHEREWITH WE WERE COMPASSED	052	11
HAST COMPASSED US ABOUT WITH SO GREAT A CLOUD	079	22
AND HAST COMPASSED US ABOUT WITH SO GREAT A	258	12
WE ALSO ARE COMPASSED ABOUT WITH SO GREAT A CLOUD OF	258	20
OF DEATH COMPASSED ME, *	359	31
AND COMPASSED ME TOGETHER ON EVERY SIDE	449	32
THEY COMPASSED ME ABOUT ALSO WITH WORDS OF HATRED,	480	07
OF DEATH COMPASSED ME ROUND ABOUT, *	486	23
10 ALL NATIONS COMPASSED ME ROUND ABOUT	488	18
UNGODLY HAVE COMPASSED ME ABOUT	494	02

COMPASSETH

AT MY HEELS COMPASSETH ME ROUND ABOUT	400	15

COMPASSION

THEE TO HAVE COMPASSION UPON OUR INFIRMITIES	049	31
AND FULL OF COMPASSION TO THE CHILDREN OF MEN	053	03
WHO HAST COMPASSION UPON ALL MEN, AND WHO WOULDEST	062	14
FULL OF COMPASSION, LONG-SUFFERING, AND OF GREAT	062	31
UP HIS COMPASSION FROM HIM, HOW DWELLETH THE LOVE OF	072	30
A HEART OF COMPASSION, KINDNESS, HUMBLENESS OF MIND,	116	04
HIS BOWELS OF COMPASSION FROM HIM, HOW DWELLETH THE	191	20
HAVING COMPASSION ONE OF ANOTHER, LOVE AS	195	20
I HAVE COMPASSION ON THE MULTITUDE, BECAUSE	199	10
AND HAD COMPASSION, AND RAN, AND FELL ON HIS	202	17
HE HAD COMPASSION ON HIM, AND WENT TO HIM, AND	208	29
HE HAD COMPASSION ON HER, AND SAID UNTO HER,	213	02
MOVED WITH COMPASSION, AND LOOSED HIM, AND FORGAVE	221	22
ALSO HAVE HAD COMPASSION ON THY FELLOW-SERVANT, EVEN	221	35
ART FULL OF COMPASSION AND MERCY, *	448	04
IS FULL OF COMPASSION AND MERCY, *	466	21
NOR TO HAVE COMPASSION UPON HIS FATHERLESS CHILDREN	480	23
MOVED WITH COMPASSION ON THEM, BECAUSE THEY FAINTED,	538	15
THEE TO HAVE COMPASSION ON OUR INFIRMITIES, AND TO	588	14
FULL OF COMPASSION	588	31

COMPASSION'S

FOR THY COMPASSION'S SAKE, TO SANCTIFY ALL OUR	594	20

COMPASSIONATE

AND COMPASSIONATE, WHO ART EVER READY TO HEAR THE	041	19

COMPASSIONS

WHOSE COMPASSIONS FAIL NOT, AND WHOSE	038	14

COMPEL

AND THEY COMPEL ONE SIMON A CYRENIAN, WHO PASSED BY,	146	05
AND HEDGES, AND COMPEL THEM TO COME IN, THAT MY HOUSE	192	19

COMPELLED

HIM THEY COMPELLED TO BEAR HIS CROSS	136	26

COMPETENT

ARE COME TO A COMPETENT AGE, AND CAN SAY THE CREED,	R 295	13
ARE COME TO A COMPETENT AGE, AND CAN SAY THE CREED,	R 582	36

COMPILING

THE FIRST COMPILING OF HER LITURGY IN THE TIME OF	V	27

COMPLAIN

WHEN MY HEART IS VEXED, I WILL COMPLAIN	311	05
WHEN MY HEART IS VEXED, I WILL COMPLAIN	433	22

COMPLAINED

AND COMPLAINED UNTO MY GOD	360	04

COMPLAINING

BONES CONSUMED AWAY THROUGH MY DAILY COMPLAINING	377	27
AND NO COMPLAINING IN OUR STREETS	520	22

COMPLAINT

THE VOICE OF MY COMPLAINT	328	05
NOT THE COMPLAINT OF THE POOR	352	14
CONSIDER MY COMPLAINT, *	358	16
AND MY COMPLAINT CAME BEFORE HIM	360	07
MY HEALTH, AND FROM THE WORDS OF MY COMPLAINT	388	06
HE HEARD THEIR COMPLAINT	475	26
LET MY COMPLAINT COME BEFORE THEE, O LORD	501	20
THE VOICE OF MY COMPLAINT	507	10
7 CONSIDER MY COMPLAINT	518	16

COMPLAINTS

POURED OUT MY COMPLAINTS BEFORE HIM, *	518	05

COMPLYING

WITH US, AND COMPLYING WITH THE RUBRICS AND CANONS OF	569	20

COMPREHEND

BE ABLE TO COMPREHEND WITH ALL SAINTS WHAT IS THE	212	17

COMPREHENDED

IS BRIEFLY COMPREHENDED IN THIS SAYING, NAMELY,	090	28
DARKNESS COMPREHENDED IT NOT	097	25

CONCEITS

BE NOT WISE IN YOUR OWN CONCEITS	112	31

CONCEIVE

A VIRGIN SHALL CONCEIVE, AND BEAR A SON, AND SHALL	235	32
THOU SHALT CONCEIVE IN THY WOMB, AND BRING FORTH A	236	15

CONCEIVED

WHO WAS CONCEIVED BY THE HOLY GHOST, BORN OF THE	015	22
WHO WAS CONCEIVED BY THE HOLY GHOST, BORN OF THE	029	27
HATH MY MOTHER CONCEIVED ME	060	21
THAT WHICH IS CONCEIVED IN HER IS OF THE HOLY GHOST	105	05
BEFORE HE WAS CONCEIVED IN THE WOMB	106	22
SHE HATH ALSO CONCEIVED A SON IN HER OLD AGE	236	26
WHO WAS CONCEIVED BY THE HOLY GHOST, BORN OF THE	284	16
HE HATH CONCEIVED MISCHIEF, AND BROUGHT FORTH	350	22
HATH MY MOTHER CONCEIVED ME	403	19
WHO WAS CONCEIVED BY THE HOLY GHOST, BORN OF THE	577	31

CONCEIVETH

AND HIS HEART CONCEIVETH FALSEHOOD WITHIN HIMSELF	392	11

CONCERN

THE THINGS WHICH CONCERN MINE INFIRMITIES	121	14

CONCERNED

OF THIS CHURCH, OR OF THE DIOCESE CONCERNED	R 037	11

CONCERNING

MULTITUDES CONCERNING JOHN, WHAT WENT YE OUT INTO THE	094	25
WAS TOLD THEM CONCERNING THIS CHILD	106	14
I SPEAK AS CONCERNING REPROACH, AS THOUGH WE HAD BEEN	120	25
THE PROPHETS CONCERNING THE SON OF MAN SHALL BE	123	19
ANGELS CHARGE CONCERNING THEE	126	34
THE THINGS CONCERNING ME HAVE AN END	150	11
UNTO HIM, CONCERNING JESUS OF NAZARETH, WHICH WAS A	167	16
THE THINGS CONCERNING HIMSELF	167	33
AND AS CONCERNING THAT HE RAISED HIM UP FROM THE	169	10
THE PSALMS, CONCERNING ME	170	10
CONCERNING SPIRITUAL GIFTS, BRETHREN, I WOULD NOT	203	16
YE ANXIOUS CONCERNING RAIMENT	211	20
YE PUT OFF CONCERNING THE FORMER CONVERSATION THE OLD	216	12
SPAKE BEFORE CONCERNING JUDAS, WHICH WAS GUIDE TO	234	10
BUT I SPEAK CONCERNING CHRIST AND THE CHURCH	267	31
CONCERNING THEM WHICH ARE ASLEEP, THAT YE	268	28
THE QUESTIONS CONCERNING THE CHURCH WHICH FOLLOW,	R 290	26
QUESTIONS CONCERNING THE MINISTRY, THE PEOPLE	R 294	03
I HAVE MADE CONCERNING THE KING	396	16
AS CONCERNING THY WORD, *	493	08
152 AS CONCERNING THY TESTIMONIES, I HAVE KNOWN LONG	500	14
HAVE INQUIRED CONCERNING THEM, AND ALSO EXAMINED	530	18
HAVE INQUIRED CONCERNING THEM, AND ALSO EXAMINED	536	19
COMFORT THEM CONCERNING THEIR TOIL	599	28
DOCTRINE CONCERNING PURGATORY, PARDONS, WORSHIPPING	607	14

CONCLUDED

SCRIPTURE HATH CONCLUDED ALL UNDER SIN, THAT THE	208	03
MAY BE CONCLUDED AND PROVED BY THE SCRIPTURE	542	08
MAY BE CONCLUDED AND PROVED BY THE SAME	554	26

CONCLUDING

THE GOSPEL, CONCLUDING WITH THE BLESSING	R 084	29
OR THE CONCLUDING PRAYER ALONE, AS IT STANDS AMONG	R 305	04
THE CONCLUDING PARAGRAPH IN THE LETTER OF	R 569	10

CONCLUSION

BROUGHT TO A CONCLUSION, IT IS HOPED THE WHOLE WILL	VI	35

CONCORD

AND LOVER OF CONCORD, IN KNOWLEDGE OF WHOM STANDETH	017	06
ELSE MAY HINDER US FROM GODLY UNION AND CONCORD	037	29
TO GIVE TO ALL NATIONS UNITY, PEACE, AND CONCORD	056	09
WITH THE SPIRIT OF TRUTH, UNITY, AND CONCORD	074	12

CONCUPISCENCE

LUST OF CONCUPISCENCE, EVEN AS THE GENTILES WHICH	127	30
THAT CONCUPISCENCE AND LUST HATH OF ITSELF THE NATURE	604	40

CONDEMN

IS HE THAT SHALL CONDEMN ME	144	21

CONDEMN   CONTINUED

THE WORLD TO CONDEMN THE WORLD   184 35
FOR IF OUR HEART CONDEMN US, GOD IS GREATER THAN OUR   191 24
IF OUR HEART CONDEMN US NOT, THEN HAVE WE CCNFIDENCE   191 26
CONDEMN NOT, AND YE SHALL NOT BE CONDEMNED   194 26
NOR CONDEMN HIM WHEN HE IS JUDGED   386 32
AND CONDEMN THE INNOCENT BLOOD   458 29

CONDEMNATION

DOTH NOTHING ELSE BUT INCREASE YOUR CONDEMNATICN   087 30
RESIST SHALL RECEIVE TO THEMSELVES CONDEMNATION   114 15
SEEING THOU ART IN THE SAME CONDEMNATION   155 04
THIS IS THE CONDEMNATION, THAT LIGHT IS COME INTC THE   185 05
OF CONDEMNATION BE GLORY, MUCH MORE DOTH THE   206 23
AND SHALL NOT COME INTO CONDEMNATION   322 02
INTO THE CONDEMNATION OF THE DEVIL   549 27
THERE IS NO CONDEMNATION FOR THEM THAT BELIEVE AND   604 39
TO THEIR CONDEMNATION, DO EAT AND DRINK THE SIGN CR   609 07

CONDEMNED

THOSE WHO ARE CONDEMNED TO DIE)   046 21
THAT HE WAS CONDEMNED, REPENTED HIMSELF, AND BROUGHT   135 03
AND THEY ALL CONDEMNED HIM TO BE GUILTY OF DEATH   143 19
HIM TO BE CONDEMNED TO DEATH, AND HAVE CRUCIFIED HIM   167 19
NOT IS CONDEMNED ALREADY, BECAUSE HE HATH NCT   185 03
HE THAT BELIEVETH ON HIM IS NOT CONDEMNED   185 03
AND YE SHALL NOT BE CONDEMNED   194 27
I SHOULD HAVE CONDEMNED THE GENERATION OF THY   429 07
SENTENCE IS GIVEN UPON HIM, LET HIM BE CONDEMNED   480 15
THEY ARE TO BE CONDEMNED, WHICH SAY, THEY CAN NC MORE   606 03

CONDEMNETH

WHO IS HE THAT CONDEMNETH   331 03

CONDEMNING

THEM IN CONDEMNING HIM   168 29

CONDESCEND

BUT CONDESCEND TO MEN OF LOW ESTATE   111 32

CONDITION

THE CONDITION OF MAN AFTER THE FALL OF ADAM IS SUCH,   604 42

CONDITIONS

ALL SORTS AND CONDITIONS OF MEN   018 27
ALL SORTS AND CONDITIONS OF MEN   032 27
FOR ALL CONDITIONS OF MEN, OR, WHEN THAT IS NOT SAID, R   035 03

CONDUCT

CONDUCT HIM IN SAFETY TO THE HAVEN WHERE HE WOULD BE,   046 14
BEEN PLEASED TO CONDUCT IN SAFETY, THROUGH THE PERILS   053 22
THE RULE OF THY CONDUCT IN DISPENSING THE DIVINE   571 26

CONFEDERATE

AND ARE CONFEDERATE AGAINST THEE   444 15

CONFER

TO CONFER HOLY ORDERS   294 09

CONFESS

ACKNOWLEDGE AND CONFESS OUR MANIFOLD SINS AND   005 30
BUT CONFESS THEM WITH AN HUMBLE, LOWLY, PENITENT, AND   005 33
LET US HUMBLY CONFESS OUR SINS UNTO ALMIGHTY GOD   006 14
O GOD, WHO CONFESS THEIR FAULTS   006 25
BUT IF WE CONFESS OUR SINS, GOD IS FAITHFUL AND JUST   022 11
LET US HUMBLY CONFESS OUR SINS UNTO ALMIGHTY GOD   023 02
ACKNOWLEDGE AND CONFESS OUR MANIFOLD SINS AND   023 05
BUT CONFESS THEM WITH AN HUMBLE, LOWLY, PENITENT, AND   023 08
O GOD, WHO CONFESS THEIR FAULTS   023 32
ALL THOSE WHO CONFESS THEIR SINS UNTO THEE   062 09
ALL THOSE WHO DO CONFESS THY HOLY NAME MAY AGREE IN   074 13
AND TO CONFESS YOURSELVES TO ALMIGHTY GOD, WITH FULL   087 20
CAUSE I WILL CONFESS TO THEE AMONG THE GENTILES, AND   092 26
IF WE CONFESS OUR SINS, HE IS FAITHFUL AND JUST TO   101 30
TONGUE SHOULD CONFESS THAT JESUS CHRIST IS LORD, TO   105 30
TONGUE SHOULD CONFESS THAT JESUS CHRIST IS LORD,   134 27
WHOSOEVER SHALL CONFESS THAT JESUS IS THE SCN OF GOD,   189 22
IF THOU SHALT CONFESS WITH THY MOUTH THE LORD JESUS,   226 26
BE ASHAMED TO CONFESS THE FAITH OF CHRIST CRUCIFIED,   280 06
YE DO NOW CONFESS IT   300 28
AND EARTH, WE CONFESS THAT WE HAVE SINNED AGAINST   323 13
6 I SAID, I WILL CONFESS MY SINS UNTO THE LORD   377 32
18 FOR I WILL CONFESS MY WICKEDNESS, *   388 28
2 LET ISRAEL NOW CONFESS THAT HE IS GRACIOUS, *   488 02
OF AARON NOW CONFESS, *   488 04
FEAR THE LORD CONFESS, *   488 06
TO CONFESS THEIR SINS UNTO THEE, AND TO ASK   566 16
TO ALL THOSE WHO CONFESS AND FCRSAKE THEIR SINS   589 28
ONE MAY SECRETLY CONFESS THE SINS AND FAILINGS CF   R   589 35
THE APOSTLE DOTH CONFESS, THAT CONCUPISCENCE AND LUST   604 40
AS WE CONFESS THAT VAIN AND RASH SWEARING IS   611 06

CONFESSED

BUT CONFESSED, I AM NOT THE CHRIST   095 23
AND HE CONFESSED, AND DENIED NOT   095 23

CONFESSING

OF JORDAN, CONFESSING THEIR SINS   112 11

CONFESSION

THAT WHEN THE CONFESSION AND ABSOLUTION ARE OMITTED, R   003 10
THAT WHEN THE CONFESSION AND ABSOLUTION ARE OMITTED, R   021 07
YOUR HUMBLE CONFESSION TO ALMIGHTY GOD, DEVOUTLY   075 13
THIS GENERAL CONFESSION BE MADE, BY THE PRIEST AND   R   075 15
BY THE CONFESSION OF A TRUE FAITH, TO   186 24
THE MOUTH CONFESSION IS MADE UNTO SALVATION   226 29
A SPECIAL CONFESSION OF HIS SINS, IF HE FEEL HIS   R   313 24
AFTER WHICH CONFESSION, ON EVIDENCE OF HIS   R   313 25
THE CONFESSION AND THE ABSOLUTION   R   323 06
THAT FOR THE CONFESSION AND ABSOLUTION THE FCLLCWING R   323 10

CONFIDE

WE DO FULLY CONFIDE, OUR LICENCE AND AUTHORITY TC   569 16

CONFIDENCE

PLACE THEIR CONFIDENCE ANYWHERE BUT IN THEE   046 24
TRUST AND CONFIDENCE IN THY MERCY, AND EVERMORE SERVE   059 25
MAY WITH SURE CONFIDENCE BEHOLD HIM WHEN HE SHALL   098 14
ACCESS WITH CONFIDENCE BY THE FAITH OF HIM   108 28
THEN HAVE WE CONFIDENCE TOWARD GOD   191 26
YOUR CONFIDENCE, WHICH HATH GREAT RECOMPENCE OF   228 14
AND SURE CONFIDENCE IN THEE, DEFEND HIM IN ALL   309 06
IN THE CONFIDENCE OF A CERTAIN FAITH   317 04
THIS IS THE CONFIDENCE THAT WE HAVE IN HIM, THAT, IF   322 15
AND MY GOD IS THE STRENGTH OF MY CONFIDENCE   458 31
TO PUT ANY CONFIDENCE IN MAN   488 15
TO PUT ANY CONFIDENCE IN PRINCES   488 17
AND IN CONFIDENCE SHALL BE OUR STRENGTH   595 20
HEART WITH CONFIDENCE, THAT THOUGH HE BE SOMETIME   597 24

CONFIDENT

BEING CONFIDENT OF THIS VERY THING, THAT HE WHICH   220 25

CONFIDENTLY

ANOTHER CONFIDENTLY AFFIRMED, SAYING, OF A TRUTH THIS   151 16

CONFIRM

PLEASE GOD TO CONFIRM AND STRENGTHEN IT IN PURITY OF   047 08
CONFIRM AND STRENGTHEN YOU IN ALL GOODNESS   076 06
TRUTH OF GOC, TO CONFIRM THE PROMISES MADE UNTO THE   092 24
WHO SHALL ALSO CONFIRM YOU UNTO THE END, THAT YE MAY   215 03
AND CONFIRM THIS FAITH IN US EVERMORE   276 11
O MERCIFUL GOD, CONFIRM AND STRENGTHEN US   588 08
ESTABLISH AND CONFIRM THEIR FAITH OF ETERNAL   606 20
STRENGTHEN AND CONFIRM OUR FAITH IN HIM   607 34

CONFIRMATION

DEFENCE AND CONFIRMATION OF THE GOSPEL, YE ALL ARE   220 29
THE GREATER CONFIRMATION OF THE FAITH, DIDST SUFFER   228 06
OR CONFIRMATION, WHEREIN, AFTER RENEWING THE   291 24
AND TO ADMINISTER CONFIRMATION   294 10
FOR THEIR CONFIRMATION, THE MINISTER OF EVERY PARISH R 583 06
IS TO SAY, CONFIRMATION, PENANCE, ORDERS, MATRIMCNY,   607 38

CONFIRMED

THAT WAS CONFIRMED BEFORE OF GOD IN CHRIST, THE LAW,   207 22
OF CHRIST WAS CONFIRMED IN YOU   214 31
BISHOP TO BE CONFIRMED BY HIM   277 16
SHOULD BE CONFIRMED BY THE BISHOP, SO SOON AFTER HIS R 281 13
YOU HAVE BEEN CONFIRMED, WHAT GREAT PRIVILEGE DCTH   291 28
AND BE CONFIRMED BY THE BISHOP, MAY RECEIVE SUCH A   294 25
BISHOP TO BE CONFIRMED BY HIM   R 295 16
THAT ARE TO BE CONFIRMED SHALL STAND IN ORDER BEFCRE R 296 05
THE PERSONS CONFIRMED TO COME, WITHOUT DELAY, TO THE R 299 06
OR BE READY AND DESIROUS TO BE CONFIRMED   R 299 09
TIME AS HE BE CONFIRMED, OR BE READY AND DESIRCUS TC R 299 09
AND BE CONFIRMED BY THE BISHOP, MAY RECEIVE SUCH A   565 25
FIT TO BE PRESENTED TO THE BISHOP TO BE CONFIRMED   R 583 09
FAITH IS CONFIRMED, AND GRACE INCREASED BY VIRTUE OF   608 29

CONFIRMING

RATIFYING AND CONFIRMING THE SAME   296 25

CONFITERI

BONUM EST CONFITERI, NUNC DIMITTIS, DEUS MISEREATUR, R 025 17

CONFORM

US GRACE SO TO CONFORM OUR LIVES TO THEIR INNOCEACY   340 31

CONFORMABLE

TO MAKE THEM CONFORMABLE TO WHAT OUGHT TC BE THE   VI 18

CONFORMED

AND BE NOT CONFORMED TO THIS WORLD   110 06
THAT IT MAY BE CONFORMED UNTO THE BODY OF HIS GLORY,   222 24

CONFORMITY

PROMISE OF CONFORMITY TO THE DOCTRINE, DISCIPLINE,   R 552 26
DO PROMISE CONFORMITY AND OBEDIENCE TO THE DOCTRINE,   552 29

CONFOUND

O LORD, CONFOUND ME NOT   491 29

CONFOUNDED

LET ME NEVER BE CONFOUNDED   011 13
THEREFORE SHALL I NOT BE CONFOUNDED   144 16
AND WERE CONFOUNDED, BECAUSE THAT EVERY MAN HEARD   180 27
AND CONFOUNDED THE JEWS WHICH DWELT AT   231 09
SHALL BE CONFOUNDED, AND SORE VEXED   349 18
PUT THEIR TRUST IN THEE, AND WERE NOT CONFOUNDED   366 13
LET ME NOT BE CONFOUNDED, NEITHER LET MINE ENEMIES   369 19
LET ME NOT BE CONFOUNDED, FOR I HAVE PUT MY TRUST IN   370 25
LET ME NOT BE CONFOUNDED, O LORD, FOR I HAVE CALLED   376 30
4 LET THEM BE CONFOUNDED, AND PUT TO SHAME, THAT SEEK   381 24
SHALL NOT BE CONFOUNDED IN THE PERILOUS TIME   385 33
AND CONFOUNDED TOGETHER, THAT SEEK AFTER MY   391 16
SEEK THEE BE CONFOUNDED THROUGH ME, O LORD GOD OF   422 15
ASHAMED AND CONFOUNDED THAT SEEK AFTER MY SOUL   424 22
LET THEM BE CONFOUNDED AND PERISH THAT ARE AGAINST MY   425 31
FOR THEY ARE CONFOUNDED AND BROUGHT UNTO SHAME THAT   426 28
LET THEM BE CONFOUNDED AND VEXED EVER MORE AND MORE   445 06
7 CONFOUNDED BE ALL THEY THAT WORSHIP CARVED IMAGES,   461 10
LET THEM BE CONFOUNDED THAT RISE UP AGAINST ME   481 27
I NOT BE CONFOUNDED, *   490 10
THE PROUD BE CONFOUNDED, FOR THEY GO WICKEDLY ABOUT   495 11
5 LET THEM BE CONFOUNDED AND TURNED BACKWARD, *   506 29

CONFUSION

SAVE US FROM VIOLENCE, DISCORD, AND CONFUSION   036 14
LET NOT THINE HERITAGE BE BROUGHT TO CONFUSION   063 04
WITHOUT A CAUSE SHALL BE PUT TO CONFUSION   369 22
LET ME NEVER BE PUT TO CONFUSION   375 23
BE PUT TO CONFUSION, AND BE PUT TO SILENCE IN THE   376 31
AND BROUGHT TO CONFUSION, THAT IMAGINE MISCHIEF FOR   381 26
THEM BE PUT TO CONFUSION AND SHAME TOGETHER, THAT   383 16
THEM TO CONFUSION THAT HATE US   395 08
PUTTEST US TO CONFUSION, *   395 11
16 MY CONFUSION IS DAILY BEFORE ME, *   395 24
PUT THEM TO CONFUSION, BECAUSE GOD HATH DESPISED   405 27
AND PUT TO CONFUSION THAT WISH ME EVIL   424 23
BE PUT TO CONFUSION, *   425 06
WITH THEIR OWN CONFUSION, AS WITH A CLOAK   481 30

CONGREGATION

THE WHOLE CONGREGATION, AFTER THE MINISTER, ALL   R 006 16
WHEN ANY DESIRE THE PRAYERS OF THE CONGREGATION   R 019 12
SAID BY THE CONGREGATION WITH THE MINISTER   R 019 34
THE WHOLE CONGREGATION, AFTER THE MINISTER, ALL   R 023 23
WHEN ANY DESIRE THE PRAYERS OF THE CONGREGATION   R 033 10
SAID BY THE CONGREGATION WITH THE MINISTER   R 033 32
OF THE CONGREGATION FOR ANY WHO HAVE DESIRED THE   R 074 02
TO THIS CONGREGATION HERE PRESENT   074 26
SO THAT THE CONGREGATION BE THEREBY OFFENDED   R 085 03
THAT THE CONGREGATION MAY THEREBY BE SATISFIED   R 085 05
THE CONGREGATION, ASSEMBLE THE ELDERS, GATHER THE   124 30
THE SUPPLICATIONS OF THY CONGREGATION   279 15
INTO THE CONGREGATION OF CHRIST'S FLOCK   280 03
AND OF THIS CONGREGATION, RENEW THE SOLEMN PROMISE   296 22
IN THE CONGREGATION OF THE RIGHTEOUS   345 20
SHALL THE CONGREGATION OF THE PEOPLES COME ABOUT   350 04
THAT THE CONGREGATION OF THE POOR MAY FALL INTO THE   353 28
OF THE CONGREGATION WILL I PRAISE THEE   367 17
25 MY PRAISE IS OF THEE IN THE GREAT CONGREGATION   367 23
HATED THE CONGREGATION OF THE WICKED   371 06
WILL I GIVE THEE THANKS IN THE GREAT CONGREGATION   382 32
THY RIGHTEOUSNESS IN THE GREAT CONGREGATION   390 34
FROM THE GREAT CONGREGATION   391 07
MINDS SET UPON RIGHTEOUSNESS, O YE CONGREGATION   410 07
10 THY CONGREGATION SHALL DWELL THEREIN   419 31
LORD IN THE CONGREGATION, *   421 06
UPON THY CONGREGATION, *   430 06
NOT THE CONGREGATION OF THE POOR FOR EVER   431 16
IN THE CONGREGATION OF PRINCES   443 18
IN THE CONGREGATION OF THE SAINTS   450 14
COVERED THE CONGREGATION OF ABIRAM   474 03
ALSO IN THE CONGREGATION OF THE PEOPLE, *   478 10
AMONG THE FAITHFUL, AND IN THE CONGREGATION   482 25
LET THE CONGREGATION OF SAINTS PRAISE HIM   525 03
OF THE CONGREGATION) SHALL, WITH THE CLERGY AND   R 530 30
OF THE CONGREGATION) SHALL, WITH THE CLERGY AND   R 537 06
CHURCH AND CONGREGATION WHOM YOU MUST SERVE, IS HIS   540 08
PRESENT CONGREGATION OF CHRIST MAY ALSO UNDERSTAND   541 24
THE CONGREGATION SHALL BE DESIRED, SECRETLY IN   R 543 23
IN THE CONGREGATION, WHERE THOU SHALT BE LAWFULLY   548 20
MOVE THE CONGREGATION PRESENT TO PRAY, SAYING THUS TO R 553 02
THAT THE CONGREGATION PRESENT MAY HAVE A TRIAL, AND   554 13
TO THE CONGREGATION, HE SHALL SAY, DEARLY BELOVED IN R 564 09
TOWARDS THE CONGREGATION.   R 565 16
INTO THE CONGREGATION OF CHRIST'S FLOCK, MAY BE   565 20
OR IN THE CONGREGATION COMMITTED TO YOUR CHARGE, TO   569 21
AND YOUR CONGREGATION, AS TO A SEPARATION AND   569 34
OF THIS CONGREGATION IS NOW COMMITTED   572 10

CONGREGATION   CONTINUED

THIS CONGREGATION WITH THY LOVE AND FAVOUR   572 26
TO THIS CONGREGATION PRESENT, GIVE THE ABUNDANCE OF   574 09
ADMINISTER THE HOLY EUCHARIST TO HIS CONGREGATION   R 574 26
BLESS THE CONGREGATION OF THY POOR   599 08
CHRIST IS A CONGREGATION OF FAITHFUL MEN, IN THE   606 38
IN THE CONGREGATION, BEFORE HE BE LAWFULLY CALLED,   607 20
THEM IN THE CONGREGATION, TO CALL AND SEND MINISTERS   607 23

CONGREGATIONS

UPON THE CONGREGATIONS COMMITTED TO THEIR CHARGE, THE   018 20
UPON THE CONGREGATIONS COMMITTED TO THEIR CHARGE, THE   032 19
BY ALL CONGREGATIONS OF THIS CHURCH, OR OF THE   R 037 10
I WILL PRAISE THE LORD IN THE CONGREGATIONS   371 21
OF THY CONGREGATIONS, *   430 12
AND THE CONGREGATIONS OF VIOLENT MEN HAVE SOUGHT   448 02

CONGRESS

IN CONGRESS ASSEMBLED   035 11

CONGRUITY

SCHOOL-AUTHORS SAY) DESERVE GRACE OF CONGRUITY   605 20

CONIES

AND SO ARE THE STONY ROCKS FOR THE CONIES   468 31

CONNECTION

SACERDOTAL CONNECTION BETWEEN YOU AND THEM, WE, YOUR   569 35

CONQUERORS

ARE MORE THAN CONQUERORS THROUGH HIM THAT LOVED US   331 09

CONSCIENCE

WITH A GOOD CONSCIENCE USE AND SUBMIT UNTO, OR WHICH   V 41
TRUST IN GOD'S MERCY, AND WITH A QUIET CONSCIENCE   088 03
QUIET HIS OWN CONSCIENCE HEREIN, BUT REQUIRETH   088 04
OF HIS CONSCIENCE, AND THE REMOVING OF ALL SCRUPLE   088 08
BUT ALSO FOR CONSCIENCE SAKE   114 23
PURGE YOUR CONSCIENCE FROM DEAD WORKS TO SERVE THE   133 02
HAD NO MORE CONSCIENCE OF SINS   157 20
FROM AN EVIL CONSCIENCE, AND OUR BODIES WASHED WITH   158 21
OF A GOOD CONSCIENCE TOWARD GOD,) BY THE RESURRECTION   161 32
IF A MAN FOR CONSCIENCE TOWARD GOD ENDURE GRIEF,   172 05
WHEREOF OUR CONSCIENCE IS AFRAID, AND GIVING US THOSE   206 08
EVERY MAN'S CONSCIENCE IN THE SIGHT OF GOD   250 32
HE FEEL HIS CONSCIENCE TROUBLED WITH ANY MATTER   R 313 25
HAVING THE TESTIMONY OF A GOOD CONSCIENCE   317 03
THE MYSTERY OF THE FAITH IN A PURE CONSCIENCE   531 29
OF A GOOD CONSCIENCE, AND CONTINUING EVER STABLE AND   535 06
WITH A CONSCIENCE VOID OF OFFENCE TOWARDS THEE, AND   590 18

CONSCIENCES

WHOSE CONSCIENCES BY SIN ARE ACCUSED, BY THY   062 10
YOUR OWN CONSCIENCES, AND THAT NOT LIGHTLY, AND AFTER   087 11
WOUNDETH THE CONSCIENCES OF THE WEAK BRETHREN   609 41

CONSECRATE

PRIEST IS TO CONSECRATE MORE, ACCORDING TO THE FORM   R 083 08
OF HEART, TO CONSECRATE THIS PLACE TO THE HONOUR OF   565 04

CONSECRATED

IN WHICH THERE IS ANY WINE TO BE CONSECRATED   R 080 34
IF THE CONSECRATED BREAD OR WINE BE SPENT BEFORE   R 083 07
OF THE CONSECRATED ELEMENTS, COVERING THE SAME WITH A R 083 12
ANY OF THE CONSECRATED BREAD AND WINE REMAIN AFTER   R 084 30
HE HATH CONSECRATED FOR US, THROUGH THE VEIL,   158 18
WHO HAST SO CONSECRATED THE STATE OF MATRIMONY THAT   303 20
ORDAINED AND CONSECRATED BISHOP   552 23
IS TO BE CONSECRATED, BROTHER, FORASMUCH AS THE HOLY R 554 06
THE NEWLY CONSECRATED BISHOP, WITH OTHERS, SHALL ALSO 559 03
ARE CONSECRATED OR ORDERED ACCORDING TO SAID FORM, WE 610 35
AND LAWFULLY CONSECRATED AND ORDERED   610 36

CONSECRATION

PRAYER OF CONSECRATION, AS FOLLOWETH   R 080 05
PRAYER OF CONSECRATION, ENDING WITH THESE WORDS,   R 323 07
EPISCOPAL CONSECRATION OR ORDINATION   529 23
FOR CONSECRATION, AND SHALL CAUSE THEM TO BE READ   R 552 25
AT THE CONSECRATION OF A BISHOP SHALL BE SAID,   R 560 32
SENTENCE OF CONSECRATION IS TO BE READ BY SOME PERSON R 566 25
AND IN THE -- YEAR OF OUR CONSECRATION   569 40
THE BOOK OF CONSECRATION OF BISHOPS, AND ORDERING OF   610 31
TO SUCH CONSECRATION AND ORDERING   610 33

CONSENT

BY COMMON CONSENT AND AUTHORITY, MAY BE ALTERED,   V 07
ALL WITH ONE CONSENT BEGAN TO MAKE EXCUSE   192 06
WITH ONE CONSENT, *   444 14

CONSENTED

HAVE CONSENTED TOGETHER IN HOLY WEDLOCK, AND HAVE   304 03

CONSENTEDST

THOU CONSENTEDST UNTO HIM   402 26

CONSEQUENCE

IN CONSEQUENCE OF THE REVOLUTION   VI 17

CONSIDER

MUST CONSIDER HOW SAINT PAUL EXHORTETH ALL   085 27
MEAN SEASON TO CONSIDER THE DIGNITY OF THAT HOLY   087 08
CONSIDER EARNESTLY WITH YOURSELVES HOW LITTLE SUCH   088 34
NEGLECT TO DO, CONSIDER WITH YOURSELVES HOW GREAT IS   089 14
IF YE EARNESTLY CONSIDER, YE WILL BY GOD'S GRACE   089 19
AND LET US CONSIDER ONE ANOTHER TO PROVOKE UNTO LCVE   158 24
CONSIDER THE LILIES OF THE FIELD, HOW THEY GROW   211 21
CONSIDER THE LILIES OF THE FIELD, HOW THEY GROW   266 19
CONSIDER HIS CONTRITION, ACCEPT HIS TEARS, ASSUAGE   314 06
WITH THINE EARS CONSIDER MY CALLING   325 06
LET THINE EARS CONSIDER WELL *   328 05
CONSIDER MY MEDITATION   347 31
3 WHEN I CONSIDER THY HEAVENS, EVEN THE WORK OF THY   351 04
CONSIDER THE TROUBLE WHICH I SUFFER OF THEM THAT HATE   352 16
5 HIS EYES CONSIDER THE POOR, *   354 28
3 CONSIDER, AND HEAR ME, O LORD MY GOD   356 02
O LORD, CONSIDER MY COMPLAINT, *   358 16
18 CONSIDER MINE ENEMIES, HOW MANY THEY ARE   370 22
WITH THINE EARS CONSIDER MY CALLING   390 02
10 HEARKEN, O DAUGHTER, AND CONSIDER   397 05
HER BULWARKS, CONSIDER HER PALACES, *   400 02
22 O CONSIDER THIS, YE THAT FORGET GOD, *   403 02
HUMBLE SHALL CONSIDER THIS, AND BE GLAD   424 08
DOTH NOT WELL CONSIDER THIS, *   456 11
RIGHTEOUS WILL CONSIDER THIS, AND REJOICE   478 30
BUT I WILL CONSIDER THY TESTIMONIES   496 16
O CONSIDER MINE ADVERSITY, AND DELIVER ME, *   500 17
159 CONSIDER, O LORD, HOW I LOVE THY COMMANDMENTS   500 29
LET THINE EARS CONSIDER WELL *   507 10
AND CONSIDER MY VOICE, WHEN I CRY UNTO THEE   517 09
7 CONSIDER MY COMPLAINT   518 16
O LORD, AND CONSIDER MY DESIRE   518 23
WHEREFORE CONSIDER WITH YOURSELVES THE END CF THE   540 14
CONSIDER HOW STUDIOUS YE OUGHT TO BE IN READING AND   541 03

CONSIDERATION

IN CONSIDERATION OF EXTREME SICKNESS, NECESSITY   R 281 17
THE GODLY CONSIDERATION OF PREDESTINATION, AND OUR   606 16

CONSIDERATIONS

IMPORTANT CONSIDERATIONS, ACCORDING TO THE VARIOUS   V 17
WEIGHTY CONSIDERATIONS HER THEREUNTO MOVING, YIELDED   V 28

CONSIDERED

WHICH ARE CONSIDERED AS WORDS OF THE SAME MEANING IN   R 015 18
WHICH ARE CONSIDERED AS WORDS OF THE SAME MEANING IN   R 029 23
I HAVE CONSIDERED THE DAYS OF OLD   310 26
I HAVE CONSIDERED THE DAYS OF OLD, AND THE YEARS THAT   311 08
FOR THOU HAST CONSIDERED MY TROUBLE, AND HAST KNCWN   376 05
AND CONSIDERED THE VOICE OF MY PRAYER   418 18
5 I HAVE CONSIDERED THE DAYS OF OLD, *   433 25
40 FOR HE CONSIDERED THAT THEY WERE BUT FLESH,   437 18
ENGLAND ARE CONSIDERED AS INAPPLICABLE TO THE   R 610 26

CONSIDERETH

HE CONSIDERETH ALL THEM THAT DWELL ON THE   379 16
IS HE THAT CONSIDERETH THE POOR AND NEEDY   391 30

CONSIDERING

DULY CONSIDERING WHOSE AUTHORITY THEY BEAR,   032 10
SERIOUSLY CONSIDERING WHAT CHRISTIANITY IS, AND WHAT   VI 38

CONSISTENTLY

CONSISTENTLY WITH THE CONSTITUTION AND LAWS O THEIR   VI 13

CONSOLATION

GRACE AND CONSOLATION OF HIS HOLY SPIRIT   024 25
PATIENCE AND CONSOLATION GRANT YOU TO BE LIKEMINDED   092 18
FOR THE CONSOLATION OF ISRAEL   232 31
UPON HIM THE HELP OF THY MERCIFUL CONSOLATION   311 23
GRACE AND CONSOLATION OF HIS HOLY SPIRIT   323 21
MAY KNOW THE CONSOLATION OF THY LOVE   342 12

CONSPIRACY

PRIVY CONSPIRACY, AND REBELLICN   055 02

CONSPIRE

WHILE THEY CONSPIRE TOGETHER AGAINST ME, AND TAKE   376 22

CONSTANCY

OUR LIVES, AND CONSTANCY OF OUR FAITH EVEN UNTO   102 25
THEE WITH CONSTANCY ON EARTH, WE MAY BE JOINED   336 07

CONSTANT

AND CONSTANT IN THEIR MINISTRATION, TO HAVE A   535 04

CONSTANT   CONTINUED

TO GIVE US THE CONSTANT ASSISTANCE OF THY HOLY   588 15
TOGETHER IN CONSTANT AFFECTION THOSE WHO, IN HOLY   598 25

CONSTANTLY

FERVENT ZEAL CONSTANTLY TO PREACH THE GOSPEL UNTC ALL   078 29
HIS EXAMPLE CONSTANTLY SPEAK THE TRUTH, BOLDLY REBUKE   242 12
THAT WE, CONSTANTLY RECEIVING THY BOUNTY, MAY   261 31
LAID) HE HATH CONSTANTLY DECREED BY HIS COUNSEL   606 07

CONSTITUTED

ORDAINED AND CONSTITUTED THE SERVICES OF ANGELS AND   251 27
REGULARLY AND LEGITIMATELY CONSTITUTED   610 42

CONSTITUTION

WITH THE CONSTITUTION AND LAWS O THEIR COUNTRY   VI 13
TO THE CONSTITUTION AND LAWS OF ENGLAND ARE   R 610 26

CONSTRAIN

THEY CONSTRAIN YOU TO BE CIRCUMCISED   210 25

CONSTRAINED

BUT THEY CONSTRAINED HIM, SAYING, ABIDE WITH US   168 03
THAT I AM CONSTRAINED TO DWELL WITH MESHECH, *   502 14

CONSTRUCTION

FAVOURABLE CONSTRUCTION AS IN COMMON EQUITY OUGHT TO   V 43

CONSULTATION

HELD A CONSULTATION WITH THE ELDERS AND SCRIBES AND   145 04

CONSULTATIONS

ALL THEIR CONSULTATIONS, TO THE ADVANCEMENT OF THY   035 12

CONSUME

HIS BEAUTY TO CONSUME AWAY, LIKE AS IT WERE A MOTH   325 03
FOR WE CONSUME AWAY IN THY DISPLEASURE, *   325 26
THE FIRE SHALL CONSUME THEM   365 24
THE LORD SHALL CONSUME AS THE FAT OF LAMBS   386 02
SMOKE SHALL THEY CONSUME AWAY   386 03
HIS BEAUTY TO CONSUME AWAY, LIKE AS IT WERE A MCTH   389 32
BEAUTY SHALL CONSUME IN THE SEPULCHRE, AND HAVE NO   401 03
8 LET THEM CONSUME AWAY LIKE A SNAIL, AND BE LIKE THE   410 23
IN THY WRATH, CONSUME THEM, THAT THEY MAY PERISH   411 32
13 CONSUME THEM IN THY WRATH, CONSUME THEM, THAT THEY   411 32
SUDDENLY DO THEY CONSUME, *   429 14
OF THY BOSOM TO CONSUME THE ENEMY   430 30
DAYS DID HE CONSUME IN VANITY, *   437 04
7 FOR WE CONSUME AWAY IN THY DISPLEASURE, *   453 31
THE EXTORTIONER CONSUME ALL THAT HE HATH   480 21
HIS TEETH, AND CONSUME AWAY   484 05
AND CONSUME THEM   520 03

CONSUMED

BE NO MORE CONSUMED WITH HUNGER IN THE LAND, NEITHER   262 18
AND MINE EYE IS CONSUMED FOR VERY HEAVINESS   376 09
AND MY BONES ARE CONSUMED   376 14
MY BONES CONSUMED AWAY THROUGH MY DAILY COMPLAINING   377 26
I AM EVEN CONSUMED BY THE MEANS OF THY HEAVY HAND   389 29
64 THE FIRE CONSUMED THEIR YOUNG MEN, *   439 04
FOR MY DAYS ARE CONSUMED AWAY LIKE SMOKE, *   464 15
THEY SHALL BE CONSUMED OUT OF THE EARTH, *   469 31
ZEAL HATH EVEN CONSUMED ME   499 17

CONSUMETH

THE FLAME THAT CONSUMETH THE MOUNTAINS   444 33

CONSUMING

AND A CONSUMING FIRE OUT OF HIS MOUTH, SO THAT CCALS   360 12
BEFORE HIM A CONSUMING FIRE, AND A MIGHTY TEMPEST   401 26

CONSUMMATION

OUR PERFECT CONSUMMATION AND BLISS, BOTH IN BODY AND   334 27

CONTAIN

ITSELF COULD NOT CONTAIN THE BOOKS THAT SHOULD BE   102 17
HOLY SCRIPTURES CONTAIN ALL DOCTRINE REQUIRED AS   533 03
HOLY SCRIPTURES CONTAIN ALL DOCTRINE REQUIRED AS   542 03
HOLY SCRIPTURES CONTAIN ALL DOCTRINE REQUIRED AS   554 20
HEAVENS CANNOT CONTAIN, MUCH LESS THE WALLS OF   564 29
WHOM THE HEAVEN OF HEAVENS CANNOT CONTAIN   567 06
DOTH CONTAIN A GODLY AND WHOLESOME DOCTRINE,   610 06
IN 1792, DOTH CONTAIN ALL THINGS NECESSARY TO SUCH   610 32

CONTAINED

AS CONTAINED IN THE APOSTLES' CREED   276 32
AS CONTAINED IN THE APOSTLES' CREED   278 09
FAITH AS CONTAINED IN THE APOSTLES' CREED   284 10
IN THE MATTER CONTAINED IN THESE OFFICES, THEY SHALL   R 295 15
THE THINGS CONTAINED IN THIS BOOK   558 22

CONTAINETH

SCRIPTURE CONTAINETH ALL THINGS NECESSARY TO   603 29

CONTAINING

OF THE JEWS, CONTAINING TWO OR THREE FIRKINS APIECE   113 19

CONTEMPT

OF HEART, AND CONTEMPT OF THY WORD AND COMMANDMENT,   055 04
OF HEART, AND CONTEMPT OF THY WORD   157 09

CONTEND

FEARLESSLY TO CONTEND AGAINST EVIL, AND TO MAKE NC   044 10
WHO WILL CONTEND WITH ME   144 19

CONTENT

AT VARIANCE, BE CONTENT TO FORGIVE FROM THE BOTTCM OF R 085 12
WILLING TO CONTENT THE PEOPLE, RELEASED BARABBAS UNTO   145 27
I AM CONTENT TO DO IT   390 32

CONTENTED

CHRIST WAS CONTENTED TO BE BETRAYED, AND GIVEN UP   156 23

CONTINUAL

UPON THEM THE CONTINUAL DEW OF THY BLESSING   018 23
UPON THEM THE CONTINUAL DEW OF THY BLESSING   032 22
US WITH THY CONTINUAL HELP   049 24
TO GRANT THEM CONTINUAL GROWTH IN THY LOVE AND   075 02
AND FOR A CONTINUAL REMEMBRANCE OF HIS DEATH, TC CUR   086 17
MOST BOUNDEN, CONTINUAL THANKS   086 20
SO BY CONTINUAL MORTIFYING OUR CORRUPT   161 15
SO BY THY CONTINUAL HELP WE MAY BRING THE SAME TC   163 26
LET THY CONTINUAL PITY CLEANSE AND DEFEND THY   212 04
THE CHURCH IN CONTINUAL GODLINESS   220 17
FOR THE CONTINUAL STRENGTHENING AND REFRESHING CF MY   291 31
FOR THE CONTINUAL REMEMBRANCE OF THE SACRIFICE CF THE   293 05
AND GIVE THEE CONTINUAL THANKS FOR THY SUSTAINING   316 22
US WITH THY CONTINUAL HELP   571 09
FOR THE CONTINUAL REMEMBRANCE OF THE SACRIFICE CF THE   582 04
FOR THY CONTINUAL CARE AND WATCHFUL PROVIDENCE CVER   591 17
COMMEND TO THY CONTINUAL CARE THE HOMES IN WHICH THY   598 20

CONTINUALLY

AND SERAPHIM CONTINUALLY DO CRY, HOLY, HOLY, HOLY,   010 13
MAY CONTINUALLY OFFER UNTO THEE OUR   052 25
TO INSPIRE CONTINUALLY THE UNIVERSAL CHURCH WITH THE   074 11
ATTENDING CONTINUALLY UPON THIS VERY THING   114 24
HOUSEHOLD CONTINUALLY IN THY TRUE RELIGICN   115 29
YEAR BY YEAR CONTINUALLY, MAKE THE COMERS THEREUNTO   157 17
AND WITH HIM CONTINUALLY DWELL, WHO LIVETH AND   177 17
AND WERE CONTINUALLY IN THE TEMPLE, PRAISING ANC   178 28
AND MAKE US CONTINUALLY TO BE GIVEN TO ALL GOOD   213 15
THE MORE CONTINUALLY WITH THY GRACE AND HOLY SPIRIT   316 11
IT LIKE THE GROUND WHICH HE HATH MADE CONTINUALLY   439 17
OURSELVES CONTINUALLY TO PRAYER, AND TO THE MINISTRY   532 13
THAT YE WILL CONTINUALLY PRAY TO GOD THE FATHER, BY   541 15
BUT AS CONTINUALLY   569 25
TO HAVE CONTINUALLY BEFORE THEIR EYES THE SENTENCE OF   606 23

CONTINUANCE

AND A LONG CONTINUANCE OF NURSING CARE AND   V 12

CONTINUE

THEE TO CONTINUE THY LOVING-KINDNESS UNTO US, THAT   052 03
THEE STILL TO CONTINUE SUCH THY MERCIES TCWARDS US,   052 13
COMMAND US TO CONTINUE, A PERPETUAL MEMORY OF THAT   080 14
THAT WE MAY CONTINUE IN THAT HOLY FELLOWSHIP,   083 27
IT CANNOT CONTINUE IN SAFETY WITHOUT THY SUCCOUR,   212 06
CONTINUE YE IN MY LOVE   238 21
THEE TO CONTINUE THY LOVING-KINDNESS TO US, THAT CUR   265 14
AND TO CONTINUE CHRIST'S FAITHFUL SOLDIER AND SERVANT   280 09
THAT I MAY CONTINUE IN THE SAME UNTO MY LIFE'S END   284 05
THAT HE MAY CONTINUE THINE FOR EVER   297 27
THY PEACE, AND CONTINUE IN THY FAVOUR, UNTO THEIR   302 20
PRESERVE AND CONTINUE THIS SICK MEMBER IN THE UNITY   314 05
10 O CONTINUE FORTH THY LOVING-KINDNESS UNTO THEM   384 16
HOUSES SHALL CONTINUE FOR EVER, AND THAT THEIR   400 26
THE RUNAGATES CONTINUE IN SCARCENESS   419 23
SERVANTS SHALL CONTINUE, *   466 05
91 THEY CONTINUE THIS DAY ACCORDING TO THINE   496 07
THE JUST SHALL CONTINUE IN THY SIGHT   517 05
THAT HE MUST CONTINUE IN THAT OFFICE OF A DEACON THE R 535 19
THAT WE MAY CONTINUE TO SHOW OURSELVES THANKFUL UNTO   545 28
AND MAY CONTINUE CHRIST'S FAITHFUL SOLDIER AND   565 21
THAT I MAY CONTINUE IN THE SAME UNTO MY LIFE'S ENC   577 26
THEE TO CONTINUE THESE THY BLESSINGS TO US, AND TC   591 20
BESEECH THEE TO CONTINUE THY GRACIOUS PROTECTION TO   591 25
INTENTION NOR CONTINUE IT WITHOUT THY BLESSING   594 23

CONTINUED

STILL BEEN CONTINUED FIRM AND UNSHAKEN   V 32
WORKS BEGUN, CONTINUED, AND ENDED IN THEE, WE MAY   049 25
WHICH HAVE CONTINUED WITH ME IN MY TEMPTATICNS   149 27
WHICH HAVE CONTINUED WITH ME IN MY TEMPTATIONS   250 12
NEITHER CONTINUED THEY STEDFAST IN HIS COVENANT   437 13
ORDERS MAY BE CONTINUED, AND REVERENTLY USED ANC   529 19

CONTINUED   CONTINUED

SAVIOUR CHRIST CONTINUED THE WHOLE NIGHT IN PRAYER,   553 05
WORKS BEGUN, CONTINUED, AND ENDED IN THEE, WE MAY   571 10

CONTINUES

BECAUSE IT CONTINUES STEDFASTLY IN THE APOSTLES'   291 14

CONTINUEST

3 AND THOU CONTINUEST HOLY, *   366 09

CONTINUETH

AND CONTINUETH THEREIN, HE BEING NOT A   176 11
AND CONTINUETH THEREIN, HE BEING NOT A   266 02
AND NEVER CONTINUETH IN ONE STAY   332 21

CONTINUING

CONTINUING INSTANT IN PRAYER   111 26
AND CONTINUING EVER STABLE AND STRONG IN THY SCN   535 06
YOU CONTINUING IN   569 19

CONTRACT

THE CIVIL CONTRACT BETWEEN THE PARTIES   R 304 20

CONTRACTED

IT MAY HAVE CONTRACTED, THROUGH THE LUSTS OF THE   317 19

CONTRADICTING

BY PAUL, CONTRADICTING AND BLASPHEMING   260 29

CONTRARIWISE

BUT CONTRARIWISE BLESSING   195 22

CONTRARY

ANY THING IN IT CONTRARY TO THE WORD OF GOD, OR TO   V 40
THINGS THAT ARE CONTRARY TO THEIR PROFESSICN, ANC   173 08
AND THESE ARE CONTRARY THE ONE TO THE OTHER   209 16
TAKE NOW MY CONTRARY PART   480 10
FIND NOT TO THE CONTRARY, BUT THAT THEY ARE LAWFULLY   536 25
DOCTRINES CONTRARY TO GOD'S WORD   542 21
DOCTRINE CONTRARY TO GOD'S WORD   555 04
IS NOT CONTRARY TO THE NEW   604 15
LUSTETH ALWAYS CONTRARY TO THE SPIRIT   604 33
THING THAT IS CONTRARY TO GOD'S WORD WRITTEN, NEITHER   607 05

CONTRITE

THAT IS OF A CONTRITE AND HUMBLE SPIRIT, TO REVIVE   003 27
HEART OF THE CONTRITE ONES   003 29
A BROKEN AND A CONTRITE HEART, O GOD, THOU WILT NOT   004 25
SIGHING OF A CONTRITE HEART, NOR THE DESIRE CF SUCH   058 16
A BROKEN AND CONTRITE HEART, O GOD, SHALT THOU ACT   061 14
IN US NEW AND CONTRITE HEARTS, THAT WE, WORTHILY   124 14
THAT ARE OF A CONTRITE HEART, *   381 04
A BROKEN AND CONTRITE HEART, O GOD, SHALT THOU ACT   404 12

CONTRITION

CONSIDER HIS CONTRITION, ACCEPT HIS TEARS, ASSUAGE   314 06
AND WORK IN US AN HEARTY CONTRITION   590 04

CONTROVERSIES

IN CONTROVERSIES OF FAITH   607 04

CONVENIENCES

AND CONVENIENCES OF LIFE   591 11

CONVENIENT

MAY SEEM MOST CONVENIENT FOR THE EDIFICATION OF THE   V 08
IN THEIR RESPECTIVE TIMES WERE THOUGHT CONVENIENT   V 30
IT MAY BE CONVENIENT, HERE FOLLOWETH THE ANTHEM   R 031 30
JUDGE MOST CONVENIENT FOR THEIR FUTURE PROSPERITY   VI 12
AS HE THINKETH MOST CONVENIENT   R 071 33
IN HIS DISCRETION, HE MAY THINK CONVENIENT   R 086 27
NOR JESTING, WHICH ARE NOT CONVENIENT   129 05
IT IS MOST CONVENIENT THAT BAPTISM SHOULD BE   R 273 04
ON SOME OTHER CONVENIENT OCCASIONS, OPENLY IN THE   R 295 08
DOWN IN SOME CONVENIENT PLACE, AS HATH BEEN   R 305 08
IT IS CONVENIENT THAT SHE RECEIVE THE HOLY COMMUNICN R 307 10
SHALL THINK CONVENIENT TO THE OCCASION   R 314 24
ON SOME OTHER CONVENIENT OCCASIONS, OPENLY IN THE   R 582 28
SHALL THINK CONVENIENT, IN SOME PART OF THIS   R 582 30
NECESSARY AND CONVENIENT TO US, WE HUMBLY BEG,   589 06
IT MAY BE CONVENIENT, IT WILL BE PROPER TO BEGIN WITH R 592 05

CONVENIENTLY

SOON AS HE CONVENIENTLY MAY   R 085 08
HE MIGHT CONVENIENTLY BETRAY HIM   140 21
BAPTISM AS CONVENIENTLY MAY BE   R 281 14
AS CAN CONVENIENTLY BE PRESENT, LET CNE OF THEM,   R 587 05
THEM MAY BE CONVENIENTLY MADE, FOR THE CLEARING CF   R 610 28

CONVENTION

OR DIOCESAN CONVENTION, THE ABOVE PRAYER MAY BE USED   R 037 09
BEFORE THE CONVENTION, THEY COULD NOT BUT, WITH   VI 22
AND DIOCESAN CONVENTION, SAYING AS FOLLCWS   R 571 24
THE GENERAL CONVENTION OF THIS CHURCH IN 1792,   610 32

CONVERSATION

HAVING YOUR CONVERSATION HONEST AMONG THE GENTILES   173 14
THE FORMER CONVERSATION THE OLD MAN, WHICH IS CCRRUPT   216 12
OF VIRTUOUS CONVERSATION, AND WITHOUT CRIME   529 27
AND GODLY CONVERSATION, TO EXERCISE THEIR MINISTRY   530 14
AND GODLY CONVERSATION, TO EXERCISE THEIR MINISTRY   536 15
IN WORD, IN CONVERSATION, IN LOVE, IN FAITH, IN   559 10

CONVERSATIONS

LIVES AND CONVERSATIONS BY THE RULE OF GOD'S   087 17

CONVERSION

HIS WONDERFUL CONVERSION IN REMEMBRANCE, MAY SHCW   229 20

CONVERT

HE SHALL CONVERT MY SOUL, *   338 21
3 HE SHALL CONVERT MY SOUL, *   368 14

CONVERTED

SHALL BE CONVERTED UNTO THEE   061 05
WHEN THOU ART CONVERTED, STRENGTHEN THY BRETHREN   149 33
HE SHOULD BE CONVERTED AND LIVE   157 06
EXCEPT YE BE CONVERTED, AND BECOME AS LITTLE   252 26
EXCEPT YE BE CONVERTED, AND BECOME AS LITTLE   339 25
SHALL BE CONVERTED UNTO THEE   404 03

CONVERTING

CONVERTING THE SOUL   363 27

CONVEYED

SEE ME WITHOUT, CONVEYED THEMSELVES FROM ME   376 18

CONVINCE

WITHSTAND AND CONVINCE THE GAINSAYERS   554 33

CONVINCETH

WHICH OF YOU CONVINCETH ME OF SIN   133 09

COOL

IN WATER, AND COOL MY TONGUE   190 15

COPPERSMITH

THE COPPERSMITH DID ME MUCH EVIL   254 07

CORDS

CAST AWAY THEIR CORDS FROM US   346 03
THE SACRIFICE WITH CORDS, YEA, EVEN UNTO THE HORNS OF   489 33
SNARE FOR ME, AND SPREAD A NET ABROAD WITH CORDS   516 19
A SCOURGE OF SMALL CORDS, HE DROVE THEM ALL OUT CF   567 28

CORINTHIANS

PAUL TO THE CORINTHIANS   R 328 19

CORN

THAN WHEN THEIR CORN AND WINE AND OIL INCREASE   347 27
PREPAREST THEIR CORN, FOR SO THOU PROVIDEST FOR THE   417 03
STAND SO THICK WITH CORN, THAT THEY SHALL LAUGH AND   417 12
SHALL BE AN HEAP OF CORN IN THE EARTH, HIGH UPON THE   427 29

CORNER

IS BECOME THE HEAD-STONE IN THE CORNER   489 13

CORNER-STONE

JESUS CHRIST HIMSELF BEING THE HEAD CORNER-STONE   254 29
JESUS CHRIST HIMSELF BEING THE CHIEF CORNER-STCNE   255 07
JESUS CHRIST HIMSELF BEING THE HEAD CORNER-STCNE   290 21
JESUS CHRIST HIMSELF BEING THE CHIEF CORNER-STONE   574 05

CORNERS

HAND ARE ALL THE CORNERS OF THE EARTH   009 09
IN THE THIEVISH CORNERS OF THE STREETS, *   353 20
HAND ARE ALL THE CORNERS OF THE EARTH   459 11
AS THE POLISHED CORNERS OF THE TEMPLE   520 16

CORRECT

WHO DOST CORRECT THOSE WHOM THOU DOST LCVE, AND   321 19

CORRECTED

CHASTENED AND CORRECTED ME   489 04

CORRECTION

THY LOVING CORRECTION SHALL MAKE ME GREAT   362 07

CORRUPT

WHERE IT IS CORRUPT, PURIFY IT   037 17
AND RUST DOTH CORRUPT, AND WHERE THIEVES BREAK   072 08
NOR RUST DOTH CORRUPT, AND WHERE THIEVES DC NOT BREAK   072 10
AND RUST DOTH CORRUPT, AND WHERE THIEVES BREAK   125 17
NOR RUST DOTH CORRUPT, AND WHERE THIEVES DO NOT BREAK   125 20
MORTIFYING OUR CORRUPT AFFECTIONS WE MAY BE BURIED   161 15
BUT A CORRUPT TREE BRINGETH FORTH EVIL FRUIT   200 19
NEITHER CAN A CORRUPT TREE BRING FORTH GOOD FRUIT   200 21
WHICH IS CORRUPT ACCORDING TO THE DECEITFUL   216 13
LET NO CORRUPT COMMUNICATION PROCEED OUT OF YOUR   216 23
2 THEY ARE CORRUPT, AND BECOME ABOMINABLE IN THEIR   356 14
AND ARE CORRUPT, *   387 30
2 CORRUPT ARE THEY, AND BECOME ABOMINABLE IN THEIR   405 14
8 THEY CORRUPT OTHER, AND SPEAK OF WICKED BLASPHEMY   428 24
PARTLY OF THE CORRUPT FOLLOWING OF THE APOSTLES,   607 40

CORRUPTIBLE

TO OBTAIN A CORRUPTIBLE CROWN   119 08
FOR THIS CORRUPTIBLE MUST PUT ON INCORRUPTION,   330 05
SO WHEN THIS CORRUPTIBLE SHALL HAVE PUT ON   330 07
AND THE CORRUPTIBLE BODIES OF THOSE WHO SLEEP IN HIM   333 20
AND THE CORRUPTIBLE BODIES OF THOSE WHO SLEEP IN HIM   337 14

CORRUPTION

TO RETURN TO CORRUPTION, HE SAID ON THIS WISE, I WILL   169 11
SHALT NOT SUFFER THINE HOLY ONE TO SEE CORRUPTICN   169 14
AND WAS LAID UNTO HIS FATHERS, AND SAW CORRUPTICN   169 17
WHOM GOD RAISED AGAIN, SAW NO CORRUPTICN   169 17
BONDAGE OF CORRUPTION INTO THE GLORIOUS LIBERTY CF   194 18
IT IS SOWN IN CORRUPTION   329 19
NEITHER DOTH CORRUPTION INHERIT INCORRUPTION   329 34
SHALT THOU SUFFER THY HOLY ONE TO SEE CORRUPTICN   358 11
WEAKNESS AND CORRUPTION OF OUR NATURE, AND THE   588 12
THE FAULT AND CORRUPTION OF THE NATURE OF EVERY MAN,   604 30

COST

FOR HIM, 8 (FOR IT COST MORE TO REDEEM THEIR SOULS,   400 20

COUCH

AND WATER MY COUCH WITH MY TEARS   349 11

COUCHES

THEM ON BEDS AND COUCHES, THAT AT THE LEAST THE   249 28

COULDEST

COULDEST NOT THOU WATCH ONE HOUR   142 04
THOU COULDEST HAVE NO POWER AT ALL AGAINST   159 16

COUNCIL

PRESIDE IN THE COUNCIL OF THE BLESSED APOSTLES, AND   036 27
TO BE WITH THE COUNCIL OF THY CHURCH HERE ASSEMBLED   036 30
AND ALL THE COUNCIL SOUGHT FOR WITNESS AGAINST JESUS   143 02
AND THE WHOLE COUNCIL, AND BOUND JESUS, AND CARRIED   145 05
HIM INTO THEIR COUNCIL, SAYING, ART THOU THE CHRIST   151 29
SHALL BE IN DANGER OF THE COUNCIL   198 06
AND THE COUNCIL OF THE WICKED LAYETH SIEGE AGAINST   367 04
AND THE PRINCES OF JUDAH THEIR COUNCIL   421 09
BE FEARED IN THE COUNCIL OF THE SAINTS, *   450 14

COUNSEL

COMFORT OR COUNSEL, LET HIM COME TO ME, OR TO SCME   088 05
SUCH GODLY COUNSEL AND ADVICE, AS MAY TEND TO THE   088 07
THE PEOPLE TOOK COUNSEL AGAINST JESUS TO PUT HIM TO   134 31
AND THEY TOOK COUNSEL, AND BOUGHT WITH THEM THE   135 11
AND TOOK COUNSEL HOW THEY MIGHT ENTANGLE HIM IN HIS   222 28
THE SPIRIT OF COUNSEL AND GHOSTLY STRENGTH, THE   297 20
WALKED IN THE COUNSEL OF THE UNGODLY, NOR STCOD IN   345 08
THE RULERS TAKE COUNSEL TOGETHER *   345 28
SHALL I SEEK COUNSEL IN MY SOUL, AND BE SO VEXED IN   355 30
A MOCK AT THE COUNSEL OF THE POOR   356 28
AND TAKE THEIR COUNSEL TO TAKE AWAY MY LIFE   376 23
BRINGETH THE COUNSEL OF THE HEATHEN TO NOUGHT, *   379 06
11 THE COUNSEL OF THE LORD SHALL ENDURE FOR EVER,   379 09
UNGODLY SEEKETH COUNSEL AGAINST THE JUST, *   385 18
15 WE TOOK SWEET COUNSEL TOGETHER, *   407 18
SOUL TAKE THEIR COUNSEL TOGETHER, SAYING, 10 GCD HATH   425 26
ME WITH THY COUNSEL, *   429 24
AND TAKEN COUNSEL AGAINST THY SECRET ONES   444 10
AND WOULD NOT ABIDE HIS COUNSEL   473 28
REGARDED THE COUNSEL OF THE MOST HIGHEST   476 27
UNTO YOU ALL THE COUNSEL OF GOD   550 26
DECREED BY HIS COUNSEL SECRET TO US, TO DELIVER FROM   606 08

COUNSELLORS

AND MY COUNSELLORS   491 14

COUNSELS

ALL GOOD COUNSELS, AND ALL JUST WORKS DO PROCEED   031 18
MANIFEST THE COUNSELS OF THE HEARTS   094 13
CASTETH OUT THE COUNSELS OF PRINCES   379 08

COUNSELS   CONTINUED

AGAINST THE MAN THAT DOETH AFTER EVIL COUNSELS   385 08
DEAR ARE THY COUNSELS UNTO ME, O GOD   515 24

COUNT

MY BRETHREN, COUNT IT ALL JOY WHEN YE FALL INTO   239 08
MOVE ME, NEITHER COUNT I MY LIFE DEAR UNTO MYSELF,   550 19

COUNTED

SO EXCUSED, BUT COUNTED UNWORTHY OF THE HEAVENLY   089 05
LIVETH IS COUNTED DEAD BEFORE THEE   122 18
THEY SHALL BE COUNTED UNTO THE LORD FOR A GENERATION   368 04
16 A HORSE IS COUNTED BUT A VAIN THING TO SAVE A MAN   379 22
AND ARE COUNTED AS SHEEP APPOINTED TO BE SLAIN   396 05
HE LIVED, HE COUNTED HIMSELF AN HAPPY MAN   401 11
3 I AM COUNTED AS ONE OF THEM THAT GO DOWN INTO THE   449 02
31 AND THAT WAS COUNTED UNTO HIM FOR RIGHTEOUSNESS,   474 31
ARE NOT TO BE COUNTED FOR SACRAMENTS OF THE GOSPEL,   607 39

COUNTENANCE

LIGHT OF HIS COUNTENANCE, AND BE MERCIFUL UNTO US   028 18
LIFT UP THY COUNTENANCE UPON HIM, AND GIVE HIM PEACE   046 05
LIFT UP HIS COUNTENANCE UPON US, AND GIVE US PEACE,   063 17
AS THE HYPOCRITES, OF A SAD COUNTENANCE   125 10
FACE OF MOSES FOR THE GLORY OF HIS COUNTENANCE   206 21
OF HIS COUNTENANCE WAS ALTERED, AND HIS RAIMENT WAS   248 26
HELP OF MY COUNTENANCE, AND MY GOD   310 19
LIFT UP HIS COUNTENANCE UPON THEE, AND GIVE THEE   314 29
OUR SECRET SINS IN THE LIGHT OF THY COUNTENANCE   325 29
LIFT UP HIS COUNTENANCE UPON YOU, AND GIVE YOU PEACE,   332 13
LIFT UP HIS COUNTENANCE UPON HIM, AND GIVE HIM PEACE,   341 17
LIGHT OF THY COUNTENANCE UPON US   347 24
HIS COUNTENANCE WILL BEHOLD THE THING THAT IS JUST   355 03
AND MAKE HIM GLAD WITH THE JOY OF THY COUNTENANCE   365 16
LIGHT OF THY COUNTENANCE, *   376 28
16 THE COUNTENANCE OF THE LORD IS AGAINST THEM THAT   380 32
HELP OF MY COUNTENANCE, AND MY GOD   393 14
HELP OF MY COUNTENANCE, AND MY GOD   393 34
HELP OF MY COUNTENANCE, AND MY GOD   394 18
AND THINE ARM, AND THE LIGHT OF THY COUNTENANCE   394 31
LIGHT OF HIS COUNTENANCE, AND BE MERCIFUL UNTO US   418 24
LIGHT OF THY COUNTENANCE, AND WE SHALL BE WHOLE   441 08
LIGHT OF THY COUNTENANCE, AND WE SHALL BE WHOLE   441 17
SHALL PERISH AT THE REBUKE OF THY COUNTENANCE   442 03
LIGHT OF THY COUNTENANCE, AND WE SHALL BE WHOLE   442 10
THEY SHALL WALK IN THE LIGHT OF THY COUNTENANCE   451 05
OUR SECRET SINS IN THE LIGHT OF THY COUNTENANCE   454 03
A CHEERFUL COUNTENANCE, AND BREAD TO STRENGTHEN MAN'S   468 25
LIGHT OF THY COUNTENANCE UPON THY SERVANT, *   499 08
LIFT UP HIS COUNTENANCE UPON US, AND GIVE US PEACE,   593 20

COUNTRIES

AND FROM ALL COUNTRIES WHITHER I HAD DRIVEN THEM   225 19
IN ALL COUNTRIES, AND FOR ALL PEOPLE   291 12
SMITE IN SUNDER THE HEADS OVER DIVERS COUNTRIES   482 20
DIVERSITY OF COUNTRIES, TIMES, AND MEN'S MANNERS,   609 34

COUNTRY

AND PROTECT THE SOLDIERS OF OUR COUNTRY   041 27
DOWN THEIR LIVES IN THE SERVICE OF OUR COUNTRY   042 17
WITH THE CONSTITUTION AND LAWS O THEIR COUNTRY   VI 14
WERE IN THE SAME COUNTRY SHEPHERDS ABIDING IN THE   099 10
INTO THEIR OWN COUNTRY ANOTHER WAY   109 25
OUT OF THE COUNTRY, THE FATHER OF ALEXANDER AND   146 06
OUT OF THE COUNTRY, AND ON HIM THEY LAID THE CROSS,   154 10
INTO A FAR COUNTRY, AND THERE WASTED HIS SUBSTANCE   202 03
AND JOINED HIMSELF TO A CITIZEN OF THAT COUNTRY   202 07
OUT OF THE NORTH COUNTRY, AND FROM ALL COUNTRIES   225 19
ALL THE HILL COUNTRY OF JUDAEA   243 28

COUNTRY'S

PROTECTION OUR COUNTRY'S NAVY, AND ALL WHO SERVE   042 06

COUNTRYMEN

BY MINE OWN COUNTRYMEN, IN PERILS BY THE HEATHEN, IN   121 05

COURAGE

ENDUE THEM WITH COURAGE AND LOYALTY   041 29
AND COURAGE TO STRENGTHEN THE WEAK AND   044 02
SING PRAISES LUSTILY UNTO HIM WITH A GOOD COURAGE   378 24
GO FORWARD WITH COURAGE, AND PERSEVERE UNTO THE END   561 09

COURSE

BUT WHEN IN THE COURSE OF DIVINE PROVIDENCE, THESE   VI 07
THAT THE COURSE OF THIS WORLD MAY BE SO   195 15
HAVE FINISHED MY COURSE, I HAVE KEPT THE FAITH   253 27
FINISHED THEIR COURSE IN FAITH, DO NOW REST FROM   334 24
AND REJOICETH AS A GIANT TO RUN HIS COURSE   363 25
THE FOUNDATIONS OF THE EARTH ARE OUT OF COURSE   443 28
I MIGHT FINISH MY COURSE WITH JOY, AND THE MINISTRY,   550 20
FULFILLING HIS COURSE, AT THE LATTER DAY HE MAY   559 12
GRANT THAT THE COURSE OF THIS WORLD MAY BE SO   574 15
THROUGH THE WHOLE COURSE OF OUR LIVES   591 18

COURT

SHALL DWELL IN THY COURT, AND SHALL BE SATISFIED WITH   416 18

COURTEOUS

LOVE AS BRETHREN, BE PITIFUL, BE COURTEOUS   195 21

COURTS

AND INTO HIS COURTS WITH PRAISE   015 11
THEE TO BLESS THE COURTS OF JUSTICE AND THE   035 32
IN THE COURTS OF THE LORD'S HOUSE   306 02
TO ENTER INTO THE COURTS OF THE LORD   445 14
ONE DAY IN THY COURTS *   445 31
FLOURISH IN THE COURTS OF THE HOUSE OF OUR GOD   456 27
BRING PRESENTS, AND COME INTO HIS COURTS   460 15
AND INTO HIS COURTS WITH PRAISE   463 12
IN THE COURTS OF THE LORD'S HOUSE   487 22
EVEN IN THE COURTS OF THE HOUSE OF OUR GOD   509 26
IN THE COURTS OF THE HOUSE OF OUR GOD   510 05

COUSIN

BEHOLD, THY COUSIN ELISABETH, SHE HATH ALSO   236 25

COUSINS

AND HER COUSINS HEARD HOW THE LORD HAD SHEWED GREAT   243 15

COVENANT

AND TO REMEMBER HIS HOLY COVENANT   014 17
THIS IS THE COVENANT THAT I WILL MAKE WITH THEM AFTER   158 11
I SAY, THAT THE COVENANT, THAT WAS CONFIRMED BEFORE   207 22
OF THE COVENANT, WHOM YE DELIGHT IN   232 06
AND TO REMEMBER HIS HOLY COVENANT   244 05
WITH THEM A COVENANT OF PEACE, AND WILL CAUSE THE   262 04
THE VOW AND COVENANT BETWIXT THEM MADE, (WHEREOF THIS   303 08
THROUGH THE BLOOD OF THE EVERLASTING COVENANT   335 18
AS KEEP HIS COVENANT AND HIS TESTIMONIES   370 05
AND HE WILL SHEW THEM HIS COVENANT   370 13
NOR BEHAVE OURSELVES FROWARDLY IN THY COVENANT   395 29
HAVE MADE A COVENANT WITH ME WITH SACRIFICE   401 31
AND TAKEST MY COVENANT IN THY MOUTH   402 23
AND HE BRAKE HIS COVENANT   407 34
21 LOOK UPON THE COVENANT   431 18
5 HE MADE A COVENANT WITH JACOB, AND GAVE ISRAEL A   435 04
KEPT NOT THE COVENANT OF GOD, *   435 20
NEITHER CONTINUED THEY STEDFAST IN HIS COVENANT   437 13
3 I HAVE MADE A COVENANT WITH MY CHOSEN   450 09
AND MY COVENANT SHALL STAND FAST WITH HIM   451 32
34 MY COVENANT WILL I NOT BREAK, NOR ALTER THE THING   452 09
HAST BROKEN THE COVENANT OF THY SERVANT, *   452 18
AS KEEP HIS COVENANT, *   467 11
MINDFUL OF HIS COVENANT AND PROMISE, *   470 18
9 EVEN THE COVENANT THAT HE MADE WITH ABRAHAM   470 20
UPON HIS COVENANT, AND PITIED THEM, ACCORDING UNTO   475 27
HE SHALL EVER BE MINDFUL OF HIS COVENANT   483 04
COMMANDED HIS COVENANT FOR EVER   483 12
WILL KEEP MY COVENANT, AND MY TESTIMONIES THAT I   508 29
THE VOW AND COVENANT BETWIXT THEM MADE, AND MAY   566 10
THROUGH THE BLOOD OF THE EVERLASTING COVENANT   573 05

COVENANTED

AND COVENANTED TO GIVE HIM MONEY   148 18

COVENANTS

FOR THESE ARE THE TWO COVENANTS   131 03

COVER

ON HIM, AND TO COVER HIS FACE, AND TO BUFFET HIM, AND   143 20
AND TO THE HILLS, COVER US   154 19
FOR CHARITY SHALL COVER THE MULTITUDE OF SINS   179 14
THICK CLOUDS TO COVER HIM   360 21
TURN AGAIN TO COVER THE EARTH   468 12
AND LET THEM COVER THEMSELVES WITH THEIR OWN   481 30
THE DARKNESS SHALL COVER ME   515 08

COVERED

AND WHOSE SIN IS COVERED   377 23
OF MY FACE HATH COVERED ME   395 25
AND COVERED US WITH THE SHADOW OF DEATH   395 33
THAT IS COVERED WITH SILVER WINGS, AND HER FEATHERS   420 07
SHAME HATH COVERED MY FACE   422 17
LET THEM BE COVERED WITH SHAME AND DISHONOUR THAT   425 32
THE HILLS WERE COVERED WITH THE SHADOW OF IT,   441 22
AND COVERED ALL THEIR SINS   446 11
AND COVERED HIM WITH DISHONOUR   452 31
AND COVERED THE CONGREGATION OF ABIRAM   474 03
THOU HAST COVERED ME IN MY MOTHER'S WOMB   515 13
THOU HAST COVERED MY HEAD IN THE DAY OF BATTLE   516 23

COVEREDST

6 THOU COVEREDST IT WITH THE DEEP LIKE AS WITH A   468 04

COVERETH

WHO COVERETH THE HEAVEN WITH CLOUDS, AND PREPARETH   264 27
AND CRUELTY COVERETH THEM AS A GARMENT   428 21
8 WHO COVERETH THE HEAVEN WITH CLOUDS, AND PREPARETH   523 10

COVERING

COVERING THE SAME WITH A FAIR LINEN CLOTH   R 083 13
BE UNDER THE COVERING OF THY WINGS   413 14
A CLOUD TO BE A COVERING, *   472 15

COVERT

HIDE THEM IN THE COVERT OF THINE OWN PRESENCE FROM   377 06

COVET

THOU SHALT NOT COVET   069 19
THOU SHALT NOT COVET THY NEIGHBOUR'S WIFE, NOR HIS   069 20
NOT BEAR FALSE WITNESS, THOU SHALT NOT COVET   090 27
THOU SHALT NOT COVET THY NEIGHBOUR'S HOUSE, THOU   287 19
THOU SHALT NOT COVET THY NEIGHBOUR'S WIFE, NOR HIS   287 20
NOT TO COVET NOR DESIRE OTHER MEN'S GOODS   289 08
THOU SHALT NOT COVET THY NEIGHBOUR'S HOUSE, THOU   579 20
THOU SHALT NOT COVET THY NEIGHBOUR'S WIFE, NOR HIS   579 21
NOT TO COVET NOR DESIRE OTHER MEN'S GOODS   580 12

COVETED

I HAVE COVETED NO MAN'S SILVER, OR GOLD, OR APPAREL   551 05

COVETOUS

NOR COVETOUS MAN, WHO IS AN IDOLATER,   129 07
TO FORSAKE ALL COVETOUS DESIRES, AND INORDINATE LOVE   250 22
WITH ALL COVETOUS DESIRES OF THE SAME, AND THE   276 26
WITH ALL COVETOUS DESIRES OF THE SAME, AND THE   277 27
GOOD OF THE COVETOUS, WHOM THE LORD ABHORRETH   353 09
NOT A BRAWLER, NOT COVETOUS   549 23

COVETOUSNESS

OR COVETOUSNESS, LET IT NOT BE ONCE NAMED AMONG YOU,   129 03
AND NOT TO COVETOUSNESS   492 12

CRAFT

EVILS WHICH THE CRAFT AND SUBTILTY OF THE DEVIL OR   058 20
MIGHT TAKE HIM BY CRAFT, AND PUT HIM TO DEATH   139 34

CRAFTILY

HAVE IMAGINED CRAFTILY AGAINST THY PEOPLE, *   444 09

CRAFTINESS

AND CUNNING CRAFTINESS, WHEREBY THEY LIE IN WAIT TO   237 27
WALKING IN CRAFTINESS, NOR HANDLING THE WORD OF GOD   250 29

CRAFTS

FROM THE CRAFTS AND ASSAULTS OF THE DEVIL   054 19

CRAFTY

BE TAKEN IN THE CRAFTY WILINESS THAT THEY HAVE   353 06

CREATE

CREATE AND MAKE IN US NEW AND CONTRITE HEARTS, THAT   124 13

CREATED

WHO HAST CREATED MAN IN THINE OWN IMAGE   044 09
HID IN GOD, WHO CREATED ALL THINGS BY JESUS CHRIST   108 23
FOR THOU HAST CREATED ALL THINGS, AND FOR THY   187 31
AND FOR THY PLEASURE THEY ARE, AND WERE CREATED   187 32
AFTER GOD IS CREATED IN RIGHTEOUSNESS AND TRUE   216 15
ALMIGHTY WHO CREATED THEE   319 21
HE COMMANDED, AND THEY WERE CREATED   524 15

CREATION

THEE FOR OUR CREATION, PRESERVATION, AND ALL THE   019 20
THEE FOR OUR CREATION, PRESERVATION, AND ALL THE   033 18
THAT THE WHOLE CREATION GROANETH AND TRAVAILETH IN   194 19
IN THY WHOLE CREATION, WE MAY LEARN TO SERVE THEE   596 20

CREATOR

O GOD, THE CREATOR AND PRESERVER OF ALL MANKIND,   018 26
O GOD, THE CREATOR AND PRESERVER OF ALL MANKIND,   032 26
GOD THE FATHER, CREATOR OF HEAVEN AND EARTH   054 05
O ETERNAL GOD, CREATOR AND PRESERVER OF ALL MANKIND,   303 03
O ALMIGHTY GOD, CREATOR OF MANKIND, WHO ONLY ART THE   303 14
OF A FAITHFUL CREATOR, AND MOST MERCIFUL SAVIOUR   317 15
OR SAY THE VENI, CREATOR SPIRITUS   R 543 27
HOLY GHOST, CREATOR BLEST, VOUCHSAFE WITHIN OUR SOULS   544 17
AND THE VENI, CREATOR SPIRITUS SHALL BE SUNG OR SAID   R 556 03
HOLY GHOST, CREATOR BLEST, VOUCHSAFE WITHIN OUR SOULS   556 25

CREATURE

WHOSE POWER NO CREATURE IS ABLE TO RESIST, TO WHOM IT   041 10
OF THE CREATURE WAITETH FOR THE MANIFESTATION OF THE   194 13
FOR THE CREATURE WAS MADE SUBJECT TO VANITY, NOT   194 15
BECAUSE THE CREATURE ITSELF ALSO SHALL BE DELIVERED   194 17
ANY THING, NOR UNCIRCUMCISION, BUT A NEW CREATURE   211 02
OF THE CREATURE WAITETH FOR THE MANIFESTATION OF THE   330 29
NOR ANY OTHER CREATURE, SHALL BE ABLE TO SEPARATE US   331 12

CREATURES

THY GIFTS AND CREATURES OF BREAD AND WINE   081 10
FOUR LIVING CREATURES, AND THE ELDERS   103 06
SHOULD BE A KIND OF FIRSTFRUITS OF HIS CREATURES   174 30
FOUR LIVING CREATURES FULL OF EYES BEFORE AND BEHIND   187 11
FOUR LIVING CREATURES HAD EACH OF THEM SIX WINGS   187 20
THOSE LIVING CREATURES GIVE GLORY AND HONOUR AND   187 24
FOUR LIVING CREATURES, AND FELL BEFORE THE THRONE ON   256 30
SHOULD BE A KIND OF FIRSTFRUITS OF HIS CREATURES   265 23
WE, THY NEEDY CREATURES, RENDER THEE OUR HUMBLE   587 20

CREDENCE

AND GAVE NO CREDENCE UNTO HIS WORD   474 18

CREED

SAID THE APOSTLES' CREED BY THE MINISTER AND THE   R 015 15
AS WORDS OF THE SAME MEANING IN THE CREED   R 015 18
OR THE CREED COMMONLY CALLED THE NICENE   R 015 32
SAID THE APOSTLES' CREED BY THE MINISTER AND THE   R 029 20
AS WORDS OF THE SAME MEANING IN THE CREED   R 029 23
OR THE CREED COMMONLY CALLED THE NICENE   R 030 03
SHALL BE SAID THE CREED COMMONLY CALLED THE NICENE,   R 070 29
BUT THE CREED MAY BE OMITTED, IF IT HATH BEEN SAID   R 070 30
OR ELSE THE APOSTLES' CREED   R 070 30
THAT THE NICENE CREED SHALL BE SAID ON CHRISTMAS DAY,   R 070 31
AFTER THE CREED, MAY BE SAID THE BIDDING PRAYER,   R 071 29
AS CONTAINED IN THE APOSTLES' CREED   276 32
CHILD LEARN THE CREED, THE LORD'S PRAYER, AND THE TEN   277 10
AS CONTAINED IN THE APOSTLES' CREED   278 09
FAITH AS CONTAINED IN THE APOSTLES' CREED   284 10
SAID THE APOSTLES' CREED BY THE MINISTER AND PEOPLE   R 284 11
AND CAN SAY THE CREED, THE LORD'S PRAYER, AND THE TEN   R 295 13
THE MINISTER, THE CREED, THE LORD'S PRAYER, THE   R 331 29
THE NICENE CREED SHALL BE SAID, AND THE BISHOP   R 546 28
FOLLOW THE NICENE CREED, AND AFTER THAT THE SERMON   R 552 16
AND CAN SAY THE CREED, THE LORD'S PRAYER, AND THE TEN   R 583 02
THE APOSTLES' CREED, OUGHT THOROUGHLY TO BE RECEIVED   604 25
THE NICENE CREED, AND THAT WHICH IS COMMONLY CALLED   604 25

CREEDS

DESCRIBED IN THE APOSTLES' AND NICENE CREEDS   291 03
DESCRIBED IN THE CREEDS AS ONE, HOLY, CATHOLIC, AND   291 04

CREEPING

ARE THINGS CREEPING INNUMERABLE, BOTH SMALL AND GREAT   469 11
CREEPING THINGS AND FLYING FOWLS   524 23

CRESCENS

CRESCENS TO GALATIA, TITUS UNTO DALMATIA   253 33

CRETES

AND PROSELYTES, CRETES AND ARABIANS, WE DO HEAR THEM   181 05

CREW

AND THE COCK CREW   143 28
AND THE SECOND TIME THE COCK CREW   143 34
WHILE HE YET SPAKE, THE COCK CREW   151 19

CRIED

AND THAT FOLLOWED, CRIED, SAYING, HOSANNA TO THE SON   091 28
THEN THEY CRIED OUT WITH A LOUD VOICE, AND STOPPED   100 09
KNEELED DOWN, AND CRIED WITH A LOUD VOICE, LORD,   100 15
THESE THINGS, HE CRIED, HE THAT HATH EARS TO HEAR,   121 27
AND HE CRIED, SAYING, JESUS, THOU SON OF DAVID, HAVE   123 29
BUT HE CRIED SO MUCH THE MORE, THOU SON OF DAVID,   123 32
SAME COASTS, AND CRIED UNTO HIM, SAYING, HAVE MERCY   128 09
BUT THEY CRIED OUT THE MORE, SAYING, LET HIM BE   136 07
NINTH HOUR JESUS CRIED WITH A LOUD VOICE, SAYING,   137 17
WHEN HE HAD CRIED AGAIN WITH A LOUD VOICE,   137 24
AND THEY CRIED OUT AGAIN, CRUCIFY HIM   145 24
AND THEY CRIED OUT THE MORE EXCEEDINGLY, CRUCIFY HIM   145 26
NINTH HOUR JESUS CRIED WITH A LOUD VOICE, SAYING,   146 27
AND JESUS CRIED WITH A LOUD VOICE, AND GAVE UP THE   146 34
SAW THAT HE SO CRIED OUT, AND GAVE UP THE GHOST, HE   147 03
AND THEY CRIED OUT ALL AT ONCE, SAYING, AWAY WITH   153 29
BUT THEY CRIED, SAYING, CRUCIFY HIM, CRUCIFY HIM   153 33
AND WHEN JESUS HAD CRIED WITH A LOUD VOICE, HE SAID,   155 12
SAW HIM, THEY CRIED OUT, SAYING, CRUCIFY HIM, CRUCIFY   159 06
BUT THE JEWS CRIED OUT, SAYING, IF THOU LET THIS MAN   159 19
BUT THEY CRIED OUT, AWAY WITH HIM, AWAY WITH HIM,   159 27
AND HE CRIED AND SAID, FATHER ABRAHAM, HAVE MERCY ON   190 13
AND HE CRIED WITH A LOUD VOICE TO THE FOUR ANGELS, TO   256 15
AND CRIED WITH A LOUD VOICE, SAYING, SALVATION TO OUR   256 27
2 O LORD MY GOD, I CRIED UNTO THEE   374 26
8 THEN CRIED I UNTO THEE, O LORD   375 08
WHEN I CRIED UNTO THEE   377 14
I HAVE CRIED DAY AND NIGHT BEFORE THEE   448 29
UNTO THEE HAVE I CRIED, O LORD   449 22
6 SO THEY CRIED UNTO THE LORD IN THEIR TROUBLE,   476 15
13 SO WHEN THEY CRIED UNTO THE LORD IN THEIR TROUBLE,   476 30
19 SO WHEN THEY CRIED UNTO THE LORD IN THEIR TROUBLE,   477 13
I CRIED UNTO THE LORD WITH MY VOICE   518 03
6 I CRIED UNTO THEE, O LORD, AND SAID, *   518 14

CRIETH

FOR SHE CRIETH AFTER US   128 13

CRIETH   CONTINUED

VOICE OF HIM THAT CRIETH IN THE WILDERNESS, PREPARE   242 20
6 LO, THE POOR CRIETH, AND THE LORD HEARETH HIM   380 13
3 THE ENEMY CRIETH SO, AND THE UNGODLY COMETH ON SO   406 23
12 FOR HE SHALL DELIVER THE POOR WHEN HE CRIETH   427 20

CRIME

OR ENVY, OR IN ANY OTHER GRIEVOUS CRIME   087 33
A MAN OF VIRTUOUS CONVERSATION, AND WITHOUT CRIME   529 27
OR NOTABLE CRIME, IN ANY OF THESE PERSONS PRESENTED   530 22
AND SHOW WHAT THE CRIME OR IMPEDIMENT IS   530 25
AND IF ANY GREAT CRIME OR IMPEDIMENT BE OBJECTED,   R 530 26
PARTY ACCUSED SHALL BE FOUND CLEAR OF THAT CRIME   R 530 28
OR NOTABLE CRIME, IN ANY OF THEM, FOR THE WHICH HE   536 28
AND SHOW WHAT THE CRIME OR IMPEDIMENT IS   536 31
AND IF ANY GREAT CRIME OR IMPEDIMENT BE OBJECTED,   R 537 02
PARTY ACCUSED SHALL BE FOUND CLEAR OF THAT CRIME   R 537 04

CROOKED

AND THE CROOKED SHALL BE MADE STRAIGHT, AND THE ROUGH   242 24

CROSS

BY THY CROSS AND PASSION   055 10
DEATH UPON THE CROSS FOR OUR REDEMPTION   080 09
THE DEATH UPON THE CROSS, FOR US, MISERABLE SINNERS,   086 09
OF HIS MERITORIOUS CROSS AND PASSION   086 32
BY DEATH UPON THE CROSS FOR YOUR SALVATION   089 11
DEATH UPON THE CROSS, THAT ALL MANKIND SHOULD FOLLOW   134 08
OBEDIENT UNTO DEATH, EVEN THE DEATH OF THE CROSS   134 22
HIM THEY COMPELLED TO BEAR HIS CROSS   136 27
THOU BE THE SON OF GOD, COME DOWN FROM THE CROSS   137 08
COME DOWN FROM THE CROSS, AND WE WILL BELIEVE HIM   137 11
IN THE WAY OF THE CROSS, MAY FIND IT NONE OTHER THAN   138 01
FATHER OF ALEXANDER AND RUFUS, TO BEAR HIS CROSS   146 07
AND COME DOWN FROM THE CROSS   146 20
NOW FROM THE CROSS, THAT WE MAY SEE AND BELIEVE   146 24
HIM THEY LAID THE CROSS, THAT HE MIGHT BEAR IT AFTER   154 10
AND TO SUFFER DEATH UPON THE CROSS   156 24
AND HE BEARING HIS CROSS WENT FORTH INTO A PLACE   159 31
AND PILATE WROTE A TITLE, AND PUT IT ON THE CROSS   159 35
THERE STOOD BY THE CROSS OF JESUS HIS MOTHER, AND HIS   160 17
REMAIN UPON THE CROSS ON THE SABBATH DAY, (FOR THAT   160 31
THE DEATH OF THE CROSS, AND BY HIS GLORIOUS   165 04
FOR THE CROSS OF CHRIST   210 26
SAVE IN THE CROSS OF OUR LORD JESUS CHRIST,   210 30
THE ENEMIES OF THE CROSS OF CHRIST   222 19
SO BY HIS CROSS AND PASSION WE MAY BE BROUGHT   235 21
HIM ENDURED THE CROSS, DESPISING THE SHAME, AND IS   258 25
THE SIGN OF THE CROSS, IN TOKEN THAT HEREAFTER HE   280 05
SHALL MAKE A CROSS UPON THE CHILD'S (OR PERSON'S)   R 280 11
WHO BY THY CROSS AND PRECIOUS BLOOD HAST   313 12
BY THY CROSS AND PASSION, BY THY PRECIOUS DEATH AND   318 04
DEATH UPON THE CROSS FOR HIM, AND SHED HIS BLOOD FOR   R 323 27

CROW

BEFORE THE COCK CROW TWICE, THOU SHALT DENY ME   141 24
BEFORE THE COCK CROW TWICE, THOU SHALT DENY ME   144 02
THE COCK SHALL NOT CROW THIS DAY, BEFORE THAT THOU   150 02
BEFORE THE COCK CROW, THOU SHALT DENY ME THRICE   151 22

CROWN

MAY RECEIVE THE CROWN OF GLORY THAT FADETH NOT AWAY   079 26
NOW THEY DO IT TO OBTAIN A CORRUPTIBLE CROWN   119 08
THEY HAD PLATTED A CROWN OF THORNS, THEY PUT IT UPON   136 18
AND PLATTED A CROWN OF THORNS, AND PUT IT ABOUT HIS   145 32
SOLDIERS PLATTED A CROWN OF THORNS, AND PUT IT ON HIS   158 31
WEARING THE CROWN OF THORNS, AND THE PURPLE   159 03
SHALL RECEIVE THE CROWN OF LIFE, WHICH THE LORD HATH   239 26
MAY RECEIVE THE CROWN OF EVERLASTING GLORY   244 27
LAID UP FOR ME A CROWN OF RIGHTEOUSNESS, WHICH THE   253 08
TO CROWN HIM WITH GLORY AND WORSHIP   351 09
AND SHALT SET A CROWN OF PURE GOLD UPON HIS HEAD   365 10
AND CAST HIS CROWN TO THE GROUND   452 19
HIMSELF SHALL HIS CROWN FLOURISH   509 11
MAY RECEIVE THE CROWN OF EVERLASTING GLORY   549 14
THE NEVER-FADING CROWN OF GLORY   558 31
HE MAY RECEIVE THE CROWN OF RIGHTEOUSNESS, LAID UP BY   559 13

CROWNEST

12 THOU CROWNEST THE YEAR WITH THY GOODNESS   417 07

CROWNETH

AND CROWNETH THEE WITH MERCY AND LOVING-KINDNESS   029 10
AND CROWNETH THEE WITH MERCY AND LOVING-KINDNESS   312 18
AND CROWNETH THEE WITH MERCY AND LOVING-KINDNESS   312 26
AND CROWNETH THEE WITH MERCY AND LOVING-KINDNESS   466 13

CROWNS

ON THEIR HEADS CROWNS OF GOLD   187 11
AND CAST THEIR CROWNS BEFORE THE THRONE, SAYING, THOU   187 28

CRUCIFIED

WAS CRUCIFIED, DEAD, AND BURIED   015 23
AND WAS CRUCIFIED ALSO FOR US UNDER PONTIUS PILATE   016 08
WAS CRUCIFIED, DEAD, AND BURIED   029 28
AND WAS CRUCIFIED ALSO FOR US UNDER PONTIUS PILATE   030 13

CRUCIFIED   CONTINUED

AND WAS CRUCIFIED ALSO FOR US UNDER PONTIUS PILATE   071 11
THEY ALL SAY UNTO HIM, LET HIM BE CRUCIFIED   136 06
CRIED OUT THE MORE, SAYING, LET HIM BE CRUCIFIED   136 08
SCOURGED JESUS, HE DELIVERED HIM TO BE CRUCIFIED   136 15
AND THEY CRUCIFIED HIM, AND PARTED HIS GARMENTS,   136 30
TWO THIEVES CRUCIFIED WITH HIM, ONE ON THE RIGHT   137 04
WHICH WERE CRUCIFIED WITH HIM, CAST THE SAME IN HIS   137 14
ENTERED NOT INTO GLORY BEFORE HE WAS CRUCIFIED   138 06
WHEN HE HAD SCOURGED HIM, TO BE CRUCIFIED   145 29
WHEN THEY HAD CRUCIFIED HIM, THEY PARTED HIS   146 10
AND THEY CRUCIFIED HIM   146 13
THEY THAT WERE CRUCIFIED WITH HIM REVILED HIM   146 25
REQUIRING THAT HE MIGHT BE CRUCIFIED   154 04
THERE THEY CRUCIFIED HIM, AND THE MALEFACTORS, ONE ON   154 23
HE HIM THEREFORE UNTO THEM TO BE CRUCIFIED   159 30
WHERE THEY CRUCIFIED HIM, AND TWO OTHER WITH HIM, ON   159 33
JESUS WAS CRUCIFIED WAS NIGH TO THE CITY   160 04
WHEN THEY HAD CRUCIFIED JESUS, TOOK HIS GARMENTS, AND   160 09
WHICH WAS CRUCIFIED WITH HIM   160 35
YE SEEK JESUS OF NAZARETH, WHICH WAS CRUCIFIED   165 29
AND HAVE CRUCIFIED HIM   167 19
OUR OLD MAN IS CRUCIFIED WITH HIM, THAT THE BODY OF   197 17
CHRIST'S HAVE CRUCIFIED THE FLESH WITH THE AFFECTIONS   209 29
THE WORLD IS CRUCIFIED UNTO ME, AND I UNTO THE WORLD   210 31
OF CHRIST CRUCIFIED, AND MANFULLY TO FIGHT UNDER HIS   280 07
WAS CRUCIFIED, DEAD, AND BURIED   284 17
WAS CRUCIFIED, DEAD, AND BURIED   577 32
WAS CRUCIFIED, DEAD, AND BURIED, TO   603 14

CRUCIFY

AND SOME OF THEM YE SHALL KILL AND CRUCIFY   100 20
LED HIM AWAY TO CRUCIFY HIM   136 25
CRIED OUT AGAIN, CRUCIFY HIM   145 25
CRUCIFY HIM   145 27
LED HIM OUT TO CRUCIFY HIM   146 04
WITH HIM THEY CRUCIFY TWO THIEVES   146 15
SAYING, CRUCIFY HIM, CRUCIFY HIM   153 33
CRUCIFY HIM, CRUCIFY HIM   153 34
CRUCIFY HIM, CRUCIFY HIM   159 06
SAYING, CRUCIFY HIM, CRUCIFY HIM   159 06
TAKE YE HIM, AND CRUCIFY HIM   159 07
I HAVE POWER TO CRUCIFY THEE, AND HAVE POWER TO   159 15
AWAY WITH HIM, CRUCIFY HIM   159 27
SHALL I CRUCIFY YOUR KING   159 28

CRUEL

ME FROM MY CRUEL ENEMIES, AND SETTETH ME UP ABOVE   363 02
UNRIGHTEOUS AND CRUEL MAN   425 12
OF DARKNESS AND CRUEL HABITATIONS   431 19

CRUELLY

WHICH CRUELLY, DISDAINFULLY, AND DESPITEFULLY SPEAK   376 33

CRUELTY

AND CRUELTY COVERETH THEM AS A GARMENT   428 21

CRUMBS

TO GATHER UP THE CRUMBS UNDER THY TABLE   082 16
DOGS EAT OF THE CRUMBS WHICH FALL FROM THEIR MASTERS'   128 18
BE FED WITH THE CRUMBS WHICH FELL FROM THE RICH MAN'S   190 07

CRY

TO THEE ALL ANGELS CRY ALOUD   010 11
CONTINUALLY DO CRY, HOLY, HOLY, HOLY, LORD GOD OF   010 13
AND LET OUR CRY COME UNTO THEE   062 06
BREAK FORTH AND CRY, THOU THAT TRAVAILEST NOT   131 10
WHEREBY WE CRY, ABBA, FATHER   200 09
TO JERUSALEM, AND CRY UNTO HER, THAT HER WARFARE IS   242 17
THE VOICE SAID, CRY   242 27
AND HE SAID, WHAT SHALL I CRY   242 28
AND LET OUR CRY COME UNTO THEE   290 15
AND LET OUR CRY COME UNTO THEE   297 12
AND LET OUR CRY COME UNTO THEE   306 22
AND LET OUR CRY COME UNTO THEE   309 02
I WILL CRY UNTO GOD WITH MY VOICE   310 29
EVEN UNTO GOD WILL I CRY WITH MY VOICE, AND HE SHALL   310 30
O LORD, WHEN I CRY UNTO THEE   326 20
WHEREBY WE CRY, ABBA, FATHER   330 22
AND LET OUR CRY COME UNTO THEE   340 21
42 THEY SHALL CRY, BUT THERE SHALL BE NONE TO HELP   362 20
THE LORD SHALL THEY CRY, BUT HE SHALL NOT HEAR THEM   362 21
2 O MY GOD, I CRY IN THE DAY-TIME, BUT THOU HEAREST   366 07
O LORD, WHEN I CRY UNTO THEE   372 12
UNTO THEE WILL I CRY, O LORD, MY STRENGTH   373 03
WHEN I CRY UNTO THEE   373 07
17 THE RIGHTEOUS CRY, AND THE LORD HEARETH THEM,   381 02
THAT CRY OVER ME, THERE   424 26
I WILL CRY UNTO GOD WITH MY VOICE   433 16
EVEN UNTO GOD WILL I CRY WITH MY VOICE, AND HE SHALL   433 17
28 SO WHEN THEY CRY UNTO THE LORD IN THEIR TROUBLE,   477 33
IN THE MORNING DO I CRY UNTO THEE   500 04
MY VOICE, WHEN I CRY UNTO THEE   517 09
ALSO WILL HEAR THEIR CRY, AND WILL HELP THEM   521 31
TO THEE, THE COMFORTER, WE CRY   544 21
TO THEE, THE COMFORTER, WE CRY   556 29
AND LET OUR CRY COME UNTO THEE   557 18
O LORD, WHEN WE CRY UNTO THEE   561 31
AND LET OUR CRY COME UNTO THEE   562 07

CRYING

INTO YOUR HEARTS, CRYING, ABBA, FATHER 005 17
THE VOICE OF ONE CRYING IN THE WILDERNESS, MAKE 095 28
INTO YOUR HEARTS, CRYING, ABBA, FATHER 104 23
THE VOICE OF ONE CRYING IN THE WILDERNESS, PREPARE YE 112 06
AND THE MULTITUDE CRYING ALOUD BEGAN TO DESIRE HIM TO 145 16
AND THE CHILDREN CRYING IN THE TEMPLE, AND SAYING, 260 11
HEAR MY CRYING, O GOD, * 413 07
3 I AM WEARY OF CRYING 422 05
AND LET MY CRYING COME UNTO THEE 464 10
NOR CRYING, NEITHER SHALL THERE BE ANY MORE 567 19

CRYSTAL

THRONE THERE WAS A SEA OF GLASS LIKE UNTO CRYSTAL 187 15

CUBIT

CAN ADD ONE CUBIT UNTO THE MEASURE OF HIS LIFE 211 19
CAN ADD ONE CUBIT UNTO THE MEASURE OF HIS LIFE 266 18

CUNNING

OF MEN, AND CUNNING CRAFTINESS, WHEREBY THEY LIE IN 237 27
LET MY RIGHT HAND FORGET HER CUNNING 513 14

CUNNINGLY

NOT FOLLOWED CUNNINGLY DEVISED FABLES, WHEN WE MADE 248 14

CUP

AND TAKE THE CUP INTO HIS HANDS, HE SHALL SAY R 080 04
AFTER SUPPER, (D) HE TOOK THE CUP 080 23
HE IS TO TAKE THE CUP INTO HIS HANDS R 080 33
WHO DELIVERETH THE CUP SHALL SAY, THE BLOOD OF OUR R 083 02
TO EAT OF THAT BREAD, AND DRINK OF THAT CUP 085 30
AND HE TOOK THE CUP, AND WHEN HE HAD GIVEN THANKS, HE 141 11
TAKE AWAY THIS CUP FROM ME 142 02
AND HE TOOK THE CUP, AND GAVE THANKS, AND SAID, TAKE 149 05
LIKEWISE ALSO THE CUP AFTER SUPPER, SAYING, THIS CUP 149 11
SAYING, THIS CUP IS THE NEW TESTAMENT IN MY 149 12
REMOVE THIS CUP FROM ME 150 19
ALSO HE TOOK THE CUP, WHEN HE HAD SUPPED, SAYING, 152 21
SAYING, THIS CUP IS THE NEW TESTAMENT IN MY 152 22
AND DRINK THIS CUP, YE DO SHEW THE LORD'S DEATH TILL 152 24
ABLE TO DRINK OF THE CUP THAT I SHALL DRINK OF, 247 12
DRINK INDEED OF MY CUP, AND BE BAPTIZED WITH THE 247 15
I WILL RECEIVE THE CUP OF SALVATION, AND CALL UPON 305 29
WITH OIL, AND MY CUP SHALL BE FULL 338 28
IS THE PORTION OF MINE INHERITANCE, AND OF MY CUP 357 32
WITH OIL, AND MY CUP SHALL BE FULL 368 21
THE LORD THERE IS A CUP, AND THE WINE IS RED 432 14
I WILL RECEIVE THE CUP OF SALVATION, * 487 11
AND LIKEWISE THE CUP OF BLESSING IS A PARTAKING OF 608 38
THE CUP OF THE LORD IS NOT TO BE DENIED TO THE 609 10

CURE

PROSPER THE MEANS MADE USE OF FOR THEIR CURE 045 07
THE MEANS WHICH SHALL BE MADE USE OF FOR HIS CURE 315 29
COMMITTED TO YOUR CURE AND CHARGE WITH ALL DILIGENCE 542 16
TO YOUR CURE, UNTIL SOME URGENT REASON OR REASONS 569 30
AND TO BLESS THE MEANS MADE USE OF FOR HIS CURE 597 23

CURES

WITHIN YOUR CURES, AS NEED SHALL REQUIRE, AND 542 23

CURIOUS

FOR CURIOUS AND CARNAL PERSONS, LACKING THE 606 22

CURSE

BLESS, AND CURSE NOT 111 29
BUT HE BEGAN TO CURSE AND TO SWEAR, SAYING, I KNOW 143 33
BLESS THEM THAT CURSE YOU, DO GOOD TO THEM THAT HATE 264 05
THEIR MOUTH, BUT CURSE WITH THEIR HEART 414 06
27 THOUGH THEY CURSE, YET BLESS THOU 481 26
TO DELIVER FROM CURSE AND DAMNATION THOSE WHOM HE 606 08

CURSED

AND THEY THAT ARE CURSED OF HIM, SHALL BE ROOTED OUT 386 07
AND CURSED ARE THEY THAT DO ERR FROM THY 491 08

CURSING

MOUTH IS FULL OF CURSING, DECEIT, AND FRAUD 353 18
THEIR TALK IS OF CURSING AND LIES 411 31
DELIGHT WAS IN CURSING, AND IT SHALL HAPPEN UNTO HIM 481 02
HIMSELF WITH CURSING LIKE AS WITH A RAIMENT, * 481 05

CURTAIN

AND SPREADEST OUT THE HEAVENS LIKE A CURTAIN 467 28

CUSTOM

AFTER THE CUSTOM OF THE FEAST 110 20
CUSTOM TO WHOM CUSTOM 114 26
CUSTOM TO WHOM CUSTOM 114 27
FOR HIM AFTER THE CUSTOM OF THE LAW, THEN TOOK HE HIM 233 04
THE RECEIPT OF CUSTOM TO BE AN APOSTLE AND 250 21

CUSTOM   CONTINUED

SITTING AT THE RECEIPT OF CUSTOM 251 13
AS HIS CUSTOM WAS, HE WENT INTO THE SYNAGOGUE ON 261 12
OF GOD, AND THE CUSTOM OF THE PRIMITIVE CHURCH, TO 607 27

CUT

OTHERS CUT DOWN BRANCHES FROM THE TREES, AND STRAWED 091 25
THE HIGH PRIEST, AND CUT OFF HIS EAR 142 23
THE HIGH PRIEST, AND CUT OFF HIS RIGHT EAR 150 33
FOOT OFFEND THEE, CUT THEM OFF, AND CAST THEM FROM 253 04
IN THE EVENING IT IS CUT DOWN, DRIED UP, AND 325 25
HE COMETH UP, AND IS CUT DOWN, LIKE A FLOWER 332 20
THEY SHALL SOON BE CUT DOWN LIKE THE GRASS, * 384 27
BURNT WITH FIRE, AND CUT DOWN 442 02
AND ARE CUT AWAY FROM THY HAND 449 06
IN THE EVENING IT IS CUT DOWN, DRIED UP, AND 453 30
CHURCH IS RIGHTLY CUT OFF FROM THE UNITY OF THE 609 26

CUTTEST

WITH LIES THOU CUTTEST LIKE A SHARP RAZOR 404 23

CUTTING

THE CUTTING OFF OCCASION, FROM THEM THAT V 37

CYMBAL

AM BECOME AS SOUNDING BRASS, OR A TINKLING CYMBAL 122 23

CYMBALS

5 PRAISE HIM UPON THE WELL-TUNED CYMBALS 525 30
PRAISE HIM UPON THE LOUD CYMBALS 525 31

CYRENE

FOUND A MAN OF CYRENE, SIMON BY NAME 136 26
OF LIBYA ABOUT CYRENE, AND STRANGERS OF ROME, 181 04

CYRENIAN

ONE SIMON A CYRENIAN, WHO PASSED BY, COMING OUT OF 146 05
ONE SIMON, A CYRENIAN, COMING OUT OF THE COUNTRY, AND 154 09

CYRENIUS

FIRST MADE WHEN CYRENIUS WAS GOVERNOR OF SYRIA 098 31

DAILY

US THIS DAY OUR DAILY BREAD 007 25
AND GRACE, MAY DAILY BE RENEWED BY THY HOLY SPIRIT 096 17
IS TO BE SAID DAILY THROUGHOUT THE OCTAVE R 096 20
AND GRACE, MAY DAILY BE RENEWED BY THY HOLY SPIRIT 104 09
IS TO BE SAID DAILY THROUGHOUT THE OCTAVE R 108 04
COMETH UPON ME DAILY, THE CARE OF ALL THE CHURCHES 121 11
I WAS DAILY WITH YOU IN THE TEMPLE TEACHING, AND YE 142 26
WHEN I WAS DAILY WITH YOU IN THE TEMPLE, YE STRETCHED 151 04
PRIEST STANDETH DAILY MINISTERING AND OFFERING 158 03
IS TO BE SAID DAILY THROUGHOUT EASTER WEEK R 163 31
GRANT US SO TO DIE DAILY FROM SIN, THAT WE MAY 165 06
AND ALSO DAILY ENDEAVOUR OURSELVES TO FOLLOW 171 32
IS TO BE SAID DAILY THROUGHOUT THE OCTAVE R 177 20
IS TO BE SAID DAILY THROUGHOUT WHITSUN WEEK R 180 15
AND HE TAUGHT DAILY IN THE TEMPLE 204 19
IS TO BE SAID DAILY THROUGHOUT THE OCTAVE R 256 12
THE COMFORTER, AND DAILY INCREASE IN THEM THY 297 18
AND DAILY INCREASE IN THY HOLY SPIRIT MORE AND MORE, 297 19
THY SERVANT MAY DAILY INCREASE IN WISDOM AND STATURE, 307 04
AWAY THROUGH MY DAILY COMPLAINING 377 27
WHILE THEY DAILY SAY UNTO ME, WHERE IS NOW THY GOD 393 05
WHILE THEY SAY DAILY UNTO ME, * 393 29
16 MY CONFUSION IS DAILY BEFORE ME, * 395 24
ENDURETH YET DAILY 404 21
HE IS DAILY FIGHTING, AND TROUBLING ME 408 15
2 MINE ENEMIES ARE DAILY AT HAND TO SWALLOW ME UP 408 16
5 THEY DAILY MISTAKE MY WORDS 408 24
THAT I MAY DAILY PERFORM MY VOWS 413 23
BE THE LORD DAILY, 420 23
14 MY MOUTH SHALL DAILY SPEAK OF THY RIGHTEOUSNESS 426 04
EVER UNTO HIM, AND DAILY SHALL HE BE PRAISED 427 28
HOW THE FOOLISH MAN BLASPHEMETH THEE DAILY 431 23
FOR I WILL CALL DAILY UPON THEE 447 09
I HAVE CALLED DAILY UPON THEE, I HAVE STRETCHED FORTH 449 15
ROUND ABOUT ME DAILY LIKE WATER, * 449 31
DELIGHT SHALL BE DAILY IN THY NAME 451 06
BY DAILY READING AND WEIGHING THE SCRIPTURES, 541 18
AND THAT WE MAY DAILY INCREASE AND GO FORWARDS IN THE 545 30
WHICH WE DAILY MEET WITH 588 14

DALMATIA

CRESCENS TO GALATIA, TITUS UNTO DALMATIA 254 02

DAMASCUS

HIM LETTERS TO DAMASCUS TO THE SYNAGOGUES, THAT IF HE 229 27
AND AS HE JOURNEYED, HE CAME NEAR DAMASCUS 229 30
HIM BY THE HAND, AND BROUGHT HIM INTO DAMASCUS 230 12
DISCIPLE AT DAMASCUS, NAMED ANANIAS 230 14
DAYS WITH THE DISCIPLES WHICH WERE AT DAMASCUS 231 03
WHICH DWELT AT DAMASCUS, PROVING THAT THIS IS VERY 231 10

DAMNATION

EVERLASTING DAMNATION, GOOD LORD, DELIVER US   054 21
IT DESERVETH GOD'S WRATH AND DAMNATION   604 34
FROM CURSE AND DAMNATION THOSE WHOM HE HATH CHOSEN IN 606 08
TO THEMSELVES DAMNATION, AS SAINT PAUL SAITH   608 05

DAMSELS

THE MIDST OF THE DAMSELS PLAYING WITH THE TIMBRELS   421 05

DANCE

3 LET THEM PRAISE HIS NAME IN THE DANCE   525 07

DANCES

4 PRAISE HIM IN THE TIMBRELS AND DANCES   525 28

DANCETH

MY HEART DANCETH FOR JOY, AND IN MY SONG WILL I   373 24

DANCING

HE HEARD MUSICK AND DANCING   202 28

DANGER

INTO NO SIN, NEITHER RUN INTO ANY KIND OF DANGER   017 17
ALL WHO ARE IN DANGER, NECESSITY, AND TRIBULATION   056 28
SO IS THE DANGER GREAT, IF WE RECEIVE THE SAME   085 32
KILL SHALL BE IN DANGER OF THE JUDGMENT   198 02
CAUSE SHALL BE IN DANGER OF THE JUDGMENT   198 04
SHALL BE IN DANGER OF THE COUNCIL   198 06
SHALL BE IN DANGER OF HELL-FIRE   198 07
YOU IN THE GREAT DANGER OF CHILD-BIRTH   305 13
DEFEND HIM IN ALL DANGER, AND KEEP HIM IN PERPETUAL 309 07
INTO NO SIN, NEITHER RUN INTO ANY KIND OF DANGER   592 23

DANGEROUS

AND SO DANGEROUS TO THOSE WHO WILL PRESUME TO RECEIVE 087 06
IS A MOST DANGEROUS DOWNFALL, WHEREBY THE DEVIL DOTH 606 24
AND DANGEROUS DECEITS   609 19

DANGERS

ALL PERILS AND DANGERS OF THIS NIGHT   031 27
HEART THE GREAT DANGERS WE ARE IN BY OUR UNHAPPY   037 27
THEM FROM THE DANGERS OF THE SEA, AND FROM THE   042 07
FROM THE DANGERS OF THE SEA, FROM SICKNESS,   046 12
AND APPARENT DANGERS WHEREWITH WE WERE COMPASSED   052 10
AND IN ALL OUR DANGERS AND NECESSITIES STRETCH FORTH 112 27
MANY AND GREAT DANGERS, THAT BY REASON OF THE FRAILTY 114 05
US IN ALL DANGERS, AND CARRY US THROUGH ALL   114 07
COMFORTED IN ALL DANGERS AND ADVERSITIES   192 27
DEFEND US IN ALL DANGERS BOTH OF SOUL AND BODY   581 02
US FROM THE DANGERS OF THE PAST NIGHT   587 23
US FROM ALL DANGERS AND ADVERSITIES   589 02
US FROM ALL DANGERS AND MISCHIEFS, AND FROM THE FEAR 591 26
ALL PERILS AND DANGERS OF THIS NIGHT   593 14
THEM FROM ALL DANGERS OF SOUL AND BODY   597 03

DARE

OUR UNWORTHINESS WE DARE NOT, AND FOR OUR BLINDNESS 050 03

DARK

WHEN IT WAS YET DARK, UNTO THE SEPULCHRE, AND SEETH 164 11
AND IT WAS DARK UNDER HIS FEET   360 16
ABOUT HIM WITH DARK WATER, AND THICK CLOUDS TO COVER 360 20
6 LET THEIR WAY BE DARK AND SLIPPERY, *   381 29
AND SHOW MY DARK SPEECH UPON THE HARP   400 13
12 SHALL THY WONDROUS WORKS BE KNOWN IN THE DARK   449 20
28 HE SENT DARKNESS, AND IT WAS DARK   471 28

DARKENED

THE SUN BE DARKENED, AND THE MOON SHALL NOT GIVE HER 118 14
AND THE SUN WAS DARKENED, AND THE VEIL OF THE TEMPLE 155 11
UNDERSTANDING DARKENED, BEING ALIENATED FROM THE LIFE 216 05

DARKLY

FOR NOW WE SEE THROUGH A GLASS, DARKLY   123 12

DARKNESS

O YE LIGHT AND DARKNESS, BLESS YE THE LORD   012 30
THAT SIT IN DARKNESS, AND IN THE SHADOW OF DEATH, * 014 31
LIGHTEN OUR DARKNESS, WE BESEECH THEE, O LORD   031 26
LIGHT OUT OF DARKNESS, AND GOOD OUT OF EVIL, GRANT TO 046 26
BRING US OUT OF DARKNESS INTO HIS OWN GLORIOUS LIGHT 077 24
BROUGHT OUT OF DARKNESS AND ERROR INTO THE CLEAR   078 31
WHO LAY IN DARKNESS AND THE SHADOW OF DEATH   086 10
THE WORKS OF DARKNESS, AND PUT UPON US THE ARMOUR OF 090 12
THE WORKS OF DARKNESS, AND LET US PUT ON THE ARMOUR 091 04
THINGS OF DARKNESS, AND WILL MAKE MANIFEST THE   094 12
AND THE DARKNESS COMPREHENDED IT NOT   097 25
AND THE LIGHT SHINETH IN DARKNESS   097 25
IN HIM IS NO DARKNESS AT ALL   101 24
AND WALK IN DARKNESS, WE LIE, AND DO NOT THE TRUTH   101 25
THE KINGDOM SHALL BE CAST OUT INTO OUTER DARKNESS   115 22
WERE SOMETIMES DARKNESS, BUT NOW ARE YE LIGHT IN THE 129 12

DARKNESS   CONTINUED

WORKS OF DARKNESS, BUT RATHER REPROVE THEM   129 17
HOUR THERE WAS DARKNESS OVER ALL THE LAND UNTO THE   137 16
THAT WALKETH IN DARKNESS, AND HATH NO LIGHT   144 24
COME, THERE WAS DARKNESS OVER THE WHOLE LAND UNTIL   146 26
AND THE POWER OF DARKNESS   151 06
AND THERE WAS A DARKNESS OVER ALL THE EARTH UNTIL THE 155 10
AND MEN LOVED DARKNESS RATHER THAN LIGHT, BECAUSE   185 06
AND CAST HIM INTO OUTER DARKNESS   218 27
RULERS OF THE DARKNESS OF THIS WORLD, AGAINST   219 09
THAT SIT IN DARKNESS AND IN THE SHADOW OF DEATH, TO 244 15
TO SHINE OUT OF DARKNESS, HATH SHINED IN OUR HEARTS, 251 08
12 HE MADE DARKNESS HIS SECRET PLACE, *   360 19
SHALL MAKE MY DARKNESS TO BE LIGHT   361 25
IS FULL OF DARKNESS AND CRUEL HABITATIONS   431 19
DO THEY UNDERSTAND, BUT WALK ON STILL IN DARKNESS   443 27
IN A PLACE OF DARKNESS, AND IN THE DEEP   449 08
THAT WALKETH IN DARKNESS, *   455 07
2 CLOUDS AND DARKNESS ARE ROUND ABOUT HIM   460 32
20 THOU MAKEST DARKNESS THAT IT MAY BE NIGHT   468 34
28 HE SENT DARKNESS, AND IT WAS DARK   471 28
SUCH AS SIT IN DARKNESS, AND IN THE SHADOW OF DEATH, 476 24
THEM OUT OF DARKNESS, AND OUT OF THE SHADOW OF DEATH, 477 02
THE GODLY THERE ARISETH UP LIGHT IN THE DARKNESS   483 24
THE DARKNESS SHALL COVER ME   515 08
DARKNESS IS NO DARKNESS WITH THEE, BUT THE NIGHT IS 515 10
11 YEA, THE DARKNESS IS NO DARKNESS WITH THEE,   515 10
THE DARKNESS AND LIGHT TO THEE ARE BOTH ALIKE   515 11
LAID ME IN THE DARKNESS, AS THE MEN THAT HAVE BEEN 518 29
LIGHTEN OUR DARKNESS, WE BESEECH THEE, O LORD   593 13
DAY FROM THE DARKNESS, AND TURNEST THE SHADOW OF   594 12
RISETH UP IN DARKNESS FOR THE GODLY   595 27
THY CHILDREN WHO ARE LIVING IN MENTAL DARKNESS   598 14

DARLING

MY DARLING FROM THE POWER OF THE DOG   367 12
ON ME, AND MY DARLING FROM THE LIONS   382 31

DARTS

ALL THE FIERY DARTS OF THE WICKED   219 17

DASH

AT ANY TIME THOU DASH THY FOOT AGAINST A STONE   127 02

DATHAN

AND SWALLOWED UP DATHAN, *   474 02

DAUGHTER

AND THY DAUGHTER, THY MAN-SERVANT, AND THY   068 28
TELL YE THE DAUGHTER OF SION, BEHOLD, THY KING COMETH 091 20
MY DAUGHTER IS GRIEVOUSLY VEXED WITH A DEVIL   128 10
AND HER DAUGHTER WAS MADE WHOLE FROM THAT VERY HOUR 128 21
SAYING, MY DAUGHTER IS EVEN NOW DEAD   224 14
HE SAID, DAUGHTER, BE OF GOOD COMFORT   224 21
THE DAUGHTER OF PHANUEL, OF THE TRIBE OF   233 16
AND THY DAUGHTER, THY MAN-SERVANT, AND THY   286 28
GATES OF THE DAUGHTER OF SION   352 20
10 HEARKEN, O DAUGHTER, AND CONSIDER   397 05
12 AND THE DAUGHTER OF TYRE SHALL BE THERE WITH A 397 09
13 THE KING'S DAUGHTER IS ALL GLORIOUS WITHIN   397 12
GATES OF THE DAUGHTER OF SION   429 34
8 O DAUGHTER OF BABYLON, WASTED WITH MISERY   513 21
AND THY DAUGHTER, THY MAN-SERVANT, AND THY   579 08

DAUGHTERS

THEM SAID, DAUGHTERS OF JERUSALEM, WEEP NOT FOR ME, 154 14
9 KINGS' DAUGHTERS ARE AMONG THY HONOURABLE WOMEN 397 02
AND THE DAUGHTERS OF JUDAH BE GLAD, *   399 31
AND THE DAUGHTERS OF JUDAH WERE GLAD, *   461 12
SONS AND THEIR DAUGHTERS UNTO DEVILS   475 10
AND OF THEIR DAUGHTERS, *   475 12
AND THAT OUR DAUGHTERS MAY BE AS THE POLISHED CORNERS 520 16

DAVID

DAY IN THE CITY OF DAVID A SAVIOUR, WHICH IS CHRIST 004 10
IN THE HOUSE OF HIS SERVANT DAVID   014 11
O SON OF DAVID, HAVE MERCY UPON US   059 14
HOSANNA TO THE SON OF DAVID   091 28
UNTO THE CITY OF DAVID, WHICH IS CALLED BETHLEHEM 099 03
BECAUSE HE WAS OF THE HOUSE AND LINEAGE OF DAVID   099 04
DAY IN THE CITY OF DAVID A SAVIOUR, WHICH IS CHRIST 099 17
THOU SON OF DAVID, FEAR NOT TO TAKE UNTO THEE MARY 105 04
THOU SON OF DAVID, HAVE MERCY ON ME   123 30
THOU SON OF DAVID, HAVE MERCY ON ME   123 33
O LORD, THOU SON OF DAVID   128 10
I WILL GIVE YOU THE SURE MERCIES OF DAVID   169 13
FOR DAVID, AFTER HE HAD SERVED HIS OWN GENERATION BY 169 15
THEY SAY UNTO HIM, THE SON OF DAVID   215 18
HOW THEN DOTH DAVID IN SPIRIT CALL HIM LORD, SAYING, 215 19
IF DAVID THEN CALL HIM LORD, HOW IS HE HIS SON   215 21
I WILL RAISE UNTO DAVID A RIGHTEOUS BRANCH, AND A 225 10
BY THE MOUTH OF DAVID SPAKE BEFORE CONCERNING JUDAS, 234 10
AND HE SAID, HEAR YE NOW, O HOUSE OF DAVID   235 29
MAN WHOSE NAME WAS JOSEPH, OF THE HOUSE OF DAVID   236 08
GIVE UNTO HIM THE THRONE OF HIS FATHER DAVID   236 18
FOR US IN THE HOUSE OF HIS SERVANT DAVID   243 35
AND SAYING, HOSANNA TO THE SON OF DAVID   260 12
UNTO DAVID HIS ANOINTED, AND UNTO HIS SEED FOR   363 08

DAVID   CONTINUED

71 HE CHOSE DAVID ALSO HIS SERVANT, *   439 19
I HAVE SWORN UNTO DAVID MY SERVANT   450 10
21 I HAVE FOUND DAVID MY SERVANT   451 15
THAT I WILL NOT FAIL DAVID   452 11
THOU SWAREST UNTO DAVID IN THY TRUTH   453 06
EVEN THE SEAT OF THE HOUSE OF DAVID   503 17
REMEMBER DAVID, *   508 05
FAITHFUL OATH UNTO DAVID, *   508 25
I MAKE THE HORN OF DAVID TO FLOURISH   509 08
AND HAST DELIVERED DAVID THY SERVANT FRCM THE PERIL   520 11

DAVID'S

FOR THY SERVANT DAVID'S SAKE, *   508 23

DAY

ON ANY DAY, SAVE A DAY OF FASTING OR ABSTINENCE,   R 003 05
OR ON ANY DAY WHEN THE LITANY OR HOLY COMMUNION IS   R 003 05
ON ANY DAY, SAVE A DAY OF FASTING OR ABSTINENCE,   R 003 05
YOU IS BORN THIS DAY IN THE CITY OF DAVID A SAVICUR,   004 10
THIS IS THE DAY WHICH THE LORD HATH MADE   005 04
GIVE US THIS DAY OUR DAILY BREAD   007 25
ON CHRISTMAS DAY AND UNTIL THE EPIPHANY   R 008 18
ON MONDAY IN EASTER WEEK AND UNTIL ASCENSION DAY   R 008 23
ON ASCENSION DAY AND UNTIL WHITSUNDAY   R 008 25
THAT ON ANY DAY WHEN THE HOLY COMMUNION IS   R 010 03
DAY BY DAY WE MAGNIFY THEE   011 06
DAY BY DAY WE MAGNIFY THEE   011 06
TO KEEP US THIS DAY WITHOUT SIN   011 08
THE THIRD DAY HE ROSE AGAIN FROM THE DEAD   015 24
AND THE THIRD DAY HE ROSE AGAIN ACCORDING TC THE   016 10
THE COLLECT FOR THE DAY, EXCEPT WHEN THE CCMMUNION   R 017 02
THE COLLECT FOR THE DAY SHALL BE OMITTED HERE   R 017 03
SAFELY BROUGHT US TO THE BEGINNING OF THIS DAY   017 15
AND GRANT THAT THIS DAY WE FALL INTO NO SIN, NEITHER   017 16
OF PSALMS FOR THE DAY, SHALL BE SUNG OR SAID THE   R 025 19
THE THIRD DAY HE ROSE AGAIN FROM THE DEAD   029 29
AND THE THIRD DAY HE ROSE AGAIN ACCORDING TO THE   030 15
THE COLLECT FOR THE DAY, AND AFTER THAT THE COLLECTS   R 031 15
AND IN THE DAY OF TROUBLE, SUFFER NOT OUR TRUST IN   036 22
SUPPORT THEM IN THE DAY OF BATTLE, AND IN THE TIME CF   041 27
BE CALLED UPON TO GIVE AT THE LAST GREAT DAY   047 21
WE HAVE HEARD THIS DAY WITH OUR OUTWARD EARS, MAY,   049 18
OF DEATH, AND IN THE DAY OF JUDGMENT, WE SINNERS DO   055 16
ON THE FIRST DAY OF LENT, THE OFFICE ENSUING MAY BE   R 060 03
BUT THE SEVENTH DAY IS THE SABBATH OF THE LCRD THY   068 26
ALL THAT IN THEM IS, AND RESTED THE SEVENTH DAY   068 31
BLESSED THE SEVENTH DAY, AND HALLOWED IT   068 32
THEN SHALL THE PRIEST SAY THE COLLECT OF THE DAY   R 070 02
BE SAID ON CHRISTMAS DAY, EASTER DAY, ASCENSICN DAY,   R 070 32
DAY, ASCENSION DAY, WHITSUNDAY, AND TRINITY SUNDAY   R 070 32
DAY, EASTER DAY, ASCENSION DAY, WHITSUNDAY, AND   R 070 32
AND THE THIRD DAY HE ROSE AGAIN ACCORDING TO THE   071 12
A GOOD REWARD IN THE DAY OF NECESSITY   072 35
UPON CHRISTMAS DAY, AND SEVEN DAYS AFTER   R 077 13
UPON EASTER DAY, AND SEVEN DAYS AFTER   R 078 06
UPON ASCENSION DAY, AND SEVEN DAYS AFTER   R 078 15
UPON ALL SAINTS' DAY, AND SEVEN DAYS AFTER   R 079 21
OR SOME HOLY DAY, IMMEDIATELY PRECEDING,) HE   R 086 25
ON -- DAY NEXT I PURPOSE, THROUGH GOD'S   086 28
SERVICE OF THE DAY BEFORE   R 090 07
THAT IN THE LAST DAY, WHEN HE SHALL COME AGAIN IN HIS   090 15
TO BE REPEATED EVERY DAY, AFTER THE OTHER CCLLECTS IN   R 090 20
THE OTHER COLLECTS IN ADVENT, UNTIL CHRISTMAS DAY   R 090 21
IS FAR SPENT, THE DAY IS AT HAND   091 03
LET US WALK HONESTLY, AS IN THE DAY   091 05
ART MY SON, THIS DAY HAVE I BEGOTTEN THEE   097 03
ON CHRISTMAS DAY, THE FOLLOWING COLLECT, EPISTLE,   R 098 08
YOU IS BORN THIS DAY IN THE CITY OF DAVID A SAVICUR,   099 16
GOSPEL FOR CHRISTMAS DAY SHALL SERVE FOR THEM   R 104 02
FOLLOWING CHRISTMAS DAY, THE FIRST EPISTLE AND GCSPEL R 104 02
OF THE LORD, AND THE DAY OF VENGEANCE OF OUR GOD   107 05
AND THE THIRD DAY THERE WAS A MARRIAGE IN CANA CF   113 11
FOR A PENNY A DAY, HE SENT THEM INTO HIS VINEYARD   119 18
YE HERE ALL THE DAY IDLE   119 25
WHICH HAVE BORNE THE BURDEN AND HEAT OF THE DAY   120 06
A NIGHT AND A DAY I HAVE BEEN IN THE DEEP   121 03
AND THE THIRD DAY HE SHALL RISE AGAIN   123 23
IS TO BE SAID EVERY DAY IN LENT, AFTER THE COLLECT   R 124 13
APPOINTED FOR THE DAY, UNTIL PALM SUNDAY   124 19
SERVE FOR EVERY DAY AFTER, UNTO THE NEXT SUNDAY,   R 125 23
AND IN THE DAY OF SALVATION HAVE I   126 06
BEHOLD, NOW IS THE DAY OF SALVATION   126 07
YOUR FATHER ABRAHAM REJOICED TO SEE MY DAY   133 29
IS TO BE SAID EVERY DAY, AFTER THE COLLECT APPOINTED   R 134 13
APPOINTED FOR THE DAY, UNTIL GOOD FRIDAY   R 134 13
THE FIELD OF BLOOD, UNTO THIS DAY   135 13
MANY THINGS THIS DAY IN A DREAM BECAUSE OF HIM   135 34
FOR THE DAY OF VENGEANCE IS IN MINE HEART, AND THE   138 20
NOT ON THE FEAST DAY, LEST THERE BE AN UPROAR OF THE   139 35
AND THE FIRST DAY OF UNLEAVENED BREAD, WHEN THEY   140 22
THE VINE, UNTIL THAT DAY THAT I DRINK IT NEW IN THE   141 15
UNTO THEE, THAT THIS DAY, EVEN IN THIS NIGHT, BEFORE   141 23
THEN CAME THE DAY OF UNLEAVENED BREAD, WHEN THE   148 21
SHALL NOT CROW THIS DAY, BEFORE THAT THOU SHALT   150 02
AS SOON AS IT WAS DAY, THE ELDERS OF THE PECPLE AND   151 21
AND THE SAME DAY PILATE AND HEROD WERE MADE FRIENDS   153 18
AS YE SEE THE DAY APPROACHING   158 28
CROSS ON THE SABBATH DAY, (FOR THAT SABBATH DAY WAS   160 32
FOR THAT SABBATH DAY WAS AN HIGH DAY,) BESOUGHT   160 32
DAY WAS AN HIGH DAY,) BESOUGHT PILATE THAT THEIR LEGS   160 32
THAT FOLLOWED THE DAY OF THE PREPARATION, THE CHIEF   162 15
NOW THE NEXT DAY, THAT FOLLOWED THE DAY OF THE   162 15

DAY   CONTINUED

SURE UNTIL THE THIRD DAY, LEST HIS DISCIPLES CCME BY   162 20
THE FIRST DAY OF THE WEEK COMETH MARY MAGDALENE   164 10
CELEBRATED ON EASTER DAY, THE FOLLOWING COLLECT,   R 164 31
MORNING THE FIRST DAY OF THE WEEK, THEY CAME UNTO THE   165 21
RAISED UP THE THIRD DAY, AND SHEWED HIM OPENLY   166 25
WENT THAT SAME DAY TO A VILLAGE CALLED EMMAUS, WHICH   167 03
TO-DAY IS THE THIRD DAY SINCE THESE THINGS WERE DCNE   167 21
AND THE DAY IS FAR SPENT   168 04
READ EVERY SABBATH DAY, THEY HAVE FULFILLED THEM IN   168 29
ART MY SON, THIS DAY HAVE I BEGOTTEN THEE   169 09
AND TO RISE FROM THE DEAD THE THIRD DAY   170 13
THE SAME DAY AT EVENING, BEING THE FIRST DAY OF THE   171 14
BEING THE FIRST DAY OF THE WEEK, WHEN THE DOORS HERE   171 14
GLORIFY GOD IN THE DAY OF VISITATION   173 17
AT THAT DAY YE SHALL ASK IN MY NAME   176 26
AND TEACH, UNTIL THE DAY IN WHICH HE WAS TAKEN UP,   177 23
SERVE FOR EVERY DAY AFTER, UNTO THE NEXT SUNDAY,   R 178 32
WHEN THE DAY OF PENTECOST WAS FULLY COME, THEY WERE   180 17
AT THAT DAY YE SHALL KNOW THAT I AM IN MY FATHER,   181 17
RAISED UP THE THIRD DAY, AND SHEWED HIM OPENLY   184 12
AND THEY REST NOT DAY AND NIGHT, SAYING, HOLY,   187 22
HAVE BOLDNESS IN THE DAY OF JUDGMENT   189 27
AND FARED SUMPTUOUSLY EVERY DAY   190 05
AND FELL IN ONE DAY THREE AND TWENTY THOUSAND   201 18
AT LEAST IN THIS THY DAY, THE THINGS WHICH BELCNG   204 08
ROSE AGAIN THE THIRD DAY ACCORDING TO THE SCRIPTURES   205 06
SUFFICIENT UNTO THE DAY IS THE EVIL THEREOF   211 34
IT CAME TO PASS THE DAY AFTER, THAT JESUS WENT INTO   212 27
BREAD ON THE SABBATH DAY, THAT THEY WATCHED HIM   213 29
IS IT LAWFUL TO HEAL ON THE SABBATH DAY   214 03
NOT STRAIGHTWAY PULL HIM OUT ON THE SABBATH DAY   214 07
BE BLAMELESS IN THE DAY OF OUR LORD JESUS CHRIST   215 04
ANY MAN FROM THAT DAY FORTH ASK HIM ANY MORE   215 23
ARE SEALED UNTO THE DAY OF REDEMPTION   216 26
IN THE EVIL DAY, AND HAVING DONE ALL, TO STAND   219 12
FROM THE FIRST DAY UNTIL NOW   220 25
PERFORM IT UNTIL THE DAY OF JESUS CHRIST   220 27
OFFENCE TILL THE DAY OF CHRIST   221 05
IN YOU, SINCE THE DAY YE HEARD OF IT, AND KNEW THE   223 29
WE ALSO, SINCE THE DAY WE HEARD IT, DO NOT CEASE TO   223 33
ISRAEL HE SAITH, ALL DAY LONG I HAVE STRETCHED FCRTH   227 21
SON WAS THIS DAY PRESENTED IN THE TEMPLE IN SUBSTANCE   231 30
WHO MAY ABIDE THE DAY OF HIS COMING   232 08
GOD WITH FASTINGS AND PRAYERS NIGHT AND DAY   233 21
UNTO THAT SAME DAY THAT HE WAS TAKEN UP FROM   234 23
THAT ON THE EIGHTH DAY THEY CAME TO CIRCUMCISE THE   243 17
THE DESERTS TILL THE DAY OF HIS SHEWING UNTO ISRAEL   244 18
THEM BEFORE OUR GOD DAY AND NIGHT   252 13
SHALL GIVE ME AT THAT DAY   253 29
AND SERVE HIM DAY AND NIGHT IN HIS TEMPLE   257 10
THE NEXT SABBATH DAY CAME ALMOST THE WHOLE CITY   260 26
ON THE SABBATH DAY, AND STOOD UP FOR TO READ   261 13
SAY UNTO THEM, THIS DAY IS THIS SCRIPTURE FULFILLED   261 24
SUFFICIENT UNTO THE DAY IS THE EVIL THEREOF   266 33
BUT SHOULD RAISE IT UP AGAIN AT THE LAST DAY   269 19
AND I WILL RAISE HIM UP AT THE LAST DAY   269 22
BAPTISM MAY BE ADMINISTERED UPON ANY OTHER DAY   R 273 07
THE THIRD DAY HE ROSE AGAIN FROM THE DEAD   284 18
BUT THE SEVENTH DAY IS THE SABBATH OF THE LORD THY   286 26
ALL THAT IN THEM IS, AND RESTED THE SEVENTH DAY   286 31
BLESSED THE SEVENTH DAY, AND HALLOWED IT   286 32
UPON THE DAY APPOINTED, ALL THAT ARE TO BE   R 296 05
AT THE DAY AND TIME APPOINTED FOR SOLEMNIZATION CF R 300 03
AT THE DREADFUL DAY OF JUDGMENT WHEN THE SECRETS OF   300 25
TO HOLD FROM THIS DAY FORWARD, FOR BETTER FCR WORSE, 301 29
TO HOLD FROM THIS DAY FORWARD, FOR BETTER FOR WCRSE, 302 05
MAY THY REST BE THIS DAY IN PEACE, AND THY   319 24
AND GOSPEL FOR THE DAY, FOR THOSE APPOINTED ABOVE   R 323 34
STAND AT THE LATTER DAY UPON THE EARTH   324 10
NOT BURN THEE BY DAY, *   327 29
IN THE LAST DAY, WE MAY BE FOUND ACCEPTABLE IN THY   335 08
PERFECTED UNTO THE DAY OF JESUS CHRIST   335 30
THAT AT THE DAY OF THE GENERAL RESURRECTICN, WE, WITH 336 23
NOT BURN THEE BY DAY, *   339 13
AND SERVE HIM DAY AND NIGHT IN HIS TEMPLE   341 21
HE EXERCISE HIMSELF DAY AND NIGHT   345 11
ART MY SON, THIS DAY HAVE I BEGOTTEN THEE   346 11
AND GOD IS PROVOKED EVERY DAY   350 16
CAME UPON ME IN THE DAY OF MY TROUBLE   361 02
2 ONE DAY TELLETH ANOTHER   363 15
HEAR THEE IN THE DAY OF TROUBLE   364 17
BEEN MY HOPE ALL THE DAY LONG   369 27
WAS HEAVY UPON ME DAY AND NIGHT, *   377 28
THY PRAISE, ALL THE DAY LONG   383 24
HATH SEEN THAT HIS DAY IS COMING   385 21
GO MOURNING ALL THE DAY LONG   388 03
DECEIT ALL THE DAY LONG   388 16
HAVE BEEN MY MEAT DAY AND NIGHT, *   393 04
OUR BOAST OF GOD ALL DAY LONG, *   395 09
WE KILLED ALL THE DAY LONG, *   396 04
10 DAY AND NIGHT THEY GO ABOUT WITHIN THE WALLS   407 06
AND REFUGE IN THE DAY OF MY TROUBLE   412 08
AND HONOUR ALL THE DAY LONG   425 22
ALL THE DAY LONG   426 28
14 ALL THE DAY LONG HAVE I BEEN PUNISHED, *   429 04
17 THE DAY IS THINE, AND THE NIGHT IS THINE   431 08
BACK IN THE DAY OF BATTLE   435 19
AND OF THE DAY WHEN HE DELIVERED THEM FROM THE HAND 437 25
10 FOR ONE DAY IN THY COURTS *   445 31
I HAVE CRIED DAY AND NIGHT BEFORE THEE   448 29
NOR FOR THE ARROW THAT FLIETH BY DAY   456 06
AND AS IN THE DAY OF TEMPTATION IN THE WILDERNESS   459 20
HIS SALVATION FROM DAY TO DAY   460 03
BE TELLING OF HIS SALVATION FROM DAY TO DAY   460 03

DAY　　　　　　　　CONTINUED

REVILE ME ALL THE DAY LONG   464 25
3 IN THE DAY OF THY POWER SHALL THY PEOPLE OFFER   482 11
EVEN KINGS IN THE DAY OF HIS WRATH   482 17
24 THIS IS THE DAY WHICH THE LORD HATH MADE   489 16
THEY CONTINUE THIS DAY ACCORDING TO THINE ORDINANCE   496 07
ALL THE DAY LONG IS MY STUDY IN IT   496 20
164 SEVEN TIMES A DAY DO I PRAISE THEE   501 09
NOT BURN THEE BY DAY, *   503 02
8 THE SUN TO RULE THE DAY   511 30
O LORD, IN THE DAY OF JERUSALEM   513 18
THEN SHALL MY NIGHT BE TURNED TO DAY   515 09
WITH THEE, BUT THE NIGHT IS AS CLEAR AS THE DAY   515 11
16 WHICH DAY BY DAY WERE FASHIONED, *   515 22
16 WHICH DAY BY DAY WERE FASHIONED, *   515 22
UP STRIFE ALL THE DAY LONG   516 12
MY HEAD IN THE DAY OF BATTLE   516 23
2 EVERY DAY WILL I GIVE THANKS UNTO THEE   520 29
UPON SOME OTHER DAY, IN THE FACE OF THE CHURCH, ADMIT   529 30
WHEN THE DAY APPOINTED BY THE BISHOP IS COME,   R 530 03
COMMUNION THE SAME DAY, WITH THE BISHOP   R 534 27
UPON SOME OTHER DAY, IN THE FACE OF THE CHURCH,   R 535 26
WHEN THE DAY APPOINTED BY THE BISHOP IS COME,   R 536 03
OF PRIESTHOOD THAT DAY, EACH OF THEM BEING DECENTLY   R 536 08
TO RECEIVE THIS DAY UNTO THE HOLY OFFICE OF   536 23
AND IF, ON THE SAME DAY, THE ORDER OF DEACONS BE   R 547 19
FROM THE FIRST DAY THAT I CAME INTO ASIA, AFTER   550 06
YOU TO RECORD THIS DAY, THAT I AM PURE FROM THE BLOOD   550 24
EVERY ONE NIGHT AND DAY WITH TEARS   551 02
THE SAME DAY AT EVENING, BEING THE FIRST DAY OF THE   551 27
BEING THE FIRST DAY OF THE WEEK, WHEN THE DOORS WERE   551 27
PERFECT AND IRREPREHENSIBLE AT THE LATTER DAY   555 33
AT THE LATTER DAY HE MAY RECEIVE THE CROWN OF   559 12
AT --, THIS -- DAY OF --, A   569 39
THE THIRD DAY HE ROSE AGAIN FROM THE DEAD   578 02
BUT THE SEVENTH DAY IS THE SABBATH OF THE LORD THY   579 06
AND RESTED THE SEVENTH DAY   579 11
BLESSED THE SEVENTH DAY, AND HALLOWED IT   579 12
HERE MAY FOLLOW THE COLLECT FOR THE DAY   R 587 16
OF OUR LIVES TO THIS DAY, AND ESPECIALLY FOR HAVING   587 22
THAT ANOTHER DAY IS ADDED TO OUR LIVES   588 05
OF THAT GREAT DAY, IN WHICH WE MUST GIVE A STRICT   588 21
THY GRACE AND PROTECTION FOR THE ENSUING DAY   588 28
HERE MAY FOLLOW THE COLLECT FOR THE DAY   R 589 23
CONFESS THE SINS AND FAILINGS OF THAT DAY   R 589 35
FOR THE MERCIES AND BENEFITS OF THE PAST DAY   591 19
AS MAY FIT US FOR THE DUTIES OF THE COMING DAY   591 29
SAFELY BROUGHT US TO THE BEGINNING OF THIS DAY   592 21
AND GRANT THAT THIS DAY WE FALL INTO NO SIN, NEITHER   592 22
WHO DIVIDEST THE DAY FROM THE DARKNESS, AND TURNEST   594 11
WHILE IT WAS DAY, WE MAY, WHEN THE NIGHT COMETH,   594 16
SUPPORT US ALL THE DAY LONG, UNTIL THE SHADOWS   594 30
BLESSINGS OF THE DAY, AND HUMBLY SUPPLICATE THY   595 07
VOUCHSAFE US THIS DAY SUCH BLESSING THROUGH OUR   595 14
WE REMEMBER THIS DAY BEFORE THEE THY FAITHFUL SERVANT   598 06
SUCH AS ARE THIS DAY DESTITUTE, HOMELESS, OR   599 07
WHICH WE MUST ONE DAY GIVE, MAY BE FAITHFUL STEWARDS   599 22
UNTIL HE RETURN TO JUDGE ALL MEN AT THE LAST DAY   603 24

DAY-SPRING

WHEREBY THE DAY-SPRING FROM ON HIGH HATH VISITED US   014 30

DAY-TIME

I CRY IN THE DAY-TIME, BUT THOU HEAREST NOT   366 07
WILL GRANT HIS LOVING-KINDNESS IN THE DAY-TIME   393 21
15 IN THE DAY-TIME ALSO HE LED THEM WITH A CLOUD,   435 28

DAY'S

WENT A DAY'S JOURNEY   110 24

DAYS

EXCEPT ON THOSE DAYS FOR WHICH OTHER CANTICLES ARE   R 008 09
ON THE DAYS HEREAFTER NAMED, IMMEDIATELY BEFORE THE   R 008 16
EPIPHANY AND SEVEN DAYS AFTER, AND ON THE FEAST OF   R 008 20
WHITSUNDAY AND SIX DAYS AFTER   R 008 27
O YE NIGHTS AND DAYS, BLESS YE THE LORD   012 28
ALL THE DAYS OF OUR LIFE   014 22
THEE IN HOLINESS AND RIGHTEOUSNESS ALL OUR DAYS   019 30
THEE IN HOLINESS AND RIGHTEOUSNESS ALL OUR DAYS   033 28
BE USED ON ROGATION SUNDAY AND THE ROGATION DAYS   R 039 02
AND OBEDIENT WALKING BEFORE THEE ALL OUR DAYS   050 28
THE RESIDUE OF HIS DAYS TO AN HUMBLE, HOLY, AND   053 06
THOU DIDST IN THEIR DAYS, AND IN THE OLD TIME BEFORE   058 30
SIX DAYS SHALT THOU LABOUR, AND DO ALL THAT THOU HAST   068 25
FOR IN SIX DAYS THE LORD MADE HEAVEN AND EARTH, THE   068 29
THAT THY DAYS MAY BE LONG IN THE LAND WHICH THE LORD   069 03
PEOPLE WHAT HOLY DAYS, OR FASTING DAYS, ARE IN THE   R 071 25
DAYS, OR FASTING DAYS, ARE IN THE WEEK FOLLOWING TO   R 071 25
ALL THE DAYS OF THEIR LIFE   074 29
AND SEVEN DAYS AFTER   R 077 13
AND SEVEN DAYS AFTER   R 077 21
AND SEVEN DAYS AFTER   R 078 06
AND SEVEN DAYS AFTER   R 078 13
AND SIX DAYS AFTER   R 078 24
AND SEVEN DAYS AFTER   R 079 21
AND OTHER HOLY DAYS, (THOUGH THERE BE NO SERMON OR   R 084 27
WITHIN FOURTEEN DAYS AFTER, AT THE FARTHEST   R 085 19
ALL THE DAYS OF OUR LIFE   086 23
HATH IN THESE LAST DAYS SPOKEN UNTO US BY HIS SON,   096 24
TO PASS IN THOSE DAYS, THAT THERE WENT OUT A DECREE   098 28
WERE THERE, THE DAYS WERE ACCOMPLISHED THAT SHE   099 06

DAYS　　　　　　　CONTINUED

THERE BE ANY MORE DAYS BEFORE THE SUNDAY FOLLOWING   R 103 34
AND WHEN EIGHT DAYS WERE ACCOMPLISHED FOR THE   106 19
OF JUDAEA, IN THE DAYS OF HEROD THE KING, BEHOLD,   108 31
HAD FULFILLED THE DAYS, AS THEY RETURNED, THE CHILD   110 21
THAT AFTER THREE DAYS THEY FOUND HIM IN THE TEMPLE,   110 28
THY PEACE ALL THE DAYS OF OUR LIFE   111 13
TO PASS IN THOSE DAYS, THAT JESUS CAME FROM NAZARETH   112 18
OF THOSE DAYS SHALL THE SUN BE DARKENED, AND THE MOON   118 14
DIDST FAST FORTY DAYS AND FORTY NIGHTS   125 27
HE HAD FASTED FORTY DAYS AND FORTY NIGHTS, HE WAS   126 25
IT IN THREE DAYS, SAVE THYSELF   137 07
THEM ALL THE DAYS OF OLD   139 04
HE REMEMBERED THE DAYS OF OLD, MOSES, AND HIS PEOPLE,   139 07
AFTER TWO DAYS WAS THE FEAST OF THE PASSOVER,   139 32
AND WITHIN THREE DAYS I WILL BUILD ANOTHER MADE   143 08
IT IN THREE DAYS, SAVE THYSELF, AND COME DOWN FROM   146 20
BEHOLD, THE DAYS ARE COMING, IN THE WHICH THEY   154 15
THEM AFTER THOSE DAYS, SAITH THE LORD, I WILL PUT MY   158 12
GOD WAITED IN THE DAYS OF NOAH, WHILE THE ARK WAS A   161 27
AFTER THREE DAYS I WILL RISE AGAIN   162 18
THINGS WHICH ARE COME TO PASS THERE IN THESE DAYS   167 15
HE WAS SEEN MANY DAYS OF THEM WHICH CAME UP WITH HIM   169 03
WORK A WORK IN YOUR DAYS, A WORK WHICH YE SHALL IN NO   169 25
SEEN OF THEM FORTY DAYS, AND SPEAKING OF THE THINGS   177 28
HOLY GHOST NOT MANY DAYS HENCE   178 04
THEN PRAYED THEY HIM TO TARRY CERTAIN DAYS   184 30
AND SEE GOOD DAYS, LET HIM REFRAIN HIS TONGUE   195 25
IN THOSE DAYS THE MULTITUDE BEING VERY GREAT,   199 08
BEEN WITH ME THREE DAYS, AND HAVE NOTHING TO EAT   199 11
AND NOT MANY DAYS AFTER THE YOUNGER SON GATHERED ALL   202 02
FOR THE DAYS SHALL COME UPON THEE, THAT THINE ENEMIES   204 10
BECAUSE THE DAYS ARE EVIL   217 24
BEHOLD, THE DAYS COME, SAITH THE LORD, THAT I WILL   225 09
IN HIS DAYS JUDAH SHALL BE SAVED, AND ISRAEL SHALL   225 12
BEHOLD, THE DAYS COME, SAITH THE LORD, THAT THEY   225 15
AND AFTER EIGHT DAYS AGAIN HIS DISCIPLES WERE WITHIN,   228 31
AND HE WAS THREE DAYS WITHOUT SIGHT, AND NEITHER DID   230 12
WAS SAUL CERTAIN DAYS WITH THE DISCIPLES WHICH WERE   231 02
THE LORD, AS IN THE DAYS OF OLD, AND AS IN FORMER   232 14
AND WHEN THE DAYS OF HER PURIFICATION ACCORDING TO   232 23
IN THOSE DAYS PETER STOOD UP IN THE MIDST OF THE   234 06
AND IN THESE DAYS CAME PROPHETS FROM JERUSALEM UNTO   241 15
CAME TO PASS IN THE DAYS OF CLAUDIUS CAESAR   241 19
BEFORE HIM, ALL THE DAYS OF OUR LIFE   244 09
THEN WERE THE DAYS OF UNLEAVENED BREAD   245 03
IN THESE DAYS CAME PROPHETS FROM JERUSALEM UNTO   246 24
CAME TO PASS IN THE DAYS OF CLAUDIUS CAESAR   246 27
PASS ABOUT AN EIGHT DAYS AFTER THESE SAYINGS, HE TOOK   248 23
NO MAN IN THOSE DAYS ANY OF THOSE THINGS WHICH THEY   249 10
BE ADMINISTERED UPON SUNDAYS AND OTHER HOLY DAYS   R 273 05
IN THE SAME ALL THE DAYS OF THY LIFE   277 06
IN THE SAME ALL THE DAYS OF THY LIFE   278 15
IN THE SAME ALL THE DAYS OF MY LIFE   283 28
SIX DAYS SHALT THOU LABOUR, AND DO ALL THAT THOU HAST   286 25
FOR IN SIX DAYS THE LORD MADE HEAVEN AND EARTH, THE   286 29
THAT THY DAYS MAY BE LONG IN THE LAND WHICH THE LORD   287 02
HIM TRULY ALL THE DAYS OF MY LIFE   288 22
SUNDAYS AND HOLY DAYS, OR ON SOME OTHER CONVENIENT   R 295 08
HAVE CONSIDERED THE DAYS OF OLD   310 26
HAVE CONSIDERED THE DAYS OF OLD, AND THE YEARS THAT   311 08
O GOD, WHOSE DAYS ARE WITHOUT END, AND WHOSE MERCIES   316 25
US IN HOLINESS AND RIGHTEOUSNESS, ALL OUR DAYS   316 29
AND THE NUMBER OF MY DAYS   324 21
THOU HAST MADE MY DAYS AS IT WERE A SPAN LONG,   324 22
ART ANGRY ALL OUR DAYS ARE GONE   325 30
THE DAYS OF OUR AGE ARE THREESCORE YEARS AND TEN   325 32
US TO NUMBER OUR DAYS, *   326 02
OF THE LORD ALL THE DAYS OF MY LIFE, TO BEHOLD THE   326 10
FOLLOW ME ALL THE DAYS OF MY LIFE   338 30
FOLLOW ME ALL THE DAYS OF MY LIFE   368 23
OF THE LORD ALL THE DAYS OF MY LIFE, TO BEHOLD THE   372 02
AND WOULD FAIN SEE GOOD DAYS   380 26
LORD KNOWETH THE DAYS OF THE GODLY   385 31
AND IN THE DAYS OF DEARTH THEY SHALL HAVE ENOUGH   385 34
AND THE NUMBER OF MY DAYS   389 16
THOU HAST MADE MY DAYS AS IT WERE A SPAN LONG, AND   389 17
I FEAR IN THE DAYS OF EVIL, *   400 14
DECEITFUL MEN SHALL NOT LIVE OUT HALF THEIR DAYS   408 09
HAVE CONSIDERED THE DAYS OF OLD, *   433 25
33 THEREFORE THEIR DAYS DID HE CONSUME IN VANITY,   437 04
HIS THRONE AS THE DAYS OF HEAVEN   451 34
44 THE DAYS OF HIS YOUTH HAST THOU SHORTENED,   452 30
ART ANGRY ALL OUR DAYS ARE GONE   454 04
10 THE DAYS OF OUR AGE ARE THREESCORE YEARS AND TEN   454 07
US TO NUMBER OUR DAYS, *   454 13
AND BE GLAD ALL THE DAYS OF OUR LIFE   454 18
3 FOR MY DAYS ARE CONSUMED AWAY LIKE SMOKE, *   464 15
11 MY DAYS ARE GONE LIKE A SHADOW, *   464 31
AND SHORTENED MY DAYS   465 27
15 THE DAYS OF MAN ARE BUT AS GRASS   467 04
7 LET HIS DAYS BE FEW   480 17
84 HOW MANY ARE THE DAYS OF THY SERVANT   495 25
IN THE SAME ALL THE DAYS OF MY LIFE   577 19
SIX DAYS SHALT THOU LABOUR, AND DO ALL THAT THOU HAST   579 05
FOR IN SIX DAYS THE LORD MADE HEAVEN AND EARTH,   579 10
THAT THY DAYS MAY BE LONG IN THE LAND WHICH THE LORD   579 13
HIM TRULY ALL THE DAYS OF MY LIFE   579 32
SUNDAYS AND HOLY DAYS, OR ON SOME OTHER CONVENIENT   R 582 28
AND ON OTHER DAYS WHEN IT MAY BE CONVENIENT, IT WILL   R 592 05
OF THEE, THAT THE DAYS TO COME MAY BE SPENT IN THY   595 15
O LORD, AS HIS DAYS INCREASE   597 28
ABIDE ALL THE DAYS OF HIS LIFE   598 03

DAYSPRING

WHEREBY THE DAYSPRING FROM ON HIGH HATH VISITED US,   244 14

DEACON

OF A PRIEST, A DEACON MAY SAY ALL THAT IS BEFORE   R 084 25
WHAT IS THE OFFICE OF A DEACON   294 16
THE OFFICE OF A DEACON IS, TO ASSIST THE PRIEST IN   294 17
OR DEACON, IN THIS CHURCH, OR SUFFERED TO   529 20
BE ADMITTED A DEACON, PRIEST, OR BISHOP, EXCEPT HE BE   529 24
ADMIT HIM A DEACON, IN SUCH MANNER AND FORM AS   529 31
THE OFFICE OF A DEACON, BEING FOUND BLAMELESS   531 31
THE OFFICE OF A DEACON WELL PURCHASE TO THEMSELVES A   532 03
THE OFFICE OF A DEACON, IN THE CHURCH WHERE HE SHALL   533 10
ONE TO BE MADE DEACON, HUMBLY KNEELING BEFORE HIM,   R 534 03
THE OFFICE OF A DEACON IN THE CHURCH OF GOD COMMITTED   534 05
DECLARED UNTO THE DEACON, THAT HE MUST CONTINUE IN   R 535 19
THAT OFFICE OF A DEACON THE SPACE OF A WHOLE YEAR,   R 535 20
TO THE OFFICE OF DEACON AND THESE THY SERVANTS NOW   547 34

DEACONS

ALL PRIESTS AND DEACONS (AND HEREIN MORE ESPECIALLY   047 26
AND DEACONS, WITH TRUE KNOWLEDGE AND   055 31
THE DEACONS, CHURCH-WARDENS, OR OTHER FIT PERSONS   R 073 27
AND DEACONS, IN LIKE MANNER, (IF ANY BE   R 082 26
PRIESTS, AND DEACONS   294 05
-- BISHOPS, PRIESTS, AND DEACONS   529 13
AND OFFICE OF SUCH AS COME TO BE ADMITTED DEACONS   R 530 05
TO BE ORDAINED DEACONS, EACH OF THEM BEING DECENTLY   R 530 08
YOU THESE PERSONS PRESENT, TO BE ADMITTED DEACONS   530 11
TO BE ORDERED DEACONS, FOR THE WHICH HE OUGHT NOT TO   530 23
TO THE ORDER OF DEACONS, AND TO POUR THY GRACE UPON   531 05
THE ORDER OF DEACONS THE FIRST MARTYR SAINT STEPHEN,   531 17
MUST THE DEACONS BE GRAVE, NOT DOUBLETONGUED,   531 27
LET THE DEACONS BE THE HUSBANDS OF ONE WIFE, RULING   531 33
THE OFFICE OF DEACONS IN THY CHURCH   535 02
THE ORDER OF DEACONS BE GIVEN TO SOME, AND THE ORDER   R 547 13
THE DEACONS SHALL BE FIRST PRESENTED, AND THEN THE   R 547 20
ARE TO BE MADE DEACONS, SHALL BE EXAMINED AND   R 547 23
THE ORDERING OF DEACONS,) THEY THAT ARE TO BE MADE   R 547 27
AND DEACONS, WITH LOVE OF THEE AND OF THY   560 19
ORDINATION OF DEACONS OR OF PRIESTS SHALL BE SAID,   R 560 25
TO THE ORDER OF DEACONS (OR PRIESTS), AND TO POUR THY   560 27
AND DEACONS, ARE NOT COMMANDED BY GOD'S LAW,   609 21
OF PRIESTS AND DEACONS, AS SET FORTH BY THE GENERAL   610 31

DEAD

WAS CRUCIFIED, DEAD, AND BURIED   015 23
THE THIRD DAY HE ROSE AGAIN FROM THE DEAD   015 25
HE SHALL COME TO JUDGE THE QUICK AND THE DEAD   015 27
WITH GLORY, TO JUDGE BOTH THE QUICK AND THE DEAD   016 13
AND I LOOK FOR THE RESURRECTION OF THE DEAD   016 21
WAS CRUCIFIED, DEAD, AND BURIED   029 28
THE THIRD DAY HE ROSE AGAIN FROM THE DEAD   029 30
HE SHALL COME TO JUDGE THE QUICK AND THE DEAD   029 32
WITH GLORY, TO JUDGE BOTH THE QUICK AND THE DEAD   030 18
AND I LOOK FOR THE RESURRECTION OF THE DEAD   030 26
IN WHOSE HANDS ARE THE LIVING AND THE DEAD   042 15
TO JUDGE BOTH THE QUICK AND THE DEAD   071 15
AND I LOOK FOR THE RESURRECTION OF THE DEAD   071 23
THE QUICK AND THE DEAD, WE MAY RISE TO THE LIFE   090 17
THE DEAF HEAR, THE DEAD ARE RAISED UP, AND THE POOR   094 22
WHEN HEROD WAS DEAD, BEHOLD, AN ANGEL OF THE LORD   107 12
FOR THEY ARE DEAD WHICH SOUGHT THE YOUNG CHILD'S   107 15
LIVETH IS COUNTED DEAD BEFORE THEE   122 18
AND ARISE FROM THE DEAD, AND CHRIST SHALL GIVE THEE   129 22
CONSCIENCE FROM DEAD WORKS TO SERVE THE LIVING GOD   133 03
ABRAHAM IS DEAD, AND THE PROPHETS   133 19
GREATER THAN OUR FATHER ABRAHAM, WHICH IS DEAD   133 22
AND THE PROPHETS ARE DEAD   133 22
FOR A TESTAMENT IS OF FORCE AFTER MEN ARE DEAD   147 16
AND SAW THAT HE WAS DEAD ALREADY, THEY BRAKE NOT HIS   161 02
SAY UNTO THE PEOPLE, HE IS RISEN FROM THE DEAD   162 22
RAISED FROM THE DEAD DIETH NO MORE   163 04
YOURSELVES TO BE DEAD INDEED UNTO SIN, *   163 08
IS RISEN FROM THE DEAD, *   163 11
BY MAN CAME ALSO THE RESURRECTION OF THE DEAD   163 14
FOR YE ARE DEAD, AND YOUR LIFE IS HID WITH CHRIST IN   164 06
THAT HE MUST RISE AGAIN FROM THE DEAD   164 28
AND DRINK WITH HIM AFTER HE ROSE FROM THE DEAD   166 28
ORDAINED OF GOD TO BE THE JUDGE OF QUICK AND DEAD   166 30
BUT GOD RAISED HIM FROM THE DEAD   169 03
HIM UP FROM THE DEAD, NOW NO MORE TO RETURN TO   169 11
TO RISE FROM THE DEAD THE THIRD DAY   170 13
THAT WE, BEING DEAD TO SINS, SHOULD LIVE UNTO   172 16
AND DRINK WITH HIM AFTER HE ROSE FROM THE DEAD   184 15
ORDAINED OF GOD TO BE THE JUDGE OF QUICK AND DEAD   184 18
UNTO THEM FROM THE DEAD, THEY WILL REPENT   190 28
THEY BE PERSUADED, THOUGH ONE ROSE FROM THE DEAD   190 31
RAISED UP FROM THE DEAD BY THE GLORY OF THE FATHER,   197 13
FOR HE THAT IS DEAD IS FREED FROM SIN   197 19
NOW IF WE BE DEAD WITH CHRIST, WE BELIEVE THAT WE   197 20
RAISED FROM THE DEAD DIETH NO MORE   197 22
YOURSELVES TO BE DEAD INDEED UNTO SIN, BUT ALIVE UNTO   197 25
FOR THIS MY SON WAS DEAD, AND IS ALIVE AGAIN   202 24
THY BROTHER WAS DEAD, AND IS ALIVE AGAIN   203 07
AND DEPARTED, LEAVING HIM HALF DEAD   208 24
BEHOLD, THERE WAS A DEAD MAN CARRIED OUT, THE ONLY   212 30
AND HE THAT WAS DEAD SAT UP, AND BEGAN TO SPEAK   213 05
MY DAUGHTER IS EVEN NOW DEAD   224 14
FOR THE MAID IS NOT DEAD, BUT SLEEPETH   224 26
RAISED HIM FROM THE DEAD, THOU SHALT BE SAVED   226 28

DEAD   CONTINUED

AND THE DEAD IN CHRIST SHALL RISE FIRST   269 07
AND THE RESURRECTION OF THE DEAD   274 11
THAT HE, BEING DEAD UNTO SIN, MAY LIVE UNTO   280 33
WAS CRUCIFIED, DEAD, AND BURIED   284 17
THE THIRD DAY HE ROSE AGAIN FROM THE DEAD   284 19
HE SHALL COME TO JUDGE THE QUICK AND THE DEAD   284 21
DID EAT MANNA IN THE WILDERNESS, AND ARE DEAD   322 24
THOUGH HE WERE DEAD, YET SHALL HE LIVE   324 06
RISEN FROM THE DEAD, AND BECOME THE FIRSTFRUITS OF   328 21
BY MAN CAME ALSO THE RESURRECTION OF THE DEAD   328 23
HOW ARE THE DEAD RAISED UP   329 05
SO ALSO IS THE RESURRECTION OF THE DEAD   329 19
AND THE DEAD SHALL BE RAISED INCORRUPTIBLE,   330 04
UP JESUS FROM THE DEAD WILL ALSO QUICKEN OUR MORTAL   333 05
THE EARTH AND THE SEA SHALL GIVE UP THEIR DEAD   333 20
BLESSED ARE THE DEAD WHO DIE IN THE LORD   333 26
AGAIN FROM THE DEAD OUR LORD JESUS CHRIST, THE GREAT   335 16
BLESSED ARE THE DEAD WHO DIE IN THE LORD   335 27
THE SEA SHALL GIVE UP HER DEAD   337 14
THOUGH HE WERE DEAD, YET SHALL HE LIVE   338 06
FORGOTTEN AS A DEAD MAN OUT OF MIND   376 19
2 THE DEAD BODIES OF THY SERVANTS HAVE THEY GIVEN TO   439 32
CAST OFF AMONG THE DEAD, LIKE UNTO THEM THAT ARE   449 04
10 DOST THOU SHOW WONDERS AMONG THE DEAD   449 16
OR SHALL THE DEAD RISE UP AGAIN, AND PRAISE THEE   449 17
AND ATE THE OFFERINGS OF THE DEAD   474 26
THE PLACES WITH THE DEAD BODIES, AND SMITE IN SUNDER   482 19
17 THE DEAD PRAISE NOT THEE, O LORD, *   486 12
AS THE MEN THAT HAVE BEEN LONG DEAD   518 29
AGAIN FROM THE DEAD OUR LORD JESUS CHRIST, THE GREAT   573 03
WAS CRUCIFIED, DEAD, AND BURIED   577 32
THE THIRD DAY HE ROSE AGAIN FROM THE DEAD   578 03
HE SHALL COME TO JUDGE THE QUICK AND THE DEAD   578 05
JUDGE OF QUICK AND DEAD, THY SON JESUS CHRIST OUR   588 24
OF THOSE WHO LABOUR, AND THE REPOSE OF THE DEAD   595 06
WAS CRUCIFIED, DEAD, AND BURIED, TO RECONCILE HIS   603 15
THE QUICK AND THE DEAD, TO HAVE REMISSION OF PAIN OR   609 18

DEADLY

US A DRINK OF DEADLY WINE   412 18
NOT EVERY DEADLY SIN WILLINGLY COMMITTED AFTER   605 39

DEAF

AND THE DEAF HEAR, THE DEAD ARE RAISED UP,   094 22
HIM ONE THAT WAS DEAF, AND HAD AN IMPEDIMENT IN HIS   206 30
HE MAKETH BOTH THE DEAF TO HEAR, AND THE DUMB TO   207 08
I WAS LIKE A DEAF MAN, AND HEARD NOT   388 17
EVEN LIKE THE DEAF ADDER, THAT STOPPETH HER EARS   410 16

DEAL

O LORD, DEAL NOT WITH US ACCORDING TO OUR SINS   058 12
THE MORE A GREAT DEAL THEY PUBLISHED IT   207 06
DEAL GRACIOUSLY, WE PRAY THEE, WITH ALL THOSE WHO   342 10
AND YOUR HANDS DEAL WITH WICKEDNESS   410 11
UNTO THE FOOLS, DEAL NOT SO MADLY   432 06
20 BUT DEAL THOU WITH ME, O LORD GOD, ACCORDING UNTO   481 12
I DEAL WITH THE THING THAT IS LAWFUL AND RIGHT   498 11
124 O DEAL WITH THY SERVANT ACCORDING UNTO THY LOVING   498 17

DEALING

MY RIGHTEOUS DEALING, *   361 06
MY RIGHTEOUS DEALING, *   361 16
AND RIGHTEOUS DEALING WAIT UPON ME   370 26
AND REJOICE, THAT FAVOUR MY RIGHTEOUS DEALING   383 20
AND THY JUST DEALING AS THE NOON-DAY   385 05

DEALINGS

TO BE TRUE AND JUST IN ALL MY DEALINGS   289 05
THE WRONGFUL DEALINGS OF MEN   499 06
TO BE TRUE AND JUST IN ALL MY DEALINGS   580 08
GRACE TO BE JUST AND UPRIGHT IN ALL OUR DEALINGS   588 31

DEALT

AS GOD HATH DEALT TO EVERY MAN THE MEASURE OF FAITH   110 12
WHY HAST THOU THUS DEALT WITH US   110 33
EVIL UNTO HIM THAT DEALT FRIENDLY WITH ME   349 29
BECAUSE HE HATH DEALT SO LOVINGLY WITH ME   356 09
10 HE HATH NOT DEALT WITH US AFTER OUR SINS   466 25
AND DEALT UNTRULY WITH HIS SERVANTS   471 23
DONE AMISS, AND DEALT WICKEDLY   473 12
O LORD, THOU HAST DEALT GRACIOUSLY WITH THY SERVANT,   494 11
20 HE HATH NOT DEALT SO WITH ANY NATION   524 02

DEAR

BLOOD OF THY DEAR SON   038 27
BY THE BLOOD OF THY DEAR SON, AND INCLINE THE HEARTS   039 18
THE FLESH OF THY DEAR SON JESUS CHRIST, AND TO DRINK   082 10
OF GOD, AS DEAR CHILDREN   128 30
WHOSE MOST DEAR SON WENT NOT UP TO JOY BUT FIRST   138 04
WHOSE DEAR SON, ON THE NIGHT BEFORE HE   152 07
OF EPAPHRAS OUR DEAR FELLOW-SERVANT, WHO IS FOR YOU A   223 30
THY SERVANT, OUR DEAR BROTHER, INTO THY HANDS,   317 14
O GOD, WHOSE MOST DEAR SON DID TAKE LITTLE CHILDREN   342 03
AND DEAR SHALL THEIR BLOOD BE IN HIS SIGHT   427 25
RIGHT DEAR IN THE SIGHT OF THE LORD IS THE DEATH OF   487 14
17 HOW DEAR ARE THY COUNSELS UNTO ME, O GOD   515 24
COUNT I MY LIFE DEAR UNTO MYSELF, SO THAT I MIGHT   550 19

DEAR   CONTINUED

AND ALL WHO ARE DEAR TO US, UNDER THY FATHERLY   589 04
ENTRUST ALL WHO ARE DEAR TO US TO THY NEVER-FAILING   597 09
FOR THE LOVE OF THY DEAR SON, OUR SAVIOUR JESUS   600 12

DEARER

OF THY MOUTH IS DEARER UNTO ME *   494 24

DEARLY

SHALL SAY, DEARLY BELOVED BRETHREN, THE SCRIPTURE   005 29
DEARLY BELOVED BRETHREN, THE SCRIPTURE MOVETH US,   023 04
THROUGH THY MOST DEARLY BELOVED SON JESUS CHRIST OUR   078 16
OF THY DEARLY BELOVED SON OUR SAVIOUR JESUS CHRIST,   080 38
DEARLY BELOVED IN THE LORD, YE WHO MIND TO COME TC   085 25
DEARLY BELOVED, ON -- DAY NEXT I PURPOSE, THROUGH   086 28
DEARLY BELOVED BRETHREN, ON -- INTEND, BY GOD'S   088 12
MOST DEARLY BELOVED IN CHRIST, TAKE YE   088 24
DEARLY BELOVED, AVENGE NOT YOURSELVES, BUT RATHER   113 03
DEARLY BELOVED, I BESEECH YOU AS STRANGERS AND   173 12
DEARLY BELOVED, FORASMUCH AS OUR SAVIOUR CHRIST   273 29
DEARLY BELOVED, YE HAVE BROUGHT THIS CHILD HERE TC BE   276 19
FOR THAT THY DEARLY BELOVED SON JESUS CHRIST,   279 09
SEEING NOW, DEARLY BELOVED BRETHREN, THAT THIS   280 13
SHALL SAY, DEARLY BELOVED, WE ARE GATHERED TOGETHER   300 08
OF THY MOST DEARLY BELOVED SON, JESUS CHRIST OUR   314 12
THY ONLY AND MOST DEARLY BELOVED SON JESUS CHRIST,   545 14
THY ONLY AND DEARLY BELOVED SCN JESUS CHRIST, TC BE   557 12
HE SHALL SAY, DEARLY BELOVED IN THE LORD   564 10
SHALL SAY, DEARLY BELOVED IN THE LORD, WE HAVE   570 12

DEARTH

THE SCARCITY AND DEARTH, WHICH WE NOW MOST JUSTLY   041 03
AND TURNED OUR DEARTH AND SCARCITY INTO PLENTY   051 32
SHOULD BE GREAT DEARTH THROUGHOUT ALL THE WORLD   241 18
SHOULD BE GREAT DEARTH THROUGHOUT ALL THE WORLD   246 26
AND TO FEED THEM IN THE TIME OF DEARTH   379 27
IN THE DAYS OF DEARTH THEY SHALL HAVE ENOUGH   385 34
HE CALLED FOR A DEARTH UPON THE LAND, *   471 04

DEATH

DESIRETH NOT THE DEATH OF A SINNER, BUT RATHER THAT   007 07
THE SHARPNESS OF DEATH, THOU DIDST OPEN THE KINGCCM   010 28
IN THE SHADOW OF DEATH, *   014 32
DESIRETH NOT THE DEATH OF A SINNER, BUT RATHER THAT   024 09
DOWN THE KINGDOM OF SIN, SATAN, AND DEATH   037 05
THE MERITS AND DEATH OF JESUS CHRIST OUR SAVIOUR   037 07
NEAR APPROACH OF DEATH, ESPECIALLY NEED OUR PRAYERS   048 09
AND FROM SUDDEN DEATH, FROM ALL SEDITION, PRIVY   054 32
BY THY PRECIOUS DEATH AND BURIAL   055 11
IN THE HOUR OF DEATH, AND IN THE DAY OF JUDGMENT,   055 16
WOULDEST NOT THE DEATH OF A SINNER, BUT RATHER THAT   062 15
WHO BY HIS DEATH HATH DESTROYED DEATH, AND BY HIS   078 11
HATH DESTROYED DEATH, AND BY HIS RISING TO LIFE AGAIN   078 11
FOR THE PRECIOUS DEATH AND MERITS OF THY SCN JESUS   079 15
CHRIST TO SUFFER DEATH UPON THE CROSS FOR CUR   080 08
THAT HIS PRECIOUS DEATH AND SACRIFICE, UNTIL HIS   080 15
AND PRECIOUS DEATH, HIS MIGHTY RESURRECTICN AND   081 03
REMEMBRANCE OF HIS DEATH AND PASSION, MAY BE   081 13
BY THE MERITS AND DEATH OF THY SON JESUS CHRIST,   081 18
HIS MOST PRECIOUS DEATH AND PASSION   083 25
THE WORLD BY THE DEATH AND PASSION OF OUR SAVIOUR   086 07
EVEN TO THE DEATH UPON THE CROSS, FOR US, MISERABLE   086 09
WHO LAY IN DARKNESS AND THE SHADOW OF DEATH   086 10
REMEMBRANCE OF HIS DEATH, TO OUR GREAT AND ENDLESS   086 18
UP HIS SOUL BY DEATH UPON THE CROSS FOR YOUR   089 10
SACRIFICE OF HIS DEATH, AS HE HIMSELF HATH COMMANDED   089 13
FAITH EVEN UNTO DEATH, WE MAY GLORIFY THY HCLY NAME   102 26
THERE UNTIL THE DEATH OF HEROD   102 32
AND THEY SHALL SCOURGE HIM, AND PUT HIM TO DEATH   123 23
THAT BY MEANS OF DEATH, FOR THE REDEMPTION CF THE   133 05
IF A MAN KEEP MY SAYING, HE SHALL NEVER SEE DEATH   133 18
MAN KEEP MY SAYING, HE SHALL NEVER TASTE OF DEATH   133 21
AND TO SUFFER DEATH UPON THE CROSS, THAT ALL MANKIND   134 07
OBEDIENT UNTO DEATH, EVEN THE DEATH OF THE CROSS   134 21
DEATH, EVEN THE DEATH OF THE CROSS   134 22
TOOK COUNSEL AGAINST JESUS TO PUT HIM TC DEATH   134 32
MIGHT TAKE HIM BY CRAFT, AND PLT HIM TO DEATH   139 35
MY SOUL IS EXCEEDING SORROWFUL UNTO DEATH   141 32
FOR WITNESS AGAINST JESUS TO PUT HIM TO DEATH   143 03
AND THEY ALL CONDEMNED HIM TO BE GUILTY OF DEATH   143 19
NECESSITY BE THE DEATH OF THE TESTATOR   147 15
BOTH INTO PRISON, AND TO DEATH   149 35
DO SHEW THE LORD'S DEATH TILL HE COME   152 25
NOTHING WORTHY OF DEATH IS DONE UNTO HIM   153 27
FOUND NO CAUSE OF DEATH IN HIM   153 35
LED WITH HIM TO BE PUT TO DEATH   154 22
AND TO SUFFER DEATH UPON THE CROSS   156 24
NOR DESIREST THE DEATH OF A SINNER, BUT RATHER THAT   157 05
BAPTIZED INTO THE DEATH OF THY BLESSED SCN, OUR   161 14
AND GATE OF DEATH, WE MAY PASS TO OUR JOYFUL   161 17
BEING PUT TO DEATH IN THE FLESH, BUT QUICKENED   161 24
DEATH HATH NO MORE DOMINION OVER HIM   163 05
SINCE BY MAN CAME DEATH, *   163 13
HAST OVERCOME DEATH, AND OPENED UNTO US THE GATE OF   163 23
SON TO THE DEATH OF THE CROSS, AND BY HIS GLORICUS   165 04
TO BE CONDEMNED TO DEATH, AND HAVE CRUCIFIED HIM   167 19
FOUND NO CAUSE OF DEATH IN HIM, YET DESIRED THEY   168 30
HAVE PASSED FROM DEATH UNTO LIFE, BECAUSE WE LOVE THE   191 12
HE THAT LOVETH NOT HIS BROTHER ABIDETH IN DEATH   191 14
INTO JESUS CHRIST WERE BAPTIZED INTO HIS DEATH   197 11
WE ARE BURIED WITH HIM BY BAPTISM INTO DEATH   197 12

DEATH   CONTINUED

LIKENESS OF HIS DEATH, WE SHALL BE ALSO IN THE   197 16
DEATH HATH NO MORE DOMINION OVER HIM   197 22
FOR THE END OF THOSE THINGS IS DEATH   199 02
FOR THE WAGES OF SIN IS DEATH   199 04
MINISTRATION OF DEATH, WRITTEN AND ENGRAVEN IN   206 18
FOR HE WAS AT THE POINT OF DEATH   219 32
HE SHOULD NOT SEE DEATH, BEFORE HE HAD SEEN THE   232 34
IN THE SHADOW OF DEATH, TO GUIDE OUR FEET INTO THE   244 16
AND THEY LOVED NOT THEIR LIVES UNTO THE DEATH   252 16
WITH CHRIST IN HIS DEATH, MAY ALSO BE PARTAKER OF HIS   281 02
IN BAPTISM IS A DEATH UNTO SIN, AND A NEW BIRTH LNTC   292 25
SACRIFICE OF THE DEATH OF CHRIST, AND OF THE BENEFITS   293 06
WITH A THANKFUL REMEMBRANCE OF HIS DEATH   293 29
TO CHERISH, TILL DEATH US DO PART, ACCORDING TO GOD'S   301 31
TO CHERISH, TILL DEATH US DO PART, ACCCRDING TC GCD'S   302 07
BY THY PRECIOUS DEATH AND BURIAL   318 05
THE POWER OF THE EVIL ONE, AND FROM ETERNAL DEATH   318 13
DESIREST NOT THE DEATH OF A SINNER   319 07
BUT IS PASSED FROM DEATH UNTO LIFE   322 03
HATH SUFFERED DEATH UPON THE CROSS FOR HIM, AND SHED R 323 27
SINCE BY MAN CAME DEATH, BY MAN CAME ALSO THE   328 23
THE LAST ENEMY THAT SHALL BE DESTROYED IS DEATH   328 31
THAT IS WRITTEN, DEATH IS SWALLOWED UP IN VICTORY   330 09
O DEATH, WHERE IS THY STING   330 10
THE STING OF DEATH IS SIN   330 11
THAT NEITHER DEATH, NOR LIFE, NOR ANGELS, NCR   331 10
IN THE MIDST OF LIFE WE ARE IN DEATH   332 22
US NOT INTO THE BITTER PAINS OF ETERNAL DEATH   332 27
FOR ANY PAINS OF DEATH, TO FALL FROM THEE   332 32
RAISE US FROM THE DEATH OF SIN UNTO THE LIFE CF   335 06
WHO BY THY DEATH DIDST TAKE AWAY THE STING OF   336 10
BY THY DEATH DIDST TAKE AWAY THE STING OF DEATH   336 11
OF THE SHADOW OF DEATH, I WILL FEAR NO EVIL   338 24
5 FOR IN DEATH NO MAN REMEMBERETH THEE   349 08
HE HATH PREPARED FOR HIM THE INSTRUMENTS OF DEATH   350 19
THOU LIFTEST ME UP FROM THE GATES OF DEATH   352 18
THAT I SLEEP NOT IN DEATH   356 03
4 THE SORROWS OF DEATH COMPASSED ME, *   359 31
THE SNARES OF DEATH OVERTOOK ME   360 02
AND THOU BRINGEST ME INTO THE DUST OF DEATH   367 03
OF THE SHADOW OF DEATH, I WILL FEAR NO EVIL   368 17
THEIR SOUL FROM DEATH, *   379 26
AND COVERED US WITH THE SHADOW OF DEATH   395 33
HE SHALL BE OUR GUIDE UNTO DEATH   400 05
DEATH IS THEIR SHEPHERD   400 34
AND THE FEAR OF DEATH IS FALLEN UPON ME   406 27
16 LET DEATH COME HASTILY UPON THEM, AND LET THEM GC   407 20
MY SOUL FROM DEATH, AND MY FEET FROM FALLING, *   409 08
GOD IS THE LORD, BY WHOM WE ESCAPE DEATH   420 26
4 FOR THEY ARE IN NO PERIL OF DEATH   428 16
AND SPARED NOT THEIR SOUL FROM DEATH   438 10
MAN IS HE THAT LIVETH, AND SHALL NOT SEE DEATH   453 03
AND PUT THE FATHERLESS TO DEATH   457 30
AND DELIVER THEM THAT ARE APPOINTED UNTO DEATH   465 21
IN THE SHADOW OF DEATH, *   476 24
OF THE SHADOW OF DEATH, *   477 03
3 THE SNARES OF DEATH COMPASSED ME RCUND ABCUT,   486 23
MY SOUL FROM DEATH, *   487 04
OF THE LORD IS THE DEATH OF HIS SAINTS   487 14
BUT HE HATH NOT GIVEN ME OVER UNTO DEATH   489 05
HE BOUGHT WITH HIS DEATH, AND FOR WHCM HE SHED HIS   540 07
REDEMPTION BY HIS DEATH, AND WAS ASCENDED INTO   545 16
REDEMPTION BY HIS DEATH, AND WAS ASCENDED INTO   557 24
SHALL BE NO MORE DEATH, NEITHER SORROW, NOR CRYING,   567 19
AND FROM EVERLASTING DEATH   581 04
A DEATH UNTO SIN, AND A NEW BIRTH UNTO   581 24
SACRIFICE OF THE DEATH OF CHRIST, AND OF THE BENEFITS   582 05
WITH A THANKFUL REMEMBRANCE OF HIS DEATH   582 25
DESIREST NOT THE DEATH OF A SINNER, LOOK UPCN HERE   589 33
SIN AND ETERNAL DEATH, AND IN GIVING US THE KNOWLEDGE   591 13
THE SHADOW OF DEATH INTO THE MORNING   594 12
RISE AGAIN FROM DEATH, AND TOOK AGAIN HIS BCDY,   603 21
A SACRAMENT OF OUR REDEMPTION BY CHRIST'S DEATH   608 36

DEATH'S

EVEN HARD AT DEATH'S DOOR   477 12

DEATHS

MADEST INFANTS TO GLORIFY THEE BY THEIR DEATHS   102 23
MORE FREQUENT, IN DEATHS OFT   120 32

DEBT

AND LOOSED HIM, AND FORGAVE HIM THE DEBT   221 22
CAST HIM INTO PRISON, TILL HE SHOULD PAY THE DEBT   221 30
THEE ALL THAT DEBT, BECAUSE THOU DESIREDST ME   221 34

DEBTORS

WE ARE DEBTORS, NOT TO THE FLESH, TO LIVE   200 03

DECALOGUE

THE DECALOGUE MAY BE OMITTED, PROVIDED IT BE SAID   R 067 28
IF THE DECALOGUE HATH BEEN OMITTED, SHALL BE   R 069 32

DECAPOLIS

THROUGH THE MIDST OF THE COASTS OF DECAPOLIS   206 29

DECAY

THAT THERE BE NO DECAY, *   520 22

DECAYED

HATH BEEN DECAYED BY THE FRAUD AND MALICE OF THE   314 04

DECAYETH

THE OUTWARD MAN DECAYETH, STRENGTHEN HIM, WE BESEECH   316 10

DECEASE

BE ABLE AFTER MY DECEASE TO HAVE THESE THINGS ALWAYS   248 12
AND SPAKE OF HIS DECEASE WHICH HE SHOULD ACCOMPLISH   248 29

DECEIT

FULL OF CURSING, DECEIT, AND FRAUD   353 18
THAT HATH USED NO DECEIT IN HIS TONGUE, NOR DONE EVIL 357 10
OF HIS MOUTH ARE UNRIGHTEOUS AND FULL OF DECEIT   383 31
AND IMAGINED DECEIT ALL THE DAY LONG   388 16
AND WITH THY TONGUE THOU HAST SET FORTH DECEIT   402 29
DECEIT AND GUILE GO NOT OUT OF HER STREETS   407 09
FOR THEY IMAGINE BUT DECEIT   498 05

DECEITFUL

TO THE DECEITFUL LUSTS   216 13
ME FROM THE DECEITFUL AND WICKED MAN   310 07
AND DECEITFUL MAN   348 12
ROOT OUT ALL DECEITFUL LIPS, *   355 12
NEITHER WILL I HAVE FELLOWSHIP WITH THE DECEITFUL   371 05
THEY IMAGINE DECEITFUL WORDS AGAINST THEM THAT ARE   383 03
ME FROM THE DECEITFUL AND WICKED MAN   394 05
AND DECEITFUL MEN SHALL NOT LIVE OUT HALF THEIR DAYS 408 08
THE CHILDREN OF MEN ARE DECEITFUL   414 16
THERE SHALL NO DECEITFUL PERSON DWELL IN MY HOUSE   464 02
MOUTH OF THE DECEITFUL IS OPENED UPON ME   480 04
AND FROM A DECEITFUL TONGUE   502 10

DECEITFULLY

NOR HANDLING THE WORD OF GOD DECEITFULLY   250 30

DECEITS

AND FROM ALL THE DECEITS OF THE WORLD, THE FLESH,   054 28
WERE BLASPHEMOUS FABLES, AND DANGEROUS DECEITS   609 19

DECEIVE

HAVE NO SIN, WE DECEIVE OURSELVES, AND THE TRUTH IS 022 10
HAVE NO SIN, WE DECEIVE OURSELVES, AND THE TRUTH IS 101 29
LET NO MAN DECEIVE YOU   117 26
THEY SHALL DECEIVE THE VERY ELECT   118 07
LET NO MAN DECEIVE YOU WITH VAIN WORDS   129 09
WHEREBY THEY LIE IN WAIT TO DECEIVE   237 28
NOR SWORN TO DECEIVE HIS NEIGHBOUR   369 04
NOR SWORN TO DECEIVE HIS NEIGHBOUR   563 19
HAVE NO SIN, WE DECEIVE OURSELVES, AND THE TRUTH IS 605 36

DECEIVED

OF TRUTH ALL SUCH AS HAVE ERRED, AND ARE DECEIVED   056 20

DECEIVER

THAT THAT DECEIVER SAID, WHILE HE WAS YET ALIVE,   162 17

DECEIVERS

AS DECEIVERS, AND YET TRUE   126 17

DECEIVETH

BUT DECEIVETH HIS OWN HEART, THIS MAN'S   176 14
WHICH DECEIVETH THE WHOLE WORLD   252 07
BUT DECEIVETH HIS OWN HEART, THIS MAN'S   266 05

DECEIVING

HEARERS ONLY, DECEIVING YOUR OWN SELVES   176 05
HEARERS ONLY, DECEIVING YOUR OWN SELVES   265 29

DECENCY

READINESS AND DECENCY BREAK THE BREAD BEFORE THE   R 080 03
OF THE NATURAL DECENCY OF THINGS, HAVE ERECTED HOUSES   564 14

DECENT

THE PEOPLE, IN A DECENT BASIN TO BE PROVIDED BY THE   R 073 29

DECENTLY

INTO THE CHURCH DECENTLY APPARELLED, AND THERE SHALL   R 305 08
OF THEM BEING DECENTLY HABITED, SAYING THESE WORDS,   R 530 09
OF THEM BEING DECENTLY HABITED, AND SHALL SAY,   R 536 09

DECK

17 I WILL DECK HER PRIESTS WITH HEALTH, *   509 06

DECKED

A RICH FEAST, DECKED HIS TABLE WITH ALL KIND OF   088 18

DECKEST

2 THOU DECKEST THYSELF WITH LIGHT AS IT WERE WITH A   467 27

DECLARATION

THE DECLARATION, WE RECEIVE THIS CHILD (OR PERSON),   R 282 05

DECLARE

TO DECLARE AND PRONOUNCE TO HIS PEOPLE,   007 09
TO DECLARE AND PRONOUNCE TO HIS PEOPLE,   024 11
AND WILL ALWAYS DECLARE THY LOVING-KINDNESS FROM   051 27
OR AT LEAST DECLARE HIMSELF TO BE IN FULL PURPOSE SO R 085 07
SEEN AND HEARD DECLARE WE UNTO YOU, THAT YE ALSO MAY 101 18
OF HIM, AND DECLARE UNTO YOU, THAT GOD IS LIGHT,   101 23
AND WE DECLARE UNTO YOU GLAD TIDINGS, HOW THAT THE   169 05
THOUGH A MAN DECLARE IT UNTO YOU   169 26
I DECLARE UNTO YOU THE GOSPEL WHICH I   204 29
YE ARE TO DECLARE IT   R 304 24
THE HEAVENS DECLARE THE GLORY OF GOD   363 13
22 I WILL DECLARE THY NAME UNTO MY BRETHREN   367 16
COME, AND SHALL DECLARE HIS RIGHTEOUSNESS *   368 06
OR SHALL IT DECLARE THY TRUTH   375 13
7 IF I SHOULD DECLARE THEM, AND SPEAK OF THEM,   390 25
HEAVENS SHALL DECLARE HIS RIGHTEOUSNESS   402 02
AND THAT DO THY WONDROUS WORKS DECLARE   431 33
I WILL DECLARE HARD SENTENCES OF OLD   434 29
3 DECLARE HIS HONOUR UNTO THE HEATHEN, *   460 04
21 THAT THEY MAY DECLARE THE NAME OF THE LORD IN   465 22
AND DECLARE THE WONDERS THAT HE DOETH FOR THE   476 20
AND DECLARE THE WONDERS THAT HE DOETH FOR THE   477 05
AND DECLARE THE WONDERS THAT HE DOETH FOR THE   477 18
AND DECLARE THE WONDERS THAT HE DOETH FOR THE   478 08
AND DECLARE THE WORKS OF THE LORD   489 02
AND DECLARE THY POWER   520 34
NOT SHUNNED TO DECLARE UNTO YOU ALL THE COUNSEL OF   550 26
BY THEM MEN DO DECLARE, THAT THEY DO NOT ONLY RENDER   605 26

DECLARED

AND HOMILIES, DECLARED THE NECESSITY AND EXPEDIENCY   V 22
TO THY PROMISES DECLARED UNTO MANKIND IN CHRIST JESUS 006 26
TO THY PROMISES DECLARED UNTO MANKIND IN CHRIST JESUS 023 33
THE LORD DECLARED HIS SALVATION   027 08
AND VIRTUE DECLARED IN ALL HIS SAINTS, WHO HAVE BEEN   048 16
FATHERS HAVE DECLARED UNTO US, THE NOBLE WORKS THAT   058 29
THEN SHALL BE DECLARED UNTO THE PEOPLE WHAT HOLY   R 071 25
HE HAVE OPENLY DECLARED HIMSELF TO HAVE TRULY   R 085 04
WHO ALSO DECLARED UNTO US YOUR LOVE IN THE SPIRIT   223 32
THIS PERSON), DECLARED BY HIS SON JESUS CHRIST   276 04
AND HAVE DECLARED THE SAME BY GIVING AND   304 06
AND VIRTUE DECLARED IN ALL THY SAINTS, WHO HAVE BEEN   336 18
11 I HAVE DECLARED THY RIGHTEOUSNESS IN THE GREAT   390 34
AND HAST DECLARED THY POWER AMONG THE PEOPLES   434 10
HEAVENS HAVE DECLARED HIS RIGHTEOUSNESS, *   461 08
3 THE LORD DECLARED HIS SALVATION   461 29
HERE IT MUST BE DECLARED UNTO THE DEACON, THAT HE   R 535 19
HAVE EXPRESSLY DECLARED UNTO US IN THE WORD OF GOD   606 29

DECLARES

AS SHE FURTHER DECLARES IN HER SAID PREFACE, TO DO   V 34
SO FAR AS IT DECLARES THE BOOKS OF HOMILIES TO BE AN R 610 24

DECLAREST

WHO DECLAREST THY GLORY AND SHOWEST FORTH THY   044 17
O GOD, WHO DECLAREST THY ALMIGHTY POWER CHIEFLY IN   204 22

DECLARING

AND DECLARING MY LOYALTY AND DEVOTION TO   291 25
DECLARING THE DUTY AND OFFICE OF SUCH AS   R 530 04
DECLARING THE DUTY AND OFFICE OF SUCH AS   R 536 04

DECREASE

AND SUFFERETH NOT THEIR CATTLE TO DECREASE   478 23

DECREE

THERE WENT OUT A DECREE FROM CAESAR AUGUSTUS, THAT   098 29
7 I WILL REHEARSE THE DECREE   346 10
HATH POWER TO DECREE RITES OR CEREMONIES, AND   607 03
IT OUGHT NOT TO DECREE ANY THING AGAINST THE SAME, SO 607 07
TO SAID FORM, WE DECREE ALL SUCH TO BE RIGHTLY,   610 35

DECREED

HATH CONSTANTLY DECREED BY HIS COUNSEL SECRET TO US,   606 07

DEDICATE

OF MANY TO DEDICATE THEMSELVES TO THE SACRED MINISTRY 039 19
WE HERE DEDICATE BOTH OUR SOULS AND OUR BODIES TO   588 05

DEDICATED

TESTAMENT WAS DEDICATED WITHOUT BLOOD   147 18
IS HERE DEDICATED TO THEE BY OUR OFFICE AND MINISTRY, 278 27

DEDICATING

AND DEDICATING IT TO THY SERVICE, FOR READING THY   565 07

DEDICATION

FOR THE DEDICATION OF THIS CHURCH   259 19
ACCEPT THE DEDICATION OF THIS PLACE TO THY SERVICE   567 06

DEED

WORD, AND DEED, AGAINST THY DIVINE MAJESTY,   075 21
BY WORD OR DEED, SO THAT THE CONGREGATION BE THEREBY R 085 02
BY WILL, WORD, OR DEED, THERE TO BEWAIL YOUR OWN   087 19
YE DO IN WORD OR DEED, DO ALL IN THE NAME OF THE LORD 116 14
A PROPHET MIGHTY IN DEED AND WORD BEFORE GOD AND ALL 167 17
THIS MAN SHALL BE BLESSED IN HIS DEED   176 13
WE MAY PLEASE THEE, BOTH IN WILL AND DEED   189 05
BUT IN DEED AND IN TRUTH   191 22
THE WORK, THIS MAN SHALL BE BLESSED IN HIS DEED   266 04
TO HURT NOBODY BY WORD OR DEED   288 32
SINNED AGAINST THEE IN THOUGHT, WORD, AND DEED   323 14
BOTH BY WORD AND DEED, HE MAY FAITHFULLY SERVE THEE   553 31
TO HURT NOBODY BY WORD OR DEED   580 07

DEEDS

WHO FOR OUR EVIL DEEDS DO WORTHILY DESERVE TO BE   130 25
FOR WE RECEIVE THE DUE REWARD OF OUR DEEDS   155 05
BECAUSE THEIR DEEDS WERE EVIL   185 07
LEST HIS DEEDS SHOULD BE REPROVED   185 09
THAT HIS DEEDS MAY BE MADE MANIFEST, THAT THEY   185 10
DO MORTIFY THE DEEDS OF THE BODY, YE SHALL LIVE   200 05
ACCORDING TO THEIR DEEDS, *   373 13
ALL OUR WORDS AND DEEDS WE MAY SEEK THY GLCRY, AND   547 11

DEEMED

AS MIGHT BE DEEMED EXPEDIENT   VI 26

DEEP

MAKING PATHS IN THE DEEP WATERS AND HIGHWAYS IN THE   038 18
ON THE GREAT DEEP OUR PRAYERS ARE DESIRED   046 11
PERILS OF THE GREAT DEEP (OF HIS WAY), THIS THY   053 23
A NIGHT AND A DAY I HAVE BEEN IN THE DEEP   121 04
THEM THROUGH THE DEEP, AS AN HORSE IN THE WILDERNESS, 139 13
LAUNCH OUT INTO THE DEEP, AND LET DOWN YOUR NETS FOR 196 14
OUT OF THE DEEP HAVE I CALLED UNTO THEE, O LORD   328 03
AND WE COMMIT HIS BODY TO THE DEEP   337 10
AND BECAUSE OF THE DEEP SIGHING OF THE POOR, 6 I WILL 355 17
AND LAYETH UP THE DEEP, AS IN A TREASURE-HOUSE   378 32
THY JUDGMENTS ARE LIKE THE GREAT DEEP   384 07
9 ONE DEEP CALLETH ANOTHER, BECAUSE OF THE NOISE OF   393 18
EVERY MAN IN THE DEEP OF HIS HEART   415 31
SOMETIME FROM THE DEEP OF THE SEA   420 32
I STICK FAST IN THE DEEP MIRE, WHERE NO GRCUND IS   422 02
I AM COME INTO DEEP WATERS, SO THAT THE FLCODS RUN   422 03
AND OUT OF THE DEEP WATERS   422 33
NEITHER LET THE DEEP SWALLOW ME UP   423 02
ME FROM THE DEEP OF THE EARTH AGAIN   426 19
IN A PLACE OF DARKNESS, AND IN THE DEEP   449 08
THY THOUGHTS ARE VERY DEEP   456 10
IT WITH THE DEEP LIKE AS WITH A GARMENT   468 04
THEM THROUGH THE DEEP, AS THROUGH A WILDERNESS   473 19
AND HIS WONDERS IN THE DEEP   477 25
UP TO THE HEAVEN, AND DOWN AGAIN TO THE DEEP   477 29
4 THE DEEP WATERS OF THE PROUD *   504 14
OUT OF THE DEEP HAVE I CALLED UNTO THEE, O LORD   507 08
THE SEA, AND IN ALL DEEP PLACES   510 14

DEEPLY

WE BESEECH THEE, DEEPLY SENSIBLE OF THE SHORTNESS AND 316 27
MAKE US DEEPLY SENSIBLE OF THE GREAT EVIL CF THEM   590 03

DEEPS

YE DRAGONS AND ALL DEEPS   524 19

DEFENCE

TRUSTING IN THY DEFENCE, MAY NCT FEAR THE PCWER CF   017 09
ARMED WITH THY DEFENCE, MAY BE PRESERVED EVERMORE   041 14
STRONG TOWER OF DEFENCE UNTO THY SERVANTS AGAINST THE 052 07
TO BE OUR DEFENCE AGAINST ALL OUR ENEMIES   128 27
AND IN THE DEFENCE AND CONFIRMATION OF THE GOSPEL, YE 220 29
BE NOW AND EVERMORE THY DEFENCE   314 18
THE LORD IS THY DEFENCE UPON THY RIGHT HAND   327 27
THE LORD IS THY DEFENCE UPON THY RIGHT HAND   339 11
ALSO WILL BE A DEFENCE FOR THE OPPRESSED, *   352 06
THE LORD IS MY STONY ROCK, AND MY DEFENCE   359 25
GIVEN ME THE DEFENCE OF THY SALVATION   362 06
IS THE WHOLESOME DEFENCE OF HIS ANOINTED   373 26
AND HOUSE OF DEFENCE, *   375 25
AND PUT THEM DOWN, O LORD OUR DEFENCE   411 28
HAST BEEN MY DEFENCE AND REFUGE IN THE DAY OF MY   412 08
HE IS MY DEFENCE, SO THAT I SHALL NOT GREATLY FALL   413 30
HE IS MY DEFENCE, SO THAT I SHALL NOT FALL   414 10
ART MY HOUSE OF DEFENCE, AND MY CASTLE   425 10
12 FOR THE LORD GOD IS A LIGHT AND DEFENCE   446 02
19 FOR THE LORD IS OUR DEFENCE   451 10
UNDER THE DEFENCE OF THE MOST HIGH, *   454 28
THINE HOUSE OF DEFENCE VERY HIGH   455 14
114 THOU ART MY DEFENCE AND SHIELD   497 26
THE LORD IS THY DEFENCE UPON THY RIGHT HAND   502 31

DEFEND

DEFEND US THY HUMBLE SERVANTS IN ALL ASSAULTS CF CUR 017 07
DEFEND US IN THE SAME WITH THY MIGHTY POWER   017 15
THY GREAT MERCY DEFEND US FROM ALL PERILS AND DANGERS 031 27
DEFEND OUR LIBERTIES, AND FASHION INTO ONE UNITED   036 15
PLEASE THEE TO DEFEND, AND PROVIDE FOR, THE   056 35
FROM OUR ENEMIES DEFEND US, O CHRIST   059 09
EVERMORE MIGHTILY DEFEND THEM   061 33
HAND TO HELP AND DEFEND US   112 28
OUR AFFLICTIONS, DEFEND US FROM ALL ERROR, AND LEAD   183 24
AND EVERMORE DEFEND US FROM ALL ADVERSITIES, WHO   186 28
PITY CLEANSE AND DEFEND THY CHURCH   212 05
MAY SUCCOUR AND DEFEND US ON EARTH   251 31
DEFEND, O LORD, THIS THY CHILD WITH THY   297 26
EVERMORE MIGHTILY DEFEND HIM   308 26
IN THEE, DEFEND HIM IN ALL DANGER, AND KEEP HIM IN   309 07
O GOD, AND DEFEND MY CAUSE AGAINST THE UNGODLY   310 05
WILT THOU DEFEND HIM AS WITH A SHIELD   348 30
THE GOD OF JACOB DEFEND THEE   364 18
O GOD, AND DEFEND MY CAUSE AGAINST THE UNGODLY   394 03
DOTH DEFEND THE EARTH, AS IT WERE WITH A   399 08
DEFEND ME FROM THEM THAT RISE UP AGAINST ME   411 04
AND DEFEND THE POOR   426 34
DEFEND THE CHILDREN OF THE POOR, AND PUNISH THE WRCNG 427 04
3 DEFEND THE POOR AND FATHERLESS   443 22
4 HE SHALL DEFEND THEE UNDER HIS WINGS, AND THOU   455 02
DEFEND THEM FROM THE SINS OF HERESY AND SCHISM   574 12
HIM TO SAVE AND DEFEND US IN ALL DANGERS BOTH CF SCUL 581 02
DEFEND US FROM ALL DANGERS AND ADVERSITIES   589 02
DEFEND US FROM ALL DANGERS AND MISCHIEFS, AND FROM   591 26
DEFEND US IN THE SAME WITH THY MIGHTY POWER   592 21
THY GREAT MERCY DEFEND US FROM ALL PERILS AND DANGERS 593 14
DEFEND THEM FROM ALL DANGERS OF SOUL AND BODY   597 03

DEFENCED

WE, BEING DEFENDED FROM THE FEAR OF OUR   031 22
MAY EVER BE DEFENDED BY THY MOST GRACIOUS AND READY   049 15
MAY EVERMORE BE DEFENDED BY THY MIGHTY POWER   115 31
POWER WE MAY BE DEFENDED AGAINST ALL ADVERSITY   120 19
THAT WE MAY BE DEFENDED FROM ALL ADVERSITIES WHICH   127 18
MIGHTY AID, BE DEFENDED AND COMFORTED IN ALL DANGERS 192 26

DEFENDER

BUT THOU, O LORD, ART MY DEFENDER   309 18
3 BUT THOU, O LORD, ART MY DEFENDER   346 29
HE IS THE DEFENDER OF ALL THEM THAT PUT THEIR TRUST   361 29
O GOD OUR DEFENDER, *   445 29
HE IS THEIR HELPER AND DEFENDER   485 29
HE IS THEIR HELPER AND DEFENDER   485 31
HE IS THEIR HELPER AND DEFENDER   485 33
MY DEFENDER IN WHOM I TRUST   519 25

DEFENDEST

BECAUSE THOU DEFENDEST THEM   348 26

DEFENDETH

AND DEFENDETH THE CAUSE OF THE WIDOWS   419 19
HE DEFENDETH THE FATHERLESS AND WIDOW   522 20

DEFENSIBLE

IS NOT FAIRLY DEFENSIBLE, IF ALLOWED SUCH JUST AND   V 42

DEFER

THAT THEY DEFER NOT THE BAPTISM OF THEIR   R 273 04

DEFIETH

AND THEREFORE DEFIETH HE ALL HIS ENEMIES   353 14

DEFILED

WHICH WERE NOT DEFILED WITH WOMEN   103 09
AND HAVE DEFILED THE DWELLING-PLACE OF THY NAME,   430 19
TEMPLE HAVE THEY DEFILED, AND MADE JERUSALEM AN HEAP 439 30
AND THE LAND WAS DEFILED WITH BLOOD   475 13

DEFILEMENTS

WHATSOEVER DEFILEMENTS IT MAY HAVE CONTRACTED,   317 19

DEFRAUD

GO BEYOND AND DEFRAUD HIS BROTHER IN ANY MATTER   127 32

DEGREE

BROTHER OF LOW DEGREE REJOICE IN THAT HE IS EXALTED   239 18
BROTHER TO SOME DEGREE OF HIS FORMER HEALTH   315 23
THEMSELVES A GOOD DEGREE, AND GREAT BOLDNESS IN THE   532 04

DELAY

AND FOLLOWED HIM WITHOUT DELAY   226 21
HE HAD, WITHOUT DELAY WAS OBEDIENT UNTO THE CALLING   246 18
TO COME, WITHOUT DELAY, TO THE LORD'S SUPPER   R 299 07

DELIGHT

WHOM YE DELIGHT IN   232 06

DELIGHT   CONTINUED   DELIVER   CONTINUED

MY DELIGHT IS IN THE LORD   305 18   20 O DELIVER NOT THE SOUL OF THY TURTLE-DOVE UNTO THE   431 15
2 BUT HIS DELIGHT IS IN THE LAW OF THE LORD   345 10   O DELIVER US, AND BE MERCIFUL UNTO OUR SINS, FOR THY   440 19
3 ALL MY DELIGHT IS UPON THE SAINTS THAT ARE IN THE   357 25   4 DELIVER THE OUTCAST AND POOR   443 24
4 DELIGHT THOU IN THE LORD, *   384 31   AND SHALL HE DELIVER HIS SOUL FROM THE POWER OF THE   453 03
THEIR DELIGHT IS IN LIES   414 05   3 FOR HE SHALL DELIVER THEE FROM THE SNARE OF THE   454 32
THE PEOPLES THAT DELIGHT IN WAR   421 17   THEREFORE WILL I DELIVER HIM   455 04
LET ALL SUCH AS DELIGHT IN THY SALVATION SAY ALWAY,   424 28   I WILL DELIVER HIM, AND BRING HIM TO HONOUR   455 27
17 THEIR DELIGHT SHALL BE DAILY IN THY NAME   451 06   HE SHALL DELIVER THEM FROM THE HAND OF THE UNGODLY   461 18
AND THAT DELIGHT IN VAIN GODS   461 11   AND DELIVER THEM THAT ARE APPOINTED UNTO DEATH   465 20
16 HIS DELIGHT WAS IN CURSING, AND IT SHALL HAPPEN   481 02   A TIME DID HE DELIVER THEM   475 22
HE HATH GREAT DELIGHT IN HIS COMMANDMENTS   483 19   45 DELIVER US, O LORD OUR GOD, AND GATHER US FROM   475 30
MY DELIGHT IS IN THE LORD   486 19   21 O DELIVER ME, FOR I AM HELPLESS AND POOR, *   481 14
HAD AS GREAT DELIGHT IN THE WAY OF THY TESTIMONIES,   490 25   I BESEECH THEE, DELIVER MY SOUL   486 26
16 MY DELIGHT SHALL BE IN THY STATUTES, *   490 29   134 O DELIVER ME FROM THE WRONGFUL DEALINGS OF MEN   499 06
ARE MY DELIGHT, *   491 14   AND DELIVER ME, *   500 17
40 BEHOLD, MY DELIGHT IS IN THY COMMANDMENTS   492 19   MY CAUSE, AND DELIVER ME   500 19
47 AND MY DELIGHT SHALL BE IN THY   493 02   DELIVER ME ACCORDING TO THY WORD   501 22
BUT MY DELIGHT HATH BEEN IN THY LAW   494 20   2 DELIVER MY SOUL, O LORD, FROM LYING LIPS, *   502 09
FOR THY LAW IS MY DELIGHT   495 10   DELIVER ME, O LORD, FROM THE EVIL MAN   516 09
92 IF MY DELIGHT HAD NOT BEEN IN THY LAW, *   496 09   8 O DELIVER ME FROM MY PERSECUTORS   518 17
MY DELIGHT SHALL BE EVER IN THY STATUTES   498 03   9 DELIVER ME, O LORD, FROM MINE ENEMIES   519 10
THY SERVANT TO DELIGHT IN THAT WHICH IS GOOD, *   498 13   DELIVER ME, AND TAKE ME OUT OF THE GREAT WATERS, FROM   520 04
FOR MY DELIGHT WAS IN THY COMMANDMENTS   498 33   11 SAVE ME, AND DELIVER ME FROM THE HAND OF   520 12
YET IS MY DELIGHT IN THY COMMANDMENTS   499 26   SHALL THE BISHOP DELIVER TO EVERY ONE OF THEM THE NEW R 534 09
AND IN THY LAW IS MY DELIGHT   501 31   THE BISHOP SHALL DELIVER TO EVERY ONE OF THEM   R 546 23
FOR I HAVE A DELIGHT THEREIN   509 03   WHAT THEY SHALL DELIVER OUT OF THY MOST HOLY WORD, CR R 547 09
BUT THE LORD'S DELIGHT IS IN THEM THAT FEAR HIM,   523 17   BISHOP SHALL DELIVER HIM THE BIBLE, SAYING, GIVE HEED R 558 20
                                                                AND DELIVER US FOR THY NAME'S SAKE   562 03
DELIGHTEST   DELIVER ME, WHEN WE DRAW NIGH TO THEE, FROM COLDNESS   594 05
                                                                SECRET TO US, TO DELIVER FROM CURSE AND DAMNATION   606 08
BUT THOU DELIGHTEST NOT IN BURNT-OFFERINGS   061 12
BUT THOU DELIGHTEST NOT IN BURNT-OFFERINGS   404 10   DELIVERANCE

DELIGHTETH   THANKS TO ALMIGHTY GOD FOR HER SAFE DELIVERANCE   R 051 04
                                                                FOR OUR DELIVERANCE FROM THOSE GREAT AND APPARENT   052 09
AND HIM THAT DELIGHTETH IN WICKEDNESS, DOTH HIS SOUL 354 31   TO PREACH DELIVERANCE TO THE CAPTIVES, AND RECOVERING   261 18
NEITHER DELIGHTETH HE IN ANY MAN'S LEGS   523 16   YOU SAFE DELIVERANCE, AND TO PRESERVE YOU IN THE   305 12
                                                                SHALT COMPASS ME ABOUT WITH SONGS OF DELIVERANCE   378 07
DELIVER
                                                                DELIVERED
BUT DELIVER US FROM EVIL   007 27
UPON THEE TO DELIVER MAN, THOU DIDST HUMBLE THYSELF   010 26   THAT WE BEING DELIVERED OUT OF THE HAND OF OUR   014 20
SAVE AND DELIVER US, WE HUMBLY BESEECH THEE, FROM THE 041 12   WE WERE NOT DELIVERED OVER AS A PREY UNTO THEM   052 12
DELIVER US, WE BESEECH THEE, IN OUR SEVERAL CALLINGS, 044 19   WERE ACCOMPLISHED THAT SHE SHOULD BE DELIVERED   099 07
DELIVER US, WE BESEECH THEE, FROM OUR PERIL   045 04   BE MERCIFULLY DELIVERED BY THY GOODNESS, FOR THE   118 30
BEEN PLEASED TO DELIVER FROM HIS BODILY SICKNESS THIS 052 31   HE SHALL BE DELIVERED UNTO THE GENTILES, AND SHALL BE   123 20
PLEASED TO DELIVER FROM HIS BODILY SICKNESS THE CHILD 053 12   HIM AWAY, AND DELIVERED HIM TO PONTIUS PILATE THE   134 33
GOOD LORD, DELIVER US   054 22   ENVY THEY HAD DELIVERED HIM   135 31
GOOD LORD, DELIVER US   055 05   HE DELIVERED HIM TO BE CRUCIFIED   136 14
HELP US, AND DELIVER US FOR THY NAME'S SAKE   058 26   HIM AWAY, AND DELIVERED HIM TO PILATE   145 06
HELP US, AND DELIVER US FOR THINE HONOUR   059 03   PRIESTS HAD DELIVERED HIM FOR ENVY   145 20
DELIVER ME FROM BLOOD-GUILTINESS, O GOD, THOU THAT   061 06   UNTO THEM, AND DELIVERED JESUS, WHEN HE HAD SCOURGED   145 28
OF THY NAME DELIVER US   062 03   WHICH ALSO I DELIVERED UNTO YOU, THAT THE LORD JESUS   152 16
PARDON AND DELIVER YOU FROM ALL YOUR SINS   076 05   BUT HE DELIVERED JESUS TO THEIR WILL   154 08
AND PROCEED TO DELIVER THE SAME TO THE BISHOPS,   R 082 26   HE THAT DELIVERED ME UNTO THEE HATH THE GREATER SIN   159 18
HELP AND DELIVER US   095 08   THEN DELIVERED HE HIM THEREFORE UNTO THEM TO BE   159 30
LET HIM DELIVER HIM NOW, IF HE WILL HAVE HIM   137 12   THEN PILATE COMMANDED THE BODY TO BE DELIVERED   162 09
THE ADVERSARY DELIVER THEE TO THE JUDGE, AND THE   198 13   HAST DELIVERED US FROM THE POWER OF OUR ENEMY   165 05
AND THE JUDGE DELIVER THEE TO THE OFFICER, AND THOU   198 14   AND OUR RULERS DELIVERED HIM TO BE CONDEMNED TO   167 18
THE RING SHALL DELIVER IT UNTO THE MAN, TO PUT IT   R 302 10   SOON AS SHE IS DELIVERED OF THE CHILD, SHE   174 11
I BESEECH THEE, DELIVER MY SOUL   305 23   ALSO SHALL BE DELIVERED FROM THE BONDAGE OF   194 17
O DELIVER ME FROM THE DECEITFUL AND WICKED MAN   310 06   FOR I DELIVERED UNTO YOU FIRST OF ALL THAT WHICH I   205 03
GOOD LORD, DELIVER HIM   318 03   AND HE DELIVERED HIM TO HIS MOTHER   213 06
PLEASE THEE TO DELIVER THE SOUL OF THY SERVANT FROM   318 11   WAS WROTH, AND DELIVERED HIM TO THE TORMENTORS,   222 03
DELIVER ME FROM ALL MINE OFFENCES   324 30   WE MAY ALL BE DELIVERED FROM THE BANDS OF THOSE SINS,   223 17
DELIVER US NOT INTO THE BITTER PAINS OF   332 26   ALL THINGS ARE DELIVERED UNTO ME OF MY FATHER   235 07
O LORD, AND DELIVER MY SOUL   349 06   FULL TIME CAME THAT SHE SHOULD BE DELIVERED   243 13
AND DELIVER ME   349 23   THAT WE BEING DELIVERED OUT OF THE HAND OF OUR   244 07
DELIVER MY SOUL FROM THE UNGODLY, BY THINE OWN SWORD 359 13   IN PRISON, AND DELIVERED HIM TO FOUR QUATERNIONS OF   245 05
44 THOU SHALT DELIVER ME FROM THE STRIVINGS OF THE   362 25   AND HATH DELIVERED ME OUT OF THE HAND OF HEROD, AND   245 27
AND THOU DIDST DELIVER THEM   366 11   THAT WE, BEING DELIVERED FROM THE DISQUIETUDE OF THIS   248 03
THAT HE WOULD DELIVER HIM   366 18   AND THERE WAS DELIVERED UNTO HIM THE BOOK OF THE   261 14
LET HIM DELIVER HIM, IF HE WILL HAVE HIM   366 19   AND DELIVERED THEM OUT OF THE HAND OF THOSE   262 13
20 DELIVER MY SOUL FROM THE SWORD, *   367 12   AFTER THEY ARE DELIVERED FROM THEIR EARTHLY PRISONS   317 12
MY SOUL, AND DELIVER ME   370 24   HE SHALL HAVE DELIVERED UP THE KINGDOM TO GOD, EVEN   328 27
21 DELIVER ISRAEL, O GOD, *   370 28   OWN SON, BUT DELIVERED HIM UP FOR US ALL, HOW SHALL   330 34
O DELIVER ME, AND BE MERCIFUL UNTO ME   371 18   AFTER THEY ARE DELIVERED FROM THE BURDEN OF THE   334 21
14 DELIVER ME NOT OVER INTO THE WILL OF MINE   372 24   I HAVE DELIVERED HIM THAT WITHOUT ANY CAUSE IS   349 30
DELIVER ME IN THY RIGHTEOUSNESS   375 23   18 HE DELIVERED ME FROM MY STRONGEST ENEMY, AND FROM   360 33
MAKE HASTE TO DELIVER ME   375 24   ANY MIGHTY MAN DELIVERED BY MUCH STRENGTH   379 20
DELIVER ME FROM THE HAND OF MINE ENEMIES, *   376 26   HE DELIVERED ME OUT OF ALL MY FEAR   380 09
NEITHER SHALL HE DELIVER ANY MAN BY HIS GREAT   379 23   BUT GOD HATH DELIVERED MY SOUL FROM THE POWER OF THE   401 05
18 TO DELIVER THEIR SOUL FROM DEATH, *   379 26   7 FOR HE HATH DELIVERED ME OUT OF ALL MY TROUBLE   406 16
O DELIVER MY SOUL FROM THE CALAMITIES WHICH THEY   382 29   HE THAT HATH DELIVERED MY SOUL IN PEACE FROM THE   407 27
HE SHALL DELIVER THEM FROM THE UNGODLY, AND SHALL   387 16   FOR THOU HAST DELIVERED MY SOUL FROM DEATH, AND MY   409 08
9 DELIVER ME FROM ALL MINE OFFENCES   389 25   5 THEREFORE WERE THY BELOVED DELIVERED   412 21
THY PLEASURE TO DELIVER ME   391 14   O LET ME BE DELIVERED FROM THEM THAT HATE ME, AND OUT   422 33
THE LORD SHALL DELIVER HIM IN THE TIME OF TROUBLE   391 31   AND SO WILL MY SOUL WHOM THOU HAST DELIVERED   426 26
AND DELIVER NOT THOU HIM INTO THE WILL OF HIS   392 02   HAST MIGHTILY DELIVERED THY PEOPLE, *   434 12
O DELIVER ME FROM THE DECEITFUL AND WICKED MAN   394 04   DAY WHEN HE DELIVERED THEM FROM THE HAND OF THE   437 26
AND DELIVER US, FOR THY MERCY'S SAKE   396 12   62 HE DELIVERED THEIR POWER INTO CAPTIVITY, *   438 34
7 BUT NO MAN MAY DELIVER HIS BROTHER, *   400 18   HIS HANDS WERE DELIVERED FROM MAKING THE POTS   442 24
THERE BE NONE TO DELIVER YOU   403 03   AND I DELIVERED THEE   442 25
14 DELIVER ME FROM BLOOD-GUILTINESS, O GOD, THOU THAT 404 04   AND THOU HAST DELIVERED MY SOUL FROM THE NETHERMOST   447 31
THE LORD WOULD DELIVER HIS PEOPLE OUT OF CAPTIVITY   405 29   KING SENT, AND DELIVERED HIM   471 12
DELIVER ME FROM MINE ENEMIES, O GOD   411 04   AND DELIVERED THEM FROM THE HAND OF THE ENEMY   473 22
2 O DELIVER ME FROM THE WICKED DOERS, *   411 06   AND DELIVERED FROM THE HAND OF THE ENEMY   476 09
O DELIVER ME, BECAUSE OF MINE ENEMIES   423 09   AND HE DELIVERED THEM FROM THEIR DISTRESS   476 16
O GOD, TO DELIVER ME   424 20   HE DELIVERED THEM OUT OF THEIR DISTRESS   476 31
BUT RID ME AND DELIVER ME IN THY RIGHTEOUSNESS   425 06   HE DELIVERED THEM OUT OF THEIR DISTRESS   477 14
3 DELIVER ME, O MY GOD, OUT OF THE HAND OF THE   425 11   6 THAT THY BELOVED MAY BE DELIVERED   479 15
THERE IS NONE TO DELIVER HIM   425 28   THOU HAST DELIVERED MY SOUL FROM DEATH, *   487 04
12 FOR HE SHALL DELIVER THE POOR WHEN HE CRIETH   427 20   THE SNARE IS BROKEN, AND WE ARE DELIVERED   504 19
14 HE SHALL DELIVER THEIR SOULS FROM FALSEHOOD AND   427 24   24 AND HATH DELIVERED US FROM OUR ENEMIES   512 30

DELIVERED   CONTINUED

AND HAST DELIVERED DAVID THY SERVANT FROM THE PERIL   520 11
THE FAITH ONCE DELIVERED TO THE SAINTS   574 12
FOR HAVING DELIVERED LS FROM THE DANGERS OF THE PAST   587 23

DELIVERER

THAT THOU ART OUR SAVIOUR AND MIGHTY DELIVERER   052 14
MY CASTLE AND DELIVERER, MY DEFENDER IN WHCM I TRUST   519 24

DELIVEREST

WHO DELIVEREST THE POOR FROM HIM THAT IS TCO   382 10

DELIVERETH

AND WHEN HE DELIVERETH THE BREAD, HE SHALL SAY,   R 082 29
MINISTER WHO DELIVERETH THE CLP SHALL SAY, THE BLCCD   R 083 02
IT IS HE THAT DELIVERETH ME FRCM MY CRUEL ENEMIES,   363 02
AND DELIVERETH THEM   380 16
AND DELIVERETH THEM OLT OF ALL THEIR TROUBLES   381 03
BUT THE LORD DELIVERETH HIM OUT OF ALL   381 07
22 THE LORD DELIVERETH THE SOULS OF HIS SERVANTS   381 12
HE DELIVERETH THEM OUT OF THEIR DISTRESS   477 34

DELIVERING

BEFORE DELIVERING THE RING TO THE MAN, THE   R 302 17

DELIVERY

TIME AFTER HER DELIVERY, SHALL COME INTO THE CHURCH   R 305 07

DEMAND

MAY DEMAND SUFFICIENT SURETY FOR HIS   R 301 03
HIS CHURCH, SHALL DEMAND OF YOU TOUCHING THE SAME   541 28
PRESIDING BISHOP DEMAND TESTIMONIALS OF THE PERSCN   R 552 24

DEMANDED

HE DEMANDED OF THEM WHERE CHRIST SHOULD BE   109 05

DEMANDS

AS OCCASION DEMANDS, THE MINISTER SHALL ADDRESS THE   R 313 15

DEMAS

FOR DEMAS HATH FORSAKEN ME, HAVING LOVED THIS PRESENT   253 31

DEN

YE HAVE MADE IT A DEN OF THIEVES   092 04
YE HAVE MADE IT A DEN OF THIEVES   204 18
YE HAVE MADE IT A DEN OF THIEVES   260 08
LURKETH HE IN HIS DEN, *   353 24

DENIED

HE CONFESSED, AND DENIED NOT   095 23
BUT HE DENIED, SAYING, I KNOW NOT, NEITHER UNDERSTAND   143 26
AND HE DENIED IT AGAIN   143 30
AND HE DENIED HIM, SAYING, WOMAN, I KNOW HIM NOT   151 12
AND HAST NOT DENIED HIM THE REQUEST OF HIS LIPS   365 08
IS NOT TO BE DENIED TO SUCH AS FALL INTO SIN AFTER   605 41
LORD IS NOT TO BE DENIED TO THE LAY-PEOPLE   609 10

DENOMINATIONS

RELIGIOUS DENOMINATIONS OF CHRISTIANS IN THESE STATES   VI 09

DENS

IN HIS LURKING DENS DOTH HE MURDER THE INNCCENT   353 21
AND LAY THEM DOWN IN THEIR DENS   469 05

DENUNCIATION

BY OPEN DENUNCIATION OF THE CHURCH IS RIGHTLY CUT OFF   609 26

DENY

THOU SHALT DENY ME THRICE   141 24
I WILL NOT DENY THEE IN ANY WISE   141 26
THOU SHALT DENY ME THRICE   144 02
THOU SHALT THRICE DENY THAT THOU KNOWEST ME   150 03
THOU SHALT DENY ME THRICE   151 22
WILL YOU DENY ALL UNGODLINESS AND WORLDLY   555 08
THEY LIVE HERE, OR DENY THE PLACE OF FORGIVENESS TO   606 04

DENYING

US THAT, DENYING UNGODLINESS AND WORLDLY LUSTS, WE   098 19

DEPART

THOU THY SERVANT DEPART IN PEACE, *   028 09
FROM INTENDING TO DEPART FROM THE CHURCH OF ENGLAND   VI 32
SHALL LET THEM DEPART WITH THIS BLESSING   R 084 17
THAT HE SHOULD DEPART OUT OF THIS WORLD UNTC THE   155 24
BUT IF I DEPART, I WILL SEND HIM UNTC YCU   175 12
THEY SHOULD NOT DEPART FROM JERUSALEM, BUT WAIT FOR   177 30
SAYING, DEPART FROM ME   196 23
THOU THY SERVANT DEPART IN PEACE, ACCORDING TC THY   233 06

DEPART   CONTINUED

DEPART, O CHRISTIAN SOUL, OUT OF THIS WORLD, IN THE   319 19
TIME THEY SHALL DEPART OUT OF THIS LIFE   R 321 03
HIS SOUL SHALL DEPART FROM THE BODY, IT MAY BE   321 24
OF THOSE WHO DEPART HENCE IN THE LORD, AND WITH WHOM   334 20
WHEN WE SHALL DEPART THIS LIFE, WE MAY REST IN HIM   335 07
HEART SHALL DEPART FROM ME   463 24
ALL THEM THAT DEPART FROM THY STATUTES   498 04
DEPART FROM ME, YE BLOOD-THIRSTY MEN   515 28
WE MAY DEPART FROM GRACE GIVEN, AND FALL INTO   605 42

DEPARTED

THE PLACE OF DEPARTED SPIRITS, WHICH ARE CONSIDERED   R 015 17
THE PLACE OF DEPARTED SPIRITS, WHICH ARE CONSIDERED   R 029 22
THY SERVANTS DEPARTED THIS LIFE IN THY FAITH AND   074 35
AND AS THEY DEPARTED, JESUS BEGAN TO SAY UNTO THE   094 24
BY NIGHT, AND DEPARTED INTO EGYPT   103 21
WHEN THEY HAD HEARD THE KING, THEY DEPARTED   109 16
TO HEROD, THEY DEPARTED INTO THEIR OWN COUNTRY   109 25
AND CEPARTED INTO THE COASTS OF TYRE AND   128 07
THE TEMPLE, AND DEPARTED, AND WENT AND HANGED   135 08
STONE TO THE DOOR OF THE SEPULCHRE, AND DEPARTED   162 13
AND DEPARTED, LEAVING HIM HALF DEAD   208 23
MORROW WHEN HE DEPARTED, HE TOOK OUT TWO PENCE,   208 33
HE AROSE, AND DEPARTED TO HIS HOUSE   217 12
WHICH DEPARTED NOT FROM THE TEMPLE, BUT SERVED   233 19
AND THE ANGEL DEPARTED FROM HER   236 30
THEN DEPARTED BARNABAS TO TARSUS, FOR TO SEEK SAUL   241 10
THE ANGEL DEPARTED FROM HIM   245 25
AS THEY DEPARTED FROM HIM, PETER SAID UNTO   248 33
AND IS DEPARTED UNTO THESSALONICA   253 32
OF THY SERVANT DEPARTED, AND GRANT HIM AN ENTRANCE   268 23
NOW DEPARTED FROM THE BODY   319 28
OF OUR BROTHER DEPARTED, AND WE COMMIT HIS BODY TO   333 15
OF THY SERVANT DEPARTED, AND GRANT HIM AN ENTRANCE   334 15
THOSE WHO ARE DEPARTED IN THE TRUE FAITH OF THY HCLY   334 26
THE FAITHFUL DEPARTED IN CHRIST, PROVIDED THAT IN ANY R 337 03
OF OUR BROTHER DEPARTED, AND WE COMMIT HIS BODY TO   337 10

DEPARTETH

SHADOW THAT DEPARTETH, *   481 16

DEPARTING

DEPARTING FROM THE COASTS OF TYRE AND SIDON,   206 27
37 EGYPT WAS GLAD AT THEIR DEPARTING   472 13
THAT AFTER MY DEPARTING SHALL GRIEVOUS WOLVES ENTER   550 30

DEPARTURE

THE TIME OF MY DEPARTURE IS AT HAND   253 26

DEPOSED

BEING FOUND GUILTY, BY JUST JUDGMENT BE DEPCSED   608 22

DEPTH

AND LENGTH, AND DEPTH, AND HEIGHT   212 19
IT EITHER IN THE DEPTH, OR IN THE HEIGHT ABOVE   235 27
DROWNED IN THE DEPTH OF THE SEA   252 33
NOR HEIGHT, NOR DEPTH, NOR ANY OTHER CREATURE,   331 12
AS IT HAD BEEN OUT OF THE GREAT DEPTH   435 32

DEPTHS

HIS KNOWLEDGE THE DEPTHS ARE BROKEN UP, AND THE   005 26
BEHOLDEST THE DEPTHS, AND DWELLEST BETWEEN THE   011 22
KNOWLEDGE THE DEPTHS ARE BROKEN UP, AND THE CLOUDS   050 19
THE DEPTHS ALSO WERE TROUBLED   434 15

DERIDED

ALSO WITH THEM DERIDED HIM, SAYING, HE SAVED OTHERS   154 28

DERISION

THE LORD SHALL HAVE THEM IN DERISION   346 05
AND HAD IN DERISION OF THEM THAT ARE ROUND ABOUT US   395 20
HAVE THEM IN DERISION, *   411 20
VERY SCORN AND DERISION UNTO THEM THAT ARE ROUND   440 07
51 THE PROUD HAVE HAD ME EXCEEDINGLY IN DERISION   493 12

DESCEND

THE LATTER RAIN DESCEND UPON THE EARTH, THAT IT MAY   051 16
KING OF ISRAEL DESCEND NOW FROM THE CROSS, THAT HE   146 23
HIMSELF SHALL DESCEND FROM HEAVEN WITH A SHOUT, WITH   269 05

DESCENDED

THE WORDS, HE DESCENDED INTO HELL, USE THE WORDS, HE   R 015 16
HE DESCENDED INTO HELL   015 24
THE WORDS, HE DESCENDED INTO HELL, USE THE WORDS, HE   R 029 31
HE DESCENDED INTO HELL   029 29
THAT HE ALSO DESCENDED FIRST INTO THE LOWER PARTS CF   237 16
HE THAT DESCENDED IS THE SAME ALSO THAT ASCENDED UP   237 17
HE DESCENDED INTO HELL   284 18
THAT HE ALSO DESCENDED FIRST INTO THE LOWER PARTS CF   538 03
HE THAT DESCENDED IS THE SAME ALSO THAT ASCENDED UP   538 04
HE DESCENDED INTO HELL   578 02

DESCENDING

LIKE A DOVE, DESCENDING UPON HIM   112 21

DESCRIBED

IS THE CHURCH DESCRIBED IN THE APOSTLES' AND NICENE 291 02
THE CHURCH IS DESCRIBED IN THE CREEDS AS ONE, HOLY, 291 04

DESERT

STRAIGHT IN THE DESERT A HIGHWAY FOR OUR GOD   004 07
IN THE DEEP WATERS AND HIGHWAYS IN THE DESERT   038 18
BEHOLD, HE IS IN THE DESERT   118 09
STRAIGHT IN THE DESERT A HIGHWAY FOR OUR GOD   242 21
AND GRIEVED HIM IN THE DESERT   437 22
AND LIKE AN OWL THAT IS IN THE DESERT   464 22
AND THEY TEMPTED GOD IN THE DESERT   473 30

DESERTS

AND WAS IN THE DESERTS TILL THE DAY OF HIS SHEWING   244 18

DESERVE

SPAREST WHEN WE DESERVE PUNISHMENT, AND IN THY WRATH 046 18
SPAREST WHEN WE DESERVE PUNISHMENT, AND IN THY WRATH 062 32
DO WORTHILY DESERVE TO BE PUNISHED, BY THE COMFORT OF 130 25
TO GIVE MORE THAN EITHER WE DESIRE OR DESERVE   206 06
SAY) DESERVE GRACE OF CONGRUITY   605 20

DESERVED

ALL THOSE EVILS THAT WE MOST JUSTLY HAVE DESERVED   059 24
PAY THEM THAT THEY HAVE DESERVED   373 16

DESERVETH

THIS WORLD, IT DESERVETH GOD'S WRATH AND DAMNATION   604 34

DESERVING

AND REWARD THE PROUD AFTER THEIR DESERVING   457 22

DESERVINGS

AND NOT FOR OUR OWN WORKS OR DESERVINGS   605 07

DESIGNATED

AT THE TIME DESIGNATED FOR THE NEW INCUMBENT'S   R 570 02

DESIGNS

UNLAWFUL DESIGNS, OR INORDINATE DESIRES, MAY REST   590 14

DESIRE

BE SAID WHEN ANY DESIRE THE PRAYERS OF THE   R 019 12
TO THOSE WHO DESIRE NOW TO OFFER UP THEIR PRAISES AND 019 18
BE SAID WHEN ANY DESIRE TO RETURN THANKS FOR MERCIES R 019 33
BE SAID WHEN ANY DESIRE THE PRAYERS OF THE   R 033 10
TO THOSE WHO DESIRE NOW TO OFFER UP THEIR PRAISES AND 033 16
BE SAID WHEN ANY DESIRE TO RETURN THANKS FOR MERCIES R 033 31
NOR THE DESIRE OF SUCH AS ARE SORROWFUL   058 16
AND WE EARNESTLY DESIRE THY FATHERLY GOODNESS,   081 15
TELL ME, YE THAT DESIRE TO BE UNDER THE LAW, DO YE   130 29
ALOUD BEGAN TO DESIRE HIM TO DO AS HE HAD EVER DONE 145 17
UNTO THEM, WITH DESIRE I HAVE DESIRED TO EAT THIS   149 02
AND DESIRE THAT WHICH THOU DOST PROMISE   174 21
GIVEN AN HEARTY DESIRE TO PRAY, MAY, BY THY MIGHTY   192 26
THY PROMISES, WHICH EXCEED ALL THAT WE CAN DESIRE   197 08
THAN EITHER WE DESIRE OR DESERVE   206 06
AS MANY AS DESIRE TO MAKE A FAIR SHEW IN THE FLESH, 210 24
BUT DESIRE TO HAVE YOU CIRCUMCISED, THAT THEY MAY   210 28
I DESIRE THAT YE FAINT NOT AT MY TRIBULATIONS FOR   212 10
FOR YOU, AND TO DESIRE THAT YE MIGHT BE FILLED WITH 224 02
AS NEWBORN BABES, DESIRE THE SINCERE MILK OF THE   259 27
THAT IS MY DESIRE   277 03
ACCEPT HIM, AND DESIRE TO FOLLOW HIM AS THY SAVIOUR 278 05
THAT IS MY DESIRE   278 12
AND DESIRE THAT WHICH THOU DOST PROMISE   285 28
NOT TO COVET NOR DESIRE OTHER MEN'S GOODS   289 08
IN HUMBLE FAITH DESIRE THE MINISTRY OF HEALING   R 320 05
8 DESIRE OF ME, AND I SHALL GIVE THEE THE NATIONS FOR 346 12
HIS OWN HEART'S DESIRE, *   353 09
HAST HEARD THE DESIRE OF THE POOR   354 13
CHILDREN AT THEIR DESIRE, *   359 17
THEE THY HEART'S DESIRE, *   364 22
HIM HIS HEART'S DESIRE, *   365 07
AND HE SHALL GIVE THEE THY HEART'S DESIRE   384 32
THOU KNOWEST ALL MY DESIRE   388 08
EYE HATH SEEN HIS DESIRE UPON MINE ENEMIES   406 17
LET ME SEE MY DESIRE UPON MINE ENEMIES   411 25
UPON EARTH THAT I DESIRE IN COMPARISON OF THEE   429 27
FOR HE GAVE THEM THEIR OWN DESIRE   436 30
2 MY SOUL HATH A DESIRE AND LONGING TO ENTER INTO THE 445 13
SHALL HEAR HIS DESIRE OF THE WICKED THAT ARISE UP   456 22
AND DESPISETH NOT THEIR DESIRE   465 14
39 AT THEIR DESIRE HE BROUGHT QUAILS   472 17
GAVE THEM THEIR DESIRE, *   473 31
UNTIL HE SEE HIS DESIRE UPON HIS ENEMIES   483 33
THE DESIRE OF THE UNGODLY SHALL PERISH   484 05
SHALL I SEE MY DESIRE UPON MINE ENEMIES   488 13
THE VERY FERVENT DESIRE *   491 06

DESIRE   CONTINUED

FOR THEREIN IS MY DESIRE   492 10
UNGODLY HAVE HIS DESIRE, O LORD   516 24
O LORD, AND CONSIDER MY DESIRE   518 23
WILL FULFIL THE DESIRE OF THEM THAT FEAR HIM   521 30
SUCH AS DESIRE TO BE ORDAINED DEACONS,   R 530 08
IF A MAN DESIRE THE OFFICE OF A BISHOP, HE   549 18
HEART THEY MAY DESIRE THE PROSPERITY OF THY HOLY   574 10
NOT TO COVET NOR DESIRE OTHER MEN'S GOODS   580 12
I DESIRE MY LORD GOD, OUR HEAVENLY FATHER,   580 29
OUT ON ALL WHO DESIRE IT, THE SPIRIT OF GRACE AND OF 594 04
THAN WE CAN DESIRE OR PRAY FOR   597 12
THE DESIRE OF VAIN-GLORY, AND THE PRIDE   598 22
SOME THE DESIRE, OF THE FLESH,) IS NOT SUBJECT TO THE 604 37

DESIRED

ESPECIALLY THOSE FOR WHOM OUR PRAYERS ARE DESIRED   019 07
ESPECIALLY THOSE FOR WHOM OUR PRAYERS ARE DESIRED   033 05
FOR WHOM OUR PRAYERS ARE DESIRED   045 15
ON THE GREAT DEEP OUR PRAYERS ARE DESIRED   046 11
SHALL HAVE DESIRE TO RETURN THANKS TO ALMIGHTY GOD R 051 03
FOR ANY WHO HAVE DESIRED THE PRAYERS OF THE CHURCH R 074 03
UNTO THEM ONE PRISONER, WHOMSOEVER THEY DESIRED   145 13
DESIRE I HAVE DESIRED TO EAT THIS PASSOVER WITH YOU 149 02
SATAN HATH DESIRED TO HAVE YOU, THAT HE MAY SIFT YOU 149 31
WAS CAST INTO PRISON, WHOM THEY HAD DESIRED   154 08
IN HIM, YET DESIRED THEY PILATE THAT HE SHOULD BE   168 30
AND KINGS HAVE DESIRED TO SEE THOSE THINGS WHICH YE 208 09
HIGH PRIEST, AND DESIRED OF HIM LETTERS TO DAMASCUS 229 27
SHALL BE ADMITTED AS SPONSORS, IF IT BE DESIRED   R 273 11
THAT WE DESIRED OF HIM   322 11
ONE THING HAVE I DESIRED OF THE LORD, WHICH I WILL   326 08
10 MORE TO BE DESIRED ARE THEY THAN GOLD, YEA,   364 04
ONE THING HAVE I DESIRED OF THE LORD, WHICH I WILL   371 32
SHALL BE DESIRED, SECRETLY IN THEIR PRAYERS, TO MAKE R 543 23

DESIREDST

BECAUSE THOU DESIREDST ME   221 34

DESIRES

THE DEVICES AND DESIRES OF OUR OWN HEARTS   006 19
O LORD, THE DESIRES AND PETITIONS OF THY   020 07
THE DEVICES AND DESIRES OF OUR OWN HEARTS   023 26
WHOM ALL HOLY DESIRES, ALL GOOD COUNSELS, AND ALL   031 18
O LORD, THE DESIRES AND PETITIONS OF THY   034 07
ARE OPEN, ALL DESIRES KNOWN, AND FROM WHOM NO SECRETS 067 17
UPON THE HEARTY DESIRES OF THY HUMBLE SERVANTS,   128 26
OUR MINDS GOOD DESIRES, SO BY THY CONTINUAL HELP WE 163 26
ALL COVETOUS DESIRES, AND INORDINATE LOVE OF RICHES, 250 22
ALL COVETOUS DESIRES OF THE SAME, AND THE SINFUL   276 26
AND THE SINFUL DESIRES OF THE FLESH, SO THAT THOU   276 27
AND THE SINFUL DESIRES OF THE FLESH, SO THAT THOU   277 28
ALL COVETOUS DESIRES OF THE SAME, AND THE SINFUL   277 28
HAST HEARD MY DESIRES, *   413 15
AND PONDER THE VOICE OF MY HUMBLE DESIRES   447 16
THE WISHES AND DESIRES OF MY WILL CENTRE IN WHAT THOU 573 18
OR INORDINATE DESIRES, MAY REST THERE   590 14
US ALL WRONG DESIRES, INCLINE OUR HEARTS TO KEEP THY 594 13
IN US THE HOLY DESIRES THOU DOST IMPART   594 19

DESIREST

FOR THOU DESIREST NO SACRIFICE, ELSE WOULD I GIVE IT 061 11
HAST MADE, NOR DESIREST THE DEATH OF A SINNER, BUT   157 05
WHO DESIREST NOT THE DEATH OF A SINNER   319 07
16 FOR THOU DESIREST NO SACRIFICE, ELSE WOULD I GIVE 404 09
WHAT DESIREST THOU OF GOD IN THIS PRAYER   580 28
WHO DESIREST NOT THE DEATH OF A SINNER,   589 33

DESIRETH

WHO DESIRETH NOT THE DEATH OF A SINNER,   007 07
WHO DESIRETH NOT THE DEATH OF A SINNER,   024 09
WHO DESIRETH NOW TO OFFER HER PRAISES AND   051 08
WHO NOW DESIRETH TO RETURN THANKS UNTO THEE, IN THE 053 02
WHO NOW DESIRETH TO RETURN HIS THANKS UNTO THEE IN   053 23
WHO DESIRETH NOW TO OFFER HER PRAISES AND   306 27
MOST EARNESTLY DESIRETH PARDON AND FORGIVENESS   314 02
AS THE HART DESIRETH THE WATER-BROOKS, *   392 29
OF A BISHOP, HE DESIRETH A GOOD WORK   549 19

DESIRING

OF SORES, AND DESIRING TO BE FED WITH THE CRUMBS   190 06
AND DESIRING A CERTAIN THING OF HIM   247 07
COME HITHER DESIRING TO RECEIVE HOLY BAPTISM   277 20

DESIROUS

FOR HE WAS DESIROUS TO SEE HIM OF A LONG SEASON,   153 11
THAT THEY WERE DESIROUS TO ASK HIM, AND SAID UNTO   174 04
OR BE READY AND DESIROUS TO BE CONFIRMED   R 299 05
AND YET IS DESIROUS TO RECEIVE THE COMMUNION IN HIS R 321 11

DESOLATE

AND ALL WHO ARE DESOLATE AND OPPRESSED   057 02
YOUR HOUSE IS LEFT UNTO YOU DESOLATE   100 31
FOR THE DESOLATE HATH MANY MORE CHILDREN THAN SHE   131 10
HABITATION BE DESOLATE, AND LET NO MAN DWELL THEREIN 234 11
FOR I AM DESOLATE, AND IN MISERY   370 10
THEY THAT HATE THE RIGHTEOUS SHALL BE DESOLATE   381 11

DESOLATE   CONTINUED

18 LET THEM BE DESOLATE, AND REWARDED WITH SHAME,   391 19
IT ALSO OUT OF DESOLATE PLACES   480 20
AND MY HEART WITHIN ME IS DESOLATE   518 31

DESOLATION

DIVIDED AGAINST ITSELF IS BROUGHT TO DESOLATION   129 30

DESPAIR

THOUGH THEY BE PERPLEXED, SAVE THEM FROM DESPAIR   599 15

DESPERATION

EITHER INTO DESPERATION, OR INTO WRETCHLESSNESS OF   606 25
NO LESS PERILOUS THAN DESPERATION   606 26

DESPISE

O GOD, THOU WILT NOT DESPISE   004 25
O GOD, SHALT THOU NOT DESPISE   061 14
LET NO MAN DESPISE THEE   098 26
TO THE ONE, AND DESPISE THE OTHER   211 11
HEED THAT YE DESPISE NOT ONE OF THESE LITTLE ONES   253 10
DESPISE NOT THEN THE WORKS OF THINE OWN HANDS   312 09
MY SON, DESPISE NOT THOU THE CHASTENING OF THE LORD,   321 28
HEED THAT YE DESPISE NOT ONE OF THESE LITTLE ONES   339 30
O GOD, SHALT THOU NOT DESPISE   404 12
DESPISE NOT THEN THE WORKS OF THINE OWN HANDS   514 15

DESPISED

AND DESPISED OTHERS   205 22
FOR HE HATH NOT DESPISED NOR ABHORRED THE LOW ESTATE   367 20
GOD HATH DESPISED THEM   405 27
FOR WE ARE UTTERLY DESPISED   504 03

DESPISERS

BEHOLD, YE DESPISERS, AND WONDER, AND PERISH   169 23

DESPISEST

WHO DESPISEST NOT THE SIGHING OF A CONTRITE   058 15

DESPISETH

THEREFORE THAT DESPISETH, DESPISETH NOT MAN, BUT GOD, 128 03
DESPISETH, DESPISETH NOT MAN, BUT GOD, WHO HATH ALSO   128 04
AND DESPISETH NOT HIS PRISONERS   424 10
AND DESPISETH NOT THEIR DESIRE   465 14

DESPISING

THE CROSS, DESPISING THE SHAME, AND IS SET DOWN AT   258 25

DESPITEFULLY

THEM WHICH DESPITEFULLY USE YOU, AND PERSECUTE YOU   264 07
AND DESPITEFULLY SPEAK AGAINST THE RIGHTEOUS   376 34

DESPITEFULNESS

WITH THE DESPITEFULNESS OF THE PROUD   504 05

DESTITUTE

BESEECH THEE, DESTITUTE OF THY MANIFOLD GIFTS, NOR   240 30
PUT THEIR TRUST IN HIM SHALL NOT BE DESTITUTE   381 13
OF THE POOR DESTITUTE, *   465 14
ALL STRANGERS DESTITUTE OF HELP   555 25
ARE THIS DAY DESTITUTE, HOMELESS, OR FORGOTTEN OF   599 07

DESTROY

YOUNG CHILD TO DESTROY HIM   103 19
THAT HE MIGHT DESTROY THE WORKS OF THE DEVIL, AND   117 05
THAT HE MIGHT DESTROY THE WORKS OF THE DEVIL   117 30
AND DESTROY JESUS   136 02
HIM SAY, I WILL DESTROY THIS TEMPLE THAT IS MADE WITH 143 06
AND TO KILL, AND TO DESTROY   186 17
6 THOU SHALT DESTROY THEM THAT SPEAK LIES   348 11
11 DESTROY THOU THEM, O GOD   348 22
AND I SHALL DESTROY THEM THAT HATE ME   362 19
THE LORD SHALL DESTROY THEM IN HIS DISPLEASURE,   365 23
NEITHER DESTROY ME WITH THE UNGODLY AND WICKED   373 10
THEIR NET TO DESTROY ME WITHOUT A CAUSE   381 31
AFTER MY SOUL TO DESTROY IT   391 17
SHALL GOD DESTROY THEE FOR EVER   404 28
DESTROY THOU THEM IN THY TRUTH   406 12
9 DESTROY THEIR TONGUES, O LORD, AND DIVIDE THEM   407 04
AND WOULD DESTROY ME GUILTLESS, ARE MIGHTY   422 09
MAYEST UTTERLY DESTROY EVERY ENEMY, *   430 10
AND FROGS TO DESTROY THEM   437 32
AND DESTROY THEM IN THEIR OWN MALICE   458 32
OUR GOD SHALL DESTROY THEM   458 34
HIM WILL I DESTROY   463 27
11 I SHALL SOON DESTROY ALL THE UNGODLY THAT ARE IN   464 04
LEST HE SHOULD DESTROY THEM   474 16
THE LORD WILL I DESTROY THEM   488 19
THE LORD WILL I DESTROY THEM   488 22
THE LORD I WILL DESTROY THEM   488 25
ABOUT TO DESTROY ME   495 12
WAIT FOR ME, TO DESTROY ME   496 15

DESTROY   CONTINUED

AND DESTROY ALL THEM THAT VEX MY SOUL   519 17
AND TO KILL, AND TO DESTROY   539 08

DESTROYED

HIS DEATH HATH DESTROYED DEATH, AND BY HIS RISING TO   078 11
SIN MIGHT BE DESTROYED, THAT HENCEFORTH WE SHOULD NOT 197 18
AND WERE DESTROYED OF SERPENTS   201 20
AND WERE DESTROYED OF THE DESTROYER   201 21
AND DESTROYED THOSE MURDERERS, AND BURNED UP   218 14
THIS HE THAT DESTROYED THEM WHICH CALLED ON THIS NAME 231 06
THIS BODY BE DESTROYED, YET SHALL I SEE GOD   324 11
THAT SHALL BE DESTROYED IS DEATH   328 31
AND DESTROYED THE UNGODLY   351 30
THOU HAST DESTROYED, WHOSE MEMORIAL IS PERISHED WITH   351 33
FOUNDATIONS BE DESTROYED, *   354 24
AND DESTROYED THEM   360 27
TILL I HAVE DESTROYED THEM   362 12
HOW THOU HAST DESTROYED THE NATIONS, AND MADE THY   394 25
THOU HAST DESTROYED ALL THEM THAT ARE UNFAITHFUL UNTO 429 31
AND DESTROYED THEM NOT   437 15
48 HE DESTROYED THEIR VINES WITH HAILSTONES, *   438 02
AND DESTROYED IT   450 26
SHALL THEY BE DESTROYED FOR EVER   456 15
ALL THE WORKERS OF WICKEDNESS SHALL BE DESTROYED   456 18
AND DESTROYED ALL THE PROVISION OF BREAD   471 05
AND DESTROYED THE TREES THAT WERE IN THEIR COASTS   472 04
HE WOULD HAVE DESTROYED THEM, HAD NOT MOSES HIS   474 14
34 NEITHER DESTROYED THEY THE HEATHEN, *   475 04
12 LET HIS POSTERITY BE DESTROYED   480 25
FOR THEY HAVE DESTROYED THY LAW   498 22

DESTROYER

AND WERE DESTROYED OF THE DESTROYER   201 22
I HAVE KEPT ME FROM THE WAYS OF THE DESTROYER   358 26

DESTROYEST

THOU THAT DESTROYEST THE TEMPLE, AND BUILDEST IT IN   137 06
THOU THAT DESTROYEST THE TEMPLE, AND BUILDEST IT   146 19
AND DESTROYEST THEM   429 13

DESTROYETH

SICKNESS THAT DESTROYETH IN THE NOON-DAY   455 08

DESTRUCTION

LIFE FROM DESTRUCTION, *   029 10
WHOSE END IS DESTRUCTION, WHOSE GOD IS THEIR BELLY,   222 19
THE LORD SAVETH THY LIFE FROM DESTRUCTION   312 17
LIFE FROM DESTRUCTION, AND CROWNETH THEE WITH MERCY   312 26
THOU TURNEST MAN TO DESTRUCTION   325 18
INTO THE DESTRUCTION THAT HE MADE FOR OTHER   350 24
BE TURNED TO DESTRUCTION, *   352 26
LET A SUDDEN DESTRUCTION COME UPON HIM UNAWARES,   382 04
WHAT DESTRUCTION HE HATH BROUGHT UPON THE EARTH   398 10
SHALT BRING THEM INTO THE PIT OF DESTRUCTION   408 07
OR THY FAITHFULNESS IN DESTRUCTION   449 19
3 THOU TURNEST MAN TO DESTRUCTION   453 23
LIFE FROM DESTRUCTION, *   466 13
AND THEY WERE SAVED FROM THEIR DESTRUCTION   477 16
NOT TO DESTRUCTION, BUT TO SALVATION   558 02

DESTRUCTIONS

THY DESTRUCTIONS ARE COME TO A PERPETUAL END   351 32

DETERMINED

BE CLEARLY DETERMINED TO BELONG TO DOCTRINE MUST BE   V 05
TRULY THE SON OF MAN GOETH, AS IT WAS DETERMINED   149 15
HIS ABILITY, DETERMINED TO SEND RELIEF UNTO THE   241 20
HIS ABILITY, DETERMINED TO SEND RELIEF UNTO THE   246 29
HAVE CLEARLY DETERMINED, BY GOD'S GRACE, TO GIVE   541 11
AND ARE YOU DETERMINED, OUT OF THE SAID SCRIPTURES TO 542 04
AND HAVE SO DETERMINED, BY GOD'S GRACE   542 09
AND ARE YOU DETERMINED OUT OF THE SAME HOLY   554 22
AND DETERMINED, BY GOD'S GRACE   554 27

DEUS

NUNC DIMITTIS, DEUS MISEREATUR, BENEDIC, ANIMA MEA,   R 025 17
OR SUNG EXSURGAT DEUS, PSALM LXVIII   R 571 30

DEVICE

IMAGINED SUCH A DEVICE AS THEY ARE NOT ABLE TO   365 28
4 THEIR DEVICE IS ONLY HOW TO PUT HIM OUT WHOM GOD   414 04

DEVICES

TOO MUCH THE DEVICES AND DESIRES OF OUR OWN HEARTS   006 19
TOO MUCH THE DEVICES AND DESIRES OF OUR OWN HEARTS   023 26
AND MAKETH THE DEVICES OF THE PEOPLE TO BE OF NONE   379 07

DEVIL

FROM THE CRAFTS AND ASSAULTS OF THE DEVIL   054 20
THE FLESH, AND THE DEVIL, FROM LIGHTNING AND TEMPEST 054 28
SUBTILTY OF THE DEVIL OR MAN WORKETH AGAINST US, MAY, 058 20
THE WORKS OF THE DEVIL, AND MAKE US THE SONS OF GOD, 117 05
HE THAT COMMITTETH SIN IS OF THE DEVIL   117 28

DEVIL   CONTINUED

FOR THE DEVIL SINNETH FROM THE BEGINNING	117 28
THAT HE MIGHT DESTROY THE WORKS OF THE DEVIL	117 31
THEN COMETH THE DEVIL, AND TAKETH AWAY THE WORD OUT	121 34
INTO THE WILDERNESS TO BE TEMPTED OF THE DEVIL	126 24
THEN THE DEVIL TAKETH HIM UP INTO THE HOLY CITY, AND	126 30
THE DEVIL TAKETH HIM UP INTO AN EXCEEDING HIGH	127 04
THEN THE DEVIL LEAVETH HIM, AND, BEHOLD, ANGELS CAME	127 11
MY DAUGHTER IS GRIEVOUSLY VEXED WITH A DEVIL	128 11
WAS CASTING OUT A DEVIL, AND IT WAS DUMB	129 24
TO PASS, WHEN THE DEVIL WAS GONE OUT, THE DUMB SPAKE	129 25
WELL THAT THOU ART A SAMARITAN, AND HAST A DEVIL	133 14
JESUS ANSWERED, I HAVE NOT A DEVIL	133 14
JEWS UNTO HIM, NOW WE KNOW THAT THOU HAST A DEVIL	133 19
BEING ENDED, THE DEVIL HAVING NOW PUT INTO THE HEART	155 27
AND HEALING ALL THAT WERE OPPRESSED OF THE DEVIL	166 21
AND HEALING ALL THAT WERE OPPRESSED OF THE DEVIL	184 09
YOUR ADVERSARY THE DEVIL, AS A ROARING LION, WALKETH	193 05
THE FLESH, AND THE DEVIL	214 25
NEITHER GIVE PLACE TO THE DEVIL	216 20
BE ABLE TO STAND AGAINST THE WILES OF THE DEVIL	219 07
CALLED THE DEVIL, AND SATAN, WHICH DECEIVETH THE	252 07
FOR THE DEVIL IS COME DOWN UNTO YOU, HAVING GREAT	252 18
RENOUNCE THE DEVIL AND ALL HIS WORKS, THE VAIN POMP	276 25
THOU RENOUNCE THE DEVIL AND ALL HIS WORKS, THE VAIN	277 26
AGAINST THE DEVIL, THE WORLD, AND THE FLESH	278 25
AGAINST SIN, THE WORLD, AND THE DEVIL	280 09
RENOUNCE THE DEVIL AND ALL HIS WORKS, THE POMPS AND	283 23
AND MALICE OF THE DEVIL, OR BY HIS OWN CARNAL WILL	314 04
PRIDE HE FALL INTO THE CONDEMNATION OF THE DEVIL	549 28
HE FALL INTO REPROACH AND THE SNARE OF THE DEVIL	549 30
RENOUNCE THE DEVIL AND ALL HIS WORKS, THE POMPS AND	577 14
WHEREBY THE DEVIL DOTH THRUST THEM EITHER INTO	606 25

DEVILS

HE CASTETH OUT DEVILS THROUGH BEELZEBUB THE CHIEF OF	129 27
DEVILS THROUGH BEELZEBUB THE CHIEF OF THE DEVILS	129 28
THAT I CAST OUT DEVILS THROUGH BEELZEBUB	129 33
CAST OUT DEVILS, BY WHOM DO YOUR SONS CAST THEM OUT	129 34
OF GOD CAST OUT DEVILS, NO DOUBT THE KINGDOM OF GOD	130 03
THEIR SONS AND THEIR DAUGHTERS UNTO DEVILS	475 10

DEVISED

CUNNINGLY DEVISED FABLES, WHEN WE MADE KNOWN UNTO YOU	248 14

DEVOTE

AND MAY HE DEVOTE THE RESIDUE OF HIS DAYS TO AN	053 06
APPROPRIATE AND DEVOTE THIS HOUSE TO THY HONOUR AND	566 30
TO THY SERVICE I DEVOTE MYSELF, BODY, SOUL, AND	573 14

DEVOTION

OF PIETY AND DEVOTION IN THE WORSHIP OF GOD	V 37
MY LOYALTY AND DEVOTION TO CHRIST AS MY MASTER, I	291 25
THY CHURCH WITH DEVOTION TO THY GLORY AND TO THE	560 22
WITH MORE DEVOTION AND HUMILITY IN HIS SERVICE	564 19
AND DEVOTION OF MIND, THAT THOU MAYEST	566 20
IN PRAYER, TO QUICKEN MY DEVOTION	573 25

DEVOTIONS

OR SUCH DEVOTIONS TAKEN FROM OTHER PARTS OF THIS	R 337 04
IN LEADING THE DEVOTIONS OF THE PEOPLE, AND IN	571 27

DEVOUR

IF A MAN DEVOUR YOU, IF A MAN TAKE OF YOU,	120 24
WALKETH ABOUT, SEEKING WHOM HE MAY DEVOUR	193 06
BEAST OF THE LAND DEVOUR THEM	262 15
2 LEST HE DEVOUR MY SOUL LIKE A LION, AND TEAR IT IN	349 25
GOETH ABOUT TO DEVOUR ME	408 15
OF THE FIELD DEVOUR IT	441 29
FEED THEM, DEVOUR THEM NOT	558 26

DEVOURED

OF THE AIR DEVOURED IT	121 22
WHICH HATH DEVOURED THY LIVING WITH HARLOTS, THOU	203 03
WE HAVE DEVOURED HIM	383 14
AMONG THEM, AND DEVOURED THEM UP	437 31
7 FOR THEY HAVE DEVOURED JACOB, *	440 14
THEIR LAND, AND DEVOURED THE FRUIT OF THEIR GROUND	472 08

DEVOUT

HAST HEARD THE DEVOUT PRAYERS OF THY CHURCH, AND	051 31
JERUSALEM JEWS, DEVOUT MEN, OUT OF EVERY NATION UNDER	180 25
TO HEAR THE DEVOUT PRAYERS OF THY CHURCH	222 11
MAN WAS JUST AND DEVOUT, WAITING FOR THE CONSOLATION	232 31
THE DEVOUT PRAISE OF THY HUMBLE SERVANT	313 05
FORASMUCH AS DEVOUT AND HOLY MEN, AS WELL UNDER THE	564 10

DEVOUTLY

THE PEOPLE DEVOUTLY KNEELING	R 016 23
THE PEOPLE DEVOUTLY KNEELING	R 030 28
ALMIGHTY GOD, DEVOUTLY KNEELING	075 14
ALL DEVOUTLY KNEELING	R 082 28
RELIGIOUSLY AND DEVOUTLY DISPOSED THE MOST	086 30
AND DEVOUTLY GIVEN TO SERVE THEE IN GOOD WORKS, TO	220 18
FAITHFULLY AND DEVOUTLY GIVE THANKS UNTO HIM, AND	276 05
FAITHFULLY AND DEVOUTLY BEG HIS BLESSING ON THIS OUR	564 24

DEW

AND THE CLOUDS DROP DOWN THE DEW	005 27
O YE SHOWERS AND DEW, BLESS YE THE LORD	012 14
THEM THE CONTINUAL DEW OF THY BLESSING	018 23
THEM THE CONTINUAL DEW OF THY BLESSING	032 22
AND THE CLOUDS DROP DOWN THE DEW	050 20
MEN COME TO THEE AS DEW FROM THE WOMB OF THE MORNING	482 13
3 LIKE AS THE DEW OF HERMON, *	509 18

DEWS

O YE DEWS AND FROSTS, BLESS YE THE LORD	012 22

DIDST

DELIVER MAN, THOU DIDST HUMBLE THYSELF TO BE BORN OF	010 26
OF DEATH, THOU DIDST OPEN THE KINGDOM OF HEAVEN TO	010 29
BY THY HOLY SPIRIT DIDST PRESIDE IN THE COUNCIL OF	036 27
WHOLE EARTH, AND DIDST SEND THY BLESSED SON TO PREACH	038 06
SON JESUS CHRIST DIDST PREPARE THE DISCIPLES FOR THE	043 19
WORKS THAT THOU DIDST IN THEIR DAYS, AND IN THE OLD	058 30
BECAUSE THOU DIDST GIVE JESUS CHRIST, THINE ONLY SON,	077 14
THY TENDER MERCY, DIDST GIVE THINE ONLY SON JESUS	080 07
THY FIRST COMING DIDST SEND THY MESSENGER TO PREPARE	093 24
LEADING OF A STAR DIDST MANIFEST THY ONLY-BEGOTTEN	107 03
UNTO HIM, SIR, DIDST NOT THOU SOW GOOD SEED IN THY	116 23
DIDST NOT THOU AGREE WITH ME FOR A PENNY	120 08
WHO FOR OUR SAKE DIDST FAST FORTY DAYS AND FORTY	125 27
SO DIDST THOU LEAD THY PEOPLE, TO MAKE THYSELF A	139 16
FOR OUR REDEMPTION DIDST GIVE THINE ONLY-BEGOTTEN SON	165 03
AS AT THIS TIME DIDST TEACH THE HEARTS OF THY	180 08
ALMIGHTY GOD, WHO DIDST GIVE SUCH GRACE UNTO THY HOLY	226 18
OF THE FAITH, DIDST SUFFER THY HOLY APOSTLE THOMAS TO	228 06
THE TRAITOR JUDAS DIDST CHOOSE THY FAITHFUL SERVANT	233 32
GOD ALMIGHTY, WHO DIDST ENDUE THY HOLY APOSTLE	240 28
SON JESUS CHRIST DIDST GIVE TO THINE APOSTLE SAINT	244 22
WHO ON THE MOUNT DIDST REVEAL TO CHOSEN WITNESSES	247 31
WHO DIDST GIVE TO THINE APOSTLE BARTHOLOMEW	249 14
BY THY BLESSED SON DIDST CALL MATTHEW FROM THE	250 20
ALMIGHTY GOD, WHO DIDST INSPIRE THY SERVANT SAINT	253 16
BUT DIDST VISIT HIM WITH COMFORTS FROM ABOVE	315 24
THY NAME THAT THOU DIDST NOT FORSAKE HIM IN HIS	315 24
DIDST SUPPORT HIM IN PATIENCE AND SUBMISSION TO THY	315 25
AND AT LAST DIDST SEND HIM SEASONABLE RELIEF	315 26
VOICE FROM HEAVEN DIDST PROCLAIM, BLESSED ARE THE	335 26
WORK WHICH THOU DIDST BEGIN IN THEM MAY BE PERFECTED	335 29
WHO BY THY DEATH DIDST TAKE AWAY THE STING OF DEATH	336 10
IN THEE, AND THOU DIDST DELIVER THEM	366 11
7 THOU DIDST TURN THY FACE FROM ME, *	375 07
AND YET THOU DIDST TURN AND REFRESH ME	426 18
14 THOU DIDST DIVIDE THE SEA THROUGH THY POWER	431 02
8 THOU DIDST CAUSE THY JUDGMENT TO BE HEARD FROM	433 04
O GOD, THOUGH THOU DIDST PUNISH THEIR WICKED DOINGS	462 33
IN THY CHURCH, AND DIDST INSPIRE THINE APOSTLES TO	531 16
SON JESUS CHRIST DIDST GIVE TO THY HOLY APOSTLES MANY	549 07
AND DIDST CHARGE THEM TO FEED THY FLOCK	549 09

DIDYMUS

CALLED DIDYMUS, WAS NOT WITH THEM WHEN JESUS	228 25

DIE

WHO ARE CONDEMNED TO DIE)	046 21
NOT ONLY TO DIE FOR US, BUT ALSO TO BE OUR	087 03
THAT THAT DISCIPLE SHOULD NOT DIE	102 10
YET JESUS SAID NOT UNTO HIM, HE SHALL NOT DIE	102 11
IF I SHOULD DIE WITH THEE, I WILL NOT DENY THEE IN	141 26
UNTO MEN ONCE TO DIE, BUT AFTER THIS THE JUDGMENT	148 27
OUR LAW HE OUGHT TO DIE, BECAUSE HE MADE HIMSELF THE	159 09
FOR AS IN ADAM ALL DIE, *	163 15
GRANT US SO TO DIE DAILY FROM SIN, THAT WE MAY	165 06
THINE ONLY SON TO DIE FOR OUR SINS, AND TO RISE AGAIN	170 20
FOR IF YE LIVE AFTER THE FLESH, YE SHALL DIE	200 05
COME DOWN ERE MY CHILD DIE	220 02
THY SERVANT) MAY DIE TO SIN AND RISE TO NEWNESS OF	278 20
AFFECTIONS MAY DIE IN HIM, AND THAT ALL THINGS	278 21
IN READINESS TO DIE, WHENSOEVER IT SHALL PLEASE	R 321 04
THAT A MAN MAY EAT THEREOF, AND NOT DIE	322 25
LIVETH AND BELIEVETH IN ME, SHALL NEVER DIE	324 08
FOR AS IN ADAM ALL DIE, EVEN SO IN CHRIST SHALL ALL	328 24
WHICH THOU SOWEST IS NOT QUICKENED, EXCEPT IT DIE	329 07
ARE THE DEAD WHO DIE IN THE LORD	333 26
SHALL LIVE, THOUGH HE DIE	334 32
IN HIM, SHALL NOT DIE ETERNALLY	335 02
ARE THE DEAD WHO DIE IN THE LORD	335 27
LIVETH AND BELIEVETH IN ME, SHALL NEVER DIE	338 08
WHEN SHALL HE DIE, AND HIS NAME PERISH	392 08
THAT WISE MEN ALSO DIE AND PERISH TOGETHER, *	400 23
PRESERVE THOU THOSE THAT ARE APPOINTED TO DIE	440 28
7 BUT YE SHALL DIE LIKE MEN, *	443 31
AND LIKE UNTO HIM THAT IS AT THE POINT TO DIE	449 27
THEIR BREATH, THEY DIE, AND ARE TURNED AGAIN TO THEIR	469 19
17 I SHALL NOT DIE, BUT LIVE, *	489 04
SUCH A STATE THAT WE MAY NEVER BE AFRAID TO DIE	591 30
PRESERVE THOU THOSE THAT ARE APPOINTED TO DIE	600 11

DIED

THE SAKE OF HIM WHO DIED AND ROSE AGAIN, AND EVER	037 2
THAT CHRIST DIED FOR THEE, AND FEED ON HIM IN THY	082 3
FOR HIS MERITS, WHO DIED, AND WAS BURIED, AND ROSE	161 1
IN THAT HE DIED, HE DIED UNTO SIN ONCE	163 0
FOR IN THAT HE DIED, HE DIED UNTO SIN ONCE	163 0
THAT THE BEGGAR DIED, AND WAS CARRIED BY THE ANGELS	190 0

DIED   CONTINUED

THE RICH MAN ALSO DIED, AND WAS BURIED   190 10
IN THAT HE DIED, HE DIED UNTO SIN ONCE   197 23
FOR IN THAT HE DIED, HE DIED UNTO SIN ONCE   197 23
HOW THAT CHRIST DIED FOR OUR SINS ACCORDING TO THE   205 04
BELIEVE THAT JESUS DIED AND ROSE AGAIN, EVEN SO THEM   268 31
THAT LIKE AS CHRIST DIED AND ROSE AGAIN, SO THIS   278 18
IT IS CHRIST THAT DIED, YEA RATHER, THAT IS RISEN   331 04
THROUGH HIM WHO DIED FOR US AND ROSE AGAIN, THY SON,   595 09
AS CHRIST DIED FOR US, AND WAS BURIED   603 18

DIETH

FROM THE DEAD DIETH NO MORE   163 04
FROM THE DEAD DIETH NO MORE   197 22
WITH HIM WHEN HE DIETH, *   401 10

DIFFERENCE

WITHOUT ANY DIFFERENCE OF INEQUALITY   079 11
THERE IS NO DIFFERENCE BETWEEN THE JEW AND THE GREEK   227 02
CASE OF ANY DIFFERENCE BETWEEN YOU AND YOUR   569 34
AND MARK OF DIFFERENCE, WHEREBY CHRISTIAN MEN ARE   608 24

DIFFERENCES

THERE ARE DIFFERENCES OF ADMINISTRATIONS, BUT THE   182 23
THERE ARE DIFFERENCES OF ADMINISTRATIONS, BUT THE   203 23

DIFFERENT

IN HIS WORSHIP DIFFERENT FORMS AND USAGES MAY WITHOUT   V 03
AIM IN THESE DIFFERENT REVIEWS AND ALTERATIONS HATH   V 33
AND THE DIFFERENT RELIGIOUS DENOMINATIONS OF   VI 09
ALL THE DIFFERENT ALTERATIONS AND AMENDMENTS   VI 28
BEING DIFFERENT IN THE SEVERAL STATES,   R 304 18

DIFFERETH

HE IS A CHILD, DIFFERETH NOTHING FROM A SERVANT,   104 15
FOR ONE STAR DIFFERETH FROM ANOTHER STAR IN GLORY   329 18

DIFFERING

THEN GIFTS DIFFERING ACCORDING TO THE GRACE THAT IS   111 15

DIFFICULT

DUTIES ARE DIFFICULT OR BURDENSOME, AND COMFORT THEM   599 27

DIFFICULTIES

SORROWS AND DIFFICULTIES OF THE WORLD   316 20

DIFFICULTY

OF SO GREAT DIFFICULTY, YE SEE WITH HOW GREAT CARE   540 25

DIGEST

AND INWARDLY DIGEST THEM, THAT BY PATIENCE AND   092 10

DIGGED

HATH GRAVEN AND DIGGED UP A PIT, *   350 23
THEY HAVE DIGGED A PIT BEFORE ME, AND ARE FALLEN INTO   409 27
UNTIL THE PIT BE DIGGED UP FOR THE UNGODLY   458 13
85 THE PROUD HAVE DIGGED PITS FOR ME, *   495 27

DIGNITY

TO CONSIDER THE DIGNITY OF THAT HOLY MYSTERY, AND THE   087 08
OF WHAT DIGNITY, AND OF HOW GREAT IMPORTANCE THIS   539 27
INTO HOW HIGH A DIGNITY, AND TO HOW WEIGHTY AN OFFICE   539 31
WHO HATH PLACED YOU IN SO HIGH A DIGNITY   540 28

DILIGENCE

DO THY DILIGENCE GLADLY TO GIVE OF THAT   072 33
HE THAT RULETH, WITH DILIGENCE   111 21
DO THY DILIGENCE TO COME SHORTLY UNTO ME   253 31
APPLY ALL YOUR DILIGENCE TO FRAME AND FASHION YOUR   533 24
YOUR CARE AND DILIGENCE, UNTIL YE HAVE DONE ALL THAT   540 17
YOUR FAITHFUL DILIGENCE ALWAYS SO TO MINISTER THE   542 11
WITH ALL DILIGENCE TO KEEP AND OBSERVE THE SAME   542 16
ALL FAITHFUL DILIGENCE, TO BANISH AND DRIVE AWAY FROM   542 19
ALL FAITHFUL DILIGENCE, TO BANISH AND DRIVE AWAY FROM   555 02
DILIGENCE, SOUND DOCTRINE, AND PRUDENCE,   569 15

DILIGENT

TO CALL FOR BY DILIGENT PRAYER   289 16
FAITHFUL AND DILIGENT, HE MAY BE ADMITTED BY HIS   R 535 23
WILL YOU BE DILIGENT IN PRAYERS, AND IN READING THE   542 26
WILL YOU BE DILIGENT TO FRAME AND FASHION YOUR OWN   542 32
BE DILIGENT IN THEM, THAT THE INCREASE COMING THEREBY   558 23
TO CALL FOR BY DILIGENT PRAYER   580 20
ALL THINGS, AND DILIGENT IN OUR SEVERAL CALLINGS   588 28
SO THAT HE BE DILIGENT TO FRAME HIS LIFE ACCORDING TO   606 33

DILIGENTLY

AND DILIGENTLY TO LIVE AFTER THY COMMANDMENTS   056 12
ALL PERSONS DILIGENTLY TO TRY AND EXAMINE THEMSELVES,   085 28
WHICH HE HAD DILIGENTLY ENQUIRED OF THE WISE MEN   103 28

DILIGENTLY   CONTINUED

OF THEM DILIGENTLY WHAT TIME THE STAR APPEARED   109 11
GO AND SEARCH DILIGENTLY FOR THE YOUNG CHILD   109 13
AND SEEK DILIGENTLY TILL SHE FIND IT   193 29
AND PASTORS DILIGENTLY TO PREACH THY HOLY WORD, AND   244 25
PARISH SHALL DILIGENTLY, UPON SUNDAYS AND HOLY DAYS,   R 295 07
SHALL DILIGENTLY FROM TIME TO TIME, BUT ESPECIALLY IN   R 321 05
THAT WE SHALL DILIGENTLY KEEP THY COMMANDMENTS   490 06
UNTO ALL MEN, DILIGENTLY READING HOLY SCRIPTURE AND   529 11
WILL YOU DILIGENTLY READ THE SAME UNTO THE PEOPLE   533 06
THAT THEY MAY DILIGENTLY PREACH THY WORD, AND DULY   549 11
AND DILIGENTLY EXERCISE SUCH DISCIPLINE AS BY THE   555 16
PARISH SHALL DILIGENTLY, UPON SUNDAYS AND HOLY DAYS,   R 582 27
DILIGENTLY AND DISTINCTLY, THAT THEY MAY   610 09

DIMINISHED

GOD'S GIFTS DIMINISHED FROM SUCH AS BY FAITH,   608 15

DIMITTIS

NUNC DIMITTIS, DEUS MISEREATUR, BENEDIC,   R 025 17
CALLED NUNC DIMITTIS, AS FOLLOWETH   R 028 06

DINNER

ARE BIDDEN, BEHOLD, I HAVE PREPARED MY DINNER   218 08

DIOCESAN

ANY GENERAL OR DIOCESAN CONVENTION, THE ABOVE PRAYER   R 037 09
ADMITTED BY HIS DIOCESAN TO THE ORDER OF PRIESTHOOD,   R 535 24
THE GENERAL AND DIOCESAN CONVENTION, SAYING AS   R 571 24

DIOCESE

OR OF THE DIOCESE CONCERNED   R 037 11
BISHOP OF THIS DIOCESE), THAT THEY MAY MINISTER   047 24
IN ANY DIOCESE, THE CONCLUDING PARAGRAPH IN THE   R 569 10
BISHOP OF THE DIOCESE IS PRESENT AT THE INSTITUTION   R 574 29

DIP

THAT HE MAY DIP THE TIP OF HIS FINGER IN   190 14
AFTER THEM, HE SHALL DIP HIM IN THE WATER DISCREETLY,   R 279 26
AND THEN SHALL DIP HIM IN THE WATER, OR POUR WATER   R 279 32

DIPPED

THY FOOT MAY BE DIPPED IN THE BLOOD OF THINE ENEMIES,   420 33

DIPPETH

THE TWELVE, THAT DIPPETH WITH ME IN THE DISH   141 05

DIRECT

BE PLEASED TO DIRECT AND PROSPER ALL THEIR   035 12
SO TO DIRECT, SANCTIFY, AND GOVERN US IN OUR   036 33
IT IS IN ERROR, DIRECT IT   037 18
MAY HAVE GRACE TO DIRECT OUR LIVES AFTER THEIR GOOD   048 19
DIRECT US, O LORD, IN ALL OUR DOINGS, WITH THY MOST   049 23
BESEECH THEE, TO DIRECT, SANCTIFY, AND GOVERN,   070 07
THEE ALSO, SO TO DIRECT AND DISPOSE THE HEARTS OF ALL   074 16
THAT HE MAY DIRECT AND RULE US ACCORDING TO THY WILL,   183 23
MAY IN ALL THINGS DIRECT AND RULE OUR HEARTS   215 29
BESEECH THEE, TO DIRECT, SANCTIFY, AND GOVERN,   298 27
OR AS THE ORDINARY SHALL DIRECT   R 305 09
MORNING WILL I DIRECT MY PRAYER UNTO THEE, AND WILL   348 05
AND SHALL DIRECT HIS GOING IN THE WAY   446 33
WAYS WERE MADE SO DIRECT, *   490 08
DIRECT US, O LORD, IN ALL OUR DOINGS, WITH THY MOST   571 08
DIRECT US IN ALL OUR WAYS   589 02

DIRECTION

UNDER THE DIRECTION OF THE PRIEST   R 073 36
UNDER THE DIRECTION OF THE BISHOP   294 19
IS LEFT TO THE DIRECTION OF THOSE LAWS, IN EVERY   R 304 19
THE DIRECTION AND ASSISTANCE OF THY HOLY   590 11

DIRECTIONS

SUCH LAWFUL DIRECTIONS AS YOU SHALL AT ANY TIME   569 21
FOR ALL THE DIRECTIONS, ASSISTANCES, AND COMFORTS OF   591 16

DISALLOWED

LIVING STONE, DISALLOWED INDEED OF MEN, BUT CHOSEN OF   259 29

DISANNUL

CANNOT DISANNUL, THAT IT SHOULD MAKE THE   207 24

DISAPPOINT

13 UP, LORD, DISAPPOINT HIM, AND CAST HIM DOWN   359 12

DISAPPOINTED

WERE NOT DISAPPOINTED OF THEIR LUST   436 30
ME NOT BE DISAPPOINTED OF MY HOPE   497 31

DISAPPOINTETH

AND DISAPPOINTETH HIM NOT, *   357 15

DISCERN

THAT THEY MAY DISCERN THE TRUTH, AND IMPARTIALLY   036 04

DISCERNED

AS A TREE DISCERNED BY THE FRUIT   605 15
MEN ARE DISCERNED FROM OTHERS THAT BE NOT CHRISTENED,   608 25

DISCERNING

TO ANOTHER DISCERNING OF SPIRITS   182 31
TO ANOTHER DISCERNING OF SPIRITS   203 31

DISCIPLE

SEETH THE DISCIPLE WHOM JESUS LOVED FOLLOWING   102 04
THAT THAT DISCIPLE SHOULD NOT DIE   102 10
THIS IS THE DISCIPLE WHICH TESTIFIETH OF THESE   102 12
AND THE DISCIPLE STANDING BY, WHOM HE LOVED,   160 20
SAITH HE TO THE DISCIPLE, BEHOLD THY MOTHER   160 22
THAT HOUR THAT DISCIPLE TOOK HER UNTO HIS OWN HOME   160 23
WHO ALSO HIMSELF WAS JESUS' DISCIPLE   162 08
TO THE OTHER DISCIPLE, WHOM JESUS LOVED, AND SAITH   164 13
AND THAT OTHER DISCIPLE, AND CAME TO THE SEPULCHRE   164 17
AND THE OTHER DISCIPLE DID OUTRUN PETER, AND CAME   164 18
ALSO THAT OTHER DISCIPLE, WHICH CAME FIRST TO THE   164 25
THE DISCIPLE IS NOT ABOVE HIS MASTER   195 04
WAS A CERTAIN DISCIPLE AT DAMASCUS, NAMED ANANIAS   230 14

DISCIPLES

PREPARE THE DISCIPLES FOR THE COMING OF THE   043 19
UPON THE DISCIPLES, TO TEACH THEM, AND TO LEAD THEM   078 28
GAVE IT TO HIS DISCIPLES, SAYING, TAKE, EAT, (C) THIS   080 20
SENT JESUS TWO DISCIPLES, SAYING UNTO THEM, GO INTO   091 13
AND THE DISCIPLES WENT, AND DID AS JESUS COMMANDED   091 22
TWO OF HIS DISCIPLES, AND SAID UNTO HIM, ART THOU HE   094 17
AND HIS DISCIPLES, TO THE MARRIAGE   113 13
AND HIS DISCIPLES BELIEVED ON HIM   113 31
AND HIS DISCIPLES ASKED HIM, SAYING, WHAT MIGHT THIS   121 28
AND HIS DISCIPLES CAME AND BESOUGHT HIM, SAYING,   128 12
A MOUNTAIN, AND THERE HE SAT WITH HIS DISCIPLES   131 25
ONE OF HIS DISCIPLES, ANDREW, SIMON PETER'S BROTHER,   131 32
TO THE DISCIPLES, AND THE DISCIPLES TO THEM THAT WERE   132 04
AND THE DISCIPLES TO THEM THAT WERE SET DOWN   132 05
SAID UNTO HIS DISCIPLES, GATHER UP THE FRAGMENTS THAT   132 07
HIS DISCIPLES SAID UNTO HIM, WHERE WILT   140 23
TWO OF HIS DISCIPLES, AND SAITH UNTO THEM, GO YE INTO   140 25
WHERE I SHALL EAT THE PASSOVER WITH MY DISCIPLES   140 30
AND HIS DISCIPLES WENT FORTH, AND CAME INTO THE CITY,   140 32
SAITH TO HIS DISCIPLES, SIT YE HERE, WHILE I SHALL   141 28
WHERE I SHALL EAT THE PASSOVER WITH MY DISCIPLES   148 30
AND HIS DISCIPLES ALSO FOLLOWED HIM   150 14
COME TO HIS DISCIPLES, HE FOUND THEM SLEEPING FOR   150 24
LEST HIS DISCIPLES COME BY NIGHT, AND STEAL HIM   162 20
THEN THE DISCIPLES WENT AWAY AGAIN UNTO THEIR OWN   164 28
TELL HIS DISCIPLES AND PETER THAT HE GOETH   165 31
HIMSELF TO HIS DISCIPLES IN THE BREAKING OF BREAD   166 07
TWO OF HIS DISCIPLES WENT THAT SAME DAY TO A VILLAGE   167 03
SHUT WHERE THE DISCIPLES WERE ASSEMBLED FOR FEAR OF   171 19
THEN WERE THE DISCIPLES GLAD WHEN THEY SAW THE LORD   171 19
SAID TO HIS DISCIPLES, A LITTLE WHILE, AND YE SHALL   173 27
SOME OF HIS DISCIPLES AMONG THEMSELVES, WHAT IS THIS   173 29
SAID UNTO HIS DISCIPLES, NOW I GO MY WAY TO HIM THAT   175 06
HIS DISCIPLES SAID UNTO HIM, LO, NOW SPEAKEST THOU   176 32
SAID UNTO HIS DISCIPLES, IF YE LOVE ME, KEEP MY   181 08
SAID TO HIS DISCIPLES, ASK, AND IT SHALL BE GIVEN   183 10
SAID UNTO HIS DISCIPLES, EXCEPT YOUR RIGHTEOUSNESS   197 28
CALLED HIS DISCIPLES UNTO HIM, AND SAITH UNTO THEM, I   199 09
AND HIS DISCIPLES ANSWERED HIM, FROM WHENCE CAN A MAN   199 14
GAVE TO HIS DISCIPLES TO SET BEFORE THEM   199 19
MANY OF HIS DISCIPLES WENT WITH HIM, AND MUCH PEOPLE   212 28
UNTO HIM THEIR DISCIPLES WITH THE HERODIANS, SAYING,   222 30
UNTO JOHN'S DISCIPLES, BEHOLD, THERE CAME A CERTAIN   224 12
AND FOLLOWED HIM, AND SO DID HIS DISCIPLES   224 16
ONE OF HIS DISCIPLES, ANDREW, SIMON PETER'S BROTHER,   225 28
TO THE DISCIPLES, AND THE DISCIPLES TO THEM THAT WERE   226 04
AND THE DISCIPLES TO THEM THAT WERE SET DOWN   226 04
SAID UNTO HIS DISCIPLES, GATHER UP THE FRAGMENTS THAT   226 06
THE OTHER DISCIPLES THEREFORE SAID UNTO HIM, WE HAVE   228 26
DAYS AGAIN HIS DISCIPLES WERE WITHIN, AND THOMAS WITH   228 31
OF HIS DISCIPLES, WHICH ARE NOT WRITTEN IN THIS BOOK   229 10
AGAINST THE DISCIPLES OF THE LORD, WENT UNTO THE HIGH   229 26
DAYS WITH THE DISCIPLES WHICH WERE AT DAMASCUS   231 03
MIDST OF THE DISCIPLES, AND SAID, (THE NUMBER OF   234 06
SO SHALL YE BE MY DISCIPLES   238 20
SAID UNTO HIS DISCIPLES, LET NOT YOUR HEART BE   239 29
AND THE DISCIPLES WERE CALLED CHRISTIANS FIRST IN   241 14
THEN THE DISCIPLES, EVERY MAN ACCORDING TO HIS   241 19
HE ASKED HIS DISCIPLES, SAYING, WHOM DO MEN SAY THAT   245 32
THEN THE DISCIPLES, EVERY MAN ACCORDING TO HIS   246 28
CAME AND SAT DOWN WITH HIM AND HIS DISCIPLES   251 17
SAID UNTO HIS DISCIPLES, WHY EATETH YOUR MASTER WITH   251 18
TIME CAME THE DISCIPLES UNTO JESUS, SAYING, WHO IS   252 22
WAS SET, HIS DISCIPLES CAME UNTO HIM   257 19
AND HIS DISCIPLES REBUKED THOSE THAT BROUGHT THEM   274 26
AND MAKE DISCIPLES OF ALL NATIONS, BAPTIZING THEM IN   275 28
TO HIS DISCIPLES, THAT THEY SHOULD GO TEACH ALL   279 12
TIME CAME THE DISCIPLES UNTO JESUS, SAYING, WHO IS   339 21
SAITH TO HIS DISCIPLES, YE NOW THEREFORE HAVE SORROW   341 09
OF THE DISCIPLES UNTO THEM, AND SAID, IT IS NOT   532 08

DISCIPLES   CONTINUED

NUMBER OF THE DISCIPLES MULTIPLIED IN JERUSALEM   532 21
HE UNTO HIS DISCIPLES, THE HARVEST TRULY IS   538 17
TO DRAW AWAY DISCIPLES AFTER THEM   550 33
SHUT WHERE THE DISCIPLES WERE ASSEMBLED FOR FEAR OF   551 28
THEN WERE THE DISCIPLES GLAD, WHEN THEY SAW THE LORD   551 32
AND HIS DISCIPLES REMEMBERED THAT IT WAS WRITTEN, THE   568 02

DISCIPLES'

TO WASH THE DISCIPLES' FEET, AND TO WIPE THEM WITH   155 33

DISCIPLINE

BELONG TO DOCTRINE MUST BE REFERRED TO DISCIPLINE   V 06
WISELY THE DISCIPLINE OF CHRIST   047 25
AND DISCIPLINE, IN SUCH MANNER AS THEY MIGHT   VI 12
OF DOCTRINE, DISCIPLINE, OR WORSHIP   VI 33
A READY WILL TO OBSERVE ALL SPIRITUAL DISCIPLINE   535 05
AND THE DISCIPLINE OF CHRIST, AS THE LORD HATH   542 13
THE GODLY DISCIPLINE THEREOF   549 12
THE DOCTRINE, DISCIPLINE, AND WORSHIP OF THE   R 552 27
THE DOCTRINE, DISCIPLINE, AND WORSHIP OF THE   552 30
EXERCISE SUCH DISCIPLINE AS BY THE AUTHORITY OF GOD'S   555 16
SO MINISTER DISCIPLINE, THAT YOU FORGET NOT MERCY   558 29
THE DISCIPLINE OF THE CHURCH   571 27
TO THE DISCIPLINE OF THE CHURCH, THAT INQUIRY BE MADE   608 19

DISCLOSED

SHALL BE DISCLOSED, THAT IF EITHER OF YOU KNOW ANY   300 26

DISCOMFIT

THEE I SHALL DISCOMFIT AN HOST OF MEN, *   361 26

DISCOMFITED

AND WERE DISCOMFITED, *   420 04

DISCOMFORT

TO THE GREAT DISCOMFORT OF MY SOUL   382 15

DISCORD

FROM VIOLENCE, DISCORD, AND CONFUSION   036 14

DISCOURAGED

HIM WHEN DISCOURAGED OR SORROWFUL   597 31
HOPE ALL DISCOURAGED AND UNHAPPY PEOPLE, AND BY THY   599 11

DISCOVERED

WORLD WERE DISCOVERED, *   360 29

DISCREETLY

IN THE WATER DISCREETLY, OR SHALL POUR WATER UPON   R 279 27
DISCREETLY, ADVISEDLY, SOBERLY, AND IN   300 18

DISCRETION

AT HIS DISCRETION, PASS AT ONCE FROM THE   R 003 07
AT HIS DISCRETION, MAY USE, INSTEAD OF WHAT FOLLOWS, R 007 04
AT HIS DISCRETION, AFTER ANY ONE OF THE FOLLOWING   R 010 04
AT HIS DISCRETION, PASS AT ONCE FROM THE   R 021 05
AT HIS DISCRETION, MAY OMIT ONE OF THE LESSONS IN   R 026 07
IN HIS DISCRETION, MAY OMIT ANY OF THE CLAUSES IN   R 047 04
AT THE DISCRETION OF THE MINISTER   R 049 04
AT HIS DISCRETION, OMIT ALL THAT FOLLOWETH,   R 058 09
OR AT HIS DISCRETION ADD OTHER PRAYERS FROM THIS   R 059 29
AT THE DISCRETION OF THE MINISTER   R 060 06
AT THE DISCRETION OF THE PRIEST   R 067 08
IN HIS DISCRETION, HE MAY THINK CONVENIENT   R 086 27
USED AT THE DISCRETION OF THE MINISTER   R 305 05
USED AT THE DISCRETION OF THE MINISTER   R 308 03
TO HIS DISCRETION, ONE OF THE PENITENTIAL PSALMS   R 308 09
AT THE DISCRETION OF THE MINISTER, BE   R 313 09
IN HIS DISCRETION, HE SHALL THINK CONVENIENT   R 314 24
AT THE DISCRETION OF THE MINISTER   R 315 04
AT THE DISCRETION OF THE MINISTER, THE CREED,   R 331 28
MORE OF THE FOLLOWING PRAYERS, AT HIS DISCRETION   R 334 13
AT HIS DISCRETION, MAY ALSO USE ANY OF THE FOLLOWING R 335 23
AT HIS DISCRETION, USE SUCH PART OF THIS OFFICE,   R 337 04
AND WILL GUIDE HIS WORDS WITH DISCRETION   483 27
THAT IN THE DISCRETION OF THE BISHOP, INSTEAD OF THE R 531 09
THAT IN THE DISCRETION OF THE BISHOP, INSTEAD OF THE R 537 15
THAT IN THE DISCRETION OF THE PRESIDING BISHOP,   R 553 23
AT THEIR OWN DISCRETION, AS THEY SHALL JUDGE THE SAME 609 23

DISDAINFULLY

DISDAINFULLY, AND DESPITEFULLY SPEAK AGAINST   376 34
SPEAK SO DISDAINFULLY, *   457 25

DISEASE

WITH A SORE DISEASE, *   388 04
8 AN EVIL DISEASE, SAY THEY, CLEAVETH FAST UNTO HIM   392 15

DISEASED

MIRACLES WHICH HE DID ON THEM THAT WERE DISEASED   131 23

DISEASED   CONTINUED

WHICH WAS DISEASED WITH AN ISSUE OF BLOOD TWELVE   224 17

DISEASES

SUDDEN PERILS, DISEASES, AND SICKNESSES, AND EVER   R 321 02

DISFIGURE

FOR THEY DISFIGURE THEIR FACES, THAT THEY MAY APPEAR   125 10

DISH

OF THE TWELVE, THAT DIPPETH WITH ME IN THE DISH   141 06

DISHONESTY

THINGS OF DISHONESTY, NOT WALKING IN CRAFTINESS,   250 29

DISHONOUR

BY HONOUR AND DISHONOUR, BY EVIL REPORT AND GOOD   126 16
AND YE DO DISHONOUR ME   133 15
IT IS SOWN IN DISHONOUR   329 20
REBUKE AND DISHONOUR, THAT BOAST THEMSELVES AGAINST   383 18
AN OPEN ENEMY THAT HATH DONE ME THIS DISHONOUR   407 12
KNOWN MY REPROACH, MY SHAME, AND MY DISHONOUR   423 12
WITH SHAME AND DISHONOUR THAT SEEK TO DO ME EVIL   425 32
HOW LONG SHALL THE ADVERSARY DO THIS DISHONOUR   430 27
AND COVERED HIM WITH DISHONOUR   452 31

DISOBEDIENCE

WRATH OF GOD UPON THE CHILDREN OF DISOBEDIENCE   129 11

DISOBEDIENT

OF THE DISOBEDIENT TO THE WISDOM OF THE JUST, THAT AT   093 28
WERE DISOBEDIENT, WHEN ONCE THE LONG-SUFFERING OF GOD   161 26
HANDS UNTO A DISOBEDIENT AND GAINSAYING PEOPLE   227 22
BUT WERE DISOBEDIENT AT THE SEA, EVEN AT THE RED SEA   473 15

DISPENSATION

OF THE DISPENSATION OF THE GRACE OF GOD, WHICH IS   108 07

DISPENSER

A FAITHFUL DISPENSER OF THE WORD OF GOD, AND OF HIS   546 13
A FAITHFUL DISPENSER OF THE WORD OF GOD, AND OF HIS   546 19

DISPENSING

CONDUCT IN DISPENSING THE DIVINE WORD, IN LEADING THE   571 26

DISPERSED

WHOLE OF THY DISPERSED SHEEP, BEING GATHERED INTO ONE   037 06
9 HE HATH DISPERSED ABROAD, AND GIVEN TO THE POOR,   483 34
SHEEP THAT ARE DISPERSED ABROAD, AND FOR HIS CHILDREN   540 02

DISPLEASED

WERE SORE DISPLEASED, AND SAID UNTO HIM, HEAREST THOU   260 12
HE WAS MUCH DISPLEASED, AND SAID UNTO THEM, SUFFER   274 27
WHO FOR OUR SINS ART JUSTLY DISPLEASED   332 24
THOU HAST ALSO BEEN DISPLEASED   412 13
TEMPTED AND DISPLEASED THE MOST HIGH GOD, *   438 24
WILT THOU BE DISPLEASED AT US FOR EVER   446 16
AND ART DISPLEASED AT HIM   452 17
SO WRATHFULLY DISPLEASED AT US   504 11

DISPLEASURE

HE SHUT UP HIS LOVING-KINDNESS IN DISPLEASURE   311 17
AWAY IN THY DISPLEASURE; *   325 26
NOR CAST THY SERVANT AWAY IN DISPLEASURE   326 25
AND VEX THEM IN HIS SORE DISPLEASURE   346 07
NEITHER CHASTEN ME IN THY DISPLEASURE   348 34
AT THE BLASTING OF THE BREATH OF THY DISPLEASURE   360 30
THEM IN HIS DISPLEASURE, AND THE FIRE SHALL CONSUME   365 23
NOR CAST THY SERVANT AWAY IN DISPLEASURE   372 17
8 LEAVE OFF FROM WRATH, AND LET GO DISPLEASURE   385 09
NEITHER CHASTEN ME IN THY HEAVY DISPLEASURE   387 22
BECAUSE OF THY DISPLEASURE   387 25
IN THY DISPLEASURE SHALT CAST THEM DOWN   408 29
THY WRATHFUL DISPLEASURE TAKE HOLD OF THEM   423 24
HE SHUT UP HIS LOVING-KINDNESS IN DISPLEASURE   433 34
UP HEAVY DISPLEASURE AGAINST ISRAEL   436 12
HIS WHOLE DISPLEASURE TO ARISE   437 17
DISPLEASURE, AND TROUBLE   438 07
HIM TO DISPLEASURE WITH THEIR IMAGES   438 29
TOOK SORE DISPLEASURE AT ISRAEL   438 31
AWAY ALL THY DISPLEASURE, *   446 12
THY WRATHFUL DISPLEASURE GOETH OVER ME, *   449 29
AWAY IN THY DISPLEASURE, +   453 31

DISPOSAL

FOR THE DISPOSAL OF THEIR TEMPORAL GOODS, AND, WHEN   R 320 22

DISPOSE

AND PRAYERS, AND DISPOSE THE WAY OF THY SERVANTS   049 12
SO TO DIRECT AND DISPOSE THE HEARTS OF ALL CHRISTIAN   074 16

DISPOSED

OR OTHERWISE DISPOSED OF, AS MAY SEEM MOST CONVENIENT   V 08
AS HE IS DISPOSED IN HIS HEART, NOT GRUDGINGLY, OR OF   072 18
AND DEVOUTLY DISPOSED THE MOST COMFORTABLE SACRAMENT   086 30

DISPOSITION

TEMPER AND DISPOSITION OF OUR SOULS   590 13

DISQUIETED

ART THOU SO DISQUIETED WITHIN ME   310 17
CAUSE TO BE DISQUIETED FOR LACK OF THE SAME   R 321 10
ART THOU SO DISQUIETED WITHIN ME   393 12
ART THOU SO DISQUIETED WITHIN ME   393 32
ART THOU SO DISQUIETED WITHIN ME   394 16
4 MY HEART IS DISQUIETED WITHIN ME, *   406 26

DISQUIETETH

AND DISQUIETETH HIMSELF IN VAIN   324 25
AND DISQUIETETH HIMSELF IN VAIN   389 20

DISQUIETNESS

THE VERY DISQUIETNESS OF MY HEART   388 07

DISQUIETUDE

FROM THE DISQUIETUDE OF THIS WORLD, MAY BE PERMITTED   248 03

DISSEMBLE

WE SHOULD NOT DISSEMBLE NOR CLOAK THEM BEFORE THE   005 31
WE SHOULD NOT DISSEMBLE NOR CLOAK THEM BEFORE THE   023 07
AND DISSEMBLE IN THEIR DOUBLE HEART   355 10

DISSEMBLED

AND DISSEMBLED WITH HIM IN THEIR TONGUE   437 11

DISSEMBLERS

MANNER OF DISSEMBLERS WITH GOD   087 12

DISSIMULATION

LET LOVE BE WITHOUT DISSIMULATION   111 22

DISSOLUTION

AND DISSOLUTION OF ALL SACERDOTAL RELATION, BETWEEN   569 32
AND DISSOLUTION OF ALL SACERDOTAL CONNECTION BETWEEN   569 35

DISTINCTLY

REHEARSE DISTINCTLY THE TEN COMMANDMENTS   R 067 22
AND DISTINCTLY, THAT THEY MAY BE UNDERSTANDED OF THE   610 09

DISTRESS

UPON THE EARTH DISTRESS OF NATIONS, WITH PERPLEXITY   093 06
THE DISTRESS OF THIS THY SERVANT   320 09
OR DISTRESS, OR PERSECUTION, OR FAMINE,   331 07
AND HE DELIVERED THEM FROM THEIR DISTRESS   476 16
HE DELIVERED THEM OUT OF THEIR DISTRESS   476 31
HE DELIVERED THEM OUT OF THEIR DISTRESS   477 14
HE DELIVERETH THEM OUT OF THEIR DISTRESS   477 34

DISTRESSED

OR DISTRESSED, IN MIND, BODY, OR ESTATE   019 05
OR DISTRESSED, IN MIND, BODY, OR ESTATE   033 03
RELIEVE THE DISTRESSED, PROTECT THE INNOCENT, AWAKEN   046 24
THE RELIEF OF DISTRESSED WOMEN IN CHILD-BED   R 307 09
SUFFER THEM NOT TO BE DISTRESSED   599 14

DISTRESSES

IN DISTRESSES, IN STRIPES, IN IMPRISONMENTS, IN   126 11

DISTRIBUTE

AND TO DISTRIBUTE, FORGET NOT   072 27

DISTRIBUTED

HE DISTRIBUTED TO THE DISCIPLES, AND THE   132 04
HE DISTRIBUTED TO THE DISCIPLES, AND THE   226 03

DISTRIBUTING

DISTRIBUTING TO THE NECESSITY OF SAINTS   111 27

DISTRIBUTION

TIME OF THE DISTRIBUTION OF THE HOLY SACRAMENT,   R 322 33
HIM IN THE DISTRIBUTION THEREOF   533 14

DITCH

SHALL THEY NOT BOTH FALL INTO THE DITCH   195 03

DIVERS

HAST APPOINTED DIVERS ORDERS IN THY CHURCH	039 08
TIMES AND IN DIVERS MANNERS SPAKE IN TIME PAST UNTO	096 22
TO ANOTHER DIVERS KINDS OF TONGUES	182 32
FOR DIVERS OF THEM CAME FROM FAR	199 13
TO ANOTHER DIVERS KINDS OF TONGUES	203 32
WHEN YE FALL INTO DIVERS TEMPTATIONS	239 08
ABOUT WITH DIVERS COLOURS	397 04
THC HEADS OVER DIVERS COUNTRIES	482 20
10 HE SMOTE DIVERS NATIONS, *	510 23
HAST APPOINTED DIVERS ORDERS OF MINISTERS IN THY	531 15
HAST APPOINTED DIVERS ORDERS OF MINISTERS IN THY	537 21
HAST APPOINTED DIVERS ORDERS OF MINISTERS IN THY	547 32
HAST APPOINTED DIVERS ORDERS OF MINISTERS IN THY	553 27
HAST APPOINTED DIVERS ORDERS IN THY CHURCH	572 08
THEY HAVE BEEN DIVERS, AND MAY BE CHANGED ACCORDING	609 33

DIVERSITIES

THERE ARE DIVERSITIES OF GIFTS, BUT THE SAME SPIRIT	182 22
THERE ARE DIVERSITIES OF OPERATIONS, BUT IT IS THE	182 24
THERE ARE DIVERSITIES OF GIFTS, BUT THE SAME SPIRIT	203 22
THERE ARE DIVERSITIES OF OPERATIONS, BUT IT IS THE	203 24

DIVERSITY

TO THE DIVERSITY OF COUNTRIES, TIMES, AND MEN'S	609 34

DIVIDE

TAKE THIS, AND DIVIDE IT AMONG YOURSELVES	149 06
O LORD, AND DIVIDE THEM	407 04
WILL REJOICE, AND DIVIDE SHECHEM, *	412 24
14 THOU DIDST DIVIDE THE SEA THROUGH THY PCWER	431 02
AND DIVIDE SHECHEM, AND METE OLT THE	479 18

DIVIDED

WHERE IT IS DIVIDED, REUNITE IT	037 20
EVERY KINGDOM DIVIDED AGAINST ITSELF IS BROUGHT TO	129 30
AND A HOUSE DIVIDED AGAINST A HOUSE FALLETH	129 31
IF SATAN ALSO BE DIVIDED AGAINST HIMSELF, HOW SHALL	129 32
AND HE DIVIDED UNTO THEM HIS LIVING	201 33
THE LAND, AND DIVIDED IT	412 15
OF THE HOUSEHOLD DIVIDED THE SPOIL	420 05
14 HE DIVIDED THE SEA, AND LET THEM GO THROUGH	435 26
THEIR LAND TO BE DIVIDED AMONG THEM FOR AN HERITAGE,	438 22
13 WHO DIVIDED THE RED SEA IN TWO PARTS	512 08
NEVER TO BE DIVIDED, WHEREOF IS ONE CHRIST, VERY GOD,	603 13

DIVIDEST

WHO DIVIDEST THE DAY FROM THE DARKNESS, AND	594 11

DIVIDETH

HE TRUSTED, AND DIVIDETH HIS SPOILS	130 08
AS A SHEPHERD DIVIDETH HIS SHEEP FROM THE GOATS	258 32
OF THE LORD DIVIDETH THE FLAMES OF FIRE	374 11

DIVIDING

GLORIOUS ARM, DIVIDING THE WATER BEFORE THEM, TC MAKE	139 11
DIVIDING TO EVERY MAN SEVERALLY AS HE WILL	182 34
DIVIDING TO EVERY MAN SEVERALLY AS HE WILL	204 03

DIVINE

FORMS OF DIVINE WORSHIP, AND THE RITES AND CEREMONIES	V 14
IT IS USED IN DIVINE SERVICE	R 007 22
WHO OF THY DIVINE PROVIDENCE HAST APPOINTED	039 08
THE POWER OF HIS DIVINE INDWELLING	043 25
IN THE COURSE OF DIVINE PROVIDENCE, THESE AMERICAN	VI 07
WE OFFER UNTO THY DIVINE MAJESTY	074 10
AGAINST THY DIVINE MAJESTY, PROVOKING MOST	075 21
HERE BEFORE THY DIVINE MAJESTY, WITH THESE THY HCLY	080 40
WHICH BEING SO DIVINE AND COMFORTABLE A THING TC THEM	087 05
THE POWER OF THE DIVINE MAJESTY TO WORSHIP THE UNITY	186 26
THE PRIEST IN DIVINE SERVICE, AND IN HIS CTHER	294 18
UNTO THY DIVINE MAJESTY	298 15
WHO BY THY DIVINE PROVIDENCE HAST APPOINTED	531 14
THE PRIEST IN DIVINE SERVICE, AND SPECIALLY WHEN HE	533 12
OF GRACE ARE THINE, O FINGER OF THE HAND DIVINE	544 26
OF GRACE ARE THINE, O FINGER OF THE HAND DIVINE	557 05
IN DISPENSING THE DIVINE WORD, IN LEADING THE	571 26

DIVISIONS

GREAT DANGERS WE ARE IN BY OLR UNHAPPY DIVISIONS	037 28

COCTORS

THE MIDST OF THE DOCTORS, BOTH HEARING THEM, AND	110 29
DOCTORS, AND PASTORS	545 18
SOME PASTORS AND DOCTORS, TO THE EDIFYING AND MAKING	557 27

DOCTRINE

TO BELONG TO DOCTRINE MUST BE REFERRED TO DISCIPLINE	V 06
OR TO SOUND DOCTRINE, OR WHICH A GODLY MAN MAY NCT	V 40
THEIR LIFE AND DOCTRINE THEY MAY SHOW FORTH THY	039 03
TRUTH OF THY DOCTRINE, AND ENDLE THEM WITH INNCCENCY	039 12
MAY ADORN THE DOCTRINE OF GOD OUR SAVIOUR	047 28
FROM ALL FALSE DOCTRINE, HERESY, AND SCHISM	055 03
POINT OF DOCTRINE, DISCIPLINE, OR WORSHIP	VI 33

DOCTRINE   CONTINUED

THEIR LIFE AND DOCTRINE, SET FORTH THY TRUE AND	074 22
BY THE DOCTRINE OF THY BLESSED APOSTLE AND EVANGELIST	101 07
THE HOLY DOCTRINE WHICH HE TAUGHT	229 22
THE HEAVENLY DOCTRINE OF THY EVANGELIST SAINT MARK	237 06
BLAST OF VAIN DOCTRINE, WE MAY BE ESTABLISHED IN THE	237 08
EVERY WIND OF DOCTRINE, BY THE SLEIGHT OF MEN, AND	237 26
TO FOLLOW HIS DOCTRINE AND HOLY LIFE, THAT WE MAY	242 10
SPIRIT BY THEIR DOCTRINE, THAT WE MAY BE MADE AN HOLY	254 30
SPIRIT BY THEIR DOCTRINE, THAT WE MAY BE MAUE AN HULY	290 22
TRUTH OF THY DOCTRINE, AND ADORN THEM WITH INNOCENCY	531 20
CONTAIN ALL DOCTRINE REQUIRED AS NECESSARY FOR	533 03
TO THE DOCTRINE OF CHRIST	533 26
TRUTH OF THY DOCTRINE, AND ADORN THEM WITH INNOCENCY	537 24
BUT WITH DOCTRINE AND EXHORTATION TAKEN OUT OF	540 35
THE RULE AND DOCTRINE OF CHRIST, THAT YE MAY BE	541 22
CONTAIN ALL DOCTRINE REQUIRED AS NECESSARY FCR	542 03
TO MINISTER THE DOCTRINE AND SACRAMENTS, AND THE	542 12
TO THE DOCTRINE OF CHRIST	542 33
TRUTH OF THY DOCTRINE, AND ADORN THEM WITH INNOCENCY	548 03
TO THE DOCTRINE, DISCIPLINE, AND WORSHIP OF THE	R 552 27
TO THE DOCTRINE, DISCIPLINE, AND WORSHIP OF THE	552 30
TRUTH OF THY DOCTRINE, AND ADORN HIM WITH INNOCENCY	553 30
CONTAIN ALL DOCTRINE REQUIRED AS NECESSARY FOR	554 21
WITH WHOLESOME DOCTRINE, AND TO WITHSTAND AND	554 32
AND STRANGE DOCTRINE CONTRARY TO GOD'S WORD	555 04
AND DOCTRINE	558 21
WITH ALL PATIENCE AND DOCTRINE	559 09
SOUND DOCTRINE, AND PRUDENCE, WE DO FULLY CCNFIDE,	569 15
TRUTH OF THY DOCTRINE, AND ENDUE HIM WITH INNOCENCY	572 11
BY MY LIFE AND DOCTRINE SET FORTH THY TRUE AND LIVELY	573 22
DOTH IT NOT APPLY THEM TO ESTABLISH ANY DOCTRINE	604 04
MOST WHOLESOME DOCTRINE, AND VERY FULL OF COMFORT, AS	605 08
THE ROMISH DOCTRINE CONCERNING PURGATORY, PARDONS,	607 14
AND WHOLESOME DOCTRINE, AND NECESSARY FOR THESE	610 06
OF CHRISTIAN DOCTRINE, AND INSTRLCTIVE IN PIETY AND	R 610 25

DOCTRINES

AND STRANGE DOCTRINES CONTRARY TO GOD'S WORD	542 21

DOER

THE WORD, AND NOT A DOER, HE IS LIKE UNTC A MAN	176 07
BUT A DOER OF THE WORK, THIS MAN SHALL BE	176 12
THE WORD, AND NOT A DOER, HE IS LIKE UNTO A MAN	265 30
BUT A DOER OF THE WORK, THIS MAN SHALL BE	266 03
AND PLENTEOUSLY REWARDETH THE PROUD DOER	377 17
AND PUNISH THE WRONG DOER	427 05

DOERS

BE YE DOERS OF THE WORD, AND NOT HEARERS ONLY,	176 05
BUT BE YE DOERS OF THE WORD, AND NOT HEARERS ONLY,	265 28
UNGODLY AND WICKED DOERS, *	373 11
NEITHER BE THOU ENVIOUS AGAINST THE EVIL DOERS	384 26
9 WICKED DOERS SHALL BE ROOTED OUT	385 11
ME FROM THE WICKED DOERS, *	411 06
AND FROM THE INSURRECTION OF WICKED DOERS	415 22
SHALL ALL WICKED DOERS SPEAK SO DISDAINFULLY,	457 25
OR WHO WILL TAKE MY PART AGAINST THE EVIL DOERS	458 19
OUT ALL WICKED DOERS FROM THE CITY OF THE LORD	464 05
LORD SHALL LEAD THEM FORTH WITH THE EVIL DOERS	505 03
AND FROM THE TRAPS OF THE WICKED DOERS	517 31

DOES

WHAT DOES OUR LORD JESUS CHRIST TEACH US	288 02
WHAT SPECIAL MEANS DOES THE CHURCH PROVIDE TO HELP	291 21

DOEST

MIRACLES THAT THOU DOEST, EXCEPT GOD BE WITH HIM	188 04
MIRACLES THAT THOU DOEST, EXCEPT GOD BE WITH HIM	275 09
SO LONG AS THOU DOEST WELL UNTO THYSELF, MEN WILL	401 14
ART THE GOD THAT DOEST WONDERS, *	434 10
THERE IS NOT ONE THAT CAN DO AS THOU DOEST	447 20
ART GREAT, AND DOEST WONDROUS THINGS	447 23

DOETH

BUT HE THAT DOETH THE WILL OF MY FATHER WHICH IS IN	072 14
UPON HIM THAT DOETH EVIL	114 21
DO THIS, AND HE DOETH IT	115 15
HE THAT DOETH RIGHTEOUSNESS IS RIGHTEOUS, EVEN AS HE	117 27
WILL THINK THAT HE DOETH GOD SERVICE	179 31
FOR EVERY ONE THAT DOETH EVIL HATETH THE LIGHT,	185 08
BUT HE THAT DOETH TRUTH COMETH TO THE LIGHT, THAT HIS	185 09
BUT HE THAT DOETH THE WILL OF MY FATHER WHICH IS IN	200 25
DWELLETH IN ME, HE DOETH THE WORKS	240 16
FOR THE SERVANT KNOWETH NOT WHAT HIS LORD DCETH	241 30
WHATSOEVER HE DOETH, IT SHALL PROSPER	345 15
THERE IS NONE THAT DOETH GOOD, NO NOT ONE	356 15
THERE IS NONE THAT DOETH GOOD, NO NOT ONE	356 20
AND DOETH THE THING WHICH IS RIGHT, AND SPEAKETH THE	357 07
7 WHOSO DOETH THESE THINGS *	357 19
THE MAN THAT DOETH AFTER EVIL COUNSELS	385 08
THERE IS NONE THAT DOETH GOOD	405 15
IS ALSO NONE THAT DOETH GOOD, NO NOT ONE	405 20
WHICH ONLY DOETH WONDROUS THINGS	428 03
UPON EARTH, HE DOETH IT HIMSELF	430 31
WONDERS THAT HE DOETH FOR THE CHILDREN OF MEN	476 20
WONDERS THAT HE DOETH FOR THE CHILDREN OF MEN	477 09
WONDERS THAT HE DOETH FOR THE CHILDREN OF MEN	477 18
WONDERS THAT HE DOETH FOR THE CHILDREN OF MEN	478 08

DOETH   CONTINUED

NOT FEAR WHAT MAN DOETH UNTO ME	488 11
4 WHO ONLY DOETH GREAT WONDERS	511 22

DOG

MY DARLING FROM THE POWER OF THE DOG	367 13
THEY GRIN LIKE A DOG, AND RUN ABOUT THROUGH THE CITY	411 17
GRIN LIKE A DOG, AND WILL GO ABOUT THE CITY	412 03

DOGS

TAKE THE CHILDREN'S BREAD, AND TO CAST IT TO DOGS	128 17
YET THE DOGS EAT OF THE CRUMBS WHICH FALL FROM THEIR	128 18
MOREOVER THE DOGS CAME AND LICKED HIS SORES	190 08
16 FOR MANY DOGS ARE COME ABOUT ME, *	367 04
THE TONGUE OF THY DOGS MAY BE RED THROUGH THE SAME	420 34

DOINGS

BUT THAT ALL OUR DOINGS, BEING ORDERED BY THY	017 17
IN ALL OUR DOINGS, WITH THY MOST GRACIOUS	049 23
US THAT ALL OUR DOINGS WITHOUT CHARITY ARE NOTHING	122 14
SHOW THE PEOPLE OF HIS DOINGS	352 12
AND BECOME ABOMINABLE IN THEIR DOINGS	356 15
AND MY TALKING SHALL BE OF THY DOINGS	434 07
THOUGH THOU DIDST PUNISH THEIR WICKED DOINGS	462 34
IN ALL OUR DOINGS, WITH THY MOST GRACIOUS	571 08
BUT THAT ALL OUR DOINGS, BEING ORDERED BY THY	592 23
IN OUR DOINGS, THAT WILL OF GOD IS TO BE	606 28

DOMINE

OR JUDICA ME, DOMINE, PSALM XXVI	R 571 31

DOMINION

YE WORKS OF HIS, IN ALL PLACES OF HIS DOMINION	029 18
HATH NO MORE DOMINION OVER HIM	163 05
BE PRAISE AND DOMINION FOR EVER AND EVER	179 22
BE GLORY AND DOMINION FOR EVER AND EVER	193 12
HATH NO MORE DOMINION OVER HIM	197 22
EXERCISE DOMINION OVER THEM, AND THEY THAT ARE GREAT	247 21
YE WORKS OF HIS, IN ALL PLACES OF HIS DOMINION	313 03
HIM TO HAVE DOMINION OF THE WORKS OF THY HANDS	351 11
THEY GET THE DOMINION OVER ME	364 11
SHALL HAVE DOMINION OVER THEM IN THE MORNING	401 02
8 HIS DOMINION SHALL BE ALSO FROM THE ONE SEA TO THE	427 12
I WILL SET HIS DOMINION ALSO IN THE SEA, *	451 25
YE WORKS OF HIS, IN ALL PLACES OF HIS DOMINION	467 21
AND ISRAEL HIS DOMINION	484 29
WICKEDNESS HAVE DOMINION OVER ME	499 05
AND THY DOMINION ENDURETH THROUGHOUT ALL AGES	521 19

DOMINO

CANTATE DOMINO, BONUM EST CONFITERI, NUNC DIMITTIS,	R 025 17

DONATION

INSTRUMENTS OF DONATION AND ENDOWMENT, IF THERE BE	R 564 08

DOOR

GREAT STONE TO THE DOOR OF THE SEPULCHRE, AND	162 13
THE STONE FROM THE DOOR OF THE SEPULCHRE	165 24
ENTERETH NOT BY THE DOOR INTO THE SHEEPFOLD, BUT	185 31
ENTERETH IN BY THE DOOR IS THE SHEPHERD OF THE SHEEP	186 03
UNTO YOU, I AM THE DOOR OF THE SHEEP	186 13
I AM THE DOOR	186 15
AND BEHOLD, A DOOR WAS OPENED IN HEAVEN	186 31
KEEPERS BEFORE THE DOOR KEPT THE PRISON	245 11
THE DOOR IS NOW SHUT, AND MY CHILDREN ARE WITH ME IN	262 31
AND THEY WERE EVEN HARD AT DEATH'S DOOR	477 12
AND KEEP THE DOOR OF MY LIPS	517 14
ENTERETH NOT BY THE DOOR INTO THE SHEEPFOLD, BUT	538 24
ENTERETH IN BY THE DOOR IS THE SHEPHERD OF THE SHEEP	538 26
UNTO YOU, I AM THE DOOR OF THE SHEEP	539 04
I AM THE DOOR	539 06

DOOR-KEEPER

RATHER BE A DOOR-KEEPER IN THE HOUSE OF MY GOD, *	445 32

DOORS

THE WEEK, WHEN THE DOORS WERE SHUT WHERE THE	171 15
CAME JESUS, THE DOORS BEING SHUT, AND STOOD IN THE	228 32
AND BE YE LIFT UP, YE EVERLASTING DOORS	369 10
AND BE YE LIFT UP, YE EVERLASTING DOORS	369 14
AND OPENED THE DOORS OF HEAVEN	436 17
THE WEEK, WHEN THE DOORS WERE SHUT WHERE THE	551 28
AND BE YE LIFT UP, YE EVERLASTING DOORS	563 25
AND BE YE LIFT UP, YE EVERLASTING DOORS	563 29

DOST

THE UNIVERSE, WHO DOST FROM THY THRONE BEHOLD ALL THE	017 28
AND DOST PROMISE THAT WHEN TWO OR THREE ARE GATHERED	020 05
AND DOST PROMISE THAT WHEN TWO OR THREE ARE GATHERED	034 05
JESUS CHRIST, WHO DOST EMBRACE CHILDREN WITH THE ARMS	043 07
OF THY MERCY, AND DOST MAKE THEM LIVING MEMBERS OF	043 08
HOLY WORD THAT THOU DOST NOT WILLINGLY AFFLICT OR	045 31
FOR THAT THOU DOST VOUCHSAFE TO FEED US WHO	083 17
AND DOST ASSURE US THEREBY OF THY FAVOUR AND GOODNESS	083 20

DOST   CONTINUED

WHO DOST GOVERN ALL THINGS IN HEAVEN AND EARTH	111 10
THOU HAST MADE, AND DOST FORGIVE THE SINS OF ALL	124 12
SAYING, DOST NOT THOU FEAR GOD, SEEING THOU ART	155 03
UNTO HIM, LORD, DOST THOU WASH MY FEET	156 02
PREVENTING US THOU DOST PUT INTO OUR MINDS GOOD	163 25
THAT WHICH THOU DOST PROMISE	174 21
THOSE WHOM THOU DOST BRING UP IN THY STEDFAST FEAR	191 05
THAT WHICH THOU DOST PROMISE, MAKE US TO LOVE THAT	209 10
THAT WHICH THOU DOST COMMAND	209 11
WHO DOST ENKINDLE THE FLAME OF THY LOVE IN THE	258 04
DOST THOU, THEREFORE, IN THE NAME OF THIS CHILD,	276 24
DOST THOU BELIEVE ALL THE ARTICLES OF THE	276 31
DOST THOU RENOUNCE THE DEVIL AND ALL HIS WORKS,	277 26
DOST THOU BELIEVE IN JESUS THE CHRIST,	278 02
DOST THOU ACCEPT HIM, AND DESIRE TO FOLLOW	278 05
DOST THOU BELIEVE ALL THE ARTICLES OF THE	278 08
LORD GOD, WHO DOST LIVE, AND GOVERN ALL THINGS,	278 30
THAT WHICH THOU DOST PROMISE	285 28
OF THY MERCIES, DOST SO PUT AWAY THE SINS OF	313 31
THOSE WHOM THOU DOST LOVE, AND CHASTISE EVERY ONE	321 19
OF MANKIND, WHO DOST CORRECT THOSE WHOM THOU DOST	321 19
EVERY ONE WHOM THOU DOST RECEIVE	321 20
THOU WITH REBUKES DOST CHASTEN MAN FOR SIN, THOU	325 02
WHO DOST GRANT TO CHILDREN AN ABUNDANT	340 29
THOU WITH REBUKES DOST CHASTEN MAN FOR SIN, THOU	389 31
6 THOU DOST BREAK THE SHIPS OF THE SEA *	399 22
WHY DOST THOU PREACH MY LAWS, AND TAKEST MY COVENANT	402 22
18 NAMELY, HOW THOU DOST SET THEM IN SLIPPERY PLACES,	429 12
10 DOST THOU SHOW WONDERS AMONG THE DEAD	449 16
SPIRIT ART, WHO DOST THY SEVENFOLD GIFTS IMPART	543 34
FATHER THOU, WHO DOST THE TONGUE WITH SPEECH ENDOW	544 28
WHOSE SINS THOU DOST FORGIVE, THEY ARE FORGIVEN	546 11
AND WHOSE SINS THOU DOST RETAIN, THEY ARE RETAINED	546 12
SPIRIT ART, WHO DOST THY SEVENFOLD GIFTS IMPART	556 09
FATHER THOU, WHO DOST THE TONGUE WITH SPEECH ENDOW	557 07
THOSE WHOM THOU DOST CALL TO THE MINISTRY OF THY	561 08
O GOD, WHO DOST EVER HALLOW AND PROTECT THY CHURCH	562 09
DOST THOU NOT THINK THAT THOU ART BOUND TO	577 20
WHAT DOST THOU CHIEFLY LEARN IN THESE	578 09
WHAT DOST THOU CHIEFLY LEARN BY THESE	579 23
HOLY DESIRES THOU DOST IMPART	594 20

DOTH

ALL THE EARTH DOTH WORSHIP THEE, THE FATHER	010 10
ALL THE WORLD DOTH ACKNOWLEDGE THEE	010 19
MY SOUL DOTH MAGNIFY THE LORD, *	026 11
IT IS THAT THE RAIN DOTH FALL, AND THE EARTH BRING	040 31
WHERE MOTH AND RUST DOTH CORRUPT, AND WHERE THIEVES	072 08
MOTH NOR RUST DOTH CORRUPT, AND WHERE THIEVES DO NOT	072 10
THE HOLY COMMUNION DOTH NOTHING ELSE BUT INCREASE	087 30
SHALL WAX OLD AS DOTH A GARMENT	097 16
AT THE BEGINNING DOTH SET FORTH GOOD WINE	113 28
SONS OF GOD, AND IT DOTH NOT YET APPEAR WHAT WE SHALL	117 17
IS NOT PUFFED UP, DOTH NOT BEHAVE ITSELF UNSEEMLY,	122 30
WHERE MOTH AND RUST DOTH CORRUPT, AND WHERE THIEVES	125 17
MOTH NOR RUST DOTH CORRUPT, AND WHERE THIEVES DO NOT	125 20
FOR WHATSOEVER DOTH MAKE MANIFEST IS LIGHT	129 20
AS HE THAT DOTH SERVE	149 24
EVEN BAPTISM, DOTH ALSO NOW SAVE US (NOT THE PUTTING	161 30
LOSE ONE OF THEM, DOTH NOT LEAVE THE NINETY AND NINE	193 19
SHE LOSE ONE PIECE, DOTH NOT LIGHT A CANDLE, AND	193 28
BE GLORY, MUCH MORE DOTH THE MINISTRATION OF	206 24
BUT IF GOD DOTH SO CLOTHE THE GRASS OF THE FIELD,	211 24
UNTO THEM, HOW THEN DOTH DAVID IN SPIRIT CALL HIM	215 18
FORTH FRUIT, AS IT DOTH ALSO IN YOU, SINCE THE DAY YE	223 28
AS HE THAT DOTH SERVE	250 09
AND THE SIN WHICH DOTH SO EASILY BESET US, AND LET US	258 22
HE DOTH EXECUTE THE JUDGMENT OF THE FATHERLESS AND	263 25
THE LORD DOTH BUILD UP JERUSALEM, *	264 21
GREAT PRIVILEGE DOTH OUR LORD PROVIDE FOR YOU	291 29
THAN AS GOD'S WORD DOTH ALLOW, THEIR MARRIAGE IS NOT	300 30
THANKS THEREFOR, HE DOTH EAT AND DRINK THE BODY AND	R 323 29
MY SOUL DOTH WAIT FOR HIM	328 11
NEITHER DOTH CORRUPTION INHERIT INCORRUPTION	329 34
FOR HIS OWN LUST, DOTH PERSECUTE THE POOR	353 05
IN HIS LURKING DENS DOTH HE MURDER THE INNOCENT	353 21
10 HE DOTH RAVISH THE POOR, *	353 25
WHILE HE DOTH SAY IN HIS HEART, TUSH, THOU GOD CAREST	354 02
IN WICKEDNESS, DOTH HIS SOUL ABHOR	354 31
AND HAVE NOT FORSAKEN MY GOD, AS THE WICKED DOTH	361 10
IN HIS TEMPLE DOTH EVERY THING SPEAK OF HIS HONOUR	374 16
NEITHER DOTH HE ABHOR ANY THING THAT IS EVIL	384 02
AT HIM WHOSE WAY DOTH PROSPER, AGAINST THE MAN THAT	385 07
THAT IS DUMB, WHO DOTH NOT OPEN HIS MOUTH	388 18
THAT MINE ENEMY DOTH NOT TRIUMPH AGAINST ME	392 22
UPON THY RIGHT HAND DOTH STAND THE QUEEN IN A VESTURE	397 03
VERY HIGH EXALTED, DOTH DEFEND THE EARTH, AS IT WERE	399 08
FOR WHO DOTH HEAR	411 19
HE DOTH SEND OUT HIS VOICE	421 23
OUT OF THE WOOD DOTH ROOT IT UP, *	441 28
6 AN UNWISE MAN DOTH NOT WELL CONSIDER THIS, *	456 11
AND A FOOL DOTH NOT UNDERSTAND IT	456 12
SHALL WAX OLD AS DOTH A GARMENT	465 35
THEREFORE DOTH MY SOUL KEEP THEM	498 28
MY SOUL DOTH WAIT FOR HIM	507 16
SO DOTH THY MEMORIAL, O LORD, FROM ONE GENERATION TO	510 28
2 THE LORD DOTH BUILD UP JERUSALEM, *	522 30
SAITH) THE CHURCH DOTH READ FOR EXAMPLE OF LIFE AND	604 02
BUT YET DOTH IT NOT APPLY THEM TO ESTABLISH ANY	604 03
INFECTION OF NATURE DOTH REMAIN, YEA IN THEM THAT ARE	604 35
YET THE APOSTLE DOTH CONFESS, THAT CONCUPISCENCE AND	604 39
AS WELL BECAUSE IT DOTH GREATLY ESTABLISH AND CONFIRM	606 20
AS BECAUSE IT DOTH FERVENTLY KINDLE THEIR LOVE	606 22

DOTH   CONTINUED

WHEREBY THE DEVIL DOTH THRUST THEM EITHER INTO   606 25
FOR HOLY SCRIPTURE DOTH SET OUT UNTO US ONLY THE NAME   606 35
BY THE WHICH HE DOTH WORK INVISIBLY IN US, AND   607 33
IN US, AND DOTH NOT ONLY QUICKEN, BUT ALSO STRENGTHEN   607 34
AND PURPOSELY, DOTH OPENLY BREAK THE TRADITIONS AND   609 36
UNDER THIS ARTICLE, DOTH CONTAIN A GODLY AND   610 06
FOR THESE TIMES, AS DOTH THE FORMER BOOK OF HOMILIES,   610 07
CHURCH IN 1792, DOTH CONTAIN ALL THINGS NECESSARY TO   610 32
CHRISTIAN RELIGION DOTH NOT PROHIBIT, BUT THAT A MAN   611 08

DOUBLE

THE LORD'S HAND DOUBLE FOR ALL HER SINS   242 19
IN THEIR DOUBLE HEART   355 11

DOUBLE-MINDED

A DOUBLE-MINDED MAN IS UNSTABLE IN ALL HIS WAYS   239 17

DOUBLETONGUED

NOT DOUBLETONGUED, NOT GIVEN TO MUCH WINE, NOT   531 27

DOUBT

OUT DEVILS, NO DOUBT THE KINGDOM OF GOD IS COME UPON   130 04
AND WITHOUT ALL DOUBT, TO BELIEVE IN THY SON JESUS   228 08
BE REASONABLE DOUBT WHETHER ANY PERSON WAS BAPTIZED   R 282 08
HAVE REASON TO DOUBT OF THE LAWFULNESS OF THE   R 301 02
LET US NOT DOUBT BUT THAT HE WILL ALSO FAVOURABLY   564 21
WAS NEVER ANY DOUBT IN THE CHURCH   603 34
TO BE DONE, WE DOUBT NOT BUT THEY HAVE THE NATURE OF   605 21

DOUBTFUL

THOMAS TO BE DOUBTFUL IN THY SON'S RESURRECTION   228 07

DOUBTFULNESS

AND THE REMOVING OF ALL SCRUPLE AND DOUBTFULNESS   088 09

DOUBTLESS

DOUBTLESS THOU ART OUR FATHER, THOUGH ABRAHAM BE   139 21
DOUBTLESS THERE IS A GOD THAT JUDGETH THE EARTH   410 33
SHALL DOUBTLESS COME AGAIN WITH JOY, AND BRING HIS   505 19

DOUBTS

IN ALL OUR DOUBTS AND UNCERTAINTIES, THE GRACE TO   595 28

DOVE

THE SPIRIT, LIKE A DOVE, DESCENDING UPON HIM   112 21
O THAT I HAD WINGS LIKE A DOVE   406 30
AS THE WINGS OF A DOVE *   420 07

DOVES

OF THEM THAT SOLD DOVES, AND SAID UNTO THEM, IT IS   092 02
OF THEM THAT SOLD DOVES, AND SAID UNTO THEM, IT IS   260 06
OXEN AND SHEEP AND DOVES, AND THE CHANGERS OF MONEY   567 27
THEM THAT SOLD DOVES, TAKE THESE THINGS HENCE   567 31

DOWN-SITTING

KNOWEST MY DOWN-SITTING, AND MINE UP-RISING   514 21

DOWNFALL

MOST DANGEROUS DOWNFALL, WHEREBY THE DEVIL DOTH   606 24

DRAGON

AND THE DRAGON FOUGHT AND HIS ANGELS, AND PREVAILED   252 04
MICHAEL AND HIS ANGELS FOUGHT AGAINST THE DRAGON   252 04
AND THE GREAT DRAGON WAS CAST OUT, THAT OLD SERPENT,   252 06
REBUKE THOU THE DRAGON AND THE BULL, WITH THE LEADERS   421 15
LION AND THE DRAGON SHALT THOU TREAD UNDER THY FEET   455 22

DRAGONS

THE PLACE OF DRAGONS, *   395 33
THE HEADS OF THE DRAGONS IN THE WATERS   431 03
YE DRAGONS AND ALL DEEPS   524 18

DRANK

AND THEY ALL DRANK OF IT   141 12
FOR THEY DRANK OF THAT SPIRITUAL ROCK THAT FOLLOWED   201 10

DRAUGHT

THE DEEP, AND LET DOWN YOUR NETS FOR A DRAUGHT   196 15
WITH HIM, AT THE DRAUGHT OF THE FISHES WHICH THEY HAD   196 25

DRAVE

67 HE DRAVE HIS ENEMIES BACKWARD, *   439 10

DRAW

DRAW NEAR WITH FAITH, AND TAKE THIS HOLY SACRAMENT TO   075 11
HE SAITH UNTO THEM, DRAW OUT NOW, AND BEAR UNTO THE   113 22

DRAW   CONTINUED

LET US DRAW NEAR WITH A TRUE HEART IN FULL ASSURANCE   158 20
BUT IF ANY MAN DRAW BACK, MY SOUL SHALL HAVE NO   228 19
ARE NOT OF THEM WHO DRAW BACK UNTO PERDITION   228 20
5 DRAW ME OUT OF THE NET THAT THEY HAVE LAID PRIVILY   375 29
19 DRAW NIGH UNTO MY SOUL, AND SAVE IT   423 09
150 THEY DRAW NIGH THAT OF MALICE PERSECUTE ME,   500 10
THIS ONE THING, AND DRAW ALL YOUR CARES AND STUDIES   541 14
PERVERSE THINGS, TO DRAW AWAY DISCIPLES AFTER THEM   550 32
WHOSOEVER SHALL DRAW NEAR UNTO THEE IN THIS PLACE,   566 14
DELIVER US, WHEN WE DRAW NIGH TO THEE, FROM COLDNESS   594 06

DRAWETH

KING AND SAVIOUR DRAWETH NIGH   R 008 16
YOUR REDEMPTION DRAWETH NIGH   093 13
AND MY LIFE DRAWETH NIGH UNTO THE GRAVE   448 32

DRAWING

OF HANDS, THAT, DRAWING NEAR WITH PENITENT AND   043 23
THEY AND WE, DRAWING NEARER TO THEE, MAY BE BOUND   597 04
AND DRAWING UP THEIR MIND TO HIGH AND   606 19

DRAWN

IN THE FIRST PLACE DRAWN TO THOSE ALTERATIONS IN THE   VI 15
MANKIND MAY BE DRAWN TO THY BLESSED KINGDOM   260 23
THE UNGODLY HAVE DRAWN OUT THE SWORD, AND HAVE BENT   385 22
WE BE DRAWN AGAIN INTO SIN, VOUCHSAFE US, WE   590 10

DREAD

TROUBLE, DREAD, OR THE NEAR APPROACH OF DEATH,   048 09
AND AN HORRIBLE DREAD HATH OVERWHELMED ME   406 29
OUR HEARTS SUCH A DREAD OF THY JUDGMENTS, AND SUCH A   588 18
FOR ALL THINGS, TO DREAD NOTHING BUT THE LOSS OF   596 04

DREADFUL

ANSWER AT THE DREADFUL DAY OF JUDGMENT WHEN THE   300 25

DREAM

TO JOSEPH IN A DREAM, SAYING, ARISE, AND TAKE THE   103 16
UNTO HIM IN A DREAM, SAYING, JOSEPH, THOU SON OF   105 03
APPEARETH IN A DREAM TO JOSEPH IN EGYPT, SAYING,   107 13
WARNED OF GOD IN A DREAM, HE TURNED ASIDE INTO THE   107 20
WARNED OF GOD IN A DREAM THAT THEY SHOULD NOT RETURN   109 24
THIS DAY IN A DREAM BECAUSE OF HIM   135 35
EVEN LIKE AS A DREAM WHEN ONE AWAKETH   429 16
THEN WERE WE LIKE UNTO THEM THAT DREAM   505 08

DREGS

10 AS FOR THE DREGS THEREOF, *   432 17

DREW

WHEN THEY DREW NIGH UNTO JERUSALEM, AND WERE COME TO   091 11
THE SERVANTS WHICH DREW THE WATER KNEW   113 25
THEM THAT STOOD BY DREW A SWORD, AND SMOTE A SERVANT   142 22
OF UNLEAVENED BREAD DREW NIGH, WHICH IS CALLED THE   148 12
BEFORE THEM, AND DREW NEAR UNTO JESUS TO KISS HIM   150 28
JESUS HIMSELF DREW NEAR, AND WENT WITH THEM   167 08
AND THEY DREW NIGH UNTO THE VILLAGE, WHITHER THEY   167 34
THEN DREW NEAR UNTO HIM ALL THE PUBLICANS AND SINNERS   193 14
AND AS HE CAME AND DREW NIGH TO THE HOUSE, HE HEARD   202 27
MY MOUTH, AND DREW IN MY BREATH   498 32

DRIED

IT IS CUT DOWN, DRIED UP, AND WITHERED   325 25
15 MY STRENGTH IS DRIED UP LIKE A POTSHERD, AND MY   366 34
IT IS CUT DOWN, DRIED UP, AND WITHERED   453 30
AND IT WAS DRIED UP   473 18
MY FLESH IS DRIED UP FOR WANT OF FATNESS   481 19

DRIEDST

THOU DRIEDST UP MIGHTY WATERS   431 07

DRIETH

AND DRIETH UP THE WATER-SPRINGS   478 12

DRINK

TO THEM, SAYING, DRINK YE ALL OF THIS   080 25
AS OFT AS YE SHALL DRINK IT, IN REMEMBRANCE OF ME   080 29
AND TO DRINK HIS BLOOD, THAT OUR SINFUL   082 19
DRINK THIS IN REMEMBRANCE THAT CHRIST'S BLOOD WAS   083 05
REVERENTLY EAT AND DRINK THE SAME   R 084 32
OF THAT BREAD, AND DRINK OF THAT CUP   085 30
IF HE THIRST, GIVE HIM DRINK   113 07
HIM VINEGAR TO DRINK MINGLED WITH GALL   136 29
WHEN HE HAD TASTED THEREOF, HE WOULD NOT DRINK   136 30
AND PUT IT ON A REED, AND GAVE HIM TO DRINK   137 23
UNTO YOU, I WILL DRINK NO MORE OF THE FRUIT OF THE   141 15
THAT DAY THAT I DRINK IT NEW IN THE KINGDOM OF GOD   141 16
THEY GAVE HIM TO DRINK WINE MINGLED WITH MYRRH   146 09
AND GAVE HIM TO DRINK, SAYING, LET ALONE   146 32
I WILL NOT DRINK OF THE FRUIT OF THE VINE,   149 07
YE MAY EAT AND DRINK AT MY TABLE IN MY KINGDOM, AND   149 29
AS OFT AS YE DRINK IT, IN REMEMBRANCE OF ME   152 23

DRINK   CONTINUED

THIS BREAD, AND DRINK THIS CUP, YE DO SHEW THE LORD'S	152 24
WHO DID EAT AND DRINK WITH HIM AFTER HE ROSE FROM THE	166 27
BEEN ALL MADE TO DRINK INTO ONE SPIRIT	183 07
WHO DID EAT AND DRINK WITH HIM AFTER HE ROSE FRCM THE	184 14
AND DID ALL DRINK THE SAME SPIRITUAL DRINK	201 09
AND DID ALL DRINK THE SAME SPIRITUAL DRINK	201 09
DOWN TO EAT AND DRINK, AND ROSE UP TO PLAY	201 16
WHAT YE SHALL EAT, OR WHAT YE SHALL DRINK	211 13
WHAT SHALL WE DRINK	211 28
AND NEITHER DID EAT NOR DRINK	230 13
CUP THAT I SHALL DRINK OF, AND TO BE BAPTIZED WITH	247 12
ARE YE ABLE TO DRINK OF THE CUP THAT I SHALL DRINK	247 12
YE SHALL DRINK INDEED OF MY CUP, AND BE	247 15
YE MAY EAT AND DRINK AT MY TABLE IN MY KINGDOM, AND	250 14
I WAS THIRSTY, AND YE GAVE ME DRINK	259 06
OR THIRSTY, AND GAVE THEE DRINK	259 11
WHAT YE SHALL EAT, OR WHAT YE SHALL DRINK	266 12
WHAT SHALL WE DRINK	266 26
HE DOTH EAT AND DRINK THE BODY AND BLOOD OF OUR	R 323 29
THIS SHALL BE THEIR PORTION TO DRINK	354 35
SHALT GIVE THEM DRINK OF THY PLEASURES, AS OUT OF THE	384 12
AND DRINK THE BLOOD OF GOATS	402 16
HAST GIVEN US A DRINK OF DEADLY WINE	412 18
WHEN I WAS THIRSTY THEY GAVE ME VINEGAR TO DRINK	423 17
OF THE EARTH SHALL DRINK THEM, AND SUCK THEM OUT	432 18
AND GAVE THEM DRINK THEREOF, AS IT HAD BEEN OUT OF	435 31
THEY MIGHT NOT DRINK OF THE RIVERS	437 30
AND GIVEST THEM PLENTEOUSNESS CF TEARS TO DRINK	441 13
AND MINGLED MY DRINK WITH WEEPING	464 28
OF THE FIELD DRINK THEREOF, *	468 15
7 HE SHALL DRINK OF THE BROOK IN THE WAY	482 21
DO EAT AND DRINK THE SIGN OR SACRAMENT OF SO GREAT A	609 07

DRINK-OFFERING

AND A DRINK-OFFERING LNTO THE LORD YOUR GOD	124 28

CRINK-OFFERINGS

5 THEIR DRINK-OFFERINGS OF BLOOD WILL I NOT OFFER,	357 29

DRINKING

EATING AND DRINKING SLCH THINGS AS THEY GIVE	254 22

DRIVE

HIM FROM SIN, AND DRIVE AWAY ALL PAIN OF SOUL AND	320 10
SO SHALT THOU DRIVE THEM AWAY	419 11
TO BANISH AND DRIVE AWAY FROM THE CHURCH ALL	542 20
DRIVE FAR AWAY OUR GHOSTLY FOE, AND THINE ABIDING	545 06
TO BANISH AND DRIVE AWAY FROM THE CHURCH ALL	555 03
DRIVE FAR AWAY OUR GHOSTLY FOE, AND THINE ABIDING	557 12
DRIVE FAR OFF FROM US ALL WRONG DESIRES, INCLINE CUR	594 13

DRIVEN

WHITHER I HAD DRIVEN THEM	225 20
A WAVE OF THE SEA DRIVEN WITH THE WIND AND TOSSED	239 15
MINE ENEMIES ARE DRIVEN BACK, *	351 26
LET THEM BE DRIVEN BACKWARD, AND PUT TO REBUKE, THAT	391 17
2 HOW THOU HAST DRIVEN OUT THE HEATHEN WITH THY HAND,	394 04
AND AM DRIVEN AWAY AS THE GRASSHOPPER	481 17
JORDAN WAS DRIVEN BACK	484 30
THAT THOU WAST DRIVEN BACK	485 03

DRIVEST

OF THY COMMAND, DRIVEST AWAY FROM MEN'S BCDIES ALL	315 07

DROP

UP, AND THE CLOUDS DROP DOWN THE DEW	005 26
UP, AND THE CLOUDS DRCP DOWN THE DEW	050 20
AND THY CLOUDS DROP FATNESS	417 08
13 THEY SHALL DROP UPON THE DWELLINGS OF THE	417 09

DROPPED

AND THE HEAVENS DROPPED AT THE PRESENCE OF GOD	419 26

DROPS

AS IT WERE GREAT DROPS OF BLOOD FALLING DOWN TO THE	150 22
IT SOFT WITH THE DROPS OF RAIN, AND BLESSEST THE	417 06
EVEN AS THE DROPS THAT WATER THE EARTH	427 09

DROPSY

WAS A CERTAIN MAN BEFORE HIM WHICH HAD THE DROPSY	213 31

CROSS

AWAY ALL THE UNGODLY CF THE EARTH LIKE DROSS	498 07

CROUGHT

WAS LIKE THE DROUGHT IN SUMMER	377 29

DROVE

OF SMALL CORDS, HE DROVE THEM ALL OUT OF THE TEMPLE,	567 29

DROWN

THE WATER-FLOOD DROWN ME, NEITHER LET THE DEEP	422 35

DROWNED

AND THAT HE WERE DROWNED IN THE DEPTH OF THE SEA	252 33
THE WATERS HAD DROWNED US, *	504 12

DRUNK

WHEN MEN HAVE WELL DRUNK, THEN THAT WHICH IS WORSE	113 28
AND MAKE THEM DRUNK IN MY FURY, AND I WILL BRING DCWN	138 26
AND BE NOT DRUNK WITH WINE, WHEREIN IS EXCESS	217 26

DRUNKARDS

AND THE DRUNKARDS MAKE SONGS UPON ME	422 27

CRUNKEN

STAGGER LIKE A DRUNKEN MAN, *	477 31

DRUNKENNESS

RIOTING AND DRUNKENNESS, NOT IN CHAMBERING AND	091 06
DRUNKENNESS, REVELLINGS, AND SUCH LIKE	209 22

DRY

HANDS PREPARED THE DRY LAND	009 12
HE WALKETH THROUGH DRY PLACES, SEEKING REST	130 11
WHAT SHALL BE DONE IN THE DRY	154 20
IN A BARREN AND DRY LAND WHERE NO WATER IS	414 28
TURNED THE SEA INTO DRY LAND, *	417 24
MY THROAT IS DRY	422 05
HANDS PREPARED THE DRY LAND	459 14
RIVERS RAN IN THE DRY PLACES	472 20
WATER-SPRINGS OF A DRY GROUND	478 17

CUE

GIVE US THAT DUE SENSE OF ALL THY MERCIES,	019 25
GIVE US THAT DUE SENSE OF ALL THY MERCIES,	033 23
THE EARTH MAY, IN DUE TIME, YIELD HER INCREASE FOR	040 27
YE SHALL PRAY FOR A DUE SUPPLY OF PERSONS FITTED TO	047 30
SO THAT IN DUE TIME WE MAY ENJOY THEM	057 11
WITH MEEK HEART AND DUE REVERENCE, THEY MAY HEAR,	074 27
TRIBUTE TO WHOM TRIBUTE IS DUE	114 26
FOR WE RECEIVE THE DUE REWARD OF OUR DEEDS	155 05
HE MAY EXALT YOU IN DUE TIME	193 03
OF ONE BORN OUT OF DUE TIME	205 12
PAY ALL THAT WAS DUE UNTO HIM	222 04
THAT SO DUE CARE MAY BE TAKEN FOR THEIR EXAMINATICN,	R 273 18
WANT OF WARNING IN DUE TIME TO THE MINISTER, CR BY	R 323 24
FORTH HIS FRUIT IN DUE SEASON	345 13
EVEN A REFUGE IN DUE TIME OF TROUBLE	352 07
THE LORD THE HONOUR DUE UNTO HIS NAME	373 32
THE LORD THE HONOUR DUE UNTO HIS NAME	460 14
GIVE THEM MEAT IN DUE SEASON	469 15
THEM THEIR MEAT IN DUE SEASON	521 23
AFTER CUE EXAMINATION, WE FIND NOT TO THE	536 24
THEIR PORTION IN DUE SEASON, HE MAY AT LAST BE	558 04
HAVING RECEIVED DUE NOTICE OF THE ELECTION OF A	R 569 04
YOU WILL GIVE US DUE NOTICE	569 34
SPIRIT WORKING IN DUE SEASON	606 12

CUES

RENDER THEREFORE TO ALL THEIR DUES	114 26

DULNESS

LIGHT THE DULNESS OF OUR BLINDED SIGHT	544 05
LIGHT THE DULNESS OF OUR BLINDED SIGHT	556 13

DULY

AND ALL THE PEOPLE, DULY CONSIDERING WHOSE AUTHORITY	032 10
MAY HIS HEART BE DULY IMPRESSED WITH A SENSE OF THY	053 04
MAY HE BE DULY SENSIBLE OF THY MERCIFUL PROVIDENCE	053 25
AND RIGHTLY AND DULY ADMINISTER THY HOLY SACRAMENTS	074 23
TO FEED US WHO HAVE DULY RECEIVED THESE HOLY	083 18
THEIR MINISTRY DULY, TO THE HONOUR OF GOD, AND THE	530 15
THAT THEY MAY DULY EXECUTE THEIR OFFICE, TO THE	531 06
THEIR MINISTRY DULY, TO THE HONOUR OF GOD, AND THE	536 16
THAT THEY MAY DULY EXERCISE THEIR OFFICE, TO THE	537 12
WHEN ALL THINGS ARE DULY PREPARED IN THE CHURCH,	R 549 03
THY WORD, AND DULY ADMINISTER THE GODLY DISCIPLINE	549 11
THAT HE MAY DULY EXECUTE THE OFFICE WHEREUNTO HE	553 19
THAT THEY MAY DULY EXECUTE THEIR OFFICE TO THE	560 28
THAT HE MAY DULY EXECUTE THE OFFICE WHEREUNTO HE	561 03
THE SACRAMENTS BE DULY MINISTERED ACCORDING TO	606 39
BUT THAT WE SHOULD DULY USE THEM	608 03

CUMB

JESUS WAS CASTING OUT A DEVIL, AND IT WAS DUMB	129 24
WAS GONE OUT, THE DUMB SPAKE	129 25
AWAY UNTO THESE DUMB IDOLS, EVEN AS YE WERE LED	203 18
TO HEAR, AND THE DUMB TO SPEAK	207 09
AND AS ONE THAT IS DUMB, WHO DOTH NOT OPEN HIS MOUTH	388 18
10 I BECAME CUMB, AND OPENED NOT MY MOUTH	389 27

DUNG

AND BECAME AS THE DUNG OF THE EARTH   444 24

DURING

TO BE USED DURING THEIR SESSION   R 035 07
DURING, OR BEFORE, THE SESSION OF ANY GENERAL OR   R 037 09

DURST

A WORD, NEITHER DURST ANY MAN FROM THAT DAY FORTH ASK   215 23
AND OF THE REST DURST NO MAN JOIN HIMSELF TO THEM   249 23

DUST

ASHES TO ASHES, DUST TO DUST   333 16
ASHES TO ASHES, DUST TO DUST   333 16
UPON THE EARTH, AND LAY MINE HONOUR IN THE DUST   349 34
AS SMALL AS THE DUST BEFORE THE WIND   362 23
ME INTO THE DUST OF DEATH   367 03
GO DOWN INTO THE DUST SHALL KNEEL BEFORE HIM   368 02
10 SHALL THE DUST GIVE THANKS UNTO THEE   375 12
LET THEM BE AS THE DUST BEFORE THE WIND, *   381 27
FOR OUR SOUL IS BROUGHT LOW, EVEN UNTO THE DUST   396 10
HIS ENEMIES SHALL LICK THE DUST   427 15
THEM AS THICK AS DUST, *   436 25
UNTO THE WHIRLING DUST, *   444 30
AND IT PITIETH THEM TO SEE HER IN THE DUST   465 08
HE REMEMBERETH THAT WE ARE BUT DUST   467 03
THEY DIE, AND ARE TURNED AGAIN TO THEIR DUST   469 20
SIMPLE OUT OF THE DUST, *   484 19
MY SOUL CLEAVETH TO THE DUST   491 17

DUTIES

PROMISE MAY THE MORE MOVE YOU TO DO YOUR DUTIES   541 27
OF ALL THE DUTIES OF MY MINISTRY   573 24
FIT US FOR THE DUTIES OF THE COMING DAY   591 28
TO ALL WHOSE DUTIES ARE DIFFICULT OR BURDENSOME,   599 27

DUTIFUL

SHOW YOURSELVES DUTIFUL AND THANKFUL UNTO THAT LORD,   540 27

DUTY

AND OUR BOUNDEN DUTY, THAT WE SHOULD AT ALL TIMES,   076 31
THIS OUR BOUNDEN DUTY AND SERVICE   081 31
WHEREFORE IT IS OUR DUTY TO RENDER MOST HUMBLE AND   086 35
MY DUTY IS TO EXHORT YOU, IN THE MEAN SEASON TO   087 07
SO IT IS YOUR DUTY TO RECEIVE THE COMMUNION IN   089 11
AND OUR BOUNDEN DUTY, THAT WE SHOULD GIVE THANKS UNTO   279 07
TOWARDS GOD, AND MY DUTY TOWARDS MY NEIGHBOUR   288 13
MY DUTY TOWARDS GOD, AND MY DUTY TOWARDS MY   288 13
WHAT IS YOUR DUTY TOWARDS GOD   288 15
MY DUTY TOWARDS GOD IS TO BELIEVE IN HIM,   288 16
WHAT IS YOUR DUTY TOWARDS YOUR NEIGHBOUR   288 23
MY DUTY TOWARDS MY NEIGHBOUR IS TO LOVE HIM   288 24
AND TO DO MY DUTY IN THAT STATE OF LIFE UNTO WHICH IT   289 10
IS YOUR BOUNDEN DUTY AS A MEMBER OF THE CHURCH   291 16
MY BOUNDEN DUTY IS TO FOLLOW CHRIST, TO WORSHIP GOD   291 18
DECLARING THE DUTY AND OFFICE OF SUCH AS COME TO BE   R 530 04
DECLARING THE DUTY AND OFFICE OF SUCH AS COME TO BE   R 536 04
TO YOUR BOUNDEN DUTY, TO BRING ALL SUCH AS ARE CR   540 18
THEIR BOUNDEN DUTY AND SERVICE, AND VOUCHSAFE TO GIVE   566 21
MY DUTY TOWARDS GOD, AND MY DUTY TOWARDS MY   579 24
TOWARDS GOD, AND MY DUTY TOWARDS MY NEIGHBOUR   579 25
WHAT IS THY DUTY TOWARDS GOD   579 26
MY DUTY TOWARDS GOD IS TO BELIEVE IN HIM,   579 27
WHAT IS THY DUTY TOWARDS THY NEIGHBOUR   579 33
MY DUTY TOWARDS MY NEIGHBOUR IS TO LOVE HIM   579 34
AND TO DO MY DUTY IN THAT STATE OF LIFE UNTO WHICH   580 14
RESTRAINED FROM SIN, AND INCITED TO OUR DUTY   588 17
AND SENSE OF OUR DUTY TOWARDS THEE   591 14
THAN OF BOUNDEN DUTY IS REQUIRED   605 28
HOLD IT TO BE THE DUTY OF ALL MEN WHO ARE PROFESSORS   610 40

DWELL

I DWELL IN THE HIGH AND HOLY PLACE, WITH HIM ALSO   003 26
WE MAY DWELL SECURE IN THY PEACE   018 09
AND HE WILL DWELL WITH THEM, AND THEY SHALL BE   021 29
AND THEY THAT DWELL THEREIN   027 20
THAT MAKEST US DWELL IN SAFETY   031 11
OF MEN FOR TO DWELL ON THE FACE OF THE WHOLE EARTH,   038 06
THAT NOW IS, AND DWELL WITH THEE IN THE LIFE THAT IS   043 13
FINALLY HE MAY DWELL WITH THEE IN LIFE EVERLASTING   045 20
THAT HE MAY DWELL IN US, AND WE IN HIM   081 28
WE MAY EVERMORE DWELL IN HIM, AND HE IN US   082 22
THE WORD OF CHRIST DWELL IN YOU RICHLY IN ALL WISDOM   116 11
THEY ENTER IN, AND DWELL THERE   130 15
FOR THEY THAT DWELL AT JERUSALEM, AND THEIR RULERS,   168 26
HIM CONTINUALLY DWELL, WHO LIVETH AND REIGNETH WITH   177 18
KNOW WE THAT HE DWELL IN HIM, AND HE IN US, BECAUSE   189 19
THAT CHRIST MAY DWELL IN YOUR HEARTS BY FAITH   212 16
AND ISRAEL SHALL DWELL SAFELY   225 13
AND THEY SHALL DWELL IN THEIR OWN LAND   225 20
AND LET NO MAN DWELL THEREIN   234 19
AND YE THAT DWELL IN THEM   252 11
THE THRONE SHALL DWELL AMONG THEM   257 11
AND THEY SHALL DWELL SAFELY IN THE WILDERNESS,   262 06
BUT THEY SHALL DWELL SAFELY, AND NONE SHALL MAKE THEM   262 16
AND TO ALL THAT DWELL IN IT   308 07
GRANT THAT HE MAY DWELL WITH THEE IN LIFE   310 24

DWELL   CONTINUED

EVEN THAT I MAY DWELL IN THE HOUSE OF THE LORD ALL   326 09
AND I WILL DWELL IN THE HOUSE OF THE LORD FOR EVER   338 30
THE THRONE SHALL DWELL AMONG THEM   341 22
THAT MAKEST ME DWELL IN SAFETY   347 29
SHALL ANY EVIL DWELL WITH THEE   348 08
WHO SHALL DWELL IN THY TABERNACLE   357 05
AND I WILL DWELL IN THE HOUSE OF THE LORD FOR EVER   368 23
AND THEY THAT DWELL THEREIN   368 29
12 HIS SOUL SHALL DWELL AT EASE, *   370 10
EVEN THAT I MAY DWELL IN THE HOUSE OF THE LORD ALL   371 33
ALL YE THAT DWELL IN THE WORLD   379 03
ALL THEM THAT DWELL ON THE EARTH   379 16
DWELL IN THE LAND, AND VERILY THOU SHALT BE FED   384 30
AND DWELL FOR EVERMORE   386 18
AND DWELL THEREIN FOR EVER   386 24
ALL YE THAT DWELL IN THE WORLD   400 08
4 I WILL DWELL IN THY TABERNACLE FOR EVER, *   413 13
7 HE SHALL DWELL BEFORE GOD FOR EVER   413 19
HE SHALL DWELL IN THY COURT, AND SHALL BE SATISFIED   416 18
8 THEY ALSO THAT DWELL IN THE UTTERMOST PARTS OF THE   416 29
CONGREGATION SHALL DWELL THEREIN   419 31
GOD'S HILL, IN THE WHICH IT PLEASETH HIM TO DWELL   420 14
THE LORD GOD MIGHT DWELL AMONG THEM   420 21
AND NO MAN TO DWELL IN THEIR TENTS   423 25
THAT MEN MAY DWELL THERE, AND HAVE IT IN POSSESSION   424 15
HIS NAME SHALL DWELL THEREIN   424 18
9 THEY THAT DWELL IN THE WILDERNESS SHALL KNEEL   427 14
OF ISRAEL TO DWELL IN THEIR TENTS   438 23
WITH THEM THAT DWELL AT TYRE   444 19
ARE THEY THAT DWELL IN THY HOUSE   445 19
THAN TO DWELL IN THE TENTS OF UNGODLINESS   445 33
THAT GLORY MAY DWELL IN OUR LAND   446 26
AND THEY THAT DWELL THEREIN   462 09
THAT THEY MAY DWELL WITH ME   463 31
DECEITFUL PERSON DWELL IN MY HOUSE   464 02
FOUND NO CITY TO DWELL IN   476 13
OF THEM THAT DWELL THEREIN   478 15
THEM A CITY TO DWELL IN   478 19
AM CONSTRAINED TO DWELL WITH MESHECH, *   502 14
HERE WILL I DWELL, FOR I HAVE A DELIGHT THEREIN   509 02
FOR BRETHREN TO DWELL TOGETHER IN UNITY   509 14
AND THEY THAT DWELL THEREIN   563 12
AND HE WILL DWELL WITH THEM, AND THEY SHALL BE   567 16
OF MEN, AND TO DWELL IN THE MIDST OF THE ASSEMBLY OF   568 08
CARE THE HOMES IN WHICH THY PEOPLE DWELL   598 21

DWELLERS

BEHOLD ALL THE DWELLERS UPON EARTH   017 29
AND THE DWELLERS IN MESOPOTAMIA, AND IN JUDAEA, AND   180 32
UNTO ALL THE DWELLERS AT JERUSALEM   234 16

DWELLEST

THE DEPTHS, AND DWELLEST BETWEEN THE CHERUBIM   011 22
O THOU THAT DWELLEST IN THE HEAVENS   503 27

DWELLETH

AND THE PLACE WHERE THINE HONOUR DWELLETH   021 15
FROM HIM, HOW DWELLETH THE LOVE OF GOD IN HIM   072 30
FOR HE DWELLETH WITH YOU, AND SHALL BE IN YOU   181 13
GOD DWELLETH IN US, AND HIS LOVE IS   189 17
SON OF GOD, GOD DWELLETH IN HIM, AND HE IN GOD   189 23
AND HE THAT DWELLETH IN LOVE DWELLETH IN GOD, AND GOD   189 25
IN LOVE DWELLETH IN GOD, AND GOD IN HIM   189 25
FROM HIM, HOW DWELLETH THE LOVE OF GOD IN HIM   191 20
COMMANDMENTS DWELLETH IN HIM, AND HE IN HIM   191 32
THE FATHER THAT DWELLETH IN ME, HE DOETH THE WORKS   240 16
HIS SPIRIT THAT DWELLETH IN US   333 06
4 HE THAT DWELLETH IN HEAVEN SHALL LAUGH THEM TO   346 04
THE LORD WHICH DWELLETH IN SION   352 11
AND THE PLACE WHERE THINE HONOUR DWELLETH   371 13
WHOSO DWELLETH UNDER THE DEFENCE OF THE MOST HIGH, *   454 28
THE LORD, WHO DWELLETH ON HIGH, IS MIGHTIER   457 14
WHO DWELLETH AT JERUSALEM   511 12

DWELLING

BRING ME UNTO THY HOLY HILL, AND TO THY DWELLING   003 23
AND THERE WERE DWELLING AT JERUSALEM JEWS, DEVOUT   180 25
CHRIST DWELLING IN YOUR HEARTS BY FAITH, YE MAY   281 10
BRING ME UNTO THY HOLY HILL, AND TO THY DWELLING   310 12
PLACE OF HIS DWELLING SHALL HE HIDE ME, AND SET ME UP   326 13
I OFFER IN HIS DWELLING AN OBLATION, WITH GREAT   326 17
PLACE OF HIS DWELLING SHALL HE HIDE ME, AND SET ME UP   372 05
I OFFER IN HIS DWELLING AN OBLATION, WITH GREAT   372 09
OF HIS DWELLING, HE CONSIDERETH ALL THEM THAT DWELL   379 16
BRING ME UNTO THY HOLY HILL, AND TO THY DWELLING   394 11
THEE OUT OF THY DWELLING, AND ROOT THEE OUT OF THE   404 29
AND HIS DWELLING IN SION   432 25
NEITHER SHALL ANY PLAGUE COME NIGH THY DWELLING   455 16
FIR-TREES ARE A DWELLING FOR THE STORK   468 29
THAT HATH HIS DWELLING SO HIGH, *   484 17

DWELLING-PLACE

AND THY DWELLING-PLACE IN THE PARADISE OF GOD   319 24
THE DWELLING-PLACE OF THY NAME, EVEN UNTO THE GROUND   430 19
AND LAID WASTE HIS DWELLING-PLACE   440 15

DWELLING-PLACES

THEIR DWELLING-PLACES SHALL ENDURE FROM ONE   400 27

DWELLINGS

IS IN THEIR DWELLINGS, AND AMONG THEM   407 21
DROP UPON THE DWELLINGS OF THE WILDERNESS   417 09
IN THE DWELLINGS OF HAM   438 13
ARE THY DWELLINGS, *   445 11
THAN ALL THE DWELLINGS OF JACOB   448 14
IS IN THE DWELLINGS OF THE RIGHTEOUS   488 30

DWELLS

THE HOLY SPIRIT DWELLS IN IT, AND SANCTIFIES ITS   291 09

DWELT

MADE FLESH, AND DWELT AMONG US   R 008 32
MADE FLESH, AND DWELT AMONG US, (AND WE BEHELD HIS 098 04
AND HE CAME AND DWELT IN A CITY CALLED NAZARETH 107 21
THE JEWS WHICH DWELT AT DAMASCUS, PROVING THAT THIS 231 10
THE BRETHREN WHICH DWELT IN JUDAEA   241 21
CAME ON ALL THAT DWELT ROUND ABOUT THEM   243 26
THE BRETHREN WHICH DWELT IN JUDAEA   246 30
4 I HAVE NOT DWELT WITH VAIN PERSONS   371 04
AND MOUNT SION, WHEREIN THOU HAST DWELT   430 09
THAT THEY MIGHT GO TO THE CITY WHERE THEY DWELT 476 18
MY SOUL HATH LONG DWELT AMONG THEM *   502 17

DYED

FROM EDOM, WITH DYED GARMENTS FROM BOZRAH   138 11

DYING

JESUS CHRIST, THUS DYING FOR US, AND THE INNUMERABLE 086 14
AS DYING, AND BEHOLD, WE LIVE   126 18
LIVING AND DYING, WE MAY BE THINE, THROUGH THE   591 31

EACH

LEAST ONE SUNDAY IN EACH MONTH   R 067 29
AND IT SAT UPON EACH OF THEM   180 22
CREATURES HAD EACH OF THEM SIX WINGS ABOUT HIM   187 20
GIVE THEIR TROTH TO EACH OTHER IN THIS MANNER   R 301 24
AND CHERISH EACH OTHER, AND SO LIVE TOGETHER   303 24
THEIR TROTH, EACH TO THE OTHER, AND HAVE DECLARED THE 304 06
AND AT THE END OF EACH PSALM SHALL BE SAID THE GLORIA R 338 15
PEACE HAVE KISSED EACH OTHER   446 28
ORDAINED DEACONS, EACH OF THEM BEING DECENTLY   R 530 09
THAT DAY, EACH OF THEM BEING DECENTLY HABITED,   R 536 09

EAGLE

AND THE FOURTH WAS LIKE A FLYING EAGLE   187 20
MAKING THEE YOUNG AND LUSTY AS AN EAGLE   466 16

EAGLES

THERE WILL THE EAGLES BE GATHERED TOGETHER   118 13

EAR

A SERVANT OF THE HIGH PRIEST, AND CUT OFF HIS EAR 142 23
GOD HATH OPENED MINE EAR, AND I WAS NOT REBELLIOUS, 144 12
AND CUT OFF HIS RIGHT EAR   150 33
AND HE TOUCHED HIS EAR, AND HEALED HIM   150 35
HE HATH INCLINED HIS EAR UNTO ME   305 20
AND THINE EAR HEARKENETH   354 14
INCLINE THINE EAR TO ME, AND HEARKEN UNTO MY WORDS 358 30
2 BOW DOWN THINE EAR TO ME   375 24
INCLINE THINE EAR   397 06
I WILL INCLINE MINE EAR TO THE PARABLE, *   400 12
GIVE EAR UNTO MY PRAYER   413 07
INCLINE THINE EAR UNTO ME, AND SAVE ME   425 07
BOW DOWN THINE EAR, O LORD, AND HEAR ME   447 05
6 GIVE EAR, LORD, UNTO MY PRAYER, *   447 15
INCLINE THINE EAR UNTO MY CALLING   448 31
AND MINE EAR SHALL HEAR HIS DESIRE OF THE WICKED THAT 456 22
HE THAT PLANTED THE EAR, SHALL HE NOT HEAR   458 04
INCLINE THINE EAR UNTO ME WHEN I CALL   464 13
HE HATH INCLINED HIS EAR UNTO ME   486 21
GIVE EAR UNTO OUR PRAYER, O MERCIFUL AND GRACIOUS 600 11

EARLIEST

CHURCH FROM THE EARLIEST TIMES   294 06

EARLY

LOVING-KINDNESS EARLY IN THE MORNING, *   027 30
WHICH WENT OUT EARLY IN THE MORNING TO HIRE LABOURERS 119 16
MARY MAGDALENE EARLY, WHEN IT WAS YET DARK, UNTO THE 164 11
AND VERY EARLY IN THE MORNING THE FIRST DAY OF THE 165 21
WHICH WERE EARLY AT THE SEPULCHRE   167 23
GOD SHALL HELP HER, AND THAT RIGHT EARLY   327 13
EARLY IN THE MORNING WILL I DIRECT MY PRAYER UNTO 348 04
GOD SHALL HELP HER, AND THAT RIGHT EARLY   398 03
I MYSELF WILL AWAKE RIGHT EARLY   409 32
EARLY WILL I SEEK THEE   414 26
AND TURNED THEM EARLY, AND INQUIRED AFTER GOD   437 07
AND EARLY SHALL MY PRAYER COME BEFORE THEE   449 22
LOVING-KINDNESS EARLY IN THE MORNING, *   456 02
I MYSELF WILL AWAKE RIGHT EARLY   479 08
147 EARLY IN THE MORNING DO I CRY UNTO THEE   500 04
HASTE TO RISE UP EARLY, AND SO LATE TAKE REST, AND 505 26

EARN

AND LABOUR TRULY TO EARN MINE OWN LIVING, AND TO DO 289 09

EARNEST

FOR THE EARNEST EXPECTATION OF THE CREATURE WAITETH 194 13
FOR THE EARNEST EXPECTATION OF THE CREATURE WAITETH 330 29
MAY NOT ONLY BE EARNEST TO REPROVE, BESEECH, AND 559 08

EARNESTLY

AND EARNESTLY BESEECHING ALMIGHTY GOD TO ACCOMPANY VI 40
DO TRULY AND EARNESTLY REPENT YOU OF YOUR SINS, 075 08
WE DO EARNESTLY REPENT, AND ARE HEARTILY SORRY FOR 075 23
AND WE EARNESTLY DESIRE THY FATHERLY GOODNESS,   081 15
CONSIDER EARNESTLY WITH YOURSELVES HOW LITTLE SUCH 088 34
THINGS IF YE EARNESTLY CONSIDER, YE WILL BY GOD'S 089 19
AND BEING IN AN AGONY HE PRAYED MORE EARNESTLY   150 22
THE FIRE, AND EARNESTLY LOOKED UPON HIM, AND SAID, 151 11
HIM EARNESTLY TO FEED THY FLOCK   244 24
HOLDING EARNESTLY THE FAITH FOR ALL TIME, IN ALL 291 11
SHALL NOT OMIT EARNESTLY TO MOVE THE PERSONS   R 299 06
WHO MOST EARNESTLY DESIRETH PARDON AND FORGIVENESS 314 02
EARNESTLY REMEMBERING THE BENEFITS HE   R 323 28
TO PRAY EARNESTLY FOR HIS HOLY SPIRIT   540 32

EARS

WITH OUR OUTWARD EARS, MAY, THROUGH THY GRACE,   049 19
TO INCLINE THINE EARS TO US WHO HAVE NOW MADE OUR 050 08
HAVE HEARD WITH OUR EARS, AND OUR FATHERS HAVE   058 28
AND STOPPED THEIR EARS, AND RAN UPON HIM WITH ONE 100 10
HE THAT HATH EARS TO HEAR, LET HIM HEAR   121 28
AND HIS EARS ARE OPEN UNTO THEIR PRAYERS   195 28
LET THY MERCIFUL EARS, O LORD, BE OPEN TO THE PRAYERS 203 11
FINGERS INTO HIS EARS, AND HE SPIT, AND TOUCHED HIS 206 32
AND STRAIGHTWAY HIS EARS WERE OPENED, AND THE STRING 207 03
CAME UNTO THE EARS OF THE CHURCH WHICH WAS IN   241 03
THIS DAY IS THIS SCRIPTURE FULFILLED IN YOUR EARS 261 25
AND WITH THINE EARS CONSIDER MY CALLING   325 06
O LET THINE EARS CONSIDER WELL *   328 05
NOT THY MERCIFUL EARS TO OUR PRAYER   332 29
IT ENTERED EVEN INTO HIS EARS   360 08
AND HIS EARS ARE OPEN UNTO THEIR PRAYERS   380 31
AND WITH THINE EARS CONSIDER MY CALLING   390 02
BUT MINE EARS HAST THOU OPENED   390 28
HAVE HEARD WITH OUR EARS, O GOD, OUR FATHERS HAVE 394 22
PONDER IT WITH YOUR EARS, ALL YE THAT DWELL IN THE 400 08
EVEN LIKE THE DEAF ADDER, THAT STOPPETH HER EARS 410 16
INCLINE YOUR EARS UNTO THE WORDS OF MY MOUTH   434 27
6 THEY HAVE EARS, AND HEAR NOT   485 22
2 O LET THINE EARS CONSIDER WELL *   507 10
17 THEY HAVE EARS, AND YET THEY HEAR NOT   511 04

EARTH

LET ALL THE EARTH KEEP SILENCE BEFORE HIM   003 15
AND UNTO THE UTTERMOST PART OF THE EARTH   005 14
THE LORD BY WISDOM HATH FOUNDED THE EARTH   005 24
WILL BE DONE, ON EARTH AS IT IS IN HEAVEN   007 24
IN HIS HAND ARE ALL THE CORNERS OF THE EARTH   009 09
LET THE WHOLE EARTH STAND IN AWE OF HIM   009 18
FOR HE COMETH TO JUDGE THE EARTH   009 19
ALL THE EARTH DOTH WORSHIP THEE, THE FATHER   010 10
HEAVEN AND EARTH ARE FULL OF THE MAJESTY OF THY 010 15
O LET THE EARTH BLESS THE LORD   013 02
THINGS UPON THE EARTH, BLESS YE THE LORD   013 06
THE FATHER ALMIGHTY, MAKER OF HEAVEN AND EARTH   015 20
OF HEAVEN AND EARTH, AND OF ALL THINGS VISIBLE AND 015 34
THY THRONE BEHOLD ALL THE DWELLERS UPON EARTH   017 29
LET ALL THE EARTH KEEP SILENCE BEFORE HIM   021 12
LET THE WHOLE EARTH STAND IN AWE OF HIM   021 20
THE WHOLE EARTH IS FULL OF HIS GLORY   022 34
ON HIGH, AND ON EARTH PEACE, GOOD WILL TOWARDS MEN 025 22
FOR HE COMETH TO JUDGE THE EARTH   027 23
MAY BE KNOWN UPON EARTH, *   028 19
AND GOVERN THE NATIONS UPON EARTH   028 25
THEN SHALL THE EARTH BRING FORTH HER INCREASE   028 28
THE FATHER ALMIGHTY, MAKER OF HEAVEN AND EARTH   029 25
OF HEAVEN AND EARTH, AND OF ALL THINGS VISIBLE AND 030 05
FORTH THY PRAISE AMONG THE NATIONS OF THE EARTH 036 21
FACE OF THE WHOLE EARTH, AND DIDST SEND THY BLESSED 038 06
AND FOR PLANTING THY CHURCH IN ALL THE EARTH   038 19
HAST BLESSED THE EARTH THAT IT SHOULD BE FRUITFUL AND 039 24
THE FRUITS OF THE EARTH, AND EVER REJOICE IN THY 039 29
GO FORTH THAT IT MAY RENEW THE FACE OF THE EARTH 040 10
THE FRUITS OF THE EARTH TO OUR COMFORT, AND TO THY 040 20
THAT THE EARTH MAY, IN DUE TIME, YIELD HER   040 27
DOTH FALL, AND THE EARTH BRING FORTH HER INCREASE 040 31
THE FRUITS OF THE EARTH BY THY HEAVENLY BENEDICTION 041 02
THY HANDIWORK IN THE HEAVENS AND IN THE EARTH   044 19
FOR THE FRUITS OF THE EARTH   048 12
DESCEND UPON THE EARTH, THAT IT MAY BRING FORTH FRUIT 051 17
CREATOR OF HEAVEN AND EARTH   054 05
FRUITS OF THE EARTH, SO THAT IN DUE TIME WE MAY ENJOY 057 11
OR IN THE WATER UNDER THE EARTH   068 10
OR IN THE EARTH BENEATH, OR IN THE WATER UNDER   068 10
MADE HEAVEN AND EARTH, THE SEA, AND ALL THAT IN THEM 068 30
OF HEAVEN AND EARTH, AND OF ALL THINGS VISIBLE AND 071 03
TREASURES UPON EARTH, WHERE MOTH AND RUST DOTH   072 07
HEAVEN AND IN THE EARTH IS THINE   073 20
HEAVEN AND EARTH ARE FULL OF THY GLORY   077 09
HEAVEN AND EARTH ARE FULL OF THY GLORY   079 33
ON HIGH, AND ON EARTH PEACE, GOOD WILL TOWARDS MEN 084 02

EARTH   CONTINUED

AND UPON THE EARTH DISTRESS OF NATIONS, WITH   093 06
AFTER THOSE THINGS WHICH ARE COMING ON THE EARTH   093 09
HEAVEN AND EARTH SHALL PASS AWAY   093 20
BEGINNING HAST LAID THE FOUNDATION OF THE EARTH   097 14
AND ON EARTH PEACE, GOOD WILL TOWARD MEN   099 21
HERE UPON EARTH FOR THE TESTIMONY OF THY TRUTH,   099 27
SHED UPON THE EARTH, FROM THE BLOOD OF RIGHTEOUS ABEL   100 23
FOUR THOUSAND, WHICH WERE REDEEMED FROM THE EARTH   103 08
AND THINGS UNDER THE EARTH   105 29
AND THINGS IN EARTH, AND THINGS UNDER THE EARTH   105 29
WHO DOST GOVERN ALL THINGS IN HEAVEN AND EARTH   111 11
THE TRIBES OF THE EARTH MOURN, AND THEY SHALL SEE THE   118 18
TREASURES UPON EARTH, WHERE MOTH AND RUST DOTH   125 17
AND THINGS IN EARTH, AND THINGS UNDER THE EARTH   134 25
AND THINGS IN EARTH, AND THINGS UNDER THE EARTH   134 26
AND THE EARTH DID QUAKE, AND THE ROCKS RENT   137 27
AND I WILL BRING DOWN THEIR STRENGTH TO THE EARTH   138 27
OVER ALL THE EARTH UNTIL THE NINTH HOUR   155 10
ON THINGS ABOVE, NOT ON THINGS ON THE EARTH   164 06
AND UNTO THE UTTERMOST PART OF THE EARTH   178 12
ORDERETH ALL THINGS IN HEAVEN AND EARTH   199 29
IN HEAVEN AND EARTH IS NAMED, THAT HE WOULD GRANT   212 13
MAN HATH POWER ON EARTH TO FORGIVE SINS, (THEN SAITH   217 09
SHALL EXECUTE JUDGMENT AND JUSTICE IN THE EARTH   225 12
WENT INTO ALL THE EARTH, AND THEIR WORDS UNTO THE   227 15
AND HE FELL TO THE EARTH, AND HEARD A VOICE SAYING   229 32
AND SAUL AROSE FROM THE EARTH   230 10
LORD OF HEAVEN AND EARTH, BECAUSE THOU HAST HID THESE   235 04
DESCENDED FIRST INTO THE LOWER PARTS OF THE EARTH   237 17
THOU SHALT BIND ON EARTH SHALL BE BOUND IN HEAVEN   246 10
SHALT LOOSE ON EARTH SHALL BE LOOSED IN HEAVEN   246 11
THEY MAY SUCCOUR AND DEFEND US ON EARTH   251 31
CAST OUT INTO THE EARTH, AND HIS ANGELS WERE CAST OUT   252 08
INHABITERS OF THE EARTH AND OF THE SEA   252 17
GIVEN TO HURT THE EARTH AND THE SEA, SAYING, HURT NCT   256 17
HURT NOT THE EARTH, NEITHER THE SEA, NOR THE TREES,   256 17
FOR THEY SHALL INHERIT THE EARTH   257 24
BE FOR SALVATION UNTO THE ENDS OF THE EARTH   261 05
ALMIGHTY GOD, LORD OF HEAVEN AND EARTH   261 29
HER FRUIT, AND THE EARTH SHALL YIELD HER INCREASE,   262 10
WITH CLOUDS, AND PREPARETH RAIN FOR THE EARTH   264 28
IN THE RETURNS OF THE FRUITS OF THE EARTH   265 13
IN PARADISE AND ON EARTH, THY LIGHT AND THY PEACE   268 16
ALL POWER IS GIVEN UNTO ME IN HEAVEN AND IN EARTH   275 27
IN HEAVEN AND EARTH IS NAMED   281 09
THE FATHER ALMIGHTY, MAKER OF HEAVEN AND EARTH   284 14
OR IN THE EARTH BENEATH, OR IN THE WATER UNDER   286 10
OR IN THE WATER UNDER THE EARTH   286 10
MADE HEAVEN AND EARTH, THE SEA, AND ALL THAT IN THEM   286 30
WHO HATH MADE HEAVEN AND EARTH   297 08
AND UNDER THE EARTH, DO BOW AND OBEY   314 17
IN HEAVEN, IN EARTH, AND UNDER THE EARTH, DO BOW AND   314 17
LORD OF HEAVEN AND EARTH, WE CONFESS THAT WE HAVE   323 12
HE SHALL STAND AT THE LATTER DAY UPON THE EARTH   324 10
OR EVER THE EARTH AND THE WORLD WERE MADE,   325 16
THOUGH THE EARTH BE MOVED, *   327 05
AND I WILL BE EXALTED IN THE EARTH   327 15
WHO HATH MADE HEAVEN AND EARTH   327 22
MAN IS OF THE EARTH, EARTHY   329 28
BE LAID INTO THE EARTH, SHALL BE SUNG OR SAID,   R 332 17
WHILE THE EARTH SHALL BE CAST UPON THE BODY   R 333 12
EARTH TO EARTH, ASHES TO ASHES, DUST TO DUST   333 16
EARTH TO EARTH, ASHES TO ASHES, DUST TO DUST   333 16
THE WORLD, THE EARTH AND THE SEA SHALL GIVE UP THEIR   333 19
SERVE THEE HERE ON EARTH, MAY AT LAST, TOGETHER WITH   335 32
WITH CONSTANCY ON EARTH, WE MAY BE JOINED HEREAFTER   336 08
WHO HATH MADE HEAVEN AND EARTH   339 06
WHILE THE EARTH IS BEING CAST UPON THE BODY   R 341 12
WIND SCATTERETH AWAY FROM THE FACE OF THE EARTH   345 18
2 THE KINGS OF THE EARTH STAND UP, AND THE RULERS   345 27
PARTS OF THE EARTH FOR THY POSSESSION   346 13
BE INSTRUCTED, YE THAT ARE JUDGES OF THE EARTH   346 18
LIFE DOWN UPON THE EARTH, AND LAY MINE HONCUR IN THE   349 33
THE MAN OF THE EARTH BE NO MORE EXALTED AGAINST THEM   354 16
WHICH FROM THE EARTH IS TRIED, AND PURIFIED SEVEN   355 21
THAT ARE IN THE EARTH, *   357 26
8 THE EARTH TREMBLED AND QUAKED, *   360 09
ROOT OUT OF THE EARTH, *   365 25
AS BE FAT UPON EARTH *   367 33
THE EARTH IS THE LORD'S, AND ALL THAT THEREIN IS   368 28
THE EARTH IS FULL OF THE GOODNESS OF THE LORD   378 27
8 LET ALL THE EARTH FEAR THE LORD   379 02
HE CONSIDERETH ALL THEM THAT DWELL ON THE EARTH   379 16
ROOT OUT THE REMEMBRANCE OF THEM FROM THE EARTH   380 34
SHALL POSSESS THE EARTH, *   385 16
KEEP HIM ALIVE, THAT HE MAY BE BLESSED UPON EARTH   392 02
THOUGH THE EARTH BE MOVED, *   397 27
HIS VOICE, AND THE EARTH SHALL MELT AWAY   398 05
WHAT DESTRUCTION HE HATH BROUGHT UPON THE EARTH   398 10
AND I WILL BE EXALTED IN THE EARTH   398 16
HE IS THE GREAT KING UPON ALL THE EARTH   398 24
7 FOR GOD IS THE KING OF ALL THE EARTH   399 02
DOTH DEFEND THE EARTH, AS IT WERE WITH A SHIELD   399 08
AND THE JOY OF THE WHOLE EARTH   399 13
THE KINGS OF THE EARTH *   399 16
AND THE EARTH, THAT HE MAY JUDGE HIS PEOPLE   401 28
AND THY GLORY ABOVE ALL THE EARTH   409 25
AND THY GLORY ABOVE ALL THE EARTH   410 05
HEART UPON THE EARTH, *   410 11
DOUBTLESS THERE IS A GOD THAT JUDGETH THE EARTH   410 34
THE ENDS OF THE EARTH WILL I CALL UPON THEE, *   413 08
THEY SHALL GO UNDER THE EARTH   415 12
THE ENDS OF THE EARTH, AND OF THEM THAT REMAIN IN THE   416 23
PARTS OF THE EARTH SHALL BE AFRAID AT THY TOKENS,   416 30

EARTH   CONTINUED

THOU VISITEST THE EARTH, AND BLESSEST IT   416 32
FOR SO THOU PROVIDEST FOR THE EARTH   417 03
MAY BE KNOWN UPON EARTH, *   418 26
AND GOVERN THE NATIONS UPON EARTH   418 32
6 THEN SHALL THE EARTH BRING FORTH HER INCREASE   419 02
8 THE EARTH SHOOK, AND THE HEAVENS   419 26
O YE KINGDOMS OF THE EARTH   421 20
35 LET HEAVEN AND EARTH PRAISE HIM   424 12
THE DEEP OF THE EARTH AGAIN   426 19
EVEN AS THE DROPS THAT WATER THE EARTH   427 09
OF CORN IN THE EARTH, HIGH UPON THE HILLS   427 29
THE CITY SHALL FLOURISH LIKE GRASS UPON THE EARTH   427 31
AND ALL THE EARTH SHALL BE FILLED WITH HIS MAJESTY   428 05
THERE IS NONE UPON EARTH THAT I DESIRE IN COMPARISON   429 27
THAT IS DONE UPON EARTH, HE DOETH IT HIMSELF   430 33
18 THOU HAST SET ALL THE BORDERS OF THE EARTH   431 10
FOR ALL THE EARTH IS FULL OF DARKNESS AND CRUEL   431 18
4 THE EARTH IS WEAK, AND ALL THE INHABITERS THEREOF   432 04
THE UNGODLY OF THE EARTH SHALL DRINK THEM, AND SUCK   432 18
THE EARTH TREMBLED, AND WAS STILL, 9 WHEN GOD AROSE   433 05
AND TO HELP ALL THE MEEK UPON EARTH   433 07
AND IS WONDERFUL AMONG THE KINGS OF THE EARTH   433 14
THE EARTH WAS MOVED, AND SHOOK WITHAL   434 19
FOUNDATIONS OF THE EARTH ARE OUT OF COURSE   443 27
O GOD, AND JUDGE THOU THE EARTH   444 02
AND BECAME AS THE DUNG OF THE EARTH   444 25
ART ONLY THE MOST HIGHEST OVER ALL THE EARTH   445 09
OUT OF THE EARTH, *   446 29
ARE THINE, THE EARTH ALSO IS THINE   450 28
HIGHER THAN THE KINGS OF THE EARTH   451 30
OR EVER THE EARTH AND THE WORLD WERE MADE,   453 21
4 IN HIS HAND ARE ALL THE CORNERS OF THE EARTH   459 11
SING UNTO THE LORD, ALL THE WHOLE EARTH   459 31
LET THE WHOLE EARTH STAND IN AWE OF HIM   460 17
AND LET THE EARTH BE GLAD   460 22
FOR HE COMETH TO JUDGE THE EARTH   460 26
LORD IS KING, THE EARTH MAY BE GLAD THEREOF   460 30
THE EARTH SAW IT, AND WAS AFRAID   461 04
AT THE PRESENCE OF THE LORD OF THE WHOLE EARTH   461 07
ART HIGHER THAN ALL THAT ARE IN THE EARTH   461 15
FOR HE IS COME TO JUDGE THE EARTH   462 12
BE THE EARTH NEVER SO UNQUIET   462 17
THE KINGS OF THE EARTH THY MAJESTY   465 10
OUT OF THE HEAVEN DID THE LORD BEHOLD THE EARTH   465 18
FOUNDATION OF THE EARTH, *   465 32
HOW HIGH THE HEAVEN IS IN COMPARISON OF THE EARTH   466 28
FOUNDATIONS OF THE EARTH, *   468 02
NEITHER TURN AGAIN TO COVER THE EARTH   468 12
THE EARTH IS FILLED WITH THE FRUIT OF THY WORKS   468 19
FOOD OUT OF THE EARTH, AND WINE THAT MAKETH GLAD THE   468 23
THE EARTH IS FULL OF THY RICHES   469 09
AND THOU SHALT RENEW THE FACE OF THE EARTH   469 22
32 THE EARTH SHALL TREMBLE AT THE LOOK OF HIM   469 25
OUT OF THE EARTH, *   469 32
17 SO THE EARTH OPENED, AND SWALLOWED UP DATHAN,   474 02
AND THY GLORY ABOVE ALL THE EARTH   479 14
ROOT OUT THE MEMORIAL OF THEM FROM OFF THE EARTH   480 31
2 HIS SEED SHALL BE MIGHTY UPON EARTH   483 20
TO BEHOLD THE THINGS THAT ARE IN HEAVEN AND EARTH   484 18
7 TREMBLE, THOU EARTH, AT THE PRESENCE OF THE LCRD   485 06
WHO MADE HEAVEN AND EARTH   486 09
THE EARTH HATH HE GIVEN TO THE CHILDREN OF MEN   486 10
19 I AM A STRANGER UPON EARTH   491 04
64 THE EARTH, O LORD, IS FULL OF THY MERCY   494 08
87 THEY HAD ALMOST MADE AN END OF ME UPON EARTH   495 31
FOUNDATION OF THE EARTH, AND IT ABIDETH   496 05
THE UNGODLY OF THE EARTH LIKE DROSS   498 06
WHO HATH MADE HEAVEN AND EARTH   502 25
WHO HATH MADE HEAVEN AND EARTH   504 21
MADE HEAVEN AND EARTH *   509 29
THAT DID HE IN HEAVEN, AND IN EARTH   510 14
6 WHO LAID OUT THE EARTH ABOVE THE WATERS   511 26
THE KINGS OF THE EARTH SHALL PRAISE THEE, O LORD   514 04
AND FASHIONED BENEATH IN THE EARTH   515 19
FULL OF WORDS SHALL NOT PROSPER UPON THE EARTH   516 33
WHEN ONE BREAKETH AND HEWETH WOOD UPON THE EARTH   517 27
TURN AGAIN TO HIS EARTH, *   522 09
MADE HEAVEN AND EARTH, THE SEA, AND ALL THAT THEREIN   522 12
WITH CLOUDS, AND PREPARETH RAIN FOR THE EARTH   523 11
COMMANDMENT UPON EARTH, *   523 25
THE LORD FROM THE EARTH, *   524 18
11 KINGS OF THE EARTH, AND ALL PEOPLES   524 25
AND HIS PRAISE ABOVE HEAVEN AND EARTH   524 29
DESCENDED FIRST INTO THE LOWER PARTS OF THE EARTH   538 04
ALL POWER IS GIVEN UNTO ME IN HEAVEN AND IN EARTH   552 10
THE EARTH IS THE LORD'S, AND ALL THAT THEREIN IS   563 11
OF THE ASSEMBLY OF THE SAINTS UPON THE EARTH   568 09
THE FATHER ALMIGHTY, MAKER OF HEAVEN AND EARTH   577 29
OR IN THE EARTH BENEATH, OR IN THE WATER UNDER   578 29
OR IN THE WATER UNDER THE EARTH   578 29
MADE HEAVEN AND EARTH, THE SEA, AND ALL THAT IN THEM   579 10
CARE REACHETH TO THE UTTERMOST PARTS OF THE EARTH   596 31

EARTHLY

I HAVE TOLD YOU EARTHLY THINGS, AND YE BELIEVE NCT,   188 22
WHO MIND EARTHLY THINGS   222 21
FROM THEIR EARTHLY PRISONS   317 13
AND THEIR EARTHLY MEMBERS, AND DRAWING UP   606 19

EARTHQUAKE

FROM EARTHQUAKE, FIRE, AND FLOOD   054 30
SAW THE EARTHQUAKE, AND THOSE THINGS THAT WERE DCNE,   137 32

EARTHY

THE FIRST MAN IS OF THE EARTH, EARTHY   329 28
AS IS THE EARTHY, SUCH ARE THEY ALSO THAT ARE EARTHY   329 29
SUCH ARE THEY ALSO THAT ARE EARTHY   329 29
THE IMAGE OF THE EARTHY, WE SHALL ALSO BEAR THE IMAGE   329 31

EASE

SOUL SHALL DWELL AT EASE, *   370 10

EASED

6 I EASED HIS SHOULDER FROM THE BURDEN, *   442 23

EASIER

FOR WHETHER IS EASIER, TO SAY, THY SINS BE FORGIVEN   217 07

EASILY

ARE NOT SO EASILY ACCEPTED AND ALLOWED BEFORE GCC   088 29
HER OWN, IS NOT EASILY PROVOKED, THINKETH NC EVIL   122 31
SIN WHICH DOTH SO EASILY BESET US, AND LET US RUN   258 22

EASINESS

AND TOO MUCH EASINESS IN ADMITTING VARIATIONS IN   V 25

EAST

WISE MEN FROM THE EAST TO JERUSALEM, SAYING, WHERE IS   108 32
HIS STAR IN THE EAST, AND ARE COME TO WORSHIP HIM   108 33
THEY SAW IN THE EAST, WENT BEFORE THEM, TILL IT CAME   109 17
SHALL COME FROM THE EAST AND WEST, AND SHALL SIT DOWN   115 19
COMETH OUT OF THE EAST, AND SHINETH EVEN UNTO THE   118 10
ASCENDING FROM THE EAST, HAVING THE SEAL OF THE   256 14
NEITHER FROM THE EAST, NOR FROM THE WEST, *   432 10
HOW WIDE ALSO THE EAST IS FROM THE WEST   466 30
THE LANDS, FROM THE EAST, AND FROM THE WEST   476 10

EAST-WIND

THROUGH THE EAST-WIND   399 23
HE CAUSED THE EAST-WIND TO BLOW UNDER HEAVEN   436 22

EASTER

ON MONDAY IN EASTER WEEK AND UNTIL ASCENSION DAY   R 008 23
ON CHRISTMAS DAY, EASTER DAY, ASCENSION DAY,   R 070 32
UPON EASTER DAY, AND SEVEN DAYS AFTER   R 078 06
DAILY THROUGHOUT EASTER WEEK   R 163 31
CELEBRATED ON EASTER DAY, THE FOLLOWING CCLLECT,   R 164 30
INTENDING AFTER EASTER TO BRING HIM FORTH TO THE   245 06

EASY

IT IS AN EASY MATTER FOR A MAN TO SAY, I WILL NCT   088 26
FOR MY YOKE IS EASY, AND MY BURDEN IS LIGHT   235 14

EAT

WITH QUIETNESS, AND EAT OUR OWN BREAD   039 27
TAKE, EAT, (C) THIS IS MY BODY, WHICH IS   080 20
GRACIOUS LORD, SO TO EAT THE FLESH OF THY DEAR SCN   082 18
TAKE AND EAT THIS IN REMEMBRANCE THAT CHRIST DIEC FOR   082 33
REVERENTLY EAT AND DRINK THE SAME   R 084 32
THEY PRESUME TO EAT OF THAT BREAD, AND DRINK OF THAT   085 29
AND HE DID EAT LOCUSTS AND WILD HONEY   112 13
YET THE DOGS EAT OF THE CRUMBS WHICH FALL FROM THEIR   128 18
WHENCE SHALL WE BUY BREAD, THAT THESE MAY EAT   131 28
THAT THOU MAYEST EAT THE PASSOVER   140 24
WHERE I SHALL EAT THE PASSOVER WITH MY DISCIPLES   140 30
AS THEY SAT AND DID EAT, JESUS SAID, VERILY I SAY   140 35
AND AS THEY DID EAT, JESUS TOOK BREAD, AND BLESSEC,   141 09
AND GAVE TO THEM, AND SAID, TAKE, EAT   141 11
THE MOTH SHALL EAT THEM UP   144 22
GO AND PREPARE US THE PASSOVER, THAT WE MAY EAT   148 24
WHERE I SHALL EAT THE PASSOVER WITH MY DISCIPLES   148 30
I HAVE DESIRED TO EAT THIS PASSOVER WITH YCU BEFCRE I   149 02
I WILL NOT ANY MORE EAT THEREOF, UNTIL IT BE   149 04
THAT YE MAY EAT AND DRINK AT MY TABLE IN MY KINGDCM,   149 29
GIVEN THANKS, HE BRAKE IT, AND SAID, TAKE, EAT   152 19
FOR AS OFTEN AS YE EAT THIS BREAD, AND DRINK THIS   152 24
EVEN TO US, WHO DID EAT AND DRINK WITH HIM AFTER HE   166 27
HE TOOK IT, AND DID EAT BEFORE THEM   170 06
EVEN TO US, WHO DID EAT AND DRINK WITH HIM AFTER HE   184 14
HAVING NOTHING TO EAT, JESUS CALLED HIS DISCIPLES   199 09
BEEN WITH ME THREE DAYS, AND HAVE NOTHING TO EAT   199 12
SO THEY DID EAT, AND WERE FILLED   199 22
AND DID ALL EAT THE SAME SPIRITUAL MEAT   201 08
PEOPLE SAT DOWN TO EAT AND DRINK, AND ROSE UP TC   201 16
HIS BELLY WITH THE HUSKS THAT THE SWINE DID EAT   202 09
AND LET US EAT, AND BE MERRY   202 24
WHAT YE SHALL EAT, OR WHAT YE SHALL DRINK   211 13
WHAT SHALL WE EAT   211 28
CHIEF PHARISEES TO EAT BREAD ON THE SABBATH DAY,   213 29
WHENCE SHALL WE BUY BREAD, THAT THESE MAY EAT   225 24
AND NEITHER DID EAT NOR DRINK   230 13
AND HONEY SHALL HE EAT, THAT HE MAY KNOW TC REFUSE   236 02
THAT YE MAY EAT AND DRINK AT MY TABLE IN MY KINGDCM,   250 14
WHAT YE SHALL EAT, OR WHAT YE SHALL DRINK   266 12
WHAT SHALL WE EAT   266 26
YOUR FATHERS DID EAT MANNA IN THE WILDERNESS, AND ARE   322 23
THAT A MAN MAY EAT THEREOF, AND NOT DIE   322 25
IF ANY MAN EAT OF THIS BREAD, HE SHALL LIVE FCR EVER   322 27

EAT   CONTINUED

HE DOTH EAT AND DRINK THE BODY AND BLCOD OF   R 323 29
26 THE POOR SHALL EAT, AND BE SATISFIED   367 25
CAME UPON ME TO EAT UP MY FLESH, *   371 28
WHO DID ALSO EAT OF MY BREAD, HATH LAID GREAT WAIT   392 18
THOU THAT I WILL EAT BULLS' FLESH, *   402 16
AS IF THEY WOULD EAT BREAD   405 23
OF HIM THAT WOULD EAT ME UP   409 18
22 THEY GAVE ME GALL TO EAT   423 16
UPON THEM FOR TO EAT, *   436 18
26 SO MAN DID EAT ANGELS' FOOD   436 20
30 SO THEY DID EAT, AND WERE WELL FILLED   436 29
SO THAT I FORGET TO EAT MY BREAD   464 18
AND DID EAT UP ALL THE GRASS IN THEIR LAND, AND   472 07
LATE TAKE REST, AND EAT THE BREAD OF CAREFULNESS   505 27
2 FOR THOU SHALT EAT THE LABOURS OF THINE HANDS   506 08
NEITHER LET ME EAT OF SUCH THINGS AS PLEASE THEM   517 17
DO EAT AND DRINK THE SIGN OR SACRAMENT   609 07

EATEN

REMAINED OVER AND ABOVE UNTO THEM THAT HAD EATEN   132 11
AND THEY THAT HAD EATEN WERE ABOUT FOUR THOUSAND   199 24
REMAINED OVER AND ABOVE UNTO THEM THAT HAD EATEN   226 10
HAVE EATEN, AND WORSHIPPED   367 33
THOU LETTEST US BE EATEN UP LIKE SHEEP, *   395 15
HOUSE HATH EVEN EATEN ME   422 20
9 FOR I HAVE EATEN ASHES AS IT WERE BREAD, *   464 27
THINE HOUSE HATH EATEN ME UP   568 03
TAKEN, AND EATEN, IN THE SUPPER, ONLY AFTER AN   608 44
IS RECEIVED AND EATEN IN THE SUPPER, IS FAITH   608 46

EATETH

ONE OF YOU WHICH EATETH WITH ME SHALL BETRAY ME   141 02
AND EATETH WITH THEM   193 16
WHY EATETH YOUR MASTER WITH PUBLICANS AND   251 18
OF A CALF THAT EATETH HAY   474 09

EATING

HOUSE REMAIN, EATING AND DRINKING SUCH THINGS AS THEY   254 22
EATING UP MY PEOPLE AS IT WERE BREAD, AND CALL NCT   356 23
EATING UP MY PEOPLE AS IF THEY WOULD EAT BREAD   405 23

ECCLESIASTICAL

THEIR ECCLESIASTICAL INDEPENDENCE WAS NECESSARILY   VI 08
TO THE ECCLESIASTICAL ADMINISTRATION   R 535 22

EDGE

THEM FALL UPON THE EDGE OF THE SWORD, *   415 13
HAST TAKEN AWAY THE EDGE OF HIS SWORD, *   452 26

EDIFICATION

FOR THE EDIFICATION OF THE PEOPLE, 'ACCORDING TO THE   V 08
AND THE EDIFICATION OF THY CHURCH   531 23
AND THE EDIFICATION OF THY CHURCH   537 27
AND THE EDIFICATION OF THY CHURCH   548 06

EDIFYING

OF GOD, AND THE EDIFYING AND WELL-GOVERNING OF THE   047 18
TO THE USE OF EDIFYING, THAT IT MAY MINISTER GRACE   216 24
FOR THE EDIFYING OF THE BODY OF CHRIST   237 21
BODY UNTO THE EDIFYING OF ITSELF IN LOVE   238 02
OF GOD, AND THE EDIFYING OF HIS CHURCH   530 16
TO THE EDIFYING OF THY CHURCH, AND THE GLORY   531 07
AND THE EDIFYING OF HIS PEOPLE   532 28
OF GOD, AND THE EDIFYING OF HIS CHURCH   536 17
TO THE EDIFYING OF THY CHURCH, AND THE GLORY   537 13
FOR THE EDIFYING OF THE BODY OF CHRIST   538 08
TO THE EDIFYING OF THY CHURCH, AND TO THE   553 19
AND THE EDIFYING AND WELL-GOVERNING OF THY   553 33
TO THE EDIFYING AND MAKING PERFECT HIS   557 27
OFFICE TO THE EDIFYING OF THY CHURCH, AND TC THE   560 29
TO THE EDIFYING OF THY CHURCH, AND TO THE   561 04
SO THAT ALL THINGS BE DONE TO EDIFYING   610 03

EDOM

THAT COMETH FROM EDOM, WITH DYED GARMENTS FROM   138 11
OVER EDOM WILL I CAST OUT MY SHOE   412 27
WHO WILL BRING ME INTO EDOM   412 30
OVER EDOM WILL I CAST OUT MY SHOE   479 22
AND WHO WILL BRING ME INTO EDOM   479 25
THE CHILDREN OF EDOM, O LORD, IN THE DAY OF   513 18

EDOMITES

OF THE EDOMITES, AND THE ISHMAELITES   444 16

EDUCATION

FOR THE GOOD EDUCATION OF ALL THE YOUTH OF THIS LAND,   047 32

EDWARD

IN THE TIME OF EDWARD THE SIXTH, UPON JUST AND   V 27
IN THE TIME OF EDWARD THE SIXTH   610 08

EFFECT

HELP WE MAY BRING THE SAME TO GOOD EFFECT 163 27
THAT IT SHOULD MAKE THE PROMISE OF NONE EFFECT 207 24
TO BE OF NONE EFFECT, AND CASTETH OUT THE COUNSELS OF 379 08
HAVE A WHOLESOME EFFECT OR OPERATION 608 04
NEITHER IS THE EFFECT OF CHRIST'S ORDINANCE TAKEN 608 14

EFFECTUAL

UNTO ME BY THE EFFECTUAL WORKING OF HIS POWER 108 17
TO THE EFFECTUAL WORKING IN THE MEASURE OF EVERY 237 32
AND EFFECTUAL SIGNS OF GRACE, AND GOD'S 607 32
WHICH BE EFFECTUAL, BECAUSE OF CHRIST'S INSTITUTION 608 17

EFFECTUALLY

MAY EFFECTUALLY BE OBTAINED, TO THE RELIEF OF 050 11
WHICH WE ASK FAITHFULLY WE MAY OBTAIN EFFECTUALLY 222 12
WE MAY BE EFFECTUALLY RESTRAINED FROM SIN, AND 588 16

EFFORTS

PROTECT THE EFFORTS OF SOBER AND HONEST INDUSTRY, AND 599 29

EFFUSION

PRICE THAN THE EFFUSION OF HIS OWN BLOOD 554 11

EGG

IF HE SHALL ASK AN EGG, WILL HE OFFER HIM A SCORPION 183 16
IF HE SHALL ASK AN EGG, WILL HE OFFER HIM A SCORPION 263 10

EGYPT

AND FLEE INTO EGYPT, AND BE THOU THERE UNTIL I BRING 103 18
AND HIS MOTHER BY NIGHT, AND DEPARTED INTO EGYPT 103 21
OUT OF EGYPT HAVE I CALLED MY SON 103 24
DREAM TO JOSEPH IN EGYPT, SAYING, ARISE, AND TAKE THE 107 13
AND PAMPHYLIA, IN EGYPT, AND IN THE PARTS OF LIBYA 181 03
THE CHILDREN OF ISRAEL OUT OF THE LAND OF EGYPT 225 17
FOR YE WERE STRANGERS IN THE LAND OF EGYPT 263 29
31 THEN SHALL THE PRINCES COME OUT OF EGYPT 421 18
IN THE LAND OF EGYPT, * 435 25
HIS MIRACLES IN EGYPT, * 437 27
THE FIRSTBORN IN EGYPT, * 438 12
8 THOU HAST BROUGHT A VINE OUR OF EGYPT 441 18
OUT OF THE LAND OF EGYPT, AND HAD HEARD A STRANGE 442 21
WHO BROUGHT THEE OUT OF THE LAND OF EGYPT 442 34
MAKE MENTION OF EGYPT AND BABYLON, * 448 18
THOU HAST SUBDUED EGYPT, AND DESTROYED IT 450 26
ALSO CAME INTO EGYPT, * 471 18
37 EGYPT WAS GLAD AT THEIR DEPARTING 472 13
NOT THY WONDERS IN EGYPT, NEITHER KEPT THEY THY GREAT 473 13
WHO HAD DONE SO GREAT THINGS IN EGYPT 474 11
ISRAEL CAME OUT OF EGYPT, * 484 27
THE FIRSTBORN OF EGYPT, * 510 18
INTO THE MIDST OF THEE, O THOU LAND OF EGYPT 510 21
10 WHO SMOTE EGYPT, WITH THEIR FIRSTBORN 512 02
OUT OF THE LAND OF EGYPT, OUT OF THE HOUSE OF 578 24

EIGHT

AND WHEN EIGHT DAYS WERE ACCOMPLISHED FOR THE 106 19
THAT IS, EIGHT SOULS WERE SAVED BY WATER 161 29
AND AFTER EIGHT DAYS AGAIN HIS DISCIPLES WERE WITHIN, 228 31
TO PASS ABOUT AN EIGHT DAYS AFTER THESE SAYINGS, HE 248 23

EIGHTEENTH

AT THE EIGHTEENTH VERSE 275 24
OUT OF THE EIGHTEENTH CHAPTER OF THE GOSPEL ACCORDING R 339 19

EIGHTH

THAT ON THE EIGHTH DAY THEY CAME TO CIRCUMCISE 243 17
IN THE EIGHTH CHAPTER OF THE ACTS OF THE 296 12

EITHER

TO TIME, SEEM EITHER NECESSARY OR EXPEDIENT V 19
TO HAVE OFFENDED, EITHER BY WILL, WORD, OR DEED, 087 19
WITH HIM, ON EITHER SIDE ONE, AND JESUS IN THE MIDST 159 34
EITHER WHAT WOMAN HAVING TEN PIECES OF SILVER, IF SHE 193 27
EITHER HOW CANST THOU SAY TO THY BROTHER, BROTHER, 195 07
TO GIVE MORE THAN EITHER WE DESIRE OR DESERVE 206 06
FOR EITHER HE WILL HATE THE ONE, AND LOVE THE OTHER 211 09
ASK IT EITHER IN THE DEPTH, OR IN THE HEIGHT ABOVE 235 26
AT THE FONT, EITHER IMMEDIATELY AFTER THE SECOND R 273 14
THAT IF EITHER OF YOU KNOW ANY IMPEDIMENT, WHY YE MAY 300 26
BUT IF A MAN, EITHER BY REASON OF EXTREMITY OF R 323 23
GOING BEFORE IT, EITHER INTO THE CHURCH OR TOWARDS R 324 03
GOING BEFORE IT, EITHER INTO THE CHURCH OR TOWARDS R 338 03
KNOWING EITHER BY HIMSELF, OR BY SUFFICIENT 529 26
LEFT AMONG YOU, EITHER FOR ERROR IN RELIGION, OR FOR 540 22
UNTO ALL, WHICH EITHER HERE OR ELSEWHERE CALL UPON 545 27
WHICH SHALL BE EITHER SAINT MATTHEW IX R 547 25
THE GOSPEL, MOVED EITHER BY THE EXPRESS COMMAND OF 564 12
PARISH SHALL EITHER BRING, OR SEND IN WRITING, WITH R 583 06
DOTH THRUST THEM EITHER INTO DESPERATION, OR INTO 606 25
BY GOD'S LAW, EITHER TO VOW THE ESTATE OF SINGLE 609 21

ELAMITES

AND MEDES, AND ELAMITES, AND THE DWELLERS IN 180 32

ELDER

NOW HIS ELDER SON WAS IN THE FIELD 202 26

ELDERS

BEFORE THE FOUR LIVING CREATURES, AND THE ELDERS 103 06
ASSEMBLE THE ELDERS, GATHER THE CHILDREN, AND THOSE 124 31
CHIEF PRIESTS AND ELDERS OF THE PEOPLE TOOK COUNSEL 134 31
CHIEF PRIESTS AND ELDERS, SAYING, I HAVE SINNED IN 135 05
CHIEF PRIESTS AND ELDERS, HE ANSWERED NOTHING 135 22
CHIEF PRIESTS AND ELDERS PERSUADED THE MULTITUDE THAT 135 35
THE SCRIBES AND ELDERS, SAID, HE SAVED OTHERS 137 09
THE CHIEF PRIESTS AND THE SCRIBES AND THE ELDERS 142 17
PRIESTS AND ELDERS AND THE SCRIBES 142 33
WITH THE ELDERS AND SCRIBES AND THE WHOLE COUNCIL, 145 04
AND THE ELDERS, WHICH WERE COME TO HIM, BE YE 151 02
IT WAS DAY, THE ELDERS OF THE PEOPLE AND THE CHIEF 151 28
FOUR AND TWENTY ELDERS SITTING, CLOTHED IN WHITE 187 10
FOUR AND TWENTY ELDERS FALL DOWN BEFORE HIM THAT SAT 187 26
SENT IT TO THE ELDERS BY THE HANDS OF BARNABAS AND 241 22
SENT IT TO THE ELDERS BY THE HANDS OF BARNABAS AND 246 31
AND ABOUT THE ELDERS AND THE FOUR LIVING CREATURES, 256 29
AND ONE OF THE ELDERS ANSWERED, SAYING UNTO ME, 257 04
AND PRAISE HIM IN THE SEAT OF THE ELDERS 478 11
AND CALLED THE ELDERS OF THE CHURCH 550 05

ELECT

AS THE ELECT OF GOD, HOLY AND BELOVED, 116 03
WERE POSSIBLE, THEY SHALL DECEIVE THE VERY ELECT 118 07
TOGETHER HIS ELECT FROM THE FOUR WINDS, FROM ONE END 118 22
TOGETHER THINE ELECT IN ONE COMMUNION AND FELLOWSHIP, 256 06
SHALL THE BISHOP ELECT PUT ON THE REST OF THE R 556 02

ELECTED

BEING ENDED, THE ELECTED BISHOP, VESTED WITH HIS R 552 17
THIS OUR BROTHER ELECTED, AND TO SEND THY GRACE UPON 553 18
THE HEAD OF THE ELECTED BISHOP, KNEELING BEFORE THEM, R 558 10
THIS OUR BROTHER ELECTED, AND TO SEND THY GRACE UPON 561 02
OF YOUR VOTE THAT HE HAS BEEN SO ELECTED 570 16

ELECTION

NOTICE OF THE ELECTION OF A MINISTER INTO A PARISH OR R 569 04
AND OUR ELECTION IN CHRIST, IS FULL OF SWEET, 606 16

ELEMENTS

THE CONSECRATED ELEMENTS, COVERING THE SAME WITH A R 083 12
UNDER THE ELEMENTS OF THE WORLD 104 18

ELEVEN

AND FOUND THE ELEVEN GATHERED TOGETHER, AND THEM THAT 168 12
NUMBERED WITH THE ELEVEN APOSTLES 234 33

ELEVENTH

AND ABOUT THE ELEVENTH HOUR HE WENT OUT, AND FOUND 119 24
HIRED ABOUT THE ELEVENTH HOUR, THEY RECEIVED EVERY 119 32

ELI

LOUD VOICE, SAYING, ELI, ELI, LAMA SABACHTHANI 137 17
SAYING, ELI, ELI, LAMA SABACHTHANI 137 18

ELIAS

ART THOU ELIAS 095 24
THAT CHRIST, NOR ELIAS, NEITHER THAT PROPHET 095 32
THIS MAN CALLETH FOR ELIAS 137 20
LET US SEE WHETHER ELIAS WILL COME TO SAVE HIM 137 23
THEY HEARD IT, SAID, BEHOLD, HE CALLETH ELIAS 146 31
LET US SEE WHETHER ELIAS WILL COME TO TAKE HIM DOWN 146 33
ELIAS 245 34
WITH HIM TWO MEN, WHICH WERE MOSES AND ELIAS 248 28
AND ONE FOR MOSES, AND ONE FOR ELIAS 249 04

ELISABETH

THY COUSIN ELISABETH, SHE HATH ALSO CONCEIVED A SON 236 25

ELISABETH'S

ELISABETH'S FULL TIME CAME THAT SHE SHOULD BE 243 13

ELOI

ELOI, ELOI, LAMA SABACHTHANI 146 28
LOUD VOICE, SAYING, ELOI, ELOI, LAMA SABACHTHANI 146 28

ELSE

AND WHERESOEVER ELSE IT IS USED IN DIVINE SERVICE R 007 21
OR ELSE HE SHALL SAY AS FOLLOWETH R 023 03
GLORIA PATRI, OR ELSE THE GLORIA IN EXCELSIS, R 025 20
AND WHATSOEVER ELSE MAY HINDER US FROM GODLY UNION 037 29
NO SACRIFICE, ELSE WOULD I GIVE IT THEE 061 11
THE NICENE, OR ELSE THE APOSTLES' CREED R 070 29
OR ELSE IMMEDIATELY SHALL BE SAID OR SUNG BY THE R 077 03
DOTH NOTHING ELSE BUT INCREASE YOUR CONDEMNATION 087 30
OF YOUR SINS, OR ELSE COME NOT TO THAT HOLY TABLE 087 34
OR ELSE THIS THAT FOLLOWETH R 155 21
OR ELSE HE WILL HOLD TO THE ONE, AND DESPISE THE 211 10

ELSE   CONTINUED

OR ELSE BELIEVE ME FOR THE VERY WORKS' SAKE   240 18
HIM NOW SPEAK, OR ELSE HEREAFTER FOR EVER HOLD HIS   300 22
BIT AND BRIDLE, ELSE THEY WILL NOT OBEY THEE   378 12
FRET NOT THYSELF, ELSE SHALT THOU BE MOVED TO DO   385 10
NO SACRIFICE, ELSE WOULD I GIVE IT THEE   404 09
TIMES APPOINTED, OR ELSE, ON URGENT OCCASION, UPCN   529 30
OR ELSE, ON URGENT OCCASION, UPON SOME OTHER DAY, IN   R 535 25
OR ELSE SAINT LUKE XII   R 547 26
AND WHATEVER ELSE THOU SHALT SEE TO BE NECESSARY AND   589 05

ELSEWHERE

PRAYERS AS ARE ELSEWHERE PROVIDED IN THIS BOOK,   R 331 30
EITHER HERE OR ELSEWHERE CALL UPON THY HOLY NAME,   545 27

EMBRACE

WHO DOST EMBRACE CHILDREN WITH THE ARMS OF   043 07
TO GOD, EMBRACE THE HAPPY OCCASION WHICH WAS OFFERED   VI 23
WE MAY EMBRACE, AND EVER HOLD FAST, THE BLESSED   092 11

EMBRACETH

MERCY EMBRACETH HIM ON EVERY SIDE   378 14

EMERALD

ABOUT THE THRONE, IN SIGHT LIKE UNTO AN EMERALD   187 08

EMMANUEL

CALL HIS NAME EMMANUEL, WHICH BEING INTERPRETED IS,   105 11

EMMAUS

A VILLAGE CALLED EMMAUS, WHICH WAS FROM JERUSALEM   167 04

EMPLOY

HELP US TO EMPLOY IT IN THE MAINTENANCE OF JUSTICE   044 12
THOSE WHOM THEY EMPLOY TO MUTUAL FORBEARANCE,   599 32

EMPLOYERS

THE HEART OF EMPLOYERS AND OF THOSE WHOM THEY EMPLOY   599 31

EMPTY

RICH HE HATH SENT EMPTY AWAY   026 25
YE SHALL NOT APPEAR BEFORE THE LORD EMPTY   073 15
HE SATISFIETH THE EMPTY SOUL, *   476 22

EMULATIONS

EMULATIONS, WRATH, STRIFE, SEDITIONS,   209 21

ENABLE

TO HEALTH, AND ENABLE HIM TO LEAD THE RESIDUE OF HIS   045 19
ENABLE WITH PERPETUAL LIGHT THE DULNESS OF OUR   544 04
ENABLE WITH PERPETUAL LIGHT THE DULNESS OF OUR   556 12

ENABLED

MAY BY THEE BE ENABLED TO LIVE ACCORDING TO THY WILL   201 02
MAY BY THEE BE ENABLED TO LIVE ACCORDING TO THY WILL   287 29
HE MAY BE ENABLED TO GO UPON HIS WAY REJOICING, AND   316 21

ENCOMPASS

WHICH ENCOMPASS US, WE BE DRAWN AGAIN INTO SIN,   590 10

ENCOURAGE

5 THEY ENCOURAGE THEMSELVES IN MISCHIEF, *   415 27
CALL UPON AND ENCOURAGE OTHERS TO THE SAME   555 05

ENCOURAGED

THAT WE, ENCOURAGED BY THE GOOD EXAMPLES OF THY   258 13

ENCOURAGEMENT

BLESSED ENCOURAGEMENT OF THY SYMPATHY, AND A CLEARER   596 13

END

TO THE END THAT WE MAY OBTAIN FORGIVENESS OF THE   005 34
IS NOW, AND EVER SHALL BE, WORLD WITHOUT END   008 06
AND LIKEWISE AT THE END OF THE VENITE, BENEDICTUS ES,   R 009 23
AND AT THE END OF EVERY PSALM, AND LIKEWISE AT THE   R 009 23
MAY BE, AND AT THE END OF THE WHOLE PORTION, OR   R 009 24
WORLD WITHOUT END   009 30
AND WE WORSHIP THY NAME EVER, WORLD WITHOUT END   011 07
WHOSE KINGDOM SHALL HAVE NO END   016 14
MINISTER MAY HERE END THE MORNING PRAYER WITH SUCH   R 017 22
AND THE HOLY GHOST, ONE GOD, WORLD WITHOUT END   018 16
BE ALL HONOUR AND GLORY, WORLD WITHOUT END   019 32
TO THE END THAT WE MAY OBTAIN FORGIVENESS OF THE   023 09
IS NOW, AND EVER SHALL BE, WORLD WITHOUT END   025 12
AND AT THE END OF EVERY PSALM, AND LIKEWISE AT THE   R 025 16
AND LIKEWISE AT THE END OF THE MAGNIFICAT, CANTATE   R 025 16
AND AT THE END OF THE WHOLE PORTION OR SELECTION CF   R 025 19
WHOSE KINGDOM SHALL HAVE NO END   030 19

END   CONTINUED

MINISTER MAY HERE END THE EVENING PRAYER WITH SUCH   R 031 31
ONE GOD, WORLD WITHOUT END   032 14
BE ALL HONOUR AND GLORY, WORLD WITHOUT END   033 30
THY CHURCH TO THE END OF THE WORLD   036 29
LOVING-KINDNESS REACHETH UNTO THE WORLD'S END   038 16
LIVEST AND REIGNEST ONE GOD, WORLD WITHOUT END   043 16
AND TO THAT END, AS WELL AS FOR THE GOOD EDUCATICN OF   047 31
AND THE HOLY GHOST, ONE GOD, WORLD WITHOUT END   049 10
BE ALL GLORY AND HONOUR, WORLD WITHOUT END   050 30
AND EVER SHALL BE, WORLD WITHOUT END   059 08
TO BE THE PROPER END OF ALL SUCH PRAYERS, NAMELY,   VI 18
THE MINISTER MAY END THE LITANY HERE, OR AT HIS   R 059 29
WORLD WITHOUT END   061 18
WHOSE KINGDOM SHALL HAVE NO END   071 16
TO THE END THAT ALL THAT BELIEVE IN HIM SHOULD   076 15
O FATHER ALMIGHTY, WORLD WITHOUT END   081 34
BE ALL HONOUR AND GLORY, WORLD WITHOUT END   083 31
APPOINTED UNTO THE END OF THE GOSPEL   R 084 26
UNTO THE END OF THE GOSPEL, CONCLUDING   R 084 29
AND TO THE END THAT WE SHOULD ALWAYS REMEMBER THE   086 12
ONE GOD, WORLD WITHOUT END   093 32
BE HONOUR AND GLORY, WORLD WITHOUT END   095 11
ONE GOD, WORLD WITHOUT END   096 19
ONE GOD, WORLD WITHOUT END   098 16
ONE GOD, WORLD WITHOUT END   104 12
AND REIGNETH EVER, ONE GOD, WORLD WITHOUT END   117 12
FOUR WINDS, FROM ONE END OF HEAVEN TO THE OTHER   118 23
ONE GOD, WORLD WITHOUT END   119 03
ONE GOD, WORLD WITHOUT END   125 32
BUT NOW ONCE IN THE END OF THE WORLD HATH HE APPEARED   148 05
FOR THE THINGS CONCERNING ME HAVE AN END   150 11
ONE GOD, WORLD WITHOUT END   152 14
HE LOVED THEM UNTO THE END   155 26
THE HOLY GHOST EVER, ONE GOD, WORLD WITHOUT END   156 26
ONE GOD, WORLD WITHOUT END   157 13
WORLD WITHOUT END   163 20
ONE GOD, WORLD WITHOUT END   163 29
ONE GOD, WORLD WITHOUT END   177 19
ONE GOD, WORLD WITHOUT END   179 10
THE END OF ALL THINGS IS AT HAND   179 12
ONE GOD, WORLD WITHOUT END   180 14
THE SAME SPIRIT EVER, ONE GOD, WORLD WITHOUT END   182 20
ONE GOD, WORLD WITHOUT END   183 27
AND THE SAME SPIRIT, ONE GOD, WORLD WITHCUT END   185 19
ONE GOD, WORLD WITHOUT END   186 29
FOR THE END OF THOSE THINGS IS DEATH   198 32
AND THE END EVERLASTING LIFE   199 04
JESUS THROUGHOUT ALL AGES, WORLD WITHOUT END   212 25
CONFIRM YOU UNTO THE END, THAT YE MAY BE BLAMELESS IN   215 03
WHOSE END IS DESTRUCTION, WHOSE GOD IS THEIR BELLY,   222 19
AND OF HIS KINGDOM THERE SHALL BE NO END   236 20
ONE GOD, WORLD WITHOUT END   248 06
ONE GOD, WORLD WITHOUT END   250 25
WORLD WITHOUT END   265 09
EVEN UNTO THE END OF THE WORLD   275 32
AND GOVERN ALL THINGS, WORLD WITHOUT END   278 31
FAITHFUL SOLDIER AND SERVANT UNTO HIS LIFE'S END   280 10
I MAY CONTINUE IN THE SAME UNTO MY LIFE'S END   284 05
AND EVER SHALL BE, WORLD WITHOLT END   285 09
THAT THEY MAY GROW IN GRACE UNTO THEIR LIFE'S END   294 27
WORLD WITHOUT END   297 10
THAT IN THE END THEY MAY OBTAIN EVERLASTING   298 22
AND REIGNETH EVER, ONE GOD, WORLD WITHOUT END   298 25
AND CONTINUE IN THY FAVOUR, UNTO THEIR LIFE'S END   302 21
ONE GOD, WORLD WITHOUT END   303 29
AND EVER SHALL BE, WORLD WITHOUT END   306 07
COME UTTERLY TO AN END FOR EVERMORE   311 15
BE ALL HONOUR AND GLORY, WORLD WITHOUT END   316 04
DAYS ARE WITHOUT END, AND WHOSE MERCIES CANNOT BE   316 25
AND THE HOLY GHOST, ONE GOD, WORLD WITHOUT END   319 13
ONE GOD, WORLD WITHOUT END   320 14
EXCEPT AT THE END OF THE WHOLE PORTION OR SELECTION   R 324 18
LET ME KNOW MINE END, AND THE NUMBER OF MY DAYS   324 20
ART GOD FROM EVERLASTING, AND WORLD WITHOUT END   325 17
OUR YEARS TO AN END, AS IT WERE A TALE THAT IS TCLD   325 31
THEN COMETH THE END, WHEN HE SHALL HAVE DELIVERED UP   328 27
ONE GOD, WORLD WITHOUT END   332 09
ONE GOD, WORLD WITHOUT END   336 15
AND AT THE END OF EACH PSALM SHALL BE SAID THE GLORIA   R 338 15
WORLD WITHOUT END   340 19
LET THE WICKEDNESS OF THE UNGODLY COME TO AN END   350 09
THY DESTRUCTIONS ARE COME TO A PERPETUAL END   351 33
ABOUT UNTO THE END OF IT AGAIN   363 25
AND THE END OF THE UNGODLY IS, THEY SHALL BE RCOTED   387 11
LET ME KNOW MINE END, AND THE NUMBER OF MY DAYS   389 15
WORLD WITHOUT END   392 26
PEOPLE GIVE THANKS UNTO THEE, WORLD WITHOUT END   397 23
SO IS THY PRAISE UNTO THE WORLD'S END   399 30
FOR I KNOW NO END THEREOF   426 05
AND FROM THE RIVER UNTO THE WORLD'S END   427 13
UNDERSTOOD I THE END OF THESE MEN   429 11
AND COME TO A FEARFUL END   429 15
COME UTTERLY TO AN END FOR EVERMORE   433 32
ART GOD FROM EVERLASTING, AND WORLD WITHOUT END   453 22
OUR YEARS TO AN END, AS IT WERE A TALE THAT IS TOLD   454 05
AND THE UNGODLY SHALL COME TO AN END   469 32
FROM EVERLASTING, AND WORLD WITHOUT END   475 34
AND ARE AT THEIR WIT'S END   477 32
AND I SHALL KEEP IT UNTO THE END   492 06
HAD ALMOST MADE AN END OF ME UPON EARTH   495 31
96 I SEE THAT ALL THINGS COME TO AN END   496 17
EVEN UNTO THE END   497 22
THERE IS NO END OF HIS GREATNESS   520 32
THE END OF THE PSALTER   R 525 33

END   CONTINUED

TO WHOM BE GLORY AND HONOUR, WORLD WITHOUT END   535 11
THEE AND THE SAME HOLY SPIRIT, WORLD WITHOUT END   537 30
WITH YOURSELVES THE END OF THE MINISTRY TOWARDS THE   540 14
UNITY OF THE SAME HOLY SPIRIT, WORLD WITHOUT END   546 05
THEE AND THE SAME HOLY SPIRIT, WORLD WITHOUT END   548 08
EVEN UNTO THE END OF THE WORLD   552 14
THEE AND THE SAME HOLY SPIRIT, WORLD WITHOUT END   554 04
TO THE END THAT THE CONGREGATION PRESENT   554 13
ONE GOD, WORLD WITHOUT END   558 08
ONE GOD, WORLD WITHOUT END   559 16
FORWARD WITH COURAGE, AND PERSEVERE UNTO THE END   561 10
ONE GOD, WORLD WITHOUT END   562 15
WORLD WITHOUT END   564 05
FAITHFUL SOLDIER AND SERVANT UNTO HIS LIFE'S END   565 22
THAT THEY MAY GROW IN GRACE UNTO THEIR LIFE'S END   565 27
IN PERFECT LOVE TOGETHER UNTO THEIR LIFE'S END   566 12
SUCCESSION TO THE END OF THE WORLD   572 18
WORSHIP AND GLORIFY AS ONE GOD, WORLD WITHOUT END   572 32
THE SAME HOLY GHOST, ONE GOD, WORLD WITHOUT END   574 23
I MAY CONTINUE IN THE SAME UNTO MY LIFE'S END   577 26
AND IN THE END BE ACCEPTED OF THEE AS THY   594 26

ENDEAVOUR

BLESSING EVERY ENDEAVOUR FOR PROMULGATING THEM TO   VI 41
AND ALSO DAILY ENDEAVOUR OURSELVES TO FOLLOW THE   171 32
I WILL ENDEAVOUR THAT YE MAY BE ABLE AFTER MY DECEASE   248 11
WILL ENDEAVOUR NOT TO FOLLOW, NOR BE LED BY   276 30
WILL ENDEAVOUR NOT TO FOLLOW, NOR BE LED BY   277 31
I WILL ENDEAVOUR SO TO DO, THE LORD BEING MY HELPER   533 34
THAT YE MAY SO ENDEAVOUR YOURSELVES, FROM TIME TO   541 19
I WILL ENDEAVOUR SO TO DO, THE LORD BEING MY HELPER   542 30

ENDEAVOURING

ENDEAVOURING TO KEEP THE UNITY OF THE SPIRIT IN THE   213 21

ENDEAVOURS

BY THEIR ENDEAVOURS, UPON THE BEST AND SUREST   035 15
TO SANCTIFY ALL OUR THOUGHTS AND ENDEAVOURS   594 21

ENDED

THIS LIFE ENDED, WE MAY BE MADE PARTAKERS WITH   048 20
AND ENDED IN THEE, WE MAY GLORIFY THY HOLY   049 25
THE EPISTLE ENDED, HE SHALL SAY, HERE ENDETH THE   R 070 20
AND SUPPER BEING ENDED, THE DEVIL HAVING NOW PUT INTO   155 27
THE SERMON BEING ENDED, A PRIEST SHALL PRESENT UNTO   R 530 07
THE COMMUNION ENDED, AFTER THE LAST COLLECT,   R 534 28
WHICH BEING ENDED, THE ELECTED BISHOP, VESTED WITH   R 552 17
THAT ENDED, THE PRESIDING BISHOP SHALL SAY,   R 557 16
AND ENDED IN THEE, WE MAY GLORIFY THY HOLY   571 10

ENDETH

HERE ENDETH THE FIRST (OR THE SECOND) LESSON   R 009 34
HERE ENDETH THE ORDER OF MORNING PRAYER   R 020 15
HERE ENDETH THE ORDER OF EVENING PRAYER   R 034 15
SHALL SAY, HERE ENDETH THE EPISTLE   R 070 20

ENDING

ALMIGHTY GOD, AND ENDING WITH THESE WORDS, PARTAKERS   R 083 09
OF CONSECRATION, ENDING WITH THESE WORDS, PARTAKERS   R 323 07
IN THIS BOOK, ENDING WITH THE BLESSING   R 331 30

ENDLESS

TO OUR GREAT AND ENDLESS COMFORT   086 18
THIS MAY BE OUR ENDLESS SONG   544 13
THIS MAY BE OUR ENDLESS SONG   556 21
THEIR GREAT AND ENDLESS COMFORT, OBTAIN REMISSION OF   565 33

ENDOR

10 WHO PERISHED AT ENDOR, *   444 24

ENDOW

THOU, WHO DOST THE TONGUE WITH SPEECH ENDOW   544 28
THOU, WHO DOST THE TONGUE WITH SPEECH ENDOW   557 07

ENDOWMENT

DONATION AND ENDOWMENT, IF THERE BE ANY, PRESENTED TO   R 564 08

ENDOWMENTS

AND ALL OTHER ENDOWMENTS AND FACULTIES OF SOUL AND   591 09

ENDS

AND ALL THE ENDS OF THE WORLD HAVE SEEN THE SALVATION   027 11
AND ALL THE ENDS OF THE WORLD SHALL FEAR HIM   028 30
UPON WHOM THE ENDS OF THE WORLD ARE COME   201 24
WORDS UNTO THE ENDS OF THE WORLD   227 15
SALVATION UNTO THE ENDS OF THE EARTH   261 05
WORDS INTO THE ENDS OF THE WORLD   363 20
27 ALL THE ENDS OF THE WORLD SHALL REMEMBER   367 28
AND UNTO THE ENDS OF THE WORLD   411 34
2 FROM THE ENDS OF THE EARTH WILL I CALL UPON THEE,   413 08
THE HOPE OF ALL THE ENDS OF THE EARTH, AND OF THEM   416 23
AND ALL THE ENDS OF THE WORLD SHALL FEAR HIM   419 04

ENDS   CONTINUED

AND ALL THE ENDS OF THE WORLD HAVE SEEN THE SALVATION   461 32
THE CLOUDS FROM THE ENDS OF THE WORLD, *   510 15

ENDUE

ENDUE THEM PLENTEOUSLY WITH HEAVENLY GIFTS   018 02
ENDUE THY MINISTERS WITH RIGHTEOUSNESS   031 06
ENDUE WITH THE SPIRIT OF WISDOM THOSE TO WHOM IN THY   036 17
THY DOCTRINE, AND ENDUE THEM WITH INNOCENCY OF LIFE,   039 12
ENDUE THEM WITH COURAGE AND LOYALTY   041 28
ENDUE THEM WITH WISDOM, PATIENCE, AND COURAGE TO   043 31
ENDUE HIS SOUL WITH PATIENCE   046 04
AND TO ENDUE US WITH THE GRACE OF THY HOLY SPIRIT TO   057 16
WHO DIDST ENDUE THY HOLY APOSTLE BARNABAS WITH   240 28
AND SO ENDUE HIM WITH THY HOLY SPIRIT, THAT HE,   559 07
MAY PLEASE THEE TO ENDUE ALL MINISTERS OF THY CHURCH   560 21
THY DOCTRINE, AND ENDUE HIM WITH INNOCENCY OF LIFE,   572 11

ENDUED

UNTIL YE BE ENDUED WITH POWER FROM ON HIGH   178 23
MAY ALSO BE ENDUED WITH HEAVENLY VIRTUES, AND   278 23
THEY WHICH BE ENDUED WITH SO EXCELLENT A BENEFIT OF   606 10

ENDUEDST

AND ENDUEDST MY SOUL WITH MUCH STRENGTH   312 02
AND ENDUEDST MY SOUL WITH MUCH STRENGTH   514 03

ENDURANCE

TO THEM THE ENDURANCE OF THEIR WRONGS   599 10

ENDURE

TOWARD GOD ENDURE GRIEF, SUFFERING WRONGFULLY   172 06
IN ALL THINGS, ENDURE AFFLICTIONS, DO THE WORK OF AN   253 23
THE LORD SHALL ENDURE FOR EVER   352 02
HEAVINESS MAY ENDURE FOR A NIGHT, BUT JOY COMETH IN   375 02
OF THE LORD SHALL ENDURE FOR EVER, *   379 09
INHERITANCE SHALL ENDURE FOR EVER   385 32
SHALL ENDURE FROM ONE GENERATION TO ANOTHER   400 27
HIS YEARS MAY ENDURE THROUGHOUT ALL GENERATIONS   413 18
17 HIS NAME SHALL ENDURE FOR EVER   427 32
WILL I MAKE TO ENDURE FOR EVER, *   451 33
35 HIS SEED SHALL ENDURE FOR EVER, *   452 12
O LORD, SHALT ENDURE FOR EVER, *   465 02
THY YEARS, THEY ENDURE THROUGHOUT ALL GENERATIONS   465 29
26 THEY SHALL PERISH, BUT THOU SHALT ENDURE   465 34
OF THE LORD SHALL ENDURE FOR EVER   469 23
THY RIGHTEOUSNESS ENDURE FOR EVERMORE   500 32
OUR SINS, AND ENDURE THE SEVERITY OF GOD'S JUDGMENT   605 12

ENDURED

SET BEFORE HIM ENDURED THE CROSS, DESPISING THE   258 25
TIME SHOULD HAVE ENDURED FOR EVER   443 11

ENDURETH

AND HIS TRUTH ENDURETH FROM GENERATION TO GENERATION   015 14
ALL THINGS, ENDURETH ALL THINGS   123 03
IS THE MAN THAT ENDURETH TEMPTATION   239 24
O LORD, ENDURETH FOR EVER   312 09
IS CLEAN, AND ENDURETH FOR EVER   363 33
5 FOR HIS WRATH ENDURETH BUT THE TWINKLING OF AN EYE,   374 32
O GOD, ENDURETH FOR EVER   396 27
ENDURETH YET DAILY   404 21
EVEN GOD, THAT ENDURETH FOR EVER, SHALL HEAR ME, AND   407 30
SUN AND MOON ENDURETH, *   427 07
SO LONG AS THE MOON ENDURETH   427 11
AND HIS TRUTH ENDURETH FROM GENERATION TO GENERATION   463 15
OF THE LORD ENDURETH FOR EVER AND EVER UPON THEM THAT   467 08
AND HIS MERCY ENDURETH FOR EVER   472 32
AND HIS MERCY ENDURETH FOR EVER   476 07
RIGHTEOUSNESS ENDURETH FOR EVER   482 29
HIS PRAISE ENDURETH FOR EVER   483 16
RIGHTEOUSNESS ENDURETH FOR EVER   483 23
OF THE LORD ENDURETH FOR EVER   487 28
HIS MERCY ENDURETH FOR EVER   487 32
THAT HIS MERCY ENDURETH FOR EVER   488 03
THAT HIS MERCY ENDURETH FOR EVER   488 05
THAT HIS MERCY ENDURETH FOR EVER   488 07
AND HIS MERCY ENDURETH FOR EVER   489 28
ENDURETH FOR EVER IN HEAVEN   496 03
O LORD, ENDURETH FOR EVER   510 28
AND HIS MERCY ENDURETH FOR EVER   511 17
FOR HIS MERCY ENDURETH FOR EVER   511 19
FOR HIS MERCY ENDURETH FOR EVER   511 20
FOR HIS MERCY ENDURETH FOR EVER   511 22
FOR HIS MERCY ENDURETH FOR EVER   511 25
FOR HIS MERCY ENDURETH FOR EVER   511 27
FOR HIS MERCY ENDURETH FOR EVER   511 28
FOR HIS MERCY ENDURETH FOR EVER   511 30
FOR HIS MERCY ENDURETH FOR EVER   511 33
FOR HIS MERCY ENDURETH FOR EVER   512 03
FOR HIS MERCY ENDURETH FOR EVER   512 05
FOR HIS MERCY ENDURETH FOR EVER   512 07
FOR HIS MERCY ENDURETH FOR EVER   512 09
FOR HIS MERCY ENDURETH FOR EVER   512 11
FOR HIS MERCY ENDURETH FOR EVER   512 13
FOR HIS MERCY ENDURETH FOR EVER   512 15
FOR HIS MERCY ENDURETH FOR EVER   512 16
FOR HIS MERCY ENDURETH FOR EVER   512 18

ENDURETH   CONTINUED

FOR HIS MERCY ENDURETH FOR EVER   512 20
FOR HIS MERCY ENDURETH FOR EVER   512 22
FOR HIS MERCY ENDURETH FOR EVER   512 25
FOR HIS MERCY ENDURETH FOR EVER   512 27
FOR HIS MERCY ENDURETH FOR EVER   512 29
FOR HIS MERCY ENDURETH FOR EVER   512 31
FOR HIS MERCY ENDURETH FOR EVER   512 32
FOR HIS MERCY ENDURETH FOR EVER   512 35
FOR HIS MERCY ENDURETH FOR EVER   513 03
O LORD, ENDURETH FOR EVER   514 15
THY DOMINION ENDURETH THROUGHOUT ALL AGES   521 19

ENEMIES

SAVED FROM OUR ENEMIES, *   014 14
THE HAND OF OUR ENEMIES *   014 20
HUMBLE SERVANTS IN ALL ASSAULTS OF OUR ENEMIES   017 08
THE FEAR OF OUR ENEMIES, MAY PASS OUR TIME IN REST   031 22
FROM THE HANDS OF OUR ENEMIES   041 13
THE VIOLENCE OF ENEMIES, AND FROM EVERY EVIL TO WHICH   046 13
THY SERVANTS AGAINST THE FACE OF THEIR ENEMIES   052 08
TO FORGIVE OUR ENEMIES, PERSECUTORS, AND SLANDERERS,   057 07
FROM OUR ENEMIES DEFEND US, O CHRIST   059 09
TO BE OUR DEFENCE AGAINST ALL OUR ENEMIES   128 28
TILL HIS ENEMIES BE MADE HIS FOOTSTOOL   158 17
THAT THINE ENEMIES SHALL CAST A TRENCH ABOUT   204 10
I MAKE THINE ENEMIES THY FOOTSTOOL   215 21
THEY ARE THE ENEMIES OF THE CROSS OF CHRIST   222 18
SAVED FROM OUR ENEMIES, AND FROM THE HAND OF ALL THAT   244 03
THE HAND OF OUR ENEMIES MIGHT SERVE HIM WITHOUT FEAR,   244 08
LOVE YOUR ENEMIES, BLESS THEM THAT CURSE YOU, DO   264 05
OF MINE ENEMIES, AND THY RIGHT HAND SHALL SAVE ME   312 06
ABOVE MINE ENEMIES ROUND ABOUT ME   326 15
HE HATH PUT ALL ENEMIES UNDER HIS FEET   328 30
SMITEST ALL MINE ENEMIES UPON THE CHEEK-BONE   347 05
IN THY RIGHTEOUSNESS, BECAUSE OF MINE ENEMIES   348 17
AND WORN AWAY BECAUSE OF ALL MINE ENEMIES   349 13
10 ALL MINE ENEMIES SHALL BE CONFOUNDED, AND SORE   349 18
BECAUSE OF THE INDIGNATION OF MINE ENEMIES   350 02
BECAUSE OF THINE ENEMIES, *   351 02
3 WHILE MINE ENEMIES ARE DRIVEN BACK, *   351 26
AND THEREFORE DEFIETH HE ALL HIS ENEMIES   353 15
MINE ENEMIES COMPASS ME ROUND ABOUT, TO TAKE AWAY MY   359 04
SO SHALL I BE SAFE FROM MINE ENEMIES   359 30
FOLLOW UPON MINE ENEMIES, AND OVERTAKE THEM   362 11
THROW DOWN MINE ENEMIES UNDER ME   362 17
HAST MADE MINE ENEMIES ALSO TO TURN THEIR BACKS UPON   362 18
ME FROM MY CRUEL ENEMIES, AND SETTETH ME UP ABOVE   363 02
8 ALL THINE ENEMIES SHALL FEEL THINE HAND   365 20
NEITHER LET MINE ENEMIES TRIUMPH OVER ME   369 20
18 CONSIDER MINE ENEMIES, HOW MANY THEY ARE   370 22
EVEN MINE ENEMIES AND MY FOES, CAME UPON ME TO EAT UP   371 27
ABOVE MINE ENEMIES ROUND ABOUT ME   372 08
LEAD ME IN THE RIGHT WAY, BECAUSE OF MINE ENEMIES   372 23
AMONG ALL MINE ENEMIES, BUT ESPECIALLY AMONG MY   376 15
THE HAND OF MINE ENEMIES, *   376 27
THAT ARE MINE ENEMIES TRIUMPH OVER ME UNGODLY   382 34
AND THE ENEMIES OF THE LORD SHALL CONSUME AS   385 35
EVEN MINE ENEMIES, SHOULD NOT TRIUMPH OVER ME   388 23
19 BUT MINE ENEMIES LIVE, AND ARE MIGHTY   388 30
DELIVER NOT THOU HIM INTO THE WILL OF HIS ENEMIES   392 03
5 MINE ENEMIES SPEAK EVIL OF ME, *   392 08
7 ALL MINE ENEMIES WHISPER TOGETHER AGAINST ME   392 13
WHILE MINE ENEMIES THAT TROUBLE ME CAST ME IN THE   393 28
WE OVERTHROW OUR ENEMIES, *   395 02
US FROM OUR ENEMIES, *   395 07
BACKS UPON OUR ENEMIES, *   395 13
OF THE KING'S ENEMIES, *   396 26
5 HE SHALL REWARD EVIL UNTO MINE ENEMIES   406 12
MINE EYE HATH SEEN HIS DESIRE UPON MINE ENEMIES   406 17
2 MINE ENEMIES ARE DAILY AT HAND TO SWALLOW ME UP   408 16
THEN SHALL MINE ENEMIES BE PUT TO FLIGHT   408 32
ME FROM MINE ENEMIES, O GOD   411 04
GOD SHALL LET ME SEE MY DESIRE UPON MINE ENEMIES   411 25
FOR IT IS HE THAT SHALL TREAD DOWN OUR ENEMIES   413 05
SHALL THINE ENEMIES BOW DOWN UNTO THEE   417 19
AND LET HIS ENEMIES BE SCATTERED   419 09
EVEN FROM THINE ENEMIES, THAT THE LORD GOD MIGHT   420 21
THE HEAD OF HIS ENEMIES, *   420 27
BLOOD OF THINE ENEMIES, *   420 34
THAT ARE MINE ENEMIES, AND WOULD DESTROY ME   422 08
O DELIVER ME, BECAUSE OF MINE ENEMIES   423 10
9 FOR MINE ENEMIES SPEAK AGAINST ME   425 25
HIS ENEMIES SHALL LICK THE DUST   427 15
THY TURTLE-DOVE UNTO THE MULTITUDE OF THE ENEMIES   431 16
24 FORGET NOT THE VOICE OF THINE ENEMIES   431 24
THEIR ENEMIES WITH THE SEA   438 15
67 HE DRAVE HIS ENEMIES BACKWARD, *   439 10
SHAME TO OUR ENEMIES, *   440 06
AND OUR ENEMIES LAUGH US TO SCORN   441 15
PUT DOWN THEIR ENEMIES, *   443 08
2 FOR LO, THINE ENEMIES MAKE A MURMURING   444 07
SCATTERED THINE ENEMIES ABROAD WITH THY MIGHTY ARM   450 27
HAND OF HIS ENEMIES, *   452 26
WHEREWITH THINE ENEMIES HAVE BLASPHEMED THEE,   453 10
LO, THINE ENEMIES SHALL PERISH   456 17
8 FOR LO, THINE ENEMIES, O LORD, LO, THINE ENEMIES   456 17
HIS LUST OF MINE ENEMIES, *   456 21
AND BURN UP HIS ENEMIES ON EVERY SIDE   461 03
8 MINE ENEMIES REVILE ME ALL THE DAY LONG   464 25
AND MADE THEM STRONGER THAN THEIR ENEMIES   471 21
41 THEIR ENEMIES OPPRESSED THEM, *   475 20
AND IT IS HE THAT SHALL TREAD DOWN OUR ENEMIES   479 31
LORD UNTO MINE ENEMIES, *   481 10

ENEMIES   CONTINUED

I MAKE THINE ENEMIES THY FOOTSTOOL   482 08
EVEN IN THE MIDST AMONG THINE ENEMIES   482 10
UNTIL HE SEE HIS DESIRE UPON HIS ENEMIES   483 33
THEREFORE SHALL I SEE MY DESIRE UPON MINE ENEMIES   488 13
HAST MADE ME WISER THAN MINE ENEMIES   496 23
BECAUSE MINE ENEMIES HAVE FORGOTTEN THY WORDS   499 18
THAT ARE ENEMIES UNTO PEACE   502 17
SPEAK WITH THEIR ENEMIES IN THE GATE   506 04
19 AS FOR HIS ENEMIES, I SHALL CLOTHE THEM WITH   509 10
24 AND HATH DELIVERED US FROM OUR ENEMIES   512 30
OF MINE ENEMIES, AND THY RIGHT HAND SHALL SAVE ME   514 12
AND THINE ENEMIES TAKE THY NAME IN VAIN   515 31
EVEN AS THOUGH THEY WERE MINE ENEMIES   516 03
O LORD, FROM MINE ENEMIES   519 10
SLAY MINE ENEMIES, *   519 17

ENEMY

AND FROM THE VIOLENCE OF THE ENEMY   042 08
PRESERVE HIM FROM THE TEMPTATIONS OF THE ENEMY   045 17
THEREFORE IF THINE ENEMY HUNGER, FEED HIM   113 06
MEN SLEPT, HIS ENEMY CAME AND SOWED TARES AMONG THE   116 20
SAID UNTO THEM, AN ENEMY HATH DONE THIS   116 25
TURNED TO BE THEIR ENEMY, AND HE FOUGHT AGAINST THEM   139 06
HAST DELIVERED US FROM THE POWER OF OUR ENEMY   165 06
SHALT LOVE THY NEIGHBOUR, AND HATE THINE ENEMY   264 04
FROM THE FACE OF HER ENEMY   306 20
LET THE ENEMY HAVE NO ADVANTAGE OF HIM   308 27
FROM THE FACE OF HIS ENEMY   308 30
WHILE THE ENEMY OPPRESSETH ME   310 10
THE LAST ENEMY THAT SHALL BE DESTROYED IS DEATH   328 30
HIM THAT WITHOUT ANY CAUSE IS MINE ENEMY   349 31
5 THEN LET MINE ENEMY PERSECUTE MY SOUL, AND TAKE ME   349 32
MIGHTEST STILL THE ENEMY AND THE AVENGER   351 03
6 O THOU ENEMY, THY DESTRUCTIONS ARE COME TO A   351 32
LONG SHALL MINE ENEMY TRIUMPH OVER ME   355 31
4 LEST MINE ENEMY SAY, I HAVE PREVAILED AGAINST HIM   356 04
FROM MY STRONGEST ENEMY, AND FROM THEM WHICH HATE ME   360 33
HAST NOT SHUT ME UP INTO THE HAND OF THE ENEMY   376 06
THAT MINE ENEMY DOTH NOT TRIUMPH AGAINST ME   392 21
WHILE THE ENEMY OPPRESSETH ME   393 26
WHILE THE ENEMY OPPRESSETH ME   394 08
FOR THE ENEMY AND AVENGER   395 27
3 THE ENEMY CRIETH SO, AND THE UNGODLY COMETH ON SO   406 23
IT IS NOT AN OPEN ENEMY THAT HATH DONE ME THIS   407 11
AND A STRONG TOWER FOR ME AGAINST THE ENEMY   413 12
PRESERVE MY LIFE FROM FEAR OF THE ENEMY   415 20
DESTROY EVERY ENEMY, *   430 11
SHALL THE ENEMY BLASPHEME THY NAME FOR EVER   430 28
RIGHT HAND OUT OF THY BOSOM TO CONSUME THE ENEMY   430 31
O LORD, HOW THE ENEMY HATH REBUKED   431 12
WHEN HE DELIVERED THEM FROM THE HAND OF THE ENEMY   437 26
23 THE ENEMY SHALL NOT BE ABLE TO DO HIM VIOLENCE   451 19
AND DELIVERED THEM FROM THE HAND OF THE ENEMY   473 22
AND DELIVERED FROM THE HAND OF THE ENEMY   476 09
12 O HELP US AGAINST THE ENEMY   479 28
3 FOR THE ENEMY HATH PERSECUTED MY SOUL   518 27
FROM OUR SPIRITUAL ENEMY, AND FROM EVERLASTING DEATH   581 04

ENEMY'S

BEAUTY INTO THE ENEMY'S HAND   438 35

ENFORCE

OUGHT IT NOT TO ENFORCE ANY THING TO BE BELIEVED FOR   607 08

ENGENDERED

NATURALLY IS ENGENDERED OF THE OFFSPRING OF ADAM   604 31

ENGLAND

THE CHURCH OF ENGLAND, TO WHICH THE PROTESTANT   V 10
BOOK OF COMMON PRAYER OF THE CHURCH OF ENGLAND   VI 31
THE CHURCH OF ENGLAND IN ANY ESSENTIAL POINT OF   VI 32
AND LAWS OF ENGLAND ARE CONSIDERED AS INAPPLICABLE TO R 610 26

ENGRAFTED

MEEKNESS THE ENGRAFTED WORD, WHICH IS ABLE TO SAVE   175 04
MEEKNESS THE ENGRAFTED WORD, WHICH IS ABLE TO SAVE   265 27

ENGRAVEN

WRITTEN AND ENGRAVEN IN STONES, WAS GLORIOUS, SO THAT   206 19

ENJOINED

WHICH GOD HATH ENJOINED UNTO YOU   147 23

ENJOY

IN DUE TIME WE MAY ENJOY THEM   057 12
THY SERVANT) MAY ENJOY THE EVERLASTING BENEDICTION OF   274 19
THAT ALL WHO SHALL ENJOY THE BENEFIT OF THIS PIOUS   566 31
YOU TO CLAIM AND ENJOY ALL THE ACCUSTOMED   569 30
THAT WE MAY ENJOY SUCH REFRESHING SLEEP AS MAY FIT US   591 27

ENJOYED

SALVATION TO BE ENJOYED THROUGH CHRIST, AS BECAUSE IT   606 21

ENKINDLE

WHO DOST ENKINDLE THE FLAME OF THY LOVE IN THE   258 04
AND SO ENKINDLE FERVENT CHARITY AMONG US ALL,   598 28

ENKINDLED

THE SAME LIGHT ENKINDLED IN OUR HEARTS MAY SHINE   106 27

ENLARGED

ENLARGED, AMENDED, OR OTHERWISE DISPOSED   V 07
16 THE SORROWS OF MY HEART ARE ENLARGED   370 18
AND THY BLESSED KINGDOM ENLARGED   546 02

ENLIGHTEN

ENLIGHTEN WITH THY WISDOM THOSE WHO TEACH AND THOSE   043 02
ENLIGHTEN THEIR MINDS MORE AND MORE WITH THE LIGHT OF   572 27
ENLIGHTEN MY UNDERSTANDING WITH THE ILLUMINATION CF   573 16

ENLIGHTENED

WE MAY BE ENLIGHTENED AND STRENGTHENED FOR THY   182 17

ENMITY

THEY WERE AT ENMITY BETWEEN THEMSELVES   153 20

ENOUGH

IT IS ENOUGH, THE HOUR IS COME   142 11
AND HE SAID UNTO THEM, IT IS ENOUGH   150 13
HAVE BREAD ENOUGH AND TO SPARE, AND I PERISH WITH   202 11
SHALT MAKE ROOM ENOUGH UNDER ME FOR TO GO, *   362 09
AND IN THE DAYS OF DEARTH THEY SHALL HAVE ENOUGH   385 34
FOR HE SENT THEM MEAT ENOUGH   436 21

ENQUIRE

THEY BEGAN TO ENQUIRE AMONG THEMSELVES, WHICH OF THEM   149 16
UNTO THEM, DO YE ENQUIRE AMONG YOURSELVES CF THAT I   174 05
AND ENQUIRE IN THE HOUSE OF JUDAS FOR ONE   230 18

ENQUIRED

HAD DILIGENTLY ENQUIRED OF THE WISE MEN   103 29
THE WISE MEN, ENQUIRED OF THEM DILIGENTLY WHAT TIME   109 11
THEN ENQUIRED HE OF THEM THE HOUR WHEN HE BEGAN TO   220 06

ENRICHED

THING YE ARE ENRICHED BY HIM, IN ALL UTTERANCE,   214 30

ENSAMPLE

AND ALSO AN ENSAMPLE OF GODLY LIFE   171 29
THEM WHICH WALK SO AS YE HAVE US FOR AN ENSAMPLE   222 16

ENSAMPLES

ALL THESE THINGS HAPPENED UNTO THEM FOR ENSAMPLES   201 23

ENSUE

SEEK PEACE, AND ENSUE IT   195 27
SEEK PEACE, AND ENSUE IT   380 29
AND ALSO THE HORRIBLE PUNISHMENT THAT WILL ENSUE   540 13

ENSUING

THE OFFICE ENSUING MAY BE READ IMMEDIATELY   R 060 03
FOR THE ENSUING DAY   588 28

ENTANGLE

HOW THEY MIGHT ENTANGLE HIM IN HIS TALK   222 29

ENTER

ENTER NOT INTO JUDGMENT WITH THY SERVANTS   062 21
LORD, SHALL ENTER INTO THE KINGDOM OF HEAVEN   072 14
AND THEY ENTER IN, AND DWELL THERE   130 15
AND PRAY, LEST YE ENTER INTO TEMPTATION   142 05
THAT WE MAY ENTER WITH JOY UPON THE MEDITATION CF   147 09
PRAY THAT YE ENTER NOT INTO TEMPTATION   150 16
AND PRAY, LEST YE ENTER INTO TEMPTATION   150 26
BOLDNESS TO ENTER INTO THE HOLIEST BY THE BLOOD OF   158 16
AND TO ENTER INTO HIS GLORY   167 31
BY ME IF ANY MAN ENTER IN, HE SHALL BE SAVED, AND   186 15
CAN HE ENTER THE SECOND TIME INTO HIS MOTHER'S WOMB,   188 08
HE CANNOT ENTER INTO THE KINGDOM OF GOD   188 11
SHALL IN NO CASE ENTER INTO THE KINGDOM OF HEAVEN   197 30
LORD, SHALL ENTER INTO THE KINGDOM OF HEAVEN   200 24
YE SHALL NOT ENTER INTO THE KINGDOM OF HEAVEN   252 27
BETTER FOR THEE TO ENTER INTO LIFE HALT OR MAIMED,   253 05
BETTER FOR THEE TO ENTER INTO LIFE WITH ONE EYE,   253 08
HOUSE YE ENTER, FIRST SAY, PEACE BE TO THIS HOUSE   254 19
MAY AT THE LAST ENTER WITH THEM INTO THINE UNENDING   268 18
NONE CAN ENTER INTO THE KINGDOM OF GOD, EXCEPT   273 30
HE SHALL NOT ENTER THEREIN   274 32
CAN HE ENTER THE SECOND TIME INTO HIS MOTHER'S WOMB,   275 13
HE CANNOT ENTER INTO THE KINGDOM OF GOD   275 16
YE SHALL NOT ENTER INTO THE KINGDOM OF HEAVEN   339 26
AND SHALL ENTER INTO THE KING'S PALACE   397 18

ENTER   CONTINUED

AND LONGING TO ENTER INTO THE COURTS OF THE LORD   445 13
O LET MY PRAYER ENTER INTO THY PRESENCE, INCLINE   448 30
THEY SHOULD NOT ENTER INTO MY REST   459 28
RIGHTEOUS SHALL ENTER INTO IT   489 09
2 AND ENTER NOT INTO JUDGMENT WITH THY SERVANT   518 25
BY ME IF ANY MAN ENTER IN, HE SHALL BE SAVED, AND   539 06
GRIEVOUS WOLVES ENTER IN AMONG YOU, NOT SPARING THE   550 31
SHALL ENTER THE CHANCEL   R 570 04

ENTERED

CHRIST IS NOT ENTERED INTO THE HOLY PLACES MADE WITH   022 22
WHEN JESUS WAS ENTERED INTO CAPERNAUM, THERE CAME   115 06
HIS OWN BLOOD HE ENTERED IN ONCE INTO THE HOLY PLACE,   132 27
AND ENTERED NOT INTO GLORY BEFORE HE WAS   138 05
CHRIST IS NOT ENTERED INTO THE HOLY PLACES MADE WITH   147 30
THEN ENTERED SATAN INTO JUDAS SURNAMED ISCARIOT,   148 15
WHEN YE ARE ENTERED INTO THE CITY, THERE SHALL A MAN   148 25
AND HE ENTERED INTO ONE OF THE SHIPS, WHICH WAS   196 10
AND AS HE ENTERED INTO A CERTAIN VILLAGE, THERE MET   210 02
JESUS ENTERED INTO A SHIP, AND PASSED OVER, AND CAME   216 33
HIS WAY, AND ENTERED INTO THE HOUSE   230 30
FEARED AS THEY ENTERED INTO THE CLOUD   249 06
NOT BY ANY TO BE ENTERED INTO UNADVISEDLY OR LIGHTLY   300 17
IT ENTERED EVEN INTO HIS EARS   360 07
THE IRON ENTERED INTO HIS SOUL   471 08

ENTERETH

THE HIGH PRIEST ENTERETH INTO THE HOLY PLACE EVERY   148 03
HOUSE WHERE HE ENTERETH IN   148 27
HE THAT ENTERETH NOT BY THE DOOR INTO THE   185 30
BUT HE THAT ENTERETH IN BY THE DOOR IS THE SHEPHERD   186 03
HE THAT ENTERETH NOT BY THE DOOR INTO THE   538 23
BUT HE THAT ENTERETH IN BY THE DOOR IS THE SHEPHERD   538 26

ENTERING

AND ENTERING INTO THE SEPULCHRE, THEY SAW A YOUNG MAN   165 26

ENTIRE

THE SUBSTANCE OF THE FAITH BE KEPT ENTIRE   V 05
BE PERFECT AND ENTIRE, WANTING NOTHING   239 11

ENTRANCE

GRANT HIM AN ENTRANCE INTO THE LAND OF LIGHT AND JOY,   268 24
GRANT HIM AN ENTRANCE INTO THE LAND OF LIGHT AND JOY,   334 16
AN ABUNDANT ENTRANCE INTO THY KINGDOM   340 30
RECEIVED AT THE ENTRANCE OF THE CHURCH, OR CHAPEL,   R 563 05

ENTREAT

WE ENTREAT THY STRENGTH AND GOODNESS IN BEHALF CF   315 15

ENTREATED

AND SPITEFULLY ENTREATED, AND SPITTED ON   123 21
AND ENTREATED THEM SPITEFULLY, AND SLEW   218 12
TO BE EVIL ENTREATED THROUGH TYRANTS, *   478 26

ENTRUST

IN THY NAME WE ENTRUST THE AUTHORITY OF GOVERNMENT,   036 18
BESEECH THEE, TO ENTRUST THE SOUL OF THIS CHILD TO   342 05
ALMIGHTY GOD, WE ENTRUST ALL WHO ARE DEAR TO US TO   597 09

ENUMERATE

UNNECESSARY TO ENUMERATE ALL THE DIFFERENT   VI 28

ENVIES

AND ENVIES, AND ALL EVIL SPEAKINGS,   259 26

ENVIETH

CHARITY ENVIETH NOT   122 29

ENVIOUS

NEITHER BE THOU ENVIOUS AGAINST THE EVIL DOERS   384 26

ENVY

FROM ENVY, HATRED, AND MALICE, AND ALL   054 24
OR BE IN MALICE, OR ENVY, OR IN ANY OTHER GRIEVOUS   087 32
HE KNEW THAT FOR ENVY THEY HAD DELIVERED HIM   135 31
THAT THE CHIEF PRIESTS HAD DELIVERED HIM FOR ENVY   145 20
WERE FILLED WITH ENVY, AND SPAKE AGAINST THOSE THINGS   260 28
OUR HEARTS FROM ENVY, HATRED, AND MALICE   590 15

ENVYING

NOT IN STRIFE AND ENVYING   091 07

ENVYINGS

ENVYINGS, MURDERS, DRUNKENNESS, REVELLINGS,   209 22

EPAPHRAS

ALSO LEARNED OF EPAPHRAS OUR DEAR FELLOW-SERVANT,   223 30

EPHESIANS

SHALL BE EPHESIANS IV   R 547 22

EPHESUS

AND TYCHICUS HAVE I SENT TO EPHESUS   254 04
PAUL SENT TO EPHESUS, AND CALLED THE ELDERS OF THE   550 04

EPHPHATHA

UNTO HIM, EPHPHATHA, THAT IS, BE OPENED   207 02

EPHRAIM

EPHRAIM ALSO IS THE STRENGTH OF MY HEAD   412 25
10 LIKE AS THE CHILDREN OF EPHRAIM   435 17
AND CHOSE NOT THE TRIBE OF EPHRAIM   439 13
2 BEFORE EPHRAIM, BENJAMIN, AND MANASSEH, *   441 06
EPHRAIM ALSO IS THE STRENGTH OF MY HEAD   479 20

EPHRATAH

OF THE SAME AT EPHRATAH, *   508 15

EPIPHANY

ON CHRISTMAS DAY AND UNTIL THE EPIPHANY   R 008 18
ON THE EPIPHANY AND SEVEN DAYS AFTER, AND ON THE   R 008 20
UPON THE EPIPHANY, AND SEVEN DAYS AFTER   R 077 21
AFTER THE EPIPHANY SHALL BE USED ON THE TWENTY-FIFTH R 224 32
AFTER THE EPIPHANY SHALL BE USED ON THE TWENTY-SIXTH, R 224 34
AFTER THE EPIPHANY ON THE TWENTY-FIFTH   R 224 35

EPISCOPAL

THE PROTESTANT EPISCOPAL CHURCH IN THESE STATES IS   V 10
OR HATH HAD EPISCOPAL CONSECRATION OR ORDINATION   529 23
THE PROTESTANT EPISCOPAL CHURCH   R 552 27
THE PROTESTANT EPISCOPAL CHURCH IN N   552 29
THE PROTESTANT EPISCOPAL CHURCH IN THE UNITED STATES   552 31
REST OF THE EPISCOPAL HABIT, AND SHALL KNEEL DOWN   R 556 02
AFFIXED OUR EPISCOPAL SEAL AND SIGNATURE, AT --, THIS 569 38

EPISTLE

WHICH A PROPER EPISTLE AND GOSPEL ARE ORDERED   R 008 33
SHALL READ THE EPISTLE, FIRST SAYING, THE EPISTLE IS R 070 18
THE EPISTLE IS WRITTEN IN THE - CHAPTER OF -,   R 070 18
THE EPISTLE ENDED, HE SHALL SAY, HERE ENDETH THE   R 070 19
HE SHALL SAY, HERE ENDETH THE EPISTLE   R 070 20
THE COLLECT, EPISTLE, AND GOSPEL, APPOINTED FOR THE R 090 04
EPISTLE, AND GOSPEL MAY BE USED AT THE FIRST   R 098 08
THE FIRST EPISTLE AND GOSPEL FOR CHRISTMAS DAY   R 104 02
THE SAME COLLECT, EPISTLE, AND GOSPEL SHALL SERVE UNTO THE R 109 26
SAME COLLECT, EPISTLE, AND GOSPEL SHALL SERVE FOR   R 125 23
EPISTLE, AND GOSPEL MAY BE USED AT THE FIRST   R 164 31
SAME COLLECT, EPISTLE, AND GOSPEL SHALL SERVE FOR   R 178 30
EPISTLE, AND GOSPEL MAY BE USED AT THE FIRST   R 182 12
THE COLLECT, EPISTLE, AND GOSPEL, HERE FOLLOWING   R 321 15
EPISTLE, AND GOSPEL   R 322 04
THE COLLECT, EPISTLE, AND GOSPEL FOR THE DAY, FOR   R 323 34
OF THE FIRST EPISTLE OF ST   R 328 19
THE COLLECT, EPISTLE, AND GOSPEL, AS FOLLOWETH   R 531 11
THE COLLECT, EPISTLE, AND GOSPEL, AS FOLLOWETH   R 537 17
THE EPISTLE SHALL BE EPHESIANS IV   R 547 22
AND ANOTHER BISHOP SHALL READ THE EPISTLE   R 549 16
BE THE COLLECT, EPISTLE, AND GOSPEL   R 567 02

EQUAL

LEFT AT FULL AND EQUAL LIBERTY TO MODEL AND ORGANIZE   VI 10
HAST MADE THEM EQUAL UNTO US, WHICH HAVE BORNE THE   120 05
NOT ROBBERY TO BE EQUAL WITH GOD   134 18
LET THINE EYES LOOK UPON THE THING THAT IS EQUAL   358 20

EQUITY

AS IN COMMON EQUITY OUGHT TO BE ALLOWED TO ALL HUMAN   V 43
AND THE PEOPLES WITH EQUITY   027 25
RIGHTEOUSNESS AND EQUITY ARE THE HABITATION OF THY   451 02
AND THE PEOPLES WITH EQUITY   462 14
HAST PREPARED EQUITY, *   462 23
AND ARE DONE IN TRUTH AND EQUITY   483 10

ERE

SIR, COME DOWN ERE MY CHILD DIE   220 02

ERECTED

OF THINGS, HAVE ERECTED HOUSES FOR THE PUBLIC WORSHIP   564 15

ERR

HAST THOU MADE US TO ERR FROM THY WAYS, AND HARDENED   139 24
DO NOT ERR, MY BELOVED BRETHREN   265 18
IS A PEOPLE THAT DO ERR IN THEIR HEARTS, FOR THEY   459 25
ARE THEY THAT DO ERR FROM THY COMMANDMENTS   491 09

ERRED

WE HAVE ERRED, AND STRAYED FROM THY WAYS LIKE LOST   006 17
WE HAVE ERRED, AND STRAYED FROM THY WAYS LIKE LOST   023 24
ALL SUCH AS HAVE ERRED, AND ARE DECEIVED   056 20
AND ANTIOCH, HAVE ERRED   606 42

ERRED   CONTINUED

OF ROME HATH ERRED, NOT ONLY IN THEIR LIVING AND   606 43

ERRONEOUS

THE CHURCH ALL ERRONEOUS AND STRANGE DOCTRINES   542 20
THE CHURCH ALL ERRONEOUS AND STRANGE DOCTRINE   555 03

ERROR

SAVE US FROM ALL ERROR, IGNORANCE, PRIDE, AND   036 31
WHERE IT IS IN ERROR, DIRECT IT   037 18
OF DARKNESS AND ERROR INTO THE CLEAR LIGHT AND TRUE   078 31
SO THE LAST ERROR SHALL BE WORSE THAN THE FIRST   162 22
THEM THAT ARE IN ERROR THE LIGHT OF THY TRUTH,   173 05
DEFEND US FROM ALL ERROR, AND LEAD US INTO ALL TRUTH   183 25
EITHER FOR ERROR IN RELIGION, OR FOR VICIOUSNESS   540 22

ERRORS

FOR ALL THE ERRORS OF HIS LIFE PAST, AND STEDFAST   316 13

ES

BENEDICTUS ES, BENEDICTUS, JUBILATE, MAY BE,   R 009 24

ESAIAS

AND AGAIN, ESAIAS SAITH, THERE SHALL BE A ROOT OF   092 30
THE WAY OF THE LORD, AS SAID THE PROPHET ESAIAS   095 30
FOR ESAIAS SAITH, LORD, WHO HATH BELIEVED OUR REPORT   227 12
BUT ESAIAS IS VERY BOLD, AND SAITH, I WAS FOUND OF   227 18
DELIVERED UNTO HIM THE BOOK OF THE PROPHET ESAIAS   261 14

ESCAPE

MAKE A WAY TO ESCAPE, THAT YE MAY BE ABLE TO BEAR IT   201 29
MAKE HASTE TO ESCAPE, *   407 02
7 SHALL THEY ESCAPE FOR THEIR WICKEDNESS   408 28
BY WHOM WE ESCAPE DEATH   420 26
AND LET ME EVER ESCAPE THEM   517 33

ESCAPED

6 OUR SOUL IS ESCAPED EVEN AS A BIRD OUT OF THE SNARE   504 18

ESCHEW

LET HIM ESCHEW EVIL, AND DO GOOD   195 26
14 ESCHEW EVIL, AND DO GOOD   380 29

ESCHEWED

AND ESCHEWED MINE OWN WICKEDNESS   361 13

ESPECIAL

TO PROMISE THY ESPECIAL PRESENCE, WHEREVER TWO OR   564 31

ESPECIALLY

MORE ESPECIALLY WE PRAY FOR THY HOLY CHURCH   018 30
ESPECIALLY THOSE FOR WHOM OUR PRAYERS ARE DESIRED   019 06
MORE ESPECIALLY WE PRAY FOR THY HOLY CHURCH   032 30
ESPECIALLY THOSE FOR WHOM OUR PRAYERS ARE DESIRED   033 04
SO ESPECIALLY FOR THEIR SENATE AND   035 10
PRISONERS (ESPECIALLY THOSE WHO ARE CONDEMNED TO   046 21
AND MORE ESPECIALLY FOR THAT BRANCH OF THE SAME   047 11
HEREIN MORE ESPECIALLY FOR THE BISHOP OF THIS   047 23
HEREIN MORE ESPECIALLY FOR THE CLERGY HERE RESIDING),   047 26
OF DEATH, ESPECIALLY NEED OUR PRAYERS   048 09
AND ESPECIALLY UNTO THEM THAT ARE OF THE HOUSEHOLD OF   072 21
AND ESPECIALLY TO THIS CONGREGATION HERE PRESENT   074 25
BUT ESPECIALLY THE PARCHMENTS   254 06
AND ESPECIALLY OF THY SERVANT (SAINT --),   258 14
TO TIME, BUT ESPECIALLY IN THE TIME OF PESTILENCE,   R 321 06
BUT ESPECIALLY AMONG MY NEIGHBOURS   376 16
AND ESPECIALLY AMONG THEM THAT ARE OR SHALL   543 08
AND ESPECIALLY TO THIS CONGREGATION PRESENT, GIVE THE   574 09
THIS DAY, AND ESPECIALLY FOR HAVING DELIVERED US FROM   587 22

ESPOUSED

WITH MARY HIS ESPOUSED WIFE, BEING GREAT WITH CHILD   099 05
MOTHER MARY WAS ESPOUSED TO JOSEPH, BEFORE THEY CAME   104 28
TO A VIRGIN ESPOUSED TO A MAN WHOSE NAME WAS JOSEPH,   236 07

ESSENTIAL

MAIN BODY AND ESSENTIAL PARTS OF THE SAME (AS WELL IN   V 30
ENGLAND IN ANY ESSENTIAL POINT OF DOCTRINE,   VI 33
WHICH ARE ESSENTIAL PARTS OF BAPTISM), SUCH PERSON   R 282 10

EST

BONUM EST CONFITERI, NUNC DIMITTIS, DEUS   R 025 17

ESTABLISH

IT IS RIGHT, ESTABLISH IT   037 19
AND TRUTH, AND ESTABLISH AMONG THEM THAT PEACE WHICH   044 29
AND TO ESTABLISH SUCH OTHER ALTERATIONS AND   VI 25
THAT HE MAY ESTABLISH THE SECOND   157 33
AND HE SHALL ESTABLISH YOUR HEART, *   377 18
APPLY THEM TO ESTABLISH ANY DOCTRINE   604 03

ESTABLISH   CONTINUED

DOTH GREATLY ESTABLISH AND CONFIRM THEIR FAITH CF   606 20

ESTABLISHED

HATH HE ESTABLISHED THE HEAVENS	005 25
ADVISEDLY ESTABLISHED, SHE HATH, IN THE REIGN OF	V 26
MAY BE ESTABLISHED AMONG US FOR ALL GENERATIONS	035 17
WE MAY BE ESTABLISHED IN THE TRUTH OF THY HOLY	237 09

ESTATE

OR DISTRESSED, IN MIND, BODY, OR ESTATE	019 06
OR DISTRESSED, IN MIND, BODY, OR ESTATE	033 04
HIGH THINGS, BUT CONDESCEND TO MEN OF LOW ESTATE	111 32
IS AN HONOURABLE ESTATE, INSTITUTED OF GOD,	300 11
WHICH HOLY ESTATE CHRIST ADORNED AND BEAUTIFIED WITH	300 13
INTO THIS HOLY ESTATE THESE TWO PERSONS PRESENT COME	300 19
IN THE HOLY ESTATE OF MATRIMONY	301 07
IN THE HOLY ESTATE OF MATRIMONY	301 16
ABHORRED THE LOW ESTATE OF THE POOR	367 20
PLACE IN THE HOLY ESTATE OF MATRIMONY, MAY FAITHFULLY	566 09
EITHER TO VOW THE ESTATE OF SINGLE LIFE, OR TO	609 22

ESTATES

THEE FOR ALL ESTATES OF MEN IN THY HOLY CHURCH, THAT   156 30

ESTEEM

PEOPLE OUGHT TO ESTEEM THEM IN THEIR OFFICE	R 530 06
PEOPLE OUGHT TO ESTEEM THEM IN THEIR OFFICE	R 536 06

ESTEEMED

USED AND ESTEEMED IN THIS CHURCH, NO MAN SHALL BE   529 19

ESTIMATION

SUCH REVEREND ESTIMATION, THAT NO MAN MIGHT PRESUME   529 14

ETERNAL

MAY COME TO HIS ETERNAL JOY	007 18
STANDETH OUR ETERNAL LIFE, WHOSE SERVICE IS PERFECT	017 06
MAY COME TO HIS ETERNAL JOY	024 20
BLESSED GIFT OF ETERNAL LIFE	038 22
O ETERNAL LORD GOD, WHO ALONE SPREADEST OUT THE	042 03
WHICH LEADETH TO ETERNAL LIFE	045 09
O ETERNAL GOD, WHO ALONE SPREADEST OUT THE HEAVENS,	046 08
O ETERNAL GOD, OUR HEAVENLY FATHER, WHO ALONE MAKEST	052 17
WITH THEE IN THY ETERNAL GODHEAD	079 18
UNTO YOU THAT ETERNAL LIFE, WHICH WAS WITH THE	101 16
ACCORDING TO THE ETERNAL PURPOSE WHICH HE PURPOSED IN	108 26
AND HEIRS OF ETERNAL LIFE	117 06
UNTO HIM IN HIS ETERNAL AND GLORIOUS KINGDOM	117 10
HAVING OBTAINED ETERNAL REDEMPTION FOR US	132 27
WHO THROUGH THE ETERNAL SPIRIT OFFERED HIMSELF	132 31
THE PROMISE OF ETERNAL INHERITANCE	133 07
HOLY MYSTERIES GIVETH US A PLEDGE OF LIFE ETERNAL	152 11
HATH GIVEN TO US ETERNAL LIFE, AND THIS LIFE IS IN	171 10
THE GLORY OF THE ETERNAL TRINITY, AND IN THE POWER OF	186 25
BUT HAVE ETERNAL LIFE	188 29
NO MURDERER HATH ETERNAL LIFE ABIDING IN HIM	191 15
US UNTO HIS ETERNAL GLORY BY CHRIST JESUS, AFTER THAT	193 09
THAT WE FINALLY LOSE NOT THE THINGS ETERNAL	194 08
GIFT OF GOD IS ETERNAL LIFE THROUGH JESUS CHRIST OUR	199 05
I DO TO INHERIT ETERNAL LIFE	208 13
THAT LEADETH TO ETERNAL LIFE	239 03
ATTAIN TO THINE ETERNAL JOY	258 17
WERE ORDAINED TO ETERNAL LIFE BELIEVED	261 08
O ETERNAL GOD, THROUGH WHOSE MIGHTY POWER OUR FATHERS	263 17
O ETERNAL GOD, WE HUMBLY BESEECH THEE, FAVOURABLY TO	267 04
O ETERNAL LORD GOD, WHO HOLDEST ALL SOULS IN LIFE	268 14
MAY COME TO THE ETERNAL KINGDOM WHICH THOU HAST	274 20
MINISTER ADD, O ETERNAL GOD, CREATOR AND PRESERVER OF	303 03
HE COME TO THY ETERNAL JOY	307 06
AND FROM ETERNAL DEATH	318 12
SAINTS IN THE ETERNAL HABITATIONS	319 10
THAT YE HAVE ETERNAL LIFE, AND THAT YE MAY BELIEVE ON	322 14
BITTER PAINS OF ETERNAL DEATH	332 27
WORTHY JUDGE ETERNAL, SUFFER US NOT, AT OUR LAST	332 31
UNTO ETERNAL LIFE, THROUGH OUR LORD JESUS CHRIST	333 17
AND SOUL, IN THY ETERNAL AND EVERLASTING GLORY	334 28
UNTO ETERNAL LIFE, THROUGH OUR LORD JESUS CHRIST	337 11
KEEPING OF THINE ETERNAL LOVE	340 27
RESURRECTION TO ETERNAL LIFE THROUGH OUR LORD JESUS	341 13
AS NECESSARY FOR ETERNAL SALVATION THROUGH FAITH IN	533 03
AS NECESSARY FOR ETERNAL SALVATION THROUGH FAITH IN	542 03
AS NECESSARY TO ETERNAL SALVATION, BUT THAT WHICH YOU	542 07
PRAISE TO THY ETERNAL MERIT, FATHER, SON, AND HOLY	544 14
TO SET FORTH THE ETERNAL PRAISE OF THY HOLY NAME	545 20
BENEFITS OF THY ETERNAL GOODNESS, AND FOR THAT THOU	545 22
AS NECESSARY FOR ETERNAL SALVATION THROUGH FAITH IN	554 21
AS NECESSARY TO ETERNAL SALVATION, BUT THAT WHICH YOU	554 25
PRAISE TO THY ETERNAL MERIT, FATHER, SON, AND HOLY	556 22
O ETERNAL GOD, MIGHTY IN POWER, AND OF MAJESTY	564 27
US FROM SIN AND ETERNAL DEATH, AND IN GIVING US THE	591 13
O GOD, THE KING ETERNAL, WHO DIVIDEST THE DAY FROM	594 11
THE ETERNAL VICTORY	598 11
THE VERY AND ETERNAL GOD, AND OF ONE SUBSTANCE WITH	603 10
VERY AND ETERNAL GOD	603 27
THEIR FAITH OF ETERNAL SALVATION TO BE ENJOYED	606 21

ETERNALLY

AND BELIEVETH IN HIM, SHALL NOT DIE ETERNALLY   335 02

ETERNITY

THAT INHABITETH ETERNITY, WHOSE NAME IS HOLY	003 25
OF ONE SUBSTANCE, POWER, AND ETERNITY	603 06

ETHIOPIA

AND TYRE, WITH ETHIOPIA   448 20

EUCHARIST

THE HOLY EUCHARIST TO HIS CONGREGATION   R 574 26

EVANGELIST

APOSTLE AND EVANGELIST SAINT JOHN, MAY SO WALK IN THE	101 07
OF THY EVANGELIST SAINT MARK	237 06
RECEIPT OF CUSTOM TO BE AN APOSTLE AND EVANGELIST	250 22
WORK OF AN EVANGELIST, MAKE FULL PROOF OF THY	253 24
WORDS OF THE EVANGELIST SAINT LUKE, IN THE EIGHTH	296 11

EVANGELISTS

AND SOME, EVANGELISTS	237 19
AND SOME, EVANGELISTS	538 06
EVANGELISTS, DOCTORS, AND PASTORS	545 18
SOME EVANGELISTS, SOME PASTORS AND DOCTORS, TO THE	557 26

EVEN

RISING OF THE SUN EVEN UNTO THE GOING DOWN OF THE	004 12
HOUSE COMETH, AT EVEN, OR AT MIDNIGHT, OR AT THE	021 25
AND GOD, EVEN OUR OWN GOD, SHALL GIVE US HIS	028 29
DID HUMBLE HIMSELF, EVEN TO THE DEATH UPON THE CROSS,	086 08
MOUTH GLORIFY GOD, EVEN THE FATHER OF OUR LORD JESUS	092 20
THEREFORE GOD, EVEN THY GOD, HATH ANOINTED THEE WITH	097 11
THE SONS OF GOD, EVEN TO THEM THAT BELIEVE ON HIS	098 02
CHILDREN TOGETHER, EVEN AS A HEN GATHERETH HER	100 29
I SUPPOSE THAT EVEN THE WORLD ITSELF COULD NOT	102 16
OF OUR FAITH EVEN UNTO DEATH, WE MAY GLORIFY THY HOLY	102 25
EVEN SO WE, WHEN WE WERE CHILDREN, WERE IN BONDAGE	104 17
LET US NOW GO EVEN UNTO BETHLEHEM, AND SEE THIS THING	106 09
EVEN AS CHRIST FORGAVE YOU, SO ALSO DO YE	116 07
PURIFY OURSELVES, EVEN AS HE IS PURE	117 07
PURIFIETH HIMSELF, EVEN AS HE IS PURE	117 21
IS RIGHTEOUS, EVEN AS HE IS RIGHTEOUS	117 27
AND SHINETH EVEN UNTO THE WEST	118 11
SO WHEN EVEN WAS COME, THE LORD OF THE VINEYARD SAITH	119 28
UNTO THIS LAST, EVEN AS UNTO THEE	120 10
THEN SHALL I KNOW EVEN AS ALSO I AM KNOWN	123 13
TURN YE EVEN TO ME, SAITH THE LORD, WITH ALL YOUR	124 21
EVEN A MEAT-OFFERING AND A DRINK-OFFERING UNTO THE	124 27
IS THE WILL OF GOD, EVEN YOUR SANCTIFICATION, THAT YE	127 27
OF CONCUPISCENCE, EVEN AS THE GENTILES WHICH KNOW NOT	127 31
BE IT UNTO THEE EVEN AS THOU WILT	128 21
FOR IT IS A SHAME EVEN TO SPEAK OF THOSE THINGS WHICH	129 18
AFTER THE SPIRIT, EVEN SO IT IS NOW	131 14
UNTO DEATH, EVEN THE DEATH OF THE CROSS	134 22
THAT THIS DAY, EVEN IN THIS NIGHT, BEFORE THE COCK	141 23
HIM AFAR OFF, EVEN INTO THE PALACE OF THE HIGH	142 34
FIGURE WHEREUNTO, EVEN BAPTISM, DOTH ALSO NOW SAVE US	161 30
WHEN THE EVEN WAS COME, THERE CAME A RICH MAN OF	162 06
EVEN SO IN CHRIST SHALL ALL BE MADE ALIVE	163 15
FOR EVEN CHRIST OUR PASSOVER IS SACRIFICED FOR US	165 12
BEFORE OF GOD, EVEN TO US, WHO DID EAT AND DRINK WITH	166 26
AND FOUND IT EVEN SO AS THE WOMEN HAD SAID	167 27
THE WORLD, EVEN OUR FAITH	170 28
BY WATER AND BLOOD, EVEN JESUS CHRIST	170 30
HATH SENT ME, EVEN SO SEND I YOU	171 21
FOR EVEN HEREUNTO WERE YE CALLED	172 09
AM KNOWN OF MINE, EVEN AS THE FATHER KNOWETH ME, AND	172 28
RECEIVED THE GIFT, EVEN SO MINISTER THE SAME ONE TO	179 16
FROM THE FATHER, EVEN THE SPIRIT OF TRUTH, WHICH	179 25
EVEN THE SPIRIT OF TRUTH	181 11
ME COMMANDMENT, EVEN SO I DO	182 10
BEFORE OF GOD, EVEN TO US, WHO DID EAT AND DRINK WITH	184 14
DOWN FROM HEAVEN, EVEN THE SON OF MAN WHICH IS IN	188 25
IN THE WILDERNESS, EVEN SO MUST THE SON OF MAN BE	188 27
OF THE SPIRIT, EVEN WE OURSELVES GROAN WITHIN	194 22
OF THE FATHER, EVEN SO WE ALSO SHOULD WALK IN NEWNESS	197 14
EVEN SO NOW YIELD YOUR MEMBERS SERVANTS TO	198 28
EVEN SO EVERY GOOD TREE BRINGETH FORTH GOOD FRUIT	200 18
THESE DUMB IDOLS, EVEN AS YE WERE LED	203 18
THOU HADST KNOWN, EVEN THOU, AT LEAST IN THIS THY	204 07
AND SHALL LAY THEE EVEN WITH THE GROUND, AND THY	204 12
OR EVEN AS THIS PUBLICAN	205 27
SAY UNTO YOU, THAT EVEN SOLOMON IN ALL HIS GLORY WAS	211 23
AND ONE SPIRIT, EVEN AS YE ARE CALLED IN ONE HOPE OF	213 23
EVEN AS THE TESTIMONY OF CHRIST WAS CONFIRMED IN YOU	214 31
ONE ANOTHER, EVEN AS GOD FOR CHRIST'S SAKE HATH	216 30
EVEN AS IT IS MEET FOR ME TO THINK THIS OF YOU ALL,	220 27
THY FELLOW-SERVANT, EVEN AS I HAD PITY ON THEE	222 02
AND NOW TELL YOU EVEN WEEPING, THAT THEY ARE THE	222 18
WHEREBY HE IS ABLE EVEN TO SUBJECT ALL THINGS UNTO	222 25
MY DAUGHTER IS EVEN NOW DEAD	224 14
THE LORD, EVEN JESUS, THAT APPEARED UNTO THEE	230 31
COME TO HIS TEMPLE, EVEN THE MESSENGER OF THE	232 05
EVEN SO, FATHER	235 06
WHICH IS THE HEAD, EVEN CHRIST	237 29
EVEN AS I HAVE KEPT MY FATHER'S COMMANDMENTS, AND	238 22
EVEN AS THE SON OF MAN CAME NOT TO BE MINISTERED	247 26

EVEN   CONTINUED

THIS MY TABERNACLE, EVEN AS OUR LORD JESUS CHRIST   248 10
FROM THE FATHER, EVEN THE SPIRIT OF TRUTH, WHICH   255 31
AND THAT THEY, EVEN THE HOUSE OF ISRAEL, ARE MY   262 21
DO NOT EVEN THE PUBLICANS THE SAME   264 12
DO NOT EVEN THE PUBLICANS SO   264 13
THEREFORE PERFECT, EVEN AS YOUR FATHER WHICH IS IN   264 14
SAY UNTO YOU, THAT EVEN SOLOMON IN ALL HIS GLORY WAS   266 21
HEAD OF THE WIFE, EVEN AS CHRIST IS THE HEAD OF THE   267 15
LOVE YOUR WIVES, EVEN AS CHRIST ALSO LOVED THE   267 19
AND CHERISHETH IT, EVEN AS THE LORD THE CHURCH   267 27
SO LOVE HIS WIFE EVEN AS HIMSELF   268 02
THAT YE SORROW NOT, EVEN AS OTHERS WHICH HAVE NC   268 29
AND ROSE AGAIN, EVEN SO THEM ALSO WHICH SLEEP IN   268 31
AM WITH YOU ALWAY, EVEN UNTO THE END OF THE WORLD   275 31
EVEN IN THE MIDST OF THEE, O JERUSALEM   306 02
THE ALTAR OF GOD, EVEN UNTO THE GOD OF MY JOY AND   310 13
EVEN UNTO GOD WILL I CRY WITH MY VOICE, AND HE SHALL   310 29
EVEN BEFORE THE GODS WILL I SING PRAISE UNTO THEE   311 29
AND MINE AGE IS EVEN AS NOTHING IN RESPECT OF THEE   324 23
TRULY MY HOPE IS EVEN IN THEE   324 29
THEM THEY ARE EVEN AS A SLEEP   325 22
EVEN THAT I MAY DWELL IN THE HOUSE OF THE LORD ALL   326 09
MY HELP COMETH EVEN FROM THE LORD, *   327 21
IT IS EVEN HE THAT SHALL KEEP THY SOUL   327 32
AS IN ADAM ALL DIE, EVEN SO IN CHRIST SHALL ALL BE   328 24
THE KINGDOM TO GOD, EVEN THE FATHER   328 28
RISEN AGAIN, WHO IS EVEN AT THE RIGHT HAND OF GCD,   331 04
EVEN SO SAITH THE SPIRIT   333 27
MY HELP COMETH EVEN FROM THE LORD, *   339 05
IT IS EVEN HE THAT SHALL KEEP THY SOUL   339 16
THY HEAVENS, EVEN THE WORK OF THY FINGERS   351 04
EVEN AS THE CITIES WHICH THOU HAST DESTROYED, WHOSE   351 13
EVEN A REFUGE IN DUE TIME OF TROUBLE   352 07
EVEN AS A LION LURKETH HE IN HIS DEN, *   353 23
EVEN AS THE SILVER WHICH FROM THE EARTH IS TRIED, AND   355 20
IN GREAT FEAR, EVEN WHERE NO FEAR WAS   356 25
2 EVEN HE THAT LEADETH AN UNCORRUPT LIFE, *   357 07
IT ENTERED EVEN INTO HIS EARS   360 07
BROUGHT ME FORTH, EVEN BECAUSE HE HAD A FAVOUR UNTO   361 05
ARMS SHALL BEND EVEN A BOW OF STEEL   362 05
EVEN UNTO THE LORD SHALL THEY CRY, BUT HE SHALL   362 21
48 EVEN THE GOD THAT SEETH THAT I BE AVENGED,   362 34
EVEN WITH THE WHOLESOME STRENGTH OF HIS RIGHT HAND   364 27
EVEN FOR EVER AND EVER   365 12
THOU ART MY GOD EVEN FROM MY MOTHER'S WOMB   366 24
MIDST OF MY BODY IS EVEN LIKE MELTING WAX   366 33
4 EVEN HE THAT HATH CLEAN HANDS, AND A PURE HEART   369 02
EVEN OF THEM THAT SEEK THY FACE, O GOD OF JACOB   369 07
STRONG AND MIGHTY, EVEN THE LORD MIGHTY IN BATTLE   369 12
EVEN THE LORD OF HOSTS, HE IS THE KING CF GLORY   369 15
2 WHEN THE WICKED, EVEN MINE ENEMIES AND MY FOES,   371 27
EVEN THAT I MAY DWELL IN THE HOUSE OF THE LORD ALL   371 33
TRUST IN THEE, EVEN BEFORE THE SONS OF MEN   377 04
EVEN WITHOUT A CAUSE HAVE THEY MADE A PIT FCR MY   382 02
AND BE WITHERED EVEN AS THE GREEN HERB   384 28
EVEN AS THE SMOKE SHALL THEY CONSUME AWAY   386 02
14 I BECAME EVEN AS A MAN THAT HEARETH NOT, *   388 19
REQUIRED THAT THEY, EVEN MINE ENEMIES, SHOULD NCT   388 23
KEPT SILENCE, YEA, EVEN FROM GOOD WORDS   389 10
AND MINE AGE IS EVEN AS NOTHING IN RESPECT OF THEE   389 18
TRULY MY HOPE IS EVEN IN THEE   389 24
I AM EVEN CONSUMED BY THE MEANS OF THY HEAVY HAND   389 29
EVEN A THANKSGIVING UNTO OUR GOD   390 14
EVEN AGAINST ME DO THEY IMAGINE THIS EVIL   392 13
9 YEA, EVEN MINE OWN FAMILIAR FRIEND WHOM I TRUSTED,   392 17
FOR GOD, YEA, EVEN FOR THE LIVING GOD   392 31
THE ALTAR OF GOD, EVEN UNTO THE GOD OF MY JOY AND   394 12
IS BROUGHT LOW, EVEN UNTO THE DUST   396 10
WHEREFORE GOD, EVEN THY GOD, HATH ANOINTED THEE WITH   396 30
EVEN THE EXCELLENCY OF JACOB, WHOM HE LOVED   398 27
CITY OF OUR GOD, EVEN UPON HIS HOLY HILL   399 11
THE LORD, EVEN THE MOST MIGHTY GOD, HATH SPOKEN,   401 21
FOR I AM GOD, EVEN THY GOD   402 05
THAT I AM EVEN SUCH A ONE AS THYSELF   402 33
14 BUT IT WAS EVEN THOU, MY COMPANION, *   407 16
20 YEA, EVEN GOD, THAT ENDURETH FOR EVER, SHALL HEAR   407 30
EVEN UNTO THE GOD THAT SHALL PERFORM THE CAUSE WHICH   409 15
5 AND I LIE EVEN AMONG THE CHILDREN OF MEN, THAT ARE   409 21
ARE FROWARD, EVEN FROM THEIR MOTHER'S WOMB   410 12
EVEN LIKE THE DEAF ADDER, THAT STOPPETH HER EARS   410 16
SHALL BE SATISFIED, EVEN AS IT WERE WITH MARROW AND   415 02
OUT THEIR ARROWS, EVEN BITTER WORDS   415 24
OF THY HOUSE, EVEN OF THY HOLY TEMPLE   416 19
AND GOD, EVEN OUR OWN GOD, SHALL GIVE US HIS   419 03
EVEN GOD IN HIS HOLY HABITATION   419 20
EVEN AS SINAI ALSO WAS MOVED AT THE PRESENCE OF GCD,   419 27
EVEN AN HIGH HILL, AS THE HILL OF BASHAN   420 11
TWENTY THOUSAND, EVEN THOUSANDS OF ANGELS   420 16
EVEN FROM THINE ENEMIES, THAT THE LORD GOD MIGHT   420 20
EVEN THE GOD WHO HELPETH US, AND POURETH HIS BENEFITS   420 23
20 HE IS OUR GOD, EVEN THE GOD OF WHOM COMETH   420 25
EVEN THE GOD OF ISRAEL, HE WILL GIVE STRENGTH AND   421 27
WATERS ARE COME IN, EVEN UNTO MY SOUL   421 32
EVEN AN ALIEN UNTO MY MOTHER'S CHILDREN   422 18
OF THINE HOUSE HATH EVEN EATEN ME   422 20
EVEN IN THE TRUTH OF THY SALVATION   422 31
THOU ART MY HOPE, EVEN FROM MY YOUTH   425 15
EVEN AS THE DROPS THAT WATER THE EARTH   427 09
BE THE LORD GOD, EVEN THE GOD OF ISRAEL, *   428 02
EVEN UNTO SUCH AS ARE OF A CLEAN HEART   428 10
AND THEY DO EVEN WHAT THEY LUST   428 22
I HAD ALMOST SAID EVEN AS THEY   429 06
20 YEA, EVEN LIKE AS A DREAM WHEN ONE AWAKETH   429 16
AND IT WENT EVEN THROUGH MY REINS   429 18

EVEN   CONTINUED

EVEN AS IT WERE A BEAST BEFORE THEE   429 20
OF THY NAME, EVEN UNTO THE GROUND   430 19
7 THOU, EVEN THOU ART TO BE FEARED   433 02
EVEN UNTO GOD WILL I CRY WITH MY VOICE, AND HE SHALL   433 16
EVEN THE SONS OF JACOB AND JOSEPH   434 12
EVEN IN THE FIELD OF ZOAN   435 25
EVEN ROUND ABOUT THEIR HABITATION   436 27
AND THAT THEY WERE EVEN A WIND THAT PASSETH AWAY,   437 19
EVEN TO THIS MOUNTAIN, WHICH HE PURCHASED WITH HIS   438 19
EVEN THE TENT THAT HE HAD PITCHED AMONG MEN   438 32
EVEN THE HILL OF SION WHICH HE LOVED   439 14
EVEN IN THE TIME APPOINTED, AND UPON OUR SOLEMN   442 16
15 PURSUE THEM EVEN SO WITH THY TEMPEST, *   445 02
EVEN THY ALTARS, O LORD OF HOSTS, MY KING AND MY GOD   445 17
AND I AM EVEN AS A MAN THAT HATH NO STRENGTH   449 03
EVEN FROM MY YOUTH UP, THY TERRORS HAVE I SUFFERED   449 27
THEM THEY ARE EVEN AS A SLEEP   453 27
AND AM EVEN AS IT WERE A SPARROW, *   464 23
EVEN SO IS THE LORD MERCIFUL UNTO THEM THAT FEAR HIM   466 32
18 EVEN UPON SUCH AS KEEP HIS COVENANT, *   467 11
EVEN UNTO THE PLACE WHICH THOU HAST APPOINTED FOR   468 09
EVEN THE CEDARS OF LEBANON WHICH HE HATH PLANTED   468 26
9 EVEN THE COVENANT THAT HE MADE WITH ABRAHAM   470 20
BUT REPROVED EVEN KINGS FOR THEIR SAKES   470 31
EVEN JOSEPH, WHO WAS SOLD TO BE A BOND-SERVANT   471 06
EVEN IN THEIR KINGS' CHAMBERS   471 32
EVEN THE CHIEF OF ALL THEIR STRENGTH   472 09
AT THE SEA, EVEN AT THE RED SEA   473 15
INNOCENT BLOOD, EVEN THE BLOOD OF THEIR SONS AND OF   475 11
AND THEY WERE EVEN HARD AT DEATH'S DOOR   477 12
BE THOU RULER, EVEN IN THE MIDST AMCNG THINE ENEMIES   482 10
SHALL WOUND EVEN KINGS IN THE DAY OF HIS WRATH   482 16
EVEN WITH THE PRINCES OF HIS PEOPLE   484 21
EVEN THE WORK OF MEN'S HANDS   485 18
EVEN HE SHALL BLESS THE HOUSE OF ISRAEL, HE SHALL   486 02
EVEN IN THE MIDST OF THEE, O JERUSALEM   487 22
AND ARE EXTINCT EVEN AS THE FIRE AMONG THE THORNS   488 23
WITH CORDS, YEA, EVEN UNTO THE HORNS OF THE ALTAR   489 23
3 EVEN THEY WHO DO NO WICKEDNESS, *   490 04
EVEN BY RULING HIMSELF AFTER THY WORD   490 17
EVEN THY SALVATION, ACCORDING UNTO THY WORD   492 23
TESTIMONIES ALSO, EVEN BEFORE KINGS, *   492 30
EVEN UNTO THE END   497 22
139 MY ZEAL HATH EVEN CONSUMED ME   499 17
146 YEA, EVEN UNTO THEE DO I CALL   500 02
EVEN MIGHTY AND SHARP ARROWS, WITH HOT BURNING CCALS   502 12
2 MY HELP COMETH EVEN FROM THE LORD, *   502 24
IT IS EVEN HE THAT SHALL KEEP THY SOUL   503 05
THE TRIBES GO UP, EVEN THE TRIBES OF THE LORD, *   503 13
EVEN THE SEAT OF THE HOUSE OF DAVID   503 16
2 BEHOLD, EVEN AS THE EYES OF SERVANTS LOOK UNTO THE   503 29
EVEN SO OUR EYES WAIT UPON THE LORD OUR GOD, UNTIL HE   503 31
HAD GONE EVEN OVER OUR SOUL   504 14
OUR SOUL IS ESCAPED EVEN AS A BIRD OUT OF THE SNARE   504 18
THE LORD SHALL BE EVEN AS THE MOUNT SION, *   504 23
EVEN SO STANDETH THE LORD ROUND ABOUT HIS PEOPLE,   504 26
EVEN SO ARE THE YOUNG CHILDREN   505 31
6 LET THEM BE EVEN AS THE GRASS UPON THE HOUSETOPS,   506 31
MY SOUL IS EVEN AS A WEANED CHILD   507 28
EVEN UNTO AARON'S BEARD, AND WENT DOWN TO THE SKIRTS   509 10
EVEN IN THE COURTS OF THE HOUSE OF OUR GOD   509 26
EVEN AN HERITAGE UNTO ISRAEL HIS PEOPLE   510 26
22 EVEN FOR AN HERITAGE UNTO ISRAEL HIS SERVANT   512 26
DOWN WITH IT, EVEN TO THE GROUND   513 20
EVEN BEFORE THE GODS WILL I SING PRAISE UNTO THEE   513 28
9 EVEN THERE ALSO SHALL THY HAND LEAD ME, *   515 06
EVEN AS THOUGH THEY WERE MINE ENEMIES   516 02
EVEN UNTO THE LORD DID I MAKE MY SUPPLICATION   518 03
EVEN THE CHILDREN OF ISRAEL, EVEN THE PEOPLE THAT   524 31
CHILDREN OF ISRAEL, EVEN THE PEOPLE THAT SERVETH HIM   524 31
EVEN SO MUST THEIR WIVES BE GRAVE, NOT SLANDERERS,   531 31
AM KNOWN OF MINE, EVEN AS THE FATHER KNOWETH ME, AND   539 17
HATH SENT ME, EVEN SO SEND I YOU   552 02
AM WITH YOU ALWAY, EVEN UNTO THE END OF THE WORLD   552 14
4 EVEN HE THAT HATH CLEAN HANDS, AND A PURE HEART   563 17
EVEN OF THEM THAT SEEK THY FACE, O JACOB   563 22
STRONG AND MIGHTY, EVEN THE LORD MIGHTY IN BATTLE   563 27
EVEN THE LORD OF HOSTS, HE IS THE KING OF GLORY   563 30

EVENING

SHALL BEGIN THE EVENING PRAYER BY READING ONE OR MORE   R 021 03
MY HANDS BE AN EVENING SACRIFICE   021 17
THE LESSONS IN EVENING PRAYER, THE LESSON READ BEING   R 026 08
BY ONE OF THE EVENING CANTICLES   R 026 08
MAY HERE END THE EVENING PRAYER WITH SUCH PRAYER,   R 031 31
THE ORDER OF EVENING PRAYER   R 034 15
OF MORNING OR EVENING PRAYER, OR COMMUNION, AT THE   R 049 03
AT MORNING OR EVENING PRAYER   R 054 03
OR EVENING PRAYER, OR AS A SEPARATE OFFICE   R 060 05
BE USED AT THE EVENING SERVICE OF THE DAY BEFORE   R 090 07
AND IN THE EVENING HE COMETH WITH THE TWELVE   140 34
FOR IT IS TOWARD EVENING, AND THE DAY IS FAR SPENT   168 04
THE SAME DAY AT EVENING, BEING THE FIRST DAY OF THE   171 14
AT MORNING OR EVENING PRAYER, OR AT SUCH OTHER TIME   R 273 15
THE MORNING OR EVENING PRAYER   R 306 10
BUT IN THE EVENING IT IS CUT DOWN, DRIED UP, AND   325 25
18 IN THE EVENING, AND MORNING, AND AT NCON-DAY WILL   407 25
AND FRO IN THE EVENING, *   411 16
14 AND IN THE EVENING THEY WILL RETURN, *   412 02
THE MORNING AND EVENING TO PRAISE THEE   416 31
BUT IN THE EVENING IT IS CUT DOWN, DRIED UP, AND   453 30
UNTIL THE EVENING   469 07
MY HANDS BE AN EVENING SACRIFICE   517 11

EVENING   CONTINUED

THE SAME DAY AT EVENING, BEING THE FIRST DAY OF THE   551 27
PRAYER OR EVENING PRAYER, OR SEPARATELY   R 563 04
PRAYER OR EVENING PRAYER, OR SEPARATELY   R 569 09
LENGTHEN AND THE EVENING COMES, AND THE BUSY WORLD IS   594 31
TO HIS WORK AND TO HIS LABOUR UNTIL THE EVENING   599 26

EVER

AND THE POWER, AND THE GLORY, FOR EVER AND EVER   007 29
AND THE GLORY, FOR EVER AND EVER   007 29
IS NOW, AND EVER SHALL BE, WORLD WITHOUT END   008 05
IS NOW, AND EVER SHALL BE, *   009 29
AND LIFT THEM UP FOR EVER   011 05
WE WORSHIP THY NAME EVER, WORLD WITHOUT END   011 07
PRAISED AND EXALTED ABOVE ALL FOR EVER   011 17
PRAISED AND EXALTED ABOVE ALL FOR EVER   011 19
PRAISED AND EXALTED ABOVE ALL FOR EVER   011 21
PRAISED AND EXALTED ABOVE ALL FOR EVER   011 24
PRAISED AND EXALTED ABOVE ALL FOR EVER   011 26
PRAISED AND EXALTED ABOVE ALL FOR EVER   011 28
PRAISE HIM, AND MAGNIFY HIM FOR EVER   011 32
PRAISE HIM, AND MAGNIFY HIM FOR EVER   012 03
PRAISE HIM, AND MAGNIFY HIM FOR EVER   012 05
PRAISE HIM, AND MAGNIFY HIM FOR EVER   012 07
PRAISE HIM, AND MAGNIFY HIM FOR EVER   012 09
PRAISE HIM, AND MAGNIFY HIM FOR EVER   012 11
PRAISE HIM, AND MAGNIFY HIM FOR EVER   012 13
PRAISE HIM, AND MAGNIFY HIM FOR EVER   012 15
PRAISE HIM, AND MAGNIFY HIM FOR EVER   012 17
PRAISE HIM, AND MAGNIFY HIM FOR EVER   012 19
PRAISE HIM, AND MAGNIFY HIM FOR EVER   012 21
PRAISE HIM, AND MAGNIFY HIM FOR EVER   012 23
PRAISE HIM, AND MAGNIFY HIM FOR EVER   012 25
PRAISE HIM, AND MAGNIFY HIM FOR EVER   012 27
PRAISE HIM, AND MAGNIFY HIM FOR EVER   012 29
PRAISE HIM, AND MAGNIFY HIM FOR EVER   012 31
PRAISE HIM, AND MAGNIFY HIM FOR EVER   012 33
LET IT PRAISE HIM, AND MAGNIFY HIM FOR EVER   013 03
PRAISE HIM, AND MAGNIFY HIM FOR EVER   013 05
PRAISE HIM, AND MAGNIFY HIM FOR EVER   013 07
PRAISE HIM, AND MAGNIFY HIM FOR EVER   013 09
PRAISE HIM, AND MAGNIFY HIM FOR EVER   013 11
PRAISE HIM, AND MAGNIFY HIM FOR EVER   013 13
PRAISE HIM, AND MAGNIFY HIM FOR EVER   013 15
PRAISE HIM, AND MAGNIFY HIM FOR EVER   013 17
PRAISE HIM, AND MAGNIFY HIM FOR EVER   013 19
PRAISE HIM, AND MAGNIFY HIM FOR EVER   013 21
PRAISE HIM, AND MAGNIFY HIM FOR EVER   013 23
PRAISE HIM, AND MAGNIFY HIM FOR EVER   013 25
PRAISE HIM, AND MAGNIFY HIM FOR EVER   013 27
PRAISE HIM, AND MAGNIFY HIM FOR EVER   013 29
PRAISE HIM, AND MAGNIFY HIM FOR EVER   013 31
AND MAKE THEM EVER MINDFUL OF THEIR CALLING TO SERVE   018 13
AND MY SIN IS EVER BEFORE ME   022 04
IS NOW, AND EVER SHALL BE, WORLD WITHOUT END   025 11
OUR FOREFATHERS, ABRAHAM AND HIS SEED, FOR EVER   026 28
LIVETH AND REIGNETH EVER, ONE GOD, WORLD WITHOUT END   032 14
AND ROSE AGAIN, AND EVER LIVETH TO MAKE INTERCESSION   037 21
OF THE EARTH, AND EVER REJOICE IN THY GOODNESS,   039 30
BE ALL HONOUR AND GLORY, NOW AND FOR EVER   041 07
WHO ART EVER READY TO HEAR THE PRAYERS OF THOSE WHO   041 19
OF HEART THEY MAY EVER LOOK UNTO THEE, WHO ART THE   042 27
LEARNING MAY FOR EVER FLOURISH AND ABOUND   047 37
THEY MAY EVER BE DEFENDED BY THY MOST GRACIOUS   049 15
TOWARDS HIM, AND EVER EXPRESS HIS THANKFULNESS BY A   053 26
PRECIOUS BLOOD, AND BE NOT ANGRY WITH US FOR EVER   054 17
IS NOW, AND EVER SHALL BE, WORLD WITHOUT END   059 07
BOTH NOW AND EVER VOUCHSAFE TO HEAR US, O CHRIST   059 15
AND MY SIN IS EVER BEFORE ME   060 15
IS NOW, AND EVER SHALL BE, *   061 17
THAT WE MAY EVER LIVE WITH THEE IN THE WORLD   062 24
AND PROPERTY IS EVER TO HAVE MERCY AND TO FORGIVE   063 09
BOTH HERE AND EVER, WE MAY BE PRESERVED IN BODY AND   070 10
GRANT THAT WE MAY EVER HEREAFTER SERVE AND PLEASE   075 28
WITH THEE AND THE HOLY GHOST, NOW AND EVER   090 19
WE MAY EMBRACE, AND EVER HOLD FAST, THE BLESSED HOPE   092 11
AND THE HOLY SPIRIT EVER, ONE GOD, WORLD WITHOUT END   093 32
AND THE SAME SPIRIT EVER, ONE GOD, WORLD WITHOUT END   096 19
O GOD, IS FOR EVER AND EVER   097 09
O GOD, IS FOR EVER AND EVER   097 09
AND THE SAME SPIRIT EVER, ONE GOD, WORLD WITHOUT END   104 11
LIVETH AND REIGNETH EVER, ONE GOD, WORLD WITHOUT END   117 11
AND THE HOLY GHOST EVER, ONE GOD, WORLD WITHOUT END   119 03
THE SPIRIT, WE MAY EVER OBEY THY GODLY MOTIONS IN   125 29
HIM TO DO AS HE HAD EVER DONE UNTO THEM   145 17
AND THE HOLY SPIRIT EVER, ONE GOD, WORLD WITHOUT END   152 13
AND THE HOLY GHOST EVER, ONE GOD, WORLD WITHOUT END   156 25
FOR SINS FOR EVER, SAT DOWN ON THE RIGHT HAND OF GOD   158 06
HATH PERFECTED FOR EVER THEM THAT ARE SANCTIFIED   158 09
IS NOW, AND EVER SHALL BE, *   163 19
AND THE HOLY GHOST EVER, ONE GOD, WITHOUT END   163 29
TO WHOM BE PRAISE AND DOMINION FOR EVER AND EVER   179 22
AND DOMINION FOR EVER AND EVER   179 22
THAT HE MAY ABIDE WITH YOU FOR EVER   181 11
OF THE SAME SPIRIT EVER, ONE GOD, WORLD WITHOUT END   182 19
ALL THAT EVER CAME BEFORE ME ARE THIEVES AND ROBBERS   186 13
LIVETH FOR EVER AND EVER, THE FOUR AND TWENTY ELDERS   187 26
WHO LIVETH FOR EVER AND EVER, THE FOUR AND TWENTY   187 26
HIM THAT LIVETH FOR EVER AND EVER, AND CAST THEIR   187 28
LIVETH FOR EVER AND EVER, AND CAST THEIR CROWNS   187 28
AND DOMINION FOR EVER AND EVER   193 12
TO HIM BE GLORY AND DOMINION FOR EVER AND EVER   193 12
SON, THOU ART EVER WITH ME, AND ALL THAT I HAVE   203 05
BUT FALL, KEEP US EVER BY THY HELP FROM ALL THINGS   210 19

EVER   CONTINUED

HE SHALL REIGN OVER THE HOUSE OF JACOB FOR EVER   236 19
BUT THE WORD OF OUR GOD SHALL STAND FOR EVER   242 32
BE UNTO OUR GOD FOR EVER AND EVER   257 02
BE UNTO OUR GOD FOR EVER AND EVER   257 02
IS NOW, AND EVER SHALL BE, *   265 08
FOR NO MAN EVER YET HATED HIS OWN FLESH   267 26
AND SO SHALL WE EVER BE WITH THE LORD   269 10
THEE AND THE SAME HOLY SPIRIT, NOW AND FOR EVER   276 15
OF THY GRACE, AND EVER REMAIN IN THE NUMBER OF THY   279 18
IS NOW, AND EVER SHALL BE, WORLD WITHOUT END   285 08
THE SPIRIT OF THY HOLY FEAR, NOW AND FOR EVER   297 22
THAT HE MAY CONTINUE THINE FOR EVER   297 27
WE BESEECH THEE, EVER BE OVER THEM   298 20
LET THY HOLY SPIRIT EVER BE WITH THEM   298 20
LIVETH AND REIGNETH EVER, ONE GOD, WORLD WITHOUT END   298 24
BOTH HERE AND EVER, WE MAY BE PRESERVED IN BODY AND   298 30
BE UPON YOU, AND REMAIN WITH YOU FOR EVER   299 05
ELSE HEREAFTER FOR EVER HOLD HIS PEACE   300 22
 AND MAY EVER REMAIN IN PERFECT LOVE AND   303 10
AND THE HOLY SPIRIT EVER, ONE GOD, WORLD WITHOUT END   303 28
IS NOW, AND EVER SHALL BE, WORLD WITHOUT END   306 06
WILL THE LORD ABSENT HIMSELF FOR EVER   311 12
IS HIS MERCY CLEAN GONE FOR EVER   311 14
O LORD, ENDURETH FOR EVER   312 09
AND SICKNESSES, AND EVER UNCERTAIN WHAT TIME THEY   R 321 03
ANY MAN EAT OF THIS BREAD, HE SHALL LIVE FOR EVER   322 27
BROUGHT FORTH, OR EVER THE EARTH AND THE WORLD WERE   325 15
AND THE HOLY GHOST EVER, ONE GOD, WORLD WITHOUT END   332 09
WHOM BE GLORY FOR EVER AND EVER   335 21
TO WHOM BE GLORY FOR EVER AND EVER   335 21
I WILL DWELL IN THE HOUSE OF THE LORD FOR EVER   338 31
THEY SHALL EVER BE GIVING OF THANKS, BECAUSE THOU   348 26
OUT THEIR NAME FOR EVER AND EVER   351 31
THOU HAST PUT OUT THEIR NAME FOR EVER AND EVER   351 31
7 BUT THE LORD SHALL ENDURE FOR EVER   352 02
ABIDING OF THE MEEK SHALL NOT PERISH FOR EVER   352 29
LORD IS KING FOR EVER AND EVER, *   354 11
KING FOR EVER AND EVER, *   354 11
SHALT PRESERVE THEM FROM THIS GENERATION FOR EVER   355 24
FOR EVER   355 28
FEAR OF THE LORD IS CLEAN, AND ENDURETH FOR EVER   363 33
EVEN FOR EVER AND EVER   365 12
EVEN FOR EVER AND EVER   365 12
BEEN LEFT UNTO THEE EVER SINCE I WAS BORN   366 23
YOUR HEART SHALL LIVE FOR EVER   367 27
I WILL DWELL IN THE HOUSE OF THE LORD FOR EVER   368 24
WHICH HAVE BEEN EVER OF OLD   369 29
14 MINE EYES ARE EVER LOOKING UNTO THE LORD   370 14
LOVING-KINDNESS IS EVER BEFORE MINE EYES   371 02
FEED THEM, AND SET THEM UP FOR EVER   373 28
AND THE LORD REMAINETH A KING FOR EVER   374 18
I WILL GIVE THANKS UNTO THEE FOR EVER   375 20
SHALL ENDURE FOR EVER, *   379 09
HIS PRAISE SHALL EVER BE IN MY MOUTH   380 04
AND THEIR INHERITANCE SHALL ENDURE FOR EVER   385 32
26 THE RIGHTEOUS IS EVER MERCIFUL, AND LENDETH   386 15
BUT THEY ARE PRESERVED FOR EVER   386 21
AND DWELL THEREIN FOR EVER   386 25
AND MY HEAVINESS IS EVER IN MY SIGHT   388 27
AND SHALT SET ME BEFORE THY FACE FOR EVER   392 24
AND WILL PRAISE THY NAME FOR EVER   395 10
AWAKE, AND BE NOT ABSENT FROM US FOR EVER   396 07
BECAUSE GOD HATH BLESSED THEE FOR EVER   396 19
6 THY SEAT, O GOD, ENDURETH FOR EVER   396 27
GOD UPHOLDETH THE SAME FOR EVER   399 26
13 FOR THIS GOD IS OUR GOD FOR EVER AND EVER   400 04
GOD IS OUR GOD FOR EVER AND EVER   400 04
SO THAT HE MUST LET THAT ALONE FOR EVER   400 21
SHALL CONTINUE FOR EVER, AND THAT THEIR   400 27
AND MY SIN IS EVER BEFORE ME   403 13
6 THEREFORE SHALL GOD DESTROY THEE FOR EVER   404 28
MERCY OF GOD FOR EVER AND EVER   405 05
IS IN THE TENDER MERCY OF GOD FOR EVER AND EVER   405 06
THAT ENDURETH FOR EVER, SHALL HEAR ME, AND BRING THEM   407 30
SHALL NOT SUFFER THE RIGHTEOUS TO FALL FOR EVER   408 05
9 OR EVER YOUR POTS BE MADE HOT WITH THORNS, *   410 26
THY TABERNACLE FOR EVER, *   413 13
7 HE SHALL DWELL BEFORE GOD FOR EVER   413 19
6 HE RULETH WITH HIS POWER FOR EVER   417 26
THE LORD WILL ABIDE IN IT FOR EVER   420 15
AND EVER BOW THOU DOWN THEIR BACKS   423 22
I BEEN HOLDEN UP EVER SINCE I WAS BORN   425 16
SHALL BE MADE UNTO HIM, AND DAILY SHALL HE BE   427 27
17 HIS NAME SHALL ENDURE FOR EVER   427 32
AND BLESSED BE THE NAME OF HIS MAJESTY FOR EVER   428 04
THE STRENGTH OF MY HEART, AND MY PORTION FOR EVER   429 29
SHALL THE ENEMY BLASPHEME THY NAME FOR EVER   430 28
FORGET NOT THE CONGREGATION OF THE POOR FOR EVER   431 17
THEE INCREASETH EVER MORE AND MORE   431 25
AND PRAISE HIM FOR EVER   432 20
7 WILL THE LORD ABSENT HIMSELF FOR EVER   433 29
8 IS HIS MERCY CLEAN GONE FOR EVER   433 31
SHALL THY JEALOUSY BURN LIKE FIRE FOR EVER   440 10
THEE THANKS FOR EVER, *   440 33
BUT THEIR TIME SHOULD HAVE ENDURED FOR EVER   443 12
AND VEXED EVER MORE AND MORE   445 06
5 WILT THOU BE DISPLEASED AT US FOR EVER   446 16
MY MOUTH WILL I EVER BE SHOWING THY TRUTH FROM ONE   450 05
MERCY SHALL BE SET UP FOR EVER   450 07
WILL I STABLISH FOR EVER, *   450 11
MAKE TO ENDURE FOR EVER, *   451 33
SHALL ENDURE FOR EVER, *   452 12
FOR EVER   452 32
BROUGHT FORTH, OR EVER THE EARTH AND THE WORLD WERE   453 20

EVER   CONTINUED

	PAGE	LN
THEN SHALL THEY BE DESTROYED FOR EVER	456	15
3 EVER SINCE THE WORLD BEGAN, HATH THY SEAT BEEN	457	09
HOLINESS BECOMETH THINE HOUSE FOR EVER	457	17
SHALT ENDURE FOR EVER, *	465	02
NEITHER KEEPETH HE HIS ANGER FOR EVER	466	24
FOR EVER AND EVER UPON THEM THAT FEAR HIM	467	09
LORD ENDURETH FOR EVER AND EVER UPON THEM THAT FEAR	467	09
MAJESTY OF THE LORD SHALL ENDURE FOR EVER	469	24
AND HIS MERCY ENDURETH FOR EVER	472	32
AND HIS MERCY ENDURETH FOR EVER	476	07
ART A PRIEST FOR EVER AFTER THE ORDER OF MELCHIZEDEK	482	15
AND HIS RIGHTEOUSNESS ENDURETH FOR EVER	482	29
HE SHALL EVER BE MINDFUL OF HIS COVENANT	483	04
THEY STAND FAST FOR EVER AND EVER, *	483	09
FAST FOR EVER AND EVER, *	483	09
HE HATH COMMANDED HIS COVENANT FOR EVER	483	12
HIS PRAISE ENDURETH FOR EVER	483	16
AND HIS RIGHTEOUSNESS ENDURETH FOR EVER	483	23
AND HIS RIGHTEOUSNESS REMAINETH FOR EVER	484	02
KINDNESS IS EVER MORE AND MORE TOWARD US	487	27
AND THE TRUTH OF THE LORD ENDURETH FOR EVER	487	28
BECAUSE HIS MERCY ENDURETH FOR EVER	487	32
AND THAT HIS MERCY ENDURETH FOR EVER	488	03
THAT HIS MERCY ENDURETH FOR EVER	488	05
THAT HIS MERCY ENDURETH FOR EVER	488	07
AND HIS MERCY ENDURETH FOR EVER	489	28
FOR EVER AND EVER	492	28
FOR EVER AND EVER	492	28
ENDURETH FOR EVER IN HEAVEN	496	03
FOR THEY ARE EVER WITH ME	496	23
HAVE I CLAIMED AS MINE HERITAGE FOR EVER	497	20
MY DELIGHT SHALL BE EVER IN THY STATUTES	498	03
THAT THOU HAST GROUNDED THEM FOR EVER	500	15
MAY NOT BE REMOVED, BUT STANDETH FAST FOR EVER	504	25
15 THIS SHALL BE MY REST FOR EVER	509	02
O LORD, ENDURETH FOR EVER	510	28
AND HIS MERCY ENDURETH FOR EVER	511	17
FOR HIS MERCY ENDURETH FOR EVER	511	19
FOR HIS MERCY ENDURETH FOR EVER	511	21
FOR HIS MERCY ENDURETH FOR EVER	511	23
FOR HIS MERCY ENDURETH FOR EVER	511	25
FOR HIS MERCY ENDURETH FOR EVER	511	27
FOR HIS MERCY ENDURETH FOR EVER	511	29
FOR HIS MERCY ENDURETH FOR EVER	511	31
FOR HIS MERCY ENDURETH FOR EVER	511	33
FOR HIS MERCY ENDURETH FOR EVER	512	03
FOR HIS MERCY ENDURETH FOR EVER	512	05
FOR HIS MERCY ENDURETH FOR EVER	512	07
FOR HIS MERCY ENDURETH FOR EVER	512	09
FOR HIS MERCY ENDURETH FOR EVER	512	11
FOR HIS MERCY ENDURETH FOR EVER	512	13
FOR HIS MERCY ENDURETH FOR EVER	512	15
FOR HIS MERCY ENDURETH FOR EVER	512	17
FOR HIS MERCY ENDURETH FOR EVER	512	19
FOR HIS MERCY ENDURETH FOR EVER	512	21
FOR HIS MERCY ENDURETH FOR EVER	512	23
FOR HIS MERCY ENDURETH FOR EVER	512	25
FOR HIS MERCY ENDURETH FOR EVER	512	27
FOR HIS MERCY ENDURETH FOR EVER	512	29
FOR HIS MERCY ENDURETH FOR EVER	512	31
FOR HIS MERCY ENDURETH FOR EVER	512	33
FOR HIS MERCY ENDURETH FOR EVER	512	35
FOR HIS MERCY ENDURETH FOR EVER	513	03
O LORD, ENDURETH FOR EVER	514	15
AND LET ME EVER ESCAPE THEM	517	33
PRAISE THY NAME FOR EVER AND EVER	520	28
AND I WILL PRAISE THY NAME FOR EVER AND EVER	520	28
AND PRAISE THY NAME FOR EVER AND EVER	520	30
PRAISE THY NAME FOR EVER AND EVER	520	30
HIS HOLY NAME FOR EVER AND EVER	521	35
GIVE THANKS UNTO HIS HOLY NAME FOR EVER AND EVER	521	35
WHO KEEPETH HIS PROMISE FOR EVER	522	13
MADE THEM FAST FOR EVER AND EVER	524	16
6 HE HATH MADE THEM FAST FOR EVER AND EVER	524	16
WITH THEE AND THE HOLY GHOST, NOW AND FOR EVER	531	25
AND CONTINUING EVER STABLE AND STRONG IN THY SON	535	07
ALL THAT EVER CAME BEFORE ME ARE THIEVES AND ROBBERS	539	04
THAT THEY MAY BE SAVED THROUGH CHRIST FOR EVER	540	04
NAME MAY BE FOR EVER GLORIFIED, AND THY BLESSED	546	02
O GOD, WHO DOST EVER HALLOW AND PROTECT THY CHURCH	562	09
OF THE SAME SPIRIT EVER, ONE GOD, WORLD WITHOUT END	562	15
IS NOW, AND EVER SHALL BE, *	564	04
TO WHOM BE GLORY FOR EVER AND EVER	573	08
WHOM BE GLORY FOR EVER AND EVER	573	08
BE EVER WITH ME IN THE PERFORMANCE OF ALL THE DUTIES	573	23
THY HANDS, WHO ART EVER READY TO RECEIVE HUMBLE AND	590	05
CHURCH THE EVIL BE EVER MINGLED WITH THE GOOD,	608	08

EVERLASTING

	PAGE	LN
EARTH DOTH WORSHIP THEE, THE FATHER EVERLASTING	010	10
THOU ART THE EVERLASTING SON OF THE FATHER	010	25
BE NUMBERED WITH THY SAINTS, IN GLORY EVERLASTING	011	03
THE LORD IS GRACIOUS, HIS MERCY IS EVERLASTING	015	13
AND THE LIFE EVERLASTING	015	30
ALMIGHTY AND EVERLASTING GOD, WHO HAST SAFELY BROUGHT	017	13
TO ATTAIN EVERLASTING JOY AND FELICITY	018	04
ALMIGHTY AND EVERLASTING GOD, FROM WHOM COMETH EVERY	018	18
AND IN THE WORLD TO COME LIFE EVERLASTING	020	10
AND THE LIFE EVERLASTING	030	02
KINGDOM IS EVERLASTING AND POWER INFINITE	032	04
ALMIGHTY AND EVERLASTING GOD, FROM WHOM COMETH EVERY	032	17
AND IN THE WORLD TO COME LIFE EVERLASTING	034	10
ALMIGHTY AND EVERLASTING GOD, WHO BY THY HOLY SPIRIT	036	26

EVERLASTING   CONTINUED

	PAGE	LN
PARTAKERS OF EVERLASTING LIFE	037	07
HE MAY DWELL WITH THEE IN LIFE EVERLASTING	045	21
GLORIOUS RESURRECTION, AND THE LIFE EVERLASTING	048	22
OF EVERLASTING SALVATION	049	13
OBTAIN EVERLASTING LIFE	049	27
PARTAKER OF EVERLASTING GLORY IN THE LIFE TO COME	051	12
PARTAKER OF EVERLASTING GLORY IN THE LIFE TO COME	053	17
AND FROM EVERLASTING DAMNATION,	054	21
AND EVERLASTING GOD, VOUCHSAFE, WE BESEECH	070	06
BRING YOU TO EVERLASTING LIFE	076	07
BUT HAVE EVERLASTING LIFE	076	16
EVERLASTING GOD	076	33
TO US EVERLASTING LIFE	078	12
SOUL UNTO EVERLASTING LIFE	082	32
SOUL UNTO EVERLASTING LIFE	083	04
HOPE OF THY EVERLASTING KINGDOM, BY THE MERITS OF HIS	083	24
EXALT US TO EVERLASTING LIFE	086	11
HOPE OF EVERLASTING LIFE, WHICH THOU HAST GIVEN US IN	092	12
THAT IT MAY AT LENGTH ATTAIN TO LIFE EVERLASTING	101	09
ALMIGHTY AND EVERLASTING GOD, WHO DOST GOVERN ALL	111	10
ALMIGHTY AND EVERLASTING GOD, MERCIFULLY LOOK UPON	112	26
ALMIGHTY AND EVERLASTING GOD, WHO HATEST NOTHING THAT	124	11
ALMIGHTY AND EVERLASTING GOD, WHO, OF THY TENDER LOVE	134	05
HIMSELF AN EVERLASTING NAME	139	12
THY NAME IS FROM EVERLASTING	139	24
ALMIGHTY AND EVERLASTING GOD, BY WHOSE SPIRIT THE	156	27
THE GATE OF EVERLASTING LIFE	163	24
TO ATTAIN TO EVERLASTING JOYS	168	21
BUT HAVE EVERLASTING LIFE	184	34
ALMIGHTY AND EVERLASTING GOD, WHO HAST GIVEN UNTO US	186	23
AND THE END EVERLASTING LIFE	199	04
ALMIGHTY AND EVERLASTING GOD, WHO ART ALWAYS MORE	206	04
ALMIGHTY AND EVERLASTING GOD, GIVE UNTO US THE	209	08
INHERIT EVERLASTING LIFE	231	21
TO KNOW IS EVERLASTING LIFE	238	29
THE CROWN OF EVERLASTING GLORY	244	27
ALMIGHTY AND EVERLASTING GOD, WHO DIDST GIVE TO THINE	249	14
O EVERLASTING GOD, WHO HAST ORDAINED AND CONSTITUTED	251	27
BE CAST INTO EVERLASTING FIRE	253	06
ALMIGHTY AND EVERLASTING GOD, WHO DOST ENKINDLE THE	258	04
UNWORTHY OF EVERLASTING LIFE, LO, WE TURN TO THE	261	02
MAY HAVE EVERLASTING LIFE	269	21
ENJOY THE EVERLASTING BENEDICTION OF THY HEAVENLY	274	19
ALMIGHTY AND EVERLASTING GOD, HEAVENLY FATHER,	276	07
AN HEIR OF EVERLASTING SALVATION	276	13
AND EVERLASTING LIFE	276	23
AND EVERLASTING LIFE	277	24
EVERLASTING GOD, FOR THAT THY DEARLY	279	09
OF THINE EVERLASTING KINGDOM	281	04
AND THE LIFE EVERLASTING	284	24
UNTO THY EVERLASTING KINGDOM	297	29
MAY OBTAIN EVERLASTING LIFE	298	23
AND EVERLASTING GOD, VOUCHSAFE, WE BESEECH	298	26
AUTHOR OF EVERLASTING LIFE	303	04
IN THE WORLD TO COME YE MAY HAVE LIFE EVERLASTING	304	16
PARTAKER OF EVERLASTING GLORY IN THE LIFE TO COME	306	31
THAT HE MAY DWELL WITH THEE IN LIFE EVERLASTING	310	24
AND EVERLASTING BLESSEDNESS	318	18
REST OF EVERLASTING PEACE, AND INTO THE GLORIOUS	320	02
HATH EVERLASTING LIFE, AND SHALL NOT COME INTO	321	34
ON ME HATH EVERLASTING LIFE	322	22
ART GOD FROM EVERLASTING, AND WORLD WITHOUT END	325	16
ETERNAL AND EVERLASTING GLORY	334	28
BLOOD OF THE EVERLASTING COVENANT	335	18
WITH THY BLESSED SAINTS IN GLORY EVERLASTING	336	09
GIVE HIM EVERLASTING FELICITY, *	365	15
LIFT UP, YE EVERLASTING DOORS	369	10
LIFT UP, YE EVERLASTING DOORS	369	14
ART GOD FROM EVERLASTING, AND WORLD WITHOUT END	453	22
THOU ART FROM EVERLASTING	457	10
THE LORD IS GRACIOUS, HIS MERCY IS EVERLASTING	463	14
FOR AN EVERLASTING TESTAMENT	470	23
FROM EVERLASTING, AND WORLD WITHOUT END	475	33
BE HAD IN EVERLASTING REMEMBRANCE	483	29
THINE EVERLASTING JUDGMENTS, O LORD, *	493	14
IS AN EVERLASTING RIGHTEOUSNESS, *	499	23
RIGHTEOUSNESS OF THY TESTIMONIES IS EVERLASTING	499	27
160 THY WORD IS TRUE FROM EVERLASTING	500	31
AND LEAD ME IN THE WAY EVERLASTING	516	07
IS AN EVERLASTING KINGDOM, *	521	18
AUTHOR OF EVERLASTING LIFE	545	15
THE CROWN OF EVERLASTING GLORY	549	14
AUTHOR OF EVERLASTING LIFE	557	23
INTO EVERLASTING JOY	558	05
OF THY EVERLASTING KINGDOM	561	20
LIFT UP, YE EVERLASTING DOORS	563	25
LIFT UP, YE EVERLASTING DOORS	563	29
OBTAIN EVERLASTING LIFE	571	12
LIGHT OF THE EVERLASTING GOSPEL	572	28
BLOOD OF THE EVERLASTING COVENANT	573	05
BE NUMBERED WITH THY SAINTS IN GLORY EVERLASTING	574	19
AND THE LIFE EVERLASTING	578	08
AND FROM EVERLASTING DEATH	581	04
ALMIGHTY AND EVERLASTING GOD, IN WHOM WE LIVE AND	587	19
ALMIGHTY AND EVERLASTING GOD, WHO HAST SAFELY BROUGHT	592	19
TRUE GOD, EVERLASTING, WITHOUT BODY, PARTS, OR	603	03
FROM EVERLASTING OF THE FATHER, THE VERY AND ETERNAL	603	09
TESTAMENT EVERLASTING LIFE IS OFFERED TO MANKIND BY	604	16
LIFE IS THE EVERLASTING PURPOSE OF GOD, WHEREBY	606	06
BY CHRIST TO EVERLASTING SALVATION, AS VESSELS MADE	606	09
ATTAIN TO EVERLASTING FELICITY	606	15

EVERLASTINGLY

AND EVERLASTINGLY REWARDED, THROUGH THY MERCY,   278 29

EVERLIVING

ALMIGHTY AND EVERLIVING GOD, WHO BY THY HOLY APOSTLE   074 06
ALMIGHTY AND EVERLIVING GOD, WE MOST HEARTILY THANK   083 16
ALMIGHTY AND EVERLIVING GOD, WHO, FOR THE GREATER   228 05
ALMIGHTY AND EVERLIVING GOD, WE HUMBLY BESEECH THY   231 28
ALMIGHTY AND EVERLIVING GOD, WHO HAST VOUCHSAFED TO   297 14
ALMIGHTY AND EVERLIVING GOD, WHO MAKEST US BOTH TO   298 13
EVERLIVING GOD, MAKER OF MANKIND, WHO DOST   321 18
ALMIGHTY AND EVERLIVING GOD, WE YIELD UNTO THEE MOST   336 16

EVERMORE

OF THE HOLY GHOST, BE WITH US ALL EVERMORE   020 14
OF THE HOLY GHOST, BE WITH US ALL EVERMORE   034 14
BE PRESERVED EVERMORE FROM ALL PERILS, TO GLORIFY   041 14
THEY MAY EVERMORE BE FILLED WITH THE POWER OF HIS   043 24
MAY EVERMORE GIVE THANKS UNTO THEE IN THY HOLY   058 23
THY MERCY, AND EVERMORE SERVE THEE IN HOLINESS AND   059 25
AND EVERMORE MIGHTILY DEFEND THEM   061 33
AND GIVE US PEACE, BOTH NOW AND EVERMORE   063 18
EVERMORE PRAISING THEE, AND SAYING, PRIEST AND   077 06
EVERMORE PRAISING THEE, AND SAYING, PRIEST AND   079 30
AND THAT WE MAY EVERMORE DWELL IN HIM, AND HE IN US   082 22
GRACE MAY EVERMORE BE DEFENDED BY THY MIGHTY POWER   115 31
IS BLESSED FOR EVERMORE, KNOWETH THAT I LIE NOT   121 16
AND PRESERVED EVERMORE, BOTH IN BODY AND SOUL   132 20
THAT WE MAY EVERMORE LIVE WITH HIM IN THE JOY OF HIS   165 07
ALL THINGS, AND EVERMORE TO REJOICE IN HIS HOLY   180 11
THIS FAITH, AND EVERMORE DEFEND US FROM ALL   186 28
PRESERVE IT EVERMORE BY THY HELP AND GOODNESS   212 07
BE ALL HONOUR AND GLORY, NOW AND FOR EVERMORE   228 12
MAY BE EVERMORE READY TO FOLLOW THY HOLY   246 20
THY BOUNTY, MAY EVERMORE GIVE THANKS UNTO THEE IN THY   261 32
AND CONFIRM THIS FAITH IN US EVERMORE   276 11
BE ALL HONOUR AND GLORY, NOW AND EVERMORE   279 21
OF THE HOLY GHOST, BE WITH US ALL EVERMORE   289 31
OF THE HOLY GHOST, BE WITH US ALL EVERMORE   295 06
AND EVERMORE MIGHTILY DEFEND HIM   308 26
HIS PROMISE COME UTTERLY TO AN END FOR EVERMORE   311 15
BE NOW AND EVERMORE THY DEFENCE   314 18
AND GIVE THEE PEACE, BOTH NOW AND EVERMORE   314 30
FROM THIS TIME FORTH FOR EVERMORE   327 34
AND GIVE YOU PEACE, BOTH NOW AND EVERMORE   332 14
AT THY RIGHT HAND THERE IS PLEASURE FOR EVERMORE   333 11
FROM THIS TIME FORTH FOR EVERMORE   339 18
OF THE HOLY GHOST, BE WITH US ALL EVERMORE   341 07
AND GIVE HIM PEACE, BOTH NOW AND EVERMORE   341 18
BLESS YOU AND KEEP YOU, NOW AND FOR EVERMORE   342 16
AT THY RIGHT HAND THERE IS PLEASURE FOR EVERMORE   358 14
HIS ANOINTED, AND UNTO HIS SEED FOR EVERMORE   363 09
AND DWELL FOR EVERMORE   386 18
HIS PROMISE COME UTTERLY TO AN END FOR EVERMORE   433 32
AND WILL PRAISE THY NAME FOR EVERMORE   447 29
FOR HIM FOR EVERMORE, *   451 31
STAND FAST FOR EVERMORE AS THE MOON, *   452 14
51 PRAISED BE THE LORD FOR EVERMORE   453 12
ART THE MOST HIGHEST FOR EVERMORE   456 16
SEEK HIS FACE EVERMORE   470 11
AMONG ALL POSTERITIES FOR EVERMORE   474 32
FROM THIS TIME FORTH FOR EVERMORE   484 11
FROM THIS TIME FORTH FOR EVERMORE   486 15
OF THY RIGHTEOUSNESS ENDURE FOR EVERMORE   500 32
FROM THIS TIME FORTH FOR EVERMORE   503 07
FROM THIS TIME FORTH FOR EVERMORE   504 28
FROM THIS TIME FORTH FOR EVERMORE   507 31
ALSO SHALL SIT UPON THY THRONE FOR EVERMORE   508 31
AND LIFE FOR EVERMORE   509 21
BE KING FOR EVERMORE, *   522 23
OFFICES WERE EVERMORE HAD IN SUCH REVEREND   529 14
THAT HE MAY EVERMORE BE READY TO SPREAD ABROAD THY   557 29
WHO IS GOD OVER ALL, BLESSED FOR EVERMORE   572 04
OF THE HOLY GHOST, BE WITH US ALL EVERMORE   589 11
OF THE HOLY GHOST, BE WITH US ALL EVERMORE   592 04
OF THE HOLY GHOST, BE WITH US ALL EVERMORE   592 29
AND GIVE US PEACE, THIS NIGHT AND EVERMORE   593 21
THAT WE BE EVERMORE KINDLY AFFECTIONED WITH   598 29

EVERY

AND IN EVERY PLACE INCENSE SHALL BE OFFERED UNTO MY   004 14
AND THAT, IN EVERY CHURCH, WHAT CANNOT BE CLEARLY   V 05
AND AT THE END OF EVERY PSALM, AND LIKEWISE AT THE   R 009 23
THAT BEFORE EVERY LESSON, THE MINISTER SHALL   R 009 32
AND AFTER EVERY LESSON, HERE ENDETH THE FIRST (OR THE   R 009 34
FROM WHOM COMETH EVERY GOOD AND PERFECT GIFT   018 19
WE HAVE TURNED EVERY ONE TO HIS OWN WAY   022 15
AND AT THE END OF EVERY PSALM, AND LIKEWISE AT THE   R 025 16
FROM WHOM COMETH EVERY GOOD AND PERFECT GIFT   032 18
AND FROM EVERY EVIL WAY   036 15
AND FROM EVERY EVIL TO WHICH HE MAY BE   046 13
THAT ALL, AND EVERY ONE OF THEM, MAY SERVE TRULY IN   047 17
AND EXAMINED BY EVERY TRUE MEMBER OF OUR CHURCH, AND   VI 36
OF OUR CHURCH, AND EVERY SINCERE CHRISTIAN, WITH A   VI 37
WITH HIS BLESSING EVERY ENDEAVOUR FOR PROMULGATING   VI 40
AFTER EVERY COMMANDMENT, ASK GOD MERCY FOR   R 067 23
NOT EVERY ONE THAT SAITH UNTO ME, LORD, LORD,   072 13
LET EVERY MAN DO ACCORDING AS HE IS DISPOSED IN HIS   072 17
EVERY MAN SHALL GIVE AS HE IS ABLE, ACCORDING TO THE   073 15
LAY HIS HAND UPON EVERY VESSEL IN WHICH THERE IS ANY   R 080 34
THAT EVERY MINISTER SO REPELLING ANY,   R 085 17
IS TO BE REPEATED EVERY DAY, AFTER THE OTHER COLLECTS   R 090 20

EVERY   CONTINUED

AND THEN SHALL EVERY MAN HAVE PRAISE OF GOD   094 13
BUT IN EVERY THING BY PRAYER AND SUPPLICATION WITH   095 15
WHICH LIGHTETH EVERY MAN THAT COMETH INTO THE WORLD   097 30
WENT TO BE TAXED, EVERY ONE INTO HIS OWN CITY   098 32
SHOULD BE WRITTEN EVERY ONE, I SUPPOSE THAT EVEN THE   102 16
WHICH IS ABOVE EVERY NAME   105 27
THE NAME OF JESUS EVERY KNEE SHOULD BOW, OF THINGS IN   105 28
AND THAT EVERY TONGUE SHOULD CONFESS THAT JESUS   105 29
GIVEN UNTO ME, TO EVERY MAN THAT IS AMONG YOU,   110 10
GOD HATH DEALT TO EVERY MAN THE MEASURE OF FAITH   110 12
IN CHRIST, AND EVERY ONE MEMBERS ONE OF ANOTHER   110 15
WENT TO JERUSALEM EVERY YEAR AT THE FEAST OF THE   110 18
SAITH UNTO HIM, EVERY MAN AT THE BEGINNING DOTH SET   113 27
LET EVERY SOUL BE SUBJECT UNTO THE HIGHER POWERS   114 11
AND EVERY MAN THAT HATH THIS HOPE IN HIM PURIFIETH   117 20
AND EVERY MAN THAT STRIVETH FOR THE MASTERY IS   119 07
THEY RECEIVED EVERY MAN A PENNY   119 32
LIKEWISE RECEIVED EVERY MAN A PENNY   120 02
COME TO HIM OUT OF EVERY CITY, HE SPAKE BY A PARABLE   121 19
IS TO BE SAID EVERY DAY IN LENT, AFTER THE COLLECT   R 124 18
SHALL SERVE FOR EVERY DAY AFTER, UNTO THE NEXT   R 125 23
BUT BY EVERY WORD THAT PROCEEDETH OUT OF THE   126 29
THAT EVERY ONE OF YOU SHOULD KNOW HOW TO POSSESS HIS   127 29
SAID UNTO THEM, EVERY KINGDOM DIVIDED AGAINST ITSELF   129 30
FOR THEM, THAT EVERY ONE OF THEM MAY TAKE A LITTLE   131 31
IS TO BE SAID EVERY DAY, AFTER THE COLLECT APPOINTED   R 134 13
THE NAME OF JESUS EVERY KNEE SHOULD BOW, OF THINGS IN   134 24
WHICH IS ABOVE EVERY NAME   134 24
AND THAT EVERY TONGUE SHOULD CONFESS THAT JESUS   134 26
UPON THEM, WHAT EVERY MAN SHOULD TAKE   146 12
MOSES HAD SPOKEN EVERY PRECEPT TO ALL THE PEOPLE   147 19
THE HOLY PLACE EVERY YEAR WITH BLOOD OF OTHERS   148 03
BUT IS CLEAN EVERY WHIT   156 10
HOLY CHURCH, THAT EVERY MEMBER OF THE SAME, IN HIS   156 31
AGAIN MADE OF SINS EVERY YEAR   157 22
AND EVERY PRIEST STANDETH DAILY MINISTERING AND   158 03
FOUR PARTS, TO EVERY SOLDIER A PART   160 10
BUT IN EVERY NATION HE THAT FEARETH HIM, AND WORKETH   166 13
WHICH ARE READ EVERY SABBATH DAY, THEY HAVE FULFILLED   168 28
YOURSELVES TO EVERY ORDINANCE OF MAN FOR THE LORD'S   173 17
EVERY GOOD GIFT AND EVERY PERFECT GIFT IS FROM ABOVE,   174 26
GOOD GIFT AND EVERY PERFECT GIFT IS FROM ABOVE,   174 26
LET EVERY MAN BE SWIFT TO HEAR, SLOW TO   174 31
BE SCATTERED, EVERY MAN TO HIS OWN, AND SHALL LEAVE   177 05
SHALL SERVE FOR EVERY DAY AFTER, UNTO THE NEXT   R 178 30
AS EVERY MAN HATH RECEIVED THE GIFT, EVEN SO MINISTER   179 16
DEVOUT MEN, OUT OF EVERY NATION UNDER HEAVEN   180 25
BECAUSE THAT EVERY MAN HEARD THEM SPEAK IN HIS OWN   180 28
AND HOW HEAR WE EVERY MAN IN OUR OWN TONGUE, WHEREIN   180 31
SPIRIT IS GIVEN TO EVERY MAN TO PROFIT WITHAL   182 26
DIVIDING TO EVERY MAN SEVERALLY AS HE WILL   182 34
FOR EVERY ONE THAT ASKETH RECEIVETH   183 12
BUT IN EVERY NATION HE THAT FEARETH HIM, AND WORKETH   183 31
FOR EVERY ONE THAT DOETH EVIL HATETH THE LIGHT,   185 07
SO IS EVERY ONE THAT IS BORN OF THE SPIRIT   188 16
AND EVERY ONE THAT LOVETH IS BORN OF GOD, AND KNOWETH   189 09
FARED SUMPTUOUSLY EVERY DAY   190 04
BUT EVERY ONE THAT IS PERFECT SHALL BE AS HIS MASTER   195 04
EVEN SO EVERY GOOD TREE BRINGETH FORTH GOOD FRUIT   200 18
EVERY TREE THAT BRINGETH NOT FORTH GOOD FRUIT IS HEWN   200 21
NOT EVERY ONE THAT SAITH UNTO ME, LORD, LORD, SHALL   200 24
SPIRIT IS GIVEN TO EVERY MAN TO PROFIT WITHAL   203 26
DIVIDING TO EVERY MAN SEVERALLY AS HE WILL   204 03
KEEP THEE IN ON EVERY SIDE, AND SHALL LAY THEE EVEN   204 12
FOR EVERY ONE THAT EXALTETH HIMSELF SHALL BE ABASED   205 32
THAT IN EVERY THING YE ARE ENRICHED BY HIM, IN ALL   214 30
AWAY LYING, SPEAK EVERY MAN TRUTH WITH HIS NEIGHBOUR   216 17
THANK MY GOD UPON EVERY REMEMBRANCE OF YOU, ALWAYS IN   220 22
OF YOU, ALWAYS IN EVERY PRAYER OF MINE FOR YOU ALL   220 23
HEARTS FORGIVE NOT EVERY ONE HIS BROTHER THEIR   222 06
BEING FRUITFUL IN EVERY GOOD WORK, AND INCREASING IN   224 05
FOR THEM, THAT EVERY ONE OF THEM MAY TAKE A LITTLE   225 27
AND EVERY ONE THAT HATH FORSAKEN HOUSES, OR BRETHREN,   231 18
LAW OF THE LORD, EVERY MALE THAT OPENETH THE WOMB   232 26
CARRIED AWAY WITH EVERY BLAST OF VAIN DOCTRINE, WE   237 08
UNTO EVERY ONE OF US IS GIVEN GRACE ACCORDING TO THE   237 12
CARRIED ABOUT WITH EVERY WIND OF DOCTRINE, BY THE   237 26
BY THAT WHICH EVERY JOINT SUPPLIETH, ACCORDING TO THE   237 31
IN THE MEASURE OF EVERY PART, MAKETH INCREASE OF THE   237 32
EVERY BRANCH IN ME THAT BEARETH NOT FRUIT HE TAKETH   238 06
AND EVERY BRANCH THAT BEARETH FRUIT, HE PURGETH IT,   238 07
THE DISCIPLES, EVERY MAN ACCORDING TO HIS ABILITY,   241 19
EVERY VALLEY SHALL BE EXALTED, AND EVERY MOUNTAIN AND   242 22
BE EXALTED, AND EVERY MOUNTAIN AND HILL SHALL BE MADE   242 22
THE DISCIPLES, EVERY MAN ACCORDING TO HIS ABILITY,   246 28
THEY WERE HEALED EVERY ONE   249 32
OURSELVES TO EVERY MAN'S CONSCIENCE IN THE SIGHT OF   250 31
HIS FACE INTO EVERY CITY AND PLACE, WHITHER HE   254 12
LET US LAY ASIDE EVERY WEIGHT, AND THE SIN WHICH DOTH   258 21
FOR EVERY ONE THAT ASKETH RECEIVETH   263 05
EVERY GOOD GIFT AND EVERY PERFECT GIFT IS FROM ABOVE,   265 18
GOOD GIFT AND EVERY PERFECT GIFT IS FROM ABOVE,   265 19
LET EVERY MAN BE SWIFT TO HEAR, SLOW TO   265 21
OWN HUSBANDS IN EVERY THING   267 18
NEVERTHELESS LET EVERY ONE OF YOU IN PARTICULAR SO   267 32
THAT SENT ME, THAT EVERY ONE WHICH SEETH THE SON,   269 20
THE MINISTER OF EVERY PARISH SHALL OFTEN ADMONISH   R 273 03
THERE SHALL BE FOR EVERY MALE-CHILD TO BE BAPTIZED,   R 273 09
AND FOR EVERY FEMALE, ONE GODFATHER AND TWO   R 273 10
SO IS EVERY ONE THAT IS BORN OF THE SPIRIT   275 21
IS EXPEDIENT THAT EVERY ADULT, THUS BAPTIZED,   R 281 13
AND AFTER EVERY COMMANDMENT THE PEOPLE SHALL SAY THE   R 285 34
TO WORSHIP GOD EVERY SUNDAY IN HIS CHURCH   291 19
THE MINISTER OF EVERY PARISH SHALL DILIGENTLY,   R 295 07

EVERY   CONTINUED

AND EVERY ONE SHALL AUDIBLY ANSWER, I DO   R 296 29
AND EVERY ONE SHALL ANSWER, I DO   R 297 05
UPON THE HEAD OF EVERY ONE SEVERALLY, SAYING, DEFEND, R 297 25
SEVERAL STATES, EVERY MINISTER IS LEFT TO THE   R 304 18
OF THOSE LAWS, IN EVERY THING THAT REGARDS THE CIVIL R 304 19
THY SERVANT FROM EVERY BOND, AND SET HIM FREE FROM   319 09
AND CHASTISE EVERY ONE WHOM THOU DOST RECEIVE   321 20
AND SCOURGETH EVERY SON WHOM HE RECEIVETH   321 30
THY SERVANT, THAT, EVERY CAUSE OF SICKNESS BEING   322 08
AND VERILY EVERY MAN LIVING IS ALTOGETHER VANITY   324 24
EVERY MAN THEREFORE IS BUT VANITY   325 04
BUT EVERY MAN IN HIS OWN ORDER   328 25
AND TO EVERY SEED ITS OWN BODY   329 11
YOU PERFECT IN EVERY GOOD WORK TO DO HIS WILL,   335 19
CASTING EVERY CARE ON THEE, THEY MAY KNOW THE   342 11
EVERY NIGHT WASH I MY BED, AND WATER MY COUCH WITH MY 349 10
GOD IS PROVOKED EVERY DAY   350 16
TALK OF VANITY EVERY ONE WITH HIS NEIGHBOUR   355 09
AND WILL HELP EVERY ONE FROM HIM THAT SWELLETH   355 18
UNGODLY WALK ON EVERY SIDE   355 25
IN OUR WAY ON EVERY SIDE, *   359 08
CLOSE ME IN ON EVERY SIDE   366 28
IN HIS TEMPLE DOTH EVERY THING SPEAK OF THY HONOUR   374 16
13 THEREFORE SHALL EVERY GOOD MAN SING OF THY PRAISE 375 18
AND FEAR IS ON EVERY SIDE   376 22
7 FOR THIS SHALL EVERY ONE THAT IS GODLY MAKE HIS   378 02
EMBRACETH HIM ON EVERY SIDE   378 15
AND VERILY EVERY MAN LIVING IS ALTOGETHER VANITY   389 19
EVERY MAN THEREFORE IS BUT VANITY   389 32
MISCHIEF AGAINST EVERY MAN   413 31
FOR THOU REWARDEST EVERY MAN ACCORDING TO HIS WORK   414 24
AMONG THEMSELVES, EVERY MAN IN THE DEEP OF HIS HEART 415 31
SHALL REJOICE ON EVERY SIDE   417 10
COMFORTED ME ON EVERY SIDE   426 21
AND CHASTENED EVERY MORNING   429 05
UTTERLY DESTROY EVERY ENEMY, *   430 11
SHED LIKE WATER ON EVERY SIDE OF JERUSALEM, *   440 04
OF GODS APPEARETH EVERY ONE OF THEM IN SION   445 26
ME TOGETHER ON EVERY SIDE   449 32
MIGHTY LORD, IS ON EVERY SIDE   450 23
UP HIS ENEMIES ON EVERY SIDE   461 03
THEY KEPT ME IN ON EVERY SIDE, THEY KEPT ME IN,   488 20
ME IN, I SAY, ON EVERY SIDE   488 21
MY FEET FROM EVERY EVIL WAY, *   496 28
2 EVERY DAY WILL I GIVE THANKS UNTO THEE   520 29
IS LOVING UNTO EVERY MAN   521 10
6 LET EVERY THING THAT HATH BREATH *   525 32
SHALL EXAMINE EVERY ONE OF THOSE WHO ARE TO BE   R 532 23
UPON THE HEAD OF EVERY ONE TO BE DEACON, HUMBLY   R 534 03
BISHOP DELIVER TO EVERY ONE OF THEM THE NEW   R 534 09
UNTO EVERY ONE OF US IS GIVEN GRACE ACCORDING TO THE 537 32
THY LIGHT TO EVERY SENSE IMPART, AND SHED THY LOVE IN 545 02
SHED THY LOVE IN EVERY HEART   545 03
UPON THE HEAD OF EVERY ONE THAT RECEIVETH THE ORDER   R 546 07
SHALL DELIVER TO EVERY ONE OF THEM KNEELING, THE   R 546 23
WITNESSETH IN EVERY CITY, SAYING THAT BONDS AND   550 17
CEASED NOT TO WARN EVERY ONE NIGHT AND DAY WITH   550 34
THY LIGHT TO EVERY SENSE IMPART, AND SHED THY LOVE IN 557 08
SHED THY LOVE IN EVERY HEART   557 09
POWER TO PERFORM EVERY ACT OF SACERDOTAL FUNCTION   569 19
YOU PERFECT IN EVERY GOOD WORK TO DO HIS WILL,   573 06
THE MINISTER OF EVERY PARISH SHALL DILIGENTLY,   R 582 27
THE MINISTER OF EVERY PARISH SHALL EITHER BRING, OR   R 583 06
SHORT PAUSE, THAT EVERY ONE MAY SECRETLY CONFESS THE R 589 34
AND GRANT THAT EVERY MEMBER OF THE SAME, IN HIS   590 25
WE BESEECH THEE, EVERY ROOT OF BITTERNESS, THE DESIRE 598 22
BE TROUBLED ON EVERY SIDE, SUFFER THEM NOT TO BE   599 13
OF THE NATURE OF EVERY MAN, THAT NATURALLY IS   604 30
AND THEREFORE IN EVERY PERSON BORN INTO THIS WORLD,   604 33
NOT EVERY DEADLY SIN WILLINGLY COMMITTED AFTER   605 39
TO SAY, THAT EVERY MAN SHALL BE SAVED BY THE LAW OR   606 32
EVERY PARTICULAR OR NATIONAL CHURCH HATH AUTHORITY TO 609 42
EVERY MAN OUGHT, OF SUCH THINGS AS   611 03

EVERYWHERE

THAT ALL MEN EVERYWHERE MAY SEEK AFTER THEE AND FIND 038 08
THY SERVANTS EVERYWHERE, THE ETERNAL VICTORY   598 10

EVIDENCE

HOPED FOR, THE EVIDENCE OF THINGS NOT SEEN   228 23
ON EVIDENCE OF HIS REPENTANCE, THE   R 313 26

EVIDENT

IT IS EVIDENT UNTO ALL MEN, DILIGENTLY READING HOLY   529 11

EVIDENTLY

MAY BE AS EVIDENTLY KNOWN AS A TREE DISCERNED BY THE 605 15

EVIL

OF GREAT KINDNESS, AND REPENTETH HIM OF THE EVIL   004 23
BUT DELIVER US FROM EVIL   007 28
AND FROM EVERY EVIL WAY   036 15
IN THE TIME OF PEACE KEEP THEM SAFE FROM ALL EVIL   041 28
AND OVERCOME EVIL, AND MAY REJOICE IN THE LIFE THAT   043 12
TO CONTEND AGAINST EVIL, AND TO MAKE NO PEACE WITH   044 11
AND FROM EVERY EVIL TO WHICH HE MAY BE EXPOSED   046 13
AND GOOD OUT OF EVIL, GRANT TO THESE THY SERVANTS,   046 27
FROM ALL EVIL AND MISCHIEF   054 19
AND DONE THIS EVIL IN THY SIGHT   060 17

EVIL   CONTINUED

OPEN AND NOTORIOUS EVIL LIVER, OR TO HAVE DONE ANY   R 084 35
AMENDED HIS FORMER EVIL LIFE, THAT THE CONGREGATION   R 085 05
ABHOR THAT WHICH IS EVIL   111 22
TO NO MAN EVIL FOR EVIL   112 32
RECOMPENSE TO NO MAN EVIL FOR EVIL   112 32
EVIL, BUT OVERCOME EVIL WITH GOOD   113 08
BE NOT OVERCOME OF EVIL, BUT OVERCOME EVIL WITH GOOD 113 08
ARE NOT A TERROR TO GOOD WORKS, BUT TO THE EVIL   114 16
DO THAT WHICH IS EVIL, BE AFRAID   114 19
TO EXECUTE WRATH UPON HIM THAT DOETH EVIL   114 22
IS THINE EYE EVIL, BECAUSE I AM GOOD   120 11
HER OWN, IS NOT EASILY PROVOKED, THINKETH NO EVIL   122 32
OF GREAT KINDNESS, AND REPENTETH HIM OF THE EVIL   124 26
AND DISHONOUR, BY EVIL REPORT AND GOOD REPORT   126 16
AND FROM ALL EVIL THOUGHTS WHICH MAY ASSAULT   127 19
WE, WHO FOR OUR EVIL DEEDS DO WORTHILY DESERVE TO BE 130 25
WHY, WHAT EVIL HATH HE DONE   136 07
WHY, WHAT EVIL HATH HE DONE   145 26
WHY, WHAT EVIL HATH HE DONE   153 35
SPRINKLED FROM AN EVIL CONSCIENCE, AND OUR BODIES   158 21
THAN FOR EVIL DOING   161 22
IF YE THEN, BEING EVIL, KNOW HOW TO GIVE GOOD GIFTS   183 17
BECAUSE THEIR DEEDS WERE EVIL   185 07
ONE THAT DOETH EVIL HATETH THE LIGHT, NEITHER COMETH 185 08
LIKEWISE LAZARUS EVIL THINGS   190 18
RENDERING EVIL FOR EVIL, OR RAILING FOR RAILING   195 22
NOT RENDERING EVIL FOR EVIL, OR RAILING FOR RAILING   195 22
HIS TONGUE FROM EVIL, AND HIS LIPS THAT THEY SPEAK NO 195 25
LET HIM ESCHEW EVIL, AND DO GOOD   195 26
THE FACE OF THE LORD IS AGAINST THEM THAT DO EVIL   195 30
CANNOT BRING FORTH EVIL FRUIT, NEITHER CAN A CORRUPT 200 20
TREE BRINGETH FORTH EVIL FRUIT   200 20
NOT LUST AFTER EVIL THINGS, AS THEY ALSO LUSTED   201 14
UNTO THE DAY IS THE EVIL THEREOF   211 35
AND CLAMOUR, AND EVIL SPEAKING, BE PUT AWAY FROM YOU, 216 28
WHEREFORE THINK YE EVIL IN YOUR HEARTS   217 07
BECAUSE THE DAYS ARE EVIL   217 24
TO WITHSTAND IN THE EVIL DAY, AND HAVING DONE ALL, TO 219 12
THIS MAN, HOW MUCH EVIL HE HATH DONE TO THY SAINTS AT 230 23
KNOW TO REFUSE THE EVIL, AND CHOOSE THE GOOD   236 03
ALEXANDER THE COPPERSMITH DID ME MUCH EVIL   254 07
SAY ALL MANNER OF EVIL AGAINST YOU FALSELY, FOR MY   257 32
AND ENVIES, AND ALL EVIL SPEAKINGS, AS NEWBORN BABES, 259 26
AND WILL CAUSE THE EVIL BEASTS TO CEASE OUT OF THE   262 05
IF YE THEN, BEING EVIL, KNOW HOW TO GIVE GOOD GIFTS   263 11
SUN TO RISE ON THE EVIL AND ON THE GOOD, AND SENDETH 264 09
UNTO THE DAY IS THE EVIL THEREOF   266 33
KEEP MY TONGUE FROM EVIL SPEAKING, LYING, AND   289 06
FROM ALL EVIL, FROM ALL SIN, FROM ALL TRIBULATION   318 02
THE POWER OF THE EVIL ONE, AND FROM ETERNAL DEATH   318 12
AND SET HIM FREE FROM ALL EVIL   319 10
THE LORD SHALL PRESERVE THEE FROM ALL EVIL   327 31
OF THE SHADOW OF DEATH, I WILL FEAR NO EVIL   338 24
THE LORD SHALL PRESERVE THEE FROM ALL EVIL   339 15
NEITHER SHALL ANY EVIL DWELL WITH THEE   348 08
IF I HAVE REWARDED EVIL UNTO HIM THAT DEALT FRIENDLY 349 29
NOR DONE EVIL TO HIS NEIGHBOUR, *   357 11
FROM THE MEN OF THE EVIL WORLD   359 14
OF THE SHADOW OF DEATH, I WILL FEAR NO EVIL   368 17
THY TONGUE FROM EVIL, *   380 27
14 ESCHEW EVIL, AND DO GOOD   380 29
THEM THAT DO EVIL, *   380 33
12 THEY REWARDED ME EVIL FOR GOOD, *   382 15
NEITHER DOTH HE ABHOR ANY THING THAT IS EVIL   384 03
ENVIOUS AGAINST THE EVIL DOERS   384 26
THAT DOETH AFTER EVIL COUNSELS   385 08
ELSE SHALT THOU BE MOVED TO DO EVIL   385 10
27 FLEE FROM EVIL, AND DO THE THING THAT IS GOOD   386 17
WENT ABOUT TO DO ME EVIL TALKED OF WICKEDNESS, AND   388 15
ALSO THAT REWARD EVIL FOR GOOD ARE AGAINST ME   388 32
AND PUT TO REBUKE, THAT WISH ME EVIL   391 18
MINE ENEMIES SPEAK EVIL OF ME, *   392 08
EVEN AGAINST ME DO THEY IMAGINE THIS EVIL   392 14
8 AN EVIL DISEASE, SAY THEY, CLEAVETH FAST UNTO HIM   392 15
FEAR IN THE DAYS OF EVIL, *   400 14
AND DONE THIS EVIL IN THY SIGHT   403 15
5 HE SHALL REWARD EVIL UNTO MINE ENEMIES   406 12
ALL THAT THEY IMAGINE IS TO DO ME EVIL   408 25
BACKWARD AND PUT TO CONFUSION THAT WISH ME EVIL   424 24
WITH SHAME AND DISHONOUR THAT SEEK TO DO ME EVIL   425 33
AND BROUGHT UNTO SHAME THAT SEEK TO DO ME EVIL   426 29
WHICH HATH DONE EVIL IN THY SANCTUARY   430 11
AND SENT EVIL ANGELS AMONG THEM   438 07
10 THERE SHALL NO EVIL HAPPEN UNTO THEE, *   455 15
MY PART AGAINST THE EVIL DOERS   458 19
SEE THAT YE HATE THE THING WHICH IS EVIL   461 17
SUFFER THEM TO BE EVIL ENTREATED THROUGH TYRANTS, *   478 26
THEY REWARDED ME EVIL FOR GOOD, *   480 11
TO THOSE THAT SPEAK EVIL AGAINST MY SOUL   481 11
BE AFRAID OF ANY EVIL TIDINGS   483 30
MY FEET FROM EVERY EVIL WAY, *   496 28
I HATE ALL EVIL WAYS   497 03
THEM THAT IMAGINE EVIL THINGS   497 24
7 THE LORD SHALL PRESERVE THEE FROM ALL EVIL   503 04
THEM FORTH WITH THE EVIL DOERS   505 03
AS MANY AS HAVE EVIL WILL AT SION   506 30
O LORD, FROM THE EVIL MAN   516 09
EVIL SHALL HUNT THE WICKED PERSON TO OVERTHROW HIM   516 33
BE INCLINED TO ANY EVIL THING   517 15
NO EVIL CAN OUR STEPS BETIDE   545 09
NO EVIL CAN OUR STEPS BETIDE   557 15
AND MY TONGUE FROM EVIL SPEAKING, LYING, AND   580 10
OF THE GREAT EVIL OF THEM   590 10
DONE OR WISH US EVIL, AND GIVE THEM REPENTANCE AND   590 33

EVIL   CONTINUED

NATURE INCLINED TO EVIL, SO THAT THE FLESH LUSTETH	604	32
VISIBLE CHURCH THE EVIL BE EVER MINGLED WITH THE	608	08
AND SOMETIMES THE EVIL HAVE CHIEF AUTHORITY IN THE	608	10
BE MINISTERED BY EVIL MEN	608	18
INQUIRY BE MADE OF EVIL MINISTERS, AND THAT THEY BE	608	20

EVILDOERS

AGAINST YOU AS EVILDOERS, THEY MAY BY YOUR GOOD	173	15
PUNISHMENT OF EVILDOERS, AND FOR THE PRAISE OF THEM	173	20

EVILS

THAT THOSE EVILS WHICH THE CRAFT AND SUBTILTY OF	058	19
FROM US ALL THOSE EVILS THAT WE MOST JUSTLY HAVE	059	23

EWES

WAS FOLLOWING THE EWES WITH THEIR YOUNG HE TCCK HIM,	439	21

EXALT

OF GOD, AND EXALT US TO EVERLASTING LIFE	086	11
OF YOU, IF A MAN EXALT HIMSELF, IF A MAN SMITE YOU ON	120	24
TO COMFORT US, AND EXALT US UNTO THE SAME PLACE	179	08
THAT HE MAY EXALT YOU IN DUE TIME	193	02
IS ONLY HOW TO PUT HIM OUT WHOM GOD WILL EXALT	414	05
NOT BE ABLE TO EXALT THEMSELVES	417	28
32 THAT THEY WOULD EXALT HIM ALSO IN THE CCNGREGATICN	478	10
13 HE SHALL EXALT THE HORN OF HIS PEOPLE	524	30

EXALTED

PRAISED AND EXALTED ABOVE ALL FOR EVER	011	17
PRAISED AND EXALTED ABOVE ALL FOR EVER	011	19
PRAISED AND EXALTED ABOVE ALL FOR EVER	011	21
PRAISED AND EXALTED ABOVE ALL FOR EVER	011	23
PRAISED AND EXALTED ABOVE ALL FOR EVER	011	26
PRAISED AND EXALTED ABOVE ALL FOR EVER	011	28
AND HATH EXALTED THE HUMBLE AND MEEK	026	23
AND THOU ART EXALTED AS HEAD ABOVE ALL	073	21
ALSO HATH HIGHLY EXALTED HIM, AND GIVEN HIM A NAME	105	26
ALSO HATH HIGHLY EXALTED HIM, AND GIVEN HIM A NAME	134	23
WHO HAST EXALTED THINE ONLY SON JESUS CHRIST	179	04
AND HE THAT HUMBLETH HIMSELF SHALL BE EXALTED	205	34
AND HE THAT HUMBLETH HIMSELF SHALL BE EXALTED	214	20
OF LOW DEGREE REJOICE IN THAT HE IS EXALTED	239	19
VALLEY SHALL BE EXALTED, AND EVERY MOUNTAIN AND HILL	242	22
I WILL BE EXALTED AMONG THE NATIONS, AND I WILL BE	327	14
AND I WILL BE EXALTED IN THE EARTH	327	15
EARTH BE NO MORE EXALTED AGAINST THEM	354	16
WHEN THEY ARE EXALTED, THE CHILDREN OF MEN ARE PUT TO	355	25
13 BE THOU EXALTED, LORD, IN THINE OWN STRENGTH	365	32
AND I WILL BE EXALTED IN THE EARTH	398	15
I WILL BE EXALTED AMONG THE NATIONS, AND I WILL BE	398	15
IS VERY HIGH EXALTED, DOTH DEFEND THE EARTH, AS IT	399	08
AND THE HORNS OF THE RIGHTEOUS SHALL BE EXALTED	432	22
I HAVE EXALTED ONE CHCSEN OUT OF THE PEOPLE	451	14
AND IN MY NAME SHALL HIS HORN BE EXALTED	451	24
MY HORN SHALL BE EXALTED LIKE THE HORN OF AN UNICCRN	456	19
THOU ART EXALTED FAR ABOVE ALL GODS	461	15
HORN SHALL BE EXALTED WITH HONOUR	484	03

EXALTETH

EVERY ONE THAT EXALTETH HIMSELF SHALL BE ABASED	205	32
FOR WHOSOEVER EXALTETH HIMSELF SHALL BE ABASED	214	19

EXAMINATION

FOR THEIR EXAMINATION, WHETHER THEY BE SUFFICIENTLY	R 273	19
AFTER EXAMINATION AND TRIAL, FINDING HIM	529	28
AFTER DUE EXAMINATION, WE FIND NOT TO THE CONTRARY,	536	24
YOUR PRIVATE EXAMINATION, AS IN THE EXHORTATION WHICH	539	24

EXAMINE

TO TRY AND EXAMINE THEMSELVES, BEFORE THEY PRESUME TO	085	28
SO TO SEARCH AND EXAMINE YOUR OWN CONSCIENCES, AND	087	10
TO EXAMINE YOUR LIVES AND CONVERSATIONS BY THE	087	16
LORD'S SUPPER TO EXAMINE THEMSELVES, WHETHER THEY	293	26
INSTRUCT OR EXAMINE THE YOUTH OF HIS PARISH	R 295	09
2 EXAMINE ME, O LORD, AND PROVE ME	370	33
PROVE ME, AND EXAMINE MY THOUGHTS	516	05
THE BISHOP SHALL EXAMINE EVERY ONE OF THOSE WHO ARE	R 532	23
WE WILL EXAMINE YOU IN CERTAIN ARTICLES, TO THE END	554	12
TO EXAMINE THEMSELVES, WHETHER THEY REPENT	582	22
INSTRUCT OR EXAMINE SO MANY CHILDREN OF HIS PARISH,	R 582	29

EXAMINED

BE RECEIVED AND EXAMINED BY EVERY TRUE MEMBER OF OUR	VI	36
HAVING EXAMINED HIM BEFORE YOU, HAVE FOUND NO	153	24
TRIED, EXAMINED, AND KNOWN TO HAVE SUCH	529	15
TRIED, EXAMINED, AND ADMITTED THEREUNTO,	529	22
AND ALSO EXAMINED THEM, AND THINK THEM SO TC	530	18
AND ALSO EXAMINED THEM, AND THINK THEM SO TO	536	19
SHALL BE EXAMINED AND ORDAINED, AS IS ABOVE	R 547	23
LIKEWISE BE EXAMINED AND ORDAINED, AS IS IN THIS	R 547	27

EXAMPLE

BY THE EXAMPLE OF THY FIRST MARTYR SAINT STEPHEN, WHO	099	30
HER A PUBLICK EXAMPLE, WAS MINDED TO PUT HER AWAY	104	31

EXAMPLE   CONTINUED

FOLLOW THE EXAMPLE OF HIS GREAT HUMILITY	134	08
BOTH FOLLOW THE EXAMPLE OF HIS PATIENCE, AND ALSC BE	134	10
GIVEN YOU AN EXAMPLE, THAT YE SHOULD DO AS I HAVE	156	17
LEAVING US AN EXAMPLE, THAT YE SHOULD FOLLOW HIS	172	11
AND AFTER HIS EXAMPLE CONSTANTLY SPEAK THE TRUTH,	242	12
WHOM, AFTER THE EXAMPLE OF THY HOLY APOSTLES, WE HAVE	298	17
SO TO FOLLOW THE EXAMPLE OF THEIR STEDFASTNESS IN THY	336	21
BY WORD AND GOOD EXAMPLE, THEY MAY FAITHFULLY SERVE	531	21
BY WORD AND GOOD EXAMPLE, THEY MAY FAITHFULLY SERVE	537	25
BY WORD AND GOOD EXAMPLE, THEY MAY FAITHFULLY SERVE	548	04
FOLLOWING THE EXAMPLE OF OUR SAVIOUR CHRIST, AND HIS	553	09
IN ALL THINGS AN EXAMPLE OF GOOD WORKS UNTO OTHERS,	555	10
A WHOLESOME EXAMPLE IN WORD, IN CONVERSATION,	559	10
MINISTRY AND EXAMPLE THY PEOPLE MAY ABIDE IN THY	562	12
FOLLOWING THE EXAMPLE OF THEIR SAVIOUR JESUS CHRIST	596	28
DOTH READ FOR EXAMPLE OF LIFE AND INSTRUCTION OF	604	02

EXAMPLES

TO DIRECT OUR LIVES AFTER THEIR GOOD EXAMPLES	048	20
THEIR GOOD EXAMPLES, THAT WITH THEM WE MAY BE	075	03
THINGS WERE OUR EXAMPLES, TO THE INTENT WE SHOULD NCT	201	13
THEIR TRIUMPHS, WE MAY PROFIT BY THEIR EXAMPLES	258	08
BY THE GOOD EXAMPLES OF THY SAINTS, AND ESPECIALLY OF	258	13
THE GOOD EXAMPLES OF THOSE WHO HAVE SERVED THEE HERE	268	17
FOR THE GOOD EXAMPLES OF ALL THOSE THY SERVANTS,	334	23
WHOLESOME EXAMPLES OF THE FLOCK OF CHRIST	533	28
AND GODLY EXAMPLES AND PATTERNS FOR THE PEOPLE TC	541	23
WHOLESOME EXAMPLES AND PATTERNS TO THE FLOCK OF	543	02

EXCEED

WHICH EXCEED ALL THAT WE CAN DESIRE	197	07
SHALL EXCEED THE RIGHTEOUSNESS OF THE SCRIBES ANC	197	29
OF RIGHTEOUSNFSS EXCEED IN GLORY	206	24

EXCEEDING

REMEMBER THE EXCEEDING GREAT LOVE OF OUR MASTER, AND	086	12
WISE MEN, WAS EXCEEDING WROTH, AND SENT FORTH, AND	103	25
REJOICED WITH EXCEEDING GREAT JOY	109	19
HIM UP INTO AN EXCEEDING HIGH MOUNTAIN, AND SHEWETH	127	05
MY SOUL IS EXCEEDING SORROWFUL UNTO DEATH	141	31
HE WAS EXCEEDING GLAD	153	11
IS ABLE TO DO EXCEEDING ABUNDANTLY ABOVE ALL THAT WE	212	21
AND BE EXCEEDING GLAD	257	33
EXCEEDING GLAD SHALL HE BE OF THY SALVATION	365	05
ART BECOME EXCEEDING GLORIOUS	467	25
COMMANDMENT IS EXCEEDING BROAD	496	18
ARE EXCEEDING RIGHTEOUS AND TRUE	499	16

EXCEEDINGLY

OUT THE MORE EXCEEDINGLY, CRUCIFY HIM	145	26
HIS PEOPLE EXCEEDINGLY, *	471	20
SO THAT THEY MULTIPLY EXCEEDINGLY	478	22
HAVE HAD ME EXCEEDINGLY IN DERISION	493	12
ANC LOVED THEM EXCEEDINGLY	501	16

EXCEL

OF HIS, YE THAT EXCEL IN STRENGTH	029	12
OF HIS, YE THAT EXCEL IN STRENGTH	312	28
AND UPON SUCH AS EXCEL IN VIRTUE	357	26
OF HIS, YE THAT EXCEL IN STRENGTH	467	15

EXCELLENCY

EVEN THE EXCELLENCY OF JACOB, WHOM HE LOVED	398	27
OF SO GREAT EXCELLENCY, AND OF SO GREAT DIFFICULTY,	540	24
CLEARNESS AND EXCELLENCY OF THY HOLY WORD	573	27

EXCELLENT

A MORE EXCELLENT NAME THAN THEY	096	31
THAT MOST EXCELLENT GIFT OF CHARITY, THE VERY BCND CF	122	16
THAT YE MAY APPROVE THINGS THAT ARE EXCELLENT	221	04
PETER MANY EXCELLENT GIFTS, AND COMMANDEDST HIM	244	23
HIM FROM THE EXCELLENT GLORY, THIS IS MY BELOVED SCN,	248	18
HOW EXCELLENT IS THY NAME IN ALL THE WORLD	350	31
HOW EXCELLENT IS THY NAME IN ALL THE WORLD	351	17
HOW EXCELLENT IS THY MERCY, O GOD	384	08
BRING IT TO AN EXCELLENT WORK	430	15
2 VERY EXCELLENT THINGS ARE SPOKEN OF THEE, *	448	16
5 WHO BY HIS EXCELLENT WISDOM MADE THE HEAVENS	511	24
WONDERFUL AND EXCELLENT FOR ME	514	29
NAME ONLY IS EXCELLENT, AND HIS PRAISE ABOVE HEAVEN	524	28
TO HIS EXCELLENT GREATNESS	525	25
APOSTLES MANY EXCELLENT GIFTS, AND DIDST CHARGE THEM	549	08
ENDUED WITH SO EXCELLENT A BENEFIT OF GOD, BE CALLED	606	11

EXCELSIS

THE GLORIA IN EXCELSIS, AS FOLLOWETH	R 025	20
THE GLORIA IN EXCELSIS, ALL STANDING, OR SOME PRCPER	R 083	32

EXCEPT

EXCEPT ON THOSE DAYS FOR WHICH OTHER CANTICLES ARE	R 008	09
AND EXCEPT ALSO, THAT PSALM 95 MAY BE USED IN THIS	R 008	10
FOR THE DAY, EXCEPT WHEN THE COMMUNION SERVICE IS	R 017	02
THEY PREACH, FXCEPT THEY BE SENT	073	09
THE NEXT SUNDAY, EXCEPT UPON THE FEAST OF ST	R 125	24
ALL AGAINST ME, EXCEPT IT WERE GIVEN THEE FROM ABOVE	159	17

EXCEPT   CONTINUED

THE NEXT SUNDAY, EXCEPT UPON THE FEAST OF ST   R 178 31
THAT THOU DOEST, EXCEPT GOD BE WITH HIM   188 04
I SAY UNTO THEE, EXCEPT A MAN BE BORN AGAIN, HE   188 05
I SAY UNTO THEE, EXCEPT HE BE BORN OF WATER AND OF   188 10
HIS DISCIPLES, EXCEPT YOUR RIGHTEOUSNESS SHALL EXCEED   197 28
JESUS UNTO HIM, EXCEPT YE SEE SIGNS AND WONDERS, YE   219 32
THEY PREACH, EXCEPT THEY BE SENT   227 08
SAID UNTO THEM, EXCEPT I SHALL SEE IN HIS HANDS THE   228 28
FRUIT OF ITSELF, EXCEPT IT ABIDE IN THE VINE   238 11
NO MORE CAN YE, EXCEPT YE ABIDE IN ME   238 11
I SAY UNTO YOU, EXCEPT YE BE CONVERTED, AND BECOME AS   252 25
WARN THEM THAT, EXCEPT FOR URGENT CAUSE, THEY SEEK   R 273 07
KINGDOM OF GOD, EXCEPT HE BE REGENERATE AND BORN ANEW   273 30
THAT THOU DOEST, EXCEPT GOD BE WITH HIM   275 09
I SAY UNTO THEE, EXCEPT A MAN BE BORN AGAIN, HE   275 10
I SAY UNTO THEE, EXCEPT A MAN BE BORN OF WATER AND OF   275 15
MAY BE OMITTED EXCEPT AT THE END OF THE WHOLE PORTION   R 324 18
IS NOT QUICKENED, EXCEPT IT DIE   329 07
I SAY UNTO YOU, EXCEPT YE BE CONVERTED, AND BECOME AS   339 24
ANY STRENGTH, EXCEPT OUR GOD   361 32
EXCEPT THE LORD BUILD THE HOUSE, *   505 22
2 EXCEPT THE LORD KEEP THE CITY, *   505 24
ANY OF THEM, EXCEPT HE WERE FIRST CALLED, TRIED,   529 15
SAID FUNCTIONS, EXCEPT HE BE CALLED, TRIED, EXAMINED,   529 21
OR BISHOP, EXCEPT HE BE OF THE AGE WHICH THE CANON IN   529 24
OF A WHOLE YEAR, (EXCEPT FOR REASONABLE CAUSES IT   R 535 20
CHANCEL OR CHOIR, EXCEPT THE BISHOP, OR THE PRIEST   R 570 05
SIN ONLY EXCEPT, FROM WHICH HE WAS CLEARLY   605 32

EXCEPTED

THAT HE IS EXCEPTED, WHICH DID PUT ALL THINGS UNDER   328 33

EXCESS

AND BE NOT DRUNK WITH WINE, WHEREIN IS EXCESS   217 27

EXCITING

AND THE EXCITING OF PIETY AND DEVOTION IN THE WORSHIP   V 36

EXCOMMUNICATED

AND EXCOMMUNICATED, OUGHT TO BE TAKEN OF THE WHOLE   609 27

EXCUSE

TO GOD, WILL YE EXCUSE YOURSELVES, AND SAY YE ARE NOT   088 33
THEY ALL WITH ONE CONSENT BEGAN TO MAKE EXCUSE   192 06

EXCUSED

WERE NOT SO EXCUSED, BUT COUNTED UNWORTHY OF THE   089 05
I PRAY THEE HAVE ME EXCUSED   192 08
I PRAY THEE HAVE ME EXCUSED   192 10

EXCUSES

BUT SUCH EXCUSES ARE NOT SO EASILY ACCEPTED AND   088 28
SUCH FEIGNED EXCUSES WILL AVAIL BEFORE GOD   089 02

EXECUTE

THEM GRACE TO EXECUTE JUSTICE, AND TO MAINTAIN TRUTH   055 27
UNDERSTANDING TO EXECUTE JUSTICE, AND TO MAINTAIN   VI 20
A REVENGER TO EXECUTE WRATH UPON HIM THAT DOETH EVIL   114 21
AND SHALL EXECUTE JUDGMENT AND JUSTICE IN THE EARTH   225 11
HE DOTH EXECUTE THE JUDGMENT OF THE FATHERLESS AND   263 25
LORD IS KNOWN TO EXECUTE JUDGMENT   352 24
9 TO EXECUTE JUDGMENT UPON THEM   525 19
MIGHT PRESUME TO EXECUTE ANY OF THEM, EXCEPT HE WERE   529 15
OR SUFFERED TO EXECUTE ANY OF THE SAID FUNCTIONS,   529 21
THEY MAY DULY EXECUTE THEIR OFFICE, TO THE EDIFYING   531 06
AUTHORITY TO EXECUTE THE OFFICE OF A DEACON IN THE   534 05
AUTHORITY TO EXECUTE THE OFFICE OF A PRIEST IN THE   546 17
THAT HE MAY DULY EXECUTE THE OFFICE WHEREUNTO HE IS   553 19
THEY MAY DULY EXECUTE THEIR OFFICE TO THE EDIFYING OF   560 28
THAT HE MAY DULY EXECUTE THE OFFICE WHEREUNTO HE IS   561 03
AND SENT TO EXECUTE THE SAME   607 21

EXECUTED

THOU HAST EXECUTED JUDGMENT AND RIGHTEOUSNESS IN   462 23

EXECUTETH

6 THE LORD EXECUTETH RIGHTEOUSNESS AND JUDGMENT *   466 17

EXECUTING

IN EXECUTING WHEREOF IF HE BE FOUND FAITHFUL AND   R 535 23

EXERCISE

OF THE GENTILES EXERCISE LORDSHIP OVER THEM   149 20
AND THEY THAT EXERCISE AUTHORITY UPON THEM ARE CALLED   149 21
OF THE GENTILES EXERCISE DOMINION OVER THEM, AND THEY   247 21
THAT ARE GREAT EXERCISE AUTHORITY UPON THEM   247 22
OF THE GENTILES EXERCISE LORDSHIP OVER THEM   250 05
AND THEY THAT EXERCISE AUTHORITY UPON THEM ARE CALLED   250 06
HIS LAW WILL HE EXERCISE HIMSELF DAY AND NIGHT   345 11
2 I DO NOT EXERCISE MYSELF IN GREAT MATTERS *   507 25
I EXERCISE MYSELF IN THE WORKS OF THY HANDS   518 33
TO EXERCISE THEIR MINISTRY DULY, TO THE HONOUR OF   530 15

EXERCISE   CONTINUED

TO EXERCISE THEIR MINISTRY DULY, TO THE HONOUR OF   536 16
THEY MAY DULY EXERCISE THEIR OFFICE, TO THE EDIFYING   537 12
THEN FAITHFULLY EXERCISE YOURSELF IN THE HOLY   554 29
AND DILIGENTLY EXERCISE SUCH DISCIPLINE AS BY THE   555 16

EXERCISED

RIGHTEOUS IS EXERCISED IN WISDOM, *   386 26

EXERCISING

AND IN EXERCISING THE DISCIPLINE OF THE CHURCH   571 27

EXHORT

MY DUTY IS TO EXHORT YOU, IN THE MEAN SEASON TO   087 08
I EXHORT YOU, AS YE LOVE YOUR OWN SALVATION,   089 08
THINGS SPEAK, AND EXHORT, AND REBUKE WITH ALL   098 25
AND EXHORT YOU BY THE LORD JESUS, THAT AS   127 23
EXHORT THEIR PARISHIONERS TO THE OFTEN   R 321 07
AND NOW AGAIN WE EXHORT YOU, IN THE NAME OF OUR LORD   539 29
THEM TO TEACH AND EXHORT WITH WHOLESOME DOCTRINE,   554 32

EXHORTATION

THE PRIEST MAY SAY THIS EXHORTATION   R 085 22
THAT THE EXHORTATION SHALL BE SAID ON THE FIRST   R 085 23
READ THIS EXHORTATION FOLLOWING   R 086 26
HE MAY USE THIS EXHORTATION   R 088 11
OR HE THAT EXHORTETH, ON EXHORTATION   111 19
A SERMON, OR EXHORTATION, DECLARING THE DUTY AND   R 530 04
A SERMON, OR EXHORTATION, DECLARING THE DUTY AND   R 536 04
AS IN THE EXHORTATION WHICH WAS NOW MADE TO YOU, AND   539 25
DOCTRINE AND EXHORTATION TAKEN OUT OF THE HOLY   540 35
EXHORTATION, AND DOCTRINE   558 21

EXHORTATIONS

AND EXHORTATIONS, AS WELL TO THE SICK AS TO THE   542 22

EXHORTED

WAS GLAD, AND EXHORTED THEM ALL, THAT WITH PURPOSE OF   241 06
THEY MAY BE EXHORTED TO PREPARE THEMSELVES, WITH   R 273 20

EXHORTETH

HOW SAINT PAUL EXHORTETH ALL PERSONS DILIGENTLY TO   085 28
OR HE THAT EXHORTETH, ON EXHORTATION   111 19

EXHORTING

BUT EXHORTING ONE ANOTHER   158 27
EXHORTING HIM TO FORGIVE, FROM THE BOTTOM OF HIS   R 313 20

EXIGENCY

TO THE VARIOUS EXIGENCY OF TIMES AND OCCASIONS   V 09
TO THE VARIOUS EXIGENCY OF TIMES AND OCCASIONS, SUCH   V 17

EXODUS

CHAPTER OF EXODUS, SAYING, I AM THE LORD THY GOD, WHO   578 23

EXPECTATION

THE EARNEST EXPECTATION OF THE CREATURE WAITETH FOR   194 13
FROM ALL THE EXPECTATION OF THE PEOPLE OF THE JEWS   245 28
THE EARNEST EXPECTATION OF THE CREATURE WAITETH FOR   330 29

EXPECTING

HENCEFORTH EXPECTING TILL HIS ENEMIES BE MADE HIS   158 07

EXPEDIENCY

NECESSITY AND EXPEDIENCY OF OCCASIONAL ALTERATIONS   V 22

EXPEDIENT

TIME TO TIME, SEEM EITHER NECESSARY OR EXPEDIENT   V 20
AS MAY BE MOST EXPEDIENT FOR THEM   020 08
AS MAY BE MOST EXPEDIENT FOR THEM   034 08
ALTERATIONS WOULD IN TIME BE FOUND EXPEDIENT   VI 03
AMENDMENTS THEREIN AS MIGHT BE DEEMED EXPEDIENT   VI 27
IT IS EXPEDIENT FOR YOU THAT I GO AWAY   175 10
IT IS EXPEDIENT THAT EVERY ADULT, THUS BAPTIZED,   R 281 13
IT IS EXPEDIENT THAT A CHILD OR PERSON SO BAPTIZED   R 281 32
TO THEE MOST EXPEDIENT FOR HIM   314 08
RENDER IT EXPEDIENT TO SHORTEN THE SERVICE, THE   R 323 04
SOMETIMES BE EXPEDIENT TO SAY UNDER SHELTER OF THE   R 336 30
SEE TO BE MOST EXPEDIENT FOR THEM   566 23

EXPERT

PERFECT AND WELL EXPERT IN THE THINGS APPERTAINING TO R 535 22

EXPLICATION

TO BE AN EXPLICATION OF CHRISTIAN DOCTRINE,   R 610 24

EXPOSED

AND FROM EVERY EVIL TO WHICH HE MAY BE EXPOSED   046 14

EXPOUND

WHICH SOME DO EXPOUND THE WISDOM, SOME SENSUALITY,   604 37
MAY IT SO EXPOUND ONE PLACE OF SCRIPTURE, THAT IT BE   607 05

EXPOUNDED

HE EXPOUNDED UNTO THEM IN ALL THE   167 32

EXPRESS

AND EVER EXPRESS HIS THANKFULNESS BY A HOLY   053 26
AND THE EXPRESS IMAGE OF HIS PERSON, AND   096 26
THEY SHOULD BE MORE THAN I AM ABLE TO EXPRESS   390 26
2 WHO CAN EXPRESS THE NOBLE ACTS OF THE LORD,   473 02
EITHER BY THE EXPRESS COMMAND OF GOD, OR BY THE   564 12

EXPRESSED

LARGELY IS EXPRESSED IN THE HOMILY OF JUSTIFICATION   605 09

EXPRESSION

THOUGHT AND EXPRESSION SUITABLE TO THE CLEARNESS AND   573 27

EXPRESSLY

WHICH WE HAVE EXPRESSLY DECLARED UNTO US IN THE WORD   606 29

EXSURGAT

BE SAID OR SUNG EXSURGAT DEUS, PSALM LXVIII   R 571 30

EXTEND

EXTEND THY ACCUSTOMED GOODNESS TO THIS THY SERVANT   309 28

EXTENDETH

MAGISTRATE EXTENDETH TO ALL MEN, AS WELL CLERGY AS   610 38

EXTINCT

AND ARE EXTINCT EVEN AS THE FIRE AMONG THE   488 23

EXTORTIONER

10 LET THE EXTORTIONER CONSUME ALL THAT HE HATH   480 21

EXTORTIONERS

MEN ARE, EXTORTIONERS, UNJUST, ADULTERERS, OR EVEN AS 205 26

EXTREME

CONSIDERATION OF EXTREME SICKNESS, NECESSITY MAY   R 281 17
IN CASES OF EXTREME SICKNESS, OR ANY IMMINENT   R 281 27
WILT BE EXTREME TO MARK WHAT IS DONE AMISS, *   328 07
WILT BE EXTREME TO MARK WHAT IS DONE AMISS, *   507 12
AND EXTREME UNCTION, ARE NOT TO BE COUNTED   607 39

EXTREMITY

BY REASON OF EXTREMITY OF SICKNESS, OR FOR WANT OF   R 323 23

EYE

IS THINE EYE EVIL, BECAUSE I AM GOOD   120 11
IS IN THY BROTHER'S EYE, BUT PERCEIVEST NOT THE BEAM   195 06
PERCEIVEST NOT THE BEAM THAT IS IN THINE OWN EYE   195 07
THAT IS IN THINE EYE, WHEN THOU THYSELF BEHOLDEST NOT 195 09
BEHOLDEST NOT THE BEAM THAT IS IN THINE OWN EYE   195 10
OUT OF THINE OWN EYE, AND THEN SHALT THOU SEE CLEARLY 195 11
TO PULL OUT THE MOTE THAT IS IN THY BROTHER'S EYE   195 12
AND IF THINE EYE OFFEND THEE, PLUCK IT OUT, AND CAST   253 07
INTO LIFE WITH ONE EYE, RATHER THAN HAVING TWO EYES   253 08
OPEN THINE EYE OF MERCY UPON THIS THY SERVANT,   313 33
THE TWINKLING OF AN EYE, AT THE LAST TRUMP   330 03
8 KEEP ME AS THE APPLE OF AN EYE   359 02
23 FOR I HAVE AN EYE UNTO ALL HIS LAWS, *   361 11
THE TWINKLING OF AN EYE, AND IN HIS PLEASURE IS LIFE   374 32
AND MINE EYE IS CONSUMED FOR VERY HEAVINESS   376 09
AND I WILL GUIDE THEE WITH MINE EYE   378 09
17 BEHOLD, THE EYE OF THE LORD IS UPON THEM THAT FEAR 379 24
5 THEY HAD AN EYE UNTO HIM, AND WERE LIGHTENED   380 11
AND MINE EYE HATH SEEN HIS DESIRE UPON MINE ENEMIES   406 17
10 MINE EYE ALSO SHALL SEE HIS LUST OF MINE ENEMIES,   456 21
OR HE THAT MADE THE EYE, SHALL HE NOT SEE   458 05

EYELIDS

AND HIS EYELIDS TRY THE CHILDREN OF MEN   354 28
NOR MINE EYELIDS TO SLUMBER   508 10

EYES

FOR MINE EYES HAVE SEEN *   028 11
UPON HIM WITH THE EYES OF THY MERCY   045 15
HAVE SEEN WITH OUR EYES, WHICH WE HAVE LOOKED UPON,   101 13
THEN LIFTED UP HIS EYES, AND SAW A GREAT COMPANY COME 131 26
(FOR THEIR EYES WERE HEAVY,) NEITHER WIST THEY   142 09
WE PRAY THEE, THE EYES OF OUR FAITH, THAT WE MAY   166 08
BUT THEIR EYES WERE HOLDEN THAT THEY SHOULD NOT KNOW   167 08
AND THEIR EYES WERE OPENED, AND THEY KNEW HIM   168 07
CREATURES FULL OF EYES BEFORE AND BEHIND   187 17
THEY WERE FULL OF EYES WITHIN   187 21

EYES   CONTINUED

HELL HE LIFT UP HIS EYES, BEING IN TORMENTS, AND   190 11
FOR THE EYES OF THE LORD ARE OVER THE RIGHTEOUS, AND   195 27
BUT NOW THEY ARE HID FROM THINE EYES   204 09
UP SO MUCH AS HIS EYES UNTO HEAVEN, BUT SMOTE UPCN   205 29
BLESSED ARE THE EYES WHICH SEE THE THINGS THAT YE   208 07
THEN LIFTED UP HIS EYES, AND SAW A GREAT COMPANY COME 225 22
AND WHEN HIS EYES WERE OPENED, HE SAW NO MAN   230 10
THERE FELL FROM HIS EYES AS IT HAD BEEN SCALES   230 34
FOR MINE EYES HAVE SEEN THY SALVATION, WHICH THOU   233 06
THAN HAVING TWO EYES TO BE CAST INTO HELL-FIRE   253 09
AND GOD SHALL WIPE AWAY ALL TEARS FROM THEIR EYES   257 16
AND THE EYES OF ALL THEM THAT WERE IN THE SYNAGOGUE   261 22
WHICH THINE EYES HAVE SEEN   263 32
UPON HIM WITH THE EYES OF THY MERCY, GIVE HIM COMFORT 309 05
THOU HOLDEST MINE EYES WAKING   311 06
AND MINE EYES SHALL BEHOLD, AND NOT AS A   324 12
I WILL LIFT UP MINE EYES UNTO THE HILLS   327 19
I WILL LIFT UP MINE EYES UNTO THE HILLS   339 03
AND GOD SHALL WIPE AWAY ALL TEARS FROM THEIR EYES   341 27
HIS EYES ARE SET AGAINST THE POOR   353 22
5 HIS EYES CONSIDER THE POOR, *   354 28
LIGHTEN MINE EYES, THAT I SLEEP NOT IN DEATH   356 03
IS LOWLY IN HIS OWN EYES, *   357 14
AND LET THINE EYES LOOK UPON THE THING THAT IS EQUAL   358 20
THE LORD IS PURE, AND GIVETH LIGHT UNTO THE EYES   363 32
14 MINE EYES ARE EVER LOOKING UNTO THE LORD   370 14
FOR THY LOVING-KINDNESS IS EVER BEFORE MINE EYES   371 02
I AM CAST OUT OF THE SIGHT OF THINE EYES   377 12
15 THE EYES OF THE LORD ARE OVER THE RIGHTEOUS,   380 30
WINK WITH THEIR EYES, THAT HATE ME WITHOUT A CAUSE   382 35
WE SAW IT WITH OUR EYES   383 06
THAT THERE IS NO FEAR OF GOD BEFORE HIS EYES   383 27
THE LIGHT OF MINE EYES IS GONE FROM ME   388 11
GOD BEFORE THEIR EYES, SEEK AFTER MY SOUL   406 08
HIS EYES BEHOLD THE NATIONS   417 26
24 LET THINE EYES BE BLINDED, THAT THEY SEE NOT   423 21
7 THEIR EYES SWELL WITH FATNESS, *   428 22
4 THOU HOLDEST MINE EYES WAKING   433 23
MY SOUL, AND HAVE NOT SET THEE BEFORE THEIR EYES   448 03
8 YEA, WITH THINE EYES SHALT THOU BEHOLD, *   455 11
8 MINE EYES LOOK UPON SUCH AS ARE FAITHFUL IN THE   463 30
EYES HAVE THEY, AND SEE NOT   485 20
MINE EYES FROM TEARS, AND MY FEET FROM FALLING   487 05
AND IT IS MARVELLOUS IN OUR EYES   489 15
18 OPEN THOU MINE EYES   491 02
37 O TURN AWAY MINE EYES, LEST THEY BEHOLD VANITY   492 13
82 MINE EYES LONG SORE FOR THY WORD   495 21
123 MINE EYES ARE WASTED AWAY WITH LOOKING FOR THY   498 15
136 MINE EYES GUSH OUT WITH WATER, *   499 10
148 MINE EYES PREVENT THE NIGHT WATCHES   500 06
I WILL LIFT UP MINE EYES UNTO THE HILLS   502 22
THEE LIFT I UP MINE EYES, *   503 27
BEHOLD, EVEN AS THE EYES OF SERVANTS LOOK UNTO THE   503 29
AND AS THE EYES OF A MAIDEN UNTO THE HAND OF   503 30
EVEN SO OUR EYES WAIT UPON THE LORD OUR GOD, UNTIL HE 503 31
NOT SUFFER MINE EYES TO SLEEP, NOR MINE EYELIDS TO   508 10
EYES HAVE THEY, BUT THEY SEE NOT   511 02
15 THINE EYES DID SEE MY SUBSTANCE, YET BEING   515 20
9 BUT MINE EYES LOOK UNTO THEE, O LORD GOD   517 28
15 THE EYES OF ALL WAIT UPON THEE, O LORD   521 22
AND GOD SHALL WIPE AWAY ALL TEARS FROM THEIR EYES   567 18
WHO ART OF PURER EYES THAN TO BEHOLD INIQUITY, AND   589 26
HAVING THE EYES OF THE MIND OPENED TO BEHOLD   594 24
BESEECH THEE, OUR EYES TO BEHOLD THY GRACIOUS HAND IN 596 18
BEFORE THEIR EYES THE SENTENCE OF GOD'S   606 23

EYESIGHT

UNTO THE CLEANNESS OF MY HANDS IN HIS EYESIGHT   361 17

EYEWITNESSES

BUT WERE EYEWITNESSES OF HIS MAJESTY   248 16

FABLES

CUNNINGLY DEVISED FABLES, WHEN WE MADE KNOWN UNTC YOU 248 14
WERE BLASPHEMOUS FABLES, AND DANGEROUS DECEITS   609 19

FACE

THEM BEFORE THE FACE OF ALMIGHTY GOD OUR HEAVENLY   005 32
SHALT GO BEFORE THE FACE OF THE LORD TO PREPARE HIS   014 25
THEM BEFORE THE FACE OF ALMIGHTY GOD OUR HEAVENLY   023 07
BEFORE THE FACE OF ALL PEOPLE   028 12
FOR TO DWELL ON THE FACE OF THE WHOLE EARTH, AND   038 06
IT MAY RENEW THE FACE OF THE EARTH   040 09
AGAINST THE FACE OF THEIR ENEMIES   052 08
TURN THY FACE FROM MY SINS, *   060 28
THE LORD MAKE HIS FACE TO SHINE UPON US, AND BE   063 16
OF THY GLORY IN THE FACE OF THY SON JESUS CHRIST OUR   078 02
BEFORE THY FACE, WHICH SHALL PREPARE THY WAY BEFORE   094 32
BEFORE THY FACE, WHICH SHALL PREPARE THY WAY BEFORE   112 05
MAN EXALT HIMSELF, IF A MAN SMITE YOU ON THE FACE   120 25
BUT THEN FACE TO FACE   123 12
BUT THEN FACE TO FACE   123 12
ANOINT THINE HEAD, AND WASH THY FACE   125 13
AND TO COVER HIS FACE, AND TO BUFFET HIM, AND TO SAY   143 20
AND HID NOT HIS FACE FROM SHAME   144 07
I HID NOT MY FACE FROM SHAME AND SPITTING   144 15
HAVE I SET MY FACE LIKE A FLINT, AND I KNOW THAT I   144 17
STRUCK HIM ON THE FACE, AND ASKED HIM, SAYING,   151 25
HIS NATURAL FACE IN A GLASS   176 08
AND THE THIRD HAD A FACE AS A MAN, AND THE FOURTH WAS 187 19

FACE   CONTINUED

BUT THE FACE OF THE LORD IS AGAINST THEM THAT DO   195 29
BEHOLD THE FACE OF MOSES FOR THE GLORY OF HIS   206 20
FELL DOWN ON HIS FACE AT HIS FEET, GIVING HIM THANKS   210 09
PREPARED BEFORE THE FACE OF ALL PEOPLE   233 08
SHALT GO BEFORE THE FACE OF THE LORD TO PREPARE HIS   244 11
GLORY OF GOD IN THE FACE OF JESUS CHRIST   251 09
ALWAYS BEHOLD THE FACE OF MY FATHER WHICH IS IN   253 12
AND TWO BEFORE HIS FACE INTO EVERY CITY AND PLACE,   254 12
HIS NATURAL FACE IN A GLASS   265 31
OF GOD, AND IN THE FACE OF THIS COMPANY, TO JOIN   300 09
FROM THE FACE OF HER ENEMY   306 20
FROM THE FACE OF HIS ENEMY   308 30
THE LORD MAKE HIS FACE TO SHINE UPON THEE, AND BE   314 28
MY HEART HATH TALKED OF THEE, SEEK YE MY FACE   326 22
THY FACE, LORD, WILL I SEEK   326 23
O HIDE NOT THOU THY FACE FROM ME, *   326 24
THE LORD MAKE HIS FACE TO SHINE UPON YOU, AND BE   332 12
ALWAYS BEHOLD THE FACE OF MY FATHER WHICH IS IN   339 31
WHOSE FACE THE ANGELS OF THY LITTLE ONES DO   340 24
THE LORD MAKE HIS FACE TO SHINE UPON HIM AND BE   341 16
AWAY FROM THE FACE OF THE EARTH   345 18
MAKE THY WAY PLAIN BEFORE MY FACE   348 17
AND HIDEST THY FACE IN THE NEEDFUL TIME OF TROUBLE   353 04
HE HIDETH AWAY HIS FACE, AND HE WILL NEVER SEE IT   353 31
WILT THOU HIDE THY FACE FROM ME   355 29
READY AGAINST THE FACE OF THEM   365 30
HE HATH NOT HID HIS FACE FROM HIM   367 21
THEM THAT SEEK THY FACE, O GOD OF JACOB   369 08
9 MY HEART HATH TALKED OF THEE, SEEK YE MY FACE   372 14
THY FACE, LORD, WILL I SEEK   372 15
O HIDE NOT THOU THY FACE FROM ME, *   372 16
THOU DIDST TURN THY FACE FROM ME, *   375 07
SET ME BEFORE THY FACE FOR EVER   392 24
AND THE SHAME OF MY FACE HATH COVERED ME   395 25
HIDEST THOU THY FACE, *   396 08
9 TURN THY FACE FROM MY SINS, *   403 27
SHAME HATH COVERED MY FACE   422 17
18 AND HIDE NOT THY FACE FROM THY SERVANT   423 07
AND LOOK UPON THE FACE OF THINE ANOINTED   445 29
AND HIDEST THOU THY FACE FROM ME   449 25
MERCY AND TRUTH SHALL GO BEFORE THY FACE   451 03
HIS FOES BEFORE HIS FACE, *   451 21
2 HIDE NOT THY FACE FROM ME IN THE TIME OF MY   464 12
THOU HIDEST THY FACE, THEY ARE TROUBLED   469 18
SHALT RENEW THE FACE OF THE EARTH   469 22
SEEK HIS FACE EVERMORE   470 11
TURN NOT AWAY THE FACE OF THINE ANOINTED   508 24
HIDE NOT THY FACE FROM ME, LEST I BE LIKE UNTO THEM   519 05
OTHER DAY, IN THE FACE OF THE CHURCH, ADMIT HIM A   529 30
OTHER DAY, IN THE FACE OF THE CHURCH, IN SUCH MANNER R 535 26
CHEER OUR SOILED FACE WITH THE ABUNDANCE OF THY   544 06
SHALL SEE MY FACE NO MORE   550 23
CHEER OUR SOILED FACE WITH THE ABUNDANCE OF THY   556 14
THEM THAT SEEK THY FACE, O JACOB   563 23
UP, AND TURNING HIS FACE TOWARDS THE CONGREGATICN,   R 565 16
THE LORD MAKE HIS FACE TO SHINE UPON US, AND BE   593 18

FACES

DISFIGURE THEIR FACES, THAT THEY MAY APPEAR UNTC MEN   125 10
THRONE ON THEIR FACES, AND WORSHIPPED GOD, SAYING,   256 31
AND THEIR FACES WERE NOT ASHAMED   380 12
16 MAKE THEIR FACES ASHAMED, O LORD, *   445 04

FACULTIES

WITH ALL THEIR POWERS AND FACULTIES   573 16
ENDOWMENTS AND FACULTIES OF SOUL AND BODY   591 09

FADE

SHALL THE RICH MAN FADE AWAY IN HIS WAYS   239 24
AND FADE AWAY SUDDENLY LIKE THE GRASS   325 23
AND FADE AWAY SUDDENLY LIKE THE GRASS   453 28

FADETH

OF GLORY THAT FADETH NOT AWAY   079 27
THE GRASS WITHERETH, THE FLOWER FADETH   242 30
THE GRASS WITHERETH, THE FLOWER FADETH   242 32

FAIL

OF TROUBLE, SUFFER NOT OUR TRUST IN THEE TO FAIL   036 23
WHOSE COMPASSIONS FAIL NOT, AND WHOSE LOVING-KINDNESS   038 14
AND THY YEARS SHALL NOT FAIL   097 18
BUT WHETHER THERE BE PROPHECIES, THEY SHALL FAIL   123 05
THAT THY FAITH FAIL NOT   149 33
THIS LIFE, THAT WE FAIL NOT FINALLY TO ATTAIN THY   207 15
THE STRANGERS SHALL FAIL, *   362 30
NOR SUFFER MY TRUTH TO FAIL   452 08
THAT I WILL NOT FAIL DAVID   452 11
THE LORD WILL NOT FAIL HIS PEOPLE   458 14
THOU ART THE SAME, AND THY YEARS SHALL NOT FAIL   466 04

FAILED

HAST NEVER FAILED THEM THAT SEEK THEE   352 09
MY STRENGTH HATH FAILED ME, *   388 10
AND MY HEART HATH FAILED ME   391 13
IT HAD NOT FAILED, BUT MY SOUL HAD BEEN PUT TO   458 20

FAILEST

WHO NEVER FAILEST TO HELP AND GOVERN THOSE WHOM   191 04

FAILETH

CHARITY NEVER FAILETH   123 04
12 MY STRENGTH FAILETH ME, BECAUSE OF MINE INIQUITY,   376 13
MY SIGHT FAILETH ME FOR WAITING SO LONG UPON MY GOD   422 06
WHEN MY STRENGTH FAILETH ME   425 24
26 MY FLESH AND MY HEART FAILETH   429 28
9 MY SIGHT FAILETH FOR VERY TROUBLE   449 14

FAILING

MEN'S HEARTS FAILING THEM FOR FEAR, AND FOR LOOKING   093 08

FAILINGS

THE SINS AND FAILINGS OF THAT DAY   R 589 35

FAIN

AND HE WOULD FAIN HAVE FILLED HIS BELLY WITH THE   202 08
AND WOULD FAIN SEE GOOD DAYS   380 25

FAINT

THEY WILL FAINT BY THE WAY   199 13
I DESIRE THAT YE FAINT NOT AT MY TRIBULATIONS FOR   212 10
RECEIVED MERCY, WE FAINT NOT   250 28
CAST DOWN AND FAINT OF HEART AMIDST THE SORROWS AND   316 19
OF THE LORD, NOR FAINT WHEN THOU ART REBUKED OF HIM   321 29
FOR MY SPIRIT WAXETH FAINT   519 05

FAINTED

UTTERLY HAVE FAINTED, *   326 28
UTTERLY HAVE FAINTED, *   372 27
THEIR SOUL FAINTED IN THEM   476 14
BECAUSE THEY FAINTED, AND WERE SCATTERED ABROAD AS   538 15

FAIR

HAVE UPON IT A FAIR WHITE LINEN CLOTH   R 067 05
THE SAME WITH A FAIR LINEN CLOTH   R 083 13
AS DESIRE TO MAKE A FAIR SHEW IN THE FLESH, THEY   210 24
TO BEHOLD THE FAIR BEAUTY OF THE LORD, AND TO   326 10
FALLEN UNTO ME IN A FAIR GROUND   358 02
TO BEHOLD THE FAIR BEAUTY OF THE LORD, AND TO   372 02
HILL OF SION IS A FAIR PLACE, AND THE JOY OF THE   399 12

FAIRER

2 THOU ART FAIRER THAN THE CHILDREN OF MEN   396 18

FAIRLY

OR WHICH IS NOT FAIRLY DEFENSIBLE, IF ALLOWED SUCH   V 42

FAIRNESS

FAIRNESS, AND GOOD-WILL   600 02

FAITH

SUBSTANCE OF THE FAITH BE KEPT ENTIRE   V 04
AND HOLD THE FAITH IN UNITY OF SPIRIT, IN THE BOND OF   019 02
AND HOLD THE FAITH IN UNITY OF SPIRIT, IN THE BCND CF   032 33
ONE LORD, ONE FAITH, ONE BAPTISM, ONE GOD AND FATHER   037 31
AND PEACE, OF FAITH AND CHARITY, AND MAY WITH ONE   037 33
THAT WITH LIVELY FAITH WE MAY LABOUR ABUNDANTLY TO   038 20
STAND FAST IN THY FAITH, TO OBEY THY WORD, AND TC   043 10
IT IN PURITY OF FAITH, IN HOLINESS OF LIFE, AND IN   047 09
LIVE IN THE TRUE FAITH AND FEAR OF GOD, AND IN   048 03
OUR SINS, BUT THE FAITH OF THY CHURCH   049 07
UNTO THEM THAT ARE OF THE HOUSEHOLD OF FAITH   072 21
THIS LIFE IN THY FAITH AND FEAR   074 35
DRAW NEAR WITH FAITH, AND TAKE THIS HOLY SACRAMENT TC   075 12
AND TRUE FAITH TURN UNTO HIM   076 04
AND THROUGH FAITH IN HIS BLOOD, WE, AND ALL THY WHCLE   081 18
IN THY HEART BY FAITH, WITH THANKSGIVING   082 34
HEART ANC LIVELY FAITH WE RECEIVE THAT HOLY   085 31
AND STEDFAST FAITH IN CHRIST OUR SAVIOUR   085 35
TO HEAVEN, AND BY FAITH BEHOLD THE GLORY THAT SHALL   099 28
CONSTANCY OF OUR FAITH EVEN UNTO DEATH, WE MAY   102 25
KNOW THEE NOW BY FAITH, MAY AFTER THIS LIFE HAVE THE   107 31
CONFIDENCE BY THE FAITH OF HIM   108 28
GOD HATH DEALT TO EVERY MAN THE MEASURE OF FAITH   110 13
US PROPHESY ACCORDING TO THE PROPORTION OF FAITH   111 17
NOT FOUND SO GREAT FAITH, NO, NOT IN ISRAEL   115 18
THOUGH I HAVE ALL FAITH, SO THAT I COULD REMOVE   122 25
AND NOW ABIDETH FAITH, HOPE, CHARITY, THESE THREE   123 14
THY FAITH HATH SAVED THEE   124 03
O WOMAN, GREAT IS THY FAITH   128 20
FOR THEE, THAT THY FAITH FAIL NOT   149 33
FULL ASSURANCE OF FAITH, HAVING OUR HEARTS SPRINKLED   158 21
PROFESSION OF OUR FAITH WITHOUT WAVERING   158 23
THE EYES OF OUR FAITH, THAT WE MAY BEHOLD THEE IN ALL   166 08
VICTORY THAT OVERCOMETH THE WORLD, EVEN OUR FAITH   170 28
TO ANOTHER FAITH BY THE SAME SPIRIT   182 29
OF A TRUE FAITH, TO ACKNOWLEDGE THE GLORY OF THE   186 25
STEDFAST IN THIS FAITH, AND EVERMORE DEFEND US FRCM   186 28
STEDFAST IN THE FAITH, KNOWING THAT THE SAME   193 06
TO ANOTHER FAITH BY THE SAME SPIRIT   203 29
THE PROMISE BY FAITH OF JESUS CHRIST MIGHT BE GIVEN   208 04

FAITH   CONTINUED

US THE INCREASE OF FAITH, HOPE, AND CHARITY   209 09
FAITH, MEEKNESS, TEMPERANCE   209 27
THY FAITH HATH MADE THEE WHOLE   210 14
HE NOT MUCH MORE CLOTHE YOU, O YE OF LITTLE FAITH   211 27
THAT CHRIST MAY DWELL IN YOUR HEARTS BY FAITH   212 16
ONE LORD, ONE FAITH, ONE BAPTISM, ONE GOD AND FATHER   213 24
SEEING THEIR FAITH, SAID UNTO THE SICK OF THE PALSY   217 03
THE SHIELD OF FAITH, WHEREWITH YE SHALL BE ABLE TO   219 16
WE HEARD OF YOUR FAITH IN CHRIST JESUS, AND OF THE   223 24
THY FAITH HATH MADE THEE WHOLE   224 22
SO THEN FAITH COMETH BY HEARING, AND HEARING BY THE   227 13
OF THE FAITH, DIDST SUFFER THY HOLY APOSTLE THOMAS TO   228 06
THAT OUR FAITH IN THY SIGHT MAY NEVER BE   228 09
NOW THE JUST SHALL LIVE BY FAITH   228 19
NOW FAITH IS THE SUBSTANCE OF THINGS HOPED FOR,   228 22
THE UNITY OF THE FAITH, AND OF THE KNOWLEDGE OF THE   237 23
THE TRYING OF YOUR FAITH WORKETH PATIENCE   239 09
BUT LET HIM ASK IN FAITH, NOTHING WAVERING   239 14
GOOD MAN, AND FULL OF THE HOLY GHOST AND OF FAITH   241 09
I HAVE FINISHED MY COURSE, I HAVE KEPT THE FAITH   253 27
THE SAME FAITH AND POWER OF LOVE   258 06
HAST CALLED US TO FAITH IN THEE, AND HAST COMPASSED   258 11
FINISHER OF THE FAITH, THY SON JESUS CHRIST OUR LORD   258 18
UNTO JESUS THE AUTHOR AND FINISHER OF OUR FAITH   258 24
HE NOT MUCH MORE CLOTHE YOU, O YE OF LITTLE FAITH   266 25
OF THY GRACE, AND FINISHER IN THE   276 10
AND CONFIRM THIS FAITH IN US EVERMORE   276 11
OF THE CHRISTIAN FAITH, AS CONTAINED IN THE APOSTLES'   276 32
WILT THOU BE BAPTIZED IN THIS FAITH   277 02
OF THE CHRISTIAN FAITH, AS CONTAINED IN THE APOSTLES'   278 09
WILT THOU BE BAPTIZED IN THIS FAITH   278 11
TO CONFESS THE FAITH OF CHRIST CRUCIFIED, AND   280 07
IN YOUR HEARTS BY FAITH, YE MAY BE FILLED WITH ALL   281 11
THE QUESTION WILT THOU BE BAPTIZED IN THIS FAITH   R 282 05
BELIEVE ALL THE ARTICLES OF THE CHRISTIAN FAITH   283 26
BELIEVE ALL THE ARTICLES OF THE CHRISTIAN FAITH   284 09
OF THE CHRISTIAN FAITH AS CONTAINED IN THE APOSTLES'   284 09
EARNESTLY THE FAITH FOR ALL TIME, IN ALL COUNTRIES,   291 12
AND FAITH, WHEREBY THEY STEDFASTLY BELIEVE THE   292 29
BY THE FAITH OF THEIR SPONSORS, INFANTS ARE   292 33
AND ARE TRAINED IN THE HOUSEHOLD OF FAITH   292 35
TO HAVE A LIVELY FAITH IN GOD'S MERCY THROUGH CHRIST,   293 28
HOLY MYSTERIES IN FAITH, AND LOVE, AND TRUE   294 31
BROUGHT UP IN THY FAITH AND FEAR, TO THE HONOUR AND   303 18
STRENGTH TO HIS FAITH, AND SERIOUSNESS TO HIS   310 23
OF THE CHRISTIAN FAITH, AND AS TO WHETHER HE REPENT   R 313 19
AND STEDFAST FAITH IN THY SON JESUS   316 13
IN THE CONFIDENCE OF A CERTAIN FAITH   317 05
SHALL IN HUMBLE FAITH DESIRE THE MINISTRY OF HEALING   R 320 05
THEIR COURSE IN FAITH, DO NOW REST FROM THEIR   334 24
IN THE TRUE FAITH OF THY HOLY NAME, MAY HAVE OUR   334 26
WHO WALK AS YET BY FAITH, THAT HAVING SERVED THEE   336 07
SO TO FOLLOW IN FAITH WHERE THOU HAST LED THE WAY,   336 12
IN THY FAITH, AND OBEDIENCE TO THY HOLY COMMANDMENTS,   336 22
AND PERFECT FAITH, THAT AT LENGTH, UNITED WITH THEM,   341 02
THE MYSTERY OF THE FAITH IN A PURE CONSCIENCE   531 29
BOLDNESS IN THE FAITH WHICH IS IN CHRIST JESUS   532 04
A MAN FULL OF FAITH AND OF THE HOLY GHOST, AND   532 16
COMPANY OF THE PRIESTS WERE OBEDIENT TO THE FAITH   532 22
SALVATION THROUGH FAITH IN JESUS CHRIST   533 04
THE UNITY OF THE FAITH, AND OF THE KNOWLEDGE OF THE   538 10
AGREEMENT IN THE FAITH AND KNOWLEDGE OF GOD, AND TO   540 20
SALVATION THROUGH FAITH IN JESUS CHRIST   542 04
THE KNOWLEDGE AND FAITH OF THEE AND THY SON, BY THE   545 31
TOWARD GOD, AND FAITH TOWARD OUR LORD JESUS CHRIST   550 14
SALVATION THROUGH FAITH IN JESUS CHRIST   554 22
IN LOVE, IN FAITH, IN CHASTITY, AND IN PURITY   559 11
ORDINANCE WITH FAITH, CHARITY, AND TRUE REPENTANCE   565 30
SUCH STEADINESS OF FAITH, AND WITH SUCH SERIOUSNESS,   566 19
MAY PROFESS THE FAITH ONCE DELIVERED TO THE SAINTS   574 12
BELIEVE ALL THE ARTICLES OF THE CHRISTIAN FAITH   577 17
AND FAITH, WHEREBY THEY STEDFASTLY BELIEVE THE   581 29
HAVE A LIVELY FAITH IN GOD'S MERCY THROUGH CHRIST,   582 24
THY GIFT OF FAITH WE BRING OUR PERPLEXITIES TO THE   596 12
FILL THEM WITH FAITH, VIRTUE, KNOWLEDGE, TEMPERANCE,   598 23
AN ARTICLE OF THE FAITH, OR BE THOUGHT REQUISITE OR   603 31
AND GOOD WORKS, TO FAITH, AND CALLING UPON GOD   604 43
JESUS CHRIST BY FAITH, AND NOT FOR OUR OWN WORKS OR   605 07
ARE JUSTIFIED BY FAITH ONLY, IS A MOST WHOLESOME   605 08
ARE THE FRUITS OF FAITH, AND FOLLOW AFTER   605 11
SPRING OUT NECESSARILY OF A TRUE AND LIVELY FAITH   605 14
BY THEM A LIVELY FAITH MAY BE AS EVIDENTLY KNOWN AS A   605 15
THEY SPRING NOT OF FAITH IN JESUS CHRIST   605 18
AND CONFIRM THEIR FAITH OF ETERNAL SALVATION TO BE   606 21
BUT ALSO IN MATTERS OF FAITH   606 44
AND AUTHORITY IN CONTROVERSIES OF FAITH   607 04
AND CONFIRM OUR FAITH IN HIM   607 35
FROM SUCH AS BY FAITH, AND RIGHTLY, DO RECEIVE THE   608 15
FAITH IS CONFIRMED, AND GRACE INCREASED BY VIRTUE OF   608 29
AND WITH FAITH, RECEIVE THE SAME, THE BREAD   608 37
IS RECEIVED AND EATEN IN THE SUPPER, IS FAITH   608 46
VOID OF A LIVELY FAITH, ALTHOUGH THEY DO CARNALLY AND   609 04
IN A CAUSE OF FAITH AND CHARITY, SO IT BE DONE   611 09

FAITHFUL

GOD IS FAITHFUL AND JUST TO FORGIVE US OUR   022 12
PENITENT AND FAITHFUL HEARTS, THEY MAY EVERMORE BE   043 23
COMPANY OF ALL FAITHFUL PEOPLE   047 08
SANCTIFIER OF THE FAITHFUL   054 09
COMPANY OF ALL FAITHFUL PEOPLE   083 23
THAT A MAN BE FOUND FAITHFUL   094 05
OUR SINS, HE IS FAITHFUL AND JUST TO FORGIVE OUR   101 30
FOR HE IS FAITHFUL THAT PROMISED   158 24

FAITHFUL   CONTINUED

HEARTS OF THY FAITHFUL PEOPLE, BY SENDING TO THEM THE   180 09
BUT GOD IS FAITHFUL, WHO WILL NOT SUFFER YOU TO BE   201 27
COMETH THAT THY FAITHFUL PEOPLE DO UNTO THEE TRUE AND   207 13
TO THY FAITHFUL PEOPLE PARDON AND PEACE, THAT   218 32
IS FOR YOU A FAITHFUL MINISTER OF CHRIST   223 31
WILLS OF THY FAITHFUL PEOPLE   225 04
CHOOSE THY FAITHFUL SERVANT MATTHIAS TO BE OF THE   233 32
AND GUIDED BY FAITHFUL AND TRUE PASTORS   234 03
NUMBER OF THY FAITHFUL CHILDREN   279 19
CHRIST'S FAITHFUL SOLDIER AND SERVANT UNTO HIS LIFE'S   280 09
RECEIVED BY THE FAITHFUL IN THE LORD'S SUPPER   293 16
THE HANDS OF A FAITHFUL CREATOR, AND MOST MERCIFUL   317 15
SOULS OF THE FAITHFUL, AFTER THEY ARE DELIVERED FROM   334 21
ONLY FOR THE FAITHFUL   R 337 02
FOR THE FAITHFUL ARE MINISHED FROM AMONG THE CHILDREN   355 07
THEM THAT ARE FAITHFUL, AND PLENTEOUSLY REWARDETH THE   377 16
AND ALL HIS WORKS ARE FAITHFUL   378 26
FED THEM WITH A FAITHFUL AND TRUE HEART, *   439 24
AND AS THE FAITHFUL WITNESS IN HEAVEN   452 15
SUCH AS ARE FAITHFUL IN THE LAND, *   463 30
AMONG THE FAITHFUL, AND IN THE CONGREGATION   482 25
OF THE FAITHFUL SHALL BE BLESSED   483 21
HATH MADE A FAITHFUL OATH UNTO DAVID, *   508 25
FAITHFUL IN ALL THINGS   531 32
IF HE BE FOUND FAITHFUL AND DILIGENT, HE MAY BE   R 535 23
THEN GIVE YOUR FAITHFUL DILIGENCE ALWAYS SO TO   542 11
WITH ALL FAITHFUL DILIGENCE, TO BANISH AND   542 19
AND BE THOU A FAITHFUL DISPENSER OF THE WORD OF GOD,   546 13
AND BE THOU A FAITHFUL DISPENSER OF THE WORD OF GOD,   546 19
WITH ALL FAITHFUL DILIGENCE, TO BANISH AND   555 02
WILL YOU BE FAITHFUL IN ORDAINING, SENDING, OR LAYING   555 20
AS A WISE AND FAITHFUL SERVANT, GIVING TO THY FAMILY   558 03
GOOD AND FAITHFUL STEWARDS OF THE MYSTERIES OF   562 10
OR THREE OF THY FAITHFUL SERVANTS SHALL ASSEMBLE IN   564 32
CHRIST'S FAITHFUL SOLDIER AND SERVANT UNTO HIS LIFE'S   565 22
FOR THESE WORDS ARE TRUE AND FAITHFUL   567 23
PROMISE TO BE A FAITHFUL SHEPHERD OVER YOU   570 34
OF THE FAITHFUL, VISIT, WE PRAY THEE, THIS   572 25
RECEIVED BY THE FAITHFUL IN THE LORD'S SUPPER   582 13
OF THEE AS THY FAITHFUL SERVANTS   594 27
LIGHT OF THE FAITHFUL, THE STRENGTH OF THOSE WHO   595 05
BEFORE THEE THY FAITHFUL SERVANT (N   598 07
MAY BE FAITHFUL STEWARDS OF THY BOUNTY   599 22
CONGREGATION OF FAITHFUL MEN, IN THE WHICH THE PURE   606 38
OF THE FAITHFUL, AS AN HEATHEN AND PUBLICAN, UNTIL HE   609 28

FAITHFULLY

MAY FAITHFULLY AND OBEDIENTLY HONOUR THEM,   032 11
NO MAN, BUT FAITHFULLY AND WISELY MAKE CHOICE OF FIT   038 30
THAT THEY MAY FAITHFULLY SERVE BEFORE THEE, TO THE   039 13
SERVE HIM FAITHFULLY, AND WORSHIP HIM ACCEPTABLY   047 14
MAY MINISTER FAITHFULLY AND WISELY THE DISCIPLINE OF   047 24
WHICH WE HAVE FAITHFULLY ASKED ACCORDING TO THY WILL,   050 10
THY HELP, MAY FAITHFULLY LIVE ACCORDING TO THY WILL   051 10
MAY BOTH FAITHFULLY LIVE IN THIS WORLD ACCORDING TO   053 15
AND POWER FAITHFULLY TO FULFIL THE SAME   109 32
WE MAY SO FAITHFULLY SERVE THEE IN THIS LIFE, THAT WE   207 15
WHICH WE ASK FAITHFULLY WE MAY OBTAIN EFFECTUALLY   222 12
LET US FAITHFULLY AND DEVOUTLY GIVE THANKS UNTO HIM,   276 05
LIVING FAITHFULLY TOGETHER, MAY SURELY PERFORM   303 07
THY HELP, MAY FAITHFULLY LIVE ACCORDING TO THY WILL   306 29
ALL SUCH AS CALL UPON HIM FAITHFULLY   521 29
THEY MAY FAITHFULLY SERVE THEE IN THIS OFFICE, TO THE   531 21
THEY MAY FAITHFULLY SERVE THEE IN THIS OFFICE, TO THE   537 26
THEY MAY FAITHFULLY SERVE THEE IN THEIR MINISTRY, TO   548 04
HE MAY FAITHFULLY SERVE THEE IN THIS OFFICE,   553 32
WILL YOU THEN FAITHFULLY EXERCISE YOURSELF IN THE   554 29
FAITHFULLY FULFILLING HIS COURSE, AT THE LATTER   559 12
AND LET US FAITHFULLY AND DEVOUTLY BEG HIS BLESSING   564 24
MAY FAITHFULLY PERFORM AND KEEP THE VOW AND COVENANT   566 10
YOU ARE FAITHFULLY TO FEED THAT PORTION OF THE FLOCK   569 24
THAT HE MAY FAITHFULLY SERVE BEFORE THEE, TO THE   572 12
THAT I MAY FAITHFULLY ADMINISTER THY HOLY SACRAMENTS,   573 21
VOCATION AND MINISTRY, MAY SERVE THEE FAITHFULLY   590 27

FAITHFULNESS

TOGETHER IN FAITHFULNESS AND PATIENCE, IN WISDOM AND   303 24
THERE IS NO FAITHFULNESS IN THEIR MOUTH   348 18
AND THY FAITHFULNESS UNTO THE CLOUDS   384 05
MERCY AND FAITHFULNESS, THAT THEY MAY PRESERVE HIM   413 20
AND THY FAITHFULNESS, O GOD, PLAYING UPON AN   426 22
OR THY FAITHFULNESS IN DESTRUCTION   449 19
HIS FAITHFULNESS AND TRUTH SHALL BE THY SHIELD AND   455 03
OF VERY FAITHFULNESS HAST CAUSED ME TO BE TROUBLED   495 05

FAITHLESS

AND BE NOT FAITHLESS, BUT BELIEVING   229 05
A FAITHLESS AND STUBBORN GENERATION   435 13
US FROM FAITHLESS FEARS AND WORLDLY ANXIETIES, AND   596 06

FALL

LET US WORSHIP AND FALL DOWN, *   009 13
THAT THIS DAY WE FALL INTO NO SIN, NEITHER RUN INTO   017 16
THAT THE RAIN DOTH FALL, AND THE EARTH BRING FORTH   040 31
STRENGTHEN THE WEAK AND RAISE UP THOSE WHO FALL   044 03
AND TO RAISE UP THOSE WHO FALL   056 24
AND THE STARS SHALL FALL FROM HEAVEN, AND THE POWERS   118 16
TIME OF TEMPTATION FALL AWAY   122 04
IF THOU WILT FALL DOWN AND WORSHIP ME   127 08
OF THE CRUMBS WHICH FALL FROM THEIR MASTERS' TABLE   128 19

FALL   CONTINUED

TO THE MOUNTAINS, FALL ON US   154 19
AND TWENTY ELDERS FALL DOWN BEFORE HIM THAT SAT ON   187 26
SHALL THEY NOT BOTH FALL INTO THE DITCH   195 03
THAT THINKETH HE STANDETH TAKE HEED LEST HE FALL   201 25
THEE CANNOT BUT FALL, KEEP US EVER BY THY HELP FROM   210 19
IS SET FOR THE FALL AND RISING AGAIN OF MANY IN   233 12
IT ALL JOY WHEN YE FALL INTO DIVERS TEMPTATIONS   239 08
PAINS OF DEATH, TO FALL FROM THEE   332 32
WE MAY AT LENGTH FALL ASLEEP PEACEFULLY IN THEE,   336 13
WICKEDNESS SHALL FALL ON HIS OWN PATE   350 26
THEY SHALL FALL AND PERISH AT THY PRESENCE   351 26
OF THE POOR MAY FALL INTO THE HANDS OF HIS CAPTAINS   353 28
SHALL NEVER FALL   357 19
THEREFORE I SHALL NOT FALL   358 07
BUT FALL UNDER MY FEET   362 15
BEEN ALSO IN THE LORD, THEREFORE SHALL I NOT FALL   370 32
THAT HE MAY FALL INTO HIS OWN MISCHIEF   382 06
24 THOUGH HE FALL, HE SHALL NOT BE CAST AWAY   386 10
THE RIGHTEOUS TO FALL FOR EVER   408 05
7 LET THEM FALL AWAY LIKE WATER THAT RUNNETH APACE   410 21
SO THAT I SHALL NOT GREATLY FALL   413 30
HE IS MY DEFENCE, SO THAT I SHALL NOT FALL   414 10
11 LET THEM FALL UPON THE EDGE OF THE SWORD, *   415 11
THEIR OWN TONGUES SHALL MAKE THEM FALL   416 02
28 LET THEM FALL FROM ONE WICKEDNESS TO ANOTHER,   423 30
11 ALL KINGS SHALL FALL DOWN BEFORE HIM   427 18
10 THEREFORE FALL THE PEOPLE UNTO THEM, *   428 28
29 HE LET IT FALL AMONG THEIR TENTS, *   436 27
AND FALL LIKE ONE OF THE PRINCES   443 31
7 A THOUSAND SHALL FALL BESIDE THEE, AND TEN THOUSAND   455 09
LET US WORSHIP AND FALL DOWN, *   459 15
LORD OUR GOD, AND FALL DOWN BEFORE HIS FOOTSTOOL   462 25
13 THOU HAST THRUST SORE AT ME, THAT I MIGHT FALL   488 26
AND FALL LOW ON OUR KNEES BEFORE HIS FOOTSTOOL   508 17
OF THEIR OWN LIPS FALL UPON THE HEAD OF THEM *   516 27
HOT BURNING COALS FALL UPON THEM   516 29
11 LET THE UNGODLY FALL INTO THEIR OWN NETS TOGETHER,   517 32
ALL SUCH AS FALL, *   521 20
UP WITH PRIDE HE FALL INTO THE CONDEMNATION OF THE   549 27
LEST HE FALL INTO REPROACH AND THE SNARE OF THE   549 29
THAT THIS DAY WE FALL INTO NO SIN, NEITHER RUN INTO   592 22
RAISE HIM UP IF HE FALL   598 02
OF MAN AFTER THE FALL OF ADAM IS SUCH, THAT HE CANNOT   604 42
DENIED TO SUCH AS FALL INTO SIN AFTER BAPTISM   605 41
GRACE GIVEN, AND FALL INTO SIN, AND BY THE GRACE OF   605 42

FALLEN

FOR ALL WHO HAVE FALLEN INTO GRIEVOUS SIN   048 07
FOR AS YET HE WAS FALLEN UPON NONE OF THEM   185 25
BUT SOME ARE FALLEN ASLEEP   205 10
AN ASS OR AN OX FALLEN INTO A PIT, AND WILL NOT   214 06
FOR AS YET HE WAS FALLEN UPON NONE OF THEM   296 11
AND IS FALLEN HIMSELF INTO THE DESTRUCTION THAT HE   350 23
7 THE LOT IS FALLEN UNTO ME IN A FAIR GROUND   358 02
8 THEY ARE BROUGHT DOWN AND FALLEN   364 31
12 THERE ARE THEY FALLEN, ALL THAT WORK WICKEDNESS   384 21
FEAR OF DEATH IS FALLEN UPON ME   406 27
AND ARE FALLEN INTO THE MIDST OF IT THEMSELVES   409 28
REBUKED THEE ARE FALLEN UPON ME   422 21
BOTH THE CHARIOT AND HORSE ARE FALLEN   432 34
8 THE LORD HELPETH THEM THAT ARE FALLEN   522 18

FALLETH

AND A HOUSE DIVIDED AGAINST A HOUSE FALLETH   129 31
OF GOODS THAT FALLETH TO ME   201 33
FLOWER THEREOF FALLETH, AND THE GRACE OF THE FASHION   239 22
11 HE FALLETH DOWN, AND HUMBLETH HIMSELF, *   353 27

FALLING

DROPS OF BLOOD FALLING DOWN TO THE GROUND   150 23
AND FALLING HEADLONG, HE BURST ASUNDER IN THE MIDST,   234 14
AND MY FEET FROM FALLING, *   409 09
THEIR WEALTH BE UNTO THEM AN OCCASION OF FALLING   423 20
MINE EYES FROM TEARS, AND MY FEET FROM FALLING   487 15
PRESERVE FROM FALLING THOSE WHOSE PENURY TEMPTETH   599 12

FALSE

FROM ALL FALSE DOCTRINE, HERESY, AND SCHISM   055 03
SHALT NOT BEAR FALSE WITNESS AGAINST THY NEIGHBOUR   069 16
SHALT NOT BEAR FALSE WITNESS, THOU SHALT NOT COVET   090 26
THERE SHALL ARISE FALSE CHRISTS, AND FALSE PROPHETS,   118 04
FALSE CHRISTS, AND FALSE PROPHETS, AND SHALL SHEW   118 05
IN PERILS AMONG FALSE BRETHREN   121 08
FOR MANY BARE FALSE WITNESS AGAINST HIM, BUT THEIR   143 04
AND BARE FALSE WITNESS AGAINST HIM, SAYING,   143 05
BEWARE OF FALSE PROPHETS, WHICH COME TO YOU IN   200 15
AND AGAINST FALSE SWEARERS, AND AGAINST THOSE THAT   232 17
PRESERVED FROM FALSE APOSTLES, MAY BE ORDERED AND   234 02
SHALT NOT BEAR FALSE WITNESS AGAINST THY NEIGHBOUR   287 15
FOR THERE ARE FALSE WITNESSES RISEN UP AGAINST ME.   372 25
11 FALSE WITNESSES DID RISE UP   382 13
O THOU FALSE TONGUE   404 27
AGAINST ME WITH FALSE TONGUES   480 06
AND ALL FALSE WAYS I UTTERLY ABHOR   498 26
UNTO THEE, THOU FALSE TONGUE   502 12
SHALT NOT BEAR FALSE WITNESS AGAINST THY NEIGHBOUR   579 18
SAVE US FROM ALL FALSE CHOICES, AND THAT IN THY LIGHT   595 30

FALSEHOOD

SUCH PLEASURE IN VANITY, AND SEEK AFTER FALSEHOOD   347 15
AND BROUGHT FORTH FALSEHOOD   350 22
CONCEIVETH FALSEHOOD WITHIN HIMSELF   392 11
AND FALSEHOOD MORE THAN RIGHTEOUSNESS   404 25
SOULS FROM FALSEHOOD AND WRONG   427 24

FALSELY

EVIL AGAINST YOU FALSELY, FOR MY SAKE   257 32
THEY PERSECUTE ME FALSELY   495 30
ANABAPTISTS DO FALSELY BOAST   611 02

FAME

AND THE FAME HEREOF WENT ABROAD INTO ALL THAT LAND   224 29

FAMILIAR

EVEN MINE OWN FAMILIAR FRIEND WHOM I TRUSTED,   392 17
AND MINE OWN FAMILIAR FRIEND   407 17

FAMILIES

LIVES OF YOUR FAMILIES, ACCORDING TO THE DOCTRINE OF   533 25
AND YOUR FAMILIES, ACCORDING TO THE DOCTRINE OF   542 33
WHO SETTEST THE SOLITARY IN FAMILIES   598 20

FAMILY

BEHOLD THIS THY FAMILY, FOR WHICH OUR LORD JESUS   156 22
OF WHOM THE WHOLE FAMILY IN HEAVEN AND EARTH IS   212 13
OF WHOM THE WHOLE FAMILY IN HEAVEN AND EARTH IS   281 08
TO FEED AND PROVIDE FOR THE LORD'S FAMILY   539 34
GIVING TO THY FAMILY THEIR PORTION IN DUE SEASON,   558 04
AS MANY OF THE FAMILY AS CAN CONVENIENTLY BE PRESENT,   R 587 04
THE FAMILY BEING TOGETHER, A LITTLE BEFORE   R 589 13
MEMBER OF THE FAMILY, SAY AS FOLLOWETH, ALL KNEELING, R 592 10
MEMBER OF THE FAMILY, SAY AS FOLLOWETH, ALL KNEELING, R 593 04

FAMINE

FROM PLAGUE, PESTILENCE, AND FAMINE   054 31
AROSE A MIGHTY FAMINE IN THAT LAND   202 05
OR FAMINE, OR NAKEDNESS, OR PERIL, OR   331 07

FAR

TO THEM THAT ARE FAR OFF AND TO THEM THAT ARE NIGH   038 07
THAT THIS CHURCH IS FAR FROM INTENDING TO DEPART FROM   VI 32
THE NIGHT IS FAR SPENT, THE DAY IS AT HAND   091 03
AND JESUS ANSWERED AND SAID, SUFFER YE THUS FAR   150 34
AND THE DAY IS FAR SPENT   168 04
HE LED THEM OUT AS FAR AS TO BETHANY, AND HE LIFTED   178 24
FOR DIVERS OF THEM CAME FROM FAR   199 14
HIS JOURNEY INTO A FAR COUNTRY, AND THERE WASTED HIS   202 03
THAT ASCENDED UP FAR ABOVE ALL HEAVENS, THAT HE MIGHT   237 18
THAT HE SHOULD GO AS FAR AS ANTIOCH   241 05
WHY STANDEST THOU SO FAR OFF, O LORD, *   353 03
THY JUDGMENTS ARE FAR ABOVE OUT OF HIS SIGHT, AND   353 13
AND ART SO FAR FROM MY HEALTH, AND FROM THE WORDS OF   366 05
19 BUT BE NOT THOU FAR FROM ME, O LORD   367 10
GO NOT FAR FROM ME, O LORD   383 08
BE NOT THOU FAR FROM ME   388 35
10 BUT NOW THOU ART FAR OFF, AND PUTTEST US TO   395 11
WOULD I GET ME AWAY FAR OFF, *   406 32
11 GO NOT FAR FROM ME, O GOD   425 29
MINE ACQUAINTANCE FAR FROM ME, *   449 11
THOU ART EXALTED FAR ABOVE ALL GODS   461 15
SO FAR HATH HE SET OUR SINS FROM US   466 31
SHALL IT BE FAR FROM HIM   481 03
AND ARE FAR FROM THY LAW   500 11
155 HEALTH IS FAR FROM THE UNGODLY   500 21
THAT ASCENDED UP FAR ABOVE ALL HEAVENS, THAT HE MIGHT   538 05
KEEP FAR OUR FOES, GIVE PEACE AT HOME   544 08
DRIVE FAR AWAY OUR GHOSTLY FOE, AND THINE ABIDING   545 06
KEEP FAR OUR FOES, GIVE PEACE AT HOME   556 16
DRIVE FAR AWAY OUR GHOSTLY FOE, AND THINE ABIDING   557 12
DRIVE FAR OFF FROM US ALL WRONG DESIRES, INCLINE OUR   594 13
PUT FAR FROM THEM, WE BESEECH THEE, EVERY ROOT OF   598 21
WHEREBY MAN IS VERY FAR GONE FROM ORIGINAL   604 32
IN THIS CHURCH, SO FAR AS IT DECLARES THE BOOKS OF   R 610 24

FARED

FINE LINEN, AND FARED SUMPTUOUSLY EVERY DAY   190 04

FARM

THEY HAD BOUGHT A FARM, OR WOULD TRY THEIR YOKES OF   089 04
ONE TO HIS FARM, ANOTHER TO HIS MERCHANDISE   218 11

FARTHEST

WITHIN FOURTEEN DAYS AFTER, AT THE FARTHEST   R 085 19

FARTHING

TILL THOU HAST PAID THE UTTERMOST FARTHING   198 17

FASHION

AND FASHION INTO ONE UNITED PEOPLE THE   036 15
BEING FOUND IN FASHION AS A MAN, HE HUMBLED HIMSELF,   134 20
THE GRACE OF THE FASHION OF IT PERISHETH   239 23

FASHION   CONTINUED

HE PRAYED, THE FASHION OF HIS COUNTENANCE WAS	248 25
TO FRAME AND FASHION YOUR OWN LIVES, AND THE LIVES OF	533 25
AND TO FASHION THEM AFTER THE RULE AND	541 21
TO FRAME AND FASHION YOUR OWN SELVES, AND YOUR	542 32

FASHIONED

MADE ME AND FASHIONED ME	494 28
AND FASHIONED BENEATH IN THE EARTH	515 19
BY DAY WERE FASHIONED, *	515 22

FASHIONETH

14 HE FASHIONETH ALL THE HEARTS OF THEM, *	379 17

FAST

PRAY THEE, TO STAND FAST IN THY FAITH, TO OBEY THY	043 10
AND EVER HOLD FAST, THE BLESSED HOPE OF EVERLASTING	092 11
IN ZION, SANCTIFY A FAST, CALL A SOLEMN ASSEMBLY	124 29
WHEN YE FAST, BE NOT, AS THE HYPOCRITES, OF A SAD	125 09
THAT THEY MAY APPEAR UNTO MEN TO FAST	125 11
NOT UNTO MEN TO FAST, BUT UNTO THY FATHER WHICH IS IN	125 14
FOR OUR SAKE DIDST FAST FORTY DAYS AND FORTY NIGHTS	125 27
LET US HOLD FAST THE PROFESSION OF OUR FAITH WITHOUT	158 23
I FAST TWICE IN THE WEEK, I GIVE TITHES OF ALL THAT I	205 27
FOR HE HATH MADE FAST THE BARS OF THY GATES, *	265 02
HE COMMANDED, AND IT STOOD FAST	379 05
THINE ARROWS STICK FAST IN ME, *	387 23
SAY THEY, CLEAVETH FAST UNTO HIM	392 15
AND THE UNGODLY COMETH ON SO FAST	406 24
STRENGTH SETTETH FAST THE MOUNTAINS, *	416 25
2 I STICK FAST IN THE DEEP MIRE, WHERE NO GROUND IS	422 02
FOR ME TO HOLD ME FAST BY GOD, TO PUT MY TRUST IN THE	429 32
8 I AM SO FAST IN PRISON *	449 13
HAND SHALL HOLD HIM FAST, *	451 17
SHALL STAND FAST WITH HIM	451 32
36 HE SHALL STAND FAST FOR EVERMORE AS THE MOON,	452 14
THE ROUND WORLD SO FAST THAT IT CANNOT BE MOVED	460 20
SEED SHALL STAND FAST IN THY SIGHT	466 06
BEING FAST BOUND IN MISERY AND IRON	476 25
8 THEY STAND FAST FOR EVER AND EVER, *	483 09
HIS HEART STANDETH FAST, AND BELIEVETH IN THE LORD	483 31
BUT STANDETH FAST FOR EVER	504 25
13 FOR HE HATH MADE FAST THE BARS OF THY GATES,	523 21
6 HE HATH MADE THEM FAST FOR EVER AND EVER	524 16

FASTED

AND WHEN HE HAD FASTED FORTY DAYS AND FORTY NIGHTS,	126 25

FASTENED

SYNAGOGUE WERE FASTENED ON HIM	261 23

FASTEST

THOU, WHEN THOU FASTEST, ANOINT THINE HEAD, AND WASH	125 12

FASTING

SAVE A DAY OF FASTING OR ABSTINENCE, OR ON ANY DAY	R 003 05
BY THY BAPTISM, FASTING, AND TEMPTATION,	055 07
THEE IN WEEPING, FASTING, AND PRAYING	062 30
HOLY DAYS, OR FASTING DAYS, ARE IN THE WEEK FOLLOWING	R 071 25
AND WITH FASTING, AND WITH WEEPING, AND WITH	124 22
I SEND THEM AWAY FASTING TO THEIR OWN HOUSES, THEY	199 12
WITH PRAYERS AND FASTING, FOR THE RECEIVING OF THIS	R 273 21
ON SACKCLOTH, AND HUMBLED MY SOUL WITH FASTING	382 18
MYSELF WITH FASTING, *	422 23
23 MY KNEES ARE WEAK THROUGH FASTING	481 18

FASTINGS

AND THIRST, IN FASTINGS OFTEN, IN COLD AND NAKEDNESS	121 09
IN WATCHINGS, IN FASTINGS	126 12
SERVED GOD WITH FASTINGS AND PRAYERS NIGHT AND DAY	233 20

FAT

IN THEIR OWN FAT, *	359 06
FAT BULLS OF BASHAN CLOSE ME IN ON EVERY SIDE	366 27
29 ALL SUCH AS BE FAT UPON EARTH *	367 33
SHALL CONSUME AS THE FAT OF LAMBS	386 02
WILL OFFER UNTO THEE FAT BURNT-SACRIFICES, WITH THE	418 10
AND SHALL BE FAT AND WELL-LIKING	456 29
70 THEIR HEART IS AS FAT AS BRAWN	494 20

FATHER

SHALL WORSHIP THE FATHER IN SPIRIT AND IN TRUTH	003 31
FOR THE FATHER SEEKETH SUCH TO WORSHIP HIM	003 32
FROM GOD OUR FATHER, AND FROM THE LORD JESUS CHRIST	004 02
AND GO TO MY FATHER, AND WILL SAY UNTO HIM, FATHER, I	004 26
SAY UNTO HIM, FATHER, I HAVE SINNED AGAINST HEAVEN,	004 27
OF HIS SON INTO YOUR HEARTS, CRYING, ABBA, FATHER,	005 17
THE FACE OF ALMIGHTY GOD OUR HEAVENLY FATHER	005 33
ALMIGHTY AND MOST MERCIFUL FATHER	006 17
O MOST MERCIFUL FATHER, FOR HIS SAKE	006 28
ALMIGHTY GOD, THE FATHER OF OUR LORD JESUS CHRIST,	007 06
OUR FATHER, WHO ART IN HEAVEN, HALLOWED BE THY NAME	007 23
GLORY BE TO THE FATHER, AND TO THE SON, AND TO THE	008 03
FATHER, SON, AND HOLY GHOST, ONE GOD	R 008 29
GLORY BE TO THE FATHER, AND TO THE SON, *	009 27

FATHER   CONTINUED

WORSHIP THEE, THE FATHER EVERLASTING	010 10
THE FATHER, OF AN INFINITE MAJESTY	010 21
THOU ART THE EVERLASTING SON OF THE FATHER	010 25
THE RIGHT HAND OF GOD, IN THE GLORY OF THE FATHER	010 31
LET US BLESS THE FATHER, AND THE SON, AND THE HOLY	013 30
IN GOD THE FATHER ALMIGHTY, MAKER OF HEAVEN AND	015 19
HAND OF GOD THE FATHER ALMIGHTY	015 26
IN ONE GOD THE FATHER ALMIGHTY, MAKER OF HEAVEN AND	015 33
BEGOTTEN OF HIS FATHER BEFORE ALL WORLDS, GOD OF GOD,	016 03
BEING OF ONE SUBSTANCE WITH THE FATHER	016 05
AND SITTETH ON THE RIGHT HAND OF THE FATHER	016 12
FROM THE FATHER AND THE SON	016 16
WHO WITH THE FATHER AND THE SON TOGETHER IS	016 17
OUR HEAVENLY FATHER, ALMIGHTY AND EVERLASTING GOD,	017 13
OUR HEAVENLY FATHER, THE HIGH AND MIGHTY RULER OF THE	017 27
ALMIGHTY GOD, FATHER OF ALL MERCIES, WE, THINE	019 14
THE FACE OF ALMIGHTY GOD OUR HEAVENLY FATHER	023 08
ALMIGHTY AND MOST MERCIFUL FATHER	023 24
O MOST MERCIFUL FATHER, FOR HIS SAKE	024 03
ALMIGHTY GOD, THE FATHER OF OUR LORD JESUS CHRIST,	024 08
GLORY BE TO THE FATHER, AND TO THE SON, AND TO THE	025 09
GOD THE FATHER ALMIGHTY	025 26
SON OF THE FATHER, THAT TAKEST AWAY THE SINS OF	025 28
HAND OF GOD THE FATHER, HAVE MERCY UPON US	025 31
ART MOST HIGH IN THE GLORY OF GOD THE FATHER	026 04
IN GOD THE FATHER ALMIGHTY, MAKER OF HEAVEN AND	029 24
HAND OF GOD THE FATHER ALMIGHTY	029 31
IN ONE GOD THE FATHER ALMIGHTY, MAKER OF HEAVEN AND	030 04
BEGOTTEN OF HIS FATHER BEFORE ALL WORLDS, GOD OF GOD,	030 08
BEING OF ONE SUBSTANCE WITH THE FATHER	030 10
AND SITTETH ON THE RIGHT HAND OF THE FATHER	030 17
FROM THE FATHER AND THE SON	030 21
WHO WITH THE FATHER AND THE SON TOGETHER IS	030 22
ALMIGHTY GOD, FATHER OF ALL MERCIES, WE, THINE	033 12
O GRACIOUS FATHER, WE HUMBLY BESEECH THEE FOR THY	037 15
O GOD, FATHER OF OUR LORD JESUS CHRIST, OUR ONLY	037 25
ONE GOD AND FATHER OF US ALL, SO WE MAY BE ALL OF ONE	037 31
OUR HEAVENLY FATHER, WHO HAST PURCHASED TO	038 25
O GRACIOUS FATHER, WHO OPENEST THINE HAND AND FILLEST	040 03
O GOD, HEAVENLY FATHER, WHO BY THY SON JESUS CHRIST	040 15
AND MOST MERCIFUL FATHER, WE HUMBLY BESEECH THEE, OF	040 23
O GOD, HEAVENLY FATHER, WHOSE GIFT IT IS THAT THE	040 30
OUR HEAVENLY FATHER, IN WHOSE HANDS ARE THE	042 14
OUR HEAVENLY FATHER, WHO HAST COMMITTED TO THY	042 30
WHO WITH THE FATHER AND THE HOLY GHOST LIVEST AND	043 15
OUR HEAVENLY FATHER, WHOSE BLESSED SON CAME NOT TO BE	043 28
OUR HEAVENLY FATHER, WHO DECLAREST THY GLORY AND	044 17
OUR HEAVENLY FATHER, GUIDE, WE BESEECH THEE, THE	044 27
O FATHER OF MERCIES AND GOD OF ALL COMFORT, OUR ONLY	045 12
O HEAVENLY FATHER, WATCH WITH US, WE PRAY THEE,	045 24
AND HEAVENLY FATHER, WHO HAST TAUGHT US IN THY	045 30
REIGNEST WITH THE FATHER AND THE HOLY GHOST, ONE GOD,	049 09
MOST MERCIFUL FATHER, THAT SHE, THROUGH THY HELP,	051 10
OUR HEAVENLY FATHER, BY WHOSE GRACIOUS	051 15
O MOST MERCIFUL FATHER, WHO OF THY GRACIOUS GOODNESS	051 30
OUR HEAVENLY FATHER, WHO ALONE MAKEST MEN TO BE	052 17
GOD AND HEAVENLY FATHER, WE GIVE THEE HUMBLE THANKS	053 10
O GRACIOUS FATHER, THAT HE, THROUGH THY HELP,	053 15
O GOD THE FATHER, CREATOR OF HEAVEN AND EARTH	054 05
BESEECH THEE, O FATHER, ETC	R 058 10
O GOD, MERCIFUL FATHER, WHO DESPISEST NOT THE SIGHING	058 15
GLORY BE TO THE FATHER, AND TO THE SON, AND TO	059 05
BESEECH THEE, O FATHER, MERCIFULLY TO LOOK UPON OUR	059 21
BESEECH THEE, O FATHER, IN THE LITANY	R 060 04
GLORY BE TO THE FATHER, AND TO THE SON, *	061 15
AND MERCIFUL FATHER, WHO HAST COMPASSION UPON	062 13
HONOUR THY FATHER AND THY MOTHER	069 02
IN ONE GOD THE FATHER ALMIGHTY, MAKER OF HEAVEN AND	071 02
BEGOTTEN OF HIS FATHER BEFORE ALL WORLDS, GOD OF GOD,	071 05
BEING OF ONE SUBSTANCE WITH THE FATHER	071 07
AND SITTETH ON THE RIGHT HAND OF THE FATHER	071 14
FROM THE FATHER AND THE SON	071 18
WHO WITH THE FATHER AND THE SON TOGETHER IS	071 19
AND GLORIFY YOUR FATHER WHICH IS IN HEAVEN	072 05
THE WILL OF MY FATHER WHICH IS IN HEAVEN	072 15
O HEAVENLY FATHER, TO ALL BISHOPS AND OTHER	074 21
GRANT THIS, O FATHER, FOR JESUS CHRIST'S SAKE,	075 05
ALMIGHTY GOD, FATHER OF OUR LORD JESUS CHRIST,	075 17
HAVE MERCY UPON US, MOST MERCIFUL FATHER	075 26
OUR HEAVENLY FATHER, WHO OF HIS GREAT MERCY HATH	076 02
ADVOCATE WITH THE FATHER, JESUS CHRIST THE RIGHTEOUS	076 22
O LORD, HOLY FATHER, ALMIGHTY, EVERLASTING GOD	076 33
OF THY GLORY, O FATHER, THE SAME WE BELIEVE OF THE	079 10
OUR HEAVENLY FATHER, FOR THAT THOU, OF THY	080 07
LORD AND HEAVENLY FATHER, ACCORDING TO THE	080 37
O MERCIFUL FATHER, TO HEAR US	081 08
BE UNTO THEE, O FATHER ALMIGHTY, WORLD WITHOUT END	081 34
O HEAVENLY FATHER, SO TO ASSIST US WITH THY	083 26
GOD THE FATHER ALMIGHTY	084 06
SON OF THE FATHER, THAT TAKEST AWAY THE SINS OF	084 08
HAND OF GOD THE FATHER, HAVE MERCY UPON US	084 11
ART MOST HIGH IN THE GLORY OF GOD THE FATHER	084 15
GOD ALMIGHTY, THE FATHER, THE SON, AND THE HOLY	084 21
TO GOD, THE FATHER, THE SON, AND THE HOLY GHOST, FOR	086 05
WITH THE FATHER AND THE HOLY GHOST, LET US GIVE, AS	086 19
OUR HEAVENLY FATHER, FOR THAT HE HATH GIVEN HIS	087 02
PETITIONS UNTO ALMIGHTY GOD, OUR HEAVENLY FATHER	089 22
EVEN THE FATHER OF OUR LORD JESUS CHRIST	092 21
REIGNEST WITH THE FATHER AND THE HOLY SPIRIT EVER,	093 31
WILL BE TO HIM A FATHER, AND HE SHALL BE TO ME A SON	097 04
BEGOTTEN OF THE FATHER,) FULL OF GRACE AND TRUTH	098 06
WAS WITH THE FATHER, AND WAS MANIFESTED UNTO US	101 17
IS WITH THE FATHER, AND WITH HIS SON JESUS CHRIST	101 20
GOVERNORS UNTIL THE TIME APPOINTED OF THE FATHER	104 17

FATHER   CONTINUED   FATHER   CONTINUED

OF HIS SON INTO YOUR HEARTS, CRYING, ABBA, FATHER   104 24   COMETH UNTO THE FATHER, BUT BY ME   240 07
CHRIST IS LORD, TO THE GLORY OF GOD THE FATHER   105 31   HAVE KNOWN MY FATHER ALSO   240 08
THE ROOM OF HIS FATHER HEROD, HE WAS AFRAID TO GO   107 19   SHEW US THE FATHER, AND IT SUFFICETH US   240 10
BEHOLD, THY FATHER AND I HAVE SOUGHT THEE SORROWING   110 33   HE THAT HATH SEEN ME HATH SEEN THE FATHER   240 12
TO GOD AND THE FATHER BY HIM   116 16   AND HOW SAYEST THOU THEN, SHEW US THE FATHER   240 13
WITH THEE, O FATHER, AND THEE, O HOLY GHOST, HE   117 10   THAT I AM IN THE FATHER, AND THE FATHER IN ME   240 14
OF LOVE THE FATHER HATH BESTOWED UPON US, THAT WE   117 14   FATHER, AND THE FATHER IN ME   240 14
THE GOD AND FATHER OF OUR LORD JESUS CHRIST, WHICH IS   121 15   BUT THE FATHER THAT DWELLETH IN ME, HE DOETH THE   240 16
BUT UNTO THY FATHER WHICH IS IN SECRET   125 14   THAT I AM IN THE FATHER, AND THE FATHER IN ME   240 17
AND THY FATHER, WHICH SEETH IN SECRET, SHALL REWARD   125 15   FATHER, AND THE FATHER IN ME   240 17
REIGNEST WITH THE FATHER AND THE HOLY GHOST, ONE GOD,   125 32   BECAUSE I GO UNTO MY FATHER   240 21
BUT I HONOUR MY FATHER, AND YE DO DISHONOUR ME   133 15   I DO, THAT THE FATHER MAY BE GLORIFIED IN THE SON   240 22
GREATER THAN OUR FATHER ABRAHAM, WHICH IS DEAD   133 21   HAVE HEARD OF MY FATHER I HAVE MADE KNOWN UNTO YOU   241 31
IT IS MY FATHER THAT HONOURETH ME   133 24   SHALL ASK OF THE FATHER IN MY NAME, HE MAY GIVE IT   242 03
YOUR FATHER ABRAHAM REJOICED TO SEE MY DAY   133 28   HIM ZACHARIAS, AFTER THE NAME OF HIS FATHER   243 19
TO THE GLORY OF GOD THE FATHER   134 28   MADE SIGNS TO HIS FATHER, HOW HE WOULD HAVE HIM   243 22
THOU ART OUR FATHER, THOUGH ABRAHAM BE IGNORANT OF   139 21   AND HIS FATHER ZACHARIAS WAS FILLED WITH THE HOLY   243 31
O LORD, ART OUR FATHER, OUR REDEEMER   139 23   HE SWARE TO OUR FATHER ABRAHAM, THAT HE WOULD GRANT   244 06
HE SAID, ABBA, FATHER, ALL THINGS ARE POSSIBLE UNTO   141 35   UNTO THEE, BUT MY FATHER WHICH IS IN HEAVEN   246 06
THE COUNTRY, THE FATHER OF ALEXANDER AND RUFUS, TO   146 06   LEAVING HIS FATHER AND ALL THAT HE HAD, WITHOUT DELAY   246 17
A KINGDOM, AS MY FATHER HATH APPOINTED UNTO ME   149 28   TO THEM FOR WHOM IT IS PREPARED OF MY FATHER   247 18
SAYING, FATHER, IF THOU BE WILLING, REMOVE   150 18   WHO WITH THEE, O FATHER, AND THEE, O HOLY GHOST,   248 05
ALMIGHTY FATHER, WHOSE DEAR SON, ON THE NIGHT BEFORE   152 07   FROM GOD THE FATHER HONOUR AND GLORY, WHEN THERE CAME   248 17
THEN SAID JESUS, FATHER, FORGIVE THEM   154 25   A KINGDOM, AS MY FATHER HATH APPOINTED UNTO ME   250 13
HE SAID, FATHER, INTO THY HANDS I COMMEND MY   155 13   THE FACE OF MY FATHER WHICH IS IN HEAVEN   253 12
WORLD UNTO THE FATHER, HAVING LOVED HIS OWN WHICH   155 25   ME HATETH MY FATHER ALSO   255 24
KNOWING THAT THE FATHER HAD GIVEN ALL THINGS INTO HIS   155 29   THEY BOTH SEEN AND HATED BOTH ME AND MY FATHER   255 27
GLORY BE TO THE FATHER, AND TO THE SON, *   163 17   UNTO YOU FROM THE FATHER, EVEN THE SPIRIT OF TRUTH,   255 31
ALMIGHTY FATHER, WHO HAST GIVEN THINE ONLY SON TO DIE   170 19   FROM THE FATHER, HE SHALL TESTIFY OF ME   255 32
AS MY FATHER HATH SENT ME, EVEN SO SEND I YOU   171 21   YE BLESSED OF MY FATHER, INHERIT THE KINGDOM PREPARED   259 04
EVEN AS THE FATHER KNOWETH ME, AND I KNOW THE   172 28   OF YOU THAT IS A FATHER, WILL HE GIVE HIM A STONE   263 08
AS THE FATHER KNOWETH ME, AND I KNOW THE FATHER   172 29   YOUR HEAVENLY FATHER GIVE THE HOLY SPIRIT TO THEM   263 12
BECAUSE I GO TO THE FATHER   173 29   CHILDREN OF YOUR FATHER WHICH IS IN HEAVEN   264 08
BECAUSE I GO TO THE FATHER   174 02   EVEN AS YOUR FATHER WHICH IS IN HEAVEN IS PERFECT   264 14
DOWN FROM THE FATHER OF LIGHTS, WITH WHOM IS NO   174 27   GLORY BE TO THE FATHER, AND TO THE SON, *   265 06
I GO TO MY FATHER, AND YE SEE ME NO MORE   175 15   O MOST MERCIFUL FATHER, WHO HAST BLESSED THE LABOURS   265 11
THINGS THAT THE FATHER HATH ARE MINE   175 23   DOWN FROM THE FATHER OF LIGHTS, WITH WHOM IS NO   265 20
GOD AND THE FATHER IS THIS, TO VISIT THE FATHERLESS   176 16   GOD AND THE FATHER IS THIS, TO VISIT THE FATHERLESS   266 07
YE SHALL ASK THE FATHER IN MY NAME, HE WILL GIVE IT   176 21   YET YOUR HEAVENLY FATHER FEEDETH THEM   266 16
BUT I SHALL SHEW YOU PLAINLY OF THE FATHER   176 26   FOR YOUR HEAVENLY FATHER KNOWETH THAT YE HAVE NEED OF   266 28
I WILL PRAY THE FATHER FOR YOU   176 27   UNTO GOD AND THE FATHER IN THE NAME OF OUR LORD JESUS   267 12
FOR THE FATHER HIMSELF LOVETH YOU, BECAUSE YE HAVE   176 28   A MAN LEAVE HIS FATHER AND MOTHER, AND SHALL BE   267 29
FORTH FROM THE FATHER, AND AM COME INTO THE WORLD   176 30   SHALL A MAN LEAVE FATHER AND MOTHER, AND SHALL CLEAVE   268 08
I LEAVE THE WORLD, AND GO TO THE FATHER   176 31   ALL THAT THE FATHER GIVETH ME SHALL COME TO ME   269 13
BECAUSE THE FATHER IS WITH ME   177 07   CALL UPON GOD THE FATHER, THROUGH OUR LORD JESUS   273 32
PROMISE OF THE FATHER, WHICH, SAITH HE, YE HAVE HEARD   177 31   THE NAME OF THE FATHER, AND OF THE SON, AND OF THE   275 29
WHICH THE FATHER HATH PUT IN HIS OWN POWER   178 08   OF OUR HEAVENLY FATHER TOWARD THIS CHILD (THIS   276 04
THE PROMISE OF MY FATHER UPON YOU   178 21   HEAVENLY FATHER, WE GIVE THEE HUMBLE THANKS,   276 07
UNTO YOU FROM THE FATHER, EVEN THE SPIRIT OF TRUTH,   179 25   O LORD, HOLY FATHER, ALMIGHTY, EVERLASTING GOD, FOR   279 08
FROM THE FATHER, HE SHALL TESTIFY OF ME   179 26   THE NAME OF THE FATHER, AND OF THE SON, AND OF THE   279 13
NOT KNOWN THE FATHER, NOR ME   180 02   THE NAME OF THE FATHER, AND OF THE SON, AND OF THE   279 28
I WILL PRAY THE FATHER, AND HE SHALL GIVE YOU ANOTHER   181 09   MOST MERCIFUL FATHER, THAT IT HATH PLEASED THEE TO   280 28
THAT I AM IN MY FATHER, AND YE IN ME, AND I IN YOU   181 17   ALMIGHTY GOD, THE FATHER OF OUR LORD JESUS CHRIST, OF   281 07
BE LOVED OF MY FATHER, AND I WILL LOVE HIM, AND WILL   181 20   THE NAME OF THE FATHER, AND OF THE SON, AND OF THE   281 21
AND MY FATHER WILL LOVE HIM, AND WE WILL COME UNTO   181 25   THE NAME OF THE FATHER, AND OF THE SON, AND OF THE   282 09 R
WHOM THE FATHER WILL SEND IN MY NAME, HE SHALL   181 31   THE NAME OF THE FATHER, AND OF THE SON, AND OF THE   282 14
BECAUSE I SAID, I GO UNTO THE FATHER   182 04   OUR HEAVENLY FATHER, THAT HE HATH CALLED ME TO THIS   284 02
FOR MY FATHER IS GREATER THAN I   182 05   IN GOD THE FATHER ALMIGHTY, MAKER OF HEAVEN AND   284 13
THAT THE WORLD MAY KNOW THAT I LOVE THE FATHER   182 09   HAND OF GOD THE FATHER ALMIGHTY   284 20
AND AS THE FATHER GAVE ME COMMANDMENT, EVEN SO I DO   182 10   IN GOD THE FATHER, WHO HATH MADE ME, AND ALL THE   284 29
OF YOU THAT IS A FATHER, WILL HE GIVE HIM A STONE   183 14   GLORY BE TO THE FATHER, AND TO THE SON, AND TO THE   285 06
YOUR HEAVENLY FATHER GIVE THE HOLY SPIRIT TO THEM   183 19   HONOUR THY FATHER AND THY MOTHER   286 35
TESTIFY THAT THE FATHER SENT THE SON TO BE THE   189 21   AND HELP MY FATHER AND MOTHER   288 27
CRIED AND SAID, FATHER ABRAHAM, HAVE MERCY ON ME,   190 13   THE NAME OF THE FATHER, AND OF THE SON, AND OF THE   292 21
THEE THEREFORE, FATHER, THAT THOU WOULDEST SEND HIM   190 23   GRANT, O FATHER, THAT WHEN WE RECEIVE THE BLESSED   294 29
AND HE SAID, NAY, FATHER ABRAHAM   190 27   REVEREND FATHER IN GOD, I PRESENT UNTO YOU THESE   296 08
O HEAVENLY FATHER, FOR THE SAKE OF JESUS CHRIST   194 09   GOD ALMIGHTY, THE FATHER, THE SON, AND THE HOLY   299 03
AS YOUR FATHER ALSO IS MERCIFUL   194 25   THE NAME OF THE FATHER, AND OF THE SON, AND OF THE   302 15
THE GLORY OF THE FATHER, EVEN SO WE ALSO SHOULD WALK   197 14   THE NAME OF THE FATHER, AND OF THE SON, AND OF THE   304 09
WHEREBY WE CRY, ABBA, FATHER   200 09   GOD THE FATHER, GOD THE SON, GOD THE HOLY GHOST,   304 11
THE WILL OF MY FATHER WHICH IS IN HEAVEN   200 26   GLORY BE TO THE FATHER, AND TO THE SON, AND TO THE   306 04
TO HIS FATHER, FATHER, GIVE ME THE PORTION OF GOODS   201 32   MOST MERCIFUL FATHER, THAT SHE, THROUGH THY HELP,   306 29
THEM SAID TO HIS FATHER, FATHER, GIVE ME THE PORTION   201 32   O HEAVENLY FATHER, THAT THE CHILD OF THIS THY   307 03
SAY UNTO HIM, FATHER, I HAVE SINNED AGAINST HEAVEN,   202 13   MOST LOVING FATHER, WHATSOEVER HATH BEEN DECAYED   314 03
AND GO TO MY FATHER, AND WILL SAY UNTO HIM, FATHER,   202 13   O FATHER OF MERCIES, AND GOD OF ALL COMFORT, OUR ONLY   316 06
AND HE AROSE, AND CAME TO HIS FATHER   202 16   O GOD THE FATHER   317 25
WAY OFF, HIS FATHER SAW HIM, AND HAD COMPASSION,   202 17   NAME OF GOD THE FATHER ALMIGHTY WHO CREATED THEE   319 20
SAID UNTO HIM, FATHER, I HAVE SINNED AGAINST HEAVEN,   202 19   REIGNEST WITH THE FATHER AND THE HOLY GHOST, ONE GOD,   320 13
BUT THE FATHER SAID TO HIS SERVANTS, BRING FORTH THE   202 21   THE NAME OF THE FATHER, AND OF THE SON, AND OF THE   320 16
AND THY FATHER HATH KILLED THE FATTED CALF, BECAUSE   202 30   O LORD, HOLY FATHER, BY WHOSE LOVING-KINDNESS OUR   322 06
CAME HIS FATHER OUT, AND INTREATED HIM   202 32   O ALMIGHTY FATHER, LORD OF HEAVEN AND EARTH, WE   323 12
SAID TO HIS FATHER, LO, THESE MANY YEARS DO I SERVE   202 33   DELIVERED UP THE KINGDOM TO GOD, EVEN THE FATHER   328 28
AND YOUR HEAVENLY FATHER FEEDETH THEM   211 17   WHEREBY WE CRY, ABBA, FATHER   330 22
FOR YOUR HEAVENLY FATHER KNOWETH THAT YE HAVE NEED OF   211 30   COMETH UNTO THE FATHER, BUT BY ME   331 26
MY KNEES UNTO THE FATHER OF OUR LORD JESUS CHRIST,   212 12   ALL THAT THE FATHER GIVETH ME SHALL COME TO ME   333 03
ONE GOD AND FATHER OF ALL, WHO IS ABOVE ALL, AND   213 25   MERCIFUL GOD, THE FATHER OF OUR LORD JESUS CHRIST,   334 30
UNTO GOD AND THE FATHER IN THE NAME OF OUR LORD JESUS   217 30   BESEECH THEE, O FATHER, TO RAISE US FROM THE DEATH OF   335 05
SO THE FATHER KNEW THAT IT WAS AT THE SAME HOUR,   220 09   CHILDREN OF MY FATHER, RECEIVE THE KINGDOM PREPARED   335 12
SHALL MY HEAVENLY FATHER DO ALSO UNTO YOU, IF YE FROM   222 05   O MERCIFUL FATHER, THROUGH JESUS CHRIST, OUR   335 14
O HEAVENLY FATHER, FOR THE SAKE OF JESUS   223 19   O HEAVENLY FATHER, VOUCHSAFE THAT WE, WHO NOW   335 31
TO GOD AND THE FATHER OF OUR LORD JESUS CHRIST,   223 22   MOST MERCIFUL FATHER, WHO HAST BEEN PLEASED TO TAKE   336 04
THANKS UNTO THE FATHER, WHICH HATH MADE US MEET TO BE   224 08   LIVEST WITH THE FATHER AND THE HOLY GHOST, ONE GOD,   336 14
ZEBEDEE THEIR FATHER, MENDING THEIR NETS   227 31   YE BLESSED OF MY FATHER, INHERIT THE KINGDOM PREPARED   336 26
SHIP AND THEIR FATHER, AND FOLLOWED HIM   227 32   GRANT THIS, O FATHER, FOR THE SAKE OF THE SAME,   336 28
OR SISTERS, OR FATHER, OR MOTHER, OR WIFE, OR   231 19   THE FACE OF MY FATHER WHICH IS IN HEAVEN   339 32
I THANK THEE, O FATHER, LORD OF HEAVEN AND EARTH,   235 04   O MERCIFUL FATHER, WHOSE FACE THE ANGELS OF THY   340 24
EVEN SO, FATHER   235 06   AND MERCIFUL FATHER, WHO DOST GRANT TO CHILDREN AN   340 29
AND NO MAN KNOWETH THE SON, BUT THE FATHER   235 08   ALMIGHTY GOD, FATHER OF MERCIES AND GIVER OF ALL   342 09
ALL THINGS ARE DELIVERED UNTO ME OF MY FATHER   235 08   ALMIGHTY GOD, THE FATHER, THE SON, AND THE HOLY   342 14
ANY MAN THE FATHER, SAVE THE SON, AND HE TO   235 09   12 WHEN MY FATHER AND MY MOTHER FORSAKE ME, *   372 20
THE THRONE OF HIS FATHER DAVID   236 18   5 HE IS A FATHER OF THE FATHERLESS, AND DEFENDETH THE   419 19
TRUE VINE, AND MY FATHER IS THE HUSBANDMAN   238 05   THOU ART MY FATHER, *   451 27
HEREIN IS MY FATHER GLORIFIED, THAT YE BEAR MUCH   238 19   13 YEA, LIKE AS A FATHER PITIETH HIS OWN CHILDREN   466 32
AS THE FATHER HATH LOVED ME, SO HAVE I LOVED YOU   238 20   REVEREND FATHER IN GOD, I PRESENT UNTO YOU   530 10

FATHER   CONTINUED

THE NAME OF THE FATHER, AND OF THE SON, AND OF THE   534 07
GOD ALMIGHTY, THE FATHER, THE SON, AND THE HOLY   535 16
REVEREND FATHER IN GOD, I PRESENT UNTO YOU THESE   536 10
EVEN AS THE FATHER KNOWETH ME, AND I KNOW THE   539 17
AS THE FATHER KNOWETH ME, AND I KNOW THE FATHER   539 18
PRAY TO GOD THE FATHER, BY THE MEDIATION OF OUR ONLY   541 16
US TO KNOW THE FATHER, SON, AND THEE, OF BOTH, TC BE   544 10
ETERNAL MERIT, FATHER, SON, AND HOLY SPIRIT   544 15
PROMISE OF THE FATHER THOU, WHO DOST THE TONGUE WITH   544 21
AND HEAVENLY FATHER, WHO, OF THINE INFINITE LOVE   545 12
THE NAME OF THE FATHER, AND OF THE SON, AND OF THE   546 15
THE NAME OF THE FATHER, AND OF THE SON, AND OF THE   546 21
MOST MERCIFUL FATHER, WE BESEECH THEE TO SEND UPON   547 04
GOD ALMIGHTY, THE FATHER, THE SON, AND THE HOLY   547 17
AS MY FATHER HATH SENT ME, EVEN SO SEND I YOU   552 02
THE NAME OF THE FATHER, AND OF THE SON, AND OF THE   552 12
REVEREND FATHER IN GOD, WE PRESENT UNTO YOU   552 21
OUR HEAVENLY FATHER, WHO HATH GIVEN YOU A GOOD   555 28
US TO KNOW THE FATHER, SON, AND THEE, OF BOTH, TC BE   556 18
ETERNAL MERIT, FATHER, SON, AND HOLY SPIRIT   556 23
PROMISE OF THE FATHER THOU, WHO DOST THE TONGUE WITH   557 06
AND MOST MERCIFUL FATHER, WHO, OF THINE INFINITE   557 20
THE NAME OF THE FATHER, AND OF THE SON, AND OF THE   558 15
MOST MERCIFUL FATHER, SEND DOWN, WE BESEECH THEE,   559 05
GOD ALMIGHTY, THE FATHER, THE SON, AND THE HOLY   559 20
O GOD THE FATHER, HAVE MERCY UPON US   560 03
GLORY BE TO THE FATHER, AND TO THE SON, *   564 02
OF AND GRACIOUSLY ACCEPTED BY OUR HEAVENLY FATHER   564 21
GOD ALMIGHTY, THE FATHER, THE SON, AND THE HOLY   568 16
THE NAME OF THE FATHER, AND OF THE SON, AND OF THE   571 02
O ALMIGHTY FATHER, IN HIS PREVAILING NAME AND   571 14
MOST GRACIOUS FATHER, THE GIVER OF ALL GOOD AND   572 06
WHOM, WITH THE FATHER AND THE SON TOGETHER, WE   572 31
OUR HEAVENLY FATHER, THAT HE HATH CALLED ME TO THIS   577 23
IN GOD THE FATHER ALMIGHTY, MAKER OF HEAVEN AND   577 28
HAND OF GOD THE FATHER ALMIGHTY   578 04
IN GOD THE FATHER, WHO HATH MADE ME, AND ALL THE   578 11
HONOUR THY FATHER AND THY MOTHER   579 13
AND SUCCOUR MY FATHER AND MOTHER   580 03
OUR HEAVENLY FATHER, WHO IS THE GIVER OF ALL   580 29
THE NAME OF THE FATHER, AND OF THE SON, AND OF THE   581 22
O GRACIOUS FATHER, THAT ANOTHER DAY IS ADDED   588 04
O GRACIOUS FATHER, WHC DESIREST NOT THE DEATH OF   589 32
OUR HEAVENLY FATHER, ALMIGHTY AND EVERLASTING GCD,   592 19
O MOST LOVING FATHER, WHO WILLEST US TO GIVE THANKS   596 03
O HEAVENLY FATHER, THOU UNDERSTANDEST ALL THY   596 11
O HEAVENLY FATHER, WHC HAST FILLED THE WORLD WITH   596 17
HEAVENLY FATHER, WHO HAST BLESSED US WITH THE   596 24
GOD OUR HEAVENLY FATHER, WE BESEECH THEE GRACIOUSLY   597 21
O HEAVENLY FATHER, WE BESEECH THEE TO HAVE MERCY UPON   598 13
OUR HEAVENLY FATHER, WHO SETTEST THE SOLITARY IN   598 19
AND GRACIOUS FATHER, FOR THE LOVE OF THY DEAR SCN,   600 12
BLESS, O FATHER, THY GIFTS TO OUR USE AND US TO THY   600 15
OUR FATHER, FOR ALL THY MERCIES, AND MAKE US   600 17
THE FATHER, THE SON, AND THE HOLY GHOST   603 07
THE WORD OF THE FATHER, BEGOTTEN FROM EVERLASTING OF   603 09
WITH THE FATHER, TOOK MAN'S NATURE IN THE WCMB OF THE   603 10
OF THE FATHER, THE VERY AND ETERNAL GOD, AND OF ONE   603 10
TO RECONCILE HIS FATHER TO US, AND TO BE A SACRIFICE,   603 15
FROM THE FATHER AND THE SON, IS OF ONE SUBSTANCE,   603 26
WITH THE FATHER AND THE SON, VERY AND ETERNAL   603 27

FATHER'S

HAVING HIS FATHER'S NAME WRITTEN IN THEIR FOREHEADS   102 31
BE ABOUT MY FATHER'S BUSINESS   111 02
BUT THE FATHER'S WHICH SENT ME   181 28
SEND HIM TO MY FATHER'S HOUSE   190 23
SERVANTS OF MY FATHER'S HAVE BREAD ENOUGH AND TO   202 11
I HAVE KEPT MY FATHER'S COMMANDMENTS, AND ABIDE IN   238 23
IN MY FATHER'S HOUSE ARE MANY MANSIONS   239 31
AND THIS IS THE FATHER'S WILL WHICH HATH SENT ME,   269 17
WOMAN AT HER FATHER'S OR FRIEND'S HANDS, SHALL CAUSE   R 301 25
IN MY FATHER'S HOUSE ARE MANY MANSIONS   331 18
AND THY FATHER'S HOUSE   397 06
MAKE NOT MY FATHER'S HOUSE AN HOUSE OF MERCHANDISE   567 32

FATHERLESS

THE FATHERLESS CHILDREN, AND WIDOWS, AND ALL WHC   057 02
TO VISIT THE FATHERLESS AND WIDOWS IN THEIR   176 16
AND THE FATHERLESS, AND THAT TURN ASIDE THE STRANGER   232 19
OF THE FATHERLESS AND WIDOW, AND LOVETH THE STRANGER,   263 26
TO VISIT THE FATHERLESS AND WIDOWS IN THEIR   266 08
TO HELP THE FATHERLESS AND POOR UNTO THEIR RIGHT,   354 15
FATHER OF THE FATHERLESS, AND DEFENDETH THE CAUSE OF   419 19
3 DEFEND THE POOR AND FATHERLESS   443 22
AND PUT THE FATHERLESS TO DEATH   457 30
CHILDREN BE FATHERLESS, *   480 18
UPON HIS FATHERLESS CHILDREN   480 24
DEFENDETH THE FATHERLESS AND WIDOW   522 21

FATHERLY

COMMEND TO THY FATHERLY GOODNESS ALL THOSE WHO   019 04
COMMEND TO THY FATHERLY GOODNESS ALL THOSE WHO   033 02
DESIRE THY FATHERLY GOODNESS, MERCIFULLY TO ACCEPT   081 15
LET THY FATHERLY HAND, WE BESEECH THEE, EVER BE CVER   298 19
UNDER THY FATHERLY CARE AND PROTECTION   589 04
O GOD, WHOSE FATHERLY CARE REACHETH TO THE UTTERMOST   596 30
LET THY FATHERLY GOODNESS BE UPON ALL THAT THOU HAST   599 05

FATHERS

O LORD GOD OF OUR FATHERS   011 16
AND OUR FATHERS HAVE DECLARED UNTO US, THE   058 28
THE SINS OF THE FATHERS UPON THE CHILDREN, UNTO THE   068 13
TO CONFIRM THE PROMISES MADE UNTO THE FATHERS   092 25
PAST UNTO THE FATHERS BY THE PROPHETS, HATH IN THESE   096 23
MADE UNTO THE FATHERS, GOD HATH FULFILLED THE SAME   169 07
LAID UNTO HIS FATHERS, AND SAW CORRUPTION   169 16
HOW THAT ALL OUR FATHERS WERE UNDER THE CLOUD,   201 06
PROMISED TO OUR FATHERS, AND TO REMEMBER HIS HOLY   244 05
MIGHTY POWER OUR FATHERS WON THEIR LIBERTIES OF CLD   263 18
THE SINS OF THE FATHERS UPON THE CHILDREN, UNTO THE   286 13
AND ALL FATHERS, MOTHERS, GUARDIANS, AND SPONSORS   R 295 10
UNTO OUR FATHERS, HAVING THE TESTIMONY OF A GOOD   317 02
YOUR FATHERS DID EAT MANNA IN THE WILDERNESS, AND ARE   322 23
AS ALL MY FATHERS WERE   325 09
4 OUR FATHERS HOPED IN THEE   366 10
AS ALL MY FATHERS WERE   390 05
O GOD, OUR FATHERS HAVE TOLD US *   394 22
AND PLANTED OUR FATHERS IN   394 25
INSTEAD OF THY FATHERS, THOU SHALT HAVE CHILDREN,   397 19
OF HIS FATHERS, *   401 14
AND SUCH AS OUR FATHERS HAVE TOLD US   434 32
9 WHEN YOUR FATHERS TEMPTED ME,   459 22
6 WE HAVE SINNED WITH OUR FATHERS   473 11
7 OUR FATHERS REGARDED NOT THY WONDERS IN EGYPT,   473 13
OF HIS FATHERS BE HAD IN REMEMBRANCE IN THE SIGHT OF   480 27
THE SINS OF THE FATHERS UPON THE CHILDREN, UNTO THE   578 31
AND ALL FATHERS, MOTHERS, MASTERS, AND MISTRESSES,   R 582 31
THE HEART OF THE FATHERS TO THE CHILDREN, AND THE   598 26
AND THE HEART OF THE CHILDREN TO THE FATHERS   598 27
THAT THE OLD FATHERS DID LOOK ONLY FOR TRANSITORY   604 18

FATLINGS

MY OXEN AND MY FATLINGS ARE KILLED, AND ALL THINGS   218 08

FATNESS

WITH MARROW AND FATNESS, *   415 03
AND THY CLOUDS DROP FATNESS   417 08
EYES SWELL WITH FATNESS, *   428 22
MY FLESH IS DRIED UP FOR WANT OF FATNESS   481 19

FATTED

BRING HITHER THE FATTED CALF, AND KILL IT   202 23
HATH KILLED THE FATTED CALF, BECAUSE HE HATH RECEIVED   202 30
FOR HIM THE FATTED CALF   203 04

FAULT

THEY ARE WITHOUT FAULT BEFORE THE THRONE OF GOD   103 13
I FIND NO FAULT IN THIS MAN   153 04
HAVE FOUND NO FAULT IN THIS MAN TOUCHING THOSE   153 24
THAT I FIND NO FAULT IN HIM   159 03
FOR I FIND NO FAULT IN HIM   159 08
ANY OFFENCE OR FAULT OF ME, O LORD   411 09
THEY RUN AND PREPARE THEMSELVES WITHOUT MY FAULT   411 11
GREATNESS OF THE FAULT, AND ALSO THE HORRIBLE   540 12
BUT IT IS THE FAULT AND CORRUPTION OF THE NATURE UF   604 30

FAULTS

SPARE THOU THOSE, O GOD, WHO CONFESS THEIR FAULTS   006 25
SPARE THOU THOSE, O GOD, WHO CONFESS THEIR FAULTS   023 32
I ACKNOWLEDGE MY FAULTS, *   060 15
REPENT US OF OUR FAULTS, AND SO MAKE HASTE TO HELP US   062 23
BUFFETED FOR YOUR FAULTS, YE SHALL TAKE IT PATIENTLY   172 07
O CLEANSE THOU ME FROM MY SECRET FAULTS   364 09
I ACKNOWLEDGE MY FAULTS, *   403 13
AND MY FAULTS ARE NOT HID FROM THEE   422 11

FAVOUR

WITH THY FAVOUR TO BEHOLD AND BLESS THY SERVANT   017 30
MINDFUL OF THY FAVOUR AND GLAD TO DO THY WILL   036 11
WITH THY GRACIOUS FAVOUR TO BEHOLD OUR UNIVERSITIES,   042 23
THY MOST GRACIOUS FAVOUR, AND FURTHER US WITH THY   049 24
US THEREBY OF THY FAVOUR AND GOODNESS TOWARDS US   083 21
AND IN FAVOUR WITH GOD AND MAN   111 07
THOU HAST FOUND FAVOUR WITH GOD   236 14
THIS SIGN, OF THY FAVOUR AND GRACIOUS GOODNESS   298 18
CONTINUE IN THY FAVOUR, UNTO THEIR LIFE'S END   302 21
WITH HIS FAVOUR LOOK UPON YOU, AND FILL YOU WITH ALL   304 13
TO TAKE HIM HENCE, TAKE HIM UNTO THY FAVOUR   314 12
IN FAVOUR WITH THEE OUR GOD, AND IN PERFECT CHARITY   317 06
ACCORDING TO THE FAVOUR WHICH THOU BEAREST UNTO THY   332 04
BECAUSE HE HAD A FAVOUR UNTO ME   361 05
AND REJOICE, THAT FAVOUR MY RIGHTEOUS DEALING   383 19
THOU HADST A FAVOUR UNTO THEM   394 31
ACCORDING TO THE FAVOUR THAT THOU BEAREST UNTO THY   473 06
MAY ABIDE IN THY FAVOUR AND BE GUIDED IN THE WAY OF   562 12
THY MOST GRACIOUS FAVOUR, AND FURTHER US WITH THY   571 09
THIS CONGREGATION WITH THY LOVE AND FAVOUR   572 26

FAVOURABLE

SUCH JUST AND FAVOURABLE CONSTRUCTION AS IN COMMON   V 43
O LORD, BE FAVOURABLE TO THY PEOPLE, WHO TURN TO THEE   062 29
BE FAVOURABLE, O LORD, BE FAVOURABLE TO THY PEOPLE,   062 29
AND WITH THY FAVOURABLE KINDNESS WILT THOU DEFEND HIM   348 29
18 O BE FAVOURABLE AND GRACIOUS UNTO SION   404 13
HE SHALL BE FAVOURABLE TO THE SIMPLE AND NEEDY,   427 22

FAVOURABLY

FAVOURABLY WITH MERCY HEAR OUR PRAYERS   059 13
BESEECH THEE FAVOURABLY TO HEAR THE PRAYERS OF THY   118 28
BESEECH THEE, FAVOURABLY TO BEHOLD THESE THY SERVANTS   267 04
HE WILL ALSO FAVOURABLY APPROVE OUR GODLY PURPOSE OF   564 22

FAVOURED

THAT ART HIGHLY FAVOURED, THE LORD IS WITH THEE   236 10

FAVOUREST

I KNOW THOU FAVOUREST ME, *   392 21

FEAR

MIGHT SERVE HIM WITHOUT FEAR   014 21
MAY NOT FEAR THE POWER OF ANY ADVERSARIES,   017 09
OF THEIR CALLING TO SERVE THIS PEOPLE IN THY FEAR   018 14
IS ON THEM THAT FEAR HIM   026 18
OF THE WORLD SHALL FEAR HIM   028 31
DEFENDED FROM THE FEAR OF OUR ENEMIES, MAY PASS OUR   031 22
THE LAW IN THE FEAR OF THEE ALONE   036 05
OF HIS LIFE IN THY FEAR, AND TO THY GLORY   045 20
THE TRUE FAITH AND FEAR OF GOD, AND IN BROTHERLY   048 03
HEART TO LOVE AND FEAR THEE, AND DILIGENTLY TO LIVE   056 12
SERVANTS DEPARTED THIS LIFE IN THY FAITH AND FEAR   074 35
FAILING THEM FOR FEAR, AND FOR LOOKING AFTER THOSE   093 08
SAID UNTO THEM, FEAR NOT   099 14
THOU SON OF DAVID, FEAR NOT TO TAKE UNTO THEE MARY   105 04
OWN SALVATION WITH FEAR AND TREMBLING   106 04
FEAR TO WHOM FEAR   114 27
FEAR TO WHOM FEAR   114 27
AND HARDENED OUR HEART FROM THY FEAR   139 25
DOST NOT THOU FEAR GOD, SEEING THOU ART IN THE SAME   155 03
WERE ASSEMBLED FOR FEAR OF THE JEWS, CAME JESUS AND   171 16
FEAR GOD   173 25
THERE IS NO FEAR IN LOVE   189 28
BUT PERFECT LOVE CASTETH OUT FEAR   189 29
BECAUSE FEAR HATH TORMENT   189 29
UP IN THY STEDFAST FEAR AND LOVE   191 05
TO HAVE A PERPETUAL FEAR AND LOVE OF THY HOLY NAME   191 08
SAID UNTO SIMON, FEAR NOT   196 28
NOT RECEIVED THE SPIRIT OF BONDAGE AGAIN TO FEAR   200 08
AND THERE CAME A FEAR ON ALL   213 07
TO ANOTHER IN THE FEAR OF GOD   217 32
FROM HIS RIGHT, AND FEAR NOT ME, SAITH THE LORD OF   232 20
SAID UNTO HER, FEAR NOT, MARY   236 13
AND FEAR CAME ON ALL THAT DWELT ROUND ABOUT THEM   243 26
SERVE HIM WITHOUT FEAR, IN HOLINESS AND RIGHTEOUSNESS   244 08
THOU SHALT FEAR THE LORD THY GOD   263 29
TO ANOTHER IN THE FEAR OF GOD   267 13
BELIEVE IN HIM, TO FEAR HIM, AND TO LOVE HIM WITH ALL   288 17
SPIRIT OF THY HOLY FEAR, NOW AND FOR EVER   297 22
AND IN THE FEAR OF GOD   300 18
UP IN THY FAITH AND FEAR, TO THE HONOUR AND GLORY OF   303 18
WHOM THEN SHALL I FEAR   326 06
WILL WE NOT FEAR, THOUGH THE EARTH BE MOVED, *   327 05
NOT RECEIVED THE SPIRIT OF BONDAGE AGAIN TO FEAR   330 21
TO ALL WHO LOVE AND FEAR THEE, SAYING, COME, YE   335 11
OF DEATH, I WILL FEAR NO EVIL   338 24
SERVE THE LORD IN FEAR, *   346 19
AND IN THY FEAR WILL I WORSHIP TOWARD THY HOLY   348 14
20 PUT THEM IN FEAR, O LORD, *   352 32
BROUGHT IN GREAT FEAR, EVEN WHERE NO FEAR WAS   356 25
FEAR, EVEN WHERE NO FEAR WAS   356 26
MUCH OF THEM THAT FEAR THE LORD   357 14
9 THE FEAR OF THE LORD IS CLEAN, AND ENDURETH FOR   363 33
THE LORD, YE THAT FEAR HIM   367 18
AND FEAR HIM, ALL YE SEED OF ISRAEL   367 19
SIGHT OF THEM THAT FEAR HIM   367 24
OF DEATH, I WILL FEAR NO EVIL   368 17
IS AMONG THEM THAT FEAR HIM   370 12
WHOM THEN SHALL I FEAR   371 25
THE MULTITUDE, AND FEAR IS ON EVERY SIDE   376 22
UP FOR THEM THAT FEAR THEE, *   377 03
8 LET ALL THE EARTH FEAR THE LORD   379 02
IS UPON THEM THAT FEAR HIM, *   379 24
HE DELIVERED ME OUT OF ALL MY FEAR   380 10
ABOUT THEM THAT FEAR HIM, *   380 16
9 O FEAR THE LORD, YE THAT ARE HIS SAINTS   380 19
FOR THEY THAT FEAR HIM LACK NOTHING   380 20
WILL TEACH YOU THE FEAR OF THE LORD   380 24
THAT THERE IS NO FEAR OF GOD BEFORE HIS EYES   383 27
SHALL SEE IT, AND FEAR, *   390 16
WILL WE NOT FEAR, THOUGH THE EARTH BE MOVED, *   397 27
5 FEAR CAME THERE UPON THEM   399 20
WHEREFORE SHOULD I FEAR IN THE DAYS OF EVIL, *   400 14
SHALL SEE THIS, AND FEAR, *   404 31
AFRAID WHERE NO FEAR WAS   405 25
AND THE FEAR OF DEATH IS FALLEN UPON ME   406 26
WILL NOT TURN, NOR FEAR GOD   407 32
AND WILL NOT FEAR WHAT FLESH CAN DO UNTO ME   408 22
A TOKEN FOR SUCH AS FEAR THEE, *   412 19
UNTO THOSE THAT FEAR THY NAME   413 16
MY LIFE FROM FEAR OF THE ENEMY   413 20
THEY HIT HIM, AND FEAR NOT   415 26
ALL YE THAT FEAR GOD   418 12
OF THE WORLD SHALL FEAR HIM   419 05
5 THEY SHALL FEAR THEE, AS LONG AS THE SUN AND MOON   427 06
THEY SHOULD NOT FEAR, *   438 17
IS NIGH THEM THAT FEAR HIM   446 25
THAT I MAY FEAR THY NAME   447 26
AND THE FEAR OF THEE HATH UNDONE ME   449 30
THE NATIONS SHALL FEAR THY NAME, O LORD   465 09

FEAR   CONTINUED

TOWARD THEM THAT FEAR HIM   466 29
UNTO THEM THAT FEAR HIM   466 33
EVER UPON THEM THAT FEAR HIM   467 09
MEAT UNTO THEM THAT FEAR HIM   483 03
10 THE FEAR OF THE LORD IS THE BEGINNING OF WISDOM   483 14
11 YE THAT FEAR THE LORD, PUT YOUR TRUST IN THE LORD   485 32
BLESS THEM THAT FEAR THE LORD, *   486 04
LET THEM NOW THAT FEAR THE LORD CONFESS, *   488 06
I WILL NOT FEAR WHAT MAN DOETH UNTO ME   488 10
THAT I MAY FEAR THEE   492 15
OF ALL THEM THAT FEAR THEE, *   494 06
74 THEY THAT FEAR THEE WILL BE GLAD WHEN THEY SEE ME   495 02
79 LET SUCH AS FEAR THEE, AND HAVE KNOWN THY   495 14
FLESH TREMBLETH FOR FEAR OF THEE   498 08
ARE ALL THEY THAT FEAR THE LORD, *   506 06
YE THAT FEAR THE LORD, PRAISE THE LORD   511 10
DESIRE OF THEM THAT FEAR HIM   521 30
IS IN THEM THAT FEAR HIM, *   523 17
WERE ASSEMBLED FOR FEAR OF THE JEWS, CAME JESUS, AND   551 29
US THE SPIRIT OF FEAR, BUT OF POWER, AND LOVE,   558 18
BELIEVE IN HIM, TO FEAR HIM, AND TO LOVE HIM WITH ALL   579 28
AND FROM THE FEAR OF THEM   591 27
THAT OTHERS MAY FEAR TO DO THE LIKE,) AS HE THAT   609 39

FEARED

WERE DONE, THEY FEARED GREATLY, SAYING, TRULY THIS   137 33
FOR THEY FEARED THE PEOPLE   148 14
AND THEY FEARED AS THEY ENTERED INTO THE CLOUD   249 06
THEREFORE SHALT THOU BE FEARED   328 10
2 FOR THE LORD IS HIGH, AND TO BE FEARED   398 23
EVEN THOU ART TO BE FEARED   433 02
BRING PRESENTS UNTO HIM THAT OUGHT TO BE FEARED   433 12
GREATLY TO BE FEARED IN THE COUNCIL OF THE SAINTS, *   450 19
HE IS MORE TO BE FEARED THAN ALL GODS   460 07
THEREFORE SHALT THOU BE FEARED   507 15

FEARETH

AMONG YOU THAT FEARETH THE LORD, THAT OBEYETH THE   144 23
NATION HE THAT FEARETH HIM, AND WORKETH   166 14
AMONG YOU FEARETH GOD, TO YOU IS THE WORD OF THIS   168 25
NATION HE THAT FEARETH HIM, AND WORKETH   183 31
HE THAT FEARETH IS NOT MADE PERFECT IN LOVE   189 29
MAN IS HE THAT FEARETH THE LORD   370 08
OR FEARETH ARIGHT THY INDIGNATION   454 12
IS THE MAN THAT FEARETH THE LORD   483 18
THAT FEARETH THE LORD   506 14

FEARFUL

AND COME TO A FEARFUL END   429 15
AND FEARFUL THINGS BY THE RED SEA   474 12

FEARFULLY

FOR I AM FEARFULLY AND WONDERFULLY MADE   515 15

FEARFULNESS

5 FEARFULNESS AND TREMBLING ARE COME UPON ME,   406 28

FEARLESSLY

US GRACE FEARLESSLY TO CONTEND AGAINST EVIL, AND TO   044 10

FEARS

US FROM FAITHLESS FEARS AND WORLDLY ANXIETIES, AND   596 06

FEAST

AND ON THE FEAST OF THE TRANSFIGURATION   R 008 20
UPON THE FEAST OF TRINITY ONLY   R 079 06
TO SUCH A HEAVENLY FEAST, IN THE MARRIAGE-GARMENT   087 13
PREPARED A RICH FEAST, DECKED HIS TABLE WITH ALL KIND   088 18
WHO REFUSED THE FEAST IN THE GOSPEL, BECAUSE THEY HAD   089 03
BUT COUNTED UNWORTHY OF THE HEAVENLY FEAST   089 06
SUNDAY OR OTHER FEAST MAY BE USED AT THE EVENING   R 090 06
EVERY YEAR AT THE FEAST OF THE PASSOVER   110 19
UP TO JERUSALEM AFTER THE CUSTOM OF THE FEAST   110 21
OUT NOW, AND BEAR UNTO THE GOVERNOR OF THE FEAST   113 23
THE RULER OF THE FEAST HAD TASTED THE WATER THAT WAS   113 24
GOVERNOR OF THE FEAST CALLED THE BRIDEGROOM, AND   113 26
EXCEPT UPON THE FEAST OF ST   R 125 24
THE PASSOVER, A FEAST OF THE JEWS, WAS NIGH   131 25
NOW AT THAT FEAST THE GOVERNOR WAS WONT TO RELEASE   135 26
TWO DAYS WAS THE FEAST OF THE PASSOVER, AND OF   139 32
NOT ON THE FEAST DAY, LEST THERE BE AN UPROAR   139 35
NOW AT THAT FEAST HE RELEASED UNTO THEM ONE PRISONER,   145 12
NOW THE FEAST OF UNLEAVENED BREAD DREW NIGH, WHICH IS   148 12
HE MUST RELEASE ONE UNTO THEM AT THE FEAST   153 29
NOW BEFORE THE FEAST OF THE PASSOVER, WHEN JESUS KNEW   155 23
LET US KEEP THE FEAST, NOT WITH OLD LEAVEN, NEITHER   162 01
LET US KEEP THE FEAST, NOT WITH OLD LEAVEN, NEITHER   165 14
THE PASCHAL FEAST, MAY BE FOUND WORTHY TO ATTAIN TO   168 20
EXCEPT UPON THE FEAST OF ST   R 178 31

FEAST-DAY

AND UPON OUR SOLEMN FEAST-DAY   442 17

FEASTS

  UPON THE FEASTS OF THE PURIFICATION, ANNUNCIATION,   R 077 28

FEATHERED

  AND FEATHERED FOWLS LIKE AS THE SAND OF THE SEA   436 26

FEATHERS

  AND HER FEATHERS LIKE GOLD   420 08
  AND THOU SHALT BE SAFE UNDER HIS FEATHERS   455 03

FED

  AND DESIRING TO BE FED WITH THE CRUMBS WHICH FELL   190 06
  THEE AN HUNGRED, AND FED THEE   259 10
  AND VERILY THOU SHALT BE FED   384 30
  73 SO HE FED THEM WITH A FAITHFUL AND TRUE HEART,   439 24
  17 I WOULD HAVE FED THEM ALSO WITH THE FINEST   443 13

FEEBLE

  I AM SO FEEBLE THAT I CANNOT SPEAK   311 06
  8 I AM FEEBLE AND SORE SMITTEN   388 06
  I AM SO FEEBLE THAT I CANNOT SPEAK   433 23
  THERE WAS NOT ONE FEEBLE PERSON AMONG THEIR TRIBES   472 12

FEED

  DIED FOR THEE, AND FEED ON HIM IN THY HEART BY FAITH, 082 34
  DOST VOUCHSAFE TO FEED US WHO HAVE DAILY RECEIVED   083 17
  WHO COME TO FEED ON THE BANQUET OF THAT MOST HEAVENLY 089 18
  THINE ENEMY HUNGER, FEED HIM   113 06
  ALL MY GOODS TO FEED THE POOR, AND THOUGH I GIVE MY 122 27
  INTO HIS FIELDS TO FEED SWINE   202 08
  HE SHALL FEED HIS FLOCK LIKE A SHEPHERD   243 08
  HIM EARNESTLY TO FEED THY FLOCK   244 24
  OF THE THRONE SHALL FEED THEM, AND SHALL LEAD THEM   257 14
  HE SHALL FEED HIS FLOCK LIKE A SHEPHERD   338 12
  HE SHALL FEED ME IN A GREEN PASTURE, *   338 19
  OF THE THRONE SHALL FEED THEM, AND SHALL LEAD THEM   341 26
  2 HE SHALL FEED ME IN A GREEN PASTURE, *   368 12
  FEED THEM, AND SET THEM UP FOR EVER   373 28
  AND TO FEED THEM IN THE TIME OF DEARTH   379 26
  THAT HE MIGHT FEED JACOB HIS PEOPLE, AND ISRAEL HIS 439 22
  TO PREMONISH, TO FEED AND PROVIDE FOR THE LORD'S   539 30
  CHARGE THEM TO FEED THY FLOCK   549 09
  YOU OVERSEERS, TO FEED THE CHURCH OF GOD, WHICH HE   550 28
  HE SAITH UNTO HIM, FEED MY LAMBS   551 16
  HE SAITH UNTO HIM, FEED MY SHEEP   551 19
  SAITH UNTO HIM, FEED MY SHEEP   551 24
  FEED THEM, DEVOUR THEM NOT   558 26
  ARE FAITHFULLY TO FEED THAT PORTION OF THE FLOCK OF 569 24

FEEDEST

  5 THOU FEEDEST THEM WITH THE BREAD OF TEARS, *   441 12

FEEDETH

  HEAVENLY FATHER FEEDETH THEM   211 17
  AND FEEDETH THE YOUNG RAVENS THAT CALL UPON HIM   264 30
  HEAVENLY FATHER FEEDETH THEM   266 16
  WHO FEEDETH THE HUNGRY   522 15
  AND FEEDETH THE YOUNG RAVENS THAT CALL UPON HIM   523 13

FEEL

  OF HIS SINS, IF HE FEEL HIS CONSCIENCE TROUBLED WITH R 313 25
  MAKE THEE KNOW AND FEEL, THAT THERE IS NONE OTHER   314 19
  THINE ENEMIES SHALL FEEL THINE HAND   365 20
  AND SUCH AS FEEL IN THEMSELVES THE WORKING OF THE   606 18

FEELING

  WHO BEING PAST FEELING HAVE GIVEN THEMSELVES OVER   216 08

FEET

  AND TO GUIDE OUR FEET INTO THE WAY OF PEACE   014 32
  AND FINALLY TO BEAT DOWN SATAN UNDER OUR FEET   056 25
  AT A YOUNG MAN'S FEET, WHOSE NAME WAS SAUL   100 12
  WASH THE DISCIPLES' FEET, AND TO WIPE THEM WITH THE 155 33
  SAITH UNTO HIM, LORD, DOST THOU WASH MY FEET   156 03
  THOU SHALT NEVER WASH MY FEET   156 05
  LORD, NOT MY FEET ONLY, BUT ALSO MY HANDS AND MY   156 07
  SAVE TO WASH HIS FEET, BUT IS CLEAN EVERY WHIT   156 09
  HE HAD WASHED THEIR FEET, AND HAD TAKEN HIS GARMENTS, 156 12
  YOUR LORD AND MASTER, HAVE WASHED YOUR FEET   156 16
  YE ALSO OUGHT TO WASH ONE ANOTHER'S FEET   156 17
  MY HANDS AND MY FEET, THAT IT IS I MYSELF   169 33
  HE SHEWED THEM HIS HANDS AND HIS FEET   170 02
  AND PUT A RING ON HIS HAND, AND SHOES ON HIS FEET   202 23
  ON HIS FACE AT HIS FEET, GIVING HIM THANKS   210 09
  AND YOUR FEET SHOD WITH THE PREPARATION OF THE GOSPEL 219 15
  FELL DOWN AT HIS FEET, AND BESOUGHT HIM, SAYING, HAVE 221 27
  BEAUTIFUL ARE THE FEET OF THEM THAT PREACH THE GOSPEL 227 09
  TO GUIDE OUR FEET INTO THE WAY OF PEACE   244 16
  TWO HANDS OR TWO FEET TO BE CAST INTO EVERLASTING   253 06
  TILL HE HATH PUT ALL ENEMIES UNDER HIS FEET   328 30
  FOR HE HATH PUT ALL THINGS UNDER HIS FEET   328 32
  HAST PUT ALL THINGS IN SUBJECTION UNDER HIS FEET   351 13
  AND IT WAS DARK UNDER HIS FEET   360 16
  MY FEET LIKE HARTS' FEET, *   362 02
  34 HE MAKETH MY FEET LIKE HARTS' FEET, *   362 02

FEET   CONTINUED

  BUT FALL UNDER MY FEET   362 15
  17 THEY PIERCED MY HANDS AND MY FEET   367 06
  HE SHALL PLUCK MY FEET OUT OF THE NET   370 15
  BUT HAST SET MY FEET IN A LARGE ROOM   376 07
  AND SET MY FEET UPON THE ROCK, AND ORDERED MY GOINGS 390 12
  AND THE NATIONS UNDER OUR FEET   398 26
  FROM DEATH, AND MY FEET FROM FALLING, *   409 09
  LAID A NET FOR MY FEET, AND PRESSED DOWN MY SOUL   409 26
  SUFFERETH NOT OUR FEET TO SLIP   417 32
  2 NEVERTHELESS, MY FEET WERE ALMOST GONE, *   428 12
  4 LIFT UP THY FEET, THAT THOU MAYEST UTTERLY DESTROY 430 10
  AND THE DRAGON SHALT THOU TREAD UNDER THY FEET   455 22
  18 WHOSE FEET THEY HURT IN THE STOCKS   471 08
  FEET HAVE THEY, AND WALK NOT   485 24
  FROM TEARS, AND MY FEET FROM FALLING   487 05
  AND TURNED MY FEET UNTO THY TESTIMONIES   493 30
  I HAVE REFRAINED MY FEET FROM EVERY EVIL WAY, *   496 28
  A LANTERN UNTO MY FEET, *   497 07
  2 OUR FEET SHALL STAND IN THY GATES, *   503 11
  AND GUIDE OUR FEET INTO THE WAY OF PEACE   594 14

FEIGN

  STRANGERS SHALL FEIGN OBEDIENCE UNTO ME   362 29
  TO BE HEARD, WHICH FEIGN THAT THE OLD FATHERS DID   604 18

FEIGNED

  HOW LITTLE SUCH FEIGNED EXCUSES WILL AVAIL BEFORE   089 02
  GOETH NOT OUT OF FEIGNED LIPS   358 18

FELICITY

  THIS LIFE, TO ATTAIN EVERLASTING JOY AND FELICITY   018 04
  THE BURDEN OF THE FLESH, ARE IN JOY AND FELICITY   334 22
  HIM EVERLASTING FELICITY, *   365 15
  I MAY SEE THE FELICITY OF THY CHOSEN, *   473 08
  THEY ATTAIN TO EVERLASTING FELICITY   606 15

FELL

  HAD SAID THIS, HE FELL ASLEEP   100 17
  HIS MOTHER, AND FELL DOWN, AND WORSHIPPED HIM   109 21
  AS HE SOWED, SOME FELL BY THE WAY-SIDE   121 21
  AND SOME FELL UPON A ROCK   121 22
  AND SOME FELL AMONG THORNS   121 24
  AND OTHER FELL ON GOOD GROUND, AND SPRANG UP, AND   121 25
  AND THAT WHICH FELL AMONG THORNS ARE THEY, WHICH,   122 05
  A LITTLE, AND FELL ON THE GROUND, AND PRAYED THAT,   141 33
  BY THE WILL OF GOD, FELL ON SLEEP, AND WAS LAID UNTO 169 16
  THE HOLY GHOST FELL ON ALL THEM WHICH HEARD THE WORD 184 21
  THE CRUMBS WHICH FELL FROM THE RICH MAN'S TABLE   190 07
  PETER SAW IT, HE FELL DOWN AT JESUS' KNEES, SAYING, 196 23
  THEM COMMITTED, AND FELL IN ONE DAY THREE AND TWENTY 201 18
  AND RAN, AND FELL ON HIS NECK, AND KISSED HIM   202 18
  TO JERICHO, AND FELL AMONG THIEVES, WHICH STRIPPED   208 22
  UNTO HIM THAT FELL AMONG THE THIEVES   209 03
  GLORIFIED GOD, AND FELL DOWN ON HIS FACE AT HIS FEET, 210 09
  SERVANT THEREFORE FELL DOWN, AND WORSHIPPED HIM,   221 19
  HIS FELLOW-SERVANT FELL DOWN AT HIS FEET, AND   221 27
  AND HE FELL TO THE EARTH, AND HEARD A VOICE SAYING   229 32
  IMMEDIATELY THERE FELL FROM HIS EYES AS IT HAD BEEN 230 34
  BY TRANSGRESSION FELL, THAT HE MIGHT GO TO HIS OWN   234 30
  AND THE LOT FELL UPON MATTHIAS   234 32
  AND HIS CHAINS FELL OFF FROM HIS HANDS   245 15
  AND FELL BEFORE THE THRONE ON THEIR FACES,   256 30
  THEY STUMBLED AND FELL   371 28
  THEIR BACKS, AND FELL AWAY LIKE THEIR FOREFATHERS   438 26
  TIME AS THE STORM FELL UPON THEE   442 26
  THEY FELL DOWN, AND THERE WAS NONE TO HELP THEM   476 29
  WHICH FELL UPON THE HILL OF SION   509 18

FELLOW

  SERVICE OF THEIR FELLOW MEN   043 31
  BENEFIT OF OUR FELLOW MEN   044 23
  OF A TRUTH THIS FELLOW ALSO WAS WITH HIM   151 17
  WE FOUND THIS FELLOW PERVERTING THE NATION, AND   152 29

FELLOW-CITIZENS

  BUT FELLOW-CITIZENS WITH THE SAINTS, AND OF THE   255 04

FELLOW-HEIRS

  SHOULD BE FELLOW-HEIRS, AND OF THE SAME BODY, AND   108 14

FELLOW-MEN

  OR FORGOTTEN OF THEIR FELLOW-MEN   599 07

FELLOW-SERVANT

  AND HIS FELLOW-SERVANT FELL DOWN AT HIS FEET, AND   221 26
  ON THY FELLOW-SERVANT, EVEN AS I HAD PITY ON THEE   222 02
  OUR DEAR FELLOW-SERVANT, WHO IS FOR YOU A FAITHFUL   223 30

FELLOW-SERVANTS

  OF HIS FELLOW-SERVANTS, WHICH OWED HIM AN HUNDRED   221 24
  WHEN HIS FELLOW-SERVANTS SAW WHAT WAS DONE, THEY WERE 221 30

FELLOWS

THEE WITH THE OIL OF GLADNESS ABOVE THY FELLOWS	097 13
THEE WITH THE OIL OF GLADNESS ABOVE THY FELLOWS	396 31
THAT BE HER FELLOWS SHALL BEAR HER COMPANY, AND SHALL	397 15

FELLOWSHIP

THE GOODLY FELLOWSHIP OF THE PROPHETS PRAISE THEE	010 17
AND THE FELLOWSHIP OF THE HOLY GHOST, BE WITH US	020 13
AND THE FELLOWSHIP OF THE HOLY GHOST, BE WITH US	034 13
IN THEIR FELLOWSHIP, MAY RUN WITH PATIENCE THE RACE	079 24
IN THAT HOLY FELLOWSHIP, AND DO ALL SUCH GCOD WCRKS	083 27
AND TRULY OUR FELLOWSHIP IS WITH THE FATHER, ANC WITH	101 19
ALSO MAY HAVE FELLOWSHIP WITH US	101 19
THAT WE HAVE FELLOWSHIP WITH HIM, AND WALK IN	101 24
WE HAVE FELLOWSHIP ONE WITH ANOTHER, AND THE BLCOD OF	101 26
WHAT IS THE FELLOWSHIP OF THE MYSTERY, WHICH FRCM THE	108 21
AND HAVE NO FELLOWSHIP WITH THE UNFRUITFUL WORKS CF	129 16
INTO THE FELLOWSHIP OF CHRIST'S RELIGION, THAT THEY	173 07
FOR YOUR FELLOWSHIP IN THE GOSPEL FROM THE FIRST	220 24
COMMUNION AND FELLOWSHIP, IN THE MYSTICAL BODY CF THY	256 06
IN THE FELLOWSHIP OF THE HOLY GHOST, BE WITH US	268 25
AND THE FELLOWSHIP OF THE HOLY GHOST, BE WITH US	289 30
IN THE APOSTLES' TEACHING AND FELLOWSHIP	291 15
AND THE FELLOWSHIP OF THE HOLY GHOST, BE WITH US	295 05
IN THE FELLOWSHIP OF THY SAINTS	334 17
AND THE FELLOWSHIP OF THE HOLY GHOST, BE WITH US	341 06
WILL I HAVE FELLOWSHIP WITH THE DECEITFUL	371 05
AND THE FELLOWSHIP OF THE HOLY GHOST, BE WITH US	589 10
AND THE FELLOWSHIP OF THE HOLY GHOST, BE WITH US	592 03
AND THE FELLOWSHIP OF THE HOLY GHOST, BE WITH US	592 28
AND IN THE FELLOWSHIP OF THY SAINTS	597 06

FEMALE

THEM MALE AND FEMALE, AND SAID, FOR THIS CAUSE SHALL	268 07
AND FOR EVERY FEMALE, ONE GODFATHER AND TWC	R 273 10

FERVENT

BOLDNESS WITH FERVENT ZEAL CONSTANTLY TC PREACH THE	078 29
FERVENT IN SPIRIT	111 25
ALL THINGS HAVE FERVENT CHARITY AMONG YOURSELVES	179 13
OUT FOR THE VERY FERVENT DESIRE *	491 06
AND SO ENKINDLE FERVENT CHARITY AMONG US ALL,	598 28

FERVENTLY

IT DOTH FERVENTLY KINDLE THEIR LCVE TCWARDS GOD	606 22

FESTIVALS

ON OTHER FESTIVALS FOR WHICH A PROPER EPISTLE ANC	R 008 33

FETCH

AND SO FETCH THEM HOME, BLESSED LORD, TO THY FOLD,	157 10
FROM ON HIGH TO FETCH ME, *	360 31

FEVER

SEVENTH HOUR THE FEVER LEFT HIM	220 08
IS HUSHED, AND THE FEVER OF LIFE IS OVER, AND CUR	594 32

FEW

TRULY IS PLENTEOUS, BLT THE LABOURERS ARE FEW	073 12
AS I WROTE AFORE IN FEW WORDS, WHEREBY, WHEN YE READ,	108 10
MANY ARE CALLED, BLT FEW CHOSEN	120 13
A PREPARING, WHEREIN FEW, THAT IS, EIGHT SOULS WERE	161 28
AND THEY HAD A FEW SMALL FISHES	199 21
MANY ARE CALLED, BUT FEW ARE CHOSEN	218 29
BUT THE LABOURERS ARE FEW	254 14
THERE WERE YET BUT A FEW OF THEM, *	470 26
7 LET HIS DAYS BE FEW	480 17
TRULY IS PLENTEOUS, BLT THE LABOURERS ARE FEW	538 18

FEWER

IF THERE BE FEWER THAN TWENTY-FIVE SUNDAYS, THE	R 224 35

FIE

FIE ON THEE	383 06
FIE ON THEE	383 06
THAT SAY UNTO ME, FIE UPON THEE	391 20
FIE UPON THEE	391 20

FIELD

ABIDING IN THE FIELD, KEEPING WATCH OVER THEIR FLOCK	099 11
UNTO A MAN WHICH SOWED GOOD SEED IN HIS FIELD	116 19
DIDST NOT THOU SOW GOOD SEED IN THY FIELD	116 24
THEM THE POTTER'S FIELD, TO BURY STRANGERS IN	135 12
WHEREFORE THAT FIELD WAS CALLED, THE FIELD CF BLCCD,	135 13
WAS CALLED, THE FIELD OF BLOOD, UNTO THIS DAY	135 13
FOR THE POTTER'S FIELD, AS THE LORD APPOINTED ME	135 18
NOW HIS ELDER SON WAS IN THE FIELD	202 26
THE LILIES OF THE FIELD, HOW THEY GROW	211 21
THE GRASS OF THE FIELD, WHICH TO-DAY IS, AND	211 25
MAN PURCHASED A FIELD WITH THE REWARD OF INIQUITY	234 13
INSOMUCH AS THAT FIELD IS CALLED IN THEIR PROPER	234 16
IS TO SAY, THE FIELD OF BLOOD	234 17
GOODLINESS THEREOF IS AS THE FLOWER OF THE FIELC	242 29
THE TREE OF THE FIELD SHALL YIELD HER FRUIT, ANC THE	262 10

FIELD   CONTINUED

THE LILIES OF THE FIELD, HOW THEY GROW	266 19
THE GRASS OF THE FIELD, WHICH TO-DAY IS, AND	266 23
AND THE BEASTS OF THE FIELD	351 14
WILD BEASTS OF THE FIELD ARE IN MY SIGHT	402 13
EVEN IN THE FIELD OF ZOAN	435 25
HIS WONDERS IN THE FIELD OF ZOAN	437 28
WILD BEASTS OF THE FIELD DEVOUR IT	441 29
12 LET THE FIELD BE JOYFUL, AND ALL THAT IS IN IT	460 24
FOR HE FLOURISHETH AS A FLOWER OF THE FIELD	467 05
ALL BEASTS OF THE FIELD DRINK THEREOF, *	468 15

FIELDS

SENT HIM INTO HIS FIELDS TO FEED SWINE	202 08
AND TEN THOUSANDS IN OUR FIELDS	520 20

FIERCE

WERE THE MORE FIERCE, SAYING, HE STIRRETH UP THE	153 04

FIERCENESS

10 THE FIERCENESS OF MAN SHALL TURN TO THY PRAISE	433 08
AND THE FIERCENESS OF THEM SHALT THOU REFRAIN	433 09

FIERY

TO QUENCH ALL THE FIERY DARTS OF THE WICKED	219 17
MAKE THEM LIKE A FIERY OVEN IN TIME OF THY WRATH	365 22

FIFTEENTH

OUT OF THE FIFTEENTH CHAPTER OF THE FIRST EPISTLE OF	R 328 18

FIFTH

SERVICE FOR THE FIFTH SUNDAY AFTER THE EPIPHANY CN	R 224 35

FIFTY

THOU ART NOT YET FIFTY YEARS OLD, AND HAST THOU SEEN	133 30

FIG

BEHOLD THE FIG TREE, AND ALL THE TREES	093 14

FIG-TREES

33 HE SMOTE THEIR VINES ALSO AND FIG-TREES	472 04

FIGHT

SO FIGHT I, NOT AS ONE THAT BEATETH THE AIR	119 10
HAVE FOUGHT A GOOD FIGHT, I HAVE FINISHED MY COURSE,	253 26
AND MANFULLY TO FIGHT UNDER HIS BANNER, AGAINST SIN,	280 08
MINE HANDS TO FIGHT, *	362 04
AGAINST THEM THAT FIGHT AGAINST ME	381 18
AND FIGHT THOU AGAINST THEM THAT FIGHT AGAINST ME	381 18
THEY BE MANY THAT FIGHT AGAINST ME, O THOU MOST	408 17
TEACHETH MY HANDS TO WAR, AND MY FINGERS TO FIGHT	519 23

FIGHTING

HE IS DAILY FIGHTING, AND TROUBLING ME	408 15

FIGS

OF THORNS, OR FIGS OF THISTLES	200 18

FIGURE

THE LIKE FIGURE WHEREUNTO, EVEN BAPTISM, DOTH ALSO	161 29

FIGURES

WHICH ARE THE FIGURES OF THE TRUE	022 23
WHICH ARE THE FIGURES OF THE TRUE	147 31

FILL

FILL THEM WITH THE LOVE OF TRUTH AND RIGHTEOUSNESS	018 12
TIME OF PROSPERITY, FILL OUR HEARTS WITH	036 22
BE PLEASED TO FILL IT WITH ALL TRUTH, IN ALL PEACE	037 17
AND SO FILL US WITH GOOD THINGS THAT THE POOR AND	040 11
NOW THE GOD OF HOPE FILL YOU WITH ALL JOY AND PEACE	092 32
SAITH UNTO THEM, FILL THE WATER-POTS WITH WATER	113 21
THAT HE MIGHT FILL ALL THINGS	237 18
AND FILL THEM, O LORD, WITH THE SPIRIT OF THY HOLY	297 21
LOOK UPON YOU, AND FILL YOU WITH ALL SPIRITUAL	304 13
AND I SHALL FILL IT	442 34
HE SHALL FILL THE PLACES WITH THE DEAD BODIES, AND	482 18
THAT HE MIGHT FILL ALL THINGS	538 05
HEAVENLY AID, AND FILL THE HEARTS WHICH THOU HAST	544 20
HEAVENLY AID, AND FILL THE HEARTS WHICH THOU HAST	556 28
IN ORDER TO FILL MEN'S MINDS WITH GREATER	564 17
FILL MY MEMORY WITH THE WORDS OF THY LAW	573 16
FILL HIS HEART WITH CONFIDENCE, THAT THOUGH HE BE	597 23
FILL THEM WITH FAITH, VIRTUE, KNOWLEDGE, TEMPERANCE,	598 23

FILLED

THY BARNS BE FILLED WITH PLENTY, AND THY PRESSES	005 22
HE HATH FILLED THE HUNGRY WITH GOOD THINGS	026 24
MAY EVERMORE BE FILLED WITH THE POWER OF HIS DIVINE	043 24

FILLED   CONTINUED

JESUS CHRIST, BE FILLED WITH THY GRACE AND HEAVENLY   081 26
AND , BEING FILLED WITH THE HOLY GHOST, MAY LEARN TO   099 29
AND THEY FILLED THEM UP TO THE BRIM   113 21
WHEN THEY WERE FILLED, HE SAID UNTO HIS DISCIPLES,   132 06
AND FILLED TWELVE BASKETS WITH THE   132 09
A SPUNGE, AND FILLED IT WITH VINEGAR, AND PUT IT ON A   137 21
AND ONE RAN AND FILLED A SPUNGE FULL OF VINEGAR, AND   146 31
AND THEY FILLED A SPUNGE WITH VINEGAR, AND PUT IT   160 26
SORROW HATH FILLED YOUR HEART   175 09
AND IT FILLED ALL THE HOUSE WHERE THEY WERE   180 20
AND THEY WERE ALL FILLED WITH THE HOLY GHOST, AND   180 23
THEM TO COME IN, THAT MY HOUSE MAY BE FILLED   192 20
THEY CAME, AND FILLED BOTH THE SHIPS, SO THAT THEY   196 21
SO THEY DID EAT, AND WERE FILLED   199 23
WOULD FAIN HAVE FILLED HIS BELLY WITH THE HUSKS THAT   202 08
THAT YE MIGHT BE FILLED WITH ALL THE FULNESS OF GOD   212 20
BUT BE FILLED WITH THE SPIRIT   217 27
BEING FILLED WITH THE FRUITS OF RIGHTEOUSNESS,   221 05
THAT YE MIGHT BE FILLED WITH THE KNOWLEDGE OF HIS   224 02
WHEN THEY WERE FILLED, HE SAID UNTO HIS DISCIPLES,   226 06
AND FILLED TWELVE BASKETS WITH THE   226 08
THY SIGHT, AND BE FILLED WITH THE HOLY GHOST   230 33
STRONG IN SPIRIT, FILLED WITH WISDOM   233 26
ZACHARIAS WAS FILLED WITH THE HOLY GHOST, AND   243 31
FOR THEY SHALL BE FILLED   257 25
THEY WERE FILLED WITH ENVY, AND SPAKE AGAINST THOSE   260 28
IS THEN TO BE FILLED WITH PURE WATER, SHALL SAY AS   R 273 24
YE MAY BE FILLED WITH ALL THE FULNESS OF GOD   281 11
OUR SINS, AND BE FILLED WITH THY GRACE AND HEAVENLY   295 02
FOR MY LOINS ARE FILLED WITH A SORE DISEASE, *   388 04
O LET MY MOUTH BE FILLED WITH THY PRAISE, *   425 21
EARTH SHALL BE FILLED WITH HIS MAJESTY   428 05
30 SO THEY DID EAT, AND WERE WELL FILLED   436 29
TAKEN ROOT, IT FILLED THE LAND   441 21
AND THE POOLS ARE FILLED WITH WATER   445 24
THE EARTH IS FILLED WITH THE FRUIT OF THY WORKS   468 19
THEY ARE FILLED WITH GOOD   469 17
AND HE FILLED THEM WITH THE BREAD OF HEAVEN   472 17
4 OUR SOUL IS FILLED WITH THE SCORNFUL REPROOF OF THE 504 04
WAS OUR MOUTH FILLED WITH LAUGHTER, *   505 09
AND BEING FILLED WITH THY GRACE AND HEAVENLY   565 31
WHO HAST FILLED THE WORLD WITH BEAUTY   596 17

FILLEST

THINE HAND AND FILLEST ALL THINGS LIVING WITH   040 04
BELLIES THOU FILLEST WITH THY HID TREASURE   359 16
AND FILLEST ALL THINGS LIVING WITH PLENTEOUSNESS   521 24

FILLETH

OF THE LORD FILLETH THE WORLD   R 008 28
AND FILLETH THEE WITH THE FLOUR OF WHEAT   265 04
AND FILLETH THE HUNGRY SOUL WITH GOODNESS   476 22
THE MOWER FILLETH NOT HIS HAND, *   507 02
AND FILLETH THEE WITH THE FLOUR OF WHEAT   523 23

FILTH

AWAY OF THE FILTH OF THE FLESH, BUT THE ANSWER OF A 161 31

FILTHINESS

NEITHER FILTHINESS, NOR FOOLISH TALKING, NOR JESTING, 129 04
LAY APART ALL FILTHINESS AND SUPERFLUITY OF   175 02
LAY APART ALL FILTHINESS AND SUPERFLUITY OF   265 26

FILTHY

NOT GREEDY OF FILTHY LUCRE   531 28
NOT GREEDY OF FILTHY LUCRE   549 22

FINAL

BEFORE THE FINAL PRAYER OF THANKSGIVING OR OF   R 035 04
BEFORE THE FINAL PRAYER OF BLESSING OF THE   R 050 16
PRAYERS BEFORE THE FINAL BLESSING   R 335 24
BEFORE THE FINAL BLESSING, THE BISHOP SHALL SAY THIS R 568 04

FINALLY

FINALLY, THE CUTTING OFF OCCASION, FROM THEM   V 37
AND FINALLY, AFTER THIS LIFE, TO ATTAIN EVERLASTING 018 03
FINALLY, WE COMMEND TO THY FATHERLY GOODNESS ALL   019 03
FINALLY, WE COMMEND TO THY FATHERLY GOODNESS ALL   032 34
AND GRANT THAT FINALLY HE MAY DWELL WITH THEE IN LIFE 045 20
FINALLY, YE SHALL YIELD UNTO GOD MOST HIGH PRAISE AND 048 15
HOLY NAME, AND FINALLY, BY THY MERCY, OBTAIN   049 26
AND FINALLY TO BEAT DOWN SATAN UNDER OUR FEET   056 24
THAT WE FINALLY LOSE NOT THE THINGS ETERNAL   194 08
THAT WE FAIL NOT FINALLY TO ATTAIN THY HEAVENLY   207 15
SO THAT FINALLY, WITH THE RESIDUE OF THY HOLY CHURCH, 281 03
HOLY NAME, AND FINALLY, BY THY MERCY, OBTAIN   571 11
AND FINALLY, BEING FOUND GUILTY, BY JUST JUDGMENT BE 608 21

FIND

OBTAIN MERCY, AND FIND GRACE TO HELP IN TIME OF NEED 005 09
AND WE FIND ACCORDINGLY, THAT, SEEKING TO KEEP THE V 24
COMING SUDDENLY HE FIND YOU SLEEPING   021 27
SEEK AFTER THEE AND FIND THEE   038 09
YE SHALL FIND AN ASS TIED, AND A COLT WITH HER   091 14
YE SHALL FIND THE BABE WRAPPED IN SWADDLING CLOTHES, 099 18
OF THE CROSS, MAY FIND IT NONE OTHER THAN THE WAY OF 138 07

FIND   CONTINUED

TO THE PEOPLE, I FIND NO FAULT IN THIS MAN   153 03
YE MAY KNOW THAT I FIND NO FAULT IN HIM   159 02
FOR I FIND NO FAULT IN HIM   159 08
AND YE SHALL FIND   183 11
GO IN AND OUT, AND FIND PASTURE   186 16
IS LOST, UNTIL HE FIND IT   193 20
DILIGENTLY TILL SHE FIND IT   193 30
AS MANY AS YE SHALL FIND, BID TO THE MARRIAGE   218 18
AND YE SHALL FIND REST UNTO YOUR SOULS   235 13
AND YE SHALL FIND   263 04
AND YE SHALL FIND   274 16
LET US WHO SEEK, FIND   274 18
UNTIL THOU FIND NONE   354 10
TRIED ME, AND SHALT FIND NO WICKEDNESS IN ME   358 22
RIGHT HAND SHALL FIND OUT THEM THAT HATE THEE   365 21
5 UNTIL I FIND OUT A PLACE FOR THE TEMPLE OF THE   508 13
HE COMETH SHALL FIND WATCHING   534 21
THIRD WATCH, AND FIND THEM SO, BLESSED ARE THOSE   534 24
DUE EXAMINATION, WE FIND NOT TO THE CONTRARY, BUT 536 24
GO IN AND OUT, AND FIND PASTURE   539 07

FINDETH

HE COMETH, HE FINDETH IT SWEPT AND GARNISHED   130 13
HE COMETH, AND FINDETH THEM SLEEPING, AND SAITH UNTO 142 03
AND HE THAT SEEKETH FINDETH   183 13
AND HE THAT SEEKETH FINDETH   263 06
AS ONE THAT FINDETH GREAT SPOILS   501 05

FINDING

AND FINDING NONE, HE SAITH, I WILL RETURN UNTO MY 130 11
AND TRIAL, FINDING HIM SUFFICIENTLY INSTRUCTED IN THE 529 28

FINE

IN PURPLE AND FINE LINEN, AND FARED SUMPTUOUSLY EVERY 190 04
THAN MUCH FINE GOLD   364 05

FINEST

ALSO WITH THE FINEST WHEAT-FLOUR   443 13

FINGER

BUT IF I WITH THE FINGER OF GOD CAST OUT DEVILS,   130 03
THE TIP OF HIS FINGER IN WATER, AND COOL MY TONGUE 190 14
AND PUT MY FINGER INTO THE PRINT OF THE NAILS,   228 29
REACH HITHER THY FINGER, AND BEHOLD MY HANDS   229 03
UPON THE FOURTH FINGER OF THE WOMAN'S LEFT HAND R 302 11
UPON THE FOURTH FINGER OF THE WOMAN'S LEFT HAND, THE R 302 23
ARE THINE, O FINGER OF THE HAND DIVINE   544 26
ARE THINE, O FINGER OF THE HAND DIVINE   557 05

FINGERS

AND PUT HIS FINGERS INTO HIS EARS, AND HE SPIT, AND 206 32
EVEN THE WORK OF THY FINGERS   351 05
TO WAR, AND MY FINGERS TO FIGHT   519 23

FINISH

SO THAT I MIGHT FINISH MY COURSE WITH JOY, AND THE 550 19

FINISHED

HAD RECEIVED THE VINEGAR, HE SAID, IT IS FINISHED 160 29
I HAVE FINISHED MY COURSE, I HAVE KEPT THE   253 27
WHO, HAVING FINISHED THEIR COURSE IN FAITH, DO NOW 334 24

FINISHER

THE AUTHOR AND FINISHER OF OUR FAITH, THY SON JESUS 258 18
THE AUTHOR AND FINISHER OF OUR FAITH   258 24

FIR-TREES

AND THE FIR-TREES ARE A DWELLING FOR THE STORK   468 28

FIRE

O YE FIRE AND HEAT, BLESS YE THE LORD   012 18
FROM EARTHQUAKE, FIRE, AND FLOOD   054 30
ANGELS SPIRITS, AND HIS MINISTERS A FLAME OF FIRE 097 08
SHALT HEAP COALS OF FIRE ON HIS HEAD   113 07
AND WARMED HIMSELF AT THE FIRE   142 35
YE THAT KINDLE A FIRE, THAT COMPASS YOURSELVES ABOUT 144 26
THE LIGHT OF YOUR FIRE, AND IN THE SPARKS THAT YE 144 27
THEY HAD KINDLED A FIRE IN THE MIDST OF THE HALL, 151 09
AS HE SAT BY THE FIRE, AND EARNESTLY LOOKED UPON HIM, 151 11
TONGUES LIKE AS OF FIRE, AND IT SAT UPON EACH OF   180 22
WERE SEVEN LAMPS OF FIRE BURNING BEFORE THE THRONE, 187 13
GOOD FRUIT IS HEWN DOWN, AND CAST INTO THE FIRE   200 23
IS LIKE A REFINER'S FIRE, AND LIKE FULLERS' SOPE   232 09
CAST THEM INTO THE FIRE, AND THEY ARE BURNED   238 16
OR TWO FEET TO BE CAST INTO EVERLASTING FIRE   253 06
SHALL RAIN SNARES, FIRE AND BRIMSTONE, STORM AND   354 33
AND PURIFIED SEVEN TIMES IN THE FIRE   355 22
AND A CONSUMING FIRE OUT OF HIS MOUTH, SO THAT COALS 360 13
HAILSTONES AND COALS OF FIRE   360 23
HAILSTONES AND COALS OF FIRE   360 25
THE WORD OF THE LORD ALSO IS TRIED IN THE FIRE   361 29
AND THE FIRE SHALL CONSUME THEM   365 24
THE VOICE OF THE LORD DIVIDETH THE FLAMES OF FIRE 374 11

FIRE   CONTINUED

WAS THUS MUSING THE FIRE KINDLED, *   389 13
IN SUNDER, AND BURNETH THE CHARIOTS IN THE FIRE   398 13
HIM A CONSUMING FIRE, AND A MIGHTY TEMPEST SHALL BE   401 26
THAT ARE SET ON FIRE, *   409 22
WE WENT THROUGH FIRE AND WATER, AND THOU BROUGHTEST   418 05
WAX MELTETH AT THE FIRE, SO LET THE UNGODLY PERISH AT   419 12
8 THEY HAVE SET FIRE UPON THY HOLY PLACES, *   430 18
AND ALL THE NIGHT THROUGH WITH A LIGHT OF FIRE   435 29
SO THE FIRE WAS KINDLED IN JACOB, AND THERE CAME UP   436 12
64 THE FIRE CONSUMED THEIR YOUNG MEN, *   439 04
JEALOUSY BURN LIKE FIRE FOR EVER   440 10
16 IT IS BURNT WITH FIRE, AND CUT DOWN   442 02
14 LIKE AS THE FIRE THAT BURNETH UP THE FOREST,   444 32
AND SHALL THY WRATH BURN LIKE FIRE   452 33
3 THERE SHALL GO A FIRE BEFORE HIM, *   461 02
AND HIS MINISTERS A FLAMING FIRE   467 33
AND FLAMES OF FIRE IN THEIR LAND   472 03
AND FIRE TO GIVE LIGHT IN THE NIGHT SEASON   472 15
18 AND THE FIRE WAS KINDLED IN THEIR COMPANY   474 04
EXTINCT EVEN AS THE FIRE AMONG THE THORNS   488 24
BE CAST INTO THE FIRE, AND INTO THE PIT, THAT THEY   516 30
8 FIRE AND HAIL, SNOW AND VAPOURS, *   524 20
SOULS INSPIRE, AND LIGHTEN WITH CELESTIAL FIRE   543 32
COMFORT, LIFE, AND FIRE OF LOVE   544 03
FOUNT OF LIFE, THE FIRE OF LOVE, THE SOUL'S ANOINTING   544 23
SOULS INSPIRE, AND LIGHTEN WITH CELESTIAL FIRE   556 07
COMFORT, LIFE, AND FIRE OF LOVE   556 11
FOUNT OF LIFE, THE FIRE OF LOVE, THE SOUL'S ANOINTING   557 02

FIREBRAND

AND MY BONES ARE BURNT UP AS IT WERE A FIREBRAND   464 16

FIRKINS

TWO OR THREE FIRKINS APIECE   113 20

FIRM

BEEN CONTINUED FIRM AND UNSHAKEN   V 32

FIRMAMENT

THOU IN THE FIRMAMENT OF HEAVEN   011 27
BE ABOVE THE FIRMAMENT, BLESS YE THE LORD   012 06
AND THE FIRMAMENT SHOWETH HIS HANDY-WORK   363 13
HIM IN THE FIRMAMENT OF HIS POWER   525 23

FIRST

THE LORD'S PRAYER, FIRST PRONOUNCING, THE LORD BE   R 003 07
UNDER GOD, FOR HER FIRST FOUNDATION AND A LONG   V 11
SINCE THE FIRST COMPILING OF HER LITURGY IN   V 27
SHALL BE READ THE FIRST LESSON, ACCORDING TO THE   R 009 31
HERE ENDETH THE FIRST (OR THE SECOND) LESSON   R 009 34
THE MINISTER FIRST PRONOUNCING,   R 016 24
SHALL BE READ THE FIRST LESSON, ACCORDING TO THE   R 026 05
THE MINISTER FIRST PRONOUNCING,   R 030 29
CHURCH WAS IN THE FIRST PLACE DRAWN TO THOSE   VI 15
ON THE FIRST DAY OF LENT, THE OFFICE ENSUING MAY BE   R 060 03
THIS IS THE FIRST AND GREAT COMMANDMENT   069 29
READ THE EPISTLE, FIRST SAYING, THE EPISTLE IS   R 070 18
READ THE GOSPEL, FIRST SAYING, THE HOLY GOSPEL IS   R 070 23
SHALL THE PRIEST FIRST RECEIVE THE HOLY COMMUNION IN   R 082 25
BE SAID ON THE FIRST SUNDAY IN ADVENT, THE FIRST   R 085 23
IN ADVENT, THE FIRST SUNDAY IN LENT, AND TRINITY   R 085 24
FIRST, TO EXAMINE YOUR LIVES AND CONVERSATIONS BY THE   087 16
WHO AT THY FIRST COMING DIDST SEND THY   093 24
MAY BE USED AT THE FIRST COMMUNION   R 098 08
THIS TAXING WAS FIRST MADE WHEN CYRENIUS WAS GOVERNOR   098 30
THE EXAMPLE OF THY FIRST MARTYR SAINT STEPHEN,   099 31
CHRISTMAS DAY, THE FIRST EPISTLE AND GOSPEL FOR   R 104 02
GATHER YE TOGETHER FIRST THE TARES, AND BIND THEM IN   116 30
BEGINNING FROM THE LAST UNTO THE FIRST   119 31
BUT WHEN THE FIRST CAME, THEY SUPPOSED THAT THEY   119 33
THE LAST SHALL BE FIRST, AND THE FIRST LAST   120 12
BE FIRST, AND THE FIRST LAST   120 12
LAST STATE OF THAT MAN IS WORSE THAN THE FIRST   130 16
WERE UNDER THE FIRST TESTAMENT, THEY WHICH ARE CALLED   133 06
NOT UP TO JOY BUT FIRST HE SUFFERED PAIN, AND ENTERED   138 05
AND THE FIRST DAY OF UNLEAVENED BREAD, WHEN THEY   140 22
NEITHER THE FIRST TESTAMENT WAS DEDICATED WITHOUT   147 17
HE TAKETH AWAY THE FIRST, THAT HE MAY ESTABLISH THE   157 32
THE LEGS OF THE FIRST, AND OF THE OTHER WHICH WAS   160 35
SO THE LAST ERROR SHALL BE WORSE THAN THE FIRST   162 23
THE FIRST DAY OF THE WEEK COMETH MARY MAGDALENE   164 10
AND CAME FIRST TO THE SEPULCHRE   164 19
WHICH CAME FIRST TO THE SEPULCHRE, AND HE SAW,   164 26
MAY BE USED AT THE FIRST COMMUNION   R 164 31
IN THE MORNING THE FIRST DAY OF THE WEEK, THEY CAME   165 21
BEING THE FIRST DAY OF THE WEEK, WHEN THE   171 14
MAY BE USED AT THE FIRST COMMUNION   R 182 12
AND THE FIRST VOICE WHICH I HEARD WAS AS IT WERE OF A   186 32
AND THE FIRST WAS LIKE A LION, AND THE SECOND LIKE A   187 18
BECAUSE HE FIRST LOVED US   189 30
THE FIRST SAID UNTO HIM, I HAVE BOUGHT A PIECE OF   192 07
CAST OUT FIRST THE BEAM OUT OF THINE OWN EYE, AND   195 10
FIRST BE RECONCILED TO THY BROTHER, AND THEN COME AND   198 10
DELIVERED UNTO YOU FIRST OF ALL THAT WHICH I ALSO   205 03
BUT SEEK YE FIRST HIS KINGDOM, AND HIS RIGHTEOUSNESS   211 31
THIS IS THE FIRST AND GREAT COMMANDMENT   215 12
GOSPEL FROM THE FIRST DAY UNTIL NOW   220 25
FIRST MOSES SAITH, I WILL PROVOKE YOU TO JEALOUSY BY   227 16
AND THE LAST SHALL BE FIRST   231 22

FIRST   CONTINUED

BUT MANY THAT ARE FIRST SHALL BE LAST   231 22
HE ALSO DESCENDED FIRST INTO THE LOWER PARTS OF THE   237 16
CALLED CHRISTIANS FIRST IN ANTIOCH   241 14
THEY WERE PAST THE FIRST AND THE SECOND WARD, THEY   245 21
HOUSE YE ENTER, FIRST SAY, PEACE BE TO THIS HOUSE   254 19
WORD OF GOD SHOULD FIRST HAVE BEEN SPOKEN TO YOU   260 31
BUT SEEK YE FIRST THE KINGDOM OF GOD, AND HIS   266 29
THAT THEY, SEEKING FIRST THY KINGDOM AND THY   267 07
AND THE DEAD IN CHRIST SHALL RISE FIRST   269 07
AT THE FIRST VERSE   275 04
THE MINISTER SHALL FIRST ASK THE QUESTIONS PROVIDED   R 281 25
THE MINISTER FIRST PRONOUNCING, THE LORD BE WITH YOU   R 283 04
FIRST, THAT I SHOULD RENOUNCE THE DEVIL AND ALL HIS   283 23
FIRST, I LEARN TO BELIEVE IN GOD THE FATHER,   284 29
THIS IS THE FIRST AND GREAT COMMANDMENT   288 08
HIS PRESENCE AND FIRST MIRACLE THAT HE WROUGHT IN   300 14
THIS IS THE FIRST (SECOND OR THIRD) TIME OF ASKING   R 304 25
THE MINISTER SHALL FIRST RECEIVE THE COMMUNION   R 322 34
CHAPTER OF THE FIRST EPISTLE OF ST   R 328 18
IT IS WRITTEN, THE FIRST MAN ADAM WAS MADE A LIVING   329 24
THAT WAS NOT FIRST WHICH IS SPIRITUAL, BUT THAT WHICH   329 26
THE FIRST MAN IS OF THE EARTH, EARTHY   329 27
THE PRAYERS, FIRST PRONOUNCING, THE LORD BE WITH YOU   R 331 31
EXCEPT HE WERE FIRST CALLED, TRIED, EXAMINED,   529 15
OF DEACONS THE FIRST MARTYR SAINT STEPHEN, WITH   531 17
AND LET THESE ALSO FIRST BE PROVED   531 30
HE ALSO DESCENDED FIRST INTO THE LOWER PARTS OF THE   538 03
DEACONS SHALL BE FIRST PRESENTED, AND THEN THE   R 547 20
YE KNOW, FROM THE FIRST DAY THAT I CAME INTO ASIA,   550 06
BEING THE FIRST DAY OF THE WEEK, WHEN THE   551 27
FIRST, THAT I SHOULD RENOUNCE THE DEVIL AND ALL HIS   577 14
FIRST, I LEARN TO BELIEVE IN GOD THE FATHER,   578 11

FIRST-BEGOTTEN

IN THE FIRST-BEGOTTEN INTO THE WORLD, HE SAITH, AND   097 05

FIRSTBORN

FORTH HER FIRSTBORN SON, AND WRAPPED HIM IN SWADDLING   099 08
FORTH HER FIRSTBORN SON   105 15
SMOTE ALL THE FIRSTBORN IN EGYPT, *   438 12
MAKE HIM MY FIRSTBORN, *   451 29
SMOTE ALL THE FIRSTBORN IN THEIR LAND   472 09
8 HE SMOTE THE FIRSTBORN OF EGYPT, *   510 18
10 WHO SMOTE EGYPT, WITH THEIR FIRSTBORN   512 02

FIRSTFRUITS

AND WITH THE FIRSTFRUITS OF ALL THINE INCREASE   005 20
BEING THE FIRSTFRUITS UNTO GOD AND TO THE LAMB   103 11
BECOME THE FIRSTFRUITS OF THEM THAT SLEPT   163 11
BE A KIND OF FIRSTFRUITS OF HIS CREATURES   174 30
HAVE THE FIRSTFRUITS OF THE SPIRIT, EVEN WE OURSELVES   194 21
BE A KIND OF FIRSTFRUITS OF HIS CREATURES   265 22
BECOME THE FIRSTFRUITS OF THEM THAT SLEPT   328 22
CHRIST THE FIRSTFRUITS   328 25

FISH

PIECE OF A BROILED FISH, AND OF AN HONEYCOMB   170 05
FISH, WILL HE FOR A FISH GIVE HIM A SERPENT   183 15
OR IF HE ASK A FISH, WILL HE FOR A FISH GIVE HIM A   183 15
OR IF HE ASK A FISH, WILL HE FOR A FISH GIVE HIM A   263 09
FISH, WILL HE FOR A FISH GIVE HIM A SERPENT   263 09
AND SLEW THEIR FISH   471 31

FISHERMEN

BUT THE FISHERMEN WERE GONE OUT OF THEM, AND WERE   196 09

FISHERS

FOR THEY WERE FISHERS   227 26
I WILL MAKE YOU FISHERS OF MEN   227 27

FISHES

HATH FIVE BARLEY LOAVES, AND TWO SMALL FISHES   131 34
LIKEWISE OF THE FISHES AS MUCH AS THEY WOULD   132 06
THEY INCLOSED A GREAT MULTITUDE OF FISHES   196 19
DRAUGHT OF THE FISHES WHICH THEY HAD TAKEN   196 25
AND THEY HAD A FEW SMALL FISHES   199 21
HATH FIVE BARLEY LOAVES, AND TWO SMALL FISHES   225 30
LIKEWISE OF THE FISHES AS MUCH AS THEY WOULD   226 05
ANOTHER OF FISHES, AND ANOTHER OF BIRDS   329 13
THE AIR, AND THE FISHES OF THE SEA   351 15

FIT

AS HE SHALL THINK FIT, OR WITH THE GRACE   R 017 23
TAKEN OUT OF THIS BOOK, AS HE SHALL THINK FIT   R 031 32
MAKE CHOICE OF FIT PERSONS, TO SERVE IN THE SACRED   038 31
OR OTHER FIT PERSONS APPOINTED FOR THAT PURPOSE,   R 075 27
AS HE SHALL THINK FIT, AND THE FOLLOWING   R 320 07
AS HE SHALL THINK FIT TO BE PRESENTED TO THE BISHOP   R 583 08
SLEEP AS MAY FIT US FOR THE DUTIES OF THE COMING DAY   591 28

FITLY

THE WHOLE BODY FITLY JOINED TOGETHER AND COMPACTED BY   237 30
ALL THE BUILDING FITLY FRAMED TOGETHER GROWETH UNTO   255 07

FITTED

SUPPLY OF PERSONS FITTED TO SERVE GOD IN THE MINISTRY   047 30

FITTING

AND SUCH OTHER FITTING PRAYERS AS ARE ELSEWHERE   R 331 30
FROM OTHER PARTS OF THIS BOOK, AS MAY BE FITTING   R 337 05
OR OTHER FITTING PRAYERS FROM THIS BOOK   R 340 22

FIVE

OF THE JEWS FIVE TIMES RECEIVED I FORTY STRIPES SAVE   120 32
WHICH HATH FIVE BARLEY LOAVES, AND TWO SMALL   131 33
IN NUMBER ABOUT FIVE THOUSAND   132 03
FRAGMENTS OF THE FIVE BARLEY LOAVES, WHICH REMAINED   132 10
FOR I HAVE FIVE BRETHREN   190 24
I HAVE BOUGHT FIVE YOKE OF OXEN, AND I GO TO   192 09
WAS SEEN OF ABOVE FIVE HUNDRED BRETHREN AT ONCE   205 08
WHICH HATH FIVE BARLEY LOAVES, AND TWO SMALL   225 30
IN NUMBER ABOUT FIVE THOUSAND   226 02
FRAGMENTS OF THE FIVE BARLEY LOAVES, WHICH REMAINED   226 09
THOSE FIVE COMMONLY CALLED SACRAMENTS, THAT IS TO   607 38

FIXED

SURELY THERE BE FIXED, WHERE TRUE JOYS ARE TO BE   174 23
BETWEEN US AND YOU THERE IS A GREAT GULF FIXED   190 20
SURELY THERE BE FIXED, WHERE TRUE JOYS ARE TO BE   285 30
8 MY HEART IS FIXED, O GOD, MY HEART IS FIXED   409 29
8 MY HEART IS FIXED, O GOD, MY HEART IS FIXED   409 29

FLAME

HIS MINISTERS A FLAME OF FIRE   097 08
FOR I AM TORMENTED IN THIS FLAME   190 16
DOST ENKINDLE THE FLAME OF THY LOVE IN THE HEARTS OF   258 05
AND AS THE FLAME THAT CONSUMETH THE MOUNTAINS   444 33
THE FLAME BURNT UP THE UNGODLY   474 05

FLAMES

LORD DIVIDETH THE FLAMES OF FIRE   374 11
AND FLAMES OF FIRE IN THEIR LAND   472 02

FLAMING

HIS MINISTERS A FLAMING FIRE   467 33

FLATTER

THEY FLATTER WITH THEIR TONGUE   348 20
THEY DO BUT FLATTER WITH THEIR LIPS, AND DISSEMBLE IN   355 10
THEY DID BUT FLATTER HIM WITH THEIR MOUTH, *   437 10

FLATTERERS

16 WITH THE FLATTERERS WERE BUSY MOCKERS, *   382 27

FLATTERETH

2 FOR HE FLATTERETH HIMSELF IN HIS OWN SIGHT,   383 28

FLED

AND THEY ALL FORSOOK HIM, AND FLED   142 28
LINEN CLOTH, AND FLED FROM THEM NAKED   142 31
OUT QUICKLY, AND FLED FROM THE SEPULCHRE   166 02
3 THE SEA SAW THAT, AND FLED   484 30

FLEDDEST

O THOU SEA, THAT THOU FLEDDEST   485 02

FLEE

WE FLEE UNTO THEE FOR SUCCOUR   045 04
AND HIS MOTHER, AND FLEE INTO EGYPT, AND BE THOU   103 18
BUT WILL FLEE FROM HIM   186 08
HELPER OF ALL WHO FLEE TO THEE FOR SUCCOUR, THE LIFE   274 10
THAT SHE SHOULD FLEE AS A BIRD UNTO THE HILL   354 20
27 FLEE FROM EVIL, AND DO THE THING THAT IS GOOD   386 17
FOR THEN WOULD I FLEE AWAY, AND BE AT REST   406 31
ALSO THAT HATE HIM FLEE BEFORE HIM   419 10
THEIR ARMIES DID FLEE, AND WERE DISCOMFITED, *   420 04
7 AT THY REBUKE THEY FLEE   468 06
5 I HAD NO PLACE TO FLEE UNTO, *   518 12
FOR I FLEE UNTO THEE TO HIDE ME   519 10
BUT WILL FLEE FROM HIM   538 31

FLEETH

AND LEAVETH THE SHEEP, AND FLEETH   172 24
THE HIRELING FLEETH, BECAUSE HE IS AN HIRELING,   172 26
MY SOUL FLEETH UNTO THE LORD BEFORE THE MORNING   328 13
HE FLEETH AS IT WERE A SHADOW, AND NEVER CONTINUETH   332 20
6 MY SOUL FLEETH UNTO THE LORD BEFORE THE MORNING   507 18
AND LEAVETH THE SHEEP, AND FLEETH   539 13
THE HIRELING FLEETH, BECAUSE HE IS AN HIRELING,   539 15

FLESH

THE WORD WAS MADE FLESH, AND DWELT AMONG US   R 008 31
SPIRIT UPON ALL FLESH, AND HASTEN THY KINGDOM   038 10
OF THE WORLD, THE FLESH, AND THE DEVIL, FROM   054 28

FLESH   CONTINUED

OF OUR MORTAL FLESH, MANIFESTED FORTH HIS   077 23
OF THE WORD MADE FLESH, THOU HAST CAUSED A NEW LIGHT   077 29
SO TO EAT THE FLESH OF THY DEAR SON JESUS CHRIST,   082 19
PROVISION FOR THE FLESH, TO FULFIL THE LUSTS THEREOF   091 08
OF THE WILL OF THE FLESH, NOR OF THE WILL OF MAN, BUT   098 03
THE WORD WAS MADE FLESH, AND DWELT AMONG US, (AND WE   098 04
OUR FLESH BEING SUBDUED TO THE SPIRIT, WE MAY   125 29
WHO WAS OF THE BONDWOMAN WAS BORN AFTER THE FLESH   131 02
WAS BORN AFTER THE FLESH PERSECUTED HIM THAT WAS BORN   131 13
SANCTIFIETH TO THE PURIFYING OF THE FLESH   132 30
TAKE UPON HIM OUR FLESH, AND TO SUFFER DEATH UPON THE   134 07
IS READY, BUT THE FLESH IS WEAK   142 06
THROUGH THE VEIL, THAT IS TO SAY, HIS FLESH   158 19
TO DEATH IN THE FLESH, BUT QUICKENED BY THE SPIRIT   161 24
THE FILTH OF THE FLESH, BUT THE ANSWER OF A GOOD   161 31
A SPIRIT HATH NOT FLESH AND BONES, AS YE SEE ME HAVE   169 34
THAT WHICH IS BORN OF THE FLESH IS FLESH   188 12
IS BORN OF THE FLESH IS FLESH   188 12
OF MEN BECAUSE OF THE INFIRMITY OF YOUR FLESH   198 27
NOT TO THE FLESH, TO LIVE AFTER THE FLESH   200 03
YE LIVE AFTER THE FLESH, YE SHALL DIE   200 04
NOT TO THE FLESH, TO LIVE AFTER THE FLESH   200 04
FOR THE FLESH LUSTETH AGAINST THE SPIRIT, AND THE   209 15
AND YE SHALL NOT FULFIL THE LUST OF THE FLESH   209 15
THE SPIRIT, AND THE SPIRIT AGAINST THE FLESH   209 16
THE WORKS OF THE FLESH ARE MANIFEST, WHICH ARE THESE   209 19
HAVE CRUCIFIED THE FLESH WITH THE AFFECTIONS AND   209 29
A FAIR SHEW IN THE FLESH, THEY CONSTRAIN YOU TO BE   210 25
THAT THEY MAY GLORY IN YOUR FLESH   210 29
OF THE WORLD, THE FLESH, AND THE DEVIL   214 24
NOT AGAINST FLESH AND BLOOD, BUT AGAINST   219 08
SUBSTANCE OF OUR FLESH, SO WE MAY BE PRESENTED UNTO   231 30
AND ALL FLESH SHALL SEE IT TOGETHER   242 27
ALL FLESH IS GRASS, AND ALL THE GOODLINESS THEREOF IS   242 28
FOR FLESH AND BLOOD HATH NOT REVEALED IT UNTO THEE,   246 05
FOR NO MAN EVER YET HATED HIS OWN FLESH   267 26
HIS BODY, OF HIS FLESH, AND OF HIS BONES   267 28
AND THEY TWO SHALL BE ONE FLESH   267 31
AND THEY TWAIN SHALL BE ONE FLESH   268 09
WHEREFORE THEY ARE NO MORE TWAIN, BUT ONE FLESH   268 10
THAT WHICH IS BORN OF THE FLESH IS FLESH   275 17
IS BORN OF THE FLESH IS FLESH   275 17
DESIRES OF THE FLESH, SO THAT THOU WILT NOT FOLLOW,   276 27
DESIRES OF THE FLESH, SO THAT THOU WILT NOT FOLLOW,   277 29
AGAINST THE DEVIL, THE WORLD, AND THE FLESH   278 26
AND ALL THE SINFUL LUSTS OF THE FLESH   283 25
THE LUSTS OF THE FLESH OR THE WILES OF SATAN, BEING   317 25
I WILL GIVE IS MY FLESH, WHICH I WILL GIVE FOR THE   322 28
ALL FLESH IS NOT THE SAME FLESH   329 11
ALL FLESH IS NOT THE SAME FLESH   329 12
IS ONE KIND OF FLESH OF MEN, ANOTHER FLESH OF BEASTS,   329 12
OF MEN, ANOTHER FLESH OF BEASTS, ANOTHER OF FISHES,   329 13
THAT FLESH AND BLOOD CANNOT INHERIT THE   329 33
MY FLESH ALSO REST IN HOPE   333 08
THE BURDEN OF THE FLESH, ARE IN JOY AND FELICITY   334 22
THE SPIRITS OF ALL FLESH, WHO BY A VOICE FROM HEAVEN   335 25
MY FLESH ALSO SHALL REST IN HOPE   358 09
ME TO EAT UP MY FLESH, *   371 28
IS NO HEALTH IN MY FLESH, BECAUSE OF THY DISPLEASURE   387 25
I WILL EAT BULLS' FLESH, *   402 16
WILL NOT FEAR WHAT FLESH CAN DO UNTO ME   408 22
FOR THEE, MY FLESH ALSO LONGETH AFTER THEE, *   414 27
THEE SHALL ALL FLESH COME   416 14
26 MY FLESH AND MY HEART FAILETH   429 28
OR PROVIDE FLESH FOR HIS PEOPLE   436 10
28 HE RAINED FLESH UPON THEM AS THICK AS DUST,   436 25
THAT THEY WERE BUT FLESH, *   437 18
AND THE FLESH OF THY SAINTS UNTO THE BEASTS OF THE   440 02
MY HEART AND MY FLESH REJOICE IN THE LIVING GOD   445 14
MY BONES WILL SCARCE CLEAVE TO MY FLESH   464 20
MY FLESH IS DRIED UP FOR WANT OF FATNESS   481 18
120 MY FLESH TREMBLETH FOR FEAR OF THEE   498 08
25 WHO GIVETH FOOD TO ALL FLESH   512 32
AND LET ALL FLESH GIVE THANKS UNTO HIS HOLY NAME FOR   521 35
LAYING ASIDE THE STUDY OF THE WORLD AND THE FLESH   542 29
AND ALL THE SINFUL LUSTS OF THE FLESH   577 16
WHO, IN HOLY WEDLOCK, HAVE BEEN MADE ONE FLESH   598 26
HIS BODY, WITH FLESH, BONES, AND ALL THINGS   603 21
SO THAT THE FLESH LUSTETH ALWAYS CONTRARY TO   604 33
THE LUST OF THE FLESH, CALLED IN GREEK, PHRONEMA   604 36
THE DESIRE, OF THE FLESH,) IS NOT SUBJECT TO THE LAW   604 38
BOTH IN HIS FLESH, AND IN HIS SPIRIT   605 32
THE WORKS OF THE FLESH, AND THEIR EARTHLY MEMBERS,   606 19

FLESHLY

ABSTAIN FROM FLESHLY LUSTS, WHICH WAR AGAINST THE   173 13

FLIES

46 HE SENT FLIES AMONG THEM, AND DEVOURED THEM UP   437 31
CAME ALL MANNER OF FLIES, *   471 35

FLIETH

THE ARROW THAT FLIETH BY DAY   455 06

FLIGHT

BODY BEING PUT TO FLIGHT, THE BLESSING OF HEALTH MAY   320 19
THOU PUT THEM TO FLIGHT, *   365 29
THEN SHALL MINE ENEMIES BE PUT TO FLIGHT   408 33

FLINT

SET MY FACE LIKE A FLINT, AND I KNOW THAT I SHALL NOT	144 17

FLINT-STONE

AND THE FLINT-STONE INTO A SPRINGING WELL	485 09

FLOCK

AND PASTORS OF THY FLOCK, THAT THEY MAY LAY HANDS	038 29
WATCH OVER THEIR FLOCK BY NIGHT	099 11
UP OUT OF THE SEA WITH THE SHEPHERD OF HIS FLOCK	139 09
MAY BE MADE ONE FLOCK UNDER ONE SHEPHERD, JESUS	157 11
THERE SHALL BE ONE FLOCK, AND ONE SHEPHERD	172 32
HE SHALL FEED HIS FLOCK LIKE A SHEPHERD	243 08
AND COMMANDEDST HIM EARNESTLY TO FEED THY FLOCK	244 24
AND YE MY FLOCK, THE FLOCK OF MY PASTURE, ARE MEN,	262 22
YE MY FLOCK, THE FLOCK OF MY PASTURE, ARE MEN, AND I	262 22
PERSON) INTO THE CONGREGATION OF CHRIST'S FLOCK	280 04
LAMB OF THINE OWN FLOCK, A SINNER OF THINE OWN	319 30
HE SHALL FEED HIS FLOCK LIKE A SHEPHERD	338 12
AND CARRIED THEM IN THE WILDERNESS LIKE A FLOCK	438 15
OF ISRAEL, THOU THAT LEADEST JOSEPH LIKE A FLOCK	441 04
HOUSEHOLDS LIKE A FLOCK OF SHEEP	478 29
EXAMPLES OF THE FLOCK OF CHRIST	533 28
THERE SHALL BE ONE FLOCK, AND ONE SHEPHERD	539 21
PATTERNS TO THE FLOCK OF CHRIST	543 03
TOGETHER A GREAT FLOCK IN ALL THE PARTS OF THE WORLD,	545 03
AND DIDST CHARGE THEM TO FEED THY FLOCK	549 09
AND TO ALL THE FLOCK, OVER THE WHICH THE HOLY GHOST	550 27
WOLVES ENTER IN AMONG YOU, NOT SPARING THE FLOCK	550 31
BE TO THE FLOCK OF CHRIST A SHEPHERD, NOT A WOLF	558 25
OF CHRIST'S FLOCK, MAY BE SANCTIFIED BY THE HOLY	565 20
PORTION OF THE FLOCK OF CHRIST WHICH IS NOW INTRUSTED	569 24
A PATTERN TO THE FLOCK COMMITTED TO THY CARE	571 29

FLOCKS

AND THEIR FLOCKS WITH HOT THUNDERBOLTS	438 05

FLOOD

FROM EARTHQUAKE, FIRE, AND FLOOD	054 31

FLOODS

O YE SEAS AND FLOODS, BLESS YE THE LORD	013 10
LET THE FLOODS CLAP THEIR HANDS, AND LET THE HILLS BE	027 21
AND STABLISHED IT UPON THE FLOODS	368 31
SO THAT THE FLOODS RUN OVER ME	422 03
AND HIS RIGHT HAND IN THE FLOODS	451 26
4 THE FLOODS ARE RISEN, O LORD, THE FLOODS HAVE LIFT	457 11
O LORD, THE FLOODS HAVE LIFT UP THEIR VOICE	457 11
THE FLOODS LIFT UP THEIR WAVES	457 12
9 LET THE FLOODS CLAP THEIR HANDS, AND LET THE HILLS	462 10
33 HE TURNETH THE FLOODS INTO A WILDERNESS, *	478 12
AND STABLISHED IT UPON THE FLOODS	563 14

FLOUR

THEE WITH THE FLOUR OF WHEAT	265 05
THEE WITH THE FLOUR OF WHEAT	523 24

FLOURISH

GOOD LEARNING FLOURISH AND ABOUND	042 25
MAY FOR EVER FLOURISH AND ABOUND	047 37
AND MADE THY PEOPLE TO FLOURISH	394 26
7 IN HIS TIME SHALL THE RIGHTEOUS FLOURISH	427 10
THE CITY SHALL FLOURISH LIKE GRASS UPON THE EARTH	427 31
11 TRUTH SHALL FLOURISH OUT OF THE EARTH, *	446 29
WICKEDNESS DO FLOURISH, *	456 14
RIGHTEOUS SHALL FLOURISH LIKE A PALM-TREE, *	456 24
SHALL FLOURISH IN THE COURTS OF THE HOUSE OF OUR GOD	456 27
THERE SHALL I MAKE THE HORN OF DAVID TO FLOURISH	509 08
BUT UPON HIMSELF SHALL HIS CROWN FLOURISH	509 11

FLOURISHETH

FOR HE FLOURISHETH AS A FLOWER OF THE FIELD	467 04

FLOURISHING

AND FLOURISHING LIKE A GREEN BAY-TREE	387 05

FLOW

HE BLOWETH WITH HIS WIND, AND THE WATERS FLOW	523 32

FLOWED

AND THE STREAMS FLOWED WITHAL	436 09
AND THE WATERS FLOWED OUT, *	472 19

FLOWER

BECAUSE AS THE FLOWER OF THE GRASS HE SHALL PASS	239 20
AND THE FLOWER THEREOF FALLETH, AND THE GRACE	239 22
THEREOF IS AS THE FLOWER OF THE FIELD	242 29
THE FLOWER FADETH	242 29
THE FLOWER FADETH	242 31
HE COMETH UP, AND IS CUT DOWN, LIKE A FLOWER	332 20
FLOURISHETH AS A FLOWER OF THE FIELD	467 05

FLY

WE FLY UNTO THEE FOR SUCCOUR IN BEHALF OF THIS THY	316 07
11 HE RODE UPON THE CHERUBIM, AND DID FLY	360 17

FLYING

FOURTH WAS LIKE A FLYING EAGLE	187 20
HE CAME FLYING UPON THE WINGS OF THE WIND	360 18
THINGS AND FLYING FOWLS	524 23

FOAL

AND A COLT THE FOAL OF AN ASS	091 21

FODDER

WHO GIVETH FODDER UNTO THE CATTLE, *	264 30
9 WHO GIVETH FODDER UNTO THE CATTLE, *	523 13

FOE

FAR AWAY OUR GHOSTLY FOE, AND THINE ABIDING PEACE	545 06
FAR AWAY OUR GHOSTLY FOE, AND THINE ABIDING PEACE	557 12

FOES

MINE ENEMIES AND MY FOES, CAME UPON ME TO EAT UP MY	371 27
AND NOT MADE MY FOES TO TRIUMPH OVER ME	374 25
WILL SMITE DOWN HIS FOES BEFORE HIS FACE, *	451 21
KEEP FAR OUR FOES, GIVE PEACE AT HOME	544 08
KEEP FAR OUR FOES, GIVE PEACE AT HOME	556 16

FOLD

GATHERED INTO ONE FOLD, SHALL BECOME PARTAKERS OF	037 06
NATIONS INTO THY FOLD, POUR OUT THY SPIRIT UPON ALL	038 10
VESTURE SHALT THOU FOLD THEM UP, AND THEY SHALL BE	097 17
TO THY FOLD, THAT THEY MAY BE MADE ONE FLOCK	157 10
WHICH ARE NOT OF THIS FOLD	172 30
SHEEP OF THINE OWN FOLD, A LAMB OF THINE OWN FLOCK,	319 30
WHICH ARE NOT OF THIS FOLD	539 19

FOLDS

NOR HE-GOATS OUT OF THY FOLDS	402 09
14 THE FOLDS SHALL BE FULL OF SHEEP	417 11

FOLK

SHALT JUDGE THE FOLK RIGHTEOUSLY, AND GOVERN THE	028 24
AND BLESSED ARE THE FOLK THAT HE HATH CHOSEN TO HIM,	379 12
SHALT JUDGE THE FOLK RIGHTEOUSLY, AND GOVERN THE	418 31
KEEP THE SIMPLE FOLK BY THEIR RIGHT, *	427 04
5 THEY COME IN NO MISFORTUNE LIKE OTHER FOLK	428 18

FOLKS

BRINGING SICK FOLKS, AND THEM WHICH WERE VEXED WITH	249 31

FOLLOW

IS IMMEDIATELY TO FOLLOW, THE MINISTER MAY, AT HIS	R 003 06
RESPONSES WHICH FOLLOW, OR, IN THE LITANY, AS THERE	R 003 14
THEN SHALL FOLLOW A PORTION OF THE PSALMS,	R 009 22
IS IMMEDIATELY TO FOLLOW, THE MINISTER AT HIS	R 010 04
BEEN SAID, SHALL FOLLOW THE LORD'S PRAYER	R 016 28
THEN SHALL FOLLOW THE COLLECT FOR THE DAY, EXCEPT	R 017 02
BE OMITTED WHEN THE HOLY COMMUNION IS TO FOLLOW	R 017 21
BEFORE THE VERSICLES AND RESPONSES WHICH FOLLOW	R 021 11
THEN SHALL FOLLOW A PORTION OF THE PSALMS,	R 025 15
BEEN SAID, SHALL FOLLOW THE LORD'S PRAYER	R 030 33
US GRACE SO TO FOLLOW THEIR GOOD EXAMPLES, THAT WITH	075 03
HERE SHALL FOLLOW THE PROPER PREFACE, ACCORDING TO	R 077 02
SAITH UNTO PETER, FOLLOW ME	102 03
FOLLOW THOU ME	102 09
ARE THEY WHICH FOLLOW THE LAMB WHITHERSOEVER HE	103 10
MANKIND SHOULD FOLLOW THE EXAMPLE OF HIS GREAT	134 08
THAT WE MAY BOTH FOLLOW THE EXAMPLE OF HIS PATIENCE,	134 10
FOLLOW HIM	140 27
FOLLOW HIM INTO THE HOUSE WHERE HE ENTERETH IN	148 27
SAW WHAT WOULD FOLLOW, THEY SAID UNTO HIM, LORD,	150 31
OURSELVES TO FOLLOW THE BLESSED STEPS OF HIS MOST	171 32
THAT YE SHOULD FOLLOW HIS STEPS	172 11
AND FOLLOW ALL SUCH THINGS AS ARE	173 09
AND THE SHEEP FOLLOW HIM	186 07
WILL THEY NOT FOLLOW, BUT WILL FLEE FROM HIM	186 08
PREVENT AND FOLLOW US, AND MAKE US CONTINUALLY TO BE	213 15
AND MINDS TO FOLLOW THEE, THE ONLY GOD	214 25
SAITH UNTO THEM, FOLLOW ME, AND I WILL MAKE YOU	227 27
MAKE US SO TO FOLLOW HIS DOCTRINE AND HOLY LIFE,	242 10
OBEDIENTLY TO FOLLOW THE SAME, THAT THEY MAY RECEIVE	244 26
ABOUT THEE, AND FOLLOW ME	245 18
EVERMORE READY TO FOLLOW THY HOLY COMMANDMENTS	246 20
OF RICHES, AND TO FOLLOW THE SAME THY SON JESUS	250 23
SAITH UNTO HIM, FOLLOW ME	251 14
US GRACE SO TO FOLLOW THY BLESSED SAINTS IN ALL	256 08
THOU WILT NOT FOLLOW, NOR BE LED BY THEM	276 27
ENDEAVOUR NOT TO FOLLOW, NOR BE LED BY THEM	276 30
THOU WILT NOT FOLLOW, NOR BE LED BY THEM	277 29
ENDEAVOUR NOT TO FOLLOW, NOR BE LED BY THEM	277 31
AND DESIRE TO FOLLOW HIM AS THY SAVIOUR AND LORD	278 05
QUESTIONS WHICH FOLLOW, THE PEOPLE READING OR	R 283 14
QUESTIONS WHICH FOLLOW, THE PEOPLE READING OR	R 287 32
THE CHURCH WHICH FOLLOW, THE PEOPLE RESPONDING	R 290 26
DUTY IS TO FOLLOW CHRIST, TO WORSHIP GOD EVERY SUNDAY	291 18

FOLLOW   CONTINUED

DO YE PROMISE TO FOLLOW JESUS CHRIST AS YOUR LORD AND   297 03
THEN SHALL FOLLOW THE LESSON, TAKEN OUT OF THE   R 328 18
SERVANTS SO TO FOLLOW IN FAITH WHERE THOU HAST LED   336 12
US GRACE SO TO FOLLOW THE EXAMPLE OF THEIR   336 21
AND MERCY SHALL FOLLOW ME ALL THE DAYS OF MY LIFE   338 29
THEN SHALL FOLLOW THE LESSON TAKEN OUT OF THE   R 339 19
38 I WILL FOLLOW UPON MINE ENEMIES, AND OVERTAKE   362 11
AND MERCY SHALL FOLLOW ME ALL THE DAYS OF MY LIFE   368 22
BECAUSE I FOLLOW THE THING THAT GOOD IS   388 33
SHALL HIS POMP FOLLOW HIM   401 10
19 HE SHALL FOLLOW THE GENERATION OF HIS FATHERS,   401 14
THE MINSTRELS FOLLOW AFTER, *   421 04
AND LET THEM FOLLOW THEIR OWN IMAGINATICNS   443 05
IN HEART SHALL FOLLOW IT   458 17
AND THE SHEEP FOLLOW HIM   538 30
WILL THEY NOT FOLLOW, BUT WILL FLEE FROM HIM   538 31
EXAMPLES AND PATTERNS FOR THE PEOPLE TO FOLLOW   541 23
MAY OBEDIENTLY FOLLOW THE SAME   549 13
THEN SHALL FOLLOW THE NICENE CREED, AND AFTER THAT   R 552 16
THEN SHALL FOLLOW THE SERMON   R 574 24
HERE MAY FOLLOW THE COLLECT FOR THE DAY   R 587 16
HERE MAY FOLLOW THE COLLECT FOR THE DAY   R 589 23
OF FAITH, AND FOLLOW AFTER JUSTIFICATION, CANNOT PUT   605 11

FOLLOWED

WE HAVE FOLLOWED TOO MUCH THE DEVICES AND DESIRES OF   006 19
WE HAVE FOLLOWED TOO MUCH THE DEVICES AND DESIRES OF   023 26
READ BEING FOLLOWED BY ONE OF THE EVENING CANTICLES   R 026 08
AND TRULY FOLLOWED, IN ALL PLACES, TO THE BREAKING   037 04
AND THAT FOLLOWED, CRIED, SAYING, HOSANNA TO THE SON   091 27
MULTITUDES FOLLOWED HIM   114 30
TO THEM THAT FOLLOWED, VERILY I SAY UNTO YOU, I HAVE   115 17
HIS SIGHT, AND FOLLOWED HIM, GLORIFYING GOD   124 04
GREAT MULTITUDE FOLLOWED HIM, BECAUSE THEY SAW HIS   131 22
AND THERE FOLLOWED HIM A CERTAIN YOUNG MAN, HAVING A   142 28
AND PETER FOLLOWED HIM AFAR OFF, EVEN INTO THE PALACE   142 33
DISCIPLES ALSO FOLLOWED HIM   150 15
AND PETER FOLLOWED AFAR OFF   151 08
AND THERE FOLLOWED HIM A GREAT COMPANY OF PEOPLE, AND   154 11
THE WOMEN THAT FOLLOWED HIM FROM GALILEE, STOOD AFAR   155 19
NEXT DAY, THAT FOLLOWED THE DAY OF THE PREPARATICN,   162 15
AND FOLLOWED HIM   196 30
ROCK THAT FOLLOWED THEM   201 10
AND FOLLOWED HIM, AND SO DID HIS DISCIPLES   224 16
AND FOLLOWED HIM WITHOUT DELAY   226 20
THEIR NETS, AND FOLLOWED HIM   227 28
AND FOLLOWED HIM   227 33
AND FOLLOWED THEE   231 14
YE WHICH HAVE FOLLOWED ME, IN THE REGENERATION WHEN   231 15
WENT OUT, AND FOLLOWED HIM   245 19
AND FOLLOWED HIM   246 19
FOR WE HAVE NOT FOLLOWED CUNNINGLY DEVISED FABLES,   248 13
HE AROSE, AND FOLLOWED HIM   251 14
OF GOD IS TO BE FOLLOWED, WHICH WE HAVE EXPRESSLY   606 29

FOLLOWERS

YE THEREFORE FOLLOWERS OF GOD, AS DEAR CHILDREN   128 30
IF YE BE FOLLOWERS OF THAT WHICH IS GOOD   195 31
BE FOLLOWERS TOGETHER OF ME, AND MARK THEM   222 15

FOLLOWETH

OR ELSE HE SHALL SAY AS FOLLOWETH   R 023 03
OR ELSE THE GLORIA IN EXCELSIS, AS FOLLOWETH   R 025 20
OR SAID THE HYMN CALLED MAGNIFICAT, AS FCLLOWETH   R 026 06
SAID THE HYMN CALLED NUNC DIMITTIS, AS FOLLOWETH   R 028 07
HERE FOLLOWETH THE ANTHEM   R 031 30
OMIT ALL THAT FOLLOWETH, TO THE PRAYER, WE HUMBLY   R 058 09
SAY THIS THAT FOLLOWETH, AFTER THE MINISTER   R 062 27
THEN FOLLOWETH THE SERMON   R 071 31
SAY THE PRAYER OF CONSECRATION, AS FOLLOWETH   R 080 05
OR ELSE THIS THAT FOLLOWETH   R 155 21
SHALL SAY AS FOLLOWETH, THE PEOPLE ALL STANDING,   R 273 25
THEN SHALL THE MINISTER PROCEED AS FOLLOWETH   R 273 28
THEN THE MINISTER SHALL SAY AS FOLLOWETH   R 274 22
AFTER WHICH THE MINISTER SHALL SAY AS FOLLOWETH   R 289 12
THE QUESTIONS ON THE SACRAMENTS, AS FOLLOWETH   R 292 03
HER RIGHT HAND, AND TO SAY AFTER HIM AS FOLLOWETH   R 301 27
THE MINISTER MAY SAY AS FOLLOWETH   R 302 18
SAY THE LORD'S PRAYER, WITH WHAT FOLLOWETH   R 306 08
PRAYER WHICH FOLLOWETH, AND SUCH OTHER FITTING   R 331 29
IN SUCH MANNER AND FORM AS FOLLOWETH   529 31
THE COLLECT, EPISTLE, AND GOSPEL, AS FOLLOWETH   R 531 12
IN SUCH MANNER AND FORM AS HEREAFTER FOLLOWETH   R 535 27
THE COLLECT, EPISTLE, AND GOSPEL, AS FOLLOWETH   R 537 18
THOSE WHO ARE TO BE ORDAINED PRIESTS AS FOLLOWETH   R 539 23
AS FOLLOWETH   R 543 29
THE COLLECT SHALL BE AS FOLLOWETH   R 547 29
SHALL ANSWER BY VERSES, AS FOLLOWETH   R 556 05
SAY AS FOLLOWETH, ALL KNEELING, AND REPEATING WITH   R 587 06
SAY AS FOLLOWETH, ALL KNEELING, AND REPEATING WITH   R 589 14
SAY AS FOLLOWETH, ALL KNEELING, AND REPEATING   R 592 10
SAY AS FOLLOWETH, ALL KNEELING, AND REPEATING   R 593 04

FOLLOWING

MORE OF THE FOLLOWING SENTENCES OF SCRIPTURE   R 003 04
OR SUNG THE FOLLOWING CANTICLE   R 008 09
OR SUNG THE FOLLOWING HYMN   R 010 02
ANY ONE OF THE FOLLOWING CANTICLES OF MORNING PRAYER   R 010 04
THAT SHALL BE SUNG OR SAID THE HYMN FOLLOWING   R 014 04
THESE PRAYERS FOLLOWING, THE PEOPLE DEVOUTLY   R 016 23

FOLLOWING   CONTINUED

THE FOLLOWING PRAYERS SHALL BE OMITTED HERE WHEN   R 017 20
OR MORE OF THE FOLLOWING SENTENCES OF SCRIPTURE   R 021 04
THESE PRAYERS FOLLOWING, THE PEOPLE DEVOUTLY   R 030 28
AND AFTER THAT THE COLLECTS AND PRAYERS FOLLOWING   R 031 16
BLESS ALL WHO, FOLLOWING IN HIS STEPS, GIVE   043 30
THEN SHALL BE SAID BY THEM THIS PSALM FOLLOWING   R 060 08
THE COLLECT FOLLOWING, THE PEOPLE KNEELING   R 067 07
IN THE WEEK FOLLOWING TO BE OBSERVED   R 071 26
SENTENCES FOLLOWING, AS HE THINKETH MOST CONVENIENT   R 071 33
A NEW LIFE, FOLLOWING THE COMMANDMENTS OF GOD, AND   075 10
RECEIVE THE COMMUNION, THIS PRAYER FOLLOWING   R 082 12
HE SHALL READ THIS EXHORTATION FOLLOWING   R 086 26
THE FOLLOWING COLLECT, EPISTLE, AND GOSPEL MAY   R 098 08
SEETH THE DISCIPLE WHOM JESUS LOVED FOLLOWING   102 04
THE SUNDAY FOLLOWING CHRISTMAS DAY, THE FIRST EPISTLE R 103 34
THE FOLLOWING SHALL BE SAID, AND MAY BE SAID   R 162 28
SIMON PETER FOLLOWING HIM, AND WENT INTO THE   164 21
THE FOLLOWING COLLECT, EPISTLE, AND GOSPEL MAY   R 164 31
THE FOLLOWING COLLECT, EPISTLE, AND GOSPEL MAY BE   R 182 12
THE SAME, BY FOLLOWING THE HOLY DOCTRINE WHICH HE   229 22
FOLLOWING THE STEPS OF THY HOLY APOSTLES, SAINT   238 31
THE FOLLOWING SHALL BE SAID OR SUNG   R 264 17
GRANT THAT WE, FOLLOWING THE GOOD EXAMPLES OF THCSE   268 17
THEN THE FOLLOWING FORM SHALL SUFFICE   R 281 18
THE FOLLOWING PRAYER, THE MINISTER FIRST   R 283 04
THE QUESTION FOLLOWING, THE PEOPLE RESPONDING   R 284 25
BE SAID THE FOLLOWING SENTENCE BY THE MINISTER AND   R 290 03
THE PEOPLE THE FOLLOWING QUESTIONS CONCERNING THE   R 294 03
OR BOTH OF THE FOLLOWING PRAYERS   R 303 13
BE IN THE FOLLOWING FORM   R 304 21
OF THEM THE FOLLOWING HYMN, THE WOMAN STILL KNEELING   R 305 15
THE FOLLOWING SERVICE, OR ANY PART THEREOF,   R 308 03
THE ANTIPHON FOLLOWING, AND THEN, ACCORDING TO HIS   R 308 08
OF THE PSALMS FOLLOWING, WITH ANTIPHON AND COLLECT   R 309 09
ANY OF THE FOLLOWING PSALMS, 20, 27, 42, 91,   R 313 09
OFFICE AS HE SHALL THINK FIT, AND THE FOLLOWING   R 320 07
THE COLLECT, EPISTLE, AND GOSPEL, HERE FOLLOWING   R 321 16
OR THE FOLLOWING COLLECT, EPISTLE, AND GOSPEL   R 322 04
THE FOLLOWING FORM SHALL SUFFICE   R 323 04
ABSOLUTION THE FOLLOWING MAY BE USED   R 323 10
OR MORE OF THE FOLLOWING SELECTIONS, TAKEN FROM THE   R 324 16
OR MORE OF THE FOLLOWING PRAYERS, AT HIS DISCRETION   R 334 12
USE ANY OF THE FOLLOWING PRAYERS BEFORE THE FINAL   R 335 23
BE SAID THE FOLLOWING PSALMS   R 338 14
BE SAID THE FOLLOWING PRAYERS, OR OTHER FITTING   R 340 22
72 AS HE WAS FOLLOWING THE EWES WITH THEIR YOUNG HE   439 21
FORM HEREAFTER FOLLOWING, OR HATH HAD EPISCOPAL   R 529 23
BE SAID THE FOLLOWING SUFFRAGE   R 531 03
OF THE PEOPLE, AFTER THIS MANNER FOLLOWING   R 532 25
FOLLOWING WITH A GLAD MIND AND WILL THEIR GODLY   R 533 33
SHALL BE SAID THIS COLLECT FOLLOWING   R 534 29
BE SAID THE FOLLOWING SUFFRAGE   R 537 09
FOLLOWING WITH A GLAD MIND AND WILL THEIR GODLY   543 14
OF HIM THE FOLLOWING PROMISE OF CONFORMITY TO THE   R 552 26
THEREFORE, FOLLOWING THE EXAMPLE OF OUR SAVIOUR   553 09
THEN SHALL BE SAID THIS PRAYER FOLLOWING   R 553 25
THE FOLLOWING OFFICE MAY BE USED WITH THE ORDER FOR   R 563 03
REPEATING THE FOLLOWING PSALM ALTERNATELY, THE BISHCP R 563 08
SHALL SAY THE FOLLOWING PRAYER   R 564 26
THE FOLLOWING SHALL BE THE COLLECT,   R 567 02
THE FOLLOWING OFFICE MAY BE USED WITH THE ORDER FOR   R 569 08
GOOD REPORT, FOLLOWING THE EXAMPLE OF THEIR SAVICUR   596 28
SUCH ARE THESE FOLLOWING   604 04
NOT IN THE FOLLOWING OF ADAM, (AS THE PELAGIANS DO   604 29
OF THE CORRUPT FOLLOWING OF THE APOSTLES, PARTLY ARE   607 40

FOLLOWS

INSTEAD OF WHAT FOLLOWS, THE ABSOLUTICN FROM THE   R 007 05
AND DIOCESAN CONVENTION, SAYING AS FOLLOWS   R 571 24

FOND

OF SAINTS, IS A FOND THING, VAINLY INVENTED, AND   607 16

FONT

BE READY AT THE FONT, EITHER IMMEDIATELY AFTER THE   R 273 14
WITH HIM AT THE FONT AT LEAST TWO WITNESSES   R 273 23
HAVING COME TO THE FONT, WHICH IS THEN TC BE FILLED   R 273 24

FOOD

WITH THE SPIRITUAL FOOD OF THE MOST PRECIOUS BODY AND   083 19
TO BE OUR SPIRITUAL FOOD AND SUSTENANCE IN THAT HOLY   087 04
TO FEED ON THE BANQUET OF THAT MOST HEAVENLY FCCD   089 18
LIFE MORE THAN THE FOOD, AND THE BODY THAN THE   211 15
IN GIVING HIM FOOD AND RAIMENT   263 27
THE LIFE MORE THAN FOOD, AND THE BODY THAN RAIMENT   266 13
AND GAVE THEM FOOD FROM HEAVEN   436 19
26 SO MAN DID EAT ANGELS' FOOD   436 20
THAT HE MAY BRING FOOD OUT OF THE EARTH, AND WINE   468 23
25 WHO GIVETH FOOD TO ALL FLESH   512 32
FRIENDS, FOOD, AND RAIMENT, AND ALL THE OTHER   591 10

FOOL

I SPEAK AS A FOOL) I AM MORE   120 30
SHALL SAY, THOU FOOL, SHALL BE IN DANGER OF   198 07
THE FOOL HATH SAID IN HIS HEART, *   356 13
AND A FOOL DOTH NOT UNDERSTAND IT   456 12

FOOLISH

NOR FOOLISH TALKING, NOR JESTING, WHICH	129 04
THE IGNORANCE OF FOOLISH MEN	173 23
AND BY A FOOLISH NATION I WILL ANGER YOU	227 18
AND MAKE ME NOT A REBUKE UNTO THE FOOLISH	324 31
THOU FOOLISH ONE, THAT WHICH THOU SOWEST IS NOT	329 06
5 SUCH AS BE FOOLISH SHALL NOT STAND IN THY SIGHT	348 09
AND MAKE ME NOT A REBLKE UNTO THE FOOLISH	389 26
THE IGNORANT AND FOOLISH, AND LEAVE THEIR RICHES FOR	400 24
THE FOOLISH BODY HATH SAID IN HIS HEART, *	405 12
22 SO FOOLISH WAS I, AND IGNORANT, *	429 20
AND HOW THE FOOLISH PEOPLE HATH BLASPHEMED THY NAME	431 13
REMEMBER HOW THE FOOLISH MAN BLASPHEMETH THEE DAILY	431 23
17 FOOLISH MEN ARE PLAGUED FOR THEIR OFFENCE,	477 09

FOOLISHLY

(I SPEAK FOOLISHLY,) I AM BOLD ALSO	120 27

FOOLISHNESS

THROUGH MY FOOLISHNESS	387 31
13 THIS THEIR WAY IS VERY FOOLISHNESS	400 32
THAT THEY TURN NOT AGAIN UNTO FOOLISHNESS	446 24

FOOLS

YE SUFFER FOOLS GLADLY, SEEING YE YOURSELVES ARE	120 22
SAID UNTO THEM, O FOOLS, AND SLOW OF HEART TO BELIEVE	167 29
NOT AS FOOLS, BUT AS WISE, REDEEMING THE TIME,	217 23
5 I SAID UNTO THE FOOLS, DEAL NCT SO MADLY	432 06
O YE FOOLS, WHEN WILL YE UNDERSTAND	458 02

FOOT

TIME THOU DASH THY FOOT AGAINST A STONE	127 02
BIND HIM HAND AND FOOT, AND TAKE HIM AWAY, AND CAST	218 26
IF THY HAND OR THY FOOT OFFEND THEE, CUT THEM OFF,	253 03
WILL NOT SUFFER THY FOOT TO BE MOVED	327 23
WILL NOT SUFFER THY FOOT TO BE MOVED	339 07
PRIVILY IS THEIR FOOT TAKEN	352 23
12 MY FOOT STANDETH RIGHT	371 20
11 O LET NOT THE FOOT OF PRIDE COME AGAINST ME	384 19
FOR WHEN MY FOOT SLIPT, THEY REJOICED GREATLY AGAINST	388 24
SO THAT THEY WENT THROUGH THE WATER ON FOOT	417 25
23 THAT THY FOOT MAY BE DIPPED IN THE BLCOD OF THINE	420 33
THOU HURT NOT THY FOOT AGAINST A STONE	455 20
BUT WHEN I SAID, MY FOOT HATH SLIPT	458 22
WILL NOT SUFFER THY FOOT TO BE MOVED	502 26
LET NOT THE FOOT OF PRIDE COME NIGH TO HURT THEM, NOR	574 13

FOOTSTEPS

THAT MY FOOTSTEPS SLIP NOT	358 28
THAT MY FOOTSTEPS SHALL NOT SLIDE	362 10
SHALL WASH HIS FOOTSTEPS IN THE BLOOD OF THE UNGCDLY	410 30
AND THY FOOTSTEPS ARE NOT KNOWN	434 22
SLANDERED THE FOOTSTEPS OF THINE ANOINTED	453 11

FOOTSTOOL

EXPECTING TILL HIS ENEMIES BE MADE HIS FOOTSTCOL	158 08
TILL I MAKE THINE ENEMIES THY FOOTSTOOL	215 21
AND FALL DOWN BEFORE HIS FOOTSTOOL	462 26
UNTIL I MAKE THINE ENEMIES THY FOOTSTOOL	482 08
AND FALL LOW ON OUR KNEES BEFORE HIS FOOTSTOOL	508 18

FORASMUCH

AND FORASMUCH AS THOU ALONE BRINGEST LIGHT OUT CF	046 25
O GOD, FORASMUCH AS WITHOUT THEE WE ARE NOT ABLE TO	215 27
BUT FORASMUCH AS HE HAD NOT TO PAY, HIS LORD	221 16
FORASMUCH AS OUR SAVIOUR CHRIST SAITH, NONE	273 29
FORASMUCH AS N	304 03
SAY UNTO HER, FORASMUCH AS IT HATH PLEASED ALMIGHTY	305 11
AND FORASMUCH AS HE PLTTETH HIS FULL TRUST CNLY IN	314 08
FORASMUCH AS ALL MORTAL MEN ARE SUBJECT TC MANY	R 321 02
OF THE LORD, FORASMUCH AS YE KNOW THAT YOUR LABOUR IS	330 15
FORASMUCH THEN AS YOUR OFFICE IS BOTH OF SO GREAT	540 24
FORASMUCH AS THE HOLY SCRIPTURE AND THE	554 07
FORASMUCH AS DEVOUT AND HOLY MEN, AS WELL UNDER THE	564 10
TO GOD, FORASMUCH AS THEY SPRING NOT OF FAITH IN	605 18
YET FORASMUCH AS THEY DO NOT THE SAME IN THEIR CWN	608 11

FORBEARANCE

TO MUTUAL FORBEARANCE, FAIRNESS, AND GOOD-WILL	599 32

FORBEARING

FORBEARING ONE ANOTHER, AND FORGIVING ONE ANOTHER, IF	116 05
FORBEARING ONE ANOTHER IN LOVE	213 21

FORBID

CAN ANY MAN FORBID WATER, THAT THESE SHOULD NOT BE	184 26
GOD FORBID	207 32
BUT GOD FORBID THAT I SHOULD GLORY, SAVE IN THE CRUSS	210 29
COME UNTO ME, AND FORBID THEM NOT	274 29
COME UNTO ME, AND FORBID THEM NOT	338 10

FORBIDDEN

SWEARING IS FORBIDDEN CHRISTIAN MEN BY CUR LORD JESUS	611 06

FORBIDDING

AND FORBIDDING TO GIVE TRIBUTE TO CAESAR,	152 29

FORCE

A TESTAMENT IS OF FORCE AFTER MEN ARE DEAD	147 16

FOREFATHER

SWARE TO OUR FOREFATHER ABRAHAM, *	014 18

FOREFATHERS

TO OUR FOREFATHERS, *	014 16
TO OUR FOREFATHERS, ABRAHAM AND HIS SEED, FOR EVER	026 27
OUR OFFENCES, NOR THE OFFENCES OF OUR FOREFATHERS	054 14
NOR THE INIQUITIES OF OUR FOREFATHERS	308 11
OUR FOREFATHERS TO TEACH THEIR CHILDREN	435 05
BE AS THEIR FOREFATHERS, A FAITHLESS AND STUBBCRN	435 13
SIGHT OF OUR FOREFATHERS, IN THE LAND OF EGYPT, *	435 24
AND FELL AWAY LIKE THEIR FOREFATHERS	438 27

FOREGOING

USING THE FOREGOING FORM	R 281 29
PARTS OF THE FOREGOING SERVICE SHALL BE USED	R 282 02
SAID WITH THE FOREGOING SERVICE, OR ANY PART THERECF,	R 315 03
PORTION OF THE FOREGOING OFFICE AS HE SHALL THINK	R 320 07

FOREHEAD

A CROSS UPON THE CHILD'S (OR PERSON'S) FOREHEAD	R 280 11

FOREHEADS

HIS FATHER'S NAME WRITTEN IN THEIR FOREHEADS	102 31
SEALED THE SERVANTS OF OUR GOD IN THEIR FOREHEADS	256 19

FOREIGNERS

STRANGERS AND FOREIGNERS, BUT FELLOW-CITIZENS WITH	255 03

FOREST

THE BEASTS OF THE FOREST ARE MINE, *	402 10
BURNETH UP THE FOREST, *	444 32
THE BEASTS OF THE FOREST DO MOVE	468 35

FORESTS

AND STRIPPETH BARE THE FORESTS	374 15

FOREWARNED

WE ALSO HAVE FOREWARNED YOU AND TESTIFIED	128 02

FORGAT

12 BUT FORGAT WHAT HE HAD DONE, *	435 22
A WHILE THEY FORGAT HIS WORKS, *	473 27
21 AND THEY FORGAT GOD THEIR SAVIOUR, *	474 10

FORGAVE

EVEN AS CHRIST FORGAVE YOU, SO ALSO DO YE	116 07
LOOSED HIM, AND FORGAVE HIM THE DEBT	221 22
I FORGAVE THEE ALL THAT DEBT, BECAUSE THOU	221 34
THAT HE FORGAVE THEIR MISDEEDS, *	437 14

FORGAVEST

AND SO THOU FORGAVEST THE WICKEDNESS OF MY SIN	377 33
THOU FORGAVEST THEM, O GOD, THOUGH THOU DIDST PUNISH	462 32

FORGET

AND FORGET NOT ALL HIS BENEFITS	029 06
THAT HE WILL FORGET YOUR WORKS, AND LABOUR THAT	072 23
TO DISTRIBUTE, FORGET NOT	072 27
O MY SOUL, AND FORGET NOT ALL HIS BENEFITS	312 22
THE PEOPLE THAT FORGET GOD	352 27
FORGET NOT THE POOR	353 32
LONG WILT THOU FORGET ME, O LORD	355 28
YET DO WE NOT FORGET THEE, *	395 29
FORGET ALSO THINE OWN PEOPLE, AND THY FATHER'S HCUSE	397 06
YE THAT FORGET GOD, *	403 02
LEST MY PEOPLE FORGET IT	411 26
AND FORGET NOT THE CONGREGATION OF THE PCOR FOR EVER	431 16
24 FORGET NOT THE VOICE OF THINE ENEMIES	431 24
AND NOT TO FORGET THE WORKS OF GOD, BUT TO KEEP HIS	435 12
SO THAT I FORGET TO EAT MY BREAD	464 18
AND FORGET NOT ALL HIS BENEFITS	466 10
AND I WILL NOT FORGET THY WORD	490 30
YET DO I NOT FORGET THY STATUTES	495 24
93 I WILL NEVER FORGET THY COMMANDMENTS	498 11
YET DO I NOT FORGET THY LAW	497 15
YET DO I NOT FORGET THY COMMANDMENTS	499 21
FOR I DO NOT FORGET THY LAW	500 18
FOR I DO NOT FORGET THY COMMANDMENTS	502 03
5 IF I FORGET THEE, O JERUSALEM, *	513 13
LET MY RIGHT HAND FORGET HER CUNNING	513 13
THAT YOU FORGET NOT MERCY	558 29

FORGETFUL

HE BEING NOT A FORGETFUL HEARER, BUT A DOER OF THE 176 11
HE BEING NOT A FORGETFUL HEARER, BUT A DOER OF THE 266 02

FORGETTEST

AND FORGETTEST OUR MISERY AND TROUBLE 396 08

FORGETTETH

STRAIGHTWAY FORGETTETH WHAT MANNER OF MAN HE WAS 176 09
STRAIGHTWAY FORGETTETH WHAT MANNER OF MAN HE WAS 265 32
AND FORGETTETH NOT THE COMPLAINT OF THE POOR 352 14

FORGIVE

AND FORGIVE US OUR TRESPASSES, AS WE FORGIVE THOSE 007 25
AS WE FORGIVE THOSE WHO TRESPASS AGAINST US 007 26
AND JUST TO FORGIVE US OUR SINS, AND TO CLEANSE US 022 12
PLEASE THEE TO FORGIVE OUR ENEMIES, PERSECUTORS, 057 07
TO FORGIVE US ALL OUR SINS, NEGLIGENCES, AND 057 15
MERCIFULLY FORGIVE THE SINS OF THY PEOPLE 059 12
MERCIFULLY FORGIVE US OUR TRESPASSES 062 16
APPERTAINETH TO FORGIVE SINS 062 19
AND PROPERTY IS EVER TO HAVE MERCY AND TO FORGIVE 063 10
CHRIST'S SAKE, FORGIVE US ALL THAT IS PAST 075 27
BE CONTENT TO FORGIVE FROM THE BOTTOM OF HIS HEART R 085 12
READY TO FORGIVE OTHERS WHO HAVE OFFENDED YOU, AS YE 087 27
AND JUST TO FORGIVE US OUR SINS, AND TO CLEANSE US 101 30
AND DOST FORGIVE THE SINS OF ALL THOSE WHO ARE 124 12
FATHER, FORGIVE THEM 154 25
FORGIVE, AND YE SHALL BE FORGIVEN 194 27
ON EARTH TO FORGIVE SINS, (THEN SAITH HE TO THE SICK 217 10
AND I FORGIVE HIM 221 10
FROM YOUR HEARTS FORGIVE NOT EVERY ONE HIS BROTHER 222 06
EXHORTING HIM TO FORGIVE, FROM THE BOTTOM OF HIS R 313 26
AND FORGIVE ME ALL MY SIN 370 20
SINS THOU DOST FORGIVE, THEY ARE FORGIVEN 546 12
UNTO US, AND FORGIVE US OUR SINS 580 35
IN MERCY, AND FORGIVE US ALL OUR TRANSGRESSIONS 590 02

FORGIVEN

AND YE SHALL BE FORGIVEN 194 28
SAKE HATH FORGIVEN YOU 216 31
THY SINS BE FORGIVEN THEE 217 04
THY SINS BE FORGIVEN THEE 217 08
IS FORGIVEN, * 377 22
2 THOU HAST FORGIVEN THE OFFENCE OF THY PEOPLE, 446 10
WHOSE SINS THOU DOST FORGIVE, THEY ARE FORGIVEN 546 12

FORGIVENESS

THE FORGIVENESS OF SINS, ACCORDING TO THE 004 34
MAY OBTAIN FORGIVENESS OF THE SAME, BY HIS INFINITE 006 02
THE FORGIVENESS OF SINS 015 29
MAY OBTAIN FORGIVENESS OF THE SAME, BY HIS INFINITE 023 10
THE FORGIVENESS OF SINS 029 34
PROMISED FORGIVENESS OF SINS TO ALL THOSE WHO WITH 076 03
WOULD HAVE FORGIVENESS OF YOUR OFFENCES AT GOD'S 087 28
PERFECT REMISSION AND FORGIVENESS 124 16
UNTO YOU THE FORGIVENESS OF SINS 169 19
FOR THE FORGIVENESS OF OUR SINS, DID SHED OUT OF HIS 279 10
THE FORGIVENESS OF SINS 284 23
UNTO THEM FORGIVENESS OF ALL THEIR SINS 297 16
HATH OFFENDED ANY OTHER, TO ASK THEM FORGIVENESS R 313 22
SHALL ASSURE HIM OF GOD'S MERCY AND FORGIVENESS R 313 27
MOST EARNESTLY DESIRETH PARDON AND FORGIVENESS 314 02
THE FORGIVENESS OF SINS 578 07
PROMISED FORGIVENESS TO ALL THOSE WHO CONFESS AND 589 27
MAY OBTAIN FORGIVENESS AT THY HANDS, WHO ART EVER 590 05
THE PLACE OF FORGIVENESS TO SUCH AS TRULY REPENT 606 04
OF THE FORGIVENESS OF SIN, AND OF OUR ADOPTION TO BE 608 28

FORGIVENESSES

AND FORGIVENESSES, THOUGH WE HAVE REBELLED AGAINST 022 06

FORGIVETH

WHO FORGIVETH ALL THY SIN, * 029 08
WHO FORGIVETH ALL THY SIN, AND HEALETH ALL THINE 312 24
3 WHO FORGIVETH ALL THY SIN, * 466 12

FORGIVING

AND FORGIVING ONE ANOTHER, IF ANY MAN HAVE A 116 06
FORGIVING US THOSE THINGS WHEREOF OUR CONSCIENCE IS 206 07
FORGIVING ONE ANOTHER, EVEN AS GOD FOR CHRIST'S SAKE 216 29

FORGOTTEN

HATH GOD FORGOTTEN TO BE GRACIOUS 311 16
18 FOR THE POOR SHALL NOT ALWAY BE FORGOTTEN 352 28
HATH SAID IN HIS HEART, TUSH, GOD HATH FORGOTTEN 353 30
14 I AM CLEAN FORGOTTEN AS A DEAD MAN OUT OF MIND 376 19
WHY HAST THOU FORGOTTEN ME 393 25
21 IF WE HAVE FORGOTTEN THE NAME OF OUR GOD, AND 395 34
9 HATH GOD FORGOTTEN TO BE GRACIOUS 433 33
IN THE LAND WHERE ALL THINGS ARE FORGOTTEN 449 21
BUT I HAVE NOT FORGOTTEN THY LAW 494 03
ENEMIES HAVE FORGOTTEN THY WORDS 499 18
OR FORGOTTEN OF THEIR FELLOW-MEN 599 07
OR BECAUSE OF POVERTY ARE FORGOTTEN 600 08

FORM

ACCORDING TO THE FORM BEFORE PRESCRIBED R 083 08
WHO, BEING IN THE FORM OF GOD, THOUGHT IT NOT ROBBERY 134 17
TOOK UPON HIM THE FORM OF A SERVANT, AND WAS MADE IN 134 19
USING THE SAME FORM OF WORDS R 279 33
THEN THE FOLLOWING FORM SHALL SUFFICE R 281 18
ADMINISTER HOLY BAPTISM, USING THE FOREGOING FORM R 281 29
BE BAPTIZED IN THE FORM BEFORE APPOINTED IN THIS R 282 11
SHALL USE THIS FORM OF WORDS R 282 12
AND VISIBLE SIGN OR FORM IN BAPTISM 292 17
AND VISIBLE SIGN OR FORM IN BAPTISM IS WATER 292 19
IT SHALL BE IN THE FOLLOWING FORM R 304 21
ACCORDING TO THE FORM BEFORE PRESCRIBED FOR THE HOLY R 322 30
THE FOLLOWING FORM SHALL SUFFICE R 323 05
ACCORDING TO THE FORM HEREAFTER FOLLOWING, OR HATH 529 22
IN SUCH MANNER AND FORM AS FOLLOWETH 529 31
IN SUCH MANNER AND FORM AS HEREAFTER FOLLOWETH R 535 26
AS BEFORE IN THE FORM FOR THE ORDERING OF DEACONS,) R 547 26
HIS SUPPLICATION FOR HIMSELF, IN THIS FORM R 573 10
THIS OFFICE IN THE FORM OF A LETTER R 574 30
VISIBLE SIGN OR FORM IN BAPTISM 581 19
ACCORDING TO SAID FORM, WE DECREE ALL SUCH TO BE 610 35

FORMER

PROVIDENCE THE FORMER AND THE LATTER RAIN DESCEND 051 16
AND AMENDED HIS FORMER EVIL LIFE, THAT THE R 085 05
INSTEAD OF THE FORMER, HE MAY USE THIS EXHORTATION R 088 11
THE FORMER TREATISE HAVE I MADE, O THEOPHILUS, 177 22
CONCERNING THE FORMER CONVERSATION THE OLD MAN, WHICH 216 12
OF OLD, AND AS IN FORMER YEARS 232 15
TRULY OF THEIR FORMER SINS, WITH STEDFAST PURPOSE TO 293 27
HIM TO HIS FORMER HEALTH, THAT HE MAY GIVE THANKS 309 30
NOT UNTO HIM HIS FORMER SINS, BUT STRENGTHEN HIM WITH 314 10
DEGREE OF HIS FORMER HEALTH 315 23
FOR THE FORMER THINGS ARE PASSED AWAY 567 20
TRULY OF THEIR FORMER SINS, STEDFASTLY PURPOSING TO 582 23
OF THE FORMER ARTICLES IS OMITTED R 607 11
AS DOTH THE FORMER BOOK OF HOMILIES, WHICH WERE SET 610 07

FORMS

WORSHIP DIFFERENT FORMS AND USAGES MAY WITHOUT V 03
THE PARTICULAR FORMS OF DIVINE WORSHIP, AND THE RITES V 14
AMENDMENTS IN HER FORMS OF PUBLIC WORSHIP V 23
AND FORMS OF WORSHIP, AND DISCIPLINE, IN VI 11

FORNICATION

THAT YE SHOULD ABSTAIN FROM FORNICATION 127 28
BUT FORNICATION, AND ALL UNCLEANNESS, OR 129 02
US COMMIT FORNICATION, AS SOME OF THEM COMMITTED, 201 17
FORNICATION, UNCLEANNESS, LASCIVIOUSNESS, 209 20

FORSAKE

US GRACE TO FORSAKE ALL COVETOUS DESIRES, AND 250 22
WHEREBY THEY FORSAKE SIN 292 28
THOU DIDST NOT FORSAKE HIM IN HIS SICKNESS 315 24
ME NOT, NEITHER FORSAKE ME, O GOD OF MY SALVATION 326 27
ME NOT, NEITHER FORSAKE ME, O GOD OF MY SALVATION 372 19
AND MY MOTHER FORSAKE ME, * 372 20
21 FORSAKE ME NOT, O LORD MY GOD 388 34
FORSAKE ME NOT WHEN MY STRENGTH FAILETH ME 425 23
17 FORSAKE ME NOT, O GOD, IN MINE OLD AGE, WHEN I AM 426 10
THEY THAT FORSAKE THEE SHALL PERISH 429 30
IF HIS CHILDREN FORSAKE MY LAW, * 452 02
NEITHER WILL HE FORSAKE HIS INHERITANCE 458 15
O FORSAKE ME NOT UTTERLY 490 14
THE UNGODLY THAT FORSAKE THY LAW 493 16
HOW YE OUGHT TO FORSAKE AND SET ASIDE, AS MUCH AS YE 541 07
WHEREBY THEY FORSAKE SIN 581 28
WHO CONFESS AND FORSAKE THEIR SINS 589 28

FORSAKEN

WHY HAST THOU FORSAKEN ME 137 19
WHY HAST THOU FORSAKEN ME 146 29
BEHOLD, WE HAVE FORSAKEN ALL, AND FOLLOWED THEE 231 13
ONE THAT HATH FORSAKEN HOUSES, OR BRETHREN, OR 231 18
FOR DEMAS HATH FORSAKEN ME, HAVING LOVED THIS PRESENT 253 32
AND HAVE NOT FORSAKEN MY GOD, AS THE WICKED DOTH 361 10
WHY HAST THOU FORSAKEN ME 366 04
THE RIGHTEOUS FORSAKEN, NOR HIS SEED BEGGING THEIR 386 13
10 GOD HATH FORSAKEN HIM 425 27
ABHORRED AND FORSAKEN THINE ANOINTED, * 452 16
HAST NOT THOU FORSAKEN US, O GOD 479 26

FORSAKETH

HE FORSAKETH NOT HIS THAT BE GODLY, BUT THEY ARE 386 20

FORSAKING

NOT FORSAKING THE ASSEMBLING OF OURSELVES TOGETHER, 158 25
SO WE, FORSAKING ALL WORLDLY AND CARNAL AFFECTIONS, 246 19
FORSAKING ALL OTHERS, KEEP THEE ONLY UNTO HER, 301 09
FORSAKING ALL OTHERS, KEEP THEE ONLY UNTO HIM, 301 17

FORSOOK

AND THEY ALL FORSOOK HIM, AND FLED 142 28
TO LAND, THEY FORSOOK ALL, AND FOLLOWED HIM 196 30
61 SO THAT HE FORSOOK THE TABERNACLE IN SHILOH, 438 32
BUT I FORSOOK NOT THY COMMANDMENTS 495 32

FORTH

GOD HATH SENT FORTH THE SPIRIT OF HIS SON INTO YOUR	005 16
HIS HANDS, TO SET FORTH HIS MOST WORTHY PRAISE,	006 07
MOUTH SHALL SHOW FORTH THY PRAISE	007 32
HATH MANIFESTED FORTH HIS GLORY	R 008 21
AND THAT WE SHOW FORTH THY PRAISE, NOT ONLY WITH OUR	019 27
MY PRAYER BE SET FORTH IN THY SIGHT AS THE INCENSE	021 16
HIS HANDS, TO SET FORTH HIS MOST WORTHY PRAISE, TC	023 19
MOUTH SHALL SHOW FORTH THY PRAISE	025 07
THE EARTH BRING FORTH HER INCREASE	028 28
AND THAT WE SHOW FORTH THY PRAISE, NOT ONLY WITH OUR	033 29
WE MAY SHOW FORTH THY PRAISE AMONG THE NATIONS	036 20
THEY MAY SHOW FORTH THY GLORY, AND SET FORWARD THE	039 19
FRUITFUL AND BRING FORTH WHATSOEVER IS NEEDFUL FOR	039 25
LET THY BREATH GO FORTH THAT IT MAY RENEW THE FACE OF	040 09
THE EARTH BRING FORTH HER INCREASE	040 31
OF HOSTS, STRETCH FORTH, WE PRAY THEE, THINE ALMIGHTY	041 25
GLORY AND SHOWEST FORTH THY HANDIWORK IN THE HEAVENS	044 18
THEY MAY BRING FORTH IN US THE FRUIT OF GOOD LIVING,	049 20
AND TO THE SETTING FORTH OF THY GLORY	050 12
THAT IT MAY BRING FORTH FRUIT FOR THE USE OF MAN	051 17
THEY MAY SET IT FORTH, AND SHOW IT ACCORDINGLY	055 33
THEE TO SEND FORTH LABOURERS INTO THY HARVEST	056 02
AND TO BRING FORTH THE FRUITS OF THE SPIRIT	056 16
THAT HE SEND FORTH LABOURERS INTO HIS HARVEST	073 13
AND DOCTRINE, SET FORTH THY TRUE AND LIVELY WORD,	074 23
MANIFESTED FORTH HIS GLORY	077 23
THEY NOW SHOOT FORTH, YE SEE AND KNOW OF YOUR OWN	093 15
AND SHE BROUGHT FORTH HER FIRSTBORN SON, AND WRAPPED	099 07
AND SENT FORTH, AND SLEW ALL THE CHILDREN THAT	103 26
WAS COME, GOD SENT FORTH HIS SON, MADE OF A WOMAN,	104 19
GOD HATH SENT FORTH THE SPIRIT OF HIS SON INTO YOUR	104 23
SHE SHALL BRING FORTH A SON, AND THOU SHALT CALL HIS	105 06
AND SHALL BRING FORTH A SON, AND THEY SHALL CALL HIS	105 10
SHE HAD BROUGHT FORTH HER FIRSTBORN SON	105 15
HEARTS MAY SHINE FORTH IN OUR LIVES	106 27
STRETCH FORTH THY RIGHT HAND TO HELP AND DEFEND US	112 28
BEGINNING DOTH SET FORTH GOOD WINE	113 28
AND MANIFESTED FORTH HIS GLORY	113 31
AND JESUS PUT FORTH HIS HAND, AND TOUCHED HIM,	114 32
UP, AND BROUGHT FORTH FRUIT, THEN APPEARED THE TARES	116 22
GO NOT FORTH	118 09
HAVE HEARD, GO FORTH, AND ARE CHOKED WITH CARES AND	122 06
KEEP IT, AND BRING FORTH FRUIT WITH PATIENCE	122 10
THE BRIDEGROOM GO FORTH OF HIS CHAMBER, AND THE BRIDE	124 32
AND STRETCH FORTH THE RIGHT HAND OF THY MAJESTY, TO	128 26
BREAK FORTH AND CRY, THOU THAT TRAVAILEST NOT	131 09
AND HE SENDETH FORTH TWO OF HIS DISCIPLES, AND SAITH	140 25
HIS DISCIPLES WENT FORTH, AND CAME INTO THE CITY, AND	140 32
YE STRETCHED FORTH NO HANDS AGAINST ME	151 05
THEREFORE WENT FORTH AGAIN, AND SAITH UNTO THEM,	158 34
I BRING HIM FORTH TO YOU, THAT YE MAY KNOW THAT I	159 02
THEN CAME JESUS FORTH, WEARING THE CROWN OF THORNS,	159 03
HE BROUGHT JESUS FORTH, AND SAT DOWN IN THE	159 23
HIS CROSS WENT FORTH INTO A PLACE CALLED THE PLACE OF	159 32
THEREFORE WENT FORTH, AND THAT OTHER DISCIPLE, AND	164 16
I CAME FORTH FROM THE FATHER, AND AM COME INTO THE	176 30
THAT THOU CAMEST FORTH FROM GOD	177 03
WHEN HE PUTTETH FORTH HIS OWN SHEEP, HE GOETH BEFORE	186 06
TREE BRINGETH FORTH EVIL FRUIT	200 19
GOOD TREE BRINGETH FORTH GOOD FRUIT	200 19
TREE CANNOT BRING FORTH EVIL FRUIT, NEITHER CAN A	200 20
CORRUPT TREE BRING FORTH GOOD FRUIT	200 21
THAT BRINGETH NOT FORTH GOOD FRUIT IS HEWN DOWN,	200 22
BRING FORTH THE BEST ROBE, AND PUT IT ON	202 11
RUMOUR OF HIM WENT FORTH THROUGHOUT ALL JUDAEA,	213 10
AND HE PUT FORTH A PARABLE TO THOSE WHICH WERE	214 08
MAN FROM THAT DAY FORTH ASK HIM ANY MORE QUESTIONS	215 23
HIS SON, AND SENT FORTH HIS SERVANTS TO CALL THEM	218 05
HE SENT FORTH OTHER SERVANTS, SAYING, TELL	218 06
AND HE SENT FORTH HIS ARMIES, AND DESTROYED THOSE	218 14
AND BRINGETH FORTH FRUIT, AS IT DOTH ALSO IN YOU,	223 28
PEOPLE WERE PUT FORTH, HE WENT IN, AND TOOK HER BY	224 28
BRINGING FORTH THE FRUIT OF GOOD WORKS, MAY BY THEE	225 05
I HAVE STRETCHED FORTH MY HANDS UNTO A DISOBEDIENT	227 22
MAY SHOW FORTH OUR THANKFULNESS UNTO THEE FOR THE	229 21
AND THEY GAVE FORTH THEIR LOTS	234 31
AND BRING FORTH A SON, AND SHALT CALL HIS NAME	236 15
THAT IT MAY BRING FORTH MORE FRUIT	238 08
THE SAME BRINGETH FORTH MUCH FRUIT	238 13
IN ME, HE IS CAST FORTH AS A BRANCH, AND IS WITHERED	238 15
AND THEY SENT FORTH BARNABAS, THAT HE SHOULD GO AS	241 04
GO AND BRING FORTH FRUIT, AND THAT YOUR FRUIT SHOULD	241 33
AND SHE BROUGHT FORTH A SON	243 14
THE KING STRETCHED FORTH HIS HANDS TO VEX CERTAIN OF	244 31
TO BRING HIM FORTH TO THE PEOPLE	245 06
HAVE BROUGHT HIM FORTH, THE SAME NIGHT PETER WAS	245 09
THE KING STRETCHED FORTH HIS HANDS TO VEX CERTAIN OF	246 32
THAT THEY BROUGHT FORTH THE SICK INTO THE STREETS,	249 27
AS JESUS PASSED FORTH FROM THENCE, HE SAW A MAN,	251 12
TO SET FORTH IN THE GOSPEL THE LOVE AND	253 17
THAT HE WOULD SEND FORTH LABOURERS INTO HIS HARVEST	254 16
BEHOLD, I SEND YOU FORTH AS LAMBS AMONG WOLVES	254 17
THEE TO POUR FORTH THY BLESSING UPON THIS LAND,	261 30
I STRETCHED FORTH MY HANDS UNTO HIM, AND CEASED NOT	311 02
THOU SHALT STRETCH FORTH THY HAND UPON THE	312 05
WERE BROUGHT FORTH, OR EVER THE EARTH AND THE WORLD	325 15
FROM THIS TIME FORTH FOR EVERMORE	327 34
AND LEAD ME FORTH BESIDE THE WATERS OF COMFORT	338 19
AND BRING ME FORTH IN THE PATHS OF RIGHTEOUSNESS FOR	338 21
FROM THIS TIME FORTH FOR EVERMORE	339 18
THAT WILL BRING FORTH HIS FRUIT IN DUE SEASON	345 13
AND BROUGHT FORTH FALSEHOOD	350 22
MY SENTENCE COME FORTH FROM THY PRESENCE	358 19
HE CAST FORTH LIGHTNINGS, AND DESTROYED THEM	360 27
20 HE BROUGHT ME FORTH ALSO INTO A PLACE OF LIBERTY	361 04
HE BROUGHT ME FORTH, EVEN BECAUSE HE HAD A FAVOUR	361 05
WHICH COMETH FORTH AS A BRIDEGROOM OUT OF HIS	363 22
6 IT GOETH FORTH FROM THE UTTERMOST PART OF THE	363 24
AND LEAD ME FORTH BESIDE THE WATERS OF COMFORT	368 13
AND BRING ME FORTH IN THE PATHS OF RIGHTEOUSNESS FOR	368 14
4 LEAD ME FORTH IN THY TRUTH, AND LEARN ME	369 25
THE HINDS TO BRING FORTH YOUNG, AND STRIPPETH BARE	374 15
3 BRING FORTH THE SPEAR, AND STOP THE WAY AGAINST	381 22
10 O CONTINUE FORTH THY LOVING-KINDNESS UNTO THEM	384 16
AND WHEN HE COMETH FORTH, HE TELLETH IT	392 12
AND BROUGHT THEM FORTH INTO THE HOUSE OF GOD	393 08
AND GOEST NOT FORTH WITH OUR ARMIES	395 12
THOU HAST SET FORTH DECEIT	402 29
4 GOD SHALL SEND FORTH HIS MERCY AND TRUTH	409 19
THE EARTH BRING FORTH HER INCREASE	419 02
WHEN THOU WENTEST FORTH BEFORE THE PEOPLE	419 24
THY GOD HATH SENT FORTH STRENGTH FOR THEE	421 11
15 I WILL GO FORTH IN THE STRENGTH OF THE LORD GOD,	426 06
9 FOR THEY STRETCH FORTH THEIR MOUTH UNTO THE HEAVEN,	428 26
I STRETCHED FORTH MY HANDS UNTO HIM, AND CEASED NOT	433 19
HE LED THEM FORTH LIKE SHEEP, *	438 14
ALWAY BE SHOWING FORTH THY PRAISE FROM GENERATION TO	440 34
THAT I CANNOT GET FORTH	449 13
I HAVE STRETCHED FORTH MY HANDS UNTO THEE	449 15
WERE BROUGHT FORTH, OR EVER THE EARTH AND THE WORLD	453 20
ALSO SHALL BRING FORTH MORE FRUIT IN THEIR AGE,	456 28
14 HE BRINGETH FORTH GRASS FOR THE CATTLE, *	468 21
23 MAN GOETH FORTH TO HIS WORK, AND TO HIS LABOUR,	469 06
THY BREATH GO FORTH, THEY SHALL BE MADE	469 21
THEIR LAND BROUGHT FORTH FROGS	471 32
36 HE BROUGHT THEM FORTH ALSO WITH SILVER AND GOLD	472 11
42 AND HE BROUGHT FORTH HIS PEOPLE WITH JOY, *	472 23
OR SHOW FORTH ALL HIS PRAISE	473 03
7 HE LED THEM FORTH BY THE RIGHT WAY, *	476 17
THOU, O GOD, GO FORTH WITH OUR HOSTS	479 27
FROM THIS TIME FORTH FOR EVERMORE	484 11
FROM THIS TIME FORTH FOR EVERMORE	486 14
THY WORD GOETH FORTH, *	498 30
FROM THIS TIME FORTH FOR EVERMORE	503 07
FROM THIS TIME FORTH FOR EVERMORE	504 27
SHALL LEAD THEM FORTH WITH THE EVIL DOERS	505 03
AND BEARETH FORTH GOOD SEED, *	505 19
FROM THIS TIME FORTH FOR EVERMORE	507 30
7 HE BRINGETH FORTH THE CLOUDS FROM THE ENDS OF THE	510 15
AND SENDETH FORTH LIGHTNINGS WITH THE RAIN, BRINGING	510 16
THOU SHALT STRETCH FORTH THY HAND UPON THE	514 11
MY PRAYER BE SET FORTH IN THY SIGHT AS THE INCENSE	517 10
6 I STRETCH FORTH MY HANDS UNTO THEE	519 02
SPIRIT LEAD ME FORTH INTO THE LAND OF RIGHTEOUSNESS	519 13
6 CAST FORTH THY LIGHTNING, AND TEAR THEM	520 02
SHEEP MAY BRING FORTH THOUSANDS, AND TEN THOUSANDS IN	520 19
OF MAN GOETH FORTH, HE SHALL TURN AGAIN TO HIS EARTH,	522 08
15 HE SENDETH FORTH HIS COMMANDMENT UPON EARTH,	523 25
17 HE CASTETH FORTH HIS ICE LIKE MORSELS	523 29
LET HIM COME FORTH IN THE NAME OF GOD, AND SHOW WHAT	530 24
AND WILL COME FORTH AND SERVE THEM	534 23
LET HIM COME FORTH IN THE NAME OF GOD, AND SHOW WHAT	536 30
THAT HE WILL SEND FORTH LABOURERS INTO HIS HARVEST	538 19
WHEN HE PUTTETH FORTH HIS OWN SHEEP, HE GOETH BEFORE	538 29
THE WORLD, TO SET FORTH THE ETERNAL PRAISE OF THY	545 20
HE CHOSE AND SENT FORTH HIS TWELVE APOSTLES	553 06
WE ADMIT AND SEND FORTH THIS PERSON PRESENTED UNTO	553 11
THY HANDS, TO SET FORTH HIS MOST WORTHY PRAISE,	566 16
MAY SHOW FORTH THEIR THANKFULNESS, BY MAKING A	566 32
THEIR LIVES SHOW FORTH THY PRAISE	567 09
AND DOCTRINE SET FORTH THY TRUE AND LIVELY WORD	573 23
WORD MAN GOETH FORTH TO HIS WORK AND TO HIS LABOUR	599 25
BE GENERALLY SET FORTH TO US IN HOLY SCRIPTURE	606 28
WHICH WERE SET FORTH IN THE TIME OF EDWARD THE SIXTH	610 08
AS SET FORTH BY THE GENERAL CONVENTION OF	610 32

FORTHWITH

HIS SIDE, AND FORTHWITH CAME THERE OUT BLOOD AND	161 04
HOLY WORD, MAY FORTHWITH GIVE UP OURSELVES OBEDIENTLY	226 22
RECEIVED SIGHT FORTHWITH, AND AROSE, AND WAS	230 35
AND FORTHWITH THE ANGEL DEPARTED FROM HIM	245 24

FORTRESS

MY HOPE AND MY FORTRESS, MY CASTLE AND DELIVERER,	519 24

FORTY

HIM AN HUNDRED FORTY AND FOUR THOUSAND, HAVING HIS	102 30
THE HUNDRED AND FORTY AND FOUR THOUSAND, WHICH WERE	103 07
TIMES RECEIVED I FORTY STRIPES SAVE ONE	120 32
SAKE DIDST FAST FORTY DAYS AND FORTY NIGHTS	125 27
FORTY DAYS AND FORTY NIGHTS	125 28
WHEN HE HAD FASTED FORTY DAYS AND FORTY NIGHTS,	126 25
FORTY DAYS AND FORTY NIGHTS, HE WAS AFTERWARD AN	126 25
BEING SEEN OF THEM FORTY DAYS, AND SPEAKING OF THE	177 28
AN HUNDRED AND FORTY AND FOUR THOUSAND OF ALL THE	366 31
10 FORTY YEARS LONG WAS I GRIEVED WITH THIS	459 24

FORWARD

AND SET FORWARD THE SALVATION OF ALL MEN	039 03
AND HE WENT FORWARD A LITTLE, AND FELL ON THE GROUND,	141 33
FROM THIS DAY FORWARD, FOR BETTER FOR WORSE, FOR	301 29
FROM THIS DAY FORWARD, FOR BETTER FOR WORSE, FOR	302 05
MAINTAIN AND SET FORWARD, AS MUCH AS SHALL LIE IN	555 14
THAT THEY MAY GO FORWARD WITH COURAGE, AND PERSEVERE	561 09

FORWARDS

AND SET FORWARDS, AS MUCH AS LIETH IN YOU, QUIETNESS,   543 06
INCREASE AND GO FORWARDS IN THE KNOWLEDGE AND FAITH   545 30

FOUGHT

AND HE FOUGHT AGAINST THEM   139 06
AND HIS ANGELS FOUGHT AGAINST THE DRAGON   252 04
AND THE DRAGON FOUGHT AND HIS ANGELS, AND PREVAILED   252 04
I HAVE FOUGHT A GOOD FIGHT, I HAVE FINISHED MY   253 26
OF HATRED, AND FOUGHT AGAINST ME WITHOUT A CAUSE   480 08
A TIME HAVE THEY FOUGHT AGAINST ME FROM MY YOUTH UP,   506 21

FOUND

WOULD IN TIME BE FOUND EXPEDIENT   VI 03
WORLD WE MAY BE FOUND AN ACCEPTABLE PEOPLE IN THY   093 30
THAT A MAN BE FOUND FAITHFUL   094 05
IN THEIR MOUTH WAS FOUND NO GUILE   103 13
SHE WAS FOUND WITH CHILD OF THE HOLY GHOST   104 29
WITH HASTE, AND FOUND MARY, AND JOSEPH, AND THE BABE   106 11
AND WHEN YE HAVE FOUND HIM, BRING ME WORD AGAIN,   109 14
AND WHEN THEY FOUND HIM NOT, THEY TURNED BACK AGAIN   110 26
THREE DAYS THEY FOUND HIM IN THE TEMPLE, SITTING IN   110 28
I HAVE NOT FOUND SO GREAT FAITH, NO, NOT IN   115 17
HE WENT OUT, AND FOUND OTHERS STANDING IDLE, AND   119 24
AND BEING FOUND IN FASHION AS A MAN, HE HUMBLED   134 20
CAME OUT, THEY FOUND A MAN OF CYRENE, SIMON BY NAME   136 25
INTO THE CITY, AND FOUND AS HE HAD SAID UNTO THEM   140 33
HE RETURNED, HE FOUND THEM ASLEEP AGAIN, (FOR THEIR   142 08
AND FOUND NONE   143 03
AND THEY WENT, AND FOUND AS HE HAD SAID UNTO THEM   148 32
HIS DISCIPLES, HE FOUND THEM SLEEPING FOR SORROW, AND   150 24
SAYING, WE FOUND THIS FELLOW PERVERTING THE   152 28
BEFORE YOU, HAVE FOUND NO FAULT IN THIS MAN TOUCHING   153 24
I HAVE FOUND NO CAUSE OF DEATH IN HIM   153 35
AND WHEN THEY FOUND NOT HIS BODY, THEY CAME, SAYING,   167 24
THE SEPULCHRE, AND FOUND IT EVEN SO AS THE WOMEN HAD   167 27
TO JERUSALEM, AND FOUND THE ELEVEN GATHERED TOGETHER,   168 12
MAY BE FOUND WORTHY TO ATTAIN TO EVERLASTING   168 21
AND THOUGH THEY FOUND NO CAUSE OF DEATH IN HIM,   168 30
NEITHER WAS GUILE FOUND IN HIS MOUTH   172 12
WHERE TRUE JOYS ARE TO BE FOUND   174 24
AND WHEN HE HATH FOUND IT, HE LAYETH IT ON HIS   193 21
FOR I HAVE FOUND MY SHEEP WHICH WAS LOST   193 24
AND WHEN SHE HATH FOUND IT, SHE CALLETH HER FRIENDS   193 30
FOR I HAVE FOUND THE PIECE WHICH I HAD LOST   193 32
HE WAS LOST, AND IS FOUND   202 25
AND WAS LOST, AND IS FOUND   203 08
THERE ARE NOT FOUND THAT RETURNED TO GIVE GLORY TO   210 12
AS MANY AS THEY FOUND, BOTH BAD AND GOOD   218 20
WENT OUT, AND FOUND ONE OF HIS FELLOW-SERVANTS, WHICH   221 23
AND SAITH, I WAS FOUND OF THEM THAT SOUGHT ME NCT   227 19
THAT IF HE FOUND ANY OF THIS WAY, WHETHER THEY WERE   229 28
FOR THOU HAST FOUND FAVOUR WITH GOD   236 14
AND WHEN HE HAD FOUND HIM, HE BROUGHT HIM UNTO   241 11
JESUS WAS FOUND ALONE   249 08
WAS THEIR PLACE FOUND ANY MORE IN HEAVEN   252 05
THE BOOK, HE FOUND THE PLACE WHERE IT WAS WRITTEN,   261 15
THERE BE FIXED, WHERE TRUE JOYS ARE TO BE FOUND   285 31
I FOUND TROUBLE AND HEAVINESS   305 22
WE MAY BE FOUND ACCEPTABLE IN THY SIGHT   335 09
WITH THEM, BE FOUND MEET TO BE PARTAKERS OF THE   335 33
IN A TIME WHEN THOU MAYEST BE FOUND   378 03
ABOMINABLE SIN BE FOUND OUT   383 29
SOUGHT HIM, BUT HIS PLACE COULD NO WHERE BE FOUND   387 07
NO MAN, NEITHER FOUND I ANY TO COMFORT ME   423 15
WERE MIGHTY HAVE FOUND NOTHING   432 31
THE SPARROW HATH FOUND HER AN HOUSE, AND THE SWALLOW   445 16
21 I HAVE FOUND DAVID MY SERVANT   451 15
AND FOUND NO CITY TO DWELL IN   476 13
4 I FOUND TROUBLE AND HEAVINESS   486 25
AND FOUND IT IN THE WOOD   508 15
ACCUSED SHALL BE FOUND CLEAR OF THAT CRIME   R 530 28
SUCH AS SHALL BE FOUND MEET TO BE ORDERED, TO THE   R 530 29
OF A DEACON, BEING FOUND BLAMELESS   531 31
THAT THEY MAY BE FOUND WORTHY TO BE CALLED UNTO THE   535 09
WHEREOF IF HE BE FOUND FAITHFUL AND DILIGENT,   R 535 23
ACCUSED SHALL BE FOUND CLEAR OF THAT CRIME   R 537 04
SUCH AS SHALL BE FOUND MEET TO BE ORDERED, TO THE   R 537 05
YOU MAY BE FOUND PERFECT AND IRREPREHENSIBLE   555 32
TO JERUSALEM, AND FOUND IN THE TEMPLE THOSE THAT SOLD   567 26
AND FINALLY, BEING FOUND GUILTY, BY JUST JUDGMENT BE   608 21

FOUNDATION

FOR HER FIRST FOUNDATION AND A LONG CONTINUANCE OF   V 11
HAST LAID THE FOUNDATION OF THE EARTH   097 14
SINCE THE FOUNDATION OF THE WORLD   148 05
UPON THE FOUNDATION OF THE APOSTLES AND PROPHETS,   254 28
UPON THE FOUNDATION OF THE APOSTLES AND PRCPHETS,   255 05
YOU FROM THE FOUNDATION OF THE WORLD   259 05
UPON THE FOUNDATION OF THE APOSTLES AND PROPHETS,   290 20
YOU FROM THE FOUNDATION OF THE WORLD   336 27
AND LAID THE FOUNDATION OF IT LIKE THE GROUND WHICH   439 17
HAST LAID THE FOUNDATION OF THE ROUND WORLD, AND ALL   450 29
HAST LAID THE FOUNDATION OF THE EARTH, *   465 31
HAST LAID THE FOUNDATION OF THE EARTH, AND IT   496 05
UPON THE FOUNDATION OF THE APOSTLES AND PRCPHETS,   574 04

FOUNDATIONS

AND SUREST FOUNDATIONS, THAT PEACE AND HAPPINESS,   035 16
3 IF THE FOUNDATIONS BE DESTROYED, *   354 24
THE VERY FOUNDATIONS ALSO OF THE HILLS SHOOK, AND   360 09

FOUNDATIONS   CONTINUED

AND THE FOUNDATIONS OF THE ROUND WORLD WERE   360 28
ALL THE FOUNDATIONS OF THE EARTH ARE OUT OF COURSE   443 27
HER FOUNDATIONS ARE UPON THE HOLY HILLS   448 13
HE LAID THE FOUNDATIONS OF THE EARTH, *   468 02
BEFORE THE FOUNDATIONS OF THE WORLD WERE LAID) HE   606 07

FOUNDED

BY WISDOM HATH FOUNDED THE EARTH   005 24
2 FOR HE HATH FOUNDED IT UPON THE SEAS, *   368 30
2 FOR HE HATH FOUNDED IT UPON THE SEAS, *   563 13

FOUNT

THE FOUNT OF LIFE, THE FIRE OF LOVE, THE SOUL'S   544 23
THE FOUNT OF LIFE, THE FIRE OF LOVE, THE SOUL'S   557 02

FOUNTAIN

O GOD, THE FOUNTAIN OF WISDOM, WHOSE STATUTES ARE   035 23
WHO ART THE FOUNTAIN OF ALL WISDOM   042 27
THE FOUNTAIN OF ALL WISDOM, WHO KNOWEST OUR   049 29
THAT ARE OF THE FOUNTAIN OF ISRAEL   421 07

FOUNTAINS

UNTO LIVING FOUNTAINS OF WATERS   257 15
UNTO LIVING FOUNTAINS OF WATERS   341 26
BROUGHTEST OUT FOUNTAINS AND WATERS OUT OF THE HARD   431 06

FOUR

HUNDRED FORTY AND FOUR THOUSAND, HAVING HIS FATHER'S   102 30
AND BEFORE THE FOUR LIVING CREATURES, AND THE ELDERS   103 05
AND FORTY AND FOUR THOUSAND, WHICH WERE REDEEMED FROM 103 07
HIS ELECT FROM THE FOUR WINDS, FROM ONE END OF HEAVEN 118 22
AND MADE FOUR PARTS, TO EVERY SOLDIER A   160 10
THE SEATS I SAW FOUR AND TWENTY ELDERS SITTING,   187 09
THE THRONE WERE FOUR AND TWENTY SEATS   187 09
THE THRONE, WERE FOUR LIVING CREATURES FULL OF EYES   187 17
AND THE FOUR LIVING CREATURES HAD EACH OF THEM SIX   187 20
EVER AND EVER, THE FOUR AND TWENTY ELDERS FALL DCWN   187 26
EATEN WERE ABOUT FOUR THOUSAND   199 25
THE LAW, WHICH WAS FOUR HUNDRED AND THIRTY YEARS   207 23
ABOUT FOURSCORE AND FOUR YEARS, WHICH DEPARTED NCT   233 19
DELIVERED HIM TO FOUR QUATERNIONS OF SOLDIERS TO KEEP 245 05
A LOUD VOICE TO THE FOUR ANGELS, TO WHCM IT WAS GIVEN 256 16
AND FORTY AND FOUR THOUSAND OF ALL THE TRIBES OF THE   256 21
THE ELDERS AND THE FOUR LIVING CREATURES, AND FELL   256 30

FOURSCORE

WIDOW OF ABOUT FOURSCORE AND FOUR YEARS, WHICH   233 19
THEY COME TO FOURSCORE YEARS, *   325 33
THEY COME TO FOURSCORE YEARS, *   454 08

FOURTEEN

WITHIN FOURTEEN DAYS AFTER, AT THE FARTHEST   R 085 19

FOURTH

THE THIRD AND FOURTH GENERATION OF THEM THAT HATE ME   068 13
AS A MAN, AND THE FOURTH WAS LIKE A FLYING EAGLE   187 19
THE THIRD AND FOURTH GENERATION OF THEM THAT HATE ME   286 13
PUT IT UPON THE FOURTH FINGER OF THE WOMAN'S LEFT   R 302 11
THE RING UPON THE FOURTH FINGER OF THE WOMAN'S LEFT R 302 23
THE THIRD AND FOURTH GENERATION OF THEM THAT HATE ME   578 32

FOWLER

EVEN AS A BIRD OUT OF THE SNARE OF THE FOWLER   504 19

FOWLS

O ALL YE FOWLS OF THE AIR, BLESS YE THE LORD   013 14
AND THE FOWLS OF THE AIR DEVOURED IT   121 22
BEHOLD THE FOWLS OF THE AIR   266 14
8 THE FOWLS OF THE AIR, AND THE FISHES OF THE SEA   351 15
11 I KNOW ALL THE FOWLS UPON THE MOUNTAINS, *   402 12
AND FEATHERED FOWLS LIKE AS THE SAND OF THE SEA   436 26
BE MEAT UNTO THE FOWLS OF THE AIR, *   440 02
THEM SHALL THE FOWLS OF THE AIR HAVE THEIR   468 17
CREEPING THINGS AND FLYING FOWLS   524 24

FOXES

THAT THEY MAY BE A PORTION FOR FOXES   415 14

FRAGMENTS

GATHER UP THE FRAGMENTS THAT REMAIN, THAT NCTHING BE   132 07
WITH THE FRAGMENTS OF THE FIVE BARLEY LOAVES, WHICH   132 09
GATHER UP THE FRAGMENTS THAT REMAIN, THAT NCTHING BE   226 07
WITH THE FRAGMENTS OF THE FIVE BARLEY LOAVES, WHICH   226 09

FRAIL

PERCEIVING HOW FRAIL AND UNCERTAIN OUR LIFE IS,   045 08

FRAILNESS

OR BY HIS OWN CARNAL WILL AND FRAILNESS   314 05

FRAILTY

BY REASON OF THE FRAILTY OF OUR NATURE WE CANNOT — 114 05
BECAUSE THE FRAILTY OF MAN WITHOUT THEE CANNOT — 210 18
WHICH BY OUR FRAILTY WE HAVE COMMITTED — 223 18
THROUGH OUR OWN FRAILTY, OR THE TEMPTATIONS WHICH — 590 09

FRAME

AS IN THE FRAME AND ORDER THEREOF) HAVE STILL BEEN — V 31
AND CHARITABLE FRAME OF MIND — VI 38
YOUR DILIGENCE TO FRAME AND FASHION YOUR OWN LIVES, — 533 24
YOU BE DILIGENT TO FRAME AND FASHION YOUR OWN SELVES, — 542 32
HE BE DILIGENT TO FRAME HIS LIFE ACCORDING TO THAT — 606 34

FRAMED

BUILDING FITLY FRAMED TOGETHER GROWETH UNTO AN HOLY — 255 08

FRAMING

AND IN FRAMING THE MANNERS BOTH OF YOURSELVES, AND OF — 541 04

FRANKINCENSE

AND FRANKINCENSE, AND MYRRH — 109 23

FRAUD

DECAYED BY THE FRAUD AND MALICE OF THE DEVIL, OR BY — 314 04
7 HIS MOUTH IS FULL OF CURSING, DECEIT, AND FRAUD — 353 18
HIRE OF THE LABOURERS TO BE KEPT BACK BY FRAUD — 599 31

FREE

CHRIST HATH MADE US FREE,* THAT IN HIS WORSHIP — V 03
THEY MAY BE SET FREE FROM THE CHAINS OF SIN, AND MAY — 046 28
ME WITH THY FREE SPIRIT — 061 03
WHICH IS ABOVE IS FREE, WHICH IS THE MOTHER OF US — 131 08
NOT CHILDREN OF THE BONDWOMAN, BUT OF THE FREE — 131 19
AS FREE, AND NOT USING YOUR LIBERTY FOR A CLOKE OF — 173 23
BE JEWS OR GENTILES, WHETHER WE BE BOND OR FREE — 183 06
OF SIN, YE WERE FREE FROM RIGHTEOUSNESS — 198 31
BUT NOW BEING MADE FREE FROM SIN, AND BECOME SERVANTS — 199 02
IT MAY BE FREE FROM ALL ADVERSITIES, AND DEVOUTLY — 220 18
AND SET HIM FREE FROM ALL EVIL — 319 09
ME WITH THY FREE SPIRIT — 403 34
6 AN OFFERING OF A FREE HEART WILL I GIVE THEE, — 406 14
THE PRINCE OF THE PEOPLE LET HIM GO FREE — 471 13
MAN WHATSOEVER IS FREE FROM THE OBEDIENCE OF THE — 604 22

FREE-WILL

108 LET THE FREE-WILL OFFERINGS OF MY MOUTH PLEASE — 497 13

FREED

HE THAT IS DEAD IS FREED FROM SIN — 197 19

FREEDOM

WHOSE SERVICE IS PERFECT FREEDOM — 017 07
USE OUR FREEDOM, HELP US TO EMPLOY IT IN THE — 044 12

FREELY

LET HIM TAKE THE WATER OF LIFE FREELY — 022 31
NOT WITH HIM ALSO FREELY GIVE US ALL THINGS — 331 02
THEY BE JUSTIFIED FREELY — 606 13

FREEWOMAN

THE ONE BY A BONDMAID, THE OTHER BY A FREEWOMAN — 130 31
BUT HE OF THE FREEWOMAN WAS BY PROMISE — 131 02
SHALL NOT BE HEIR WITH THE SON OF THE FREEWOMAN — 131 17

FREQUENT

IN PRISONS MORE FREQUENT, IN DEATHS OFT — 120 31

FRESH

ALL MY FRESH SPRINGS ARE IN THEE — 448 27
I AM ANOINTED WITH FRESH OIL — 456 20

FRET

FRET NOT THYSELF BECAUSE OF THE UNGODLY — 384 25
FRET NOT THYSELF, ELSE SHALT THOU BE MOVED TO DO — 385 09

FRETTING

IT WERE A MOTH FRETTING A GARMENT — 325 04
IT WERE A MOTH FRETTING A GARMENT — 389 33

FRIDAY

AND GOOD FRIDAY THE VENITE MAY BE OMITTED — R 008 12
COLLECT APPOINTED FOR THE DAY, UNTIL GOOD FRIDAY — R 134 14

FRIEND

AND SAID, FRIEND, I DO THEE NO WRONG — 120 07
THOU ART NOT CAESAR'S FRIEND — 159 21
SAY UNTO THEE, FRIEND, GO UP HIGHER — 214 17
SAITH UNTO HIM, FRIEND, HOW CAMEST THOU IN HITHER NOT — 218 24

FRIEND   CONTINUED

YOU SHALL HAVE A FRIEND, AND SHALL GO UNTO HIM AT — 262 27
FOR A FRIEND OF MINE IN HIS JOURNEY IS COME TO ME, — 262 28
AND SAY UNTO HIM, FRIEND, LEND ME THREE LOAVES — 262 28
BECAUSE HE IS HIS FRIEND, YET BECAUSE OF HIS — 263 02
IT HAD BEEN MY FRIEND OR MY BROTHER — 382 20
MINE OWN FAMILIAR FRIEND WHOM I TRUSTED, * — 392 17
MY GUIDE, AND MINE OWN FAMILIAR FRIEND — 407 17

FRIEND'S

HER FATHER'S OR FRIEND'S HANDS, SHALL CAUSE THE MAN — R 301 25

FRIENDLESS

THE FRIENDLESS, AND THE NEEDY — 044 05
FOR THOU ART THE HELPER OF THE FRIENDLESS — 354 08

FRIENDLY

HIM THAT DEALT FRIENDLY WITH ME — 349 29
WHICH SPEAK FRIENDLY TO THEIR NEIGHBOURS, BUT IMAGINE — 373 11
RATHER SMITE ME FRIENDLY, AND REPROVE ME — 517 19

FRIENDS

HEROD WERE MADE FRIENDS TOGETHER — 153 19
TOGETHER HIS FRIENDS AND NEIGHBOURS, SAYING UNTO — 193 23
SHE CALLETH HER FRIENDS AND HER NEIGHBOURS TOGETHER, — 193 30
THAT I MIGHT MAKE MERRY WITH MY FRIENDS — 203 02
THAT A MAN LAY DOWN HIS LIFE FOR HIS FRIENDS — 241 27
YE ARE MY FRIENDS, IF YE DO WHATSOEVER I COMMAND YOU — 241 28
BUT I HAVE CALLED YOU FRIENDS — 241 30
WITH THEIR FRIENDS AND NEIGHBOURS — R 300 05
AND WALKED IN THE HOUSE OF GOD AS FRIENDS — 407 19
18 MY LOVERS AND FRIENDS HAST THOU PUT AWAY FROM ME, — 449 33
OUR RELATIONS, FRIENDS, AND NEIGHBOURS — 590 31
FOR OUR HEALTH, FRIENDS, FOOD, AND RAIMENT, AND ALL — 591 10

FRO

TOSSED TO AND FRO, AND CARRIED ABOUT WITH EVERY WIND — 237 26
6 THEY GO TO AND FRO IN THE EVENING, * — 411 16
27 THEY REEL TO AND FRO, AND STAGGER LIKE A DRUNKEN — 477 31

FROGS

AND FROGS TO DESTROY THEM — 437 32
30 THEIR LAND BROUGHT FORTH FROGS — 471 32

FROST

O YE FROST AND COLD, BLESS YE THE LORD — 012 24
AND THEIR MULBERRY-TREES WITH THE FROST — 438 03
WHO IS ABLE TO ABIDE HIS FROST — 523 30

FROSTS

O YE DEWS AND FROSTS, BLESS YE THE LORD — 012 22

FROWARD

AND WITH THE FROWARD THOU SHALT BE FROWARD — 361 21
AND WITH THE FROWARD THOU SHALT BE FROWARD — 361 21
THE UNGODLY ARE FROWARD, EVEN FROM THEIR MOTHER'S — 410 12
TOGETHER OF THE FROWARD, * — 415 21
5 A FROWARD HEART SHALL DEPART FROM ME — 463 24

FROWARDLY

OURSELVES FROWARDLY IN THY COVENANT — 395 29

FROWARDNESS

STILL IN HIS FROWARDNESS AND MALICE — R 085 15

FRUIT

PEACE WHICH IS THE FRUIT OF RIGHTEOUSNESS, THAT THEY — 044 30
FORTH IN US THE FRUIT OF GOOD LIVING, TO THE HONOUR — 049 20
IT MAY BRING FORTH FRUIT FOR THE USE OF MAN — 051 17
AND BROUGHT FORTH FRUIT, THEN APPEARED THE TARES — 116 22
UP, AND BARE FRUIT AN HUNDREDFOLD — 121 26
AND BRING NO FRUIT TO PERFECTION — 122 07
AND BRING FORTH FRUIT WITH PATIENCE — 122 10
FOR THE FRUIT OF THE SPIRIT IS IN ALL GOODNESS AND — 129 14
NO MORE OF THE FRUIT OF THE VINE, UNTIL THAT DAY THAT — 141 15
NOT DRINK OF THE FRUIT OF THE VINE, UNTIL THE KINGDOM — 149 07
WHAT FRUIT HAD YE THEN IN THOSE THINGS WHEREOF YE ARE — 198 31
YE HAVE YOUR FRUIT UNTO HOLINESS, AND THE END — 199 03
EVEN SO EVERY GOOD TREE BRINGETH FORTH GOOD FRUIT — 200 19
BUT A CORRUPT TREE BRINGETH FORTH EVIL FRUIT — 200 20
BRING FORTH EVIL FRUIT, NEITHER CAN A CORRUPT TREE — 200 20
NEITHER CAN A CORRUPT TREE BRING FORTH GOOD FRUIT — 200 21
NOT FORTH GOOD FRUIT IS HEWN DOWN, AND CAST INTO THE — 200 22
BUT THE FRUIT OF THE SPIRIT IS LOVE, JOY, PEACE, — 209 26
AND BRINGETH FORTH FRUIT, AS IT DOTH ALSO IN YOU, — 223 28
BRINGING FORTH THE FRUIT OF GOOD WORKS, MAY BY THEE — 225 06
THAT BEARETH NOT FRUIT HE TAKETH AWAY — 238 06
THAT BEARETH FRUIT, HE PURGETH IT, THAT IT MAY BRING — 238 07
HE PURGETH IT, THAT IT MAY BRING FORTH MORE FRUIT — 238 08
BRANCH CANNOT BEAR FRUIT OF ITSELF, EXCEPT IT ABIDE — 238 10
THE SAME BRINGETH FORTH MUCH FRUIT — 238 14
IS MY FATHER GLORIFIED, THAT YE BEAR MUCH FRUIT — 238 20
GO AND BRING FORTH FRUIT, AND THAT YOUR FRUIT SHOULD — 241 33

FRUIT   CONTINUED

AND THAT YOUR FRUIT SHOULD REMAIN   242 02
SHALL YIELD HER FRUIT, AND THE EARTH SHALL YIELD HER   262 10
BRING FORTH HIS FRUIT IN DUE SEASON   345 13
10 THEIR FRUIT SHALT THOU ROOT OUT OF THE EARTH,   365 25
LIKE THE UNTIMELY FRUIT OF A WOMAN   410 24
THE FRUIT THEREOF SHALL SHAKE LIKE LEBANON   427 30
47 HE GAVE THEIR FRUIT UNTO THE CATERPILLAR, *   437 33
BRING FORTH MORE FRUIT IN THEIR AGE, *   456 28
IS FILLED WITH THE FRUIT OF THY WORKS   468 20
AND DEVOURED THE FRUIT OF THEIR GROUND   472 08
AND THE FRUIT OF THE WOMB, *   505 29
12 OF THE FRUIT OF THY BODY *   508 27
EVIDENTLY KNOWN AS A TREE DISCERNED BY THE FRUIT   605 15

FRUITFUL

IT SHOULD BE FRUITFUL AND BRING FORTH WHATSOEVER IS   039 25
BEING FRUITFUL IN EVERY GOOD WORK, AND   224 05
TO GIVE US A FRUITFUL SEASON   261 31
34 A FRUITFUL LAND MAKETH HE BARREN, *   478 14
SHALL BE AS THE FRUITFUL VINE *   506 10
FRUITFUL TREES AND ALL CEDARS   524 22

FRUITION

LIFE HAVE THE FRUITION OF THY GLORIOUS GODHEAD   108 02

FRUITS

MAY GATHER IN THE FRUITS OF THE EARTH, AND EVER   039 29
MAY RECEIVE THE FRUITS OF THE EARTH TO OUR COMFORT,   040 20
INCREASE THE FRUITS OF THE EARTH BY THY HEAVENLY   041 02
FOR THE FRUITS OF THE EARTH   048 12
IN OF THE FRUITS THEREOF, AND FOR ALL THE OTHER   050 23
MAY YIELD US HER FRUITS OF INCREASE, TO THY GLORY AND   052 04
BRING FORTH THE FRUITS OF THE SPIRIT   056 16
USE THE KINDLY FRUITS OF THE EARTH, SO THAT IN DUE   057 11
YE SHALL KNOW THEM BY THEIR FRUITS   200 17
BY THEIR FRUITS YE SHALL KNOW THEM   200 23
FILLED WITH THE FRUITS OF RIGHTEOUSNESS, WHICH ARE BY   221 05
RETURNS OF THE FRUITS OF THE EARTH   265 12
TO YIELD THEM FRUITS OF INCREASE   478 21
WHICH ARE THE FRUITS OF FAITH, AND FOLLOW AFTER   605 11

FULFIL

FULFIL NOW, O LORD, THE DESIRES AND PETITIONS OF THY   020 07
YE THAT FULFIL HIS COMMANDMENT, AND HEARKEN UNTO THE   029 13
FULFIL NOW, O LORD, THE DESIRES AND PETITIONS OF THY   034 07
FOR THE FLESH, TO FULFIL THE LUSTS THEREOF   091 09
FAITHFULLY TO FULFIL THE SAME   109 13
AND YE SHALL NOT FULFIL THE LUST OF THE FLESH   209 14
OBEDIENTLY TO FULFIL THY HOLY COMMANDMENTS   226 23
YE THAT FULFIL HIS COMMANDMENT, AND HEARKEN UNTO THE   312 29
AND FULFIL ALL THY MIND   364 22
THAT I SHOULD FULFIL THY WILL, O MY GOD   390 32
YE THAT FULFIL HIS COMMANDMENT, AND HEARKEN UNTO THE   467 16
MY HEART TO FULFIL THY STATUTES ALWAY, *   497 21
19 HE WILL FULFIL THE DESIRE OF THEM THAT FEAR HIM   521 30
AND STRENGTH TO FULFIL THE SAME   566 06

FULFILLED

ANOTHER HATH FULFILLED THE LAW   090 24
IT MIGHT BE FULFILLED WHICH WAS SPOKEN BY THE   091 18
SHALL NOT PASS AWAY, TILL ALL BE FULFILLED   093 20
IT MIGHT BE FULFILLED WHICH WAS SPOKEN OF THE LORD BY   103 22
THEN WAS FULFILLED THAT WHICH WAS SPOKEN BY JEREMY   103 29
IT MIGHT BE FULFILLED WHICH WAS SPOKEN OF THE LORD BY   105 08
IT MIGHT BE FULFILLED WHICH WAS SPOKEN BY THE   107 22
WHEN THEY HAD FULFILLED THE DAYS, AS THEY RETURNED,   110 21
THEN WAS FULFILLED THAT WHICH WAS SPOKEN BY JEREMY   135 14
IT MIGHT BE FULFILLED WHICH WAS SPOKEN BY THE   136 31
BUT THE SCRIPTURES MUST BE FULFILLED   142 27
SCRIPTURE WAS FULFILLED, WHICH SAITH, AND HE WAS   146 16
UNTIL IT BE FULFILLED IN THE KINGDOM OF GOD   149 04
MIGHT BE FULFILLED, WHICH SAITH, THEY PARTED MY   160 14
MIGHT BE FULFILLED, SAITH, I THIRST   160 25
SHOULD BE FULFILLED, A BONE OF HIM SHALL NOT BE   161 08
THEY HAVE FULFILLED THEM IN CONDEMNING HIM   168 29
WHEN THEY HAD FULFILLED ALL THAT WAS WRITTEN OF HIM,   168 32
GOD HATH FULFILLED THE SAME UNTO US THEIR CHILDREN,   169 07
THINGS MUST BE FULFILLED, WHICH WERE WRITTEN IN THE   170 08
HAVE BEEN FULFILLED, WHICH THE HOLY GHOST BY THE   234 09
WORD MIGHT BE FULFILLED THAT IS WRITTEN IN THEIR LAW,   255 28
THIS SCRIPTURE FULFILLED IN YOUR EARS   261 25

FULFILLING

LOVE IS THE FULFILLING OF THE LAW   090 30
AND STORM, FULFILLING HIS WORD   524 21
FAITHFULLY FULFILLING HIS COURSE, AT THE LATTER DAY   559 12

FULFILMENT

TO HASTEN THE FULFILMENT OF THY PURPOSE, THAT THY   561 16

FULL

AND EARTH ARE FULL OF THE MAJESTY OF THY GLORY   010 15
THE WHOLE EARTH IS FULL OF HIS GLORY   022 34
THOU, O LORD, AND FULL OF COMPASSION TO THE CHILDREN   053 03
STATES WERE LEFT AT FULL AND EQUAL LIBERTY TO MODEL   VI 10
ART A MERCIFUL GOD, FULL OF COMPASSION,   062 31

FULL   CONTINUED

AND EARTH ARE FULL OF THY GLORY   077 09
AND EARTH ARE FULL OF THY GLORY   079 33
ONCE OFFERED) A FULL, PERFECT, AND SUFFICIENT   080 10
HIMSELF TO BE IN FULL PURPOSE SO TO DO, AS SOON AS HE R 085 07
ALMIGHTY GOD, WITH FULL PURPOSE OF AMENDMENT OF LIFE   087 21
BUT WITH A FULL TRUST IN GOD'S MERCY, AND WITH A   088 02
OF THE FATHER,) FULL OF GRACE AND TRUTH   098 06
BEING FULL OF THE HOLY GHOST, LOOKED UP   100 05
THAT YOUR JOY MAY BE FULL   101 22
PRESENT TIME, IN FULL ASSURANCE OF THE GLORY THAT   144 09
AND FILLED A SPUNGE FULL OF VINEGAR, AND PUT IT ON A   146 32
A TRUE HEART IN FULL ASSURANCE OF FAITH, HAVING OUR   158 20
WAS SET A VESSEL FULL OF VINEGAR   160 26
THAT YOUR JOY MAY BE FULL   176 23
LIVING CREATURES FULL OF EYES BEFORE AND BEHIND   187 17
AND THEY WERE FULL OF EYES WITHIN   187 21
LAID AT HIS GATE, FULL OF SORES, AND DESIRING TO BE   190 06
AND THAT YOUR JOY MIGHT BE FULL   238 25
WAS A GOOD MAN, AND FULL OF THE HOLY GHOST AND OF   241 08
ELISABETH'S FULL TIME CAME THAT SHE SHOULD BE   243 13
AN EVANGELIST, MAKE FULL PROOF OF THY MINISTRY   253 24
AS HE PUTTETH HIS FULL TRUST ONLY IN THY MERCY,   314 09
TO LIVE, AND IS FULL OF MISERY   332 19
MY HEAD WITH OIL, AND MY CUP SHALL BE FULL   338 28
7 HIS MOUTH IS FULL OF CURSING, DECEIT, AND FRAUD   353 18
MY HEAD WITH OIL, AND MY CUP SHALL BE FULL   368 21
THEIR RIGHT HAND IS FULL OF GIFTS   371 17
THE EARTH IS FULL OF THE GOODNESS OF THE LORD   378 28
ARE UNRIGHTEOUS AND FULL OF DECEIT   383 30
6 WHY ART THOU SO FULL OF HEAVINESS, O MY SOUL   393 11
FULL OF GRACE ARE THY LIPS, BECAUSE GOD HATH BLESSED   396 18
THY RIGHT HAND IS FULL OF RIGHTEOUSNESS   399 30
THE RIVER OF GOD IS FULL OF WATER   417 02
THE FOLDS SHALL BE FULL OF SHEEP   417 11
I AM FULL OF HEAVINESS   423 13
ALL THE EARTH IS FULL OF DARKNESS AND CRUEL   431 18
IT IS FULL MIXT, AND HE POURETH OUT OF THE SAME   432 15
O LORD GOD, ART FULL OF COMPASSION AND MERCY, *   448 04
2 FOR MY SOUL IS FULL OF TROUBLE, *   448 32
8 THE LORD IS FULL OF COMPASSION AND MERCY, *   466 21
THE LORD ALSO ARE FULL OF SAP   468 26
THE EARTH IS FULL OF THY RICHES   469 09
O LORD, IS FULL OF THY MERCY   494 08
HATH HIS QUIVER FULL OF THEM   506 02
11 A MAN FULL OF WORDS SHALL NOT PROSPER UPON THE   516 32
OUR GARNERS MAY BE FULL AND PLENTEOUS WITH ALL MANNER   520 18
OF HONEST REPORT, FULL OF THE HOLY GHOST AND WISDOM,   532 12
A MAN FULL OF FAITH AND OF THE HOLY GHOST,   532 16
POSSESSED OF FULL POWER TO PERFORM EVERY ACT OF   569 18
FULL OF COMPASSION   588 31
AND VERY FULL OF COMFORT, AS MORE LARGELY   605 09
IN CHRIST, IS FULL OF SWEET, PLEASANT, AND   606 17

FULLERS'

AND LIKE FULLERS' SOPE   232 09

FULLY

OF PENTECOST WAS FULLY COME, THEY WERE ALL WITH ONE   180 17
WE DO FULLY CONFIDE, OUR LICENCE AND   569 15

FULNESS

BUT WHEN THE FULNESS OF THE TIME WAS COME, GOD SENT   104 19
WITH ALL THE FULNESS OF GOD   212 21
STATURE OF THE FULNESS OF CHRIST   237 24
MAY RECEIVE THE FULNESS OF THY GRACE, AND EVER REMAIN   279 18
WITH ALL THE FULNESS OF GOD   281 11
PRESENCE IS THE FULNESS OF JOY, AND AT THY RIGHT HAND   333 10
THY PRESENCE IN FULNESS OF JOY   341 03
PRESENCE IS THE FULNESS OF JOY, *   358 13
STATURE OF THE FULNESS OF CHRIST   538 11

FUNCTION

TO ANY HOLY FUNCTION, GIVE THY GRACE AND HEAVENLY   038 32
CALLED TO THEIR FUNCTION AND MINISTRY, AND THAT THEY   536 25
OF SACERDOTAL FUNCTION AMONG THE PEOPLE OF THE SAME   569 19

FUNCTIONS

OF THE SAID FUNCTIONS, EXCEPT HE BE CALLED, TRIED,   529 21

FURIOUSLY

THE HEATHEN SO FURIOUSLY RAGE TOGETHER   345 25

FURIOUSNESS

UPON THE FURIOUSNESS OF MINE ENEMIES, AND THY RIGHT   312 06
THEM THE FURIOUSNESS OF HIS WRATH, ANGER,   438 06
UPON THE FURIOUSNESS OF MINE ENEMIES, AND THY RIGHT   514 12

FURLONGS

WAS FROM JERUSALEM ABOUT THREESCORE FURLONGS   167 05

FURNISHED

UPPER ROOM FURNISHED AND PREPARED   140 31
HE SHALL SHEW YOU A LARGE UPPER ROOM FURNISHED   148 31
WEDDING WAS FURNISHED WITH GUESTS   218 21

FURROWS

11 THOU WATEREST HER FURROWS   417 04
AND MADE LONG FURROWS   506 26

FURTHER

AS SHE FURTHER DECLARES IN HER SAID PREFACE,   V 34
AND FURTHER US WITH THY CONTINUAL HELP   049 24
BE SUPPOSED THAT FURTHER ALTERATIONS WOULD IN TIME BE VI 03
TO TAKE A FURTHER REVIEW OF THE PUBLIC SERVICE,   VI 25
OR FURTHER THAN LOCAL CIRCUMSTANCES REQUIRE   VI 33
BUT REQUIRETH FURTHER COMFORT OR COUNSEL, LET HIM 088 05
WHAT NEED WE ANY FURTHER WITNESSES   143 17
WHAT NEED WE ANY FURTHER WITNESS   152 02
AND HE MADE AS THOUGH HE WOULD HAVE GONE FURTHER   168 02
HE PROCEEDED FURTHER TO TAKE PETER ALSO   245 02
HE PROCEEDED FURTHER TO TAKE PETER ALSO   247 04
AND NOTE FURTHER, THAT THE PART OF THE COMMANDMENT R 286 03
AND NOTE FURTHER, THAT IN THE DISCRETION OF THE   R 531 09
AND NOTE FURTHER, THAT IN THE DISCRETION OF THE   R 537 15
WE PROCEED NO FURTHER, BECAUSE WE WOULD NOT THAT AN 570 18
AND FURTHER US WITH THY CONTINUAL HELP   571 09

FURTHERANCE

AND THE FURTHERANCE OF OUR HAPPINESS BOTH TEMPORAL 565 13

FURTHERMORE

AND FURTHERMORE, IT IS HIS OFFICE, WHERE PROVISION IS 533 18
FURTHERMORE, WE MUST RECEIVE GOD'S PROMISES IN SUCH 606 27

FURY

AND TRAMPLE THEM IN MY FURY   138 19
AND MY FURY, IT UPHELD ME   138 25
THEM DRUNK IN MY FURY, AND I WILL BRING DOWN THEIR 138 26

FUTURE

FOR THEIR FUTURE PROSPERITY   VI 13

GABBATHA

BUT IN THE HEBREW, GABBATHA   159 24

GABRIEL

MONTH THE ANGEL GABRIEL WAS SENT FROM GOD UNTO A CITY 236 05

GAINSAYERS

AND TO WITHSTAND AND CONVINCE THE GAINSAYERS   554 33

GAINSAYING

AND GAINSAYING PEOPLE   227 22

GALATIA

CRESCENS TO GALATIA, TITUS UNTO DALMATIA   253 33

GALILAEAN

FOR THOU ART A GALILAEAN, AND THY SPEECH AGREETH   143 32
FOR HE IS A GALILAEAN   151 17
HE ASKED WHETHER THE MAN WERE A GALILAEAN   153 07

GALILAEANS

ARE NOT ALL THESE WHICH SPEAK GALILAEANS   180 30

GALILEE

THIS IS JESUS THE PROPHET OF NAZARETH OF GALILEE   091 32
WENT UP FROM GALILEE, OUT OF THE CITY OF NAZARETH, 099 02
HE TURNED ASIDE INTO THE PARTS OF GALILEE   107 21
FROM NAZARETH OF GALILEE, AND WAS BAPTIZED OF JOHN IN 112 19
THIRD DAY THERE WAS A MARRIAGE IN CANA OF GALILEE 113 12
JESUS IN CANA OF GALILEE, AND MANIFESTED FORTH HIS 113 31
OVER THE SEA OF GALILEE, WHICH IS THE SEA OF   131 21
I AM RISEN, I WILL GO BEFORE YOU INTO GALILEE   141 21
BEGINNING FROM GALILEE TO THIS PLACE   153 06
PILATE HEARD OF GALILEE, HE ASKED WHETHER THE MAN 153 07
HIM FROM GALILEE, STOOD AFAR OFF, BEHOLDING THESE 155 20
AND PETER THAT HE GOETH BEFORE YOU INTO GALILEE   165 32
AND BEGAN FROM GALILEE, AFTER THE BAPTISM WHICH JOHN 166 18
UP WITH HIM FROM GALILEE TO JERUSALEM, WHO ARE HIS 169 04
YE MEN OF GALILEE, WHY STAND YE GAZING UP INTO   178 16
AND BEGAN FROM GALILEE, AFTER THE BAPTISM WHICH JOHN 184 05
UNTO THE SEA OF GALILEE, THROUGH THE MIDST OF   206 28
PASSED THROUGH THE MIDST OF SAMARIA AND GALILEE   209 32
OF JUDAEA INTO GALILEE, HE WENT UNTO HIM, AND   219 30
WHEN HE WAS COME OUT OF JUDAEA INTO GALILEE   220 13
BY THE SEA OF GALILEE, SAW TWO BRETHREN, SIMON CALLED 227 24
RETURNED INTO GALILEE, TO THEIR OWN CITY NAZARETH 233 25
INTO A CITY OF GALILEE, NAMED NAZARETH, TO A VIRGIN 236 06
IN CANA OF GALILEE, AND IS COMMENDED OF SAINT PAUL TO 300 15

GALL

THEY GAVE HIM VINEGAR TO DRINK MINGLED WITH GALL   136 29
22 THEY GAVE ME GALL TO EAT   423 16

GAP

BEFORE HIM IN THE GAP, *   474 15

GAPE

13 THEY GAPE UPON ME WITH THEIR MOUTHS, *   366 29

GAPED

21 THEY GAPED UPON ME WITH THEIR MOUTHS, AND SAID, 383 05

GARMENT

AND THEY ALL SHALL WAX OLD AS DOTH A GARMENT   097 16
THE GARMENT OF PRAISE FOR THE SPIRIT OF   107 08
THEY ALL SHALL WAX OLD AS A GARMENT   144 22
LET HIM SELL HIS GARMENT, AND BUY ONE   150 08
CLOTHED IN A LONG WHITE GARMENT   165 27
BEHIND HIM, AND TOUCHED THE HEM OF HIS GARMENT   224 19
BUT TOUCH HIS GARMENT, I SHALL BE WHOLE   224 20
CAST THY GARMENT ABOUT THEE, AND FOLLOW ME   245 18
LIKE AS IT WERE A MOTH FRETTING A GARMENT   325 04
LIKE AS IT WERE A MOTH FRETTING A GARMENT   389 33
AND CRUELTY COVERETH THEM AS A GARMENT   428 21
THEY ALL SHALL WAX OLD AS DOTH A GARMENT   465 35
IT WERE WITH A GARMENT, *   467 27
COVEREDST IT WITH THE DEEP LIKE AS WITH A GARMENT 468 04

GARMENTS

THY BEAUTIFUL GARMENTS, O JERUSALEM   004 19
AND NOT YOUR GARMENTS, AND TURN UNTO THE LORD YOUR 004 20
SPREAD THEIR GARMENTS IN THE WAY   091 25
AND NOT YOUR GARMENTS, AND TURN UNTO THE LORD YOUR 124 23
AND PARTED HIS GARMENTS, CASTING LOTS   136 31
THEY PARTED MY GARMENTS AMONG THEM, AND UPON MY   136 33
WITH DYED GARMENTS FROM BOZRAH   138 12
AND THY GARMENTS LIKE HIM THAT TREADETH IN THE   138 15
UPON MY GARMENTS, AND I WILL STAIN ALL MY RAIMENT 138 20
THEY PARTED HIS GARMENTS, CASTING LOTS UPON THEM, 146 11
AND LAID ASIDE HIS GARMENTS   155 31
HAD TAKEN HIS GARMENTS, AND WAS SET DOWN AGAIN,   156 13
TOOK HIS GARMENTS, AND MADE FOUR PARTS,   160 10
18 THEY PART MY GARMENTS AMONG THEM, *   367 08
8 ALL THY GARMENTS SMELL OF MYRRH, ALOES, AND CASSIA 396 32

GARNERS

13 THAT OUR GARNERS MAY BE FULL AND PLENTEOUS WITH 520 18

GARNISHED

HE FINDETH IT SWEPT AND GARNISHED   130 13

GASPETH

MY SOUL GASPETH UNTO THEE AS A THIRSTY LAND   519 02

GAT

AND GAT ME TO MY LORD RIGHT HUMBLY   375 08
3 FOR THEY GAT NOT THE LAND IN POSSESSION THROUGH 394 27
THE PAINS OF HELL GAT HOLD UPON ME   486 24

GATE

THE GRAVE, AND GATE OF DEATH, WE MAY PASS TO OUR   161 16
OPENED UNTO US THE GATE OF EVERLASTING LIFE   163 24
WAS LAID AT HIS GATE, FULL OF SORES, AND DESIRING TO 190 06
HE CAME NIGH TO THE GATE OF THE CITY, BEHOLD, THERE 212 30
CAME UNTO THE IRON GATE THAT LEADETH UNTO THE CITY 245 22
OPEN THE GATE UNTO US WHO KNOCK   274 18
THAT SIT IN THE GATE SPEAK AGAINST ME, *   422 26
20 THIS IS THE GATE OF THE LORD, *   489 08
WHEN THEY SPEAK WITH THEIR ENEMIES IN THE GATE   506 04

GATES

YOUR WAY INTO HIS GATES WITH THANKSGIVING, AND INTO 015 10
AND THE STRANGER THAT IS WITHIN THY GATES   068 29
AND THE GATES OF HELL SHALL NOT PREVAIL AGAINST IT 246 08
THE BARS OF THY GATES, *   265 02
AND THE STRANGER THAT IS WITHIN THY GATES   286 29
ME UP FROM THE GATES OF DEATH   352 18
PRAISES WITHIN THE GATES OF THE DAUGHTER OF SION   352 19
7 LIFT UP YOUR HEADS, O YE GATES   369 09
9 LIFT UP YOUR HEADS, O YE GATES   369 13
THY WORKS IN THE GATES OF THE DAUGHTER OF SION   429 34
LORD LOVETH THE GATES OF SION MORE THAN ALL THE   448 14
YOUR WAY INTO HIS GATES WITH THANKSGIVING, AND INTO 463 11
HE HATH BROKEN THE GATES OF BRASS, *   477 07
19 OPEN ME THE GATES OF RIGHTEOUSNESS, *   489 06
SHALL STAND IN THY GATES, *   503 11
THE BARS OF THY GATES, *   523 21
7 LIFT UP YOUR HEADS, O YE GATES   563 24
9 LIFT UP YOUR HEADS, O YE GATES   563 28
AND THE STRANGER THAT IS WITHIN THY GATES   579 09
OPENED TO HIM THE GATES OF LARGER LIFE, THOU WILT 598 08

GATHER

THAT WE MAY GATHER IN THE FRUITS OF THE EARTH,   039 29
SO MUCH AS TO GATHER UP THE CRUMBS UNDER THY TABLE 082 16
THAT WE GO AND GATHER THEM UP   116 26

GATHER CONTINUED

	PAGE	LN
LEST WHILE YE GATHER UP THE TARES, YE ROOT UP ALSO	116	27
TO THE REAPERS, GATHER YE TOGETHER FIRST THE TARES,	116	30
BUT GATHER THE WHEAT INTO MY BARN	116	31
AND THEY SHALL GATHER TOGETHER HIS ELECT FROM THE	118	22
GATHER THE PEOPLE, SANCTIFY THE CONGREGATION,	124	30
THE ELDERS, GATHER THE CHILDREN, AND THOSE THAT SUCK	124	31
HIS DISCIPLES, GATHER UP THE FRAGMENTS THAT REMAIN,	132	07
DO MEN GATHER GRAPES OF THORNS, OR FIGS OF THISTLES	200	17
DO THEY REAP, NOR GATHER INTO BARNS	211	17
HIS DISCIPLES, GATHER UP THE FRAGMENTS THAT REMAIN,	226	06
AND MEN GATHER THEM, AND CAST THEM INTO THE FIRE,	238	16
HE SHALL GATHER THE LAMBS WITH HIS ARM, AND CARRY	243	09
AND GATHER TOGETHER THE OUTCASTS OF ISRAEL	264	21
DO THEY REAP, NOR GATHER INTO BARNS	266	15
TELL WHO SHALL GATHER THEM	324	27
HE SHALL GATHER THE LAMBS WITH HIS ARMS, AND CARRY	338	12
TELL WHO SHALL GATHER THEM	389	22
5 GATHER MY SAINTS TOGETHER UNTO ME	401	30
21 THEY GATHER THEM TOGETHER AGAINST THE SOUL OF THE	458	28
IT THEM, THEY GATHER IT	469	16
LORD OUR GOD, AND GATHER US FROM AMONG THE HEATHEN	475	30
AND GATHER TOGETHER THE OUTCASTS OF ISRAEL	522	30

GATHERED

	PAGE	LN
OR THREE ARE GATHERED TOGETHER IN THY NAME THOU WILT	020	06
OR THREE ARE GATHERED TOGETHER IN THY NAME THOU WILT	034	06
BEING GATHERED INTO ONE FOLD, SHALL BECOME	037	06
WOULD I HAVE GATHERED THY CHILDREN TOGETHER, EVEN AS	100	29
AND WHEN HE HAD GATHERED ALL THE CHIEF PRIESTS AND	109	04
THE EAGLES BE GATHERED TOGETHER	118	13
PEOPLE WERE GATHERED TOGETHER, AND WERE COME TO HIM	121	18
THEREFORE THEY GATHERED THEM TOGETHER, AND FILLED	132	08
WHEN THEY WERE GATHERED TOGETHER, PILATE SAID UNTO	135	29
AND GATHERED UNTO HIM THE WHOLE BAND OF	136	16
THE ELEVEN GATHERED TOGETHER, AND THEM THAT WERE WITH	168	12
BEING GATHERED TOGETHER IN UNITY BY THY HOLY	185	15
THE YOUNGER SON GATHERED ALL TOGETHER, AND TOOK HIS	202	02
THEY WERE GATHERED TOGETHER	215	07
PHARISEES WERE GATHERED TOGETHER, JESUS ASKED THEM,	215	16
AND GATHERED TOGETHER ALL AS MANY AS THEY	218	20
THEREFORE THEY GATHERED THEM TOGETHER, AND FILLED	226	08
HIM SHALL BE GATHERED ALL NATIONS	258	30
WE ARE GATHERED TOGETHER HERE IN THE SIGHT	300	08
WE MAY BE GATHERED UNTO OUR FATHERS, HAVING THE	317	02
AND GATHERED THEMSELVES TOGETHER	382	23
WERE GATHERED, AND GONE BY TOGETHER	399	16
MIGHTY MEN ARE GATHERED AGAINST ME, WITHOUT ANY	411	09
THE PEOPLES ARE GATHERED TOGETHER, *	465	24
3 AND GATHERED THEM OUT OF THE LANDS, FROM THE EAST,	476	10
AND MINISTRY HE GATHERED TOGETHER A GREAT FLOCK IN	545	19
WHO ARE HERE GATHERED TOGETHER WITH ALL HUMILITY AND	565	03

GATHEREST

	PAGE	LN
FOR SO GATHEREST THOU THYSELF A GOOD REWARD IN THE	072	34

GATHERETH

	PAGE	LN
EVEN AS A HEN GATHERETH HER CHICKENS UNDER HER WINGS,	100	30
AND HE THAT GATHERETH NOT WITH ME SCATTERETH	130	09
7 HE GATHERETH THE WATERS OF THE SEA TOGETHER, AS IT	378	31

GATHERING

	PAGE	LN
GROUND AND THE GATHERING IN OF THE FRUITS THEREOF,	050	23
ME FROM THE GATHERING TOGETHER OF THE FROWARD,	415	21

GAVE

	PAGE	LN
THE WORLD, THAT HE GAVE HIS ONLY-BEGOTTEN SON, TO THE	076	14
HE BRAKE IT, AND GAVE IT TO HIS DISCIPLES, SAYING,	080	19
GIVEN THANKS, HE GAVE IT TO THEM, SAYING, DRINK YE	080	24
TO THEM GAVE HE POWER TO BECOME THE SONS OF GOD,	097	34
WHO GAVE HIMSELF FOR US, THAT HE MIGHT REDEEM US FROM	098	23
WHEN THEY SAW IT, GAVE PRAISE UNTO GOD	124	06
COMMANDMENTS WE GAVE YOU BY THE LORD JESUS	127	26
AND GAVE THEM FOR THE POTTER'S FIELD, AS THE LORD	135	17
OF A SKULL, THEY GAVE HIM VINEGAR TO DRINK MINGLED	136	34
IT ON A REED, AND GAVE HIM TO DRINK	137	22
AND BRAKE IT, AND GAVE TO THEM, AND SAID, TAKE,	141	10
GIVEN THANKS, HE GAVE IT TO THEM	141	12
OUR SAVIOUR, GAVE HIS BACK TO THE SMITERS AND	144	06
I GAVE MY BACK TO THE SMITERS, AND MY CHEEKS TO THEM	144	13
AND THEY GAVE HIM TO DRINK WINE MINGLED WITH MYRRH	146	09
IT ON A REED, AND GAVE HIM TO DRINK, SAYING, LET	146	32
A LOUD VOICE, AND GAVE UP THE GHOST	146	35
SO CRIED OUT, AND GAVE UP THE GHOST, HE SAID, TRULY	147	04
TOOK THE CUP, AND GAVE THANKS, AND SAID, TAKE THIS,	149	05
AND BRAKE IT, AND GAVE UNTO THEM, SAYING, THIS IS MY	149	09
HE TOOK BREAD, AND GAVE THANKS, AND BRAKE IT, AND	149	09
AND PILATE GAVE SENTENCE THAT IT SHOULD BE AS THEY	154	05
PAPS WHICH NEVER GAVE SUCK	154	18
SAID THUS, HE GAVE UP THE GHOST	155	14
BUT JESUS GAVE HIM NO ANSWER	159	13
BOWED HIS HEAD, AND GAVE UP THE GHOST	160	29
AND BRAKE, AND GAVE TO THEM	168	07
AND THEY GAVE HIM A PIECE OF A BROILED FISH, AND OF	170	05
THE RECORD THAT GOD GAVE OF HIS SON	171	09
AS THE SPIRIT GAVE THEM UTTERANCE	180	24
AND AS THE FATHER GAVE ME COMMANDMENT, EVEN SO I DO	182	10
THE WORLD, THAT HE GAVE HIS ONLY-BEGOTTEN SON, THAT	184	32
ONE ANOTHER, AS HE GAVE US COMMANDMENT	191	31
AND BRAKE, AND GAVE TO HIS DISCIPLES TO SET BEFORE	199	19

GAVE CONTINUED

	PAGE	LN
SEVEN LOAVES, AND GAVE THANKS, AND BRAKE, AND GAVE TO	199	19
AND NO MAN GAVE UNTO HIM	202	09
BUT GOD GAVE IT TO ABRAHAM BY PROMISE	207	26
OUT TWO PENCE, AND GAVE THEM TO THE HOST, AND SAID	208	33
IN THAT INSTANT GAVE THANKS LIKEWISE UNTO THE LORD,	233	22
AND THEY GAVE FORTH THEIR LOTS	234	31
AND GAVE GIFTS UNTO MEN	237	15
AND HE GAVE SOME, APOSTLES	237	19
AN HUNGRED, AND YE GAVE ME MEAT	259	06
WAS THIRSTY, AND YE GAVE ME DRINK	259	06
OR THIRSTY, AND GAVE THEE DRINK	259	11
THE BOOK, AND HE GAVE IT AGAIN TO THE MINISTER,	261	22
THE CHURCH, AND GAVE HIMSELF FOR IT	267	20
AND GAVE COMMANDMENT TO HIS DISCIPLES, THAT THEY	279	11
WHO GAVE YOU THIS NAME	283	17
MY SPONSORS GAVE ME THIS NAME IN BAPTISM	283	18
THE LORD GAVE, AND THE LORD HATH TAKEN AWAY	324	14
AND THE HIGHEST GAVE HIS THUNDER	360	25
AND GAVE HIM PRAISES WITH MY TONGUE	418	14
11 THE LORD GAVE THE WORD	420	02
22 THEY GAVE ME GALL TO EAT	423	16
I WAS THIRSTY THEY GAVE ME VINEGAR TO DRINK	423	17
WITH JACOB, AND GAVE ISRAEL A LAW, *	435	04
AND GAVE THEM DRINK THEREOF, AS IT HAD BEEN OUT OF	435	31
AND GAVE THEM FOOD FROM HEAVEN	436	19
FOR HE GAVE THEM THEIR OWN DESIRE	436	29
47 HE GAVE THEIR FRUIT UNTO THE CATERPILLAR, *	437	33
BUT GAVE THEIR LIFE OVER TO THE PESTILENCE	438	10
63 HE GAVE HIS PEOPLE OVER ALSO UNTO THE SWORD,	439	02
13 SO I GAVE THEM UP UNTO THEIR OWN HEARTS' LUSTS,	443	04
4 HIS LIGHTNINGS GAVE SHINE UNTO THE WORLD,	461	04
AND THE LAW THAT HE GAVE THEM	462	31
32 HE GAVE THEM HAILSTONES FOR RAIN	472	02
43 AND GAVE THEM THE LANDS OF THE HEATHEN	472	25
15 AND HE GAVE THEM THEIR DESIRE, *	473	31
AND GAVE NO CREDENCE UNTO HIS WORD	474	18
40 AND HE GAVE THEM OVER INTO THE HAND OF THE	475	18
12 AND GAVE THEIR LAND TO BE AN HERITAGE, *	510	26
21 AND GAVE AWAY THEIR LAND FOR AN HERITAGE	512	24
AND GAVE GIFTS UNTO MEN	538	02
AND HE GAVE SOME, APOSTLES	538	06
WHO GAVE YOU THIS NAME	577	08

GAVEST

	PAGE	LN
YET THOU NEVER GAVEST ME A KID, THAT I MIGHT MAKE	202	35
AND THOU GAVEST HIM A LONG LIFE, *	365	11
AND GAVEST HIM TO BE MEAT FOR THE PEOPLE OF THE	431	05
WHO ALONE GAVEST US THE BREATH OF LIFE, AND	594	18

GAZED

	PAGE	LN
OF CHRIST TO BE GAZED UPON, OR TO BE CARRIED ABOUT,	608	02

GAZING

	PAGE	LN
WHY STAND YE GAZING UP INTO HEAVEN	178	17

GEBAL

	PAGE	LN
7 GEBAL, AND AMMON, AND AMALEK	444	18

GENDERETH

	PAGE	LN
WHICH GENDERETH TO BONDAGE, WHICH IS AGAR	131	04

GENERAL

	PAGE	LN
HER GENERAL AIM IN THESE DIFFERENT REVIEWS AND	V	33
PRAYER WITH SUCH GENERAL INTERCESSIONS TAKEN OUT OF	R 017	23
THAT THE GENERAL THANKSGIVING MAY BE SAID BY	R 019	34
THAT THE GENERAL THANKSGIVING MAY BE SAID BY	R 033	32
UNITED STATES IN GENERAL, SO ESPECIALLY FOR THEIR	035	09
SESSION OF ANY GENERAL OR DIOCESAN CONVENTION,	R 037	09
USED AFTER THE GENERAL THANKSGIVING, OR, WHEN THAT IS	R 050	15
THEN SHALL THIS GENERAL CONFESSION BE MADE, BY THE	R 075	15
AND THAT, AT THE GENERAL RESURRECTION IN THE LAST	335	08
THE DAY OF THE GENERAL RESURRECTION, WE, WITH ALL	336	23
OF CANONS OF THE GENERAL AND DIOCESAN CONVENTION,	R 571	24
SET FORTH BY THE GENERAL CONVENTION OF THIS CHURCH IN	610	32

GENERALLY

	PAGE	LN
AS GENERALLY NECESSARY TO SALVATION	292	07
TWO ONLY, AS GENERALLY NECESSARY TO SALVATION	581	09
AS THEY BE GENERALLY SET FORTH TO US IN HOLY	606	28

GENERATION

	PAGE	LN
ENDURETH FROM GENERATION TO GENERATION	015	14
HIS TRUTH ENDURETH FROM GENERATION TO GENERATION	015	14
THEE FROM GENERATION TO GENERATION	043	04
THEE AND SERVE THEE FROM GENERATION TO GENERATION	043	05
THY LOVING-KINDNESS FROM GENERATION TO GENERATION	051	27
FROM GENERATION TO GENERATION	051	27
AND FOURTH GENERATION OF THEM THAT HATE ME	068	14
THIS GENERATION SHALL NOT PASS AWAY, TILL ALL BE	093	19
ALL THESE THINGS SHALL COME UPON THIS GENERATION	100	27
HIS OWN GENERATION BY THE WILL OF GOD, FELL ON SLEEP,	169	15
AND FOURTH GENERATION OF THEM THAT HATE ME	286	14
THEE IN OUR GENERATION, WE MAY BE GATHERED UNTO OUR	317	02
FROM ONE GENERATION TO ANOTHER	325	13
FROM THIS GENERATION FOR EVER	355	24
GOD IS IN THE GENERATION OF THE RIGHTEOUS	356	26

GENERATION   CONTINUED

SHALL BE COUNTED UNTO THE LORD FOR A GENERATION	368 05
6 THIS IS THE GENERATION OF THEM THAT SEEK HIM	369 07
HEART FROM GENERATION TO GENERATION	379 10
OF HIS HEART FROM GENERATION TO GENERATION	379 10
FROM ONE GENERATION TO ANOTHER	397 22
FROM ONE GENERATION TO ANOTHER	400 28
FOLLOW THE GENERATION OF HIS FATHERS, *	401 14
UNTO THIS GENERATION, AND THY POWER TO ALL THEM THAT	426 12
FROM ONE GENERATION TO ANOTHER	427 07
CONDEMNED THE GENERATION OF THY CHILDREN	429 07
A FAITHLESS AND STUBBORN GENERATION	435 14
A GENERATION THAT SET NOT THEIR HEART ARIGHT, AND	435 14
PRAISE FROM GENERATION TO GENERATION	440 34
FORTH THY PRAISE FROM GENERATION TO GENERATION	440 34
FROM ONE GENERATION TO ANOTHER	446 17
FROM ONE GENERATION TO ANOTHER	450 06
FROM ONE GENERATION TO ANOTHER	450 12
FROM ONE GENERATION TO ANOTHER	453 18
WITH THIS GENERATION, AND SAID, *	459 24
HIS TRUTH ENDURETH FROM GENERATION TO GENERATION	463 15
ENDURETH FROM GENERATION TO GENERATION	463 15
IN THE NEXT GENERATION LET HIS NAME BE CLEAN PUT OUT	480 25
THE GENERATION OF THE FAITHFUL SHALL BE BLESSED	483 20
FROM ONE GENERATION TO ANOTHER	496 04
FROM ONE GENERATION TO ANOTHER	510 29
4 ONE GENERATION SHALL PRAISE THY WORKS UNTO ANOTHER,	520 33
6 THIS IS THE GENERATION OF THEM THAT SEEK HIM	563 22
AND FOURTH GENERATION OF THEM THAT HATE ME	578 32

GENERATIONS

ALL GENERATIONS SHALL CALL ME BLESSED	026 14
THROUGHOUT ALL GENERATIONS	026 19
MAY BE ESTABLISHED AMONG US FOR ALL GENERATIONS	035 18
LIGHTS OF THE WORLD IN THEIR SEVERAL GENERATIONS	048 18
LIGHTS OF THE WORLD IN THEIR SEVERAL GENERATIONS	336 20
HIS YEARS MAY ENDURE THROUGHOUT ALL GENERATIONS	413 18
OF THE GENERATIONS TO COME	435 02
AND THY REMEMBRANCE THROUGHOUT ALL GENERATIONS	465 03
THEY ENDURE THROUGHOUT ALL GENERATIONS	465 30
THAT HE MADE TO A THOUSAND GENERATIONS	470 19
AND THROUGHOUT ALL GENERATIONS	522 24
IN TRUTH AND PURITY THROUGH ALL GENERATIONS	568 11

GENNESARET

THE LAKE OF GENNESARET, AND SAW TWO SHIPS STANDING BY	196 07

GENTILES

SAME MY NAME SHALL BE GREAT AMONG THE GENTILES	004 14
THE GENTILES SHALL COME TO THY LIGHT,	022 02
TO LIGHTEN THE GENTILES, *	028 13
AND THAT THE GENTILES MIGHT GLORIFY GOD FOR HIS	092 25
THEE AMONG THE GENTILES, AND SING UNTO THY NAME	092 27
YE GENTILES, WITH HIS PEOPLE	092 28
PRAISE THE LORD, ALL YE GENTILES	092 29
AND HE THAT SHALL RISE TO REIGN OVER THE GENTILES	092 31
HIM SHALL THE GENTILES TRUST	092 32
MANIFEST THY ONLY-BEGOTTEN SON TO THE GENTILES	107 30
CHRIST FOR YOU GENTILES, IF YE HAVE HEARD OF THE	108 07
THAT THE GENTILES SHOULD BE FELLOW-HEIRS, AND OF THE	108 14
AMONG THE GENTILES THE UNSEARCHABLE RICHES OF CHRIST	108 20
UNTO THE GENTILES, AND SHALL BE MOCKED, AND	123 21
EVEN AS THE GENTILES WHICH KNOW NOT GOD	127 31
KINGS OF THE GENTILES EXERCISE LORDSHIP OVER THEM	149 20
YOUR CONVERSATION HONEST AMONG THE GENTILES	173 14
WE BE JEWS OR GENTILES, WHETHER WE BE BOND OR FREE	183 05
THAT ON THE GENTILES ALSO WAS POURED OUT THE GIFT OF	184 23
THAT YE WERE GENTILES, CARRIED AWAY UNTO THESE DUMB	203 17
THINGS DO THE GENTILES SEEK	211 29
NOT AS OTHER GENTILES WALK, IN THE VANITY OF THEIR	216 04
NAME BEFORE THE GENTILES, AND KINGS, AND THE CHILDREN	230 27
TO LIGHTEN THE GENTILES, AND THE GLORY OF THY PEOPLE	233 08
PRINCES OF THE GENTILES EXERCISE DOMINION OVER THEM,	247 21
KINGS OF THE GENTILES EXERCISE LORDSHIP OVER THEM	250 05
OF EVERLASTING LIFE, LO, WE TURN TO THE GENTILES	261 03
A LIGHT OF THE GENTILES, THAT THOU SHOULDEST BE FOR	261 04
AND WHEN THE GENTILES HEARD THIS, THEY WERE GLAD,	261 06
THINGS DO THE GENTILES SEEK	266 27
AMONG THE GENTILES, *	363 06

GENTLE

AND SUCH AS ARE GENTLE, THEM SHALL HE LEARN HIS WAY	370 03
YOU SHOW YOURSELF GENTLE, AND BE MERCIFUL FOR	555 23

GENTLENESS

GENTLENESS, GOODNESS, FAITH, MEEKNESS, TEMPERANCE	209 27

GENTLY

AND SHALL GENTLY LEAD THOSE THAT ARE WITH	243 10

GET

JESUS UNTO HIM, GET THEE HENCE, SATAN	127 08
GOOD TIDINGS, GET THEE UP INTO THE HIGH MOUNTAIN	243 02
LEST THEY GET THE DOMINION OVER ME	364 11
7 LO, THEN WOULD I GET ME AWAY FAR OFF, *	406 32
THAT I CANNOT GET FORTH	449 13
AND THEY GET THEM AWAY TOGETHER, *	469 04
THY COMMANDMENTS I GET UNDERSTANDING	497 02

GET   CONTINUED

AND LABOUR TRULY TO GET MINE OWN LIVING, AND TO DO MY	580 13

GETHSEMANE

THEY CAME TO A PLACE WHICH WAS NAMED GETHSEMANE	141 28

GETTETH

WHEN HE GETTETH HIM INTO HIS NET	353 25

GHOST

THAT THE HOLY GHOST IS COME UPON YOU	005 12
AND TO THE SON, AND TO THE HOLY GHOST	008 04
AND HOLY GHOST, ONE GOD	R 008 29
AND TO THE HOLY GHOST	009 28
ALSO THE HOLY GHOST, THE COMFORTER	010 23
AND THE SON, AND THE HOLY GHOST	013 31
BY THE HOLY GHOST, BORN OF THE VIRGIN MARY	015 22
I BELIEVE IN THE HOLY GHOST	015 28
BY THE HOLY GHOST OF THE VIRGIN MARY, AND WAS MADE	016 07
IN THE HOLY GHOST, THE LORD, AND GIVER OF LIFE, WHO	016 15
THEE AND THE HOLY GHOST, ONE GOD, WORLD WITHOUT END	018 15
THEE AND THE HOLY GHOST, BE ALL HONOUR AND GLORY,	019 31
OF THE HOLY GHOST, BE WITH US ALL EVERMORE	020 13
AND TO THE SON, AND TO THE HOLY GHOST	025 10
WITH THE HOLY GHOST, ART MOST HIGH IN THE GLORY OF	026 03
BY THE HOLY GHOST, BORN OF THE VIRGIN MARY	029 27
I BELIEVE IN THE HOLY GHOST	029 33
BY THE HOLY GHOST OF THE VIRGIN MARY, AND WAS MADE	030 12
IN THE HOLY GHOST, THE LORD, AND GIVER OF LIFE, WHO	030 20
THEE AND THE HOLY GHOST LIVETH AND REIGNETH EVER, ONE	032 13
THEE AND THE HOLY GHOST, BE ALL HONOUR AND GLORY,	033 29
OF THE HOLY GHOST, BE WITH US ALL EVERMORE	034 13
POWER OF THE HOLY GHOST, THAT THE COMFORTABLE GOSPEL	037 02
THEE AND THE HOLY GHOST, BE ALL HONOUR AND GLORY, NOW	041 06
AND THE HOLY GHOST LIVEST AND REIGNEST ONE GOD,	043 15
AND THE HOLY GHOST, ONE GOD, WORLD WITHOUT END	049 09
THEE AND THE HOLY GHOST, BE ALL GLORY AND HONOUR,	050 29
O GOD THE HOLY GHOST, SANCTIFIER OF THE FAITHFUL	054 09
COMING OF THE HOLY GHOST,	055 13
AND TO THE SON, AND TO THE HOLY GHOST	059 06
AND TO THE HOLY GHOST	061 16
BY THE HOLY GHOST OF THE VIRGIN MARY, AND WAS MADE	071 10
IN THE HOLY GHOST, THE LORD, AND GIVER OF LIFE, WHO	071 17
OF THE HOLY GHOST, WAS MADE VERY MAN, OF THE	077 16
THE HOLY GHOST CAME DOWN AS AT THIS TIME	078 26
AND THE HOLY GHOST, ART ONE GOD, ONE LORD,	079 08
AND OF THE HOLY GHOST, WITHOUT ANY DIFFERENCE OF	079 11
TO US OF THE HOLY GHOST, THE COMFORTER	079 17
UNITY OF THE HOLY GHOST, ALL HONOUR AND GLORY BE UNTO	081 33
THEE AND THE HOLY GHOST, BE ALL HONOUR AND GLORY,	083 30
WITH THE HOLY GHOST, ART MOST HIGH IN THE GLORY OF	084 14
AND THE HOLY GHOST, BE AMONGST YOU, AND REMAIN	084 22
AND THE HOLY GHOST, FOR THE REDEMPTION OF THE	086 06
AND THE HOLY GHOST, LET US GIVE, AS WE ARE MOST	086 19
THEE AND THE HOLY GHOST, NOW AND EVER	090 18
THROUGH THE POWER OF THE HOLY GHOST	093 03
THEE AND THE HOLY GHOST, BE HONOUR AND GLORY, WORLD	095 10
THEE AND THE HOLY GHOST, ONE GOD, WORLD WITHOUT END	098 16
WITH THE HOLY GHOST, MAY LEARN TO LOVE AND BLESS OUR	099 29
FULL OF THE HOLY GHOST, LOOKED UP STEDFASTLY INTO	100 05
SHE WAS FOUND WITH CHILD OF THE HOLY GHOST	104 29
WHICH IS CONCEIVED IN HER IS OF THE HOLY GHOST	105 06
BUT HE SHALL BAPTIZE YOU WITH THE HOLY GHOST	112 18
AND THEE, O HOLY GHOST, HE LIVETH AND REIGNETH EVER,	117 11
THEE AND THE HOLY GHOST EVER, ONE GOD, WORLD WITHOUT	119 03
SEND THY HOLY GHOST, AND POUR INTO OUR HEARTS THAT	122 15
AND THE HOLY GHOST, ONE GOD, WORLD WITHOUT END	125 32
BY THE HOLY GHOST, BY LOVE UNFEIGNED, BY THE WORD OF	126 13
AGAIN WITH A LOUD VOICE, YIELDED UP THE GHOST	137 25
CRIED WITH A LOUD VOICE, AND GAVE UP THE GHOST	146 35
AND GAVE UP THE GHOST, HE SAID, TRULY THIS MAN WAS	147 04
AND HAVING SAID THUS, HE GAVE UP THE GHOST	155 14
THEE AND THE HOLY GHOST EVER, ONE GOD, WORLD WITHOUT	156 25
WHEREOF THE HOLY GHOST ALSO IS A WITNESS TO US	158 09
AND HE BOWED HIS HEAD, AND GAVE UP THE GHOST	160 29
AND TO THE HOLY GHOST	163 18
THEE AND THE HOLY GHOST EVER, ONE GOD, WORLD WITHOUT	163 29
WITH THE HOLY GHOST AND WITH POWER	166 20
RECEIVE YE THE HOLY GHOST	171 23
THEE AND THE HOLY GHOST, ONE GOD, WORLD WITHOUT END	177 19
THROUGH THE HOLY GHOST HAD GIVEN COMMANDMENTS UNTO	177 25
WITH THE HOLY GHOST NOT MANY DAYS HENCE	178 03
THAT THE HOLY GHOST IS COME UPON YOU	178 09
TO US THINE HOLY GHOST TO COMFORT US, AND EXALT US	179 07
AND THE SAME HOLY GHOST, ONE GOD, WORLD WITHOUT END	179 10
WITH THE HOLY GHOST, AND BEGAN TO SPEAK WITH OTHER	180 23
WHICH IS THE HOLY GHOST, WHOM THE FATHER WILL SEND IN	181 31
WITH THE HOLY GHOST AND WITH POWER	184 07
THE HOLY GHOST FELL ON ALL THEM WHICH HEARD	184 21
ALSO WAS POURED OUT THE GIFT OF THE HOLY GHOST	184 24
RECEIVED THE HOLY GHOST AS WELL AS WE	184 28
THAT THEY MIGHT RECEIVE THE HOLY GHOST	185 25
HANDS ON THEM, AND THEY RECEIVED THE HOLY GHOST	185 28
SAY THAT JESUS IS THE LORD, BUT BY THE HOLY GHOST	203 22
THEE AND THE HOLY GHOST, BE ALL HONOUR AND GLORY, NOW	228 11
AND BE FILLED WITH THE HOLY GHOST	230 34
AND THE HOLY GHOST WAS UPON HIM	232 32
HIM BY THE HOLY GHOST, THAT HE SHOULD NOT SEE DEATH,	232 33
WHICH THE HOLY GHOST BY THE MOUTH OF DAVID SPAKE	234 09
UNTO HER, THE HOLY GHOST SHALL COME UPON THEE,	236 22
BARNABAS WITH SINGULAR GIFTS OF THE HOLY GHOST	240 30
FULL OF THE HOLY GHOST AND OF FAITH	241 09

GHOST   CONTINUED

WITH THE HOLY GHOST, AND PROPHESIED, SAYING, BLESSED	243 32
AND THEE, O HOLY GHOST, LIVETH AND REIGNETH, ONE GOD,	248 05
THEE AND THE HOLY GHOST, ONE GOD, WORLD WITHOUT END	250 25
AND TO THE HOLY GHOST	265 07
AND BORN ANEW OF WATER AND OF THE HOLY GHOST	273 32
WATER AND THE HOLY GHOST, AND RECEIVED INTO CHRIST'S	274 05
AND OF THE SON, AND OF THE HOLY GHOST	275 30
HIM WITH THE HOLY GHOST, TO GIVE HIM THE KINGDOM OF	276 22
YOU WITH THE HOLY GHOST, TO GIVE YOU THE KINGDOM OF	277 24
THE FATHER, AND OF THE SON, AND OF THE HOLY GHOST	279 14
THE FATHER, AND OF THE SON, AND OF THE HOLY GHOST	279 29
THE FATHER, AND OF THE SON, AND OF THE HOLY GHOST	281 22
AND OF THE HOLY GHOST, (WHICH ARE ESSENTIAL PARTS OF	R 282 09
AND OF THE SON, AND OF THE HOLY GHOST	282 15
BY THE HOLY GHOST, BORN OF THE VIRGIN MARY	284 16
I BELIEVE IN THE HOLY GHOST	284 22
IN GOD THE HOLY GHOST, WHO SANCTIFIETH ME, AND ALL	285 02
THE FATHER, AND TO THE SON, AND TO THE HOLY GHOST	285 07
OF THE HOLY GHOST, BE WITH US ALL EVERMORE	289 30
AND OF THE SON, AND OF THE HOLY GHOST	292 21
OF THE HOLY GHOST, BE WITH US ALL EVERMORE	295 05
THAT THEY MIGHT RECEIVE THE HOLY GHOST	296 17
AND THEY RECEIVED THE HOLY GHOST	296 20
WATER AND THE HOLY GHOST, AND HAST GIVEN UNTO THEM	297 16
WITH THE HOLY GHOST, THE COMFORTER, AND DAILY	297 18
AND THE HOLY GHOST, BE UPON YOU, AND REMAIN WITH	299 04
AND OF THE SON, AND OF THE HOLY GHOST	302 15
AND OF THE SON, AND OF THE HOLY GHOST	304 09
GOD THE HOLY GHOST, BLESS, PRESERVE, AND KEEP	304 11
AND TO THE SON, AND TO THE HOLY GHOST	306 05
O GOD THE HOLY GHOST	317 29
AND BY THE COMING OF THE HOLY GHOST	318 08
THEE AND THE HOLY GHOST, ONE GOD, WORLD WITHOUT END	319 12
NAME OF THE HOLY GHOST WHO SANCTIFIETH THEE	319 23
AND THE HOLY GHOST, ONE GOD, WORLD WITHOUT END	320 13
AND OF THE SON, AND OF THE HOLY GHOST	320 17
THEE AND THE HOLY GHOST EVER, ONE GOD, WORLD WITHOUT	332 08
AND THE HOLY GHOST, ONE GOD, WORLD WITHOUT END	336 15
OF THE HOLY GHOST, BE WITH US ALL EVERMORE	341 06
AND THE HOLY GHOST, BLESS YOU AND KEEP YOU,	342 15
THEE AND THE HOLY GHOST, NOW AND FOR EVER	531 25
FULL OF THE HOLY GHOST AND WISDOM, WHOM WE MAY	532 12
AND OF THE HOLY GHOST, AND PHILIP, AND PROCHORUS, AND	532 16
MOVED BY THE HOLY GHOST TO TAKE UPON YOU THIS OFFICE	532 27
AND OF THE SON, AND OF THE HOLY GHOST	534 07
AND THE HOLY GHOST, BE AMONGST YOU, AND REMAIN	535 17
FOR THE HEAVENLY ASSISTANCE OF THE HOLY GHOST	541 17
COME, HOLY GHOST, OUR SOULS INSPIRE, AND LIGHTEN WITH	543 31
COME, HOLY GHOST, CREATOR BLEST, VOUCHSAFE WITHIN OUR	544 17
RECEIVE THE HOLY GHOST FOR THE OFFICE AND WORK OF A	546 09
AND OF THE SON, AND OF THE HOLY GHOST	546 15
AND OF THE SON, AND OF THE HOLY GHOST	546 21
AND THE HOLY GHOST, BE AMONGST YOU, AND REMAIN	547 18
SAVE THAT THE HOLY GHOST WITNESSETH IN EVERY CITY,	550 17
THE WHICH THE HOLY GHOST HATH MADE YOU OVERSEERS,	550 28
AND SAITH UNTO THEM, RECEIVE YE THE HOLY GHOST	552 04
AND OF THE SON, AND OF THE HOLY GHOST	552 12
WE TRUST THE HOLY GHOST HATH CALLED HIM	553 12
COME, HOLY GHOST, OUR SOULS INSPIRE, AND LIGHTEN WITH	556 06
COME, HOLY GHOST, CREATOR BLEST, VOUCHSAFE WITHIN OUR	556 25
THEE AND THE HOLY GHOST, LIVETH AND REIGNETH, ONE	558 07
RECEIVE THE HOLY GHOST FOR THE OFFICE AND WORK OF A	558 12
AND OF THE SON, AND OF THE HOLY GHOST	558 15
AND THE HOLY GHOST, BE AMONGST YOU, AND REMAIN	559 21
O GOD THE HOLY GHOST, O HOLY TRINITY,	560 07
AND TO THE HOLY GHOST	564 03
BY THE HOLY GHOST, AND MAY CONTINUE CHRIST'S FAITHFUL	565 21
AND THE HOLY GHOST, BE AMONGST YOU, AND REMAIN	568 17
AND OF THE SON, AND OF THE HOLY GHOST	571 03
O GOD, HOLY GHOST, SANCTIFIER OF THE FAITHFUL,	572 25
WITH THE ILLUMINATION OF THE HOLY GHOST	573 18
OF THE HOLY GHOST, ALL CHRISTIANS MAY BE SO JOINED	574 06
AND THE SAME HOLY GHOST, ONE GOD, WORLD WITHOUT END	574 22
BY THE HOLY GHOST, BORN OF THE VIRGIN MARY	577 31
I BELIEVE IN THE HOLY GHOST	578 06
IN GOD THE HOLY GHOST, WHO SANCTIFIETH ME, AND ALL	578 15
AND OF THE SON, AND OF THE HOLY GHOST	581 22
OF THE HOLY GHOST, BE WITH US ALL EVERMORE	589 10
OF THE HOLY GHOST, BE WITH US ALL EVERMORE	592 03
OF THE HOLY GHOST, BE WITH US ALL EVERMORE	592 28
THE SON, AND THE HOLY GHOST	603 07
THE HOLY GHOST, PROCEEDING FROM THE FATHER AND THE	603 26
AGAINST THE HOLY GHOST, AND UNPARDONABLE	605 40
RECEIVED THE HOLY GHOST, WE MAY DEPART FROM GRACE	605 42
OF GOD BY THE HOLY GHOST, ARE VISIBLY SIGNED AND	608 29

GHOSTLY

OF COUNSEL AND GHOSTLY STRENGTH, THE SPIRIT OF	297 20
FAR AWAY OUR GHOSTLY FOE, AND THINE ABIDING PEACE	545 06
FAR AWAY OUR GHOSTLY FOE, AND THINE ABIDING PEACE	557 12

GIANT

AND REJOICETH AS A GIANT TO RUN HIS COURSE	363 23
AND LIKE A GIANT REFRESHED WITH WINE	439 09
IN THE HAND OF THE GIANT, *	505 31

GIFT

FROM WHOM COMETH EVERY GOOD AND PERFECT GIFT	018 19
FROM WHOM COMETH EVERY GOOD AND PERFECT GIFT	032 18
ALL MEN THY BLESSED GIFT OF ETERNAL LIFE	038 22
WHOSE GIFT IT IS THAT THE RAIN DOTH FALL, AND	040 30

GIFT   CONTINUED

STRENGTHENED BY THE GIFT OF THE HOLY SPIRIT THROUGH	043 22
ACCORDING TO THE GIFT OF THE GRACE OF GOD GIVEN UNTO	108 17
AND OFFER THE GIFT THAT MOSES COMMANDED, FOR A	115 05
THAT MOST EXCELLENT GIFT OF CHARITY, THE VERY BOND OF	122 16
THOUGH I HAVE THE GIFT OF PROPHECY, AND UNDERSTAND	122 23
AND EVERY PERFECT GIFT IS FROM ABOVE, AND COMETH DOWN	174 26
EVERY GOOD GIFT AND EVERY PERFECT GIFT IS FROM ABOVE,	174 26
HATH RECEIVED THE GIFT, EVEN SO MINISTER THE SAME ONE	179 16
WAS POURED OUT THE GIFT OF THE HOLY GHOST	184 24
IF THOU BRING THY GIFT TO THE ALTAR, AND THERE	198 08
LEAVE THERE THY GIFT BEFORE THE ALTAR, AND GO THY	198 10
AND THEN COME AND OFFER THY GIFT	198 11
BUT THE GIFT OF GOD IS ETERNAL LIFE THROUGH JESUS	199 05
OF WHOSE ONLY GIFT IT COMETH THAT THY FAITHFUL	207 12
SO THAT YE COME BEHIND IN NO GIFT	214 32
THE MEASURE OF THE GIFT OF CHRIST	237 13
EVERY GOOD GIFT AND EVERY PERFECT GIFT IS FROM ABOVE,	265 18
AND EVERY PERFECT GIFT IS FROM ABOVE, AND COMETH DOWN	265 19
IT BE THY WILL, THE GIFT AND HERITAGE OF CHILDREN	303 16
THE DAUGHTER OF TYRE SHALL BE THERE WITH A GIFT	397 10
ARE AN HERITAGE AND GIFT THAT COMETH OF THE LORD	505 30
THE MEASURE OF THE GIFT OF CHRIST	537 33
TO THEE, THE GIFT OF GOD MOST HIGH	544 25
TO THEE, THE GIFT OF GOD MOST HIGH	556 30
THROUGH THY GIFT OF FAITH WE BRING OUR PERPLEXITIES	596 12

GIFTS

ENDUE THEM PLENTEOUSLY WITH HEAVENLY GIFTS	018 02
GIVER OF ALL GOOD GIFTS, WHO OF THY DIVINE PROVIDENCE	039 07
FOR ALL HIS GOOD GIFTS, TEMPORAL AND SPIRITUAL,	048 13
THESE THY HOLY GIFTS, WHICH WE NOW OFFER UNTO THEE,	080 40
THESE THY GIFTS AND CREATURES OF BREAD AND	081 10
THEY PRESENTED UNTO HIM GIFTS	109 23
HAVING THEN GIFTS DIFFERING ACCORDING TO THE GRACE	111 15
ARE DIVERSITIES OF GIFTS, BUT THE SAME SPIRIT	182 22
TO ANOTHER THE GIFTS OF HEALING BY THE SAME SPIRIT	182 29
HOW TO GIVE GOOD GIFTS UNTO YOUR CHILDREN	183 18
SPIRITUAL GIFTS, BRETHREN, I WOULD NOT HAVE YOU	203 16
ARE DIVERSITIES OF GIFTS, BUT THE SAME SPIRIT	203 22
TO ANOTHER THE GIFTS OF HEALING BY THE SAME SPIRIT	203 30
AND GAVE GIFTS UNTO MEN	237 15
WITH SINGULAR GIFTS OF THE HOLY GHOST	240 29
OF THY MANIFOLD GIFTS, NOR YET OF GRACE TO USE THEM	240 31
MANY EXCELLENT GIFTS, AND COMMANDEDST HIM EARNESTLY	244 23
HOW TO GIVE GOOD GIFTS UNTO YOUR CHILDREN	263 11
THE STRENGTHENING GIFTS OF THE HOLY SPIRIT	291 27
THEM THY MANIFOLD GIFTS OF GRACE	297 19
AND THEIR RIGHT HAND IS FULL OF GIFTS	371 17
AND RECEIVED GIFTS FROM MEN	420 20
THE KINGS OF ARABIA AND SABA SHALL BRING GIFTS	427 17
AND GAVE GIFTS UNTO MEN	538 02
DOST THY SEVENFOLD GIFTS IMPART	543 34
THE SEVENFOLD GIFTS OF GRACE ARE THINE, O FINGER OF	544 25
MANY EXCELLENT GIFTS, AND DIDST CHARGE HIM TO FEED	549 08
DOST THY SEVENFOLD GIFTS IMPART	556 09
THE SEVENFOLD GIFTS OF GRACE ARE THINE, O FINGER OF	557 04
POURED DOWN HIS GIFTS ABUNDANTLY UPON MEN, MAKING	557 25
GOOD AND PERFECT GIFTS, WHO OF THY WISE PROVIDENCE	572 07
GLORY BE TO THEE FOR ALL THY GRACIOUS GIFTS	596 15
THOSE WHO ADMINISTER TO HIM OF THY HEALING GIFTS	597 17
O FATHER, THY GIFTS TO OUR USE AND US TO THY SERVICE	600 15
THE GRACE OF GOD'S GIFTS DIMINISHED FROM SUCH AS BY	608 15

GILEAD

7 GILEAD IS MINE, AND MANASSEH IS MINE	412 25
8 GILEAD IS MINE, AND MANASSEH IS MINE	479 20

GIRD

SAID UNTO HIM, GIRD THYSELF, AND BIND ON THY SANDALS	245 16
3 GIRD THEE WITH THY SWORD UPON THY THIGH, O THOU	396 20
THAT HE SHALL GIRD HIMSELF, AND MAKE THEM TO SIT	534 22

GIRDED

TOOK A TOWEL, AND GIRDED HIMSELF	155 32
WIPE THEM WITH THE TOWEL WHEREWITH HE WAS GIRDED	155 33
40 THOU HAST GIRDED ME WITH STRENGTH UNTO THE BATTLE	362 16
MY SACKCLOTH, AND GIRDED ME WITH GLADNESS	375 17
AND IS GIRDED ABOUT WITH POWER	416 26
HIS APPAREL, AND GIRDED HIMSELF WITH STRENGTH	457 05
THAT HE IS ALWAY GIRDED WITHAL	481 09
LET YOUR LOINS BE GIRDED ABOUT, AND YOUR LIGHTS	534 22

GIRDETH

IT IS GOD THAT GIRDETH ME WITH STRENGTH OF WAR,	361 33

GIRDLE

AND WITH A GIRDLE OF A SKIN ABOUT HIS LOINS	112 13
AND AS THE GIRDLE THAT HE IS ALWAY GIRDED WITHAL	481 09

GIRT

HAVING YOUR LOINS GIRT ABOUT WITH TRUTH, AND HAVING	219 13

GIVE

GIVE US THIS DAY OUR DAILY BREAD	007 25
THAT HE WOULD GIVE US	014 19
TO GIVE KNOWLEDGE OF SALVATION UNTO HIS PEOPLE *	014 27

GIVE   CONTINUED

TO GIVE LIGHT TO THEM THAT SIT IN DARKNESS, AND IN — 014 31
DO GIVE THEE MOST HUMBLE AND HEARTY THANKS — 019 15
WE BESEECH THEE, GIVE US THAT DUE SENSE OF ALL THY — 019 25
WE GLORIFY THEE, WE GIVE THANKS TO THEE FOR THY GREAT — 025 24
REJOICE, AND GIVE THANKS — 027 14
IS A GOOD THING TO GIVE THANKS UNTO THE LORD, — 027 28
OUR OWN GOD, SHALL GIVE US HIS BLESSING — 028 29
GIVE PEACE IN OUR TIME, O LORD — 031 10
GIVE UNTO THY SERVANTS THAT PEACE WHICH THE WORLD — 031 19
SERVANTS THAT PEACE WHICH THE WORLD CANNOT GIVE — 031 20
DO GIVE THEE MOST HUMBLE AND HEARTY THANKS — 033 13
WE BESEECH THEE, GIVE US THAT DUE SENSE OF ALL THY — 033 23
AND GIVE UNTO THEM THE SPIRIT OF WISDOM AND — 036 02
GIVE US GRACE SERIOUSLY TO LAY TO HEART THE GREAT — 037 26
WE GIVE THEE HUMBLE THANKS FOR OPENING HEATHEN LANDS — 038 16
ANY HOLY FUNCTION, GIVE THY GRACE AND HEAVENLY — 039 02
GIVE THY GRACE, WE HUMBLY BESEECH THEE, TO ALL THOSE — 039 09
THAT OUR LAND MAY GIVE HER INCREASE — 040 11
POOR AND NEEDY MAY GIVE THANKS UNTO THY NAME — 040 12
WE GIVE THEE THANKS FOR ALL THOSE THY SERVANTS WHO — 042 15
GIVE THEM GRACE, WE PRAY THEE, TO STAND FAST IN THY — 043 09
IN HIS STEPS, GIVE THEMSELVES TO THE SERVICE CF THEIR — 043 30
GIVE STRENGTH AND SKILL TO ALL THOSE WHO MINISTER TO — 045 05
AND GIVE HIM PATIENCE UNDER HIS AFFLICTION — 045 17
PERFECT HEALTH WHICH IT IS THINE ALONE TO GIVE — 045 27
UPON HIM, AND GIVE HIM PEACE — 046 05
GIVE THEM A RIGHT UNDERSTANDING OF THEMSELVES, AND CF — 046 21
BE CALLED UPON TO GIVE AT THE LAST GREAT DAY — 047 20
MY PEACE I GIVE UNTO YOU — 049 06
VOUCHSAFE TO GIVE US, FOR THE WORTHINESS OF THY — 050 04
WE BESEECH THEE, GIVE US A JUST SENSE OF THESE GREAT — 050 25
O ALMIGHTY GOD, WE GIVE THEE HUMBLE THANKS FOR THAT — 051 05
WE GIVE THEE HUMBLE THANKS THAT IT HATH PLEASED THEE — 051 18
WE GIVE THEE HUMBLE THANKS FOR THIS THY SPECIAL — 051 32
HEAVENLY FATHER, WE GIVE THEE HUMBLE THANKS FOR THAT — 053 10
MAY PLEASE THEE TO GIVE TO ALL NATIONS UNITY, — 056 08
MAY PLEASE THEE TO GIVE US AN HEART TO LOVE AND FEAR — 056 11
MAY PLEASE THEE TO GIVE TO ALL THY PEOPLE INCREASE CF — 056 14
MAY PLEASE THEE TO GIVE AND PRESERVE TO OUR USE THE — 057 10
MAY PLEASE THEE TO GIVE US TRUE REPENTANCE — 057 14
MAY EVERMORE GIVE THANKS UNTO THEE IN THY HOLY — 058 23
O GIVE ME THE COMFORT OF THY HELP AGAIN, * — 061 02
ELSE WOULD I GIVE IT THEE — 061 11
UPON US, AND GIVE US PEACE, BOTH NOW AND EVERMORE — 063 17
IS MORE BLESSED TO GIVE THAN TO RECEIVE — 072 03
IF THOU HAST MUCH, GIVE PLENTEOUSLY — 072 32
DILIGENCE GLADLY TO GIVE OF THAT LITTLE — 072 34
EVERY MAN SHALL GIVE AS HE IS ABLE, ACCORDING TC THE — 073 16
AND TO GIVE THANKS FOR ALL MEN — 074 08
GIVE GRACE, O HEAVENLY FATHER, TO ALL BISHOPS AND — 074 21
TO ALL THY PEOPLE GIVE THY HEAVENLY GRACE — 074 25
AND SERVICE, AND TO GIVE US GRACE SO TO FOLLOW THEIR — 075 03
LET US GIVE THANKS UNTO OUR LORD GOD — 076 28
AND IN ALL PLACES, GIVE THANKS UNTO THEE, O LORD, — 076 32
BECAUSE THOU DIDST GIVE JESUS CHRIST, THINE ONLY SON, — 077 14
IN OUR HEARTS, TO GIVE THE KNOWLEDGE OF THY GLORY IN — 078 02
TENDER MERCY, DIDST GIVE THINE ONLY SCN JESUS CHRIST — 080 08
WE GLORIFY THEE, WE GIVE THANKS TO THEE FOR THY GREAT — 084 04
SHALL BE OBLIGED TO GIVE AN ACCOUNT OF THE SAME TO — R 085 18
ALL THINGS YE MUST GIVE MOST HUMBLE AND HEARTY THANKS — 086 05
HOLY GHOST, LET US GIVE, AS WE ARE MOST BOUNDEN, — 086 20
ALMIGHTY GOD, GIVE US GRACE THAT WE MAY CAST AWAY THE — 090 11
THAT WE MAY GIVE AN ANSWER TO THEM THAT SENT US — 095 27
MOURN IN ZION, TO GIVE UNTO THEM BEAUTY FCR ASHES, — 107 07
BUT RATHER GIVE PLACE UNTO WRATH — 113 04
IF HE THIRST, GIVE HIM DRINK — 113 06
THE MOON SHALL NOT GIVE HER LIGHT, AND THE STARS — 118 15
IS RIGHT I WILL GIVE YOU — 119 22
THE LABOURERS, AND GIVE THEM THEIR HIRE, BEGINNING — 119 30
I WILL GIVE UNTO THIS LAST, EVEN AS UNTO THEE — 120 09
AND THOUGH I GIVE MY BODY TO BE BURNED, AND — 122 27
O LORD, AND GIVE NOT THINE HERITAGE TO — 125 04
GIVE US GRACE TO USE SUCH ABSTINENCE, THAT, OUR FLESH — 125 28
HE SHALL GIVE HIS ANGELS CHARGE CONCERNING — 126 33
THESE THINGS WILL I GIVE THEE, IF THOU WILT FALL DOWN — 127 07
AND CHRIST SHALL GIVE THEE LIGHT — 129 22
AND PROMISED TO GIVE HIM MONEY — 140 20
AND COVENANTED TO GIVE HIM MONEY — 148 19
AND FORBIDDEN TO GIVE TRIBUTE TO CAESAR, SAYING THAT — 152 29
REDEMPTION DIDST GIVE THINE ONLY-BEGOTTEN SCN TC THE — 165 03
TO HIM GIVE ALL THE PROPHETS WITNESS, THAT THROUGH — 166 30
THIS WISE, I WILL GIVE YOU THE SURE MERCIES OF DAVID — 169 12
GIVE US GRACE THAT WE MAY ALWAYS MOST THANKFULLY — 171 30
IN MY NAME, HE WILL GIVE IT YOU — 176 21
AND HE SHALL GIVE YOU ANOTHER COMFORTER, THAT HE MAY — 181 10
MY PEACE I GIVE UNTO YOU — 181 34
THE WORLD GIVETH, GIVE I UNTO YOU — 181 35
A FATHER, WILL HE GIVE HIM A STONE — 183 15
WILL HE FOR A FISH GIVE HIM A SERPENT — 183 16
KNOW HOW TO GIVE GOOD GIFTS UNTO YOUR CHILDREN — 183 17
HEAVENLY FATHER GIVE THE HOLY SPIRIT TO THEM THAT ASK — 183 19
TO HIM GIVE ALL THE PROPHETS WITNESS, THAT THROUGH — 184 18
LIVING CREATURES GIVE GLORY AND HONOUR AND THANKS TO — 187 24
GIVE, AND IT SHALL BE GIVEN UNTO YOU — 194 28
SHALL MEN GIVE INTO YOUR BOSOM — 194 30
AND TO GIVE US THOSE THINGS WHICH ARE — 199 31
HIS FATHER, FATHER, GIVE ME THE PORTION OF GOODS THAT — 201 32
WHEREFORE I GIVE YOU TO UNDERSTAND, THAT NO MAN — 203 19
IN THE WEEK, I GIVE TITHES OF ALL THAT I POSSESS — 205 27
AND ART WONT TO GIVE MORE THAN EITHER WE DESIRE OR — 206 05
EVERLASTING GOD, GIVE UNTO US THE INCREASE OF FAITH, — 209 08
THAT RETURNED TO GIVE GLORY TO GOD, SAVE THIS — 210 12
AND SAY TO THEE, GIVE THIS MAN PLACE — 214 13
NEITHER GIVE PLACE TO THE DEVIL — 216 19

THAT HE MAY HAVE TO GIVE TO HIM THAT NEEDETH — 216 22
IS IT LAWFUL TO GIVE TRIBUTE UNTO CAESAR, OR NCT — 223 04
WE GIVE THANKS TO GOD AND THE FATHER OF OUR LORD — 223 22
HE SAID UNTO THEM, GIVE PLACE — 224 25
WHO DIDST GIVE SUCH GRACE UNTO THY HOLY APOSTLE — 226 18
MAY FORTHWITH GIVE UP OURSELVES OBEDIENTLY TC — 226 22
AND I WILL GIVE YOU REST — 235 11
LORD HIMSELF SHALL GIVE YOU A SIGN — 235 31
THE LORD GOD SHALL GIVE UNTO HIM THE THRONE OF HIS — 236 17
GIVE US GRACE THAT, BEING NOT LIKE CHILDREN CARRIED — 237 07
IN MY NAME, HE MAY GIVE IT YOU — 242 03
TO GIVE KNOWLEDGE OF SALVATION UNTO HIS PEOPLE BY THE — 244 12
HATH VISITED US, TO GIVE LIGHT TO THEM THAT SIT IN — 244 15
JESUS CHRIST DIDST GIVE TO THY APOSTLE SAINT PETER — 244 23
AND I WILL GIVE UNTO THEE THE KEYS OF THE KINGDOM OF — 246 09
IS NOT MINE TO GIVE, BUT IT SHALL BE GIVEN TC THEM — 247 17
TO MINISTER, AND TO GIVE HIS LIFE A RANSOM FOR MANY — 247 27
WHO DIDST GIVE TO THINE APOSTLE BARTHOLOMEW — 249 14
IN OUR HEARTS, TO GIVE THE LIGHT OF THE KNOWLEDGE OF — 251 08
SHALL GIVE ME AT THAT DAY — 253 29
EATING AND DRINKING SUCH THINGS AS THEY GIVE — 254 23
THIS LAND, AND TO GIVE US A FRUITFUL SEASON — 261 31
MAY EVERMORE GIVE THANKS UNTO THEE IN THY HOLY — 261 32
I CANNOT RISE AND GIVE THEE — 262 32
WILL NOT RISE AND GIVE HIM, BECAUSE HE IS HIS FRIEND, — 262 33
HE WILL RISE AND GIVE HIM AS MANY AS HE NEEDETH — 263 02
A FATHER, WILL HE GIVE HIM A STONE — 263 08
WILL HE FOR A FISH GIVE HIM A SERPENT — 263 09
KNOW HOW TO GIVE GOOD GIFTS UNTO YOUR CHILDREN — 263 11
HEAVENLY FATHER GIVE THE HOLY SPIRIT TO THEM THAT ASK — 263 12
WE GIVE THEE HUMBLE AND HEARTY THANKS FOR THIS THY — 265 13
GIVE THANKS ALWAYS FOR ALL THINGS UNTO GOD AND THE — 267 11
OR SPONSORS SHALL GIVE KNOWLEDGE THEREOF TO THE — R 273 12
SO GIVE NOW UNTO US WHO ASK — 274 17
AND DEVOUTLY GIVE THANKS UNTO HIM, AND SAY, — 276 06
HEAVENLY FATHER, WE GIVE THEE HUMBLE THANKS, THAT — 276 08
GIVE THY HOLY SPIRIT TO THIS CHILD (THIS THY — 276 11
THE HOLY GHOST, TO GIVE HIM THE KINGDOM OF HEAVEN, — 276 22
THE HOLY GHOST, TO GIVE YOU THE KINGDOM OF HEAVEN, — 277 24
LET US GIVE THANKS UNTO OUR LORD GOD — 279 04
THAT WE SHOULD GIVE THANKS UNTO THEE, O LORD, HOLY — 279 08
LET US GIVE THANKS UNTO ALMIGHTY GOD FOR — 280 15
I PRAY UNTO GOD TO GIVE ME HIS GRACE, THAT I MAY — 284 04
TO WORSHIP HIM, TO GIVE HIM THANKS — 288 19
WORK AND PRAY AND GIVE FOR THE SPREAD OF HIS KINGDOM — 291 20
THEN SHALL THEY GIVE THEIR TROTH TO EACH OTHER IN — R 301 24
AND THERETO I GIVE THEE MY TROTH — 302 08
AND THE MAN SHALL GIVE UNTO THE WOMAN A RING CN THIS — R 302 09
OF HIS GOODNESS, TO GIVE YOU SAFE DELIVERANCE, — 305 12
YOU SHALL THEREFORE GIVE HEARTY THANKS UNTO GOD, — 305 14
WHAT REWARD SHALL I GIVE UNTO THE LORD FCR ALL THE — 305 27
O ALMIGHTY GOD, WE GIVE THEE HUMBLE THANKS FOR THAT — 306 24
THAT COMETH TO GIVE HER THANKS, MUST OFFER ACCUSTOMED R 307 12
EYES OF THY MERCY, GIVE HIM COMFORT AND SURE — 309 06
THAT HE MAY GIVE THANKS UNTO THEE IN THY HOLY — 309 31
GIVE SENTENCE WITH ME, O GOD, AND DEFEND MY CAUSE — 310 05
THE HARP WILL I GIVE THANKS UNTO THEE, O GOD, MY GOD — 310 14
FOR I WILL YET GIVE THEE THANKS, WHICH IS THE HELP OF — 310 18
I WILL GIVE THANKS UNTO THEE, O LORD, WITH MY WHOLE — 311 28
UPON THEE, AND GIVE THEE PEACE, BOTH NOW AND — 314 30
GIVE HIM UNFEIGNED REPENTANCE FOR ALL THE ERRORS OF — 316 12
WAY REJOICING, AND GIVE THEE CONTINUAL THANKS FOR THY — 316 22
MAY PLEASE THEE TO GIVE HIM JOY AND GLADNESS IN THY — 318 20
THEN HE MUST GIVE TIMELY NOTICE TO THE MINISTER, — R 321 12
BREAD THAT I WILL GIVE IS MY FLESH, WHICH I WILL GIVE — 322 22
WHICH I WILL GIVE FOR THE LIFE OF THE WORLD — 322 28
HIM ALSO FREELY GIVE US ALL THINGS — 331 03
UPON YOU, AND GIVE YOU PEACE, BOTH NOW AND EVERMORE — 332 13
AND THE SEA SHALL GIVE UP THEIR DEAD — 333 19
WE GIVE THEE HEARTY THANKS FOR THE GOOD EXAMPLES OF — 334 22
BESEECHING THEE TO GIVE US GRACE SO TO FOLLOW THE — 336 21
THE SEA SHALL GIVE UP HER DEAD — 337 13
UPON HIM, AND GIVE HIM PEACE, BOTH NOW AND EVERMORE — 341 18
GIVE US GRACE, WE BESEECH THEE, TO ENTRUST THE SOUL — 342 04
OF ME, AND I SHALL GIVE THEE THE NATIONS FOR THINE — 346 12
THOU, LORD, WILT GIVE THY BLESSING UNTO THE — 348 28
AND WHO WILL GIVE THEE THANKS IN THE PIT — 349 09
GIVE SENTENCE WITH ME, O LORD, * — 350 06
18 I WILL GIVE THANKS UNTO THE LORD, ACCORDING TC HIS — 350 27
I WILL GIVE THANKS UNTO THEE, O LORD, WITH MY WHOLE — 351 22
8 WHO SHALL GIVE SALVATION UNTO ISRAEL OUT OF SION — 356 30
THIS CAUSE WILL I GIVE THANKS UNTO THEE, O LORD, — 363 05
6 FOR THOU SHALT GIVE HIM EVERLASTING FELICITY, — 365 15
THY PEOPLE, AND GIVE THY BLESSING UNTO THINE — 373 27
10 THE LORD SHALL GIVE STRENGTH UNTO HIS PEOPLE — 374 19
THE LORD SHALL GIVE HIS PEOPLE THE BLESSING CF PEACE — 374 20
AND GIVE THANKS UNTO HIM, FOR A REMEMBRANCE OF HIS — 374 31
10 SHALL THE DUST GIVE THANKS UNTO THEE — 375 12
O MY GOD, I WILL GIVE THANKS UNTO THEE FOR EVER — 375 19
I WILL ALWAY GIVE THANKS UNTO THE LORD — 380 03
18 SO WILL I GIVE THEE THANKS IN THE GREAT — 382 32
AND THOU SHALT GIVE THEM DRINK OF THY PLEASURES, — 384 12
AND HE SHALL GIVE THEE THY HEART'S DESIRE — 384 31
GIVE SENTENCE WITH ME, O GOD, AND DEFEND MY CAUSE — 394 03
THE HARP WILL I GIVE THANKS UNTO THEE, O GOD, MY GOD — 394 14
FOR I WILL YET GIVE THEE THANKS, WHICH IS THE HELP OF — 394 17
SHALL THE PEOPLE GIVE THANKS UNTO THEE, WORLD WITHOUT — 397 22
NOR GIVE A RANSOM UNTO GOD FOR HIM — 400 18
12 O GIVE ME THE COMFORT OF THY HELP AGAIN, * — 403 33
ELSE WOULD I GIVE IT THEE — 404 09
10 I WILL ALWAY GIVE THANKS UNTO THEE FOR THAT THOU — 405 07
A FREE HEART WILL I GIVE THEE, AND PRAISE THY NAME, C — 406 14
UNTO THEE WILL I GIVE THANKS — 409 07
I WILL SING AND GIVE PRAISE — 409 30

GIVE   CONTINUED

10 I WILL GIVE THANKS UNTO THEE, O LORD, AMONG THE   409 33
GIVE EAR UNTO MY PRAYER   413 07
THEY GIVE GOOD WORDS WITH THEIR MOUTH, BUT CURSE WITH   414 05
GIVE NOT YOURSELVES UNTO VANITY   414 18
OUR OWN GOD, SHALL GIVE US HIS BLESSING   419 03
26 GIVE THANKS UNTO GOD THE LORD IN THE CONGREGATION,   421 06
OF ISRAEL, HE WILL GIVE STRENGTH AND POWER UNTO HIS   421 28
GIVE THE KING THY JUDGMENTS, O GOD, *   426 31
OF THE ISLES SHALL GIVE PRESENTS   427 16
THE POOR AND NEEDY GIVE PRAISE UNTO THY NAME   431 21
O GOD, DO WE GIVE THANKS   431 30
UNTO THEE DO WE GIVE THANKS   431 31
BUT CAN HE GIVE BREAD ALSO, OR PROVIDE FLESH FOR HIS   436 10
THY PASTURE, SHALL GIVE THEE THANKS FOR EVER, *   440 33
2 HOW LONG WILL YE GIVE WRONG JUDGMENT, *   443 20
THE LORD WILL GIVE GRACE AND WORSHIP   446 03
AND OUR LAND SHALL GIVE HER INCREASE   446 32
6 GIVE EAR, LORD, UNTO MY PRAYER, *   447 15
GIVE THY STRENGTH UNTO THY SERVANT, AND HELP THE SON   448 07
11 FOR HE SHALL GIVE HIS ANGELS CHARGE OVER THEE,   455 17
IS A GOOD THING TO GIVE THANKS UNTO THE LORD,   455 32
13 THAT THOU MAYEST GIVE HIM PATIENCE IN TIME OF   458 12
AND GIVE THANKS FOR A REMEMBRANCE OF HIS HOLINESS   461 21
REJOICE, AND GIVE THANKS   462 03
3 THEY SHALL GIVE THANKS UNTO THY NAME, *   462 20
THAT THOU MAYEST GIVE THEM MEAT IN DUE SEASON   469 14
O GIVE THANKS UNTO THE LORD, AND CALL UPON HIS NAME   470 05
UNTO THEE WILL I GIVE THE LAND OF CANAAN, *   470 24
AND FIRE TO GIVE LIGHT IN THE NIGHT SEASON   472 16
O GIVE THANKS UNTO THE LORD   472 31
OF THY PEOPLE, AND GIVE THANKS WITH THINE   473 09
THAT WE MAY GIVE THANKS UNTO THY HOLY NAME, AND MAKE   475 31
THE PEOPLE SAY, O GIVE THANKS UNTO THE LORD, FOR HE   476 06
2 LET THEM GIVE THANKS WHOM THE LORD HATH REDEEMED,   476 08
I WILL SING, AND GIVE PRAISE WITH THE BEST MEMBER   479 05
3 I WILL GIVE THANKS UNTO THEE, O LORD, AMONG THE   479 09
BUT I GIVE MYSELF UNTO PRAYER   480 10
AS FOR ME, I WILL GIVE GREAT THANKS UNTO THE LORD   481 32
I WILL GIVE THANKS UNTO THE LORD WITH MY WHOLE HEART,   482 24
THAT HE MAY GIVE THEM THE HERITAGE OF THE HEATHEN   483 06
BUT UNTO THY NAME GIVE THE PRAISE   485 12
WHAT REWARD SHALL I GIVE UNTO THE LORD *   487 09
O GIVE THANKS UNTO THE LORD, FOR HE IS GRACIOUS   487 31
GO INTO THEM, AND GIVE THANKS UNTO THE LORD   489 07
29 O GIVE THANKS UNTO THE LORD   489 27
34 GIVE ME UNDERSTANDING, AND I SHALL KEEP THY LAW   492 07
I WILL RISE TO GIVE THANKS UNTO THEE, *   494 04
O GIVE ME UNDERSTANDING, THAT I MAY LEARN THY   494 28
O GIVE ME NOT OVER UNTO MINE OPPRESSORS   498·11
GIVE ME UNDERSTANDING ACCORDING TO THY WORD   501 20
UNTO ISRAEL, TO GIVE THANKS UNTO THE NAME OF   503 14
GIVE THEE BLESSING OUT OF SION   509 29
O GIVE THANKS UNTO THE LORD, FOR HE IS GRACIOUS   511 16
2 O GIVE THANKS UNTO THE GOD OF ALL GODS   511 18
26 O GIVE THANKS UNTO THE GOD OF HEAVEN   512 34
27 O GIVE THANKS UNTO THE LORD OF LORDS   513 02
I WILL GIVE THANKS UNTO THEE, O LORD, WITH MY WHOLE   513 27
13 I WILL GIVE THANKS UNTO THEE, FOR I AM FEARFULLY   515 15
ALSO SHALL GIVE THANKS UNTO THY NAME   517 04
THAT I MAY GIVE THANKS UNTO THY NAME   518 19
2 EVERY DAY WILL I GIVE THANKS UNTO THEE   520 29
AND THY SAINTS GIVE THANKS UNTO THINE   521 13
AND LET ALL FLESH GIVE THANKS UNTO HIS HOLY NAME FOR   521 35
BUT WE WILL GIVE OURSELVES CONTINUALLY TO PRAYER, AND   532 13
BY GOD'S GRACE, TO GIVE YOURSELVES WHOLLY TO THIS   541 11
WILL YOU THEN GIVE YOUR FAITHFUL DILIGENCE ALWAYS SO   542 11
KEEP FAR OUR FOES, GIVE PEACE AT HOME   544 08
JESUS CHRIST DIDST GIVE TO THY HOLY APOSTLES MANY   549 08
GIVE GRACE, WE BESEECH THEE, TO ALL BISHOPS, THE   549 09
YOU UP, AND TO GIVE YOU AN INHERITANCE AMONG ALL THEM   551 04
IS MORE BLESSED TO GIVE THAN TO RECEIVE   551 11
KEEP FAR OUR FOES, GIVE PEACE AT HOME   556 16
THE BIBLE, SAYING, GIVE HEED UNTO READING,   558 21
IN THIS PLACE, TO GIVE THEE THANKS FOR THE BENEFITS   566 14
AND VOUCHSAFE TO GIVE WHATEVER IN THY INFINITE WISDOM   566 21
BY THESE PRESENTS GIVE AND GRANT UNTO YOU, IN WHOSE   569 14
ALL WHICH YOU WILL GIVE US DUE NOTICE   569 33
IN TOKEN THEREOF, GIVE INTO YOUR HANDS THE KEYS OF   570 29
GIVE THY GRACE, WE BESEECH THEE, TO THY SERVANT, TO   572 08
IN PREACHING, TO GIVE A READINESS OF THOUGHT AND   573 26
GIVE THE ABUNDANCE OF THY GRACE   574 09
I PRAY UNTO GOD TO GIVE ME HIS GRACE, THAT I MAY   577 25
TO WORSHIP HIM, TO GIVE HIM THANKS   579 30
THE BISHOP SHALL GIVE KNOWLEDGE FOR CHILDREN TO BE   R 583 05
AND TO GIVE US THE CONSTANT ASSISTANCE   588 15
IN WHICH WE MUST GIVE A STRICT ACCOUNT OF OUR   588 22
GIVE US GRACE TO BE JUST AND UPRIGHT IN ALL OUR   588 30
WISH US EVIL, AND GIVE THEM REPENTANCE AND BETTER   590 33
TO US, AND TO GIVE US GRACE TO SHOW OUR THANKFULNESS   591 21
UPON US, AND GIVE US PEACE, THIS NIGHT AND EVERMORE   593 20
REJOICE TO GIVE THEE THANKS   594 16
WHO WILLEST US TO GIVE THANKS FOR ALL THINGS, TO   596 03
GIVE US LIGHT AND STRENGTH SO TO TRAIN THEM, THAT   596 25
OF SPIRIT, AND GIVE THEM HEALTH AND PEACE   598 16
WE MUST ONE DAY GIVE, MAY BE FAITHFUL STEWARDS OF THY 599 22
GIVE THE SPIRIT OF GOVERNANCE AND OF A SOUND MIND TO   600 02
GIVE EAR UNTO OUR PRAYER, O MERCIFUL AND GRACIOUS   600 11
GIVE US GRATEFUL HEARTS, OUR FATHER, FOR ALL THY   600 17
LIBERALLY TO GIVE ALMS TO THE POOR, ACCORDING TO HIS   611 04

GIVEN

AND LIVE, HATH GIVEN POWER, AND COMMANDMENT, TO HIS   007 08
WHO HAST GIVEN US GRACE AT THIS TIME WITH ONE   020 03

GIVEN   CONTINUED

AND LIVE, HATH GIVEN POWER, AND COMMANDMENT, TO HIS   024 10
WHO HAST GIVEN US GRACE AT THIS TIME WITH ONE   034 03
WHO HAST GIVEN US THIS GOOD LAND FOR OUR   036 09
SHALL NOTICE BE GIVEN OF THE COMMUNION, AND OF THE   R 071 27
GOD WHICH HE HATH GIVEN THEE   073 17
THINE OWN HAVE WE GIVEN THEE   073 24
AND WHEN HE HAD GIVEN THANKS, (B) HE BRAKE IT, AND   080 18
MY BODY, WHICH IS GIVEN FOR YOU   080 21
AND WHEN HE HAD GIVEN THANKS, HE GAVE IT TO THEM,   080 24
SHALL BE GIVEN TO THOSE PRESENT TO COMMUNICATE   R 082 29
WHICH WAS GIVEN FOR THEE, PRESERVE THY BODY   082 31
FOR THAT HE HATH GIVEN HIS SON OUR SAVIOUR JESUS   087 02
WHICH THOU HAST GIVEN US IN OUR SAVIOUR JESUS CHRIST 092 12
WHO HAST GIVEN US THY ONLY-BEGOTTEN SON TO TAKE   096 13
WHO HAST GIVEN US THY ONLY-BEGOTTEN SON TO TAKE   104 05
EXALTED HIM, AND GIVEN HIM A NAME WHICH IS ABOVE   105 26
OF GOD, WHICH IS GIVEN ME TO YOU-WARD   108 08
THE GRACE OF GOD GIVEN UNTO ME BY THE EFFECTUAL   108 17
IS THIS GRACE GIVEN, THAT I SHOULD PREACH AMONG THE   108 19
THROUGH THE GRACE GIVEN UNTO ME, TO EVERY MAN THAT IS 110 09
THE GRACE THAT IS GIVEN TO US, WHETHER PROPHECY,   111 16
GIVEN TO HOSPITALITY   111 28
UNTO YOU IT IS GIVEN TO KNOW THE MYSTERIES OF THE   121 30
WHO HATH ALSO GIVEN UNTO US HIS HOLY SPIRIT   128 04
LOVED US, AND HATH GIVEN HIMSELF FOR US AN OFFERING   128 32
AND WHEN HE HAD GIVEN THANKS, HE DISTRIBUTED TO THE   132 04
EXALTED HIM, AND GIVEN HIM A NAME WHICH IS ABOVE   134 23
AND HAVE BEEN GIVEN TO THE POOR   140 09
AND WHEN HE HAD GIVEN THANKS, HE GAVE IT TO THEM   141 12
BETRAYED HIM HAD GIVEN THEM A TOKEN, SAYING,   142 17
WHEREBY THOU HAST GIVEN UNTO US LIFE AND IMMORTALITY 147 10
MY BODY WHICH IS GIVEN FOR YOU   149 10
AND WHEN HE HAD GIVEN THANKS, HE BRAKE IT, AND SAID, 152 18
THE FATHER HAD GIVEN ALL THINGS INTO HIS HANDS,   155 29
FOR I HAVE GIVEN YOU AN EXAMPLE, THAT YE SHOULD DO AS 156 17
BE BETRAYED, AND GIVEN UP INTO THE HANDS OF WICKED   156 23
EXCEPT IT WERE GIVEN THEE FROM ABOVE   159 17
THE HOLY GHOST HAD GIVEN COMMANDMENTS UNTO THE   177 25
OF THE SPIRIT IS GIVEN TO EVERY MAN TO PROFIT WITHAL 182 26
FOR TO ONE IS GIVEN BY THE SPIRIT THE WORD OF WISDOM 182 27
AND IT SHALL BE GIVEN YOU   183 10
WHO HAST GIVEN UNTO US THY SERVANTS GRACE, BY   186 23
BECAUSE HE HATH GIVEN US OF HIS SPIRIT   189 19
WHICH HE HATH GIVEN US   191 34
TO WHOM THOU HAST GIVEN AN HEARTY DESIRE TO PRAY,   192 25
AND IT SHALL BE GIVEN UNTO YOU   194 28
OF THE SPIRIT IS GIVEN TO EVERY MAN TO PROFIT WITHAL 203 26
FOR TO ONE IS GIVEN BY THE SPIRIT THE WORD OF WISDOM 203 27
HAD BEEN A LAW GIVEN WHICH COULD HAVE GIVEN LIFE,   207 32
WHICH COULD HAVE GIVEN LIFE, VERILY RIGHTEOUSNESS   208 02
CHRIST MIGHT BE GIVEN TO THEM THAT BELIEVE   208 04
CONTINUALLY TO BE GIVEN TO ALL GOOD WORKS   213 15
OF GOD WHICH IS GIVEN YOU BY JESUS CHRIST   214 29
PAST FEELING HAVE GIVEN THEMSELVES OVER UNTO   216 08
WHICH HAD GIVEN SUCH POWER UNTO MEN   217 14
UTTERANCE MAY BE GIVEN UNTO ME, THAT I MAY OPEN MY   219 22
AND DEVOUTLY GIVEN TO SERVE THEE IN GOOD WORKS,   220 19
AND WHEN HE HAD GIVEN THANKS, HE DISTRIBUTED TO THE   226 03
EVERY ONE OF US IS GIVEN GRACE ACCORDING TO THE   237 12
AND IT SHALL BE GIVEN HIM   239 13
BUT IT SHALL BE GIVEN TO THEM FOR WHOM IT IS PREPARED 247 17
TO WHOM IT WAS GIVEN TO HURT THE EARTH AND THE SEA,   256 16
AND IT SHALL BE GIVEN YOU   263 04
ALL WHICH HE HATH GIVEN ME I SHOULD LOSE NOTHING,   269 18
NOTICE SHALL BE GIVEN TO THE MINISTER   R 273 18
ALL POWER IS GIVEN UNTO ME IN HEAVEN AND IN EARTH   275 27
TEN COMMANDMENTS, GIVEN IN OLD TIME BY GOD TO THE   285 16
SPIRITUAL GRACE GIVEN UNTO US   292 11
AND HAST GIVEN UNTO THEM FORGIVENESS OF ALL   297 16
WHEREOF THIS RING GIVEN AND RECEIVED IS A TOKEN AND   303 09
AND THERETO HAVE GIVEN AND PLEDGED THEIR TROTH, EACH 304 05
NOTICE SHALL BE GIVEN THEREOF TO THE MINISTER OF THE R 308 05
FOR ANY OF THOSE GIVEN ABOVE   313 10
NAME UNDER HEAVEN GIVEN TO MAN, IN WHOM, AND THROUGH 314 20
6 HE THAT HATH NOT GIVEN HIS MONEY UPON USURY,   357 17
36 THOU HAST GIVEN ME THE DEFENCE OF THY SALVATION   362 06
2 THOU HAST GIVEN HIM HIS HEART'S DESIRE,   365 07
THE SALVATION WERE GIVEN UNTO ISRAEL OUT OF SION   405 28
THOU HAST GIVEN US A DRINK OF DEADLY WINE   412 18
4 THOU HAST GIVEN A TOKEN FOR SUCH AS FEAR THEE,   412 19
AND HAST GIVEN AN HERITAGE UNTO THOSE THAT FEAR THY   413 16
UNTO HIM SHALL BE GIVEN OF THE GOLD OF ARABIA   427 26
MAIDENS WERE NOT GIVEN IN MARRIAGE   439 05
SERVANTS HAVE THEY GIVEN TO BE MEAT UNTO THE FOWLS OF 439 32
6 WHEN SENTENCE IS GIVEN UPON HIM, LET HIM BE   480 15
5 HE HATH GIVEN MEAT UNTO THEM THAT FEAR HIM   483 03
AND GIVEN TO THE POOR, *   483 34
THE EARTH HATH HE GIVEN TO THE CHILDREN OF MEN   486 11
BUT HE HATH NOT GIVEN ME OVER UNTO DEATH   489 05
REWARD SHALL BE GIVEN OR DONE UNTO THEE, THOU FALSE   502 11
WHO HATH NOT GIVEN US OVER FOR A PREY UNTO THEIR   504 16
10 THOU HAST GIVEN VICTORY UNTO KINGS, *   520 10
HE HATH GIVEN THEM A LAW WHICH SHALL NOT BE BROKEN   524 17
NOT GIVEN TO MUCH WINE, NOT GREEDY OF   531 28
EVERY ONE OF US IS GIVEN GRACE ACCORDING TO THE   537 32
AND ABILITY IS GIVEN OF GOD ALONE   540 31
AND OCCASION SHALL BE GIVEN   542 24
WHO HATH GIVEN YOU THIS WILL TO DO ALL THESE   543 18
TOWARDS US, HAST GIVEN TO US THY ONLY AND MOST DEARLY 545 13
OF DEACONS BE GIVEN TO SOME, AND THE ORDER OF   R 547 19
OF GOOD BEHAVIOUR, GIVEN TO HOSPITALITY, APT TO   549 21

GIVEN   CONTINUED

	PAGE	LN
NOT GIVEN TO WINE, NO STRIKER, NOT GREEDY OF FILTHY	549	22
ALL POWER IS GIVEN UNTO ME IN HEAVEN AND IN EARTH	552	10
WHO HATH GIVEN YOU A GOOD WILL TO DO ALL	555	29
HAST GIVEN THY ONLY AND DEARLY BELOVED SON	557	21
USE THE AUTHORITY GIVEN HIM, NOT TO DESTRUCTION, BUT	558	02
OF GOD, WHICH IS GIVEN THEE BY THIS IMPOSITION CF OUR	558	17
FOR GOD HATH NOT GIVEN US THE SPIRIT OF FEAR, BUT OF	558	18
THE LAW WAS GIVEN BY MOSES	571	32
SPIRITUAL GRACE GIVEN UNTO US	581	13
LOVING HAND HATH GIVEN US ALL THAT WE POSSESS	599	19
ALTHOUGH THE LAW GIVEN FROM GOD BY MOSES, AS TOUCHING	604	19
DEPART FROM GRACE GIVEN, AND FALL INTO SIN, AND BY	605	42
PUBLIC AUTHORITY GIVEN UNTO THEM IN THE CONGREGATION,	607	23
AND HATH GIVEN OCCASION TO MANY SUPERSTITIONS	608	43
BODY OF CHRIST IS GIVEN, TAKEN, AND EATEN, IN THE	608	44

GIVER

	PAGE	LN
THE LORD, AND GIVER OF LIFE, WHO PROCEEDETH FROM THE	016	15
THE LORD, AND GIVER OF LIFE, WHO PROCEEDETH FROM THE	030	20
ALMIGHTY GOD, THE GIVER OF ALL GOOD GIFTS, WHO CF THY	039	07
WHO ART THE ONLY GIVER OF ALL VICTORY	041	15
O GOD, WHO ART THE GIVER OF LIFE, OF HEALTH, AND OF	052	29
THE LORD, AND GIVER OF LIFE, WHO PROCEEDETH FROM THE	071	17
FOR GOD LOVETH A CHEERFUL GIVER	072	19
ART THE AUTHOR AND GIVER OF ALL GOOD THINGS	198	21
ART THE AUTHOR AND GIVER OF ALL GOOD THINGS	283	09
OF ALL MANKIND, GIVER OF ALL SPIRITUAL GRACE, THE	303	04
WHO ART THE GIVER OF ALL HEALTH, AND THE AID OF	315	13
OF MERCIES AND GIVER OF ALL COMFORT	342	09
ALMIGHTY GOD, GIVER OF ALL GOOD THINGS, WHO OF THY	534	30
ALMIGHTY GOD, GIVER OF ALL GOOD THINGS, WHO BY THY	537	20
ALMIGHTY GOD, GIVER OF ALL GOOD THINGS, WHO BY THY	547	31
ALMIGHTY GOD, GIVER OF ALL GOOD THINGS, WHC BY THY	553	26
THE GIVER OF ALL GOOD AND PERFECT GIFTS, WHO	572	06
WHO IS THE GIVER OF ALL GOODNESS, TO SEND HIS	580	30
O MERCIFUL GOD, GIVER OF LIFE AND HEALTH	597	15

GIVES

	PAGE	LN
THAT HE WHO GIVES IT AND SHE WHO WEARS IT MAY	302	19

GIVEST

	PAGE	LN
WORK WHICH THOU GIVEST US TO DO, IN TRUTH, IN BEAUTY,	044	21
AND GIVEST THEM PLENTEOUSNESS OF TEARS TO DRINK	441	12
AND GIVEST HIM NOT VICTORY IN THE BATTLE	452	27
28 WHEN THOU GIVEST IT THEM, THEY GATHER IT	469	16
AND THOU GIVEST THEM THEIR MEAT IN DUE SEASCN	521	23

GIVETH

	PAGE	LN
BE TO GOD, WHICH GIVETH US THE VICTORY THROUGH CUR	022	17
THE LORD THY GOD GIVETH THEE	069	04
WHEN THE MINISTER GIVETH WARNING FOR THE CELEBRATION	R 086	24
HE THAT GIVETH, LET HIM DO IT WITH SIMPLICITY	111	20
HOLY MYSTERIES GIVETH US A PLEDGE OF LIFE ETERNAL	152	11
THE GOOD SHEPHERD GIVETH HIS LIFE FOR THE SHEEP	172	22
LET HIM DO IT AS OF THE ABILITY WHICH GOD GIVETH	179	20
NOT AS THE WORLD GIVETH, GIVE I UNTO YOU	181	35
THE PROUD, AND GIVETH GRACE TO THE HUMBLE	192	32
BUT THE SPIRIT GIVETH LIFE	206	18
ASK OF GOD, THAT GIVETH TO ALL MEN LIBERALLY, ANC	239	12
AND GIVETH MEDICINE TO HEAL THEIR SICKNESS	264	23
WHO GIVETH FODDER UNTO THE CATTLE, *	264	30
THAT THE FATHER GIVETH ME SHALL COME TO ME	269	13
THE LORD THY GOD GIVETH THEE	287	03
MINISTER SAY, WHO GIVETH THIS WOMAN TO BE MARRIED TO	301	23
BUT GOD GIVETH IT A BODY AS IT HATH PLEASED HIM, AND	329	10
BE TO GOD, WHICH GIVETH US THE VICTORY THROUGH CUR	330	13
THAT THE FATHER GIVETH ME SHALL COME TO ME	333	03
GREAT PROSPERITY GIVETH HE UNTO HIS KING, *	363	07
LORD IS SURE, AND GIVETH WISDOM UNTO THE SIMPLE	363	28
LORD IS PURE, AND GIVETH LIGHT UNTO THE EYES	363	31
IT GIVETH LIGHT AND UNDERSTANDING UNTO THE SIMPLE	498	30
FOR SO HE GIVETH HIS BELOVED SLEEP	505	28
25 WHO GIVETH FOOD TO ALL FLESH	512	32
THE LORD GIVETH SIGHT TO THE BLIND	522	17
AND GIVETH MEDICINE TO HEAL THEIR SICKNESS	522	33
9 WHO GIVETH FODDER UNTO THE CATTLE, *	523	13
16 HE GIVETH SNOW LIKE WOOL, *	523	27
THE GOOD SHEPHERD GIVETH HIS LIFE FOR THE SHEEP	539	11
THE LORD THY GOD GIVETH THEE	579	14

GIVING

	PAGE	LN
GIVING THEM PATIENCE UNDER THEIR SUFFERINGS, AND A	019	09
IN OUR LIVES, BY GIVING UP OUR SELVES TO THY SERVICE,	019	28
I WILL REJOICE IN GIVING PRAISE FOR THE OPERATIONS OF	028	03
GIVING THEM PATIENCE UNDER THEIR SUFFERINGS, AND A	033	07
IN OUR LIVES, BY GIVING UP OUR SELVES TO THY SERVICE,	033	26
AND MAGISTRATES, GIVING THEM GRACE TO EXECUTE	055	27
GIVING THEM BOLDNESS WITH FERVENT ZEAL CONSTANTLY TO	078	29
THE LORD JESUS, GIVING THANKS TO GOD AND THE FATHER	116	15
GIVING NO OFFENCE IN ANY THING, THAT THE MINISTRY BE	126	08
BUT RATHER GIVING OF THANKS	129	06
IS AFRAID, AND GIVING US THOSE GOOD THINGS WHICH WE	206	08
FACE AT HIS FEET, GIVING HIM THANKS	210	09
GIVING THANKS ALWAYS FOR ALL THINGS UNTO GOD ANC THE	217	29
GIVING THANKS UNTO THE FATHER, WHICH HATH MADE US	224	08
THE STRANGER, IN GIVING HIM FOOD AND RAIMENT	263	27
THE SAME BY GIVING AND RECEIVING A RING, AND BY	304	07
HATH THEREBY, AND GIVING HIM HEARTY THANKS THEREFOR,	R 323	29
SHALL EVER BE GIVING OF THANKS, BECAUSE THOU	348	26

GIVING   CONTINUED

	PAGE	LN
THE LORD FOR GIVING ME WARNING	358	04
I WILL REJOICE IN GIVING PRAISE FOR THE OPERATIONS OF	456	07
FAITHFUL SERVANT, GIVING TO THY FAMILY THEIR PCRTION	558	04
AND IN GIVING US THE KNOWLEDGE AND SENSE OF	591	13

GLAD

	PAGE	LN
I WAS GLAD WHEN THEY SAID UNTO ME, WE WILL GO INTO	003	17
WILL REJOICE AND BE GLAD IN IT	005	05
AND SHOW OURSELVES GLAD IN HIM WITH PSALMS	009	06
WHEREOF SHALL MAKE GLAD THE CITY OF GOD, THE HOLY	022	27
HAST MADE ME GLAD THROUGH THY WORKS	028	02
O LET THE NATIONS REJOICE AND BE GLAD	028	23
OF THY FAVOUR AND GLAD TO DO THY WILL	036	12
WHO MAKEST US GLAD WITH THE YEARLY REMEMBRANCE	098	11
AND HE SAW IT, AND WAS GLAD	133	29
HEARD IT, THEY WERE GLAD, AND PROMISED TO GIVE HIM	140	20
AND THEY WERE GLAD, AND COVENANTED TO GIVE HIM MCNEY	148	18
AND WHEN HEROD SAW JESUS, HE WAS EXCEEDING GLAD	153	11
WE DECLARE UNTO YOU GLAD TIDINGS, HOW THAT THE	169	06
WERE THE DISCIPLES GLAD WHEN THEY SAW THE LORD	171	19
WAS MEET THAT WE SHOULD MAKE MERRY, AND BE GLAD	203	07
OF PEACE, AND BRING GLAD TIDINGS OF GOOD THINGS	227	10
GRACE OF GOD, WAS GLAD, AND EXHORTED THEM ALL, THAT	241	06
AND BE EXCEEDING GLAD	257	33
THEY WERE GLAD, AND GLORIFIED THE WORD OF THE	261	06
WHEREOF MAKE GLAD THE CITY OF GOD	327	09
MY HEART IS GLAD, AND MY GLORY REJOICETH	333	07
2 I WILL BE GLAD AND REJOICE IN THEE	351	24
SHALL JACOB REJOICE, AND ISRAEL SHALL BE GLAD	356	32
MY HEART IS GLAD, AND MY GLORY REJOICETH	358	08
EXCEEDING GLAD SHALL HE BE OF THY SALVATION	365	06
AND MAKE HIM GLAD WITH THE JOY OF THY COUNTENANCE	365	16
8 I WILL BE GLAD AND REJOICE IN THY MERCY	376	04
12 BE GLAD, O YE RIGHTEOUS, AND REJOICE IN THE LORD	378	16
THE HUMBLE SHALL HEAR THEREOF, AND BE GLAD	380	06
27 LET THEM BE GLAD AND REJOICE, THAT FAVOUR MY	383	19
BE JOYFUL AND GLAD IN THEE	391	21
WHEREBY THEY HAVE MADE THEE GLAD	396	34
WHEREOF MAKE GLAD THE CITY OF GOD	397	32
OF JUDAH BE GLAD, *	399	32
AND ISRAEL SHOULD BE RIGHT GLAD	405	32
BE THOU GLAD OF ME	412	28
AND ALL THEY THAT ARE TRUE OF HEART SHALL BE GLAD	416	08
4 O LET THE NATIONS REJOICE AND BE GLAD	418	30
THE RIGHTEOUS BE GLAD, AND REJOICE BEFORE GOD	419	14
33 THE HUMBLE SHALL CONSIDER THIS, AND BE GLAD	424	08
THEE BE JOYFUL AND GLAD IN THEE	424	27
22 MY LIPS WILL BE GLAD WHEN I SING UNTO THEE	426	25
WE REJOICE AND BE GLAD ALL THE DAYS OF OUR LIFE	454	18
HAST MADE ME GLAD THROUGH THY WORKS	456	06
AND SHOW OURSELVES GLAD IN HIM WITH PSALMS	459	08
AND LET THE EARTH BE GLAD	460	22
THE EARTH MAY BE GLAD THEREOF	460	30
OF THE ISLES MAY BE GLAD THEREOF	460	31
OF JUDAH WERE GLAD, *	461	13
WINE THAT MAKETH GLAD THE HEART OF MAN	468	24
37 EGYPT WAS GLAD AT THEIR DEPARTING	472	13
30 THEN ARE THEY GLAD, BECAUSE THEY ARE AT REST	478	04
WILL REJOICE AND BE GLAD IN IT	489	17
FEAR THEE WILL BE GLAD WHEN THEY SEE ME	495	02
162 I AM AS GLAD OF THY WORD, *	501	05
I WAS GLAD WHEN THEY SAID UNTO ME, *	503	09
FOLLOWING WITH A GLAD MIND AND WILL THEIR GODLY	533	33
FOLLOWING WITH A GLAD MIND AND WILL THEIR GODLY	543	14
WERE THE DISCIPLES GLAD, WHEN THEY SAW THE LORD	551	32
THY GOSPEL, THE GLAD TIDINGS OF RECONCILIATION WITH	557	30
WHO MAKEST US GLAD WITH THE WEEKLY REMEMBRANCE	595	12

GLADLY

	PAGE	LN
DO THY DILIGENCE GLADLY TO GIVE OF THAT LITTLE	072	33
YE SUFFER FOOLS GLADLY, SEEING YE YOURSELVES ARE	120	22
WILL YOU DO THIS GLADLY AND WILLINGLY	533	21

GLADNESS

	PAGE	LN
THE LORD WITH GLADNESS, AND COME BEFORE HIS PRESENCE	015	05
HEAR OF JOY AND GLADNESS, *	060	26
WITH THE OIL OF GLADNESS ABOVE THY FELLOWS	097	12
UNTO THE GOD OF MY JOY AND GLADNESS	310	03
OF GOD, EVEN UNTO THE GOD OF MY JOY AND GLADNESS	310	14
MOURNING INTO GLADNESS, BY RESTORING THIS OUR BRCTHER	315	22
WITH GREAT GLADNESS, AND TO BLESS THY HOLY NAME FOR	315	32
HIM JOY AND GLADNESS IN THY KINGDOM, WITH THY SAINTS	318	20
IN HIS DWELLING AN OBLATION, WITH GREAT GLADNESS	326	18
8 THOU HAST PUT GLADNESS IN MY HEART	347	26
IN HIS DWELLING AN OBLATION, WITH GREAT GLADNESS	372	10
AND GIRDED ME WITH GLADNESS	375	17
OF GOD, EVEN UNTO THE GOD OF MY JOY AND GLADNESS	394	13
WITH THE OIL OF GLADNESS ABOVE THY FELLOWS	396	31
15 WITH JOY AND GLADNESS SHALL THEY BE BROUGHT,	397	17
HEAR OF JOY AND GLADNESS, *	403	25
AND JOYFUL GLADNESS FOR SUCH AS ARE TRUE-HEARTED	401	20
THE LORD WITH GLADNESS, AND COME BEFORE HIS PRESENCE	463	06
AND HIS CHOSEN WITH GLADNESS	472	24
REJOICE IN THE GLADNESS OF THY PEOPLE, AND GIVE	473	09
AND TELL OUT HIS WORKS WITH GLADNESS	477	21
WE MAY LEARN TO SERVE THEE WITH GLADNESS	596	20

GLASS

	PAGE	LN
WE SEE THROUGH A GLASS, DARKLY	123	12
UNTO A MAN BEHOLDING HIS NATURAL FACE IN A GLASS	176	08

GLASS   CONTINUED

THERE WAS A SEA OF GLASS LIKE UNTO CRYSTAL   187 15
UNTO A MAN BEHOLDING HIS NATURAL FACE IN A GLASS   265 31

GLISTERING

IN RAIMENT WHITE AND GLISTERING   248 02
AND HIS RAIMENT WAS WHITE AND GLISTERING   248 27

GLORIA

SUNG OR SAID THE GLORIA PATRI   R 009 26
SUNG OR SAID THE GLORIA PATRI   R 025 18
SUNG OR SAID THE GLORIA PATRI, OR ELSE THE GLORIA IN   R 025 20
OR ELSE THE GLORIA IN EXCELSIS, AS FOLLOWETH   R 025 20
SHALL BE SAID THE GLORIA IN EXCELSIS, ALL STANDING,   R 083 32
THE GLORIA PATRI MAY BE OMITTED EXCEPT AT THE END OF   R 324 17
SHALL BE SAID THE GLORIA PATRI   R 338 15

GLORIFIED

AND THE SON TOGETHER IS WORSHIPPED AND GLORIFIED   016 18
AND THE SON TOGETHER IS WORSHIPPED AND GLORIFIED   030 23
AND THE SON TOGETHER IS WORSHIPPED AND GLORIFIED   071 20
THAT HE MIGHT BE GLORIFIED   107 10
WAS DONE, HE GLORIFIED GOD, SAYING, CERTAINLY THIS   155 15
THINGS MAY BE GLORIFIED THROUGH JESUS CHRIST, TO WHOM   179 21
WE MAY BE ALSO GLORIFIED TOGETHER   200 13
A LOUD VOICE GLORIFIED GOD, AND FELL DOWN ON HIS FACE   210 09
AND THEY GLORIFIED GOD, SAYING, THAT A GREAT PROPHET   213 07
AND GLORIFIED GOD, WHICH HAD GIVEN SUCH   217 13
IS MY FATHER GLORIFIED, THAT YE BEAR MUCH FRUIT   238 19
FATHER MAY BE GLORIFIED IN THE SON   240 23
WERE GLAD, AND GLORIFIED THE WORD OF THE LORD   261 06
WE MAY BE ALSO GLORIFIED TOGETHER   330 26
BE FOR EVER GLORIFIED, AND THY BLESSED KINGDOM   546 02

GLORIFY

WORSHIP THEE, WE GLORIFY THEE, WE GIVE THANKS TO THEE   025 24
AND ONE MOUTH GLORIFY THEE   038 02
ALL PERILS, TO GLORIFY THEE, WHO ART THE ONLY GIVER   041 15
IN THEE, WE MAY GLORIFY THY HOLY NAME, AND FINALLY,   049 26
WE PRAISE AND GLORIFY THY HOLY NAME FOR THIS THY   051 26
GOOD WORKS, AND GLORIFY YOUR FATHER WHICH IS IN   072 05
WORSHIP THEE, WE GLORIFY THEE, WE GIVE THANKS TO THEE   084 04
AND ONE MOUTH GLORIFY GOD, EVEN THE FATHER OF OUR   092 20
GENTILES MIGHT GLORIFY GOD FOR HIS MERCY   092 25
INFANTS TO GLORIFY THEE BY THEIR DEATHS   102 23
WE MAY GLORIFY THY HOLY NAME   102 26
SHALL BEHOLD, GLORIFY GOD IN THE DAY OF VISITATION   173 16
HE SHALL GLORIFY ME   175 22
AND SHALL GLORIFY THY NAME   447 22
IN THEE, WE MAY GLORIFY THY HOLY NAME, AND FINALLY,   571 11
WE WORSHIP AND GLORIFY AS ONE GOD, WORLD WITHOUT END   572 32

GLORIFYING

GLORIFYING AND PRAISING GOD FOR ALL THE   106 17
FOLLOWED HIM, GLORIFYING GOD   124 05

GLORIOUS

THE LORD IS GLORIOUS IN HIS SAINTS   R 008 34
THE GLORIOUS COMPANY OF THE APOSTLES PRAISE THEE   010 16
ART THOU ON THE GLORIOUS THRONE OF THY KINGDOM   011 25
THEM OF THE GLORIOUS RESURRECTION, AND THE LIFE   048 21
AND GLORIOUS TRINITY, ONE GOD   054 11
BY THY GLORIOUS RESURRECTION AND ASCENSION   055 11
AND MAGNIFY THY GLORIOUS NAME   077 06
INTO HIS OWN GLORIOUS LIGHT   077 25
THEE FOR THE GLORIOUS RESURRECTION OF THY SON JESUS   078 08
AFTER HIS MOST GLORIOUS RESURRECTION, MANIFESTLY   078 17
AND MAGNIFY THY GLORIOUS NAME   079 29
AND GLORIOUS ASCENSION   081 03
AGAIN IN HIS GLORIOUS MAJESTY TO JUDGE BOTH THE QUICK   090 16
AND THE GLORIOUS APPEARING OF THE GREAT GOD AND   098 22
FRUITION OF THY GLORIOUS GODHEAD   108 02
HIS ETERNAL AND GLORIOUS KINGDOM   117 10
THIS THAT IS GLORIOUS IN HIS APPAREL, TRAVELLING IN   138 12
MOSES WITH HIS GLORIOUS ARM, DIVIDING THE WATER   139 11
MAKE THYSELF A GLORIOUS NAME   139 17
AND BY HIS GLORIOUS RESURRECTION HAST DELIVERED US   165 05
INTO THE GLORIOUS LIBERTY OF THE CHILDREN OF GOD   194 18
IN STONES, WAS GLORIOUS, SO THAT THE CHILDREN OF   206 19
THE MINISTRATION OF THE SPIRIT BE RATHER GLORIOUS   206 23
TO HIS GLORIOUS POWER, UNTO ALL PATIENCE AND   224 07
LIGHT OF THE GLORIOUS GOSPEL OF CHRIST, WHO IS THE   251 04
IT TO HIMSELF A GLORIOUS CHURCH, NOT HAVING SPOT, OR   267 22
BY THY GLORIOUS RESURRECTION AND ASCENSION, AND BY   318 07
AND INTO THE GLORIOUS COMPANY OF THE SAINTS IN LIGHT   320 02
WHOSE COMING IN GLORIOUS MAJESTY TO JUDGE THE WORLD,   333 18
UNTO HIS OWN GLORIOUS BODY   333 22
WHOSE COMING IN GLORIOUS MAJESTY TO JUDGE THE WORLD,   337 13
LIKE UNTO HIS GLORIOUS BODY   337 15
IT IS THE GLORIOUS GOD THAT MAKETH THE THUNDER   374 03
THE LORD IS A GLORIOUS VOICE   374 06
DAUGHTER IS ALL GLORIOUS WITHIN   397 12
MAKE HIS PRAISE TO BE GLORIOUS   417 16
4 THOU ART GLORIOUS IN MIGHT, *   432 28
17 AND THE GLORIOUS MAJESTY OF THE LORD OUR GOD BE   454 24
5 O LORD, HOW GLORIOUS ARE THY WORKS   456 09
AND HATH PUT ON GLORIOUS APPAREL   457 04
O LORD MY GOD, THOU ART BECOME EXCEEDING GLORIOUS   467 25
31 THE GLORIOUS MAJESTY OF THE LORD SHALL ENDURE FOR   469 23

GLORIOUS   CONTINUED

FOR HIS GLORIOUS MAJESTY, AND AFFECT THEIR HEARTS   564 18
OFFERING TO THY GLORIOUS MAJESTY THE SACRIFICES OF   565 09
O MOST GLORIOUS GOD, WHOM THE HEAVEN OF HEAVENS   567 05
AND MAGNIFY THY GLORIOUS NAME   587 24
OF THE GLORIOUS RESURRECTION OF THY SON OUR LORD   595 13

GLORY

SOBER LIFE, TO THE GLORY OF THY HOLY NAME   006 29
THE POWER, AND THE GLORY, FOR EVER AND EVER   007 29
SHALL SAY, GLORY BE TO THE FATHER, AND TO THE SON,   008 03
THE LORD HATH MANIFESTED FORTH HIS GLORY   R 008 21
GLORY BE TO THE FATHER, AND TO THE SON, *   009 27
AND EARTH ARE FULL OF THE MAJESTY OF THY GLORY   010 15
ART THE KING OF GLORY, O CHRIST   010 24
OF GOD, IN THE GLORY OF THE FATHER   010 30
THY SAINTS, IN GLORY EVERLASTING   011 02
COME AGAIN, WITH GLORY, TO JUDGE BOTH THE QUICK AND   016 12
WHOSE GLORY IS IN ALL THE WORLD   018 07
AND FOR THE HOPE OF GLORY   019 24
BE ALL HONOUR AND GLORY, WORLD WITHOUT END   019 31
THE WHOLE EARTH IS FULL OF HIS GLORY   022 34
SOBER LIFE, TO THE GLORY OF THY HOLY NAME   024 04
SHALL SAY, GLORY BE TO THE FATHER, AND TO THE SON,   025 09
GLORY BE TO GOD ON HIGH, AND ON EARTH PEACE, GOOD   025 22
THEE FOR THY GREAT GLORY, O LORD GOD, HEAVENLY KING,   025 25
MOST HIGH IN THE GLORY OF GOD THE FATHER   026 04
AND TO BE THE GLORY OF THY PEOPLE ISRAEL   028 14
COME AGAIN, WITH GLORY, TO JUDGE BOTH THE QUICK AND   030 17
MAY ABOVE ALL THINGS SEEK THY HONOUR AND GLORY   032 09
AND FOR THE HOPE OF GLORY   033 22
BE ALL HONOUR AND GLORY, WORLD WITHOUT END   033 29
ADVANCEMENT OF THY GLORY, THE GOOD OF THY CHURCH,   035 13
TO THE GLORY OF THY NAME AND THE WELFARE OF THE   035 27
MAY SHOW FORTH THY GLORY, AND SET FORWARD THE   039 03
TO THE GLORY OF THY GREAT NAME, AND THE BENEFIT   039 13
BE ALL HONOUR AND GLORY, NOW AND FOR EVER   041 07
OUR GOD, TO THE GLORY OF THY NAME   042 11
TO THE GLORY OF THY HOLY NAME   044 14
WHO DECLAREST THY GLORY AND SHOWEST FORTH THY   044 18
RESIDUE OF HIS LIFE IN THY FEAR, AND TO THY GLORY   045 20
CALLINGS TO THE GLORY OF GOD, AND THE EDIFYING AND   047 18
AND TO THE SETTING FORTH OF THY GLORY   050 12
HOLY GHOST, BE ALL GLORY AND HONOUR, WORLD WITHOUT   050 29
OF EVERLASTING GLORY IN THE LIFE TO COME   051 12
AND TO THE GLORY OF THY HOLY NAME   051 19
TO THY GLORY AND OUR COMFORT   052 04
OF EVERLASTING GLORY IN THE LIFE TO COME   053 17
HE MAY ABOVE ALL THINGS SEEK THY HONOUR AND GLORY   055 24
GLORY BE TO THE FATHER, AND TO THE SON, AND TO THE   059 05
FOR THE GLORY OF THY NAME, TURN FROM US ALL   059 22
AND PURENESS OF LIVING, TO THY HONOUR AND GLORY   059 27
GLORY BE TO THE FATHER, AND TO THE SON, *   061 15
AND FOR THE GLORY OF THY NAME DELIVER US   062 03
SHALL BE SAID, GLORY BE TO THEE, O LORD   070 26
COME AGAIN, WITH GLORY, TO JUDGE BOTH THE QUICK AND   071 15
THE POWER, AND THE GLORY, AND THE VICTORY, AND THE   073 19
TO THE HONOUR AND GLORY OF THY NAME   075 30
GLORY BE TO THEE, O LORD MOST HIGH   077 10
HEAVEN AND EARTH ARE FULL OF THY GLORY   077 10
MANIFESTED FORTH HIS GLORY   077 24
KNOWLEDGE OF THY GLORY IN THE FACE OF THY SON JESUS   078 02
AND REIGN WITH HIM IN GLORY   078 21
WE BELIEVE OF THY GLORY, O FATHER, THE SAME WE   079 10
THE CROWN OF GLORY THAT FADETH NOT AWAY   079 26
HEAVEN AND EARTH ARE FULL OF THY GLORY   079 34
GLORY BE TO THEE, O LORD MOST HIGH   079 34
ALL GLORY BE TO THEE, ALMIGHTY GOD, OUR HEAVENLY   080 06
ALL HONOUR AND GLORY BE UNTO THEE, O FATHER ALMIGHTY,   081 34
BEGINNING AT, ALL GLORY BE TO THEE, ALMIGHTY GOD,   R 083 09
BE ALL HONOUR AND GLORY, WORLD WITHOUT END   083 30
GLORY BE TO GOD ON HIGH, AND ON EARTH PEACE, GOOD   084 02
THEE FOR THY GREAT GLORY, O LORD GOD, HEAVENLY KING,   084 05
MOST HIGH IN THE GLORY OF GOD THE FATHER   084 15
RECEIVED US TO THE GLORY OF GOD   092 22
MAN COMING IN A CLOUD WITH POWER AND GREAT GLORY   093 11
BE HONOUR AND GLORY, WORLD WITHOUT END   095 10
BRIGHTNESS OF HIS GLORY, AND THE EXPRESS IMAGE OF HIS   096 26
HIS GLORY, THE GLORY AS OF THE ONLY BEGOTTEN OF THE   098 05
AND WE BEHELD HIS GLORY, THE GLORY AS OF THE ONLY   098 05
UPON THEM, AND THE GLORY OF THE LORD SHONE ROUND   099 13
AND SAYING, GLORY TO GOD IN THE HIGHEST, AND ON   099 21
FAITH BEHOLD THE GLORY THAT SHALL BE REVEALED   099 28
AND SAW THE GLORY OF GOD, AND JESUS STANDING ON THE   100 06
IS LORD, TO THE GLORY OF GOD THE FATHER   105 30
AND MANIFESTED FORTH HIS GLORY   113 31
POWER AND GREAT GLORY, WE MAY BE MADE LIKE UNTO HIM   117 09
THE CLOUDS OF HEAVEN WITH POWER AND GREAT GLORY   118 20
FOR THE GLORY OF THY NAME   118 31
IF I MUST NEEDS GLORY, I WILL GLORY OF THE THINGS   121 13
GLORY, I WILL GLORY OF THE THINGS WHICH CONCERN MINE   121 13
TO THY HONOUR AND GLORY, WHO LIVEST AND REIGNEST WITH   125 31
THE WORLD, AND THE GLORY OF THEM   127 06
AND I SEEK NOT MINE OWN GLORY   133 16
IS LORD, TO THE GLORY OF GOD THE FATHER   134 27
ENTERED NOT INTO GLORY BEFORE HE WAS CRUCIFIED   138 06
THE HABITATION OF THY HOLINESS AND OF THY GLORY   139 19
ASSURANCE OF THE GLORY THAT SHALL BE REVEALED   144 09
GLORY BE TO THE FATHER, AND TO THE SON, *   163 17
THEN SHALL YE ALSO APPEAR WITH HIM IN GLORY   164 08
AND TO ENTER INTO HIS GLORY   167 31
FOR WHAT GLORY IS IT, IF, WHEN YE BE BUFFETED FOR   172 06
O GOD, THE KING OF GLORY, WHO HAST EXALTED THINE ONLY   179 04
TO THE GLORY OF THY NAME   185 17

GLORY   CONTINUED

TO ACKNOWLEDGE THE GLORY OF THE ETERNAL TRINITY,	186 25
CREATURES GIVE GLORY AND HONOUR AND THANKS TO HIM	187 24
O LORD, TO RECEIVE GLORY AND HONOUR AND POWER	187 30
UNTO HIS ETERNAL GLORY BY CHRIST JESUS, AFTER THAT YE	193 09
TO HIM BE GLORY AND DOMINION FOR EVER AND EVER	193 11
COMPARED WITH THE GLORY WHICH SHALL BE REVEALED IN	194 12
THE DEAD BY THE GLORY OF THE FATHER, EVEN SO WE ALSO	197 13
OF MOSES FOR THE GLORY OF HIS COUNTENANCE	206 21
WHICH GLORY WAS TO BE DONE AWAY	206 21
OF CONDEMNATION BE GLORY, MUCH MORE DOTH THE	206 23
THE MINISTRATION OF RIGHTEOUSNESS EXCEED IN GLORY	206 25
RETURNED TO GIVE GLORY TO GOD, SAVE THIS STRANGER	210 12
THAT I SHOULD GLORY, SAVE IN THE CROSS OF OUR LORD	210 29
THAT THEY MAY GLORY IN YOUR FLESH	210 29
SOLOMON IN ALL HIS GLORY WAS NCT ARRAYED LIKE ONE OF	211 23
AT MY TRIBULATIONS FOR YOU, WHICH IS YOUR GLORY	212 11
THE RICHES OF HIS GLORY, TO BE STRENGTHENED WITH	212 14
IN US, UNTO HIM BE GLORY IN THE CHURCH BY CHRIST	212 23
GOOD WORKS, TO THE GLORY OF THY NAME	220 19
UNTO THE GLORY AND PRAISE OF GOD	221 06
AND WHOSE GLORY IS IN THEIR SHAME, WHO MIND	222 20
THE BODY OF HIS GLORY, ACCORDING TO THE WORKING	222 24
BE ALL HONOUR AND GLORY, NOW AND FOR EVERMORE	228 12
THE THRONE OF HIS GLORY, YE ALSO SHALL SIT UPON	231 16
AND THE GLORY OF THY PEOPLE ISRAEL	233 09
BROUGHT UNTO THE GLORY OF HIS RESURRECTION	235 21
GRACE TO USE THEM ALWAY TO THY HONOUR AND GLORY	240 32
AND THE GLORY OF THE LORD SHALL BE REVEALED, AND ALL	242 25
THEY MAY RECEIVE THE CROWN OF EVERLASTING GLORY	244 28
FATHER HONOUR AND GLORY, WHEN THERE CAME SUCH A VOICE	248 17
FROM THE EXCELLENT GLORY, THIS IS MY BELOVED SON,	248 18
WHO APPEARED IN GLORY, AND SPAKE OF HIS DECEASE WHICH	248 28
THEY SAW HIS GLORY, AND THE TWO MEN THAT STOOD WITH	248 31
KNOWLEDGE OF THE GLORY OF GOD IN THE FACE OF JESUS	251 09
AND GLORY, AND WISDOM, AND THANKSGIVING,	256 32
SHALL COME IN HIS GLORY, AND ALL THE HOLY ANGELS WITH	258 28
THEN SHALL HE SIT UPON THE THRONE OF HIS GLORY	258 30
GLORY BE TO THE FATHER, AND TO THE SON, *	265 06
TO THY GLORY AND OUR COMFORT	265 15
SOLOMON IN ALL HIS GLORY WAS NOT ARRAYED LIKE ONE OF	266 21
THE VAIN POMP AND GLORY OF THE WORLD, WITH ALL	276 25
THE VAIN POMP AND GLORY OF THE WORLD, WITH ALL	277 27
BE ALL HONOUR AND GLORY, NOW AND EVERMORE	279 21
GLORY BE TO THE FATHER,	285 06
AND THEIR CHILDREN THY GLORY	290 09
TO THE HONOUR AND GLORY OF THY NAME	303 18
GLORY BE TO THE FATHER, AND TO THE SON, AND TO THE	306 04
OF EVERLASTING GLORY IN THE LIFE TO COME	306 31
OF HIS INFIRMITIES, TO THINE HONOUR AND GLORY	315 17
BE ALL HONOUR AND GLORY, WORLD WITHOUT END	316 04
BUT THE GLORY OF THE CELESTIAL IS ONE, AND THE GLORY	329 15
IS ONE, AND THE GLORY OF THE TERRESTRIAL IS ANOTHER	329 15
THERE IS ONE GLORY OF THE SUN, AND ANOTHER GLORY OF	329 16
AND ANOTHER GLORY OF THE STARS	329 17
AND ANOTHER GLORY OF THE MOON, AND ANOTHER GLORY	329 17
FOR ONE STAR DIFFERETH FROM ANOTHER STAR IN GLORY	329 18
IT IS RAISED IN GLORY	329 21
COMPARED WITH THE GLORY WHICH SHALL BE REVEALED IN	330 28
IS GLAD, AND MY GLORY REJOICETH	333 07
IN THY ETERNAL AND EVERLASTING GLORY	334 28
TO WHOM BE GLORY FOR EVER AND EVER	335 21
BLESSED SAINTS IN GLORY EVERLASTING	336 09
THAT HAST SET THY GLORY ABOVE THE HEAVENS	350 32
TO CROWN HIM WITH GLORY AND WORSHIP	351 12
IS GLAD, AND MY GLORY REJOICETH	358 08
DECLARE THE GLORY OF GOD	363 13
GLORY AND GREAT WORSHIP SHALT THOU LAY UPON HIM	365 13
AND THE KING OF GLORY SHALL COME IN	369 10
8 WHO IS THIS KING OF GLORY	369 14
AND THE KING OF GLORY SHALL COME IN	369 15
10 WHO IS THIS KING OF GLORY	369 15
EVEN THE LORD OF HOSTS, HE IS THE KING OF GLORY	369 16
OR IF THE GLORY OF HIS HOUSE BE INCREASED	401 08
AND THY GLORY ABOVE ALL THE EARTH	409 25
9 AWAKE UP, MY GLORY	409 31
AND THY GLORY ABOVE ALL THE EARTH	410 05
7 IN GOD IS MY HEALTH AND MY GLORY	414 11
THAT I MIGHT BEHOLD THY POWER AND GLORY	414 30
I MAY SING OF THY GLORY AND HONOUR ALL THE DAY LONG	425 22
AND AFTER THAT RECEIVE ME WITH GLORY	429 25
FOR THE GLORY OF THY NAME	440 18
THAT GLORY MAY DWELL IN OUR LAND	446 26
FOR THOU ART THE GLORY OF THEIR STRENGTH, *	451 08
HAST PUT OUT HIS GLORY, *	452 28
AND THEIR CHILDREN THY GLORY	454 23
6 GLORY AND WORSHIP ARE BEFORE HIM	460 10
AND ALL THE PEOPLES HAVE SEEN HIS GLORY	461 09
AND WHEN HIS GLORY SHALL APPEAR	465 12
THEY TURNED THEIR GLORY *	474 08
AND THY GLORY ABOVE ALL THE EARTH	479 14
AND HIS GLORY ABOVE THE HEAVENS	484 14
THAT GREAT IS THE GLORY OF THE LORD	514 07
THY GLORY, THY PRAISE, AND WONDROUS WORKS	521 03
11 THEY SHOW THE GLORY OF THY KINGDOM, *	521 14
THY POWER, THY GLORY, AND MIGHTINESS OF THY KINGDOM,	521 16
9 LET THE SAINTS BE JOYFUL WITH GLORY	525 11
AND THE GLORY OF THY HOLY NAME	531 07
TO THE GLORY OF THY NAME, AND THE EDIFICATION	531 22
PROMOTING OF HIS GLORY, AND THE EDIFYING OF HIS	532 28
TO WHOM BE GLORY AND HONOUR, WORLD WITHOUT	535 11
AND THE GLORY OF THY HOLY NAME	537 13
TO THE GLORY OF THY NAME, AND THE EDIFICATION	537 26
WE MAY SEEK THY GLORY, AND THE INCREASE OF THY	547 12
TO THE GLORY OF THY NAME, AND THE	548 05

GLORY   CONTINUED

ALL MAY RECEIVE THE CROWN OF EVERLASTING GLORY	549 14
AND GLORY OF THY NAME	553 20
TO THE GLORY OF THY NAME, AND THE EDIFYING	553 32
YOU MAY RECEIVE THE NEVER-FADING CROWN OF GLORY	558 31
DEVOTION TO THY GLORY AND TO THE SALVATION OF SOULS	560 22
AND TO THE GLORY OF THY HOLY NAME	560 29
AND GLORY OF THY NAME	561 05
AND THE KING OF GLORY SHALL COME IN	563 25
8 WHO IS THIS KING OF GLORY	563 26
AND THE KING OF GLORY SHALL COME IN	563 29
10 WHO IS THIS KING OF GLORY	563 30
EVEN THE LORD OF HOSTS, HE IS THE KING OF GLORY	563 31
GLORY BE TO THE FATHER, AND TO THE SON, *	564 02
TEND MOST TO THY GLORY, AND THE FURTHERANCE OF OUR	565 13
USE OF IT, TO THE GLORY OF THY BLESSED NAME	566 33
TO THE GLORY OF THY GREAT NAME, AND THE BENEFIT	572 13
TO WHOM BE GLORY FOR EVER AND EVER	573 08
WITH THY SAINTS IN GLORY EVERLASTING	574 19
GLORY BE TO THEE FOR ALL THY GRACIOUS GIFTS	596 15
AND GLORY, WITH THE FATHER AND THE SON, VERY	603 27

GNASH

HE SHALL GNASH WITH HIS TEETH, AND CONSUME AWAY	484 05

GNASHED

WHO GNASHED UPON ME WITH THEIR TEETH	382 27

GNASHETH

AND GNASHETH UPON HIM WITH HIS TEETH	385 19

GNASHING

BE WEEPING AND GNASHING OF TEETH	115 22
BE WEEPING AND GNASHING OF TEETH	218 28

GO

SAID UNTO ME, WE WILL GO INTO THE HOUSE OF THE LORD	003 17
I WILL ARISE AND GO TO MY FATHER, AND WILL SAY UNTO	004 26
FOR THOU SHALT GO BEFORE THE FACE OF THE LORD TO	014 25
O GO YOUR WAY INTO HIS GATES WITH THANKSGIVING	015 10
LET THY BREATH GO FORTH THAT IT MAY RENEW THE FACE OF	040 09
SAYING UNTO THEM, GO INTO THE VILLAGE OVER AGAINST	091 13
AND SAID UNTO THEM, GO AND SHEW JOHN AGAIN THOSE	094 19
LET US NOW GO EVEN UNTO BETHLEHEM, AND SEE	106 09
AND HIS MOTHER, AND GO INTO THE LAND OF ISRAEL	107 14
HE WAS AFRAID TO GO THITHER	107 19
AND SAID, GO AND SEARCH DILIGENTLY FOR THE	109 13
BUT GO THY WAY, SHEW THYSELF TO THE PRIEST, AND OFFER	115 04
I SAY TO THIS MAN, GO, AND HE GOETH	115 14
UNTO THE CENTURION, GO THY WAY	115 23
THOU THEN THAT WE GO AND GATHER THEM UP	116 26
GO NOT FORTH	118 09
GO YE ALSO INTO THE VINEYARD, AND WHATSOEVER IS RIGHT	119 21
HE SAITH UNTO THEM, GO YE ALSO INTO THE VINEYARD	119 27
THAT THINE IS, AND GO THY WAY	120 09
WHEN THEY HAVE HEARD, GO FORTH, AND ARE CHOKED WITH	122 06
UNTO THEM, BEHOLD, WE GO UP TO JERUSALEM, AND ALL	123 18
LET THE BRIDEGROOM GO FORTH OF HIS CHAMBER, AND THE	124 32
THAT NO MAN GO BEYOND AND DEFRAUD HIS BROTHER IN ANY	127 32
WILT THOU THAT WE GO AND PREPARE THAT THOU MAYEST EAT	140 24
AND SAITH UNTO THEM, GO YE INTO THE CITY, AND THERE	140 26
WHERESOEVER HE SHALL GO IN, SAY YE TO THE GOODMAN OF	140 28
I AM RISEN, I WILL GO BEFORE YOU INTO GALILEE	141 21
RISE UP, LET US GO	142 13
AND JOHN, SAYING, GO AND PREPARE US THE PASSOVER,	148 23
I AM READY TO GO WITH THEE, BOTH INTO PRISON,	149 35
ASK YOU, YE WILL NOT ANSWER ME, NOR LET ME GO	151 32
I WILL THEREFORE CHASTISE HIM, AND LET HIM GO	154 02
IF THOU LET THIS MAN GO, THOU ART NOT CAESAR'S	159 20
GO YOUR WAY, MAKE IT AS SURE AS YE CAN	162 23
BUT GO YOUR WAY, TELL HIS DISCIPLES AND PETER THAT HE	165 31
SEE ME, BECAUSE I GO TO THE FATHER	173 29
BECAUSE I GO TO THE FATHER	173 32
HIS DISCIPLES, NOW I GO MY WAY TO HIM THAT SENT ME	175 06
FOR YOU THAT I GO AWAY	175 10
FOR IF I GO NOT AWAY, THE COMFORTER WILL NOT COME	175 10
BECAUSE I GO TO MY FATHER, AND YE SEE ME NO MORE	175 15
LEAVE THE WORLD, AND GO TO THE FATHER	176 31
AS YE HAVE SEEN HIM GO INTO HEAVEN	178 19
I SAID UNTO YOU, I GO AWAY, AND COME AGAIN UNTO YOU	182 03
BECAUSE I SAID, I GO UNTO THE FATHER	182 04
BE SAVED, AND SHALL GO IN AND OUT, AND FIND PASTURE	186 16
AND I MUST NEEDS GO AND SEE IT	192 08
YOKE OF OXEN, AND I GO TO PROVE THEM	192 09
SAID TO HIS SERVANT, GO OUT QUICKLY INTO THE STREETS	192 14
UNTO THE SERVANT, GO OUT INTO THE HIGHWAYS AND	192 18
THE WILDERNESS, AND GO AFTER THAT WHICH IS LOST,	193 20
BEFORE THE ALTAR, AND GO THY WAY	198 10
I WILL ARISE AND GO TO MY FATHER, AND WILL SAY UNTO	202 12
AND WOULD NOT GO IN	202 32
SAID JESUS UNTO HIM, GO, AND DO THOU LIKEWISE	209 05
HE SAID UNTO THEM, GO SHEW YOURSELVES UNTO THE	210 05
SAID UNTO HIM, ARISE, GO THY WAY	210 13
AND HEALED HIM, AND LET HIM GO	214 04
WHEN THOU ART BIDDEN, GO AND SIT DOWN IN THE LOWEST	214 15
UNTO THEE, FRIEND, GO UP HIGHER	214 17
LET NOT THE SUN GO DOWN UPON YOUR WRATH	216 19
TAKE UP THY BED, AND GO UNTO THINE HOUSE	217 11
GO YE THEREFORE INTO THE HIGHWAYS, AND AS MANY AS YE	218 17
JESUS SAITH UNTO HIM, GO THY WAY	220 03

GO   CONTINUED

UNTO HIM, ARISE, AND GO INTO THE CITY, AND IT SHALL	230 07
UNTO HIM, ARISE, AND GO INTO THE STREET WHICH IS	230 17
LORD SAID UNTO HIM, GO THY WAY	230 25
THAT HE MIGHT GO TO HIS OWN PLACE	234 31
I GO TO PREPARE A PLACE FOR YOU	239 32
AND IF I GO AND PREPARE A PLACE FOR YOU, I WILL COME	239 33
AND WHITHER I GO YE KNOW, AND THE WAY YE KNOW	240 03
BECAUSE I GO UNTO MY FATHER	240 21
THAT HE SHOULD GO AS FAR AS ANTIOCH	241 05
THAT YE SHOULD GO AND BRING FORTH FRUIT,	241 33
FOR THOU SHALT GO BEFORE THE FACE OF THE LORD TO	244 11
BUT GO YE AND LEARN WHAT THAT MEANETH, I WILL HAVE	251 21
GO YOUR WAYS	254 16
A FRIEND, AND SHALL GO UNTO HIM AT MIDNIGHT, AND SAY	262 27
GO YE THEREFORE, AND MAKE DISCIPLES OF ALL NATIONS,	275 27
THAT THEY SHOULD GO TEACH ALL NATIONS, AND BAPTIZE	279 12
I WILL GO UNTO THE ALTAR OF GOD	310 02
AND WHY GO I SO HEAVILY, WHILE THE ENEMY OPPRESSETH	310 09
AND THAT I MAY GO UNTO THE ALTAR OF GOD, EVEN UNTO	310 13
HE MAY BE ABLE TO GO TO THINE HOUSE, TO OFFER THEE AN	315 31
HE MAY BE ENABLED TO GO UPON HIS WAY REJOICING, AND	316 21
BEFORE I GO HENCE, AND BE NO MORE SEEN	325 11
AND IF I GO AND PREPARE A PLACE FOR YOU, I WILL CCME	331 20
I GO TO PREPARE A PLACE FOR YOU	331 20
AND WHITHER I GO YE KNOW, AND THE WAY YE KNOW	331 23
LOVE OF THEE, HE MAY GO FROM STRENGTH TO STRENGTH, IN	332 05
UNDER ME FOR TO GO, *	362 09
11 O GO NOT FROM ME	366 25
30 ALL THEY THAT GO DOWN INTO THE DUST SHALL KNEEL	368 02
AND SO WILL I GO TO THINE ALTAR	371 09
BECOME LIKE THEM THAT GO DOWN INTO THE PIT	373 05
THAT I SHOULD NOT GO DOWN INTO THE PIT	374 29
WHEN I GO DOWN INTO THE PIT	375 10
AND TEACH THEE IN THE WAY WHEREIN THOU SHALT GO	378 09
GO NOT FAR FROM ME, O LORD	383 08
FROM WRATH, AND LET GO DISPLEASURE	385 09
15 THEIR SWORD SHALL GO THROUGH THEIR OWN HEART,	385 25
THAT I GO MOURNING ALL THE DAY LONG	388 03
BEFORE I GO HENCE, AND BE NO MORE SEEN	390 07
AND TO SUCH AS GO ABOUT WITH LIES	390 19
WHY GO I THUS HEAVILY, WHILE THE ENEMY OPPRESSETH ME	393 25
AND WHY GO I SO HEAVILY, WHILE THE ENEMY CPPRESSETH	394 07
4 AND THAT I MAY GO UNTO THE ALTAR OF GOD, EVEN UNTO	394 12
WALK ABOUT SION, AND GO ROUND ABOUT HER	399 33
THERE SHALL GO BEFORE HIM A CONSUMING FIRE, AND A	401 26
10 DAY AND NIGHT THEY GO ABOUT WITHIN THE WALLS	407 06
DECEIT AND GUILE GO NOT OUT OF HER STREETS	407 09
AND LET THEM GO DOWN ALIVE INTO THE PIT	407 20
THEY ARE BORN, THEY GO ASTRAY, AND SPEAK LIES	410 13
6 THEY GO TO AND FRO IN THE EVENING, *	411 16
LIKE A DOG, AND WILL GO ABOUT THE CITY	412 03
WILT NOT THOU, O GOD, GO OUT WITH OUR HOSTS	412 32
THEY SHALL GO UNDER THE EARTH	415 12
12 I WILL GO INTO THINE HOUSE WITH BURNT-OFFERINGS,	418 07
25 THE SINGERS GO BEFORE, THE MINSTRELS FOLLOW AFTER,	421 04
11 GO NOT FAR FROM ME, O GOD	425 29
15 I WILL GO FORTH IN THE STRENGTH OF THE LORD GOD,	426 06
O LET NOT THE SIMPLE GO AWAY ASHAMED	431 20
THE SEA, AND LET THEM GO THROUGH	435 26
THAT ALL THEY THAT GO BY PLUCK OFF HER GRAPES	441 27
18 AND SO WILL NOT WE GO BACK FROM THEE	442 07
7 THEY WILL GO FROM STRENGTH TO STRENGTH, *	445 25
RIGHTEOUSNESS SHALL GO BEFORE HIM, *	446 33
AS ONE OF THEM THAT GO DOWN INTO THE PIT, *	449 02
MERCY AND TRUTH SHALL GO BEFORE THY FACE	451 03
40 ALL THEY THAT GO BY SPOIL HIM, *	452 22
13 THOU SHALT GO UPON THE LION AND ADDER	455 21
3 THERE SHALL GO A FIRE BEFORE HIM, *	461 02
3 O GO YOUR WAY INTO HIS GATES WITH THANKSGIVING,	463 11
8 THEY GO UP AS HIGH AS THE HILLS, AND DOWN TO THE	468 08
26 THERE GO THE SHIPS, AND THERE IS THAT LEVIATHAN,	469 12
LETTEST THY BREATH GO FORTH, THEY SHALL BE MADE	469 21
OF THE PEOPLE LET HIM GO FREE	471 13
THAT THEY MIGHT GO TO THE CITY WHERE THEY DWELT	476 18
23 THEY THAT GO DOWN TO THE SEA IN SHIPS, *	477 22
WILT NOT THOU, O GOD, GO FORTH WITH OUR HOSTS	479 27
22 I GO HENCE LIKE THE SHADOW THAT DEPARTETH,	481 16
NEITHER ALL THEY THAT GO DOWN INTO SILENCE	486 13
THAT I MAY GO INTO THEM, AND GIVE THANKS UNTO THE	489 06
O LET ME NOT GO WRONG OUT OF THY COMMANDMENTS	490 19
35 MAKE ME TO GO IN THE PATH OF THY COMMANDMENTS	492 09
FOR THEY GO WICKEDLY ABOUT TO DESTROY ME	495 11
WE WILL GO INTO THE HOUSE OF THE LORD	503 09
THITHER THE TRIBES GO UP, EVEN THE TRIBES OF THE	503 13
8 SO THAT THEY WHO GO BY SAY NOT SO MUCH AS, THE LORD	507 04
7 WE WILL GO INTO HIS TABERNACLE, *	508 17
14 AND MADE ISRAEL TO GO THROUGH THE MIDST OF IT	512 10
6 WHITHER SHALL I GO THEN FROM THY SPIRIT	514 31
OR WHITHER SHALL I GO THEN FROM THY PRESENCE	514 32
IF I GO DOWN TO HELL, THOU ART THERE ALSO	515 02
LIKE UNTO THEM THAT GO DOWN INTO THE PIT	519 06
BE SAVED, AND SHALL GO IN AND OUT, AND FIND PASTURE	539 07
DAILY INCREASE AND GO FORWARDS IN THE KNOWLEDGE AND	545 30
AND THE BISHOP SHALL GO ON IN THE SERVICE CF THE	R 546 29
AND NOW, BEHOLD, I GO BOUND IN THE SPIRIT UNTO	550 15
GO YE THEREFORE, AND TEACH ALL NATIONS, BAPTIZING	552 10
THAT THEY MAY GO FORWARD WITH COURAGE, AND PERSEVERE	561 09
WHO ARE PRESENT SHALL GO UP THE AISLE OF THE CHURCH,	R 563 07
THE BISHOP SHALL GO WITHIN THE RAILS, WITH SUCH CF	R 564 06
WHO SHALL GO WITHIN THE RAILS OF THE	R 570 06
CHOOSING TO GO ON WITH THE SERVICE, THEN SHALL BE	R 570 23
SUFFER THE SUN TO GO DOWN UPON OUR WRATH	590 16
BUT MAY ALWAYS GO TO OUR REST IN PEACE, CHARITY,	590 17

GOATS

BY THE BLOOD OF GOATS AND CALVES, BUT BY HIS CWN	132 26
OF BULLS AND OF GOATS, AND THE ASHES OF AN HEIFER	132 28
OF CALVES AND OF GOATS, WITH WATER, AND SCARLET WCOL,	147 20
OF BULLS AND OF GOATS SHOULD TAKE AWAY SINS	157 23
AS A SHEPHERD DIVIDETH HIS SHEEP FROM THE GOATS	258 32
BUT THE GOATS ON THE LEFT	259 02
AND DRINK THE BLOOD OF GOATS	402 17
I WILL OFFER BULLOCKS AND GOATS	418 11
18 THE HIGH HILLS ARE A REFUGE FOR THE WILD GOATS	468 30

GOD

AND PEACE, FROM GOD OUR FATHER, AND FROM THE	004 02
MAKE STRAIGHT IN THE DESERT A HIGHWAY FOR OUR GCC	004 07
YOUR GARMENTS, AND TURN UNTO THE LORD YOUR GOD	004 21
THE SACRIFICES OF GOD ARE A BROKEN SPIRIT	004 24
A CONTRITE HEART, O GOD, THOU WILT NCT DESPISE	004 25
JESUS THE SON OF GOD, LET US COME BOLDLY UNTO THE	005 07
IS INDEBTED, UNDER GOD, FOR HER FIRST FOUNDATION AND	V 11
BECAUSE YE ARE SONS, GOD HATH SENT FORTH THE SPIRIT	005 16
HOLY, LORD GOD ALMIGHTY, WHICH WAS, AND IS, AND	005 18
THE FACE OF ALMIGHTY GOD OUR HEAVENLY FATHER	005 32
OF PIETY AND DEVOTION IN THE WORSHIP OF GOD	V 37
TO THE WORD OF GOD, OR TO SOUND DOCTRINE, CR WHICH A	V 40
HUMBLY TO ACKNOWLEDGE OUR SINS BEFORE GOD	006 04
LET US HUMBLY CONFESS OUR SINS UNTO ALMIGHTY GOD	006 14
SPARE THOU THOSE, O GOD, WHO CONFESS THEIR FAULTS	006 25
ALMIGHTY GOD, THE FATHER OF OUR LORD JESUS CHRIST,	007 06
AND HOLY GHOST, ONE GOD	R 008 29
FOR THE LORD IS A GREAT GOD	009 07
FOR HE IS THE LORD OUR GOD	009 15
WE PRAISE THEE, O GOD	010 08
HOLY, LORD GOD OF SABAOTH	010 14
AT THE RIGHT HAND OF GOD, IN THE GLORY OF THE FATHER	010 30
ART THOU, O LORD GOD OF OUR FATHERS	011 16
O YE WINDS OF GOD, BLESS YE THE LORD	012 16
BLESSED BE THE LORD GOD OF ISRAEL	014 08
THEIR SINS, THROUGH THE TENDER MERCY OF OUR GOD	014 29
BE YE SURE THAT THE LORD HE IS GOD	015 07
I BELIEVE IN GOD THE FATHER ALMIGHTY, MAKER OF HEAVEN	015 19
ON THE RIGHT HAND OF GOD THE FATHER ALMIGHTY	015 26
I BELIEVE IN ONE GOD THE FATHER ALMIGHTY, MAKER CF	015 33
ALL WORLDS, GOD OF GOD, LIGHT OF LIGHT, VERY GCD OF	016 03
BEFORE ALL WORLDS, GOD OF GOD, LIGHT OF LIGHT, VERY	016 03
THE ONLY-BEGOTTEN SON OF GOD	016 03
GOD OF GOD, LIGHT OF LIGHT, VERY GOD OF VERY GOD	016 04
LIGHT OF LIGHT, VERY GOD OF VERY GOD	016 04
O GOD, MAKE CLEAN OUR HEARTS WITHIN US	016 31
O GOD, WHO ART THE AUTHOR OF PEACE AND LOVER OF	017 05
AND EVERLASTING GOD, WHO HAST SAFELY BROUGHT US TO	017 14
THE HOLY GHOST, ONE GOD, WORLD WITHOUT END	018 16
AND EVERLASTING GOD, FROM WHOM COMETH EVERY GOCD AND	018 18
O GOD, THE CREATOR AND PRESERVER OF ALL MANKIND,	018 26
ALMIGHTY GOD, FATHER OF ALL MERCIES, WE, THINE	019 14
ALMIGHTY GOD, WHO HAST GIVEN US GRACE AT THIS TIME	020 03
AND THE LOVE OF GOD, AND THE FELLOWSHIP OF THE HCLY	020 13
THE TABERNACLE OF GOD IS WITH MEN, AND HE WILL DWELL	021 28
BE HIS PEOPLE, AND GOD HIMSELF SHALL BE WITH THEM,	021 30
GOD HIMSELF SHALL BE WITH THEM, AND BE THEIR GCD	021 31
TO THE LORD OUR GOD BELONG MERCIES AND FORGIVENESSES,	022 06
OF THE LORD OUR GOD, TO WALK IN HIS LAWS WHICH HE SET	022 08
WE CONFESS OUR SINS, GOD IS FAITHFUL AND JUST TO	022 11
THANKS BE TO GOD, WHICH GIVETH US THE VICTORY THRCUGH	022 17
WHERE CHRIST SITTETH ON THE RIGHT HAND OF GOD	022 20
IN THE PRESENCE OF GOD FOR US	022 25
GLAD THE CITY OF GOD, THE HOLY PLACE OF THE	022 27
LET US HUMBLY CONFESS OUR SINS UNTO ALMIGHTY GCD	023 02
THE FACE OF ALMIGHTY GOD OUR HEAVENLY FATHER	023 08
HUMBLY TO ACKNOWLEDGE OUR SINS BEFORE GOD	023 13
SPARE THOU THOSE, O GOD, WHO CONFESS THEIR FAULTS	023 32
ALMIGHTY GOD, THE FATHER OF OUR LORD JESUS CHRIST,	024 08
GLORY BE TO GOD ON HIGH, AND ON EARTH PEACE, GCCD	025 22
GREAT GLORY, O LORD GOD, HEAVENLY KING, GOD THE	025 25
GOD, HEAVENLY KING, GOD THE FATHER ALMIGHTY	025 25
O LORD GOD, LAMB OF GOD, SON OF THE FATHER, THAT	025 28
O LORD GOD, LAMB OF GOD, SON OF THE FATHER, THAT	025 28
AT THE RIGHT HAND OF GOD THE FATHER, HAVE MERCY UPON	025 31
HIGH IN THE GLORY OF GOD THE FATHER	026 04
HATH REJOICED IN GOD MY SAVIOUR	026 12
OF THE WORLD HAVE SEEN THE SALVATION OF OUR GOD	027 12
GOD BE MERCIFUL UNTO US, AND BLESS US, *	028 17
LET THE PEOPLES PRAISE THEE, O GOD	028 21
LET THE PEOPLES PRAISE THEE, O GOD	028 26
AND GOD, EVEN OUR OWN GOD, SHALL GIVE US HIS	028 28
GOD, EVEN OUR OWN GOD, SHALL GIVE US HIS BLESSING	028 29
GOD SHALL BLESS US	028 30
I BELIEVE IN GOD THE FATHER ALMIGHTY, MAKER OF HEAVEN	029 24
ON THE RIGHT HAND OF GOD THE FATHER ALMIGHTY	029 31
I BELIEVE IN ONE GOD THE FATHER ALMIGHTY, MAKER CF	030 04
ALL WORLDS, GOD OF GOD, LIGHT OF LIGHT, VERY GCD OF	030 08
BEFORE ALL WORLDS, GOD OF GOD, LIGHT OF LIGHT, VERY	030 08
THE ONLY-BEGOTTEN SON OF GOD	030 08
LIGHT OF LIGHT, VERY GOD OF VERY GOD	030 09
GOD OF GOD, LIGHT OF LIGHT, VERY GOD OF VERY GCD	030 09
O GOD, MAKE CLEAN OUR HEARTS WITHIN US	031 13
O GOD, FROM WHOM ALL HOLY DESIRES, ALL GOOD COUNSELS,	031 18
ALMIGHTY GOD, WHOSE KINGDOM IS EVERLASTING AND PCWER	032 04
REIGNETH EVER, ONE GOD, WORLD WITHOUT END	032 14
AND EVERLASTING GOD, FROM WHOM COMETH EVERY GOOD AND	032 17
O GOD, THE CREATOR AND PRESERVER OF ALL MANKIND,	032 26
ALMIGHTY GOD, FATHER OF ALL MERCIES, WE, THINE	033 12
ALMIGHTY GOD, WHO HAST GIVEN US GRACE AT THIS TIME	034 03
AND THE LOVE OF GOD, AND THE FELLOWSHIP OF THE HCLY	034 13
MOST GRACIOUS GOD, WE HUMBLY BESEECH THEE, AS FOR THE	035 08

GOD CONTINUED

	PAGE LN
O GOD, THE FOUNTAIN OF WISDOM, WHOSE STATUTES ARE	035 23
ALMIGHTY GOD, WHO SITTEST IN THE THRONE JUDGING	035 31
ALMIGHTY GOD, WHO HAST GIVEN US THIS GOOD LAND FOR	036 09
AND EVERLASTING GOD, WHO BY THY HOLY SPIRIT DIDST	036 26
O GOD, THE FATHER OF OUR LORD JESUS CHRIST, OUR ONLY	037 25
ONE BAPTISM, ONE GOD AND FATHER OF US ALL, SO WE MAY	037 31
O GOD, WHO HAST MADE OF ONE BLOOD ALL NATIONS OF MEN	038 05
ALMIGHTY GOD, WHOSE COMPASSIONS FAIL NOT, AND WHOSE	038 14
ALMIGHTY GOD, OUR HEAVENLY FATHER, WHO HAST PURCHASED	038 25
ALMIGHTY GOD, THE GIVER OF ALL GOOD GIFTS, WHO OF THY	039 07
O ALMIGHTY GOD, LOOK MERCIFULLY UPON THE WORLD WHICH	039 17
ALMIGHTY GOD, WHO HAST BLESSED THE EARTH THAT IT	039 24
O GOD, HEAVENLY FATHER, WHO BY THY SON JESUS CHRIST	040 15
O GOD, HEAVENLY FATHER, WHOSE GIFT IT IS THAT THE	040 30
O ALMIGHTY GOD, THE SUPREME GOVERNOR OF ALL THINGS,	041 09
O GOD, MERCIFUL AND COMPASSIONATE, WHO ART EVER READY	041 19
O LORD GOD OF HOSTS, STRETCH FORTH, WE PRAY THEE,	041 25
O ETERNAL LORD GOD, WHO ALONE SPREADEST OUT THE	042 03
SERVE THEE OUR GOD, TO THE GLORY OF THY NAME	042 11
ALMIGHTY GOD, OUR HEAVENLY FATHER, IN WHOSE HANDS ARE	042 14
ALMIGHTY GOD, WE BESEECH THEE, WITH THY GRACIOUS	042 22
ALMIGHTY GOD, OUR HEAVENLY FATHER, WHO HAST COMMITTED	042 30
AND REIGNEST ONE GOD, WORLD WITHOUT END	043 15
O GOD, WHO THROUGH THE TEACHING OF THY SON JESUS	043 18
ALMIGHTY GOD, WHO HAST CREATED MAN IN THINE OWN	044 09
ALMIGHTY GOD, OUR HEAVENLY FATHER, WHO DECLAREST THY	044 17
ALMIGHTY GOD, OUR HEAVENLY FATHER, GUIDE, WE BESEECH	044 27
MIGHTY AND MERCIFUL GOD, IN THIS TIME OF GRIEVOUS	045 03
OF MERCIES AND GOD OF ALL COMFORT, OUR ONLY HELP IN	045 12
O MERCIFUL GOD, AND HEAVENLY FATHER, WHO HAST TAUGHT	045 30
O ETERNAL GOD, WHO ALONE SPREADEST OUT THE HEAVENS,	046 08
O GOD, WHO SPAREST WHEN WE DESERVE PUNISHMENT,	046 18
THAT IT MAY PLEASE GOD TO CONFIRM AND STRENGTHEN IT	047 08
THE SAME PLANTED BY GOD IN THIS LAND, WHEREOF WE ARE	047 12
TO THE GLORY OF GOD, AND THE EDIFYING AND	047 18
THE DOCTRINE OF GOD OUR SAVIOUR	047 28
FITTED TO SERVE GOD IN THE MINISTRY AND IN THE STATE	047 31
FAITH AND FEAR OF GOD, AND IN BROTHERLY CHARITY ONE	048 03
YE SHALL ALSO PRAISE GOD FOR RAIN AND SUNSHINE	048 11
YE SHALL YIELD UNTO GOD MOST HIGH PRAISE AND HEARTY	048 15
AND PRAY UNTO GOD, THAT WE MAY HAVE GRACE TO DIRECT	048 19
THE HOLY GHOST, ONE GOD, WORLD WITHOUT END	049 10
ALMIGHTY GOD, THAT THE WORDS WHICH WE HAVE	049 17
ALMIGHTY GOD, THE FOUNTAIN OF ALL WISDOM, WHO KNOWEST	049 29
ALMIGHTY GOD, WHO HAST PROMISED TO HEAR THE PETITIONS	050 06
MOST GRACIOUS GOD, BY WHOSE KNOWLEDGE THE DEPTHS ARE	050 19
THANKS TO ALMIGHTY GOD FOR HER SAFE DELIVERANCE	R 051 04
O ALMIGHTY GOD, WE GIVE THEE HUMBLE THANKS FOR THAT	051 05
O GOD, OUR HEAVENLY FATHER, BY WHOSE GRACIOUS	051 15
O LORD GOD, WHO HAST JUSTLY HUMBLED US BY THY LATE	051 22
O ALMIGHTY GOD, WHO ART A STRONG TOWER OF DEFENCE	052 07
O ETERNAL GOD, OUR HEAVENLY FATHER, WHO ALONE MAKEST	052 17
O GOD, WHO ART THE GIVER OF LIFE, OF HEALTH, AND OF	052 29
ALMIGHTY GOD AND HEAVENLY FATHER, WE GIVE THEE HUMBLE	053 10
O GOD THE FATHER, CREATOR OF HEAVEN AND EARTH	054 05
O GOD THE SON, REDEEMER OF THE WORLD	054 07
O GOD THE HOLY GHOST, SANCTIFIER OF THE FAITHFUL	054 09
AND GLORIOUS TRINITY, ONE GOD	054 11
WE SINNERS DO BESEECH THEE TO HEAR US, O LORD GOD	055 18
SON OF GOD, WE BESEECH THEE TO HEAR US	057 19
O GOD, MERCIFUL FATHER, WHO DESPISEST NOT THE SIGHING	058 15
O GOD, WE HAVE HEARD WITH OUR EARS, AND OUR FATHERS	058 28
WITH GRATITUDE TO GOD, EMBRACE THE HAPPY OCCASION	VI 23
BESEECHING ALMIGHTY GOD TO ACCOMPANY WITH HIS	VI 40
MERCY UPON ME, O GOD, AFTER THY GREAT GOODNESS	060 10
ME A CLEAN HEART, O GOD, *	060 30
O GOD, THOU THAT ART THE GOD OF MY	061 06
THOU THAT ART THE GOD OF MY HEALTH	061 07
THE SACRIFICE OF GOD IS A TROUBLED SPIRIT	061 13
CONTRITE HEART, O GOD, SHALT THOU NOT DESPISE	061 14
HELP US, O GOD OUR SAVIOUR	062 02
O MOST MIGHTY GOD, AND MERCIFUL FATHER, WHO HAST	062 13
THOU ART A MERCIFUL GOD, FULL OF COMPASSION,	062 31
SHALL SAY, O GOD, WHOSE NATURE AND PROPERTY IS EVER	063 09
ALMIGHTY GOD, UNTO WHOM ALL HEARTS ARE OPEN, ALL	067 16
ASK GOD MERCY FOR THEIR TRANSGRESSIONS	R 067 24
GOD SPAKE THESE WORDS, AND SAID	068 03
I AM THE LORD THY GOD	068 04
FOR I THE LORD THY GOD AM A JEALOUS GOD, AND VISIT	068 12
THY GOD AM A JEALOUS GOD, AND VISIT THE SINS OF THE	068 12
NAME OF THE LORD THY GOD IN VAIN	068 18
SEVENTH DAY IS THE SABBATH OF THE LORD THY GOD	068 26
WHICH THE LORD THY GOD GIVETH THEE	069 04
LOVE THE LORD THY GOD WITH ALL THY HEART, AND WITH	069 27
AND EVERLASTING GOD, VOUCHSAFE, WE BESEECH THEE, TO	070 06
I BELIEVE IN ONE GOD THE FATHER ALMIGHTY, MAKER OF	071 02
ALL WORLDS, GOD OF GOD, LIGHT OF LIGHT, VERY GOD OF	071 05
THE ONLY-BEGOTTEN SON OF GOD	071 05
BEFORE ALL WORLDS, GOD OF GOD, LIGHT OF LIGHT, VERY	071 05
GOD OF GOD, LIGHT OF LIGHT, VERY GOD OF VERY GOD	071 06
LIGHT OF LIGHT, VERY GOD OF VERY GOD	071 06
FOR GOD LOVETH A CHEERFUL GIVER	072 19
GOD IS NOT UNRIGHTEOUS, THAT HE WILL FORGET YOUR	072 23
WITH SUCH SACRIFICES GOD IS WELL PLEASED	072 28
DWELLETH THE LOVE OF GOD IN HIM	072 31
OF THE LORD THY GOD WHICH HE HATH GIVEN THEE	073 17
AND EVERLIVING GOD, WHO BY THY HOLY APOSTLE HAST	074 06
THE COMMANDMENTS OF GOD, AND WALKING FROM HENCEFORTH	075 11
TO ALMIGHTY GOD, DEVOUTLY KNEELING	075 13
ALMIGHTY GOD, FATHER OF OUR LORD JESUS CHRIST,	075 17
ALMIGHTY GOD, OUR HEAVENLY FATHER, WHO OF HIS	076 02
SO GOD LOVED THE WORLD, THAT HE GAVE HIS	076 14
LET US GIVE THANKS UNTO OUR LORD GOD	076 28
EVERLASTING GOD	076 33

GOD CONTINUED

	PAGE LN
HOLY, LORD GOD OF HOSTS, HEAVEN AND EARTH ARE	077 08
HOLY GHOST, ART ONE GOD, ONE LORD, IN TRINITY OF	079 08
HOLY, LORD GOD OF HOSTS, HEAVEN AND EARTH ARE	079 32
BE TO THEE, ALMIGHTY GOD, OUR HEAVENLY FATHER, FOR	080 06
BE TO THEE, ALMIGHTY GOD, AND ENDING WITH THESE	R 083 09
AND EVERLIVING GOD, WE MOST HEARTILY THANK THEE, FOR	083 16
GLORY BE TO GOD ON HIGH, AND ON EARTH PEACE, GOOD	084 02
GOD, HEAVENLY KING, GOD THE FATHER ALMIGHTY	084 05
GREAT GLORY, O LORD GOD, HEAVENLY KING, GOD THE	084 05
O LORD GOD, LAMB OF GOD, SON OF THE FATHER, THAT	084 08
O LORD GOD, LAMB OF GOD, SON OF THE FATHER, THAT	084 08
AT THE RIGHT HAND OF GOD THE FATHER, HAVE MERCY UPON	084 11
HIGH IN THE GLORY OF GOD THE FATHER	084 15
THE PEACE OF GOD, WHICH PASSETH ALL UNDERSTANDING,	084 18
AND LOVE OF GOD, AND OF HIS SON JESUS CHRIST OUR	084 20
AND THE BLESSING OF GOD ALMIGHTY, THE FATHER, THE	084 21
AND HEARTY THANKS TO GOD, THE FATHER, THE SON, AND	086 05
SAVIOUR CHRIST, BOTH GOD AND MAN	086 08
US THE CHILDREN OF GOD, AND EXALT US TO EVERLASTING	086 11
THANKS TO ALMIGHTY GOD, OUR HEAVENLY FATHER, FOR THAT	087 02
AND AFTER THE MANNER OF DISSEMBLERS WITH GOD	087 12
REQUIRED BY GOD IN HOLY SCRIPTURE, AND BE RECEIVED AS	087 14
TO ALMIGHTY GOD, WITH FULL PURPOSE OF AMENDMENT OF	087 21
ARE NOT ONLY AGAINST GOD, BUT ALSO AGAINST YOUR	087 23
BE A BLASPHEMER OF GOD, AN HINDERER OR SLANDERER OF	087 31
CALLED AND BIDDEN BY GOD HIMSELF	088 17
ARE NOT SO EASILY ACCEPTED AND ALLOWED BEFORE GOD	088 29
WHEN GOD CALLETH YOU, ARE YE NOT ASHAMED TO SAY YE	088 32
YE SHOULD RETURN TO GOD, WILL YE EXCUSE YOURSELVES,	088 33
LITTLE SUCH FEIGNED EXCUSES WILL AVAIL BEFORE GOD	089 03
YOU IN THE NAME OF GOD, I CALL YOU IN CHRIST'S	089 07
AND AS THE SON OF GOD DID VOUCHSAFE TO YIELD UP HIS	089 10
YOUR INGRATITUDE TO GOD, AND HOW SORE PUNISHMENT	089 15
UNTO ALMIGHTY GOD, OUR HEAVENLY FATHER	089 22
ALMIGHTY GOD, GIVE US GRACE THAT WE MAY CAST AWAY THE	090 11
INTO THE TEMPLE OF GOD, AND CAST OUT ALL THEM THAT	091 33
NOW THE GOD OF PATIENCE AND CONSOLATION GRANT YOU TO	092 18
ONE MOUTH GLORIFY GOD, EVEN THE FATHER OF OUR LORD	092 20
AS CHRIST ALSO RECEIVED US TO THE GLORY OF GOD	092 23
FOR THE TRUTH OF GOD, TO CONFIRM THE PROMISES MADE	092 24
MIGHT GLORIFY GOD FOR HIS MERCY	092 26
NOW THE GOD OF HOPE FILL YOU WITH ALL JOY AND PEACE	092 32
THAT THE KINGDOM OF GOD IS NIGH AT HAND	093 18
SPIRIT EVER, ONE GOD, WORLD WITHOUT END	093 32
AND STEWARDS OF THE MYSTERIES OF GOD	094 04
AND THEN SHALL EVERY MAN HAVE PRAISE OF GOD	094 14
LET YOUR REQUESTS BE MADE KNOWN UNTO GOD	095 17
AND THE PEACE OF GOD, WHICH PASSETH ALL	095 17
ALMIGHTY GOD, WHO HAST GIVEN US THY ONLY-BEGOTTEN SON	096 13
SPIRIT EVER, ONE GOD, WORLD WITHOUT END	096 19
GOD, WHO AT SUNDRY TIMES AND IN DIVERS MANNERS SPAKE	096 22
ALL THE ANGELS OF GOD WORSHIP HIM	097 06
THY THRONE, O GOD, IS FOR EVER AND EVER	097 09
THEREFORE GOD, EVEN THY GOD, HATH ANOINTED THEE WITH	097 11
GOD, EVEN THY GOD, HATH ANOINTED THEE WITH THE OIL OF	097 12
AND THE WORD WAS WITH GOD, AND THE WORD WAS GOD	097 21
THE WORD WAS WITH GOD, AND THE WORD WAS GOD	097 21
THE SAME WAS IN THE BEGINNING WITH GOD	097 22
WAS A MAN SENT FROM GOD, WHOSE NAME WAS JOHN	097 26
BECOME THE SONS OF GOD, EVEN TO THEM THAT BELIEVE ON	097 34
NOR OF THE WILL OF MAN, BUT OF GOD	098 04
O GOD, WHO MAKEST US GLAD WITH THE YEARLY REMEMBRANCE	098 11
THE HOLY GHOST, ONE GOD, WORLD WITHOUT END	098 16
THE GRACE OF GOD THAT BRINGETH SALVATION HATH	098 18
OF THE GREAT GOD AND OUR SAVIOUR JESUS CHRIST	098 22
HOST PRAISING GOD, AND SAYING, GLORY TO GOD IN THE	099 20
AND SAYING, GLORY TO GOD IN THE HIGHEST, AND ON EARTH	099 21
AT THE RIGHT HAND OF GOD TO SUCCOUR ALL THOSE WHO	100 02
AND SAW THE GLORY OF GOD, AND JESUS STANDING ON THE	100 06
ON THE RIGHT HAND OF GOD, AND SAID, BEHOLD, I SEE THE	100 07
THE SON OF MAN STANDING ON THE RIGHT HAND OF GOD	100 09
CALLING UPON GOD, AND SAYING, LORD JESUS, RECEIVE MY	100 14
UNTO YOU, THAT GOD IS LIGHT, AND IN HIM IS NO	101 23
O ALMIGHTY GOD, WHO OUT OF THE MOUTHS OF BABES AND	102 21
THE FIRSTFRUITS UNTO GOD AND TO THE LAMB	103 12
THEY ARE WITHOUT FAULT BEFORE THE THRONE OF GOD	103 14
ALMIGHTY GOD, WHO HAST GIVEN US THY ONLY-BEGOTTEN SON	104 05
SPIRIT EVER, ONE GOD, WORLD WITHOUT END	104 11
THE TIME WAS COME, GOD SENT FORTH HIS SON, MADE OF A	104 19
BECAUSE YE ARE SONS, GOD HATH SENT FORTH THE SPIRIT	104 22
THEN AN HEIR OF GOD THROUGH CHRIST	104 25
INTERPRETED IS, GOD WITH US	105 12
ALMIGHTY GOD, WHO MADEST THY BLESSED SON TO BE	105 19
GOD ALSO HATH HIGHLY EXALTED HIM, AND GIVEN HIM A	105 26
TO THE GLORY OF GOD THE FATHER	105 31
FOR IT IS GOD WHICH WORKETH IN YOU BOTH TO WILL AND	106 04
AND PRAISING GOD FOR ALL THE THINGS THAT THEY HAD	106 18
ALMIGHTY GOD, WHO HAST POURED UPON US THE NEW LIGHT	106 25
SPIRIT OF THE LORD GOD IS UPON ME	106 30
AND THE DAY OF VENGEANCE OF OUR GOD	107 05
BEING WARNED OF GOD IN A DREAM, HE TURNED ASIDE INTO	107 20
O GOD, WHO BY THE LEADING OF A STAR DIDST MANIFEST	107 29
OF THE GRACE OF GOD, WHICH IS GIVEN ME TO YOU-WARD	108 08
GIFT OF THE GRACE OF GOD GIVEN UNTO ME BY THE	108 17
HATH BEEN HID IN GOD, WHO CREATED ALL THINGS BY JESUS	108 22
MANIFOLD WISDOM OF GOD, ACCORDING TO THE ETERNAL	108 25
AND BEING WARNED OF GOD IN A DREAM THAT THEY SHOULD	109 24
BY THE MERCIES OF GOD, THAT YE PRESENT YOUR BODIES A	110 04
ACCEPTABLE UNTO GOD, WHICH IS YOUR REASONABLE	110 05
AND PERFECT, WILL OF GOD	110 09
ACCORDING AS GOD HATH DEALT TO EVERY MAN THE MEASURE	110 12
AND IN FAVOUR WITH GOD AND MAN	111 07
AND EVERLASTING GOD, WHO DOST GOVERN ALL THINGS IN	111 10
OF THE GOSPEL OF JESUS CHRIST, THE SON OF GOD	112 04

GOD   CONTINUED

AND EVERLASTING GOD, MERCIFULLY LOOK UPCN OUR	112 26
O GOD, WHO KNOWEST US TO BE SET IN THE MIDST OF SC	114 04
FOR THERE IS NO POWER BUT OF GCD	114 12
THE POWERS THAT BE ARE ORDAINED OF GOD	114 13
THE POWER, RESISTETH THE ORDINANCE OF GOD	114 14
IS THE MINISTER OF GOD TO THEE FOR GOOD	114 18
IS THE MINISTER OF GOD, A REVENGER TO EXECUTE WRATH	114 21
AS THE ELECT OF GOD, HOLY AND BELOVED, A HEART OF	116 03
AND LET THE PEACE OF GOD RULE IN YOUR HEARTS, IC THE	116 09
GIVING THANKS TO GOD AND THE FATHER BY HIM	116 15
O GOD, WHOSE BLESSED SON WAS MANIFESTED THAT HE MIGHT	117 04
MAKE US THE SONS OF GOD, AND HEIRS OF ETERNAL LIFE	117 06
REIGNETH EVER, ONE GOD, WORLD WITHOUT END	117 12
THAT WE SHOULD BE CALLED THE SCNS OF GOD	117 16
ARE WE THE SONS OF GOD, AND IT DOTH NOT YET APPEAR	117 17
PURPOSE THE SON OF GOD WAS MANIFESTED, THAT HE MIGHT	117 29
HOLY GHOST EVER, ONE GOD, WORLD WITHOUT END	119 03
O LORD GOD, WHO SEEST THAT WE PUT NOT OUR TRUST IN	120 17
THE GOD AND FATHER OF OUR LORD JESUS CHRIST, WHICH IS	121 14
GIVEN TO KNOW THE MYSTERIES OF THE KINGDOM OF GCD	121 30
THE SEED IS THE WORD OF GOD	121 33
HIS SIGHT, AND FOLLOWED HIM, GLORIFYING GOD	124 05
WHEN THEY SAW IT, GAVE PRAISE UNTO GOD	124 06
AND EVERLASTING GOD, WHO HATEST NOTHING THAT THOU	124 11
OBTAIN OF THEE, THE GOD OF ALL MERCY, PERFECT	124 16
YOUR GARMENTS, AND TURN UNTO THE LORD YOUR GOD	124 24
AND A DRINK-OFFERING UNTO THE LORD YOUR GOD	124 28
THEY SAY AMONG THE PEOPLE, WHERE IS THEIR GOD	125 07
THE HOLY GHOST, ONE GOD, WORLD WITHOUT END	125 32
NOT THE GRACE OF GOD IN VAIN	126 04
AS THE MINISTERS OF GOD, IN MUCH PATIENCE, IN	126 10
BY THE POWER OF GOD, BY THE ARMOUR OF RIGHTEOUSNESS	126 15
THOU BE THE SON OF GOD, COMMAND THAT THESE STONES BE	126 27
WORD THAT PROCEEDETH OUT OF THE MOUTH OF GOD	126 30
THOU BE THE SON OF GOD, CAST THYSELF DCWN	126 32
THOU SHALT NOT TEMPT THE LORD THY GOD	127 04
WORSHIP THE LORD THY GOD, AND HIM ONLY SHALT THCU	127 10
ALMIGHTY GOD, WHO SEEST THAT WE HAVE NO PCWER OF	127 15
WALK AND TO PLEASE GOD, SO YE WOULD ABOUND MORE AND	127 25
THIS IS THE WILL OF GOD, EVEN YOUR SANCTIFICATICN,	127 27
EVEN AS THE GENTILES WHICH KNOW NOT GOD	127 31
FOR GOD HATH NOT CALLED US UNTO UNCLEANNESS, BUT UNTO	128 02
NOT MAN, BUT GOD, WHO HATH ALSO GIVEN UNTO US HIS	128 04
ALMIGHTY GOD, LOOK UPON THE HEARTY DESIRES OF	128 25
FOLLOWERS OF GOD, AS DEAR CHILDREN	128 30
AND A SACRIFICE TO GOD FOR A SWEET-SMELLING SAVOUR	128 32
INHERITANCE IN THE KINGDOM OF CHRIST AND OF GOD	129 09
COMETH THE WRATH OF GOD UPON THE CHILDREN OF	129 10
I WITH THE FINGER OF GOD CAST CUT DEVILS, NO DOUBT	130 03
DOUBT THE KINGDOM OF GOD IS COME UPON YOU	130 04
HEAR THE WORD OF GOD, AND KEEP IT	130 21
ALMIGHTY GOD, THAT WE, WHO FOR OUR EVIL DEEDS	130 24
ALMIGHTY GOD, MERCIFULLY TO LOOK UPON THY	132 18
WITHOUT SPOT AND DEAD, PURGE YOUR CONSCIENCE FROM CEAD	133 02
FROM DEAD WORKS TO SERVE THE LIVING GOD	133 03
HE THAT IS OF GOD HEARETH GOD'S WORDS	133 11
HEAR THEM NOT, BECAUSE YE ARE NOT OF GOD	133 12
OF WHOM YE SAY, THAT HE IS YOUR GOD	133 25
AND EVERLASTING GOD, WHO, OF THY TENDER LOVE TOWARDS	134 05
BEING IN THE FORM OF GOD, THOUGHT IT NCT RCBBERY TO	134 17
THOUGHT IT NOT ROBBERY TO BE EQUAL WITH GCD	134 18
WHEREFORE GOD ALSO HATH HIGHLY EXALTED HIM, AND GIVEN	134 22
TO THE GLORY OF GOD THE FATHER	134 27
THOU BE THE SON OF GOD, COME DOWN FROM THE CROSS	137 08
HE TRUSTED IN GOD	137 12
FOR HE SAID, I AM THE SON OF GOD	137 13
TO SAY, MY GOD, MY GOD, WHY HAST THOU FORSAKEN ME	137 18
THAT IS TO SAY, MY GOD, MY GOD, WHY HAST THCU	137 18
TRULY THIS WAS THE SON OF GOD	137 34
ALMIGHTY GOD, WHOSE MOST DEAR SON WENT NOT UP TC JOY	138 04
DAY THAT I DRINK IT NEW IN THE KINGDOM OF GOD	141 16
O LORD GOD, WHOSE BLESSED SON, OUR SAVIOUR, GAVE HIS	144 06
THE LORD GOD HATH OPENED MINE EAR, AND I WAS NOT	144 12
FOR THE LORD GOD WILL HELP ME	144 16
BEHOLD, THE LORD GOD WILL HELP ME	144 20
IN THE NAME OF THE LORD, AND STAY UPON HIS GOD	144 26
MY GOD, MY GOD, WHY HAST THOU FORSAKEN ME	146 29
MY GOD, MY GOD, WHY HAST THOU FORSAKEN	146 29
TRULY THIS MAN WAS THE SON OF GOD	147 05
THY HELP, O LORD GOD OF OUR SALVATION	147 08
THE TESTAMENT WHICH GOD HATH ENJOINED UNTO YOU	147 23
IN THE PRESENCE OF GOD FOR US	147 32
UNTIL IT BE FULFILLED IN THE KINGDOM OF GOD	149 05
UNTIL THE KINGDOM OF GOD SHALL COME	149 08
OF MAN SIT ON THE RIGHT HAND OF THE POWER OF GOD	151 33
ART THOU THEN THE SON OF GOD	151 34
SPIRIT EVER, ONE GOD, WORLD WITHOUT END	152 13
IF HE BE CHRIST, THE CHOSEN OF GOD	154 29
DOST NOT THOU FEAR GOD, SEEING THOU ART IN THE SAME	155 03
HE GLORIFIED GOD, SAYING, CERTAINLY THIS WAS A	155 15
AND THAT HE WAS COME FROM GOD, AND WENT TO GOD	155 30
HE WAS COME FROM GOD, AND WENT TO GOD	155 30
ALMIGHTY GOD, WE BESEECH THEE GRACIOUSLY TO BEHOLC	156 21
HOLY GHOST EVER, ONE GOD, WORLD WITHOUT END	156 26
AND EVERLASTING GOD, BY WHOSE SPIRIT THE WHOLE BCDY	156 27
O MERCIFUL GOD, WHO HAST MADE ALL MEN, AND HATEST	157 04
THE HOLY SPIRIT, ONE GOD, WORLD WITHOUT END	157 13
BOOK IT IS WRITTEN OF ME,) TO DO THY WILL, O GOD	157 28
THEN SAID HE, LO, I COME TO DO THY WILL, O GOD	157 32
SAT DOWN ON THE RIGHT HAND OF GOD	158 07
AND HAVING AN HIGH PRIEST OVER THE HOUSE OF GOD	158 20
TO DIE, BECAUSE HE MADE HIMSELF THE SON OF GOD	159 10
IF THE WILL OF GOD BE SO, THAT YE SUFFER FOR WELL	161 21
HE MIGHT BRING US TO GOD, BEING PUT TO DEATH IN THE	161 24

GOD   CONTINUED

LONG-SUFFERING OF GOD WAITED IN THE DAYS OF NOAH,	161 27
CONSCIENCE TOWARD GOD,) BY THE RESURRECTICN OF JESUS	161 32
AND IS ON THE RIGHT HAND OF GOD	162 03
BUT IN THAT HE LIVETH, HE LIVETH UNTO GOD	163 07
BUT ALIVE UNTO GOD THROUGH JESUS CHRIST OUR LORD	163 09
ALMIGHTY GOD, WHO THROUGH THINE ONLY-BEGCTTEN SCN	163 22
HOLY GHOST EVER, ONE GOD, WORLD WITHOUT END	163 29
WHERE CHRIST SITTETH ON THE RIGHT HAND OF GOD	164 05
AND YOUR LIFE IS HID WITH CHRIST IN GOD	164 07
O GOD, WHO FOR OUR REDEMPTION DIDST GIVE THINE	165 03
O GOD, WHOSE BLESSED SON DID MANIFEST HIMSELF TC HIS	166 06
I PERCEIVE THAT GOD IS NO RESPECTER OF PERSONS	166 13
THE WORD WHICH GOD SENT UNTO THE CHILDREN CF ISRAEL,	166 15
HOW GOD ANOINTED JESUS OF NAZARETH WITH THE HOLY	166 19
FOR GOD WAS WITH HIM	166 22
HIM GOD RAISED UP THE THIRD DAY, AND SHEWED HIM	166 24
CHOSEN BEFORE OF GOD, EVEN TO US, WHO DID EAT AND	166 26
WAS ORDAINED OF GOD TO BE THE JUDGE OF QUICK ANC	166 29
DEED AND WORD BEFORE GOD AND ALL THE PEOPLE	167 17
ALMIGHTY GOD, THAT WE WHO CELEBRATE WITH	168 19
AMONG YOU FEARETH GOD, TO YOU IS THE WORD OF THIS	168 25
BUT GOD RAISED HIM FROM THE DEAD	169 02
UNTO THE FATHERS, GOD HATH FULFILLED THE SAME UNTO US	169 07
BY THE WILL OF GOD, FELL ON SLEEP, AND WAS LAID UNTO	169 16
BUT HE, WHOM GOD RAISED AGAIN, SAW NC CORRUPTION	169 17
IS BORN OF GOD OVERCOMETH THE WORLD	170 26
HE THAT BELIEVETH THAT JESUS IS THE SON OF GOD	170 29
THE WITNESS OF GOD IS GREATER	171 05
IS THE WITNESS OF GOD WHICH HE HATH TESTIFIED CF HIS	171 05
ON THE SON OF GOD HATH THE WITNESS IN HIMSELF	171 07
THAT BELIEVETH NOT GOD HATH MADE HIM A LIAR	171 08
NOT THE RECORD THAT GOD GAVE OF HIS SON	171 09
IS THE RECORD, THAT GOD HATH GIVEN TO US ETERNAL	171 10
HATH NOT THE SON OF GOD HATH NOT LIFE	171 12
ALMIGHTY GOD, WHO HAST GIVEN THINE ONLY SON TO BE	171 28
CONSCIENCE TOWARD GOD ENDURE GRIEF, SUFFERING	172 06
THIS IS ACCEPTABLE WITH GOD	172 09
ALMIGHTY GOD, WHO SHOWEST TO THEM THAT ARE IN ERROR	173 04
BEHOLD, GLORIFY GOD IN THE DAY OF VISITATION	173 17
SO IS THE WILL OF GOD, THAT WITH WELL DOING YE MAY	173 21
BUT AS THE SERVANTS OF GOD	173 24
FEAR GOD	173 25
O ALMIGHTY GOD, WHO ALONE CANST ORDER THE UNRULY	174 18
WRATH OF MAN WORKETH NOT THE RIGHTEOUSNESS CF GCD	175 02
AND UNDEFILED BEFORE GOD AND THE FATHER IS THIS,	176 16
AND HAVE BELIEVED THAT I CAME OUT FROM GOD	176 30
THIS WE BELIEVE THAT THOU CAMEST FORTH FROM GOD	177 03
ALMIGHTY GOD, THAT LIKE AS WE DO BELIEVE THY	177 14
THE HOLY GHOST, ONE GOD, WORLD WITHOUT END	177 19
OF THE THINGS PERTAINING TO THE KINGDOM OF GOD	177 29
IN THE TEMPLE, PRAISING AND BLESSING GOD	178 29
O GOD, THE KING OF GLORY, WHO HAST EXALTED THINE CNLY	179 04
SAME HOLY GHOST, ONE GOD, WORLD WITHOUT END	179 10
AS GOOD STEWARDS OF THE MANIFOLD GRACE OF GCD	179 18
MAN SPEAK, LET HIM SPEAK AS THE ORACLES OF GOD	179 19
THAT GOD IN ALL THINGS MAY BE GLORIFIED THROUGH JESUS	179 20
OF THE ABILITY WHICH GOD GIVETH	179 20
THINK THAT HE DOETH GOD SERVICE	179 31
O GOD, WHO AS AT THIS TIME DIDST TEACH THE HEARTS CF	180 08
THE SAME SPIRIT, ONE GOD, WORLD WITHOUT END	180 14
SPEAK IN OUR TONGUES THE WONDERFUL WORKS OF GOD	181 06
AND MOST MERCIFUL GOD, GRANT, WE BESEECH THEE, THAT	182 15
SPIRIT EVER, ONE GOD, WORLD WITHOUT END	182 19
BUT IT IS THE SAME GOD WHICH WORKETH ALL IN ALL	182 25
ALMIGHTY GOD, THY HOLY SPIRIT INTO OUR HEARTS,	183 22
AND REIGNETH, ONE GOD, WORLD WITHOUT END	183 27
I PERCEIVE THAT GOD IS NO RESPECTER OF PERSCNS	183 30
THE WORD WHICH GOD SENT UNTO THE CHILDREN CF ISRAEL,	184 02
HOW GOD ANOINTED JESUS OF NAZARETH WITH THE HOLY	184 06
FOR GOD WAS WITH HIM	184 09
HIM GOD RAISED UP THE THIRD DAY, AND SHEWED HIM	184 12
CHOSEN BEFORE OF GOD, EVEN TO US, WHO DID EAT ANC	184 14
WAS ORDAINED OF GOD TO BE THE JUDGE OF QUICK AND	184 17
HEARD THEM SPEAK WITH TONGUES, AND MAGNIFY GOD	184 25
GOD SO LOVED THE WORLD, THAT HE GAVE HIS	184 32
FOR GOD SENT NOT HIS SON INTO THE WORLD TO CONDEMN	184 34
IN THE NAME OF THE ONLY-BEGOTTEN SON OF GOD	185 05
THAT THEY ARE WROUGHT IN GOD	185 11
MERCIFUL GOD, THAT THY CHURCH, BEING GATHERED	185 14
THE SAME SPIRIT, ONE GOD, WORLD WITHOUT END	185 19
RECEIVED THE WORD OF GOD, THEY SENT UNTO THEM PETER	185 22
AND EVERLASTING GOD, WHO HAST GIVEN UNTO US THY	186 23
AND REIGNEST, ONE GOD, WORLD WITHOUT END	186 29
WHICH ARE THE SEVEN SPIRITS OF GOD	187 14
HOLY, LORD GOD ALMIGHTY, WHICH WAS, AND IS, AND	187 23
WE KNOW THAT THOU ART A TEACHER COME FROM GCD	188 03
THOU DOEST, EXCEPT GOD BE WITH HIM	188 04
HE CANNOT SEE THE KINGDOM OF GOD	188 06
HE CANNOT ENTER INTO THE KINGDOM OF GOD	188 11
O GOD, THE STRENGTH OF ALL THOSE WHO PUT THEIR TRUST	188 32
FOR LOVE IS OF GOD	189 08
LOVETH IS BORN OF GOD, AND KNOWETH GOD	189 09
ONE THAT LOVETH IS BORN OF GOD, AND KNOWETH GOD	189 10
HE THAT LOVETH NOT KNOWETH NOT GOD	189 10
FOR GOD IS LOVE	189 10
THE LOVE OF GOD TOWARD US, BECAUSE THAT GOD SENT HIS	189 11
BECAUSE THAT GOD SENT HIS ONLY-BEGOTTEN SON INTO	189 12
NOT THAT WE LOVED GOD, BUT THAT HE LOVED US, AND SENT	189 14
IF GOD SO LOVED US, WE OUGHT ALSO TO LOVE	189 15
WE LOVE ONE ANOTHER, GOD DWELLETH IN US, AND HIS LOVE	189 17
NO MAN HATH SEEN GOD AT ANY TIME	189 17
IS THE SON OF GOD, GOD DWELLETH IN HIM, AND HE IN	189 22
JESUS IS THE SON OF GOD, GOD DWELLETH IN HIM, AND HE	189 22
SON OF GOD, GOD DWELLETH IN HIM, AND HE IN GOD	189 23

GOD   CONTINUED   GOD   CONTINUED

THE LOVE THAT GOD HATH TO US   189 24   FOR THOU HAST FOUND FAVOUR WITH GOD   236 14
GOD IS LOVE   189 24   AND THE LORD GOD SHALL GIVE UNTO HIM THE THRONE CF   236 17
IN LOVE DWELLETH IN GOD, AND GOD IN HIM   189 25   BE BORN OF THEE SHALL BE CALLED THE SON OF GOD   236 25
DWELLETH IN GOD, AND GOD IN HIM   189 25   FOR WITH GOD NOTHING SHALL BE IMPOSSIBLE   236 27
IF A MAN SAY, I LOVE GOD, AND HATETH HIS BROTHER, 189 31   O ALMIGHTY GOD, WHO HAST INSTRUCTED THY HOLY CHURCH 237 05
HOW CAN HE LOVE GOD WHOM HE HATH NOT SEEN   189 33   OF THE SON OF GOD, UNTO A PERFECT MAN, UNTO THE   237 23
THAT HE WHO LOVETH GOD LOVE HIS BROTHER ALSO   189 35   O ALMIGHTY GOD, WHOM TRULY TO KNOW IS EVERLASTING   238 29
WE THE LOVE OF GOD, BECAUSE HE LAID DOWN HIS LIFE FOR 191 16 A SERVANT OF GOD AND OF THE LORD JESUS CHRIST,   239 06
DWELLETH THE LOVE OF GOD IN HIM   191 21   LET HIM ASK OF GOD, THAT GIVETH TO ALL MEN LIBERALLY, 239 12
HEART CONDEMN US, GOD IS GREATER THAN OUR HEART, AND 191 24 YE BELIEVE IN GOD, BELIEVE ALSO IN ME   239 30
THEN HAVE WE CONFIDENCE TOWARD GOD   191 27   O LORD GOD ALMIGHTY, WHO DIDST ENDUE THY HOLY APOSTLE 240 28
FOR GOD RESISTETH THE PROUD, AND GIVETH GRACE TC THE 192 31 SEEN THE GRACE OF GOD, WAS GLAD, AND EXHORTED THEM   241 06
THE MIGHTY HAND OF GOD, THAT HE MAY EXALT YCU IN DUE 193 02 ALMIGHTY GOD, BY WHOSE PROVIDENCE THY SERVANT JCHN   242 07
BUT THE GOD OF ALL GRACE, WHO HATH CALLED US UNTO HIS 193 08 COMFORT YE MY PEOPLE, SAITH YOUR GOD   242 16
OF THE ANGELS OF GOD OVER ONE SINNER THAT REPENTETH 193 33 MAKE STRAIGHT IN THE DESERT A HIGHWAY FOR OUR GOD   242 22
O GOD, THE PROTECTOR OF ALL THAT TRUST IN THEE,   194 04   BUT THE WORD OF OUR GOD SHALL STAND FOR EVER   242 32
WAITETH FOR THE MANIFESTATION OF THE SONS OF GOD 194 14   SAY UNTO THE CITIES OF JUDAH, BEHOLD YOUR GCD   243 05
INTO THE GLORIOUS LIBERTY OF THE CHILDREN OF GOD 194 19   BEHOLD, THE LORD GOD WILL COME WITH STRONG HAND,   243 06
SANCTIFY THE LORD GOD IN YOUR HEARTS   196 04   HIS TONGUE LOOSED, AND HE SPAKE, AND PRAISED GOD   243 26
TO HEAR THE WORD OF GOD, HE STOOD BY THE LAKE OF 196 07   BLESSED BE THE LORD GOD OF ISRAEL   243 33
O GOD, WHO HAST PREPARED FOR THOSE WHO LOVE THEE SUCH 197 04 THROUGH THE TENDER MERCY OF OUR GOD   244 13
BUT IN THAT HE LIVETH, HE LIVETH UNTO GOD   197 24   O ALMIGHTY GOD, WHO BY THY SON JESUS CHRIST DIDST   244 22
BUT ALIVE UNTO GOD THROUGH JESUS CHRIST OUR   197 26   OF THE CHURCH UNTO GOD FOR HIM   245 08
BECOME SERVANTS TO GOD, YE HAVE YOUR FRUIT UNTO   199 03   THE SON OF THE LIVING GOD   246 03
BUT THE GIFT OF GOD IS ETERNAL LIFE THROUGH JESUS 199 05   GRANT, O MERCIFUL GOD, THAT, AS THINE HOLY APOSTLE   246 16
O GOD, WHOSE NEVER-FAILING PROVIDENCE ORDERETH ALL 199 28   O GOD, WHO ON THE MOUNT DIDST REVEAL TO CHOSEN   247 31
BY THE SPIRIT OF GOD, THEY ARE THE SONS OF GOD   200 07   AND REIGNETH, ONE GOD, WORLD WITHOUT END   248 06
LED BY THE SPIRIT OF GOD, THEY ARE THE SCNS OF GCD 200 07   FOR HE RECEIVED FROM GOD THE FATHER HONOUR AND GLORY, 248 17
WITH OUR SPIRIT, THAT WE ARE THE CHILDREN CF GOD 200 11   AND EVERLASTING GOD, WHO DIDST GIVE TO THINE APCSTLE 249 14
HEIRS OF GOD, AND JOINT-HEIRS WITH CHRIST   200 12   O ALMIGHTY GOD, WHO BY THY BLESSED SON DIDST CALL   250 20
WITH MANY OF THEM GOD WAS NOT WELL PLEASED   201 11   THE HOLY GHOST, ONE GOD, WORLD WITHOUT END   250 25
BUT GOD IS FAITHFUL, WHO WILL NOT SUFFER YCU TO BE 201 27   HANDLING THE WORD OF GOD DECEITFULLY   250 30
BY THE SPIRIT OF GOD CALLETH JESUS ACCURSED   203 20   TO EVERY MAN'S CONSCIENCE IN THE SIGHT OF GOD   250 32
BUT IT IS THE SAME GOD WHICH WORKETH ALL IN ALL   203 25   IN WHOM THE GOD OF THIS WORLD HATH BLINDED THE MINDS 251 02
O GOD, WHO DECLAREST THY ALMIGHTY POWER CHIEFLY IN 204 22   WHO IS THE IMAGE OF GOD, SHOULD SHINE UNTO THEM   251 05
BECAUSE I PERSECUTED THE CHURCH OF GOD   205 14   FOR GOD, WHO COMMANDED THE LIGHT TO SHINE OUT OF   251 07
BUT BY THE GRACE OF GOD I AM WHAT I AM   205 15   OF THE GLORY OF GOD IN THE FACE OF JESUS CHRIST   251 09
BUT THE GRACE OF GOD WHICH WAS WITH ME   205 17   O EVERLASTING GOD, WHO HAST ORDAINED AND CONSTITUTED 251 27
THUS WITH HIMSELF, GOD, I THANK THEE, THAT I AM NOT 205 25 THE KINGDOM OF OUR GOD, AND THE POWER OF HIS CHRIST 252 11
HIS BREAST, SAYING, GOD BE MERCIFUL TO ME A SINNER 205 30   THEM BEFORE OUR GOD DAY AND NIGHT   252 13
AND EVERLASTING GOD, WHO ART ALWAYS MORE READY TC 206 04   ALMIGHTY GOD, WHO DIDST INSPIRE THY SERVANT SAINT   253 16
BUT OUR SUFFICIENCY IS OF GOD   206 15   O ALMIGHTY GOD, WHO HAST BUILT THY CHURCH UPON THE   254 27
AND MERCIFUL GOD, OF WHOSE ONLY GIFT IT COMETH THAT 207 12 WITH THE SAINTS, AND OF THE HOUSEHOLD OF GOD   255 05
CONFIRMED BEFORE OF GOD IN CHRIST, THE LAW, WHICH WAS 207 22 FOR AN HABITATION OF GOD THROUGH THE SPIRIT   255 10
BUT GOD GAVE IT TO ABRAHAM BY PROMISE   207 26   O ALMIGHTY GOD, WHO HAST KNIT TOGETHER THINE ELECT IN 256 05
MEDIATOR OF ONE, BUT GOD IS ONE   207 30   FROM THE EAST, HAVING THE SEAL OF THE LIVING GOD   256 15
IS THE LAW THEN AGAINST THE PROMISES OF GOD   207 31   THE SERVANTS OF OUR GOD IN THEIR FOREHEADS   256 19
GOD FORBID   207 31   SALVATION TO OUR GOD WHICH SITTETH UPON THE THRONE, 256 27
LOVE THE LORD THY GOD WITH ALL THY HEART, AND WITH 208 15   AND WORSHIPPED GOD, SAYING, AMEN   256 31
AND EVERLASTING GOD, GIVE UNTO US THE INCREASE CF 209 08   BE UNTO OUR GOD FOR EVER AND EVER   257 02
SUCH THINGS SHALL NOT INHERIT THE KINGDOM CF GCD 209 25   BEFORE THE THRONE OF GOD, AND SERVE HIM DAY AND NIGHT 257 10
LOUD VOICE GLORIFIED GOD, AND FELL DOWN ON HIS FACE 210 09 AND GOD SHALL WIPE AWAY ALL TEARS FROM THEIR EYES   257 15
TO GIVE GLORY TO GOD, SAVE THIS STRANGER   210 13   FOR THEY SHALL SEE GOD   257 27
BUT GOD FORBID THAT I SHOULD GLORY, SAVE IN THE CROSS 210 29 FOR THEY SHALL BE CALLED THE CHILDREN OF GOD   257 28
BE ON THEM, AND MERCY, AND UPON THE ISRAEL CF GCD 211 04   AND EVERLASTING GOD, WHO DOST ENKINDLE THE FLAME CF 258 04
YE CANNOT SERVE GOD AND MAMMON   211 11   O ALMIGHTY GOD, WHO HAST CALLED US TO FAITH IN THEE, 258 11
BUT IF GOD DOTH SO CLOTHE THE GRASS OF THE FIELD, 211 24   SET DOWN AT THE RIGHT HAND OF THE THRONE OF GOD   258 26
YE MIGHT BE FILLED WITH ALL THE FULNESS OF GOD   212 21   O GOD, WHOM YEAR BY YEAR WE PRAISE FOR THE DEDICATICN 259 19
AND THEY GLORIFIED GOD, SAYING, THAT A GREAT PROPHET 213 07 BUT CHOSEN OF GOD, AND PRECIOUS, YE ALSO,   259 30
THAT GOD HATH VISITED HIS PEOPLE   213 08   ACCEPTABLE TO GOD BY JESUS CHRIST   259 32
ONE BAPTISM, ONE GOD AND FATHER OF ALL, WHO IS ABCVE 213 24 INTO THE TEMPLE OF GOD, AND CAST OUT ALL THEM THAT   260 03
HEARTS AND MINDS TO FOLLOW THEE, THE ONLY GCD   214 26   O ALMIGHTY GOD, WHO HAST COMMITTED TO THE HANDS CF   260 19
I THANK MY GOD ALWAYS ON YOUR BEHALF, FOR THE GRACE 214 28 THE WHOLE CITY TOGETHER TO HEAR THE WORD OF GOD   260 27
FOR THE GRACE OF GOD WHICH IS GIVEN YCU BY JESUS 214 29   THAT THE WORD OF GOD SHOULD FIRST HAVE BEEN SPOKEN TO 260 31
LOVE THE LORD THY GOD WITH ALL THY HEART, AND WITH 215 11   ALMIGHTY GOD, LORD OF HEAVEN AND EARTH   261 29
O GOD, FORASMUCH AS WITHOUT THEE WE ARE NOT ABLE TO 215 27 I THE LORD THEIR GOD AM WITH THEM, AND THAT THEY,   262 20
FROM THE LIFE OF GOD THROUGH THE IGNORANCE THAT IS IN 216 06 OF ISRAEL, ARE MY PEOPLE, SAITH THE LORD GOD   262 22
NEW MAN, WHICH AFTER GOD IS CREATED IN RIGHTEOUSNESS 216 15 AND I AM YOUR GOD, SAITH THE LORD GOD   262 23
THE HOLY SPIRIT OF GOD, WHEREBY YE ARE SEALED UNTO 216 26   AND I AM YOUR GOD, SAITH THE LORD GOD   262 24
ONE ANOTHER, EVEN AS GOD FOR CHRIST'S SAKE HATH   216 30   O ETERNAL GOD, THROUGH WHOSE MIGHTY POWER OUR FATHERS 263 17
AND GLORIFIED GOD, WHICH HAD GIVEN SUCH POWER UNTO 217 13   THE LORD YOUR GOD IS GOD OF GODS, AND LORD OF LCRDS, 263 23
AND MOST MERCIFUL GOD, OF THY BOUNTIFUL GOODNESS KEEP 217 17 THE LORD YOUR GOD IS GOD OF GODS, AND LORD OF LORDS, 263 23
FOR ALL THINGS UNTO GOD AND THE FATHER IN THE NAME OF 217 30 OF LORDS, A GREAT GOD, A MIGHTY, AND A TERRIBLE,   263 24
YOURSELVES ONE TO ANOTHER IN THE FEAR OF GCD   217 32   THOU SHALT FEAR THE LORD THY GOD   263 29
THE WHOLE ARMOUR OF GOD, THAT YE MAY BE ABLE TO STAND 219 06 AND HE IS THY GOD, THAT HATH DONE FOR THEE THESE   263 31
THE WHOLE ARMOUR OF GOD, THAT YE MAY BE ABLE TO   219 11   IT IS A GOOD THING TO SING PRAISES UNTO OUR GOD   264 19
THE SWORD OF THE SPIRIT, WHICH IS THE WORD OF GCC 219 19   SING PRAISES UPON THE HARP UNTO OUR GOD   264 26
I THANK MY GOD UPON EVERY REMEMBRANCE OF YOU,   220 22   PRAISE THY GOD, O SION   264 32
FOR GOD IS MY RECORD, HOW GREATLY I LONG AFTER YOU 220 31   WRATH OF MAN WORKETH NOT THE RIGHTEOUSNESS OF GOD   265 25
UNTO THE GLORY AND PRAISE OF GOD   221 07   AND UNDEFILED BEFORE GOD AND THE FATHER IS THIS,   266 07
O GOD, OUR REFUGE AND STRENGTH, WHO ART THE AUTHCR OF 222 09 IF GOD SO CLOTHE THE GRASS OF THE FIELD,   266 22
WHOSE GOD IS THEIR BELLY, AND WHOSE   222 19   FIRST THE KINGDOM OF GOD, AND HIS RIGHTEOUSNESS   266 29
TEACHEST THE WAY OF GOD IN TRUTH, NEITHER CAREST THCU 222 31 O ETERNAL GOD, WE HUMBLY BESEECH THEE, FAVOURABLY TO 267 04
AND UNTO GOD THE THINGS THAT ARE GOD'S   223 10   FOR ALL THINGS UNTO GOD AND THE FATHER IN THE NAME CF 267 11
WE GIVE THANKS TO GOD AND THE FATHER OF OUR LORD 223 22   YOURSELVES ONE TO ANOTHER IN THE FEAR OF GOD   267 13
KNEW THE GRACE OF GOD IN TRUTH   223 29   WHAT THEREFORE GOD HATH JOINED TOGETHER, LET NOT MAN 268 10
AND INCREASING IN THE KNOWLEDGE OF GOD   224 06   O ETERNAL LORD GOD, WHO HOLDEST ALL SOULS IN LIFE   268 14
ALMIGHTY GOD, WHO DIDST GIVE SUCH GRACE UNTO THY HOLY 226 18 O GOD, WHOSE MERCIES CANNOT BE NUMBERED   268 22
IN THINE HEART THAT GOD HATH RAISED HIM FRCM THE 226 27   SLEEP IN JESUS WILL GOD BRING WITH HIM   269 02
AND HEARING BY THE WORD OF GOD   227 13   VOICE OF THE ARCHANGEL, AND WITH THE TRUMP OF GOD   269 07
AND EVERLIVING GOD, WHO, FOR THE GREATER CONFIRMATION 228 05 INTO THE KINGDOM OF GOD, EXCEPT HE BE REGENERATE AND 273 30
DONE THE WILL OF GOD, YE MIGHT RECEIVE THE PROMISE 228 16   YOU TO CALL UPON GOD THE FATHER, THROUGH OUR LORD   273 32
ANSWERED AND SAID UNTO HIM, MY LORD AND MY GCD   229 07   AND IMMORTAL GOD, THE AID OF ALL WHO NEED, THE HELPER 274 09
BELIEVE THAT JESUS IS THE CHRIST, THE SON OF GOD 229 12   FOR OF SUCH IS THE KINGDOM OF GOD   274 30
O GOD, WHO, THROUGH THE PREACHING OF THE BLESSED 229 17   THE KINGDOM OF GOD AS A LITTLE CHILD, HE SHALL NOT   274 31
THAT HE IS THE SON OF GOD   231 05   WE KNOW THAT THOU ART A TEACHER COME FROM GOD   275 08
AND EVERLIVING GOD, WE HUMBLY BESEECH THY MAJESTY, 231 28   THOU DOEST, EXCEPT GOD BE WITH HIM   275 09
AND BLESSED GOD, AND SAID, LORD, NOW LETTEST   233 05   HE CANNOT SEE THE KINGDOM OF GOD   275 11
BUT SERVED GOD WITH FASTINGS AND PRAYERS   233 20   HE CANNOT ENTER INTO THE KINGDOM OF GOD   275 16
AND THE GRACE OF GOD WAS UPON HIM   233 27   AND EVERLASTING GOD, HEAVENLY FATHER, WE GIVE THEE   276 07
O ALMIGHTY GOD, WHO INTO THE PLACE OF THE TRAITOR 233 31   I WILL, GOD BEING MY HELPER   277 17
SAYING, ASK THEE A SIGN OF THE LORD THY GOD   235 26   IN JESUS THE CHRIST, THE SON OF THE LIVING GOD   278 03
BUT WILL YE WEARY MY GOD ALSO   235 30   O MERCIFUL GOD, GRANT THAT LIKE AS CHRIST DIED   278 18
WAS SENT FROM GOD UNTO A CITY OF GALILEE, NAMED   236 06   O BLESSED LORD GOD, WHO DOST LIVE, AND GOVERN ALL   278 30

GOD   CONTINUED

LET US GIVE THANKS UNTO OUR LORD GOD   279 04
EVERLASTING GOD, FOR THAT THY DEARLY BELOVED SON   279 09
THANKS UNTO ALMIGHTY GOD FOR THESE BENEFITS   280 15
THE ALMIGHTY GOD, THE FATHER OF OUR LORD JESUS   281 07
YE MAY BE FILLED WITH ALL THE FULNESS OF GOD   281 12
THE CHILD OF GOD, AND AN INHERITOR OF THE   283 19
AND I PRAY UNTO GOD TO GIVE ME HIS GRACE, THAT I MAY   284 04
I BELIEVE IN GOD THE FATHER ALMIGHTY, MAKER OF HEAVEN   284 13
ON THE RIGHT HAND OF GOD THE FATHER ALMIGHTY   284 20
LEARN TO BELIEVE IN GOD THE FATHER, WHO HATH MADE ME,   284 29
IN GOD THE SON, WHO HATH REDEEMED ME,   284 31
IN GOD THE HOLY GHOST, WHO SANCTIFIETH ME,   285 02
WHO SANCTIFIETH ME, AND ALL THE PEOPLE OF GOD   285 03
HOLY TRINITY, ONE GOD, I PRAISE AND MAGNIFY, SAYING,   285 04
GIVEN IN OLD TIME BY GOD TO THE PEOPLE OF ISRAEL   285 17
O ALMIGHTY GOD, WHO ALONE CANST ORDER THE UNRULY   285 25
FOR I THE LORD THY GOD AM A JEALOUS GOD, AND VISIT   286 12
THY GOD AM A JEALOUS GOD, AND VISIT THE SINS OF THE   286 12
NAME OF THE LORD THY GOD IN VAIN   286 19
SEVENTH DAY IS THE SABBATH OF THE LORD THY GOD   286 26
WHICH THE LORD THY GOD GIVETH THEE   287 03
LOVE THE LORD THY GOD WITH ALL THY HEART, WITH ALL   288 06
MY DUTY TOWARDS GOD, AND MY DUTY TOWARDS MY   288 13
WHAT IS YOUR DUTY TOWARDS GOD   288 15
MY DUTY TOWARDS GOD IS TO BELIEVE IN HIM, TO FEAR   288 16
AND REVERENCE WHICH BECOMETH A SERVANT OF GOD   288 31
IT SHALL PLEASE GOD TO CALL ME   289 11
THE COMMANDMENTS OF GOD, AND TO SERVE HIM, WITHOUT   289 14
AND THE LOVE OF GOD, AND THE FELLOWSHIP OF THE HOLY   289 30
O ALMIGHTY GOD, WHO HAST BUILT THY CHURCH UPON THE   290 19
TO WORSHIP GOD EVERY SUNDAY IN HIS CHURCH   291 19
THE PROMISES OF GOD TO THEM IN THAT SACRAMENT   292 30
TO PREACH THE WORD OF GOD   294 13
AND THE LOVE OF GOD, AND THE FELLOWSHIP OF THE HOLY   295 05
REVEREND FATHER IN GOD, I PRESENT UNTO YOU THESE   296 08
RECEIVED THE WORD OF GOD, THEY SENT UNTO THEM PETER   296 14
IN THE PRESENCE OF GOD, AND OF THIS CONGREGATION,   296 22
AND EVERLIVING GOD, WHO HAST VOUCHSAFED TO REGENERATE   297 14
AND EVERLIVING GOD, WHO MAKEST US BOTH TO WILL AND TO   298 13
REIGNETH EVER, ONE GOD, WORLD WITHOUT END   298 25
AND EVERLASTING GOD, VOUCHSAFE, WE BESEECH THEE, TO   298 26
THE BLESSING OF GOD ALMIGHTY, THE FATHER, THE SON,   299 03
HERE IN THE SIGHT OF GOD, AND IN THE FACE OF THIS   300 09
INSTITUTED OF GOD, SIGNIFYING UNTO US THE MYSTICAL   300 11
AND IN THE FEAR OF GOD   300 19
O ETERNAL GOD, CREATOR AND PRESERVER OF ALL   303 03
O ALMIGHTY GOD, CREATOR OF MANKIND, WHO ONLY ART THE   303 14
O GOD, WHO HAST SO CONSECRATED THE STATE OF MATRIMONY   303 20
SPIRIT EVER, ONE GOD, WORLD WITHOUT END   303 28
AND SAY, THOSE WHOM GOD HATH JOINED TOGETHER LET NO   303 31
THE SAME BEFORE GOD AND THIS COMPANY, AND THERETO   304 05
GOD THE SON, GOD THE HOLY GHOST, BLESS,   304 11
GOD THE FATHER, GOD THE SON, GOD THE HOLY GHOST,   304 11
GOD THE FATHER, GOD THE SON, GOD THE HOLY GHOST,   304 11
PLEASED ALMIGHTY GOD, OF HIS GOODNESS, TO GIVE YOU   305 11
HEARTY THANKS UNTO GOD, AND SAY, THEN SHALL BE SAID   305 14
OUR GOD IS MERCIFUL   305 25
O ALMIGHTY GOD, WE GIVE THEE HUMBLE THANKS FOR THAT   306 24
OF MY SOUL, THERE IS NO HELP FOR HIM IN HIS GOD   309 17
AND MOST MERCIFUL GOD AND SAVIOUR   309 27
I WILL GO UNTO THE ALTAR OF GOD   310 02
UNTO THE GOD OF MY JOY AND GLADNESS   310 03
SENTENCE WITH ME, O GOD, AND DEFEND MY CAUSE AGAINST   310 05
FOR THOU ART THE GOD OF MY STRENGTH   310 08
GO UNTO THE ALTAR OF GOD, EVEN UNTO THE GOD OF MY JOY   310 13
GOD, EVEN UNTO THE GOD OF MY JOY AND GLADNESS   310 14
THANKS UNTO THEE, O GOD, MY GOD   310 15
HARP WILL I GIVE THANKS UNTO THEE, O GOD, MY GOD   310 15
O PUT THY TRUST IN GOD   310 18
WHICH IS THE HELP OF MY COUNTENANCE, AND MY GOD   310 19
EVEN UNTO GOD WILL I CRY WITH MY VOICE, AND HE SHALL   310 29
I WILL CRY UNTO GOD WITH MY VOICE   310 29
WHEN I AM IN HEAVINESS, I WILL THINK UPON GOD   311 04
HATH GOD FORGOTTEN TO BE GRACIOUS   311 16
O GOD, THE STRENGTH OF THE WEAK AND THE COMFORT OF   312 12
O MOST MERCIFUL GOD, WHO, ACCORDING TO THE   313 30
O GOD OF HEAVENLY POWERS, WHO, BY THE MIGHT OF THY   315 06
O ALMIGHTY GOD, WHO ART THE GIVER OF ALL HEALTH,   315 13
GREAT AND MIGHTY GOD, WHO BRINGEST DOWN TO THE GRAVE,   315 19
OF MERCIES, AND GOD OF ALL COMFORT, OUR ONLY HELP IN   316 06
MOST GRACIOUS GOD, THIS THY SERVANT, CAST DOWN   316 18
O GOD, WHOSE DAYS ARE WITHOUT END, AND WHOSE MERCIES   316 25
FAVOUR WITH THEE OUR GOD, AND IN PERFECT CHARITY WITH   317 06
O ALMIGHTY GOD, WITH WHOM DO LIVE THE SPIRITS OF JUST   317 11
O GOD THE FATHER   317 25
O GOD THE SON   317 27
O GOD THE HOLY GHOST   317 29
O HOLY TRINITY, ONE GOD   317 31
WE SINNERS DO BESEECH THEE TO HEAR US, O LORD GOD   318 10
O LAMB OF GOD, WHO TAKEST AWAY THE SINS OF THE WORLD   318 23
THE HOLY GHOST, ONE GOD, WORLD WITHOUT END   319 12
IN THE NAME OF GOD THE FATHER ALMIGHTY WHO CREATED   319 20
AND THY DWELLING-PLACE IN THE PARADISE OF GOD   319 25
THE HOLY GHOST, ONE GOD, WORLD WITHOUT END   320 13
PLEASE ALMIGHTY GOD TO CALL THEM, THE MINISTERS SHALL R   321 05
EVERLIVING GOD, MAKER OF MANKIND, WHO DOST   321 18
YOU THAT BELIEVE ON THE NAME OF THE SON OF GOD   322 13
THAT YE MAY BELIEVE ON THE NAME OF THE SON OF GOD   322 15
MERCY UPON US, O GOD, AFTER THY GREAT GOODNESS   323 14
THIS BODY BE DESTROYED, YET SHALL I SEE GOD   324 11
THOU ART GOD FROM EVERLASTING, AND WORLD WITHOUT END   325 16
FORSAKE ME, O GOD OF MY SALVATION   326 27
GOD IS OUR HOPE AND STRENGTH, *   327 03
THE STREAMS WHEREOF MAKE GLAD THE CITY OF GOD   327 10

GOD   CONTINUED

GOD IS IN THE MIDST OF HER, THEREFORE SHALL SHE NOT   327 12
GOD SHALL HELP HER, AND THAT RIGHT EARLY   327 13
BE STILL THEN, AND KNOW THAT I AM GOD   327 14
THE GOD OF JACOB IS OUR REFUGE   327 16
UP THE KINGDOM TO GOD, EVEN THE FATHER   328 28
UNDER HIM, THAT GOD MAY BE ALL IN ALL   329 03
BUT GOD GIVETH IT A BODY AS IT HATH PLEASED HIM, AND   329 10
FLESH AND BLOOD CANNOT INHERIT THE KINGDOM OF GOD   329 34
BUT THANKS BE TO GOD, WHICH GIVETH US THE VICTORY   330 12
LED BY THE SPIRIT OF GOD, THEY ARE THE SONS OF GOD   330 19
BY THE SPIRIT OF GOD, THEY ARE THE SONS OF GOD   330 20
THAT WE ARE THE CHILDREN OF GOD   330 24
HEIRS OF GOD, AND JOINT-HEIRS WITH CHRIST   330 24
WAITETH FOR THE MANIFESTATION OF THE SONS OF GOD   330 30
TO THEM THAT LOVE GOD, TO THEM WHO ARE THE CALLED   330 31
IF GOD BE FOR US, WHO CAN BE AGAINST US   330 33
AT THE RIGHT HAND OF GOD, WHO ALSO MAKETH   331 05
US FROM THE LOVE OF GOD, WHICH IS IN CHRIST JESUS OUR   331 13
YE BELIEVE IN GOD, BELIEVE ALSO IN ME   331 18
HOLY GHOST EVER, ONE GOD, WORLD WITHOUT END   332 09
O LORD GOD MOST HOLY, O LORD MOST MIGHTY,   332 25
LORD MOST HOLY, O GOD MOST MIGHTY, O HOLY AND   332 30
UNTO ALMIGHTY GOD WE COMMEND THE SOUL OF OUR   333 14
O GOD, WHOSE MERCIES CANNOT BE NUMBERED   334 14
ALMIGHTY GOD, WITH WHOM DO LIVE THE SPIRITS OF THOSE   334 19
O MERCIFUL GOD, THE FATHER OF OUR LORD JESUS CHRIST,   334 30
THE GOD OF PEACE, WHO BROUGHT AGAIN FROM THE DEAD OUR   335 16
O ALMIGHTY GOD, THE GOD OF THE SPIRITS OF ALL FLESH,   335 25
O ALMIGHTY GOD, THE GOD OF THE SPIRITS OF ALL FLESH,   335 25
THE HOLY GHOST, ONE GOD, WORLD WITHOUT END   336 15
AND EVERLIVING GOD, WE YIELD UNTO THEE MOST HIGH   336 16
UNTO ALMIGHTY GOD WE COMMEND THE SOUL OF OUR   337 09
FOR OF SUCH IS THE KINGDOM OF GOD   338 11
FOR THEY SHALL SEE GOD   340 17
AND THE LOVE OF GOD, AND THE FELLOWSHIP OF THE HOLY   341 06
BEFORE THE THRONE OF GOD, AND SERVE HIM DAY AND NIGHT   341 20
AND GOD SHALL WIPE AWAY ALL TEARS FROM THEIR EYES   341 27
O GOD, WHOSE MOST DEAR SON DID TAKE LITTLE CHILDREN   342 03
ALMIGHTY GOD, FATHER OF MERCIES AND GIVER OF ALL   342 09
MAY ALMIGHTY GOD, THE FATHER, THE SON, AND THE HOLY   342 14
THERE IS NO HELP FOR HIM IN HIS GOD   346 28
AND HELP ME, O MY GOD, *   347 04
ME WHEN I CALL, O GOD OF MY RIGHTEOUSNESS   347 10
UNTO THE VOICE OF MY CALLING, MY KING AND MY GOD   348 02
4 FOR THOU ART THE GOD THAT HAST NO PLEASURE IN   348 07
11 DESTROY THOU THEM, O GOD   348 22
O LORD MY GOD, IN THEE HAVE I PUT MY TRUST   349 22
3 O LORD MY GOD, IF I HAVE DONE ANY SUCH THING   349 27
10 FOR THE RIGHTEOUS GOD *   350 11
11 MY HELP COMETH OF GOD, *   350 13
12 GOD IS A RIGHTEOUS JUDGE, STRONG, AND PATIENT   350 15
AND GOD IS PROVOKED EVERY DAY   350 16
AND ALL THE PEOPLE THAT FORGET GOD   352 27
HE CARETH NOT FOR GOD, *   353 11
NEITHER IS GOD IN ALL HIS THOUGHTS   353 12
IN HIS HEART, TUSH, GOD HATH FORGOTTEN   353 30
13 ARISE, O LORD GOD, AND LIFT UP THINE HAND   353 32
THE WICKED BLASPHEME GOD, *   353 34
TUSH, THOU GOD CAREST NOT FOR IT   354 02
AND FEAR ME, O LORD MY GOD   356 02
THERE IS NO GOD   356 13
ANY THAT WOULD UNDERSTAND, AND SEEK AFTER GOD   356 18
FOR GOD IS IN THE GENERATION OF THE RIGHTEOUS   356 26
PRESERVE ME, O GOD   357 21
THOU ART MY GOD   357 24
RUN AFTER ANOTHER GOD *   357 27
CALLED UPON THEE, O GOD, FOR THOU SHALT HEAR ME   358 29
2 MY SAVIOUR, MY GOD, AND MY MIGHT, IN WHOM I WILL   359 26
AND COMPLAINED UNTO MY GOD   360 05
HAVE NOT FORSAKEN MY GOD, AS THE WICKED DOTH   361 10
THE LORD MY GOD SHALL MAKE MY DARKNESS TO BE LIGHT   361 24
WITH THE HELP OF MY GOD I SHALL LEAP OVER THE WALL   361 27
31 THE WAY OF GOD IS AN UNDEFILED WAY   361 28
32 FOR WHO IS GOD, BUT THE LORD   361 31
OR WHO HATH ANY STRENGTH, EXCEPT OUR GOD   361 32
33 IT IS GOD THAT GIRDETH ME WITH STRENGTH OF WAR,   361 33
AND PRAISED BE THE GOD OF MY SALVATION   362 33
48 EVEN THE GOD THAT SEETH THAT I BE AVENGED,   362 34
THE HEAVENS DECLARE THE GLORY OF GOD   363 13
THE NAME OF THE GOD OF JACOB DEFEND THEE   364 18
AND TRIUMPH IN THE NAME OF THE LORD OUR GOD   364 24
BUT WE WILL REMEMBER THE NAME OF THE LORD OUR GOD   364 30
MY GOD, MY GOD, LOOK UPON ME   366 04
MY GOD, MY GOD, LOOK UPON ME   366 04
2 O MY GOD, I CRY IN THE DAY-TIME, BUT THOU HEAREST   366 07
THOU ART MY GOD EVEN FROM MY MOTHER'S WOMB   366 24
FROM THE GOD OF HIS SALVATION   369 06
SEEK THY FACE, O GOD OF JACOB   369 08
MY GOD, I HAVE PUT MY TRUST IN THEE   369 18
FOR THOU ART THE GOD OF MY SALVATION   369 26
21 DELIVER ISRAEL, O GOD, *   370 28
FORSAKE ME, O GOD OF MY SALVATION   372 19
IT IS THE GLORIOUS GOD THAT MAKETH THE THUNDER   374 03
2 O LORD MY GOD, I CRIED UNTO THEE   374 26
O MY GOD, I WILL GIVE THANKS UNTO THEE FOR EVER   375 19
O LORD, THOU GOD OF TRUTH   375 32
I HAVE SAID, THOU ART MY GOD   376 25
ARE THE PEOPLE WHOSE GOD IS THE LORD JEHOVAH   379 11
THOU MY CAUSE, MY GOD AND MY LORD   383 10
JUDGE ME, O LORD MY GOD, ACCORDING TO THY   383 11
THERE IS NO FEAR OF GOD BEFORE HIS EYES   383 27
HOW EXCELLENT IS THY MERCY, O GOD   384 09
AS ARE BLESSED OF GOD, SHALL POSSESS THE LAND   386 06
32 THE LAW OF HIS GOD IS IN HIS HEART, *   386 28

GOD   CONTINUED

THOU SHALT ANSWER FOR ME, O LORD MY GOD   388 22
21 FORSAKE ME NOT, O LORD MY GOD   388 34
O LORD GOD OF MY SALVATION   389 03
EVEN A THANKSGIVING UNTO OUR GOD   390 15
6 O LORD MY GOD, GREAT ARE THE WONDROUS WORKS WHICH   390 31
OF ME, THAT I SHOULD FULFIL THY WILL, O MY GOD   390 32
MAKE NO LONG TARRYING, O MY GOD   391 27
BLESSED BE THE LORD GOD OF ISRAEL, *   392 25
SO LONGETH MY SOUL AFTER THEE, O GOD   392 30
SOUL IS ATHIRST FOR GOD, YEA, EVEN FOR THE LIVING   392 31
EVEN FOR THE LIVING GOD   393 02
SHALL I COME TO APPEAR BEFORE THE PRESENCE OF GOD   393 03
THEY DAILY SAY UNTO ME, WHERE IS NOW THY GOD   393 05
AND BROUGHT THEM FORTH INTO THE HOUSE OF GOD   393 08
7 O PUT THY TRUST IN GOD   393 13
WHICH IS THE HELP OF MY COUNTENANCE, AND MY GOD   393 14
MY PRAYER UNTO THE GOD OF MY LIFE   393 23
I WILL SAY UNTO THE GOD OF MY STRENGTH, WHY HAST THOU   393 24
WHERE IS NOW THY GOD   393 30
15 O PUT THY TRUST IN GOD   393 33
WHICH IS THE HELP OF MY COUNTENANCE, AND MY GOD   393 34
SENTENCE WITH ME, O GOD, AND DEFEND MY CAUSE AGAINST   394 03
2 FOR THOU ART THE GOD OF MY STRENGTH   394 06
GO UNTO THE ALTAR OF GOD, EVEN UNTO THE GOD OF MY JOY   394 12
GOD, EVEN UNTO THE GOD OF MY JOY AND GLADNESS   394 13
HARP WILL I GIVE THANKS UNTO THEE, O GOD, MY GOD   394 14
THANKS UNTO THEE, O GOD, MY GOD   394 14
6 O PUT THY TRUST IN GOD   394 17
WHICH IS THE HELP OF MY COUNTENANCE, AND MY GOD   394 18
WITH OUR EARS, O GOD, OUR FATHERS HAVE TOLD US *   394 22
5 THOU ART MY KING, O GOD   394 32
WE MAKE OUR BOAST OF GOD ALL DAY LONG, *   395 09
THE NAME OF OUR GOD, AND HOLDEN UP OUR HANDS TO ANY   395 34
HANDS TO ANY STRANGE GOD, *   396 02
SHALL NOT GOD SEARCH IT OUT   396 02
THY LIPS, BECAUSE GOD HATH BLESSED THEE FOR EVER   396 19
6 THY SEAT, O GOD, ENDURETH FOR EVER   396 27
GOD, EVEN THY GOD, HATH ANOINTED THEE WITH THE OIL OF   396 30
WHEREFORE GOD, EVEN THY GOD, HATH ANOINTED THEE WITH   396 30
GOD IS OUR HOPE AND STRENGTH, *   397 25
THE STREAMS WHEREOF MAKE GLAD THE CITY OF GOD   397 33
5 GOD IS IN THE MIDST OF HER, THEREFORE SHALL SHE NOT   398 02
GOD SHALL HELP HER, AND THAT RIGHT EARLY   398 03
BUT GOD HATH SHOWED HIS VOICE, AND THE EARTH SHALL   398 05
THE GOD OF JACOB IS OUR REFUGE   398 07
10 BE STILL THEN, AND KNOW THAT I AM GOD   398 14
THE GOD OF JACOB IS OUR REFUGE   398 17
O SING UNTO GOD WITH THE VOICE OF MELODY   398 22
5 GOD IS GONE UP WITH A MERRY NOISE, *   398 29
SING PRAISES UNTO OUR GOD   398 31
7 FOR GOD IS THE KING OF ALL THE EARTH   399 02
8 GOD REIGNETH OVER THE NATIONS   399 04
GOD SITTETH UPON HIS HOLY SEAT   399 04
FOR GOD, WHICH IS VERY HIGH EXALTED, DOTH DEFEND THE   399 07
THE PEOPLE OF THE GOD OF ABRAHAM   399 07
IN THE CITY OF OUR GOD, EVEN UPON HIS HOLY HILL   399 11
GOD IS WELL KNOWN IN HER PALACES AS A SURE REFUGE   399 14
GOD UPHOLDETH THE SAME FOR EVER   399 25
CITY OF THE LORD OF HOSTS, IN THE CITY OF OUR GOD   399 25
O GOD, *   399 27
9 O GOD, ACCORDING TO THY NAME, SO IS THY PRAISE UNTO   399 29
13 FOR THIS GOD IS OUR GOD FOR EVER AND EVER   400 04
FOR THIS GOD IS OUR GOD FOR EVER AND EVER   400 04
GIVE A RANSOM UNTO GOD FOR HIM,   400 19
15 BUT GOD HATH DELIVERED MY SOUL FROM THE POWER OF   401 05
EVEN THE MOST MIGHTY GOD, HATH SPOKEN, *   401 21
2 OUT OF SION HATH GOD APPEARED *   401 24
3 OUR GOD SHALL COME, AND SHALL NOT KEEP SILENCE   401 25
FOR GOD IS JUDGE HIMSELF   402 03
FOR I AM GOD, EVEN THY GOD   402 05
FOR I AM GOD, EVEN THY GOD   402 05
14 OFFER UNTO GOD THANKSGIVING, *   402 18
THE UNGODLY SAITH GOD, *   402 22
YE THAT FORGET GOD, *   403 02
HIS WAY ARIGHT, WILL I SHOW THE SALVATION OF GOD   403 06
MERCY UPON ME, O GOD, AFTER THY GREAT GOODNESS   403 08
ME A CLEAN HEART, O GOD, *   403 29
O GOD, THOU THAT ART THE GOD OF MY   404 04
THOU THAT ART THE GOD OF MY HEALTH   404 05
17 THE SACRIFICE OF GOD IS A TROUBLED SPIRIT   404 11
CONTRITE HEART, O GOD, SHALT THOU NOT DESPISE   404 12
THE GOODNESS OF GOD *   404 21
6 THEREFORE SHALL GOD DESTROY THEE FOR EVER   404 28
MAN THAT TOOK NOT GOD FOR HIS STRENGTH   404 33
THE MERCY OF GOD FOR EVER AND EVER   405 05
I AM LIKE A GREEN OLIVE-TREE IN THE HOUSE OF GOD   405 05
THERE IS NO GOD   405 13
3 GOD LOOKED DOWN FROM HEAVEN UPON THE CHILDREN OF   405 16
ANY THAT WOULD UNDERSTAND, AND SEEK AFTER GOD   405 18
THEY HAVE NOT CALLED UPON GOD   405 24
FOR GOD HATH BROKEN THE BONES OF HIM THAT BESIEGED   405 25
BECAUSE GOD HATH DESPISED THEM   405 27
SAVE ME, O GOD, FOR THY NAME'S SAKE, *   406 03
2 HEAR MY PRAYER, O GOD, *   406 05
WHICH HAVE NOT GOD BEFORE THEIR EYES, SEEK AFTER MY   406 08
4 BEHOLD, GOD IS MY HELPER   406 10
HEAR MY PRAYER, O GOD, *   406 19
IN THE HOUSE OF GOD AS FRIENDS   407 19
I WILL CALL UPON GOD, *   407 23
20 YEA, EVEN GOD, THAT ENDURETH FOR EVER, SHALL HEAR   407 30
FOR THEY WILL NOT TURN, NOR FEAR GOD   407 32
THOU, O GOD, SHALT BRING THEM INTO THE PIT OF   408 06
MERCIFUL UNTO ME, O GOD, FOR MAN GOETH ABOUT TO   408 14
4 I WILL PRAISE GOD, BECAUSE OF HIS WORD   408 21

GOD   CONTINUED

HAVE PUT MY TRUST IN GOD, AND WILL NOT FEAR WHAT   408 22
THOU, O GOD, IN THY DISPLEASURE SHALT CAST THEM DOWN   408 28
FOR GOD IS ON MY SIDE   408 33
11 YEA, IN GOD HAVE I PUT MY TRUST   409 04
12 UNTO THEE, O GOD, WILL I PAY MY VOWS   409 06
I MAY WALK BEFORE GOD IN THE LIGHT OF THE LIVING   409 09
MERCIFUL UNTO ME, O GOD, BE MERCIFUL UNTO ME   409 12
UNTO THE MOST HIGH GOD, *   409 15
EVEN UNTO THE GOD THAT SHALL PERFORM THE CAUSE WHICH   409 16
4 GOD SHALL SEND FORTH HIS MERCY AND TRUTH   409 19
6 SET UP THYSELF, O GOD, ABOVE THE HEAVENS   409 24
MY HEART IS FIXED, O GOD, MY HEART IS FIXED   409 29
12 SET UP THYSELF, O GOD, ABOVE THE HEAVENS   410 04
BREAK THEIR TEETH, O GOD, IN THEIR MOUTHS   410 19
DOUBTLESS THERE IS A GOD THAT JUDGETH THE EARTH   410 33
DELIVER ME FROM MINE ENEMIES, O GOD   411 04
5 STAND UP, O LORD GOD OF HOSTS, THOU GOD OF ISRAEL,   411 13
GOD OF HOSTS, THOU GOD OF ISRAEL, TO VISIT ALL THE   411 13
FOR THOU ART THE GOD OF MY REFUGE   411 23
AND GOD SHALL LET ME SEE MY DESIRE UPON MINE ENEMIES   411 24
10 GOD SHOWETH ME HIS GOODNESS PLENTEOUSLY   411 24
AND KNOW THAT IT IS GOD THAT RULETH IN JACOB, AND   411 33
ART MY REFUGE, AND MY MERCIFUL GOD   412 10
FOR THOU, O GOD, ART MY REFUGE, AND MY MERCIFUL GOD   412 10
O GOD, THOU HAST CAST US OUT, AND SCATTERED US   412 12
6 GOD HATH SPOKEN IN HIS HOLINESS, I WILL REJOICE,   412 23
10 HAST NOT THOU CAST US OUT, O GOD   412 31
WILT NOT THOU, O GOD, GO OUT WITH OUR HOSTS   412 32
12 THROUGH GOD WILL WE DO GREAT ACTS   413 04
HEAR MY CRYING, O GOD, *   413 07
SHALL DWELL BEFORE GOD FOR EVER   413 19
MY SOUL TRULY WAITETH STILL UPON GOD   413 27
TO PUT HIM OUT WHOM GOD WILL EXALT   414 04
MY SOUL, WAIT THOU STILL UPON GOD   414 07
7 IN GOD IS MY HEALTH AND MY GLORY   414 11
AND IN GOD IS MY TRUST   414 12
BEFORE HIM, FOR GOD IS OUR HOPE   414 14
11 GOD SPAKE ONCE, AND TWICE I HAVE ALSO HEARD THE   414 21
THAT POWER BELONGETH UNTO GOD   414 22
O GOD, THOU ART MY GOD   414 26
O GOD, THOU ART MY GOD   414 26
12 BUT THE KING SHALL REJOICE IN GOD   415 15
HEAR MY VOICE, O GOD, IN MY PRAYER   415 19
7 BUT GOD SHALL SUDDENLY SHOOT AT THEM WITH A SWIFT   415 33
SHALL SAY, THIS HATH GOD DONE   416 04
THOU, O GOD, ART PRAISED IN SION   416 11
THY RIGHTEOUSNESS, O GOD OF OUR SALVATION   416 22
10 THE RIVER OF GOD IS FULL OF WATER   417 02
O BE JOYFUL IN GOD, ALL YE LANDS   417 15
2 SAY UNTO GOD, O HOW WONDERFUL ART THOU IN THY   417 17
AND BEHOLD THE WORKS OF GOD   417 22
7 O PRAISE OUR GOD, YE PEOPLES, *   417 29
9 FOR THOU, O GOD, HAST PROVED US   417 33
AND HEARKEN, ALL YE THAT FEAR GOD   418 12
17 BUT GOD HATH HEARD ME   418 18
18 PRAISED BE GOD, WHO HATH NOT CAST OUT MY PRAYER,   418 20
GOD BE MERCIFUL UNTO US, AND BLESS US, *   418 23
3 LET THE PEOPLES PRAISE THEE, O GOD   418 28
5 LET THE PEOPLES PRAISE THEE, O GOD   418 33
AND GOD, EVEN OUR OWN GOD, SHALL GIVE US HIS   419 03
GOD, EVEN OUR OWN GOD, SHALL GIVE US HIS BLESSING   419 03
7 GOD SHALL BLESS US   419 04
LET GOD ARISE, AND LET HIS ENEMIES BE SCATTERED   419 09
SO LET THE UNGODLY PERISH AT THE PRESENCE OF GOD   419 13
LET THE RIGHTEOUS BE GLAD, AND REJOICE BEFORE GOD   419 14
4 O SING UNTO GOD, AND SING PRAISES UNTO HIS NAME   419 16
EVEN GOD IN HIS HOLY HABITATION   419 20
6 HE IS THE GOD THAT MAKETH MEN TO BE OF ONE MIND IN   419 21
7 O GOD, WHEN THOU WENTEST FORTH BEFORE THE PEOPLE   419 24
AND THE HEAVENS DROPPED AT THE PRESENCE OF GOD   419 27
OF GOD, WHO IS THE GOD OF ISRAEL   419 28
AT THE PRESENCE OF GOD, WHO IS THE GOD OF ISRAEL   419 28
9 THOU, O GOD, SENTEST A GRACIOUS RAIN UPON THINE   419 29
FOR THOU, O GOD, HAST OF THY GOODNESS PREPARED FOR   419 32
17 THE CHARIOTS OF GOD ARE TWENTY THOUSAND, EVEN   420 16
THAT THE LORD GOD MIGHT DWELL AMONG THEM   420 21
EVEN THE GOD WHO HELPETH US, AND POURETH HIS BENEFITS   420 23
20 HE IS OUR GOD, EVEN THE GOD OF WHOM COMETH   420 25
IS OUR GOD, EVEN THE GOD OF WHOM COMETH SALVATION   420 25
GOD IS THE LORD, BY WHOM WE ESCAPE DEATH   420 26
21 GOD SHALL WOUND THE HEAD OF HIS ENEMIES, *   420 27
IT IS WELL SEEN, O GOD, HOW THOU GOEST   421 02
HOW THOU, MY GOD AND KING, GOEST IN THE SANCTUARY   421 03
26 GIVE THANKS UNTO GOD THE LORD IN THE CONGREGATION,   421 06
28 THY GOD HATH SENT STRENGTH FOR THEE   421 11
THE THING, O GOD, THAT THOU HAST WROUGHT IN US, 29   421 12
LAND SHALL SOON STRETCH OUT HER HANDS UNTO GOD   421 19
32 SING UNTO GOD, O YE KINGDOMS OF THE EARTH   421 20
YE THE POWER TO GOD OVER ISRAEL   421 25
35 O GOD, WONDERFUL ART THOU IN THY HOLY PLACES   421 27
EVEN THE GOD OF ISRAEL, HE WILL GIVE STRENGTH AND   421 28
BLESSED BE GOD   421 29
SAVE ME, O GOD   421 32
SIGHT FAILETH ME FOR WAITING SO LONG UPON MY GOD   422 06
GOD, THOU KNOWEST MY SIMPLENESS; AND MY FAULTS ARE   422 10
IN THEE, O LORD GOD OF HOSTS, BE ASHAMED FOR MY   422 13
THROUGH GOD, O LORD GOD OF ISRAEL   422 15
14 HEAR ME, O GOD, IN THE MULTITUDE OF THY MERCY,   422 30
THY HELP, O GOD, SHALL LIFT ME UP   424 03
PRAISE THE NAME OF GOD WITH A SONG, *   424 04
SEEK YE AFTER GOD, AND YOUR SOUL SHALL LIVE   424 09
36 FOR GOD WILL SAVE SION, AND BUILD THE CITIES OF   424 14
HASTE THEE, O GOD, TO DELIVER ME   424 20
HASTE THEE UNTO ME, O GOD   424 31

GOD CONTINUED

3 DELIVER ME, O MY GOD, OUT OF THE HAND OF THE — 425 11
4 FOR THOU, O LORD GOD, ART THE THING THAT I LONG — 425 14
SAYING, 10 GOD HATH FORSAKEN HIM — 425 27
MY GOD, HASTE THEE TO HELP ME — 425 29
11 GO NOT FAR FROM ME, O GOD — 425 29
STRENGTH OF THE LORD GOD, * — 426 06
16 THOU, O GOD, HAST TAUGHT ME FROM MY YOUTH UP UNTIL — 426 08
17 FORSAKE ME NOT, O GOD, IN MINE OLD AGE, WHEN I AM — 426 10
THY RIGHTEOUSNESS, O GOD, IS VERY HIGH, * — 426 14
O GOD, WHO IS LIKE UNTO THEE — 426 15
THY FAITHFULNESS, O GOD, PLAYING UPON AN INSTRUMENT — 426 23
THY JUDGMENTS, O GOD, * — 426 31
BLESSED BE THE LORD GOD, EVEN THE GOD OF ISRAEL, — 428 02
LORD GOD, EVEN THE GOD OF ISRAEL, * — 428 02
TRULY GOD IS LOVING UNTO ISRAEL — 428 10
SAY THEY, HOW SHOULD GOD PERCEIVE IT — 428 30
FOR ME, 17 UNTIL I WENT INTO THE SANCTUARY OF GCD — 429 10
BUT GOD IS THE STRENGTH OF MY HEART, AND MY PORTICN — 429 28
TO HOLD ME FAST BY GOD, TO PUT MY TRUST IN THE LCRD — 429 32
MY TRUST IN THE LORD GOD, * — 429 33
O GOD, WHEREFORE ART THOU ABSENT FROM US SC LONG — 430 03
UP ALL THE HOUSES OF GOD IN THE LAND — 430 23
11 O GOD, HOW LONG SHALL THE ADVERSARY DO THIS — 430 27
13 FOR GOD IS MY KING OF OLD — 430 32
23 ARISE, O GOD, MAINTAIN THINE OWN CAUSE — 431 22
UNTO THEE, O GOD, DO WE GIVE THANKS — 431 30
SAITH GOD, * — 432 02
GOD IS THE JUDGE — 432 12
I WILL TALK OF THE GOD OF JACOB, * — 432 19
IN JUDAH IS GOD KNOWN — 432 24
6 AT THY REBUKE, O GOD OF JACOB, * — 432 33
WAS STILL, 9 WHEN GOD AROSE TO JUDGMENT, * — 433 06
UNTO THE LORD YOUR GOD, AND KEEP IT, ALL YE THAT ARE — 433 10
EVEN UNTO GOD WILL I CRY WITH MY VOICE, AND HE SHALL — 433 16
I WILL CRY UNTO GOD WITH MY VOICE — 433 16
3 WHEN I AM IN HEAVINESS, I WILL THINK UPCN GOD — 433 21
9 HATH GOD FORGOTTEN TO BE GRACIOUS — 433 33
WHO IS SO GREAT A GOD AS OUR GOD — 434 08
13 THY WAY, O GOD, IS HOLY — 434 08
WHO IS SO GREAT A GOD AS OUR GOD — 434 09
14 THOU ART THE GOD THAT DOEST WONDERS, * — 434 10
WATERS SAW THEE, O GOD, THE WATERS SAW THEE, ANC WERE — 434 14
8 THAT THEY MIGHT PUT THEIR TRUST IN GOD — 435 11
FORGET THE WORKS OF GOD, BUT TO KEEP HIS — 435 12
AND WHOSE SPIRIT CLAVE NOT STEDFASTLY UNTO GOD — 435 16
NOT THE COVENANT OF GOD, * — 435 20
19 THEY TEMPTED GOD IN THEIR HEARTS, * — 436 04
THEY SPAKE AGAINST GOD ALSO, SAYING, * — 436 06
SHALL GOD PREPARE A TABLE IN THE WILDERNESS — 436 06
THEY BELIEVED NOT IN GOD, * — 436 14
THE HEAVY WRATH OF GOD CAME UPON THEM, AND SLEW THE — 436 33
AND TURNED THEM EARLY, AND INQUIRED AFTER GOD — 437 07
THEY REMEMBERED THAT GOD WAS THEIR STRENGTH, * — 437 08
AND THAT THE HIGH GOD WAS THEIR REDEEMER — 437 09
AND TEMPTED GOD, * — 437 23
THE MOST HIGH GOD, * — 438 25
60 WHEN GOD HEARD THIS, HE WAS WROTH, * — 438 30
O GOD, THE HEATHEN ARE COME INTO THINE INHERITANCE — 439 29
9 HELP US, O GOD OF OUR SALVATION, FOR THE GLORY OF — 440 18
WHERE IS NOW THEIR GOD — 440 22
3 TURN US AGAIN, O GOD — 441 08
4 O LORD GOD OF HOSTS, * — 441 10
TURN US AGAIN, THOU GOD OF HOSTS — 441 16
THEE AGAIN, THOU GOD CF HOSTS, LOOK DOWN FROM HEAVEN, — 441 30
US AGAIN, O LORD GOD OF HOSTS — 442 09
SING WE MERRILY UNTO GOD OUR STRENGTH — 442 12
NOISE UNTO THE GOD OF JACOB — 442 13
AND A LAW OF THE GOD OF JACOB — 442 19
SHALL NO STRANGE GOD BE IN THEE, * — 442 31
NEITHER SHALT THOU WORSHIP ANY OTHER GOD — 442 32
11 I AM THE LORD THY GOD, WHO BROUGHT THEE OUT OF THE — 442 33
GOD STANDETH IN THE CONGREGATION OF PRINCES — 443 18
8 ARISE, O GOD, AND JUDGE THOU THE EARTH — 444 02
NOT THY TONGUE, O GOD, KEEP NOT STILL SILENCE — 444 05
REFRAIN NOT THYSELF, O GOD — 444 06
THE HOUSES OF GOD IN POSSESSION — 444 29
13 O MY GOD, MAKE THEM LIKE UNTO THE WHIRLING DUST, — 444 30
MY HEART AND MY FLESH REJOICE IN THE LIVING GOD — 445 15
O LORD OF HOSTS, MY KING AND MY GOD — 445 18
AND UNTO THE GOD OF GODS APPEARETH EVERY ONE CF THEM — 445 26
8 O LORD GOD OF HOSTS, HEAR MY PRAYER — 445 27
HEARKEN, O GOD OF JACOB — 445 28
9 BEHOLD, O GOD OUR DEFENDER, * — 445 29
IN THE HOUSE OF MY GOD, * — 445 33
12 FOR THE LORD GOD IS A LIGHT AND DEFENCE — 446 02
13 O LORD GOD OF HOSTS, * — 446 05
4 TURN US THEN, O GOD OUR SAVIOUR, * — 446 14
WHAT THE LORD GOD WILL SAY — 446 22
MY GOD, SAVE THY SERVANT THAT PUTTETH HIS TRUST IN — 447 07
THOU ART GOD ALONE — 447 24
O LORD MY GOD, WITH ALL MY HEART — 447 28
14 O GOD, THE PROUD ARE RISEN AGAINST ME — 447 32
15 BUT THOU, O LORD GOD, ART FULL OF COMPASSION AND — 448 04
THOU CITY OF GOD — 448 17
O LORD GOD OF MY SALVATION, I HAVE CRIED DAY ANC — 448 29
8 GOD IS VERY GREATLY TO BE FEARED IN THE COUNCIL OF — 450 14
9 O LORD GOD OF HOSTS, WHO IS LIKE UNTO THEE — 450 22
MY GOD, AND MY STRONG SALVATION — 451 27
THOU ART GOD FROM EVERLASTING, AND WORLD WITHOUT END — 453 21
OF THE LORD OUR GOD BE UPON US — 454 24
MY GOD, IN HIM WILL I TRUST — 454 31
FLOURISH IN THE COURTS OF THE HOUSE OF OUR GOD — 456 27
O LORD GOD, TO WHOM VENGEANCE BELONGETH, * — 457 19
THOU GOD, TO WHOM VENGEANCE BELONGETH, SHOW THYSELF — 457 20

GOD CONTINUED

NEITHER SHALL THE GOD OF JACOB REGARD IT — 457 32
AND MY GOD IS THE STRENGTH OF MY CONFIDENCE — 458 30
THE LORD OUR GOD SHALL DESTROY THEM — 458 33
3 FOR THE LORD IS A GREAT GOD — 459 09
7 FOR HE IS THE LORD OUR GOD — 459 17
OF THE WORLD HAVE SEEN THE SALVATION OF OUR GOD — 461 33
MAGNIFY THE LORD OUR GOD, AND FALL DOWN BEFORE HIS — 462 05
8 THOU HEARDEST THEM, O LORD OUR GOD — 462 32
FORGAVEST THEM, O GOD, THOUGH THOU DIDST PUNISH THEIR — 462 33
MAGNIFY THE LORD OUR GOD, AND WORSHIP HIM UPON HIS — 463 02
FOR THE LORD OUR GOD IS HOLY — 463 03
2 BE YE SURE THAT THE LORD HE IS GOD — 463 08
24 BUT I SAID, O MY GOD, TAKE ME NOT AWAY IN THE — 465 28
O LORD MY GOD, THOU ART BECOME EXCEEDING GLORIOUS — 467 24
DO SEEK THEIR MEAT FROM GOD — 469 03
I WILL PRAISE MY GOD WHILE I HAVE MY BEING — 469 28
7 HE IS THE LORD OUR GOD — 470 16
AND THEY TEMPTED GOD IN THE DESERT — 473 30
21 AND THEY FORGAT GOD THEIR SAVIOUR, * — 474 10
O LORD OUR GOD, AND GATHER US FROM AMONG THE — 475 30
BLESSED BE THE LORD GOD OF ISRAEL, FROM EVERLASTING, — 475 33
O GOD, MY HEART IS READY, MY HEART IS READY — 479 04
5 SET UP THYSELF, O GOD, ABOVE THE HEAVENS, * — 479 13
7 GOD HATH SPOKEN IN HIS HOLINESS — 479 17
11 HAST NOT THOU FORSAKEN US, O GOD — 479 26
AND WILT NOT THOU, O GOD, GO FORTH WITH OUR HOSTS — 479 27
13 THROUGH GOD WE SHALL DO GREAT ACTS — 479 30
NOT THY TONGUE, O GOD OF MY PRAISE — 480 03
THOU WITH ME, O LORD GOD, ACCORDING UNTO THY NAME — 481 12
25 HELP ME, O LORD MY GOD — 481 22
UNTO THE LORD OUR GOD, THAT HATH HIS DWELLING SC — 484 16
THE PRESENCE OF THE GOD OF JACOB — 485 07
WHERE IS NOW THEIR GOD — 485 15
3 AS FOR OUR GOD, HE IS IN HEAVEN — 485 16
OUR GOD IS MERCIFUL — 486 28
27 GOD IS THE LORD, WHO HATH SHOWED US LIGHT — 489 22
28 THOU ART MY GOD, AND I WILL THANK THEE — 489 25
THOU ART MY GOD, AND I WILL PRAISE THEE — 489 26
I WILL KEEP THE COMMANDMENTS OF MY GOD — 497 29
OF THE LORD OUR GOD, * — 503 24
UPON THE LORD OUR GOD, UNTIL HE HAVE MERCY UPON US — 503 32
UNTO THE ALMIGHTY GOD OF JACOB — 508 07
FOR THE MIGHTY GOD OF JACOB — 508 14
EVEN IN THE COURTS OF THE HOUSE OF OUR GOD — 509 26
IN THE COURTS OF THE HOUSE OF OUR GOD — 510 06
GIVE THANKS UNTO THE GOD OF ALL GODS — 511 18
GIVE THANKS UNTO THE GOD OF HEAVEN — 512 34
17 HOW DEAR ARE THY COUNSELS UNTO ME, O GOD — 515 24
19 WILT THOU NOT SLAY THE WICKED, O GOD — 515 28
23 TRY ME, O GOD, AND SEEK THE GROUND OF MY HEART — 516 04
THOU ART MY GOD, * — 516 20
7 O LORD GOD, THOU STRENGTH OF MY HEALTH — 516 22
9 BUT MINE EYES LOOK UNTO THEE, O LORD GOD — 517 28
FOR THOU ART MY GOD — 519 13
9 I WILL SING A NEW SONG UNTO THEE, O GOD — 520 08
ARE THE PEOPLE WHO HAVE THE LORD FOR THEIR GOD — 520 25
WILL MAGNIFY THEE, O GOD, MY KING — 520 27
I HAVE ANY BEING, I WILL SING PRAISES UNTO MY GOD — 522 05
IS HE THAT HATH THE GOD OF JACOB FOR HIS HELP, — 522 10
AND WHOSE HOPE IS IN THE LORD HIS GOD — 522 11
10 THE LORD THY GOD, O SION, SHALL BE KING FOR — 522 23
IT IS A GOOD THING TO SING PRAISES UNTO OUR GOD — 522 28
SING PRAISES UPON THE HARP UNTO OUR GOD — 523 09
PRAISE THY GOD, O SION — 523 19
6 LET THE PRAISES OF GOD BE IN THEIR MOUTH — 525 13
O PRAISE GOD IN HIS SANCTUARY — 525 22
REVEREND FATHER IN GOD, I PRESENT UNTO YOU THESE — 530 10
TO THE HONOUR OF GOD, AND THE EDIFYING OF HIS CHURCH — 530 16
FORTH IN THE NAME OF GOD, AND SHOW WHAT THE CRIME CR — 530 25
ALMIGHTY GOD, WHO BY THY DIVINE PROVIDENCE HAST — 531 14
LEAVE THE WORD OF GOD, AND SERVE TABLES — 532 10
AND THE WORD OF GOD INCREASED — 532 20
TO SERVE GOD FOR THE PROMOTING OF HIS GLORY, AND THE — 532 28
I WILL SO DO, BY THE HELP OF GOD — 533 23
IN THE CHURCH OF GOD COMMITTED UNTO THEE — 534 06
IN THE CHURCH OF GOD, AND TO PREACH THE SAME, IF THCU — 534 12
ALMIGHTY GOD, GIVER OF ALL GOOD THINGS, WHC OF THY — 534 30
THE PEACE OF GOD, WHICH PASSETH ALL UNDERSTANDING, — 535 13
AND LOVE OF GOD, AND OF HIS SON JESUS CHRIST OUR — 535 15
AND THE BLESSING OF GOD ALMIGHTY, THE FATHER, THE — 535 16
REVEREND FATHER IN GOD, I PRESENT UNTO YOU THESE — 536 10
TO THE HONOUR OF GOD, AND THE EDIFYING OF HIS CHURCH — 536 17
WHOM WE PURPOSE, GOD WILLING, TO RECEIVE THIS DAY — 536 22
FORTH IN THE NAME OF GOD, AND SHOW WHAT THE CRIME CR — 536 30
ALMIGHTY GOD, GIVER OF ALL GOOD THINGS, WHO BY THY — 537 20
OF THE SON OF GOD, UNTO A PERFECT MAN, UNTO THE — 538 10
THE CHILDREN OF GOD, TOWARDS THE SPOUSE AND BODY OF — 540 14
AND KNOWLEDGE OF GOD, AND TO THAT RIPENESS AND — 540 20
ABILITY IS GIVEN OF GOD ALONE — 540 31
IT HATH PLEASED GOD TO CALL YOU — 541 12
CONTINUALLY PRAY TO GOD THE FATHER, BY THE MEDIATICN — 541 15
WE, IN THE NAME OF GOD, AND OF HIS CHURCH, SHALL — 541 28
ACCORDING TO THE COMMANDMENTS OF GOD — 542 15
BISHOP SAY, ALMIGHTY GOD, WHO HATH GIVEN YOU THIS — 542 34
SUPPLICATIONS TO GOD FOR ALL THESE THINGS — R 543 24
TO THEE, THE GIFT OF GOD MOST HIGH — 544 22
AND SAY, ALMIGHTY GOD, AND HEAVENLY FATHER, WHO, — 545 12
IN THE CHURCH OF GOD, NOW COMMITTED UNTO THEE BY THE — 546 10
OF THE WORD OF GOD, AND OF HIS HOLY SACRAMENTS — 546 14
IN THE CHURCH OF GOD, NOW COMMITTED TO THEE BY THE — 546 18
OF THE WORD OF GOD, AND OF HIS HOLY SACRAMENTS — 546 20
PREACH THE WORD OF GOD, AND TO MINISTER THE HOLY — 546 25
THE PEACE OF GOD, WHICH PASSETH ALL UNDERSTANDING, — 547 14
AND LOVE OF GOD, AND OF HIS SON JESUS CHRIST OUR — 547 16

GOD   CONTINUED

AND THE BLESSING OF GOD ALMIGHTY, THE FATHER, THE   547 17
ALMIGHTY GOD, GIVER OF ALL GOOD THINGS, WHO BY THY   547 31
ALMIGHTY GOD, WHO BY THE SON JESUS CHRIST DIDST GIVE   549 07
HOW SHALL HE TAKE CARE OF THE CHURCH OF GOD   549 26
REPENTANCE TOWARD GOD, AND FAITH TOWARD OUR LORD   550 14
TO TESTIFY THE GOSPEL OF THE GRACE OF GOD   550 21
THE KINGDOM OF GOD, SHALL SEE MY FACE NO MORE   550 23
TO DECLARE UNTO YOU ALL THE COUNSEL OF GOD   550 26
FEED THE CHURCH OF GOD, WHICH HE HATH PURCHASED WITH   550 29
I COMMEND YOU TO GOD, AND TO THE WORD OF HIS GRACE,   551 03
REVEREND FATHER IN GOD, WE PRESENT UNTO YOU THIS   552 21
IN THE NAME OF GOD, AMEN   552 28
SO HELP ME GOD, THROUGH JESUS CHRIST   552 32
PRAYERS TO ALMIGHTY GOD, BEFORE WE ADMIT AND SEND   553 10
ALMIGHTY GOD, GIVER OF ALL GOOD THINGS, WHO BY THY   553 26
MINDED TO BEHAVE YOURSELF IN THE CHURCH OF GOD   554 15
AND CALL UPON GOD BY PRAYER FOR THE TRUE   554 30
I WILL SO DO, BY THE HELP OF GOD   554 34
I WILL SO DO, BY THE HELP OF GOD   555 19
I WILL SO BE, BY THE HELP OF GOD   555 22
SHALL SAY, ALMIGHTY GOD, OUR HEAVENLY FATHER, WHO   555 28
TO THEE, THE GIFT OF GOD MOST HIGH   556 30
ALMIGHTY GOD, AND MOST MERCIFUL FATHER, WHO, OF THINE   557 20
AND REIGNETH, ONE GOD, WORLD WITHOUT END   558 07
IN THE CHURCH OF GOD, NOW COMMITTED UNTO THEE BY THE   558 13
STIR UP THE GRACE OF GOD, WHICH IS GIVEN THEE BY THIS   558 16
FOR GOD HATH NOT GIVEN US THE SPIRIT OF FEAR, BUT OF   558 17
HOLY SPIRIT, ONE GOD, WORLD WITHOUT END   559 15
THE PEACE OF GOD, WHICH PASSETH ALL UNDERSTANDING,   559 17
AND LOVE OF GOD, AND OF HIS SON JESUS CHRIST OUR   559 19
AND THE BLESSING OF GOD ALMIGHTY, THE FATHER, THE   559 20
O GOD THE FATHER, HAVE MERCY UPON US   560 03
O GOD THE SON, O GOD THE HOLY GHOST,   560 05
O GOD THE SON, O GOD THE HOLY GHOST,   560 07
O HOLY TRINITY, ONE GOD, WE BESEECH THEE TO HEAR US,   560 09
O GOD, WHO DOST EVER HALLOW AND PROTECT THY CHURCH   562 09
SPIRIT EVER, ONE GOD, WORLD WITHOUT END   562 15
FROM THE GOD OF HIS SALVATION   563 21
EXPRESS COMMAND OF GOD, OR BY THE SECRET INSPIRATION   564 12
PUBLIC WORSHIP OF GOD, AND SEPARATED THEM FROM ALL   564 16
O ETERNAL GOD, MIGHTY IN POWER, AND OF MAJESTY   564 27
O MOST GLORIOUS GOD, WHOM THE HEAVEN OF HEAVENS   567 05
COMING DOWN FROM GOD OUT OF HEAVEN, PREPARED AS A   567 13
THE TABERNACLE OF GOD IS WITH MEN, AND HE WILL DWELL   567 15
BE HIS PEOPLE, AND GOD HIMSELF SHALL BE WITH THEM,   567 17
GOD HIMSELF SHALL BE WITH THEM, AND BE THEIR GOD   567 17
AND GOD SHALL WIPE AWAY ALL TEARS FROM THEIR EYES   567 18
BE THY NAME, O LORD GOD, FOR THAT IT HATH PLEASED   568 06
THE PEACE OF GOD, WHICH PASSETH ALL UNDERSTANDING,   568 13
AND LOVE OF GOD, AND OF HIS SON JESUS CHRIST OUR   568 15
AND THE BLESSING OF GOD ALMIGHTY, THE FATHER, THE   568 16
KEYS OF THE HOUSE OF GOD AT YOUR HANDS, AS THE   570 32
WHO IS GOD OVER ALL, BLESSED FOR EVERMORE   572 03
O GOD, HOLY GHOST, SANCTIFIER OF THE FAITHFUL,   572 25
AND GLORIFY AS ONE GOD, WORLD WITHOUT END   572 32
THE GOD OF PEACE, WHO BROUGHT AGAIN FROM THE DEAD OUR   573 03
O LORD MY GOD, I AM NOT WORTHY THAT THOU SHOULDEST   573 11
O ALMIGHTY GOD, WHO HAST BUILT THY CHURCH UPON THE   574 03
SAME HOLY GHOST, ONE GOD, WORLD WITHOUT END   574 22
THE CHILD OF GOD, AND AN INHERITOR OF THE   577 10
AND I PRAY UNTO GOD TO GIVE ME HIS GRACE, THAT I MAY   577 25
I BELIEVE IN GOD THE FATHER ALMIGHTY, MAKER OF HEAVEN   577 28
ON THE RIGHT HAND OF GOD THE FATHER ALMIGHTY   578 04
LEARN TO BELIEVE IN GOD THE FATHER, WHO HATH MADE ME,   578 11
IN GOD THE SON, WHO HATH REDEEMED ME,   578 13
IN GOD THE HOLY GHOST, WHO SANCTIFIETH ME,   578 15
WHO SANCTIFIETH ME, AND ALL THE PEOPLE OF GOD   578 16
THE SAME WHICH GOD SPAKE IN THE TWENTIETH CHAPTER OF   578 22
I AM THE LORD THY GOD, WHO BROUGHT THEE OUT OF THE   578 23
THY GOD AM A JEALOUS GOD, AND VISIT THE SINS OF THE   578 31
FOR I THE LORD THY GOD AM A JEALOUS GOD, AND VISIT   578 31
NAME OF THE LORD THY GOD IN VAIN   578 35
SEVENTH DAY IS THE SABBATH OF THE LORD THY GOD   579 06
WHICH THE LORD THY GOD GIVETH THEE   579 14
MY DUTY TOWARDS GOD, AND MY DUTY TOWARDS MY   579 24
WHAT IS THY DUTY TOWARDS GOD   579 26
MY DUTY TOWARDS GOD IS TO BELIEVE IN HIM, TO FEAR   579 27
IT SHALL PLEASE GOD TO CALL ME   580 14
THE COMMANDMENTS OF GOD, AND TO SERVE HIM, WITHOUT   580 18
DESIREST THOU OF GOD IN THIS PRAYER   580 28
I DESIRE MY LORD GOD, OUR HEAVENLY FATHER, WHO IS THE   580 29
AND I PRAY UNTO GOD, THAT HE WILL SEND US ALL THINGS   580 33
THE PROMISES OF GOD MADE TO THEM IN THAT SACRAMENT   581 29
AND EVERLASTING GOD, IN WHOM WE LIVE AND MOVE AND   587 19
DO THOU, O MERCIFUL GOD, CONFIRM AND STRENGTHEN US   588 08
O GOD, WHO KNOWEST THE WEAKNESS AND CORRUPTION   588 12
AND THE LOVE OF GOD, AND THE FELLOWSHIP OF THE HOLY   589 10
MOST MERCIFUL GOD, WHO ART OF PURER EYES THAN TO   589 26
AND DO THOU, THE GOD OF PITY, ADMINISTER TO THEM   591 03
AND THE LOVE OF GOD, AND THE FELLOWSHIP OF THE HOLY   592 03
AND EVERLASTING GOD, WHO HAST SAFELY BROUGHT US TO   592 20
AND THE LOVE OF GOD, AND THE FELLOWSHIP OF THE HOLY   592 28
O ALMIGHTY GOD, WHO POUREST OUT ON ALL WHO DESIRE IT,   594 04
O GOD, THE KING ETERNAL, WHO DIVIDEST THE DAY FROM   594 11
ALMIGHTY GOD, WHO ALONE GAVEST US THE BREATH OF LIFE,   594 18
O GOD, WHO ART THE LIFE OF MORTAL MEN, THE LIGHT OF   595 04
O GOD, WHO MAKEST US GLAD WITH THE WEEKLY REMEMBRANCE   595 12
O GOD OF PEACE, WHO HAST TAUGHT US THAT IN RETURNING   595 19
WHERE WE MAY BE STILL AND KNOW THAT THOU ART GOD   595 23
O GOD, BY WHOM THE MEEK ARE GUIDED IN JUDGMENT,   595 26
ALMIGHTY GOD, HEAVENLY FATHER, WHO HAST BLESSED US   596 24
O GOD, WHOSE FATHERLY CARE REACHETH TO THE UTTERMOST   596 30
ALMIGHTY GOD, WE ENTRUST ALL WHO ARE DEAR TO US TO   597 09
O MERCIFUL GOD, GIVER OF LIFE AND HEALTH   597 15

GOD   CONTINUED

ALMIGHTY GOD OUR HEAVENLY FATHER, WE BESEECH THEE   597 21
ALMIGHTY GOD, WE REMEMBER THIS DAY BEFORE THEE THY   598 06
ALMIGHTY GOD, OUR HEAVENLY FATHER, WHO SETTEST THE   598 19
O GOD, ALMIGHTY AND MERCIFUL, WHO HEALEST THOSE THAT   599 03
ALMIGHTY GOD, WHOSE LOVING HAND HATH GIVEN US ALL   599 19
O GOD, AT WHOSE WORD MAN GOETH FORTH TO HIS WORK AND   599 25
ONE LIVING AND TRUE GOD, EVERLASTING, WITHOUT BODY,   603 03
THE VERY AND ETERNAL GOD, AND OF ONE SUBSTANCE WITH   603 10
IS ONE CHRIST, VERY GOD, AND VERY MAN   603 14
WITH THE FATHER AND THE SON, VERY AND ETERNAL GOD   603 27
MEDIATOR BETWEEN GOD AND MAN, BEING BOTH GOD AND MAN   604 17
AND MAN, BEING BOTH GOD AND MAN   604 17
THE LAW GIVEN FROM GOD BY MOSES, AS TOUCHING   604 19
IS NOT SUBJECT TO THE LAW OF GOD   604 38
AND GOOD WORKS, TO FAITH, AND CALLING UPON GOD   604 44
WITHOUT THE GRACE OF GOD BY CHRIST PREVENTING US,   605 02
AND ACCEPTABLE TO GOD, WITHOUT THE GRACE OF GOD BY   605 02
RIGHTEOUS BEFORE GOD, ONLY FOR THE MERIT OF OUR LORD   605 06
AND ACCEPTABLE TO GOD IN CHRIST, AND DO SPRING OUT   605 13
ARE NOT PLEASANT TO GOD, FORASMUCH AS THEY SPRING NOT   605 18
THEY ARE NOT DONE AS GOD HATH WILLED AND COMMANDED   605 21
NOT ONLY RENDER UNTO GOD AS MUCH AS THEY ARE BOUND TO   605 26
AND BY THE GRACE OF GOD WE MAY ARISE AGAIN, AND AMEND   606 02
PURPOSE OF GOD, WHEREBY (BEFORE THE FOUNDATIONS OF   606 06
A BENEFIT OF GOD, BE CALLED ACCORDING TO GOD'S   606 11
THEY BE MADE SONS OF GOD BY ADOPTION   606 13
IT DOTH FERVENTLY KINDLE THEIR LOVE TOWARDS GOD   606 22
THAT WILL OF GOD IS TO BE FOLLOWED, WHICH WE   606 29
EXPRESSLY DECLARED UNTO US IN THE WORD OF GOD   606 30
THE PURE WORD OF GOD IS PREACHED, AND THE SACRAMENTS   606 39
BUT RATHER REPUGNANT TO THE WORD OF GOD   607 17
TO THE WORD OF GOD, AND THE CUSTOM OF THE PRIMITIVE   607 27
NOT ANY VISIBLE SIGN OR CEREMONY ORDAINED OF GOD   607 43
HEARING THE WORD OF GOD, AND IN RECEIVING THE   608 13
TO BE THE SONS OF GOD BY THE HOLY GHOST, ARE VISIBLY   608 28
AND GRACE INCREASED BY VIRTUE OF PRAYER UNTO GOD   608 30
TO THE WORD OF GOD, AND BE ORDAINED AND APPROVED BY   609 37

GOD-SPEED

SALUTE AND WELCOME HIM, BIDDING HIM GOD-SPEED   R 574 28

GOD-WARD

SUCH TRUST HAVE WE THROUGH CHRIST TO GOD-WARD   206 13

GOD'S

WORK ACCORDING TO GOD'S WILL, SERVE HIM FAITHFULLY,   047 13
THE MINISTERS OF GOD'S HOLY WORD AND SACRAMENTS   047 22
I PURPOSE, THROUGH GOD'S ASSISTANCE, TO ADMINISTER TO   086 29
BY THE RULE OF GOD'S COMMANDMENTS   087 17
YOUR OFFENCES AT GOD'S HAND   087 28
A FULL TRUST IN GOD'S MERCY, AND WITH A QUIET   088 02
OTHER MINISTER OF GOD'S WORD, AND OPEN HIS GRIEF   088 06
ON -- INTEND, BY GOD'S GRACE, TO CELEBRATE THE LORD'S   088 12
UNTO WHICH, IN GOD'S BEHALF, I BID YOU ALL WHO ARE   088 14
PROVOKE GOD'S INDIGNATION AGAINST YOU   088 26
YE WILL BY GOD'S GRACE RETURN TO A BETTER MIND   089 19
FOR THEY ARE GOD'S MINISTERS, ATTENDING CONTINUALLY   114 24
IS OF GOD HEARETH GOD'S WORDS   133 11
AND UNTO GOD THE THINGS THAT ARE GOD'S   223 15
BY GOD'S HELP, WILL ENDEAVOUR NOT TO FOLLOW, NOR   276 29
OBEDIENTLY KEEP GOD'S HOLY WILL AND COMMANDMENTS, AND   277 04
I WILL, BY GOD'S HELP   277 07
I WILL, BY GOD'S HELP   277 13
BY GOD'S HELP, WILL ENDEAVOUR NOT TO FOLLOW, NOR   277 30
OBEDIENTLY KEEP GOD'S HOLY WILL AND COMMANDMENTS, AND   278 13
I WILL, BY GOD'S HELP   278 16
THAT I SHOULD KEEP GOD'S HOLY WILL AND COMMANDMENTS,   283 27
AND BY GOD'S HELP SO I WILL   283 30
YOU SHOULD KEEP GOD'S HOLY WILL AND COMMANDMENTS   285 14
LET US ASK GOD'S HELP TO KNOW AND TO KEEP THEM   285 19
A LIVELY FAITH IN GOD'S MERCY THROUGH CHRIST, WITH A   293 28
AND BLESSING IN GOD'S NAME   294 15
OTHERWISE THAN AS GOD'S WORD DOTH ALLOW, THEIR   300 30
TOGETHER AFTER GOD'S ORDINANCE IN THE HOLY ESTATE OF   301 07
TOGETHER AFTER GOD'S ORDINANCE IN THE HOLY ESTATE OF   301 15
ACCORDING TO GOD'S HOLY ORDINANCE   301 31
ACCORDING TO GOD'S HOLY ORDINANCE   302 07
ASSURE HIM OF GOD'S MERCY AND FORGIVENESS   R 313 26
SHALL SAY, UNTO GOD'S GRACIOUS MERCY AND PROTECTION   314 26
UNTO GOD'S GRACIOUS MERCY AND PROTECTION WE COMMIT   332 10
10 IN GOD'S WORD WILL I REJOICE   409 02
OF BASHAN, SO IS GOD'S HILL   420 11
THIS IS GOD'S HILL, IN THE WHICH IT PLEASETH HIM TO   420 13
BY GOD'S GRACE, TO GIVE YOURSELVES WHOLLY   541 11
SO DETERMINED, BY GOD'S GRACE   542 10
CONTRARY TO GOD'S WORD   542 21
AND DETERMINED, BY GOD'S GRACE   554 27
CONTRARY TO GOD'S WORD   555 04
THE AUTHORITY OF GOD'S WORD, AND BY THE ORDER OF THIS   555 17
SO SHOW MYSELF, BY GOD'S HELP   555 26
THAT I SHOULD KEEP GOD'S HOLY WILL AND COMMANDMENTS,   577 19
AND BY GOD'S HELP SO I WILL   577 22
YOU SHOULD KEEP GOD'S COMMANDMENTS   578 18
A LIVELY FAITH IN GOD'S MERCY THROUGH CHRIST, WITH A   582 24
IT DESERVETH GOD'S WRATH AND DAMNATION   604 34
THE SEVERITY OF GOD'S JUDGMENT YET ARE THEY PLEASING   605 12
OVER AND ABOVE, GOD'S COMMANDMENTS, WHICH THEY CALL   605 24
ACCORDING TO GOD'S PURPOSE BY HIS SPIRIT WORKING IN   606 11
AND AT LENGTH, BY GOD'S MERCY, THEY ATTAIN TO   606 15
THE SENTENCE OF GOD'S PREDESTINATION, IS A MOST   606 24
WE MUST RECEIVE GOD'S PROMISES IN SUCH WISE, AS THEY   606 27

GOD'S   CONTINUED

IS CONTRARY TO GOD'S WORD WRITTEN, NEITHER MAY IT SO   607 05
OF GRACE, AND GOD'S GOOD WILL TOWARDS US, BY THE   607 33
NOR THE GRACE OF GOD'S GIFTS DIMINISHED FROM SUCH AS   608 15
NOT COMMANDED BY GOD'S LAW, EITHER TO VOW THE ESTATE   609 21
ORDAINED AGAINST GOD'S WORD   609 35

GODFATHER

ONE GODFATHER AND TWO GODMOTHERS   R 273 10

GODFATHERS

BE HAD, TWO GODFATHERS AND ONE GODMOTHER   R 273 10
AND THEN THE GODFATHERS AND GODMOTHERS, AND THE   R 273 13
UNTO THE GODFATHERS AND GODMOTHERS ON THIS WISE   R 276 18
SAY TO THE GODFATHERS AND GODMOTHERS,   R 279 24

GODHEAD

WHO ARE ONE WITH THEE IN THY ETERNAL GODHEAD   079 18
LIFE HAVE THE FRUITION OF THY GLORIOUS GODHEAD   108 02
IN UNITY OF THIS GODHEAD THERE BE THREE PERSONS,   603 06
IS TO SAY, THE GODHEAD AND MANHOOD, WERE JOINED   603 12

GODLINESS

LIFE IN ALL GODLINESS AND HONESTY, MAY CONTINUALLY   052 25
IN ALL GODLINESS AND HONESTY   VI 21
THY HOUSEHOLD THE CHURCH IN CONTINUAL GODLINESS   220 17
WHO ART THE AUTHOR OF ALL GODLINESS   222 10
THE SPIRIT OF KNOWLEDGE AND TRUE GODLINESS   297 21
AND TRUE GODLINESS, THAT THEIR HOME MAY BE A HAVEN OF   303 25
IN THE WAY OF GODLINESS   463 19
PATIENCE, GODLINESS   598 24
SHALL JUDGE THE SAME TO SERVE BETTER TO GODLINESS   609 24

GODLY

OR WHICH A GODLY MAN MAY NOT WITH A GOOD CONSCIENCE   V 41
HEREAFTER LIVE A GODLY, RIGHTEOUS, AND SOBER LIFE,   006 29
HEREAFTER LIVE A GODLY, RIGHTEOUS, AND SOBER LIFE,   024 04
MAY HINDER US FROM GODLY UNION AND CONCORD   037 29
OF SOUND AND GODLY LEARNING, AND FOR ALL WHOSE HANDS   047 34
LIVE IN UNITY AND GODLY LOVE   074 15
BE PERSUADED TO A GODLY UNITY, BUT REMAIN STILL IN   R 085 14
MAY RECEIVE SUCH GODLY COUNSEL AND ADVICE, AS MAY   088 07
AND GODLY, IN THIS PRESENT WORLD   098 20
MAY EVER OBEY THY GODLY MOTIONS IN RIGHTEOUSNESS,   125 30
MAY TRULY AND GODLY SERVE THEE   157 02
AN ENSAMPLE OF GODLY LIFE   171 30
SERVE THEE IN ALL GODLY QUIETNESS   195 18
ALL VIRTUOUS AND GODLY LIVING, THAT WE MAY COME TO   256 08
LORD HATH CHOSEN TO HIMSELF THE MAN THAT IS GODLY   347 17
THERE IS NOT ONE GODLY MAN LEFT   355 06
EVERY ONE THAT IS GODLY MAKE HIS PRAYER UNTO THEE, IN   378 02
18 THE LORD KNOWETH THE DAYS OF THE GODLY   385 31
NOT HIS THAT BE GODLY, BUT THEY ARE PRESERVED FOR   386 20
THEM THAT LIVE A GODLY LIFE   446 04
9 WHOSO LEADETH A GODLY LIFE, *   463 32
4 UNTO THE GODLY THERE ARISETH UP LIGHT IN THE   483 24
THEIR LEARNING AND GODLY CONVERSATION, TO EXERCISE   530 14
AND WILL THEIR GODLY ADMONITIONS   533 33
THEIR LEARNING AND GODLY CONVERSATION, TO EXERCISE   536 15
BE WHOLESOME AND GODLY EXAMPLES AND PATTERNS FOR THE   541 22
AND WILL THEIR GODLY ADMONITIONS, AND SUBMITTING   543 14
TO THEIR GODLY JUDGMENTS   543 15
ADMINISTER THE GODLY DISCIPLINE THEREOF   549 12
UNTO YOU THIS GODLY AND WELL-LEARNED MAN, TO BE   552 22
AND GODLY IN THIS PRESENT WORLD   555 09
APPROVE OUR GODLY PURPOSE OF SETTING APART THIS PLACE   564 22
SERVE THEE IN ALL GODLY QUIETNESS   574 17
AND GODLY LIFE   588 07
AND LIGHT RISETH UP IN DARKNESS FOR THE GODLY   595 27
AS THE GODLY CONSIDERATION OF PREDESTINATION,   606 16
COMFORT TO GODLY PERSONS, AND SUCH AS FEEL IN   606 17
DOTH CONTAIN A GODLY AND WHOLESOME DOCTRINE, AND   610 06

GODMOTHER

THEY CAN BE HAD, TWO GODFATHERS AND ONE GODMOTHER   R 273 10

GODMOTHERS

EVERY FEMALE, ONE GODFATHER AND TWO GODMOTHERS   R 273 11
AND GODMOTHERS, AND THE PEOPLE WITH THE CHILDREN,   R 273 13
AND GODMOTHERS ON THIS WISE   R 276 18
AND GODMOTHERS, NAME THIS CHILD   R 279 24

GODS

AND A GREAT KING ABOVE ALL GODS   009 08
HAVE NONE OTHER GODS BUT ME   068 05
YOUR GOD IS GOD OF GODS, AND LORD OF LORDS, A GREAT   263 23
HAVE NONE OTHER GODS BUT ME   286 05
EVEN BEFORE THE GODS WILL I SING PRAISE UNTO THEE   311 29
HE IS A JUDGE AMONG GODS   443 05
I HAVE SAID, YE ARE GODS, *   443 29
AND UNTO THE GOD OF GODS APPEARETH EVERY ONE OF THEM   445 26
8 AMONG THE GODS THERE IS NONE LIKE UNTO THEE,   447 19
IS HE AMONG THE GODS, *   450 17
AND A GREAT KING ABOVE ALL GODS   459 10
HE IS MORE TO BE FEARED THAN ALL GODS   460 07
5 AS FOR ALL THE GODS OF THE HEATHEN, THEY ARE BUT   460 08
WORSHIP HIM, ALL YE GODS   461 11

GODS   CONTINUED

CARVED IMAGES, AND THAT DELIGHT IN VAIN GODS   461 11
THOU ART EXALTED FAR ABOVE ALL GODS   461 15
AND THAT OUR LORD IS ABOVE ALL GODS   510 12
2 O GIVE THANKS UNTO THE GOD OF ALL GODS   511 18
EVEN BEFORE THE GODS WILL I SING PRAISE UNTO THEE   513 28
HAVE NONE OTHER GODS BUT ME   578 26

GOEST

ASKETH ME, WHITHER GOEST THOU   175 07
WE KNOW NOT WHITHER THOU GOEST   240 05
WE KNOW NOT WHITHER THOU GOEST   331 24
AND GOEST NOT FORTH WITH OUR ARMIES   395 12
24 IT IS WELL SEEN, O GOD, HOW THOU GOEST   421 02
MY GOD AND KING, GOEST IN THE SANCTUARY   421 03

GOETH

THEY WHICH FOLLOW THE LAMB WHITHERSOEVER HE GOETH   103 10
AND I SAY TO THIS MAN, GO, AND HE GOETH   115 14
THEN GOETH HE, AND TAKETH TO HIM SEVEN OTHER SPIRITS   130 14
AS A BEAST GOETH DOWN INTO THE VALLEY, THE SPIRIT OF   139 15
SON OF MAN INDEED GOETH, AS IT IS WRITTEN OF HIM   141 06
AS HE WAS COME, HE GOETH STRAIGHTWAY TO HIM, AND   142 20
THE SON OF MAN GOETH, AS IT WAS DETERMINED   149 14
AND PETER THAT HE GOETH BEFORE YOU INTO GALILEE   165 32
AND GOETH HIS WAY, AND STRAIGHTWAY   176 08
HIS OWN SHEEP, HE GOETH BEFORE THEM, AND THE SHEEP   186 06
NOT TELL WHENCE IT COMETH, AND WHITHER IT GOETH   188 16
AND GOETH HIS WAY, AND STRAIGHTWAY   265 32
NOT TELL WHENCE IT COMETH, AND WHITHER IT GOETH   275 21
MY PRAYER, THAT GOETH NOT OUT OF FEIGNED LIPS   358 17
6 IT GOETH FORTH FROM THE UTTERMOST PART OF THE   363 24
O GOD, FOR MAN GOETH ABOUT TO DEVOUR ME   408 14
OF SUCH A ONE AS GOETH ON STILL IN HIS WICKEDNESS   420 28
AND THEIR TONGUE GOETH THROUGH THE WORLD   428 27
DISPLEASURE GOETH OVER ME, *   449 29
SOON AS THE WIND GOETH OVER IT, IT IS GONE   467 06
23 MAN GOETH FORTH TO HIS WORK, AND TO HIS LABOUR,   469 06
130 WHEN THY WORD GOETH FORTH, *   498 30
7 HE THAT NOW GOETH ON HIS WAY WEEPING, AND BEARETH   505 18
THE BREATH OF MAN GOETH FORTH, HE SHALL TURN AGAIN TO 522 08
HIS OWN SHEEP, HE GOETH BEFORE THEM, AND THE SHEEP   538 29
AT WHOSE WORD MAN GOETH FORTH TO HIS WORK AND TO HIS   599 25

GOING

SUN EVEN UNTO THE GOING DOWN OF THE SAME MY NAME   004 12
YE WERE AS SHEEP GOING ASTRAY   172 18
AND AS HE WAS NOW GOING DOWN, HIS SERVANTS MET HIM,   220 05
AND GOING ON FROM THENCE, HE SAW OTHER TWO BRETHREN,   227 28
THE BODY, AND GOING BEFORE IT, EITHER INTO THE CHURCH R 324 03
SHALL PRESERVE THY GOING OUT, AND THY COMING IN, *   327 33
THE BODY, AND GOING BEFORE IT, EITHER INTO THE CHURCH R 338 03
SHALL PRESERVE THY GOING OUT, AND THY COMING IN, *   339 17
A GOOD MAN'S GOING, *   386 08
THE SUN UNTO THE GOING DOWN THEREOF   401 23
6 WHO GOING THROUGH THE VALE OF MISERY USE IT FOR A   445 23
SHALL DIRECT HIS GOING IN THE WAY   446 34
SUN KNOWETH HIS GOING DOWN   468 33
THE SUN UNTO THE GOING DOWN OF THE SAME   484 13
SHALL PRESERVE THY GOING OUT, AND THY COMING IN, *   503 06

GOINGS

O HOLD THOU UP MY GOINGS IN THY PATHS, *   358 27
AND HIS GOINGS SHALL NOT SLIDE   386 28
SET MY FEET UPON THE ROCK, AND ORDERED MY GOINGS   390 13
WHO ARE PURPOSED TO OVERTHROW MY GOINGS   516 17

GOLD

GOLD, AND FRANKINCENSE, AND MYRRH   109 23
AND THEY HAD ON THEIR HEADS CROWNS OF GOLD   187 11
AND PURGE THEM AS GOLD AND SILVER, THAT THEY MAY   232 11
ARE THEY THAN GOLD, YEA, THAN MUCH FINE GOLD   364 04
ARE THEY THAN GOLD, YEA, THAN MUCH FINE GOLD   364 05
SET A CROWN OF PURE GOLD UPON HIS HEAD   365 10
IN A VESTURE OF GOLD, WROUGHT ABOUT WITH DIVERS   397 04
HER CLOTHING IS OF WROUGHT GOLD   397 13
AND HER FEATHERS LIKE GOLD   420 08
BE GIVEN OF THE GOLD OF ARABIA   427 27
HE BROUGHT THEM FORTH ALSO WITH SILVER AND GOLD   472 11
ARE SILVER AND GOLD, *   485 18
THAN THOUSANDS OF GOLD AND SILVER   494 25
ABOVE GOLD AND PRECIOUS STONES   498 23
THEY ARE BUT SILVER AND GOLD   510 33
NO MAN'S SILVER, OR GOLD, OR APPAREL   551 06

GOLGOTHA

A PLACE CALLED GOLGOTHA, THAT IS TO SAY, A PLACE OF A 136 28
UNTO THE PLACE GOLGOTHA, WHICH IS, BEING INTERPRETED, 146 08
A SKULL, WHICH IS CALLED IN THE HEBREW GOLGOTHA   159 33

GONE

WE LIKE SHEEP HAVE GONE ASTRAY   022 14
AS THE ANGELS WERE GONE AWAY FROM THEM INTO HEAVEN,   106 07
WHEN THE DEVIL WAS GONE OUT, THE DUMB SPAKE   129 25
UNCLEAN SPIRIT IS GONE OUT OF A MAN, HE WALKETH   130 10
WHO IS GONE INTO HEAVEN, AND IS ON THE RIGHT HAND OF   162 02
HE WOULD HAVE GONE FURTHER   168 02
SAVIOUR CHRIST IS GONE BEFORE, WHO LIVETH AND   179 09

GONE   CONTINUED

THE FISHERMEN WERE GONE OUT OF THEM, AND WERE WASHING   196 09
IS HIS MERCY CLEAN GONE FOR EVER   311 10
FOR WHEN THOU ART ANGRY ALL OUR DAYS ARE GCNE   325 30
SO SOON PASSETH IT AWAY, AND WE ARE GCNE   325 35
7 MY BEAUTY IS GONE FOR VERY TROUBLE, *   349 12
4 BUT THEY ARE ALL GONE OUT OF THE WAY, THEY ARE   356 19
4 THEIR SOUND IS GONE OUT INTO ALL LANDS   363 19
AND THE UNGODLY SHALL BE CLEAN GONE   385 14
37 I WENT BY, AND LO, HE WAS GONE   387 06
MY WICKEDNESSES ARE GONE OVER MY HEAD, *   387 28
OF MINE EYES IS GONE FROM ME   388 11
AND STORMS ARE GONE OVER ME   393 19
NEITHER OUR STEPS GONE OUT OF THY WAY   395 31
5 GOD IS GONE UP WITH A MERRY NOISE, *   398 29
WERE GATHERED, AND GONE BY TOGETHER   399 17
4 BUT THEY ARE ALL GONE OUT OF THE WAY, THEY ARE   405 19
18 THOU ART GONE UP ON HIGH, THOU HAST LED CAPTIVITY   420 19
MY FEET WERE ALMOST GONE, *   428 12
IS HIS MERCY CLEAN GONE FOR EVER   433 31
THE THING THAT IS GONE OUT OF MY LIPS   452 10
9 FOR WHEN THOU ART ANGRY ALL OUR DAYS ARE GONE   454 04
SO SOON PASSETH IT AWAY, AND WE ARE GCNE   454 10
11 MY DAYS ARE GONE LIKE A SHADOW, *   464 31
FOR AS SOON AS THE WIND GOETH OVER IT, IT IS GONE   467 06
176 I HAVE GONE ASTRAY LIKE A SHEEP THAT IS LOST   502 02
AND THE STREAM HAD GONE OVER OUR SOUL   504 13
HAD GONE EVEN OVER OUR SOUL   504 14
AMONG WHOM I HAVE GONE PREACHING THE KINGDOM OF GCD,   550 23
MAN IS VERY FAR GONE FROM ORIGINAL RIGHTEOUSNESS,   604 32

GOOD

BEHOLD, I BRING YOU GOOD TIDINGS OF GREAT JOY,   004 08
MAN MAY NOT WITH A GOOD CONSCIENCE USE AND SUBMIT   V 41
ASH WEDNESDAY AND GOOD FRIDAY THE VENITE MAY BE   R 008 12
UNTO HIM, AND SPEAK GOOD OF HIS NAME   015 12
WHOM COMETH EVERY GOOD AND PERFECT GIFT   018 19
AND GOVERNED BY THY GOOD SPIRIT, THAT ALL WHO PRCFESS   018 31
AND ON EARTH PEACE, GOOD WILL TOWARDS MEN   025 22
THE HUNGRY WITH GOOD THINGS   026 24
IT IS A GOOD THING TO GIVE THANKS UNTO THE LORD,   027 28
O SPEAK GOOD OF THE LORD, ALL YE WORKS OF HIS,   029 17
HOLY DESIRES, ALL GOOD COUNSELS, AND ALL JUST WCRKS   031 18
WHOM COMETH EVERY GOOD AND PERFECT GIFT   032 18
AND GOVERNED BY THY GUUD SPIRIT, THAT ALL WHO PRCFESS   032 31
OF THY GLORY, THE GOOD OF THY CHURCH, THE SAFETY,   035 13
WHOSE STATUTES ARE GOOD AND GRACIOUS AND WHOSE LAW IS   035 24
HAST GIVEN US THIS GOOD LAND FOR OUR HERITAGE   036 09
THE GIVER OF ALL GOOD GIFTS, WHO OF THY DIVINE   039 07
AND SO FILL US WITH GOOD THINGS THAT THE PCOR AND   040 11
THAT THE GOOD WORK WHICH THOU HAST BEGUN IN   042 18
AMONG US, AND ALL GOOD LEARNING FLOURISH AND ABCUND   042 25
IN THY GOOD TIME, RESTORE HIM TO HEALTH, AND ENABLE   045 18
OF DARKNESS, AND GOOD OUT OF EVIL, GRANT TO THESE THY   046 26
GOOD CHRISTIAN PEOPLE, I BID YOUR PRAYERS FOR   047 06
AS WELL AS FOR THE GOOD EDUCATION OF ALL THE YOUTH OF   047 32
AND FOR ALL HIS GOOD GIFTS, TEMPORAL AND SPIRITUAL,   048 13
LIVES AFTER THEIR GOOD EXAMPLES   048 20
IN US THE FRUIT OF GOOD LIVING, TO THE HONCUR AND   049 21
SPARE US, GOOD LORD, SPARE THY PEOPLE, WHOM THOU HAST   054 15
SPARE US, GOOD LORD   054 18
GOOD LORD, DELIVER US   054 22
AND COMMANDMENT, GOOD LORD, DELIVER US   055 05
THEE TO HEAR US, GOOD LORD   055 21
THEE TO HEAR US, GOOD LORD   056 04
THEE TO HEAR US, GOOD LORD   057 04
MAY, BY THY GOOD PROVIDENCE, BE BROUGHT TO   058 21
BUT THIS GREAT AND GOOD WORK MISCARRIED AT THAT TIME   VI 17
SPARE US THEREFORE, GOOD LORD, SPARE THY PEOPLE,   062 20
TURN THOU US, O GOOD LORD, AND SO SHALL WE BE TURNED   062 28
SPARE THY PEOPLE, GOOD LORD, SPARE THEM, AND LET NOT   063 03
THEY MAY SEE YOUR GOOD WORKS, AND GLORIFY YCUR FATHER   072 05
LET US DO GOOD UNTO ALL MEN   072 20
TO DO GOOD, AND TO DISTRIBUTE, FORGET NOT   072 27
HATH THIS WORLD'S GOOD, AND SEETH HIS BROTHER HAVE   072 29
THOU THYSELF A GOOD REWARD IN THE DAY OF NECESSITY   072 34
SO TO FOLLOW THEIR GOOD EXAMPLES, THAT WITH THEM WE   075 04
AND DO ALL SUCH GOOD WORKS AS THOU HAST PREPARED FOR   083 28
AND ON EARTH PEACE, GOOD WILL TOWARDS MEN   084 02
IN CHRIST, TAKE YE GOOD HEED, LEST YE, WITHDRAWING   088 24
ZEALOUS OF GOOD WORKS   098 25
BEHOLD, I BRING YOU GOOD TIDINGS OF GREAT JOY,   099 15
AND ON EARTH PEACE, GOOD WILL TOWARD MEN   099 22
AND TO DO OF HIS GOOD PLEASURE   106 05
ME TO PREACH GOOD TIDINGS UNTO THE MEEK   106 31
PROVE WHAT IS THAT GOOD, AND ACCEPTABLE, AND PERFECT,   110 08
CLEAVE TO THAT WHICH IS GOOD   113 23
BUT OVERCOME EVIL WITH GOOD   113 09
DOTH SET FORTH GOOD WINE   113 28
THOU HAST KEPT THE GOOD WINE UNTIL NOW   113 29
ARE NOT A TERROR TO GOOD WORKS, BUT TO THE EVIL   114 16
DO THAT WHICH IS GOOD, AND THOU SHALT HAVE PRAISE OF   114 17
FOR HE IS THE MINISTER OF GOD TO THEE FOR GOOD   114 19
A MAN WHICH SOWED GOOD SEED IN HIS FIELD   116 19
DIDST NOT THOU SOW GOOD SEED IN THY FIELD   116 24
IS THINE EYE EVIL, BECAUSE I AM GOOD   120 11
AND OTHER FELL ON GOOD GROUND, AND SPRANG UP, AND   121 26
BUT THAT ON THE GOOD GROUND ARE THEY, WHICH IN AN   122 08
IN AN HONEST AND GOOD HEART, HAVING HEARD THE WCRD,   122 09
BY EVIL REPORT AND GOOD REPORT   126 17
AN HIGH PRIEST OF GOOD THINGS TO COME, BY A GREATER   132 23
FOR THE DAY, UNTIL GOOD FRIDAY   R 134 14
SHE HATH WROUGHT A GOOD WORK ON ME   140 11
AND WHENSOEVER YE WILL YE MAY DO THEM GOOD   140 13

GOOD WERE IT FOR THAT MAN IF HE HAD NEVER BEEN BCRN   141 08
HAVING A SHADOW OF GOOD THINGS TO COME, AND NOT THE   157 15
UNTO LOVE AND TO GOOD WORKS   158 25
BUT THE ANSWER OF A GOOD CONSCIENCE TOWARD GOD,) BY   161 31
PUT INTO OUR MINDS GOOD DESIRES, SO BY THY CCNTINUAL   163 26
BRING THE SAME TO GOOD EFFECT   163 27
WENT ABOUT DOING GOOD, AND HEALING ALL THAT WERE   166 21
I AM THE GOOD SHEPHERD   172 21
THE GOOD SHEPHERD GIVETH HIS LIFE FOR THE SHEEP   172 21
I AM THE GOOD SHEPHERD   172 27
THEY MAY BY YOUR GOOD WORKS, WHICH THEY SHALL BEHCLD   173 16
EVERY GOOD GIFT AND EVERY PERFECT GIFT IS FROM ABOVE,   174 26
FROM WHOM ALL GOOD THINGS DO COME   175 29
THINGS THAT ARE GOOD, AND BY THY MERCIFUL GUIDING MAY   175 31
BUT BE OF GOOD CHEER   177 09
ONE TO ANOTHER, AS GOOD STEWARDS OF THE MANIFOLD   179 17
KNOW HOW TO GIVE GOOD GIFTS UNTO YOUR CHILDREN   183 18
WENT ABOUT DOING GOOD, AND HEALING ALL THAT WERE   184 08
WE CAN DO NO GOOD THING WITHOUT THEE, GRANT US THE   189 03
RECEIVEDST THY GOOD THINGS, AND LIKEWISE LAZARUS EVIL   190 17
PROTECTION OF THY GOOD PROVIDENCE, AND MAKE US TC   191 07
HATH THIS WORLD'S GOOD, AND SEETH HIS BROTHER HAVE   191 19
GOOD MEASURE, PRESSED DOWN, AND SHAKEN TOGETHER, AND   194 28
LOVE LIFE, AND SEE GOOD DAYS, LET HIM REFRAIN HIS   195 25
LET HIM ESCHEW EVIL, AND DO GOOD   195 27
IF YE BE FOLLOWERS OF THAT WHICH IS GOOD   195 31
WHO LOVE THEE SUCH GOOD THINGS AS PASS MAN'S   197 05
AND GIVER OF ALL GOOD THINGS   198 21
EVEN SO EVERY GOOD TREE BRINGETH FORTH GCOD FRUIT   200 18
TREE BRINGETH FORTH GOOD FRUIT   200 19
A GOOD TREE CANNOT BRING FORTH EVIL FRUIT, NEITHER   200 20
TREE BRING FORTH GOOD FRUIT   200 21
BRINGETH NOT FORTH GOOD FRUIT IS HEWN DOWN, AND CAST   200 22
ANY THING THAT IS GOOD WITHOUT THEE, MAY BY THEE BE   200 31
AND GIVING US THOSE GOOD THINGS WHICH WE ARE NOT   206 08
TO BE GIVEN TO ALL GOOD WORKS   213 16
THE THING WHICH IS GOOD, THAT HE MAY HAVE TO GIVE TC   216 22
BUT THAT WHICH IS GOOD TO THE USE OF EDIFYING, THAT   216 24
BE OF GOOD CHEER   217 03
ALL AS MANY AS THEY FOUND, BOTH BAD AND GOOD   218 21
TO SERVE THEE IN GOOD WORKS, TO THE GLORY OF THY   220 19
WHICH HATH BEGUN A GOOD WORK IN YOU WILL PERFORM IT   220 26
FRUITFUL IN EVERY GOOD WORK, AND INCREASING IN THE   224 05
BE OF GOOD COMFORT   224 22
FORTH THE FRUIT OF GOOD WORKS, MAY BY THEE BE   225 06
GLAD TIDINGS OF GOOD THINGS   227 11
FOR SO IT SEEMED GOOD IN THY SIGHT   235 07
MAY KNOW TO REFUSE THE EVIL, AND CHOOSE THE GCOD   236 03
FOR HE WAS A GOOD MAN, AND FULL OF THE HOLY GHOST AND   241 08
THAT BRINGEST GOOD TIDINGS, GET THEE UP INTO   243 02
THAT BRINGEST GOOD TIDINGS, LIFT UP THY VOICE WITH   243 03
IT IS GOOD FOR US TO BE HERE   249 02
I HAVE FOUGHT A GOOD FIGHT, I HAVE FINISHED MY   253 26
ENCOURAGED BY THE GOOD EXAMPLES OF THY SAINTS, AND   258 13
KNOW HOW TO GIVE GOOD GIFTS UNTO YOUR CHILDREN   263 11
THAT CURSE YOU, DO GOOD TO THEM THAT HATE YCU,   264 06
THE EVIL AND ON THE GOOD, AND SENDETH RAIN ON THE   264 09
FOR IT IS A GOOD THING TO SING PRAISES UNTO CUR   264 18
EVERY GOOD GIFT AND EVERY PERFECT GIFT IS FRCM ABOVE,   265 18
WE, FOLLOWING THE GOOD EXAMPLES OF THOSE WHO HAVE   268 17
PERSUADED OF THE GOOD WILL OF OUR HEAVENLY FATHER   276 03
AND GIVER OF ALL GOOD THINGS   283 09
ANY THING THAT IS GOOD WITHOUT THEE, MAY BY THEE BE   287 28
THINGS WHICH ARE GOOD, AND ACCEPTABLE UNTO THY DIVINE   298 14
THE LORD SHALL MAKE GOOD HIS LOVING-KINDNESS TCWARD   312 08
O SPEAK GOOD OF THE LORD, ALL YE WORKS OF HIS,   313 02
THE TESTIMONY OF A GOOD CONSCIENCE   317 03
GOOD LORD, DELIVER HIM   318 03
THEE TO HEAR US, GOOD LORD   318 14
WORK TOGETHER FOR GOOD TO THEM THAT LOVE GOD, TO THEM   330 31
THANKS FOR THE GOOD EXAMPLES OF ALL THOSE THY   334 23
PERFECT IN EVERY GOOD WORK TO DO HIS WILL, WORKING IN   335 19
THY LOVE, THAT THE GOOD WORK WHICH THOU DIDST BEGIN   335 29
WHO WILL SHOW US ANY GOOD   347 23
AND SPEAKETH GOOD OF THE COVETOUS, WHOM THE LORD   353 09
IS NONE THAT DOETH GOOD, NO NOT ONE   356 15
IS NONE THAT DOETH GOOD, NO NOT ONE   356 21
I HAVE NO GOOD LIKE UNTO THEE   357 24
SHALL EVERY GOOD MAN SING OF THY PRAISE WITHCUT   375 18
UNTO HIM WITH A GOOD COURAGE   378 24
LORD SHALL WANT NO MANNER OF THING THAT IS GOOD   380 22
AND WOULD FAIN SEE GOOD DAYS   380 26
14 ESCHEW EVIL, AND DO GOOD   380 29
ME EVIL FOR GOOD, *   382 15
LEFT OFF TO BEHAVE HIMSELF WISELY, AND TO DC GOOD   383 32
SET HIMSELF IN NO GOOD WAY   384 02
PUT THOU THY TRUST IN THE LORD, AND BE DOING GCCD   384 29
THE LORD ORDERETH A GOOD MAN'S GOING, *   386 08
AND DO THE THING THAT IS GOOD   386 17
REWARD EVIL FOR GOOD ARE AGAINST ME   388 32
THE THING THAT GOOD IS   388 33
EVEN FROM GOOD WORDS   389 10
OVERFLOWETH WITH A GOOD MATTER   396 15
4 GOOD LUCK HAVE THOU WITH THINE HONCUR   396 22
MEN WILL SPEAK GOOD OF THEE   401 13
THERE IS NONE THAT DOETH GOOD   405 15
NONE THAT DOETH GOOD, NO NOT ONE   405 21
THEY GIVE GOOD WORDS WITH THEIR MOUTH, BUT CURSE WITH 414 05
28 BUT IT IS GOOD FOR ME TO HOLD ME FAST BY GOD,   429 32
AND NO GOOD THING SHALL HE WITHHOLD FROM THEM THAT   446 03
FOR THOU, LORD, ART GOOD AND GRACIOUS, *   447 13
17 SHOW SOME TOKEN UPON ME FOR GOOD   448 09
IT IS A GOOD THING TO GIVE THANKS UNTO THE LORD,   455 32
UNTO HIM, AND SPEAK GOOD OF HIS NAME   463 13

GOOD   CONTINUED

THY MOUTH WITH GOOD THINGS, *   466 15
22 O SPEAK GOOD OF THE LORD, ALL YE WORKS OF HIS,   467 20
THEY ARE FILLED WITH GOOD   469 17
ME EVIL FOR GOOD, *   480 11
AND HATRED FOR MY GOOD WILL   480 12
BECAUSE HIS MIND WAS NOT TO DO GOOD   480 32
A GOOD UNDERSTANDING HAVE ALL THEY THAT DO   483 15
5 A GOOD MAN IS MERCIFUL, AND LENDETH   483 26
WE HAVE WISHED YOU GOOD LUCK, WE THAT ARE OF THE   489 20
FOR THY JUDGMENTS ARE GOOD   492 18
68 THOU ART GOOD AND GRACIOUS   494 17
71 IT IS GOOD FOR ME THAT I HAVE BEEN IN TROUBLE   494 22
AND I HAVE A GOOD HOPE BECAUSE OF THY WORD   495 20
IN THAT WHICH IS GOOD, *   498 14
I WILL SEEK TO DO THINE GOOD   503 25
UNTO THOSE THAT ARE GOOD AND TRUE OF HEART   504 32
AND BEARETH FORTH GOOD SEED, *   505 19
WE WISH YOU GOOD LUCK IN THE NAME OF THE LORD   507 05
BEHOLD, HOW GOOD AND JOYFUL A THING IT IS, *   509 13
THE LORD SHALL MAKE GOOD HIS LOVING-KINDNESS TOWARD   514 14
FOR IT IS A GOOD THING TO SING PRAISES UNTO OUR   522 27
BOTH BY WORD AND GOOD EXAMPLE, THEY MAY FAITHFULLY   531 21
TO THEMSELVES A GOOD DEGREE, AND GREAT BOLDNESS IN   532 04
GIVER OF ALL GOOD THINGS, WHO OF THY GREAT   534 30
THE TESTIMONY OF A GOOD CONSCIENCE, AND CONTINUING   535 06
OTHERWISE SEEM GOOD UNTO THE BISHOP,) TO THE INTENT   R 535 21
UNTO THE PEOPLE, GOOD PEOPLE, THESE ARE THEY WHOM WE   536 22
GIVER OF ALL GOOD THINGS, WHO BY THY HOLY SPIRIT   537 20
BOTH BY WORD AND GOOD EXAMPLE, THEY MAY FAITHFULLY   537 25
I AM THE GOOD SHEPHERD   539 10
THE GOOD SHEPHERD GIVETH HIS LIFE FOR THE SHEEP   539 10
I AM THE GOOD SHEPHERD   539 16
WE HAVE GOOD HOPE THAT YE HAVE WELL WEIGHED THESE   541 09
GIVER OF ALL GOOD THINGS, WHO BY THY HOLY SPIRIT   547 31
BOTH BY WORD AND GOOD EXAMPLE, THEY MAY FAITHFULLY   548 04
HE DESIRETH A GOOD WORK   549 19
SOBER, OF GOOD BEHAVIOUR, GIVEN TO   549 21
HE MUST HAVE A GOOD REPORT OF THEM WHICH ARE WITHOUT   549 28
THEE TO HEAR US, GOOD LORD   553 22
GIVER OF ALL GOOD THINGS, WHO BY THY HOLY SPIRIT   553 26
AN EXAMPLE OF GOOD WORKS UNTO OTHERS, THAT   555 11
HATH GIVEN YOU A GOOD WILL TO DO ALL THESE THINGS   555 29
IN YOU THE GOOD WORK WHICH HE HATH BEGUN, YOU MAY BE   555 31
THEE TO HEAR US, GOOD LORD   560 11
THEE TO HEAR US, GOOD LORD   560 14
THEE TO HEAR US, GOOD LORD   561 06
THROUGH THY SPIRIT, GOOD AND FAITHFUL STEWARDS OF THE   562 10
THE GIVER OF ALL GOOD AND PERFECT GIFTS, WHO OF THY   572 06
PERFECT IN EVERY GOOD WORK TO DO HIS WILL, WORKING IN   573 06
MY GOOD CHILD, KNOW THIS   580 16
AND READY TO DO GOOD TO ALL MEN, ACCORDING TO OUR   588 32
WHO HAVE DONE US GOOD, AND PARDON ALL THOSE WHO HAVE   590 32
WENT ABOUT DOING GOOD, THY SON OUR SAVIOUR JESUS   591 05
AND LOVELY AND OF GOOD REPORT, FOLLOWING THE EXAMPLE   596 27
OR IN SCHOOLS OF GOOD LEARNING   600 04
STRENGTH AND GOOD WORKS, TO FAITH, AND CALLING UPON   604 43
HAVE NO POWER TO DO GOOD WORKS PLEASANT AND   604 44
WHEN WE HAVE THAT GOOD WILL   605 03
THAT WE MAY HAVE A GOOD WILL, AND WORKING WITH US,   605 03
ALBEIT THAT GOOD WORKS, WHICH ARE THE FRUITS OF   605 11
WALK RELIGIOUSLY IN GOOD WORKS, AND AT LENGTH,   606 15
OF GRACE, AND GOD'S GOOD WILL TOWARDS US, BY THE   607 33
MINGLED WITH THE GOOD, AND SOMETIMES THE EVIL HAVE   608 08

GOOD-WILL

AND GOOD-WILL, WITH A CONSCIENCE VOID OF   590 17
TO MUTUAL FORBEARANCE, FAIRNESS, AND GOOD-WILL   600 02

GOODLINESS

AND ALL THE GOODLINESS THEREOF IS AS THE FLOWER OF   242 28

GOODLY

THE GOODLY FELLOWSHIP OF THE PROPHETS PRAISE THEE   010 17
I HAVE A GOODLY HERITAGE   358 03
WERE LIKE THE GOODLY CEDAR-TREES   441 23

GOODMAN

AGAINST THE GOODMAN OF THE HOUSE, SAYING, THESE LAST   120 04
SAY YE TO THE GOODMAN OF THE HOUSE, THE MASTER SAITH,   140 28
SAY UNTO THE GOODMAN OF THE HOUSE, THE MASTER SAITH   148 28

GOODNESS

BY HIS INFINITE GOODNESS AND MERCY   006 02
TO THY FATHERLY GOODNESS ALL THOSE WHO ARE ANY WAYS   019 04
FOR ALL THY GOODNESS AND LOVING-KINDNESS TO US, AND   019 16
BY HIS INFINITE GOODNESS AND MERCY   023 11
TO THY FATHERLY GOODNESS ALL THOSE WHO ARE ANY WAYS   033 02
FOR ALL THY GOODNESS AND LOVING-KINDNESS TO US, AND   033 13
REJOICE IN THY GOODNESS, TO THE PRAISE OF THY HOLY   039 30
THINE INFINITE GOODNESS TO HEAR US, WHO NOW MAKE OUR   040 05
OF THY GREAT GOODNESS, TO RESTRAIN THOSE IMMODERATE   040 24
THROUGH THY GOODNESS, BE MERCIFULLY TURNED INTO   041 04
COMFORT HIM WITH A SENSE OF THY GOODNESS   045 16
COMFORT HIM WITH A SENSE OF THY GOODNESS   046 05
OF THY GOODNESS, TO COMFORT AND SUCCOUR ALL   046 20
OF THY GRACIOUS GOODNESS HAST HEARD THE DEVOUT   051 30
IT THY GOODNESS THAT WE WERE NOT DELIVERED OVER AS A   052 11
OF THY MERCIFUL GOODNESS, AND MAY HE DEVOTE THE   053 05
O GOD, AFTER THY GREAT GOODNESS   060 10

GOODNESS   CONTINUED

OF THY GOODNESS, O LORD, TO COMFORT AND SUCCOUR   074 30
CONFIRM AND STRENGTHEN YOU IN ALL GOODNESS   076 06
OF THY ALMIGHTY GOODNESS, VOUCHSAFE TO BLESS AND   081 09
THY FATHERLY GOODNESS, MERCIFULLY TO ACCEPT THIS OUR   081 15
THY FAVOUR AND GOODNESS TOWARDS US   083 21
BY THY GOODNESS, FOR THE GLORY OF THY NAME   118 31
IS IN ALL GOODNESS AND RIGHTEOUSNESS AND TRUTH   129 14
BY THY GREAT GOODNESS THEY MAY BE GOVERNED AND   132 19
AND THE GREAT GOODNESS TOWARD THE HOUSE OF ISRAEL,   138 30
US WITH ALL GOODNESS, AND OF THY GREAT MERCY KEEP US   198 23
GOODNESS, FAITH, MEEKNESS, TEMPERANCE   209 27
PRESERVE IT EVERMORE BY THY HELP AND GOODNESS   212 07
THY BOUNTIFUL GOODNESS KEEP US, WE BESEECH THEE,   217 18
THY BOUNTIFUL GOODNESS WE MAY ALL BE DELIVERED FROM   223 16
US WITH ALL GOODNESS, AND OF THY GREAT MERCY KEEP US   283 11
AND GRACIOUS GOODNESS TOWARDS THEM   298 19
OF HIS GOODNESS, TO GIVE YOU SAFE DELIVERANCE,   305 12
THY ACCUSTOMED GOODNESS TO THIS THY SERVANT WHO IS   309 28
PRESENT IN THY GOODNESS WITH THIS THY SERVANT, THAT   315 08
STRENGTH AND GOODNESS IN BEHALF OF THIS THY SERVANT,   315 15
THY WONDERFUL GOODNESS, FOR HAVING TURNED OUR   315 21
FOR ALL THY GOODNESS TOWARDS HIM   316 02
MERCY UPON US, O GOD, AFTER THY GREAT GOODNESS   323 15
TO SEE THE GOODNESS OF THE LORD IN THE LAND OF THE   326 29
BLESSINGS OF GOODNESS, *   365 09
THINK THOU UPON ME, O LORD, FOR THY GOODNESS   369 32
TO SEE THE GOODNESS OF THE LORD IN THE LAND OF THE   372 28
OF THY GOODNESS, HAST MADE MY HILL SO STRONG   375 05
IS THY GOODNESS, WHICH THOU HAST LAID UP FOR THEM   377 02
IS FULL OF THE GOODNESS OF THE LORD   378 28
O GOD, AFTER THY GREAT GOODNESS   403 08
2 WHEREAS THE GOODNESS OF GOD *   404 21
MORE THAN GOODNESS, *   404 24
SHOWETH ME HIS GOODNESS PLENTEOUSLY   411 24
12 THOU CROWNEST THE YEAR WITH THY GOODNESS   417 07
HAST OF THY GOODNESS PREPARED FOR THE POOR   419 32
PLENTEOUS IN GOODNESS AND TRUTH   448 05
AND OF GREAT GOODNESS   466 29
THE MERCIFUL GOODNESS OF THE LORD ENDURETH FOR EVER   467 08
THEY THY GREAT GOODNESS IN REMEMBRANCE   473 11
WOULD THEREFORE PRAISE THE LORD FOR HIS GOODNESS   476 20
AND FILLETH THE HUNGRY SOUL WITH GOODNESS   476 23
WOULD THEREFORE PRAISE THE LORD FOR HIS GOODNESS   477 05
WOULD THEREFORE PRAISE THE LORD FOR HIS GOODNESS   477 18
WOULD THEREFORE PRAISE THE LORD FOR HIS GOODNESS   478 08
12 AND OF THY GOODNESS SLAY MINE ENEMIES, *   519 17
AND OF GREAT GOODNESS   521 09
OF THY GREAT GOODNESS HAST VOUCHSAFED TO ACCEPT AND   534 31
LOVE AND GOODNESS TOWARDS US, HAST GIVEN TO US THY   545 13
OF THY ETERNAL GOODNESS, AND FOR THAT THOU HAST   545 22
THINE INFINITE GOODNESS, HAST GIVEN THY ONLY AND   557 21
NOURISH THEM WITH ALL GOODNESS   572 29
GIVER OF ALL GOODNESS, TO SEND HIS GRACE UNTO ME, AND   580 30
HIS MERCY AND GOODNESS, THROUGH OUR LORD JESUS   581 05
SENSE OF THY GOODNESS TO US, AS MAY MAKE US BOTH   588 19
THY FATHERLY GOODNESS BE UPON ALL THAT THOU HAST   599 05
OF INFINITE POWER, WISDOM, AND GOODNESS   603 04

GOODS

I BESTOW ALL MY GOODS TO FEED THE POOR, AND THOUGH I   122 27
HIS PALACE, HIS GOODS ARE IN PEACE   130 05
ME THE PORTION OF GOODS THAT FALLETH TO ME   201 33
NOT TO COVET NOR DESIRE OTHER MEN'S GOODS   289 08
OF THEIR TEMPORAL GOODS, AND, WHEN OF ABILITY,   R 320 23
SO THAT THEY WHICH HATE US SPOIL OUR GOODS   395 14
TRUST IN THEIR GOODS, *   400 16
NOT TO COVET NOR DESIRE OTHER MEN'S GOODS   580 12
THE RICHES AND GOODS OF CHRISTIANS ARE NOT COMMON,   610 44

GORGEOUS

HIM IN A GORGEOUS ROBE, AND SENT HIM AGAIN TO PILATE   153 17

GOSPEL

AND UNFEIGNEDLY BELIEVE HIS HOLY GOSPEL   007 13
EPISTLE AND GOSPEL ARE ORDERED   R 008 33
AND UNFEIGNEDLY BELIEVE HIS HOLY GOSPEL   024 15
THE COMFORTABLE GOSPEL OF CHRIST MAY BE TRULY   037 02
THE TRUTHS OF THE GOSPEL ARE   VI 39
SHALL READ THE GOSPEL, FIRST SAYING, THE HOLY GOSPEL R 070 22
THE HOLY GOSPEL IS WRITTEN IN THE - CHAPTER   R 070 23
AND AFTER THE GOSPEL MAY BE SAID, PRAISE BE TO THEE, R 070 27
TO PREACH THE GOSPEL UNTO ALL NATIONS   078 30
AND IN HIS HOLY GOSPEL COMMAND US TO CONTINUE,   080 14
IS BEFORE APPOINTED UNTO THE END OF THE GOSPEL   R 084 26
THE END OF THE GOSPEL, CONCLUDING WITH THE BLESSING   R 084 29
THE FEAST IN THE GOSPEL, BECAUSE THEY HAD BOUGHT A   089 07
AND GOSPEL, APPOINTED FOR THE SUNDAY,   R 090 07
THE POOR HAVE THE GOSPEL PREACHED TO THEM   094 2
AND GOSPEL MAY BE USED AT THE FIRST   R 098 07
FIRST EPISTLE AND GOSPEL FOR CHRISTMAS DAY SHALL   R 104 0
PARTAKERS OF HIS PROMISE IN CHRIST BY THE GOSPEL   108 14
SAME EPISTLE AND GOSPEL SHALL SERVE UNTO THE NEXT   R 109 26
BEGINNING OF THE GOSPEL OF JESUS CHRIST, THE SON OF   112 0
AND GOSPEL SHALL SERVE FOR EVERY DAY AFTER,   R 125 2
WHERESOEVER THIS GOSPEL SHALL BE PREACHED THROUGHOUT   140 1
REVEALED IN THE GOSPEL OF THY SON   157 0
AND GOSPEL MAY BE USED AT THE FIRST   R 164 3
AND GOSPEL SHALL SERVE FOR EVERY DAY AFTER,   R 178 3
AND GOSPEL MAY BE USED AT THE FIRST   R 182 1
UNTO YOU THE GOSPEL WHICH I PREACHED UNTO YOU, WHICH   204 2
OF THE GOSPEL OF PEACE   219 1

GOSPEL   CONTINUED

MYSTERY OF THE GOSPEL, FOR WHICH I AM AN AMBASSADOR   219 24
FELLOWSHIP IN THE GOSPEL FROM THE FIRST DAY UNTIL   220 24
OF THE GOSPEL, YE ALL ARE PARTAKERS OF MY GRACE   220 30
BEFORE IN THE WORD OF THE TRUTH OF THE GOSPEL   223 27
THAT PREACH THE GOSPEL OF PEACE, AND BRING GLAD   227 10
BUT THEY HAVE NOT ALL OBEYED THE GOSPEL   227 11
THE LIGHT OF THE GOSPEL TO SHINE THROUGHOUT THE   229 18
BE ESTABLISHED IN THE TRUTH OF THY HOLY GOSPEL   237 09
BUT IF OUR GOSPEL BE HID, IT IS HID TO THEM THAT ARE   250 32
OF THE GLORIOUS GOSPEL OF CHRIST, WHO IS THE IMAGE OF   251 04
SET FORTH IN THE GOSPEL THE LOVE AND HEALING POWER OF   253 17
ME TO PREACH THE GOSPEL TO THE POOR   261 17
THE WORDS OF THE GOSPEL, WRITTEN BY SAINT MARK,   274 23
THE WORDS OF THE GOSPEL, WRITTEN BY SAINT JOHN,   275 03
THE WORDS OF THE GOSPEL, WRITTEN BY SAINT MATTHEW,   275 23
THE GOSPEL, THE QUESTIONS (OMITTING THE QUESTION WILT R 282 04
TO PREACH THE GOSPEL TO THE WHOLE WORLD   291 13
AND GOSPEL, HERE FOLLOWING   R 321 16
OR THE FOLLOWING COLLECT, EPISTLE, AND GOSPEL   R 322 04
AND GOSPEL FOR THE DAY, FOR THOSE APPOINTED   R 323 34
CHAPTER OF THE GOSPEL ACCORDING TO ST   R 339 20
AND GOSPEL, AS FOLLOWETH   R 531 12
TO READ THE GOSPEL IN THE CHURCH OF GOD, AND TO   R 534 11
APPOINTED BY THE BISHOP, SHALL READ THE GOSPEL   R 534 14
AND GOSPEL, AS FOLLOWETH   R 537 18
TAKEN OUT OF THE GOSPEL, AND THE WRITINGS OF THE   539 26
HAVING READ THE GOSPEL, (WHICH SHALL BE EITHER SAINT   R 547 24
TO TESTIFY THE GOSPEL OF THE GRACE OF GOD   550 21
THEN ANOTHER BISHOP SHALL READ THE GOSPEL   R 551 12
IS WRITTEN IN THE GOSPEL OF SAINT LUKE, THAT OUR   553 04
SPREAD ABROAD THY GOSPEL, THE GLAD TIDINGS OF   557 30
THAT THE GOSPEL MAY BE PREACHED TO ALL   561 13
LAW AS UNDER THE GOSPEL, MOVED EITHER BY THE EXPRESS   564 12
SHALL BE THE COLLECT, EPISTLE, AND GOSPEL   R 567 03
AND MORE WITH THE LIGHT OF THE EVERLASTING GOSPEL   572 28
THE LIGHT OF THY GOSPEL SHINE UPON ALL NATIONS   590 23
OUR LORD IN THE GOSPEL, THAT IS TO SAY, BAPTISM, AND   607 36
SACRAMENTS OF THE GOSPEL, BEING SUCH AS HAVE GROWN   607 40
PROFESSORS OF THE GOSPEL, TO PAY RESPECTFUL OBEDIENCE   610 41

GOTTEN

HATH HE GOTTEN HIMSELF THE VICTORY   027 07
HATH HE GOTTEN HIMSELF THE VICTORY   461 28

GOVERN

GOVERN THEM, AND LIFT THEM UP FOR EVER   011 05
AND GOVERN THE NATIONS UPON EARTH   028 24
SANCTIFY, AND GOVERN US IN OUR WORK, BY THE MIGHTY   036 33
AND THE CLAUSE, GOVERN US IN OUR WORK, TO GOVERN THEM R 037 13
IN OUR WORK, TO GOVERN THEM IN THEIR WORK   R 037 13
TIME SO GUIDE AND GOVERN THE MINDS OF THY SERVANTS   038 28
THEE TO RULE AND GOVERN THY HOLY CHURCH UNIVERSAL IN   055 19
SANCTIFY, AND GOVERN, BOTH OUR HEARTS AND BODIES, IN   070 07
WHO DOST GOVERN ALL THINGS IN HEAVEN AND EARTH   111 10
TO HELP AND GOVERN THOSE WHOM THOU DOST BRING UP IN   191 04
DOST LIVE, AND GOVERN ALL THINGS, WORLD WITHOUT END   278 30
SANCTIFY, AND GOVERN, BOTH OUR HEARTS AND BODIES, IN   298 27
AND GOVERN THE NATIONS UPON EARTH   418 31
AND THE STARS TO GOVERN THE NIGHT   511 32

GOVERNANCE

BY THY GOVERNANCE, MAY BE RIGHTEOUS IN THY SIGHT   017 18
FOR OUR GOVERNANCE ONLY SUCH THINGS AS PLEASE THEE,   035 26
BY THY GOVERNANCE, THAT THY CHURCH MAY JOYFULLY SERVE   195 16
BY THY GOVERNANCE, THAT THY CHURCH MAY JOYFULLY SERVE   574 16
BY THY GOVERNANCE, MAY BE RIGHTEOUS IN THY SIGHT   592 24
THE SPIRIT OF GOVERNANCE AND OF A SOUND MIND TO ALL   600 02

GOVERNED

SO GUIDED AND GOVERNED BY THY GOOD SPIRIT, THAT ALL   018 31
SO GUIDED AND GOVERNED BY THY GOOD SPIRIT, THAT ALL   032 31
THEY MAY BE GOVERNED AND PRESERVED EVERMORE, BOTH IN   132 20
THE CHURCH IS GOVERNED AND SANCTIFIED   156 28

GOVERNMENT

AUTHORITY OF GOVERNMENT, THAT THERE MAY BE JUSTICE   036 18
TO CIVIL GOVERNMENT, THEIR ECCLESIASTICAL   VI 08
CHARGE AND GOVERNMENT OVER YOU   533 32
CHARGE AND GOVERNMENT OVER YOU   543 13
ANY PERSON TO GOVERNMENT IN THE CHURCH OF CHRIST,   554 09

GOVERNOR

O LORD OUR GOVERNOR, WHOSE GLORY IS IN ALL THE WORLD   018 07
THE GOVERNOR OF THIS STATE, AND ALL OTHERS IN   032 07
THE SUPREME GOVERNOR OF ALL THINGS, WHOSE POWER NO   041 09
AND FOR THE GOVERNOR OF THIS STATE, AND FOR ALL THAT   047 16
CYRENIUS WAS GOVERNOR OF SYRIA   098 31
SHALL COME A GOVERNOR, THAT SHALL RULE MY PEOPLE   109 09
BEAR UNTO THE GOVERNOR OF THE FEAST   113 23
THE GOVERNOR OF THE FEAST CALLED THE BRIDEGROOM,   113 26
AND DELIVERED HIM TO PONTIUS PILATE THE GOVERNOR   134 33
AND JESUS STOOD BEFORE THE GOVERNOR   135 19
AND THE GOVERNOR ASKED HIM, SAYING, ART THOU THE KING   135 19
THAT THE GOVERNOR MARVELLED GREATLY   135 25
THAT FEAST THE GOVERNOR WAS WONT TO RELEASE UNTO THE   135 26
THE GOVERNOR ANSWERED AND SAID UNTO THEM, WHETHER OF   136 02
AND THE GOVERNOR SAID, WHY, WHAT EVIL HATH HE DONE   136 06
SOLDIERS OF THE GOVERNOR TOOK JESUS INTO THE COMMON   136 15

GOVERNOR   CONTINUED

O LORD OUR GOVERNOR, HOW EXCELLENT IS THY NAME IN ALL   350 31
9 O LORD OUR GOVERNOR, *   351 17
AND HE IS THE GOVERNOR AMONG THE NATIONS   367 32

GOVERNORS

TUTORS AND GOVERNORS UNTIL THE TIME APPOINTED OF THE   104 16
OR UNTO GOVERNORS, AS UNTO THEM THAT ARE SENT BY HIM   173 19
TO ALL MY GOVERNORS, TEACHERS, SPIRITUAL PASTORS AND   288 29
TO ALL MY GOVERNORS, TEACHERS, SPIRITUAL PASTORS AND   580 05

GRACE

GRACE BE UNTO YOU, AND PEACE, FROM GOD OUR FATHER,   004 02
ACCORDING TO THE RICHES OF HIS GRACE   004 34
UNTO THE THRONE OF GRACE, THAT WE MAY OBTAIN MERCY,   005 08
AND FIND GRACE TO HELP IN TIME OF NEED   005 09
OF THE HEAVENLY GRACE, SAYING OR HE SHALL SAY,   006 12
AS HE SHALL THINK FIT, OR WITH THE GRACE   R 017 24
THEM WITH THE GRACE OF THY HOLY SPIRIT, THAT THEY MAY   017 32
THE HEALTHFUL SPIRIT OF THY GRACE   018 21
FOR THE MEANS OF GRACE, AND FOR THE HOPE OF GLORY   019 24
WHO HAST GIVEN US GRACE AT THIS TIME WITH ONE ACCORD   020 03
THE GRACE OF OUR LORD JESUS CHRIST, AND THE LOVE OF   020 12
OF THE HEAVENLY GRACE, SAYING   023 21
OF LIFE, AND THE GRACE AND CONSOLATION OF HIS HOLY   024 25
THE HEALTHFUL SPIRIT OF THY GRACE   032 20
FOR THE MEANS OF GRACE, AND FOR THE HOPE OF GLORY   033 22
WHO HAST GIVEN US GRACE AT THIS TIME WITH ONE ACCORD   034 03
THE GRACE OF OUR LORD JESUS CHRIST, AND THE LOVE OF   034 12
THANKSGIVING OR OF BLESSING, OR BEFORE THE GRACE   R 035 05
GIVE US GRACE SERIOUSLY TO LAY TO HEART THE GREAT   037 26
GIVE THY GRACE AND HEAVENLY BENEDICTION   039 02
GIVE THY GRACE, WE HUMBLY BESEECH THEE, TO ALL THOSE   039 09
GIVE THEM GRACE, WE PRAY THEE, TO STAND FAST IN THY   043 09
GRANT US GRACE FEARLESSLY TO CONTEND AGAINST EVIL,   044 10
FOR THE WONDERFUL GRACE AND VIRTUE DECLARED IN ALL   048 16
VESSELS OF HIS GRACE AND THE LIGHTS OF THE WORLD IN   048 18
THAT WE MAY HAVE GRACE TO DIRECT OUR LIVES AFTER   048 19
THROUGH THY GRACE, BE SO GRAFTED INWARDLY IN OUR   049 19
GRANT TO ALL OF US GRACE, THAT WE MAY HENCEFORTH   052 22
GIVING THEM GRACE TO EXECUTE JUSTICE, AND TO MAINTAIN   055 27
PEOPLE INCREASE OF GRACE TO HEAR MEEKLY THY WORD,   056 15
ENDUE US WITH THE GRACE OF THY HOLY SPIRIT TO AMEND   057 16
RULERS MAY HAVE GRACE, WISDOM, AND UNDERSTANDING TO   VI 19
THE TIME PAST, AND GRACE TO KEEP THE LAW FOR THE TIME R 067 25
GIVE GRACE, O HEAVENLY FATHER, TO ALL BISHOPS AND   074 21
AND TO ALL THY PEOPLE GIVE THY HEAVENLY GRACE   074 25
AND TO GIVE US GRACE SO TO FOLLOW THEIR GOOD   075 03
BE FILLED WITH THY GRACE AND HEAVENLY BENEDICTION,   081 26
ASSIST US WITH THY GRACE, THAT WE MAY CONTINUE IN   083 27
BY GOD'S GRACE, TO CELEBRATE THE LORD'S   088 13
YE WILL BY GOD'S GRACE RETURN TO A BETTER MIND   089 19
GIVE US GRACE THAT WE MAY CAST AWAY THE WORKS OF   090 11
THY BOUNTIFUL GRACE AND MERCY MAY SPEEDILY HELP   095 08
BY ADOPTION AND GRACE, MAY DAILY BE RENEWED BY THY   096 16
FULL OF GRACE AND TRUTH   098 06
THE GRACE OF GOD THAT BRINGETH SALVATION HATH   098 18
US BY THY GRACE, THAT BY THE INNOCENCY OF OUR LIVES,   102 24
BY ADOPTION AND GRACE, MAY DAILY BE RENEWED BY THY   104 08
OF THE GRACE OF GOD, WHICH IS GIVEN ME TO YOU-WARD   108 08
TO THE GIFT OF THE GRACE OF GOD GIVEN UNTO ME BY THE   108 17
IS THIS GRACE GIVEN, THAT I SHOULD PREACH   108 19
AND ALSO MAY HAVE GRACE AND POWER FAITHFULLY TO   109 32
I SAY, THROUGH THE GRACE GIVEN UNTO ME, TO EVERY MAN   110 09
ACCORDING TO THE GRACE THAT IS GIVEN TO US, WHETHER   111 15
OF THY HEAVENLY GRACE MAY EVERMORE BE DEFENDED BY THY   115 30
SINGING WITH GRACE IN YOUR HEARTS TO THE LORD   116 13
GIVE US GRACE TO USE SUCH ABSTINENCE, THAT, OUR FLESH   125 28
YE RECEIVE NOT THE GRACE OF GOD IN VAIN   126 04
THE COMFORT OF THY GRACE MAY MERCIFULLY BE RELIEVED   130 26
GRANT US GRACE TO TAKE JOYFULLY THE SUFFERINGS OF THE   144 08
AS BY THY SPECIAL GRACE PREVENTING US THOU DOST PUT   163 25
GIVE US GRACE THAT WE MAY ALWAYS MOST THANKFULLY   171 30
OF THE MANIFOLD GRACE OF GOD   179 18
US THY SERVANTS GRACE, BY THE CONFESSION OF A TRUE   186 24
US THE HELP OF THY GRACE, THAT IN KEEPING THY   189 04
AND GIVETH GRACE TO THE HUMBLE   192 32
BUT THE GOD OF ALL GRACE, WHO HATH CALLED US UNTO HIS   193 09
A MEASURE OF THY GRACE, THAT WE, RUNNING THE WAY OF   204 24
AND HIS GRACE WHICH WAS BESTOWED UPON ME WAS NOT IN   205 15
BUT BY THE GRACE OF GOD I AM WHAT I AM   205 15
YET NOT I, BUT THE GRACE OF GOD WHICH WAS WITH ME   205 17
THE GRACE OF OUR LORD JESUS CHRIST BE WITH   211 06
PRAY THEE THAT THY GRACE MAY ALWAYS PREVENT AND   213 14
GRANT THY PEOPLE GRACE TO WITHSTAND THE TEMPTATIONS   214 23
FOR THE GRACE OF GOD WHICH IS GIVEN YOU BY   214 28
IT MAY MINISTER GRACE UNTO THE HEARERS   216 25
YE ALL ARE PARTAKERS OF MY GRACE   220 30
AND KNEW THE GRACE OF GOD IN TRUTH   223 29
DIDST GIVE SUCH GRACE UNTO THY HOLY APOSTLE SAINT   226 18
AND THE GRACE OF GOD WAS UPON HIM   233 27
O LORD, POUR THY GRACE INTO OUR HEARTS   235 18
GIVE US GRACE THAT, BEING NOT LIKE CHILDREN CARRIED   237 07
ONE OF US IS GIVEN GRACE ACCORDING TO THE MEASURE OF   237 12
AND THE GRACE OF THE FASHION OF IT   239 23
NOR YET OF GRACE TO USE THEM ALWAY TO THY   240 31
AND HAD SEEN THE GRACE OF GOD, WAS GLAD, AND EXHORTED   241 06
BARTHOLOMEW GRACE TRULY TO BELIEVE AND TO PREACH THY   249 15
GRANT US GRACE TO FORSAKE ALL COVETOUS DESIRES,   250 22
GRANT US GRACE SO TO FOLLOW THY BLESSED SAINTS IN ALL   256 07
THIS LAND MAY HAVE GRACE TO MAINTAIN THESE LIBERTIES   263 19
MAY OBTAIN THE MANIFOLD BLESSINGS OF THY GRACE   267 08
KNOWLEDGE OF THY GRACE, AND FAITH IN THEE   276 10

GRACE   CONTINUED

THE FULNESS OF THY GRACE, AND EVER REMAIN IN THE   279 18
GOD TO GIVE ME HIS GRACE, THAT I MAY CONTINUE IN THE   284 04
WITHOUT HIS SPECIAL GRACE   289 15
ALL KNEELING, THE GRACE OF OUR LORD JESUS CHRIST,   289 29
AND SPIRITUAL GRACE GIVEN UNTO US   292 11
WE RECEIVE THIS GRACE, AND A PLEDGE TO ASSURE US   292 13
AND THE INWARD AND SPIRITUAL GRACE   292 16
AND SPIRITUAL GRACE IN BAPTISM   292 22
AND SPIRITUAL GRACE IN BAPTISM IS A DEATH UNTO SIN,   292 24
WHEREBY WE ARE MADE THE CHILDREN OF GRACE   292 26
RECIPIENTS OF HIS GRACE, AND ARE TRAINED IN THE   292 35
THEY MAY GROW IN GRACE UNTO THEIR LIFE'S END   294 27
BE FILLED WITH THY GRACE AND HEAVENLY BENEDICTION   295 02
THE GRACE OF OUR LORD JESUS CHRIST, AND THE LOVE OF   295 04
INCREASE IN THEM THY MANIFOLD GIFTS OF GRACE   297 19
THIS THY CHILD WITH THY HEAVENLY GRACE   297 27
OF ALL SPIRITUAL GRACE, THE AUTHOR OF EVERLASTING   303 04
FILL YOU WITH ALL SPIRITUAL BENEDICTION AND GRACE   304 14
WITH THY GRACE AND HOLY SPIRIT IN THE INNER MAN   316 11
THY SINS, AND THE GRACE AND COMFORT OF THE HOLY   319 16
OF LIFE, AND THE GRACE AND CONSOLATION OF HIS HOLY   323 21
FOR THE WONDERFUL GRACE AND VIRTUE DECLARED IN ALL   336 18
VESSELS OF THY GRACE, AND THE LIGHTS OF THE WORLD IN   336 19
THEE TO GIVE US GRACE SO TO FOLLOW THE EXAMPLE OF   336 21
GRANT US GRACE SO TO CONFORM OUR LIVES TO THEIR   340 31
THE GRACE OF OUR LORD JESUS CHRIST, AND THE LOVE OF   341 05
GIVE US GRACE, WE BESEECH THEE, TO ENTRUST THE SOUL   342 04
FULL OF GRACE ARE THY LIPS, BECAUSE GOD HATH BLESSED   396 19
THE LORD WILL GIVE GRACE AND WORSHIP   446 03
AND TO POUR THY GRACE UPON THEM   531 06
AND TO POUR THY GRACE UPON THEM   537 12
ONE OF US IS GIVEN GRACE ACCORDING TO THE MEASURE OF   537 32
BY GOD'S GRACE, TO GIVE YOURSELVES WHOLLY TO THIS   541 11
AND HAVE SO DETERMINED, BY GOD'S GRACE   542 10
OUR SOILED FACE WITH THE ABUNDANCE OF THY GRACE   544 07
COME WITH THY GRACE AND HEAVENLY AID, AND FILL THE   544 19
SEVENFOLD GIFTS OF GRACE ARE THINE, O FINGER OF THE   544 25
THAT WE MAY HAVE GRACE TO HEAR AND RECEIVE WHAT THEY   547 09
GIVE GRACE, WE BESEECH THEE, TO ALL BISHOPS, THE   549 09
THE GOSPEL OF THE GRACE OF GOD   550 21
TO THE WORD OF HIS GRACE, WHICH IS ABLE TO BUILD YOU   551 03
AND TO SEND THY GRACE UPON HIM, THAT HE MAY DULY   553 18
AND DETERMINED, BY GOD'S GRACE   554 28
OUR SOILED FACE WITH THE ABUNDANCE OF THY GRACE   556 15
COME WITH THY GRACE AND HEAVENLY AID, AND FILL THE   556 27
SEVENFOLD GIFTS OF GRACE ARE THINE, O FINGER OF THE   557 04
THY SERVANT, SUCH GRACE, THAT HE MAY EVERMORE BE   557 29
THOU STIR UP THE GRACE OF GOD, WHICH IS GIVEN THEE BY   558 16
AND TO POUR THY GRACE UPON THEM   560 28
AND TO SEND THY GRACE UPON HIM, THAT HE MAY DULY   561 03
THEY MAY GROW IN GRACE UNTO THEIR LIFE'S END   565 27
FILLED WITH THY GRACE AND HEAVENLY BENEDICTION,   565 32
BUT GRACE AND TRUTH CAME BY JESUS CHRIST   572 02
GIVE THY GRACE, WE BESEECH THEE, TO THY SERVANT, TO   572 08
GIVE THE ABUNDANCE OF THY GRACE   574 10
GOD TO GIVE ME HIS GRACE, THAT I MAY CONTINUE IN THE   577 25
WITHOUT HIS SPECIAL GRACE   580 19
TO SEND HIS GRACE UNTO ME, AND TO ALL PEOPLE   580 30
AND SPIRITUAL GRACE GIVEN UNTO US   581 13
VISIBLE SIGN, AND THE INWARD SPIRITUAL GRACE   581 18
WHAT IS THE INWARD AND SPIRITUAL GRACE   581 23
WE ARE HEREBY MADE THE CHILDREN OF GRACE   581 26
WE MAY GROW IN GRACE, AND IN THE KNOWLEDGE OF OUR   588 09
WE IMPLORE THY GRACE AND PROTECTION FOR THE ENSUING   588 27
GIVE US GRACE TO BE JUST AND UPRIGHT IN ALL OUR   588 30
THE GRACE OF OUR LORD JESUS CHRIST, AND THE LOVE OF   589 09
AND TO GIVE US GRACE TO SHOW OUR THANKFULNESS IN   591 21
AND GRANT US GRACE ALWAYS TO LIVE IN SUCH A STATE   591 29
THE GRACE OF OUR LORD JESUS CHRIST, AND THE LOVE OF   592 02
THE GRACE OF OUR LORD JESUS CHRIST, AND THE LOVE OF   592 27
THE SPIRIT OF GRACE AND OF SUPPLICATION   594 05
THE GRACE TO ASK WHAT THOU WOULDEST   595 28
BY THY HEAVENLY GRACE PRESERVE FROM FALLING THOSE   599 12
GRANT US GRACE THAT WE MAY HONOUR THEE WITH OUR   599 20
WITHOUT THE GRACE OF GOD BY CHRIST PREVENTING   605 02
DONE BEFORE THE GRACE OF CHRIST, AND THE INSPIRATION   605 17
MEET TO RECEIVE GRACE, OR (AS THE SCHOOL-AUTHORS SAY)   605 19
SAY) DESERVE GRACE OF CONGRUITY   605 20
WE MAY DEPART FROM GRACE GIVEN, AND FALL INTO SIN,   605 42
AND BY THE GRACE OF GOD WE MAY ARISE AGAIN, AND   605 42
THEY THROUGH GRACE OBEY THE CALLING   606 12
EFFECTUAL SIGNS OF GRACE, AND GOD'S GOOD WILL TOWARDS   607 33
NOR THE GRACE OF GOD'S GIFTS DIMINISHED FROM SUCH AS   608 15
IS CONFIRMED, AND GRACE INCREASED BY VIRTUE OF PRAYER   608 29

GRACIOUS

FOR HE IS GRACIOUS AND MERCIFUL, SLOW TO ANGER, AND   004 21
FOR THE LORD IS GRACIOUS, HIS MERCY IS EVERLASTING   015 13
MOST GRACIOUS GOD, WE HUMBLY BESEECH THEE, AS FOR THE   035 08
ARE GOOD AND GRACIOUS AND WHOSE LAW IS TRUTH   035 24
O GRACIOUS FATHER, WE HUMBLY BESEECH THEE FOR THY   037 15
O GRACIOUS FATHER, WHO OPENEST THINE HAND AND FILLEST   040 15
AND MOST GRACIOUS PROTECTION OUR COUNTRY'S NAVY, AND   042 05
WITH THY GRACIOUS FAVOUR TO BEHOLD OUR   042 22
BY THY MOST GRACIOUS AND READY HELP   049 15
WITH THY MOST GRACIOUS FAVOUR, AND FURTHER US WITH   049 24
MOST GRACIOUS GOD, BY WHOSE KNOWLEDGE THE DEPTHS ARE   050 31
BY WHOSE GRACIOUS PROVIDENCE THE FORMER AND THE   051 15
WHO OF THY GRACIOUS GOODNESS HAST HEARD THE DEVOUT   051 30
GRACIOUS ART THOU, O LORD, AND FULL OF COMPASSION TO   053 03
BESEECH THEE, O GRACIOUS FATHER, THAT HE, THROUGH THY   053 14
MOST GRACIOUS LORD, WHOSE MERCY IS OVER ALL THY   053 20
UPON US, AND BE GRACIOUS UNTO US   063 16

GRACIOUS   CONTINUED

US THEREFORE, GRACIOUS LORD, SO TO EAT THE FLESH OF   082 18
FOR HE IS GRACIOUS AND MERCIFUL, SLOW TO ANGER, AND   124 24
MAY OBTAIN THY GRACIOUS PROMISES, AND BE MADE   204 25
IF SO BE YE HAVE TASTED THAT THE LORD IS GRACIOUS   259 28
THY FAVOUR AND GRACIOUS GOODNESS TOWARDS THEM   298 19
GRACIOUS IS THE LORD, AND RIGHTEOUS   305 25
HATH GOD FORGOTTEN TO BE GRACIOUS   311 16
UNTO GOD'S GRACIOUS MERCY AND PROTECTION WE   314 26
AND BE GRACIOUS UNTO THEE   314 28
MOST GRACIOUS GOD, THIS THY SERVANT, CAST DOWN   316 18
IF IT BE THY GRACIOUS WILL   321 23
UNTO GOD'S GRACIOUS MERCY AND PROTECTION WE COMMIT   332 10
AND BE GRACIOUS UNTO YOU   332 12
UPON HIM AND BE GRACIOUS UNTO HIM, THE LORD LIFT UP   341 17
7 GRACIOUS AND RIGHTEOUS IS THE LORD   369 33
AND SEE, HOW GRACIOUS THE LORD IS   380 17
FAVOURABLE AND GRACIOUS UNTO SION   404 13
SENTEST A GRACIOUS RAIN UPON THINE INHERITANCE,   419 29
9 HATH GOD FORGOTTEN TO BE GRACIOUS   433 33
THOU ART BECOME GRACIOUS UNTO THY LAND   446 08
ART GOOD AND GRACIOUS, *   447 13
AND BE GRACIOUS UNTO THY SERVANTS   454 15
FOR THE LORD IS GRACIOUS, HIS MERCY IS EVERLASTING   463 14
FOR HE IS GRACIOUS, *   472 31
FOR HE IS GRACIOUS, *   476 06
MERCIFUL AND GRACIOUS LORD HATH SO DONE HIS   482 30
5 GRACIOUS IS THE LORD, AND RIGHTEOUS   486 28
O GIVE THANKS UNTO THE LORD, FOR HE IS GRACIOUS   487 31
THAT HE IS GRACIOUS, *   488 02
FOR HE IS GRACIOUS, *   489 27
68 THOU ART GOOD AND GRACIOUS   494 17
3 O PRAISE THE LORD, FOR THE LORD IS GRACIOUS   510 07
AND BE GRACIOUS UNTO HIS SERVANTS   510 30
O GIVE THANKS UNTO THE LORD, FOR HE IS GRACIOUS   511 16
8 THE LORD IS GRACIOUS AND MERCIFUL   521 08
WITH THY MOST GRACIOUS FAVOUR, AND FURTHER US WITH   571 09
MOST GRACIOUS FATHER, THE GIVER OF ALL GOOD AND   572 06
THE GRACIOUS BISHOP AND SHEPHERD OF OUR   574 21
OF THY MERCY, O GRACIOUS FATHER, THAT ANOTHER DAY IS   588 04
O GRACIOUS FATHER, WHO DESIREST NOT THE DEATH OF   589 32
BE GRACIOUS UNTO THY CHURCH   590 25
TO CONTINUE THY GRACIOUS PROTECTION TO US THIS NIGHT   591 25
UPON US, AND BE GRACIOUS UNTO US   593 19
FOR ALL THY GRACIOUS GIFTS   596 15
TO BEHOLD THY GRACIOUS HAND IN ALL THY WORKS   596 19
O MERCIFUL AND GRACIOUS FATHER, FOR THE LOVE OF THY   600 12

GRACIOUSLY

GRACIOUSLY HEARKEN TO US WHO CALL UPON THEE, AND   041 21
HAST BEEN GRACIOUSLY PLEASED TO PRESERVE, THROUGH THE   051 06
HAST BEEN GRACIOUSLY PLEASED TO DELIVER FROM HIS   053 11
AND GRACIOUSLY HEAR US, THAT THOSE EVILS WHICH THE   058 19
GRACIOUSLY LOOK UPON OUR AFFLICTIONS   059 10
GRACIOUSLY HEAR US, O CHRIST   059 16
GRACIOUSLY HEAR US, O LORD CHRIST   059 16
BESEECH THEE GRACIOUSLY TO BEHOLD THIS THY FAMILY,   156 21
HAST BEEN GRACIOUSLY PLEASED TO PRESERVE, THROUGH THE   306 25
LOOK GRACIOUSLY UPON HIM, O LORD   316 09
DEAL GRACIOUSLY, WE PRAY THEE, WITH ALL THOSE WHO   342 10
HAST DEALT GRACIOUSLY WITH THY SERVANT, *   494 11
OF AND GRACIOUSLY ACCEPTED BY OUR HEAVENLY FATHER   564 20
YET HAST BEEN GRACIOUSLY PLEASED TO PROMISE THY   564 30
GRACIOUSLY ACCEPT THE DEDICATION OF THIS PLACE TO THY   567 06
BE GRACIOUSLY PLEASED TO BLESS THE MINISTRY AND   572 19
AND BE GRACIOUSLY PLEASED TO TAKE US, AND ALL WHO ARE   589 03
BESEECH THEE GRACIOUSLY TO BEHOLD AND BLESS THOSE   596 31
BESEECH THEE GRACIOUSLY TO COMFORT THY SERVANT IN HIS   597 22

GRAFT

GRAFT IN OUR HEARTS THE LOVE OF THY NAME, INCREASE IN   198 21
GRAFT IN OUR HEARTS THE LOVE OF THY NAME, INCREASE IN   283 09
GRAFT IN THEIR HEARTS A LOVE OF THE TRUTH   572 28

GRAFTED

THY GRACE, BE SO GRAFTED INWARDLY IN OUR HEARTS, THAT   049 19
AND GRAFTED INTO THE BODY OF CHRIST'S   280 14
RIGHTLY ARE GRAFTED INTO THE CHURCH   608 27

GRAFTING

THY HOLY SPIRIT GRAFTING IT INWARDLY IN THE HEART,   566 04

GRAIN

SHALL BE, BUT BARE GRAIN, IT MAY CHANCE OF WHEAT,   329 09
IT MAY CHANCE OF WHEAT, OR OF SOME OTHER GRAIN   329 10

GRANT

AND GRANT, O MOST MERCIFUL FATHER, FOR HIS SAKE   006 27
US BESEECH HIM TO GRANT US TRUE REPENTANCE, AND HIS   007 14
AND GRANT US THY SALVATION   016 30
AND GRANT THAT THIS DAY WE FALL INTO NO SIN, NEITHER   017 16
GRANT THEM IN HEALTH AND PROSPERITY LONG TO LIVE   018 02
GRANT TO THE PRESIDENT OF THE UNITED STATES, AND TO   018 10
GRANT THIS, O LORD, FOR THE HONOUR OF OUR ADVOCATE   018 23
THY NAME THOU WILT GRANT THEIR REQUESTS   020 01
AND GRANT, O MOST MERCIFUL FATHER, FOR HIS SAKE   024 02
US BESEECH HIM TO GRANT US TRUE REPENTANCE, AND HIS   024 16
AND MERCIFUL LORD GRANT YOU ABSOLUTION AND REMISSION   024 23
AND GRANT US THY SALVATION   031 03

GRANT   CONTINUED

GRANT THIS, O LORD, FOR THE HONOUR OF OUR ADVOCATE   032 22
THY NAME THOU WILT GRANT THEIR REQUESTS   034 06
GRANT THAT ALL MEN EVERYWHERE MAY SEEK AFTER THEE AND   038 08
GRANT, WE BESEECH THEE, UNTO US THY SERVANTS, THAT   038 19
AND GRANT SUCH SEASONABLE WEATHER THAT WE   039 28
AND GRANT THAT THE SCARCITY AND DEARTH, WHICH WE NOW   041 02
UPON THEE, AND GRANT US THY HELP IN THIS OUR NEED   041 21
AND GRANT THAT IN ALL THINGS THEY MAY SERVE WITHOUT   041 29
GRANT TO THEM THY MERCY AND THE LIGHT OF THY   042 17
AND GRANT THAT IN HUMILITY OF HEART THEY MAY EVER   042 26
GRANT US GRACE FEARLESSLY TO CONTEND AGAINST EVIL,   044 10
AND GRANT THAT, PERCEIVING HOW FRAIL AND UNCERTAIN   045 07
AND GRANT THAT FINALLY HE MAY DWELL WITH THEE IN LIFE   045 20
ARE OFFERED, AND GRANT THAT HE MAY BE RESTORED TO   045 26
GOOD OUT OF EVIL, GRANT TO THESE THY SERVANTS,   046 27
AND GRANT TO IT THAT PEACE AND UNITY WHICH IS   049 07
GRANT, WE BESEECH THEE, ALMIGHTY GOD, THAT THE WORDS   049 17
AND GRANT THAT THOSE THINGS WHICH WE HAVE FAITHFULLY   050 10
GRANT, WE BESEECH THEE, MOST MERCIFUL FATHER, THAT   051 09
BESEECHING THEE TO GRANT TO ALL OF US GRACE, THAT WE   052 22
GRANT, WE BESEECH THEE, O GRACIOUS FATHER, THAT HE,   053 14
GRANT US THY PEACE   057 22
AND GRANT, THAT IN ALL OUR TROUBLES WE MAY PUT OUR   059 24
AND GRANT THAT ALL THOSE WHO DO CONFESS THY HOLY NAME   074 13
BESEECHING THEE TO GRANT THEM CONTINUAL GROWTH IN THY   075 02
GRANT THIS, O FATHER, FOR JESUS CHRIST'S SAKE,   075 04
AND GRANT THAT WE MAY EVER HEREAFTER SERVE AND PLEASE   075 28
BESEECHING THEE TO GRANT THAT, BY THE MERITS AND   081 17
GRANT US THEREFORE, GRACIOUS LORD, SO TO EAT THE   082 18
GRANT THAT WE MAY IN SUCH WISE HEAR THEM, READ, MARK,   092 08
AND CONSOLATION GRANT YOU TO BE LIKEMINDED ONE TOWARD   092 18
GRANT THAT THE MINISTERS AND STEWARDS OF THY   093 26
GRANT THAT WE BEING REGENERATE, AND MADE THY CHILDREN   096 15
GRANT THAT AS WE JOYFULLY RECEIVE HIM FOR OUR   098 13
GRANT, O LORD, THAT, IN ALL OUR SUFFERINGS HERE UPON   099 26
GRANT THAT WE BEING REGENERATE, AND MADE THY CHILDREN   104 07
GRANT US THE TRUE CIRCUMCISION OF THE SPIRIT   105 20
GRANT THAT THE SAME LIGHT ENKINDLED IN OUR HEARTS MAY   106 26
MERCIFULLY GRANT THAT WE, WHO KNOW THEE NOW BY FAITH,   107 30
AND GRANT THAT THEY MAY BOTH PERCEIVE AND KNOW WHAT   109 30
OF THY PEOPLE, AND GRANT US THY PEACE ALL THE DAYS OF   111 12
GRANT TO US SUCH STRENGTH AND PROTECTION, AS MAY   114 06
GRANT US, WE BESEECH THEE, THAT, HAVING THIS HOPE, WE   117 06
MERCIFULLY GRANT THAT BY THY POWER WE MAY BE DEFENDED   120 18
GRANT THIS FOR THINE ONLY SON JESUS CHRIST'S SAKE   122 18
GRANT, WE BESEECH THEE, ALMIGHTY GOD, THAT WE,   130 24
MERCIFULLY GRANT, THAT WE MAY BOTH FOLLOW THE EXAMPLE   134 09
MERCIFULLY GRANT THAT WE, WALKING IN THE WAY OF THE   138 06
GRANT US GRACE TO TAKE JOYFULLY THE SUFFERINGS OF THE   144 08
MERCIFULLY GRANT THAT WE MAY THANKFULLY RECEIVE THE   152 09
GRANT, O LORD, THAT AS WE ARE BAPTIZED INTO THE DEATH   161 13
GRANT US SO TO DIE DAILY FROM SIN, THAT WE MAY   165 06
GRANT, WE BESEECH THEE, ALMIGHTY GOD, THAT WE WHO   168 19
GRANT US SO TO PUT AWAY THE LEAVEN OF MALICE AND   170 21
GRANT UNTO ALL THOSE WHO ARE ADMITTED INTO THE   173 06
GRANT UNTO THY PEOPLE, THAT THEY MAY LOVE THE THING   174 19
GRANT TO US THY HUMBLE SERVANTS, THAT BY THY HOLY   175 29
GRANT, WE BESEECH THEE, ALMIGHTY GOD, THAT LIKE AS WE   177 14
GRANT US BY THE SAME SPIRIT TO HAVE A RIGHT JUDGMENT   180 10
MOST MERCIFUL GOD, GRANT, WE BESEECH THEE, THAT BY   182 15
GRANT, WE BESEECH THEE, MERCIFUL GOD, THAT THY   185 14
WITHOUT THEE, GRANT US THE HELP OF THY GRACE, THAT IN   189 03
AND GRANT THAT WE, TO WHOM THOU HAST GIVEN AN HEARTY   192 25
GRANT THIS, O HEAVENLY FATHER, FOR THE SAKE OF JESUS   194 08
GRANT, O LORD, WE BESEECH THEE, THAT THE COURSE OF   195 15
GRANT TO US, LORD, WE BESEECH THEE, THE SPIRIT TO   200 29
MERCIFULLY GRANT UNTO US SUCH A MEASURE OF THY GRACE,   204 23
GRANT, WE BESEECH THEE, THAT WE MAY SO FAITHFULLY   207 14
THAT HE WOULD GRANT YOU, ACCORDING TO THE RICHES OF   212 14
WE BESEECH THEE, GRANT THY PEOPLE GRACE TO WITHSTAND   214 23
MERCIFULLY GRANT THAT THY HOLY SPIRIT MAY IN ALL   215 28
GRANT, WE BESEECH THEE, MERCIFUL LORD, TO THY   218 32
AND GRANT THAT THOSE THINGS WHICH WE ASK FAITHFULLY   222 11
GRANT THIS, O HEAVENLY FATHER, FOR THE SAKE OF JESUS   223 18
GRANT UNTO US ALL, THAT WE, BEING CALLED BY THY HOLY   226 21
GRANT US SO PERFECTLY, AND WITHOUT ALL DOUBT, TO   228 07
GRANT, WE BESEECH THEE, THAT WE, HAVING HIS WONDERFUL   229 19
GRANT THAT THY CHURCH, BEING ALWAY PRESERVED FROM   233 33
GRANT US PERFECTLY TO KNOW THY SON JESUS CHRIST TO BE   238 30
THAT HE WOULD GRANT UNTO US, THAT WE BEING DELIVERED   244 06
GRANT, O MERCIFUL GOD, THAT, AS THINE HOLY APOSTLE   246 16
SAITH UNTO HIM, GRANT THAT THESE MY TWO SONS MAY SIT,   247 09
MERCIFULLY GRANT THAT WE, BEING DELIVERED FROM THE   248 02
GRANT, WE BESEECH THEE, UNTO THY CHURCH, TO LOVE THAT   249 16
GRANT US GRACE TO FORSAKE ALL COVETOUS DESIRES,   250 22
MERCIFULLY GRANT THAT, AS THY HOLY ANGELS ALWAYS DO   251 29
GRANT US SO TO BE JOINED TOGETHER IN UNITY OF SPIRIT   254 29
GRANT US GRACE SO TO FOLLOW THY BLESSED SAINTS IN ALL   256 07
GRANT TO US, THY HUMBLE SERVANTS, THE SAME FAITH AND   258 06
GRANT THAT WE, ENCOURAGED BY THE GOOD EXAMPLES OF THY   258 13
OF THY PEOPLE, AND GRANT THAT WHOSOEVER SHALL WORSHIP   259 21
GRANT, WE BESEECH THEE, THAT WE AND ALL THE PEOPLE OF   263 18
AND GRANT THAT THEY, SEEKING FIRST THY KINGDOM AND   267 07
AND GRANT THAT WE, FOLLOWING THE GOOD EXAMPLES OF   268 16
AND GRANT HIM AN ENTRANCE INTO THE LAND OF   269 04
MERCY HE WILL GRANT TO THIS CHILD (THIS PERSON) THAT   274 03
O MERCIFUL GOD, GRANT THAT LIKE AS CHRIST DIED AND   278 18
GRANT THAT ALL SINFUL AFFECTIONS MAY DIE IN HIM,   278 21
GRANT THAT HE MAY HAVE POWER AND STRENGTH TO HAVE   278 24
GRANT THAT WHOSOEVER IS HERE DEDICATED TO THEE BY OUR   278 27
AND GRANT THAT THIS CHILD (THIS THY SERVANT), NOW TO   279 16
WE BESEECH THEE TO GRANT, THAT HE, BEING DEAD UNTO   280 32
GRANT YOU TO BE STRENGTHENED WITH MIGHT BY HIS SPIRIT   281 09
GRANT UNTO THY PEOPLE, THAT THEY MAY LOVE THE THING   285 26

GRANT   CONTINUED

THE MINISTER SAY, GRANT TO US, LORD, WE BESEECH THEE,   287 26
GRANT US SO TO BE JOINED TOGETHER IN UNITY OF SPIRIT   290 21
GRANT, O LORD, THAT THEY WHO SHALL RENEW THE PROMISES   294 24
GRANT, O FATHER, THAT WHEN WE RECEIVE THE BLESSED   294 29
AND GRANT THAT THEY MAY SEE THEIR CHILDREN BROUGHT UP   303 11
GRANT, WE BESEECH THEE, MOST MERCIFUL FATHER, THAT   306 28
THEN MAY BE SAID, GRANT, WE BESEECH THEE, O HEAVENLY   307 03
AND GRANT THAT HE MAY DWELL WITH THEE IN LIFE   310 24
OUR PRAYERS, AND GRANT TO THY SERVANT THE HELP OF THY   312 13
AND GRANT HIM AN ABIDING SENSE OF THY   313 06
AND GRANT THAT, BY THE POWER OF THY HOLY SPIRIT, HE   316 20
MAY PLEASE THEE TO GRANT HIM A PLACE OF REFRESHMENT   318 17
GRANT HIM THY PEACE   318 28
AND MERCIFUL LORD GRANT THEE PARDON AND REMISSION OF   319 15
THINE HAND, AND TO GRANT THAT HE MAY TAKE HIS   321 22
AND MERCIFUL LORD GRANT YOU ABSOLUTION AND REMISSION   323 19
THY PEOPLE, AND GRANT THAT, INCREASING IN KNOWLEDGE   332 04
AND GRANT HIM AN ENTRANCE INTO THE LAND OF   334 16
GRANT THIS, WE BESEECH THEE, O MERCIFUL FATHER,   335 13
GRANT TO US WHO ARE STILL IN OUR PILGRIMAGE, AND WHO   336 06
GRANT UNTO US THY SERVANTS SO TO FOLLOW IN FAITH   336 11
GRANT THIS, O FATHER, FOR THE SAKE OF THE SAME,   336 28
GRANT US STEDFASTLY TO BELIEVE THAT THIS THY CHILD   340 25
WHO DOST GRANT TO CHILDREN AN ABUNDANT   340 29
GRANT US GRACE SO TO CONFORM OUR LIVES TO THEIR   340 31
4 GRANT THEE THY HEART'S DESIRE, *   364 22
10 THE LORD WILL GRANT HIS LOVING-KINDNESS IN THE   393 21
6 THOU SHALT GRANT THE KING A LONG LIFE, *   413 17
AND GRANT US THY SALVATION   446 20
O GRANT ME UNDERSTANDING, *   498 19
O GRANT ME UNDERSTANDING, AND I SHALL LIVE   499 28
THING IF THOU WILT GRANT ME, THEN SHALL THE RIGHTEOUS   518 20
GRANT ALSO UNTO YOU STRENGTH AND POWER TO PERFORM THE   543 19
BLESSED SON, TO GRANT UNTO ALL, WHICH EITHER HERE OR   545 27
GRANT ALSO, THAT WE MAY HAVE GRACE TO HEAR AND   547 08
AND GRANT TO THE PEOPLE, THAT THEY MAY OBEDIENTLY   549 12
GRANT ALSO UNTO YOU STRENGTH AND POWER TO PERFORM THE   555 29
GRANT, WE BESEECH THEE, TO THIS THY SERVANT, SUCH   557 28
MAY PLEASE THEE TO GRANT PEACE TO THE WHOLE WORLD,   560 12
MAY PLEASE THEE TO GRANT THAT WE, WITH ALL THY   561 19
THY SERVANTS, AND GRANT THAT WHOSOEVER IN THIS HOUSE   565 19
GRANT, O LORD, THAT THEY WHO AT THIS PLACE SHALL IN   565 23
GRANT, O LORD, THAT WHOSOEVER SHALL RECEIVE IN THIS   565 28
GRANT, O LORD, THAT BY THY HOLY WORD WHICH SHALL BE   566 02
GRANT, O LORD, THAT WHOSOEVER SHALL BE JOINED   566 08
GRANT, WE BESEECH THEE, BLESSED LORD, THAT WHOSOEVER   566 13
AND GRANT THAT ALL WHO SHALL ENJOY THE BENEFIT OF   566 31
AND GRANT THAT ALL WHO SHALL CALL UPON THEE HERE MAY   567 07
GRANT, WE BESEECH THEE, THAT IN THIS PLACE NOW SET   568 09
PRESENTS GIVE AND GRANT UNTO YOU, IN WHOSE LEARNING,   569 14
TO MY CHARGE, GRANT THAT I MAY FAITHFULLY ADMINISTER   573 21
GRANT THIS FOR THE SAKE OF JESUS CHRIST THY SON OUR   573 28
GRANT THAT, BY THE OPERATION OF THE HOLY GHOST, ALL   574 05
AND GRANT THAT THE COURSE OF THIS WORLD MAY BE SO   574 15
GRANT US PATIENCE UNDER OUR AFFLICTIONS   588 29
AND GRANT THAT EVERY MEMBER OF THE SAME, IN HIS   590 25
AND GRANT US GRACE ALWAYS TO LIVE IN SUCH A STATE   591 29
AND GRANT THAT THIS DAY WE FALL INTO NO SIN, NEITHER   592 22
AND GRANT THAT, HAVING THE EYES OF THE MIND OPENED TO   594 23
THEN IN THY MERCY GRANT US A SAFE LODGING, AND A HOLY   595 02
GRANT US, IN ALL OUR DOUBTS AND UNCERTAINTIES, THE   595 27
AND GRANT THAT NO CLOUDS OF THIS MORTAL   596 07
AND GRANT THAT BOTH THEY AND WE, DRAWING NEARER TO   597 04
GRANT THIS, O LORD, FOR THE LOVE OF HIM, WHO FOR OUR   599 15
GRANT US GRACE THAT WE MAY HONOUR THEE WITH OUR   599 20
WHEREFORE THE GRANT OF REPENTANCE IS NOT TO BE DENIED   605 40

GRANTING

GRANTING US IN THIS WORLD KNOWLEDGE OF THY TRUTH, AND   020 08
GRANTING US IN THIS WORLD KNOWLEDGE OF THY TRUTH, AND   034 08

GRAPES

DO MEN GATHER GRAPES OF THORNS, OR FIGS OF THISTLES   200 18
THAT ALL THEY THAT GO BY PLUCK OFF HER GRAPES   441 27

GRASS

NOW THERE WAS MUCH GRASS IN THE PLACE   132 02
DOTH SO CLOTHE THE GRASS OF THE FIELD, WHICH TO-DAY   211 24
NOW THERE WAS MUCH GRASS IN THE PLACE   225 32
THE FLOWER OF THE GRASS HE SHALL PASS AWAY   239 20
IT WITHERETH THE GRASS, AND THE FLOWER THEREOF   239 22
ALL FLESH IS GRASS, AND ALL THE GOODLINESS THEREOF IS   242 28
THE GRASS WITHERETH, THE FLOWER FADETH   242 29
THE GRASS WITHERETH, THE FLOWER FADETH   242 31
SURELY THE PEOPLE IS GRASS   242 31
AND MAKETH THE GRASS TO GROW UPON THE MOUNTAINS, AND   264 28
GOD SO CLOTHE THE GRASS OF THE FIELD, WHICH TO-DAY   266 23
AND FADE AWAY SUDDENLY LIKE THE GRASS   325 23
CUT DOWN LIKE THE GRASS, *   384 27
RAIN UPON THE MOWN GRASS, *   427 09
FLOURISH LIKE GRASS UPON THE EARTH   427 31
AND FADE AWAY SUDDENLY LIKE THE GRASS   453 28
ARE GREEN AS THE GRASS, AND WHEN ALL THE WORKERS OF   456 13
MY HEART IS SMITTEN DOWN, AND WITHERED LIKE GRASS   464 17
AND I AM WITHERED LIKE GRASS   464 32
15 THE DAYS OF MAN ARE BUT AS GRASS   467 14
HE BRINGETH FORTH GRASS FOR THE CATTLE, *   468 21
DID EAT UP ALL THE GRASS IN THEIR LAND, AND DEVOURED   472 07
BE EVEN AS THE GRASS UPON THE HOUSETOPS, *   506 31
AND MAKETH THE GRASS TO GROW UPON THE MOUNTAINS, AND   523 11

GRASSHOPPER

AND THEIR LABOUR UNTO THE GRASSHOPPER   437 34
AND AM DRIVEN AWAY AS THE GRASSHOPPER   481 17

GRASSHOPPERS

AND THE GRASSHOPPERS CAME, AND CATERPILLARS   472 06

GRATEFUL

WITH A GRATEFUL SENSE OF THY MERCIES   046 15
AND SUCH A GRATEFUL SENSE OF THY GOODNESS TO US,   588 19
GIVE US GRATEFUL HEARTS, OUR FATHER, FOR ALL THY   600 17

GRATITUDE

NOT BUT, WITH GRATITUDE TO GOD, EMBRACE THE HAPPY   VI 23
TO HEIGHTEN MY LOVE AND GRATITUDE   573 26

GRAVE

THAT THROUGH THE GRAVE, AND GATE OF DEATH, WE MAY   161 16
DOWN TO THE GRAVE, AND BRINGEST UP AGAIN   315 20
OR TOWARDS THE GRAVE, SHALL SAY OR SING, I AM THE   R 324 04
O GRAVE, WHERE IS THY VICTORY   330 10
THEY COME TO THE GRAVE, WHILE THE BODY IS MADE READY   R 332 16
TO BE SAID AT THE GRAVE, THE SAME IS HEREBY ALLOWED   R 336 31
OR TOWARDS THE GRAVE, SHALL SAY, I AM THE   R 338 04
ARE COME TO THE GRAVE SHALL BE SAID OR SUNG, JESUS   R 341 08
TO CONFUSION, AND BE PUT TO SILENCE IN THE GRAVE   376 32
AND NOT SEE THE GRAVE   400 22
14 THEY LIE IN THE GRAVE LIKE SHEEP   400 34
DELIVERED MY SOUL FROM THE POWER OF THE GRAVE   401 06
AND MY LIFE DRAWETH NIGH UNTO THE GRAVE   448 13
AND LIE IN THE GRAVE, *   449 05
SHALL THY LOVING-KINDNESS BE SHOWED IN THE GRAVE   449 18
HE DELIVER HIS SOUL FROM THE POWER OF THE GRAVE   453 04
THE DEACONS BE GRAVE, NOT DOUBLETONGUED, NOT GIVEN TO   531 27
THEIR WIVES BE GRAVE, NOT SLANDERERS, SOBER, FAITHFUL   531 32
LAY DOWN IN THE GRAVE, AND ROSE AGAIN FOR US, THY SON   587 27

GRAVEN

TO THYSELF ANY GRAVEN IMAGE, NOR THE LIKENESS OF ANY   068 08
TO THYSELF ANY GRAVEN IMAGE, NOR THE LIKENESS OF ANY   286 08
16 HE HATH GRAVEN AND DIGGED UP A PIT, *   350 23
TO THYSELF ANY GRAVEN IMAGE, NOR THE LIKENESS OF ANY   578 27

GRAVES

AND THE GRAVES WERE OPENED   137 27
CAME OUT OF THE GRAVES AFTER HIS RESURRECTION,   137 29

GRAVITY

HIS CHILDREN IN SUBJECTION WITH ALL GRAVITY   549 25

GRAY-HEADED

WHEN I AM GRAY-HEADED, *   426 11

GREAT

GOOD TIDINGS OF GREAT JOY, WHICH SHALL BE TO ALL   004 08
MY NAME SHALL BE GREAT AMONG THE GENTILES   004 13
MY NAME SHALL BE GREAT AMONG THE HEATHEN, SAITH THE   004 16
TO ANGER, AND OF GREAT KINDNESS, AND REPENTETH HIM OF   004 22
THAT WE HAVE A GREAT HIGH PRIEST, THAT IS PASSED INTO   005 06
THANKS FOR THE GREAT BENEFITS THAT WE HAVE RECEIVED   006 06
AND A GREAT KING ABOVE ALL GODS   009 07
FOR THE LORD IS A GREAT GOD   009 07
THANKS FOR THE GREAT BENEFITS THAT WE HAVE RECEIVED   023 14
TO THEE FOR THY GREAT GLORY, O LORD GOD, HEAVENLY   025 25
AND BY THY GREAT MERCY DEFEND US FROM ALL PERILS AND   031 27
AND OF THY GREAT MERCY VOUCHSAFE, WE BESEECH THEE, SO   036 32
LAY TO HEART THE GREAT DANGERS WE ARE IN BY OUR   037 27
THE GLORY OF THY GREAT NAME, AND THE BENEFIT OF THY   039 13
OF THY GREAT GOODNESS, TO RESTRAIN THOSE   040 24
ON THE GREAT DEEP OUR PRAYERS ARE DESIRED   046 11
GIVE AT THE LAST GREAT DAY   047 20
SENSE OF THESE GREAT MERCIES   050 26
THROUGH THE GREAT PAIN AND PERIL OF CHILD-BIRTH, THIS   051 07
US ABOUT WITH SO GREAT COMFORT, AND TO THE GLORY OF THY 051 19
FROM THOSE GREAT AND APPARENT DANGERS WHEREWITH WE   052 10
THE PERILS OF THE GREAT DEEP (OF HIS WAY), THIS THY   053 22
BUT THIS GREAT AND GOOD WORK MISCARRIED AT THAT TIME   VI 05
O GOD, AFTER THY GREAT GOODNESS   060 10
AND OF GREAT PITY   062 32
FOR THY MERCY IS GREAT, AND AFTER THE MULTITUDE OF   063 05
PITIFULNESS OF THY GREAT MERCY LOOSE US   063 12
IS THE FIRST AND GREAT COMMANDMENT   069 29
WHO OF HIS GREAT MERCY HATH PROMISED   076 02
US ABOUT WITH SO GREAT A CLOUD OF WITNESSES   079 23
THY MANIFOLD AND GREAT MERCIES   082 15
TO THEE FOR THY GREAT GLORY, O LORD GOD, HEAVENLY   084 05
AS THE BENEFIT IS GREAT, IF WITH A TRUE PENITENT   085 30
SO IS THE DANGER GREAT, IF WE RECEIVE THE SAME   085 32
THE EXCEEDING GREAT LOVE OF OUR MASTER, AND ONLY   086 13
HIS DEATH, TO OUR GREAT AND ENDLESS COMFORT   086 18
AND THE GREAT PERIL OF THE UNWORTHY   087 09
WOULD NOT THINK A GREAT INJURY AND WRONG DONE UNTO   088 23
YOURSELVES HOW GREAT IS YOUR INGRATITUDE TO GOD, AND   089 14
TO VISIT US IN GREAT HUMILITY   090 14
AND A VERY GREAT MULTITUDE SPREAD THEIR GARMENTS IN   091 24
WITH POWER AND GREAT GLORY   093 11

GREAT   CONTINUED

AMONG US, AND WITH GREAT MIGHT SUCCOUR US   095 05
APPEARING OF THE GREAT GOD AND OUR SAVIOUR JESUS   098 22
BEING GREAT WITH CHILD   099 05
GOOD TIDINGS OF GREAT JOY, WHICH SHALL BE TO ALL   099 15
AS THE VOICE OF A GREAT THUNDER   103 03
AND WEEPING, AND GREAT MOURNING, RACHEL WEEPING FOR   103 31
WITH EXCEEDING GREAT JOY   109 19
OF SO MANY AND GREAT DANGERS, THAT BY REASON OF THE   114 05
FROM THE MOUNTAIN, GREAT MULTITUDES FOLLOWED HIM   114 29
HAVE NOT FOUND SO GREAT FAITH, NO, NOT IN ISRAEL   115 17
WITH POWER AND GREAT GLORY, WE MAY BE MADE LIKE UNTO   117 09
AND SHALL SHEW GREAT SIGNS AND WONDERS   118 05
WITH POWER AND GREAT GLORY   118 20
HIS ANGELS WITH A GREAT SOUND OF A TRUMPET, AND THEY   118 21
TO ANGER, AND OF GREAT KINDNESS, AND REPENTETH HIM OF   124 25
UNTO HER, O WOMAN, GREAT IS THY FAITH   128 20
AND A GREAT MULTITUDE FOLLOWED HIM, BECAUSE THEY SAW   131 22
AND SAW A GREAT COMPANY COME UNTO HIM, HE SAITH   131 26
THAT BY THY GREAT GOODNESS THEY MAY BE GOVERNED AND   132 19
THE EXAMPLE OF HIS GREAT HUMILITY   134 09
ON US, AND THE GREAT GOODNESS TOWARD THE HOUSE OF   138 30
AND WITH HIM A GREAT MULTITUDE WITH SWORDS AND   142 15
WAS AS IT WERE GREAT DROPS OF BLOOD FALLING DOWN TO   150 22
FOLLOWED HIM A GREAT COMPANY OF PEOPLE, AND OF WOMEN,   154 12
AND HE ROLLED A GREAT STONE TO THE DOOR OF THE   162 12
FOR IT WAS VERY GREAT   165 26
TO JERUSALEM WITH GREAT JOY   178 28
JESUS CHRIST WITH GREAT TRIUMPH UNTO THY KINGDOM IN   179 05
AND YOU THERE IS A GREAT GULF FIXED   190 20
CERTAIN MAN MADE A GREAT SUPPER, AND BADE MANY   192 03
THEY INCLOSED A GREAT MULTITUDE OF FISHES   196 18
AND OF THY GREAT MERCY KEEP US IN THE SAME   198 23
BEING VERY GREAT, AND HAVING NOTHING TO EAT, JESUS   199 08
WHEN HE WAS YET A GREAT WAY OFF, HIS FATHER SAW HIM,   202 17
SO MUCH THE MORE A GREAT DEAL THEY PUBLISHED IT   207 06
THAT A GREAT PROPHET IS RISEN UP AMONG US   213 08
WHICH IS THE GREAT COMMANDMENT IN THE LAW   215 09
IS THE FIRST AND GREAT COMMANDMENT   215 12
AND SAW A GREAT COMPANY COME UNTO HIM, HE SAITH   225 22
WHICH HATH GREAT RECOMPENCE OF REWARD   228 15
WILL SHEW HIM HOW GREAT THINGS HE MUST SUFFER FOR MY   230 28
SHE WAS OF A GREAT AGE, AND HAD LIVED WITH AN HUSBAND   233 17
HE SHALL BE GREAT, AND SHALL BE CALLED THE SON OF THE   236 16
THERE SHOULD BE GREAT DEARTH THROUGHOUT ALL THE   241 18
LORD HAD SHEWED GREAT MERCY UPON HER   243 16
THERE SHOULD BE GREAT DEARTH THROUGHOUT ALL THE   246 26
AND THEY THAT ARE GREAT EXERCISE AUTHORITY UPON THEM   247 22
WHOSOEVER WILL BE GREAT AMONG YOU, LET HIM BE YOUR   247 24
AND THE GREAT DRAGON WAS CAST OUT, THAT OLD SERPENT,   252 06
UNTO YOU, HAVING GREAT WRATH, BECAUSE HE KNOWETH THAT   252 19
HARVEST TRULY IS GREAT, BUT THE LABOURERS ARE FEW   254 14
AND, LO, A GREAT MULTITUDE, WHICH NO MAN   256 23
WHICH CAME OUT OF GREAT TRIBULATION, AND HAVE WASHED   257 07
FOR GREAT IS YOUR REWARD IN HEAVEN   257 33
US ABOUT WITH SO GREAT A CLOUD OF WITNESSES   258 12
ABOUT WITH SO GREAT A CLOUD OF WITNESSES, LET US LAY   258 20
LORD OF LORDS, A GREAT GOD, A MIGHTY, AND A TERRIBLE,   263 24
FOR THEE THESE GREAT AND TERRIBLE THINGS, WHICH THINE   263 32
THIS IS A GREAT MYSTERY   267 31
AND OF THY GREAT MERCY KEEP US IN THE SAME   283 11
IS THE FIRST AND GREAT COMMANDMENT   288 08
WHAT GREAT PRIVILEGE DOTH OUR LORD PROVIDE   291 28
YOU IN THE GREAT DANGER OF CHILD-BIRTH   305 13
THROUGH THE GREAT PAIN AND PERIL OF CHILD-BIRTH, THIS   306 26
GREAT AND MIGHTY GOD, WHO BRINGEST DOWN TO THE GRAVE,   315 19
AN OBLATION WITH GREAT GLADNESS, AND TO BLESS THY   315 32
HERE LYING IN GREAT WEAKNESS OF BODY   316 08
O GOD, AFTER THY GREAT GOODNESS   323 15
AN OBLATION, WITH GREAT GLADNESS   326 18
JESUS CHRIST, THE GREAT SHEPHERD OF THE SHEEP,   335 17
THEY BROUGHT IN GREAT FEAR, EVEN WHERE NO FEAR WAS   356 25
SHALL HAVE GREAT TROUBLE   357 27
AND THY LOVING CORRECTION SHALL MAKE ME GREAT   362 08
51 GREAT PROSPERITY GIVETH HE UNTO HIS KING, *   363 07
OF THEM THERE IS GREAT REWARD   364 07
INNOCENT FROM THE GREAT OFFENCE   364 12
GLORY AND GREAT WORSHIP SHALT THOU LAY UPON HIM   365 13
5 HIS HONOUR IS GREAT IN THY SALVATION   365 13
IS OF THEE IN THE GREAT CONGREGATION   367 23
FOR IT IS GREAT   370 07
AN OBLATION, WITH GREAT GLADNESS   372 10
ME MARVELLOUS GREAT KINDNESS IN A STRONG CITY   377 10
SURELY THE GREAT WATER-FLOODS SHALL NOT COME NIGH   378 04
11 GREAT PLAGUES REMAIN FOR THE UNGODLY   378 13
ANY MAN BY HIS GREAT STRENGTH   379 23
19 GREAT ARE THE TROUBLES OF THE RIGHTEOUS   381 06
TO THE GREAT DISCOMFORT OF MY SOUL   382 15
THEE THANKS IN THE GREAT CONGREGATION   382 32
ARE LIKE THE GREAT DEEP   384 07
IS BETTER THAN GREAT RICHES OF THE UNGODLY   385 28
THE UNGODLY IN GREAT POWER, *   387 04
AM BROUGHT INTO SO GREAT TROUBLE AND MISERY, *   388 02
6 O LORD MY GOD, GREAT ARE THE WONDROUS WORKS WHICH   390 21
IN THE GREAT CONGREGATION   390 34
FROM THE GREAT CONGREGATION   391 07
HATH LAID GREAT WAIT FOR ME   392 18
HE IS THE GREAT KING UPON ALL THE EARTH   398 24
GREAT IS THE LORD, AND HIGHLY TO BE PRAISED *   399 10
THE CITY OF THE GREAT KING   399 14
O GOD, AFTER THY GREAT GOODNESS   403 08
GOD WILL WE DO GREAT ACTS   413 04
GREAT WAS THE COMPANY OF WOMEN THAT BARE THE TIDINGS   420 02
AND GREAT THINGS ARE THEY THAT THOU HAST DONE   426 14
19 O WHAT GREAT TROUBLES AND ADVERSITIES HAST THOU   426 17

GREAT   CONTINUED

HAST BROUGHT ME TO GREAT HONOUR, *   426 20
HIS NAME IS GREAT IN ISRAEL   432 24
WHO IS SO GREAT A GOD AS OUR GOD   434 08
THY PATHS IN THE GREAT WATERS, *   434 21
BEEN OUT OF THE GREAT DEPTH   435 31
FOR WE ARE COME TO GREAT MISERY   440 17
AND OF GREAT MERCY UNTO ALL THEM THAT CALL UPON THEE   447 13
10 FOR THOU ART GREAT, AND DOEST WONDROUS THINGS   447 23
13 FOR GREAT IS THY MERCY TOWARD ME   447 30
FOR THE LORD IS A GREAT GOD   459 09
AND A GREAT KING ABOVE ALL GODS   459 09
4 FOR THE LORD IS GREAT, AND CANNOT WORTHILY BE   460 06
2 THE LORD IS GREAT IN SION, *   462 19
WHICH IS GREAT, WONDERFUL, AND HOLY   462 21
AND OF GREAT GOODNESS   466 22
SO GREAT IS HIS MERCY ALSO TOWARD THEM THAT FEAR HIM   466 28
25 SO IS THE GREAT AND WIDE SEA ALSO   469 10
BOTH SMALL AND GREAT BEASTS   469 11
KEPT THEY THY GREAT GOODNESS IN REMEMBRANCE   473 14
WHO HAD DONE SO GREAT THINGS IN EGYPT   474 11
AND THE PLAGUE WAS GREAT AMONG THEM   474 28
THEIR BUSINESS IN GREAT WATERS   477 23
GOD WE SHALL DO GREAT ACTS   479 30
I WILL GIVE GREAT THANKS UNTO THE LORD WITH MY   481 32
OF THE LORD ARE GREAT, *   482 26
HE HATH GREAT DELIGHT IN HIS COMMANDMENTS   483 19
BOTH SMALL AND GREAT   486 05
14 I HAVE HAD AS GREAT DELIGHT IN THE WAY CF THY   490 25
156 GREAT IS THY MERCY, O LORD   500 23
ONE THAT FINDETH GREAT SPOILS   501 06
165 GREAT IS THE PEACE THAT THEY HAVE WHO LOVE THY   501 11
THE LORD HATH DONE GREAT THINGS FOR THEM   505 12
THE LORD HATH DONE GREAT THINGS FOR US ALREADY   505 13
EXERCISE MYSELF IN GREAT MATTERS *   507 25
THAT THE LORD IS GREAT, *   510 11
4 WHO ONLY DOETH GREAT WONDERS   511 22
7 WHO HATH MADE GREAT LIGHTS   511 28
17 WHO SMOTE GREAT KINGS   512 16
THAT GREAT IS THE GLORY OF THE LORD   514 07
O HOW GREAT IS THE SUM OF THEM   515 25
TAKE ME OUT OF THE GREAT WATERS, FROM THE HAND CF   520 05
3 GREAT IS THE LORD, AND MARVELLCUS WORTHY TO BE   520 31
AND OF GREAT GOODNESS   521 09
IS OUR LORD, AND GREAT IS HIS POWER   523 04
5 GREAT IS OUR LORD, AND GREAT IS HIS POWER   523 04
AND IF ANY GREAT CRIME OR IMPEDIMENT BE OBJECTCC,   R 530 26
A GOOD DEGREE, AND GREAT BOLDNESS IN THE FAITH WHICH   532 04
AND A GREAT COMPANY OF THE PRIESTS WERE OBEDIENT TO   532 21
WHO OF THY GREAT GOODNESS HAST VOUCHSAFED TO   534 31
AND IF ANY GREAT CRIME OR IMPEDIMENT BE OBJECTEC,   R 537 02
AND OF HOW GREAT IMPORTANCE THIS OFFICE IS, WHEREUNTO   539 28
HOW GREAT A TREASURE IS COMMITTED TO   540 05
IS BOTH OF SO GREAT EXCELLENCY, AND OF SO GREAT   540 24
AND OF SO GREAT DIFFICULTY, YE SEE WITH HOW GREAT   540 25
YE SEE WITH HOW GREAT CARE AND STUDY YE OUGHT TO   540 25
TOGETHER A GREAT FLOCK IN ALL THE PARTS OF THE WCRLD,   545 19
FOR THESE SO GREAT BENEFITS OF THY ETERNAL GOODNESS,   545 21
THE HONOUR OF THY GREAT NAME   565 05
TO THEIR GREAT AND ENDLESS COMFORT, OBTAIN   565 32
AND I HEARD A GREAT VOICE OUT OF HEAVEN SAYING,   567 14
THE GLORY OF THY GREAT NAME, AND THE BENEFIT OF THY   572 13
AND OF THY GREAT MERCY KEEP THEM IN THE SAME,   572 30
JESUS CHRIST, THE GREAT SHEPHERD OF THE SHEEP,   573 04
OF THAT GREAT DAY, IN WHICH WE MUST GIVE A STRICT   588 21
SENSIBLE OF THE GREAT EVIL OF THEM   590 03
OUR MANY AND GREAT PROVOCATIONS   591 15
AND BY THY GREAT MERCY DEFEND US FROM ALL PERILS ANC   593 14
OR SACRAMENT OF SO GREAT A THING   609 08

GREATER

TO COME, BY A GREATER AND MORE PERFECT TABERNACLE,   132 24
ART THOU GREATER THAN OUR FATHER ABRAHAM, WHICH IS   133 21
FOR WHETHER IS GREATER, HE THAT SITTETH AT MEAT,   149 24
THEE HATH THE GREATER SIN   159 18
THE WITNESS OF MEN, THE WITNESS OF GOD IS GREATER   171 05
FOR MY FATHER IS GREATER THAN I   182 05
GOD IS GREATER THAN OLR HEART, AND KNOWETH ALL   191 25
OF WHOM THE GREATER PART REMAIN UNTO THIS PRESENT,   205 09
WHO, FOR THE GREATER CONFIRMATION OF THE FAITH, CIDST   228 05
AND GREATER WORKS THAN THESE SHALL HE DC   240 20
GREATER LOVE HATH NO MAN THAN THIS, THAT A MAN LAY   241 26
FOR WHETHER IS GREATER, HE THAT SITTETH AT MEAT, OR   250 09
SERVANT IS NOT GREATER THAN HIS LORD   255 18
FOR THY MERCY IS GREATER THAN THE HEAVENS, *   479 11
MEN'S MINDS WITH GREATER REVERENCE FOR HIS GLORICUS   564 17

GREATEST

BUT THE GREATEST OF THESE IS CHARITY   123 15
WHICH OF THEM SHOULD BE ACCOUNTED THE GREATEST   149 19
BUT HE THAT IS GREATEST AMONG YOU, LET HIM BE AS THE   149 22
WHICH OF THEM SHOULD BE ACCOUNTED THE GREATEST   250 04
BUT HE THAT IS GREATEST AMONG YOU, LET HIM BE AS THE   250 08
WHO IS THE GREATEST IN THE KINGDOM OF HEAVEN   252 23
THE SAME IS GREATEST IN THE KINGDOM OF HEAVEN   252 28
WHO IS THE GREATEST IN THE KINGDOM OF HEAVEN   339 22
THE SAME IS THE GREATEST IN THE KINGDOM OF HEAVEN   339 27

GREATLY

INSOMUCH THAT THE GOVERNOR MARVELLED GREATLY   135 25
THEY FEARED GREATLY, SAYING, TRULY THIS WAS THE SCN   137 33
MY RECORD, HOW GREATLY I LONG AFTER YOU ALL IN THE   220 31

GREATLY   CONTINUED

FOR HE HATH GREATLY WITHSTOOD OUR WORDS   254 09
THEY REJOICED GREATLY AGAINST ME   388 25
THAT I SHALL NOT GREATLY FALL   413 30
8 GOD IS VERY GREATLY TO BE FEARED IN THE COUNCIL CF   450 19
OF THE DISCIPLES MULTIPLIED IN JERUSALEM GREATLY   532 21
BECAUSE IT DOTH GREATLY ESTABLISH AND CONFIRM THEIR   606 20

GREATNESS

O LORD, IS THE GREATNESS, AND THE POWER, AND THE   073 18
IN THE GREATNESS OF HIS STRENGTH   138 13
11 FOR THE GREATNESS OF THY MERCY REACHETH UNTO THE   410 02
THROUGH THE GREATNESS OF THY POWER SHALL THINE   417 18
TO THE GREATNESS OF THY POWER, PRESERVE THOU THOSE   440 27
THERE IS NO END OF HIS GREATNESS   520 32
AND I WILL ALSO TELL OF THY GREATNESS   521 05
PRAISE HIM ACCORDING TO HIS EXCELLENT GREATNESS   525 25
YE KNOW THE GREATNESS OF THE FAULT, AND ALSO THE   540 12
TO THE GREATNESS OF THY POWER, PRESERVE THCU THOSE   600 10

GREEDINESS

TO WORK ALL UNCLEANNESS WITH GREEDINESS   216 09

GREEDY

AS A LION THAT IS GREEDY OF HIS PREY, *   359 10
TO MUCH WINE, NOT GREEDY OF FILTHY LUCRE   531 28
NO STRIKER, NOT GREEDY OF FILTHY LUCRE   549 22

GREEK

IN LETTERS OF GREEK, AND LATIN, AND HEBREW,   154 33
IN HEBREW, AND GREEK, AND LATIN   160 05
IS NO DIFFERENCE BETWEEN THE JEW AND THE GREEK   227 02
CALLED IN GREEK, PHRONEMA SARKOS, (WHICH SOME   604 36

GREEKS

AND ALSO TO THE GREEKS, REPENTANCE TOWARD GOD, AND   550 13

GREEN

O ALL YE GREEN THINGS UPON THE EARTH, BLESS YE THE   013 06
THESE THINGS IN A GREEN TREE, WHAT SHALL BE DONE IN   154 30
THE MORNING IT IS GREEN, AND GROWETH UP   325 24
SHALL FEED ME IN A GREEN PASTURE, *   338 19
SHALL FEED ME IN A GREEN PASTURE, *   368 12
EVEN AS THE GREEN HERB   384 28
FLOURISHING LIKE A GREEN BAY-TREE   387 05
I AM LIKE A GREEN OLIVE-TREE IN THE HOUSE OF GOD   405 04
A WHIRLWIND, THE GREEN AND THE BURNING ALIKE   410 27
THE MORNING IT IS GREEN, AND GROWETH UP   453 29
THE UNGODLY ARE GREEN AS THE GRASS, AND WHEN ALL THE   456 13
AND GREEN HERB FOR THE SERVICE OF MEN   468 21

GREETING

TRIBES WHICH ARE SCATTERED ABROAD, GREETING   239 07
GREETING   569 13

GREW

AND THE CHILD GREW, AND WAXED STRONG IN SPIRIT   233 26
AND THE CHILD GREW, AND WAXED STRONG IN SPIRIT,   244 17

GRIEF

GRIEF, TROUBLE, DREAD, OR THE NEAR   048 08
OTHER MINISTER OF GOD'S WORD, AND OPEN HIS GRIEF   088 07
TOWARD GOD ENDURE GRIEF, SUFFERING WRONGFULLY   172 06
IT WAS PAIN AND GRIEF TO ME   389 10

GRIEVE

AFFLICT OR GRIEVE THE CHILDREN OF MEN   045 32
AND GRIEVE NOT THE HOLY SPIRIT OF GCD, WHEREBY YE ARE   216 25
BUT GRIEVE NOT THYSELF AT HIM WHOSE WAY DOTH PROSPER,   385 07
AND IT SHALL GRIEVE HIM   484 04

GRIEVED

WHO ARE GRIEVED AND WEARIED WITH THE BURDEN CF   062 17
SERVANT WHO IS GRIEVED WITH SICKNESS   309 29
I WAS GRIEVED AT THE WICKED   428 14
MY HEART WAS GRIEVED, *   429 18
AND GRIEVED HIM IN THE DESERT   437 22
59 FOR THEY GRIEVED HIM WITH THEIR HILL-ALTARS,   438 28
YEARS LONG WAS I GRIEVED WITH THIS GENERATION,   459 24
AND AM NOT I GRIEVED WITH THOSE THAT RISE UP AGAINST   515 33
PETER WAS GRIEVED BECAUSE HE SAID UNTO HIM THE THIRD   551 21

GRIEVETH

169 IT GRIEVETH ME WHEN I SEE THE TRANSGRESSORS   500 27

GRIEVOUS

IN THIS TIME OF GRIEVOUS SICKNESS, WE FLEE UNTO THEE   045 04
FALLEN INTO GRIEVOUS SIN   048 07
OF THEM IS GRIEVOUS UNTO US   075 24
OR IN ANY OTHER GRIEVOUS CRIME   087 33
YE KNOW HOW GRIEVOUS AND UNKIND A THING IT IS, WHEN A   088 17
MAN SAY, I AM A GRIEVOUS SINNER, AND THEREFORE AN   088 30

GRIEVOUS   CONTINUED

	PAGE	LN
5 HIS WAYS ARE ALWAY GRIEVOUS	353	13
DEPARTING SHALL GRIEVOUS WOLVES ENTER IN AMONG YOU,	550	30

GRIEVOUSLY

	PAGE	LN
TO TIME, MOST GRIEVOUSLY HAVE COMMITTED, BY THOUGHT,	075	20
OF THE PALSY, GRIEVOUSLY TORMENTED	115	09
DAUGHTER IS GRIEVOUSLY VEXED WITH A DEVIL	128	11

GRIN

	PAGE	LN
THEY GRIN LIKE A DOG, AND RUN ABOUT THROUGH THE CITY	411	16
GRIN LIKE A DOG, AND WILL GO ABOUT THE CITY	412	02

GROAN

	PAGE	LN
EVEN WE OURSELVES GROAN WITHIN OURSELVES, WAITING FOR	194	22

GROANETH

	PAGE	LN
WHOLE CREATION GROANETH AND TRAVAILETH IN PAIN	194	19

GROANING

	PAGE	LN
6 I AM WEARY OF MY GROANING	349	10
AND MY GROANING IS NOT HID FROM THEE	388	08
THE VOICE OF MY GROANING, *	464	19

GROUND

	PAGE	LN
INCREASE OF THE GROUND AND THE GATHERING IN OF THE	050	22
FELL ON GOOD GROUND, AND SPRANG UP, AND BARE FRUIT AN	121	26
THAT ON THE GOOD GROUND ARE THEY, WHICH IN AN HONEST	122	08
AND FELL ON THE GROUND, AND PRAYED THAT, IF IT WERE	141	33
GREAT DROPS OF BLOOD FALLING DOWN TO THE GROUND	150	23
BOUGHT A PIECE OF GROUND, AND I MUST NEEDS GO AND SEE	192	07
HE COMMANDED THE PEOPLE TO SIT DOWN ON THE GROUND	199	18
EVEN WITH THE GROUND, AND THY CHILDREN WITHIN THEE	204	12
AND WE COMMIT HIS BODY TO THE GROUND	333	16
WE COMMIT THE BODY OF THIS CHILD TO THE GROUND	341	15
7 THE LOT IS FALLEN UNTO ME IN A FAIR GROUND	358	02
WATCHING TO CAST US DOWN TO THE GROUND	359	09
OUR BELLY CLEAVETH UNTO THE GROUND	396	11
WHERE NO GROUND IS	422	02
DWELLING-PLACE OF THY NAME, EVEN UNTO THE GROUND	430	20
THE LIGHTNINGS SHONE UPON THE GROUND	434	19
OF IT LIKE THE GROUND WHICH HE HATH MADE CONTINUALLY	439	17
AND CAST HIS CROWN TO THE GROUND	452	19
AND CAST HIS THRONE DOWN TO THE GROUND	452	20
AND DEVOURED THE FRUIT OF THEIR GROUND	472	08
AND WATER-SPRINGS OF A DRY GROUND	478	17
DOWN WITH IT, DOWN WITH IT, EVEN TO THE GROUND	513	20
AND SEEK THE GROUND OF MY HEART	516	04
HE HATH SMITTEN MY LIFE DOWN TO THE GROUND	518	28
AND BRINGETH THE UNGODLY DOWN TO THE GROUND	523	07

GROUNDED

	PAGE	LN
ROOTED AND GROUNDED IN LOVE, MAY BE ABLE TO	212	17
THAT THOU HAST GROUNDED THEM FOR EVER	500	15
AND GROUNDED UPON NO WARRANTY OF SCRIPTURE,	607	16

GROW

	PAGE	LN
LET BOTH GROW TOGETHER UNTIL THE HARVEST	116	28
CONSIDER THE LILIES OF THE FIELD, HOW THEY GROW	211	22
TRUTH IN LOVE, MAY GROW UP INTO HIM IN ALL THINGS,	237	29
THAT YE MAY GROW THEREBY	259	27
MAKETH THE GRASS TO GROW UPON THE MOUNTAINS, AND HERB	264	28
CONSIDER THE LILIES OF THE FIELD, HOW THEY GROW	266	20
SPIRIT MAY LIVE AND GROW IN HIM	278	22
THAT THEY MAY GROW IN GRACE UNTO THEIR LIFE'S END	294	27
AND STATURE, AND GROW IN THY LOVE AND SERVICE, UNTIL	307	05
THAT OUR SONS MAY GROW UP AS THE YOUNG PLANTS,	520	15
MAKETH THE GRASS TO GROW UPON THE MOUNTAINS, AND HERB	523	11
THAT THEY MAY GROW IN GRACE UNTO THEIR LIFE'S END	565	27
GROW IN AGE, WE MAY GROW IN GRACE, AND IN THE	588	09
AS WE GROW IN AGE, WE MAY GROW IN GRACE,	588	09

GROWETH

	PAGE	LN
FRAMED TOGETHER GROWETH UNTO AN HOLY TEMPLE IN THE	255	08
IT IS GREEN, AND GROWETH UP	325	24
IT IS GREEN, AND GROWETH UP	453	29

GROWN

	PAGE	LN
AFORE IT BE GROWN UP	506	32
BEING SUCH AS HAVE GROWN PARTLY OF THE CORRUPT	607	40

GROWTH

	PAGE	LN
THEM CONTINUAL GROWTH IN THY LOVE AND SERVICE,	075	02

GRUDGE

	PAGE	LN
AND GRUDGE IF THEY BE NOT SATISFIED	412	04

GRUDGING

	PAGE	LN
USE HOSPITALITY ONE TO ANOTHER WITHOUT GRUDGING	179	16

GRUDGINGLY

	PAGE	LN
NOT GRUDGINGLY, OR OF NECESSITY	072	18

GUARD

	PAGE	LN
GUARD HIM, WE BESEECH THEE, FROM THE DANGERS OF THE	046	11

GUARDIANS

	PAGE	LN
GUARDIANS, AND SPONSORS SHALL BRING THOSE,	R 295	10

GUEST-CHAMBER

	PAGE	LN
IS THE GUEST-CHAMBER, WHERE I SHALL EAT THE PASSOVER	140	29
IS THE GUEST-CHAMBER, WHERE I SHALL EAT THE PASSOVER	148	29

GUESTS

	PAGE	LN
NOTHING BUT THE GUESTS TO SIT DOWN	088	20
AND THE WEDDING WAS FURNISHED WITH GUESTS	218	21
IN TO SEE THE GUESTS, HE SAW THERE A MAN WHICH HAD	218	22

GUIDE

	PAGE	LN
AND TO GUIDE OUR FEET INTO THE WAY OF PEACE	014	32
BESEECH THEE SO TO GUIDE AND BLESS THE LEGISLATURE OF	035	25
AT THIS TIME SO GUIDE AND GOVERN THE MINDS OF THY	038	28
HEAVENLY FATHER, GUIDE, WE BESEECH THEE, THE NATIONS	044	27
IS COME, HE WILL GUIDE YOU INTO ALL TRUTH	175	19
OUR RULER AND GUIDE, WE MAY SO PASS THROUGH THINGS	194	07
WHICH WAS GUIDE TO THEM THAT TOOK JESUS	234	11
OF DEATH, TO GUIDE OUR FEET INTO THE WAY OF PEACE	244	16
BUT GUIDE THOU THE JUST	350	10
ARE MEEK SHALL HE GUIDE IN JUDGMENT	370	02
BE THOU ALSO MY GUIDE, AND LEAD ME FOR THY NAME'S	375	28
AND I WILL GUIDE THEE WITH MINE EYE	378	09
HE SHALL BE OUR GUIDE UNTO DEATH	400	05
MY GUIDE, AND MINE OWN FAMILIAR FRIEND	407	16
24 THOU SHALT GUIDE ME WITH THY COUNSEL, *	429	24
AND WILL GUIDE HIS WORDS WITH DISCRETION	483	26
WHERE THOU ART GUIDE, NO ILL CAN COME	544	09
BE OUR PREVENTING GUIDE, NO EVIL CAN OUR STEPS	545	08
WHERE THOU ART GUIDE, NO ILL CAN COME	556	17
BE OUR PREVENTING GUIDE, NO EVIL CAN OUR STEPS	557	14
MAY PLEASE THEE TO GUIDE BY THY INDWELLING SPIRIT	561	07
KEEP THY LAW, AND GUIDE OUR FEET INTO THE WAY OF	594	14
BLESS AND GUIDE HIM WHEREVER HE MAY BE, KEEPING HIM	597	29

GUIDED

	PAGE	LN
THAT BEING GUIDED BY THY PROVIDENCE, WE MAY	018	09
THAT IT MAY BE SO GUIDED AND GOVERNED BY THY GOOD	018	31
THAT IT MAY BE SO GUIDED AND GOVERNED BY THY GOOD	032	31
BE ORDERED AND GUIDED BY FAITHFUL AND TRUE PASTORS	234	03
THY FAVOUR AND BE GUIDED IN THE WAY OF TRUTH	562	13
WHOM THE MEEK ARE GUIDED IN JUDGMENT, AND LIGHT	595	26

GUIDING

	PAGE	LN
BY THY MERCIFUL GUIDING MAY PERFORM THE SAME	176	02

GUILE

	PAGE	LN
AND IN THEIR MOUTH WAS FOUND NO GUILE	103	13
NEITHER WAS GUILE FOUND IN HIS MOUTH	172	12
FROM EVIL, AND HIS LIPS THAT THEY SPEAK NO GUILE	195	26
AND ALL GUILE, AND HYPOCRISIES, AND ENVIES,	259	25
AND IN WHOSE SPIRIT THERE IS NO GUILE	377	25
AND THY LIPS, THAT THEY SPEAK NO GUILE	380	28
DECEIT AND GUILE GO NOT OUT OF HER STREETS	407	09

GUILT

	PAGE	LN
ONLY FOR ORIGINAL GUILT, BUT ALSO FOR ACTUAL SINS OF	603	16
OF PAIN OR GUILT, WERE BLASPHEMOUS FABLES, AND	609	18

GUILTLESS

	PAGE	LN
NOT HOLD HIM GUILTLESS, THAT TAKETH HIS NAME IN VAIN	068	20
NOT HOLD HIM GUILTLESS, THAT TAKETH HIS NAME IN VAIN	286	20
DESTROY ME GUILTLESS, ARE MIGHTY	422	09
NOT HOLD HIM GUILTLESS, THAT TAKETH HIS NAME IN VAIN	579	02

GUILTY

	PAGE	LN
PROTECT THE INNOCENT, AWAKEN THE GUILTY	046	25
HIM TO BE GUILTY OF DEATH	143	19
BEING FOUND GUILTY, BY JUST JUDGMENT BE DEPOSED	608	21

GULF

	PAGE	LN
THERE IS A GREAT GULF FIXED	190	20

GUMS

	PAGE	LN
CLEAVETH TO MY GUMS, *	367	02

GUSH

	PAGE	LN
136 MINE EYES GUSH OUT WITH WATER, *	499	10

GUSHED

	PAGE	LN
ALL HIS BOWELS GUSHED OUT	234	15
SO THAT IT GUSHED OUT LIKE THE RIVERS	435	34

GUSHED   CONTINUED

THAT THE WATER GUSHED OUT, AND THE STREAMS FLOWED   436 09

HABIT

OF THE EPISCOPAL HABIT, AND SHALL KNEEL DOWN   R 556 02

HABITATION

LOVED THE HABITATION OF THY HOUSE, AND THE PLACE   021 14
FROM THE HABITATION OF THY HOLINESS AND OF THY GLORY   139 18
LET HIS HABITATION BE DESOLATE, AND LET NO MAN DWELL   234 19
FOR AN HABITATION OF GOD THROUGH THE SPIRIT   255 09
LOVED THE HABITATION OF THY HOUSE, *   371 12
FROM THE HABITATION OF HIS DWELLING, HE CONSIDERETH   379 15
EVEN GOD IN HIS HOLY HABITATION   419 20
26 LET THEIR HABITATION BE VOID, *   423 25
EVEN ROUND ABOUT THEIR HABITATION   436 28
ARE THE HABITATION OF THY SEAT   451 02
ARE THE HABITATION OF HIS SEAT   460 33
HAVE THEIR HABITATION, *   468 18
TO HAVE MY HABITATION AMONG THE TENTS OF KEDAR   502 15
AN HABITATION FOR THE MIGHTY GOD OF JACOB   508 14
SION TO BE AN HABITATION FOR HIMSELF   508 32
TO HAVE THY HABITATION AMONG THE SONS OF MEN, AND TO   568 07

HABITATIONS

WITH ALL THY SAINTS IN THE ETERNAL HABITATIONS   319 11
EARTH IS FULL OF DARKNESS AND CRUEL HABITATIONS   431 19

HABITED

BEING DECENTLY HABITED, SAYING THESE WORDS, REVEREND   R 530 09
BEING DECENTLY HABITED, AND SHALL SAY, REVEREND   R 536 09

HAD

AND WHEN HE HAD GIVEN THANKS, (B) HE BRAKE IT, AND   080 18
AND WHEN HE HAD GIVEN THANKS, HE GAVE IT TO THEM,   080 23
BECAUSE THEY HAD BOUGHT A FARM, OR WOULD TRY   089 04
NOW WHEN JOHN HAD HEARD IN THE PRISON THE WORKS OF   094 16
HIS POWER, WHEN HE HAD BY HIMSELF PURGED OUR SINS,   096 28
AND WHEN HE HAD SAID THIS, HE FELL ASLEEP   100 16
TO THE TIME WHICH HE HAD DILIGENTLY ENQUIRED OF THE   103 28
ANGEL OF THE LORD HAD BIDDEN HIM, AND TOOK UNTO HIM   105 13
HER NOT TILL SHE HAD BROUGHT FORTH HER FIRSTBORN SON   105 14
AND WHEN THEY HAD SEEN IT, THEY MADE KNOWN ABROAD THE   106 13
THE THINGS THAT THEY HAD HEARD AND SEEN, AS IT WAS   106 18
WHEN HEROD THE KING HAD HEARD THESE THINGS, HE WAS   109 02
AND WHEN HE HAD GATHERED ALL THE CHIEF PRIESTS AND   109 04
THEN HEROD, WHEN HE HAD PRIVILY CALLED THE WISE MEN,   109 10
WHEN THEY HAD HEARD THE KING, THEY DEPARTED   109 15
AND WHEN THEY HAD OPENED THEIR TREASURES, THEY   109 22
AND WHEN THEY HAD FULFILLED THE DAYS, AS THEY   110 21
RULER OF THE FEAST HAD TASTED THE WATER THAT WAS MADE   113 24
AND WHEN HE HAD AGREED WITH THE LABOURERS FOR A PENNY   119 17
AND WHEN THEY HAD RECEIVED IT, THEY MURMURED AGAINST   120 03
AS THOUGH WE HAD BEEN WEAK   120 26
AND WHEN HE HAD SAID THESE THINGS, HE CRIED, HE THAT   121 27
AND WHEN HE HAD FASTED FORTY DAYS AND FORTY NIGHTS,   126 24
THAT ABRAHAM HAD TWO SONS, THE ONE BY A BONDMAID, THE   130 30
AND WHEN HE HAD GIVEN THANKS, HE DISTRIBUTED TO THE   132 04
THOSE MEN, WHEN THEY HAD SEEN THE MIRACLE THAT JESUS   132 11
ABOVE UNTO THEM THAT HAD EATEN   132 11
AND WHEN THEY HAD BOUND HIM, THEY LED HIM AWAY, AND   134 32
THEN JUDAS, WHICH HAD BETRAYED HIM, WHEN HE SAW THAT   135 02
AND THEY HAD THEN A NOTABLE PRISONER, CALLED   135 27
THAT FOR ENVY THEY HAD DELIVERED HIM   135 31
AND WHEN HE HAD SCOURGED JESUS, HE DELIVERED HIM TO   136 14
AND WHEN THEY HAD PLATTED A CROWN OF THORNS, THEY PUT   136 18
AND AFTER THAT THEY HAD MOCKED HIM, THEY TOOK THE   136 23
AND WHEN HE HAD TASTED THEREOF, HE WOULD NOT DRINK   136 29
WHEN HE HAD CRIED AGAIN WITH A LOUD VOICE,   137 24
THERE WERE SOME THAT HAD INDIGNATION WITHIN   140 06
AND FOUND AS HE HAD SAID UNTO THEM   140 33
FOR THAT MAN IF HE HAD NEVER BEEN BORN   141 09
THE CUP, AND WHEN HE HAD GIVEN THANKS, HE GAVE IT TO   141 12
AND WHEN THEY HAD SUNG AN HYMN, THEY WENT OUT INTO   141 17
HE THAT BETRAYED HIM HAD GIVEN THEM A TOKEN, SAYING,   142 17
BOUND WITH THEM THAT HAD MADE INSURRECTION WITH HIM,   145 15
WITH HIM, WHO HAD COMMITTED MURDER IN THE   145 15
HIM TO DO AS HE HAD EVER DONE UNTO THEM   145 17
THE CHIEF PRIESTS HAD DELIVERED HIM FOR ENVY   145 20
WHEN HE HAD SCOURGED HIM, TO BE CRUCIFIED   145 29
AND WHEN THEY HAD MOCKED HIM, THEY TOOK OFF THE   146 03
AND WHEN THEY HAD CRUCIFIED HIM, THEY PARTED HIS   146 10
FOR WHEN MOSES HAD SPOKEN EVERY PRECEPT TO ALL THE   147 19
AND FOUND AS HE HAD SAID UNTO THEM   148 32
AND WHEN THEY HAD KINDLED A FIRE IN THE MIDST OF THE   151 08
OF THE LORD, HOW HE HAD SAID UNTO HIM, BEFORE THE   151 21
AND WHEN THEY HAD BLINDFOLDED HIM, THEY STRUCK HIM ON   151 24
AND WHEN HE HAD GIVEN THANKS, HE BRAKE IT, AND SAID,   152 18
THE CUP, WHEN HE HAD SUPPED, SAYING, THIS CUP IS THE   152 21
BECAUSE HE HAD HEARD MANY THINGS OF HIM   153 12
AND PILATE, WHEN HE HAD CALLED TOGETHER THE CHIEF   153 21
WHOM THEY HAD DESIRED   154 07
AND WHEN JESUS HAD CRIED WITH A LOUD VOICE, HE SAID,   155 12
THAT THE FATHER HAD GIVEN ALL THINGS INTO HIS HANDS,   155 29
THEIR FEET, AND HAD TAKEN HIS GARMENTS, AND WAS SET   156 12
SO AFTER HE HAD WASHED THEIR FEET, AND HAD TAKEN HIS   156 12
PURGED SHOULD HAVE HAD NO MORE CONSCIENCE OF SINS   157 20
FOR SIN THOU HAST HAD NO PLEASURE   157 26
THIS MAN, AFTER HE HAD OFFERED ONE SACRIFICE FOR SINS   158 05
FOR AFTER THAT HE HAD SAID BEFORE, THIS IS THE   158 10

HAD   CONTINUED

WHEN THEY HAD CRUCIFIED JESUS, TOOK HIS   160 09
WHEN JESUS THEREFORE HAD RECEIVED THE VINEGAR,   160 28
AND WHEN JOSEPH HAD TAKEN THE BODY, HE WRAPPED IT IN   162 10
NEW TOMB, WHICH HE HAD HEWN OUT IN THE ROCK   162 12
AND SALOME, HAD BOUGHT SWEET SPICES, THAT THEY   165 19
THESE THINGS WHICH HAD HAPPENED   167 06
WE TRUSTED THAT IT HAD BEEN HE WHICH SHOULD HAVE   167 20
THAT THEY HAD ALSO SEEN A VISION OF ANGELS,   167 25
EVEN SO AS THE WOMEN HAD SAID   167 28
AND WHEN THEY HAD FULFILLED ALL THAT WAS WRITTEN OF   168 31
FOR DAVID, AFTER HE HAD SERVED HIS OWN GENERATION BY   169 15
SUPPOSED THAT THEY HAD SEEN A SPIRIT   169 30
AND WHEN HE HAD THUS SPOKEN, HE SHEWED THEM HIS HANDS   170 02
AND WHEN HE HAD SO SAID, HE SHEWED UNTO THEM HIS   171 18
AND WHEN HE HAD SAID THIS, HE BREATHED ON THEM,   171 22
THE HOLY GHOST HAD GIVEN COMMANDMENTS UNTO THE   177 25
THE APOSTLES WHOM HE HAD CHOSEN   177 26
AND WHEN HE HAD SPOKEN THESE THINGS, WHILE THEY   178 12
HEARD THAT SAMARIA HAD RECEIVED THE WORD OF GOD,   185 22
AND THEY HAD ON THEIR HEADS CROWNS OF GOLD   187 11
AND THE THIRD HAD A FACE AS A MAN, AND THE   187 19
LIVING CREATURES HAD EACH OF THEM SIX WINGS ABOUT   187 20
THE PIECE WHICH I HAD LOST   193 32
NOW WHEN HE HAD LEFT SPEAKING, HE SAID UNTO SIMON,   196 13
AND WHEN THEY HAD THIS DONE, THEY INCLOSED A GREAT   196 18
FISHES WHICH THEY HAD TAKEN   196 26
AND WHEN HE HAD BROUGHT THEIR SHIPS TO LAND,   196 29
WHAT FRUIT HAD YE THEN IN THOSE THINGS WHEREOF YE ARE   198 31
AND THEY HAD A FEW SMALL FISHES   199 21
AND THEY THAT HAD EATEN WERE ABOUT FOUR THOUSAND   199 24
A CERTAIN MAN HAD TWO SONS   201 31
AND WHEN HE HAD SPENT ALL, THERE AROSE A MIGHTY   202 05
FATHER SAW HIM, AND HAD COMPASSION, AND RAN, AND FELL   202 17
THAT WAS DEAF, AND HAD AN IMPEDIMENT IN HIS SPEECH   206 30
FOR IF THERE HAD BEEN A LAW GIVEN WHICH COULD HAVE   207 32
WHEN HE SAW HIM, HE HAD COMPASSION ON HIM, AND WENT   208 29
THE LORD SAW HER, HE HAD COMPASSION ON HER, AND SAID   213 02
MAN BEFORE HIM WHICH HAD THE DROPSY   213 31
WHEN THE PHARISEES HAD HEARD THAT JESUS HAD PUT THE   215 06
HAD HEARD THAT JESUS HAD PUT THE SADDUCEES TO   215 06
GLORIFIED GOD, WHICH HAD GIVEN SUCH POWER UNTO MEN   217 13
THERE A MAN WHICH HAD NOT ON A WEDDING-GARMENT   218 23
THE WORD THAT JESUS HAD SPOKEN UNTO HIM, AND HE WENT   220 04
AND WHEN HE HAD BEGUN TO RECKON, ONE WAS BROUGHT UNTO   221 14
BUT FORASMUCH AS HE HAD NOT TO PAY, HIS LORD   221 16
AND ALL THAT HE HAD, AND PAYMENT TO BE MADE   221 18
AFTER THAT HE HAD CALLED HIM, SAID UNTO HIM,   221 33
NOT THOU ALSO HAVE HAD COMPASSION ON THY   221 35
EVEN AS I HAD PITY ON THEE   222 02
WHEN THEY HAD HEARD THESE WORDS, THEY MARVELLED, AND   223 11
COUNTRIES WHITHER I HAD DRIVEN THEM   225 20
AND WHEN HE HAD GIVEN THANKS, HE DISTRIBUTED TO THE   226 03
ABOVE UNTO THEM THAT HAD EATEN   226 10
THOSE MEN, WHEN THEY HAD SEEN THE MIRACLE THAT JESUS   226 11
FROM HIS EYES AS IT HAD BEEN SCALES   230 35
AND WHEN HE HAD RECEIVED MEAT, HE WAS STRENGTHENED   230 36
SEE DEATH, BEFORE HE HAD SEEN THE LORD'S CHRIST   232 34
OF A GREAT AGE, AND HAD LIVED WITH AN HUSBAND SEVEN   233 17
AND WHEN THEY HAD PERFORMED ALL THINGS ACCORDING TO   233 24
WITH US, AND HAD OBTAINED PART OF THIS MINISTRY   234 12
IF YE HAD KNOWN ME, YE SHOULD HAVE KNOWN MY FATHER   240 07
WHEN HE CAME, AND HAD SEEN THE GRACE OF GOD, WAS   241 06
AND WHEN HE HAD FOUND HIM, HE BROUGHT HIM UNTO   241 11
HEARD HOW THE LORD HAD SHEWED GREAT MERCY UPON HER   243 15
AND WHEN HE HAD APPREHENDED HIM, HE PUT HIM IN   245 04
AND ALL THAT HE HAD, WITHOUT DELAY WAS OBEDIENT UNTO   246 17
THINGS WHICH THEY HAD SEEN   249 10
IF I HAD NOT COME AND SPOKEN UNTO THEM, THEY HAD NOT   255 22
UNTO THEM, THEY HAD NOT HAD SIN   255 23
THEY HAD NOT HAD SIN   255 23
IF I HAD NOT DONE AMONG THEM THE WORKS WHICH NONE   255 25
THEY HAD NOT HAD SIN   255 26
OTHER MAN DID, THEY HAD NOT HAD SIN   255 26
WHERE HE HAD BEEN BROUGHT UP   261 11
AND WHEN HE HAD OPENED THE BOOK, HE FOUND THE PLACE   261 15
WHEN THEY CAN BE HAD, TWO GODFATHERS AND ONE   R 273 09
HEARD THAT SAMARIA HAD RECEIVED THE WORD OF GOD,   296 14
EVEN BECAUSE YOU HAD A FAVOUR UNTO ME   361 05
5 THEY HAD AN EYE UNTO HIM, AND WERE LIGHTENED   380 11
MYSELF AS THOUGH IT HAD BEEN MY FRIEND OR MY BROTHER   382 20
TO SCORN, AND HAD IN DERISION OF THEM THAT ARE ROUND   395 20
AND I SAID, O THAT I HAD WINGS LIKE A DOVE   406 30
MY TREADINGS HAD WELL-NIGH SLIPT   428 13
15 YEA, AND I HAD ALMOST SAID EVEN AS THEY   429 06
BUT FORGAT WHAT HE HAD DONE, *   435 22
WORKS THAT HE HAD SHOWED FOR THEM   435 23
DRINK THEREOF, AS IT HAD BEEN OUT OF THE GREAT DEPTH   435 31
44 HOW HE HAD WROUGHT HIS MIRACLES IN EGYPT, *   437 27
THE TENT THAT HE HAD PITCHED AMONG MEN   438 33
AND WHEN IT HAD TAKEN ROOT, IT FILLED THE LAND   441 20
LAND OF EGYPT, AND HAD HEARD A STRANGE LANGUAGE   442 21
FOR IF ISRAEL HAD WALKED IN MY WAYS, 15 I SHOULD SOON   443 07
11 I HAD RATHER BE A DOOR-KEEPER IN THE HOUSE OF MY   445 32
AND TO BE HAD IN REVERENCE OF ALL THEM THAT ARE ROUND   450 20
17 IF THE LORD HAD NOT HELPED ME, *   458 20
IT HAD NOT FAILED, BUT MY SOUL HAD BEEN PUT TO   458 20
BUT MY SOUL HAD BEEN PUT TO SILENCE   458 21
THE SORROWS THAT I HAD IN MY HEART, *   458 24
17 BUT HE HAD SENT A MAN BEFORE THEM, *   471 06
AND AARON WHOM HE HAD CHOSEN   471 25
WHO HAD DONE SO GREAT THINGS IN EGYPT   474 10
HAVE DESTROYED THEM, HAD NOT MOSES HIS CHOSEN STOOD   474 14
AND HAD THEM IN SUBJECTION   475 20
FOR THE LOVE THAT I HAD UNTO THEM, LO, THEY TAKE NOW   480 09

HAD   CONTINUED

OF HIS FATHERS BE HAD IN REMEMBRANCE IN THE SIGHT OF	480 27
TO BE PRAISED AND HAD IN HONOUR, *	482 28
THEY OUGHT TO BE HAD IN REMEMBRANCE	483 02
RIGHTEOUS SHALL BE HAD IN EVERLASTING REMEMBRANCE	483 29
14 I HAVE HAD AS GREAT DELIGHT IN THE WAY OF THY	490 25
51 THE PROUD HAVE HAD ME EXCEEDINGLY IN DERISION	493 12
56 THIS I HAD, *	493 22
87 THEY HAD ALMOST MADE AN END OF ME UPON EARTH	495 31
92 IF MY DELIGHT HAD NOT BEEN IN THY LAW, *	496 09
IF THE LORD HIMSELF HAD NOT BEEN ON OUR SIDE,	504 07
IF THE LORD HIMSELF HAD NOT BEEN ON OUR SIDE, WHEN	504 08
2 THEY HAD SWALLOWED US UP ALIVE	504 10
3 YEA, THE WATERS HAD DROWNED US, *	504 12
AND THE STREAM HAD GONE OVER OUR SOUL	504 13
HAD GONE EVEN OVER OUR SOUL	504 14
5 I HAD NO PLACE TO FLEE UNTO, *	518 12
WERE EVERMORE HAD IN SUCH REVEREND ESTIMATION,	529 14
OR HATH HAD EPISCOPAL CONSECRATION OR	529 23
AND WHEN THEY HAD PRAYED, THEY LAID THEIR HANDS ON	532 19
WHO, AFTER HE HAD MADE PERFECT OUR REDEMPTION BY HIS	545 16
AND WHEN HE HAD SO SAID, HE SHEWED UNTO THEM HIS	551 31
AND WHEN HE HAD SAID THIS, HE BREATHED ON THEM,	552 03
WHO, AFTER THAT HE HAD MADE PERFECT OUR REDEMPTION BY	557 23
AND WHEN HE HAD MADE A SCOURGE OF SMALL CORDS,	567 28
THEY ALSO ARE TO BE HAD ACCURSED THAT PRESUME TO SAY,	606 32

HADST

WHEN THOU HADST OVERCOME THE SHARPNESS OF DEATH,	010 28
NEITHER HADST PLEASURE THEREIN	157 30
IF THOU HADST KNOWN, EVEN THOU, AT LEAST IN	204 07
BECAUSE THOU HADST A FAVOUR UNTO THEM	394 31

HAGARENES

THE MOABITES, AND HAGARENES	444 17

HAIL

MOCKED HIM, SAYING, HAIL, KING OF THE JEWS	136 21
TO SALUTE HIM, HAIL, KING OF THE JEWS	145 33
AND SAID, HAIL, KING OF THE JEWS	158 32
UNTO HER, AND SAID, HAIL, THOU THAT ART HIGHLY	236 09
8 FIRE AND HAIL, SNOW AND VAPOURS, *	524 20

HAILSTONES

HAILSTONES AND COALS OF FIRE	360 23
HAILSTONES AND COALS OF FIRE	360 25
VINES WITH HAILSTONES, *	438 02
ALSO WITH HAILSTONES, *	438 04
HE GAVE THEM HAILSTONES FOR RAIN	472 02

HAIR

WITH CAMEL'S HAIR, AND WITH A GIRDLE OF A SKIN ABOUT	112 12
AND MY CHEEKS TO THEM THAT PLUCKED OFF THE HAIR	144 15

HAIRS

IN NUMBER THAN THE HAIRS OF MY HEAD, AND MY HEART	391 12
ARE MORE THAN THE HAIRS OF MY HEAD	422 08

HAIRY

AND THE HAIRY SCALP OF SUCH A ONE AS GOETH ON STILL	420 28

HALF

LEAVING HIM HALF DEAD	208 24
SHALL NOT LIVE OUT HALF THEIR DAYS	408 09

HALL

INTO THE COMMON HALL, AND GATHERED UNTO HIM THE WHOLE	136 16
HIM AWAY INTO THE HALL, CALLED PRAETORIUM	145 30
IN THE MIDST OF THE HALL, AND WERE SET DOWN TOGETHER,	151 09
INTO THE JUDGMENT HALL, AND SAITH UNTO JESUS, WHENCE	159 12

HALLOW

WHO DOST EVER HALLOW AND PROTECT THY CHURCH	562 09

HALLOWED

ART IN HEAVEN, HALLOWED BE THY NAME	007 23
AND HALLOWED IT	068 32
AND HALLOWED IT	286 32
AND HALLOWED IT	579 12

HALT

THE MAIMED, AND THE HALT, AND THE BLIND	192 16
TO ENTER INTO LIFE HALT OR MAIMED, RATHER THAN HAVING	253 05

HAM

PRINCIPAL AND MIGHTIEST IN THE DWELLINGS OF HAM	438 13
AND JACOB WAS A STRANGER IN THE LAND OF HAM	471 19
AND WONDERS IN THE LAND OF HAM	471 27
22 WONDROUS WORKS IN THE LAND OF HAM	474 12

HAMMERS

WITH AXES AND HAMMERS	430 17

HAND

FOR THE KINGDOM OF HEAVEN IS AT HAND	004 04
IN HIS HAND ARE ALL THE CORNERS OF THE EARTH	009 09
AND THE SHEEP OF HIS HAND	009 16
AT THE RIGHT HAND OF GOD, IN THE GLORY OF THE FATHER	010 30
AND FROM THE HAND OF ALL THAT HATE US	014 15
OUT OF THE HAND OF OUR ENEMIES *	014 20
ON THE RIGHT HAND OF GOD THE FATHER ALMIGHTY	015 26
ON THE RIGHT HAND OF THE FATHER	016 11
ON THE RIGHT HAND OF GOD	022 20
AT THE RIGHT HAND OF GOD THE FATHER, HAVE MERCY UPON	025 31
WITH HIS OWN RIGHT HAND, AND WITH HIS HOLY ARM,	027 06
ON THE RIGHT HAND OF GOD THE FATHER ALMIGHTY	029 31
ON THE RIGHT HAND OF THE FATHER	030 16
WHO OPENEST THINE HAND AND FILLEST ALL THINGS LIVING	040 03
ON THE RIGHT HAND OF THE FATHER	071 14
AND HERE TO LAY HIS HAND UPON ALL THE BREAD	R 080 32
HE IS TO LAY HIS HAND UPON EVERY VESSEL IN WHICH	R 080 34
AT THE RIGHT HAND OF GOD THE FATHER, HAVE MERCY UPON	084 11
HAVE FORGIVENESS OF YOUR OFFENCES AT GOD'S HAND	087 29
THE NIGHT IS FAR SPENT, THE DAY IS AT HAND	091 03
YOUR OWN SELVES THAT SUMMER IS NOW NIGH AT HAND	093 16
KNOW YE THAT THE KINGDOM OF GOD IS NIGH AT HAND	093 18
THE LORD IS AT HAND	095 15
DOWN ON THE RIGHT HAND OF THE MAJESTY ON HIGH	096 29
AT THE RIGHT HAND OF GOD TO SUCCOUR ALL THOSE WHO	100 02
ON THE RIGHT HAND OF GOD, AND SAID, BEHOLD, I SEE THE	100 07
ON THE RIGHT HAND OF GOD	100 09
FORTH THY RIGHT HAND TO HELP AND DEFEND US	112 28
JESUS PUT FORTH HIS HAND, AND TOUCHED HIM, SAYING, I	114 32
ON THE RIGHT HAND AND ON THE LEFT, BY HONOUR AND	126 15
FORTH THE RIGHT HAND OF THY MAJESTY, TO BE OUR	128 27
AND A REED IN HIS RIGHT HAND	136 20
ONE ON THE RIGHT HAND, AND ANOTHER ON THE LEFT	137 04
THEM BY THEIR HAND OF MOSES WITH HIS GLORIOUS	139 11
HE THAT BETRAYETH ME IS AT HAND	142 14
ON THE RIGHT HAND OF POWER, AND COMING IN THE CLOUDS	143 15
THIS SHALL YE HAVE OF MINE HAND	144 29
ONE ON HIS RIGHT HAND, AND THE OTHER ON HIS LEFT	146 15
BEHOLD, THE HAND OF HIM THAT BETRAYETH ME IS	149 13
SIT ON THE RIGHT HAND OF THE POWER OF GOD	151 33
ONE ON THE RIGHT HAND, AND THE OTHER ON THE LEFT	154 24
DOWN ON THE RIGHT HAND OF GOD	158 06
AND IS ON THE RIGHT HAND OF GOD	162 02
ON THE RIGHT HAND OF GOD	164 04
THE END OF ALL THINGS IS AT HAND	179 12
UNDER THE MIGHTY HAND OF GOD, THAT HE MAY EXALT YOU	193 02
PUT A RING ON HIS HAND, AND SHOES ON HIS FEET	202 22
HIM TO PUT HIS HAND UPON HIM	206 31
BY ANGELS IN THE HAND OF A MEDIATOR	207 29
LETTER I HAVE WRITTEN UNTO YOU WITH MINE OWN HAND	210 24
THOU ON MY RIGHT HAND, TILL I MAKE THINE ENEMIES THY	215 20
BIND HIM HAND AND FOOT, AND TAKE HIM AWAY,	218 26
COME AND LAY THY HAND UPON HER, AND SHE SHALL LIVE	224 15
AND TOOK HER BY THE HAND, AND THE MAID AROSE	224 28
AND THRUST MY HAND INTO HIS SIDE, I WILL NOT BELIEVE	228 30
REACH HITHER THY HAND, AND THRUST IT INTO MY SIDE	229 04
THEY LED HIM BY THE HAND, AND BROUGHT HIM INTO	230 11
AND PUTTING HIS HAND ON HIM, THAT HE MIGHT	230 20
OF THE LORD'S HAND DOUBLE FOR ALL HER SINS	242 19
COME WITH STRONG HAND, AND HIS ARM SHALL RULE FOR	243 06
AND THE HAND OF THE LORD WAS WITH HIM	243 30
AND FROM THE HAND OF ALL THAT HATE US	244 03
OUT OF THE HAND OF OUR ENEMIES MIGHT SERVE HIM	244 07
ME OUT OF THE HAND OF HEROD, AND FROM ALL THE	245 28
ONE ON THY RIGHT HAND, AND THE OTHER ON THE LEFT, IN	247 10
TO SIT ON MY RIGHT HAND, AND ON MY LEFT, IS NOT MINE	247 16
WHEREFORE IF THY HAND OR THY FOOT OFFEND THEE, CUT	253 03
AND THE TIME OF MY DEPARTURE IS AT HAND	253 26
DOWN AT THE RIGHT HAND OF THE THRONE OF GOD	258 26
SHEEP ON HIS RIGHT HAND, BUT THE GOATS ON THE LEFT	259 02
THEM ON HIS RIGHT HAND, COME, YE BLESSED OF MY	259 03
THEM OUT OF THE HAND OF THOSE THAT SERVED THEMSELVES	262 13
TAKE HIM BY THE HAND, AND SHALL ASK THE WITNESSES THE	R 279 31
ON THE RIGHT HAND OF GOD THE FATHER ALMIGHTY	284 20
HE SHALL LAY HIS HAND UPON THE HEAD OF EVERY ONE	R 297 24
LET THY FATHERLY HAND, WE BESEECH THEE, EVER BE OVER	298 19
MAN ON THE RIGHT HAND, AND THE WOMAN ON THE LEFT, THE	R 300 06
MAN WITH HIS RIGHT HAND TO TAKE THE WOMAN BY HER	R 301 26
WOMAN BY HER RIGHT HAND, AND TO SAY AFTER HIM AS	R 301 26
WITH HER RIGHT HAND TAKING THE MAN BY HIS RIGHT HAND,	R 302 02
MAN BY HIS RIGHT HAND, SHALL LIKEWISE SAY AFTER THE	R 302 03
UPON THE FOURTH FINGER OF THE WOMAN'S LEFT HAND	R 302 12
OF THE WOMAN'S LEFT HAND, THE MINISTER SHALL SAY,	R 302 24
YEARS OF THE RIGHT HAND OF THE MOST HIGHEST	311 19
STRETCH FORTH THY HAND UPON THE FURIOUSNESS OF MINE	312 05
AND THY RIGHT HAND SHALL SAVE ME	312 06
OIL (OR I LAY MY HAND UPON THEE), IN THE NAME OF THE	320 15
VISITED WITH THINE HAND, AND TO GRANT THAT HE MAY	321 22
THE LORD IS THY DEFENCE UPON THY RIGHT HAND	327 28
EVEN AT THE RIGHT HAND OF GOD, WHO ALSO MAKETH	331 05
AND AT THY RIGHT HAND THERE IS PLEASURE FOR EVERMORE	333 10
BE SET ON HIS RIGHT HAND, AND HEAR THAT HIS MOST	336 25
THE LORD IS THY DEFENCE UPON THY RIGHT HAND	339 12
AND LET NOT MAN HAVE THE UPPER HAND	352 30
O LORD GOD, AND LIFT UP THINE HAND	353 32
THAT THOU MAYEST TAKE THE MATTER INTO THY HAND	354 06
HE IS ON MY RIGHT HAND, THEREFORE I SHALL NOT FALL	358 07
AND AT THY RIGHT HAND THERE IS PLEASURE FOR EVERMORE	358 13
FROM SUCH AS RESIST THY RIGHT HAND	358 33
14 YEA, BY THY HAND, O LORD	359 14

HAND   CONTINUED

THY RIGHT HAND ALSO SHALL HOLD ME UP, AND THY LCVING   362 07
WITH THE WHOLESOME STRENGTH OF HIS RIGHT HAND   364 28
8 ALL THINE ENEMIES SHALL FEEL THINE HAND   365 20
THY RIGHT HAND SHALL FIND OUT THEM THAT HATE THEE   365 21
TROUBLE IS HARD AT HAND,   366 25
AND THEIR RIGHT HAND IS FULL OF GIFTS   371 16
SHUT ME UP INTO THE HAND OF THE ENEMY   376 26
17 MY TIMES ARE IN THY HAND   376 26
DELIVER ME FROM THE HAND OF MINE ENEMIES, *   376 26
4 FOR THY HAND WAS HEAVY UPON ME DAY AND NIGHT,   377 28
2 LAY HAND UPON THE SHIELD AND BUCKLER, *   381 20
AND LET NOT THE HAND OF THE UNGODLY CAST ME DOWN   384 20
FOR THE LORD UPHOLDETH HIM WITH HIS HAND   386 11
LEAVE HIM IN HIS HAND, *   386 32
AND THY HAND PRESSETH ME SORE   387 23
I AM EVEN CONSUMED BY THE MEANS OF THY HEAVY HAND   389 07
HEATHEN WITH THY HAND, AND PLANTED OUR FATHERS IN   394 24
4 BUT THY RIGHT HAND, AND THINE ARM, AND THE LIGHT OF   394 30
AND THY RIGHT HAND SHALL TEACH THEE TERRIBLE THINGS   396 24
UPON THY RIGHT HAND DOTH STAND THE QUEEN IN A VESTURE   397 03
THY RIGHT HAND IS FULL OF RIGHTEOUSNESS   399 30
ARE DAILY AT HAND TO SWALLOW ME UP   408 16
THAT SHALL PERFORM THE CAUSE WHICH I HAVE IN HAND   409 16
ME WITH THY RIGHT HAND, AND HEAR ME   412 22
THY RIGHT HAND HATH UPHOLDEN ME   415 09
MY GOD, OUT OF THE HAND OF THE UNGODLY, *   425 11
OUT OF THE HAND OF THE UNRIGHTEOUS AND CRUEL MAN   425 12
FOR THOU HAST HOLDEN ME BY MY RIGHT HAND   429 23
12 WHY WITHDRAWEST THOU THY HAND   430 29
THOU NOT THY RIGHT HAND OUT OF THY BOSCM TC CONSUME   430 30
9 FOR IN THE HAND OF THE LORD THERE IS A CUP,   432 14
YEARS OF THE RIGHT HAND OF THE MOST HIGHEST   434 03
BY THE HAND OF MOSES AND AARCN   434 23
THOUGHT NOT OF HIS HAND, *   437 25
THEM FROM THE HAND OF THE ENEMY   437 26
WHICH HE PURCHASED WITH HIS RIGHT HAND   438 20
AND THEIR BEAUTY INTO THE ENEMY'S HAND   438 35
THAT THY RIGHT HAND HATH PLANTED, *   441 32
MAN OF THY RIGHT HAND,   442 04
17 LET THY HAND BE UPON THE MAN OF THY RIGHT HANC,   442 04
AND TURNED MY HAND AGAINST THEIR ADVERSARIES   443 09
SAVE THEM FROM THE HAND OF THE UNGODLY   443 25
OF REMEMBRANCE, AND ARE CUT AWAY FROM THY HAND   449 06
STRONG IS THY HAND, AND HIGH IS THY RIGHT HAND   450 33
STRONG IS THY HAND, AND HIGH IS THY RIGHT HAND   450 34
22 MY HAND SHALL HOLD HIM FAST, *   451 17
AND HIS RIGHT HAND IN THE FLOODS   451 26
SET UP THE RIGHT HAND OF HIS ENEMIES, *   452 24
BESIDE THEE, AND TEN THOUSAND AT THY RIGHT HAND   455 10
4 IN HIS HAND ARE ALL THE CORNERS OF THE EARTH   459 11
AND THE SHEEP OF HIS HAND   459 18
THEM FROM THE HAND OF THE UNGODLY   461 18
WITH HIS OWN RIGHT HAND, AND WITH HIS HOLY ARM,   461 27
4 I WILL TAKE NO WICKED THING IN HAND   463 02
THOU OPENEST THY HAND, THEY ARE FILLED WITH GCOD   469 17
THE ADVERSARY'S HAND, *   473 20
THEM FROM THE HAND OF THE ENEMY   473 22
THEN LIFT HE UP HIS HAND AGAINST THEM, *   474 21
THEM OVER INTO THE HAND OF THE HEATHEN   475 18
DELIVERED FROM THE HAND OF THE ENEMY   476 09
LET THY RIGHT HAND SAVE THEM, AND HEAR THOU ME   479 16
AND LET AN ADVERSARY STAND AT HIS RIGHT HAND   480 14
THAT THIS IS THY HAND, *   481 24
STAND AT THE RIGHT HAND OF THE POOR, *   482 02
THOU ON MY RIGHT HAND, UNTIL I MAKE THINE ENEMIES THY   482 08
LORD UPON THY RIGHT HAND, *   482 16
THE RIGHT HAND OF THE LORD BRINGETH MIGHTY THINGS TO   488 31
16 THE RIGHT HAND OF THE LORD HATH THE PRE-EMINENCE   488 33
THE RIGHT HAND OF THE LORD BRINGETH MIGHTY THINGS TO   488 34
109 MY SOUL IS ALWAY IN MY HAND   497 15
TO LAY TO THINE HAND   498 21
151 BE THOU NIGH AT HAND, O LORD   500 12
173 LET THINE HAND HELP ME   501 28
THE LORD IS THY DEFENCE UPON THY RIGHT HAND   502 31
LOOK UNTO THE HAND OF THEIR MASTERS, AND AS THE EYES   503 30
A MAIDEN UNTO THE HAND OF HER MISTRESS, *   503 31
RIGHTEOUS PUT THEIR HAND UNTO WICKEDNESS   504 30
THE ARROWS IN THE HAND OF THE GIANT, *   505 31
FILLETH NOT HIS HAND, *   507 02
12 WITH A MIGHTY HAND AND STRETCHED-OUT ARM   512 06
LET MY RIGHT HAND FORGET HER CUNNING   513 13
STRETCH FORTH THY HAND UPON THE FURIOUSNESS OF MINE   514 11
AND THY RIGHT HAND SHALL SAVE ME   514 12
ALSO SHALL THY RIGHT HAND LEAD ME, *   515 06
AND THY RIGHT HAND SHALL HOLD ME   515 07
ALSO UPON MY RIGHT HAND, *   518 10
7 SEND DOWN THINE HAND FROM ABOVE   520 04
FROM THE HAND OF STRANGERS   520 05
AND THEIR RIGHT HAND IS A RIGHT HAND OF WICKEDNESS   520 06
HAND IS A RIGHT HAND OF WICKEDNESS   520 07
DELIVER ME FROM THE HAND OF STRANGERS, *   520 12
AND THEIR RIGHT HAND IS A RIGHT HAND OF INIQUITY   520 13
HAND IS A RIGHT HAND OF INIQUITY   520 14
THOU OPENEST THINE HAND, *   521 24
O FINGER OF THE HAND DIVINE,   544 26
THE BIBLE INTO HIS HAND, SAYING,   R 546 24
O FINGER OF THE HAND DIVINE   557 05
PASSOVER WAS AT HAND, AND JESUS WENT UP TO JERUSALEM,   557 25
THE CHURCH IN HIS HAND, IN OPEN VIEW, THE BISHOP,   R 570 10
HURT THEM, NOR THE HAND OF THE UNGODLY TO CAST THEM   574 14
ON THE RIGHT HAND OF GOD THE FATHER ALMIGHTY   578 04
WITH HIS HAND SUBSCRIBED THEREUNTO, THE   R 583 07
BEHOLD THY GRACIOUS HAND IN ALL THY WORKS   596 19

HAND   CONTINUED

WHOSE LOVING HAND HATH GIVEN US ALL THAT WE   599 19

HANDIWORK

FORTH THY HANDIWORK IN THE HEAVENS AND IN THE EARTH   044 18

HANDLE

HANDLE ME, AND SEE   169 33
HAVE HANDS, AND HANDLE NOT   485 24

HANDLED

OUR HANDS HAVE HANDLED, OF THE WORD OF LIFE   101 14

HANDLING

NOR HANDLING THE WORD OF GOD DECEITFULLY   250 30

HANDMAID

BEHOLD THE HANDMAID OF THE LORD   236 28
THY SERVANT, AND HELP THE SON OF THINE HANDMAID   448 08
AND THE SON OF THINE HANDMAID   487 17

HANDMAIDEN

THE LOWLINESS OF HIS HANDMAIDEN   026 13

HANDS

RECEIVED AT HIS HANDS, TO SET FORTH HIS MOST WORTHY   006 06
AND HIS HANDS PREPARED THE DRY LAND   009 11
LIFTING UP OF MY HANDS BE AN EVENING SACRIFICE   021 17
PLACES MADE WITH HANDS, WHICH ARE THE FIGURES OF THE   022 23
RECEIVED AT HIS HANDS, TO SET FORTH HIS MOST WORTHY   023 15
FLOODS CLAP THEIR HANDS, AND LET THE HILLS BE JCYFUL   027 21
IN GIVING PRAISE FOR THE OPERATIONS OF THY HANDS   028 04
THAT THEY MAY LAY HANDS SUDDENLY ON NO MAN, BUT   038 29
FROM THE HANDS OF OUR ENEMIES   041 13
IN WHOSE HANDS ARE THE LIVING AND THE DEAD   042 14
THE LAYING ON OF HANDS, THAT, DRAWING NEAR WITH   043 23
AND FOR ALL WHOSE HANDS ARE OPEN FOR THEIR   047 34
THE CUP INTO HIS HANDS, HE SHALL SAY THE PRAYER CF   R 080 04
THE PRIEST IS TO TAKE THE PATEN INTO HIS HANDS   R 080 30
D) HERE HE IS TO TAKE THE CUP INTO HIS HANDS   R 080 33
INTO THEIR HANDS, ALL DEVOUTLY KNEELING   R 082 28
AND THE HEAVENS ARE THE WORKS OF THINE HANDS   097 15
AND OUR HANDS HAVE HANDLED, OF THE WORD OF   101 14
AND IN THEIR HANDS THEY SHALL BEAR THEE UP, LEST AT   126 34
NOT MADE WITH HANDS, THAT IS TO SAY, NCT OF THIS   132 25
AND WASHED HIS HANDS BEFORE THE MULTITUDE, SAYING,   136 10
BETRAYED INTO THE HANDS OF SINNERS   142 13
THEY LAID THEIR HANDS ON HIM, AND TOOK HIM   142 21
THAT IS MADE WITH HANDS, AND WITHIN THREE DAYS I WILL   143 07
DAYS I WILL BUILD ANOTHER MADE WITHOUT HANDS   143 08
DID STRIKE HIM WITH THE PALMS OF THEIR HANDS   143 22
PLACES MADE WITH HANDS, WHICH ARE THE FIGURES OF THE   147 31
STRETCHED FORTH NO HANDS AGAINST ME   151 05
INTO THY HANDS I COMMEND MY SPIRIT   155 13
THINGS INTO HIS HANDS, AND THAT HE WAS COME FRCM GOD,   155 29
BUT ALSO MY HANDS AND MY HEAD   156 08
GIVEN UP INTO THE HANDS OF WICKED MEN, AND TC SUFFER   156 23
AND THEY SMOTE HIM WITH THEIR HANDS   158 33
BEHOLD MY HANDS AND MY FEET, THAT IT IS I MYSELF   169 32
HE SHEWED THEM HIS HANDS AND HIS FEET   170 02
UNTO THEM HIS HANDS AND HIS SIDE   171 18
HE LIFTED UP HIS HANDS, AND BLESSED THEM   178 24
LAID THEY THEIR HANDS ON THEM, AND THEY RECEIVED THE   185 27
WORKING WITH HIS HANDS THE THING WHICH IS GOOD, THAT   216 21
AND HE LAID HANDS ON HIM, AND TOOK HIM BY THE THRCAT,   221 25
STRETCHED FORTH MY HANDS UNTO A DISOBEDIENT AND   227 22
I SHALL SEE IN HIS HANDS THE PRINT OF THE NAILS, AND   228 28
REACH HITHER THY FINGER, AND BEHOLD MY HANDS   229 04
AND PUTTING HIS HANDS ON HIM SAID, BROTHER SAUL, THE   230 30
THE ELDERS BY THE HANDS OF BARNABAS AND SAUL   241 22
FORTH HIS HANDS TO VEX CERTAIN OF THE CHURCH   244 32
AND HIS CHAINS FELL OFF FROM HIS HANDS   245 15
THE ELDERS BY THE HANDS OF BARNABAS AND SAUL   246 31
FORTH HIS HANDS TO VEX CERTAIN OF THE CHURCH   246 32
BY THE HANDS OF THE APOSTLES WERE MANY SIGNS AND   249 21
THAN HAVING TWO HANDS OR TWO FEET TO BE CAST INTC   253 06
WITH WHITE ROBES, AND PALMS IN THEIR HANDS   256 26
COMMITTED TO THE HANDS OF MEN THE MINISTRY OF   260 19
HIS ARMS, PUT HIS HANDS UPON THEM, AND BLESSED THEM   274 33
TO KEEP MY HANDS FROM PICKING AND STEALING   289 04
THE LAYING ON OF HANDS, OR CONFIRMATION, WHEREIN,   291 23
THESE PERSONS TO RECEIVE THE LAYING ON OF HANDS   296 09
LAID THEY THEIR HANDS ON THEM, AND THEY RECEIVED THE   296 19
HAVE NOW LAID OUR HANDS, TO CERTIFY THEM, BY THIS   298 19
OR FRIEND'S HANDS, SHALL CAUSE THE MAN WITH HIS RIGHT   R 301 25
THEN SHALL THEY LOOSE THEIR HANDS   R 302 02
THEN SHALL THEY AGAIN LOOSE THEIR HANDS   R 302 09
JOIN THEIR RIGHT HANDS TOGETHER, AND SAY, THOSE WHOM   R 303 30
GIVING AND RECEIVING A RING, AND BY JOINING HANDS   304 07
STRETCHED FORTH MY HANDS UNTO HIM, AND CEASED NOT IN   311 02
DESPISE NOT THEN THE WORKS OF THINE OWN HANDS   312 10
INTO THY HANDS, AS INTO THE HANDS OF A   317 14
HANDS, AS INTO THE HANDS OF A FAITHFUL CREATOR,   317 15
INTO THY HANDS, O MERCIFUL SAVIOUR, WE COMMEND THE   319 27
OR LAYING ON OF HANDS, THE MINISTER MAY USE SUCH   R 320 06
OR IF THERE BE ANY WICKEDNESS IN MY HANDS   349 28
HIM TO HAVE DOMINION OF THE WORKS OF THY HANDS   351 12
UNGODLY IS TRAPPED IN THE WORK OF HIS OWN HANDS   352 25

HANDS   CONTINUED

MAY FALL INTO THE HANDS OF HIS CAPTAINS   353 28
CLEANNESS OF MY HANDS DID HE RECOMPENSE ME   361 07
CLEANNESS OF MY HANDS IN HIS EYESIGHT   361 16
HE TEACHETH MINE HANDS TO FIGHT, *   362 04
17 THEY PIERCED MY HANDS AND MY FEET   367 06
HE THAT HATH CLEAN HANDS, AND A PURE HEART   369 02
6 I WILL WASH MY HANDS IN INNOCENCY, O LORD   371 08
10 IN WHOSE HANDS IS WICKEDNESS, *   371 16
WHEN I HOLD UP MY HANDS TOWARDS THE MERCY-SEAT OF THY   373 08
5 RECOMPENSE THEM AFTER THE WORK OF THEIR HANDS   373 15
NOR THE OPERATION OF HIS HANDS   373 18
6 INTO THY HANDS I COMMEND MY SPIRIT   375 31
AND HOLDEN UP OUR HANDS TO ANY STRANGE GOD, *   396 02
O CLAP YOUR HANDS TOGETHER, ALL YE PEOPLES   398 21
21 HE LAID HIS HANDS UPON SUCH AS BE AT PEACE WITH   407 33
AND YOUR HANDS DEAL WITH WICKEDNESS   410 11
AND LIFT UP MY HANDS IN THY NAME   414 34
STRETCH OUT HER HANDS UNTO GOD   421 19
AND WASHED MY HANDS IN INNOCENCY   429 03
ALL THE MEN WHOSE HANDS WERE MIGHTY HAVE FOUND   432 31
STRETCHED FORTH MY HANDS UNTO HIM, AND CEASED NOT IN   433 19
AND HIS HANDS WERE DELIVERED FROM MAKING THE POTS   442 23
STRETCHED FORTH MY HANDS UNTO THEE   449 15
THE WORK OF OUR HANDS UPON US   454 25
BEAR THEE IN THEIR HANDS, *   455 19
IN GIVING PRAISE FOR THE OPERATIONS OF THY HANDS   456 08
AND HIS HANDS PREPARED THE DRY LAND   459 13
FLOODS CLAP THEIR HANDS, AND LET THE HILLS BE JOYFUL   462 10
AND THE HEAVENS ARE THE WORK OF THY HANDS   465 33
7 THE WORKS OF HIS HANDS ARE VERITY AND JUDGMENT   483 07
EVEN THE WORK OF MEN'S HANDS   485 19
7 THEY HAVE HANDS, AND HANDLE NOT   485 24
48 MY HANDS ALSO WILL I LIFT UP UNTO THY   493 04
THY HANDS HAVE MADE ME AND FASHIONED ME   494 28
2 FOR THOU SHALT EAT THE LABOURS OF THINE HANDS   506 08
3 LIFT UP YOUR HANDS IN THE SANCTUARY, *   509 27
THE WORK OF MEN'S HANDS   510 33
DESPISE NOT THEN THE WORKS OF THINE OWN HANDS   514 16
O LORD, FROM THE HANDS OF THE UNGODLY   516 15
LIFTING UP OF MY HANDS BE AN EVENING SACRIFICE   517 11
I EXERCISE MYSELF IN THE WORKS OF THY HANDS   518 33
I STRETCH FORTH MY HANDS UNTO THEE   519 02
WHO TEACHETH MY HANDS TO WAR, AND MY FINGERS TO   519 23
AND A TWO-EDGED SWORD IN THEIR HANDS   525 14
WITH IMPOSITION OF HANDS, WERE APPROVED AND ADMITTED   529 17
THEY LAID THEIR HANDS ON THEM   532 19
SHALL LAY THEIR HANDS SEVERALLY UPON THE HEAD OF EVERY   R 534 02
SHALL LAY THEIR HANDS SEVERALLY UPON THE HEAD OF   R 546 07
UNTO THEE BY THE IMPOSITION OF OUR HANDS   546 11
COMMITTED TO THEE BY THE IMPOSITION OF OUR HANDS   546 19
SAME PLACE WHERE HANDS WERE LAID UPON THEM, UNTIL   R 546 30
THAT THESE HANDS HAVE MINISTERED UNTO MY   551 07
UNTO THEM HIS HANDS AND HIS SIDE   551 31
HASTY IN LAYING ON HANDS, AND ADMITTING ANY PERSON TO   554 09
OR LAYING HANDS UPON OTHERS   555 21
SHALL LAY THEIR HANDS UPON THE HEAD OF THE ELECTED   R 558 09
UNTO THEE BY THE IMPOSITION OF OUR HANDS   558 14
IS GIVEN THEE BY THIS IMPOSITION OF OUR HANDS   558 17
HE THAT HATH CLEAN HANDS, AND A PURE HEART   563 17
MUCH LESS THE WALLS OF TEMPLES MADE WITH HANDS   564 30
SERVICE AT OUR HANDS, AND BLESS IT WITH SUCH SUCCESS   565 12
RECEIVED AT THY HANDS, TO SET FORTH THY MOST WORTHY   566 16
GIVE INTO YOUR HANDS THE KEYS OF THIS CHURCH   570 30
OF GOD AT YOUR HANDS, AS THE PLEDGES OF MY   570 33
TO KEEP MY HANDS FROM PICKING AND STEALING, AND MY   580 09
FORGIVENESS AT THY HANDS, WHO ART EVER READY TO   590 05
STRENGTHEN THEIR HANDS, THAT THEY MAY PUNISH   590 28

HANDY-WORK

AND THE FIRMAMENT SHOWETH HIS HANDY-WORK   363 14
O PROSPER THOU OUR HANDY-WORK   454 26

HANG

TWO COMMANDMENTS HANG ALL THE LAW AND THE PROPHETS   069 31
TWO COMMANDMENTS HANG ALL THE LAW AND THE PROPHETS   215 15

HANGED

AND WENT AND HANGED HIMSELF   135 08
WHICH WERE HANGED RAILED ON HIM, SAYING, IF THOU BE   154 35
THEY SLEW AND HANGED ON A TREE   166 24
THEY SLEW AND HANGED ON A TREE   184 11
A MILLSTONE WERE HANGED ABOUT HIS NECK, AND THAT HE   252 32
MY HOPE, WHEN I HANGED YET UPON MY MOTHER'S BREASTS   366 21
FOR OUR HARPS, WE HANGED THEM UP *   513 07

HANGETH

SORE PUNISHMENT HANGETH OVER YOUR HEADS FOR THE SAME   089 15
9 MY SOUL HANGETH UPON THEE   415 09

HAPPEN

WHICH MAY HAPPEN TO THE BODY, AND FROM ALL EVIL   127 18
SHALL NO HARM HAPPEN UNTO ME   353 17
SHALL NO EVIL HAPPEN UNTO THEE, *   455 15
AND IT SHALL HAPPEN UNTO HIM   481 02
19 LET IT THUS HAPPEN FROM THE LORD UNTO MINE   481 10
AND IF IT SHALL HAPPEN THAT THE SAME CHURCH, OR ANY   540 10

HAPPENED

TOGETHER OF ALL THESE THINGS WHICH HAD HAPPENED   167 06
THESE THINGS HAPPENED UNTO THEM FOR ENSAMPLES   201 22

HAPPINESS

THAT PEACE AND HAPPINESS, TRUTH AND JUSTICE, RELIGION   035 16
OF OUR HAPPINESS BOTH TEMPORAL AND SPIRITUAL   565 13

HAPPY

TO KEEP THE HAPPY MEAN BETWEEN TOO MUCH STIFFNESS IN   V 24
AND A HAPPY ISSUE OUT OF ALL THEIR   019 10
AND A HAPPY ISSUE OUT OF ALL THEIR   033 08
EMBRACE THE HAPPY OCCASION WHICH WAS OFFERED TO   VI 23
HAPPY ARE YE   196 02
COUNTED HIMSELF AN HAPPY MAN   401 11
6 HAPPY IS THE MAN THAT HATH HIS QUIVER FULL OF THEM   506 02
WELL IS THEE, AND HAPPY SHALT THOU BE   506 09
HAPPY SHALL HE BE THAT REWARDETH THEE AS THOU   513 22
15 HAPPY ARE THE PEOPLE THAT ARE IN SUCH A CASE   520 24

HARD

IT IS HARD FOR THEE TO KICK AGAINST THE PRICKS   230 04
FOR TROUBLE IS HARD AT HAND, *   366 25
BUT IT WAS TOO HARD FOR ME,   429 09
WATERS OUT OF THE HARD ROCKS   431 07
I WILL DECLARE HARD SENTENCES OF OLD   434 30
16 HE CLAVE THE HARD ROCKS IN THE WILDERNESS,   435 30
INDIGNATION LIETH HARD UPON ME, *   449 09
AND THEY WERE EVEN HARD AT DEATH'S DOOR   477 12
8 WHO TURNED THE HARD ROCK INTO A STANDING WATER,   485 08

HARDEN

HEAR HIS VOICE, HARDEN NOT YOUR HEARTS *   459 19

HARDENED

THY WAYS, AND HARDENED OUR HEART FROM THY FEAR   139 25

HARDNESS

FROM HARDNESS OF HEART, AND CONTEMPT OF THY WORD AND   055 03
ALL IGNORANCE, HARDNESS OF HEART, AND CONTEMPT OF THY   157 09

HARLOTS

THY LIVING WITH HARLOTS, THOU HAST KILLED FOR HIM THE   203 04

HARM

WHO IS HE THAT WILL HARM YOU, IF YE BE FOLLOWERS OF   195 30
THERE SHALL NO HARM HAPPEN UNTO ME   353 17
AND DO MY PROPHETS NO HARM   471 03
BODILY ACCIDENT AND HARM THE WORKMEN AT THEIR WORK   599 29

HARNESSED

WHO BEING HARNESSED, AND CARRYING BOWS, TURNED   435 17

HARP

PRAISE THE LORD UPON THE HARP   027 15
SING TO THE HARP WITH A PSALM OF THANKSGIVING   027 15
UPON A LOUD INSTRUMENT, AND UPON THE HARP   027 33
PRAISES UPON THE HARP UNTO OUR GOD   264 26
AND UPON THE HARP WILL I GIVE THANKS UNTO THEE, O   310 14
2 PRAISE THE LORD WITH HARP   378 21
AND UPON THE HARP WILL I GIVE THANKS UNTO THEE, O   394 13
AND SHOW MY DARK SPEECH UPON THE HARP   400 13
AWAKE, LUTE AND HARP   409 31
I SING UPON THE HARP, O THOU HOLY ONE OF ISRAEL   426 24
THE MERRY HARP WITH THE LUTE   442 15
UPON A LOUD INSTRUMENT, AND UPON THE HARP   456 05
6 PRAISE THE LORD UPON THE HARP   462 04
SING TO THE HARP WITH A PSALM OF THANKSGIVING   462 04
2 AWAKE, THOU LUTE AND HARP   479 07
PRAISES UPON THE HARP UNTO OUR GOD   523 09
THEM SING PRAISES UNTO HIM WITH TABRET AND HARP   525 08
PRAISE HIM UPON THE LUTE AND HARP   525 27

HARPERS

THE VOICE OF HARPERS HARPING WITH THEIR HARPS   103 04

HARPING

VOICE OF HARPERS HARPING WITH THEIR HARPS   103 04

HARPS

THE VOICE OF HARPERS HARPING WITH THEIR HARPS   103 04
2 AS FOR OUR HARPS, WE HANGED THEM UP *   513 07

HART

LIKE AS THE HART DESIRETH THE WATER-BROOKS, *   392 29

HARTS'

MY FEET LIKE HARTS' FEET, *   362 02

HARVEST

OF SEED—TIME AND HARVEST, FOR THE INCREASE OF THE   050 22
THEE TO SEND FORTH LABOURERS INTO THY HARVEST   056 03
UNTO THEM, THE HARVEST TRULY IS PLENTEOUS, BUT THE   073 11
THAT HE SEND FORTH LABOURERS INTO HIS HARVEST   073 13
THE LORD OF THE HARVEST, THAT HE SEND FORTH LABOURERS   073 13
IN THE TIME OF HARVEST I WILL SAY TO THE REAPERS,   116 29
LET BOTH GROW TOGETHER UNTIL THE HARVEST   116 29
UNTO THEM, THE HARVEST TRULY IS GREAT, BUT THE   254 14
THE LORD OF THE HARVEST, THAT HE WOULD SEND FORTH   254 15
HE WOULD SEND FORTH LABOURERS INTO HIS HARVEST   254 16
THE HARVEST TRULY IS PLENTEOUS, BUT THE   538 17
HE WILL SEND FORTH LABOURERS INTO HIS HARVEST   538 19
THE LORD OF THE HARVEST, THAT HE WILL SEND FORTH   538 19

HARVESTS

MULTIPLY THE HARVESTS OF THE WORLD   040 08

HAS

OF MORNING PRAYER HAS BEEN SAID OR SUNG, MAY PASS AT   R 010 05
THE CIVIL AUTHORITY HAS NOT SINCE THOUGHT PROPER TO   VI 06
OF YOUR VOTE THAT HE HAS BEEN SO ELECTED   570 15

HAST

WHOM THOU HAST REDEEMED WITH THY PRECIOUS   010 34
WHO HAST SAFELY BROUGHT US TO THE BEGINNING OF   017 14
ALMIGHTY GOD, WHO HAST GIVEN US GRACE AT THIS TIME   020 03
FOR THOU, LORD, HAST MADE ME GLAD THROUGH THY WORKS   028 02
WHICH THOU HAST PREPARED *   028 12
ALMIGHTY GOD, WHO HAST GIVEN US GRACE AT THIS TIME   034 03
ALMIGHTY GOD, WHO HAST GIVEN US THIS GOOD LAND FOR   036 09
AND HAST PROMISED, THROUGH THY SON JESUS   036 28
O GOD, WHO HAST MADE OF ONE BLOOD ALL NATIONS OF MEN   038 05
WHO HAST PURCHASED TO THYSELF AN UNIVERSAL   038 25
DIVINE PROVIDENCE HAST APPOINTED DIVERS ORDERS IN THY   039 08
WORLD WHICH THOU HAST REDEEMED BY THE BLOOD OF THY   039 18
ALMIGHTY GOD, WHO HAST BLESSED THE EARTH THAT IT   039 24
LIFE OF MAN, AND HAST COMMANDED US TO WORK WITH   039 26
SON JESUS CHRIST HAST PROMISED TO ALL THOSE WHO SEEK   040 16
WHEREWITH THOU HAST AFFLICTED US   040 25
WORK WHICH THOU HAST BEGUN IN THEM MAY BE PERFECTED   042 18
WHO HAST COMMITTED TO THY HOLY CHURCH THE   042 30
ALMIGHTY GOD, WHO HAST CREATED MAN IN THINE OWN   044 09
WHO HAST TAUGHT US IN THY HOLY WORD THAT THOU   045 30
ALMIGHTY GOD, WHO HAST PROMISED TO HEAR THE PETITIONS   050 06
FOR THAT THOU HAST BEEN GRACIOUSLY PLEASED TO   051 06
O LORD GOD, WHO HAST JUSTLY HUMBLED US BY THY LATE   051 22
AND IN THY MERCY HAST RELIEVED AND COMFORTED OUR   051 24
GRACIOUS GOODNESS HAST HEARD THE DEVOUT PRAYERS OF   051 31
THY NAME, THAT THOU HAST BEEN PLEASED TO DELIVER FROM   052 30
FOR THAT THOU HAST BEEN GRACIOUSLY PLEASED TO DELIVER   053 11
HOLY NAME THAT THOU HAST BEEN PLEASED TO CONDUCT IN   053 21
WHOM THOU HAST REDEEMED WITH THY MOST   054 16
BONES WHICH THOU HAST BROKEN MAY REJOICE   060 27
WHO HAST COMPASSION UPON ALL MEN, AND WHO   062 13
WHOM THOU HAST REDEEMED   062 20
DO ALL THAT THOU HAST TO DO   068 25
IF THOU HAST MUCH, GIVE PLENTEOUSLY   072 32
IF THOU HAST LITTLE, DO THY DILIGENCE GLADLY TO GIVE   072 33
BY THY HOLY APOSTLE HAST TAUGHT US TO MAKE PRAYERS,   074 07
MADE FLESH, THOU HAST CAUSED A NEW LIGHT TO SHINE IN   077 30
OF THY SAINTS, HAST COMPASSED US ABOUT WITH SO GREAT   079 22
GOOD WORKS AS THOU HAST PREPARED FOR US TO WALK IN   083 28
BLESSED LORD, WHO HAST CAUSED ALL HOLY SCRIPTURES TO   092 07
WHICH THOU HAST GIVEN US IN OUR SAVIOUR JESUS   092 12
ALMIGHTY GOD, WHO HAST GIVEN US THY ONLY—BEGOTTEN SON   096 13
THOU HAST LOVED RIGHTEOUSNESS, AND HATED INIQUITY   097 10
IN THE BEGINNING HAST LAID THE FOUNDATION OF THE   097 13
BABES AND SUCKLINGS HAST ORDAINED STRENGTH, AND   102 22
ALMIGHTY GOD, WHO HAST GIVEN US THY ONLY—BEGOTTEN SON   104 05
ALMIGHTY GOD, WHO HAST POURED UPON US THE NEW LIGHT   106 25
UNTO HIM, SON, WHY HAST THOU THUS DEALT WITH US   110 32
BUT THOU HAST KEPT THE GOOD WINE UNTIL NOW   113 29
AND AS THOU HAST BELIEVED, SO BE IT DONE UNTO THEE   115 24
ONE HOUR, AND THOU HAST MADE THEM EQUAL UNTO US,   120 05
O LORD, WHO HAST TAUGHT US THAT ALL OUR DOINGS   122 14
NOTHING THAT THOU HAST MADE, AND DOST FORGIVE THE   124 12
THE PAPS WHICH THOU HAST SUCKED   130 20
A SAMARITAN, AND HAST A DEVIL   133 14
WE KNOW THAT THOU HAST A DEVIL   133 19
YEARS OLD, AND HAST THOU SEEN ABRAHAM   133 30
TOWARDS MANKIND, HAST SENT THY SON, OUR SAVIOUR JESUS   134 06
MY GOD, MY GOD, WHY HAST THOU FORSAKEN ME   137 19
O LORD, WHY HAST THOU MADE US TO ERR FROM THY WAYS,   139 24
MY GOD, MY GOD, WHY HAST THOU FORSAKEN ME   146 29
WHEREBY THOU HAST GIVEN UNTO US LIFE AND   147 10
WASH THEE NOT, THOU HAST NO PART WITH ME   156 04
O MERCIFUL GOD, WHO HAST MADE ALL MEN, AND HATEST   157 04
NOTHING THAT THOU HAST MADE, NOR DESIREST THE DEATH   157 05
BUT A BODY HAST THOU PREPARED ME   157 25
FOR SIN THOU HAST HAD NO PLEASURE   157 26
SON JESUS CHRIST HAST OVERCOME DEATH, AND OPENED UNTO   163 23
RESURRECTION HAST DELIVERED US FROM THE POWER OF OUR   165 05
IN JERUSALEM, AND HAST NOT KNOWN THE THINGS WHICH ARE   167 13
WHO HAST GIVEN THINE ONLY SON TO DIE FOR OUR   170 19
ALMIGHTY GOD, WHO HAST GIVEN THINE ONLY SON TO OUR   171 28
KING OF GLORY, WHO HAST EXALTED THINE ONLY SON JESUS   179 04
WHO HAST GIVEN UNTO US THY SERVANTS GRACE, BY   186 23
FOR THOU HAST CREATED ALL THINGS, AND FOR THY   187 30
IT IS DONE AS THOU HAST COMMANDED, AND YET THERE IS   192 17
WE, TO WHOM THOU HAST GIVEN AN HEARTY DESIRE TO PRAY,   192 25

HAST   CONTINUED

O GOD, WHO HAST PREPARED FOR THOSE WHO LOVE THEE SUCH   197 04
TILL THOU HAST PAID THE UTTERMOST FARTHING   198 16
WITH HARLOTS, THOU HAST KILLED FOR HIM THE FATTED   203 04
SAID UNTO HIM, THOU HAST ANSWERED RIGHT   208 18
BECAUSE THOU HAST SEEN ME, THOU HAST BELIEVED   229 07
HAST SEEN ME, THOU HAST BELIEVED   229 07
APOSTLE SAINT PAUL, HAST CAUSED THE LIGHT OF THE   229 18
WHICH THOU HAST PREPARED BEFORE THE FACE OF ALL   233 07
OF THESE TWO HAST THOU CHOSEN, THAT HE MAY TAKE PART   234 28
BECAUSE THOU HAST HID THESE THINGS FROM THE   235 04
AND PRUDENT, AND HAST REVEALED THEM UNTO BABES   235 05
FOR THOU HAST FOUND FAVOUR WITH GOD   236 14
O ALMIGHTY GOD, WHO HAST INSTRUCTED THY HOLY CHURCH   237 05
WITH YOU, AND YET HAST THOU NOT KNOWN ME, PHILIP   240 11
WHO HAST ORDAINED AND CONSTITUTED THE SERVICES   251 27
O ALMIGHTY GOD, WHO HAST BUILT THY CHURCH UPON THE   254 27
O ALMIGHTY GOD, WHO HAST KNIT TOGETHER THINE ELECT IN   256 05
JOYS WHICH THOU HAST PREPARED FOR THOSE WHO   256 10
O ALMIGHTY GOD, WHO HAST CALLED US TO FAITH IN THEE,   258 11
FAITH IN THEE, AND HAST COMPASSED US ABOUT WITH SO   258 12
AND SUCKLINGS THOU HAST PERFECTED PRAISE   260 15
O ALMIGHTY GOD, WHO HAST COMMITTED TO THE HANDS OF   260 19
WHO HAST BLESSED THE LABOURS OF THE   265 11
O LORD, AS THOU HAST PROMISED BY THY WELL—BELOVED   274 14
KINGDOM WHICH THOU HAST PROMISED BY CHRIST OUR LORD   274 21
THAT THOU HAST VOUCHSAFED TO CALL US TO THE   276 09
DO ALL THAT THOU HAST TO DO   286 25
O ALMIGHTY GOD, WHO HAST BUILT THY CHURCH UPON THE   290 19
EVERLIVING GOD, WHO HAST VOUCHSAFED TO REGENERATE   297 14
THE HOLY GHOST, AND HAST GIVEN UNTO THEM FORGIVENESS   297 16
O GOD, WHO HAST SO CONSECRATED THE STATE OF MATRIMONY   303 20
FOR THAT THOU HAST BEEN GRACIOUSLY PLEASED TO   306 25
WHY HAST THOU PUT ME FROM THEE   310 08
FOR THOU HAST MAGNIFIED THY NAME, AND THY WORD,   311 32
AND PRECIOUS BLOOD HAST REDEEMED US   313 13
BEHOLD, THOU HAST MADE MY DAYS AS IT WERE A SPAN   324 22
THOU HAST BEEN OUR REFUGE, *   325 13
THOU HAST SET OUR MISDEEDS BEFORE THEE   325 28
THOU HAST BEEN MY SUCCOUR   326 26
WHO HAST BEEN PLEASED TO TAKE UNTO THYSELF   336 04
IN FAITH WHERE THOU HAST LED THE WAY, THAT WE MAY AT   336 12
THOU HAST ANOINTED MY HEAD WITH OIL, AND MY CUP SHALL   338 27
THOU HAST BROKEN THE TEETH OF THE UNGODLY   347 05
THOU HAST SET ME AT LIBERTY WHEN I WAS IN TROUBLE   347 11
8 THOU HAST PUT GLADNESS IN MY HEART   347 26
ART THE GOD THAT HAST NO PLEASURE IN WICKEDNESS   348 07
JUDGMENT THAT THOU HAST COMMANDED   350 03
THOU THAT HAST SET THY GLORY ABOVE THE HEAVENS   350 32
BABES AND SUCKLINGS HAST THOU ORDAINED STRENGTH,   350 34
STARS WHICH THOU HAST ORDAINED   351 05
AND THOU HAST PUT ALL THINGS IN SUBJECTION UNDER HIS   351 12
4 FOR THOU HAST MAINTAINED MY RIGHT AND MY CAUSE   351 28
5 THOU HAST REBUKED THE HEATHEN, AND DESTROYED THE   351 30
THOU HAST PUT OUT THEIR NAME FOR EVER AND EVER   351 31
CITIES WHICH THOU HAST DESTROYED, WHOSE MEMORIAL IS   351 33
FOR THOU, LORD, HAST NEVER FAILED THEM THAT SEEK   352 09
15 SURELY THOU HAST SEEN IT   354 04
19 LORD, THOU HAST HEARD THE DESIRE OF THE POOR   354 13
2 O MY SOUL, THOU HAST SAID UNTO THE LORD, *   357 23
3 THOU HAST PROVED AND VISITED MINE HEART IN THE   358 21
THOU HAST TRIED ME, AND SHALT FIND NO WICKEDNESS IN   358 22
36 THOU HAST GIVEN ME THE DEFENCE OF THY SALVATION   362 06
40 THOU HAST GIRDED ME WITH STRENGTH UNTO THE BATTLE   362 16
41 THOU HAST MADE MINE ENEMIES ALSO TO TURN THEIR   362 18
AND HAST NOT DENIED HIM THE REQUEST OF HIS LIPS   365 07
2 THOU HAST GIVEN HIM HIS HEART'S DESIRE, *   365 07
WHY HAST THOU FORSAKEN ME   366 04
THOU HAST HEARD ME ALSO FROM AMONG THE HORNS OF THE   367 14
THOU HAST ANOINTED MY HEAD WITH OIL, AND MY CUP SHALL   368 20
11 THOU HAST BEEN MY SUCCOUR   372 18
FOR THOU HAST SET ME UP, *   374 24
AND THOU HAST HEALED ME   374 26
3 THOU, LORD, HAST BROUGHT MY SOUL OUT OF HELL   374 28
THOU HAST KEPT MY LIFE, THAT I SHOULD NOT GO DOWN   374 29
OF THY GOODNESS, HAST MADE MY HILL SO STRONG   375 05
THOU HAST PUT OFF MY SACKCLOTH, AND GIRDED ME WITH   375 16
12 THOU HAST TURNED MY HEAVINESS INTO JOY   375 16
FOR THOU HAST REDEEMED ME, O LORD, THOU GOD OF TRUTH   375 31
FOR THOU HAST CONSIDERED MY TROUBLE, AND HAST KNOWN   376 04
MY TROUBLE, AND HAST KNOWN MY SOUL IN ADVERSITIES   376 05
9 THOU HAST NOT SHUT ME UP INTO THE HAND OF THE   376 06
BUT HAST SET MY FEET IN A LARGE ROOM   376 07
WHICH THOU HAST LAID UP FOR THEM THAT FEAR THEE, *   377 02
AND THAT THOU HAST PREPARED FOR THEM THAT PUT THEIR   377 03
22 THIS THOU HAST SEEN, O LORD   383 07
6 BEHOLD, THOU HAST MADE MY DAYS AS IT WERE A SPAN   389 17
WORKS WHICH THOU HAST DONE, LIKE AS BE ALSO THY   390 22
BUT MINE EARS HAST THOU OPENED   390 28
SACRIFICE FOR SIN HAST THOU NOT REQUIRED   390 29
OF MY STRENGTH, WHY HAST THOU FORGOTTEN ME   393 24
WHY HAST THOU PUT ME FROM THEE   394 06
WHAT THOU HAST DONE IN THEIR TIME OF OLD   394 23
2 HOW THOU HAST DRIVEN OUT THE HEATHEN WITH THY HAND,   394 24
HOW THOU HAST DESTROYED THE NATIONS, AND MADE THY   394 25
AND HAST SCATTERED US AMONG THE HEATHEN   395 15
NOT WHEN THOU HAST SMITTEN US INTO THE PLACE OF   395 32
7 THOU HAST LOVED RIGHTEOUSNESS, AND HATED INIQUITY   396 29
AND HAST CAST MY WORDS BEHIND THEE   402 24
AND HAST BEEN PARTAKER WITH THE ADULTERERS   402 27
19 THOU HAST LET THY MOUTH SPEAK WICKEDNESS, *   402 28
THY TONGUE THOU HAST SET FORTH DECEIT   402 29
AND HAST SLANDERED THINE OWN MOTHER'S SON   402 31
21 THESE THINGS HAST THOU DONE, AND I HELD MY TONGUE,   402 32
THINGS THAT THOU HAST DONE   402 35

HAST   CONTINUED

BONES WHICH THOU HAST BROKEN MAY REJOICE   403 26
4 THOU HAST LOVED UNRIGHTEOUSNESS MORE THAN GOODNESS,   404 24
5 THOU HAST LOVED TO SPEAK ALL WORDS THAT MAY DO   404 26
THEE FOR THAT THOU HAST DONE   405 08
THOU HAST PUT THEM TO CONFUSION, BECAUSE GOD HATH   405 26
13 FOR THOU HAST DELIVERED MY SOUL FROM DEATH,   409 08
FOR THOU HAST BEEN MY DEFENCE AND REFUGE IN THE DAY   412 07
O GOD, THOU HAST CAST US OUT, AND SCATTERED US   412 12
THOU HAST ALSO BEEN DISPLEASED   412 13
2 THOU HAST MOVED THE LAND, AND DIVIDED IT   412 15
3 THOU HAST SHOWED THY PEOPLE HEAVY THINGS   412 17
THOU HAST GIVEN US A DRINK OF DEADLY WINE   412 18
4 THOU HAST GIVEN A TOKEN FOR SUCH AS FEAR THEE,   412 19
10 HAST NOT THOU CAST US OUT, O GOD   412 31
FOR THOU HAST BEEN MY HOPE, AND A STRONG TOWER FCR ME   413 11
AND HAST GIVEN AN HERITAGE UNTO THOSE THAT FEAR THY   413 15
5 FOR THOU, O LORD, HAST HEARD MY DESIRES, *   413 15
8 BECAUSE THOU HAST BEEN MY HELPER   415 07
9 FOR THOU, O GOD, HAST PROVED US   417 33
THOU ALSO HAST TRIED US, LIKE AS SILVER IS TRIED   417 33
FOR THOU, O GOD, HAST OF THY GOODNESS PREPARED FOR   419 32
UP ON HIGH, THOU HAST LED CAPTIVITY CAPTIVE, AND   420 19
O GOD, THAT THOU HAST WROUGHT IN US, 29 FOR THY   421 12
20 THOU HAST KNOWN MY REPROACH, MY SHAME, AND MY   423 11
HIM WHOM THOU HAST SMITTEN   423 27
VEX THEM WHOM THOU HAST WOUNDED   423 28
THOU HAST PROMISED TO HELP ME, FOR THOU ART MY HOUSE   425 09
16 THOU, O GOD, HAST TAUGHT ME FROM MY YOUTH UP UNTIL   426 08
ARE THEY THAT THOU HAST DONE   426 15
AND ADVERSITIES HAST THOU SHOWED ME   426 17
20 THOU HAST BROUGHT ME TO GREAT HONOUR, *   426 20
MY SOUL WHOM THOU HAST DELIVERED   426 26
FOR THOU HAST HOLDEN ME BY MY RIGHT HAND   429 22
THOU HAST DESTROYED ALL THEM THAT ARE UNFAITHFUL UNTO   429 31
WHOM THOU HAST PURCHASED, AND REDEEMED OF OLD   430 06
WHEREIN THOU HAST DWELT   430 09
THOU HAST PREPARED THE LIGHT AND THE SUN   431 08
18 THOU HAST SET ALL THE BORDERS OF THE EARTH   431 10
THOU HAST MADE SUMMER AND WINTER   431 11
AND HAST DECLARED THY POWER AMONG THE PEOPLES   434 10
15 THOU HAST MIGHTILY DELIVERED THY PEOPLE, *   434 12
6 THOU HAST MADE US A VERY STRIFE UNTO OUR   441 14
THOU HAST CAST OUT THE HEATHEN, AND PLANTED IT   441 18
8 THOU HAST BROUGHT A VINE OUR OF EGYPT   441 18
12 WHY HAST THOU THEN BROKEN DOWN HER HEDGE, *   441 26
THOU HAST TURNED AWAY THE CAPTIVITY OF JACOB   446 09
2 THOU HAST FORGIVEN THE OFFENCE OF THY PEOPLE,   446 10
3 THOU HAST TAKEN AWAY ALL THY DISPLEASURE, *   446 12
NATIONS WHOM THOU HAST MADE SHALL COME AND WORSHIP   447 21
AND THOU HAST DELIVERED MY SOUL FROM THE NETHERMOST   447 30
BECAUSE THOU, LORD, HAST HOLPEN ME, AND COMFORTED ME   448 11
5 THOU HAST LAID ME IN THE LOWEST PIT, *   449 07
AND THOU HAST VEXED ME WITH ALL THY STORMS   449 10
7 THOU HAST PUT AWAY MINE ACQUAINTANCE FAR FROM ME,   449 11
LOVERS AND FRIENDS HAST THOU PUT AWAY FROM ME,   449 33
11 THOU HAST SUBDUED EGYPT, AND DESTROYED IT   450 26
THOU HAST SCATTERED THINE ENEMIES ABROAD WITH THY   450 27
THOU HAST LAID THE FOUNDATION OF THE ROUND WORLD, AND   450 29
13 THOU HAST MADE THE NORTH AND THE SOUTH   450 31
14 THOU HAST A MIGHTY ARM   450 33
37 BUT THOU HAST ABHORRED AND FORSAKEN THINE   452 16
38 THOU HAST BROKEN THE COVENANT OF THY SERVANT,   452 18
39 THOU HAST OVERTHROWN ALL HIS HEDGES, *   452 20
41 THOU HAST SET UP THE RIGHT HAND OF HIS ENEMIES,   452 24
42 THOU HAST TAKEN AWAY THE EDGE OF HIS SWORD,   452 26
43 THOU HAST PUT OUT HIS GLORY, *   452 28
DAYS OF HIS YOUTH HAST THOU SHORTENED, *   452 30
WHEREFORE HAST THOU MADE ALL MEN FOR NOUGHT   452 34
THOU HAST BEEN OUR REFUGE, *   453 18
8 THOU HAST SET OUR MISDEEDS BEFORE THEE   454 02
THE TIME THAT THOU HAST PLAGUED US   454 19
THOU HAST SET THINE HOUSE OF DEFENCE VERY HIGH   455 13
4 FOR THOU, LORD, HAST MADE ME GLAD THROUGH THY   456 06
THOU HAST PREPARED EQUITY, *   462 22
THOU HAST EXECUTED JUDGMENT AND RIGHTEOUSNESS IN   462 23
FOR THOU HAST TAKEN ME UP, AND CAST ME DOWN   464 30
IN THE BEGINNING HAST LAID THE FOUNDATION OF THE   465 31
PLACE WHICH THOU HAST APPOINTED FOR THEM   468 09
9 THOU HAST SET THEM THEIR BOUNDS, WHICH THEY SHALL   468 11
IN WISDOM HAST THOU MADE THEM ALL   469 09
WHOM THOU HAST MADE TO TAKE HIS PASTIME THEREIN   469 13
11 HAST NOT THOU FORSAKEN US, O GOD   479 26
THAT THOU, LORD, HAST DONE IT   481 25
THOU HAST DELIVERED MY SOUL FROM DEATH, *   487 04
THOU HAST BROKEN MY BONDS IN SUNDER   487 17
13 THOU HAST THRUST SORE AT ME, THAT I MIGHT FALL   488 26
FOR THOU HAST HEARD ME, *   489 10
4 THOU HAST CHARGED *   490 06
21 THOU HAST REBUKED THE PROUD   491 08
WHEN THOU HAST SET MY HEART AT LIBERTY   491 32
WHEREIN THOU HAST CAUSED ME TO PUT MY TRUST   493 09
O LORD, THOU HAST DEALT GRACIOUSLY WITH THY SERVANT,   494 11
VERY FAITHFULNESS HAST CAUSED ME TO BE TROUBLED   495 05
THOU HAST LAID THE FOUNDATION OF THE EARTH, AND IT   496 05
FOR WITH THEM THOU HAST QUICKENED ME   496 12
THY COMMANDMENTS, HAST MADE ME WISER THAN MINE   496 22
118 THOU HAST TRODDEN DOWN ALL THEM THAT DEPART FROM   498 04
THAT THOU HAST COMMANDED *   499 15
THAT THOU HAST GROUNDED THEM FOR EVER   500 15
WHEN THOU HAST TAUGHT ME THY STATUTES   501 24
THEE AS THOU HAST SERVED US   513 22
FOR THOU HAST MAGNIFIED THY NAME, AND THY WORD,   513 32
O LORD, THOU HAST SEARCHED ME OUT, AND KNOWN ME   514 20
4 THOU HAST BESET ME BEHIND AND BEFORE, *   514 27

HAST   CONTINUED

THOU HAST COVERED ME IN MY MOTHER'S WOMB   515 13
THOU HAST COVERED MY HEAD IN THE DAY OF BATTLE   516 22
IS MAN, THAT THOU HAST SUCH RESPECT UNTO HIM   519 27
AND HAST DELIVERED DAVID THY SERVANT FROM THE PERIL   520 10
10 THOU HAST GIVEN VICTORY UNTO KINGS, *   520 10
DIVINE PROVIDENCE HAST APPOINTED DIVERS ORDERS OF   531 14
THY GREAT GOODNESS HAST VOUCHSAFED TO ACCEPT AND TAKE   534 31
BY THY HOLY SPIRIT HAST APPOINTED DIVERS ORDERS CF   537 21
HEARTS WHICH THOU HAST MADE   544 20
TOWARDS US, HAST GIVEN TO US THY ONLY AND MOST DEARLY   545 13
AND FOR THAT THOU HAST VOUCHSAFED TO CALL THESE THY   545 22
BY THY HOLY SPIRIT HAST APPOINTED DIVERS ORDERS CF   547 32
BY THY HOLY SPIRIT HAST APPOINTED DIVERS ORDERS CF   553 27
HEARTS WHICH THOU HAST MADE   556 28
INFINITE GOODNESS, HAST GIVEN THY ONLY AND DEARLY   557 21
AND WHO YET HAST BEEN GRACIOUSLY PLEASED TO PROMISE   564 30
THY WISE PROVIDENCE HAST APPOINTED DIVERS ORDERS IN   572 07
O HOLY JESUS, WHO HAST PURCHASED TO THYSELF AN   572 16
AND HAST PROMISED TO BE WITH THE MINISTERS OF   572 17
YET THOU HAST HONOURED THY SERVANT WITH APPOINTING   573 12
CENTRE IN WHAT THOU HAST COMMANDED   573 19
O ALMIGHTY GOD, WHO HAST BUILT THY CHURCH UPON THE   574 03
DO ALL THAT THOU HAST TO DO   579 05
TO HIM WHOM THOU HAST APPOINTED THE JUDGE OF QUICK   588 23
AND HAST PROMISED FORGIVENESS TO ALL THOSE   589 27
WHO HAST SAFELY BROUGHT US TO THE BEGINNING OF   592 20
O GOD OF PEACE, WHO HAST TAUGHT US THAT IN RETURNING   595 19
AND WHICH THOU HAST MANIFESTED UNTO US IN THY SON,   596 09
WHO HAST FILLED THE WORLD WITH BEAUTY   596 17
WHO HAST BLESSED US WITH THE JOY AND CARE OF   596 24
UPON ALL THAT THOU HAST MADE   599 06

HASTE

AND SO MAKE HASTE TO HELP US IN THIS WORLD, THAT WE   062 24
AND THEY CAME WITH HASTE, AND FOUND MARY, AND JOSEPH,   106 11
ART MY SUCCOUR, HASTE THEE TO HELP ME   367 11
MAKE HASTE TO DELIVER ME   375 24
24 BUT IN MY HASTE I SAID, *   377 11
22 HASTE THEE TO HELP ME, *   389 03
MAKE HASTE, O LORD, TO HELP ME   391 15
8 I WOULD MAKE HASTE TO ESCAPE, *   407 02
O HASTE THEE, AND HEAR ME   423 08
HASTE THEE, O GOD, TO DELIVER ME   424 20
MAKE HASTE TO HELP ME, O LORD   424 20
HASTE THEE UNTO ME, O GOD   424 30
MY GOD, HASTE THEE TO HELP ME   425 29
THY THUNDER THEY HASTE AWAY   468 07
I SAID IN MY HASTE, ALL MEN ARE LIARS   487 08
60 I MADE HASTE, AND PROLONGED NOT THE TIME, *   493 31
LABOUR THAT YE HASTE TO RISE UP EARLY, AND SO LATE   505 26
HASTE THEE UNTO ME, *   517 08

HASTEN

ALL FLESH, AND HASTEN THY KINGDOM   038 10
PLEASE THEE TO HASTEN THE FULFILMENT OF THY PURPOSE,   561 16

HASTILY

LET DEATH COME HASTILY UPON THEM, AND LET THEM GO   407 20

HASTY

WE SHOULD NOT BE HASTY IN LAYING ON HANDS, AND   554 08

HATE

HAND OF ALL THAT HATE US   014 15
OF THEM THAT HATE ME   068 14
IF THE WORLD HATE YOU   191 11
FOR EITHER HE WILL HATE THE ONE, AND LOVE THE OTHER   211 09
HAND OF ALL THAT HATE US   244 04
IF THE WORLD HATE YOU, YE KNOW THAT IT HATED ME   255 13
THY NEIGHBOUR, AND HATE THINE ENEMY   264 04
GOOD TO THEM THAT HATE YOU, AND PRAY FOR THEM WHICH   264 06
OF THEM THAT HATE ME   286 14
SUFFER OF THEM THAT HATE ME, *   352 17
AND FROM THEM WHICH HATE ME   360 34
DESTROY THEM THAT HATE ME   362 19
FIND OUT THEM THAT HATE THEE   365 21
BEAR A TYRANNOUS HATE AGAINST ME   370 23
AND THEY THAT HATE THE RIGHTEOUS SHALL BE DESOLATE   381 11
THEIR EYES, THAT HATE ME WITHOUT A CAUSE   382 36
AND THEY THAT HATE ME WRONGFULLY ARE MANY IN NUMBER   388 31
TO CONFUSION THAT HATE US   395 08
SO THAT THEY WHICH HATE US SPOIL OUR GOODS   395 14
LET THEM ALSO THAT HATE HIM FLEE BEFORE HIM   419 10
4 THEY THAT HATE ME WITHOUT A CAUSE ARE MORE THAN THE   422 07
FROM THEM THAT HATE ME, AND OUT OF THE DEEP WATERS   422 33
OF THEM THAT HATE THEE INCREASETH EVER MORE AND MORE   431 25
AND THEY THAT HATE THEE HAVE LIFT UP THEIR HEAD   444 08
THAT THEY WHO HATE ME MAY SEE IT, AND BE ASHAMED,   448 10
PLAGUE THEM THAT HATE HIM   451 22
SEE THAT YE HATE THE THING WHICH IS EVIL   461 16
I HATE THE SINS OF UNFAITHFULNESS   463 22
THEREFORE I HATE ALL EVIL WAYS   497 03
I HATE THEM THAT IMAGINE EVIL THINGS   497 24
163 AS FOR LIES, I HATE AND ABHOR THEM   501 07
O LORD, THAT HATE THEE   515 32
21 DO NOT I HATE THEM, O LORD, THAT HATE THEE   515 32
22 YEA, I HATE THEM RIGHT SORE   516 02
OF THEM THAT HATE ME   578 33

HATED

AND HATED INIQUITY	097 11
YE KNOW THAT IT HATED ME BEFORE IT HATED YOU	255 13
HATED ME BEFORE IT HATED YOU	255 14
THEY BOTH SEEN AND HATED BOTH ME AND MY FATHER	255 27
IN THEIR LAW, THEY HATED ME WITHOUT A CAUSE	255 29
NO MAN EVER YET HATED HIS OWN FLESH	267 26
5 I HAVE HATED THE CONGREGATION OF THE WICKED	371 06
7 I HAVE HATED THEM THAT HOLD OF LYING VANITIES,	376 02
AND HATED INIQUITY	396 29
THAT THEY HATED HIS PEOPLE, *	471 22
AND THEY THAT HATED THEM WERE LORDS OVER THEM	475 19

HATERS

16 THE HATERS OF THE LORD SHOULD HAVE SUBMITTED	443 10

HATEST

WHO HATEST NOTHING THAT THOU HAST MADE, AND DOST	124 11
MADE ALL MEN, AND HATEST NOTHING THAT THOU HAST MADE,	157 04
FOR THOU HATEST ALL THEM THAT WORK INIQUITY	348 10
17 WHEREAS THOU HATEST TO BE REFORMED, *	402 24

HATETH

THAT DOETH EVIL HATETH THE LIGHT, NEITHER COMETH TO	185 08
I LOVE GOD, AND HATETH HIS BROTHER, HE IS A LIAR	189 31
WHOSOEVER HATETH HIS BROTHER IS A MURDERER	191 14
THE WORLD HATETH YOU	255 17
HE THAT HATETH ME HATETH MY FATHER ALSO	255 24
HE THAT HATETH ME HATETH MY FATHER ALSO	255 24

HATH

WHEREWITH THE LORD HATH AFFLICTED ME	004 31
WHEREWITH CHRIST HATH MADE US FREE,' THAT IN HIS	V 03
DAY WHICH THE LORD HATH MADE	005 04
AND PROTECTION, HATH, IN THE PREFACE OF HER BOOK OF	V 12
YE ARE SONS, GOD HATH SENT FORTH THE SPIRIT OF HIS	005 16
THE SAME CHURCH HATH NOT ONLY IN HER PREFACE,	V 21
THE LORD BY WISDOM HATH FOUNDED THE EARTH	005 24
BY UNDERSTANDING HATH HE ESTABLISHED THE HEAVENS	005 25
SHE HATH, IN THE REIGN OF SEVERAL	V 26
AND ALTERATIONS HATH BEEN, AS SHE FURTHER DECLARES IN	V 33
AND LIVE, HATH GIVEN POWER, AND COMMANDMENT, TO HIS	007 08
THE LORD HATH MANIFESTED FORTH HIS GLORY	R 008 21
FOR HE HATH VISITED AND REDEEMED HIS PEOPLE	014 08
AND HATH RAISED UP A MIGHTY SALVATION FOR US,	014 10
FROM ON HIGH HATH VISITED US	014 30
IT IS HE THAT HATH MADE US, AND NOT WE OURSELVES	015 07
IF IT HATH NOT ALREADY BEEN SAID, SHALL	R 016 28
AND THE LORD HATH LAID ON HIM THE INIQUITY OF US ALL	022 10
AND LIVE, HATH GIVEN POWER, AND COMMANDMENT, TO HIS	024 10
AND MY SPIRIT HATH REJOICED IN GOD MY SAVIOUR	026 11
FOR HE HATH REGARDED *	026 16
HE THAT IS MIGHTY HATH MAGNIFIED ME	026 16
HE HATH SHOWED STRENGTH WITH HIS ARM	026 20
HE HATH SCATTERED THE PROUD IN THE IMAGINATION OF	026 20
HE HATH PUT DOWN THE MIGHTY FROM THEIR SEAT, *	026 22
AND HATH EXALTED THE HUMBLE AND MEEK	026 23
HE HATH FILLED THE HUNGRY WITH GOOD THINGS	026 24
AND THE RICH HE HATH SENT EMPTY AWAY	026 25
HIS MERCY HATH HOLPEN HIS SERVANT ISRAEL	026 26
FOR HE HATH DONE MARVELLOUS THINGS	027 04
HATH HE GOTTEN HIMSELF THE VICTORY	027 06
HIS RIGHTEOUSNESS HATH OPENLY SHOWED IN THE SIGHT	027 09
HE HATH REMEMBERED HIS MERCY AND TRUTH TOWARD THE	027 10
IF IT HATH NOT ALREADY BEEN SAID, SHALL	R 030 33
WORDS WHICH CHRIST HATH TAUGHT US, WE MAKE BOLD TO	048 24
THANKS THAT IT HATH PLEASED THEE TO SEND US RAIN TO	051 18
HOLY NAME, THAT IT HATH PLEASED THEE TO APPEASE THE	052 20
AND IN SIN HATH MY MOTHER CONCEIVED ME	060 20
IF THE LITANY HATH BEEN ALREADY SAID, THE MINISTER	R 061 19
IF THE DECALOGUE HATH BEEN OMITTED, SHALL BE SAID,	R 069 32
BE OMITTED, IF IT HATH BEEN SAID IMMEDIATELY BEFORE	R 070 30
WHOSO HATH THIS WORLD'S GOOD, AND SEETH HIS BROTHER	072 29
THY GOD WHICH HE HATH GIVEN THEE	073 17
OF HIS GREAT MERCY HATH PROMISED FORGIVENESS OF SINS	076 03
OFFERED FOR US, AND HATH TAKEN AWAY THE SIN OF THE	078 10
WHO BY HIS DEATH HATH DESTROYED DEATH, AND BY HIS	078 11
TO LIFE AGAIN HATH RESTORED TO US EVERLASTING LIFE	078 12
THE HOLY TABLE, HATH SO ORDERED THE BREAD AND WINE,	R 080 02
MEMORIAL THY SON HATH COMMANDED US TO MAKE	080 41
OUR SAVIOUR CHRIST HATH TAUGHT US, WE ARE BOLD TO	082 02
AND THAT HE HATH RECOMPENSED THE PARTIES TO WHOM HE	R 085 06
PARTIES TO WHOM HE HATH DONE WRONG	085 07
ALL THAT THE OTHER HATH TRESPASSED AGAINST HIM,	R 085 13
WHEREIN HE HIMSELF HATH OFFENDED	R 085 14
BLOOD-SHEDDING HE HATH OBTAINED FOR US	086 15
HE HATH INSTITUTED AND ORDAINED HOLY MYSTERIES,	086 16
FOR THAT HE HATH GIVEN HIS SON OUR SAVIOUR	087 02
IT IS, WHEN A MAN HATH PREPARED A RICH FEAST, DECKED	088 13
AS HE HIMSELF HATH COMMANDED	089 13
THAT LOVETH ANOTHER HATH FULFILLED THE LAW	090 24
SHALL SAY, THE LORD HATH NEED OF THEM	091 17
BY THE PROPHETS, HATH IN THESE LAST DAYS SPOKEN UNTO	096 23
BY HIS SON, WHOM HE HATH APPOINTED HEIR OF ALL	096 24
THE ANGELS, AS HE HATH BY INHERITANCE OBTAINED A MORE	096 30
EVEN THY GOD, HATH ANOINTED THEE WITH THE OIL OF	097 12
BRINGETH SALVATION HATH APPEARED TO ALL MEN, TEACHING	098 18
YE ARE SONS, GOD HATH SENT FORTH THE SPIRIT OF HIS	104 22
GOD ALSO HATH HIGHLY EXALTED HIM, AND GIVEN HIM A	105 26
WHICH THE LORD HATH MADE KNOWN UNTO US	106 10
BECAUSE THE LORD HATH ANOINTED ME TO PREACH GOOD	106 31

HATH   CONTINUED

HE HATH SENT ME TO BIND UP THE BROKENHEARTED, TO	107 02
OF THE WORLD HATH BEEN HID IN GOD, WHO CREATED ALL	108 22
ACCORDING AS GOD HATH DEALT TO EVERY MAN THE MEASURE	110 12
FROM WHENCE THEN HATH IT TARES	116 24
UNTO THEM, AN ENEMY HATH DONE THIS	116 25
OF LOVE THE FATHER HATH BESTOWED UPON US, THAT WE	117 14
AND EVERY MAN THAT HATH THIS HOPE IN HIM PURIFIETH	117 20
WHOSOEVER SINNETH HATH NOT SEEN HIM, NEITHER KNOWN	117 25
BECAUSE NO MAN HATH HIRED US	119 26
HE CRIED, HE THAT HATH EARS TO HEAR, LET HIM HEAR	121 27
THY FAITH HATH SAVED THEE	124 03
FOR GOD HATH NOT CALLED US UNTO UNCLEANNESS, BUT UNTO	128 02
BUT GOD, WHO HATH ALSO GIVEN UNTO US HIS HOLY	128 04
AS CHRIST ALSO HATH LOVED US, AND HATH GIVEN HIMSELF	128 31
HATH LOVED US, AND HATH GIVEN HIMSELF FOR US AN	128 31
WHO IS AN IDOLATER, HATH ANY INHERITANCE IN THE	129 08
FOR THE DESOLATE HATH MANY MORE CHILDREN THAN SHE	131 10
THAN SHE WHICH HATH AN HUSBAND	131 11
A LAD HERE, WHICH HATH FIVE BARLEY LOAVES, AND TWO	131 33
WHEREFORE GOD ALSO HATH HIGHLY EXALTED HIM, AND GIVEN	134 22
WHAT EVIL HATH HE DONE	136 07
ALL THAT THE LORD HATH BESTOWED ON US, AND THE GREAT	138 29
OF ISRAEL, WHICH HE HATH BESTOWED ON THEM ACCORDING	138 31
SHE HATH WROUGHT A GOOD WORK ON ME	140 11
SHE HATH DONE WHAT SHE COULD	140 14
THIS ALSO THAT SHE HATH DONE SHALL BE SPOKEN OF FOR A	140 17
THE LORD GOD HATH OPENED MINE EAR, AND I WAS NOT	144 12
IN DARKNESS, AND HATH NO LIGHT	144 24
WHAT EVIL HATH HE DONE	145 26
TESTAMENT WHICH GOD HATH ENJOINED UNTO YOU	147 23
END OF THE WORLD HE HATH APPEARED TO PUT AWAY SIN BY	148 06
AS MY FATHER HATH APPOINTED UNTO ME	149 28
BEHOLD, SATAN HATH DESIRED TO HAVE YOU, THAT HE MAY	149 31
BUT NOW, HE THAT HATH A PURSE, LET HIM TAKE IT, AND	150 06
AND HE THAT HATH NO SWORD, LET HIM SELL HIS GARMENT,	150 08
WHAT EVIL HATH HE DONE	153 35
BUT THIS MAN HATH DONE NOTHING AMISS	155 05
BY ONE OFFERING HE HATH PERFECTED FOR EVER THEM THAT	158 08
WHICH HE HATH CONSECRATED FOR US, THROUGH THE	158 18
ME UNTO THEE HATH THE GREATER SIN	159 18
FOR CHRIST ALSO HATH ONCE SUFFERED FOR SINS, THE JUST	161 22
DEATH HATH NO MORE DOMINION OVER HIM	163 05
RISEN INDEED, AND HATH APPEARED TO SIMON	168 14
THE FATHERS, GOD HATH FULFILLED THE SAME UNTO US	169 07
IN THAT HE HATH RAISED UP JESUS AGAIN	169 08
FOR A SPIRIT HATH NOT FLESH AND BONES, AS YE SEE ME	169 34
OF GOD WHICH HE HATH TESTIFIED OF HIS SON	171 06
ON THE SON OF GOD HATH THE WITNESS IN HIMSELF	171 07
BELIEVETH NOT GOD HATH MADE HIM A LIAR	171 08
THAT GOD HATH GIVEN TO US ETERNAL LIFE,	171 10
HE THAT HATH THE SON HATH LIFE	171 11
THAT HATH THE SON HATH LIFE	171 11
AND HE THAT HATH NOT THE SON OF GOD HATH NOT LIFE	171 11
NOT THE SON OF GOD HATH NOT LIFE	171 12
AS MY FATHER HATH SENT ME, EVEN SO SEND I YOU	171 21
SHE IS IN TRAVAIL HATH SORROW, BECAUSE HER HOUR IS	174 10
UNTO YOU, SORROW HATH FILLED YOUR HEART	175 09
THAT THE FATHER HATH ARE MINE	175 23
WHICH THE FATHER HATH PUT IN HIS OWN POWER	178 08
AS EVERY MAN HATH RECEIVED THE GIFT, EVEN SO MINISTER	179 16
HE THAT HATH MY COMMANDMENTS, AND KEEPETH THEM, HE IT	181 18
WORLD COMETH, AND HATH NOTHING IN ME	182 08
BODY IS ONE, AND HATH MANY MEMBERS, AND ALL THE	183 02
BECAUSE HE HATH NOT BELIEVED IN THE NAME OF	185 04
AND NO MAN HATH ASCENDED UP TO HEAVEN, BUT HE THAT	188 24
NO MAN HATH SEEN GOD AT ANY TIME	189 16
IN US, BECAUSE HE HATH GIVEN US OF HIS SPIRIT	189 19
THE LOVE THAT GOD HATH TO US	189 24
BECAUSE FEAR HATH TORMENT	189 29
HIS BROTHER WHOM HE HATH SEEN, HOW CAN HE LOVE GOD	189 33
HE LOVE GOD WHOM HE HATH NOT SEEN	189 33
THAT NO MURDERER HATH ETERNAL LIFE ABIDING IN HIM	191 15
BUT WHOSO HATH THIS WORLD'S GOOD, AND SEETH HIS	191 18
THE SPIRIT WHICH HE HATH GIVEN US	191 34
OF ALL GRACE, WHO HATH CALLED US UNTO HIS ETERNAL	193 09
AND WHEN HE HATH FOUND IT, HE LAYETH IT ON HIS	193 21
AND WHEN SHE HATH FOUND IT, SHE CALLETH HER FRIENDS	193 30
REASON OF HIM WHO HATH SUBJECTED THE SAME IN HOPE,	194 16
DEATH HATH NO MORE DOMINION OVER HIM	197 22
THAT THY BROTHER HATH OUGHT AGAINST THEE	198 09
THERE HATH NO TEMPTATION TAKEN YOU BUT SUCH AS IS	201 25
AND THY FATHER HATH KILLED THE FATTED CALF, BECAUSE	202 30
BECAUSE HE HATH RECEIVED HIM SAFE AND SOUND	202 31
SON WAS COME, WHICH HATH DEVOURED THY LIVING WITH	203 03
WHO ALSO HATH MADE US ABLE MINISTERS OF THE NEW	206 16
HE HATH DONE ALL THINGS WELL	207 08
BUT THE SCRIPTURE HATH CONCLUDED ALL UNDER SIN,	208 03
THY FAITH HATH MADE THEE WHOLE	210 14
THAT GOD HATH VISITED HIS PEOPLE	213 09
FOR CHRIST'S SAKE HATH FORGIVEN YOU	216 30
THAT THE SON OF MAN HATH POWER ON EARTH TO FORGIVE	217 09
THAT HE WHICH HATH BEGUN A GOOD WORK IN YOU WILL	220 26
THE FATHER, WHICH HATH MADE US MEET TO BE PARTAKERS	224 09
THY FAITH HATH MADE THEE WHOLE	224 22
A LAD HERE, WHICH HATH FIVE BARLEY LOAVES, AND TWO	225 30
HEART THAT GOD HATH RAISED HIM FROM THE DEAD, THOU	226 27
LORD, WHO HATH BELIEVED OUR REPORT	227 12
WHICH HATH GREAT RECOMPENCE OF REWARD	228 14
HE PRAYETH, AND HATH SEEN IN A VISION A MAN NAMED	230 19
HOW MUCH EVIL HE HATH DONE TO THY SAINTS AT	230 23
AND HERE HE HATH AUTHORITY FROM THE CHIEF PRIESTS TO	230 24
WAY AS THOU CAMEST, HATH SENT ME, THAT THOU MIGHTEST	230 32
AND EVERY ONE THAT HATH FORSAKEN HOUSES, OR BRETHREN,	231 18
SHE HATH ALSO CONCEIVED A SON IN HER OLD	236 25

HATH   CONTINUED   HATH   CONTINUED

AS THE FATHER HATH LOVED ME, SO HAVE I LOVED YOU	238 20
WHICH THE LORD HATH PROMISED TO THEM THAT LOVE HIM	239 26
THAT HATH SEEN ME HATH SEEN THE FATHER	240 12
HE THAT HATH SEEN ME HATH SEEN THE FATHER	240 12
GREATER LOVE HATH NO MAN THAN THIS, THAT A MAN LAY	241 26
FOR SHE HATH RECEIVED OF THE LORD'S HAND DOUBLE FOR	242 19
MOUTH OF THE LORD HATH SPOKEN IT	242 26
FOR HE HATH VISITED AND REDEEMED HIS PEOPLE, AND HATH	243 33
HIS PEOPLE, AND HATH RAISED UP AN HORN OF SALVATION	243 34
FROM ON HIGH HATH VISITED US, TO GIVE LIGHT TO THEM	244 14
SENT HIS ANGEL, AND HATH DELIVERED ME OUT OF THE HAND	245 27
THAT THE LORD HATH SENT HIS ANGEL, AND HATH DELIVERED	245 27
FOR FLESH AND BLOOD HATH NOT REVEALED IT UNTO THEE,	246 05
LORD JESUS CHRIST HATH SHEWED ME	248 11
AS MY FATHER HATH APPOINTED UNTO ME	250 13
GOD OF THIS WORLD HATH BLINDED THE MINDS OF THEM	251 03
OUT OF DARKNESS, HATH SHINED IN OUR HEARTS, TO GIVE	251 08
HE KNOWETH THAT HE HATH BUT A SHORT TIME	252 19
FOR DEMAS HATH FORSAKEN ME, HAVING LOVED THIS PRESENT	253 31
FOR HE HATH GREATLY WITHSTOOD OUR WORDS	254 09
FOR SO HATH THE LORD COMMANDED US, SAYING, I HAVE SET	261 03
UPON ME, BECAUSE HE HATH ANOINTED ME TO PREACH THE	261 17
HE HATH SENT ME TO HEAL THE BROKENHEARTED, TO PREACH	261 18
HE IS THY GOD, THAT HATH DONE FOR THEE THESE GREAT	263 31
HAVE HEARD THAT IT HATH BEEN SAID, THOU SHALT LOVE	264 03
FOR HE HATH MADE FAST THE BARS OF THY GATES, *	265 02
AND HATH BLESSED THY CHILDREN WITHIN THEE	265 03
WHAT THEREFORE GOD HATH JOINED TOGETHER, LET NOT MAN	268 10
FATHER'S WILL WHICH HATH SENT ME, THAT OF ALL WHICH	269 17
OF ALL WHICH HE HATH GIVEN ME, I SHOULD LOSE NOTHING,	269 18
ALL STANDING, HATH THIS CHILD (PERSON) BEEN ALREADY	273 26
THAT IT HATH PLEASED THEE TO REGENERATE THIS	280 29
THAT HE HATH CALLED ME TO THIS STATE OF	284 02
GOD THE FATHER, WHO HATH MADE ME, AND ALL THE WORLD	284 30
IN GOD THE SON, WHO HATH REDEEMED ME, AND ALL	284 31
OUR SAVIOUR CHRIST HATH TAUGHT US, AND SAY,	289 19
HOW MANY SACRAMENTS HATH CHRIST ORDAINED IN HIS	292 04
CHRIST HATH ORDAINED TWO SACRAMENTS ONLY,	292 06
WHICH THE LORD HATH COMMANDED TO BE RECEIVED	293 11
WHO HATH MADE HEAVEN AND EARTH	297 08
THOSE WHOM GOD HATH JOINED TOGETHER LET NO MAN	303 31
AS HATH BEEN ACCUSTOMED, OR AS THE ORDINARY	R 305 09
FORASMUCH AS IT HATH PLEASED ALMIGHTY GOD, OF HIS	305 11
BECAUSE HE HATH HEARD THE VOICE OF MY PRAYER	305 18
BECAUSE HE HATH INCLINED HIS EAR UNTO ME	305 20
BENEFITS THAT HE HATH DONE UNTO ME	305 28
HATH GOD FORGOTTEN TO BE GRACIOUS	311 16
AND IF HE HATH OFFENDED ANY OTHER, TO ASK THEM	R 313 21
AND WHERE HE HATH DONE INJURY OR WRONG TO ANY MAN,	R 313 22
WHATSOEVER HATH BEEN DECAYED BY THE FRAUD AND	314 03
HIM THAT SENT ME, HATH EVERLASTING LIFE, AND SHALL	321 34
BELIEVETH ON ME HATH EVERLASTING LIFE	322 22
THAT JESUS CHRIST HATH SUFFERED DEATH UPON THE CROSS	R 323 27
THE BENEFITS HE HATH THEREBY, AND GIVING HIM HEARTY	R 323 29
AND THE LORD HATH TAKEN AWAY	324 15
MY HEART HATH SAID OF THEE, SEEK YE MY FACE	326 22
WHO HATH MADE HEAVEN AND EARTH	327 21
MUST REIGN, TILL HE HATH PUT ALL ENEMIES UNDER HIS	328 30
FOR HE HATH PUT ALL THINGS UNDER HIS FEET	328 31
IT A BODY AS IT HATH PLEASED HIM, AND TO EVERY SEED	329 10
IS BORN OF A WOMAN, HATH BUT A SHORT TIME TO LIVE,	332 18
WHO ALSO HATH TAUGHT US, BY HIS HOLY APOSTLE SAINT	335 03
WHO HATH MADE HEAVEN AND EARTH	339 05
THAT THIS THY CHILD HATH BEEN TAKEN INTO THE SAFE	340 26
IS THE MAN THAT HATH NOT WALKED IN THE COUNSEL OF THE	345 07
AND HATH NOT SAT IN THE SEAT OF THE SCORNFUL	345 09
THE LORD HATH SAID UNTO ME, THOU ART MY SON, THIS DAY	346 10
THAT THE LORD HATH CHOSEN TO HIMSELF THE MAN	347 16
FOR THE LORD HATH HEARD THE VOICE OF MY WEEPING	349 15
9 THE LORD HATH HEARD MY PETITION	349 16
HE HATH BENT HIS BOW, AND MADE IT READY	350 18
14 HE HATH PREPARED FOR HIM THE INSTRUMENTS OF DEATH	350 19
HE HATH CONCEIVED MISCHIEF, AND BROUGHT FORTH	350 22
16 HE HATH GRAVEN AND DIGGED UP A PIT, *	350 23
HE HATH ALSO PREPARED HIS SEAT FOR JUDGMENT	352 02
3 FOR THE UNGODLY HATH MADE BOAST OF HIS OWN HEART'S	353 08
6 FOR HE HATH SAID IN HIS HEART, TUSH, I SHALL NEVER	353 16
12 HE HATH SAID IN HIS HEART, TUSH, GOD HATH	353 30
TUSH, GOD HATH FORGOTTEN	353 30
BECAUSE HE HATH DEALT SO LOVINGLY WITH ME	356 09
THE FOOL HATH SAID IN HIS HEART, *	356 13
3 HE THAT HATH USED NO DECEIT IN HIS TONGUE, NOR DONE	357 10
AND HATH NOT SLANDERED HIS NEIGHBOUR	357 11
6 HE THAT HATH NOT GIVEN HIS MONEY UPON USURY,	357 17
OR WHO HATH ANY STRENGTH, EXCEPT OUR GOD	361 31
5 IN THEM HATH HE SET A TABERNACLE FOR THE SUN	363 21
24 FOR HE HATH NOT DESPISED NOR ABHORRED THE LOW	367 20
HE HATH NOT HID HIS FACE FROM HIM	367 21
AND NO MAN HATH QUICKENED HIS OWN SOUL	368 03
WHOM THE LORD HATH MADE	368 08
2 FOR HE HATH FOUNDED IT UPON THE SEAS, *	368 30
4 EVEN HE THAT HATH CLEAN HANDS, AND A PURE HEART	369 02
AND THAT HATH NOT LIFT UP HIS MIND UNTO VANITY, NOR	369 03
IN THEE HATH BEEN MY HOPE ALL THE DAY LONG	369 26
FOR MY HOPE HATH BEEN IN THEE	370 27
MY TRUST HATH BEEN ALSO IN THE LORD, THEREFORE SHALL	370 31
9 MY HEART HATH TALKED OF THEE, SEEK YE MY FACE	372 14
FOR HE HATH HEARD THE VOICE OF MY HUMBLE PETITIONS	373 20
MY HEART HATH TRUSTED IN HIM, AND I AM HELPED	373 23
AND MY TRUST HATH BEEN IN THE LORD	376 03
16 BUT MY HOPE HATH BEEN IN THEE, O LORD	376 24
FOR HE HATH SHOWED ME MARVELLOUS GREAT KINDNESS IN A	377 09
THE FOLK THAT HE HATH CHOSEN TO HIM, TO BE HIS	379 12
19 OUR SOUL HATH PATIENTLY TARRIED FOR THE LORD	379 28

AND HIS NET THAT HE HATH LAID PRIVILY CATCH HIMSELF	382 05
BE THE LORD, WHO HATH PLEASURE IN THE PROSPERITY OF	383 21
HE HATH LEFT OFF TO BEHAVE HIMSELF WISELY, AND TO DO	383 31
UPON HIS BED, AND HATH SET HIMSELF IN NO GOOD WAY	383 33
FOR HE HATH SEEN THAT HIS DAY IS COMING	385 20
THAT THE RIGHTEOUS HATH, *	385 27
MY STRENGTH HATH FAILED ME, *	388 10
3 AND HE HATH PUT A NEW SONG IN MY MOUTH, *	390 14
IS THE MAN THAT HATH SET HIS HOPE IN THE LORD, *	390 18
MY TALK HATH BEEN OF THY TRUTH, AND OF THY SALVATION	391 05
AND MY HEART HATH FAILED ME	391 13
EAT OF MY BREAD, HATH LAID GREAT WAIT FOR ME	392 18
SHAME OF MY FACE HATH COVERED ME	395 25
BECAUSE GOD HATH BLESSED THEE FOR EVER	396 19
EVEN THY GOD, HATH ANOINTED THEE WITH THE OIL OF	396 30
BUT GOD HATH SHOWED HIS VOICE, AND THE EARTH SHALL	398 05
WHAT DESTRUCTION HE HATH BROUGHT UPON THE EARTH	398 10
15 BUT GOD HATH DELIVERED MY SOUL FROM THE POWER OF	401 05
IS IN HONOUR BUT HATH NO UNDERSTANDING *	401 16
MOST MIGHTY GOD, HATH SPOKEN, *	401 21
2 OUT OF SION HATH GOD APPEARED *	401 24
AND IN SIN HATH MY MOTHER CONCEIVED ME	403 18
THE FOOLISH BODY HATH SAID IN HIS HEART, *	405 12
FOR GOD HATH BROKEN THE BONES OF HIM THAT BESIEGED	405 25
BECAUSE GOD HATH DESPISED THEM	405 27
7 FOR HE HATH DELIVERED ME OUT OF ALL MY TROUBLE	406 16
AND MINE EYE HATH SEEN HIS DESIRE UPON MINE ENEMIES	406 17
AN HORRIBLE DREAD HATH OVERWHELMED ME	406 29
AN OPEN ENEMY THAT HATH DONE ME THIS DISHONOUR	407 11
19 IT IS HE THAT HATH DELIVERED MY SOUL IN PEACE FROM	407 27
6 GOD HATH SPOKEN IN HIS HOLINESS, I WILL REJOICE,	412 23
THY RIGHT HAND HATH UPHOLDEN ME	415 09
IT SHALL SAY, THIS HATH GOD DONE	416 04
TELL YOU WHAT HE HATH DONE FOR MY SOUL	418 13
17 BUT GOD HATH HEARD ME	418 18
PRAISED BE GOD, WHO HATH NOT CAST OUT MY PRAYER,	418 20
22 THE LORD HATH SAID, I WILL BRING MY PEOPLE AGAIN,	420 30
28 THY GOD HATH SENT FORTH STRENGTH FOR THEE	421 11
SHAME HATH COVERED MY FACE	422 17
ZEAL OF THINE HOUSE HATH EVEN EATEN ME	422 20
21 REPROACH HATH BROKEN MY HEART	423 13
THAN A BULLOCK THAT HATH HORNS AND HOOFS	424 07
10 GOD HATH FORSAKEN HIM	425 27
AND HIM THAT HATH NO HELPER	427 21
WHICH THOU HAST DONE EVIL IN THY SANCTUARY	430 11
HOW THE ENEMY HATH REBUKED	431 12
THE FOOLISH PEOPLE HATH BLASPHEMED THY NAME	431 13
9 HATH GOD FORGOTTEN TO BE GRACIOUS	433 33
WORKS THAT HE HATH DONE	435 03
THE GROUND WHICH HE HATH MADE CONTINUALLY	439 17
THAT THY RIGHT HAND HATH PLANTED, *	441 33
2 MY SOUL HATH A DESIRE AND LONGING TO ENTER INTO THE	445 13
3 YEA, THE SPARROW HATH FOUND HER AN HOUSE, AND THE	445 16
AND RIGHTEOUSNESS HATH LOOKED DOWN FROM HEAVEN	446 30
EVEN AS A MAN THAT HATH NO STRENGTH	449 03
THE FEAR OF THEE HATH UNDONE ME	449 30
14 BECAUSE HE HATH SET HIS LOVE UPON ME, THEREFORE	455 23
HIM UP, BECAUSE HE HATH KNOWN MY NAME	455 24
LORD IS KING, AND HATH PUT ON GLORIOUS APPAREL	457 04
THE LORD HATH PUT ON HIS APPAREL, AND GIRDED HIMSELF	457 05
2 HE HATH MADE THE ROUND WORLD SO SURE, *	457 07
THE WORLD BEGAN, HATH THY SEAT BEEN PREPARED	457 09
I SAID, MY FOOT HATH SLIPT	458 22
THAT IT IS HE WHO HATH MADE THE ROUND WORLD SO FAST	460 19
FOR HE HATH DONE MARVELLOUS THINGS	461 25
HATH HE GOTTEN HIMSELF THE VICTORY	461 28
HIS RIGHTEOUSNESS HATH HE OPENLY SHOWED IN THE SIGHT	461 30
4 HE HATH REMEMBERED HIS MERCY AND TRUTH TOWARD THE	461 31
IT IS HE THAT HATH MADE US, AND NOT WE OURSELVES	463 09
7 WHOSO HATH ALSO A HAUGHTY LOOK AND A PROUD HEART,	463 28
19 FOR HE HATH LOOKED DOWN FROM HIS SANCTUARY	465 17
10 HE HATH NOT DEALT WITH US AFTER OUR SINS	466 25
SO FAR HATH HE SET OUR SINS FROM US	466 31
19 THE LORD HATH PREPARED HIS SEAT IN HEAVEN,	467 13
OF LEBANON WHICH HE HATH PLANTED	468 27
WHAT THINGS HE HATH DONE	470 06
WORKS THAT HE HATH DONE	470 12
8 HE HATH BEEN ALWAY MINDFUL OF HIS COVENANT AND	470 18
WHOM THE LORD HATH REDEEMED, *	476 08
16 FOR HE HATH BROKEN THE GATES OF BRASS, *	477 07
7 GOD HATH SPOKEN IN HIS HOLINESS	479 17
10 LET THE EXTORTIONER CONSUME ALL THAT HE HATH	480 21
THE CLOAK THAT HE HATH UPON HIM, *	481 08
AND GRACIOUS LORD HATH SO DONE HIS MARVELLOUS WORKS,	482 30
5 HE HATH GIVEN MEAT UNTO THEM THAT FEAR HIM	483 03
6 HE HATH SHOWED HIS PEOPLE THE POWER OF HIS WORKS,	483 05
HE HATH COMMANDED HIS COVENANT FOR EVER	483 11
HE HATH GREAT DELIGHT IN HIS COMMANDMENTS	483 18
9 HE HATH DISPERSED ABROAD, AND GIVEN TO THE POOR,	483 34
LORD OUR GOD, THAT HATH HIS DWELLING SO HIGH, *	484 16
HE HATH DONE WHATSOEVER PLEASED HIM	485 16
12 THE LORD HATH BEEN MINDFUL OF US, AND HE SHALL	485 34
THE EARTH HATH HE GIVEN TO THE CHILDREN OF MEN	486 11
BECAUSE HE HATH HEARD THE VOICE OF MY PRAYER	486 19
2 BECAUSE HE HATH INCLINED HIS EAR UNTO ME	486 21
FOR THE LORD HATH REWARDED THEE	487 03
BENEFITS THAT HE HATH DONE UNTO ME	487 10
HAND OF THE LORD HATH THE PRE-EMINENCE	488 33
18 THE LORD HATH CHASTENED AND CORRECTED ME	489 04
BUT HE HATH NOT GIVEN ME OVER UNTO DEATH	489 05
DAY WHICH THE LORD HATH MADE	489 16
IS THE LORD, WHO HATH SHOWED US LIGHT	489 22
THAT IT HATH ALWAY UNTO THY JUDGMENTS	491 07
FOR THY WORD HATH QUICKENED ME	493 11

HATH	CONTINUED		HAVE	CONTINUED	

BUT MY DELIGHT HATH BEEN IN THY LAW 494 20
MY SOUL HATH LONGED FOR THY SALVATION, * 495 19
139 MY ZEAL HATH EVEN CONSUMED ME 499 17
167 MY SOUL HATH KEPT THY TESTIMONIES, * 501 15
5 MY SOUL HATH LONG DWELT AMONG THEM * 502 17
WHO HATH MADE HEAVEN AND EARTH 502 24
WHO HATH NOT GIVEN US OVER FOR A PREY UNTO THEIR 504 16
WHO HATH MADE HEAVEN AND EARTH 504 21
THE LORD HATH DONE GREAT THINGS FOR THEM 505 11
4 YEA, THE LORD HATH DONE GREAT THINGS FOR US 505 13
IS THE MAN THAT HATH HIS QUIVER FULL OF THEM 506 02
HATH HEWN THE SNARES OF THE UNGODLY IN PIECES 506 27
11 THE LORD HATH MADE A FAITHFUL OATH UNTO DAVID, 508 25
14 FOR THE LORD HATH CHOSEN SION TO BE AN HABITATION 508 32
HE HATH LONGED FOR HER 508 33
THE LORD HATH CHOSEN JACOB UNTO HIMSELF, * 510 09
9 HE HATH SENT TOKENS AND WONDERS INTO THE MIDST OF 510 20
7 WHO HATH MADE GREAT LIGHTS 511 28
24 AND HATH DELIVERED US FROM OUR ENEMIES 512 30
LORD BE HIGH, YET HATH HE RESPECT UNTO THE LOWLY 514 08
HE HATH SMITTEN MY LIFE DOWN TO THE GROUND 518 27
3 FOR THE ENEMY HATH PERSECUTED MY SOUL 518 27
HE HATH LAID ME IN THE DARKNESS, AS THE MEN THAT HAVE 518 28
BLESSED IS HE THAT HATH THE GOD OF JACOB FOR HIS 522 10
10 HE HATH NO PLEASURE IN THE STRENGTH OF AN HORSE 523 15
13 FOR HE HATH MADE FAST THE BARS OF THY GATES, 523 21
AND HATH BLESSED THY CHILDREN WITHIN THEE 523 22
20 HE HATH NOT DEALT SO WITH ANY NATION 524 02
6 HE HATH MADE THEM FAST FOR EVER AND EVER 524 16
HE HATH GIVEN THEM A LAW WHICH SHALL NOT BE BROKEN 524 16
4 FOR THE LORD HATH PLEASURE IN HIS PEOPLE, * 525 09
EVERY THING THAT HATH BREATH * 525 32
OR HATH HAD EPISCOPAL CONSECRATION OR 529 23
UNTO THAT LORD, WHO HATH PLACED YOU IN SO HIGH A 540 28
WHEREUNTO IT HATH PLEASED GOD TO CALL YOU 541 12
AS THE LORD HATH COMMANDED, AND AS THIS 542 13
AND AS THIS CHURCH HATH RECEIVED THE SAME, ACCORDING 542 14
ALMIGHTY GOD, WHO HATH GIVEN YOU THIS WILL TO DO ALL 543 18
HIS WORK WHICH HE HATH BEGUN IN YOU 543 21
THE HOLY GHOST HATH MADE YOU OVERSEERS, TO FEED THE 550 28
OF GOD, WHICH HE HATH PURCHASED WITH HIS OWN BLOOD 550 29
AS MY FATHER HATH SENT ME, EVEN SO SEND I YOU 552 02
THE HOLY GHOST HATH CALLED HIM 553 12
OF CHRIST, WHICH HE HATH PURCHASED WITH NO LESS PRICE 554 10
WHO HATH GIVEN YOU A GOOD WILL TO DO ALL 555 28
GOOD WORK WHICH HE HATH BEGUN, YOU MAY BE FOUND 555 31
FOR GOD HATH NOT GIVEN US THE SPIRIT OF FEAR, BUT OF 558 17
2 FOR HE HATH FOUNDED IT UPON THE SEAS, * 563 13
4 EVEN HE THAT HATH CLEAN HANDS, AND A PURE HEART 563 17
AND THAT HATH NOT LIFT UP HIS MIND UNTO VANITY, NOR 563 18
O LORD, THAT IT HATH PLEASED THEE TO PUT IT INTO THE 566 28
ZEAL OF THINE HOUSE HATH EATEN ME UP 568 03
FOR THAT IT HATH PLEASED THEE TO HAVE THY 568 06
AND AS THE LORD HATH ORDAINED THAT THEY WHO SERVE AT 569 28
OUR LORD, WHO HATH TAUGHT US TO PRAY UNTO THEE, 571 17
THAT HE HATH CALLED ME TO THIS STATE OF 577 23
GOD THE FATHER, WHO HATH MADE ME, AND ALL THE WORLD 578 12
IN GOD THE SON, WHO HATH REDEEMED ME, AND ALL 578 13
HOW MANY SACRAMENTS HATH CHRIST ORDAINED IN HIS 581 07
WHICH THE LORD HATH COMMANDED TO BE RECEIVED 582 09
WHOSE LOVING HAND HATH GIVEN US ALL THAT WE POSSESS 599 19
AND LUST HATH OF ITSELF THE NATURE OF SIN 604 40
ARE NOT DONE AS GOD HATH WILLED AND COMMANDED THEM TO 605 21
WORLD WERE LAID) HE HATH CONSTANTLY DECREED BY HIS 606 07
THOSE WHOM HE HATH CHOSEN IN CHRIST OUT OF MANKIND, 606 09
THE CHURCH OF ROME HATH ERRED, NOT ONLY IN THEIR 606 43
THE CHURCH HATH POWER TO DECREE RITES OR CEREMONIES, 607 03
OF A SACRAMENT, AND HATH GIVEN OCCASION TO MANY 608 43
BY A JUDGE THAT HATH AUTHORITY THEREUNTO 609 30
OR NATIONAL CHURCH HATH AUTHORITY TO ORDAIN, CHANGE, 609 42
NEITHER HATH IT ANY THING THAT, OF ITSELF, IS 610 33
BUT HATH NO AUTHORITY IN THINGS PURELY SPIRITUAL 610 39

HATRED

TAKE AWAY ALL HATRED AND PREJUDICE, AND WHATSOEVER 037 28
FROM ENVY, HATRED, AND MALICE, AND ALL 054 24
MALICE AND HATRED TO REIGN R 085 10
HATRED, VARIANCE, EMULATIONS, WRATH, 209 21
NO MALICE NOR HATRED IN MY HEART 288 33
WITH WORDS OF HATRED, AND FOUGHT AGAINST ME WITHOUT A 480 07
AND HATRED FOR MY GOOD WILL 480 12
NO MALICE NOR HATRED IN MY HEART 580 08
HEARTS FROM ENVY, HATRED, AND MALICE 590 15

HAUGHTY

HATH ALSO A HAUGHTY LOOK AND A PROUD HEART, * 463 28

HAVE

UNTO HIM, FATHER, I HAVE SINNED AGAINST HEAVEN, 004 27
IN WHOM WE HAVE REDEMPTION THROUGH HIS BLOOD, 004 33
SEEING THAT WE HAVE A GREAT HIGH PRIEST, THAT IS 005 06
AND ORDER THEREOF) HAVE STILL BEEN CONTINUED FIRM AND V 32
BENEFITS THAT WE HAVE RECEIVED AT HIS HANDS, TO SET 006 06
WE HAVE ERRED, AND STRAYED FROM THY WAYS LIKE LOST 006 17
WE HAVE FOLLOWED TOO MUCH THE DEVICES AND DESIRES OF 006 18
WE HAVE OFFENDED AGAINST THY HOLY LAWS 006 20
WE HAVE LEFT UNDONE THOSE THINGS WHICH WE OUGHT TO 006 20
WHICH WE OUGHT TO HAVE DONE 006 21
AND WE HAVE DONE THOSE THINGS WHICH WE OUGHT NOT TO 006 22
WE OUGHT NOT TO HAVE DONE 006 23
BUT THOU, O LORD, HAVE MERCY UPON US, MISERABLE 006 24

HAVE MERCY UPON US, HAVE MERCY UPON US 011 09
O LORD, HAVE MERCY UPON US, HAVE MERCY UPON US 011 09
O LORD, IN THEE HAVE I TRUSTED 011 12
WHICH HAVE BEEN SINCE THE WORLD BEGAN 014 13
WHOSE KINGDOM SHALL HAVE NO END 016 13
I HAVE LOVED THE HABITATION OF THY HOUSE, 021 14
THOUGH WE HAVE REBELLED AGAINST HIM 022 07
NEITHER HAVE WE OBEYED THE VOICE OF THE LORD OUR GOD, 022 07
IF WE SAY THAT WE HAVE NO SIN, WE DECEIVE OURSELVES, 022 10
ALL WE LIKE SHEEP HAVE GONE ASTRAY 022 14
WE HAVE TURNED EVERY ONE TO HIS OWN WAY 022 14
BENEFITS THAT WE HAVE RECEIVED AT HIS HANDS, TO SET 023 15
WE HAVE ERRED, AND STRAYED FROM THY WAYS LIKE LOST 023 24
WE HAVE FOLLOWED TOO MUCH THE DEVICES AND DESIRES OF 023 25
WE HAVE OFFENDED AGAINST THY HOLY LAWS 023 27
WE HAVE LEFT UNDONE THOSE THINGS WHICH WE OUGHT TO 023 27
WHICH WE OUGHT TO HAVE DONE 023 28
AND WE HAVE DONE THOSE THINGS WHICH WE OUGHT NOT TO 023 29
WE OUGHT NOT TO HAVE DONE 023 30
BUT THOU, O LORD, HAVE MERCY UPON US, MISERABLE 023 31
SINS OF THE WORLD, HAVE MERCY UPON US 025 29
OF GOD THE FATHER, HAVE MERCY UPON US 025 31
ENDS OF THE WORLD HAVE SEEN THE SALVATION OF OUR GOD 027 11
FOR MINE EYES HAVE SEEN * 028 11
WHOSE KINGDOM SHALL HAVE NO END 030 18
HAVE MERCY UPON THIS WHOLE LAND 032 05
THY SERVANTS WHO HAVE LAID DOWN THEIR LIVES IN THE 042 16
FOR ALL WHO HAVE FALLEN INTO GRIEVOUS SIN 048 07
ALL HIS SAINTS, WHO HAVE BEEN THE CHOICE VESSELS OF 048 17
THAT WE MAY HAVE GRACE TO DIRECT OUR LIVES AFTER 048 19
THE WORDS WHICH WE HAVE HEARD THIS DAY WITH OUR 049 18
WE BESEECH THEE TO HAVE COMPASSION UPON OUR 049 31
EARS TO US WHO HAVE NOW MADE OUR PRAYERS AND 050 08
THINGS WHICH WE HAVE FAITHFULLY ASKED ACCORDING TO 050 10
IN CHURCH, SHALL HAVE DESIRED TO RETURN THANKS TO R 051 03
TUMULTS WHICH HAVE BEEN LATELY RAISED UP AMONGST US 052 21
HAVE MERCY UPON US 054 06
TRUTH ALL SUCH AS HAVE ERRED, AND ARE DECEIVED 056 20
MAY PLEASE THEE TO HAVE MERCY UPON ALL MEN 057 05
HAVE MERCY UPON US 057 24
HAVE MERCY UPON US 057 27
HAVE MERCY UPON US 057 29
O GOD, WE HAVE HEARD WITH OUR EARS, AND OUR FATHERS 058 28
AND OUR FATHERS HAVE DECLARED UNTO US, THE NOBLE 058 29
O SON OF DAVID, HAVE MERCY UPON US 059 14
THAT 'RULERS MAY HAVE GRACE, WISDOM, AND VI 19
THAT WE MOST JUSTLY HAVE DESERVED 059 23
HAVE MERCY UPON ME, O GOD, AFTER THY GREAT GOODNESS 060 10
AGAINST THEE ONLY HAVE I SINNED, AND DONE THIS EVIL 060 17
HAVE MERCY UPON US 061 21
HAVE MERCY UPON US 061 22
IS ALWAYS TO HAVE MERCY 062 18
PROPERTY IS EVER TO HAVE MERCY AND TO FORGIVE 063 09
HOLY TABLE SHALL HAVE UPON IT A FAIR WHITE LINEN R 067 05
THOU SHALT HAVE NONE OTHER GODS BUT ME 068 04
HAVE MERCY UPON US, AND INCLINE OUR HEARTS TO 068 06
HAVE MERCY UPON US, AND INCLINE OUR HEARTS TO 069 05
HAVE MERCY UPON US, AND WRITE ALL THESE THY 069 23
BE SAID, LORD, HAVE MERCY UPON US 070 02
HAVE MERCY UPON US THEN THE PRIEST MAY SAY, 070 03
WHOSE KINGDOM SHALL HAVE NO END 071 16
WHILE WE HAVE TIME, LET US DO GOOD UNTO ALL MEN 072 20
WHICH LOVE YE HAVE SHOWED FOR HIS NAME'S SAKE, WHO 072 24
NAME'S SAKE, WHO HAVE MINISTERED UNTO THE SAINTS, AND 072 25
SEETH HIS BROTHER HAVE NEED, AND SHUTTETH UP HIS 072 29
INASMUCH AS YE HAVE DONE IT UNTO ONE OF THE 073 03
MY BRETHREN, YE HAVE DONE IT UNTO ME 073 04
ON HIM IN WHOM THEY HAVE NOT BELIEVED 073 06
IN HIM OF WHOM THEY HAVE NOT HEARD 073 08
AND OF THINE OWN HAVE WE GIVEN THEE 073 23
FOR ANY WHO HAVE DESIRED THE PRAYERS OF THE CHURCH R 074 03
MOST GRIEVOUSLY HAVE COMMITTED, BY THOUGHT, WORD, AND 075 20
HAVE MERCY UPON US, HAVE MERCY UPON US, MOST MERCIFUL 075 25
HAVE MERCY UPON US, HAVE MERCY UPON US, MOST MERCIFUL 075 26
HAVE MERCY UPON YOU 076 05
NOT PERISH, BUT HAVE EVERLASTING LIFE 076 16
IF ANY MAN SIN, WE HAVE AN ADVOCATE WITH THE FATHER, 076 22
WHEREBY WE HAVE BEEN BROUGHT OUT OF DARKNESS AND 078 30
IS ALWAYS TO HAVE MERCY 082 17
BE SPENT BEFORE ALL HAVE COMMUNICATED, THE PRIEST IS R 083 07
WHEN ALL HAVE COMMUNICATED, THE PRIEST SHALL RETURN R 083 11
TO FEED US WHO HAVE DULY RECEIVED THESE HOLY 083 18
SINS OF THE WORLD, HAVE MERCY UPON US 084 09
OF GOD THE FATHER, HAVE MERCY UPON US 084 11
EVIL LIVER, OR TO HAVE DONE ANY WRONG TO HIS R 085 02
UNTIL HE HAVE OPENLY DECLARED HIMSELF TO HAVE R 085 04
DECLARED HIMSELF TO HAVE TRULY REPENTED AND AMENDED R 085 05
HAVE A LIVELY AND STEDFAST FAITH IN CHRIST OUR 085 35
YOURSELVES TO HAVE OFFENDED, EITHER BY WILL, WORD, 087 19
FORGIVE OTHERS WHO HAVE OFFENDED YOU, AS YE WOULD 087 27
AS YE WOULD HAVE FORGIVENESS OF YOUR OFFENCES AT 087 28
BUT YE HAVE MADE IT A DEN OF THIEVES 092 03
SCRIPTURES MIGHT HAVE HOPE 092 17
SHALL EVERY MAN HAVE PRAISE OF GOD 094 15
UP, AND THE POOR HAVE THE GOSPEL PREACHED TO THEM 094 23
MY SON, THIS DAY HAVE I BEGOTTEN THEE 097 03
HOW OFTEN WOULD I HAVE GATHERED THY CHILDREN 100 29
WHICH WE HAVE HEARD, WHICH WE HAVE SEEN 101 12
WHICH WE HAVE SEEN WITH OUR EYES, WHICH WE 101 13
AND OUR HANDS HAVE HANDLED, OF THE WORD OF 101 14
OUR EYES, WHICH WE HAVE LOOKED UPON, AND OUR HANDS 101 14
AND WE HAVE SEEN IT, AND BEAR WITNESS, 101 15
THAT WHICH WE HAVE SEEN AND HEARD DECLARE WE UNTO 101 18
THAT YE ALSO MAY HAVE FELLOWSHIP WITH US 101 19

HAVE CONTINUED

	PAGE	LN
MESSAGE WHICH WE HAVE HEARD OF HIM, AND DECLARE UNTO	101	22
IF WE SAY THAT WE HAVE FELLOWSHIP WITH HIM, AND WALK	101	24
IS IN THE LIGHT, WE HAVE FELLOWSHIP ONE WITH ANOTHER,	101	26
IF WE SAY THAT WE HAVE NO SIN, WE DECEIVE OURSELVES,	101	28
IF WE SAY THAT WE HAVE NOT SINNED, WE MAKE HIM A	101	32
OUT OF EGYPT HAVE I CALLED MY SON	103	24
MY BELOVED, AS YE HAVE ALWAYS OBEYED, NOT AS IN MY	105	31
MAY AFTER THIS LIFE HAVE THE FRUITION OF THY GLORIOUS	108	02
YOU GENTILES, IF YE HAVE HEARD OF THE DISPENSATION OF	108	07
IN WHOM WE HAVE BOLDNESS AND ACCESS WITH CONFIDENCE	108	27
FOR WE HAVE SEEN HIS STAR IN THE EAST, AND ARE COME	108	33
AND WHEN YE HAVE FOUND HIM, BRING ME WORD AGAIN,	109	14
TO DO, AND ALSO MAY HAVE GRACE AND POWER FAITHFULLY	109	32
FOR AS WE HAVE MANY MEMBERS IN ONE BODY, AND ALL	110	13
AND ALL MEMBERS HAVE NOT THE SAME OFFICE	110	14
SUPPOSING HIM TO HAVE BEEN IN THE COMPANY, WENT A	110	24
THY FATHER AND I HAVE SOUGHT THEE SORROWING	110	33
I INDEED HAVE BAPTIZED YOU WITH WATER	112	16
UNTO HIM, THEY HAVE NO WINE	113	15
WOMAN, WHAT HAVE I TO DO WITH THEE	113	16
AND WHEN MEN HAVE WELL DRUNK, THEN THAT WHICH IS	113	28
AND THOU SHALT HAVE PRAISE OF THE SAME	114	18
I SAY UNTO YOU, I HAVE NOT FOUND SO GREAT FAITH, NO,	115	17
IF ANY MAN HAVE A QUARREL AGAINST ANY	116	06
BEHOLD, I HAVE TOLD YOU BEFORE	118	07
ANY MEANS, WHEN I HAVE PREACHED TO OTHERS, I MYSELF	119	12
THAT THEY SHOULD HAVE RECEIVED MORE	120	02
THESE LAST HAVE WROUGHT BUT ONE HOUR, AND	120	04
UNTO US, WHICH HAVE BORNE THE BURDEN AND HEAT OF THE	120	06
A NIGHT AND A DAY I HAVE BEEN IN THE DEEP	121	04
AND THESE HAVE NO ROOT, WHICH FOR A WHILE BELIEVE,	122	03
WHEN THEY HAVE HEARD, GO FORTH, AND ARE CHOKED	122	06
AND OF ANGELS, AND HAVE NOT CHARITY, I AM BECOME AS	122	22
AND THOUGH I HAVE THE GIFT OF PROPHECY, AND	122	23
AND THOUGH I HAVE ALL FAITH, SO THAT I COULD REMOVE	122	25
AND HAVE NOT CHARITY, I AM NOTHING	122	26
TO BE BURNED, AND HAVE NOT CHARITY, IT PROFITETH ME	122	28
THOU SON OF DAVID, HAVE MERCY ON ME	123	30
THOU SON OF DAVID, HAVE MERCY ON ME	123	33
SAY UNTO YOU, THEY HAVE THEIR REWARD	125	12
FOR HE SAITH, I HAVE HEARD THEE IN A TIME ACCEPTED,	126	05
DAY OF SALVATION HAVE I SUCCOURED THEE	126	06
WHO SEEST THAT WE HAVE NO POWER OF OURSELVES TO HELP	127	15
THAT AS YE HAVE RECEIVED OF US HOW YE OUGHT TO	127	24
AS WE ALSO HAVE FOREWARNED YOU AND TESTIFIED	127	32
UNTO HIM, SAYING, HAVE MERCY ON ME, O LORD, THOU SON	128	09
AND HAVE NO FELLOWSHIP WITH THE UNFRUITFUL WORKS OF	129	16
JESUS ANSWERED, I HAVE NOT A DEVIL	133	14
YET YE HAVE NOT KNOWN HIM	133	25
SINNED IN THAT I HAVE BETRAYED THE INNOCENT BLOOD	135	05
SAYING, I HAVE SINNED IN THAT I HAVE BETRAYED	135	05
UNTO HIM, SAYING, HAVE THOU NOTHING TO DO WITH THAT	135	33
FOR I HAVE SUFFERED MANY THINGS THIS DAY IN A DREAM	135	34
HIM NOW, IF HE WILL HAVE HIM	137	13
I HAVE TRODDEN THE WINEPRESS ALONE	138	16
OF THY HOLINESS HAVE POSSESSED IT BUT A LITTLE WHILE	139	27
OUR ADVERSARIES HAVE TRODDEN DOWN THY SANCTUARY	139	28
FOR IT MIGHT HAVE BEEN SOLD FOR MORE THAN THREE	140	08
HUNDRED PENCE, AND HAVE BEEN GIVEN TO THE POOR	140	09
FOR YE HAVE THE POOR WITH YOU ALWAYS, AND WHENSOEVER	140	12
BUT ME YE HAVE NOT ALWAYS	140	13
YE HAVE HEARD THE BLASPHEMY	143	18
THEREFORE HAVE I SET MY FACE LIKE A FLINT, AND I KNOW	144	17
THE SPARKS THAT YE HAVE KINDLED	144	28
THIS SHALL YE HAVE OF MINE HAND	144	28
THEN MUST HE OFTEN HAVE SUFFERED SINCE THE FOUNDATION	148	04
WITH DESIRE I HAVE DESIRED TO EAT THIS PASSOVER	149	02
YE ARE THEY WHICH HAVE CONTINUED WITH ME IN MY	149	26
HATH DESIRED TO HAVE YOU, THAT HE MAY SIFT YOU AS	149	31
BUT I HAVE PRAYED FOR THEE, THAT THY FAITH FAIL NOT	149	32
CONCERNING ME HAVE AN END	150	11
FOR WE OURSELVES HAVE HEARD OF HIS OWN MOUTH	152	02
I HAVE RECEIVED OF THE LORD THAT WHICH ALSO I	152	16
AND HE HOPED TO HAVE SEEN SOME MIRACLE DONE BY HIM	153	13
SAID UNTO THEM, YE HAVE BROUGHT THIS MAN UNTO ME, AS	153	22
HIM BEFORE YOU, HAVE FOUND NO FAULT IN THIS MAN	153	24
I HAVE FOUND NO CAUSE OF DEATH IN HIM	153	35
KNOW YE WHAT I HAVE DONE TO YOU	156	14
LORD AND MASTER, HAVE WASHED YOUR FEET	156	16
FOR I HAVE GIVEN YOU AN EXAMPLE, THAT YE SHOULD DO AS	156	17
YE SHOULD DO AS I HAVE DONE TO YOU	156	18
HAVE MERCY UPON ALL WHO KNOW THEE NOT AS THOU ART	157	07
THEN WOULD THEY NOT HAVE CEASED TO BE OFFERED	157	19
ONCE PURGED SHOULD HAVE HAD NO MORE CONSCIENCE OF	157	20
ANSWERED HIM, WE HAVE A LAW, AND BY OUR LAW HE OUGHT	159	09
THOU NOT THAT I HAVE POWER TO CRUCIFY THEE, AND HAVE	159	14
CRUCIFY THEE, AND HAVE POWER TO RELEASE THEE	159	15
THOU COULDEST HAVE NO POWER AT ALL AGAINST ME, EXCEPT	159	16
WE HAVE NO KING BUT CAESAR	159	29
WHAT I HAVE WRITTEN I HAVE WRITTEN	160	08
I HAVE WRITTEN I HAVE WRITTEN	160	09
SAID UNTO THEM, YE HAVE A WATCH	162	23
UNTO THEM, THEY HAVE TAKEN AWAY THE LORD OUT OF THE	164	14
KNOW NOT WHERE THEY HAVE LAID HIM	164	16
ARE THESE THAT YE HAVE ONE TO ANOTHER, AS YE WALK,	167	11
TO DEATH, AND HAVE CRUCIFIED HIM	167	19
HE WHICH SHOULD HAVE REDEEMED ISRAEL	167	20
OUGHT NOT CHRIST TO HAVE SUFFERED THESE THINGS, AND	167	30
THAT THE PROPHETS HAVE SPOKEN	167	30
AS THOUGH HE WOULD HAVE GONE FURTHER	168	02
SABBATH DAY, THEY HAVE FULFILLED THEM IN CONDEMNING	168	29
MY SON, THIS DAY HAVE I BEGOTTEN THEE	169	10
HATH NOT FLESH AND BONES, AS YE SEE ME HAVE	169	34
HE SAID UNTO THEM, HAVE YE HERE ANY MEAT	170	04

HAVE CONTINUED

	PAGE	LN
AND OTHER SHEEP I HAVE, WHICH ARE NOT OF THIS FOLD	172	30
YE NOW THEREFORE HAVE SORROW	174	13
BUT BECAUSE I HAVE SAID THESE THINGS UNTO YOU,	175	08
I HAVE YET MANY THINGS TO SAY UNTO YOU, BUT YE CANNOT	175	17
HITHERTO HAVE YE ASKED NOTHING IN MY NAME	176	22
THESE THINGS HAVE I SPOKEN UNTO YOU IN PROVERBS	176	23
BECAUSE YE HAVE LOVED ME, AND HAVE BELIEVED THAT	176	29
HAVE LOVED ME, AND HAVE BELIEVED THAT I CAME OUT FROM	176	29
THESE THINGS I HAVE SPOKEN UNTO YOU, THAT IN ME YE	177	08
THAT IN ME YE MIGHT HAVE PEACE	177	08
THE WORLD YE SHALL HAVE TRIBULATION	177	09
I HAVE OVERCOME THE WORLD	177	10
JESUS CHRIST TO HAVE ASCENDED INTO THE HEAVENS	177	16
THE FORMER TREATISE HAVE I MADE, O THEOPHILUS,	177	22
SAITH HE, YE HAVE HEARD OF ME	178	02
LIKE MANNER AS YE HAVE SEEN HIM GO INTO HEAVEN	178	19
ABOVE ALL THINGS HAVE FERVENT CHARITY AMONG	179	13
BECAUSE YE HAVE BEEN WITH ME FROM THE	179	27
THESE THINGS HAVE I SPOKEN UNTO YOU, THAT YE SHOULD	179	28
BECAUSE THEY HAVE NOT KNOWN THE FATHER, NOR ME	179	32
BUT THESE THINGS HAVE I TOLD YOU, THAT WHEN THE TIME	180	02
THE SAME SPIRIT TO HAVE A RIGHT JUDGMENT IN ALL	180	10
THESE THINGS HAVE I SPOKEN UNTO YOU, BEING YET	181	29
WHATSOEVER I HAVE SAID UNTO YOU	181	33
YE HAVE HEARD HOW I SAID UNTO YOU, I GO AWAY, AND	182	02
AND NOW I HAVE TOLD YOU BEFORE IT COME TO PASS, THAT,	182	05
AND HAVE BEEN ALL MADE TO DRINK INTO ONE SPIRIT	183	06
BE BAPTIZED, WHICH HAVE RECEIVED THE HOLY GHOST AS	184	27
NOT PERISH, BUT HAVE EVERLASTING LIFE	184	34
THAT THEY MIGHT HAVE LIFE, AND THAT THEY MIGHT HAVE	186	18
AND THAT THEY MIGHT HAVE IT MORE ABUNDANTLY	186	19
AND TESTIFY THAT WE HAVE SEEN	188	21
IF I HAVE TOLD YOU EARTHLY THINGS, AND YE BELIEVE	188	22
NOT PERISH, BUT HAVE ETERNAL LIFE	188	29
AND WE HAVE SEEN AND DO TESTIFY THAT THE FATHER SENT	189	20
AND WE HAVE KNOWN AND BELIEVED THE LOVE THAT GOD HATH	189	23
THAT WE MAY HAVE BOLDNESS IN THE DAY OF JUDGMENT	189	26
THIS COMMANDMENT HAVE WE FROM HIM, THAT HE WHO LOVETH	189	34
FATHER ABRAHAM, HAVE MERCY ON ME, AND SEND LAZARUS,	190	13
FOR I HAVE FIVE BRETHREN	190	24
UNTO HIM, THEY HAVE MOSES AND THE PROPHETS	190	26
AND MAKE US TO HAVE A PERPETUAL FEAR AND LOVE OF THY	191	07
WE KNOW THAT WE HAVE PASSED FROM DEATH UNTO LIFE,	191	12
SEETH HIS BROTHER HAVE NEED, AND SHUTTETH UP HIS	191	19
US NOT, THEN HAVE WE CONFIDENCE TOWARD GOD	191	26
SAID UNTO HIM, I HAVE BOUGHT A PIECE OF GROUND,	192	07
I PRAY THEE HAVE ME EXCUSED	192	08
AND ANOTHER SAID, I HAVE BOUGHT FIVE YOKE OF OXEN,	192	09
I PRAY THEE HAVE ME EXCUSED	192	10
AND ANOTHER SAID, I HAVE MARRIED A WIFE, AND	192	11
AFTER THAT YE HAVE SUFFERED A WHILE, MAKE YOU	193	10
FOR I HAVE FOUND MY SHEEP WHICH WAS LOST	193	24
FOR I HAVE FOUND THE PIECE WHICH I HAD LOST	193	32
WHICH HAVE THE FIRSTFRUITS OF THE SPIRIT, EVEN	194	21
MASTER, WE HAVE TOILED ALL THE NIGHT, AND HAVE	196	16
ALL THE NIGHT, AND HAVE TAKEN NOTHING	196	16
FOR IF WE HAVE BEEN PLANTED TOGETHER IN THE LIKENESS	197	15
YE HAVE HEARD THAT IT WAS SAID BY THEM OF OLD TIME,	197	31
FOR AS YE HAVE YIELDED YOUR MEMBERS SERVANTS TO	198	27
SERVANTS TO GOD, YE HAVE YOUR FRUIT UNTO HOLINESS,	199	03
SAITH UNTO THEM, I HAVE COMPASSION ON THE MULTITUDE,	199	10
ME THREE DAYS, AND HAVE NOTHING TO EAT	199	11
BECAUSE THEY HAVE NOW BEEN WITH ME THREE DAYS,	199	11
HOW MANY LOAVES HAVE YE	199	16
FOR YE HAVE NOT RECEIVED THE SPIRIT OF BONDAGE AGAIN	200	07
BUT YE HAVE RECEIVED THE SPIRIT OF ADOPTION, WHEREBY	200	08
AND HE WOULD FAIN HAVE FILLED HIS BELLY WITH THE	202	08
OF MY FATHER'S HAVE BREAD ENOUGH AND TO SPARE, AND I	202	11
UNTO HIM, FATHER, I HAVE SINNED AGAINST HEAVEN, AND	202	13
UNTO HIM, FATHER, I HAVE SINNED AGAINST HEAVEN,	202	19
AND ALL THAT I HAVE IS THINE	203	06
I WOULD NOT HAVE YOU IGNORANT	203	17
BUT YE HAVE MADE IT A DEN OF THIEVES	204	18
WHICH ALSO YE HAVE RECEIVED, AND WHEREIN YE	204	30
UNTO YOU, UNLESS YE HAVE BELIEVED IN VAIN	205	02
SUCH TRUST HAVE WE THROUGH CHRIST TO GOD-WARD	206	13
GIVEN WHICH COULD HAVE GIVEN LIFE, VERILY	207	32
SHOULD HAVE BEEN BY THE LAW	208	02
WHICH YE SEE, AND HAVE NOT SEEN THEM	208	09
PROPHETS AND KINGS HAVE DESIRED TO SEE THOSE THINGS	208	09
WHICH YE HEAR, AND HAVE NOT HEARD THEM	208	11
YOU BEFORE, AS I HAVE ALSO TOLD YOU IN TIME PAST,	209	24
THAT ARE CHRIST'S HAVE CRUCIFIED THE FLESH WITH THE	209	28
MASTER, HAVE MERCY ON US	210	04
LARGE A LETTER I HAVE WRITTEN UNTO YOU WITH MINE OWN	210	23
BUT DESIRE TO HAVE YOU CIRCUMCISED, THAT THEY MAY	210	28
KNOWETH THAT YE HAVE NEED OF ALL THESE THINGS	211	30
WHICH OF YOU SHALL HAVE AN ASS OR AN OX FALLEN INTO A	214	05
THEN SHALT THOU HAVE WORSHIP IN THE PRESENCE OF THEM	214	18
BEING PAST FEELING HAVE GIVEN THEMSELVES OVER UNTO	216	08
IF SO BE THAT YE HAVE HEARD HIM, AND HAVE BEEN TAUGHT	216	10
BUT YE HAVE NOT SO LEARNED CHRIST	216	10
HAVE HEARD HIM, AND HAVE BEEN TAUGHT BY HIM, AS THE	216	11
THAT HE MAY HAVE TO GIVE TO HIM THAT NEEDETH	216	22
BEHOLD, I HAVE PREPARED MY DINNER	218	08
YOU ALL, BECAUSE I HAVE YOU IN MY HEART	220	28
SAYING, LORD, HAVE PATIENCE WITH ME, AND I WILL	221	20
SAYING, HAVE PATIENCE WITH ME, AND I WILL PAY	221	27
NOT THOU ALSO HAVE HAD COMPASSION ON THY	221	35
WHICH WALK SO AS YE HAVE US FOR AN ENSAMPLE	222	16
OF WHOM I HAVE TOLD YOU OFTEN, AND NOW TELL YOU	222	17
BY OUR FRAILTY WE HAVE COMMITTED	223	18
THE LOVE WHICH YE HAVE TO ALL THE SAINTS, FOR THE	223	25
ON HIM IN WHOM THEY HAVE NOT BELIEVED	227	06

HAVE   CONTINUED   HAVE   CONTINUED

IN HIM OF WHOM THEY HAVE NOT HEARD   227 07   TO COME YE MAY HAVE LIFE EVERLASTING   304 15
BUT THEY HAVE NOT ALL OBEYED THE GOSPEL   227 11   SHALL SAY, LORD, HAVE MERCY UPON US   308 14
BUT I SAY, HAVE THEY NOT HEARD   227 14   HAVE MERCY UPON US   308 15
ALL DAY LONG I HAVE STRETCHED FORTH MY HANDS UNTC A 227 21   LET THE ENEMY HAVE NO ADVANTAGE OF HIM   308 27
FOR YE HAVE NEED OF PATIENCE, THAT, AFTER YE HAVE   228 15   I HAVE CONSIDERED THE DAYS OF OLD   310 26
AFTER YE HAVE DONE THE WILL OF GOD, YE MIGHT   228 16   I HAVE CONSIDERED THE DAYS OF OLD, AND THE YEARS THAT 311 08
MY SOUL SHALL HAVE NO PLEASURE IN HIM   228 19   ALL PERSONS THAT HAVE OFFENDED HIM   R 313 21
SAID UNTO HIM, WE HAVE SEEN THE LORD   228 27   WHEN WE SHALL HAVE SERVED THEE IN OUR   316 29
ARE THEY THAT HAVE NOT SEEN, AND YET HAVE BELIEVED   229 08   DEFILEMENTS IT MAY HAVE CONTRACTED, THROUGH THE LUSTS 317 19
NOT SEEN, AND YET HAVE BELIEVED   229 09   HAVE MERCY UPON THE SOUL OF THY SERVANT   317 26
BELIEVING YE MIGHT HAVE LIFE THROUGH HIS NAME   229 13   HAVE MERCY UPON HIM   318 24
WHAT WILT THOU HAVE ME TO DO   230 06   HAVE MERCY   318 29
LORD, I HAVE HEARD BY MANY OF THIS MAN, HOW   230 22   HAVE MERCY   318 30
BEHOLD, WE HAVE FORSAKEN ALL, AND FOLLOWED   231 12   SUDDEN VISITATION, HAVE THE LESS CAUSE TO BE   R 321 10
WHAT SHALL WE HAVE THEREFORE   231 13   WE BESEECH THEE TO HAVE MERCY UPON THIS THY SERVANT 321 21
THAT YE WHICH HAVE FOLLOWED ME, IN THE   231 15   THESE THINGS HAVE I WRITTEN UNTO YOU THAT BELIEVE CN 322 12
FOR MINE EYES HAVE SEEN THY SALVATION, WHICH THOU   233 06   YE MAY KNOW THAT YE HAVE ETERNAL LIFE, AND THAT YE   322 14
MUST NEEDS HAVE BEEN FULFILLED, WHICH THE HOLY GHOST 234 09   CONFIDENCE THAT WE HAVE IN HIM, THAT, IF WE ASK ANY 322 16
OF THESE MEN WHICH HAVE COMPANIED WITH US ALL THE   234 21   WE KNOW THAT WE HAVE THE PETITIONS THAT WE DESIRED CF 322 18
AS WE HAVE KNOWN THE INCARNATION OF THY SCN   235 19   WE CONFESS THAT WE HAVE SINNED AGAINST THEE IN   323 13
THE WORD WHICH I HAVE SPOKEN UNTO YOU   238 09   HAVE MERCY UPON US, O GOD, AFTER THY GREAT GOODNESS 323 14
HATH LOVED ME, SO HAVE I LOVED YOU   238 21   HOW LONG I HAVE TO LIVE   324 21
EVEN AS I HAVE KEPT MY FATHER'S COMMANDMENTS, AND   238 23   ONE THING HAVE I DESIRED OF THE LORD, WHICH I WILL 326 08
THESE THINGS HAVE I SPOKEN UNTO YOU, THAT MY JOY   238 24   HAVE MERCY UPON ME, AND HEAR ME   326 21
BUT LET PATIENCE HAVE HER PERFECT WORK, THAT YE MAY 239 10   I SHOULD UTTERLY HAVE FAINTED, *   326 28
NOT SO, I WOULD HAVE TOLD YOU   239 32   OUT OF THE DEEP HAVE I CALLED UNTO THEE, O LORD   328 03
KNOWN ME, YE SHOULD HAVE KNOWN MY FATHER ALSO   240 08   WHEN HE SHALL HAVE DELIVERED UP THE KINGDOM TO   328 27
YE KNOW HIM, AND HAVE SEEN HIM   240 09   WHEN HE SHALL HAVE PUT DOWN ALL RULE AND ALL   328 28
SAITH UNTO HIM, HAVE I BEEN SO LONG TIME WITH YOU,   240 10   AND AS WE HAVE BORNE THE IMAGE OF THE EARTHY,   329 31
ONE ANOTHER, AS I HAVE LOVED YOU   241 26   CORRUPTIBLE SHALL HAVE PUT ON INCORRUPTION, AND THIS 330 07
BUT I HAVE CALLED YOU FRIENDS   241 30   THIS MORTAL SHALL HAVE PUT ON IMMORTALITY, THEN SHALL 330 08
OF MY FATHER I HAVE MADE KNOWN UNTO YOU   241 31   FOR YE HAVE NOT RECEIVED THE SPIRIT OF BONDAGE AGAIN 330 20
ALL THINGS THAT I HAVE HEARD OF MY FATHER I HAVE MADE 241 31   BUT YE HAVE RECEIVED THE SPIRIT OF ADOPTION, WHEREBY 330 21
CHOSEN ME, BUT I HAVE CHOSEN YOU, AND ORDAINED YOU, 241 32   NOT SO, I WOULD HAVE TOLD YOU   331 19
YE HAVE NOT CHOSEN ME, BUT I HAVE CHOSEN YOU, AND   241 32   HAVE MERCY UPON US   334 03
HOW HE WOULD HAVE HIM CALLED   243 22   HAVE MERCY UPON US   334 04
WHICH HAVE BEEN SINCE THE WORLD BEGAN   244 02   THY HOLY NAME, MAY HAVE OUR PERFECT CONSUMMATION AND 334 27
WHEN HEROD WOULD HAVE BROUGHT HIM FORTH, THE SAME   245 09   ALL THY SAINTS, WHO HAVE BEEN THE CHOICE VESSELS OF 336 18
AFTER MY DECEASE TO HAVE THESE THINGS ALWAYS IN   248 12   HAVE MERCY UPON US   340 06
FOR WE HAVE NOT FOLLOWED CUNNINGLY DEVISED FABLES,   248 13   HAVE MERCY UPON US   340 07
YE ARE THEY WHICH HAVE CONTINUED WITH ME IN MY   250 12   YE NOW THEREFORE HAVE SORROW   341 09
AS WE HAVE RECEIVED MERCY, WE FAINT NOT   250 27   THE LORD SHALL HAVE THEM IN DERISION   346 05
THEREFORE SEEING WE HAVE THIS MINISTRY, AS WE HAVE   250 27   6 YET HAVE I SET MY KING *   346 08
BUT HAVE RENOUNCED THE HIDDEN THINGS OF DISHONESTY, 250 28   MY SON, THIS DAY HAVE I BEGOTTEN THEE   346 11
I WILL HAVE MERCY, AND NOT SACRIFICE   251 22   THAT HAVE SET THEMSELVES AGAINST ME ROUND ABOUT   347 03
A GOOD FIGHT, I HAVE FINISHED MY COURSE, I HAVE KEPT 253 26   HAVE MERCY UPON ME, AND HEARKEN UNTO MY PRAYER   347 12
I HAVE FOUGHT A GOOD FIGHT, I HAVE FINISHED MY   253 26   AND HAVE SUCH PLEASURE IN VANITY, AND SEEK AFTER   347 14
MY COURSE, I HAVE KEPT THE FAITH   253 27   FOR THEY HAVE REBELLED AGAINST THEE   348 24
AND TYCHICUS HAVE I SENT TO EPHESUS   254 04   2 HAVE MERCY UPON ME, O LORD, FOR I AM WEAK   349 02
OF THE WORLD, BUT I HAVE CHOSEN YOU OUT OF THE WCRLD, 255 16   MY GOD, IN THEE HAVE I PUT MY TRUST   349 22
IF THEY HAVE PERSECUTED ME, THEY WILL ALSO PERSECUTE 255 18   O LORD MY GOD, IF I HAVE DONE ANY SUCH THING   349 27
IF THEY HAVE KEPT MY SAYING, THEY WILL KEEP YOUR'S   255 19   4 IF I HAVE REWARDED EVIL UNTO HIM THAT DEALT   349 29
BUT NOW THEY HAVE NO CLOKE FOR THEIR SIN   255 23   I HAVE DELIVERED HIM THAT WITHOUT ANY CAUSE IS   349 30
BUT NOW HAVE THEY BOTH SEEN AND HATED BOTH ME AND MY 255 26   THOU MAKEST HIM TO HAVE DOMINION OF THE WORKS OF THY 351 11
BECAUSE YE HAVE BEEN WITH ME FROM THE   255 33   13 HAVE MERCY UPON ME, O LORD   352 16
THE TREES, TILL WE HAVE SEALED THE SERVANTS OF OUR   256 18   AND LET NOT MAN HAVE THE UPPER HAND   352 30
AND HAVE WASHED THEIR ROBES, AND MADE   257 08   WILINESS THAT THEY HAVE IMAGINED   353 07
INASMUCH AS YE HAVE DONE IT UNTO ONE OF THE   259 15   4 WHICH HAVE SAID, WITH OUR TONGUE WILL WE PREVAIL 355 14
MY BRETHREN, YE HAVE DONE IT UNTO ME   259 16   MINE ENEMY SAY, I HAVE PREVAILED AGAINST HIM   356 04
IF SO BE YE HAVE TASTED THAT THE LORD IS GRACIOUS   259 28   5 HAVE THEY NO KNOWLEDGE, THAT THEY ARE ALL SUCH   356 22
BUT YE HAVE MADE IT A DEN OF THIEVES   260 07   7 AS FOR YOU, YE HAVE MADE A MOCK AT THE COUNSEL CF 356 28
HAVE YE NEVER READ, OUT OF THE MOUTH OF BABES AND   260 14   FOR IN THEE HAVE I PUT MY TRUST   357 21
OF GOD SHOULD FIRST HAVE BEEN SPOKEN TO YOU   260 32   I HAVE NO GOOD LIKE UNTO THEE   357 24
SAYING, I HAVE SET THEE TO BE A LIGHT OF THE   261 04   SHALL HAVE GREAT TROUBLE   357 27
AM THE LORD, WHEN I HAVE BROKEN THE BANDS OF THEIR   262 12   I HAVE A GOODLY HERITAGE   358 03
WHICH OF YOU SHALL HAVE A FRIEND, AND SHALL GO UNTO 262 26   9 I HAVE SET THE LORD ALWAY BEFORE ME   358 06
COME TO ME, AND I HAVE NOTHING TO SET BEFORE HIM   262 29   WORD OF THY LIPS I HAVE KEPT ME FROM THE WAYS OF THE 358 26
OF THIS LAND MAY HAVE GRACE TO MAINTAIN THESE   263 19   6 I HAVE CALLED UPON THEE, O GOD, FOR THOU SHALT HEAR 358 29
WHICH THINE EYES HAVE SEEN   263 32   WHICH HAVE THEIR PORTION IN THIS LIFE, WHOSE BELLIES 359 15
JESUS SAID, YE HAVE HEARD THAT IT HATH BEEN SAID,   264 03   15 THEY HAVE CHILDREN AT THEIR DESIRE, *   359 17
WHAT REWARD HAVE YE   264 11   22 BECAUSE I HAVE KEPT THE WAYS OF THE LORD, *   361 09
KNOWETH THAT YE HAVE NEED OF ALL THESE THINGS   266 28   AND HAVE NOT FORSAKEN MY GOD, AS THE WICKED DOTH   361 10
AND SAID UNTO THEM, HAVE YE NOT READ, THAT HE WHICH 268 05   23 FOR I HAVE AN EYE UNTO ALL HIS LAWS, *   361 11
OF THOSE WHO HAVE SERVED THEE HERE AND ARE NOW AT   268 17   I TURN AGAIN TILL I HAVE DESTROYED THEM   362 12
I WOULD NOT HAVE YOU TO BE IGNORANT, BRETHREN,   268 28   A PEOPLE WHOM I HAVE NOT KNOWN SHALL SERVE ME   362 27
AS OTHERS WHICH HAVE NO HOPE   268 30   IF HE WILL HAVE HIM   366 19
ON HIM, MAY HAVE EVERLASTING LIFE   269 21   10 I HAVE BEEN LEFT UNTO THEE EVER SINCE I WAS BCRN 366 23
THEY SEEK NOT TO HAVE THEIR CHILDREN BAPTIZED IN   R 273 08   HAVE EATEN, AND WORSHIPPED   367 33
THIS PERSON) THAT WHICH BY NATURE HE CANNOT HAVE   274 04   MY GOD, I HAVE PUT MY TRUST IN THEE   369 19
ASK, AND YE SHALL HAVE   274 16   WHICH HAVE BEEN EVER OF OLD   369 29
THINGS WHATSOEVER I HAVE COMMANDED YOU   275 31   THEE UNTO ME, AND HAVE MERCY UPON ME   370 16
DEARLY BELOVED, YE HAVE BROUGHT THIS CHILD HERE TO BE 276 19   FOR I HAVE PUT MY TRUST IN THEE   370 25
YE HAVE PRAYED THAT OUR LORD JESUS CHRIST WOULD   276 20   O LORD, FOR I HAVE WALKED INNOCENTLY   370 30
YOU HAVE COME HITHER DESIRING TO   277 20   4 I HAVE NOT DWELT WITH VAIN PERSONS   371 04
WE HAVE PRAYED THAT OUR LORD JESUS CHRIST WCULD   277 21   NEITHER WILL I HAVE FELLOWSHIP WITH THE DECEITFUL   371 05
GRANT THAT HE MAY HAVE POWER AND STRENGTH TO HAVE   278 24   5 I HAVE HATED THE CONGREGATION OF THE WICKED   371 06
AND STRENGTH TO HAVE VICTORY, AND TO TRIUMPH, AGAINST 278 24   8 LORD, I HAVE LOVED THE HABITATION OF THY HCUSE, 371 12
THOU SHALT HAVE NONE OTHER GODS BUT ME   286 05   4 ONE THING HAVE I DESIRED OF THE LORD, WHICH I WILL 371 32
HAVE MERCY UPON US, AND INCLINE OUR HEARTS TO   286 06   HAVE MERCY UPON ME, AND HEAR ME   372 13
HAVE MERCY UPON US, AND INCLINE OUR HEARTS TO   287 04   15 I SHOULD UTTERLY HAVE FAINTED, *   372 27
HAVE MERCY UPON US, AND WRITE ALL THESE THY   287 23   PAY THEM THAT THEY HAVE DESERVED   373 16
AFTER YOU HAVE BEEN CONFIRMED, WHAT GREAT PRIVILEGE 291 28   HEAR, O LORD, AND HAVE MERCY UPON ME   375 14
TO HAVE A LIVELY FAITH IN GOD'S MERCY THROUGH CHRIST, 293 28   IN THEE, O LORD, HAVE I PUT MY TRUST   375 22
WHICH ORDERS HAVE BEEN IN THE CHURCH FROM THE   294 06   THE NET THAT THEY HAVE LAID PRIVILY FOR ME   375 29
HOLY APOSTLES, WE HAVE NOW LAID OUR HANDS, TO CERTIFY 298 17   7 I HAVE HATED THEM THAT HOLD OF LYING VANITIES,   376 07
IF HE SHALL HAVE REASON TO DOUBT OF THE LAWFULNESS OF R 301 02   10 HAVE MERCY UPON ME, O LORD, FOR I AM IN TROUBLE, 376 08
WILT THOU HAVE THIS WOMAN TO THY WEDDED WIFE, TC LIVE 301 06   15 FOR I HAVE HEARD THE BLASPHEMY OF THE MULTITUDE, 376 21
WILT THOU HAVE THIS MAN TO THY WEDDED HUSBAND,   301 14   I HAVE SAID, THOU ART MY GOD   376 24
MY WEDDED WIFE, TO HAVE AND TO HOLD FROM THIS DAY   301 28   O LORD, FOR I HAVE CALLED UPON THEE   376 30
WEDDED HUSBAND, TO HAVE AND TO HOLD FROM THIS DAY   302 04   UNRIGHTEOUSNESS HAVE I NOT HID   377 31
HAVE CONSENTED TOGETHER IN HOLY WEDLOCK, AND HAVE   304 03   AND MULE, WHICH HAVE NO UNDERSTANDING   378 10
HOLY WEDLOCK, AND HAVE WITNESSED THE SAME BEFORE GOD 304 04   BECAUSE WE HOPED IN HIS HOLY NAME   379 30
AND THERETO HAVE GIVEN AND PLEDGED THEIR TROTH, EACH 304 05   7 FOR THEY HAVE PRIVILY LAID THEIR NET TO DESTROY ME 381 31
TO THE OTHER, AND HAVE DECLARED THE SAME BY GIVING   304 06   WITHOUT A CAUSE HAVE THEY MADE A PIT FOR MY SOUL   382 02

HAVE CONTINUED	PAGE	LN
SO WOULD WE HAVE IT	383	14
LET THEM SAY, WE HAVE DEVOURED HIM	383	14
OUT THE SWORD, AND HAVE BENT THEIR BOW, *	385	22
14 THE UNGODLY HAVE DRAWN OUT THE SWORD, AND HAVE	385	22
DEARTH THEY SHALL HAVE ENOUGH	385	34
25 I HAVE BEEN YOUNG, AND NOW AM OLD	386	12
36 I MYSELF HAVE SEEN THE UNGODLY IN GREAT POWER,	387	04
I HAVE ROARED FOR THE VERY DISQUIETNESS OF MY HEART	388	06
IN THEE, O LORD, HAVE I PUT MY TRUST	388	21
16 I HAVE REQUIRED THAT THEY, EVEN MINE ENEMIES,	388	23
HOW LONG I HAVE TO LIVE	389	16
11 I HAVE DECLARED THY RIGHTEOUSNESS IN THE GREAT	390	34
12 I HAVE NOT HID THY RIGHTEOUSNESS WITHIN MY HEART	391	04
13 I HAVE NOT KEPT BACK THY LOVING MERCY AND TRUTH *	391	06
MY SINS HAVE TAKEN SUCH HOLD UPON ME, THAT I AM NOT	391	11
HEAL MY SOUL, FOR I HAVE SINNED AGAINST THEE	392	07
3 MY TEARS HAVE BEEN MY MEAT DAY AND NIGHT, *	393	04
WE HAVE HEARD WITH OUR EARS, O GOD, OUR FATHERS HAVE	394	22
O GOD, OUR FATHERS HAVE TOLD US *	394	22
21 IF WE HAVE FORGOTTEN THE NAME OF OUR GOD, AND	395	34
THE THINGS WHICH I HAVE MADE CONCERNING THE KING	396	16
4 GOOD LUCK HAVE THOU WITH THINE HONOUR	396	22
WHEREBY THEY HAVE MADE THEE GLAD	396	33
SO SHALL THE KING HAVE PLEASURE IN THY BEAUTY	397	07
THOU SHALT HAVE CHILDREN, *	397	19
7 LIKE AS WE HAVE HEARD, SO HAVE WE SEEN IN THE CITY	399	24
WE HAVE HEARD, SO HAVE WE SEEN IN THE CITY OF THE	399	24
THE RIGHTEOUS SHALL HAVE DOMINION OVER THEM IN THE	401	02
THE SEPULCHRE, AND HAVE NO ABIDING	401	04
THOSE THAT HAVE MADE A COVENANT WITH ME WITH	401	30
HAVE MERCY UPON ME, O GOD, AFTER THY GREAT GOODNESS	403	08
4 AGAINST THEE ONLY HAVE I SINNED, AND DONE THIS EVIL	403	15
THEY HAVE NOT CALLED UPON GOD	405	24
AND TYRANTS, WHICH HAVE NOT GOD BEFORE THEIR EYES,	406	08
FOR I HAVE SPIED UNRIGHTEOUSNESS AND STRIFE IN THE	407	05
FOR THEN I COULD HAVE BORNE IT	407	12
I WOULD HAVE HID MYSELF FROM HIM	407	14
I HAVE PUT MY TRUST IN GOD, AND WILL NOT FEAR WHAT	408	21
11 YEA, IN GOD HAVE I PUT MY TRUST	409	04
THE CAUSE WHICH I HAVE IN HAND	409	16
7 THEY HAVE LAID A NET FOR MY FEET, AND PRESSED DOWN	409	26
THEY HAVE DIGGED A PIT BEFORE ME, AND ARE FALLEN INTO	409	27
THOU, O LORD, SHALT HAVE THEM IN DERISION, *	411	20
AND TWICE I HAVE ALSO HEARD THE SAME, *	414	21
3 THUS HAVE I LOOKED FOR THEE IN THE SANCTUARY,	414	29
7 HAVE I NOT REMEMBERED THEE IN MY BED, *	415	05
3 WHO HAVE WHET THEIR TONGUE LIKE A SWORD, *	415	23
13 THOUGH YE HAVE LAIN AMONG THE SHEEP-FOLDS,	420	06
FOR THY SAKE HAVE I SUFFERED REPROOF	422	16
LOOKED FOR SOME TO HAVE PITY ON ME, BUT THERE WAS NO	423	14
THINGS THAT SHOULD HAVE BEEN FOR THEIR WEALTH BE UNTO	423	19
DWELL THERE, AND HAVE IT IN POSSESSION	424	15
IN THEE, O LORD, HAVE I PUT MY TRUST	425	05
5 THROUGH THEE HAVE I BEEN HOLDEN UP EVER SINCE I WAS	425	16
UNTIL I HAVE SHOWED THY STRENGTH UNTO THIS	426	11
AND THESE HAVE RICHES IN POSSESSION	428	33
13 AND I SAID, THEN HAVE I CLEANSED MY HEART IN VAIN,	429	02
14 ALL THE DAY LONG HAVE I BEEN PUNISHED, *	429	04
THEN I SHOULD HAVE CONDEMNED THE GENERATION OF	429	07
25 WHOM HAVE I IN HEAVEN BUT THEE	429	26
AND HAVE DEFILED THE DWELLING-PLACE OF THY NAME, EVEN	430	18
8 THEY HAVE SET FIRE UPON THY HOLY PLACES, *	430	18
THUS HAVE THEY BURNT UP ALL THE HOUSES OF GOD IN THE	430	22
ARE ROBBED, THEY HAVE SLEPT THEIR SLEEP	432	30
HANDS WERE MIGHTY HAVE FOUND NOTHING	432	31
5 I HAVE CONSIDERED THE DAYS OF OLD, *	433	25
3 WHICH WE HAVE HEARD AND KNOWN, *	434	31
SUCH AS OUR FATHERS HAVE TOLD US	434	32
THY HOLY TEMPLE HAVE THEY DEFILED, AND MADE JERUSALEM	439	30
OF THY SERVANTS HAVE THEY GIVEN TO BE MEAT UNTO THE	439	32
3 THEIR BLOOD HAVE THEY SHED LIKE WATER ON EVERY SIDE	440	04
THE KINGDOMS THAT HAVE NOT CALLED UPON THY NAME	440	12
THE HEATHEN THAT HAVE NOT KNOWN THEE	440	12
7 FOR THEY HAVE DEVOURED JACOB, *	440	14
OUR OLD SINS, BUT HAVE MERCY UPON US, AND THAT SOON	440	16
OUR NEIGHBOURS HAVE BLASPHEMED THEE, *	440	30
MY PEOPLE WOULD HAVE HEARKENED UNTO ME	443	06
15 I SHOULD SOON HAVE PUT DOWN THEIR ENEMIES, *	443	08
OF THE LORD SHOULD HAVE SUBMITTED THEMSELVES UNTO	443	10
THEIR TIME SHOULD HAVE ENDURED FOR EVER	443	11
17 I WOULD HAVE FED THEM ALSO WITH THE FINEST	443	13
STONY ROCK WOULD I HAVE SATISFIED THEE	443	14
NEED AND NECESSITY HAVE RIGHT	443	23
6 I HAVE SAID, YE ARE GODS, *	443	29
THEY THAT HATE THEE HAVE LIFT UP THEIR HEAD	444	08
3 THEY HAVE IMAGINED CRAFTILY AGAINST THY PEOPLE,	444	09
4 THEY HAVE SAID, COME, AND LET US ROOT THEM OUT,	444	11
5 FOR THEY HAVE CAST THEIR HEADS TOGETHER WITH ONE	444	14
THEY HAVE HOLPEN THE CHILDREN OF LOT	444	20
AND PEACE HAVE KISSED EACH OTHER	446	28
OF VIOLENT MEN HAVE SOUGHT AFTER MY SOUL, AND HAVE	448	02
AFTER MY SOUL, AND HAVE NOT SET THEE BEFORE THEIR	448	03
THEN UNTO ME, AND HAVE MERCY UPON ME	448	06
OF MY SALVATION, I HAVE CRIED DAY AND NIGHT BEFORE	448	29
I HAVE CALLED DAILY UPON THEE, I HAVE STRETCHED	449	14
DAILY UPON THEE, I HAVE STRETCHED FORTH MY HANDS UNTO	449	15
13 UNTO THEE HAVE I CRIED, O LORD	449	22
UP, THY TERRORS HAVE I SUFFERED WITH A TROUBLED MIND	449	27
2 FOR I HAVE SAID, MERCY SHALL BE SET UP FOR EVER	450	07
3 I HAVE MADE A COVENANT WITH MY CHOSEN	450	09
I HAVE SWORN UNTO DAVID MY SERVANT	450	09
I HAVE LAID HELP UPON ONE THAT IS MIGHTY, I HAVE	451	13
THAT IS MIGHTY, I HAVE EXALTED ONE CHOSEN OUT OF THE	451	14
21 I HAVE FOUND DAVID MY SERVANT	451	15

HAVE CONTINUED	PAGE	LN
WITH MY HOLY OIL HAVE I ANOINTED HIM	451	16
I HAVE SWORN ONCE BY MY HOLINESS, THAT I WILL NOT	452	10
THAT THY SERVANTS HAVE, *	453	08
THINE ENEMIES HAVE BLASPHEMED THEE, *	453	10
YEARS WHEREIN WE HAVE SUFFERED ADVERSITY	454	20
O LORD, THE FLOODS HAVE LIFT UP THEIR VOICE	457	11
THY COMFORTS HAVE REFRESHED MY SOUL	458	25
20 WILT THOU HAVE ANY THING TO DO WITH THE THRONE OF	458	26
FOR THEY HAVE NOT KNOWN MY WAYS	459	26
6 THE HEAVENS HAVE DECLARED HIS RIGHTEOUSNESS,	461	08
AND ALL THE PEOPLES HAVE SEEN HIS GLORY	461	09
ENDS OF THE WORLD HAVE SEEN THE SALVATION OF OUR GOD	461	32
2 O LET ME HAVE UNDERSTANDING *	463	19
7 I HAVE WATCHED, AND AM EVEN AS IT WERE A SPARROW,	464	23
9 FOR I HAVE EATEN ASHES AS IT WERE BREAD, *	464	27
SHALT ARISE, AND HAVE MERCY UPON SION	465	04
IS TIME THAT THOU HAVE MERCY UPON HER, YEA, THE TIME	465	05
FOWLS OF THE AIR HAVE THEIR HABITATION, *	468	17
MY GOD WHILE I HAVE MY BEING	469	28
6 WE HAVE SINNED WITH OUR FATHERS	473	11
WE HAVE DONE AMISS, AND DEALT WICKEDLY	473	11
SO HE SAID HE WOULD HAVE DESTROYED THEM, HAD NOT	474	14
AND GIVE PRAISE WITH THE BEST MEMBER THAT I HAVE	479	06
2 AND THEY HAVE SPOKEN AGAINST ME WITH FALSE TONGUES	480	06
4 THUS HAVE THEY REWARDED ME EVIL FOR GOOD, *	480	11
NOR TO HAVE COMPASSION UPON HIS FATHERLESS CHILDREN	480	23
OF ALL THEM THAT HAVE PLEASURE THEREIN	482	27
GOOD UNDERSTANDING HAVE ALL THEY THAT DO THEREAFTER	483	15
5 THEY HAVE MOUTHS, AND SPEAK NOT	485	20
EYES HAVE THEY, AND SEE NOT	485	20
NOSES HAVE THEY, AND SMELL NOT	485	22
6 THEY HAVE EARS, AND HEAR NOT	485	22
FEET HAVE THEY, AND WALK NOT	485	24
7 THEY HAVE HANDS, AND HANDLE NOT	485	24
WE HAVE WISHED YOU GOOD LUCK, WE THAT ARE OF THE	489	20
WHILE I HAVE RESPECT UNTO ALL THY COMMANDMENTS	490	10
WHEN I SHALL HAVE LEARNED THE JUDGMENTS OF THY	490	13
WITH MY WHOLE HEART HAVE I SOUGHT THEE	490	18
11 THY WORD HAVE I HID WITHIN MY HEART, *	490	20
13 WITH MY LIPS HAVE I BEEN TELLING *	490	23
14 I HAVE HAD AS GREAT DELIGHT IN THE WAY OF THY	490	25
AND HAVE RESPECT UNTO THY WAYS	490	27
FOR I HAVE KEPT THY TESTIMONIES	491	10
26 I HAVE ACKNOWLEDGED MY WAYS, AND THOU HEARDEST ME	491	19
30 I HAVE CHOSEN THE WAY OF TRUTH, *	491	27
AND THY JUDGMENTS HAVE I LAID BEFORE ME	491	28
31 I HAVE STUCK UNTO THY TESTIMONIES	491	29
WHICH I HAVE LOVED	493	03
WHICH I HAVE LOVED	493	05
51 THE PROUD HAVE HAD ME EXCEEDINGLY IN DERISION	493	12
YET HAVE I NOT SHRINKED FROM THY LAW	493	13
54 THY STATUTES HAVE BEEN MY SONGS, *	493	18
55 I HAVE THOUGHT UPON THY NAME, O LORD, IN THE NIGHT	493	20
AND HAVE KEPT THY LAW	493	21
I HAVE PROMISED TO KEEP THY LAW	493	24
OF THE UNGODLY HAVE COMPASSED ME ABOUT	494	02
BUT I HAVE NOT FORGOTTEN THY LAW	494	03
FOR I HAVE BELIEVED THY COMMANDMENTS	494	14
BUT NOW HAVE I KEPT THY WORD	494	15
69 THE PROUD HAVE IMAGINED A LIE AGAINST ME	494	18
GOOD FOR ME THAT I HAVE BEEN IN TROUBLE	494	22
THY HANDS HAVE MADE ME AND FASHIONED ME	494	28
BECAUSE I HAVE PUT MY TRUST IN THY WORD	495	03
AS FEAR THEE, AND HAVE KNOWN THY TESTIMONIES,	495	14
AND I HAVE A GOOD HOPE BECAUSE OF THY WORD	495	19
85 THE PROUD HAVE DIGGED PITS FOR ME, *	495	27
I SHOULD HAVE PERISHED IN MY TROUBLE	496	10
FOR I HAVE SOUGHT THY COMMANDMENTS	496	13
WHAT LOVE HAVE I UNTO THY LAW	496	20
99 I HAVE MORE UNDERSTANDING THAN MY TEACHERS	496	24
101 I HAVE REFRAINED MY FEET FROM EVERY EVIL WAY,	496	28
102 I HAVE NOT SHRUNK FROM THY JUDGMENTS	496	30
106 I HAVE SWORN, AND AM STEDFASTLY PURPOSED,	497	09
110 THE UNGODLY HAVE LAID A SNARE FOR ME	497	17
111 THY TESTIMONIES HAVE I CLAIMED AS MINE HERITAGE	497	19
112 I HAVE APPLIED MY HEART TO FULFIL THY STATUTES	497	21
FOR THEY HAVE DESTROYED THY LAW	498	22
SHALL NO WICKEDNESS HAVE DOMINION OVER ME	499	05
MINE ENEMIES HAVE FORGOTTEN THY WORDS	499	18
AND HEAVINESS HAVE TAKEN HOLD UPON ME	499	25
THY TESTIMONIES, I HAVE KNOWN LONG SINCE, *	500	14
PRINCES HAVE PERSECUTED ME WITHOUT A CAUSE	501	03
THE PEACE THAT THEY HAVE WHO LOVE THY LAW	501	11
AND THEY HAVE NONE OCCASION OF STUMBLING	501	12
166 LORD, I HAVE LOOKED FOR THY SAVING HEALTH,	501	13
168 I HAVE KEPT THY COMMANDMENTS AND TESTIMONIES	501	17
FOR I HAVE CHOSEN THY COMMANDMENTS	501	28
174 I HAVE LONGED FOR THY SAVING HEALTH, O LORD	501	30
176 I HAVE GONE ASTRAY LIKE A SHEEP THAT IS LOST	502	02
AND TO HAVE MY HABITATION AMONG THE TENTS OF KEDAR	502	15
OUR GOD, UNTIL HE HAVE MERCY UPON US	503	32
3 HAVE MERCY UPON US, O LORD, HAVE MERCY UPON US	504	02
UPON US, O LORD, HAVE MERCY UPON US	504	02
MANY A TIME HAVE THEY FOUGHT AGAINST ME FROM MY YOUTH	506	21
2 YEA, MANY A TIME HAVE THEY VEXED ME FROM MY YOUTH	506	23
BUT THEY HAVE NOT PREVAILED AGAINST ME	506	24
AS MANY AS HAVE EVIL WILL AT SION	506	30
OUT OF THE DEEP HAVE I CALLED UNTO THEE, O LORD	507	08
I HAVE NO PROUD LOOKS	507	24
WILL I DWELL, FOR I HAVE A DELIGHT THEREIN	509	03
I HAVE ORDAINED A LANTERN FOR MINE ANOINTED	509	09
16 THEY HAVE MOUTHS, AND SPEAK NOT	511	02
EYES HAVE THEY, BUT THEY SEE NOT	511	02
17 THEY HAVE EARS, AND YET THEY HEAR NOT	511	04

HAVE   CONTINUED

FOR THEY HAVE HEARD THE WORDS OF THY MOUTH	514 05
3 THEY HAVE SHARPENED THEIR TONGUES LIKE A SERPENT	516 13
5 THE PROUD HAVE LAID A SNARE FOR ME, AND SPREAD A	516 18
LET NOT THE UNGODLY HAVE HIS DESIRE, O LORD	516 24
THE SNARE THAT THEY HAVE LAID FOR ME, *	517 30
WHEREIN I WALKED, HAVE THEY PRIVILY LAID A SNARE FOR	518 08
AS THE MEN THAT HAVE BEEN LONG DEAD	518 29
ARE THE PEOPLE WHO HAVE THE LORD FOR THEIR GOD	520 25
AS LONG AS I HAVE ANY BEING, I WILL SING PRAISES	522 04
NEITHER HAVE THE HEATHEN KNOWLEDGE OF HIS LAWS	524 02
SUCH HONOUR HAVE ALL HIS SAINTS	525 20
TIME THERE HAVE BEEN THESE ORDERS OF MINISTERS IN	529 12
AND KNOWN TO HAVE SUCH QUALITIES AS ARE REQUISITE FOR	529 16
SHALL ANSWER, I HAVE INQUIRED CONCERNING THEM,	530 18
FOR THEY THAT HAVE USED THE OFFICE OF A DEACON WELL	532 02
OF THE CHURCH, MAY HAVE THE CHARGE AND GOVERNMENT	533 32
TO HAVE A READY WILL TO OBSERVE ALL	535 04
SHALL ANSWER, I HAVE INQUIRED CONCERNING THEM,	536 19
AND THAT THEY MIGHT HAVE IT MORE ABUNDANTLY	539 09
THAT THEY MIGHT HAVE LIFE, AND THAT THEY MIGHT HAVE	539 09
AND OTHER SHEEP I HAVE, WHICH ARE NOT OF THIS FOLD	539 19
YE HAVE HEARD, BRETHREN, AS WELL IN YOUR PRIVATE	539 24
THAT YE HAVE IN REMEMBRANCE, INTO HOW HIGH A	539 30
HAVE ALWAYS THEREFORE PRINTED IN YOUR REMEMBRANCE,	540 05
UNTIL YE HAVE DONE ALL THAT LIETH IN YOU,	540 17
YE CANNOT HAVE A MIND AND WILL THERETO OF	540 30
YE OUGHT, AND HAVE NEED, TO PRAY EARNESTLY FOR HIS	540 32
WE HAVE GOOD HOPE THAT YE HAVE WELL WEIGHED THESE	541 09
GOOD HOPE THAT YE HAVE WELL WEIGHED THESE THINGS WITH	541 09
AND THAT YE HAVE CLEARLY DETERMINED, BY GOD'S GRACE,	541 11
SO PERSUADED, AND HAVE SO DETERMINED, BY GOD'S GRACE	542 09
OF THE CHURCH, MAY HAVE THE CHARGE AND GOVERNMENT	543 13
SUCH TIME AS THEY HAVE RECEIVED THE COMMUNION	R 546 31
BY THEIR MOUTHS MAY HAVE SUCH SUCCESS, THAT IT MAY	547 07
THAT WE MAY HAVE GRACE TO HEAR AND RECEIVE WHAT	547 08
MOREOVER HE MUST HAVE A GOOD REPORT OF THEM WHICH ARE	549 28
AFTER WHAT MANNER I HAVE BEEN WITH YOU AT ALL	550 07
SHEWED YOU, AND HAVE TAUGHT YOU, AND FROM	550 11
UNTO YOU, BUT HAVE SHEWED YOU, AND HAVE TAUGHT YOU	550 11
WHICH I HAVE RECEIVED OF THE LORD JESUS, TO	550 20
AMONG WHOM I HAVE GONE PREACHING THE KINGDOM OF	550 22
FOR I HAVE NOT SHUNNED TO DECLARE UNTO YOU ALL THE	550 25
I HAVE COVETED NO MAN'S SILVER, OR GOLD, OR APPAREL	551 05
THAT THESE HANDS HAVE MINISTERED UNTO MY NECESSITIES,	551 07
I HAVE SHEWED YOU ALL THINGS, HOW THAT SO LABOURING	551 08
THINGS WHATSOEVER I HAVE COMMANDED YOU	552 13
PRESENT MAY HAVE A TRIAL, AND BEAR WITNESS, HOW YOU	554 14
O GOD THE FATHER, HAVE MERCY UPON US	560 04
HAVE MERCY UPON US	561 22
HAVE MERCY UPON US	561 23
HAVE MERCY UPON US AND HEAR US	561 33
IN HIS CHAIR, SHALL HAVE THE INSTRUMENTS OF DONATION	R 564 07
DECENCY OF THINGS, HAVE ERECTED HOUSES FOR THE PUBLIC	564 15
WHICH PIOUS WORKS HAVE BEEN APPROVED OF AND	564 20
TO DO, AND MAY HAVE POWER AND STRENGTH TO FULFIL THE	566 06
BENEFITS WHICH THEY HAVE RECEIVED AT THY HANDS, TO	566 15
PLEASED THEE TO THY HABITATION AMONG THE SONS OF	568 07
WITNESS WHEREOF, WE HAVE HEREUNTO AFFIXED OUR	569 38
IN THE LORD, WE HAVE ASSEMBLED FOR THE PURPOSE OF	570 12
AND TO DO, AS THEY HAVE PROMISED FOR THEE	577 21
THOU SHALT HAVE NONE OTHER GODS BUT ME	578 26
HAVE A LIVELY FAITH IN GOD'S MERCY THROUGH CHRIST,	582 26
WHO HAVE NOT LEARNED THEIR CATECHISM,	R 582 32
SUCH TIME AS THEY HAVE LEARNED ALL THAT IS HERE	R 582 34
LIVE AND MOVE AND HAVE OUR BEING	587 20
BESEECH THEE TO HAVE COMPASSION ON OUR INFIRMITIES,	588 14
AND MAY AS MANY AS HAVE RECEIVED IT, LIVE AS BECOMES	590 24
ALL THOSE WHO HAVE DONE OR WISH US EVIL, AND GIVE	590 32
REWARD ALL WHO HAVE DONE US GOOD, AND PARDON ALL	590 32
WHAT THOU WOULDEST HAVE US TO DO, THAT THE SPIRIT OF	595 29
WE BESEECH THEE TO HAVE MERCY UPON ALL THY CHILDREN	598 13
IN HOLY WEDLOCK, HAVE BEEN MADE ONE FLESH	598 26
WHEREFORE WE HAVE NO POWER TO DO GOOD WORKS PLEASANT	604 44
THAT WE MAY HAVE A GOOD WILL, AND WORKING WITH	605 03
WITH US, WHEN WE HAVE THAT GOOD WILL	605 03
DOUBT NOT BUT THEY HAVE THE NATURE OF SIN	605 22
WHEN YE HAVE DONE ALL THAT ARE COMMANDED TO	605 28
AND IF WE SAY WE HAVE NO SIN, WE DECEIVE OURSELVES,	605 36
AFTER WE HAVE RECEIVED THE HOLY GHOST, WE MAY DEPART	605 41
OF CHRIST, TO HAVE CONTINUALLY BEFORE THEIR EYES THE	606 23
WHICH WE HAVE EXPRESSLY DECLARED UNTO US IN	606 29
AND ANTIOCH, HAVE ERRED	606 42
WORK BY MEN WHO HAVE PUBLIC AUTHORITY GIVEN UNTO THEM	607 22
TO HAVE PUBLIC PRAYER IN THE CHURCH, OR TO	607 28
BEING SUCH AS HAVE GROWN PARTLY OF THE CORRUPT	607 40
BUT YET HAVE NOT LIKE NATURE OF SACRAMENTS WITH	607 42
FOR THAT THEY HAVE NOT ANY VISIBLE SIGN OR CEREMONY	607 43
THE SAME, THEY HAVE A WHOLESOME EFFECT OR OPERATION	608 04
SOMETIMES THE EVIL HAVE CHIEF AUTHORITY IN THE	608 10
BY THOSE THAT HAVE KNOWLEDGE OF THEIR OFFENCES	608 20
CHRISTIANS OUGHT TO HAVE AMONG THEMSELVES ONE TO	608 35
AND THE DEAD, TO HAVE REMISSION OF PAIN OR GUILT,	609 18
AT ALL TIMES THEY HAVE BEEN DIVERS, AND MAY BE	609 33
TITLES WHEREOF WE HAVE JOINED UNDER THIS ARTICLE,	610 05

HAVEN

IN SAFETY TO THE HAVEN WHERE HE WOULD BE, WITH A	046 14
HOME MAY BE A HAVEN OF BLESSING AND OF PEACE	303 26
THEM UNTO THE HAVEN WHERE THEY WOULD BE	478 05

HAVING

HAVING IN REMEMBRANCE HIS BLESSED PASSION AND	081 02

HAVING   CONTINUED

FOUR THOUSAND, HAVING HIS FATHER'S NAME WRITTEN IN	102 30
HAVING THEN GIFTS DIFFERING ACCORDING TO THE GRACE	111 15
UNDER AUTHORITY, HAVING SOLDIERS UNDER ME	115 13
THAT, HAVING THIS HOPE, WE MAY PURIFY	117 07
AND GOOD HEART, HAVING HEARD THE WORD, KEEP IT,	122 09
AS HAVING NOTHING, AND YET POSSESSING ALL THINGS	126 20
THE HOLY PLACE, HAVING OBTAINED ETERNAL REDEMPTION	132 27
CAME A WOMAN HAVING AN ALABASTER BOX OF OINTMENT OF	140 04
YOUNG MAN, HAVING A LINEN CLOTH CAST ABOUT HIS NAKED	142 29
BEHOLD, I, HAVING EXAMINED HIM BEFORE YOU, HAVE	153 23
AND HAVING SAID THUS, HE GAVE UP THE GHOST	155 14
UNTO THE FATHER, HAVING LOVED HIS OWN WHICH WERE IN	155 25
THE DEVIL HAVING NOW PUT INTO THE HEART OF	155 27
THE LAW HAVING A SHADOW OF GOOD THINGS TO COME,	157 15
HAVING THEREFORE, BRETHREN, BOLDNESS TO ENTER INTO	158 16
AND HAVING AN HIGH PRIEST OVER THE HOUSE OF GOD	158 19
OF FAITH, HAVING OUR HEARTS SPRINKLED FROM AN EVIL	158 21
HAVING YOUR CONVERSATION HONEST AMONG THE GENTILES	173 14
WHAT MAN OF YOU, HAVING AN HUNDRED SHEEP, IF HE LOSE	193 18
EITHER WHAT WOMAN HAVING TEN PIECES OF SILVER, IF SHE	193 27
ALL OF ONE MIND, HAVING COMPASSION ONE OF ANOTHER,	195 20
VERY GREAT, AND HAVING NOTHING TO EAT, JESUS CALLED	199 08
OF THEIR MIND, HAVING THE UNDERSTANDING DARKENED,	216 05
IN HITHER NOT HAVING A WEDDING-GARMENT	218 24
THE EVIL DAY, AND HAVING DONE ALL, TO STAND	219 12
STAND THEREFORE, HAVING YOUR LOINS GIRT ABOUT WITH	219 13
WITH TRUTH, AND HAVING ON THE BREASTPLATE OF	219 14
THAT WE, HAVING HIS WONDERFUL CONVERSION IN	229 20
DOWN UNTO YOU, HAVING GREAT WRATH, BECAUSE HE KNOWETH	252 19
RATHER THAN HAVING TWO HANDS OR TWO FEET TO BE CAST	253 05
RATHER THAN HAVING TWO EYES TO BE CAST INTO	253 09
HATH FORSAKEN ME, HAVING LOVED THIS PRESENT WORLD,	253 32
FROM THE EAST, HAVING THE SEAL OF THE LIVING GOD	256 14
NOT HAVING SPOT, OR WRINKLE, OR ANY SUCH	267 22
THE MINISTER, HAVING COME TO THE FONT, WHICH IS	R 273 24
HAVING NOW, IN THE NAME OF THIS CHILD,	277 08
FOR HAVING TURNED OUR HEAVINESS INTO JOY	315 21
UNTO OUR FATHERS, HAVING THE TESTIMONY OF A GOOD	317 03
WHO, HAVING FINISHED THEIR COURSE IN FAITH,	334 24
BY FAITH, THAT HAVING SERVED THEE WITH CONSTANCY ON	336 07
THAN BUTTER, HAVING WAR IN HIS HEART	408 02
THAT THEY, HAVING ALWAYS THE TESTIMONY OF A GOOD	535 05
ABROAD AS SHEEP HAVING NO SHEPHERD	538 16
THEN ONE OF THEM HAVING READ THE GOSPEL, (WHICH SHALL	R 547 24
HIS OWN HOUSE, HAVING HIS CHILDREN IN SUBJECTION WITH	549 24
MAY BE ASHAMED, HAVING NOTHING TO SAY AGAINST YOU	555 12
THE BISHOP HAVING RECEIVED DUE NOTICE OF THE	R 569 04
OR MISTRESS HAVING CALLED TOGETHER AS MANY OF THE	R 587 04
ESPECIALLY FOR HAVING DELIVERED US FROM THE DANGERS	587 23
THAT HAVING DONE THY WILL WITH CHEERFULNESS WHILE IT	594 15
AND GRANT THAT, HAVING THE EYES OF THE MIND OPENED TO	594 23
PRAY THEE THAT, HAVING OPENED TO HIM THE GATES OF	598 08

HAVOC

LET US MAKE HAVOC OF THEM ALTOGETHER	430 21

HAY

INTO THE SIMILITUDE OF A CALF THAT EATETH HAY	474 09

HE-GOATS

NOR HE-GOATS OUT OF THY FOLDS	402 08

HEAD

THOU ART EXALTED AS HEAD ABOVE ALL	073 21
DOING THOU SHALT HEAP COALS OF FIRE ON HIS HEAD	113 08
ANOINT THINE HEAD, AND WASH THY FACE	125 13
PUT IT UPON HIS HEAD, AND A REED IN HIS RIGHT HAND	136 19
AND SMOTE HIM ON THE HEAD	136 22
AND SET UP OVER HIS HEAD HIS ACCUSATION WRITTEN,	137 02
AND POURED IT ON HIS HEAD	140 05
PUT IT ABOUT HIS HEAD, AND BEGAN TO SALUTE HIM,	145 33
SMOTE HIM ON THE HEAD WITH A REED, AND DID SPIT UPON	145 34
NOT MY FEET ONLY, BUT ALSO MY HANDS AND MY HEAD	156 08
AND PUT IT ON HIS HEAD, AND THEY PUT ON HIM A PURPLE	158 32
AND HE BOWED HIS HEAD, AND GAVE UP THE GHOST	160 29
THAT WAS ABOUT HIS HEAD, NOT LYING WITH THE LINEN	164 23
WHICH IS THE HEAD, EVEN CHRIST	237 29
HIMSELF BEING THE HEAD CORNER-STONE	254 29
THE HUSBAND IS THE HEAD OF THE WIFE, EVEN AS CHRIST	267 15
AS CHRIST IS THE HEAD OF THE CHURCH	267 16
HIMSELF BEING THE HEAD CORNER-STONE	290 21
JESUS CHRIST IS THE HEAD, AND ALL BAPTIZED PEOPLE ARE	290 33
BECAUSE IT IS ONE BODY UNDER ONE HEAD	291 08
HIS HAND UPON THE HEAD OF EVERY ONE SEVERALLY,	R 297 25
THOU ART MY WORSHIP, AND THE LIFTER UP OF MY HEAD	309 19
HE LIFT UP MINE HEAD *	326 15
HAST ANOINTED MY HEAD WITH OIL, AND MY CUP SHALL BE	338 27
AND THE LIFTER UP OF MY HEAD	346 30
COME UPON HIS OWN HEAD, *	350 25
SHALT MAKE ME THE HEAD OF THE NATIONS	362 26
AND SHALT SET A CROWN OF PURE GOLD UPON HIS HEAD	365 10
HAST ANOINTED MY HEAD WITH OIL, AND MY CUP SHALL BE	368 20
HE LIFT UP MINE HEAD *	372 07
ARE GONE OVER MY HEAD, *	387 28
THE HAIRS OF MY HEAD, AND MY HEART HATH FAILED ME	391 13
EPHRAIM ALSO IS THE STRENGTH OF MY HEAD	412 26
GOD SHALL WOUND THE HEAD OF HIS ENEMIES, *	420 27
A CAUSE ARE MORE THAN THE HAIRS OF MY HEAD	422 08
AND THEY THAT HATE THEE HAVE LIFT UP THEIR HEAD	444 08
EPHRAIM ALSO IS THE STRENGTH OF MY HEAD	479 21

HEAD CONTINUED

THEREFORE SHALL HE LIFT UP HIS HEAD	482 22
THE TEMPLES OF MY HEAD TO TAKE ANY REST	508 11
OIL UPON THE HEAD, THAT RAN DOWN UNTO THE BEARD, *	509 15
HAST COVERED MY HEAD IN THE DAY OF BATTLE	516 23
LIPS FALL UPON THE HEAD OF THEM *	516 27
LET NOT MY HEAD REFUSE THEIR PRECIOUS BALMS	517 20
SEVERALLY UPON THE HEAD OF EVERY ONE TO BE MADE	R 534 03
SEVERALLY UPON THE HEAD OF EVERY ONE THAT RECEIVETH	R 546 07
HANDS UPON THE HEAD OF THE ELECTED BISHOP, KNEELING	R 558 10
LET THE HEAD OF THE HOUSEHOLD, OR SOME	R 592 09
LET THE HEAD OF THE HOUSEHOLD, OR SOME	R 593 03

HEAD-STONE

IS BECOME THE HEAD-STONE IN THE CORNER	489 13

HEADLONG

AND FALLING HEADLONG, HE BURST ASUNDER IN THE MIDST,	234 14

HEADS

HANGETH OVER YOUR HEADS FOR THE SAME	089 16
TO PASS, THEN LOOK UP, AND LIFT UP YOUR HEADS	093 13
WAGGING THEIR HEADS, AND SAYING, THOU THAT	137 06
WAGGING THEIR HEADS, AND SAYING, AH, THOU THAT	146 18
THEY HAD ON THEIR HEADS CROWNS OF GOLD	187 11
AND SHAKE THEIR HEADS, SAYING, 8 HE TRUSTED IN THE	366 17
7 LIFT UP YOUR HEADS, O YE GATES	369 09
9 LIFT UP YOUR HEADS, O YE GATES	369 13
SHAKE THEIR HEADS AT US	395 23
11 THOU SUFFEREDST MEN TO RIDE OVER OUR HEADS	418 04
THOU BRAKEST THE HEADS OF THE DRAGONS IN THE WATERS	431 03
THOU SMOTEST THE HEADS OF LEVIATHAN IN PIECES,	431 04
HAVE CAST THEIR HEADS TOGETHER WITH ONE CONSENT,	444 14
THEY THAT LOOK UPON ME SHAKE THEIR HEADS	481 21
IN SUNDER THE HEADS OVER DIVERS COUNTRIES	482 19
7 LIFT UP YOUR HEADS, O YE GATES	563 24
9 LIFT UP YOUR HEADS, O YE GATES	563 28

HEAL

I WILL COME AND HEAL HIM	115 10
IS IT LAWFUL TO HEAL ON THE SABBATH DAY	214 03
COME DOWN, AND HEAL HIS SON	219 31
HE HATH SENT ME TO HEAL THE BROKENHEARTED, TO PREACH	261 18
GIVETH MEDICINE TO HEAL THEIR SICKNESS	264 24
O LORD, HEAL ME, FOR MY BONES ARE VEXED	349 03
HEAL MY SOUL, FOR I HAVE SINNED AGAINST THEE	392 06
HEAL THE SORES THEREOF, FOR IT SHAKETH	412 15
GIVETH MEDICINE TO HEAL THEIR SICKNESS	522 33
HOLD UP THE WEAK, HEAL THE SICK, BIND UP THE BROKEN,	558 27

HEALED

AND MY SERVANT SHALL BE HEALED	115 12
HIS SERVANT WAS HEALED IN THE SELFSAME HOUR	115 25
HIS EAR, AND HEALED HIM	150 35
BY WHOSE STRIPES YE WERE HEALED	172 17
SAW THAT HE WAS HEALED, TURNED BACK, AND WITH A LOUD	210 04
HE TOOK HIM, AND HEALED HIM, AND LET HIM GO	214 04
AND THEY WERE HEALED EVERY ONE	249 32
AND HE HEALED THEM	260 09
THAT HE MAY BE HEALED OF HIS INFIRMITIES, TO THINE	315 16
AND THOU HAST HEALED ME	374 27
HIS WORD, AND HEALED THEM	477 15

HEALEST

WHO HEALEST THOSE THAT ARE BROKEN IN HEART,	599 03

HEALETH

AND HEALETH ALL THINE INFIRMITIES	029 08
HE HEALETH THOSE THAT ARE BROKEN IN HEART, *	264 23
ALL THY SIN, AND HEALETH ALL THINE INFIRMITIES	312 24
AND HEALETH ALL THINE INFIRMITIES	466 12
3 HE HEALETH THOSE THAT ARE BROKEN IN HEART, *	522 32

HEALING

DOING GOOD, AND HEALING ALL THAT WERE OPPRESSED OF	166 21
THE GIFTS OF HEALING BY THE SAME SPIRIT	182 30
DOING GOOD, AND HEALING ALL THAT WERE OPPRESSED OF	184 08
THE GIFTS OF HEALING BY THE SAME SPIRIT	203 30
THE LOVE AND HEALING POWER OF THY SON	253 18
AND LOVE, TO THE HEALING OF OUR BODIES AND OUR SOULS	253 19
THE MINISTRY OF HEALING THROUGH ANOINTING OR LAYING	R 320 05
TO HIM OF THY HEALING GIFTS	597 17

HEALTH

AND THERE IS NO HEALTH IN US	006 23
GRANT THEM IN HEALTH AND PROSPERITY LONG TO LIVE	018 03
THY SAVING HEALTH UNTO ALL NATIONS	018 29
AND THERE IS NO HEALTH IN US	023 30
THY SAVING HEALTH AMONG ALL NATIONS	028 20
THY SAVING HEALTH UNTO ALL NATIONS	032 29
RESTORE HIM TO HEALTH, AND ENABLE HIM TO LEAD THE	045 19
TO THAT PERFECT HEALTH WHICH IT IS THINE ALONE TO	045 26
GIVER OF LIFE, OF HEALTH, AND OF SAFETY	052 29
O GOD, THOU THAT ART THE GOD OF MY HEALTH	061 07
OUGHT TO KNOW AND BELIEVE TO HIS SOUL'S HEALTH	277 12
AND KEEP HER IN SICKNESS AND IN HEALTH	301 09

HEALTH CONTINUED

AND KEEP HIM IN SICKNESS AND IN HEALTH	301 17
SICKNESS AND IN HEALTH, TO LOVE AND TO CHERISH, TILL	301 30
SICKNESS AND IN HEALTH, TO LOVE AND TO CHERISH, TILL	302 06
HIM TO HIS FORMER HEALTH, THAT HE MAY GIVE THANKS	309 31
BE TURNED INTO HEALTH, AND OUR SORROW INTO JOY	312 15
MAYEST RECEIVE HEALTH AND SALVATION, BUT ONLY THE	314 21
THAT HIS HEALTH BEING THEREUPON RESTORED, HE MAY	315 10
THE GIVER OF ALL HEALTH, AND THE AID OF THEM THAT	315 13
OUR BROTHER TO SOME DEGREE OF HIS FORMER HEALTH	315 23
BEING RESTORED TO HEALTH OF BODY, VIGOUR OF MIND, AND	315 29
TO SOUNDNESS OF HEALTH, HE MAY OFFER THEE PRAISE AND	320 11
THE BLESSING OF HEALTH MAY BE RESTORED UNTO THEE	320 19
THEY ARE IN HEALTH, TO MAKE WILLS ARRANGING FOR THE	R 320 22
HIS BODILY HEALTH, IF IT BE THY GRACIOUS WILL	321 23
HE MAY BE RESTORED TO SOUNDNESS OF HEALTH	322 09
TO HIS SOUL'S HEALTH, ALTHOUGH HE DO NOT RECEIVE THE	R 323 30
SO FAR FROM MY HEALTH, AND FROM THE WORDS OF MY	366 05
3 THERE IS NO HEALTH IN MY FLESH, BECAUSE OF THY	387 25
O GOD, THOU THAT ART THE GOD OF MY HEALTH	404 05
7 IN GOD IS MY HEALTH AND MY GLORY	414 11
THY SAVING HEALTH AMONG ALL NATIONS	418 27
VOICE OF JOY AND HEALTH IS IN THE DWELLINGS OF THE	488 30
LOOKING FOR THY HEALTH, *	498 16
155 HEALTH IS FAR FROM THE UNGODLY	500 21
FOR THY SAVING HEALTH, *	501 13
FOR THY SAVING HEALTH, O LORD	501 30
HER PRIESTS WITH HEALTH, *	509 06
THOU STRENGTH OF MY HEALTH	516 22
FOR OUR HEALTH, FRIENDS, FOOD, AND RAIMENT, AND ALL	591 10
O MERCIFUL GOD, GIVER OF LIFE AND HEALTH	597 15
BE RESTORED TO HEALTH OF BODY AND OF MIND	597 18
AND GIVE THEM HEALTH AND PEACE	598 16

HEALTHFUL

THE HEALTHFUL SPIRIT OF THY GRACE	018 21
THE HEALTHFUL SPIRIT OF THY GRACE	032 20

HEAP

SO DOING THOU SHALT HEAP COALS OF FIRE ON HIS HEAD	113 07
OF THE SEA TOGETHER, AS IT WERE UPON AN HEAP	378 32
THERE SHALL BE AN HEAP OF CORN IN THE EARTH, HIGH	427 29
HE MADE THE WATERS TO STAND ON AN HEAP	435 27
MADE JERUSALEM AN HEAP OF STONES	439 31

HEAPETH

HE HEAPETH UP RICHES, AND CANNOT TELL WHO SHALL	324 26
HE HEAPETH UP RICHES, AND CANNOT TELL WHO SHALL	389 21

HEAR

WORTHY PRAISE, TO HEAR HIS MOST HOLY WORD, AND TO ASK	006 07
WORTHY PRAISE, TO HEAR HIS MOST HOLY WORD, AND TO ASK	023 16
AND MERCIFULLY HEAR US WHEN WE CALL UPON THEE	031 05
GOODNESS TO HEAR US, WHO NOW MAKE OUR PRAYERS AND	040 05
ART EVER READY TO HEAR THE PRAYERS OF THOSE WHO PUT	041 20
HAST PROMISED TO HEAR THE PETITIONS OF THOSE WHO ASK	050 06
DO BESEECH THEE TO HEAR US, O LORD GOD	055 18
WE BESEECH THEE TO HEAR US, GOOD LORD	055 21
WE BESEECH THEE TO HEAR US, GOOD LORD	056 04
OF GRACE TO HEAR MEEKLY THY WORD, AND TO RECEIVE IT	056 15
WE BESEECH THEE TO HEAR US, GOOD LORD	057 04
WE BESEECH THEE TO HEAR US	057 19
O CHRIST, HEAR US	057 25
AND GRACIOUSLY HEAR US, THAT THOSE EVILS WHICH THE	058 19
WITH MERCY HEAR OUR PRAYERS	059 13
EVER VOUCHSAFE TO HEAR US, O CHRIST	059 15
GRACIOUSLY HEAR US, O CHRIST	059 16
GRACIOUSLY HEAR US, O LORD CHRIST	059 16
THOU SHALT MAKE ME HEAR OF JOY AND GLADNESS, *	060 26
O LORD, HEAR OUR PRAYER	062 05
MERCIFULLY HEAR OUR PRAYERS, AND SPARE ALL	062 08
HEAR US, O LORD, FOR THY MERCY IS GREAT, AND AFTER	063 04
THE LAW, BEGINNING, HEAR WHAT OUR LORD JESUS CHRIST	R 067 30
MAY THE PRIEST SAY, HEAR WHAT OUR LORD JESUS CHRIST	069 26
AND HOW SHALL THEY HEAR WITHOUT A PREACHER	073 08
THEY MAY HEAR, AND RECEIVE THY HOLY WORD	074 27
THE PRIEST SAY, HEAR WHAT COMFORTABLE WORDS OUR	076 10
HEAR ALSO WHAT SAINT PAUL SAITH	076 17
HEAR ALSO WHAT SAINT JOHN SAITH	076 21
MERCIFUL FATHER, TO HEAR US	081 08
WE MAY IN SUCH WISE HEAR THEM, READ, MARK, LEARN,	092 10
THINGS WHICH YE DO HEAR AND SEE	094 20
AND THE DEAF HEAR, THE DEAD ARE RAISED UP, AND THE	094 22
MERCIFULLY HEAR THE SUPPLICATIONS OF THY PEOPLE, AND	111 11
THEE FAVOURABLY TO HEAR THE PRAYERS OF THY PEOPLE	118 28
HE CRIED, HE THAT HATH EARS TO HEAR, LET HIM HEAR	121 28
THAT HATH EARS TO HEAR, LET HIM HEAR	121 28
THOSE BY THE WAY-SIDE ARE THEY THAT HEAR	121 34
WHEN THEY HEAR, RECEIVE THE WORD WITH JOY	122 03
ARE THEY THAT HEAR THE WORD OF GOD, AND KEEP IT	130 21
THE LAW, DO YE NOT HEAR THE LAW	130 30
YE THEREFORE HEAR THEM NOT, BECAUSE YE ARE NOT OF	133 11
AND THEY SHALL HEAR MY VOICE	172 31
MAN BE SWIFT TO HEAR, SLOW TO SPEAK, SLOW TO WRATH	174 31
WHATSOEVER HE SHALL HEAR, THAT SHALL HE SPEAK	175 20
AND HOW HEAR WE EVERY MAN IN OUR OWN TONGUE, WHEREIN	180 31
AND ARABIANS, WE DO HEAR THEM SPEAK IN OUR TONGUES	181 05
THE WORD WHICH YE HEAR IS NOT MINE, BUT THE FATHER'S	181 28
AND THE SHEEP HEAR HIS VOICE	186 04
THE SHEEP DID NOT HEAR THEM	186 14
LET THEM HEAR THEM	190 27

HEAR   CONTINUED

	PAGE	LN
UNTO HIM, IF THEY HEAR NOT MOSES AND THE PROPHETS,	190	29
THEE MERCIFULLY TO HEAR US	192	24
AND SINNERS FOR TO HEAR HIM	193	15
PRESSED UPON HIM TO HEAR THE WORD OF GOD, HE STOOD BY	196	07
MORE READY TO HEAR THAN WE TO PRAY, AND ART WONT TO	206	05
BOTH THE DEAF TO HEAR, AND THE DUMB TO SPEAK	207	08
AND TO HEAR THOSE THINGS WHICH YE HEAR, AND HAVE NOT	208	10
THINGS WHICH YE HEAR, AND HAVE NOT HEARD THEM	208	10
WE BESEECH THEE, TO HEAR THE DEVOUT PRAYERS OF THY	222	10
AND HOW SHALL THEY HEAR WITHOUT A PREACHER	227	07
HEAR US, O LORD, THROUGH THE SAME JESUS CHRIST,	228	10
AND HE SAID, HEAR YE NOW, O HOUSE OF DAVID	235	28
HEAR HIM	249	08
HEAR, WE BESEECH THEE, THE PRAYERS OF THY PEOPLE, AND	259	20
CITY TOGETHER TO HEAR THE WORD OF GOD	260	27
MAN BE SWIFT TO HEAR, SLOW TO SPEAK, SLOW TO WRATH	265	24
HEAR THE WORDS OF THE GOSPEL, WRITTEN BY SAINT MARK,	274	23
HEAR THE WORDS OF THE GOSPEL, WRITTEN BY SAINT JOHN,	275	03
HEAR THE WORDS OF THE GOSPEL, WRITTEN BY SAINT	275	23
	290	14
BY HIM, MAY SAY, HEAR THE WORDS OF THE EVANGELIST	296	11
HEAR OUR PRAYER	297	11
HEAR OUR PRAYER	306	21
O LORD, HEAR OUR PRAYER	308	31
HEAR US, ALMIGHTY AND MOST MERCIFUL GOD AND SAVIOUR	309	27
HEAR, O LORD, WE BESEECH THEE, THESE OUR PRAYERS,	311	21
DO BESEECH THEE TO HEAR US, O LORD GOD	318	10
WE BESEECH THEE TO HEAR US, GOOD LORD	318	14
IF WE KNOW THAT HE HEAR US, WHATSOEVER WE ASK, WE	322	17
HEAR MY PRAYER, O LORD, AND WITH THINE EARS CONSIDER	325	06
MERCY UPON ME, AND HEAR ME	326	21
HEAR MY VOICE	328	04
HIS RIGHT HAND, AND HEAR THAT HIS MOST JOYFUL VOICE	336	25
HEAR OUR PRAYER	340	20
HEAR ME WHEN I CALL, O GOD OF MY RIGHTEOUSNESS	347	10
THE LORD HE WILL HEAR ME	347	18
MY VOICE SHALT THOU HEAR BETIMES, O LORD	348	04
3 CONSIDER, AND HEAR ME, O LORD MY GOD	356	02
HEAR THE RIGHT, O LORD, CONSIDER MY COMPLAINT,	358	16
FOR THOU SHALT HEAR ME	358	29
BUT HE SHALL NOT HEAR THEM	362	22
45 AS SOON AS THEY HEAR OF ME, THEY SHALL OBEY ME	362	28
THE LORD HEAR THEE IN THE DAY OF TROUBLE	364	17
AND WILL HEAR HIM FROM HIS HOLY HEAVEN,	364	27
AND HEAR US, O KING OF HEAVEN, *	365	02
MERCY UPON ME, AND HEAR ME	372	13
2 HEAR THE VOICE OF MY HUMBLE PETITIONS, WHEN I CRY	373	07
11 HEAR, O LORD, AND HAVE MERCY UPON ME	375	14
THE HUMBLE SHALL HEAR THEREOF, AND BE GLAD	380	06
13 HEAR MY PRAYER, O LORD, AND WITH THINE EARS	390	07
O HEAR YE THIS, ALL YE PEOPLE	400	07
7 HEAR, O MY PEOPLE, AND I WILL SPEAK	402	04
SO WILL I HEAR THEE, AND THOU SHALT PRAISE ME	402	21
THOU SHALT MAKE ME HEAR OF JOY AND GLADNESS, *	403	25
2 HEAR MY PRAYER, O GOD, *	406	05
HEAR MY PRAYER, O GOD, *	406	19
HEED UNTO ME, AND HEAR ME, *	406	21
AND HE SHALL HEAR MY VOICE	407	26
FOR EVER, SHALL HEAR ME, AND BRING THEM DOWN	407	30
5 WHICH REFUSETH TO HEAR THE VOICE OF THE CHARMER,	410	17
FOR WHO DOTH HEAR	411	19
THY RIGHT HAND, AND HEAR ME	412	22
HEAR MY CRYING, O GOD, *	413	07
HEAR MY VOICE, O GOD, IN MY PRAYER	415	19
THE LORD WILL NOT HEAR ME	418	17
14 HEAR ME, O GOD, IN THE MULTITUDE OF THY MERCY,	422	30
17 HEAR ME, O LORD, FOR THY LOVING-KINDNESS IS	423	04
O HASTE THEE, AND HEAR ME	423	08
HEAR MY LAW, O MY PEOPLE	434	27
HEAR, O THOU SHEPHERD OF ISRAEL, THOU THAT LEADEST	441	03
9 HEAR, O MY PEOPLE	442	29
MY PEOPLE WOULD NOT HEAR MY VOICE	443	02
LORD GOD OF HOSTS, HEAR MY PRAYER	445	27
O LORD, AND HEAR ME	447	05
UPON ME, AND I WILL HEAR HIM	455	26
AND MINE EAR SHALL HEAR HIS DESIRE OF THE WICKED THAT	456	22
9 HE THAT PLANTED THE EAR, SHALL HE NOT HEAR	458	04
8 TO-DAY IF YE WILL HEAR HIS VOICE, HARDEN NOT YOUR	459	19
HEAR MY PRAYER, O LORD, *	464	10
O HEAR ME, AND THAT RIGHT SOON	464	13
20 THAT HE MIGHT HEAR THE MOURNINGS OF SUCH AS ARE IN	465	19
HAND SAVE THEM, AND HEAR THOU ME	479	16
THEY HAVE EARS, AND HEAR NOT	485	22
HEAR ME, O LORD	499	31
149 HEAR MY VOICE, O LORD, ACCORDING UNTO THY	500	08
HEAR MY VOICE	507	09
AND YET THEY HEAR NOT	511	04
HEAR THE VOICE OF MY PRAYERS, O LORD	516	20
THAT THEY MAY HEAR MY WORDS	517	25
HEAR MY PRAYER, O LORD, AND CONSIDER MY DESIRE	518	23
7 HEAR ME, O LORD, AND THAT SOON	519	04
8 O LET ME HEAR THY LOVING-KINDNESS BETIMES IN THE	519	07
HE ALSO WILL HEAR THEIR CRY, AND WILL HELP THEM	521	31
AND THE SHEEP HEAR HIS VOICE	538	27
THE SHEEP DID NOT HEAR THEM	539	05
AND THEY SHALL HEAR MY VOICE	539	20
MAY HAVE GRACE TO HEAR AND RECEIVE WHAT THEY SHALL	547	09
WE BESEECH THEE TO HEAR US, GOOD LORD	553	22
SHALL SAY, LORD, HEAR OUR PRAYER	557	17
AND THEM THAT HEAR THEE	558	25
WE BESEECH THEE TO HEAR US, GOOD LORD	560	11
WE BESEECH THEE TO HEAR US, GOOD LORD	560	14
WE BESEECH THEE TO HEAR US, GOOD LORD	561	06
MERCY UPON US AND HEAR US	561	33

HEAR   CONTINUED

	PAGE	LN
HEAR OUR PRAYER	562	06
LET ME HEAR, THEREFORE, IF THOU CANST SAY THE LORD'S	580	20
AND OBEDIENTLY TO HEAR AND TO BE ORDERED BY THE	R 582	33

HEARD

	PAGE	LN
WHICH WE HAVE HEARD THIS DAY WITH OUR OUTWARD EARS,	049	18
GOODNESS HAST HEARD THE DEVOUT PRAYERS OF THY CHURCH,	051	31
O GOD, WE HAVE HEARD WITH OUR EARS, AND OUR FATHERS	058	28
THEY BELIEVE IN HIM OF WHOM THEY HAVE NOT HEARD	073	08
NOW WHEN JOHN HAD HEARD IN THE PRISON THE WORKS OF	094	16
WHICH WE HAVE HEARD, WHICH WE HAVE SEEN WITH OUR	101	13
WE HAVE SEEN AND HEARD DECLARE WE UNTO YOU, THAT YE	101	18
WHICH WE HAVE HEARD OF HIM, AND DECLARE UNTO YOU,	101	22
AND I HEARD A VOICE FROM HEAVEN, AS THE VOICE OF MANY	102	31
AND I HEARD THE VOICE OF HARPERS HARPING WITH THEIR	103	03
WAS THERE A VOICE HEARD, LAMENTATION, AND WEEPING,	103	31
AND ALL THEY THAT HEARD IT WONDERED AT THOSE THINGS	106	14
THAT THEY HAD HEARD AND SEEN, AS IT WAS TOLD UNTO	106	18
BUT WHEN HE HEARD THAT ARCHELAUS DID REIGN IN JUDAEA	107	18
IF YE HAVE HEARD OF THE DISPENSATION OF THE GRACE OF	108	07
HEROD THE KING HAD HEARD THESE THINGS, HE WAS	109	03
WHEN THEY HAD HEARD THE KING, THEY DEPARTED	109	15
AND ALL THAT HEARD HIM WERE ASTONISHED AT HIS	110	30
WHEN JESUS HEARD IT, HE MARVELLED, AND SAID TO THEM	115	16
WHEN THEY HAVE HEARD, GO FORTH, AND ARE CHOKED WITH	122	06
GOOD HEART, HAVING HEARD THE WORD, KEEP IT, AND BRING	122	09
HE SAITH, I HAVE HEARD THEE IN A TIME ACCEPTED,	126	05
WHEN THEY HEARD THAT, SAID, THIS MAN CALLETH	137	20
AND WHEN THEY HEARD IT, THEY WERE GLAD, AND PROMISED	140	20
SAYING, WE HEARD HIM SAY, I WILL DESTROY THIS	143	06
YE HAVE HEARD THE BLASPHEMY	143	18
WHEN THEY HEARD IT, SAID, BEHOLD, HE CALLETH	146	30
WE OURSELVES HAVE HEARD OF HIS OWN MOUTH	152	02
WHEN PILATE HEARD OF GALILEE, HE ASKED WHETHER THE	153	06
BECAUSE HE HAD HEARD MANY THINGS OF HIM	153	12
PILATE THEREFORE HEARD THAT SAYING, HE WAS THE MORE	159	10
PILATE THEREFORE HEARD THAT SAYING, HE BROUGHT JESUS	159	22
SAITH HE, YE HAVE HEARD OF ME	178	02
THAT EVERY MAN HEARD THEM SPEAK IN HIS OWN LANGUAGE	180	28
YE HAVE HEARD HOW I SAID UNTO YOU, I GO AWAY, AND	182	02
ON ALL THEM WHICH HEARD THE WORD	184	01
FOR THEY HEARD THEM SPEAK WITH TONGUES, AND MAGNIFY	184	25
WERE AT JERUSALEM HEARD THAT SAMARIA HAD RECEIVED THE	185	21
VOICE WHICH I HEARD WAS AS IT WERE OF A TRUMPET	186	32
YE HAVE HEARD THAT IT WAS SAID BY THEM OF OLD TIME,	197	31
TO THE HOUSE, HE HEARD MUSICK AND DANCING	202	27
HEAR, AND HAVE NOT HEARD THEM	208	11
THE PHARISEES HAD HEARD THAT JESUS HAD PUT THE	215	06
SO BE THAT YE HAVE HEARD HIM, AND HAVE BEEN TAUGHT BY	216	10
BUT WHEN THE KING HEARD THEREOF, HE WAS WROTH	218	13
WHEN HE HEARD THAT JESUS WAS COME OUT OF JUDAEA INTO	219	29
WHEN THEY HAD HEARD THESE WORDS, THEY MARVELLED, AND	223	11
FOR YOU, SINCE WE HEARD OF YOUR FAITH IN CHRIST	223	23
WHEREOF YE HEARD BEFORE IN THE WORD OF THE	223	26
SINCE THE DAY YE HEARD OF IT, AND KNEW THE GRACE OF	223	29
SINCE THE DAY WE HEARD IT, DO NOT CEASE TO PRAY FOR	223	33
THEY BELIEVE IN HIM OF WHOM THEY HAVE NOT HEARD	227	07
BUT I SAY, HAVE THEY NOT HEARD	227	14
TO THE EARTH, AND HEARD A VOICE SAYING UNTO HIM,	229	32
I HAVE HEARD BY MANY OF THIS MAN, HOW MUCH EVIL	230	22
BUT ALL THAT HEARD HIM WERE AMAZED, AND SAID	231	05
THINGS THAT I HAVE HEARD OF MY FATHER I HAVE MADE	241	31
AND HER COUSINS HEARD HOW THE LORD HAD SHEWED GREAT	243	15
AND ALL THEY THAT HEARD THEM LAID THEM UP IN THEIR	243	29
AND WHEN THE TEN HEARD IT, THEY WERE MOVED WITH	247	19
FROM HEAVEN WE HEARD, WHEN WE WERE WITH HIM IN THE	248	20
BUT WHEN JESUS HEARD THAT, HE SAID UNTO THEM,	251	19
AND I HEARD A LOUD VOICE SAYING IN HEAVEN, NOW IS	252	09
AND I HEARD THE NUMBER OF THEM WHICH WERE SEALED	256	19
WHEN THE GENTILES HEARD THIS, THEY WERE GLAD,	261	06
YE HAVE HEARD THAT IT HATH BEEN SAID, THOU	264	03
WERE AT JERUSALEM HEARD THAT SAMARIA HAD RECEIVED THE	296	13
BECAUSE HE HATH HEARD THE VOICE OF MY PRAYER	305	18
AND HE HEARD ME OUT OF HIS HOLY HILL	309	12
MY VOICE, AND HE HEARD ME OUT OF HIS HOLY HILL	309	20
BE SAID OR SUNG, I HEARD A VOICE FROM HEAVEN, SAYING	333	25
AND HE HEARD ME OUT OF HIS HOLY HILL	346	32
FOR THE LORD HATH HEARD THE VOICE OF MY WEEPING	349	15
9 THE LORD HATH HEARD MY PETITION	349	16
19 LORD, THOU HAST HEARD THE DESIRE OF THE POOR	354	13
7 SO HE HEARD MY VOICE OUT OF HIS HOLY TEMPLE,	360	06
THEIR VOICES ARE HEARD AMONG THEM	363	18
THOU HAST HEARD ME ALSO FROM AMONG THE HORNS OF THE	367	14
CALLED UNTO HIM HE HEARD HIM	367	22
FOR HE HATH HEARD THE VOICE OF MY HUMBLE PETITIONS	373	20
15 FOR I HAVE HEARD THE BLASPHEMY OF THE MULTITUDE,	376	21
THE LORD, AND HE HEARD ME	380	09
A DEAF MAN, AND HEARD NOT	388	17
UNTO ME, AND HEARD MY CALLING	390	10
WE HAVE HEARD WITH OUR EARS, O GOD, OUR FATHERS HAVE	394	22
7 LIKE AS WE HAVE HEARD, SO HAVE WE SEEN IN THE CITY	399	24
THOU, O LORD, HAST HEARD MY DESIRES, *	413	15
TWICE I HAVE ALSO HEARD THE SAME, *	414	21
AND MAKE THE VOICE OF HIS PRAISE TO BE HEARD	417	30
17 BUT GOD HATH HEARD ME	418	18
THY JUDGMENT TO BE HEARD FROM HEAVEN	433	04
OF THY THUNDER WAS HEARD ROUND ABOUT	434	18
3 WHICH WE HAVE HEARD AND KNOWN, *	434	31
22 WHEN THE LORD HEARD THIS, HE WAS WROTH	436	11
60 WHEN GOD HEARD THIS, HE WAS WROTH, *	438	30
OF EGYPT, AND HAD HEARD A STRANGE LANGUAGE	442	21
AND HEARD THEE WHAT TIME AS THE STORM FELL UPON THEE	442	26
8 SION HEARD OF IT, AND REJOICED	461	12

HEARD   CONTINUED

THE LORD, AND HE HEARD THEM   462 29
HE HEARD THEIR COMPLAINT   475 25
BECAUSE HE HATH HEARD THE VOICE OF MY PRAYER   486 19
AND THE LORD HEARD ME AT LARGE   488 09
FOR THOU HAST HEARD ME, *   489 10
AND HE HEARD ME   502 08
6 LO, WE HEARD OF THE SAME AT EPHRATAH, *   508 15
FOR THEY HAVE HEARD THE WORDS OF THY MOUTH   514 05
YE HAVE HEARD, BRETHREN, AS WELL IN YOUR PRIVATE   539 24
AND I HEARD A GREAT VOICE OUT OF HEAVEN SAYING,   567 14
THEY ARE NOT TO BE HEARD, WHICH FEIGN THAT THE CLD   604 18

HEARDEST

UPON THEE, THOU HEARDEST ME   312 02
THOU HEARDEST THE VOICE OF MY PRAYER, *   377 13
8 THOU HEARDEST THEM, O LORD OUR GOD   462 32
AND THOU HEARDEST ME   491 19
UPON THEE, THOU HEARDEST ME   514 02

HEARER

FOR IF ANY BE A HEARER OF THE WORD, AND NOT A DCER,   176 06
NOT A FORGETFUL HEARER, BUT A DOER OF THE WCRK, THIS   176 11
FOR IF ANY BE A HEARER OF THE WORD, AND NOT A DCER,   265 30
NOT A FORGETFUL HEARER, BUT A DOER OF THE WORK,   266 03

HEARERS

AND NOT HEARERS ONLY, DECEIVING YOUR OWN   176 05
THAT IT MAY MINISTER GRACE UNTO THE HEARERS   216 25
AND NOT HEARERS ONLY, DECEIVING YOUR OWN   265 29
THE HEART, THE HEARERS THEREOF MAY BOTH PERCEIVE AND   566 04

HEAREST

PILATE UNTO HIM, HEAREST THOU NOT HOW MANY THINGS   135 23
AND THOU HEAREST THE SOUND THEREOF, BUT CANST NCT   188 15
SAID UNTO HIM, HEAREST THOU WHAT THESE SAY   260 13
AND THOU HEAREST THE SOUND THEREOF, BUT CANST NCT   275 19
BUT THOU HEAREST NOT   366 07
AS THOUGH THOU HEAREST NOT, I BECOME LIKE THEM THAT   373 05
2 THOU THAT HEAREST THE PRAYER, *   416 13
FOR THOU HEAREST ME   447 18

HEARETH

AND LET HIM THAT HEARETH SAY, COME   022 30
THAT IS OF GOD HEARETH GOD'S WORDS   133 11
HE THAT HEARETH MY WORD, AND BELIEVETH CN HIM   321 33
TO HIS WILL, HE HEARETH US   322 17
AND THE LORD HEARETH HIM   380 13
AND THE LORD HEARETH THEM, *   381 02
AS A MAN THAT HEARETH NOT, *   388 19
34 FOR THE LORD HEARETH THE POOR, *   424 10

HEARING

BOTH HEARING THEM, AND ASKING THEM   110 29
NOT SEE, AND HEARING THEY MIGHT NOT UNDERSTAND   121 32
AND HEARING THE MULTITUDE PASS BY, HE ASKED WHAT IT   123 27
BY HEARING, AND HEARING BY THE WORD OF GOD   227 13
FAITH COMETH BY HEARING, AND HEARING BY THE WORD OF   227 13
HEARING A VOICE, BUT SEEING NO MAN   230 09
BOTH IN HEARING THE WORD OF GOD, AND IN RECEIVING THE   608 13

HEARKEN

AND HEARKEN UNTO THE VOICE OF HIS WORD   029 13
GRACIOUSLY HEARKEN TO US WHO CALL UPON THEE, AND   041 21
AND HE SHALL HEARKEN UNTO ME   310 30
AND HEARKEN UNTO THE VOICE OF HIS WORD   312 29
HEARKEN UNTO MY VOICE, O LORD, WHEN I CRY UNTO THEE   326 20
UPON ME, AND HEARKEN UNTO MY PRAYER   347 12
2 O HEARKEN THOU UNTO THE VOICE OF MY CALLING,   347 32
AND HEARKEN UNTO MY PRAYER, THAT GOETH NOT OUT CF   358 17
EAR TO ME, AND HEARKEN UNTO MY WORDS   358 30
8 HEARKEN UNTO MY VOICE, O LORD, WHEN I CRY UNTO   372 12
YE CHILDREN, AND HEARKEN UNTO ME   380 23
10 HEARKEN, O DAUGHTER, AND CONSIDER   397 05
AND HEARKEN UNTO THE WORDS OF MY MOUTH   406 05
COME HITHER, AND HEARKEN, ALL YE THAT FEAR GOD   418 12
AND HE SHALL HEARKEN UNTO ME   433 17
IF THOU WILT HEARKEN UNTO ME, LO THERE SHALL NO   442 30
HEARKEN, O GOD OF JACOB   445 27
8 I WILL HEARKEN WHAT THE LORD GOD WILL SAY   446 22
AND HEARKEN UNTO THE VOICE OF HIS WORD   467 16
HEARKEN UNTO ME FOR THY TRUTH AND RIGHTEOUSNESS'   518 24
HEARKEN UNTO OUR VOICE, O LORD, WHEN WE   561 31

HEARKENED

WOULD HAVE HEARKENED UNTO ME   443 06
AND HEARKENED NOT UNTO THE VOICE OF THE LORD   474 19

HEARKENETH

PREPAREST THEIR HEART, AND THINE EAR HEARKENETH   354 14

HEART

MEDITATION OF MY HEART, BE ALWAYS ACCEPTABLE IN THY   003 20
AND TO REVIVE THE HEART OF THE CONTRITE ONES   003 28
REND YOUR HEART, AND NOT YOUR GARMENTS,   004 20

HEART   CONTINUED

AND A CONTRITE HEART, O GOD, THOU WILT NOT DESPISE   004 25
AND OBEDIENT HEART   005 34
ME WITH A PURE HEART, AND HUMBLE VOICE, UNTO THE   006 11
AND HUMBLE MEN OF HEART, BLESS YE THE LORD   013 28
MEDITATION OF MY HEART, BE ALWAY ACCEPTABLE IN THY   021 22
AND OBEDIENT HEART   023 09
ME WITH A PURE HEART, AND HUMBLE VOICE, UNTO THE   023 20
TO LAY TO HEART THE GREAT DANGERS WE ARE IN BY CUR   037 27
MAY BE ALL OF ONE HEART AND OF ONE SOUL, UNITED IN   037 32
IN HUMILITY OF HEART THEY MAY EVER LOOK UNTO THEE,   042 26
WITH SINGLENESS OF HEART AS THY SERVANTS, AND TC THE   042 32
MAY HIS HEART BE DULY IMPRESSED WITH A SENSE OF THY   053 04
FROM ALL BLINDNESS OF HEART   054 23
FROM HARDNESS OF HEART, AND CONTEMPT OF THY WORD AND   055 04
SO TO RULE THE HEART OF THY SERVANT, THE PRESIDENT CF   055 22
THEE TO GIVE US AN HEART TO LOVE AND FEAR THEE, AND   056 11
OF A CONTRITE HEART, NOR THE DESIRE OF SUCH AS ARE   058 16
MAKE ME A CLEAN HEART, O GOD, *   060 30
AND CONTRITE HEART, O GOD, SHALT THOU NOT DESPISE   061 14
GOD WITH ALL THY HEART, AND WITH ALL THY SOUL, AND   069 27
IS DISPOSED IN HIS HEART, NOT GRUDGINGLY, OR OF   072 18
WITH MEEK HEART AND DUE REVERENCE, THEY MAY   074 27
FEED ON HIM IN THY HEART BY FAITH, WITH THANKSGIVING   082 34
THE BOTTOM OF HIS HEART ALL THAT THE OTHER HATH   R 085 12
A TRUE PENITENT HEART AND LIVELY FAITH WE RECEIVE   085 31
ALL THESE THINGS, AND PONDERED THEM IN HER HEART   106 17
HIS MOTHER KEPT ALL THESE SAYINGS IN HER HEART   111 06
AND BELOVED, A HEART OF COMPASSION, KINDNESS,   116 04
AN HONEST AND GOOD HEART, HAVING HEARD THE WORD,   122 09
WITH ALL YOUR HEART, AND WITH FASTING, AND WITH   124 22
AND REND YOUR HEART, AND NOT YOUR GARMENTS, AND TURN   124 23
THERE WILL YOUR HEART BE ALSO   125 21
IS IN MINE HEART, AND THE YEAR OF MY REDEEMED IS   138 21
AND HARDENED OUR HEART FROM THY FEAR   139 25
NOW PUT INTO THE HEART OF JUDAS ISCARIOT, SIMON'S   155 27
HARDNESS OF HEART, AND CONTEMPT OF THY WORD   157 09
NEAR WITH A TRUE HEART IN FULL ASSURANCE OF FAITH,   158 20
AND SLOW OF HEART TO BELIEVE ALL THAT THE   167 29
DID NOT OUR HEART BURN WITHIN US, WHILE HE TALKED   168 09
AND YOUR HEART SHALL REJOICE, AND YOUR JOY NO   174 14
THINGS UNTO YOU, SORROW HATH FILLED YOUR HEART   175 09
DECEIVETH HIS OWN HEART, THIS MAN'S RELIGION IS VAIN   176 14
SO WE MAY ALSO IN HEART AND MIND THITHER ASCEND,   177 17
LET NOT YOUR HEART BE TROUBLED, NEITHER LET IT BE   181 35
FOR IF OUR HEART CONDEMN US, GOD IS GREATER THAN CUR   191 24
GREATER THAN OUR HEART, AND KNOWETH ALL THINGS   191 25
IF OUR HEART CONDEMN US NOT, THEN HAVE WE   191 26
GOD WITH ALL THY HEART, AND WITH ALL THY SOUL, AND   208 15
GOD WITH ALL THY HEART, AND WITH ALL THY SOUL, AND   215 11
BECAUSE OF THE BLINDNESS OF THEIR HEART   216 07
MELODY IN YOUR HEART TO THE LORD   217 29
BECAUSE I HAVE YOU IN MY HEART   220 28
BELIEVE IN THINE HEART THAT GOD HATH RAISED HIM FRCM   226 27
FOR WITH THE HEART MAN BELIEVETH UNTO RIGHTECUSNESS   226 28
FOR I AM MEEK AND LOWLY IN HEART   235 13
LET NOT YOUR HEART BE TROUBLED   239 29
WITH PURPOSE OF HEART THEY WOULD CLEAVE UNTC THE   241 07
BLESSED ARE THE PURE IN HEART   257 27
THAT ARE BROKEN IN HEART, *   264 23
DECEIVETH HIS OWN HEART, THIS MAN'S RELIGION IS VAIN   266 06
GOD WITH ALL THY HEART, WITH ALL THY MIND, WITH ALL   288 06
HIM WITH ALL MY HEART, WITH ALL MY MIND, WITH ALL MY   288 17
TO BEAR NO MALICE NOR HATRED IN MY HEART   288 33
WHEN MY HEART IS VEXED, I WILL COMPLAIN   311 05
WITH MINE OWN HEART, AND SEARCH OUT MY SPIRIT   311 11
O LORD, WITH MY WHOLE HEART   311 29
THE BOTTOM OF HIS HEART, ALL PERSONS THAT HAVE   R 313 21
DOWN AND FAINT OF HEART AMIDST THE SORROWS AND   316 19
MY HEART HATH TALKED OF THEE, SEEK YE MY FACE   326 22
BE STRONG, AND HE SHALL COMFORT THINE HEART   326 31
LET NOT YOUR HEART BE TROUBLED   331 17
WHEREFORE MY HEART IS GLAD, AND MY GLORY REJOICETH   333 07
BLESSED ARE THE PURE IN HEART   340 16
AND YOUR HEART SHALL REJOICE, AND YOUR JOY NO   341 10
WITH YOUR OWN HEART, AND IN YOUR CHAMBER, AND BE   347 20
8 THOU HAST PUT GLADNESS IN MY HEART   347 26
WHO PRESERVETH THEM THAT ARE TRUE OF HEART   350 14
O LORD, WITH MY WHOLE HEART   351 23
HATH SAID IN HIS HEART, TUSH, I SHALL NEVER BE CAST   353 16
HATH SAID IN HIS HEART, TUSH, GOD HATH FORGOTTEN   353 30
HE DOTH SAY IN HIS HEART, TUSH, THOU GOD CAREST NOT   354 02
PREPAREST THEIR HEART, AND THINE EAR HEARKENETH   354 14
MAY PRIVILY SHOOT AT THEM WHICH ARE TRUE OF HEART   354 23
AND DISSEMBLE IN THEIR DOUBLE HEART   355 11
COUNSEL IN MY SOUL, AND BE SO VEXED IN MY HEART   355 31
AND MY HEART IS JOYFUL IN THY SALVATION   356 07
HATH SAID IN HIS HEART, *   356 13
AND SPEAKETH THE TRUTH FROM HIS HEART   357 09
10 WHEREFORE MY HEART IS GLAD, AND MY GLORY   358 08
AND VISITED MINE HEART IN THE NIGHT SEASON   358 21
OF THE LORD ARE RIGHT, AND REJOICE THE HEART   363 31
MEDITATION OF MY HEART, BE ALWAY ACCEPTABLE IN THY   364 14
MY HEART ALSO IN THE MIDST OF MY BODY IS EVEN LIKE   366 32
YOUR HEART SHALL LIVE FOR EVER   367 26
4 EVEN HE THAT HATH CLEAN HANDS, AND A PURE HEART   369 02
THE SORROWS OF MY HEART ARE ENLARGED   370 14
TRY OUT MY REINS AND MY HEART   370 34
YET SHALL NOT MY HEART BE AFRAID   371 30
9 MY HEART HATH TALKED OF THEE, SEEK YE MY FACE   372 14
BE STRONG, AND HE SHALL COMFORT THINE HEART   372 31
MY HEART HATH TRUSTED IN HIM, AND I AM HELPED   373 22
THEREFORE MY HEART DANCETH FOR JOY, AND IN MY SONG   373 23
ESTABLISH YOUR HEART, *   377 18
ALL YE THAT ARE TRUE OF HEART   378 17

HEART   CONTINUED

THOUGHTS OF HIS HEART FROM GENERATION TO GENERATICN   379 10
20 FOR OUR HEART SHALL REJOICE IN HIM   379 30
ARE OF A CONTRITE HEART, *   381 05
MY HEART SHOWETH ME THE WICKEDNESS OF THE UNGODLY,   383 26
RIGHTEOUSNESS UNTO THEM THAT ARE TRUE OF HEART   384 18
THROUGH THEIR OWN HEART, *   385 25
HIS GOD IS IN HIS HEART, *   386 28
HAVE ROARED FOR THE VERY DISQUIETNESS OF MY HEART   388 07
10 MY HEART PANTETH, MY STRENGTH HATH FAILED ME,   388 10
4 MY HEART WAS HOT WITHIN ME   389 12
THY LAW IS WITHIN MY HEART   390 33
I HAVE NOT HID THY RIGHTEOUSNESS WITHIN MY HEART   391 04
OF MY HEAD, AND MY HEART HATH FAILED ME   391 13
AND HIS HEART CONCEIVETH FALSEHOOD WITHIN HIMSELF   392 11
I POUR OUT MY HEART BY MYSELF   393 06
19 OUR HEART IS NOT TLRNED BACK, *   395 30
FOR HE KNOWETH THE VERY SECRETS OF THE HEART   396 03
MY HEART OVERFLOWETH WITH A GOOD MATTER   396 15
VERY SHARP IN THE HEART OF THE KING'S ENEMIES, *   396 25
AND MY HEART SHALL MUSE OF UNDERSTANDING   400 10
10 MAKE ME A CLEAN HEART, O GOD, *   403 29
AND CONTRITE HEART, O GOD, SHALT THOU NCT DESPISE   404 12
HATH SAID IN HIS HEART, *   405 12
OFFERING OF A FREE HEART WILL I GIVE THEE, AND PRAISE   406 14
4 MY HEART IS DISQUIETED WITHIN ME, *   406 26
WERE SOFTER THAN BUTTER, HAVING WAR IN HIS HEART   408 02
8 MY HEART IS FIXED, O GOD, MY HEART IS FIXED   409 29
O GOD, MY HEART IS FIXED   409 29
MISCHIEF IN YOUR HEART UPON THE EARTH, *   410 10
WHEN MY HEART IS IN HEAVINESS   413 09
BUT CURSE WITH THEIR HEART   414 06
SET NOT YOUR HEART UPON THEM   414 19
EVERY MAN IN THE DEEP OF HIS HEART   415 32
THAT ARE TRUE OF HEART SHALL BE GLAD   416 07
WITH MINE HEART, *   418 16
21 REPROACH HATH BROKEN MY HEART   423 13
EVEN SUCH AS ARE OF A CLEAN HEART   428 11
HAVE I CLEANSED MY HEART IN VAIN, *   429 02
21 THUS MY HEART WAS GRIEVED, *   429 18
26 MY FLESH AND MY HEART FAILETH   429 28
THE STRENGTH OF MY HEART, AND MY PORTION FCR EVER   429 29
WHEN MY HEART IS VEXED, I WILL COMPLAIN   433 22
WITH MINE OWN HEART, AND SEARCH OUT MY SPIRIT   433 28
THAT SET NOT THEIR HEART ARIGHT, AND WHOSE SPIRIT   435 11
37 FOR THEIR HEART WAS NOT WHOLE WITH HIM, *   437 12
FAITHFUL AND TRUE HEART   439 24
MY HEART AND MY FLESH REJOICE IN THE LIVING GOD   445 14
IN WHOSE HEART ARE THY WAYS   445 22
O KNIT MY HEART UNTO THEE, THAT I MAY FEAR THY NAME   447 26
O LORD MY GOD, WITH ALL MY HEART   447 29
AS ARE TRUE IN HEART SHALL FOLLOW IT   458 17
THAT I HAD IN MY HEART, *   458 25
I WILL WALK IN MY HOUSE WITH A PERFECT HEART   463 21
5 A FROWARD HEART SHALL DEPART FROM ME   463 24
LOOK AND A PROUD HEART, *   463 28
4 MY HEART IS SMITTEN DOWN, AND WITHERED LIKE GRASS   464 17
MAKETH GLAD THE HEART OF MAN   468 24
AND BREAD TO STRENGTHEN MAN'S HEART   468 25
LET THE HEART OF THEM REJOICE THAT SEEK THE LORD   470 09
25 WHOSE HEART TURNED SO, THAT THEY HATED HIS PECPLE,   471 22
BROUGHT DOWN THEIR HEART THROUGH HEAVINESS   476 28
O GOD, MY HEART IS READY, MY HEART IS READY   479 04
HEART IS READY, MY HEART IS READY   479 04
HE MIGHT SLAY HIM THAT WAS VEXED AT THE HEART   480 34
AND MY HEART IS WOUNDED WITHIN ME   481 15
LORD WITH MY WHOLE HEART, *   482 24
FOR HIS HEART STANDETH FAST, AND BELIEVETH IN THE   483 30
8 HIS HEART IS STABLISHED, AND WILL NOT SHRINK,   483 32
AND SEEK HIM WITH THEIR WHOLE HEART   490 03
WITH AN UNFEIGNED HEART, *   490 12
10 WITH MY WHOLE HEART HAVE I SOUGHT THEE   490 18
I HID WITHIN MY HEART, *   490 20
THOU HAST SET MY HEART AT LIBERTY   491 32
I SHALL KEEP IT WITH MY WHOLE HEART   492 08
36 INCLINE MY HEART UNTO THY TESTIMONIES, *   492 11
PETITION IN THY PRESENCE WITH MY WHOLE HEART   493 27
I WILL KEEP THY COMMANDMENTS WITH MY WHOLE HEART   494 19
70 THEIR HEART IS AS FAT AS BRAWN   494 20
80 O LET MY HEART BE SOUND IN THY STATUTES, *   495 16
THEY ARE THE VERY JOY OF MY HEART   497 20
I HAVE APPLIED MY HEART TO FULFIL THY STATUTES ALWAY,   497 21
I CALL WITH MY WHOLE HEART   499 31
BUT MY HEART STANDETH IN AWE OF THY WORD   501 04
UNTO THOSE THAT ARE GOOD AND TRUE OF HEART   504 33
O LORD, WITH MY WHOLE HEART   513 28
AND SEEK THE GROUND OF MY HEART   516 04
4 O LET NOT MINE HEART BE INCLINED TO ANY EVIL THING   517 15
AND MY HEART WITHIN ME IS DESOLATE   518 31
THAT ARE BROKEN IN HEART, *   522 32
YOU THINK IN YOUR HEART, THAT YOU ARE TRULY CALLED,   541 30
SENSE IMPART, AND SHED THY LOVE IN EVERY HEART   545 03
SENSE IMPART, AND SHED THY LOVE IN EVERY HEART   557 09
4 EVEN HE THAT HATH CLEAN HANDS, AND A PURE HEART   563 17
AND READINESS OF HEART, TO CONSECRATE THIS PLACE TO   565 04
IT INWARDLY IN THE HEART, THE HEARERS THEREOF MAY   566 04
MEDITATION OF HIS HEART, BE ALWAY ACCEPTABLE IN THY   572 23
THAT WITH ONE HEART THEY MAY DESIRE THE PROSPERITY OF   574 10
HIM WITH ALL MY HEART, WITH ALL MY MIND, WITH ALL MY   579 28
TO BEAR NO MALICE NOR HATRED IN MY HEART   580 09
FROM COLDNESS OF HEART AND WANDERINGS OF MIND, THAT   594 06
WE MAY IN HEART BE INSPIRED BY THY WISDOM   594 25
FILL HIS HEART WITH CONFIDENCE, THAT THOUGH HE BE   597 24
AND IN HIS HEART MAY THY PEACE WHICH PASSETH   598 02
TURN THE HEART OF THE FATHERS TO THE CHILDREN, AND   598 26

HEART   CONTINUED

AND THE HEART OF THE CHILDREN TO THE   598 27
THAT ARE BROKEN IN HEART, AND TURNEST THE SADNESS CF   599 04
INCLINE THE HEART OF EMPLOYERS AND OF THOSE WHOM THEY   599 31

HEART'S

BOAST OF HIS OWN HEART'S DESIRE, *   353 08
4 GRANT THEE THY HEART'S DESIRE, *   364 22
GIVEN HIM HIS HEART'S DESIRE, *   365 07
GIVE THEE THY HEART'S DESIRE   384 32

HEARTILY

LET US HEARTILY REJOICE IN THE STRENGTH OF OUR   009 03
MOST HEARTILY WE BESEECH THEE, WITH THY FAVOUR TC   017 29
AND ARE HEARTILY SORRY FOR THESE OUR   075 23
WE MOST HEARTILY THANK THEE, FOR THAT THOU DOST   083 16
AND I HEARTILY THANK OUR HEAVENLY FATHER, THAT HE   284 02
LET US HEARTILY REJOICE IN THE STRENGTH OF OUR   459 05
AND I HEARTILY THANK OUR HEAVENLY FATHER, THAT HE   577 23

HEARTS

HIS SON INTO YOUR HEARTS, CRYING, ABBA, FATHER   005 17
MUCH THE DEVICES AND DESIRES OF OUR OWN HEARTS   006 20
MAKE CLEAN OUR HEARTS WITHIN US   016 31
THAT OUR HEARTS MAY BE UNFEIGNEDLY THANKFUL   019 26
MUCH THE DEVICES AND DESIRES OF OUR OWN HEARTS   023 27
THE PROUD IN THE IMAGINATION OF THEIR HEARTS   026 21
MAKE CLEAN OUR HEARTS WITHIN US   031 13
THAT OUR HEARTS MAY BE SET TO OBEY THY COMMANDMENTS,   031 20
AND SO RULE THE HEARTS OF THY SERVANTS THE PRESIDENT   032 06
THAT OUR HEARTS MAY BE UNFEIGNEDLY THANKFUL   033 24
FILL OUR HEARTS WITH THANKFULNESS, AND IN THE DAY OF   036 22
AND INCLINE THE HEARTS OF MANY TO DEDICATE THEMSELVES   039 19
BESEECH THEE, THE HEARTS AND MINDS OF THY SERVANTS   043 20
AND FAITHFUL HEARTS, THEY MAY EVERMORE BE FILLED WITH   043 24
WE MAY APPLY OUR HEARTS UNTO THAT HEAVENLY WISDOM   045 09
INWARDLY IN OUR HEARTS, THAT THEY MAY BRING FORTH IN   049 20
AND SLANDERERS, AND TO TURN THEIR HEARTS   057 08
WITH PITY BEHOLD THE SORROWS OF OUR HEARTS   059 11
UNTO WHOM ALL HEARTS ARE OPEN, ALL DESIRES KNOWN, AND   067 16
THOUGHTS OF OUR HEARTS BY THE INSPIRATION OF THY HOLY   067 18
AND INCLINE OUR HEARTS TO KEEP THIS LAW   068 06
AND INCLINE OUR HEARTS TO KEEP THIS LAW   069 05
THY LAWS IN OUR HEARTS, WE BESEECH THEE   069 24
BOTH OUR HEARTS AND BODIES, IN THE WAYS OF   070 08
AND DISPOSE THE HEARTS OF ALL CHRISTIAN RULERS, THAT   074 16
PRIEST SHALL PROCEED, SAYING, LIFT UP YOUR HEARTS   076 26
TO SHINE IN OUR HEARTS, TO GIVE THE KNOWLEDGE OF THY   077 30
KEEP YOUR HEARTS AND MINDS IN THE KNOWLEDGE AND   084 19
MEN'S HEARTS FAILING THEM FOR FEAR, AND FOR LOOKING   093 08
BY TURNING THE HEARTS OF THE DISOBEDIENT TO THE   093 28
AND WILL MAKE MANIFEST THE COUNSELS OF THE HEARTS   094 13
SHALL KEEP YOUR HEARTS AND MINDS THROUGH CHRIST   095 18
HIS SON INTO YOUR HEARTS, CRYING, ABBA, FATHER   104 23
OUR HEARTS, AND ALL OUR MEMBERS, BEING   105 21
ENKINDLED IN OUR HEARTS MAY SHINE FORTH IN OUR LIVES   106 27
GOD RULE IN YOUR HEARTS, TO THE WHICH ALSO YE ARE   116 09
GRACE IN YOUR HEARTS TO THE LORD   116 13
WORD OUT OF THEIR HEARTS, LEST THEY SHOULD BELIEVE   121 35
AND POUR INTO OUR HEARTS THAT MOST EXCELLENT GIFT OF   122 16
NEW AND CONTRITE HEARTS, THAT WE, WORTHILY LAMENTING   124 14
LAWS INTO THEIR HEARTS, AND IN THEIR MINDS WILL I   158 12
HAVING OUR HEARTS SPRINKLED FROM AN EVIL   158 21
AND WHY DO THOUGHTS ARISE IN YOUR HEARTS   169 32
OF THE WORLD, OUR HEARTS MAY SURELY THERE BE FIXED,   174 23
DIDST TEACH THE HEARTS OF THY FAITHFUL PEOPLE, BY   180 08
SPIRIT INTO OUR HEARTS, THAT HE MAY DIRECT AND RULE   183 23
SHALL ASSURE OUR HEARTS BEFORE HIM   191 24
BUT SANCTIFY THE LORD GOD IN YOUR HEARTS   196 04
POUR INTO OUR HEARTS SUCH LOVE TOWARD THEE, THAT WE,   197 06
GRAFT IN OUR HEARTS THE LOVE OF THY NAME, INCREASE IN   198 21
MAY DWELL IN YOUR HEARTS BY FAITH   212 16
AND WITH PURE HEARTS AND MINDS TO FOLLOW THEE,   214 25
MAY IN ALL THINGS DIRECT AND RULE OUR HEARTS   215 29
WHEREFORE THINK YE EVIL IN YOUR HEARTS   217 07
IF YE FROM YOUR HEARTS FORGIVE NOT EVERY ONE HIS   222 06
PURE AND CLEAN HEARTS, BY THE SAME THY SON JESUS   231 31
THOUGHTS OF MANY HEARTS MAY BE REVEALED   233 15
WHICH KNOWEST THE HEARTS OF ALL MEN, SHEW WHETHER OF   234 28
POUR THY GRACE INTO OUR HEARTS   235 19
THEM UP IN THEIR HEARTS, SAYING, WHAT MANNER OF CHILD   243 29
SHINED IN OUR HEARTS, TO GIVE THE LIGHT OF THE   251 08
THY LOVE IN THE HEARTS OF THE SAINTS   258 05
PUT IT INTO THE HEARTS OF MANY TO OFFER THEMSELVES   260 22
LIFT UP YOUR HEARTS   279 02
DWELLING IN YOUR HEARTS BY FAITH, YE MAY BE FILLED   281 11
GRAFT IN OUR HEARTS THE LOVE OF THY NAME, INCREASE IN   283 09
OF THE WORLD, OUR HEARTS MAY SURELY THERE BE FIXED,   285 30
AND INCLINE OUR HEARTS TO KEEP THIS LAW   286 06
AND INCLINE OUR HEARTS TO KEEP THIS LAW   287 04
THY LAWS IN OUR HEARTS, WE BESEECH THEE   287 24
BOTH OUR HEARTS AND BODIES, IN THE WAYS OF   298 28
SECRETS OF ALL HEARTS SHALL BE DISCLOSED, THAT IF   300 26
LIFT UP YOUR HEARTS, ETC   R 323 06
WE MAY APPLY OUR HEARTS UNTO WISDOM   326 03
THE SECRETS OF OUR HEARTS   332 28
TRIETH THE VERY HEARTS AND REINS   350 11
BUT IMAGINE MISCHIEF IN THEIR HEARTS   373 12
ALL THE HEARTS OF THEM, *   379 17
NOT SAY IN THEIR HEARTS, THERE   383 13
POUR OUT YOUR HEARTS BEFORE HIM, FOR GOD IS OUR HOPE   414 14
SAID IN THEIR HEARTS, LET US MAKE HAVOC OF THEM   430 21

HEARTS   CONTINUED

GOD IN THEIR HEARTS, *   436 04
WE MAY APPLY OUR HEARTS UNTO WISDOM   454 14
HARDEN NOT YOUR HEARTS *   459 20
DO ERR IN THEIR HEARTS, FOR THEY HAVE NOT KNOWN MY   459 25
MISCHIEF IN THEIR HEARTS, *   516 11
KEEP YOUR HEARTS AND MINDS IN THE KNOWLEDGE AND   535 14
AND FILL THE HEARTS WHICH THOU HAST MADE   544 20
KEEP YOUR HEARTS AND MINDS IN THE KNOWLEDGE AND LOVE   547 15
AND FILL THE HEARTS WHICH THOU HAST MADE   556 28
KEEP YOUR HEARTS AND MINDS IN THE KNOWLEDGE AND LOVE   559 18
AND AFFECT THEIR HEARTS WITH MORE DEVOTION AND   564 18
PUT IT INTO THE HEARTS OF THY SERVANTS TO APPROPRIATE   566 29
KEEP YOUR HEARTS AND MINDS IN THE KNOWLEDGE AND   568 14
GRAFT IN THEIR HEARTS A LOVE OF THE TRUTH   572 28
IMPRINT UPON OUR HEARTS SUCH A DREAD OF THY   588 18
PURGE OUR HEARTS FROM ENVY, HATRED, AND MALICE   590 15
AND SO RULE THEIR HEARTS AND STRENGTHEN THEIR HANDS,   590 28
INCLINE OUR HEARTS TO KEEP THY LAW, AND GUIDE OUR   594 14
GIVE US GRATEFUL HEARTS, OUR FATHER, FOR ALL THY   600 17

HEARTS'

UNTO THEIR OWN HEARTS' LUSTS, *   443 04

HEARTY

MOST HUMBLE AND HEARTY THANKS FOR ALL THY GOODNESS   019 16
MOST HUMBLE AND HEARTY THANKS FOR ALL THY GOODNESS   033 14
HIGH PRAISE AND HEARTY THANKS FOR THE WONDERFUL GRACE   048 16
THOSE WHO WITH HEARTY REPENTANCE AND TRUE FAITH TURN   076 04
UNTO THEE MOST HEARTY THANKS FOR THE INNUMERABLE   081 04
MOST HUMBLE AND HEARTY THANKS TO GOD, THE FATHER,   086 05
MOST HUMBLE AND HEARTY THANKS TO ALMIGHTY GOD, OUR   086 35
LOOK UPON THE HEARTY DESIRES OF THY HUMBLE SERVANTS,   128 25
HAST GIVEN AN HEARTY DESIRE TO PRAY, MAY, BY THY   192 25
THEE HUMBLE AND HEARTY THANKS FOR THIS THY BOUNTY   265 13
WE YIELD THEE HEARTY THANKS, MOST MERCIFUL FATHER,   280 28
WE YIELD THEE HEARTY THANKS, ETC   R 281 24
THEREFORE GIVE HEARTY THANKS UNTO GOD, AND SAY, THEN   305 14
AND GIVING HIM HEARTY THANKS THEREFOR, HE DOTH EAT   R 323 29
WE GIVE THEE HEARTY THANKS FOR THE GOOD EXAMPLES OF   334 23
HIGH PRAISE AND HEARTY THANKS, FOR THE WONDERFUL   336 17
UNTO THEE MOST HEARTY THANKS, WE PRAISE AND WORSHIP   545 25
AND WORK IN US AN HEARTY CONTRITION   590 04

HEAT

O YE FIRE AND HEAT, BLESS YE THE LORD   012 18
THE BURDEN AND HEAT OF THE DAY   120 06
WITH A BURNING HEAT, BUT IT WITHERETH THE GRASS, AND   239 21
NEITHER SHALL THE SUN LIGHT ON THEM, NOR ANY HEAT   257 13
NEITHER SHALL THE SUN LIGHT ON THEM, NOR ANY HEAT   341 24
HID FROM THE HEAT THEREOF   363 26

HEATHEN

GREAT AMONG THE HEATHEN, SAITH THE LORD OF HOSTS   004 16
HATH HE OPENLY SHOWED IN THE SIGHT OF THE HEATHEN   027 09
FOR OPENING HEATHEN LANDS TO THE LIGHT OF THY TRUTH   038 16
IN PERILS BY THE HEATHEN, IN PERILS IN THE CITY,   121 06
THAT THE HEATHEN SHOULD RULE OVER THEM   125 05
BE A PREY TO THE HEATHEN, NEITHER SHALL THE BEAST OF   262 15
THE SHAME OF THE HEATHEN ANY MORE   262 19
WHY DO THE HEATHEN SO FURIOUSLY RAGE TOGETHER   345 25
HAST REBUKED THE HEATHEN, AND DESTROYED THE UNGODLY   351 30
15 THE HEATHEN ARE SUNK DOWN IN THE PIT THAT THEY   352 15
LET THE HEATHEN BE JUDGED IN THY SIGHT   352 31
THAT THE HEATHEN MAY KNOW THEMSELVES TO BE BUT MEN   352 32
AND THE HEATHEN ARE PERISHED OUT OF THE LAND   354 11
COUNSEL OF THE HEATHEN TO NOUGHT, *   379 06
DRIVEN OUT THE HEATHEN WITH THY HAND, AND PLANTED OUR   394 24
AND HAST SCATTERED US AMONG THE HEATHEN   395 16
TO VISIT ALL THE HEATHEN, *   411 14
LAUGH ALL THE HEATHEN TO SCORN   411 21
LEADERS OF THE HEATHEN, SO THAT THEY HUMBLY BRING   421 16
HE CAST OUT THE HEATHEN ALSO BEFORE THEM, *   438 21
O GOD, THE HEATHEN ARE COME INTO THINE INHERITANCE   439 29
UPON THE HEATHEN THAT HAVE NOT KNOWN THEE   440 11
WHEREFORE DO THE HEATHEN SAY, *   440 21
SHOWED UPON THE HEATHEN, IN OUR SIGHT   440 24
CAST OUT THE HEATHEN, AND PLANTED IT   441 19
INSTRUCTETH THE HEATHEN, *   458 06
HONOUR UNTO THE HEATHEN, *   460 04
THE GODS OF THE HEATHEN, THEY ARE BUT IDOLS   460 08
IT OUT AMONG THE HEATHEN, THAT THE LORD IS KING, AND   460 18
HATH HE OPENLY SHOWED IN THE SIGHT OF THE HEATHEN   461 30
43 AND GAVE THEM THE LANDS OF THE HEATHEN   472 25
THEY THE HEATHEN, *   475 04
AMONG THE HEATHEN, *   475 06
HE GAVE THEM OVER INTO THE HAND OF THE HEATHEN   475 18
AND GATHER US FROM AMONG THE HEATHEN   475 31
6 HE SHALL JUDGE AMONG THE HEATHEN   482 18
THAT HE MAY GIVE THEM THE HERITAGE OF THE HEATHEN   483 06
SHALL THE HEATHEN SAY, *   485 14
THEY AMONG THE HEATHEN, *   505 11
IMAGES OF THE HEATHEN, THEY ARE BUT SILVER AND GOLD   510 32
NEITHER HAVE THE HEATHEN KNOWLEDGE OF HIS LAWS   524 03
AS AN HEATHEN AND PUBLICAN, UNTIL HE BE   609 28

HEAVEN

THE KINGDOM OF HEAVEN IS AT HAND   004 04
SINNED AGAINST HEAVEN, AND BEFORE THEE, AND AM NO   004 27
WHO ART IN HEAVEN, HALLOWED BE THY NAME   007 23

HEAVEN   CONTINUED

THY WILL BE DONE, ON EARTH AS IT IS IN HEAVEN   007 25
CHRIST THE LORD ASCENDETH INTO HEAVEN   R 008 26
HEAVEN AND EARTH ARE FULL OF THE MAJESTY OF THY   010 15
THE KINGDOM OF HEAVEN TO ALL BELIEVERS   010 29
BLESSED ART THOU IN THE FIRMAMENT OF HEAVEN   011 27
O YE STARS OF HEAVEN, BLESS YE THE LORD   012 12
MAKER OF HEAVEN AND EARTH   015 19
HE ASCENDED INTO HEAVEN, AND SITTETH ON THE RIGHT   015 25
MAKER OF HEAVEN AND EARTH, AND OF ALL THINGS VISIBLE   015 34
CAME DOWN FROM HEAVEN, AND WAS INCARNATE BY THE HOLY   016 07
AND ASCENDED INTO HEAVEN, AND SITTETH ON THE RIGHT   016 11
BUT INTO HEAVEN ITSELF, NOW TO APPEAR IN THE PRESENCE   022 24
MAKER OF HEAVEN AND EARTH   029 24
HE ASCENDED INTO HEAVEN, AND SITTETH ON THE RIGHT   029 30
MAKER OF HEAVEN AND EARTH, AND OF ALL THINGS VISIBLE   030 05
CAME DOWN FROM HEAVEN, AND WAS INCARNATE BY THE HOLY   030 12
AND ASCENDED INTO HEAVEN, AND SITTETH ON THE RIGHT   030 16
CREATOR OF HEAVEN AND EARTH   054 05
THING THAT IS IN HEAVEN ABOVE, OR IN THE EARTH   068 05
THE LORD MADE HEAVEN AND EARTH, THE SEA, AND ALL THAT   068 30
MAKER OF HEAVEN AND EARTH, AND OF ALL THINGS VISIBLE   071 03
CAME DOWN FROM HEAVEN, AND WAS INCARNATE BY THE HOLY   071 09
AND ASCENDED INTO HEAVEN, AND SITTETH ON THE RIGHT   071 13
AND GLORIFY YOUR FATHER WHICH IS IN HEAVEN   072 06
TREASURES IN HEAVEN, WHERE NEITHER MOTH NOR RUST DOTH   072 10
SHALL ENTER INTO THE KINGDOM OF HEAVEN   072 14
DOETH THE WILL OF MY FATHER WHICH IS IN HEAVEN   072 15
THAT IS IN THE HEAVEN AND IN THE EARTH IS THINE   073 20
THE COMPANY OF HEAVEN, WE LAUD AND MAGNIFY THY   077 05
GOD OF HOSTS, HEAVEN AND EARTH ARE FULL OF THY   077 09
ASCENDED UNTO HEAVEN, TO PREPARE A PLACE FOR US   078 19
AT THIS TIME FROM HEAVEN, LIGHTING UPON THE   078 27
THE COMPANY OF HEAVEN, WE LAUD AND MAGNIFY THY   079 29
GOD OF HOSTS, HEAVEN AND EARTH ARE FULL OF   079 33
AND ARE MADE PARTAKERS OF THE KINGDOM OF HEAVEN   086 34
FOR THE POWERS OF HEAVEN SHALL BE SHAKEN   093 10
HEAVEN AND EARTH SHALL PASS AWAY   093 20
LOOK UP TO HEAVEN, AND BY FAITH BEHOLD THE GLORY THAT   099 28
STEDFASTLY INTO HEAVEN, AND SAW THE GLORY OF GOD,   100 06
A VOICE FROM HEAVEN, AS THE VOICE OF MANY WATERS,   103 02
OF THINGS IN HEAVEN, AND THINGS IN EARTH, AND   105 28
FROM THEM INTO HEAVEN, THE SHEPHERDS SAID ONE TO   106 08
ALL THINGS IN HEAVEN AND EARTH   111 11
CAME A VOICE FROM HEAVEN, SAYING, THOU ART MY BELOVED   112 22
AND JACOB, IN THE KINGDOM OF HEAVEN   115 20
THE KINGDOM OF HEAVEN IS LIKENED UNTO A MAN WHICH   116 18
SHALL FALL FROM HEAVEN, AND THE POWERS OF THE HEAVENS   118 16
SHALL APPEAR THE SIGN OF THE SON OF MAN IN HEAVEN   118 18
IN THE CLOUDS OF HEAVEN WITH POWER AND GREAT GLORY   118 20
FROM ONE END OF HEAVEN TO THE OTHER   118 23
THE KINGDOM OF HEAVEN IS LIKE UNTO A MAN THAT IS AN   119 15
TREASURES IN HEAVEN, WHERE NEITHER MOTH NOR RUST DOTH   125 19
SOUGHT OF HIM A SIGN FROM HEAVEN   129 29
OF THINGS IN HEAVEN, AND THINGS IN EARTH,   134 25
LOOK DOWN FROM HEAVEN, AND BEHOLD FROM THE HABITATION   139 18
AND COMING IN THE CLOUDS OF HEAVEN   143 16
BUT INTO HEAVEN ITSELF, NOW TO APPEAR IN THE PRESENCE   147 32
UNTO HIM FROM HEAVEN, STRENGTHENING HIM   150 20
WHO IS GONE INTO HEAVEN, AND IS ON THE RIGHT HAND OF   162 02
STEDFASTLY TOWARD HEAVEN AS HE WENT UP, BEHOLD,   178 15
OF GALILEE, WHY STAND YE GAZING UP INTO HEAVEN   178 17
UP FROM YOU INTO HEAVEN, SHALL SO COME IN LIKE MANNER   178 18
IN LIKE MANNER AS YE HAVE SEEN HIM GO INTO HEAVEN   178 19
AND CARRIED UP INTO HEAVEN   178 26
WITH GREAT TRIUMPH UNTO THY KINGDOM IN HEAVEN   179 06
CAME A SOUND FROM HEAVEN AS OF A RUSHING MIGHTY WIND,   180 19
OUT OF EVERY NATION UNDER HEAVEN   180 26
A DOOR WAS OPENED IN HEAVEN   186 32
THRONE WAS SET IN HEAVEN, AND ONE SAT ON THE THRONE   187 05
CAME DOWN FROM HEAVEN, EVEN THE SON OF MAN WHICH IS   188 25
ASCENDED UP TO HEAVEN, BUT HE THAT CAME DOWN FROM   188 25
HEAVEN, EVEN THE SON OF MAN WHICH IS IN HEAVEN   188 26
JOY SHALL BE IN HEAVEN OVER ONE SINNER THAT   193 26
SHALL IN NO CASE ENTER INTO THE KINGDOM OF HEAVEN   197 30
THINGS BOTH IN HEAVEN AND EARTH   199 29
SHALL ENTER INTO THE KINGDOM OF HEAVEN   200 25
DOETH THE WILL OF MY FATHER WHICH IS IN HEAVEN   200 26
SINNED AGAINST HEAVEN, AND BEFORE THEE, AND AM NO   202 14
SINNED AGAINST HEAVEN, AND IN THY SIGHT, AND AM NO   202 19
AS HIS EYES UNTO HEAVEN, BUT SMOTE UPON HIS BREAST,   205 29
AND LOOKING UP TO HEAVEN, HE SIGHED, AND SAITH UNTO   207 02
THE BIRDS OF THE HEAVEN, THAT THEY SOW NOT, NEITHER   211 16
WHOLE FAMILY IN HEAVEN AND EARTH IS NAMED, THAT HE   212 13
THE KINGDOM OF HEAVEN IS LIKE UNTO A CERTAIN KING,   218 03
IS THE KINGDOM OF HEAVEN LIKENED UNTO A CERTAIN KING,   221 13
FOR OUR CITIZENSHIP IS IN HEAVEN   222 21
UP FOR YOU IN HEAVEN, WHEREOF YE HEARD BEFORE IN THE   223 26
THERE SHINED ROUND ABOUT HIM A LIGHT FROM HEAVEN   229 32
O FATHER, LORD OF HEAVEN AND EARTH, BECAUSE THOU HAST   235 04
BUT MY FATHER WHICH IS IN HEAVEN   246 06
GIVE UNTO THEE THE KEYS OF THE KINGDOM OF HEAVEN   246 10
THOU SHALT BIND ON EARTH SHALL BE BOUND IN HEAVEN   246 11
SHALT LOOSE ON EARTH SHALL BE LOOSED IN HEAVEN   246 12
WHICH CAME FROM HEAVEN WE HEARD, WHEN WE WERE WITH   248 20
THEE SERVICE IN HEAVEN, SO, BY THY APPOINTMENT,   251 30
THERE WAS WAR IN HEAVEN   252 03
NEITHER WAS THEIR PLACE FOUND ANY MORE IN HEAVEN   252 06
VOICE SAYING IN HEAVEN, NOW IS COME SALVATION,   252 10
WHO IS THE GREATEST IN THE KINGDOM OF HEAVEN   252 23
YE SHALL NOT ENTER INTO THE KINGDOM OF HEAVEN   252 27
THE SAME IS GREATEST IN THE KINGDOM OF HEAVEN   252 29
UNTO YOU, THAT IN HEAVEN THEIR ANGELS DO ALWAYS   253 11
BEHOLD THE FACE OF MY FATHER WHICH IS IN HEAVEN   253 12
FOR THEIR'S IS THE KINGDOM OF HEAVEN   257 22

HEAVEN   CONTINUED

FOR THEIR'S IS THE KINGDOM OF HEAVEN   257 30
FOR GREAT IS YOUR REWARD IN HEAVEN   257 34
LORD OF HEAVEN AND EARTH   261 29
BE THE CHILDREN OF YOUR FATHER WHICH IS IN HEAVEN   264 08
WHICH IS IN HEAVEN IS PERFECT   264 15
WHO COVERETH THE HEAVEN WITH CLOUDS, AND PREPARETH   264 27
DESCEND FROM HEAVEN WITH A SHOUT, WITH THE VOICE CF   269 05
I CAME DOWN FROM HEAVEN, NOT TO DO MINE OWN WILL, BUT   269 15
GIVEN UNTO ME IN HEAVEN AND IN EARTH   275 27
THE KINGDOM OF HEAVEN, AND EVERLASTING LIFE   276 23
THE KINGDOM OF HEAVEN, AND EVERLASTING LIFE   277 24
WHOLE FAMILY IN HEAVEN AND EARTH IS NAMED   281 08
OF GOD, AND AN INHERITOR OF THE KINGDOM OF HEAVEN   283 20
MAKER OF HEAVEN AND EARTH   284 14
HE ASCENDED INTO HEAVEN, AND SITTETH ON THE RIGHT   284 19
THING THAT IS IN HEAVEN ABOVE, OR IN THE EARTH   286 09
THE LORD MADE HEAVEN AND EARTH, THE SEA, AND ALL THAT   286 30
WHO HATH MADE HEAVEN AND EARTH   297 08
LOOK DOWN FROM HEAVEN, BEHOLD, VISIT, AND RELIEVE   309 04
ALL THINGS IN HEAVEN, IN EARTH, AND UNDER THE EARTH,   314 17
OTHER NAME UNDER HEAVEN GIVEN TO MAN, IN WHOM, AND   314 19
AND HIS PARDON SEALED IN HEAVEN   316 15
COMETH DOWN FROM HEAVEN, THAT A MAN MAY EAT THEREOF,   322 25
I AM THE LIVING BREAD WHICH CAME DOWN FROM HEAVEN   322 26
LORD OF HEAVEN AND EARTH, WE CONFESS THAT WE   323 12
WHO HATH MADE HEAVEN AND EARTH   327 22
THE SECOND MAN IS THE LORD FROM HEAVEN   329 28
A VOICE FROM HEAVEN, SAYING UNTO ME, WRITE, FROM   333 25
BY A VOICE FROM HEAVEN DIDST PROCLAIM, BLESSED ARE   335 26
WHO HATH MADE HEAVEN AND EARTH   339 06
WHO IS THE GREATEST IN THE KINGDOM OF HEAVEN   339 22
YE SHALL NOT ENTER INTO THE KINGDOM OF HEAVEN   339 26
THE SAME IS GREATEST IN THE KINGDOM OF HEAVEN   339 28
UNTO YOU, THAT IN HEAVEN THEIR ANGELS DO ALWAYS   339 31
BEHOLD THE FACE OF MY FATHER WHICH IS IN HEAVEN   339 32
OF THY LITTLE ONES DO ALWAYS BEHOLD IN HEAVEN   340 25
THAT DWELLETH IN HEAVEN SHALL LAUGH THEM TO SCORN   346 04
THE LORD'S SEAT IS IN HEAVEN   354 27
LOOKED DOWN FROM HEAVEN UPON THE CHILDREN OF MEN, *   356 16
THUNDERED OUT OF HEAVEN, AND THE HIGHEST GAVE HIS   360 24
PART OF THE HEAVEN, AND RUNNETH ABOUT UNTO THE END OF   363 24
HIM FROM HIS HOLY HEAVEN, *   364 27
O KING OF HEAVEN, *   365 02
LOOKETH DOWN FROM HEAVEN, AND BEHOLDETH ALL THE   379 14
HE SHALL CALL THE HEAVEN FROM ABOVE, *   401 28
LOOKED DOWN FROM HEAVEN UPON THE CHILDREN OF MEN, *   405 16
SHALL SEND FROM HEAVEN, *   409 17
35 LET HEAVEN AND EARTH PRAISE HIM   424 12
MOUTH UNTO THE HEAVEN, *   428 26
25 WHOM HAVE I IN HEAVEN BUT THEE   429 26
DIDST CAUSE THY JUDGMENT TO BE HEARD FROM HEAVEN   433 05
AND OPENED THE DOORS OF HEAVEN   436 17
AND GAVE THEM FOOD FROM HEAVEN   436 19
27 HE CAUSED THE EAST-WIND TO BLOW UNDER HEAVEN   436 22
LOOK DOWN FROM HEAVEN, *   441 31
AND RIGHTEOUSNESS HATH LOOKED DOWN FROM HEAVEN   446 30
AND HIS THRONE AS THE DAYS OF HEAVEN   451 34
AND AS THE FAITHFUL WITNESS IN HEAVEN   452 15
OUT OF THE HEAVEN DID THE LORD BEHOLD THE EARTH   465 18
LOOK HOW HIGH THE HEAVEN IS IN COMPARISON OF THE   466 27
HIS SEAT IN HEAVEN, *   467 13
AND HE FILLED THEM WITH THE BREAD OF HEAVEN   472 18
CARRIED UP TO THE HEAVEN, AND DOWN AGAIN TO THE DEEP   477 28
THAT ARE IN HEAVEN AND EARTH   484 18
3 AS FOR OUR GOD, HE IS IN HEAVEN   485 16
WHO MADE HEAVEN AND EARTH   486 08
ENDURETH FOR EVER IN HEAVEN   496 03
WHO HATH MADE HEAVEN AND EARTH   502 25
WHO HATH MADE HEAVEN AND EARTH   504 21
LORD THAT MADE HEAVEN AND EARTH *   509 29
THAT DID HE IN HEAVEN, AND IN EARTH   510 13
26 O GIVE THANKS UNTO THE GOD OF HEAVEN   512 34
I CLIMB UP INTO HEAVEN, THOU ART THERE   515 02
5 MADE HEAVEN AND EARTH, THE SEA, AND ALL THAT   522 12
WHO COVERETH THE HEAVEN WITH CLOUDS, AND PREPARETH   523 10
HIS PRAISE ABOVE HEAVEN AND EARTH   524 29
WAS ASCENDED INTO HEAVEN, SENT ABROAD INTO THE WORLD   545 17
GIVEN UNTO ME IN HEAVEN AND IN EARTH   552 10
WAS ASCENDED INTO HEAVEN, POURED DOWN HIS GIFTS   557 25
WHOM THE HEAVEN OF HEAVENS CANNOT CONTAIN, MUCH LESS   564 28
WHOM THE HEAVEN OF HEAVENS CANNOT CONTAIN   567 05
FROM GOD OUT OF HEAVEN, PREPARED AS A BRIDE ADORNED   567 13
VOICE OUT OF HEAVEN SAYING, BEHOLD, THE TABERNACLE OF   567 15
OF GOD, AND AN INHERITOR OF THE KINGDOM OF HEAVEN   577 11
MAKER OF HEAVEN AND EARTH   577 29
HE ASCENDED INTO HEAVEN, AND SITTETH ON THE RIGHT   578 01
THING THAT IS IN HEAVEN ABOVE, OR IN THE EARTH   578 28
THE LORD MADE HEAVEN AND EARTH, THE SEA, AND ALL THAT   579 10
HE ASCENDED INTO HEAVEN, AND THERE SITTETH, UNTIL HE   603 23

HEAVENLY

GOD OUR HEAVENLY FATHER   005 33
THRONE OF THE HEAVENLY GRACE, SAYING OR   006 12
O LORD, OUR HEAVENLY FATHER, ALMIGHTY AND EVERLASTING   017 13
O LORD, OUR HEAVENLY FATHER, THE HIGH AND MIGHTY   017 27
WITH HEAVENLY GIFTS   018 02
GOD OUR HEAVENLY FATHER   023 08
THRONE OF THE HEAVENLY GRACE, SAYING   023 21
O LORD GOD, HEAVENLY KING, GOD THE FATHER ALMIGHTY   025 25
OUR HEAVENLY FATHER, WHO HAST PURCHASED TO   038 25
THY GRACE AND HEAVENLY BENEDICTION   039 02
O GOD, HEAVENLY FATHER, WHO BY THY SON JESUS CHRIST   040 15
O GOD, HEAVENLY FATHER, WHOSE GIFT IT IS THAT THE   040 30

HEAVENLY   CONTINUED

EARTH BY THY HEAVENLY BENEDICTION   041 02
OUR HEAVENLY FATHER, IN WHOSE HANDS ARE THE   042 14
OUR HEAVENLY FATHER, WHO HAST COMMITTED TO THY   042 30
O LORD, OUR HEAVENLY FATHER, WHOSE BLESSED SON CAME   043 28
OUR HEAVENLY FATHER, WHO DECLAREST THY GLORY AND   044 17
OUR HEAVENLY FATHER, GUIDE, WE BESEECH THEE, THE   044 27
UNTO THAT HEAVENLY WISDOM WHICH LEADETH TO ETERNAL   045 09
O HEAVENLY FATHER, WATCH WITH US, WE PRAY THEE,   045 24
AND HEAVENLY FATHER, WHO HAST TAUGHT US IN THY   045 30
O GOD, OUR HEAVENLY FATHER, BY WHOSE GRACIOUS   051 15
OUR HEAVENLY FATHER, WHO ALONE MAKEST MEN TO BE   052 17
GOD AND HEAVENLY FATHER, WE GIVE THEE HUMBLE THANKS   053 10
GIVE GRACE, O HEAVENLY FATHER, TO ALL BISHOPS AND   074 21
PEOPLE GIVE THY HEAVENLY GRACE   074 25
OF THY HEAVENLY KINGDOM   075 04
OUR HEAVENLY FATHER, WHO OF HIS GREAT MERCY HATH   076 02
OUR HEAVENLY FATHER, FOR THAT THOU, OF THY   080 06
O LORD AND HEAVENLY FATHER, ACCORDING TO THE   080 36
THY GRACE AND HEAVENLY BENEDICTION, AND MADE ONE BODY   081 27
BESEECH THEE, O HEAVENLY FATHER, SO TO ASSIST US WITH   083 26
O LORD GOD, HEAVENLY KING, GOD THE FATHER ALMIGHTY   084 05
OUR HEAVENLY FATHER, FOR THAT HE HATH GIVEN HIS   087 02
CLEAN TO SUCH A HEAVENLY FEAST, IN THE   087 13
UNWORTHY OF THE HEAVENLY FEAST   089 06
OF THAT MOST HEAVENLY FOOD   089 18
OUR HEAVENLY FATHER   089 22
OF THE HEAVENLY HOST PRAISING GOD, AND SAYING, GLORY   099 20
AND POWERS IN HEAVENLY PLACES MIGHT BE KNOWN BY THE   108 24
THE HOPE OF THY HEAVENLY GRACE MAY EVERMORE BE   115 30
BUT THE HEAVENLY THINGS THEMSELVES WITH BETTER   147 29
MORE SHALL YOUR HEAVENLY FATHER GIVE THE HOLY SPIRIT   183 19
I TELL YOU OF HEAVENLY THINGS   188 24
GRANT THIS, O HEAVENLY FATHER, FOR THE SAKE OF JESUS   194 08
OF THY HEAVENLY TREASURE   204 26
TO ATTAIN THY HEAVENLY PROMISES   207 16
AND YOUR HEAVENLY FATHER FEEDETH THEM   211 17
FOR YOUR HEAVENLY FATHER KNOWETH THAT YE HAVE NEED OF   211 30
SHALL MY HEAVENLY FATHER DO ALSO UNTO YOU, IF YE FROM   222 05
GRANT THIS, O HEAVENLY FATHER, FOR THE SAKE OF JESUS   223 18
CHURCH WITH THE HEAVENLY DOCTRINE OF THY EVANGELIST   237 06
MORE SHALL YOUR HEAVENLY FATHER GIVE THE HOLY SPIRIT   263 12
YET YOUR HEAVENLY FATHER FEEDETH THEM   266 16
FOR YOUR HEAVENLY FATHER KNOWETH THAT YE HAVE NEED OF   266 28
OF THY HEAVENLY WASHING, AND MAY COME TO THE ETERNAL   274 20
WILL OF OUR HEAVENLY FATHER TOWARD THIS CHILD (THIS   276 04
HEAVENLY FATHER, WE GIVE THEE HUMBLE THANKS,   276 07
BE ENDUED WITH HEAVENLY VIRTUES, AND EVERLASTINGLY   278 28
THANK OUR HEAVENLY FATHER, THAT HE HATH CALLED ME TO   284 02
THY GRACE AND HEAVENLY BENEDICTION   295 02
CHILD WITH THY HEAVENLY GRACE   297 26
BESEECH THEE, O HEAVENLY FATHER, THAT THE CHILD OF   307 03
O GOD OF HEAVENLY POWERS, WHO, BY THE MIGHT OF THY   315 06
AND AS IS THE HEAVENLY, SUCH ARE THEY ALSO THAT ARE   329 30
SUCH ARE THEY ALSO THAT ARE HEAVENLY   329 30
WE SHALL ALSO BEAR THE IMAGE OF THE HEAVENLY   329 32
IN THY HEAVENLY KINGDOM   332 07
OF THY MERCY, O HEAVENLY FATHER, VOUCHSAFE THAT WE,   335 31
US ALL TO THY HEAVENLY KINGDOM   342 06
FOR THE HEAVENLY ASSISTANCE OF THE HOLY   541 17
THY GRACE AND HEAVENLY AID, AND FILL THE HEARTS WHICH   544 19
AND HEAVENLY FATHER, WHO, OF THINE INFINITE LOVE   545 12
SERVANTS THY HEAVENLY BLESSING   547 05
OUR HEAVENLY FATHER, WHO HATH GIVEN YOU A GOOD   555 28
THY GRACE AND HEAVENLY AID, AND FILL THE HEARTS WHICH   556 27
THY SERVANT THY HEAVENLY BLESSING   559 06
ACCEPTED BY OUR HEAVENLY FATHER   564 21
THY GRACE AND HEAVENLY BENEDICTION, MAY, TO THEIR   565 32
THANK OUR HEAVENLY FATHER, THAT HE HATH CALLED ME TO   577 23
LORD GOD, OUR HEAVENLY FATHER, WHO IS THE GIVER OF   580 29
O LORD, OUR HEAVENLY FATHER, ALMIGHTY AND EVERLASTING   592 19
O HEAVENLY FATHER, THOU UNDERSTANDEST ALL THY   596 11
O HEAVENLY FATHER, WHO HAST FILLED THE WORLD WITH   596 17
ALMIGHTY GOD, HEAVENLY FATHER, WHO HAST BLESSED US   596 24
GOD OUR HEAVENLY FATHER, WE BESEECH THEE GRACIOUSLY   597 21
O HEAVENLY FATHER, WE BESEECH THEE TO HAVE MERCY UPON   598 13
OUR HEAVENLY FATHER, WHO SETTEST THE SOLITARY IN   598 19
AND BY THY HEAVENLY GRACE PRESERVE FROM FALLING THOSE   599 12
TO HIGH AND HEAVENLY THINGS, AS WELL BECAUSE IT DOTH   606 20
ONLY AFTER AN HEAVENLY AND SPIRITUAL MANNER   608 45

HEAVENS

PASSED INTO THE HEAVENS, JESUS THE SON OF GOD, LET US   005 07
BY UNDERSTANDING HATH HE ESTABLISHED THE HEAVENS   005 25
THE HEAVENS, AND ALL THE POWERS THEREIN   010 11
O YE HEAVENS, BLESS YE THE LORD   012 04
OUT THE HEAVENS, AND RULEST THE RAGING OF THE SEA   042 04
HANDIWORK IN THE HEAVENS AND IN THE EARTH   044 19
OUT THE HEAVENS, AND RULEST THE RAGING OF THE SEA   046 08
AND THE HEAVENS ARE THE WORKS OF THINE HANDS   097 14
I SEE THE HEAVENS OPENED, AND THE SON OF MAN STANDING   100 08
HE SAW THE HEAVENS OPENED, AND THE SPIRIT, LIKE A   112 21
POWERS OF THE HEAVENS SHALL BE SHAKEN   118 16
OF THINGS IN THE HEAVENS SHOULD BE PURIFIED WITH   147 28
JESUS CHRIST TO HAVE ASCENDED INTO THE HEAVENS   177 16
UP FAR ABOVE ALL HEAVENS, THAT HE MIGHT FILL ALL   237 18
YE HEAVENS, AND YE THAT DWELL IN THEM   252 16
THOU THAT HAST SET THY GLORY ABOVE THE HEAVENS   350 33
I CONSIDER THY HEAVENS, EVEN THE WORK OF THY FINGERS   351 04
10 HE BOWED THE HEAVENS ALSO, AND CAME DOWN, *   360 15
THE HEAVENS DECLARE THE GLORY OF GOD   363 13
LORD WERE THE HEAVENS MADE   378 29
UNTO THE HEAVENS, *   384 04
6 AND THE HEAVENS SHALL DECLARE HIS RIGHTEOUSNESS   402 02

HEAVENS   CONTINUED

6 SET UP THYSELF, O GOD, ABOVE THE HEAVENS   409 24
UNTO THE HEAVENS, *   410 03
12 SET UP THYSELF, O GOD, ABOVE THE HEAVENS   410 04
MAGNIFY HIM THAT RIDETH UPON THE HEAVENS   419 17
AND THE HEAVENS DROPPED AT THE PRESENCE OF   419 26
SITTETH IN THE HEAVENS OVER ALL, FROM THE BEGINNING   421 22
THY TRUTH SHALT THOU STABLISH IN THE HEAVENS   450 08
O LORD, THE VERY HEAVENS SHALL PRAISE THY WONDROUS   450 13
12 THE HEAVENS ARE THINE, THE EARTH ALSO IS THINE   450 28
BUT IT IS THE LORD THAT MADE THE HEAVENS   460 09
11 LET THE HEAVENS REJOICE, AND LET THE EARTH BE   460 22
6 THE HEAVENS HAVE DECLARED HIS RIGHTEOUSNESS,   461 08
AND THE HEAVENS ARE THE WORK OF THY HANDS   465 32
OUT THE HEAVENS LIKE A CURTAIN   467 28
GREATER THAN THE HEAVENS, *   479 11
O GOD, ABOVE THE HEAVENS, *   479 13
AND HIS GLORY ABOVE THE HEAVENS   484 15
16 ALL THE WHOLE HEAVENS ARE THE LORD'S   486 10
O THOU THAT DWELLEST IN THE HEAVENS   503 28
5 WHO BY HIS EXCELLENT WISDOM MADE THE HEAVENS   511 24
5 BOW THY HEAVENS, O LORD, AND COME DOWN   519 31
O PRAISE THE LORD FROM THE HEAVENS   524 05
ALL YE HEAVENS, *   524 11
AND YE WATERS THAT ARE ABOVE THE HEAVENS   524 12
UP FAR ABOVE ALL HEAVENS, THAT HE MIGHT FILL ALL   538 05
THE HEAVEN OF HEAVENS CANNOT CONTAIN, MUCH LESS THE   564 28
THE HEAVEN OF HEAVENS CANNOT CONTAIN   567 05

HEAVILY

AND WHY GO I SO HEAVILY, WHILE THE ENEMY OPPRESSETH   310 09
I WENT HEAVILY, AS ONE THAT MOURNETH FOR HIS MOTHER   382 21
WHY GO I THUS HEAVILY, WHILE THE ENEMY OPPRESSETH ME 393 25
AND WHY GO I SO HEAVILY, WHILE THE ENEMY OPPRESSETH   394 07

HEAVINESS

THE GARMENT OF PRAISE FOR THE SPIRIT OF HEAVINESS   107 08
I FOUND TROUBLE AND HEAVINESS   305 22
WHEN I AM IN HEAVINESS, I WILL THINK UPON GOD   311 04
TURNED OUR HEAVINESS INTO JOY AND OUR MOURNING INTO   315 21
HEAVINESS MAY ENDURE FOR A NIGHT, BUT JOY COMETH IN   375 02
HAST TURNED MY HEAVINESS INTO JOY   375 16
AND MINE EYE IS CONSUMED FOR VERY HEAVINESS   376 09
WAXEN OLD WITH HEAVINESS, *   376 11
AND MY HEAVINESS IS EVER IN MY SIGHT   388 26
SO FULL OF HEAVINESS, O MY SOUL   393 11
WHEN MY HEART IS IN HEAVINESS   413 09
I AM FULL OF HEAVINESS   423 13
AM POOR AND IN HEAVINESS, *   424 02
3 WHEN I AM IN HEAVINESS, I WILL THINK UPON GOD   433 21
ALSO BROUGHT DOWN THEIR HEART THROUGH HEAVINESS   476 28
4 I FOUND TROUBLE AND HEAVINESS   486 25
28 MY SOUL MELTETH AWAY FOR VERY HEAVINESS   491 23
TROUBLE AND HEAVINESS HAVE TAKEN HOLD UPON ME   499 25
AND MELODY IN OUR HEAVINESS   513 10
SPIRIT WAS IN HEAVINESS, THOU KNEWEST MY PATH   518 07

HEAVY

TRAVAIL AND ARE HEAVY LADEN, AND I WILL REFRESH YOU   076 12
AND BEGAN TO BE SORE AMAZED, AND TO BE VERY HEAVY   141 31
THEIR EYES WERE HEAVY,) NEITHER WIST THEY WHAT TO   142 09
LABOUR AND ARE HEAVY LADEN, AND I WILL GIVE YOU REST 235 11
WERE WITH HIM WERE HEAVY WITH SLEEP   248 30
WHY ART THOU SO HEAVY, O MY SOUL   310 16
4 FOR THY HAND WAS HEAVY UPON ME DAY AND NIGHT,   377 28
CHASTEN ME IN THY HEAVY DISPLEASURE   387 22
A SORE BURDEN, TOO HEAVY FOR ME TO BEAR   387 29
THE MEANS OF THY HEAVY HAND   389 30
5 WHY ART THOU SO HEAVY, O MY SOUL   394 15
SHOWED THY PEOPLE HEAVY THINGS   412 17
AND THERE CAME UP HEAVY DISPLEASURE AGAINST ISRAEL   436 12
THEIR MOUTHS, THE HEAVY WRATH OF GOD CAME UPON THEM, 436 33

HEBREW

AND LATIN, AND HEBREW, THIS IS THE KING OF THE JEWS   154 33
BUT IN THE HEBREW, GABBATHA   159 24
IS CALLED IN THE HEBREW GOLGOTHA   159 33
IT WAS WRITTEN IN HEBREW, AND GREEK, AND LATIN   160 05

HEBREWS

ARE THEY HEBREWS   120 28

HEDGE

WALL SHALL YE BE, AND LIKE A BROKEN HEDGE   414 03
BROKEN DOWN HER HEDGE, *   441 26

HEDGES

THE HIGHWAYS AND HEDGES, AND COMPEL THEM TO COME IN, 192 19
ALL HIS HEDGES, *   452 20

HEED

TAKE YE GOOD HEED, LEST YE, WITHDRAWING YOURSELVES   088 25
HE STANDETH TAKE HEED LEST HE FALL   201 25
TAKE HEED THAT YE DESPISE NOT ONE OF THESE LITTLE   253 09
ON THY PART TAKE HEED THAT THIS CHILD LEARN THE   277 09
WILT THOU TAKE HEED THAT THIS CHILD, SO SOON AS   277 14
TAKE HEED THAT YE DESPISE NOT ONE OF THESE LITTLE   339 29

HEED   CONTINUED

AND TAKE HEED UNTO THE THING THAT IS   387 08
I SAID, I WILL TAKE HEED TO MY WAYS, *   389 05
2 TAKE HEED UNTO ME, AND HEAR ME, *   406 21
8 TAKE HEED, YE UNWISE AMONG THE PEOPLE   458 02
TAKE HEED THAT THE PERSONS, WHOM YE PRESENT UNTO US, 530 13
TAKE HEED THAT THE PERSONS, WHOM YE PRESENT UNTO US, 536 14
TAKE HEED THEREFORE UNTO YOURSELVES, AND TO ALL THE   550 26
SAYING, GIVE HEED UNTO READING, EXHORTATION,   558 21

HEELS

WICKEDNESS AT MY HEELS COMPASSETH ME ROUND ABOUT   400 15

HEIFER

THE ASHES OF AN HEIFER SPRINKLING THE UNCLEAN,   132 29

HEIGHT

IS THE BREADTH, AND LENGTH, AND DEPTH, AND HEIGHT   212 19
OR IN THE HEIGHT ABOVE   235 27
TO COME, NOR HEIGHT, NOR DEPTH, NOR ANY OTHER   331 12

HEIGHTEN

IN PRAISES, TO HEIGHTEN MY LOVE AND GRATITUDE   573 25

HEIGHTS

PRAISE HIM IN THE HEIGHTS   524 06

HEIR

HE HATH APPOINTED HEIR OF ALL THINGS, BY WHOM ALSO HE 096 25
NOW I SAY, THAT THE HEIR, AS LONG AS HE IS A CHILD,   104 14
IF A SON, THEN AN HEIR OF GOD THROUGH CHRIST   104 25
SHALL NOT BE HEIR WITH THE SON OF THE FREEWOMAN   131 17
AND BE MADE AN HEIR OF EVERLASTING SALVATION   276 13

HEIRS

AND ARE ALSO HEIRS THROUGH HOPE OF THY EVERLASTING   083 24
SONS OF GOD, AND HEIRS OF ETERNAL LIFE   117 06
HEIRS OF GOD, AND JOINT-HEIRS WITH CHRIST   200 11
AND IF CHILDREN, THEN HEIRS   200 11
AND IF CHILDREN, THEN HEIRS   330 24
HEIRS OF GOD, AND JOINT-HEIRS WITH CHRIST   330 24

HELD

BUT HE HELD HIS PEACE, AND ANSWERED NOTHING   143 12
THE CHIEF PRIESTS HELD A CONSULTATION WITH THE ELDERS 145 03
AND THE MEN THAT HELD JESUS MOCKED HIM, AND SMOTE   151 23
AND THEY HELD THEIR PEACE   214 03
3 FOR WHILST I HELD MY TONGUE, *   377 26
MOUTHS MUST BE HELD WITH BIT AND BRIDLE, ELSE THEY   378 11
3 I HELD MY TONGUE, AND SPAKE NOTHING   389 09
THOU DONE, AND I HELD MY TONGUE, AND THOU THOUGHTEST 402 32
THY MERCY, O LORD, HELD ME UP   458 23

HELL

HE DESCENDED INTO HELL, USE THE WORDS, HE WENT INTO   R 015 17
HE DESCENDED INTO HELL   015 24
HE DESCENDED INTO HELL, USE THE WORDS, HE WENT INTO   R 029 22
HE DESCENDED INTO HELL   029 29
AND IN HELL HE LIFT UP HIS EYES, BEING IN TORMENTS,   190 11
AND THE GATES OF HELL SHALL NOT PREVAIL AGAINST IT   246 08
HE DESCENDED INTO HELL   284 18
THOU SHALT NOT LEAVE MY SOUL IN HELL   358 10
5 THE PAINS OF HELL CAME ABOUT ME   360 02
HAST BROUGHT MY SOUL OUT OF HELL   374 28
HAST DELIVERED MY SOUL FROM THE NETHERMOST HELL   447 31
AND THE PAINS OF HELL GAT HOLD UPON ME   486 24
IF I GO DOWN TO HELL, THOU ART THERE ALSO   515 03
HE DESCENDED INTO HELL   578 02
IS IT TO BE BELIEVED, THAT HE WENT DOWN INTO HELL   603 19

HELL-FIRE

SHALL BE IN DANGER OF HELL-FIRE   198 07
THAN HAVING TWO EYES TO BE CAST INTO HELL-FIRE   253 09

HELMET

AND TAKE THE HELMET OF SALVATION, AND THE SWORD OF   219 18

HELP

AND FIND GRACE TO HELP IN TIME OF NEED   005 09
PRAY THEE, HELP THY SERVANTS, WHOM THOU HAST REDEEMED 010 33
AND GRANT US THY HELP IN THIS OUR NEED   041 22
USE OUR FREEDOM, HELP US TO EMPLOY IT IN THE   044 12
COMFORT, OUR ONLY HELP IN TIME OF NEED   045 13
BE DEFENDED BY THY MOST GRACIOUS AND READY HELP   049 15
AND FURTHER US WITH THY CONTINUAL HELP   049 25
THROUGH THY HELP, MAY FAITHFULLY LIVE ACCORDING   051 10
THROUGH THY HELP, MAY BOTH FAITHFULLY LIVE IN   053 15
AND TO COMFORT AND HELP THE WEAK-HEARTED   056 23
THEE TO SUCCOUR, HELP, AND COMFORT, ALL WHO ARE IN   056 27
O LORD, ARISE, HELP US, AND DELIVER US FOR THY NAME'S 058 26
O LORD, ARISE, HELP US, AND DELIVER US FOR THINE   059 03
THE COMFORT OF THY HELP AGAIN, *   061 02
SEND UNTO THEM HELP FROM ABOVE   061 32

HELP   CONTINUED

HELP US, O GOD OUR SAVIOUR	062 02
SO MAKE HASTE TO HELP US IN THIS WORLD, THAT WE MAY	062 24
MERCY MAY SPEEDILY HELP AND DELIVER US	095 08
THY RIGHT HAND TO HELP AND DEFEND US	112 28
OF OURSELVES TO HELP OURSELVES	127 16
SAYING, LORD, HELP ME	128 16
AND THERE WAS NONE TO HELP	138 23
THE LORD GOD WILL HELP ME	144 16
THE LORD GOD WILL HELP ME	144 21
MERCIFULLY WITH THY HELP, O LORD GOD OF OUR	147 08
SO BY THY CONTINUAL HELP WE MAY BRING THE SAME TO	163 26
GRANT US THE HELP OF THY GRACE, THAT IN KEEPING	189 03
NEVER FAILEST TO HELP AND GOVERN THOSE WHOM THOU DOST	191 04
SHOULD COME AND HELP THEM	196 21
KEEP US EVER BY THY HELP FROM ALL THINGS HURTFUL, AND	210 19
IT EVERMORE BY THY HELP AND GOODNESS	212 07
BY GOD'S HELP, WILL ENDEAVOUR NOT TO FOLLOW, NOR	276 29
I WILL, BY GOD'S HELP	277 07
I WILL, BY GOD'S HELP	277 13
BY GOD'S HELP, WILL ENDEAVOUR NOT TO FOLLOW, NOR	277 30
I WILL, BY GOD'S HELP	278 16
AND BY GOD'S HELP SO I WILL	283 30
LET US ASK GOD'S HELP TO KNOW AND TO KEEP THEM	285 19
HONOUR, AND HELP MY FATHER AND MOTHER	288 27
CHURCH PROVIDE TO HELP YOU TO DO ALL THESE THINGS	291 22
OUR HELP IS IN THE NAME OF THE LORD	297 10
THROUGH THY HELP, MAY FAITHFULLY LIVE ACCORDING	306 29
SEND HIM HELP FROM THY HOLY PLACE	308 25
THERE IS NO HELP FOR HIM IN HIS GOD	309 17
WHICH IS THE HELP OF MY COUNTENANCE, AND MY GOD	310 19
BESTOW UPON HIM THE HELP OF THY MERCIFUL CONSOLATION	311 23
TO THY SERVANT THE HELP OF THY POWER, THAT HIS	312 14
SAVE US, AND HELP US, WE HUMBLY BESEECH THEE, O LORD	313 13
COMFORT, OUR ONLY HELP IN TIME OF NEED	316 07
A VERY PRESENT HELP IN TROUBLE	327 03
GOD SHALL HELP HER, AND THAT RIGHT EARLY	327 13
FROM WHENCE COMETH MY HELP	327 20
MY HELP COMETH EVEN FROM THE LORD, *	327 21
FROM WHENCE COMETH MY HELP	339 04
MY HELP COMETH EVEN FROM THE LORD, *	339 05
THERE IS NO HELP FOR HIM IN HIS GOD	346 28
7 UP, LORD, AND HELP ME, O MY GOD, *	347 04
WHILE THERE IS NONE TO HELP	349 26
11 MY HELP COMETH OF GOD, *	350 13
20 TO HELP THE FATHERLESS AND POOR UNTO THEIR RIGHT,	354 15
HELP ME, LORD, FOR THERE IS NOT ONE GODLY MAN LEFT	355 06
AND WILL HELP EVERY ONE FROM HIM THAT SWELLETH	355 18
AND WITH THE HELP OF MY GOD I SHALL LEAP OVER THE	361 27
SHALL BE NONE TO HELP THEM	362 20
2 SEND THEE HELP FROM THE SANCTUARY, *	364 19
THERE IS NONE TO HELP ME	366 26
HASTE THEE TO HELP ME	367 11
FOR HE IS OUR HELP AND OUR SHIELD	379 29
AND STAND UP TO HELP ME	381 21
22 HASTE THEE TO HELP ME, *	389 03
O LORD, TO HELP ME	391 15
WHICH IS THE HELP OF MY COUNTENANCE, AND MY GOD	393 14
WHICH IS THE HELP OF MY COUNTENANCE, AND MY GOD	393 34
WHICH IS THE HELP OF MY COUNTENANCE, AND MY GOD	394 18
SEND HELP UNTO JACOB	394 32
MY SWORD THAT SHALL HELP ME	395 06
26 ARISE, AND HELP US, *	396 12
A VERY PRESENT HELP IN TROUBLE	397 25
GOD SHALL HELP HER, AND THAT RIGHT EARLY	398 03
THE COMFORT OF THY HELP AGAIN, *	403 33
THOU THEREFORE IS MY HELP, AND BEHOLD	411 12
HELP ME WITH THY RIGHT HAND, AND HEAR ME	412 21
FOR VAIN IS THE HELP OF MAN	413 02
11 O BE THOU OUR HELP IN TROUBLE	413 02
THY HELP, O GOD, SHALL LIFT ME UP	424 03
MAKE HASTE TO HELP ME, O LORD	424 21
HAST PROMISED TO HELP ME, FOR THOU ART MY HOUSE OF	425 09
HASTE THEE TO HELP ME	425 30
THE HELP THAT IS DONE UPON EARTH, HE DOETH IT	430 32
AND TO HELP ALL THE MEEK UPON EARTH	433 06
AND PUT NOT THEIR TRUST IN HIS HELP	436 15
9 HELP US, O GOD OF OUR SALVATION, FOR THE GLORY OF	440 18
AND COME AND HELP US	441 07
THY SERVANT, AND HELP THE SON OF THINE HANDMAID	448 07
I HAVE LAID HELP UPON ONE THAT IS MIGHTY, I HAVE	451 13
THERE WAS NONE TO HELP THEM	476 29
FOR VAIN IS THE HELP OF MAN	479 28
12 O HELP US AGAINST THE ENEMY	479 28
25 HELP ME, O LORD MY GOD	481 22
PART WITH THEM THAT HELP ME	488 12
BUT THE LORD WAS MY HELP	488 27
25 HELP ME NOW, O LORD	489 18
O BE THOU MY HELP	495 30
HELP ME, AND I SHALL KEEP THY TESTIMONIES	500 02
173 LET THINE HAND HELP ME	501 28
THY JUDGMENTS SHALL HELP ME	501 33
FROM WHENCE COMETH MY HELP	502 23
2 MY HELP COMETH EVEN FROM THE LORD, *	502 24
7 OUR HELP STANDETH IN THE NAME OF THE LORD, *	504 20
THEIR CRY, AND WILL HELP THEM	501 01
FOR THERE IS NO HELP IN THEM	522 07
OF JACOB FOR HIS HELP, *	522 10
AND TO HELP HIM IN THE DISTRIBUTION	533 13
WILL SO DO, BY THE HELP OF GOD	533 23
WILL SO DO, BY THE HELP OF THE LORD	542 18
IN SUCH STUDIES AS HELP TO THE KNOWLEDGE OF THE SAME,	542 27
SO HELP ME GOD, THROUGH JESUS CHRIST	552 32
WILL SO DO, BY THE HELP OF GOD	554 34
WILL SO DO, BY THE HELP OF GOD	555 19

HELP   CONTINUED

WILL SO BE, BY THE HELP OF GOD	555 22
AND TO ALL STRANGERS DESTITUTE OF HELP	555 25
I WILL SO SHOW MYSELF, BY GOD'S HELP	555 26
NOT TO HURT, BUT TO HELP	558 03
O LORD, ARISE, HELP US	562 02
AND FURTHER US WITH THY CONTINUAL HELP	571 10
AND BY GOD'S HELP SO I WILL	577 22

HELPED

MY HEART HATH TRUSTED IN HIM, AND I AM HELPED	373 23
OWN ARM THAT HELPED THEM	394 28
THE LORD HAD NOT HELPED ME, *	458 20
HE HELPED THEM FOR HIS NAME'S SAKE,	473 16
IN MISERY, AND HE HELPED ME	486 31

HELPER

ALL WHO NEED, THE HELPER OF ALL WHO FLEE TO THEE FOR	274 10
I WILL, GOD BEING MY HELPER	277 17
FOR THOU ART THE HELPER OF THE FRIENDLESS	354 08
BE MY STRONG HELPER, *	362 32
BE THOU MY HELPER	375 15
21 THOU ART MY HELPER AND REDEEMER	391 26
4 BEHOLD, GOD IS MY HELPER	406 10
8 BECAUSE THOU HAST BEEN MY HELPER	415 07
6 THOU ART MY HELPER, AND MY REDEEMER	424 32
AND HIM THAT HATH NO HELPER	427 21
HE IS THEIR HELPER AND DEFENDER	485 29
HE IS THEIR HELPER AND DEFENDER	485 31
HE IS THEIR HELPER AND DEFENDER	485 33
I WILL SO DO, THE LORD BEING MY HELPER	533 29
WILL ENDEAVOUR SO TO DO, THE LORD BEING MY HELPER	533 35
I WILL, THE LORD BEING MY HELPER	542 25
WILL ENDEAVOUR SO TO DO, THE LORD BEING MY HELPER	542 31
APPLY MYSELF THERETO, THE LORD BEING MY HELPER	543 05
I WILL SO DO, THE LORD BEING MY HELPER	543 10
I WILL SO DO, THE LORD BEING MY HELPER	543 16
I AM READY, THE LORD BEING MY HELPER	555 07
I WILL SO DO, THE LORD BEING MY HELPER	555 13

HELPETH

I THAT THE LORD HELPETH HIS ANOINTED, AND WILL HEAR	364 26
EVEN THE GOD WHO HELPETH US, AND POURETH HIS BENEFITS	420 23
41 YET HELPETH HE THE POOR OUT OF MISERY, *	478 28
6 WHO HELPETH THEM TO RIGHT THAT SUFFER WRONG	522 14
8 THE LORD HELPETH THEM THAT ARE FALLEN	522 18
AND HELPETH THE MEEK-HEARTED	525 09

HELPLESS

THE POOR HELPLESS MAN, THAT HE MIGHT SLAY HIM THAT	480 33
FOR I AM HELPLESS AND POOR, *	481 14
AND MAINTAIN THE CAUSE OF THE HELPLESS	517 03

HELPLESSNESS

HELPLESSNESS, GRIEF, TROUBLE, DREAD, OR	048 08

HEM

AND TOUCHED THE HEM OF HIS GARMENT	224 19

HEN

EVEN AS A HEN GATHERETH HER CHICKENS UNDER	100 30

HENCE

UNTO HIM, GET THEE HENCE, SATAN	127 09
BAPTIZED WITH THE HOLY GHOST NOT MANY DAYS HENCE	178 04
WOULD PASS FROM HENCE TO YOU CANNOT	190 21
TO TAKE HIM HENCE, TAKE HIM UNTO THY FAVOUR	314 11
BEFORE I GO HENCE, AND BE NO MORE SEEN	325 11
THOSE WHO DEPART HENCE IN THE LORD, AND WITH WHOM THE	334 20
BEFORE I GO HENCE, AND BE NO MORE SEEN	390 07
22 I GO HENCE LIKE THE SHADOW THAT DEPARTETH,	481 16
THEM THAT SOLD DOVES, TAKE THESE THINGS HENCE	567 32

HENCEFORTH

BEHOLD, FROM HENCEFORTH *	026 14
THAT WE MAY HENCEFORTH OBEDIENTLY WALK IN THY HOLY	052 23
WALKING FROM HENCEFORTH IN HIS HOLY WAYS	075 11
NOT SEE ME HENCEFORTH, TILL YE SHALL SAY, BLESSED IS	100 32
FROM HENCEFORTH EXPECTING TILL HIS ENEMIES BE MADE	158 07
FROM HENCEFORTH THOU SHALT CATCH MEN	196 28
THAT HENCEFORTH WE SHOULD NOT SERVE SIN	197 18
FROM HENCEFORTH LET NO MAN TROUBLE ME	211 04
THAT YE HENCEFORTH WALK NOT AS OTHER GENTILES	216 04
THAT WE HENCEFORTH BE NO MORE CHILDREN, TOSSED TO AND	237 25
AND FROM HENCEFORTH YE KNOW HIM, AND HAVE SEEN HIM	240 08
HENCEFORTH I CALL YOU NOT SERVANTS	241 28
HENCEFORTH THERE IS LAID UP FOR ME A CROWN OF	253 27
HENCEFORTH, WORLD WITHOUT END	297 10
FROM HENCEFORTH BLESSED ARE THE DEAD WHO DIE	333 26
HENCEFORTH, WORLD WITHOUT END	340 19
SEPARATING IT HENCEFORTH FROM ALL UNHALLOWED,	565 06

HERB

THE MOUNTAINS, AND HERB FOR THE USE OF MEN	264 29
AND BE WITHERED EVEN AS THE GREEN HERB	384 28

HERB CONTINUED

AND GREEN HERB FOR THE SERVICE OF MEN	468 22
THE MOUNTAINS, AND HERB FOR THE USE OF MEN	523 12

HEREAFTER

THAT WE MAY HEREAFTER LIVE A GODLY, RIGHTEOUS, AND	006 28
OF OUR LIFE HEREAFTER MAY BE PURE AND HOLY	007 17
ON THE DAYS HEREAFTER NAMED, IMMEDIATELY BEFORE THE	R 008 14
THAT WE MAY HEREAFTER LIVE A GODLY, RIGHTEOUS, AND	024 03
OF OUR LIFE HEREAFTER MAY BE PURE AND HOLY	024 19
WE MAY EVER HEREAFTER SERVE AND PLEASE THEE IN	075 28
HEREAFTER SHALL THE SON OF MAN SIT ON THE RIGHT HAND	151 32
BUT THOU SHALT KNOW HEREAFTER	156 04
HEREAFTER I WILL NOT TALK MUCH WITH YOU	182 07
I WILL SHEW THEE THINGS WHICH MUST BE HEREAFTER	187 03
IN TOKEN THAT HEREAFTER HE SHALL NOT BE ASHAMED TO	280 05
OR ELSE HEREAFTER FOR EVER HOLD HIS PEACE	300 22
MAY BE JOINED HEREAFTER WITH THY BLESSED SAINTS IN	336 08
TO THE FORM HEREAFTER FOLLOWING, OR HATH HAD	529 22
AND FORM AS HEREAFTER FOLLOWETH	R 535 26
BISHOP AND SOVEREIGN JUDGE OF ALL, HEREAFTER	569 27

HEREBY

YET AM I NOT HEREBY JUSTIFIED	094 09
HEREBY KNOW WE THAT WE DWELL IN HIM, AND HE IN US,	189 18
HEREBY PERCEIVE WE THE LOVE OF GOD, BECAUSE HE LAID	191 16
AND HEREBY WE KNOW THAT WE ARE OF THE TRUTH, AND	191 23
AND HEREBY WE KNOW THAT HE ABIDETH IN US, BY THE	191 33
THE SAME IS HEREBY ALLOWED FOR WEIGHTY CAUSE	R 336 32
AND ALSO HEREBY DO INSTITUTE YOU INTO SAID PARISH,	569 17
OF WRATH, WE ARE HEREBY MADE THE CHILDREN OF GRACE	581 26

HEREIN

FOR BISHOPS (AND HEREIN MORE ESPECIALLY FOR THE	047 23
AND DEACONS (AND HEREIN MORE ESPECIALLY FOR THE	047 26
PRINCIPAL CARE HEREIN WAS TO MAKE THEM CONFORMABLE TO	VI 18
AS IS HEREIN SPECIFIED, SHALL BE OBLIGED TO GIVE	R 085 18
OWN CONSCIENCE HEREIN, BUT REQUIRETH FURTHER COMFORT	088 05
HEREIN IS LOVE, NOT THAT WE LOVED GOD, BUT THAT HE	189 13
HEREIN IS OUR LOVE MADE PERFECT, THAT WE MAY HAVE	189 26
HEREIN IS MY FATHER GLORIFIED, THAT YE BEAR MUCH	238 19

HEREOF

AND THE FAME HEREOF WENT ABROAD INTO ALL THAT LAND	224 29

HERESIES

HERESIES, ENVYINGS, MURDERS, DRUNKENNESS,	209 22

HERESY

FALSE DOCTRINE, HERESY, AND SCHISM	055 03
FROM THE SINS OF HERESY AND SCHISM	574 13

HEREUNTO

FOR EVEN HEREUNTO WERE YE CALLED	172 09
WE HAVE HEREUNTO AFFIXED OUR EPISCOPAL SEAL AND	569 38

HERITAGE

SAVE THY PEOPLE, AND BLESS THINE HERITAGE	011 04
WHO HAST GIVEN US THIS GOOD LAND FOR OUR HERITAGE	036 10
LET NOT THINE HERITAGE BE BROUGHT TO CONFUSION	063 03
GIVE NOT THINE HERITAGE TO REPROACH, THAT THE HEATHEN	125 04
THE GIFT AND HERITAGE OF CHILDREN	303 16
I HAVE A GOODLY HERITAGE	358 03
CHOOSE OUT AN HERITAGE FOR US, *	398 27
HAST GIVEN AN HERITAGE UNTO THOSE THAT FEAR THY NAME	413 16
THEM FOR AN HERITAGE, AND MADE THE TRIBES OF ISRAEL	438 22
AND TROUBLE THINE HERITAGE	457 28
GIVE THEM THE HERITAGE OF THE HEATHEN	483 06
CLAIMED AS MINE HERITAGE FOR EVER	497 19
ARE AN HERITAGE AND GIFT THAT COMETH OF THE LORD	505 29
LAND TO BE AN HERITAGE, *	510 26
EVEN AN HERITAGE UNTO ISRAEL HIS PEOPLE	510 27
21 AND GAVE AWAY THEIR LAND FOR AN HERITAGE	512 24
22 EVEN FOR AN HERITAGE UNTO ISRAEL HIS SERVANT	512 26

HERMON

OF JORDAN, FROM HERMON AND THE LITTLE HILL	393 16
TABOR AND HERMON SHALL REJOICE IN THY NAME	450 32
AS THE DEW OF HERMON, *	509 18

HEROD

FOR HEROD WILL SEEK THE YOUNG CHILD TO DESTROY HIM	103 19
AND WAS THERE UNTIL THE DEATH OF HEROD	103 22
THEN HEROD, WHEN HE SAW THAT HE WAS MOCKED OF THE	103 24
WHEN HEROD WAS DEAD, BEHOLD, AN ANGEL OF THE LORD	107 12
ROOM OF HIS FATHER HEROD, HE WAS AFRAID TO GO	107 19
IN THE DAYS OF HEROD THE KING, BEHOLD, THERE CAME	108 31
WHEN HEROD THE KING HAD HEARD THESE THINGS, HE WAS	109 02
THEN HEROD, WHEN HE HAD PRIVILY CALLED THE WISE MEN,	109 10
NOT RETURN TO HEROD, THEY DEPARTED INTO THEIR OWN	109 24
HE SENT HIM TO HEROD, WHO HIMSELF ALSO WAS AT	153 09
AND WHEN HEROD SAW JESUS, HE WAS EXCEEDING GLAD	153 10
AND HEROD WITH HIS MEN OF WAR SET HIM AT NOUGHT, AND	153 16
DAY PILATE AND HEROD WERE MADE FRIENDS TOGETHER	153 19
NOR YET HEROD	153 26

HEROD CONTINUED

ABOUT THAT TIME HEROD THE KING STRETCHED FORTH HIS	244 31
AND WHEN HEROD WOULD HAVE BROUGHT HIM FORTH, THE SAME	245 09
OUT OF THE HAND OF HEROD, AND FROM ALL THE	245 28
ABOUT THAT TIME HEROD THE KING STRETCHED FORTH HIS	246 32

HEROD'S

HE BELONGED UNTO HEROD'S JURISDICTION, HE SENT HIM TO	153 08

HERODIANS

WITH THE HERODIANS, SAYING, MASTER, WE KNOW THAT THOU	222 30

HERSELF

SHE SAID WITHIN HERSELF, IF I MAY BUT TOUCH HIS	224 19

HEWED

6 HE THAT HEWED TIMBER AFORE OUT OF THE THICK TREES,	430 14

HEWETH

ONE BREAKETH AND HEWETH WOOD UPON THE EARTH	517 27

HEWN

WHICH HE HAD HEWN OUT IN THE ROCK	162 12
FORTH GOOD FRUIT IS HEWN DOWN, AND CAST INTO THE	200 22
HATH HEWN THE SNARES OF THE UNGODLY IN PIECES	506 27

HID

AND FROM WHOM NO SECRETS ARE HID	067 17
THE WORLD HATH BEEN HID IN GOD, WHO CREATED ALL	108 22
AND THIS SAYING WAS HID FROM THEM, NEITHER KNEW THEY	123 24
BUT JESUS HID HIMSELF, AND WENT OUT OF THE TEMPLE	133 33
TO THE SMITERS AND HID NOT HIS FACE FROM SHAME	144 07
I HID NOT MY FACE FROM SHAME AND SPITTING	144 15
AND YOUR LIFE IS HID WITH CHRIST IN GOD	164 06
BUT NOW THEY ARE HID FROM THINE EYES	204 09
BECAUSE THOU HAST HID THESE THINGS FROM THE WISE AND	235 05
BUT IF OUR GOSPEL BE HID, IT IS HID TO THEM THAT ARE	250 32
GOSPEL BE HID, IT IS HID TO THEM THAT ARE LOST	251 02
SAME NET WHICH THEY HID PRIVILY IS THEIR FOOT TAKEN	352 22
FILLEST WITH THY HID TREASURE	359 16
AND THERE IS NOTHING HID FROM THE HEAT THEREOF	363 26
HE HATH NOT HID HIS FACE FROM HIM	367 21
AND MINE UNRIGHTEOUSNESS HAVE I NOT HID	377 31
MY GROANING IS NOT HID FROM THEE	388 09
12 I HAVE NOT HID THY RIGHTEOUSNESS WITHIN MY HEART	391 04
I WOULD HAVE HID MYSELF FROM HIM	407 14
MY FAULTS ARE NOT HID FROM THEE	422 11
AND HID MINE ACQUAINTANCE OUT OF MY SIGHT	449 34
11 THY WORD HAVE I HID WITHIN MY HEART, *	490 20
14 MY BONES ARE NOT HID FROM THEE, *	515 18

HIDDEN

TO LIGHT THE HIDDEN THINGS OF DARKNESS, AND WILL MAKE	094 12
RENOUNCED THE HIDDEN THINGS OF DISHONESTY, NOT	250 29

HIDE

OF TROUBLE HE SHALL HIDE ME IN HIS TABERNACLE	326 12
DWELLING SHALL HE HIDE ME, AND SET ME UP UPON A ROCK	326 14
O HIDE NOT THOU THY FACE FROM ME	326 24
HOW LONG WILT THOU HIDE THY FACE FROM ME	355 29
HIDE ME UNDER THE SHADOW OF THY WINGS,	359 02
OF TROUBLE HE SHALL HIDE ME IN HIS TABERNACLE	372 04
DWELLING SHALL HE HIDE ME, AND SET ME UP UPON A ROCK	372 06
10 O HIDE NOT THOU THY FACE FROM ME, *	372 16
22 THOU SHALT HIDE THEM IN THE COVERT OF THINE OWN	377 06
THOU ART A PLACE TO HIDE ME IN	378 05
AND HIDE NOT THYSELF FROM MY PETITION	406 19
2 HIDE ME FROM THE GATHERING TOGETHER OF THE FROWARD,	415 21
18 AND HIDE NOT THY FACE FROM THY SERVANT	423 07
THAT WE SHOULD NOT HIDE THEM FROM THE CHILDREN OF THE	434 33
HOW LONG WILT THOU HIDE THYSELF	452 32
2 HIDE NOT THY FACE FROM ME IN THE TIME OF MY	464 12
O HIDE NOT THY COMMANDMENTS FROM ME	491 04
HIDE NOT THY FACE FROM ME, LEST I BE LIKE UNTO THEM	519 05
I FLEE UNTO THEE TO HIDE ME	519 11
MORTAL LIFE MAY HIDE FROM US THE LIGHT OF THAT LOVE	596 07

HIDEST

AND HIDEST THY FACE IN THE NEEDFUL TIME OF TROUBLE	353 03
24 WHEREFORE HIDEST THOU THY FACE, *	396 08
AND HIDEST THOU THY FACE FROM ME	449 24
29 WHEN THOU HIDEST THY FACE, THEY ARE TROUBLED	469 18

HIDETH

HE HIDETH AWAY HIS FACE, AND HE WILL NEVER SEE IT	353 31

HIEROME

OTHER BOOKS (AS HIEROME SAITH) THE CHURCH DOTH READ	604 02

HIGH

THUS SAITH THE HIGH AND LOFTY ONE THAT INHABITETH	003 25
I DWELL IN THE HIGH AND HOLY PLACE, WITH HIM ALSO	003 26

HIGH   CONTINUED

WE HAVE A GREAT HIGH PRIEST, THAT IS PASSED INTO THE   005 06
DAY-SPRING FROM ON HIGH HATH VISITED US   014 30
THE HIGH AND MIGHTY RULER OF THE UNIVERSE,   017 27
HOLY PLACE OF THE TABERNACLES OF THE MOST HIGH   022 28
GLORY BE TO GOD ON HIGH, AND ON EARTH PEACE, GOOD   025 22
ART MOST HIGH IN THE GLORY OF GOD THE FATHER   026 03
YIELD UNTO GOD MOST HIGH PRAISE AND HEARTY THANKS FOR   048 15
GLORY BE TO THEE, O LORD MOST HIGH   077 10
GLORY BE TO THEE, O LORD MOST HIGH   079 34
GLORY BE TO GOD ON HIGH, AND ON EARTH PEACE, GOOD   084 02
ART MOST HIGH IN THE GLORY OF GOD THE FATHER   084 14
THAT NOW IT IS HIGH TIME TO AWAKE OUT OF SLEEP   090 31
SAT DOWN ON THE RIGHT HAND OF THE MAJESTY ON HIGH   096 29
MIND NOT HIGH THINGS, BUT CONDESCEND TO MEN OF LOW   111 31
INTO AN EXCEEDING HIGH MOUNTAIN, AND SHEWETH HIM ALL   127 05
BEING COME AN HIGH PRIEST OF GOOD THINGS TO COME, BY   132 23
A SERVANT OF THE HIGH PRIEST, AND CUT OFF HIS EAR   142 23
JESUS AWAY TO THE HIGH PRIEST   142 32
THE PALACE OF THE HIGH PRIEST   142 34
AND THE HIGH PRIEST STOOD UP IN THE MIDST, AND ASKED   143 09
AGAIN THE HIGH PRIEST ASKED HIM, AND SAID UNTO HIM,   143 13
THEN THE HIGH PRIEST RENT HIS CLOTHES, AND SAITH,   143 16
OF THE MAIDS OF THE HIGH PRIEST   143 24
AS THE HIGH PRIEST ENTERETH INTO THE HOLY   148 02
THE SERVANT OF THE HIGH PRIEST, AND CUT OFF HIS RIGHT   150 33
HIM INTO THE HIGH PRIEST'S HOUSE   151 07
AND HAVING AN HIGH PRIEST OVER THE HOUSE OF GOD   158 19
SABBATH DAY WAS AN HIGH DAY,) BESOUGHT PILATE THAT   160 32
UNTIL YE BE ENDUED WITH POWER FROM ON HIGH   178 23
WICKEDNESS IN HIGH PLACES   219 10
WENT UNTO THE HIGH PRIEST, AND DESIRED OF HIM   229 26
HE ASCENDED UP ON HIGH, HE LED CAPTIVITY CAPTIVE,   237 14
THEE UP INTO THE HIGH MOUNTAIN   243 03
DAYSPRING FROM ON HIGH HATH VISITED US, TO GIVE LIGHT   244 14
UNTO THE MOST HIGH PRAISE AND HEARTY THANKS, FOR THE   336 17
AND I WILL PRAISE THE NAME OF THE LORD MOST HIGH   350 29
SENT DOWN FROM HIGH TO FETCH ME, *   360 31
BRING DOWN THE HIGH LOOKS OF THE PROUD   361 23
AND SETTETH ME UP ON HIGH   362 03
2 FOR THE LORD IS HIGH, AND TO BE FEARED   398 23
WHICH IS VERY HIGH EXALTED, DOTH DEFEND THE   399 07
2 HIGH AND LOW, RICH AND POOR, *   400 09
CALL UNTO THE MOST HIGH GOD, *   409 15
EVEN AN HIGH HILL, AS THE HILL OF BASHAN   420 11
WHY MOCK YE SO, YE HIGH HILLS   420 13
THOU ART GONE UP ON HIGH, THOU HAST LED CAPTIVITY   420 19
O GOD, IS VERY HIGH, *   426 14
CORN IN THE EARTH, HIGH UPON THE HILLS   427 29
THEIR TALKING IS AGAINST THE MOST HIGH   428 25
IS THERE KNOWLEDGE IN THE MOST HIGH   428 31
NOT UP YOUR HORN ON HIGH, *   432 08
AND THAT THE HIGH GOD WAS THEIR REDEEMER   437 09
DISPLEASED THE MOST HIGH GOD, *   438 24
BUILT HIS TEMPLE ON HIGH, *   439 16
AND THE MOST HIGH SHALL STABLISH HER   448 23
IS THY HAND, AND HIGH IS THY RIGHT HAND   450 34
DEFENCE OF THE MOST HIGH,   454 29
THOU HAST SET THINE HOUSE OF DEFENCE VERY HIGH   455 14
WHO DWELLETH ON HIGH, IS MIGHTIER   457 14
AND HIGH ABOVE ALL PEOPLE   462 19
11 FOR LOOK HOW HIGH THE HEAVEN IS IN COMPARISON OF   466 27
8 THEY GO UP AS HIGH AS THE HILLS, AND DOWN TO THE   468 08
18 THE HIGH HILLS ARE A REFUGE FOR THE WILD GOATS   468 30
4 THE LORD IS HIGH ABOVE ALL NATIONS, *   484 14
HIS DWELLING SO HIGH, *   484 17
WHICH ARE TOO HIGH FOR ME   507 26
THOUGH THE LORD BE HIGH, YET HATH HE RESPECT UNTO THE   514 08
HE ASCENDED UP ON HIGH, HE LED CAPTIVITY CAPTIVE,   537 34
INTO HOW HIGH A DIGNITY, AND TO HOW WEIGHTY AN OFFICE   539 30
PLACED YOU IN SO HIGH A DIGNITY   540 28
THE GIFT OF GOD MOST HIGH   544 22
THE GIFT OF GOD MOST HIGH   556 30
UP THEIR MIND TO HIGH AND HEAVENLY THINGS, AS WELL   606 19

HIGH-MINDED

I AM NOT HIGH-MINDED   507 24

HIGHER

SUBJECT UNTO THE HIGHER POWERS   114 11
HE MAY SAY UNTO THEE, FRIEND, GO UP HIGHER   214 17
THE ROCK THAT IS HIGHER THAN I   413 10
HIGHER THAN THE KINGS OF THE EARTH   451 29
THOU, LORD, ART HIGHER THAN ALL THAT ARE IN THE   461 14
CALLED UNTO THE HIGHER MINISTRIES IN THY CHURCH   535 09

HIGHEST

SHALT BE CALLED THE PROPHET OF THE HIGHEST   014 24
AND TO SING PRAISES UNTO THY NAME, O MOST HIGHEST   027 29
HOSANNA IN THE HIGHEST   091 30
TO GOD IN THE HIGHEST, AND ON EARTH PEACE, GOOD WILL   099 21
NOT DOWN IN THE HIGHEST SEAT   214 11
AND SHALL BE CALLED THE SON OF THE HIGHEST   236 17
THE POWER OF THE HIGHEST SHALL OVERSHADOW THEE   236 23
SHALT BE CALLED THE PROPHET OF THE HIGHEST   244 10
THE YEARS OF THE RIGHT HAND OF THE MOST HIGHEST   311 19
HOLY PLACE OF THE TABERNACLE OF THE MOST HIGHEST   327 11
WILL I MAKE OF THY NAME, O THOU MOST HIGHEST   351 25
I WILL PRAISE THE NAME OF THE LORD MOST HIGHEST   356 11
AND THE HIGHEST GAVE HIS THUNDER   360 25
OF THE MOST HIGHEST HE SHALL NOT MISCARRY   365 18
HOLY PLACE OF THE TABERNACLE OF THE MOST HIGHEST   397 34

HIGHEST   CONTINUED

AND PAY THY VOWS UNTO THE MOST HIGHEST   402 19
MANY THAT FIGHT AGAINST ME, O THOU MOST HIGHEST   408 18
THE YEARS OF THE RIGHT HAND OF THE MOST HIGHEST   434 03
THE MOST HIGHEST IN THE WILDERNESS   436 03
AND YE ARE ALL THE CHILDREN OF THE MOST HIGHEST   443 30
ONLY THE MOST HIGHEST OVER ALL THE EARTH   445 09
AND TO SING PRAISES UNTO THY NAME, O MOST HIGHEST   455 33
ART THE MOST HIGHEST FOR EVERMORE   456 15
LIGHTLY REGARDED THE COUNSEL OF THE MOST HIGHEST   476 27

HIGHLY

GOD ALSO HATH HIGHLY EXALTED HIM, AND GIVEN HIM A   105 26
OF HIMSELF MORE HIGHLY THAN HE OUGHT TO THINK   110 11
GOD ALSO HATH HIGHLY EXALTED HIM, AND GIVEN HIM A   134 23
THOU THAT ART HIGHLY FAVOURED, THE LORD IS WITH THEE   236 09
IS THE LORD, AND HIGHLY TO BE PRAISED *   399 10

HIGHWAY

IN THE DESERT A HIGHWAY FOR OUR GOD   004 07
IN THE DESERT A HIGHWAY FOR OUR GOD   242 22

HIGHWAYS

DEEP WATERS AND HIGHWAYS IN THE DESERT   038 18
GO OUT INTO THE HIGHWAYS AND HEDGES, AND COMPEL THEM   192 18
INTO THE HIGHWAYS, AND AS MANY AS YE SHALL FIND,   218 18
OUT INTO THE HIGHWAYS, AND GATHERED TOGETHER ALL AS   218 19

HILL

ME UNTO THY HOLY HILL, AND TO THY DWELLING   003 23
EVERY MOUNTAIN AND HILL SHALL BE MADE LOW   242 23
THROUGHOUT ALL THE HILL COUNTRY OF JUDAEA   243 28
ROUND ABOUT MY HILL A BLESSING   262 07
AND HE HEARD ME OUT OF HIS HOLY HILL   309 12
MY VOICE, AND HE HEARD ME OUT OF HIS HOLY HILL   309 21
ME UNTO THY HOLY HILL, AND TO THY DWELLING   310 12
UPON MY HOLY HILL OF SION   346 08
AND HE HEARD ME OUT OF HIS HOLY HILL   346 32
THAT SHE SHOULD FLEE AS A BIRD UNTO THE HILL   354 20
OR WHO SHALL REST UPON THY HOLY HILL   357 06
ASCEND INTO THE HILL OF THE LORD   368 32
HAST MADE MY HILL SO STRONG   375 05
LAND OF JORDAN, FROM HERMON AND THE LITTLE HILL   393 17
ME UNTO THY HOLY HILL, AND TO THY DWELLING   394 10
IN THE CITY OF OUR GOD, EVEN UPON HIS HOLY HILL   399 11
2 THE HILL OF SION IS A FAIR PLACE, AND THE JOY OF   399 12
15 AS THE HILL OF BASHAN, SO IS GOD'S HILL   420 11
15 AS THE HILL OF BASHAN, SO IS GOD'S HILL   420 11
HIGH HILL, AS THE HILL OF BASHAN   420 12
EVEN AN HIGH HILL, AS THE HILL OF BASHAN   420 12
THIS IS GOD'S HILL, IN THE WHICH IT PLEASETH HIM TO   420 13
EVEN THE HILL OF SION WHICH HE LOVED   439 14
AND WORSHIP HIM UPON HIS HOLY HILL   463 03
WHICH FELL UPON THE HILL OF SION   509 18
ASCEND INTO THE HILL OF THE LORD   563 15

HILL-ALTARS

WITH THEIR HILL-ALTARS, *   438 28

HILLS

STRENGTH OF THE HILLS IS HIS ALSO   009 10
O YE MOUNTAINS AND HILLS, BLESS YE THE LORD   013 04
AND LET THE HILLS BE JOYFUL TOGETHER BEFORE   027 21
AND TO THE HILLS, COVER US   154 19
AND THOUGH THE HILLS BE CARRIED INTO THE MIDST OF THE   327 06
I WILL LIFT UP MINE EYES UNTO THE HILLS   327 19
I WILL LIFT UP MINE EYES UNTO THE HILLS   339 03
ALSO OF THE HILLS SHOOK, AND WERE REMOVED, BECAUSE HE   360 10
AND THOUGH THE HILLS BE CARRIED INTO THE MIDST OF THE   397 28
AND SO ARE THE CATTLE UPON A THOUSAND HILLS   402 11
AND THE LITTLE HILLS SHALL REJOICE ON EVERY SIDE   417 10
16 WHY MOCK YE SO, YE HIGH HILLS   420 13
AND THE LITTLE HILLS RIGHTEOUSNESS UNTO THE PEOPLE   427 03
AN HEAP OF CORN IN THE EARTH, HIGH UPON THE HILLS   427 30
COMEST FROM THE HILLS OF THE ROBBERS   432 29
10 THE HILLS WERE COVERED WITH THE SHADOW OF IT,   441 22
HER FOUNDATIONS ARE UPON THE HOLY HILLS   448 13
STRENGTH OF THE HILLS IS HIS ALSO   459 12
5 THE HILLS MELTED LIKE WAX AT THE PRESENCE OF THE   461 06
AND LET THE HILLS BE JOYFUL TOGETHER BEFORE   462 10
THE WATERS STAND ABOVE THE HILLS   468 05
UP AS HIGH AS THE HILLS, AND DOWN TO THE VALLEYS   468 08
WHICH RUN AMONG THE HILLS   468 14
13 HE WATERETH THE HILLS FROM ABOVE   468 19
18 THE HIGH HILLS ARE A REFUGE FOR THE WILD GOATS   468 30
DO BUT TOUCH THE HILLS, THEY SHALL SMOKE   469 26
AND THE LITTLE HILLS LIKE YOUNG SHEEP   484 32
AND YE LITTLE HILLS, LIKE YOUNG SHEEP   485 05
I WILL LIFT UP MINE EYES UNTO THE HILLS   502 22
A THE HILLS STAND ABOUT JERUSALEM   504 26
9 MOUNTAINS AND ALL HILLS   524 22

HIMSELF

AND GOD HIMSELF SHALL BE WITH THEM, AND BE   021 30
HATH HE GOTTEN HIMSELF THE VICTORY   027 07
ONE OBLATION OF HIMSELF ONCE OFFERED) A FULL,   080 10
IN BOTH KINDS HIMSELF, AND PROCEED TO DELIVER THE   R 082 25
OPENLY DECLARED HIMSELF TO HAVE TRULY REPENTED AND   R 085 04

HIMSELF   CONTINUED

AT LEAST DECLARE HIMSELF TO BE IN FULL PURPOSE SC TO   R 085 07
THAT WHEREIN HE HIMSELF HATH OFFENDED   R 085 14
WHO DID HUMBLE HIMSELF, EVEN TC THE DEATH UPCN THE   086 08
SO LOVINGLY CALLED AND BIDDEN BY GOD HIMSELF   088 17
HIS DEATH, AS HE HIMSELF HATH COMMANDED   089 13
WHEN HE HAD BY HIMSELF PURGED OUR SINS, SAT DOWN ON   096 28
WHO GAVE HIMSELF FOR LS, THAT HE MIGHT REDEEM US FROM   098 23
AND PURIFY UNTO HIMSELF A PECULIAR PEOPLE, ZEALCUS OF   098 24
NOT TO THINK OF HIMSELF MORE HIGHLY THAN HE OUGHT TO   110 10
IN HIM PURIFIETH HIMSELF, EVEN AS HE IS PURE   117 21
IF A MAN EXALT HIMSELF, IF A MAN SMITE YOU ON THE   120 24
AND HATH GIVEN HIMSELF FOR US AN OFFERING AND A   128 32
DIVIDED AGAINST HIMSELF, HOW SHALL HIS KINGDOM STAND   129 32
HIM SEVEN OTHER SPIRITS MORE WICKED THAN HIMSELF   130 15
FOR HE HIMSELF KNEW WHAT HE WOULD DO   131 29
SPIRIT OFFERED HIMSELF WITHOUT SPOT TO GOD, PURGE   133 02
BUT JESUS HID HIMSELF, AND WENT OUT OF THE TEMPLE   133 33
BUT MADE HIMSELF OF NO REPUTATION, AND TOCK UPCN HIM   134 18
HE HUMBLED HIMSELF, AND BECAME OBEDIENT UNTO   134 21
REPENTED HIMSELF, AND BROUGHT AGAIN THE THIRTY PIECES   135 03
AND WENT AND HANGED HIMSELF   135 08
HIMSELF HE CANNOT SAVE   137 10
TO MAKE HIMSELF AN EVERLASTING NAME   139 12
AND WARMED HIMSELF AT THE FIRE   142 35
PETER WARMING HIMSELF, SHE LOOKED UPON HIM, AND SAID,   143 24
HIMSELF HE CANNOT SAVE   146 22
HE SHOULD OFFER HIMSELF OFTEN, AS THE HIGH PRIEST   148 02
TO PUT AWAY SIN BY THE SACRIFICE OF HIMSELF   148 07
SAYING THAT HE HIMSELF IS CHRIST A KING   152 30
TO HEROD, WHO HIMSELF ALSO WAS AT JERUSALEM AT THAT   153 09
LET HIM SAVE HIMSELF, IF HE BE CHRIST, THE CHOSEN OF   154 29
AND TOOK A TOWEL, AND GIRDED HIMSELF   155 32
BECAUSE HE MADE HIMSELF THE SON OF GOD   159 10
WHOSOEVER MAKETH HIMSELF A KING, SPEAKETH AGAINST   159 21
WHO ALSO HIMSELF WAS JESUS' DISCIPLE   162 07
SON DID MANIFEST HIMSELF TO HIS DISCIPLES IN THE   166 06
JESUS HIMSELF DREW NEAR, AND WENT WITH   167 07
ALL THE SCRIPTURES THE THINGS CONCERNING HIMSELF   167 33
JESUS HIMSELF STOOD IN THE MIDST OF THEM, AND SAITH   169 28
ON THE SON OF GOD HATH THE WITNESS IN HIMSELF   171 07
BUT COMMITTED HIMSELF TO HIM THAT JUDGETH   172 14
FOR HE SHALL NOT SPEAK OF HIMSELF   175 20
FOR HE BEHOLDETH HIMSELF, AND GOETH HIS WAY, AND   176 08
AND TO KEEP HIMSELF UNSPOTTED FROM THE WORLD   176 17
FOR THE FATHER HIMSELF LOVETH YOU, BECAUSE YE HAVE   176 28
ALSO HE SHEWED HIMSELF ALIVE AFTER HIS PASSION BY   177 26
THE SPIRIT HIMSELF BEARETH WITNESS WITH OUR SPIRIT,   200 10
WENT AND JOINED HIMSELF TO A CITIZEN OF THAT COUNTRY   202 06
WHEN HE CAME TO HIMSELF, HE SAID, HOW MANY HIRED   202 10
PRAYED THUS WITH HIMSELF, GOD, I THANK THEE, THAT I   205 25
THAT EXALTETH HIMSELF SHALL BE ABASED   205 33
HE THAT HUMBLETH HIMSELF SHALL BE EXALTED   205 33
TO JUSTIFY HIMSELF, SAID UNTO JESUS, AND WHO IS MY   208 19
EXALTETH HIMSELF SHALL BE ABASED   214 19
HE THAT HUMBLETH HIMSELF SHALL BE EXALTED   214 20
AND HIMSELF BELIEVED, AND HIS WHOLE HOUSE   220 10
IS ABLE EVEN TO SUBJECT ALL THINGS UNTO HIMSELF   222 26
FOR HE HIMSELF KNEW WHAT HE WOULD DO   225 25
THE LORD HIMSELF SHALL GIVE YOU A SIGN   235 31
WAS COME TO HIMSELF, HE SAID, NOW I KNOW OF A SURETY,   245 26
NO MAN JOIN HIMSELF TO THEM   249 24
SHALL HUMBLE HIMSELF AS THIS LITTLE CHILD, THE SAME   252 28
WHITHER HE HIMSELF WOLD COME   254 13
JESUS CHRIST HIMSELF BEING THE HEAD CORNER-STONE   254 29
JESUS CHRIST HIMSELF BEING THE CHIEF CORNER-STONE   255 06
FOR HE BEHOLDETH HIMSELF, AND GOETH HIS WAY, AND   265 31
AND TO KEEP HIMSELF UNSPOTTED FROM THE WORLD   266 08
AND GAVE HIMSELF FOR IT   267 20
PRESENT IT TO HIMSELF A GLORIOUS CHURCH, NOT HAVING   267 22
HE THAT LOVETH HIS WIFE LOVETH HIMSELF   267 26
IN PARTICULAR SO LOVE HIS WIFE EVEN AS HIMSELF   268 02
FOR THE LORD HIMSELF SHALL DESCEND FROM HEAVEN WITH A   269 05
JESUS CHRIST HIMSELF BEING THE HEAD CORNER-STONE   290 21
BY CHRIST HIMSELF, AS A MEANS WHEREBY WE RECEIVE THIS   292 12
THE LORD ABSENT HIMSELF FOR EVER   311 12
THE COMMUNION HIMSELF, AND AFTER MINISTER UNTO THOSE   R 322 34
AND DISQUIETETH HIMSELF IN VAIN   324 25
THE LORD HIMSELF IS THY KEEPER   327 27
THE SON ALSO HIMSELF BE SUBJECT UNTO HIM THAT PUT ALL   329 02
THE SPIRIT HIMSELF BEARETH WITNESS WITH OUR SPIRIT,   330 22
HE IS ABLE TO SUBDUE ALL THINGS UNTO HIMSELF   333 23
HE IS ABLE TO SUBDUE ALL THINGS UNTO HIMSELF   337 17
THE LORD HIMSELF IS THY KEEPER   339 11
SHALL HUMBLE HIMSELF AS THIS LITTLE CHILD, THE SAME   339 27
WILL HE EXERCISE HIMSELF DAY AND NIGHT   345 11
HATH CHOSEN TO HIMSELF THE MAN THAT IS GODLY   347 16
AND IS FALLEN HIMSELF INTO THE DESTRUCTION THAT HE   350 24
AND HUMBLETH HIMSELF, *   353 27
POOR COMMITTETH HIMSELF UNTO THEE   354 07
SETTETH NOT BY HIMSELF, BUT IS LOWLY IN HIS OWN EYES,   357 13
6 THE LORD HIMSELF IS THE PORTION OF MINE   357 31
HIS NET THAT HE HATH LAID PRIVILY CATCH HIMSELF   382 05
HE FLATTERETH HIMSELF IN HIS OWN SIGHT, *   383 28
OFF TO BEHAVE HIMSELF WISELY, AND TO DO GCCD   383 31
AND HATH SET HIMSELF IN NO GOOD WAY   384 02
AND MAKETH HIS WAY ACCEPTABLE TO HIMSELF   386 09
AND DISQUIETETH HIMSELF IN VAIN   389 21
AND HIS HEART CONCEIVETH FALSEHOOD WITHIN HIMSELF   392 11
HE COUNTED HIMSELF AN HAPPY MAN   401 11
FOR GOD IS JUDGE HIMSELF   402 03
AND STRENGTHENED HIMSELF IN HIS WICKEDNESS   405 03
THAT DID MAGNIFY HIMSELF AGAINST ME   407 13
HELP THAT IS DONE UPON EARTH, HE DOETH IT HIMSELF   430 33
THE LORD ABSENT HIMSELF FOR EVER   433 29

HIMSELF   CONTINUED

AND GIRDED HIMSELF WITH STRENGTH   457 05
HATH HE GOTTEN HIMSELF THE VICTORY   461 28
17 HE CLOTHED HIMSELF WITH CURSING LIKE AS WITH A   481 05
AND YET HUMBLETH HIMSELF TO BEHOLD THE THINGS THAT   484 17
EVEN BY RULING HIMSELF AFTER THY WORD   490 17
5 THE LORD HIMSELF IS THY KEEPER   502 30
IF THE LORD HIMSELF HAD NOT BEEN ON OUR SIDE,   504 07
IF THE LORD HIMSELF HAD NOT BEEN ON OUR SIDE, WHEN   504 08
HATH CHOSEN SION TO BE AN HABITATION FOR HIMSELF   508 33
BUT UPON HIMSELF SHALL HIS CROWN FLOURISH   509 11
JACOB UNTO HIMSELF, *   510 09
EITHER BY HIMSELF, OR BY SUFFICIENT TESTIMONY,   529 26
IF THOU BE THERETO LICENSED BY THE BISHOP HIMSELF   534 13
HE SHALL GIRD HIMSELF, AND MAKE THEM TO SIT DOWN TO   534 22
AND GOD HIMSELF SHALL BE WITH THEM, AND BE   567 17
SUPPLICATION FOR HIMSELF, IN THIS FORM   R 573 10
JESUS CHRIST HIMSELF BEING THE CHIEF CORNER-STONE   574 05
BY CHRIST HIMSELF, AS A MEANS WHEREBY WE RECEIVE THE   581 14
TURN AND PREPARE HIMSELF, BY HIS OWN NATURAL STRENGTH   604 43
BY SACRIFICE OF HIMSELF ONCE MADE, SHOULD TAKE AWAY   605 33

HINDER

ELSE MAY HINDER US FROM GODLY UNION AND CONCORD   037 29

HINDERED

I AM OTHERWISE HINDERED WITH WORLDLY BUSINESS   088 28
SORE LET AND HINDERED IN RUNNING THE RACE THAT IS SET   095 07

HINDERER

OF GOD, AN HINDERER OR SLANDERER OF HIS WORD, AN   087 31

HINDRANCE

THOUGH IT WERE TO HIS OWN HINDRANCE   357 16
ANY HURT OR HINDRANCE BY REASON OF YOUR NEGLIGENCE,   540 11

HINDS

LORD MAKETH THE HINDS TO BRING FORTH YOUNG, AND   374 14

FIRE

IN THE MORNING TO HIRE LABOURERS INTO HIS VINEYARD   119 17
AND GIVE THEM THEIR HIRE, BEGINNING FROM THE LAST   119 30
FOR THE LABOURER IS WORTHY OF HIS HIRE   254 23
AND SUFFER NOT THE HIRE OF THE LABOURERS TO BE KEPT   599 30

HIRED

NO MAN HATH HIRED US   119 26
CAME THAT WERE HIRED ABOUT THE ELEVENTH HOUR, THEY   119 31
HE SAID, HOW MANY HIRED SERVANTS OF MY FATHER'S HAVE   202 11
ME AS ONE OF THY HIRED SERVANTS   202 15

HIRELING

HE THAT IS AN HIRELING, AND NOT THE SHEPHERD, WHCSE   172 22
THE HIRELING FLEETH, BECAUSE HE IS AN HIRELING, AND   172 25
HE IS AN HIRELING, AND CARETH NOT FOR THE SHEEP   172 26
OPPRESS THE HIRELING IN HIS WAGES, THE WIDOW, AND THE   232 18
HE THAT IS AN HIRELING, AND NOT THE SHEPHERD, WHCSE   539 11
THE HIRELING FLEETH, BECAUSE HE IS AN HIRELING, AND   539 14
HE IS AN HIRELING, AND CARETH NOT FOR THE SHEEP   539 15

HIT

SUDDENLY DO THEY HIT HIM, AND FEAR NOT   415 26

HITHER

BROUGHT HITHER OUT OF MANY KINDREDS AND TONGUES   036 16
COME UP HITHER, AND I WILL SHEW THEE THINGS   187 03
AND BRING IN HITHER THE POOR, AND THE MAIMED, AND THE   192 15
AND BRING HITHER THE FATTED CALF, AND KILL IT   202 23
CAMEST THOU IN HITHER NOT HAVING A WEDDING-GARMENT   218 24
TO THOMAS, REACH HITHER THY FINGER, AND BEHOLD MY   229 03
AND REACH HITHER THY HAND, AND THRUST IT INTO MY   229 04
AND CAME HITHER FOR THAT INTENT, THAT HE MIGHT BRING   231 07
YOU HAVE COME HITHER DESIRING TO RECEIVE HOLY   277 20
8 O COME HITHER, AND BEHOLD THE WORKS OF THE LCRD,   398 09
4 O COME HITHER, AND BEHOLD THE WORKS OF GOD   417 22
14 O COME HITHER, AND HEARKEN, ALL YE THAT FEAR GOD   418 12
THE PSALM, BRING HITHER THE TABRET, *   442 14

HITHERTO

HITHERTO HAVE YE ASKED NOTHING IN MY NAME   176 22

HOAR-FROST

THE HOAR-FROST LIKE ASHES   523 27

HOLD

WAY OF TRUTH, AND HOLD THE FAITH IN UNITY OF SPIRIT,   019 02
WAY OF TRUTH, AND HOLD THE FAITH IN UNITY OF SPIRIT,   032 33
THE LORD WILL NOT HOLD HIM GUILTLESS, THAT TAKETH HIS   068 12
AND EVER HOLD FAST, THE BLESSED HOPE OF   092 11
THAT HE SHOULD HOLD HIS PEACE   123 31
THE YOUNG MEN LAID HOLD ON HIM   142 30
HIM AWAY, THEY LAID HOLD UPON ONE SIMON, A CYRENIAN,   154 09

HOLD CONTINUED

LET US HOLD FAST THE PROFESSION OF OUR FAITH WITHOUT	158 23
OR ELSE HE WILL HOLD TO THE ONE, AND DESPISE THE	211 10
THE LORD WILL NOT HOLD HIM GUILTLESS, THAT TAKETH HIS	286 20
HEREAFTER FOR EVER HOLD HIS PEACE	300 22
TO HAVE AND TO HOLD FROM THIS DAY FORWARD, FOR BETTER	301 29
TO HAVE AND TO HOLD FROM THIS DAY FORWARD, FOR BETTER	302 05
HOLD NOT THY PEACE AT MY TEARS	325 07
5 O HOLD THOU UP MY GOINGS IN THY PATHS, *	358 27
HAND ALSO SHALL HOLD ME UP, AND THY LOVING CORRECTION	362 07
WHEN I HOLD UP MY HANDS TOWARDS THE MERCY-SEAT OF THY	373 08
HATED THEM THAT HOLD OF LYING VANITIES, *	376 02
HOLD NOT THY TONGUE THEN	383 07
7 HOLD THEE STILL IN THE LORD, AND ABIDE PATIENTLY	385 16
HOLD NOT THY PEACE AT MY TEARS	390 03
HAVE TAKEN SUCH HOLD UPON ME, THAT I AM NOT ABLE TO	391 11
6 THEY HOLD ALL TOGETHER, AND KEEP THEMSELVES CLOSE,	408 26
DISPLEASURE TAKE HOLD OF THEM	423 24
IS GOOD FOR ME TO HOLD ME FAST BY GOD, TO PUT MY	429 32
HOLD NOT THY TONGUE, O GOD, KEEP NOT STILL SILENCE	444 05
22 MY HAND SHALL HOLD HIM FAST, *	451 17
HOLD NOT THY TONGUE, O GOD OF MY PRAISE	480 03
PAINS OF HELL GAT HOLD UPON ME	486 24
117 HOLD THOU ME UP, AND I SHALL BE SAFE	498 02
128 THEREFORE HOLD I STRAIGHT ALL THY COMMANDMENTS	498 25
HAVE TAKEN HOLD UPON ME	499 25
RIGHT HAND SHALL HOLD ME	515 07
HOLD UP THE WEAK, HEAL THE SICK, BIND UP THE BROKEN,	558 26
THE LORD WILL NOT HOLD HIM GUILTLESS, THAT TAKETH HIS	579 02
AND WE HOLD IT TO BE THE DUTY OF ALL MEN WHO ARE	610 40

HOLDEN

THEIR EYES WERE HOLDEN THAT THEY SHOULD NOT KNOW HIM	167 09
OF OUR GOD, AND HOLDEN UP OUR HANDS TO ANY STRANGE	396 02
THEE HAVE I BEEN HOLDEN UP EVER SINCE I WAS BORN	425 16
THAT THEY ARE SO HOLDEN WITH PRIDE, *	428 20
FOR THOU HAST HOLDEN ME BY MY RIGHT HAND	429 23

HOLDEST

LORD GOD, WHO HOLDEST ALL SOULS IN LIFE	268 14
THOU HOLDEST MINE EYES WAKING	311 06
4 THOU HOLDEST MINE EYES WAKING	433 23

HOLDETH

8 WHO HOLDETH OUR SOUL IN LIFE	417 31

HOLDING

IT IS UNIVERSAL, HOLDING EARNESTLY THE FAITH FOR ALL	291 11
AND THE MAN HOLDING THE RING THERE, AND TAUGHT BY THE	R 302 12
HOLDING THE MYSTERY OF THE FAITH IN A PURE	531 29
HIS PLACE) HOLDING THE KEYS OF THE CHURCH IN HIS	R 570 09

HOLIEST

ENTER INTO THE HOLIEST BY THE BLOOD OF JESUS, BY A	158 17

HOLINESS

O WORSHIP THE LORD IN THE BEAUTY OF HOLINESS	009 17
BLESSED ART THOU IN THE TEMPLE OF THY HOLINESS	011 20
IN HOLINESS AND RIGHTEOUSNESS BEFORE HIM, *	014 22
BEFORE THEE IN HOLINESS AND RIGHTEOUSNESS ALL OUR	019 29
O WORSHIP THE LORD IN THE BEAUTY OF HOLINESS	021 19
BEFORE THEE IN HOLINESS AND RIGHTEOUSNESS ALL OUR	033 27
OF FAITH, IN HOLINESS OF LIFE, AND IN PERFECTNESS OF	047 09
SERVE THEE IN HOLINESS AND PURENESS OF LIVING, TO THY	059 26
SERVING THEE IN HOLINESS AND RIGHTEOUSNESS ALL THE	074 28
HIM IN TRUE HOLINESS AND RIGHTEOUSNESS ALL THE DAYS	086 22
AND TRUE HOLINESS, TO THY HONOUR AND GLORY, WHO	125 30
NOT CALLED US UNTO UNCLEANNESS, BUT UNTO HOLINESS	128 03
OF THY HOLINESS AND OF THY GLORY	139 18
PEOPLE OF THY HOLINESS HAVE POSSESSED IT BUT A LITTLE	139 27
MEMBERS SERVANTS TO RIGHTEOUSNESS UNTO HOLINESS	198 30
YOUR FRUIT UNTO HOLINESS, AND THE END EVERLASTING	199 03
GOD IS CREATED IN RIGHTEOUSNESS AND TRUE HOLINESS	216 16
IN HOLINESS AND RIGHTEOUSNESS BEFORE HIM, ALL	244 08
LEAD US IN HOLINESS AND RIGHTEOUSNESS, ALL OUR DAYS	316 28
FOR A REMEMBRANCE OF HIS HOLINESS	374 31
SPOKEN IN HIS HOLINESS, I WILL REJOICE, AND DIVIDE	412 23
ONCE BY MY HOLINESS, THAT I WILL NOT FAIL DAVID	452 11
HOLINESS BECOMETH THINE HOUSE FOR EVER	457 16
9 O WORSHIP THE LORD IN THE BEAUTY OF HOLINESS	460 16
AND GIVE THANKS FOR A REMEMBRANCE OF HIS HOLINESS	461 22
7 GOD HATH SPOKEN IN HIS HOLINESS	479 17

HOLPEN

HIS MERCY HATH HOLPEN HIS SERVANT ISRAEL	026 26
5 THEY CALLED UPON THEE, AND WERE HOLPEN	366 12
THEY HAVE HOLPEN THE CHILDREN OF LOT	444 20
THOU, LORD, HAST HOLPEN ME, AND COMFORTED ME	448 11

HOLY

WHEN THE LITANY OR HOLY COMMUNION IS IMMEDIATELY TO	R 003 06
THE LORD IS IN HIS HOLY TEMPLE	003 15
BRING ME UNTO THY HOLY HILL, AND TO THY DWELLING	003 23
IN THE HIGH AND HOLY PLACE, WITH HIM ALSO THAT IS OF	003 26
ONE THAT INHABITETH ETERNITY, WHOSE NAME IS HOLY	003 26
AFTER THAT THE HOLY GHOST IS COME UPON YOU	005 11
HOLY, HOLY, HOLY, LORD GOD ALMIGHTY,	005 18

HOLY CONTINUED

HOLY, HOLY, HOLY, LORD GOD ALMIGHTY, WHICH WAS, AND	005 18
HOLY, HOLY, HOLY, LORD GOD ALMIGHTY, WHICH WAS, AND	005 18
TO HEAR HIS MOST HOLY WORD, AND TO ASK THOSE THINGS	006 07
AGAINST THY HOLY LAWS	006 20
TO THE GLORY OF THY HOLY NAME	006 29
THE ORDER FOR THE HOLY COMMUNION	R 007 05
BELIEVE HIS HOLY GOSPEL	007 12
REPENTANCE, AND HIS HOLY SPIRIT, THAT THOSE THINGS	007 15
REST OF OUR LIFE HEREAFTER MAY BE PURE AND HOLY	007 17
THE SON, AND TO THE HOLY GHOST	008 03
SON, AND HOLY GHOST, ONE GOD	R 008 29
AND TO THE HOLY GHOST	009 28
ON ANY DAY WHEN THE HOLY COMMUNION IS IMMEDIATELY TO	R 010 03
CONTINUALLY DO CRY, HOLY, HOLY, HOLY, LORD GOD OF	010 14
DO CRY, HOLY, HOLY, HOLY, LORD GOD OF SABAOTH	010 14
DO CRY, HOLY, HOLY, HOLY, LORD GOD OF SABAOTH	010 14
THE HOLY CHURCH THROUGHOUT ALL THE WORLD DOTH	010 19
ALSO THE HOLY GHOST, THE COMFORTER	010 23
O YE HOLY AND HUMBLE MEN OF HEART, BLESS YE THE LORD	013 28
THE SON, AND THE HOLY GHOST	013 30
BY THE MOUTH OF HIS HOLY PROPHETS, *	014 12
AND TO REMEMBER HIS HOLY COVENANT	014 17
CONCEIVED BY THE HOLY GHOST, BORN OF THE VIRGIN MARY	015 22
THE HOLY CATHOLIC CHURCH	015 28
I BELIEVE IN THE HOLY GHOST	015 28
INCARNATE BY THE HOLY GHOST OF THE VIRGIN MARY, AND	016 07
I BELIEVE IN THE HOLY GHOST, THE LORD, AND GIVER OF	016 15
AND TAKE NOT THY HOLY SPIRIT FROM US	016 32
BE OMITTED WHEN THE HOLY COMMUNION IS TO FOLLOW	R 017 21
THE GRACE OF THY HOLY SPIRIT, THAT THEY MAY ALWAYS	017 32
WITH THEE AND THE HOLY GHOST, ONE GOD, WORLD WITHOUT	018 15
WE PRAY FOR THY HOLY CHURCH UNIVERSAL	018 30
WITH THEE AND THE HOLY GHOST, BE ALL HONOUR AND	019 31
FELLOWSHIP OF THE HOLY GHOST, BE WITH US ALL	020 13
THE LORD IS IN HIS HOLY TEMPLE	021 12
ENTERED INTO THE HOLY PLACES MADE WITH HANDS, WHICH	022 22
CITY OF GOD, THE HOLY PLACE OF THE TABERNACLES OF THE	022 27
HOLY, HOLY, HOLY, IS THE LORD OF	022 33
HOLY, HOLY, HOLY, IS THE LORD OF HOSTS	022 33
HOLY, HOLY, HOLY, IS THE LORD OF HOSTS	022 33
TO HEAR HIS MOST HOLY WORD, AND TO ASK THOSE THINGS	023 16
AGAINST THY HOLY LAWS	023 27
TO THE GLORY OF THY HOLY NAME	024 04
BELIEVE HIS HOLY GOSPEL	024 14
REPENTANCE, AND HIS HOLY SPIRIT, THAT THOSE THINGS	024 17
REST OF OUR LIFE HEREAFTER MAY BE PURE AND HOLY	024 19
CONSOLATION OF HIS HOLY SPIRIT	024 26
THE SON, AND TO THE HOLY GHOST	025 09
FOR THOU ONLY ART HOLY	026 02
O CHRIST, WITH THE HOLY GHOST, ART MOST HIGH IN THE	026 03
AND HOLY IS HIS NAME	026 16
AND WITH HIS HOLY ARM, *	027 06
PRAISE HIS HOLY NAME	029 05
CONCEIVED BY THE HOLY GHOST, BORN OF THE VIRGIN MARY	029 27
I BELIEVE IN THE HOLY GHOST	029 33
THE HOLY CATHOLIC CHURCH	029 33
INCARNATE BY THE HOLY GHOST OF THE VIRGIN MARY, AND	030 12
I BELIEVE IN THE HOLY GHOST, THE LORD, AND GIVER OF	030 20
AND TAKE NOT THY HOLY SPIRIT FROM US	031 14
FROM WHOM ALL HOLY DESIRES, ALL GOOD COUNSELS,	031 18
WITH THEE AND THE HOLY GHOST LIVETH AND REIGNETH	032 13
WE PRAY FOR THY HOLY CHURCH UNIVERSAL	032 30
WITH THEE AND THE HOLY GHOST, BE ALL HONOUR AND	033 29
FELLOWSHIP OF THE HOLY GHOST, BE WITH US ALL	034 13
WHO BY THY HOLY SPIRIT DIDST PRESIDE IN THE	036 26
MIGHTY POWER OF THE HOLY GHOST, THAT THE COMFORTABLE	037 02
THEE FOR THY HOLY CATHOLIC CHURCH	037 16
UNITED IN ONE HOLY BOND OF TRUTH AND PEACE,	037 33
BE ORDAINED TO ANY HOLY FUNCTION, GIVE THY GRACE AND	038 32
THE BENEFIT OF THY HOLY CHURCH	039 14
THE PRAISE OF THY HOLY NAME	039 30
WITH THEE AND THE HOLY GHOST, BE ALL HONOUR AND	041 06
COMMITTED TO THY HOLY CHURCH THE CARE AND NURTURE OF	042 31
MADE STRONG BY THY HOLY SPIRIT, THEY MAY RESIST	043 11
THE FATHER AND THE HOLY GHOST LIVEST AND REIGNEST ONE	043 15
BY THE GIFT OF THE HOLY SPIRIT THROUGH THE LAYING ON	043 22
TO THE GLORY OF THY HOLY NAME	044 14
TAUGHT US IN THY HOLY WORD THAT THOU DOST NOT	045 31
BY THE POWER OF THY HOLY SPIRIT THEY MAY BE SET FREE	046 28
FOR CHRIST'S HOLY CATHOLIC CHURCH, THE BLESSED	047 07
MINISTERS OF GOD'S HOLY WORD AND SACRAMENTS	047 22
THE FATHER AND THE HOLY GHOST, ONE GOD, WORLD WITHOUT	049 09
WE MAY GLORIFY THY HOLY NAME, AND FINALLY, BY THY	049 26
LIVES BY AN HUMBLE, HOLY, AND OBEDIENT WALKING BEFORE	050 27
WITH THEE AND THE HOLY GHOST, BE ALL GLORY AND	050 29
TO THE GLORY OF THY HOLY NAME	051 20
AND GLORIFY THY HOLY NAME FOR THIS THY MERCY, AND	051 26
WE BLESS THY HOLY NAME, THAT IT HATH PLEASED THEE TO	052 20
WALK IN THY HOLY COMMANDMENTS	052 23
DAYS TO AN HUMBLE, HOLY, AND OBEDIENT WALKING BEFORE	053 06
WE PRAISE THY HOLY NAME THAT THOU HAST BEEN PLEASED	053 21
UNTO THEE IN THY HOLY CHURCH	053 24
THANKFULNESS BY A HOLY TRUST IN THEE, AND OBEDIENCE	053 26
OR BEFORE THE HOLY COMMUNION	R 054 04
O GOD THE HOLY GHOST, SANCTIFIER OF THE FAITHFUL	054 09
O HOLY, BLESSED, AND GLORIOUS TRINITY, ONE GOD	054 11
BY THY HOLY NATIVITY AND CIRCUMCISION	055 06
THE MYSTERY OF THY HOLY INCARNATION	055 06
THE COMING OF THE HOLY GHOST,	055 13
RULE AND GOVERN THY HOLY CHURCH UNIVERSAL IN THE	055 20
THE GRACE OF THY HOLY SPIRIT TO AMEND OUR LIVES	057 16
ACCORDING TO THY HOLY WORD	057 17
UNTO THEE IN THY HOLY CHURCH	058 23
THE SON, AND TO THE HOLY GHOST	059 05

HOLY   CONTINUED

AND TAKE NOT THY HOLY SPIRIT FROM ME   060 33
AND TO THE HOLY GHOST   061 15
COMMUNION-TIME THE HOLY TABLE SHALL HAVE UPON IT A   R 067 05
BEFORE THE HOLY TABLE, SHALL SAY THE LORD'S PRAYER   R 067 06
INSPIRATION OF THY HOLY SPIRIT, THAT WE MAY PERFECTLY   067 19
MAGNIFY THY HOLY NAME   067 20
THAT THOU KEEP HOLY THE SABBATH-DAY   068 24
FIRST SAYING, THE HOLY GOSPEL IS WRITTEN IN THE -   R 070 23
INCARNATE BY THE HOLY GHOST OF THE VIRGIN MARY, AND   071 09
I BELIEVE IN THE HOLY GHOST, THE LORD, AND GIVER OF   071 17
THE PEOPLE WHAT HOLY DAYS, OR FASTING DAYS, ARE IN   R 071 25
SHALL RETURN TO THE HOLY TABLE, AND BEGIN THE   R 071 32
PLACE IT UPON THE HOLY TABLE   R 073 28
PLACE UPON THE HOLY TABLE, THE BREAD AND THE WINE   R 073 32
IN THE WORDS OF HOLY SCRIPTURE OR OF THE BOOK OF   R 073 35
WHO BY THY HOLY APOSTLE HAST TAUGHT US TO MAKE   074 06
WHO DO CONFESS THY HOLY NAME MAY AGREE IN THE TRUTH   074 13
IN THE TRUTH OF THY HOLY WORD, AND LIVE IN UNITY AND   074 14
DULY ADMINISTER THY HOLY SACRAMENTS   074 24
AND RECEIVE THY HOLY WORD   074 28
WE ALSO BLESS THY HOLY NAME FOR ALL THY SERVANTS   074 34
COME TO RECEIVE THE HOLY COMMUNION, YE WHO DO TRULY   R 075 07
HENCEFORTH IN HIS HOLY WAYS   075 11
AND TAKE THIS HOLY SACRAMENT TO YOUR COMFORT   075 12
TO RECEIVE THE HOLY COMMUNION, HUMBLY KNEELING   R 075 16
PRIEST TURN TO THE HOLY TABLE, AND SAY, IT IS VERY   R 076 30
UNTO THEE, O LORD, HOLY FATHER, ALMIGHTY, EVERLASTING   076 33
HOLY, HOLY, HOLY, LORD GOD OF HOSTS, HEAVEN AND EARTH   077 08
HOLY, HOLY, HOLY, LORD GOD OF HOSTS, HEAVEN AND EARTH   077 08
HOLY, HOLY, HOLY, LORD GOD OF HOSTS, HEAVEN AND EARTH   077 08
OPERATION OF THE HOLY GHOST, WAS MADE VERY MAN,   077 16
TRUE PROMISE, THE HOLY GHOST CAME DOWN AS AT THIS   078 26
AND THE HOLY GHOST, ART ONE GOD, ONE LORD, IN   079 07
THE SON, AND OF THE HOLY GHOST, WITHOUT ANY   079 11
TO US OF THE HOLY GHOST, THE COMFORTER   079 17
HOLY, HOLY, HOLY, LORD GOD OF HOSTS, HEAVEN AND EARTH   079 32
HOLY, HOLY, HOLY, LORD GOD OF HOSTS, HEAVEN AND EARTH   079 32
HOLY, HOLY, HOLY, LORD GOD OF HOSTS, HEAVEN AND EARTH   079 32
STANDING BEFORE THE HOLY TABLE, HATH SO ORDERED THE   R 080 02
AND IN HIS HOLY GOSPEL COMMAND US TO CONTINUE, A   080 13
WITH THESE THY HOLY GIFTS, WHICH WE NOW OFFER UNTO   080 40
WITH THY WORD AND HOLY SPIRIT, THESE THY GIFTS AND   081 10
JESUS CHRIST'S HOLY INSTITUTION, IN REMEMBRANCE OF   081 12
TO BE A REASONABLE, HOLY, AND LIVING SACRIFICE UNTO   081 22
PARTAKERS OF THIS HOLY COMMUNION, MAY WORTHILY   081 24
IN THE UNITY OF THE HOLY GHOST, ALL HONOUR AND GLORY   081 33
FIRST RECEIVE THE HOLY COMMUNION IN BOTH KINDS   R 082 25
DULY RECEIVED THESE HOLY MYSTERIES, WITH THE   083 18
CONTINUE IN THAT HOLY FELLOWSHIP, AND DO ALL SUCH   083 27
WITH THEE AND THE HOLY GHOST, BE ALL HONOUR AND   083 30
FOR THOU ONLY ART HOLY   084 13
O CHRIST, WITH THE HOLY GHOST, ART MOST HIGH IN THE   084 14
THE SON, AND THE HOLY GHOST, BE AMONGST YOU, AND   084 22
SUNDAYS AND OTHER HOLY DAYS, (THOUGH THERE BE NO   R 084 27
BE PARTAKERS OF THE HOLY COMMUNION, THE MINISTER   R 084 34
PERSON TO THE HOLY COMMUNION, AND NOT HIM THAT IS   085 16
MIND TO COME TO THE HOLY COMMUNION OF THE BODY AND   085 26
WE RECEIVE THAT HOLY SACRAMENT   085 32
PARTAKERS OF THOSE HOLY MYSTERIES   086 04
THE SON, AND OF THE HOLY GHOST, FOR THE REDEMPTION OF   086 06
AND ORDAINED HOLY MYSTERIES, AS PLEDGES OF HIS LOVE,   086 16
THE FATHER AND THE HOLY GHOST, LET US GIVE, AS WE ARE   086 19
WHOLLY TO HIS HOLY WILL AND PLEASURE, AND STUDYING TO   086 21
CELEBRATION OF THE HOLY COMMUNION, (WHICH HE SHALL   R 086 24
THE SUNDAY, OR SOME HOLY DAY, IMMEDIATELY PRECEDING,)   R 086 25
SUSTENANCE IN THAT HOLY SACRAMENT   087 04
THE DIGNITY OF THAT HOLY MYSTERY, AND THE GREAT PERIL   087 09
SO THAT YE MAY COME HOLY AND CLEAN TO SUCH A HEAVENLY   087 12
REQUIRED BY GOD IN HOLY SCRIPTURE, AND BE RECEIVED AS   087 14
PARTAKERS OF THAT HOLY TABLE   087 15
RECEIVING OF THE HOLY COMMUNION DOTH NOTHING ELSE BUT   087 29
COME NOT TO THAT HOLY TABLE   087 34
SHOULD COME TO THE HOLY COMMUNION, BUT WITH A FULL   088 02
TO COME TO THE HOLY COMMUNION, INSTEAD OF THE FORMER,   R 088 10
FROM THIS HOLY SUPPER, PROVOKE GOD'S INDIGNATION   088 25
PARTAKERS OF THIS HOLY COMMUNION   089 09
WITH THEE AND THE HOLY GHOST, NOW AND EVER   090 18
WHO HAST CAUSED ALL HOLY SCRIPTURES TO BE WRITTEN FOR   092 07
AND COMFORT OF THY HOLY WORD, WE MAY EMBRACE, AND   092 10
THE POWER OF THE HOLY GHOST   093 03
THE FATHER AND THE HOLY SPIRIT EVER, ONE GOD, WORLD   093 31
WITH THEE AND THE HOLY GHOST, BE HONOUR AND GLORY,   095 10
BE RENEWED BY THY HOLY SPIRIT   096 17
IN ANY CHURCH THE HOLY COMMUNION BE TWICE CELEBRATED   R 098 07
WITH THEE AND THE HOLY GHOST, ONE GOD, WORLD WITHOUT   098 16
FILLED WITH THE HOLY GHOST, MAY LEARN TO LOVE AND   099 29
BEING FULL OF THE HOLY GHOST, LOOKED UP STEDFASTLY   100 05
WE MAY GLORIFY THY HOLY NAME   102 26
BE RENEWED BY THY HOLY SPIRIT   104 09
WITH CHILD OF THE HOLY GHOST   104 29
IN HER IS OF THE HOLY GHOST   105 06
REVEALED UNTO HIS HOLY APOSTLES AND PROPHETS BY THE   108 13
A LIVING SACRIFICE, HOLY, ACCEPTABLE UNTO GOD,   110 05
YOU WITH THE HOLY GHOST   112 17
THE ELECT OF GOD, HOLY AND BELOVED, A HEART OF   116 03
AND THEE, O HOLY GHOST, HE LIVETH AND   117 11
WITH THEE AND THE HOLY GHOST EVER, ONE GOD, WORLD   119 03
SEND THY HOLY GHOST, AND POUR INTO OUR HEARTS THAT   122 15
THE FATHER AND THE HOLY GHOST, ONE GOD, WORLD WITHOUT   125 32
BY KINDNESS, BY THE HOLY GHOST, BY LOVE UNFEIGNED, BY   126 13
HIM UP INTO THE HOLY CITY, AND SETTETH HIM ON A   126 31
GIVEN UNTO US HIS HOLY SPIRIT   128 05
IN ONCE INTO THE HOLY PLACE, HAVING OBTAINED ETERNAL   132 27
AND WENT INTO THE HOLY CITY, AND APPEARED UNTO MANY   137 30

HOLY   CONTINUED

AND VEXED HIS HOLY SPIRIT   139 05
IS HE THAT PUT HIS HOLY SPIRIT WITHIN HIM   139 10
ENTERED INTO THE HOLY PLACES MADE WITH HANDS, WHICH   147 30
ENTERETH INTO THE HOLY PLACE EVERY YEAR WITH BLOOD OF   148 03
WHO IN THESE HOLY MYSTERIES GIVETH US A PLEDGE   152 11
WITH THEE AND THE HOLY SPIRIT EVER, ONE GOD, WORLD   152 13
WITH THEE AND THE HOLY GHOST EVER, ONE GOD, WORLD   156 25
OF MEN IN THY HOLY CHURCH, THAT EVERY MEMBER OF THE   156 30
WITH THEE AND THE HOLY SPIRIT, ONE GOD, WORLD WITHOUT   157 13
WHEREOF THE HOLY GHOST ALSO IS A WITNESS TO US   158 09
AND TO THE HOLY GHOST   163 18
WITH THEE AND THE HOLY GHOST EVER, ONE GOD, WORLD   163 29
IN ANY CHURCH THE HOLY COMMUNION BE TWICE CELEBRATED   R 164 30
NAZARETH WITH THE HOLY GHOST AND WITH POWER   166 20
NOT SUFFER THINE HOLY ONE TO SEE CORRUPTION   169 14
RECEIVE YE THE HOLY GHOST   171 23
STEPS OF HIS MOST HOLY LIFE   172 02
THAT BY THY HOLY INSPIRATION WE MAY THINK THOSE   175 30
WITH THEE AND THE HOLY GHOST, ONE GOD, WORLD WITHOUT   177 18
THAT HE THROUGH THE HOLY GHOST HAD GIVEN COMMANDMENTS   177 24
BAPTIZED WITH THE HOLY GHOST NOT MANY DAYS HENCE   178 03
AFTER THAT THE HOLY GHOST IS COME UPON YOU   178 09
SEND TO US THINE HOLY GHOST TO COMFORT US, AND EXALT   179 07
THEE AND THE SAME HOLY GHOST, ONE GOD, WORLD WITHOUT   179 10
THE LIGHT OF THY HOLY SPIRIT   180 10
TO REJOICE IN HIS HOLY COMFORT   180 12
ALL FILLED WITH THE HOLY GHOST, AND BEGAN TO SPEAK   180 23
WHICH IS THE HOLY GHOST, WHOM THE FATHER WILL SEND IN   181 30
IN ANY CHURCH THE HOLY COMMUNION BE TWICE CELEBRATED   R 182 11
INDWELLING OF THY HOLY SPIRIT, WE MAY BE ENLIGHTENED   182 16
FATHER GIVE THE HOLY SPIRIT TO THEM THAT ASK HIM   183 19
ALMIGHTY GOD, THY HOLY SPIRIT INTO OUR HEARTS, THAT   183 22
THEE AND THE SAME HOLY SPIRIT LIVETH AND REIGNETH,   183 26
NAZARETH WITH THE HOLY GHOST AND WITH POWER   184 07
THESE WORDS, THE HOLY GHOST FELL ON ALL THEM WHICH   184 21
OUT THE GIFT OF THE HOLY GHOST   184 24
HAVE RECEIVED THE HOLY GHOST AS WELL AS WE   184 28
IN UNITY BY THY HOLY SPIRIT, MAY MANIFEST THY POWER   185 16
MIGHT RECEIVE THINE HOLY GHOST   185 25
THEY RECEIVED THE HOLY GHOST   185 28
AND NIGHT, SAYING, HOLY, HOLY, HOLY, LORD GOD   187 22
HOLY, HOLY, HOLY, LORD GOD ALMIGHTY, WHICH   187 23
HOLY, HOLY, HOLY, LORD GOD ALMIGHTY, WHICH   187 23
AND LOVE OF THY HOLY NAME   191 08
WITHOUT WHOM NOTHING IS STRONG, NOTHING IS HOLY   194 05
BUT BY THE HOLY GHOST   203 21
GRANT THAT THY HOLY SPIRIT MAY IN ALL THINGS DIRECT   215 28
AND GRIEVE NOT THE HOLY SPIRIT OF GOD, WHEREBY YE ARE   216 25
SUCH GRACE UNTO THY HOLY APOSTLE SAINT ANDREW,   226 19
BEING CALLED BY THY HOLY WORD, MAY FORTHWITH GIVE UP   226 22
TO FULFIL THY HOLY COMMANDMENTS   226 23
DIDST SUFFER THY HOLY APOSTLE THOMAS TO BE DOUBTFUL   228 06
WITH THEE AND THE HOLY GHOST, BE ALL HONOUR AND   228 11
BY FOLLOWING THE HOLY DOCTRINE WHICH HE TAUGHT   229 22
BE FILLED WITH THE HOLY GHOST   230 34
SHALL BE CALLED HOLY TO THE LORD   232 27
AND THE HOLY GHOST WAS UPON HIM   232 32
UNTO HIM BY THE HOLY GHOST, THAT HE SHOULD NOT SEE   232 33
WHICH THE HOLY GHOST BY THE MOUTH OF DAVID SPAKE   234 09
SAID UNTO HER, THE HOLY GHOST SHALL COME UPON THEE,   236 22
THEREFORE ALSO THAT HOLY THING WHICH SHALL BE BORN OF   236 24
HAST INSTRUCTED THY HOLY CHURCH WITH THE HEAVENLY   237 05
IN THE TRUTH OF THY HOLY GOSPEL   237 09
THE STEPS OF THY HOLY APOSTLES, SAINT PHILIP AND   238 32
WHO DIDST ENDUE THY HOLY APOSTLE BARNABAS WITH   240 28
GIFTS OF THE HOLY GHOST   240 29
AND FULL OF THE HOLY GHOST AND OF FAITH   241 09
HIS DOCTRINE AND HOLY LIFE, THAT WE MAY TRULY REPENT   242 10
WAS FILLED WITH THE HOLY GHOST, AND PROPHESIED,   243 32
BY THE MOUTH OF HIS HOLY PROPHETS, WHICH HAVE BEEN   243 35
AND TO REMEMBER HIS HOLY COVENANT   244 05
TO PREACH THY HOLY WORD, AND THE PEOPLE OBEDIENTLY TO   244 26
THAT, AS THINE HOLY APOSTLE SAINT JAMES, LEAVING   246 16
READY TO FOLLOW THY HOLY COMMANDMENTS   246 21
AND THEE, O HOLY GHOST, LIVETH AND REIGNETH,   248 05
WITH HIM IN THE HOLY MOUNT   248 21
WITH THEE AND THE HOLY GHOST, ONE GOD, WORLD WITHOUT   250 25
GRANT THAT, AS THY HOLY ANGELS ALWAYS DO THEE SERVICE   251 29
WE MAY BE MADE AN HOLY TEMPLE ACCEPTABLE UNTO THEE   254 31
GROWETH UNTO AN HOLY TEMPLE IN THE LORD   255 08
AND ALL THE HOLY ANGELS WITH HIM, THEN SHALL   258 29
SPIRITUAL HOUSE, AN HOLY PRIESTHOOD, TO OFFER UP   259 31
INSPIRATION OF THY HOLY SPIRIT, TO PUT IT INTO THE   260 21
UNTO THEE IN THY HOLY CHURCH   262 02
FATHER GIVE THE HOLY SPIRIT TO THEM THAT ASK HIM   263 13
AND TO THE HOLY GHOST   265 07
ACCORDING TO THY HOLY ORDINANCE   267 06
THAT IT SHOULD BE HOLY AND WITHOUT BLEMISH   R 267 24
SUNDAYS AND OTHER HOLY DAYS   R 273 05
RECEIVING OF THIS HOLY SACRAMENT   R 273 21
OF WATER AND OF THE HOLY GHOST   273 31
INTO CHRIST'S HOLY CHURCH, AND BE MADE A LIVING   274 05
WITH WATER AND THE HOLY GHOST, AND RECEIVED INTO   274 05
COMING TO THY HOLY BAPTISM, MAY RECEIVE REMISSION   274 13
THE SON, AND OF THE HOLY GHOST   275 29
GIVE THY HOLY SPIRIT TO THIS CHILD (THIS THY   276 11
THEE AND THE SAME HOLY SPIRIT, NOW AND FOR EVER   276 15
HIM WITH THE HOLY GHOST, TO GIVE HIM THE KINGDOM OF   276 22
KEEP GOD'S HOLY WILL AND COMMANDMENTS, AND WALK IN   277 04
DESIRING TO RECEIVE HOLY BAPTISM   277 21
YOU WITH THE HOLY GHOST, TO GIVE YOU THE KINGDOM OF   277 23
KEEP GOD'S HOLY WILL AND COMMANDMENTS, AND WALK IN   278 13
UNTO THEE, O LORD, HOLY FATHER, ALMIGHTY, EVERLASTING   279 08
THE SON, AND OF THE HOLY GHOST   279 14

HOLY   CONTINUED   HOLY   CONTINUED

IN THE UNITY OF THE HOLY SPIRIT, BE ALL HONOUR AND   279 21
THE SON, AND OF THE HOLY GHOST   279 29
SERVANT) WITH THY HOLY SPIRIT, TO RECEIVE HIM FOR   280 30
HIM INTO THY HOLY CHURCH   280 31
THE RESIDUE OF THY HOLY CHURCH, HE MAY BE AN   281 04
BE ADMITTED TO THE HOLY COMMUNION   R 281 15
THE SON, AND OF THE HOLY GHOST   281 22
MAY ADMINISTER HOLY BAPTISM, USING THE FOREGOING   R 281 28
THE SON, AND OF THE HOLY GHOST, (WHICH ARE ESSENTIAL   R 282 09
THE SON, AND OF THE HOLY GHOST   282 15
I SHOULD KEEP GOD'S HOLY WILL AND COMMANDMENTS,   283 27
CONCEIVED BY THE HOLY GHOST, BORN OF THE VIRGIN MARY   284 16
I BELIEVE IN THE HOLY GHOST   284 22
THE HOLY CATHOLIC CHURCH   284 22
IN GOD THE HOLY GHOST, WHO SANCTIFIETH ME,   285 02
AND THIS HOLY TRINITY, ONE GOD, I PRAISE AND MAGNIFY,   285 04
THE SON, AND TO THE HOLY GHOST   285 07
SHOULD KEEP GOD'S HOLY WILL AND COMMANDMENTS   285 14
THAT THOU KEEP HOLY THE SABBATH-DAY   286 24
TO HONOUR HIS HOLY NAME AND HIS WORD   288 21
FELLOWSHIP OF THE HOLY GHOST, BE WITH US ALL   289 30
WE MAY BE MADE AN HOLY TEMPLE ACCEPTABLE UNTO THEE   290 23
THE CREEDS AS ONE, HOLY, CATHOLIC, AND APOSTOLIC   291 05
HOLY   291 09
BECAUSE THE HOLY SPIRIT DWELLS IN IT, AND SANCTIFIES   291 09
GIFTS OF THE HOLY SPIRIT   291 27
LORD'S SUPPER, OR HOLY COMMUNION, FOR THE CONTINUAL   291 31
THE SON, AND OF THE HOLY GHOST   292 21
TO CONFER HOLY ORDERS   294 09
TO CELEBRATE THE HOLY COMMUNION   294 14
A MEASURE OF THY HOLY SPIRIT, THAT THEY MAY GROW IN   294 26
COMING TO THOSE HOLY MYSTERIES IN FAITH, AND LOVE,   294 31
FELLOWSHIP OF THE HOLY GHOST, BE WITH US ALL   295 05
UPON SUNDAYS AND HOLY DAYS, OR ON SOME OTHER   R 295 07
CHAIR NEAR TO THE HOLY TABLE, THE PEOPLE ALL STANDING   R 296 06
MIGHT RECEIVE THE HOLY GHOST   296 17
THEY RECEIVED THE HOLY GHOST   296 20
BY WATER AND THE HOLY GHOST, AND HAST GIVEN UNTO THEM   297 16
O LORD, WITH THY HOLY GHOST, THE COMFORTER, AND DAILY   297 18
THE SPIRIT OF THY HOLY FEAR, NOW AND FOR EVER   297 22
INCREASE IN THY HOLY SPIRIT MORE AND MORE, UNTIL HE   297 28
THE EXAMPLE OF THY HOLY APOSTLES, WE HAVE NOW LAID   298 17
LET THY HOLY SPIRIT EVER BE WITH THEM   298 20
THEE AND THE SAME HOLY SPIRIT LIVETH AND REIGNETH   298 24
THE SON, AND OF THE HOLY GHOST, BE UPON YOU, AND REMAIN   299 04
BE ADMITTED TO THE HOLY COMMUNION, UNTIL SUCH TIME AS   R 299 08
AND THIS WOMAN IN HOLY MATRIMONY   300 10
WHICH HOLY ESTATE CHRIST ADORNED AND BEAUTIFIED WITH   300 13
INTO THIS HOLY ESTATE THESE TWO PERSONS PRESENT COME   300 19
ORDINANCE IN THE HOLY ESTATE OF MATRIMONY   301 07
ORDINANCE IN THE HOLY ESTATE OF MATRIMONY   301 15
ACCORDING TO GOD'S HOLY ORDINANCE   301 31
ACCORDING TO GOD'S HOLY ORDINANCE   302 07
THE SON, AND OF THE HOLY GHOST   302 15
WITH THEE AND THE HOLY SPIRIT EVER, ONE GOD, WORLD   303 28
TOGETHER IN HOLY WEDLOCK, AND HAVE WITNESSED THE SAME   304 04
THE SON, AND OF THE HOLY GHOST   304 09
THE SON, GOD THE HOLY GHOST, BLESS, PRESERVE, AND   304 11
JOINED TOGETHER IN HOLY MATRIMONY, YE ARE TO DECLARE   R 304 24
THE SON, AND TO THE HOLY GHOST   306 04
SHE RECEIVE THE HOLY COMMUNION   R 307 10
HIM HELP FROM THY HOLY PLACE   308 25
HEARD ME OUT OF HIS HOLY HILL   309 12
HEARD ME OUT OF HIS HOLY HILL   309 21
UNTO THEE IN THY HOLY CHURCH   309 31
BRING ME UNTO THY HOLY HILL, AND TO THY DWELLING   310 12
WORSHIP TOWARD THY HOLY TEMPLE, AND PRAISE THY NAME,   311 30
PRAISE HIS HOLY NAME   312 21
HE MAY BLESS THY HOLY NAME   315 11
AND TO BLESS THY HOLY NAME FOR ALL THY GOODNESS   315 32
WITH THEE AND THE HOLY SPIRIT, BE ALL HONOUR AND   316 03
WITH THY GRACE AND HOLY SPIRIT IN THE INNER MAN   316 12
BY THE POWER OF THY HOLY SPIRIT, HE MAY BE ENABLED TO   316 21
AND LET THY HOLY SPIRIT LEAD US IN HOLINESS AND   316 28
AND HOLY HOPE   317 06
O GOD THE HOLY GHOST   317 29
O HOLY TRINITY, ONE GOD   317 31
BY THY HOLY INCARNATION, BY THY CROSS AND PASSION,   318 04
THE COMING OF THE HOLY GHOST   318 08
WITH THEE AND THE HOLY GHOST, ONE GOD, WORLD WITHOUT   319 12
AND COMFORT OF THE HOLY SPIRIT   319 17
IN THE NAME OF THE HOLY GHOST WHO SANCTIFIETH THEE   319 23
THE FATHER AND THE HOLY GHOST, ONE GOD, WORLD WITHOUT   320 13
THE SON, AND OF THE HOLY GHOST   320 17
RECEIVING OF THE HOLY COMMUNION OF THE BODY AND BLOOD   R 321 07
THERE CELEBRATE THE HOLY COMMUNION, BEGINNING WITH   R 321 15
O LORD, HOLY FATHER, BY WHOSE LOVING-KINDNESS OUR   322 06
PRESCRIBED FOR THE HOLY COMMUNION, BEGINNING AT THESE   R 322 31
DISTRIBUTION OF THE HOLY SACRAMENT, THE MINISTER   R 322 33
CONSOLATION OF HIS HOLY SPIRIT   323 22
THE HOLY PLACE OF THE TABERNACLE OF THE MOST HIGHEST   327 10
WITH THEE AND THE HOLY GHOST EVER, ONE GOD, WORLD   332 08
O LORD GOD MOST HOLY, O LORD MOST MIGHTY, O HOLY AND   332 25
LORD MOST MIGHTY, O HOLY AND MOST MERCIFUL SAVIOUR,   332 26
GOD MOST MIGHTY, O HOLY AND MERCIFUL SAVIOUR,   332 30
SPARE US, LORD MOST HOLY, O GOD MOST MIGHTY, O HOLY   332 30
TRUE FAITH OF THY HOLY NAME, MAY HAVE OUR PERFECT   334 26
TAUGHT US, BY HIS HOLY APOSTLE SAINT PAUL, NOT TO BE   335 03
THE FATHER AND THE HOLY GHOST, ONE GOD, WORLD WITHOUT   336 15
OBEDIENCE TO THY HOLY COMMANDMENTS, THAT AT THE DAY   336 22
FELLOWSHIP OF THE HOLY GHOST, BE WITH US ALL   341 06
THE SON, AND THE HOLY GHOST, BLESS YOU AND KEEP YOU,   342 15
UPON MY HOLY HILL OF SION   346 08
HEARD ME OUT OF HIS HOLY HILL   346 32

WORSHIP TOWARD THY HOLY TEMPLE   348 15
THE LORD IS IN HIS HOLY TEMPLE   354 26
SHALL REST UPON THY HOLY HILL   357 06
THOU SUFFER THY HOLY ONE TO SEE CORRUPTION   358 11
MY VOICE OUT OF HIS HOLY TEMPLE, *   360 06
HOLY THOU SHALT BE HOLY, *   361 18
26 WITH THE HOLY THOU SHALT BE HOLY, *   361 18
HEAR HIM FROM HIS HOLY HEAVEN, *   364 27
AND THOU CONTINUEST HOLY, *   366 09
RISE UP IN HIS HOLY PLACE   368 33
MERCY-SEAT OF THY HOLY TEMPLE   373 09
THE LORD WITH HOLY WORSHIP   373 33
HAVE HOPED IN HIS HOLY NAME   379 31
BRING ME UNTO THY HOLY HILL, AND TO THY DWELLING   394 10
THE HOLY PLACE OF THE TABERNACLE OF THE MOST HIGHEST   397 33
SITTETH UPON HIS HOLY SEAT   399 05
EVEN UPON HIS HOLY HILL   399 11
AND TAKE NOT THY HOLY SPIRIT FROM ME   403 32
EVEN OF THY HOLY TEMPLE   416 19
EVEN GOD IN HIS HOLY HABITATION   419 20
THEM AS IN THE HOLY PLACE OF SINAI   420 18
ART THOU IN THY HOLY PLACES   421 27
THE HARP, O THOU HOLY ONE OF ISRAEL   426 24
SET FIRE UPON THY HOLY PLACES, *   430 18
13 THY WAY, O GOD, IS HOLY   434 08
AND PROVOKED THE HOLY ONE IN ISRAEL   437 24
THY HOLY TEMPLE HAVE THEY DEFILED, AND MADE JERUSALEM   439 30
2 PRESERVE THOU MY SOUL, FOR I AM HOLY   447 07
ARE UPON THE HOLY HILLS   448 13
THE HOLY ONE OF ISRAEL IS OUR KING   451 10
WITH MY HOLY OIL HAVE I ANOINTED HIM   451 15
AND WITH HIS HOLY ARM, *   461 27
WHICH IS GREAT, WONDERFUL, AND HOLY   462 21
FOR HE IS HOLY   462 26
FOR THE LORD OUR GOD IS HOLY   463 03
HIM UPON HIS HOLY HILL   463 03
PRAISE HIS HOLY NAME   466 09
3 REJOICE IN HIS HOLY NAME   470 09
HE REMEMBERED HIS HOLY PROMISE   472 21
THANKS UNTO THY HOLY NAME, AND MAKE OUR BOAST OF THY   475 32
WILLINGLY WITH AN HOLY WORSHIP   482 12
HOLY AND REVEREND IS HIS NAME   483 12
WORSHIP TOWARD THY HOLY TEMPLE, AND PRAISE THY NAME,   513 30
AND HOLY IN ALL HIS WORKS   521 26
THANKS UNTO HIS HOLY NAME FOR EVER AND EVER   521 35
DILIGENTLY READING HOLY SCRIPTURE AND ANCIENT   529 11
INSTRUCTED IN THE HOLY SCRIPTURE, AND OTHERWISE   529 28
CHAIR NEAR TO THE HOLY TABLE, SUCH AS DESIRE TO BE   R 530 08
THE GLORY OF THY HOLY NAME   531 08
WITH THEE AND THE HOLY GHOST, NOW AND FOR EVER   531 25
FULL OF THE HOLY GHOST AND WISDOM, WHOM WE   532 12
OF FAITH AND OF THE HOLY GHOST, AND PHILIP, AND   532 16
MOVED BY THE HOLY GHOST TO TAKE UPON YOU THIS OFFICE   532 26
PERSUADED THAT THE HOLY SCRIPTURES CONTAIN ALL   533 02
HE MINISTERETH THE HOLY COMMUNION, AND TO HELP HIM IN   533 13
AND TO READ HOLY SCRIPTURES AND HOMILIES IN THE   533 14
THE SON, AND OF THE HOLY GHOST   534 07
AND RECEIVE THE HOLY COMMUNION THE SAME DAY, WITH THE R   534 27
THE SON, AND THE HOLY GHOST, BE AMONGST YOU, AND   535 17
CHAIR NEAR TO THE HOLY TABLE, ALL THOSE WHO ARE TO   R 536 08
THIS DAY UNTO THE HOLY OFFICE OF PRIESTHOOD   536 23
RECEIVED INTO THIS HOLY MINISTRY, LET HIM COME FORTH   536 29
THE GLORY OF THY HOLY NAME   537 14
WHO BY THY HOLY SPIRIT HAST APPOINTED DIVERS   537 21
THEE AND THE SAME HOLY SPIRIT, WORLD WITHOUT END   537 29
TO YOU, AND IN THE HOLY LESSONS TAKEN OUT OF THE   539 26
EARNESTLY FOR HIS HOLY SPIRIT   540 33
TAKEN OUT OF THE HOLY SCRIPTURES, AND WITH A LIFE   541 02
ASSISTANCE OF THE HOLY GHOST   541 17
PERSUADED THAT THE HOLY SCRIPTURES CONTAIN ALL   542 02
AND IN READING THE HOLY SCRIPTURES, AND IN SUCH   542 27
COME, HOLY GHOST, OUR SOULS INSPIRE, AND LIGHTEN WITH   543 31
SON, AND HOLY SPIRIT   544 15
COME, HOLY GHOST, CREATOR BLEST, VOUCHSAFE WITHIN OUR   544 17
PRAISE OF THY HOLY NAME   545 21
CALL UPON THY HOLY NAME, THAT WE MAY CONTINUE TO SHOW   545 28
AND THY SON, BY THY HOLY SPIRIT   545 31
THY MINISTERS, THY HOLY NAME MAY BE FOR EVER   545 33
UNITY OF THE SAME HOLY SPIRIT, WORLD WITHOUT END   546 04
RECEIVE THE HOLY GHOST FOR THE OFFICE AND   546 09
OF GOD, AND OF HIS HOLY SACRAMENTS   546 14
THE SON, AND OF THE HOLY GHOST   546 15
OF GOD, AND OF HIS HOLY SACRAMENTS   546 20
THE SON, AND OF THE HOLY GHOST   546 21
AND TO MINISTER THE HOLY SACRAMENTS IN THE   546 26
OUT OF THY MOST HOLY WORD, OR AGREEABLE TO THE SAME,   547 10
THE SON, AND THE HOLY GHOST, BE AMONGST YOU, AND   547 17
WHO BY THY HOLY SPIRIT HAST APPOINTED DIVERS   547 32
THEE AND THE SAME HOLY SPIRIT, WORLD WITHOUT END   548 08
DIDST GIVE TO THY HOLY APOSTLES MANY EXCELLENT GIFTS,   549 08
SAVE THAT THE HOLY GHOST WITNESSETH IN EVERY CITY,   550 16
OVER THE WHICH THE HOLY GHOST HATH MADE YOU   550 28
RECEIVE YE THE HOLY GHOST   552 04
THE SON, AND OF THE HOLY GHOST   552 12
HIS CHAIR, NEAR THE HOLY TABLE   R 553 10
THAT THE HOLY APOSTLES PRAYED BEFORE THEY   553 07
WE TRUST THE HOLY GHOST HATH CALLED HIM   553 12
WHO BY THY HOLY SPIRIT HAST APPOINTED DIVERS   553 27
THEE AND THE SAME HOLY SPIRIT, WORLD WITHOUT END   554 03
FORASMUCH AS THE HOLY SCRIPTURE AND THE ANCIENT   554 07
PERSUADED THAT THE HOLY SCRIPTURES CONTAIN ALL   554 20
OUT OF THE SAME HOLY SCRIPTURES TO INSTRUCT THE   554 23
YOURSELF IN THE HOLY SCRIPTURES, AND CALL UPON GOD BY   554 30
COME, HOLY GHOST, OUR SOULS INSPIRE, AND LIGHTEN WITH   556 06

HOLY   CONTINUED

SON, AND HOLY SPIRIT   556 23
COME, HOLY GHOST, CREATOR BLEST, VOUCHSAFE WITHIN OUR   556 25
WITH THEE AND THE HOLY GHOST, LIVETH AND REIGNETH,   558 07
RECEIVE THE HOLY GHOST FOR THE OFFICE AND   558 12
THE SON, AND OF THE HOLY GHOST   558 15
ENDUE HIM WITH THY HOLY SPIRIT, THAT HE, PREACHING   559 07
THEE AND THE SAME HOLY SPIRIT, ONE GOD, WORLD WITHOUT   559 15
THE SON, AND THE HOLY GHOST, BE AMONGST YOU, AND   559 20
THE SON, O GOD THE HOLY GHOST,   560 07
THE HOLY GHOST, O HOLY TRINITY, ONE GOD,   560 09
TO THE GLORY OF THY HOLY NAME   560 30
THE ORDER FOR THE HOLY COMMUNION, OR AT MORNING   R 563 03
OR CHAPEL, TO THE HOLY TABLE, REPEATING THE FOLLOWING   R 563 08
RISE UP IN HIS HOLY PLACE   563 16
AND TO THE HOLY GHOST   564 03
AS DEVOUT AND HOLY MEN, AS WELL UNDER THE LAW AS   564 11
FOR READING THY HOLY WORD, FOR CELEBRATING THY HOLY   565 08
FOR CELEBRATING THY HOLY SACRAMENTS, FOR OFFERING TO   565 08
AND FOR ALL OTHER HOLY OFFICES   565 11
SANCTIFIED BY THE HOLY GHOST, AND MAY CONTINUE   565 21
A MEASURE OF THY HOLY SPIRIT, THAT THEY MAY GROW IN   565 26
MAY COME TO THAT HOLY ORDINANCE WITH FAITH, CHARITY,   565 30
O LORD, THAT BY THY HOLY WORD WHICH SHALL BE READ AND   566 02
AND BY THY HOLY SPIRIT GRAFTING IT INWARDLY IN   566 03
THIS PLACE IN THE HOLY ESTATE OF MATRIMONY, MAY   566 09
AND I JOHN SAW THE HOLY CITY, NEW JERUSALEM, COMING   567 12
TO THY SERVICE, THY HOLY NAME MAY BE WORSHIPPED IN   568 10
THE SON, AND THE HOLY GHOST, BE AMONGST YOU, AND   568 17
THE ORDER FOR THE HOLY COMMUNION, OR AT MORNING   R 569 08
THE SON, AND OF THE HOLY GHOST   571 03
WE MAY GLORIFY THY HOLY NAME, AND FINALLY, BY THY   571 11
THE BENEFIT OF THY HOLY CHURCH   572 13
O HOLY JESUS, WHO HAST PURCHASED TO THYSELF AN   572 16
O GOD, HOLY GHOST, SANCTIFIER OF THE FAITHFUL,   572 25
AND TO SERVE AT THY HOLY ALTAR   573 14
ILLUMINATION OF THE HOLY GHOST   573 18
ADMINISTER THY HOLY SACRAMENTS, AND BY MY LIFE AND   573 22
EXCELLENCY OF THY HOLY WORD   573 28
OPERATION OF THE HOLY GHOST, ALL CHRISTIANS MAY BE SO   574 06
THAT THEY MAY BE AN HOLY TEMPLE ACCEPTABLE UNTO THEE   574 08
PROSPERITY OF THY HOLY APOSTOLIC CHURCH, AND WITH ONE   574 11
THEE AND THE SAME HOLY GHOST, ONE GOD, WORLD WITHOUT   574 22
TO ADMINISTER THE HOLY EUCHARIST TO HIS CONGREGATION   R 574 26
I SHOULD KEEP GOD'S HOLY WILL AND COMMANDMENTS,   577 18
CONCEIVED BY THE HOLY GHOST, BORN OF THE VIRGIN MARY   577 31
THE HOLY CATHOLIC CHURCH   578 06
I BELIEVE IN THE HOLY GHOST   578 06
IN GOD THE HOLY GHOST, WHO SANCTIFIETH ME,   578 15
THAT THOU KEEP HOLY THE SABBATH-DAY   579 04
TO HONOUR HIS HOLY NAME AND HIS WORD   579 31
THE SON, AND OF THE HOLY GHOST   581 22
UPON SUNDAYS AND HOLY DAYS, OR ON SOME OTHER   R 582 27
ASSISTANCE OF THY HOLY SPIRIT   588 16
FELLOWSHIP OF THE HOLY GHOST, BE WITH US ALL   589 10
ASSISTANCE OF THY HOLY SPIRIT   590 12
AND COMFORTS OF THY HOLY SPIRIT   591 17
FELLOWSHIP OF THE HOLY GHOST, BE WITH US ALL   592 03
A BRIEF PORTION OF HOLY SCRIPTURE, LET THE HEAD OF   R 592 09
FELLOWSHIP OF THE HOLY GHOST, BE WITH US ALL   592 28
A BRIEF PORTION OF HOLY SCRIPTURE, LET THE HEAD OF   R 593 03
ALIVE IN US THE HOLY DESIRES THOU DOST IMPART   594 19
SAFE LODGING, AND A HOLY REST, AND PEACE AT THE LAST   595 02
COMMUNION OF THY HOLY SPIRIT, AND IN THE FELLOWSHIP   597 06
THOSE WHO, IN HOLY WEDLOCK, HAVE BEEN MADE ONE FLESH   598 25
THE SON, AND THE HOLY GHOST   603 07
THE HOLY GHOST, PROCEEDING FROM THE FATHER AND THE   603 26
HOLY SCRIPTURE CONTAINETH ALL THINGS NECESSARY TO   603 29
IN THE NAME OF THE HOLY SCRIPTURE WE DO UNDERSTAND   603 32
CERTAIN WARRANTS OF HOLY SCRIPTURE   604 27
IS SIN AGAINST THE HOLY GHOST, AND UNPARDONABLE   605 40
HAVE RECEIVED THE HOLY GHOST, WE MAY DEPART FROM   605 41
SET FORTH TO US IN HOLY SCRIPTURE   606 28
FOR HOLY   606 34
AND A KEEPER OF HOLY WRIT, YET, AS IT OUGHT NOT TO   607 07
SONS OF GOD BY THE HOLY GHOST, ARE VISIBLY SIGNED AND   608 28
CANNOT BE PROVED BY HOLY WRIT   608 41

HOLY-DAY

AMONG SUCH AS KEEP HOLY-DAY   393 10

HOME

AND PEACE AT HOME, AND THAT, THROUGH OBEDIENCE TO THY   036 19
MY SERVANT LIETH AT HOME SICK OF THE PALSY,   115 08
AND SO FETCH THEM HOME, BLESSED LORD, TO THY FOLD,   157 10
HOUR THAT DISCIPLE TOOK HER UNTO HIS OWN HOME   160 23
THE DISCIPLES WENT AWAY AGAIN UNTO THEIR OWN HOME   164 29
AND WHEN HE COMETH HOME, HE CALLETH TOGETHER HIS   193 22
THAT THEIR HOME MAY BE A HAVEN OF BLESSING AND OF   303 25
KEEP FAR OUR FOES, GIVE PEACE AT HOME   544 08
KEEP FAR OUR FOES, GIVE PEACE AT HOME   556 16

HOMELESS

DAY DESTITUTE, HOMELESS, OR FORGOTTEN OF THEIR   599 07

HOMES

CONTINUAL CARE THE HOMES IN WHICH THY PEOPLE DWELL   598 21

HOMILIES

ARTICLES AND HOMILIES, DECLARED THE NECESSITY AND   V 22

HOMILIES   CONTINUED

SCRIPTURES AND HOMILIES IN THE CHURCH   533 15
SECOND BOOK OF HOMILIES, THE SEVERAL TITLES WHEREOF   610 05
FORMER BOOK OF HOMILIES, WHICH WERE SET FORTH IN THE   610 07
THE BOOKS OF HOMILIES TO BE AN EXPLICATION OF   R 610 24
READING OF SAID HOMILIES IN CHURCHES, UNTIL A   R 610 27

HOMILY

EXPRESSED IN THE HOMILY OF JUSTIFICATION   605 09

HONEST

PRODUCTS OF ALL HONEST INDUSTRY   048 12
PROVIDE THINGS HONEST IN THE SIGHT OF ALL MEN   112 32
WHICH IN AN HONEST AND GOOD HEART, HAVING HEARD   122 09
YOUR CONVERSATION HONEST AMONG THE GENTILES   173 14
YOU SEVEN MEN OF HONEST REPORT, FULL OF THE HOLY   532 11
OF SOBER AND HONEST INDUSTRY, AND SUFFER NOT THE HIRE   599 30

HONESTLY

LET US WALK HONESTLY, AS IN THE DAY   091 05

HONESTY

GODLINESS AND HONESTY, MAY CONTINUALLY OFFER UNTO   052 25
IN ALL GODLINESS AND HONESTY   VI 21

HONEY

AND HE DID EAT LOCUSTS AND WILD HONEY   112 14
BUTTER AND HONEY SHALL HE EAT, THAT HE MAY KNOW TO   236 02
SWEETER ALSO THAN HONEY, AND THE HONEYCOMB   364 05
AND WITH HONEY OUT OF THE STONY ROCK WOULD I HAVE   443 14
SWEETER THAN HONEY UNTO MY MOUTH   496 33

HONEYCOMB

A PIECE OF A BROILED FISH, AND OF AN HONEYCOMB   170 05
SWEETER ALSO THAN HONEY, AND THE HONEYCOMB   364 05

HONOUR

HONOUR THE LORD WITH THY SUBSTANCE, AND WITH THE   005 20
O LORD, FOR THE HONOUR OF OUR ADVOCATE AND MEDIATOR,   018 24
BE ALL HONOUR AND GLORY, WORLD WITHOUT END   019 31
PLACE WHERE THINE HONOUR DWELLETH   021 15
THINGS SEEK THY HONOUR AND GLORY   032 09
AND OBEDIENTLY HONOUR THEM, ACCORDING TO THY BLESSED   032 11
O LORD, FOR THE HONOUR OF OUR ADVOCATE AND MEDIATOR,   032 23
BE ALL HONOUR AND GLORY, WORLD WITHOUT END   033 29
THE SAFETY, HONOUR, AND WELFARE OF THY PEOPLE   035 14
OF THE EARTH TO OUR COMFORT, AND TO THY HONOUR   040 20
BE ALL HONOUR AND GLORY, NOW AND FOR EVER   041 06
TO THE HONOUR AND PRAISE OF THY NAME   049 21
BE ALL GLORY AND HONOUR, WORLD WITHOUT END   050 29
THINGS SEEK THY HONOUR AND GLORY   055 24
AND DELIVER US FOR THINE HONOUR   059 03
OF LIVING, TO THY HONOUR AND GLORY   059 26
FOR THE HONOUR OF JESUS CHRIST, OUR MEDIATOR AND   063 13
HONOUR THY FATHER AND THY MOTHER   069 02
OF LIFE, TO THE HONOUR AND GLORY OF THY NAME   075 29
HOLY GHOST, ALL HONOUR AND GLORY BE UNTO THEE, O   081 33
BE ALL HONOUR AND GLORY, WORLD WITHOUT END   083 30
HOLY GHOST, BE HONOUR AND GLORY, WORLD WITHOUT END   095 10
IN HONOUR PREFERRING ONE ANOTHER   111 24
HONOUR TO WHOM HONOUR   114 27
HONOUR TO WHOM HONOUR   114 27
TO THY HONOUR AND GLORY, WHO LIVEST AND   125 31
ON THE LEFT, BY HONOUR AND DISHONOUR, BY EVIL REPORT   126 16
POSSESS HIS VESSEL IN SANCTIFICATION AND HONOUR   127 30
BUT I HONOUR MY FATHER, AND YE DO DISHONOUR ME   133 15
IF I HONOUR MYSELF, MY HONOUR IS NOTHING   133 23
HONOUR MYSELF, MY HONOUR IS NOTHING   133 24
HONOUR ALL MEN   173 24
HONOUR THE KING   173 25
GIVE GLORY AND HONOUR AND THANKS TO HIM THAT SAT ON   187 25
RECEIVE GLORY AND HONOUR AND POWER   187 30
BE ALL HONOUR AND GLORY, NOW AND FOR EVERMORE   228 11
THEM ALWAY TO THY HONOUR AND GLORY   240 32
GOD THE FATHER HONOUR AND GLORY, WHEN THERE CAME SUCH   248 17
AND HONOUR, AND POWER, AND MIGHT, BE   256 32
BE ALL HONOUR AND GLORY, NOW AND EVERMORE   279 21
HONOUR THY FATHER AND THY MOTHER   286 35
TO HONOUR HIS HOLY NAME AND HIS WORD   288 21
TO LOVE, HONOUR, AND HELP MY FATHER AND MOTHER   288 27
TO HONOUR AND OBEY THE CIVIL AUTHORITY   288 28
COMFORT HER, HONOUR, AND KEEP HER IN SICKNESS   301 08
COMFORT HIM, HONOUR, AND KEEP HIM IN SICKNESS   301 17
AND FEAR, TO THE HONOUR AND GLORY OF THY NAME   303 18
THEY MAY LOVE, HONOUR, AND CHERISH EACH OTHER, AND SO   303 23
TO THINE HONOUR AND GLORY   315 17
BE ALL HONOUR AND GLORY, WORLD WITHOUT END   316 03
YE BLASPHEME MINE HONOUR, *   347 14
AND LAY MINE HONOUR IN THE DUST   349 34
5 HIS HONOUR IS GREAT IN THY SALVATION   365 13
PLACE WHERE THINE HONOUR DWELLETH   371 13
UNTO THE LORD THE HONOUR DUE UNTO HIS NAME   373 32
HIS TEMPLE DOTH EVERY THING SPEAK OF HIS HONOUR   374 16
4 GOOD LUCK HAVE THOU WITH THINE HONOUR   396 22
MAN BEING IN HONOUR ABIDETH NOT, *   400 30
20 MAN THAT IS IN HONOUR BUT HATH NO UNDERSTANDING *   401 16
PRAISES UNTO THE HONOUR OF HIS NAME   417 16
OF THY GLORY AND HONOUR ALL THE DAY LONG   425 22

HONOUR   CONTINUED

ME TO GREAT HONOUR, *   426 20
BUT TO SHOW THE HONOUR OF THE LORD, HIS MIGHTY AND   435 02
I WILL DELIVER HIM, AND BRING HIM TO HONOUR   455 28
3 DECLARE HIS HONOUR UNTO THE HEATHEN, *   460 04
POWER AND HONOUR ARE IN HIS SANCTUARY   460 10
UNTO THE LORD THE HONOUR DUE UNTO HIS NAME   460 14
THOU ART CLOTHED WITH MAJESTY AND HONOUR   467 26
AND HAD IN HONOUR, *   482 28
HIS HORN SHALL BE EXALTED WITH HONOUR   484 03
SUCH HONOUR HAVE ALL HIS SAINTS   525 20
TO THE HONOUR OF GOD, AND THE EDIFYING OF HIS   530 15
WHOM BE GLORY AND HONOUR, WORLD WITHOUT END   535 11
TO THE HONOUR OF GOD, AND THE EDIFYING OF HIS   536 16
AND TO THE HONOUR, PRAISE, AND GLORY OF THY NAME   553 20
AND TO THE HONOUR, PRAISE, AND GLORY OF THY NAME   561 05
THIS PLACE TO THE HONOUR OF THY GREAT NAME   565 05
THIS HOUSE TO THY HONOUR AND WORSHIP   566 30
HONOUR THY FATHER AND THY MOTHER   579 13
TO HONOUR HIS HOLY NAME AND HIS WORD   579 31
TO LOVE, HONOUR, AND SUCCOUR MY FATHER AND MOTHER   580 03
TO HONOUR AND OBEY THE CIVIL AUTHORITY   580 04
GRACE THAT WE MAY HONOUR THEE WITH OUR SUBSTANCE, AND   599 20
AS VESSELS MADE TO HONOUR   606 10

HONOURABLE

OUR LAND WITH HONOURABLE INDUSTRY, SOUND LEARNING,   036 12
LEST A MORE HONOURABLE MAN THAN THOU BE BIDDEN OF   214 12
WHICH IS AN HONOURABLE ESTATE, INSTITUTED OF GOD,   300 11
PAUL TO BE HONOURABLE AMONG ALL MEN   300 16
ARE AMONG THY HONOURABLE WOMEN   397 02

HONOURED

YET THOU HAST HONOURED THY SERVANT WITH APPOINTING   573 12

HONOURETH

MY FATHER THAT HONOURETH ME   133 24
AND PRAISE, HE HONOURETH ME   403 04

HOOFS

BETTER THAN A BULLOCK THAT HATH HORNS AND HOOFS   424 07

HOPE

AND FOR THE HOPE OF GLORY   019 24
AND FOR THE HOPE OF GLORY   033 22
ONE SPIRIT, AND ONE HOPE OF OUR CALLING, ONE LORD,   037 30
ALSO HEIRS THROUGH HOPE OF THY EVERLASTING KINGDOM,   083 24
THE BLESSED HOPE OF EVERLASTING LIFE, WHICH   092 12
AND COMFORT OF THE SCRIPTURES MIGHT HAVE HOPE   092 17
NOW THE GOD OF HOPE FILL YOU WITH ALL JOY AND PEACE   092 32
YE MAY ABOUND IN HOPE, THROUGH THE POWER OF THE HOLY   093 03
FOR THAT BLESSED HOPE, AND THE GLORIOUS APPEARING OF   098 21
REJOICING IN HOPE   111 26
LEAN ONLY UPON THE HOPE OF THY HEAVENLY GRACE MAY   115 30
HAVING THIS HOPE, WE MAY PURIFY OURSELVES,   117 07
MAN THAT HATH THIS HOPE IN HIM PURIFIETH HIMSELF,   117 20
NOW ABIDETH FAITH, HOPE, CHARITY, THESE THREE   123 14
THE SAME IN HOPE, BECAUSE THE CREATURE ITSELF ALSO   194 16
INCREASE OF FAITH, HOPE, AND CHARITY   209 09
ARE CALLED IN ONE HOPE OF YOUR CALLING   213 23
THE SAINTS, FOR THE HOPE WHICH IS LAID UP FOR YOU IN   223 25
YE SORROW NOT, EVEN AS OTHERS WHICH HAVE NO HOPE   268 30
COMFORT OF A REASONABLE, RELIGIOUS, AND HOLY HOPE   317 06
AND NOW, LORD, WHAT IS MY HOPE   324 28
TRULY MY HOPE IS EVEN IN THEE   324 28
GOD IS OUR HOPE AND STRENGTH, *   327 03
MY FLESH ALSO SHALL REST IN HOPE   333 08
IN SURE AND CERTAIN HOPE OF THE RESURRECTION UNTO   333 17
AS MEN WITHOUT HOPE, FOR THOSE WHO SLEEP IN HIM   335 04
IN SURE AND CERTAIN HOPE OF THE RESURRECTION UNTO   337 11
IN SURE AND CERTAIN HOPE OF THE RESURRECTION TO   341 13
MY FLESH ALSO SHALL REST IN HOPE   358 09
THOU WAST MY HOPE, WHEN I HANGED YET UPON MY MOTHER'S   366 21
2 FOR ALL THEY THAT HOPE IN THEE SHALL NOT BE   369 21
THEE HATH BEEN MY HOPE ALL THE DAY LONG   369 26
FOR MY HOPE HATH BEEN IN THEE   370 27
16 BUT MY HOPE HATH BEEN IN THEE, O LORD   376 24
35 HOPE THOU IN THE LORD, AND KEEP HIS WAY, AND HE   386 34
8 AND NOW, LORD, WHAT IS MY HOPE   389 23
TRULY MY HOPE IS EVEN IN THEE   389 23
THAT HATH SET HIS HOPE IN THE LORD, *   390 18
GOD IS OUR HOPE AND STRENGTH, *   397 25
AND I WILL HOPE IN THY NAME, FOR THY SAINTS LIKE IT   405 08
THOU HAST BEEN MY HOPE, AND A STRONG TOWER FOR ME   413 11
FOR MY HOPE IS IN HIM   414 08
OUT YOUR HEARTS BEFORE HIM, FOR GOD IS OUR HOPE   414 14
THOU THAT ART THE HOPE OF ALL THE ENDS OF THE EARTH,   416 22
THOU ART MY HOPE, EVEN FROM MY YOUTH   425 15
THOU ART MY HOPE, AND MY STRONGHOLD   454 30
9 FOR THOU, LORD, ART MY HOPE   455 13
FOR MY HOPE IS IN THY JUDGMENTS   492 27
AND I HAVE A GOOD HOPE BECAUSE OF THY WORD   495 20
AND LET ME NOT BE DISAPPOINTED OF MY HOPE   497 31
THOU ART MY HOPE, AND MY PORTION IN THE LAND OF THE   518 15
2 MY HOPE AND MY FORTRESS, MY CASTLE AND DELIVERER,   519 24
AND WHOSE HOPE IS IN THE LORD HIS GOD   522 11
WE HAVE GOOD HOPE THAT YE HAVE WELL WEIGHED THESE   541 09
CHEER WITH HOPE ALL DISCOURAGED AND UNHAPPY PEOPLE,   599 11

HOPED

AND IT IS TO BE HOPED, THE REASONS OF THEM ALSO, UPON   VI 29
IT IS HOPED THE WHOLE WILL BE RECEIVED   VI 36
AND HE HOPED TO HAVE SEEN SOME MIRACLE DONE BY HIM   153 13
OF THINGS HOPED FOR, THE EVIDENCE OF THINGS NOT SEEN   228 22
4 OUR FATHERS HOPED IN THEE   366 10
BECAUSE WE HAVE HOPED IN HIS HOLY NAME   379 31

HOPETH

ALL THINGS, HOPETH ALL THINGS, ENDURETH ALL THINGS   123 03

HOREB

MADE A CALF IN HOREB, *   474 06

HORN

HATH RAISED UP AN HORN OF SALVATION FOR US IN THE   243 34
MY BUCKLER, THE HORN ALSO OF MY SALVATION, AND MY   359 27
AND TO THE UNGODLY, SET NOT UP YOUR HORN   432 07
6 SET NOT UP YOUR HORN ON HIGH, *   432 08
MY NAME SHALL HIS HORN BE EXALTED   451 24
BE EXALTED LIKE THE HORN OF AN UNICORN   456 19
9 BUT MY HORN SHALL BE EXALTED LIKE THE HORN OF AN   456 19
HIS HORN SHALL BE EXALTED WITH HONOUR   484 02
SHALL I MAKE THE HORN OF DAVID TO FLOURISH   509 08
HE SHALL EXALT THE HORN OF HIS PEOPLE   524 30

HORNS

FROM AMONG THE HORNS OF THE UNICORNS   367 15
BULLOCK THAT HATH HORNS AND HOOFS   424 07
12 ALL THE HORNS OF THE UNGODLY ALSO WILL I BREAK,   432 21
AND THE HORNS OF THE RIGHTEOUS SHALL BE EXALTED   432 22
THY LOVING-KINDNESS THOU SHALT LIFT UP OUR HORNS   451 09
EVEN UNTO THE HORNS OF THE ALTAR   489 23

HORRIBLE

ALSO OUT OF THE HORRIBLE PIT, OUT OF THE MIRE AND   390 11
AND AN HORRIBLE DREAD HATH OVERWHELMED ME   406 29
AND ALSO THE HORRIBLE PUNISHMENT THAT WILL ENSUE   540 13

HORRIBLY

WAVES OF THE SEA ARE MIGHTY, AND RAGE HORRIBLY   457 13
53 I AM HORRIBLY AFRAID, *   493 16

HORSE

THE DEEP, AS AN HORSE IN THE WILDERNESS, THAT THEY   139 14
BE YE NOT LIKE TO HORSE AND MULE, WHICH HAVE NO   378 10
16 A HORSE IS COUNTED BUT A VAIN THING TO SAVE A MAN   379 22
THE CHARIOT AND HORSE ARE FALLEN   432 34
HE HATH NO PLEASURE IN THE STRENGTH OF AN HORSE   523 15

HORSES

PUT THEIR TRUST IN CHARIOTS, AND SOME IN HORSES   364 29

HOSANNA

SAYING, HOSANNA TO THE SON OF DAVID   091 28
HOSANNA IN THE HIGHEST   091 29
AND SAYING, HOSANNA TO THE SON OF DAVID   260 11

HOSPITALITY

GIVEN TO HOSPITALITY   111 28
USE HOSPITALITY ONE TO ANOTHER WITHOUT GRUDGING   179 15
GIVEN TO HOSPITALITY, APT TO TEACH   549 21

HOST

OF THE HEAVENLY HOST PRAISING GOD, AND SAYING, GLORY   099 20
GAVE THEM TO THE HOST, AND SAID UNTO HIM, TAKE CARE   208 34
SHALL DISCOMFIT AN HOST OF MEN, *   361 26
3 THOUGH AN HOST OF MEN WERE LAID AGAINST ME,   371 29
AND ALL THE HOST OF THEM BY THE BREATH OF HIS MOUTH   378 30
THAT CAN BE SAVED BY THE MULTITUDE OF AN HOST   379 20
FOR PHARAOH AND HIS HOST, HE OVERTHREW THEM IN THE   512 12
PRAISE HIM, ALL HIS HOST   524 08

HOSTS

GREAT AMONG THE HEATHEN, SAITH THE LORD OF HOSTS   004 16
IS THE LORD OF HOSTS   022 33
O PRAISE THE LORD, ALL YE HIS HOSTS   029 15
O LORD GOD OF HOSTS, STRETCH FORTH, WE PRAY THEE,   041 25
LORD GOD OF HOSTS, HEAVEN AND EARTH ARE FULL OF   077 09
LORD GOD OF HOSTS, HEAVEN AND EARTH ARE FULL OF   079 33
BEHOLD, HE SHALL COME, SAITH THE LORD OF HOSTS   232 07
AND FEAR NOT ME, SAITH THE LORD OF HOSTS   232 01
O PRAISE THE LORD, ALL YE HIS HOSTS   312 31
THE LORD OF HOSTS IS WITH US   327 16
EVEN THE LORD OF HOSTS, HE IS THE KING OF GLORY   369 15
7 THE LORD OF HOSTS IS WITH US   398 07
11 THE LORD OF HOSTS IS WITH US   398 17
OF THE LORD OF HOSTS, IN THE CITY OF OUR GOD   399 25
UP, O LORD GOD OF HOSTS, THOU GOD OF ISRAEL, TO VISIT   411 13
WILT NOT THOU, O GOD, GO OUT WITH OUR HOSTS   412 32
O LORD GOD OF HOSTS, BE ASHAMED FOR MY CAUSE   422 13
4 O LORD GOD OF HOSTS, *   441 10

HOSTS   CONTINUED

7 TURN US AGAIN, THOU GOD OF HOSTS   441 16
THOU GOD OF HOSTS, LOOK DOWN FROM HEAVEN, *   441 30
19 TURN US AGAIN, O LORD GOD OF HOSTS   442 09
THOU LORD OF HOSTS   445 12
O LORD OF HOSTS, MY KING AND MY GOD   445 18
8 O LORD GOD OF HOSTS, HEAR MY PRAYER   445 27
13 O LORD GOD OF HOSTS, *   446 05
9 O LORD GOD OF HOSTS, WHO IS LIKE UNTO THEE   450 22
21 O PRAISE THE LORD, ALL YE HIS HOSTS   467 18
O GOD, GO FORTH WITH OUR HOSTS   479 27
EVEN THE LORD OF HOSTS, HE IS THE KING OF GLORY   563 30

HOT

4 MY HEART WAS HOT WITHIN ME   389 12
YOUR POTS BE MADE HOT WITH THORNS, *   410 26
WHY IS THY WRATH SO HOT AGAINST THE SHEEP OF THY   430 04
THEIR FLOCKS WITH HOT THUNDERBOLTS   438 05
SHARP ARROWS, WITH HOT BURNING COALS   502 12
10 LET HOT BURNING COALS FALL UPON THEM   516 29

HOUR

THE HOUR COMETH, AND NOW IS, WHEN THE TRUE   003 30
IN THE HOUR OF DEATH, AND IN THE DAY OF JUDGMENT,   055 16
MINE HOUR IS NOT YET COME   113 11
AND HIS SERVANT WAS HEALED IN THE SELFSAME HOUR   115 25
OUT ABOUT THE THIRD HOUR, AND SAW OTHERS STANDING   119 19
THE SIXTH AND NINTH HOUR, AND DID LIKEWISE   119 23
ABOUT THE ELEVENTH HOUR HE WENT OUT, AND FOUND OTHERS   119 24
ABOUT THE ELEVENTH HOUR, THEY RECEIVED EVERY MAN A   119 32
WROUGHT BUT ONE HOUR, AND THOU HAST MADE THEM EQUAL   120 05
HER DAUGHTER WAS MADE WHOLE FROM THAT VERY HOUR   128 22
NOW FROM THE SIXTH HOUR THERE WAS DARKNESS OVER ALL   137 15
DARKNESS OVER ALL THE LAND UNTO THE NINTH HOUR   137 16
AND ABOUT THE NINTH HOUR JESUS CRIED WITH A LOUD   137 17
WERE POSSIBLE, THE HOUR MIGHT PASS FROM HIM   141 34
COULDEST NOT THOU WATCH ONE HOUR   142 05
IT IS ENOUGH, THE HOUR IS COME   142 12
IT WAS THE THIRD HOUR, AND THEY CRUCIFIED HIM   146 12
AND WHEN THE SIXTH HOUR WAS COME, THERE WAS DARKNESS   146 25
AND AT THE NINTH HOUR JESUS CRIED WITH A LOUD VOICE,   146 27
DARKNESS OVER THE WHOLE LAND UNTIL THE NINTH HOUR   146 27
AND WHEN THE HOUR WAS COME, HE SAT DOWN, AND THE   148 33
BUT THIS IS YOUR HOUR, AND THE POWER OF DARKNESS   151 06
THE SPACE OF ONE HOUR AFTER ANOTHER CONFIDENTLY   151 16
WAS ABOUT THE SIXTH HOUR, AND THERE WAS A DARKNESS   155 09
DARKNESS OVER ALL THE EARTH UNTIL THE NINTH HOUR   155 10
JESUS KNEW THAT HIS HOUR WAS COME THAT HE SHOULD   155 24
OF THE PASSOVER, AND ABOUT THE SIXTH HOUR   159 26
AND FROM THAT HOUR THAT DISCIPLE TOOK HER UNTO HIS   160 22
ROSE UP THE SAME HOUR, AND RETURNED TO JERUSALEM, AND   168 11
BECAUSE HER HOUR IS COME   174 11
BEHOLD, THE HOUR COMETH, YEA, IS NOW COME, THAT YE   177 04
HE OF THEM THE HOUR WHEN HE BEGAN TO AMEND   220 07
AT THE SEVENTH HOUR THE FEVER LEFT HIM   220 08
IT WAS AT THE SAME HOUR, IN THE WHICH JESUS SAID UNTO   220 09
AND THE WOMAN WAS MADE WHOLE FROM THAT HOUR   224 23
US NOT, AT OUR LAST HOUR, FOR ANY PAINS OF DEATH,   332 32

HOURS

WE BESEECH THEE, IN SAFETY TO THE MORNING HOURS   595 09

HOUSE

WILL GO INTO THE HOUSE OF THE LORD   003 18
IN THE HOUSE OF HIS SERVANT DAVID   014 11
HABITATION OF THY HOUSE, AND THE PLACE WHERE THINE   021 14
THE MASTER OF THE HOUSE COMETH, AT EVEN, OR AT   021 25
TRUTH TOWARD THE HOUSE OF ISRAEL   027 11
OF ONE MIND IN A HOUSE, AND STILLEST THE OUTRAGE OF A   052 18
THY NEIGHBOUR'S HOUSE, THOU SHALT NOT COVET THY   069 20
IT IS WRITTEN, MY HOUSE SHALL BE CALLED THE HOUSE OF   092 02
BE CALLED THE HOUSE OF PRAYER   092 03
HE WAS OF THE HOUSE AND LINEAGE OF DAVID   099 04
BEHOLD, YOUR HOUSE IS LEFT UNTO YOU DESOLATE   100 31
WERE COME INTO THE HOUSE, THEY SAW THE YOUNG CHILD   109 20
THE GOODMAN OF THE HOUSE, SAYING, THESE LAST HAVE   120 04
LOST SHEEP OF THE HOUSE OF ISRAEL   128 15
AND A HOUSE DIVIDED AGAINST A HOUSE FALLETH   129 31
DIVIDED AGAINST A HOUSE FALLETH   129 31
RETURN UNTO MY HOUSE WHENCE I CAME OUT   130 12
TOWARD THE HOUSE OF ISRAEL, WHICH HE HATH BESTOWED ON   138 30
IN BETHANY IN THE HOUSE OF SIMON THE LEPER, AS HE SAT   140 02
THE GOODMAN OF THE HOUSE, THE MASTER SAITH, WHERE IS   140 29
HIM INTO THE HOUSE WHERE HE ENTERETH IN   148 27
THE GOODMAN OF THE HOUSE, THE MASTER SAITH UNTO THEE,   148 28
AND BROUGHT HIM INTO THE HIGH PRIEST'S HOUSE   151 08
PRIEST OVER THE HOUSE OF GOD   158 19
IT FILLED ALL THE HOUSE WHERE THEY WERE SITTING   180 20
THAT THOU WOULDEST SEND HIM TO MY FATHER'S HOUSE   190 24
THE MASTER OF THE HOUSE BEING ANGRY SAID TO HIS   192 13
COME IN, THAT MY HOUSE MAY BE FILLED   192 19
AND SWEEP THE HOUSE, AND SEEK DILIGENTLY TILL SHE   193 29
DREW NIGH TO THE HOUSE, HE HEARD MUSICK AND DANCING   202 27
IT IS WRITTEN, MY HOUSE IS THE HOUSE OF PRAYER   204 17
MY HOUSE IS THE HOUSE OF PRAYER   204 18
WENT DOWN TO HIS HOUSE JUSTIFIED RATHER THAN THE   205 31
WENT INTO THE HOUSE OF ONE OF THE CHIEF PHARISEES TO   213 28
TAKE UP THY BED, AND GO UNTO THINE HOUSE   217 11
AND DEPARTED TO HIS HOUSE   217 12
AND HIMSELF BELIEVED, AND HIS WHOLE HOUSE   220 11
INTO THE RULER'S HOUSE, AND SAW THE MINSTRELS AND THE   224 24

HOUSE   CONTINUED

THE SEED OF THE HOUSE OF ISRAEL OUT OF THE NORTH   225 18
AND ENQUIRE IN THE HOUSE OF JUDAS FOR ONE CALLED   230 18
ANANIAS WENT HIS WAY, AND ENTERED INTO THE HOUSE   230 30
HEAR YE NOW, O HOUSE OF DAVID   235 29
WAS JOSEPH, OF THE HOUSE OF DAVID   236 08
REIGN OVER THE HOUSE OF JACOB FOR EVER   236 19
IN MY FATHER'S HOUSE ARE MANY MANSIONS   239 31
FOR US IN THE HOUSE OF HIS SERVANT DAVID   243 34
SAT AT MEAT IN THE HOUSE, BEHOLD, MANY PUBLICANS AND   251 15
INTO WHATSOEVER HOUSE YE ENTER, FIRST SAY, PEACE BE   254 19
FIRST SAY, PEACE BE TO THIS HOUSE   254 20
AND IN THE SAME HOUSE REMAIN, EATING AND DRINKING   254 22
UP A SPIRITUAL HOUSE, AN HOLY PRIESTHOOD, TO OFFER UP   259 31
IT IS WRITTEN, MY HOUSE SHALL BE CALLED THE HOUSE OF   260 06
BE CALLED THE HOUSE OF PRAYER   260 07
EVEN THE HOUSE OF ISRAEL, ARE MY PEOPLE, SAITH   262 21
THY NEIGHBOUR'S HOUSE, THOU SHALT NOT COVET THY   287 20
IN SOME PROPER HOUSE, WITH THEIR FRIENDS AND   R 300 05
ALL HIS PEOPLE, IN THE COURTS OF THE LORD'S HOUSE   306 02
PEACE BE TO THIS HOUSE, AND TO ALL THAT DWELL IN IT   308 07
TO GO TO THINE HOUSE, TO OFFER THEE AN OBLATION WITH   315 31
IS DESIROUS TO RECEIVE THE COMMUNION IN HIS HOUSE   R 321 12
I MAY DWELL IN THE HOUSE OF THE LORD ALL THE DAYS OF   326 09
IN MY FATHER'S HOUSE ARE MANY MANSIONS   331 18
WILL DWELL IN THE HOUSE OF THE LORD FOR EVER   338 30
OF THY MERCY I WILL COME INTO THINE HOUSE   348 14
WILL DWELL IN THE HOUSE OF THE LORD FOR EVER   368 23
HABITATION OF THY HOUSE, *   371 12
I MAY DWELL IN THE HOUSE OF THE LORD ALL THE DAYS OF   371 33
STRONG ROCK, AND HOUSE OF DEFENCE, *   375 25
BE SATISFIED WITH THE PLENTEOUSNESS OF THY HOUSE   384 12
FORTH INTO THE HOUSE OF GOD   393 08
ALSO THINE OWN PEOPLE, AND THY FATHER'S HOUSE   397 06
THE GLORY OF HIS HOUSE BE INCREASED   401 08
OUT OF THINE HOUSE, *   402 08
OLIVE-TREE IN THE HOUSE OF GOD   405 04
AND WALKED IN THE HOUSE OF GOD AS FRIENDS   407 19
PLEASURES OF THY HOUSE, EVEN OF THY HOLY TEMPLE   416 19
WILL GO INTO THINE HOUSE WITH BURNT-OFFERINGS,   418 07
OF ONE MIND IN AN HOUSE, AND BRINGETH THE PRISONERS   419 22
THE ZEAL OF THINE HOUSE HATH EVEN EATEN ME   422 20
FOR THOU ART MY HOUSE OF DEFENCE, AND MY CASTLE   425 10
HATH FOUND HER AN HOUSE, AND THE SWALLOW A NEST,   445 16
4 BLESSED ARE THEY THAT DWELL IN THY HOUSE   445 19
DOOR-KEEPER IN THE HOUSE OF MY GOD, *   445 32
HAST SET THINE HOUSE OF DEFENCE VERY HIGH   455 14
ARE PLANTED IN THE HOUSE OF THE LORD, *   456 26
THE COURTS OF THE HOUSE OF OUR GOD   456 27
BECOMETH THINE HOUSE FOR EVER   457 17
TRUTH TOWARD THE HOUSE OF ISRAEL   461 32
I WILL WALK IN MY HOUSE WITH A PERFECT HEART   463 21
THERE SHALL NO DECEITFUL PERSON DWELL IN MY HOUSE   464 02
LORD ALSO OF HIS HOUSE, *   471 14
3 RICHES AND PLENTEOUSNESS SHALL BE IN HIS HOUSE   483 22
WOMAN TO KEEP HOUSE, *   484 23
AND THE HOUSE OF JACOB FROM AMONG THE STRANGE PEOPLE,   484 27
9 BUT THOU, HOUSE OF ISRAEL, TRUST THOU IN THE LORD   485 28
10 YE HOUSE OF AARON, PUT YOUR TRUST IN THE LORD   485 30
HE SHALL BLESS THE HOUSE OF ISRAEL, HE SHALL BLESS   486 02
HE SHALL BLESS THE HOUSE OF AARON   486 03
IN THE COURTS OF THE LORD'S HOUSE   487 22
3 LET THE HOUSE OF AARON NOW CONFESS, *   488 04
WE THAT ARE OF THE HOUSE OF THE LORD   489 20
IN THE HOUSE OF MY PILGRIMAGE   493 18
WILL GO INTO THE HOUSE OF THE LORD   503 10
THE SEAT OF THE HOUSE OF DAVID   503 17
BECAUSE OF THE HOUSE OF THE LORD OUR GOD, *   503 24
THE LORD BUILD THE HOUSE, *   505 22
UPON THE WALLS OF THINE HOUSE   506 11
TABERNACLE OF MINE HOUSE, *   508 08
NIGHT STAND IN THE HOUSE OF THE LORD, *   509 25
THE COURTS OF THE HOUSE OF OUR GOD   509 26
THAT STAND IN THE HOUSE OF THE LORD, *   510 05
THE COURTS OF THE HOUSE OF OUR GOD   510 06
THE LORD, YE HOUSE OF ISRAEL   511 08
THE LORD, YE HOUSE OF AARON   511 09
THE LORD, YE HOUSE OF LEVI   511 10
WELL HIS OWN HOUSE, HAVING HIS CHILDREN IN SUBJECTION   549 24
TO RULE HIS OWN HOUSE, HOW SHALL HE TAKE CARE OF THE   549 25
AND FROM HOUSE TO HOUSE, TESTIFYING BOTH TO THE JEWS,   550 12
AND FROM HOUSE TO HOUSE, TESTIFYING BOTH TO THE JEWS,   550 12
WHOSOEVER IN THIS HOUSE SHALL BE RECEIVED BY BAPTISM   565 19
AND DEVOTE THIS HOUSE TO THY HONOUR AND WORSHIP   566 30
NOT MY FATHER'S HOUSE AN HOUSE OF MERCHANDISE   567 32
FATHER'S HOUSE AN HOUSE OF MERCHANDISE   567 32
THE ZEAL OF THINE HOUSE HATH EATEN ME UP   568 03
THESE KEYS OF THE HOUSE OF GOD AT YOUR HANDS, AS THE   570 32
TO THEE IN THIS HOUSE, WHICH IS CALLED BY THY NAME   572 21
TO STAND IN THY HOUSE, AND TO SERVE AT THY HOLY   573 13
OUT OF THE HOUSE OF BONDAGE   578 24
THY NEIGHBOUR'S HOUSE, THOU SHALT NOT COVET THY   579 20

HOUSEHOLD

ARE OF THE HOUSEHOLD OF FAITH   072 21
THY CHURCH AND HOUSEHOLD CONTINUALLY IN THY TRUE   115 29
TO KEEP THY HOUSEHOLD THE CHURCH IN CONTINUAL   220 16
AND OF THE HOUSEHOLD OF GOD   255 05
TRAINED IN THE HOUSEHOLD OF FAITH   292 35
THEY OF THE HOUSEHOLD DIVIDED THE SPOIL   420 05
HEAD OF THE HOUSEHOLD, OR SOME OTHER MEMBER OF THE   R 592 10
HEAD OF THE HOUSEHOLD, OR SOME OTHER MEMBER OF THE   R 593 04

HOUSEHOLDER

OF THE HOUSEHOLDER CAME AND SAID UNTO HIM, SIR,   116 23
THAT IS AN HOUSEHOLDER, WHICH WENT OUT EARLY IN THE   119 16

HOUSEHOLDS

MAKETH HIM HOUSEHOLDS LIKE A FLOCK OF SHEEP   478 29

HOUSES

THEY THAT WEAR SOFT CLOTHING ARE IN KINGS' HOUSES   094 29
TO THEIR OWN HOUSES, THEY WILL FAINT BY THE WAY   199 13
HATH FORSAKEN HOUSES, OR BRETHREN, OR SISTERS, CR   231 18
TO HAVE THEIR CHILDREN BAPTIZED IN THEIR HOUSES   R 273 08
THINK THAT THEIR HOUSES SHALL CONTINUE FOR EVER, AND   400 26
BURNT UP ALL THE HOUSES OF GOD IN THE LAND   430 22
THE HOUSES OF GOD IN POSSESSION   444 28
AND THEIR OWN HOUSES WELL   532 02
HAVE ERECTED HOUSES FOR THE PUBLIC WORSHIP OF GOD,   564 15

HOUSETOP

THAT SITTETH ALONE UPON THE HOUSETOP   464 24

HOUSETOPS

GRASS UPON THE HOUSETOPS, *   506 31

HOW

PERCEIVING HOW FRAIL AND UNCERTAIN OUR LIFE IS,   045 08
OF THE LORD JESUS, HOW HE SAID, IT IS MORE BLESSED TO 072 02
COMPASSION FROM HIM, HOW DWELLETH THE LOVE OF GOD IN   072 30
HOW THEN SHALL THEY CALL ON HIM IN WHOM THEY HAVE NOT 073 06
AND HOW SHALL THEY BELIEVE IN HIM OF WHOM THEY HAVE   073 07
AND HOW SHALL THEY HEAR WITHOUT A PREACHER   073 08
AND HOW SHALL THEY PREACH, EXCEPT THEY BE SENT   073 09
MUST CONSIDER HOW SAINT PAUL EXHORTETH ALL PERSONS   085 27
YE KNOW HOW GRIEVOUS AND UNKIND A THING IT IS, WHEN A 088 17
WITH YOURSELVES HOW LITTLE SUCH FEIGNED EXCUSES WILL   089 02
WITH YOURSELVES HOW GREAT IS YOUR INGRATITUDE TO GOD, 089 14
TO GOD, AND HOW SORE PUNISHMENT HANGETH OVER YOUR   089 15
ARE SENT UNTO THEE, HOW OFTEN WOULD I HAVE GATHERED   100 28
HOW THAT BY REVELATION HE MADE KNOWN UNTO ME THE   108 08
HE SAID UNTO THEM, HOW IS IT THAT YE SOUGHT ME   110 34
HAVE RECEIVED OF US HOW YE OUGHT TO WALK AND TO   127 24
OF YOU SHOULD KNOW HOW TO POSSESS HIS VESSEL IN   127 29
AGAINST HIMSELF, HOW SHALL HIS KINGDOM STAND   129 32
HOW MUCH MORE SHALL THE BLOOD OF CHRIST, WHO THROUGH   132 30
HEAREST THOU NOT HOW MANY THINGS THEY WITNESS AGAINST 135 23
THE SCRIBES SOUGHT HOW THEY MIGHT TAKE HIM BY CRAFT,   139 34
AND HE SOUGHT HOW HE MIGHT CONVENIENTLY BETRAY HIM   140 21
BEHOLD HOW MANY THINGS THEY WITNESS AGAINST THEE   145 10
AND SCRIBES SOUGHT HOW THEY MIGHT KILL HIM   148 14
AND CAPTAINS, HOW HE MIGHT BETRAY HIM UNTO THEM   148 17
WORD OF THE LORD, HOW HE HAD SAID UNTO HIM, BEFORE   151 21
HOW GOD ANOINTED JESUS OF NAZARETH WITH THE HOLY   166 19
AND HOW THE CHIEF PRIESTS AND OUR RULERS DELIVERED   167 18
DONE IN THE WAY, AND HOW HE WAS KNOWN OF THEM IN   168 15
YOU GLAD TIDINGS, HOW THAT THE PROMISE WHICH WAS MADE 169 06
AND HOW HEAR WE EVERY MAN IN OUR OWN TONGUE, WHEREIN   180 30
NOT ISCARIOT, LORD, HOW IS IT THAT THOU WILT MANIFEST 181 22
YE HAVE HEARD HOW I SAID UNTO YOU, I GO AWAY, AND   182 02
BEING EVIL, KNOW HOW TO GIVE GOOD GIFTS UNTO YOUR   183 17
HOW MUCH MORE SHALL YOUR HEAVENLY FATHER GIVE THE   183 18
HOW GOD ANOINTED JESUS OF NAZARETH WITH THE HOLY   184 06
SAITH UNTO HIM, HOW CAN A MAN BE BORN WHEN HE IS OLD   188 07
AND SAID UNTO HIM, HOW CAN THESE THINGS BE   188 18
AND YE BELIEVE NOT, HOW SHALL YE BELIEVE, IF I TELL   188 23
WHOM HE HATH SEEN, HOW CAN HE LOVE GOD WHOM HE HATH   189 33
COMPASSION FROM HIM, HOW DWELLETH THE LOVE OF GOD IN   191 20
EITHER HOW CANST THOU SAY TO THY BROTHER, BROTHER,   195 07
AND HE ASKED THEM, HOW MANY LOAVES HAVE YE   199 16
SHOULD BE IGNORANT, HOW THAT ALL OUR FATHERS WERE   201 06
TO HIMSELF, HE SAID, HOW MANY HIRED SERVANTS OF MY   202 10
I ALSO RECEIVED, HOW THAT CHRIST DIED FOR OUR SINS   205 04
HOW SHALL NOT THE MINISTRATION OF THE SPIRIT BE   206 22
HOW READEST THOU   208 14
YE SEE HOW LARGE A LETTER I HAVE WRITTEN UNTO YOU   210 23
LILIES OF THE FIELD, HOW THEY GROW   211 21
WHEN HE MARKED HOW THEY CHOSE OUT THE CHIEF SEATS   214 09
HE SAITH UNTO THEM, HOW THEN DOTH DAVID IN SPIRIT   215 18
THEN CALL HIM LORD, HOW IS HE HIS SON   215 21
UNTO HIM, FRIEND, HOW CAMEST THOU IN HITHER NOT   218 24
GOD IS MY RECORD, HOW GREATLY I LONG AFTER YOU ALL IN 220 31
UNTO JESUS, LORD, HOW OFT SHALL MY BROTHER SIN   221 09
AND TOOK COUNSEL HOW THEY MIGHT ENTANGLE HIM IN HIS   222 28
HOW THEN SHALL THEY CALL ON HIM IN WHOM THEY HAVE NOT 227 05
AND HOW SHALL THEY BELIEVE IN HIM OF WHOM THEY HAVE   227 06
AND HOW SHALL THEY HEAR WITHOUT A PREACHER   227 07
AND HOW SHALL THEY PREACH, EXCEPT THEY BE SENT   227 08
AS IT IS WRITTEN, HOW BEAUTIFUL ARE THE FEET OF THEM   227 09
BY MANY OF THIS MAN, HOW MUCH EVIL HE HATH DONE TO   230 22
FOR I WILL SHEW HIM HOW GREAT THINGS HE MUST SUFFER   230 28
MARY UNTO THE ANGEL, HOW SHALL THIS BE, SEEING I KNOW 236 20
AND HOW CAN WE KNOW THE WAY   240 05
AND HOW SAYEST THOU THEN, SHEW US THE FATHER   240 13
HER COUSINS HEARD HOW THE LORD HAD SHEWED GREAT MERCY 243 15
SIGNS TO HIS FATHER, HOW HE WOULD HAVE HIM CALLED   243 22
BEING EVIL, KNOW HOW TO GIVE GOOD GIFTS UNTO YOUR   263 11
HOW MUCH MORE SHALL YOUR HEAVENLY FATHER GIVE THE   263 12
LILIES OF THE FIELD, HOW THEY GROW   266 19
SAITH UNTO HIM, HOW CAN A MAN BE BORN WHEN HE IS OLD   275 27
TELL ME HOW MANY COMMANDMENTS THERE ARE   285 15

HOW   CONTINUED

HOW IS THE CHURCH DESCRIBED IN THE   291 02
HOW MANY SACRAMENTS HATH CHRIST ORDAINED IN HIS   292 04
HOW MANY PARTS ARE THERE IN A SACRAMENT   292 05
HOW ARE THEY INCREASED THAT TROUBLE ME   309 14
SIGNIFYING ALSO HOW MANY THERE ARE TO COMMUNICATE   R 321 13
I MAY BE CERTIFIED HOW LONG I HAVE TO LIVE   324 21
SOME MAN WILL SAY, HOW ARE THE DEAD RAISED UP   329 05
HIM UP FOR US ALL, HOW SHALL HE NOT WITH HIM ALSO   331 02
AND HOW CAN WE KNOW THE WAY   331 24
HOW ARE THEY INCREASED THAT TROUBLE ME   346 25
2 O YE SONS OF MEN, HOW LONG WILL YE BLASPHEME MINE   347 13
LORD, HOW LONG WILT THOU PUNISH ME   349 04
O LORD OUR GOVERNOR, HOW EXCELLENT IS THY NAME IN ALL 350 31
HOW EXCELLENT IS THY NAME IN ALL THE WORLD   351 17
HOW SAY YE THEN TO MY SOUL, THAT SHE SHOULD FLEE AS A 354 19
HOW LONG WILT THOU FORGET ME, O LORD   355 28
HOW LONG WILT THOU HIDE THY FACE FROM ME   355 29
2 HOW LONG SHALL I SEEK COUNSEL IN MY SOUL, AND BE SO 355 30
HOW LONG SHALL MINE ENEMY TRIUMPH OVER ME   355 31
12 WHO CAN TELL HOW OFT HE OFFENDETH   364 08
MINE ENEMIES, HOW MANY THEY ARE   370 22
21 O HOW PLENTIFUL IS THY GOODNESS, WHICH THOU HAST   377 02
8 O TASTE, AND SEE, HOW GRACIOUS THE LORD IS   380 17
17 LORD, HOW LONG WILT THOU LOOK UPON THIS   382 29
HOW EXCELLENT IS THY MERCY, O GOD   384 08
I MAY BE CERTIFIED HOW LONG I HAVE TO LIVE   389 16
2 HOW THOU HAST DRIVEN OUT THE HEATHEN WITH THY HAND, 394 24
HOW THOU HAST DESTROYED THE NATIONS, AND MADE THY   394 24
HOW I MOURN IN MY PRAYER, AND AM VEXED   406 21
3 HOW LONG WILL YE IMAGINE MISCHIEF AGAINST EVERY   413 31
THEIR DEVICE IS ONLY HOW TO PUT HIM OUT WHOM GOD WILL 414 04
AMONG THEMSELVES, HOW THEY MAY LAY SNARES   415 28
2 SAY UNTO GOD, O HOW WONDERFUL ART THOU IN THY   417 17
HOW WONDERFUL HE IS IN HIS DOING TOWARD THE CHILDREN   417 22
HOW THOU, MY GOD AND KING, GOEST IN THE SANCTUARY   421 02
IS WELL SEEN, O GOD, HOW THOU GOEST   421 02
AND THEY TALK HOW THEY MAY VEX THEM WHOM THOU HAST   423 28
11 TUSH, SAY THEY, HOW SHOULD GOD PERCEIVE IT   428 30
18 NAMELY, HOW THOU DOST SET THEM IN SLIPPERY PLACES, 429 12
19 O HOW SUDDENLY DO THEY CONSUME, *   429 14
11 O GOD, HOW LONG SHALL THE ADVERSARY DO THIS   430 27
O LORD, HOW THE ENEMY HATH REBUKED   431 12
AND HOW THE FOOLISH PEOPLE HATH BLASPHEMED THY NAME   431 13
REMEMBER HOW THE FOOLISH MAN BLASPHEMETH THEE DAILY   431 23
44 HOW HE HAD WROUGHT HIS MIRACLES IN EGYPT, *   437 27
5 LORD, HOW LONG WILT THOU BE ANGRY   440 09
HOW LONG WILT THOU BE ANGRY WITH THY PEOPLE THAT   441 10
2 HOW LONG WILT YE GIVE WRONG JUDGMENT, *   443 20
O HOW AMIABLE ARE THY DWELLINGS, *   445 11
45 LORD, HOW LONG WILT THOU HIDE THYSELF   452 32
46 O REMEMBER HOW SHORT MY TIME IS   452 34
AND HOW I DO BEAR IN MY BOSOM THE REBUKES OF MANY   453 08
5 O LORD, HOW GLORIOUS ARE THY WORKS   456 09
THAT THEY MAY SHOW HOW TRUE THE LORD MY STRENGTH IS,   456 30
HOW LONG SHALL THE UNGODLY TRIUMPH   457 23
3 LORD, HOW LONG SHALL THE UNGODLY, *   457 23
4 HOW LONG SHALL ALL WICKED DOERS SPEAK SO   457 25
AND HOW THAT HE SHALL JUDGE THE PEOPLES RIGHTEOUSLY   460 20
11 FOR LOOK HOW HIGH THE HEAVEN IS IN COMPARISON OF   466 27
12 LOOK HOW WIDE ALSO THE EAST IS FROM THE WEST   466 30
24 O LORD, HOW MANIFOLD ARE THY WORKS   469 08
AND THEY SHALL KNOW HOW THAT THIS IS THY HAND,   481 24
14 BEHOLD, O LORD, HOW THAT I AM THY SERVANT   487 16
84 HOW LOVE I THE DAYS OF THY SERVANT   495 25
103 O HOW SWEET ARE THY WORDS UNTO MY THROAT   496 32
O LORD, HOW I LOVE THY COMMANDMENTS   500 29
2 HOW HE SWARE UNTO THE LORD, *   508 06
BEHOLD, HOW GOOD AND JOYFUL A THING IT IS, *   509 13
4 HOW SHALL WE SING THE LORD'S SONG *   513 12
HOW THEY SAID, DOWN WITH IT, DOWN WITH IT, EVEN TO   513 19
17 HOW DEAR ARE THY COUNSELS UNTO ME, O GOD   515 24
O HOW GREAT IS THE SUM OF THEM   515 25
HOW NECESSARY THAT ORDER IS IN THE CHURCH OF CHRIST, R 530 05
OF CHRIST, AND ALSO, HOW THE PEOPLE OUGHT TO ESTEEM   R 530 06
HOW NECESSARY THAT ORDER IS IN THE CHURCH OF CHRIST, R 536 05
OF CHRIST, AND ALSO, HOW THE PEOPLE OUGHT TO ESTEEM   R 536 06
WHAT DIGNITY, AND OF HOW GREAT IMPORTANCE THIS OFFICE   539 28
IN REMEMBRANCE, INTO HOW HIGH A DIGNITY, AND TO HOW   539 30
A DIGNITY, AND, TO HOW WEIGHTY AN OFFICE AND CHARGE YE 539 31
IN YOUR REMEMBRANCE, HOW GREAT A TREASURE IS   540 06
YE SEE WITH HOW GREAT CARE AND STUDY YE OUGHT TO   540 25
CONSIDER HOW STUDIOUS YE OUGHT TO BE IN READING AND   541 03
SELF-SAME CAUSE, HOW READY YE OUGHT TO FORSAKE AND SET 541 07
IF A MAN KNOW NOT HOW TO RULE HIS OWN HOUSE, HOW   549 25
RULE HIS OWN HOUSE, HOW SHALL HE TAKE CARE OF THE   549 26
AND HOW I KEPT BACK NOTHING THAT WAS PROFITABLE UNTO   550 10
YOU ALL THINGS, HOW THAT SO LABOURING YE OUGHT TO   551 08
OF THE LORD JESUS, HOW HE SAID, IT IS MORE BLESSED TO 551 10
AND BEAR WITNESS, HOW YOU ARE MINDED TO BEHAVE   554 14
TELL ME HOW MANY THERE ARE   578 19
HOW MANY SACRAMENTS HATH CHRIST ORDAINED   581 07
HOW MANY PARTS ARE THERE IN A SACRAMENT   581 16

HOWBEIT

HOWBEIT WHEREINSOEVER ANY IS BOLD, (I SPEAK   120 26
HOWBEIT WHEN HE, THE SPIRIT OF TRUTH, IS COME, HE   175 18
HOWBEIT THAT WAS NOT FIRST WHICH IS SPIRITUAL, BUT   329 25
HOWBEIT, YE CANNOT HAVE A MIND AND WILL THERETO OF   540 30

HUMAN

BE ALLOWED TO ALL HUMAN WRITINGS   YET UPON THE   VI 02
AND UNCERTAINTY OF HUMAN LIFE   316 27

HUMBLE

OF A CONTRITE AND HUMBLE SPIRIT, TO REVIVE THE SPIRIT   003 27
THE SPIRIT OF THE HUMBLE, AND TO REVIVE THE HEART OF   003 28
THEM WITH AN HUMBLE, LOWLY, PENITENT, AND OBEDIENT   005 33
A PURE HEART, AND HUMBLE VOICE, UNTO THE THRONE OF   006 11
THOU DIDST HUMBLE THYSELF TO BE BORN OF A   010 27
O YE HOLY AND HUMBLE MEN OF HEART, BLESS YE THE LORD   013 28
DEFEND US THY HUMBLE SERVANTS IN ALL ASSAULTS OF OUR   017 08
DO GIVE THEE MOST HUMBLE AND HEARTY THANKS FOR ALL   019 15
THEM WITH AN HUMBLE, LOWLY, PENITENT, AND OBEDIENT   023 09
A PURE HEART, AND HUMBLE VOICE, UNTO THE THRONE OF   023 20
HATH EXALTED THE HUMBLE AND MEEK   026 23
DO GIVE THEE MOST HUMBLE AND HEARTY THANKS FOR ALL   033 13
WE GIVE THEE HUMBLE THANKS FOR OPENING HEATHEN LANDS   038 16
OUR LIVES BY AN HUMBLE, HOLY, AND OBEDIENT WALKING   050 27
WE GIVE THEE HUMBLE THANKS FOR THAT THOU HAST   051 05
WE GIVE THEE HUMBLE THANKS THAT IT HATH PLEASED THEE   051 18
WE GIVE THEE HUMBLE THANKS FOR THIS THY SPECIAL   052 02
OF HIS DAYS TO AN HUMBLE, HOLY, AND OBEDIENT WALKING   053 06
WE GIVE THEE HUMBLE THANKS FOR THAT THOU HAST BEEN   053 11
RECEIVE OUR HUMBLE PETITIONS   063 10
AND MAKE YOUR HUMBLE CONFESSION TO ALMIGHTY GOD,   075 13
WE, THY HUMBLE SERVANTS, DO CELEBRATE AND   080 39
YE MUST GIVE MOST HUMBLE AND HEARTY THANKS TO GCD,   086 05
WHO DID HUMBLE HIMSELF, EVEN TO THE DEATH UPCN THE   086 08
TO RENDER MOST HUMBLE AND HEARTY THANKS TO ALMIGHTY   086 35
CEASE TO MAKE OUR HUMBLE PETITIONS UNTO ALMIGHTY GOD,   089 21
DESIRES OF THY HUMBLE SERVANTS, AND STRETCH FORTH   128 26
GRANT TO US THY HUMBLE SERVANTS, THAT BY THY HOLY   175 30
HUMBLE YOURSELVES THEREFORE UNDER THE MIGHTY HAND OF   192 32
THE PROUD, AND GIVETH GRACE TO THE HUMBLE   192 32
PRAYERS OF THY HUMBLE SERVANTS   203 12
THEREFORE SHALL HUMBLE HIMSELF AS THIS LITTLE CHILD,   252 28
GRANT TO US, THY HUMBLE SERVANTS, THE SAME FAITH ANC   258 06
WE GIVE THEE HUMBLE AND HEARTY THANKS FOR THIS THY   265 13
WE GIVE THEE HUMBLE THANKS, THAT THOU HAST   276 08
WE MAKE OUR HUMBLE SUPPLICATIONS UNTO THEE FOR THESE   298 15
WE GIVE THEE HUMBLE THANKS FOR THAT THOU HAST   306 24
PRAISE OF THY HUMBLE SERVANT   313 06
PERSON SHALL IN HUMBLE FAITH DESIRE THE MINISTRY OF   R 320 05
THE PRAYER OF HUMBLE ACCESS   R 323 08
THEREFORE SHALL HUMBLE HIMSELF AS THIS LITTLE CHILD,   339 27
THE VOICE OF MY HUMBLE PETITIONS, WHEN I CRY UNTC   373 07
THE VOICE OF MY HUMBLE PETITIONS   373 21
THE HUMBLE SHALL HEAR THEREOF, AND BE GLAD   380 06
SUCH AS BE OF AN HUMBLE SPIRIT   381 05
33 THE HUMBLE SHALL CONSIDER THIS, AND BE GLAD   424 08
THE VOICE OF MY HUMBLE DESIRES   447 16
58 I MADE MY HUMBLE PETITION IN THY PRESENCE WITH MY   493 26
TO BE MODEST, HUMBLE, AND CONSTANT IN THEIR   535 03
TO MAKE THEIR HUMBLE SUPPLICATIONS TO GOD FOR ALL   R 543 24
RENDER THEE OUR HUMBLE PRAISES, FOR THY PRESERVATION   587 21
BEFORE THEE IN AN HUMBLE SENSE OF OUR OWN   589 29
READY TO RECEIVE HUMBLE AND PENITENT SINNERS   590 06

HUMBLED

WHO HAST JUSTLY HUMBLED US BY THY LATE VISITATICN OF   051 22
AS A MAN, HE HUMBLED HIMSELF, AND BECAME OBEDIENT   134 21
AND HUMBLED MY SOUL WITH FASTING   382 18

HUMBLENESS

HUMBLENESS OF MIND, MEEKNESS,   116 04

HUMBLETH

AND HE THAT HUMBLETH HIMSELF SHALL BE EXALTED   205 33
AND HE THAT HUMBLETH HIMSELF SHALL BE EXALTED   214 20
AND HUMBLETH HIMSELF, *   353 27
AND YET HUMBLETH HIMSELF TO BEHOLD THE THINGS THAT   484 17

HUMBLY

AT ALL TIMES, HUMBLY TO ACKNOWLEDGE OUR SINS BEFORE   006 03
SHALL SAY, LET US HUMBLY CONFESS OUR SINS UNTO   006 14
ALL MANKIND, WE HUMBLY BESEECH THEE FOR ALL SORTS AND   018 27
LET US HUMBLY CONFESS OUR SINS UNTO ALMIGHTY GOC   023 02
AT ALL TIMES, HUMBLY TO ACKNOWLEDGE OUR SINS BEFORE   023 12
ALL MANKIND, WE HUMBLY BESEECH THEE FOR ALL SORTS AND   032 27
GRACIOUS GOD, WE HUMBLY BESEECH THEE, AS FOR THE   035 08
WHOLE CHURCH, WE HUMBLY BEG IN THE NAME AND MEDIATION   035 19
WE HUMBLY BESEECH THEE TO BLESS THE COURTS OF JUSTICE   035 32
WE HUMBLY BESEECH THEE THAT WE MAY ALWAYS PROVE   036 10
WE HUMBLY BESEECH THEE FOR THY HOLY CATHOLIC   037 15
THY GRACE, WE HUMBLY BESEECH THEE, TO ALL THOSE WHO   039 09
WE HUMBLY BESEECH THEE, OF THY GREAT   040 23
DELIVER US, WE HUMBLY BESEECH THEE, FROM THE HANDS OF   041 12
WE HUMBLY BESEECH THEE TO BEHOLD, VISIT, AND RELIEVE   045 13
WE HUMBLY BESEECH THEE, OF THY GOODNESS, TC CCMFCRT   046 19
MOST HUMBLY BESEECHING THEE TO GRANT TO ALL OF US   052 22
TO THE PRAYER, WE HUMBLY BESEECH THEE, O FATHER,   R 058 10
WE HUMBLY BESEECH THEE, O FATHER, MERCIFULLY TO LCOK   059 '21
THE PRAYER, WE HUMBLY BESEECH THEE, O FATHER, IN THE   R 060 04
WHO SHALL HUMBLY PRESENT AND PLACE IT UPON   R 073 30
WE HUMBLY BESEECH THEE MOST MERCIFULLY TO ACCEPT OUR   074 08
AND WE MOST HUMBLY BESEECH THEE, OF THY GOODNESS,   074 30
HOLY COMMUNION, HUMBLY KNEELING   R 075 16
AND WE MOST HUMBLY BESEECH THEE, O MERCIFUL FATHER,   081 07
MOST HUMBLY BESEECHING THEE TO GRANT THAT, BY THE   081 17
HUMBLY BESEECHING THEE, THAT WE, AND ALL OTHERS WHO   081 23
AND WE HUMBLY BESEECH THEE, O HEAVENLY FATHER,   083 26
WE HUMBLY BESEECH THEE THAT, AS BY THY SPECIAL GRACE   163 24
WE HUMBLY BESEECH THEE TO PUT AWAY FROM US ALL   199 29
WE HUMBLY BESEECH THY MAJESTY, THAT, AS THY   231 28

HUMBLY   CONTINUED

WE HUMBLY BESEECH THEE, BY THE INSPIRATION OF THY   260 20
O ETERNAL GOD, WE HUMBLY BESEECH THEE, FAVOURABLY TO   267 04
AND HUMBLY WE BESEECH THEE TO GRANT, THAT HE, BEING   280 32
AND HELP US, WE HUMBLY BESEECH THEE, O LORD   313 14
WE HUMBLY COMMEND THE SOUL OF THIS THY SERVANT, CUR   317 13
WE HUMBLY BESEECH THEE, A SHEEP OF THINE   319 29
WE HUMBLY BESEECH THEE, O FATHER, TO RAISE US FROM   335 05
MOST HUMBLY BESEECHING THEE TO GIVE US GRACE SC TO   336 20
AND GAT ME TO MY LORD RIGHT HUMBLY   375 09
SO THAT THEY HUMBLY BRING PIECES OF SILVER   421 16
BE MADE DEACON, HUMBLY KNEELING BEFORE HIM, AND SHALL R   534 03
AND WE HUMBLY BESEECH THEE, BY THE SAME THY BLESSED   545 26
THE RECEIVERS HUMBLY KNEELING, AND THE BISHOP SAYING, R   546 08
HUMBLY BESEECHING THEE TO ACCEPT THIS OUR MORNING   587 25
WE HUMBLY BESEECH THEE TO HAVE COMPASSION ON OUR   588 14
TO US, WE HUMBLY BEG, THROUGH THE MERITS AND   589 06
OF THE DAY, AND HUMBLY SUPPLICATE THY MERCIFUL   595 07
WE HUMBLY BESEECH THEE GRACIOUSLY TO BEHOLD AND BLESS   596 31

HUMILIATION

BODY OF OUR HUMILIATION THAT IT MAY BE CONFORMED UNTO   222 23

HUMILITY

GRANT THAT IN HUMILITY OF HEART THEY MAY EVER LOOK   042 26
JESUS CHRIST CAME TO VISIT US IN GREAT HUMILITY   090 15
SHOULD FOLLOW THE EXAMPLE OF HIS GREAT HUMILITY   134 09
ONE TO ANOTHER, AND BE CLOTHED WITH HUMILITY   192 31
LORD WITH ALL HUMILITY OF MIND, AND WITH MANY TEARS,   550 08
DEVOTION AND HUMILITY IN HIS SERVICE   564 19
WITH ALL HUMILITY AND READINESS OF HEART, TO   565 04

HUNDRED

AND WITH HIM AN HUNDRED FORTY AND FOUR THOUSAND,   102 30
SONG BUT THE HUNDRED AND FORTY AND FOUR THOUSAND,   103 07
TWO HUNDRED PENNYWORTH OF BREAD IS NOT   131 30
MORE THAN THREE HUNDRED PENCE, AND HAVE BEEN GIVEN TC   140 08
HAVING AN HUNDRED SHEEP, IF HE LOSE ONE OF THEM,   193 18
OF ABOVE FIVE HUNDRED BRETHREN AT ONCE   205 08
WHICH WAS FOUR HUNDRED AND THIRTY YEARS AFTER,   207 23
OWED HIM AN HUNDRED PENCE   221 24
TWO HUNDRED PENNYWORTH OF BREAD IS NOT   225 26
WERE ABOUT AN HUNDRED AND TWENTY,) MEN AND BRETHREN,   234 08
WERE SEALED AN HUNDRED AND FORTY AND FOUR THOUSAND CF   256 21

HUNDREDFOLD

AND BARE FRUIT AN HUNDREDFOLD   121 26
RECEIVE AN HUNDREDFOLD, AND SHALL INHERIT EVERLASTING   231 20

HUNGER

IF THINE ENEMY HUNGER, FEED HIM   113 06
IN HUNGER AND THIRST, IN FASTINGS OFTEN, IN   121 09
ENOUGH AND TO SPARE, AND I PERISH WITH HUNGER   202 12
THEY SHALL HUNGER NO MORE, NEITHER THIRST ANY MORE   257 12
ARE THEY WHICH DO HUNGER AND THIRST AFTER   257 12
CONSUMED WITH HUNGER IN THE LAND, NEITHER BEAR THE   262 18
THEY SHALL HUNGER NO MORE, NEITHER THIRST ANY MORE   341 23
10 THE LIONS DO LACK, AND SUFFER HUNGER   380 21

HUNGRED

HE WAS AFTERWARD AN HUNGRED   126 25
FOR I WAS AN HUNGRED, AND YE GAVE ME MEAT   259 05
SAW WE THEE AN HUNGRED, AND FED THEE   259 10

HUNGRY

HATH FILLED THE HUNGRY WITH GOOD THINGS   026 24
12 IF I BE HUNGRY, I WILL NOT TELL THEE   402 14
5 HUNGRY AND THIRSTY, *   476 14
AND FILLETH THE HUNGRY SOUL WITH GOODNESS   476 23
HE SETTETH THE HUNGRY, *   478 18
WHO FEEDETH THE HUNGRY   522 15

HUNT

EVIL SHALL HUNT THE WICKED PERSON TO OVERTHROW HIM   516 33

HUNTER

THE SNARE OF THE HUNTER, *   454 33

HURT

THY SERVANTS, BEING HURT BY NO PERSECUTIONS, MAY   058 22
MAY ASSAULT AND HURT THE SOUL   127 20
ALL THINGS THAT MAY HURT US   217 19
IT WAS GIVEN TO HURT THE EARTH AND THE SEA, SAYING,   256 17
THE SEA, SAYING, HURT NOT THE EARTH, NEITHER THE SEA,   256 17
TO HURT NOBODY BY WORD OR DEED   288 32
WICKED APPROACH TO HURT HIM   308 28
WORDS THAT MAY DO HURT, *   404 27
ALSO THAT SEEK THE HURT OF MY SOUL, *   415 11
SHALL NOT HURT HIM   451 20
THAT THOU HURT NOT THY FOOT AGAINST A STONE   455 20
18 WHOSE FEET THEY HURT IN THE STOCKS   471 08
DO TAKE ANY HURT OR HINDRANCE BY REASON OF YOUR   540 11
NOT TO HURT, BUT TO HELP   558 03
PRIDE COME NIGH TO HURT THEM, NOR THE HAND OF THE   574 14
TO HURT NOBODY BY WORD OR DEED   580 07

HURTETH

THE CHURCH, AND HURTETH THE AUTHORITY OF THE   609 40

HURTFUL

AWAY FROM US ALL HURTFUL THINGS, AND TO GIVE US THOSE   199 30
FROM ALL THINGS HURTFUL, AND LEAD US TO ALL THINGS   210 20

HUSBAND

THEN JOSEPH HER HUSBAND, BEING A JUST MAN, AND NOT   104 30
MANY MORE CHILDREN THAN SHE WHICH HATH AN HUSBAND   131 11
LIVED WITH AN HUSBAND SEVEN YEARS FROM HER VIRGINITY   233 18
FOR THE HUSBAND IS THE HEAD OF THE WIFE, EVEN AS   267 15
AND THE WIFE SEE THAT SHE REVERENCE HER HUSBAND   268 03
TO THY WEDDED HUSBAND, TO LIVE TOGETHER AFTER GCD'S   301 14
TO MY WEDDED HUSBAND, TO HAVE AND TO HOLD FROM THIS   302 04
THE HUSBAND OF ONE WIFE, VIGILANT,   549 20
PREPARED AS A BRIDE ADORNED FOR HER HUSBAND   567 14

HUSBANDMAN

OF THE HUSBANDMAN, AND GRANT SUCH SEASONABLE WEATHER   039 28
AND MY FATHER IS THE HUSBANDMAN   238 05
OF THE HUSBANDMAN IN THE RETURNS OF THE FRUITS CF THE   265 12

HUSBANDS

UNTO YOUR OWN HUSBANDS, AS UNTO THE LORD   267 14
BE TO THEIR OWN HUSBANDS IN EVERY THING   267 18
HUSBANDS, LOVE YOUR WIVES, EVEN AS CHRIST ALSC LCVED   267 19
DEACONS BE THE HUSBANDS OF ONE WIFE, RULING THEIR   531 33

HUSHED

THE BUSY WORLD IS HUSHED, AND THE FEVER OF LIFE IS   594 32

HUSKS

HIS BELLY WITH THE HUSKS THAT THE SWINE DID EAT   202 09

HYMN

HERE SHALL BE SAID OR SUNG THE FOLLOWING HYMN   R 010 02
BE SUNG OR SAID THE HYMN FOLLOWING   R 014 04
BE SUNG OR SAID THE HYMN CALLED MAGNIFICAT, AS   R 026 06
BE SUNG OR SAID THE HYMN CALLED NUNC DIMITTIS,   R 028 06
HERE MAY BE SUNG A HYMN OR AN ANTHEM   R 070 21
THERE MAY BE SUNG A HYMN, OR AN OFFERTORY ANTHEM IN   R 073 35
HERE MAY BE SUNG A HYMN   R 082 24
ALL STANDING, OR SOME PROPER`HYMN   R 083 33
THEY HAD SUNG AN HYMN, THEY WENT OUT INTO THE MOUNT   141 17
THE SINGING OF A HYMN, SHALL BE SAID BY THE MINISTER   R 283 03
HERE MAY BE SUNG A HYMN, AFTER WHICH THE MINISTER,   R 285 11
SHALL BE SUNG A HYMN, AFTER WHICH THE MINISTER SHALL   R 289 12
THE SINGING OF A HYMN, THERE SHALL BE SAID THE   R 290 03
HERE MAY BE SUNG A HYMN, AFTER WHICH, THE PEOPLE   R 290 25
AFTER ANOTHER HYMN, THE MINISTER SHALL PROCEED WITH   R 292 02
HERE MAY BE SUNG A HYMN, AFTER WHICH THE MINISTER   R 294 02
THEM THE FOLLOWING HYMN, THE WOMAN STILL KNEELING   R 305 15
HERE MAY BE SUNG A HYMN OR ANTHEM   R 331 28
HERE MAY BE SUNG A HYMN OR AN ANTHEM   R 340 02

HYMNS

IN PSALMS AND HYMNS AND SPIRITUAL SONGS, SINGING WITH   116 13
IN PSALMS AND HYMNS AND SPIRITUAL SONGS, SINGING AND   217 28

HYPOCRISIES

AND HYPOCRISIES, AND ENVIES, AND ALL EVIL   259 25

HYPOCRISY

FROM PRIDE, VAINGLORY, AND HYPOCRISY   054 24

HYPOCRITE

THOU HYPOCRITE, CAST OUT FIRST THE BEAM OUT OF THINE   195 10

HYPOCRITES

AS THE HYPOCRITES, OF A SAD COUNTENANCE   125 09
AND SAID, WHY TEMPT YE ME, YE HYPOCRITES   223 06

HYSSOP

PURGE ME WITH HYSSOP, AND I SHALL BE CLEAN   060 24
SCARLET WOOL, AND HYSSOP, AND SPRINKLED BOTH THE BOOK   147 21
AND PUT IT UPON HYSSOP, AND PUT IT TO HIS MOUTH   160 27
PURGE ME WITH HYSSOP, AND I SHALL BE CLEAN   403 22

ICE

O YE ICE AND SNOW, BLESS YE THE LORD   012 26
HE CASTETH FORTH HIS ICE LIKE MORSELS   523 29

IDLE

SAW OTHERS STANDING IDLE IN THE MARKET-PLACE, AND   119 20
OTHERS STANDING IDLE, AND SAITH UNTO THEM, WHY STAND   119 25
WHY STAND YE HERE ALL THE DAY IDLE   119 26

IDOLATER

WHO IS AN IDOLATER, HATH ANY INHERITANCE IN THE   129 07

IDOLATERS

NEITHER BE YE IDOLATERS, AS WERE SOME OF THEM   201 15

IDOLATRY

IDOLATRY, WITCHCRAFT, HATRED,   209 21

IDOLS

UNTO THESE DUMB IDOLS, EVEN AS YE WERE LED   203 18
ALL THE GODS OF THE HEATHEN, THEY ARE BUT IDOLS   460 08
WORSHIPPED THEIR IDOLS, WHICH BECAME A SNARE UNTC   475 08
OFFERED UNTO THE IDOLS OF CANAAN   475 13
4 THEIR IDOLS ARE SILVER AND GOLD, *   485 18

IGNORANCE

ALL ERROR, IGNORANCE, PRIDE, AND PREJUDICE   036 31
IGNORANCE, HELPLESSNESS, GRIEF, TROUBLE,   048 08
AND OUR IGNORANCE IN ASKING   049 30
FROM THEM ALL IGNORANCE, HARDNESS OF HEART, AND   157 09
TO SILENCE THE IGNORANCE OF FOOLISH MEN   173 22
THROUGH THE IGNORANCE THAT IS IN THEM, BECAUSE OF THE   216 06

IGNORANCES

AND IGNORANCES   057 15

IGNORANT

ABRAHAM BE IGNORANT OF US, AND ISRAEL ACKNOWLEDGE US   139 22
YE SHOULD BE IGNORANT, HOW THAT ALL OUR FATHERS WERE   201 05
I WOULD NOT HAVE YOU IGNORANT   203 17
HAVE YOU TO BE IGNORANT, BRETHREN, CONCERNING THEM   268 28
AS WELL AS THE IGNORANT AND FOOLISH, AND LEAVE THEIR   400 24
WAS I, AND IGNORANT, *   429 20

ILL

LOVE WORKETH NO ILL TO HIS NEIGHBOUR   090 29
THOU ART GUIDE, NO ILL CAN COME   544 09
THOU ART GUIDE, NO ILL CAN COME   556 17

ILLUMINATE

THEE TO ILLUMINATE ALL BISHOPS, PRIESTS, AND DEACCNS,   055 30
THEE TO ILLUMINATE ALL BISHOPS, ETC   R 531 02
THEE TO ILLUMINATE ALL BISHOPS, ETC   R 537 08
THEE TO ILLUMINATE ALL BISHOPS, ETC   R 553 15

ILLUMINATION

WITH THE ILLUMINATION OF THE HOLY GHOST   573 17

ILLUMINED

THAT IT, BEING ILLUMINED BY THE DOCTRINE OF THY   101 06

IMAGE

WHO HAST CREATED MAN IN THINE OWN IMAGE   044 10
THYSELF ANY GRAVEN IMAGE, NOR THE LIKENESS OF ANY   068 08
AND THE EXPRESS IMAGE OF HIS PERSON, AND UPHOLDING   096 27
AND NOT THE VERY IMAGE OF THE THINGS, CAN NEVER WITH   157 16
WHOSE IS THIS IMAGE AND SUPERSCRIPTION   223 08
WHO IS THE IMAGE OF GOD, SHOULD SHINE UNTO   251 04
THYSELF ANY GRAVEN IMAGE, NOR THE LIKENESS OF ANY   286 08
WE HAVE BORNE THE IMAGE OF THE EARTHY, WE SHALL ALSC   329 31
ALSO BEAR THE IMAGE OF THE HEAVENLY   329 32
THOU MAKE THEIR IMAGE TO VANISH OUT OF THE CITY   429 17
AND WORSHIPPED THE MOLTEN IMAGE   474 07
THYSELF ANY GRAVEN IMAGE, NOR THE LIKENESS OF ANY   578 27
BE MADE LIKE THE IMAGE OF HIS ONLY-BEGOTTEN SCN JESUS   606 14

IMAGES

AND PROVOKED HIM TO DISPLEASURE WITH THEIR IMAGES   438 29
WORSHIP CARVED IMAGES, AND THAT DELIGHT IN VAIN GODS   461 10
15 AS FOR THE IMAGES OF THE HEATHEN, THEY ARE BUT   510 32
AS WELL OF IMAGES AS OF RELICS, AND ALSO INVOCATION   607 15

IMAGINATION

PROUD IN THE IMAGINATION OF THEIR HEARTS   026 21
MISCHIEVOUS IMAGINATION PROSPER, LEST THEY BE TCC   516 25

IMAGINATIONS

LET THEM PERISH THROUGH THEIR OWN IMAGINATICNS   348 23
AND LET THEM FOLLOW THEIR OWN IMAGINATIONS   443 05

IMAGINE

DO THE PEOPLE IMAGINE A VAIN THING   345 26
BUT IMAGINE MISCHIEF IN THEIR HEARTS   373 12
THAT IMAGINE MISCHIEF FOR ME   381 26
BUT THEY IMAGINE DECEITFUL WORDS AGAINST THEM THAT   383 03
ME DO THEY IMAGINE THIS EVIL   392 14
ALL THAT THEY IMAGINE IS TO DO ME EVIL   408 24
2 YEA, YE IMAGINE MISCHIEF IN YOUR HEART UPON THE   410 10
HOW LONG WILL YE IMAGINE MISCHIEF AGAINST EVERY MAN   413 31

IMAGINE   CONTINUED

6 THEY IMAGINE WICKEDNESS, AND PRACTISE IT   415 30
I HATE THEM THAT IMAGINE EVIL THINGS   497 24
FOR THEY IMAGINE BUT DECEIT   498 05
2 WHO IMAGINE MISCHIEF IN THEIR HEARTS, *   516 11

IMAGINED

IN THE CRAFTY WILINESS THAT THEY HAVE IMAGINED   353 07
AND IMAGINED SUCH A DEVICE AS THEY ARE NOT ABLE TC   365 27
AND IMAGINED DECEIT ALL THE DAY LONG   388 16
3 THEY HAVE IMAGINED CRAFTILY AGAINST THY PEOPLE,   444 09
THE PROUD HAVE IMAGINED A LIE AGAINST ME   494 18

IMAGINETH

4 HE IMAGINETH MISCHIEF UPON HIS BED, AND HATH SET   383 33
3 THY TONGUE IMAGINETH WICKEDNESS, *   404 22
WHICH IMAGINETH MISCHIEF AS A LAW   458 27

IMMACULATE

BLOOD OF THAT IMMACULATE LAMB, THAT WAS SLAIN TO TAKE 317 17

IMMANUEL

AND SHALL CALL HIS NAME IMMANUEL   235 32

IMMEDIATELY

COMMUNION IS IMMEDIATELY TO FOLLOW, THE MINISTER MAY, R 003 06
IMMEDIATELY AFTER THE LORD BE WITH YOU, ETC   R 003 13
IMMEDIATELY BEFORE THE VENITE MAY BE SUNG CR   R 008 14
COMMUNION IS IMMEDIATELY TO FOLLOW, THE MINISTER AT R 010 03
IMMEDIATELY AFTER THE LORD BE WITH YOU, ETC   R 021 10
MAY BE READ IMMEDIATELY AFTER THE PRAYER, WE HUMBLY R 060 03
BEEN SAID IMMEDIATELY BEFORE IN MORNING PRAYER   R 070 30
OR IMMEDIATELY AFTER THE CREED, MAY BE SAID   R 071 29
OR ELSE IMMEDIATELY SHALL BE SAID OR SUNG BY THE   R 077 03
IMMEDIATELY AFTER THE BLESSING, REVERENTLY EAT   R 084 32
HOLY DAY, IMMEDIATELY PRECEDING,) HE SHALL READ THIS R 086 26
AND IMMEDIATELY HIS LEPROSY WAS CLEANSED   115 02
IMMEDIATELY AFTER THE TRIBULATION OF THOSE DAYS SHALL 118 13
AND IMMEDIATELY HE RECEIVED HIS SIGHT, AND FOLLCWED   124 04
AND IMMEDIATELY, WHILE HE YET SPAKE, COMETH JUDAS,   142 14
AND IMMEDIATELY, WHILE HE YET SPAKE, THE COCK CREW   151 18
AND IMMEDIATELY I WAS IN THE SPIRIT   187 04
AND THEY IMMEDIATELY LEFT THE SHIP AND THEIR FATHER, 227 32
AND IMMEDIATELY THERE FELL FROM HIS EYES AS IT HAD   230 34
WAS OPENED IMMEDIATELY, AND HIS TONGUE LOOSED, AND HE 243 25
EITHER IMMEDIATELY AFTER THE SECOND LESSON AT   R 273 14
THEY MAY OPEN UNTO HIM IMMEDIATELY   534 19
AND IMMEDIATELY BEFORE THE BENEDICTION,   R 534 28
AND IMMEDIATELY BEFORE THE BENEDICTION,   R 547 02
IMMEDIATELY AFTER   R 547 22
AND IMMEDIATELY BEFORE THE BENEDICTION, SHALL BE   R 559 04
AND IMMEDIATELY BEFORE THE FINAL BLESSING, THE   R 568 04

IMMERSION

AT THE IMMERSION OR THE POURING OF WATER, THE   R 282 11

IMMINENT

OR ANY IMMINENT PERIL, IF A MINISTER CANNOT BE   R 281 27

IMMODERATE

THOSE IMMODERATE RAINS, WHEREWITH THOU HAST AFFLICTED 040 25
OF US WITH IMMODERATE RAIN AND WATERS, AND IN THY   051 23

IMMORTAL

TO THE LIFE IMMORTAL, THROUGH HIM WHO LIVETH AND   090 17
ALMIGHTY AND IMMORTAL GOD, THE AID OF ALL WHO NEED,   274 09
LOVE WHICH IS IMMORTAL, AND WHICH THOU HAST   596 08

IMMORTALITY

THOU HAST GIVEN UNTO US LIFE AND IMMORTALITY   147 11
AND THIS MORTAL MUST PUT ON IMMORTALITY   330 06
HAVE PUT ON IMMORTALITY, THEN SHALL BE BROUGHT TC   330 08

IMPART

SPIRIT ART, WHO DOST THY SEVENFOLD GIFTS IMPART   543 34
TO EVERY SENSE IMPART, AND SHED THY LOVE IN EVERY   545 02
SPIRIT ART, WHO DOST THY SEVENFOLD GIFTS IMPART   556 09
TO EVERY SENSE IMPART, AND SHED THY LOVE IN EVERY   557 08
ALIVE IN US THE HOLY DESIRES THOU DOST IMPART   594 20

IMPARTIALLY

AND IMPARTIALLY ADMINISTER THE LAW IN THE FEAR   036 04
TRULY AND IMPARTIALLY ADMINISTER JUSTICE, TO THE   074 17

IMPATIENT

BE THE PEOPLE NEVER SO IMPATIENT   462 16

IMPEDIMENT

AND HAD AN IMPEDIMENT IN HIS SPEECH   206 30
YOU KNOW ANY IMPEDIMENT, WHY YE MAY NOT BE LAWFULLY   300 27
BUT IF NO IMPEDIMENT SHALL BE ALLEGED, OR SUSPECTED, R 301 04

IMPEDIMENT   CONTINUED

OR JUST IMPEDIMENT, WHY THESE TWO PERSONS SHOULD NCT R 304 23
OTHER JUST IMPEDIMENT, DO NOT RECEIVE THE SACRAMENT R 323 24
KNOWETH ANY IMPEDIMENT, OR NOTABLE CRIME, IN ANY OF   530 22
THE CRIME OR IMPEDIMENT IS   530 25
CRIME OR IMPEDIMENT BE OBJECTED, THE BISHOP SHALL   R 530 26
KNOWETH ANY IMPEDIMENT, OR NOTABLE CRIME, IN ANY OF   536 28
THE CRIME OR IMPEDIMENT IS   536 31
CRIME OR IMPEDIMENT BE OBJECTED, THE BISHOP SHALL   R 537 02

IMPERFECT

EYES DID SEE MY SUBSTANCE, YET BEING IMPERFECT   515 20
UP THESE OUR IMPERFECT PRAYERS   591 33

IMPIETY

CANNOT BE TAUGHT WITHOUT ARROGANCY AND IMPIETY   605 26

IMPLORE

WE IMPLORE THY GRACE AND PROTECTION FOR   588 27

IMPORTANCE

OF HOW GREAT IMPORTANCE THIS OFFICE IS, WHEREUNTC YE 539 28

IMPORTANT

WEIGHTY AND IMPORTANT CONSIDERATIONS, ACCORDING TO   V 16
AND NOW, THIS IMPORTANT WORK BEING BROUGHT TO A   VI 35

IMPORTUNITY

OF HIS IMPORTUNITY HE WILL RISE AND GIVE HIM AS MANY 263 02

IMPOSITION

WITH IMPOSITION OF HANDS, WERE APPROVED AND   529 17
THEE BY THE IMPOSITION OF OUR HANDS   546 11
THEE BY THE IMPOSITION OF OUR HANDS   546 19
THEE BY THE IMPOSITION OF OUR HANDS   558 14
THEE BY THIS IMPOSITION OF OUR HANDS   558 17

IMPOSSIBLE

FOR WITH GOD NOTHING SHALL BE IMPOSSIBLE   236 28

IMPOTENT

POOR, AND IMPOTENT PEOPLE OF THE PARISH, THAT   533 19

IMPRESSED

HEART BE DULY IMPRESSED WITH A SENSE OF THY MERCIFUL 053 04

IMPRINT

IMPRINT UPON OUR HEARTS SUCH A DREAD OF THY   588 17

IMPRISONMENTS

IN IMPRISONMENTS, IN TUMULTS, IN LABOURS, IN   126 11

IMPUTE

IN THY MERCY, IMPUTE NOT UNTO HIM HIS FORMER SINS,   314 09

IMPUTETH

WHOM THE LORD IMPUTETH NO SIN, *   377 24

INAPPLICABLE

AS INAPPLICABLE TO THE CIRCUMSTANCES OF THIS CHURCH R 610 26

INASMUCH

I SAY UNTO YOU, INASMUCH AS YE HAVE DONE IT UNTC CNE 073 03
INASMUCH AS BOTH IN MY BONDS, AND IN THE DEFENCE AND 220 28
I SAY UNTO YOU, INASMUCH AS YE HAVE DONE IT UNTO ONE 259 15
INASMUCH AS IT MAY SOMETIMES BE EXPEDIENT TO SAY   R 336 30

INCARNATE

AND WAS INCARNATE BY THE HOLY GHOST OF THE VIRGIN   016 07
AND WAS INCARNATE BY THE HOLY GHOST OF THE VIRGIN   030 12
AND WAS INCARNATE BY THE HOLY GHOST OF THE VIRGIN   071 09
LIGHT OF THINE INCARNATE WORD   106 26

INCARNATION

BY THE MYSTERY OF THY HOLY INCARNATION   055 06
KNOWN THE INCARNATION OF THY SON JESUS CHRIST BY THE 235 19
BY THY HOLY INCARNATION, BY THY CROSS AND PASSION,   318 04

INCENSE

IN EVERY PLACE INCENSE SHALL BE OFFERED UNTO MY NAME, 004 14
PRAYER BE SET FORTH IN THY SIGHT AS THE INCENSE   021 16
WITH THE INCENSE OF RAMS   418 11
PRAYER BE SET FORTH IN THY SIGHT AS THE INCENSE   517 10

INCITED

FROM SIN, AND INCITED TO OUR DUTY   588 17

INCLINE

THEY MAY ALWAYS INCLINE TO THY WILL, AND WALK IN THY   017 33
DEAR SON, AND INCLINE THE HEARTS OF MANY TO DEDICATE   039 19
MERCIFULLY TO INCLINE THINE EARS TO US WHO HAVE NOW   050 08
UPON US, AND INCLINE OUR HEARTS TO KEEP THIS LAW   068 06
UPON US, AND INCLINE OUR HEARTS TO KEEP THIS LAW   069 05
UPON US, AND INCLINE OUR HEARTS TO KEEP THIS LAW   286 06
UPON US, AND INCLINE OUR HEARTS TO KEEP THIS LAW   287 04
INCLINE THINE EAR TO ME, AND HEARKEN UNTO MY WORDS   358 30
INCLINE THINE EAR   397 05
4 I WILL INCLINE MINE EAR TO THE PARABLE, *   400 12
16 IF I INCLINE UNTO WICKEDNESS WITH MINE HEART,   418 16
INCLINE THINE EAR UNTO ME, AND SAVE ME   425 07
INCLINE YOUR EARS UNTO THE WORDS OF MY MOUTH   434 27
THY PRESENCE, INCLINE THINE EAR UNTO MY CALLING   448 31
INCLINE THINE EAR UNTO ME WHEN I CALL   464 13
36 INCLINE MY HEART UNTO THY TESTIMONIES, *   492 11
WRONG DESIRES, INCLINE OUR HEARTS TO KEEP THY LAW,   594 13
INCLINE THE HEART OF EMPLOYERS AND OF THOSE WHOM THEY   599 31

INCLINED

BECAUSE HE HATH INCLINED HIS EAR UNTO ME   305 20
AND HE INCLINED UNTO ME, AND HEARD MY CALLING   390 09
BECAUSE HE HATH INCLINED HIS EAR UNTO ME   486 21
MINE HEART BE INCLINED TO ANY EVIL THING   517 15
HIS OWN NATURE INCLINED TO EVIL, SO THAT THE FLESH   604 32

INCLOSED

THIS DONE, THEY INCLOSED A GREAT MULTITUDE OF FISHES   196 18
10 THEY ARE INCLOSED IN THEIR OWN FAT, *   359 06

INCLUDED

INDEPENDENCE WAS NECESSARILY INCLUDED   VI 09

INCOMPREHENSIBLE

MAJESTY INCOMPREHENSIBLE, WHOM THE HEAVEN OF HEAVENS   564 28

INCORPORATE

VERY MEMBERS INCORPORATE IN THE MYSTICAL BODY OF THY   083 22
AND TO INCORPORATE HIM INTO THY HOLY CHURCH   280 31

INCORRUPTIBLE

BUT WE AN INCORRUPTIBLE   119 09
BE RAISED INCORRUPTIBLE, AND WE SHALL BE CHANGED   330 04

INCORRUPTION

IT IS RAISED IN INCORRUPTION   329 20
NEITHER DOTH CORRUPTION INHERIT INCORRUPTION   329 35
MUST PUT ON INCORRUPTION, AND THIS MORTAL MUST PUT ON   330 05
HAVE PUT ON INCORRUPTION, AND THIS MORTAL SHALL HAVE   330 07

INCREASE

AND WITH THE FIRSTFRUITS OF ALL THINE INCREASE   005 21
THEN SHALL THE EARTH BRING FORTH HER INCREASE   028 28
THAT OUR LAND MAY GIVE HER INCREASE   040 11
YIELD HER INCREASE FOR OUR USE AND BENEFIT   040 27
AND THE EARTH BRING FORTH HER INCREASE   040 31
INCREASE THE FRUITS OF THE EARTH BY THY HEAVENLY   040 32
FOR THE INCREASE OF THE GROUND AND THE GATHERING IN   050 22
HER FRUITS OF INCREASE, TO THY GLORY AND OUR COMFORT   052 04
ALL THY PEOPLE INCREASE OF GRACE TO HEAR MEEKLY THY   056 14
ELSE BUT INCREASE YOUR CONDEMNATION   087 30
INCREASE AND MULTIPLY UPON US THY MERCY   194 05
OF THY NAME, INCREASE IN US TRUE RELIGION, NOURISH US   198 22
UNTO US THE INCREASE OF FAITH, HOPE, AND CHARITY   209 08
MAKETH INCREASE OF THE BODY UNTO THE EDIFYING   238 02
SHALL YIELD HER INCREASE, AND THEY SHALL BE SAFE IN   262 11
STILL YIELD HER INCREASE, TO THY GLORY AND OUR   265 15
INCREASE THIS KNOWLEDGE, AND CONFIRM THIS FAITH IN US   276 10
OF THY NAME, INCREASE IN US TRUE RELIGION, NOURISH US   283 10
AND DAILY INCREASE IN THEM THY MANIFOLD GIFTS OF   297 18
AND DAILY INCREASE IN THY HOLY SPIRIT MORE AND MORE,   297 28
MAY DAILY INCREASE IN WISDOM AND STATURE, AND GROW IN   307 04
THAN WHEN THEIR CORN AND WINE AND OIL INCREASE   347 27
IF RICHES INCREASE, SET NOT YOUR HEART UPON THEM   414 19
BLESSEST THE INCREASE OF IT   417 06
6 THEN SHALL THE EARTH BRING FORTH HER INCREASE   419 02
AND OUR LAND SHALL GIVE HER INCREASE   446 32
TO YIELD THEM FRUITS OF INCREASE   478 21
THE LORD SHALL INCREASE YOU MORE AND MORE, *   486 06
VICTUALS WITH INCREASE, *   509 04
WE MAY DAILY INCREASE AND GO FORWARDS IN THE   545 30
AND THE INCREASE OF THY KINGDOM   547 12
THAT THE INCREASE COMING THEREBY MAY BE   558 23
PLEASE THEE TO INCREASE THE NUMBER OF THE MINISTERS   561 12
INCREASE IN THEM TRUE RELIGION   572 29
O LORD, AS HIS DAYS INCREASE   597 28

INCREASED

MAY BE INCREASED AMONG US, AND ALL GOOD LEARNING   042 24
AND JESUS INCREASED IN WISDOM AND STATURE, AND IN   111 06
BUT SAUL INCREASED THE MORE IN STRENGTH, AND   231 08

INCREASED   CONTINUED

HOW ARE THEY INCREASED THAT TROUBLE ME   309 14
HOW ARE THEY INCREASED THAT TROUBLE ME   346 25
OR IF THE GLORY OF HIS HOUSE BE INCREASED   401 08
24 AND HE INCREASED HIS PEOPLE EXCEEDINGLY, *   471 20
AND THE WORD OF GOD INCREASED   532 20
AND GRACE INCREASED BY VIRTUE OF PRAYER UNTO GOD   608 29

INCREASETH

HATE THEE INCREASETH EVER MORE AND MORE   431 25

INCREASING

AND INCREASING IN THE KNOWLEDGE OF GOD   224 05
GRANT THAT, INCREASING IN KNOWLEDGE AND LOVE OF THEE,   332 05

INCUMBENT

BY THE NEW INCUMBENT, AND BY THE OTHER CLERGY   R 570 03
TO THE NEW INCUMBENT, SAYING, IN THE NAME AND BEHALF   R 570 26
THEN THE NEW INCUMBENT SHALL SAY, I, A   R 570 31
RECEIVE THE INCUMBENT WITHIN THE RAILS OF THE ALTAR,   R 571 22

INCUMBENT'S

FOR THE NEW INCUMBENT'S INSTITUTION, THE BISHOP,   R 570 02

INDEBTED

THESE STATES IS INDEBTED, UNDER GOD, FOR HER FIRST   V 11

INDEMNIFICATION

DEMAND SUFFICIENT SURETY FOR HIS INDEMNIFICATION   R 301 03

INDEPENDENCE

INDEPENDENCE WAS NECESSARILY INCLUDED   VI 09

INDEPENDENT

BECAME INDEPENDENT WITH RESPECT TO CIVIL GOVERNMENT,   VI 08

INDIFFERENT

OWN NATURE INDIFFERENT, AND ALTERABLE, AND SO   V 15

INDIGNATION

WRATH AND INDIGNATION AGAINST US   075 22
GOD'S INDIGNATION AGAINST YOU   088 26
THAT HAD INDIGNATION WITHIN THEMSELVES, AND SAID, WHY   140 06
MOVED WITH INDIGNATION AGAINST THE TWO BRETHREN   247 19
AND ARE AFRAID AT THY WRATHFUL INDIGNATION   325 27
NOT IN THINE INDIGNATION, *   348 33
OF THE INDIGNATION OF MINE ENEMIES   350 02
OUT THINE INDIGNATION UPON THEM, *   423 23
A WAY TO HIS INDIGNATION, AND SPARED NOT THEIR SOUL   438 09
OUT THINE INDIGNATION UPON THE HEATHEN THAT HAVE NOT   440 11
AND TURNED THYSELF FROM THY WRATHFUL INDIGNATION   446 13
6 THINE INDIGNATION LIETH HARD UPON ME, *   449 09
AND ARE AFRAID AT THY WRATHFUL INDIGNATION   453 32
OR FEARETH ARIGHT THY INDIGNATION   454 12
OF THINE INDIGNATION AND WRATH   464 29
HIS WRATHFUL INDIGNATION, LEST HE SHOULD DESTROY   474 16

INDUSTRY

WITH HONOURABLE INDUSTRY, SOUND LEARNING, AND PURE   036 12
FOR THE PRODUCTS OF ALL HONEST INDUSTRY   048 12
AND HONEST INDUSTRY, AND SUFFER NOT THE HIRE OF THE   599 30

INDWELLING

BE FILLED WITH THE POWER OF HIS DIVINE INDWELLING   043 25
THAT BY THE INDWELLING OF THY HOLY SPIRIT, WE MAY BE   182 16
BY THY INDWELLING POWER, THE DISTRESS OF THIS   320 09
GUIDE BY THY INDWELLING SPIRIT THOSE WHOM THOU DOST   561 07

INEQUALITY

WITHOUT ANY DIFFERENCE OF INEQUALITY   079 12

INESTIMABLE

FOR THINE INESTIMABLE LOVE IN THE REDEMPTION OF THE   019 22
FOR THINE INESTIMABLE LOVE IN THE REDEMPTION OF THE   033 20
THAT HIS INESTIMABLE BENEFIT, AND ALSO DAILY   171 31

INFALLIBLE

BY MANY INFALLIBLE PROOFS, BEING SEEN OF THEM FORTY   177 27

INFANTS

AND MADEST INFANTS TO GLORIFY THEE BY THEIR DEATHS   102 23
WHY THEN ARE INFANTS BAPTIZED, WHEN BY REASON OF   292 31
THEIR SPONSORS, INFANTS ARE RECEIVED INTO CHRIST'S   292 33
IN THE ABSENCE OF THE PRIEST TO BAPTIZE INFANTS   533 16
WHY THEN ARE INFANTS BAPTIZED, WHEN BY REASON OF   581 31

INFECTION

AND THIS INFECTION OF NATURE DOTH REMAIN, YEA IN THEM   604 35

INFECTIOUS

OR OTHER INFECTIOUS SICKNESS, EXHORT THEIR   R 321 06

INFERIOR

IN THIS INFERIOR OFFICE, THAT THEY MAY BE FOUND   535 08

INFINITE

BY HIS INFINITE GOODNESS AND MERCY   006 02
OF AN INFINITE MAJESTY   010 21
BY HIS INFINITE GOODNESS AND MERCY   023 11
WHOSE KINGDOM IS EVERLASTING AND POWER INFINITE   032 05
THEE OF THINE INFINITE GOODNESS TO HEAR US, WHO NOW   040 05
AND HIS WISDOM IS INFINITE   523 05
WHO, OF THINE INFINITE LOVE AND GOODNESS TOWARDS US,   545 13
WHO, OF THINE INFINITE GOODNESS, HAST GIVEN THY ONLY   557 21
WHATEVER IN THY INFINITE WISDOM THOU SHALT SEE TO BE   566 22
OF INFINITE POWER, WISDOM, AND GOODNESS   603 04

INFIRMITIES

AND HEALETH ALL THINE INFIRMITIES   029 08
THEE TO HAVE COMPASSION UPON OUR INFIRMITIES   050 02
MERCIFULLY TO LOOK UPON OUR INFIRMITIES   059 22
UPON OUR INFIRMITIES, AND IN ALL OUR DANGERS AND   112 27
OF THE THINGS WHICH CONCERN MINE INFIRMITIES   121 14
AND HEALETH ALL THINE INFIRMITIES   312 24
OF HIS INFIRMITIES, TO THINE HONOUR AND GLORY   315 16
AND HEALETH ALL THINE INFIRMITIES   466 12
ON OUR INFIRMITIES, AND TO GIVE US THE CONSTANT   588 15

INFIRMITY

BECAUSE OF THE INFIRMITY OF YOUR FLESH   198 26
AND I SAID, IT IS MINE OWN INFIRMITY   311 18
FROM MEN'S BODIES ALL SICKNESS AND ALL INFIRMITY   315 08
10 AND I SAID, IT IS MINE OWN INFIRMITY   434 02
MIGHT SUPPLY TO STRENGTHEN OUR INFIRMITY   545 05
MIGHT SUPPLY TO STRENGTHEN OUR INFIRMITY   557 11

INFORM

9 I WILL INFORM THEE, AND TEACH THEE IN THE WAY   378 08
22 THAT HE MIGHT INFORM HIS PRINCES AFTER HIS WILL,   471 16

INGRATITUDE

IS YOUR INGRATITUDE TO GOD, AND HOW SORE PUNISHMENT   089 15

INHABITANTS

THAT THE INHABITANTS OF OUR LAND MAY IN PEACE AND   042 10

INHABITERS

WOE TO THE INHABITERS OF THE EARTH AND OF THE SEA   252 17
AND ALL THE INHABITERS THEREOF   432 04

INHABITETH

ONE THAT INHABITETH ETERNITY, WHOSE NAME IS HOLY   003 25

INHERIT

THAT YE SHOULD INHERIT A BLESSING   195 24
SHALL I DO TO INHERIT ETERNAL LIFE   208 13
THINGS SHALL NOT INHERIT THE KINGDOM OF GOD   209 25
AND SHALL INHERIT EVERLASTING LIFE   231 21
FOR THEY SHALL INHERIT THE EARTH   257 23
OF MY FATHER, INHERIT THE KINGDOM PREPARED FOR YOU   259 04
AND BLOOD CANNOT INHERIT THE KINGDOM OF GOD   329 33
DOTH CORRUPTION INHERIT INCORRUPTION   329 34
OF MY FATHER, INHERIT THE KINGDOM PREPARED FOR YOU   336 26
HIS SEED SHALL INHERIT THE LAND   370 10
THOSE SHALL INHERIT THE LAND   385 12
RIGHTEOUS SHALL INHERIT THE LAND, *   386 24
SERVANTS SHALL INHERIT IT   424 17

INHERITANCE

AND BLESS THINE INHERITANCE   031 09
HE HATH BY INHERITANCE OBTAINED A MORE EXCELLENT NAME   096 31
HATH ANY INHERITANCE IN THE KINGDOM OF CHRIST AND OF   129 08
MIGHT RECEIVE THE PROMISE OF ETERNAL INHERITANCE   133 07
THE TRIBES OF THINE INHERITANCE   139 26
FOR IF THE INHERITANCE BE OF THE LAW, IT IS NO MORE   207 25
OF THE INHERITANCE OF THE SAINTS IN LIGHT   224 09
OF THE INHERITANCE OF THE SAINTS IN LIGHT   335 33
FOR THINE INHERITANCE, *   346 13
OF MINE INHERITANCE, AND OF MY CUP   357 31
AND GIVE THY BLESSING UNTO THINE INHERITANCE   373 28
THAT HE HATH CHOSEN TO HIM, TO BE HIS INHERITANCE   379 13
AND THEIR INHERITANCE SHALL ENDURE FOR EVER   385 32
UPON THINE INHERITANCE, *   419 29
OF THINE INHERITANCE, *   430 08
AND WAS WROTH WITH HIS INHERITANCE   439 03
FEED JACOB HIS PEOPLE, AND ISRAEL HIS INHERITANCE   439 23
THE HEATHEN ARE COME UNTO THINE INHERITANCE   439 29
THOU SHALT TAKE ALL NATIONS TO THINE INHERITANCE   444 03
NEITHER WILL HE FORSAKE HIS INHERITANCE   458 15
THE LOT OF YOUR INHERITANCE   470 25
AND GIVE THANKS WITH THINE INHERITANCE   473 10
INSOMUCH THAT HE ABHORRED HIS OWN INHERITANCE   475 17
GIVE YOU AN INHERITANCE AMONG ALL THEM WHICH ARE   551 04

INHERITOR

HE MAY BE AN INHERITOR OF THINE EVERLASTING KINGDOM   281 04
OF GOD, AND AN INHERITOR OF THE KINGDOM OF HEAVEN   283 20
OF GOD, AND AN INHERITOR OF THE KINGDOM OF HEAVEN   577 10

INIQUITIES

NEITHER REWARD US ACCORDING TO OUR INIQUITIES   058 13
SINS AND INIQUITIES WILL I REMEMBER NO MORE   158 14
REMEMBER NOT, LORD, OUR INIQUITIES   308 10
NOR THE INIQUITIES OF OUR FOREFATHERS   308 11

INIQUITY

LAID ON HIM THE INIQUITY OF US ALL   022 16
THOU HAST LOVED RIGHTEOUSNESS, AND HATED INIQUITY   097 11
US FROM ALL INIQUITY, AND PURIFY UNTO HIMSELF A   098 24
NOT IN INIQUITY, BUT REJOICETH IN THE TRUTH   122 32
TO UNCLEANNESS AND TO INIQUITY UNTO INIQUITY   198 28
AND TO INIQUITY UNTO INIQUITY   198 28
MAN PURCHASED A FIELD WITH THE REWARD OF INIQUITY   234 13
THAT HER INIQUITY IS PARDONED   242 18
FOR THOU HATEST ALL THEM THAT WORK INIQUITY   348 10
ALL YE THAT WORK INIQUITY   349 14
THE UNGODLY TRAVAILETH WITH INIQUITY   350 21
BECAUSE OF MINE INIQUITY, *   376 13
THOU HAST LOVED RIGHTEOUSNESS, AND HATED INIQUITY   396 29
AND THEIR RIGHT HAND IS A RIGHT HAND OF INIQUITY   520 14
THAN TO BEHOLD INIQUITY, AND HAST PROMISED   589 27

INJURIES

FOR ALL INJURIES AND WRONGS DONE BY YOU TO   087 26

INJURY

NOT THINK A GREAT INJURY AND WRONG DONE UNTO HIM   088 23
HE HATH DONE INJURY OR WRONG TO ANY MAN, THAT HE MAKE   R 313 22

INN

BECAUSE THERE WAS NO ROOM FOR THEM IN THE INN   099 10
BROUGHT HIM TO AN INN, AND TOOK CARE OF HIM   208 32

INNER

HIS SPIRIT IN THE INNER MAN   212 15
HIS SPIRIT IN THE INNER MAN   281 10
HOLY SPIRIT IN THE INNER MAN   316 12

INNOCENCY

THEM WITH INNOCENCY OF LIFE, THAT THEY MAY FAITHFULLY   039 12
THAT BY THE INNOCENCY OF OUR LIVES, AND CONSTANCY OF   102 25
LIVES TO THEIR INNOCENCY AND PERFECT FAITH, THAT AT   340 31
TO THE INNOCENCY THAT IS IN ME   350 08
MY HANDS IN INNOCENCY, O LORD   371 08
38 KEEP INNOCENCY, AND TAKE HEED UNTO THE THING THAT   387 08
12 AND IN MY INNOCENCY THOU UPHOLDEST ME, *   392 23
AND WASHED MY HANDS IN INNOCENCY   429 03
THEM WITH INNOCENCY OF LIFE, THAT, BOTH BY WORD AND   531 20
THEM WITH INNOCENCY OF LIFE, THAT, BOTH BY WORD AND   537 25
THEM WITH INNOCENCY OF LIFE, THAT, BOTH BY WORD AND   548 03
ADORN HIM WITH INNOCENCY OF LIFE, THAT, BOTH BY WORD   553 31
ENDUE HIM WITH INNOCENCY OF LIFE, THAT HE MAY   572 11

INNOCENT

PROTECT THE INNOCENT, AWAKEN THE GUILTY   046 25
BETRAYED THE INNOCENT BLOOD   135 06
I AM INNOCENT OF THE BLOOD OF THIS JUST   136 11
IN HIS LURKING DENS DOTH HE MURDER THE INNOCENT   353 22
NOR TAKEN REWARD AGAINST THE INNOCENT   357 18
AND INNOCENT FROM THE GREAT OFFENCE   364 12
AND CONDEMN THE INNOCENT BLOOD   458 29
37 AND SHED INNOCENT BLOOD, EVEN THE BLOOD OF THEIR   475 11
BEFRIEND INNOCENT SUFFERERS, AND SANCTIFY TO THEM THE   599 09

INNOCENTLY

FOR I HAVE WALKED INNOCENTLY   370 30
11 BUT AS FOR ME, I WILL WALK INNOCENTLY   371 18

INNUMERABLE

FOR THE INNUMERABLE BENEFITS PROCURED UNTO US BY THE   081 05
AND THE INNUMERABLE BENEFITS WHICH BY HIS   086 14
15 FOR INNUMERABLE TROUBLES ARE COME ABOUT ME   391 10
CREEPING INNUMERABLE, BOTH SMALL AND GREAT BEASTS   469 11
CATERPILLARS INNUMERABLE, *   472 07

INORDINATE

FROM ALL INORDINATE AND SINFUL AFFECTIONS   054 27
AND INORDINATE LOVE OF RICHES, AND TO FOLLOW   250 23
OR INORDINATE DESIRES, MAY REST THERE   590 14

INQUIRE

MAY THE MINISTER INQUIRE OF THE SICK PERSON AS TO HIS   R 313 18

INQUIRED

THEM EARLY, AND INQUIRED AFTER GOD   437 07
I HAVE INQUIRED CONCERNING THEM, AND ALSO   530 18

INQUIRED   CONTINUED

I HAVE INQUIRED CONCERNING THEM, AND ALSO   536 19

INQUIRY

THE CHURCH, THAT INQUIRY BE MADE OF EVIL MINISTERS,   608 19

INQUISITION

HE MAKETH INQUISITION FOR BLOOD, HE REMEMBERETH THEM,   352 13

INSET

OMIT THAT PART OF THE COMMANDMENT WHICH IS INSET   R 067 27
WHICH IS INSET MAY BE OMITTED   R 286 04

INSOMUCH

INSOMUCH THAT, IF IT WERE POSSIBLE, THEY SHALL   118 06
INSOMUCH THAT THE GOVERNOR MARVELLED GREATLY   135 24
INSOMUCH AS THAT FIELD IS CALLED IN THEIR PROPER   234 16
INSOMUCH THAT THEY BROUGHT FORTH THE SICK INTO THE   249 26
INSOMUCH THAT WHOSO SEETH THEM SHALL LAUGH THEM TO   416 02
36 INSOMUCH THAT THEY WORSHIPPED THEIR IDOLS,   475 08
INSOMUCH THAT HE ABHORRED HIS OWN INHERITANCE   475 17
INSOMUCH THAT BY THEM A LIVELY FAITH MAY BE AS   605 14
INSOMUCH THAT TO SUCH AS RIGHTLY, WORTHILY, AND WITH   608 36

INSPIRATION

BY THE INSPIRATION OF THY HOLY SPIRIT, THAT WE MAY   067 18
BY THY HOLY INSPIRATION WE MAY THINK THOSE THINGS   175 30
BY THE INSPIRATION OF THY HOLY SPIRIT, TO PUT   260 21
THE SECRET INSPIRATION OF THE BLESSED SPIRIT,   564 13
AND THE INSPIRATION OF HIS SPIRIT, ARE NOT PLEASANT   605 17

INSPIRE

THEE TO INSPIRE CONTINUALLY THE UNIVERSAL CHURCH WITH   074 11
WHO DIDST INSPIRE THY SERVANT SAINT LUKE THE   253 16
AND DIDST INSPIRE THINE APOSTLES TO CHOOSE INTO THE   531 16
OUR SOULS INSPIRE, AND LIGHTEN WITH CELESTIAL   543 31
OUR SOULS INSPIRE, AND LIGHTEN WITH CELESTIAL   556 06
PLEASE THEE TO INSPIRE ALL BISHOPS, PRIESTS, AND   560 18

INSPIRED

BEING INSPIRED BY THY LOVE, THEY MAY WORTHILY   044 03
MAY IN HEART BE INSPIRED BY THY WISDOM, AND IN WORK   594 25

INSTANT

CONTINUING INSTANT IN PRAYER   111 27
AND THEY WERE INSTANT WITH LOUD VOICES, REQUIRING   154 03
COMING IN THAT INSTANT GAVE THANKS LIKEWISE UNTO THE   233 21

INSTANTLY

AND AT NOON-DAY WILL I PRAY, AND THAT INSTANTLY   407 26

INSTEAD

MAY USE, INSTEAD OF WHAT FOLLOWS, THE ABSOLUTION FROM   R 007 04
CHURCHES MAY, INSTEAD OF THE WORDS, HE DESCENDED INTO   R 015 16
CHURCHES MAY, INSTEAD OF THE WORDS, HE DESCENDED INTO   R 029 21
HOLY COMMUNION, INSTEAD OF THE FORMER, HE MAY USE   R 088 11
MORNING PRAYER, INSTEAD OF THE VENITE, THE FOLLOWING   R 162 28
INSTEAD OF THE VENITE, THE FOLLOWING SHALL BE SAID   R 264 17
BUT INSTEAD OF THE SENTENCE OF COMMITTAL, THE   R 337 07
16 INSTEAD OF THY FATHERS, THOU SHALT HAVE CHILDREN,   397 19
OF THE BISHOP, INSTEAD OF THE LITANY APPOINTED, MAY   R 531 09
OF THE BISHOP, INSTEAD OF THE LITANY APPOINTED, MAY   R 537 15
INSTEAD OF THE LITANY, MAY BE SAID THE LITANY   R 553 23

INSTITUTE

AND DID INSTITUTE, AND IN HIS HOLY GOSPEL COMMAND US   080 13
DID INSTITUTE THE SACRAMENT OF HIS BODY AND   152 08
MAY PROCEED TO INSTITUTE HIM INTO THE PARISH   R 569 06
ALSO HEREBY DO INSTITUTE YOU INTO SAID PARISH, (CR   569 17

INSTITUTED

HE HATH INSTITUTED AND ORDAINED HOLY MYSTERIES,   086 16
INSTITUTED OF GOD, SIGNIFYING UNTO US THE   300 11
A CANONICALLY INSTITUTED PRIEST INTO THE OFFICE OF   569 23
HE MAY NOT BE INSTITUTED, WE PROCEED NO FURTHER,   570 18
SHALL THE INSTITUTED MINISTER KNEEL AT THE ALTAR,   R 573 09
THE INSTITUTED MINISTER, STANDING UP, SHALL SAY,   R 573 30
THE INSTITUTED MINISTER SHALL PROCEED TO THAT   R 574 25

INSTITUTING

PURPOSE OF INSTITUTING THE REV   570 13

INSTITUTION

TO THE INSTITUTION OF THY DEARLY BELOVED SON OUR   080 37
HOLY INSTITUTION, IN REMEMBRANCE OF HIS DEATH AND   081 12
LETTER OF INSTITUTION MAY BE OMITTED, WHERE IT   R 569 10
INCUMBENT'S INSTITUTION, THE BISHOP, OR THE   R 570 02
AS ALSO OF THE PRESCRIBED LETTER OF INSTITUTION   570 15
THEN SHALL BE READ THE LETTER OF INSTITUTION   R 570 24
OF MY INSTITUTION, AND OF YOUR PAROCHIAL RECOGNITION,   570 33
AT THE INSTITUTION OF A MINISTER, HE SHALL MAKE TO   R 574 29

INSTITUTION   CONTINUED

OF CHRIST'S INSTITUTION AND PROMISE, ALTHOUGH THEY BE   608 17
WITH THE INSTITUTION OF CHRIST   608 32

INSTITUTOR

OR THE INSTITUTOR APPOINTED BY HIM, ATTENDED BY THE   R 570 03
WHO ACTS AS INSTITUTOR, WHO SHALL GO WITHIN THE RAILS   R 570 06
ACTS AS THE INSTITUTOR, SHALL SAY,   R 570 11
ACTS AS THE INSTITUTOR, SHALL JUDGE WHETHER IT AFFORD   R 570 21
OR THE INSTITUTOR CHOOSING TO GO ON WITH THE SERVICE,   R 570 23
HERE THE INSTITUTOR SHALL BEGIN THE OFFICE   R 571 04
SHALL THE INSTITUTOR RECEIVE THE INCUMBENT WITHIN THE   R 571 22

INSTRUCT

IN THE CHURCH, INSTRUCT OR EXAMINE THE YOUTH OF HIS   R 295 08
MINISTER SHALL INSTRUCT HIM, THAT IF HE DO TRULY   R 323 26
AND TO INSTRUCT THE YOUTH IN THE CATECHISM   533 15
SCRIPTURES TO INSTRUCT THE PEOPLE COMMITTED TO YOUR   542 05
SCRIPTURES TO INSTRUCT THE PEOPLE COMMITTED TO YOUR   554 23
IN THE CHURCH, INSTRUCT OR EXAMINE SO MANY CHILDREN   R 582 28

INSTRUCTED

WHO HAST INSTRUCTED THY HOLY CHURCH WITH THE   237 05
SUFFICIENTLY INSTRUCTED IN THE PRINCIPLES OF THE   R 273 19
SUFFICIENTLY INSTRUCTED, BE BROUGHT TO THE BISHOP TO   277 15
THAT WHERE SO INSTRUCTED, THE PEOPLE MAY REPEAT THE   R 286 02
SUFFICIENTLY INSTRUCTED IN THE MATTER CONTAINED IN   R 295 15
BE INSTRUCTED, YE THAT ARE JUDGES OF THE EARTH   346 17
SUFFICIENTLY INSTRUCTED IN THE HOLY SCRIPTURE, AND   529 28

INSTRUCTETH

OR HE THAT INSTRUCTETH THE HEATHEN, *   458 06

INSTRUCTION

TO RECEIVE INSTRUCTION BY THE MINISTER   R 295 12
OF LIFE AND INSTRUCTION OF MANNERS   604 03

INSTRUCTIVE

AND INSTRUCTIVE IN PIETY AND MORALS   R 610 25

INSTRUMENT

UPON AN INSTRUMENT OF TEN STRINGS, AND UPON THE LUTE   027 32
UPON A LOUD INSTRUMENT, AND UPON THE HARP   027 33
THE LUTE, AND INSTRUMENT OF TEN STRINGS   378 22
UPON AN INSTRUMENT OF MUSIC   426 23
3 UPON AN INSTRUMENT OF TEN STRINGS, AND UPON THE   456 04
UPON A LOUD INSTRUMENT, AND UPON THE HARP   456 05
AS BY AN INSTRUMENT, THEY THAT RECEIVE BAPTISM   608 26

INSTRUMENTAL

TO MAKE ME INSTRUMENTAL IN PROMOTING THE SALVATION OF   573 19

INSTRUMENTS

FOR HIM THE INSTRUMENTS OF DEATH   350 19
HAVE THE INSTRUMENTS OF DONATION AND ENDOWMENT, IF   R 564 07

INSURRECTION

HAD MADE INSURRECTION WITH HIM, WHO HAD COMMITTED   145 15
WHO HAD COMMITTED MURDER IN THE INSURRECTION   145 16
FROM THE INSURRECTION OF WICKED DOERS   415 22

INTEND

AND INTEND TO LEAD A NEW LIFE, FOLLOWING   075 10
ON -- INTEND, BY GOD'S GRACE, TO CELEBRATE   088 12

INTENDED

11 FOR THEY INTENDED MISCHIEF AGAINST THEE, *   365 27

INTENDING

IS FAR FROM INTENDING TO DEPART FROM THE CHURCH OF   VI 32
INTENDING AFTER EASTER TO BRING HIM FORTH TO THE   245 06

INTENT

TO THE INTENT THAT NOW UNTO THE PRINCIPALITIES AND   108 23
THY TRUTH, TO THE INTENT THAT THEY MAY RETURN INTO   173 05
TO THE INTENT WE SHOULD NOT LUST AFTER EVIL   201 13
HITHER FOR THAT INTENT, THAT HE MIGHT BRING THEM   231 07
TO THE INTENT THEY MAY BE ALWAYS IN   R 321 04
7 TO THE INTENT THAT WHEN THEY CAME UP, *   435 09
TO THE INTENT THAT THESE ORDERS MAY BE   529 18
  TO THE INTENT HE MAY BE PERFECT AND WELL   R 535 21

INTENTION

WITHOUT A PURE INTENTION NOR CONTINUE IT WITHOUT THY   594 22

INTERCESSION

TO MAKE INTERCESSION FOR US, JESUS CHRIST, THY SON,   037 22
ALSO MAKETH INTERCESSION FOR US   331 05
MERITS AND INTERCESSION WE RECEIVED THEM ALL, THY SON   591 22

INTERCESSIONS

GENERAL INTERCESSIONS TAKEN OUT OF THIS BOOK, R 017 23
OR OTHER AUTHORIZED PRAYERS AND INTERCESSIONS R 071 30
THE SECRET INTERCESSIONS OF THE CONGREGATION FOR ANY R 074 02
OUR INTERCESSIONS FOR ALL MANKIND 590 22

INTERFERES

WHERE IT INTERFERES WITH THE USAGES, LAWS, OR R 569 11

INTERPOSED

30 THEN STOOD UP PHINEHAS, AND INTERPOSED 474 29

INTERPRETATION

THE INTERPRETATION OF TONGUES 182 33
THE INTERPRETATION OF TONGUES 204 02

INTERPRETED

WHICH BEING INTERPRETED IS, GOD WITH US 105 12
BEING INTERPRETED, THE PLACE OF A SKULL 146 08
BEING INTERPRETED, MY GOD, MY GOD, WHY HAST THOU 146 29

INTOLERABLE

THE BURDEN OF THEM IS INTOLERABLE 075 25

INTREATED

AND INTREATED HIM 202 32
AND WILL HE BE NO MORE INTREATED 311 13
AND WILL HE BE NO MORE INTREATED 433 30

INTRUSTED

WHICH IS NOW INTRUSTED TO YOU 569 25

INVALUABLE

IT IS A MOST INVALUABLE PART OF THAT BLESSED 'LIBERTY V 02

INVENTED

VAINLY INVENTED, AND GROUNDED UPON NO WARRANTY 607 16

INVENTIONS

TO THE WICKEDNESS OF THEIR OWN INVENTIONS 373 14
PROVOKED HIM TO`ANGER WITH THEIR OWN INVENTIONS 474 28
AND WENT A WHORING WITH THEIR OWN INVENTIONS 475 15
THEIR OWN INVENTIONS, AND WERE BROUGHT DOWN IN THEIR 475 23

INVISIBLE

AND OF ALL THINGS VISIBLE AND INVISIBLE 015 34
AND OF ALL THINGS VISIBLE AND INVISIBLE 030 05
AND OF ALL THINGS VISIBLE AND INVISIBLE 071 03
BEHOLD THINGS INVISIBLE AND UNSEEN, WE MAY IN HEART 594 24
OF ALL THINGS BOTH VISIBLE AND INVISIBLE 603 05

INVISIBLY

HE DOTH WORK INVISIBLY IN US, AND DOTH NOT CNLY 607 34

INVOCATION

AND ALSO INVOCATION OF SAINTS, IS A FCND THING, 607 15

INWARD

TRUTH IN THE INWARD PARTS, * 060 22
SIGN OF AN INWARD AND SPIRITUAL GRACE GIVEN UNTO US 292 11
AND THE INWARD AND SPIRITUAL GRACE 292 16
WHAT IS THE INWARD AND SPIRITUAL GRACE IN BAPTISM 292 22
THE INWARD AND SPIRITUAL GRACE IN BAPTISM IS 292 24
WHAT IS THE INWARD PART, OR THING SIGNIFIED 293 13
THE INWARD PART, OR THING SIGNIFIED 293 14
THEIR INWARD PARTS ARE VERY WICKEDNESS 348 19
TRUTH IN THE INWARD PARTS, * 403 20
SIGN OF AN INWARD AND SPIRITUAL GRACE GIVEN UNTC US 581 12
AND THE INWARD SPIRITUAL GRACE 581 17
WHAT IS THE INWARD AND SPIRITUAL GRACE 581 23
WHAT IS THE INWARD PART, OR THING SIGNIFIED 582 11

INWARDLY

BE SO GRAFTED INWARDLY IN OUR HEARTS, THAT THEY MAY 049 19
AND INWARDLY DIGEST THEM, THAT BY PATIENCE AND 092 09
OUR BODIES, AND INWARDLY IN OUR SOULS 127 17
BUT INWARDLY THEY ARE RAVENING WOLVES 200 16
THAT YOU ARE INWARDLY MOVED BY THE HOLY GHOST TO TAKE 532 26
GRAFTING IT INWARDLY IN THE HEART, THE HEARERS 566 04

IRON

THEY CAME UNTO THE IRON GATE THAT LEADETH UNTO THE 245 22
THEM WITH A ROD OF IRON, * 346 15
THE IRON ENTERED INTO HIS SOUL 471 08
BEING FAST BOUND IN MISERY AND IRON 476 25
SMITTEN THE BARS OF IRON IN SUNDER 477 08
AND THEIR NOBLES WITH LINKS OF IRON 525 18

IRREPREHENSIBLE

AND IRREPREHENSIBLE AT THE LATTER DAY 555 32

ISAAC

WITH ABRAHAM, AND ISAAC, AND JACOB, IN THE KINGDCM CF 115 20
WE, BRETHREN, AS ISAAC WAS, ARE THE CHILDREN OF 131 12
AND THE OATH THAT HE SWARE UNTO ISAAC 470 21

ISCARIOT

AND JUDAS ISCARIOT, ONE OF THE TWELVE, WENT UNTO THE 140 18
JUDAS SURNAMED ISCARIOT, BEING OF THE NUMBER OF THE 148 15
HEART OF JUDAS ISCARIOT, SIMON'S SON, TO BETRAY HIM 155 28
UNTO HIM, NOT ISCARIOT, LORD, HOW IS IT THAT THOU 181 22

ISHMAELITES

TABERNACLES OF THE EDOMITES, AND THE ISHMAELITES 444 16

ISLES

AND OF THE ISLES SHALL GIVE PRESENTS 427 16
MULTITUDE OF THE ISLES MAY BE GLAD THEREOF 460 31

ISRAEL

O LET ISRAEL BLESS THE LORD 013 20
BLESSED BE THE LORD GOD OF ISRAEL 014 08
HIS MERCY HATH HOLPEN HIS SERVANT ISRAEL 026 27
HIS MERCY AND TRUTH TOWARD THE HOUSE OF ISRAEL 027 11
AND TO BE THE GLORY OF THY PEOPLE ISRAEL 028 14
AND HIS MOTHER, AND GO INTO THE LAND OF ISRAEL 107 15
AND CAME INTO THE LAND OF ISRAEL 107 17
COME A GOVERNOR, THAT SHALL RULE MY PEOPLE ISRAEL 109 10
HAVE NOT FOUND SO GREAT FAITH, NO, NOT IN ISRAEL 115 18
BUT UNTO THE LOST SHEEP OF THE HOUSE OF ISRAEL 128 15
THE CHILDREN OF ISRAEL DID VALUE 135 17
HE BE THE KING OF ISRAEL, LET HIM NOW COME DOWN FROM 137 11
THE.HOUSE OF ISRAEL, WHICH HE HATH BESTOWED CN THEM 138 30
OF US, AND ISRAEL ACKNOWLEDGE US NOT 139 22
THE KING OF ISRAEL DESCEND NOW FROM THE CROSS, THAT 146 23
JUDGING THE TWELVE TRIBES OF ISRAEL 149 30
THE CHILDREN OF ISRAEL, PREACHING PEACE BY JESUS 166 16
IT HAD BEEN HE WHICH SHOULD HAVE REDEEMED ISRAEL 167 21
AT THIS TIME RESTORE AGAIN THE KINGDOM TO ISRAEL 178 06
THE CHILDREN OF ISRAEL, PREACHING PEACE BY JESUS 184 03
THOU A MASTER OF ISRAEL, AND KNOWEST NOT THESE 188 19
THE CHILDREN OF ISRAEL COULD NOT STEDFASTLY BEHCLD 206 20
AND UPON THE ISRAEL OF GOD 211 04
BE SAVED, AND ISRAEL SHALL DWELL SAFELY 225 12
THE CHILDREN OF ISRAEL OUT OF THE LAND OF EGYPT 225 17
OF THE HOUSE OF ISRAEL OUT OF THE NORTH COUNTRY, AND 225 18
I SAY, DID NOT ISRAEL KNOW 227 16
BUT TO ISRAEL HE SAITH, ALL DAY LONG I HAVE STRETCHED 227 21
AND THE CHILDREN OF ISRAEL 230 28
JUDGING THE TWELVE TRIBES OF ISRAEL 231 18
WAITING FOR THE CONSOLATION OF ISRAEL 232 32
THE GENTILES, AND THE GLORY OF THY PEOPLE ISRAEL 233 09
FOR THE FALL AND RISING AGAIN OF MANY IN ISRAEL 233 13
BLESSED BE THE LORD GOD OF ISRAEL 243 33
DESERTS TILL THE DAY OF HIS SHEWING UNTO ISRAEL 244 18
ON THRONES JUDGING THE TWELVE TRIBES OF ISRAEL 250 16
OF ALL THE TRIBES OF THE CHILDREN OF ISRAEL 256 22
EVEN THE HOUSE OF ISRAEL, ARE MY PEOPLE, SAITH THE 262 21
AND GATHER TOGETHER THE OUTCASTS OF ISRAEL 264 22
GIVEN IN OLD TIME BY GOD TO THE PEOPLE OF ISRAEL 285 17
HE THAT KEEPETH ISRAEL * 327 25
O ISRAEL, TRUST IN THE LORD, FOR WITH THE LCRD THERE 328 15
HE SHALL REDEEM ISRAEL * 328 17
HE THAT KEEPETH ISRAEL * 339 09
SALVATION UNTO ISRAEL OUT OF SION 356 30
AND ISRAEL SHALL BE GLAD 356 32
O THOU WORSHIP OF ISRAEL 366 09
AND FEAR HIM, ALL YE SEED OF ISRAEL 367 19
21 DELIVER ISRAEL, O GOD, * 370 28
THE LORD GOD OF ISRAEL, * 392 25
I MYSELF WILL TESTIFY AGAINST THEE, O ISRAEL 402 05
WERE GIVEN UNTO ISRAEL OUT OF SION 405 28
ANC ISRAEL SHOULD BE RIGHT GLAD 405 31
THOU GOD OF ISRAEL, TO VISIT ALL THE HEATHEN, * 411 13
AT THE PRESENCE OF GOD, WHO IS THE GOD OF ISRAEL 419 28
YE THAT ARE OF THE FOUNTAIN OF ISRAEL 421 07
34 ASCRIBE YE THE POWER TO GOD OVER ISRAEL 421 25
EVEN THE GOD OF ISRAEL, HE WILL GIVE STRENGTH AND 421 28
BE CONFOUNDED THROUGH ME, O LORD GOD OF ISRAEL 422 15
O THOU HOLY ONE OF ISRAEL 426 24
EVEN THE GOD OF ISRAEL, * 428 02
TRULY GOD IS LOVING UNTO ISRAEL 428 10
HIS NAME IS GREAT IN ISRAEL 432 24
AND GAVE ISRAEL A LAW, * 435 04
THERE CAME UP HEAVY DISPLEASURE AGAINST ISRAEL 436 13
AND SMOTE DOWN THE CHOSEN MEN THAT WERE IN ISRAEL 436 35
AND PROVOKED THE HOLY ONE IN ISRAEL 437 24
THE TRIBES OF ISRAEL TO DWELL IN THEIR TENTS 438 23
AND TOOK SORE DISPLEASURE AT ISRAEL 438 31
HIS PEOPLE, AND ISRAEL HIS INHERITANCE 439 23
THOU SHEPHERD OF ISRAEL, THOU THAT LEADEST JOSEPH 441 03
A STATUTE FOR ISRAEL, * 442 18
ASSURE THEE, O ISRAEL, * 442 29
AND ISRAEL WOULD NOT OBEY ME 443 02
FOR IF ISRAEL HAD WALKED IN MY WAYS, 15 I SHOULD SCCN 443 07
THAT THE NAME OF ISRAEL MAY BE NO MORE IN 444 12
THE HOLY ONE OF ISRAEL IS OUR KING 451 11

ISRAEL   CONTINUED

HIS MERCY AND TRUTH TOWARD THE HOUSE OF ISRAEL   461 32
HIS WORKS UNTO THE CHILDREN OF ISRAEL   466 20
AND TO ISRAEL FOR AN EVERLASTING TESTAMENT   470 23
23 ISRAEL ALSO CAME INTO EGYPT, *   471 18
THE LORD GOD OF ISRAEL, FROM EVERLASTING, AND WCRLD 475 33
WHEN ISRAEL CAME OUT OF EGYPT, *   484 27
AND ISRAEL HIS DOMINION   484 29
THOU, HOUSE OF ISRAEL, TRUST THOU IN THE LORD   485 28
THE HOUSE OF ISRAEL, HE SHALL BLESS THE HOUSE OF   486 02
2 LET ISRAEL NOW CONFESS THAT HE IS GRACIOUS,   488 02
HE THAT KEEPETH ISRAEL *   502 28
TO TESTIFY UNTO ISRAEL, TO GIVE THANKS UNTO THE NAME 503 14
OUR SIDE, NOW MAY ISRAEL SAY   504 08
BUT PEACE SHALL BE UPCN ISRAEL   505 04
AND PEACE UPON ISRAEL   506 19
MAY ISRAEL NOW SAY   506 22
7 O ISRAEL, TRUST IN THE LORD   507 20
HE SHALL REDEEM ISRAEL *   507 22
4 O ISRAEL, TRUST IN THE LORD *   507 30
AND ISRAEL FOR HIS OWN POSSESSION   510 10
AN HERITAGE UNTO ISRAEL HIS PEOPLE   510 27
19 PRAISE THE LORD, YE HOUSE OF ISRAEL   511 08
AND BROUGHT OUT ISRAEL FROM AMONG THEM   512 04
14 AND MADE ISRAEL TO GO THROUGH THE MIDST OF IT   512 10
AN HERITAGE UNTO ISRAEL HIS SERVANT   512 26
AND GATHER TOGETHER THE OUTCASTS OF ISRAEL   522 31
HIS STATUTES AND ORDINANCES UNTO ISRAEL   523 34
THE CHILDREN OF ISRAEL, EVEN THE PEOPLE THAT SERVETH 524 31
2 LET ISRAEL REJOICE IN HIM THAT MADE HIM, *   525 05

ISRAELITES

ARE THEY ISRAELITES   120 28

ISSUE

AND A HAPPY ISSUE OUT OF ALL THEIR AFFLICTIONS   019 10
AND A HAPPY ISSUE OUT OF ALL THEIR AFFLICTIONS   033 08
DISEASED WITH AN ISSUE OF BLOOD TWELVE YEARS, CAME   224 17

ISSUED

FOR A REVIEW WAS ISSUED IN THE YEAR 1689   VI 04

ITS

AND SANCTIFIES ITS MEMBERS   291 10
AND TO EVERY SEED ITS OWN BODY   329 11

ITSELF

BUT INTO HEAVEN ITSELF, NOW TO APPEAR IN THE PRESENCE 022 24
EVEN THE WORLD ITSELF COULD NOT CONTAIN THE BOOKS   102 17
VAUNTETH NOT ITSELF, IS NOT PUFFED UP, DOTH NCT   122 30
DOTH NOT BEHAVE ITSELF UNSEEMLY, SEEKETH NCT HER CWN, 122 31
DIVIDED AGAINST ITSELF IS BROUGHT TO DESOLATION   129 30
BUT INTO HEAVEN ITSELF, NOW TO APPEAR IN THE PRESENCE 147 32
BUT WRAPPED TOGETHER IN A PLACE BY ITSELF   164 25
THE CREATURE ITSELF ALSO SHALL BE DELIVERED FROM THE 194 17
FOR THE MORROW WILL BE ANXIOUS FOR ITSELF   211 34
THE EDIFYING OF ITSELF IN LOVE   238 02
BEAR FRUIT OF ITSELF, EXCEPT IT ABIDE IN THE VINE   238 10
SHALL TAKE THOUGHT FOR THE THINGS OF ITSELF   266 32
THEY ARE ALTOGETHER LIGHTER THAN VANITY ITSELF   414 17
LOVING-KINDNESS IS BETTER THAN THE LIFE ITSELF   414 31
THAT IS AT UNITY IN ITSELF   503 12
AND LUST HATH OF ITSELF THE NATURE OF SIN   604 40
THING THAT, OF ITSELF, IS SUPERSTITIOUS AND UNGCDLY 610 34

IVORY

OUT OF THE IVORY PALACES, WHEREBY THEY HAVE MADE THEE 396 33

JABIN

AND UNTO JABIN AT THE BROOK OF KISHON   444 23

JACOB

AND ISAAC, AND JACOB, IN THE KINGDOM OF HEAVEN   115 20
OVER THE HOUSE OF JACOB FOR EVER   236 19
THE GOD OF JACOB IS OUR REFUGE   327 16
THEN SHALL JACOB REJOICE, AND ISRAEL SHALL BE   356 32
NAME OF THE GOD OF JACOB DEFEND THEE   364 18
MAGNIFY HIM, ALL YE OF THE SEED OF JACOB   367 19
EVEN OF THEM THAT SEEK THY FACE, O GOD OF JACOB   369 08
SEND HELP UNTO JACOB   394 32
THE GOD OF JACOB IS OUR REFUGE   398 07
THE GOD OF JACOB IS OUR REFUGE   398 17
THE EXCELLENCY OF JACOB, WHOM HE LOVED   398 28
8 THEN SHOULD JACOB REJOICE, *   405 31
GOD THAT RULETH IN JACOB, AND UNTO THE ENDS OF THE   411 34
TALK OF THE GOD OF JACOB, *   432 19
O GOD OF JACOB, *   432 33
EVEN THE SONS OF JACOB AND JOSEPH   434 15
A COVENANT WITH JACOB, AND GAVE ISRAEL A LAW, *   435 04
WAS KINDLED IN JACOB, AND THERE CAME UP HEAVY   436 12
THAT HE MIGHT FEED JACOB HIS PEOPLE, AND ISRAEL HIS 439 22
THEY HAVE DEVOURED JACOB, *   440 14
MAKE A CHEERFUL NOISE UNTO THE GOD OF JACOB   442 15
AND A LAW OF THE GOD OF JACOB   442 19
HEARKEN, O GOD OF JACOB   445 28
THOU HAST TURNED AWAY THE CAPTIVITY OF JACOB   446 09
OF SION MORE THAN ALL THE DWELLINGS OF JACCB   448 15

JACOB   CONTINUED

SHALL THE GOD OF JACOB REGARD IT   457 32
HAST EXECUTED JUDGMENT AND RIGHTEOUSNESS IN JACOB   462 24
YE CHILDREN OF JACOB HIS CHOSEN   470 15
THE SAME UNTO JACOB FOR A LAW, *   470 22
AND JACOB WAS A STRANGER IN THE LAND OF HAM   471 18
AND THE HOUSE OF JACOB FROM AMONG THE STRANGE PECPLE, 484 28
AT THE PRESENCE OF THE GOD OF JACOB   485 07
AND VOWED A VOW UNTO THE ALMIGHTY GOD OF JACCB   508 07
AN HABITATION FOR THE MIGHTY GOD OF JACOB   508 14
LORD HATH CHOSEN JACOB UNTO HIMSELF, *   510 09
HATH THE GOD OF JACOB FOR HIS HELP, *   522 10
HIS WORD UNTO JACOB, *   523 33
EVEN OF THEM THAT SEEK THY FACE, O JACOB   563 23

JAH

HIM IN HIS NAME JAH, AND REJOICE BEFORE HIM   419 18

JAMES

WITH HIM PETER AND JAMES AND JOHN, AND BEGAN TO BE   141 30
MARY THE MOTHER OF JAMES, AND SALOME, HAD BOUGHT   165 19
JAMES   R 178 31
AND SO WAS ALSO JAMES, AND JOHN, THE SONS OF ZEBEDEE, 196 26
AFTER THAT, HE WAS SEEN OF JAMES   205 11
TWO BRETHREN, JAMES THE SON OF ZEBEDEE, AND JCHN HIS 227 29
PHILIP AND SAINT JAMES, WE MAY STEDFASTLY WALK IN THE 239 02
JAMES, A SERVANT OF GOD AND OF THE LORD JESUS CHRIST, 239 06
AND HE KILLED JAMES THE BROTHER OF JOHN WITH THE   244 33
HOLY APOSTLE SAINT JAMES, LEAVING HIS FATHER AND ALL 246 17
AND HE KILLED JAMES THE BROTHER OF JOHN WITH THE   247 02
PETER AND JOHN AND JAMES, AND WENT UP INTO A MCUNTAIN 248 24
JESUS CHRIST, AND JAMES HIS APOSTLE, SO WE JUDGE,   611 07

JASPER

LOOK UPON LIKE A JASPER AND A SARDINE STONE   187 06

JAW-BONES

SMITE THE JAW-BONES OF THE LIONS, O LORD   410 20

JEALOUS

THY GOD AM A JEALOUS GOD, AND VISIT THE SINS OF THE 068 12
THY GOD AM A JEALOUS GOD, AND VISIT THE SINS OF THE 286 12
THY GOD AM A JEALOUS GOD, AND VISIT THE SINS OF THE 578 31

JEALOUSY

PROVOKE YOU TO JEALOUSY BY THEM THAT ARE NO PECPLE, 227 17
SHALL THY JEALOUSY BURN LIKE FIRE FOR EVER   440 09

JEHOVAH

ARE THE PEOPLE WHOSE GOD IS THE LORD JEHOVAH   379 12
WHOSE NAME IS JEHOVAH, *   445 09

JEREMIAS

AND OTHERS, JEREMIAS, OR ONE OF THE PROPHETS   245 34

JEREMY

WAS SPOKEN BY JEREMY THE PROPHET, SAYING, IN RAMA WAS 103 30
WAS SPOKEN BY JEREMY THE PROPHET, SAYING, AND THEY   135 14

JERICHO

COME NIGH UNTO JERICHO, A CERTAIN BLIND MAN SAT BY   123 26
JERUSALEM TO JERICHO, AND FELL AMONG THIEVES, WHICH 208 22

JERUSALEM

PUT ON THY BEAUTIFUL GARMENTS, O JERUSALEM   004 19
ME BOTH IN JERUSALEM, AND IN ALL JUDAEA, AND IN   005 13
DREW NIGH UNTO JERUSALEM, AND WERE CCME TO BETHPHAGE, 091 11
WAS COME INTO JERUSALEM, ALL THE CITY WAS MOVED,   091 30
LEVITES FROM JERUSALEM TO ASK HIM, WHO ART THOU   095 22
O JERUSALEM, JERUSALEM, THOU THAT KILLEST THE   100 27
O JERUSALEM, JERUSALEM, THOU THAT KILLEST THE   100 27
THE EAST TO JERUSALEM, SAYING, WHERE IS HE THAT IS   108 32
AND ALL JERUSALEM WITH HIM   109 03
WENT TO JERUSALEM EVERY YEAR AT THE FEAST OF THE   110 18
WENT UP TO JERUSALEM AFTER THE CUSTOM OF THE FEAST   110 20
THE CHILD JESUS TARRIED BEHIND IN JERUSALEM   110 22
BACK AGAIN TO JERUSALEM, SEEKING HIM   110 26
AND THEY OF JERUSALEM, AND WERE ALL BAPTIZED OF HIM 112 10
WE GO UP TO JERUSALEM, AND ALL THINGS THAT ARE   123 18
ANSWERETH TO JERUSALEM WHICH NOW IS, AND IS IN   131 06
BUT JERUSALEM WHICH IS ABOVE IS FREE, WHICH IS THE   131 07
ALSO WAS AT JERUSALEM AT THAT TIME   153 09
DAUGHTERS OF JERUSALEM, WEEP NOT FOR ME, BUT WEEP FCR 154 14
BOTH IN THE LAND OF THE JEWS, AND IN JERUSALEM   166 23
WHICH WAS FROM JERUSALEM ABOUT THREESCORE FURLONGS   167 04
A STRANGER IN JERUSALEM, AND HAST NOT KNCWN THE   167 13
RETURNED TO JERUSALEM, AND FOUND THE ELEVEN GATHERED 168 12
THAT DWELT AT JERUSALEM, AND THEIR RULERS, BECAUSE   168 26
GALILEE TO JERUSALEM, WHO ARE HIS WITNESSES UNTO THE 169 04
NAME AMONG ALL NATIONS, BEGINNING AT JERUSALEM   170 15
DEPART FROM JERUSALEM, BUT WAIT FOR THE PROMISE CF   177 30
ME BOTH IN JERUSALEM, AND IN ALL JUDAEA, AND IN   178 10
IN THE CITY OF JERUSALEM, UNTIL YE BE ENDUED WITH   178 22
RETURNED TO JERUSALEM WITH GREAT JOY   178 27

JERUSALEM   CONTINUED

DWELLING AT JERUSALEM JEWS, DEVOUT MEN, OUT OF EVERY   180 25
BOTH IN THE LAND OF THE JEWS, AND IN JERUSALEM   184 11
WHICH WERE AT JERUSALEM HEARD THAT SAMARIA HAD   185 21
WENT DOWN FROM JERUSALEM TO JERICHO, AND FELL AMONG   208 21
JESUS WENT TO JERUSALEM, THAT HE PASSED THROUGH THE   209 31
HE MIGHT BRING THEM BOUND UNTO JERUSALEM   229 30
MUCH EVIL HE HATH DONE TO THY SAINTS AT JERUSALEM   230 23
THIS NAME IN JERUSALEM, AND CAME HITHER FOR THAT   231 07
OF JUDAH AND JERUSALEM BE PLEASANT UNTO THE LORD, AS   232 13
BROUGHT HIM TO JERUSALEM, TO PRESENT HIM TO THE LORD   232 21
WAS A MAN IN JERUSALEM, WHOSE NAME WAS SIMEON   232 30
ALL THEM THAT LOOKED FOR REDEMPTION IN JERUSALEM   233 23
IT WAS KNOWN UNTO ALL THE DWELLERS AT JERUSALEM   234 16
THE EARS OF THE CHURCH WHICH WAS IN JERUSALEM   241 04
PROPHETS FROM JERUSALEM UNTO ANTIOCH   241 15
COMFORTABLY TO JERUSALEM, AND CRY UNTO HER, THAT HER   242 17
O JERUSALEM, THAT BRINGEST GOOD TIDINGS, LIFT UP THY   243 03
PROPHETS FROM JERUSALEM UNTO ANTIOCH   246 24
DECEASE WHICH HE SHOULD ACCOMPLISH AT JERUSALEM   248 29
ABOUT UNTO JERUSALEM, BRINGING SICK FOLKS, AND THEM   249 30
DOTH BUILD UP JERUSALEM, *   264 21
PRAISE THE LORD, O JERUSALEM   264 32
WHICH WERE AT JERUSALEM HEARD THAT SAMARIA HAD   296 13
EVEN IN THE MIDST OF THEE, O JERUSALEM   306 03
BUILD THOU THE WALLS OF JERUSALEM   404 14
UNTO THEE SHALL THE VOW BE PERFORMED IN JERUSALEM   416 12
IN US, 29 FOR THY TEMPLE'S SAKE AT JERUSALEM   421 13
AND MADE JERUSALEM AN HEAP OF STONES   439 30
EVERY SIDE OF JERUSALEM, *   440 05
AND HIS WORSHIP AT JERUSALEM   465 23
EVEN IN THE MIDST OF THEE, O JERUSALEM   487 23
O JERUSALEM   503 11
3 JERUSALEM IS BUILT AS A CITY *   503 12
6 O PRAY FOR THE PEACE OF JERUSALEM   503 18
2 THE HILLS STAND ABOUT JERUSALEM   504 26
THOU SHALT SEE JERUSALEM IN PROSPERITY ALL THY LIFE   506 17
WHO DWELLETH AT JERUSALEM   511 13
FORGET THEE, O JERUSALEM, *   513 13
I PREFER NOT JERUSALEM ABOVE MY CHIEF JOY   513 16
O LORD, IN THE DAY OF JERUSALEM   513 19
DOTH BUILD UP JERUSALEM, *   522 30
12 PRAISE THE LORD, O JERUSALEM   523 19
MULTIPLIED IN JERUSALEM GREATLY   532 21
SPIRIT UNTO JERUSALEM, NOT KNOWING THE THINGS THAT   550 15
HOLY CITY, NEW JERUSALEM, COMING DOWN FROM GOD OUT OF   567 12
WENT UP TO JERUSALEM, AND FOUND IN THE TEMPLE THOSE   567 26
THE CHURCH OF JERUSALEM, ALEXANDRIA, AND ANTIOCH,   606 42

JESSE

SHALL BE A ROOT OF JESSE, AND HE THAT SHALL RISE TO   092 31

JESTED

AND THEY JESTED UPON ME   422 25

JESTING

NOR JESTING, WHICH ARE NOT CONVENIENT   129 05

JESUS

AND FROM THE LORD JESUS CHRIST   004 03
INTO THE HEAVENS, JESUS THE SON OF GOD, LET US COME   005 07
MANKIND IN CHRIST JESUS OUR LORD   006 27
FATHER OF OUR LORD JESUS CHRIST, WHO DESIRETH NOT THE   007 06
THROUGH JESUS CHRIST OUR LORD   007 18
AND IN JESUS CHRIST HIS ONLY SON OUR LORD   015 21
AND IN ONE LORD JESUS CHRIST, THE ONLY-BEGOTTEN SON   016 02
THE MIGHT OF JESUS CHRIST OUR LORD   017 10
THROUGH JESUS CHRIST OUR LORD   017 19
THROUGH JESUS CHRIST OUR LORD   018 04
THROUGH JESUS CHRIST OUR LORD, WHO LIVETH AND   018 14
AND MEDIATOR, JESUS CHRIST   018 24
THIS WE BEG FOR JESUS CHRIST'S SAKE   019 11
WORLD BY OUR LORD JESUS CHRIST   019 23
THROUGH JESUS CHRIST OUR LORD, TO WHOM, WITH THEE AND   019 30
GRACE OF OUR LORD JESUS CHRIST, AND THE LOVE OF GOD,   020 12
THROUGH OUR LORD JESUS CHRIST   022 18
MANKIND IN CHRIST JESUS OUR LORD   024 02
FATHER OF OUR LORD JESUS CHRIST, WHO DESIRETH NOT THE   024 08
THROUGH JESUS CHRIST OUR LORD   024 20
ONLY-BEGOTTEN SON, JESUS CHRIST   025 27
AND IN JESUS CHRIST HIS ONLY SON OUR LORD   029 26
AND IN ONE LORD JESUS CHRIST, THE ONLY-BEGOTTEN SON   030 07
THE MERITS OF JESUS CHRIST OUR SAVIOUR   031 24
OUR SAVIOUR, JESUS CHRIST   031 29
THROUGH JESUS CHRIST OUR LORD, WHO WITH THEE AND THE   032 12
AND MEDIATOR, JESUS CHRIST   032 23
THIS WE BEG FOR JESUS CHRIST'S SAKE   033 09
WORLD BY OUR LORD JESUS CHRIST   033 21
THROUGH JESUS CHRIST OUR LORD, TO WHOM, WITH THEE AND   033 28
GRACE OF OUR LORD JESUS CHRIST, AND THE LOVE OF GOD,   034 12
AND MEDIATION OF JESUS CHRIST, OUR MOST BLESSED LORD   035 20
THROUGH JESUS CHRIST, THY SON, OUR LORD   035 28
OUR SAVIOUR JESUS CHRIST   036 06
WE ASK THROUGH JESUS CHRIST OUR LORD   036 24
THROUGH THY SON JESUS CHRIST, TO BE WITH THY CHURCH   036 28
AND DEATH OF JESUS CHRIST OUR SAVIOUR   037 08
FOR US, JESUS CHRIST, THY SON, OUR LORD   037 22
FATHER OF OUR LORD JESUS CHRIST, OUR ONLY SAVIOUR,   037 25
THROUGH JESUS CHRIST OUR LORD   038 03
THE SAME THY SON JESUS CHRIST OUR LORD   038 11
THROUGH JESUS CHRIST OUR LORD   038 22

JESUS   CONTINUED

THROUGH JESUS CHRIST OUR LORD   039 04
THROUGH JESUS CHRIST OUR LORD   039 14
THE SAME THY SON JESUS CHRIST OUR LORD   039 21
THROUGH JESUS CHRIST OUR LORD   039 31
WHO BY THY SON JESUS CHRIST HAST PROMISED TO ALL   040 15
THROUGH JESUS CHRIST OUR LORD   040 21
THROUGH JESUS CHRIST OUR LORD   040 28
FOR THE LOVE OF JESUS CHRIST OUR LORD, TO WHOM, WITH   041 05
MERITS OF THY SON, JESUS CHRIST OUR LORD   041 16
THROUGH JESUS CHRIST OUR LORD   041 22
THROUGH JESUS CHRIST OUR LORD   041 30
THROUGH JESUS CHRIST OUR LORD   042 12
THROUGH JESUS CHRIST THY SON OUR LORD   042 19
THROUGH JESUS CHRIST OUR LORD   042 28
THROUGH JESUS CHRIST OUR LORD   043 05
O LORD JESUS CHRIST, WHO DOST EMBRACE CHILDREN WITH   043 07
OF THY SON JESUS CHRIST DIDST PREPARE THE DISCIPLES   043 18
THROUGH THE SAME JESUS CHRIST OUR LORD   043 25
OUR SAVIOUR JESUS CHRIST   044 07
THROUGH JESUS CHRIST OUR LORD   044 14
THY SON JESUS CHRIST OUR LORD   044 25
LORD AND SAVIOUR JESUS CHRIST   044 31
THROUGH JESUS CHRIST OUR LORD   045 10
THROUGH JESUS CHRIST OUR LORD   045 21
THROUGH JESUS CHRIST OUR LORD   045 27
THROUGH JESUS CHRIST OUR LORD   046 06
THROUGH JESUS CHRIST OUR LORD   046 16
THROUGH JESUS CHRIST OUR LORD   046 29
O LORD JESUS CHRIST, WHO SAIDST UNTO THINE APOSTLES,   049 05
THROUGH JESUS CHRIST OUR LORD   049 16
THROUGH JESUS CHRIST OUR LORD   049 22
THROUGH JESUS CHRIST OUR LORD   049 27
OF THY SON JESUS CHRIST OUR LORD   050 04
THROUGH JESUS CHRIST OUR LORD   050 13
THROUGH JESUS CHRIST OUR LORD, TO WHOM, WITH THEE AND   050 28
THROUGH JESUS CHRIST OUR LORD   051 12
THROUGH JESUS CHRIST OUR LORD   051 20
THROUGH JESUS CHRIST OUR LORD   051 28
THROUGH JESUS CHRIST OUR LORD   052 05
THROUGH JESUS CHRIST OUR LORD   052 15
THROUGH JESUS CHRIST OUR LORD   052 27
THROUGH JESUS CHRIST OUR LORD   053 07
THROUGH JESUS CHRIST OUR LORD   053 17
THROUGH JESUS CHRIST OUR LORD   053 27
THROUGH JESUS CHRIST OUR LORD   058 24
AND ADVOCATE, JESUS CHRIST OUR LORD   059 27
FOR THE SAKE OF JESUS CHRIST, OUR BLESSED LORD AND   VI 42
THROUGH JESUS CHRIST OUR LORD   062 25
THY BLESSED SON, JESUS CHRIST OUR LORD   063 06
FOR THE HONOUR OF JESUS CHRIST, OUR MEDIATOR AND   063 13
HEAR WHAT OUR LORD JESUS CHRIST SAITH   R 067 30
HEAR WHAT OUR LORD JESUS CHRIST SAITH   069 26
LORD AND SAVIOUR JESUS CHRIST   070 12
AND IN ONE LORD JESUS CHRIST, THE ONLY-BEGOTTEN SON   071 04
WORDS OF THE LORD JESUS, HOW HE SAID, IT IS MORE   072 02
JESUS SAID UNTO THEM, THE HARVEST TRULY IS PLENTEOUS,   073 11
O FATHER, FOR JESUS CHRIST'S SAKE, OUR ONLY MEDIATOR   075 05
FATHER OF OUR LORD JESUS CHRIST, MAKER OF ALL THINGS,   075 17
THY SON OUR LORD JESUS CHRIST'S SAKE, FORGIVE US ALL   075 27
THROUGH JESUS CHRIST OUR LORD   075 30
THROUGH JESUS CHRIST OUR LORD   076 07
THAT CHRIST JESUS CAME INTO THE WORLD TO SAVE   076 19
WITH THE FATHER, JESUS CHRIST THE RIGHTEOUS   076 23
THOU DIDST GIVE JESUS CHRIST, THINE ONLY SON, TO BE   077 14
THROUGH JESUS CHRIST OUR LORD   077 22
FACE OF THY SON JESUS CHRIST OUR LORD   078 03
OF THY SON JESUS CHRIST OUR LORD   078 08
DEARLY BELOVED SON JESUS CHRIST OUR LORD   078 16
THROUGH JESUS CHRIST OUR LORD   078 25
AND OF THY SON JESUS CHRIST   079 02
MERITS OF THY SON JESUS CHRIST OUR LORD, AND FOR THE   079 15
THINE ONLY SON JESUS CHRIST TO SUFFER DEATH UPON THE   080 08
SON OUR SAVIOUR JESUS CHRIST, WE, THY HUMBLE   080 38
SON OUR SAVIOUR JESUS CHRIST'S HOLY INSTITUTION,   081 12
DEATH OF THY SON JESUS CHRIST, AND THROUGH FAITH IN   081 18
BLOOD OF THY SON JESUS CHRIST, BE FILLED WITH THY   081 26
THROUGH JESUS CHRIST OUR LORD   081 32
OF THY DEAR SON JESUS CHRIST, AND TO DRINK HIS BLOOD,   082 19
BODY OF OUR LORD JESUS CHRIST, WHICH WAS GIVEN FOR   082 31
BLOOD OF OUR LORD JESUS CHRIST, WHICH WAS SHED FOR   083 03
SON OUR SAVIOUR JESUS CHRIST   083 20
THROUGH JESUS CHRIST OUR LORD, TO WHOM, WITH THEE AND   083 29
ONLY-BEGOTTEN SON, JESUS CHRIST   084 07
AND OF HIS SON JESUS CHRIST OUR LORD   084 20
AND ONLY SAVIOUR, JESUS CHRIST, THUS DYING FOR US,   086 13
SON OUR SAVIOUR JESUS CHRIST, NOT ONLY TO DIE FOR US,   087 03
FOR THE LORD JESUS CHRIST'S SAKE, THAT YE WILL   088 15
IN WHICH THY SON JESUS CHRIST CAME TO VISIT US IN   090 14
PUT YE ON THE LORD JESUS CHRIST, AND MAKE NOT   091 08
THEN SENT JESUS TWO DISCIPLES, SAYING UNTO   091 13
AND DID AS JESUS COMMANDED THEM, AND BROUGHT   091 22
THIS IS JESUS THE PROPHET OF NAZARETH OF   091 32
AND JESUS WENT INTO THE TEMPLE OF GOD, AND CAST OUT   091 33
US IN OUR SAVIOUR JESUS CHRIST   092 13
ONE TOWARD ANOTHER ACCORDING TO CHRIST JESUS   092 19
FATHER OF OUR LORD JESUS CHRIST   092 21
NOW I SAY THAT JESUS CHRIST WAS A MINISTER OF THE   092 23
O LORD JESUS CHRIST, WHO AT THY FIRST COMING DIDST   093 24
JESUS ANSWERED AND SAID UNTO THEM, GO AND SHEW JOHN   094 19
AS THEY DEPARTED, JESUS BEGAN TO SAY UNTO THE   094 25
THROUGH JESUS CHRIST OUR LORD, TO WHOM, WITH THEE AND   095 09
KEEP YOUR HEARTS AND MINDS THROUGH CHRIST JESUS   095 19
THE SAME OUR LORD JESUS CHRIST, WHO LIVETH AND   096 18
OF THINE ONLY SON JESUS CHRIST   098 12

JESUS   CONTINUED

AND OUR SAVIOUR JESUS CHRIST   098 22
TO THEE, O BLESSED JESUS, WHO STANDEST AT THE RIGHT   099 32
GLORY OF GOD, AND JESUS STANDING ON THE RIGHT HAND OF   100 06
AND SAYING, LORD JESUS, RECEIVE MY SPIRIT   100 14
THROUGH JESUS CHRIST OUR LORD   101 09
AND WITH HIS SON JESUS CHRIST   101 20
AND THE BLOOD OF JESUS CHRIST HIS SON CLEANSETH US   101 27
JESUS SAITH UNTO PETER, FOLLOW ME   102 03
THE DISCIPLE WHOM JESUS LOVED FOLLOWING   102 04
JESUS SAITH UNTO HIM, IF I WILL THAT HE TARRY TILL I   102 07
HIM SAITH TO JESUS, LORD, AND WHAT SHALL THIS MAN DO   102 07
YET JESUS SAID NOT UNTO HIM, HE SHALL NOT DIE   102 10
OTHER THINGS WHICH JESUS DID, THE WHICH, IF THEY   102 15
THROUGH JESUS CHRIST OUR LORD   102 26
THE SAME OUR LORD JESUS CHRIST, WHO LIVETH AND   104 10
THE BIRTH OF JESUS CHRIST WAS ON THIS WISE   104 27
FORTH A SON, AND THOU SHALT CALL HIS NAME JESUS   105 07
AND HE CALLED HIS NAME JESUS   105 15
THE SAME THY SON JESUS CHRIST OUR LORD   105 24
AT THE NAME OF JESUS EVERY KNEE SHOULD BOW, OF THINGS   105 28
CONFESS THAT JESUS CHRIST IS LORD, TO THE GLORY OF   105 30
NAME WAS CALLED JESUS, WHICH WAS SO NAMED OF THE   106 21
THROUGH JESUS CHRIST OUR LORD   106 28
THE SAME THY SON JESUS CHRIST OUR LORD   108 03
THE PRISONER OF JESUS CHRIST FOR YOU GENTILES, IF YE   108 06
ALL THINGS BY JESUS CHRIST   108 23
PURPOSED IN CHRIST JESUS OUR LORD   108 27
WHEN JESUS WAS BORN IN BETHLEHEM OF JUDAEA, IN THE   108 30
THROUGH JESUS CHRIST OUR LORD   109 33
THE CHILD JESUS TARRIED BEHIND IN JERUSALEM   110 22
AND JESUS INCREASED IN WISDOM AND STATURE, AND IN   111 06
THROUGH JESUS CHRIST OUR LORD   111 13
OF THE GOSPEL OF JESUS CHRIST, THE SON OF GOD   112 03
THOSE DAYS, THAT JESUS CAME FROM NAZARETH OF GALILEE,   112 18
THROUGH JESUS CHRIST OUR LORD   112 29
AND THE MOTHER OF JESUS WAS THERE   113 12
AND BOTH JESUS WAS CALLED, AND HIS DISCIPLES, TO THE   113 13
THE MOTHER OF JESUS SAITH UNTO HIM, THEY HAVE NO   113 14
JESUS SAITH UNTO HER, WOMAN, WHAT HAVE I TO DO WITH   113 15
JESUS SAITH UNTO THEM, FILL THE WATER-POTS WITH   113 20
OF MIRACLES DID JESUS IN CANA OF GALILEE, AND   113 30
THROUGH JESUS CHRIST OUR LORD   114 08
AND JESUS PUT FORTH HIS HAND, AND TOUCHED HIM,   114 32
AND JESUS SAITH UNTO HIM, SEE THOU TELL NO MAN   115 03
AND WHEN JESUS WAS ENTERED INTO CAPERNAUM, THERE CAME   115 06
AND JESUS SAITH UNTO HIM, I WILL COME AND HEAL HIM   115 09
WHEN JESUS HEARD IT, HE MARVELLED, AND SAID TO THEM   115 16
AND JESUS SAID UNTO THE CENTURION, GO THY WAY   115 23
THROUGH JESUS CHRIST OUR LORD   115 32
NAME OF THE LORD JESUS, GIVING THANKS TO GOD AND THE   116 15
THROUGH JESUS CHRIST OUR SAVIOUR, WHO LIVETH AND   118 31
THROUGH JESUS CHRIST OUR LORD   120 20
FATHER OF OUR LORD JESUS CHRIST, WHICH IS BLESSED FOR   121 15
FOR THINE ONLY SON JESUS CHRIST'S SAKE   122 19
THEN JESUS TOOK UNTO HIM THE TWELVE, AND SAID UNTO   123 17
TOLD HIM, THAT JESUS OF NAZARETH PASSETH BY   123 29
HE CRIED, SAYING, JESUS, THOU SON OF DAVID, HAVE   123 30
AND JESUS STOOD, AND COMMANDED HIM TO BE BROUGHT UNTO   123 33
AND JESUS SAID UNTO HIM, RECEIVE THY SIGHT   124 03
THROUGH JESUS CHRIST OUR LORD   124 17
THEN WAS JESUS LED UP OF THE SPIRIT INTO THE   126 23
JESUS SAID UNTO HIM, IT IS WRITTEN AGAIN, THOU SHALT   127 03
THEN SAITH JESUS UNTO HIM, GET THEE HENCE, SATAN   127 08
THROUGH JESUS CHRIST OUR LORD   127 20
YOU BY THE LORD JESUS, THAT AS YE HAVE RECEIVED OF US   127 24
WHAT COMMANDMENTS WE GAVE YOU BY THE LORD JESUS   127 27
JESUS WENT THENCE, AND DEPARTED INTO THE COASTS OF   128 07
THEN JESUS ANSWERED AND SAID UNTO HER, O WOMAN, GREAT   128 19
THROUGH JESUS CHRIST OUR LORD   128 28
JESUS WAS CASTING OUT A DEVIL, AND IT WAS DUMB   129 24
LORD AND SAVIOUR JESUS CHRIST   130 27
JESUS WENT OVER THE SEA OF GALILEE, WHICH IS THE SEA   131 21
AND JESUS WENT UP INTO A MOUNTAIN, AND THERE HE SAT   131 24
WHEN JESUS THEN LIFTED UP HIS EYES, AND SAW A GREAT   131 26
AND JESUS SAID, MAKE THE MEN SIT DOWN   131 35
AND JESUS TOOK THE LOAVES   132 03
THE MIRACLE THAT JESUS DID, SAID, THIS IS OF A TRUTH   132 12
THROUGH JESUS CHRIST OUR LORD   132 21
JESUS SAID, WHICH OF YOU CONVINCETH ME OF SIN   133 09
JESUS ANSWERED, I HAVE NOT A DEVIL   133 14
JESUS ANSWERED, IF I HONOUR MYSELF, MY HONOUR IS   133 23
JESUS SAITH UNTO THEM, VERILY, VERILY, I SAY UNTO YOU,   133 31
BUT JESUS HID HIMSELF, AND WENT OUT OF THE TEMPLE   133 33
OUR SAVIOUR JESUS CHRIST, TO TAKE UPON HIM OUR   134 07
THROUGH THE SAME JESUS CHRIST OUR LORD   134 11
WHICH WAS ALSO IN CHRIST JESUS   134 16
AT THE NAME OF JESUS EVERY KNEE SHOULD BOW, OF THINGS   134 24
CONFESS THAT JESUS CHRIST IS LORD, TO THE GLORY OF   134 27
COUNSEL AGAINST JESUS TO PUT HIM TO DEATH   134 31
AND JESUS STOOD BEFORE THE GOVERNOR   135 18
AND JESUS SAID UNTO HIM, THOU SAYEST   135 20
OR JESUS WHICH IS CALLED CHRIST   135 30
THAT THEY SHOULD ASK BARABBAS, AND DESTROY JESUS   136 02
I DO THEN WITH JESUS WHICH IS CALLED CHRIST   136 05
HE HAD SCOURGED JESUS, HE DELIVERED HIM TO BE   136 14
THE GOVERNOR TOOK JESUS INTO THE COMMON HALL, AND   136 16
THIS IS JESUS THE KING OF THE JEWS   137 02
THE NINTH HOUR JESUS CRIED WITH A LOUD VOICE, SAYING,   137 17
JESUS, WHEN HE HAD CRIED AGAIN WITH A LOUD VOICE,   137 24
WITH HIM, WATCHING JESUS, SAW THE EARTHQUAKE, AND   137 32
THE SAME THY SON JESUS CHRIST OUR LORD   138 09
AND JESUS SAID, LET HER ALONE   140 10
SAT AND DID EAT, JESUS SAID, VERILY I SAY UNTO YOU,   140 35
AS THEY DID EAT, JESUS TOOK BREAD, AND BLESSED, AND   141 09

JESUS   CONTINUED

AND JESUS SAITH UNTO THEM, ALL YE SHALL BE OFFENDED   141 18
AND JESUS SAITH UNTO HIM, VERILY I SAY UNTO THEE,   141 22
AND JESUS ANSWERED AND SAID UNTO THEM, ARE YE COME   142 24
AND THEY LED JESUS AWAY TO THE HIGH PRIEST   142 31
WITNESS AGAINST JESUS TO PUT HIM TO DEATH   143 03
AND ASKED JESUS, SAYING, ANSWEREST THOU   143 10
AND JESUS SAID, I AM   143 14
ALSO WAST WITH JESUS OF NAZARETH   143 26
MIND THE WORD THAT JESUS SAID UNTO HIM, BEFORE THE   143 35
THE SAME THY SON JESUS CHRIST OUR LORD   144 10
AND BOUND JESUS, AND CARRIED HIM AWAY,   145 05
BUT JESUS YET ANSWERED NOTHING   145 11
AND DELIVERED JESUS, WHEN HE HAD SCOURGED HIM, TO BE   145 28
AT THE NINTH HOUR JESUS CRIED WITH A LOUD VOICE,   146 27
AND JESUS CRIED WITH A LOUD VOICE, AND GAVE UP THE   146 34
THROUGH JESUS CHRIST OUR LORD   147 11
AND DREW NEAR UNTO JESUS TO KISS HIM   150 28
BUT JESUS SAID UNTO HIM, JUDAS, BETRAYEST THOU THE   150 29
AND JESUS ANSWERED AND SAID, SUFFER YE THUS FAR   150 34
THEN JESUS SAID UNTO THE CHIEF PRIESTS, AND CAPTAINS   150 35
THE MEN THAT HELD JESUS MOCKED HIM, AND SMOTE HIM   151 23
THE SAME THY SON JESUS CHRIST OUR LORD, WHO NOW   152 12
THAT THE LORD JESUS THE SAME NIGHT IN WHICH HE   152 17
AND WHEN HEROD SAW JESUS, HE WAS EXCEEDING GLAD   153 10
WILLING TO RELEASE JESUS, SPAKE AGAIN TO THEM   153 32
BUT HE DELIVERED JESUS TO THEIR WILL   154 08
LAID THE CROSS, THAT HE MIGHT BEAR IT AFTER JESUS   154 11
BUT JESUS TURNING UNTO THEM SAID, DAUGHTERS OF   154 13
THEN SAID JESUS, FATHER, FORGIVE THEM   154 25
AND HE SAID UNTO JESUS, LORD, REMEMBER ME WHEN THOU   155 06
AND JESUS SAID UNTO HIM, VERILY I SAY UNTO THEE,   155 07
AND WHEN JESUS HAD CRIED WITH A LOUD VOICE, HE SAID,   155 12
THE PASSOVER, WHEN JESUS KNEW THAT HIS HOUR WAS COME   155 23
JESUS KNOWING THAT THE FATHER HAD GIVEN ALL THINGS   155 28
JESUS ANSWERED AND SAID UNTO HIM, WHAT I DO THOU   156 03
JESUS ANSWERED HIM, IF I WASH THEE NOT, THOU HAST NO   156 05
JESUS SAITH TO HIM, HE THAT IS WASHED NEEDETH NOT   156 08
FOR WHICH OUR LORD JESUS CHRIST WAS CONTENTED TO BE   156 22
LORD AND SAVIOUR JESUS CHRIST   157 03
ONE SHEPHERD, JESUS CHRIST OUR LORD, WHO LIVETH AND   157 11
OF THE BODY OF JESUS CHRIST ONCE FOR ALL   158 02
BY THE BLOOD OF JESUS, BY A NEW AND LIVING WAY,   158 17
THEREFORE TOOK JESUS, AND SCOURGED HIM   158 30
THEN CAME JESUS FORTH, WEARING THE CROWN OF THORNS,   159 03
AND SAITH UNTO JESUS, WHENCE ART THOU   159 12
BUT JESUS GAVE HIM NO ANSWER   159 13
JESUS ANSWERED, THOU COULDEST HAVE NO POWER AT ALL   159 16
HE BROUGHT JESUS FORTH, AND SAT DOWN IN THE   159 23
AND THEY TOOK JESUS, AND LED HIM AWAY   159 31
SIDE ONE, AND JESUS IN THE MIDST   159 34
THE WRITING WAS, JESUS OF NAZARETH THE KING OF THE   160 02
THE PLACE WHERE JESUS WAS CRUCIFIED WAS NIGH TO THE   160 04
THEY HAD CRUCIFIED JESUS, TOOK HIS GARMENTS, AND MADE   160 10
BY THE CROSS OF JESUS HIS MOTHER, AND HIS MOTHER'S   160 17
WHEN JESUS THEREFORE SAW HIS MOTHER, AND THE DISCIPLE   160 19
AFTER THIS, JESUS KNOWING THAT ALL THINGS WERE NOW   160 23
WHEN JESUS THEREFORE HAD RECEIVED THE VINEGAR,   160 28
WHEN THEY CAME TO JESUS, AND SAW THAT HE WAS DEAD   161 02
OUR SAVIOUR JESUS CHRIST, SO BY CONTINUAL   161 14
THE SAME THY SON JESUS CHRIST OUR LORD   161 19
RESURRECTION OF JESUS CHRIST   161 32
AND BEGGED THE BODY OF JESUS   162 09
UNTO GOD THROUGH JESUS CHRIST OUR LORD   163 09
ONLY-BEGOTTEN SON JESUS CHRIST HAST OVERCOME DEATH,   163 23
THROUGH THE SAME JESUS CHRIST OUR LORD, WHO LIVETH   163 28
WHOM JESUS LOVED, AND SAITH UNTO THEM,   164 14
YE SEEK JESUS OF NAZARETH, WHICH WAS CRUCIFIED   165 29
THE SAME THY SON JESUS CHRIST OUR LORD   166 09
PREACHING PEACE BY JESUS CHRIST   166 16
HOW GOD ANOINTED JESUS OF NAZARETH WITH THE HOLY   166 19
AND REASONED, JESUS HIMSELF DREW NEAR, AND WENT WITH   167 07
CONCERNING JESUS OF NAZARETH, WHICH WAS A   167 16
THROUGH JESUS CHRIST OUR LORD   168 21
HE HATH RAISED UP JESUS AGAIN   169 08
JESUS HIMSELF STOOD IN THE MIDST OF THEM, AND SAITH   169 28
THE SAME THY SON JESUS CHRIST OUR LORD   170 23
BELIEVETH THAT JESUS IS THE SON OF GOD   170 29
AND BLOOD, EVEN JESUS CHRIST   170 30
OF THE JEWS, CAME JESUS AND STOOD IN THE MIDST, AND   171 16
THEN SAID JESUS TO THEM AGAIN, PEACE BE UNTO YOU   171 20
THE SAME THY SON JESUS CHRIST OUR LORD   172 02
JESUS SAID, I AM THE GOOD SHEPHERD   172 21
THROUGH OUR LORD JESUS CHRIST   173 10
JESUS SAID TO HIS DISCIPLES, A LITTLE WHILE, AND YE   173 27
NOW JESUS KNEW THAT THEY WERE DESIROUS TO ASK HIM,   174 03
THROUGH JESUS CHRIST OUR LORD   174 24
JESUS SAID UNTO HIS DISCIPLES, NOW I GO MY WAY TO HIM   175 06
THROUGH OUR LORD JESUS CHRIST   176 03
JESUS ANSWERED THEM, DO YE NOW BELIEVE   177 03
SON OUR LORD JESUS CHRIST TO HAVE ASCENDED INTO THE   177 15
OF ALL THAT JESUS BEGAN BOTH TO DO AND TEACH, UNTIL   177 23
THIS SAME JESUS, WHICH IS TAKEN UP FROM YOU INTO   178 17
JESUS SAID, BEHOLD, I SEND THE PROMISE OF MY FATHER   178 21
THINE ONLY SON JESUS CHRIST WITH GREAT TRIUMPH UNTO   179 05
GLORIFIED THROUGH JESUS CHRIST, TO WHOM BE PRAISE AND   179 21
MERITS OF CHRIST JESUS OUR SAVIOUR, WHO LIVETH AND   180 12
JESUS SAID UNTO HIS DISCIPLES, IF YE LOVE ME,   181 08
JESUS ANSWERED AND SAID UNTO HIM, IF A MAN LOVE ME,   181 23
THROUGH JESUS CHRIST OUR LORD, WHO LIVETH AND   182 18
JESUS SAID TO HIS DISCIPLES, ASK, AND IT SHALL BE   183 10
THROUGH JESUS CHRIST OUR LORD, WHO WITH THEE AND THE   183 25
PREACHING PEACE BY JESUS CHRIST   184 03
HOW GOD ANOINTED JESUS OF NAZARETH WITH THE HOLY   184 07
THROUGH JESUS CHRIST OUR LORD, WHO LIVETH AND   185 17

JESUS   CONTINUED

THEY WERE BAPTIZED IN THE NAME OF THE LORD JESUS   185 26
THIS PARABLE SPAKE JESUS UNTO THEM   186 10
THEN SAID JESUS UNTO THEM AGAIN, VERILY, VERILY,   186 12
THE SAME CAME TO JESUS BY NIGHT, AND SAID UNTO HIM,   187 35
JESUS ANSWERED AND SAID UNTO HIM, VERILY, VERILY, I   188 04
JESUS ANSWERED, VERILY, VERILY, I SAY UNTO THEE,   188 09
JESUS ANSWERED AND SAID UNTO HIM, ART THOU A MASTER   188 18
THROUGH JESUS CHRIST OUR LORD   189 05
SHALL CONFESS THAT JESUS IS THE SON OF GOD, GOD   189 22
THROUGH JESUS CHRIST OUR LORD   191 08
NAME OF HIS SON JESUS CHRIST, AND LOVE ONE ANOTHER,   191 31
THROUGH JESUS CHRIST OUR LORD   192 27
GLORY BY CHRIST JESUS, AFTER THAT YE HAVE SUFFERED A   193 10
FOR THE SAKE OF JESUS CHRIST OUR LORD   194 09
THROUGH JESUS CHRIST OUR LORD   195 18
AND JESUS SAID UNTO SIMON, FEAR NOT   196 27
THROUGH JESUS CHRIST OUR LORD   197 08
WERE BAPTIZED INTO JESUS CHRIST WERE BAPTIZED INTO   197 11
UNTO GOD THROUGH JESUS CHRIST OUR LORD   197 26
JESUS SAID UNTO HIS DISCIPLES, EXCEPT YOUR   197 28
THROUGH JESUS CHRIST OUR LORD   198 24
LIFE THROUGH JESUS CHRIST OUR LORD   199 05
NOTHING TO EAT, JESUS CALLED HIS DISCIPLES UNTO HIM,   199 09
THROUGH JESUS CHRIST OUR LORD   199 32
THROUGH JESUS CHRIST OUR LORD   201 03
JESUS SAID, A CERTAIN MAN HAD TWO SONS   201 31
THROUGH JESUS CHRIST OUR LORD   203 14
OF GOD CALLETH JESUS ACCURSED   203 20
MAN CAN SAY THAT JESUS IS THE LORD, BUT BY THE HOLY   203 21
THROUGH JESUS CHRIST OUR LORD   204 27
JESUS SPAKE THIS PARABLE UNTO CERTAIN WHICH TRUSTED   205 21
AND MEDIATION OF JESUS CHRIST, THY SON, OUR LORD   206 10
JESUS, DEPARTING FROM THE COASTS OF TYRE AND SIDON,   206 27
THE MERITS OF JESUS CHRIST OUR LORD   207 17
BY FAITH OF JESUS CHRIST MIGHT BE GIVEN TO THEM THAT   208 04
AND JESUS ANSWERING SAID, A CERTAIN MAN WENT DOWN   208 20
SAID UNTO JESUS, AND WHO IS MY NEIGHBOUR   208 20
THEN SAID JESUS UNTO HIM, GO, AND DO THOU LIKEWISE   209 04
THROUGH JESUS CHRIST OUR LORD   209 11
CAME TO PASS, AS JESUS WENT TO JERUSALEM, THAT HE   209 31
AND SAID, JESUS, MASTER, HAVE MERCY ON US   210 04
AND JESUS ANSWERING SAID, WERE THERE NOT TEN   210 10
THROUGH JESUS CHRIST OUR LORD   210 21
CROSS OF OUR LORD JESUS CHRIST, BY WHOM THE WORLD IS   210 30
FOR IN CHRIST JESUS NEITHER CIRCUMCISION AVAILETH ANY   210 32
GRACE OF OUR LORD JESUS CHRIST BE WITH YOUR SPIRIT   211 06
FOR I BEAR IN MY BODY THE MARKS OF THE LORD JESUS   211 06
THROUGH JESUS CHRIST OUR LORD   212 07
FATHER OF OUR LORD JESUS CHRIST, OF WHOM THE WHOLE   212 12
CHURCH BY CHRIST JESUS THROUGHOUT ALL AGES, WORLD   212 24
DAY AFTER, THAT JESUS WENT INTO A CITY CALLED NAIN   212 27
THROUGH JESUS CHRIST OUR LORD   213 16
CAME TO PASS, AS JESUS WENT INTO THE HOUSE OF ONE OF   213 28
AND JESUS ANSWERING SPAKE UNTO THE LAWYERS AND   213 31
THROUGH JESUS CHRIST OUR LORD   214 26
IS GIVEN YOU BY JESUS CHRIST   214 29
COMING OF OUR LORD JESUS CHRIST   215 02
DAY OF OUR LORD JESUS CHRIST   215 04
HAD HEARD THAT JESUS HAD PUT THE SADDUCEES TO   215 06
JESUS SAID UNTO HIM, THOU SHALT LOVE THE LORD THY GOD   215 10
GATHERED TOGETHER, JESUS ASKED THEM, SAYING, WHAT   215 16
THROUGH JESUS CHRIST OUR LORD   215 29
HAVE BEEN TAUGHT BY HIM, AS THE TRUTH IS IN JESUS   216 11
JESUS ENTERED INTO A SHIP, AND PASSED OVER, AND CAME   216 33
AND JESUS, SEEING THEIR FAITH, SAID UNTO THE SICK OF   217 02
AND JESUS KNOWING THEIR THOUGHTS SAID, WHEREFORE   217 06
THROUGH JESUS CHRIST OUR LORD   217 21
NAME OF OUR LORD JESUS CHRIST   217 31
JESUS SAID, THE KINGDOM OF HEAVEN IS LIKE UNTO A   218 03
THROUGH JESUS CHRIST OUR LORD   219 03
WHEN HE HEARD THAT JESUS WAS COME OUT OF JUDAEA INTO   219 29
THEN SAID JESUS UNTO HIM, EXCEPT YE SEE SIGNS AND   219 32
JESUS SAID UNTO HIM, GO THY WAY   220 04
THE WORD THAT JESUS HAD SPOKEN UNTO HIM, AND HE WENT   220 10
IN THE WHICH JESUS SAID UNTO HIM, THY SON   220 12
MIRACLE THAT JESUS DID, WHEN HE WAS COME OUT OF   220 20
THROUGH JESUS CHRIST OUR LORD   220 27
UNTIL THE DAY OF JESUS CHRIST   220 32
YOU ALL IN THE TENDER MERCIES OF CHRIST JESUS   221 06
WHICH ARE BY JESUS CHRIST, UNTO THE GLORY AND PRAISE   221 09
PETER SAID UNTO JESUS, LORD, HOW OFT SHALL MY BROTHER   221 11
JESUS SAITH UNTO HIM, I SAY NOT UNTO THEE, UNTIL   222 13
THROUGH JESUS CHRIST OUR LORD   222 22
THE LORD JESUS CHRIST   223 05
BUT JESUS PERCEIVED THEIR WICKEDNESS, AND SAID,   223 19
FOR THE SAKE OF JESUS CHRIST, OUR BLESSED LORD AND   223 23
FATHER OF OUR LORD JESUS CHRIST, PRAYING ALWAYS FOR   223 24
FAITH IN CHRIST JESUS, AND OF THE LOVE WHICH YE HAVE   224 12
WHILE JESUS SPAKE THESE THINGS UNTO JOHN'S DISCIPLES,   224 16
AND JESUS AROSE, AND FOLLOWED HIM, AND SO DID HIS   224 24
BUT JESUS TURNED HIM ABOUT, AND WHEN HE SAW HER, HE   225 07
AND WHEN JESUS CAME INTO THE RULER'S HOUSE, AND SAW   225 22
THROUGH JESUS CHRIST OUR LORD   225 31
WHEN JESUS THEN LIFTED UP HIS EYES, AND SAW A GREAT   226 02
AND JESUS SAID, MAKE THE MEN SIT DOWN   226 11
AND JESUS TOOK THE LOAVES   226 20
THE MIRACLE THAT JESUS DID, SAID, THIS IS OF A TRUTH   226 23
CALLING OF THY SON JESUS CHRIST, AND FOLLOWED HIM   226 26
THROUGH THE SAME JESUS CHRIST OUR LORD   227 24
THY MOUTH THE LORD JESUS, AND SHALT BELIEVE IN THINE   228 09
JESUS, WALKING BY THE SEA OF GALILEE, SAW TWO   228 10
BELIEVE IN THY SON JESUS CHRIST, THAT OUR FAITH IN   228 26
THROUGH THE SAME JESUS CHRIST, TO WHOM, WITH THEE AND
NOT WITH THEM WHEN JESUS CAME

JESUS   CONTINUED

THEN CAME JESUS, THE DOORS BEING SHUT, AND STOOD IN   228 32
JESUS SAITH UNTO HIM, THOMAS, BECAUSE THOU HAST SEEN   229 07
SIGNS TRULY DID JESUS IN THE PRESENCE OF HIS   229 09
MIGHT BELIEVE THAT JESUS IS THE CHRIST, THE SON OF   229 12
THROUGH JESUS CHRIST OUR LORD   229 23
LORD SAID, I AM JESUS WHOM THOU PERSECUTEST   230 03
THE LORD, EVEN JESUS, THAT APPEARED UNTO THEE IN THE   230 31
AND SAID UNTO JESUS, BEHOLD, WE HAVE FORSAKEN ALL,   231 12
AND JESUS SAID UNTO THEM, VERILY I SAY UNTO YOU, THAT   231 14
THE SAME THY SON JESUS CHRIST OUR LORD   231 32
IN THE CHILD JESUS, TO DO FOR HIM AFTER THE CUSTOM OF   233 03
THROUGH JESUS CHRIST OUR LORD   234 04
WHICH WAS GUIDE TO THEM THAT TOOK JESUS   234 11
TIME THAT THE LORD JESUS WENT IN AND OUT AMONG US,   234 22
AT THAT TIME JESUS ANSWERED AND SAID, I THANK THEE,   235 03
OF THY SON JESUS CHRIST BY THE MESSAGE OF AN ANGEL,   235 20
THROUGH THE SAME JESUS CHRIST OUR LORD   235 22
BRING FORTH A SON, AND SHALT CALL HIS NAME JESUS   236 16
THROUGH JESUS CHRIST OUR LORD   237 09
TO KNOW THY SON JESUS CHRIST TO BE THE WAY, THE   238 30
THE SAME THY SON JESUS CHRIST OUR LORD   239 03
AND OF THE LORD JESUS CHRIST, TO THE TWELVE TRIBES   239 06
AND JESUS SAID UNTO HIS DISCIPLES, LET NOT YOUR HEART   239 29
JESUS SAITH UNTO HIM, I AM THE WAY, THE TRUTH, AND   240 05
JESUS SAITH UNTO HIM, HAVE I BEEN SO LONG TIME WITH   240 10
THROUGH JESUS CHRIST OUR LORD   240 32
TH SAME THY SON JESUS CHRIST OUR LORD   242 14
WHO BY THY SON JESUS CHRIST DIDST GIVE TO THY APOSTLE   244 22
THE SAME THY SON JESUS CHRIST OUR LORD   244 28
WHEN JESUS CAME INTO THE COASTS OF CAESAREA PHILIPPI,   245 31
AND JESUS ANSWERED AND SAID UNTO HIM, BLESSED ART   246 04
CALLING OF THY SON JESUS CHRIST, AND FOLLOWED HIM   246 19
THROUGH THE SAME JESUS CHRIST OUR LORD   246 21
BUT JESUS ANSWERED AND SAID, YE KNOW NOT WHAT YE ASK   247 11
BUT JESUS CALLED THEM UNTO HIM, AND SAID, YE KNOW   247 20
EVEN AS OUR LORD JESUS CHRIST HATH SHEWED ME   248 11
COMING OF OUR LORD JESUS CHRIST, BUT WERE   248 15
PETER SAID UNTO JESUS, MASTER, IT IS GOOD FOR US TO   248 33
VOICE WAS PAST, JESUS WAS FOUND ALONE   249 08
THROUGH JESUS CHRIST OUR LORD   249 18
THE SAME THY SON JESUS CHRIST, WHO LIVETH AND   250 24
BUT CHRIST JESUS THE LORD   251 06
GOD IN THE FACE OF JESUS CHRIST   251 09
AND AS JESUS PASSED FORTH FROM THENCE, HE SAW A MAN,   251 12
CAME TO PASS, AS JESUS SAT AT MEAT IN THE HOUSE,   251 15
BUT WHEN JESUS HEARD THAT, HE SAID UNTO THEM, THEY   251 19
THROUGH JESUS CHRIST OUR LORD   251 31
THE DISCIPLES UNTO JESUS, SAYING, WHO IS THE GREATEST   252 22
AND JESUS CALLED A LITTLE CHILD UNTO HIM, AND SET HIM   252 24
THE SAME THY SON JESUS CHRIST OUR LORD   253 20
AND PROPHETS, JESUS CHRIST HIMSELF BEING THE HEAD   254 28
THROUGH THE SAME JESUS CHRIST OUR LORD   254 32
AND PROPHETS, JESUS CHRIST HIMSELF BEING THE CHIEF   255 06
THE SAME THY SON JESUS CHRIST OUR LORD   256 11
JESUS SEEING THE MULTITUDES, WENT UP INTO A MOUNTAIN   257 18
THROUGH JESUS CHRIST OUR LORD   258 08
OUR FAITH, THY SON JESUS CHRIST OUR LORD   258 18
LOOKING UNTO JESUS THE AUTHOR AND FINISHER OF OUR   258 23
THROUGH JESUS CHRIST OUR LORD   259 23
TO GOD BY JESUS CHRIST   259 32
JESUS WENT INTO THE TEMPLE OF GOD, AND CAST OUT ALL   260 03
AND JESUS SAITH UNTO THEM, YEA   260 13
THROUGH JESUS CHRIST OUR LORD   260 24
JESUS CAME TO NAZARETH, WHERE HE HAD BEEN BROUGHT UP   261 10
THROUGH JESUS CHRIST OUR LORD   262 02
JESUS SAID UNTO THEM, WHICH OF YOU SHALL HAVE A   262 26
THROUGH JESUS CHRIST OUR LORD   263 21
JESUS SAID, YE HAVE HEARD THAT IT HATH BEEN SAID,   264 03
THROUGH JESUS CHRIST OUR LORD   265 16
JESUS SAID, BE NOT ANXIOUS FOR YOUR LIFE, WHAT YE   266 11
THROUGH JESUS CHRIST OUR LORD   267 09
NAME OF OUR LORD JESUS CHRIST   267 12
JESUS ANSWERED AND SAID UNTO THEM, HAVE YE NOT READ,   268 05
THROUGH JESUS CHRIST OUR LORD   268 19
THROUGH JESUS CHRIST OUR LORD   268 25
IF WE BELIEVE THAT JESUS DIED AND ROSE AGAIN, EVEN SO   268 30
WHICH SLEEP IN JESUS WILL GOD BRING WITH HIM   268 31
JESUS SAID UNTO THEM, ALL THAT THE FATHER GIVETH ME   269 13
THROUGH OUR LORD JESUS CHRIST, THAT OF HIS BOUNTEOUS   274 02
BUT WHEN JESUS SAW IT, HE WAS MUCH DISPLEASED,   274 27
THE SAME CAME TO JESUS BY NIGHT, AND SAID UNTO HIM,   275 06
JESUS ANSWERED AND SAID UNTO HIM, VERILY, VERILY, I   275 09
JESUS ANSWERED, VERILY, VERILY, I SAY UNTO THEE,   275 14
JESUS CAME AND SPAKE UNTO THEM, SAYING, ALL POWER IS   275 26
BY HIS SON JESUS CHRIST   276 05
THROUGH OUR LORD JESUS CHRIST, WHO LIVETH AND   276 14
THAT OUR LORD JESUS CHRIST WOULD VOUCHSAFE TO RECEIVE   276 20
THAT OUR LORD JESUS CHRIST WOULD VOUCHSAFE TO RECEIVE   277 22
THOU BELIEVE IN JESUS THE CHRIST, THE SON OF THE   278 02
DEARLY BELOVED SON JESUS CHRIST, FOR THE FORGIVENESS   279 10
THROUGH THE SAME JESUS CHRIST OUR LORD, TO WHOM,   279 20
FATHER OF OUR LORD JESUS CHRIST, OF WHOM THE WHOLE   281 07
THROUGH JESUS CHRIST OUR LORD   283 12
THROUGH JESUS CHRIST OUR SAVIOUR   284 03
AND IN JESUS CHRIST HIS ONLY SON OUR LORD   284 15
THROUGH JESUS CHRIST OUR LORD   285 31
THROUGH JESUS CHRIST OUR LORD   287 30
WHAT DOES OUR LORD JESUS CHRIST TEACH US ABOUT THESE   288 02
OUR LORD JESUS CHRIST TEACHES US THAT THEY   288 04
GRACE OF OUR LORD JESUS CHRIST, AND THE LOVE OF GOD,   289 29
AND PROPHETS, JESUS CHRIST HIMSELF BEING THE HEAD   290 20
THROUGH THE SAME JESUS CHRIST OUR LORD   290 24
THE BODY OF WHICH JESUS CHRIST IS THE HEAD, AND ALL   290 32
THROUGH JESUS CHRIST OUR LORD   294 28

JESUS   CONTINUED

THROUGH JESUS CHRIST OUR LORD   295 03
GRACE OF OUR LORD JESUS CHRIST, AND THE LOVE OF GOD, 295 04
THEY WERE BAPTIZED IN THE NAME OF THE LORD JESUS   296 18
PROMISE TO FOLLOW JESUS CHRIST AS YOUR LORD AND   297 03
THROUGH OUR LORD JESUS CHRIST, WHO WITH THEE AND THE 298 23
LORD AND SAVIOUR JESUS CHRIST   298 32
THROUGH JESUS CHRIST OUR LORD   302 21
THROUGH JESUS CHRIST OUR LORD   303 11
THROUGH JESUS CHRIST OUR LORD   303 19
THROUGH THE SAME JESUS CHRIST OUR LORD, WHO LIVETH   303 27
THROUGH JESUS CHRIST OUR LORD   306 32
THROUGH JESUS CHRIST OUR LORD   307 06
THROUGH JESUS CHRIST OUR LORD   309 08
THROUGH JESUS CHRIST OUR LORD   309 32
THROUGH JESUS CHRIST OUR LORD   310 25
THROUGH JESUS CHRIST OUR LORD   311 24
THROUGH JESUS CHRIST OUR LORD   312 16
THROUGH JESUS CHRIST OUR LORD   313 07
BELOVED SON, JESUS CHRIST OUR LORD   314 13
NAME OF OUR LORD JESUS CHRIST   314 22
THROUGH JESUS CHRIST OUR LORD   315 11
THROUGH JESUS CHRIST OUR LORD   315 17
THROUGH JESUS CHRIST OUR SAVIOUR, TO WHOM, WITH THEE 316 02
AND STEDFAST FAITH IN THY SON JESUS   316 14
THROUGH JESUS CHRIST OUR LORD   316 23
WE ASK THROUGH JESUS CHRIST OUR LORD   317 08
THE MERITS OF JESUS CHRIST THINE ONLY SON OUR LORD   317 22
THROUGH JESUS CHRIST OUR LORD, WHO LIVETH AND   319 11
IN THE NAME OF JESUS CHRIST WHO REDEEMED THEE   319 22
MERCY OF OUR LORD JESUS CHRIST, THAT ALL THY PAIN AND 320 17
THROUGH JESUS CHRIST OUR LORD   321 25
THROUGH JESUS CHRIST OUR LORD   322 10
JESUS SAID, VERILY, VERILY, I SAY UNTO YOU, HE THAT 322 21
FOR JESUS CHRIST'S SAKE   323 17
BELIEVE THAT JESUS CHRIST HATH SUFFERED DEATH UPON R 323 27
THROUGH OUR LORD JESUS CHRIST   330 13
WHICH IS IN CHRIST JESUS OUR LORD   331 14
JESUS SAID, LET NOT YOUR HEART BE TROUBLED   331 17
JESUS SAITH UNTO HIM, I AM THE WAY, THE TRUTH, AND   331 25
THROUGH JESUS CHRIST OUR LORD, WHO LIVETH AND   332 07
HE THAT RAISED UP JESUS FROM THE DEAD WILL ALSO   333 05
THROUGH OUR LORD JESUS CHRIST   333 18
THROUGH JESUS CHRIST OUR LORD   334 17
THROUGH JESUS CHRIST OUR LORD   334 29
FATHER OF OUR LORD JESUS CHRIST, WHO IS THE   334 30
THROUGH JESUS CHRIST, OUR MEDIATOR AND   335 14
THE DEAD OUR LORD JESUS CHRIST, THE GREAT SHEPHERD OF 335 17
THROUGH JESUS CHRIST, TO WHOM BE GLORY FOR EVER AND 335 21
THOSE WHO REST IN JESUS, THE MANIFOLD BLESSINGS OF   335 28
UNTO THE DAY OF JESUS CHRIST   335 30
THE SAME THY SON JESUS CHRIST OUR LORD   336 02
THROUGH JESUS CHRIST OUR LORD   336 09
O LORD JESUS CHRIST, WHO BY THY DEATH DIDST TAKE AWAY 336 10
THE SAME, THY SON JESUS CHRIST, OUR ONLY MEDIATOR AND 336 29
THROUGH OUR LORD JESUS CHRIST   337 12
JESUS CALLED THEM UNTO HIM AND SAID, SUFFER THE   338 09
THE DISCIPLES UNTO JESUS, SAYING, WHO IS THE GREATEST 339 21
AND JESUS CALLED A LITTLE CHILD UNTO HIM, AND SET HIM 339 23
THROUGH JESUS CHRIST OUR LORD   340 27
THROUGH JESUS CHRIST OUR LORD   341 03
GRACE OF OUR LORD JESUS CHRIST, AND THE LOVE OF GOD, 341 05
BE SAID OR SUNG, JESUS SAITH TO HIS DISCIPLES,   341 09
THROUGH OUR LORD JESUS CHRIST, WE COMMIT THE BODY OF 341 14
THE SAME THY SON, JESUS CHRIST OUR LORD   342 07
THROUGH JESUS CHRIST OUR LORD   342 12
OF OUR SAVIOUR JESUS CHRIST, WHO LIVETH AND REIGNETH 531 24
BOLDNESS IN THE FAITH WHICH IS IN CHRIST JESUS   532 05
WILL OF OUR LORD JESUS CHRIST, AND ACCORDING TO THE 532 32
THROUGH FAITH IN JESUS CHRIST   533 04
SON OUR SAVIOUR JESUS CHRIST, TO WHOM BE GLORY AND   535 10
AND OF HIS SON JESUS CHRIST OUR LORD   535 15
OF OUR SAVIOUR JESUS CHRIST, WHO LIVETH AND REIGNETH 537 28
WHEN JESUS SAW THE MULTITUDES, HE WAS MOVED WITH   538 14
THIS PARABLE SPAKE JESUS UNTO THEM   538 33
THEN SAID JESUS UNTO THEM AGAIN, VERILY, VERILY,   539 03
NAME OF OUR LORD JESUS CHRIST, THAT YE HAVE IN   539 30
OUR ONLY SAVIOUR JESUS CHRIST, FOR THE HEAVENLY   541 16
WILL OF OUR LORD JESUS CHRIST, AND ACCORDING TO THE 541 31
THROUGH FAITH IN JESUS CHRIST   542 04
THROUGH JESUS CHRIST OUR LORD   543 21
DEARLY BELOVED SON JESUS CHRIST, TO BE OUR REDEEMER, 545 14
THE SAME THY SON JESUS CHRIST OUR LORD, WHO LIVETH   546 03
THROUGH JESUS CHRIST OUR LORD   547 13
AND OF HIS SON JESUS CHRIST OUR LORD   547 16
OF OUR SAVIOUR JESUS CHRIST, WHO LIVETH AND REIGNETH 548 07
WHO BY THE SON JESUS CHRIST DIDST GIVE TO THY HOLY   549 07
THE SAME THY SON JESUS CHRIST OUR LORD   549 15
TOWARD OUR LORD JESUS CHRIST   550 14
OF THE LORD JESUS, TO TESTIFY THE GOSPEL OF THE GRACE 550 21
WORDS OF THE LORD JESUS, HOW HE SAID, IT IS MORE   551 10
JESUS SAITH TO SIMON PETER, SIMON, SON OF JONAS,   551 14
JESUS SAITH UNTO HIM, FEED MY SHEEP   551 24
OF THE JEWS, CAME JESUS, AND STOOD IN THE MIDST, AND 551 29
THEN SAITH JESUS TO THEM AGAIN, PEACE BE UNTO YOU   551 33
JESUS CAME AND SPAKE UNTO THEM, SAYING, ALL POWER IS 552 09
ME GOD, THROUGH JESUS CHRIST   552 32
OF OUR SAVIOUR JESUS CHRIST, WHO LIVETH AND REIGNETH 554 02
WILL OF OUR LORD JESUS CHRIST, AND THE ORDER OF THIS 554 17
THROUGH FAITH IN JESUS CHRIST   554 22
THROUGH JESUS CHRIST OUR LORD   555 33
DEARLY BELOVED SON JESUS CHRIST, TO BE OUR REDEEMER, 557 22
THROUGH THE SAME JESUS CHRIST OUR LORD, WHO, WITH   558 06
THROUGH JESUS CHRIST OUR LORD   558 32
UP BY THE LORD JESUS, THE RIGHTEOUS JUDGE, WHO LIVETH 559 14

JESUS   CONTINUED

AND OF HIS SON JESUS CHRIST OUR LORD   559 19
THROUGH JESUS CHRIST OUR LORD, WHO LIVETH AND   562 13
THROUGH JESUS CHRIST OUR BLESSED LORD AND SAVIOUR   565 14
WHICH WE BEG FOR JESUS CHRIST'S SAKE, OUR MOST   566 23
THROUGH JESUS CHRIST OUR LORD   566 34
THROUGH JESUS CHRIST OUR LORD   567 09
WAS AT HAND, AND JESUS WENT UP TO JERUSALEM, AND   567 25
THROUGH JESUS CHRIST OUR LORD   568 12
AND OF HIS SON JESUS CHRIST OUR LORD   568 15
THROUGH JESUS CHRIST OUR LORD, WHO HATH TAUGHT US TO 571 12
AND TRUTH CAME BY JESUS CHRIST   572 02
THROUGH JESUS CHRIST, OUR ONLY MEDIATOR AND REDEEMER 572 14
O HOLY JESUS, WHO HAST PURCHASED TO THYSELF AN   572 16
THE DEAD OUR LORD JESUS CHRIST, THE GREAT SHEPHERD OF 573 04
THROUGH JESUS CHRIST, TO WHOM BE GLORY FOR EVER AND 573 07
FOR THE SAKE OF JESUS CHRIST THY SON OUR SAVIOUR   573 28
AND PROPHETS, JESUS CHRIST HIMSELF BEING THE CHIEF   574 04
THY BLESSED SON JESUS CHRIST, THE GRACIOUS BISHOP AND 574 20
THROUGH JESUS CHRIST OUR SAVIOUR   577 24
AND IN JESUS CHRIST HIS ONLY SON OUR LORD   577 30
THROUGH OUR LORD JESUS CHRIST   581 06
SON OUR SAVIOUR JESUS CHRIST   587 28
LORD AND SAVIOUR JESUS CHRIST   588 10
AND DEAD, THY SON JESUS CHRIST OUR LORD   588 24
OF THY SON JESUS CHRIST, OUR LORD AND SAVIOUR   589 07
GRACE OF OUR LORD JESUS CHRIST, AND THE LOVE OF GOD, 589 09
SAKE OF THY SON JESUS CHRIST, OUR ONLY SAVIOUR AND   590 06
LORD AND SAVIOUR JESUS CHRIST   590 20
SON OUR SAVIOUR JESUS CHRIST   591 05
SON OUR SAVIOUR JESUS CHRIST   591 23
OF THY SON CHRIST JESUS, IN WHOSE NAME WE OFFER UP   591 32
GRACE OF OUR LORD JESUS CHRIST, AND THE LOVE OF GOD, 592 02
THROUGH JESUS CHRIST OUR LORD   592 25
GRACE OF OUR LORD JESUS CHRIST, AND THE LOVE OF GOD, 592 27
OUR SAVIOUR, JESUS CHRIST   593 16
THROUGH JESUS CHRIST OUR LORD   594 09
THROUGH JESUS CHRIST OUR LORD   594 17
THROUGH JESUS CHRIST OUR SAVIOUR   594 27
OUR SAVIOUR JESUS CHRIST   595 10
THROUGH THE SAME JESUS CHRIST OUR LORD   595 16
THROUGH JESUS CHRIST OUR LORD   595 23
THROUGH JESUS CHRIST OUR LORD   595 32
US IN THY SON, JESUS CHRIST OUR LORD   596 09
THY SON, JESUS CHRIST OUR LORD   596 22
OF THEIR SAVIOUR JESUS CHRIST   596 28
THROUGH JESUS CHRIST OUR LORD   597 07
THROUGH JESUS CHRIST OUR LORD   597 12
THROUGH JESUS CHRIST OUR LORD   597 18
THROUGH JESUS CHRIST OUR LORD   597 25
THROUGH JESUS CHRIST OUR LORD   598 04
THROUGH JESUS CHRIST OUR LORD   598 11
THROUGH JESUS CHRIST OUR LORD   598 16
THROUGH JESUS CHRIST OUR LORD   598 30
OUR SAVIOUR JESUS CHRIST   599 17
THROUGH JESUS CHRIST OUR LORD   599 23
OUR SAVIOUR JESUS CHRIST   600 13
THROUGH JESUS CHRIST OUR LORD   600 19
LORD AND SAVIOUR JESUS CHRIST BY FAITH, AND NOT FOR 605 07
NOT OF FAITH IN JESUS CHRIST   605 18
ONLY-BEGOTTEN SON JESUS CHRIST   606 14
ONLY THE NAME OF JESUS CHRIST, WHEREBY MEN MUST BE   606 35
MEN BY OUR LORD JESUS CHRIST, AND JAMES HIS APOSTLE, 611 07

JESUS'

ALSO HIMSELF WAS JESUS' DISCIPLE   162 08
HE FELL DOWN AT JESUS' KNEES, SAYING, DEPART FROM ME 196 23
YOUR SERVANTS FOR JESUS' SAKE   251 07

JEW

BETWEEN THE JEW AND THE GREEK   227 02

JEWRY

THROUGHOUT ALL JEWRY, BEGINNING FROM GALILEE TO THIS 153 05

JEWS

OF JOHN, WHEN THE JEWS SENT PRIESTS AND LEVITES FROM 095 21
WHERE IS HE THAT IS BORN KING OF THE JEWS   108 33
PURIFYING OF THE JEWS, CONTAINING TWO OR THREE   113 19
OF THE JEWS FIVE TIMES RECEIVED I FORTY STRIPES SAVE 120 32
A FEAST OF THE JEWS, WAS NIGH   131 25
THEN ANSWERED THE JEWS, AND SAID UNTO HIM, SAY WE NOT 133 12
THEN SAID THE JEWS UNTO HIM, NOW WE KNOW THAT THOU   133 18
THEN SAID THE JEWS UNTO HIM, THOU ART NOT YET FIFTY 133 29
ASKED HIM, SAYING, ART THOU THE KING OF THE JEWS   135 20
HAIL, KING OF THE JEWS   136 21
THIS IS JESUS THE KING OF THE JEWS   137 03
PILATE ASKED HIM, ART THOU THE KING OF THE JEWS   145 07
YE THAT I RELEASE UNTO YOU THE KING OF THE JEWS   145 19
DO UNTO HIM WHOM YE CALL THE KING OF THE JEWS   145 24
AND BEGAN TO SALUTE HIM, HAIL, KING OF THE JEWS   145 33
ACCUSATION WAS WRITTEN OVER, THE KING OF THE JEWS   146 14
ART THOU THE KING OF THE JEWS   153 02
BE THE KING OF THE JEWS, SAVE THYSELF   154 31
AND HEBREW, THIS IS THE KING OF THE JEWS   154 34
A PURPLE ROBE, AND SAID, HAIL, KING OF THE JEWS   158 33
THE JEWS ANSWERED HIM, WE HAVE A LAW, AND BY OUR LAW 159 08
BUT THE JEWS CRIED OUT, SAYING, IF THOU LET THIS MAN 159 19
HE SAITH UNTO THE JEWS, BEHOLD YOUR KING   159 26
JESUS OF NAZARETH THE KING OF THE JEWS   160 03
THIS TITLE THEN READ MANY OF THE JEWS   160 04

JEWS CONTINUED

PRIESTS OF THE JEWS TO PILATE, WRITE NOT, THE KING OF	160 06
JEWS TO PILATE, WRITE NOT, THE KING OF THE JEWS	160 07
BUT THAT HE SAID, I AM KING OF THE JEWS	160 08
THE JEWS THEREFORE, BECAUSE IT WAS THE PREPARATION,	160 30
IN THE LAND OF THE JEWS, AND IN JERUSALEM	166 23
FOR FEAR OF THE JEWS, CAME JESUS AND STOOD IN THE	171 16
AT JERUSALEM JEWS, DEVOUT MEN, OUT OF EVERY NATION	180 25
STRANGERS OF ROME, JEWS AND PROSELYTES, CRETES AND	181 05
WHETHER WE BE JEWS OR GENTILES, WHETHER WE BE	183 05
IN THE LAND OF THE JEWS, AND IN JERUSALEM	184 11
NAMED NICODEMUS, A RULER OF THE JEWS	187 35
AND CONFOUNDED THE JEWS WHICH DWELT AT DAMASCUS,	231 09
SAW IT PLEASED THE JEWS, HE PROCEEDED FURTHER TO TAKE	245 02
ALL THE EXPECTATION OF THE PEOPLE OF THE JEWS	245 29
SAW IT PLEASED THE JEWS, HE PROCEEDED FURTHER TO TAKE	247 04
BUT WHEN THE JEWS SAW THE MULTITUDES, THEY WERE	260 27
NAMED NICODEMUS, A RULER OF THE JEWS	275 06
WHICH BEFELL ME BY THE LYING IN WAIT OF THE JEWS	550 10
BOTH TO THE JEWS, AND ALSO TO THE GREEKS, REPENTANCE	550 13
FOR FEAR OF THE JEWS, CAME JESUS, AND STOOD IN THE	551 29

JEWS'

AND THE JEWS' PASSOVER WAS AT HAND, AND JESUS WENT UP	567 25

JOHN

ALSO WHAT SAINT JOHN SAITH	076 21
NOW WHEN JOHN HAD HEARD IN THE PRISON THE WORKS OF	094 16
GO AND SHEW JOHN AGAIN THOSE THINGS WHICH YE DO	094 19
CONCERNING JOHN, WHAT WENT YE OUT INTO THE WILDERNESS	094 26
IS THE RECORD OF JOHN, WHEN THE JEWS SENT PRIESTS AND	095 21
JOHN ANSWERED THEM, SAYING, I BAPTIZE WITH WATER	096 02
WHERE JOHN WAS BAPTIZING	096 07
WAS A MAN SENT FROM GOD, WHOSE NAME WAS JOHN	097 26
EVANGELIST SAINT JOHN, MAY SO WALK IN THE LIGHT OF	101 08
JOHN DID BAPTIZE IN THE WILDERNESS, AND PREACH THE	112 07
AND JOHN WAS CLOTHED WITH CAMEL'S HAIR, AND WITH A	112 12
AND WAS BAPTIZED OF JOHN IN JORDAN	112 19
PETER AND JAMES AND JOHN, AND BEGAN TO BE SORE	141 30
HE SENT PETER AND JOHN, SAYING, GO AND PREPARE US THE	148 23
THE BAPTISM WHICH JOHN PREACHED	166 19
FOR JOHN TRULY BAPTIZED WITH WATER	178 02
THE BAPTISM WHICH JOHN PREACHED	184 06
WORD OF GOD, THEY SENT UNTO THEM PETER AND JOHN	185 23
WAS ALSO JAMES, AND JOHN, THE SONS OF ZEBEDEE, WHICH	196 26
SON OF ZEBEDEE, AND JOHN HIS BROTHER, IN A SHIP WITH	227 30
FROM THE BAPTISM OF JOHN, UNTO THAT SAME DAY THAT HE	234 23
THY SERVANT JOHN BAPTIST WAS WONDERFULLY BORN,	242 08
BUT HE SHALL BE CALLED JOHN	243 20
AND WROTE, SAYING, HIS NAME IS JOHN	243 24
THE BROTHER OF JOHN WITH THE SWORD	244 33
SAY THAT THOU ART JOHN THE BAPTIST	245 34
THE BROTHER OF JOHN WITH THE SWORD	247 03
HE TOOK PETER AND JOHN AND JAMES, AND WENT UP INTO A	248 24
WRITTEN BY SAINT JOHN, IN THE THIRD CHAPTER, AT THE	275 03
WORD OF GOD, THEY SENT UNTO THEM PETER AND JOHN	296 15
AND I JOHN SAW THE HOLY CITY, NEW JERUSALEM, COMING	567 12
AND SIN (AS SAINT JOHN SAITH) WAS NOT IN HIM	605 34

JOHN'S

THESE THINGS UNTO JOHN'S DISCIPLES, BEHOLD, THERE	224 12

JOIN

REST DURST NO MAN JOIN HIMSELF TO THEM	249 24
OF THIS COMPANY, TO JOIN TOGETHER THIS MAN AND THIS	300 10
SHALL THE MINISTER JOIN THEIR RIGHT HANDS TOGETHER,	R 303 30
O LORD, WE JOIN OUR UNFEIGNED THANKS FOR ALL	591 07

JOINED

AND HE WENT AND JOINED HIMSELF TO A CITIZEN OF THAT	202 06
WHOLE BODY FITLY JOINED TOGETHER AND COMPACTED BY	237 30
GRANT US SO TO BE JOINED TOGETHER IN UNITY OF SPIRIT	254 30
OR ABOUT TO BE) JOINED IN WEDLOCK ACCORDING TO THY	267 06
AND SHALL BE JOINED UNTO HIS WIFE, AND THEY TWO SHALL	267 30
GOD HATH JOINED TOGETHER, LET NOT MAN PUT ASUNDER	268 10
GRANT US SO TO BE JOINED TOGETHER IN UNITY OF SPIRIT	290 22
THESE TWO PERSONS PRESENT COME NOW TO BE JOINED	300 20
NOT LAWFULLY BE JOINED TOGETHER, LET HIM NOW SPEAK,	300 21
NOT BE LAWFULLY JOINED TOGETHER IN MATRIMONY, YE DO	300 27
ANY PERSONS ARE JOINED TOGETHER OTHERWISE THAN AS	300 29
WHOM GOD HATH JOINED TOGETHER LET NO MAN PUT ASUNDER	303 31
SHOULD NOT BE JOINED TOGETHER IN HOLY MATRIMONY,	R 304 24
WE MAY BE JOINED HEREAFTER WITH THY BLESSED	336 08
THE PEOPLES ARE JOINED UNTO THE PEOPLE OF THE GOD OF	399 06
8 ASSYRIA ALSO IS JOINED WITH THEM	444 20
28 THEY JOINED THEMSELVES UNTO BAAL-PEOR, *	474 25
SHALL BE JOINED TOGETHER IN THIS PLACE IN THE HOLY	566 08
MAY BE SO JOINED TOGETHER IN UNITY OF SPIRIT, AND IN	574 07
AND MANHOOD, WERE JOINED TOGETHER IN ONE PERSON,	603 13
WHEREOF WE HAVE JOINED UNDER THIS ARTICLE, DOTH	610 05

JOINING

A RING, AND BY JOINING HANDS	304 07

JOINT

THAT WHICH EVERY JOINT SUPPLIETH, ACCORDING TO THE	237 31
AND ALL MY BONES ARE OUT OF JOINT	366 32

JOINT-HEIRS

OF GOD, AND JOINT-HEIRS WITH CHRIST	200 12
OF GOD, AND JOINT-HEIRS WITH CHRIST	330 24

JONAS

SON OF JONAS, LOVEST THOU ME MORE THAN THESE	551 14
SON OF JONAS, LOVEST THOU ME	551 18
SON OF JONAS, LOVEST THOU ME	551 21

JORDAN

BETHABARA BEYOND JORDAN, WHERE JOHN WAS BAPTIZING	096 06
IN THE RIVER OF JORDAN, CONFESSING THEIR SINS	112 11
AND WAS BAPTIZED OF JOHN IN JORDAN	112 19
FROM THE LAND OF JORDAN, FROM HERMON AND THE LITTLE	393 16
JORDAN WAS DRIVEN BACK	484 30
AND THOU JORDAN, THAT THOU WAST DRIVEN BACK	485 03

JOSEPH

AND JOSEPH ALSO WENT UP FROM GALILEE, OUT OF THE CITY	098 32
LORD APPEARETH TO JOSEPH IN A DREAM, SAYING, ARISE,	103 16
WAS ESPOUSED TO JOSEPH, BEFORE THEY CAME TOGETHER,	104 28
THEN JOSEPH HER HUSBAND, BEING A JUST MAN, AND NOT	104 30
A DREAM, SAYING, JOSEPH, THOU SON OF DAVID, FEAR NOT	105 04
THEN JOSEPH BEING RAISED FROM SLEEP DID AS THE ANGEL	105 12
FOUND MARY, AND JOSEPH, AND THE BABE LYING IN A	106 12
IN A DREAM TO JOSEPH IN EGYPT, SAYING, ARISE, AND	107 13
AND JOSEPH AND HIS MOTHER KNEW NOT OF IT	110 22
NAMED JOSEPH, WHO ALSO HIMSELF WAS JESUS'	162 07
AND WHEN JOSEPH HAD TAKEN THE BODY, HE WRAPPED IT IN	162 10
AND JOSEPH AND HIS MOTHER MARVELLED AT THOSE THINGS	233 09
APPOINTED TWO, JOSEPH CALLED BARSABAS, WHO WAS	234 25
WHOSE NAME WAS JOSEPH, OF THE HOUSE OF DAVID	236 07
EVEN THE SONS OF JACOB AND JOSEPH	434 13
THE TABERNACLE OF JOSEPH, *	439 12
THOU THAT LEADEST JOSEPH LIKE A FLOCK	441 04
HE ORDAINED IN JOSEPH FOR A TESTIMONY, *	442 20
EVEN JOSEPH, WHO WAS SOLD TO BE A BOND-SERVANT	471 06

JOURNEY

TO HAVE BEEN IN THE COMPANY, WENT A DAY'S JOURNEY	110 24
AND TOOK HIS JOURNEY INTO A FAR COUNTRY, AND THERE	202 03
OF MINE IN HIS JOURNEY IS COME TO ME, AND I HAVE	262 29
STRENGTH IN MY JOURNEY, *	465 26

JOURNEYED

AS HE JOURNEYED, CAME WHERE HE WAS	208 28
AND AS HE JOURNEYED, HE CAME NEAR DAMASCUS	229 30
THE MEN WHICH JOURNEYED WITH HIM STOOD SPEECHLESS,	230 08

JOURNEYINGS

IN JOURNEYINGS OFTEN, IN PERILS OF WATERS, IN PERILS	121 04

JOY

TIDINGS OF GREAT JOY, WHICH SHALL BE TO ALL PEOPLE	004 08
THAT AT THE LAST WE MAY COME TO HIS ETERNAL JOY	007 18
ATTAIN EVERLASTING JOY AND FELICITY	018 04
THAT AT THE LAST WE MAY COME TO HIS ETERNAL JOY	024 20
MAKE ME HEAR OF JOY AND GLADNESS, *	060 26
FILL YOU WITH ALL JOY AND PEACE IN BELIEVING, THAT YE	093 02
TIDINGS OF GREAT JOY, WHICH SHALL BE TO ALL PEOPLE	099 15
UNTO YOU, THAT YOUR JOY MAY BE FULL	101 21
THE OIL OF JOY FOR MOURNING, THE GARMENT OF	107 07
THE STAR, THEY REJOICED WITH EXCEEDING GREAT JOY	109 19
RECEIVE THE WORD WITH JOY	122 03
SON WENT NOT UP TO JOY BUT FIRST HE SUFFERED PAIN,	138 05
WE MAY ENTER WITH JOY UPON THE MEDITATION OF THOSE	147 09
LIVE WITH HIM IN THE JOY OF HIS RESURRECTION	165 07
YET BELIEVED NOT FOR JOY, AND WONDERED, HE SAID UNTO	170 03
BUT YOUR SORROW SHALL BE TURNED INTO JOY	174 10
THE ANGUISH, FOR JOY THAT A MAN IS BORN INTO THE	174 12
AND YOUR JOY NO MAN TAKETH FROM YOU	174 15
THAT YOUR JOY MAY BE FULL	176 23
AND RETURNED TO JERUSALEM WITH GREAT JOY	178 28
THAT LIKEWISE JOY SHALL BE IN HEAVEN OVER ONE	193 25
UNTO YOU, THERE IS JOY IN THE PRESENCE OF THE ANGELS	193 33
THE SPIRIT IS LOVE, JOY, PEACE, LONG-SUFFERING,	209 26
MAKING REQUEST WITH JOY, FOR YOUR FELLOWSHIP IN THE	220 24
UNTO YOU, THAT MY JOY MIGHT REMAIN IN YOU, AND THAT	238 25
AND THAT YOUR JOY MIGHT BE FULL	238 25
COUNT IT ALL JOY WHEN YE FALL INTO DIVERS	239 08
WE, WITH THEM, ATTAIN TO THINE ETERNAL JOY	258 17
WHO FOR THE JOY THAT WAS SET BEFORE HIM ENDURED THE	258 24
THE LAST ENTER WITH THEM INTO THINE UNENDING JOY	268 19
LAND OF LIGHT AND JOY, IN THE FELLOWSHIP OF THY	268 25
AND SERVICE, UNTIL HE COME TO THY ETERNAL JOY	307 06
UNTO THE GOD OF MY JOY AND GLADNESS	310 03
UNTO THE GOD OF MY JOY AND GLADNESS	310 14
BE TURNED INTO HEALTH, AND OUR SORROW INTO JOY	312 15
OUR HEAVINESS INTO JOY AND OUR MOURNING INTO	315 21
THEE TO GIVE HIM JOY AND GLADNESS IN THY KINGDOM,	318 20
IS THE FULNESS OF JOY, AND AT THY RIGHT HAND THERE IS	333 10
LAND OF LIGHT AND JOY, IN THE FELLOWSHIP OF THY	334 17
OF THE FLESH, ARE IN JOY AND FELICITY	334 22
WE MAY STAND IN THY PRESENCE IN FULNESS OF JOY	341 03
AND YOUR JOY NO MAN TAKETH FROM YOU	341 11
IS THE FULNESS OF JOY, *	358 13
HIM GLAD WITH THE JOY OF THY COUNTENANCE	365 16
MY HEART DANCETH FOR JOY, AND IN MY SONG WILL I	373 24

JOY   CONTINUED

FOR A NIGHT, BUT JOY COMETH IN THE MORNING   375 03
12 THOU HAST TURNED MY HEAVINESS INTO JOY   375 16
UNTO THE GOD OF MY JOY AND GLADNESS   394 13
15 WITH JOY AND GLADNESS SHALL THEY BE BROUGHT,   397 17
FAIR PLACE, AND THE JOY OF THE WHOLE EARTH   399 12
MAKE ME HEAR OF JOY AND GLADNESS, *   403 25
MY JOY SHALL BE IN THE LORD   469 29
HIS PEOPLE WITH JOY, *   472 23
15 THE VOICE OF JOY AND HEALTH IS IN THE DWELLINGS OF 488 30
THEY ARE THE VERY JOY OF MY HEART   497 20
AND OUR TONGUE WITH JOY   505 10
SHALL REAP IN JOY   505 17
COME AGAIN WITH JOY, AND BRING HIS SHEAVES WITH HIM 505 19
IF I PREFER NOT JERUSALEM ABOVE MY CHIEF JOY   513 17
MY COURSE WITH JOY, AND THE MINISTRY, WHICH I HAVE 550 20
HE MAY AT LAST BE RECEIVED INTO EVERLASTING JOY   558 05
BLESSED US WITH THE JOY AND CARE OF CHILDREN   596 25
AND TURNEST THE SADNESS OF THE SORROWFUL TO JOY   599 05

JOYFUL

O BE JOYFUL IN THE LORD, ALL YE LANDS   015 04
SHOW YOURSELVES JOYFUL UNTO THE LORD, ALL YE LANDS 027 13
O SHOW YOURSELVES JOYFUL BEFORE THE LORD, THE KING 027 18
LET THE HILLS BE JOYFUL TOGETHER BEFORE THE LORD   027 21
AND MAKE THY CHOSEN PEOPLE JOYFUL   031 07
MAY PASS TO OUR JOYFUL RESURRECTION   161 17
A JOYFUL AND PLEASANT THING IT IS TO BE   264 19
THAT HIS MOST JOYFUL VOICE   336 26
THY NAME SHALL BE JOYFUL IN THEE   348 27
AND MY HEART IS JOYFUL IN THY SALVATION   356 07
AND BE JOYFUL, ALL YE THAT ARE TRUE OF HEART   378 17
MY SOUL SHALL BE JOYFUL IN THE LORD   382 07
SEEK THEE, BE JOYFUL AND GLAD IN THEE   391 21
THEE WITH JOYFUL LIPS   415 03
O BE JOYFUL IN GOD, ALL YE LANDS   417 15
LET THEM ALSO BE MERRY AND JOYFUL   419 15
THAT SEEK THEE BE JOYFUL AND GLAD IN THEE   424 27
LET THE FIELD BE JOYFUL, AND ALL THAT IS IN IT   460 24
AND JOYFUL GLADNESS FOR SUCH AS ARE TRUE-HEARTED   461 20
5 SHOW YOURSELVES JOYFUL UNTO THE LORD, ALL YE LANDS 462 02
O SHOW YOURSELVES JOYFUL BEFORE THE LORD, THE KING 462 07
LET THE HILLS BE JOYFUL TOGETHER BEFORE THE LORD   462 11
O BE JOYFUL IN THE LORD, ALL YE LANDS   463 05
AND TO BE A JOYFUL MOTHER OF CHILDREN   484 24
HOW GOOD AND JOYFUL A THING IT IS, *   509 13
A JOYFUL AND PLEASANT THING IT IS TO BE   522 28
OF SION BE JOYFUL IN THEIR KING   525 06
LET THE SAINTS BE JOYFUL WITH GLORY   525 11
AND MORE INTO THY JOYFUL SERVICE   598 09

JOYFULLY

THAT AS WE JOYFULLY RECEIVE HIM FOR OUR REDEEMER,   098 13
GRACE TO TAKE JOYFULLY THE SUFFERINGS OF THE PRESENT 144 08
THY CHURCH MAY JOYFULLY SERVE THEE IN ALL GODLY   195 17
THY CHURCH MAY JOYFULLY SERVE THEE IN ALL GODLY   574 17

JOYFULNESS

ALL PATIENCE AND LONG-SUFFERING WITH JOYFULNESS   224 08
AND LET THY SAINTS SING WITH JOYFULNESS   508 22
AND LET THY SAINTS SING WITH JOYFULNESS   562 05

JOYS

MAY BE FOUND WORTHY TO ATTAIN TO EVERLASTING JOYS   168 21
WHERE TRUE JOYS ARE TO BE FOUND   174 23
THOSE UNSPEAKABLE JOYS WHICH THOU HAST PREPARED FOR 256 09
WHERE TRUE JOYS ARE TO BE FOUND   285 31

JUBILATE

BENEDICTUS, JUBILATE, MAY BE, AND AT THE END OF   R 009 24

JUDA

IN THE LAND OF JUDA, ART NOT THE LEAST AMONG THE   109 08
ART NOT THE LEAST AMONG THE PRINCES OF JUDA   109 09

JUDAEA

AND IN ALL JUDAEA, AND IN SAMARIA, AND UNTO THE   005 13
OF NAZARETH, INTO JUDAEA, UNTO THE CITY OF DAVID,   099 02
DID REIGN IN JUDAEA IN THE ROOM OF HIS FATHER HEROD, 107 18
IN BETHLEHEM OF JUDAEA, IN THE DAYS OF HEROD THE   108 30
AND THEY SAID UNTO HIM, IN BETHLEHEM OF JUDAEA   109 07
ALL THE LAND OF JUDAEA, AND THEY OF JERUSALEM,   112 10
THROUGHOUT ALL JUDAEA, AND BEGAN FROM GALILEE,   166 18
AND IN ALL JUDAEA, AND IN SAMARIA, AND UNTO THE   178 11
AND IN JUDAEA, AND CAPPADOCIA, IN PONTUS, AND ASIA, 181 02
THROUGHOUT ALL JUDAEA, AND BEGAN FROM GALILEE,   184 05
THROUGHOUT ALL JUDAEA, AND THROUGHOUT ALL THE REGION 213 10
WAS COME OUT OF JUDAEA INTO GALILEE, HE WENT UNTO   219 30
WAS COME OUT OF JUDAEA INTO GALILEE   220 12
RELIEF UNTO THE BRETHREN WHICH DWELT IN JUDAEA   241 21
ABROAD THROUGHOUT ALL THE HILL COUNTRY OF JUDAEA   243 28
RELIEF UNTO THE BRETHREN WHICH DWELT IN JUDAEA   246 30

JUDAH

IN HIS DAYS JUDAH SHALL BE SAVED, AND ISRAEL SHALL 225 12
THE OFFERING OF JUDAH AND JERUSALEM BE PLEASANT UNTO 232 13
UNTO THE CITIES OF JUDAH, BEHOLD YOUR GOD   243 05

JUDAH   CONTINUED

THE DAUGHTERS OF JUDAH BE GLAD, *   399 32
JUDAH IS MY LAW-GIVER   412 26
AND THE PRINCES OF JUDAH THEIR COUNCIL   421 09
THE CITIES OF JUDAH, *   424 15
IN JUDAH IS GOD KNOWN   432 24
CHOSE THE TRIBE OF JUDAH, *   439 14
THE DAUGHTERS OF JUDAH WERE GLAD, *   461 13
JUDAH IS MY LAWGIVER   479 21
STRANGE PEOPLE, 2 JUDAH WAS HIS SANCTUARY, *   484 29

JUDAS

THEN JUDAS, WHICH HAD BETRAYED HIM, WHEN HE SAW THAT 135 02
AND JUDAS ISCARIOT, ONE OF THE TWELVE, WENT UNTO THE 140 18
YET SPAKE, COMETH JUDAS, ONE OF THE TWELVE, AND WITH 142 15
ENTERED SATAN INTO JUDAS SURNAMED ISCARIOT, BEING OF 148 15
HE THAT WAS CALLED JUDAS, ONE OF THE TWELVE, WENT   150 27
SAID UNTO HIM, JUDAS, BETRAYEST THOU THE SON OF MAN 150 29
INTO THE HEART OF JUDAS ISCARIOT, SIMON'S SON,   155 28
JUDAS SAITH UNTO HIM, NOT ISCARIOT, LORD, HOW IS IT 181 21
IN THE HOUSE OF JUDAS FOR ONE CALLED SAUL, OF TARSUS 230 18
OF THE TRAITOR JUDAS DIDST CHOOSE THY FAITHFUL   233 32
BEFORE CONCERNING JUDAS, WHICH WAS GUIDE TO THEM THAT 234 10
FROM WHICH JUDAS BY TRANSGRESSION FELL, THAT HE MIGHT 234 30

JUDGE

FOR HE COMETH TO JUDGE THE EARTH   009 19
RIGHTEOUSNESS TO JUDGE THE WORLD, AND THE PEOPLES   009 20
WE BELIEVE THAT THOU SHALT COME TO BE OUR JUDGE   010 32
HE SHALL COME TO JUDGE THE QUICK AND THE DEAD   015 27
WITH GLORY, TO JUDGE BOTH THE QUICK AND THE DEAD   016 12
FOR HE COMETH TO JUDGE THE EARTH   027 22
SHALL HE JUDGE THE WORLD, *   027 24
FOR THOU SHALT JUDGE THE FOLK RIGHTEOUSLY, AND GOVERN 028 24
HE SHALL COME TO JUDGE THE QUICK AND THE DEAD   029 32
WITH GLORY, TO JUDGE BOTH THE QUICK AND THE DEAD   030 17
COME TO BE OUR JUDGE, THY SON, OUR SAVIOUR JESUS   036 06
AS THEY MIGHT JUDGE MOST CONVENIENT FOR THEIR FUTURE VI 12
WITH GLORY, TO JUDGE BOTH THE QUICK AND THE DEAD   071 15
OF ALL THINGS, JUDGE OF ALL MEN   075 18
JUDGE THEREFORE YOURSELVES, BRETHREN, THAT YE BE NOT 085 33
MAJESTY TO JUDGE BOTH THE QUICK AND THE DEAD, WE MAY 090 16
SECOND COMING TO JUDGE THE WORLD WE MAY BE FOUND AN 093 29
I JUDGE NOT MINE OWN SELF   094 07
THEREFORE JUDGE NOTHING BEFORE THE TIME, UNTIL THE 094 10
COME TO BE OUR JUDGE, WHO LIVETH AND REIGNETH WITH 098 15
OF GOD TO BE THE JUDGE OF QUICK AND DEAD   166 30
OF GOD TO BE THE JUDGE OF QUICK AND DEAD   184 17
JUDGE NOT, AND YE SHALL NOT BE JUDGED   194 26
THE JUDGE, AND THE JUDGE DELIVER THEE TO THE OFFICER, 198 14
THEE TO THE JUDGE, AND THE JUDGE DELIVER THEE TO THE 198 14
THE RIGHTEOUS JUDGE, SHALL GIVE ME AT THAT DAY   253 29
IT FROM YOU, AND JUDGE YOURSELVES UNWORTHY OF   261 02
HE SHALL COME TO JUDGE THE QUICK AND THE DEAD   284 21
THOU MOST WORTHY JUDGE ETERNAL, SUFFER US NOT, AT OUR 332 31
MAJESTY TO JUDGE THE WORLD, THE EARTH AND THE SEA   333 19
MAJESTY TO JUDGE THE WORLD, THE SEA SHALL GIVE UP HER 337 13
8 THEY SHALL JUDGE THE PEOPLES   350 06
GOD IS A RIGHTEOUS JUDGE, STRONG, AND PATIENT   350 15
8 FOR HE SHALL JUDGE THE WORLD IN RIGHTEOUSNESS,   352 04
BE THOU MY JUDGE, O LORD, FOR I HAVE WALKED   370 30
AND STAND UP TO JUDGE MY QUARREL   383 09
24 JUDGE ME, O LORD MY GOD, ACCORDING TO THY   383 11
THAT HE MAY JUDGE HIS PEOPLE   401 29
FOR GOD IS JUDGE HIMSELF   402 03
IN THY SAYING, AND CLEAR WHEN THOU SHALT JUDGE   403 17
AND DO YE JUDGE THE THING THAT IS RIGHT, O YE SONS OF 410 08
FOR THOU SHALT JUDGE THE FOLK RIGHTEOUSLY, AND GOVERN 418 31
2 THEN SHALL HE JUDGE THY PEOPLE ACCORDING UNTO   426 33
I SHALL JUDGE ACCORDING UNTO RIGHT   432 02
GOD IS THE JUDGE   432 12
HE IS A JUDGE AMONG GODS   443 19
ARISE, O GOD, AND JUDGE THOU THE EARTH   444 02
2 ARISE, THOU JUDGE OF THE WORLD, *   457 21
HOW THAT HE SHALL JUDGE THE PEOPLES RIGHTEOUSLY   460 21
FOR HE COMETH TO JUDGE THE EARTH   460 26
RIGHTEOUSNESS TO JUDGE THE WORLD, AND THE PEOPLES   460 27
FOR HE IS COME TO JUDGE THE EARTH   462 11
SHALL HE JUDGE THE WORLD, *   462 13
6 HE SHALL JUDGE AMONG THE HEATHEN   482 18
THE RIGHTEOUS JUDGE, WHO LIVETH AND REIGNETH WITH   559 14
AND SOVEREIGN JUDGE OF ALL, HEREAFTER   569 27
ARE TO BE THE ULTIMATE ARBITER AND JUDGE   569 37
SHALL JUDGE WHETHER IT AFFORD JUST CAUSE   R 570 22
HE SHALL COME TO JUDGE THE QUICK AND THE DEAD   578 05
HAST APPOINTED THE JUDGE OF QUICK AND DEAD, THY SON 588 23
UNTIL HE RETURN TO JUDGE ALL MEN AT THE LAST DAY   603 23
THOSE WE OUGHT TO JUDGE LAWFULLY CALLED AND SENT,   607 21
AS THEY SHALL JUDGE THE SAME TO SERVE BETTER TO   609 24
THE CHURCH BY A JUDGE THAT HATH AUTHORITY THEREUNTO 609 29
AND THEREFORE WE JUDGE THEM TO BE READ IN CHURCHES BY 610 08
HIS APOSTLE, SO WE JUDGE, THAT CHRISTIAN RELIGION   611 07

JUDGED

IN THY SAYING, AND CLEAR WHEN THOU ART JUDGED   060 19
THAT YE BE NOT JUDGED OF THE LORD   085 34
THAT I SHOULD BE JUDGED OF YOU, OR OF MAN'S JUDGMENT 094 07
BECAUSE THE PRINCE OF THIS WORLD IS JUDGED   175 17
AND YE SHALL NOT BE JUDGED   194 26
THE HEATHEN BE JUDGED IN THY SIGHT   352 31
NOR CONDEMN HIM WHEN HE IS JUDGED   386 33

JUDGES

THEREFORE SHALL THEY BE YOUR JUDGES	130 03
YE THAT ARE JUDGES OF THE EARTH	346 18
TO SAVE HIS SOUL FROM UNRIGHTEOUS JUDGES	482 03
7 LET THEIR JUDGES BE OVERTHROWN IN STONY PLACES,	517 24
AND ALL JUDGES OF THE WORLD	524 26

JUDGEST

THE THRONE THAT JUDGEST RIGHT	351 29

JUDGETH

BUT HE THAT JUDGETH ME IS THE LORD	094 09
THERE IS ONE THAT SEEKETH AND JUDGETH	133 16
TO HIM THAT JUDGETH RIGHTEOUSLY	172 14
IS A GOD THAT JUDGETH THE EARTH	410 33

JUDGING

IN THE THRONE JUDGING RIGHT	035 31
SIT ON THRONES, JUDGING THE TWELVE TRIBES OF ISRAEL	149 30
TWELVE THRONES, JUDGING THE TWELVE TRIBES OF ISRAEL	231 17
SIT ON THRONES JUDGING THE TWELVE TRIBES OF ISRAEL	250 15

JUDGMENT

TO HER JUDGMENT, THERE BE NOT ANY THING IN IT	V 39
IN THE DAY OF JUDGMENT, WE SINNERS DO BESEECH THEE TO	055 16
ENTER NOT INTO JUDGMENT WITH THY SERVANTS	062 21
I SHOULD BE JUDGED OF YOU, OR OF MAN'S JUDGMENT	094 07
UNTO MEN ONCE TO DIE, BUT AFTER THIS THE JUDGMENT	148 08
AGAIN INTO THE JUDGMENT HALL, AND SAITH UNTO JESUS,	159 12
AND OF RIGHTEOUSNESS, AND OF JUDGMENT	175 14
OF JUDGMENT, BECAUSE THE PRINCE OF THIS WORLD IS	175 16
TO HAVE A RIGHT JUDGMENT IN ALL THINGS, AND EVERMORE	180 11
THAT WE MAY HAVE BOLDNESS IN THE DAY OF JUDGMENT	189 27
SHALL KILL SHALL BE IN DANGER OF THE JUDGMENT	198 03
A CAUSE SHALL BE IN DANGER OF THE JUDGMENT	198 05
MORE AND MORE IN KNOWLEDGE AND IN ALL JUDGMENT	221 03
SHALL EXECUTE JUDGMENT AND JUSTICE IN THE EARTH	225 11
AND I WILL COME NEAR TO YOU TO JUDGMENT	232 15
EXECUTE THE JUDGMENT OF THE FATHERLESS AND WIDOW,	263 26
DREADFUL DAY OF JUDGMENT WHEN THE SECRETS OF ALL	300 25
TO STAND IN THE JUDGMENT, *	345 20
FOR ME IN THE JUDGMENT THAT THOU HAST COMMANDED	350 03
HE HATH ALSO PREPARED HIS SEAT FOR JUDGMENT	352 03
MINISTER TRUE JUDGMENT UNTO THE PEOPLE	352 05
16 THE LORD IS KNOWN TO EXECUTE JUDGMENT	352 24
8 THEM THAT ARE MEEK SHALL HE GUIDE IN JUDGMENT	370 02
5 HE LOVETH RIGHTEOUSNESS AND JUDGMENT	378 27
AND HIS TONGUE WILL BE TALKING OF JUDGMENT	386 27
DIDST CAUSE THY JUDGMENT TO BE HEARD FROM HEAVEN	433 04
GOD AROSE TO JUDGMENT, *	433 06
YE GIVE WRONG JUDGMENT, *	443 20
15 UNTIL RIGHTEOUSNESS TURN AGAIN UNTO JUDGMENT	458 16
AND JUDGMENT ARE THE HABITATION OF HIS SEAT	460 33
4 THE KING'S POWER LOVETH JUDGMENT	462 22
HAST EXECUTED JUDGMENT AND RIGHTEOUSNESS IN JACOB	462 23
MY SONG SHALL BE OF MERCY AND JUDGMENT	463 17
AND JUDGMENT *	466 17
THAT ALWAY KEEP JUDGMENT, *	473 04
7 THE WORKS OF HIS HANDS ARE VERITY AND JUDGMENT	483 07
IS THE SEAT OF JUDGMENT, *	503 16
ENTER NOT INTO JUDGMENT WITH THY SERVANT	518 25
9 TO EXECUTE JUDGMENT UPON THEM	525 19
ARE GUIDED IN JUDGMENT, AND LIGHT RISETH UP IN	595 26
OF GOD'S JUDGMENT YET ARE THEY PLEASING AND	605 12
BY JUST JUDGMENT BE DEPOSED	608 21
HIS PRIVATE JUDGMENT, WILLINGLY AND PURPOSELY,	609 36
IN JUSTICE, JUDGMENT, AND TRUTH	611 10

JUDGMENT-SEAT

ON THE JUDGMENT-SEAT, HIS WIFE SENT UNTO HIM, SAYING,	135 32
IN THE JUDGMENT-SEAT IN A PLACE THAT IS CALLED THE	159 23

JUDGMENTS

THY JUDGMENTS ARE FAR ABOVE OUT OF HIS SIGHT, AND	353 13
THE JUDGMENTS OF THE LORD ARE TRUE, AND RIGHTEOUS	364 02
THY JUDGMENTS ARE LIKE THE GREAT DEEP	384 07
BECAUSE OF THY JUDGMENTS	399 32
THE KING THY JUDGMENTS, O GOD, *	426 31
AND WALK NOT IN MY JUDGMENTS	452 03
BECAUSE OF THY JUDGMENTS, O LORD	461 13
AND THE JUDGMENTS OF HIS MOUTH	470 13
HIS JUDGMENTS ARE IN ALL THE WORLD	470 16
LEARNED THE JUDGMENTS OF THY RIGHTEOUSNESS	490 13
OF ALL THE JUDGMENTS OF THY MOUTH	490 23
THAT IT HATH ALWAY UNTO THY JUDGMENTS	491 07
AND THY JUDGMENTS HAVE I LAID BEFORE ME	491 27
FOR THY JUDGMENTS ARE GOOD	492 18
FOR MY HOPE IS IN THY JUDGMENTS	492 27
EVERLASTING JUDGMENTS, O LORD, *	493 14
BECAUSE OF THY RIGHTEOUS JUDGMENTS,	494 05
THAT THY JUDGMENTS ARE RIGHT, *	495 04
102 I HAVE NOT SHRUNK FROM THY JUDGMENTS	496 30
TO KEEP THY RIGHTEOUS JUDGMENTS	497 10
AND TEACH ME THY JUDGMENTS	497 14
AND I AM AFRAID OF THY JUDGMENTS	498 09
AND TRUE ARE THY JUDGMENTS	499 14
ACCORDING TO THY JUDGMENTS	500 09
ALL THE JUDGMENTS OF THY RIGHTEOUSNESS ENDURE FOR	500 31
BECAUSE OF THY RIGHTEOUS JUDGMENTS	501 10

JUDGMENTS   CONTINUED

AND THY JUDGMENTS SHALL HELP ME	501 33
SUBMITTING YOURSELVES TO THEIR GODLY JUDGMENTS	543 15
A DREAD OF THY JUDGMENTS, AND SUCH A GRATEFUL SENSE	588 18

JUDICA

OR JUDICA ME, DOMINE, PSALM XXVI	R 571 30

JURISDICTION

HEROD'S JURISDICTION, HE SENT HIM TO HEROD, WHO	153 08

JUST

THE SIXTH, UPON JUST AND WEIGHTY CONSIDERATIONS HER	V 28
IF ALLOWED SUCH JUST AND FAVOURABLE CONSTRUCTION AS	V 42
GOD IS FAITHFUL AND JUST TO FORGIVE US OUR SINS,	022 12
AND ALL JUST WORKS DO PROCEED	031 19
GIVE US A JUST SENSE OF THESE GREAT MERCIES	050 25
THE WISDOM OF THE JUST, THAT AT THY SECOND COMING TO	093 29
HE IS FAITHFUL AND JUST TO FORGIVE US OUR SINS, AND	101 30
BEING A JUST MAN, AND NOT WILLING TO MAKE	104 30
TO DO WITH THAT JUST MAN	135 34
THE BLOOD OF THIS JUST PERSON	136 11
FOR SINS, THE JUST FOR THE UNJUST, THAT HE MIGHT	161 23
NINETY AND NINE JUST PERSONS, WHICH NEED NO	193 26
NOW THE JUST SHALL LIVE BY FAITH	228 18
THE SAME MAN WAS JUST AND DEVOUT, WAITING FOR THE	232 31
SENDETH RAIN ON THE JUST AND ON THE UNJUST	264 10
TO BE TRUE AND JUST IN ALL MY DEALINGS	289 05
IF ANY MAN CAN SHOW JUST CAUSE, WHY THEY MAY NOT	300 20
YOU KNOW CAUSE, OR JUST IMPEDIMENT, WHY THESE TWO	R 304 23
LIVE THE SPIRITS OF JUST MEN MADE PERFECT, AFTER THEY	317 12
OR BY ANY OTHER JUST IMPEDIMENT, DO NOT RECEIVE THE	R 323 24
BUT GUIDE THOU THE JUST	350 10
COUNTENANCE WILL BEHOLD THE THING THAT IS JUST	355 03
BECOMETH WELL THE JUST TO BE THANKFUL	378 20
AND THY JUST DEALING AS THE NOON-DAY	385 05
COUNSEL AGAINST THE JUST, *	385 18
AND THE JUST SHALL CONTINUE IN THY SIGHT	517 05
ANY OF YOU CAN SHOW JUST CAUSE WHY HE MAY NOT BE	570 17
WHETHER IT AFFORD JUST CAUSE TO SUSPEND THE SERVICE	R 570 22
TO BE TRUE AND JUST IN ALL MY DEALINGS	580 08
GIVE US GRACE TO BE JUST AND UPRIGHT IN ALL OUR	588 30
FOUND GUILTY, BY JUST JUDGMENT BE DEPOSED	608 21

JUSTICE

TRUTH AND JUSTICE, RELIGION AND PIETY, MAY BE	035 17
THE COURTS OF JUSTICE AND THE MAGISTRATES IN ALL THIS	036 02
THERE MAY BE JUSTICE AND PEACE AT HOME, AND THAT,	036 19
MAINTENANCE OF JUSTICE AMONG MEN AND NATIONS,	044 13
INTO THE WAY OF JUSTICE AND TRUTH, AND ESTABLISH	044 29
GRACE TO EXECUTE JUSTICE, AND TO MAINTAIN TRUTH	055 28
TO EXECUTE JUSTICE, AND TO MAINTAIN TRUTH	VI 20
ADMINISTER JUSTICE, TO THE PUNISHMENT OF WICKEDNESS	074 18
JUDGMENT AND JUSTICE IN THE EARTH	225 11
IN JUSTICE, JUDGMENT, AND TRUTH	611 10

JUSTIFICATION

AND TO RISE AGAIN FOR OUR JUSTIFICATION	170 20
IS EXPRESSED IN THE HOMILY OF JUSTIFICATION	605 09
AFTER JUSTIFICATION,	605 11

JUSTIFIED

MIGHTEST BE JUSTIFIED IN THY SAYING, AND CLEAR WHEN	060 18
YET AM I NOT HEREBY JUSTIFIED	094 09
BELIEVE ARE JUSTIFIED FROM ALL THINGS, FROM WHICH YE	169 20
COULD NOT BE JUSTIFIED BY THE LAW OF MOSES	169 21
TO HIS HOUSE JUSTIFIED RATHER THAN THE OTHER	205 31
MIGHTEST BE JUSTIFIED IN THY SAYING, AND CLEAR WHEN	403 16
FOR IN THY SIGHT SHALL NO MAN LIVING BE JUSTIFIED	518 26
THAT WE ARE JUSTIFIED BY FAITH ONLY, IS A MOST	605 08
THEY BE JUSTIFIED FREELY	606 13

JUSTIFIETH

IS NEAR THAT JUSTIFIETH ME	144 18

JUSTIFY

WILLING TO JUSTIFY HIMSELF, SAID UNTO JESUS, AND	208 19

JUSTLY

WHICH WE NOW MOST JUSTLY SUFFER FOR OUR SINS, MAY,	041 03
WHOM IT BELONGETH JUSTLY TO PUNISH SINNERS, AND TO BE	041 11
WHO HAST JUSTLY HUMBLED US BY THY LATE	051 22
THAT WE MOST JUSTLY HAVE DESERVED	059 23
PROVOKING MOST JUSTLY THY WRATH AND INDIGNATION	075 22
THAT WE, WHO ARE JUSTLY PUNISHED FOR OUR OFFENCES,	118 29
AND WE INDEED JUSTLY	155 04
FOR OUR SINS ART JUSTLY DISPLEASED	332 24

JUSTUS

WHO WAS SURNAMED JUSTUS, AND MATTHIAS	234 26

KADESH

THE LORD SHAKETH THE WILDERNESS OF KADESH	374 13

KEDAR

TO HAVE MY HABITATION AMONG THE TENTS OF KEDAR   502 16

KEEP

LET ALL THE EARTH KEEP SILENCE BEFORE HIM   003 16
SEEKING TO KEEP THE HAPPY MEAN BETWEEN TOO MUCH   V 24
O LORD, TO KEEP US THIS DAY WITHOUT SIN   011 08
LET ALL THE EARTH KEEP SILENCE BEFORE HIM   021 13
THE TIME OF PEACE KEEP THEM SAFE FROM ALL EVIL   041 28
THEE TO BLESS AND KEEP ALL THY PEOPLE   056 05
LORD BLESS US, AND KEEP US   063 15
AND GRACE TO KEEP THE LAW FOR THE TIME TO COME   R 067 25
OUR HEARTS TO KEEP THIS LAW   068 06
THAT LOVE ME AND KEEP MY COMMANDMENTS   068 15
REMEMBER THAT THOU KEEP HOLY THE SABBATH-DAY   068 24
OUR HEARTS TO KEEP THIS LAW   069 05
ALL UNDERSTANDING, KEEP YOUR HEARTS AND MINDS IN THE 084 19
SHALL KEEP YOUR HEARTS AND MINDS THROUGH CHRIST   095 18
WE BESEECH THEE TO KEEP THY CHURCH AND HOUSEHOLD   115 28
BUT I KEEP UNDER MY BODY, AND BRING IT INTO   119 10
HEARD THE WORD, KEEP IT, AND BRING FORTH FRUIT WITH   122 09
KEEP US BOTH OUTWARDLY IN OUR BODIES, AND INWARDLY IN 127 16
WORD OF GOD, AND KEEP IT   130 21
UNTO YOU, IF A MAN KEEP MY SAYING, HE SHALL NEVER SEE 133 17
IF A MAN KEEP MY SAYING, HE SHALL NEVER TASTE   133 20
BUT I KNOW HIM, AND KEEP HIS SAYING   133 28
THEREFORE LET US KEEP THE FEAST,   162 31
THEREFORE LET US KEEP THE FEAST, NOT WITH OLD LEAVEN, 165 13
AND TO KEEP HIMSELF UNSPOTTED FROM THE   176 17
IF YE LOVE ME, KEEP MY COMMANDMENTS   181 08
LOVE ME, HE WILL KEEP MY WORDS   181 25
THAT THOU WOULDEST KEEP US STEDFAST IN THIS FAITH,   186 27
KEEP US, WE BESEECH THEE, UNDER THE PROTECTION OF THY 191 06
OF HIM, BECAUSE WE KEEP HIS COMMANDMENTS, AND DO   191 28
OF THY GREAT MERCY KEEP US IN THE SAME   198 23
THEE ROUND, AND KEEP THEE IN ON EVERY SIDE, AND SHALL 204 11
YE ARE SAVED, IF YE KEEP IN MEMORY WHAT I PREACHED   204 31
KEEP, WE BESEECH THEE, O LORD, THY CHURCH WITH THY   210 17
CANNOT BUT FALL, KEEP US EVER BY THY HELP FROM ALL   210 19
WHO ARE CIRCUMCISED KEEP THE LAW   210 28
ENDEAVOURING TO KEEP THE UNITY OF THE SPIRIT IN THE   213 21
BOUNTIFUL GOODNESS KEEP US, WE BESEECH THEE, FROM ALL 217 18
WE BESEECH THEE TO KEEP THY HOUSEHOLD THE CHURCH IN   220 16
IF YE KEEP MY COMMANDMENTS, YE SHALL ABIDE IN MY   238 22
OF SOLDIERS TO KEEP HIM   245 05
THEY WILL KEEP YOUR'S ALSO   255 20
AND TO KEEP HIMSELF UNSPOTTED FROM THE   266 08
THEN OBEDIENTLY KEEP GOD'S HOLY WILL AND   277 04
THEN OBEDIENTLY KEEP GOD'S HOLY WILL AND   278 13
OF THY GREAT MERCY KEEP US IN THE SAME   283 11
THAT I SHOULD KEEP GOD'S HOLY WILL AND COMMANDMENTS, 283 27
THAT YOU SHOULD KEEP GOD'S HOLY WILL AND   285 14
HELP TO KNOW AND TO KEEP THEM   285 19
OUR HEARTS TO KEEP THIS LAW   286 06
THAT LOVE ME AND KEEP MY COMMANDMENTS   286 15
REMEMBER THAT THOU KEEP HOLY THE SABBATH-DAY   286 24
OUR HEARTS TO KEEP THIS LAW   287 04
TO KEEP MY BODY IN TEMPERANCE, SOBERNESS, AND   289 02
TO KEEP MY HANDS FROM PICKING AND STEALING   289 04
TO KEEP MY TONGUE FROM EVIL SPEAKING, LYING, AND   289 06
HONOUR, AND KEEP HER IN SICKNESS AND IN HEALTH   301 09
ALL OTHERS, KEEP THEE ONLY UNTO HER, SO LONG AS YE   301 10
HONOUR, AND KEEP HIM IN SICKNESS AND IN HEALTH   301 17
ALL OTHERS, KEEP THEE ONLY UNTO HIM, SO LONG AS YE   301 18
SURELY PERFORM AND KEEP THE VOW AND COVENANT BETWIXT 303 08
AND KEEP YOU   304 12
IN ALL DANGER, AND KEEP HIM IN PERPETUAL PEACE AND   309 07
BLESS THEE, AND KEEP THEE   314 27
EVEN HE THAT SHALL KEEP THY SOUL   327 32
LORD BLESS YOU AND KEEP YOU   332 11
EVEN HE THAT SHALL KEEP THY SOUL   339 16
LORD BLESS HIM AND KEEP HIM, THE LORD MAKE HIS FACE   341 16
BLESS YOU AND KEEP YOU, NOW AND FOR EVERMORE   342 15
8 THOU SHALT KEEP THEM, O LORD   355 23
8 KEEP ME AS THE APPLE OF AN EYE   359 02
13 KEEP THY SERVANT ALSO FROM PRESUMPTUOUS SINS,   364 10
UNTO SUCH AS KEEP HIS COVENANT AND HIS TESTIMONIES   370 05
19 O KEEP MY SOUL, AND DELIVER ME   370 24
THOU SHALT KEEP THEM SECRETLY IN THY TABERNACLE FROM 377 07
13 KEEP THY TONGUE FROM EVIL, *   380 27
IN THE LORD, AND KEEP HIS WAY, AND HE SHALL PROMOTE   386 34
38 KEEP INNOCENCY, AND TAKE HEED UNTO THE THING THAT 387 08
2 I WILL KEEP MY MOUTH AS IT WERE WITH A BRIDLE,   389 07
PRESERVE HIM, AND KEEP HIM ALIVE, THAT HE MAY BE   391 32
AMONG SUCH AS KEEP HOLY-DAY   393 10
COME, AND SHALL NOT KEEP SILENCE   401 25
ALL TOGETHER, AND KEEP THEMSELVES CLOSE, *   408 26
THAT THEY KEEP SECRET AMONG THEMSELVES, EVERY MAN IN 415 31
4 HE SHALL KEEP THE SIMPLE FOLK BY THEIR RIGHT,   427 04
LORD YOUR GOD, AND KEEP IT, ALL YE THAT ARE ROUND   433 10
OF GOD, BUT TO KEEP HIS COMMANDMENTS   435 12
THY TONGUE, O GOD, KEEP NOT STILL SILENCE   444 05
29 MY MERCY WILL I KEEP FOR HIM FOR EVERMORE,   451 31
MY STATUTES, AND KEEP NOT MY COMMANDMENTS   452 04
TO KEEP THEE IN ALL THY WAYS   455 18
EVEN UPON SUCH AS KEEP HIS COVENANT, *   467 11
44 THAT THEY MIGHT KEEP HIS STATUTES, *   472 27
ARE THEY THAT ALWAY KEEP JUDGMENT, *   473 04
THE BARREN WOMAN TO KEEP HOUSE, *   484 23
ARE THEY THAT KEEP HIS TESTIMONIES, *   490 02
WE SHALL DILIGENTLY KEEP THY COMMANDMENTS   490 06
THAT I MIGHT KEEP THY STATUTES   490 09
8 I WILL KEEP THY STATUTES   490 14
I MAY LIVE, AND KEEP THY WORD   490 33

KEEP   CONTINUED

AND I SHALL KEEP IT UNTO THE END   492 06
AND I SHALL KEEP THY LAW   492 07
I SHALL KEEP IT WITH MY WHOLE HEART   492 08
44 SO SHALL I ALWAY KEEP THY LAW   492 28
I HAVE PROMISED TO KEEP THY LAW   493 25
TO KEEP THY COMMANDMENTS   493 32
AND KEEP THY COMMANDMENTS   494 07
BUT I WILL KEEP THY COMMANDMENTS WITH MY WHOLE HEART 494 19
AND SO SHALL I KEEP THE TESTIMONIES OF THY MOUTH   495 34
BECAUSE I KEEP THY COMMANDMENTS   496 26
THAT I MAY KEEP THY WORD   496 29
TO KEEP THY RIGHTEOUS JUDGMENTS   497 09
I WILL KEEP THE COMMANDMENTS OF MY GOD   497 28
DOTH MY SOUL KEEP THEM   498 29
AND SO SHALL I KEEP THY COMMANDMENTS   499 07
BECAUSE MEN KEEP NOT THY LAW   499 10
I WILL KEEP THY STATUTES   499 32
AND I SHALL KEEP THY TESTIMONIES   500 03
BECAUSE THEY KEEP NOT THY LAW   500 28
EVEN HE THAT SHALL KEEP THY SOUL   503 05
2 EXCEPT THE LORD KEEP THE CITY, *   505 24
MY SOUL, AND KEEP IT LOW, LIKE AS A CHILD THAT IS   507 27
THY CHILDREN WILL KEEP MY COVENANT, AND MY   508 29
4 KEEP ME, O LORD, FROM THE HANDS OF THE UNGODLY   516 15
AND KEEP THE DOOR OF MY LIPS   517 13
10 KEEP ME FROM THE SNARE THAT THEY HAVE LAID FOR ME, 517 30
ALL UNDERSTANDING, KEEP YOUR HEARTS AND MINDS IN THE 535 14
ALL DILIGENCE TO KEEP AND OBSERVE THE SAME   542 17
KEEP FAR OUR FOES, GIVE PEACE AT HOME   544 08
KEEP YOUR HEARTS AND MINDS IN THE   547 15
ALL UNDERSTANDING, KEEP YOUR HEARTS AND MINDS IN THE 547 15
KEEP FAR OUR FOES, GIVE PEACE AT HOME   556 16
ALL UNDERSTANDING, KEEP YOUR HEARTS AND MINDS IN THE 559 18
PERFORM AND KEEP THE VOW AND COVENANT BETWIXT THEM   566 10
ALL UNDERSTANDING, KEEP YOUR HEARTS AND MINDS IN THE 568 14
OF THY GREAT MERCY KEEP THEM IN THE SAME, O BLESSED   572 30
THAT I SHOULD KEEP GOD'S HOLY WILL AND COMMANDMENTS, 577 18
THAT YOU SHOULD KEEP GOD'S COMMANDMENTS   578 18
THAT LOVE ME AND KEEP MY COMMANDMENTS   578 34
REMEMBER THAT THOU KEEP HOLY THE SABBATH-DAY   579 04
TO KEEP MY HANDS FROM PICKING AND STEALING, AND MY   580 09
TO KEEP MY BODY IN TEMPERANCE, SOBERNESS, AND   580 11
AND THAT HE WILL KEEP US FROM ALL SIN AND WICKEDNESS, 581 03
ABOVE ALL, KEEP IN OUR MINDS A LIVELY   588 20
KEEP US TEMPERATE IN ALL THINGS, AND DILIGENT IN OUR 588 28
LORD BLESS US AND KEEP US   593 18
OUR HEARTS TO KEEP THY LAW, AND GUIDE OUR FEET INTO   594 14
AND ALONE CANST KEEP ALIVE IN US THE HOLY DESIRES   594 19

KEEPER

THE LORD HIMSELF IS THY KEEPER   327 27
THE LORD HIMSELF IS THY KEEPER   339 11
5 THE LORD HIMSELF IS THY KEEPER   502 30
A WITNESS AND A KEEPER OF HOLY WRIT, YET, AS IT OUGHT 607 07

KEEPERS

AND THE KEEPERS BEFORE THE DOOR KEPT THE PRISON   245 11

KEEPETH

STRONG MAN ARMED KEEPETH HIS PALACE, HIS GOODS ARE IN 130 05
AND KEEPETH THEM, HE IT IS THAT LOVETH ME   181 19
LOVETH ME NOT KEEPETH NOT MY SAYINGS   181 27
AND HE THAT KEEPETH HIS COMMANDMENTS DWELLETH IN HIM, 191 32
AND HE THAT KEEPETH THEE WILL NOT SLEEP   327 24
BEHOLD, HE THAT KEEPETH ISRAEL *   327 25
AND HE THAT KEEPETH THEE WILL NOT SLEEP   339 08
BEHOLD, HE THAT KEEPETH ISRAEL *   339 09
20 HE KEEPETH ALL HIS BONES, *   381 08
NEITHER KEEPETH HE HIS ANGER FOR EVER   466 23
AND HE THAT KEEPETH THEE WILL NOT SLEEP   502 27
BEHOLD, HE THAT KEEPETH ISRAEL *   502 28
WHO KEEPETH HIS PROMISE FOR EVER   522 13

KEEPING

IN THE FIELD, KEEPING WATCH OVER THEIR FLOCK BY   099 11
THAT IN KEEPING THY COMMANDMENTS WE MAY PLEASE   189 04
INTO THE SAFE KEEPING OF THINE ETERNAL LOVE   340 27
AND IN KEEPING OF THEM THERE IS GREAT REWARD   364 07
HE MAY BE, KEEPING HIM UNSPOTTED FROM THE WORLD   597 29

KEPT

OF THE FAITH BE KEPT ENTIRE   V 04
BUT MARY KEPT ALL THESE THINGS, AND PONDERED THEM IN 106 16
BUT HIS MOTHER KEPT ALL THESE SAYINGS IN HER HEART   111 06
BUT THOU HAST KEPT THE GOOD WINE UNTIL NOW   113 29
EVEN AS I HAVE KEPT MY FATHER'S COMMANDMENTS, AND   238 23
PETER THEREFORE WAS KEPT IN PRISON   245 07
BEFORE THE DOOR KEPT THE PRISON   245 12
AND THEY KEPT IT CLOSE, AND TOLD NO MAN IN THOSE DAYS 249 09
MY COURSE, I HAVE KEPT THE FAITH   253 27
IF THEY HAVE KEPT MY SAYING, THEY WILL KEEP YOUR'S   255 19
OF THY LIPS I HAVE KEPT ME FROM THE WAYS OF THE   358 26
22 BECAUSE I HAVE KEPT THE WAYS OF THE LORD, *   361 09
THOU HAST KEPT MY LIFE, THAT I SHOULD NOT GO DOWN   374 29
I KEPT SILENCE, YEA, EVEN FROM GOOD WORDS   389 09
13 I HAVE NOT KEPT BACK THY LOVING MERCY AND TRUTH * 391 06
11 THEY KEPT NOT THE COVENANT OF GOD, *   435 20
AND KEPT NOT HIS TESTIMONIES   438 25
FOR THEY KEPT HIS TESTIMONIES, AND THE LAW THAT HE   462 31
IN EGYPT, NEITHER KEPT THEY THY GREAT GOODNESS IN   473 14

KEPT   CONTINUED

11 THEY KEPT ME IN ON EVERY SIDE, THEY KEPT ME IN,	488	20
ON EVERY SIDE, THEY KEPT ME IN, I SAY, ON EVERY SIDE	488	20
FOR I HAVE KEPT THY TESTIMONIES	491	10
AND HAVE KEPT THY LAW	493	21
BECAUSE I KEPT THY COMMANDMENTS	493	22
BUT NOW HAVE I KEPT THY WORD	494	16
167 MY SOUL HATH KEPT THY TESTIMONIES, *	501	15
168 I HAVE KEPT THY COMMANDMENTS AND TESTIMONIES	501	17
SHALL BE SILENCE KEPT FOR A SPACE	R 543	25
AND HOW I KEPT BACK NOTHING THAT WAS PROFITABLE UNTO	550	10
THE LABOURERS TO BE KEPT BACK BY FRAUD	599	31

KEYS

GIVE UNTO THEE THE KEYS OF THE KINGDOM OF HEAVEN	246	09
PLACE) HOLDING THE KEYS OF THE CHURCH IN HIS HAND, IN	R 570	09
PLACE) PRESENT THE KEYS OF THE CHURCH TO THE NEW	R 570	26
INTO YOUR HANDS THE KEYS OF THIS CHURCH	570	30
RECEIVE THESE KEYS OF THE HOUSE OF GOD AT YOUR HANDS,	570	32

KICK

IS HARD FOR THEE TO KICK AGAINST THE PRICKS	230	04

KID

NEVER GAVEST ME A KID, THAT I MIGHT MAKE MERRY WITH	203	02

KILL

THOU SHALT NOT KILL, THOU SHALT NOT STEAL, THOU SHALT	090	25
OF THEM YE SHALL KILL AND CRUCIFY	100	20
MORTIFY AND KILL ALL VICES IN US, AND SO STRENGTHEN	102	23
HOW THEY MIGHT KILL HIM	148	14
TO STEAL, AND TO KILL, AND TO DESTROY	186	17
AND WHOSOEVER SHALL KILL SHALL BE IN DANGER OF THE	198	02
WAS SAID BY THEM OF OLD TIME, THOU SHALT NOT KILL	198	02
FATTED CALF, AND KILL IT	202	23
TO STEAL, AND TO KILL, AND TO DESTROY	539	08

KILLED

AS CHASTENED, AND NOT KILLED	126	19
WHEN THEY KILLED THE PASSOVER, HIS DISCIPLES	140	23
WHEN THE PASSOVER MUST BE KILLED	148	22
THY FATHER HATH KILLED THE FATTED CALF, BECAUSE HE	202	30
THOU HAST KILLED FOR HIM THE FATTED CALF	203	04
MY FATLINGS ARE KILLED, AND ALL THINGS ARE READY	218	09
AND HE KILLED JAMES THE BROTHER OF JOHN WITH THE	244	32
AND HE KILLED JAMES THE BROTHER OF JOHN WITH THE	247	02
SAKE ALSO ARE WE KILLED ALL THE DAY LONG, *	396	04

KILLEST

THOU THAT KILLEST THE PROPHETS, AND STONEST THEM	100	27

KILLETH

THAT WHOSOEVER KILLETH YOU WILL THINK THAT HE DOETH	179	31
FOR THE LETTER KILLETH, BUT THE SPIRIT GIVETH LIFE	206	17

KIND

RUN INTO ANY KIND OF DANGER	017	17
HIS TABLE WITH ALL KIND OF PROVISION, SO THAT THERE	088	19
CHARITY SUFFERETH LONG, AND IS KIND	122	29
THAT WE SHOULD BE A KIND OF FIRSTFRUITS OF HIS	174	30
AND BE YE KIND ONE TO ANOTHER, TENDER-HEARTED,	216	29
THAT WE SHOULD BE A KIND OF FIRSTFRUITS OF HIS	265	22
BUT THERE IS ONE KIND OF FLESH OF MEN, ANOTHER FLESH	329	12
RUN INTO ANY KIND OF DANGER	592	23

KINDLE

ALL YE THAT KINDLE A FIRE, THAT COMPASS YOURSELVES	144	26
IT DOTH FERVENTLY KINDLE THEIR LOVE TOWARDS GOD	606	22

KINDLED

YOUR FIRE, AND IN THE SPARKS THAT YE HAVE KINDLED	144	28
WHEN THEY HAD KINDLED A FIRE IN THE MIDST OF THE	151	09
IF HIS WRATH BE KINDLED, YEA BUT A LITTLE	346	22
THAT COALS WERE KINDLED AT IT	360	13
MUSING THE FIRE KINDLED, *	389	13
SO THE FIRE WAS KINDLED IN JACOB, AND THERE CAME UP	436	12
AND THE FIRE WAS KINDLED IN THEIR COMPANY	474	04
OF THE LORD KINDLED AGAINST HIS PEOPLE, *	475	16
THOUGHTS AND KINDLED AFFECTIONS, WE MAY WORSHIP THEE	594	08

KINDLY

TO OUR USE THE KINDLY FRUITS OF THE EARTH, SO THAT IN	057	11
BE KINDLY AFFECTIONED ONE TO ANOTHER WITH BROTHERLY	111	23
WE BE EVERMORE KINDLY AFFECTIONED WITH BROTHERLY	598	29

KINDNESS

AND OF GREAT KINDNESS, AND REPENTETH HIM OF THE EVIL	004	22
OF COMPASSION, KINDNESS, HUMBLENESS OF MIND,	116	04
AND OF GREAT KINDNESS, AND REPENTETH HIM OF THE EVIL	124	25
BY KINDNESS, BY THE HOLY GHOST, BY LOVE UNFEIGNED, BY	126	13
THY MERCIFUL KINDNESS, O LORD, BE UPON US	290	10
THY FAVOURABLE KINDNESS WILT THOU DEFEND HIM AS WITH	348	29
GREAT KINDNESS IN A STRONG CITY	377	10

KINDNESS   CONTINUED

THY MERCIFUL KINDNESS, O LORD, BE UPON US, *	379	32
HIS MERCIFUL KINDNESS IS EVER MORE AND MORE TOWARD	487	27
THY MERCIFUL KINDNESS BE MY COMFORT, *	495	07
THINE ABUNDANT KINDNESS SHALL BE SHOWED	521	06

KINDRED

IS NONE OF THY KINDRED THAT IS CALLED BY THIS NAME	243	21

KINDREDS

OUT OF MANY KINDREDS AND TONGUES	036	17
AND KINDREDS, AND PEOPLES, AND TONGUES,	256	24
AND ALL THE KINDREDS OF THE NATIONS SHALL WORSHIP	367	29
THE LORD, O YE KINDREDS OF THE PEOPLES, *	460	12

KINDS

COMMUNION IN BOTH KINDS HIMSELF, AND PROCEED TO	R 082	25
TO ANOTHER DIVERS KINDS OF TONGUES	182	32
TO ANOTHER DIVERS KINDS OF TONGUES	203	32

KING

OUR KING AND SAVIOUR DRAWETH NIGH	R 008	16
AND A GREAT KING ABOVE ALL GODS	009	07
THOU ART THE KING OF GLORY, O CHRIST	010	24
LORD GOD, HEAVENLY KING, GOD THE FATHER ALMIGHTY	025	25
SHOW YOURSELVES JOYFUL BEFORE THE LORD, THE KING	027	18
AND THE KING SHALL ANSWER AND SAY UNTO THEM, VERILY I	073	02
LORD GOD, HEAVENLY KING, GOD THE FATHER ALMIGHTY	084	05
BEHOLD, THY KING COMETH UNTO THEE, MEEK, AND	091	20
DAYS OF HEROD THE KING, BEHOLD, THERE CAME WISE MEN	108	31
IS HE THAT IS BORN KING OF THE JEWS	108	33
WHEN HEROD THE KING HAD HEARD THESE THINGS, HE WAS	109	02
THEY HAD HEARD THE KING, THEY DEPARTED	109	16
ART THOU THE KING OF THE JEWS	135	20
SAYING, HAIL, KING OF THE JEWS	136	21
THIS IS JESUS THE KING OF THE JEWS	137	03
IF HE BE THE KING OF ISRAEL, LET HIM NOW COME DOWN	137	11
ART THOU THE KING OF THE JEWS	145	07
UNTO YOU THE KING OF THE JEWS	145	19
WHOM YE CALL THE KING OF THE JEWS	145	24
SALUTE HIM, HAIL, KING OF THE JEWS	145	33
WRITTEN OVER, THE KING OF THE JEWS	146	14
LET CHRIST THE KING OF ISRAEL DESCEND NOW FROM THE	146	23
SAYING THAT HE HIMSELF IS CHRIST A KING	152	30
ART THOU THE KING OF THE JEWS	152	31
IF THOU BE THE KING OF THE JEWS, SAVE THYSELF	154	31
THIS IS THE KING OF THE JEWS	154	34
AND SAID, HAIL, KING OF THE JEWS	158	33
MAKETH HIMSELF A KING, SPEAKETH AGAINST CAESAR	159	21
AND HE SAITH UNTO THE JEWS, BEHOLD YOUR KING	159	26
SHALL I CRUCIFY YOUR KING	159	28
WE HAVE NO KING BUT CAESAR	159	29
OF NAZARETH THE KING OF THE JEWS	160	03
WRITE NOT, THE KING OF THE JEWS	160	07
THAT HE SAID, I AM KING OF THE JEWS	160	08
IT BE TO THE KING, AS SUPREME	173	19
HONOUR THE KING	173	25
O GOD, THE KING OF GLORY, WHO HAST EXALTED THINE ONLY	179	04
LIKE UNTO A CERTAIN KING, WHICH MADE A MARRIAGE FOR	218	04
BUT WHEN THE KING HEARD THEREOF, HE WAS WROTH	218	13
AND WHEN THE KING CAME IN TO SEE THE GUESTS, HE SAW	218	22
THEN SAID THE KING TO THE SERVANTS, BIND HIM HAND AND	218	26
UNTO A CERTAIN KING, WHICH WOULD TAKE ACCOUNT OF HIS	221	13
AND A KING SHALL REIGN AND PROSPER, AND SHALL	225	10
THAT TIME HEROD THE KING STRETCHED FORTH HIS HANDS TO	244	31
THAT TIME HEROD THE KING STRETCHED FORTH HIS HANDS TO	246	32
TO BEHOLD THE KING IN HIS BEAUTY, WHO WITH THEE, C	248	04
THEN SHALL THE KING SAY UNTO THEM ON HIS RIGHT HAND,	259	03
AND THE KING SHALL ANSWER AND SAY UNTO THEM, VERILY I	259	14
6 YET HAVE I SET MY KING *	346	08
OF MY CALLING, MY KING AND MY GOD	348	02
18 THE LORD IS KING FOR EVER AND EVER, *	354	11
GIVETH HE UNTO HIS KING, *	363	07
AND HEAR US, O KING OF HEAVEN, *	365	02
THE KING SHALL REJOICE IN THY STRENGTH, O LORD	365	05
BECAUSE THE KING PUTTETH HIS TRUST IN THE LORD	365	17
AND THE KING OF GLORY SHALL COME IN	369	10
8 WHO IS THIS KING OF GLORY	369	11
AND THE KING OF GLORY SHALL COME IN	369	14
10 WHO IS THIS KING OF GLORY	369	15
OF HOSTS, HE IS THE KING OF GLORY	369	16
LORD REMAINETH A KING FOR EVER	374	18
15 THERE IS NO KING THAT CAN BE SAVED BY THE	379	19
5 THOU ART MY KING, O GOD	394	32
THE THINGS WHICH I HAVE MADE CONCERNING THE KING	396	16
11 SO SHALL THE KING HAVE PLEASURE IN THY BEAUTY	397	07
BE BROUGHT UNTO THE KING IN RAIMENT OF NEEDLEWORK	397	14
HE IS THE GREAT KING UPON ALL THE EARTH	398	24
SING PRAISES UNTO OUR KING	398	32
7 FOR GOD IS THE KING OF ALL THE EARTH	399	02
THE NORTH SIDE LIETH THE CITY OF THE GREAT KING	399	14
SHALT GRANT THE KING A LONG LIFE, *	413	17
12 BUT THE KING SHALL REJOICE IN GOD	415	15
THOU, MY GOD AND KING, GOEST IN THE SANCTUARY	421	03
GIVE THE KING THY JUDGMENTS, O GOD, *	426	31
13 FOR GOD IS MY KING OF OLD	430	32
O LORD OF HOSTS, MY KING AND MY GOD	445	18
THE HOLY ONE OF ISRAEL IS OUR KING	451	11
THE LORD IS KING, AND HATH PUT ON GLORIOUS APPAREL	457	04
AND A GREAT KING ABOVE ALL GODS	459	09
THAT THE LORD IS KING, AND THAT IT IS HE WHO HATH	460	19

KING   CONTINUED

	PAGE	LN
THE LORD IS KING, THE EARTH MAY BE GLAD THEREOF	460	30
SHOW YOURSELVES JOYFUL BEFORE THE LORD, THE KING	462	07
THE LORD IS KING, BE THE PEOPLE NEVER SO IMPATIENT	462	16
20 THE KING SENT, AND DELIVERED HIM	471	12
AND OG, THE KING OF BASHAN	510	24
11 SIHON, KING OF THE AMORITES	510	24
19 SIHON, KING OF THE AMORITES	512	20
20 AND OG, THE KING OF BASHAN	512	22
I WILL MAGNIFY THEE, O GOD, MY KING	520	27
O SION, SHALL BE KING FOR EVERMORE, *	522	23
LET THE CHILDREN OF SION BE JOYFUL IN THEIR KING	525	06
AND THE KING OF GLORY SHALL COME IN	563	25
8 WHO IS THIS KING OF GLORY	563	26
AND THE KING OF GLORY SHALL COME IN	563	29
10 WHO IS THIS KING OF GLORY	563	30
OF HOSTS, HE IS THE KING OF GLORY	563	31
O GOD, THE KING ETERNAL, WHO DIVIDEST THE DAY FROM	594	11

KING'S

	PAGE	LN
THE HEART OF THE KING'S ENEMIES, *	396	25
13 THE KING'S DAUGHTER IS ALL GLORIOUS WITHIN	397	12
ENTER INTO THE KING'S PALACE	397	18
UNTO THE KING'S SON	426	32
4 THE KING'S POWER LOVETH JUDGMENT	462	22

KINGDOM

	PAGE	LN
FOR THE KINGDOM OF HEAVEN IS AT HAND	004	04
THY KINGDOM COME	007	24
FOR THINE IS THE KINGDOM, AND THE POWER, AND THE	007	28
DIDST OPEN THE KINGDOM OF HEAVEN TO ALL BELIEVERS	010	29
ART THOU ON THE GLORIOUS THRONE OF THY KINGDOM	011	25
WHOSE KINGDOM SHALL HAVE NO END	016	13
WHOSE KINGDOM SHALL HAVE NO END	030	18
WHOSE KINGDOM IS EVERLASTING AND POWER INFINITE	032	04
DOWN THE KINGDOM OF SIN, SATAN, AND DEATH	037	04
THY SPIRIT UPON ALL FLESH, AND HASTEN THY KINGDOM	038	11
WHO SEEK THY KINGDOM, AND THE RIGHTEOUSNESS THEREOF,	040	16
MAY BECOME THE KINGDOM OF OUR LORD AND SAVIOUR JESUS	044	31
WHOSE KINGDOM SHALL HAVE NO END	071	16
ENTER INTO THE KINGDOM OF HEAVEN	072	14
THINE IS THE KINGDOM, O LORD, AND THOU ART EXALTED AS	073	20
THEM WE MAY BE PARTAKERS OF THY HEAVENLY KINGDOM	075	04
THY EVERLASTING KINGDOM, BY THE MERITS OF HIS MOST	083	24
PARTAKERS OF THE KINGDOM OF HEAVEN	086	34
KNOW YE THAT THE KINGDOM OF GOD IS NIGH AT HAND	093	18
OF RIGHTEOUSNESS IS THE SCEPTRE OF THY KINGDOM	097	10
IN THE KINGDOM OF HEAVEN	115	20
CHILDREN OF THE KINGDOM SHALL BE CAST INTO OUTER	115	21
THE KINGDOM OF HEAVEN IS LIKENED UNTO A MAN WHICH	116	18
LIKE UNTO HIM IN HIS ETERNAL AND GLORIOUS KINGDOM	117	10
THE KINGDOM OF HEAVEN IS LIKE UNTO A MAN THAT IS AN	119	15
MYSTERIES OF THE KINGDOM OF GOD	121	30
IN THE KINGDOM OF CHRIST AND OF GOD	129	08
UNTO THEM, EVERY KINGDOM DIVIDED AGAINST ITSELF IS	129	30
HOW SHALL HIS KINGDOM STAND	129	32
NO DOUBT THE KINGDOM OF GOD IS COME UPON YOU	130	04
IT NEW IN THE KINGDOM OF GOD	141	16
FULFILLED IN THE KINGDOM OF GOD	149	05
UNTIL THE KINGDOM OF GOD SHALL COME	149	08
UNTO YOU A KINGDOM, AS MY FATHER HATH APPOINTED UNTO	149	28
MY TABLE IN MY KINGDOM, AND SIT ON THRONES, JUDGING	149	29
REMEMBER ME WHEN THOU COMEST INTO THY KINGDOM	155	07
TO THE KINGDOM OF GOD	177	29
AGAIN THE KINGDOM TO ISRAEL	178	06
TRIUMPH UNTO THY KINGDOM IN HEAVEN	179	05
CANNOT SEE THE KINGDOM OF GOD	188	06
ENTER INTO THE KINGDOM OF GOD	188	11
ENTER INTO THE KINGDOM OF HEAVEN	197	30
ENTER INTO THE KINGDOM OF HEAVEN	200	25
NOT INHERIT THE KINGDOM OF GOD	209	25
YE FIRST HIS KINGDOM, AND HIS RIGHTEOUSNESS	211	31
JESUS SAID, THE KINGDOM OF HEAVEN IS LIKE UNTO A	218	03
THEREFORE IS THE KINGDOM OF HEAVEN LIKENED UNTO A	221	13
AND OF HIS KINGDOM THERE SHALL BE NO END	236	19
THE KEYS OF THE KINGDOM OF HEAVEN	246	09
AND THE OTHER ON THE LEFT, IN THY KINGDOM	247	10
UNTO YOU A KINGDOM, AS MY FATHER HATH APPOINTED UNTO	250	13
MY TABLE IN MY KINGDOM, AND SIT ON THRONES JUDGING	250	15
AND THE KINGDOM OF OUR GOD, AND THE POWER OF HIS	252	11
GREATEST IN THE KINGDOM OF HEAVEN	252	23
ENTER INTO THE KINGDOM OF HEAVEN	252	27
GREATEST IN THE KINGDOM OF HEAVEN	252	29
THEIR'S IS THE KINGDOM OF HEAVEN	257	21
THEIR'S IS THE KINGDOM OF HEAVEN	257	30
INHERIT THE KINGDOM PREPARED FOR YOU FROM THE	259	04
MANKIND MAY BE DRAWN TO THY BLESSED KINGDOM	260	24
YE FIRST THE KINGDOM OF GOD, AND HIS RIGHTEOUSNESS	266	29
FIRST THY KINGDOM AND THY RIGHTEOUSNESS, MAY OBTAIN	267	07
ENTER INTO THE KINGDOM OF GOD, EXCEPT HE BE	273	30
TO THE ETERNAL KINGDOM WHICH THOU HAST PROMISED BY	274	20
OF SUCH IS THE KINGDOM OF GOD	274	30
NOT RECEIVE THE KINGDOM OF GOD AS A LITTLE CHILD, HE	274	31
CANNOT SEE THE KINGDOM OF GOD	275	11
ENTER INTO THE KINGDOM OF GOD	275	16
TO GIVE HIM THE KINGDOM OF HEAVEN, AND EVERLASTING	276	23
TO GIVE YOU THE KINGDOM OF HEAVEN, AND EVERLASTING	277	24
MAY BE AN INHERITER OF THINE EVERLASTING KINGDOM	281	05
INHERITOR OF THE KINGDOM OF HEAVEN	283	20
AND PRAY AND GIVE FOR THE SPREAD OF HIS KINGDOM	291	20
UNTIL HE COME UNTO THY EVERLASTING KINGDOM	297	29
GLADNESS IN THY KINGDOM, WITH THY SAINTS IN LIGHT	318	21
DELIVERED UP THE KINGDOM TO GOD, EVEN THE FATHER	328	27

KINGDOM   CONTINUED

	PAGE	LN
INHERIT THE KINGDOM OF GOD	329	34
LIFE OF PERFECT SERVICE, IN THY HEAVENLY KINGDOM	332	07
RECEIVE THE KINGDOM PREPARED FOR YOU FROM THE	335	12
INHERIT THE KINGDOM PREPARED FOR YOU FROM THE	336	27
OF SUCH IS THE KINGDOM OF GOD	338	11
GREATEST IN THE KINGDOM OF HEAVEN	339	22
ENTER INTO THE KINGDOM OF HEAVEN	339	26
GREATEST IN THE KINGDOM OF HEAVEN	339	28
TO CHILDREN AN ABUNDANT ENTRANCE INTO THY KINGDOM	340	30
AND BRING US ALL TO THY HEAVENLY KINGDOM	342	07
28 FOR THE KINGDOM IS THE LORD'S, *	367	31
SCEPTRE OF THY KINGDOM IS A RIGHT SCEPTRE	396	28
AND HIS KINGDOM RULETH OVER ALL	467	14
FROM ONE KINGDOM TO ANOTHER PEOPLE	470	29
THE GLORY OF THY KINGDOM, *	521	14
OF THY KINGDOM, *	521	17
13 THY KINGDOM IS AN EVERLASTING KINGDOM, *	521	18
AN EVERLASTING KINGDOM, *	521	18
AND THY BLESSED KINGDOM ENLARGED	546	02
AND THE INCREASE OF THY KINGDOM	547	12
PREACHING THE KINGDOM OF GOD, SHALL SEE MY FACE NO	550	23
MAY BE PARTAKERS OF THY EVERLASTING KINGDOM	561	20
INHERITOR OF THE KINGDOM OF HEAVEN	577	11

KINGDOMS

	PAGE	LN
HIM ALL THE KINGDOMS OF THE WORLD, AND THE GLORY OF	127	06
AND THE KINGDOMS ARE MOVED	398	04
UNTO GOD, O YE KINGDOMS OF THE EARTH	421	20
AND UPON THE KINGDOMS THAT HAVE NOT CALLED UPON THY	440	12
AND THE KINGDOMS ALSO, TO SERVE THE LORD	465	25
AND ALL THE KINGDOMS OF CANAAN	510	25

KINGS

	PAGE	LN
TO THY LIGHT, AND KINGS TO THE BRIGHTNESS OF THY	022	02
UNTO THEM, THE KINGS OF THE GENTILES EXERCISE	149	19
MANY PROPHETS AND KINGS HAVE DESIRED TO SEE THOSE	208	08
THE GENTILES, AND KINGS, AND THE CHILDREN OF ISRAEL	230	27
UNTO THEM, THE KINGS OF THE GENTILES EXERCISE	250	05
2 THE KINGS OF THE EARTH STAND UP, AND THE RULERS	345	27
10 BE WISE NOW THEREFORE, O YE KINGS	346	17
3 FOR LO, THE KINGS OF THE EARTH *	399	16
12 KINGS WITH THEIR ARMIES DID FLEE, AND WERE	420	04
ALMIGHTY SCATTERED KINGS FOR THEIR SAKE, *	420	09
SO SHALL KINGS BRING PRESENTS UNTO THEE	421	13
10 THE KINGS OF TARSHISH AND OF THE ISLES SHALL GIVE	427	16
THE KINGS OF ARABIA AND SABA SHALL BRING GIFTS	427	17
11 ALL KINGS SHALL FALL DOWN BEFORE HIM	427	18
AMONG THE KINGS OF THE EARTH	433	14
HIGHER THAN THE KINGS OF THE EARTH	451	30
AND ALL THE KINGS OF THE EARTH THY MAJESTY	465	10
BUT REPROVED EVEN KINGS FOR THEIR SAKES	470	31
SHALL WOUND EVEN KINGS IN THE DAY OF HIS WRATH	482	17
EVEN BEFORE KINGS, *	492	31
AND SLEW MIGHTY KINGS	510	23
17 WHO SMOTE GREAT KINGS	512	16
18 YEA, AND SLEW MIGHTY KINGS	512	18
4 ALL THE KINGS OF THE EARTH SHALL PRAISE THEE,	514	04
GIVEN VICTORY UNTO KINGS, *	520	10
11 KINGS OF THE EARTH, AND ALL PEOPLES	524	25
8 TO BIND THEIR KINGS IN CHAINS, *	525	17

KINGS'

	PAGE	LN
CLOTHING ARE IN KINGS' HOUSES	094	29
9 KINGS' DAUGHTERS ARE AMONG THY HONOURABLE WOMEN	397	02
EVEN IN THEIR KINGS' CHAMBERS	471	33

KINSFOLK

	PAGE	LN
HIM AMONG THEIR KINSFOLK AND ACQUAINTANCE	110	25

KINSMEN

	PAGE	LN
AND MY KINSMEN STOOD AFAR OFF	388	13

KISHON

	PAGE	LN
AND UNTO JABIN AT THE BROOK OF KISHON	444	23

KISS

	PAGE	LN
WHOMSOEVER I SHALL KISS, THAT SAME IS HE	142	18
NEAR UNTO JESUS TO KISS HIM	150	29
BETRAYEST THOU THE SON OF MAN WITH A KISS	150	30
12 KISS THE SON, LEST HE BE ANGRY, AND SO YE PERISH	346	21

KISSED

	PAGE	LN
AND KISSED HIM	142	21
ON HIS NECK, AND KISSED HIM	202	18
AND PEACE HAVE KISSED EACH OTHER	446	28

KNAPPETH

	PAGE	LN
THE BOW, AND KNAPPETH THE SPEAR IN SUNDER, AND	398	12

KNEE

	PAGE	LN
NAME OF JESUS EVERY KNEE SHOULD BOW, OF THINGS IN	105	28
NAME OF JESUS EVERY KNEE SHOULD BOW, OF THINGS IN	134	24
AND THEY BOWED THE KNEE BEFORE HIM, AND MOCKED HIM,	136	20

KNEEL

THE MINISTER SHALL KNEEL, AND SAY THE LORD'S PRAYER	R 007 20
AND KNEEL BEFORE THE LORD OUR MAKER	009 13
THE MINISTER SHALL KNEEL, AND SAY THE LORD'S PRAYER	R 024 27
AND THERE SHALL KNEEL DOWN IN SOME CONVENIENT PLACE,	R 305 08
THE DUST SHALL KNEEL BEFORE HIM	368 02
WILDERNESS SHALL KNEEL BEFORE HIM	427 14
AND KNEEL BEFORE THE LORD OUR MAKER	459 15
AND SHALL KNEEL DOWN	R 556 03
MINISTER KNEEL AT THE ALTAR, TO PRESENT HIS	R 573 09

KNEELED

AND HE KNEELED DOWN, AND CRIED WITH A LOUD VOICE,	100 15
AND KNEELED DOWN, AND PRAYED, SAYING, FATHER,	150 17

KNEELING

AFTER THE MINISTER, ALL KNEELING	R 006 16
THE PEOPLE STILL KNEELING	R 007 07
PEOPLE STILL KNEELING, AND REPEATING IT WITH HIM,	R 007 21
THE PEOPLE DEVOUTLY KNEELING	R 016 23
AFTER THE MINISTER, ALL KNEELING	R 023 23
THE PEOPLE STILL KNEELING	R 024 07
PEOPLE STILL KNEELING, AND REPEATING IT WITH HIM	R 024 28
THE PEOPLE DEVOUTLY KNEELING	R 030 28
AND THE PEOPLE KNEELING, THEN SHALL BE SAID BY THEM	R 060 07
AND THE COLLECT FOLLOWING, THE PEOPLE KNEELING	R 067 07
STILL KNEELING, SHALL, AFTER EVERY	R 067 23
CONFESSION TO ALMIGHTY GOD, DEVOUTLY KNEELING	075 14
TO RECEIVE THE HOLY COMMUNION, HUMBLY KNEELING	R 075 16
THE PRIEST, KNEELING DOWN AT THE LORD'S TABLE,	R 082 11
INTO THEIR HANDS, ALL DEVOUTLY KNEELING	R 082 28
THE PEOPLE KNEELING, THE PRIEST (THE BISHOP IF HE BE	R 084 04
ALL KNEELING, THE FOLLOWING PRAYER, THE	R 283 04
BY THE MINISTER AND PEOPLE TOGETHER, ALL KNEELING	R 285 24
ALL KNEELING, THE GRACE OF OUR LORD JESUS	R 289 21
THEM IN ORDER KNEELING BEFORE THE BISHOP, HE SHALL	R 297 24
THE PEOPLE KNEELING AND REPEATING IT WITH HIM	R 298 13
MAN AND WIFE KNEELING, THE MINISTER SHALL ADD THIS	R 304 10
THEM THE FOLLOWING HYMN, THE WOMAN STILL KNEELING	R 305 16
HUMBLY KNEELING BEFORE HIM, AND SHALL SAY,	R 534 03
PRIESTS KNEELING, AND OTHERS STANDING, THE BISHOP	R 543 26
HUMBLY KNEELING, AND THE BISHOP SAYING, RECEIVE THE	R 546 08
ONE OF THEM KNEELING, THE BIBLE INTO HIS HAND,	R 546 23
ELECTED BISHOP, KNEELING BEFORE THEM, THE PRESIDING	R 558 10
THE BISHOP, KNEELING, SHALL SAY THE FOLLOWING PRAYER	R 564 26
ALL KNEELING, AND REPEATING WITH HIM THE	R 587 06
ALL KNEELING, AND REPEATING WITH HIM THE	R 589 14
ALL KNEELING, AND REPEATING WITH HIM THE	R 592 10
ALL KNEELING, AND REPEATING WITH HIM THE	R 593 04

KNEES

AND BOWING THEIR KNEES WORSHIPPED HIM	146 02
DOWN AT JESUS' KNEES, SAYING, DEPART FROM ME	196 23
CAUSE I BOW MY KNEES UNTO THE FATHER OF OUR LORD	212 11
23 MY KNEES ARE WEAK THROUGH FASTING	481 18
FALL LOW ON OUR KNEES BEFORE HIS FOOTSTOOL	508 18

KNEW

AND THE WORLD KNEW HIM NOT	097 32
AND KNEW HER NOT TILL SHE HAD BROUGHT FORTH HER	105 14
AND HIS MOTHER KNEW NOT OF IT	110 23
WAS MADE WINE, AND KNEW NOT WHENCE IT WAS	113 25
BUT THE SERVANTS WHICH DREW THE WATER KNEW	113 26
US NOT, BECAUSE IT KNEW HIM NOT	117 16
FROM THEM, NEITHER KNEW THEY THE THINGS WHICH WERE	123 25
FOR HE HIMSELF KNEW WHAT HE WOULD DO	131 29
FOR HE KNEW THAT FOR ENVY THEY HAD DELIVERED HIM	135 31
FOR HE KNEW THAT THE CHIEF PRIESTS HAD DELIVERED HIM	145 19
AND AS SOON AS HE KNEW THAT HE BELONGED UNTO HEROD'S	153 08
WHEN JESUS KNEW THAT HIS HOUR WAS COME THAT HE SHOULD	155 23
FOR HE KNEW WHO SHOULD BETRAY HIM	156 11
FOR AS YET THEY KNEW NOT THE SCRIPTURE, THAT HE MUST	164 27
AND THEY KNEW HIM	168 07
BECAUSE THEY KNEW HIM NOT, NOR YET THE VOICES OF THE	168 27
NOW JESUS KNEW THAT THEY WERE DESIROUS TO ASK HIM,	174 03
SO THE FATHER KNEW THAT IT WAS AT THE SAME HOUR,	220 09
YE HEARD OF IT, AND KNEW THE GRACE OF GOD IN TRUTH	223 29
FOR HE HIMSELF KNEW WHAT HE WOULD DO	225 25
THINGS THAT I KNEW NOT	382 14

KNEWEST

BECAUSE THOU KNEWEST NOT THE TIME OF THY VISITATION	204 14
THOU KNEWEST MY PATH	518 07

KNIT

WHO HAST KNIT TOGETHER THINE ELECT IN ONE	256 05
O KNIT MY HEART UNTO THEE, THAT I MAY FEAR THY NAME	447 26
KNIT TOGETHER IN CONSTANT AFFECTION THOSE WHO, IN	598 24

KNOCK

KNOCK, AND IT SHALL BE OPENED UNTO YOU	183 11
KNOCK, AND IT SHALL BE OPENED UNTO YOU	263 04
KNOCK, AND IT SHALL BE OPENED UNTO YOU	274 16
OPEN THE GATE UNTO US WHO KNOCK	274 18

KNOCKETH

AND TO HIM THAT KNOCKETH IT SHALL BE OPENED	183 13

KNOCKETH   CONTINUED

AND TO HIM THAT KNOCKETH IT SHALL BE OPENED	263 07
HE COMETH AND KNOCKETH, THEY MAY OPEN UNTO HIM	534 19

KNOW

AND STRENGTH TO KNOW AND TO DO THY WILL	018 11
WATCH YE, FOR YE KNOW NOT WHEN THE MASTER OF THE	021 24
ALL THE WORLD MAY KNOW THAT THOU ART OUR SAVIOUR AND	052 14
THE MINISTER SHALL KNOW ANY TO BE AN OPEN AND	R 084 35
UNTIL HE KNOW THEM TO BE RECONCILED	R 085 11
YE KNOW HOW GRIEVOUS AND UNKIND A THING IT IS, WHEN A	088 17
YE SEE AND KNOW OF YOUR OWN SELVES THAT SUMMER	093 16
COME TO PASS, KNOW YE THAT THE KINGDOM OF GOD IS NIGH	093 17
FOR I KNOW NOTHING AGAINST MYSELF	094 08
AMONG YOU, WHOM YE KNOW NOT	096 04
AND WE KNOW THAT HIS TESTIMONY IS TRUE	102 14
GRANT THAT WE, WHO KNOW THEE NOW BY FAITH, MAY AFTER	107 31
BOTH PERCEIVE AND KNOW WHAT THINGS THEY OUGHT TO DO,	109 31
BUT WE KNOW THAT, WHEN HE SHALL APPEAR, WE SHALL BE	117 18
AND YE KNOW THAT HE WAS MANIFESTED TO TAKE AWAY OUR	117 23
KNOW YE NOT THAT THEY WHICH RUN IN A RACE RUN ALL,	119 05
YOU IT IS GIVEN TO KNOW THE MYSTERIES OF THE KINGDOM	121 30
FOR WE KNOW IN PART, AND WE PROPHESY IN PART	123 06
BUT THEN SHALL I KNOW EVEN AS ALSO I AM KNOWN	123 13
NOW I KNOW IN PART	123 13
FOR YE KNOW WHAT COMMANDMENTS WE GAVE YOU BY THE LORD	127 26
ONE OF YOU SHOULD KNOW HOW TO POSSESS HIS VESSEL IN	127 29
THE GENTILES WHICH KNOW NOT GOD	127 31
FOR THIS YE KNOW, THAT NO WHOREMONGER, NOR UNCLEAN	129 06
UNTO HIM, NOW WE KNOW THAT THOU HAST A DEVIL	133 19
IF I SHOULD SAY, I KNOW HIM NOT, I SHALL BE A LIAR	133 26
BUT I KNOW HIM	133 26
BUT I KNOW HIM, AND KEEP HIS SAYING	133 27
SAYING, I KNOW NOT, NEITHER UNDERSTAND I WHAT	143 26
TO SWEAR, SAYING, I KNOW NOT THIS MAN OF WHOM YE	143 33
LIKE A FLINT, AND I KNOW THAT I SHALL NOT BE ASHAMED	144 17
WOMAN, I KNOW HIM NOT	151 13
PETER SAID, MAN, I KNOW NOT WHAT THOU SAYEST	151 18
FOR THEY KNOW NOT WHAT THEY DO	154 25
BUT THOU SHALT KNOW HEREAFTER	156 04
HE SAID UNTO THEM, KNOW YE WHAT I HAVE DONE TO YOU	156 14
MERCY UPON ALL WHO KNOW THEE NOT AS THOU ART REVEALED	157 07
TO YOU, THAT YE MAY KNOW THAT I FIND NO FAULT IN HIM	159 02
AND WE KNOW NOT WHERE THEY HAVE LAID HIM	164 15
KNOW YE NOT THAT A LITTLE LEAVEN LEAVENETH THE WHOLE	165 10
I SAY, YE KNOW, WHICH WAS PUBLISHED THROUGHOUT	166 17
THEY SHOULD NOT KNOW HIM	167 09
AND KNOW MY SHEEP, AND AM KNOWN OF MINE, EVEN AS THE	172 27
KNOWETH ME, AND I KNOW THE FATHER	172 29
IS NOT FOR YOU TO KNOW THE TIMES OR THE SEASONS,	178 07
BUT YE KNOW HIM	181 13
THAT DAY YE SHALL KNOW THAT I AM IN MY FATHER,	181 17
THAT THE WORLD MAY KNOW THAT I LOVE THE FATHER	182 09
BEING EVIL, KNOW HOW TO GIVE GOOD GIFTS UNTO	183 17
I SAY, YE KNOW, WHICH WAS PUBLISHED THROUGHOUT	184 04
FOR THEY KNOW HIS VOICE	186 07
FOR THEY KNOW NOT THE VOICE OF STRANGERS	186 09
UNTO HIM, RABBI, WE KNOW THAT THOU ART A TEACHER COME	188 02
WE SPEAK THAT WE DO KNOW, AND TESTIFY THAT WE HAVE	188 21
HEREBY KNOW WE THAT WE DWELL IN HIM, AND HE IN US,	189 18
WE KNOW THAT WE HAVE PASSED FROM DEATH UNTO LIFE,	191 12
AND YE KNOW THAT NO MURDERER HATH ETERNAL LIFE	191 15
AND HEREBY WE KNOW THAT WE ARE OF THE TRUTH, AND	191 23
AND HEREBY WE KNOW THAT HE ABIDETH IN US, BY THE	191 33
FOR WE KNOW THAT THE WHOLE CREATION GROANETH AND	194 19
KNOW YE NOT, THAT SO MANY OF US AS WERE BAPTIZED INTO	197 10
YE SHALL KNOW THEM BY THEIR FRUITS	200 17
FRUITS YE SHALL KNOW THEM	200 23
YE KNOW THAT YE WERE GENTILES, CARRIED AWAY UNTO	203 17
AND TO KNOW THE LOVE OF CHRIST, WHICH PASSETH	212 19
BUT THAT YE MAY KNOW THAT THE SON OF MAN HATH POWER	217 09
MASTER, WE KNOW THAT THOU ART TRUE, AND	222 31
BUT I SAY, DID NOT ISRAEL KNOW	227 16
HE EAT, THAT HE MAY KNOW TO REFUSE THE EVIL, AND	236 02
THIS BE, SEEING I KNOW NOT A MAN	236 21
WHOM TRULY TO KNOW IS EVERLASTING LIFE	238 29
US PERFECTLY TO KNOW THY SON JESUS CHRIST TO BE THE	238 30
AND WHITHER I GO YE KNOW, AND THE WAY YE KNOW	240 03
AND WHITHER I GO YE KNOW, AND THE WAY YE KNOW	240 03
UNTO HIM, LORD, WE KNOW NOT WHITHER THOU GOEST	240 04
AND HOW CAN WE KNOW THE WAY	240 05
FROM HENCEFORTH YE KNOW HIM, AND HAVE SEEN HIM	240 08
HE SAID, NOW I KNOW OF A SURETY, THAT THE LORD HATH	245 26
AND SAID, YE KNOW NOT WHAT YE ASK	247 11
AND SAID, YE KNOW THAT THE PRINCES OF THE	247 21
WORLD HATE YOU, YE KNOW THAT IT HATED ME BEFORE IT	255 13
BECAUSE THEY KNOW NOT HIM THAT SENT ME	255 22
AND SHALL KNOW THAT I AM THE LORD, WHEN I HAVE	262 11
THUS SHALL THEY KNOW THAT I THE LORD THEIR GOD AM	262 20
BEING EVIL, KNOW HOW TO GIVE GOOD GIFTS UNTO	263 11
UNTO HIM, RABBI, WE KNOW THAT THOU ART A TEACHER COME	275 07
CHRISTIAN OUGHT TO KNOW AND BELIEVE TO HIS SOUL'S	277 12
ASK GOD'S HELP TO KNOW AND TO KEEP THEM	285 19
KNOW THIS	289 13
IF EITHER OF YOU KNOW ANY IMPEDIMENT, WHY YE MAY NOT	300 26
IF ANY OF YOU KNOW CAUSE, OR JUST IMPEDIMENT, WHY	R 304 23
AND MAKE THEE KNOW AND FEEL, THAT THERE IS NONE OTHER	314 18
THAT YE MAY KNOW THAT YE HAVE ETERNAL LIFE, AND THAT	322 13
AND IF WE KNOW THAT HE HEAR US, WHATSOEVER WE ASK, WE	322 17
WE ASK, WE KNOW THAT WE HAVE THE PETITIONS THAT WE	322 18
I KNOW THAT MY REDEEMER LIVETH, AND THAT HE SHALL	324 09
LET ME KNOW MINE END, AND THE NUMBER OF MY	324 20
BE STILL THEN, AND KNOW THAT I AM GOD	327 14
FORASMUCH AS YE KNOW THAT YOUR LABOUR IS NOT IN VAIN	330 16

KNOW   CONTINUED

WE KNOW THAT ALL THINGS WORK TOGETHER FOR GOOD TO	330 30
AND WHITHER I GO YE KNOW, AND THE WAY YE KNOW	331 23
AND WHITHER I GO YE KNOW, AND THE WAY YE KNOW	331 23
UNTO HIM, LORD, WE KNOW NOT WHITHER THOU GOEST	331 24
AND HOW CAN WE KNOW THE WAY	331 25
ON THEE, THEY MAY KNOW THE CONSOLATION OF THY LOVE	342 12
3 KNOW THIS ALSO, THAT THE LORD HATH CHOSEN TO	347 16
10 AND THEY THAT KNOW THY NAME WILL PUT THEIR TRUST	352 08
THE HEATHEN MAY KNOW THEMSELVES TO BE BUT MEN	352 33
6 NOW KNOW I THAT THE LORD HELPETH HIS ANOINTED,	364 26
UNTO THEM THAT KNOW THEE, *	384 17
5 LORD, LET ME KNOW MINE END, AND THE NUMBER OF MY	389 15
11 BY THIS I KNOW THOU FAVOUREST ME, *	392 21
BE STILL THEN, AND KNOW THAT I AM GOD	398 14
11 I KNOW ALL THE FOWLS UPON THE MOUNTAINS, *	402 12
THIS I KNOW	408 33
AND KNOW THAT IT IS GOD THAT RULETH IN JACOB, AND	411 33
FOR I KNOW NO END THEREOF	426 05
POSTERITY MIGHT KNOW IT, *	435 07
5 THEY KNOW NOT, NEITHER DO THEY UNDERSTAND, BUT WALK	443 26
18 AND THEY SHALL KNOW THAT THOU, WHOSE NAME IS	445 08
AMONG THEM THAT KNOW ME	448 19
I WILL NOT KNOW A WICKED PERSON	463 25
PLACE THEREOF SHALL KNOW IT NO MORE	467 07
26 AND THEY SHALL KNOW HOW THAT THIS IS THY HAND,	481 24
75 I KNOW, O LORD, THAT THY JUDGMENTS ARE RIGHT,	495 04
THAT I MAY KNOW THY TESTIMONIES	498 20
5 FOR I KNOW THAT THE LORD IS GREAT, *	510 11
NO MAN THAT WOULD KNOW ME	518 11
FOR THEY KNOW HIS VOICE	538 30
FOR THEY KNOW NOT THE VOICE OF STRANGERS	538 32
AND KNOW MY SHEEP, AND AM KNOWN OF MINE, EVEN AS THE	539 16
KNOWETH ME, AND I KNOW THE FATHER	539 18
YOUR NEGLIGENCE, YE KNOW THE GREATNESS OF THE FAULT,	540 12
TEACH US TO KNOW THE FATHER, SON, AND THEE, OF BOTH,	544 10
FOR IF A MAN KNOW NOT HOW TO RULE HIS OWN HOUSE,	549 25
SAID UNTO THEM, YE KNOW, FROM THE FIRST DAY THAT I	550 06
AND NOW, BEHOLD, I KNOW THAT YE ALL, AMONG WHOM I	550 22
FOR I KNOW THIS, THAT AFTER MY DEPARTING SHALL	550 30
YE YOURSELVES KNOW, THAT THESE HANDS HAVE	551 06
TEACH US TO KNOW THE FATHER, SON, AND THEE, OF BOTH,	556 18
BOTH PERCEIVE AND KNOW WHAT THINGS THEY OUGHT TO DO,	566 05
MY GOOD CHILD, KNOW THIS	580 16
WE MAY BE STILL AND KNOW THAT THOU ART GOD	595 23

KNOWEST

ALL WISDOM, WHO KNOWEST OUR NECESSITIES BEFORE WE	049 29
O GOD, WHO KNOWEST US TO BE SET IN THE MIDST OF SO	114 04
DENY THAT THOU KNOWEST ME	150 03
WHAT I DO THOU KNOWEST NOT NOW	156 04
KNOWEST THOU NOT THAT I HAVE POWER TO CRUCIFY THEE,	159 14
SURE THAT THOU KNOWEST ALL THINGS, AND NEEDEST NOT	176 33
OF ISRAEL, AND KNOWEST NOT THESE THINGS	188 19
WHICH KNOWEST THE HEARTS OF ALL MEN, SHEW	234 27
AND I SAID UNTO HIM, SIR, THOU KNOWEST	257 06
THOU KNOWEST, LORD, THE SECRETS OF OUR HEARTS	332 28
9 LORD, THOU KNOWEST ALL MY DESIRE	388 07
REFRAIN MY LIPS, O LORD, AND THAT THOU KNOWEST	391 03
THOU KNOWEST MY SIMPLENESS, AND MY FAULTS ARE	422 11
THOU KNOWEST MY DOWN-SITTING, AND MINE UP-RISING	514 21
THOU, O LORD, KNOWEST IT ALTOGETHER	514 26
THOU KNOWEST THAT I LOVE THEE	551 16
THOU KNOWEST THAT I LOVE THEE	551 19
THOU KNOWEST THAT I LOVE THEE	551 23
LORD, THOU KNOWEST ALL THINGS	551 23
O GOD, WHO KNOWEST THE WEAKNESS AND CORRUPTION	588 12

KNOWETH

THE WORLD KNOWETH US NOT, BECAUSE IT KNEW HIM NOT	117 16
FOR EVERMORE, KNOWETH THAT I LIE NOT	121 16
WHO KNOWETH IF HE WILL RETURN AND REPENT, AND LEAVE A	124 26
AND HE KNOWETH THAT HE SAITH TRUE, THAT YE MIGHT	161 06
AS THE FATHER KNOWETH ME, AND I KNOW THE FATHER	172 28
HIM NOT, NEITHER KNOWETH HIM	181 13
BORN OF GOD, AND KNOWETH GOD	189 09
THAT LOVETH NOT KNOWETH NOT GOD	189 10
OUR HEART, AND KNOWETH ALL THINGS	191 25
HEAVENLY FATHER KNOWETH THAT YE HAVE NEED OF ALL	211 30
AND NO MAN KNOWETH THE SON, BUT THE FATHER	235 08
NEITHER KNOWETH ANY MAN THE FATHER, SAVE THE SON,	235 09
FOR THE SERVANT KNOWETH NOT WHAT HIS LORD DOETH	241 29
BECAUSE HE KNOWETH THAT HE HATH BUT A SHORT TIME	252 19
HEAVENLY FATHER KNOWETH THAT YE HAVE NEED OF ALL	266 28
7 BUT THE LORD KNOWETH THE WAY OF THE RIGHTEOUS	345 22
18 THE LORD KNOWETH THE DAYS OF THE GODLY	385 31
FOR HE KNOWETH THE VERY SECRETS OF THE HEART	396 03
11 THE LORD KNOWETH THE THOUGHTS OF MAN, *	458 08
14 FOR HE KNOWETH WHEREOF WE ARE MADE	467 02
AND THE SUN KNOWETH HIS GOING DOWN	468 33
AND THAT MY SOUL KNOWETH RIGHT WELL	515 17
ANY OF YOU WHO KNOWETH ANY IMPEDIMENT, OR NOTABLE	530 21
ANY OF YOU WHO KNOWETH ANY IMPEDIMENT, OR NOTABLE	536 27
AS THE FATHER KNOWETH ME, AND I KNOW THE FATHER	539 17

KNOWING

THAT THEY, KNOWING WHOSE MINISTERS THEY ARE, MAY	032 08
AND THAT, KNOWING THE TIME, THAT NOW IT IS HIGH TIME	090 31
BUT HE, KNOWING THEIR THOUGHTS, SAID UNTO THEM,	129 29
JESUS KNOWING THAT THE FATHER HAD GIVEN ALL THINGS	155 28
JESUS KNOWING THAT ALL THINGS WERE NOW	160 24
IN THE FAITH, KNOWING THAT THE SAME AFFLICTIONS ARE	193 07

KNOWING   CONTINUED

KNOWING THAT YE ARE THEREUNTO CALLED, THAT YE SHOULD	195 23
KNOWING THIS, THAT OUR OLD MAN IS CRUCIFIED WITH HIM,	197 17
KNOWING THAT CHRIST BEING RAISED FROM THE DEAD DIETH	197 21
AND JESUS KNOWING THEIR THOUGHTS SAID, WHEREFORE	217 06
KNOWING THIS, THAT THE TRYING OF YOUR FAITH WORKETH	239 09
KNOWING THAT SHORTLY I MUST PUT OFF THIS MY	248 09
NOT KNOWING WHAT HE SAID	249 04
AND THE BISHOP, KNOWING EITHER BY HIMSELF, OR BY	529 26
NOT KNOWING THE THINGS THAT SHALL BEFALL	550 15
KNOWING THAT THOU ART DOING FOR THEM BETTER THINGS	597 11

KNOWLEDGE

BY HIS KNOWLEDGE THE DEPTHS ARE BROKEN UP, AND THE	005 25
TO GIVE KNOWLEDGE OF SALVATION UNTO HIS PEOPLE *	014 27
OF CONCORD, IN KNOWLEDGE OF WHOM STANDETH OUR ETERNAL	017 06
IN THIS WORLD KNOWLEDGE OF THY TRUTH, AND IN THE	020 09
IN THIS WORLD KNOWLEDGE OF THY TRUTH, AND IN THE	034 09
THAT KNOWLEDGE MAY BE INCREASED AMONG US,	042 24
IN THE KNOWLEDGE OF THY TRUTH, THEY MAY WORSHIP THEE	043 03
BY WHOSE KNOWLEDGE THE DEPTHS ARE BROKEN UP, AND	050 19
WITH TRUE KNOWLEDGE AND UNDERSTANDING OF THY WORD	055 31
TO GIVE THE KNOWLEDGE OF THY GLORY IN THE FACE OF THY	078 02
LIGHT AND TRUE KNOWLEDGE OF THEE, AND OF THY SON	079 02
MINDS IN THE KNOWLEDGE AND LOVE OF GOD, AND OF HIS	084 19
UNDERSTAND MY KNOWLEDGE IN THE MYSTERY OF CHRIST)	108 11
AND UNDERSTAND ALL MYSTERIES, AND ALL KNOWLEDGE	122 24
THERE BE KNOWLEDGE, IT SHALL VANISH AWAY	123 06
BY KNOWLEDGE, BY LONG-SUFFERING, BY	126 12
THE WORD OF KNOWLEDGE BY THE SAME SPIRIT	182 28
THE WORD OF KNOWLEDGE BY THE SAME SPIRIT	203 28
WHICH PASSETH KNOWLEDGE, THAT YE MIGHT BE FILLED WITH	212 20
IN ALL UTTERANCE, AND IN ALL KNOWLEDGE	214 31
AND MORE IN KNOWLEDGE AND IN ALL JUDGMENT	221 02
WITH THE KNOWLEDGE OF HIS WILL IN ALL WISDOM AND	224 02
IN THE KNOWLEDGE OF GOD	224 06
AND OF THE KNOWLEDGE OF THE SON OF GOD, UNTO A	237 23
TO GIVE KNOWLEDGE OF SALVATION UNTO HIS PEOPLE BY THE	244 12
LIGHT OF THE KNOWLEDGE OF THE GLORY OF GOD IN THE	251 09
SHALL GIVE KNOWLEDGE THEREOF TO THE MINISTER	R 273 13
CALL US TO THE KNOWLEDGE OF THY GRACE, AND FAITH IN	276 09
INCREASE THIS KNOWLEDGE, AND CONFIRM THIS FAITH IN US	276 10
THE SPIRIT OF KNOWLEDGE AND TRUE GODLINESS	297 21
THEM IN THE KNOWLEDGE AND OBEDIENCE OF THY WORD, THAT	298 21
INCREASING IN KNOWLEDGE AND LOVE OF THEE, HE MAY GO	332 05
5 HAVE THEY NO KNOWLEDGE, THAT THEY ARE ALL SUCH	356 22
IS THERE KNOWLEDGE IN THE MOST HIGH	428 31
IT IS HE THAT TEACHETH MAN KNOWLEDGE	458 07
66 O TEACH ME TRUE UNDERSTANDING AND KNOWLEDGE	494 13
5 SUCH KNOWLEDGE IS TOO WONDERFUL AND EXCELLENT FOR	514 29
THE HEATHEN IN THE KNOWLEDGE OF HIS LAWS	524 03
MINDS IN THE KNOWLEDGE AND LOVE OF GOD, AND OF HIS	535 14
AND OF THE KNOWLEDGE OF THE SON OF GOD, UNTO A	538 10
THE FAITH AND KNOWLEDGE OF GOD, AND TO THAT RIPENESS	540 20
AS HELP TO THE KNOWLEDGE OF THE SAME, LAYING ASIDE	542 28
IN THE KNOWLEDGE AND FAITH OF THEE AND THY SON, BY	545 30
MINDS IN THE KNOWLEDGE AND LOVE OF GOD, AND OF HIS	547 15
MINDS IN THE KNOWLEDGE AND LOVE OF GOD, AND OF HIS	559 18
MINDS IN THE KNOWLEDGE AND LOVE OF GOD, AND OF HIS	568 14
SHALL GIVE KNOWLEDGE FOR CHILDREN TO BE BROUGHT UNTO	R 583 05
AND IN THE KNOWLEDGE OF OUR LORD AND SAVIOUR JESUS	588 09
GIVING US THE KNOWLEDGE AND SENSE OF OUR DUTY TOWARDS	591 13
AND A CLEARER KNOWLEDGE OF THY WILL	596 14
VIRTUE, KNOWLEDGE, TEMPERANCE, PATIENCE,	598 24
THAT HAVE KNOWLEDGE OF THEIR OFFENCES	608 21

KNOWN

TO MAKE THY WAYS KNOWN UNTO THEM, THY SAVING HEALTH	018 29
THY WAY MAY BE KNOWN UPON EARTH, *	028 19
TO MAKE THY WAYS KNOWN UNTO THEM, THY SAVING HEALTH	032 29
ABUNDANTLY TO MAKE KNOWN TO ALL MEN THY BLESSED GIFT	038 21
OPEN, ALL DESIRES KNOWN, AND FROM WHOM NO SECRETS ARE	067 17
YOUR MODERATION BE KNOWN UNTO ALL MEN	095 14
REQUESTS BE MADE KNOWN UNTO GOD	095 17
THE LORD HATH MADE KNOWN UNTO US	106 10
SEEN IT, THEY MADE KNOWN ABROAD THE SAYING WHICH WAS	106 13
REVELATION HE MADE KNOWN UNTO ME THE MYSTERY	108 09
AGES WAS NOT MADE KNOWN UNTO THE SONS OF MEN, AS IT	108 12
PLACES MIGHT BE KNOWN BY THE CHURCH THE MANIFOLD	108 25
SEEN HIM, NEITHER KNOWN HIM	117 26
BUT THEN SHALL I KNOW EVEN AS ALSO I AM KNOWN	123 14
AS UNKNOWN, AND YET WELL KNOWN	126 18
YET YE HAVE NOT KNOWN HIM	133 26
AND HAST NOT KNOWN THE THINGS WHICH ARE COME TO PASS	167 14
AND HOW HE WAS KNOWN OF THEM IN BREAKING OF BREAD	168 15
BE IT KNOWN UNTO YOU THEREFORE, MEN AND BRETHREN,	169 18
MY SHEEP, AND AM KNOWN OF MINE, EVEN AS THE FATHER	172 28
THEY HAVE NOT KNOWN THE FATHER, NOR ME	180 02
AND WE HAVE KNOWN AND BELIEVED THE LOVE THAT GOD HATH	189 23
IF THOU HADST KNOWN, EVEN THOU, AT LEAST IN THIS THY	204 07
TO MAKE KNOWN THE MYSTERY OF THE GOSPEL, FOR	219 23
AND IT WAS KNOWN UNTO ALL THE DWELLERS AT JERUSALEM	234 15
AS WE HAVE KNOWN THE INCARNATION OF THY SON	235 19
IF YE HAD KNOWN ME, YE SHOULD HAVE KNOWN MY FATHER	240 07
YE SHOULD HAVE KNOWN MY FATHER ALSO	240 08
YET HAST THOU NOT KNOWN ME, PHILIP	240 11
FATHER I HAVE MADE KNOWN UNTO YOU	241 31
WHEN WE MADE KNOWN UNTO YOU THE POWER AND COMING OF	248 14
16 THE LORD IS KNOWN TO EXECUTE JUDGMENT	352 24
WHOM I HAVE NOT KNOWN SHALL SERVE ME	362 27
AND HAST KNOWN MY SOUL IN ADVERSITIES	376 05
GOD IS WELL KNOWN IN HER PALACES AS A SURE REFUGE	399 14
THY WAY MAY BE KNOWN UPON EARTH, *	418 26

KNOWN   CONTINUED

20 THOU HAST KNOWN MY REPROACH, MY SHAME, AND MY	423	11
WAS KNOWN TO BRING IT TO AN EXCELLENT WORK	430	15
IN JUDAH IS GOD KNOWN	432	24
AND THY FOOTSTEPS ARE NOT KNOWN	434	22
WE HAVE HEARD AND KNOWN, *	434	31
THAT HAVE NOT KNOWN THEE	440	12
WONDROUS WORKS BE KNOWN IN THE DARK	449	20
BECAUSE HE HATH KNOWN MY NAME	455	24
FOR THEY HAVE NOT KNOWN MY WAYS	459	26
19 UNTIL THE TIME CAME THAT HIS CAUSE WAS KNOWN	471	10
THAT HE MIGHT MAKE HIS POWER TO BE KNOWN	473	17
AND HAVE KNOWN THY TESTIMONIES, *	495	14
I HAVE KNOWN LONG SINCE, *	500	14
ME OUT, AND KNOWN ME	514	20
MIGHT BE KNOWN UNTO MEN	521	17
AND KNOWN TO HAVE SUCH QUALITIES AS ARE	529	16
MY SHEEP, AND AM KNOWN OF MINE, EVEN AS THE FATHER	539	17
BE AS EVIDENTLY KNOWN AS A TREE DISCERNED BY THE	605	15

LABOUR

FAITH WE MAY LABOUR ABUNDANTLY TO MAKE KNOWN TO ALL	038	21
DAYS SHALT THOU LABOUR, AND DO ALL THAT THOU HAST TO	068	25
YOUR WORKS, AND LABOUR THAT PROCEEDETH OF LOVE	072	24
RATHER LET HIM LABOUR, WORKING WITH HIS HANDS THE	216	21
ALL YE THAT LABOUR AND ARE HEAVY LADEN, AND I	235	11
DAYS SHALT THOU LABOUR, AND DO ALL THAT THOU HAST TO	286	25
BUT TO LEARN AND LABOR TRULY TO EARN MINE OWN	289	09
STRENGTH THEN BUT LABOUR AND SORROW	325	34
YE KNOW THAT YOUR LABOUR IS NOT IN VAIN IN THE LORD	330	16
AND THEIR LABOUR UNTO THE GRASSHOPPER	437	34
STRENGTH THEN BUT LABOUR AND SORROW	454	09
AND TO HIS LABOUR, *	469	06
AND LET THE STRANGER SPOIL HIS LABOUR	480	22
6 I LABOUR FOR PEACE	502	19
THEIR LABOUR IS BUT LOST THAT BUILD IT	505	22
3 IT IS BUT LOST LABOUR THAT YE HASTE TO RISE UP	505	26
14 THAT OUR OXEN MAY BE STRONG TO LABOUR	520	21
NEVER CEASE YOUR LABOR, YOUR CARE AND DILIGENCE,	540	16
BY WHOSE LABOUR AND MINISTRY HE GATHERED TOGETHER A	545	19
DAYS SHALT THOU LABOUR, AND DO ALL THAT THOU HAST TO	579	05
BUT TO LEARN AND LABOR TRULY TO GET MINE OWN LIVING,	580	13
OF THOSE WHO LABOUR, AND THE REPOSE OF THE DEAD	595	05
WORK AND TO HIS LABOUR UNTIL THE EVENING	599	26
ALL THOSE WHO LABOUR IN WORKS OF MERCY OR IN SCHOOLS	600	04

LABOURED

BUT I LABOURED MORE ABUNDANTLY THAN THEY ALL	205	16

LABOURER

FOR THE LABOURER IS WORTHY OF HIS HIRE	254	23

LABOURERS

TO SEND FORTH LABOURERS INTO THY HARVEST	056	02
BUT THE LABOURERS ARE FEW	073	12
HE SEND FORTH LABOURERS INTO HIS HARVEST	073	13
TO HIRE LABOURERS INTO HIS VINEYARD	119	17
WITH THE LABOURERS FOR A PENNY A DAY, HE SENT THEM	119	18
CALL THE LABOURERS, AND GIVE THEM THEIR HIRE,	119	30
BUT THE LABOURERS ARE FEW	254	14
SEND FORTH LABOURERS INTO HIS HARVEST	254	16
BUT THE LABOURERS ARE FEW	538	18
SEND FORTH LABOURERS INTO HIS HARVEST	538	19
HIRE OF THE LABOURERS TO BE KEPT BACK BY FRAUD	599	30

LABOURING

HOW THAT SO LABOURING YE OUGHT TO SUPPORT THE WEAK,	551	09

LABOURS

BLESS THE LABOURS OF THE HUSBANDMAN, AND GRANT SUCH	039	28
IN LABOURS MORE ABUNDANT, IN STRIPES ABOVE MEASURE,	120	30
IN TUMULTS, IN LABOURS, IN WATCHINGS, IN FASTINGS	126	12
HAST BLESSED THE LABOURS OF THE HUSBANDMAN IN THE	265	11
FOR THEY REST FROM THEIR LABOURS	333	28
COURSE IN FAITH, DO NOW REST FROM THEIR LABOURS	334	25
THEY TOOK THE LABOURS OF THE PEOPLE IN POSSESSION	472	26
SHALT EAT THE LABOURS OF THINE HANDS	506	08

LACK

IF ANY OF YOU LACK WISDOM, LET HIM ASK OF GOD,	239	12
BE DISQUIETED FOR LACK OF THE SAME	R 321	10
THEREFORE CAN I LACK NOTHING	338	17
THEREFORE CAN I LACK NOTHING	368	10
THEY THAT FEAR HIM LACK NOTHING	380	20
10 THE LIONS DO LACK, AND SUFFER HUNGER	380	21

LACKED

BECAUSE IT LACKED MOISTURE	121	24
AND SHOES, LACKED YE ANY THING	150	05

LACKETH

SO THAT THERE LACKETH NOTHING BUT THE GUESTS TO SIT	088	19

LACKING

CARNAL PERSONS, LACKING THE SPIRIT OF CHRIST, TO HAVE	606	23

LAD

UNTO HIM, THERE IS A LAD HERE, WHICH HATH FIVE BARLEY	131	33
UNTO HIM, THERE IS A LAD HERE, WHICH HATH FIVE BARLEY	225	29

LADEN

AND ARE HEAVY LADEN, AND I WILL REFRESH YOU	076	12
AND ARE HEAVY LADEN, AND I WILL GIVE YOU REST	235	11

LAID

OF COMMON PRAYER, LAID IT DOWN AS A RULE, THAT 'THE	V	13
AND THE LORD HATH LAID ON HIM THE INIQUITY OF US ALL	022	16
SERVANTS WHO HAVE LAID DOWN THEIR LIVES IN THE	042	16
THE SAKE OF HIM WHO LAID DOWN HIS LIFE FOR US,	044	06
PRINCIPLES ALREADY LAID DOWN, IT CANNOT BUT BE	VI	02
THE BEGINNING HAST LAID THE FOUNDATION OF THE EARTH	097	13
AND LAID HIM IN A MANGER	099	09
AND THE WITNESSES LAID DOWN THEIR CLOTHES AT A YOUNG	100	12
AND THEY LAID THEIR HANDS ON HIM, AND TOOK HIM	142	21
AND THE YOUNG MEN LAID HOLD ON HIM	142	30
LED HIM AWAY, THEY LAID HOLD UPON ONE SIMON, A	154	09
AND ON HIM THEY LAID THE CROSS, THAT HE MIGHT BEAR IT	154	10
FROM SUPPER, AND LAID ASIDE HIS GARMENTS	155	31
LINEN CLOTH, AND LAID IT IN HIS OWN NEW TOMB,	162	11
NOT WHERE THEY HAVE LAID HIM	164	16
PLACE WHERE THEY LAID HIM	165	31
FROM THE TREE, AND LAID HIM IN A SEPULCHRE	169	02
ON SLEEP, AND WAS LAID UNTO HIS FATHERS, AND SAW	169	16
THEN LAID THEY THEIR HANDS ON THEM, AND THEY RECEIVED	185	27
WHICH WAS LAID AT HIS GATE, FULL OF SORES,	190	06
OF GOD, BECAUSE HE LAID DOWN HIS LIFE FOR US	191	17
AND HE LAID HANDS ON HIM, AND TOOK HIM BY THE THROAT,	221	25
THE HOPE WHICH IS LAID UP FOR YOU IN HEAVEN, WHEREOF	223	25
THAT HEARD THEM LAID THEM UP IN THEIR HEARTS, SAYING,	243	29
THE STREETS, AND LAID THEM ON BEDS AND COUCHES, THAT	249	27
HENCEFORTH THERE IS LAID UP FOR ME A CROWN OF	253	28
THEN LAID THEY THEIR HANDS ON THEM, AND THEY RECEIVED	296	19
WE HAVE NOW LAID OUR HANDS, TO CERTIFY THEM, BY THIS	298	17
I LAID ME DOWN AND SLEPT, AND ROSE UP AGAIN	309	22
IS MADE READY TO BE LAID INTO THE EARTH, SHALL BE	R 332	16
5 I LAID ME DOWN AND SLEPT, AND ROSE UP AGAIN	346	33
AN HOST OF MEN WERE LAID AGAINST ME, YET SHALL NOT MY	371	29
NET THAT THEY HAVE LAID PRIVILY FOR ME	375	29
WHICH THOU HAST LAID UP FOR THEM THAT FEAR THEE, *	377	02
THEY HAVE PRIVILY LAID THEIR NET TO DESTROY ME	381	31
NET THAT HE HATH LAID PRIVILY CATCH HIMSELF	382	05
THEY LAID TO MY CHARGE THINGS THAT I KNEW NOT	382	13
AFTER MY LIFE LAID SNARES FOR ME	388	14
OF MY BREAD, HATH LAID GREAT WAIT FOR ME	392	18
21 HE LAID HIS HANDS UPON SUCH AS BE AT PEACE WITH	407	33
7 THEY HAVE LAID A NET FOR MY FEET, AND PRESSED DOWN	409	26
AND LAID THE FOUNDATION OF IT LIKE THE GROUND WHICH	439	16
AND LAID WASTE HIS DWELLING-PLACE	440	14
5 THOU HAST LAID ME IN THE LOWEST PIT, *	449	07
THOU HAST LAID THE FOUNDATION OF THE ROUND WORLD, AND	450	29
I HAVE LAID HELP UPON ONE THAT IS MIGHTY, I HAVE	451	13
THE BEGINNING HAST LAID THE FOUNDATION OF THE EARTH,	465	31
5 HE LAID THE FOUNDATIONS OF THE EARTH, *	468	02
JUDGMENTS HAVE I LAID BEFORE ME	491	28
THOU HAST LAID THE FOUNDATION OF THE EARTH, AND IT	496	05
95 THE UNGODLY LAID WAIT FOR ME, TO DESTROY ME	496	15
THE UNGODLY HAVE LAID A SNARE FOR ME	497	17
6 WHO LAID OUT THE EARTH ABOVE THE WATERS	511	26
AND LAID THINE HAND UPON ME	514	27
5 THE PROUD HAVE LAID A SNARE FOR ME, AND SPREAD A	516	18
THAT THEY HAVE LAID FOR ME, *	517	30
HAVE THEY PRIVILY LAID A SNARE FOR ME	518	09
HE HATH LAID ME IN THE DARKNESS, AS THE MEN THAT HAVE	518	28
HAD PRAYED, THEY LAID THEIR HANDS ON THEM	532	19
WHERE HANDS WERE LAID UPON THEM, UNTIL SUCH TIME AS	R 546	30
OF RIGHTEOUSNESS, LAID UP BY THE LORD JESUS, THE	559	13
BY HIM, AND THEN LAID BY HIM UPON THE COMMUNION	R 566	26
OF THE WORLD WERE LAID) HE HATH CONSTANTLY DECREED BY	606	07

LAIDEST

AND LAIDEST TROUBLE UPON OUR LOINS	418	02

LAIN

13 THOUGH YE HAVE LAIN AMONG THE SHEEP-FOLDS,	420	06

LAITY

AS WELL CLERGY AS LAITY, IN ALL THINGS TEMPORAL	610	39

LAKE

HE STOOD BY THE LAKE OF GENNESARET, AND SAW TWO SHIPS	196	07
AND SAW TWO SHIPS STANDING BY THE LAKE	196	08

LAMA

ELI, ELI, LAMA SABACHTHANI	137	18
ELOI, ELOI, LAMA SABACHTHANI	146	28

LAMB

O LORD GOD, LAMB OF GOD, SON OF THE FATHER, THAT	025	28
IS THE VERY PASCHAL LAMB, WHICH WAS OFFERED FOR US,	078	09
O LORD GOD, LAMB OF GOD, SON OF THE FATHER, THAT	084	08
AND, LO, A LAMB STOOD ON THE MOUNT SION,	102	29
WHICH FOLLOW THE LAMB WHITHERSOEVER HE GOETH	103	10
BEING THE FIRSTFRUITS UNTO GOD AND TO THE LAMB	103	12

LAMB   CONTINUED

BY THE BLOOD OF THE LAMB, AND BY THE WORD OF THEIR	252 14
AND BEFORE THE LAMB, CLOTHED WITH WHITE ROBES, AND	256 25
WHICH SITTETH UPON THE THRONE, AND UNTO THE LAMB	256 28
AND MADE THEM WHITE IN THE BLOOD OF THE LAMB	257 09
FOR THE LAMB WHICH IS IN THE MIDST OF THE THRONE	257 13
OF THAT IMMACULATE LAMB, THAT WAS SLAIN TO TAKE AWAY	317 17
O LAMB OF GOD, WHO TAKEST AWAY THE SINS OF THE WORLD	318 23
THINE OWN FOLD, A LAMB OF THINE OWN FLOCK, A SINNER	319 30
FOR THE LAMB WHICH IS IN THE MIDST OF THE THRONE	341 25
HE CAME TO BE THE LAMB WITHOUT SPOT, WHO, BY	605 33

LAMBS

SHALL GATHER THE LAMBS WITH HIS ARM, AND CARRY THEM	243 09
SEND YOU FORTH AS LAMBS AMONG WOLVES	254 17
SHALL GATHER THE LAMBS WITH HIS ARMS, AND CARRY THEM	338 13
OF THE LORD SHALL CONSUME AS THE FAT OF LAMBS	386 02
HE SAITH UNTO HIM, FEED MY LAMBS	551 17

LAME

AND THE LAME WALK, THE LEPERS ARE CLEANSED,	094 21
THE BLIND AND THE LAME CAME TO HIM IN THE TEMPLE	260 08

LAMENT

YE SHALL WEEP AND LAMENT, BUT THE WORLD SHALL	174 08

LAMENTATION

VOICE HEARD, LAMENTATION, AND WEEPING, AND GREAT	103 31
AND THERE WERE NO WIDOWS TO MAKE LAMENTATION	439 07

LAMENTED

BEWAILED AND LAMENTED HIM	154 13

LAMENTING

WE, WORTHILY LAMENTING OUR SINS AND ACKNOWLEDGING OUR	124 14

LAMPS

THERE WERE SEVEN LAMPS OF FIRE BURNING BEFORE THE	187 13

LAND

AND HIS HANDS PREPARED THE DRY LAND	009 12
HAVE MERCY UPON THIS WHOLE LAND	032 05
OF JUSTICE AND THE MAGISTRATES IN ALL THIS LAND	036 02
GIVEN US THIS GOOD LAND FOR OUR HERITAGE	036 09
BLESS OUR LAND WITH HONOURABLE INDUSTRY, SOUND	036 12
THAT OUR LAND MAY GIVE HER INCREASE	040 10
INHABITANTS OF OUR LAND MAY LIVE IN PEACE AND QUIETNESS	042 10
BY GOD IN THIS LAND, WHEREOF WE ARE MEMBERS	047 12
THE YOUTH OF THIS LAND, YE SHALL PRAY FOR ALL	047 33
ALL WHO TRAVEL BY LAND, SEA, OR AIR	048 05
UNTO US, THAT OUR LAND MAY YIELD US HER FRUITS OF	057 03
ALL WHO TRAVEL BY LAND, BY WATER, OR BY AIR, ALL	056 31
MAY BE LONG IN THE LAND WHICH THE LORD THY GOD GIVETH	069 03
AND GO INTO THE LAND OF ISRAEL	107 15
AND CAME INTO THE LAND OF ISRAEL	107 17
IN THE LAND OF JUDA, ART NOT THE LEAST	109 08
UNTO HIM ALL THE LAND OF JUDAEA, AND THEY OF	112 10
OVER ALL THE LAND UNTO THE NINTH HOUR	137 16
OVER THE WHOLE LAND UNTIL THE NINTH HOUR	146 26
HE DID BOTH IN THE LAND OF THE JEWS, AND IN	166 23
HE DID BOTH IN THE LAND OF THE JEWS, AND IN	184 10
THAT HE WOULD THRUST OUT A LITTLE FROM THE LAND	196 12
THEIR SHIPS TO LAND, THEY FORSOOK ALL, AND FOLLOWED	196 29
THERE AROSE A MIGHTY FAMINE IN THAT LAND	202 05
THE FAME HEREOF WENT ABROAD INTO ALL THAT LAND	224 30
ISRAEL OUT OF THE LAND OF EGYPT	225 17
AND THEY SHALL DWELL IN THEIR OWN LAND	225 20
BLESSING UPON THIS LAND, AND TO GIVE US A FRUITFUL	261 30
CAUSE THE EVIL BEASTS TO CEASE OUT OF THE LAND	262 05
BE SAFE IN THEIR LAND, AND SHALL KNOW THAT I AM THE	262 11
THE BEAST OF THE LAND DEVOUR THEM	262 15
WITH HUNGER IN THE LAND, NEITHER BEAR THE SHAME OF	262 19
THE PEOPLE OF THIS LAND MAY HAVE GRACE TO MAINTAIN	263 19
STRANGERS IN THE LAND OF EGYPT	263 28
TO US, THAT OUR LAND MAY STILL YIELD HER INCREASE, TO	265 15
ENTRANCE INTO THE LAND OF LIGHT AND JOY, IN THE	268 24
MAY BE LONG IN THE LAND WHICH THE LORD THY GOD GIVETH	287 02
OF THE LORD IN THE LAND OF THE LIVING	326 29
ENTRANCE INTO THE LAND OF LIGHT AND JOY, IN THE	334 16
AND THE HEATHEN ARE PERISHED OUT OF THE LAND	354 12
AND HIS SEED SHALL INHERIT THE LAND	370 11
OF THE LORD IN THE LAND OF THE LIVING	372 28
WORDS AGAINST THEM THAT ARE QUIET IN THE LAND	383 04
DWELL IN THE LAND, AND VERILY THOU SHALT BE FED	384 30
THOSE SHALL INHERIT THE LAND	385 12
AS ARE BLESSED OF GOD, SHALL POSSESS THE LAND	386 06
SHALL INHERIT THE LAND, *	386 24
THAT THOU SHALT POSSESS THE LAND	387 02
THEE FROM THE LAND OF JORDAN, FROM HERMON AND THE	393 16
THEY GAT NOT THE LAND IN POSSESSION THROUGH THEIR OWN	394 27
THEE OUT OF THE LAND OF THE LIVING	404 30
THOU HAST MOVED THE LAND, AND DIVIDED IT	412 15
IN A BARREN AND DRY LAND WHERE NO WATER IS	414 28
THE SEA INTO DRY LAND, *	417 26
THE MORIANS' LAND SHALL SOON STRETCH OUT HER HANDS	421 19
THEY BURNT UP ALL THE HOUSES OF GOD IN THE LAND	430 23
IN THE LAND OF EGYPT, *	435 25

LAND   CONTINUED

CAUSED THEIR LAND TO BE DIVIDED AMONG THEM FOR AN	438 22
FLESH OF THY SAINTS UNTO THE BEASTS OF THE LAND	440 03
AND WHEN IT HAD TAKEN ROOT, IT FILLED THE LAND	441 21
HE CAME OUT OF THE LAND OF EGYPT, AND HAD HEARD A	442 21
THEE OUT OF THE LAND OF EGYPT	442 34
THOU ART BECOME GRACIOUS UNTO THY LAND	446 08
THAT GLORY MAY DWELL IN OUR LAND	446 26
AND OUR LAND SHALL GIVE HER INCREASE	446 32
IN THE LAND WHERE ALL THINGS ARE FORGOTTEN	449 21
AND HIS HANDS PREPARED THE DRY LAND	459 14
ARE FAITHFUL IN THE LAND, *	463 30
SOON DESTROY ALL THE UNGODLY THAT ARE IN THE LAND	464 05
WILL I GIVE THE LAND OF CANAAN, *	470 24
AND THEY STRANGERS IN THE LAND	470 27
A DEARTH UPON THE LAND, *	471 04
A STRANGER IN THE LAND OF HAM	471 19
AND WONDERS IN THE LAND OF HAM	471 27
30 THEIR LAND BROUGHT FORTH FROGS	471 32
AND FLAMES OF FIRE IN THEIR LAND	472 03
THE GRASS IN THEIR LAND, AND DEVOURED THE FRUIT OF	472 08
35 HE SMOTE ALL THE FIRSTBORN IN THEIR LAND	472 09
WORKS IN THE LAND OF HAM	474 12
OF THAT PLEASANT LAND, *	474 17
AND THE LAND WAS DEFILED WITH BLOOD	475 13
34 A FRUITFUL LAND MAKETH HE BARREN, *	478 14
THEY MAY SOW THEIR LAND, AND PLANT VINEYARDS,	478 20
IN THE LAND OF THE LIVING	487 06
OF THEE, O THOU LAND OF EGYPT	510 21
12 AND GAVE THEIR LAND TO BE AN HERITAGE, *	510 26
AND GAVE AWAY THEIR LAND FOR AN HERITAGE	512 24
IN A STRANGE LAND	513 12
MY PORTION IN THE LAND OF THE LIVING	518 15
MY SOUL GASPETH UNTO THEE AS A THIRSTY LAND	519 03
ME FORTH INTO THE LAND OF RIGHTEOUSNESS	519 14
THEE OUT OF THE LAND OF EGYPT, OUT OF THE HOUSE OF	578 24
MAY BE LONG IN THE LAND WHICH THE LORD THY GOD GIVETH	579 14
THOSE WHO TRAVEL BY LAND OR BY SEA	600 06

LANDS

O BE JOYFUL IN THE LORD, ALL YE LANDS	015 04
YOURSELVES JOYFUL UNTO THE LORD, ALL YE LANDS	027 13
OPENING HEATHEN LANDS TO THE LIGHT OF THY TRUTH	038 17
TO BLESS THE LANDS AND MULTIPLY THE HARVESTS OF THE	040 08
OR CHILDREN, OR LANDS, FOR MY NAME'S SAKE, SHALL	231 20
4 THEIR SOUND IS GONE OUT INTO ALL LANDS	363 19
WHOM THOU MAYEST MAKE PRINCES IN ALL LANDS	397 20
AND CALL THE LANDS AFTER THEIR OWN NAMES	400 28
O BE JOYFUL IN GOD, ALL YE LANDS	417 15
YOURSELVES JOYFUL UNTO THE LORD, ALL YE LANDS	462 02
O BE JOYFUL IN THE LORD, ALL YE LANDS	463 05
AND GAVE THEM THE LANDS OF THE HEATHEN	472 25
AND TO SCATTER THEM IN THE LANDS	474 24
THEM OUT OF THE LANDS, FROM THE EAST, AND FROM THE	476 10

LANES

THE STREETS AND LANES OF THE CITY, AND BRING IN	192 14

LANGUAGE

EVERY MAN HEARD THEM SPEAK IN HIS OWN LANGUAGE	180 28
3 THERE IS NEITHER SPEECH NOR LANGUAGE	363 17
AND HAD HEARD A STRANGE LANGUAGE	442 22

LANTERN

THY WORD IS A LANTERN UNTO MY FEET, *	497 07
HAVE ORDAINED A LANTERN FOR MINE ANOINTED	509 09

LARGE

HE WILL SHEW YOU A LARGE UPPER ROOM FURNISHED AND	140 31
SHALL SHEW YOU A LARGE UPPER ROOM FURNISHED	148 31
YE SEE HOW LARGE A LETTER I HAVE WRITTEN UNTO YOU	210 23
SET MY FEET IN A LARGE ROOM	376 07
AND THE LORD HEARD ME AT LARGE	488 09

LARGELY

COMFORT, AS MORE LARGELY IS EXPRESSED IN THE HOMILY	605 09

LARGER

HIM THE GATES OF LARGER LIFE, THOU WILT RECEIVE HIM	598 08

LASCIVIOUSNESS

LASCIVIOUSNESS, IDOLATRY, WITCHCRAFT, HATRED,	209 20
OVER UNTO LASCIVIOUSNESS, TO WORK ALL UNCLEANNESS	216 08

LAST

SO THAT AT THE LAST WE MAY COME TO HIS ETERNAL JOY	007 17
SO THAT AT THE LAST WE MAY COME TO HIS ETERNAL JOY	024 19
UPON TO GIVE AT THE LAST GREAT DAY	047 20
THAT IN THE LAST DAY, WHEN HE SHALL COME AGAIN IN HIS	090 15
HATH IN THESE LAST DAYS SPOKEN UNTO US BY HIS SON,	096 24
BEGINNING FROM THE LAST UNTO THE FIRST	119 31
THESE LAST HAVE WROUGHT BUT ONE HOUR, AND	120 04
WILL GIVE UNTO THIS LAST, EVEN AS UNTO THEE	120 09
SO THE LAST SHALL BE FIRST, AND THE FIRST LAST	120 12
SO THE LAST SHALL BE FIRST, AND THE FIRST LAST	120 12
AND THE LAST STATE OF THAT MAN IS WORSE THAN THE	130 16

LAST   CONTINUED

SO THE LAST ERROR SHALL BE WORSE THAN THE FIRST   162 22
AND LAST OF ALL HE WAS SEEN OF ME ALSO, AS OF ONE   205 11
BUT MANY THAT ARE FIRST SHALL BE LAST   231 22
AND THE LAST SHALL BE FIRST   231 22
AT REST, MAY AT THE LAST ENTER WITH THEM INTO THINE   268 18
IT UP AGAIN AT THE LAST DAY   269 19
RAISE HIM UP AT THE LAST DAY   269 22
AND AT LAST DIDST SEND HIM SEASONABLE RELIEF   315 26
WITH THE SICK, AND LAST OF ALL TO THE SICK PERSON   R 323 02
THE LAST ENEMY THAT SHALL BE DESTROYED IS DEATH   328 30
THE LAST ADAM WAS MADE A QUICKENING SPIRIT   329 24
OF AN EYE, AT THE LAST TRUMP   330 03
US NOT, AT OUR LAST HOUR, FOR ANY PAINS OF DEATH, TO   332 31
RESURRECTION IN THE LAST DAY, WE MAY BE FOUND   335 08
ON EARTH, MAY AT LAST, TOGETHER WITH THEM, BE FOUND   335 32
FOR THAT SHALL BRING A MAN PEACE AT THE LAST   387 09
THEY SHALL BE ROOTED OUT AT THE LAST   387 12
AND AT THE LAST I SPAKE WITH MY TONGUE   389 13
O LORD, AT THE LAST, *   454 15
AFTER THE LAST COLLECT, AND IMMEDIATELY BEFORE   R 534 28
AFTER THE LAST COLLECT, AND IMMEDIATELY BEFORE   R 547 02
HE MAY AT LAST BE RECEIVED INTO EVERLASTING   558 05
AND PEACE, AND AT LAST BE NUMBERED WITH THY SAINTS IN 574 18
AND A HOLY REST, AND PEACE AT THE LAST   595 03
ALL MEN AT THE LAST DAY   603 24

LATCHET

WHOSE SHOE'S LATCHET I AM NOT WORTHY TO UNLOOSE   096 05
I AFTER ME, THE LATCHET OF WHOSE SHOES I AM NOT   112 15

LATE

FOR THY LATE MERCIES VOUCHSAFED UNTO THEM   019 19
FOR THY LATE MERCIES VOUCHSAFED UNTO THEM   033 17
HUMBLED US BY THY LATE VISITATION OF US WITH   051 22
UP EARLY, AND SO LATE TAKE REST, AND EAT THE BREAD OF 505 27

LATELY

WHICH HAVE BEEN LATELY RAISED UP AMONGST US   052 21

LATIN

OF GREEK, AND LATIN, AND HEBREW, THIS IS THE KING OF   154 33
IT WAS WRITTEN IN HEBREW, AND GREEK, AND LATIN   160 06

LATTER

IN ADVENT, THE LATTER PORTION THEREOF MAY BE OMITTED R 014 05
FORMER AND THE LATTER RAIN DESCEND UPON THE EARTH,   051 16
STAND AT THE LATTER DAY UPON THE EARTH   324 10
AT THE LATTER DAY   555 33
AT THE LATTER DAY HE MAY RECEIVE THE CROWN OF   559 12

LAUD

OF HEAVEN, WE LAUD AND MAGNIFY THY GLORIOUS NAME   077 05
OF HEAVEN, WE LAUD AND MAGNIFY THY GLORIOUS NAME   079 29
AND LAUD HIM, ALL YE PEOPLE   092 29
O PRAISE THE LORD, LAUD YE THE NAME OF THE LORD   510 03

LAUDABLE

THEE TRUE AND LAUDABLE SERVICE   207 14

LAUGH

IN HEAVEN SHALL LAUGH THEM TO SCORN   346 04
THEY THAT SEE ME LAUGH ME TO SCORN   366 16
13 THE LORD SHALL LAUGH HIM TO SCORN   385 20
AND SHALL LAUGH HIM TO SCORN   404 32
AND THOU SHALT LAUGH ALL THE HEATHEN TO SCORN   411 21
SEETH THEM SHALL LAUGH THEM TO SCORN   416 03
THAT THEY SHALL LAUGH AND SING   417 12
AND OUR ENEMIES LAUGH US TO SCORN   441 15

LAUGHED

AND THEY LAUGHED HIM TO SCORN   224 27
TO BE LAUGHED TO SCORN, AND HAD IN DERISION OF THEM   395 20

LAUGHTER

FILLED WITH LAUGHTER, *   505 09

LAUNCH

SAID UNTO SIMON, LAUNCH OUT INTO THE DEEP, AND LET   196 14

LAW

GRACIOUS AND WHOSE LAW IS TRUTH   035 24
ADMINISTER THE LAW IN THE FEAR OF THEE ALONE   036 05
OBEDIENCE TO THY LAW, WE MAY SHOW FORTH THY PRAISE   036 20
GRACE TO KEEP THE LAW FOR THE TIME TO COME   R 067 25
THE SUMMARY OF THE LAW, BEGINNING, HEAR WHAT OUR LORD R 067 30
AND INCLINE OUR HEARTS TO KEEP THIS LAW   068 07
AND INCLINE OUR HEARTS TO KEEP THIS LAW   069 06
HANG ALL THE LAW AND THE PROPHETS   069 31
FOR HE THAT LOVETH ANOTHER HATH FULFILLED THE LAW   090 24
THEREFORE LOVE IS THE FULFILLING OF THE LAW   090 30
MADE UNDER THE LAW, TO REDEEM THEM THAT WERE UNDER   104 20
THAT WERE UNDER THE LAW, THAT WE MIGHT RECEIVE THE   104 21

LAW   CONTINUED

AND OBEDIENT TO THE LAW FOR MAN   105 20
COMMITTETH SIN TRANSGRESSETH ALSO THE LAW   117 22
FOR SIN IS THE TRANSGRESSION OF THE LAW   117 23
TO BE UNDER THE LAW, DO YE NOT HEAR THE LAW   130 29
TO BE UNDER THE LAW, DO YE NOT HEAR THE LAW   130 30
ACCORDING TO THE LAW, HE TOOK THE BLOOD OF CALVES AND 147 20
THINGS ARE BY THE LAW PURGED WITH BLOOD   147 25
THE LAW HAVING A SHADOW OF GOOD THINGS TO COME,   157 15
WHICH ARE OFFERED BY THE LAW   157 31
WE HAVE A LAW, AND BY OUR LAW HE OUGHT TO DIE,   159 09
A LAW, AND BY OUR LAW HE OUGHT TO DIE, BECAUSE HE   159 09
BE JUSTIFIED BY THE LAW OF MOSES   169 22
WERE WRITTEN IN THE LAW OF MOSES, AND IN THE   170 09
INTO THE PERFECT LAW OF LIBERTY, AND CONTINUETH   176 10
GOD IN CHRIST, THE LAW, WHICH WAS FOUR HUNDRED AND   207 23
BE OF THE LAW, IT IS NO MORE OF PROMISE   207 25
WHEREFORE THEN SERVETH THE LAW   207 27
IS THE LAW THEN AGAINST THE PROMISES OF GOD   207 31
IF THERE HAD BEEN A LAW GIVEN WHICH COULD HAVE GIVEN   207 32
VERILY RIGHTEOUSNESS SHOULD HAVE BEEN BY THE LAW   208 03
HE SAID UNTO HIM, WHAT IS WRITTEN IN THE LAW   208 14
YE BE LED OF THE SPIRIT, YE ARE NOT UNDER THE LAW   209 19
AGAINST SUCH THERE IS NO LAW   209 28
THEY THEMSELVES WHO ARE CIRCUMCISED KEEP THE LAW   210 28
WHICH IS THE GREAT COMMANDMENT IN THE LAW   215 10
HANG ALL THE LAW AND THE PROPHETS   215 15
ACCORDING TO THE LAW OF MOSES WERE ACCOMPLISHED,   232 24
IT IS WRITTEN IN THE LAW OF THE LORD, EVERY MALE THAT 232 26
WHICH IS SAID IN THE LAW OF THE LORD, A PAIR OF   232 28
THE CUSTOM OF THE LAW, THEN TOOK HE HIM UP IN HIS   233 04
ACCORDING TO THE LAW OF THE LORD, THEY RETURNED INTO   233 24
IS WRITTEN IN THEIR LAW, THEY HATED ME WITHOUT A   255 29
INTO THE PERFECT LAW OF LIBERTY, AND CONTINUETH   266 02
AND INCLINE OUR HEARTS TO KEEP THIS LAW   286 07
AND INCLINE OUR HEARTS TO KEEP THIS LAW   287 05
AND THE STRENGTH OF SIN IS THE LAW   330 12
DELIGHT IS IN THE LAW OF THE LORD   345 12
AND IN HIS LAW WILL HE EXERCISE HIMSELF DAY AND   345 11
LORD IS AN UNDEFILED LAW, CONVERTING THE SOUL   363 27
7 THE LAW OF THE LORD IS AN UNDEFILED LAW, CONVERTING 363 27
32 THE LAW OF HIS GOD IS IN HIS HEART, *   386 28
THY LAW IS WITHIN MY HEART   390 33
HEAR MY LAW, O MY PEOPLE   434 27
AND GAVE ISRAEL A LAW, *   435 05
AND WOULD NOT WALK IN HIS LAW   435 21
AND A LAW OF THE GOD OF JACOB   442 18
CHILDREN FORSAKE MY LAW, *   452 02
AND TEACHEST HIM IN THY LAW   458 11
WHICH IMAGINETH MISCHIEF AS A LAW   458 27
AND THE LAW THAT HE GAVE THEM   462 31
UNTO JACOB FOR A LAW, *   470 22
AND WALK IN THE LAW OF THE LORD   489 32
THAT I MAY SEE THE WONDROUS THINGS OF THY LAW   491 03
AND CAUSE THOU ME TO MAKE MUCH OF THY LAW   491 26
GIVE ME UNDERSTANDING, AND I SHALL KEEP THY LAW   492 07
44 SO SHALL I ALWAY KEEP THY LAW   492 28
YET HAVE I NOT SHRINKED FROM THY LAW   493 13
FOR THE UNGODLY THAT FORSAKE THY LAW   493 17
AND HAVE KEPT THY LAW   493 21
I HAVE PROMISED TO KEEP THY LAW   493 25
BUT I HAVE NOT FORGOTTEN THY LAW   494 03
BUT MY DELIGHT HATH BEEN IN THY LAW   494 21
72 THE LAW OF THY MOUTH IS DEARER UNTO ME *   494 24
FOR THY LAW IS MY DELIGHT   495 10
WHICH ARE NOT AFTER THY LAW   495 28
HAD NOT BEEN IN THY LAW, *   496 09
WHAT LOVE HAVE I UNTO THY LAW   496 20
YET DO I NOT FORGET THY LAW   497 16
BUT THY LAW DO I LOVE   497 24
FOR THEY HAVE DESTROYED THY LAW   498 22
BECAUSE MEN KEEP NOT THY LAW   499 11
AND THY LAW IS THE TRUTH   499 24
AND ARE FAR FROM THY LAW   500 11
FOR I DO NOT FORGET THY LAW   500 18
BECAUSE THEY KEEP NOT THY LAW   500 28
BUT THY LAW DO I LOVE   501 07
IS THE PEACE THAT THEY HAVE WHO LOVE THY LAW   501 12
AND IN THY LAW IS MY DELIGHT   501 31
HE HATH GIVEN THEM A LAW WHICH SHALL NOT BE BROKEN   524 17
AS WELL UNDER THE LAW AS UNDER THE GOSPEL, MOVED   564 11
THE LAW WAS GIVEN BY MOSES   571 32
FILL MY MEMORY WITH THE WORDS OF THY LAW   573 16
HEARTS TO KEEP THY LAW, AND GUIDE OUR FEET INTO THE   594 14
ALTHOUGH THE LAW GIVEN FROM GOD BY MOSES, AS TOUCHING 604 19
NOT SUBJECT TO THE LAW OF GOD   604 38
BE SAVED BY THE LAW OR SECT WHICH HE PROFESSETH, SO   606 33
ACCORDING TO THAT LAW, AND THE LIGHT OF NATURE   606 34
COMMANDED BY GOD'S LAW, EITHER TO VOW THE ESTATE OF   609 21

LAW-GIVER

JUDAH IS MY LAW-GIVER   412 26

LAWFUL

SEAS UPON THEIR LAWFUL OCCASIONS   042 10
IS IT NOT LAWFUL FOR ME TO DO WHAT I WILL WITH MINE   120 10
IS IT NOT LAWFUL FOR ME TO PUT THEM INTO THE   135 09
IS IT LAWFUL TO HEAL ON THE SABBATH DAY   214 02
IS IT LAWFUL TO GIVE TRIBUTE UNTO CAESAR, OR NOT   223 04
THEIR MARRIAGE IS NOT LAWFUL   300 30
THE THING THAT IS LAWFUL AND RIGHT   498 11
THEREUNTO BY LAWFUL AUTHORITY   529 18
OR TAKEN TO BE A LAWFUL BISHOP, PRIEST, OR DEACON,   529 20

LAWFUL   CONTINUED

AND WITH SUCH LAWFUL DIRECTIONS AS YOU SHALL AT ANY	569 21
AND YET IT IS NOT LAWFUL FOR THE CHURCH TO ORDAIN ANY	607 04
IT IS NOT LAWFUL FOR ANY MAN TC TAKE UPON HIM THE	607 19
THEREFORE IT IS LAWFUL	609 22

LAWFULLY

THEY MAY NOT LAWFULLY BE JOINED TOGETHER, LET HIM NOW	300 21
YE MAY NOT BE LAWFULLY JOINED TOGETHER IN MATRIMONY,	300 27
THAT THEY ARE LAWFULLY CALLED TO THEIR FUNCTION AND	536 25
THOU SHALT BE LAWFULLY APPOINTED THEREUNTO	546 27
BEFORE HE BE LAWFULLY CALLED, AND SENT TO EXECUTE THE	607 20
OUGHT TO JUDGE LAWFULLY CALLED AND SENT, WHICH BE	607 21
AND LAWFULLY CONSECRATED AND ORDERED	610 36

LAWFULNESS

DOUBT OF THE LAWFULNESS OF THE PROPOSED MARRIAGE, MAY R 301 02	

LAWGIVER

JUDAH IS MY LAWGIVER	479 21

LAWS

WE HAVE OFFENDED AGAINST THY HOLY LAWS	006 20
TO WALK IN HIS LAWS WHICH HE SET BEFORE US	022 08
WE HAVE OFFENDED AGAINST THY HOLY LAWS	023 27
A HOLY TRUST IN THEE, AND OBEDIENCE TO THY LAWS	053 27
CONSTITUTION AND LAWS O THEIR COUNTRY	VI 13
WRITE ALL THESE THY LAWS IN OUR HEARTS, WE BESEECH	069 23
IN THE WAYS OF THY LAWS, AND IN THE WORKS OF THY	070 08
I WILL PUT MY LAWS INTO THEIR HEARTS, AND IN	158 12
WRITE ALL THESE THY LAWS IN OUR HEARTS, WE BESEECH	287 23
IN THE WAYS OF THY LAWS, AND IN THE WORKS OF THY	298 28
PEACE TOGETHER, AND LIVE ACCORDING TO THY LAWS	303 11
THE LAWS RESPECTING MATRIMONY, WHETHER BY	R 304 17
DIRECTION OF THOSE LAWS, IN EVERY THING THAT REGARDS	R 304 19
AN EYE UNTO ALL THY LAWS, *	361 11
DOST THOU PREACH MY LAWS, AND TAKEST MY COVENANT IN	402 23
AND OBSERVE HIS LAWS	472 28
NEITHER HAVE THE HEATHEN KNOWLEDGE OF HIS LAWS	524 03
WITH THE USAGES, LAWS, OR CHARTERS OF THE CHURCH IN	R 569 11
OUR MANIFOLD TRANSGRESSIONS OF THY RIGHTEOUS LAWS	589 32
OBEDIENCE TO HIS LAWS, THROUGH WHOSE MERITS AND	591 22
CONSTITUTION AND LAWS OF ENGLAND ARE CONSIDERED AS	R 610 26

LAWYER

BEHOLD, A CERTAIN LAWYER STOOD UP, AND TEMPTED HIM,	208 11
WHICH WAS A LAWYER, ASKED HIM A QUESTION,	215 08

LAWYERS

SPAKE UNTO THE LAWYERS AND PHARISEES, SAYING, IS IT	214 02

LAY

GRACE SERIOUSLY TO LAY TO HEART THE GREAT DANGERS WE	037 27
THAT THEY MAY LAY HANDS SUDDENLY ON NO MAN,	038 29
LAY NOT UP FOR YOURSELVES TREASURES UPON EARTH,	072 07
BUT LAY UP FOR YOURSELVES TREASURES IN HEAVEN, WHERE	072 09
C) AND HERE TO LAY HIS HAND UPON ALL THE BREAD	R 080 32
AND HERE HE IS TO LAY HIS HAND UPON EVERY VESSEL IN	R 080 34
WHO LAY IN DARKNESS AND THE SHADOW OF DEATH	086 09
A LOUD VOICE, LORD, LAY NOT THIS SIN TO THEIR CHARGE	100 15
LAY NOT UP FOR YOURSELVES TREASURES UPON EARTH, WHERE	125 16
BUT LAY UP FOR YOURSELVES TREASURES IN HEAVEN, WHERE	125 18
WHICH LAY BOUND WITH THEM THAT HAD MADE	145 14
AND I LAY DOWN MY LIFE FOR THE SHEEP	172 29
WHEREFORE LAY APART ALL FILTHINESS AND SUPERFLUITY OF	175 02
AND WE OUGHT TO LAY DOWN OUR LIVES FOR THE BRETHREN	191 17
AND SHALL LAY THEE EVEN WITH THE GROUND,	204 12
BUT COME AND LAY THY HAND UPON HER, AND SHE SHALL	224 15
THAT A MAN LAY DOWN HIS LIFE FOR HIS FRIENDS	241 27
OF WITNESSES, LET US LAY ASIDE EVERY WEIGHT, AND THE	258 21
WHEREFORE LAY APART ALL FILTHINESS AND SUPERFLUITY OF	265 26
THE BISHOP, HE SHALL LAY HIS HAND UPON THE HEAD OF	R 297 24
THEE WITH OIL (OR I LAY MY HAND UPON THEE), IN THE	320 15
9 I WILL LAY ME DOWN IN PEACE, AND TAKE MY REST	347 28
UPON THE EARTH, AND LAY MINE HONOUR IN THE DUST	349 34
WORSHIP SHALT THOU LAY UPON HIM	365 14
2 LAY HAND UPON THE SHIELD AND BUCKLER, *	381 20
MY STEPS, WHEN THEY LAY WAIT FOR MY SOUL	408 27
HOW THEY MAY LAY SNARES	415 28
AND THEY THAT LAY WAIT FOR MY SOUL TAKE THEIR COUNSEL	425 26
WHERE SHE MAY LAY HER YOUNG	445 12
AND LAY THEM DOWN IN THEIR DENS	469 05
FOR THEE, LORD, TO LAY TO THINE HAND	498 21
THE BISHOP SHALL LAY HIS HANDS SEVERALLY UPON THE	R 534 02
AND I LAY DOWN MY LIFE FOR THE SHEEP	539 18
SHALL LAY HIS HANDS SEVERALLY UPON THE	R 546 06
PRESENT SHALL LAY THEIR HANDS UPON THE HEAD OF THE	R 558 09
FOR HIS SAKE WHO LAY DOWN IN THE GRAVE, AND ROSE	587 26

LAY-PEOPLE

OF THE LORD IS NOT TO BE DENIED TO THE LAY-PEOPLE	609 10

LAYETH

HATH FOUND IT, HE LAYETH IT ON HIS SHOULDERS,	193 21
OF THE WICKED LAYETH SIEGE AGAINST ME	367 05
AND LAYETH UP THE DEEP, AS IN A TREASURE-HOUSE	378 32

LAYETH   CONTINUED

3 WHO LAYETH THE BEAMS OF HIS CHAMBERS IN THE WATERS,	467 29

LAYING

THROUGH THE LAYING ON OF HANDS, THAT, DRAWING NEAR	043 22
LAYING ASIDE ALL MALICE, AND ALL GUILE, AND	259 25
PROVIDES THE LAYING ON OF HANDS, OR CONFIRMATION,	291 23
TO RECEIVE THE LAYING ON OF HANDS	296 09
ANOINTING OR LAYING ON OF HANDS, THE MINISTER MAY USE R 320 06	
OF THE SAME, LAYING ASIDE THE STUDY OF THE WORLD AND	542 28
NOT BE HASTY IN LAYING ON HANDS, AND ADMITTING ANY	554 09
OR LAYING HANDS UPON OTHERS	555 21

LAZARUS

BEGGAR NAMED LAZARUS, WHICH WAS LAID AT HIS GATE,	190 05
AFAR OFF, AND LAZARUS IN HIS BOSOM	190 12
ON ME, AND SEND LAZARUS, THAT HE MAY DIP THE TIP CF	190 14
AND LIKEWISE LAZARUS EVIL THINGS	190 17

LEAD

THAT THEY MAY LEAD ME, AND BRING ME UNTO THY HOLY	003 22
AND LEAD US NOT INTO TEMPTATION, BUT DELIVER US FROM	007 27
AND ENABLE HIM TO LEAD THE RESIDUE OF HIS LIFE IN THY	045 19
THE PEOPLE 'MAY LEAD QUIET AND PEACEABLE LIVES,	VI 21
AND INTEND TO LEAD A NEW LIFE, FOLLOWING THE	075 10
TEACH THEM, AND TO LEAD THEM INTO ALL TRUTH	078 28
SO DIDST THOU LEAD THY PEOPLE, TO MAKE THYSELF A	139 16
TAKE HIM, AND LEAD HIM AWAY SAFELY	142 19
FROM ALL ERROR, AND LEAD US INTO ALL TRUTH	183 25
CAN THE BLIND LEAD THE BLIND	195 03
THINGS HURTFUL, AND LEAD US TO ALL THINGS PROFITABLE	210 20
AND SHALL GENTLY LEAD THOSE THAT ARE WITH YOUNG	243 10
AND SHALL LEAD THEM UNTO LIVING FOUNTAINS OF	257 15
THIS PERSON) MAY LEAD THE REST OF HIS LIFE ACCORDING	280 17
STEDFAST PURPOSE TO LEAD A NEW LIFE	293 27
AND SO LEAD THEM IN THE KNOWLEDGE AND OBEDIENCE CF	298 21
THAT THEY MAY LEAD ME, AND BRING ME UNTO THY HOLY	310 11
LET THY HOLY SPIRIT LEAD US IN HOLINESS AND	316 28
AND LEAD ME FORTH BESIDE THE WATERS OF COMFORT	338 19
AND SHALL LEAD THEM UNTO LIVING FOUNTAINS OF	341 26
8 LEAD ME, O LORD, IN THY RIGHTEOUSNESS, BECAUSE OF	348 16
AND LEAD ME FORTH BESIDE THE WATERS OF COMFORT	368 12
4 LEAD ME FORTH IN THY TRUTH, AND LEARN ME	369 25
AND LEAD ME IN THE RIGHT WAY, BECAUSE OF MINE	372 22
ALSO MY GUIDE, AND LEAD ME FOR THY NAME'S SAKE	375 28
THAT THEY MAY LEAD ME, *	394 10
9 WHO WILL LEAD ME INTO THE STRONG CITY	412 29
10 WHO WILL LEAD ME INTO THE STRONG CITY	479 24
THE LORD SHALL LEAD THEM FORTH WITH THE EVIL DOERS	505 03
ALSO SHALL THY HAND LEAD ME, *	515 06
AND LEAD ME IN THE WAY EVERLASTING	516 07
THY LOVING SPIRIT LEAD ME FORTH INTO THE LAND OF	519 13
PURPOSING TO LEAD A NEW LIFE	582 23

LEADERS

WITH THE LEADERS OF THE HEATHEN, SO THAT THEY	421 15

LEADEST

THOU THAT LEADEST JOSEPH LIKE A FLOCK	441 03

LEADETH

WISDOM WHICH LEADETH TO ETERNAL LIFE	045 09
BY NAME, AND LEADETH THEM OUT	186 05
IN THE WAY THAT LEADETH TO ETERNAL LIFE	239 02
IRON GATE THAT LEADETH UNTO THE CITY	245 22
2 EVEN HE THAT LEADETH AN UNCORRUPT LIFE, *	357 07
9 WHOSO LEADETH A GODLY LIFE, *	463 32
BY NAME, AND LEADETH THEM OUT	538 28

LEADING

LEADING A QUIET AND PEACEABLE LIFE IN ALL	052 24
WHO BY THE LEADING OF A STAR DIDST MANIFEST THY	107 29
NO LEADING INTO CAPTIVITY, AND NO COMPLAINING IN CUR	520 22
DIVINE WORD, IN LEADING THE DEVOTIONS OF THE PEOPLE,	571 26

LEAF

4 HIS LEAF ALSO SHALL NOT WITHER	345 14

LEAN

THAT THEY WHO DO LEAN ONLY UPON THE HOPE OF THY	115 30

LEANED

WHICH ALSO LEANED ON HIS BREAST AT SUPPER, AND SAID,	102 05

LEANNESS

AND SENT LEANNESS WITHAL INTO THEIR SOUL	473 31

LEAP

OF MY GOD I SHALL LEAP OVER THE WALL	361 27

LEARN

BLESS ALL WHO TEACH AND ALL WHO LEARN	042 26

LEARN   CONTINUED

AND THOSE WHO LEARN, THAT, REJOICING IN THE KNOWLEDGE	043	03
READ, MARK, LEARN, AND INWARDLY DIGEST THEM,	092	09
HOLY GHOST, MAY LEARN TO LOVE AND BLESS OUR	099	30
AND NO MAN COULD LEARN THAT SONG BUT THE HUNDRED AND	103	06
YOKE UPON YOU, AND LEARN OF ME	235	12
BUT GO YE AND LEARN WHAT THAT MEANETH, I WILL HAVE	251	21
THAT THIS CHILD LEARN THE CREED, THE LORD'S PRAYER,	277	10
DO YOU CHIEFLY LEARN IN THESE ARTICLES OF YOUR	284	27
I LEARN TO BELIEVE IN GOD THE FATHER,	284	29
DO YOU CHIEFLY LEARN FROM THE TEN COMMANDMENTS	288	10
I LEARN TWO THINGS FROM THESE COMMANDMENTS	288	12
BUT TO LEARN AND LABOR TRULY TO EARN MINE CWN	289	09
WHICH YOU MUST LEARN AT ALL TIMES TO CALL FOR BY	289	16
IN THY TRUTH, AND LEARN ME	369	25
THEM SHALL HE LEARN HIS WAY	370	31
THAT I MAY LEARN THY STATUTES	494	23
THAT I MAY LEARN THY COMMANDMENTS	494	29
DOST THOU CHIEFLY LEARN IN THESE ARTICLES OF THY	578	09
I LEARN TO BELIEVE IN GOD THE FATHER,	578	11
DOST THOU CHIEFLY LEARN BY THESE COMMANDMENTS	579	21
I LEARN TWO THINGS	579	24
BUT TO LEARN AND LABOR TRULY TO GET MINE OWN LIVING,	580	12
WHICH THOU MUST LEARN AT ALL TIMES TO CALL FOR BY	580	19
ALL THAT IS HERE APPOINTED FOR THEM TO LEARN	R 582	35
WE MAY LEARN TO SERVE THEE WITH GLADNESS	596	20

LEARNED

YE HAVE NOT SO LEARNED CHRIST	216	10
AS YE ALSO LEARNED OF EPAPHRAS OUR DEAR	223	30
AND LEARNED THEIR WORKS	475	06
I SHALL HAVE LEARNED THE JUDGMENTS OF THY	490	13
AND OTHERWISE LEARNED AS THE CANONS REQUIRE, MAY,	529	29
WHO HAVE NOT LEARNED THEIR CATECHISM, TO COME TC THE	R 582	32
AS THEY HAVE LEARNED ALL THAT IS HERE APPOINTED FOR	R 582	34

LEARNING

SOUND LEARNING, AND PURE MANNERS	036	13
AND ALL GOOD LEARNING FLOURISH AND ABOUND	042	25
SOUND AND GODLY LEARNING, AND FOR ALL WHOSE HANDS ARE	047	34
AND USEFUL LEARNING MAY FOR EVER FLOURISH AND ABOUND	047	36
HOLY SCRIPTURES TO BE WRITTEN FOR OUR LEARNING	092	08
WRITTEN FOR OUR LEARNING, THAT WE THROUGH PATIENCE	092	16
FOR THEIR LEARNING AND GODLY CONVERSATION,	530	14
FOR THEIR LEARNING AND GODLY CONVERSATION,	536	15
IN READING AND LEARNING THE SCRIPTURES, AND IN	541	04
IN WHOSE LEARNING, DILIGENCE, SOUND DOCTRINE,	569	14
IN WORKS OF MERCY OR IN SCHOOLS OF GOOD LEARNING	600	04

LEAST

IT BE SAID AT LEAST ONE SUNDAY IN EACH MONTH	R 067	28
IT UNTO ONE OF THE LEAST OF THESE MY BRETHREN,	073	04
OR AT LEAST DECLARE HIMSELF TO BE IN FULL PURPOSE SO	R 085	07
AM LESS THAN THE LEAST OF ALL SAINTS, IS THIS GRACE	108	18
ART NOT THE LEAST AMONG THE PRINCES OF JUDA	109	08
EVEN THOU, AT LEAST IN THIS THY DAY, THE THINGS WHICH	204	08
FOR I AM THE LEAST OF THE APOSTLES, THAT AM NOT MEET	205	13
THAT AT THE LEAST THE SHADOW OF PETER PASSING BY	249	28
IT UNTO ONE OF THE LEAST OF THESE MY BRETHREN, YE	259	15
HIM AT THE FONT AT LEAST TWO WITNESSES	R 273	23

LEAVE

PEACE I LEAVE WITH YOU, MY PEACE I GIVE	049	06
AND REPENT, AND LEAVE A BLESSING BEHIND HIM	124	27
I LEAVE THE WORLD, AND GO TO THE FATHER	176	31
HIS OWN, AND SHALL LEAVE ME ALONE	177	06
WE BESEECH THEE, LEAVE US NOT COMFORTLESS	179	06
I WILL NOT LEAVE YOU COMFORTLESS	181	14
PEACE I LEAVE WITH YOU, MY PEACE I GIVE UNTO YOU	181	33
OF THEM, DOTH NOT LEAVE THE NINETY AND NINE IN THE	193	19
LEAVE THERE THY GIFT BEFORE THE ALTAR, AND GO THY	198	09
AND THEY SHALL NOT LEAVE IN THEE ONE STONE UPON	204	13
LEAVE US NOT, WE BESEECH THEE, DESTITUTE OF THY	240	30
CAUSE SHALL A MAN LEAVE HIS FATHER AND MOTHER,	267	29
CAUSE SHALL A MAN LEAVE FATHER AND MOTHER, AND SHALL	268	07
OF ABILITY, TO LEAVE BEQUESTS FOR RELIGIOUS AND	R 320	23
LEAVE ME NOT, NEITHER FORSAKE ME, O GOD OF MY	326	26
THOU SHALT NOT LEAVE MY SOUL IN HELL	358	10
AND LEAVE THE REST OF THEIR SUBSTANCE FOR THEIR	359	17
LEAVE ME NOT, NEITHER FORSAKE ME, O GOD OF MY	372	18
8 LEAVE OFF FROM WRATH, AND LET GO DISPLEASURE	385	09
THE LORD WILL NOT LEAVE HIM IN HIS HAND, *	386	32
AND FOOLISH, AND LEAVE THEIR RICHES FOR OTHER	400	24
THAT WE SHOULD LEAVE THE WORD OF GOD, AND SERVE	532	10

LEAVEN

NEITHER WITH THE LEAVEN OF MALICE AND WICKEDNESS	162	32
NOT WITH OLD LEAVEN, NEITHER WITH THE LEAVEN OF	162	32
NOT THAT A LITTLE LEAVEN LEAVENETH THE WHOLE LUMP	165	10
THEREFORE THE OLD LEAVEN, THAT YE MAY BE A NEW LUMP,	165	11
NOT WITH OLD LEAVEN, NEITHER WITH THE LEAVEN OF	165	14
NEITHER WITH THE LEAVEN OF MALICE AND WICKEDNESS	165	14
TO PUT AWAY THE LEAVEN OF MALICE AND WICKEDNESS,	170	21

LEAVENETH

LITTLE LEAVEN LEAVENETH THE WHOLE LUMP	165	10

LEAVETH

THEN THE DEVIL LEAVETH HIM, AND, BEHOLD, ANGELS CAME	127	11
WOLF COMING, AND LEAVETH THE SHEEP, AND FLEETH	172	24
WOLF COMING, AND LEAVETH THE SHEEP, AND FLEETH	539	13

LEAVING

SUFFERED FOR US, LEAVING US AN EXAMPLE, THAT YE	172	10
AND DEPARTED, LEAVING HIM HALF DEAD	208	23
SAINT JAMES, LEAVING HIS FATHER AND ALL THAT HE HAD,	246	17
THE MAN LEAVING THE RING UPON THE FOURTH	R 302	23

LEBANON

THE LORD BREAKETH THE CEDARS OF LEBANON	374	08
LEBANON ALSO, AND SIRION, LIKE A YOUNG UNICORN	374	09
THE FRUIT THEREOF SHALL SHAKE LIKE LEBANON	427	30
AND SHALL SPREAD ABROAD LIKE A CEDAR IN LEBANON	456	25
THE CEDARS OF LEBANON WHICH HE HATH PLANTED	468	27

LED

CHRISTIANS MAY BE LED INTO THE WAY OF TRUTH, AND HOLD	018	32
CHRISTIANS MAY BE LED INTO THE WAY OF TRUTH, AND HOLD	032	32
THEN WAS JESUS LED UP OF THE SPIRIT INTO THE	126	23
HAD BOUND HIM, THEY LED HIM AWAY, AND DELIVERED HIM	134	33
RAIMENT ON HIM, AND LED HIM AWAY TO CRUCIFY HIM	136	24
THAT LED THEM BY THE RIGHT HAND OF MOSES WITH HIS	139	10
THAT LED THEM THROUGH THE DEEP, AS AN HORSE IN THE	139	13
AND THEY LED JESUS AWAY TO THE HIGH PRIEST	142	31
AND THE SOLDIERS LED HIM AWAY INTO THE HALL, CALLED	145	30
CLOTHES ON HIM, AND LED HIM OUT TO CRUCIFY HIM	146	04
TOOK THEY HIM, AND LED HIM, AND BROUGHT HIM INTO	151	07
CAME TOGETHER, AND LED HIM INTO THEIR COUNCIL,	151	29
OF THEM AROSE, AND LED HIM UNTO PILATE	152	27
AND AS THEY LED HIM AWAY, THEY LAID HOLD UPON ONE	154	09
MALEFACTORS, LED WITH HIM TO BE PUT TO DEATH	154	21
THEY TOOK JESUS, AND LED HIM AWAY	159	31
AND HE LED THEM OUT AS FAR AS TO BETHANY, AND HE	178	23
FOR AS MANY AS ARE LED BY THE SPIRIT OF GOD, THEY ARE	200	06
AWAY UNTO THESE DUMB IDOLS, EVEN AS YE WERE LED	203	18
BUT IF YE BE LED OF THE SPIRIT, YE ARE NOT UNDER THE	209	18
BROUGHT UP AND WHICH LED THE SEED OF THE HOUSE CF	225	18
BUT THEY LED HIM BY THE HAND, AND BROUGHT HIM INTO	230	11
UP ON HIGH, HE LED CAPTIVITY CAPTIVE, AND GAVE GIFTS	237	14
NOT FOLLOW, NOR BE LED BY THEM	276	27
TO FOLLOW, NOR BE LED BY THEM	276	30
NOT FOLLOW, NOR BE LED BY THEM	277	29
TO FOLLOW, NOR BE LED BY THEM	277	31
AS MANY AS ARE LED BY THE SPIRIT OF GOD, THEY ARE THE	330	19
WHERE THOU HAST LED THE WAY, THAT WE MAY AT LENGTH	336	12
ON HIGH, THOU HAST LED CAPTIVITY CAPTIVE, AND	420	19
THE DAY-TIME ALSO HE LED THEM WITH A CLOUD, *	435	28
HIS OWN PEOPLE, HE LED THEM FORTH LIKE SHEEP, *	438	14
SO HE LED THEM THROUGH THE DEEP, AS THROUGH A	473	19
MADE ALL THOSE THAT LED THEM AWAY CAPTIVE TO PITY	475	29
7 HE LED THEM FORTH BY THE RIGHT WAY, *	476	17
16 WHO LED HIS PEOPLE THROUGH THE WILDERNESS	512	14
3 FOR THEY THAT LED US AWAY CAPTIVE, REQUIRED OF US	513	09
UP ON HIGH, HE LED CAPTIVITY CAPTIVE, AND GAVE GIFTS	537	34

LEDDEST

20 THOU LEDDEST THY PEOPLE LIKE SHEEP, *	434	23

LEFT

WE HAVE LEFT UNDONE THOSE THINGS WHICH WE OUGHT TO	006	21
WE HAVE LEFT UNDONE THOSE THINGS WHICH WE OUGHT TO	023	28
THESE STATES WERE LEFT AT FULL AND EQUAL LIBERTY TO	VI	10
YOUR HOUSE IS LEFT UNTO YOU DESOLATE	100	31
HAND AND ON THE LEFT, BY HONOUR AND DISHONOUR,	126	16
ONE ON THE RIGHT HAND, AND ANOTHER ON THE LEFT	137	05
AND HE LEFT THE LINEN CLOTH, AND FLED FROM THEM	142	30
ONE ON HIS RIGHT HAND, AND THE OTHER ON HIS LEFT	146	16
AND THE OTHER ON THE LEFT	154	25
NOW WHEN HE HAD LEFT SPEAKING, HE SAID UNTO SIMON,	196	13
MEAT THAT WAS LEFT SEVEN BASKETS	199	24
HOUR THE FEVER LEFT HIM	220	09
THEY MARVELLED, AND LEFT HIM, AND WENT THEIR WAY	223	12
THEY STRAIGHTWAY LEFT THEIR NETS, AND FOLLOWED HIM	227	28
THEY IMMEDIATELY LEFT THE SHIP AND THEIR FATHER,	227	32
THE OTHER ON THE LEFT, IN THY KINGDOM	247	10
AND ON MY LEFT, IS NOT MINE TO GIVE, BUT IT	247	17
THE CLOKE THAT I LEFT AT TROAS WITH CARPUS, WHEN THOU	254	04
BUT THE GOATS ON THE LEFT	259	02
THE WOMAN ON THE LEFT, THE MINISTER SHALL SAY,	R 300	07
OF THE WOMAN'S LEFT HAND	R 302	11
OF THE WOMAN'S LEFT HAND, THE MINISTER SHALL SAY,	R 302	24
EVERY MINISTER IS LEFT TO THE DIRECTICN OF THOSE	R 304	19
FOR THERE IS NOT ONE GODLY MAN LEFT	355	06
10 I HAVE BEEN LEFT UNTO THEE EVER SINCE I WAS BCRN	366	23
HE HATH LEFT OFF TO BEHAVE HIMSELF WISELY, AND TC DC	383	31
THERE WAS NOT ONE OF THEM LEFT	473	24
THERE BE NO PLACE LEFT AMONG YOU, EITHER FOR ERRCR IN	540	21
ON THE RIGHT AND LEFT OF THE ALTAR, WITHOUT THE	R 570	08

LEGISLATURE

BLESS THE LEGISLATURE OF THIS STATE, THAT IT MAY	035	25

LEGITIMATELY

AND LEGITIMATELY CONSTITUTED	610	4?

LEGS

PILATE THAT THEIR LEGS MIGHT BE BROKEN, AND THAT THEY   160 33
AND BRAKE THE LEGS OF THE FIRST, AND OF THE OTHER   160 34
THAT HE WAS DEAD ALREADY, THEY BRAKE NOT HIS LEGS   161 03
NEITHER DELIGHTETH HE IN ANY MAN'S LEGS   523 16

LEISURE

O TARRY THOU THE LORD'S LEISURE   326 30
16 O TARRY THOU THE LORD'S LEISURE   372 30

LEND

UNTO HIM, FRIEND, LEND ME THREE LOAVES   262 28

LENDETH

26 THE RIGHTEOUS IS EVER MERCIFUL, AND LENDETH   386 15
5 A GOOD MAN IS MERCIFUL, AND LENDETH   483 26

LENGTH

TILL AT LENGTH THE WHOLE OF THY DISPERSED SHEEP,   037 05
THAT IT MAY AT LENGTH ATTAIN TO LIFE EVERLASTING   101 19
THE BREADTH, AND LENGTH, AND DEPTH, AND HEIGHT   212 18
UNTIL AT LENGTH, THROUGH THY MERCY, WE, WITH   258 16
THAT WE MAY AT LENGTH FALL ASLEEP PEACEFULLY IN THEE,   336 13
THAT AT LENGTH, UNITED WITH THEM, WE MAY STAND   341 02
AND AT LENGTH, BY GOD'S MERCY, THEY ATTAIN TO   606 15

LENGTHEN

THE SHADOWS LENGTHEN AND THE EVENING COMES, AND THE   594 31

LENT

ON THE FIRST DAY OF LENT, THE OFFICE ENSUING MAY BE   R 060 03
THE FIRST SUNDAY IN LENT, AND TRINITY SUNDAY   R 085 24
SAID EVERY DAY IN LENT, AFTER THE COLLECT APPOINTED   R 124 18

LEPER

THERE CAME A LEPER AND WORSHIPPED HIM, SAYING,   114 31
HOUSE OF SIMON THE LEPER, AS HE SAT AT MEAT, THERE   140 03

LEPERS

LAME WALK, THE LEPERS ARE CLEANSED, AND THE DEAF   094 21
TEN MEN THAT WERE LEPERS, WHICH STOOD AFAR OFF   210 03

LEPROSY

IMMEDIATELY HIS LEPROSY WAS CLEANSED   115 03

LESS

UNTO ME, WHO AM LESS THAN THE LEAST OF ALL SAINTS, IS   108 18
HAVE THE LESS CAUSE TO BE DISQUIETED FOR LACK OF THE   R 321 10
PURCHASED WITH NO LESS PRICE THAN THE EFFUSION OF HIS   554 11
MUCH LESS THE WALLS OF TEMPLES MADE WITH   564 29
UNCLEAN LIVING, NO LESS PERILOUS THAN DESPERATION   606 26

LESSON

BE READ THE FIRST LESSON, ACCORDING TO THE TABLE OR   R 009 31
THAT BEFORE EVERY LESSON, THE MINISTER SHALL SAY,   R 009 32
HERE ENDETH THE FIRST (OR THE SECOND) LESSON   R 009 34
AND AFTER EVERY LESSON, HERE ENDETH THE FIRST (OR THE   R 009 34
THE SECOND LESSON, TAKEN OUT OF THE NEW TESTAMENT,   R 014 02
BE READ THE FIRST LESSON, ACCORDING TO THE TABLE OR   R 026 06
THE LESSON READ BEING FOLLOWED BY ONE OF THE   R 026 08
THEN A LESSON OF THE NEW TESTAMENT, AS IT IS   R 028 05
AFTER THE SECOND LESSON AT MORNING OR EVENING PRAYER,   R 273 15
SHALL FOLLOW THE LESSON, TAKEN OUT OF THE FIFTEENTH   R 328 18
SHALL FOLLOW THE LESSON TAKEN OUT OF THE EIGHTEENTH   R 339 19

LESSONS

OMIT ONE OF THE LESSONS IN EVENING PRAYER, THE LESSON   R 026 07
AND IN THE HOLY LESSONS TAKEN OUT OF THE GOSPEL,   539 26

LEST

LEST COMING SUDDENLY HE FIND YOU SLEEPING   021 26
TAKE YE GOOD HEED, LEST YE, WITHDRAWING YOURSELVES   088 25
LEST WHILE YE GATHER UP THE TARES, YE ROOT UP ALSO   116 27
LEST THAT BY ANY MEANS, WHEN I HAVE PREACHED TO   119 11
OF THEIR HEARTS, LEST THEY SHOULD BELIEVE AND BE   121 35
SHALL BEAR THEE UP, LEST AT ANY TIME THOU DASH THY   127 02
ON THE FEAST DAY, LEST THERE BE AN UPROAR OF THE   139 35
WATCH YE AND PRAY, LEST YE ENTER INTO TEMPTATION   142 05
RISE AND PRAY, LEST YE ENTER INTO TEMPTATION   150 26
THE THIRD DAY, LEST HIS DISCIPLES COME BY NIGHT,   162 20
BEWARE THEREFORE, LEST THAT COME UPON YOU, WHICH IS   169 22
TO THE LIGHT, LEST HIS DEEDS SHOULD BE REPROVED   185 09
TESTIFY UNTO THEM, LEST THEY ALSO COME INTO THIS   190 25
LEST AT ANY TIME THE ADVERSARY DELIVER THEE TO THE   198 13
STANDETH TAKE HEED LEST HE FALL   201 25
ONLY LEST THEY SHOULD SUFFER PERSECUTION FOR THE   210 26
LEST A MORE HONOURABLE MAN THAN THOU BE BIDDEN OF   214 12
WHICH BELIEVE NOT, LEST THE LIGHT OF THE GLORIOUS   251 03
12 KISS THE SON, LEST HE BE ANGRY, AND SO YE PERISH   346 21
2 LEST HE DEVOUR MY SOUL LIKE A LION, AND TEAR IT IN   349 25
4 LEST MINE ENEMY SAY, I HAVE PREVAILED AGAINST THEE   356 04
PRESUMPTUOUS SINS, LEST THEY GET THE DOMINION OVER   364 10

LEST   CONTINUED

LEST, IF THOU MAKE AS THOUGH THOU HEAREST NOT, I   373 04
LEST I PLUCK YOU AWAY, AND THERE BE NONE TO DELIVER   403 02
11 SLAY THEM NOT, LEST MY PEOPLE FORGET IT   411 26
LEST HE SHOULD DESTROY THEM   474 16
AWAY MINE EYES, LEST THEY BEHOLD VANITY   492 13
LEST THE RIGHTEOUS PUT THEIR HAND UNTO WICKEDNESS   504 30
LEST THEY BE TOO PROUD   516 25
THY FACE FROM ME, LEST I BE LIKE UNTO THEM THAT GO   519 05
NOT A NOVICE, LEST BEING LIFTED UP WITH PRIDE HE   549 27
LEST HE FALL INTO REPROACH AND THE SNARE OF THE   549 29
AND LEST, THROUGH OUR OWN FRAILTY, OR THE TEMPTATIONS   590 09

LET

LET US PRAY   R 003 09
LET ALL THE EARTH KEEP SILENCE BEFORE HIM   003 15
LET THE WORDS OF MY MOUTH, AND THE MEDITATION OF MY   003 19
THE SON OF GOD, LET US COME BOLDLY UNTO THE THRONE OF   005 08
OR HE SHALL SAY, LET US HUMBLY CONFESS OUR SINS UNTO   006 14
WHEREFORE LET US BESEECH HIM TO GRANT US TRUE   007 14
O COME, LET US ADORE HIM   R 008 17
O COME, LET US ADORE HIM   R 008 19
O COME, LET US ADORE HIM   R 008 21
O COME, LET US ADORE HIM   R 008 24
O COME, LET US ADORE HIM   R 008 26
O COME, LET US ADORE HIM   R 008 28
O COME, LET US ADORE HIM   R 008 30
O COME, LET US ADORE HIM   R 008 32
O COME, LET US ADORE HIM   R 008 34
LET US HEARTILY REJOICE IN THE STRENGTH OF OUR   009 03
O COME, LET US SING UNTO THE LORD   009 03
LET US COME BEFORE HIS PRESENCE WITH THANKSGIVING   009 05
O COME, LET US WORSHIP AND FALL DOWN, *   009 13
LET THE WHOLE EARTH STAND IN AWE OF HIM   009 17
O LORD, LET THY MERCY BE UPON US, AS OUR TRUST IS IN   011 10
LET ME NEVER BE CONFOUNDED   011 12
O LET THE EARTH BLESS THE LORD   013 02
LET IT PRAISE HIM, AND MAGNIFY HIM FOR EVER   013 02
O LET ISRAEL BLESS THE LORD   013 20
LET US BLESS THE FATHER, AND THE SON, AND THE HOLY   013 30
LET US PRAY   016 27
LET ALL THE EARTH KEEP SILENCE BEFORE HIM   021 12
LET MY PRAYER BE SET FORTH IN THY SIGHT AS THE   021 16
AND LET THE LIFTING UP OF MY HANDS BE AN EVENING   021 17
LET THE WHOLE EARTH STAND IN AWE OF HIM   021 19
LET THE WORDS OF MY MOUTH, AND THE MEDITATION OF MY   021 21
AND LET HIM THAT HEARETH SAY, COME   022 29
AND LET HIM THAT IS ATHIRST COME   022 30
AND WHOSOEVER WILL, LET HIM TAKE THE WATER OF LIFE   022 31
LET US HUMBLY CONFESS OUR SINS UNTO ALMIGHTY GOD   023 02
WHEREFORE LET US BESEECH HIM TO GRANT US TRUE   024 16
LET THE SEA MAKE A NOISE, AND ALL THAT THEREIN IS   027 16
LET THE FLOODS CLAP THEIR HANDS, AND LET THE HILLS BE   027 21
THEIR HANDS, AND LET THE HILLS BE JOYFUL TOGETHER   027 21
LET ALL THE PEOPLES PRAISE THEE   028 21
LET THE PEOPLES PRAISE THEE, O GOD   028 21
O LET THE NATIONS REJOICE AND BE GLAD   028 23
LET THE PEOPLES PRAISE THEE, O GOD   028 26
LET ALL THE PEOPLES PRAISE THEE   028 26
LET THY BREATH GO FORTH THAT IT MAY RENEW THE FACE OF   040 09
O LORD, LET THY MERCY BE SHOWED UPON US   059 18
AND LET OUR CRY COME UNTO THEE   062 06
SPARE THEM, AND LET NOT THINE HERITAGE BE BROUGHT TO   063 03
OF OUR SINS, YET LET THE PITIFULNESS OF THY GREAT   063 12
LET YOUR LIGHT SO SHINE BEFORE MEN, THAT THEY MAY SEE   072 04
LET EVERY MAN DO ACCORDING AS HE IS DISPOSED IN HIS   072 17
WHILE WE HAVE TIME, LET US DO GOOD UNTO ALL MEN   072 20
THE PRIEST SAY, LET US PRAY FOR THE WHOLE STATE OF   074 05
LET US GIVE THANKS UNTO OUR LORD GOD   076 28
HE BE PRESENT) SHALL LET THEM DEPART WITH THIS   R 084 17
AND THE HOLY GHOST, LET US GIVE, AS WE ARE MOST   086 19
COMFORT OR COUNSEL, LET HIM COME TO ME, OR TO SOME   088 05
LET US THEREFORE CAST OFF THE WORKS OF DARKNESS, AND   091 03
OF DARKNESS, AND LET US PUT ON THE ARMOUR OF LIGHT   091 04
LET US WALK HONESTLY, AS IN THE DAY   091 05
LET A MAN SO ACCOUNT OF US, AS OF THE MINISTERS OF   094 04
WE ARE SORE LET AND HINDERED IN RUNNING THE RACE THAT   095 06
LET YOUR MODERATION BE KNOWN UNTO ALL MEN   095 14
WITH THANKSGIVING LET YOUR REQUESTS BE MADE KNOWN   095 16
HE SAITH, AND LET ALL THE ANGELS OF GOD   097 06
LET NO MAN DESPISE THEE   098 26
SAID ONE TO ANOTHER, LET US NOW GO EVEN UNTO   106 09
WHETHER PROPHECY, LET US PROPHESY ACCORDING TO THE   111 11
OR MINISTRY, LET US WAIT ON OUR MINISTERING   111 18
HE THAT GIVETH, LET HIM DO IT WITH SIMPLICITY   111 20
LET LOVE BE WITHOUT DISSIMULATION   111 21
LET EVERY SOUL BE SUBJECT UNTO THE HIGHER POWERS   114 11
AND LET THE PEACE OF GOD RULE IN YOUR HEARTS,   116 09
LET THE WORD OF CHRIST DWELL IN YOU RICHLY IN ALL   116 11
LET BOTH GROW TOGETHER UNTIL THE HARVEST   116 28
LITTLE CHILDREN, LET NO MAN DECEIVE YOU   117 26
HATH EARS TO HEAR, LET HIM HEAR   121 28
LET THE BRIDEGROOM GO FORTH OF HIS CHAMBER, AND THE   124 32
LET THE PRIESTS, THE MINISTERS OF THE LORD, WEEP   125 02
AND THE ALTAR, AND LET THEM SAY, SPARE THY PEOPLE, O   125 03
OR COVETOUSNESS, LET IT NOT BE ONCE NAMED AMONG YOU,   129 03
LET NO MAN DECEIVE YOU WITH VAIN WORDS   129 09
LET THIS MIND BE IN YOU, WHICH WAS ALSO IN CHRIST   134 16
ALL SAY UNTO HIM, LET HIM BE CRUCIFIED   136 06
THE MORE, SAYING, LET HIM BE CRUCIFIED   136 08
THE KING OF ISRAEL, LET HIM NOW COME DOWN FROM THE   137 11
LET HIM DELIVER HIM NOW, IF HE WILL HAVE HIM   137 12
THE REST SAID, LET BE, LET US SEE WHETHER ELIAS WILL   137 23
REST SAID, LET BE, LET US SEE WHETHER ELIAS WILL COME   137 23

LET CONTINUED

AND JESUS SAID, LET HER ALONE	140	10
RISE UP, LET US GO	142	13
LET US STAND TOGETHER	144	19
LET HIM COME NEAR TO ME	144	20
LET HIM TRUST IN THE NAME OF THE LORD, AND STAY UPON	144	25
LET CHRIST THE KING OF ISRAEL DESCEND NOW FROM THE	146	23
TO DRINK, SAYING, LET ALONE	146	33
LET US SEE WHETHER ELIAS WILL COME TO TAKE HIM DOWN	146	33
GREATEST AMONG YOU, LET HIM BE AS THE YOUNGER	149	22
THAT HATH A PURSE, LET HIM TAKE IT, AND LIKEWISE HIS	150	07
THAT HATH NO SWORD, LET HIM SELL HIS GARMENT, AND BUY	150	08
NOT ANSWER ME, NOR LET ME GO	151	32
CHASTISE HIM, AND LET HIM GO	154	02
LET HIM SAVE HIMSELF, IF HE BE CHRIST, THE CHOSEN OF	154	28
LET US DRAW NEAR WITH A TRUE HEART IN FULL ASSURANCE	158	20
LET US HOLD FAST THE PROFESSION OF OUR FAITH WITHOUT	158	22
AND LET US CONSIDER ONE ANOTHER TO PROVOKE UNTO LOVE	158	24
SAYING, IF THOU LET THIS MAN GO, THOU ART NOT	159	20
AMONG THEMSELVES, LET US NOT REND IT, BUT CAST LOTS	160	13
THEREFORE LET US KEEP THE FEAST,	162	31
THEREFORE LET US KEEP THE FEAST, NOT WITH OLD LEAVEN,	165	13
MY BELOVED BRETHREN, LET EVERY MAN BE SWIFT TO HEAR,	174	31
IF ANY MAN SPEAK, LET HIM SPEAK AS THE ORACLES OF	179	18
IF ANY MAN MINISTER, LET HIM DO IT AS OF THE ABILITY	179	19
LET NOT YOUR HEART BE TROUBLED, NEITHER LET IT BE	181	35
BE TROUBLED, NEITHER LET IT BE AFRAID	182	02
LET US LOVE ONE ANOTHER	189	08
LET THEM HEAR THEM	190	27
MY LITTLE CHILDREN, LET US NOT LOVE IN WORD, NEITHER	191	21
BROTHER, LET ME PULL OUT THE MOTE THAT IS IN	195	08
AND SEE GOOD DAYS, LET HIM REFRAIN HIS TONGUE FROM	195	25
LET HIM ESCHEW EVIL, AND DO GOOD	195	26
LET HIM SEEK PEACE, AND ENSUE IT	195	27
INTO THE DEEP, AND LET DOWN YOUR NETS FOR A DRAUGHT	196	14
AT THY WORD I WILL LET DOWN THE NET	196	17
NEITHER LET US COMMIT FORNICATION, AS SOME OF THEM	201	17
NEITHER LET US TEMPT CHRIST, AS SOME OF THEM ALSO	201	19
WHEREFORE LET HIM THAT THINKETH HE STANDETH TAKE HEED	201	24
AND LET US EAT, AND BE MERRY	202	24
LET THY MERCIFUL EARS, O LORD, BE OPEN TO THE PRAYERS	203	11
FROM HENCEFORTH LET NO MAN TROUBLE ME	211	04
WE BESEECH THEE, LET THY CONTINUAL PITY CLEANSE AND	212	04
AND HEALED HIM, AND LET HIM GO	214	04
LET NOT THE SUN GO DOWN UPON YOUR WRATH	216	18
LET HIM THAT STOLE STEAL NO MORE	216	20
BUT RATHER LET HIM LABOUR, WORKING WITH HIS HANDS THE	216	21
LET NO CORRUPT COMMUNICATION PROCEED OUT OF YOUR	216	22
LET ALL BITTERNESS, AND WRATH, AND ANGER, AND	216	27
THE BOOK OF PSALMS, LET HIS HABITATION BE DESOLATE,	234	18
BE DESOLATE, AND LET NO MAN DWELL THEREIN	234	19
AND HIS BISHOPRICK LET ANOTHER TAKE	234	20
BUT LET PATIENCE HAVE HER PERFECT WORK, THAT YE MAY	239	10
OF YOU LACK WISDOM, LET HIM ASK OF GOD, THAT GIVETH	239	12
BUT LET HIM ASK IN FAITH, NOTHING WAVERING	239	14
FOR LET NOT THAT MAN THINK THAT HE SHALL RECEIVE ANY	239	16
LET THE BROTHER OF LOW DEGREE REJOICE IN THAT HE IS	239	18
UNTO HIS DISCIPLES, LET NOT YOUR HEART BE TROUBLED	239	29
BE GREAT AMONG YOU, LET HIM BE YOUR MINISTER	247	24
BE CHIEF AMONG YOU, LET HIM BE YOUR SERVANT	247	25
AND LET US MAKE THREE TABERNACLES	249	02
GREATEST AMONG YOU, LET HIM BE AS THE YOUNGER	250	08
CLOUD OF WITNESSES, LET US LAY ASIDE EVERY WEIGHT,	258	21
EASILY BESET US, AND LET US RUN WITH PATIENCE THE	258	22
MY BELOVED BRETHREN, LET EVERY MAN BE SWIFT TO HEAR,	265	23
UNTO CHRIST, SO LET THE WIVES BE TO THEIR OWN	267	18
NEVERTHELESS LET EVERY ONE OF YOU IN PARTICULAR SO	267	32
JOINED TOGETHER, LET NOT MAN PUT ASUNDER	268	11
LET US WHO SEEK, FIND	274	17
LET US FAITHFULLY AND DEVOUTLY GIVE THANKS UNTO HIM,	276	05
LET US GIVE THANKS UNTO OUR LORD GOD	279	04
OF CHRIST'S CHURCH, LET US GIVE THANKS UNTO ALMIGHTY	280	15
THE MINISTER SAY, LET US ASK GOD'S HELP TO KNOW AND	285	19
LET US PRAY, AS OUR SAVIOUR CHRIST HATH	289	19
COME YE, AND LET US WALK IN THE LIGHT OF THE LORD	290	05
LET THY MERCIFUL KINDNESS, O LORD,	290	10
AND LET OUR CRY COME UNTO THEE	290	15
AND LET OUR CRY COME UNTO THEE	297	12
LET THY FATHERLY HAND, WE BESEECH THEE, EVER BE OVER	298	19
LET THY HOLY SPIRIT EVER BE WITH THEM	298	20
BE JOINED TOGETHER, LET HIM NOW SPEAK, OR ELSE	300	21
HATH JOINED TOGETHER LET NO MAN PUT ASUNDER	303	31
AND LET OUR CRY COME UNTO THEE	306	22
LET THE ENEMY HAVE NO ADVANTAGE OF HIM	308	27
AND LET OUR CRY COME UNTO THEE	309	02
AND LET THY HOLY SPIRIT LEAD US IN HOLINESS AND	316	28
LET ME KNOW MINE END, AND THE NUMBER OF MY	324	20
O LET THINE EARS CONSIDER WELL *	328	05
JESUS SAID, LET NOT YOUR HEART BE TROUBLED	331	17
AND LET OUR CRY COME UNTO THEE	340	21
3 LET US BREAK THEIR BONDS ASUNDER, *	346	02
LET THEM PERISH THROUGH THEIR OWN IMAGINATIONS	348	22
12 AND LET ALL THEM THAT PUT THEIR TRUST IN THEE	348	25
5 THEN LET MINE ENEMY PERSECUTE MY SOUL, AND TAKE ME	349	32
LET HIM TREAD MY LIFE DOWN UPON THE EARTH,	349	33
9 O LET THE WICKEDNESS OF THE UNGODLY COME TO AN END	350	09
19 UP, LORD, AND LET NOT MAN HAVE THE UPPER HAND	352	30
LET THE HEATHEN BE JUDGED IN THY SIGHT	352	31
LET THEM BE TAKEN IN THE CRAFTY WILINESS THAT THEY	353	06
2 LET MY SENTENCE COME FORTH FROM THY PRESENCE	358	19
AND LET THINE EYES LOOK UPON THE THING THAT IS EQUAL	358	20
14 LET THE WORDS OF MY MOUTH, AND THE MEDITATION OF	364	13
LET HIM DELIVER HIM, IF HE WILL HAVE HIM	366	19
O LET ME NOT BE CONFOUNDED, NEITHER LET MINE ENEMIES	369	19
NEITHER LET MINE ENEMIES TRIUMPH OVER ME	369	20

LET CONTINUED

LET ME NOT BE CONFOUNDED, FOR I HAVE PUT MY TRUST IN	370	24
20 LET PERFECTNESS AND RIGHTEOUS DEALING WAIT UPON	370	26
LET ME NEVER BE PUT TO CONFUSION	375	22
19 LET ME NOT BE CONFOUNDED, O LORD, FOR I HAVE	376	30
LET THE UNGODLY BE PUT TO CONFUSION, AND BE PUT TO	376	31
20 LET THE LYING LIPS BE PUT TO SILENCE, *	376	33
8 LET ALL THE EARTH FEAR THE LORD	379	02
21 LET THY MERCIFUL KINDNESS, O LORD, BE UPON US,	379	32
AND LET US MAGNIFY HIS NAME TOGETHER	380	07
4 LET THEM BE CONFOUNDED, AND PUT TO SHAME, THAT SEEK	381	24
LET THEM BE TURNED BACK, AND BROUGHT TO CONFUSION,	381	25
5 LET THEM BE AS THE DUST BEFORE THE WIND, *	381	27
6 LET THEIR WAY BE DARK AND SLIPPERY, *	381	29
AND LET THE ANGEL OF THE LORD PURSUE THEM	381	29
8 LET A SUDDEN DESTRUCTION COME UPON HIM UNAWARES,	382	04
19 O LET NOT THEM THAT ARE MINE ENEMIES TRIUMPH OVER	382	34
NEITHER LET THEM WINK WITH THEIR EYES, THAT HATE ME	382	35
AND LET THEM NOT TRIUMPH OVER ME	383	12
25 LET THEM NOT SAY IN THEIR HEARTS, THERE	383	13
NEITHER LET THEM SAY, WE HAVE DEVOURED HIM	383	14
26 LET THEM BE PUT TO CONFUSION AND SHAME TOGETHER,	383	16
LET THEM BE CLOTHED WITH REBUKE AND DISHONOUR, THAT	383	17
27 LET THEM BE GLAD AND REJOICE, THAT FAVOUR MY	383	19
LET THEM SAY ALWAY, BLESSED BE THE LORD, WHO	383	20
11 O LET NOT THE FOOT OF PRIDE COME AGAINST ME	384	19
AND LET NOT THE HAND OF THE UNGODLY CAST ME DOWN	384	20
OFF FROM WRATH, AND LET GO DISPLEASURE	385	09
5 LORD, LET ME KNOW MINE END, AND THE NUMBER OF MY	389	15
LET THY LOVING-KINDNESS AND THY TRUTH ALWAY PRESERVE	391	09
16 O LORD, LET IT BE THY PLEASURE TO DELIVER ME	391	14
17 LET THEM BE ASHAMED, AND CONFOUNDED TOGETHER,	391	16
LET THEM BE DRIVEN BACKWARD, AND PUT TO REBUKE, THAT	391	17
18 LET THEM BE DESOLATE, AND REWARDED WITH SHAME,	391	19
19 LET ALL THOSE THAT SEEK THEE, BE JOYFUL AND GLAD	391	21
AND LET SUCH AS LOVE THY SALVATION, SAY ALWAY,	391	22
10 LET THE MOUNT SION REJOICE, AND THE DAUGHTERS OF	399	31
SO THAT HE MUST LET THAT ALONE FOR EVER	400	21
19 THOU HAST LET THY MOUTH SPEAK WICKEDNESS, *	402	28
16 LET DEATH COME HASTILY UPON THEM, AND LET THEM GO	407	20
UPON THEM, AND LET THEM GO DOWN ALIVE INTO THE PIT	407	20
7 LET THEM FALL AWAY LIKE WATER THAT RUNNETH APACE	410	21
SHOOT THEIR ARROWS, LET THEM BE ROOTED OUT	410	22
8 LET THEM CONSUME AWAY LIKE A SNAIL, AND BE LIKE THE	410	23
AND LET THEM NOT SEE THE SUN	410	24
AND GOD SHALL LET ME SEE MY DESIRE UPON MINE ENEMIES	411	25
11 LET THEM FALL UPON THE EDGE OF THE SWORD, *	415	13
LET ALL THE PEOPLES PRAISE THEE	418	28
3 LET THE PEOPLES PRAISE THEE, O GOD	418	28
4 O LET THE NATIONS REJOICE AND BE GLAD	418	30
LET ALL THE PEOPLES PRAISE THEE	418	33
5 LET THE PEOPLES PRAISE THEE, O GOD	418	33
LET THEM ALSO THAT HATE HIM FLEE BEFORE HIM	419	09
LET GOD ARISE, AND LET HIS ENEMIES BE SCATTERED	419	09
LET GOD ARISE, AND LET HIS ENEMIES BE SCATTERED	419	09
AT THE FIRE, SO LET THE UNGODLY PERISH AT THE	419	12
3 BUT LET THE RIGHTEOUS BE GLAD, AND REJOICE BEFORE	419	14
LET THEM ALSO BE MERRY AND JOYFUL	419	15
6 LET NOT THEM THAT TRUST IN THEE, O LORD GOD OF	422	13
LET NOT THOSE THAT SEEK THEE BE CONFOUNDED THROUGH	422	14
O LET ME BE DELIVERED FROM THEM THAT HATE ME, AND OUT	422	32
16 LET NOT THE WATER-FLOOD DROWN ME, NEITHER LET THE	422	35
DROWN ME, NEITHER LET THE DEEP SWALLOW ME UP	422	35
AND LET NOT THE PIT SHUT HER MOUTH UPON ME	423	02
23 LET THEIR TABLE BE MADE A SNARE TO TAKE THEMSELVES	423	18
AND LET THE THINGS THAT SHOULD HAVE BEEN FOR THEIR	423	19
24 LET THEIR EYES BE BLINDED, THAT THEY SEE NOT	423	21
AND LET THY WRATHFUL DISPLEASURE TAKE HOLD OF THEM	423	23
26 LET THEIR HABITATION BE VOID, *	423	25
28 LET THEM FALL FROM ONE WICKEDNESS TO ANOTHER,	423	30
29 LET THEM BE WIPED OUT OF THE BOOK OF THE LIVING,	423	32
35 LET HEAVEN AND EARTH PRAISE HIM	424	12
2 LET THEM BE ASHAMED AND CONFOUNDED THAT SEEK AFTER	424	22
LET THEM BE TURNED BACKWARD AND PUT TO CONFUSION THAT	424	23
3 LET THEM FOR THEIR REWARD BE SOON BROUGHT TO SHAME,	424	25
4 BUT LET ALL THOSE THAT SEEK THEE BE JOYFUL AND GLAD	424	27
AND LET ALL SUCH AS DELIGHT IN THY SALVATION SAY	424	28
LET ME NEVER BE PUT TO CONFUSION, *	425	05
7 O LET MY MOUTH BE FILLED WITH THY PRAISE, *	425	21
12 LET THEM BE CONFOUNDED AND PERISH THAT ARE AGAINST	425	31
LET THEM BE COVERED WITH SHAME AND DISHONOUR THAT	425	32
IN THEIR HEARTS, LET US MAKE HAVOC OF THEM	430	21
BUT LET THE POOR AND NEEDY GIVE PRAISE UNTO THY NAME	431	20
22 O LET NOT THE SIMPLE GO AWAY ASHAMED	431	20
DIVIDED THE SEA, AND LET THEM GO THROUGH	435	26
29 HE LET IT FALL AMONG THEIR TENTS, *	436	27
11 O LET THE VENGEANCE OF THY SERVANTS' BLOOD THAT IS	440	23
12 O LET THE SORROWFUL SIGHING OF THE PRISONERS COME	440	26
17 LET THY HAND BE UPON THE MAN OF THY RIGHT HAND,	442	04
O LET US LIVE, AND WE SHALL CALL UPON THY NAME	442	07
AND LET THEM FOLLOW THEIR OWN IMAGINATIONS	443	05
HAVE SAID, COME, AND LET US ROOT THEM OUT, THAT THEY	444	11
12 WHO SAY, LET US TAKE TO OURSELVES *	444	28
17 LET THEM BE CONFOUNDED AND VEXED EVER MORE AND	445	06
LET THEM BE PUT TO SHAME, AND PERISH	445	07
AND LET THINE ANGER CEASE FROM US	446	14
O LET MY PRAYER ENTER INTO THY PRESENCE, INCLINE	448	30
O COME, LET US SING UNTO THE LORD	459	05
LET US HEARTILY REJOICE IN THE STRENGTH OF OUR	459	05
2 LET US COME BEFORE HIS PRESENCE WITH THANKSGIVING	459	07
6 O COME, LET US WORSHIP AND FALL DOWN, *	459	15
LET THE WHOLE EARTH STAND IN AWE OF HIM	460	16
11 LET THE HEAVENS REJOICE, AND LET THE EARTH BE	460	22
HEAVENS REJOICE, AND LET THE EARTH BE GLAD	460	22
LET THE SEA MAKE A NOISE, AND ALL THAT THEREIN IS	460	23

LET   CONTINUED

12 LET THE FIELD BE JOYFUL, AND ALL THAT IS IN IT   460 24
8 LET THE SEA MAKE A NOISE, AND ALL THAT THEREIN IS   462 08
THEIR HANDS, AND LET THE HILLS BE JOYFUL TOGETHER   462 10
9 LET THE FLOODS CLAP THEIR HANDS, AND LET THE HILLS   462 10
2 O LET ME HAVE UNDERSTANDING *   463 19
AND LET MY CRYING COME UNTO THEE   464 10
2 O LET YOUR SONGS BE OF HIM, AND PRAISE HIM   470 07
AND LET YOUR TALKING BE OF ALL HIS WONDROUS WORKS   470 08
LET THE HEART OF THEM REJOICE THAT SEEK THE LORD   470 09
PRINCE OF THE PEOPLE LET HIM GO FREE   471 13
AND LET ALL THE PEOPLE SAY, O GIVE THANKS UNTO THE   475 34
2 LET THEM GIVE THANKS WHOM THE LORD HATH REDEEMED,   476 08
AND LET THEM WANDER OUT OF THE WAY IN THE WILDERNESS   478 27
LET THY RIGHT HAND SAVE THEM, AND HEAR THOU ME   479 15
AND LET AN ADVERSARY STAND AT HIS RIGHT HAND   480 14
IS GIVEN UPON HIM, LET HIM BE CONDEMNED   480 15
AND LET HIS PRAYER BE TURNED INTO SIN   480 16
AND LET ANOTHER TAKE HIS OFFICE   480 17
7 LET HIS DAYS BE FEW   480 17
8 LET HIS CHILDREN BE FATHERLESS, *   480 18
9 LET HIS CHILDREN BE VAGABONDS, AND BEG THEIR BREAD   480 19
LET THEM SEEK IT ALSO OUT OF DESOLATE PLACES   480 20
10 LET THE EXTORTIONER CONSUME ALL THAT HE HATH   480 21
AND LET THE STRANGER SPOIL HIS LABOUR   480 22
11 LET THERE BE NO MAN TO PITY HIM, *   480 23
12 LET HIS POSTERITY BE DESTROYED   480 25
THE NEXT GENERATION LET HIS NAME BE CLEAN PUT OUT   480 26
13 LET THE WICKEDNESS OF HIS FATHERS BE HAD IN   480 27
AND LET NOT THE SIN OF HIS MOTHER BE DONE AWAY   480 28
14 LET THEM ALWAY BE BEFORE THE LORD, *   480 30
18 LET IT BE UNTO HIM AS THE CLOAK THAT HE HATH UPON   481 08
19 LET IT THUS HAPPEN FROM THE LORD UNTO MINE   481 10
AND LET THEM BE CONFOUNDED THAT RISE UP AGAINST ME   481 26
BUT LET THY SERVANT REJOICE   481 27
28 LET MINE ADVERSARIES BE CLOTHED WITH SHAME   481 29
AND LET THEM COVER THEMSELVES WITH THEIR OWN   481 30
2 LET ISRAEL NOW CONFESS THAT HE IS GRACIOUS,   488 02
3 LET THE HOUSE OF AARON NOW CONFESS, *   488 04
4 YEA, LET THEM NOW THAT FEAR THE LORD CONFESS,   488 06
O LET ME NOT GO WRONG OUT OF THY COMMANDMENTS   490 18
LET THY LOVING MERCY COME ALSO UNTO ME, O LORD,   492 22
76 O LET THY MERCIFUL KINDNESS BE MY COMFORT,   495 07
77 O LET THY LOVING MERCIES COME UNTO ME, THAT I MAY   495 09
78 LET THE PROUD BE CONFOUNDED, FOR THEY GO WICKEDLY   495 11
79 LET SUCH AS FEAR THEE, AND HAVE KNOWN THY   495 14
80 O LET MY HEART BE SOUND IN THY STATUTES, *   495 16
108 LET THE FREE-WILL OFFERINGS OF MY MOUTH PLEASE   497 13
AND LET ME NOT BE DISAPPOINTED OF MY HOPE   497 31
LET MY COMPLAINT COME BEFORE THEE, O LORD   501 20
170 LET MY SUPPLICATION COME BEFORE THEE   501 22
173 LET THINE HAND HELP ME   501 28
175 O LET MY SOUL LIVE, AND IT SHALL PRAISE THEE   501 32
5 LET THEM BE CONFOUNDED AND TURNED BACKWARD,   506 29
6 LET THEM BE EVEN AS THE GRASS UPON THE HOUSETOPS,   506 31
2 O LET THINE EARS CONSIDER WELL *   507 10
9 LET THY PRIESTS BE CLOTHED WITH RIGHTEOUSNESS   508 21
AND LET THY SAINTS SING WITH JOYFULNESS   508 22
LET MY RIGHT HAND FORGET HER CUNNING   513 13
NOT REMEMBER THEE, LET MY TONGUE CLEAVE TO THE ROOF   513 15
8 LET NOT THE UNGODLY HAVE HIS DESIRE, O LORD   516 24
LET NOT HIS MISCHIEVOUS IMAGINATION PROSPER, LEST   516 24
9 LET THE MISCHIEF OF THEIR OWN LIPS FALL UPON THE   516 27
LET THEM BE CAST INTO THE FIRE, AND INTO THE PIT,   516 29
10 LET HOT BURNING COALS FALL UPON THEM   516 29
2 LET MY PRAYER BE SET FORTH IN THY SIGHT AS THE   517 10
AND LET THE LIFTING UP OF MY HANDS BE AN EVENING   517 11
4 O LET NOT MINE HEART BE INCLINED TO ANY EVIL THING   517 15
LET ME NOT BE OCCUPIED IN UNGODLY WORKS WITH THE MEN   517 16
NEITHER LET ME EAT OF SUCH THINGS AS   517 17
5 LET THE RIGHTEOUS RATHER SMITE ME FRIENDLY,   517 19
LET NOT MY HEAD REFUSE THEIR PRECIOUS BALMS   517 20
7 LET THEIR JUDGES BE OVERTHROWN IN STONY PLACES,   517 24
11 LET THE UNGODLY FALL INTO THEIR OWN NETS TOGETHER,   517 32
AND LET ME EVER ESCAPE THEM   517 33
8 O LET ME HEAR THY LOVING-KINDNESS BETIMES IN THE   519 07
LET THY LOVING SPIRIT LEAD ME FORTH INTO THE LAND OF   519 13
AND LET ALL FLESH GIVE THANKS UNTO HIS HOLY NAME FOR   521 34
5 LET THEM PRAISE THE NAME OF THE LORD   524 13
LET THE CONGREGATION OF SAINTS PRAISE HIM   525 03
2 LET ISRAEL REJOICE IN HIM THAT MADE HIM, *   525 05
AND LET THE CHILDREN OF SION BE JOYFUL IN THEIR KING   525 05
3 LET THEM PRAISE HIS NAME IN THE DANCE   525 07
LET THEM SING PRAISES UNTO HIM WITH TABRET AND HARP   525 07
5 LET THE SAINTS BE JOYFUL WITH GLORY   525 11
LET THEM REJOICE IN THEIR BEDS   525 11
6 LET THE PRAISES OF GOD BE IN THEIR MOUTH   525 13
6 LET EVERY THING THAT HATH BREATH *   525 32
TO THAT OFFICE, LET HIM COME FORTH IN THE NAME OF   530 24
THEN LET THEM USE THE OFFICE OF A DEACON, BEING FOUND   531 30
AND LET THESE ALSO FIRST BE PROVED   531 30
LET THE DEACONS BE THE HUSBANDS OF ONE WIFE, RULING   531 33
LET YOUR LOINS BE GIRDED ABOUT, AND YOUR LIGHTS   534 16
THIS HOLY MINISTRY, LET HIM COME FORTH IN THE NAME OF   536 30
LET US, THEREFORE, FOLLOWING THE EXAMPLE OF OUR   553 08
AND LET OUR CRY COME UNTO THEE   557 19
LET THY PRIESTS BE CLOTHED WITH   562 04
AND LET THY SAINTS SING WITH JOYFULNESS   562 05
AND LET OUR CRY COME UNTO THEE   562 07
LET US NOT DOUBT BUT THAT HE WILL ALSO FAVOURABLY   564 21
AND LET US FAITHFULLY AND DEVOUTLY BEG HIS   564 24
AND LET THEM BE THE RULE OF THY CONDUCT IN DISPENSING   571 25
LET NOT THE FOOT OF PRIDE COME NIGH TO HURT THEM, NOR   574 13
LET ME HEAR, THEREFORE, IF THOU CANST SAY THE LORD'S   580 20
BE PRESENT, LET ONE OF THEM, OR ANY OTHER WHO MAY BE   R 587 05

LET   CONTINUED

BEFORE BED-TIME, LET THE MASTER OR MISTRESS, OR ANY   R 589 13
LOOK UPON HERE LET HIM WHO READS MAKE A SHORT PAUSE,   R 589 34
LET THE LIGHT OF THY GOSPEL SHINE UPON ALL NATIONS   590 23
OF HOLY SCRIPTURE, LET THE HEAD OF THE HOUSEHOLD, OR   R 592 09
OF HOLY SCRIPTURE, LET THE HEAD OF THE HOUSEHOLD, OR   R 593 03
LET THY FATHERLY GOODNESS BE UPON ALL THAT THOU HAST   599 05
LET THE SORROWFUL SIGHING OF THE PRISONERS COME   600 08

LETTER

NOT OF THE LETTER, BUT OF THE SPIRIT   206 17
FOR THE LETTER KILLETH, BUT THE SPIRIT GIVETH LIFE   206 17
SEE HOW LARGE A LETTER I HAVE WRITTEN UNTO YOU WITH   210 23
PARAGRAPH IN THE LETTER OF INSTITUTION MAY BE   R 569 10
OF THE PRESCRIBED LETTER OF INSTITUTION   570 16
SHALL BE READ THE LETTER OF INSTITUTION   R 570 24
PRESCRIBED IN THIS OFFICE IN THE FORM OF A LETTER   R 574 31

LETTERS

OVER HIM, IN LETTERS OF GREEK, AND LATIN, AND HEBREW,   154 33
DESIRED OF HIM LETTERS TO DAMASCUS TO THE SYNAGOGUES,   229 27

LETTEST

NOW LETTEST THOU THY SERVANT DEPART IN PEACE,   028 09
LORD, NOW LETTEST THOU THY SERVANT DEPART IN   233 05
12 THOU LETTEST US BE EATEN UP LIKE SHEEP, *   395 15
30 WHEN THOU LETTEST THY BREATH GO FORTH, THEY SHALL   469 21

LETTETH

BUT LETTETH THE RUNAGATES CONTINUE IN SCARCENESS   419 23

LEVI

PURIFY THE SONS OF LEVI, AND PURGE THEM AS GOLD AND   232 11
20 PRAISE THE LORD, YE HOUSE OF LEVI   511 10

LEVIATHAN

THE HEADS OF LEVIATHAN IN PIECES, *   431 04
THERE IS THAT LEVIATHAN, *   469 12

LEVITE

AND LIKEWISE A LEVITE, WHEN HE WAS AT THE PLACE,   208 26

LEVITES

SENT PRIESTS AND LEVITES FROM JERUSALEM TO ASK HIM,   095 22

LIAR

WE MAKE HIM A LIAR, AND HIS WORD IS NOT IN US   101 32
I SHALL BE A LIAR LIKE UNTO YOU   133 27
HE THAT BELIEVETH NOT GOD HATH MADE HIM A LIAR   171 08
AND HATETH HIS BROTHER, HE IS A LIAR   189 32

LIARS

I SAID IN MY HASTE, ALL MEN ARE LIARS   487 08

LIBERAL

BUT THE RIGHTEOUS IS MERCIFUL AND LIBERAL   386 05

LIBERALLY

TO ALL MEN LIBERALLY, AND UPBRAIDETH NOT   239 13
HE POSSESSETH, LIBERALLY TO GIVE ALMS TO THE POOR,   611 03

LIBERTIES

DEFEND OUR LIBERTIES, AND FASHION INTO ONE UNITED   036 15
WON THEIR LIBERTIES OF OLD   263 18
MAINTAIN THESE LIBERTIES IN RIGHTEOUSNESS AND PEACE   263 20

LIBERTY

OF THAT BLESSED 'LIBERTY WHEREWITH CHRIST HATH MADE   V 02
FULL AND EQUAL LIBERTY TO MODEL AND ORGANIZE THEIR   VI 10
TO PROCLAIM LIBERTY TO THE CAPTIVES, AND THE OPENING   107 03
NOT USING YOUR LIBERTY FOR A CLOKE OF MALICIOUSNESS,   173 23
PERFECT LAW OF LIBERTY, AND CONTINUETH THEREIN, HE   176 10
THE GLORIOUS LIBERTY OF THE CHILDREN OF GOD   194 18
TO SET AT LIBERTY THEM THAT ARE BRUISED,   261 20
PERFECT LAW OF LIBERTY, AND CONTINUETH THEREIN,   266 02
HAST SET ME AT LIBERTY WHEN I WAS IN TROUBLE   347 11
HE BROUGHT ME FORTH ALSO INTO A PLACE OF LIBERTY   361 04
WHEN THOU HAST SET MY HEART AT LIBERTY   491 32
45 AND I WILL WALK AT LIBERTY   492 29

LIBYA

IN THE PARTS OF LIBYA ABOUT CYRENE, AND STRANGERS OF   181 04

LICE

AND LICE IN ALL THEIR QUARTERS   471 35

LICENCE

OR BY LICENCE, BEING DIFFERENT IN THE   R 304 18

LICENCE   CONTINUED

OUR LICENCE AND AUTHORITY TO PERFORM THE   569 16

LICENSED

THOU BE THERETO LICENSED BY THE BISHOP HIMSELF   534 13

LICK

HIS ENEMIES SHALL LICK THE DUST   427 15

LICKED

THE DOGS CAME AND LICKED HIS SORES   190 08

LIE

WALK IN DARKNESS, WE LIE, AND DO NOT THE TRUTH   101 25
KNOWETH THAT I LIE NOT   121 16
THEY ARE MY PEOPLE, CHILDREN THAT WILL NOT LIE   138 34
YE SHALL LIE DOWN IN SORROW   144 29
THE LINEN CLOTHES LIE, AND THE NAPKIN, THAT WAS ABOUT   164 23
WHEREBY THEY LIE IN WAIT TO DECEIVE   237 28
11 THEY LIE WAITING IN OUR WAY ON EVERY SIDE,   359 08
14 THEY LIE IN THE GRAVE LIKE SHEEP   400 34
5 AND I LIE EVEN AMONG THE CHILDREN OF MEN, THAT ARE   409 21
3 FOR LO, THEY LIE WAITING FOR MY SOUL   411 08
THAT ARE SLAIN, AND LIE IN THE GRAVE, *   449 05
HAVE IMAGINED A LIE AGAINST ME   494 18
8 OUR BONES LIE SCATTERED BEFORE THE PIT, *   517 26
AS MUCH AS SHALL LIE IN YOU, QUIETNESS, LOVE, AND   555 15

LIES

6 THOU SHALT DESTROY THEM THAT SPEAK LIES   348 11
UNTO THE PROUD, AND TO SUCH AS GO ABOUT WITH LIES   390 20
AND WITH LIES THOU CUTTEST LIKE A SHARP RAZOR   404 22
THEY GO ASTRAY, AND SPEAK LIES   410 14
THEIR TALK IS OF CURSING AND LIES   411 31
THEIR DELIGHT IS IN LIES   414 05
OF THEM THAT SPEAK LIES SHALL BE STOPPED   415 17
HE THAT TELLETH LIES SHALL NOT TARRY IN MY SIGHT   464 03
163 AS FOR LIES, I HATE AND ABHOR THEM   501 07

LIETH

AS MUCH AS LIETH IN YOU, LIVE PEACEABLY WITH ALL MEN   113 02
MY SERVANT LIETH AT HOME SICK OF THE PALSY,   115 08
9 FOR HE LIETH WAITING SECRETLY   353 23
HIM WHEN HE LIETH SICK UPON HIS BED   392 04
AND NOW THAT HE LIETH, HE SHALL RISE UP NO MORE   392 16
THE NORTH SIDE LIETH THE CITY OF THE GREAT KING   399 13
THINE INDIGNATION LIETH HARD UPON ME, *   449 09
AS MUCH AS IN YOU LIETH, WHOLESOME EXAMPLES OF THE   533 27
HAVE DONE ALL THAT LIETH IN YOU, ACCORDING TO YOUR   540 17
AS MUCH AS LIETH IN YOU, YE WILL APPLY   541 13
AS MUCH AS IN YOU LIETH, WHOLESOME EXAMPLES AND   543 02
AS MUCH AS LIETH IN YOU, QUIETNESS, PEACE, AND LOVE,   543 07

LIFE

AND SOBER LIFE, TO THE GLORY OF THY HOLY NAME   006 29
THE REST OF OUR LIFE HEREAFTER MAY BE PURE AND HOLY   007 16
ALL THE DAYS OF OUR LIFE   014 23
AND THE LIFE EVERLASTING   015 30
AND GIVER OF LIFE, WHO PROCEEDETH FROM THE   016 16
AND THE LIFE OF THE WORLD TO COME   016 21
OUR ETERNAL LIFE, WHOSE SERVICE IS PERFECT FREEDOM   017 07
AFTER THIS LIFE, TO ATTAIN EVERLASTING JOY   018 03
AND IN RIGHTEOUSNESS OF LIFE   019 03
AND ALL THE BLESSINGS OF THIS LIFE   019 22
THE WORLD TO COME LIFE EVERLASTING   020 10
TAKE THE WATER OF LIFE FREELY   022 31
AND SOBER LIFE, TO THE GLORY OF THY HOLY NAME   024 04
THE REST OF OUR LIFE HEREAFTER MAY BE PURE AND HOLY   024 18
AMENDMENT OF LIFE, AND THE GRACE AND CONSOLATION OF   024 25
WHO SAVETH THY LIFE FROM DESTRUCTION, *   029 10
AND THE LIFE EVERLASTING   030 02
AND GIVER OF LIFE, WHO PROCEEDETH FROM THE   030 21
AND THE LIFE OF THE WORLD TO COME   030 26
AND IN RIGHTEOUSNESS OF LIFE   032 34
AND ALL THE BLESSINGS OF THIS LIFE   033 20
THE WORLD TO COME LIFE EVERLASTING   034 10
SHALL BECOME PARTAKERS OF EVERLASTING LIFE   037 07
KNOWN TO ALL MEN THY BLESSED GIFT OF ETERNAL LIFE   038 22
THAT BOTH BY THEIR LIFE AND DOCTRINE THEY MAY SHOW   039 03
WITH INNOCENCY OF LIFE, THAT THEY MAY FAITHFULLY   039 12
IS NEEDFUL FOR THE LIFE OF MAN, AND HAST COMMANDED US   039 26
WITH THEE IN THE LIFE THAT IS TO COME   043 13
MAY REJOICE IN THE LIFE THAT NOW IS, AND DWELL WITH   043 13
WHO LAID DOWN HIS LIFE FOR US, THE SAME THY SON, OUR   044 06
AND UNCERTAIN OUR LIFE IS, WE MAY APPLY OUR HEARTS   045 08
HEAVENLY WISDOM WHICH LEADETH TO ETERNAL LIFE   045 10
THE RESIDUE OF HIS LIFE IN THY FEAR, AND TO THY   045 19
DWELL WITH THEE IN LIFE EVERLASTING   045 21
OF SIN, AND MAY BE BROUGHT TO NEWNESS OF LIFE   046 29
IN HOLINESS OF LIFE, AND IN PERFECTNESS OF LOVE, AND   047 09
THIS LIFE ENDED, WE MAY BE MADE PARTAKERS WITH   048 20
AND THE LIFE EVERLASTING   048 22
OF THE MORTAL LIFE, THEY MAY EVER BE DEFENDED BY THY   049 14
BY THY MERCY, OBTAIN EVERLASTING LIFE   049 27
TO THY WILL IN THIS LIFE, AND ALSO MAY BE PARTAKER OF   051 11
GLORY IN THE LIFE TO COME   051 12
QUIET AND PEACEABLE LIFE IN ALL GODLINESS AND   052 24
ART THE GIVER OF LIFE, OF HEALTH, AND OF SAFETY   052 29

LIFE   CONTINUED

GLORY IN THE LIFE TO COME   053 17
AND GIVER OF LIFE, WHO PROCEEDETH FROM THE   071 18
AND THE LIFE OF THE WORLD TO COME   071 23
BOTH BY THEIR LIFE AND DOCTRINE, SET FORTH THY   074 22
AND RIGHTEOUSNESS ALL THE DAYS OF THEIR LIFE   074 29
IN THIS TRANSITORY LIFE, ARE IN TROUBLE, SORROW,   074 32
DEPARTED THIS LIFE IN THY FAITH AND FEAR   074 35
TO LEAD A NEW LIFE, FOLLOWING THE COMMANDMENTS OF   075 10
THEE IN NEWNESS OF LIFE, TO THE HONOUR AND GLORY OF   075 29
AND BRING YOU TO EVERLASTING LIFE   076 07
HIM SHOULD NOT PERISH, BUT HAVE EVERLASTING LIFE   076 16
LIFE AGAIN HATH RESTORED TO US EVERLASTING LIFE   078 12
BY HIS RISING TO LIFE AGAIN HATH RESTORED TO US   078 12
PRESERVE THY BODY AND SOUL UNTO EVERLASTING LIFE   082 33
PRESERVE THY BODY AND SOUL UNTO EVERLASTING LIFE   083 05
HIS FORMER EVIL LIFE, THAT THE CONGREGATION MAY   R 085 05
AND EXALT US TO EVERLASTING LIFE   086 11
AND RIGHTEOUSNESS ALL THE DAYS OF OUR LIFE   086 23
WITH FULL PURPOSE OF AMENDMENT OF LIFE   087 21
TIME OF THIS MORTAL LIFE, IN WHICH THY SON JESUS   090 13
WE MAY RISE TO THE LIFE IMMORTAL, THROUGH HIM WHO   090 17
HOPE OF EVERLASTING LIFE, WHICH THOU HAST GIVEN US IN   092 12
AND THE LIFE WAS THE LIGHT OF MEN   097 24
IN HIM WAS LIFE   097 24
AT LENGTH ATTAIN TO LIFE EVERLASTING   101 09
AND OUR HANDS HAVE HANDLED, OF THE WORD OF LIFE   101 15
FOR THE LIFE WAS MANIFESTED, AND WE HAVE SEEN IT,   101 15
YOU THAT ETERNAL LIFE, WHICH WAS WITH THE FATHER, AND   101 16
THEY ARE DEAD WHICH SOUGHT THE YOUNG CHILD'S LIFE   107 16
MAY AFTER THIS LIFE HAVE THE FRUITION OF THY GLORIOUS   107 31
AND GRANT US THY PEACE ALL THE DAYS OF OUR LIFE   111 13
AND HEIRS OF ETERNAL LIFE   117 06
PLEASURES OF THIS LIFE, AND BRING NO FRUIT TO   122 07
THAN THE WAY OF LIFE AND PEACE   138 08
HAST GIVEN UNTO US LIFE AND IMMORTALITY   147 11
US A PLEDGE OF LIFE ETERNAL   152 11
AND OPENED UNTO US THE GATE OF EVERLASTING LIFE   163 24
ARE DEAD, AND YOUR LIFE IS HID WITH CHRIST IN GOD   164 06
WHO IS OUR LIFE, SHALL APPEAR, THEN SHALL YE   164 07
LIFE, AND THIS LIFE IS IN HIS SON   171 10
GIVEN TO US ETERNAL LIFE, AND THIS LIFE IS IN HIS   171 10
HE THAT HATH THE SON HATH LIFE   171 11
AND HE THAT HATH NOT THE SON OF GOD HATH NOT LIFE   171 12
AND ALSO AN ENSAMPLE OF GODLY LIFE   171 30
TO FOLLOW THE BLESSED STEPS OF HIS MOST HOLY LIFE   172 02
SHEPHERD GIVETH HIS LIFE FOR THE SHEEP   172 22
AND I LAY DOWN MY LIFE FOR THE SHEEP   172 29
HIM SHOULD NOT PERISH, BUT HAVE EVERLASTING LIFE   184 34
THEY MIGHT HAVE LIFE, AND THAT THEY MIGHT HAVE IT   186 18
IN HIM SHOULD NOT PERISH, BUT HAVE ETERNAL LIFE   188 29
FROM DEATH UNTO LIFE, BECAUSE WE LOVE THE BRETHREN   191 13
HATH ETERNAL LIFE ABIDING IN HIM   191 16
HE LAID DOWN HIS LIFE FOR US   191 17
HE THAT WILL LOVE LIFE, AND SEE GOOD DAYS, LET HIM   195 24
EVEN SO WE ALSO SHOULD WALK IN NEWNESS OF LIFE   197 14
FRUIT UNTO HOLINESS, AND THE END EVERLASTING LIFE   199 04
OF GOD IS ETERNAL LIFE THROUGH JESUS CHRIST OUR LORD   199 05
THE LETTER KILLETH, BUT THE SPIRIT GIVETH LIFE   206 18
SERVE THEE IN THIS LIFE, THAT WE FAIL NOT FINALLY TO   207 15
COULD HAVE GIVEN LIFE, VERILY RIGHTEOUSNESS SHOULD   208 02
WHAT SHALL I DO TO INHERIT ETERNAL LIFE   208 13
ANXIOUS FOR YOUR LIFE, WHAT YE SHALL EAT, OR WHAT YE   211 13
IS NOT THE LIFE MORE THAN THE FOOD, AND THE BODY THAN   211 14
CAN ADD ONE CUBIT UNTO THE MEASURE OF HIS LIFE   211 20
ALIENATED FROM THE LIFE OF GOD THROUGH THE IGNORANCE   216 06
YE MIGHT HAVE LIFE THROUGH HIS NAME   229 13
AND SHALL INHERIT EVERLASTING LIFE   231 21
WHOM TRULY TO KNOW IS EVERLASTING LIFE   238 30
CHRIST TO BE THE WAY, THE TRUTH, AND THE LIFE   238 31
WALK IN THE WAY THAT LEADETH TO ETERNAL LIFE   239 03
THE CROWN OF LIFE, WHICH THE LORD HATH PROMISED TO   239 26
I AM THE WAY, THE TRUTH, AND THE LIFE   240 06
A MAN LAY DOWN HIS LIFE FOR HIS FRIENDS   241 27
DOCTRINE AND HOLY LIFE, THAT WE MAY TRULY REPENT   242 10
BEFORE HIM, ALL THE DAYS OF OUR LIFE   244 09
AND TO GIVE HIS LIFE A RANSOM FOR MANY   247 27
THEE TO ENTER INTO LIFE HALT OR MAIMED, RATHER THAN   253 05
THEE TO ENTER INTO LIFE WITH ONE EYE, RATHER THAN   253 08
OF EVERLASTING LIFE, LO, WE TURN TO THE GENTILES   261 02
ORDAINED TO ETERNAL LIFE BELIEVED   261 08
ANXIOUS FOR YOUR LIFE, WHAT YE SHALL EAT, OR WHAT YE   266 11
IS NOT THE LIFE MORE THAN FOOD, AND THE BODY THAN   266 13
CAN ADD ONE CUBIT UNTO THE MEASURE OF HIS LIFE   266 18
WHO HOLDEST ALL SOULS IN LIFE   268 14
MAY HAVE EVERLASTING LIFE   269 21
FOR SUCCOUR, THE LIFE OF THOSE WHO BELIEVE, AND THE   274 10
HIM THE KINGDOM OF HEAVEN, AND EVERLASTING LIFE   276 23
YOU THE KINGDOM OF HEAVEN, AND EVERLASTING LIFE   277 25
AND WALK IN THE SAME ALL THE DAYS OF THY LIFE   277 06
AND WALK IN THE SAME ALL THE DAYS OF THY LIFE   278 15
MAY DIE TO SIN AND RISE TO NEWNESS OF LIFE   278 20
THE REST OF HIS LIFE ACCORDING TO THIS BEGINNING   280 18
AND WALK IN THE SAME ALL THE DAYS OF MY LIFE   283 28
AND THE LIFE EVERLASTING   284 24
AND TO SERVE HIM TRULY ALL THE DAYS OF MY LIFE   288 22
IN THAT STATE OF LIFE UNTO WHICH IT SHALL PLEASE GOD   289 10
WITH STEDFAST PURPOSE TO LEAD A NEW LIFE   293 28
THAT IN THE END THEY MAY OBTAIN EVERLASTING LIFE   298 23
THE AUTHOR OF EVERLASTING LIFE   303 05
OF MANKIND, WHO ONLY ART THE WELL-SPRING OF LIFE   303 15
TO COME YE MAY HAVE LIFE EVERLASTING   304 10
TOGETHER IN THIS LIFE, THAT IN THE WORLD TO COME YE   304 15
TO THY WILL IN THIS LIFE, AND ALSO MAY BE PARTAKER OF   306 30
GLORY IN THE LIFE TO COME   306 31

LIFE   CONTINUED   LIFE'S

DWELL WITH THEE IN LIFE EVERLASTING   310 24
THE LORD SAVETH THY LIFE FROM DESTRUCTION   312 17
WHO SAVETH THY LIFE FROM DESTRUCTION, AND CROWNETH   312 26
THE ERRORS OF HIS LIFE PAST, AND STEDFAST FAITH IN   316 13
OF THE SHORTNESS AND UNCERTAINTY OF HUMAN LIFE   316 28
WHAT TIME THEY SHALL DEPART OUT OF THIS LIFE   R 321 04
HATH EVERLASTING LIFE, AND SHALL NOT COME INTO   322 02
BUT IS PASSED FROM DEATH UNTO LIFE   322 03
YE HAVE ETERNAL LIFE, AND THAT YE MAY BELIEVE ON THE   322 14
HE THAT BELIEVETH ON ME HATH EVERLASTING LIFE   322 22
I AM THAT BREAD OF LIFE   322 23
I WILL GIVE FOR THE LIFE OF THE WORLD   322 28
AMENDMENT OF LIFE, AND THE GRACE AND CONSOLATION OF   323 21
AND THE LIFE, SAITH THE LORD   324 05
THE LORD IS THE STRENGTH OF MY LIFE   326 06
ALL THE DAYS OF MY LIFE, TO BEHOLD THE FAIR BEAUTY OF   326 10
NEITHER DEATH, NOR LIFE, NOR ANGELS, NOR   331 10
UNTO HIM, I AM THE WAY, THE TRUTH, AND THE LIFE   331 26
TO STRENGTH, IN THE LIFE OF PERFECT SERVICE, IN THY   332 06
IN THE MIDST OF LIFE WE ARE IN DEATH   332 22
THOU SHALT SHOW ME THE PATH OF LIFE   333 09
UNTO ETERNAL LIFE, THROUGH OUR LORD JESUS CHRIST   333 17
WHO IS THE RESURRECTION AND THE LIFE   334 31
OF SIN UNTO THE LIFE OF RIGHTEOUSNESS   335 06
SHALL DEPART THIS LIFE, WE MAY REST IN HIM   335 07
UNTO ETERNAL LIFE, THROUGH OUR LORD JESUS CHRIST   337 12
AND THE LIFE, SAITH THE LORD   338 05
AND MERCY SHALL FOLLOW ME ALL THE DAYS OF MY LIFE   338 30
TO ETERNAL LIFE THROUGH OUR LORD JESUS CHRIST,   341 14
LET HIM TREAD MY LIFE DOWN UPON THE EARTH, AND LAY   349 33
AN UNCORRUPT LIFE, *   357 07
12 THOU SHALT SHOW ME THE PATH OF LIFE   358 12
PORTION IN THIS LIFE, WHOSE BELLIES THOU FILLEST WITH   359 15
GAVEST HIM A LONG LIFE, *   365 11
4 HE ASKED LIFE OF THEE   365 11
AND MERCY SHALL FOLLOW ME ALL THE DAYS OF MY LIFE   368 23
NOR MY LIFE WITH THE BLOOD-THIRSTY   371 14
THE LORD IS THE STRENGTH OF MY LIFE   371 25
ALL THE DAYS OF MY LIFE, TO BEHOLD THE FAIR BEAUTY OF   372 02
THOU HAST KEPT MY LIFE, THAT I SHOULD NOT GO DOWN   374 29
TWINKLING OF AN EYE, AND IN HIS PLEASURE IS LIFE   375 02
11 FOR MY LIFE IS WAXEN OLD WITH HEAVINESS, *   376 11
AND TAKE THEIR COUNSEL TO TAKE AWAY MY LIFE   376 23
9 FOR WITH THEE IS THE WELL OF LIFE   384 14
SOUGHT AFTER MY LIFE LAID SNARES FOR ME   388 14
AND MAKE MY PRAYER UNTO THE GOD OF MY LIFE   393 23
THE KING A LONG LIFE, *   413 17
IS BETTER THAN THE LIFE ITSELF   414 31
PRESERVE MY LIFE FROM FEAR OF THE ENEMY   415 20
8 WHO HOLDETH OUR SOUL IN LIFE   417 31
BUT GAVE THEIR LIFE OVER TO THE PESTILENCE   438 10
HE WITHHOLD FROM THEM THAT LIVE A GODLY LIFE   446 04
AND MY LIFE DRAWETH NIGH UNTO THE GRAVE   448 32
WE REJOICE AND BE GLAD ALL THE DAYS OF OUR LIFE   454 18
16 WITH LONG LIFE WILL I SATISFY HIM, *   455 29
LEADETH A GODLY LIFE, *   463 32
4 WHO SAVETH THY LIFE FROM DESTRUCTION, *   466 13
PROSPERITY ALL THY LIFE LONG   506 17
AND LIFE FOR EVERMORE   509 20
HE HATH SMITTEN MY LIFE DOWN TO THE GROUND   518 28
WITH INNOCENCY OF LIFE, THAT, BOTH BY WORD AND GOOD   531 20
WITH INNOCENCY OF LIFE, THAT, BOTH BY WORD AND GOOD   537 25
THEY MIGHT HAVE LIFE, AND THAT THEY MIGHT HAVE IT   539 09
SHEPHERD GIVETH HIS LIFE FOR THE SHEEP   539 11
AND I LAY DOWN MY LIFE FOR THE SHEEP   539 18
OR FOR VICIOUSNESS IN LIFE   540 23
AND WITH A LIFE AGREEABLE TO THE SAME   541 02
IS COMFORT, LIFE, AND FIRE OF LOVE   544 03
THE FOUNT OF LIFE, THE FIRE OF LOVE, THE SOUL'S   544 23
AND THE AUTHOR OF EVERLASTING LIFE   545 15
WITH INNOCENCY OF LIFE, THAT, BOTH BY WORD AND GOOD   548 04
NEITHER COUNT I MY LIFE DEAR UNTO MYSELF, SO THAT I   550 19
WITH INNOCENCY OF LIFE, THAT, BOTH BY WORD AND DEED,   553 11
IS COMFORT, LIFE, AND FIRE OF LOVE   556 11
THE FOUNT OF LIFE, THE FIRE OF LOVE, THE SOUL'S   557 02
OUR REDEEMER, AND THE AUTHOR OF EVERLASTING LIFE   557 23
BY THY MERCY, OBTAIN EVERLASTING LIFE   571 12
WITH INNOCENCY OF LIFE, THAT HE MAY FAITHFULLY SERVE   572 12
AND BY MY LIFE AND DOCTRINE SET FORTH THY TRUE AND   573 22
AND WALK IN THE SAME ALL THE DAYS OF MY LIFE   577 19
AND THE LIFE EVERLASTING   578 08
AND TO SERVE HIM TRULY ALL THE DAYS OF MY LIFE   579 32
IN THAT STATE OF LIFE UNTO WHICH IT SHALL PLEASE GOD   580 14
STEDFASTLY PURPOSING TO LEAD A NEW LIFE   582 24
AND GODLY LIFE   588 07
ALL THE OTHER COMFORTS AND CONVENIENCES OF LIFE   591 11
US THE BREATH OF LIFE, AND ALONE CANST KEEP ALIVE IN   594 19
AND THE FEVER OF LIFE IS OVER, AND OUR WORK IS DONE   594 32
O GOD, WHO ART THE LIFE OF MORTAL MEN, THE LIGHT OF   595 04
OF THIS MORTAL LIFE MAY HIDE FROM US THE LIGHT OF   596 07
AND LOVE, FOR THIS LIFE AND THE LIFE TO COME   597 10
THIS LIFE AND THE LIFE TO COME   597 11
GIVER OF LIFE AND HEALTH   597 15
UNDERSTANDING ABIDE ALL THE DAYS OF HIS LIFE   598 03
THE GATES OF LARGER LIFE, THOU WILT RECEIVE HIM MORE   598 08
THE DESIRE OF VAIN-GLORY, AND THE PRIDE OF LIFE   598 23
READ FOR EXAMPLE OF LIFE AND INSTRUCTION OF MANNERS   604 03
EVERLASTING LIFE IS OFFERED TO MANKIND BY CHRIST,   604 16
PREDESTINATION TO LIFE IS THE EVERLASTING PURPOSE OF   606 06
TO FRAME HIS LIFE ACCORDING TO THAT LAW, AND THE   606 34
ARE STATES OF LIFE ALLOWED IN THE SCRIPTURES   607 41
ESTATE OF SINGLE LIFE, OR TO ABSTAIN FROM MARRIAGE   609 22

SERVANT UNTO HIS LIFE'S END   280 10
THE SAME UNTO MY LIFE'S END   284 05
GRACE UNTO THEIR LIFE'S END   294 27
UNTO THEIR LIFE'S END   302 21
SERVANT UNTO HIS LIFE'S END   565 22
GRACE UNTO THEIR LIFE'S END   565 27
UNTO THEIR LIFE'S END   566 12
THE SAME UNTO MY LIFE'S END   577 26

LIFETIME

THOU IN THY LIFETIME RECEIVEDST THY GOOD THINGS,   190 17

LIFT

GOVERN THEM, AND LIFT THEM UP FOR EVER   011 05
LIFT UP THY COUNTENANCE UPON HIM, AND GIVE HIM PEACE   046 05
THE LORD LIFT UP HIS COUNTENANCE UPON US, AND GIVE US   063 17
SAYING, LIFT UP YOUR HEARTS   076 26
WE LIFT THEM UP UNTO THE LORD   076 27
THEN LOOK UP, AND LIFT UP YOUR HEADS   093 13
AND IN HELL HE LIFT UP HIS EYES, BEING IN TORMENTS,   190 11
AFAR OFF, WOULD NOT LIFT UP SO MUCH AS HIS EYES UNTO   205 29
LIFT IT UP, BE NOT AFRAID   243 04
GOOD TIDINGS, LIFT UP THY VOICE WITH STRENGTH   243 04
LIFT UP YOUR HEARTS   279 02
WE LIFT THEM UP UNTO THE LORD   279 03
THE LORD LIFT UP HIS COUNTENANCE UPON THEE, AND GIVE   314 29
LIFT UP YOUR HEARTS, ETC   R 323 06
AND NOW SHALL HE LIFT UP MINE HEAD *   326 15
I WILL LIFT UP MINE EYES UNTO THE HILLS   327 19
THE LORD LIFT UP HIS COUNTENANCE UPON YOU, AND GIVE   332 13
I WILL LIFT UP MINE EYES UNTO THE HILLS   339 03
UNTO HIM, THE LORD LIFT UP HIS COUNTENANCE UPON HIM,   341 17
7 LORD, LIFT THOU UP *   347 24
IN THY WRATH, AND LIFT UP THYSELF, BECAUSE OF THE   349 35
SAKES THEREFORE LIFT UP THYSELF AGAIN   350 05
O LORD GOD, AND LIFT UP THINE HAND   353 32
AND THAT HATH NOT LIFT UP HIS MIND UNTO VANITY, NOR   369 03
AND BE YE LIFT UP, YE EVERLASTING DOORS   369 09
7 LIFT UP YOUR HEADS, O YE GATES   369 09
9 LIFT UP YOUR HEADS, O YE GATES   369 13
AND BE YE LIFT UP, YE EVERLASTING DOORS   369 13
O LORD, WILL I LIFT UP MY SOUL   369 18
6 AND NOW SHALL HE LIFT UP MINE HEAD *   372 07
AND LIFT UP MY HANDS IN THY NAME   414 34
O GOD, SHALL LIFT ME UP   424 03
4 LIFT UP THY FEET, THAT THOU MAYEST UTTERLY DESTROY   430 10
THAT HATE THEE HAVE LIFT UP THEIR HEAD   444 08
O LORD, DO I LIFT UP MY SOUL   447 12
THOU SHALT LIFT UP OUR HORNS   451 09
THE FLOODS HAVE LIFT UP THEIR VOICE   457 11
THE FLOODS LIFT UP THEIR WAVES   457 12
26 THEN LIFT HE UP HIS HAND AGAINST THEM, *   474 21
THEREFORE SHALL HE LIFT UP HIS HEAD   482 22
HANDS ALSO WILL I LIFT UP UNTO THY COMMANDMENTS,   493 04
I WILL LIFT UP MINE EYES UNTO THE HILLS   502 22
UNTO THEE LIFT I UP MINE EYES, *   503 27
3 LIFT UP YOUR HANDS IN THE SANCTUARY, *   509 27
FOR I LIFT UP MY SOUL UNTO THEE   519 09
AND THAT HATH NOT LIFT UP HIS MIND UNTO VANITY, NOR   563 18
7 LIFT UP YOUR HEADS, O YE GATES   563 24
AND BE YE LIFT UP, YE EVERLASTING DOORS   563 24
AND BE YE LIFT UP, YE EVERLASTING DOORS   563 28
9 LIFT UP YOUR HEADS, O YE GATES   563 28
THE LORD LIFT UP HIS COUNTENANCE UPON US, AND GIVE US   593 20
MIGHT OF THY SPIRIT LIFT US, WE PRAY THEE, TO THY   595 22

LIFTED

OF THE COMPANY LIFTED UP HER VOICE, AND SAID UNTO   130 18
WHEN JESUS THEN LIFTED UP HIS EYES, AND SAW A GREAT   131 26
AND HE LIFTED UP HIS HANDS, AND BLESSED   178 24
AND AS MOSES LIFTED UP THE SERPENT IN THE WILDERNESS,   188 26
THE SON OF MAN BE LIFTED UP   188 28
AND THEY LIFTED UP THEIR VOICES, AND SAID, JESUS,   210 03
WHEN JESUS THEN LIFTED UP HIS EYES, AND SAW A GREAT   225 22
LEST BEING LIFTED UP WITH PRIDE HE FALL INTO THE   549 27
CARRIED ABOUT, LIFTED UP, OR WORSHIPPED   608 48

LIFTER

AND THE LIFTER UP OF MY HEAD   309 19
AND THE LIFTER UP OF MY HEAD   346 30

LIFTEST

THOU THAT LIFTEST ME UP FROM THE GATES OF DEATH   352 17

LIFTETH

WHICH LIFTETH UP THE WAVES THEREOF   477 27
AND LIFTETH THE POOR OUT OF THE MIRE   484 19
AND LIFTETH UP ALL THOSE THAT ARE DOWN   521 20

LIFTING

AND LET THE LIFTING UP OF MY HANDS BE AN EVENING   021 17
AND LET THE LIFTING UP OF MY HANDS BE AN EVENING   517 11

LIGHT

O SEND OUT THY LIGHT AND THY TRUTH, THAT THEY MAY   003 22

LIGHT   CONTINUED

O YE LIGHT AND DARKNESS, BLESS YE THE LORD   012 30
TO GIVE LIGHT TO THEM THAT SIT IN DARKNESS, AND IN   014 31
OF GOD, LIGHT OF LIGHT, VERY GOD OF VERY GOD   016 04
GOD OF GOD, LIGHT OF LIGHT, VERY GOD OF VERY GOD   016 04
SHALL COME TO THY LIGHT, AND KINGS TO THE BRIGHTNESS   022 02
TO BE A LIGHT TO LIGHTEN THE GENTILES, *   028 13
AND SHOW US THE LIGHT OF HIS COUNTENANCE, AND BE   028 18
OF GOD, LIGHT OF LIGHT, VERY GOD OF VERY GOD   030 09
GOD OF GOD, LIGHT OF LIGHT, VERY GOD OF VERY GOD   030 09
LANDS TO THE LIGHT OF THY TRUTH   038 17
THY MERCY AND THE LIGHT OF THY PRESENCE, THAT THE   042 18
ALONE BRINGEST LIGHT OUT OF DARKNESS, AND GOOD OUT OF   046 26
OF GOD, LIGHT OF LIGHT, VERY GOD OF VERY GOD   071 06
GOD OF GOD, LIGHT OF LIGHT, VERY GOD OF VERY GOD   071 06
LET YOUR LIGHT SO SHINE BEFORE MEN, THAT THEY MAY SEE   072 04
US OUT OF DARKNESS INTO HIS OWN GLORIOUS LIGHT   077 25
HAST CAUSED A NEW LIGHT TO SHINE IN OUR HEARTS,   077 30
INTO THE CLEAR LIGHT AND TRUE KNOWLEDGE OF THEE,   079 02
US THE ARMOUR OF LIGHT, NOW IN THE TIME OF THIS   090 13
AND LET US PUT ON THE ARMOUR OF LIGHT   091 05
BOTH WILL BRING TO LIGHT THE HIDDEN THINGS OF   094 11
AND THE LIGHT SHINETH IN DARKNESS   097 24
THE LIFE WAS THE LIGHT OF MEN   097 24
WITNESS OF THE LIGHT, THAT ALL MEN THROUGH HIM MIGHT   097 27
HE WAS NOT THAT LIGHT, BUT WAS SENT TO BEAR WITNESS   097 29
BUT WAS SENT TO BEAR WITNESS OF THAT LIGHT   097 29
THAT WAS THE TRUE LIGHT, WHICH LIGHTETH EVERY MAN   097 30
BRIGHT BEAMS OF LIGHT UPON THY CHURCH, THAT IT,   101 06
MAY SO WALK IN THE LIGHT OF THY TRUTH, THAT IT MAY AT   101 08
THAT GOD IS LIGHT, AND IN HIM IS NO DARKNESS AT   101 23
AS HE IS IN THE LIGHT, WE HAVE FELLOWSHIP ONE WITH   101 26
IF WE WALK IN THE LIGHT, AS HE IS IN THE LIGHT,   101 26
UPON US THE NEW LIGHT OF THINE INCARNATE WORD   106 26
THAT THE SAME LIGHT ENKINDLED IN OUR HEARTS MAY SHINE   106 27
SHALL NOT GIVE HER LIGHT, AND THE STARS SHALL FALL   118 15
BUT NOW ARE YE LIGHT IN THE LORD   129 13
WALK AS CHILDREN OF LIGHT   129 13
THAT ARE REPROVED ARE MADE MANIFEST BY THE LIGHT   129 20
FOR WHATSOEVER DOTH MAKE MANIFEST IS LIGHT   129 21
AND CHRIST SHALL GIVE THEE LIGHT   129 22
THAT WALKETH IN DARKNESS, AND HATH NO LIGHT   144 25
WALK IN THE LIGHT OF YOUR FIRE, AND IN THE SPARKS   144 27
ARE IN ERROR THE LIGHT OF THY TRUTH, TO THE INTENT   173 05
TO THEM THE LIGHT OF THY HOLY SPIRIT   180 09
THAT LIGHT IS COME INTO THE WORLD,   185 06
RATHER THAN LIGHT, BECAUSE THEIR DEEDS WERE EVIL   185 07
EVIL HATETH THE LIGHT, NEITHER COMETH TO THE LIGHT,   185 08
COMETH TO THE LIGHT, LEST HIS DEEDS SHOULD BE   185 09
COMETH TO THE LIGHT, THAT HIS DEEDS MAY BE MADE   185 10
DOTH NOT LIGHT A CANDLE, AND SWEEP THE HOUSE,   193 28
BUT THEY MADE LIGHT OF IT, AND WENT THEIR WAYS, ONE   218 10
OF THE INHERITANCE OF THE SAINTS IN LIGHT   224 10
HAST CAUSED THE LIGHT OF THE GOSPEL TO SHINE   229 18
ROUND ABOUT HIM A LIGHT FROM HEAVEN   229 31
A LIGHT TO LIGHTEN THE GENTILES, AND THE GLORY OF THY   233 08
FOR MY YOKE IS EASY, AND MY BURDEN IS LIGHT   235 14
TO GIVE LIGHT TO THEM THAT SIT IN DARKNESS AND IN   244 15
UPON HIM, AND A LIGHT SHINED IN THE PRISON   245 13
LEST THE LIGHT OF THE GLORIOUS GOSPEL OF CHRIST,   251 04
WHO COMMANDED THE LIGHT TO SHINE OUT OF DARKNESS   251 07
TO GIVE THE LIGHT OF THE KNOWLEDGE OF THE GLORY OF   251 08
SHALL THE SUN SHINE ON THEM, NOR ANY HEAT   257 13
SET THEE TO BE A LIGHT OF THE GENTILES, THAT THOU   261 04
AND ON EARTH, THY LIGHT AND THY PEACE   268 16
INTO THE LAND OF LIGHT AND JOY, IN THE FELLOWSHIP OF   268 24
LET US WALK IN THE LIGHT OF THE LORD   290 05
O SEND OUT THY LIGHT AND THY TRUTH, THAT THEY MAY   310 11
GLADNESS IN THY KINGDOM, WITH THY SAINTS IN LIGHT   318 21
INTO THE GLORIOUS COMPANY OF THE SAINTS IN LIGHT   320 03
SECRET SINS IN THE LIGHT OF THY COUNTENANCE   325 29
THE LORD IS MY LIGHT AND MY SALVATION   326 05
INTO THE LAND OF LIGHT AND JOY, IN THE FELLOWSHIP OF   334 16
OF THE INHERITANCE OF THE SAINTS IN LIGHT   336 02
SHALL THE SUN LIGHT ON THEM, NOR ANY HEAT   341 24
THE LIGHT OF THY COUNTENANCE UPON US   347 24
29 THOU ALSO SHALT LIGHT MY CANDLE   361 24
LORD MY GOD SHALL MAKE MY DARKNESS TO BE LIGHT   361 25
AND GIVETH LIGHT UNTO THE EYES   363 32
THE LORD IS MY LIGHT AND MY SALVATION   371 24
THY SERVANT THE LIGHT OF THY COUNTENANCE, *   376 28
AND IN THY LIGHT SHALL WE SEE LIGHT   384 14
AND IN THY LIGHT SHALL WE SEE LIGHT   384 15
AS CLEAR AS THE LIGHT, *   385 04
AND THE LIGHT OF MINE EYES IS GONE FROM ME   388 11
3 O SEND OUT THY LIGHT AND THY TRUTH, THAT THEY   394 09
THINE ARM, AND THE LIGHT OF THY COUNTENANCE   394 09
AND SHALL NEVER SEE LIGHT   401 15
BEFORE GOD IN THE LIGHT OF THE LIVING   409 10
AND SHOW US THE LIGHT OF HIS COUNTENANCE, AND BE   418 24
HAST PREPARED THE LIGHT AND THE SUN   431 09
THROUGH WITH A LIGHT OF FIRE   435 29
SHOW THE LIGHT OF THY COUNTENANCE, AND WE SHALL BE   441 08
SHOW THE LIGHT OF THY COUNTENANCE, AND WE SHALL BE   441 16
SHOW THE LIGHT OF THY COUNTENANCE, AND WE SHALL BE   442 09
THE LORD GOD IS A LIGHT AND DEFENCE   446 02
SHALL WALK IN THE LIGHT OF THY COUNTENANCE   451 05
SECRET SINS IN THE LIGHT OF THY COUNTENANCE   454 03
IS SPRUNG UP A LIGHT FOR THE RIGHTEOUS, *   461 19
THYSELF WITH LIGHT AS IT WERE WITH A GARMENT,   467 27
AND FIRE TO GIVE LIGHT IN THE NIGHT SEASON   472 16
THERE ARISETH UP LIGHT IN THE DARKNESS   483 24
27 GOD IS THE LORD, WHO HATH SHOWED US LIGHT   489 22
AND A LIGHT UNTO MY PATHS   497 07
IT GIVETH LIGHT AND UNDERSTANDING UNTO THE SIMPLE   498 30

135 SHOW THE LIGHT OF THY COUNTENANCE UPON THY   499 08
THE DARKNESS AND LIGHT TO THEE ARE BOTH ALIKE   515 11
PRAISE HIM, ALL YE STARS AND LIGHT   524 10
WITH PERPETUAL LIGHT THE DULNESS OF OUR BLINDED   544 04
THY LIGHT TO EVERY SENSE IMPART, AND SHED THY LOVE IN   545 02
WITH PERPETUAL LIGHT THE DULNESS OF OUR BLINDED   556 12
THY LIGHT TO EVERY SENSE IMPART, AND SHED THY LOVE IN   557 08
AND MORE WITH THE LIGHT OF THE EVERLASTING GOSPEL   572 27
LET THE LIGHT OF THY GOSPEL SHINE UPON ALL NATIONS   590 23
OF MORTAL MEN, THE LIGHT OF THE FAITHFUL, THE   595 04
IN JUDGMENT, AND LIGHT RISETH UP IN DARKNESS FOR THE   595 27
LIGHT WE MAY SEE LIGHT, AND IN THY STRAIGHT PATH MAY   595 31
AND THAT IN THY LIGHT WE MAY SEE LIGHT, AND IN THY   595 31
HIDE FROM US THE LIGHT OF THAT LOVE WHICH IS   596 06
TO THE LIGHT OF THY WISDOM, AND RECEIVE THE BLESSED   596 13
GIVE US LIGHT AND STRENGTH SO TO TRAIN THEM, THAT   596 25
THAT LAW, AND THE LIGHT OF NATURE   606 34

LIGHTEN

TO BE A LIGHT TO LIGHTEN THE GENTILES, *   028 13
LIGHTEN OUR DARKNESS, WE BESEECH THEE, O LORD   031 26
A LIGHT TO LIGHTEN THE GENTILES, AND THE GLORY OF THY   233 08
LIGHTEN MINE EYES, THAT I SLEEP NOT IN DEATH   356 02
AND LIGHTEN WITH CELESTIAL FIRE   543 32
AND LIGHTEN WITH CELESTIAL FIRE   556 07
LIGHTEN OUR DARKNESS, WE BESEECH THEE, O LORD   593 13

LIGHTENED

5 THEY HAD AN EYE UNTO HIM, AND WERE LIGHTENED   380 11

LIGHTER

ARE ALTOGETHER LIGHTER THAN VANITY ITSELF   414 17

LIGHTETH

WHICH LIGHTETH EVERY MAN THAT COMETH INTO THE   097 30

LIGHTING

FROM HEAVEN, LIGHTING UPON THE DISCIPLES, TO TEACH   078 27

LIGHTLY

AND THAT NOT LIGHTLY, AND AFTER THE MANNER OF   087 11
BY ANY TO BE ENTERED INTO UNADVISEDLY OR LIGHTLY   300 17
AND LIGHTLY REGARDED THE COUNSEL OF THE MOST HIGHEST   476 27

LIGHTNING

FROM LIGHTNING AND TEMPEST   054 30
FOR AS THE LIGHTNING COMETH OUT OF THE EAST, AND   118 10
CAST FORTH THY LIGHTNING, AND TEAR THEM   520 02

LIGHTNINGS

O YE LIGHTNINGS AND CLOUDS, BLESS YE THE LORD   012 32
PROCEEDED LIGHTNINGS AND THUNDERINGS AND VOICES   187 12
HE CAST FORTH LIGHTNINGS, AND DESTROYED THEM   360 27
THE LIGHTNINGS SHONE UPON THE GROUND   434 19
4 HIS LIGHTNINGS GAVE SHINE UNTO THE WORLD   461 04
SENDETH FORTH LIGHTNINGS WITH THE RAIN, BRINGING THE   510 16

LIGHTS

THEY MAY SHINE AS LIGHTS IN THE WORLD, AND IN ALL   047 27
HIS GRACE AND THE LIGHTS OF THE WORLD IN THEIR   048 18
THE FATHER OF LIGHTS, WITH WHOM IS NO VARIABLENESS,   174 27
THE FATHER OF LIGHTS, WITH WHOM IS NO VARIABLENESS,   265 20
AND THE LIGHTS OF THE WORLD IN THEIR SEVERAL   336 19
7 WHO HATH MADE GREAT LIGHTS   511 28
AND YOUR LIGHTS BURNING   534 16

LIKE

THERE BE ANY SORROW LIKE UNTO MY SORROW WHICH IS DONE   004 30
FROM THY WAYS LIKE LOST SHEEP   006 18
SHALL BE READ, IN LIKE MANNER, THE SECOND LESSON,   R 014 02
ALL WE LIKE SHEEP HAVE GONE ASTRAY   022 14
FROM THY WAYS LIKE LOST SHEEP   023 25
AND THE SECOND IS LIKE UNTO IT   069 29
AND DEACONS, IN LIKE MANNER, (IF ANY BE   R 082 27
AND THE SPIRIT, LIKE A DOVE, DESCENDING UPON HIM   112 21
WE MAY BE MADE LIKE UNTO HIM IN HIS ETERNAL AND   117 09
WE SHALL BE LIKE HIM   117 19
OF HEAVEN IS LIKE UNTO A MAN THAT IS AN HOUSEHOLDER,   119 15
I SHALL BE A LIAR LIKE UNTO YOU   133 27
AND THY GARMENTS LIKE HIM THAT TREADETH IN THE   138 15
HAVE I SET MY FACE LIKE A FLINT, AND I KNOW THAT I   144 11
THE LIKE FIGURE WHEREUNTO, EVEN BAPTISM, DOTH ALSO   161 29
NOT A DOER, HE IS LIKE UNTO A MAN BEHOLDING HIS   176 07
ALMIGHTY GOD, THAT LIKE AS WE DO BELIEVE THY   177 14
SHALL SO COME IN LIKE MANNER AS YE HAVE SEEN HIM GO   178 19
THEM CLOVEN TONGUES LIKE AS OF FIRE, AND IT SAT UPON   180 21
WAS TO LOOK UPON LIKE A JASPER AND A SARDINE STONE   187 06
IN SIGHT LIKE UNTO AN EMERALD   187 08
WAS A SEA OF GLASS LIKE UNTO CRYSTAL   187 15
AND THE FIRST WAS LIKE A LION, AND THE SECOND LIKE A   187 18
AND THE SECOND LIKE A CALF, AND THE THIRD HAD A FACE   187 18
AND THE FOURTH WAS LIKE A FLYING EAGLE   187 19
THAT LIKE AS CHRIST WAS RAISED UP FROM THE DEAD BY   197 13
DRUNKENNESS, REVELLINGS, AND SUCH LIKE   209 23

LIKE   CONTINUED

WAS NOT ARRAYED LIKE ONE OF THESE   211 24
AND THE SECOND IS LIKE UNTO IT, THOU SHALT LOVE THY   215 13
OF HEAVEN IS LIKE UNTO A CERTAIN KING, WHICH MADE A   218 03
FOR HE IS LIKE A REFINER'S FIRE, AND LIKE FULLERS'   232 09
REFINER'S FIRE, AND LIKE FULLERS' SOPE   232 09
BEING NOT LIKE CHILDREN CARRIED AWAY WITH EVERY   237 07
HE THAT WAVERETH IS LIKE A WAVE OF THE SEA DRIVEN   239 15
FEED HIS FLOCK LIKE A SHEPHERD   243 08
IN THY CHURCH THE LIKE POWER AND LOVE, TO THE HEALING   253 19
NOT A DOER, HE IS LIKE UNTO A MAN BEHOLDING HIS   265 30
WAS NOT ARRAYED LIKE ONE OF THESE   266 22
GRANT THAT LIKE AS CHRIST DIED AND ROSE AGAIN,   278 18
TO CONSUME AWAY, LIKE AS IT WERE A MOTH FRETTING A   325 03
FADE AWAY SUDDENLY LIKE THE GRASS   325 23
AND IS CUT DOWN, LIKE A FLOWER   332 20
AND MADE LIKE UNTO HIS OWN GLORIOUS BODY   333 21
AND MADE LIKE UNTO HIS GLORIOUS BODY   337 15
FEED HIS FLOCK LIKE A SHEPHERD   338 12
3 AND HE SHALL BE LIKE A TREE PLANTED BY THE   345 12
BUT THEY ARE LIKE THE CHAFF, WHICH THE WIND   345 17
THEM IN PIECES LIKE A POTTER'S VESSEL   346 16
HE DEVOUR MY SOUL LIKE A LION, AND TEAR IT IN PIECES,   349 25
I HAVE NO GOOD LIKE UNTO THEE   357 24
12 LIKE AS A LION THAT IS GREEDY OF HIS PREY,   359 10
HE MAKETH MY FEET LIKE HARTS' FEET, *   362 02
SHALT MAKE THEM LIKE A FIERY OVEN IN TIME OF THY   365 22
14 I AM POURED OUT LIKE WATER, AND ALL MY BONES ARE   366 31
OF MY BODY IS EVEN LIKE MELTING WAX   366 33
IS DRIED UP LIKE A POTSHERD, AND MY TONGUE CLEAVETH   366 34
I BECOME LIKE THEM THAT GO DOWN INTO THE PIT   373 05
THEM ALSO TO SKIP LIKE A CALF   374 09
AND SIRION, LIKE A YOUNG UNICORN   374 10
I AM BECOME LIKE A BROKEN VESSEL   376 20
AND MY MOISTURE WAS LIKE THE DROUGHT IN SUMMER   377 29
10 BE YE NOT LIKE TO HORSE AND MULE, WHICH HAVE NC   378 10
LIKE AS WE DO PUT OUR TRUST IN THEE   379 33
LORD, WHO IS LIKE UNTO THEE, WHO DELIVEREST THE   382 09
STANDETH LIKE THE STRONG MOUNTAINS   384 06
THY JUDGMENTS ARE LIKE THE GREAT DEEP   384 07
SOON BE CUT DOWN LIKE THE GRASS, *   384 27
AND FLOURISHING LIKE A GREEN BAY-TREE   387 05
AND ARE LIKE A SORE BURDEN, TOO HEAVY FOR ME TO BEAR   387 29
13 AS FOR ME, I WAS LIKE A DEAF MAN, AND HEARD NOT   388 17
TO CONSUME AWAY, LIKE AS IT WERE A MOTH FRETTING A   389 32
THOU HAST DONE, LIKE AS BE ALSO THY THOUGHTS, WHICH   390 22
LIKE AS THE HART DESIRETH THE WATER-BROOKS, *   392 29
US BE EATEN UP LIKE SHEEP, *   395 15
LIKE AS THE RICH ALSO AMONG THE PEOPLE SHALL MAKE   397 10
7 LIKE AS WE HAVE HEARD, SO HAVE WE SEEN IN THE CITY   399 24
LIE IN THE GRAVE LIKE SHEEP   400 34
LIES THOU CUTTEST LIKE A SHARP RAZOR   404 23
9 AS FOR ME, I AM LIKE A GREEN OLIVE-TREE IN THE   405 04
FOR THY SAINTS LIKE IT WELL   405 09
O THAT I HAD WINGS LIKE A DOVE   406 30
EVEN LIKE THE DEAF ADDER, THAT STOPPETH HER EARS   410 16
LET THEM FALL AWAY LIKE WATER THAT RUNNETH APACE   410 21
THEM CONSUME AWAY LIKE A SNAIL, AND BE LIKE THE   410 23
A SNAIL, AND BE LIKE THE UNTIMELY FRUIT OF A WOMAN   410 23
THEY GRIN LIKE A DOG, AND RUN ABOUT THROUGH THE CITY   411 16
GRIN LIKE A DOG, AND WILL GO ABOUT THE CITY   412 02
SHALL YE BE, AND LIKE A BROKEN HEDGE   414 03
WHET THEIR TONGUE LIKE A SWORD, *   415 23
ALSO HAST TRIED US, LIKE AS SILVER IS TRIED   417 34
2 LIKE AS THE SMOKE VANISHETH, SO SHALT THOU DRIVE   419 11
AND LIKE AS WAX MELTETH AT THE FIRE, SO LET THE   419 12
AND HER FEATHERS LIKE GOLD   420 08
O GOD, WHO IS LIKE UNTO THEE   426 15
HE SHALL COME DOWN LIKE THE RAIN UPON THE MOWN GRASS,   427 08
THEREOF SHALL SHAKE LIKE LEBANON   427 30
CITY SHALL FLOURISH LIKE GRASS UPON THE EARTH   427 31
IN NO MISFORTUNE LIKE OTHER FOLK   428 18
ARE THEY PLAGUED LIKE OTHER MEN   428 19
20 YEA, EVEN LIKE AS A DREAM WHEN ONE AWAKETH   429 16
LEDDEST THY PEOPLE LIKE SHEEP, *   434 23
10 LIKE AS THE CHILDREN OF EPHRAIM   435 17
THAT IT GUSHED OUT LIKE THE RIVERS   435 34
AND FEATHERED FOWLS LIKE AS THE SAND OF THE SEA   436 26
HE LED THEM FORTH LIKE SHEEP, *   438 14
IN THE WILDERNESS LIKE A FLOCK   438 15
AND FELL AWAY LIKE THEIR FOREFATHERS   438 26
STARTING ASIDE LIKE A BROKEN BOW   438 27
AND LIKE A GIANT REFRESHED WITH WINE   439 08
FOUNDATION OF IT LIKE THE GROUND WHICH HE HATH MADE   439 17
HAVE THEY SHED LIKE WATER ON EVERY SIDE OF JERUSALEM,   440 04
THY JEALOUSY BURN LIKE FIRE FOR EVER   440 10
THAT LEADEST JOSEPH LIKE A FLOCK   441 04
BOUGHS THEREOF WERE LIKE THE GOODLY CEDAR-TREES   441 23
7 BUT YE SHALL DIE LIKE MEN, *   443 31
AND FALL LIKE ONE OF THE PRINCES   443 31
AND THEIR PRINCES LIKE OREB AND ZEEB   444 26
ALL THEIR PRINCES LIKE AS ZEBAH AND ZALMUNNA   444 27
O MY GOD, MAKE THEM LIKE UNTO THE WHIRLING DUST,   444 30
14 LIKE AS THE FIRE THAT BURNETH UP THE FOREST,   444 32
GODS THERE IS NONE LIKE UNTO THEE, O LORD   447 19
OFF AMONG THE DEAD, LIKE UNTO THEM THAT ARE SLAIN,   449 04
I AM IN MISERY, AND LIKE UNTO HIM THAT IS AT THE   449 26
ABOUT ME DAILY LIKE WATER, *   449 31
THAT SHALL BE LIKE UNTO THE LORD   450 17
OF HOSTS, WHO IS LIKE UNTO THEE   450 22
AND HIS THRONE IS LIKE AS THE SUN BEFORE ME   452 13
THY WRATH BURN LIKE FIRE   452 33
FADE AWAY SUDDENLY LIKE THE GRASS   453 28
SHALL BE EXALTED LIKE THE HORN OF AN UNICORN   456 19
SHALL FLOURISH LIKE A PALM-TREE, *   456 24

LILIES

CONSIDER THE LILIES OF THE FIELD, HOW THEY GROW 211 21
CONSIDER THE LILIES OF THE FIELD, HOW THEY GROW 266 19

LINEAGE

OF THE HOUSE AND LINEAGE OF DAVID 099 04

LINEN

IT A FAIR WHITE LINEN CLOTH .... R 067 06
SAME WITH A FAIR LINEN CLOTH .... R 083 13
HAVING A LINEN CLOTH CAST ABOUT HIS NAKED BODY 142 29
AND HE LEFT THE LINEN CLOTH, AND FLED FROM THEM 142 30
IT IN A CLEAN LINEN CLOTH, AND LAID IT IN HIS OWN NEW 162 11
SAW THE LINEN CLOTHES LYING 164 20
AND SEETH THE LINEN CLOTHES LIE, AND THE NAPKIN, THAT 164 22
NOT LYING WITH THE LINEN CLOTHES, BUT WRAPPED 164 24
IN PURPLE AND FINE LINEN, AND FARED SUMPTUOUSLY EVERY 190 04

LINKS

THEIR NOBLES WITH LINKS OF IRON 525 18

LION

FIRST WAS LIKE A LION, AND THE SECOND LIKE A CALF, ... 187 18
AS A ROARING LION, WALKETH ABOUT, SEEKING WHOM 193 05
MY SOUL LIKE A LION, AND TEAR IT IN PIECES, * 349 25
EVEN AS A LION LURKETH HE IN HIS DEN, * 353 23
12 LIKE AS A LION THAT IS GREEDY OF HIS PREY, ... 359 10
AS IT WERE A RAMPING AND A ROARING LION 366 30
SHALT GO UPON THE LION AND ADDER 455 21
THE YOUNG LION AND THE DRAGON SHALT THOU TREAD UNDER 455 22

LION'S

AND AS IT WERE A LION'S WHELP LURKING IN SECRET 359 11
SAVE ME FROM THE LION'S MOUTH 367 14

LIONS

10 THE LIONS DO LACK, AND SUFFER HUNGER 380 21
THEY BRING ON ME, AND MY DARLING FROM THE LIONS 382 31
MY SOUL IS AMONG LIONS 409 20
JAW-BONES OF THE LIONS, O LORD 410 20
21 THE LIONS, ROARING AFTER THEIR PREY, * 469 02

LIPS

OPEN THOU OUR LIPS, ETC .... R 003 12
LIKEWISE HE SHALL SAY, O LORD, OPEN THOU OUR LIPS 007 31
NOT ONLY WITH OUR LIPS, BUT IN OUR LIVES, BY GIVING 019 27
OPEN THOU OUR LIPS, ETC .... R 021 09
LIKEWISE HE SHALL SAY, O LORD, OPEN THOU OUR LIPS 025 06
NOT ONLY WITH OUR LIPS, BUT IN OUR LIVES, BY GIVING 033 25
THOU SHALT OPEN MY LIPS, O LORD, * 061 09
FROM EVIL, AND HIS LIPS THAT THEY SPEAK NO GUILE 195 26
FLATTER WITH THEIR LIPS, AND DISSEMBLE IN THEIR 355 10
OUT ALL DECEITFUL LIPS, * 355 12
MAKE MENTION OF THEIR NAMES WITHIN MY LIPS 357 30
THAT GOETH NOT OUT OF FEIGNED LIPS 358 18
BY THE WORD OF THY LIPS I HAVE KEPT ME FROM THE WAYS 358 25
SHOOT OUT THEIR LIPS, AND SHAKE THEIR HEADS, SAYING, ... 365 08
20 LET THE LYING LIPS BE PUT TO SILENCE, * 376 13
AND THY LIPS, THAT THEY SPEAK NO GUILE 380 27
WILL NOT REFRAIN MY LIPS, O LORD, AND THAT THOU 391 02
OF GRACE ARE THY LIPS, BECAUSE GOD HATH BLESSED THEE 396 19
THOU SHALT OPEN MY LIPS, O LORD, * 404 07
WITH THEIR MOUTH, AND SWORDS ARE IN THEIR LIPS 411 19
THE WORDS OF THEIR LIPS, THEY SHALL BE TAKEN IN THEIR 411 30
MY LIPS SHALL PRAISE THEE 414 32
WHEN MY MOUTH PRAISETH THEE WITH JOYFUL LIPS 415 04
I PROMISED WITH MY LIPS, AND SPAKE WITH MY MOUTH, ... 418 08
22 MY LIPS WILL BE GLAD WHEN I SING UNTO THEE 426 25
NOR ALTER THE THING THAT IS GONE OUT OF MY LIPS 452 10
SO THAT HE SPAKE UNADVISEDLY WITH HIS LIPS 475 03
13 WITH MY LIPS HAVE I BEEN TELLING * 490 23
171 MY LIPS SHALL SPEAK OF THY PRAISE, * 501 24
O LORD, FROM LYING LIPS, * 502 09
ADDER'S POISON IS UNDER THEIR LIPS 516 14
OF THEIR OWN LIPS FALL UPON THE HEAD OF THEM * 516 27
AND KEEP THE DOOR OF MY LIPS 517 14

LISTETH

BLOWETH WHERE IT LISTETH, AND THOU HEAREST THE SOUND 188 14
BLOWETH WHERE IT LISTETH, AND THOU HEAREST THE SOUND 275 19

LITANY

ANY DAY WHEN THE LITANY OR HOLY COMMUNION IS .... R 003 06
IN THE LITANY, AS THERE APPOINTED .... R 003 14
HERE WHEN THE LITANY IS SAID, AND MAY BE OMITTED WHEN .... R 017 20
MAY END THE LITANY HERE, OR AT HIS DISCRETION ADD .... R 059 29
WE HUMBLY BESEECH THEE, O FATHER, IN THE LITANY .... R 060 04
IF THE LITANY HATH BEEN ALREADY SAID, THE MINISTER .... R 061 19
THE CLERGY AND PEOPLE PRESENT, SAY THE LITANY .... R 530 31
MAY BE SAID THE LITANY FOR ORDINATIONS .... R 531 10
INSTEAD OF THE LITANY APPOINTED, MAY BE SAID THE .... R 531 10
THE CLERGY AND PEOPLE PRESENT, SAY THE LITANY .... R 537 07
MAY BE SAID THE LITANY FOR ORDINATIONS .... R 537 16
INSTEAD OF THE LITANY APPOINTED, MAY BE SAID THE .... R 537 16
SUFFICE THAT THE LITANY BE ONCE SAID FOR BOTH .... R 547 21

LITANY   CONTINUED

AND THEN SHALL BE SAID THE LITANY .... R 553 14
INSTEAD OF THE LITANY, MAY BE SAID THE LITANY FOR .... R 553 24
MAY BE SAID THE LITANY FOR ORDINATIONS .... R 553 24

LITTLE

HE THAT SOWETH LITTLE SHALL REAP LITTLE 072 16
HE THAT SOWETH LITTLE SHALL REAP LITTLE 072 16
IF THOU HAST LITTLE, DO THY DILIGENCE GLADLY TO GIVE 072 33
DO THY DILIGENCE GLADLY TO GIVE OF THAT LITTLE 072 34
YOURSELVES HOW LITTLE SUCH FEIGNED EXCUSES WILL AVAIL 089 02
LITTLE CHILDREN, LET NO MAN DECEIVE YOU 117 26
THAT EVERY ONE OF THEM MAY TAKE A LITTLE 131 31
IT BUT A LITTLE WHILE 139 27
HE WENT FORWARD A LITTLE, AND FELL ON THE GROUND, ... 141 33
AND A LITTLE AFTER, THEY THAT STOOD BY SAID AGAIN TO 143 30
AND AFTER A LITTLE WHILE ANOTHER SAW HIM, AND SAID, ... 151 13
YE NOT THAT A LITTLE LEAVEN LEAVENETH THE WHOLE LUMP 165 10
HIS DISCIPLES, A LITTLE WHILE, AND YE SHALL NOT SEE 173 27
AND AGAIN, A LITTLE WHILE, AND YE SHALL SEE ME, ... 173 28
AND AGAIN, A LITTLE WHILE, AND YE SHALL SEE ME 173 31
SAITH UNTO US, A LITTLE WHILE, AND YE SHALL NOT SEE 173 31
THAT HE SAITH, A LITTLE WHILE 174 03
OF THAT I SAID, A LITTLE WHILE, AND YE SHALL NOT SEE 174 05
AND AGAIN, A LITTLE WHILE, AND YE SHALL SEE ME 174 06
YET A LITTLE WHILE, AND THE WORLD SEETH ME NO MORE 181 15
MY LITTLE CHILDREN, LET US NOT LOVE IN WORD, NEITHER 191 21
THRUST OUT A LITTLE FROM THE LAND 196 11
O YE OF LITTLE FAITH 211 26
THAT EVERY ONE OF THEM MAY TAKE A LITTLE 225 28
FOR YET A LITTLE WHILE, AND HE THAT SHALL COME WILL 228 17
JESUS CALLED A LITTLE CHILD UNTO HIM, AND SET HIM IN 252 24
AND BECOME AS LITTLE CHILDREN, YE SHALL NOT ENTER 252 26
HIMSELF AS THIS LITTLE CHILD, THE SAME IS GREATEST IN 252 28
RECEIVE ONE SUCH LITTLE CHILD IN MY NAME RECEIVETH 252 30
ONE OF THESE LITTLE ONES WHICH BELIEVE IN ME, ... 252 31
NOT ONE OF THESE LITTLE ONES 253 10
O YE OF LITTLE FAITH 266 25
SUFFER THE LITTLE CHILDREN TO COME UNTO ME, AND 274 28
OF GOD AS A LITTLE CHILD, HE SHALL NOT ENTER THEREIN 274 31
O SPARE ME A LITTLE, THAT I MAY RECOVER MY STRENGTH, ... 325 10
SUFFER THE LITTLE CHILDREN TO COME UNTO ME, AND 338 09
JESUS CALLED A LITTLE CHILD UNTO HIM, AND SET HIM IN 339 23
AND BECOME AS LITTLE CHILDREN, YE SHALL NOT ENTER 339 25
HIMSELF AS THIS LITTLE CHILD, THE SAME IS GREATEST IN 339 27
RECEIVE ONE SUCH LITTLE CHILD IN MY NAME RECEIVETH 339 29
NOT ONE OF THESE LITTLE ONES 339 30
THE ANGELS OF THY LITTLE ONES DO ALWAYS BEHOLD IN 340 25
DEAR SON DID TAKE LITTLE CHILDREN INTO HIS ARMS AND 342 03
IF HIS WRATH BE KINDLED, YEA BUT A LITTLE 346 22
10 YET A LITTLE WHILE, AND THE UNGODLY SHALL BE CLEAN 385 13
15 O SPARE ME A LITTLE, THAT I MAY RECOVER MY 390 06
HERMON AND THE LITTLE HILL 393 17
RAIN INTO THE LITTLE VALLEYS THEREOF 417 05
AND THE LITTLE HILLS SHALL REJOICE ON EVERY SIDE 417 10
27 THERE IS LITTLE BENJAMIN THEIR RULER, AND THE 421 08
AND THE LITTLE HILLS RIGHTEOUSNESS UNTO THE PEOPLE 427 02
AND THE LITTLE HILLS LIKE YOUNG SHEEP 484 31
AND YE LITTLE HILLS, LIKE YOUNG SHEEP 485 05
BEING TOGETHER, A LITTLE BEFORE BED-TIME, LET THE .... R 589 13
AND ALL LITTLE CHILDREN, THE SICK AND THE 600 05

LITURGY

COMPILING OF HER LITURGY IN THE TIME OF EDWARD THE .... V 27
OF CAVIL OR QUARREL AGAINST HER LITURGY .... V 39
IN THE LITURGY WHICH BECAME NECESSARY IN THE PRAYERS .... VI 16

LIVE

WE MAY HEREAFTER LIVE A GODLY, RIGHTEOUS, AND SOBER 006 28
HIS WICKEDNESS AND LIVE, HATH GIVEN POWER, AND 007 08
GRANT THEM IN HEALTH AND PROSPERITY LONG TO LIVE 018 03
WE MAY HEREAFTER LIVE A GODLY, RIGHTEOUS, AND SOBER 024 03
HIS WICKEDNESS AND LIVE, HATH GIVEN POWER, AND 024 10
THAT THEY MAY LIVE IN THE TRUE FAITH AND FEAR OF GOD, ... 048 03
MAY FAITHFULLY LIVE ACCORDING TO THY WILL IN THIS 051 10
MAY BOTH FAITHFULLY LIVE IN THIS WORLD ACCORDING TO 053 15
AND DILIGENTLY TO LIVE AFTER THY COMMANDMENTS 056 12
THAT WE MAY EVER LIVE WITH THEE IN THE WORLD TO COME 062 24
THY HOLY WORD, AND LIVE IN UNITY AND GODLY LOVE 074 14
WE SHOULD LIVE SOBERLY, RIGHTEOUSLY, AND MEN 098 20
AS LIETH IN YOU, LIVE PEACEABLY WITH ALL MEN 113 02
AS DYING, AND BEHOLD, WE LIVE 126 18
MAN SHALL NOT LIVE BY BREAD ALONE, BUT BY EVERY WORD 126 29
BUT RATHER THAT HE SHOULD BE CONVERTED AND LIVE 157 07
WE MAY EVERMORE LIVE WITH HIM IN THE JOY OF HIS 165 07
TO SINS, SHOULD LIVE UNTO RIGHTEOUSNESS 172 16
I LIVE, YE SHALL LIVE ALSO 181 16
BECAUSE I LIVE, YE SHALL LIVE ALSO 181 16
THAT WE MIGHT LIVE THROUGH HIM 189 13
THAT WE SHALL ALSO LIVE WITH HIM 197 21
TO THE FLESH, TO LIVE AFTER THE FLESH 200 03
FOR IF YE LIVE AFTER THE FLESH, YE SHALL DIE 200 04
DO MORTIFY THE DEEDS OF THE BODY, YE SHALL LIVE 200 06
THEE BE ENABLED TO LIVE ACCORDING TO THY WILL 201 02
THIS DO, AND THOU SHALT LIVE 208 19
AND LAY THY HAND UPON HER, AND SHE SHALL LIVE 224 15
NOW THE JUST SHALL LIVE BY FAITH 228 18
TO THE SPIRIT MAY LIVE AND GROW IN HIM 278 22
LORD GOD, WHO DOST LIVE, AND GOVERN ALL THINGS, ... 278 30
DEAD UNTO SIN, MAY LIVE UNTO RIGHTEOUSNESS, AND BEING 280 33
THEE BE ENABLED TO LIVE ACCORDING TO THY WILL 287 29
THY WEDDED WIFE, TO LIVE TOGETHER AFTER GOD'S 301 07

LIVE   CONTINUED

	PAGE	LN
SO LONG AS YE BOTH SHALL LIVE	301	10
WEDDED HUSBAND, TO LIVE TOGETHER AFTER GOD'S	301	15
THEE ONLY UNTO HIM, SO LONG AS YE BOTH SHALL LIVE	301	19
PEACE TOGETHER, AND LIVE ACCORDING TO THY LAWS	303	11
EACH OTHER, AND SO LIVE TOGETHER IN FAITHFULNESS AND	303	24
THAT YE MAY SO LIVE TOGETHER IN THIS LIFE, THAT IN	304	14
THEREFORE WILL I CALL UPON HIM AS LONG AS I LIVE	305	21
MAY FAITHFULLY LIVE ACCORDING TO THY WILL IN THIS	306	30
WITH WHOM DO LIVE THE SPIRITS OF JUST MEN MADE	317	11
HE SHALL LIVE FOR EVER	322	27
THOUGH HE WERE DEAD, YET SHALL HE LIVE	324	07
THAT I MAY BE CERTIFIED HOW LONG I HAVE TO LIVE	324	21
BUT A SHORT TIME TO LIVE, AND IS FULL OF MISERY	332	19
WITH WHOM DO LIVE THE SPIRITS OF THOSE WHO	334	19
SHALL LIVE, THOUGH HE DIE	334	32
THOUGH HE WERE DEAD, YET SHALL HE LIVE	338	07
YOUR HEART SHALL LIVE FOR EVER	367	26
HE THAT LUSTETH TO LIVE, *	380	25
19 BUT MINE ENEMIES LIVE, AND ARE MIGHTY	388	30
THAT I MAY BE CERTIFIED HOW LONG I HAVE TO LIVE	389	16
9 THAT HE SHALL LIVE ALWAY, *	400	22
MEN SHALL NOT LIVE OUT HALF THEIR DAYS	408	08
5 AS LONG AS I LIVE WILL I MAGNIFY THEE IN THIS	414	33
SEEK YE AFTER GOD, AND YOUR SOUL SHALL LIVE	424	09
15 HE SHALL LIVE, AND UNTO HIM SHALL BE GIVEN OF THE	427	26
O LET US LIVE, AND WE SHALL CALL UPON THY NAME	442	07
FROM THEM THAT LIVE A GODLY LIFE	446	04
33 I WILL SING UNTO THE LORD AS LONG AS I LIVE	469	27
THEREFORE WILL I CALL UPON HIM AS LONG AS I LIVE	486	22
SHALL NOT DIE, BUT LIVE, *	489	02
THAT I MAY LIVE, AND KEEP THY WORD	490	32
THY LOVING MERCIES COME UNTO ME, THAT I MAY LIVE	495	10
ME ACCORDING TO THY WORD, THAT I MAY LIVE	497	31
O GRANT ME UNDERSTANDING, AND I SHALL LIVE	499	28
175 O LET MY SOUL LIVE, AND IT SHALL PRAISE THEE	501	32
WHILE I LIVE, WILL I PRAISE THE LORD	522	03
WORLDLY LUSTS, AND LIVE SOBERLY, RIGHTEOUSLY, AND	555	09
AT THE ALTAR SHOULD LIVE OF THE THINGS BELONGING TO	569	29
IN WHOM WE LIVE AND MOVE AND HAVE OUR BEING	587	19
HAVE RECEIVED IT, LIVE AS BECOMES IT	590	24
US GRACE ALWAYS TO LIVE IN SUCH A STATE THAT WE MAY	591	29
SIN AS LONG AS THEY LIVE HERE, OR DENY THE PLACE OF	606	03

LIVED

	PAGE	LN
GREAT AGE, AND HAD LIVED WITH AN HUSBAND SEVEN YEARS	233	17
18 FOR WHILE HE LIVED, HE COUNTED HIMSELF AN HAPPY	401	11

LIVELY

	PAGE	LN
THAT WITH LIVELY FAITH WE MAY LABOUR ABUNDANTLY TO	038	20
THY TRUE AND LIVELY WORD, AND RIGHTLY AND DULY	074	23
HEART AND LIVELY FAITH WE RECEIVE THAT HOLY	085	31
HAVE A LIVELY AND STEDFAST FAITH IN CHRIST OUR	085	35
YE ALSO, AS LIVELY STONES, ARE BUILT UP A SPIRITUAL	259	30
TO HAVE A LIVELY FAITH IN GOD'S MERCY THROUGH CHRIST,	293	28
THY TRUE AND LIVELY WORD	573	23
HAVE A LIVELY FAITH IN GOD'S MERCY THROUGH CHRIST,	582	24
IN OUR MINDS A LIVELY REMEMBRANCE OF THAT GREAT DAY,	588	21
THAT BY THEM A LIVELY FAITH MAY BE AS EVIDENTLY KNOWN	605	14
OF A TRUE AND LIVELY FAITH	605	14
AS BE VOID OF A LIVELY FAITH, ALTHOUGH THEY DO	609	04

LIVER

	PAGE	LN
AND NOTORIOUS EVIL LIVER, OR TO HAVE DONE ANY WRONG	R 084	35

LIVES

	PAGE	LN
BUT IN OUR LIVES, BY GIVING UP OUR SELVES TO	019	28
BUT IN OUR LIVES, BY GIVING UP OUR SELVES TO	033	26
LAID DOWN THEIR LIVES IN THE SERVICE OF OUR COUNTRY	042	16
TO DIRECT OUR LIVES AFTER THEIR GOOD EXAMPLES	048	20
MAY APPEAR IN OUR LIVES BY AN HUMBLE, HOLY, AND	050	26
TO AMEND OUR LIVES ACCORDING TO THY HOLY WORD	057	17
AND PEACEABLE LIVES, IN ALL GODLINESS AND HONESTY	VI	21
AMEND YOUR LIVES, AND BE IN PERFECT CHARITY WITH ALL	086	02
TO EXAMINE YOUR LIVES AND CONVERSATIONS BY THE RULE	087	17
INNOCENCY OF OUR LIVES, AND CONSTANCY OF OUR FAITH	102	25
IN OUR HEARTS MAY SHINE FORTH IN OUR LIVES	106	27
TO LAY DOWN OUR LIVES FOR THE BRETHREN	191	18
LOVED NOT THEIR LIVES UNTO THE DEATH	252	15
SO TO CONFORM OUR LIVES TO THEIR INNOCENCY AND	340	31
OWN LIVES, AND THE LIVES OF YOUR FAMILIES, ACCORDING	533	25
FASHION YOUR OWN LIVES, AND THE LIVES OF YOUR	533	25
TO SANCTIFY THE LIVES OF YOU AND YOURS, AND TO	541	20
AND MAY IN THEIR LIVES SHOW FORTH THY PRAISE	567	09
BEGINNING OF OUR LIVES TO THIS DAY, AND ESPECIALLY	587	22
THAT ANOTHER DAY IS ADDED TO OUR LIVES	588	05
OVER US THROUGH THE WHOLE COURSE OF OUR LIVES	591	18
OF GOD WE MAY ARISE AGAIN, AND AMEND OUR LIVES	606	02

LIVEST

	PAGE	LN
THE HOLY GHOST LIVEST AND REIGNEST ONE GOD, WORLD	043	15
TO THY WILL, WHO LIVEST AND REIGNEST WITH THE FATHER	049	09
IN THY SIGHT, WHO LIVEST AND REIGNEST WITH THE FATHER	093	31
AND GLORY, WHO LIVEST AND REIGNEST WITH THE FATHER	125	32
WHO LIVEST AND REIGNEST, ONE GOD,	186	29
WHO LIVEST AND REIGNEST WITH THE FATHER AND THE HOLY	320	12
THY MERCY, WHO LIVEST WITH THE FATHER AND THE HOLY	336	14

LIVETH

	PAGE	LN
OUR LORD, WHO LIVETH AND REIGNETH WITH THEE AND THE	018	15
THE HOLY GHOST LIVETH AND REIGNETH EVER, ONE GOD,	032	14
AND EVER LIVETH TO MAKE INTERCESSION FOR US,	037	21
THROUGH HIM WHO LIVETH AND REIGNETH WITH THEE AND THE	090	18
JESUS CHRIST, WHO LIVETH AND REIGNETH WITH THEE AND	096	18
BE OUR JUDGE, WHO LIVETH AND REIGNETH WITH THEE AND	098	15
JESUS CHRIST, WHO LIVETH AND REIGNETH WITH THEE AND	104	10
O HOLY GHOST, HE LIVETH AND REIGNETH WITH THEE AND	117	11
OUR SAVIOUR, WHO LIVETH AND REIGNETH WITH THEE AND	119	02
WHICH WHOSOEVER LIVETH IS COUNTED DEAD BEFORE THEE	122	18
OF NO STRENGTH AT ALL WHILE THE TESTATOR LIVETH	147	17
OUR LORD, WHO NOW LIVETH AND REIGNETH WITH THEE AND	152	12
WHO NOW LIVETH AND REIGNETH WITH THEE AND THE HOLY	156	25
OUR LORD, WHO LIVETH AND REIGNETH WITH THEE AND THE	157	12
BUT IN THAT HE LIVETH, HE LIVETH UNTO GOD	163	07
HE LIVETH, HE LIVETH UNTO GOD	163	07
OUR LORD, WHO LIVETH AND REIGNETH WITH THEE AND THE	163	28
WHO LIVETH AND REIGNETH WITH THEE AND THE HOLY	177	18
GONE BEFORE, WHO LIVETH AND REIGNETH WITH THEE AND	179	09
OUR SAVIOUR, WHO LIVETH AND REIGNETH WITH THEE,	180	13
OUR LORD, WHO LIVETH AND REIGNETH WITH THEE IN THE	182	18
SAME HOLY SPIRIT LIVETH AND REIGNETH, ONE GOD,	183	27
OUR LORD, WHO LIVETH AND REIGNETH WITH THEE AND,	185	18
THE THRONE, WHO LIVETH FOR EVER AND EVER, THE FOUR	187	26
WORSHIP HIM THAT LIVETH FOR EVER AND EVER, AND CAST	187	28
HE LIVETH, HE LIVETH UNTO GOD	197	24
BUT IN THAT HE LIVETH, HE LIVETH UNTO GOD	197	24
THY SON LIVETH	220	03
AND TOLD HIM, SAYING, THY SON LIVETH	220	06
IN THE WHICH JESUS SAID UNTO HIM, THY SON LIVETH	220	10
THE LORD LIVETH, WHICH BROUGHT UP THE CHILDREN	225	16
THE LORD LIVETH, WHICH BROUGHT UP AND WHICH LED	225	17
O HOLY GHOST, LIVETH AND REIGNETH, ONE GOD, WORLD	248	05
JESUS CHRIST, WHO LIVETH AND REIGNETH WITH THEE AND	250	24
JESUS CHRIST, WHO LIVETH AND REIGNETH WITH THEE AND	276	14
SAME HOLY SPIRIT LIVETH AND REIGNETH EVER, ONE GOD,	298	24
OUR LORD, WHO LIVETH AND REIGNETH WITH THEE AND THE	303	27
OUR LORD, WHO LIVETH AND REIGNETH WITH THEE AND THE	319	11
AND WHOSOEVER LIVETH AND BELIEVETH IN ME, SHALL NEVER	324	07
THAT MY REDEEMER LIVETH, AND THAT HE SHALL STAND AT	324	09
OUR LORD, WHO LIVETH AND REIGNETH WITH THEE AND THE	332	08
AND WHOSOEVER LIVETH, AND BELIEVETH IN HIM, SHALL NOT	335	02
AND WHOSOEVER LIVETH AND BELIEVETH IN ME, SHALL NEVER	338	07
47 THE LORD LIVETH	362	32
MAN IS HE THAT LIVETH, AND SHALL NOT SEE DEATH	453	02
JESUS CHRIST, WHO LIVETH AND REIGNETH WITH THEE AND	531	24
JESUS CHRIST, WHO LIVETH AND REIGNETH WITH THEE AND	537	28
OUR LORD, WHO LIVETH AND REIGNETH WITH THEE IN THE	546	03
JESUS CHRIST, WHO LIVETH AND REIGNETH WITH THEE AND	548	07
JESUS CHRIST, WHO LIVETH AND REIGNETH WITH THEE AND	554	02
THE HOLY GHOST, LIVETH AND REIGNETH, ONE GOD, WORLD	558	07
WHO LIVETH AND REIGNETH WITH THEE AND THE SAME	559	14
OUR LORD, WHO LIVETH AND REIGNETH WITH THEE IN THE	562	14
OF OUR SOULS, WHO LIVETH AND REIGNETH WITH THEE AND	574	21

LIVING

	PAGE	LN
ALL THINGS LIVING WITH PLENTEOUSNESS	040	04
HANDS ARE THE LIVING AND THE DEAD	042	15
DOST MAKE THEM LIVING MEMBERS OF THY CHURCH	043	08
THE FRUIT OF GOOD LIVING, TO THE HONOUR AND PRAISE OF	049	21
PREACHING AND LIVING THEY MAY SET IT FORTH, AND SHOW	055	33
AND PURENESS OF LIVING, TO THY HONOUR AND GLORY	059	26
AND LIVING SACRIFICE UNTO THEE	081	23
BEFORE THE FOUR LIVING CREATURES, AND THE ELDERS	103	05
YOUR BODIES A LIVING SACRIFICE, HOLY, ACCEPTABLE UNTO	110	04
TO SERVE THE LIVING GOD	133	03
BY A NEW AND LIVING WAY, WHICH HE HATH CONSECRATED	158	17
IN PURENESS OF LIVING AND TRUTH	170	22
WERE FOUR LIVING CREATURES FULL OF EYES	187	17
AND THE FOUR LIVING CREATURES HAD EACH OF THEM SIX	187	20
AND WHEN THOSE LIVING CREATURES GIVE GLORY AND HONOUR	187	24
AND HE DIVIDED UNTO THEM HIS LIVING	202	02
THERE WASTED HIS SUBSTANCE WITH RIOTOUS LIVING	202	04
HATH DEVOURED THY LIVING WITH HARLOTS, THOU HAST	203	03
THE SON OF THE LIVING GOD	246	03
AND GODLY LIVING, THAT WE MAY COME TO THOSE	256	09
THE SEAL OF THE LIVING GOD	256	15
AND THE FOUR LIVING CREATURES, AND FELL BEFORE THE	256	30
LEAD THEM UNTO LIVING FOUNTAINS OF WATERS	257	15
AS UNTO A LIVING STONE, DISALLOWED INDEED OF	259	29
AND BE MADE A LIVING MEMBER OF THE SAME	274	06
THE SON OF THE LIVING GOD	278	03
TO EARN MINE OWN LIVING, AND TO DO MY DUTY IN THAT	289	09
THAT THEY, LIVING FAITHFULLY TOGETHER, MAY SURELY	303	07
I AM THE LIVING BREAD WHICH CAME DOWN FROM HEAVEN	322	26
VERILY EVERY MAN LIVING IS ALTOGETHER VANITY	324	24
GOODNESS OF GOD IN THE LAND OF THE LIVING	326	29
ADAM WAS MADE A LIVING SOUL	329	24
LEAD THEM UNTO LIVING FOUNTAINS OF WATERS	341	26
GOODNESS OF THE LORD IN THE LAND OF THE LIVING	372	29
VERILY EVERY MAN LIVING IS ALTOGETHER VANITY	389	19
EVEN FOR THE LIVING GOD	392	31
AND ROOT THEE OUT OF THE LAND OF THE LIVING	404	30
I MAY WALK BEFORE GOD IN THE LIGHT OF THE LIVING	409	10
THE BOOK OF THE LIVING, *	423	32
REJOICE IN THE LIVING GOD	445	15
IN THE LAND OF THE LIVING	487	06
AND MY PORTION IN THE LAND OF THE LIVING	518	15
SHALL NO MAN LIVING BE JUSTIFIED	518	26
ALL THINGS LIVING WITH PLENTEOUSNESS	521	25
TO GET MINE OWN LIVING, AND TO DO MY DUTY IN THAT	580	13
SO THAT, LIVING AND DYING, WE MAY BE THINE, THROUGH	591	30
CHILDREN WHO ARE LIVING IN MENTAL DARKNESS	598	14

LIVING   CONTINUED

THERE IS BUT ONE LIVING AND TRUE GOD, EVERLASTING,   603 03
OF MOST UNCLEAN LIVING, NO LESS PERILOUS THAN   606 26
NOT ONLY IN THEIR LIVING AND MANNER OF CEREMONIES,   606 43

LO

BUT LO, THOU REQUIREST TRUTH IN THE INWARD PARTS,   060 22
LO, THE ANGEL OF THE LORD CAME UPON THEM,   099 12
I LOOKED, AND, LO, A LAMB STOOD ON THE MOUNT SION,   102 29
LO, THE STAR, WHICH THEY SAW IN THE EAST, WENT   109 16
SHALL SAY UNTO YOU, LO, HERE IS CHRIST, OR THERE   118 03
LO, HE THAT BETRAYETH ME IS AT HAND   142 13
LO, THEY ALL SHALL WAX OLD AS A GARMENT   144 21
LO, NOTHING WORTHY OF DEATH IS DONE UNTO HIM   153 26
THEN SAID I, LO, I COME (IN THE VOLUME OF THE BOOK IT   157 27
THEN SAID HE, LO, I COME TO DO THY WILL, O GOD   157 31
SAID UNTO HIM, LO, NOW SPEAKEST THOU PLAINLY,   176 32
SAID TO HIS FATHER, LO, THESE MANY YEARS DO I SERVE   202 33
THIS I BEHELD, AND, LO, A GREAT MULTITUDE, WHICH NO   256 23
OF EVERLASTING LIFE, LO, WE TURN TO THE GENTILES   261 02
LO, I AM WITH YOU ALWAY, EVEN UNTO THE END OF   275 31
2 FOR LO, THE UNGODLY BEND THEIR BOW, AND MAKE READY   354 21
6 LO, THE POOR CRIETH, AND THE LORD HEARETH HIM   380 13
37 I WENT BY, AND LO, HE WAS GONE   387 06
THEN SAID I, LO, I COME   390 30
LO, I WILL NOT REFRAIN MY LIPS, O LORD, AND THAT THOU   391 02
3 FOR LO, THE KINGS OF THE EARTH *   399 16
6 BUT LO, THOU REQUIREST TRUTH IN THE INWARD PARTS,   403 20
8 LO, THIS IS THE MAN THAT TOOK NOT GOD FOR HIS   404 33
7 LO, THEN WOULD I GET ME AWAY FAR OFF, *   406 32
3 FOR LO, THEY LIE WAITING FOR MY SOUL   411 08
LO, HE DOTH SEND OUT HIS VOICE   421 23
12 LO, THESE ARE THE UNGODLY, *   428 32
BUT LO, THEN I SHOULD HAVE CONDEMNED THE GENERATION   429 06
27 FOR LO, THEY THAT FORSAKE THEE SHALL PERISH   429 30
2 FOR LO, THINE ENEMIES MAKE A MURMURING   444 07
LO, IN SION WERE THEY BORN   448 20
LO, IN SION WERE THEY BORN   448 25
8 FOR LO, THINE ENEMIES, O LORD, LO, THINE ENEMIES   456 17
O LORD, LO, THINE ENEMIES SHALL PERISH   456 17
THAT I HAD UNTO THEM, LO, THEY TAKE NOW MY CONTRARY   480 09
4 LO, CHILDREN, AND THE FRUIT OF THE WOMB, *   505 29
5 LO, THUS SHALL THE MAN BE BLESSED *   506 14
6 LO, WE HEARD OF THE SAME AT EPHRATAH, *   508 15
3 FOR LO, THERE IS NOT A WORD IN MY TONGUE, *   514 25
LO, I AM WITH YOU ALWAY, EVEN UNTO THE END OF   552 14

LOAVES

HATH FIVE BARLEY LOAVES, AND TWO SMALL FISHES   131 33
AND JESUS TOOK THE LOAVES   132 03
THE FIVE BARLEY LOAVES, WHICH REMAINED OVER AND ABOVE   132 10
HOW MANY LOAVES HAVE YE   199 16
HE TOOK THE SEVEN LOAVES, AND GAVE THANKS, AND BRAKE,   199 18
HATH FIVE BARLEY LOAVES, AND TWO SMALL FISHES   225 30
AND JESUS TOOK THE LOAVES   226 03
THE FIVE BARLEY LOAVES, WHICH REMAINED OVER AND ABOVE   226 09
LEND ME THREE LOAVES   262 28

LOCAL

OR FURTHER THAN LOCAL CIRCUMSTANCES REQUIRE   VI 33
IT IS PARTLY OF A LOCAL AND CIVIL NATURE,   R 607 11
AS FROM THE LOCAL REFERENCES   R 610 29

LOCUSTS

AND HE DID EAT LOCUSTS AND WILD HONEY   112 13

LODGING

GRANT US A SAFE LODGING, AND A HOLY REST, AND PEACE   595 02

LOFTY

SAITH THE HIGH AND LOFTY ONE THAT INHABITETH   003 25

LOINS

AND WITH A GIRDLE OF A SKIN ABOUT HIS LOINS   112 13
HAVING YOUR LOINS GIRT ABOUT WITH TRUTH, AND HAVING   219 13
7 FOR MY LOINS ARE FILLED WITH A SORE DISEASE,   388 04
AND LAIDEST TROUBLE UPON OUR LOINS   418 03
LET YOUR LOINS BE GIRDED ABOUT, AND YOUR LIGHTS   534 16

LONG

FOUNDATION AND A LONG CONTINUANCE OF NURSING CARE AND   V 11
AND PROSPERITY LONG TO LIVE   018 03
THY DAYS MAY BE LONG IN THE LAND WHICH THE LORD THY   069 03
THAT THE HEIR, AS LONG AS HE IS A CHILD, DIFFERETH   104 14
CHARITY SUFFERETH LONG, AND IS KIND   122 29
TO SEE HIM OF A LONG SEASON, BECAUSE HE HAD HEARD   153 11
CLOTHED IN A LONG WHITE GARMENT   165 27
HOW GREATLY I LONG AFTER YOU ALL IN THE TENDER   220 31
HE SAITH, ALL DAY LONG I HAVE STRETCHED FORTH MY   227 21
HAVE I BEEN SO LONG TIME WITH YOU, AND YET HAST   240 11
I THINK IT MEET, AS LONG AS I AM IN THIS TABERNACLE,   248 08
THY DAYS MAY BE LONG IN THE LAND WHICH THE LORD THY   287 02
ONLY UNTO HER, SO LONG AS YE BOTH SHALL LIVE   301 10
ONLY UNTO HIM, SO LONG AS YE BOTH SHALL LIVE   301 18
I CALL UPON HIM AS LONG AS I LIVE   305 21
BE CERTIFIED HOW LONG I HAVE TO LIVE   324 21
AS IT WERE A SPAN LONG, AND MINE AGE IS EVEN AS   324 22

LONG   CONTINUED

YE SONS OF MEN, HOW LONG WILL YE BLASPHEME MINE   347 13
LORD, HOW LONG WILT THOU PUNISH ME   349 04
HOW LONG WILT THOU FORGET ME, O LORD   355 28
HOW LONG WILT THOU HIDE THY FACE FROM ME   355 29
2 HOW LONG SHALL I SEEK COUNSEL IN MY SOUL, AND BE SO   355 30
HOW LONG SHALL MINE ENEMY TRIUMPH OVER ME   355 31
THOU GAVEST HIM A LONG LIFE, *   365 11
IN THEE HATH BEEN MY HOPE ALL THE DAY LONG   369 27
17 LORD, HOW LONG WILT THOU LOOK UPON THIS   382 29
AND OF THY PRAISE, ALL THE DAY LONG   383 24
THAT I GO MOURNING ALL THE DAY LONG   388 03
AND IMAGINED DECEIT ALL THE DAY LONG   388 16
BE CERTIFIED HOW LONG I HAVE TO LIVE   389 16
AS IT WERE A SPAN LONG, AND MINE AGE IS EVEN AS   389 18
MAKE NO LONG TARRYING, O MY GOD   391 26
OF GOD ALL DAY LONG, *   395 09
KILLED ALL THE DAY LONG, *   396 04
AND SO LONG AS THOU DOEST WELL UNTO THYSELF, MEN WILL   401 12
GRANT THE KING A LONG LIFE, *   413 17
3 HOW LONG WILL YE IMAGINE MISCHIEF AGAINST EVERY   413 31
5 AS LONG AS I LIVE WILL I MAGNIFY THEE IN THIS   414 33
ME FOR WAITING SO LONG UPON MY GOD   422 06
O LORD, MAKE NO LONG TARRYING   424 33
THE THING THAT I LONG FOR   425 14
MAY SING OF THY GLORY AND HONOUR ALL THE DAY LONG   425 22
SHALL TALK OF THY RIGHTEOUSNESS ALL THE DAY LONG   426 28
SHALL FEAR THEE, AS LONG AS THE SUN AND MOON   427 06
OF PEACE, SO LONG AS THE MOON ENDURETH   427 11
14 ALL THE DAY LONG HAVE I BEEN PUNISHED, *   429 04
WHEREFORE ART THOU ABSENT FROM US SO LONG   430 03
11 O GOD, HOW LONG SHALL THE ADVERSARY DO THIS   430 27
5 LORD, HOW LONG WILT THOU BE ANGRY   440 09
HOW LONG WILT THOU BE ANGRY WITH THY PEOPLE THAT   441 10
2 HOW LONG WILL YE GIVE WRONG JUDGMENT, *   443 20
45 LORD, HOW LONG WILT THOU HIDE THYSELF   452 32
16 WITH LONG LIFE WILL I SATISFY HIM, *   455 29
3 LORD, HOW LONG SHALL THE UNGODLY, *   457 23
HOW LONG SHALL THE UNGODLY TRIUMPH   457 23
4 HOW LONG SHALL ALL WICKED DOERS SPEAK SO   457 25
10 FORTY YEARS LONG WAS I GRIEVED WITH THIS   459 24
8 MINE ENEMIES REVILE ME ALL THE DAY LONG   464 25
UNTO THE LORD AS LONG AS I LIVE   469 27
I CALL UPON HIM AS LONG AS I LIVE   486 22
82 MINE EYES LONG SORE FOR THY WORD   495 21
ALL THE DAY LONG IS MY STUDY IN IT   496 21
I HAVE KNOWN LONG SINCE, *   500 14
5 MY SOUL HATH LONG DWELT AMONG THEM *   502 17
SEE JERUSALEM IN PROSPERITY ALL THY LIFE LONG   506 17
AND MADE LONG FURROWS   506 26
MY THOUGHTS LONG BEFORE   514 22
AND STIR UP STRIFE ALL THE DAY LONG   516 12
MEN THAT HAVE BEEN LONG DEAD   518 29
AS LONG AS I HAVE ANY BEING, I WILL SING PRAISES   522 04
WITH YOURSELVES, LONG BEFORE THIS TIME   541 10
THY DAYS MAY BE LONG IN THE LAND WHICH THE LORD THY   579 14
US ALL THE DAY LONG, UNTIL THE SHADOWS LENGTHEN AND   594 30
CAN NO MORE SIN AS LONG AS THEY LIVE HERE, OR DENY   606 03

LONG-SUFFERING

LONG-SUFFERING, AND OF GREAT PITY   062 31
HUMBLENESS OF MIND, MEEKNESS, LONG-SUFFERING   116 05
BY LONG-SUFFERING, BY KINDNESS, BY THE HOLY GHOST, BY   126 13
ONCE THE LONG-SUFFERING OF GOD WAITED IN THE DAYS OF   161 27
LONG-SUFFERING, GENTLENESS, GOODNESS, FAITH,   209 26
WITH LONG-SUFFERING, FORBEARING ONE ANOTHER IN LOVE   213 20
AND LONG-SUFFERING WITH JOYFULNESS   224 07
LONG-SUFFERING, PLENTEOUS IN GOODNESS AND TRUTH   448 05
LONG-SUFFERING, AND OF GREAT GOODNESS   466 21
LONG-SUFFERING, AND OF GREAT GOODNESS   521 08

LONGED

MY SOUL HATH LONGED FOR THY SALVATION, *   495 19
174 I HAVE LONGED FOR THY SAVING HEALTH, O LORD   501 30
HE HATH LONGED FOR HER   508 33

LONGETH

SO LONGETH MY SOUL AFTER THEE, O GOD   392 29
MY FLESH ALSO LONGETH AFTER THEE, *   414 27

LONGING

A DESIRE AND LONGING TO ENTER INTO THE COURTS OF THE   445 13

LOOK

AND I LOOK FOR THE RESURRECTION OF THE DEAD   016 20
AND I LOOK FOR THE RESURRECTION OF THE DEAD   030 25
MERCIFULLY LOOK UPON THE SAME, AND AT THIS TIME SO   038 27
O ALMIGHTY GOD, LOOK MERCIFULLY UPON THE WORLD WHICH   039 17
HEART THEY MAY EVER LOOK UNTO THEE, WHO ART THE   042 27
LOOK UPON HIM WITH THE EYES OF THY MERCY   045 15
LOOK WITH PITY, WE BESEECH THEE, UPON THE SORROWS OF   045 32
GRACIOUSLY LOOK UPON OUR AFFLICTIONS   059 10
MERCIFULLY TO LOOK UPON OUR INFIRMITIES   059 21
OF THY MERCIES LOOK UPON US   063 05
AND I LOOK FOR THE RESURRECTION OF THE DEAD   071 22
COME TO PASS, THEN LOOK UP, AND LIFT UP YOUR HEADS   093 12
COME, OR DO WE LOOK FOR ANOTHER   094 18
WE MAY STEDFASTLY LOOK UP TO HEAVEN, AND BY FAITH   099 28
MERCIFULLY LOOK UPON OUR INFIRMITIES, AND IN ALL   112 26
ALMIGHTY GOD, LOOK UPON THE HEARTY DESIRES OF   128 25

LOOK   CONTINUED   LORD

MERCIFULLY TO LOOK UPON THY PEOPLE   132 18
LOOK DOWN FROM HEAVEN, AND BEHOLD FROM THE HABITATION 139 17
AND UNTO THEM THAT LOOK FOR HIM SHALL HE APPEAR THE   148 09
THEY SHALL LOOK ON HIM WHOM THEY PIERCED   161 09
HE THAT SAT WAS TO LOOK UPON LIKE A JASPER AND A   187 06
FROM WHENCE ALSO WE LOOK FOR THE SAVIOUR, THE LCRD   222 09
LOOK MERCIFULLY UPON THESE THY SERVANTS, THAT THEY   303 22
WITH HIS FAVOUR LOOK UPON YOU, AND FILL YOU WITH ALL 304 13
O LORD, LOOK DOWN FROM HEAVEN, BEHOLD, VISIT,   309 04
LOOK UPON HIM WITH THE EYES OF THY MERCY, GIVE HIM   309 05
LOOK GRACIOUSLY UPON HIM, O LORD   316 09
MERCIFULLY LOOK UPON THIS THY SERVANT, THAT, EVERY   322 07
I LOOK FOR THE LORD   328 11
AND LOOK, WHATSOEVER HE DOETH, IT SHALL PROSPER   345 14
UNTO THEE, AND WILL LOOK UP   348 06
AND LET THINE EYES LOOK UPON THE THING THAT IS EQUAL 358 20
MY GOD, MY GOD, LOOK UPON ME   366 04
17 LOOK UPON MY ADVERSITY AND MISERY, *   370 20
HOW LONG WILT THOU LOOK UPON THIS   382 29
THOU SHALT LOOK AFTER HIS PLACE, AND HE SHALL BE   385 14
I AM NOT ABLE TO LOOK UP   391 12
21 LOOK UPON THE COVENANT   431 18
THOU GOD OF HOSTS, LOOK DOWN FROM HEAVEN, *   441 30
AND LOOK UPON THE FACE OF THINE ANOINTED   445 29
HATH ALSO A HAUGHTY LOOK AND A PROUD HEART, *   463 28
8 MINE EYES LOOK UPON SUCH AS ARE FAITHFUL IN THE   463 30
11 FOR LOOK HOW HIGH THE HEAVEN IS IN COMPARISON OF   466 27
12 LOOK HOW WIDE ALSO THE EAST IS FROM THE WEST   466 30
TREMBLE AT THE LOOK OF HIM   469 25
THEY THAT LOOK UPON ME SHAKE THEIR HEADS   481 21
132 O LOOK THOU UPON ME, AND BE MERCIFUL UNTO ME,   499 02
EYES OF SERVANTS LOOK UNTO THE HAND OF THEIR MASTERS, 503 29
5 I LOOK FOR THE LORD   507 16
24 LOOK WELL IF THERE BE ANY WAY OF WICKEDNESS IN ME 516 06
9 BUT MINE EYES LOOK UNTO THEE, O LORD GOD   517 28
LOOK YE OUT AMONG YOU SEVEN MEN OF HONEST   532 11
DEATH OF A SINNER, LOOK UPON HERE LET HIM WHO READS   589 33
THE OLD FATHERS DID LOOK ONLY FOR TRANSITORY   604 18

LOOKED

THE HOLY GHOST, LOOKED UP STEDFASTLY INTO HEAVEN, AND 100 05
WHICH WE HAVE LOOKED UPON,   101 14
I LOOKED, AND, LO, A LAMB STOOD ON THE MOUNT SICN,   102 29
AND I LOOKED, AND THERE WAS NONE TO HELP   138 22
SHE LOOKED UPON HIM, AND SAID, AND THOU ALSO   143 25
AND EARNESTLY LOOKED UPON HIM, AND SAID, THIS MAN WAS 151 11
LORD TURNED, AND LOOKED UPON PETER   151 20
AND WHEN THEY LOOKED, THEY SAW THAT THE STONE WAS   165 24
AND WHILE THEY LOOKED STEDFASTLY TOWARD HEAVEN AS HE 178 14
AFTER THIS I LOOKED, AND BEHOLD, A DOOR WAS OPENED IN 186 31
CAME AND LOOKED ON HIM, AND PASSED BY ON THE   208 27
TO ALL THEM THAT LOOKED FOR REDEMPTION IN JERUSALEM   233 23
3 THE LORD LOOKED DOWN FROM HEAVEN UPON THE CHILDREN 356 16
3 GOD LOOKED DOWN FROM HEAVEN UPON THE CHILDREN OF   405 16
3 THUS HAVE I LOOKED FOR THEE IN THE SANCTUARY,   414 29
I LOOKED FOR SOME TO HAVE PITY ON ME, BUT THERE WAS   423 14
19 FOR HE HATH LOOKED DOWN FROM HIS SANCTUARY   465 17
166 LORD, I HAVE LOOKED FOR THY SAVING HEALTH,   501 13
4 I LOOKED ALSO UPON MY RIGHT HAND, *   518 10

LOOKETH

BUT WHOSO LOOKETH INTO THE PERFECT LAW OF LIBERTY,   176 10
BUT WHOSO LOOKETH INTO THE PERFECT LAW OF LIBERTY,   265 33
13 THE LORD LOOKETH DOWN FROM HEAVEN, AND BEHOLDETH   379 14

LOOKING

AND FOR LOOKING AFTER THOSE THINGS WHICH ARE   093 08
LOOKING FOR THAT BLESSED HOPE, AND THE GLORIOUS   098 21
AND LOOKING IN, SAW THE LINEN CLOTHES LYING   164 20
AND LOOKING UP TO HEAVEN, HE SIGHED, AND SAITH UNTO 206 33
SET BEFORE US, LOOKING UNTO JESUS THE AUTHOR AND   258 23
STARING AND LOOKING UPON ME   367 07
EYES ARE EVER LOOKING UNTO THE LORD   370 14
DID STAND LOOKING UPON MY TROUBLE, *   388 12
WASTED AWAY WITH LOOKING FOR THY HEALTH, *   498 15

LOOKS

DOWN THE HIGH LOOKS OF THE PROUD   361 23
I HAVE NO PROUD LOOKS   507 24

LOOSE

OF THY GREAT MERCY LOOSE US   063 12
LOOSE THEM, AND BRING THEM UNTO ME   091 15
THOU SHALT LOOSE ON EARTH SHALL BE LOOSED IN HEAVEN 246 11
THEN SHALL THEY LOOSE THEIR HANDS   R 302 02
SHALL THEY AGAIN LOOSE THEIR HANDS   R 302 09
WE BESEECH THEE TO LOOSE THE SPIRIT OF THIS THY   319 08

LOOSED

OF HIS TONGUE WAS LOOSED, AND HE SPAKE PLAIN   207 04
AND LOOSED HIM, AND FCRGAVE HIM THE DEBT   221 22
AND HIS TONGUE LOOSED, AND HE SPAKE, AND PRAISED GOD 243 25
ON EARTH SHALL BE LOOSED IN HEAVEN   246 12

LOOSETH

7 THE LORD LOOSETH MEN OUT OF PRISON   522 16

THE LORD BE WITH YOU   R 003 08
TO THE VERSICLES, O LORD, OPEN THOU OUR LIPS, ETC R 003 11
AFTER THE LORD BE WITH YOU, ETC   R 003 13
THE LORD IS IN HIS HOLY TEMPLE   003 15
UNTO ME, WE WILL GO INTO THE HOUSE OF THE LORD   003 18
IN THY SIGHT, O LORD, MY STRENGTH AND MY REDEEMER   003 20
AND FROM THE LORD JESUS CHRIST   004 03
YE THE WAY OF THE LORD, MAKE STRAIGHT IN THE DESERT A 004 06
CITY OF DAVID A SAVIOUR, WHICH IS CHRIST THE LORD   004 11
SAITH THE LORD OF HOSTS   004 16
AND TURN UNTO THE LORD YOUR GOD   004 21
WHEREWITH THE LORD HATH AFFLICTED ME   004 31
THE LORD IS RISEN INDEED   005 02
THE DAY WHICH THE LORD HATH MADE   005 04
HOLY, HOLY, LORD GOD ALMIGHTY, WHICH WAS, AND   005 18
HONOUR THE LORD WITH THY SUBSTANCE, AND WITH THE   005 20
THE LORD BY WISDOM HATH FOUNDED THE EARTH   005 24
BUT THOU, O LORD, HAVE MERCY UPON US, MISERABLE   006 23
DECLARED UNTO MANKIND IN CHRIST JESUS OUR LORD   006 27
THE FATHER OF OUR LORD JESUS CHRIST, WHO DESIRETH NCT 007 06
THROUGH JESUS CHRIST OUR LORD   007 18
HE SHALL SAY, O LORD, OPEN THOU OUR LIPS   007 31
PRAISE YE THE LORD   008 07
THE LORD HATH MANIFESTED FORTH HIS GLORY   R 008 21
THE LORD IS   R 008 23
CHRIST THE LORD ASCENDETH INTO HEAVEN   R 008 25
THE SPIRIT OF THE LORD FILLETH THE WORLD   R 008 27
THE LORD IS GLORIOUS IN HIS SAINTS   R 008 34
LET US SING UNTO THE LORD   009 03
FOR THE LORD IS A GREAT GOD   009 07
KNEEL BEFORE THE LORD OUR MAKER   009 14
FOR HE IS THE LORD OUR GOD   009 15
O WORSHIP THE LORD IN THE BEAUTY OF HOLINESS   009 17
WE ACKNOWLEDGE THEE TO BE THE LORD   010 09
HOLY, HOLY, LORD GOD OF SABAOTH   010 14
O LORD, SAVE THY PEOPLE, AND BLESS THINE HERITAGE   011 04
VOUCHSAFE, O LORD, TO KEEP US THIS DAY WITHOUT SIN   011 08
O LORD, HAVE MERCY UPON US, HAVE MERCY UPON US   011 09
O LORD, LET THY MERCY BE UPON US, AS OUR TRUST IS IN 011 10
O LORD, IN THEE HAVE I TRUSTED   011 12
BLESSED ART THOU, O LORD GOD OF OUR FATHERS   011 16
O ALL YE WORKS OF THE LORD, BLESS YE THE LORD   011 31
ALL YE WORKS OF THE LORD, BLESS YE THE LORD   011 31
O YE ANGELS OF THE LORD, BLESS YE THE LORD   012 02
O YE ANGELS OF THE LORD, BLESS YE THE LORD   012 02
O YE HEAVENS, BLESS YE THE LORD   012 04
THAT BE ABOVE THE FIRMAMENT, BLESS YE THE LORD   012 07
O ALL YE POWERS OF THE LORD, BLESS YE THE LORD   012 08
YE POWERS OF THE LORD, BLESS YE THE LORD   012 08
O YE SUN AND MOON, BLESS YE THE LORD   012 10
O YE STARS OF HEAVEN, BLESS YE THE LORD   012 12
O YE SHOWERS AND DEW, BLESS YE THE LORD   012 14
O YE WINDS OF GOD, BLESS YE THE LORD   012 16
O YE FIRE AND HEAT, BLESS YE THE LORD   012 18
O YE WINTER AND SUMMER, BLESS YE THE LORD   012 20
O YE DEWS AND FROSTS, BLESS YE THE LORD   012 22
O YE FROST AND COLD, BLESS YE THE LORD   012 24
O YE ICE AND SNOW, BLESS YE THE LORD   012 26
O YE NIGHTS AND DAYS, BLESS YE THE LORD   012 28
O YE LIGHT AND DARKNESS, BLESS YE THE LORD   012 30
O YE LIGHTNINGS AND CLOUDS, BLESS YE THE LORD   012 32
O LET THE EARTH BLESS THE LORD   013 02
O YE MOUNTAINS AND HILLS, BLESS YE THE LORD   013 04
YE GREEN THINGS UPON THE EARTH, BLESS YE THE LORD   013 07
O YE WELLS, BLESS YE THE LORD   013 08
O YE SEAS AND FLOODS, BLESS YE THE LORD   013 10
ALL THAT MOVE IN THE WATERS, BLESS YE THE LORD   013 13
O ALL YE FOWLS OF THE AIR, BLESS YE THE LORD   013 14
O ALL YE BEASTS AND CATTLE, BLESS YE THE LORD   013 16
O YE CHILDREN OF MEN, BLESS YE THE LORD   013 18
O LET ISRAEL BLESS THE LORD   013 20
O YE PRIESTS OF THE LORD, BLESS YE THE LORD   013 22
O YE PRIESTS OF THE LORD, BLESS YE THE LORD   013 22
O YE SERVANTS OF THE LORD, BLESS YE THE LORD   013 24
YE SERVANTS OF THE LORD, BLESS YE THE LORD   013 24
AND SOULS OF THE RIGHTEOUS, BLESS YE THE LORD   013 27
HOLY AND HUMBLE MEN OF HEART, BLESS YE THE LORD   013 29
BLESSED BE THE LORD GOD OF ISRAEL   014 08
THE FACE OF THE LORD TO PREPARE HIS WAYS   014 25
SERVE THE LORD WITH GLADNESS, AND COME BEFORE HIS   015 04
O BE JOYFUL IN THE LORD, ALL YE LANDS   015 04
BE YE SURE THAT THE LORD HE IS GOD   015 07
FOR THE LORD IS GRACIOUS, HIS MERCY IS EVERLASTING   015 15
AND IN JESUS CHRIST HIS ONLY SON OUR LORD   015 21
AND IN ONE LORD JESUS CHRIST, THE ONLY-BEGOTTEN SON 016 02
THE HOLY GHOST, THE LORD, AND GIVER OF LIFE, WHO   016 15
THE LORD BE WITH YOU   016 25
O LORD, SHOW THY MERCY UPON US   016 29
THROUGH THE MIGHT OF JESUS CHRIST OUR LORD   017 11
O LORD, OUR HEAVENLY FATHER, ALMIGHTY AND EVERLASTING 017 13
THROUGH JESUS CHRIST OUR LORD   017 19
O LORD, OUR HEAVENLY FATHER, THE HIGH AND MIGHTY   017 27
THROUGH JESUS CHRIST OUR LORD   018 05
O LORD OUR GOVERNOR, WHOSE GLORY IS IN ALL THE WORLD 018 07
JESUS CHRIST OUR LORD, WHO LIVETH AND REIGNETH WITH 018 14
GRANT THIS, O LORD, FOR THE HONOUR OF OUR ADVOCATE   018 23
OF THE WORLD BY OUR LORD JESUS CHRIST   019 23
JESUS CHRIST OUR LORD, TO WHOM, WITH THEE AND THE   019 30
FULFIL NOW, O LORD, THE DESIRES AND PETITIONS OF THY 020 07
THE GRACE OF OUR LORD JESUS CHRIST, AND THE LOVE OF 020 12
TO THE VERSICLES, O LORD, OPEN THOU OUR LIPS, ETC R 021 08
AFTER THE LORD BE WITH YOU, ETC   R 021 10
THE LORD IS IN HIS HOLY TEMPLE   021 12
LORD, I HAVE LOVED THE HABITATION OF THY HOUSE,   021 14

LORD   CONTINUED   LORD   CONTINUED

O WORSHIP THE LORD IN THE BEAUTY OF HOLINESS	021 19
IN THY SIGHT, O LORD, MY STRENGTH AND MY REDEEMER	021 22
TO THE LORD OUR GOD BELONG MERCIES AND FORGIVENESSES,	022 06
THE VOICE OF THE LORD OUR GOD, TO WALK IN HIS LAWS	022 08
AND THE LORD HATH LAID ON HIM THE INIQUITY OF US ALL	022 16
VICTORY THROUGH OUR LORD JESUS CHRIST	022 18
HOLY, IS THE LORD OF HOSTS	022 33
BUT THOU, O LORD, HAVE MERCY UPON US, MISERABLE	023 30
DECLARED UNTO MANKIND IN CHRIST JESUS OUR LORD	024 02
THE FATHER OF OUR LORD JESUS CHRIST, WHO DESIRETH NOT	024 08
THROUGH JESUS CHRIST OUR LORD	024 20
AND MERCIFUL LORD GRANT YOU ABSOLUTION AND REMISSION	024 23
HE SHALL SAY, O LORD, OPEN THOU OUR LIPS	025 06
PRAISE YE THE LORD	025 13
THY GREAT GLORY, O LORD GOD, HEAVENLY KING, GOD THE	025 25
O LORD, THE ONLY-BEGOTTEN SON, JESUS CHRIST	025 27
O LORD GOD, LAMB OF GOD, SON OF THE FATHER, THAT	025 27
THOU ONLY ART THE LORD	026 02
DOTH MAGNIFY THE LORD, *	026 11
O SING UNTO THE LORD A NEW SONG	027 04
THE LORD DECLARED HIS SALVATION	027 08
JOYFUL UNTO THE LORD, ALL YE LANDS	027 13
PRAISE THE LORD UPON THE HARP	027 15
JOYFUL BEFORE THE LORD, THE KING	027 18
LET THE HILLS BE JOYFLL TOGETHER BEFORE THE LORD	027 22
THANKS UNTO THE LORD, *	027 28
FOR THOU, LORD, HAST MADE ME GLAD THROUGH THY WORKS	028 02
LORD, NOW LETTEST THOU THY SERVANT DEPART IN PEACE,	028 09
PRAISE THE LORD, O MY SOUL	029 04
PRAISE THE LORD, O MY SOUL, *	029 06
O PRAISE THE LORD, YE ANGELS OF HIS, YE THAT EXCEL IN	029 12
O PRAISE THE LORD, ALL YE HIS HOSTS	029 15
O SPEAK GOOD OF THE LORD, ALL YE WORKS OF HIS,	029 17
PRAISE THOU THE LORD, O MY SOUL	029 18
AND IN JESUS CHRIST HIS ONLY SON OUR LORD	029 26
AND IN ONE LORD JESUS CHRIST, THE ONLY-BEGOTTEN SCN	030 07
THE HOLY GHOST, THE LCRD, AND GIVER OF LIFE, WHO	030 20
THE LORD BE WITH YOU	030 30
O LORD, SHOW THY MERCY UPON US	031 02
O LORD, SAVE THE STATE	031 04
O LORD, SAVE THY PEOPLE	031 08
GIVE PEACE IN OUR TIME, O LORD	031 10
FOR IT IS THOU, LORD, ONLY, THAT MAKEST US DWELL IN	031 11
LIGHTEN OUR DARKNESS, WE BESEECH THEE, O LORD	031 26
JESUS CHRIST OUR LORD, WHO WITH THEE AND THE HOLY	032 13
GRANT THIS, O LORD, FOR THE HONOUR OF OUR ADVOCATE	032 22
OF THE WORLD BY OUR LORD JESUS CHRIST	033 17
JESUS CHRIST OUR LORD, TO WHOM, WITH THEE AND THE	033 28
FULFIL NOW, O LORD, THE DESIRES AND PETITIONS OF THY	034 07
THE GRACE OF OUR LORD JESUS CHRIST, AND THE LOVE OF	034 12
OUR MOST BLESSED LORD AND SAVIOUR	035 21
THROUGH JESUS CHRIST, THY SON, OUR LORD	035 29
ALL WHICH WE ASK THROUGH JESUS CHRIST OUR LORD	036 24
JESUS CHRIST, THY SON, OUR LORD	037 23
THE FATHER OF OUR LORD JESUS CHRIST, OUR CNLY	037 25
OF OUR CALLING, ONE LORD, ONE FAITH, ONE BAPTISM,	037 31
THROUGH JESUS CHRIST OUR LORD	038 03
THROUGH THE SAME THY SON JESUS CHRIST OUR LORD	038 12
THROUGH JESUS CHRIST OUR LORD	038 22
THROUGH JESUS CHRIST OUR LORD	039 05
THROUGH JESUS CHRIST OUR LORD	039 15
THROUGH THE SAME THY SON JESUS CHRIST OUR LORD	039 21
THROUGH JESUS CHRIST OUR LORD	039 31
THROUGH CHRIST OUR LORD	040 13
THROUGH JESUS CHRIST OUR LORD	040 21
THROUGH JESUS CHRIST OUR LORD	040 28
OF JESUS CHRIST OUR LORD, TO WHOM, WITH THEE AND THE	041 05
THE MERITS OF THY SON, JESUS CHRIST OUR LORD	041 16
THROUGH JESUS CHRIST CUR LORD	041 22
O LORD GOD OF HOSTS, STRETCH FORTH, WE PRAY THEE,	041 25
THROUGH JESUS CHRIST OUR LORD	041 31
O ETERNAL LORD GOD, WHO ALONE SPREADEST OUT THE	042 03
THROUGH JESUS CHRIST OUR LORD	042 12
THROUGH JESUS CHRIST THY SON OUR LORD	042 20
THROUGH JESUS CHRIST OUR LORD	042 28
THROUGH JESUS CHRIST CUR LORD	043 05
O LORD JESUS CHRIST, WHO DOST EMBRACE CHILDREN WITH	043 07
THROUGH THE SAME JESUS CHRIST OUR LORD	043 26
O LORD, OUR HEAVENLY FATHER, WHOSE BLESSED SON CAME	043 28
THROUGH JESUS CHRIST OUR LORD	044 14
ONE THAT SERVETH, THY SON JESUS CHRIST OUR LORD	044 25
THE KINGDOM OF OUR LORD AND SAVIOUR JESUS CHRIST	044 31
THROUGH JESUS CHRIST OUR LORD	045 10
THROUGH JESUS CHRIST CUR LORD	045 21
THROUGH JESUS CHRIST CUR LORD	045 28
REMEMBER HIM, O LORD, IN MERCY	046 03
THROUGH JESUS CHRIST CUR LORD	046 06
THROUGH JESUS CHRIST CUR LORD	046 16
THROUGH JESUS CHRIST CUR LORD	046 30
O LORD JESUS CHRIST, WHO SAIDST UNTO THINE APOSTLES,	049 05
US MERCIFULLY, O LORD, IN THESE OUR SUPPLICATIONS AND	049 11
THROUGH JESUS CHRIST OUR LORD	049 16
THROUGH JESUS CHRIST CUR LORD	049 22
DIRECT US, O LORD, IN ALL OUR DOINGS, WITH THY MOST	049 23
THROUGH JESUS CHRIST CUR LORD	049 28
THE WORTHINESS OF THY SON JESUS CHRIST OUR LORD	050 05
THROUGH JESUS CHRIST OUR LORD	050 13
JESUS CHRIST OUR LORD, TO WHOM, WITH THEE AND THE	050 28
THROUGH JESUS CHRIST CUR LORD	051 13
THROUGH JESUS CHRIST CUR LORD	051 20
O LORD GOD, WHO HAST JUSTLY HUMBLED US BY THY LATE	051 22
THROUGH JESUS CHRIST CUR LORD	051 28
THROUGH JESUS CHRIST CUR LORD	052 05
THROUGH JESUS CHRIST CUR LORD	052 15

THROUGH JESUS CHRIST OUR LORD	052 27
ART THOU, O LORD, AND FULL OF COMPASSION TO THE	053 03
THROUGH JESUS CHRIST OUR LORD	053 07
THROUGH JESUS CHRIST OUR LORD	053 18
MOST GRACIOUS LORD, WHOSE MERCY IS OVER ALL THY	053 20
THROUGH JESUS CHRIST OUR LORD	053 27
REMEMBER NOT, LORD, OUR OFFENCES, NOR THE OFFENCES OF	054 13
SPARE US, GOOD LORD, SPARE THY PEOPLE, WHOM THOU HAST	054 15
SPARE US, GOOD LORD	054 18
GOOD LORD, DELIVER US	054 22
GOOD LORD, DELIVER US	055 05
THEE TO HEAR US, O LORD GOD	055 18
WE BESEECH THEE TO HEAR US, GOOD LORD	055 21
WE BESEECH THEE TO HEAR US, GOOD LORD	056 04
WE BESEECH THEE TO HEAR US, GOOD LORD	057 04
LORD, HAVE MERCY UPON US	057 27
O LORD, DEAL NOT WITH US ACCORDING TO OUR SINS	058 12
THROUGH JESUS CHRIST OUR LORD	058 24
O LORD, ARISE, HELP US, AND DELIVER US FOR THY NAME'S	058 26
O LORD, ARISE, HELP US, AND DELIVER US FOR THINE	059 03
HEAR US, O LORD CHRIST	059 16
O LORD, LET THY MERCY BE SHOWED UPON US	059 18
ONLY MEDIATOR AND ADVOCATE, JESUS CHRIST OUR LORD	059 28
OUR BLESSED LORD AND SAVIOUR	VI 43
OPEN MY LIPS, O LORD, *	061 09
PASS AT ONCE TO O LORD, SAVE THY SERVANTS	R 061 20
LORD, HAVE MERCY UPON US	061 21
O LORD, SAVE THY SERVANTS	061 30
O LORD, HEAR OUR PRAYER	062 05
O LORD, WE BESEECH THEE, MERCIFULLY HEAR OUR PRAYERS,	062 08
THROUGH CHRIST OUR LORD	062 11
US THEREFORE, GOOD LORD, SPARE THY PEOPLE, WHOM THOU	062 20
THROUGH JESUS CHRIST OUR LORD	062 26
THOU US, O GOOD LORD, AND SO SHALL WE BE TURNED	062 28
BE FAVOURABLE, O LORD, BE FAVOURABLE TO THY PEOPLE,	062 29
THY PEOPLE, GOOD LORD, SPARE THEM, AND LET NOT THINE	063 03
HEAR US, O LORD, FOR THY MERCY IS GREAT, AND AFTER	063 04
OF THY BLESSED SON, JESUS CHRIST OUR LORD	063 07
THE LORD BLESS US, AND KEEP US	063 15
THE LORD MAKE HIS FACE TO SHINE UPON US, AND BE	063 15
THE LORD LIFT UP HIS COUNTENANCE UPON US, AND GIVE US	063 17
THROUGH CHRIST OUR LORD	067 21
HEAR WHAT OUR LORD JESUS CHRIST SAITH	R 067 30
I AM THE LORD THY GOD	068 04
LORD, HAVE MERCY UPON US, AND INCLINE OUR HEARTS TO	068 06
FOR I THE LORD THY GOD AM A JEALOUS GOD, AND VISIT	068 12
THE NAME OF THE LORD THY GOD IN VAIN	068 18
FOR THE LORD WILL NOT HOLD HIM GUILTLESS, THAT TAKETH	068 20
THE SABBATH OF THE LORD THY GOD	068 26
FOR IN SIX DAYS THE LORD MADE HEAVEN AND EARTH,	068 30
WHEREFORE THE LORD BLESSED THE SEVENTH DAY, AND	068 31
THE LAND WHICH THE LORD THY GOD GIVETH THEE	069 03
LORD, HAVE MERCY UPON US, AND INCLINE OUR HEARTS TO	069 05
LORD, HAVE MERCY UPON US, AND WRITE ALL THESE THY	069 23
HEAR WHAT OUR LORD JESUS CHRIST SAITH	069 26
THOU SHALT LOVE THE LORD THY GOD WITH ALL THY HEART,	069 27
SHALL BE SAID, LORD, HAVE MERCY UPON US	070 02
MAY SAY, O ALMIGHTY LORD, AND EVERLASTING GOD,	070 06
THROUGH OUR LORD AND SAVIOUR JESUS CHRIST	070 11
SHALL BE SAID, THE LORD BE WITH YOU	070 14
HERE SHALL BE SAID, GLORY BE TO THEE, O LORD	070 26
AND IN ONE LORD JESUS CHRIST, THE ONLY-BEGOTTEN SCN	071 04
THE HOLY GHOST, THE LORD, AND GIVER OF LIFE, WHO	071 17
THE WORDS OF THE LORD JESUS, HOW HE SAID, IT IS MORE	072 02
UNTO ME, LORD, LORD, SHALL ENTER INTO THE KINGDOM OF	072 13
THAT SAITH UNTO ME, LORD, LORD, SHALL ENTER INTO THE	072 13
YE THEREFORE THE LORD OF THE HARVEST, THAT HE SEND	073 12
APPEAR BEFORE THE LORD EMPTY	073 15
THE BLESSING OF THE LORD THY GOD WHICH HE HATH GIVEN	073 17
O LORD, IS THE GREATNESS, AND THE POWER,	073 18
IS THE KINGDOM, O LORD, AND THOU ART EXALTED AS HEAD	073 21
COME OF THEE, O LORD, AND OF THINE OWN HAVE WE GIVEN	073 23
OF THY GOODNESS, O LORD, TO COMFORT AND SUCCOUR ALL	074 31
FATHER OF OUR LORD JESUS CHRIST, MAKER OF ALL	075 17
FOR THY SON OUR LORD JESUS CHRIST'S SAKE, FORGIVE US	075 27
THROUGH JESUS CHRIST OUR LORD	075 30
THROUGH JESUS CHRIST OUR LORD	076 08
WE LIFT THEM UP UNTO THE LORD	076 27
THANKS UNTO OUR LORD GOD	076 28
THANKS UNTO THEE, O LORD, HOLY FATHER, ALMIGHTY,	076 33
HOLY, HOLY, LORD GOD OF HOSTS, HEAVEN AND EARTH	077 08
GLORY BE TO THEE, O LORD MOST HIGH	077 10
THROUGH JESUS CHRIST OUR LORD	077 22
IN THE FACE OF THY SON JESUS CHRIST OUR LORD	078 03
RESURRECTION OF THY SON JESUS CHRIST OUR LORD	078 09
THY MOST DEARLY BELOVED SON JESUS CHRIST OUR LORD	078 17
THROUGH JESUS CHRIST OUR LORD	078 25
ART ONE GOD, ONE LORD, IN TRINITY OF PERSONS AND IN	079 08
JESUS CHRIST OUR LORD, AND FOR THE SENDING TO US OF	079 16
HOLY, HOLY, LORD GOD OF HOSTS, HEAVEN AND EARTH	079 32
GLORY BE TO THEE, O LORD MOST HIGH	079 34
O LORD AND HEAVENLY FATHER, ACCORDING TO	080 36
UNTO THEE, O LORD, OUR SELVES, OUR SOULS AND BODIES,	081 21
THROUGH JESUS CHRIST OUR LORD	081 32
O MERCIFUL LORD, TRUSTING IN OUR OWN	082 14
THOU ART THE SAME LORD, WHOSE PROPERTY IS ALWAYS TO	082 17
GRACIOUS LORD, SO TO EAT THE FLESH OF THY	082 18
THE BODY OF OUR LORD JESUS CHRIST, WHICH WAS GIVEN	082 31
THE BLOOD OF OUR LORD JESUS CHRIST, WHICH WAS SHED	083 03
JESUS CHRIST OUR LORD, TO WHOM, WITH THEE AND THE	083 29
THY GREAT GLORY, O LORD GOD, HEAVENLY KING, GOD THE	084 05
O LORD GOD, LAMB OF GOD, SON OF THE FATHER, THAT	084 07
O LORD, THE ONLY-BEGOTTEN SON, JESUS CHRIST	084 07
THOU ONLY ART THE LORD	084 13

LORD   CONTINUED

AND OF HIS SON JESUS CHRIST OUR LORD   084 20
BELOVED IN THE LORD, YE WHO MIND TO COME TO THE HOLY   085 25
THAT YE BE NOT JUDGED OF THE LORD   085 34
FOR THE LORD JESUS CHRIST'S SAKE, THAT YE WILL   088 15
BUT PUT YE ON THE LORD JESUS CHRIST, AND MAKE NOT   091 08
YE SHALL SAY, THE LORD HATH NEED OF THEM   091 17
BLESSED IS HE THAT COMETH IN THE NAME OF THE LORD   091 29
BLESSED LORD, WHO HAST CAUSED ALL HOLY SCRIPTURES TO   092 07
THE FATHER OF OUR LORD JESUS CHRIST   092 21
PRAISE THE LORD, ALL YE GENTILES   092 29
O LORD JESUS CHRIST, WHO AT THY FIRST COMING DIDST   093 24
BUT HE THAT JUDGETH ME IS THE LORD   094 10
THE TIME, UNTIL THE LORD COME, WHO BOTH WILL BRING TO   094 11
O LORD, RAISE UP, WE PRAY THEE, THY POWER, AND COME   095 04
JESUS CHRIST OUR LORD, TO WHOM, WITH THEE AND THE   095 09
REJOICE IN THE LORD ALWAY   095 13
THE LORD IS AT HAND   095 15
THE WAY OF THE LORD, AS SAID THE PROPHET ESAIAS   095 29
THE SAME OUR LORD JESUS CHRIST, WHO LIVETH AND   096 18
THOU, LORD, IN THE BEGINNING HAST LAID THE   097 13
THE ANGEL OF THE LORD CAME UPON THEM, AND THE GLORY   099 12
THE GLORY OF THE LORD SHONE ROUND ABOUT THEM   099 13
CITY OF DAVID A SAVIOUR, WHICH IS CHRIST THE LORD   099 17
GRANT, O LORD, THAT, IN ALL OUR SUFFERINGS HERE UPON   099 26
AND SAYING, LORD JESUS, RECEIVE MY SPIRIT   100 14
WITH A LOUD VOICE, LORD, LAY NOT THIS SIN TO THEIR   100 15
BLESSED IS HE THAT COMETH IN THE NAME OF THE LORD   100 34
MERCIFUL LORD, WE BESEECH THEE TO CAST THY BRIGHT   101 05
THROUGH JESUS CHRIST OUR LORD   101 10
AND SAID, LORD, WHICH IS HE THAT BETRAYETH   102 05
HIM SAITH TO JESUS, LORD, AND WHAT SHALL THIS MAN DO   102 07
THROUGH JESUS CHRIST OUR LORD   102 27
THE ANGEL OF THE LORD APPEARETH TO JOSEPH IN A DREAM,   103 16
WAS SPOKEN OF THE LORD BY THE PROPHET, SAYING, OUT OF   103 23
THE SAME OUR LORD JESUS CHRIST, WHO LIVETH AND   104 10
THOUGH HE BE LORD OF ALL   104 15
THE ANGEL OF THE LORD APPEARED UNTO HIM IN A DREAM,   105 03
WAS SPOKEN OF THE LORD BY THE PROPHET, SAYING,   105 09
AS THE ANGEL OF THE LORD HAD BIDDEN HIM, AND TOOK   105 13
THROUGH THE SAME THY SON JESUS CHRIST OUR LORD   105 24
JESUS CHRIST IS LORD, TO THE GLORY OF GOD THE FATHER   105 30
TO PASS, WHICH THE LORD HATH MADE KNOWN UNTO US   106 10
THROUGH JESUS CHRIST OUR LORD   106 28
THE SPIRIT OF THE LORD GOD IS UPON ME   106 30
BECAUSE THE LORD HATH ANOINTED ME TO PREACH GOOD   106 31
YEAR OF THE LORD, AND THE DAY OF VENGEANCE OF OUR   107 05
THE PLANTING OF THE LORD, THAT HE MIGHT BE GLORIFIED   107 10
AN ANGEL OF THE LORD APPEARETH IN A DREAM TO JOSEPH   107 12
THROUGH THE SAME THY SON JESUS CHRIST OUR LORD   108 03
WHICH HE PURPOSED IN CHRIST JESUS OUR LORD   108 27
O LORD, WE BESEECH THEE MERCIFULLY TO RECEIVE THE   109 29
THROUGH JESUS CHRIST OUR LORD   109 33
THROUGH JESUS CHRIST OUR LORD   111 13
SERVING THE LORD   111 26
YE THE WAY OF THE LORD, MAKE HIS PATHS STRAIGHT   112 07
THROUGH JESUS CHRIST OUR LORD   112 29
I WILL REPAY, SAITH THE LORD   113 05
THROUGH JESUS CHRIST OUR LORD   114 09
SAYING, LORD, IF THOU WILT, THOU CANST MAKE ME   114 31
AND SAYING, LORD, MY SERVANT LIETH AT HOME SICK   115 08
ANSWERED AND SAID, LORD, I AM NOT WORTHY THAT THOU   115 10
O LORD, WE BESEECH THEE TO KEEP THY CHURCH AND   115 28
THROUGH JESUS CHRIST OUR LORD   115 32
SINGING WITH GRACE IN YOUR HEARTS TO THE LORD   116 14
IN THE NAME OF THE LORD JESUS, GIVING THANKS TO GOD   116 15
O LORD, WE BESEECH THEE FAVOURABLY TO HEAR THE   118 28
EVEN WAS COME, THE LORD OF THE VINEYARD SAITH UNTO   119 29
O LORD GOD, WHO SEEST THAT WE PUT NOT OUR TRUST IN   120 17
THROUGH JESUS CHRIST OUR LORD   120 20
AND FATHER OF OUR LORD JESUS CHRIST, WHICH IS BLESSED   121 15
O LORD, WHO HAST TAUGHT US THAT ALL OUR DOINGS   122 14
AND HE SAID, LORD, THAT I MAY RECEIVE MY SIGHT   124 02
THROUGH JESUS CHRIST OUR LORD   124 17
TO ME, SAITH THE LORD, WITH ALL YOUR HEART, AND WITH   124 21
AND TURN UNTO THE LORD YOUR GOD   124 24
UNTO THE LORD YOUR GOD   124 28
MINISTERS OF THE LORD, WEEP BETWEEN THE PORCH AND THE   125 02
SPARE THY PEOPLE, O LORD, AND GIVE NOT THINE HERITAGE   125 04
O LORD, WHO FOR OUR SAKE DIDST FAST FORTY DAYS AND   125 27
SHALT NOT TEMPT THE LORD THY GOD   127 04
SHALT WORSHIP THE LORD THY GOD, AND HIM ONLY SHALT   127 10
THROUGH JESUS CHRIST OUR LORD   127 20
EXHORT YOU BY THE LORD JESUS, THAT AS YE HAVE   127 24
WE GAVE YOU BY THE LORD JESUS   127 27
BECAUSE THAT THE LORD IS THE AVENGER OF ALL SUCH,   127 32
HAVE MERCY ON ME, O LORD, THOU SON OF DAVID   128 10
SAYING, LORD, HELP ME   128 16
AND SHE SAID, TRUTH, LORD   128 18
THROUGH JESUS CHRIST OUR LORD   128 28
BUT NOW ARE YE LIGHT IN THE LORD   129 13
PROVING WHAT IS ACCEPTABLE UNTO THE LORD   129 16
THROUGH OUR LORD AND SAVIOUR JESUS CHRIST   130 27
THROUGH JESUS CHRIST OUR LORD   132 21
THROUGH THE SAME JESUS CHRIST OUR LORD   134 12
JESUS CHRIST IS LORD, TO THE GLORY OF GOD THE FATHER   134 27
AS THE LORD APPOINTED ME   135 18
THROUGH THE SAME THY SON JESUS CHRIST OUR LORD   138 09
OF THE LORD, AND THE PRAISES OF THE LORD, ACCORDING   138 28
TO ALL THAT THE LORD HATH BESTOWED ON US, AND THE   138 29
THE PRAISES OF THE LORD, ACCORDING TO ALL THAT THE   138 29
THE SPIRIT OF THE LORD CAUSED HIM TO REST   139 16
THOU, O LORD, ART OUR FATHER, OUR REDEEMER   139 23
O LORD, WHY HAST THOU MADE US TO ERR FROM THY WAYS,   139 24
O LORD GOD, WHOSE BLESSED SON, OUR SAVIOUR, GAVE HIS   144 06

THROUGH THE SAME THY SON JESUS CHRIST OUR LORD   144 10
THE LORD GOD HATH OPENED MINE EAR, AND I WAS NOT   144 12
FOR THE LORD GOD WILL HELP ME   144 16
BEHOLD, THE LORD GOD WILL HELP ME   144 20
THAT FEARETH THE LORD, THAT OBEYETH THE VOICE OF HIS   144 23
IN THE NAME OF THE LORD, AND STAY UPON HIS GOD   144 25
WITH THY HELP, O LORD GOD OF OUR SALVATION   147 08
THROUGH JESUS CHRIST OUR LORD   147 11
AND THE LORD SAID, SIMON, SIMON, BEHOLD, SATAN HATH   149 31
HE SAID UNTO HIM, LORD, I AM READY TO GO WITH THEE,   149 34
AND THEY SAID, LORD, BEHOLD, HERE ARE TWO SWORDS   150 12
THEY SAID UNTO HIM, LORD, SHALL WE SMITE WITH THE   150 31
AND THE LORD TURNED, AND LOOKED UPON PETER   151 19
THE WORD OF THE LORD, HOW HE HAD SAID UNTO HIM,   151 21
JESUS CHRIST OUR LORD, WHO NOW LIVETH AND REIGNETH   152 12
RECEIVED OF THE LORD THAT WHICH ALSO I DELIVERED UNTO   152 16
UNTO YOU, THAT THE LORD JESUS THE SAME NIGHT IN WHICH   152 17
HE SAID UNTO JESUS, LORD, REMEMBER ME WHEN THOU   155 06
SAITH UNTO HIM, LORD, DOST THOU WASH MY FEET   156 02
SAITH UNTO HIM, LORD, NOT MY FEET ONLY, BUT ALSO MY   156 07
IF I THEN, YOUR LORD AND MASTER, HAVE WASHED YOUR   156 15
YE CALL ME MASTER AND LORD   156 15
FOR WHICH OUR LORD JESUS CHRIST WAS CONTENTED TO BE   156 22
THROUGH OUR LORD AND SAVIOUR JESUS CHRIST   157 02
THEM HOME, BLESSED LORD, TO THY FOLD, THAT THEY MAY   157 10
JESUS CHRIST OUR LORD, WHO LIVETH AND REIGNETH WITH   157 12
SAITH THE LORD, I WILL PUT MY LAWS INTO THEIR   158 12
GRANT, O LORD, THAT AS WE ARE BAPTIZED INTO THE DEATH   161 13
FOR US, THE SAME THY SON JESUS CHRIST OUR LORD   161 19
BUT ALIVE UNTO GOD THROUGH JESUS CHRIST OUR LORD   163 10
JESUS CHRIST OUR LORD, WHO LIVETH AND REIGNETH WITH   163 28
HAVE TAKEN AWAY THE LORD OUT OF THE SEPULCHRE,   164 15
THROUGH THE SAME THY SON JESUS CHRIST OUR LORD   165 08
THROUGH THE SAME THY SON JESUS CHRIST OUR LORD   166 02
HE IS LORD OF ALL   166 16
SAYING, THE LORD IS RISEN INDEED, AND HATH   168 13
THROUGH JESUS CHRIST OUR LORD   168 22
MERITS OF THE SAME THY SON JESUS CHRIST OUR LORD   170 24
WERE THE DISCIPLES GLAD WHEN THEY SAW THE LORD   171 20
THROUGH THE SAME THY SON JESUS CHRIST OUR LORD   172 03
THROUGH OUR LORD JESUS CHRIST   173 10
THROUGH JESUS CHRIST OUR LORD   174 24
O LORD, FROM WHOM ALL GOOD THINGS DO COME   175 29
THROUGH OUR LORD JESUS CHRIST   176 02
SON OUR LORD JESUS CHRIST TO HAVE ASCENDED INTO THE   177 15
OF HIM, SAYING, LORD, WILT THOU AT THIS TIME RESTORE   178 05
NOT ISCARIOT, LORD, HOW IS IT THAT THOU WILT   181 22
JESUS CHRIST OUR LORD, WHO LIVETH AND REIGNETH WITH   182 18
DIFFERENCES OF ADMINISTRATIONS, BUT THE SAME LORD   182 24
JESUS CHRIST OUR LORD, WHO WITH THEE AND THE SAME   183 26
HE IS LORD OF ALL   184 04
THEM TO BE BAPTIZED IN THE NAME OF THE LORD   184 29
JESUS CHRIST OUR LORD, WHO LIVETH AND REIGNETH WITH   185 17
IN THE NAME OF THE LORD JESUS   185 26
HOLY, HOLY, LORD GOD ALMIGHTY, WHICH WAS,   187 23
THOU ART WORTHY, O LORD, TO RECEIVE GLORY AND HONOUR   187 29
THROUGH JESUS CHRIST OUR LORD   189 06
O LORD, WHO NEVER FAILEST TO HELP AND GOVERN THOSE   191 04
THROUGH JESUS CHRIST OUR LORD   191 09
AND SHEWED HIS LORD THESE THINGS   192 12
THE SERVANT SAID, LORD, IT IS DONE AS THOU HAST   192 16
AND THE LORD SAID UNTO THE SERVANT, GO OUT INTO THE   192 18
O LORD, WE BESEECH THEE MERCIFULLY TO HEAR US   192 24
THROUGH JESUS CHRIST OUR LORD   192 28
FOR THE SAKE OF JESUS CHRIST OUR LORD   194 09
GRANT, O LORD, WE BESEECH THEE, THAT THE COURSE OF   195 15
THROUGH JESUS CHRIST OUR LORD   195 18
FOR THE EYES OF THE LORD ARE OVER THE RIGHTEOUS,   195 28
BUT THE FACE OF THE LORD IS AGAINST THEM THAT DO   195 29
BUT SANCTIFY THE LORD GOD IN YOUR HEARTS   196 03
FOR I AM A SINFUL MAN, O LORD   196 24
THROUGH JESUS CHRIST OUR LORD   197 08
BUT ALIVE UNTO GOD THROUGH JESUS CHRIST OUR LORD   197 26
LORD OF ALL POWER AND MIGHT, WHO ART THE AUTHOR AND   198 20
THROUGH JESUS CHRIST OUR LORD   198 24
GOD IS ETERNAL LIFE THROUGH JESUS CHRIST OUR LORD   199 06
THROUGH JESUS CHRIST OUR LORD   199 32
UNTO ME, LORD, LORD, SHALL ENTER INTO THE KINGDOM OF   200 24
THAT SAITH UNTO ME, LORD, LORD, SHALL ENTER INTO THE   200 24
GRANT TO US, LORD, WE BESEECH THEE, THE SPIRIT TO   200 29
THROUGH JESUS CHRIST OUR LORD   201 03
MERCIFUL EARS, O LORD, BE OPEN TO THE PRAYERS OF THY   203 11
THROUGH JESUS CHRIST OUR LORD   203 14
THAT JESUS IS THE LORD, BUT BY THE HOLY GHOST   203 21
DIFFERENCES OF ADMINISTRATIONS, BUT THE SAME LORD   203 24
THROUGH JESUS CHRIST OUR LORD   204 27
AND MEDIATION OF JESUS CHRIST, THY SON, OUR LORD   206 10
THROUGH THE MERITS OF JESUS CHRIST OUR LORD   207 17
THOU SHALT LOVE THE LORD THY GOD WITH ALL THY HEART,   208 15
THROUGH JESUS CHRIST OUR LORD   209 11
WE BESEECH THEE, O LORD, THY CHURCH WITH THY   210 17
THROUGH JESUS CHRIST OUR LORD   210 21
IN THE CROSS OF OUR LORD JESUS CHRIST, BY WHOM THE   210 30
THE MARKS OF THE LORD JESUS   211 05
THE GRACE OF OUR LORD JESUS CHRIST BE WITH YOUR   211 06
O LORD, WE BESEECH THEE, LET THY CONTINUAL PITY   212 04
THROUGH JESUS CHRIST OUR LORD   212 08
THE FATHER OF OUR LORD JESUS CHRIST, OF WHOM THE   212 12
AND WHEN THE LORD SAW HER, HE HAD COMPASSION ON HER,   213 02
LORD, WE PRAY THEE THAT THY GRACE MAY ALWAYS PREVENT   213 14
THROUGH JESUS CHRIST OUR LORD   213 16
THE PRISONER OF THE LORD, BESEECH YOU THAT YE WALK   213 18
ONE LORD, ONE FAITH, ONE BAPTISM, ONE GOD AND FATHER   213 24
LORD, WE BESEECH THEE, GRANT THY PEOPLE GRACE TO   214 23

LORD   CONTINUED

THROUGH JESUS CHRIST OUR LORD   214 26
THE COMING OF OUR LORD JESUS CHRIST   215 02
IN THE DAY OF OUR LORD JESUS CHRIST   215 04
THOU SHALT LOVE THE LORD THY GOD WITH ALL THY HEART,   215 11
LORD, SAYING, THE LORD SAID UNTO MY LORD, SIT THOU ON   215 19
IN SPIRIT CALL HIM LORD, SAYING, THE LORD SAID UNTO   215 19
LORD SAID UNTO MY LORD, SIT THOU ON MY RIGHT HAND,   215 20
DAVID THEN CALL HIM LORD, HOW IS HE HIS SON   215 21
THROUGH JESUS CHRIST OUR LORD   215 30
AND TESTIFY IN THE LORD, THAT YE HENCEFORTH WALK NOT   216 03
THROUGH JESUS CHRIST OUR LORD   217 21
THE WILL OF THE LORD IS   217 26
AND MAKING MELODY IN YOUR HEART TO THE LORD   217 29
IN THE NAME OF OUR LORD JESUS CHRIST   217 31
MERCIFUL LORD, TO THY FAITHFUL PEOPLE PARDON   218 32
THROUGH JESUS CHRIST OUR LORD   219 03
BE STRONG IN THE LORD, AND IN THE POWER OF HIS MIGHT   219 05
LORD, WE BESEECH THEE TO KEEP THY HOUSEHOLD THE   220 16
THROUGH JESUS CHRIST OUR LORD   220 20
SAID UNTO JESUS, LORD, HOW OFT SHALL MY BROTHER SIN   221 09
HAD NOT TO PAY, HIS LORD COMMANDED HIM TO BE SOLD,   221 17
SAYING, LORD, HAVE PATIENCE WITH ME, AND I WILL   221 20
THEN THE LORD OF THAT SERVANT WAS MOVED WITH   221 21
AND TOLD UNTO THEIR LORD ALL THAT WAS DONE   221 32
THEN HIS LORD, AFTER THAT HE HAD CALLED HIM, SAID   221 32
AND HIS LORD WAS WROTH, AND DELIVERED HIM TO THE   222 02
THROUGH JESUS CHRIST OUR LORD   222 13
THE SAVIOUR, THE LORD JESUS CHRIST   222 22
O LORD, WE BESEECH THEE, ABSOLVE THY PEOPLE FROM   223 15
OUR BLESSED LORD AND SAVIOUR   223 19
THE FATHER OF OUR LORD JESUS CHRIST, PRAYING ALWAYS   223 22
WALK WORTHY OF THE LORD UNTO ALL PLEASING, BEING   224 04
WE BESEECH THEE, O LORD, THE WILLS OF THY FAITHFUL   225 04
THROUGH JESUS CHRIST OUR LORD   225 07
COME, SAITH THE LORD, THAT I WILL RAISE UNTO DAVID A   225 09
BE CALLED, THE LORD OUR RIGHTEOUSNESS   225 14
COME, SAITH THE LORD, THAT THEY SHALL NO MORE SAY,   225 15
NO MORE SAY, THE LORD LIVETH, WHICH BROUGHT UP THE   225 16
THE LORD LIVETH, WHICH BROUGHT UP AND WHICH LED   225 17
THROUGH THE SAME JESUS CHRIST OUR LORD   226 24
WITH THY MOUTH THE LORD JESUS, AND SHALT BELIEVE IN   226 26
FOR THE SAME LORD OVER ALL IS RICH UNTO ALL THAT CALL   227 03
THE NAME OF THE LORD SHALL BE SAVED   227 04
FOR ESAIAS SAITH, LORD, WHO HATH BELIEVED OUR REPORT   227 12
HEAR US, O LORD, THROUGH THE SAME JESUS CHRIST,   228 10
THEREFORE SAID UNTO HIM, WE HAVE SEEN THE LORD   228 27
SAID UNTO HIM, MY LORD AND MY GOD   229 06
THROUGH JESUS CHRIST OUR LORD   229 23
DISCIPLES OF THE LORD, WENT UNTO THE HIGH PRIEST, AND   229 26
AND HE SAID, WHO ART THOU, LORD   230 03
AND THE LORD SAID, I AM JESUS WHOM THOU PERSECUTEST   230 03
ASTONISHED SAID, LORD, WHAT WILT THOU HAVE ME TO DO   230 05
AND THE LORD SAID UNTO HIM, ARISE, AND GO INTO THE   230 06
AND TO HIM SAID THE LORD IN A VISION, ANANIAS   230 15
AND THE LORD SAID UNTO HIM, ARISE, AND GO INTO THE   230 16
AND HE SAID, BEHOLD, I AM HERE, LORD   230 16
ANANIAS ANSWERED, LORD, I HAVE HEARD BY MANY OF THIS   230 22
BUT THE LORD SAID UNTO HIM, GO THY WAY   230 25
BROTHER SAUL, THE LORD, EVEN JESUS, THAT APPEARED   230 31
BY THE SAME THY SON JESUS CHRIST OUR LORD   231 32
AND THE LORD, WHOM YE SEEK, SHALL SUDDENLY COME TO   232 04
COME, SAITH THE LORD OF HOSTS   232 07
MAY OFFER UNTO THE LORD AN OFFERING IN RIGHTEOUSNESS   232 12
PLEASANT UNTO THE LORD, AS IN THE DAYS OF OLD,   232 14
NOT ME, SAITH THE LORD OF HOSTS   232 20
TO PRESENT HIM TO THE LORD   232 25
IN THE LAW OF THE LORD, EVERY MALE THAT OPENETH THE   232 26
OPENETH THE WOMB SHALL BE CALLED HOLY TO THE LORD   232 27
IN THE LAW OF THE LORD, A PAIR OF TURTLE-DOVES, OR   232 28
AND SAID, LORD, NOW LETTEST THOU THY SERVANT   233 05
LIKEWISE UNTO THE LORD, AND SPAKE OF HIM TO ALL THEM   233 22
TO THE LAW OF THE LORD, THEY RETURNED INTO GALILEE,   233 25
THROUGH JESUS CHRIST OUR LORD   234 04
THE TIME THAT THE LORD JESUS WENT IN AND OUT AMONG   234 21
AND SAID, THOU, LORD, WHICH KNOWEST THE HEARTS OF ALL   234 27
O FATHER, LORD OF HEAVEN AND EARTH, BECAUSE   235 04
WE BESEECH THEE, O LORD, POUR THY GRACE INTO OUR   235 18
THROUGH THE SAME JESUS CHRIST OUR LORD   235 22
MOREOVER THE LORD SPAKE AGAIN UNTO AHAZ, SAYING,   235 25
THEE A SIGN OF THE LORD THY GOD   235 26
NEITHER WILL I TEMPT THE LORD   235 28
THEREFORE THE LORD HIMSELF SHALL GIVE YOU A SIGN   235 31
THE LORD IS WITH THEE   236 10
AND THE LORD GOD SHALL GIVE UNTO HIM THE THRONE OF   236 17
BEHOLD THE HANDMAID OF THE LORD   236 29
THROUGH JESUS CHRIST OUR LORD   237 10
THROUGH THE SAME THY SON JESUS CHRIST OUR LORD   239 04
OF GOD AND OF THE LORD JESUS CHRIST, TO THE TWELVE   239 06
THINK THAT HE SHALL RECEIVE ANY THING OF THE LORD   239 17
OF LIFE, WHICH THE LORD HATH PROMISED TO THEM THAT   239 26
SAITH UNTO HIM, LORD, WE KNOW NOT WHITHER THOU GOEST   240 04
SAITH UNTO HIM, LORD, SHEW US THE FATHER, AND IT   240 09
O LORD GOD ALMIGHTY, WHO DIDST ENDUE THY HOLY APOSTLE   240 28
THROUGH JESUS CHRIST OUR LORD   240 32
PURPOSE OF HEART THEY WOULD CLEAVE UNTO THE LORD   241 08
AND MUCH PEOPLE WAS ADDED UNTO THE LORD   241 10
NOT WHAT HIS LORD DOETH   241 30
THROUGH TH   SAME THY SON JESUS CHRIST OUR LORD   242 14
YE THE WAY OF THE LORD, MAKE STRAIGHT IN THE DESERT   242 21
THE GLORY OF THE LORD SHALL BE REVEALED, AND ALL   242 25
THE MOUTH OF THE LORD HATH SPOKEN IT   242 26
THE SPIRIT OF THE LORD BLOWETH UPON IT   242 30
BEHOLD, THE LORD GOD WILL COME WITH STRONG HAND,   243 06
HEARD HOW THE LORD HAD SHEWED GREAT MERCY UPON HER   243 15

LORD   CONTINUED

AND THE HAND OF THE LORD WAS WITH HIM   243 30
BLESSED BE THE LORD GOD OF ISRAEL   243 32
THE FACE OF THE LORD TO PREPARE HIS WAYS   244 11
THROUGH THE SAME THY SON JESUS CHRIST OUR LORD   244 28
THE ANGEL OF THE LORD CAME UPON HIM, AND A LIGHT   245 12
A SURETY, THAT THE LORD HATH SENT HIS ANGEL, AND HATH   245 26
THROUGH THE SAME JESUS CHRIST OUR LORD   246 22
EVEN AS OUR LORD JESUS CHRIST HATH SHEWED ME   248 11
AND COMING OF OUR LORD JESUS CHRIST, BUT WERE   248 15
THROUGH JESUS CHRIST OUR LORD   249 19
MORE ADDED TO THE LORD, MULTITUDES BOTH OF MEN AND   249 25
PREACH NOT OURSELVES, BUT CHRIST JESUS THE LORD   251 06
THROUGH JESUS CHRIST OUR LORD   251 32
THROUGH THE SAME THY SON JESUS CHRIST OUR LORD   253 20
WHICH THE LORD, THE RIGHTEOUS JUDGE, SHALL GIVE ME AT   253 28
THE LORD REWARD HIM ACCORDING TO HIS WORKS   254 07
THE LORD APPOINTED OTHER SEVENTY ALSO, AND SENT THEM   254 11
YE THEREFORE THE LORD OF THE HARVEST, THAT HE WOULD   254 15
THROUGH THE SAME JESUS CHRIST OUR LORD   254 32
TOGETHER GROWETH UNTO AN HOLY TEMPLE IN THE LORD   255 09
THE SERVANT IS NOT GREATER THAN HIS LORD   255 18
IN THE MYSTICAL BODY OF THY SON CHRIST OUR LORD   256 07
THROUGH THE SAME THY SON JESUS CHRIST OUR LORD   256 11
THROUGH JESUS CHRIST OUR LORD   258 09
THY SON JESUS CHRIST OUR LORD   258 18
ANSWER HIM, SAYING, LORD, WHEN SAW WE THEE AN   259 10
THROUGH JESUS CHRIST OUR LORD   259 23
TASTED THAT THE LORD IS GRACIOUS   259 28
THROUGH JESUS CHRIST OUR LORD   260 24
FOR SO HATH THE LORD COMMANDED US, SAYING, I HAVE SET   261 03
WERE GLAD, AND GLORIFIED THE WORD OF THE LORD   261 07
AND THE WORD OF THE LORD WAS PUBLISHED THROUGHOUT ALL   261 08
THE SPIRIT OF THE LORD IS UPON ME, BECAUSE HE HATH   261 16
TO PREACH THE ACCEPTABLE YEAR OF THE LORD   261 21
ALMIGHTY GOD, LORD OF HEAVEN AND EARTH   261 29
THROUGH JESUS CHRIST OUR LORD   262 02
KNOW THAT I AM THE LORD, WHEN I HAVE BROKEN THE BANDS   262 12
KNOW THAT I THE LORD THEIR GOD AM WITH THEM, AND THAT   262 20
SAITH THE LORD GOD   262 22
YOUR GOD, SAITH THE LORD GOD   262 23
THROUGH JESUS CHRIST OUR LORD   263 21
IS GOD OF GODS, AND LORD OF LORDS, A GREAT GOD, A   263 23
THE LORD YOUR GOD IS GOD OF GODS, AND LORD OF LORDS,   263 23
THOU SHALT FEAR THE LORD THY GOD   263 29
O PRAISE THE LORD, FOR IT IS A GOOD THING TO SING   264 18
THE LORD DOTH BUILD UP JERUSALEM, *   264 21
O SING UNTO THE LORD WITH THANKSGIVING   264 25
PRAISE THE LORD, O JERUSALEM   264 32
THROUGH JESUS CHRIST OUR LORD   265 16
THROUGH JESUS CHRIST OUR LORD   267 09
IN THE NAME OF OUR LORD JESUS CHRIST   267 12
UNTO YOUR OWN HUSBANDS, AS UNTO THE LORD   267 15
EVEN AS THE LORD THE CHURCH   267 27
O ETERNAL LORD GOD, WHO HOLDEST ALL SOULS IN LIFE   268 14
THROUGH JESUS CHRIST OUR LORD   268 20
THROUGH JESUS CHRIST OUR LORD   268 26
BY THE WORD OF THE LORD, THAT WE WHICH ARE ALIVE AND   269 03
THE COMING OF THE LORD SHALL NOT PREVENT THEM WHICH   269 04
FOR THE LORD HIMSELF SHALL DESCEND FROM HEAVEN WITH A   269 05
TO MEET THE LORD IN THE AIR   269 09
AND SO SHALL WE EVER BE WITH THE LORD   269 10
THROUGH OUR LORD JESUS CHRIST, THAT OF HIS   274 02
RECEIVE HIM, O LORD, AS THOU HAST PROMISED BY THY   274 14
WHICH THOU HAST PROMISED BY CHRIST OUR LORD   274 21
THROUGH OUR LORD JESUS CHRIST, WHO LIVETH AND   276 14
PRAYED THAT OUR LORD JESUS CHRIST WOULD VOUCHSAFE TO   276 20
PRAYED THAT OUR LORD JESUS CHRIST WOULD VOUCHSAFE TO   277 22
AND DESIRE TO FOLLOW HIM AS THY SAVIOUR AND LORD   278 06
O BLESSED LORD GOD, WHO DOST LIVE, AND GOVERN   278 30
THE LORD BE WITH YOU   278 32
WE LIFT THEM UP UNTO THE LORD   279 03
THANKS UNTO OUR LORD GOD   279 04
THANKS UNTO THEE, O LORD, HOLY FATHER, ALMIGHTY,   279 08
JESUS CHRIST OUR LORD, TO WHOM, WITH THEE, IN THE   279 20
THROUGH CHRIST OUR LORD   281 05
THE FATHER OF OUR LORD JESUS CHRIST, OF WHOM THE   281 07
THE LORD BE WITH YOU   283 05
LORD OF ALL POWER AND MIGHT, WHO ART THE AUTHOR AND   283 08
THROUGH JESUS CHRIST OUR LORD   283 12
AND IN CHRIST HIS ONLY SON OUR LORD   284 15
THE LORD BE WITH YOU   285 20
THROUGH JESUS CHRIST OUR LORD   285 31
LORD, HAVE MERCY UPON US, AND INCLINE OUR HEARTS TO   286 06
FOR I THE LORD THY GOD AM A JEALOUS GOD, AND VISIT   286 12
THE NAME OF THE LORD THY GOD IN VAIN   286 18
FOR THE LORD WILL NOT HOLD HIM GUILTLESS, THAT TAKETH   286 20
THE SABBATH OF THE LORD THY GOD   286 26
FOR IN SIX DAYS THE LORD MADE HEAVEN AND EARTH,   286 30
WHEREFORE THE LORD BLESSED THE SEVENTH DAY, AND   286 31
THE LAND WHICH THE LORD THY GOD GIVETH THEE   287 02
LORD, HAVE MERCY UPON US, AND INCLINE OUR HEARTS TO   287 04
LORD, HAVE MERCY UPON US, AND WRITE ALL THESE THY   287 23
GRANT TO US, LORD, WE BESEECH THEE, THE SPIRIT   287 26
THROUGH JESUS CHRIST OUR LORD   287 30
WHAT DOES OUR LORD JESUS CHRIST TEACH US ABOUT THESE   288 02
OUR LORD JESUS CHRIST TEACHES US THAT THEY   288 04
THOU SHALT LOVE THE LORD THY GOD WITH ALL THY HEART,   288 06
THE PRAYER THAT OUR LORD TAUGHT US TO PRAY   289 17
THE GRACE OF OUR LORD JESUS CHRIST, AND THE LOVE OF   289 29
AND LET US WALK IN THE LIGHT OF THE LORD   290 05
O LORD, BE UPON US   290 10
NOT UNTO US, O LORD, NOT UNTO US, BUT UNTO THY   290 12
LORD, HEAR OUR PRAYER   290 14
THE LORD BE WITH YOU   290 16

LORD   CONTINUED

THROUGH THE SAME JESUS CHRIST OUR LORD   290 24
PRIVILEGE DOTH OUR LORD PROVIDE FOR YOU   291 29
OUR LORD PROVIDES THE SACRAMENT OF THE LORD'S   291 30
IS TO SAY, BAPTISM, AND THE SUPPER OF THE LORD   292 08
AND WINE, WHICH THE LORD HATH COMMANDED TO BE   293 11
MINISTER ADD, THE LORD BE WITH YOU   294 21
GRANT, O LORD, THAT THEY WHO SHALL RENEW THE PROMISES   294 24
THROUGH JESUS CHRIST OUR LORD   294 28
THROUGH JESUS CHRIST OUR LORD   295 03
THE GRACE OF OUR LORD JESUS CHRIST, AND THE LOVE OF   295 04
IN THE NAME OF THE LORD JESUS   296 16
CHRIST AS YOUR LORD AND SAVIOUR   297 03
OUR HELP IS IN THE NAME OF THE LORD   297 07
BLESSED BE THE NAME OF THE LORD   297 09
LORD, HEAR OUR PRAYER   297 11
WE BESEECH THEE, O LORD, WITH THE HOLY GHOST, THE   297 17
AND FILL THEM, O LORD, WITH THE SPIRIT OF THY HOLY   297 22
DEFEND, O LORD, THIS THY CHILD WITH THY   297 26
THE BISHOP SAY, THE LORD BE WITH YOU   297 31
THROUGH OUR LORD JESUS CHRIST, WHO WITH THEE AND THE   298 23
O ALMIGHTY LORD, AND EVERLASTING GOD, VOUCHSAFE,   298 26
THROUGH OUR LORD AND SAVIOUR JESUS CHRIST   298 31
BLESS, O LORD, THIS RING, THAT HE WHO GIVES IT AND   302 19
THROUGH JESUS CHRIST OUR LORD   302 22
THROUGH JESUS CHRIST OUR LORD   303 12
THROUGH JESUS CHRIST OUR LORD   303 19
JESUS CHRIST OUR LORD, WHO LIVETH AND REIGNETH WITH   303 27
THE LORD MERCIFULLY WITH HIS FAVOUR LOOK UPON YOU,   304 12
MY DELIGHT IS IN THE LORD   305 18
THEN CALLED I UPON THE NAME OF THE LORD   305 23
O LORD, I BESEECH THEE, DELIVER MY SOUL   305 23
GRACIOUS IS THE LORD, AND RIGHTEOUS   305 25
I GIVE UNTO THE LORD FOR ALL THE BENEFITS THAT HE   305 27
OF SALVATION, AND CALL UPON THE NAME OF THE LORD   305 30
PRAISE THE LORD   306 03
O LORD, SAVE THIS WOMAN THY SERVANT   306 17
LORD, HEAR OUR PRAYER   306 21
THROUGH JESUS CHRIST OUR LORD   306 32
THROUGH JESUS CHRIST OUR LORD   307 06
REMEMBER NOT, LORD, OUR INIQUITIES   308 10
MINISTER SHALL SAY, LORD, HAVE MERCY UPON US   308 14
O LORD, SAVE THY SERVANT   308 23
BE UNTO HIM, O LORD, A STRONG TOWER   308 29
O LORD, HEAR OUR PRAYER   308 31
O LORD, LOOK DOWN FROM HEAVEN, BEHOLD, VISIT,   309 04
THROUGH JESUS CHRIST OUR LORD   309 08
I DID CALL UPON THE LORD WITH MY VOICE   309 11
LORD, HOW ARE THEY INCREASED THAT TROUBLE ME   309 14
BUT THOU, O LORD, ART MY DEFENDER   309 18
I DID CALL UPON THE LORD WITH MY VOICE, AND HE HEARD   309 20
FOR THE LORD SUSTAINED ME   309 23
SALVATION BELONGETH UNTO THE LORD   309 24
VISIT HIM, O LORD, WITH THY LOVING MERCY, AND SO   309 29
THROUGH JESUS CHRIST OUR LORD   309 32
WE BESEECH THEE, O LORD, THE SICKNESS OF THIS THY   310 21
THROUGH JESUS CHRIST OUR LORD   310 25
IN THE TIME OF MY TROUBLE I SOUGHT THE LORD   310 31
WILL THE LORD ABSENT HIMSELF FOR EVER   311 12
HEAR, O LORD, WE BESEECH THEE, THESE OUR PRAYERS,   311 21
THROUGH JESUS CHRIST OUR LORD   311 24
THANKS UNTO THEE, O LORD, WITH MY WHOLE HEART   311 28
THE LORD SHALL MAKE GOOD HIS LOVING-KINDNESS TOWARD   312 08
THY MERCY, O LORD, ENDURETH FOR EVER   312 09
THROUGH JESUS CHRIST OUR LORD   312 16
THE LORD SAVETH THY LIFE FROM DESTRUCTION   312 17
PRAISE THE LORD, O MY SOUL   312 20
PRAISE THE LORD, O MY SOUL, AND FORGET NOT ALL HIS   312 22
O PRAISE THE LORD, YE ANGELS OF HIS, YE THAT EXCEL IN   312 28
O PRAISE THE LORD, ALL YE HIS HOSTS   312 31
O SPEAK GOOD OF THE LORD, ALL YE WORKS OF HIS,   313 02
PRAISE THOU THE LORD, O MY SOUL   313 03
MERCIFUL LORD, THE DEVOUT PRAISE OF THY HUMBLE   313 05
THROUGH JESUS CHRIST OUR LORD   313 08
WE HUMBLY BESEECH THEE, O LORD   313 14
MOST DEARLY BELOVED SON, JESUS CHRIST OUR LORD   314 13
THE ALMIGHTY LORD, WHO IS A MOST STRONG TOWER TO   314 15
THE NAME OF OUR LORD JESUS CHRIST   314 22
THE LORD BLESS THEE, AND KEEP THEE   314 27
THE LORD MAKE HIS FACE TO SHINE UPON THEE, AND BE   314 28
THE LORD LIFT UP HIS COUNTENANCE UPON THEE, AND GIVE   314 29
THROUGH JESUS CHRIST OUR LORD   315 11
THROUGH JESUS CHRIST OUR LORD   315 17
LOOK GRACIOUSLY UPON HIM, O LORD   316 09
SAME THY SON, OUR LORD AND SAVIOUR   316 16
THROUGH JESUS CHRIST OUR LORD   316 23
ALL WHICH WE ASK THROUGH JESUS CHRIST OUR LORD   317 08
MERITS OF JESUS CHRIST THINE ONLY SON OUR LORD   317 23
GOOD LORD, DELIVER HIM   318 03
THEE TO HEAR US, O LORD GOD   318 10
WE BESEECH THEE TO HEAR US, GOOD LORD   318 14
LORD, HAVE MERCY   318 29
O SOVEREIGN LORD, WHO DESIREST NOT THE DEATH OF A   319 07
JESUS CHRIST OUR LORD, WHO LIVETH AND REIGNETH WITH   319 11
AND MERCIFUL LORD GRANT THEE PARDON AND REMISSION OF   319 15
THE MERCY OF OUR LORD JESUS CHRIST, THAT ALL THY PAIN   320 17
THROUGH JESUS CHRIST OUR LORD   321 26
CHASTENING OF THE LORD, NOR FAINT WHEN THOU ART   321 28
FOR WHOM THE LORD LOVETH HE CHASTENETH, AND SCOURGETH   321 30
O LORD, HOLY FATHER, BY WHOSE LOVING-KINDNESS OUR   322 06
THROUGH JESUS CHRIST OUR LORD   322 10
O ALMIGHTY FATHER, LORD OF HEAVEN AND EARTH, WE   323 12
AND MERCIFUL LORD GRANT YOU ABSOLUTION AND REMISSION   323 19
AM THE RESURRECTION AND THE LIFE, SAITH THE LORD   324 05
LORD GAVE, AND THE LORD HATH TAKEN AWAY   324 14

LORD   CONTINUED

THE LORD GAVE, AND THE LORD HATH TAKEN AWAY   324 14
BLESSED BE THE NAME OF THE LORD   324 15
LORD, LET ME KNOW MINE END, AND THE NUMBER OF MY   324 20
AND NOW, LORD, WHAT IS MY HOPE   324 28
HEAR MY PRAYER, O LORD, AND WITH THINE EARS CONSIDER   325 06
LORD, THOU HAST BEEN OUR REFUGE, *   325 13
THE LORD IS MY LIGHT AND MY SALVATION   326 05
THE LORD IS THE STRENGTH OF MY LIFE   326 06
I DESIRED OF THE LORD, WHICH I WILL REQUIRE   326 08
IN THE HOUSE OF THE LORD ALL THE DAYS OF MY LIFE, TO   326 09
FAIR BEAUTY OF THE LORD, AND TO VISIT HIS TEMPLE   326 10
I WILL SING AND SPEAK PRAISES UNTO THE LORD   326 19
UNTO MY VOICE, O LORD, WHEN I CRY UNTO THEE   326 20
THY FACE, LORD, WILL I SEEK   326 23
THE GOODNESS OF THE LORD IN THE LAND OF THE LIVING   326 29
AND PUT THOU THY TRUST IN THE LORD   326 31
THE LORD OF HOSTS IS WITH US   327 16
EVEN FROM THE LORD, *   327 21
THE LORD HIMSELF IS THY KEEPER   327 27
THE LORD IS THY DEFENCE UPON THY RIGHT HAND   327 27
THE LORD SHALL PRESERVE THEE FROM ALL EVIL   327 31
THE LORD SHALL PRESERVE THY GOING OUT, AND THY COMING   327 33
OUT OF THE DEEP HAVE I CALLED UNTO THEE, O LORD   328 03
LORD, HEAR MY VOICE   328 04
IF THOU, LORD, WILT BE EXTREME TO MARK WHAT IS DONE   328 07
O LORD, WHO MAY ABIDE IT   328 08
I LOOK FOR THE LORD   328 11
FLEETH UNTO THE LORD BEFORE THE MORNING WATCH   328 13
TRUST IN THE LORD, FOR WITH THE LORD THERE IS MERCY,   328 15
LORD, FOR WITH THE LORD THERE IS MERCY, *   328 15
SECOND MAN IS THE LORD FROM HEAVEN   329 28
VICTORY THROUGH OUR LORD JESUS CHRIST   330 13
IN THE WORK OF THE LORD, FORASMUCH AS YE KNOW THAT   330 15
KNOW THAT YOUR LABOUR IS NOT IN VAIN IN THE LORD   330 16
LOVE OF GOD, WHICH IS IN CHRIST JESUS OUR LORD   331 14
SAITH UNTO HIM, LORD, WE KNOW NOT WHITHER THOU GOEST   331 24
THE LORD BE WITH YOU   331 32
THY SERVANT, O LORD, ACCORDING TO THE FAVOUR WHICH   332 03
JESUS CHRIST OUR LORD, WHO LIVETH AND REIGNETH WITH   332 07
THE LORD MAKE HIS FACE TO SHINE UPON YOU, AND BE   332 11
THE LORD BLESS YOU AND KEEP YOU   332 11
THE LORD LIFT UP HIS COUNTENANCE UPON YOU, AND GIVE   332 13
BUT OF THEE, O LORD, WHO FOR OUR SINS ART JUSTLY   332 23
GOD MOST HOLY, O LORD MOST MIGHTY, O HOLY AND MOST   332 25
O LORD GOD MOST HOLY, O LORD MOST MIGHTY,   332 25
THOU KNOWEST, LORD, THE SECRETS OF OUR HEARTS   332 28
BUT SPARE US, LORD MOST HOLY, O GOD MOST MIGHTY, O   332 32
THROUGH OUR LORD JESUS CHRIST   333 18
BLESSED ARE THE DEAD WHO DIE IN THE LORD   333 27
SHALL SAY, THE LORD BE WITH YOU   333 30
LORD, HAVE MERCY UPON US   334 03
THROUGH JESUS CHRIST OUR LORD   334 18
DEPART HENCE IN THE LORD, AND WITH WHOM THE SOULS OF   334 20
THROUGH JESUS CHRIST OUR LORD   334 29
THE FATHER OF OUR LORD JESUS CHRIST, WHO IS THE   334 30
FROM THE DEAD OUR LORD JESUS CHRIST, THE GREAT   335 17
BLESSED ARE THE DEAD WHO DIE IN THE LORD   335 27
SAKE OF THE SAME THY SON JESUS CHRIST OUR LORD   336 03
THROUGH JESUS CHRIST OUR LORD   336 09
O LORD JESUS CHRIST, WHO BY THY DEATH DIDST TAKE AWAY   336 10
THROUGH OUR LORD JESUS CHRIST   337 12
AM THE RESURRECTION AND THE LIFE, SAITH THE LORD   338 05
THE LORD IS MY SHEPHERD   338 17
IN THE HOUSE OF THE LORD FOR EVER   338 31
EVEN FROM THE LORD, *   339 05
THE LORD IS THY DEFENCE UPON THY RIGHT HAND   339 11
THE LORD HIMSELF IS THY KEEPER   339 11
THE LORD SHALL PRESERVE THEE FROM ALL EVIL   339 15
THE LORD SHALL PRESERVE THY GOING OUT, AND THY COMING   339 17
MINISTER SAY, THE LORD BE WITH YOU   340 03
LORD, HAVE MERCY UPON US   340 06
BLESSED BE THE NAME OF THE LORD   340 18
LORD, HEAR OUR PRAYER   340 20
THROUGH JESUS CHRIST OUR LORD   340 28
THROUGH JESUS CHRIST OUR LORD   341 04
THE GRACE OF OUR LORD JESUS CHRIST, AND THE LOVE OF   341 05
LIFE THROUGH OUR LORD JESUS CHRIST, WE COMMIT THE   341 14
THE LORD BLESS HIM AND KEEP HIM, THE LORD MAKE HIS   341 15
AND KEEP HIM, THE LORD MAKE HIS FACE TO SHINE UPON   341 16
UNTO HIM, THE LORD LIFT UP HIS COUNTENANCE UPON HIM,   341 17
MINISTER SAY, THE LORD BE WITH YOU   341 29
THROUGH THE SAME THY SON, JESUS CHRIST OUR LORD   342 08
THROUGH JESUS CHRIST OUR LORD   342 13
2 BUT HIS DELIGHT IS IN THE LAW OF THE LORD   345 10
7 BUT THE LORD KNOWETH THE WAY OF THE RIGHTEOUS   345 22
AGAINST THE LORD, AND AGAINST HIS ANOINTED   345 28
THE LORD SHALL HAVE THEM IN DERISION   346 05
THE LORD HATH SAID UNTO ME, THOU ART MY SON, THIS DAY   346 10
11 SERVE THE LORD IN FEAR, *   346 19
LORD, HOW ARE THEY INCREASED THAT TROUBLE ME   346 25
3 BUT THOU, O LORD, ART MY DEFENDER   346 29
I DID CALL UPON THE LORD WITH MY VOICE, *   346 31
FOR THE LORD SUSTAINED ME   346 34
7 UP, LORD, AND HELP ME, O MY GOD, *   347 04
8 SALVATION BELONGETH UNTO THE LORD   347 07
THIS ALSO, THAT THE LORD HATH CHOSEN TO HIMSELF THE   347 16
I CALL UPON THE LORD HE WILL HEAR ME   347 17
AND PUT YOUR TRUST IN THE LORD   347 22
7 LORD, LIFT THOU UP *   347 24
FOR IT IS THOU, LORD, ONLY, THAT MAKEST ME DWELL IN   347 29
PONDER MY WORDS, O LORD, *   347 31
3 MY VOICE SHALT THOU HEAR BETIMES, O LORD   348 04
THE LORD WILL ABHOR BOTH THE BLOOD-THIRSTY AND   348 11
8 LEAD ME, O LORD, IN THY RIGHTEOUSNESS, BECAUSE OF   348 16

LORD   CONTINUED

	PAGE	LN
13 FOR THOU, LORD, WILT GIVE THY BLESSING UNTO THE	348	28
O LORD, REBUKE ME NOT IN THINE INDIGNATION, *	348	33
MERCY UPON ME, O LORD, FOR I AM WEAK	349	02
O LORD, HEAL ME, FOR MY BONES ARE VEXED	349	03
LORD, HOW LONG WILT THOU PUNISH ME	349	04
4 TURN THEE, O LORD, AND DELIVER MY SOUL	349	06
FOR THE LORD HATH HEARD THE VOICE OF MY WEEPING	349	15
THE LORD WILL RECEIVE MY PRAYER	349	16
9 THE LORD HATH HEARD MY PETITION	349	16
O LORD MY GOD, IN THEE HAVE I PUT MY TRUST	349	22
3 O LORD MY GOD, IF I HAVE DONE ANY SUCH THING	349	27
6 STAND UP, O LORD, IN THY WRATH, AND LIFT UP	349	35
8 THE LORD SHALL JUDGE THE PEOPLES	350	06
SENTENCE WITH ME, O LORD, *	350	07
THANKS UNTO THE LORD, ACCORDING TO HIS RIGHTEOUSNESS	350	27
THE NAME OF THE LORD MOST HIGH	350	28
O LORD OUR GOVERNOR, HOW EXCELLENT IS THY NAME IN ALL	350	31
9 O LORD OUR GOVERNOR, *	351	17
THANKS UNTO THEE, O LORD, WITH MY WHOLE HEART	351	22
7 BUT THE LORD SHALL ENDURE FOR EVER	352	02
9 THE LORD ALSO WILL BE A DEFENCE FOR THE OPPRESSED,	352	06
FOR THOU, LORD, HAST NEVER FAILED THEM THAT SEEK	352	09
11 O PRAISE THE LORD WHICH DWELLETH IN SION	352	11
13 HAVE MERCY UPON ME, O LORD	352	16
16 THE LORD IS KNOWN TO EXECUTE JUDGMENT	352	24
19 UP, LORD, AND LET NOT MAN HAVE THE UPPER HAND	352	30
PUT THEM IN FEAR, O LORD, *	352	32
THOU SO FAR OFF, O LORD, *	353	03
WHOM THE LORD ABHORRETH	353	10
13 ARISE, O LORD GOD, AND LIFT UP THINE HAND	353	32
18 THE LORD IS KING FOR EVER AND EVER, *	354	11
19 LORD, THOU HAST HEARD THE DESIRE OF THE POOR	354	13
IN THE LORD PUT I MY TRUST	354	19
4 THE LORD IS IN HIS HOLY TEMPLE	354	26
6 THE LORD APPROVETH THE RIGHTEOUS	354	30
8 FOR THE RIGHTEOUS LORD LOVETH RIGHTEOUSNESS	355	02
HELP ME, LORD, FOR THERE IS NOT ONE GODLY MAN LEFT	355	06
3 THE LORD SHALL ROOT OUT ALL DECEITFUL LIPS,	355	12
WHO IS LORD OVER US	355	15
SIGHING OF THE POOR, 6 I WILL UP, SAITH THE LORD	355	18
7 THE WORDS OF THE LORD ARE PURE WORDS	355	20
8 THOU SHALT KEEP THEM, O LORD	355	23
HOW LONG WILT THOU FORGET ME, O LORD	355	28
AND HEAR ME, O LORD MY GOD	356	02
I WILL SING OF THE LORD, BECAUSE HE HATH DEALT SO	356	09
THE NAME OF THE LORD MOST HIGHEST	356	10
3 THE LORD LOOKED DOWN FROM HEAVEN UPON THE CHILDREN	356	16
AS IT WERE BREAD, AND CALL NOT UPON THE LORD	356	24
BECAUSE HE PUTTETH HIS TRUST IN THE LORD	356	29
WHEN THE LORD TURNETH THE CAPTIVITY OF HIS PEOPLE,	356	31
LORD, WHO SHALL DWELL IN THY TABERNACLE	357	05
AND MAKETH MUCH OF THEM THAT FEAR THE LORD	357	14
HAST SAID UNTO THE LORD, *	357	23
6 THE LORD HIMSELF IS THE PORTION OF MINE	357	31
8 I WILL THANK THE LORD FOR GIVING ME WARNING	358	04
9 I HAVE SET THE LORD ALWAY BEFORE ME	358	06
HEAR THE RIGHT, O LORD, CONSIDER MY COMPLAINT,	358	16
13 UP, LORD, DISAPPOINT HIM, AND CAST HIM DOWN	359	12
14 YEA, BY THY HAND, O LORD	359	14
THE LORD IS MY STONY ROCK, AND MY DEFENCE	359	24
I WILL LOVE THEE, O LORD, MY STRENGTH	359	24
WILL CALL UPON THE LORD, WHICH IS WORTHY TO BE	359	29
I CALLED UPON THE LORD, *	360	04
14 THE LORD ALSO THUNDERED OUT OF HEAVEN, AND THE	360	24
AT THY CHIDING, O LORD, AT THE BLASTING OF THE BREATH	360	30
BUT THE LORD WAS MY UPHOLDER	361	03
21 THE LORD REWARDED ME AFTER MY RIGHTEOUS DEALING,	361	06
THE WAYS OF THE LORD, *	361	09
25 THEREFORE THE LORD REWARDED ME AFTER MY RIGHTEOUS	361	15
THE LORD MY GOD SHALL MAKE MY DARKNESS TO BE LIGHT	361	24
THE WORD OF THE LORD ALSO IS TRIED IN THE FIRE	361	29
32 FOR WHO IS GOD, BUT THE LORD	361	31
EVEN UNTO THE LORD SHALL THEY CRY, BUT HE SHALL	362	21
47 THE LORD LIVETH	362	32
THANKS UNTO THEE, O LORD, AMONG THE GENTILES, *	363	05
7 THE LAW OF THE LORD IS AN UNDEFILED LAW, CONVERTING	363	27
TESTIMONY OF THE LORD IS SURE, AND GIVETH WISDOM UNTO	363	28
THE STATUTES OF THE LORD ARE RIGHT, AND REJOICE THE	363	30
COMMANDMENT OF THE LORD IS PURE, AND GIVETH LIGHT	363	31
9 THE FEAR OF THE LORD IS CLEAN, AND ENDURETH FOR	363	33
JUDGMENTS OF THE LORD ARE TRUE, AND RIGHTEOUS	364	02
O LORD, MY STRENGTH AND MY REDEEMER	364	14
THE LORD HEAR THEE IN THE DAY OF TROUBLE	364	17
IN THE NAME OF THE LORD OUR GOD	364	24
THE LORD PERFORM ALL THY PETITIONS	364	24
NOW KNOW I THAT THE LORD HELPETH HIS ANOINTED,	364	26
THE NAME OF THE LORD OUR GOD	364	30
9 SAVE, LORD	365	02
THE KING SHALL REJOICE IN THY STRENGTH, O LORD	365	05
BECAUSE THE KING PUTTETH HIS TRUST IN THE LORD	365	18
THE LORD SHALL DESTROY THEM IN HIS DISPLEASURE,	365	23
13 BE THOU EXALTED, LORD, IN THINE OWN STRENGTH	365	32
8 HE TRUSTED IN THE LORD, THAT HE WOULD DELIVER HIM	366	18
19 BUT BE NOT THOU FAR FROM ME, O LORD	367	10
23 O PRAISE THE LORD, YE THAT FEAR HIM	367	18
THAT SEEK AFTER THE LORD SHALL PRAISE HIM	367	26
REMEMBER THEMSELVES, AND BE TURNED UNTO THE LORD	367	29
BE COUNTED UNTO THE LORD FOR A GENERATION	368	05
BE BORN, WHOM THE LORD HATH MADE	368	07
THE LORD IS MY SHEPHERD	368	10
IN THE HOUSE OF THE LORD FOR EVER	368	24
3 WHO SHALL ASCEND INTO THE HILL OF THE LORD	368	32
BLESSING FROM THE LORD, *	369	05
IT IS THE LORD STRONG AND MIGHTY, EVEN THE LORD	369	11

LORD   CONTINUED

	PAGE	LN
EVEN THE LORD MIGHTY IN BATTLE	369	12
EVEN THE LORD OF HOSTS, HE IS THE KING OF GLORY	369	15
UNTO THEE, O LORD, WILL I LIFT UP MY SOUL	369	18
SHOW ME THY WAYS, O LORD, *	369	24
TO REMEMBRANCE, O LORD, THY TENDER MERCIES, *	369	28
THOU UPON ME, O LORD, FOR THY GOODNESS	369	31
7 GRACIOUS AND RIGHTEOUS IS THE LORD	369	33
THE PATHS OF THE LORD ARE MERCY AND TRUTH, *	370	04
THY NAME'S SAKE, O LORD, *	370	06
11 WHAT MAN IS HE THAT FEARETH THE LORD	370	08
THE SECRET OF THE LORD IS AMONG THEM THAT FEAR HIM	370	12
14 MINE EYES ARE EVER LOOKING UNTO THE LORD	370	14
BE THOU MY JUDGE, O LORD, FOR I HAVE WALKED	370	30
BEEN ALSO IN THE LORD, THEREFORE SHALL I NOT FALL	370	31
2 EXAMINE ME, O LORD, AND PROVE ME	370	33
6 I WILL WASH MY HANDS IN INNOCENCY, O LORD	371	12
8 LORD, I HAVE LOVED THE HABITATION OF THY HOUSE,	371	12
I WILL PRAISE THE LORD IN THE CONGREGATIONS	371	20
THE LORD IS MY LIGHT AND MY SALVATION	371	24
THE LORD IS THE STRENGTH OF MY LIFE	371	25
I DESIRED OF THE LORD, WHICH I WILL REQUIRE	371	32
IN THE HOUSE OF THE LORD ALL THE DAYS OF MY LIFE, TO	371	33
FAIR BEAUTY OF THE LORD, AND TO VISIT HIS TEMPLE	372	03
I WILL SING AND SPEAK PRAISES UNTO THE LORD	372	11
UNTO MY VOICE, O LORD, WHEN I CRY UNTO THEE	372	12
THY FACE, LORD, WILL I SEEK	372	15
THE LORD TAKETH ME UP	372	21
TEACH ME THY WAY, O LORD, *	372	22
THE GOODNESS OF THE LORD IN THE LAND OF THE LIVING	372	28
AND PUT THY TRUST IN THE LORD	372	32
THEE WILL I CRY, O LORD, MY STRENGTH	373	03
THE WORKS OF THE LORD, NOR THE OPERATION OF HIS	373	18
7 PRAISED BE THE LORD	373	20
8 THE LORD IS MY STRENGTH, AND MY SHIELD	373	22
9 THE LORD IS MY STRENGTH, *	373	25
ASCRIBE UNTO THE LORD, O YE MIGHTY, *	373	30
ASCRIBE UNTO THE LORD WORSHIP AND STRENGTH	373	31
2 ASCRIBE UNTO THE LORD THE HONOUR DUE UNTO HIS NAME	373	32
WORSHIP THE LORD WITH HOLY WORSHIP	373	33
3 THE VOICE OF THE LORD IS UPON THE WATERS	374	02
4 IT IS THE LORD THAT RULETH THE SEA	374	04
THE VOICE OF THE LORD IS MIGHTY IN OPERATION	374	05
THE VOICE OF THE LORD IS A GLORIOUS VOICE	374	05
5 THE VOICE OF THE LORD BREAKETH THE CEDAR-TREES	374	07
THE LORD BREAKETH THE CEDARS OF LEBANON	374	08
7 THE VOICE OF THE LORD DIVIDETH THE FLAMES OF FIRE	374	11
THE VOICE OF THE LORD SHAKETH THE WILDERNESS	374	12
THE LORD SHAKETH THE WILDERNESS OF KADESH	374	13
8 THE VOICE OF THE LORD MAKETH THE HINDS TO BRING	374	14
9 THE LORD SITTETH ABOVE THE WATER-FLOOD, *	374	17
AND THE LORD REMAINETH A KING FOR EVER	374	18
10 THE LORD SHALL GIVE STRENGTH UNTO HIS PEOPLE	374	19
THE LORD SHALL GIVE HIS PEOPLE THE BLESSING OF PEACE	374	20
I WILL MAGNIFY THEE, O LORD	374	24
2 O LORD MY GOD, I CRIED UNTO THEE	374	26
3 THOU, LORD, HAST BROUGHT MY SOUL OUT OF HELL	374	28
PRAISES UNTO THE LORD, O YE SAINTS OF HIS	374	30
THOU, LORD, OF THY GOODNESS, HAST MADE MY HILL SO	375	05
8 THEN CRIED I UNTO THEE, O LORD	375	08
AND GAT ME TO MY LORD RIGHT HUMBLY	375	09
LORD, BE THOU MY HELPER	375	14
11 HEAR, O LORD, AND HAVE MERCY UPON ME	375	14
IN THEE, O LORD, HAVE I PUT MY TRUST	375	22
HAST REDEEMED ME, O LORD, THOU GOD OF TRUTH	375	32
AND MY TRUST HATH BEEN IN THE LORD	376	03
MERCY UPON ME, O LORD, FOR I AM IN TROUBLE, *	376	08
16 BUT MY HOPE HATH BEEN IN THEE, O LORD	376	24
BE CONFOUNDED, O LORD, FOR I HAVE CALLED UPON THEE	376	30
23 THANKS BE TO THE LORD	377	09
FOR THE LORD PRESERVETH THEM THAT ARE FAITHFUL, AND	377	15
26 O LOVE THE LORD, ALL YE HIS SAINTS	377	15
ALL YE THAT PUT YOUR TRUST IN THE LORD	377	19
MAN UNTO WHOM THE LORD IMPUTETH NO SIN, *	377	24
I WILL CONFESS MY SINS UNTO THE LORD	377	32
HIS TRUST IN THE LORD, MERCY EMBRACETH HIM ON EVERY	378	14
O YE RIGHTEOUS, AND REJOICE IN THE LORD	378	16
REJOICE IN THE LORD, O YE RIGHTEOUS	378	19
2 PRAISE THE LORD WITH HARP	378	21
3 SING UNTO THE LORD A NEW SONG	378	23
FOR THE WORD OF THE LORD IS TRUE	378	25
THE EARTH IS FULL OF THE GOODNESS OF THE LORD	378	28
BY THE WORD OF THE LORD WERE THE HEAVENS MADE	378	29
8 LET ALL THE EARTH FEAR THE LORD	379	02
10 THE LORD BRINGETH THE COUNSEL OF THE HEATHEN TO	379	06
THE COUNSEL OF THE LORD SHALL ENDURE FOR EVER,	379	11
WHOSE GOD IS THE LORD JEHOVAH	379	14
13 THE LORD LOOKETH DOWN FROM HEAVEN, AND BEHOLDETH	379	24
THE EYE OF THE LORD IS UPON THEM THAT FEAR HIM, *	379	28
19 OUR SOUL HATH PATIENTLY TARRIED FOR THE LORD	379	32
O LORD, BE UPON US, *	380	03
I WILL ALWAY GIVE THANKS UNTO THE LORD	380	05
2 MY SOUL SHALL MAKE HER BOAST IN THE LORD	380	07
3 O PRAISE THE LORD WITH ME, *	380	09
4 I SOUGHT THE LORD, AND HE HEARD ME	380	15
AND THE LORD HEARETH HIM	380	17
7 THE ANGEL OF THE LORD TARRIETH ROUND ABOUT THEM	380	19
HOW GRACIOUS THE LORD IS	380	22
9 O FEAR THE LORD, YE THAT ARE HIS SAINTS	380	24
THEY WHO SEEK THE LORD SHALL WANT NO MANNER OF THING	380	30
I WILL TEACH YOU THE FEAR OF THE LORD	380	32
15 THE EYES OF THE LORD ARE OVER THE RIGHTEOUS,	381	02
COUNTENANCE OF THE LORD IS AGAINST THEM THAT DO EVIL,	381	04
AND THE LORD HEARETH THEM, *		
18 THE LORD IS NIGH UNTO THEM THAT ARE OF A CONTRITE		

LORD   CONTINUED

BUT THE LORD DELIVERETH HIM OUT OF ALL	381 07
22 THE LORD DELIVERETH THE SOULS OF HIS SERVANTS	381 12
THOU MY CAUSE, O LORD, WITH THEM THAT STRIVE WITH ME,	381 17
THE ANGEL OF THE LORD SCATTERING THEM	381 28
THE ANGEL OF THE LORD PURSUE THEM	381 30
9 AND MY SOUL SHALL BE JOYFUL IN THE LORD	382 07
MY BONES SHALL SAY, LORD, WHO IS LIKE UNTO THEE,	382 09
17 LORD, HOW LONG WILT THOU LOOK UPON THIS	382 29
22 THIS THOU HAST SEEN, O LORD	383 07
GO NOT FAR FROM ME, O LORD	383 08
AVENGE THOU MY CAUSE, MY GOD AND MY LORD	383 10
24 JUDGE ME, O LORD MY GOD, ACCORDING TO THY	383 11
BLESSED BE THE LORD, WHO HATH PLEASURE IN THE	383 21
5 THY MERCY, O LORD, REACHETH UNTO THE HEAVENS,	384 04
7 THOU, LORD, SHALT SAVE BOTH MAN AND BEAST	384 08
THY TRUST IN THE LORD, AND BE DOING GOOD	384 29
DELIGHT THOU IN THE LORD, *	384 31
THY WAY UNTO THE LORD, AND PUT THY TRUST IN HIM, *	385 02
THEE STILL IN THE LORD, AND ABIDE PATIENTLY UPON HIM	385 06
PATIENTLY ABIDE THE LORD, THOSE SHALL INHERIT THE	385 12
13 THE LORD SHALL LAUGH HIM TO SCORN	385 20
AND THE LORD UPHOLDETH THE RIGHTEOUS	385 30
18 THE LORD KNOWETH THE DAYS OF THE GODLY	385 31
THE ENEMIES OF THE LORD SHALL CONSUME AS THE FAT OF	386 02
23 THE LORD ORDERETH A GOOD MAN'S GOING, *	386 08
FOR THE LORD UPHOLDETH HIM WITH HIS HAND	386 11
28 FOR THE LORD LOVETH THE THING THAT IS RIGHT	386 19
34 THE LORD WILL NOT LEAVE HIM IN HIS HAND, *	386 32
35 HOPE THOU IN THE LORD, AND KEEP HIS WAY, AND HE	386 34
THE SALVATION OF THE RIGHTEOUS COMETH OF THE LORD	387 14
41 AND THE LORD SHALL STAND BY THEM, AND SAVE THEM	387 15
ME NOT TO REBUKE, O LORD, IN THINE ANGER	387 21
9 LORD, THOU KNOWEST ALL MY DESIRE	388 08
15 FOR IN THEE, O LORD, HAVE I PUT MY TRUST	388 21
ANSWER FOR ME, O LORD MY GOD	388 22
FORSAKE ME NOT, O LORD MY GOD	388 34
O LORD GOD OF MY SALVATION	389 03
5 LORD, LET ME KNOW MINE END, AND THE NUMBER OF MY	389 15
8 AND NOW, LORD, WHAT IS MY HOPE	389 23
HEAR MY PRAYER, O LORD, AND WITH THINE EARS CONSIDER	390 02
PATIENTLY FOR THE LORD, *	390 09
AND SHALL PUT THEIR TRUST IN THE LORD	390 17
SET HIS HOPE IN THE LORD, *	390 19
6 O LORD MY GOD, GREAT ARE THE WONDROUS WORKS WHICH	390 21
REFRAIN MY LIPS, O LORD, AND THAT THOU KNOWEST	391 02
14 WITHDRAW NOT THOU THY MERCY FROM ME, O LORD	391 08
16 O LORD, LET IT BE THY PLEASURE TO DELIVER ME	391 14
MAKE HASTE, O LORD, TO HELP ME	391 15
SAY ALWAY, THE LORD BE PRAISED	391 23
BUT THE LORD CARETH FOR ME	391 24
THE LORD SHALL DELIVER HIM IN THE TIME OF TROUBLE	391 31
2 THE LORD PRESERVE HIM, AND KEEP HIM ALIVE, THAT HE	391 32
3 THE LORD COMFORT HIM WHEN HE LIETH SICK UPON HIS	392 04
4 I SAID, LORD, BE MERCIFUL UNTO ME	392 06
10 BUT BE THOU MERCIFUL UNTO ME, O LORD	392 19
13 BLESSED BE THE LORD GOD OF ISRAEL, *	392 25
10 THE LORD SHALL GRANT HIS LOVING-KINDNESS IN THE	393 21
23 UP, LORD, WHY SLEEPEST THOU	396 06
FOR HE IS THY LORD, AND WORSHIP THOU HIM	397 08
7 THE LORD OF HOSTS IS WITH US	398 07
THE WORKS OF THE LORD, *	398 09
11 THE LORD OF HOSTS IS WITH US	398 17
2 FOR THE LORD IS HIGH, AND TO BE FEARED	398 23
AND THE LORD WITH THE SOUND OF THE TRUMP	398 29
GREAT IS THE LORD, AND HIGHLY TO BE PRAISED *	399 10
IN THE CITY OF THE LORD OF HOSTS, IN THE CITY OF OUR	399 25
THE LORD, EVEN THE MOST MIGHTY GOD, HATH SPOKEN,	401 21
OPEN MY LIPS, O LORD, *	404 07
O THAT THE LORD WOULD DELIVER HIS PEOPLE OUT OF	405 29
THE LORD IS WITH THEM THAT UPHOLD MY SOUL	406 10
WILL I GIVE THEE, AND PRAISE THY NAME, O LORD	406 15
THEIR TONGUES, O LORD, AND DIVIDE THEM	407 04
AND THE LORD SAVE ME	407 23
THY BURDEN UPON THE LORD, AND HE SHALL NOURISH THEE,	408 04
MY TRUST SHALL BE IN THEE, O LORD	408 10
THANKS UNTO THEE, O LORD, AMONG THE PEOPLES	409 33
SMITE THE JAW-BONES OF THE LIONS, O LORD	410 20
WITHOUT ANY OFFENCE OR FAULT OF ME, O LORD	411 10
5 STAND UP, O LORD GOD OF HOSTS, THOU GOD OF ISRAEL,	411 13
8 BUT THOU, O LORD, SHALT HAVE THEM IN DERISION,	411 20
PUT THEM DOWN, O LORD OUR DEFENCE	411 28
5 FOR THOU, O LORD, HAST HEARD MY DESIRES, *	413 15
12 AND THAT THOU, LORD, ART MERCIFUL	414 23
REJOICE IN THE LORD, AND PUT HIS TRUST IN HIM	416 06
THE LORD WILL NOT HEAR ME	418 17
11 THE LORD GAVE THE WORD	420 15
THE LORD WILL ABIDE IN IT FOR EVER	420 17
AND THE LORD IS AMONG THEM AS IN THE HOLY PLACE OF	420 17
THAT THE LORD GOD MIGHT DWELL AMONG THEM	420 21
19 PRAISED BE THE LORD DAILY, *	420 23
GOD IS THE LORD, BY WHOM WE ESCAPE DEATH	420 26
22 THE LORD HATH SAID, I WILL BRING MY PEOPLE AGAIN,	420 30
THANKS UNTO GOD THE LORD IN THE CONGREGATION, *	421 06
O SING PRAISES UNTO THE LORD	421 21
TRUST IN THEE, O LORD GOD OF HOSTS, BE ASHAMED FOR MY	422 13
THROUGH ME, O LORD GOD OF ISRAEL	422 15
13 BUT, LORD, I MAKE MY PRAYER UNTO THEE *	422 28
17 HEAR ME, O LORD, FOR THY LOVING-KINDNESS IS	423 04
SHALL PLEASE THE LORD	424 04
34 FOR THE LORD HEARETH THE POOR, *	424 10
MAKE HASTE TO HELP ME, O LORD	424 21
SAY ALWAY, THE LORD BE PRAISED	424 29
O LORD, MAKE NO LONG TARRYING	424 32
IN THEE, O LORD, HAVE I PUT MY TRUST	425 05

LORD   CONTINUED

4 FOR THOU, O LORD GOD, ART THE THING THAT I LONG	425 14
THE STRENGTH OF THE LORD GOD, *	426 06
18 BLESSED BE THE LORD GOD, EVEN THE GOD OF ISRAEL,	428 02
PUT MY TRUST IN THE LORD GOD, *	429 33
19 REMEMBER THIS, O LORD, HOW THE ENEMY HATH REBUKED	431 12
IN THE HAND OF THE LORD THERE IS A CUP, AND THE WINE	432 14
11 PROMISE UNTO THE LORD YOUR GOD, AND KEEP IT,	433 10
2 IN THE TIME OF MY TROUBLE I SOUGHT THE LORD	433 18
7 WILL THE LORD ABSENT HIMSELF FOR EVER	433 29
THE WORKS OF THE LORD, *	434 04
THE HONOUR OF THE LORD, HIS MIGHTY AND WONDERFUL	435 03
22 WHEN THE LORD HEARD THIS, HE WAS WROTH	436 11
66 SO THE LORD AWAKED AS ONE OUT OF SLEEP, *	439 08
5 LORD, HOW LONG WILT THOU BE ANGRY	440 09
REWARD THOU THEM, O LORD, SEVEN-FOLD INTO THEIR	440 30
4 O LORD GOD OF HOSTS, *	441 10
19 TURN US AGAIN, O LORD GOD OF HOSTS	442 09
11 I AM THE LORD THY GOD, WHO BROUGHT THEE OUT OF THE	442 33
THE HATERS OF THE LORD SHOULD HAVE SUBMITTED	443 10
FACES ASHAMED, O LORD, *	445 04
THOU LORD OF HOSTS	445 11
AND LONGING TO ENTER INTO THE COURTS OF THE LORD	445 14
EVEN THY ALTARS, O LORD OF HOSTS, MY KING AND MY GOD	445 18
8 O LORD GOD OF HOSTS, HEAR MY PRAYER	445 27
THE LORD WILL GIVE GRACE AND WORSHIP	446 02
12 FOR THE LORD GOD IS A LIGHT AND DEFENCE	446 02
13 O LORD GOD OF HOSTS, *	446 05
LORD, THOU ART BECOME GRACIOUS UNTO THY LAND	446 08
US THY MERCY, O LORD, *	446 20
HEARKEN WHAT THE LORD GOD WILL SAY	446 22
12 YEA, THE LORD SHALL SHOW LOVING-KINDNESS	446 31
DOWN THINE EAR, O LORD, AND HEAR ME	447 05
3 BE MERCIFUL UNTO ME, O LORD	447 09
FOR UNTO THEE, O LORD, DO I LIFT UP MY SOUL	447 12
5 FOR THOU, LORD, ART GOOD AND GRACIOUS, *	447 13
6 GIVE EAR, LORD, UNTO MY PRAYER, *	447 15
THE GODS THERE IS NONE LIKE UNTO THEE, O LORD	447 20
HAST MADE SHALL COME AND WORSHIP THEE, O LORD	447 22
TEACH ME THY WAY, O LORD, AND I WILL WALK IN THY	447 25
WILL THANK THEE, O LORD MY GOD, WITH ALL MY HEART	447 28
15 BUT THOU, O LORD GOD, ART FULL OF COMPASSION AND	448 04
BECAUSE THOU, LORD, HAST HOLPEN ME, AND COMFORTED ME	448 10
THE LORD LOVETH THE GATES OF SION MORE THAN ALL THE	448 24
6 THE LORD SHALL RECORD IT, WHEN HE WRITETH UP THE	448 24
O LORD GOD OF MY SALVATION, I HAVE CRIED DAY AND	448 29
LORD, I HAVE CALLED DAILY UPON THEE, I HAVE STRETCHED	449 14
13 UNTO THEE HAVE I CRIED, O LORD	449 22
14 LORD, WHY ABHORREST THOU MY SOUL, *	449 24
SHALL BE ALWAY OF THE LOVING-KINDNESS OF THE LORD	450 05
5 O LORD, THE VERY HEAVENS SHALL PRAISE THY WONDROUS	450 13
THAT SHALL BE COMPARED UNTO THE LORD	450 16
THAT SHALL BE LIKE UNTO THE LORD	450 18
9 O LORD GOD OF HOSTS, WHO IS LIKE UNTO THEE	450 22
MOST MIGHTY LORD, IS ON EVERY SIDE	450 23
IS THE PEOPLE, O LORD, THAT CAN REJOICE IN THEE	451 04
19 FOR THE LORD IS OUR DEFENCE	451 10
45 LORD, HOW LONG WILT THOU HIDE THYSELF	452 32
48 LORD, WHERE ARE THY OLD LOVING-KINDNESSES,	453 05
49 REMEMBER, LORD, THE REBUKE THAT THY SERVANTS HAVE,	453 07
51 PRAISED BE THE LORD FOR EVERMORE	453 12
LORD, THOU HAST BEEN OUR REFUGE, *	453 18
TURN THEE AGAIN, O LORD, AT THE LAST, *	454 15
MAJESTY OF THE LORD OUR GOD BE UPON US	454 24
I WILL SAY UNTO THE LORD, THOU ART MY HOPE, AND MY	454 30
9 FOR THOU, LORD, ART MY HOPE	455 13
THANKS UNTO THE LORD, *	455 32
4 FOR THOU, LORD, HAST MADE ME GLAD THROUGH THY	456 06
5 O LORD, HOW GLORIOUS ARE THY WORKS	456 09
BUT THOU, LORD, ART THE MOST HIGHEST FOR EVERMORE	456 15
THINE ENEMIES, O LORD, LO, THINE ENEMIES SHALL	456 17
IN THE HOUSE OF THE LORD, *	456 26
SHOW HOW TRUE THE LORD MY STRENGTH IS, *	456 30
THE LORD IS KING, AND HATH PUT ON GLORIOUS APPAREL	457 04
THE LORD HATH PUT ON HIS APPAREL, AND GIRDED HIMSELF	457 05
FLOODS ARE RISEN, O LORD, THE FLOODS HAVE LIFT UP	457 11
BUT YET THE LORD, WHO DWELLETH ON HIGH, IS MIGHTIER	457 14
THY TESTIMONIES, O LORD, ARE VERY SURE	457 16
O LORD GOD, TO WHOM VENGEANCE BELONGETH, *	457 19
3 LORD, HOW LONG SHALL THE UNGODLY, *	457 23
DOWN THY PEOPLE, O LORD, *	457 27
THEY SAY, TUSH, THE LORD SHALL NOT SEE, *	457 31
11 THE LORD KNOWETH THE THOUGHTS OF MAN, *	458 08
THOU CHASTENEST, O LORD	458 10
14 FOR THE LORD WILL NOT FAIL HIS PEOPLE	458 14
17 IF THE LORD HAD NOT HELPED ME, *	458 20
THY MERCY, O LORD, HELD ME UP	458 23
22 BUT THE LORD IS MY REFUGE, *	458 30
THE LORD OUR GOD SHALL DESTROY THEM	458 33
LET US SING UNTO THE LORD	459 05
3 FOR THE LORD IS A GREAT GOD	459 09
KNEEL BEFORE THE LORD OUR MAKER	459 16
7 FOR HE IS THE LORD OUR GOD	459 17
O SING UNTO THE LORD A NEW SONG	459 30
SING UNTO THE LORD, ALL THE WHOLE EARTH	459 31
2 SING UNTO THE LORD, AND PRAISE HIS NAME	460 02
4 FOR THE LORD IS GREAT, AND CANNOT WORTHILY BE	460 06
BUT IT IS THE LORD THAT MADE THE HEAVENS	460 09
7 ASCRIBE UNTO THE LORD, O YE KINDREDS OF THE	460 12
ASCRIBE UNTO THE LORD WORSHIP AND POWER	460 13
8 ASCRIBE UNTO THE LORD THE HONOUR DUE UNTO HIS NAME	460 14
9 O WORSHIP THE LORD IN THE BEAUTY OF HOLINESS	460 16
THAT THE LORD IS KING, AND THAT IT IS HE WHO	460 18
ALL THE TREES OF THE WOOD REJOICE BEFORE THE LORD	460 25
THE LORD IS KING, THE EARTH MAY BE GLAD THEREOF	460 30

LORD   CONTINUED   LORD   CONTINUED

THE PRESENCE OF THE LORD OF THE WHOLE EARTH   461 07   O PRAISE THE NAME OF THE LORD   484 09
HILLS MELTED LIKE WAX AT THE PRESENCE OF THE LORD   461 07   BE THE NAME OF THE LORD *   484 10
BECAUSE OF THY JUDGMENTS, O LORD   461 13   4 THE LORD IS HIGH ABOVE ALL NATIONS, *   484 14
9 FOR THOU, LORD, ART HIGHER THAN ALL THAT ARE IN THE 461 14   IS LIKE UNTO THE LORD OUR GOD, THAT HATH HIS DWELLING 484 16
O YE THAT LOVE THE LORD, SEE THAT YE HATE THE THING 461 16   AT THE PRESENCE OF THE LORD   485 06
THE LORD PRESERVETH THE SOULS OF HIS SAINTS   461 17   NOT UNTO US, O LORD, NOT UNTO US, BUT UNTO THY NAME 485 11
12 REJOICE IN THE LORD, YE RIGHTEOUS   461 21   HOUSE OF ISRAEL, TRUST THOU IN THE LORD   485 28
O SING UNTO THE LORD A NEW SONG   461 25   PUT YOUR TRUST IN THE LORD   485 30
3 THE LORD DECLARED HIS SALVATION   461 29   11 YE THAT FEAR THE LORD, PUT YOUR TRUST IN THE LORD 485 32
JOYFUL UNTO THE LORD, ALL YE LANDS   462 02   PUT YOUR TRUST IN THE LORD   485 32
6 PRAISE THE LORD UPON THE HARP   462 04   12 THE LORD HATH BEEN MINDFUL OF US, AND HE SHALL   485 34
JOYFUL BEFORE THE LORD, THE KING   462 07   THEM THAT FEAR THE LORD, *   486 04
LET THE HILLS BE JOYFUL TOGETHER BEFORE THE LORD   462 11   14 THE LORD SHALL INCREASE YOU MORE AND MORE,   486 06
THE LORD IS KING, BE THE PEOPLE NEVER SO IMPATIENT   462 16   THE BLESSED OF THE LORD, *   486 08
2 THE LORD IS GREAT IN SION, *   462 19   PRAISE NOT THEE, O LORD, *   486 12
5 O MAGNIFY THE LORD OUR GOD, AND FALL DOWN BEFORE   462 25   WE WILL PRAISE THE LORD, *   486 14
CALLED UPON THE LORD, AND HE HEARD THEM   462 29   PRAISE THE LORD   486 15
HEARDEST THEM, O LORD OUR GOD   462 32   MY DELIGHT IS IN THE LORD   486 19
9 O MAGNIFY THE LORD OUR GOD, AND WORSHIP HIM UPON   463 02   THEN CALLED I UPON THE NAME OF THE LORD   486 26
FOR THE LORD OUR GOD IS HOLY   463 03   O LORD, I BESEECH THEE, DELIVER MY SOUL   486 26
SERVE THE LORD WITH GLADNESS, AND COME BEFORE HIS   463 05   5 GRACIOUS IS THE LORD, AND RIGHTEOUS   486 28
O BE JOYFUL IN THE LORD, ALL YE LANDS   463 05   6 THE LORD PRESERVETH THE SIMPLE   486 30
BE YE SURE THAT THE LORD HE IS GOD   463 08   FOR THE LORD HATH REWARDED THEE   487 06
4 FOR THE LORD IS GRACIOUS, HIS MERCY IS EVERLASTING 463 14   WALK BEFORE THE LORD *   487 06
UNTO THEE, O LORD, WILL I SING   463 18   I GIVE UNTO THE LORD *   487 09
OUT ALL WICKED DOERS FROM THE CITY OF THE LORD   464 06   AND CALL UPON THE NAME OF THE LORD   487 12
HEAR MY PRAYER, O LORD, *   464 10   IN THE SIGHT OF THE LORD IS THE DEATH OF HIS SAINTS 487 14
12 BUT THOU, O LORD, SHALT ENDURE FOR EVER, *   465 02   14 BEHOLD, O LORD, HOW THAT I AM THY SERVANT   487 16
15 THE NATIONS SHALL FEAR THY NAME, O LORD   465 09   AND WILL CALL UPON THE NAME OF THE LORD   487 20
16 WHEN THE LORD SHALL BUILD UP SION, *   465 11   MY VOWS UNTO THE LORD, IN THE SIGHT OF ALL HIS   487 21
PEOPLE WHICH SHALL BE BORN SHALL PRAISE THE LORD   465 16   PRAISE THE LORD   487 23
THE HEAVEN DID THE LORD BEHOLD THE EARTH   465 18   O PRAISE THE LORD, ALL YE NATIONS   487 25
THE NAME OF THE LORD IN SION, *   465 22   THE TRUTH OF THE LORD ENDURETH FOR EVER   487 28
AND THE KINGDOMS ALSO, TO SERVE THE LORD   465 25   PRAISE THE LORD   487 29
25 THOU, LORD, IN THE BEGINNING HAST LAID THE   465 31   THANKS UNTO THE LORD, FOR HE IS GRACIOUS   487 31
PRAISE THE LORD, O MY SOUL   466 08   NOW THAT FEAR THE LORD CONFESS, *   488 06
2 PRAISE THE LORD, O MY SOUL, *   466 10   AND THE LORD HEARD ME AT LARGE   488 08
6 THE LORD EXECUTETH RIGHTEOUSNESS AND JUDGMENT *   466 17   5 I CALLED UPON THE LORD IN TROUBLE   488 08
8 THE LORD IS FULL OF COMPASSION AND MERCY, *   466 21   6 THE LORD IS ON MY SIDE   488 10
EVEN SO IS THE LORD MERCIFUL UNTO THEM THAT FEAR HIM 466 33   7 THE LORD TAKETH MY PART WITH THEM THAT HELP ME   488 12
GOODNESS OF THE LORD ENDURETH FOR EVER AND EVER UPON 467 08   TO TRUST IN THE LORD, *   488 14
19 THE LORD HATH PREPARED HIS SEAT IN HEAVEN,   467 13   TO TRUST IN THE LORD, *   488 16
20 O PRAISE THE LORD, YE ANGELS OF HIS, YE THAT EXCEL 467 15   IN THE NAME OF THE LORD WILL I DESTROY THEM   488 19
21 O PRAISE THE LORD, ALL YE HIS HOSTS   467 18   IN THE NAME OF THE LORD WILL I DESTROY THEM   488 21
O SPEAK GOOD OF THE LORD, ALL YE WORKS OF HIS,   467 20   IN THE NAME OF THE LORD I WILL DESTROY THEM   488 25
PRAISE THOU THE LORD, O MY SOUL   467 21   BUT THE LORD WAS MY HELP   488 27
O LORD MY GOD, THOU ART BECOME EXCEEDING GLORIOUS   467 24   14 THE LORD IS MY STRENGTH, AND MY SONG   488 28
PRAISE THE LORD, O MY SOUL   467 24   RIGHT HAND OF THE LORD BRINGETH MIGHTY THINGS TO   488 31
16 THE TREES OF THE LORD ALSO ARE FULL OF SAP   468 26   RIGHT HAND OF THE LORD HATH THE PRE-EMINENCE   488 33
24 O LORD, HOW MANIFOLD ARE THY WORKS   469 08   RIGHT HAND OF THE LORD BRINGETH MIGHTY THINGS TO   488 34
MAJESTY OF THE LORD SHALL ENDURE FOR EVER   469 23   AND DECLARE THE WORKS OF THE LORD   489 03
THE LORD SHALL REJOICE IN HIS WORKS   469 24   18 THE LORD HATH CHASTENED AND CORRECTED ME   489 04
WILL SING UNTO THE LORD AS LONG AS I LIVE   469 27   AND GIVE THANKS UNTO THE LORD   489 07
MY JOY SHALL BE IN THE LORD   469 30   IS THE GATE OF THE LORD   489 08
PRAISE THE LORD   469 33   THE DAY WHICH THE LORD HATH MADE   489 16
36 PRAISE THOU THE LORD, O MY SOUL   469 33   25 HELP ME NOW, O LORD   489 18
THANKS UNTO THE LORD, AND CALL UPON HIS NAME   470 05   O LORD, SEND US NOW PROSPERITY   489 18
LET THE HEART OF THEM REJOICE THAT SEEK THE LORD   470 10   BLESSED BE HE THAT COMETH IN THE NAME OF THE LORD   489 19
4 SEEK THE LORD AND HIS STRENGTH   470 11   WE THAT ARE OF THE HOUSE OF THE LORD   489 21
7 HE IS THE LORD OUR GOD   470 16   27 GOD IS THE LORD, WHO HATH SHOWED US LIGHT   489 22
THE WORD OF THE LORD TRIED HIM   471 11   29 O GIVE THANKS UNTO THE LORD   489 27
21 HE MADE HIM LORD ALSO OF HIS HOUSE, *   471 14   AND WALK IN THE LAW OF THE LORD   489 32
O GIVE THANKS UNTO THE LORD   472 31   12 BLESSED ART THOU, O LORD   490 22
NOBLE ACTS OF THE LORD, *   473 02   O LORD, CONFOUND ME NOT   491 29
4 REMEMBER ME, O LORD, ACCORDING TO THE FAVOUR THAT 473 06   TEACH ME, O LORD, THE WAY OF THY STATUTES, *   492 05
AND AARON THE SAINT OF THE LORD   473 34   ALSO UNTO ME, O LORD, *   492 22
AND HEARKENED NOT UNTO THE VOICE OF THE LORD   474 20   O LORD, *   493 15
AS THE LORD COMMANDED THEM   475 04   UPON THY NAME, O LORD, IN THE NIGHT SEASON,   493 20
THE WRATH OF THE LORD KINDLED AGAINST HIS PEOPLE, * 475 16   THOU ART MY PORTION, O LORD   493 24
45 DELIVER US, O LORD OUR GOD, AND GATHER US FROM   475 30   64 THE EARTH, O LORD, IS FULL OF THY MERCY   494 08
46 BLESSED BE THE LORD GOD OF ISRAEL, FROM   475 33   O LORD, THOU HAST DEALT GRACIOUSLY WITH THY SERVANT 494 11
THANKS UNTO THE LORD, FOR HE IS GRACIOUS, *   476 06   75 I KNOW, O LORD, THAT THY JUDGMENTS ARE RIGHT,   495 04
THANKS WHOM THE LORD HATH REDEEMED, *   476 08   O LORD, THY WORD *   496 03
THEY CRIED UNTO THE LORD IN THEIR TROUBLE, *   476 15   LORD, WHAT LOVE HAVE I UNTO THY LAW   496 20
PRAISE THE LORD FOR HIS GOODNESS   476 19   QUICKEN ME, O LORD, ACCORDING TO THY WORD   497 12
THE WORDS OF THE LORD, *   476 26   OFFERINGS OF MY MOUTH PLEASE THEE, O LORD   497 14
THEY CRIED UNTO THE LORD IN THEIR TROUBLE, *   476 30   IS TIME FOR THEE, LORD, TO LAY TO THINE HAND   498 21
PRAISE THE LORD FOR HIS GOODNESS   477 04   RIGHTEOUS ART THOU, O LORD   499 13
THEY CRIED UNTO THE LORD IN THEIR TROUBLE, *   477 13   HEAR ME, O LORD   499 31
PRAISE THE LORD FOR HIS GOODNESS   477 17   HEAR MY VOICE, O LORD, ACCORDING UNTO THY   500 08
THE WORKS OF THE LORD, *   477 24   151 BE THOU NIGH AT HAND, O LORD   500 12
THEY CRY UNTO THE LORD IN THEIR TROUBLE, *   477 33   156 GREAT IS THY MERCY, O LORD   500 23
PRAISE THE LORD FOR HIS GOODNESS   478 07   159 CONSIDER, O LORD, HOW I LOVE THY COMMANDMENTS   500 29
SHALL UNDERSTAND THE LOVING-KINDNESS OF THE LORD   478 33   166 LORD, I HAVE LOOKED FOR THY SAVING HEALTH,   501 13
THANKS UNTO THEE, O LORD, AMONG THE PEOPLES   479 09   LET MY COMPLAINT COME BEFORE THEE, O LORD   501 20
BE HAD IN REMEMBRANCE IN THE SIGHT OF THE LORD   480 28   174 I HAVE LONGED FOR THY SAVING HEALTH, O LORD   501 30
ALWAY BE BEFORE THE LORD, *   480 30   I CALLED UPON THE LORD, *   502 07
HAPPEN FROM THE LORD UNTO MINE ENEMIES, *   481 10   DELIVER MY SOUL, O LORD, FROM LYING LIPS, *   502 09
THOU WITH ME, O LORD GOD, ACCORDING UNTO THY NAME   481 12   EVEN FROM THE LORD, *   502 24
25 HELP ME, O LORD MY GOD   481 22   5 THE LORD HIMSELF IS THY KEEPER   502 30
AND THAT THOU, LORD, HAST DONE IT   481 25   THE LORD IS THY DEFENCE UPON THY RIGHT HAND   502 30
THANKS UNTO THE LORD WITH MY MOUTH, *   481 32   7 THE LORD SHALL PRESERVE THEE FROM ALL EVIL   503 04
THE LORD SAID UNTO MY LORD, *   482 07   8 THE LORD SHALL PRESERVE THY GOING OUT, AND THY   503 06
LORD SAID UNTO MY LORD, *   482 07   WE WILL GO INTO THE HOUSE OF THE LORD   503 10
2 THE LORD SHALL SEND THE ROD OF THY POWER OUT OF   482 09   THE TRIBES OF THE LORD, *   503 14
4 THE LORD SWARE, AND WILL NOT REPENT, *   482 14   TO GIVE THANKS UNTO THE NAME OF THE LORD   503 15
5 THE LORD UPON THY RIGHT HAND *   482 16   OF THE HOUSE OF THE LORD OUR GOD, *   503 24
THANKS UNTO THE LORD WITH MY WHOLE HEART, *   482 24   EYES WAIT UPON THE LORD OUR GOD, UNTIL HE HAVE MERCY 503 32
2 THE WORKS OF THE LORD ARE GREAT, *   482 26   MERCY UPON US, O LORD, HAVE MERCY UPON US   504 02
AND GRACIOUS LORD HATH SO DONE HIS MARVELLOUS WORKS, 482 30   IF THE LORD HIMSELF HAD NOT BEEN ON OUR SIDE,   504 07
10 THE FEAR OF THE LORD IS THE BEGINNING OF WISDOM   483 14   IF THE LORD HIMSELF HAD NOT BEEN ON OUR SIDE, WHEN 504 08
BLESSED IS THE MAN THAT FEARETH THE LORD   483 18   BUT PRAISED BE THE LORD, *   504 16
AND BELIEVETH IN THE LORD   483 31   IN THE NAME OF THE LORD, *   504 20
PRAISE THE LORD, YE SERVANTS   484 08   THEIR TRUST IN THE LORD SHALL BE EVEN AS THE MOUNT 504 23

LORD   CONTINUED

SO STANDETH THE LORD ROUND ABOUT HIS PEOPLE, FROM   504 27
4 DO WELL, O LORD, *   504 32
THE LORD SHALL LEAD THEM FORTH WITH THE EVIL DOERS   505 03
WHEN THE LORD TURNED AGAIN THE CAPTIVITY OF SION,   505 07
THE LORD HATH DONE GREAT THINGS FOR THEM   505 11
4 YEA, THE LORD HATH DONE GREAT THINGS FOR US   505 13
OUR CAPTIVITY, O LORD, *   505 15
EXCEPT THE LORD BUILD THE HOUSE, *   505 22
2 EXCEPT THE LORD KEEP THE CITY, *   505 24
ARE AN HERITAGE AND GIFT THAT COMETH OF THE LORD   505 30
THEY THAT FEAR THE LORD, *   506 06
THAT FEARETH THE LORD   506 15
6 THE LORD FROM OUT OF SION SHALL SO BLESS THEE,   506 16
4 BUT THE RIGHTEOUS LORD, *   506 27
NOT SO MUCH AS, THE LORD PROSPER YOU   507 05
WE WISH YOU GOOD LUCK IN THE NAME OF THE LORD   507 06
OUT OF THE DEEP HAVE I CALLED UNTO THEE, O LORD   507 08
LORD, HEAR MY VOICE   507 09
3 IF THOU, LORD, WILT BE EXTREME TO MARK WHAT IS DONE 507 12
O LORD, WHO MAY ABIDE IT   507 13
5 I LOOK FOR THE LORD   507 16
FLEETH UNTO THE LORD BEFORE THE MORNING WATCH   507 18
FOR WITH THE LORD THERE IS MERCY, *   507 20
7 O ISRAEL, TRUST IN THE LORD   507 20
LORD, I AM NOT HIGH-MINDED   507 24
TRUST IN THE LORD *   507 30
LORD, REMEMBER DAVID, *   508 05
HE SWARE UNTO THE LORD, *   508 06
I FIND OUT A PLACE FOR THE TEMPLE OF THE LORD   508 13
8 ARISE, O LORD, INTO THY RESTING-PLACE   508 19
11 THE LORD HATH MADE A FAITHFUL OATH UNTO DAVID,   508 25
14 FOR THE LORD HATH CHOSEN SION TO BE AN HABITATION 508 32
4 FOR THERE THE LORD PROMISED HIS BLESSING, *   509 20
PRAISE THE LORD, *   509 23
ALL YE SERVANTS OF THE LORD   509 24
IN THE HOUSE OF THE LORD, *   509 25
AND PRAISE THE LORD   509 28
4 THE LORD THAT MADE HEAVEN AND EARTH *   509 29
O PRAISE THE LORD, LAUD YE THE NAME OF THE LORD   510 03
LAUD YE THE NAME OF THE LORD   510 03
O YE SERVANTS OF THE LORD   510 04
IN THE HOUSE OF THE LORD, *   510 05
THE LORD, FOR THE LORD IS GRACIOUS   510 07
3 O PRAISE THE LORD, FOR THE LORD IS GRACIOUS   510 07
THE LORD HATH CHOSEN JACOB UNTO HIMSELF, *   510 09
AND THAT OUR LORD IS ABOVE ALL GODS   510 11
FOR I KNOW THAT THE LORD IS GREAT, *   510 11
6 WHATSOEVER THE LORD PLEASED, THAT DID HE IN HEAVEN, 510 13
13 THY NAME, O LORD, ENDURETH FOR EVER   510 28
THY MEMORIAL, O LORD, FROM ONE GENERATION TO ANOTHER 510 29
14 FOR THE LORD WILL AVENGE HIS PEOPLE, *   510 30
PRAISE THE LORD, YE HOUSE OF AARON   511 08
19 PRAISE THE LORD, YE HOUSE OF ISRAEL   511 08
20 PRAISE THE LORD, YE HOUSE OF LEVI   511 10
YE THAT FEAR THE LORD, PRAISE THE LORD   511 11
YE THAT FEAR THE LORD, PRAISE THE LORD   511 11
21 PRAISED BE THE LORD OUT OF SION, *   511 12
THANKS UNTO THE LORD, FOR HE IS GRACIOUS   511 16
3 O THANK THE LORD OF ALL LORDS   511 20
THANKS UNTO THE LORD OF LORDS   513 02
CHILDREN OF EDOM, O LORD, IN THE DAY OF JERUSALEM   513 18
THANKS UNTO THEE, O LORD, WITH MY WHOLE HEART   513 27
THE KINGS OF THE EARTH SHALL PRAISE THEE, O LORD   514 04
OF THE WAYS OF THE LORD, *   514 06
THAT GREAT IS THE GLORY OF THE LORD   514 07
6 FOR THOUGH THE LORD BE HIGH, YET HATH HE RESPECT   514 08
8 THE LORD SHALL MAKE GOOD HIS LOVING-KINDNESS TOWARD 514 14
THY MERCY, O LORD, ENDURETH FOR EVER   514 15
O LORD, THOU HAST SEARCHED ME OUT, AND KNOWN ME   514 20
BUT THOU, O LORD, KNOWEST IT ALTOGETHER   514 26
NOT I HATE THEM, O LORD, THAT HATE THEE   515 32
DELIVER ME, O LORD, FROM THE EVIL MAN   516 09
4 KEEP ME, O LORD, FROM THE HANDS OF THE UNGODLY   516 15
6 I SAID UNTO THE LORD, THOU ART MY GOD, *   516 20
HEAR THE VOICE OF MY PRAYERS, O LORD   516 21
7 O LORD GOD, THOU STRENGTH OF MY HEALTH   516 22
8 LET NOT THE UNGODLY HAVE HIS DESIRE, O LORD   516 24
SURE I AM THAT THE LORD WILL AVENGE THE POOR,   517 02
LORD, I CALL UPON THEE   517 08
3 SET A WATCH, O LORD, BEFORE MY MOUTH, *   517 17
LOOK UNTO THEE, O LORD GOD   517 28
I CRIED UNTO THE LORD WITH MY VOICE   518 03
EVEN UNTO THE LORD DID I MAKE MY SUPPLICATION   518 04
CRIED UNTO THEE, O LORD, AND SAID, *   518 14
HEAR MY PRAYER, O LORD, AND CONSIDER MY DESIRE   518 23
7 HEAR ME, O LORD, AND THAT SOON   519 04
9 DELIVER ME, O LORD, FROM MINE ENEMIES   519 10
11 QUICKEN ME, O LORD, FOR THY NAME'S SAKE   519 15
BLESSED BE THE LORD MY STRENGTH, *   519 22
3 LORD, WHAT IS MAN, THAT THOU HAST SUCH RESPECT UNTO 519 27
BOW THY HEAVENS, O LORD, AND COME DOWN   519 31
PEOPLE WHO HAVE THE LORD FOR THEIR GOD   520 25
3 GREAT IS THE LORD, AND MARVELLOUS WORTHY TO BE   520 31
8 THE LORD IS GRACIOUS AND MERCIFUL   521 08
9 THE LORD IS LOVING UNTO EVERY MAN   521 10
10 ALL THY WORKS PRAISE THEE, O LORD   521 12
14 THE LORD UPHOLDETH ALL SUCH AS FALL, *   521 20
15 THE EYES OF ALL WAIT UPON THEE, O LORD   521 22
17 THE LORD IS RIGHTEOUS IN ALL HIS WAYS, *   521 26
18 THE LORD IS NIGH UNTO ALL THEM THAT CALL UPON HIM 521 28
20 THE LORD PRESERVETH ALL THEM THAT LOVE HIM   521 32
21 MY MOUTH SHALL SPEAK THE PRAISE OF THE LORD   521 34
PRAISE THE LORD, O MY SOUL   522 03
WHILE I LIVE, WILL I PRAISE THE LORD   522 04

HOPE IS IN THE LORD HIS GOD   522 11
THE LORD GIVETH SIGHT TO THE BLIND   522 16
7 THE LORD LOOSETH MEN OUT OF PRISON   522 16
THE LORD CARETH FOR THE RIGHTEOUS   522 18
8 THE LORD HELPETH THEM THAT ARE FALLEN   522 18
9 THE LORD CARETH FOR THE STRANGERS   522 20
10 THE LORD THY GOD, O SION, SHALL BE KING FOR   522 23
O PRAISE THE LORD, FOR IT IS A GOOD THING TO SING   522 27
2 THE LORD DOTH BUILD UP JERUSALEM, *   522 30
5 GREAT IS OUR LORD, AND GREAT IS HIS POWER   523 04
6 THE LORD SETTETH UP THE MEEK, *   523 06
7 O SING UNTO THE LORD WITH THANKSGIVING   523 08
12 PRAISE THE LORD, O JERUSALEM   523 19
O PRAISE THE LORD FROM THE HEAVENS   524 05
5 LET THEM PRAISE THE NAME OF THE LORD   524 13
7 PRAISE THE LORD FROM THE EARTH, *   524 18
OLD MEN AND CHILDREN, PRAISE THE NAME OF THE LORD   524 28
O SING UNTO THE LORD A NEW SONG   525 03
4 FOR THE LORD HATH PLEASURE IN HIS PEOPLE, *   525 09
PRAISE THE LORD   525 32
TO THE WILL OF OUR LORD JESUS CHRIST, AND ACCORDING 532 32
I WILL SO DO, THE LORD BEING MY HELPER   533 29
SO TO DO, THE LORD BEING MY HELPER   533 34
THAT WAIT FOR THEIR LORD, WHEN HE WILL RETURN FROM   534 18
WHOM THE LORD WHEN HE COMETH SHALL FIND   534 20
WE BESEECH THEE, O LORD, TO BE MODEST, HUMBLE,   535 03
AND OF HIS SON JESUS CHRIST OUR LORD   535 15
YE THEREFORE THE LORD OF THE HARVEST, THAT HE WILL   538 18
IN THE NAME OF OUR LORD JESUS CHRIST, THAT YE HAVE IN 539 29
BE MESSENGERS, WATCHMEN, AND STEWARDS OF THE LORD   539 33
THANKFUL UNTO THAT LORD, WHO HATH PLACED YOU IN SO   540 27
TO THE WILL OF OUR LORD JESUS CHRIST, AND ACCORDING 541 31
OF CHRIST, AS THE LORD HATH COMMANDED, AND AS THIS   542 13
I WILL SO DO, BY THE HELP OF THE LORD   542 18
I WILL, THE LORD BEING MY HELPER   542 25
SO TO DO, THE LORD BEING MY HELPER   542 30
MYSELF THERETO, THE LORD BEING MY HELPER   543 04
I WILL SO DO, THE LORD BEING MY HELPER   543 10
I WILL SO DO, THE LORD BEING MY HELPER   543 16
THROUGH JESUS CHRIST OUR LORD   543 22
JESUS CHRIST OUR LORD, WHO LIVETH AND REIGNETH WITH 546 03
THROUGH JESUS CHRIST OUR LORD   547 13
AND OF HIS SON JESUS CHRIST OUR LORD   547 16
THROUGH THE SAME THY SON JESUS CHRIST OUR LORD   549 15
SERVING THE LORD WITH ALL HUMILITY OF MIND, AND WITH 550 10
FAITH TOWARD OUR LORD JESUS CHRIST   550 14
RECEIVED OF THE LORD JESUS, TO TESTIFY THE GOSPEL OF 550 21
THE WORDS OF THE LORD JESUS, HOW HE SAID, IT IS MORE 551 10
HE SAITH UNTO HIM, YEA, LORD   551 15
HE SAITH UNTO HIM, YEA, LORD   551 18
HE SAID UNTO HIM, LORD, THOU KNOWEST ALL THINGS   551 23
WERE THE DISCIPLES GLAD, WHEN THEY SAW THE LORD   551 33
WE BESEECH THEE TO HEAR US, GOOD LORD   553 22
TO THE WILL OF OUR LORD JESUS CHRIST, AND THE ORDER 554 17
I AM READY, THE LORD BEING MY HELPER   555 07
I WILL SO DO, THE LORD BEING MY HELPER   555 13
THROUGH JESUS CHRIST OUR LORD   555 33
BISHOP SHALL SAY, LORD, HEAR OUR PRAYER   557 17
JESUS CHRIST OUR LORD, WHO, WITH THEE AND THE HOLY   558 06
THROUGH JESUS CHRIST OUR LORD   558 32
LAID UP BY THE LORD JESUS, THE RIGHTEOUS JUDGE, WHO 559 13
AND OF HIS SON JESUS CHRIST OUR LORD   559 19
ONE GOD, WE BESEECH THEE TO HEAR US, GOOD LORD   560 11
WE BESEECH THEE TO HEAR US, GOOD LORD   560 14
WE BESEECH THEE TO HEAR US, GOOD LORD   561 06
LORD, HAVE MERCY UPON US   561 22
UNTO OUR VOICE, O LORD, WHEN WE CRY UNTO THEE   561 31
O LORD, ARISE, HELP US   562 02
LORD, HEAR OUR PRAYER   562 06
JESUS CHRIST OUR LORD, WHO LIVETH AND REIGNETH WITH 562 14
3 WHO SHALL ASCEND INTO THE HILL OF THE LORD   563 15
BLESSING FROM THE LORD, *   563 20
IT IS THE LORD STRONG AND MIGHTY, EVEN THE LORD   563 26
EVEN THE LORD MIGHTY IN BATTLE   563 27
EVEN THE LORD OF HOSTS, HE IS THE KING OF GLORY   563 30
HE SHALL SAY, DEARLY BELOVED IN THE LORD   564 10
VOUCHSAFE, O LORD, TO BE PRESENT WITH US, WHO ARE   565 03
ACCEPT, O LORD, THIS SERVICE AT OUR HANDS, AND BLESS 565 11
CHRIST OUR BLESSED LORD AND SAVIOUR   565 14
REGARD, O LORD, THE SUPPLICATIONS OF THY   565 18
GRANT, O LORD, THAT THEY WHO AT THIS PLACE SHALL IN 565 23
GRANT, O LORD, THAT WHOSOEVER SHALL RECEIVE IN THIS 565 28
GRANT, O LORD, THAT BY THY HOLY WORD WHICH SHALL BE 566 02
GRANT, O LORD, THAT WHOSOEVER SHALL BE JOINED   566 08
BLESSED LORD, THAT WHOSOEVER SHALL DRAW NEAR TO   566 13
OUR MOST BLESSED LORD AND SAVIOUR   566 24
BE THY NAME, O LORD, THAT IT HATH PLEASED THEE TO PUT 566 28
THROUGH JESUS CHRIST OUR LORD   566 34
THROUGH JESUS CHRIST OUR LORD   567 10
BE THY NAME, O LORD GOD, FOR THAT IT HATH PLEASED   568 06
THROUGH JESUS CHRIST OUR LORD   568 12
AND OF HIS SON JESUS CHRIST OUR LORD   568 15
AND AS THE LORD HATH ORDAINED THAT THEY WHO SERVE AT 569 28
BELOVED IN THE LORD, WE HAVE ASSEMBLED FOR THE   570 12
THE LORD BE WITH YOU   571 05
DIRECT US, O LORD, IN ALL OUR DOINGS, WITH THY MOST 571 08
JESUS CHRIST OUR LORD, WHO HATH TAUGHT US TO PRAY   571 13
IN THY SIGHT, O LORD, OUR STRENGTH AND OUR REDEEMER 572 23
FROM THE DEAD OUR LORD JESUS CHRIST, THE GREAT   573 04
O LORD MY GOD, I AM NOT WORTHY THAT THOU SHOULDEST   573 11
UP, SHALL SAY, THE LORD BE WITH YOU   573 31
AND IN JESUS CHRIST HIS ONLY SON OUR LORD   577 30
I AM THE LORD THY GOD, WHO BROUGHT THEE OUT   578 23
FOR I THE LORD THY GOD AM A JEALOUS GOD, AND VISIT   578 30

LORD   CONTINUED

THE NAME OF THE LORD THY GOD IN VAIN   578 35
FOR THE LORD WILL NOT HOLD HIM GUILTLESS, THAT TAKETH   579 02
THE SABBATH OF THE LORD THY GOD   579 06
FOR IN SIX DAYS THE LORD MADE HEAVEN AND EARTH,   579 10
WHEREFORE THE LORD BLESSED THE SEVENTH DAY, AND   579 12
THE LAND WHICH THE LORD THY GOD GIVETH THEE   579 14
I DESIRE MY LORD GOD, OUR HEAVENLY FATHER, WHO IS THE   580 29
THROUGH OUR LORD JESUS CHRIST   581 06
AND THE SUPPER OF THE LORD   581 10
AND WINE, WHICH THE LORD HATH COMMANDED TO BE   582 09
KNOWLEDGE OF OUR LORD AND SAVIOUR JESUS CHRIST   588 10
THY SON JESUS CHRIST OUR LORD   588 24
JESUS CHRIST, OUR LORD AND SAVIOUR   589 08
THE GRACE OF OUR LORD JESUS CHRIST, AND THE LOVE OF   589 09
THE COMING OF OUR LORD AND SAVIOUR JESUS CHRIST   590 20
AND ACCEPT, O LORD, OUR INTERCESSIONS FOR ALL   590 22
TO OUR PRAYERS, O LORD, WE JOIN OUR UNFEIGNED THANKS   591 07
THE GRACE OF OUR LORD JESUS CHRIST, AND THE LOVE OF   592 02
O LORD, OUR HEAVENLY FATHER, ALMIGHTY AND EVERLASTING   592 19
THROUGH JESUS CHRIST OUR LORD   592 25
THE GRACE OF OUR LORD JESUS CHRIST, AND THE LOVE OF   592 27
LIGHTEN OUR DARKNESS, WE BESEECH THEE, O LORD   593 13
THE LORD MAKE HIS FACE TO SHINE UPON US, AND BE   593 18
THE LORD BLESS US AND KEEP US   593 18
THE LORD LIFT UP HIS COUNTENANCE UPON US, AND GIVE US   593 19
THROUGH JESUS CHRIST OUR LORD   594 09
THROUGH JESUS CHRIST OUR LORD   594 17
O LORD, SUPPORT US ALL THE DAY LONG, UNTIL THE   594 30
OF THE GLORIOUS RESURRECTION OF THY SON OUR LORD   595 14
THROUGH THE SAME JESUS CHRIST OUR LORD   595 16
THROUGH JESUS CHRIST OUR LORD   595 24
THROUGH JESUS CHRIST OUR LORD   595 32
UNTO US IN THY SON, JESUS CHRIST OUR LORD   596 09
THINGS WERE MADE, THY SON, JESUS CHRIST OUR LORD   596 22
THROUGH JESUS CHRIST OUR LORD   597 07
THROUGH JESUS CHRIST OUR LORD   597 13
THROUGH JESUS CHRIST OUR LORD   597 19
THROUGH JESUS CHRIST OUR LORD   597 26
OVER THY CHILD, O LORD, AS HIS DAYS INCREASE   597 28
THROUGH JESUS CHRIST OUR LORD   598 04
THROUGH JESUS CHRIST OUR LORD   598 11
THROUGH JESUS CHRIST OUR LORD   598 17
THROUGH JESUS CHRIST OUR LORD   598 30
GRANT THIS, O LORD, FOR THE LOVE OF HIM, WHO FOR OUR   599 15
THROUGH JESUS CHRIST OUR LORD   599 23
THROUGH JESUS CHRIST OUR LORD   600 19
THE MERIT OF OUR LORD AND SAVIOUR JESUS CHRIST BY   605 06
OF CHRIST OUR LORD IN THE GOSPEL, THAT IS TO SAY,   607 36
AND THE SUPPER OF THE LORD   607 37
THE SUPPER OF THE LORD IS NOT ONLY A SIGN OF THE LOVE   608 34
THE SUPPER OF THE LORD, CANNOT BE PROVED BY HOLY   608 41
THE CUP OF THE LORD IS NOT TO BE DENIED TO THE   609 10
MEN BY OUR LORD JESUS CHRIST, AND JAMES HIS APOSTLE,   611 07

LORD'S

SENTENCES TO THE LORD'S PRAYER, FIRST PRONOUNCING,   R 003 07
IN WHICH CASE THE LORD'S PRAYER SHALL BE SAID WITH   R 003 12
AND SAY THE LORD'S PRAYER   R 007 20
THE LORD'S NAME BE PRAISED   008 08
SHALL FOLLOW THE LORD'S PRAYER   R 016 28
SENTENCES TO THE LORD'S PRAYER   R 021 06
IN WHICH CASE THE LORD'S PRAYER SHALL BE SAID WITH   R 021 09
AND SAY THE LORD'S PRAYER   R 024 27
THE LORD'S NAME BE PRAISED   025 14
SHALL FOLLOW THE LORD'S PRAYER   R 030 33
WITH HIM, SAY THE LORD'S PRAYER   R 058 02
SHALL SAY THE LORD'S PRAYER AND THE COLLECT   R 067 07
BUT THE LORD'S PRAYER MAY BE OMITTED AT THE   R 067 08
DOWN AT THE LORD'S TABLE, SAY, IN THE NAME OF ALL   R 082 11
RETURN TO THE LORD'S TABLE, AND REVERENTLY PLACE UPON   R 083 11
TO COME TO THE LORD'S TABLE, UNTIL HE HAVE OPENLY   R 085 04
PARTAKERS OF THE LORD'S TABLE, UNTIL HE KNOW THEM TO   R 085 11
TO CELEBRATE THE LORD'S SUPPER   088 13
ABSTAIN FROM THE LORD'S TABLE, AND SEPARATE FROM YOUR   089 17
YE DO SHEW THE LORD'S DEATH TILL HE COME   152 25
OF MAN FOR THE LORD'S SAKE   173 18
HE HAD SEEN THE LORD'S CHRIST   232 34
RECEIVED OF THE LORD'S HAND DOUBLE FOR ALL HER SINS   242 19
THE CREED, THE LORD'S PRAYER, AND THE TEN   277 10
SHALL BE SAID THE LORD'S PRAYER, AND THE THANKSGIVING   R 281 23
THE LORD'S PRAYER   289 18
SACRAMENT OF THE LORD'S SUPPER, OR HOLY COMMUNION,   291 31
SACRAMENT OF THE LORD'S SUPPER ORDAINED   293 02
SACRAMENT OF THE LORD'S SUPPER WAS ORDAINED FOR THE   293 04
OR SIGN OF THE LORD'S SUPPER   293 08
OR SIGN OF THE LORD'S SUPPER IS, BREAD AND WINE,   293 10
FAITHFUL IN THE LORD'S SUPPER   293 16
PARTAKERS IN THE LORD'S SUPPER   293 18
PARTAKERS IN THE LORD'S SUPPER ARE THE STRENGTHENING   293 20
WHO COME TO THE LORD'S SUPPER   293 24
WHO COME TO THE LORD'S SUPPER TO EXAMINE THEMSELVES,   293 25
THE CREED, THE LORD'S PRAYER, AND THE TEN   R 295 14
UNTIL THE LORD'S PRAYER   R 296 07
BISHOP SAY THE LORD'S PRAYER, THE PEOPLE KNEELING AND   R 298 03
TO THE LORD'S SUPPER   R 299 07
SAY THE LORD'S PRAYER   302 26
THE COURTS OF THE LORD'S HOUSE   306 02
MINISTER SAY THE LORD'S PRAYER, WITH WHAT FOLLOWETH   R 306 08
BUT THE LORD'S PRAYER MAY BE OMITTED, IF THIS BE USED   R 306 09
THE LORD'S PRAYER   R 323 09
O TARRY THOU THE LORD'S LEISURE   326 30
THE CREED, THE LORD'S PRAYER, THE PRAYER WHICH   R 331 29
THE LORD'S SEAT IS IN HEAVEN   354 26

LORD'S   CONTINUED

KINGDOM IS THE LORD'S, *   367 31
THE EARTH IS THE LORD'S, AND ALL THAT THEREIN IS   368 28
O TARRY THOU THE LORD'S LEISURE   372 30
IN THE LORD'S WORD WILL I COMFORT ME   409 02
3 THE LORD'S NAME IS PRAISED *   484 12
16 ALL THE WHOLE HEAVENS ARE THE LORD'S   486 10
THE COURTS OF THE LORD'S HOUSE   487 22
23 THIS IS THE LORD'S DOING, *   489 14
SHALL WE SING THE LORD'S SONG *   513 12
11 BUT THE LORD'S DELIGHT IS IN THEM THAT FEAR HIM,   523 17
PROVIDE FOR THE LORD'S FAMILY   539 34
THE EARTH IS THE LORD'S, AND ALL THAT THEREIN IS   563 11
CANST SAY THE LORD'S PRAYER   580 21
SACRAMENT OF THE LORD'S SUPPER ORDAINED   582 02
OR SIGN OF THE LORD'S SUPPER   582 07
FAITHFUL IN THE LORD'S SUPPER   582 13
WHO COME TO THE LORD'S SUPPER   582 21
THE CREED, THE LORD'S PRAYER, AND THE TEN   R 583 02
WITH HIM THE LORD'S PRAYER   R 587 06
WITH HIM THE LORD'S PRAYER   R 589 15
WITH HIM THE LORD'S PRAYER   R 592 11
WITH HIM THE LORD'S PRAYER   R 593 05
INTO THE LORD'S VINEYARD   607 24
AND THE LORD'S SUPPER, FOR THAT THEY HAVE   607 42
SACRAMENT OF THE LORD'S SUPPER WAS NOT BY CHRIST'S   608 47
THE PARTS OF THE LORD'S SACRAMENT, BY CHRIST'S   609 11

LORDS

AND LORD OF LORDS, A GREAT GOD, A MIGHTY, AND A   263 23
HATED THEM WERE LORDS OVER THEM   475 19
3 O THANK THE LORD OF ALL LORDS   511 20
27 O GIVE THANKS UNTO THE LORD OF LORDS   513 02

LORDSHIP

EXERCISE LORDSHIP OVER THEM   149 20
EXERCISE LORDSHIP OVER THEM   250 05

LOSE

IF HE LOSE ONE OF THEM, DOTH NOT LEAVE THE   193 18
OF SILVER, IF SHE LOSE ONE PIECE, DOTH NOT LIGHT A   193 28
THAT WE FINALLY LOSE NOT THE THINGS ETERNAL   194 08
GIVEN ME I SHOULD LOSE NOTHING, BUT SHOULD RAISE IT   269 18

LOSS

NOTHING BUT THE LOSS OF THEE, AND TO CAST ALL OUR   596 04

LOST

FROM THY WAYS LIKE LOST SHEEP   006 18
FROM THY WAYS LIKE LOST SHEEP   023 25
SENT BUT UNTO THE LOST SHEEP OF THE HOUSE OF ISRAEL   128 14
THE FRAGMENTS THAT REMAIN, THAT NOTHING BE LOST   132 08
AFTER THAT WHICH IS LOST, UNTIL HE FIND IT   193 20
FOR I HAVE FOUND MY SHEEP WHICH WAS LOST   193 24
FOR I HAVE FOUND THE PIECE WHICH I HAD LOST   193 32
HE WAS LOST, AND IS FOUND   202 25
AND WAS LOST, AND IS FOUND   203 08
THE FRAGMENTS THAT REMAIN, THAT NOTHING BE LOST   226 07
GOSPEL BE HID, IT IS HID TO THEM THAT ARE LOST   251 02
176 I HAVE GONE ASTRAY LIKE A SHEEP THAT IS LOST   502 02
THEIR LABOUR IS BUT LOST THAT BUILD IT   505 23
3 IT IS BUT LOST LABOUR THAT YE HASTE TO RISE UP   505 26
BRING AGAIN THE OUTCASTS, SEEK THE LOST   558 28

LOT

AND THE LOT FELL UPON MATTHIAS   234 32
THOU SHALT MAINTAIN MY LOT   357 32
7 THE LOT IS FALLEN UNTO ME IN A FAIR GROUND   358 02
THEY HAVE HOLPEN THE CHILDREN OF LOT   444 21
THE LOT OF YOUR INHERITANCE   470 25
NOT ABIDE UPON THE LOT OF THE RIGHTEOUS   504 30

LOTS

AND PARTED HIS GARMENTS, CASTING LOTS   136 31
AND UPON MY VESTURE DID THEY CAST LOTS   136 34
CASTING LOTS UPON THEM, WHAT EVERY MAN   146 11
AND THEY PARTED HIS RAIMENT, AND CAST LOTS   154 27
REND IT, BUT CAST LOTS FOR IT, WHOSE IT SHALL BE   160 13
AMONG THEM, AND FOR MY VESTURE THEY DID CAST LOTS   160 16
AND THEY GAVE FORTH THEIR LOTS   234 31
AND CAST LOTS UPON MY VESTURE   367 08

LOUD

UPON A LOUD INSTRUMENT, AND UPON THE HARP   027 33
CRIED OUT WITH A LOUD VOICE, AND STOPPED THEIR EARS,   100 09
AND CRIED WITH A LOUD VOICE, LORD, LAY NOT THIS SIN   100 15
JESUS CRIED WITH A LOUD VOICE, SAYING, ELI, ELI, LAMA   137 17
CRIED AGAIN WITH A LOUD VOICE, YIELDED UP THE GHOST   137 25
JESUS CRIED WITH A LOUD VOICE, SAYING, ELOI, ELOI,   146 27
JESUS CRIED WITH A LOUD VOICE, AND GAVE UP THE GHOST   146 34
WERE INSTANT WITH LOUD VOICES, REQUIRING THAT HE   154 03
HAD CRIED WITH A LOUD VOICE, HE SAID, FATHER, INTO   155 12
AND WITH A LOUD VOICE GLORIFIED GOD, AND FELL   210 08
AND I HEARD A LOUD VOICE SAYING IN HEAVEN, NOW IS   252 10
AND HE CRIED WITH A LOUD VOICE TO THE FOUR ANGELS,   256 16
AND CRIED WITH A LOUD VOICE, SAYING, SALVATION TO OUR   256 27
UPON A LOUD INSTRUMENT, AND UPON THE HARP   456 05

LOUD   CONTINUED   LOVE   CONTINUED

PRAISE HIM UPON THE LOUD CYMBALS   525 31   ALL THEM ALSO THAT LOVE HIS APPEARING   253 30
                                                               THAT YE LOVE ONE ANOTHER   255 12
LOVE   THE WORLD WOULD LOVE HIS OWN   255 15
                                                               WHO UNFEIGNEDLY LOVE THEE   256 10
FILL THEM WITH THE LOVE OF TRUTH AND RIGHTEOUSNESS 018 12   THE FLAME OF THY LOVE IN THE HEARTS OF THE SAINTS   258 05
THINE INESTIMABLE LOVE IN THE REDEMPTION OF THE WORLD 019 22   THE SAME FAITH AND POWER OF LOVE   258 07
AND THE LOVE OF GOD, AND THE FELLOWSHIP OF   020 12   LOVE YE THEREFORE THE STRANGER   263 27
FOR THE LOVE OF THY ONLY SON, OUR SAVIOUR, JESUS   031 28   THOU SHALT LOVE THY NEIGHBOUR, AND HATE THINE   264 04
THINE INESTIMABLE LOVE IN THE REDEMPTION OF THE WORLD 033 20   BUT I SAY UNTO YOU, LOVE YOUR ENEMIES, BLESS THEM   264 05
AND THE LOVE OF GOD, AND THE FELLOWSHIP OF   034 12   FOR IF YE LOVE THEM WHICH LOVE YOU, WHAT REWARD HAVE 264 11
FOR THE LOVE OF JESUS CHRIST OUR LORD, TO WHOM, WITH 041 05   YE LOVE THEM WHICH LOVE YOU, WHAT REWARD HAVE YE   264 11
AND TO ABIDE IN THY LOVE   043 11   LOVE YOUR WIVES, EVEN AS CHRIST ALSO LOVED   267 19
INSPIRED BY THY LOVE, THEY MAY WORTHILY MINISTER IN 044 04   SO OUGHT MEN TO LOVE THEIR WIVES AS THEIR OWN BODIES 267 24
IN PERFECTNESS OF LOVE, AND TO RESTORE TO IT THE   047 10   IN PARTICULAR SO LOVE HIS WIFE EVEN AS HIMSELF   268 02
GIVE US AN HEART TO LOVE AND FEAR THEE, AND   056 11   IN OUR HEARTS THE LOVE OF THY NAME, INCREASE IN US 283 09
WE MAY PERFECTLY LOVE THEE, AND WORTHILY MAGNIFY THY 067 19   THAT THEY MAY LOVE THE THING WHICH THOU COMMANDEST, 285 27
IN THEM THAT LOVE ME AND KEEP MY COMMANDMENTS   068 15   IN THEM THAT LOVE ME AND KEEP MY COMMANDMENTS   286 15
THOU SHALT LOVE THE LORD THY GOD WITH ALL THY HEART, 069 27   THOU SHALT LOVE THE LORD THY GOD WITH ALL THY HEART, 288 06
THOU SHALT LOVE THY NEIGHBOUR AS THYSELF   069 30   THOU SHALT LOVE THY NEIGHBOUR AS THYSELF   288 09
WHICH LOVE YE HAVE SHOWED FOR HIS NAME'S SAKE, WHO 072 24   TO FEAR HIM, AND TO LOVE HIM WITH ALL MY HEART,   288 17
YOUR WORKS, AND LABOUR THAT PROCEEDETH OF LOVE   072 24   MY NEIGHBOUR IS TO LOVE HIM AS MYSELF, AND TO DO TO 288 24
HOW DWELLETH THE LOVE OF GOD IN HIM   072 31   TO LOVE, HONOUR, AND HELP MY FATHER AND MOTHER   288 27
THY HOLY WORD, AND LIVE IN UNITY AND GODLY LOVE   074 15   AND THE LOVE OF GOD, AND THE FELLOWSHIP OF   289 29
GROWTH IN THY LOVE AND SERVICE, AND TO GIVE US GRACE 075 02   IN FAITH, AND LOVE, AND TRUE REPENTANCE, WE MAY   294 31
AND ARE IN LOVE AND CHARITY WITH YOUR   075 09   AND THE LOVE OF GOD, AND THE FELLOWSHIP OF   295 04
THE KNOWLEDGE AND LOVE OF GOD, AND OF HIS SON JESUS 084 20   WILT THOU LOVE HER, COMFORT HER, HONOUR, AND KEEP HER 301 08
THE EXCEEDING GREAT LOVE OF OUR MASTER, AND ONLY   086 13   WILT THOU LOVE HIM, COMFORT HIM, HONOUR, AND KEEP HIM 301 16
AS PLEDGES OF HIS LOVE, AND FOR A CONTINUAL   086 17   AND IN HEALTH, TO LOVE AND TO CHERISH, TILL DEATH US 301 30
I EXHORT YOU, AS YE LOVE YOUR OWN SALVATION, THAT YE 089 08   AND IN HEALTH, TO LOVE AND TO CHERISH, TILL DEATH US 302 06
ANY THING, BUT TO LOVE ONE ANOTHER   090 23   REMAIN IN PERFECT LOVE AND PEACE TOGETHER, AND LIVE 303 10
THOU SHALT LOVE THY NEIGHBOUR AS THYSELF   090 29   THAT THEY MAY LOVE, HONOUR, AND CHERISH EACH OTHER, 303 23
LOVE WORKETH NO ILL TO HIS NEIGHBOUR   090 29   AND GROW IN THY LOVE AND SERVICE, UNTIL HE COME TO 307 05
THEREFORE LOVE IS THE FULFILLING OF THE LAW   090 30   WHOM THOU DOST LOVE, AND CHASTISE EVERY ONE WHOM THOU 321 15
MAY LEARN TO LOVE AND BLESS OUR PERSECUTORS BY   099 30   GOOD TO THEM THAT LOVE GOD, TO THEM WHO ARE THE   330 31
LET LOVE BE WITHOUT DISSIMULATION   111 22   US FROM THE LOVE OF CHRIST   331 06
AFFECTIONED ONE TO ANOTHER WITH BROTHERLY LOVE   111 24   US FROM THE LOVE OF GOD, WHICH IS IN CHRIST JESUS OUR 331 13
WHAT MANNER OF LOVE THE FATHER HATH BESTOWED UPON US, 117 14   IN KNOWLEDGE AND LOVE OF THEE, HE MAY GO FROM   332 05
THE HOLY GHOST, BY LOVE UNFEIGNED, BY THE WORD OF   126 14   TO ALL WHO LOVE AND FEAR THEE, SAYING, COME, YE   335 11
AND WALK IN LOVE, AS CHRIST ALSO HATH LOVED US,   128 31   BLESSINGS OF THY LOVE, THAT THE GOOD WORK WHICH THOU 335 29
WHO, OF THY TENDER LOVE TOWARDS MANKIND, HAST SENT 134 06   TAKEN INTO THE SAFE KEEPING OF THINE ETERNAL LOVE   340 27
IN HIS LOVE AND IN HIS PITY HE REDEEMED THEM   139 03   AND THE LOVE OF GOD, AND THE FELLOWSHIP OF   341 05
TO PROVOKE UNTO LOVE AND TO GOOD WORKS   158 25   CARE AND LOVE, AND BRING US ALL TO THY HEAVENLY   342 06
LOVE THE BROTHERHOOD   173 25   THEY MAY KNOW THE CONSOLATION OF THY LOVE   342 12
THAT THEY MAY LOVE THE THING WHICH THOU COMMANDEST, 174 20   THEY THAT LOVE THY NAME SHALL BE JOYFUL IN THEE   348 27
IF YE LOVE ME, KEEP MY COMMANDMENTS   181 08   I WILL LOVE THEE, O LORD, MY STRENGTH   359 24
AND I WILL LOVE HIM, AND WILL MANIFEST MYSELF   181 21   26 O LOVE THE LORD, ALL YE HIS SAINTS   377 15
UNTO HIM, IF A MAN LOVE ME, HE WILL KEEP MY WORDS   181 24   AND LET SUCH AS LOVE THY SALVATION, SAY ALWAY,   391 12
AND MY FATHER WILL LOVE HIM, AND WE WILL COME UNTO 181 25   AND THEY THAT LOVE HIS NAME SHALL DWELL THEREIN   424 18
MAY KNOW THAT I LOVE THE FATHER   182 09   HE HATH SET HIS LOVE UPON ME, THEREFORE WILL I   455 23
LET US LOVE ONE ANOTHER   189 08   10 O YE THAT LOVE THE LORD, SEE THAT YE HATE THE   461 16
FOR LOVE IS OF GOD   189 08   3 FOR THE LOVE THAT I HAD UNTO THEM, LO, THEY TAKE 480 09
WAS MANIFESTED THE LOVE OF GOD TOWARD US, BECAUSE   189 11   WHAT LOVE HAVE I UNTO THY LAW   496 20
FOR GOD IS LOVE   189 11   BUT THY LAW DO I LOVE   497 25
HEREIN IS LOVE, NOT THAT WE LOVED GOD, BUT THAT HE 189 13   THEREFORE I LOVE THY TESTIMONIES   498 07
WE OUGHT ALSO TO LOVE ONE ANOTHER   189 16   127 FOR I LOVE THY COMMANDMENTS *   498 23
IF WE LOVE ONE ANOTHER, GOD DWELLETH IN US, AND HIS 189 17   DO UNTO THOSE THAT LOVE THY NAME   499 03
IN US, AND HIS LOVE IS PERFECTED IN US   189 18   O LORD, HOW I LOVE THY COMMANDMENTS   500 29
GOD IS LOVE   189 24   BUT THY LAW DO I LOVE   501 08
AND BELIEVED THE LOVE THAT GOD HATH TO US   189 24   THAT THEY HAVE WHO LOVE THY LAW   501 11
HE THAT DWELLETH IN LOVE DWELLETH IN GOD, AND GOD IN 189 25   SHALL PROSPER THAT LOVE THEE   503 19
HEREIN IS OUR LOVE MADE PERFECT, THAT WE MAY HAVE   189 26   ALL THEM THAT LOVE HIM   521 32
BUT PERFECT LOVE CASTETH OUT FEAR   189 28   THE KNOWLEDGE AND LOVE OF GOD, AND OF HIS SON JESUS 535 15
THERE IS NO FEAR IN LOVE   189 28   AND LOVE, AMONG ALL CHRISTIAN PEOPLE, AND   543 07
WE LOVE HIM, BECAUSE HE FIRST LOVED US   189 30   FROM ABOVE, IS COMFORT, LIFE, AND FIRE OF LOVE   544 03
HE THAT FEARETH IS NOT MADE PERFECT IN LOVE   189 30   THE FIRE OF LOVE, THE SOUL'S ANOINTING FROM   544 23
IF A MAN SAY, I LOVE GOD, AND HATETH HIS BROTHER,   189 31   AND SHED THY LOVE IN EVERY HEART   545 03
HOW CAN HE LOVE GOD WHOM HE HATH NOT SEEN   189 33   OF THINE INFINITE LOVE AND GOODNESS TOWARDS US,   545 13
HE WHO LOVETH GOD LOVE HIS BROTHER ALSO   189 35   THE KNOWLEDGE AND LOVE OF GOD, AND OF HIS SON JESUS 547 15
THOU DOST BRING UP IN THY STEDFAST FEAR AND LOVE   191 06   THOU KNOWEST THAT I LOVE THEE   551 16
PERPETUAL FEAR AND LOVE OF THY HOLY NAME   191 08   THOU KNOWEST THAT I LOVE THEE   551 19
BECAUSE WE LOVE THE BRETHREN   191 13   THOU KNOWEST THAT I LOVE THEE   551 24
PERCEIVE WE THE LOVE OF GOD, BECAUSE HE LAID DOWN HIS 191 16   IN YOU, QUIETNESS, LOVE, AND PEACE AMONG ALL MEN   555 15
LET US NOT LOVE IN WORD, NEITHER IN TONGUE   191 21   FROM ABOVE, IS COMFORT, LIFE, AND FIRE OF LOVE   556 11
HOW DWELLETH THE LOVE OF GOD IN HIM   191 21   THE FIRE OF LOVE, THE SOUL'S ANOINTING FROM   557 02
JESUS CHRIST, AND LOVE ONE ANOTHER, AS HE GAVE US   191 31   AND SHED THY LOVE IN EVERY HEART   557 09
ONE OF ANOTHER, LOVE AS BRETHREN, BE PITIFUL, BE   195 21   BUT OF POWER, AND LOVE, AND SOBERNESS   558 18
FOR HE THAT WILL LOVE LIFE, AND SEE GOOD DAYS, LET 195 24   IN CONVERSATION, IN LOVE, IN FAITH, IN CHASTITY,   559 11
FOR THOSE WHO LOVE THEE SUCH GOOD THINGS AS PASS   197 04   THE KNOWLEDGE AND LOVE OF GOD, AND OF HIS SON JESUS 559 18
OUR HEARTS SUCH LOVE TOWARD THEE, THAT WE, LOVING   197 06   AND DEACONS, WITH LOVE OF THEE AND OF THY TRUTH   560 19
IN OUR HEARTS THE LOVE OF THY NAME, INCREASE IN US 198 21   REMAIN IN PERFECT LOVE TOGETHER UNTO THEIR LIFE'S 566 11
THOU SHALT LOVE THE LORD THY GOD WITH ALL THY   208 15   THE KNOWLEDGE AND LOVE OF GOD, AND OF HIS SON JESUS 568 15
MAKE US TO LOVE THAT WHICH THOU DOST   209 10   WITH THY LOVE AND FAVOUR   572 26
OF THE SPIRIT IS LOVE, JOY, PEACE, LONG-SUFFERING, 209 26   IN THEIR HEARTS A LOVE OF THE TRUTH   572 28
HATE THE ONE, AND LOVE THE OTHER   211 10   TO HEIGHTEN MY LOVE AND GRATITUDE   573 25
AND GROUNDED IN LOVE, MAY BE ABLE TO COMPREHEND WITH 212 17   IN THEM THAT LOVE ME AND KEEP MY COMMANDMENTS   578 14
AND TO KNOW THE LOVE OF CHRIST, WHICH PASSETH   212 19   TO FEAR HIM, AND TO LOVE HIM WITH ALL MY HEART,   579 28
FORBEARING ONE ANOTHER IN LOVE   213 21   MY NEIGHBOUR IS TO LOVE HIM AS MYSELF, AND TO DO TO 579 34
THOU SHALT LOVE THE LORD THY GOD WITH ALL THY   215 11   TO LOVE, HONOUR, AND SUCCOUR MY FATHER AND MOTHER 580 03
UNTO IT, THOU SHALT LOVE THY NEIGHBOUR AS THYSELF   215 13   AND THE LOVE OF GOD, AND THE FELLOWSHIP OF   589 09
I PRAY, THAT YOUR LOVE MAY ABOUND YET MORE AND MORE 221 02   AND THE LOVE OF GOD, AND THE FELLOWSHIP OF   592 02
AND OF THE LOVE WHICH YE HAVE TO ALL THE   223 24   AND THE LOVE OF GOD, AND THE FELLOWSHIP OF   592 27
UNTO US YOUR LOVE IN THE SPIRIT   223 32   FOR THE LOVE OF THY ONLY SON, OUR SAVIOUR, JESUS   593 15
THE TRUTH IN LOVE, MAY GROW UP INTO HIM IN ALL   237 28   THE LIGHT OF THAT LOVE WHICH IS IMMORTAL, AND WHICH 596 08
OF THE BODY UNTO THE EDIFYING OF ITSELF IN LOVE   238 03   THAT THEY MAY LOVE WHATSOEVER THINGS ARE TRUE   596 26
CONTINUE YE IN MY LOVE   238 21   BLESS THOSE WHOM WE LOVE, NOW ABSENT FROM US   597 02
YE SHALL ABIDE IN MY LOVE   238 22   TOGETHER BY THY LOVE IN THE COMMUNION OF THY HOLY   597 05
MY FATHER'S COMMANDMENTS, AND ABIDE IN HIS LOVE   238 24   CARE AND LOVE, FOR THIS LIFE AND THE LIFE TO COME   597 10
TO THEM THAT LOVE HIM   239 27   EVERMORE KINDLY AFFECTIONED WITH BROTHERLY LOVE   598 29
THAT YE LOVE ONE ANOTHER, AS I HAVE LOVED YOU   241 25   O LORD, FOR THE LOVE OF HIM, WHO FOR OUR SAKES BECAME 599 16
GREATER LOVE HATH NO MAN THAN THIS, THAT A MAN LAY 241 26   FOR THE LOVE OF THY DEAR SON, OUR SAVIOUR   600 12
UNTO THY CHURCH, TO LOVE THAT WORD WHICH HE BELIEVED, 249 17   KINDLE THEIR LOVE TOWARDS GOD   606 22
AND INORDINATE LOVE OF RICHES, AND TO FOLLOW THE SAME 250 23   ONLY A SIGN OF THE LOVE THAT CHRISTIANS OUGHT TO HAVE 608 34
IN THE GOSPEL THE LOVE AND HEALING POWER OF THY SON 253 18
THE LIKE POWER AND LOVE, TO THE HEALING OF OUR BODIES 253 19

LOVED

I HAVE LOVED THE HABITATION OF THY HOUSE,	021 14
SO GOD LOVED THE WORLD, THAT HE GAVE HIS	076 14
THOU HAST LOVED RIGHTEOUSNESS, AND HATED INIQUITY	097 10
WHOM JESUS LOVED FOLLOWING	102 04
CHRIST ALSO HATH LOVED US, AND HATH GIVEN HIMSELF FOR	128 31
THE FATHER, HAVING LOVED HIS OWN WHICH WERE IN THE	155 25
IN THE WORLD, HE LOVED THEM UNTO THE END	155 26
WHOM HE LOVED, HE SAITH UNTO HIS MOTHER, WOMAN,	160 20
WHOM JESUS LOVED, AND SAITH UNTO THEM, THEY HAVE	164 14
BECAUSE YE HAVE LOVED ME, AND HAVE BELIEVED THAT I	176 29
LOVETH ME SHALL BE LOVED OF MY FATHER, AND I WILL	181 20
IF YE LOVED ME, YE WOULD REJOICE, BECAUSE I SAID, I	182 03
GOD SO LOVED THE WORLD, THAT HE GAVE HIS	184 32
THE WORLD, AND MEN LOVED DARKNESS RATHER THAN LIGHT,	185 06
NOT THAT WE LOVED GOD, BUT THAT HE LOVED US,	189 14
BUT THAT HE LOVED US, AND SENT HIS SON TO BE THE	189 14
IF GOD SO LOVED US, WE OUGHT ALSO TO LOVE	189 16
BECAUSE HE FIRST LOVED US	189 31
AS THE FATHER HATH LOVED ME, SO HAVE I LOVED YOU	238 20
SO HAVE I LOVED YOU	238 21
AS I HAVE LOVED YOU	241 26
AND THEY LOVED NOT THEIR LIVES UNTO THE DEATH	252 15
HAVING LOVED THIS PRESENT WORLD, AND IS DEPARTED	253 32
AS CHRIST ALSO LOVED THE CHURCH, AND GAVE HIMSELF FOR	267 19
THROUGH HIM THAT LOVED US	331 09
8 LORD, I HAVE LOVED THE HABITATION OF THY HOUSE,	371 12
7 THOU HAST LOVED RIGHTEOUSNESS, AND HATED INIQUITY	396 29
EVEN THE EXCELLENCY OF JACOB, WHOM HE LOVED	398 28
4 THOU HAST LOVED UNRIGHTEOUSNESS MORE THAN GOODNESS,	404 24
5 THOU HAST LOVED TO SPEAK EVIL WORDS THAT MAY DO	404 26
EVEN THE HILL OF SION WHICH HE LOVED	439 15
HE LOVED NOT BLESSING, THEREFORE SHALL IT BE FAR FROM	481 03
WHICH I HAVE LOVED	493 03
LIFT UP UNTO THY COMMANDMENTS, WHICH I HAVE LOVED	493 05
AND LOVED THEM EXCEEDINGLY	501 15

LOVELY

O SING PRAISES UNTO HIS NAME, FOR IT IS LOVELY	510 08
TRUE AND PURE AND LOVELY AND OF GOOD REPORT,	596 27

LOVER

OF PEACE AND LOVER OF CONCORD, IN KNOWLEDGE OF WHOM	017 05

LOVERS

11 MY LOVERS AND MY NEIGHBOURS DID STAND LOOKING UPON	388 12
18 MY LOVERS AND FRIENDS HAST THOU PUT AWAY FROM ME,	449 33

LOVEST

SON OF JONAS, LOVEST THOU ME MORE THAN THESE	551 14
SON OF JONAS, LOVEST THOU ME	551 18
SON OF JONAS, LOVEST THOU ME	551 21
THE THIRD TIME, LOVEST THOU ME	551 22

LOVETH

FOR GOD LOVETH A CHEERFUL GIVER	072 19
FOR HE THAT LOVETH ANOTHER HATH FULFILLED THE LAW	090 24
FATHER HIMSELF LOVETH YOU, BECAUSE YE HAVE LOVED ME,	176 28
HE IT IS THAT LOVETH ME	181 19
AND HE THAT LOVETH ME SHALL BE LOVED OF MY FATHER,	181 20
HE THAT LOVETH ME NOT KEEPETH NOT MY SAYINGS	181 21
EVERY ONE THAT LOVETH IS BORN OF GOD, AND KNOWETH	189 09
HE THAT LOVETH NOT KNOWETH NOT GOD	189 10
FOR HE THAT LOVETH NOT HIS BROTHER WHOM HE HATH SEEN,	189 32
THAT HE WHO LOVETH GOD LOVE HIS BROTHER ALSO	189 35
HE THAT LOVETH NOT HIS BROTHER ABIDETH IN DEATH	191 11
AND WIDOW, AND LOVETH THE STRANGER, IN GIVING HIM	263 26
LOVETH HIS WIFE LOVETH HIMSELF	267 25
HE THAT LOVETH HIS WIFE LOVETH HIMSELF	267 25
FOR WHOM THE LORD LOVETH HE CHASTENETH, AND SCOURGETH	321 30
RIGHTEOUS LORD LOVETH RIGHTEOUSNESS	355 02
5 HE LOVETH RIGHTEOUSNESS AND JUDGMENT	378 27
28 FOR THE LORD LOVETH THE THING THAT IS RIGHT	386 19
THE LORD LOVETH THE GATES OF SION MORE THAN ALL THE	448 14
THE KING'S POWER LOVETH JUDGMENT	462 22
AND THY SERVANT LOVETH IT	499 20

LOVING

THAT WE, LOVING THEE ABOVE ALL THINGS, MAY	197 06
O LORD, WITH THY LOVING MERCY, AND SO RESTORE HIM TO	309 30
IN HIM, MOST LOVING FATHER, WHATSOEVER HATH BEEN	314 03
ME UP, AND THY LOVING CORRECTION SHALL MAKE ME GREAT	362 07
NOT KEPT BACK THY LOVING MERCY AND TRUTH *	391 06
O PREPARE THY LOVING MERCY AND FAITHFULNESS, THAT	413 20
TRULY GOD IS LOVING UNTO ISRAEL	428 10
HE IS MERCIFUL, LOVING, AND RIGHTEOUS	483 25
FOR THY LOVING MERCY, AND FOR THY TRUTH'S SAKE	485 12
LET THY LOVING MERCY COME ALSO UNTO ME, O LORD,	492 22
77 O LET THY LOVING MERCIES COME UNTO ME, THAT I MAY	495 09
UNTO THY LOVING MERCY, *	498 17
LET THY LOVING SPIRIT LEAD ME FORTH INTO THE LAND OF	519 13
9 THE LORD IS LOVING UNTO EVERY MAN	521 10
O MOST LOVING FATHER, WHO WILLEST US TO GIVE THANKS	596 03
WHOSE LOVING HAND HATH GIVEN US ALL THAT WE	599 19

LOVING-KINDNESS

AND LOVING-KINDNESS TO US, AND TO ALL MEN	019 16

LOVING-KINDNESS   CONTINUED

OF THY LOVING-KINDNESS EARLY IN THE MORNING, *	027 30
AND CROWNETH THEE WITH MERCY AND LOVING-KINDNESS	029 11
AND LOVING-KINDNESS TO US, AND TO ALL MEN	033 14
WHOSE LOVING-KINDNESS REACHETH UNTO THE WORLD'S END	038 15
SHOW THY LOVING-KINDNESS, THAT OUR LAND MAY GIVE HER	040 10
THY LOVING-KINDNESS FROM GENERATION TO GENERATION	051 27
THY LOVING-KINDNESS UNTO US, THAT OUR LAND MAY YIELD	052 13
THY LOVING-KINDNESS TO US, THAT OUR LAND MAY STILL	265 14
UP HIS LOVING-KINDNESS IN DISPLEASURE	311 17
OF THY LOVING-KINDNESS AND TRUTH	311 31
GOOD HIS LOVING-KINDNESS TOWARD ME	312 08
AND CROWNETH THEE WITH MERCY AND LOVING-KINDNESS	312 18
AND CROWNETH THEE WITH MERCY AND LOVING-KINDNESS	312 27
GRANT HIM AN ABIDING SENSE OF THY LOVING-KINDNESS	313 07
BY WHOSE LOVING-KINDNESS OUR SOULS AND BODIES ARE	322 06
THY LOVING-KINDNESS AND MERCY SHALL FOLLOW ME ALL THE	338 29
LOVING-KINDNESS, THOU THAT ART THE SAVIOUR OF THEM	358 31
SHOWETH LOVING-KINDNESS UNTO DAVID HIS ANOINTED,	363 08
THY LOVING-KINDNESS AND MERCY SHALL FOLLOW ME ALL THE	368 22
FOR THY LOVING-KINDNESS IS EVER BEFORE MINE EYES	371 02
THY LOVING-KINDNESS UNTO THEM THAT KNOW THEE, *	384 11
LET THY LOVING-KINDNESS AND THY TRUTH ALWAY PRESERVE	391 09
HIS LOVING-KINDNESS IN THE DAY-TIME	393 21
FOR THY LOVING-KINDNESS, O GOD, *	399 27
FOR THY LOVING-KINDNESS IS BETTER THAN THE LIFE	414 31
FOR THY LOVING-KINDNESS IS COMFORTABLE	423 04
UP HIS LOVING-KINDNESS IN DISPLEASURE	433 34
THE LORD SHALL SHOW LOVING-KINDNESS	446 31
THY LOVING-KINDNESS BE SHOWED IN THE GRAVE	449 18
OF THE LOVING-KINDNESS OF THE LORD	450 04
IN THY LOVING-KINDNESS THOU SHALT LIFT UP OUR HORNS	451 09
MY LOVING-KINDNESS WILL I NOT UTTERLY TAKE FROM HIM,	452 07
OF THY LOVING-KINDNESS EARLY IN THE MORNING, *	456 02
AND CROWNETH THEE WITH MERCY AND LOVING-KINDNESS	466 14
THE LOVING-KINDNESS OF THE LORD	478 33
88 O QUICKEN ME AFTER THY LOVING-KINDNESS	495 33
ACCORDING UNTO THY LOVING-KINDNESS	500 08
ACCORDING TO THY LOVING-KINDNESS	500 30
OF THY LOVING-KINDNESS AND TRUTH	513 31
GOOD HIS LOVING-KINDNESS TOWARD ME	514 14
HEAR THY LOVING-KINDNESS BETIMES IN THE MORNING	519 07

LOVING-KINDNESSES

THY LOVING-KINDNESSES, WHICH HAVE BEEN EVER OF OLD	369 29
OLD LOVING-KINDNESSES, *	453 05

LOVINGKINDNESSES

THE LOVINGKINDNESSES OF THE LORD, AND THE PRAISES OF	138 28
TO THE MULTITUDE OF HIS LOVINGKINDNESSES	138 32

LOVINGLY

BEING SO LOVINGLY CALLED AND BIDDEN BY GOD HIMSELF	088 16
HATH DEALT SO LOVINGLY WITH ME	356 09

LOW

CONDESCEND TO MEN OF LOW ESTATE	111 32
LET THE BROTHER OF LOW DEGREE REJOICE IN THAT HE IS	239 18
BUT THE RICH, IN THAT HE IS MADE LOW	239 19
AND EVERY MOUNTAIN AND HILL SHALL BE MADE LOW	242 23
NOR ABHORRED THE LOW ESTATE OF THE POOR	367 20
OUR SOUL IS BROUGHT LOW, EVEN UNTO THE DUST	396 10
2 HIGH AND LOW, RICH AND POOR, *	400 09
MINISHED AND BROUGHT LOW *	478 25
MY SOUL, AND KEEP IT LOW, LIKE AS A CHILD THAT IS	507 27
AND FALL LOW ON OUR KNEES BEFORE HIS FOOTSTOOL	508 17
FOR I AM BROUGHT VERY LOW	518 16

LOWER

FIRST INTO THE LOWER PARTS OF THE EARTH	237 16
5 THOU MADEST HIM LOWER THAN THE ANGELS, *	351 09
FIRST INTO THE LOWER PARTS OF THE EARTH	538 03

LOWEST

SHAME TO TAKE THE LOWEST PLACE	214 15
SIT DOWN IN THE LOWEST PLACE	214 16
LAID ME IN THE LOWEST PIT, *	449 07

LOWLINESS

THE LOWLINESS OF HIS HANDMAIDEN	026 13
WITH ALL LOWLINESS AND MEEKNESS, WITH LONG-SUFFERING,	213 20
MYSELF IN THAT LOWLINESS AND REVERENCE WHICH BECOMETH	288 30

LOWLY

WITH AN HUMBLE, LOWLY, PENITENT, AND OBEDIENT HEART	005 34
WITH AN HUMBLE, LOWLY, PENITENT, AND OBEDIENT HEART	023 09
FOR I AM MEEK AND LOWLY IN HEART	235 13
BY HIMSELF, BUT IS LOWLY IN HIS OWN EYES, *	357 13
YET HATH HE RESPECT UNTO THE LOWLY	514 09
TO ORDER MYSELF LOWLY AND REVERENTLY TO ALL MY	580 06

LOYALTY

ENDUE THEM WITH COURAGE AND LOYALTY	041 29
AND DECLARING MY LOYALTY AND DEVOTION TO CHRIST AS MY	291 25

LUCK

4 GOOD LUCK HAVE THOU WITH THINE HONOUR	396 22
WISHED YOU GOOD LUCK, WE THAT ARE OF THE HOUSE CF THE	489 20
WE WISH YOU GOOD LUCK IN THE NAME OF THE LORD	507 05

LUCRE

NOT GREEDY OF FILTHY LUCRE	531 28
NOT GREEDY OF FILTHY LUCRE	549 22

LUKE

THY SERVANT SAINT LUKE THE PHYSICIAN, TO SET FORTH IN	253 17
ONLY LUKE IS WITH ME	254 02
EVANGELIST SAINT LUKE, IN THE EIGHTH CHAPTER OF THE	296 11
OR ELSE SAINT LUKE XII	R 547 26
THE GOSPEL OF SAINT LLKE, THAT OUR SAVIOUR CHRIST	553 04

LUMP

NOT THAT A LITTLE LEAVEN LEAVENETH THE WHOLE LUMP	165 11
YE MAY BE A NEW LUMP, AS YE ARE UNLEAVENED	165 12

LURKETH

EVEN AS A LION LURKETH HE IN HIS DEN, *	353 23

LURKING

8 HE SITTETH LURKING IN THE THIEVISH CORNERS CF THE	353 20
PRIVILY IN HIS LURKING DENS DOTH HE MURDER THE	353 21
A LION'S WHELP LURKING IN SECRET PLACES	359 11

LUST

NOT IN THE LUST OF CONCUPISCENCE, EVEN AS THE	127 30
WE SHOULD NOT LUST AFTER EVIL THINGS, AS THEY ALSO	201 14
NOT FULFIL THE LUST OF THE FLESH	209 15
FOR HIS OWN LUST, DOTH PERSECUTE THE POOR	353 05
AND THEY DO EVEN WHAT THEY LUST	428 23
AND REQUIRED MEAT FOR THEIR LUST	436 05
THEY WERE NOT DISAPPOINTED OF THEIR LUST	436 31
ALSO SHALL SEE HIS LUST OF MINE ENEMIES, *	456 21
14 BUT LUST CAME UPON THEM IN THE WILDERNESS,	473 29
WHEREBY THE LUST OF THE FLESH, CALLED IN GREEK,	604 36
CONCUPISCENCE AND LUST HATH OF ITSELF THE NATURE OF	604 40

LUSTED

NOT LUST AFTER EVIL THINGS, AS THEY ALSO LUSTED	201 14

LUSTETH

FOR THE FLESH LUSTETH AGAINST THE SPIRIT, AND THE	209 15
MAN IS HE THAT LUSTETH TO LIVE, *	380 25
THAT THE FLESH LUSTETH ALWAYS CONTRARY TO THE SPIRIT	604 33

LUSTILY

SING PRAISES LUSTILY UNTO HIM WITH A GOOD COURAGE	378 23

LUSTS

TO FULFIL THE LUSTS THEREOF	091 09
AND WORLDLY LUSTS, WE SHOULD LIVE SOBERLY,	098 20
WORLDLY AND CARNAL LUSTS, WE MAY IN ALL THINGS OBEY	105 23
FROM FLESHLY LUSTS, WHICH WAR AGAINST THE SOUL	173 13
CRUCIFIED THE FLESH WITH THE AFFECTIONS AND LUSTS	209 29
WHICH IS CORRUPT ACCORDING TO THE DECEITFUL LUSTS	216 13
AND ALL THE SINFUL LUSTS OF THE FLESH	283 25
THROUGH THE LUSTS OF THE FLESH OR THE WILES OF SATAN,	317 20
THEIR OWN HEARTS' LUSTS, *	443 04
AND WORLDLY LUSTS, AND LIVE SOBERLY, RIGHTEOUSLY, AND	555 08
AND ALL THE SINFUL LUSTS OF THE FLESH	577 16

LUSTY

BUT ARE LUSTY AND STRONG	428 16
THEE YOUNG AND LUSTY AS AN EAGLE	466 16

LUTE

AN INSTRUMENT OF TEN STRINGS, AND UPON THE LUTE	027 32
UNTO HIM WITH THE LUTE, AND INSTRUMENT OF TEN	378 22
AWAKE, LUTE AND HARP	409 31
THE MERRY HARP WITH THE LUTE	442 15
AN INSTRUMENT OF TEN STRINGS, AND UPON THE LUTE	456 05
2 AWAKE, THOU LUTE AND HARP	479 07
SING PRAISES UNTO THEE UPON A TEN-STRINGED LUTE	520 09
PRAISE HIM UPON THE LUTE AND HARP	525 27

LYING

SWADDLING CLOTHES, LYING IN A MANGER	099 19
AND THE BABE LYING IN A MANGER	100 13
SAW THE LINEN CLOTHES LYING	164 20
HIS HEAD, NOT LYING WITH THE LINEN CLOTHES, BUT	164 23
PUTTING AWAY LYING, SPEAK EVERY MAN TRUTH WITH HIS	216 16
SICK OF THE PALSY, LYING ON A BED	217 02
EVIL SPEAKING, LYING, AND SLANDERING	289 06
THY SERVANT, HERE LYING IN GREAT WEAKNESS OF BODY	316 08
THEM THAT HOLD OF LYING VANITIES, *	376 02
20 LET THE LYING LIPS BE PUT TO SILENCE, *	376 33
FROM ME THE WAY OF LYING, *	491 25

LYING   CONTINUED

O LORD, FROM LYING LIPS, *	502 09
BEFELL ME BY THE LYING IN WAIT OF THE JEWS	550 10
EVIL SPEAKING, LYING, AND SLANDERING	580 10

MAD

AND THEY THAT ARE MAD UPON ME ARE SWORN TOGETHER	464 26

MADE

CHRIST HATH MADE US FREE,' THAT IN HIS WORSHIP	V 03
THIS IS THE DAY WHICH THE LORD HATH MADE	005 04
SHOULD BE MADE THEREIN, AS TO THOSE THAT ARE IN PLACE	V 18
TO BE MADE BY THE PRIEST ALONE, STANDING	R 007 03
THE WORD WAS MADE FLESH, AND DWELT AMONG US	R 008 31
SEA IS HIS, AND HE MADE IT	009 11
IT IS HE THAT HATH MADE US, AND NOT WE OURSELVES	015 08
NOT MADE	016 04
BY WHOM ALL THINGS WERE MADE	016 06
AND WAS MADE MAN	016 08
THE HOLY PLACES MADE WITH HANDS, WHICH ARE THE	022 22
TO BE MADE BY THE PRIEST ALONE, STANDING	R 024 07
THOU, LORD, HAST MADE ME GLAD THROUGH THY WCRKS	028 02
NOT MADE	030 09
BY WHOM ALL THINGS WERE MADE	030 11
AND WAS MADE MAN	030 13
O GOD, WHO HAST MADE OF ONE BLOOD ALL NATIONS OF MEN	038 05
BEING MADE STRONG BY THY HOLY SPIRIT, THEY MAY	043 11
PROSPER THE MEANS MADE USE OF FOR THEIR CURE	045 07
WE MAY BE MADE PARTAKERS WITH THEM OF THE	048 21
TO US WHO HAVE NOW MADE OUR PRAYERS AND SUPPLICATIONS	050 29
SIX DAYS THE LORD MADE HEAVEN AND EARTH, THE SEA,	068 30
NOT MADE	071 06
BY WHOM ALL THINGS WERE MADE	071 08
AND WAS MADE MAN	071 10
CONFESSION BE MADE, BY THE PRIEST AND ALL THOSE WHO	R 075 15
THE HOLY GHOST, WAS MADE VERY MAN, OF THE SUBSTANCE	077 16
MYSTERY OF THE WORD MADE FLESH, THOU HAST CAUSED A	077 29
WHO MADE THERE (BY HIS ONE OBLATION OF HIMSELF ONCE	080 09
AND MADE ONE BODY WITH HIM, THAT HE MAY	081 27
BODIES MAY BE MADE CLEAN BY HIS BODY, AND OUR SOULS	082 20
OUR SINS, AND ARE MADE PARTAKERS OF THE KINGDOM CF	086 34
BUT YE HAVE MADE IT A DEN OF THIEVES	092 03
THE PROMISES MADE UNTO THE FATHERS	092 25
YOUR REQUESTS BE MADE KNOWN UNTO GOD	095 17
AND MADE THY CHILDREN BY ADOPTION AND	096 16
BY WHOM ALSO HE MADE THE WORLDS	096 25
BEING MADE SO MUCH BETTER THAN THE ANGELS, AS HE HATH	096 30
ALL THINGS WERE MADE BY HIM	097 22
WITHOUT HIM WAS NOT ANY THING MADE THAT WAS MADE	097 23
WAS NOT ANY THING MADE THAT WAS MADE	097 23
AND THE WORLD WAS MADE BY HIM, AND THE WORLD KNEW HIM	097 31
AND THE WORD WAS MADE FLESH, AND DWELT AMONG US, (AND	098 04
TAXING WAS FIRST MADE WHEN CYRENIUS WAS GOVERNOR OF	098 30
AND MADE THY CHILDREN BY ADOPTION AND	104 08
SENT FORTH HIS SON, MADE OF A WOMAN, MADE UNDER THE	104 20
MADE OF A WOMAN, MADE UNDER THE LAW, TO REDEEM THEM	104 20
WHICH THE LORD HATH MADE KNOWN UNTO US	106 10
HAD SEEN IT, THEY MADE KNOWN ABROAD THE SAYING WHICH	106 13
BY REVELATION HE MADE KNOWN UNTO ME THE MYSTERY	108 09
OTHER AGES WAS NOT MADE KNOWN UNTO THE SONS OF MEN,	108 12
WHEREOF I WAS MADE A MINISTER, ACCORDING TO THE GIFT	108 16
THE WATER THAT WAS MADE WINE, AND KNEW NOT WHENCE IT	113 24
WE MAY BE MADE LIKE UNTO HIM IN HIS ETERNAL	117 09
AND THOU HAST MADE THEM EQUAL UNTO US, WHICH	120 05
THAT THOU HAST MADE, AND DOST FORGIVE THE SINS OF ALL	124 12
THESE STONES BE MADE BREAD	126 27
HER DAUGHTER WAS MADE WHOLE FROM THAT VERY HOUR	128 21
ARE REPROVED ARE MADE MANIFEST BY THE LIGHT	129 19
NOT MADE WITH HANDS, THAT IS TO SAY,	132 25
AND ALSO BE MADE PARTAKERS OF HIS RESURRECTICN	134 10
BUT MADE HIMSELF OF NO REPUTATION, AND TOOK UPCN HIM	134 18
A SERVANT, AND WAS MADE IN THE LIKENESS OF MEN	134 19
RATHER A TUMULT WAS MADE, HE TOOK WATER, AND WASHED	136 09
WHY HAST THOU MADE US TO ERR FROM THY WAYS, AND	139 24
WHY WAS THIS WASTE OF THE OINTMENT MADE	140 07
AND THEY MADE READY THE PASSOVER	140 33
THIS TEMPLE THAT IS MADE WITH HANDS, AND WITHIN THREE	143 07
WILL BUILD ANOTHER MADE WITHOUT HANDS	143 08
WITH THEM THAT HAD MADE INSURRECTION WITH HIM,	145 15
THE HOLY PLACES MADE WITH HANDS, WHICH ARE THE	147 30
AND THEY MADE READY THE PASSOVER	148 33
AND HEROD WERE MADE FRIENDS TOGETHER	153 19
A CERTAIN SEDITION MADE IN THE CITY, AND FOR MURDER,	153 31
WHO HAST MADE ALL MEN, AND HATEST NOTHING THAT	157 04
THAT THOU HAST MADE, NOR DESIREST THE DEATH OF A	157 05
THAT THEY MAY BE MADE ONE FLOCK UNDER ONE SHEPHERD,	157 11
A REMEMBRANCE AGAIN MADE OF SINS EVERY YEAR	157 22
TILL HIS ENEMIES BE MADE HIS FOOTSTOOL	158 08
TO DIE, BECAUSE HE MADE HIMSELF THE SON OF GOD	159 10
HIS GARMENTS, AND MADE FOUR PARTS, TO EVERY SOLDIER	160 10
AND POWERS BEING MADE SUBJECT UNTO HIM	162 03
THE SEPULCHRE BE MADE SURE UNTIL THE THIRD DAY, LEST	162 19
SO THEY WENT, AND MADE THE SEPULCHRE SURE, SEALING	162 24
CHRIST SHALL ALL BE MADE ALIVE	163 16
ALSO OF OUR COMPANY MADE US ASTONISHED, WHICH WERE	167 23
AND HE MADE AS THOUGH HE WOULD HAVE GONE FURTHER	168 02
PROMISE WHICH WAS MADE UNTO THE FATHERS, GOD HATH	169 06
NOT GOD HATH MADE HIM A LIAR	171 08
TREATISE HAVE I MADE, O THEOPHILUS, OF ALL THAT JESUS	177 22
AND HAVE BEEN ALL MADE TO DRINK INTO ONE SPIRIT	183 06
HIS DEEDS MAY BE MADE MANIFEST, THAT THEY ARE WRCUGHT	185 10
HEREIN IS OUR LOVE MADE PERFECT, THAT WE MAY HAVE	189 26
THAT FEARETH IS NOT MADE PERFECT IN LOVE	189 30

MADE   CONTINUED

A CERTAIN MAN MADE A GREAT SUPPER, AND BADE MANY   192 03
THE CREATURE WAS MADE SUBJECT TO VANITY, NOT   194 15
BUT NOW BEING MADE FREE FROM SIN, AND BECOME SERVANTS   199 02
BUT YE HAVE MADE IT A DEN OF THIEVES   204 18
AND BE MADE PARTAKERS OF THY HEAVENLY   204 26
WHO ALSO HATH MADE US ABLE MINISTERS OF THE NEW   206 16
TO ABRAHAM AND HIS SEED WERE THE PROMISES MADE   207 19
THE SEED SHOULD COME TO WHOM THE PROMISE WAS MADE   207 29
THY FAITH HATH MADE THEE WHOLE   210 11
CERTAIN KING, WHICH MADE A MARRIAGE FOR HIS SON,   218 04
BUT THEY MADE LIGHT OF IT, AND WENT THEIR WAYS, ONE   218 10
AND ALL THAT HE HAD, AND PAYMENT TO BE MADE   221 19
WHICH HATH MADE US MEET TO BE PARTAKERS OF   224 09
THY FAITH HATH MADE THEE WHOLE   224 22
AND THE WOMAN WAS MADE WHOLE FROM THAT HOUR   224 23
MOUTH CONFESSION IS MADE UNTO SALVATION   226 30
I WAS MADE MANIFEST UNTO THEM THAT ASKED NOT AFTER   227 20
IN THAT HE IS MADE LOW   239 19
OF MY FATHER I HAVE MADE KNOWN UNTO YOU   241 31
AND HILL SHALL BE MADE LOW   242 23
CROOKED SHALL BE MADE STRAIGHT, AND THE ROUGH PLACES   242 24
AND THEY MADE SIGNS TO HIS FATHER, HOW HE WOULD HAVE   243 22
BUT PRAYER WAS MADE WITHOUT CEASING OF THE CHURCH   245 08
WHEN WE MADE KNOWN UNTO YOU THE POWER AND   248 14
THAT WE MAY BE MADE AN HOLY TEMPLE ACCEPTABLE UNTO   254 31
THEIR ROBES, AND MADE THEM WHITE IN THE BLOOD OF THE   257 08
BUT YE HAVE MADE IT A DEN OF THIEVES   260 07
FOR HE HATH MADE FAST THE BARS OF THY GATES, *   265 02
AT THE BEGINNING MADE THEM MALE AND FEMALE, AND SAID,   268 06
THAT HE WHICH MADE THEM AT THE BEGINNING MADE   268 06
HOLY CHURCH, AND BE MADE A LIVING MEMBER OF THE SAME   274 06
BORN AGAIN, AND BE MADE AN HEIR OF EVERLASTING   276 13
NAME OF THIS CHILD, MADE THESE PROMISES, WILT THOU   277 08
WHEREIN I WAS MADE A MEMBER OF CHRIST, THE CHILD OF   283 19
WHO HATH MADE ME, AND ALL THE WORLD   284 30
SIX DAYS THE LORD MADE HEAVEN AND EARTH, THE SEA,   286 30
THAT WE MAY BE MADE AN HOLY TEMPLE ACCEPTABLE UNTO   290 23
WHEN WERE YOU MADE A MEMBER OF THE CHURCH   290 28
I WAS MADE A MEMBER OF THE CHURCH WHEN I WAS   290 29
WHEREBY WE ARE MADE THE CHILDREN OF GRACE   292 06
AND VOW THAT YE MADE, OR THAT WAS MADE IN YOUR NAME,   296 24
MADE, OR THAT WAS MADE IN YOUR NAME, AT YOUR BAPTISM   296 24
WHO HATH MADE HEAVEN AND EARTH   297 08
BETWIXT THEM MADE, (WHEREOF THIS RING GIVEN AND   303 08
WHICH SHALL BE MADE USE OF FOR HIS CURE   315 29
SPIRITS OF JUST MEN MADE PERFECT, AFTER THEY ARE   317 12
BEHOLD, THOU HAST MADE MY DAYS AS IT WERE A SPAN   324 22
AND THE WORLD WERE MADE, *   325 16
WHO HATH MADE HEAVEN AND EARTH   327 21
CHRIST SHALL ALL BE MADE ALIVE   328 24
FIRST MAN ADAM WAS MADE A LIVING SOUL   329 24
THE LAST ADAM WAS MADE A QUICKENING SPIRIT   329 25
WHILE THE BODY IS MADE READY TO BE LAID INTO THE   R 332 16
BE CHANGED, AND MADE LIKE UNTO HIS OWN GLORIOUS BODY   333 21
BE CHANGED, AND MADE LIKE UNTO HIS GLORIOUS BODY   337 15
WHO HATH MADE HEAVEN AND EARTH   339 05
BENT HIS BOW, AND MADE IT READY   350 18
DESTRUCTION THAT HE MADE FOR OTHER   350 24
HEATHEN ARE SUNK DOWN IN THE PIT THAT THEY MADE   352 02
THE UNGODLY HATH MADE BOAST OF HIS OWN HEART'S   353 08
AS FOR YOU, YE HAVE MADE A MOCK AT THE COUNSEL OF THE   356 28
OF UNGODLINESS MADE ME AFRAID   359 32
12 HE MADE DARKNESS HIS SECRET PLACE, *   360 19
41 THOU HAST MADE MINE ENEMIES ALSO TO TURN THEIR   362 18
THAT SHALL BE BORN, WHOM THE LORD HATH MADE   368 08
AND NOT MADE MY FOES TO TRIUMPH OVER ME   374 25
THY GOODNESS, HAST MADE MY HILL SO STRONG   375 05
6 BY THE WORD OF THE LORD WERE THE HEAVENS MADE   378 29
A CAUSE HAVE THEY MADE A PIT FOR MY SOUL   382 03
6 BEHOLD, THOU HAST MADE MY DAYS AS IT WERE A SPAN   389 17
THE NATIONS, AND MADE THY PEOPLE TO FLOURISH   394 26
THINGS WHICH I HAVE MADE CONCERNING THE KING   396 16
WHEREBY THEY HAVE MADE THEE GLAD   396 33
THOUGH ONE BE MADE RICH, *   401 07
THOSE THAT HAVE MADE A COVENANT WITH ME WITH   401 31
EVER YOUR POTS BE MADE HOT WITH THORNS, *   410 26
LET THEIR TABLE BE MADE A SNARE TO TAKE THEMSELVES   423 18
PRAYER SHALL BE MADE EVER UNTO HIM, AND DAILY SHALL   427 27
THOU HAST MADE SUMMER AND WINTER   431 11
5 HE MADE A COVENANT WITH JACOB, AND GAVE ISRAEL A   435 04
HE MADE THE WATERS TO STAND ON AN HEAP   435 27
51 HE MADE A WAY TO HIS INDIGNATION, AND SPARED NOT   438 09
AN HERITAGE, AND MADE THE TRIBES OF ISRAEL TO DWELL   438 23
WHICH HE HATH MADE CONTINUALLY   439 17
THEY DEFILED, AND MADE JERUSALEM AN HEAP OF STONES   439 30
6 THOU HAST MADE US A VERY STRIFE UNTO OUR   441 14
4 FOR THIS WAS MADE A STATUTE FOR ISRAEL, *   442 18
WHOM THOU HAST MADE SHALL COME AND WORSHIP THEE, O   447 21
AND MADE ME TO BE ABHORRED OF THEM   449 12
3 I HAVE MADE A COVENANT WITH MY CHOSEN   450 09
13 THOU HAST MADE THE NORTH AND THE SOUTH   450 31
AND MADE ALL HIS ADVERSARIES TO REJOICE   452 25
WHEREFORE HAST THOU MADE ALL MEN FOR NOUGHT   452 35
AND THE WORLD WERE MADE, *   453 21
THOU, LORD, HAST MADE ME GLAD THROUGH THY WORKS   456 06
2 HE MADE THE ROUND WORLD SO SURE, *   457 07
OR HE THAT MADE THE EYE, SHALL HE NOT SEE   458 05
SEA IS HIS, AND HE MADE IT   459 13
IT IS THE LORD THAT MADE THE HEAVENS   460 09
IT IS HE WHO HATH MADE THE ROUND WORLD SO FAST THAT   460 19
IT IS HE THAT HATH MADE US, AND NOT WE OURSELVES   463 09
14 FOR HE KNOWETH WHEREOF WE ARE MADE   467 02
IN WISDOM HAST THOU MADE THEM ALL   469 09
WHOM THOU HAST MADE TO TAKE HIS PASTIME THEREIN   469 13

MADE   CONTINUED

LETTEST THY BREATH GO FORTH, THEY SHALL BE MADE   469 22
THAT HE MADE TO A THOUSAND GENERATIONS   470 19
COVENANT THAT HE MADE WITH ABRAHAM   470 20
21 HE MADE HIM LORD ALSO OF HIS HOUSE, *   471 14
AND MADE THEM STRONGER THAN THEIR ENEMIES   471 20
19 THEY MADE A CALF IN HOREB, *   474 06
HE MADE ALL THOSE THAT LED THEM AWAY CAPTIVE TO   475 09
WHO MADE HEAVEN AND EARTH   486 08
24 THIS IS THE DAY WHICH THE LORD HATH MADE   489 16
O THAT MY WAYS WERE MADE SO DIRECT, *   490 08
58 I MADE MY HUMBLE PETITION IN THY PRESENCE WITH MY   493 26
60 I MADE HASTE, AND PROLONGED NOT THE TIME, *   493 31
THY HANDS HAVE MADE ME AND FASHIONED ME   494 28
87 THEY HAD ALMOST MADE AN END OF ME UPON EARTH   495 31
HAST MADE ME WISER THAN MINE ENEMIES   496 22
WHO HATH MADE HEAVEN AND EARTH   502 25
WHO HATH MADE HEAVEN AND EARTH   504 21
AND MADE LONG FURROWS   506 25
11 THE LORD HATH MADE A FAITHFUL OATH UNTO DAVID,   508 25
4 THE LORD THAT MADE HEAVEN AND EARTH *   509 29
EXCELLENT WISDOM MADE THE HEAVENS   511 24
7 WHO HATH MADE GREAT LIGHTS   511 28
14 AND MADE ISRAEL TO GO THROUGH THE MIDST OF IT   512 10
FOR I AM FEARFULLY AND WONDERFULLY MADE   515 16
THOUGH I BE MADE SECRETLY, AND FASHIONED BENEATH IN   515 18
5 WHO MADE HEAVEN AND EARTH, THE SEA, AND ALL THAT   522 12
13 FOR HE HATH MADE FAST THE BARS OF THY GATES,   523 21
FOR HE SPAKE THE WORD, AND THEY WERE MADE   524 14
6 HE HATH MADE THEM FAST FOR EVER AND EVER   524 16
REJOICE IN HIM THAT MADE HIM, *   525 05
PROVISION IS SO MADE, TO SEARCH FOR THE SICK, POOR,   533 19
OF EVERY ONE TO BE MADE DEACON, HUMBLY KNEELING   R 534 03
WHICH WAS NOW MADE TO YOU, AND IN THE HOLY LESSONS   539 25
AND FILL THE HEARTS WHICH THOU HAST MADE   544 20
WHO, AFTER HE HAD MADE PERFECT OUR REDEMPTION BY HIS   545 16
THEY THAT ARE TO BE MADE DEACONS, SHALL BE EXAMINED   R 547 23
THEY THAT ARE TO BE MADE PRIESTS SHALL LIKEWISE BE   R 547 27
THE HOLY GHOST HATH MADE YOU OVERSEERS, TO FEED THE   550 28
AND FILL THE HEARTS WHICH THOU HAST MADE   556 28
AFTER THAT HE HAD MADE PERFECT OUR REDEMPTION BY HIS   557 23
WALLS OF TEMPLES MADE WITH HANDS   564 29
BETWIXT THEM MADE, AND MAY REMAIN IN PERFECT LOVE   566 11
AND WHEN HE HAD MADE A SCOURGE OF SMALL CORDS,   567 28
WHEREIN I WAS MADE A MEMBER OF CHRIST, THE CHILD OF   577 10
WHO HATH MADE ME, AND ALL THE WORLD   578 12
SIX DAYS THE LORD MADE HEAVEN AND EARTH, THE SEA, AND   579 10
WE ARE HEREBY MADE THE CHILDREN OF GRACE   581 26
THE PROMISES OF GOD MADE TO THEM IN THAT SACRAMENT   581 30
ALL THINGS WERE MADE, THY SON, JESUS CHRIST OUR LORD   596 21
TO BLESS THE MEANS MADE USE OF FOR HIS CURE   597 23
HAVE BEEN MADE ONE FLESH   598 26
FATHERLY GOODNESS BE UPON ALL THAT THOU HAST MADE   599 06
OF OUR NATURE WAS MADE LIKE UNTO US IN ALL THINGS,   605 31
OF HIMSELF ONCE MADE, SHOULD TAKE AWAY THE SINS OF   605 34
AS VESSELS MADE TO HONOUR   606 10
THEY BE MADE LIKE   606 13
THEY BE MADE SONS OF GOD BY ADOPTION   606 13
THAT INQUIRY BE MADE OF EVIL MINISTERS, AND THAT THEY   608 20
OF CHRIST ONCE MADE IS THAT PERFECT REDEMPTION,   609 14
MAY BE CONVENIENTLY MADE, FOR THE CLEARING OF THEM,   R 610 28

MADEST

AND MADEST INFANTS TO GLORIFY THEE BY THEIR   102 22
ALMIGHTY GOD, WHO MADEST THY BLESSED SON TO BE   105 19
5 THOU MADEST HIM LOWER THAN THE ANGELS, *   351 09
9 THOU MADEST ROOM FOR IT   441 20
BRANCH THAT THOU MADEST SO STRONG FOR THYSELF   441 33
OF MAN, WHOM THOU MADEST SO STRONG FOR THINE OWN   442 05

MADLY

5 I SAID UNTO THE FOOLS, DEAL NOT SO MADLY   432 06

MADNESS

AND THE MADNESS OF THE PEOPLES   416 28

MAGDALENE

MARY THE WIFE OF CLEOPHAS, AND MARY MAGDALENE   160 19
THERE WAS MARY MAGDALENE, AND THE OTHER MARY, SITTING   162 14
COMETH MARY MAGDALENE EARLY, WHEN IT WAS YET DARK,   164 10
WAS PAST, MARY MAGDALENE, AND MARY THE MOTHER OF   165 18

MAGISTRATE

OF THE MAGISTRATE, AND WOUNDETH THE CONSCIENCES OF   609 40
OF THE CIVIL MAGISTRATE EXTENDETH TO ALL MEN,   610 38
WHEN THE MAGISTRATE REQUIRETH, IN A CAUSE OF FAITH   611 08

MAGISTRATES

AND THE MAGISTRATES IN ALL THIS LAND   036 02
RULERS AND MAGISTRATES, GIVING THEM GRACE TO EXECUTE   055 27

MAGNIFICAT

END OF THE MAGNIFICAT, CANTATE DOMINO, BONUM EST   R 025 17
HYMN CALLED MAGNIFICAT, AS FOLLOWETH   R 026 06

MAGNIFIED

IS MIGHTY HATH MAGNIFIED ME   026 16

MAGNIFIED   CONTINUED

BUT THE PEOPLE MAGNIFIED THEM   249 24
FOR THOU HAST MAGNIFIED THY NAME, AND THY WORD,   311 32
FOR THOU HAST MAGNIFIED THY NAME, AND THY WORD,   513 32

MAGNIFY

DAY BY DAY WE MAGNIFY THEE   011 06
PRAISE HIM, AND MAGNIFY HIM FOR EVER   011 32
PRAISE HIM, AND MAGNIFY HIM FOR EVER   012 03
PRAISE HIM, AND MAGNIFY HIM FOR EVER   012 05
PRAISE HIM, AND MAGNIFY HIM FOR EVER   012 07
PRAISE HIM, AND MAGNIFY HIM FOR EVER   012 09
PRAISE HIM, AND MAGNIFY HIM FOR EVER   012 11
PRAISE HIM, AND MAGNIFY HIM FOR EVER   012 13
PRAISE HIM, AND MAGNIFY HIM FOR EVER   012 15
PRAISE HIM, AND MAGNIFY HIM FOR EVER   012 17
PRAISE HIM, AND MAGNIFY HIM FOR EVER   012 19
PRAISE HIM, AND MAGNIFY HIM FOR EVER   012 21
PRAISE HIM, AND MAGNIFY HIM FOR EVER   012 23
PRAISE HIM, AND MAGNIFY HIM FOR EVER   012 25
PRAISE HIM, AND MAGNIFY HIM FOR EVER   012 27
PRAISE HIM, AND MAGNIFY HIM FOR EVER   012 29
PRAISE HIM, AND MAGNIFY HIM FOR EVER   012 31
PRAISE HIM, AND MAGNIFY HIM FOR EVER   012 33
PRAISE HIM, AND MAGNIFY HIM FOR EVER   013 03
PRAISE HIM, AND MAGNIFY HIM FOR EVER   013 05
PRAISE HIM, AND MAGNIFY HIM FOR EVER   013 07
PRAISE HIM, AND MAGNIFY HIM FOR EVER   013 08
PRAISE HIM, AND MAGNIFY HIM FOR EVER   013 11
PRAISE HIM, AND MAGNIFY HIM FOR EVER   013 13
PRAISE HIM, AND MAGNIFY HIM FOR EVER   013 15
PRAISE HIM, AND MAGNIFY HIM FOR EVER   013 17
PRAISE HIM, AND MAGNIFY HIM FOR EVER   013 19
PRAISE HIM, AND MAGNIFY HIM FOR EVER   013 20
PRAISE HIM, AND MAGNIFY HIM FOR EVER   013 23
PRAISE HIM, AND MAGNIFY HIM FOR EVER   013 25
PRAISE HIM, AND MAGNIFY HIM FOR EVER   013 27
PRAISE HIM, AND MAGNIFY HIM FOR EVER   013 29
PRAISE HIM, AND MAGNIFY HIM FOR EVER   013 31
MY SOUL DOTH MAGNIFY THE LORD, *   026 11
AND WORTHILY MAGNIFY THY HOLY NAME   067 20
WE LAUD AND MAGNIFY THY GLORIOUS NAME   077 05
WE LAUD AND MAGNIFY THY GLORIOUS NAME   079 29
AND MAGNIFY GOD   184 25
I PRAISE AND MAGNIFY, SAYING,   285 04
MAGNIFY HIM, ALL YE OF THE SEED OF JACOB   367 18
I WILL MAGNIFY THEE, O LORD   374 24
AND LET US MAGNIFY HIS NAME TOGETHER   380 07
THAT DID MAGNIFY HIMSELF AGAINST ME   407 13
AS I LIVE WILL I MAGNIFY THEE IN THIS MANNER, *   414 33
MAGNIFY HIM THAT RIDETH UPON THE HEAVENS   419 17
AND MAGNIFY IT WITH THANKSGIVING   424 05
5 O MAGNIFY THE LORD OUR GOD, AND FALL DOWN BEFORE   462 25
9 O MAGNIFY THE LORD OUR GOD, AND WORSHIP HIM UPON   463 02
I WILL MAGNIFY THEE, O GOD, MY KING   520 27
WE BLESS AND MAGNIFY THY GLORIOUS NAME   587 24

MAID

NOR HIS MAID, NOR HIS OX, NOR HIS ASS,   069 21
AND A MAID SAW HIM AGAIN, AND BEGAN TO SAY TO THEM   143 28
BUT A CERTAIN MAID BEHELD HIM AS HE SAT BY THE FIRE,   151 14
FOR THE MAID IS NOT DEAD, BUT SLEEPETH   224 26
THE HAND, AND THE MAID AROSE   224 29
NOR HIS MAID, NOR HIS OX, NOR HIS ASS,   287 21
NOR HIS MAID, NOR HIS OX, NOR HIS ASS,   579 22

MAID-SERVANT

AND THY MAID-SERVANT, THY CATTLE, AND THE STRANGER   068 28
AND THY MAID-SERVANT, THY CATTLE, AND THE STRANGER   286 28
AND THY MAID-SERVANT, THY CATTLE, AND THE STRANGER   579 08

MAIDEN

AS THE EYES OF A MAIDEN UNTO THE HAND OF HER   503 30

MAIDENS

AND THEIR MAIDENS WERE NOT GIVEN IN MARRIAGE   439 05
12 YOUNG MEN AND MAIDENS, OLD MEN AND CHILDREN,   524 27

MAIDS

COMETH ONE OF THE MAIDS OF THE HIGH PRIEST   143 23

MAIMED

THE POOR, AND THE MAIMED, AND THE HALT, AND THE   192 15
INTO LIFE HALT OR MAIMED, RATHER THAN HAVING TWO   253 05

MAIN

YET SO AS THAT THE MAIN BODY AND ESSENTIAL PARTS OF   V 30

MAINTAIN

AND TO MAINTAIN TRUTH   055 28
AND TO MAINTAIN TRUTH   VI 20
HAVE GRACE TO MAINTAIN THESE LIBERTIES IN   263 20
THOU SHALT MAINTAIN MY LOT   357 32
ARISE, O GOD, MAINTAIN THINE OWN CAUSE   431 22
AND MAINTAIN THE CAUSE OF THE HELPLESS   517 03
WILL YOU MAINTAIN AND SET FORWARDS, AS MUCH AS LIETH   543 06

MAINTAIN   CONTINUED

AND TO TEACH OR MAINTAIN NOTHING, AS NECESSARY TO   554 24
WILL YOU MAINTAIN AND SET FORWARD, AS MUCH AS SHALL   555 14
AND VICE, AND MAINTAIN THY TRUE RELIGION AND VIRTUE   590 29

MAINTAINED

FOR THOU HAST MAINTAINED MY RIGHT AND MY CAUSE   351 28

MAINTENANCE

IT IN THE MAINTENANCE OF JUSTICE AMONG MEN AND   044 13
ALL WHOSE HANDS ARE OPEN FOR THEIR MAINTENANCE   047 35
AND TO THE MAINTENANCE OF THY TRUE RELIGION, AND   074 19

MAJESTIC

AFFECTING AND MAJESTIC MANNER, FOR THE SAKE OF JESUS   VI 42

MAJESTY

ARE FULL OF THE MAJESTY OF THY GLORY   010 15
THE FATHER, OF AN INFINITE MAJESTY   010 21
BLESSED ART THOU FOR THE NAME OF THY MAJESTY   011 18
AND THE VICTORY, AND THE MAJESTY   073 19
WHICH WE OFFER UNTO THY DIVINE MAJESTY   074 11
THY DIVINE MAJESTY, PROVOKING MOST JUSTLY THY WRATH   075 21
THY DIVINE MAJESTY, WITH THESE THY HOLY GIFTS, WHICH   080 40
IN HIS GLORIOUS MAJESTY TO JUDGE BOTH THE QUICK AND   090 16
HAND OF THE MAJESTY ON HIGH   096 29
HAND OF THY MAJESTY, TO BE OUR DEFENCE AGAINST ALL   128 27
OF THE DIVINE MAJESTY TO WORSHIP THE UNITY   186 26
BESEECH THY MAJESTY, THAT, AS THY ONLY-BEGOTTEN SON   231 29
BUT WERE EYEWITNESSES OF HIS MAJESTY   248 16
ARE GOOD, AND ACCEPTABLE UNTO THY DIVINE MAJESTY   298 15
IN GLORIOUS MAJESTY TO JUDGE THE WORLD, THE EARTH AND   333 19
IN GLORIOUS MAJESTY TO JUDGE THE WORLD, THE SEA SHALL   337 13
THE NAME OF HIS MAJESTY FOR EVER   428 04
ALL THE EARTH SHALL BE FILLED WITH HIS MAJESTY   428 05
AND THE GLORIOUS MAJESTY OF THE LORD OUR GOD BE UPON   454 24
AND ALL THE KINGS OF THE EARTH THY MAJESTY   465 10
ART CLOTHED WITH MAJESTY AND HONOUR   467 26
31 THE GLORIOUS MAJESTY OF THE LORD SHALL ENDURE FOR   469 23
FOR HIS GLORIOUS MAJESTY, AND AFFECT THEIR HEARTS   564 18
IN POWER, AND OF MAJESTY INCOMPREHENSIBLE, WHOM THE   564 27
TO THY GLORIOUS MAJESTY THE SACRIFICES OF PRAYER AND   565 09
ONE SUBSTANCE, MAJESTY, AND GLORY, WITH THE FATHER   603 27

MAKE

WAY OF THE LORD, MAKE STRAIGHT IN THE DESERT A   004 06
YIELDED TO MAKE SUCH ALTERATIONS IN SOME   V 29
MAKE THEM TO BE NUMBERED WITH THY SAINTS, IN GLORY   011 02
O GOD, MAKE CLEAN OUR HEARTS WITHIN US   016 31
AND MAKE THEM EVER MINDFUL OF THEIR CALLING TO SERVE   018 13
BE PLEASED TO MAKE THY WAYS KNOWN UNTO THEM, THY   018 28
WITH ONE ACCORD TO MAKE OUR COMMON SUPPLICATIONS   020 04
WHEREOF SHALL MAKE GLAD THE CITY OF GOD, THE HOLY   022 27
LET THE SEA MAKE A NOISE, AND ALL THAT THEREIN IS   027 19
AND MAKE THY CHOSEN PEOPLE JOYFUL   031 07
O GOD, MAKE CLEAN OUR HEARTS WITHIN US   031 13
BE PLEASED TO MAKE THY WAYS KNOWN UNTO THEM, THY   032 28
WITH ONE ACCORD TO MAKE OUR COMMON SUPPLICATIONS   034 04
AND EVER LIVETH TO MAKE INTERCESSION FOR US, JESUS   037 22
ABUNDANTLY TO MAKE KNOWN TO ALL MEN THY BLESSED GIFT   038 21
AND WISELY MAKE CHOICE OF FIT PERSONS, TO SERVE IN   038 30
TO HEAR US, WHO NOW MAKE OUR PRAYERS AND   040 06
THY MERCY, AND DOST MAKE THEE LIVING MEMBERS OF THY   043 08
MAKE READY, WE BESEECH THEE, THE HEARTS AND MINDS OF   043 20
AND TO MAKE NO PEACE WITH OPPRESSION   044 11
HATH TAUGHT US, WE MAKE BOLD TO SAY,   048 25
PRAYERS WHICH WE MAKE BEFORE THEE IN ALL OUR TROUBLES   058 17
CARE HEREIN WAS TO MAKE THEM CONFORMABLE TO WHAT   VI 18
AND SHALT MAKE ME TO UNDERSTAND WISDOM SECRETLY   060 23
THOU SHALT MAKE ME HEAR OF JOY AND GLADNESS, *   060 26
MAKE ME A CLEAN HEART, O GOD, *   060 30
OUR FAULTS, AND SO MAKE HASTE TO HELP US IN THIS   062 24
THE LORD MAKE HIS FACE TO SHINE UPON US, AND BE   063 15
THOU SHALT NOT MAKE TO THYSELF ANY GRAVEN IMAGE,   068 08
HAST TAUGHT US TO MAKE PRAYERS, AND SUPPLICATIONS,   074 07
AND MAKE YOUR HUMBLE CONFESSION TO ALMIGHTY GOD,   075 13
SPOT OF SIN, TO MAKE US CLEAN FROM ALL SIN   077 18
DO CELEBRATE AND MAKE HERE BEFORE THY DIVINE MAJESTY,   080 39
THE MEMORIAL THY SON HATH COMMANDED US TO MAKE   081 02
AGAINST HIM, AND TO MAKE AMENDS FOR THAT WHEREIN HE   R 085 13
THAT HE MIGHT MAKE US THE CHILDREN OF GOD, AND EXALT   086 10
BEING READY TO MAKE RESTITUTION AND SATISFACTION,   087 24
SHALL NOT CEASE TO MAKE OUR HUMBLE PETITIONS UNTO   089 21
JESUS CHRIST, AND MAKE NOT PROVISION FOR THE FLESH,   091 08
SO PREPARE AND MAKE READY THY WAY, BY TURNING THE   093 27
AND WILL MAKE MANIFEST THE COUNSELS OF THE   094 12
IN THE WILDERNESS, MAKE STRAIGHT THE WAY OF THE LORD,   095 29
HAVE NOT SINNED, WE MAKE HIM A LIAR, AND HIS WORD IS   101 32
AND NOT WILLING TO MAKE HER A PUBLICK EXAMPLE,   104 31
AND TO MAKE ALL MEN SEE WHAT IS THE FELLOWSHIP OF THE   108 20
WAY OF THE LORD, MAKE HIS PATHS STRAIGHT   112 07
THOU CANST MAKE ME CLEAN   114 32
OF THE DEVIL, AND MAKE US THE SONS OF GOD, AND HEIRS   117 05
CREATE AND MAKE IN US NEW AND CONTRITE HEARTS, THAT   124 13
FOR WHATSOEVER DOTH MAKE MANIFEST IS LIGHT   129 20
AND JESUS SAID, MAKE THE MEN SIT DOWN   131 35
IN MINE ANGER, AND MAKE THEM DRUNK IN MY FURY,   138 26
BEFORE THEM, TO MAKE HIMSELF AN EVERLASTING NAME   139 12
LEAD THY PEOPLE, TO MAKE THYSELF A GLORIOUS NAME   139 17
THERE MAKE READY FOR US   140 31

MAKE   CONTINUED   MAKE   CONTINUED

THERE MAKE READY   148 31   AND OIL TO MAKE HIM A CHEERFUL COUNTENANCE, AND BREAD   468 24
YEAR CONTINUALLY, MAKE THE COMERS THEREUNTO PERFECT   157 18   WHEREIN THE BIRDS MAKE THEIR NESTS   468 28
THAT I WILL MAKE WITH THEM AFTER THOSE DAYS, SAITH   158 11   THAT HE MIGHT MAKE HIS POWER TO BE KNOWN   473 17
GO YOUR WAY, MAKE IT AS SURE AS YE CAN   162 24   THY HOLY NAME, AND MAKE OUR BOAST OF THY PRAISE   475 32
COME UNTO HIM, AND MAKE YOUR ABODE WITH HIM   181 26   RIGHT HAND, UNTIL I MAKE THINE ENEMIES THY FOOTSTCCL   482 08
AND MAKE US TO HAVE A PERPETUAL FEAR AND   191 07   8 THEY THAT MAKE THEM ARE LIKE UNTO THEM   485 26
CONSENT BEGAN TO MAKE EXCUSE   192 06   27 MAKE ME TO UNDERSTAND THE WAY OF THY COMMANDMENTS   491 21
SUFFERED A WHILE, MAKE YOU PERFECT, STABLISH,   193 10   CAUSE THOU ME TO MAKE MUCH OF THY LAW   491 26
THE TEMPTATION ALSO MAKE A WAY TO ESCAPE, THAT YE MAY   201 29   35 MAKE ME TO GO IN THE PATH OF THY COMMANDMENTS   492 09
MAKE ME AS ONE OF THY HIRED SERVANTS   202 15   42 SO SHALL I MAKE ANSWER UNTO MY BLASPHEMERS   492 24
A KID, THAT I MIGHT MAKE MERRY WITH MY FRIENDS   203 02   122 MAKE THOU THY SERVANT TO DELIGHT IN THAT WHICH IS   498 13
MEET THAT WE SHOULD MAKE MERRY, AND BE GLAD   203 06   THEY MAKE THEM READY TO BATTLE   502 20
THEIR PETITIONS, MAKE THEM TO ASK SUCH THINGS AS   203 13   18 THERE SHALL I MAKE THE HORN OF DAVID TO FLOURISH   509 08
THAT IT SHOULD MAKE THE PROMISE OF NONE EFFECT   207 24   18 THEY THAT MAKE THEM ARE LIKE UNTO THEM   511 06
THOU DOST PROMISE, MAKE US TO LOVE THAT WHICH THOU   209 10   8 THE LORD SHALL MAKE GOOD HIS LOVING-KINDNESS TOWARD   514 14
MANY AS DESIRE TO MAKE A FAIR SHEW IN THE FLESH, THEY   210 24   UNTO THE LORD DID I MAKE MY SUPPLICATION   518 04
AND FOLLOW US, AND MAKE US CONTINUALLY TO BE GIVEN   213 15   AND TO MAKE BOTH YOURSELVES AND THEM, AS MUCH AS IN   533 26
RIGHT HAND, TILL I MAKE THINE ENEMIES THY FCOTSTCOL   215 20   GIRD HIMSELF, AND MAKE THEM TO SIT DOWN TO MEAT,   534 22
MY MOUTH BOLDLY, TO MAKE KNOWN THE MYSTERY OF THE   219 23   MAKE THEM, WE BESEECH THEE, O LORD, TO BE MODEST,   535 01
AND JESUS SAID, MAKE THE MEN SIT DOWN   225 31   AND TO MAKE BOTH YOURSELVES AND THEM, AS MUCH AS IN   542 34
AND I WILL MAKE YOU FISHERS OF MEN   227 27   THEIR PRAYERS, TO MAKE THEIR HUMBLE SUPPLICATICNS TO R 543 24
MAKE US SO TO FOLLOW HIS DOCTRINE AND HOLY LIFE,   242 10   BEHOLD, I MAKE ALL THINGS NEW   567 22
WAY OF THE LORD, MAKE STRAIGHT IN THE DESERT A   242 11   MAKE NOT MY FATHER'S HOUSE AN HOUSE OF MERCHANDISE   567 32
MAKE, WE BESEECH THEE, ALL BISHOPS AND PASTORS   244 24   MAKE YOU PERFECT IN EVERY GOOD WORK TO DO HIS WILL,   573 05
AND LET US MAKE THREE TABERNACLES   249 02   TO MAKE ME INSTRUMENTAL IN PROMOTING THE   573 19
OF AN EVANGELIST, MAKE FULL PROOF OF THY MINISTRY   253 24   HE SHALL MAKE TO HIM THE ADDRESS, AS   R 574 30
I WILL MAKE WITH THEM A COVENANT OF PEACE, AND WILL   262 04   THOU SHALT NOT MAKE TO THYSELF ANY GRAVEN IMAGE,   578 27
AND I WILL MAKE THEM AND THE PLACES ROUND ABOUT MY   262 07   TO US, AS MAY MAKE US BOTH AFRAID AND ASHAMED TC   588 19
AND NONE SHALL MAKE THEM AFRAID   262 16   LET HIM WHO READS MAKE A SHORT PAUSE, THAT EVERY CNE R 589 34
YE THEREFORE, AND MAKE DISCIPLES OF ALL NATIONS,   275 28   MAKE US DEEPLY SENSIBLE OF THE GREAT EVIL OF THEM   590 03
THE MINISTER SHALL MAKE A CROSS UPON THE CHILD'S (OR R 280 11   THE LORD MAKE HIS FACE TO SHINE UPON US, AND BE   593 18
AND WITH ONE ACCORD MAKE OUR PRAYERS UNTO HIM, THAT   280 16   THY MERCIES, AND MAKE US MINDFUL OF THE NEEDS OF   600 18
THOU SHALT NOT MAKE TO THYSELF ANY GRAVEN IMAGE,   286 08   NEITHER DO THEY MAKE MEN MEET TO RECEIVE GRACE,   605 19
WE MAKE OUR HUMBLE SUPPLICATIONS UNTO THEE FOR THESE   298 15
THE LORD SHALL MAKE GOOD HIS LOVING-KINDNESS TOWARD   312 08 MAKER
TO ANY MAN, THAT HE MAKE AMENDS TO THE UTTERMOST OF   R 313 23
PERSON BE MOVED TO MAKE A SPECIAL CONFESSICN OF HIS   R 313 24   AND KNEEL BEFORE THE LORD OUR MAKER   009 14
AND MAKE THEE KNOW AND FEEL, THAT THERE IS NONE OTHER   314 18   FATHER ALMIGHTY, MAKER OF HEAVEN AND EARTH   015 19
THE LORD MAKE HIS FACE TO SHINE UPON THEE, AND BE   314 28   FATHER ALMIGHTY, MAKER OF HEAVEN AND EARTH, AND OF   015 33
MAKE US, WE BESEECH THEE, DEEPLY SENSIBLE CF THE   316 26   FATHER ALMIGHTY, MAKER OF HEAVEN AND EARTH   029 24
ARE IN HEALTH, TO MAKE WILLS ARRANGING FOR THE   R 320 22   FATHER ALMIGHTY, MAKER OF HEAVEN AND EARTH, AND CF   030 04
AND MAKE ME NOT A REBLKE UNTO THE FOOLISH   324 30   FATHER ALMIGHTY, MAKER OF HEAVEN AND EARTH, AND CF   071 02
THE STREAMS WHEREOF MAKE GLAD THE CITY OF GOD   327 09   LORD JESUS CHRIST, MAKER OF ALL THINGS, JUDGE OF ALL   075 18
THE LORD MAKE HIS FACE TO SHINE UPON YOU, AND BE   332 12   FATHER ALMIGHTY, MAKER OF HEAVEN AND EARTH   284 13
MAKE YOU PERFECT IN EVERY GOOD WORK TO DO HIS WILL,   335 19   EVERLIVING GOD, MAKER OF MANKIND, WHO DOST CORRECT   321 18
KEEP HIM, THE LORD MAKE HIS FACE TO SHINE UPON HIM   341 16   AND KNEEL BEFORE THE LORD OUR MAKER   459 16
UNTO THEE WILL I MAKE MY PRAYER   348 02   FATHER ALMIGHTY, MAKER OF HEAVEN AND EARTH   577 28
MAKE THY WAY PLAIN BEFORE THY FACE   348 17   THE MAKER, AND PRESERVER OF ALL THINGS BOTH VISIBLE   603 04
MY SONGS WILL I MAKE OF THY NAME, O THOU MOST   351 12
BEND THEIR BOW, AND MAKE READY THEIR ARROWS WITHIN   354 21 MAKEST
NEITHER MAKE MENTION OF THEIR NAMES WITHIN MY LIPS   357 30
LORD MY GOD SHALL MAKE MY DARKNESS TO BE LIGHT   361 25   ONLY, THAT MAKEST US DWELL IN SAFETY   031 11
CORRECTION SHALL MAKE ME GREAT   362 08   WHO ALONE MAKEST MEN TO BE OF ONE MIND IN A   052 18
37 THOU SHALT MAKE ROOM ENOUGH UNDER ME FOR TO GC,   362 09   O GOD, WHO MAKEST US GLAD WITH THE YEARLY REMEMBRANCE   098 11
AND THOU SHALT MAKE ME THE HEAD OF THE NATIONS   362 26   WHOM MAKEST THOU THYSELF   133 23
AND MAKE HIM GLAD WITH THE JOY OF THY COUNTENANCE   365 16   WHO MAKEST US BOTH TO WILL AND TO DO THOSE   298 13
9 THOU SHALT MAKE THEM LIKE A FIERY OVEN IN TIME OF   365 22   MAN FOR SIN, THOU MAKEST HIS BEAUTY TO CONSUME AWAY,   325 03
THY BOW SHALT THOU MAKE READY AGAINST THE FACE CF   365 30   ONLY, THAT MAKEST ME DWELL IN SAFETY   347 29
IF THOU MAKE AS THOUGH THOU HEAREST NOT, I   373 04   6 THOU MAKEST HIM TO HAVE DOMINION OF THE WORKS CF   351 11
MAKE HASTE TO DELIVER ME   375 24   MAN FOR SIN, THOU MAKEST HIS BEAUTY TO CONSUME AWAY,   389 32
ONE THAT IS GODLY MAKE HIS PRAYER UNTO THEE, IN A   378 02   11 THOU MAKEST US TO TURN OUR BACKS UPON OUR ENEMIES,   395 13
2 MY SOUL SHALL MAKE HER BOAST IN THE LORD   380 05   14 THOU MAKEST US TO BE REBUKED OF OUR NEIGHBOURS,   395 19
6 HE SHALL MAKE THY RIGHTEOUSNESS AS CLEAR AS THE   385 04   15 THOU MAKEST US TO BE A BY-WORD AMONG THE NATICNS,   395 22
AND MAKE ME NOT A REBLKE UNTO THE FOOLISH   389 25   THOU THAT MAKEST THE OUT-GOINGS OF THE MORNING AND   416 30
MAKE HASTE, O LORD, TO HELP ME   391 14   THOU MAKEST IT VERY PLENTEOUS   416 32
MAKE NO LONG TARRYING, O MY GOD   391 26   THOU MAKEST IT SOFT WITH THE DROPS OF RAIN, AND   417 05
MAKE THOU ALL HIS BED IN HIS SICKNESS   392 05   20 THOU MAKEST DARKNESS THAT IT MAY BE NIGHT   468 34
I SING OF HIM, AND MAKE MY PRAYER UNTO THE GOD OF MY   393 23   O GOD, WHO MAKEST US GLAD WITH THE WEEKLY REMEMBRANCE   595 12
9 WE MAKE OUR BOAST OF GOD ALL DAY LONG, *   395 09
THE PEOPLE SHALL MAKE THEIR SUPPLICATION BEFORE THEE   397 10 MAKETH
WHOM THOU MAYEST MAKE PRINCES IN ALL LANDS   397 20
17 I WILL MAKE THY NAME TO BE REMEMBERED FROM ONE   397 21   HE SAITH, WHO MAKETH HIS ANGELS SPIRITS, AND HIS   097 07
THE STREAMS WHEREOF MAKE GLAD THE CITY OF GOD   397 32   WHOSOEVER MAKETH HIMSELF A KING, SPEAKETH AGAINST   159 14
6 THE NATIONS MAKE MUCH ADO, AND THE KINGDOMS ARE   398 04   HE MAKETH BOTH THE DEAF TO HEAR, AND THE DUMB TO   207 08
AND SHALT MAKE ME TO UNDERSTAND WISDOM SECRETLY   403 21   OF EVERY PART, MAKETH INCREASE OF THE BODY UNTO THE   238 02
8 THOU SHALT MAKE ME HEAR OF JOY AND GLADNESS,   403 25   FOR HE MAKETH HIS SUN TO RISE ON THE EVIL AND ON THE   264 09
10 MAKE ME A CLEAN HEART, O GOD, *   403 29   AND MAKETH THE GRASS TO GROW UPON THE MOUNTAINS, AND   264 28
8 I WOULD MAKE HASTE TO ESCAPE, *   407 02   HE MAKETH PEACE IN THY BORDERS, *   265 04
OWN TONGUES SHALL MAKE THEM FALL   416 02   OF GOD, WHO ALSO MAKETH INTERCESSION FOR US   331 05
MAKE HIS PRAISE TO BE GLORIOUS   417 16   12 FOR WHEN HE MAKETH INQUISITION FOR BLOOD, HE   352 13
AND MAKE THE VOICE OF HIS PRAISE TO BE HEARD   417 29   AND MAKETH MUCH OF THEM THAT FEAR THE LORD   357 14
AND THE DRUNKARDS MAKE SONGS UPON ME   422 27   AND MAKETH MY WAY PERFECT   361 34
13 BUT, LORD, I MAKE MY PRAYER UNTO THEE *   422 28   34 HE MAKETH MY FEET LIKE HARTS' FEET, *   362 02
MAKE HASTE TO HELP ME, O LORD   424 20   GLORIOUS GOD THAT MAKETH THE THUNDER   374 03
O LORD, MAKE NO LONG TARRYING   424 34   6 HE MAKETH THEM ALSO TO SKIP LIKE A CALF   374 04
AND WILL MAKE MENTION OF THY RIGHTEOUSNESS CNLY   426 07   VOICE OF THE LORD MAKETH THE HINDS TO BRING FORTH   374 14
SO SHALT THOU MAKE THEIR IMAGE TO VANISH OUT OF THE   429 17   AND MAKETH THE DEVICES OF THE PEOPLE TO BE OF NONE   379 07
LET US MAKE HAVOC OF THEM ALTOGETHER   430 21   AND MAKETH HIS WAY ACCEPTABLE TO HIMSELF   386 09
WERE NO WIDOWS TO MAKE LAMENTATION   439 07   9 HE MAKETH WARS TO CEASE IN ALL THE WCRLD   398 11
MAKE A CHEERFUL NOISE UNTO THE GOD OF JACCB   442 12   IS THE GOD THAT MAKETH MEN TO BE OF ONE MIND IN AN   419 21
THINE ENEMIES MAKE A MURMURING   444 07   AND MAKETH THE CLOUDS HIS CHARIOT, AND WALKETH UPON   467 30
11 MAKE THEM AND THEIR PRINCES LIKE OREB AND ZEEB   444 26   4 HE MAKETH HIS ANGELS WINDS, *   467 32
MAKE ALL THEIR PRINCES LIKE AS ZEBAH AND   444 27   AND WINE THAT MAKETH GLAD THE HEART OF MAN   468 24
13 O MY GOD, MAKE THEM LIKE UNTO THE WHIRLING DUST,   444 30   29 FOR HE MAKETH THE STORM TO CEASE, *   478 02
AND MAKE THEM AFRAID WITH THY STORM   445 02   A FRUITFUL LAND MAKETH HE BARREN, *   478 14
16 MAKE THEIR FACES ASHAMED, O LORD, *   445 04   35 AGAIN, HE MAKETH THE WILDERNESS A STANDING WATER,   478 16
3 I WILL MAKE MENTION OF EGYPT AND BABYLCN, *   448 18   AND MAKETH HIM HOUSEHOLDS LIKE A FLOCK OF SHEEP   478 28
TRUMPETERS SHALL MAKE ANSWER   448 26   8 HE MAKETH THE BARREN WOMAN TO KEEP HOUSE, *   484 23
SHALL MAKE THEIR BOAST   451 07   AND MAKETH THE GRASS TO GROW UPON THE MOUNTAINS, AND   523 11
28 AND I WILL MAKE HIM MY FIRSTBORN, *   451 29   14 HE MAKETH PEACE IN THY BORDERS, *   523 23
SEED ALSO WILL I MAKE TO ENDURE FOR EVER, *   451 33
AND MAKE SUCH PROUD BOASTING   457 26 MAKING
LET THE SEA MAKE A NOISE, AND ALL THAT THEREIN IS   460 23
8 LET THE SEA MAKE A NOISE, AND ALL THAT THEREIN IS   462 08   FOR MAKING PATHS IN THE DEEP WATERS AND HIGHWAYS IN   038 17

MAKING   CONTINUED

	PAGE	LN
AS POOR, YET MAKING MANY RICH	126	20
SINGING AND MAKING MELODY IN YOUR HEART TO THE LORD	217	29
MINE FOR YOU ALL MAKING REQUEST WITH JOY, FOR YOUR	220	23
AND THE PEOPLE MAKING A NOISE, HE SAID UNTO THEM,	224	25
ME UNAWARES, MAKING MOUTHS AT ME, AND CEASED NOT	382	25
DELIVERED FROM MAKING THE POTS	442	24
MAKING THEE YOUNG AND LUSTY AS AN EAGLE	466	15
UPON MEN, MAKING SOME APOSTLES, SOME PROPHETS, SOME	557	25
THE EDIFYING AND MAKING PERFECT HIS CHURCH	557	27
BY MAKING A RIGHT USE OF IT, TO THE	566	32

MALE

OF THE LORD, EVERY MALE THAT OPENETH THE WOMB SHALL	232	26
BEGINNING MADE THEM MALE AND FEMALE, AND SAID,	268	07

MALE-CHILD

BE FOR EVERY MALE-CHILD TO BE BAPTIZED, WHEN THEY CAN R	273	09

MALEFACTORS

TWO OTHER, MALEFACTORS, LED WITH HIM TO BE PUT TC	154	21
AND THE MALEFACTORS, ONE ON THE RIGHT HAND,	154	24
ONE OF THE MALEFACTORS WHICH WERE HANGED RAILED ON	154	34

MALICE

HATRED, AND MALICE, AND ALL UNCHARITABLENESS,	054	24
HE PERCEIVETH MALICE AND HATRED TO REIGN	R 085	10
BUT REMAIN STILL IN HIS FROWARDNESS AND MALICE	R 085	10
OR BE IN MALICE, OR IN ENVY, OR IN ANY OTHER GRIEVOUS	087	32
THE LEAVEN OF MALICE AND WICKEDNESS	162	32
THE LEAVEN OF MALICE AND WICKEDNESS	165	14
THE LEAVEN OF MALICE AND WICKEDNESS, THAT WE MAY	170	21
BE PUT AWAY FROM YOU, WITH ALL MALICE	216	29
LAYING ASIDE ALL MALICE, AND ALL GUILE, AND	259	25
TO BEAR NO MALICE NOR HATRED IN MY HEART	288	32
BY THE FRAUD AND MALICE OF THE DEVIL, OR BY HIS OWN	314	04
AND DESTROY THEM IN THEIR OWN MALICE	458	33
DRAW NIGH THAT OF MALICE PERSECUTE ME, *	500	10
TO BEAR NO MALICE NOR HATRED IN MY HEART	580	08
PURGE OUR HEARTS FROM ENVY, HATRED, AND MALICE	590	15

MALICIOUS

BREAK THOU THE POWER OF THE UNGODLY AND MALICIOUS	354	09
THAT OFFEND OF MALICIOUS WICKEDNESS	411	15

MALICIOUSLY

SO MALICIOUSLY ARE THEY SET AGAINST ME	406	25

MALICIOUSNESS

A CLOKE OF MALICIOUSNESS, BUT AS THE SERVANTS OF GOD	173	24

MAMMON

THE SERVICE OF MAMMON, THAT WE MAY DO THE WORK WHICH	044	20
YE CANNOT SERVE GOD AND MAMMON	211	12

MAN

OR WHICH A GODLY MAN MAY NOT WITH A GOOD CONSCIENCE	V	41
UPON THEE TO DELIVER MAN, THOU DIDST HUMBLE THYSELF	010	26
HOLY GHOST OF THE VIRGIN MARY, AND WAS MADE MAN	016	08
HOLY GHOST OF THE VIRGIN MARY, AND WAS MADE MAN	030	13
HANDS SUDDENLY ON NO MAN, BUT FAITHFULLY AND WISELY	038	30
FOR THE LIFE OF MAN, AND HAST COMMANDED US TO WORK	039	26
WHO HAST CREATED MAN IN THINE OWN IMAGE	044	19
THAT IT MAY BRING FORTH FRUIT FOR THE USE OF MAN	051	17
OF THE DEVIL OR MAN WORKETH AGAINST US, MAY, BY THY	058	20
HOLY GHOST OF THE VIRGIN MARY, AND WAS MADE MAN	071	10
LET EVERY MAN DO ACCORDING AS HE IS DISPOSED IN HIS	072	17
EVERY MAN SHALL GIVE AS HE IS ABLE, ACCORDING TO THE	073	15
IF ANY MAN SIN, WE HAVE AN ADVOCATE WITH THE FATHER,	076	22
WAS MADE VERY MAN, OF THE SUBSTANCE OF THE	077	16
PASSION OF OUR SAVIOUR CHRIST, BOTH GOD AND MAN	086	08
IS REQUISITE THAT NO MAN SHOULD COME TO THE HOLY	087	35
THING IT IS, WHEN A MAN HATH PREPARED A RICH FEAST,	088	18
AN EASY MATTER FOR A MAN TO SAY, I WILL NOT	088	27
IF ANY MAN SAY, I AM A GRIEVOUS SINNER, AND THEREFORE	088	30
OWE NO MAN ANY THING, BUT TO LOVE ONE ANOTHER	090	23
AND IF ANY MAN SAY OUGHT UNTO YOU, YE SHALL SAY, THE	091	16
THEY SEE THE SON OF MAN COMING IN A CLOUD WITH POWER	093	11
LET A MAN SO ACCOUNT OF US, AS OF THE MINISTERS OF	094	03
IN STEWARDS, THAT A MAN BE FOUND FAITHFUL	094	05
AND THEN SHALL EVERY MAN HAVE PRAISE OF GOD	094	13
A MAN CLOTHED IN SOFT RAIMENT	094	28
THERE WAS A MAN SENT FROM GOD, WHOSE NAME WAS JCHN	097	26
WHICH LIGHTETH EVERY MAN THAT COMETH INTO THE WCRLD	097	30
NOR OF THE WILL OF MAN, BUT OF GOD	098	04
LET NO MAN DESPISE THEE	098	26
AND THE SON OF MAN STANDING ON THE RIGHT HAND OF GOD	100	08
AND WHAT SHALL THIS MAN DO	102	07
AND NO MAN COULD LEARN THAT SONG BUT THE HUNDRED AND	103	06
BEING A JUST MAN, AND NOT WILLING TO MAKE HER A	104	30
AND OBEDIENT TO THE LAW FOR MAN	105	20
UNTO HIM, TO EVERY MAN THAT IS AMONG YOU, NOT TO THINK	110	10
HATH DEALT TO EVERY MAN THE MEASURE OF FAITH	110	12
AND IN FAVOUR WITH GOD AND MAN	111	07
RECOMPENSE TO NO MAN EVIL FOR EVIL	112	32
UNTO HIM, EVERY MAN AT THE BEGINNING DOTH SET FORTH	113	27

MAN   CONTINUED

	PAGE	LN
AND JESUS SAITH UNTO HIM, SEE THOU TELL NO MAN	115	04
FOR I AM A MAN UNDER AUTHORITY, HAVING SOLDIERS UNDER	115	13
AND I SAY TO THIS MAN, GO, AND HE GOETH	115	14
ONE ANOTHER, IF ANY MAN HAVE A QUARREL AGAINST ANY	116	06
IS LIKENED UNTO A MAN WHICH SOWED GOOD SEED IN HIS	116	18
AND EVERY MAN THAT HATH THIS HOPE IN HIM PURIFIETH	117	20
LET NO MAN DECEIVE YOU	117	26
THEN IF ANY MAN SHALL SAY UNTO YOU, LO, HERE IS	118	03
COMING OF THE SON OF MAN BE	118	12
SIGN OF THE SON OF MAN IN HEAVEN	118	17
SHALL SEE THE SON OF MAN COMING IN THE CLOUDS OF	118	19
AND EVERY MAN THAT STRIVETH FOR THE MASTERY IS	119	07
IS LIKE UNTO A MAN THAT IS AN HOUSEHOLDER, WHICH WENT	119	15
UNTO HIM, BECAUSE NO MAN HATH HIRED US	119	26
THEY RECEIVED EVERY MAN A PENNY	119	32
RECEIVED EVERY MAN A PENNY	120	02
FOR YE SUFFER, IF A MAN BRING YOU INTO BONDAGE,	120	23
TAKE OF YOU, IF A MAN EXALT HIMSELF, IF A MAN SMITE	120	24
MAN DEVOUR YOU, IF A MAN TAKE OF YOU, IF A MAN EXALT	120	24
INTO BONDAGE, IF A MAN DEVOUR YOU, IF A MAN TAKE OF	120	24
EXALT HIMSELF, IF A MAN SMITE YOU ON THE FACE	120	25
BUT WHEN I BECAME A MAN, I PUT AWAY CHILDISH THINGS	123	11
THE SON OF MAN SHALL BE ACCOMPLISHED	123	20
A CERTAIN BLIND MAN SAT BY THE WAY-SIDE BEGGING	123	27
IT IS WRITTEN, MAN SHALL NOT LIVE BY BREAD	126	28
THAT NO MAN GO BEYOND AND DEFRAUD HIS BROTHER IN ANY	127	31
DESPISETH NOT MAN, BUT GOD, WHO HATH ALSO GIVEN UNTO	128	04
NOR COVETOUS MAN, WHO IS AN IDOLATER, HATH	129	07
LET NO MAN DECEIVE YOU WITH VAIN WORDS	129	09
WHEN A STRONG MAN ARMED KEEPETH HIS PALACE, HIS GCODS	130	05
IS GONE OUT OF A MAN, HE WALKETH THROUGH DRY PLACES,	130	10
LAST STATE OF THAT MAN IS WORSE THAN THE FIRST	130	16
I SAY UNTO YOU, IF A MAN KEEP MY SAYING, HE SHALL	133	17
THOU SAYEST, IF A MAN KEEP MY SAYING, HE SHALL NEVER	133	20
IN FASHION AS A MAN, HE HUMBLED HIMSELF, AND BECAME	134	21
HAVE NOTHING TO DO WITH THAT JUST MAN	135	34
THEY FOUND A MAN OF CYRENE, SIMON BY NAME	136	26
SAID, THIS MAN CALLETH FOR ELIAS	137	20
SHALL MEET YOU A MAN BEARING A PITCHER OF WATER	140	27
THE SON OF MAN INDEED GOETH, AS IT IS WRITTEN OF HIM	141	06
BUT WOE TO THAT MAN BY WHOM THE SON OF MAN IS	141	07
WERE IT FOR THAT MAN IF HE HAD NEVER BEEN BORN	141	08
BY WHOM THE SON OF MAN IS BETRAYED	141	08
BEHOLD, THE SON OF MAN IS BETRAYED INTO THE HANDS OF	142	12
HIM A CERTAIN YOUNG MAN, HAVING A LINEN CLOTH CAST	142	29
SHALL SEE THE SON OF MAN SITTING ON THE RIGHT HAND OF	143	15
I KNOW NOT THIS MAN OF WHOM YE SPEAK	143	33
WHAT EVERY MAN SHOULD TAKE	146	12
HE SAID, TRULY THIS MAN WAS THE SON OF GOD	147	04
THERE SHALL A MAN MEET YOU, BEARING A PITCHER	148	26
AND TRULY THE SON OF MAN GOETH, AS IT WAS DETERMINED	149	14
BUT WOE UNTO THAT MAN BY WHOM HE IS BETRAYED	149	15
THOU THE SON OF MAN WITH A KISS	150	30
AND SAID, THIS MAN WAS ALSO WITH HIM	151	12
AND PETER SAID, MAN, I AM NOT	151	15
AND PETER SAID, MAN, I KNOW NOT WHAT THOU SAYEST	151	18
SHALL THE SON OF MAN SIT ON THE RIGHT HAND OF THE	151	33
AND TO THE PEOPLE, I FIND NO FAULT IN THIS MAN	153	04
HE ASKED WHETHER THE MAN WERE A GALILAEAN	153	07
YE HAVE BROUGHT THIS MAN UNTO ME, AS ONE THAT	153	22
NO FAULT IN THIS MAN TOUCHING THOSE THINGS WHERECF YE	153	25
AWAY WITH THIS MAN, AND RELEASE UNTO US BARABBAS	153	30
BUT THIS MAN HATH DONE NOTHING AMISS	155	05
SAYING, CERTAINLY THIS WAS A RIGHTEOUS MAN	155	16
BUT THIS MAN, AFTER HE HAD OFFERED ONE SACRIFICE FOR	158	05
AND PILATE SAITH UNTO THEM, BEHOLD THE MAN	159	05
IF THOU LET THIS MAN GO, THOU ART NOT CAESAR'S	159	20
THERE CAME A RICH MAN OF ARIMATHAEA, NAMED JOSEPH,	162	06
BY MAN CAME ALSO THE RESURRECTION OF THE DEAD	163	13
FOR SINCE BY MAN CAME DEATH, *	163	13
THEY SAW A YOUNG MAN SITTING ON THE RIGHT SIDE,	165	27
NEITHER SAID THEY ANY THING TO ANY MAN	166	03
THAT THROUGH THIS MAN IS PREACHED UNTO YOU THE	169	19
THOUGH A MAN DECLARE IT UNTO YOU	169	26
IS THANKWORTHY, IF A MAN FOR CONSCIENCE TOWARD GOD	172	05
EVERY ORDINANCE OF MAN FOR THE LORD'S SAKE	173	18
FOR JOY THAT A MAN IS BORN INTO THE WORLD	174	13
AND YOUR JOY NO MAN TAKETH FROM YOU	174	15
LET EVERY MAN BE SWIFT TO HEAR, SLOW TO	174	31
FOR THE WRATH OF MAN WORKETH NOT THE RIGHTEOUSNESS CF	174	32
HE IS LIKE UNTO A MAN BEHOLDING HIS NATURAL FACE IN A	176	07
WHAT MANNER OF MAN HE WAS	176	09
OF THE WORK, THIS MAN SHALL BE BLESSED IN HIS DEED	176	12
IF ANY MAN AMONG YOU SEEM TO BE RELIGIOUS, AND	176	13
NEEDEST NOT THAT ANY MAN SHOULD ASK THEE	177	02
BE SCATTERED, EVERY MAN TO HIS OWN, AND SHALL LEAVE	177	06
AS EVERY MAN HATH RECEIVED THE GIFT, EVEN SO MINISTER	179	16
IF ANY MAN SPEAK, LET HIM SPEAK AS THE ORACLES OF	179	18
IF ANY MAN MINISTER, LET HIM DO IT AS OF THE ABILITY	179	19
BECAUSE THAT EVERY MAN HEARD THEM SPEAK IN HIS OWN	180	28
HOW HEAR WE EVERY MAN IN OUR OWN TONGUE, WHEREIN WE	180	31
SAID UNTO HIM, IF A MAN LOVE ME, HE WILL KEEP MY	181	24
IS GIVEN TO EVERY MAN TO PROFIT WITHAL	182	26
DIVIDING TO EVERY MAN SEVERALLY AS HE WILL	182	34
CAN ANY MAN FORBID WATER, THAT THESE SHOULD	184	26
BY ME IF ANY MAN ENTER IN, HE SHALL BE SAVED, AND	186	15
HAD A FACE AS A MAN, AND THE FOURTH WAS LIKE A FLYING	187	19
THERE WAS A MAN OF THE PHARISEES, NAMED NICODEMUS,	187	34
FOR NO MAN CAN DO THESE MIRACLES THAT THOU DOEST,	188	03
UNTO THEE, EXCEPT A MAN BE BORN AGAIN, HE CANNOT SEE	188	06
UNTO HIM, HOW CAN A MAN BE BORN WHEN HE IS OLD	188	07
UNTO THEE, EXCEPT A MAN BE BORN OF WATER AND OF THE	188	10
AND NO MAN HATH ASCENDED UP TO HEAVEN, BUT HE THAT	188	24
EVEN THE SON OF MAN WHICH IS IN HEAVEN	188	26

SO MUST THE SON OF MAN BE LIFTED UP	188 28
NO MAN HATH SEEN GOD AT ANY TIME	189 16
IF A MAN SAY, I LOVE GOD, AND HATETH HIS BROTHER,	189 31
WAS A CERTAIN RICH MAN, WHICH WAS CLOTHED IN PURPLE	190 03
THE RICH MAN ALSO DIED, AND WAS BURIED	190 10
A CERTAIN MAN MADE A GREAT SUPPER, AND BADE MANY	192 03
THIS MAN RECEIVETH SINNERS, AND EATETH WITH	193 16
SAYING, WHAT MAN OF YOU, HAVING AN HUNDRED	193 18
FOR I AM A SINFUL MAN, O LORD	196 24
THAT OUR OLD MAN IS CRUCIFIED WITH HIM,	197 17
FROM WHENCE CAN A MAN SATISFY THESE MEN WITH BREAD	199 15
TEMPTATION TAKEN YOU BUT SUCH AS IS COMMON TO MAN	201 26
A CERTAIN MAN HAD TWO SONS	201 31
AND NO MAN GAVE UNTO HIM	202 09
THAT NO MAN SPEAKING BY THE SPIRIT OF GOD	203 19
AND THAT NO MAN CAN SAY THAT JESUS IS THE LORD,	203 21
IS GIVEN TO EVERY MAN TO PROFIT WITHAL	203 26
DIVIDING TO EVERY MAN SEVERALLY AS HE WILL	204 03
I TELL YOU, THIS MAN WENT DOWN TO HIS HOUSE JUSTIFIED	205 31
AND HE CHARGED THEM THAT THEY SHOULD TELL NO MAN	207 05
A CERTAIN MAN WENT DOWN FROM JERUSALEM TO	208 21
THE FRAILTY OF MAN WITHOUT THEE CANNOT BUT FALL, KEEP	210 18
HENCEFORTH LET NO MAN TROUBLE ME	211 04
NO MAN CAN SERVE TWO MASTERS	211 09
WITH MIGHT BY HIS SPIRIT IN THE INNER MAN	212 15
THERE WAS A DEAD MAN CARRIED OUT, THE ONLY SON OF HIS	212 30
AND HE SAID, YOUNG MAN, I SAY UNTO THEE, ARISE	213 04
THERE WAS A CERTAIN MAN BEFORE HIM WHICH HAD THE	213 31
ART BIDDEN OF ANY MAN TO A WEDDING, SIT NOT DOWN IN	214 11
A MORE HONOURABLE MAN THAN THOU BE BIDDEN OF HIM	214 12
TO THEE, GIVE THIS MAN PLACE	214 14
AND NO MAN WAS ABLE TO ANSWER HIM A WORD, NEITHER	215 22
NEITHER DURST ANY MAN FROM THAT DAY FORTH ASK HIM ANY	215 23
CONVERSATION THE OLD MAN, WHICH IS CORRUPT ACCORDING	216 13
YE PUT ON THE NEW MAN, WHICH AFTER GOD IS CREATED IN	216 15
SPEAK EVERY MAN TRUTH WITH HIS NEIGHBOUR	216 17
BROUGHT TO HIM A MAN SICK OF THE PALSY, LYING ON A	217 02
THIS MAN BLASPHEMETH	217 05
KNOW THAT THE SON OF MAN HATH POWER ON EARTH TO	217 09
HE SAW THERE A MAN WHICH HAD NOT ON A	218 23
AND THE MAN BELIEVED THE WORD THAT JESUS HAD SPOKEN	220 03
NEITHER CAREST THOU FOR ANY MAN	223 02
FOR WITH THE HEART MAN BELIEVETH UNTO RIGHTEOUSNESS	226 28
BUT IF ANY MAN DRAW BACK, MY SOUL SHALL HAVE NO	228 19
HEARING A VOICE, BUT SEEING NO MAN	230 09
AND WHEN HIS EYES WERE OPENED, HE SAW NO MAN	230 11
SEEN IN A VISION A MAN NAMED ANANIAS COMING IN,	230 20
BY MANY OF THIS MAN, HOW MUCH EVIL HE HATH DONE TO	230 22
WHEN THE SON OF MAN SHALL SIT IN THE THRONE OF HIS	231 16
BEHOLD, THERE WAS A MAN IN JERUSALEM, WHOSE NAME WAS	232 30
AND THE SAME MAN WAS JUST AND DEVOUT, WAITING FOR THE	232 31
NOW THIS MAN PURCHASED A FIELD WITH THE REWARD OF	234 13
AND LET NO MAN DWELL THEREIN	234 19
AND NO MAN KNOWETH THE SON, BUT THE FATHER	235 08
NEITHER KNOWETH ANY MAN THE FATHER, SAVE THE SON,	235 09
VIRGIN ESPOUSED TO A MAN WHOSE NAME WAS JOSEPH,	236 07
HOW SHALL THIS BE, SEEING I KNOW NOT A MAN	236 21
UNTO A PERFECT MAN, UNTO THE MEASURE OF THE	237 24
IF A MAN ABIDE NOT IN ME, HE IS CAST FORTH AS A	238 14
FOR LET NOT THAT MAN THINK THAT HE SHALL RECEIVE ANY	239 16
A DOUBLE-MINDED MAN IS UNSTABLE IN ALL HIS WAYS	239 17
ALSO SHALL THE RICH MAN FADE AWAY IN HIS WAYS	239 24
BLESSED IS THE MAN THAT ENDURETH TEMPTATION	239 24
NO MAN COMETH UNTO THE FATHER, BUT BY ME	240 06
FOR HE WAS A GOOD MAN, AND FULL OF THE HOLY GHOST AND	241 08
THE DISCIPLES, EVERY MAN ACCORDING TO HIS ABILITY,	241 20
GREATER LOVE HATH NO MAN THAN THIS, THAT A MAN LAY	241 26
THAN THIS, THAT A MAN LAY DOWN HIS LIFE FOR HIS	241 27
THAT I THE SON OF MAN AM	245 33
THE DISCIPLES, EVERY MAN ACCORDING TO HIS ABILITY,	246 28
EVEN AS THE SON OF MAN CAME NOT TO BE MINISTERED	247 26
AND TOLD NO MAN IN THOSE DAYS ANY OF THOSE	249 09
OF THE REST DURST NO MAN JOIN HIMSELF TO THEM	249 24
HE SAW A MAN, NAMED MATTHEW, SITTING AT THE	251 12
BUT WOE TO THAT MAN BY WHOM THE OFFENCE COMETH	253 02
AND SALUTE NO MAN BY THE WAY	254 18
WHICH NONE OTHER MAN DID, THEY HAD NOT HAD SIN	255 26
WHICH NO MAN COULD NUMBER, OF ALL NATIONS,	256 24
WHEN THE SON OF MAN SHALL COME IN HIS GLORY, AND ALL	258 28
LET EVERY MAN BE SWIFT TO HEAR, SLOW TO	265 24
FOR THE WRATH OF MAN WORKETH NOT THE RIGHTEOUSNESS OF	265 25
HE IS LIKE UNTO A MAN BEHOLDING HIS NATURAL FACE IN A	265 30
WHAT MANNER HE WAS	265 33
OF THE WORK, THIS MAN SHALL BE BLESSED IN HIS DEED	266 03
IF ANY MAN AMONG YOU SEEM TO BE RELIGIOUS, AND	266 04
FOR NO MAN EVER YET HATED HIS OWN FLESH	267 26
THIS CAUSE SHALL A MAN LEAVE HIS FATHER AND MOTHER,	267 29
THIS CAUSE SHALL A MAN LEAVE FATHER AND MOTHER, AND	268 07
LET NOT MAN PUT ASUNDER	268 11
THERE WAS A MAN OF THE PHARISEES, NAMED NICODEMUS,	275 05
FOR NO MAN CAN DO THESE MIRACLES THAT THOU DOEST,	275 08
UNTO THEE, EXCEPT A MAN BE BORN AGAIN, HE CANNOT SEE	275 10
UNTO HIM, HOW CAN A MAN BE BORN WHEN HE IS OLD	275 12
UNTO THEE, EXCEPT A MAN BE BORN OF WATER AND OF THE	275 15
WITH MIGHT BY HIS SPIRIT IN THE INNER MAN	281 10
THE MAN ON THE RIGHT HAND, AND THE WOMAN ON	R 300 06
JOIN TOGETHER THIS MAN AND THIS WOMAN IN HOLY	300 10
IF ANY MAN CAN SHOW JUST CAUSE, WHY THEY MAY NOT	300 20
SHALL SAY TO THE MAN, N	R 301 05
THE MAN SHALL ANSWER, I WILL	R 301 11
WILT THOU HAVE THIS MAN TO THY WEDDED HUSBAND,	301 14
WHO GIVETH THIS WOMAN TO BE MARRIED TO THIS MAN	301 23
SHALL CAUSE THE MAN WITH HIS RIGHT HAND TO TAKE THE	R 301 26
HAND TAKING THE MAN BY HIS RIGHT HAND, SHALL LIKEWISE	R 302 03

AND THE MAN SHALL GIVE UNTO THE WOMAN A RING ON THIS	R 302 09
DELIVER IT UNTO THE MAN, TO PUT IT UPON THE FOURTH	R 302 11
AND THE MAN HOLDING THE RING THERE, AND TAUGHT BY THE	R 302 12
THE RING TO THE MAN, THE MINISTER MAY SAY AS	R 302 17
THE MAN LEAVING THE RING UPON THE FOURTH	R 302 23
THY SERVANTS, THIS MAN AND THIS WOMAN, WHOM WE BLESS	303 06
TOGETHER LET NO MAN PUT ASUNDER	303 31
THAT THEY ARE MAN AND WIFE, IN THE NAME OF THE	304 08
THE MAN AND WIFE KNEELING, THE MINISTER SHALL ADD	R 304 10
O DELIVER ME FROM THE DECEITFUL AND WICKED MAN	310 07
OR WRONG TO ANY MAN, THAT HE MAKE AMENDS TO THE	R 313 23
HEAVEN GIVEN TO MAN, IN WHOM, AND THROUGH WHOM,	314 20
THE MORE THE OUTWARD MAN DECAYETH, STRENGTHEN HIM,	316 10
WITH THY GRACE AND HOLY SPIRIT IN THE INNER MAN	316 12
FROM HEAVEN, THAT A MAN MAY EAT THEREOF, AND NOT DIE	322 25
IF ANY MAN EAT OF THIS BREAD, HE SHALL LIVE FOR EVER	322 27
BUT IF A MAN, EITHER BY REASON OF EXTREMITY OF	R 323 23
AND VERILY EVERY MAN LIVING IS ALTOGETHER VANITY	324 24
FOR MAN WALKETH IN A VAIN SHADOW, AND DISQUIETETH	324 25
REBUKES DOST CHASTEN MAN FOR SIN, THOU MAKEST HIS	325 02
EVERY MAN THEREFORE IS BUT VANITY	325 04
THOU TURNEST MAN TO DESTRUCTION	325 18
FOR SINCE BY MAN CAME DEATH, BY MAN CAME ALSO THE	328 22
MAN CAME DEATH, BY MAN CAME ALSO THE RESURRECTION OF	328 23
BUT EVERY MAN IN HIS OWN ORDER	328 25
BUT SOME MAN WILL SAY, HOW ARE THE DEAD RAISED UP	329 05
THE FIRST MAN ADAM WAS MADE A LIVING SOUL	329 24
THE FIRST MAN IS OF THE EARTH, EARTHY	329 27
THE SECOND MAN IS THE LORD FROM HEAVEN	329 28
NO MAN COMETH UNTO THE FATHER, BUT BY ME	331 26
BE SUNG OR SAID, MAN, THAT IS BORN OF A WOMAN,	332 18
AND YOUR JOY NO MAN TAKETH FROM YOU	341 11
BLESSED IS THE MAN THAT HATH NOT WALKED IN THE	345 07
TO HIMSELF THE MAN THAT IS GODLY	347 17
ABHOR BOTH THE BLOOD-THIRSTY AND DECEITFUL MAN	348 12
5 FOR IN DEATH NO MAN REMEMBERETH THEE	349 08
13 IF A MAN WILL NOT TURN, HE WILL WHET HIS SWORD	350 17
4 WHAT IS MAN, THAT THOU ART MINDFUL OF HIM	351 07
AND THE SON OF MAN, THAT THOU VISITEST HIM	351 08
AND LET NOT MAN HAVE THE UPPER HAND	352 30
THAT THE MAN OF THE EARTH BE NO MORE EXALTED AGAINST	354 16
IS NOT ONE GODLY MAN LEFT	355 06
AND WITH A PERFECT MAN THOU SHALT BE PERFECT	361 19
THOU SHALT RID ME FROM THE WICKED MAN	363 04
6 BUT AS FOR ME, I AM A WORM, AND NO MAN	366 14
AND NO MAN HATH QUICKENED HIS OWN SOUL	368 03
11 WHAT MAN IS HE THAT FEARETH THE LORD	370 08
SHALL EVERY GOOD MAN SING OF THY PRAISE WITHOUT	375 18
FORGOTTEN AS A DEAD MAN OUT OF MIND	376 19
2 BLESSED IS THE MAN UNTO WHOM THE LORD IMPUTETH NO	377 24
IS ANY MIGHTY MAN DELIVERED BY MUCH STRENGTH	379 20
A HORSE IS COUNTED BUT A VAIN THING TO SAVE A MAN	379 22
SHALL HE DELIVER ANY MAN BY HIS GREAT STRENGTH	379 23
BLESSED IS THE MAN THAT TRUSTETH IN HIM	380 18
12 WHAT MAN IS HE THAT LUSTETH TO LIVE, *	380 25
SHALT SAVE BOTH MAN AND BEAST	384 08
AGAINST THE MAN THAT DOETH AFTER EVIL	385 08
THAT SHALL BRING A MAN PEACE AT THE LAST	387 09
I WAS LIKE A DEAF MAN, AND HEARD NOT	388 17
I BECAME EVEN AS A MAN THAT HEARETH NOT, *	388 19
AND VERILY EVERY MAN LIVING IS ALTOGETHER VANITY	389 19
7 FOR MAN WALKETH IN A VAIN SHADOW, AND DISQUIETETH	389 20
REBUKES DOST CHASTEN MAN FOR SIN, THOU MAKEST HIS	389 31
EVERY MAN THEREFORE IS BUT VANITY	389 33
5 BLESSED IS THE MAN THAT HATH SET HIS HOPE IN THE	390 18
AND YET THERE IS NO MAN THAT ORDERETH THEM UNTO THEE	390 23
O DELIVER ME FROM THE DECEITFUL AND WICKED MAN	394 05
7 BUT NO MAN MAY DELIVER HIS BROTHER, *	400 18
12 NEVERTHELESS, MAN BEING IN HONOUR ABIDETH NOT,	400 30
HE COUNTED HIMSELF AN HAPPY MAN	401 12
20 MAN THAT IS IN HONOUR BUT HATH NO UNDERSTANDING *	401 16
8 LO, THIS IS THE MAN THAT TOOK NOT GOD FOR HIS	404 33
UNTO ME, O GOD, FOR MAN GOETH ABOUT TO DEVOUR ME	408 14
NOT BE AFRAID WHAT MAN CAN DO UNTO ME	409 05
11 SO THAT A MAN SHALL SAY, VERILY THERE IS A REWARD	410 32
FOR VAIN IS THE HELP OF MAN	413 03
LONG WILL YE IMAGINE MISCHIEF AGAINST EVERY MAN	414 02
THOU REWARDEST EVERY MAN ACCORDING TO HIS WORK	414 24
AND SAY, THAT NO MAN SHALL SEE THEM	415 29
EVERY MAN IN THE DEEP OF HIS HEART	415 31
4 BLESSED IS THE MAN WHOM THOU CHOOSEST, AND	416 17
BUT THERE WAS NO MAN, NEITHER FOUND I ANY TO	423 15
AND NO MAN TO DWELL IN THEIR TENTS	423 25
OUT OF THE HAND OF THE UNRIGHTEOUS AND CRUEL MAN	425 13
HOW THE FOOLISH MAN BLASPHEMETH THEE DAILY	431 23
10 THE FIERCENESS OF MAN SHALL TURN TO THY PRAISE	433 08
26 SO MAN DID EAT ANGELS' FOOD	436 20
AND THERE WAS NO MAN TO BURY THEM	440 05
THY HAND BE UPON THE MAN OF THY RIGHT HAND, *	442 04
AND UPON THE SON OF MAN, WHOM THOU MADEST SO STRONG	442 05
5 BLESSED IS THE MAN WHOSE STRENGTH IS IN THEE	445 21
BLESSED IS THE MAN THAT PUTTETH HIS TRUST IN THEE	446 05
AND I AM EVEN AS A MAN THAT HATH NO STRENGTH	449 03
47 WHAT MAN IS HE THAT LIVETH, AND SHALL NOT SEE	453 02
3 THOU TURNEST MAN TO DESTRUCTION	453 23
6 AN UNWISE MAN DOTH NOT WELL CONSIDER THIS, *	456 11
IS HE THAT TEACHETH MAN KNOWLEDGE	458 07
THE THOUGHTS OF MAN, *	458 08
12 BLESSED IS THE MAN WHOM THOU CHASTENEST, O LORD,	458 10
15 THE DAYS OF MAN ARE BUT AS GRASS	467 04
AND WINE THAT MAKETH GLAD THE HEART OF MAN	468 24
23 MAN GOETH FORTH TO HIS WORK, AND TO HIS LABOUR,	469 06
14 HE SUFFERED NO MAN TO DO THEM WRONG, *	470 30
17 BUT HE HAD SENT A MAN BEFORE THEM, *	471 06

MAN   CONTINUED

LIKE A DRUNKEN MAN, *	477 32
FOR VAIN IS THE HELP OF MAN	479 29
SET THOU AN UNGODLY MAN TO BE RULER OVER HIM,	480 13
11 LET THERE BE NO MAN TO PITY HIM, *	480 23
THE POOR HELPLESS MAN, THAT HE MIGHT SLAY HIM THAT	480 33
BLESSED IS THE MAN THAT FEARETH THE LORD	483 18
5 A GOOD MAN IS MERCIFUL, AND LENDETH	483 26
I WILL NOT FEAR WHAT MAN DOETH UNTO ME	488 10
THAN TO PUT ANY CONFIDENCE IN MAN	488 15
SHALL A YOUNG MAN CLEANSE HIS WAY	490 16
6 HAPPY IS THE MAN THAT HATH HIS QUIVER FULL OF THEM	506 02
5 LO, THUS SHALL THE MAN BE BLESSED *	506 14
BOTH OF MAN AND BEAST	510 18
O LORD, FROM THE EVIL MAN	516 09
AND PRESERVE ME FROM THE WICKED MAN	516 10
11 A MAN FULL OF WORDS SHALL NOT PROSPER UPON THE	516 32
AND SAW THERE WAS NO MAN THAT WOULD KNOW ME	518 11
AND NO MAN CARED FOR MY SOUL	518 12
THY SIGHT SHALL NO MAN LIVING BE JUSTIFIED	518 26
3 LORD, WHAT IS MAN, THAT THOU HAST SUCH RESPECT UNTO	519 27
OR THE SON OF MAN, THAT THOU SO REGARDEST HIM	519 28
4 MAN IS LIKE A THING OF NOUGHT	519 29
9 THE LORD IS LOVING UNTO EVERY MAN	521 10
NOR IN ANY CHILD OF MAN	522 07
WHEN THE BREATH OF MAN GOETH FORTH, HE SHALL TURN	522 08
THAT NO MAN MIGHT PRESUME TO EXECUTE ANY	529 14
IN THIS CHURCH, NO MAN SHALL BE ACCOUNTED OR TAKEN TO	529 19
ANY PERSON TO BE A MAN OF VIRTUOUS CONVERSATION, AND	529 27
CHOSE STEPHEN, A MAN FULL OF FAITH AND OF THE HOLY	532 16
UNTO A PERFECT MAN, UNTO THE MEASURE OF THE	538 11
BY ME IF ANY MAN ENTER IN, HE SHALL BE SAVED, AND	539 06
TO THE SALVATION OF MAN, BUT WITH DOCTRINE AND	540 35
A TRUE SAYING, IF A MAN DESIRE THE OFFICE OF A	549 18
FOR IF A MAN KNOW NOT HOW TO RULE HIS OWN HOUSE,	549 25
AND WELL-LEARNED MAN, TO BE ORDAINED AND CONSECRATED	552 22
O GOD, AT WHOSE WORD MAN GOETH FORTH TO HIS WORK AND	599 25
WHEREOF IS ONE CHRIST, VERY GOD, AND VERY MAN	603 14
BE REQUIRED OF ANY MAN, THAT IT SHOULD BE BELIEVED AS	603 31
BETWEEN GOD AND MAN, BEING BOTH GOD AND MAN	604 17
BETWEEN GOD AND MAN, BEING BOTH GOD AND MAN	604 17
NO CHRISTIAN MAN WHATSOEVER IS FREE FROM THE	604 22
THE NATURE OF EVERY MAN, THAT NATURALLY IS ENGENDERED	604 30
WHEREBY MAN IS VERY FAR GONE FROM ORIGINAL	604 31
THE CONDITION OF MAN AFTER THE FALL OF ADAM IS SUCH,	604 42
TO SAY, THAT EVERY MAN SHALL BE SAVED BY THE LAW OR	606 32
NOT LAWFUL FOR ANY MAN TO TAKE UPON HIM THE OFFICE OF	607 19
EVERY MAN OUGHT, OF SUCH THINGS AS HE POSSESSETH,	611 03
BUT THAT A MAN MAY SWEAR WHEN THE	611 08

MAN-PLEASER

NOT AS A MAN-PLEASER, BUT AS CONTINUALLY BEARING IN	569 25

MAN-SERVANT

THY MAN-SERVANT, AND THY MAID-SERVANT, THY CATTLE,	068 28
THY MAN-SERVANT, AND THY MAID-SERVANT, THY CATTLE,	286 28
THY MAN-SERVANT, AND THY MAID-SERVANT, THY CATTLE,	579 08

MAN'S

OF YOU, OR OF MAN'S JUDGMENT	094 07
CLOTHES AT A YOUNG MAN'S FEET, WHOSE NAME WAS SAUL	100 12
OWN HEART, THIS MAN'S RELIGION IS VAIN	176 15
FELL FROM THE RICH MAN'S TABLE	190 07
THINGS AS PASS MAN'S UNDERSTANDING	197 05
OURSELVES TO EVERY MAN'S CONSCIENCE IN THE SIGHT OF	250 31
OWN HEART, THIS MAN'S RELIGION IS VAIN	266 06
ORDERETH A GOOD MAN'S GOING, *	386 08
TO STRENGTHEN MAN'S HEART	468 25
HE IN ANY MAN'S LEGS	523 16
I HAVE COVETED NO MAN'S SILVER, OR GOLD, OR APPAREL	551 05
THE FATHER, TOOK MAN'S NATURE IN THE WOMB OF THE	603 11
THE PERFECTION OF MAN'S NATURE	603 22
ORDAINED ONLY BY MAN'S AUTHORITY, SO THAT ALL THINGS	610 02

MANASSEH

IS MINE, AND MANASSEH IS MINE	412 25
AND MANASSEH, *	441 06
IS MINE, AND MANASSEH IS MINE	479 20

MANFULLY

AND MANFULLY TO FIGHT UNDER HIS BANNER,	280 07

MANGER

IN SWADDLING CLOTHES, AND LAID HIM IN A MANGER	099 09
WRAPPED IN SWADDLING CLOTHES, LYING IN A MANGER	099 19
AND THE BABE LYING IN A MANGER	106 12

MANHOOD

THE GODHEAD AND MANHOOD, WERE JOINED TOGETHER IN ONE	603 12

MANIFEST

AND WILL MAKE MANIFEST THE COUNSELS OF THE HEARTS	094 12
OF A STAR DIDST MANIFEST THY ONLY-BEGOTTEN SON TO THE	107 29
ARE MADE MANIFEST BY THE LIGHT	129 19
DOTH MAKE MANIFEST IS LIGHT	129 20
BLESSED SON DID MANIFEST HIMSELF TO HIS DISCIPLES IN	166 06
AND WILL MANIFEST MYSELF TO HIM	181 21

MANIFEST   CONTINUED

THAT THOU WILT MANIFEST THYSELF UNTO US, AND NOT UNTO	181 23
MAY BE MADE MANIFEST, THAT THEY ARE WROUGHT IN GOD	185 11
MAY MANIFEST THY POWER AMONG ALL PEOPLES,	185 16
THE FLESH ARE MANIFEST, WHICH ARE THESE	209 19
I WAS MADE MANIFEST UNTO THEM THAT ASKED NOT AFTER	227 20
MANIFEST IN THY CHURCH THE LIKE POWER AND LOVE, TO	253 18
IT IS MANIFEST THAT HE IS EXCEPTED, WHICH DID	328 33
THEREBY MAY BE MANIFEST UNTO ALL MEN	558 24

MANIFESTATION

BUT THE MANIFESTATION OF THE SPIRIT IS GIVEN TO EVERY	182 25
FOR THE MANIFESTATION OF THE SONS OF GOD	194 14
BUT THE MANIFESTATION OF THE SPIRIT IS GIVEN TO EVERY	203 25
BUT BY MANIFESTATION OF THE TRUTH COMMENDING	250 30
FOR THE MANIFESTATION OF THE SONS OF GOD	330 29

MANIFESTED

THE LORD HATH MANIFESTED FORTH HIS GLORY	R 008 21
MORTAL FLESH, MANIFESTED FORTH HIS GLORY	077 23
THE LIFE WAS MANIFESTED, AND WE HAVE SEEN IT,	101 15
AND WAS MANIFESTED UNTO US	101 17
AND MANIFESTED FORTH HIS GLORY	113 31
SON WAS MANIFESTED THAT HE MIGHT DESTROY THE WORKS OF	117 04
THAT HE WAS MANIFESTED TO TAKE AWAY OUR SINS	117 23
OF GOD WAS MANIFESTED, THAT HE MIGHT DESTROY THE	117 30
IN THIS WAS MANIFESTED THE LOVE OF GOD TOWARD US,	189 11
THOU HAST MANIFESTED UNTO US IN THY SON, JESUS CHRIST	596 09

MANIFESTLY

MANIFESTLY APPEARED TO ALL HIS	078 18

MANIFOLD

AND CONFESS OUR MANIFOLD SINS AND WICKEDNESS	005 30
AND CONFESS OUR MANIFOLD SINS AND WICKEDNESS	023 06
AND BEWAIL OUR MANIFOLD SINS AND WICKEDNESS, WHICH	075 19
THROUGH OUR MANIFOLD SINS, TO OFFER UNTO THEE ANY	081 29
BUT IN THY MANIFOLD AND GREAT MERCIES	082 15
THE CHURCH THE MANIFOLD WISDOM OF GOD, ACCORDING TO	108 25
THE SUNDRY AND MANIFOLD CHANGES OF THE WORLD,	174 22
STEWARDS OF THE MANIFOLD GRACE OF GOD	179 18
OF THY MANIFOLD GIFTS, NOR YET OF GRACE TO USE THEM	240 31
MAY OBTAIN THE MANIFOLD BLESSINGS OF THY GRACE	267 08
THE SUNDRY AND MANIFOLD CHANGES OF THE WORLD, OUR	285 29
IN THEM THY MANIFOLD GIFTS OF GRACE	297 19
IN JESUS, THE MANIFOLD BLESSINGS OF THY LOVE, THAT	335 28
24 O LORD, HOW MANIFOLD ARE THY WORKS	469 08
AND THE MANIFOLD TEMPTATIONS WHICH WE DAILY	588 13
OUR MANIFOLD TRANSGRESSIONS OF THY RIGHTEOUS	589 31

MANKIND

DECLARED UNTO MANKIND IN CHRIST JESUS OUR LORD	006 27
PRESERVER OF ALL MANKIND, WE HUMBLY BESEECH THEE FOR	018 31
DECLARED UNTO MANKIND IN CHRIST JESUS OUR LORD	024 02
PRESERVER OF ALL MANKIND, WE HUMBLY BESEECH THEE FOR	032 26
THEM TO MANKIND IN THE CLEAREST, PLAINEST, MOST	VI 41
LOVE TOWARDS MANKIND, HAST SENT THY SON, OUR SAVIOUR	134 06
THAT ALL MANKIND SHOULD FOLLOW THE EXAMPLE OF	134 08
THAT THEREBY MANKIND MAY BE DRAWN TO THY BLESSED	260 23
WHO HATH REDEEMED ME, AND ALL MANKIND	284 32
PRESERVER OF ALL MANKIND, GIVER OF ALL SPIRITUAL	303 03
CREATOR OF MANKIND, WHO ONLY ART THE WELL-SPRING	303 14
MAKER OF MANKIND, WHO DOST CORRECT THOSE WHOM	321 18
THE SALVATION OF MANKIND, WE RENDER UNTO THEE MOST	545 24
WHO HATH REDEEMED ME, AND ALL MANKIND	578 14
OUR INTERCESSIONS FOR ALL MANKIND	590 22
IS OFFERED TO MANKIND BY CHRIST, WHO IS THE ONLY	604 16
IN CHRIST OUT OF MANKIND, AND TO BRING THEM BY CHRIST	606 09

MANNA

FATHERS DID EAT MANNA IN THE WILDERNESS, AND ARE	322 23
25 HE RAINED DOWN MANNA ALSO UPON THEM FOR TO EAT,	436 18

MANNER

BE READ, IN LIKE MANNER, THE SECOND LESSON, TAKEN OUT	R 014 02
IN SUCH MANNER AS THEY MIGHT JUDGE MOST CONVENIENT	VI 12
AND MAJESTIC MANNER, FOR THE SAKE OF JESUS CHRIST,	VI 42
THOU SHALT DO NO MANNER OF WORK	068 27
IN LIKE MANNER, (IF ANY BE PRESENT,) AND,	R 082 27
AND AFTER THE MANNER OF DISSEMBLERS WITH GOD	087 11
AFTER THE MANNER OF THE PURIFYING OF THE JEWS,	113 19
BEHOLD, WHAT MANNER OF LOVE THE FATHER HATH BESTOWED	117 14
AFTER THE SAME MANNER ALSO HE TOOK THE CUP, WHEN HE	152 21
AS THE MANNER OF SOME IS	158 26
UNTO THEM, WHAT MANNER OF COMMUNICATIONS ARE THESE	167 10
FORGETTETH WHAT MANNER OF MAN HE WAS	176 09
SO COME IN LIKE MANNER AS YE HAVE SEEN HIM GO INTO	178 19
I SPEAK AFTER THE MANNER OF MEN BECAUSE OF THE	190 06
IN HER MIND WHAT MANNER OF SALUTATION THIS SHOULD BE	236 12
WHAT MANNER OF CHILD SHALL THIS BE	243 30
AND SHALL SAY ALL MANNER OF EVIL AGAINST YOU FALSELY,	257 32
FORGETTETH WHAT MANNER OF MAN HE WAS	265 33
THOU SHALT DO NO MANNER OF WORK	286 27
GIVE THEIR TROTH TO EACH OTHER IN THIS MANNER	R 301 24
SHALL WANT NO MANNER OF THING THAT IS GOOD	380 22
THEE IN THIS MANNER, *	414 33
THERE CAME ALL MANNER OF FLIES, *	471 34
SOUL ABHORRED ALL MANNER OF MEAT, *	477 11

MANNER   CONTINUED

AS IN ALL MANNER OF RICHES   490 26
WITH ALL MANNER OF STORE   520 19
A DEACON, IN SUCH MANNER AND FORM AS FOLLOWETH   529 31
AFTER THIS MANNER FOLLOWING   R 532 24
IN SUCH MANNER AND FORM AS HEREAFTER   R 535 36
AFTER WHAT MANNER I HAVE BEEN WITH YOU AT ALL   550 07
PLACE IN SOLEMN MANNER, FOR THE SEVERAL OFFICES CF   564 23
THOU SHALT DO NO MANNER OF WORK   579 07
THEIR LIVING AND MANNER OF CEREMONIES, BUT ALSO IN   606 43
ONLY AFTER AN HEAVENLY AND SPIRITUAL MANNER   608 45

MANNERS

SOUND LEARNING, AND PURE MANNERS   036 13
AND IN DIVERS MANNERS SPAKE IN TIME PAST UNTO THE   096 22
IN FRAMING THE MANNERS BOTH OF YOURSELVES, AND OF   541 04
FOR EXAMPLE OF LIFE AND INSTRUCTION OF MANNERS   604 03
AND MEN'S MANNERS, SO THAT NOTHING BE ORDAINED   609 34

MANSIONS

IN MY FATHER'S HOUSE ARE MANY MANSIONS   239 31
IN MY FATHER'S HOUSE ARE MANY MANSIONS   331 19

MANY

AND BESEECH YOU, AS MANY AS ARE HERE PRESENT, TO   006 10
AND BESEECH YOU, AS MANY AS ARE HERE PRESENT, TO   023 19
HITHER OUT OF MANY KINDREDS AND TONGUES   036 16
THE HEARTS OF MANY TO DEDICATE THEMSELVES TO THE   039 19
FOR YOU, AND FOR MANY, FOR THE REMISSION OF SINS   080 27
BUT AS MANY AS RECEIVED HIM, TO THEM GAVE HE POWER TO   097 33
AND THERE ARE ALSO MANY OTHER THINGS WHICH JESUS DID,   102 15
AS THE VOICE OF MANY WATERS, AND AS THE VOICE OF A   103 02
FOR AS WE HAVE MANY MEMBERS IN ONE BODY, AND ALL   110 13
SO WE, BEING MANY, ARE ONE BODY IN CHRIST, AND EVERY   110 14
IN THE MIDST OF SO MANY AND GREAT DANGERS, THAT BY   114 05
SAY UNTO YOU, THAT MANY SHALL COME FROM THE EAST AND   115 18
FOR MANY BE CALLED, BUT FEW CHOSEN   120 12
AS POOR, YET MAKING MANY RICH   126 20
THE DESOLATE HATH MANY MORE CHILDREN THAN SHE WHICH   131 10
BUT WHAT ARE THEY AMONG SO MANY   131 34
THOU NOT HOW MANY THINGS THEY WITNESS AGAINST THEE   135 23
FOR I HAVE SUFFERED MANY THINGS THIS DAY IN A DREAM   135 34
AND MANY BODIES OF THE SAINTS WHICH SLEPT AROSE, AND   137 28
WENT INTO THE HOLY CITY, AND APPEARED UNTO MANY   137 30
OF THE NEW TESTAMENT, WHICH IS SHED FOR MANY   141 14
FOR MANY BARE FALSE WITNESS AGAINST HIM, BUT THEIR   143 04
ACCUSED HIM OF MANY THINGS   145 08
BEHOLD HOW MANY THINGS THEY WITNESS AGAINST THEE   145 10
CHRIST WAS ONCE OFFERED TO BEAR THE SINS OF MANY   148 09
AND MANY OTHER THINGS BLASPHEMOUSLY SPAKE THEY   151 26
HE HAD HEARD MANY THINGS OF HIM   153 12
WITH HIM IN MANY WORDS   153 14
TITLE THEN READ MANY OF THE JEWS   160 03
AND HE WAS SEEN MANY DAYS OF THEM WHICH CAME UP WITH   169 03
I HAVE YET MANY THINGS TO SAY UNTO YOU, BUT YE CANNOT   175 17
HIS PASSION BY MANY INFALLIBLE PROOFS, BEING SEEN OF   177 27
THE HOLY GHOST NOT MANY DAYS HENCE   178 04
IS ONE, AND HATH MANY MEMBERS, AND ALL THE MEMBERS OF   183 02
ONE BODY, BEING MANY, ARE ONE BODY   183 03
FOR THE BODY IS NOT ONE MEMBER, BUT MANY   183 08
WERE ASTONISHED, AS MANY AS CAME WITH PETER, BECAUSE   184 23
A CERTAIN MAN MADE A GREAT SUPPER, AND BADE MANY   192 04
YE NOT, THAT SO MANY OF US AS WERE BAPTIZED INTO   197 10
HE ASKED THEM, HOW MANY LOAVES HAVE YE   199 16
FOR AS MANY AS ARE LED BY THE SPIRIT OF GOD, THEY ARE   200 06
BUT WITH MANY OF THEM GOD WAS NOT WELL PLEASED   201 11
AND NOT MANY DAYS AFTER THE YOUNGER SON GATHERED ALL   202 02
HE SAID, HOW MANY HIRED SERVANTS OF MY FATHER'S HAVE   202 11
LO, THESE MANY YEARS DO I SERVE THEE, NEITHER   202 34
HE SAITH NOT, AND TO SEEDS, AS OF MANY   207 20
I TELL YOU, THAT MANY PROPHETS AND KINGS HAVE DESIRED   208 08
AS MANY AS DESIRE TO MAKE A FAIR SHEW IN THE FLESH,   210 24
AND AS MANY AS WALK ACCORDING TO THIS RULE, PEACE BE   211 02
AND MANY OF HIS DISCIPLES WENT WITH HIM, AND MUCH   212 28
AND AS MANY AS YE SHALL FIND, BID TO THE   218 18
TOGETHER ALL AS MANY AS THEY FOUND, BOTH BAD AND   218 20
FOR MANY ARE CALLED, BUT FEW ARE CHOSEN   218 28
FOR MANY WALK, OF WHOM I HAVE TOLD YOU OFTEN,   222 17
BUT WHAT ARE THEY AMONG SO MANY   225 31
AND MANY OTHER SIGNS TRULY DID JESUS IN THE PRESENCE   229 09
I HAVE HEARD BY MANY OF THIS MAN, HOW MUCH EVIL HE   230 22
BUT MANY THAT ARE FIRST SHALL BE LAST   231 21
AND RISING AGAIN OF MANY IN ISRAEL   233 12
THE THOUGHTS OF MANY HEARTS MAY BE REVEALED   233 15
FATHER'S HOUSE ARE MANY MANSIONS   239 31
APOSTLE SAINT PETER MANY EXCELLENT GIFTS, AND   244 23
AND TO GIVE HIS LIFE A RANSOM FOR MANY   247 27
THE APOSTLES WERE MANY SIGNS AND WONDERS WROUGHT   249 21
THE HOUSE, BEHOLD, MANY PUBLICANS AND SINNERS CAME   251 16
INTO THE HEARTS OF MANY TO OFFER THEMSELVES FOR THIS   260 22
AND AS MANY AS WERE ORDAINED TO ETERNAL LIFE   261 07
AND GIVE HIM AS MANY AS HE NEEDETH   263 03
TELL ME HOW MANY COMMANDMENTS THERE ARE   285 15
HOW MANY SACRAMENTS HATH CHRIST ORDAINED IN HIS   292 04
HOW MANY PARTS ARE THERE IN A SACRAMENT   292 14
MANY ARE THEY THAT RISE AGAINST ME   309 14
MANY ONE THERE BE THAT SAY OF MY SOUL, THERE IS NO   309 16
MEN ARE SUBJECT TO MANY SUDDEN PERILS, DISEASES,   R 321 02
SIGNIFYING ALSO HOW MANY THERE ARE TO COMMUNICATE   R 321 13
AS MANY AS ARE LED BY THE SPIRIT OF GOD, THEY ARE THE   330 19
FATHER'S HOUSE ARE MANY MANSIONS   331 19
MANY ARE THEY THAT RISE AGAINST ME   346 25

MANY   CONTINUED

2 MANY ONE THERE BE THAT SAY OF MY SOUL, *   346 27
6 THERE BE MANY THAT SAY, *   347 23
AND TOOK ME OUT OF MANY WATERS   360 32
12 MANY OXEN ARE COME ABOUT ME   366 27
16 FOR MANY DOGS ARE COME ABOUT ME, *   367 04
MINE ENEMIES, HOW MANY THEY ARE   370 22
ME WRONGFULLY ARE MANY IN NUMBER   388 15
4 MANY SHALL SEE IT, AND FEAR, *   390 16
FOR THERE WERE MANY THAT STROVE WITH ME   407 28
FOR THEY BE MANY THAT FIGHT AGAINST ME, O THOU MOST   408 17
WERE A MONSTER UNTO MANY, *   425 19
39 YEA, MANY A TIME TURNED HE HIS WRATH AWAY,   437 16
41 MANY A TIME DID THEY PROVOKE HIM IN THE   437 21
THE REBUKES OF MANY PEOPLE   453 09
42 MANY A TIME DID HE DELIVER THEM   475 22
84 HOW MANY ARE THE DAYS OF THY SERVANT   495 25
157 MANY THERE ARE THAT TROUBLE ME, AND PERSECUTE ME   500 25
MANY A TIME HAVE THEY FOUGHT AGAINST ME FROM MY YOUTH   506 21
2 YEA, MANY A TIME HAVE THEY VEXED ME FROM MY YOUTH   506 23
AS MANY AS HAVE EVIL WILL AT SION   506 30
THY HOLY APOSTLES MANY EXCELLENT GIFTS, AND DIDST   549 08
OF MIND, AND WITH MANY TEARS, AND TEMPTATIONS,   550 09
TELL ME HOW MANY THERE ARE   578 19
HOW MANY SACRAMENTS HATH CHRIST ORDAINED   581 07
HOW MANY PARTS ARE THERE IN A SACRAMENT   581 16
OR EXAMINE SO MANY CHILDREN OF HIS PARISH, SENT UNTO   R 582 29
CALLED TOGETHER AS MANY OF THE FAMILY AS CAN   R 587 04
AND MAY AS MANY AS HAVE RECEIVED IT, LIVE AS BECOMES   590 24
NOTWITHSTANDING OUR MANY AND GREAT PROVOCATIONS   591 15
YET OFFEND IN MANY THINGS   605 36
GIVEN OCCASION TO MANY SUPERSTITIONS   608 43

MARK

HEAR THEM, READ, MARK, LEARN, AND INWARDLY DIGEST   092 09
TOGETHER OF ME, AND MARK THEM WHICH WALK SO AS YE   222 15
HEAVENLY DOCTRINE OF THY EVANGELIST SAINT MARK   237 07
TAKE MARK, AND BRING HIM WITH THEE   254 12
WRITTEN BY SAINT MARK, IN THE TENTH CHAPTER, AT THE   274 23
WILT BE EXTREME TO MARK WHAT IS DONE AMISS, *   328 17
12 MARK WELL HER BULWARKS, CONSIDER HER PALACES,   400 02
AND MARK MY STEPS, WHEN THEY LAY WAIT FOR MY SOUL   408 27
WILT BE EXTREME TO MARK WHAT IS DONE AMISS, *   507 12
OF PROFESSION, AND MARK OF DIFFERENCE, WHEREBY   608 24

MARKED

WHEN HE MARKED HOW THEY CHOSE OUT THE CHIEF   214 09

MARKET-PLACE

IDLE IN THE MARKET-PLACE, AND SAID UNTO THEM   119 20

MARKS

IN MY BODY THE MARKS OF THE LORD JESUS   211 05

MARRIAGE

DAY THERE WAS A MARRIAGE IN CANA OF GALILEE   113 11
AND HIS DISCIPLES, TO THE MARRIAGE   113 13
WHICH MADE A MARRIAGE FOR HIS SON, AND SENT FORTH HIS   218 04
COME UNTO THE MARRIAGE   218 10
AND AS MANY AS YE SHALL FIND, BID TO THE MARRIAGE   218 18
THEIR MARRIAGE IS NOT LAWFUL   300 30
OF THE PROPOSED MARRIAGE, MAY DEMAND SUFFICIENT   R 301 03
THE SPIRITUAL MARRIAGE AND UNITY BETWIXT CHRIST AND   303 21
THE BANNS OF MARRIAGE BETWEEN N   R 304 22
AND THEIR MAIDENS WERE NOT GIVEN IN MARRIAGE   439 05
OR TO ABSTAIN FROM MARRIAGE   609 22

MARRIAGE-GARMENT

IN THE MARRIAGE-GARMENT REQUIRED BY GOD IN HOLY   087 13

MARRIED

THEY WERE MARRIED, WERE NOT SO EXCUSED, BUT COUNTED   089 05
I HAVE MARRIED A WIFE, AND THEREFORE I CANNOT   192 11
PERSONS TO BE MARRIED SHALL COME INTO THE BODY OF THE   R 300 04
WHO ARE TO BE MARRIED, HE SHALL SAY, I REQUIRE AND   R 300 23
THIS WOMAN TO BE MARRIED TO THIS MAN   301 23

MARROW

AS IT WERE WITH MARROW AND FATNESS, *   415 02

MARRY

CHRISTIAN MEN, TO MARRY AT THEIR OWN DISCRETION,   609 23

MARTYR

OF THY FIRST MARTYR SAINT STEPHEN, WHO PRAYED FOR HIS   099 31
DEACONS THE FIRST MARTYR SAINT STEPHEN, WITH OTHERS   531 17

MARTYRS

NOBLE ARMY OF MARTYRS PRAISE THEE   010 18

MARVEL

MARVEL NOT THAT I SAID UNTO THEE, YE MUST BE BORN   188 13
MARVEL NOT, MY BRETHREN, IF THE WORLD HATE YOU   191 11

MARVEL   CONTINUED

MARVEL NOT THAT I SAID UNTO THEE, YE MUST BE BORN   275 18

MARVELLED

HEARD IT, HE MARVELLED, AND SAID TO THEM THAT   115 16
THE GOVERNOR MARVELLED GREATLY   135 25
SO THAT PILATE MARVELLED   145 12
ALL AMAZED AND MARVELLED, SAYING ONE TO ANOTHER,   180 29
SAW IT, THEY MARVELLED, AND GLORIFIED GOD, WHICH HAD   217 13
THEY MARVELLED, AND LEFT HIM, AND WENT THEIR   223 12
AND HIS MOTHER MARVELLED AT THOSE THINGS WHICH WERE   233 10
AND THEY MARVELLED ALL   243 24
4 THEY MARVELLED TO SEE SUCH THINGS   399 18

MARVELLOUS

HE HATH DONE MARVELLOUS THINGS   027 05
OF ALL THY MARVELLOUS WORKS   351 23
7 SHOW THY MARVELLOUS LOVING-KINDNESS, THOU THAT ART   358 31
SHOWED ME MARVELLOUS GREAT KINDNESS IN A STRONG CITY   377 10
13 MARVELLOUS THINGS DID HE IN THE SIGHT CF OUR   435 24
HE HATH DONE MARVELLOUS THINGS   461 26
REMEMBER THE MARVELLOUS WORKS THAT HE HATH DONE   470 12
SO DONE HIS MARVELLOUS WORKS, *   482 30
AND IT IS MARVELLOUS IN OUR EYES   489 14
MARVELLOUS ARE THY WORKS, AND THAT MY SOUL KNOWETH   515 16
THE LORD, AND MARVELLOUS WORTHY TO BE PRAISED   520 31
MIGHT OF THY MARVELLOUS ACTS   521 04

MARY

BY THE HOLY GHOST, BORN OF THE VIRGIN MARY   015 22
GHOST OF THE VIRGIN MARY, AND WAS MADE MAN   016 08
BY THE HOLY GHOST, BORN OF THE VIRGIN MARY   029 27
GHOST OF THE VIRGIN MARY, AND WAS MADE MAN   030 13
GHOST OF THE VIRGIN MARY, AND WAS MADE MAN   071 10
OF THE VIRGIN MARY HIS MOTHER   077 17
TO BE TAXED WITH MARY HIS ESPOUSED WIFE, BEING GREAT   099 04
WHEN AS HIS MOTHER MARY WAS ESPOUSED TO JOSEPH,   104 28
TO TAKE UNTO THEE MARY THY WIFE   105 05
AND FOUND MARY, AND JCSEPH, AND THE BABE LYING   106 11
BUT MARY KEPT ALL THESE THINGS, AND PONDERED THEM IN   106 16
YOUNG CHILD WITH MARY HIS MOTHER, AND FELL DOWN, AND   109 20
MOTHER'S SISTER, MARY THE WIFE OF CLEOPHAS, AND MARY   160 18
OF CLEOPHAS, AND MARY MAGDALENE   160 19
AND THE OTHER MARY, SITTING OVER AGAINST THE   162 14
AND THERE WAS MARY MAGDALENE, AND THE OTHER MARY,   162 14
OF THE WEEK COMETH MARY MAGDALENE EARLY, WHEN IT WAS   164 10
SABBATH WAS PAST, MARY MAGDALENE, AND MARY THE MOTHER   165 18
MARY MAGDALENE, AND MARY THE MOTHER OF JAMES, ANC   165 19
AND SAID UNTO MARY HIS MOTHER, BEHOLD, THIS   233 11
AND THE VIRGIN'S NAME WAS MARY   236 08
AND THE ANGEL SAID UNTO HER, FEAR NOT, MARY   236 13
THEN SAID MARY UNTO THE ANGEL, HOW SHALL THIS BE,   236 20
AND MARY SAID, BEHOLD THE HANDMAID OF THE LORD   236 28
BY THE HOLY GHOST, BORN OF THE VIRGIN MARY   284 16
BY THE HOLY GHOST, BORN OF THE VIRGIN MARY   577 31

MASSES

THE SACRIFICES OF MASSES, IN THE WHICH IT WAS   609 17

MASTER

KNOW NOT WHEN THE MASTER OF THE HOUSE COMETH, AT   021 24
GREAT LOVE OF OUR MASTER, AND ONLY SAVIOUR, JESUS   086 13
OF THE HOUSE, THE MASTER SAITH, WHERE IS THE   140 29
AND SAITH, MASTER, MASTER   142 20
AND SAITH, MASTER, MASTER   142 21
OF THE HOUSE, THE MASTER SAITH UNTO THEE, WHERE IS   148 29
YE CALL ME MASTER AND LORD   156 14
YOUR LORD AND MASTER, HAVE WASHED YOUR FEET   156 16
ART THOU A MASTER OF ISRAEL, AND KNOWEST NOT   188 19
THEN THE MASTER OF THE HOUSE BEING ANGRY SAID TC HIS   192 13
THE DISCIPLE IS NOT ABOVE HIS MASTER   195 04
EVERY ONE THAT IS PERFECT SHALL BE AS HIS MASTER   195 05
SAID UNTO HIM, MASTER, WE HAVE TOILED ALL THE NIGHT,   196 16
SAYING, MASTER, WHAT SHALL I DC TO INHERIT   208 12
AND SAID, JESUS, MASTER, HAVE MERCY ON US   210 04
AND SAYING, MASTER, WHICH IS THE GREAT   215 09
MASTER, WE KNOW THAT THOU ART TRUE, AND   222 30
SAID UNTO JESUS, MASTER, IT IS GCOD FOR US TO BE   249 02
WHY EATETH YOUR MASTER WITH PUBLICANS AND SINNERS   251 18
TO CHRIST AS MY MASTER, I RECEIVE THE STRENGTHENING   291 26
THE MASTER OR MISTRESS HAVING CALLED TOGETHER AS   R 587 04
LET THE MASTER OR MISTRESS, OR ANY OTHER   R 589 13

MASTERS

NO MAN CAN SERVE TWO MASTERS   211 09
SPIRITUAL PASTORS AND MASTERS   288 29
HAND OF THEIR MASTERS, AND AS THE EYES OF A MAICEN   503 30
SPIRITUAL PASTORS AND MASTERS   580 06
MASTERS, AND MISTRESSES, SHALL CAUSE THEIR   R 582 31

MASTERS'

FALL FROM THEIR MASTERS' TABLE   128 19

MASTERY

STRIVETH FOR THE MASTERY IS TEMPERATE IN ALL THINGS   119 07

MATERIALS

THE CHIEFEST MATERIALS, AS IN THE FRAME AND ORDER   V 31

MATRIMONY

THE BANNS OF MATRIMONY, AND OF OTHER MATTERS TO BE   R 071 27
OF MATRIMONY, THE PERSONS TO BE MARRIED SHALL COME   R 300 03
THIS MAN AND THIS WOMAN IN HOLY MATRIMONY   300 10
TOGETHER IN MATRIMONY, YE DO NOW CONFESS IT   300 28
GOD'S ORDINANCE IN THE HOLY ESTATE OF MATRIMONY   301 08
GOD'S ORDINANCE IN THE HOLY ESTATE OF MATRIMONY   301 16
THE STATE OF MATRIMONY THAT IN IT IS REPRESENTED THE   303 20
RESPECTING MATRIMONY, WHETHER BY PUBLISHING THE BANNS R 304 17
IN HOLY MATRIMONY, YE ARE TO DECLARE IT   R 304 24
HOLY ESTATE OF MATRIMONY, MAY FAITHFULLY PERFORM AND   566 09
MATRIMONY, AND EXTREME UNCTION, ARE NOT TO BE   607 39

MATTER

IT IS AN EASY MATTER FOR A MAN TO SAY, I WILL NCT   088 26
GO BEYOND AND DEFRAUD HIS BROTHER IN ANY MATTER   127 32
INSTRUCTED IN THE MATTER CONTAINED IN THESE OFFICES,   R 295 15
HE FEEL HIS CONSCIENCE TROUBLED WI TH ANY MATTER   R 313 25
MAYEST TAKE THE MATTER INTO THY HAND   354 05
MY HEART OVERFLOWETH WITH A GOOD MATTER   396 15

MATTERS

AND OF OTHER MATTERS TO BE PUBLISHED   R 071 28
MYSELF IN GREAT MATTERS *   507 25
BUT ALSO IN MATTERS OF FAITH   606 44

MATTHEW

SON DIDST CALL MATTHEW FROM THE RECEIPT OF CUSTOM TC   250 21
SAW A MAN, NAMED MATTHEW, SITTING AT THE RECEIPT OF   251 13
WRITTEN BY SAINT MATTHEW, IN THE TWENTY-EIGHTH   275 23
MATTHEW   R 339 20
BE EITHER SAINT MATTHEW IX   R 547 25

MATTHIAS

MATTHIAS   R 125 24
SERVANT MATTHIAS TO BE OF THE NUMBER OF THE TWELVE   233 32
WHO WAS SURNAMED JUSTUS, AND MATTHIAS   234 26
AND THE LOT FELL UPON MATTHIAS   234 32
THEY ORDAINED MATTHIAS TO BE OF THE NUMBER OF THE   553 08

MAYEST

PREPARE THAT THOU MAYEST EAT THE PASSOVER   140 24
WHOM, THOU MAYEST RECEIVE HEALTH AND SALVATION, BUT   314 20
THAT THOU MAYEST TAKE THE MATTER INTO THY   354 05
THAT THOU MAYEST SAVE ME   375 26
A TIME WHEN THOU MAYEST BE FOUND   378 03
WHOM THOU MAYEST MAKE PRINCES IN ALL LANDS   397 20
THAT THOU MAYEST UTTERLY DESTROY EVERY ENEMY, *   430 10
13 THAT THOU MAYEST GIVE HIM PATIENCE IN TIME OF   458 12
THAT THOU MAYEST GIVE THEM MEAT IN DUE SEASON   469 14
THAT THOU MAYEST ACCEPT THEIR BOUNDEN DUTY AND   566 20

MEA

ANIMA MEA, MAY BE SUNG OR SAID THE GLORIA   R 025 18

MEAN

TO KEEP THE HAPPY MEAN BETWEEN TOO MUCH STIFFNESS IN   V 24
EXHORT YOU, IN THE MEAN SEASON TO CONSIDER THE   087 08
WHAT DO WE MEAN BY THESE WORDS   291 06
WE MEAN THAT THE CHURCH IS ONE   291 07
WHAT DO YOU MEAN BY THIS WORD SACRAMENT   292 09
I MEAN BY THIS WORD SACRAMENT AN OUTWARD AND   292 10
I MEAN AN OUTWARD AND VISIBLE SIGN OF AN   581 12
AND THE MEAN WHEREBY THE BODY OF CHRIST IS RECEIVED   608 45

MEANEST

WHAT MEANEST THOU BY THIS WORD SACRAMENT   581 11

MEANETH

LEARN WHAT THAT MEANETH, I WILL HAVE MERCY, AND NOT   251 21

MEANING

OF THE SAME MEANING IN THE CREED   R 015 18
OF THE SAME MEANING IN THE CREED   R 029 23
PERSON ON THE MEANING AND USE OF THE TIME OF   R 313 16

MEANS

FOR THE MEANS OF GRACE, AND FOR THE HOPE OF GLORY   019 24
FOR THE MEANS OF GRACE, AND FOR THE HOPE OF GLORY   033 22
PROSPER THE MEANS MADE USE OF FOR THEIR CURE   045 07
THE WAY AND MEANS THERETO IS   087 16
WHO BY THIS MEANS CANNOT QUIET HIS CWN   088 04
LEST THAT BY ANY MEANS, WHEN I HAVE PREACHED TO   119 12
THAT BY MEANS OF DEATH, FOR THE REDEMPTION   133 04
THOU SHALT BY NO MEANS COME OUT THENCE, TILL THOU   198 16
WHAT SPECIAL MEANS DOES THE CHURCH PROVIDE TO HELP   291 21
AS A MEANS WHEREBY WE RECEIVE THIS GRACE,   292 12
AND PROSPER THE MEANS WHICH SHALL BE MADE USE OF FOR   315 28
CONSUMED BY THE MEANS OF THY HEAVY HAND   389 30

MEANS CONTINUED

BY ANY OTHER MEANS COMPASS THE DOING OF SO WEIGHTY A 540 34
THE SAME, AS THE MEANS OF OUR SALVATION 547 10
AS A MEANS WHEREBY WE RECEIVE THE SAME, AND 581 14
AND TO BLESS THE MEANS MADE USE OF FOR HIS CURE 597 23

MEANT

THE MULTITUDE PASS BY, HE ASKED WHAT IT MEANT 123 28
THE SERVANTS, AND ASKED WHAT THESE THINGS MEANT 202 29

MEASURE

TO EVERY MAN THE MEASURE OF FAITH 110 12
IN STRIPES ABOVE MEASURE, IN PRISONS MORE FREQUENT, 120 31
GOOD MEASURE, PRESSED DOWN, AND SHAKEN TOGETHER, 194 29
WITH THE SAME MEASURE THAT YE METE WITHAL IT SHALL BE 194 31
UNTO US SUCH A MEASURE OF THY GRACE, THAT WE, RUNNING 204 24
AND WERE BEYOND MEASURE ASTONISHED, SAYING, HE HATH 207 07
CUBIT UNTO THE MEASURE OF HIS LIFE 211 20
ACCORDING TO THE MEASURE OF THE GIFT OF CHRIST 237 13
UNTO THE MEASURE OF THE STATURE OF THE FULNESS 237 24
WORKING IN THE MEASURE OF EVERY PART, MAKETH INCREASE 237 32
CUBIT UNTO THE MEASURE OF HIS LIFE 266 18
RECEIVE SUCH A MEASURE OF THY HOLY SPIRIT, THAT THEY 294 26
107 I AM TROUBLED ABOVE MEASURE 497 11
ACCORDING TO THE MEASURE OF THE GIFT OF CHRIST 537 33
UNTO THE MEASURE OF THE STATURE OF THE FULNESS 538 11
RECEIVE SUCH A MEASURE OF THY HOLY SPIRIT, THAT THEY 565 26

MEASURED

IT SHALL BE MEASURED TO YOU AGAIN 194 31

MEAT

AS HE SAT AT MEAT, THERE CAME A WOMAN HAVING 140 03
HE THAT SITTETH AT MEAT, OR HE THAT SERVETH 149 24
IS NOT HE THAT SITTETH AT MEAT 149 25
AS HE SAT AT MEAT WITH THEM, HE TOOK BREAD, AND 168 05
HE SAID UNTO THEM, HAVE YE HERE ANY MEAT 170 04
UP OF THE BROKEN MEAT THAT WAS LEFT SEVEN BASKETS 199 23
AND DID ALL EAT THE SAME SPIRITUAL MEAT 201 09
OF THEM THAT SIT AT MEAT WITH THEE 214 19
HE HAD RECEIVED MEAT, HE WAS STRENGTHENED 230 36
HE THAT SITTETH AT MEAT, OR HE THAT SERVETH 250 10
IS NOT HE THAT SITTETH AT MEAT 250 11
AS JESUS SAT AT MEAT IN THE HOUSE, BEHOLD, MANY 251 15
FOR I WAS AN HUNGRED, AND YE GAVE ME MEAT 259 06
TEARS HAVE BEEN MY MEAT DAY AND NIGHT, * 393 04
HERE AND THERE FOR MEAT, * 412 04
GAVEST HIM TO BE MEAT FOR THE PEOPLE OF THE 431 05
AND REQUIRED MEAT FOR THEIR LUST 436 05
FOR HE SENT THEM MEAT ENOUGH 436 20
31 BUT WHILE THE MEAT WAS YET IN THEIR MOUTHS, 436 32
THEY GIVEN TO BE MEAT UNTO THE FOWLS OF THE AIR, 440 02
DO SEEK THEIR MEAT FROM GOD 469 03
MAYEST GIVE THEM MEAT IN DUE SEASON 469 15
ALL MANNER OF MEAT, * 477 11
5 HE HATH GIVEN MEAT UNTO THEM THAT FEAR HIM 483 05
GIVEST THEM THEIR MEAT IN DUE SEASON 521 23
THEM TO SIT DOWN TO MEAT, AND WILL COME FORTH AND 534 22

MEAT-OFFERING

EVEN A MEAT-OFFERING AND A DRINK-OFFERING UNTO THE 124 27

MEDES

AND MEDES, AND ELAMITES, AND THE DWELLERS 180 32

MEDIATION

THE NAME AND MEDIATION OF JESUS CHRIST, OUR MOST 035 20
THE MERITS AND MEDIATION OF THY BLESSED SON, JESUS 063 06
THE MERITS AND MEDIATION OF JESUS CHRIST, THY SON, 206 10
BY THE MEDIATION OF OUR ONLY SAVIOUR JESUS 541 16
THE MERITS AND MEDIATION OF THY SON JESUS CHRIST, 589 07

MEDIATOR

ADVOCATE AND MEDIATOR, JESUS CHRIST 018 24
ADVOCATE AND MEDIATOR, JESUS CHRIST 032 23
OUR ONLY MEDIATOR AND ADVOCATE, JESUS CHRIST OUR 059 27
OUR MEDIATOR AND ADVOCATE 063 13
OUR ONLY MEDIATOR AND ADVOCATE 075 05
OUR ONLY MEDIATOR AND ADVOCATE 100 03
CAUSE HE IS THE MEDIATOR OF THE NEW TESTAMENT, 133 04
WAS ORDAINED BY ANGELS IN THE HAND OF A MEDIATOR 207 29
NOW A MEDIATOR IS NOT A MEDIATOR OF ONE, BUT GOD IS 207 30
IS NOT A MEDIATOR OF ONE, BUT GOD IS ONE 207 30
OUR MEDIATOR AND REDEEMER 335 15
OUR ONLY MEDIATOR AND ADVOCATE 336 29
OUR ONLY MEDIATOR AND REDEEMER 572 14
WHO IS THE ONLY MEDIATOR BETWEEN GOD AND MAN, BEING 604 17

MEDICINE

AND GIVETH MEDICINE TO HEAL THEIR SICKNESS 264 24
AND GIVETH MEDICINE TO HEAL THEIR SICKNESS 522 33

MEDITATION

AND THE MEDITATION OF MY HEART, BE ALWAYS ACCEPTABLE 003 19
AND THE MEDITATION OF MY HEART, BE ALWAY ACCEPTABLE 021 21

MEDITATION CONTINUED

JOY UPON THE MEDITATION OF THOSE MIGHTY ACTS, WHEREBY 147 09
CONSIDER MY MEDITATION 347 31
AND THE MEDITATION OF MY HEART, BE ALWAY ACCEPTABLE 364 13
AND THE MEDITATION OF HIS HEART, BE ALWAY ACCEPTABLE 572 22

MEEK

AND HATH EXALTED THE HUMBLE AND MEEK 026 23
WITH A MEEK, CANDID, AND CHARITABLE FRAME VI 37
WITH MEEK HEART AND DUE REVERENCE, THEY MAY 074 26
COMETH UNTO THEE, MEEK, AND SITTING UPON AN ASS, 091 21
ANOINTED ME TO PREACH GOOD TIDINGS UNTO THE MEEK 107 02
FOR I AM MEEK AND LOWLY IN HEART 235 13
BLESSED ARE THE MEEK 257 23
ABIDING OF THE MEEK SHALL NOT PERISH FOR EVER 352 29
8 THEM THAT ARE MEEK SHALL HE GUIDE IN JUDGMENT 370 02
AND TO HELP ALL THE MEEK UPON EARTH 433 07
LORD SETTETH UP THE MEEK, * 523 06
O GOD, BY WHOM THE MEEK ARE GUIDED IN JUDGMENT, 595 26

MEEK-HEARTED

AND HELPETH THE MEEK-HEARTED 525 10

MEEK-SPIRITED

11 BUT THE MEEK-SPIRITED SHALL POSSESS THE EARTH, 385 16

MEEKLY

OF GRACE TO HEAR MEEKLY THY WORD, AND TO RECEIVE IT 056 15
FROM US, WHO MEEKLY ACKNOWLEDGE OUR TRANSGRESSIONS, 062 22

MEEKNESS

OF MIND, MEEKNESS, LONG-SUFFERING 116 05
RECEIVE WITH MEEKNESS THE ENGRAFTED WORD, WHICH IS 175 03
MEEKNESS, TEMPERANCE 209 27
LOWLINESS AND MEEKNESS, WITH LONG-SUFFERING, 213 20
RECEIVE WITH MEEKNESS THE ENGRAFTED WORD, WHICH IS 265 27
OF TRUTH, OF MEEKNESS, AND RIGHTEOUSNESS 396 23

MEET

WE ASSEMBLE AND MEET TOGETHER TO RENDER THANKS FOR 006 05
WE ASSEMBLE AND MEET TOGETHER TO RENDER THANKS FOR 023 14
IT IS MEET AND RIGHT SO TO DO 076 29
AND SAY, IT IS VERY MEET, RIGHT, AND OUR BOUNDEN 076 31
SO SHALL YE BE MEET PARTAKERS OF THOSE HOLY 086 03
AND SAID, IT IS NOT MEET TO TAKE THE CHILDREN'S 128 17
AND THERE SHALL MEET YOU A MAN BEARING A PITCHER OF 140 26
THERE SHALL A MAN MEET YOU, BEARING A PITCHER OF 148 26
IT WAS MEET THAT WE SHOULD MAKE MERRY, AND BE GLAD 203 06
THAT AM NOT MEET TO BE CALLED AN APOSTLE, BECAUSE I 205 13
EVEN AS IT IS MEET FOR ME TO THINK THIS OF YOU ALL, 220 27
WHICH HATH MADE US MEET TO BE PARTAKERS OF THE 224 09
I THINK IT MEET, AS LONG AS I AM IN THIS TABERNACLE, 248 08
IN THE CLOUDS, TO MEET THE LORD IN THE AIR 269 09
IT IS MEET AND RIGHT SO TO DO 279 05
IT IS VERY MEET, RIGHT, AND OUR BOUNDEN DUTY, 279 07
WITH THEM, BE FOUND MEET TO BE PARTAKERS OF THE 335 33
3 FOR THOU SHALT MEET HIM WITH THE BLESSINGS OF 365 09
UNTO US, BE APT AND MEET, FOR THEIR LEARNING AND 530 14
AS SHALL BE FOUND MEET TO BE ORDERED, TO THE PRAYERS R 530 29
UNTO US, BE APT AND MEET, FOR THEIR LEARNING AND 536 15
THEY ARE PERSONS MEET FOR THE SAME 536 26
AS SHALL BE FOUND MEET TO BE ORDERED, TO THE PRAYERS R 537 05
WHICH WE DAILY MEET WITH 588 14
DO THEY MAKE MEN MEET TO RECEIVE GRACE, OR (AS THE 605 19

MEETING

THE MINISTER, MEETING THE BODY, AND GOING BEFORE R 324 03
THE MINISTER, MEETING THE BODY, AND GOING BEFORE R 338 03

MELCHIZEDEK

A PRIEST FOR EVER AFTER THE ORDER OF MELCHIZEDEK 482 15

MELODY

AND MAKING MELODY IN YOUR HEART TO THE LORD 217 29
O SING UNTO GOD WITH THE VOICE OF MELODY 398 22
THEN A SONG, AND MELODY IN OUR HEAVINESS 513 10

MELT

AND THE EARTH SHALL MELT AWAY 398 06

MELTED

5 THE HILLS MELTED LIKE WAX AT THE PRESENCE OF THE 461 06

MELTETH

AND LIKE AS WAX MELTETH AT THE FIRE, SO LET THE 419 12
THEIR SOUL MELTETH AWAY BECAUSE OF THE TROUBLE 477 29
28 MY SOUL MELTETH AWAY FOR VERY HEAVINESS 491 23
HIS WORD, AND MELTETH THEM 523 31

MELTING

IS EVEN LIKE MELTING WAX 366 33

MEMBER

BY EVERY TRUE MEMBER OF OUR CHURCH, AND EVERY SINCERE	VI 36
THAT EVERY MEMBER OF THE SAME, IN HIS VOCATION AND	156 31
BODY IS NOT ONE MEMBER, BUT MANY	183 07
BE MADE A LIVING MEMBER OF THE SAME	274 06
I WAS MADE A MEMBER OF CHRIST, THE CHILD OF GOD,	283 19
WERE YOU MADE A MEMBER OF THE CHURCH	290 28
I WAS MADE A MEMBER OF THE CHURCH WHEN I WAS	290 29
BOUNDEN DUTY AS A MEMBER OF THE CHURCH	291 16
THIS SICK MEMBER IN THE UNITY OF THE CHURCH	314 06
WITH THE BEST MEMBER THAT I HAVE	479 05
OR ANY MEMBER THEREOF, DO TAKE ANY HURT OR	540 11
WARDEN (OR THE MEMBER OF THE VESTRY SUPPLYING HIS	R 570 09
WARDEN (OR THE MEMBER OF THE VESTRY SUPPLYING HIS	R 570 25
I WAS MADE A MEMBER OF CHRIST, THE CHILD OF GOD,	577 10
GRANT THAT EVERY MEMBER OF THE SAME, IN HIS VOCATION	590 25
OR SOME OTHER MEMBER OF THE FAMILY, SAY AS FOLLOWETH,	R 592 10
OR SOME OTHER MEMBER OF THE FAMILY, SAY AS FOLLOWETH,	R 593 04

MEMBERS

MAKE THEM LIVING MEMBERS OF THY CHURCH	043 09
BY GOD IN THIS LAND, WHEREOF WE ARE MEMBERS	047 12
THAT WE ARE VERY MEMBERS INCORPORATE IN THE MYSTICAL	083 22
AND ALL OUR MEMBERS, BEING MORTIFIED FROM ALL WORLDLY	105 22
AS WE HAVE MANY MEMBERS IN ONE BODY, AND ALL MEMBERS	110 13
AND ALL MEMBERS HAVE NOT THE SAME OFFICE	110 14
AND EVERY ONE MEMBERS ONE OF ANOTHER	110 15
AND HATH MANY MEMBERS, AND ALL THE MEMBERS OF THAT	183 02
AND ALL THE MEMBERS OF THAT ONE BODY, BEING MANY, ARE	183 03
YIELDED YOUR MEMBERS SERVANTS TO UNCLEANNESS AND TO	198 27
NOW YIELD YOUR MEMBERS SERVANTS TO RIGHTEOUSNESS UNTO	198 29
FOR WE ARE MEMBERS ONE OF ANOTHER	216 18
FOR WE ARE MEMBERS OF HIS BODY, OF HIS FLESH,	267 28
AND ALL BAPTIZED PEOPLE ARE THE MEMBERS	290 33
SPIRIT DWELLS IN IT, AND SANCTIFIES ITS MEMBERS	291 10
BOOK WERE ALL MY MEMBERS WRITTEN	515 21
TWO MEMBERS OF THE VESTRY) STANDING ON THE	R 570 07
THEIR EARTHLY MEMBERS, AND DRAWING UP THEIR MIND TO	606 19

MEMORIAL

UNTO THEE, THE MEMORIAL THY SON HATH COMMANDED US TO	080 41
SPOKEN OF FOR A MEMORIAL OF HER	140 18
WHOSE MEMORIAL IS PERISHED WITH THEM	351 34
ROOT OUT THE MEMORIAL OF THEM FROM OFF THE EARTH	480 31
SO DOTH THY MEMORIAL, O LORD, FROM ONE GENERATION TO	510 29
7 THE MEMORIAL OF THINE ABUNDANT KINDNESS SHALL BE	521 06

MEMORY

A PERPETUAL MEMORY OF THAT HIS PRECIOUS DEATH	080 15
IF YE KEEP IN MEMORY WHAT I PREACHED UNTO YOU,	205 02
FILL MY MEMORY WITH THE WORDS OF THY LAW	573 16

MEN

O YE CHILDREN OF MEN, BLESS YE THE LORD	013 18
O YE HOLY AND HUMBLE MEN OF HEART, BLESS YE THE LORD	013 28
WHO FOR US MEN AND FOR OUR SALVATION CAME DOWN FROM	016 06
BESEECH THEE FOR ALL SORTS AND CONDITIONS OF MEN	018 28
AND LOVING-KINDNESS TO US, AND TO ALL MEN	019 17
OF GOD IS WITH MEN, AND HE WILL DWELL WITH THEM, AND	021 28
AND ON EARTH PEACE, GOOD WILL TOWARDS MEN	025 23
WHO FOR US MEN AND FOR OUR SALVATION CAME DOWN FROM	030 11
BESEECH THEE FOR ALL SORTS AND CONDITIONS OF MEN	032 28
AND LOVING-KINDNESS TO US, AND TO ALL MEN	033 11
ALL CONDITIONS OF MEN, OR, WHEN THAT IS NOT SAID,	R 035 03
BLOOD ALL NATIONS OF MEN FOR TO DWELL ON THE FACE OF	038 05
GRANT THAT ALL MEN EVERYWHERE MAY SEEK AFTER THEE AND	038 08
TO MAKE KNOWN TO ALL MEN THY BLESSED GIFT OF ETERNAL	038 21
AND SET FORWARD THE SALVATION OF ALL MEN	039 04
THEMSELVES TO THE SERVICE OF THEIR FELLOW MEN	043 31
OF JUSTICE AMONG MEN AND NATIONS, TO THE GLORY OF THY	044 14
AND TO THE BENEFIT OF OUR FELLOW MEN	044 23
WILLINGLY AFFLICT OR GRIEVE THE CHILDREN OF MEN	045 32
TEMPORAL AND SPIRITUAL, TO US AND TO ALL MEN	048 14
WHO ALONE MAKEST MEN TO BE OF ONE MIND IN A HOUSE,	052 18
AND FULL OF COMPASSION TO THE CHILDREN OF MEN	053 04
IT MAY PLEASE THEE TO HAVE MERCY UPON ALL MEN	057 05
COMPASSION UPON ALL MEN, AND WHO WOULDEST NOT	062 14
WHO FOR US MEN AND FOR OUR SALVATION CAME DOWN FROM	071 08
SO SHINE BEFORE MEN, THAT THEY MAY SEE YOUR GOOD	072 04
LET US DO GOOD UNTO ALL MEN	072 20
AND SUPPLICATIONS, AND TO GIVE THANKS FOR ALL MEN	074 08
MAKER OF ALL THINGS, JUDGE OF ALL MEN	075 18
AND WORTHY OF ALL MEN TO BE RECEIVED, THAT CHRIST	076 18
AND ON EARTH PEACE, GOOD WILL TOWARDS MEN	084 03
AND BE IN PERFECT CHARITY WITH ALL MEN	086 03
LET YOUR MODERATION BE KNOWN UNTO ALL MEN	095 14
AND THE LIFE WAS THE LIGHT OF MEN	097 14
THE LIGHT, THAT ALL MEN THROUGH HIM MIGHT BELIEVE	097 28
HATH APPEARED TO ALL MEN, TEACHING US THAT, DENYING	098 19
AND ON EARTH PEACE, GOOD WILL TOWARD MEN	099 22
AND WISE MEN, AND SCRIBES	100 19
REDEEMED FROM AMONG MEN, BEING THE FIRSTFRUITS UNTO	102 11
MOCKED OF THE WISE MEN, WAS EXCEEDING WROTH, AND SENT	103 25
WHICH HE HAD DILIGENTLY ENQUIRED OF THE WISE MEN	103 29
UNTO THE SONS OF MEN, AS IT IS NOW REVEALED UNTO HIS	108 13
AND TO MAKE ALL MEN SEE WHAT IS THE FELLOWSHIP OF THE	108 21
THERE CAME WISE MEN FROM THE EAST TO JERUSALEM,	108 32
CALLED THE WISE MEN, ENQUIRED OF THEM DILIGENTLY WHAT	109 11
BUT CONDESCEND TO MEN OF LOW ESTATE	111 32
PROVIDE THINGS HONEST IN THE SIGHT OF ALL MEN	113 02
MUCH AS LIETH IN YOU, LIVE PEACEABLY WITH ALL MEN	113 03

MEN   CONTINUED

AND WHEN MEN HAVE WELL DRUNK, THEN THAT WHICH IS	113 28
BUT WHILE MEN SLEPT, HIS ENEMY CAME AND SOWED TARES	116 19
WITH THE TONGUES OF MEN AND OF ANGELS, AND HAVE NOT	122 21
THEY MAY APPEAR UNTO MEN TO FAST	125 11
THOU APPEAR NOT UNTO MEN TO FAST, BUT UNTO THY FATHER	125 14
JESUS SAID, MAKE THE MEN SIT DOWN	131 35
SO THE MEN SAT DOWN, IN NUMBER ABOUT FIVE THOUSAND	132 02
THEN THOSE MEN, WHEN THEY HAD SEEN THE MIRACLE THAT	132 11
OF A SERVANT, AND WAS MADE IN THE LIKENESS OF MEN	134 20
AND THE YOUNG MEN LAID HOLD ON HIM	142 30
IS OF FORCE AFTER MEN ARE DEAD	147 16
IT IS APPOINTED UNTO MEN ONCE TO DIE, BUT AFTER THIS	148 07
AND THE MEN THAT HELD JESUS MOCKED HIM, AND SMOTE	151 23
AND HEROD WITH HIS MEN OF WAR SET HIM AT NOUGHT, AND	153 16
THE HANDS OF WICKED MEN, AND TO SUFFER DEATH UPON THE	156 24
FOR ALL ESTATES OF MEN IN THY HOLY CHURCH, THAT EVERY	156 30
WHO HAST MADE ALL MEN, AND HATEST NOTHING THAT THOU	157 04
MEN AND BRETHREN, CHILDREN OF THE STOCK OF ABRAHAM,	168 24
UNTO YOU THEREFORE, MEN AND BRETHREN, THAT THROUGH	169 18
THE WITNESS OF MEN, THE WITNESS OF GOD IS GREATER	171 04
MAY PUT TO SILENCE THE IGNORANCE OF FOOLISH MEN	173 23
HONOUR ALL MEN	173 25
THE UNRULY WILLS AND AFFECTIONS OF SINFUL MEN	174 19
WENT UP, BEHOLD, TWO MEN STOOD BY THEM IN WHITE	178 15
WHICH ALSO SAID, YE MEN OF GALILEE, WHY STAND YE	178 16
DEVOUT MEN, OUT OF EVERY NATION UNDER HEAVEN	180 25
INTO THE WORLD, AND MEN LOVED DARKNESS RATHER THAN	185 06
THAT NONE OF THOSE MEN WHICH WERE BIDDEN SHALL TASTE	192 20
RUNNING OVER, SHALL MEN GIVE INTO YOUR BOSOM	194 30
FROM HENCEFORTH THOU SHALT CATCH MEN	196 29
AFTER THE MANNER OF MEN BECAUSE OF THE INFIRMITY OF	198 26
A MAN SATISFY THESE MEN WITH BREAD HERE IN THE	199 15
DO MEN GATHER GRAPES OF THORNS, OR FIGS OF THISTLES	200 17
TWO MEN WENT UP INTO THE TEMPLE TO PRAY	205 23
I AM NOT AS OTHER MEN ARE, EXTORTIONERS, UNJUST,	205 26
THERE MET HIM TEN MEN THAT WERE LEPERS, WHICH STOOD	210 03
WHICH HAD GIVEN SUCH POWER UNTO MEN	217 14
FOR THOU REGARDEST NOT THE PERSON OF MEN	223 03
JESUS SAID, MAKE THE MEN SIT DOWN	225 31
SO THE MEN SAT DOWN, IN NUMBER ABOUT FIVE THOUSAND	225 32
THEN THOSE MEN, WHEN THEY HAD SEEN THE MIRACLE THAT	226 11
AND I WILL MAKE YOU FISHERS OF MEN	227 27
WHETHER THEY WERE MEN OR WOMEN, HE MIGHT BRING THEM	229 29
AND THE MEN WHICH JOURNEYED WITH HIM STOOD	230 08
HUNDRED AND TWENTY,) MEN AND BRETHREN, THIS SCRIPTURE	234 08
WHEREFORE OF THESE MEN WHICH HAVE COMPANIED WITH US	234 20
THE HEARTS OF ALL MEN, SHEW WHETHER OF THESE TWO THOU	234 28
FOR YOU TO WEARY MEN, BUT WILL YE WEARY MY GOD ALSO	235 30
HE LED CAPTIVITY CAPTIVE, AND GAVE GIFTS UNTO MEN	237 15
BY THE SLEIGHT OF MEN, AND CUNNING CRAFTINESS,	237 27
AND MEN GATHER THEM, AND CAST THEM INTO THE FIRE,	238 16
THAT GIVETH TO ALL MEN LIBERALLY, AND UPBRAIDETH NOT	239 13
WHOM DO MEN SAY THAT I THE SON OF MAN AM	245 32
TALKED WITH HIM TWO MEN, WHICH WERE MOSES AND ELIAS	248 27
AND THE TWO MEN THAT STOOD WITH HIM	248 32
MULTITUDES BOTH OF MEN AND WOMEN	249 26
OF ANGELS AND MEN IN A WONDERFUL ORDER	251 28
BLESSED ARE YE, WHEN MEN SHALL REVILE YOU, AND	257 31
DISALLOWED INDEED OF MEN, BUT CHOSEN OF GOD, AND	259 30
TO THE HANDS OF MEN THE MINISTRY OF RECONCILIATION	260 20
OF MY PASTURE, ARE MEN, AND I AM YOUR GOD, SAITH THE	262 23
AND HERB FOR THE USE OF MEN	264 29
SO OUGHT MEN TO LOVE THEIR WIVES AS THEIR OWN BODIES	267 24
THE UNRULY WILLS AND AFFECTIONS OF SINFUL MEN	285 26
AND TO DO TO ALL MEN AS I WOULD THEY SHOULD DO UNTO	288 25
AND TO BE IN CHARITY WITH ALL MEN	293 30
OF SAINT PAUL TO BE HONOURABLE AMONG ALL MEN	300 16
THE SPIRITS OF JUST MEN MADE PERFECT, AFTER THEY ARE	317 12
AS ALL MORTAL MEN ARE SUBJECT TO MANY SUDDEN PERILS,	R 321 02
AGAIN THOU SAYEST, COME AGAIN, YE CHILDREN OF MEN	325 19
AND THOUGH MEN BE SO STRONG THAT THEY COME TO	325 33
ONE KIND OF FLESH OF MEN, ANOTHER FLESH OF BEASTS,	329 12
NOT TO BE SORRY, AS MEN WITHOUT HOPE, FOR THOSE WHO	335 04
2 O YE SONS OF MEN, HOW LONG WILL YE BLASPHEME MINE	347 13
THE HEATHEN MAY KNOW THEMSELVES TO BE BUT MEN	352 33
AND HIS EYELIDS TRY THE CHILDREN OF MEN	354 29
ARE MINISHED FROM AMONG THE CHILDREN OF MEN	355 08
THE CHILDREN OF MEN ARE PUT TO REBUKE	355 26
UPON THE CHILDREN OF MEN, *	356 17
AS FOR THE WORKS OF MEN, *	358 25
FROM THE MEN OF THE EVIL WORLD	359 14
DISCOMFIT AN HOST OF MEN, *	361 26
AND THEIR SEED FROM AMONG THE CHILDREN OF MEN	365 26
A VERY SCORN OF MEN, AND THE OUTCAST OF THE PEOPLE	366 15
3 THOUGH AN HOST OF MEN WERE LAID AGAINST ME,	371 29
EVEN BEFORE THE SONS OF MEN	377 05
OF THINE OWN PRESENCE FROM THE PLOTTINGS OF MEN	377 07
AND BEHOLDETH ALL THE CHILDREN OF MEN	379 15
AND THE CHILDREN OF MEN SHALL PUT THEIR TRUST UNDER	384 09
2 THOU ART FAIRER THAN THE CHILDREN OF MEN	396 18
HE SEETH THAT WISE MEN ALSO DIE AND PERISH TOGETHER,	400 23
WELL UNTO THYSELF, MEN WILL SPEAK GOOD OF THEE	401 12
UPON THE CHILDREN OF MEN, *	405 17
AND DECEITFUL MEN SHALL NOT LIVE OUT HALF THEIR DAYS	408 08
THE CHILDREN OF MEN, THAT ARE SET ON FIRE, *	409 21
JUDGE THE THING THAT IS RIGHT, O YE SONS OF MEN	410 09
AND SAVE ME FROM THE BLOOD-THIRSTY MEN	411 07
THE MIGHTY MEN ARE GATHERED AGAINST ME, WITHOUT ANY	411 08
FOR THE CHILDREN OF MEN, THEY ARE BUT VANITY	414 15
THE CHILDREN OF MEN ARE DECEITFUL	414 16
9 AND ALL MEN THAT SEE IT SHALL SAY, THIS HATH GOD	416 04
HE IS IN HIS DOING TOWARD THE CHILDREN OF MEN	417 23
11 THOU SUFFEREDST MEN TO RIDE OVER OUR HEADS	418 04
THE GOD THAT MAKETH MEN TO BE OF ONE MIND IN AN	419 21

MEN   CONTINUED

AND RECEIVED GIFTS FROM MEN   420 20
THAT MEN MAY DWELL THERE, AND HAVE IT IN POSSESSICN   424 15
NEITHER ARE THEY PLAGUED LIKE OTHER MEN   428 19
THEN UNDERSTOOD I THE END OF THESE MEN   429 11
AND ALL THE MEN WHOSE HANDS WERE MIGHTY HAVE FOUND   432 31
DOWN THE CHOSEN MEN THAT WERE IN ISRAEL   436 35
EVEN THE TENT THAT HE HAD PITCHED AMONG MEN   438 33
CONSUMED THEIR YOUNG MEN, *   439 04
YE SHALL DIE LIKE MEN, *   443 31
OF VIOLENT MEN HAVE SOUGHT AFTER MY SOUL, AND HAVE   448 02
HAST THOU MADE ALL MEN FOR NOUGHT   452 35
AGAIN THOU SAYEST, COME AGAIN, YE CHILDREN CF MEN   453 24
AND THOUGH MEN BE SO STRONG THAT THEY COME TO   454 08
AND GREEN HERB FOR THE SERVICE OF MEN   468 22
8 O THAT MEN WOULD THEREFORE PRAISE THE LORD FOR HIS   476 19
THE WONDERS THAT HE DOETH FOR THE CHILDREN OF MEN   476 21
15 O THAT MEN WOULD THEREFORE PRAISE THE LORD FOR HIS   477 04
THE WONDERS THAT HE DOETH FOR THE CHILDREN OF MEN   477 06
17 FOOLISH MEN ARE PLAGUED FOR THEIR OFFENCE,   477 09
21 O THAT MEN WOULD THEREFCRE PRAISE THE LCRD FOR HIS   477 17
THE WONDERS THAT HE DOETH FOR THE CHILDREN OF MEN   477 19
24 THESE MEN SEE THE WORKS OF THE LORD, *   477 24
31 O THAT MEN WOULD THEREFORE PRAISE THE LORD FCR HIS   478 07
THE WONDERS THAT HE DOETH FOR THE CHILDREN OF MEN   478 09
THY YOUNG MEN COME TO THEE AS DEW FROM THE WOMB CF   482 12
THE EARTH HATH HE GIVEN TO THE CHILDREN OF MEN   486 11
IN MY HASTE, ALL MEN ARE LIARS   487 08
O DELIVER ME FROM THE WRONGFUL DEALINGS OF MEN   499 06
BECAUSE MEN KEEP NOT THY LAW   499 10
ON OUR SIDE, WHEN MEN ROSE UP AGAINST US   504 09
DEPART FROM ME, YE BLOOD-THIRSTY MEN   515 29
ME FROM THE WICKED MEN, WHO ARE PURPOSED TO OVERTHROW   516 16
WORKS WITH THE MEN THAT WORK WICKEDNESS, NEITHER LET   517 16
THE DARKNESS, AS THE MEN THAT HAVE BEEN LONG DEAD   518 29
6 SO THAT MEN SHALL SPEAK OF THE MIGHT OF THY   521 04
AND MEN SHALL SING OF THY RIGHTEOUSNESS   521 07
MIGHT BE KNOWN UNTO MEN   521 17
7 THE LORD LOOSETH MEN OUT OF PRISON   522 16
AND HERB FOR THE USE OF MEN   523 12
12 YOUNG MEN AND MAIDENS, OLD MEN AND CHILDREN,   524 27
MEN AND MAIDENS, OLD MEN AND CHILDREN, PRAISE THE   524 27
IS EVIDENT UNTO ALL MEN, DILIGENTLY READING HOLY   529 11
OUT AMONG YOU SEVEN MEN OF HONEST REPORT, FULL OF THE   532 11
YOURSELVES LIKE UNTO MEN THAT WAIT FOR THEIR LORD,   534 17
HE LED CAPTIVITY CAPTIVE, AND GAVE GIFTS UNTO MEN   538 02
THAT I AM PURE FROM THE BLOOD OF ALL MEN   550 25
OWN SELVES SHALL MEN ARISE, SPEAKING PERVERSE THINGS,   550 32
AND PEACE AMONG ALL MEN   555 15
ABUNDANTLY UPON MEN, MAKING SOME APOSTLES, SOME   557 25
COMING THEREBY MAY BE MANIFEST UNTO ALL MEN   558 24
AS DEVOUT AND HOLY MEN, AS WELL UNDER THE LAW AS   564 11
OF GOD IS WITH MEN, AND HE WILL DWELL WITH THEM, AND   567 15
AMONG THE SONS OF MEN, AND TO DWELL IN THE MIDST OF   568 08
AND TO DO TO ALL MEN AS I WOULD THEY SHOULD DO UNTO   580 02
AND BE IN CHARITY WITH ALL MEN   582 26
TO DO GOOD TO ALL MEN, ACCORDING TO OUR ABILITIES AND   588 32
VOID OF OFFENCE TOWARDS THEE, AND TOWARDS MEN   590 19
THE LIFE OF MORTAL MEN, THE LIGHT OF THE FAITHFUL,   595 04
BUT ALSO FOR ACTUAL SINS OF MEN   603 16
RETURN TO JUDGE ALL MEN AT THE LAST DAY   603 24
NOT BIND CHRISTIAN MEN, NOR THE CIVIL PRECEPTS   604 20
NEITHER DO THEY MAKE MEN MEET TO RECEIVE GRACE,   605 19
FOR BY THEM MEN DO DECLARE, THAT THEY DO NOT ONLY   606 26
WHEREBY MEN MUST BE SAVED   606 35
OF FAITHFUL MEN, IN THE WHICH THE PURE WORD OF GCC IS   606 38
TO THIS WORK BY MEN WHO HAVE PUBLIC AUTHORITY GIVEN   607 22
ALTHOUGH THEY BE MINISTERED BY EVIL MEN   608 18
WHEREBY CHRISTIAN MEN ARE DISCERNED FROM OTHERS THAT   608 25
TO ALL CHRISTIAN MEN ALIKE   609 12
ALL OTHER CHRISTIAN MEN, TO MARRY AT THEIR CWN   609 23
EXTENDETH TO ALL MEN, AS WELL CLERGY AS LAITY, IN ALL   610 38
BE THE DUTY OF ALL MEN WHO ARE PROFESSORS OF THE   610 40
FORBIDDEN CHRISTIAN MEN BY OUR LORD JESUS CHRIST, AND   611 06

MEN'S

MEN'S HEARTS FAILING THEM FOR FEAR, AND FOR LCOKING   093 07
NOR DESIRE OTHER MEN'S GOODS   289 08
DRIVEST AWAY FROM MEN'S BODIES ALL SICKNESS AND ALL   315 07
EVEN THE WORK OF MEN'S HANDS   485 19
THE WORK OF MEN'S HANDS   510 33
IN ORDER TO FILL MEN'S MINDS WITH GREATER REVERENCE   564 17
NOR DESIRE OTHER MEN'S GOODS   580 12
OF CHRISTIAN MEN'S PROFESSION, BUT RATHER THEY BE   607 32
AND MEN'S MANNERS, SO THAT NOTHING BE ORDAINED   609 34

MENDING

THEIR FATHER, MENDING THEIR NETS   227 31

MENTAL

WHO ARE LIVING IN MENTAL DARKNESS   598 14

MENTION

I WILL MENTION THE LOVINGKINDNESSES OF THE LORD, AND   138 27
NEITHER MAKE MENTION OF THEIR NAMES WITHIN MY LIPS   357 30
AND WILL MAKE MENTION OF THY RIGHTEOUSNESS ONLY   426 07
3 I WILL MAKE MENTION OF EGYPT AND BABYLON, *   448 18

MERCHANDISE

ANOTHER TO HIS MERCHANDISE   218 11

MERCHANDISE   CONTINUED

NOT MY FATHER'S HOUSE AN HOUSE OF MERCHANDISE   568 02

MERCIES

FATHER OF ALL MERCIES, WE, THINE UNWORTHY SERVANTS,   019 14
FOR THY LATE MERCIES VOUCHSAFED UNTO THEM   019 19
SENSE OF ALL THY MERCIES, THAT OUR HEARTS MAY BE   019 25
THANKS FOR MERCIES VOUCHSAFED TO THEM   R 019 33
OUR GOD BELONG MERCIES AND FORGIVENESSES, THOUGH WF   022 06
FATHER OF ALL MERCIES, WE, THINE UNWORTHY SERVANTS,   033 12
FOR THY LATE MERCIES VOUCHSAFED UNTO THEM   033 17
SENSE OF ALL THY MERCIES, THAT OUR HEARTS MAY BE   033 23
THANKS FOR MERCIES VOUCHSAFED TO THEM   R 033 31
O FATHER OF MERCIES AND GOD OF ALL COMFORT, OUR CNLY   045 12
WITH A GRATEFUL SENSE OF THY MERCIES   046 15
GIVE US A JUST SENSE OF THESE GREAT MERCIES   050 26
SUCH THY MERCIES TOWARDS US, THAT ALL THE WORLD MAY   052 13
FOR THESE THY MERCIES TOWARDS US   052 27
MULTITUDE OF THY MERCIES DO AWAY MINE OFFENCES   060 11
MULTITUDE OF THY MERCIES LOOK UPON US   063 05
BUT IN THY MANIFOLD AND GREAT MERCIES   082 15
BY THE MERCIES OF GOD, THAT YE PRESENT YOUR   110 03
ACCORDING TO HIS MERCIES, AND ACCORDING TO THE   138 31
AND OF THY MERCIES TOWARD ME   139 20
YOU THE SURE MERCIES OF DAVID   169 12
IN THE TENDER MERCIES OF CHRIST JESUS   220 32
O GOD, WHOSE MERCIES CANNOT BE NUMBERED   268 22
MULTITUDE OF THY MERCIES, DOST SO PUT AWAY THE SINS   313 31
O FATHER OF MERCIES, AND GOD OF ALL COMFORT, OUR ONLY   316 06
AND WHOSE MERCIES CANNOT BE NUMBERED   316 25
MULTITUDE OF THY MERCIES, DO AWAY OUR OFFENCES AND   323 15
O GOD, WHOSE MERCIES CANNOT BE NUMBERED   334 14
FATHER OF MERCIES AND GIVER OF ALL COMFORT   342 09
THY TENDER MERCIES, *   369 28
MULTITUDE OF THY MERCIES DO AWAY MINE OFFENCES   403 09
UNTO ME ACCORDING TO THE MULTITUDE OF THY MERCIES   423 06
ACCORDING UNTO THE MULTITUDE OF HIS MERCIES   475 28
O LET THY LOVING MERCIES COME UNTO ME, THAT I MAY   495 09
FOR THESE THY MERCIES, WE BLESS AND MAGNIFY THY   587 24
WE JOIN OUR UNFEIGNED THANKS FOR ALL THY MERCIES   591 08
FOR THE MERCIES AND BENEFITS OF THE PAST DAY   591 19
FOR ALL THY MERCIES, AND MAKE US MINDFUL OF THE NEECS   600 17

MERCIFUL

IS GRACIOUS AND MERCIFUL, SLOW TO ANGER, AND OF GREAT   004 21
AND MOST MERCIFUL FATHER   006 17
GRANT, O MOST MERCIFUL FATHER, FOR HIS SAKE   006 27
NATION TO THY MERCIFUL CARE, THAT BEING GUIDED BY THY   018 08
AND MOST MERCIFUL FATHER   023 24
GRANT, O MOST MERCIFUL FATHER, FOR HIS SAKE   024 02
ALMIGHTY AND MERCIFUL LORD GRANT YOU ABSOLUTION AND   024 23
GOD BE MERCIFUL UNTO US, AND BLESS US, *   028 17
AND BE MERCIFUL UNTO US   028 18
AND MOST MERCIFUL FATHER, WE HUMBLY BESEECH THEE, OF   040 23
AND TO BE MERCIFUL TO THOSE WHO TRULY REPENT   041 11
O GOD, MERCIFUL AND COMPASSIONATE, WHO ART EVER READY   041 19
THY MERITS, O MERCIFUL SAVIOUR, WHO WITH THE FATHER   043 14
MOST MIGHTY AND MERCIFUL GOD, IN THIS TIME OF   045 03
O MERCIFUL GOD, AND HEAVENLY FATHER, WHO HAST TAUGHT   045 30
OF HIS MERCIFUL PROVIDENCE   050 18
OF THY MERCIFUL PROVIDENCE BESTOWED UPON THIS NATION   050 24
MOST MERCIFUL FATHER, THAT SHE, THROUGH THY   051 09
O MOST MERCIFUL FATHER, WHO OF THY GRACIOUS GCODNESS   051 30
A SENSE OF THY MERCIFUL GOODNESS, AND MAY HE DEVCTE   053 05
SENSIBLE OF THY MERCIFUL PROVIDENCE TOWARDS HIM,   053 25
O GOD, MERCIFUL FATHER, WHO DESPISEST NOT THE SIGHING   058 15
BE MERCIFUL TO US SINNERS, FOR THY NAME'S SAKE   062 03
BY THY MERCIFUL PARDON MAY BE ABSOLVED   062 11
MIGHTY GOD, AND MERCIFUL FATHER, WHO HAST COMPASSION   062 13
FOR THOU ART A MERCIFUL GOD, FULL OF COMPASSION,   062 31
BE MERCIFUL AFTER THY POWER   072 32
UPON US, MOST MERCIFUL FATHER   075 26
BESEECH THEE, O MERCIFUL FATHER, TO HEAR US   081 08
THY TABLE, O MERCIFUL LORD, TRUSTING IN OUR OWN   082 14
MERCIFUL LORD, WE BESEECH THEE TO CAST THY BRIGHT   101 05
IS GRACIOUS AND MERCIFUL, SLOW TO ANGER, AND OF GREAT   124 25
O MERCIFUL GOD, WHO HAST MADE ALL MEN, AND HATEST   157 04
AND BY THY MERCIFUL GUIDING MAY PERFORM THE SAME   176 02
AND MOST MERCIFUL GOD, GRANT, WE BESEECH THEE, THAT   182 15
BESEECH THEE, MERCIFUL GOD, THAT THY CHURCH, BEING   185 14
AS YOUR FATHER ALSO IS MERCIFUL   194 25
BE YE THEREFORE MERCIFUL, AS YOUR FATHER ALSO IS   194 25
LET THY MERCIFUL EARS, O LORD, BE OPEN TO THE PRAYERS   203 11
GOD BE MERCIFUL TO ME A SINNER   205 30
ALMIGHTY AND MERCIFUL GOD, OF WHOSE ONLY GIFT IT   207 12
AND MOST MERCIFUL GOD, OF THY BOUNTIFUL GOODNESS KEEP   217 17
BESEECH THEE, MERCIFUL LORD, TO THY FAITHFUL PECPLE   218 32
GRANT, O MERCIFUL GOD, THAT, AS THINE HOLY APOSTLE   246 16
BLESSED ARE THE MERCIFUL   257 26
MAY OBTAIN THY MERCIFUL AID AND PROTECTICN   259 22
O MOST MERCIFUL FATHER, WHO HAST BLESSED THE LABCURS   265 11
MINISTER SAY, O MERCIFUL GOD, GRANT THAT LIKE AS   278 18
MOST MERCIFUL FATHER, THAT IT HATH PLEASED   280 28
LET THY MERCIFUL KINDNESS, O LORD, BE UPON US   290 10
OUR GOD IS MERCIFUL   305 26
MOST MERCIFUL FATHER, THAT SHE, THROUGH THY   306 29
AND MOST MERCIFUL GOD AND SAVIOUR   309 27
THE HELP OF THY MERCIFUL CONSOLATION   311 23
BESEECH THEE, MERCIFUL LORD, THE DEVOUT PRAISE CF THY   313 05
O MOST MERCIFUL GOD, WHO, ACCORDING TO THE   313 30
AND MOST MERCIFUL SAVIOUR   317 15
ALMIGHTY AND MERCIFUL LORD GRANT THEE PARDON AND   319 15
THY HANDS, O MERCIFUL SAVIOUR, WE COMMEND THE SOUL OF   319 27

MERCIFUL   CONTINUED

ALMIGHTY AND MERCIFUL LORD GRANT YOU ABSOLUTION AND	323 19
O HOLY AND MOST MERCIFUL SAVIOUR, DELIVER US NOT INTO	332 26
SHUT NOT THY MERCIFUL EARS TO OUR PRAYER	332 29
O HOLY AND MERCIFUL SAVIOUR, THOU MOST WORTHY JUDGE	332 30
O MERCIFUL GOD, THE FATHER OF OUR LORD JESUS CHRIST,	334 30
BESEECH THEE, O MERCIFUL FATHER, THROUGH JESUS	335 14
MOST MERCIFUL FATHER, WHO HAST BEEN PLEASED TO TAKE	336 04
O MERCIFUL FATHER, WHOSE FACE THE ANGELS OF THY	340 24
ALMIGHTY AND MERCIFUL FATHER, WHO DOST GRANT TO	340 29
BE MERCIFUL UNTO MY SIN	370 06
AND BE MERCIFUL UNTO ME	371 19
21 LET THY MERCIFUL KINDNESS, O LORD, BE UPON US,	379 32
RIGHTEOUS IS MERCIFUL AND LIBERAL	386 05
IS EVER MERCIFUL, AND LENDETH	386 15
LORD, BE MERCIFUL UNTO ME	392 06
10 BUT BE THOU MERCIFUL UNTO ME, O LORD	392 19
BE MERCIFUL UNTO ME, O GOD, FOR MAN GOETH ABOUT TO	408 14
BE MERCIFUL UNTO ME, O GOD, BE MERCIFUL UNTO ME	409 12
O GOD, BE MERCIFUL UNTO ME	409 12
AND BE NOT MERCIFUL UNTO THEM THAT OFFEND OF	411 14
AND MY MERCIFUL GOD	412 10
12 AND THAT THOU, LORD, ART MERCIFUL	414 23
O BE THOU MERCIFUL UNTO OUR SINS	416 16
GOD BE MERCIFUL UNTO US, AND BLESS US, *	418 23
AND BE MERCIFUL UNTO US	418 24
BUT HE WAS SO MERCIFUL, THAT HE FORGAVE THEIR	437 14
AND BE MERCIFUL UNTO OUR SINS, FOR THY NAME'S	440 19
3 BE MERCIFUL UNTO ME, O LORD	447 09
SO IS THE LORD MERCIFUL UNTO THEM THAT FEAR HIM	466 33
17 BUT THE MERCIFUL GOODNESS OF THE LORD ENDURETH FOR	467 08
4 THE MERCIFUL AND GRACIOUS LORD HATH SO DONE HIS	482 30
HE IS MERCIFUL, LOVING, AND RIGHTEOUS	483 25
5 A GOOD MAN IS MERCIFUL, AND LENDETH	483 26
OUR GOD IS MERCIFUL	486 29
2 FOR HIS MERCIFUL KINDNESS IS EVER MORE AND MORE	487 27
O BE MERCIFUL UNTO ME, ACCORDING TO THY WORD	493 27
76 O LET THY MERCIFUL KINDNESS BE MY COMFORT,	495 07
UPON ME, AND BE MERCIFUL UNTO ME, *	499 02
8 THE LORD IS GRACIOUS AND MERCIFUL	521 08
MOST MERCIFUL FATHER, WE BESEECH THEE TO SEND UPON	547 04
AND BE MERCIFUL FOR CHRIST'S SAKE TO POOR AND	555 23
AND MOST MERCIFUL FATHER, WHO, OF THINE INFINITE	557 20
BE SO MERCIFUL, THAT YE BE NOT TOO REMISS	558 28
MOST MERCIFUL FATHER, SEND DOWN, WE BESEECH THEE,	559 05
THAT HE WILL BE MERCIFUL UNTO US, AND FORGIVE US OUR	580 34
DO THOU, O MERCIFUL GOD, CONFIRM AND STRENGTHEN US	588 08
MOST MERCIFUL GOD, WHO ART OF PURER EYES THAN TO	589 26
BE MERCIFUL TO ALL WHO ARE IN ANY TROUBLE	591 02
SUPPLICATE THY MERCIFUL PROTECTION ALL THIS NIGHT	595 07
O MERCIFUL GOD, GIVER OF LIFE AND HEALTH	597 15
ALMIGHTY AND MERCIFUL, WHO HEALEST THOSE THAT ARE	599 03
BE MERCIFUL TO ALL WHOSE DUTIES ARE DIFFICULT OR	599 26
OUR PRAYER, O MERCIFUL AND GRACIOUS FATHER, FOR THE	600 11

MERCIFULLY

AND MERCIFULLY HEAR US WHEN WE CALL UPON	031 05
MERCIFULLY LOOK UPON THE SAME, AND AT THIS TIME SO	038 27
LOOK MERCIFULLY UPON THE WORLD WHICH THOU HAST	039 17
BE MERCIFULLY TURNED INTO PLENTY	041 04
ASSIST US MERCIFULLY, O LORD, IN THESE OUR	049 11
BESEECH THEE MERCIFULLY TO INCLINE THINE EARS TO US	050 08
MERCIFULLY ASSIST OUR PRAYERS WHICH WE MAKE BEFORE	058 17
MERCIFULLY FORGIVE THE SINS OF THY PEOPLE	059 12
O FATHER, MERCIFULLY TO LOOK UPON OUR INFIRMITIES	059 21
BESEECH THEE, MERCIFULLY HEAR OUR PRAYERS, AND SPARE	062 08
MERCIFULLY FORGIVE US OUR TRESPASSES	062 16
THEE MOST MERCIFULLY TO ACCEPT OUR (ALMS AND)	074 09
MERCIFULLY TO ACCEPT THIS OUR SACRIFICE OF	081 15
MERCIFULLY GRANT THAT WE, WHO KNOW THEE NOW BY FAITH,	107 30
BESEECH THEE MERCIFULLY TO RECEIVE THE PRAYERS OF THY	109 29
MERCIFULLY HEAR THE SUPPLICATIONS OF THY PEOPLE, AND	111 11
MERCIFULLY LOOK UPON OUR INFIRMITIES, AND IN ALL	112 26
MAY BE MERCIFULLY DELIVERED BY THY GOODNESS, FOR THE	118 30
MERCIFULLY GRANT THAT BY THY POWER WE MAY BE DEFENDED	120 18
THY GRACE MAY MERCIFULLY BE RELIEVED	130 26
ALMIGHTY GOD, MERCIFULLY TO LOOK UPON THY PEOPLE	132 18
MERCIFULLY GRANT, THAT WE MAY BOTH FOLLOW THE EXAMPLE	134 09
MERCIFULLY GRANT THAT WE, WALKING IN THE WAY OF THE	138 06
ASSIST US MERCIFULLY WITH THY HELP, O LORD GOD OF OUR	147 08
MERCIFULLY GRANT THAT WE MAY THANKFULLY RECEIVE THE	152 09
MERCIFULLY ACCEPT OUR PRAYERS	188 33
BESEECH THEE MERCIFULLY TO HEAR US	192 24
MERCIFULLY GRANT UNTO US SUCH A MEASURE OF THY GRACE,	204 23
MERCIFULLY GRANT THAT THY HOLY SPIRIT MAY IN ALL	215 28
MERCIFULLY GRANT THAT WE, BEING DELIVERED FROM THE	248 02
MERCIFULLY GRANT THAT, AS THY HOLY ANGELS ALWAYS DO	251 29
LOOK MERCIFULLY UPON THESE THY SERVANTS, THAT THEY	303 22
THE LORD MERCIFULLY WITH HIS FAVOUR LOOK UPON YOU,	304 12
MERCIFULLY ACCEPT OUR PRAYERS, AND GRANT TO THY	312 13
PLEASE THEE MERCIFULLY TO PARDON ALL HIS SINS	318 15
MERCIFULLY LOOK UPON THIS THY SERVANT, THAT, EVERY	322 07
MERCIFULLY BEHOLD THESE THY SERVANTS NOW CALLED TO	531 18
MERCIFULLY BEHOLD THESE THY SERVANTS NOW CALLED TO	537 22
MERCIFULLY BEHOLD THESE THY SERVANTS NOW CALLED TO	547 33
MERCIFULLY BEHOLD THIS THY SERVANT, NOW CALLED TO THE	553 28

MERCY

THAT WE MAY OBTAIN MERCY, AND FIND GRACE TO HELP IN	005 09
BY HIS INFINITE GOODNESS AND MERCY	006 03
THOU, O LORD, HAVE MERCY UPON US, MISERABLE	006 24
O LORD, HAVE MERCY UPON US, HAVE MERCY UPON US	011 09
UPON US, HAVE MERCY UPON US	011 09

MERCY   CONTINUED

O LORD, LET THY MERCY BE UPON US, AS OUR TRUST IS IN	011 10
TO PERFORM THE MERCY PROMISED TO OUR FOREFATHERS,	014 16
THROUGH THE TENDER MERCY OF OUR GOD	014 29
IS GRACIOUS, HIS MERCY IS EVERLASTING	015 13
O LORD, SHOW THY MERCY UPON US	016 29
OF THE SAME, BY HIS INFINITE GOODNESS AND MERCY	023 11
THOU, O LORD, HAVE MERCY UPON US, MISERABLE	023 31
OF THE WORLD, HAVE MERCY UPON US	025 29
THE FATHER, HAVE MERCY UPON US	025 32
AND HIS MERCY IS ON THEM THAT FEAR HIM *	026 18
HE REMEMBERING HIS MERCY HATH HOLPEN HIS SERVANT	026 26
REMEMBERED HIS MERCY AND TRUTH TOWARD THE HOUSE OF	027 10
CROWNETH THEE WITH MERCY AND LOVING-KINDNESS	029 11
O LORD, SHOW THY MERCY UPON US	031 02
AND BY THY GREAT MERCY DEFEND US FROM ALL PERILS AND	031 27
HAVE MERCY UPON THIS WHOLE LAND	032 05
AND OF THY GREAT MERCY VOUCHSAFE, WE BESEECH THEE, SO	036 32
BUT THY PROMISES OF MERCY	040 07
GRANT TO THEM THY MERCY AND THE LIGHT OF THY	042 17
THE ARMS OF THY MERCY, AND DOST MAKE THEM LIVING	043 08
LOOK UPON HIM WITH THE EYES OF THY MERCY	045 16
REMEMBER HIM, O LORD, IN MERCY	046 03
AND IN THY WRATH REMEMBEREST MERCY	046 19
WHOLLY IN THY MERCY, THEY MAY NOT PLACE THEIR	046 23
BY THY MERCY, OBTAIN EVERLASTING LIFE	049 27
AND IN THY MERCY HAST RELIEVED AND COMFORTED	051 24
NAME FOR THIS THY MERCY, AND WILL ALWAYS DECLARE THY	051 26
WHOSE MERCY IS OVER ALL THY WORKS	053 20
HAVE MERCY UPON US	054 06
THEE TO HAVE MERCY UPON ALL MEN	057 05
HAVE MERCY UPON US	057 24
HAVE MERCY UPON US	057 27
HAVE MERCY UPON US	057 29
FAVOURABLY WITH MERCY HEAR OUR PRAYERS	059 13
SON OF DAVID, HAVE MERCY UPON US	059 14
O LORD, LET THY MERCY BE SHOWED UPON US	059 18
CONFIDENCE IN THY MERCY, AND EVERMORE SERVE THEE IN	059 25
HAVE MERCY UPON ME, O GOD, AFTER THY GREAT GOODNESS	060 10
HAVE MERCY UPON US	061 21
HAVE MERCY UPON US	061 22
THY PROPERTY IS ALWAYS TO HAVE MERCY	062 18
AND IN THY WRATH THINKEST UPON MERCY	063 02
O LORD, FOR THY MERCY IS GREAT, AND AFTER THE	063 04
IS EVER TO HAVE MERCY AND TO FORGIVE	063 10
OF THY GREAT MERCY LOOSE US	063 12
ASK GOD MERCY FOR THEIR TRANSGRESSIONS FOR THE TIME	R 067 24
HAVE MERCY UPON US, AND INCLINE OUR HEARTS TO	068 06
AND SHOW MERCY UNTO THOUSANDS IN THEM THAT LOVE ME	068 14
HAVE MERCY UPON US, AND INCLINE OUR HEARTS TO	069 05
HAVE MERCY UPON US, AND WRITE ALL THESE THY	069 23
LORD, HAVE MERCY UPON US	070 02
HAVE MERCY UPON US THEN THE PRIEST MAY SAY,	070 03
HAVE MERCY UPON US, HAVE MERCY UPON US, MOST MERCIFUL	075 25
UPON US, HAVE MERCY UPON US, MOST MERCIFUL FATHER	075 26
WHO OF HIS GREAT MERCY HATH PROMISED FORGIVENESS OF	076 03
HAVE MERCY UPON YOU	076 05
OF THY TENDER MERCY, DIDST GIVE THINE ONLY SON JESUS	080 07
WHOSE PROPERTY IS ALWAYS TO HAVE MERCY	082 18
OF THE WORLD, HAVE MERCY UPON US	084 09
THE FATHER, HAVE MERCY UPON US	084 11
TRUST IN GOD'S MERCY, AND WITH A QUIET CONSCIENCE	088 02
THAT THE GENTILES MIGHT GLORIFY GOD FOR HIS MERCY	092 26
GRACE AND MERCY MAY SPEEDILY HELP AND DELIVER US	095 08
HE THAT SHEWETH MERCY, WITH CHEERFULNESS	111 21
SON OF DAVID, HAVE MERCY ON ME	123 30
SON OF DAVID, HAVE MERCY ON ME	123 33
THE GOD OF ALL MERCY, PERFECT REMISSION AND	124 16
SAYING, HAVE MERCY ON ME, O LORD, THOU SON OF	128 10
HAVE MERCY UPON ALL WHO KNOW THEE NOT AS THOU ART	157 07
HAVE MERCY ON ME, AND SEND LAZARUS, THAT HE	190 13
INCREASE AND MULTIPLY UPON US THY MERCY	194 06
AND OF THY GREAT MERCY KEEP US IN THE SAME	198 23
CHIEFLY IN SHOWING MERCY AND PITY	204 23
POUR DOWN UPON US THE ABUNDANCE OF THY MERCY	206 07
HE THAT SHEWED MERCY ON HIM	209 04
HAVE MERCY ON US	210 04
THY CHURCH WITH THY PERPETUAL MERCY	210 18
BE ON THEM, AND MERCY, AND UPON THE ISRAEL OF GOD	211 03
HAD SHEWED GREAT MERCY UPON HER	243 16
TO PERFORM THE MERCY PROMISED TO OUR FATHERS, AND TO	244 04
THROUGH THE TENDER MERCY OF OUR GOD	244 13
WE HAVE RECEIVED MERCY, WE FAINT NOT	250 28
I WILL HAVE MERCY, AND NOT SACRIFICE	251 22
FOR THEY SHALL OBTAIN MERCY	257 26
THROUGH THY MERCY, WE, WITH THEM, ATTAIN TO THINE	258 16
OF HIS BOUNTEOUS MERCY HE WILL GRANT TO THIS CHILD	274 02
THROUGH THY MERCY, O BLESSED LORD GOD, WHO DOST LIVE,	278 29
AND OF THY GREAT MERCY KEEP US IN THE SAME	283 11
HAVE MERCY UPON US, AND INCLINE OUR HEARTS TO	286 06
AND SHOW MERCY UNTO THOUSANDS IN THEM THAT LOVE ME	286 14
HAVE MERCY UPON US, AND INCLINE OUR HEARTS TO	287 04
HAVE MERCY UPON US, AND WRITE ALL THESE THY	287 23
FAITH IN GOD'S MERCY THROUGH CHRIST, WITH A THANKFUL	293 28
LORD, HAVE MERCY UPON US	308 14
HAVE MERCY UPON US	308 15
THE EYES OF THY MERCY, GIVE HIM COMFORT AND SURE	309 06
WITH THY LOVING MERCY, AND SO RESTORE HIM TO HIS	309 30
IS HIS MERCY CLEAN GONE FOR EVER	311 14
THY MERCY, O LORD, ENDURETH FOR EVER	312 09
CROWNETH THEE WITH MERCY AND LOVING-KINDNESS	312 18
CROWNETH THEE WITH MERCY AND LOVING-KINDNESS	312 27
HIM OF GOD'S MERCY AND FORGIVENESS	R 313 27
OPEN THINE EYE OF MERCY UPON THIS THY SERVANT,	313 33
TRUST ONLY IN THY MERCY, IMPUTE NOT UNTO HIM HIS	314 09

MERCY   CONTINUED

GOD'S GRACIOUS MERCY AND PROTECTION WE COMMIT THEE   314 26
THIS THY MERCY TOWARDS HIM   315 28
DONE AWAY BY THY MERCY, AND HIS PARDON SEALED IN   316 15
HAVE MERCY UPON THE SOUL OF THY SERVANT   317 26
HAVE MERCY UPON HIM   318 24
HAVE MERCY   318 29
HAVE MERCY   318 30
THE ARMS OF THY MERCY, INTO THE BLESSED REST OF   319 31
BESEECHING THE MERCY OF OUR LORD JESUS CHRIST, THAT   320 17
THEE TO HAVE MERCY UPON THIS THY SERVANT VISITED WITH 321 21
HAVE MERCY UPON US, O GOD, AFTER THY GREAT GOODNESS   323 14
HAVE MERCY UPON ME, AND HEAR ME   326 21
FOR THERE IS MERCY WITH THEE   328 09
THE LORD THERE IS MERCY, *   328 16
GOD'S GRACIOUS MERCY AND PROTECTION WE COMMIT YOU   332 10
HAVE MERCY UPON US   334 03
HAVE MERCY UPON US   334 04
AND OF THY MERCY, O HEAVENLY FATHER, VOUCHSAFE THAT   335 31
THROUGH THY MERCY, WHO LIVEST WITH THE FATHER AND THE 336 14
AND MERCY SHALL FOLLOW ME ALL THE DAYS OF MY LIFE   338 29
HAVE MERCY UPON US   340 06
HAVE MERCY UPON US   340 07
HAVE MERCY UPON ME, AND HEARKEN UNTO MY PRAYER   347 12
MULTITUDE OF THY MERCY I WILL COME INTO THINE HOUSE   348 13
2 HAVE MERCY UPON ME, O LORD, FOR I AM WEAK   349 02
13 HAVE MERCY UPON ME, O LORD   352 16
MY TRUST IS IN THY MERCY, *   356 07
AND IN THE MERCY OF THE MOST HIGHEST HE SHALL NOT   365 18
AND MERCY SHALL FOLLOW ME ALL THE DAYS OF MY LIFE   368 22
ACCORDING TO THY MERCY THINK THOU UPON ME, O LORD,   369 31
OF THE LORD ARE MERCY AND TRUTH, *   370 04
UNTO ME, AND HAVE MERCY UPON ME   370 16
HAVE MERCY UPON ME, AND HEAR ME   372 13
O LORD, AND HAVE MERCY UPON ME   375 14
8 I WILL BE GLAD AND REJOICE IN THY MERCY   376 04
10 HAVE MERCY UPON ME, O LORD, FOR I AM IN TROUBLE,   376 08
TRUST IN THE LORD, MERCY EMBRACETH HIM ON EVERY SIDE   378 14
AND UPON THEM THAT PUT THEIR TRUST IN HIS MERCY   379 25
5 THY MERCY, O LORD, REACHETH UNTO THE HEAVENS,   384 04
EXCELLENT IS THY MERCY, O GOD   384 09
BACK THY LOVING MERCY AND TRUTH *   391 06
NOT THOU THY MERCY FROM ME, O LORD   391 08
HAVE MERCY UPON ME, O GOD, AFTER THY GREAT GOODNESS   403 08
IS IN THE TENDER MERCY OF GOD FOR EVER AND EVER   405 05
SEND FORTH HIS MERCY AND TRUTH   409 19
GREATNESS OF THY MERCY REACHETH UNTO THE HEAVENS, *   410 02
WILL PRAISE THY MERCY BETIMES IN THE MORNING   412 07
PREPARE THY LOVING MERCY AND FAITHFULNESS, THAT THEY   413 20
NOR TURNED HIS MERCY FROM ME   418 21
MULTITUDE OF THY MERCY, *   422 30
8 IS HIS MERCY CLEAN GONE FOR EVER   433 31
OLD SINS, BUT HAVE MERCY UPON US, AND THAT SOON   440 16
7 SHOW US THY MERCY, O LORD, *   446 20
10 MERCY AND TRUTH ARE MET TOGETHER   446 27
AND OF GREAT MERCY UNTO ALL THEM THAT CALL UPON THEE   447 14
FOR GREAT IS THY MERCY TOWARD ME   447 30
OF COMPASSION AND MERCY, *   448 05
UNTO ME, AND HAVE MERCY UPON ME   448 06
2 FOR I HAVE SAID, MERCY SHALL BE SET UP FOR EVER   450 07
MERCY AND TRUTH SHALL GO BEFORE THY FACE   451 03
TRUTH ALSO AND MY MERCY SHALL BE WITH HIM   451 23
29 MY MERCY WILL I KEEP FOR HIM FOR EVERMORE,   451 31
US WITH THY MERCY, AND THAT SOON   454 17
THY MERCY, O LORD, HELD ME UP   458 22
REMEMBERED HIS MERCY AND TRUTH TOWARD THE HOUSE OF   461 31
IS GRACIOUS, HIS MERCY IS EVERLASTING   463 14
SONG SHALL BE OF MERCY AND JUDGMENT   463 17
ARISE, AND HAVE MERCY UPON SION   465 04
THAT THOU HAVE MERCY UPON HER, YEA, THE TIME IS COME   465 05
CROWNETH THEE WITH MERCY AND LOVING-KINDNESS   466 14
OF COMPASSION AND MERCY, *   466 21
SO GREAT IS HIS MERCY ALSO TOWARD THEM THAT FEAR HIM   466 28
AND HIS MERCY ENDURETH FOR EVER   472 32
AND HIS MERCY ENDURETH FOR EVER   476 07
4 FOR THY MERCY IS GREATER THAN THE HEAVENS, *   479 11
FOR SWEET IS THY MERCY   481 13
O SAVE ME ACCORDING TO THY MERCY   481 23
FOR THY LOVING MERCY, AND FOR THY TRUTH'S SAKE   485 12
BECAUSE HIS MERCY ENDURETH FOR EVER   487 32
AND THAT HIS MERCY ENDURETH FOR EVER   488 03
THAT HIS MERCY ENDURETH FOR EVER   488 04
THAT HIS MERCY ENDURETH FOR EVER   488 07
AND HIS MERCY ENDURETH FOR EVER   489 28
LET THY LOVING MERCY COME ALSO UNTO ME, O LORD,   492 22
O LORD, IS FULL OF THY MERCY   494 08
UNTO THY LOVING MERCY, *   498 18
156 GREAT IS THY MERCY, O LORD   500 23
UNTIL HE HAVE MERCY UPON US   503 32
3 HAVE MERCY UPON US, O LORD, HAVE MERCY UPON US   504 02
O LORD, HAVE MERCY UPON US   504 02
4 FOR THERE IS MERCY WITH THEE   507 14
THE LORD THERE IS MERCY, *   507 21
AND HIS MERCY ENDURETH FOR EVER   511 17
FOR HIS MERCY ENDURETH FOR EVER   511 19
FOR HIS MERCY ENDURETH FOR EVER   511 20
FOR HIS MERCY ENDURETH FOR EVER   511 22
FOR HIS MERCY ENDURETH FOR EVER   511 25
FOR HIS MERCY ENDURETH FOR EVER   511 27
FOR HIS MERCY ENDURETH FOR EVER   511 28
FOR HIS MERCY ENDURETH FOR EVER   511 30
FOR HIS MERCY ENDURETH FOR EVER   511 33
FOR HIS MERCY ENDURETH FOR EVER   512 03
FOR HIS MERCY ENDURETH FOR EVER   512 05
FOR HIS MERCY ENDURETH FOR EVER   512 07

MERCY   CONTINUED

FOR HIS MERCY ENDURETH FOR EVER   512 09
FOR HIS MERCY ENDURETH FOR EVER   512 11
FOR HIS MERCY ENDURETH FOR EVER   512 13
FOR HIS MERCY ENDURETH FOR EVER   512 15
FOR HIS MERCY ENDURETH FOR EVER   512 16
FOR HIS MERCY ENDURETH FOR EVER   512 18
FOR HIS MERCY ENDURETH FOR EVER   512 20
FOR HIS MERCY ENDURETH FOR EVER   512 22
FOR HIS MERCY ENDURETH FOR EVER   512 25
FOR HIS MERCY ENDURETH FOR EVER   512 27
FOR HIS MERCY ENDURETH FOR EVER   512 29
FOR HIS MERCY ENDURETH FOR EVER   512 31
FOR HIS MERCY ENDURETH FOR EVER   512 32
FOR HIS MERCY ENDURETH FOR EVER   512 35
FOR HIS MERCY ENDURETH FOR EVER   513 02
THY MERCY, O LORD, ENDURETH FOR EVER   514 15
AND HIS MERCY IS OVER ALL HIS WORKS   521 10
AND PUT THEIR TRUST IN HIS MERCY   523 18
THAT YOU FORGET NOT MERCY   558 30
THE FATHER, HAVE MERCY UPON US   560 04
HAVE MERCY UPON US   561 22
HAVE MERCY UPON US   561 23
HAVE MERCY UPON US AND HEAR US   561 33
BY THY MERCY, OBTAIN EVERLASTING LIFE   571 12
AND OF THY GREAT MERCY KEEP THEM IN THE SAME,   572 30
AND SHOW MERCY UNTO THOUSANDS IN THEM THAT LOVE ME   578 33
HE WILL DO OF HIS MERCY AND GOODNESS, THROUGH OUR   581 05
FAITH IN GOD'S MERCY THROUGH CHRIST, WITH A THANKFUL   582 24
SINCE IT IS OF THY MERCY, O GRACIOUS FATHER, THAT   588 04
BESEECH THEE, IN MERCY, AND FORGIVE US ALL OUR   590 02
WE ADORE THY MERCY IN SENDING THY ONLY SON INTO   591 11
AND BY THY GREAT MERCY DEFEND US FROM ALL PERILS AND   593 14
THEN IN THY MERCY GRANT US A SAFE LODGING, AND A HOLY 595 02
THEE TO HAVE MERCY UPON ALL THY CHILDREN WHO ARE   598 13
LABOUR IN WORKS OF MERCY OR IN SCHOOLS OF GOOD   600 04
BY GOD'S MERCY, THEY ATTAIN TO EVERLASTING   606 15

MERCY-SEAT

TOWARDS THE MERCY-SEAT OF THY HOLY TEMPLE   373 08

MERCY'S

SAVE ME, FOR THY MERCY'S SAKE   349 07
SAVE ME FOR THY MERCY'S SAKE   376 29
FOR THY MERCY'S SAKE   396 12

MERIT

TO THY ETERNAL MERIT, FATHER, SON, AND HOLY SPIRIT   544 14
TO THY ETERNAL MERIT, FATHER, SON, AND HOLY SPIRIT   556 22
ONLY FOR THE MERIT OF OUR LORD AND SAVIOUR JESUS   605 06

MERITORIOUS

OF HIS MERITORIOUS CROSS AND PASSION   086 32

MERITS

THROUGH THE MERITS OF JESUS CHRIST OUR SAVIOUR   031 23
THROUGH THE MERITS AND DEATH OF JESUS CHRIST OUR   037 07
THROUGH THE MERITS OF THY SON, JESUS CHRIST OUR LORD   041 16
THROUGH THY MERITS, O MERCIFUL SAVIOUR, WHO WITH THE   043 14
THROUGH THE MERITS AND MEDIATION OF THY BLESSED SON,   063 06
DEATH AND MERITS OF THY SON JESUS CHRIST OUR LORD,   079 15
BY THE MERITS AND DEATH OF THY SON JESUS   081 18
NOT WEIGHING OUR MERITS, BUT PARDONING OUR OFFENCES,   081 31
BY THE MERITS OF HIS MOST PRECIOUS DEATH AND   083 25
FOR HIS MERITS, WHO DIED, AND WAS BURIED, AND ROSE   161 18
THROUGH THE MERITS OF THE SAME THY SON JESUS CHRIST   170 23
THROUGH THE MERITS OF CHRIST JESUS OUR SAVIOUR, WHO   180 12
BUT THROUGH THE MERITS AND MEDIATION OF JESUS CHRIST, 206 10
THROUGH THE MERITS OF JESUS CHRIST OUR LORD   207 16
THROUGH THE MERITS OF THY MOST DEARLY BELOVED SON,   314 12
THROUGH THE MERITS OF JESUS CHRIST THINE ONLY SON OUR 317 22
THROUGH THE MERITS OF OUR SAVIOUR JESUS CHRIST, WHO   531 23
THROUGH THE MERITS OF OUR SAVIOUR JESUS CHRIST,   537 28
THROUGH THE MERITS OF OUR SAVIOUR JESUS CHRIST, WHO   548 06
THROUGH THE MERITS OF OUR SAVIOUR JESUS CHRIST,   554 02
THROUGH THE MERITS OF THE SAME THY BLESSED SON JESUS   574 20
THROUGH THE MERITS AND MEDIATION OF THY SON   589 07
THROUGH WHOSE MERITS AND INTERCESSION WE RECEIVED   591 22
THROUGH THE MERITS AND SATISFACTION OF THY SON CHRIST 591 31

MERRILY

SING WE MERRILY UNTO GOD OUR STRENGTH   442 12

MERRY

AND LET US EAT, AND BE MERRY   202 24
AND THEY BEGAN TO BE MERRY   202 26
THAT I MIGHT MAKE MERRY WITH MY FRIENDS   203 02
WE SHOULD MAKE MERRY, AND BE GLAD   203 06
IS GONE UP WITH A MERRY NOISE, *   398 29
LET THEM ALSO BE MERRY AND JOYFUL   419 15
THE MERRY HARP WITH THE LUTE   442 14

MESHECH

TO DWELL WITH MESHECH, *   502 15

MESOPOTAMIA

DWELLERS IN MESOPOTAMIA, AND IN JUDAEA, AND   181 02

MESSAGE

THIS THEN IS THE MESSAGE WHICH WE HAVE HEARD OF HIM,   101 22
CHRIST BY THE MESSAGE OF AN ANGEL, SO BY HIS CROSS   235 20

MESSENGER

DIDST SEND THY MESSENGER TO PREPARE THY WAY BEFORE   093 25
I SEND MY MESSENGER BEFORE THY FACE, WHICH SHALL   094 32
I SEND MY MESSENGER BEFORE THY FACE, WHICH SHALL   112 05
I WILL SEND MY MESSENGER, AND HE SHALL PREPARE THE   232 03
EVEN THE MESSENGER OF THE COVENANT, WHOM YE DELIGHT   232 05

MESSENGERS

TO SAY, TO BE MESSENGERS, WATCHMEN, AND STEWARDS OF   539 32

MET

THERE MET HIM TEN MEN THAT WERE LEPERS,   210 02
HIS SERVANTS MET HIM, AND TOLD HIM, SAYING,   220 06
MERCY AND TRUTH ARE MET TOGETHER   446 27

METE

MEASURE THAT YE METE WITHAL IT SHALL BE MEASURED TO   194 31
AND METE OUT THE VALLEY OF SUCCOTH   412 24
DIVIDE SHECHEM, AND METE OUT THE VALLEY OF SUCCOTH   479 18

MICHAEL

MICHAEL AND HIS ANGELS FOUGHT AGAINST THE DRAGON   252 03

MIDIANITES

9 BUT DO THOU TO THEM AS UNTO THE MIDIANITES   444 22

MIDNIGHT

AT EVEN, OR AT MIDNIGHT, OR AT THE COCK-CROWING, OR   021 25
GO UNTO HIM AT MIDNIGHT, AND SAY UNTO HIM, FRIEND,   262 27
62 AT MIDNIGHT I WILL RISE TO GIVE THANKS UNTO THEE,   494 04

MIDST

SITTING IN THE MIDST OF THE DOCTORS, BOTH HEARING   110 28
TO BE SET IN THE MIDST OF SO MANY AND GREAT DANGERS,   114 04
STOOD UP IN THE MIDST, AND ASKED JESUS, SAYING,   143 10
A FIRE IN THE MIDST OF THE HALL, AND WERE SET DOWN   151 09
AND THE VEIL OF THE TEMPLE WAS RENT IN THE MIDST   155 12
ON EITHER SIDE ONE, AND JESUS IN THE MIDST   159 35
STOOD IN THE MIDST OF THEM, AND SAITH UNTO THEM,   169 28
AND STOOD IN THE MIDST, AND SAITH UNTO THEM, PEACE BE 171 17
AND IN THE MIDST OF THE THRONE, AND ROUND ABOUT THE   187 16
THROUGH THE MIDST OF THE COASTS OF DECAPOLIS   206 28
PASSED THROUGH THE MIDST OF SAMARIA AND GALILEE   209 32
AND STOOD IN THE MIDST, AND SAID, PEACE BE UNTO YOU   229 02
STOOD UP IN THE MIDST OF THE DISCIPLES, AND SAID,   234 06
ASUNDER IN THE MIDST, AND ALL HIS BOWELS GUSHED OUT   234 14
AND SET HIM IN THE MIDST OF THEM, AND SAID, VERILY I   252 25
WHICH IS IN THE MIDST OF THE THRONE SHALL FEED THEM,   257 14
EVEN IN THE MIDST OF THEE, O JERUSALEM   306 02
I WALK IN THE MIDST OF TROUBLE   311 25
I WALK IN THE MIDST OF TROUBLE, YET SHALT THOU   312 04
CARRIED INTO THE MIDST OF THE SEA   327 06
GOD IS IN THE MIDST OF HER, THEREFORE SHALL SHE NOT   327 12
IN THE MIDST OF LIFE WE ARE IN DEATH   332 22
AND SET HIM IN THE MIDST OF THEM, AND SAID, VERILY I   339 24
WHICH IS IN THE MIDST OF THE THRONE SHALL FEED THEM,   341 25
HEART ALSO IN THE MIDST OF MY BODY IS EVEN LIKE   366 32
IN THE MIDST OF THE CONGREGATION WILL I PRAISE THEE   367 17
CARRIED INTO THE MIDST OF THE SEA   397 28
5 GOD IS IN THE MIDST OF HER, THEREFORE SHALL SHE NOT 398 02
IN THE MIDST OF THY TEMPLE   399 28
SORROW ARE IN THE MIDST OF IT   407 07
FALLEN INTO THE MIDST OF IT THEMSELVES   409 28
IN THE MIDST OF THE DAMSELS PLAYING WITH THE   421 05
ROAR IN THE MIDST OF THY CONGREGATIONS, *   430 12
ME NOT AWAY IN THE MIDST OF MINE AGE   465 28
EVEN IN THE MIDST AMONG THINE ENEMIES   482 10
EVEN IN THE MIDST OF THEE, O JERUSALEM   487 23
WONDERS INTO THE MIDST OF THEE, O THOU LAND OF EGYPT   510 20
TO GO THROUGH THE MIDST OF IT   512 10
I WALK IN THE MIDST OF TROUBLE, YET SHALT THOU   514 10
WHO ARE IN THE MIDST OF THIS NAUGHTY WORLD, THAT THEY 540 03
AND STOOD IN THE MIDST, AND SAITH UNTO THEM, PEACE BE 551 30
TO DWELL IN THE MIDST OF THE ASSEMBLY OF THE SAINTS   568 08

MIGHT

MIGHT MOST TEND TO THE PRESERVATION OF   V 35
MIGHT SERVE HIM WITHOUT FEAR   014 21
THROUGH THE MIGHT OF JESUS CHRIST OUR LORD   017 10
MANNER AS THEY MIGHT JUDGE MOST CONVENIENT FOR THEIR   VI 12
THEREIN AS MIGHT BE DEEMED EXPEDIENT   VI 26
THAT HE MIGHT BRING US OUT OF DARKNESS INTO HIS OWN   077 24
HE IS, THITHER WE MIGHT ALSO ASCEND, AND REIGN WITH   078 20
THAT HE MIGHT MAKE US THE CHILDREN OF GOD, AND EXALT   086 10
WAS DONE, THAT IT MIGHT BE FULFILLED WHICH WAS SPOKEN 091 18
OF THE SCRIPTURES MIGHT HAVE HOPE   092 17
THAT THE GENTILES MIGHT GLORIFY GOD FOR HIS MERCY   092 25
AND WITH GREAT MIGHT SUCCOUR US   095 05

MIGHT   CONTINUED

MEN THROUGH HIM MIGHT BELIEVE   097 28
FOR US, THAT HE MIGHT REDEEM US FROM ALL INIQUITY,   098 23
THAT IT MIGHT BE FULFILLED WHICH WAS SPOKEN OF THE   103 22
THE LAW, THAT WE MIGHT RECEIVE THE ADOPTION OF SONS   104 21
WAS DONE, THAT IT MIGHT BE FULFILLED WHICH WAS SPOKEN 105 08
THAT THEY MIGHT BE CALLED TREES OF RIGHTEOUSNESS,   107 09
THE LORD, THAT HE MIGHT BE GLORIFIED   107 10
THAT IT MIGHT BE FULFILLED WHICH WAS SPOKEN BY THE   107 22
IN HEAVENLY PLACES MIGHT BE KNOWN BY THE CHURCH THE   108 24
MANIFESTED THAT HE MIGHT DESTROY THE WORKS OF THE   117 05
THAT HE MIGHT DESTROY THE WORKS OF THE DEVIL   117 30
SAYING, WHAT MIGHT THIS PARABLE BE   121 29
THAT SEEING THEY MIGHT NOT SEE, AND HEARING THEY   121 31
AND HEARING MIGHT NOT UNDERSTAND   121 32
WHICH ARE CALLED MIGHT RECEIVE THE PROMISE OF ETERNAL 133 06
THAT IT MIGHT BE FULFILLED WHICH WAS SPOKEN BY THE   136 31
SOUGHT HOW THEY MIGHT TAKE HIM BY CRAFT, AND PUT HIM   139 34
FOR IT MIGHT HAVE BEEN SOLD FOR MORE THAN THREE   140 08
HE SOUGHT HOW HE MIGHT CONVENIENTLY BETRAY HIM   140 21
THE HOUR MIGHT PASS FROM HIM   141 34
SOUGHT HOW THEY MIGHT KILL HIM   148 14
HOW HE MIGHT BETRAY HIM UNTO THEM   148 18
REQUIRING THAT HE MIGHT BE CRUCIFIED   154 03
THE CROSS, THAT HE MIGHT BEAR IT AFTER JESUS   154 11
THAT THE SCRIPTURE MIGHT BE FULFILLED, WHICH SAITH   160 14
THAT THE SCRIPTURE MIGHT BE FULFILLED, SAITH, I   160 25
AND THAT THEY MIGHT BE TAKEN AWAY   160 33
THAT THEIR LEGS MIGHT BE BROKEN, AND THAT THEY MIGHT   160 33
THAT YE MIGHT BELIEVE   161 07
THAT HE MIGHT BRING US TO GOD, BEING PUT TO   161 23
THAT THEY MIGHT COME AND ANOINT HIM   165 20
THAT THEY MIGHT UNDERSTAND THE SCRIPTURES, AND SAID   170 11
THAT IN ME YE MIGHT HAVE PEACE   177 08
COME TO PASS, YE MIGHT BELIEVE   182 06
WORLD THROUGH HIM MIGHT BE SAVED   185 02
THAT THEY MIGHT RECEIVE THE HOLY GHOST   185 24
AM COME THAT THEY MIGHT HAVE LIFE, AND THAT THEY   186 18
AND THAT THEY MIGHT HAVE IT MORE ABUNDANTLY   186 18
THE WORLD, THAT WE MIGHT LIVE THROUGH HIM   189 13
THE BODY OF SIN MIGHT BE DESTROYED, THAT HENCEFORTH   197 18
OF ALL POWER AND MIGHT, WHO ART THE AUTHOR AND GIVER   198 20
ME A KID, THAT I MIGHT MAKE MERRY WITH MY FRIENDS   203 02
OF JESUS CHRIST MIGHT BE GIVEN TO THEM THAT BELIEVE   208 04
STRENGTHENED WITH MIGHT BY HIS SPIRIT IN THE INNER   212 15
THAT YE MIGHT BE FILLED WITH ALL THE   212 20
STRONG IN THE LORD, AND IN THE POWER OF HIS MIGHT   219 06
COUNSEL HOW THEY MIGHT ENTANGLE HIM IN HIS TALK   222 29
TO DESIRE THAT YE MIGHT BE FILLED WITH THE KNOWLEDGE   224 02
THAT YE MIGHT WALK WORTHY OF THE LORD UNTO ALL   224 04
WITH ALL MIGHT, ACCORDING TO HIS GLORIOUS POWER, UNTO 224 06
WILL OF GOD, YE MIGHT RECEIVE THE PROMISE   228 16
THAT YE MIGHT BELIEVE THAT JESUS IS THE   229 11
THAT BELIEVING YE MIGHT HAVE LIFE THROUGH HIS NAME   229 13
MEN OR WOMEN, HE MIGHT BRING THEM BOUND UNTO   229 29
ON HIM, THAT HE MIGHT RECEIVE HIS SIGHT   230 21
THAT HE MIGHT BRING THEM BOUND UNTO THE CHIEF   231 07
THAT HE MIGHT GO TO HIS OWN PLACE   234 30
THAT HE MIGHT FILL ALL THINGS   237 18
AND THAT YOUR JOY MIGHT BE FULL   238 21
THAT MY JOY MIGHT REMAIN IN YOU, AND THAT YOUR   238 25
OF OUR ENEMIES MIGHT SERVE HIM WITHOUT FEAR, IN   244 08
PETER PASSING BY MIGHT OVERSHADOW SOME OF THEM   249 29
THAT THE WORD MIGHT BE FULFILLED THAT IS WRITTEN IN   255 28
AND POWER, AND MIGHT, BE UNTO OUR GOD FOR EVER AND   257 02
THAT HE MIGHT SANCTIFY AND CLEANSE IT WITH THE   267 20
THE WORD, THAT HE MIGHT PRESENT IT TO HIMSELF A   267 22
STRENGTHENED WITH MIGHT BY HIS SPIRIT IN THE INNER   281 09
OF ALL POWER AND MIGHT, WHO ART THE AUTHOR AND GIVER   283 08
THAT THEY MIGHT RECEIVE THE HOLY GHOST   296 16
WHO, BY THE MIGHT OF THY COMMAND, DRIVEST AWAY FROM   315 06
MY GOD, AND MY MIGHT, IN WHOM I WILL TRUST   359 26
THE ROCK OF MY MIGHT   414 12
THAT I MIGHT BEHOLD THY POWER AND GLORY   414 30
THAT THE LORD GOD MIGHT DWELL AMONG THEM   420 21
ART GLORIOUS IN MIGHT, *   432 28
THEIR POSTERITY MIGHT KNOW IT, *   435 07
THEY MIGHT SHOW THEIR CHILDREN THE SAME   435 09
8 THAT THEY MIGHT PUT THEIR TRUST IN GOD   435 11
SO THAT THEY MIGHT NOT DRINK OF THE RIVERS   437 30
THAT HE MIGHT FEED JACOB HIS PEOPLE, AND ISRAEL HIS   439 22
20 THAT HE MIGHT HEAR THE MOURNINGS OF SUCH AS ARE IN 465 19
22 THAT HE MIGHT INFORM HIS PRINCES AFTER HIS WILL,   471 16
44 THAT THEY MIGHT KEEP HIS STATUTES, *   472 27
THAT HE MIGHT MAKE HIS POWER TO BE KNOWN   473 17
THAT THEY MIGHT GO TO THE CITY WHERE THEY DWELT   476 17
THAT HE MIGHT SLAY HIM THAT WAS VEXED AT THE   480 33
SORE AT ME, THAT I MIGHT FALL   488 26
THAT I MIGHT KEEP THY STATUTES   490 08
THAT I MIGHT BE OCCUPIED IN THY WORD   500 06
SHALL SPEAK OF THE MIGHT OF THY MARVELLOUS ACTS   521 04
MIGHT BE KNOWN UNTO MEN   521 17
THAT NO MAN MIGHT PRESUME TO EXECUTE ANY OF THEM,   529 14
THAT HE MIGHT FILL ALL THINGS   538 05
AND THAT THEY MIGHT HAVE IT MORE ABUNDANTLY   539 00
AM COME THAT THEY MIGHT HAVE LIFE, AND THAT THEY   539 09
OWN UNFAILING MIGHT SUPPLY TO STRENGTHEN OUR   545 04
SO THAT I MIGHT FINISH MY COURSE WITH JOY,   550 19
OWN UNFAILING MIGHT SUPPLY TO STRENGTHEN OUR   557 10
BY THE MIGHT OF THY SPIRIT LIFT US, WE PRAY THEE, TO   595 21

MIGHTEST

THAT THOU MIGHTEST BE JUSTIFIED IN THY SAYING,   060 18
THAT THOU MIGHTEST RECEIVE THY SIGHT, AND BE   230 33

MIGHTEST   CONTINUED

THAT THOU MIGHTEST STILL THE ENEMY AND THE AVENGER	351 03
THAT THOU MIGHTEST BE JUSTIFIED IN THY SAYING,	403 16

MIGHTIER

COMETH ONE MIGHTIER THAN I AFTER ME, THE LATCHET OF	112 14
WHO DWELLETH ON HIGH, IS MIGHTIER	457 14

MIGHTIEST

PRINCIPAL AND MIGHTIEST IN THE DWELLINGS OF HAM	438 13

MIGHTILY

AND EVERMORE MIGHTILY DEFEND THEM	061 33
AND EVERMORE MIGHTILY DEFEND HIM	308 26
15 THOU HAST MIGHTILY DELIVERED THY PEOPLE, *	434 12
MIGHTILY BEFRIEND INNOCENT SUFFERERS, AND SANCTIFY TO	599 09

MIGHTINESS

AND MIGHTINESS OF THY KINGDOM, *	521 16

MIGHTY

HATH RAISED UP A MIGHTY SALVATION FOR US, *	014 10
THE SAME WITH THY MIGHTY POWER	017 15
THE HIGH AND MIGHTY RULER OF THE UNIVERSE, WHO DOST	017 27
FOR HE THAT IS MIGHTY HATH MAGNIFIED ME	026 16
HATH PUT DOWN THE MIGHTY FROM THEIR SEAT,	026 22
OUR WORK, BY THE MIGHTY POWER OF THE HOLY GHOST,	037 02
O MOST MIGHTY AND MERCIFUL GOD, IN THIS TIME OF	045 03
OUR SAVIOUR AND MIGHTY DELIVERER	052 14
O MOST MIGHTY GOD, AND MERCIFUL FATHER, WHO HAST	062 13
THROUGH THY MOST MIGHTY PROTECTION, BOTH HERE AND	070 10
HIS MIGHTY RESURRECTION AND GLORIOUS	081 03
DEFENDED BY THY MIGHTY POWER	115 31
IN RIGHTEOUSNESS, MIGHTY TO SAVE	138 14
OF THOSE MIGHTY ACTS, WHEREBY THOU HAST GIVEN UNTO US	147 10
WAS A PROPHET MIGHTY IN DEED AND WORD BEFORE GOD AND	167 17
AS OF A RUSHING MIGHTY WIND, AND IT FILLED ALL THE	180 20
MAY, BY THY MIGHTY AID, BE DEFENDED AND	192 26
UNDER THE MIGHTY HAND OF GOD, THAT HE MAY EXALT YOU	193 02
THERE AROSE A MIGHTY FAMINE IN THAT LAND	202 05
THROUGH WHOSE MIGHTY POWER OUR FATHERS WON THEIR	263 17
A GREAT GOD, A MIGHTY, AND A TERRIBLE, WHICH	263 24
THROUGH THY MOST MIGHTY PROTECTION, BOTH HERE AND	298 30
GREAT AND MIGHTY GOD, WHO BRINGEST DOWN TO THE GRAVE,	315 19
O LORD MOST MIGHTY, O HOLY AND MOST MERCIFUL	332 25
O GOD MOST MIGHTY, O HOLY AND MERCIFUL SAVIOUR,	332 30
ACCORDING TO THE MIGHTY WORKING WHEREBY HE IS ABLE TO	333 22
ACCORDING TO THE MIGHTY WORKING WHEREBY HE IS ABLE TO	337 16
FOR THEY WERE TOO MIGHTY FOR ME	360 34
LORD STRONG AND MIGHTY, EVEN THE LORD MIGHTY IN	369 12
EVEN THE LORD MIGHTY IN BATTLE	369 12
THE LORD, O YE MIGHTY, *	373 30
OF THE LORD IS MIGHTY IN OPERATION	374 05
NEITHER IS ANY MIGHTY MAN DELIVERED BY MUCH STRENGTH	379 20
19 BUT MINE ENEMIES LIVE, AND ARE MIGHTY	388 30
O THOU MOST MIGHTY, *	396 21
EVEN THE MOST MIGHTY GOD, HATH SPOKEN, *	401 21
AND A MIGHTY TEMPEST SHALL BE STIRRED UP ROUND	401 26
THE MIGHTY MEN ARE GATHERED AGAINST ME, WITHOUT ANY	411 08
AND THAT A MIGHTY VOICE	421 24
AND WOULD DESTROY ME GUILTLESS, ARE MIGHTY	422 09
THOU DRIEDST UP MIGHTY WATERS	431 07
WHOSE HANDS WERE MIGHTY HAVE FOUND NOTHING	432 31
OF THE LORD, HIS MIGHTY AND WONDERFUL WORKS THAT HE	435 03
THY TRUTH, MOST MIGHTY LORD, IS ON EVERY SIDE	450 23
ABROAD WITH THY MIGHTY ARM	450 27
14 THOU HAST A MIGHTY ARM	450 33
UPON ONE THAT IS MIGHTY, I HAVE EXALTED ONE CHOSEN	451 13
OF THE SEA ARE MIGHTY, AND RAGE HORRIBLY	457 13
HIS SEED SHALL BE MIGHTY UPON EARTH	483 20
THE LORD BRINGETH MIGHTY THINGS TO PASS	488 31
THE LORD BRINGETH MIGHTY THINGS TO PASS	488 34
EVEN MIGHTY AND SHARP ARROWS, WITH HOT BURNING COALS	502 12
FOR THE MIGHTY GOD OF JACOB	508 14
AND SLEW MIGHTY KINGS	510 23
12 WITH A MIGHTY HAND AND STRETCHED-OUT ARM	512 06
18 YEA, AND SLEW MIGHTY KINGS	512 18
LORD STRONG AND MIGHTY, EVEN THE LORD MIGHTY IN	563 27
EVEN THE LORD MIGHTY IN BATTLE	563 27
O ETERNAL GOD, MIGHTY IN POWER, AND OF MAJESTY	564 27
THE SAME WITH THY MIGHTY POWER	592 21

MILETUS

FROM MILETUS PAUL SENT TO EPHESUS, AND CALLED THE	550 04

MILK

DESIRE THE SINCERE MILK OF THE WORD, THAT YE MAY GROW	259 27

MILLSTONE

FOR HIM THAT A MILLSTONE WERE HANGED ABOUT HIS NECK,	252 32

MIND

OR DISTRESSED, IN MIND, BODY, OR ESTATE	019 05
OR DISTRESSED, IN MIND, BODY, OR ESTATE	033 03
AND MAY WITH ONE MIND AND ONE MOUTH GLORIFY THEE	038 02
MEN TO BE OF ONE MIND IN A HOUSE, AND STILLEST THE	052 18

MIND   CONTINUED

AND CHARITABLE FRAME OF MIND	VI 38
AND WITH ALL THY SOUL, AND WITH ALL THY MIND	069 28
IN THE LORD, YE WHO MIND TO COME TO THE HOLY	085 25
YE WILL BY GOD'S GRACE RETURN TO A BETTER MIND	089 20
YE MAY WITH ONE MIND AND ONE MOUTH GLORIFY GOD, EVEN	092 20
RENEWING OF YOUR MIND, THAT YE MAY PROVE WHAT IS THAT	110 07
BE OF THE SAME MIND ONE TOWARD ANOTHER	111 31
MIND NOT HIGH THINGS, BUT CONDESCEND TO MEN OF LOW	111 31
HUMBLENESS OF MIND, MEEKNESS, LONG-SUFFERING	116 05
LET THIS MIND BE IN YOU, WHICH WAS ALSO IN CHRIST	134 16
AND PETER CALLED TO MIND THE WORD THAT JESUS SAID	143 35
ALSO IN HEART AND MIND THITHER ASCEND, AND WITH HIM	177 17
BE YE ALL OF ONE MIND, HAVING COMPASSION ONE OF	195 20
AND WITH ALL THY STRENGTH, AND WITH ALL THY MIND	208 17
AND WITH ALL THY SOUL, AND WITH ALL THY MIND	215 12
THE VANITY OF THEIR MIND, HAVING THE UNDERSTANDING	216 05
AND BE RENEWED IN THE SPIRIT OF YOUR MIND	216 14
AND SERVE THEE WITH A QUIET MIND	219 03
IN THEIR SHAME, WHO MIND EARTHLY THINGS	222 20
AND CAST IN HER MIND WHAT MANNER OF SALUTATION THIS	236 12
WITH ALL THY MIND, WITH ALL THY SOUL, AND WITH	288 07
WITH ALL MY MIND, WITH ALL MY SOUL, AND WITH	288 18
OF BODY, VIGOUR OF MIND, AND CHEERFULNESS OF SPIRIT,	315 30
AND FULFIL ALL THY MIND	364 22
NOT LIFT UP HIS MIND UNTO VANITY, NOR SWORN TO	369 03
REGARD NOT IN THEIR MIND THE WORKS OF THE LORD, NOR	373 17
14 I AM CLEAN FORGOTTEN AS A DEAD MAN OUT OF MIND	376 19
MEN TO BE OF ONE MIND IN AN HOUSE, AND BRINGETH THE	419 21
AND CALL TO MIND THY WONDERS OF OLD TIME	434 05
THY TERRORS HAVE I SUFFERED WITH A TROUBLED MIND	449 28
BECAUSE HIS MIND WAS NOT TO DO GOOD	480 32
WITH A GLAD MIND AND WILL THEIR GODLY ADMONITIONS	533 33
YE CANNOT HAVE A MIND AND WILL THERETO OF YOURSELVES	540 30
WITH A GLAD MIND AND WILL THEIR GODLY ADMONITIONS,	543 14
ALL HUMILITY OF MIND, AND WITH MANY TEARS, AND	550 08
NOT LIFT UP HIS MIND UNTO VANITY, NOR SWORN TO	563 18
AND DEVOTION OF MIND, THAT THOU MAYEST ACCEPT THEIR	566 20
BEARING IN MIND THAT YOU ARE ACCOUNTABLE TO US HERE,	569 26
WITH ALL MY MIND, WITH ALL MY SOUL, AND WITH	579 29
AND WANDERINGS OF MIND, THAT YE WITH STEDFAST THOUGHTS	594 07
THE EYES OF THE MIND OPENED TO BEHOLD THINGS	594 24
HE MAY BE RESTORED TO HEALTH OF BODY AND OF MIND	597 18
THEM TO STRENGTH OF MIND AND CHEERFULNESS OF SPIRIT,	598 15
AND OF A SOUND MIND TO ALL IN PLACES OF AUTHORITY	600 03
DRAWING UP THEIR MIND TO HIGH AND HEAVENLY THINGS, AS	606 19

MINDED

ALL THOSE WHO ARE MINDED TO RECEIVE THE HOLY	R 075 16
WAS MINDED TO PUT HER AWAY PRIVILY	104 31
FOR THEY ARE MINDED TO DO ME SOME MISCHIEF, SO	406 24
HOW YOU ARE MINDED TO BEHAVE YOURSELF IN THE CHURCH	554 15

MINDFUL

MAKE THEM EVER MINDFUL OF THEIR CALLING TO SERVE THIS	018 13
A PEOPLE MINDFUL OF THY FAVOUR AND GLAD TO DO THY	036 11
THAT THOU ART MINDFUL OF HIM	351 07
HATH BEEN ALWAY MINDFUL OF HIS COVENANT AND PROMISE,	470 18
HE SHALL EVER BE MINDFUL OF HIS COVENANT	483 04
LORD HATH BEEN MINDFUL OF US, AND HE SHALL BLESS US	485 34
AND MAKE US MINDFUL OF THE NEEDS OF OTHERS	600 18

MINDS

AND GOVERN THE MINDS OF THY SERVANTS THE BISHOPS AND	038 28
THE HEARTS AND MINDS OF THY SERVANTS WHO AT THIS TIME	043 21
YOUR HEARTS AND MINDS IN THE KNOWLEDGE AND LOVE OF	084 19
YOUR HEARTS AND MINDS THROUGH CHRIST JESUS	095 19
AND IN THEIR MINDS WILL I WRITE THEM	158 13
DOST PUT INTO OUR MINDS GOOD DESIRES, SO BY THY	163 26
PURE HEARTS AND MINDS TO FOLLOW THEE, THE ONLY GOD	214 25
HATH BLINDED THE MINDS OF THEM WHICH BELIEVE NOT,	251 03
ARE YOUR MINDS SET UPON RIGHTEOUSNESS, O YE	410 07
YOUR HEARTS AND MINDS IN THE KNOWLEDGE AND LOVE OF	535 14
UNDERSTAND YOUR MINDS AND WILLS IN THESE THINGS,	541 25
YOUR HEARTS AND MINDS IN THE KNOWLEDGE AND LOVE OF	547 15
YOUR HEARTS AND MINDS IN THE KNOWLEDGE AND LOVE OF	559 18
TO FILL MEN'S MINDS WITH GREATER REVERENCE FOR HIS	564 17
YOUR HEARTS AND MINDS IN THE KNOWLEDGE AND LOVE OF	568 14
ENLIGHTEN THEIR MINDS MORE AND MORE WITH THE LIGHT OF	572 27
KEEP IN OUR MINDS A LIVELY REMEMBRANCE OF THAT	588 21
AND GIVE THEM REPENTANCE AND BETTER MINDS	591 02

MINE

FOR MINE EYES HAVE SEEN *	028 11
THY MERCIES DO AWAY MINE OFFENCES	060 12
ACCORDING TO MINE OFFICE, I BID YOU IN THE NAME OF	089 07
I JUDGE NOT MINE OWN SELF	094 08
FOR IT IS WRITTEN, VENGEANCE IS MINE	113 05
MINE HOUR IS NOT YET COME	113 16
DO WHAT I WILL WITH MINE OWN	120 11
IN PERILS BY MINE OWN COUNTRYMEN, IN PERILS BY THE	121 05
WHICH CONCERN MINE INFIRMITIES	121 14
AND I SEEK NOT MINE OWN GLORY	133 16
WILL TREAD THEM IN MINE ANGER, AND TRAMPLE THEM IN MY	138 18
OF VENGEANCE IS IN MINE HEART, AND THE YEAR OF MY	138 21
THEREFORE MINE OWN ARM BROUGHT SALVATION UNTO ME	138 24
DOWN THE PEOPLE IN MINE ANGER, AND MAKE THEM DRUNK IN	138 26
GOD HATH OPENED MINE EAR, AND I WAS NOT REBELLIOUS,	144 12
WHO IS MINE ADVERSARY	144 19
SHALL YE HAVE OF MINE HAND	144 29
AND AM KNOWN OF MINE, EVEN AS THE FATHER KNOWETH ME,	172 28

MINE   CONTINUED

HE SHALL RECEIVE OF MINE, AND SHALL SHEW IT UNTC YOU   175 22
ALL THINGS THAT THE FATHER HATH ARE MINE   175 23
HE SHALL TAKE OF MINE, AND SHALL SHEW IT UNTO YCU   175 24
YE HEAR IS NOT MINE, BUT THE FATHER'S WHICH SENT ME   181 28
UNTO YOU WITH MINE OWN HAND   210 24
IN EVERY PRAYER OF MINE FOR YOU ALL MAKING REQUEST   220 23
FOR MINE EYES HAVE SEEN THY SALVATION, WHICH THCU   233 06
ON MY LEFT, IS NOT MINE TO GIVE, BUT IT SHALL BE   247 17
FOR A FRIEND OF MINE IN HIS JCURNEY IS COME TO ME,   262 28
NOT TO DO MINE OWN WILL, BLT THE WILL OF HIM   269 16
TRULY TO EARN MINE OWN LIVING, AND TO DO MY DUTY IN   289 09
THOU HOLDEST MINE EYES WAKING   311 06
I COMMUNE WITH MINE OWN HEART, AND SEARCH OUT MY   311 11
AND I SAID, IT IS MINE OWN INFIRMITY   311 18
THE FURIOUSNESS OF MINE ENEMIES, AND THY RIGHT HAND   312 06
SEE FOR MYSELF, AND MINE EYES SHALL BEHCLD, AND NOT   324 12
LET ME KNOW MINE END, AND THE NUMBER OF MY   324 20
A SPAN LONG, AND MINE AGE IS EVEN AS NOTHING IN   324 23
DELIVER ME FROM ALL MINE OFFENCES   324 30
ABOVE MINE ENEMIES ROUND ABOUT ME   326 15
SHALL HE LIFT UP MINE HEAD *   326 15
I WILL LIFT UP MINE EYES UNTO THE HILLS   327 19
I WILL LIFT UP MINE EYES UNTO THE HILLS   339 03
THOU SMITEST ALL MINE ENEMIES UPON THE CHEEK-BONE   347 05
WILL YE BLASPHEME MINE HONOUR, *   347 13
BECAUSE OF MINE ENEMIES   348 11
AWAY BECAUSE OF ALL MINE ENEMIES   349 13
10 ALL MINE ENEMIES SHALL BE CCNFOUNDED, AND SORE   349 18
ANY CAUSE IS MINE ENEMY   349 31
5 THEN LET MINE ENEMY PERSECLTE MY SOUL, AND TAKE ME   349 32
THE EARTH, AND LAY MINE HONOUR IN THE DUST   349 34
THE INDIGNATION OF MINE ENEMIES   350 02
3 WHILE MINE ENEMIES ARE DRIVEN BACK, *   351 26
HOW LONG SHALL MINE ENEMY TRIUMPH OVER ME   355 31
LIGHTEN MINE EYES, THAT I SLEEP NOT IN DEATH   356 03
4 LEST MINE ENEMY SAY, I HAVE PREVAILED AGAINST HIM   356 04
IS THE PORTION OF MINE INHERITANCE, AND OF MY CUP   357 31
PROVED AND VISITED MINE HEART IN THE NIGHT SEASCN   358 21
MINE ENEMIES COMPASS ME ROUND ABOUT, TO TAKE AWAY MY   359 04
I BE SAFE FROM MINE ENEMIES   359 30
AND ESCHEWED MINE OWN WICKEDNESS   361 14
AND MINE ARMS SHALL BEND EVEN A BOW OF STEEL   362 04
35 HE TEACHETH MINE HANDS TO FIGHT, *   362 04
I WILL FOLLOW UPON MINE ENEMIES, AND OVERTAKE THEM   362 11
SHALT THROW DOWN MINE ENEMIES UNDER ME   362 17
41 THOU HAST MADE MINE ENEMIES ALSO TO TURN THEIR   362 18
SETTETH ME UP ABOVE MINE ADVERSARIES   363 03
NEITHER LET MINE ENEMIES TRIUMPH OVER ME   369 20
14 MINE EYES ARE EVER LOOKING UNTO THE LORD   370 14
18 CONSIDER MINE ENEMIES, HOW MANY THEY ARE   370 22
IS EVER BEFORE MINE EYES   371 02
THE WICKED, EVEN MINE ENEMIES AND MY FOES, CAME UPCN   371 27
SHALL HE LIFT UP MINE HEAD *   372 07
ABOVE MINE ENEMIES ROUND ABOUT ME   372 07
BECAUSE OF MINE ENEMIES   372 23
INTO THE WILL OF MINE ADVERSARIES   372 24
AND MINE EYE IS CONSUMED FOR VERY HEAVINESS   376 09
BECAUSE OF MINE INIQUITY, *   376 13
REPROACH AMONG ALL MINE ENEMIES, BUT ESPECIALLY AMONG   376 15
AND THEY OF MINE ACQUAINTANCE WERE AFRAID OF ME   376 16
ME FROM THE HAND OF MINE ENEMIES, *   376 27
AND MINE UNRIGHTEOUSNESS HAVE I NOT HID   377 30
GUIDE THEE WITH MINE EYE   378 09
SHALL LIVE UNTO MINE OWN BOSOM   382 19
15 BUT IN MINE ADVERSITY THEY REJOICED, AND GATHERED   382 23
NOT THEM THAT ARE MINE ENEMIES TRIUMPH OVER ME   382 34
AND THE LIGHT OF MINE EYES IS GONE FROM ME   388 11
THAT THEY, EVEN MINE ENEMIES, SHOULD NOT TRIUMPH CVER   388 23
19 BUT MINE ENEMIES LIVE, AND ARE MIGHTY   388 30
5 LORD, LET ME KNOW MINE END, AND THE NUMBER OF MY   389 15
A SPAN LONG, AND MINE AGE IS EVEN AS NOTHING IN   389 18
DELIVER ME FROM ALL MINE OFFENCES   389 25
BUT MINE EARS HAST THCU OPENED   390 27
5 MINE ENEMIES SPEAK EVIL OF ME, *   392 08
7 ALL MINE ENEMIES WHISPER TOGETHER AGAINST ME   392 13
9 YEA, EVEN MINE OWN FAMILIAR FRIEND WHOM I TRUSTED,   392 17
THAT MINE ENEMY DOTH NOT TRIUMPH AGAINST ME   392 21
WHILE MINE ENEMIES THAT TROUBLE ME CAST ME IN THE   393 28
4 I WILL INCLINE MINE EAR TO THE PARABLE, *   400 12
OF THE FOREST ARE MINE, *   402 10
THE WHOLE WORLD IS MINE, AND ALL THAT IS THEREIN   402 15
THY MERCIES DO AWAY MINE OFFENCES   403 10
REWARD EVIL UNTO MINE ENEMIES   406 12
HIS DESIRE UPON MINE ENEMIES   406 17
AND MINE EYE HATH SEEN HIS DESIRE UPON MINE ENEMIES   406 17
13 NEITHER WAS IT MINE ADVERSARY THAT DID MAGNIFY   407 13
MY GUIDE, AND MINE OWN FAMILIAR FRIEND   407 17
2 MINE ENEMIES ARE DAILY AT HAND TO SWALLOW ME UP   408 16
THEN SHALL MINE ENEMIES BE PUT TO FLIGHT   408 32
DELIVER ME FROM MINE ENEMIES, O GOD   411 04
SEE MY DESIRE UPON MINE ENEMIES   411 25
7 GILEAD IS MINE, AND MANASSEH IS MINE   412 25
7 GILEAD IS MINE, AND MANASSEH IS MINE   412 25
WICKEDNESS WITH MINE HEART, *   418 16
MINE OWN WILL I BRING AGAIN, AS I DID SOMETIME FRCM   420 31
THEY THAT ARE MINE ENEMIES, AND WOULD DESTROY ME   422 08
BECAUSE OF MINE ENEMIES   423 10
MINE ADVERSARIES ARE ALL IN THY SIGHT   423 12
9 FOR MINE ENEMIES SPEAK AGAINST ME   425 25
ME NOT, O GOD, IN MINE OLD AGE, WHEN I AM   426 10
4 THOU HOLDEST MINE EYES WAKING   433 23
I COMMUNE WITH MINE OWN HEART, AND SEARCH OUT MY   433 28
AND I SAID, IT IS MINE OWN INFIRMITY   434 02
THOU HAST PUT AWAY MINE ACQUAINTANCE FAR FRCM ME,   449 11

MINE   CONTINUED

AND HID MINE ACQUAINTANCE OUT OF MY SIGHT   449 34
SEE HIS LUST OF MINE ENEMIES, *   456 21
10 MINE EYE ALSO SHALL SEE HIS LUST OF MINE ENEMIES,   456 21
AND MINE EAR SHALL HEAR HIS DESIRE OF THE WICKED THAT   456 22
8 MINE EYES LOOK UPON SUCH AS ARE FAITHFUL IN THE   463 30
8 MINE ENEMIES REVILE ME ALL THE DAY LONG   464 25
IN THE MIDST OF MINE AGE   465 29
15 TOUCH NOT MINE ANOINTED, *   471 02
8 GILEAD IS MINE, AND MANASSEH IS MINE   479 20
8 GILEAD IS MINE, AND MANASSEH IS MINE   479 20
FROM THE LORD UNTO MINE ENEMIES, *   481 10
28 LET MINE ADVERSARIES BE CLOTHED WITH SHAME   481 29
MINE EYES FROM TEARS, AND MY FEET FROM FALLING   487 05
SEE MY DESIRE UPON MINE ENEMIES   488 13
18 OPEN THOU MINE EYES   491 02
37 O TURN AWAY MINE EYES, LEST THEY BEHOLD VANITY   492 13
59 I CALLED MINE OWN WAYS TO REMEMBRANCE, *   493 29
82 MINE EYES LONG SORE FOR THY WORD   495 21
MADE ME WISER THAN MINE ENEMIES   496 23
HAVE I CLAIMED AS MINE HERITAGE FOR EVER   497 19
ME NOT OVER UNTO MINE OPPRESSORS   498 12
123 MINE EYES ARE WASTED AWAY WITH LOOKING FOR THY   498 15
136 MINE EYES GUSH OUT WITH WATER, *   499 10
BECAUSE MINE ENEMIES HAVE FORGOTTEN THY WORDS   499 17
148 MINE EYES PREVENT THE NIGHT WATCHES   500 06
O CONSIDER MINE ADVERSITY, AND DELIVER ME, *   500 17
I WILL LIFT UP MINE EYES UNTO THE HILLS   502 22
UNTO THEE LIFT I UP MINE EYES, *   503 27
THE TABERNACLE OF MINE HOUSE, *   508 08
4 I WILL NOT SUFFER MINE EYES TO SLEEP, NOR MINE   508 10
EYES TO SLEEP, NOR MINE EYELIDS TO SLUMBER   508 10
A LANTERN FOR MINE ANOINTED   509 09
THE FURIOUSNESS OF MINE ENEMIES, AND THY RIGHT HAND   514 12
AND MINE UP-RISING   514 21
AS THOUGH THEY WERE MINE ENEMIES   516 03
4 O LET NOT MINE HEART BE INCLINED TO ANY EVIL THING   517 15
9 BUT MINE EYES LOOK UNTO THEE, O LORD GOD   517 28
O LORD, FROM MINE ENEMIES   519 10
THY GOODNESS SLAY MINE ENEMIES, *   519 17
AND AM KNOWN OF MINE, EVEN AS THE FATHER KNCWETH ME,   539 17
LABOUR TRULY TO GET MINE OWN LIVING, AND TO DO MY   580 13

MINGLED

VINEGAR TO DRINK MINGLED WITH GALL   136 29
TO DRINK WINE MINGLED WITH MYRRH   146 09
AND MINGLED MY DRINK WITH WEEPING   464 27
35 BUT WERE MINGLED AMONG THE HEATHEN, *   475 06
THE EVIL BE EVER MINGLED WITH THE GCCD, AND SOMETIMES   608 08

MINISHED

FAITHFUL ARE MINISHED FROM AMONG THE CHILDREN CF MEN   355 07
WHEN THEY ARE MINISHED AND BROUGHT LOW *   478 24

MINISTER

THE MINISTER SHALL BEGIN THE MORNING PRAYER BY   R 003 03
TO FOLLOW, THE MINISTER MAY, AT HIS DISCRETICN, PASS   R 003 06
THE MINISTER MAY, AFTER THE SENTENCES,   R 003 11
THEN THE MINISTER SHALL SAY, DEARLY BELOVED   R 005 28
AFTER THE MINISTER, ALL KNEELING   R 006 16
THEN THE MINISTER SHALL KNEEL, AND SAY THE LCRD'S   R 007 20
UP, THE MINISTER SHALL SAY, GLORY BE TC THE FATHER,   R 008 02
THE MINISTER SHALL SAY, HERE BEGINNETH SUCH A   R 009 32
TO FOLLOW, THE MINISTER AT HIS DISCRETION, AFTER ANY   R 010 04
CREED BY THE MINISTER AND THE PEOPLE, STANDING   R 015 15
THE MINISTER FIRST PRONOUNCING,   R 016 24
THAT THE MINISTER MAY HERE END THE MORNING   R 017 22
MAY BE SAID BY THE CONGREGATION WITH THE MINISTER   R 019 35
THE MINISTER SHALL BEGIN THE EVENING PRAYER BY   R 021 03
THE MINISTER MAY, AFTER THE SENTENCES,   R 021 08
AFTER THE MINISTER, ALL KNEELING   R 023 23
THEN THE MINISTER SHALL KNEEL, AND SAY THE LORD'S   R 024 27
UP, THE MINISTER SHALL SAY, GLORY BE TC THE FATHER,   R 025 08
THAT THE MINISTER, AT HIS DISCRETION, MAY OMIT   R 026 07
CREED BY THE MINISTER AND THE PEOPLE, STANDING   R 029 20
THE MINISTER FIRST PRONOUNCING,   R 030 29
THE MINISTER MAY HERE END THE EVENING PRAYER WITH   R 031 31
MAY BE SAID BY THE CONGREGATION WITH THE MINISTER   R 033 33
CAME NOT TO BE MINISTERED UNTO, BUT TO MINISTER   043 29
MAY WORTHILY MINISTER IN THY NAME TO THE SUFFERING,   044 04
ALL THOSE WHO MINISTER TO THE SICK   045 06
THAT THE MINISTER, IN HIS DISCRETION, MAY OMIT   R 047 04
THAT THEY MAY MINISTER FAITHFULLY AND WISELY THE   047 24
OR COMMUNION, AT THE DISCRETION OF THE MINISTER   R 049 04
THEN SHALL THE MINISTER, AND THE PEOPLE WITH HIM,   R 058 02
THE MINISTER MAY, AT HIS DISCRETION, OMIT ALL THAT   R 058 09
MINISTER AND PEOPLE   R 058 25
MINISTER AND PEOPLE   R 059 02
THE MINISTER MAY END THE LITANY HERE, CR AT HIS   R 059 29
AT THE DISCRETION OF THE MINISTER   R 060 06
THE MINISTER AND THE PEOPLE KNEELING, THEN SHALL BE   R 060 07
THE MINISTER MAY PASS AT ONCE TO O LORD, SAVE   R 061 19
SAY THIS THAT FOLLOWETH, AFTER THE MINISTER   R 062 27
THEN THE MINISTER SHALL SAY, O GOD, WHOSE NATURE AND   R 063 08
THE COLLECT THE MINISTER APPOINTED SHALL READ THE   R 070 18
THE MINISTER APPOINTED SHALL READ THE   R 070 22
MINISTERED UNTO THE SAINTS, AND YET DO MINISTER   072 26
AND THE MINISTER WHO DELIVERETH THE CUP SHALL SAY,   R 083 02
BUT THE MINISTER AND OTHER COMMUNICANTS SHALL,   R 084 31
THE MINISTER SHALL KNOW ANY TO BE AN OPEN   R 084 35
ORDER SHALL THE MINISTER USE WITH THOSE, BETWIXT WHCM   R 085 09
THE MINISTER IN THAT CASE OUGHT TO ADMIT THE PENITENT   R 085 15

MINISTER   CONTINUED

THAT EVERY MINISTER SO REPELLING ANY, AS IS HEREIN   R 085 17
WHEN THE MINISTER GIVETH WARNING FOR THE   R 086 24
TO SOME OTHER MINISTER OF GOD'S WORD, AND OPEN HIS   088 06
CHRIST WAS A MINISTER OF THE CIRCUMCISION FOR THE   092 23
I WAS MADE A MINISTER, ACCORDING TO THE GIFT OF THE   108 16
FOR HE IS THE MINISTER OF GOD TO THEE FOR GOOD   114 18
FOR HE IS THE MINISTER OF GOD, A REVENGER TO EXECUTE   114 20
EVEN SO MINISTER THE SAME ONE TO ANOTHER,   179 17
IF ANY MAN MINISTER, LET HIM DO IT AS OF THE ABILITY   179 19
THAT IT MAY MINISTER GRACE UNTO THE HEARERS   216 25
YOU A FAITHFUL MINISTER OF CHRIST   223 31
WILL BE GREAT AMONG YOU, LET HIM BE YOUR MINISTER   247 24
BUT TO MINISTER, AND TO GIVE HIS LIFE A RANSOM   247 27
IT AGAIN TO THE MINISTER, AND SAT DOWN   261 22
THE MINISTER OF EVERY PARISH SHALL OFTEN ADMONISH   R 273 03
SHALL GIVE KNOWLEDGE THEREOF TO THE MINISTER   R 273 13
TIME AS THE MINISTER SHALL APPOINT   R 273 16
TIMELY NOTICE SHALL BE GIVEN TO THE MINISTER   R 273 18
THE MINISTER, HAVING COME TO THE FONT, WHICH IS   R 273 24
THEN SHALL THE MINISTER PROCEED AS FOLLOWETH   R 273 28
THEN SHALL THE MINISTER SAY, ALMIGHTY AND IMMORTAL   R 274 07
THEN THE MINISTER SAY AS FOLLOWETH   R 274 22
THEN SHALL THE MINISTER SAY, AND NOW, BEING PERSUADED   R 276 02
MINISTER AND PEOPLE   R 276 16
THE MINISTER SHALL SPEAK UNTO THE   R 276 17
FOR ADULTS, THE MINISTER SHALL ADDRESS THEM ON THIS   R 277 18
THEN SHALL THE MINISTER SAY, O MERCIFUL GOD, GRANT   R 278 17
THEN SHALL THE MINISTER SAY, IT IS VERY MEET, RIGHT,   R 279 06
THEN THE MINISTER SHALL TAKE THE CHILD INTO HIS   R 279 23
AN ADULT, THE MINISTER SHALL TAKE HIM BY THE HAND,   R 279 30
THEN THE MINISTER SHALL SAY   R 280 02
HERE THE MINISTER SHALL MAKE A CROSS UPON THE   R 280 11
THEN SHALL THE MINISTER SAY, SEEING NOW, DEARLY   R 280 12
THEN SHALL THE MINISTER SAY, WE YIELD THEE HEARTY   R 280 27
THEN THE MINISTER SHALL ADD, THE ALMIGHTY GOD, THE   R 281 06
IS PRESENT, THE MINISTER SHALL POUR WATER UPON HIM,   R 281 19
AN ADULT, THE MINISTER SHALL FIRST ASK THE QUESTIONS   R 281 25
IF A MINISTER CANNOT BE PROCURED, THEN ANY   R 281 27
OF WATER, THE MINISTER SHALL USE THIS FORM OF WORDS   R 282 12
BE SAID BY THE MINISTER AND PEOPLE TOGETHER, ALL   R 283 03
THE MINISTER FIRST PRONOUNCING, THE LORD BE   R 283 04
THE MINISTER SHALL ASK THEM THE QUESTIONS   R 283 13
THEN THE MINISTER SHALL SAY, YOU SAID THAT YOUR   R 284 06
CREED BY THE MINISTER AND PEOPLE   R 284 11
THE MINISTER, TURNING TO THE PEOPLE, SHALL   R 284 25
MINISTER AND PEOPLE   R 285 10
AFTER WHICH THE MINISTER, TURNING TO THE PEOPLE,   R 285 11
THEN SHALL THE MINISTER SAY, LET US ASK GOD'S HELP TO   R 285 18
PRAYER BY THE MINISTER AND PEOPLE TOGETHER, ALL   R 285 23
THEN SHALL THE MINISTER REPEAT THE TEN COMMANDMENTS,   R 285 33
THE MINISTER SAYING THE RESPONSE   R 286 03
THEN SHALL THE MINISTER SAY, GRANT TO US, LORD, WE   R 287 25
THE MINISTER, TURNING TO THEM, SHALL ASK THE   R 287 31
AFTER WHICH THE MINISTER SAY AS FOLLOWETH   R 289 12
BE SAID BY THE MINISTER AND PEOPLE TOGETHER, ALL   R 289 21
SENTENCE BY THE MINISTER AND PEOPLE TOGETHER   R 290 04
THE MINISTER SHALL ASK THEM THE QUESTIONS   R 290 25
THE MINISTER SHALL PROCEED WITH THE QUESTIONS   R 292 02
AFTER WHICH THE MINISTER SHALL ASK THE PEOPLE THE   R 294 02
A PRIEST IS, TO MINISTER TO THE PEOPLE COMMITTED TO   294 12
THEN SHALL THE MINISTER ADD, THE LORD BE WITH YOU   R 294 20
THE MINISTER OF EVERY PARISH SHALL DILIGENTLY   R 295 07
TO RECEIVE INSTRUCTION BY THE MINISTER   R 295 12
AND THE MINISTER SHALL SAY, REVEREND FATHER IN GOD, I   R 296 07
OR SOME MINISTER APPOINTED BY HIM, MAY SAY,   R 296 10
THE MINISTER SHALL NOT OMIT EARNESTLY TO MOVE THE   R 299 06
THE LEFT, THE MINISTER SHALL SAY, DEARLY BELOVED, WE   R 300 07
THE MINISTER, IF HE SHALL HAVE REASON TO DOUBT OF   R 301 02
THE MINISTER SHALL SAY TO THE MAN,   R 301 04
THEN SHALL THE MINISTER SAY UNTO THE WOMAN, N   R 301 13
THEN SHALL THE MINISTER SAY, WHO GIVETH THIS WOMAN TO   R 301 22
THE MINISTER,   R 301 24
SAY AFTER THE MINISTER, I N   R 302 03
THE MINISTER TAKING THE RING SHALL DELIVER IT UNTO   R 302 10
TAUGHT BY THE MINISTER, SHALL SAY,   R 302 12
TO THE MAN, THE MINISTER MAY SAY AS FOLLOWETH   R 302 17
LEFT HAND, THE MINISTER SHALL SAY, THEN SHALL THE   R 302 24
THEN SHALL THE MINISTER AND THE PEOPLE, STILL   R 302 26
THEN SHALL THE MINISTER ADD, O ETERNAL GOD, CREATOR   R 303 02
THE MINISTER MAY ADD ONE OR BOTH OF THE FOLLOWING   R 303 13
THEN SHALL THE MINISTER JOIN THEIR RIGHT HANDS   R 303 30
THEN SHALL THE MINISTER SPEAK UNTO THE COMPANY   R 304 02
THE MINISTER SHALL ADD THIS BLESSING   R 304 10
EVERY MINISTER IS LEFT TO THE DIRECTION OF   R 304 18
MAY BE USED AT THE DISCRETION OF THE MINISTER   R 305 06
THE MINISTER SHALL THEN SAY UNTO HER, FORASMUCH AS   R 305 10
THEN SHALL THE MINISTER SAY THE LORD'S PRAYER,   R 306 08
APPLIED BY THE MINISTER AND THE CHURCH-WARDENS TO THE   R 307 08
MAY BE USED AT THE DISCRETION OF THE MINISTER   R 308 04
THEREOF TO THE MINISTER OF THE PARISH   R 308 05
THEN THE MINISTER SHALL SAY, LORD, HAVE MERCY UPON   R 308 12
OF THE MINISTER, BE SUBSTITUTED FOR ANY OF THOSE   R 313 10
THE MINISTER SHALL ADDRESS THE SICK PERSON   R 313 15
HERE MAY THE MINISTER INQUIRE OF THE SICK PERSON AS   R 313 18
REPENTANCE, THE MINISTER SHALL ASSURE HIM OF GOD'S   R 313 26
THEN THE MINISTER SHALL SAY, O MOST MERCIFUL GOD,   R 313 28
THEN SHALL THE MINISTER SAY, THE ALMIGHTY LORD, WHO   R 314 14
HERE THE MINISTER MAY USE ANY PART OF THE SERVICE   R 314 23
PART THEREOF, AT THE DISCRETION OF THE MINISTER   R 315 04
OF HANDS, THE MINISTER MAY USE SUCH PORTION OF THE   R 320 06
THE MINISTER IS ORDERED, FROM TIME TO TIME,   R 320 21
NOTICE TO THE MINISTER, SIGNIFYING ALSO HOW MANY   R 321 13
THE MINISTER SHALL THERE CELEBRATE THE HOLY   R 321 14
AFTER WHICH THE MINISTER SHALL PROCEED ACCORDING TO   R 322 30

MINISTER   CONTINUED

THE MINISTER SHALL FIRST RECEIVE THE   R 322 33
AND AFTER MINISTER UNTO THOSE WHO ARE APPOINTED TO   R 322 34
DUE TIME TO THE MINISTER, OR BY ANY OTHER JUST   R 323 24
AND BLOOD, THE MINISTER SHALL INSTRUCT HIM, THAT IF   R 323 25
THE MINISTER, MEETING THE BODY, AND GOING BEFORE   R 324 03
OF THE MINISTER,   R 331 28
THE MINISTER, BEFORE THE PRAYERS, FIRST PRONOUNCING,   R 331 31
THE MINISTER SHALL SAY,   R 333 13
THEN THE MINISTER SHALL SAY, THE LORD BE WITH YOU   R 333 29
THEN THE MINISTER SHALL SAY ONE OR MORE OF THE   R 334 12
THE MINISTER, AT HIS DISCRETION, MAY ALSO USE ANY   R 335 23
OTHER CASE THE MINISTER MAY, AT HIS DISCRETION, USE   R 337 03
THE MINISTER SHALL SAY,   R 337 08
THE MINISTER, MEETING THE BODY, AND GOING BEFORE   R 338 03
THEN SHALL THE MINISTER SAY, THE LORD BE WITH YOU   R 340 02
BE SAID BY THE MINISTER AND PEOPLE, BLESSED   R 340 09
THE BODY, THE MINISTER SHALL SAY, IN SURE AND CERTAIN   R 341 12
THEN SHALL THE MINISTER SAY, THE LORD BE WITH YOU   R 341 28
AND MINISTER TRUE JUDGMENT UNTO THE PEOPLE   352 05
ALWAYS SO TO MINISTER THE DOCTRINE AND SACRAMENTS,   542 12
OF GOD, AND TO MINISTER THE HOLY SACRAMENTS IN THE   546 26
SO MINISTER DISCIPLINE, THAT YOU FORGET NOT MERCY   558 29
ELECTION OF A MINISTER INTO A PARISH OR CHURCH, AS   R 569 04
IS A QUALIFIED MINISTER OF THIS CHURCH, MAY PROCEED   R 569 06
PERSON SHOULD MINISTER AMONG YOU   570 19
THE INSTITUTED MINISTER KNEEL AT THE ALTAR, TO   R 573 09
THE INSTITUTED MINISTER, STANDING UP, SHALL SAY,   R 573 30
THE INSTITUTED MINISTER SHALL PROCEED TO THAT   R 574 25
OF A MINISTER, HE   R 574 29
THE MINISTER OF EVERY PARISH SHALL DILIGENTLY,   R 582 27
ORDERED BY THE MINISTER, UNTIL SUCH TIME AS THEY HAVE   R 582 34
THE MINISTER OF EVERY PARISH SHALL EITHER BRING, OR   R 583 06
OR TO MINISTER THE SACRAMENTS, IN A TONGUE   607 28
AND SO MINISTER BY HIS COMMISSION AND AUTHORITY,   608 12

MINISTERED

NOT TO BE MINISTERED UNTO, BUT TO MINISTER   043 29
WHO HAVE MINISTERED UNTO THE SAINTS, AND YET DO   072 25
CAME AND MINISTERED UNTO HIM   127 11
NOT TO BE MINISTERED UNTO, BUT TO MINISTER, AND TO   247 26
HANDS HAVE MINISTERED UNTO MY NECESSITIES, AND TO   551 07
BE DULY MINISTERED ACCORDING TO CHRIST'S ORDINANCE,   606 39
SACRAMENTS MINISTERED UNTO THEM   608 16
THEY BE MINISTERED BY EVIL MEN   608 18
OUGHT TO BE MINISTERED TO ALL CHRISTIAN MEN ALIKE   609 12

MINISTERETH

WHEN HE MINISTERETH THE HOLY COMMUNION, AND TO HELP   533 12

MINISTERING

OR MINISTRY, LET US WAIT ON OUR MINISTERING   111 18
DAILY MINISTERING AND OFFERING OFTENTIMES THE SAME   158 03
OR MINISTERING THE SACRAMENTS IN THE CONGREGATION,   607 20

MINISTERS

TO HIS MINISTERS, TO DECLARE AND PRONOUNCE TO HIS   007 09
TO HIS MINISTERS, TO DECLARE AND PRONOUNCE TO HIS   024 11
ENDUE THY MINISTERS WITH RIGHTEOUSNESS   031 06
KNOWING WHOSE MINISTERS THEY ARE, MAY ABOVE ALL   032 08
PRAY FOR THE MINISTERS OF GOD'S HOLY WORD AND   047 22
AND OTHER MINISTERS, THAT THEY MAY, BOTH BY THEIR   074 22
GRANT THAT THE MINISTERS AND STEWARDS OF THY   093 26
AS OF THE MINISTERS OF CHRIST, AND STEWARDS OF   094 03
AND HIS MINISTERS A FLAME OF FIRE   097 08
THEY ARE GOD'S MINISTERS, ATTENDING CONTINUALLY UPON   114 24
ARE THEY MINISTERS OF CHRIST   120 29
THE MINISTERS OF THE LORD, WEEP BETWEEN THE   125 02
AS THE MINISTERS OF GOD, IN MUCH PATIENCE, IN   126 09
MADE US ABLE MINISTERS OF THE NEW TESTAMENT   206 16
WHAT ORDERS OF MINISTERS ARE THERE IN THE CHURCH   294 04
CALL THEM, THE MINISTERS SHALL DILIGENTLY FROM TIME   R 321 05
AND HIS MINISTERS A FLAMING FIRE   467 32
ORDERS OF MINISTERS IN CHRIST'S CHURCH, -- BISHOPS,   529 13
ORDERS OF MINISTERS IN THY CHURCH, AND DIDST INSPIRE   531 15
OTHER CHIEF MINISTERS, WHO, ACCORDING TO THE CANONS   533 31
ORDERS OF MINISTERS IN THY CHURCH   537 21
OTHER CHIEF MINISTERS, WHO, ACCORDING TO THE CANONS   543 12
BY THESE THY MINISTERS, AS BY THEM OVER WHOM THEY   545 32
APPOINTED THY MINISTERS, THY HOLY NAME MAY BE FOR   545 33
ORDERS OF MINISTERS IN THY CHURCH   547 32
ORDERS OF MINISTERS IN THY CHURCH   553 27
TO ENDUE ALL MINISTERS OF THY CHURCH WITH DEVOTION TO   560 21
NUMBER OF THE MINISTERS OF THY CHURCH, THAT THE   561 13
TO BE WITH THE MINISTERS OF APOSTOLIC SUCCESSION TO   572 18
CALL AND SEND MINISTERS INTO THE LORD'S VINEYARD   607 23
MADE OF EVIL MINISTERS, AND THAT THEY BE ACCUSED BY   608 20
BY THE MINISTERS, DILIGENTLY AND DISTINCTLY, THAT   610 09

MINISTRATION

BUT IF THE MINISTRATION OF DEATH, WRITTEN AND   206 18
NOT THE MINISTRATION OF THE SPIRIT BE RATHER   206 22
FOR IF THE MINISTRATION OF CONDEMNATION BE GLORY,   206 23
DOTH THE MINISTRATION OF RIGHTEOUSNESS EXCEED IN   206 24
THE PUBLIC MINISTRATION IN CHURCH, SUBSTITUTING THE   R 323 33
OFFICE AND MINISTRATION, TO SERVE GOD FOR THE   532 27
IN THEIR MINISTRATION, TO HAVE A READY WILL TO   535 04
TO THIS MINISTRATION, ACCORDING TO THE WILL OF OUR   554 17
IN THE MINISTRATION OF THE WORD AND SACRAMENTS, YET   608 10

MINISTRATIONS

HIS OTHER MINISTRATIONS, UNDER THE DIRECTICN CF THE   294 18

MINISTRIES

THE HIGHER MINISTRIES IN THY CHURCH   535 09

MINISTRY

IN THE SACRED MINISTRY OF THY CHURCH	038 31
TO THE SACRED MINISTRY OF THY CHURCH	039 20
GOD IN THE MINISTRY AND IN THE STATE	047 31
OR MINISTRY, LET US WAIT ON CUR MINISTERING	111 17
THAT THE MINISTRY BE NOT BLAMED	126 08
AND ALL THE VESSELS OF THE MINISTRY	147 25
VOCATION AND MINISTRY, MAY TRULY AND GODLY SERVE	156 31
AND HAD OBTAINED PART OF THIS MINISTRY	234 12
PART OF THIS MINISTRY AND APOSTLESHIP, FRCM WHICH	234 29
THE WORK OF THE MINISTRY, FOR THE EDIFYING OF THE	237 21
WE HAVE THIS MINISTRY, AS WE HAVE RECEIVED MERCY, WE	250 27
MAKE FULL PROOF OF THY MINISTRY	253 24
FOR HE IS PROFITABLE TO ME FOR THE MINISTRY	254 03
OF MEN THE MINISTRY OF RECONCILIATION	260 20
OF MANY TO OFFER THEMSELVES FOR THIS MINISTRY	260 22
OUR OFFICE AND MINISTRY, MAY ALSO BE ENDUED WITH	278 28
CONCERNING THE MINISTRY, THE PEOPLE RESPONDING	R 294 03
DESIRE THE MINISTRY OF HEALING THROUGH ANCINTING CR	R 320 05
EXERCISE THEIR MINISTRY DULY, TO THE HONOUR OF GCC,	530 15
AND TO THE MINISTRY OF THE WORD	532 14
TO THE MINISTRY OF THE SAME	532 33
EXERCISE THEIR MINISTRY DULY, TO THE HONOUR OF GCC,	536 16
FUNCTION AND MINISTRY, AND THAT THEY ARE PERSCNS MEET	536 26
INTO THIS HOLY MINISTRY, LET HIM COME FORTH IN THE	536 29
THE WORK OF THE MINISTRY, FOR THE EDIFYING OF THE	538 08
THE END OF THE MINISTRY TOWARDS THE CHILDREN OF GCD,	540 14
YE MAY WAX RIPER AND STRONGER IN YOUR MINISTRY	541 19
THE ORDER AND MINISTRY OF PRIESTHOOD	541 33
LABOUR AND MINISTRY HE GATHERED TOGETHER A GREAT	545 19
SAME OFFICE AND MINISTRY, APPOINTED FOR THE SALVATICN	545 23
THEE IN THEIR MINISTRY, TO THE GLORY OF THY NAME,	548 05
AND THE MINISTRY, WHICH I HAVE RECEIVED OF THE	550 20
TO THE WORK AND MINISTRY OF A BISHOP	553 29
CALL TO THE MINISTRY OF THY CHURCH	561 08
THAT BY THEIR MINISTRY AND EXAMPLE THY PEOPLE MAY	562 11
TO BLESS THE MINISTRY AND SERVICE OF HIM WHO IS NCW	572 19
THE PERFORMANCE OF ALL THE DUTIES OF MY MINISTRY	573 24
VOCATION AND MINISTRY, MAY SERVE THEE FAITHFULLY	590 26
MAY USE THEIR MINISTRY, BOTH IN HEARING THE WORD OF	608 13

MINSTRELS

AND SAW THE MINSTRELS AND THE PEOPLE MAKING A NCISE,   224 24
GO BEFORE, THE MINSTRELS FOLLOW AFTER, *   421 04

MIRACLE

HAD SEEN THE MIRACLE THAT JESUS DID, SAID, THIS IS OF	132 12
HAVE SEEN SOME MIRACLE DONE BY HIM	153 13
AGAIN THE SECOND MIRACLE THAT JESUS DID, WHEN HE WAS	220 12
HAD SEEN THE MIRACLE THAT JESUS DID, SAID, THIS IS CF	226 11
AND FIRST MIRACLE THAT HE WROUGHT IN CANA OF GALILEE,	300 14

MIRACLES

BEGINNING OF MIRACLES DID JESUS IN CANA OF GALILEE,	113 30
THEY SAW HIS MIRACLES WHICH HE DID ON THEM THAT WERE	131 23
TO ANOTHER THE WORKING OF MIRACLES	182 31
CAN DO THESE MIRACLES THAT THOU DOEST, EXCEPT GCD BE	188 03
TO ANOTHER THE WORKING OF MIRACLES	203 31
CAN DO THESE MIRACLES THAT THOU DOEST, EXCEPT GCC BE	275 08
HAD WROUGHT HIS MIRACLES IN EGYPT, *	437 27

MIRE

OUT OF THE MIRE AND CLAY, *	390 12
FAST IN THE DEEP MIRE, WHERE NO GROUND IS	422 02
TAKE ME OUT OF THE MIRE, THAT I SINK NOT	422 32
AND LIFTETH THE POOR CUT OF THE MIRE	484 20

MISCARRIED

AND GOOD WORK MISCARRIED AT THAT TIME   VI 05

MISCARRY

MERCY OF THE MOST HIGHEST HE SHALL NOT MISCARRY   365 19

MISCHIEF

FROM ALL EVIL AND MISCHIEF	054 19
HATH CONCEIVED MISCHIEF, AND BROUGHT FORTH FALSEHCOD	350 22
SUCH WORKERS OF MISCHIEF, *	356 23
THEY INTENDED MISCHIEF AGAINST THEE, *	365 27
BUT IMAGINE MISCHIEF IN THEIR HEARTS	373 12
THAT IMAGINE MISCHIEF FOR ME	381 26
THAT HE MAY FALL INTO HIS OWN MISCHIEF	382 06
4 HE IMAGINETH MISCHIEF UPON HIS BED, AND HATH SET	383 33
THAT THOU CANST DO MISCHIEF	404 20
TO DO ME SOME MISCHIEF, SO MALICIOUSLY ARE THEY SET	406 24
MISCHIEF ALSO AND SORROW ARE IN THE MIDST CF IT	407 07
YE IMAGINE MISCHIEF IN YOUR HEART UPCN THE	410 10
WILL YE IMAGINE MISCHIEF AGAINST EVERY MAN	413 31
THEMSELVES IN MISCHIEF, *	415 27
WHICH IMAGINETH MISCHIEF AS A LAW	458 27
2 WHO IMAGINE MISCHIEF IN THEIR HEARTS, *	516 11

MISCHIEF   CONTINUED

9 LET THE MISCHIEF OF THEIR OWN LIPS FALL UPCN THE   516 27

MISCHIEFS

DANGERS AND MISCHIEFS, AND FROM THE FEAR OF THEM   591 27

MISCHIEVOUS

LET NOT HIS MISCHIEVOUS IMAGINATION PROSPER, LEST   516 25

MISDEEDS

AND PUT OUT ALL MY MISDEEDS	060 28
HAST SET OUR MISDEEDS BEFORE THEE	325 28
AND PUT OUT ALL MY MISDEEDS	403 27
3 MY MISDEEDS PREVAIL AGAINST ME	416 15
FORGAVE THEIR MISDEEDS, *	437 14
HAST SET OUR MISDEEDS BEFORE THEE	454 02

MISDOINGS

AND ARE HEARTILY SORRY FOR THESE OUR MISDCINGS   075 24

MISERABLE

MERCY UPON US, MISERABLE OFFENDERS	006 24
MERCY UPON US, MISERABLE OFFENDERS	023 31
FOR US, MISERABLE SINNERS, WHO LAY IN DARKNESS	086 09

MISEREATUR

DEUS MISEREATUR, BENEDIC, ANIMA MEA, MAY BE SUNG OR   R 025 18

MISERY

BUT A SHORT TIME TO LIVE, AND IS FULL OF MISERY	332 19
FOR I AM DESOLATE, AND IN MISERY	370 17
MY ADVERSITY AND MISERY, *	370 20
HIM THAT IS IN MISERY, FROM HIM THAT SPOILETH HIM	382 11
GREAT TROUBLE AND MISERY, *	388 02
FORGETTEST OUR MISERY AND TROUBLE	396 09
5 AS FOR ME, I AM POOR AND IN MISERY	424 30
FOR WE ARE COME TO GREAT MISERY	440 17
THE VALE OF MISERY USE IT FOR A WELL	445 23
FOR I AM POOR, AND IN MISERY	447 06
15 I AM IN MISERY, AND LIKE UNTO HIM THAT IS AT THE	449 26
FAST BOUND IN MISERY AND IRON	476 25
THE POOR OUT OF MISERY, *	478 28
I WAS IN MISERY, AND HE HELPED ME	486 30
8 O DAUGHTER OF BABYLON, WASTED WITH MISERY	513 21

MISFORTUNE

21 BUT MISFORTUNE SHALL SLAY THE UNGODLY   381 10
COME IN NO MISFORTUNE LIKE OTHER FOLK   428 18

MISTAKE

5 THEY DAILY MISTAKE MY WORDS   408 24

MISTRESS

THE HAND OF HER MISTRESS, *	503 31
THE MASTER OR MISTRESS HAVING CALLED TOGETHER AS MANY	R 587 04
THE MASTER OR MISTRESS, OR ANY OTHER WHO MAY BE	R 589 13

MISTRESSES

AND MISTRESSES, SHALL CAUSE THEIR CHILDREN,   R 582 31

MIXT

IT IS FULL MIXT, AND HE POURETH OUT OF THE SAME   432 15

MOAB

8 MOAB IS MY WASH-POT   412 27
9 MOAB IS MY WASH-POT   479 22

MOABITES

THE MOABITES, AND HAGARENES   444 17

MOCK

YE HAVE MADE A MOCK AT THE COUNSEL OF THE PCOR   356 28
16 WHY MOCK YE SO, YE HIGH HILLS   420 13

MOCKED

SAW THAT HE WAS MOCKED OF THE WISE MEN, WAS EXCEEDING	103 25
AND SHALL BE MOCKED, AND SPITEFULLY ENTREATED,	123 21
BEFORE HIM, AND MOCKED HIM, SAYING, HAIL, KING CF THE	136 20
THAT THEY HAD MOCKED HIM, THEY TOOK THE ROBE OFF FROM	136 23
AND WHEN THEY HAD MOCKED HIM, THEY TOOK OFF THE	146 03
THAT HELD JESUS MOCKED HIM, AND SMOTE HIM	151 23
AT NOUGHT, AND MOCKED HIM, AND ARRAYED HIM IN A	153 17
THE SOLDIERS ALSO MOCKED HIM, COMING TO HIM, AND	154 30

MOCKERS

WERE BUSY MOCKERS, *   382 27

MOCKING

CHIEF PRIESTS MOCKING HIM, WITH THE SCRIBES AND   137 09
CHIEF PRIESTS MOCKING SAID AMONG THEMSELVES WITH THE   146 21

MODEL

EQUAL LIBERTY TO MODEL AND ORGANIZE THEIR RESPECTIVE   VI 11

MODERATE

SUCH MODERATE RAIN AND SHOWERS, THAT WE   040 19

MODERATION

LET YOUR MODERATION BE KNOWN UNTO ALL MEN   095 14

MODEST

O LORD, TO BE MODEST, HUMBLE, AND CONSTANT IN THEIR   535 03

MOISTURE

IT WITHERED AWAY, BECAUSE IT LACKED MOISTURE   121 24
AND MY MOISTURE WAS LIKE THE DROUGHT IN SUMMER   377 29

MOLTEN

WORSHIPPED THE MOLTEN IMAGE   474 07

MOMENT

BE CHANGED, IN A MOMENT, IN THE TWINKLING OF AN EYE,   330 02

MONDAY

ON MONDAY IN EASTER WEEK AND UNTIL ASCENSION DAY   R 008 23

MONEY

AND PROMISED TO GIVE HIM MONEY   140 21
THEY WERE GLAD, AND COVENANTED TO GIVE HIM MONEY   148 19
SHEW ME THE TRIBUTE MONEY   223 06
HATH NOT GIVEN HIS MONEY UPON USURY, *   357 17
AND TAKEST NO MONEY FOR THEM   395 18
THE CHANGERS OF MONEY SITTING   567 27
OUT THE CHANGERS' MONEY, AND OVERTHREW THE TABLES   567 30

MONEY-CHANGERS

OF THE MONEY-CHANGERS, AND THE SEATS OF THEM THAT   091 35
OF THE MONEY-CHANGERS, AND THE SEATS OF THEM THAT   260 05

MONITIONS

AND PRIVATE MONITIONS AND EXHORTATIONS, AS WELL TO   542 22

MONSTER

AS IT WERE A MONSTER UNTO MANY, *   425 19

MONTH

IT BE SAID AT LEAST ONE SUNDAY IN EACH MONTH   R 067 29
AND IN THE SIXTH MONTH THE ANGEL GABRIEL WAS SENT   236 05
THIS IS THE SIXTH MONTH WITH HER, WHO WAS CALLED   236 27

MOON

O YE SUN AND MOON, BLESS YE THE LORD   012 10
THE SUN, AND IN THE MOON, AND IN THE STARS   093 05
AND THE MOON SHALL NOT GIVE HER LIGHT,   118 15
NEITHER THE MOON BY NIGHT   327 30
GLORY OF THE MOON, AND ANOTHER GLORY OF THE STARS   329 17
NEITHER THE MOON BY NIGHT   339 14
THE MOON AND THE STARS WHICH THOU HAST ORDAINED   351 05
LONG AS THE SUN AND MOON ENDURETH, *   427 06
SO LONG AS THE MOON ENDURETH   427 11
TRUMPET IN THE NEW MOON, *   442 16
FOR EVERMORE AS THE MOON, *   452 14
19 HE APPOINTED THE MOON FOR CERTAIN SEASONS, *   468 32
NEITHER THE MOON BY NIGHT   503 03
9 THE MOON AND THE STARS TO GOVERN THE NIGHT   511 32
3 PRAISE HIM, SUN AND MOON   524 09

MORAL

OF THE COMMANDMENTS WHICH ARE CALLED MORAL   604 23

MORALS

AND INSTRUCTIVE IN PIETY AND MORALS   R 610 25

MORE

BY READING ONE OR MORE OF THE FOLLOWING SENTENCES OF   R 003 03
AND AM NO MORE WORTHY TO BE CALLED THY SON   004 28
MORE ESPECIALLY WE PRAY FOR THY HOLY CHURCH   018 29
BY READING ONE OR MORE OF THE FOLLOWING SENTENCES OF   R 021 03
MORE ESPECIALLY WE PRAY FOR THY HOLY CHURCH   032 29
AND MORE ESPECIALLY FOR THAT BRANCH OF THE SAME   047 11
BISHOPS (AND HEREIN MORE ESPECIALLY FOR THE BISHOP OF   047 23
DEACONS (AND HEREIN MORE ESPECIALLY FOR THE CLERGY   047 26
ONE OR MORE OF THESE SENTENCES FOLLOWING, AS HE   R 071 33
HOW HE SAID, IT IS MORE BLESSED TO GIVE THAN TO   072 03

MORE   CONTINUED

HE MAY WITH THE MORE READINESS AND DECENCY BREAK THE   R 080 03
IS TO CONSECRATE MORE, ACCORDING TO THE FORM BEFORE   R 083 08
I SAY UNTO YOU, AND MORE THAN A PROPHET   094 30
OBTAINED A MORE EXCELLENT NAME THAN THEY   096 31
IF THERE BE ANY MORE DAYS BEFORE THE SUNDAY   R 103 34
THOU ART NO MORE A SERVANT, BUT A SON   104 24
BUT NOW MUCH MORE IN MY ABSENCE, WORK OUT YOUR   106 03
TO THINK OF HIMSELF MORE HIGHLY THAN HE OUGHT TO   110 11
THEY SUPPOSED THAT THEY SHOULD HAVE RECEIVED MORE   120 02
IN LABOURS MORE ABUNDANT, IN STRIPES ABOVE MEASURE,   120 30
I SPEAK AS A FOOL) I AM MORE   120 30
IN PRISONS MORE FREQUENT, IN DEATHS OFT   120 31
CRIED SO MUCH THE MORE, THOU SON OF DAVID, HAVE MERCY   123 32
SO YE WOULD ABOUND MORE AND MORE   127 25
SO YE WOULD ABOUND MORE AND MORE   127 26
SEVEN OTHER SPIRITS MORE WICKED THAN HIMSELF   130 15
DESOLATE HATH MANY MORE CHILDREN THAN SHE WHICH HATH   131 11
BY A GREATER AND MORE PERFECT TABERNACLE, NOT MADE   132 24
HOW MUCH MORE SHALL THE BLOOD OF CHRIST, WHO THROUGH   132 30
THEY CRIED OUT THE MORE, SAYING, LET HIM BE   136 07
HAVE BEEN SOLD FOR MORE THAN THREE HUNDRED PENCE, AND   140 08
I WILL DRINK NO MORE OF THE FRUIT OF THE VINE, UNTIL   141 15
BUT HE SPAKE THE MORE VEHEMENTLY, IF I SHOULD DIE   141 25
THEY CRIED OUT THE MORE EXCEEDINGLY, CRUCIFY HIM   145 26
I WILL NOT ANY MORE EAT THEREOF, UNTIL IT BE   149 04
AN AGONY HE PRAYED MORE EARNESTLY   150 21
AND THEY WERE THE MORE FIERCE, SAYING, HE STIRRETH UP   153 04
SHOULD HAVE HAD NO MORE CONSCIENCE OF SINS   157 20
THEIR SINS AND INIQUITIES WILL I REMEMBER NO MORE   158 14
THERE IS NO MORE OFFERING FOR SIN   158 15
AND SO MUCH THE MORE, AS YE SEE THE DAY APPROACHING   158 28
HE WAS THE MORE AFRAID   159 11
CHRIST BEING RAISED FROM THE DEAD DIETH NO MORE   163 04
DEATH HATH NO MORE DOMINION OVER HIM   163 05
THE DEAD, NOW NO MORE TO RETURN TO CORRUPTION,   169 11
SHE REMEMBERETH NO MORE THE ANGUISH, FOR JOY THAT A   174 12
BECAUSE I GO TO MY FATHER, AND YE SEE ME NO MORE   175 16
WHEN I SHALL NO MORE SPEAK UNTO YOU IN PROVERBS,   176 25
AND THE WORLD SEETH ME NO MORE   181 16
HOW MUCH MORE SHALL YOUR HEAVENLY FATHER GIVE THE   183 18
THEY MIGHT HAVE IT MORE ABUNDANTLY   186 19
THAT REPENTETH, MORE THAN OVER NINETY AND NINE JUST   193 26
CHRIST BEING RAISED FROM THE DEAD DIETH NO MORE   197 22
DEATH HATH NO MORE DOMINION OVER HIM   197 22
AND AM NO MORE WORTHY TO BE CALLED THY SON   202 14
AND AM NO MORE WORTHY TO BE CALLED THY SON   202 20
BUT I LABOURED MORE ABUNDANTLY THAN THEY ALL   205 16
WHO ART ALWAYS MORE READY TO HEAR THAN WE TO   206 04
ART WONT TO GIVE MORE THAN EITHER WE DESIRE OR   206 06
BE GLORY, MUCH MORE DOTH THE MINISTRATION OF   206 24
BUT THE MORE HE CHARGED THEM, SO MUCH THE MORE A   207 05
SO MUCH THE MORE A GREAT DEAL THEY PUBLISHED   207 06
THE LAW, IT IS NO MORE OF PROMISE   207 25
THOU SPENDEST MORE, WHEN I COME AGAIN, I WILL REPAY   208 35
IS NOT THE LIFE MORE THAN THE FOOD, AND THE BODY THAN   211 14
ARE NOT YE OF MUCH MORE VALUE THAN THEY   211 18
SHALL HE NOT MUCH MORE CLOTHE YOU, O YE OF LITTLE   211 26
LEST A MORE HONOURABLE MAN THAN THOU BE BIDDEN OF   214 12
FORTH ASK HIM ANY MORE QUESTIONS   215 24
LET HIM THAT STOLE STEAL NO MORE   216 20
LOVE MAY ABOUND YET MORE AND MORE IN KNOWLEDGE AND IN   221 02
ABOUND YET MORE AND MORE IN KNOWLEDGE AND IN ALL   221 02
THAT THEY SHALL NO MORE SAY, THE LORD LIVETH, WHICH   225 15
SAUL INCREASED THE MORE IN STRENGTH, AND CONFOUNDED   231 09
WE HENCEFORTH BE NO MORE CHILDREN, TOSSED TO AND FRO,   237 25
IT MAY BRING FORTH MORE FRUIT   238 08
NO MORE CAN YE, EXCEPT YE ABIDE IN ME   238 11
BELIEVERS WERE THE MORE ADDED TO THE LORD, MULTITUDES   249 25
PLACE FOUND ANY MORE IN HEAVEN   252 06
THEREFORE YE ARE NO MORE STRANGERS AND FOREIGNERS,   255 03
SHALL HUNGER NO MORE, NEITHER THIRST ANY MORE   257 12
SHALL HUNGER NO MORE, NEITHER THIRST ANY MORE   257 12
AND THEY SHALL NO MORE BE A PREY TO THE HEATHEN,   262 14
THEY SHALL BE NO MORE CONSUMED WITH HUNGER IN THE   262 18
NEITHER BEAR THE SHAME OF THE HEATHEN ANY MORE   262 20
HOW MUCH MORE SHALL YOUR HEAVENLY FATHER GIVE THE   263 12
WHAT DO YE MORE THAN OTHERS   264 13
IS NOT THE LIFE MORE THAN FOOD, AND THE BODY THAN   266 13
SHALL HE NOT MUCH MORE CLOTHE YOU, O YE OF LITTLE   266 24
THEY ARE NO MORE TWAIN, BUT ONE FLESH   268 09
IN THY HOLY SPIRIT MORE AND MORE, UNTIL HE COME UNTO   297 28
SPIRIT MORE AND MORE, UNTIL HE COME UNTO THY   297 28
BE SAID ANY ONE OR MORE OF THE PSALMS FOLLOWING,   R 309 09
AND WILL HE BE NO MORE INTREATED   311 13
THAT THOU REMEMBEREST THEM NO MORE   313 33
AND THE MORE THE OUTWARD MAN DECAYETH, STRENGTHEN   316 10
SO MUCH THE MORE CONTINUALLY WITH THY GRACE AND   316 11
BE SAID ONE OR MORE OF THE FOLLOWING SELECTIONS,   R 324 16
GO HENCE, AND BE NO MORE SEEN   325 11
THESE THINGS WE ARE MORE THAN CONQUERORS THROUGH HIM   331 09
SHALL SAY ONE OR MORE OF THE FOLLOWING PRAYERS,   R 334 12
SHALL HUNGER NO MORE, NEITHER THIRST ANY MORE   341 23
SHALL HUNGER NO MORE, NEITHER THIRST ANY MORE   341 23
MORE THAN WHEN THEIR CORN AND WINE AND OIL   347 26
OF THE EARTH BE NO MORE EXALTED AGAINST THEM   354 16
10 MORE TO BE DESIRED ARE THEY THAN GOLD, YEA,   364 04
GO HENCE, AND BE NO MORE SEEN   390 07
THEY SHOULD BE MORE THAN I AM ABLE TO EXPRESS   390 26
THEY ARE MORE IN NUMBER THAN THE HAIRS OF MY   391 12
AND NOW THAT HE LIETH, HE SHALL RISE UP NO MORE   392 16
8 (FOR IT COST MORE TO REDEEM THEIR SOULS,   400 20
UNRIGHTEOUSNESS MORE THAN GOODNESS, *   404 24
AND FALSEHOOD MORE THAN RIGHTEOUSNESS   404 25
WITHOUT A CAUSE ARE MORE THAN THE HAIRS OF MY HEAD   422 07

MORE   CONTINUED

WILL PRAISE THEE MORE AND MORE	426 03
AND WILL PRAISE THEE MORE AND MORE	426 03
THERE IS NOT ONE PROPHET MORE	430 25
THAT UNDERSTANDETH ANY MORE	430 26
INCREASETH EVER MORE AND MORE	431 25
THEM THAT HATE THEE INCREASETH EVER MORE AND MORE	431 26
AND WILL HE BE NO MORE INTREATED	433 30
THIS THEY SINNED MORE AGAINST HIM, *	436 02
THEY SINNED YET MORE, *	437 02
THAT THEY BE NO MORE A PEOPLE, *	444 12
OF ISRAEL MAY BE NO MORE IN REMEMBRANCE	444 13
AND VEXED EVER MORE AND MORE	445 06
THEM BE CONFOUNDED AND VEXED EVER MORE AND MORE	445 07
THE GATES OF SION MORE THAN ALL THE DWELLINGS OF	448 14
SHALL BRING FORTH MORE FRUIT IN THEIR AGE, *	456 28
HE IS MORE TO BE FEARED THAN ALL GODS	460 07
AND THE PLACE THEREOF SHALL KNOW IT NO MORE	467 07
YOU MORE AND MORE, *	486 06
SHALL INCREASE YOU MORE AND MORE, *	486 06
KINDNESS IS EVER MORE AND MORE TOWARD US	487 27
IS EVER MORE AND MORE TOWARD US	487 27
99 I HAVE MORE UNDERSTANDING THAN MY TEACHERS	496 24
TELL THEM, THEY ARE MORE IN NUMBER THAN THE SAND	515 26
THEY MIGHT HAVE IT MORE ABUNDANTLY	539 09
PROMISE MAY THE MORE MOVE YOU TO DO YOUR DUTIES	541 26
SHALL SEE MY FACE NO MORE	550 24
HOW HE SAID, IT IS MORE BLESSED TO GIVE THAN TO	551 10
LOVEST THOU ME MORE THAN THESE	551 11
THEIR HEARTS WITH MORE DEVOTION AND HUMILITY IN HIS	564 19
THERE SHALL BE NO MORE DEATH, NEITHER SORROW, NOR	567 19
SHALL THERE BE ANY MORE PAIN	567 20
THEIR MINDS MORE AND MORE WITH THE LIGHT OF THE	572 27
MINDS MORE AND MORE WITH THE LIGHT OF THE EVERLASTING	572 27
HIM MORE AND MORE INTO THY JOYFUL SERVICE	598 09
WILT RECEIVE HIM MORE AND MORE INTO THY JOYFUL	598 09
FULL OF COMFORT, AS MORE LARGELY IS EXPRESSED IN THE	605 09
BUT THAT THEY DO MORE FOR HIS SAKE, THAN OF BOUNDEN	605 27
THEY CAN NO MORE SIN AS LONG AS THEY LIVE HERE,	606 03

MORIANS'

THE MORIANS' LAND SHALL SOON STRETCH OUT HER HANDS	421 19

MORNING

SHALL BEGIN THE MORNING PRAYER BY READING ONE OR MORE	R 003 03
CANTICLES OF MORNING PRAYER HAS BEEN SAID OR SUNG,	R 010 05
MAY HERE END THE MORNING PRAYER WITH SUCH GENERAL	R 017 22
THE ORDER OF MORNING PRAYER	R 020 15
OR AT THE COCK-CROWING, OR IN THE MORNING	021 26
EARLY IN THE MORNING, *	027 30
THE COLLECTS OF MORNING OR EVENING PRAYER, OR	R 049 03
THIRD COLLECT AT MORNING OR EVENING PRAYER	R 054 03
MAY BE USED WITH MORNING PRAYER, OR EVENING PRAYER,	R 060 05
BEFORE IN MORNING PRAYER	R 070 31
OUT EARLY IN THE MORNING TO HIRE LABOURERS INTO HIS	119 16
WHEN THE MORNING WAS COME, ALL THE CHIEF PRIESTS AND	134 30
IN THE MORNING THE CHIEF PRIESTS HELD A CONSULTATION	145 03
AT MORNING PRAYER, INSTEAD OF THE VENITE, THE	R 162 28
EARLY IN THE MORNING THE FIRST DAY OF THE WEEK,	165 21
SECOND LESSON AT MORNING OR EVENING PRAYER, OR AT	R 273 15
BE USED WITH THE MORNING OR EVENING PRAYER	R 306 09
IN THE MORNING IT IS GREEN, AND GROWETH UP	325 24
LORD BEFORE THE MORNING WATCH	328 13
BEFORE THE MORNING WATCH	328 14
EARLY IN THE MORNING WILL I DIRECT MY PRAYER UNTO	348 05
BUT JOY COMETH IN THE MORNING	375 03
SHALL HAVE DOMINION OVER THEM IN THE MORNING	401 03
THE EVENING, AND MORNING, AND AT NOON-DAY WILL I	407 25
AND WILL PRAISE THY MERCY BETIMES IN THE MORNING	412 07
OF THE MORNING AND EVENING TO PRAISE THEE	416 31
AND CHASTENED EVERY MORNING	429 05
6 IN THE MORNING IT IS GREEN, AND GROWETH UP	453 29
EARLY IN THE MORNING, *	456 02
COME TO THEE AS DEW FROM THE WOMB OF THE MORNING	482 13
147 EARLY IN THE MORNING DO I CRY UNTO THEE	500 04
LORD BEFORE THE MORNING WATCH	507 18
BEFORE THE MORNING WATCH	507 19
THE WINGS OF THE MORNING, *	515 04
HEAR THY LOVING-KINDNESS BETIMES IN THE MORNING	519 08
OR AT MORNING PRAYER OR EVENING PRAYER,	R 563 04
OR AT MORNING PRAYER OR EVENING PRAYER,	R 569 09
ACCEPT THIS OUR MORNING SACRIFICE OF PRAISE AND	587 25
AND TURNEST THE SHADOW OF DEATH INTO THE MORNING	594 13
IN SAFETY TO THE MORNING HOURS	595 09

MORROW

AND ON THE MORROW WHEN HE DEPARTED, HE TOOK OUT TWO	208 32
BE NOT THEREFORE ANXIOUS FOR THE MORROW	211 33
FOR THE MORROW WILL BE ANXIOUS FOR ITSELF	211 34
BE NOT THEREFORE ANXIOUS FOR THE MORROW	266 31
FOR THE MORROW SHALL TAKE THOUGHT FOR THE THINGS OF	266 32

MORSELS

17 HE CASTETH FORTH HIS ICE LIKE MORSELS	523 29

MORTAL

CHANCES OF THE MORTAL LIFE, THEY MAY EVER BE DEFENDED	049 14
SUBSTANCE OF OUR MORTAL FLESH, MANIFESTED FORTH HIS	077 23
THE TIME OF THIS MORTAL LIFE, IN WHICH THY SON JESUS	090 13
WEAKNESS OF OUR MORTAL NATURE, WE CAN DO NO GOOD	189 02

MORTAL   CONTINUED

FORASMUCH AS ALL MORTAL MEN ARE SUBJECT TO MANY	R 321 02
AND THIS MORTAL MUST PUT ON IMMORTALITY,	330 06
AND THIS MORTAL SHALL HAVE PUT ON IMMORTALITY,	330 08
ALSO QUICKEN OUR MORTAL BODIES, BY HIS SPIRIT THAT	333 06
ART THE LIFE OF MORTAL MEN, THE LIGHT OF THE	595 04
NO CLOUDS OF THIS MORTAL LIFE MAY HIDE FROM US THE	596 07

MORTIFIED

BEING MORTIFIED FROM ALL WORLDLY AND CARNAL	105 22

MORTIFY

MORTIFY AND KILL ALL VICES IN US, AND SO STRENGTHEN	102 23
THE SPIRIT DO MORTIFY THE DEEDS OF THE BODY, YE SHALL	200 05

MORTIFYING

BY CONTINUAL MORTIFYING OUR CORRUPT AFFECTIONS WE MAY	161 15
OF CHRIST, MORTIFYING THE WORKS OF THE FLESH, AND	606 18

MOSES

THE GIFT THAT MOSES COMMANDED, FOR A TESTIMONY UNTO	115 05
THE DAYS OF OLD, MOSES, AND HIS PEOPLE, SAYING, WHERE	139 07
THE RIGHT HAND OF MOSES WITH HIS GLORIOUS ARM,	139 11
FOR WHEN MOSES HAD SPOKEN EVERY PRECEPT TO ALL THE	147 18
AND BEGINNING AT MOSES AND ALL THE PROPHETS, HE	167 32
YE COULD NOT BE JUSTIFIED BY THE LAW OF MOSES,	169 07
IN THE LAW OF MOSES, AND IN THE PROPHETS, AND IN THE	170 09
AND AS MOSES LIFTED UP THE SERPENT IN THE WILDERNESS,	188 26
THEY HAVE MOSES AND THE PROPHETS	190 26
IF THEY HEAR NOT MOSES AND THE PROPHETS, NEITHER WILL	190 29
ALL BAPTIZED UNTO MOSES IN THE CLOUD AND IN THE SEA	201 07
BEHOLD THE FACE OF MOSES FOR THE GLORY OF HIS	206 20
FIRST MOSES SAITH, I WILL PROVOKE YOU TO JEALOUSY BY	227 16
TO THE LAW OF MOSES WERE ACCOMPLISHED, THEY BROUGHT	232 24
WHICH WERE MOSES AND ELIAS	248 28
AND ONE FOR MOSES, AND ONE FOR ELIAS	249 03
BY THE HAND OF MOSES AND AARON	434 24
6 MOSES AND AARON AMONG HIS PRIESTS, AND SAMUEL AMONG	462 27
HIS WAYS UNTO MOSES, *	466 19
26 THEN SENT HE MOSES HIS SERVANT, *	471 24
16 THEY ANGERED MOSES ALSO IN THE TENTS, *	473 33
HAD NOT MOSES HIS CHOSEN STOOD BEFORE HIM IN	474 15
THAT HE PUNISHED MOSES FOR THEIR SAKES	474 34
THE LAW WAS GIVEN BY MOSES	571 32
GIVEN FROM GOD BY MOSES, AS TOUCHING CEREMONIES AND	604 19

MOST

IT IS A MOST INVALUABLE PART OF THAT BLESSED 'LIBERTY	V 02
AS MAY SEEM MOST CONVENIENT FOR THE EDIFICATION	V 08
MIGHT MOST TEND TO THE PRESERVATION OF PEACE AND	V 35
TO SET FORTH HIS MOST WORTHY PRAISE, TO HEAR HIS MOST	006 07
TO HEAR HIS MOST HOLY WORD, AND TO ASK THOSE	006 07
ALMIGHTY AND MOST MERCIFUL FATHER	006 17
AND GRANT, O MOST MERCIFUL FATHER, FOR HIS SAKE	006 17
MOST HEARTILY WE BESEECH THEE, WITH THY FAVOUR TO	017 29
DO GIVE THEE MOST HUMBLE AND HEARTY THANKS FOR ALL	019 15
AS MAY BE MOST EXPEDIENT FOR THEM	020 08
TABERNACLES OF THE MOST HIGH	022 28
TO HEAR HIS MOST HOLY WORD, AND TO ASK THOSE	023 16
TO SET FORTH HIS MOST WORTHY PRAISE, TO HEAR HIS MOST	023 16
ALMIGHTY AND MOST MERCIFUL FATHER	023 24
AND GRANT, O MOST MERCIFUL FATHER, FOR HIS SAKE	024 02
THE HOLY GHOST, ART MOST HIGH IN THE GLORY OF GOD THE	026 03
UNTO THY NAME, O MOST HIGHEST	027 29
DO GIVE THEE MOST HUMBLE AND HEARTY THANKS FOR ALL	033 13
AS MAY BE MOST EXPEDIENT FOR THEM	034 08
MOST GRACIOUS GOD, WE HUMBLY BESEECH THEE, AS FOR THE	035 08
JESUS CHRIST, OUR MOST BLESSED LORD AND SAVIOUR	035 20
ALMIGHTY AND MOST MERCIFUL FATHER, WE HUMBLY BESEECH	040 23
WHICH WE NOW MOST JUSTLY SUFFER FOR OUR SINS, MAY,	041 03
THY ALMIGHTY AND MOST GRACIOUS PROTECTION OUR	042 05
O MOST MIGHTY AND MERCIFUL GOD, IN THIS TIME OF	045 03
YIELD UNTO GOD MOST HIGH PRAISE AND HEARTY THANKS FOR	048 15
BE DEFENDED BY THY MOST GRACIOUS AND READY HELP	049 15
WITH THY MOST GRACIOUS FAVOUR, AND FURTHER US	049 23
MOST GRACIOUS GOD, BY WHOSE KNOWLEDGE THE DEPTHS ARE	050 19
WE BESEECH THEE, MOST MERCIFUL FATHER, THAT SHE	051 09
O MOST MERCIFUL FATHER, WHO OF THY GRACIOUS GOODNESS	051 30
MOST HUMBLY BESEECHING THEE TO GRANT TO ALL OF US	052 22
MOST GRACIOUS LORD, WHOSE MERCY IS OVER ALL THY	053 20
REDEEMED WITH THY MOST PRECIOUS BLOOD, AND BE NOT	054 16
AS THEY MIGHT JUDGE MOST CONVENIENT FOR THEIR FUTURE	VI 12
THOSE EVILS THAT WE MOST JUSTLY HAVE DESERVED	059 23
PLAINEST, MOST AFFECTING AND MAJESTIC	VI 42
O MOST MIGHTY GOD, AND MERCIFUL FATHER, WHO HAST	062 13
THROUGH THY MOST MIGHTY PROTECTION, BOTH HERE	070 09
AS HE THINKETH MOST CONVENIENT	R 071 33
HUMBLY BESEECH THEE MOST MERCIFULLY TO ACCEPT OUR	074 09
AND WE MOST HUMBLY BESEECH THEE, OF THY GOODNESS,	074 30
FROM TIME TO TIME, MOST GRIEVOUSLY HAVE COMMITTED,	075 20
PROVOKING MOST JUSTLY THY WRATH AND	075 22
HAVE MERCY UPON US, MOST MERCIFUL FATHER	075 26
BE TO THEE, O LORD MOST HIGH	077 10
THROUGH THY MOST DEARLY BELOVED SON JESUS CHRIST OUR	078 16
WHO, AFTER HIS MOST GLORIOUS RESURRECTION, MANIFESTLY	078 17
ACCORDING TO WHOSE MOST TRUE PROMISE, THE HOLY GHOST	078 26
BE TO THEE, O LORD MOST HIGH	079 34
RENDERING UNTO THEE MOST HEARTY THANKS FOR THE	081 04
AND WE MOST HUMBLY BESEECH THEE, O MERCIFUL FATHER,	081 07
BE PARTAKERS OF HIS MOST BLESSED BODY AND BLOOD	081 14

MOST   CONTINUED

```
MOST HUMBLY BESEECHING THEE TO GRANT THAT, BY THE      081 17
RECEIVE THE MOST PRECIOUS BODY AND BLOOD OF THY SON    081 25
WASHED THROUGH HIS MOST PRECIOUS BLOOD, AND THAT WE    082 21
PARTAKERS OF HIS MOST BLESSED BODY AND BLOOD         R 083 10
EVERLIVING GOD, WE MOST HEARTILY THANK THEE, FOR THAT  083 16
FOOD OF THE MOST PRECIOUS BODY AND BLOOD OF THY SON    083 19
THE MERITS OF HIS MOST PRECIOUS DEATH AND PASSION      083 25
THE HOLY GHOST, ART MOST HIGH IN THE GLORY OF GOD THE  084 14
THINGS YE MUST GIVE MOST HUMBLE AND HEARTY THANKS TO   086 05
US GIVE, AS WE ARE MOST BOUNDEN, CONTINUAL THANKS      086 20
DISPOSED THE MOST COMFORTABLE SACRAMENT OF THE BODY    086 30
OUR DUTY TO RENDER MOST HUMBLE AND HEARTY THANKS TO    086 35
WITHOUT ANY CAUSE, MOST UNTHANKFULLY REFUSE TO COME    088 21
MOST DEARLY BELOVED IN CHRIST, TAKE YE                 088 24
THE BANQUET OF THAT MOST HEAVENLY FOOD                 089 18
OUR HEARTS THAT MOST EXCELLENT GIFT OF CHARITY,        122 16
ALMIGHTY GOD, WHOSE MOST DEAR SON WENT NOT UP TO JOY   138 04
THAT WE MAY ALWAYS MOST THANKFULLY RECEIVE THAT HIS    171 30
STEPS OF HIS MOST HOLY LIFE                            172 02
ALMIGHTY AND MOST MERCIFUL GOD, GRANT, WE BESEECH      182 15
O ALMIGHTY AND MOST MERCIFUL GOD, OF THY BOUNTIFUL     217 17
O MOST MERCIFUL FATHER, WHO HAST BLESSED THE LABOURS   265 11
AND THAT IT IS MOST CONVENIENT THAT BAPTISM SHOULD BE R 273 04
DID SHED OUT OF HIS MOST PRECIOUS SIDE BOTH WATER AND  279 11
THEE HEARTY THANKS, MOST MERCIFUL FATHER, THAT IT      280 28
THROUGH THY MOST MIGHTY PROTECTION, BOTH HERE          298 29
WE BESEECH THEE, MOST MERCIFUL FATHER, THAT SHE,       306 28
ALMIGHTY AND MOST MERCIFUL GOD AND SAVIOUR             309 27
RIGHT HAND OF THE MOST HIGHEST                         311 19
SHALL SAY, O MOST MERCIFUL GOD, WHO, ACCORDING TO      313 30
THY SERVANT, WHO MOST EARNESTLY DESIRETH PARDON AND    314 02
RENEW IN HIM, MOST LOVING FATHER, WHATSOEVER HATH      314 03
SHALL SEEM TO THEE MOST EXPEDIENT FOR HIM              314 08
THE MERITS OF THY MOST DEARLY BELOVED SON, JESUS       314 12
WHO IS A MOST STRONG TOWER TO ALL THOSE WHO PUT        314 15
WE BESEECH THEE, MOST GRACIOUS GOD, THIS THY SERVANT,  316 18
AND MOST MERCIFUL SAVIOUR                              317 15
PARTAKERS OF HIS MOST BLESSED BODY AND BLOOD         R 323 08
TABERNACLE OF THE MOST HIGHEST                         327 10
MOST HOLY, O LORD MOST MIGHTY, O HOLY AND MOST         332 25
O LORD GOD MOST HOLY, O LORD MOST MIGHTY,              332 25
O HOLY AND MOST MERCIFUL SAVIOUR, DELIVER US           332 26
BUT SPARE US, LORD MOST HOLY, O GOD MOST MIGHTY, O     332 29
MOST HOLY, O GOD MOST MIGHTY, O HOLY AND MERCIFUL      332 30
THOU MOST WORTHY JUDGE ETERNAL, SUFFER US              332 31
MOST MERCIFUL FATHER, WHO HAST BEEN PLEASED TO TAKE    336 04
WE YIELD UNTO THEE MOST HIGH PRAISE AND HEARTY         336 17
MOST HUMBLY BESEECHING THEE TO GIVE US GRACE SO TO     336 20
AND HEAR THAT HIS MOST JOYFUL VOICE                    336 25
O GOD, WHOSE MOST DEAR SON DID TAKE LITTLE CHILDREN    342 03
NAME OF THE LORD MOST HIGH                             350 29
OF THY NAME, O THOU MOST HIGHEST                       351 25
NAME OF THE LORD MOST HIGHEST                          356 11
IN THE MERCY OF THE MOST HIGHEST HE SHALL NOT          365 18
THY THIGH, O THOU MOST MIGHTY, *                       396 21
TABERNACLE OF THE MOST HIGHEST                         397 33
THE LORD, EVEN THE MOST MIGHTY GOD, HATH SPOKEN,       401 21
THY VOWS UNTO THE MOST HIGHEST                         402 19
AGAINST ME, O THOU MOST HIGHEST                        408 17
WILL CALL UNTO THE MOST HIGH GOD, *                    409 15
IS AGAINST THE MOST HIGH                               428 25
KNOWLEDGE IN THE MOST HIGH                             428 31
RIGHT HAND OF THE MOST HIGH                            434 03
AND PROVOKED THE MOST HIGHEST IN THE WILDERNESS        436 03
THE MOST PRINCIPAL AND MIGHTIEST IN THE DWELLINGS OF   438 12
AND DISPLEASED THE MOST HIGH GOD, *                    438 24
THE CHILDREN OF THE MOST HIGHEST                       443 30
ART ONLY THE MOST HIGHEST OVER ALL THE EARTH           445 09
AND THE MOST HIGH SHALL STABLISH HER                   448 23
THY TRUTH, MOST MIGHTY LORD, IS ON EVERY SIDE          450 23
THE DEFENCE OF THE MOST HIGH, *                        454 28
UNTO THY NAME, O MOST HIGHEST                          455 33
THOU, LORD, ART THE MOST HIGHEST FOR EVERMORE          456 15
THE COUNSEL OF THE MOST HIGHEST                        476 27
THE GIFT OF GOD MOST HIGH                              544 22
TO US THY ONLY AND MOST DEARLY BELOVED SON JESUS       545 14
WE RENDER UNTO THEE MOST HEARTY THANKS, WE PRAISE AND  545 25
MOST MERCIFUL FATHER, WE BESEECH THEE TO SEND UPON     547 04
DELIVER OUT OF THY MOST HOLY WORD, OR AGREEABLE TO     547 10
THE GIFT OF GOD MOST HIGH                              556 30
ALMIGHTY GOD, AND MOST MERCIFUL FATHER, WHO, OF THINE  557 17
MOST MERCIFUL FATHER, SEND DOWN, WE BESEECH THEE,      559 05
SUCCESS AS MAY TEND MOST TO THY GLORY, AND THE         565 12
TO SET FORTH THY MOST WORTHY PRAISE, TO CONFESS THEIR  566 16
SHALT SEE TO BE MOST EXPEDIENT FOR THEM                566 22
CHRIST'S SAKE, OUR MOST BLESSED LORD AND SAVIOUR       566 24
O MOST GLORIOUS GOD, WHOM THE HEAVEN OF HEAVENS        567 05
WITH THY MOST GRACIOUS FAVOUR, AND FURTHER US          571 08
MOST GRACIOUS FATHER, THE GIVER OF ALL GOOD AND        572 06
MOST MERCIFUL GOD, WHO ART OF PURER EYES THAN TO       589 26
O MOST LOVING FATHER, WHO WILLEST US TO GIVE THANKS    596 03
MAY BE PROVED BY MOST CERTAIN WARRANTS OF HOLY         604 27
BY FAITH ONLY, IS A MOST WHOLESOME DOCTRINE, AND VERY  605 08
IS A MOST DANGEROUS DOWNFALL, WHEREBY THE DEVIL DOTH   606 24
WRETCHLESSNESS OF MOST UNCLEAN LIVING, NO LESS         606 26
IN THE CHURCH, AS MOST AGREEABLE WITH THE INSTITUTION  608 32
```

MOTE

```
BEHOLDEST THOU THE MOTE THAT IS IN THY BROTHER'S EYE,  195 06
LET ME PULL OUT THE MOTE THAT IS IN THINE EYE, WHEN    195 08
TO PULL OUT THE MOTE THAT IS IN THY BROTHER'S EYE      195 12
```

MOTH

```
UPON EARTH, WHERE MOTH AND RUST DOTH CORRUPT, AND      072 08
WHERE NEITHER MOTH NOR RUST DOTH CORRUPT, AND WHERE    072 10
UPON EARTH, WHERE MOTH AND RUST DOTH CORRUPT, AND      125 17
WHERE NEITHER MOTH NOR RUST DOTH CORRUPT, AND WHERE    125 19
THE MOTH SHALL EAT THEM UP                             144 22
LIKE AS IT WERE A MOTH FRETTING A GARMENT              325 04
LIKE AS IT WERE A MOTH FRETTING A GARMENT              389 33
```

MOTHER

```
IN SIN HATH MY MOTHER CONCEIVED ME                     060 21
HONOUR THY FATHER AND THY MOTHER                       069 02
OF THE SUBSTANCE OF THE VIRGIN MARY HIS MOTHER         077 17
CHILD AND HIS MOTHER, AND FLEE INTO EGYPT, AND BE      103 18
CHILD AND HIS MOTHER BY NIGHT, AND DEPARTED INTO       103 21
WHEN AS HIS MOTHER MARY WAS ESPOUSED TO JOSEPH,        104 28
CHILD AND HIS MOTHER, AND GO INTO THE LAND OF ISRAEL   107 14
CHILD AND HIS MOTHER, AND CAME INTO THE LAND OF        107 17
WITH MARY HIS MOTHER, AND FELL DOWN, AND WORSHIPPED    109 21
JOSEPH AND HIS MOTHER KNEW NOT OF IT                   110 23
AND HIS MOTHER SAID UNTO HIM, SON, WHY HAST THOU THUS  110 32
BUT HIS MOTHER KEPT ALL THESE SAYINGS IN HER HEART     111 05
AND THE MOTHER OF JESUS WAS THERE                      113 12
WANTED WINE, THE MOTHER OF JESUS SAITH UNTO HIM, THEY  113 14
HIS MOTHER SAITH UNTO THE SERVANTS, WHATSOEVER HE      113 17
WHICH IS THE MOTHER OF US ALL                          131 08
OF JESUS HIS MOTHER, AND HIS MOTHER'S SISTER, MARY     160 18
THEREFORE SAW HIS MOTHER, AND THE DISCIPLE STANDING    160 20
HE SAITH UNTO HIS MOTHER, WOMAN, BEHOLD THY SON        160 21
THEN SAITH HE TO THE DISCIPLE, BEHOLD THY MOTHER       160 22
AND MARY THE MOTHER OF JAMES, AND SALOME, HAD BOUGHT   165 19
ONLY SON OF HIS MOTHER, AND SHE WAS A WIDOW            212 31
AND HE DELIVERED HIM TO HIS MOTHER                     213 06
OR FATHER, OR MOTHER, OR WIFE, OR CHILDREN, OR LANDS,  231 19
JOSEPH AND HIS MOTHER MARVELLED AT THOSE THINGS WHICH  233 09
UNTO MARY HIS MOTHER, BEHOLD, THIS CHILD IS SET FOR    233 11
AND HIS MOTHER ANSWERED AND SAID, NOT SO              243 19
CAME TO HIM THE MOTHER OF ZEBEDEE'S CHILDREN WITH HER  247 06
HIS FATHER AND MOTHER, AND SHALL BE JOINED UNTO HIS    267 29
LEAVE FATHER AND MOTHER, AND SHALL CLEAVE TO HIS       268 08
HONOUR THY FATHER AND THY MOTHER                       286 35
AND HELP MY FATHER AND MOTHER                          288 27
MY FATHER AND MY MOTHER FORSAKE ME, *                  372 20
AS ONE THAT MOURNETH FOR HIS MOTHER                    382 22
IN SIN HATH MY MOTHER CONCEIVED ME                     403 19
THE SIN OF HIS MOTHER BE DONE AWAY                     480 29
TO BE A JOYFUL MOTHER OF CHILDREN                      484 24
LIKE AS A CHILD THAT IS WEANED FROM HIS MOTHER         507 28
HONOUR THY FATHER AND THY MOTHER                       579 13
AND SUCCOUR MY FATHER AND MOTHER                       580 04
```

MOTHER'S

```
AND HIS MOTHER'S SISTER, MARY THE WIFE OF              160 18
TIME INTO HIS MOTHER'S WOMB, AND BE BORN               188 08
TIME INTO HIS MOTHER'S WOMB, AND BE BORN               275 13
ME OUT OF MY MOTHER'S WOMB                             366 20
YET UPON MY MOTHER'S BREASTS                           366 22
EVEN FROM MY MOTHER'S WOMB                             366 24
THINE OWN MOTHER'S SON                                 402 31
EVEN FROM THEIR MOTHER'S WOMB                          410 12
ALIEN UNTO MY MOTHER'S CHILDREN                        422 19
ME OUT OF MY MOTHER'S WOMB                             425 17
ME IN MY MOTHER'S WOMB                                 515 14
```

MOTHERS

```
AND ALL FATHERS, MOTHERS, GUARDIANS, AND SPONSORS    R 295 10
AND ALL FATHERS, MOTHERS, MASTERS, AND MISTRESSES,   R 582 31
```

MOTIONS

```
OBEY THY GODLY MOTIONS IN RIGHTEOUSNESS, AND TRUE      125 30
```

MOUNT

```
UNTO THE MOUNT OF OLIVES, THEN SENT JESUS TWO          091 12
LAMB STOOD ON THE MOUNT SION, AND WITH HIM AN HUNDRED  102 29
THE ONE FROM THE MOUNT SINAI, WHICH GENDERETH TO       131 04
FOR THIS AGAR IS MOUNT SINAI IN ARABIA, AND ANSWERETH  131 05
WENT OUT INTO THE MOUNT OF OLIVES                      141 17
WAS WONT, TO THE MOUNT OF OLIVES                       150 14
O GOD, WHO ON THE MOUNT DIDST REVEAL TO CHOSEN         247 31
WE HEARD, WHEN WE WERE WITH HIM IN THE HOLY MOUNT      248 21
10 LET THE MOUNT SION REJOICE, AND THE DAUGHTERS OF    399 31
AND MOUNT SION, WHEREIN THOU HAST DWELT                430 08
BE EVEN AS THE MOUNT SION, *                           504 24
```

MOUNTAIN

```
DOWN FROM THE MOUNTAIN, GREAT MULTITUDES FOLLOWED      114 29
EXCEEDING HIGH MOUNTAIN, AND SHEWETH HIM ALL THE       127 05
WENT UP INTO A MOUNTAIN, AND THERE HE SAT WITH HIS     131 24
AND EVERY MOUNTAIN AND HILL SHALL BE MADE LOW          242 23
GET THEE UP INTO THE HIGH MOUNTAIN                     243 03
WENT UP INTO A MOUNTAIN TO PRAY                        248 25
SEEING THE MULTITUDES, WENT UP INTO A MOUNTAIN         257 18
EVEN TO THIS MOUNTAIN, WHICH HE PURCHASED WITH HIS     438 19
```

MOUNTAINS

```
O YE MOUNTAINS AND HILLS, BLESS YE THE LORD            013 04
I COULD REMOVE MOUNTAINS, AND HAVE NOT CHARITY, I AM   122 25
```

MOUNTAINS   CONTINUED

TO SAY TO THE MOUNTAINS, FALL CN US	154 18
GROW UPON THE MOUNTAINS, AND HERB FOR THE USE OF MEN	264 29
BEFORE THE MOUNTAINS WERE BROUGHT FORTH, OR EVER THE	325 15
AND THOUGH THE MOUNTAINS SHAKE AT THE TEMPEST OF THE	327 08
RIGHTEOUSNESS STANDETH LIKE THE STRONG MOUNTAINS	384 06
AND THOUGH THE MOUNTAINS SHAKE AT THE TEMPEST OF THE	397 31
FOWLS UPON THE MOUNTAINS, *	402 12
FAST THE MOUNTAINS, *	416 25
3 THE MOUNTAINS ALSO SHALL BRING PEACE, *	427 02
AND AS THE FLAME THAT CONSUMETH THE MOUNTAINS	444 33
2 BEFORE THE MOUNTAINS WERE BROUGHT FORTH, OR EVER	453 20
4 THE MOUNTAINS SKIPPED LIKE RAMS, *	484 31
6 YE MOUNTAINS, THAT YE SKIPPED LIKE RAMS	485 04
TOUCH THE MOUNTAINS, AND THEY SHALL SMOKE	519 32
GROW UPON THE MOUNTAINS, AND HERB FOR THE USE OF MEN	523 12
9 MOUNTAINS AND ALL HILLS	524 22

MOURN

TO COMFORT ALL THAT MOURN	107 06
UNTO THEM THAT MOURN IN ZION, TO GIVE UNTC THEM	107 06
OF THE EARTH MOURN, AND THEY SHALL SEE THE SCN OF MAN	118 18
BLESSED ARE THEY THAT MOURN	257 22
WITH ALL THOSE WHO MOLRN, THAT, CASTING EVERY CARE ON	342 11
HOW I MOURN IN MY PRAYER, AND AM VEXED	406 21

MOURNETH

AS ONE THAT MOURNETH FOR HIS MCTHER	382 21

MOURNING

AND GREAT MOURNING, RACHEL WEEPING FOR HER CHILDREN,	103 32
OIL OF JOY FOR MOURNING, THE GARMENT OF PRAISE FOR	107 08
AND WITH WEEPING, AND WITH MOURNING	124 23
JOY AND OUR MOURNING INTO GLADNESS, BY RESTCRING THIS	315 22
AND MY YEARS WITH MOURNING	376 12
THAT I GO MOURNING ALL THE DAY LONG	388 03

MOURNINGS

MIGHT HEAR THE MOURNINGS OF SUCH AS ARE IN CAPTIVITY,	465 19

MOUTH

THE WORDS OF MY MOUTH, AND THE MEDITATICN OF MY	003 19
AND OUR MOUTH SHALL SHOW FORTH THY PRAISE	007 32
AS HE SPAKE BY THE MOLTH OF HIS HOLY PROPHETS,	014 12
THE WORDS OF MY MOUTH, AND THE MEDITATICN OF MY	021 21
AND OUR MOUTH SHALL SHOW FORTH THY PRAISE	025 07
ONE MIND AND ONE MOUTH GLORIFY THEE	038 02
AND MY MOUTH SHALL SHCW THY PRAISE	061 09
ONE MIND AND ONE MOUTH GLORIFY GOD, EVEN THE FATHER	092 20
AND IN THEIR MOUTH WAS FOUND NO GUILE	103 12
OUT OF THE MOUTH OF GOD	126 30
FOR WE OURSELVES HAVE HEARD OF HIS OWN MOUTH	152 03
AND PUT IT UPON HYSSOP, AND PUT IT TO HIS MOUTH	160 27
PETER OPENED HIS MOUTH, AND SAID, OF A TRUTH I	166 12
NEITHER WAS GUILE FOUND IN HIS MCUTH	172 12
PETER OPENED HIS MOUTH, AND SAID, OF A TRUTH I	183 29
OUT OF YOUR MOUTH, BUT THAT WHICH IS GOOD TO THE USE	216 23
THAT I MAY OPEN MY MOLTH BOLDLY, TO MAKE KNCWN THE	219 23
CONFESS WITH THY MOUTH THE LCRD JESUS, AND SHALT	226 26
AND WITH THE MOUTH CONFESSION IS MADE UNTO SALVATION	226 29
HOLY GHOST BY THE MOUTH OF DAVID SPAKE BEFORE	234 10
FOR THE MOUTH OF THE LORD HATH SPOKEN IT	242 26
AND HIS MOUTH WAS OPENED IMMEDIATELY, AND HIS TCNGUE	243 24
AS HE SPAKE BY THE MOLTH OF HIS HOLY PROPHETS, WHICH	243 35
AND HE OPENED HIS MOUTH, AND TAUGHT THEM, SAYING,	257 20
OUT OF THE MOUTH OF BABES AND SUCKLINGS THOU	260 14
HE DO NOT RECEIVE THE SACRAMENT WITH HIS MCUTH	R 323 31
9 FOR THERE IS NO FAITHFULNESS IN THEIR MOUTH	348 18
2 OUT OF THE MOUTH OF VERY BABES AND SUCKLINGS HAST	350 34
7 HIS MOUTH IS FULL OF CURSING, DECEIT, AND FRAUC	353 18
PURPOSED THAT MY MOUTH SHALL NOT OFFEND	358 23
AND THEIR MOUTH SPEAKETH PROUD THINGS	359 06
FIRE OUT OF HIS MOUTH, SO THAT COALS WERE KINDLEC AT	360 13
THE WORDS OF MY MOUTH, AND THE MEDITATICN CF MY	364 13
21 SAVE ME FROM THE LION'S MOUTH	367 14
ALL THE HOST OF THEM BY THE BREATH OF HIS MOUTH	378 30
HIS PRAISE SHALL EVER BE IN MY MOUTH	380 04
3 THE WORDS OF HIS MOLTH ARE UNRIGHTECUS AND FULL OF	383 30
31 THE MOUTH OF THE RIGHTEOUS IS EXERCISED IN WISDOM,	386 26
WHO DOTH NOT OPEN HIS MOUTH	388 18
AND IN WHOSE MOUTH ARE NO REPROOFS	388 20
2 I WILL KEEP MY MOUTH AS IT WERE WITH A BRIDLE,	389 07
10 I BECAME DUMB, AND OPENED NOT MY MOUTH	389 27
A NEW SONG IN MY MOUTH, *	390 14
3 MY MOUTH SHALL SPEAK OF WISDOM, *	400 10
AND TAKEST MY COVENANT IN THY MOUTH	402 23
THOU HAST LET THY MOUTH SPEAK WICKEDNESS, *	402 28
AND MY MOUTH SHALL SHOW THY PRAISE	404 07
AND HEARKEN UNTO THE WORDS OF MY MOUTH	406 06
THE WORDS OF HIS MOUTH WERE SOFTER THAN BUTTER,	407 35
SPEAK WITH THEIR MOUTH, AND SWORDS ARE IN THEIR LIPS	411 18
THE SIN OF THEIR MOUTH, AND FOR THE WORDS CF THEIR	411 29
WORDS WITH THEIR MOUTH, BUT CURSE WITH THEIR HEART	414 06
WHEN MY MOUTH PRAISETH THEE WITH JOYFUL LIPS	415 03
FOR THE MOUTH OF THEM THAT SPEAK LIES SHALL BE	415 16
AND SPAKE WITH MY MOUTH, WHEN I WAS IN TROUBLE	418 09
UNTO HIM WITH MY MOUTH, *	418 14
THE PIT SHUT HER MOUTH UPON ME	423 02
7 O LET MY MOUTH BE FILLED WITH THY PRAISE, *	425 21
14 MY MOUTH SHALL DAILY SPEAK OF THY RIGHTEOUSNESS	426 04

MOUTH   CONTINUED

FORTH THEIR MOUTH UNTO THE HEAVEN, *	428 26
INCLINE YOUR EARS UNTO THE WORDS OF MY MOUTH	434 28
2 I WILL OPEN MY MOUTH IN A PARABLE	434 29
HIM WITH THEIR MOUTH, *	437 11
OPEN THY MOUTH WIDE, AND I SHALL FILL IT	442 34
WITH MY MOUTH WILL I EVER BE SHOWING THY TRUTH FRCM	450 05
WHO SATISFIETH THY MOUTH WITH GOOD THINGS, *	466 15
AND THE JUDGMENTS OF HIS MOUTH	470 13
AND THE MOUTH OF ALL WICKEDNESS SHALL BE STCPPED	478 31
FOR THE MOUTH OF THE UNGODLY, YEA, THE MOUTH OF THE	480 04
YEA, THE MOUTH OF THE DECEITFUL IS OPENED	480 04
THE LORD WITH MY MOUTH, *	481 33
OF ALL THE JUDGMENTS OF THY MOUTH	490 24
NOT THE WORD OF THY TRUTH UTTERLY OUT OF MY MCUTH	492 27
72 THE LAW OF THY MOUTH IS DEARER UNTO ME *	494 14
AND SO SHALL I KEEP THE TESTIMONIES OF THY MOUTH	495 34
SWEETER THAN HONEY UNTO MY MOUTH	496 33
OFFERINGS OF MY MOUTH PLEASE THEE, O LORD	497 13
131 I OPENED MY MOUTH, AND DREW IN MY BREATH	498 32
2 THEN WAS OUR MOUTH FILLED WITH LAUGHTER, *	505 09
LET MY TONGUE CLEAVE TO THE ROOF OF MY MOUTH	513 16
FOR THEY HAVE HEARD THE WORDS OF THY MOUTH	514 05
O LORD, BEFORE MY MOUTH, *	517 13
8 WHOSE MOUTH TALKETH OF VANITY, *	520 06
WHOSE MOUTH TALKETH OF VANITY, AND THEIR RIGHT HAND	520 13
21 MY MOUTH SHALL SPEAK THE PRAISE OF THE LCRD	521 34
6 LET THE PRAISES OF GOD BE IN THEIR MOUTH	525 13
THE WORDS OF HIS MOUTH, AND THE MEDITATICN CF HIS	572 22
AND WITH ONE MOUTH MAY PROFESS THE FAITH ONCE	574 11

MOUTHS

WHO OUT OF THE MOUTHS OF BABES AND SUCKLINGS HAST	102 21
ME WITH THEIR MOUTHS, *	366 29
WHOSE MOUTHS MUST BE HELD WITH BIT AND BRIDLE, ELSE	378 11
MAKING MOUTHS AT ME, AND CEASED NOT	382 25
ME WITH THEIR MOUTHS, AND SAID, *	383 05
6 BREAK THEIR TEETH, O GOD, IN THEIR MOUTHS	410 19
WAS YET IN THEIR MOUTHS, THE HEAVY WRATH OF GCD CAME	436 32
5 THEY HAVE MOUTHS, AND SPEAK NOT	485 20
16 THEY HAVE MOUTHS, AND SPEAK NOT	511 02
NEITHER IS THERE ANY BREATH IN THEIR MOUTHS	511 05
SPOKEN BY THEIR MOUTHS MAY HAVE SUCH SUCCESS, THAT IT	547 07

MOVE

AND ALL THAT MOVE IN THE WATERS, BLESS YE THE LCRD	013 12
OMIT EARNESTLY TO MOVE THE PERSONS CCNFIRMED TC COME,	R 299 06
IT NEVER SHOULD MOVE AT ANY TIME	468 03
WHEREIN ALL THE BEASTS OF THE FOREST DO MOVE	468 35
MAY THE MORE MOVE YOU TO DO YOUR DUTIES	541 26
OF THESE THINGS MOVE ME, NEITHER COUNT I MY LIFE DEAR	550 18
BISHOP SHALL MOVE THE CONGREGATION PRESENT TC PRAY,	R 553 02
IN WHOM WE LIVE AND MOVE AND HAVE OUR BEING	587 20

MOVED

WHICH OF YOU IN SUCH A CASE WOULD NOT BE MOVED	088 22
ALL THE CITY WAS MOVED, SAYING, WHO IS THIS	091 31
THE CHIEF PRIESTS MOVED THE PEOPLE, THAT HE SHCULD	145 21
THAT SERVANT WAS MOVED WITH COMPASSION, AND LOOSED	221 21
THEY WERE MOVED WITH INDIGNATION AGAINST THE TWC	247 19
THE SICK PERSON BE MOVED TO MAKE A SPECIAL CCNFESSICN	R 313 24
THE EARTH BE MOVED, *	327 05
HE WILL NOT SUFFER THY FOOT TO BE MOVED	327 23
HE WILL NOT SUFFER THY FOOT TO BE MOVED	339 07
ELSE SHALT THOU BE MOVED TO DO EVIL	385 10
THE EARTH BE MOVED, *	397 28
AND THE KINGDOMS ARE MOVED	398 05
2 THOU HAST MOVED THE LAND, AND DIVIDED IT	412 15
AS SINAI ALSO WAS MOVED AT THE PRESENCE OF GOD, WHO	419 27
THE EARTH WAS MOVED, AND SHOOK WITHAL	434 20
THAT IT CANNOT BE MOVED	457 08
THE ROUND WORLD SO FAST THAT IT CANNCT BE MOVED	460 20
6 FOR HE SHALL NEVER BE MOVED	483 28
3 HE WILL NOT SUFFER THY FOOT TO BE MOVED	502 26
YOU ARE INWARDLY MOVED BY THE HOLY GHOST TO TAKE UPCN	532 26
HE WAS MOVED WITH COMPASSION CN THEM,	538 14
UNDER THE GOSPEL, MOVED EITHER BY THE EXPRESS CCMMANC	564 12

MOVETH

THE SCRIPTURE MOVETH US, IN SUNDRY PLACES, TC	005 29
THE SCRIPTURE MOVETH US, IN SUNDRY PLACES, TO	023 04
AND ALL THAT MOVETH THEREIN	424 13

MOVING

HER THEREUNTO MOVING, YIELDED TO MAKE SUCH	V 28

MOWER

7 WHEREOF THE MOWER FILLETH NOT HIS HAND, *	507 02

MOWN

THE RAIN UPON THE MOWN GRASS, *	427 08

MUCH

MEAN BETWEEN TOO MUCH STIFFNESS IN REFUSING, ANC TCC	V 24
AND TOO MUCH EASINESS IN ADMITTING	V 25
HAVE FOLLOWED TOO MUCH THE DEVICES AND DESIRES OF OUR	006 19
HAVE FOLLOWED TOO MUCH THE DEVICES AND DESIRES CF CUR	023 26

MUCH   CONTINUED

IF THOU HAST MUCH, GIVE PLENTEOUSLY   072 32
ARE NOT WORTHY SO MUCH AS TO GATHER UP THE CRUMBS   082 16
OR SO MUCH THEREOF AS, IN HIS DISCRETION, HE MAY   R 086 27
BEING MADE SO MUCH BETTER THAN THE ANGELS, AS HE HATH   096 30
BUT NOW MUCH MORE IN MY ABSENCE, WORK OUT YOUR   106 02
IT BE POSSIBLE, AS MUCH AS LIETH IN YOU, LIVE   113 02
WHEN MUCH PEOPLE WERE GATHERED TOGETHER, AND WERE   121 18
BUT HE CRIED SO MUCH THE MORE, THOU SON OF DAVID,   123 32
OF GOD, IN MUCH PATIENCE, IN AFFLICTIONS, IN   126 10
NOW THERE WAS MUCH GRASS IN THE PLACE   132 02
OF THE FISHES AS MUCH AS THEY WOULD   132 06
HOW MUCH MORE SHALL THE BLOOD OF CHRIST, WHO THROUGH   132 30
AND SO MUCH THE MORE, AS YE SEE THE DAY APPROACHING   158 27
I WILL NOT TALK MUCH WITH YOU   182 07
HOW MUCH MORE SHALL YOUR HEAVENLY FATHER GIVE THE   183 18
NOT LIFT UP SO MUCH AS HIS EYES UNTO HEAVEN, BUT   205 29
BE GLORY, MUCH MORE DOTH THE MINISTRATION OF   206 24
HE CHARGED THEM, SO MUCH THE MORE A GREAT DEAL THEY   207 06
ARE NOT YE OF MUCH MORE VALUE THAN THEY   211 18
SHALL HE NOT MUCH MORE CLOTHE YOU, O YE OF   211 26
WENT WITH HIM, AND MUCH PEOPLE   212 29
AND MUCH PEOPLE OF THE CITY WAS WITH HER   212 32
NOW THERE WAS MUCH GRASS IN THE PLACE   225 32
OF THE FISHES AS MUCH AS THEY WOULD   226 05
OF THIS MAN, HOW MUCH EVIL HE HATH DONE TO THY SAINTS   230 23
SAME BRINGETH FORTH MUCH FRUIT   238 13
THAT YE BEAR MUCH FRUIT   238 19
AND MUCH PEOPLE WAS ADDED UNTO THE LORD   241 09
AND TAUGHT MUCH PEOPLE   241 13
COPPERSMITH DID ME MUCH EVIL   254 07
HOW MUCH MORE SHALL YOUR HEAVENLY FATHER GIVE THE   263 12
ARE YE NOT MUCH BETTER THAN THEY   266 16
SHALL HE NOT MUCH MORE CLOTHE YOU, O YE OF   266 24
SAW IT, HE WAS MUCH DISPLEASED, AND SAID UNTO THEM,   274 27
MY SOUL WITH MUCH STRENGTH   312 03
WE BESEECH THEE, SO MUCH THE MORE CONTINUALLY WITH   316 11
AND MAKETH MUCH OF THEM THAT FEAR THE LORD   357 14
YEA, THAN MUCH FINE GOLD   364 05
MAN DELIVERED BY MUCH STRENGTH   379 20
PRAISE THEE AMONG MUCH PEOPLE   382 33
6 THE NATIONS MAKE MUCH ADO, AND THE KINGDOMS ARE   398 04
THOU ME TO MAKE MUCH OF THY LAW   491 26
GO BY SAY NOT SO MUCH AS, THE LORD PROSPER YOU   507 04
MY SOUL WITH MUCH STRENGTH   514 03
NOT GIVEN TO MUCH WINE, NOT GREEDY OF FILTHY LUCRE   531 28
AND THEM, AS MUCH AS IN YOU LIETH, WHOLESOME EXAMPLES   533 27
AND SET ASIDE, AS MUCH AS YE MAY, ALL WORLDLY CARES   541 08
SO THAT, AS MUCH AS LIETH IN YOU, YE WILL APPLY   541 13
AND THEM, AS MUCH AS IN YOU LIETH, WHOLESOME EXAMPLES   542 34
SET FORWARDS, AS MUCH AS LIETH IN YOU, QUIETNESS,   543 06
AND SET FORWARD, AS MUCH AS SHALL LIE IN YOU,   555 14
CANNOT CONTAIN, MUCH LESS THE WALLS OF TEMPLES MADE   564 29
RENDER UNTO GOD AS MUCH AS THEY ARE BOUND TO DO,   605 27

MULBERRY-TREES

AND THEIR MULBERRY-TREES WITH THE FROST   438 03

MULE

LIKE TO HORSE AND MULE, WHICH HAVE NO UNDERSTANDING   378 10

MULTIPLIED

THE DISCIPLES MULTIPLIED IN JERUSALEM GREATLY   532 21

MULTIPLY

THE LANDS AND MULTIPLY THE HARVESTS OF THE WORLD   040 08
INCREASE AND MULTIPLY UPON US THY MERCY   194 06
MULTIPLY, WE BESEECH THEE, TO THOSE WHO REST IN   335 27
SO THAT THEY MULTIPLY EXCEEDINGLY   478 22

MULTITUDE

TO THE MULTITUDE OF THY MERCIES DO AWAY MINE   060 11
AND AFTER THE MULTITUDE OF THY MERCIES LOOK UPON US   063 05
WHO, IN THE MULTITUDE OF THY SAINTS, HAST COMPASSED   079 22
A VERY GREAT MULTITUDE SPREAD THEIR GARMENTS IN THE   091 24
AND THE MULTITUDE SAID, THIS IS JESUS THE PROPHET OF   091 31
THE ANGEL A MULTITUDE OF THE HEAVENLY HOST PRAISING   099 20
HEARING THE MULTITUDE PASS BY, HE ASKED WHAT IT   123 28
AND A GREAT MULTITUDE FOLLOWED HIM, BECAUSE THEY SAW   131 22
PERSUADED THE MULTITUDE THAT THEY SHOULD ASK   135 36
BEFORE THE MULTITUDE, SAYING, I AM INNOCENT OF THE   136 10
TO THE MULTITUDE OF HIS LOVINGKINDNESSES   138 32
HIM A GREAT MULTITUDE WITH SWORDS AND STAVES, FROM   142 15
AND THE MULTITUDE CRYING ALOUD BEGAN TO DESIRE HIM TO   145 16
HIM UNTO THEM IN THE ABSENCE OF MULTITUDE   148 21
BEHOLD A MULTITUDE, AND HE THAT WAS CALLED JUDAS, ONE   150 27
THE WHOLE MULTITUDE OF THEM AROSE, AND LED HIM UNTO   152 27
COVER THE MULTITUDE OF SINS   179 15
THE MULTITUDE CAME TOGETHER, AND WERE   180 27
A GREAT MULTITUDE OF FISHES   196 18
THOSE DAYS THE MULTITUDE BEING VERY GREAT, AND HAVING   199 08
ON THE MULTITUDE, BECAUSE THEY HAVE NOW BEEN WITH ME   199 10
ASIDE FROM THE MULTITUDE, AND PUT HIS FINGERS INTO   206 32
CAME ALSO A MULTITUDE OUT OF THE CITIES ROUND ABOUT   249 30
A GREAT MULTITUDE, WHICH NO MAN COULD NUMBER, OF   256 23
TO THE MULTITUDE OF THY MERCIES, DOST SO PUT AWAY THE   313 30
TO THE MULTITUDE OF THY MERCIES, DO AWAY OUR OFFENCES   323 15
FOR ME, IN THE MULTITUDE OF THY MERCY I WILL COME   348 13
OUT IN THE MULTITUDE OF THEIR UNGODLINESS   348 23
OF THE MULTITUDE, AND FEAR IS ON EVERY SIDE   376 21

MULTITUDE   CONTINUED

SAVED BY THE MULTITUDE OF AN HOST   379 19
IN THE MULTITUDE OF PEACE   385 17
WENT WITH THE MULTITUDE, AND BROUGHT THEM FORTH INTO   393 07
IN THE MULTITUDE OF THEIR RICHES   400 17
TO THE MULTITUDE OF THY MERCIES DO AWAY MINE   403 09
UNTO THE MULTITUDE OF HIS RICHES, AND STRENGTHENED   405 02
O GOD, IN THE MULTITUDE OF THY MERCY, *   422 30
TO THE MULTITUDE OF THY MERCIES   423 05
UNTO THE MULTITUDE OF THE ENEMIES   431 16
19 IN THE MULTITUDE OF THE SORROWS THAT I HAD IN MY   458 24
THE MULTITUDE OF THE ISLES MAY BE GLAD THEREOF   460 31
UNTO THE MULTITUDE OF HIS MERCIES   475 28
AND PRAISE HIM AMONG THE MULTITUDE   481 33
CALLED THE MULTITUDE OF THE DISCIPLES UNTO THEM, AND   532 08
AND THE SAYING PLEASED THE WHOLE MULTITUDE   532 15
OF THE WHOLE MULTITUDE OF THE FAITHFUL, AS AN HEATHEN   609 28

MULTITUDES

PEOPLE THE MULTITUDES BROUGHT HITHER OUT OF MANY   036 16
AND THE MULTITUDES THAT WENT BEFORE, AND THAT   091 27
SAY UNTO THE MULTITUDES CONCERNING JOHN, WHAT WENT YE   094 25
GREAT MULTITUDES FOLLOWED HIM   114 30
BUT WHEN THE MULTITUDES SAW IT, THEY MARVELLED, AND   217 12
TO THE LORD, MULTITUDES BOTH OF MEN AND WOMEN   249 26
SEEING THE MULTITUDES, WENT UP INTO A MOUNTAIN   257 18
JEWS SAW THE MULTITUDES, THEY WERE FILLED WITH ENVY,   260 28
JESUS SAW THE MULTITUDES, HE WAS MOVED WITH   538 14

MURDER

FROM BATTLE AND MURDER, AND FROM SUDDEN DEATH,   054 32
THOU SHALT DO NO MURDER   069 07
WHO HAD COMMITTED MURDER IN THE INSURRECTION   145 16
THE CITY, AND FOR MURDER, WAS CAST INTO PRISON   153 31
FOR SEDITION AND MURDER WAS CAST INTO PRISON, WHOM   154 07
THOU SHALT DO NO MURDER   287 06
DENS DOTH HE MURDER THE INNOCENT   353 21
6 THEY MURDER THE WIDOW AND THE STRANGER, *   457 29
THOU SHALT DO NO MURDER   579 15

MURDERER

WHOSOEVER HATETH HIS BROTHER IS A MURDERER   191 15
YE KNOW THAT NO MURDERER HATH ETERNAL LIFE ABIDING IN   191 15

MURDERERS

PRAYED FOR HIS MURDERERS TO THEE, O BLESSED JESUS,   099 31
THOSE MURDERERS, AND BURNED UP THEIR CITY   218 15

MURDERS

MURDERS, DRUNKENNESS, REVELLINGS, AND SUCH   209 22

MURMUR

NEITHER MURMUR YE, AS SOME OF THEM ALSO MURMURED, AND   201 20

MURMURED

THEY MURMURED AGAINST THE GOODMAN OF THE HOUSE,   120 03
AND THEY MURMURED AGAINST HER   140 09
AND SCRIBES MURMURED, SAYING, THIS MAN RECEIVETH   193 16
OF THEM ALSO MURMURED, AND WERE DESTROYED OF THE   201 21
25 BUT MURMURED IN THEIR TENTS, *   474 19

MURMURING

THINE ENEMIES MAKE A MURMURING   444 07

MUSE

AND MY HEART SHALL MUSE OF UNDERSTANDING   400 11
I MUSE UPON ALL THY WORKS   518 32

MUSIC

PLAYING UPON AN INSTRUMENT OF MUSIC   426 23

MUSICK

HE HEARD MUSICK AND DANCING   202 27

MUSING

WHILE I WAS THUS MUSING THE FIRE KINDLED, *   389 13

MUST

BELONG TO DOCTRINE MUST BE REFERRED TO DISCIPLINE   V 06
OUR SAVIOUR CHRIST, MUST CONSIDER HOW SAINT PAUL   085 27
ABOVE ALL THINGS YE MUST GIVE MOST HUMBLE AND HEARTY   086 04
WIST YE NOT THAT I MUST BE ABOUT MY FATHER'S   111 02
WHEREFORE YE MUST NEEDS BE SUBJECT, NOT ONLY FOR   114 22
IF I MUST NEEDS GLORY, I WILL GLORY OF THE THINGS   121 13
BUT THE SCRIPTURES MUST BE FULFILLED   142 27
TESTAMENT IS, THERE MUST ALSO OF NECESSITY BE THE   147 14
FOR THEN MUST HE OFTEN HAVE SUFFERED SINCE THE   148 04
WHEN THE PASSOVER MUST BE KILLED   148 22
THAT IS WRITTEN MUST YET BE ACCOMPLISHED IN ME, AND   150 09
OF NECESSITY HE MUST RELEASE ONE UNTO THEM AT THE   153 28
THAT HE MUST RISE AGAIN FROM THE DEAD   164 27
THAT ALL THINGS MUST BE FULFILLED, WHICH WERE WRITTEN   170 08

MUST CONTINUED

	PAGE	LN
THEM ALSO I MUST BRING, AND THEY SHALL HEAR MY VOICE	172	31
THEE THINGS WHICH MUST BE HEREAFTER	187	03
SAID UNTO THEE, YE MUST BE BORN AGAIN	188	14
EVEN SO MUST THE SON OF MAN BE LIFTED UP	188	27
OF GROUND, AND I MUST NEEDS GO AND SEE IT	192	08
TOLD THEE WHAT THOU MUST DO	230	08
HOW GREAT THINGS HE MUST SUFFER FOR MY NAME'S SAKE	230	28
THIS SCRIPTURE MUST NEEDS HAVE BEEN FULFILLED,	234	09
TAKEN UP FROM US, MUST ONE BE ORDAINED TO BE A	234	24
THAT SHORTLY I MUST PUT OFF THIS MY TABERNACLE, EVEN	248	10
FOR IT MUST NEEDS BE THAT OFFENCES COME	252	34
WITH THE CHILDREN, MUST BE READY AT THE FONT,	R 273	14
SAID UNTO THEE, YE MUST BE BORN AGAIN	275	18
WHICH YOU MUST LEARN AT ALL TIMES TO CALL FOR BY	289	16
TO GIVE HER THANKS, MUST OFFER ACCUSTOMED OFFERINGS,	R 307	07
THEN HE MUST GIVE TIMELY NOTICE TO THE MINISTER,	R 321	12
FOR HE MUST REIGN, TILL HE HATH PUT ALL ENEMIES UNDER	328	29
THIS CORRUPTIBLE MUST PUT ON INCORRUPTION, AND THIS	330	05
AND THIS MORTAL MUST PUT ON IMMORTALITY	330	06
WHOSE MOUTHS MUST BE HELD WITH BIT AND BRIDLE, ELSE	378	11
SO THAT HE MUST LET THAT ALONE FOR EVER	400	21
LIKEWISE MUST THE DEACONS BE GRAVE, NOT	531	27
EVEN SO MUST THEIR WIVES BE GRAVE, NOT SLANDERERS,	531	31
THE DEACON, THAT HE MUST CONTINUE IN THAT OFFICE OF A	R 535	19
AND HERE IT MUST BE DECLARED UNTO THE DEACON,	R 535	19
THEM ALSO I MUST BRING, AND THEY SHALL HEAR MY VOICE	539	20
WHOM YOU MUST SERVE, IS HIS SPOUSE, AND HIS BODY	540	09
A BISHOP THEN MUST BE BLAMELESS, THE HUSBAND OF ONE	549	19
MOREOVER HE MUST HAVE A GOOD REPORT OF THEM WHICH ARE	549	28
WHICH THOU MUST LEARN AT ALL TIMES TO CALL FOR BY	580	19
IN WHICH WE MUST GIVE A STRICT ACCOUNT OF OUR	588	22
ACCOUNT WHICH WE MUST ONE DAY GIVE, MAY BE FAITHFUL	599	22
WE MUST RECEIVE GOD'S PROMISES IN SUCH	606	27
WHEREBY MEN MUST BE SAVED	606	36

MUTUAL

	PAGE	LN
THEY EMPLOY TO MUTUAL FORBEARANCE, FAIRNESS, AND	599	32

MYRRH

	PAGE	LN
AND FRANKINCENSE, AND MYRRH	109	23
THEY GAVE HIM TO DRINK WINE MINGLED WITH MYRRH	146	10
GARMENTS SMELL OF MYRRH, ALOES, AND CASSIA	396	32

MYSELF

	PAGE	LN
FOR I KNOW NOTHING AGAINST MYSELF	094	08
TO OTHERS, I MYSELF SHOULD BE A CASTAWAY	119	12
IF I HONOUR MYSELF, MY HONOUR IS NOTHING	133	23
BEHOLD MY HANDS AND MY FEET, THAT IT IS I MYSELF	169	33
AND WILL MANIFEST MYSELF TO HIM	181	21
I WILL COME AGAIN, AND RECEIVE YOU UNTO MYSELF	240	02
WORDS THAT I SPEAK UNTO YOU I SPEAK NOT OF MYSELF	240	15
IS TO LOVE HIM AS MYSELF, AND TO DO TO ALL MEN AS I	288	25
TO SUBMIT MYSELF TO ALL MY GOVERNORS, TEACHERS,	288	28
AND TO ORDER MYSELF IN THAT LOWLINESS AND REVERENCE	288	30
I SHALL SEE FOR MYSELF, AND MINE EYES SHALL BEHOLD,	324	11
AND RECEIVE YOU UNTO MYSELF	331	21
14 I BEHAVED MYSELF AS THOUGH IT HAD BEEN MY FRIEND	382	20
36 I MYSELF HAVE SEEN THE UNGODLY IN GREAT POWER,	387	04
I POUR OUT MY HEART BY MYSELF	393	07
I MYSELF WILL TESTIFY AGAINST THEE, O ISRAEL	402	04
I WOULD HAVE HID MYSELF FROM HIM	407	15
I MYSELF WILL AWAKE RIGHT EARLY	409	31
AND CHASTENED MYSELF WITH FASTING, *	422	23
I MYSELF WILL AWAKE RIGHT EARLY	479	07
BUT I GIVE MYSELF UNTO PRAYER	480	10
I DO NOT EXERCISE MYSELF IN GREAT MATTERS *	507	25
I EXERCISE MYSELF IN THE WORKS OF THY HANDS	518	33
I WILL APPLY MYSELF THERETO, THE LORD BEING MY	543	04
MY LIFE DEAR UNTO MYSELF, SO THAT I MIGHT FINISH MY	550	19
I WILL SO SHOW MYSELF, BY GOD'S HELP	555	26
SERVICE I DEVOTE MYSELF, BODY, SOUL, AND SPIRIT,	573	15
IS TO LOVE HIM AS MYSELF, AND TO DO TO ALL MEN AS I	580	02
TO SUBMIT MYSELF TO ALL MY GOVERNORS, TEACHERS,	580	05
TO ORDER MYSELF LOWLY AND REVERENTLY TO ALL MY	580	06

MYSTERIES

	PAGE	LN
THESE HOLY MYSTERIES, WITH THE SPIRITUAL FOOD OF THE	083	18
YE BE MEET PARTAKERS OF THOSE HOLY MYSTERIES	086	04
ORDAINED HOLY MYSTERIES, AS PLEDGES OF HIS LOVE, AND	086	16
OF THY MYSTERIES MAY LIKEWISE SO PREPARE AND MAKE	093	26
OF THE MYSTERIES OF GOD	094	04
TO KNOW THE MYSTERIES OF THE KINGDOM OF GOD	121	30
UNDERSTAND ALL MYSTERIES, AND ALL KNOWLEDGE	122	24
IN THESE HOLY MYSTERIES GIVETH US A PLEDGE OF LIFE	152	11
TO THOSE HOLY MYSTERIES IN FAITH, AND LOVE, AND TRUE	294	31
OF THE MYSTERIES OF CHRIST, THAT BY THEIR MINISTRY	562	11

MYSTERY

	PAGE	LN
BY THE MYSTERY OF THY HOLY INCARNATION	055	06
BECAUSE IN THE MYSTERY OF THE WORD MADE FLESH,	077	29
OF THAT HOLY MYSTERY, AND THE GREAT PERIL OF THE	087	09
BY REVELATION HE MADE KNOWN UNTO ME THE MYSTERY	108	09
KNOWLEDGE IN THE MYSTERY OF CHRIST) WHICH IN OTHER	108	11
OF THE MYSTERY, WHICH FROM THE BEGINNING OF THE WORLD	108	21
MAKE KNOWN THE MYSTERY OF THE GOSPEL, FOR WHICH I AM	219	24
THIS IS A GREAT MYSTERY	267	31
BEHOLD, I SHEW YOU A MYSTERY	329	35
HOLDING THE MYSTERY OF THE FAITH IN A PURE	531	29

MYSTICAL

	PAGE	LN
IN THE MYSTICAL BODY OF THY SON, WHICH IS THE BLESSED	083	22
IN THE MYSTICAL BODY OF THY SON CHRIST OUR LORD	256	06
WATER TO THE MYSTICAL WASHING AWAY OF SIN	279	16
UNTO US THE MYSTICAL UNION THAT IS BETWIXT CHRIST AND	300	12
WHO ARE OF THE MYSTICAL BODY OF THY SON, MAY BE SET	336	24

NAILS

	PAGE	LN
THE PRINT OF THE NAILS, AND PUT MY FINGER INTO THE	228	29
THE PRINT OF THE NAILS, AND THRUST MY HAND INTO HIS	228	29

NAIN

	PAGE	LN
THAT JESUS WENT INTO A CITY CALLED NAIN	212	28

NAKED

	PAGE	LN
CAST ABOUT HIS NAKED BODY	142	29
HE LEFT THE LINEN CLOTH, AND FLED FROM THEM NAKED	142	31
NAKED, AND YE CLOTHED ME	259	07
OR NAKED, AND CLOTHED THEE	259	12

NAKEDNESS

	PAGE	LN
IN FASTINGS OFTEN, IN COLD AND NAKEDNESS	121	10
OR FAMINE, OR NAKEDNESS, OR PERIL, OR SWORD	331	07

NAME

	PAGE	LN
WHOSE NAME IS HOLY	003	26
DOWN OF THE SAME MY NAME SHALL BE GREAT AMONG THE	004	13
FOR MY NAME SHALL BE GREAT AMONG THE HEATHEN, SAITH	004	15
BE OFFERED UNTO MY NAME, AND A PURE OFFERING	004	15
TO THE GLORY OF THY HOLY NAME	006	30
WHO ART IN HEAVEN, HALLOWED BE THY NAME	007	23
THE LORD'S NAME BE PRAISED	008	08
AND WE WORSHIP THY NAME EVER, WORLD WITHOUT END	011	07
ART THOU FOR THE NAME OF THY MAJESTY	011	18
BE THANKFUL UNTO HIM, AND SPEAK GOOD OF HIS NAME	015	12
TOGETHER IN THY NAME THOU WILT GRANT THEIR REQUESTS	020	06
TO THE GLORY OF THY HOLY NAME	024	05
THE LORD'S NAME BE PRAISED	025	14
AND HOLY IS HIS NAME	026	17
PRAISES UNTO THY NAME, O MOST HIGHEST	027	29
AND ALL THAT IS WITHIN ME, PRAISE HIS HOLY NAME	029	05
TOGETHER IN THY NAME THOU WILT GRANT THEIR REQUESTS	034	06
HUMBLY BEG IN THE NAME AND MEDIATION OF JESUS CHRIST,	035	20
TO THE GLORY OF THY NAME AND THE WELFARE OF THE	035	27
TO WHOM IN THY NAME WE ENTRUST THE AUTHORITY OF	036	18
ASSEMBLED IN THY NAME AND PRESENCE	036	31
ASSEMBLED IN THY NAME, BEING CHANGED TO NOW ASSEMBLED	R 037	11
TO ASSEMBLE) IN THY NAME AND PRESENCE	R 037	12
GLORY OF THY GREAT NAME, AND THE BENEFIT OF THY HOLY	039	14
TO THE PRAISE OF THY HOLY NAME	039	31
THE POOR AND NEEDY MAY GIVE THANKS UNTO THY NAME	040	12
SERVE THEE OUR GOD, TO THE GLORY OF THY NAME	042	12
MINISTER IN THY NAME TO THE SUFFERING, THE	044	04
MEN AND NATIONS, TO THE GLORY OF THY HOLY NAME	044	14
TO THE HONOUR AND PRAISE OF THY NAME	049	21
GLORIFY THY HOLY NAME, AND FINALLY, BY THY MERCY,	049	26
THE PETITIONS OF THOSE WHO ASK IN THY SON'S NAME	050	07
AND TO THE GLORY OF THY HOLY NAME	051	20
GLORIFY THY HOLY NAME FOR THIS THY MERCY, AND WILL	051	26
WE BLESS THY HOLY NAME, THAT IT HATH PLEASED THEE TO	052	20
WE BLESS THY NAME, THAT THOU HAST BEEN PLEASED TO	052	30
AND PRAISE THY NAME, IN THE PRESENCE OF ALL THY	053	13
WE PRAISE THY HOLY NAME THAT THOU HAST BEEN PLEASED	053	21
THE GLORY OF THY NAME, TURN FROM US ALL THOSE EVILS	059	23
TO THE PRAISE OF THY HOLY NAME DELIVER US	062	03
LOVE THEE, AND WORTHILY MAGNIFY THY HOLY NAME	067	20
SHALT NOT TAKE THE NAME OF THE LORD THY GOD IN VAIN	068	18
THAT TAKETH HIS NAME IN VAIN	068	20
DO CONFESS THY HOLY NAME MAY AGREE IN THE TRUTH OF	074	14
ALSO BLESS THY HOLY NAME FOR ALL THY SERVANTS	074	34
OF LIFE, TO THE HONOUR AND GLORY OF THY NAME	075	30
WE LAUD AND MAGNIFY THY GLORIOUS NAME	077	06
WE LAUD AND MAGNIFY THY GLORIOUS NAME	079	30
SAY, IN THE NAME OF ALL THOSE WHO SHALL	R 082	11
I BID YOU IN THE NAME OF GOD, I CALL YOU IN CHRIST'S	089	07
THAT COMETH IN THE NAME OF THE LORD	091	29
THEE AMONG THE GENTILES, AND SING UNTO THY NAME	092	27
A MORE EXCELLENT NAME THAN THEY	096	31
FROM GOD, WHOSE NAME WAS JOHN	097	26
OF GOD, EVEN TO THEM THAT BELIEVE ON HIS NAME	098	02
MAN'S FEET, WHOSE NAME WAS SAUL	100	13
THAT COMETH IN THE NAME OF THE LORD	100	33
WE MAY GLORIFY THY HOLY NAME	102	26
HAVING HIS FATHER'S NAME WRITTEN IN THEIR FOREHEADS	102	31
THOU SHALT CALL HIS NAME JESUS	105	07
THEY SHALL CALL HIS NAME EMMANUEL, WHICH BEING	105	11
AND HE CALLED HIS NAME JESUS	105	15
THAT AT THE NAME OF JESUS EVERY KNEE SHOULD BOW, OF	105	27
AND GIVEN HIM A NAME WHICH IS ABOVE EVERY NAME	105	27
AND GIVEN HIM A NAME WHICH IS ABOVE EVERY NAME	105	27
OF THE CHILD, HIS NAME WAS CALLED JESUS, WHICH WAS SO	106	21
DO ALL IN THE NAME OF THE LORD JESUS, GIVING	116	15
FOR THE GLORY OF THY NAME	118	31
AND GIVEN HIM A NAME WHICH IS ABOVE EVERY NAME	134	23
AND GIVEN HIM A NAME WHICH IS ABOVE EVERY NAME	134	24
THAT AT THE NAME OF JESUS EVERY KNEE SHOULD BOW, OF	134	24
THEY FOUND A MAN OF CYRENE, SIMON BY NAME	136	26
TO MAKE HIMSELF AN EVERLASTING NAME	139	13
TO MAKE THYSELF A GLORIOUS NAME	139	17
THY NAME IS FROM EVERLASTING	139	23

NAME   CONTINUED

	PAGE	LN
THEY WERE NOT CALLED BY THY NAME	139	30
HIM TRUST IN THE NAME OF THE LORD, AND STAY UPON HIS	144	25
THAT THROUGH HIS NAME WHOSOEVER BELIEVETH IN HIM	166	31
ONE OF THEM, WHOSE NAME WAS CLEOPAS, ANSWERING SAID	167	12
BE PREACHED IN HIS NAME AMONG ALL NATIONS, BEGINNING	170	15
THE FATHER IN MY NAME, HE WILL GIVE IT YOU	176	21
HITHERTO HAVE YE ASKED NOTHING IN MY NAME	176	22
AT THAT DAY YE SHALL ASK IN MY NAME	176	27
WILL SEND IN MY NAME, HE SHALL TEACH YOU ALL THINGS,	181	31
THAT THROUGH HIS NAME WHOSOEVER BELIEVETH IN HIM	184	19
BE BAPTIZED IN THE NAME OF THE LORD	184	29
NOT BELIEVED IN THE NAME OF THE ONLY-BEGOTTEN SON OF	185	04
POWER AMONG ALL PEOPLES, TO THE GLORY OF THY NAME	185	17
BAPTIZED IN THE NAME OF THE LORD JESUS	185	26
HIS OWN SHEEP BY NAME, AND LEADETH THEM OUT	186	05
HAVE A PERPETUAL FEAR AND LOVE OF THY HOLY NAME	191	08
BELIEVE ON THE NAME OF HIS SON JESUS CHRIST, AND LOVE	191	30
THE LOVE OF THY NAME, INCREASE IN US TRUE RELIGION,	198	22
THE FATHER IN THE NAME OF OUR LORD JESUS CHRIST	217	31
TO THE GLORY OF THY NAME	220	20
AND THIS IS HIS NAME WHEREBY HE SHALL BE CALLED,	225	13
SHALL CALL UPON THE NAME OF THE LORD SHALL BE SAVED	227	04
BELIEVING YE MIGHT HAVE LIFE THROUGH HIS NAME	229	13
CHIEF PRIESTS TO BIND ALL THAT CALL ON THY NAME	230	25
UNTO ME, TO BEAR MY NAME BEFORE THE GENTILES, AND	230	27
CALLED ON THIS NAME IN JERUSALEM, AND CAME HITHER FOR	231	06
IN JERUSALEM, WHOSE NAME WAS SIMEON	232	30
AND SHALL CALL HIS NAME IMMANUEL	235	32
TO A MAN WHOSE NAME WAS JOSEPH, OF THE HOUSE OF	236	07
AND THE VIRGIN'S NAME WAS MARY	236	08
AND SHALT CALL HIS NAME JESUS	236	16
YE SHALL ASK IN MY NAME, THAT WILL I DO, THAT THE	240	22
ASK ANY THING IN MY NAME, I WILL DO IT	240	23
OF THE FATHER IN MY NAME, HE MAY GIVE IT YOU	242	03
AFTER THE NAME OF HIS FATHER	243	19
NONE OF THY KINDRED THAT IS CALLED BY THIS NAME	243	21
SAYING, HIS NAME IS JOHN	243	24
LITTLE CHILD IN MY NAME RECEIVETH ME	252	30
TO HIM SHALT THOU CLEAVE, AND SWEAR BY HIS NAME	263	30
THE FATHER IN THE NAME OF OUR LORD JESUS CHRIST	267	12
THEM IN THE NAME OF THE FATHER, AND OF THE SON,	275	29
IN THE NAME OF THIS CHILD, RENOUNCE THE	276	24
HAVING NOW, IN THE NAME OF THIS CHILD, MADE THESE	277	08
BAPTIZE THEM IN THE NAME OF THE FATHER, AND OF THE	279	13
AND GODMOTHERS, NAME THIS CHILD	279	25
BAPTIZE THEE IN THE NAME OF THE FATHER, AND OF THE	279	28
AND SHALL ASK THE WITNESSES THE NAME	R 279	31
BAPTIZE THEE IN THE NAME OF THE FATHER, AND OF THE	281	21
WITH WATER, IN THE NAME OF THE FATHER, AND OF THE	R 282	09
BAPTIZE THEE IN THE NAME OF THE FATHER, AND OF THE	282	14
THE LOVE OF THY NAME, INCREASE IN US TRUE RELIGION,	283	10
WHAT IS YOUR CHRISTIAN NAME	283	15
MY CHRISTIAN NAME IS --	283	17
WHO GAVE YOU THIS NAME	283	18
GAVE ME THIS NAME IN BAPTISM	283	23
DID PROMISE AND VOW THREE THINGS IN MY NAME	286	18
SHALT NOT TAKE THE NAME OF THE LORD THY GOD IN VAIN	286	20
THAT TAKETH HIS NAME IN VAIN	288	21
TO HONOUR HIS HOLY NAME AND HIS WORD	290	18
BUT UNTO THY NAME BE THE PRAISE	292	20
IS BAPTIZED, IN THE NAME OF THE FATHER, AND OF THE	294	15
PRONOUNCE ABSOLUTION AND BLESSING IN GOD'S NAME	296	18
BAPTIZED IN THE NAME OF THE LORD JESUS	296	24
WAS MADE IN YOUR NAME, AT YOUR BAPTISM	297	07
OUR HELP IS IN THE NAME OF THE LORD	297	09
BLESSED BE THE NAME OF THE LORD	302	14
IN THE NAME OF THE FATHER, AND OF THE SON, AND OF THE	303	06
WHOM WE BLESS IN THY NAME	303	19
TO THE HONOUR AND GLORY OF THY NAME	304	08
AND WIFE, IN THE NAME OF THE FATHER, AND OF THE SON,	305	23
CALLED I UPON THE NAME OF THE LORD	305	30
AND CALL UPON THE NAME OF THE LORD	311	31
AND PRAISE THY NAME, BECAUSE OF THY LOVING-KINDNESS	311	32
HAST MAGNIFIED THY NAME, AND THY WORD, ABOVE ALL	312	21
AND ALL THAT IS WITHIN ME, PRAISE HIS HOLY NAME	314	19
THERE IS NONE OTHER NAME UNDER HEAVEN GIVEN TO MAN,	314	21
BUT ONLY THE NAME OF OUR LORD JESUS CHRIST	315	11
THEREUPON RESTORED, HE MAY BLESS THY HOLY NAME	315	23
BLESSED BE THY NAME THAT THOU DIDST NOT FORSAKE HIM	315	32
TO BLESS THY HOLY NAME FOR ALL THY GOODNESS TOWARDS	319	20
THIS WORLD, IN THE NAME OF GOD THE FATHER ALMIGHTY	319	22
IN THE NAME OF JESUS CHRIST WHO REDEEMED THEE	319	23
IN THE NAME OF THE HOLY GHOST WHO SANCTIFIETH THEE	320	16
UPON THEE), IN THE NAME OF THE FATHER, AND OF THE	322	13
THAT BELIEVE ON THE NAME OF THE SON OF GOD	322	14
MAY BELIEVE ON THE NAME OF THE SON OF GOD	324	15
BLESSED BE THE NAME OF THE LORD	334	27
FAITH OF THY HOLY NAME, MAY HAVE OUR PERFECT	339	29
LITTLE CHILD IN MY NAME RECEIVETH ME	340	18
BLESSED BE THE NAME OF THE LORD	348	27
THEY THAT LOVE THY NAME SHALL BE JOYFUL IN THEE	350	28
I WILL PRAISE THE NAME OF THE LORD MOST HIGH	350	31
EXCELLENT IS THY NAME IN ALL THE WORLD	351	17
EXCELLENT IS THY NAME IN ALL THE WORLD	351	25
WILL I MAKE OF THY NAME, O THOU MOST HIGHEST	351	31
HAST PUT OUT THEIR NAME FOR EVER AND EVER	352	08
THEY THAT KNOW THY NAME WILL PUT THEIR TRUST IN THEE	356	10
I WILL PRAISE THE NAME OF THE LORD MOST HIGHEST	363	06
AND SING PRAISES UNTO THY NAME	364	17
THE NAME OF THE GOD OF JACOB DEFEND THEE	364	24
AND TRIUMPH IN THE NAME OF THE LORD OUR GOD	364	30
WILL REMEMBER THE NAME OF THE LORD OUR GOD	367	16
I WILL DECLARE THY NAME UNTO MY BRETHREN	373	33
UNTO THE LORD THE HONOUR DUE UNTO HIS NAME		

NAME   CONTINUED

	PAGE	LN
BECAUSE WE HAVE HOPED IN HIS HOLY NAME	379	31
LET US MAGNIFY HIS NAME TOGETHER	380	08
HE DIE, AND HIS NAME PERISH	392	09
AND IN THY NAME WILL WE TREAD THEM UNDER THAT RISE UP	395	03
AND WILL PRAISE THY NAME FOR EVER	395	10
HAVE FORGOTTEN THE NAME OF OUR GOD, AND HOLDEN UP OUR	395	34
17 I WILL MAKE THY NAME TO BE REMEMBERED FROM ONE	397	21
ACCORDING TO THY NAME, SO IS THY PRAISE UNTO THE	399	29
I WILL HOPE IN THY NAME, FOR THY SAINTS LIKE IT WELL	405	08
AND PRAISE THY NAME, O LORD	406	15
GIVEN AN HERITAGE UNTO THOSE THAT FEAR THY NAME	413	16
PRAISE UNTO THY NAME, *	413	22
AND LIFT UP MY HANDS IN THY NAME	414	34
SING PRAISES UNTO THE HONOUR OF HIS NAME	417	16
SING OF THEE, AND PRAISE THY NAME	417	21
AND SING PRAISES UNTO HIS NAME	419	16
PRAISE HIM IN HIS NAME JAH, AND REJOICE BEFORE HIM	419	18
I WILL PRAISE THE NAME OF GOD WITH A SONG, *	424	04
THEY THAT LOVE HIS NAME SHALL DWELL THEREIN	424	18
HIS NAME SHALL REMAIN UNDER THE SUN AMONG THE	427	32
17 HIS NAME SHALL ENDURE FOR EVER	427	32
AND BLESSED BE THE NAME OF HIS MAJESTY FOR EVER	428	04
OF THY NAME, EVEN UNTO THE GROUND	430	19
ENEMY BLASPHEME THY NAME FOR EVER	430	28
HOW THE FOOLISH PEOPLE HATH BLASPHEMED THY NAME	431	14
LET THE POOR AND NEEDY GIVE PRAISE UNTO THY NAME	431	21
2 THY NAME ALSO IS SO NIGH	431	32
HIS NAME IS GREAT IN ISRAEL	432	24
THE KINGDOMS THAT HAVE NOT CALLED UPON THY NAME	440	13
FOR THE GLORY OF THY NAME	440	19
O LET US LIVE, AND WE SHALL CALL UPON THY NAME	442	08
AND THAT THE NAME OF ISRAEL MAY BE NO MORE IN	444	12
THAT THEY MAY SEEK THY NAME	445	05
THAT THOU, WHOSE NAME IS JEHOVAH, *	445	08
AND SHALL GLORIFY THY NAME	447	22
THAT I MAY FEAR THY NAME	447	27
AND WILL PRAISE THY NAME FOR EVERMORE	447	29
TABOR AND HERMON SHALL REJOICE IN THY NAME	450	32
17 THEIR DELIGHT SHALL BE DAILY IN THY NAME	451	06
AND IN MY NAME SHALL HIS HORN BE EXALTED	451	24
BECAUSE HE HATH KNOWN MY NAME	455	25
PRAISES UNTO THY NAME, O MOST HIGHEST	455	33
2 SING UNTO THE LORD, AND PRAISE HIS NAME	460	02
UNTO THE LORD THE HONOUR DUE UNTO HIS NAME	460	15
THANKS UNTO THY NAME, *	462	20
AND SAMUEL AMONG SUCH AS CALL UPON HIS NAME	462	28
BE THANKFUL UNTO HIM, AND SPEAK GOOD OF HIS NAME	463	13
SHALL FEAR THY NAME, O LORD	465	09
MAY DECLARE THE NAME OF THE LORD IN SION, *	465	22
AND ALL THAT IS WITHIN ME, PRAISE HIS HOLY NAME	466	09
GIVE THANKS UNTO THE LORD, AND CALL UPON HIS NAME	470	06
3 REJOICE IN HIS HOLY NAME	470	09
UNTO THY HOLY NAME, AND MAKE OUR BOAST OF THY PRAISE	475	32
GENERATION LET HIS NAME BE CLEAN PUT OUT	480	26
O LORD GOD, ACCORDING UNTO THY NAME	481	13
HOLY AND REVEREND IS HIS NAME	483	13
O PRAISE THE NAME OF THE LORD	484	08
2 BLESSED BE THE NAME OF THE LORD *	484	10
3 THE LORD'S NAME IS PRAISED *	484	12
BUT UNTO THY NAME GIVE THE PRAISE	485	11
CALLED I UPON THE NAME OF THE LORD	486	26
AND CALL UPON THE NAME OF THE LORD	487	12
WILL CALL UPON THE NAME OF THE LORD	487	20
BUT IN THE NAME OF THE LORD WILL I DESTROY THEM	488	19
BUT IN THE NAME OF THE LORD WILL I DESTROY THEM	488	21
FOR IN THE NAME OF THE LORD I WILL DESTROY THEM	488	24
THAT COMETH IN THE NAME OF THE LORD	489	19
THOUGHT UPON THY NAME, O LORD, IN THE NIGHT SEASON, *	493	20
AS THOU USEST TO DO UNTO THOSE THAT LOVE THY NAME	499	03
THANKS UNTO THE NAME OF THE LORD	503	15
STANDETH IN THE NAME OF THE LORD, *	504	20
GOOD LUCK IN THE NAME OF THE LORD	507	05
LAUD YE THE NAME OF THE LORD	510	03
PRAISES UNTO HIS NAME, FOR IT IS LOVELY	510	08
13 THY NAME, O LORD, ENDURETH FOR EVER	510	28
AND PRAISE THY NAME, BECAUSE OF THY LOVING-KINDNESS	513	31
HAST MAGNIFIED THY NAME, AND THY WORD, ABOVE ALL	513	32
ENEMIES TAKE THY NAME IN VAIN	515	31
RIGHTEOUS ALSO SHALL GIVE THANKS UNTO THY NAME	517	05
THAT I MAY GIVE THANKS UNTO THY NAME	518	20
I WILL PRAISE THY NAME FOR EVER AND EVER	520	28
AND PRAISE THY NAME FOR EVER AND EVER	520	30
UNTO HIS HOLY NAME FOR EVER AND EVER	521	35
LET THEM PRAISE THE NAME OF THE LORD	524	13
FOR HIS NAME ONLY IS EXCELLENT, AND HIS PRAISE ABOVE	524	28
PRAISE THE NAME OF THE LORD	524	28
LET THEM PRAISE HIS NAME IN THE DANCE	525	07
COME FORTH IN THE NAME OF GOD, AND SHOW WHAT THE	530	25
OF THY CHURCH, AND THE GLORY OF THY HOLY NAME	531	08
TO THE GLORY OF THY NAME, AND THE EDIFICATION OF THY	531	22
IN THE NAME OF THE FATHER, AND OF THE SON, AND OF THE	534	07
COME FORTH IN THE NAME OF GOD, AND SHOW WHAT THE	536	30
OF THY CHURCH, AND THE GLORY OF THY HOLY NAME	537	14
TO THE GLORY OF THY NAME, AND THE EDIFICATION OF THY	537	27
HIS OWN SHEEP BY NAME, AND LEADETH THEM OUT	538	28
EXHORT YOU, IN THE NAME OF OUR LORD JESUS CHRIST,	539	29
WHICH WE, IN THE NAME OF GOD, AND OF HIS CHURCH,	541	28
TO SET FORTH THE ETERNAL PRAISE OF THY HOLY NAME	545	21
CALL UPON THY HOLY NAME, THAT WE MAY CONTINUE TO SHOW	545	28
THY HOLY NAME MAY BE FOR EVER GLORIFIED,	545	33
IN THE NAME OF THE FATHER, AND OF THE SON, AND OF THE	546	14
IN THE NAME OF THE FATHER, AND OF THE SON, AND OF THE	546	21
TO THE GLORY OF THY NAME, AND THE EDIFICATION OF THY	548	05
THEM IN THE NAME OF THE FATHER, AND OF THE SON, AND	552	11

NAME   CONTINUED

IN THE NAME OF GOD, AMEN   552 28
AND TO THE HONOUR, PRAISE, AND GLORY OF THY NAME   553 21
TO THE GLORY OF THY NAME, AND THE EDIFYING AND   553 33
IN THE NAME OF THE FATHER, AND OF THE SON, AND OF THE   558 14
OF THY CHURCH, AND TO THE GLORY OF THY HOLY NAME   560 30
AND GLORY OF THY NAME   561 05
ASSEMBLE IN THY NAME, TO OFFER UP THEIR PRAISES AND   564 32
THIS PLACE TO THE HONOUR OF THY GREAT NAME   565 05
THY PEOPLE IN THY NAME, AND FOR ALL OTHER HOLY   565 10
BLESSED BE THY NAME, O LORD, THAT IT HATH   566 28
TO THE GLORY OF THY BLESSED NAME   566 33
BLESSED BE THY NAME, O LORD GOD, FOR THAT IT HATH   568 06
THY HOLY NAME MAY BE WORSHIPPED IN TRUTH AND   568 10
IN THE NAME AND BEHALF OF -- PARISH (OR   570 27
IN THE NAME OF THE FATHER, AND OF THE SON, AND OF THE   571 02
GLORIFY THY HOLY NAME, AND FINALLY, BY THY MERCY,   571 11
IN HIS PREVAILING NAME AND WORDS, THEN SHALL THE   571 14
GLORY OF THY GREAT NAME, AND THE BENEFIT OF THY HOLY   572 13
WHICH IS CALLED BY THY NAME   572 22
WHAT IS YOUR NAME   577 06
WHO GAVE YOU THIS NAME   577 08
THEY DID PROMISE AND VOW THREE THINGS IN MY NAME   577 14
SHALT NOT TAKE THE NAME OF THE LORD THY GOD IN VAIN   578 35
THAT TAKETH HIS NAME IN VAIN   579 03
TO HONOUR HIS HOLY NAME AND HIS WORD   579 31
IS BAPTIZED, IN THE NAME OF THE FATHER, AND OF THE   581 22
WE BLESS AND MAGNIFY THY GLORIOUS NAME   587 25
IN WHOSE NAME WE OFFER UP THESE OUR IMPERFECT   591 32
IN THE NAME OF THE HOLY SCRIPTURE WE DO UNDERSTAND   603 32
UNTO US ONLY THE NAME OF JESUS CHRIST, WHEREBY MEN   606 35
SAME IN THEIR OWN NAME, BUT IN CHRIST'S, AND DO   608 11

NAME'S

US FOR THY NAME'S SAKE   058 26
FOR THY NAME'S SAKE   062 04
SHOWED FOR HIS NAME'S SAKE, WHO HAVE MINISTERED UNTO   072 25
SUFFER FOR MY NAME'S SAKE   230 29
OR LANDS, FOR MY NAME'S SAKE, SHALL RECEIVE AN   231 20
UNTO YOU FOR MY NAME'S SAKE, BECAUSE THEY KNOW NOT   255 21
FOR HIS NAME'S SAKE   338 22
FOR HIS NAME'S SAKE   368 15
10 FOR THY NAME'S SAKE, O LORD, *   370 06
LEAD ME FOR THY NAME'S SAKE   375 28
O GOD, FOR THY NAME'S SAKE, *   406 03
OUR SINS, FOR THY NAME'S SAKE   440 20
THEM FOR HIS NAME'S SAKE, *   473 16
O LORD, FOR THY NAME'S SAKE   519 15
US FOR THY NAME'S SAKE   562 03

NAMED

THE DAYS HEREAFTER NAMED, IMMEDIATELY BEFORE THE   R 008 14
WHICH WAS SO NAMED OF THE ANGEL BEFORE HE WAS   106 21
LET IT NOT BE ONCE NAMED AMONG YOU, AS BECOMETH   129 03
A PLACE WHICH WAS NAMED GETHSEMANE   141 28
AND THERE WAS ONE NAMED BARABBAS, WHICH LAY BOUND   145 14
MAN OF ARIMATHAEA, NAMED JOSEPH, WHO ALSO HIMSELF WAS   162 07
OF THE PHARISEES, NAMED NICODEMUS, A RULER OF THE   187 34
A CERTAIN BEGGAR NAMED LAZARUS, WHICH WAS LAID AT HIS   190 05
AND EARTH IS NAMED, THAT HE WOULD GRANT YOU,   212 13
AT DAMASCUS, NAMED ANANIAS   230 14
IN A VISION A MAN NAMED ANANIAS COMING IN, AND   230 20
A CITY OF GALILEE, NAMED NAZARETH, TO A VIRGIN   236 06
UP ONE OF THEM NAMED AGABUS, AND SIGNIFIED BY THE   241 16
UP ONE OF THEM NAMED AGABUS, AND SIGNIFIED BY THE   246 25
HE SAW A MAN, NAMED MATTHEW, SITTING AT THE RECEIPT   251 13
OF THE PHARISEES, NAMED NICODEMUS, A RULER OF THE   275 05
THE WHOLE FAMILY IN HEAVEN AND EARTH IS NAMED   281 09
OR PERSON) BEING NAMED BY SOME ONE WHO IS PRESENT,   R 281 19

NAMELY

ALL SUCH PRAYERS, NAMELY, THAT 'RULERS MAY HAVE   VI 19
IN THIS SAYING, NAMELY, THOU SHALT LOVE THY NEIGHBOUR   090 28
13 NAMELY, WHILE THEY SAY DAILY UNTO ME, *   393 29
18 NAMELY, HOW THOU DOST SET THEM IN SLIPPERY PLACES,   429 12

NAMES

THE NUMBER OF NAMES TOGETHER WERE ABOUT AN HUNDRED   234 07
MENTION OF THEIR NAMES WITHIN MY LIPS   357 30
AND CALL THE LANDS AFTER THEIR OWN NAMES   400 29
AND CALLETH THEM ALL BY THEIR NAMES   523 03
THE NAMES OF ALL SUCH PERSONS WITHIN HIS   R 583 07

NAMING

AND THEN, NAMING THE CHILD AFTER THEM, HE SHALL DIP   R 279 26

NAPHTHALI

PRINCES OF ZEBULON, AND THE PRINCES OF NAPHTHALI   421 10

NAPKIN

AND THE NAPKIN, THAT WAS ABOUT HIS HEAD, NOT   164 23

NATION

WE COMMEND THIS NATION TO THY MERCIFUL CARE, THAT   018 08
UPON THIS NATION AND PEOPLE   050 24
PERVERTING THE NATION, AND FORBIDDING TO GIVE TRIBUTE   152 29
BUT IN EVERY NATION HE THAT FEARETH HIM, AND WORKETH   166 13

NATION   CONTINUED

OUT OF EVERY NATION UNDER HEAVEN   180 25
BUT IN EVERY NATION HE THAT FEARETH HIM, AND WORKETH   183 31
AND BY A FOOLISH NATION I WILL ANGER YOU   227 18
WENT FROM ONE NATION TO ANOTHER, *   470 28
20 HE HATH NOT DEALT SO WITH ANY NATION   524 02

NATIONAL

PARTICULAR OR NATIONAL CHURCH HATH AUTHORITY TO   609 42

NATIONS

THY SAVING HEALTH UNTO ALL NATIONS   018 29
THY SAVING HEALTH AMONG ALL NATIONS   028 20
O LET THE NATIONS REJOICE AND BE GLAD   028 23
AND GOVERN THE NATIONS UPON EARTH   028 24
THY SAVING HEALTH UNTO ALL NATIONS   032 29
PRAISE AMONG THE NATIONS OF THE EARTH   036 21
OF ONE BLOOD ALL NATIONS OF MEN FOR TO DWELL ON THE   038 05
BRING THE NATIONS INTO THY FOLD, POUR OUT THY SPIRIT   038 09
AMONG MEN AND NATIONS, TO THE GLORY OF THY HOLY NAME   044 13
THE NATIONS OF THE WORLD INTO THE WAY OF   044 28
TO GIVE TO ALL NATIONS UNITY, PEACE, AND CONCORD   056 08
CONSTANTLY TO PREACH THE GOSPEL UNTO ALL NATIONS   078 30
DISTRESS OF NATIONS, WITH PERPLEXITY   093 06
NAME AMONG ALL NATIONS, BEGINNING AT JERUSALEM   170 15
OF ALL NATIONS, AND KINDREDS, AND PEOPLES,   256 24
AND BEFORE HIM SHALL BE GATHERED ALL NATIONS   258 31
DISCIPLES OF ALL NATIONS, BAPTIZING THEM IN THE NAME   275 28
GO TEACH ALL NATIONS, AND BAPTIZE THEM IN THE NAME OF   279 13
AMONG THE NATIONS, AND I WILL BE EXALTED IN THE   327 15
GIVE THEE THE NATIONS FOR THINE INHERITANCE, *   346 12
AND THOU SHALT MAKE ME THE HEAD OF THE NATIONS   362 26
KINDREDS OF THE NATIONS SHALL WORSHIP BEFORE HIM   367 30
AND HE IS THE GOVERNOR AMONG THE NATIONS   367 32
DESTROYED THE NATIONS, AND MADE THY PEOPLE TO   394 26
AMONG THE NATIONS, *   395 22
6 THE NATIONS MAKE MUCH ADO, AND THE KINGDOMS ARE   398 04
AMONG THE NATIONS, AND I WILL BE EXALTED IN THE   398 15
AND THE NATIONS UNDER OUR FEET   398 25
8 GOD REIGNETH OVER THE NATIONS   399 04
AND I WILL SING UNTO THEE AMONG THE NATIONS   409 34
HIS EYES BEHOLD THE NATIONS   417 27
THY SAVING HEALTH AMONG ALL NATIONS   418 27
4 O LET THE NATIONS REJOICE AND BE GLAD   418 30
AND GOVERN THE NATIONS UPON EARTH   418 31
ALL NATIONS SHALL DO HIM SERVICE   427 18
AND ALL THE NATIONS SHALL PRAISE HIM   427 34
SHALT TAKE ALL NATIONS TO THINE INHERITANCE   444 03
9 ALL NATIONS WHOM THOU HAST MADE SHALL COME AND   447 21
15 THE NATIONS SHALL FEAR THY NAME, O LORD   465 09
SEED AMONG THE NATIONS, *   474 23
I WILL SING PRAISES UNTO THEE AMONG THE NATIONS   479 10
HIGH ABOVE ALL NATIONS, *   484 14
O PRAISE THE LORD, ALL YE NATIONS   487 25
10 ALL NATIONS COMPASSED ME ROUND ABOUT   488 18
HE SMOTE DIVERS NATIONS, *   510 23
AVENGED OF THE NATIONS, *   525 15
AND TEACH ALL NATIONS, BAPTIZING THEM IN THE NAME OF   552 11
THE LIGHT OF THY GOSPEL SHINE UPON ALL NATIONS   590 23

NATIVITY

BY THY HOLY NATIVITY AND CIRCUMCISION   055 07

NATURAL

BEHOLDING HIS NATURAL FACE IN A GLASS   176 08
BEHOLDING HIS NATURAL FACE IN A GLASS   265 31
IT IS SOWN A NATURAL BODY   329 22
THERE IS A NATURAL BODY, AND THERE IS A SPIRITUAL   329 23
BUT THAT WHICH IS NATURAL   329 26
AND SENSE OF THE NATURAL DECENCY OF THINGS, HAVE   564 14
BY HIS OWN NATURAL STRENGTH AND GOOD WORKS, TO FAITH, 604 43

NATURALLY

THAT NATURALLY IS ENGENDERED OF THE OFFSPRING OF   604 31

NATURE

IN THEIR OWN NATURE INDIFFERENT, AND ALTERABLE,   V 15
O GOD, WHOSE NATURE AND PROPERTY IS EVER TO HAVE   063 09
SON TO TAKE OUR NATURE UPON HIM, AND AS AT THIS TIME   096 14
SON TO TAKE OUR NATURE UPON HIM, AND AS AT THIS TIME   104 06
FRAILTY OF OUR NATURE WE CANNOT ALWAYS STAND UPRIGHT   114 06
OF OUR MORTAL NATURE, WE CAN DO NO GOOD THING WITHOUT 189 02
THAT WHICH BY NATURE HE CANNOT HAVE   274 03
FOR BEING BY NATURE BORN IN SIN, AND THE CHILDREN OF   581 25
CORRUPTION OF OUR NATURE, AND THE MANIFOLD   588 13
TOOK MAN'S NATURE IN THE WOMB OF THE BLESSED VIRGIN,   603 11
APPERTAINING TO THE PERFECTION OF MAN'S NATURE   603 22
CORRUPTION OF THE NATURE OF EVERY MAN, THAT NATURALLY 604 30
AND IS OF HIS OWN NATURE INCLINED TO EVIL, SO THAT   604 32
THIS INFECTION OF NATURE DOTH REMAIN, YEA IN THEM   604 35
OF ITSELF THE NATURE OF SIN   604 40
BUT THEY HAVE THE NATURE OF SIN   605 22
THE TRUTH OF OUR NATURE WAS MADE LIKE UNTO US IN ALL   605 31
ACCORDING TO THAT LAW, AND THE LIGHT OF NATURE   606 34
A LOCAL AND CIVIL NATURE, AND IS PROVIDED   R 607 11
YET HAVE NOT LIKE NATURE OF SACRAMENTS WITH BAPTISM,   607 42
OVERTHROWETH THE NATURE OF A SACRAMENT, AND HATH   608 42

NATURES

AND PERFECT NATURES, THAT IS TO SAY, THE GODHEAD AND   603 12

NAUGHTINESS

OF NAUGHTINESS, AND RECEIVE WITH MEEKNESS THE   175 03
OF NAUGHTINESS, AND RECEIVE WITH MEEKNESS THE   265 26

NAUGHTY

MIDST OF THIS NAUGHTY WORLD, THAT THEY MAY BE SAVED   540 03

NAVY

OUR COUNTRY'S NAVY, AND ALL WHO SERVE THEREIN   042 06

NAY

BUT HE SAID, NAY   116 27
AND HE SAID, NAY, FATHER ABRAHAM   190 27
NAY, IN ALL THESE THINGS WE ARE MORE THAN CONQUERORS   331 08

NAZARENE

HE SHALL BE CALLED A NAZARENE   107 23

NAZARETH

THE PROPHET OF NAZARETH OF GALILEE   091 32
OF THE CITY OF NAZARETH, INTO JUDAEA, UNTO THE CITY   099 02
AND HE CAME AND DWELT IN A CITY CALLED NAZARETH   107 22
AND CAME TO NAZARETH, AND WAS SUBJECT UNTO THEM   111 05
JESUS CAME FROM NAZARETH OF GALILEE, AND WAS BAPTIZED   112 19
THAT JESUS OF NAZARETH PASSETH BY   123 29
AND THOU ALSO WAST WITH JESUS OF NAZARETH   143 26
JESUS OF NAZARETH THE KING OF THE JEWS   160 02
SEEK JESUS OF NAZARETH, WHICH WAS CRUCIFIED   165 29
JESUS OF NAZARETH WITH THE HOLY GHOST AND WITH POWER   166 19
JESUS OF NAZARETH, WHICH WAS A PROPHET MIGHTY IN DEED   167 16
JESUS OF NAZARETH WITH THE HOLY GHOST AND WITH POWER   184 07
TO THEIR OWN CITY NAZARETH   233 25
NAMED NAZARETH, TO A VIRGIN ESPOUSED TO A   236 06
JESUS CAME TO NAZARETH, WHERE HE HAD BEEN BROUGHT UP   261 11

NEAR

DRAWING NEAR WITH PENITENT AND FAITHFUL HEARTS,   043 23
OR THE NEAR APPROACH OF DEATH, ESPECIALLY NEED   048 09
DRAW NEAR WITH FAITH, AND TAKE THIS HOLY SACRAMENT TO   075 12
WHEN HE WAS COME NEAR, HE ASKED HIM, SAYING, WHAT   123 34
HE IS NEAR THAT JUSTIFIETH ME   144 18
LET HIM COME NEAR TO ME   144 20
AND DREW NEAR UNTO JESUS TO KISS HIM   150 28
LET US DRAW NEAR WITH A TRUE HEART IN FULL ASSURANCE   158 20
JESUS HIMSELF DREW NEAR, AND WENT WITH THEM   167 08
THEN DREW NEAR UNTO HIM ALL THE PUBLICANS AND SINNERS   193 14
WHEN HE WAS COME NEAR, HE BEHELD THE CITY, AND WEPT   204 06
HE CAME NEAR DAMASCUS   229 30
AND I WILL COME NEAR TO YOU TO JUDGMENT   232 15
IN HIS CHAIR NEAR TO THE HOLY TABLE, THE PEOPLE ALL   R 296 06
IN HIS CHAIR NEAR TO THE HOLY TABLE, SUCH AS DESIRE   R 530 08
IN HIS CHAIR NEAR TO THE HOLY TABLE, ALL THOSE WHO   R 536 07
IN HIS CHAIR, NEAR THE HOLY TABLE   R 552 19
SHALL DRAW NEAR TO THEE IN THIS PLACE, TO GIVE THEE   566 14

NEARER

IS OUR SALVATION NEARER THAN WHEN WE BELIEVED   091 02
AND WE, DRAWING NEARER TO THEE, MAY BE BOUND TOGETHER   597 04

NECESSARIES

ALL OTHER NECESSARIES, FOR THEM, FOR US, AND THY   035 18

NECESSARILY

WAS NECESSARILY INCLUDED   VI 09
SPRING OUT NECESSARILY OF A TRUE AND LIVELY FAITH   605 14

NECESSARY

SEEM EITHER NECESSARY OR EXPEDIENT   V 20
REQUISITE AND NECESSARY, AS WELL FOR THE BODY AS THE   006 08
REQUISITE AND NECESSARY, AS WELL FOR THE BODY AS THE   023 17
ALL THINGS NECESSARY TO THEIR BODILY SUSTENANCE   040 17
WHICH BECAME NECESSARY IN THE PRAYERS FOR OUR CIVIL   VI 16
WAS THEREFORE NECESSARY THAT THE PATTERNS OF THINGS   147 27
IT WAS NECESSARY THAT THE WORD OF GOD SHOULD   260 31
AS GENERALLY NECESSARY TO SALVATION   292 07
AND ALL THINGS NECESSARY BEING PREPARED, THE MINISTER   R 321 14
HOW NECESSARY THAT ORDER IS IN THE CHURCH OF CHRIST,   R 530 05
REQUIRED AS NECESSARY FOR ETERNAL SALVATION THROUGH   533 03
HOW NECESSARY THAT ORDER IS IN THE CHURCH OF CHRIST,   R 536 05
REQUIRED AS NECESSARY FOR ETERNAL SALVATION THROUGH   542 03
AS NECESSARY TO ETERNAL SALVATION, BUT THAT   542 06
REQUIRED AS NECESSARY FOR ETERNAL SALVATION THROUGH   554 21
AS NECESSARY TO ETERNAL SALVATION, BUT THAT   554 25
REQUISITE AND NECESSARY, AS WELL FOR THE BODY AS FOR   566 18
CASE OF THEIR NECESSARY ABSENCE, TWO MEMBERS OF THE   R 570 07
AS GENERALLY NECESSARY TO SALVATION   581 09
SEE TO BE NECESSARY AND CONVENIENT TO US, WE HUMBLY   589 06
ALL THINGS NECESSARY TO SALVATION   603 29
REQUISITE OR NECESSARY TO SALVATION   603 32
IT IS NOT NECESSARY THAT TRADITIONS AND CEREMONIES BE   609 32

NECESSARY   CONTINUED

AND NECESSARY FOR THESE TIMES, AS DOTH THE   610 06
ALL THINGS NECESSARY TO SUCH CONSECRATION AND   610 33

NECESSITIES

ACCORDING TO THEIR SEVERAL NECESSITIES   019 09
ACCORDING TO THEIR SEVERAL NECESSITIES   033 07
KNOWEST OUR NECESSITIES BEFORE WE ASK, AND OUR   049 30
DANGERS AND NECESSITIES STRETCH FORTH THY RIGHT HAND   112 27
IN NECESSITIES, IN DISTRESSES, IN STRIPES, IN   126 10
UNTO MY NECESSITIES, AND TO THEM THAT WERE WITH ME   551 07
TO THEM ACCORDING TO THEIR SEVERAL NECESSITIES   591 04

NECESSITY

DECLARED THE NECESSITY AND EXPEDIENCY OF OCCASIONAL   V 22
IN THIS OUR NECESSITY, SUCH MODERATE RAIN AND   040 18
RELIEF OF OUR NECESSITY, AND TO THE SETTING FORTH OF   050 12
ARE IN DANGER, NECESSITY, AND TRIBULATION   056 28
NOT GRUDGINGLY, OR OF NECESSITY   072 19
THYSELF A GOOD REWARD IN THE DAY OF NECESSITY   072 35
TO THE NECESSITY OF SAINTS   111 27
MUST ALSO OF NECESSITY BE THE DEATH OF THE TESTATOR   147 14
FOR OF NECESSITY HE MUST RELEASE ONE UNTO THEM AT THE   153 28
IF NECESSITY SO REQUIRE, BAPTISM MAY BE ADMINISTERED   R 273 06
NECESSITY MAY REQUIRE, THEN THE FOLLOWING   R 281 17
IN NEED AND NECESSITY HAVE RIGHT   443 23
OUGHT OF NECESSITY TO BE RECEIVED IN ANY   604 21
THINGS THAT OF NECESSITY ARE REQUISITE TO THE SAME   606 40
BELIEVED FOR NECESSITY OF SALVATION   607 09

NECK

AND FELL ON HIS NECK, AND KISSED HIM   202 18
HANGED ABOUT HIS NECK, AND THAT HE WERE DROWNED IN   252 32
AND SPEAK NOT WITH A STIFF NECK   432 09

NEED

AND FIND GRACE TO HELP IN TIME OF NEED   005 09
UPON THEE, AND GRANT US THY HELP IN THIS OUR NEED   041 22
GOD OF ALL COMFORT, OUR ONLY HELP IN TIME OF NEED   045 13
ESPECIALLY NEED OUR PRAYERS   048 10
HIS BROTHER HAVE NEED, AND SHUTTETH UP HIS COMPASSION   072 30
IN TROUBLE, SORROW, NEED, SICKNESS, OR ANY OTHER   074 32
THE LORD HATH NEED OF THEM   091 17
AND SAITH, WHAT NEED WE ANY FURTHER WITNESSES   143 17
AND THEY SAID, WHAT NEED WE ANY FURTHER WITNESS   151 35
HIS BROTHER HAVE NEED, AND SHUTTETH UP HIS BOWELS OF   191 19
JUST PERSONS, WHICH NEED NO REPENTANCE   193 27
THAT YE HAVE NEED OF ALL THESE THINGS   211 30
FOR YE HAVE NEED OF PATIENCE, THAT, AFTER YE HAVE   228 15
THEY THAT BE WHOLE NEED NOT A PHYSICIAN, BUT THEY   251 20
THAT YE HAVE NEED OF ALL THESE THINGS   266 28
THE AID OF ALL WHO NEED, THE HELPER OF ALL WHO FLEE   274 09
GOD OF ALL COMFORT, OUR ONLY HELP IN TIME OF NEED   316 07
THAT SUCH AS ARE IN NEED AND NECESSITY HAVE RIGHT   443 23
YE OUGHT, AND HAVE NEED, TO PRAY EARNESTLY FOR HIS   540 32
YOUR CURES, AS NEED SHALL REQUIRE, AND OCCASION SHALL   542 24

NEEDEST

ALL THINGS, AND NEEDEST NOT THAT ANY MAN SHOULD ASK   177 02

NEEDETH

THAT IS WASHED NEEDETH NOT SAVE TO WASH HIS FEET, BUT   156 09
THAT HE MAY HAVE TO GIVE TO HIM THAT NEEDETH   216 22
HE WILL RISE AND GIVE HIM AS MANY AS HE NEEDETH   263 03

NEEDFUL

WHATSOEVER IS NEEDFUL FOR THE LIFE OF MAN, AND HAST   039 26
THY FACE IN THE NEEDFUL TIME OF TROUBLE   353 04
THINGS THAT ARE NEEDFUL BOTH FOR OUR SOULS AND   580 33

NEEDLEWORK

BE BROUGHT UNTO THE KING IN RAIMENT OF NEEDLEWORK   397 15

NEEDS

WHEREFORE YE MUST NEEDS BE SUBJECT, NOT ONLY FOR   114 22
IF I MUST NEEDS GLORY, I WILL GLORY OF THE THINGS   121 13
AND I MUST NEEDS GO AND SEE IT   192 08
SCRIPTURE MUST NEEDS HAVE BEEN FULFILLED, WHICH THE   234 09
FOR IT MUST NEEDS BE THAT OFFENCES COME   252 34
US MINDFUL OF THE NEEDS OF OTHERS   600 18

NEEDY

THAT THE POOR AND NEEDY MAY GIVE THANKS UNTO THY   040 12
TO THE SUFFERING, THE FRIENDLESS, AND THE NEEDY   044 05
SAKE OF THE NEEDY, *   355 16
DOWN THE POOR AND NEEDY, AND TO SLAY SUCH AS BE   385 23
20 AS FOR ME, I AM POOR AND NEEDY   391 24
BLESSED IS HE THAT CONSIDERETH THE POOR AND NEEDY   391 30
THE NEEDY ALSO, AND HIM THAT HATH NO HELPER   427 21
TO THE SIMPLE AND NEEDY, *   427 22
LET THE POOR AND NEEDY GIVE PRAISE UNTO THY NAME   431 21
SAKE TO POOR AND NEEDY PEOPLE, AND TO ALL STRANGERS   555 24
WE, THY NEEDY CREATURES, RENDER THEE OUR HUMBLE   587 20

NEGLECT

IF YE SHALL NEGLECT TO DO, CONSIDER WITH YOURSELVES   089 14

NEGLIGENCE

OF YOUR NEGLIGENCE, YE KNOW THE GREATNESS OF THE   540 12

NEGLIGENCES

OUR SINS, NEGLIGENCES, AND IGNORANCES   057 15

NEGLIGENT

SEE THE PEOPLE NEGLIGENT TO COME TO THE HOLY   R 088 10

NEIGHBOUR

NOT BEAR FALSE WITNESS AGAINST THY NEIGHBOUR   069 16
SHALT LOVE THY NEIGHBOUR AS THYSELF   069 30
SHALT LOVE THY NEIGHBOUR AS THYSELF   090 29
LOVE WORKETH NO ILL TO HIS NEIGHBOUR   090 30
AND THY NEIGHBOUR AS THYSELF   208 17
SAID UNTO JESUS, AND WHO IS MY NEIGHBOUR   208 20
THOU, WAS NEIGHBOUR UNTO HIM THAT FELL AMONG THE   209 03
SHALT LOVE THY NEIGHBOUR AS THYSELF   215 14
SPEAK EVERY MAN TRUTH WITH HIS NEIGHBOUR   216 17
SHALT LOVE THY NEIGHBOUR, AND HATE THINE ENEMY   264 04
NOT BEAR FALSE WITNESS AGAINST THY NEIGHBOUR   287 15
SHALT LOVE THY NEIGHBOUR AS THYSELF   288 09
AND MY DUTY TOWARDS MY NEIGHBOUR   288 13
WHAT IS YOUR DUTY TOWARDS YOUR NEIGHBOUR   288 24
TOWARDS MY NEIGHBOUR IS TO LOVE HIM AS MYSELF, AND TO   288 24
THEY TALK OF VANITY EVERY ONE WITH HIS NEIGHBOUR   355 09
AND HATH NOT SLANDERED HIS NEIGHBOUR   357 11
EVIL TO HIS NEIGHBOUR, *   357 11
UNTO HIS NEIGHBOUR, AND DISAPPOINTETH HIM NOT, *   357 15
UNTO VANITY, NOR SWORN TO DECEIVE HIS NEIGHBOUR   369 04
SLANDERETH HIS NEIGHBOUR, *   463 26
UNTO VANITY, NOR SWORN TO DECEIVE HIS NEIGHBOUR   563 19
NOT BEAR FALSE WITNESS AGAINST THY NEIGHBOUR   579 18
TOWARDS GOD, AND MY DUTY TOWARDS MY NEIGHBOUR   579 25
WHAT IS THY DUTY TOWARDS THY NEIGHBOUR   579 33
TOWARDS MY NEIGHBOUR IS TO LOVE HIM AS MYSELF, AND TO   579 34

NEIGHBOUR'S

COVET THY NEIGHBOUR'S WIFE, NOR HIS SERVANT, NOR HIS   069 20
THY NEIGHBOUR'S HOUSE, THOU SHALT NOT COVET THY   069 20
COVET THY NEIGHBOUR'S HOUSE, THOU SHALT NOT COVET THY   287 20
COVET THY NEIGHBOUR'S WIFE, NOR HIS SERVANT, NOR HIS   287 20
COVET THY NEIGHBOUR'S HOUSE, THOU SHALT NOT COVET THY   579 20
COVET THY NEIGHBOUR'S WIFE, NOR HIS SERVANT, NOR HIS   579 21

NEIGHBOURS

WITH YOUR NEIGHBOURS, AND INTEND TO LEAD A NEW LIFE,   075 09
WRONG TO HIS NEIGHBOURS BY WORD OR DEED, SO THAT THE   R 085 02
BUT ALSO AGAINST YOUR NEIGHBOURS   087 23
FRIENDS AND NEIGHBOURS, SAYING UNTO THEM, REJOICE   193 23
AND HER NEIGHBOURS TOGETHER, SAYING, REJOICE WITH ME   193 31
AND HER NEIGHBOURS AND HER COUSINS HEARD HOW THE LORD   243 14
WITH THEIR FRIENDS AND NEIGHBOURS   R 300 05
TO THEIR NEIGHBOURS, BUT IMAGINE MISCHIEF IN THEIR   373 12
MINE ENEMIES, BUT ESPECIALLY AMONG MY NEIGHBOURS   376 16
LOVERS AND MY NEIGHBOURS DID STAND LOOKING UPON MY   388 12
OF OUR NEIGHBOURS, *   395 19
WHEREWITH OUR NEIGHBOURS HAVE BLASPHEMED THEE, *   440 29
UNTO OUR NEIGHBOURS, *   441 14
AND HE IS BECOME A REPROACH TO HIS NEIGHBOURS   452 23
UPON ALL OUR RELATIONS, FRIENDS, AND NEIGHBOURS   590 31

NEITHER

INTO NO SIN, NEITHER RUN INTO ANY KIND OF DANGER   017 16
NEITHER HAVE WE OBEYED THE VOICE OF THE LORD OUR GOD,   022 07
NEITHER TAKE THOU VENGEANCE OF OUR SINS   054 14
NEITHER REWARD US ACCORDING TO OUR INIQUITIES   058 13
IN HEAVEN, WHERE NEITHER MOTH NOR RUST DOTH CORRUPT,   072 10
NOR ELIAS, NEITHER THAT PROPHET   096 02
NOT SEEN HIM, NEITHER KNOWN HIM   117 25
HID FROM THEM, NEITHER KNEW THEY THE THINGS WHICH   123 25
IN HEAVEN, WHERE NEITHER MOTH NOR RUST DOTH CORRUPT,   125 19
NEITHER FILTHINESS, NOR FOOLISH TALKING, NOR JESTING,   129 04
NEITHER BY THE BLOOD OF GOATS AND CALVES, BUT BY HIS   132 12
WERE HEAVY,) NEITHER WIST THEY WHAT TO ANSWER HIM   142 09
BUT NEITHER SO DID THEIR WITNESS AGREE TOGETHER   143 08
I KNOW NOT, NEITHER UNDERSTAND I WHAT THOU SAYEST   143 26
NOT REBELLIOUS, NEITHER TURNED AWAY BACK   144 13
WHEREUPON NEITHER THE FIRST TESTAMENT WAS DEDICATED   147 17
WOULDEST NOT, NEITHER HADST PLEASURE THEREIN   157 30
WITH OLD LEAVEN, NEITHER WITH THE LEAVEN OF MALICE   162 32
WITH OLD LEAVEN, NEITHER WITH THE LEAVEN OF MALICE   165 14
NEITHER SAID THEY ANY THING TO ANY MAN   166 03
WHO DID NO SIN, NEITHER WAS GUILE FOUND IN HIS MOUTH   172 12
NO VARIABLENESS, NEITHER SHADOW OF TURNING   174 28
SEETH HIM NOT, NEITHER KNOWETH HIM   181 18
BE TROUBLED, NEITHER LET IT BE AFRAID   182 02
THE LIGHT, NEITHER COMETH TO THE LIGHT, LEST HIS   185 08
NEITHER CAN THEY PASS TO US, THAT WOULD COME FROM   190 21
THE PROPHETS, NEITHER WILL THEY BE PERSUADED, THOUGH   190 30
LOVE IN WORD, NEITHER IN TONGUE   191 22
OF THEIR TERROR, NEITHER BE TROUBLED   196 03
EVIL FRUIT, NEITHER CAN A CORRUPT TREE BRING FORTH   200 20
NEITHER BE YE IDOLATERS, AS WERE SOME OF THEM   201 14

NEITHER   CONTINUED

NEITHER LET US COMMIT FORNICATION, AS SOME OF THEM   201 17
NEITHER LET US TEMPT CHRIST, AS SOME OF THEM ALSO   201 19
NEITHER MURMUR YE, AS SOME OF THEM ALSO MURMURED, AND   201 20
DO I SERVE THEE, NEITHER TRANSGRESSED I AT ANY TIME   202 34
FOR NEITHER THEY THEMSELVES WHO ARE CIRCUMCISED KEEP   210 27
IN CHRIST JESUS NEITHER CIRCUMCISION AVAILETH ANY   210 32
THEY SOW NOT, NEITHER DO THEY REAP, NOR GATHER INTO   211 16
THEY TOIL NOT, NEITHER DO THEY SPIN   211 22
HIM A WORD, NEITHER DURST ANY MAN FROM THAT DAY FORTH   215 23
NEITHER GIVE PLACE TO THE DEVIL   216 19
OF GOD IN TRUTH, NEITHER CAREST THOU FOR ANY MAN   223 02
AND NEITHER DID EAT NOR DRINK   230 13
NEITHER KNOWETH ANY MAN THE FATHER, SAVE THE SON,   235 09
I WILL NOT ASK, NEITHER WILL I TEMPT THE LORD   235 28
NEITHER WAS THEIR PLACE FOUND ANY MORE IN HEAVEN   252 05
CARRY NEITHER PURSE, NOR SCRIP, NOR SHOES   254 17
NOT THE EARTH, NEITHER THE SEA, NOR THE TREES,   256 18
HUNGER NO MORE, NEITHER THIRST ANY MORE   257 12
NEITHER SHALL THE SUN LIGHT ON THEM, NOR ANY HEAT   257 12
TO THE HEATHEN, NEITHER SHALL THE BEAST OF THE LAND   262 15
IN THE LAND, NEITHER BEAR THE SHAME OF THE HEATHEN   262 19
NO VARIABLENESS, NEITHER SHADOW OF TURNING   265 21
THEY SOW NOT, NEITHER DO THEY REAP, NOR GATHER INTO   266 15
THEY TOIL NOT, NEITHER DO THEY SPIN   266 20
LEAVE ME NOT, NEITHER FORSAKE ME, O GOD OF MY   326 26
SHALL NEITHER SLUMBER NOR SLEEP   327 25
NEITHER THE MOON BY NIGHT   327 29
NEITHER DOTH CORRUPTION INHERIT INCORRUPTION   329 34
THAT NEITHER DEATH, NOR LIFE, NOR ANGELS,   331 10
SHALL NEITHER SLUMBER NOR SLEEP   339 09
NEITHER THE MOON BY NIGHT   339 13
HUNGER NO MORE, NEITHER THIRST ANY MORE   341 23
NEITHER SHALL THE SUN LIGHT ON THEM, NOR ANY HEAT   341 24
NEITHER THE SINNERS IN THE CONGREGATION OF THE   345 20
NEITHER SHALL ANY EVIL DWELL WITH THEE   348 08
NEITHER CHASTEN ME IN THY DISPLEASURE   348 33
NEITHER IS GOD IN ALL HIS THOUGHTS   353 12
NEITHER MAKE MENTION OF THEIR NAMES WITHIN MY LIPS   357 29
NEITHER SHALT THOU SUFFER THY HOLY ONE TO SEE   358 11
NEITHER WILL I TURN AGAIN TILL I HAVE DESTROYED THEM   362 12
3 THERE IS NEITHER SPEECH NOR LANGUAGE   363 17
BE CONFOUNDED, NEITHER LET MINE ENEMIES TRIUMPH OVER   369 20
NEITHER WILL I HAVE FELLOWSHIP WITH THE DECEITFUL   371 04
LEAVE ME NOT, NEITHER FORSAKE ME, O GOD OF MY   372 18
ME NOT AWAY, NEITHER DESTROY ME WITH THE UNGODLY AND   373 10
NEITHER IS ANY MIGHTY MAN DELIVERED BY MUCH STRENGTH   379 20
NEITHER SHALL HE DELIVER ANY MAN BY HIS GREAT   379 23
NEITHER LET THEM WINK WITH THEIR EYES, THAT HATE ME   382 35
NEITHER LET THEM SAY, WE HAVE DEVOURED HIM   383 14
NEITHER DOTH HE ABHOR ANY THING THAT IS EVIL   384 02
NEITHER BE THOU ENVIOUS AGAINST THE EVIL DOERS   384 25
NEITHER CHASTEN ME IN THY HEAVY DISPLEASURE   387 22
NEITHER IS THERE ANY REST IN MY BONES, BY REASON OF   387 26
NEITHER WAS IT THEIR OWN ARM THAT HELPED THEM   394 28
NEITHER OUR STEPS GONE OUT OF THY WAY   395 30
NEITHER SHALL HIS POMP FOLLOW HIM   401 10
13 NEITHER WAS IT MINE ADVERSARY THAT DID MAGNIFY   407 13
DROWN ME, NEITHER LET THE DEEP SWALLOW ME UP   422 35
WAS NO MAN, NEITHER FOUND I ANY TO COMFORT ME   423 15
NEITHER ARE THEY PLAGUED LIKE OTHER MEN   428 18
PROMOTION COMETH NEITHER FROM THE EAST, NOR FROM THE   432 10
NEITHER CONTINUED THEY STEDFAST IN HIS COVENANT   437 12
NEITHER SHALT THOU WORSHIP ANY OTHER GOD   442 31
5 THEY KNOW NOT, NEITHER DO THEY UNDERSTAND, BUT WALK   443 26
NEITHER SHALL ANY PLAGUE COME NIGH THY DWELLING   455 15
NEITHER SHALL THE GOD OF JACOB REGARD IT   457 32
NEITHER WILL HE FORSAKE HIS INHERITANCE   458 14
NEITHER KEEPETH HE HIS ANGER FOR EVER   466 25
NEITHER TURN AGAIN TO COVER THE EARTH   468 12
IN EGYPT, NEITHER KEPT THEY THY GREAT GOODNESS IN   473 13
34 NEITHER DESTROYED THEY THE HEATHEN, *   475 04
NEITHER SPEAK THEY THROUGH THEIR THROAT   485 25
NEITHER ALL THEY THAT GO DOWN INTO SILENCE   486 12
SHALL NEITHER SLUMBER NOR SLEEP   502 28
NEITHER THE MOON BY NIGHT   503 02
NEITHER HE THAT BINDETH UP THE SHEAVES HIS BOSOM   507 02
NEITHER THE TEMPLES OF MY HEAD TO TAKE ANY REST   508 11
NEITHER IS THERE ANY BREATH IN THEIR MOUTHS   511 04
WORK WICKEDNESS, NEITHER LET ME EAT OF SUCH THINGS AS   517 17
NEITHER DELIGHTETH HE IN ANY MAN'S LEGS   523 16
NEITHER HAVE THE HEATHEN KNOWLEDGE OF HIS LAWS   524 02
TO BEWARE THAT NEITHER YOU YOURSELVES OFFEND, NOR BE   540 29
THINGS MOVE ME, NEITHER COUNT I MY LIFE DEAR UNTO   550 18
NOR CRYING, NEITHER SHALL THERE BE ANY MORE PAIN   567 19
NO MORE DEATH, NEITHER SORROW, NOR CRYING, NEITHER   567 19
INTO NO SIN, NEITHER RUN INTO ANY KIND OF DANGER   592 22
THAT WE MAY NEITHER BEGIN AN ACTION WITHOUT A PURE   594 22
NEITHER DO THEY MAKE MEN MEET TO RECEIVE GRACE,   605 19
WORD WRITTEN, NEITHER MAY IT SO EXPOUND ONE PLACE OF   607 05
NEITHER IS THE EFFECT OF CHRIST'S ORDINANCE TAKEN   608 14
NEITHER HATH IT ANY THING THAT, OF ITSELF, IS   610 33

NEST

AND THE SWALLOW A NEST, WHERE SHE MAY LAY HER YOUNG   445 17

NESTS

17 WHEREIN THE BIRDS MAKE THEIR NESTS   468 28

NET

NEVERTHELESS AT THY WORD I WILL LET DOWN THE NET   196 17
AND THEIR NET BRAKE   196 19

NET   CONTINUED

	PAGE	LN
CASTING A NET INTO THE SEA	227	26
IN THE SAME NET WHICH THEY HID PRIVILY IS THEIR FCOT	352	22
WHEN HE GETTETH HIM INTO HIS NET	353	26
FOR HE SHALL PLUCK MY FEET OUT OF THE NET	370	15
5 DRAW ME OUT OF THE NET THAT THEY HAVE LAID PRIVILY	375	29
PRIVILY LAID THEIR NET TO DESTROY ME WITHOUT A CAUSE	381	31
AND HIS NET THAT HE HATH LAID PRIVILY CATCH	382	05
7 THEY HAVE LAID A NET FOR MY FEET, AND PRESSED DOWN	409	26
FOR ME, AND SPREAD A NET ABROAD WITH CURDS	516	18

NETHERMOST

	PAGE	LN
SOUL FROM THE NETHERMOST HELL	447	31

NETS

	PAGE	LN
AND WERE WASHING THEIR NETS	196	10
AND LET DOWN YOUR NETS FOR A DRAUGHT	196	15
LEFT THEIR NETS, AND FOLLOWED HIM	227	28
WITH ZEBEDEE THEIR FATHER, MENDING THEIR NETS	227	31
FALL INTO THEIR OWN NETS TOGETHER, *	517	32

NEVER

	PAGE	LN
LET ME NEVER BE CONFOUNDED	011	12
CHARITY NEVER FAILETH	123	04
HE SHALL NEVER SEE DEATH	133	18
HE SHALL NEVER TASTE OF DEATH	133	21
HE ANSWERED HIM TO NEVER A WORD	135	24
THOU NEVER BAREST RULE OVER THEM	139	29
THAT MAN IF HE HAD NEVER BEEN BORN	141	09
AND THE PAPS WHICH NEVER GAVE SUCK	154	17
AND THE WOMBS THAT NEVER BARE, AND THE PAPS WHICH	154	17
THOU SHALT NEVER WASH MY FEET	156	05
OF THE THINGS, CAN NEVER WITH THOSE SACRIFICES, WHICH	157	16
WHICH CAN NEVER TAKE AWAY SINS	158	05
O LORD, WHO NEVER FAILEST TO HELP AND GOVERN THOSE	191	04
AND YET THOU NEVER GAVEST ME A KID, THAT I MIGHT MAKE	202	35
IN THY SIGHT MAY NEVER BE REPROVED	228	09
HAVE YE NEVER READ, OUT OF THE MOUTH OF BABES AND	260	14
IN ME, SHALL NEVER DIE	324	08
WERE A SHADOW, AND NEVER CONTINUETH IN ONE STAY	332	21
IN ME, SHALL NEVER DIE	338	08
THOU, LORD, HAST NEVER FAILED THEM THAT SEEK THEE	352	09
I SHALL NEVER BE CAST DOWN, *	353	16
AND HE WILL NEVER SEE IT	353	31
SHALL NEVER FALL	357	19
I SAID, I SHALL NEVER BE REMOVED	375	04
LET ME NEVER BE PUT TO CONFUSICN	375	22
AND YET SAW I NEVER THE RIGHTEOUS FORSAKEN, NOR HIS	386	13
AND SHALL NEVER SEE LIGHT	401	15
CHARM HE NEVER SO WISELY	410	18
THE THINGS THAT I NEVER TOOK	422	10
LET ME NEVER BE PUT TO CONFUSION, *	425	05
BE THE PEOPLE NEVER SO IMPATIENT	462	16
BE THE EARTH NEVER SO UNQUIET	462	17
THAT IT NEVER SHOULD MOVE AT ANY TIME	468	02
6 FOR HE SHALL NEVER BE MOVED	483	28
93 I WILL NEVER FORGET THY COMMANDMENTS	496	11
THE PIT, THAT THEY NEVER RISE UP AGAIN	516	30
AND SEE THAT YE NEVER CEASE YOUR LABOUR, YOUR CARE	540	16
THAT IT MAY NEVER BE SPOKEN IN VAIN	547	08
THAT WE MAY NEVER SUFFER THE SUN TO GO DOWN UPON CUR	590	16
STATE THAT WE MAY NEVER BE AFRAID TO DIE	591	30
IN ONE PERSON, NEVER TO BE DIVIDED, WHEREOF IS CNE	603	13
AUTHORITY WAS NEVER ANY DOUBT IN THE CHURCH	603	34

NEVER-FADING

	PAGE	LN
RECEIVE THE NEVER-FADING CROWN OF GLORY	558	31

NEVER-FAILING

	PAGE	LN
WHOSE NEVER-FAILING PROVIDENCE ORDERETH ALL	199	28
TO THY NEVER-FAILING CARE AND LOVE, AND BRING US ALL	342	05
US TO THY NEVER-FAILING CARE AND LOVE, FOR THIS LIFE	597	10

NEW

	PAGE	LN
SHALL BURST OUT WITH NEW WINE	005	23
TAKEN OUT OF THE NEW TESTAMENT, ACCORDING TO THE	R 014	03
SING UNTO THE LORD A NEW SONG	027	04
THEN A LESSON OF THE NEW TESTAMENT, AS IT IS	R 028	05
TO REVIVE IT BY ANY NEW COMMISSION	VI	06
AND INTEND TO LEAD A NEW LIFE, FOLLOWING THE	075	10
THOU HAST CAUSED A NEW LIGHT TC SHINE IN OUR HEARTS,	077	30
IS MY BLOOD OF THE NEW TESTAMENT, WHICH IS	080	26
SUNG AS IT WERE A NEW SONG BEFORE THE THRONE, AND	103	05
POURED UPON US THE NEW LIGHT OF THINE INCARNATE WORD	106	25
AND MAKE IN US NEW AND CONTRITE HEARTS, THAT WE,	124	13
THE MEDIATOR OF THE NEW TESTAMENT, THAT BY MEANS OF	133	04
IS MY BLOOD OF THE NEW TESTAMENT, WHICH IS SHED FCR	141	13
DAY THAT I DRINK IT NEW IN THE KINGDOM OF GOD	141	16
THIS CUP IS THE NEW TESTAMENT IN MY BLOOD, WHICH IS	149	12
THIS CUP IS THE NEW TESTAMENT IN MY BLOOD	152	22
BLOOD OF JESUS, BY A NEW AND LIVING WAY, WHICH HE	158	17
LAID IT IN HIS OWN NEW TOMB, WHICH HE HAD HEWN CUT IN	162	11
THAT YE MAY BE A NEW LUMP, AS YE ARE UNLEAVENED	165	12
MINISTERS OF THE NEW TESTAMENT	206	16
BUT A NEW CREATURE	211	02
THAT YE PUT ON THE NEW MAN, WHICH AFTER GOD IS	216	15
UNTO SIN, AND A NEW BIRTH UNTO RIGHTEOUSNESS	292	25
PURPOSE TO LEAD A NEW LIFE	293	28
SING UNTO THE LORD A NEW SONG	378	23

NEW   CONTINUED

	PAGE	LN
3 AND HE HATH PUT A NEW SONG IN MY MOUTH, *	390	14
THE TRUMPET IN THE NEW MOON, *	442	16
SING UNTO THE LORD A NEW SONG	459	30
SING UNTO THE LORD A NEW SONG	461	25
9 I WILL SING A NEW SONG UNTO THEE, O GOD	520	08
SING UNTO THE LORD A NEW SONG	525	03
ONE OF THEM THE NEW TESTAMENT, SAYING,	R 534	09
SAW THE HOLY CITY, NEW JERUSALEM, COMING DOWN FROM	567	12
THE THRONE SAID, BEHOLD, I MAKE ALL THINGS NEW	567	22
DESIGNATED FOR THE NEW INCUMBENT'S INSTITUTICN,	R 570	02
ATTENDED BY THE NEW INCUMBENT, AND BY THE OTHER	R 570	03
OF THE CHURCH TO THE NEW INCUMBENT, SAYING, IN THE	R 570	26
THEN THE NEW INCUMBENT SHALL SAY, I, A	R 570	31
UNTO SIN, AND A NEW BIRTH UNTO RIGHTEOUSNESS	581	24
PURPOSING TO LEAD A NEW LIFE	582	24
A CHAPTER, FROM THE NEW TESTAMENT	R 592	06
BOOKS OF THE OLD AND NEW TESTAMENT, OF WHOSE	603	33
ALL THE BOOKS OF THE NEW TESTAMENT, AS THEY ARE	604	12
THE OLD TESTAMENT IS NOT CONTRARY TO THE NEW	604	14
BOTH IN THE OLD AND NEW TESTAMENT EVERLASTING LIFE IS	604	15

NEW-BIRTH

	PAGE	LN
OR NEW-BIRTH, WHEREBY, AS BY AN INSTRUMENT, THEY THAT	608	26

NEWBORN

	PAGE	LN
AS NEWBORN BABES, DESIRE THE SINCERE MILK	259	26

NEWLY

	PAGE	LN
WITH WHOM THE NEWLY CONSECRATED BISHOP, WITH CTHERS,	R 559	03

NEWNESS

	PAGE	LN
BE BROUGHT TO NEWNESS OF LIFE	046	29
PLEASE THEE IN NEWNESS OF LIFE, TO THE HONOUR AND	075	29
SHOULD WALK IN NEWNESS OF LIFE	197	14
SIN AND RISE TO NEWNESS OF LIFE	278	20

NEXT

	PAGE	LN
ON -- DAY NEXT I PURPOSE, THROUGH GOD'S	086	28
SERVE UNTO THE NEXT SUNDAY	R 109	26
DAY AFTER, UNTO THE NEXT SUNDAY, EXCEPT UPON THE	R 125	24
NOW THE NEXT DAY, THAT FOLLOWED THE DAY OF THE	162	15
DAY AFTER, UNTO THE NEXT SUNDAY, EXCEPT UPON THE	R 178	31
THE NEXT SABBATH DAY CAME ALMOST THE WHOLE CITY	260	26
AND IN THE NEXT GENERATION LET HIS NAME BE CLEAN PUT	480	25

NICANOR

	PAGE	LN
AND NICANOR, AND TIMON, AND PARMENAS, AND	532	17

NICENE

	PAGE	LN
OR THE CREED COMMONLY CALLED THE NICENE	R 015	32
OR THE CREED COMMONLY CALLED THE NICENE	R 030	03
CALLED THE NICENE, OR ELSE THE APOSTLES' CREED	R 070	29
THAT THE NICENE CREED SHALL BE SAID ON CHRISTMAS DAY,	R 070	31
THE APOSTLES' AND NICENE CREEDS	291	03
THIS IS DONE, THE NICENE CREED SHALL BE SAID, AND THE	R 546	28
SHALL FOLLOW THE NICENE CREED, AND AFTER THAT THE	R 552	16
THE NICENE CREED, AND THAT WHICH IS COMMONLY CALLED	604	25

NICODEMUS

	PAGE	LN
NAMED NICODEMUS, A RULER OF THE JEWS	187	34
NICODEMUS SAITH UNTO HIM, HOW CAN A MAN BE BORN WHEN	188	07
NICODEMUS ANSWERED AND SAID UNTO HIM, HOW CAN THESE	188	17
NAMED NICODEMUS, A RULER OF THE JEWS	275	05
NICODEMUS SAITH UNTO HIM, HOW CAN A MAN BE BORN WHEN	275	11

NICOLAS

	PAGE	LN
AND NICOLAS A PROSELYTE OF ANTIOCH	532	18

NIGH

	PAGE	LN
OUR KING AND SAVIOUR DRAWETH NIGH	R 008	16
THEM THAT ARE FAR OFF AND TO THEM THAT ARE NIGH	038	08
WHEN THEY DREW NIGH UNTO JERUSALEM, AND WERE COME TO	091	11
FOR YOUR REDEMPTION DRAWETH NIGH	093	14
THAT SUMMER IS NOW NIGH AT HAND	093	16
KINGDOM OF GOD IS NIGH AT HAND	093	18
THAT AS HE WAS COME NIGH UNTO JERICHO, A CERTAIN	123	26
A FEAST OF THE JEWS, WAS NIGH	131	26
BREAD DREW NIGH, WHICH IS CALLED THE PASSOVER	148	12
WAS CRUCIFIED WAS NIGH TO THE CITY	160	04
AND THEY DREW NIGH UNTO THE VILLAGE, WHITHER THEY	167	34
AS HE CAME AND DREW NIGH TO THE HOUSE, HE HEARD	202	27
NOW WHEN HE CAME NIGH TO THE GATE OF THE CITY,	212	29
SHALL NOT COME NIGH HIM	378	04
18 THE LORD IS NIGH UNTO THEM THAT ARE OF A CONTRITE	381	04
19 DRAW NIGH UNTO MY SOUL, AND SAVE IT	423	09
2 THY NAME ALSO IS SO NIGH	431	32
HIS SALVATION IS NIGH THEM THAT FEAR HIM	446	25
AND MY LIFE DRAWETH NIGH UNTO THE GRAVE	448	33
IT SHALL NOT COME NIGH THEE	455	10
ANY PLAGUE COME NIGH THY DWELLING	455	16
150 THEY DRAW NIGH THAT OF MALICE PERSECUTE ME,	500	10
151 BE THOU NIGH AT HAND, O LORD	500	12
18 THE LORD IS NIGH UNTO ALL THEM THAT CALL UPON HIM	521	28
FOOT OF PRIDE COME NIGH TO HURT THEM, NOR THE HAND CF	574	14

NIGH CONTINUED

WHEN WE DRAW NIGH TO THEE, FROM COLDNESS OF HEART	594 06

NIGHT

THY TRUTH IN THE NIGHT SEASON	027 31
US FROM ALL PERILS AND DANGERS OF THIS NIGHT	031 28
FOR IN THE NIGHT IN WHICH HE WAS BETRAYED,	080 17
THE NIGHT IS FAR SPENT, THE DAY IS AT HAND	091 03
KEEPING WATCH OVER THEIR FLOCK BY NIGHT	099 11
AND HIS MOTHER BY NIGHT, AND DEPARTED INTO EGYPT	103 21
A NIGHT AND A DAY I HAVE BEEN IN THE DEEP	121 03
ALL YE SHALL BE OFFENDED BECAUSE OF ME THIS NIGHT	141 19
EVEN IN THIS NIGHT, BEFORE THE COCK CROW TWICE,	141 24
DEAR SON, ON THE NIGHT BEFORE HE SUFFERED, DID	152 07
JESUS THE SAME NIGHT IN WHICH HE WAS BETRAYED TOOK	152 17
DISCIPLES COME BY NIGHT, AND STEAL HIM AWAY, AND SAY	162 20
REST DAY AND NIGHT, SAYING, HOLY, HOLY, HOLY,	187 22
CAME TO JESUS BY NIGHT, AND SAID UNTO HIM, RABBI, WE	187 35
TOILED ALL THE NIGHT, AND HAVE TAKEN NOTHING	196 16
AND PRAYERS NIGHT AND DAY	233 21
THE SAME NIGHT PETER WAS SLEEPING BETWEEN TWO	245 10
WHICH ACCUSED THEM BEFORE OUR GOD DAY AND NIGHT	252 13
SERVE HIM DAY AND NIGHT IN HIS TEMPLE	257 10
CAME TO JESUS BY NIGHT, AND SAID UNTO HIM, RABBI,.WE	275 06
CEASED NOT IN THE NIGHT SEASON	311 02
AND IN THE NIGHT I COMMUNE WITH MINE OWN HEART,	311 10
AND AS A WATCH IN THE NIGHT	325 21
NEITHER THE MOON BY NIGHT	327 30
NEITHER THE MOON BY NIGHT	339 14
SERVE HIM DAY AND NIGHT IN HIS TEMPLE	341 21
IN HIS LAW WILL HE EXERCISE HIMSELF DAY AND NIGHT	345 11
EVERY NIGHT WASH I MY BED, AND WATER MY COUCH WITH MY	349 10
CHASTEN ME IN THE NIGHT SEASON	358 05
MINE HEART IN THE NIGHT SEASON	358 21
AND ONE NIGHT CERTIFIETH ANOTHER	363 15
AND IN THE NIGHT SEASON ALSO I TAKE NO REST	366 08
MAY ENDURE FOR A NIGHT, BUT JOY COMETH IN THE	375 03
UPON ME DAY AND NIGHT, *	377 28
MY MEAT DAY AND NIGHT, *	393 04
AND IN THE NIGHT SEASON WILL I SING OF HIM, AND MAKE	393 22
10 DAY AND NIGHT THEY GO ABOUT WITHIN THE WALLS	407 06
IS THINE, AND THE NIGHT IS THINE	431 08
CEASED NOT IN THE NIGHT SEASON	433 20
AND IN THE NIGHT I COMMUNE WITH MINE OWN HEART, AND	433 27
AND ALL THE NIGHT THROUGH WITH A LIGHT OF FIRE	435 29
HAVE CRIED DAY AND NIGHT BEFORE THEE	448 30
AND AS A WATCH IN THE NIGHT	453 26
FOR ANY TERROR BY NIGHT, *	455 05
THY TRUTH IN THE NIGHT SEASON	456 03
20 THOU MAKEST DARKNESS THAT IT MAY BE NIGHT	468 34
GIVE LIGHT IN THE NIGHT SEASON	472 16
O LORD, IN THE NIGHT SEASON, *	493 21
EYES PREVENT THE NIGHT WATCHES	500 06
NEITHER THE MOON BY NIGHT	503 03
2 YE THAT BY NIGHT STAND IN THE HOUSE OF THE LORD,	509 25
9 THE MOON AND THE STARS TO GOVERN THE NIGHT	511 32
THEN SHALL MY NIGHT BE TURNED TO DAY	515 09
WITH THEE, BUT THE NIGHT IS AS CLEAR AS THE DAY	515 11
TO WARN EVERY ONE NIGHT AND DAY WITH TEARS	551 02
THE WHOLE NIGHT IN PRAYER, BEFORE HE CHOSE AND SENT	553 05
DELIVERED US FROM THE DANGERS OF THE PAST NIGHT	587 23
CONTINUE THY GRACIOUS PROTECTION TO US THIS NIGHT	591 26
US FROM ALL PERILS AND DANGERS OF THIS NIGHT	593 15
US PEACE, THIS NIGHT AND EVERMORE	593 21
WE MAY, WHEN THE NIGHT COMETH, REJOICE TO GIVE THEE	594 16
SUPPLICATE THY MERCIFUL PROTECTION ALL THIS NIGHT	595 08

NIGHTS

O YE NIGHTS AND DAYS, BLESS YE THE LORD	012 28
OUR SAKE DIDST FAST FORTY DAYS AND FORTY NIGHTS	125 28
DAYS AND FORTY NIGHTS, HE WAS AFTERWARD AN HUNGRED	126 25

NINE

THE NINETY AND NINE IN THE WILDERNESS, AND GO AFTER	193 19
OVER NINETY AND NINE JUST PERSONS, WHICH NEED NO	193 26
BUT WHERE ARE THE NINE	210 12

NINETY

NOT LEAVE THE NINETY AND NINE IN THE WILDERNESS,	193 19
MORE THAN OVER NINETY AND NINE JUST PERSONS, WHICH	193 26

NINTH

THE SIXTH AND NINTH HOUR, AND DID LIKEWISE	119 23
THE LAND UNTO THE NINTH HOUR	137 16
AND ABOUT THE NINTH HOUR JESUS CRIED WITH A LOUD	137 17
AND AT THE NINTH HOUR JESUS CRIED WITH A LOUD VOICE,	146 27
LAND UNTIL THE NINTH HOUR	146 27
EARTH UNTIL THE NINTH HOUR	155 10

NO

BEFORE THEE, AND AM NO MORE WORTHY TO BE CALLED THY	004 28
AND THERE IS NO HEALTH IN US	006 23
KINGDOM SHALL HAVE NO END	016 13
THIS DAY WE FALL INTO NO SIN, NEITHER RUN INTO ANY	017 16
WE SAY THAT WE HAVE NO SIN, WE DECEIVE OURSELVES,	022 10
AND THERE IS NO HEALTH IN US	023 30
KINGDOM SHALL HAVE NO END	030 18
LAY HANDS SUDDENLY ON NO MAN, BUT FAITHFULLY AND	038 30
WHOSE POWER NO CREATURE IS ABLE TO RESIST,	041 10

NO CONTINUED

AND TO MAKE NO PEACE WITH OPPRESSION	044 11
BEING HURT BY NO PERSECUTIONS, MAY EVERMORE GIVE	058 22
FOR THOU DESIREST NO SACRIFICE, ELSE WOULD I GIVE IT	061 11
AND FROM WHOM NO SECRETS ARE HID	067 17
IN IT THOU SHALT DO NO MANNER OF WORK	068 27
THOU SHALT DO NO MURDER	069 07
KINGDOM SHALL HAVE NO END	071 16
THOUGH THERE BE NO SERMON OR COMMUNION,) MAY BE SAID R	084 27
IT IS REQUISITE THAT NO MAN SHOULD COME TO THE HOLY	087 35
OWE NO MAN ANY THING, BUT TO LOVE ONE ANOTHER	090 23
LOVE WORKETH NO ILL TO HIS NEIGHBOUR	090 29
AND HE ANSWERED, NO	095 26
LET NO MAN DESPISE THEE	098 26
BECAUSE THERE WAS NO ROOM FOR THEM IN THE INN	099 09
AND IN HIM IS NO DARKNESS AT ALL	101 23
WE SAY THAT WE HAVE NO SIN, WE DECEIVE OURSELVES, AND	101 28
AND NO MAN COULD LEARN THAT SONG BUT THE HUNDRED AND	103 06
THEIR MOUTH WAS FOUND NO GUILE	103 13
WHEREFORE THOU ART NO MORE A SERVANT, BUT A SON	104 24
RECOMPENSE TO NO MAN EVIL FOR EVIL	112 31
UNTO HIM, THEY HAVE NO WINE	113 15
FOR THERE IS NO POWER BUT OF GOD	114 12
SEE THOU TELL NO MAN	115 04
FOUND SO GREAT FAITH, NO, NOT IN ISRAEL	115 18
AND IN HIM IS NO SIN	117 24
LITTLE CHILDREN, LET NO MAN DECEIVE YOU	117 26
SAY UNTO HIM, BECAUSE NO MAN HATH HIRED US	119 26
I DO THEE NO WRONG	120 07
AND THESE HAVE NO ROOT, WHICH FOR A WHILE BELIEVE,	122 03
THIS LIFE, AND BRING NO FRUIT TO PERFECTION	122 07
THINKETH NO EVIL	122 32
GIVING NO OFFENCE IN ANY THING, THAT THE MINISTRY BE	126 08
SEEST THAT WE HAVE NO POWER OF OURSELVES TO HELP	127 15
THAT NO MAN GO BEYOND AND DEFRAUD HIS BROTHER IN ANY	127 31
THIS YE KNOW, THAT NO WHOREMONGER, NOR UNCLEAN	129 06
LET NO MAN DECEIVE YOU WITH VAIN WORDS	129 11
AND HAVE NO FELLOWSHIP WITH THE UNFRUITFUL WORKS OF	129 16
GOD CAST OUT DEVILS, NO DOUBT THE KINGDOM OF GOD IS	130 03
BUT MADE HIMSELF OF NO REPUTATION, AND TOOK UPON HIM	134 18
I WILL DRINK NO MORE OF THE FRUIT OF THE VINE,	141 15
IN DARKNESS, AND HATH NO LIGHT	144 24
OTHERWISE IT IS OF NO STRENGTH AT ALL WHILE THE	147 16
SHEDDING OF BLOOD IS NO REMISSION	147 26
AND HE THAT HATH NO SWORD, LET HIM SELL HIS GARMENT,	150 08
YE STRETCHED FORTH NO HANDS AGAINST ME	151 05
TO THE PEOPLE, I FIND NO FAULT IN THIS MAN	153 03
HAVE FOUND NO FAULT IN THIS MAN TOUCHING THOSE	153 24
NO, NOR YET HEROD	153 25
I HAVE FOUND NO CAUSE OF DEATH IN HIM	153 35
THEE NOT, THOU HAST NO PART WITH ME	156 06
SHOULD HAVE HAD NO MORE CONSCIENCE OF SINS	157 20
FOR SIN THOU HAST HAD NO PLEASURE	157 27
WILL I REMEMBER NO MORE	158 14
OF THESE IS, THERE IS NO MORE OFFERING FOR SIN	158 15
MAY KNOW THAT I FIND NO FAULT IN HIM	159 03
FOR I FIND NO FAULT IN HIM	159 08
BUT JESUS GAVE HIM NO ANSWER	159 13
THOU COULDEST HAVE NO POWER AT ALL AGAINST ME, EXCEPT	159 16
WE HAVE NO KING BUT CAESAR	159 29
FROM THE DEAD DIETH NO MORE	163 04
DEATH HATH NO MORE DOMINION OVER HIM	163 05
PERCEIVE THAT GOD IS NO RESPECTER OF PERSONS	166 13
AND THOUGH THEY FOUND NO CAUSE OF DEATH IN HIM,	168 30
UP FROM THE DEAD, NOW NO MORE TO RETURN TO	169 11
GOD RAISED AGAIN, SAW NO CORRUPTION	169 17
WHICH YE KNOW IN NO WISE BELIEVE, THOUGH A MAN	169 25
WHO DID NO SIN, NEITHER WAS GUILE FOUND IN HIS MOUTH	172 11
SHE REMEMBERETH NO MORE THE ANGUISH, FOR JOY THAT A	174 12
AND YOUR JOY NO MAN TAKETH FROM YOU	174 15
WITH WHOM IS NO VARIABLENESS, NEITHER SHADOW	174 28
AND YE SEE ME NO MORE	175 16
WHEN I SHALL NO MORE SPEAK UNTO YOU IN	176 25
AND SPEAKEST NO PROVERB	176 33
THE WORLD SEETH ME NO MORE	181 16
PERCEIVE THAT GOD IS NO RESPECTER OF PERSONS	183 30
FOR NO MAN CAN DO THESE MIRACLES THAT THOU DOEST,	188 03
AND NO MAN HATH ASCENDED UP TO HEAVEN, BUT HE THAT	188 24
WE CAN DO NO GOOD THING WITHOUT THEE, GRANT	189 03
NO MAN HATH SEEN GOD AT ANY TIME	189 16
THERE IS NO FEAR IN LOVE	189 28
AND YE KNOW THAT NO MURDERER HATH ETERNAL LIFE	191 15
WHICH NEED NO REPENTANCE	193 27
LIPS THAT THEY SPEAK NO GUILE	195 26
DEATH HATH NO MORE DOMINION OVER HIM	197 22
FROM THE DEAD DIETH NO MORE	197 22
YE SHALL IN NO CASE ENTER INTO THE KINGDOM OF HEAVEN	197 30
THOU SHALT BY NO MEANS COME OUT THENCE, TILL	198 16
THERE HATH NO TEMPTATION TAKEN YOU BUT SUCH AS IS	201 26
AND NO MAN GAVE UNTO HIM	202 09
BEFORE THEE, AND AM NO MORE WORTHY TO BE CALLED THY	202 14
IN THY SIGHT, AND AM NO MORE WORTHY TO BE CALLED THY	202 20
TO UNDERSTAND, THAT NO MAN SPEAKING BY THE SPIRIT OF	203 19
AND THAT NO MAN CAN SAY THAT JESUS IS THE LORD,	203 21
THAT THEY SHOULD TELL NO MAN	207 03
BE OF THE LAW, IT IS NO MORE OF PROMISE	207 25
AGAINST SUCH THERE IS NO LAW	209 28
FROM HENCEFORTH LET NO MAN TROUBLE ME	211 04
NO MAN CAN SERVE TWO MASTERS	211 09
YE COME BEHIND IN NO GIFT	214 32
AND NO MAN WAS ABLE TO ANSWER HIM A WORD, NEITHER	215 22
HIM THAT STOLE STEAL NO MORE	216 20
LET NO CORRUPT COMMUNICATION PROCEED OUT OF YOUR	216 23
THAT THEY SHALL NO MORE SAY, THE LORD LIVETH,	225 15
FOR THERE IS NO DIFFERENCE BETWEEN THE JEW AND THE	227 02

NO CONTINUED

	PAGE	LN
BY THEM THAT ARE NO PEOPLE, AND BY A FOOLISH NATION I	227	17
MY SOUL SHALL HAVE NO PLEASURE IN HIM	228	19
A VOICE, BUT SEEING NO MAN	230	09
WERE OPENED, HE SAW NO MAN	230	11
BE DESOLATE, AND LET NO MAN DWELL THEREIN	234	19
AND NO MAN KNOWETH THE SON, BUT THE FATHER	235	08
THERE SHALL BE NO END	236	20
THAT WE HENCEFORTH BE NO MORE CHILDREN, TOSSED TO AND	237	25
AND NO MORE CAN YE, EXCEPT YE ABIDE IN ME	238	11
FOR THE SUN IS NO SOONER RISEN WITH A BURNING HEAT,	239	21
NO MAN COMETH UNTO THE FATHER, BUT BY ME	240	06
GREATER LOVE HATH NO MAN THAN THIS, THAT A MAN LAY	241	26
IT CLOSE, AND TOLD NO MAN IN THOSE DAYS ANY OF THOSE	249	09
AND OF THE REST DURST NO MAN JOIN HIMSELF TO THEM	249	24
AND SALUTE NO MAN BY THE WAY	254	18
NOW THEREFORE YE ARE NO MORE STRANGERS AND	255	03
BUT NOW THEY HAVE NO CLOKE FOR THEIR SIN	255	23
WHICH NO MAN COULD NUMBER, OF ALL NATIONS,	256	23
THEY SHALL HUNGER NO MORE, NEITHER THIRST ANY MORE	257	12
AND THEY SHALL NO MORE BE A PREY TO THE HEATHEN,	262	14
AND THEY SHALL BE NO MORE CONSUMED WITH HUNGER IN THE	262	18
WITH WHOM IS NO VARIABLENESS, NEITHER SHADOW	265	20
FOR NO MAN EVER YET HATED HIS OWN FLESH	267	26
WHEREFORE THEY ARE NO MORE TWAIN, BUT ONE FLESH	268	09
AS OTHERS WHICH HAVE NO HOPE	268	30
TO ME I WILL IN NO WISE CAST OUT	269	15
THIS CHILD (PERSON) BEEN ALREADY BAPTIZED, OR NO	273	27
IF THEY ANSWER, NO	R 273	27
FOR NO MAN CAN DO THESE MIRACLES THAT THOU DOEST,	275	08
IN IT THOU SHALT DO NO MANNER OF WORK	286	27
THOU SHALT DO NO MURDER	287	06
TO BEAR NO MALICE NOR HATRED IN MY HEART	288	32
BUT IF NO IMPEDIMENT SHALL BE ALLEGED, OR SUSPECTED,	R 301	04
JOINED TOGETHER LET NO MAN PUT ASUNDER	303	31
LET THE ENEMY HAVE NO ADVANTAGE OF HIM	308	27
OF MY SOUL, THERE IS NO HELP FOR HIM IN HIS GOD	309	16
AND WILL HE BE NO MORE INTREATED	311	13
THOU REMEMBEREST THEM NO MORE	313	32
I GO HENCE, AND BE NO MORE SEEN	325	11
NO MAN COMETH UNTO THE FATHER, BUT BY ME	331	26
TO ME I WILL IN NO WISE CAST OUT	333	04
OF DEATH, I WILL FEAR NO EVIL	338	24
AND YOUR JOY NO MAN TAKETH FROM YOU	341	11
THEY SHALL HUNGER NO MORE, NEITHER THIRST ANY MORE	341	23
THERE IS NO HELP FOR HIM IN HIS GOD	346	27
ART THE GOD THAT HAST NO PLEASURE IN WICKEDNESS	348	07
9 FOR THERE IS NO FAITHFULNESS IN THEIR MOUTH	348	18
5 FOR IN DEATH NO MAN REMEMBERETH THEE	349	08
THERE SHALL NO HARM HAPPEN UNTO ME	353	17
MAN OF THE EARTH BE NO MORE EXALTED AGAINST THEM	354	16
THERE IS NO GOD	356	13
NONE THAT DOETH GOOD, NO NOT ONE	356	15
NONE THAT DOETH GOOD, NO NOT ONE	356	21
5 HAVE THEY NO KNOWLEDGE, THAT THEY ARE ALL SUCH	356	22
EVEN WHERE NO FEAR WAS	356	26
3 HE THAT HATH USED NO DECEIT IN HIS TONGUE, NOR DONE	357	10
I HAVE NO GOOD LIKE UNTO THEE	357	24
AND SHALT FIND NO WICKEDNESS IN ME	358	22
SEASON ALSO I TAKE NO REST	366	08
I AM A WORM, AND NO MAN	366	14
AND NO MAN HATH QUICKENED HIS OWN SOUL	368	03
OF DEATH, I WILL FEAR NO EVIL	368	17
THINK NO SCORN OF ME	373	04
THE LORD IMPUTETH NO SIN, *	377	24
WHOSE SPIRIT THERE IS NO GUILE	377	25
AND MULE, WHICH HAVE NO UNDERSTANDING	378	10
15 THERE IS NO KING THAT CAN BE SAVED BY THE	379	19
THE LORD SHALL WANT NO MANNER OF THING THAT IS GOOD	380	22
THAT THEY SPEAK NO GUILE	380	28
THAT THERE IS NO FEAR OF GOD BEFORE HIS EYES	383	27
HATH SET HIMSELF IN NO GOOD WAY	384	02
BUT HIS PLACE COULD NO WHERE BE FOUND	387	07
3 THERE IS NO HEALTH IN MY FLESH, BECAUSE OF THY	387	25
AND THERE IS NO WHOLE PART IN MY BODY	388	05
IN WHOSE MOUTH ARE NO REPROOFS	388	20
I GO HENCE, AND BE NO MORE SEEN	390	07
AND YET THERE IS NO MAN THAT ORDERETH THEM UNTO THEE	390	23
MAKE NO LONG TARRYING, O MY GOD	391	26
HE SHALL RISE UP NO MORE	392	16
AND TAKEST NO MONEY FOR THEM	395	17
20 NO, NOT WHEN THOU HAST SMITTEN US INTO THE PLACE	395	32
7 BUT NO MAN MAY DELIVER HIS BROTHER, *	400	18
AND HAVE NO ABIDING	401	04
IS IN HONOUR BUT HATH NO UNDERSTANDING *	401	16
9 I WILL TAKE NO BULLOCK OUT OF THINE HOUSE, *	402	08
16 FOR THOU DESIREST NO SACRIFICE, ELSE WOULD I GIVE	404	09
THERE IS NO GOD	405	12
NONE THAT DOETH GOOD, NO NOT ONE	405	21
WERE AFRAID WHERE NO FEAR WAS	405	25
AND DRY LAND WHERE NO WATER IS	414	28
AND SAY, THAT NO MAN SHALL SEE THEM	415	29
THE DEEP MIRE, WHERE NO GROUND IS	422	02
ON ME, BUT THERE WAS NO MAN, NEITHER FOUND I ANY TO	423	15
AND NO MAN TO DWELL IN THEIR TENTS	423	25
O LORD, MAKE NO LONG TARRYING	424	33
FOR I KNOW NO END THEREOF	426	05
AND HIM THAT HATH NO HELPER	427	21
4 FOR THEY ARE IN NO PERIL OF DEATH	428	16
5 THEY COME IN NO MISFORTUNE LIKE OTHER FOLK	428	18
THEREOUT SUCK THEY NO SMALL ADVANTAGE	428	29
NO, NOT ONE IS THERE AMONG US, THAT UNDERSTANDETH ANY	430	25
AND WILL HE BE NO MORE INTREATED	433	30
AND THERE WERE NO WIDOWS TO MAKE LAMENTATION	439	07
AND THERE WAS NO MAN TO BURY THEM	440	05
10 THERE SHALL NO STRANGE GOD BE IN THEE, *	442	31
THAT THEY BE NO MORE A PEOPLE, *	444	12
NAME OF ISRAEL MAY BE NO MORE IN REMEMBRANCE	444	13
AND NO GOOD THING SHALL HE WITHHOLD FROM THEM THAT	446	03
AS A MAN THAT HATH NO STRENGTH	449	03
10 THERE SHALL NO EVIL HAPPEN UNTO THEE, *	455	15
AND THAT THERE IS NO UNRIGHTEOUSNESS IN HIM	456	31
4 I WILL TAKE NO WICKED THING IN HAND	463	22
THERE SHALL NO SUCH CLEAVE UNTO ME	463	23
10 THERE SHALL NO DECEITFUL PERSON DWELL IN MY HOUSE	464	02
THEREOF SHALL KNOW IT NO MORE	467	07
14 HE SUFFERED NO MAN TO DO THEM WRONG, *	470	30
AND DO MY PROPHETS NO HARM	471	03
AND GAVE NO CREDENCE UNTO HIS WORD	474	18
AND FOUND NO CITY TO DWELL IN	476	13
11 LET THERE BE NO MAN TO PITY HIM, *	480	23
3 EVEN THEY WHO DO NO WICKEDNESS, *	490	04
THAT THE PROUD DO ME NO WRONG	498	14
AND SO SHALL NO WICKEDNESS HAVE DOMINION OVER ME	499	04
141 I AM SMALL AND OF NO REPUTATION	499	21
I HAVE NO PROUD LOOKS	507	24
THE DARKNESS IS NO DARKNESS WITH THEE, BUT THE	515	10
AND SAW THERE WAS NO MAN THAT WOULD KNOW ME	518	11
5 I HAD NO PLACE TO FLEE UNTO, *	518	12
AND NO MAN CARED FOR MY SOUL	518	12
IN THY SIGHT SHALL NO MAN LIVING BE JUSTIFIED	518	26
NO LEADING INTO CAPTIVITY, AND NO COMPLAINING IN OUR	520	22
INTO CAPTIVITY, AND NO COMPLAINING IN OUR STREETS	520	22
THAT THERE BE NO DECAY, *	520	22
THERE IS NO END OF HIS GREATNESS	520	32
FOR THERE IS NO HELP IN THEM	522	07
10 HE HATH NO PLEASURE IN THE STRENGTH OF AN HORSE	523	15
THAT NO MAN MIGHT PRESUME TO EXECUTE ANY	529	14
IN THIS CHURCH, NO MAN SHALL BE ACCOUNTED OR TAKEN TO	529	19
AS SHEEP HAVING NO SHEPHERD	538	16
THAT THERE BE NO PLACE LEFT AMONG YOU, EITHER	540	21
WHERE THOU ART GUIDE, NO ILL CAN COME	544	09
OUR PREVENTING GUIDE, NO EVIL CAN OUR STEPS BETIDE	545	09
NOT GIVEN TO WINE, NO STRIKER, NOT GREEDY OF FILTHY	549	22
SHALL SEE MY FACE NO MORE	550	23
I HAVE COVETED NO MAN'S SILVER, OR GOLD, OR APPAREL	551	05
HATH PURCHASED WITH NO LESS PRICE THAN THE EFFUSION	554	11
WHERE THOU ART GUIDE, NO ILL CAN COME	556	17
OUR PREVENTING GUIDE, NO EVIL CAN OUR STEPS BETIDE	557	15
AND THERE SHALL BE NO MORE DEATH, NEITHER SORROW,	567	19
WE PROCEED NO FURTHER, BECAUSE WE WOULD NOT THAT AN	570	18
NO OBJECTION BEING OFFERED, OR THE INSTITUTOR	R 570	23
IN IT THOU SHALT DO NO MANNER OF WORK	579	07
THOU SHALT DO NO MURDER	579	15
TO BEAR NO MALICE NOR HATRED IN MY HEART	580	08
THAT NO UNCLEAN THOUGHTS, UNLAWFUL DESIGNS, OR	590	13
THIS DAY WE FALL INTO NO SIN, NEITHER RUN INTO ANY	592	22
AND GRANT THAT NO CLOUDS OF THIS MORTAL LIFE MAY HIDE	596	07
YET NOTWITHSTANDING, NO CHRISTIAN MAN WHATSOEVER IS	604	22
AND ALTHOUGH THERE IS NO CONDEMNATION FOR THEM THAT	604	38
WHEREFORE WE HAVE NO POWER TO DO GOOD WORKS PLEASANT	604	44
AND IF WE SAY WE HAVE NO SIN, WE DECEIVE OURSELVES,	605	36
WHICH SAY, THEY CAN NO MORE SIN AS LONG AS THEY LIVE	606	03
MOST UNCLEAN LIVING, NO LESS PERILOUS THAN	606	26
AND GROUNDED UPON NO WARRANTY OF SCRIPTURE, BUT	607	16
YET IN NO WISE ARE THEY PARTAKERS OF CHRIST	609	06
BUT HATH NO AUTHORITY IN THINGS PURELY SPIRITUAL	610	39

NOAH

	PAGE	LN
IN THE DAYS OF NOAH, WHILE THE ARK WAS A PREPARING,	161	28

NOBLE

	PAGE	LN
THE NOBLE ARMY OF MARTYRS PRAISE THEE	010	18
UNTO US, THE NOBLE WORKS THAT THOU DIDST IN THEIR	058	29
CAN EXPRESS THE NOBLE ACTS OF THE LORD, *	473	02
PRAISE HIM IN HIS NOBLE ACTS	525	24

NOBLEMAN

	PAGE	LN
WAS A CERTAIN NOBLEMAN, WHOSE SON WAS SICK AT	219	28
THE NOBLEMAN SAITH UNTO HIM, SIR, COME DOWN ERE MY	219	33

NOBLES

	PAGE	LN
AND THEIR NOBLES WITH LINKS OF IRON	525	17

NOBODY

	PAGE	LN
TO HURT NOBODY BY WORD OR DEED	288	32
TO HURT NOBODY BY WORD OR DEED	580	07

NOISE

	PAGE	LN
LET THE SEA MAKE A NOISE, AND ALL THAT THEREIN IS	027	19
PEOPLE MAKING A NOISE, HE SAID UNTO THEM, GIVE PLACE	224	25
BECAUSE OF THE NOISE OF THY WATER-FLOODS	393	18
UP WITH A MERRY NOISE, *	398	29
AND THE NOISE OF HIS WAVES, AND THE MADNESS OF THE	416	27
MAKE A CHEERFUL NOISE UNTO THE GOD OF JACOB	442	13
LET THE SEA MAKE A NOISE, AND ALL THAT THEREIN IS	460	23
LET THE SEA MAKE A NOISE, AND ALL THAT THEREIN IS	462	08

NOISED

	PAGE	LN
NOW WHEN THIS WAS NOISED ABROAD, THE MULTITUDE CAME	180	26
SAYINGS WERE NOISED ABROAD THROUGHOUT ALL THE HILL	243	27

NOISOME

AND FROM THE NOISOME PESTILENCE	454 33

NONE

THOU SHALT HAVE NONE OTHER GODS BUT ME	068 04
AND THEY UNDERSTOOD NONE OF THESE THINGS	123 24
AND FINDING NONE, HE SAITH, I WILL RETURN UNTO MY	130 12
MAY FIND IT NONE OTHER THAN THE WAY OF LIFE	138 07
PEOPLE THERE WAS NONE WITH ME	138 11
AND THERE WAS NONE TO HELP	138 22
THAT THERE WAS NONE TO UPHOLD	138 23
AND FOUND NONE	143 03
AND NONE OF YOU ASKETH ME, WHITHER GOEST THOU	175 07
HE WAS FALLEN UPON NONE OF THEM	185 25
SAY UNTO YOU, THAT NONE OF THOSE MEN WHICH WERE	192 20
MAKE THE PROMISE OF NONE EFFECT	207 24
UNTO HER, THERE IS NONE OF THY KINDRED THAT IS CALLED	243 21
THE WORKS WHICH NONE OTHER MAN DID, THEY HAD NOT HAD	255 25
DWELL SAFELY, AND NONE SHALL MAKE THEM AFRAID	262 16
CHRIST SAITH, NONE CAN ENTER INTO THE KINGDOM OF GOD,	273 30
THOU SHALT HAVE NONE OTHER GODS BUT ME	286 05
HE WAS FALLEN UPON NONE OF THEM	296 17
AND THERE SHALL NONE BE ADMITTED TO THE HOLY	R 299 08
THAT THERE IS NONE OTHER NAME UNDER HEAVEN	314 19
WHILE THERE IS NONE TO HELP	349 26
SEARCH OUT HIS UNGODLINESS, UNTIL THOU FIND NONE	354 10
THERE IS NONE THAT DOETH GOOD, NO NOT ONE	356 15
THERE IS NONE THAT DOETH GOOD, NO NOT ONE	356 20
BUT THERE SHALL BE NONE TO HELP THEM	362 20
AND THERE IS NONE TO HELP ME	366 26
THE PEOPLE TO BE OF NONE EFFECT, AND CASTETH OUT THE	379 08
AND THERE BE NONE TO DELIVER YOU	403 03
THERE IS NONE THAT DOETH GOOD	405 15
THERE IS ALSO NONE THAT DOETH GOOD, NO NOT ONE	405 20
FOR THERE IS NONE TO DELIVER HIM	425 28
AND THERE IS NONE UPON EARTH THAT I DESIRE IN	429 27
THE GODS THERE IS NONE LIKE UNTO THEE, O LORD	447 19
AND THERE WAS NONE TO HELP THEM	476 29
AND THEY HAVE NONE OCCASION OF STUMBLING	501 12
AS YET THERE WAS NONE OF THEM	515 23
AND NONE SHALL BE ADMITTED A DEACON, PRIEST, OR	529 24
BUT NONE OF THESE THINGS MOVE ME, NEITHER COUNT I MY	550 18
THOU SHALT HAVE NONE OTHER GODS BUT ME	578 26
AND THERE IS NONE OTHER SATISFACTION FOR SIN,	609 16

NOON-DAY

AND THY JUST DEALING AS THE NOON-DAY	385 05
AND AT NOON-DAY WILL I PRAY, AND THAT	407 25
FOR THE SICKNESS THAT DESTROYETH IN THE NOON-DAY	455 08

NOR

SHOULD NOT DISSEMBLE NOR CLOAK THEM BEFORE THE FACE	005 32
SHOULD NOT DISSEMBLE NOR CLOAK THEM BEFORE THE FACE	023 07
OUR OFFENCES, NOR THE OFFENCES OF OUR	054 13
OF A CONTRITE HEART, NOR THE DESIRE OF SUCH AS ARE	058 16
ANY GRAVEN IMAGE, NOR THE LIKENESS OF ANY THING THAT	068 08
BOW DOWN TO THEM, NOR WORSHIP THEM	068 11
NEIGHBOUR'S WIFE, NOR HIS SERVANT, NOR HIS MAID,	069 21
HIS OX, NOR HIS ASS, NOR ANY THING THAT IS HIS	069 21
HIS SERVANT, NOR HIS MAID, NOR HIS OX, NOR HIS	069 21
NOR HIS OX, NOR HIS ASS, NOR ANY THING THAT IS	069 21
NOR HIS MAID, NOR HIS OX, NOR HIS ASS, NOR ANY THING	069 21
WHERE NEITHER MOTH NOR RUST DOTH CORRUPT, AND WHERE	072 10
DO NOT BREAK THROUGH NOR STEAL	072 11
BE NOT THAT CHRIST, NOR ELIAS, NEITHER THAT PROPHET	095 32
WILL OF THE FLESH, NOR OF THE WILL OF MAN, BUT OF	098 03
NOT OF BLOOD, NOR OF THE WILL OF THE FLESH,	098 03
WHERE NEITHER MOTH NOR RUST DOTH CORRUPT, AND WHERE	125 19
DO NOT BREAK THROUGH NOR STEAL	125 20
NEITHER FILTHINESS, NOR FOOLISH TALKING, NOR JESTING,	129 04
NOR FOOLISH TALKING, NOR JESTING, WHICH ARE NOT	129 05
NOR UNCLEAN PERSON, NOR COVETOUS MAN, WHO IS AN	129 07
THAT NO WHOREMONGER, NOR UNCLEAN PERSON, NOR COVETOUS	129 07
NOR YET THAT HE SHOULD OFFER HIMSELF OFTEN, AS THE	148 02
WILL NOT ANSWER ME, NOR LET ME GO	151 32
NOR YET HEROD	153 25
THAT THOU HAST MADE, NOR DESIREST THE DEATH OF A	157 05
THEY KNEW HIM NOT, NOR YET THE VOICES OF THE PROPHETS	168 27
KNOWN THE FATHER, NOR ME	180 02
AVAILETH ANY THING, NOR UNCIRCUMCISION, BUT A NEW	210 32
NOR YET FOR YOUR BODY, WHAT YE SHALL PUT ON	211 13
DO THEY REAP, NOR GATHER INTO BARNS	211 17
AND NEITHER DID EAT NOR DRINK	230 13
THY MANIFOLD GIFTS, NOR YET OF GRACE TO USE THEM	240 31
IN CRAFTINESS, NOR HANDLING THE WORD OF GOD	250 29
NOR SCRIP, NOR SHOES	254 18
CARRY NEITHER PURSE, NOR SCRIP, NOR SHOES	254 18
NEITHER THE SEA, NOR THE TREES, TILL WE HAVE SEALED	256 18
SUN LIGHT ON THEM, NOR ANY HEAT	257 13
NOT PERSONS, NOR TAKETH REWARD	263 25
NOR YET FOR YOUR BODY, WHAT YE SHALL PUT ON	266 12
DO THEY REAP, NOR GATHER INTO BARNS	266 15
WILT NOT FOLLOW, NOR BE LED BY THEM	276 27
NOT TO FOLLOW, NOR BE LED BY THEM	276 30
WILT NOT FOLLOW, NOR BE LED BY THEM	277 29
NOT TO FOLLOW, NOR BE LED BY THEM	277 31
ANY GRAVEN IMAGE, NOR THE LIKENESS OF ANY THING THAT	286 09
BOW DOWN TO THEM, NOR WORSHIP THEM	286 11
HIS OX, NOR HIS ASS, NOR ANY THING THAT IS HIS	287 21
NEIGHBOUR'S WIFE, NOR HIS SERVANT, NOR HIS MAID,	287 21
NOR HIS SERVANT, NOR HIS MAID, NOR HIS OX, NOR HIS	287 21
NOR HIS OX, NOR HIS ASS, NOR ANY THING THAT IS	287 21

NOR   CONTINUED

NOR HIS MAID, NOR HIS OX, NOR HIS ASS, NOR ANY THING	287 21
TO BEAR NO MALICE NOR HATRED IN MY HEART	288 33
NOT TO COVET NOR DESIRE OTHER MEN'S GOODS	289 08
THINGS OF YOURSELF, NOR TO WALK IN THE COMMANDMENTS	289 14
NOR THE INIQUITIES OF OUR FOREFATHERS	308 10
NOR THE WICKED APPROACH TO HURT HIM	308 28
OF THE LORD, NOR FAINT WHEN THOU ART REBUKED OF HIM	321 29
NOR CAST THY SERVANT AWAY IN DISPLEASURE	326 24
NEITHER SLUMBER NOR SLEEP	327 26
THAT NEITHER DEATH, NOR LIFE, NOR ANGELS, NOR	331 10
NOR LIFE, NOR ANGELS, NOR PRINCIPALITIES, NOR	331 10
NOR ANGELS, NOR PRINCIPALITIES, NOR POWERS, NOR	331 10
NOR POWERS, NOR THINGS PRESENT, NOR THINGS TO COME,	331 11
NOR THINGS PRESENT, NOR THINGS TO COME, NOR HEIGHT,	331 11
NOR PRINCIPALITIES, NOR POWERS, NOR THINGS PRESENT,	331 11
TO COME, NOR HEIGHT, NOR DEPTH, NOR ANY OTHER	331 12
NOR THINGS TO COME, NOR HEIGHT, NOR DEPTH, NOR ANY	331 12
NOR DEPTH, NOR ANY OTHER CREATURE, SHALL BE	331 12
NEITHER SLUMBER NOR SLEEP	339 10
SUN LIGHT ON THEM, NOR ANY HEAT	341 24
OF THE UNGODLY, NOR STOOD IN THE WAY OF SINNERS, *	345 08
IN HIS TONGUE, NOR DONE EVIL TO HIS NEIGHBOUR, *	357 10
NOR TAKEN REWARD AGAINST THE INNOCENT	357 17
IS NEITHER SPEECH NOR LANGUAGE	363 17
HE HATH NOT DESPISED NOR ABHORRED THE LOW ESTATE OF	367 20
MIND UNTO VANITY, NOR SWORN TO DECEIVE MY NEIGHBOUR	369 03
NOR MY LIFE WITH THE BLOOD-THIRSTY	371 14
NOR CAST THY SERVANT AWAY IN DISPLEASURE	372 16
WORKS OF THE LORD, NOR THE OPERATION OF HIS HANDS	373 18
RIGHTEOUS FORSAKEN, NOR HIS SEED BEGGING THEIR BREAD	386 13
NOR CONDEMN HIM WHEN HE IS JUDGED	386 32
NOR BEHAVE OURSELVES FROWARDLY IN THY COVENANT	395 29
NOR GIVE A RANSOM UNTO GOD FOR HIM,	400 18
NOR HE-GOATS OUT OF THY FOLDS	402 08
THEY WILL NOT TURN, NOR FEAR GOD	407 31
NOR TURNED HIS MERCY FROM ME	418 21
FROM THE EAST, NOR FROM THE WEST, *	432 10
NOR YET FROM THE SOUTH	432 11
NOR SUFFER MY TRUTH TO FAIL	452 08
WILL I NOT BREAK, NOR ALTER THE THING THAT IS GONE	452 09
NOR FOR THE ARROW THAT FLIETH BY DAY	455 05
NOR FOR THE SICKNESS THAT DESTROYETH IN THE NOON-DAY	455 07
NOR REWARDED US ACCORDING TO OUR WICKEDNESSES	466 25
NOR TO HAVE COMPASSION UPON HIS FATHERLESS CHILDREN	480 23
NEITHER SLUMBER NOR SLEEP	502 29
NOR CLIMB UP INTO MY BED	508 09
MINE EYES TO SLEEP, NOR MINE EYELIDS TO SLUMBER	508 10
TRUST IN PRINCES, NOR IN ANY CHILD OF MAN	522 06
YOURSELVES OFFEND, NOR BE OCCASION THAT OTHERS	540 29
MIND UNTO VANITY, NOR SWORN TO DECEIVE HIS NEIGHBOUR	563 18
NEITHER SORROW, NOR CRYING, NEITHER SHALL THERE BE	567 19
NIGH TO HURT THEM, NOR THE HAND OF THE UNGODLY TO	574 14
ANY GRAVEN IMAGE, NOR THE LIKENESS OF ANY THING THAT	578 27
BOW DOWN TO THEM, NOR WORSHIP THEM	578 30
NOR HIS SERVANT, NOR HIS MAID, NOR HIS OX, NOR HIS	579 21
NEIGHBOUR'S WIFE, NOR HIS SERVANT, NOR HIS MAID, NOR	579 21
NOR HIS OX, NOR HIS ASS, NOR ANY THING THAT IS	579 22
HIS OX, NOR HIS ASS, NOR ANY THING THAT IS HIS	579 22
NOR HIS MAID, NOR HIS OX, NOR HIS ASS, NOR ANY THING	579 22
TO BEAR NO MALICE NOR HATRED IN MY HEART	580 08
NOT TO COVET NOR DESIRE OTHER MEN'S GOODS	580 12
THINGS OF THYSELF, NOR TO WALK IN THE COMMANDMENTS OF	580 17
A PURE INTENTION NOR CONTINUE IT WITHOUT THY	594 22
IS NOT READ THEREIN, NOR MAY BE PROVED THEREBY,	603 30
BIND CHRISTIAN MEN, NOR THE CIVIL PRECEPTS THEREOF	604 20
BY THEIR WICKEDNESS, NOR THE GRACE OF GOD'S GIFTS	608 15

NORTH

ISRAEL OUT OF THE NORTH COUNTRY, AND FROM ALL	225 19
UPON THE NORTH SIDE LIETH THE CITY OF THE GREAT KING	399 13
THOU HAST MADE THE NORTH AND THE SOUTH	450 31
FROM THE NORTH, AND FROM THE SOUTH	476 11

NOSES

NOSES HAVE THEY, AND SMELL NOT	485 22

NOTABLE

THEY HAD THEN A NOTABLE PRISONER, CALLED BARABBAS	135 27
OR NOTABLE CRIME, IN ANY OF THESE PERSONS	530 22
OR NOTABLE CRIME, IN ANY OF THEM, FOR THE	536 28

NOTE

AND NOTE, THAT WHEN THE CONFESSION AND ABSOLUTION	R 003 10
BUT NOTE, THAT THE PRIEST, AT HIS DISCRETION,	R 007 04
BUT NOTE, THAT ON ASH WEDNESDAY AND GOOD FRIDAY THE	R 008 12
AND NOTE, THAT BEFORE EVERY LESSON, THE MINISTER	R 009 32
BUT NOTE, THAT ON ANY DAY WHEN THE HOLY COMMUNION	R 010 03
BUT NOTE, THAT, SAVE ON THE SUNDAYS IN ADVENT,	R 014 05
AND NOTE, THAT THE MINISTER MAY HERE END THE	R 017 22
NOTE, THAT THE GENERAL THANKSGIVING MAY BE SAID BY	R 019 34
AND NOTE, THAT WHEN THE CONFESSION AND ABSOLUTION	R 021 07
BUT NOTE, THAT THE MINISTER, AT HIS DISCRETION,	R 026 07
NOTE, THAT THE GENERAL THANKSGIVING MAY BE SAID BY	R 033 32
AND NOTE, THAT THE MINISTER, IN HIS DISCRETION,	R 047 04
AND NOTE, THAT IN REHEARSING THE TEN COMMANDMENTS,	R 067 02
BUT NOTE, THAT WHENEVER IT IS OMITTED, THE PRIEST	R 067 29
AND NOTE, THAT THESE SENTENCES MAY BE USED ON ANY	R 073 25
AND NOTE, THAT THE EXHORTATION SHALL BE SAID ON THE	R 085 23
AND NOTE, THAT AT THE TIME OF THE BAPTISM OF AN	R 273 22
BUT NOTE, THAT IF THE PERSON TO BE BAPTIZED BE AN	R 279 30

NOTE   CONTINUED

BUT NOTE, THAT IN THE CASE OF AN ADULT, THE	R 281 25
BUT NOTE, THAT WHERE SO INSTRUCTED, THE PEOPLE MAY	R 285 30
AND NOTE FURTHER, THAT THE PART OF THE COMMANDMENT	R 286 03
AND NOTE, THAT FOR THE CONFESSION AND ABSOLUTION THE	R 323 09
AND NOTE, THAT AFTER THE SUFFRAGE, THAT IT MAY	R 531 02
AND NOTE FURTHER, THAT IN THE DISCRETION OF THE	R 531 09
AND NOTE, THAT AFTER THE SUFFRAGE, THAT IT MAY	R 537 08
AND NOTE FURTHER, THAT IN THE DISCRETION OF THE	R 537 15
AND NOTE, THAT IN THE DISCRETION OF THE PRESIDING	R 553 23

NOTED

IT IS TO BE NOTED THAT THIS OFFICE IS APPROPRIATE	R 337 02
NOT THESE THINGS NOTED IN THY BOOK	408 31

NOTHING

IS IT NOTHING TO YOU, ALL YE THAT PASS BY	004 29
COMMUNION DOTH NOTHING ELSE BUT INCREASE YOUR	087 30
THERE LACKETH NOTHING BUT THE GUESTS TO SIT DOWN	088 19
FOR I KNOW NOTHING AGAINST MYSELF	094 08
THEREFORE JUDGE NOTHING BEFORE THE TIME, UNTIL THE	094 10
BE CAREFUL FOR NOTHING	095 15
DIFFERETH NOTHING FROM A SERVANT, THOUGH HE BE	104 15
CHARITY ARE NOTHING WORTH	122 15
AND HAVE NOT CHARITY, I AM NOTHING	122 26
AND HAVE NOT CHARITY, IT PROFITETH ME NOTHING	122 29
WHO HATEST NOTHING THAT THOU HAST MADE, AND DOST	124 11
AS HAVING NOTHING, AND YET POSSESSING ALL THINGS	126 20
THAT NOTHING BE LOST	132 08
IF I HONOUR MYSELF, MY HONOUR IS NOTHING	133 24
THE CHIEF PRIESTS AND ELDERS, HE ANSWERED NOTHING	135 22
HAVE THOU NOTHING TO DO WITH THAT JUST MAN	135 33
HE COULD PREVAIL NOTHING, BUT THAT RATHER A TUMULT	136 09
AND ASKED JESUS, SAYING, ANSWEREST THOU NOTHING	143 11
BUT HE HELD HIS PEACE, AND ANSWERED NOTHING	143 12
BUT HE ANSWERED NOTHING	145 09
ANSWEREST THOU NOTHING	145 10
BUT JESUS YET ANSWERED NOTHING	145 12
AND THEY SAID, NOTHING	150 06
BUT HE ANSWERED HIM NOTHING	153 15
LO, NOTHING WORTHY OF DEATH IS DONE UNTO HIM	153 26
MAN HATH DONE NOTHING AMISS	155 05
AND HATEST NOTHING THAT THOU HAST MADE, NOR	157 05
HAVE YE ASKED NOTHING IN MY NAME	176 22
AND HATH NOTHING IN ME	182 08
IS STRONG, NOTHING IS HOLY	194 05
WITHOUT WHOM NOTHING IS STRONG, NOTHING IS HOLY	194 05
HAVE TOILED ALL THE NIGHT, AND HAVE TAKEN NOTHING	196 16
AND HAVING NOTHING TO EAT, JESUS CALLED HIS DISCIPLES	199 09
AND HAVE NOTHING TO EAT	199 12
THAT NOTHING BE LOST	226 07
FOR WITH GOD NOTHING SHALL BE IMPOSSIBLE	236 27
FOR WITHOUT ME YE CAN DO NOTHING	238 14
YE MAY BE PERFECT AND ENTIRE, WANTING NOTHING	239 11
ASK IN FAITH, NOTHING WAVERING	239 14
AND I HAVE NOTHING TO SET BEFORE HIM	262 29
ME I SHOULD LOSE NOTHING, BUT SHOULD RAISE IT UP	269 18
WE BROUGHT NOTHING INTO THIS WORLD, AND IT IS CERTAIN	324 13
WE CAN CARRY NOTHING OUT	324 14
AGE IS EVEN AS NOTHING IN RESPECT OF THEE	324 23
THEREFORE CAN I LACK NOTHING	338 17
AND THERE IS NOTHING HID FROM THE HEAT THEREOF	363 26
THEREFORE CAN I LACK NOTHING	368 11
FOR THEY THAT FEAR HIM LACK NOTHING	380 20
3 I HELD MY TONGUE, AND SPAKE NOTHING	389 09
AGE IS EVEN AS NOTHING IN RESPECT OF THEE	389 18
HE SHALL CARRY NOTHING AWAY WITH HIM WHEN HE DIETH, *	401 09
MEN WHOSE HANDS WERE MIGHTY HAVE FOUND NOTHING	432 32
AND TO TEACH NOTHING, AS NECESSARY TO ETERNAL	542 06
HOW I KEPT BACK NOTHING THAT WAS PROFITABLE UNTO YOU,	550 10
OR MAINTAIN NOTHING, AS NECESSARY TO ETERNAL	554 24
HAVING NOTHING TO SAY AGAINST YOU	555 12
TO DREAD NOTHING BUT THE LOSS OF THEE,	596 04
SO THAT NOTHING BE ORDAINED AGAINST GOD'S	609 35

NOTICE

BE) SHALL NOTICE BE GIVEN OF THE COMMUNION, AND OF	R 071 26
TIMELY NOTICE SHALL BE GIVEN TO THE	R 273 18
PERSON IS SICK, NOTICE SHALL BE GIVEN THEREOF TO THE	R 308 05
MUST GIVE TIMELY NOTICE TO THE MINISTER, SIGNIFYING	R 321 12
RECEIVED DUE NOTICE OF THE ELECTION OF A MINISTER	R 569 04
OF ALL WHICH YOU WILL GIVE US DUE NOTICE	569 34

NOTORIOUS

BE AN OPEN AND NOTORIOUS EVIL LIVER, OR TO HAVE DONE	R 084 35

NOTWITHSTANDING

NOTWITHSTANDING, BEING WARNED OF GOD IN A DREAM, HE	107 19
WITH US, NOTWITHSTANDING OUR MANY AND GREAT	591 15
YET NOTWITHSTANDING, NO	604 21
NOTWITHSTANDING, EVERY MAN OUGHT, OF SUCH THINGS AS	611 03

NOUGHT

BY THY GOOD PROVIDENCE, BE BROUGHT TO NOUGHT	058 21
OF WAR SET HIM AT NOUGHT, AND MOCKED HIM, AND ARRAYED	153 17
OF THE HEATHEN TO NOUGHT, *	379 07
THY PEOPLE FOR NOUGHT, *	395 17
WHEREFORE HAST THOU MADE ALL MEN FOR NOUGHT	452 35
4 MAN IS LIKE A THING OF NOUGHT	519 29

NOURISH

TRUE RELIGION, NOURISH US WITH ALL GOODNESS, AND OF	198 22
TRUE RELIGION, NOURISH US WITH ALL GOODNESS, AND OF	283 10
AND HE SHALL NOURISH THEE, *	408 04
NOURISH THEM WITH ALL GOODNESS	572 29

NOURISHETH

BUT NOURISHETH AND CHERISHETH IT, EVEN AS THE LORD	267 27

NOVICE

NOT A NOVICE, LEST BEING LIFTED UP WITH PRIDE HE FALL	549 26

NUMBER

MEN SAT DOWN, IN NUMBER ABOUT FIVE THOUSAND	132 02
BEING OF THE NUMBER OF THE TWELVE	148 16
MEN SAT DOWN, IN NUMBER ABOUT FIVE THOUSAND	226 02
TO BE OF THE NUMBER OF THE TWELVE APOSTLES	233 33
AND SAID, (THE NUMBER OF NAMES TOGETHER WERE ABOUT AN	234 07
AND I HEARD THE NUMBER OF THEM WHICH WERE SEALED	256 19
NO MAN COULD NUMBER, OF ALL NATIONS, AND KINDREDS,	256 24
REMAIN IN THE NUMBER OF THY FAITHFUL CHILDREN	279 19
MINE END, AND THE NUMBER OF MY DAYS	324 20
SO TEACH US TO NUMBER OUR DAYS, *	326 02
THEY THAT HATE ME WRONGFULLY ARE MANY IN NUMBER	388 31
MINE END, AND THE NUMBER OF MY DAYS	389 15
THEY ARE MORE IN NUMBER THAN THE HAIRS OF MY HEAD,	391 12
12 SO TEACH US TO NUMBER OUR DAYS, *	454 13
THEY ARE MORE IN NUMBER THAN THE SAND	515 26
4 HE TELLETH THE NUMBER OF THE STARS, *	523 02
AND THE NUMBER OF THE DISCIPLES MULTIPLIED IN	532 20
TO BE OF THE NUMBER OF THE TWELVE	553 08
TO INCREASE THE NUMBER OF THE MINISTERS OF THY	561 12

NUMBERED

MAKE THEM TO BE NUMBERED WITH THY SAINTS, IN GLORY	011 02
AND HE WAS NUMBERED WITH THE TRANSGRESSORS	146 17
FOR HE WAS NUMBERED WITH US, AND HAD OBTAINED PART OF	234 11
AND HE WAS NUMBERED WITH THE ELEVEN APOSTLES	234 32
WHOSE MERCIES CANNOT BE NUMBERED	268 22
WITHOUT END, AND WHOSE MERCIES CANNOT BE NUMBERED	316 26
WHOSE MERCIES CANNOT BE NUMBERED	334 14
AND AT LAST BE NUMBERED WITH THY SAINTS IN GLORY	574 19

NUNC

EST CONFITERI, NUNC DIMITTIS, DEUS MISEREATUR,	R 025 17
THE HYMN CALLED NUNC DIMITTIS, AS FOLLOWETH	R 028 06

NURSING

CONTINUANCE OF NURSING CARE AND PROTECTION, HATH, IN	V 12

NURTURE

THE CARE AND NURTURE OF THY CHILDREN	042 31
WHOSE RELIGIOUS NURTURE THEY ARE RESPONSIBLE,	R 295 11

OATH

TO PERFORM THE OATH WHICH HE SWARE TO OUR FOREFATHER	014 18
THE OATH WHICH HE SWARE TO OUR FATHER ABRAHAM, THAT	244 05
AND THE OATH THAT HE SWARE UNTO ISAAC	470 21
MADE A FAITHFUL OATH UNTO DAVID, *	508 25

OBEDIENCE

THROUGH OBEDIENCE TO THY LAW, WE MAY SHOW FORTH	036 20
IN THEE, AND OBEDIENCE TO THY LAWS	053 27
KNOWLEDGE AND OBEDIENCE OF THY WORD, THAT IN THE END	298 22
THY FAITH, AND OBEDIENCE TO THY HOLY COMMANDMENTS,	336 22
SHALL FEIGN OBEDIENCE UNTO ME	362 29
CONFORMITY AND OBEDIENCE TO THE DOCTRINE, DISCIPLINE,	552 30
IN A SINCERE OBEDIENCE TO HIS LAWS, THROUGH WHOSE	591 21
FREE FROM THE OBEDIENCE OF THE COMMANDMENTS WHICH ARE	604 22
PAY RESPECTFUL OBEDIENCE TO THE CIVIL AUTHORITY,	610 41

OBEDIENT

AND OBEDIENT HEART	005 34
AND OBEDIENT HEART	023 09
AND OBEDIENT WALKING BEFORE THEE ALL OUR DAYS	050 27
AND OBEDIENT WALKING BEFORE THEE	053 06
AND OBEDIENT TO THE LAW FOR MAN	105 20
AND BECAME OBEDIENT UNTO DEATH, EVEN THE DEATH OF THE	134 21
DELAY WAS OBEDIENT UNTO THE CALLING OF THY SON JESUS	246 18
THEY WERE NOT OBEDIENT UNTO HIS WORD	471 29
PRIESTS WERE OBEDIENT TO THE FAITH	532 22

OBEDIENTLY

AND OBEDIENTLY HONOUR THEM, ACCORDING TO THY BLESSED	032 11
HENCEFORTH OBEDIENTLY WALK IN THY HOLY COMMANDMENTS	052 23
UP OURSELVES OBEDIENTLY TO FULFIL THY HOLY	226 22
THE PEOPLE OBEDIENTLY TO FOLLOW THE SAME, THAT THEY	244 26
THOU THEN OBEDIENTLY KEEP GOD'S HOLY WILL AND	277 04
THOU THEN OBEDIENTLY KEEP GOD'S HOLY WILL AND	278 13
THAT THEY MAY OBEDIENTLY FOLLOW THE SAME	549 13
AND OBEDIENTLY TO HEAR AND TO BE ORDERED BY THE	R 582 33

OBEY

MAY BE SET TO OBEY THY COMMANDMENTS, AND ALSO THAT BY	031 21
IN THY FAITH, TO OBEY THY WORD, AND TO ABIDE IN THY	043 10
MAY IN ALL THINGS OBEY THY BLESSED WILL	105 23
WE MAY EVER OBEY THY GODLY MOTIONS IN	125 30
TO HONOUR AND OBEY THE CIVIL AUTHORITY	288 28
AND UNDER THE EARTH, DO BOW AND OBEY	314 17
OF ME, THEY SHALL OBEY ME	362 28
ELSE THEY WILL NOT OBEY THEE	378 12
ISRAEL WOULD NOT OBEY ME	443 03
WILL YOU REVERENTLY OBEY YOUR BISHOP, AND OTHER CHIEF	533 30
WILL YOU REVERENTLY OBEY YOUR BISHOP, AND OTHER CHIEF	543 11
TO HONOUR AND OBEY THE CIVIL AUTHORITY	580 04
SERVE HIM, AND OBEY HIM, AS WE OUGHT TO DO	580 32
THEY THROUGH GRACE OBEY THE CALLING	606 12

OBEYED

NEITHER HAVE WE OBEYED THE VOICE OF THE LORD OUR GOD,	022 08
AS YE HAVE ALWAYS OBEYED, NOT AS IN MY PRESENCE ONLY,	106 02
THAT HE READILY OBEYED THE CALLING OF THY SON JESUS	226 19
THEY HAVE NOT ALL OBEYED THE GOSPEL	227 11

OBEYETH

THE LORD, THAT OBEYETH THE VOICE OF HIS SERVANT, THAT	144 23

OBJECTED

IMPEDIMENT BE OBJECTED, THE BISHOP SHALL CEASE FROM	R 530 26
IMPEDIMENT BE OBJECTED, THE BISHOP SHALL CEASE FROM	R 537 02

OBJECTION

IF ANY OBJECTION BE OFFERED, THE BISHOP, OR THE	R 570 21
NO OBJECTION BEING OFFERED, OR THE INSTITUTOR	R 570 23

OBLATION

BY HIS ONE OBLATION OF HIMSELF ONCE OFFERED) A FULL,	080 10
OBLATION, AND SATISFACTION, FOR THE SINS	080 11
OFFER THEE AN OBLATION WITH GREAT GLADNESS, AND TO	315 31
HIS DWELLING AN OBLATION, WITH GREAT GLADNESS	326 17
HIS DWELLING AN OBLATION, WITH GREAT GLADNESS	372 09

OBLATIONS

THE ALMS AND OBLATIONS ARE BEING RECEIVED AND	R 073 34
OUR (ALMS AND) OBLATIONS, AND TO RECEIVE THESE OUR	074 09
WITH THE BURNT-OFFERINGS AND OBLATIONS	404 16

OBLIGED

SHALL BE OBLIGED TO GIVE AN ACCOUNT OF THE SAME TO	R 085 18

OBSERVE

TEACHING THEM TO OBSERVE ALL THINGS WHATSOEVER I HAVE	275 30
AND OBSERVE HIS LAWS	472 27
A READY WILL TO OBSERVE ALL SPIRITUAL DISCIPLINE	535 05
TO KEEP AND OBSERVE THE SAME	542 17
TEACHING THEM TO OBSERVE ALL THINGS WHATSOEVER I HAVE	552 13

OBSERVED

ARE IN THE WEEK FOLLOWING TO BE OBSERVED	R 071 26

OBSOLETE

AS WELL FROM OBSOLETE WORDS AND PHRASES, AS FROM THE	R 610 28

OBSTINATE

THE HOLY COMMUNION, AND NOT HIM THAT IS OBSTINATE	R 085 17

OBTAIN

THAT WE MAY OBTAIN MERCY, AND FIND GRACE TO HELP IN	005 09
END THAT WE MAY OBTAIN FORGIVENESS OF THE SAME,	006 02
END THAT WE MAY OBTAIN FORGIVENESS OF THE SAME,	023 10
BY THY MERCY, OBTAIN EVERLASTING LIFE	049 27
WHOLE CHURCH, MAY OBTAIN REMISSION OF OUR SINS, AND	081 19
WHEREBY ALONE WE OBTAIN REMISSION OF OUR SINS,	086 33
SO RUN, THAT YE MAY OBTAIN	119 06
NOW THEY DO IT TO OBTAIN A CORRUPTIBLE CROWN	119 08
MAY OBTAIN OF THEE, THE GOD OF ALL	124 15
ALL THINGS, MAY OBTAIN THY PROMISES, WHICH EXCEED ALL	197 07
THAT THEY MAY OBTAIN THEIR PETITIONS, MAKE THEM TO	203 12
MAY OBTAIN THY GRACIOUS PROMISES,	204 25
THAT WE MAY OBTAIN THAT WHICH THOU DOST PROMISE,	209 10
FAITHFULLY WE MAY OBTAIN EFFECTUALLY	222 12
FOR THEY SHALL OBTAIN MERCY	257 26
THIS PLACE, MAY OBTAIN THY MERCIFUL AID AND	259 22
MAY OBTAIN THE MANIFOLD BLESSINGS OF THY GRACE	267 08
THE END THEY MAY OBTAIN EVERLASTING LIFE	298 22
ENDLESS COMFORT, OBTAIN REMISSION OF THEIR SINS, AND	565 33
BY THY MERCY, OBTAIN EVERLASTING LIFE	571 10
THAT WE MAY OBTAIN FORGIVENESS AT THY HANDS, WHO ART	590 04

OBTAINED

EFFECTUALLY BE OBTAINED, TO THE RELIEF OF OUR	050 11
HE HATH OBTAINED FOR US	086 15
BY INHERITANCE OBTAINED A MORE EXCELLENT NAME THAN	096 31
HAVING OBTAINED ETERNAL REDEMPTION FOR US	132 27

OBTAINED　　　　　CONTINUED

AND HAD OBTAINED PART OF THIS MINISTRY	234 12

OBTAINING

FOR THE OBTAINING WHEREOF WE SHALL NOT CEASE TO MAKE	089 20

OCCASION

THE CUTTING OFF OCCASION, FROM THEM THAT SEEK	V 38
THEM THAT SEEK OCCASION, OF CAVIL OR QUARREL AGAINST	V 38
ADD OTHERS, AS OCCASION MAY REQUIRE	R 047 05
THE HAPPY OCCASION WHICH WAS OFFERED TO THEM	VI 23
AND (IF OCCASION BE) SHALL NOTICE BE GIVEN OF THE	R 071 26
ON ANY OTHER OCCASION OF PUBLIC WORSHIP WHEN THE	R 073 25
AS OCCASION DEMANDS, THE MINISTER SHALL ADDRESS THE	R 313 15
HE SHALL THINK CONVENIENT TO THE OCCASION	R 314 24
AND SEEKETH OCCASION TO SLAY HIM	386 31
BE UNTO THEM AN OCCASION OF FALLING	423 20
THEY HAVE NONE OCCASION OF STUMBLING	501 12
ON URGENT OCCASION, UPON SOME OTHER DAY,	529 30
ON URGENT OCCASION, UPON SOME OTHER DAY, IN THE	R 535 25
NOR BE OCCASION THAT OTHERS OFFEND	540 29
AND OCCASION SHALL BE GIVEN	542 24
OR REASONS OCCASION A WISH IN YOU, OR IN THE	569 31
AND HATH GIVEN OCCASION TO MANY SUPERSTITIONS	608 43

OCCASIONAL

EXPEDIENCY OF OCCASIONAL ALTERATIONS AND AMENDMENTS	V 22
AMONG THE OCCASIONAL PRAYERS AND THANKSGIVINGS, MAY	R 305 04

OCCASIONS

TO THE VARIOUS EXIGENCY OF TIMES AND OCCASIONS	V 09
OF TIMES AND OCCASIONS, SUCH CHANGES AND ALTERATIONS	V 18
AS PASS ON THE SEAS UPON THEIR LAWFUL OCCASIONS	042 10
BE USED BEFORE SERMONS, OR ON SPECIAL OCCASIONS	R 047 03
CONVENIENT OCCASIONS, OPENLY IN THE CHURCH, INSTRUCT	R 295 08
CONVENIENT OCCASIONS, OPENLY IN THE CHURCH, INSTRUCT	R 582 28

OCCUPIED

THY SERVANT IS OCCUPIED IN THY STATUTES	491 13
BUT I WILL BE OCCUPIED IN THY COMMANDMENTS	495 12
THAT I MIGHT BE OCCUPIED IN THY WORD	500 07
LET ME NOT BE OCCUPIED IN UNGODLY WORKS WITH THE MEN	517 16

OCCUPY

AND OCCUPY THEIR BUSINESS IN GREAT WATERS	477 22

OCTAVE

COLLECT IS TO BE SAID DAILY THROUGHOUT THE OCTAVE	R 096 20
COLLECT IS TO BE SAID DAILY THROUGHOUT THE OCTAVE	R 108 04
BE SAID, AND MAY BE SAID THROUGHOUT THE OCTAVE	R 162 29
COLLECT IS TO BE SAID DAILY THROUGHOUT THE OCTAVE	R 177 20
COLLECT IS TO BE SAID DAILY THROUGHOUT THE OCTAVE	R 256 12

OCTOBER

OCTOBER, 1789	VI 44

OFFENCE

MAY WITHOUT OFFENCE BE ALLOWED, PROVIDED THE	V 04
GIVING NO OFFENCE IN ANY THING, THAT THE MINISTRY BE	126 08
AND WITHOUT OFFENCE TILL THE DAY OF CHRIST	221 04
MAN BY WHOM THE OFFENCE COMETH	253 02
BE UNDEFILED, AND INNOCENT FROM THE GREAT OFFENCE	364 12
WITHOUT ANY OFFENCE OR FAULT OF ME, O LORD	411 09
FORGIVEN THE OFFENCE OF THY PEOPLE, *	446 10
FOR THEIR OFFENCE, *	477 09
VOID OF OFFENCE TOWARDS THEE, AND TOWARDS MEN	590 18

OFFENCES

NOR THE OFFENCES OF OUR FOREFATHERS	054 13
LORD, OUR OFFENCES, NOR THE OFFENCES OF OUR	054 13
MULTITUDE OF THY MERCIES DO AWAY MINE OFFENCES	060 12
PARDONING OUR OFFENCES, THROUGH JESUS CHRIST OUR	081 32
PERCEIVE YOUR OFFENCES TO BE SUCH AS ARE NOT ONLY	087 22
OF YOUR OFFENCES AT GOD'S HAND	087 28
FOR OUR OFFENCES, MAY BE MERCIFULLY DELIVERED BY THY	118 30
ABSOLVE THY PEOPLE FROM THEIR OFFENCES	223 16
WOE UNTO THE WORLD BECAUSE OF OFFENCES	252 34
NEEDS BE THAT OFFENCES COME	253 02
DO AWAY OUR OFFENCES AND CLEANSE US FROM OUR SINS	323 16
DELIVER ME FROM ALL MINE OFFENCES	324 30
THE SINS AND OFFENCES OF MY YOUTH	369 30
9 DELIVER ME FROM ALL MINE OFFENCES	389 25
MULTITUDE OF THY MERCIES DO AWAY MINE OFFENCES	403 10
VISIT THEIR OFFENCES WITH THE ROD, AND THEIR SIN WITH	452 05
BY THOSE THAT HAVE KNOWLEDGE OF THEIR OFFENCES	608 21

OFFEND

BUT WHOSO SHALL OFFEND ONE OF THESE LITTLE ONES WHICH	252 31
HAND OR THY FOOT OFFEND THEE, CUT THEM OFF, AND CAST	253 03
AND IF THINE EYE OFFEND THEE, PLUCK IT OUT, AND CAST	253 07
UTTERLY PURPOSED THAT MY MOUTH SHALL NOT OFFEND	358 24
THAT I OFFEND NOT IN MY TONGUE	389 05
UNTO THEM THAT OFFEND OF MALICIOUS WICKEDNESS	411 15
YOU YOURSELVES OFFEND, NOR BE OCCASION THAT OTHERS	540 29

OFFEND   CONTINUED

NOR BE OCCASION THAT OTHERS OFFEND   540 30
AND ASHAMED TO OFFEND THEE   588 20
IN CHRIST, YET OFFEND IN MANY THINGS   605 36

OFFENDED

WE HAVE OFFENDED AGAINST THY HOLY LAWS   006 20
WE HAVE OFFENDED AGAINST THY HOLY LAWS   023 27
SO THAT THE CONGREGATION BE THEREBY OFFENDED   R 085 03
AMENDS FOR THAT WHEREIN HE HIMSELF HATH OFFENDED   R 085 14
TO HAVE OFFENDED, EITHER BY WILL, WORD, OR DEED,   087 19
OTHERS WHO HAVE OFFENDED YOU, AS YE WOULD HAVE   087 27
SHALL NOT BE OFFENDED IN ME   094 24
WHO IS OFFENDED, AND I BURN NOT   121 12
ALL YE SHALL BE OFFENDED BECAUSE OF ME THIS NIGHT   141 18
ALL SHALL BE OFFENDED, YET WILL NOT I   141 22
THAT YE SHOULD NOT BE OFFENDED   179 29
THAT HAVE OFFENDED HIM   R 313 21
AND IF HE HATH OFFENDED ANY OTHER, TO ASK THEM   R 313 22

OFFENDERS

O LORD, HAVE MERCY UPON US, MISERABLE OFFENDERS   006 24
O LORD, HAVE MERCY UPON US, MISERABLE OFFENDERS   023 31

OFFENDETH

12 WHO CAN TELL HOW OFT HE OFFENDETH   364 08
AS HE THAT OFFENDETH AGAINST THE COMMON ORDER OF THE   609 39

OFFER

WHO DESIRE NOW TO OFFER UP THEIR PRAISES AND   019 18
WHO DESIRE NOW TO OFFER UP THEIR PRAISES AND   033 16
DESIRETH NOW TO OFFER HER PRAISES AND THANKSGIVINGS   051 08
MAY CONTINUALLY OFFER UNTO THEE OUR SACRIFICE OF   052 25
PRIEST SHALL THEN OFFER, AND SHALL PLACE UPON THE   R 073 32
WHICH WE OFFER UNTO THY DIVINE MAJESTY   074 10
WHICH WE NOW OFFER UNTO THEE, THE MEMORIAL THY SON   080 41
AND HERE WE OFFER AND PRESENT UNTO THEE, O LORD,   081 21
MANIFOLD SINS, TO OFFER UNTO THEE ANY SACRIFICE   081 29
TO THE PRIEST, AND OFFER THE GIFT THAT MOSES   115 05
YET THAT HE SHOULD OFFER HIMSELF OFTEN, AS THE HIGH   148 02
WHICH WE OFFER BEFORE THEE FOR ALL ESTATES   156 29
AN EGG, WILL HE OFFER HIM A SCORPION   183 16
AND THEN COME AND OFFER THY GIFT   198 11
THAT THEY MAY OFFER UNTO THE LORD AN OFFERING IN   232 12
AND TO OFFER A SACRIFICE ACCORDING TO THAT WHICH IS   232 27
TO OFFER UP SPIRITUAL SACRIFICES,   259 32
HEARTS OF MANY TO OFFER THEMSELVES FOR THIS MINISTRY   260 22
AN EGG, WILL HE OFFER HIM A SCORPION   263 10
DESIRETH NOW TO OFFER HER PRAISES AND THANKSGIVINGS   306 27
HER THANKS, MUST OFFER ACCUSTOMED OFFERINGS, WHICH   R 307 07
TO THINE HOUSE, TO OFFER THEE AN OBLATION WITH GREAT   315 31
OF HEALTH, HE MAY OFFER THEE PRAISE AND THANKSGIVING   320 12
THEREFORE WILL I OFFER IN HIS DWELLING AN OBLATION,   326 17
5 OFFER THE SACRIFICE OF RIGHTEOUSNESS, *   347 21
BLOOD WILL I NOT OFFER, *   357 32
7 THEREFORE WILL I OFFER IN HIS DWELLING AN OBLATION,   372 09
14 OFFER UNTO GOD THANKSGIVING, *   402 18
THEN SHALL THEY OFFER YOUNG BULLOCKS UPON THINE   404 17
13 I WILL OFFER UNTO THEE FAT BURNT-SACRIFICES,   418 10
I WILL OFFER BULLOCKS AND GOATS   418 11
22 THAT THEY WOULD OFFER UNTO HIM THE SACRIFICE OF   477 20
SHALL THY PEOPLE OFFER THEMSELVES WILLINGLY WITH AN   482 11
15 I WILL OFFER TO THEE THE SACRIFICE OF   487 19
AND HIS APOSTLES, OFFER UP OUR PRAYERS TO ALMIGHTY   553 10
IN THY NAME, TO OFFER UP THEIR PRAISES AND   564 32
NOW APPOINTED TO OFFER THE SACRIFICES OF PRAYER AND   572 20
IN WHOSE NAME WE OFFER UP THESE OUR IMPERFECT   591 32
THE PRIEST DID OFFER CHRIST FOR THE QUICK AND THE   609 18

OFFERED

INCENSE SHALL BE OFFERED UNTO MY NAME, AND A PURE   004 14
OUR PRAYERS ARE OFFERED, AND GRANT THAT HE MAY BE   045 25
OF THY SERVANT FOR WHOM OUR PRAYERS ARE OFFERED   046 03
WHICH WAS OFFERED TO THEM (UNINFLUENCED AND   VI 24
WHICH WAS OFFERED FOR US, AND HATH TAKEN AWAY   078 09
OF HIMSELF ONCE OFFERED) A FULL, PERFECT, AND   080 10
ETERNAL SPIRIT OFFERED HIMSELF WITHOUT SPOT TO GOD,   132 31
CHRIST WAS ONCE OFFERED TO BEAR THE SINS OF MANY   148 08
WHICH THEY OFFERED YEAR BY YEAR CONTINUALLY, MAKE THE   157 17
FOR THEN WOULD THEY NOT HAVE CEASED TO BE OFFERED   157 19
WHICH ARE OFFERED BY THE LAW   157 31
AFTER HE HAD OFFERED ONE SACRIFICE FOR SINS FOR EVER,   158 05
NOW READY TO BE OFFERED, AND THE TIME OF MY DEPARTURE   253 25
THEY OFFERED THEIR SONS AND THEIR DAUGHTERS UNTO   475 09
WHOM THEY OFFERED UNTO THE IDOLS OF CANAAN   475 12
ANY OBJECTION BE OFFERED, THE BISHOP, OR THE PRIEST   R 570 21
OBJECTION BEING OFFERED, OR THE INSTITUTOR CHOOSING   R 570 23
LIFE IS OFFERED TO MANKIND BY CHRIST, WHO IS THE ONLY   604 16

OFFERETH

23 WHOSO OFFERETH ME THANKS AND PRAISE, HE HONOURETH   403 04

OFFERING

BE OFFERED UNTO MY NAME, AND A PURE OFFERING   004 15
FOR US AN OFFERING AND A SACRIFICE TO GOD FOR A   128 32
TO HIM, AND OFFERING HIM VINEGAR, AND SAYING, IF THOU   154 30
SACRIFICE AND OFFERING THOU WOULDEST NOT, BUT A BODY   157 25
SACRIFICE AND OFFERING AND BURNT-OFFERINGS AND   157 29

OFFERING   CONTINUED

AND OFFERING FOR SIN THOU WOULDEST NOT, NEITHER HADST   157 30
THROUGH THE OFFERING OF THE BODY OF JESUS CHRIST ONCE   158 02
MINISTERING AND OFFERING OFTENTIMES THE SAME   158 04
FOR BY ONE OFFERING HE HATH PERFECTED FOR EVER THEM   158 08
IS NO MORE OFFERING FOR SIN   158 15
THE LORD AN OFFERING IN RIGHTEOUSNESS   232 12
THEN SHALL THE OFFERING OF JUDAH AND JERUSALEM BE   232 13
8 SACRIFICE AND OFFERING THOU WOULDEST NOT, *   390 27
6 AN OFFERING OF A FREE HEART WILL I GIVE THEE,   406 14
FOR OFFERING TO THY GLORIOUS MAJESTY   565 04
THE OFFERING OF CHRIST ONCE MADE IS THAT PERFECT   609 14

OFFERINGS

WHEN THE OFFERINGS OF THE PEOPLE ARE TO BE RECEIVED   R 073 26
AND OTHER OFFERINGS OF THE PEOPLE, IN A DECENT BASIN   R 073 28
ACCUSTOMED OFFERINGS, WHICH SHALL BE APPLIED BY THE   R 307 07
ALL THY OFFERINGS, *   364 21
AND ATE THE OFFERINGS OF THE DEAD   474 26
THE FREE-WILL OFFERINGS OF MY MOUTH PLEASE THEE,   497 13

OFFERTORY

AND BEGIN THE OFFERTORY, SAYING ONE OR MORE OF THESE   R 071 32
A HYMN, OR AN OFFERTORY ANTHEM IN THE WORDS OF HOLY   R 073 35

OFFICE

BE CALLED TO ANY OFFICE AND ADMINISTRATION IN THE   039 10
DAY OF LENT, THE OFFICE ENSUING MAY BE READ   R 060 03
OR EVENING PRAYER, OR AS A SEPARATE OFFICE   R 060 05
THE SAME OFFICE MAY BE READ AT OTHER TIMES,   R 060 06
ACCORDING TO MINE OFFICE, I BID YOU IN THE NAME OF   089 07
AND ALL MEMBERS HAVE NOT THE SAME OFFICE   110 14
WHEN THE OFFICE IS USED FOR CHILDREN, THE MINISTER   R 276 17
WHEN THE OFFICE IS USED FOR ADULTS, THE MINISTER   R 277 18
TO THEE BY OUR OFFICE AND MINISTRY, MAY ALSO BE   278 28
FROM THIS OFFICE, BEGINNING, WE YIELD THEE HEARTY   R 281 24
PROVIDED IN THIS OFFICE FOR THE BAPTISM OF ADULTS   R 281 26
AND THE REMAINDER OF THE OFFICE   R 282 06
IN THE FORM BEFORE APPOINTED IN THIS OFFICE   R 282 11
WHAT IS THE OFFICE OF A BISHOP   294 07
THE OFFICE OF A BISHOP IS, TO BE A CHIEF   294 08
WHAT IS THE OFFICE OF A PRIEST   294 11
THE OFFICE OF A PRIEST IS, TO MINISTER TO   294 12
WHAT IS THE OFFICE OF A DEACON   294 16
THE OFFICE OF A DEACON IS, TO ASSIST THE   294 17
OF THE FOREGOING OFFICE AS HE SHALL THINK FIT, AND   R 320 07
THIS OFFICE MAY BE USED WITH AGED AND BED-RIDDEN   R 323 32
NOTED THAT THIS OFFICE IS APPROPRIATE TO BE USED ONLY R 337 02
SUCH PART OF THIS OFFICE, OR SUCH DEVOTIONS TAKEN   R 337 04
THE SAME OFFICE MAY BE USED   R 337 07
AND LET ANOTHER TAKE HIS OFFICE   480 17
THE DUTY AND OFFICE OF SUCH AS COME TO BE ADMITTED   R 530 04
THE PEOPLE OUGHT TO ESTEEM THEM IN THEIR OFFICE   R 530 06
ADMITTED TO THAT OFFICE, LET HIM COME FORTH IN THE   530 24
EXECUTE THEIR OFFICE, TO THE EDIFYING OF THY CHURCH,   531 07
TO THE LIKE OFFICE AND ADMINISTRATION   531 19
THEE IN THIS OFFICE, TO THE GLORY OF THY NAME,   531 22
LET THEM USE THE OFFICE OF A DEACON, BEING FOUND   531 30
HAVE USED THE OFFICE OF A DEACON WELL PURCHASE TO   532 03
UPON YOU THIS OFFICE AND MINISTRATION, TO SERVE GOD   532 27
TO THE OFFICE OF A DEACON, IN THE CHURCH WHERE HE   533 10
IT IS HIS OFFICE, WHERE PROVISION IS SO MADE, TO   533 18
TO EXECUTE THE OFFICE OF A DEACON IN THE CHURCH OF   534 05
SERVANTS UNTO THE OFFICE OF DEACONS IN THY CHURCH   535 02
IN THIS INFERIOR OFFICE, THAT THEY MAY BE FOUND   535 08
CONTINUE IN THAT OFFICE OF A DEACON THE SPACE OF A   R 535 20
THE DUTY AND OFFICE OF SUCH AS COME TO BE ADMITTED   R 536 04
THE PEOPLE OUGHT TO ESTEEM THEM IN THEIR OFFICE   R 536 06
DAY UNTO THE HOLY OFFICE OF PRIESTHOOD   536 23
EXERCISE THEIR OFFICE, TO THE EDIFYING OF THY CHURCH, 537 13
NOW CALLED TO THE OFFICE OF PRIESTHOOD   537 23
THEE IN THIS OFFICE, TO THE GLORY OF THY NAME, AND   537 26
IMPORTANCE THIS OFFICE IS, WHEREUNTO YE ARE CALLED   539 28
TO HOW WEIGHTY AN OFFICE AND CHARGE YE ARE CALLED   539 31
THEN AS YOUR OFFICE IS BOTH OF SO GREAT EXCELLENCY,   540 24
WHOLLY TO THIS OFFICE, WHEREUNTO IT HATH PLEASED GOD   541 12
TO THE SAME OFFICE AND MINISTRY, APPOINTED FOR THE   545 23
GHOST FOR THE OFFICE AND WORK OF A PRIEST IN THE   546 09
TO EXECUTE THE OFFICE OF A PRIEST IN THE CHURCH OF   546 17
7 TO 13, AS BEFORE IN THIS OFFICE   R 547 22
36 TO 38, AS BEFORE IN THIS OFFICE   R 547 25
AS IS IN THIS OFFICE BEFORE APPOINTED   R 547 28
NOW CALLED TO THE OFFICE OF DEACON AND THESE THY   547 34
NOW CALLED TO THE OFFICE OF PRIEST   548 02
A MAN DESIRE THE OFFICE OF A BISHOP, HE DESIRETH A   549 18
DULY EXECUTE THE OFFICE WHEREUNTO HE IS CALLED, TO   553 19
THEE IN THIS OFFICE, TO THE GLORY OF THY NAME, AND   553 32
GHOST FOR THE OFFICE AND WORK OF A BISHOP IN THE   558 12
EXECUTE THEIR OFFICE TO THE EDIFYING OF THY CHURCH,   560 29
DULY EXECUTE THE OFFICE WHEREUNTO HE IS CALLED,   561 04
THE FOLLOWING OFFICE MAY BE USED WITH THE ORDER FOR   R 563 03
THE FOLLOWING OFFICE MAY BE USED WITH THE ORDER FOR   R 569 09
TO PERFORM THE OFFICE OF A PRIEST, IN THE PARISH (OR   569 16
PRIEST INTO THE OFFICE OF RECTOR OF -- PARISH, (OR   569 23
HERE THE INSTITUTOR SHALL BEGIN THE OFFICE   R 571 04
IN THIS OFFICE IN THE FORM OF A LETTER   R 574 30
TAKE UPON HIM THE OFFICE OF PUBLIC PREACHING, OR   607 19

OFFICER

THEE TO THE OFFICER, AND THOU BE CAST INTO PRISON   198 14

OFFICERS

THEREFORE AND OFFICERS SAW HIM, THEY CRIED OUT,   159 05

OFFICES

IN THESE OFFICES, THEY SHALL BE BROUGHT TO THE BISHOP   R 295 15
WHICH OFFICES WERE EVERMORE HAD IN SUCH REVEREND   529 14
FOR THE SEVERAL OFFICES OF RELIGIOUS WORSHIP, AND LET   564 23
IN THY NAME, AND FOR ALL OTHER HOLY OFFICES   565 11

OFFSPRING

OF THE OFFSPRING OF ADAM   604 31

OFT

DO THIS, AS OFT AS YE SHALL DRINK IT, IN REMEMBRANCE   080 28
IN PRISONS MORE FREQUENT, IN DEATHS OFT   120 32
THIS DO YE, AS OFT AS YE DRINK IT, IN REMEMBRANCE OF   152 23
LORD, HOW OFT SHALL MY BROTHER SIN AGAINST ME,   221 09
12 WHO CAN TELL HOW OFT HE OFFENDETH   364 08

OFTEN

UNTO THEE, HOW OFTEN WOULD I HAVE GATHERED THY   100 29
IN JOURNEYINGS OFTEN, IN PERILS OF WATERS, IN PERILS   121 04
IN FASTINGS OFTEN, IN COLD AND NAKEDNESS   121 09
IN WATCHINGS OFTEN, IN HUNGER AND THIRST, IN FASTINGS   121 09
OFFER HIMSELF OFTEN, AS THE HIGH PRIEST ENTERETH INTO   148 02
FOR THEN MUST HE OFTEN HAVE SUFFERED SINCE THE   148 04
FOR AS OFTEN AS YE EAT THIS BREAD, AND DRINK THIS   152 24
I HAVE TOLD YOU OFTEN, AND NOW TELL YOU EVEN WEEPING,   222 17
EVERY PARISH SHALL OFTEN ADMONISH THE PEOPLE, THAT   R 273 03
TO THE OFTEN RECEIVING OF THE HOLY COMMUNION OF THE   R 321 07

OFTENTIMES

AND OFFERING OFTENTIMES THE SAME SACRIFICES, WHICH   158 04

OG

AND OG, THE KING OF BASHAN   510 24
20 AND OG, THE KING OF BASHAN   512 22

OIL

THEE WITH THE OIL OF GLADNESS ABOVE THY FELLOWS   097 12
FOR ASHES, THE OIL OF JOY FOR MOURNING, THE GARMENT   107 07
POURING IN OIL AND WINE, AND SET HIM ON HIS   208 31
I ANOINT THEE WITH OIL (OR I LAY MY HAND UPON THEE),   320 15
MY HEAD WITH OIL, AND MY CUP SHALL BE FULL   338 28
CORN AND WINE AND OIL INCREASE   347 27
MY HEAD WITH OIL, AND MY CUP SHALL BE FULL   368 21
THEE WITH THE OIL OF GLADNESS ABOVE THY FELLOWS   396 31
WERE SMOOTHER THAN OIL, AND YET BE THEY VERY SWORDS   408 03
WITH MY HOLY OIL HAVE I ANOINTED HIM   451 15
FOR I AM ANOINTED WITH FRESH OIL   456 20
AND OIL TO MAKE HIM A CHEERFUL COUNTENANCE, AND BREAD   468 24
LIKE WATER, AND LIKE OIL INTO HIS BONES   481 07
IS LIKE THE PRECIOUS OIL UPON THE HEAD, THAT RAN DOWN   509 15

OINTMENT

BOX OF OINTMENT OF SPIKENARD VERY PRECIOUS   140 04
WASTE OF THE OINTMENT MADE   140 07

OLD

AND IN THE OLD TIME BEFORE THEM   058 30
THEY ALL SHALL WAX OLD AS DOTH A GARMENT   097 16
FROM TWO YEARS OLD AND UNDER, ACCORDING TO THE TIME   103 27
HE WAS TWELVE YEARS OLD, THEY WENT UP TO JERUSALEM   110 20
NOT YET FIFTY YEARS OLD, AND HAST THOU SEEN ABRAHAM   133 30
AND CARRIED THEM ALL THE DAYS OF OLD   139 04
THE DAYS OF OLD, MOSES, AND HIS PEOPLE, SAYING, WHERE   139 07
THEY ALL SHALL WAX OLD AS A GARMENT   144 22
THE FEAST, NOT WITH OLD LEAVEN, NEITHER WITH THE   162 32
OUT THEREFORE THE OLD LEAVEN, THAT YE MAY BE A NEW   165 11
THE FEAST, NOT WITH OLD LEAVEN, NEITHER WITH THE   165 14
HOW CAN A MAN BE BORN WHEN HE IS OLD   188 08
THAT OUR OLD MAN IS CRUCIFIED WITH HIM,   197 17
WAS SAID BY THEM OF OLD TIME, THOU SHALT NOT KILL   197 31
CONVERSATION THE OLD MAN, WHICH IS CORRUPT ACCORDING   216 13
AS IN THE DAYS OF OLD, AND AS IN FORMER YEARS   232 14
A SON IN HER OLD AGE   236 26
WAS CAST OUT, THAT OLD SERPENT, CALLED THE DEVIL,   252 07
POWER OUR FATHERS WON THEIR LIBERTIES OF OLD   263 18
HOW CAN A MAN BE BORN WHEN HE IS OLD   275 12
GIVEN IN OLD TIME BY GOD TO THE PEOPLE OF ISRAEL   285 16
I HAVE CONSIDERED THE DAYS OF OLD   310 26
THE DAYS OF OLD, AND THE YEARS THAT ARE PAST   311 08
WHICH HAVE BEEN EVER OF OLD   369 29
FOR MY LIFE IS WAXEN OLD WITH HEAVINESS, *   376 11
25 I HAVE BEEN YOUNG, AND NOW AM OLD   386 12
WHAT THOU HAST DONE IN THEIR TIME OF OLD   394 23
O GOD, IN MINE OLD AGE, WHEN I AM GRAY-HEADED, *   426 10
WHOM THOU HAST PURCHASED, AND REDEEMED OF OLD   430 07
13 FOR GOD IS MY KING OF OLD   430 32
THE DAYS OF OLD, *   433 25
MIND THY WONDERS OF OLD TIME   434 05
I WILL DECLARE HARD SENTENCES OF OLD   434 30
8 O REMEMBER NOT OUR OLD SINS, BUT HAVE MERCY UPON   440 16
WHERE ARE THY OLD LOVING-KINDNESSES, *   453 05
THEY ALL SHALL WAX OLD AS DOTH A GARMENT   465 35
MEN AND MAIDENS, OLD MEN AND CHILDREN, PRAISE THE   524 27

OLD   CONTINUED

BOOKS OF THE OLD AND NEW TESTAMENT, OF WHOSE   603 33
THE OLD TESTAMENT IS NOT CONTRARY TO THE NEW   604 15
FOR BOTH IN THE OLD AND NEW TESTAMENT EVERLASTING   604 15
WHICH FEIGN THAT THE OLD FATHERS DID LOOK ONLY FOR   604 18

OLIVE-BRANCHES

LIKE THE OLIVE-BRANCHES *   506 12

OLIVE-TREE

LIKE A GREEN OLIVE-TREE IN THE HOUSE OF GOD   405 04

OLIVES

UNTO THE MOUNT OF OLIVES, THEN SENT JESUS TWO   091 12
THEY WENT OUT INTO THE MOUNT OF OLIVES   141 17
AND WENT, AS HE WAS WONT, TO THE MOUNT OF OLIVES   150 14

OMIT

HIS DISCRETION, MAY OMIT ONE OF THE LESSONS IN   R 026 07
HIS DISCRETION, MAY OMIT ANY OF THE CLAUSES IN THIS   R 047 04
AT HIS DISCRETION, OMIT ALL THAT FOLLOWETH, TO THE   R 058 09
THE PRIEST MAY OMIT THAT PART OF THE COMMANDMENT   R 067 27
MINISTER SHALL NOT OMIT EARNESTLY TO MOVE THE PERSONS R 299 06

OMITTED

ABSOLUTION ARE OMITTED, THE MINISTER MAY, AFTER THE   R 003 10
AND GOOD FRIDAY THE VENITE MAY BE OMITTED   R 008 13
THE LATTER PORTION THEREOF MAY BE OMITTED   R 014 06
THE DAY SHALL BE OMITTED HERE   R 017 03
PRAYERS SHALL BE OMITTED HERE WHEN THE LITANY IS   R 017 20
AND MAY BE OMITTED WHEN THE HOLY COMMUNION IS   R 017 21
ABSOLUTION ARE OMITTED, THE MINISTER MAY, AFTER THE   R 021 07
PRAYER MAY BE OMITTED AT THE DISCRETION OF THE   R 067 08
DECALOGUE MAY BE OMITTED, PROVIDED IT BE SAID AT   R 067 28
WHENEVER IT IS OMITTED, THE PRIEST SHALL SAY THE   R 067 29
HATH BEEN OMITTED, SHALL BE SAID, LORD, HAVE MERCY   R 069 32
THE CREED MAY BE OMITTED, IF IT HATH BEEN SAID   R 070 30
THE OVERPLUS SHALL BE OMITTED   R 224 36
OF THE COMMANDMENT WHICH IS INSET MAY BE OMITTED   R 286 04
PRAYER MAY BE OMITTED, IF THIS BE USED WITH THE   R 306 09
PATRI MAY BE OMITTED EXCEPT AT THE END OF THE WHOLE   R 324 11
MAY BE OMITTED, WHERE IT INTERFERES WITH THE USAGES,   R 569 11
TWENTY-FIRST OF THE FORMER ARTICLES IS OMITTED   R 607 11

OMITTING

THE QUESTIONS (OMITTING THE QUESTION WILT THOU BE   R 282 04

ONCE

PASS AT ONCE FROM THE SENTENCES TO THE   R 003 07
IN THINGS ONCE ADVISEDLY ESTABLISHED, SHE HATH,   V 26
MAY PASS AT ONCE TO THE COMMUNION SERVICE   R 010 05
PASS AT ONCE FROM THE SENTENCES TO THE   R 021 05
MAY PASS AT ONCE TO O LORD, SAVE THY SERVANTS   R 061 19
OBLATION OF HIMSELF ONCE OFFERED) A FULL, PERFECT,   080 10
I BEATEN WITH RODS, ONCE WAS I STONED, THRICE I   121 02
LET IT NOT BE ONCE NAMED AMONG YOU, AS BECOMETH   129 03
BLOOD HE ENTERED IN ONCE INTO THE HOLY PLACE, HAVING   132 27
BUT NOW ONCE IN THE END OF THE WORLD HATH HE APPEARED   148 05
APPOINTED UNTO MEN ONCE TO DIE, BUT AFTER THIS THE   148 07
SO CHRIST WAS ONCE OFFERED TO BEAR THE SINS OF MANY   148 08
CRIED OUT ALL AT ONCE, SAYING, AWAY WITH THIS MAN,   153 29
THE WORSHIPPERS ONCE PURGED SHOULD HAVE HAD NO MORE   157 20
OF JESUS CHRIST ONCE FOR ALL   158 03
CHRIST ALSO HATH ONCE SUFFERED FOR SINS, THE JUST FOR   161 22
WHEN ONCE THE LONG-SUFFERING OF GOD   161 27
FOR IN THAT HE DIED, HE DIED UNTO SIN ONCE   163 06
FOR IN THAT HE DIED, HE DIED UNTO SIN ONCE   197 23
WAS SEEN OF ABOVE FIVE HUNDRED BRETHREN AT ONCE   205 09
11 GOD SPAKE ONCE, AND TWICE I HAVE ALSO HEARD THE   414 21
I HAVE SWORN ONCE BY MY HOLINESS, THAT I WILL NOT   452 10
THAT THE LITANY BE ONCE SAID FOR BOTH   R 547 21
PROFESS THE FAITH ONCE DELIVERED TO THE SAINTS   574 12
OF HIMSELF ONCE MADE, SHOULD TAKE AWAY THE SINS OF   605 34
OFFERING OF CHRIST ONCE MADE IS THAT PERFECT   609 14

ONE

PRAYER BY READING ONE OR MORE OF THE FOLLOWING   R 003 03
THE HIGH AND LOFTY ONE THAT INHABITETH ETERNITY,   003 25
AND HOLY GHOST, ONE GOD   R 008 29
AFTER ANY ONE OF THE FOLLOWING CANTICLES OF MORNING   R 010 04
I BELIEVE IN ONE GOD THE FATHER ALMIGHTY, MAKER OF   015 33
AND IN ONE LORD JESUS CHRIST, THE ONLY-BEGOTTEN SON   016 02
BEING OF ONE SUBSTANCE WITH THE FATHER   016 05
I ACKNOWLEDGE ONE BAPTISM FOR THE REMISSION OF SINS   016 19
AND I BELIEVE ONE CATHOLIC AND APOSTOLIC CHURCH   016 19
AND THE HOLY GHOST, ONE GOD, WORLD WITHOUT END   018 15
AT THIS TIME WITH ONE ACCORD TO MAKE OUR COMMON   020 04
PRAYER BY READING ONE OR MORE OF THE FOLLOWING   R 021 03
WE HAVE TURNED EVERY ONE TO HIS OWN WAY   022 15
MAY OMIT ONE OF THE LESSONS IN EVENING   R 026 07
BEING FOLLOWED BY ONE OF THE EVENING CANTICLES   R 026 08
I BELIEVE IN ONE GOD THE FATHER ALMIGHTY, MAKER OF   030 04
AND IN ONE LORD JESUS CHRIST, THE ONLY-BEGOTTEN SON   030 07
BEING OF ONE SUBSTANCE WITH THE FATHER   030 10
I ACKNOWLEDGE ONE BAPTISM FOR THE REMISSION OF SINS   030 24
AND I BELIEVE ONE CATHOLIC AND APOSTOLIC CHURCH   030 24
AND REIGNETH EVER, ONE GOD, WORLD WITHOUT END   032 14

AT THIS TIME WITH ONE ACCORD TO MAKE OUR COMMON   034 04
AND FASHION INTO ONE UNITED PEOPLE THE MULTITUDES   036 15
BEING GATHERED INTO ONE FOLD, SHALL BECOME PARTAKERS   037 06
THAT AS THERE IS BUT ONE BODY AND ONE SPIRIT, AND ONE   037 30
AND ONE SPIRIT, AND ONE HOPE OF OUR CALLING, ONE   037 30
IS BUT ONE BODY AND ONE SPIRIT, AND ONE HOPE OF OUR   037 30
ONE LORD, ONE FAITH, ONE BAPTISM, ONE GOD AND FATHER   037 31
ONE BAPTISM, ONE GOD AND FATHER OF US ALL, SO   037 31
HOPE OF OUR CALLING, ONE LORD, ONE FAITH, ONE   037 31
ONE LORD, ONE FAITH, ONE BAPTISM, ONE GOD   037 31
SO WE MAY BE ALL OF ONE HEART AND OF ONE SOUL,   037 32
OF ONE HEART AND OF ONE SOUL, UNITED IN ONE HOLY BOND   037 32
ONE SOUL, UNITED IN ONE HOLY BOND OF TRUTH AND PEACE,   037 33
WITH ONE MIND AND ONE MOUTH GLORIFY THEE   038 02
AND MAY WITH ONE MIND AND ONE MOUTH GLORIFY THEE   038 02
WHO HAST MADE OF ONE BLOOD ALL NATIONS OF MEN FOR TO   038 05
LIVEST AND REIGNEST ONE GOD, WORLD WITHOUT END   043 15
WHO CAME AMONG US AS ONE THAT SERVETH, THY SON JESUS   044 24
THAT ALL, AND EVERY ONE OF THEM, MAY SERVE TRULY IN   047 17
IN BROTHERLY CHARITY ONE TOWARDS ANOTHER   048 04
AND THE HOLY GHOST, ONE GOD, WORLD WITHOUT END   049 10
MAKEST MEN TO BE OF ONE MIND IN A HOUSE, AND STILLEST   052 18
GLORIOUS TRINITY, ONE GOD   054 11
IT BE SAID AT LEAST ONE SUNDAY IN EACH MONTH   R 067 28
I BELIEVE IN ONE GOD THE FATHER ALMIGHTY, MAKER OF   071 02
AND IN ONE LORD JESUS CHRIST, THE ONLY-BEGOTTEN SON   071 04
BEING OF ONE SUBSTANCE WITH THE FATHER   071 07
I ACKNOWLEDGE ONE BAPTISM FOR THE REMISSION OF SINS   071 21
AND I BELIEVE ONE CATHOLIC AND APOSTOLIC CHURCH   071 21
THE OFFERTORY, SAYING ONE OR MORE OF THESE SENTENCES   R 071 32
NOT EVERY ONE THAT SAITH UNTO ME, LORD, LORD,   072 13
YE HAVE DONE IT UNTO ONE OF THE LEAST OF THESE MY   073 03
ART ONE GOD, ONE LORD, IN TRINITY OF   079 08
THE HOLY GHOST, ART ONE GOD, ONE LORD, IN TRINITY OF   079 08
WHO ARE ONE WITH THEE IN THY ETERNAL GODHEAD   079 17
MADE THERE (BY HIS ONE OBLATION OF HIMSELF ONCE   080 10
AND MADE ONE BODY WITH HIM, THAT HE MAY DWELL IN US,   081 27
AND IF ONE OF THE PARTIES, SO AT VARIANCE, BE CONTENT   R 085 11
BUT TO LOVE ONE ANOTHER   090 23
YOU TO BE LIKEMINDED ONE TOWARD ANOTHER ACCORDING TO   092 19
THAT YE MAY WITH ONE MIND AND ONE MOUTH GLORIFY GOD,   092 20
WITH ONE MIND AND ONE MOUTH GLORIFY GOD, EVEN THE   092 20
WHEREFORE RECEIVE YE ONE ANOTHER, AS CHRIST ALSO   092 22
HOLY SPIRIT EVER, ONE GOD, WORLD WITHOUT END   093 32
I AM THE VOICE OF ONE CRYING IN THE WILDERNESS, MAKE   095 28
BUT THERE STANDETH ONE AMONG YOU, WHOM YE KNOW NOT   096 03
SAME SPIRIT EVER, ONE GOD, WORLD WITHOUT END   096 19
AND THE HOLY GHOST, ONE GOD, WORLD WITHOUT END   098 16
TO BE TAXED, EVERY ONE INTO HIS OWN CITY   098 32
RAN UPON HIM WITH ONE ACCORD, AND CAST HIM OUT OF THE   100 10
WE HAVE FELLOWSHIP ONE WITH ANOTHER, AND THE BLOOD OF   101 27
BE WRITTEN EVERY ONE, I SUPPOSE THAT EVEN THE WORLD   102 16
SAME SPIRIT EVER, ONE GOD, WORLD WITHOUT END   104 11
THE SHEPHERDS SAID ONE TO ANOTHER, LET US NOW GO EVEN   106 08
HAVE MANY MEMBERS IN ONE BODY, AND ALL MEMBERS HAVE   110 13
EVERY ONE MEMBERS ONE OF ANOTHER   110 15
IN CHRIST, AND EVERY ONE MEMBERS ONE OF ANOTHER   110 15
WE, BEING MANY, ARE ONE BODY IN CHRIST, AND EVERY ONE   110 15
KINDLY AFFECTIONED ONE TO ANOTHER WITH BROTHERLY   111 23
IN HONOUR PREFERRING ONE ANOTHER   111 24
BE OF THE SAME MIND ONE TOWARD ANOTHER   111 31
THE VOICE OF ONE CRYING IN THE WILDERNESS, PREPARE YE   112 06
THERE COMETH ONE MIGHTIER THAN I AFTER ME,   112 14
FORBEARING ONE ANOTHER, AND FORGIVING ONE ANOTHER, IF   116 05
AND FORGIVING ONE ANOTHER, IF ANY MAN HAVE A QUARREL   116 06
YE ARE CALLED IN ONE BODY   116 10
AND ADMONISHING ONE ANOTHER IN PSALMS AND HYMNS AND   116 12
AND REIGNETH EVER, ONE GOD, WORLD WITHOUT END   117 11
THE FOUR WINDS, FROM ONE END OF HEAVEN TO THE OTHER   118 22
THE HOLY GHOST EVER, ONE GOD, WORLD WITHOUT END   119 03
A RACE RUN ALL, BUT ONE RECEIVETH THE PRIZE   119 06
SO FIGHT I, NOT AS ONE THAT BEATETH THE AIR   119 10
HAVE WROUGHT BUT ONE HOUR, AND THOU HAST MADE THEM   120 05
BUT HE ANSWERED ONE OF THEM, AND SAID, FRIEND,   120 07
JEWS FIVE TIMES RECEIVED I FORTY STRIPES SAVE ONE   121 02
AND THE HOLY GHOST, ONE GOD, WORLD WITHOUT END   125 32
THAT EVERY ONE OF YOU SHOULD KNOW HOW TO POSSESS HIS   127 29
HAD TWO SONS, THE ONE BY A BONDMAID, THE OTHER BY A   130 31
THE ONE FROM THE MOUNT SINAI, WHICH GENDERETH TO   131 04
FOR THEM, THAT EVERY ONE OF THEM MAY TAKE A LITTLE   131 31
ONE OF HIS DISCIPLES, ANDREW, SIMON PETER'S BROTHER,   131 32
THERE IS ONE THAT SEEKETH AND JUDGETH   133 16
CRUCIFIED WITH HIM, ONE ON THE RIGHT HAND, AND   137 04
AND STRAIGHTWAY ONE OF THEM RAN, AND TOOK A SPUNGE,   137 21
AND JUDAS ISCARIOT, ONE OF THE TWELVE, AND SMOTE   140 18
I SAY UNTO YOU, ONE OF YOU WHICH EATETH WITH ME SHALL   141 02
SAY UNTO HIM ONE BY ONE, IS IT I   141 04
AND TO SAY UNTO HIM ONE BY ONE, IS IT I   141 04
UNTO THEM, IT IS ONE OF THE TWELVE, THAT DIPPETH WITH   141 05
NOT THOU WATCH ONE HOUR   142 05
COMETH JUDAS, ONE OF THE TWELVE, AND WITH HIM   142 15
AND ONE OF THEM THAT STOOD BY DREW A SWORD, AND SMOTE   142 22
THERE COMETH ONE OF THE MAIDS OF THE HIGH   143 23
STOOD BY, THIS IS ONE OF THEM   143 29
SURELY THOU ART ONE OF THEM   143 31
RELEASED UNTO THEM ONE PRISONER, WHOMSOEVER THEY   145 13
AND THERE WAS ONE NAMED BARABBAS, WHICH LAY BOUND   145 14
AND THEY COMPEL ONE SIMON A CYRENIAN, WHO PASSED BY,   146 05
THE ONE ON HIS RIGHT HAND, AND THE OTHER ON HIS LEFT   146 15
AND ONE RAN AND FILLED A SPUNGE FULL OF VINEGAR, AND   146 31
LET HIM SELL HIS GARMENT, AND BUY ONE   150 08
WAS CALLED JUDAS, ONE OF THE TWELVE, WENT BEFORE   150 27
AND ONE OF THEM SMOTE THE SERVANT OF THE HIGH PRIEST,   150 32
ABOUT THE SPACE OF ONE HOUR AFTER ANOTHER CONFIDENTLY   151 15

HOLY SPIRIT EVER, ONE GOD, WORLD WITHOUT END   152 13
THIS MAN UNTO ME, AS ONE THAT PERVERTETH THE PEOPLE   153 23
HE MUST RELEASE ONE UNTO THEM AT THE FEAST   153 28
THEY LAID HOLD UPON ONE SIMON, A CYRENIAN, COMING OUT   154 09
AND THE MALEFACTORS, ONE ON THE RIGHT HAND, AND THE   154 24
AND ONE OF THE MALEFACTORS WHICH WERE HANGED RAILED   154 34
ALSO OUGHT TO WASH ONE ANOTHER'S FEET   156 16
THE HOLY GHOST EVER, ONE GOD, WORLD WITHOUT END   156 26
THEY MAY BE MADE ONE FLOCK UNDER ONE SHEPHERD, JESUS   157 11
MADE ONE FLOCK UNDER ONE SHEPHERD, JESUS CHRIST OUR   157 11
AND THE HOLY SPIRIT, ONE GOD, WORLD WITHOUT END   157 13
AFTER YE HAD OFFERED ONE SACRIFICE FOR SINS FOR EVER,   158 06
FOR BY ONE OFFERING HE HATH PERFECTED FOR EVER THEM   158 08
AND LET US CONSIDER ONE ANOTHER TO PROVOKE UNTO LOVE   158 24
BUT EXHORTING ONE ANOTHER   158 27
ON EITHER SIDE ONE, AND JESUS IN THE MIDST   159 34
BUT ONE OF THE SOLDIERS WITH A SPEAR PIERCED HIS   161 03
THE HOLY GHOST EVER, ONE GOD, WORLD WITHOUT END   163 29
THESE THAT YE HAVE ONE TO ANOTHER, AS YE WALK,   167 11
AND THE ONE OF THEM, WHOSE NAME WAS CLEOPAS,   167 11
AND THEY SAID ONE TO ANOTHER, DID NOT OUR HEART BURN   168 04
SUFFER THINE HOLY ONE TO SEE CORRUPTION   169 14
AND THESE THREE AGREE IN ONE   171 04
BE ONE FLOCK, AND ONE SHEPHERD   172 32
AND THERE SHALL BE ONE FLOCK, AND ONE SHEPHERD   172 32
AND THE HOLY GHOST, ONE GOD, WORLD WITHOUT END   177 19
THE SAME HOLY GHOST, ONE GOD, WORLD WITHOUT END   179 10
USE HOSPITALITY ONE TO ANOTHER WITHOUT GRUDGING   179 15
SO MINISTER THE SAME ONE TO ANOTHER, AS GOOD STEWARDS   179 17
OF THE SAME SPIRIT, ONE GOD, WORLD WITHOUT END   180 14
WITH ONE ACCORD IN ONE PLACE   180 18
THEY WERE ALL WITH ONE ACCORD IN ONE PLACE   180 18
SAYING ONE TO ANOTHER, BEHOLD, ARE NOT ALL   180 29
SAME SPIRIT EVER, ONE GOD, WORLD WITHOUT END   182 19
FOR TO ONE IS GIVEN BY THE SPIRIT THE WORD OF WISDOM   182 27
THESE WORKETH THAT ONE AND THE SELFSAME SPIRIT,   182 33
FOR AS THE BODY IS ONE, AND HATH MANY MEMBERS,   183 02
THE MEMBERS OF THAT ONE BODY, BEING MANY, ARE ONE   183 03
BEING MANY, ARE ONE BODY   183 03
FOR BY ONE SPIRIT ARE WE ALL BAPTIZED INTO ONE BODY,   183 04
WE ALL BAPTIZED INTO ONE BODY, WHETHER WE BE JEWS OR   183 05
MADE TO DRINK INTO ONE SPIRIT   183 07
FOR THE BODY IS NOT ONE MEMBER, BUT MANY   183 07
FOR EVERY ONE THAT ASKETH RECEIVETH   183 12
LIVETH AND REIGNETH, ONE GOD, WORLD WITHOUT END   183 27
FOR EVERY ONE THAT DOETH EVIL HATETH THE LIGHT,   185 08
AND THE SAME SPIRIT, ONE GOD, WORLD WITHOUT END   185 19
LIVEST AND REIGNEST, ONE GOD, WORLD WITHOUT END   186 29
SET IN HEAVEN, AND ONE SAT ON THE THRONE   187 05
SO IS EVERY ONE THAT IS BORN OF THE SPIRIT   188 16
LET US LOVE ONE ANOTHER   189 08
AND EVERY ONE THAT LOVETH IS BORN OF GOD, AND KNOWETH   189 09
OUGHT ALSO TO LOVE ONE ANOTHER   189 16
IF WE LOVE ONE ANOTHER, GOD DWELLETH IN US, AND HIS   189 17
BUT IF ONE WENT UNTO THEM FROM THE DEAD, THEY WILL   190 28
BE PERSUADED, THOUGH ONE ROSE FROM THE DEAD   190 30
AND LOVE ONE ANOTHER, AS HE GAVE US   191 31
AND THEY ALL WITH ONE CONSENT BEGAN TO MAKE EXCUSE   192 06
OF YOU BE SUBJECT ONE TO ANOTHER, AND BE CLOTHED WITH   192 30
IF HE LOSE ONE OF THEM, DOTH NOT LEAVE THE   193 18
BE IN HEAVEN OVER ONE SINNER THAT REPENTETH, MORE   193 25
IF SHE LOSE ONE PIECE, DOTH NOT LIGHT A   193 28
ANGELS OF GOD OVER ONE SINNER THAT REPENTETH   193 34
BUT EVERY ONE THAT IS PERFECT SHALL BE AS HIS MASTER   195 04
HAVING COMPASSION ONE OF ANOTHER, LOVE AS BRETHREN,   195 20
BE YE ALL OF ONE MIND, HAVING COMPASSION ONE OF   195 20
AND HE ENTERED INTO ONE OF THE SHIPS, WHICH WAS   196 10
NOT EVERY ONE THAT SAITH UNTO ME, LORD, LORD, SHALL   200 24
AND FELL IN ONE DAY THREE AND TWENTY THOUSAND   201 18
MAKE ME AS ONE OF THY HIRED SERVANTS   202 15
AND HE CALLED ONE OF THE SERVANTS, AND ASKED WHAT   202 28
FOR TO ONE IS GIVEN BY THE SPIRIT THE WORD OF WISDOM   203 27
THESE WORKETH THAT ONE AND THE SELFSAME SPIRIT,   204 03
NOT LEAVE IN THEE ONE STONE UPON ANOTHER   204 14
OF ME ALSO, AS OF ONE BORN OUT OF DUE TIME   205 12
THE ONE A PHARISEE, AND THE OTHER A PUBLICAN   205 24
FOR EVERY ONE THAT EXALTETH HIMSELF SHALL BE ABASED   205 32
THEY BRING UNTO HIM ONE THAT WAS DEAF, AND HAD AN   206 29
BUT AS OF ONE, AND TO THY SEED, WHICH IS CHRIST   207 20
IS NOT A MEDIATOR OF ONE, BUT GOD IS ONE   207 30
MEDIATOR IS NOT A MEDIATOR OF ONE, BUT GOD IS ONE   207 31
ARE CONTRARY THE ONE TO THE OTHER   209 17
AND ONE OF THEM, WHEN HE SAW THAT HE WAS HEALED,   210 07
HE WILL HATE THE ONE, AND LOVE THE OTHER   211 10
HE WILL HOLD TO THE ONE, AND DESPISE THE OTHER   211 11
ANXIOUS CAN ADD ONE CUBIT UNTO THE MEASURE OF HIS   211 19
WAS NOT ARRAYED LIKE ONE OF THESE   211 24
FORBEARING ONE ANOTHER IN LOVE   213 21
THERE IS ONE BODY, AND ONE SPIRIT, EVEN AS YE ARE   213 22
IS ONE BODY, AND ONE SPIRIT, EVEN AS YE ARE CALLED IN   213 23
AS YE ARE CALLED IN ONE HOPE OF YOUR CALLING   213 23
ONE LORD, ONE FAITH, ONE BAPTISM, ONE GOD AND FATHER   213 24
ONE LORD, ONE FAITH, ONE BAPTISM, ONE GOD AND FATHER   213 24
ONE BAPTISM, ONE GOD AND FATHER OF ALL, WHO IS   213 24
INTO THE HOUSE OF ONE OF THE CHIEF PHARISEES TO EAT   213 28
THEN ONE OF THEM, WHICH WAS A LAWYER, ASKED HIM A   215 08
FOR WE ARE MEMBERS ONE OF ANOTHER   216 18
AND BE YE KIND ONE TO ANOTHER, TENDER-HEARTED,   216 29
FORGIVING ONE ANOTHER, EVEN AS GOD FOR CHRIST'S SAKE   216 30
YOURSELVES ONE TO ANOTHER IN THE FEAR OF GOD   217 32
AND WENT THEIR WAYS, ONE TO HIS FARM, ANOTHER TO HIS   218 11
HAD BEGUN TO RECKON, ONE WAS BROUGHT UNTO HIM,   221 15
WENT OUT, AND FOUND ONE OF HIS FELLOW-SERVANTS, WHICH   221 23

ONE   CONTINUED

FORGIVE NOT EVERY ONE HIS BROTHER THEIR TRESPASSES   222 06
FOR THEM, THAT EVERY ONE OF THEM MAY TAKE A LITTLE   225 27
ONE OF HIS DISCIPLES, ANDREW, SIMON PETER'S BROTHER,   225 28
ONE OF THE TWELVE, CALLED DIDYMUS, WAS NOT   228 25
HOUSE OF JUDAS FOR ONE CALLED SAUL, OF TARSUS   230 18
AND EVERY ONE THAT HATH FORSAKEN HOUSES, OR BRETHREN,   231 18
AND THERE WAS ONE ANNA, A PROPHETESS, THE DAUGHTER OF   233 16
UP FROM US, MUST BE ORDAINED TO BE A WITNESS WITH   234 24
UNTO EVERY ONE OF US IS GIVEN GRACE ACCORDING TO THE   237 12
AND THERE STOOD UP ONE OF THEM NAMED AGABUS, AND   241 16
THAT YE LOVE ONE ANOTHER, AS I HAVE LOVED YOU   241 25
PASSED ON THROUGH ONE STREET   245 24
JEREMIAS, OR ONE OF THE PROPHETS   245 35
AND THERE STOOD UP ONE OF THEM NAMED AGABUS, AND   246 25
SONS MAY SIT, THE ONE ON THY RIGHT HAND, AND THE   247 10
LIVETH AND REIGNETH, ONE GOD, WORLD WITHOUT END   248 06
ONE FOR MOSES, AND ONE FOR ELIAS   249 03
ONE FOR THEE, AND ONE FOR MOSES, AND ONE FOR ELIAS   249 03
ONE FOR THEE, AND ONE FOR MOSES, AND CNE FOR ELIAS   249 03
THEY WERE ALL WITH ONE ACCORD IN SOLOMON'S PORCH   249 23
AND THEY WERE HEALED EVERY ONE   249 32
AND THE HOLY GHOST, ONE GOD, WORLD WITHOUT END   250 25
WHOSO SHALL RECEIVE ONE SUCH LITTLE CHILD IN MY NAME   252 29
WHOSO SHALL OFFEND ONE OF THESE LITTLE ONES WHICH   252 31
ENTER INTO LIFE WITH ONE EYE, RATHER THAN HAVING TWO   253 08
THAT YE DESPISE NOT ONE OF THESE LITTLE ONES   253 10
THAT YE LOVE ONE ANOTHER   255 12
THINE ELECT IN ONE COMMUNION AND FELLOWSHIP, IN THE   256 06
AND ONE OF THE ELDERS ANSWERED, SAYING UNTO ME,   257 04
SHALL SEPARATE THEM ONE FROM ANOTHER, AS A SHEPHERD   258 31
YE HAVE DONE IT UNTO ONE OF THE LEAST OF THESE MY   259 15
FOR EVERY ONE THAT ASKETH RECEIVETH   263 05
ANXIOUS CAN ADD ONE CUBIT UNTO THE MEASURE OF HIS   266 17
WAS NOT ARRAYED LIKE ONE OF THESE   266 22
YOURSELVES ONE TO ANOTHER IN THE FEAR OF GOD   267 13
THEY TWO SHALL BE ONE FLESH   267 31
LET EVERY ONE OF YOU IN PARTICULAR SO LOVE HIS WIFE   267 32
THEY TWAIN SHALL BE ONE FLESH   268 09
NO MORE TWAIN, BUT ONE FLESH   268 10
WHEREFORE COMFORT ONE ANOTHER WITH THESE WORDS   269 10
SENT ME, THAT EVERY ONE WHICH SEETH THE SON, AND   269 20
TWO GODFATHERS AND ONE GODMOTHER   R 273 10
FOR EVERY FEMALE, ONE GODFATHER AND TWO GODMOTHERS   R 273 10
SO IS EVERY ONE THAT IS BORN OF THE SPIRIT   275 21
AND WITH ONE ACCORD MAKE OUR PRAYERS UNTO HIM, THAT   280 16
BEING NAMED BY SOME ONE WHO IS PRESENT, THE MINISTER   R 281 19
THIS HOLY TRINITY, ONE GOD, I PRAISE AND MAGNIFY,   285 04
IN THE CREEDS AS ONE, HOLY, CATHOLIC, AND APOSTOLIC   291 04
IT IS ONE BODY UNDER ONE HEAD   291 08
WE MEAN THAT THE CHURCH IS ONE   291 08
BECAUSE IT IS ONE BODY UNDER ONE HEAD   291 08
AND EVERY ONE SHALL AUDIBLY ANSWER, I DO   R 296 29
AND EVERY ONE SHALL ANSWER, I DO   R 297 05
THE HEAD OF EVERY ONE SEVERALLY, SAYING, DEFEND, O   R 297 25
AND REIGNETH EVER, ONE GOD, WORLD WITHOUT END   298 25
THE MINISTER MAY ADD ONE OR BOTH OF THE FOLLOWING   R 303 13
HOLY SPIRIT EVER, ONE GOD, WORLD WITHOUT END   303 28
TO HIS DISCRETION, ONE OF THE PENITENTIAL PSALMS   R 308 09
HERE MAY BE SAID ANY ONE OR MORE OF THE PSALMS   R 309 09
MANY ONE THERE BE THAT SAY OF MY SOUL, THERE IS NO   309 16
O HOLY TRINITY, ONE GOD   317 31
POWER OF THE EVIL ONE, AND FROM ETERNAL DEATH   318 12
AND THE HOLY GHOST, ONE GOD, WORLD WITHOUT END   319 12
AND THE HOLY GHOST, ONE GOD, WORLD WITHOUT END   320 13
AND CHASTISE EVERY ONE WHOM THOU DOST RECEIVE   321 20
SHALL BE SAID ONE OR MORE OF THE FOLLOWING   R 324 16
FROM ONE GENERATION TO ANOTHER   325 13
ONE THING HAVE I DESIRED OF THE LORD, WHICH I WILL   326 08
THOU FOOLISH ONE, THAT WHICH THOU SOWEST IS NOT   329 06
BUT THERE IS ONE KIND OF FLESH OF MEN, ANOTHER FLESH   329 12
OF THE CELESTIAL IS ONE, AND THE GLORY OF THE   329 15
THERE IS ONE GLORY OF THE SUN, AND ANOTHER GLORY OF   329 16
FOR ONE STAR DIFFERETH FROM ANOTHER STAR IN GLORY   329 18
THE HOLY GHOST EVER, ONE GOD, WORLD WITHOUT END   332 09
NEVER CONTINUETH IN ONE STAY   332 21
MINISTER SHALL SAY ONE OR MORE OF THE FOLLOWING   R 334 12
AND THE HOLY GHOST, ONE GOD, WORLD WITHOUT END   336 15
WHOSO SHALL RECEIVE ONE SUCH LITTLE CHILD IN MY NAME   339 28
THAT YE DESPISE NOT ONE OF THESE LITTLE ONES   339 30
2 MANY ONE THERE BE THAT SAY OF MY SOUL, *   346 27
FOR THERE IS NOT ONE GODLY MAN LEFT   355 06
TALK OF VANITY EVERY ONE WITH HIS NEIGHBOUR   355 09
AND WILL HELP EVERY ONE FROM HIM THAT SWELLETH   355 18
THERE IS NONE THAT DOETH GOOD, NO NOT ONE   356 15
THERE IS NONE THAT DOETH GOOD, NO NOT ONE   356 21
THOU SUFFER THY HOLY ONE TO SEE CORRUPTION   358 11
AND ONE NIGHT CERTIFIETH ANOTHER   363 15
2 ONE DAY TELLETH ANOTHER   363 15
4 ONE THING HAVE I DESIRED OF THE LORD, WHICH I WILL   371 32
FOR THIS SHALL EVERY ONE THAT IS GODLY MAKE HIS   378 02
SO THAT NOT ONE OF THEM IS BROKEN   381 08
I WENT HEAVILY, AS ONE THAT MOURNETH FOR HIS MOTHER   382 21
AND AS ONE THAT IS DUMB, WHO DOTH NOT OPEN HIS MOUTH   388 18
9 ONE DEEP CALLETH ANOTHER, BECAUSE OF THE NOISE OF   393 18
BE REMEMBERED FROM ONE GENERATION TO ANOTHER   397 21
ONE WITH ANOTHER   400 07
SHALL ENDURE FROM ONE GENERATION TO ANOTHER   400 28
THOU AFRAID, THOUGH ONE BE MADE RICH, *   401 07
I AM EVEN SUCH A ONE AS THYSELF   402 33
THERE IS ALSO NONE THAT DOETH GOOD, NO NOT ONE   405 21
MAKETH MEN TO BE OF ONE MIND IN AN HOUSE, AND   419 25
SCALP OF SUCH A ONE AS GOETH ON STILL IN HIS   420 28
LET THEM FALL FROM ONE WICKEDNESS TO ANOTHER,   423 30
O THOU HOLY ONE OF ISRAEL   426 24

ONE   CONTINUED

FROM ONE GENERATION TO ANOTHER   427 07
BE ALSO FROM THE ONE SEA TO THE OTHER, *   427 12
LIKE AS A DREAM WHEN ONE AWAKETH   429 16
THERE IS NOT ONE PROPHET MORE   430 24
NOT ONE IS THERE AMONG US, THAT UNDERSTANDETH ANY   430 25
HE PUTTETH DOWN ONE, AND SETTETH UP ANOTHER   432 12
PROVOKED THE HOLY ONE IN ISRAEL   437 24
THE LORD AWAKED AS ONE OUT OF SLEEP, *   439 08
AND FALL LIKE ONE OF THE PRINCES   443 31
HEADS TOGETHER WITH ONE CONSENT, *   444 14
GODS APPEARETH EVERY ONE OF THEM IN SION   445 26
10 FOR ONE DAY IN THY COURTS *   445 31
OUT THY WRATH FROM ONE GENERATION TO ANOTHER   446 17
THERE IS NOT ONE THAT CAN DO AS THOU DOEST   447 20
BE REPORTED, THIS ONE AND THAT ONE WERE BORN IN HER   448 22
THIS ONE AND THAT ONE WERE BORN IN HER   448 22
3 I AM COUNTED AS ONE OF THEM THAT GO DOWN INTO THE   449 02
THY TRUTH FROM ONE GENERATION TO ANOTHER   450 06
UP THY THRONE FROM ONE GENERATION TO ANOTHER   450 12
THE HOLY ONE OF ISRAEL IS OUR KING   451 10
HAVE LAID HELP UPON ONE THAT IS MIGHTY, I HAVE   451 13
I HAVE EXALTED ONE CHOSEN OUT OF THE PEOPLE   451 14
FROM ONE GENERATION TO ANOTHER   453 18
AS THEY WENT FROM ONE NATION TO ANOTHER, *   470 28
FROM ONE KINGDOM TO ANOTHER PEOPLE   470 29
THERE WAS NOT ONE FEEBLE PERSON AMONG THEIR TRIBES   472 12
THERE WAS NOT ONE OF THEM LEFT   473 24
ALSO REMAINETH FROM ONE GENERATION TO ANOTHER   496 04
AS ONE THAT FINDETH GREAT SPOILS   501 05
O LORD, FROM ONE GENERATION TO ANOTHER   510 29
SING US ONE OF THE SONGS OF SION   513 10
LIKE AS WHEN ONE BREAKETH AND HEWETH WOOD UPON THE   517 27
4 ONE GENERATION SHALL PRAISE THY WORKS UNTO ANOTHER,   520 33
BE THE HUSBANDS OF ONE WIFE, RULING THEIR CHILDREN   531 33
SHALL EXAMINE EVERY ONE OF THOSE WHO ARE TO BE   R 532 23
THE HEAD OF EVERY ONE TO BE MADE DEACON, HUMBLY   R 534 03
DELIVER TO EVERY ONE OF THEM THE NEW TESTAMENT,   R 534 09
THEN ONE OF THEM, APPOINTED BY THE BISHOP, SHALL   R 534 14
UNTO EVERY ONE OF US IS GIVEN GRACE ACCORDING TO THE   537 32
AND THERE SHALL BE ONE FLOCK, AND ONE SHEPHERD   539 21
BE ONE FLOCK, AND ONE SHEPHERD   539 21
WHOLLY TO THIS ONE THING, AND DRAW ALL YOUR CARES AND   541 14
THE FATHER, SON, AND THEE, OF BOTH, TO BE BUT ONE   544 11
THE HEAD OF EVERY ONE THAT RECEIVETH THE ORDER OF   R 546 07
DELIVER TO EVERY ONE OF THEM KNEELING, (THE BIBLE INTO R 546 23
THEN ONE OF THEM HAVING READ THE GOSPEL, (WHICH SHALL R 547 24
THE HUSBAND OF ONE WIFE, VIGILANT, SOBER, OF GOOD   549 20
ONE THAT RULETH WELL HIS OWN HOUSE, HAVING HIS   549 23
NOT TO WARN EVERY ONE NIGHT AND DAY WITH TEARS   551 02
THE FATHER, SON, AND THEE, OF BOTH, TO BE BUT ONE   556 19
LIVETH AND REIGNETH, ONE GOD, WORLD WITHOUT END   558 07
SAME HOLY SPIRIT, ONE GOD, WORLD WITHOUT END   559 15
O HOLY TRINITY, ONE GOD, WE BESEECH THEE TO HEAR US,   560 09
THAT THY CHURCH MAY BE ONE   561 17
SAME SPIRIT EVER, ONE GOD, WORLD WITHOUT END   562 15
THE BISHOP ONE VERSE AND THE CLERGY ANOTHER   R 563 09
AND GLORIFY AS ONE GOD, WORLD WITHOUT END   572 32
THAT WITH ONE HEART THEY MAY DESIRE THE PROSPERITY OF   574 10
AND WITH ONE MOUTH MAY PROFESS THE FAITH ONCE   574 11
THE SAME HOLY GHOST, ONE GOD, WORLD WITHOUT END   574 22
BE PRESENT, LET ONE OF THEM, OR ANY OTHER WHO MAY BE   R 587 05
THAT EVERY ONE MAY SECRETLY CONFESS THE SINS   R 589 34
HAVE BEEN MADE ONE FLESH   598 26
WHICH WE MUST ONE DAY GIVE, MAY BE FAITHFUL STEWARDS   599 22
THERE IS BUT ONE LIVING AND TRUE GOD, EVERLASTING,   603 03
BE THREE PERSONS, OF ONE SUBSTANCE, POWER, AND   603 06
ETERNAL GOD, AND OF ONE SUBSTANCE WITH THE FATHER,   603 10
JOINED TOGETHER IN ONE PERSON, NEVER TO BE DIVIDED,   603 13
WHEREOF IS ONE CHRIST, VERY GOD, AND VERY   603 14
AND THE SON, IS OF ONE SUBSTANCE, MAJESTY, AND GLORY,   603 26
MAY IT SO EXPOUND ONE PLACE OF SCRIPTURE, THAT IT BE   607 05
AMONG THEMSELVES ONE TO ANOTHER   608 35
BE IN ALL PLACES ONE, OR UTTERLY LIKE   609 32

ONES

AND TO REVIVE THE HEART OF THE CONTRITE ONES   003 29
ONE OF THESE LITTLE ONES WHICH BELIEVE IN ME, IT WERE   252 31
HEED THAT YE DESPISE NOT ONE OF THESE LITTLE ONES   253 10
HEED THAT YE DESPISE NOT ONE OF THESE LITTLE ONES   339 30
OF THY LITTLE ONES DO ALWAYS BEHOLD IN HEAVEN   340 05
AND TAKEN COUNSEL AGAINST THY SECRET ONES   444 10

ONLY

CHURCH HATH NOT ONLY IN HER PREFACE, BUT LIKEWISE IN   V 21
TRUE, AND ONLY SON   010 22
IN JESUS CHRIST HIS ONLY SON OUR LORD   015 21
THY PRAISE, NOT ONLY WITH OUR LIPS, BUT IN OUR LIVES,   019 27
THOU ONLY ART THE LORD   026 02
FOR THOU ONLY ART HOLY   026 02
THOU ONLY, O CHRIST, WITH THE HOLY GHOST, ART MOST   026 03
IN JESUS CHRIST HIS ONLY SON OUR LORD   029 26
IT IS THOU, LORD, ONLY, THAT MAKEST US DWELL IN   031 11
FOR THE LOVE OF THY ONLY SON, OUR SAVIOUR, JESUS   031 28
THY PRAISE, NOT ONLY WITH OUR LIPS, BUT IN OUR LIVES,   033 25
FOR OUR GOVERNANCE ONLY SUCH THINGS AS PLEASE THEE,   035 26
JESUS CHRIST, OUR ONLY SAVIOUR, THE PRINCE OF PEACE   037 25
WHO ART THE ONLY GIVER OF ALL VICTORY   041 15
OF ALL COMFORT, OUR ONLY HELP IN TIME OF NEED   045 12
THROUGH OUR ONLY MEDIATOR AND ADVOCATE, JESUS CHRIST   059 27
AGAINST THEE ONLY HAVE I SINNED, AND DONE THIS EVIL   060 17
TO THEE ONLY IT APPERTAINETH TO FORGIVE SINS   062 19
CHRIST'S SAKE, OUR ONLY MEDIATOR AND ADVOCATE   075 05

ONLY   CONTINUED

JESUS CHRIST, THINE ONLY SON, TO BE BORN AS AT THIS	077 14
UPON THE FEAST OF TRINITY ONLY	R 079 06
DIDST GIVE THINE ONLY SON JESUS CHRIST TO SUFFER	080 08
THOU ONLY ART THE LORD	084 13
FOR THOU ONLY ART HOLY	084 13
THOU ONLY, O CHRIST, WITH THE HOLY GHOST, ART MOST	084 14
OF OUR MASTER, AND ONLY SAVIOUR, JESUS CHRIST, THUS	086 13
JESUS CHRIST, NOT ONLY TO DIE FOR US, BUT ALSO TO BE	087 03
BE SUCH AS ARE NOT ONLY AGAINST GOD, BUT ALSO AGAINST	087 22
THE GLORY AS OF THE ONLY BEGOTTEN OF THE	098 06
THE BIRTH OF THINE ONLY SON JESUS CHRIST	098 12
FOR THEE, OUR ONLY MEDIATOR AND ADVOCATE	100 03
AS IN MY PRESENCE ONLY, BUT NOW MUCH MORE IN MY	106 02
BE SUBJECT, NOT ONLY FOR WRATH, BUT ALSO FOR	114 22
BUT SPEAK THE WORD ONLY, AND MY SERVANT SHALL BE	115 12
THEY WHO DO LEAN ONLY UPON THE HOPE OF THY HEAVENLY	115 30
THIS FOR THINE ONLY SON JESUS CHRIST'S SAKE	122 19
THY GOD, AND HIM ONLY SHALT THOU SERVE	127 10
NOT MY FEET ONLY, BUT ALSO MY HANDS AND MY	156 07
UNTO HIM, ART THOU ONLY A STRANGER IN JERUSALEM,	167 13
HAST GIVEN THINE ONLY SON TO DIE FOR OUR SINS, AND TO	170 19
NOT BY WATER ONLY, BUT BY WATER AND BLOOD	170 31
HAST GIVEN THINE ONLY SON TO BE UNTO US BOTH A	171 28
AND NOT HEARERS ONLY, DECEIVING YOUR OWN SELVES	176 05
HAST EXALTED THINE ONLY SON JESUS CHRIST WITH GREAT	179 04
ONLY THEY WERE BAPTIZED IN THE NAME OF THE LORD	185 26
AND NOT ONLY THEY, BUT OURSELVES ALSO, WHICH HAVE THE	194 20
OF WHOSE ONLY GIFT IT COMETH THAT THY FAITHFUL	207 12
ONLY LEST THEY SHOULD SUFFER PERSECUTION FOR THE	210 26
CARRIED OUT, THE ONLY SON OF HIS MOTHER, AND SHE WAS	212 31
TO FOLLOW THEE, THE ONLY GOD	214 26
AND NOT TO ME ONLY, BUT UNTO ALL THEM ALSO THAT LOVE	253 30
ONLY LUKE IS WITH ME	254 02
YOUR BRETHREN ONLY, WHAT DO YE MORE THAN OTHERS	264 13
AND NOT HEARERS ONLY, DECEIVING YOUR OWN SELVES	265 29
IN JESUS CHRIST HIS ONLY SON OUR LORD	284 15
TWO SACRAMENTS ONLY, AS GENERALLY NECESSARY TO	292 06
ONLY THEY WERE BAPTIZED IN THE NAME OF THE LORD	296 18
KEEP THEE ONLY UNTO HER, SO LONG AS YE BOTH	301 10
KEEP THEE ONLY UNTO HIM, SO LONG AS YE BOTH	301 18
OF MANKIND, WHO ONLY ART THE WELL-SPRING OF LIFE	303 14
HIS FULL TRUST ONLY IN THY MERCY, IMPUTE NOT UNTO HIM	314 09
AND SALVATION, BUT ONLY THE NAME OF OUR LORD JESUS	314 21
OF ALL COMFORT, OUR ONLY HELP IN TIME OF NEED	316 07
JESUS CHRIST THINE ONLY SON OUR LORD	317 23
JESUS CHRIST, OUR ONLY MEDIATOR AND ADVOCATE	336 29
TO BE USED ONLY FOR THE FAITHFUL DEPARTED IN CHRIST,	R 337 02
IT IS THOU, LORD, ONLY, THAT MAKEST ME DWELL IN	347 29
4 AGAINST THEE ONLY HAVE I SINNED, AND DONE THIS EVIL	403 15
4 THEIR DEVICE IS ONLY HOW TO PUT HIM OUT WHOM GOD	414 04
AND WILL MAKE MENTION OF THY RIGHTEOUSNESS ONLY	426 07
WHICH ONLY DOETH WONDROUS THINGS	428 03
ART ONLY THE MOST HIGHEST OVER ALL THE EARTH	445 09
4 WHO ONLY DOETH GREAT WONDERS	511 22
FOR HIS NAME ONLY IS EXCELLENT, AND HIS PRAISE ABOVE	524 28
MEDIATION OF OUR ONLY SAVIOUR JESUS CHRIST, FOR THE	541 16
GIVEN TO US THY ONLY AND MOST DEARLY BELOVED SON	545 14
SAVE ONLY, THAT AFTER THIS PLACE, THAT IT MAY PLEASE	R 553 14
HAST GIVEN THY ONLY AND DEARLY BELOVED SON JESUS	557 21
THY WORD, MAY NOT ONLY BE EARNEST TO REPROVE,	559 08
JESUS CHRIST, OUR ONLY MEDIATOR AND REDEEMER	572 14
IN JESUS CHRIST HIS ONLY SON OUR LORD	577 30
TWO ONLY, AS GENERALLY NECESSARY TO	581 09
JESUS CHRIST, OUR ONLY SAVIOUR AND REDEEMER	590 07
IN SENDING THY ONLY SON INTO THE WORLD, TO REDEEM US	591 12
FOR THE LOVE OF THY ONLY SON, OUR SAVIOUR, JESUS	593 15
BE A SACRIFICE, NOT ONLY FOR ORIGINAL GUILT, BUT ALSO	603 16
WHO IS THE ONLY MEDIATOR BETWEEN GOD AND MAN,	604 16
FATHERS DID LOOK ONLY FOR TRANSITORY PROMISES	604 18
BEFORE GOD, ONLY FOR THE MERIT OF OUR LORD AND	605 06
JUSTIFIED BY FAITH ONLY, IS A MOST WHOLESOME	605 08
THAT THEY DO NOT ONLY RENDER UNTO GOD AS MUCH AS THEY	605 26
IN ALL THINGS, SIN ONLY EXCEPT, FROM WHICH HE WAS	605 32
SET OUT UNTO US ONLY THE NAME OF JESUS CHRIST,	606 35
HATH ERRED, NOT ONLY IN THEIR LIVING AND MANNER OF	606 43
OF CHRIST BE NOT ONLY BADGES OR TOKENS OF CHRISTIAN	607 31
IN US, AND DOTH NOT ONLY QUICKEN, BUT ALSO STRENGTHEN	607 34
AND IN SUCH ONLY AS WORTHILY RECEIVE THE SAME, THEY	608 03
BAPTISM IS NOT ONLY A SIGN OF PROFESSION, AND MARK OF	608 24
OF THE LORD IS NOT ONLY A SIGN OF THE LOVE THAT	608 34
IN THE SUPPER, ONLY AFTER AN HEAVENLY AND SPIRITUAL	608 44
THE CHURCH ORDAINED ONLY BY MAN'S AUTHORITY, SO THAT	610 02

ONLY-BEGOTTEN

THE ONLY-BEGOTTEN SON OF GOD	016 02
THE ONLY-BEGOTTEN SON, JESUS CHRIST	025 27
THE ONLY-BEGOTTEN SON OF GOD	030 07
THE ONLY-BEGOTTEN SON OF GOD	071 04
GAVE HIS ONLY-BEGOTTEN SON, TO THE END THAT ALL THAT	076 14
WITH THINE ONLY-BEGOTTEN SON, AND THE HOLY GHOST, ART	079 07
THE ONLY-BEGOTTEN SON, JESUS CHRIST	084 07
US THY ONLY-BEGOTTEN SON TO TAKE OUR NATURE UPON HIM,	096 13
US THY ONLY-BEGOTTEN SON TO TAKE OUR NATURE UPON HIM,	104 05
THY ONLY-BEGOTTEN SON TO THE GENTILES	107 30
THINE ONLY-BEGOTTEN SON JESUS CHRIST HAST OVERCOME	163 22
GIVE THINE ONLY-BEGOTTEN SON TO THE DEATH OF THE	165 03
THY ONLY-BEGOTTEN SON OUR LORD JESUS CHRIST TO HAVE	177 15
GAVE HIS ONLY-BEGOTTEN SON, THAT WHOSOEVER BELIEVETH	184 32
OF THE ONLY-BEGOTTEN SON OF GOD	185 05
SENT HIS ONLY-BEGOTTEN SON INTO THE WORLD, THAT WE	189 12
AS THY ONLY-BEGOTTEN SON WAS THIS DAY PRESENTED IN	231 29
THINE ONLY-BEGOTTEN SON WONDERFULLY TRANSFIGURED, IN	247 32
OF HIS ONLY-BEGOTTEN SON JESUS CHRIST	606 14

OPEN

O LORD, OPEN THOU OUR LIPS, ETC	R 003 11
SHALL SAY, O LORD, OPEN THOU OUR LIPS	007 31
THOU DIDST OPEN THE KINGDOM OF HEAVEN TO ALL	010 29
O LORD, OPEN THOU OUR LIPS, ETC	R 021 08
SHALL SAY, O LORD, OPEN THOU OUR LIPS	025 06
ALL WHOSE HANDS ARE OPEN FOR THEIR MAINTENANCE	047 35
THOU SHALT OPEN MY LIPS, O LORD,	061 09
WHOM ALL HEARTS ARE OPEN, ALL DESIRES KNOWN, AND FROM	067 16
KNOW ANY TO BE AN OPEN AND NOTORIOUS EVIL LIVER,	R 084 35
OF GOD'S WORD, AND OPEN HIS GRIEF	088 07
OPEN, WE PRAY THEE, THE EYES OF OUR FAITH, THAT WE	166 07
AND HIS EARS ARE OPEN UNTO THEIR PRAYERS	195 28
O LORD, BE OPEN TO THE PRAYERS OF THY HUMBLE	203 11
UNTO ME, THAT I MAY OPEN MY MOUTH BOLDLY, TO MAKE	219 23
OPEN THE GATE UNTO US WHO KNOCK	274 18
OPEN THINE EYE OF MERCY UPON THIS THY SERVANT,	313 33
THEIR THROAT IS AN OPEN SEPULCHRE	348 20
AND HIS EARS ARE OPEN UNTO THEIR PRAYERS	380 31
WHO DOTH NOT OPEN HIS MOUTH	388 18
15 THOU SHALT OPEN MY LIPS, O LORD,	404 07
12 FOR IT IS NOT AN OPEN ENEMY THAT HATH DONE ME THIS	407 11
2 I WILL OPEN MY MOUTH IN A PARABLE	434 29
4 WE ARE BECOME AN OPEN SHAME TO OUR ENEMIES,	440 06
OPEN THY MOUTH WIDE, AND I SHALL FILL IT	442 34
19 OPEN ME THE GATES OF RIGHTEOUSNESS,	489 06
18 OPEN THOU MINE EYES	491 02
THEY MAY OPEN UNTO HIM IMMEDIATELY	534 19
IN HIS HAND, IN OPEN VIEW, THE BISHOP, OR THE PRIEST	R 570 10
OPEN, WE BESEECH THEE, OUR EYES TO BEHOLD THY	596 18
PERSON WHICH BY OPEN DENUNCIATION OF THE CHURCH IS	609 26

OPENED

I SEE THE HEAVENS OPENED, AND THE SON OF MAN STANDING	100 08
AND WHEN THEY HAD OPENED THEIR TREASURES, THEY	109 22
SAW THE HEAVENS OPENED, AND THE SPIRIT, LIKE A DOVE,	112 21
AND THE GRAVES WERE OPENED	137 28
THE LORD GOD HATH OPENED MINE EAR, AND I WAS NOT	144 12
AND OPENED UNTO US THE GATE OF EVERLASTING	163 23
PETER OPENED HIS MOUTH, AND SAID, OF A TRUTH I	166 12
THEIR EYES WERE OPENED, AND THEY KNEW HIM	168 07
AND WHILE HE OPENED TO US THE SCRIPTURES	168 10
THEN OPENED HE THEIR UNDERSTANDING, THAT THEY MIGHT	170 10
AND IT SHALL BE OPENED UNTO YOU	183 11
AND TO HIM THAT KNOCKETH IT SHALL BE OPENED	183 13
THEN PETER OPENED HIS MOUTH, AND SAID, OF A TRUTH I	183 29
A DOOR WAS OPENED IN HEAVEN	186 31
HIS EARS WERE OPENED, AND THE STRING OF HIS TONGUE	207 03
THAT IS, BE OPENED	207 03
HIS EYES WERE OPENED, HE SAW NO MAN	230 11
AND HIS MOUTH WAS OPENED IMMEDIATELY, AND HIS TONGUE	243 25
WHICH OPENED TO THEM OF HIS OWN ACCORD	245 23
AND HE OPENED HIS MOUTH, AND TAUGHT THEM, SAYING,	257 20
AND WHEN HE HAD OPENED THE BOOK, HE FOUND THE PLACE	261 15
AND IT SHALL BE OPENED UNTO YOU	263 05
AND TO HIM THAT KNOCKETH IT SHALL BE OPENED	263 07
AND IT SHALL BE OPENED UNTO YOU	274 16
BECAME DUMB, AND OPENED NOT MY MOUTH	389 27
BUT MINE EARS HAST THOU OPENED	390 28
AND OPENED THE DOORS OF HEAVEN	436 16
40 HE OPENED THE ROCK OF STONE, AND THE WATERS FLOWED	472 19
17 SO THE EARTH OPENED, AND SWALLOWED UP DATHAN,	474 02
THE DECEITFUL IS OPENED UPON ME	480 05
131 I OPENED MY MOUTH, AND DREW IN MY BREATH	498 32
EYES OF THE MIND OPENED TO BEHOLD THINGS INVISIBLE	594 24
THEE THAT, HAVING OPENED TO HIM THE GATES OF LARGER	598 08

OPENEST

WHO OPENEST THINE HAND AND FILLEST ALL THINGS	040 03
AND WHEN THOU OPENEST THY HAND, THEY ARE FILLED WITH	469 17
16 THOU OPENEST THINE HAND,	521 24

OPENETH

TO HIM THE PORTER OPENETH	186 04
EVERY MALE THAT OPENETH THE WOMB SHALL BE CALLED HOLY	232 26
TO HIM THE PORTER OPENETH	538 27

OPENING

THANKS FOR OPENING HEATHEN LANDS TO THE LIGHT OF THY	038 16
AND THE OPENING OF THE PRISON TO THEM THAT ARE BOUND	107 03

OPENLY

HATH HE OPENLY SHOWED IN THE SIGHT OF THE HEATHEN	027 09
UNTIL HE HAVE OPENLY DECLARED HIMSELF TO HAVE TRULY	R 085 04
WHICH SEETH IN SECRET, SHALL REWARD THEE OPENLY	125 16
RAISED UP THE THIRD DAY, AND SHEWED HIM OPENLY	166 25
RAISED UP THE THIRD DAY, AND SHEWED HIM OPENLY	184 13
OPENLY IN THE CHURCH, INSTRUCT OR EXAMINE	R 295 08
BE OPENLY SHOWED UPON THE HEATHEN, IN OUR SIGHT	440 24
HATH HE OPENLY SHOWED IN THE SIGHT OF THE HEATHEN	461 30
PRIVATELY AND OPENLY TO CALL UPON AND ENCOURAGE	555 05
OPENLY IN THE CHURCH, INSTRUCT OR EXAMINE	R 582 28
UNTIL HE BE OPENLY RECONCILED BY PENANCE, AND	609 29
DOTH OPENLY BREAK THE TRADITIONS AND	609 36
TO BE REBUKED OPENLY, (THAT OTHERS MAY FEAR TO DO THE	609 38

OPERATION

WHO, BY THE OPERATION OF THE HOLY GHOST, WAS MADE	077 16
NOR THE OPERATION OF HIS HANDS	373 18

OPERATION   CONTINUED

THE VOICE OF THE LORD IS MIGHTY IN OPERATION   374 05
BY THE OPERATION OF THE HOLY GHOST, ALL   574 06
THEY HAVE A WHOLESOME EFFECT OR OPERATION   608 04

OPERATIONS

FOR THE OPERATIONS OF THY HANDS   028 03
OF OPERATIONS, BUT IT IS THE SAME GOD WHICH WORKETH   182 24
OF OPERATIONS, BUT IT IS THE SAME GOD WHICH WORKETH   203 24
FOR THE OPERATIONS OF THY HANDS   456 07

OPPORTUNITIES

ACCORDING TO OUR ABILITIES AND OPPORTUNITIES   588 32

OPPORTUNITY

SUFFICIENT OPPORTUNITY SHALL BE GIVEN TO THOSE   R 082 28
AND SOUGHT OPPORTUNITY TO BETRAY HIM UNTO THEM IN THE 148 20
AND THE OPPORTUNITY IT AFFORDS FOR SPIRITUAL PROFIT   R 313 16

OPPRESS

WHENSOEVER THEY OPPRESS US   058 19
THOSE THAT OPPRESS THE HIRELING IN HIS WAGES,   232 18

OPPRESSED

AND ALL WHO ARE DESOLATE AND OPPRESSED   057 03
ALL THAT WERE OPPRESSED OF THE DEVIL   166 21
ALL THAT WERE OPPRESSED OF THE DEVIL   184 09
FOR THE OPPRESSED, *   352 06
THEM THAT ARE OPPRESSED WITH WRONG   466 18
THEIR ENEMIES OPPRESSED THEM, *   475 20

OPPRESSETH

THE ENEMY OPPRESSETH ME   310 10
THE ENEMY OPPRESSETH ME   393 26
THE ENEMY OPPRESSETH ME   394 08

OPPRESSION

AND TO MAKE NO PEACE WITH OPPRESSION   044 11
THROUGH OPPRESSION, THROUGH ANY PLAGUE OR TROUBLE   478 25

OPPRESSORS

O GIVE ME NOT OVER UNTO MINE OPPRESSORS   498 12

ORACLES

HIM SPEAK AS THE ORACLES OF GOD   179 19

ORDAIN

THAT IT MAY ORDAIN FOR OUR GOVERNANCE ONLY SUCH   035 26
FOR THE CHURCH TO ORDAIN ANY THING THAT IS CONTRARY   607 04
HATH AUTHORITY TO ORDAIN, CHANGE, AND ABOLISH,   609 42

ORDAINED

WHO SHALL BE ORDAINED TO ANY HOLY FUNCTION, GIVE THY 038 32
INSTITUTED AND ORDAINED HOLY MYSTERIES, AS PLEDGES OF 086 16
SUCKLINGS HAST ORDAINED STRENGTH, AND MADEST INFANTS 102 22
THAT BE ARE ORDAINED OF GOD   114 13
IS HE WHICH WAS ORDAINED OF GOD TO BE THE JUDGE OF   166 29
IS HE WHICH WAS ORDAINED OF GOD TO BE THE JUDGE OF   184 17
AND IT WAS ORDAINED BY ANGELS IN THE HAND OF A   207 29
MUST ONE BE ORDAINED TO BE A WITNESS WITH US OF   234 24
CHOSEN YOU, AND ORDAINED YOU, THAT YE SHOULD GO AND   241 33
WHO HAST ORDAINED AND CONSTITUTED THE SERVICES   251 27
AS MANY AS WERE ORDAINED TO ETERNAL LIFE BELIEVED   261 07
HATH CHRIST ORDAINED IN HIS CHURCH   292 04
CHRIST HATH ORDAINED TWO SACRAMENTS ONLY, AS   292 06
ORDAINED BY CHRIST HIMSELF, AS A MEANS WHEREBY WE   292 12
WAS THE SACRAMENT OF THE LORD'S SUPPER ORDAINED   293 03
SUPPER WAS ORDAINED FOR THE CONTINUAL REMEMBRANCE OF 293 04
HAST THOU ORDAINED STRENGTH, BECAUSE OF THINE   351 02
THE MOON AND THE STARS WHICH THOU HAST ORDAINED   351 05
5 THIS HE ORDAINED IN JOSEPH FOR A TESTIMONY,   442 20
I HAVE ORDAINED A LANTERN FOR MINE ANOINTED   509 09
AS DESIRE TO BE ORDAINED DEACONS, EACH OF THEM BEING R 530 08
WHO ARE TO BE ORDAINED PRIESTS AS FOLLOWETH   R 539 23
PERSONS TO BE ORDAINED PRIESTS KNEELING, AND OTHERS   R 543 26
BE EXAMINED AND ORDAINED, AS IS ABOVE PRESCRIBED   R 547 24
BE EXAMINED AND ORDAINED, AS IS IN THIS OFFICE BEFORE R 547 28
TO BE ORDAINED AND CONSECRATED BISHOP   552 22
BEFORE THEY ORDAINED MATTHIAS TO BE OF THE NUMBER OF 553 08
THE LORD HATH ORDAINED THAT THEY WHO SERVE AT THE   569 28
HATH CHRIST ORDAINED IN HIS CHURCH   581 07
ORDAINED BY CHRIST HIMSELF, AS A MEANS WHEREBY WE   581 13
WAS THE SACRAMENT OF THE LORD'S SUPPER ORDAINED   582 03
SACRAMENTS ORDAINED OF CHRIST BE NOT ONLY BADGES OR   607 31
TWO SACRAMENTS ORDAINED OF CHRIST OUR LORD IN THE   607 36
OR CEREMONY ORDAINED OF GOD   607 43
WERE NOT ORDAINED OF CHRIST TO BE GAZED UPON,   608 02
THAT NOTHING BE ORDAINED AGAINST GOD'S WORD   609 35
OF GOD, AND BE ORDAINED AND APPROVED BY COMMON   609 38
OF THE CHURCH ORDAINED ONLY BY MAN'S AUTHORITY,   610 02

ORDAINETH

HE ORDAINETH HIS ARROWS AGAINST THE PERSECUTORS   350 20

ORDAINING

BE FAITHFUL IN ORDAINING, SENDING, OR LAYING HANDS   555 20

ORDER

IN THE FRAME AND ORDER THEREOF) HAVE STILL BEEN   V 31
FROM THE ORDER FOR THE HOLY COMMUNION   R 007 05
HERE ENDETH THE ORDER OF MORNING PRAYER   R 020 15
HERE ENDETH THE ORDER OF EVENING PRAYER   R 034 15
THE PEOPLE ALSO IN ORDER, INTO THEIR HANDS, ALL   R 082 28
THE SAME ORDER SHALL THE MINISTER USE WITH THOSE,   R 085 09
WHO ALONE CANST ORDER THE UNRULY WILLS AND AFFECTIONS 174 18
SERVICES OF ANGELS AND MEN IN A WONDERFUL ORDER   251 29
WHO ALONE CANST ORDER THE UNRULY WILLS AND AFFECTIONS 285 25
AND TO ORDER MYSELF IN THAT LOWLINESS AND REVERENCE   288 30
SHALL STAND IN ORDER BEFORE THE BISHOP, SITTING IN   R 296 05
ALL OF THEM IN ORDER KNEELING BEFORE THE BISHOP,   R 297 24
BUT EVERY MAN IN HIS OWN ORDER   328 25
FOR EVER AFTER THE ORDER OF MELCHIZEDEK   482 15
133 ORDER MY STEPS IN THY WORD   499 04
HOW NECESSARY THAT ORDER IS IN THE CHURCH OF CHRIST, R 530 05
BE ADMITTED TO THE ORDER OF DEACONS, AND TO POUR THY R 531 05
TO CHOOSE INTO THE ORDER OF DEACONS THE FIRST MARTYR R 531 16
DIOCESAN TO THE ORDER OF PRIESTHOOD, AT THE TIMES   R 535 24
HOW NECESSARY THAT ORDER IS IN THE CHURCH OF CHRIST, R 536 05
ARE TO RECEIVE THE ORDER OF PRIESTHOOD THAT DAY,   R 536 08
BE ADMITTED TO THE ORDER OF PRIESTHOOD   R 536 11
BE ADMITTED TO THE ORDER OF PRIESTS, AND TO POUR THY R 537 11
TO THE ORDER AND MINISTRY OF PRIESTHOOD   R 541 32
THAT RECEIVETH THE ORDER OF PRIESTHOOD   R 546 07
THE SAME DAY, THE ORDER OF DEACONS BE GIVEN TO SCME, R 547 19
TO SOME, AND THE ORDER OF PRIESTHOOD TO OTHERS   R 547 20
AND SET IN ORDER, THE PRESIDING BISHOP, OR   R 549 03
AND THE ORDER OF THIS CHURCH   554 18
AND BY THE ORDER OF THIS CHURCH, IS COMMITTED   555 17
BE ADMITTED TO THE ORDER OF DEACONS (OR PRIESTS),   560 27
BE USED WITH THE ORDER FOR THE HOLY COMMUNION,   R 563 03
COMMON USES, IN ORDER TO FILL MEN'S MINDS WITH   564 17
BE USED WITH THE ORDER FOR THE HOLY COMMUNION,   R 569 08
TO ORDER MYSELF LOWLY AND REVERENTLY TO ALL MY   580 06
AGAINST THE COMMON ORDER OF THE CHURCH, AND HURTETH   609 40
ALSO SUSPENDS THE ORDER FOR THE READING OF SAID   R 610 27

ORDERED

FOR WHICH A PROPER EPISTLE AND GOSPEL ARE ORDERED   R 008 33
BEING ORDERED BY THY GOVERNANCE, MAY BE   017 18
THINGS MAY BE SO ORDERED AND SETTLED BY THEIR   035 15
HATH SO ORDERED THE BREAD AND WINE, THAT HE   R 080 02
WHERE IT IS NOT IN THIS BOOK OTHERWISE ORDERED   R 090 05
BE SO PEACEABLY ORDERED BY THY GOVERNANCE, THAT THY   195 16
MAY BE ORDERED AND GUIDED BY FAITHFUL AND   234 03
THE MINISTER IS ORDERED, FROM TIME TO TIME, TO ADVISE R 320 21
THE ROCK, AND ORDERED MY GOINGS   390 13
PRESENTED TO BE ORDERED DEACONS, FOR THE WHICH HE   530 23
FOUND MEET TO BE ORDERED, TO THE PRAYERS OF THE   R 530 29
WHO ARE TO BE ORDERED, IN THE PRESENCE OF THE PEOPLE, R 532 24
AND ALL WHO ARE ORDERED SHALL TARRY, AND RECEIVE THE R 534 26
FOUND MEET TO BE ORDERED, TO THE PRAYERS OF THE   R 537 05
BE SO PEACEABLY ORDERED BY THY GOVERNANCE, THAT THY   574 16
HEAR AND TO BE ORDERED BY THE MINISTER, UNTIL SUCH   R 582 34
BEING ORDERED BY THY GOVERNANCE, MAY BE   592 24
CONSECRATED OR ORDERED ACCORDING TO SAID FORM,   610 35
AND LAWFULLY CONSECRATED AND ORDERED   610 36

ORDERETH

PROVIDENCE ORDERETH ALL THINGS BOTH IN HEAVEN AND   199 28
23 THE LORD ORDERETH A GOOD MAN'S GOING, *   386 08
IS NO MAN THAT ORDERETH THEM UNTO THEE   390 23
AND TO HIM THAT ORDERETH HIS WAY ARIGHT, WILL I SHOW 403 05

ORDERING

CEASE FROM ORDERING THAT PERSON, UNTIL SUCH TIME AS R 530 27
CEASE FROM ORDERING THAT PERSON, UNTIL SUCH TIME AS R 537 03
FORM FOR THE ORDERING OF DEACONS,) THEY THAT ARE TO R 547 26
OF BISHOPS, AND ORDERING OF PRIESTS AND DEACONS,   610 31
NECESSARY TO SUCH CONSECRATION AND ORDERING   610 33

ORDERLY

TO BE RIGHTLY, ORDERLY, AND LAWFULLY CONSECRATED AND 610 36

ORDERS

APPOINTED DIVERS ORDERS IN THY CHURCH   039 08
WHAT ORDERS OF MINISTERS ARE THERE IN THE CHURCH   294 04
WHICH ORDERS HAVE BEEN IN THE CHURCH FROM THE   294 05
TO CONFER HOLY ORDERS   294 09
HAVE BEEN THESE ORDERS OF MINISTERS IN CHRIST'S   529 12
INTENT THAT THESE ORDERS MAY BE CONTINUED, AND   529 18
APPOINTED DIVERS ORDERS OF MINISTERS IN THY CHURCH,   531 15
APPOINTED DIVERS ORDERS OF MINISTERS IN THY CHURCH   537 21
THEY WHO RECEIVE ORDERS SHALL TAKE TOGETHER, AND   R 546 20
APPOINTED DIVERS ORDERS OF MINISTERS IN THY CHURCH   547 32
APPOINTED DIVERS ORDERS OF MINISTERS IN THY CHURCH   553 27
APPOINTED DIVERS ORDERS IN THY CHURCH   572 08
ORDERS, MATRIMONY, AND EXTREME UNCTION,   607 39

ORDINANCE

ACCORDING TO THY BLESSED WORD AND ORDINANCE   032 12
RESISTETH THE ORDINANCE OF GOD   114 14
TO EVERY ORDINANCE OF MAN FOR THE LORD'S SAKE   173 18

ORDINANCE   CONTINUED

JOINED IN WEDLOCK ACCORDING TO THY HOLY ORDINANCE   267 06
AFTER GOD'S ORDINANCE IN THE HOLY ESTATE CF   301 07
AFTER GOD'S ORDINANCE IN THE HOLY ESTATE OF   301 15
ACCORDING TO GOD'S HOLY ORDINANCE   301 32
ACCORDING TO GOD'S HOLY ORDINANCE   302 08
CONTINUE THIS DAY ACCORDING TO THINE ORDINANCE   496 07
TO THAT HOLY ORDINANCE WITH FAITH, CHARITY, AND TRUE   565 30
TO CHRIST'S ORDINANCE, IN ALL THOSE THINGS THAT CF   606 40
OF CHRIST'S ORDINANCE TAKEN AWAY BY THEIR WICKEDNESS,   608 14
BY CHRIST'S ORDINANCE RESERVED, CARRIED ABOUT, LIFTED   608 47
BY CHRIST'S ORDINANCE AND COMMANDMENT, OUGHT TO BE   609 11

ORDINANCES

STATUTES AND ORDINANCES UNTO ISRAEL   523 34

ORDINARY

THE SAME TO THE ORDINARY, WITHIN FOURTEEN DAYS AFTER, R 085 18
OR AS THE ORDINARY SHALL DIRECT   R 305 09
ALL UNHALLOWED, ORDINARY, AND COMMON USES   565 06

ORDINATION

WEEKS PRECEDING THE STATED TIMES OF ORDINATION   R 038 24
OR HATH HAD EPISCOPAL CONSECRATION OR ORDINATION   529 23
AT THE ORDINATION OF DEACONS OR OF PRIESTS   R 560 25

ORDINATIONS

MAY BE SAID THE LITANY FOR ORDINATIONS   R 531 10
MAY BE SAID THE LITANY FOR ORDINATIONS   R 537 16
MAY BE SAID THE LITANY FOR ORDINATIONS   R 553 24

OREB

THEIR PRINCES LIKE OREB AND ZEEB   444 26

ORGANIZE

TO MODEL AND ORGANIZE THEIR RESPECTIVE CHURCHES, AND   VI 11

ORIGINAL

NOT ONLY FOR ORIGINAL GUILT, BUT ALSO FOR ACTUAL SINS   603 16
ORIGINAL SIN STANDETH NOT IN THE FOLLOWING OF ADAM,   604 29
FAR GONE FROM ORIGINAL RIGHTEOUSNESS, AND IS OF HIS   604 32
BOTH ORIGINAL AND ACTUAL   609 15

OTHER

BE SAID WITH THE OTHER PRAYERS, IMMEDIATELY AFTER THE R 003 12
DAYS FOR WHICH OTHER CANTICLES ARE APPOINTED   R 008 10
ON OTHER FESTIVALS FOR WHICH A PROPER EPISTLE AND   R 008 33
OUR BISHOPS, AND OTHER CLERGY, AND UPCN THE   018 20
BE SAID WITH THE OTHER PRAYERS, IMMEDIATELY AFTER THE R 021 09
OUR BISHOPS, AND OTHER CLERGY, AND UPCN THE   032 19
THESE AND ALL OTHER NECESSARIES, FOR THEM, FOR US,   035 18
AND ALL THE OTHER BLESSINGS OF HIS MERCIFUL   050 18
AND FOR ALL THE OTHER BLESSINGS OF THY MERCIFUL   050 23
TO ESTABLISH SUCH OTHER ALTERATIONS AND AMENDMENTS   VI 26
HIS DISCRETION ADD OTHER PRAYERS FROM THIS BOOK   R 059 29
MAY BE READ AT OTHER TIMES, AT THE DISCRETION OF THE   R 060 06
SHALT HAVE NONE OTHER GODS BUT ME   068 05
AND OF OTHER MATTERS TO BE PUBLISHED   R 071 27
BIDDING PRAYER, OR OTHER AUTHORIZED PRAYERS AND   R 071 30
MAY BE USED ON ANY OTHER OCCASION OF PUBLIC WORSHIP   R 073 25
OR OTHER FIT PERSONS APPOINTED FOR   R 073 27
FOR THE POOR, AND OTHER OFFERINGS OF THE PEOPLE, IN A R 073 28
TO ALL BISHOPS AND OTHER MINISTERS, THAT THEY MAY,   074 21
OR ANY OTHER ADVERSITY   074 32
OUR SINS, AND ALL OTHER BENEFITS OF HIS PASSION   081 20
THE SUNDAYS AND OTHER HOLY DAYS, (THOUGH THERE BE NO   084 21
THE MINISTER AND OTHER COMMUNICANTS SHALL,   084 31
HEART ALL THAT THE OTHER HATH TRESPASSED AGAINST HIM, R 085 13
AND THE OTHER PARTY WILL NOT BE PERSUADED TO A GODLY   R 085 14
ALL INJURIES AND WRONGS DONE BY YOU TO ANY OTHER   087 26
OR ENVY, OR IN ANY OTHER GRIEVOUS CRIME   087 33
TO ME, OR TO SOME OTHER MINISTER OF GOD'S WORD,   088 06
FOR ANY SUNDAY OR OTHER FEAST MAY BE USED AT THE   R 090 06
AFTER THE OTHER COLLECTS IN ADVENT, UNTIL   R 090 20
IF THERE BE ANY OTHER COMMANDMENT, IT IS BRIEFLY   090 27
ARE ALSO MANY OTHER THINGS WHICH JESUS DID, THE   102 15
CHRIST) WHICH IN OTHER AGES WAS NOT MADE KNOWN UNTO   108 12
FOUR WINDS, FROM ONE END OF HEAVEN TO THE OTHER   118 23
AND OTHER FELL ON GOOD GROUND, AND SPRANG UP, AND   121 25
TO HIM SEVEN OTHER SPIRITS MORE WICKED THAN HIMSELF   130 14
BY A BONDMAID, THE OTHER BY A FREEWOMAN   130 31
MAY FIND IT NONE OTHER THAN THE WAY OF LIFE AND   138 07
AND THE OTHER ON HIS LEFT   146 16
AND MANY OTHER THINGS BLASPHEMOUSLY SPAKE THEY   151 26
WERE ALSO TWO OTHER, MALEFACTORS, LED WITH HIM TO BE   154 21
AND THE OTHER ON THE LEFT   154 24
BUT THE OTHER ANSWERING REBUKED HIM, SAYING, DOST NOT   155 02
AND TWO OTHER WITH HIM, ON EITHER SIDE ONE,   159 34
AND OF THE OTHER WHICH WAS CRUCIFIED WITH HIM   160 35
AND THE OTHER MARY, SITTING OVER AGAINST   162 14
AND TO THE OTHER DISCIPLE, WHOM JESUS LOVED,   164 13
AND THAT OTHER DISCIPLE, AND CAME TO THE   164 17
AND THE OTHER DISCIPLE DID OUTRUN PETER, AND CAME   164 18
WENT IN ALSO THAT OTHER DISCIPLE, WHICH CAME FIRST TO   164 25
AND OTHER SHEEP I HAVE, WHICH ARE NOT OF THIS FOLD   172 30
TO SPEAK WITH OTHER TONGUES, AS THE SPIRIT GAVE THEM   180 23
CLIMBETH UP SOME OTHER WAY, THE SAME IS A THIEF AND A   186 02

OTHER   CONTINUED

WHICH WERE IN THE OTHER SHIP, THAT THEY SHOULD CCME   196 20
AND THE OTHER A PUBLICAN   205 24
THAT I AM NOT AS OTHER MEN ARE, EXTORTIONERS, UNJUST,   205 26
DOWN TO HIS HOUSE JUSTIFIED RATHER THAN THE OTHER   205 32
PASSED BY ON THE OTHER SIDE   208 26
PASSED BY ON THE OTHER SIDE   208 27
AND THESE ARE CONTRARY THE ONE TO THE OTHER   209 17
EITHER HE WILL HATE THE ONE, AND LOVE THE OTHER   211 10
HE WILL HOLD TO THE ONE, AND DESPISE THE OTHER   211 11
WALK NOT AS OTHER GENTILES WALK, IN THE VANITY CF   216 04
HE SENT FORTH OTHER SERVANTS, SAYING, TELL THEM WHICH   218 07
HE SAW OTHER TWO BRETHREN, JAMES THE SON OF   227 29
THE OTHER DISCIPLES THEREFORE SAID UNTO HIM, WE HAVE   228 26
AND MANY OTHER SIGNS TRULY DID JESUS IN THE PRESENCE   229 09
AND THE OTHER ON THE LEFT, IN THY KINGDOM   247 10
THE LORD APPOINTED OTHER SEVENTY ALSO, AND SENT THEM   254 11
WORKS WHICH NONE OTHER MAN DID, THEY HAD NOT HAD SIN   255 26
UPON SUNDAYS AND OTHER HOLY DAYS   R 273 05
UPON ANY OTHER DAY   R 273 07
OR AT SUCH OTHER TIME AS THE MINISTER SHALL   R 273 16
AND ALL OTHER THINGS WHICH A CHRISTIAN OUGHT TO KNOW   277 11
SHALT HAVE NONE OTHER GODS BUT ME   286 05
COVET NOR DESIRE OTHER MEN'S GOODS   289 08
AND IN HIS OTHER MINISTRATIONS, UNDER THE DIRECTICN   294 18
OR ON SOME OTHER CONVENIENT OCCASIONS, OPENLY   R 295 08
TROTH TO EACH OTHER IN THIS MANNER   R 301 24
AND CHERISH EACH OTHER, AND SO LIVE TOGETHER IN   303 24
EACH TO THE OTHER, AND HAVE DECLARED THE SAME   304 06
HATH OFFENDED ANY OTHER, TO ASK THEM FORGIVENESS   R 313 22
THAT THERE IS NONE OTHER NAME UNDER HEAVEN GIVEN TO   314 19
OF PESTILENCE, OR OTHER INFECTIOUS SICKNESS, EXHORT   R 321 06
OR BY ANY OTHER JUST IMPEDIMENT, DO NOT RECEIVE THE   R 323 24
OR OF SOME OTHER GRAIN   329 10
NOR DEPTH, NOR ANY OTHER CREATURE, SHALL BE ABLE TO   331 12
AND SUCH OTHER FITTING PRAYERS AS ARE ELSEWHERE   R 331 30
THAT IN ANY OTHER CASE THE MINISTER MAY, AT HIS   R 337 03
TAKEN FROM OTHER PARTS OF THIS BOOK, AS MAY BE   R 337 05
OR OTHER FITTING PRAYERS FROM THIS BOOK   R 340 22
INTO THE DESTRUCTION THAT HE MADE FOR OTHER   350 24
AND FOOLISH, AND LEAVE THEIR RICHES FOR OTHER   400 25
THE ONE SEA TO THE OTHER, *   427 13
NO MISFORTUNE LIKE OTHER FOLK   428 18
THEY PLAGUED LIKE OTHER MEN   428 19
8 THEY CORRUPT OTHER, AND SPEAK OF WICKED BLASPHEMY   428 24
THOU WORSHIP ANY OTHER GOD   442 32
RIGHTEOUSNESS AND PEACE HAVE KISSED EACH OTHER   446 28
UPON SOME OTHER DAY, IN THE FACE OF THE CHURCH, ADMIT   529 30
YOUR BISHOP, AND OTHER CHIEF MINISTERS, WHO,   533 31
UPON SOME OTHER DAY, IN THE FACE OF THE CHURCH, IN   R 535 25
CLIMBETH UP SOME OTHER WAY, THE SAME IS A THIEF AND A   538 25
AND OTHER SHEEP I HAVE, WHICH ARE NOT OF THIS FOLD   539 19
YE CANNOT BY ANY OTHER MEANS COMPASS THE DOING OF SO   540 33
YOUR BISHOP, AND OTHER CHIEF MINISTERS, WHO   543 12
THESE AND ALL THY OTHER BENEFITS   545 29
OR SOME OTHER BISHOP APPOINTED BY THE BISHOPS   R 549 04
OR SOME OTHER PERSONS APPOINTED FOR THAT   R 563 06
AND FOR ALL OTHER HOLY OFFICES   565 11
AND ALL OTHER BENEFITS OF HIS PASSION   565 34
AND BY THE OTHER CLERGY PRESENT, SHALL ENTER THE   R 570 04
SHALT HAVE NONE OTHER GODS BUT ME   578 26
COVET NOR DESIRE OTHER MEN'S GOODS   580 12
OR ON SOME OTHER CONVENIENT OCCASIONS, OPENLY   R 582 28
CAN ANSWER TO THE OTHER QUESTIONS OF THIS SHORT   R 583 03
OF THEM, OR ANY OTHER WHO MAY BE APPOINTED, SAY AS   R 587 05
OR ANY OTHER WHO MAY BE APPOINTED, SAY AS   R 589 14
AND ALL OTHER ENDOWMENTS AND FACULTIES OF   591 09
AND ALL THE OTHER COMFORTS AND CONVENIENCES OF LIFE   591 10
ON SUNDAYS, AND ON OTHER DAYS WHEN IT MAY BE   R 592 05
OR SOME OTHER MEMBER OF THE FAMILY,   R 592 10
OR SOME OTHER MEMBER OF THE FAMILY,   R 593 04
AND THE OTHER BOOKS (AS HIEROME SAITH) THE CHURCH   604 02
PARTS OF IT, IN OTHER ARTICLES   R 607 12
AND THERE IS NONE OTHER SATISFACTION FOR SIN,   609 16
AS FOR ALL OTHER CHRISTIAN MEN, TO MARRY AT   609 23

OTHERS

AND ALL OTHERS IN AUTHORITY   017 31
AND ALL OTHERS IN AUTHORITY, THAT THEY,   032 07
OR MAY ADD OTHERS, AS OCCASION MAY REQUIRE   R 047 05
THAT WE, AND ALL OTHERS WHO SHALL BE PARTAKERS CF   081 24
READY TO FORGIVE OTHERS WHO HAVE OFFENDED YOU, AS YE   087 27
OTHERS CUT DOWN BRANCHES FROM THE TREES, AND STRAWED   091 25
HAVE PREACHED TO OTHERS, I MYSELF SHOULD BE A   119 12
AND SAW OTHERS STANDING IDLE IN THE   119 20
AND FOUND OTHERS STANDING IDLE, AND SAITH UNTO   119 24
BUT TO OTHERS IN PARABLES   121 31
AND OTHERS, TEMPTING HIM, SOUGHT OF HIM A SIGN FROM   129 28
THE SCRIBES AND ELDERS, SAID, HE SAVED OTHERS   137 10
THEMSELVES WITH THE SCRIBES, HE SAVED OTHERS   146 22
THE HOLY PLACE EVERY YEAR WITH BLOOD OF OTHERS   148 04
WITH THEM DERIDED HIM, SAYING, HE SAVED OTHERS   154 28
THAT THEY WERE RIGHTEOUS, AND DESPISED OTHERS   205 23
AND OTHERS, JEREMIAS, OR ONE OF THE PROPHETS   245 34
WHAT DO YE MORE THAN OTHERS   264 13
EVEN AS OTHERS WHICH HAVE NO HOPE   268 30
FORSAKING ALL OTHERS, KEEP THEE ONLY UNTO HER,   301 10
FORSAKING ALL OTHERS, KEEP THEE ONLY UNTO HIM,   301 18
THE FIRST MARTYR SAINT STEPHEN, WITH OTHERS   531 17
WITH THE ALMS OF THE PARISHIONERS, CR OTHERS   533 21
BE OCCASION THAT OTHERS OFFEND   540 29
AND OTHERS STANDING, THE BISHOP SHALL SING   R 543 26
THE PRIESTS, AND OTHERS THAT ARE PRESENT, ANSWERING   R 543 28
TO SOME, AND THE ORDER OF PRIESTHOOD TO OTHERS   R 547 26

OTHERS   CONTINUED

AND ENCOURAGE OTHERS TO THE SAME   555 05
GOOD WORKS UNTO OTHERS, THAT THE ADVERSARY MAY BE   555 11
SENDING, OR LAYING HANDS UPON OTHERS   555 21
AND THE OTHERS THAT ARE PRESENT, STANDING,   R 556 05
WITH OTHERS, SHALL ALSO COMMUNICATE   R 559 03
AND OTHERS, SHALL SALUTE AND WELCOME HIM,   R 574 27
AND MAKE US MINDFUL OF THE NEEDS OF OTHERS   600 18
DISCERNED FROM OTHERS THAT BE NOT CHRISTENED,   608 25
(THAT OTHERS MAY FEAR TO DO THE LIKE,) AS HE   609 39

OTHERWISE

OR OTHERWISE DISPOSED OF, AS MAY SEEM MOST   V 08
FOR OTHERWISE THE RECEIVING OF THE HOLY COMMUNICN   087 29
BECAUSE I AM OTHERWISE HINDERED WITH WORLDLY   088 28
IN THIS BOOK OTHERWISE ORDERED   R 090 05
OTHERWISE IT IS OF NO STRENGTH AT ALL WHILE THE   147 16
TOGETHER OTHERWISE THAN AS GOD'S WORD DOTH ALLOW,   300 29
AND OTHERWISE LEARNED AS THE CANONS   529 29
IT SHALL OTHERWISE SEEM GOOD UNTO THE   R 535 21

OUGHT

IN COMMON EQUITY OUGHT TO BE ALLOWED TO ALL HUMAN   V 43
AND ALTHOUGH WE OUGHT, AT ALL TIMES, HUMBLY TO   006 03
YET OUGHT WE CHIEFLY SO TO DO, WHEN WE ASSEMBLE AND   006 04
THINGS WHICH WE OUGHT TO HAVE DONE   006 21
THINGS WHICH WE OUGHT NOT TO HAVE DONE   006 22
AND ALTHOUGH WE OUGHT, AT ALL TIMES, HUMBLY TO   023 11
YET OUGHT WE CHIEFLY SO TO DO, WHEN WE ASSEMBLE AND   023 13
THINGS WHICH WE OUGHT TO HAVE DONE   023 28
THINGS WHICH WE OUGHT NOT TO HAVE DONE   023 29
TO WHAT OUGHT TO BE THE PROPER END OF ALL SUCH   VI 18
IN THAT CASE OUGHT TO ADMIT THE PENITENT PERSON TO   R 085 16
AND IF ANY MAN SAY OUGHT UNTO YOU, YE SHALL SAY, THE   091 16
WHAT THINGS THEY OUGHT TO DO, AND ALSO MAY HAVE GRACE   109 32
HIGHLY THAN HE OUGHT TO THINK   110 11
OF US HOW YE OUGHT TO WALK AND TO PLEASE GOD, SO YE   127 25
YE ALSO OUGHT TO WASH ONE ANOTHER'S FEET   156 16
AND BY OUR LAW HE OUGHT TO DIE, BECAUSE HE MADE   159 09
OUGHT NOT CHRIST TO HAVE SUFFERED THESE THINGS, AND   167 30
SO LOVED US, WE OUGHT ALSO TO LOVE ONE ANOTHER   189 16
AND WE OUGHT TO LAY DOWN OUR LIVES FOR THE BRETHREN   191 17
THY BROTHER HATH OUGHT AGAINST THEE   198 09
SPEAK BOLDLY, AS I OUGHT TO SPEAK   219 25
SO OUGHT MEN TO LOVE THEIR WIVES AS THEIR CWN BODIES   267 24
WHICH A CHRISTIAN OUGHT TO KNOW AND BELIEVE TO HIS   277 12
WE ARE THEY THAT OUGHT TO SPEAK   355 15
UNTO HIM THAT OUGHT TO BE FEARED   433 12
THAT THEY OUGHT TO BE HAD IN REMEMBRANCE   483 02
HOW THE PEOPLE OUGHT TO ESTEEM THEM IN THEIR OFFICE   R 530 06
FOR THE WHICH HE OUGHT NOT TO BE ADMITTED TO THAT   530 23
HOW THE PEOPLE OUGHT TO ESTEEM THEM IN THEIR OFFICE   R 536 06
FOR THE WHICH HE OUGHT NOT TO BE RECEIVED INTO THIS   536 29
CARE AND STUDY YE OUGHT TO APPLY YOURSELVES, AS WELL   540 26
THEREFORE YE OUGHT, AND HAVE NEED, TO PRAY EARNESTLY   540 32
HOW STUDIOUS YE OUGHT TO BE IN READING AND LEARNING   541 03
HOW YE OUGHT TO FORSAKE AND SET ASIDE,   541 07
SO LABOURING YE OUGHT TO SUPPORT THE WEAK, AND TO   551 09
WHAT THINGS THEY OUGHT TO DO, AND MAY HAVE POWER AND   566 05
OBEY HIM, AS WE OUGHT TO DO   580 32
PRECEPTS THEREOF OUGHT OF NECESSITY TO BE RECEIVED IN   604 21
APOSTLES' CREED, OUGHT THOROUGHLY TO BE RECEIVED AND   604 26
YET, AS IT OUGHT NOT TO DECREE ANY THING   607 07
BESIDES THE SAME OUGHT IT NOT TO ENFORCE ANY THING TO   607 08
AND THOSE WE OUGHT TO JUDGE LAWFULLY CALLED AND SENT,   607 21
THAT CHRISTIANS OUGHT TO HAVE AMONG THEMSELVES CNE TO   608 34
AND COMMANDMENT, OUGHT TO BE MINISTERED TO ALL   609 12
OUGHT TO BE TAKEN OF THE WHOLE   609 27
COMMON AUTHORITY, OUGHT TO BE REBUKED OPENLY,   609 38
EVERY MAN OUGHT, OF SUCH THINGS AS HE POSSESSETH,   611 03

OURSELVES

AND SHOW OURSELVES GLAD IN HIM WITH PSALMS   009 06
IT IS HE THAT HATH MADE US, AND NOT WE OURSELVES   015 08
WE DECEIVE OURSELVES, AND THE TRUTH IS NOT IN US   022 10
ALWAYS PROVE OURSELVES A PEOPLE MINDFUL OF THY FAVOUR   036 11
SUBMITTING OURSELVES WHOLLY TO HIS HOLY WILL AND   086 21
WE DECEIVE OURSELVES, AND THE TRUTH IS NOT IN US   101 29
WE MAY PURIFY OURSELVES, EVEN AS HE IS PURE   117 07
APPROVING OURSELVES AS THE MINISTERS OF GOD, IN MUCH   126 09
WE HAVE NO POWER OF OURSELVES TO HELP OURSELVES   127 16
NO POWER OF OURSELVES TO HELP OURSELVES   127 16
FOR WE OURSELVES HAVE HEARD OF HIS OWN MOUTH   152 02
ASSEMBLING OF OURSELVES TOGETHER, AS THE MANNER CF   158 26
ENDEAVOUR OURSELVES TO FOLLOW THE BLESSED STEPS OF   171 32
ONLY THEY, BUT OURSELVES ALSO, WHICH HAVE THE   194 21
GROAN WITHIN OURSELVES, WAITING FOR THE ADOPTION, TO   194 22
EVEN WE OURSELVES GROAN WITHIN OURSELVES, WAITING FOR   194 22
SUFFICIENT OF OURSELVES TO THINK ANY THING AS OF   206 14
OF OURSELVES TO THINK ANY THING AS OF OURSELVES   206 15
GIVE UP OURSELVES OBEDIENTLY TO FULFIL THY HOLY   226 22
COMMENDING OURSELVES TO EVERY MAN'S CONSCIENCE IN THE   250 31
WE PREACH NOT OURSELVES, BUT CHRIST JESUS THE LCRD   251 05
AND OURSELVES YOUR SERVANTS FOR JESUS' SAKE   251 06
NOR BEHAVE OURSELVES FROWARDLY IN THY COVENANT   395 29
LET US TAKE TO OURSELVES *   444 28
AND SHOW OURSELVES GLAD IN HIM WITH PSALMS   459 08
IT IS HE THAT HATH MADE US, AND NOT WE OURSELVES   463 09
WE WILL GIVE OURSELVES CONTINUALLY TO PRAYER, AND TO   532 13
TO SHOW OURSELVES THANKFUL UNTO THEE FOR THESE ANC   545 28
WE DECEIVE OURSELVES, AND THE TRUTH IS NOT IN US   605 37

OUT-GOINGS

MAKEST THE OUT-GOINGS OF THE MORNING AND EVENING TO   416 31

OUTCAST

OF MEN, AND THE OUTCAST OF THE PEOPLE   366 15
4 DELIVER THE OUTCAST AND POOR   443 24

OUTCASTS

TOGETHER THE OUTCASTS OF ISRAEL   264 22
TOGETHER THE OUTCASTS OF ISRAEL   522 31
BRING AGAIN THE OUTCASTS, SEEK THE LOST   558 28

OUTER

BE CAST OUT INTO OUTER DARKNESS   115 21
AND CAST HIM INTO OUTER DARKNESS   218 27

OUTRAGE

AND STILLEST THE OUTRAGE OF A VIOLENT AND UNRULY   052 19

OUTRUN

DISCIPLE DID OUTRUN PETER, AND CAME FIRST TO THE   164 18

OUTWARD

DAY WITH OUR OUTWARD EARS, MAY, THROUGH THY GRACE, BE   049 18
SACRAMENT AN OUTWARD AND VISIBLE SIGN OF AN INWARD   292 10
THE OUTWARD AND VISIBLE SIGN, AND THE INWARD AND   292 15
WHAT IS THE OUTWARD AND VISIBLE SIGN OR FORM IN   292 17
THE OUTWARD AND VISIBLE SIGN OR FORM IN   292 19
WHAT IS THE OUTWARD PART OR SIGN OF THE LORD'S   293 08
THE OUTWARD PART OR SIGN OF THE LORD'S   293 10
ANC THE MORE THE OUTWARD MAN DECAYETH, STRENGTHEN   316 10
I MEAN AN OUTWARD AND VISIBLE SIGN OF AN INWARD AND   581 12
THE OUTWARD VISIBLE SIGN, AND THE INWARD SPIRITUAL   581 17
WHAT IS THE OUTWARD VISIBLE SIGN OR FORM IN BAPTISM   581 19
WHAT IS THE OUTWARD PART OR SIGN OF THE LORD'S   582 07

OUTWARDLY

KEEP US BOTH OUTWARDLY IN OUR BODIES, AND INWARDLY IN   127 16

OVEN

IS CAST INTO THE OVEN, SHALL HE NOT MUCH MORE CLOTHE   211 26
IS CAST INTO THE OVEN, SHALL HE NOT MUCH MORE CLCTHE   266 24
THEM LIKE A FIERY OVEN IN TIME OF THY WRATH   365 22

OVERCAME

AND THEY OVERCAME HIM BY THE BLOOD OF THE LAMB,   252 14

OVERCOME

WHEN THOU HADST OVERCOME THE SHARPNESS OF DEATH,   010 28
TEMPTATION AND OVERCOME EVIL, AND MAY REJOICE IN THE   043 12
BE NOT OVERCOME OF EVIL, BUT OVERCOME EVIL WITH GCOD   113 08
OF EVIL, BUT OVERCOME EVIL WITH GOOD   113 08
UPON HIM, AND OVERCOME HIM, HE TAKETH FROM HIM ALL   130 07
CHRIST HAST OVERCOME DEATH, AND OPENED UNTO US THE   163 23
I HAVE OVERCOME THE WORLD   177 10

OVERCOMETH

BORN OF GOD OVERCOMETH THE WORLD   170 26
VICTORY THAT OVERCOMETH THE WORLD, EVEN OUR FAITH   170 27
IS HE THAT OVERCOMETH THE WORLD, BUT HE THAT   170 28

OVERFLOWETH

MY HEART OVERFLOWETH WITH A GOOD MATTER   396 15

OVERFLOWINGS

AND THE OVERFLOWINGS OF UNGODLINESS MADE ME AFRAID   359 31

OVERPAST

UNTIL THIS TYRANNY BE OVERPAST   409 14

OVERPLUS

THE OVERPLUS SHALL BE OMITTED   R 224 36

OVERSEERS

HATH MADE YOU OVERSEERS, TO FEED THE CHURCH OF GOD,   550 28

OVERSHADOW

HIGHEST SHALL OVERSHADOW THEE   236 23
BY MIGHT OVERSHADOW SOME OF THEM   249 29

OVERSHADOWED

AND OVERSHADOWED THEM   249 05

OVERTAKE

AND OVERTAKE THEM   362 11

OVERTASKED

WEAKNESS ARE OVERTASKED, OR BECAUSE OF POVERTY ARE   600 07

OVERTHREW

AND OVERTHREW THE TABLES OF THE   091 34
AND OVERTHREW THE TABLES OF THE   260 04
HIS HOST, HE OVERTHREW THEM IN THE RED SEA   512 12
AND OVERTHREW THE TABLES   567 30

OVERTHROW

THEE WILL WE OVERTHROW OUR ENEMIES, *   395 02
TO OVERTHROW THEM IN THE WILDERNESS   474 21
PURPOSED TO OVERTHROW MY GOINGS   516 17
PERSON TO OVERTHROW HIM   516 33

OVERTHROWETH

OVERTHROWETH THE NATURE OF A SACRAMENT,   608 42

OVERTHROWN

FOR THEY WERE OVERTHROWN IN THE WILDERNESS   201 12
39 THOU HAST OVERTHROWN ALL HIS HEDGES, *   452 20
JUDGES BE OVERTHROWN IN STONY PLACES, *   517 24

OVERTOOK

SNARES OF DEATH OVERTOOK ME   360 03

OVERWHELMED

DREAD HATH OVERWHELMED ME   406 29
AND OVERWHELMED THEIR ENEMIES WITH THE SEA   438 17
THE WATERS OVERWHELMED THEM   473 23

OWE

OWE NO MAN ANY THING, BUT TO LOVE ONE ANOTHER   090 23

OWED

UNTO HIM, WHICH OWED HIM TEN THOUSAND TALENTS   221 15
WHICH OWED HIM AN HUNDRED PENCE   221 24

OWEST

HIM BY THE THROAT, SAYING, PAY ME THAT THOU OWEST   221 26

OWL

AND LIKE AN OWL THAT IS IN THE DESERT   464 22

OWN

THINGS IN THEIR OWN NATURE INDIFFERENT, AND   V 15
AND DESIRES OF OUR OWN HEARTS   006 19
EVERY ONE TO HIS OWN WAY   022 15
AND DESIRES OF OUR OWN HEARTS   023 26
WITH HIS OWN RIGHT HAND, AND WITH HIS HOLY ARM,   027 06
AND GOD, EVEN OUR OWN GOD, SHALL GIVE US HIS   028 29
AND EAT OUR OWN BREAD   039 27
CREATED MAN IN THINE OWN IMAGE   044 09
O LORD, AND OF THINE OWN HAVE WE GIVEN THEE   073 23
OF DARKNESS INTO HIS OWN GLORIOUS LIGHT   077 25
TRUSTING IN OUR OWN RIGHTEOUSNESS, BUT IN THY   082 14
AND EXAMINE YOUR OWN CONSCIENCES, AND THAT NOT   087 10
THERE TO BEWAIL YOUR OWN SINFULNESS, AND TO CONFESS   087 20
CANNOT QUIET HIS OWN CONSCIENCE HEREIN, BUT REQUIRETH   088 04
AS YE LOVE YOUR OWN SALVATION, THAT YE WILL BE   089 08
SEE AND KNOW OF YOUR OWN SELVES THAT SUMMER IS NOW   093 16
I JUDGE NOT MINE OWN SELF   094 08
HE CAME UNTO HIS OWN, AND HIS OWN RECEIVED HIM NOT   097 32
HIS OWN, AND HIS OWN RECEIVED HIM NOT   097 33
EVERY ONE INTO HIS OWN CITY   098 32
WORK OUT YOUR OWN SALVATION WITH FEAR AND TREMBLING   106 03
DEPARTED INTO THEIR OWN COUNTRY ANOTHER WAY   109 25
BE NOT WISE IN YOUR OWN CONCEITS   112 31
NOT LAWFUL FOR ME TO DO WHAT I WILL WITH MINE OWN   120 11
IN PERILS BY MINE OWN COUNTRYMEN, IN PERILS BY THE   121 05
SEEKETH NOT HER OWN, IS NOT EASILY PROVOKED, THINKETH   122 31
BUT BY HIS OWN BLOOD HE ENTERED IN ONCE INTO   126 26
AND I SEEK NOT MINE OWN GLORY   133 16
AND PUT HIS OWN RAIMENT ON HIM, AND LED HIM AWAY   136 24
THEREFORE MINE OWN ARM BROUGHT SALVATION UNTO ME   138 24
AND PUT HIS OWN CLOTHES ON HIM, AND LED HIM OUT   146 04
HAVE HEARD OF HIS OWN MOUTH   152 03
HAVING LOVED HIS OWN WHICH WERE IN THE WORLD, HE   155 25
TOOK HER UNTO HIS OWN HOME   160 23
AND LAID IT IN HIS OWN NEW TOMB, WHICH HE HAD HEWN   162 11
AGAIN UNTO THEIR OWN HOME   164 29
HE HAD SERVED HIS OWN GENERATION BY THE WILL OF GOD,   169 15
WHO HIS OWN SELF BARE OUR SINS IN HIS OWN BODY ON THE   172 15
BARE OUR SINS IN HIS OWN BODY ON THE TREE, THAT WE,   172 15
THE SHEPHERD, WHOSE OWN THE SHEEP ARE NOT, SEETH THE   172 23
OF HIS OWN WILL BEGAT HE US WITH THE WORD OF TRUTH,   174 29
DECEIVING YOUR OWN SELVES   176 06
BUT DECEIVETH HIS OWN HEART, THIS MAN'S RELIGION IS   176 14
EVERY MAN TO HIS OWN, AND SHALL LEAVE ME ALONE   177 06
HATH PUT IN HIS OWN POWER   178 08
THEM SPEAK IN HIS OWN LANGUAGE   180 28
WE EVERY MAN IN OUR OWN TONGUE, WHEREIN WE WERE BORN   180 31
AND HE CALLETH HIS OWN SHEEP BY NAME, AND LEADETH   186 05
HE PUTTETH FORTH HIS OWN SHEEP, HE GOETH BEFORE THEM,   186 06

OWN   CONTINUED

THAT IS IN THINE OWN EYE   195 07
THAT IS IN THINE OWN EYE   195 10
BEAM OUT OF THINE OWN EYE, AND THEN SHALT THOU SEE   195 11
FASTING TO THEIR OWN HOUSES, THEY WILL FAINT BY THE   199 13
AND SET HIM ON HIS OWN BEAST, AND BROUGHT HIM TO AN   208 31
UNTO YOU WITH MINE OWN HAND   210 24
AND CAME INTO HIS OWN CITY   216 34
SHALL DWELL IN THEIR OWN LAND   225 20
PIERCE THROUGH THY OWN SOUL ALSO,) THAT THE THOUGHTS   233 14
TO THEIR OWN CITY NAZARETH   233 25
HE MIGHT GO TO HIS OWN PLACE   234 31
TO THEM OF HIS OWN ACCORD   245 23
WERE OF THE WORLD, THE WORLD WOULD LOVE HIS OWN   255 15
OF HIS OWN WILL BEGAT HE US WITH THE WORD OF TRUTH,   265 21
DECEIVING YOUR OWN SELVES   265 29
BUT DECEIVETH HIS OWN HEART, THIS MAN'S RELIGION IS   266 06
YOURSELVES UNTO YOUR OWN HUSBANDS, AS UNTO THE LORD   267 14
WIVES BE TO THEIR OWN HUSBANDS IN EVERY THING   267 18
THEIR WIVES AS THEIR OWN BODIES   267 25
EVER YET HATED HIS OWN FLESH   267 26
NOT TO DO MINE OWN WILL, BUT THE WILL OF HIM THAT   269 16
HIM FOR THINE OWN CHILD, AND TO INCORPORATE HIM INTO   280 31
TRULY TO EARN MINE OWN LIVING, AND TO DO MY DUTY IN   289 09
I COMMUNE WITH MINE OWN HEART, AND SEARCH OUT MY   311 11
I SAID, IT IS MINE OWN INFIRMITY   311 18
THE WORKS OF THINE OWN HANDS   312 10
THE DEVIL, OR BY HIS OWN CARNAL WILL AND FRAILNESS   314 05
A SHEEP OF THINE OWN FOLD, A LAMB OF THINE OWN FLOCK,   319 29
A SINNER OF THINE OWN REDEEMING   319 30
A LAMB OF THINE OWN FLOCK, A SINNER OF THINE OWN   319 30
BUT EVERY MAN IN HIS OWN ORDER   328 25
TO EVERY SEED ITS OWN BODY   329 11
THAT SPARED NOT HIS OWN SON, BUT DELIVERED HIM UP FOR   330 34
MADE LIKE UNTO HIS OWN GLORIOUS BODY   333 21
COMMUNE WITH YOUR OWN HEART, AND IN YOUR CHAMBER, AND   347 19
PERISH THROUGH THEIR OWN IMAGINATIONS   348 23
SHALL COME UPON HIS OWN HEAD, *   350 25
SHALL FALL ON HIS OWN PATE   350 26
IN THE WORK OF HIS OWN HANDS   352 25
THE UNGODLY, FOR HIS OWN LUST, DOTH PERSECUTE THE   353 05
MADE BOAST OF HIS OWN HEART'S DESIRE, *   353 08
BUT IS LOWLY IN HIS OWN EYES, *   357 13
IT WERE TO HIS OWN HINDRANCE   357 17
INCLOSED IN THEIR OWN FAT, *   359 06
BY THINE OWN SWORD   359 13
AND ESCHEWED MINE OWN WICKEDNESS   361 14
IN THINE OWN STRENGTH   365 32
HATH QUICKENED HIS OWN SOUL   368 03
WICKEDNESS OF THEIR OWN INVENTIONS   373 14
THE COVERT OF THINE OWN PRESENCE FROM THE PLOTTINGS   377 06
HE MAY FALL INTO HIS OWN MISCHIEF   382 06
SHALL TURN INTO MINE OWN BOSOM   382 19
HIMSELF IN HIS OWN SIGHT, *   383 28
GO THROUGH THEIR OWN HEART, *   385 25
9 YEA, EVEN MINE OWN FAMILIAR FRIEND WHOM I TRUSTED,   392 17
THROUGH THEIR OWN SWORD, *   394 28
NEITHER WAS IT THEIR OWN ARM THAT HELPED THEM   394 28
FORGET ALSO THINE OWN PEOPLE, AND THY FATHER'S HOUSE   397 06
LANDS AFTER THEIR OWN NAMES   400 29
HAST SLANDERED THINE OWN MOTHER'S SON   402 31
MY GUIDE, AND MINE OWN FAMILIAR FRIEND   407 17
8 YEA, THEIR OWN TONGUES SHALL MAKE THEM FALL   416 02
AND GOD, EVEN OUR OWN GOD, SHALL GIVE US HIS   419 03
MINE OWN WILL I BRING AGAIN, AS I DID SOMETIME FROM   420 31
MAINTAIN THINE OWN CAUSE   431 22
I COMMUNE WITH MINE OWN HEART, AND SEARCH OUT MY   433 28
I SAID, IT IS MINE OWN INFIRMITY   434 02
HE GAVE THEM THEIR OWN DESIRE   436 30
53 BUT AS FOR HIS OWN PEOPLE, HE LED THEM FORTH LIKE   438 14
SO STRONG FOR THINE OWN SELF   442 06
THEM UP UNTO THEIR OWN HEARTS' LUSTS, *   443 04
THEM FOLLOW THEIR OWN IMAGINATIONS   443 05
THEM IN THEIR OWN MALICE   458 33
2 WITH HIS OWN RIGHT HAND, AND WITH HIS HOLY ARM,   461 27
A FATHER PITIETH HIS OWN CHILDREN   466 32
TO ANGER WITH THEIR OWN INVENTIONS   474 27
STAINED WITH THEIR OWN WORKS, *   475 14
A WHORING WITH THEIR OWN INVENTIONS   475 15
THAT HE ABHORRED HIS OWN INHERITANCE   475 17
HIM WITH THEIR OWN INVENTIONS, AND WERE BROUGHT DOWN   475 23
WITH THEIR OWN CONFUSION, AS WITH A CLOAK   481 30
59 I CALLED MINE OWN WAYS TO REMEMBRANCE, *   493 29
TURN BACK UNTO THEIR OWN WICKEDNESS, *   505 02
AND ISRAEL FOR HIS OWN POSSESSION   510 10
THE WORKS OF THINE OWN HANDS   514 16
MISCHIEF OF THEIR OWN LIPS FALL UPON THE HEAD OF THEM   516 27
FALL INTO THEIR OWN NETS TOGETHER, *   517 32
CHILDREN AND THEIR OWN HOUSES WELL   532 02
AND FASHION YOUR OWN LIVES, AND THE LIVES OF YOUR   533 25
AND HE CALLETH HIS OWN SHEEP BY NAME, AND LEADETH   538 28
HE PUTTETH FORTH HIS OWN SHEEP, HE GOETH BEFORE THEM,   538 29
THE SHEPHERD, WHOSE OWN THE SHEEP ARE NOT, SEETH THE   539 12
AND FASHION YOUR OWN SELVES, AND YOUR FAMILIES,   542 33
THINE OWN UNFAILING MIGHT SUPPLY TO STRENGTHEN OUR   545 04
THAT RULETH WELL HIS OWN HOUSE, HAVING HIS CHILDREN   549 24
NOT HOW TO RULE HIS OWN HOUSE, HOW SHALL HE TAKE CARE   549 25
PURCHASED WITH HIS OWN BLOOD   550 29
ALSO OF YOUR OWN SELVES SHALL MEN ARISE, SPEAKING   550 31
THE EFFUSION OF HIS OWN BLOOD   554 11
THINE OWN UNFAILING MIGHT SUPPLY TO STRENGTHEN OUR   557 10
AGREEABLY TO THEIR OWN REASON AND SENSE OF THE   564 14
PLACE SHALL IN THEIR OWN PERSONS RENEW THE PROMISES   565 24
TRULY TO GET MINE OWN LIVING, AND TO DO MY DUTY IN   580 13
HUMBLE SENSE OF OUR OWN UNWORTHINESS, ACKNOWLEDGING   589 30

OWN   CONTINUED

THROUGH OUR OWN FRAILTY, OR THE TEMPTATIONS 590 09
AND IS OF HIS OWN NATURE INCLINED TO EVIL, SO THAT 604 32
BY HIS OWN NATURAL STRENGTH AND GOOD WORKS, 604 43
AND NOT FOR OUR OWN WORKS OR DESERVINGS 605 07
THE SAME IN THEIR OWN NAME, BUT IN CHRIST'S, AND DO 608 11
TO MARRY AT THEIR OWN DISCRETION, AS THEY SHALL JUDGE 609 23

OX

NOR HIS MAID, NOR HIS OX, NOR HIS ASS, NOR ANY THING 069 21
HAVE AN ASS OR AN OX FALLEN INTO A PIT, AND WILL NOT 214 06
NOR HIS MAID, NOR HIS OX, NOR HIS ASS, NOR ANY THING 287 21
NOR HIS MAID, NOR HIS OX, NOR HIS ASS, NOR ANY THING 579 22

OXEN

TRY THEIR YOKES OF OXEN, OR BECAUSE THEY WERE 089 04
BOUGHT FIVE YOKE OF OXEN, AND I GO TO PROVE THEM 192 09
MY OXEN AND MY FATLINGS ARE KILLED, AND ALL THINGS 218 08
7 ALL SHEEP AND OXEN 351 14
12 MANY OXEN ARE COME ABOUT ME 366 27
14 THAT OUR OXEN MAY BE STRONG TO LABOUR 520 21
THOSE THAT SOLD OXEN AND SHEEP AND DOVES, AND THE 567 27
AND THE SHEEP, AND THE OXEN 567 30

PAID

TILL THOU HAST PAID THE UTTERMOST FARTHING 198 16
5 I PAID THEM THE THINGS THAT I NEVER TOOK 422 10

PAIN

THROUGH THE GREAT PAIN AND PERIL OF CHILD-BIRTH, THIS 051 07
FIRST HE SUFFERED PAIN, AND ENTERED NOT INTO GLORY 138 05
AND TRAVAILETH IN PAIN TOGETHER UNTIL NOW 194 20
THROUGH THE GREAT PAIN AND PERIL OF CHILD-BIRTH, THIS 306 26
ASSUAGE HIS PAIN, AS SHALL SEEM TO THEE MOST 314 07
AND DRIVE AWAY ALL PAIN OF SOUL AND BODY, THAT BEING 320 10
THAT ALL THY PAIN AND SICKNESS OF BODY BEING PUT TO 320 18
BUT IT WAS PAIN AND GRIEF TO ME 389 10
NOR CRYING, NEITHER SHALL THERE BE ANY MORE PAIN 567 20
HAVE REMISSION OF PAIN OR GUILT, WERE BLASPHEMOUS 609 18

PAINFULNESS

AND PAINFULNESS, IN WATCHINGS OFTEN, IN HUNGER AND 121 08

PAINS

INTO THE BITTER PAINS OF ETERNAL DEATH 332 27
LAST HOUR, FOR ANY PAINS OF DEATH, TO FALL FROM THEE 332 32
5 THE PAINS OF HELL CAME ABOUT ME 360 02
AND THE PAINS OF HELL GAT HOLD UPON ME 486 24

PAIR

LAW OF THE LORD, A PAIR OF TURTLE-DOVES, OR TWO YOUNG 232 29

PALACE

ARMED KEEPETH HIS PALACE, HIS GOODS ARE IN PEACE 130 05
EVEN INTO THE PALACE OF THE HIGH PRIEST 142 34
BENEATH IN THE PALACE, THERE COMETH ONE OF THE MAIDS 143 23
AND SHALL ENTER INTO THE KING'S PALACE 397 18

PALACES

OUT OF THE IVORY PALACES, WHEREBY THEY HAVE MADE THEE 396 33
KNOWN IN HER PALACES AS A SURE REFUGE 399 14
CONSIDER HER PALACES, * 400 02
AND PLENTEOUSNESS WITHIN THY PALACES 503 21

PALM

FOR THE DAY, UNTIL PALM SUNDAY R 124 19

PALM-TREE

LIKE A PALM-TREE, * 456 24

PALMS

HIM WITH THE PALMS OF THEIR HANDS 143 22
WHITE ROBES, AND PALMS IN THEIR HANDS 256 26

PALSY

HOME SICK OF THE PALSY, GRIEVOUSLY TORMENTED 115 08
A MAN SICK OF THE PALSY, LYING ON A BED 217 02
SAID UNTO THE SICK OF THE PALSY 217 03
TO THE SICK OF THE PALSY,) ARISE, TAKE UP THY BED, 217 10

PAMPHYLIA

AND PAMPHYLIA, IN EGYPT, AND IN THE PARTS OF 181 03

PANTETH

10 MY HEART PANTETH, MY STRENGTH HATH FAILED ME, 388 10

PAPS

BARE THEE, AND THE PAPS WHICH THOU HAST SUCKED 130 19
NEVER BARE, AND THE PAPS WHICH NEVER GAVE SUCK 154 17

PARABLE

AND HE SPAKE TO THEM A PARABLE 093 14
TO HIM OUT OF EVERY CITY, HE SPAKE BY A PARABLE 121 19
WHAT MIGHT THIS PARABLE BE 121 29
NOW THE PARABLE IS THIS 121 32
THIS PARABLE SPAKE JESUS UNTO THEM 186 10
HE SPAKE THIS PARABLE UNTO THEM, SAYING, WHAT MAN OF 193 17
AND HE SPAKE A PARABLE UNTO THEM, CAN THE BLIND LEAD 195 02
JESUS SPAKE THIS PARABLE UNTO CERTAIN WHICH TRUSTED 205 21
HE PUT FORTH A PARABLE TO THOSE WHICH WERE BIDDEN, 214 08
MINE EAR TO THE PARABLE. * 400 12
2 I WILL OPEN MY MOUTH IN A PARABLE 434 29
THIS PARABLE SPAKE JESUS UNTO THEM 538 33

PARABLES

BUT TO OTHERS IN PARABLES 121 31

PARADISE

TO-DAY SHALT THOU BE WITH ME IN PARADISE 155 09
WHOLE CHURCH IN PARADISE AND ON EARTH, THY LIGHT AND 268 16
IN THE PARADISE OF GOD 319 25

PARAGRAPH

THE CONCLUDING PARAGRAPH IN THE LETTER OF INSTITUTION R 569 10

PARCHMENTS

BUT ESPECIALLY THE PARCHMENTS 254 06

PARDON

BY THY MERCIFUL PARDON MAY BE ABSOLVED 062 11
PARDON AND DELIVER YOU FROM ALL YOUR SINS 076 05
FAITHFUL PEOPLE PARDON AND PEACE, THAT THEY MAY BE 218 33
DESIRETH PARDON AND FORGIVENESS 314 02
AND HIS PARDON SEALED IN HEAVEN 316 15
MERCIFULLY TO PARDON ALL HIS SINS 318 15
LORD GRANT THEE PARDON AND REMISSION OF ALL THY SINS, 319 15
DONE US GOOD, AND PARDON ALL THOSE WHO HAVE DONE OR 590 32

PARDONED

THAT HER INIQUITY IS PARDONED 242 18

PARDONETH

HE PARDONETH AND ABSOLVETH ALL THOSE WHO TRULY 007 11
HE PARDONETH AND ABSOLVETH ALL THOSE WHO TRULY 024 13

PARDONING

BUT PARDONING OUR OFFENCES, THROUGH JESUS 081 31

PARDONS

PARDONS, WORSHIPPING AND ADORATION, AS 607 14

PARENTS

NOW HIS PARENTS WENT TO JERUSALEM EVERY YEAR AT THE 110 18
AND WHEN THE PARENTS BROUGHT IN THE CHILD JESUS, TO 233 02
AND PARENTS SHALL BE ADMITTED AS SPONSORS, IF IT BE R 273 11
BE BAPTIZED, THE PARENTS OR SPONSORS SHALL GIVE R 273 12

PARISH

IN A DECENT BASIN TO BE PROVIDED BY THE PARISH R 073 29
MINISTER OF EVERY PARISH SHALL OFTEN ADMONISH THE R 273 03
REPORTED TO THE PARISH AUTHORITIES R 281 30
MINISTER OF EVERY PARISH SHALL DILIGENTLY, UPON R 295 07
INSTRUCT OR EXAMINE THE YOUTH OF HIS PARISH R 295 09
BE GIVEN THEREOF TO THE MINISTER OF THE PARISH R 308 06
PEOPLE OF THE PARISH, THAT THEY MAY BE RELIEVED WITH 533 20
A MINISTER INTO A PARISH OR CHURCH, AS PRESCRIBED BY R 569 05
MAY PROCEED TO INSTITUTE HIM INTO THE PARISH R 569 07
A PRIEST, IN THE PARISH (OR CHURCH) OF E 569 17
YOU INTO SAID PARISH, (OR CHURCH,) POSSESSED OF FULL 569 18
OF RECTOR OF -- PARISH, (OR CHURCH,) YOU ARE 569 24
INTO THIS PARISH, (OR CHURCH,) AS PRIEST AND RECTOR 570 14
AND BEHALF OF -- PARISH (OR CHURCH) I DO RECEIVE AND 570 27
MINISTER OF EVERY PARISH SHALL DILIGENTLY, UPON R 582 27
CHILDREN OF HIS PARISH, SENT UNTO HIM, AS HE SHALL R 582 29
MINISTER OF EVERY PARISH SHALL EITHER BRING, OR SEND R 583 06
WITHIN HIS PARISH, AS HE SHALL THINK FIT TO BE R 583 08

PARISHIONERS

THEIR PARISHIONERS TO THE OFTEN RECEIVING OF THE HOLY R 321 07
ALMS OF THE PARISHIONERS, OR OTHERS 533 21

PARMENAS

AND TIMON, AND PARMENAS, AND NICOLAS A PROSELYTE OF 532 17

PAROCHIAL

AND OF YOUR PAROCHIAL RECOGNITION, AND PROMISE TO BE 570 33

PART

A MOST INVALUABLE PART OF THAT BLESSED 'LIBERTY V 02
UNTO THE UTTERMOST PART OF THE EARTH 005 14

PART   CONTINUED

MAY OMIT THAT PART OF THE COMMANDMENT WHICH IS INSET   R 067 27
FOR WE KNOW IN PART, AND WE PROPHESY IN PART   123 07
FOR WE KNOW IN PART, AND WE PROPHESY IN PART   123 07
THAT WHICH IS IN PART SHALL BE DONE AWAY   123 08
NOW I KNOW IN PART   123 13
THOU HAST NO PART WITH ME   156 06
AND MADE FOUR PARTS, TO EVERY SOLDIER A PART   160 11
UNTO THE UTTERMOST PART OF THE EARTH   178 12
OF WHOM THE GREATER PART REMAIN UNTO THIS PRESENT,   205 09
AND HAD OBTAINED PART OF THIS MINISTRY   234 12
THAT HE MAY TAKE PART OF THIS MINISTRY AND   234 29
MEASURE OF EVERY PART, MAKETH INCREASE OF THE BODY   237 32
THOU ALSO ON THY PART TAKE HEED THAT THIS CHILD LEARN   277 09
THAT THE PART OF THE COMMANDMENT WHICH IS   R 286 03
WHAT IS THE OUTWARD PART OR SIGN OF THE LORD'S   293 08
THE OUTWARD PART OR SIGN OF THE LORD'S SUPPER IS,   293 10
WHAT IS THE INWARD PART, OR THING SIGNIFIED   293 13
THE INWARD PART, OR THING SIGNIFIED, IS THE BODY AND   293 14
TILL DEATH US DO PART, ACCORDING TO GOD'S HOLY   301 31
TILL DEATH US DO PART, ACCORDING TO GOD'S HOLY   302 07
OR ANY PART THEREOF, MAY BE USED AT THE   R 308 03
MAY USE ANY PART OF THE SERVICE OF THIS BCCK,   R 314 23
OR ANY PART THEREOF, AT THE DISCRETION OF   R 315 03
THE WHOLE OR A PART OF THE SERVICE APPOINTED TO BE   R 336 31
USE SUCH PART OF THIS OFFICE, OR SUCH DEVOTIONS TAKEN R 337 04
FROM THE UTTERMOST PART OF THE HEAVEN, AND RUNNETH   363 24
18 THEY PART MY GARMENTS AMONG THEM, *   367 08
THERE IS NO WHOLE PART IN MY BODY   388 05
OR WHO WILL TAKE MY PART AGAINST THE EVIL DOERS   458 19
HAD UNTO THEM, LO, THEY TAKE NCW MY CONTRARY PART   480 10
THE LORD TAKETH MY PART WITH THEM THAT HELP ME   488 12
WHAT IS THE OUTWARD PART OR SIGN OF THE LORD'S   582 07
WHAT IS THE INWARD PART, OR THING SIGNIFIED   582 11
IN SOME PART OF THIS CATECHISM   R 582 30
WITH A CHAPTER, OR PART OF A CHAPTER, FROM THE NEW   R 592 06

PARTAKER

AND ALSO MAY BE PARTAKER OF EVERLASTING GLORY IN THE   051 11
AND ALSO MAY BE PARTAKER OF EVERLASTING GLORY IN THE   053 16
MAY ALSO BE PARTAKER OF HIS RESURRECTION   281 02
AND ALSO MAY BE PARTAKER OF EVERLASTING GLORY IN THE   306 30
AND HAST BEEN PARTAKER WITH THE ADULTERERS   402 27

PARTAKERS

SHALL BECOME PARTAKERS OF EVERLASTING LIFE   037 07
WE MAY BE MADE PARTAKERS WITH THEM OF THE GLORICUS   048 21
THEM WE MAY BE PARTAKERS OF THY HEAVENLY KINGDOM   075 04
MAY BE PARTAKERS OF HIS MOST BLESSED BODY AND BLCOD   081 13
WHO SHALL BE PARTAKERS OF THIS HOLY COMMUNION,   081 24
THESE WORDS, PARTAKERS OF HIS MOST BLESSED BODY AND   R 083 10
WHO COME TO BE PARTAKERS OF THE HOLY COMMUNION,   R 084 34
THEM TO BE PARTAKERS OF THE LORD'S TABLE, UNTIL HE   R 085 17
YE BE MEET PARTAKERS CF THOSE HOLY MYSTERIES   086 03
AND ARE MADE PARTAKERS OF THE KINGDOM OF HEAVEN   086 34
AS WORTHY PARTAKERS OF THAT HOLY TABLE   087 15
YE WILL BE PARTAKERS OF THIS HOLY COMMUNICN   089 09
SAME BODY, AND PARTAKERS OF HIS PROMISE IN CHRIST BY   108 15
YE THEREFORE PARTAKERS WITH THEM   129 11
ALSO BE MADE PARTAKERS OF HIS RESURRECTION   134 10
AND BE MADE PARTAKERS OF THY HEAVENLY TREASURE   204 26
YE ALL ARE PARTAKERS OF MY GRACE   220 30
US MEET TO BE PARTAKERS OF THE INHERITANCE CF THE   224 09
WHEREOF WE ARE PARTAKERS IN THE LORD'S SUPPER   293 17
WHEREOF WE ARE PARTAKERS IN THE LORD'S SUPPER ARE THE   293 19
THESE WORDS, PARTAKERS OF HIS MOST BLESSED BODY AND   R 323 07
MEET TO BE PARTAKERS OF THE INHERITANCE OF THE SAINTS   335 33
MAY BE PARTAKERS OF THY EVERLASTING KINGDOM   561 20
WHEREOF WE ARE PARTAKERS THEREBY   582 15
WISE ARE THEY PARTAKERS OF CHRIST   609 06

PARTAKING

WE BREAK IS A PARTAKING OF THE BODY OF CHRIST   608 37
BLESSING IS A PARTAKING OF THE BLOOD OF CHRIST   608 38

PARTED

AND PARTED HIS GARMENTS, CASTING LOTS   136 31
THE PROPHET, THEY PARTED MY GARMENTS AMONG THEM, AND   136 32
THEY PARTED HIS GARMENTS, CASTING LOTS UPON   146 11
AND THEY PARTED HIS RAIMENT, AND CAST LOTS   154 26
WHICH SAITH, THEY PARTED MY RAIMENT AMCNG THEM,   160 15
HE WAS PARTED FROM THEM, AND CARRIED UP INTO   178 26

PARTHIANS

PARTHIANS, AND MEDES, AND ELAMITES, AND THE DWELLERS   180 32

PARTICULAR

THAT 'THE PARTICULAR FORMS OF DIVINE WORSHIP, ANC THE   V 13
ONE OF YOU IN PARTICULAR SO LOVE HIS WIFE EVEN AS   268 02
IN PARTICULAR, WE IMPLORE THY GRACE AND PROTECTION   588 27
IN PARTICULAR, WE BESEECH THEE TO CONTINUE THY   591 25
EVERY PARTICULAR OR NATIONAL CHURCH HATH AUTHORITY TO   609 42

PARTICULARLY

PARTICULARLY TO THOSE WHO DESIRE NOW TO OFFER UP   019 17
PARTICULARLY TO THOSE WHO DESIRE NOW TO OFFER UP   033 15
AND PARTICULARLY FOR THE MERCIES AND BENEFITS OF THE   591 19

PARTICULARS

IN SOME PARTICULARS, AS IN THEIR RESPECTIVE TIMES   V 29

PARTIES

RECOMPENSED THE PARTIES TO WHOM HE HATH DONE WRONG   R 085 06
IF ONE OF THE PARTIES, SO AT VARIANCE, BE CONTENT TC   R 085 11
REGARDS THE CIVIL CONTRACT BETWEEN THE PARTIES   R 304 20

PARTLY

BECAUSE IT IS PARTLY OF A LOCAL AND CIVIL NATURE,   R 607 11
AS HAVE GROWN PARTLY OF THE CORRUPT FOLLOWING OF THE   607 40
OF THE APOSTLES, PARTLY ARE STATES OF LIFE ALLOWED IN   607 41

PARTNERS

UNTO THEIR PARTNERS, WHICH WERE IN THE OTHER SHIP,   196 20
WHICH WERE PARTNERS WITH SIMON   196 27

PARTS

BODY AND ESSENTIAL PARTS OF THE SAME (AS WELL IN THE   V 30
IN THE INWARD PARTS, *   060 22
ASIDE INTO THE PARTS OF GALILEE   107 21
AND MADE FOUR PARTS, TO EVERY SOLDIER A PART   160 10
AND IN THE PARTS OF LIBYA ABOUT CYRENE,   181 04
INTO THE LOWER PARTS OF THE EARTH   237 16
WHICH TIME THESE PARTS OF THE FOREGOING SERVICE SHALL R 282 02
ARE ESSENTIAL PARTS OF BAPTISM), SUCH PERSON MAY BE   R 282 10
HOW MANY PARTS ARE THERE IN A SACRAMENT   292 14
THERE ARE TWO PARTS IN A SACRAMENT   292 15
TAKEN FROM OTHER PARTS OF THIS BOOK, AS MAY BE   R 337 05
AND THE UTMOST PARTS OF THE EARTH FCR THY POSSESSION   346 13
THEIR INWARD PARTS ARE VERY WICKEDNESS   348 19
IN THE INWARD PARTS, *   403 20
IN THE UTTERMOST PARTS OF THE EARTH SHALL BE AFRAID   416 29
13 WHO DIVIDED THE RED SEA IN TWO PARTS   512 08
IN THE UTTERMOST PARTS OF THE SEA   515 05
INTO THE LOWER PARTS OF THE EARTH   538 03
FLOCK IN ALL THE PARTS OF THE WORLD, TO SET FORTH THE   545 20
HOW MANY PARTS ARE THERE IN A SACRAMENT   581 16
TO THE UTTERMOST PARTS OF THE EARTH   596 31
WITHOUT BODY, PARTS, OR PASSIONS   603 03
TO THE REMAINING PARTS OF IT, IN OTHER ARTICLES   R 607 12
FOR BOTH THE PARTS OF THE LORD'S SACRAMENT, BY   609 11

PARTY

AND THE OTHER PARTY WILL NOT BE PERSUADED TO A GCDLY   R 085 14
SUCH TIME AS THE PARTY ACCUSED SHALL BE FOUND CLEAR   R 530 27
SUCH TIME AS THE PARTY ACCUSED SHALL BE FOUND CLEAR   R 537 03

PASCHAL

HE IS THE VERY PASCHAL LAMB, WHICH WAS OFFERED FCR   078 09
REVERENCE THE PASCHAL FEAST, MAY BE FOUND WORTHY TO   168 20

PASS

AT HIS DISCRETION, PASS AT ONCE FROM THE SENTENCES TO R 003 07
THE SENTENCES, PASS TO THE VERSICLES, O LORD,   R 003 11
TO YOU, ALL YE THAT PASS BY   004 29
SAID OR SUNG, MAY PASS AT ONCE TO THE COMMUNION   R 010 05
AT HIS DISCRETION, PASS AT ONCE FROM THE SENTENCES TC R 021 05
THE SENTENCES, PASS TO THE VERSICLES, O LORD,   R 021 08
OF OUR ENEMIES, MAY PASS OUR TIME IN REST AND   031 23
FOR SUCH AS PASS ON THE SEAS UPON THEIR LAWFUL   042 09
THE MINISTER MAY PASS AT ONCE TO O LORD, SAVE THY   R 061 19
BEGIN TO COME TO PASS, THEN LOOK UP, AND LIFT UP YOUR 093 12
THINGS COME TO PASS, KNOW YE THAT THE KINGDOM OF GOD   093 17
SHALL NOT PASS AWAY, TILL ALL BE FULFILLED   093 19
AND EARTH SHALL PASS AWAY   093 20
MY WORDS SHALL NOT PASS AWAY   093 21
AND IT CAME TO PASS IN THOSE DAYS, THAT THERE WENT   098 28
AND IT CAME TO PASS, AS THE ANGELS WERE GONE AWAY   106 07
WHICH IS COME TO PASS, WHICH THE LORD HATH MADE KNOWN 106 10
AND IT CAME TO PASS, THAT AFTER THREE DAYS THEY FOUND 110 27
AND IT CAME TO PASS IN THOSE DAYS, THAT JESUS CAME   112 18
AND IT CAME TO PASS, THAT AS HE WAS COME NIGH UNTC   123 26
THE MULTITUDE PASS BY, HE ASKED WHAT IT MEANT   123 28
AND IT CAME TO PASS, WHEN THE DEVIL WAS GONE OUT,   129 25
AND IT CAME TO PASS, AS HE SPAKE THESE THINGS,   130 17
THE HOUR MIGHT PASS FROM HIM   141 34
OF DEATH, WE MAY PASS TO OUR JOYFUL RESURRECTICN   161 17
AND IT CAME TO PASS, THAT, WHILE THEY COMMUNED   167 06
WHICH ARE COME TO PASS THERE IN THESE DAYS   167 14
AND IT CAME TO PASS, AS HE SAT AT MEAT WITH THEM, HE   168 05
AND IT CAME TO PASS, WHILE HE BLESSED THEM, HE WAS   178 25
WHEN IT IS COME TO PASS, YE MIGHT BELIEVE   182 06
BEFORE IT COME TO PASS, THAT, WHEN IT IS COME TC   182 06
AND IT CAME TO PASS, THAT THE BEGGAR DIED, AND WAS   190 09
THEY WHICH WOULD PASS FROM HENCE TO YOU CANNOT   190 20
NEITHER CAN THEY PASS TO US, THAT WOULD COME FROM   190 21
WE MAY SO PASS THROUGH THINGS TEMPCRAL,   194 07
IT CAME TO PASS, THAT, AS THE PEOPLE PRESSED UPON HIM 196 06
SUCH GOOD THINGS AS PASS MAN'S UNDERSTANDING   197 05
AND IT CAME TO PASS, AS JESUS WENT TO JERUSALEM,   209 31
AND IT CAME TO PASS, THAT, AS THEY WENT, THEY WERE   210 06
AND IT CAME TO PASS THE DAY AFTER, THAT JESUS WENT   212 27
IT CAME TO PASS, AS JESUS WENT INTO THE HOUSE OF ONE   213 28
THE GRASS HE SHALL PASS AWAY   239 20
AND IT CAME TO PASS, THAT A WHOLE YEAR THEY ASSEMBLED 241 12
WHICH CAME TO PASS IN THE DAYS OF CLAUDIUS CAESAR   241 18
AND IT CAME TO PASS, THAT ON THE EIGHTH DAY THEY CAME 243 17

PASS   CONTINUED

	PAGE	LN
WHICH CAME TO PASS IN THE DAYS OF CLAUDIUS CAESAR	246	27
AND IT CAME TO PASS ABOUT AN EIGHT DAYS AFTER THESE	248	23
AND IT CAME TO PASS, AS THEY DEPARTED FROM HIM,	248	33
AND IT CAME TO PASS, AS JESUS SAT AT MEAT IN THE	251	15
BUT THIS COMETH TO PASS, THAT THE WORD MIGHT BE	255	28
SHALL BE BROUGHT TO PASS THE SAYING THAT IS WRITTEN,	330	09
AND HE SHALL BRING IT TO PASS	385	03
THEY SHALL NOT PASS, *	468	12
HAND OF THE LORD BRINGETH MIGHTY THINGS TO PASS	488	32
HAND OF THE LORD BRINGETH MIGHTY THINGS TO PASS	488	35

PASSED

	PAGE	LN
THAT IS PASSED INTO THE HEAVENS, JESUS THE	005	07
AND THEY THAT PASSED BY REVILED HIM, WAGGING THEIR	137	05
A CYRENIAN, WHO PASSED BY, COMING OUT OF THE COUNTRY,	146	05
AND THEY THAT PASSED BY RAILED ON HIM, WAGGING THEIR	146	18
KNOW THAT WE HAVE PASSED FROM DEATH UNTO LIFE,	191	12
AND ALL PASSED THROUGH THE SEA	201	07
HE SAW HIM, HE PASSED BY ON THE OTHER SIDE	208	25
ON HIM, AND PASSED BY ON THE OTHER SIDE	208	27
THAT HE PASSED THROUGH THE MIDST OF SAMARIA AND	209	32
INTO A SHIP, AND PASSED OVER, AND CAME INTO HIS OWN	216	33
WENT OUT, AND PASSED ON THROUGH ONE STREET	245	24
AND AS JESUS PASSED FORTH FROM THENCE, HE SAW A MAN,	251	12
BUT IS PASSED FROM DEATH UNTO LIFE	322	03
FORMER THINGS ARE PASSED AWAY	567	21

PASSETH

	PAGE	LN
OF GOD, WHICH PASSETH ALL UNDERSTANDING, KEEP YOUR	084	18
OF GOD, WHICH PASSETH ALL UNDERSTANDING, SHALL KEEP	095	18
OF NAZARETH PASSETH BY	123	29
OF CHRIST, WHICH PASSETH KNOWLEDGE, THAT YE MIGHT BE	212	20
SO SOON PASSETH IT AWAY, AND WE ARE GONE	325	35
EVEN A WIND THAT PASSETH AWAY, AND COMETH NOT AGAIN	437	19
SO SOON PASSETH IT AWAY, AND WE ARE GONE	454	10
HIS TIME PASSETH AWAY LIKE A SHADOW	519	29
OF GOD, WHICH PASSETH ALL UNDERSTANDING, KEEP YOUR	535	13
OF GOD, WHICH PASSETH ALL UNDERSTANDING, KEEP YOUR	547	14
OF GOD, WHICH PASSETH ALL UNDERSTANDING, KEEP YOUR	559	17
OF GOD, WHICH PASSETH ALL UNDERSTANDING, KEEP YOUR	568	13
THY PEACE WHICH PASSETH UNDERSTANDING ABIDE ALL THE	598	03

PASSING

	PAGE	LN
SHADOW OF PETER PASSING BY MIGHT OVERSHADOW SOME OF	249	28

PASSION

	PAGE	LN
BY THY CROSS AND PASSION	055	11
HIS BLESSED PASSION AND PRECIOUS DEATH, HIS MIGHTY	081	02
OF HIS DEATH AND PASSION, MAY BE PARTAKERS OF HIS	081	13
AND ALL OTHER BENEFITS OF HIS PASSION	081	20
THE MERITS OF HIS MOST PRECIOUS DEATH AND PASSION	083	25
BY THE DEATH AND PASSION OF OUR SAVIOUR CHRIST,	086	07
REMEMBRANCE OF HIS MERITORIOUS CROSS AND PASSION	086	32
ALIVE AFTER HIS PASSION BY MANY INFALLIBLE PROOFS,	177	27
BY HIS CROSS AND PASSION WE MAY BE BROUGHT UNTO THE	235	21
BY THY CROSS AND PASSION, BY THY PRECIOUS DEATH AND	318	04
THEIR SINS, AND ALL OTHER BENEFITS OF HIS PASSION	565	34

PASSIONS

	PAGE	LN
WITHOUT BODY, PARTS, OR PASSIONS	603	04

PASSOVER

	PAGE	LN
JERUSALEM EVERY YEAR AT THE FEAST OF THE PASSOVER	110	19
AND THE PASSOVER, A FEAST OF THE JEWS, WAS NIGH	131	25
FEAST OF THE PASSOVER, AND OF UNLEAVENED BREAD	139	32
THEY KILLED THE PASSOVER, HIS DISCIPLES SAID UNTO	140	23
GO AND PREPARE THAT THOU MAYEST EAT THE PASSOVER	140	25
I SHALL EAT THE PASSOVER WITH MY DISCIPLES	140	30
AND THEY MADE READY THE PASSOVER	140	34
BREAD DREW NIGH, WHICH IS CALLED THE PASSOVER	148	13
WHEN THE PASSOVER MUST BE KILLED	148	22
PREPARE US THE PASSOVER, THAT WE MAY EAT	148	23
I SHALL EAT THE PASSOVER WITH MY DISCIPLES	148	30
AND THEY MADE READY THE PASSOVER	148	33
TO EAT THIS PASSOVER WITH YOU BEFORE I SUFFER	149	03
FEAST OF THE PASSOVER, WHEN JESUS KNEW THAT HIS HOUR	155	23
OF THE PASSOVER, AND ABOUT THE SIXTH HOUR	159	25
CHRIST OUR PASSOVER IS SACRIFICED FOR US	162	30
EVEN CHRIST OUR PASSOVER IS SACRIFICED FOR US	165	13
AND THE JEWS' PASSOVER WAS AT HAND, AND JESUS WENT UP	567	25

PAST

	PAGE	LN
FOR THE TIME PAST, AND GRACE TO KEEP THE LAW FOR THE	R 067	24
JESUS CHRIST'S SAKE, FORGIVE US ALL THAT IS PAST	075	28
REPENT YOU TRULY FOR YOUR SINS PAST	085	35
SPAKE IN TIME PAST UNTO THE FATHERS BY THE PROPHETS,	096	23
THE SABBATH WAS PAST, MARY MAGDALENE, AND MARY THE	165	18
TOLD YOU IN TIME PAST, THAT THEY WHICH DO SUCH THINGS	209	24
WHO BEING PAST FEELING HAVE GIVEN THEMSELVES OVER	218	08
WHEN THEY WERE PAST THE FIRST AND THE SECOND WARD,	245	21
WHEN THE VOICE WAS PAST, JESUS WAS FOUND ALONE	249	08
AND THE YEARS THAT ARE PAST	310	27
AND THE YEARS THAT ARE PAST	311	09
ERRORS OF HIS LIFE PAST, AND STEDFAST FAITH IN THY	316	13
WHEN IT IS PAST, *	325	21
AND THE YEARS THAT ARE PAST	433	26
WHEN IT IS PAST, *	453	26

PAST   CONTINUED

	PAGE	LN
5 YET DO I REMEMBER THE TIME PAST	518	32
THE DANGERS OF THE PAST NIGHT	587	23
AND BENEFITS OF THE PAST DAY	591	19

PASTIME

	PAGE	LN
MADE TO TAKE HIS PASTIME THEREIN	469	13

PASTOR

	PAGE	LN
TO BE A CHIEF PASTOR IN THE CHURCH	294	08

PASTORS

	PAGE	LN
THE BISHOPS AND PASTORS OF THY FLOCK, THAT THEY MAY	038	29
ORDERED AND GUIDED BY FAITHFUL AND TRUE PASTORS	234	03
AND SOME, PASTORS AND TEACHERS	237	20
ALL BISHOPS AND PASTORS DILIGENTLY TO PREACH THY HOLY	244	25
SPIRITUAL PASTORS AND MASTERS	288	29
AND SOME, PASTORS AND TEACHERS	538	07
DOCTORS, AND PASTORS	545	18
ALL BISHOPS, THE PASTORS OF THY CHURCH, THAT THEY MAY	549	10
SOME PASTORS AND DOCTORS, TO THE EDIFYING AND MAKING	557	27
SPIRITUAL PASTORS AND MASTERS	580	05

PASTURE

	PAGE	LN
PEOPLE OF HIS PASTURE, AND THE SHEEP OF HIS HAND	009	16
WE ARE HIS PEOPLE, AND THE SHEEP OF HIS PASTURE	015	09
AND SHALL GO IN AND OUT, AND FIND PASTURE	186	16
THE FLOCK OF MY PASTURE, ARE MEN, AND I AM YOUR GOD,	262	23
ME IN A GREEN PASTURE, *	338	19
ME IN A GREEN PASTURE, *	368	12
THY WRATH SO HOT AGAINST THE SHEEP OF THY PASTURE	430	05
AND SHEEP OF THY PASTURE, SHALL GIVE THEE THANKS FOR	440	32
PEOPLE OF HIS PASTURE, AND THE SHEEP OF HIS HAND	459	18
WE ARE HIS PEOPLE, AND THE SHEEP OF HIS PASTURE	463	10
AND SHALL GO IN AND OUT, AND FIND PASTURE	539	07

PATE

	PAGE	LN
AND HIS WICKEDNESS SHALL FALL ON HIS OWN PATE	350	26

PATEN

	PAGE	LN
IS TO TAKE THE PATEN INTO HIS HANDS	R 080	30

PATH

	PAGE	LN
SHALT SHOW ME THE PATH OF LIFE	333	09
SHALT SHOW ME THE PATH OF LIFE	358	12
ME TO GO IN THE PATH OF THY COMMANDMENTS	492	09
2 THOU ART ABOUT MY PATH, AND ABOUT MY BED	514	23
MY SPIRIT WAS IN HEAVINESS, THOU KNEWEST MY PATH	518	08
AND IN THY STRAIGHT PATH MAY NOT STUMBLE	595	31

PATHS

	PAGE	LN
FOR MAKING PATHS IN THE DEEP WATERS AND HIGHWAYS IN	038	17
THE LORD, MAKE HIS PATHS STRAIGHT	112	07
AND WE WILL WALK IN HIS PATHS	290	07
ME FORTH IN THE PATHS OF RIGHTEOUSNESS FOR HIS NAME'S	338	22
THROUGH THE PATHS OF THE SEAS	351	16
MY GOINGS IN THY PATHS, *	358	27
ME FORTH IN THE PATHS OF RIGHTEOUSNESS FOR HIS NAME'S	368	15
AND TEACH ME THY PATHS	369	24
9 ALL THE PATHS OF THE LORD ARE MERCY AND TRUTH,	370	04
THE SEA, AND THY PATHS IN THE GREAT WATERS, *	434	21
AND A LIGHT UNTO MY PATHS	497	08

PATIENCE

	PAGE	LN
GIVING THEM PATIENCE UNDER THEIR SUFFERINGS, AND A	019	09
GIVING THEM PATIENCE UNDER THEIR SUFFERINGS, AND A	033	07
WITH WISDOM, PATIENCE, AND COURAGE TO STRENGTHEN THE	044	02
AND GIVE HIM PATIENCE UNDER HIS AFFLICTION	045	17
ENDUE HIS SOUL WITH PATIENCE	046	04
MAY RUN WITH PATIENCE THE RACE THAT IS SET BEFORE US,	079	25
THAT BY PATIENCE AND COMFORT OF THY HOLY WORD,	092	10
THAT WE THROUGH PATIENCE AND COMFORT OF THE	092	16
NOW THE GOD OF PATIENCE AND CONSOLATION GRANT YOU TO	092	18
KEEP IT, AND BRING FORTH FRUIT WITH PATIENCE	122	10
OF GOD, IN MUCH PATIENCE, IN AFFLICTIONS, IN	126	10
EXAMPLE OF HIS PATIENCE, AND ALSO BE MADE PARTAKERS	134	10
HAVE PATIENCE WITH ME, AND I WILL PAY THEE ALL	221	20
HAVE PATIENCE WITH ME, AND I WILL PAY THEE	221	28
UNTO ALL PATIENCE AND LONG-SUFFERING WITH	224	07
YE HAVE NEED OF PATIENCE, THAT, AFTER YE HAVE DONE	228	15
BUT LET PATIENCE HAVE HER PERFECT WORK, THAT YE MAY	239	10
THAT THE TRYING OF YOUR FAITH WORKETH PATIENCE	239	10
LET US RUN WITH PATIENCE THE RACE THAT IS SET BEFORE	258	23
AND PATIENCE, IN WISDOM AND TRUE GODLINESS, THAT	303	25
SUPPORT HIM IN PATIENCE AND SUBMISSION TO THY WILL	315	26
MAYEST GIVE HIM PATIENCE IN TIME OF ADVERSITY,	458	12
WITH ALL PATIENCE AND DOCTRINE	533	09
GRANT US PATIENCE UNDER OUR AFFLICTIONS	588	29
THEE FOR THY PATIENCE WITH US, NOTWITHSTANDING OUR	591	14
PATIENCE, GODLINESS	598	24

PATIENT

	PAGE	LN
PATIENT IN TRIBULATION	111	26
12 GOD IS A RIGHTEOUS JUDGE, STRONG, AND PATIENT	350	15
THE PATIENT ABIDING OF THE MEEK SHALL NOT PERISH FOR	352	28

PATIENT   CONTINUED

BUT PATIENT, NOT A BRAWLER, NOT COVETOUS   549 23

PATIENTLY

FOR YOUR FAULTS, YE SHALL TAKE IT PATIENTLY   172 08
YE TAKE IT PATIENTLY, THIS IS ACCEPTABLE WITH   172 09
AND PATIENTLY SUFFER FOR THE TRUTH'S SAKE   242 13
HIS SICKNESS PATIENTLY, AND RECOVER HIS BODILY   321 22
OUR SOUL HATH PATIENTLY TARRIED FOR THE LORD   379 28
AND ABIDE PATIENTLY UPON HIM   385 06
AND THEY THAT PATIENTLY ABIDE THE LORD, THOSE SHALL   385 12
I WAITED PATIENTLY FOR THE LORD, *   390 09
FOR ME, I WILL PATIENTLY ABIDE ALWAY, *   426 02

PATRI

SHALL BE SUNG OR SAID THE GLORIA PATRI   R 009 26
MAY BE SUNG OR SAID THE GLORIA PATRI   R 025 18
OR SAID THE GLORIA PATRI, OR ELSE THE GLORIA IN   R 025 20
THE GLORIA PATRI MAY BE OMITTED EXCEPT AT THE END OF   R 324 17
END OF EACH PSALM SHALL BE SAID THE GLORIA PATRI   R 338 15

PATTERN

IN ALL THINGS A PATTERN TO THE FLOCK COMMITTED TC THY   571 28

PATTERNS

THAT THE PATTERNS OF THINGS IN THE HEAVENS SHOULC BE   147 27
EXAMPLES AND PATTERNS FOR THE PEOPLE TO FCLLOW   541 23
EXAMPLES AND PATTERNS TO THE FLOCK OF CHRIST   543 02

PAUL

ALSO WHAT SAINT PAUL SAITH   076 17
CONSIDER HOW SAINT PAUL EXHORTETH ALL PERSONS   085 27
FOR THIS CAUSE I PAUL, THE PRISONER OF JESUS CHRIST   108 00
APOSTLE SAINT PAUL, HAST CAUSED THE LIGHT CF THE   229 18
WERE SPOKEN BY PAUL, CONTRADICTING AND BLASPHEMING   260 29
THEN PAUL AND BARNABAS WAXED BOLD, AND SAID, IT WAS   260 30
COMMENDED OF SAINT PAUL TO BE HCNOURABLE AMONG ALL   300 16
PAUL TO THE CORINTHIANS   R 328 19
HOLY APOSTLE SAINT PAUL, NOT TO BE SORRY, AS MEN   335 04
FROM MILETUS PAUL SENT TO EPHESUS, AND CALLED THE   550 04
AS SAINT PAUL SAITH   608 05

PAUSE

READS MAKE A SHORT PALSE, THAT EVERY ONE MAY SECRETLY   R 589 34

PAVEMENT

IS CALLED THE PAVEMENT, BUT IN THE HEBREW, GABBATHA   159 24

PAVILION

HIS PAVILION ROUND ABOUT HIM WITH DARK WATER, ANC   360 19

PAY

FOR FOR THIS CAUSE PAY YE TRIBUTE ALSO   114 23
AS HE HAD NOT TO PAY, HIS LORD COMMANDED HIM TO BE   221 17
WITH ME, AND I WILL PAY THEE ALL   221 20
THE THROAT, SAYING, PAY ME THAT THOU OWEST   221 26
WITH ME, AND I WILL PAY THEE ALL   221 28
TILL HE SHOULD PAY THE DEBT   221 30
TILL HE SHOULD PAY ALL THAT WAS DUE UNTO HIM   222 04
I WILL PAY MY VOWS NOW IN THE PRESENCE OF ALL HIS   305 31
PAY THEM THAT THEY HAVE DESERVED   373 15
AND PAY THY VOWS UNTO THE MOST HIGHEST   402 18
O GOD, WILL I PAY MY VOWS   409 06
AND WILL PAY THEE MY VOWS, *   418 08
13 I WILL PAY MY VOWS NOW IN THE PRESENCE OF ALL HIS   487 13
16 I WILL PAY MY VOWS UNTO THE LORD, IN THE SIGHT OF   487 21
OF THE GOSPEL, TO PAY RESPECTFUL OBEDIENCE TO THE   610 41

PAYETH

AND PAYETH NOT AGAIN   386 04

PAYMENT

THAT HE HAD, AND PAYMENT TO BE MADE   221 18

PEACE

BE UNTO YOU, AND PEACE, FROM GCD OUR FATHER, ANC FROM   004 02
PRESERVATION OF PEACE AND UNITY IN THE CHURCH   V 35
AND TO GUIDE OUR FEET INTO THE WAY OF PEACE   014 33
ART THE AUTHOR OF PEACE AND LOVER OF CONCORD, IN   017 05
WE MAY DWELL SECURE IN THY PEACE   018 10
IN THE BOND OF PEACE, AND IN RIGHTEOUSNESS OF LIFE   019 03
AND ON EARTH PEACE, GOOD WILL TOWARDS MEN   025 22
SERVANT DEPART IN PEACE, *   028 09
GIVE PEACE IN OUR TIME, O LORD   031 10
THY SERVANTS THAT PEACE WHICH THE WORLD CANNOT GIVE   031 20
IN THE BOND OF PEACE, AND IN RIGHTEOUSNESS OF LIFE   032 34
THAT PEACE AND HAPPINESS, TRUTH AND   035 16
MAY BE JUSTICE AND PEACE AT HOME, AND THAT, THRCUGH   036 19
PLEASED TO FILL IT WITH ALL TRUTH, IN ALL PEACE   037 17
OUR ONLY SAVIOUR, THE PRINCE OF PEACE   037 26
BOND OF TRUTH AND PEACE, OF FAITH AND CHARITY,   037 33
SON TO PREACH PEACE TO THEM THAT ARE FAR OFF AND TO   038 07
AND IN THE TIME OF PEACE KEEP THEM SAFE FROM ALL   041 28

PEACE   CONTINUED

OF OUR LAND MAY IN PEACE AND QUIETNESS SERVE THEE OUR   042 11
AND TO MAKE NO PEACE WITH OPPRESSION   044 11
AMONG THEM THAT PEACE WHICH IS THE FRUIT OF   044 29
UP THY COUNTENANCE UPON HIM, AND GIVE HIM PEACE   046 06
THINE APOSTLES, PEACE I LEAVE WITH YOU, MY PEACE I   049 06
LEAVE WITH YOU, MY PEACE I GIVE UNTO YOU   049 06
GRANT TO IT THAT PEACE AND UNITY WHICH IS ACCORDING   049 08
ALL NATIONS UNITY, PEACE, AND CONCORD   056 09
GRANT US THY PEACE   057 22
AND GIVE US PEACE, BOTH NOW AND EVERMORE   063 17
AND ON EARTH PEACE, GOOD WILL TOWARDS MEN   084 02
THE PEACE OF GOD, WHICH PASSETH ALL UNDERSTANDING,   084 18
WITH ALL JOY AND PEACE IN BELIEVING, THAT YE MAY   093 02
AND THE PEACE OF GOD, WHICH PASSETH ALL   095 17
AND ON EARTH PEACE, GOOD WILL TOWARD MEN   099 21
AND GRANT US THY PEACE ALL THE DAYS OF OUR LIFE   111 12
AND LET THE PEACE OF GOD RULE IN YOUR HEARTS,   116 09
THE VERY BOND OF PEACE AND OF ALL VIRTUES, WITHOUT   122 17
THAT WE SHOULD HOLD HIS PEACE   123 32
ARMED KEEPETH HIS PALACE, HIS GOODS ARE IN PEACE   130 06
FIND IT NONE OTHER THAN THE WAY OF LIFE AND PEACE   138 08
BUT HE HELD HIS PEACE, AND ANSWERED NOTHING   143 12
PREACHING PEACE BY JESUS CHRIST   166 16
SAITH UNTO THEM, PEACE BE UNTO YOU   169 29
SAITH UNTO THEM, PEACE BE UNTO YOU   171 17
TO THEM AGAIN, PEACE BE UNTO YOU   171 20
THAT IN ME YE MIGHT HAVE PEACE   177 08
PEACE I LEAVE WITH YOU, MY PEACE I GIVE UNTO YOU   181 33
LEAVE WITH YOU, MY PEACE I GIVE UNTO YOU   181 34
PREACHING PEACE BY JESUS CHRIST   184 03
LET HIM SEEK PEACE, AND ENSUE IT   195 27
THE THINGS WHICH BELONG UNTO THY PEACE   204 09
IS LOVE, JOY, PEACE, LONG-SUFFERING, GENTLENESS,   209 26
TO THIS RULE, PEACE BE ON THEM, AND MERCY, AND UPCN   211 03
KEEP THE UNITY OF THE SPIRIT IN THE BOND OF PEACE   213 22
AND THEY HELD THEIR PEACE   214 03
PEOPLE PARDON AND PEACE, THAT THEY MAY BE CLEANSED   218 33
SHOD WITH THE PREPARATION OF THE GOSPEL OF PEACE   219 16
THE GOSPEL OF PEACE, AND BRING GLAD TIDINGS OF GOOD   227 10
AND SAID, PEACE BE UNTO YOU   229 02
SERVANT DEPART IN PEACE, ACCORDING TO THY WCRD   233 06
TO GUIDE OUR FEET INTO THE WAY OF PEACE   244 16
FIRST SAY, PEACE BE TO THIS HOUSE   254 19
BE THERE, YOUR PEACE SHALL REST UPON IT   254 20
AND IF THE SON OF PEACE BE THERE, YOUR PEACE SHALL   254 20
THEM A COVENANT OF PEACE, AND WILL CAUSE THE EVIL   262 04
THESE LIBERTIES IN RIGHTEOUSNESS AND PEACE   263 20
HE MAKETH PEACE IN THY BORDERS, *   265 04
IN PARADISE AND ON EARTH, THY LIGHT AND THY PEACE   268 16
OR ELSE HEREAFTER FOR EVER HOLD HIS PEACE   300 22
MAY ABIDE IN THY PEACE, AND CONTINUE IN THY FAVOUR,   302 20
PERFECT LOVE AND PEACE TOGETHER, AND LIVE ACCORDING   303 10
HOME MAY BE A HAVEN OF BLESSING AND OF PEACE   303 26
SHALL SAY, PEACE BE TO THIS HOUSE, AND TO ALL THAT   308 07
HIM IN PERPETUAL PEACE AND SAFETY   309 08
AND GIVE THEE PEACE, BOTH NOW AND EVERMORE   314 30
GRANT HIM THY PEACE   318 28
BE THIS DAY IN PEACE, AND THY DWELLING-PLACE IN THE   319 24
OF EVERLASTING PEACE, AND INTO THE GLORIOUS COMPANY   320 02
HOLD NOT THY PEACE AT MY TEARS   325 07
AND GIVE YOU PEACE, BOTH NOW AND EVERMORE   332 14
THE GOD OF PEACE, WHO BROUGHT AGAIN FROM THE DEAC OUR   335 16
AND GIVE HIM PEACE, BOTH NOW AND EVERMORE   341 18
LAY ME DOWN IN PEACE, AND TAKE MY REST   347 28
LORD SHALL GIVE HIS PEOPLE THE BLESSING OF PEACE   374 20
SEEK PEACE, AND ENSUE IT   380 29
THEIR COMMUNING IS NOT FOR PEACE   383 02
AND SHALL BE REFRESHED IN THE MULTITUDE OF PEACE   385 17
SHALL BRING A MAN PEACE AT THE LAST   387 09
HOLD NOT THY PEACE AT MY TEARS   390 03
MY SOUL IN PEACE FROM THE BATTLE THAT WAS AGAINST ME   407 27
UPON SUCH AS BE AT PEACE WITH HIM, *   407 33
ALSO SHALL BRING PEACE, *   427 02
AND ABUNDANCE OF PEACE, SO LONG AS THE MOON ENDURETH   427 11
FOR HE SHALL SPEAK PEACE UNTO HIS PEOPLE, AND TO HIS   446 23
RIGHTEOUSNESS AND PEACE HAVE KISSED EACH OTHER   446 28
165 GREAT IS THE PEACE THAT THEY HAVE WHO LOVE THY   501 11
THAT ARE ENEMIES UNTO PEACE   502 18
6 I LABOUR FOR PEACE   502 19
6 O PRAY FOR THE PEACE OF JERUSALEM   503 18
7 PEACE BE WITHIN THY WALLS, *   503 20
BUT PEACE SHALL BE UPON ISRAEL   505 04
AND PEACE UPON ISRAEL   506 19
14 HE MAKETH PEACE IN THY BORDERS, *   523 23
THE PEACE OF GOD, WHICH PASSETH ALL UNDERSTANDING,   535 13
IN YOU, QUIETNESS, PEACE, AND LOVE, AMONG ALL   543 07
FAR OUR FOES, GIVE PEACE AT HOME   544 08
AND THINE ABIDING PEACE BESTOW   545 07
THE PEACE OF GOD, WHICH PASSETH ALL UNDERSTANDING,   547 14
SAITH UNTO THEM, PEACE BE UNTO YOU   551 30
TO THEM AGAIN, PEACE BE UNTO YOU   551 33
AND PEACE AMONG ALL MEN   555 15
FAR OUR FOES, GIVE PEACE AT HOME   556 16
AND THINE ABIDING PEACE BESTOW   557 13
THE PEACE OF GOD, WHICH PASSETH ALL UNDERSTANDING,   559 17
THEE TO GRANT PEACE TO THE WHOLE WORLD, AND TO THY   560 12
THE PEACE OF GOD, WHICH PASSETH ALL UNDERSTANDING,   568 13
THE GOD OF PEACE, WHO BROUGHT AGAIN FROM THE DEAD CUR   573 03
AND IN THE BOND OF PEACE, THAT THEY MAY BE AN HOLY   574 07
WAYS OF TRUTH AND PEACE, AND AT LAST BE NUMBERED WITH   574 18
GO TO OUR REST IN PEACE, CHARITY, AND GOOD-WILL,   590 17
AND GIVE US PEACE, THIS NIGHT AND EVERMORE   593 20
AND GUIDE OUR FEET INTO THE WAY OF PEACE   594 15
A HOLY REST, AND PEACE AT THE LAST   595 03

PEACE   CONTINUED

O GOD OF PEACE, WHO HAST TAUGHT US THAT IN RETURNING   595 19
HIS HEART MAY THY PEACE WHICH PASSETH UNDERSTANDING   598 02
AND GIVE THEM HEALTH AND PEACE   598 16

PEACEABLE

A QUIET AND PEACEABLE LIFE IN ALL GODLINESS AND   052 24
LEAD QUIET AND PEACEABLE LIVES, IN ALL GODLINESS AND   VI 21
QUIET AND PEACEABLE   588 31

PEACEABLY

IN YOU, LIVE PEACEABLY WITH ALL MEN   113 03
MAY BE SO PEACEABLY ORDERED BY THY GOVERNANCE,   195 16
MAY BE SO PEACEABLY ORDERED BY THY GOVERNANCE, THAT   574 16

PEACEFULLY

FALL ASLEEP PEACEFULLY IN THEE, AND AWAKE UP AFTER   336 13

PEACEMAKERS

BLESSED ARE THE PEACEMAKERS   257 27

PECULIAR

UNTO HIMSELF A PECULIAR PEOPLE, ZEALOUS OF GOOD   098 24

PELAGIANS

(AS THE PELAGIANS DO VAINLY TALK   604 29

PELICAN

AM BECOME LIKE A PELICAN IN THE WILDERNESS, *   464 21

PEN

MY TONGUE IS THE PEN CF A READY WRITER   396 17

PENANCE

PENANCE, ORDERS, MATRIMONY, AND EXTREME   607 38
RECONCILED BY PENANCE, AND RECEIVED INTO THE CHURCH   609 29

PENCE

THAN THREE HUNDRED PENCE, AND HAVE BEEN GIVEN TO THE   140 09
HE TOOK OUT TWO PENCE, AND GAVE THEM TO THE HOST, AND   208 33
WHICH OWED HIM AN HUNDRED PENCE   221 24

PENITENT

LOWLY, PENITENT, AND OBEDIENT HEART   005 34
RESTORE THOU THOSE WHO ARE PENITENT   006 26
BEING PENITENT, THE ABSOLUTION AND REMISSION   007 10
LOWLY, PENITENT, AND OBEDIENT HEART   023 09
RESTORE THOU THOSE WHO ARE PENITENT   023 33
BEING PENITENT, THE ABSOLUTION AND REMISSION   024 12
NEAR WITH PENITENT AND FAITHFUL HEARTS, THEY MAY   043 23
TO ADMIT THE PENITENT PERSON TO THE HOLY COMMUNICN,   R 085 24
IF WITH A TRUE PENITENT HEART AND LIVELY FAITH WE   085 31
FORGIVE THE SINS OF ALL THOSE WHO ARE PENITENT   124 13
HUMBLE AND PENITENT SINNERS   590 06

PENITENTIAL

ONE OF THE PENITENTIAL PSALMS   R 308 09

PENNY

LABOURERS FOR A PENNY A DAY, HE SENT THEM INTO HIS   119 18
THEY RECEIVED EVERY MAN A PENNY   119 32
AND THEY LIKEWISE RECEIVED EVERY MAN A PENNY   120 03
DIDST NOT THOU AGREE WITH ME FOR A PENNY   120 08
AND THEY BROUGHT UNTO HIM A PENNY   223 07

PENNYWORTH

TWO HUNDRED PENNYWORTH OF BREAD IS NOT SUFFICIENT FOR   131 30
TWO HUNDRED PENNYWORTH OF BREAD IS NOT SUFFICIENT FOR   225 26

PENTECOST

THE DAY OF PENTECOST WAS FULLY COME, THEY WERE ALL   180 17

PENURY

THOSE WHOSE PENURY TEMPTETH THEM TO SIN   599 12

PEOPLE

OF GREAT JOY, WHICH SHALL BE TO ALL PEOPLE   004 09
OF THE PEOPLE, 'ACCORDING TO THE VARIOUS EXIGENCY OF   V 09
THE PEOPLE STILL KNEELING   R 007 03
PRONOUNCE TO HIS PEOPLE, BEING PENITENT, THE   007 10
THE PEOPLE   R 007 20
AND WE ARE THE PEOPLE OF HIS PASTURE, AND THE SHEEP   009 15
O LORD, SAVE THY PEOPLE, AND BLESS THINE HERITAGE   011 04
FOR HE HATH VISITED AND REDEEMED HIS PEOPLE   014 09
UNTO HIS PEOPLE *   014 27
WE ARE HIS PEOPLE, AND THE SHEEP OF HIS PASTURE   015 08
MINISTER AND THE PEOPLE, STANDING   R 015 15
THE PEOPLE DEVOUTLY KNEELING   R 016 23

PEOPLE   CONTINUED

TO SERVE THIS PEOPLE IN THY FEAR   018 14
THEY SHALL BE HIS PEOPLE, AND GOD HIMSELF SHALL BE   021 30
THE PEOPLE STILL KNEELING   R 024 07
PRONOUNCE TO HIS PEOPLE, BEING PENITENT, THE   024 12
THE PEOPLE STILL   R 024 27
BEFORE THE FACE OF ALL PEOPLE   028 12
THE GLORY OF THY PEOPLE ISRAEL   028 14
MINISTER AND THE PEOPLE, STANDING   R 029 20
THE PEOPLE DEVOUTLY KNEELING   R 030 28
MAKE THY CHOSEN PEOPLE JOYFUL   031 07
O LORD, SAVE THY PEOPLE   031 08
WE AND ALL THE PEOPLE, DULY CONSIDERING WHOSE   032 10
AS FOR THE PEOPLE OF THESE UNITED STATES IN   035 09
AND WELFARE OF THY PEOPLE   035 14
GLORY OF THY NAME AND THE WELFARE OF THE PEOPLE   035 28
PROVE OURSELVES A PEOPLE MINDFUL OF THY FAVOUR AND   036 11
INTO ONE UNITED PEOPLE THE MULTITUDES BROUGHT HITHER   036 16
THE AFFLICTIONS OF THY PEOPLE   040 32
GOOD CHRISTIAN PEOPLE, I BID YOUR PRAYERS FCR   047 06
THE BLESSED COMPANY OF ALL FAITHFUL PEOPLE   047 08
OF THE PEOPLE, REMEMBERING THE ACCOUNT THEY SHALL BE   047 19
PRAY FOR ALL THE PEOPLE OF THESE UNITED STATES,   048 02
PROVIDENCE BESTOWED UPON THIS NATION AND PEOPLE   050 25
THE OUTRAGE OF A VIOLENT AND UNRULY PEOPLE   052 19
IN THE PRESENCE OF ALL THY PEOPLE   053 03
THY NAME, IN THE PRESENCE OF ALL THY PEOPLE   053 14
SPARE THY PEOPLE, WHOM THOU HAST REDEEMED WITH   054 15
MAY PLEASE THEE TO BLESS AND KEEP ALL THY PEOPLE   056 06
GIVE TO ALL THY PEOPLE INCREASE OF GRACE TO HEAR   056 14
AND THE PEOPLE WITH HIM, SAY THE LORD'S   R 058 02
MINISTER AND PEOPLE   R 058 25
MINISTER AND PEOPLE   R 059 02
MERCIFULLY FORGIVE THE SINS OF THY PEOPLE   059 12
AND THAT THE PEOPLE 'MAY LEAD QUIET AND PEACEABLE   VI 21
MINISTER AND THE PEOPLE KNEELING, THEN SHALL BE SAID R 060 07
SPARE THY PEOPLE, WHOM THOU HAST REDEEMED   062 20
THEN SHALL THE PEOPLE SAY THIS THAT FOLLOWETH,   R 062 27
FAVOURABLE TO THY PEOPLE, WHO TURN TO THEE IN   062 29
SPARE THY PEOPLE, GOOD LORD, SPARE THEM, AND LET NCT   063 02
THE PEOPLE KNEELING   R 067 07
TURNING TO THE PEOPLE, REHEARSE DISTINCTLY THE TEN   R 067 22
AND THE PEOPLE, STILL KNEELING, SHALL, AFTER EVERY   R 067 23
ALL THE PEOPLE STANDING, THE MINISTER   R 070 22
DECLARED UNTO THE PEOPLE WHAT HOLY DAYS, OR FASTING   071 25
OFFERINGS OF THE PEOPLE ARE TO BE RECEIVED   R 073 26
OFFERINGS OF THE PEOPLE, IN A DECENT BASIN TO BE   R 073 29
AND TO ALL THY PEOPLE GIVE THY HEAVENLY GRACE   074 25
TURNING TO THE PEOPLE, SAY,   R 075 33
PRAISING THEE, AND SAYING, PRIEST AND PEOPLE   R 077 07
PRAISING THEE, AND SAYING, PRIEST AND PEOPLE   R 079 31
BREAD BEFORE THE PEOPLE, AND TAKE THE CUP INTO HIS   R 080 04
TO THE PEOPLE ALSO IN ORDER, INTO THEIR HANDS,   R 082 27
IS THE BLESSED COMPANY OF ALL FAITHFUL PEOPLE   083 23
THE PEOPLE KNEELING, THE PRIEST (THE BISHOP   R 084 16
HE SHALL SEE THE PEOPLE NEGLIGENT TO COME TO THE HOLY R 088 10
YE GENTILES, WITH HIS PEOPLE   092 28
AND LAUD HIM, ALL YE PEOPLE   092 30
AN ACCEPTABLE PEOPLE IN THY SIGHT, WHO LIVEST AND   093 30
A PECULIAR PEOPLE, ZEALOUS OF GOOD WORKS   098 24
OF GREAT JOY, WHICH SHALL BE TO ALL PEOPLE   099 16
HE SHALL SAVE HIS PEOPLE FROM THEIR SINS   105 07
SCRIBES OF THE PEOPLE TOGETHER, HE DEMANDED OF THEM   109 05
SHALL RULE MY PEOPLE ISRAEL   109 10
PRAYERS OF THY PEOPLE WHO CALL UPON THEE   109 30
OF THY PEOPLE, AND GRANT US THY PEACE ALL THE DAYS OF 111 12
THEE FAVOURABLY TO HEAR THE PRAYERS OF THY PEOPLE   118 29
WHEN MUCH PEOPLE WERE GATHERED TOGETHER, AND WERE   121 18
AND ALL THE PEOPLE, WHEN THEY SAW IT, GAVE PRAISE   124 05
GATHER THE PEOPLE, SANCTIFY THE CONGREGATION,   124 30
SPARE THY PEOPLE, O LORD, AND GIVE NOT THINE   125 04
SAY AMONG THE PEOPLE, WHERE IS THEIR GOD   125 06
AND THE PEOPLE WONDERED   129 26
MERCIFULLY TO LOOK UPON THY PEOPLE   132 19
AND ELDERS OF THE PEOPLE TOOK COUNSEL AGAINST JESUS   134 31
RELEASE UNTO THE PEOPLE A PRISONER, WHOM THEY WOULD   135 26
ANSWERED ALL THE PEOPLE, AND SAID, HIS BLCOD BE CN   136 12
AND OF THE PEOPLE THERE WAS NONE WITH ME   138 17
TREAD DOWN THE PEOPLE IN MINE ANGER, AND MAKE THEM   138 25
THEY ARE MY PEOPLE, CHILDREN THAT WILL NOT LIE   138 33
AND HIS PEOPLE, SAYING, WHERE IS HE THAT   139 08
THOU LEAD THY PEOPLE, TO MAKE THYSELF A GLORIOUS   139 17
THE PEOPLE OF THY HOLINESS HAVE POSSESSED IT BUT A   139 27
FEAST DAY, LEST THERE BE AN UPROAR OF THE PEOPLE   140 02
PRIESTS MOVED THE PEOPLE, THAT HE SHOULD RATHER   145 21
TO CONTENT THE PEOPLE, RELEASED BARABBAS UNTO THEM,   145 28
TO ALL THE PEOPLE ACCORDING TO THE LAW, HE TOOK THE   147 19
BOOK AND ALL THE PEOPLE, SAYING, THIS IS THE BLCOD OF 147 22
FOR THEY FEARD THE PEOPLE   148 14
THE ELDERS OF THE PEOPLE AND THE CHIEF PRIESTS AND   151 28
AND TO THE PEOPLE, I FIND NO FAULT IN THIS MAN   153 03
STIRRETH UP THE PEOPLE, TEACHING THROUGHOUT ALL   153 05
RULERS AND THE PEOPLE, SAID UNTO THEM, YE HAVE   153 22
AS ONE THAT PERVERTETH THE PEOPLE   153 23
GREAT COMPANY OF PEOPLE, AND OF WOMEN, WHICH ALSO   154 12
AND THE PEOPLE STOOD BEHOLDING   154 27
AND ALL THE PEOPLE THAT CAME TOGETHER TO THAT SIGHT,   155 16
AND SAY UNTO THE PEOPLE, HE IS RISEN FROM THE DEAD   162 21
NOT TO ALL THE PEOPLE, BUT UNTO WITNESSES CHOSEN   166 26
PREACH UNTO THE PEOPLE, AND TO TESTIFY THAT IT IS HE   166 28
IN DEED AND WORD BEFORE GOD AND ALL THE PEOPLE   167 18
WHO ARE HIS WITNESSES UNTO THE PEOPLE   169 05
GRANT UNTO THY WITNESSES, THAT THEY MAY LOVE THE THING 174 20
OF THY FAITHFUL PEOPLE, BY SENDING TO THEM THE LIGHT   180 09
NOT TO ALL THE PEOPLE, BUT UNTO WITNESSES CHOSEN   184 13

PEOPLE   CONTINUED

PREACH UNTO THE PEOPLE, AND TO TESTIFY THAT IT IS HE   184 16
AS THE PEOPLE PRESSED UPON HIM TO HEAR THE WORD   196 06
AND TAUGHT THE PEOPLE OUT OF THE SHIP   196 12
HE COMMANDED THE PEOPLE TO SIT DOWN ON THE GROUND   199 17
AND THEY DID SET THEM BEFORE THE PEOPLE   199 20
IS WRITTEN, THE PEOPLE SAT DOWN TO EAT AND DRINK,   201 16
THAT THY FAITHFUL PEOPLE DO UNTO THEE TRUE AND   207 13
OF HIS DISCIPLES WENT WITH HIM, AND MUCH PEOPLE   212 29
AND MUCH PEOPLE OF THE CITY WAS WITH HER   212 32
THAT GOD HATH VISITED HIS PEOPLE   213 09
GRANT THY PEOPLE GRACE TO WITHSTAND THE   214 23
TO THY FAITHFUL PEOPLE PARDON AND PEACE, THAT THEY   218 33
ABSOLVE THY PEOPLE FROM THEIR OFFENCES   223 15
MINSTRELS AND THE PEOPLE MAKING A NOISE, HE SAID UNTO   224 25
BUT WHEN THE PEOPLE WERE PUT FORTH, HE WENT IN, AND   224 27
THE WILLS OF THY FAITHFUL PEOPLE   225 05
THEM THAT ARE NO PEOPLE, AND BY A FOOLISH NATION I   227 18
MY HANDS UNTO A DISOBEDIENT AND GAINSAYING PEOPLE   227 22
THOU HAST PREPARED BEFORE THE FACE OF ALL PEOPLE   233 08
THE GLORY OF THY PEOPLE ISRAEL   233 09
AND MUCH PEOPLE WAS ADDED UNTO THE LORD   241 09
WITH THE CHURCH, AND TAUGHT MUCH PEOPLE   241 14
COMFORT YE MY PEOPLE, SAITH YOUR GOD   242 16
SURELY THE PEOPLE IS GRASS   242 31
AND REDEEMED HIS PEOPLE, AND HATH RAISED UP AN HORN   243 33
UNTO HIS PEOPLE BY THE REMISSION OF THEIR SINS,   244 12
AND THE PEOPLE OBEDIENTLY TO FOLLOW THE SAME,   244 26
AFTER EASTER TO BRING HIM FORTH TO THE PEOPLE   245 07
OF THE PEOPLE OF THE JEWS   245 28
MANY SIGNS AND WONDERS WROUGHT AMONG THE PEOPLE   249 22
BUT THE PEOPLE MAGNIFIED THEM   249 24
PRAYERS OF THY PEOPLE, AND GRANT THAT WHOSOEVER SHALL   259 21
OF ISRAEL, ARE MY PEOPLE, SAITH THE LORD GOD   262 22
WE AND ALL THE PEOPLE OF THIS LAND MAY HAVE GRACE TO   263 19
ADMONISH THE PEOPLE, THAT THEY DEFER NOT THE BAPTISM   R 273 03
AND THE PEOPLE WITH THE CHILDREN, MUST BE READY AT   R 273 14
AS FOLLOWETH, THE PEOPLE ALL STANDING, HATH THIS   R 273 25
MINISTER AND PEOPLE   R 276 16
THE MINISTER AND PEOPLE TOGETHER, ALL KNEELING, THE   R 283 03
THE PEOPLE BEING SEATED, THE MINISTER SHALL   R 283 13
WHICH FOLLOW, THE PEOPLE READING OR REPEATING THE   R 283 14
THE APOSTLES' CREED BY THE MINISTER AND PEOPLE   R 284 12
TURNING TO THE PEOPLE, SHALL ASK THE QUESTION   R 284 25
THE PEOPLE RESPONDING   R 284 26
AND ALL THE PEOPLE OF GOD   285 03
MINISTER AND PEOPLE   R 285 10
TURNING TO THE PEOPLE, SHALL SAY,   R 285 11
BY GOD TO THE PEOPLE OF ISRAEL   285 17
THE MINISTER AND PEOPLE TOGETHER, ALL KNEELING   R 285 23
GRANT UNTO THY PEOPLE, THAT THEY MAY LOVE THE THING   R 285 27
COMMANDMENT THE PEOPLE SHALL SAY THE RESPONSE   R 285 34
THE PEOPLE MAY REPEAT THE COMMANDMENTS,   R 286 02
AFTER THIS, THE PEOPLE BEING SEATED, THE MINISTER   R 287 31
WHICH FOLLOW, THE PEOPLE READING OR REPEATING THE   R 287 32
THE MINISTER AND PEOPLE TOGETHER, ALL KNEELING,   R 289 21
THE MINISTER AND PEOPLE TOGETHER   R 290 04
AFTER WHICH, THE PEOPLE BEING SEATED, THE MINISTER   R 290 25
WHICH FOLLOW, THE PEOPLE RESPONDING   R 290 27
AND ALL BAPTIZED PEOPLE ARE THE MEMBERS   290 33
IN ALL COUNTRIES, AND FOR ALL PEOPLE   291 12
SHALL ASK THE PEOPLE THE FOLLOWING QUESTIONS   R 294 02
THE MINISTRY, THE PEOPLE RESPONDING   R 294 03
MINISTER TO THE PEOPLE COMMITTED TO HIS CARE   294 13
HOLY TABLE, THE PEOPLE ALL STANDING UNTIL THE LORD'S   R 296 06
THE PEOPLE KNEELING AND REPEATING IT WITH   R 298 03
MINISTER AND THE PEOPLE, STILL STANDING, SAY THE   R 302 26
OF ALL HIS PEOPLE, IN THE COURTS OF THE LORD'S HOUSE   305 31
AND THY BLESSING IS UPON THY PEOPLE   309 25
AND DEFEND MY CAUSE AGAINST THE UNGODLY PEOPLE   310 06
TO ADVISE THE PEOPLE, WHILST THEY ARE IN HEALTH, TO   R 320 21
BEAREST UNTO THY PEOPLE, AND GRANT THAT, INCREASING   332 04
THE MINISTER AND PEOPLE, BLESSED ARE THE   R 340 09
AND WHY DO THE PEOPLE IMAGINE A VAIN THING   345 26
THOUSANDS OF THE PEOPLE, *   347 02
AND THY BLESSING IS UPON THY PEOPLE   347 08
AND MINISTER TRUE JUDGMENT UNTO THE PEOPLE   352 05
SHOW THE PEOPLE OF HIS DOINGS   352 12
AND ALL THE PEOPLE THAT FORGET GOD   352 27
EATING UP MY PEOPLE AS IT WERE BREAD, AND CALL NOT   356 23
CAPTIVITY OF MY PEOPLE, THEN SHALL JACOB REJOICE,   356 31
SHALT SAVE THE PEOPLE THAT ARE IN ADVERSITY, *   361 22
STRIVINGS OF THE PEOPLE, *   362 26
A PEOPLE WHOM I HAVE NOT KNOWN SHALL SERVE ME   362 27
AND SUBDUETH THE PEOPLE UNTO ME   362 35
AND THE OUTCAST OF THE PEOPLE   366 15
UNTO A PEOPLE THAT SHALL BE BORN, WHOM THE LORD HATH   368 07
10 O SAVE THY PEOPLE, AND GIVE THY BLESSING UNTO   373 27
10 THE LORD SHALL GIVE STRENGTH UNTO HIS PEOPLE   374 19
SHALL GIVE HIS PEOPLE THE BLESSING OF PEACE   374 20
DEVICES OF THE PEOPLE TO BE OF NONE EFFECT, AND   379 07
BLESSED ARE THE PEOPLE WHOSE GOD IS THE LORD JEHOVAH   379 11
I WILL PRAISE THEE AMONG MUCH PEOPLE   382 33
AND DEFEND MY CAUSE AGAINST THE UNGODLY PEOPLE   394 04
AND MADE THY PEOPLE TO FLOURISH   394 26
THOU SELLEST THY PEOPLE FOR NOUGHT, *   395 17
AND THE PEOPLE SHALL BE SUBDUED UNTO THEE   396 26
ALSO THINE OWN PEOPLE, AND THY FATHER'S HOUSE   397 06
ALSO AMONG THE PEOPLE SHALL MAKE THEIR SUPPLICATION   397 10
SHALL THE PEOPLE GIVE THANKS UNTO THEE, WORLD WITHOUT   397 22
JOINED UNTO THE PEOPLE OF THE GOD OF ABRAHAM   399 06
O HEAR YE THIS, ALL YE PEOPLE   400 07
AND THE EARTH, THAT HE MAY JUDGE HIS PEOPLE   401 29
7 HEAR, O MY PEOPLE, AND I WILL SPEAK   402 04
EATING UP MY PEOPLE AS IF THEY WOULD EAT BREAD   405 23

PEOPLE   CONTINUED

WOULD DELIVER HIS PEOPLE OUT OF CAPTIVITY   405 29
THEM NOT, LEST MY PEOPLE FORGET IT   411 26
ABROAD AMONG THE PEOPLE, AND PUT THEM DOWN, O LORD   411 27
HAST SHOWED THY PEOPLE HEAVY THINGS   412 17
8 O PUT YOUR TRUST IN HIM ALWAY, YE PEOPLE   414 13
WHEN THOU WENTEST FORTH BEFORE THE PEOPLE   419 24
I WILL BRING MY PEOPLE AGAIN, AS I DID FROM BASHAN   420 30
HE WILL GIVE STRENGTH AND POWER UNTO HIS PEOPLE   421 29
HE JUDGE THY PEOPLE ACCORDING UNTO RIGHT, *   426 33
THE LITTLE HILLS RIGHTEOUSNESS UNTO THE PEOPLE   427 03
FALL THE PEOPLE UNTO THEM, *   428 28
BE MEAT FOR THE PEOPLE OF THE WILDERNESS   431 05
HOW THE FOOLISH PEOPLE HATH BLASPHEMED THY NAME   431 13
DELIVERED THY PEOPLE, *   434 12
THOU LEDDEST THY PEOPLE LIKE SHEEP, *   434 23
HEAR MY LAW, O MY PEOPLE   434 27
OR PROVIDE FLESH FOR HIS PEOPLE   436 10
AS FOR HIS OWN PEOPLE, HE LED THEM FORTH LIKE SHEEP,   438 14
63 HE GAVE HIS PEOPLE OVER ALSO UNTO THE SWORD,   439 02
FEED JACOB HIS PEOPLE, AND ISRAEL HIS INHERITANCE   439 22
WE, THAT ARE THY PEOPLE, AND SHEEP OF THY PASTURE,   440 32
BE ANGRY WITH THY PEOPLE THAT PRAYETH   441 11
9 HEAR, O MY PEOPLE   442 29
12 BUT MY PEOPLE WOULD NOT HEAR MY VOICE   443 02
14 O THAT MY PEOPLE WOULD HAVE HEARKENED UNTO ME   443 06
AGAINST THY PEOPLE, *   444 09
THEY BE NO MORE A PEOPLE, *   444 12
OFFENCE OF THY PEOPLE, *   446 10
THAT THY PEOPLE MAY REJOICE IN THEE   446 19
PEACE UNTO HIS PEOPLE, AND TO HIS SAINTS, THAT THEY   446 23
16 BLESSED IS THE PEOPLE, O LORD, THAT CAN REJOICE IN   451 04
I HAVE EXALTED ONE CHOSEN OUT OF THE PEOPLE   451 14
I DO BEAR IN MY BOSOM THE REBUKES OF MANY PEOPLE   453 09
SMITE DOWN THY PEOPLE, O LORD, *   457 27
YE UNWISE AMONG THE PEOPLE   458 02
14 FOR THE LORD WILL NOT FAIL HIS PEOPLE   458 14
AND WE ARE THE PEOPLE OF HIS PASTURE, AND THE SHEEP   459 17
IT IS A PEOPLE THAT DO ERR IN THEIR HEARTS, FOR THEY   459 25
IS KING, BE THE PEOPLE NEVER SO IMPATIENT   462 16
AND HIGH ABOVE ALL PEOPLE   462 19
WE ARE HIS PEOPLE, AND THE SHEEP OF HIS PASTURE   463 09
AND THE PEOPLE WHICH SHALL BE BORN SHALL PRAISE THE   465 16
TELL THE PEOPLE WHAT THINGS HE HATH DONE   470 06
FROM ONE KINGDOM TO ANOTHER PEOPLE   470 29
THE PRINCE OF THE PEOPLE LET HIM GO FREE   471 13
HE INCREASED HIS PEOPLE EXCEEDINGLY, *   471 20
THEY HATED HIS PEOPLE, *   471 22
BROUGHT FORTH HIS PEOPLE WITH JOY, *   472 23
LABOURS OF THE PEOPLE IN POSSESSION   472 26
TO THE FAVOUR THAT THOU BEAREST UNTO THY PEOPLE   473 07
GLADNESS OF THY PEOPLE, AND GIVE THANKS WITH THINE   473 09
AGAINST HIS PEOPLE, *   475 17
AND LET ALL THE PEOPLE SAY, O GIVE THANKS UNTO THE   475 34
OF THE PEOPLE, *   478 11
POWER SHALL THY PEOPLE OFFER THEMSELVES WILLINGLY   482 11
HATH SHOWED HIS PEOPLE THE POWER OF HIS WORKS,   483 05
9 HE SENT REDEMPTION UNTO HIS PEOPLE   483 11
EVEN WITH THE PRINCES OF HIS PEOPLE   484 22
AMONG THE STRANGE PEOPLE, 2 JUDAH WAS HIS SANCTUARY,   484 28
PAY MY VOWS NOW IN THE PRESENCE OF ALL HIS PEOPLE   487 14
SIGHT OF ALL HIS PEOPLE, *   487 22
ROUND ABOUT HIS PEOPLE, FROM THIS TIME FORTH FOR   504 27
EVEN AN HERITAGE UNTO ISRAEL HIS PEOPLE   510 27
WILL AVENGE HIS PEOPLE, *   510 30
16 WHO LED HIS PEOPLE THROUGH THE WILDERNESS   512 14
WHO SUBDUED MY PEOPLE THAT IS UNDER ME   519 25
15 HAPPY ARE THE PEOPLE THAT ARE IN SUCH A CASE   520 24
BLESSED ARE THE PEOPLE WHO HAVE THE LORD FOR THEIR   520 25
13 HE SHALL EXALT THE HORN OF HIS PEOPLE   524 30
EVEN THE PEOPLE THAT SERVETH HIM   524 32
PLEASURE IN HIS PEOPLE, *   525 09
AND ALSO, HOW THE PEOPLE OUGHT TO ESTEEM THEM IN   R 530 06
SAY UNTO THE PEOPLE, BRETHREN, IF THERE BE ANY OF YOU R 530 20
THE CLERGY AND PEOPLE PRESENT, SAY THE LITANY   R 530 30
THE PEOPLE BEING SEATED, THE BISHOP SHALL   R 532 23
PRESENCE OF THE PEOPLE, AFTER THIS MANNER FOLLOWING   R 532 24
OF HIS GLORY, AND THE EDIFYING OF HIS PEOPLE   R 532 29
THE SAME UNTO THE PEOPLE ASSEMBLED IN THE CHURCH   533 07
AND IMPOTENT PEOPLE OF THE PARISH, THAT THEY MAY BE   533 19
THE PEOPLE STANDING, THE BISHOP SHALL LAY HIS   R 534 02
AND ALSO, HOW THE PEOPLE OUGHT TO ESTEEM THEM IN   R 536 06
SAY UNTO THE PEOPLE, GOOD PEOPLE, THESE ARE THEY WHOM R 536 21
THE PEOPLE, GOOD PEOPLE, THESE ARE THEY WHOM WE   536 22
THE CLERGY AND PEOPLE PRESENT, SAY THE LITANY   R 537 06
THE PEOPLE BEING SEATED, THE BISHOP SHALL SAY   R 539 22
PATTERNS FOR THE PEOPLE TO FOLLOW   541 23
TO INSTRUCT THE PEOPLE COMMITTED TO YOUR CHARGE   542 05
YOU MAY TEACH THE PEOPLE COMMITTED TO YOUR CURE AND   542 15
ALL CHRISTIAN PEOPLE, AND ESPECIALLY AMONG THEM THAT   543 08
AND GRANT TO THE PEOPLE, THAT THEY MAY OBEDIENTLY   549 13
THE PEOPLE BEING SEATED, THE PRESIDING   R 554 08
TO INSTRUCT THE PEOPLE COMMITTED TO YOUR CHARGE   554 23
TO POOR AND NEEDY PEOPLE, AND TO ALL STRANGERS   555 24
THAT THE GOSPEL MAY BE PREACHED TO ALL PEOPLE   561 14
AND EXAMPLE THY PEOPLE MAY ABIDE IN THY FAVOUR AND BE   562 12
FOR BLESSING THY PEOPLE IN THY NAME, AND FOR ALL   565 10
THEY SHALL BE HIS PEOPLE, AND GOD HIMSELF SHALL BE   567 16
AMONG THE PEOPLE OF THE SAME   569 19
DEVOTIONS OF THE PEOPLE, AND IN EXERCISING THE   571 27
SALVATION OF THE PEOPLE NOW COMMITTED TO MY CHARGE,   573 20
AND ALL THE PEOPLE OF GOD   578 16
TO SEND HIS GRACE UNTO ME, AND TO ALL PEOPLE   580 31
IN WHICH THY PEOPLE DWELL   598 21
AND UNHAPPY PEOPLE, AND BY THY HEAVENLY GRACE   599 11

PEOPLE   CONTINUED

IN A TONGUE NOT UNDERSTANDED OF THE PEOPLE	607 29
THAT THEY MAY BE UNDERSTANDED OF THE PEOPLE	610 10

PEOPLES

AND THE PEOPLES WITH HIS TRUTH	009 20
AND THE PEOPLES WITH EQUITY	027 25
LET THE PEOPLES PRAISE THEE, O GOD	028 21
LET ALL THE PEOPLES PRAISE THEE	028 22
LET THE PEOPLES PRAISE THEE, O GOD	028 26
LET ALL THE PEOPLES PRAISE THEE	028 27
POWER AMONG ALL PEOPLES, TO THE GLORY OF THY NAME	185 16
AND PEOPLES, AND TONGUES, STOOD BEFORE THE	256 24
OF THE PEOPLES COME ABOUT THEE	350 04
8 THE LORD SHALL JUDGE THE PEOPLES	350 06
AND THAT THE PEOPLES SHAKE THEIR HEADS AT US	395 23
O CLAP YOUR HANDS TOGETHER, ALL YE PEOPLES	398 21
SHALL SUBDUE THE PEOPLES UNDER US, *	398 25
PRINCES OF THE PEOPLES ARE JOINED UNTO THE PEOPLE OF	399 06
GIVE THANKS UNTO THEE, O LORD, AMONG THE PEOPLES	409 34
AND THE MADNESS OF THE PEOPLES	416 28
OUR GOD, YE PEOPLES, *	417 29
3 LET THE PEOPLES PRAISE THEE, O GOD	418 28
LET ALL THE PEOPLES PRAISE THEE	418 29
5 LET THE PEOPLES PRAISE THEE, O GOD	418 33
LET ALL THE PEOPLES PRAISE THEE	418 34
SCATTER THOU THE PEOPLES THAT DELIGHT IN WAR	421 17
AND HAST DECLARED THY POWER AMONG THE PEOPLES	434 11
WHEN HE WRITETH UP THE PEOPLES	448 25
AND HIS WONDERS UNTO ALL PEOPLES	460 05
KINDREDS OF THE PEOPLES, *	460 12
SHALL JUDGE THE PEOPLES RIGHTEOUSLY	460 21
AND THE PEOPLES WITH HIS TRUTH	460 27
AND ALL THE PEOPLES HAVE SEEN HIS GLORY	461 09
AND THE PEOPLES WITH EQUITY	462 14
22 WHEN THE PEOPLES ARE GATHERED TOGETHER, *	465 24
O LORD, AMONG THE PEOPLES	479 09
PRAISE HIM, ALL YE PEOPLES	487 26
11 KINGS OF THE EARTH, AND ALL PEOPLES	524 25
AND TO REBUKE THE PEOPLES	525 16

PERADVENTURE

FOR THEN PERADVENTURE I WOULD HAVE HID MYSELF FROM	407 14
IF I SAY, PERADVENTURE THE DARKNESS SHALL COVER ME	515 08

PERCEIVE

YE SHALL PERCEIVE YOURSELVES TO HAVE OFFENDED, EITHER	087 18
AND IF YE SHALL PERCEIVE YOUR OFFENCES TO BE SUCH AS	087 22
THEY MAY BOTH PERCEIVE AND KNOW WHAT THINGS THEY	109 31
OF A TRUTH I PERCEIVE THAT GOD IS NO RESPECTER CF	166 12
OF A TRUTH I PERCEIVE THAT GOD IS NO RESPECTER CF	183 30
HEREBY PERCEIVE WE THE LOVE OF GOD, BECAUSE HE LAID	191 16
FOR THEY SHALL PERCEIVE THAT IT IS HIS WORK	416 05
HOW SHOULD GOD PERCEIVE IT	428 30
MAY BOTH PERCEIVE AND KNOW WHAT THINGS THEY OUGHT TO	566 05

PERCEIVED

BUT JESUS PERCEIVED THEIR WICKEDNESS, AND SAID,	223 05

PERCEIVEST

BUT PERCEIVEST NOT THE BEAM THAT IS IN THINE OWN	195 06

PERCEIVETH

WHOM HE PERCEIVETH MALICE AND HATRED TO REIGN	R 085 09

PERCEIVING

GRANT THAT, PERCEIVING HOW FRAIL AND UNCERTAIN OUR	045 07

PERDITION

WE ARE NOT OF THEM WHO DRAW BACK UNTO PERDITION	228 21

PERFECT

WHOSE SERVICE IS PERFECT FREEDOM	017 07
EVERY GOOD AND PERFECT GIFT	018 19
EVERY GOOD AND PERFECT GIFT	032 18
RESTORED TO THAT PERFECT HEALTH WHICH IT IS THINE	045 26
OFFERED) A FULL, PERFECT, AND SUFFICIENT SACRIFICE,	080 11
AND BE IN PERFECT CHARITY WITH ALL MEN	086 02
AND PERFECT, WILL OF GOD	110 08
THAT WHICH IS PERFECT IS COME, THEN THAT WHICH IS IN	123 08
OF ALL MERCY, PERFECT REMISSION AND FORGIVENESS	124 16
GREATER AND MORE PERFECT TABERNACLE, NOT MADE WITH	132 24
MAKE THE COMERS THEREUNTO PERFECT	157 18
GIFT AND EVERY PERFECT GIFT IS FROM ABOVE, AND COMETH	174 26
LOOKETH INTO THE PERFECT LAW OF LIBERTY, AND	176 10
IS OUR LOVE MADE PERFECT, THAT WE MAY HAVE BOLDNESS	189 26
BUT PERFECT LOVE CASTETH OUT FEAR	189 28
IS NOT MADE PERFECT IN LOVE	189 30
MAKE YOU PERFECT, STABLISH, STRENGTHEN, SETTLE	193 10
ONE THAT IS PERFECT SHALL BE AS HIS MASTER	195 04
OF GOD, UNTO A PERFECT MAN, UNTO THE MEASURE OF THE	237 24
HAVE HER PERFECT WORK, THAT YE MAY BE PERFECT AND	239 10
THAT YE MAY BE PERFECT AND ENTIRE, WANTING NOTHING	239 11
BE YE THEREFORE PERFECT, EVEN AS YOUR FATHER WHICH IS	264 14
EVEN AS YOUR FATHER WHICH IS IN HEAVEN IS PERFECT	264 15
GIFT AND EVERY PERFECT GIFT IS FROM ABOVE, AND COMETH	265 19

PERFECT   CONTINUED

LOOKETH INTO THE PERFECT LAW OF LIBERTY, AND	265 33
EVER REMAIN IN PERFECT LOVE AND PEACE TOGETHER,	303 10
PERFECT, WE BESEECH THEE, THIS THY MERCY TOWARDS HIM	315 27
OUR GOD, AND IN PERFECT CHARITY WITH THE WORLD	317 06
OF JUST MEN MADE PERFECT, AFTER THEY ARE DELIVERED	317 12
IN THE LIFE OF PERFECT SERVICE, IN THY HEAVENLY	332 06
MAY MAKE OUR PERFECT CONSUMMATION AND BLISS, BOTH IN	334 27
MAKE YOU PERFECT IN EVERY GOOD WORK TO DO HIS WILL,	335 19
INNOCENCY AND PERFECT FAITH, THAT AT LENGTH, UNITED	341 02
AND WITH A PERFECT MAN THOU SHALT BE PERFECT	361 18
AND WITH A PERFECT MAN THOU SHALT BE PERFECT	361 19
AND MAKETH MY WAY PERFECT	361 34
IN PERFECT BEAUTY	401 24
THEY MAY PRIVILY SHOOT AT HIM THAT IS PERFECT	415 25
MY HOUSE WITH A PERFECT HEART	463 21
INTENT HE MAY BE PERFECT AND WELL EXPERT IN THE	R 535 22
OF GOD, UNTO A PERFECT MAN, UNTO THE MEASURE OF THE	538 11
HE HAD MADE PERFECT OUR REDEMPTION BY HIS DEATH,	545 16
YOU MAY BE FOUND PERFECT AND IRREPREHENSIBLE AT THE	555 32
THAT HE HAD MADE PERFECT OUR REDEMPTION BY HIS DEATH,	557 23
AND MAKING PERFECT HIS CHURCH	557 27
MAY REMAIN IN PERFECT LOVE TOGETHER UNTO THEIR LIFE'S	566 11
OF ALL GOOD AND PERFECT GIFTS, WHO OF THY WISE	572 06
MAKE YOU PERFECT IN EVERY GOOD WORK TO DO HIS WILL,	573 06
TWO WHOLE AND PERFECT NATURES, THAT IS TO SAY,	603 12
MADE IS THAT PERFECT REDEMPTION, PROPITIATION,	609 14

PERFECTED

WHICH THOU HAST BEGUN IN THEM MAY BE PERFECTED	042 19
HE HATH PERFECTED FOR EVER THEM THAT ARE SANCTIFIED	158 08
HIS LOVE IS PERFECTED IN US	189 18
THOU HAST PERFECTED PRAISE	260 15
IN THEM MAY BE PERFECTED UNTO THE DAY OF JESUS	335 30

PERFECTING

FOR THE PERFECTING OF THE SAINTS, FOR THE WORK OF THE	237 20
FOR THE PERFECTING OF THE SAINTS, FOR THE WORK OF THE	538 07

PERFECTION

AND BRING NO FRUIT TO PERFECTION	122 08
TO THE PERFECTION OF MAN'S NATURE	603 22

PERFECTLY

THAT WE MAY PERFECTLY LOVE THEE, AND WORTHILY MAGNIFY	067 19
GRANT US SO PERFECTLY, AND WITHOUT ALL DOUBT, TO	228 08
GRANT US PERFECTLY TO KNOW THY SON JESUS CHRIST TO BE	238 30

PERFECTNESS

AND IN PERFECTNESS OF LOVE, AND TO RESTORE TO	047 09
WHICH IS THE BOND OF PERFECTNESS	116 08
20 LET PERFECTNESS AND RIGHTEOUS DEALING WAIT UPCN	370 26
RIPENESS AND PERFECTNESS OF AGE IN CHRIST, THAT THERE	540 21

PERFORM

TO PERFORM THE MERCY PROMISED TO OUR FOREFATHERS,	014 16
TO PERFORM THE OATH WHICH HE SWARE TO OUR FOREFATHER	014 18
GUIDING MAY PERFORM THE SAME	176 02
WORK IN YOU WILL PERFORM IT UNTIL THE DAY OF JESUS	220 26
TO PERFORM THE MERCY PROMISED TO OUR FATHERS, AND TO	244 04
AGE THEY CANNOT PERFORM THEM	292 32
MAY SURELY PERFORM AND KEEP THE VOW AND COVENANT	303 07
THE LORD PERFORM ALL THY PETITIONS	364 24
SUCH A DEVICE AS THEY ARE NOT ABLE TO PERFORM	365 28
MY VOWS WILL I PERFORM IN THE SIGHT OF THEM THAT FEAR	367 24
GOD THAT SHALL PERFORM THE CAUSE WHICH I HAVE IN	409 16
THAT I MAY DAILY PERFORM MY VOWS	413 23
AND POWER TO PERFORM THE SAME, THAT HE MAY ACCOMPLISH	543 20
AND POWER TO PERFORM THE SAME	555 30
MAY FAITHFULLY PERFORM AND KEEP THE VOW AND COVENANT	566 10
AND AUTHORITY TO PERFORM THE OFFICE OF A PRIEST, IN	569 16
OF FULL POWER TO PERFORM EVERY ACT OF SACERDOTAL	569 18
AGE THEY CANNOT PERFORM THEM	581 32
THEY COME TO AGE, THEMSELVES ARE BOUND TO PERFORM	581 35

PERFORMANCE

ME IN THE PERFORMANCE OF ALL THE DUTIES OF MY	573 24

PERFORMED

WHEN THEY HAD PERFORMED ALL THINGS ACCORDING TO THE	233 24
THE VOW BE PERFORMED IN JERUSALEM	416 12

PERIL

WE BESEECH THEE, FROM OUR PERIL	045 05
THE GREAT PAIN AND PERIL OF CHILD-BIRTH, THIS WOMAN,	051 07
AND THE GREAT PERIL OF THE UNWORTHY RECEIVING	087 00
OR ANY IMMINENT PERIL, IF A MINISTER CANNOT BE	R 281 27
THE GREAT PAIN AND PERIL OF CHILD-BIRTH, THIS WOMAN,	306 26
OR NAKEDNESS, OR PERIL, OR SWORD	331 08
FOR THEY ARE IN NO PERIL OF DEATH	428 16
SERVANT FROM THE PERIL OF THE SWORD	520 11

PERILOUS

IN THE PERILOUS TIME	385 33
NO LESS PERILOUS THAN DESPERATION	606 26

PERILS

US FROM ALL PERILS AND DANGERS OF THIS NIGHT   031 27
EVERMORE FROM ALL PERILS, TO GLORIFY THEE, WHO ART   041 15
THROUGH THE PERILS OF THE GREAT DEEP (OF HIS WAY),   053 22
IN PERILS OF WATERS, IN PERILS OF ROBBERS, IN   121 04
OF WATERS, IN PERILS OF ROBBERS, IN PERILS BY MINE   121 05
OF ROBBERS, IN PERILS BY MINE OWN COUNTRYMEN,   121 05
THE HEATHEN, IN PERILS IN THE CITY, IN PERILS IN THE   121 06
IN PERILS BY THE HEATHEN, IN PERILS IN   121 06
IN THE SEA, IN PERILS AMONG FALSE BRETHREN   121 07
IN PERILS IN THE SEA, IN PERILS AMONG   121 07
IN THE CITY, IN PERILS IN THE WILDERNESS, IN PERILS   121 07
TO MANY SUDDEN PERILS, DISEASES, AND SICKNESSES, AND   R 321 02
US FROM ALL PERILS AND DANGERS OF THIS NIGHT   593 14

PERISH

IN HIM SHOULD NOT PERISH, BUT HAVE EVERLASTING LIFE   076 15
THEY SHALL PERISH   097 15
BEHOLD, YE DESPISERS, AND WONDER, AND PERISH   169 24
IN HIM SHOULD NOT PERISH, BUT HAVE EVERLASTING LIFE   184 33
IN HIM SHOULD NOT PERISH, BUT HAVE ETERNAL LIFE   188 29
TO SPARE, AND I PERISH WITH HUNGER   202 12
AND THE WAY OF THE UNGODLY SHALL PERISH   345 23
AND SO YE PERISH FROM THE RIGHT WAY, IF HIS   346 21
LET THEM PERISH THROUGH THEIR OWN IMAGINATIONS   348 22
SHALL FALL AND PERISH AT THY PRESENCE   351 21
MEEK SHALL NOT PERISH FOR EVER   352 29
THEY SHALL PERISH, AND THE ENEMIES OF THE LORD SHALL   385 35
THE UNGODLY SHALL PERISH, THOU SHALT SEE IT   387 03
THEY SHALL PERISH TOGETHER   387 10
WHEN SHALL HE DIE, AND HIS NAME PERISH   392 09
MEN ALSO DIE AND PERISH TOGETHER, *   400 23
HE MAY BE COMPARED UNTO THE BEASTS THAT PERISH   400 31
IS COMPARED UNTO THE BEASTS THAT PERISH   401 17
CONSUME THEM, THAT THEY MAY PERISH   411 33
LET THE UNGODLY PERISH AT THE PRESENCE OF GOD   419 13
BE CONFOUNDED AND PERISH THAT ARE AGAINST MY SOUL   425 31
PERISH, AND COME TO A FEARFUL END   429 14
THEY THAT FORSAKE THEE SHALL PERISH   429 30
AND THEY SHALL PERISH AT THE REBUKE OF THY   442 03
LET THEM BE PUT TO SHAME, AND PERISH   445 07
THINE ENEMIES SHALL PERISH   456 18
26 THEY SHALL PERISH, BUT THOU SHALT ENDURE   465 34
THE DESIRE OF THE UNGODLY SHALL PERISH   484 06
AND THEN ALL HIS THOUGHTS PERISH   522 09

PERISHED

MEMORIAL IS PERISHED WITH THEM   351 34
THE HEATHEN ARE PERISHED OUT OF THE LAND   354 12
10 WHO PERISHED AT ENDOR, *   444 24
I SHOULD HAVE PERISHED IN MY TROUBLE   496 10

PERISHETH

AND THE GRACE OF THE FASHION OF IT PERISHETH   239 23

PERMITTED

MAY BE PERMITTED TO BEHOLD THE KING IN HIS   248 04

PERPETUAL

TO CONTINUE, A PERPETUAL MEMORY OF THAT HIS PRECIOUS   080 14
US TO HAVE A PERPETUAL FEAR AND LOVE OF THY HOLY   191 07
WITH THY PERPETUAL MERCY   210 18
KEEP HIM IN PERPETUAL PEACE AND SAFETY   309 07
ARE COME TO A PERPETUAL END   351 32
PUT THEM TO A PERPETUAL SHAME   439 11
ENABLE WITH PERPETUAL LIGHT THE DULNESS OF OUR   544 04
ENABLE WITH PERPETUAL LIGHT THE DULNESS OF OUR   556 12

PERPLEXED

THOUGH THEY BE PERPLEXED, SAVE THEM FROM DESPAIR   599 14

PERPLEXITIES

BRING OUR PERPLEXITIES TO THE LIGHT OF THY WISDOM,   596 12

PERPLEXITY

THE EARTH DISTRESS OF NATIONS, WITH PERPLEXITY   093 07

PERSECUTE

AND PERSECUTE THEM FROM CITY TO CITY   100 21
THEM WHICH PERSECUTE YOU   111 28
THEY WILL ALSO PERSECUTE YOU   255 19
AND PERSECUTE YOU, AND SHALL SAY ALL MANNER OF   257 31
USE YOU, AND PERSECUTE YOU   264 07
ALL THEM THAT PERSECUTE ME, AND DELIVER ME   349 23
LET MINE ENEMY PERSECUTE MY SOUL, AND TAKE ME   349 32
OWN LUST, DOTH PERSECUTE THE POOR   353 05
FROM THEM THAT PERSECUTE ME   376 27
27 FOR THEY PERSECUTE HIM WHOM THOU HAST SMITTEN   423 27
PERSECUTE HIM, AND TAKE HIM, FOR THERE IS NONE TO   425 27
OF THEM THAT PERSECUTE ME   495 26
THEY PERSECUTE ME FALSELY   495 29
THAT OF MALICE PERSECUTE ME, *   500 10
AND PERSECUTE ME   500 25

PERSECUTED

THE FLESH PERSECUTED HIM THAT WAS BORN AFTER THE   131 13
BECAUSE I PERSECUTED THE CHURCH OF GOD   205 14
IF THEY HAVE PERSECUTED ME, THEY WILL ALSO PERSECUTE   255 18
WHICH ARE PERSECUTED FOR RIGHTEOUSNESS' SAKE   257 29
FOR SO PERSECUTED THEY THE PROPHETS WHICH WERE BEFORE   257 34
BUT PERSECUTED THE POOR HELPLESS MAN, THAT HE MIGHT   480 33
PRINCES HAVE PERSECUTED ME WITHOUT A CAUSE   501 03
ENEMY HATH PERSECUTED MY SOUL   518 27

PERSECUTEST

WHY PERSECUTEST THOU ME   230 02
THE LORD SAID, I AM JESUS WHOM THOU PERSECUTEST   230 04

PERSECUTION

SUFFER PERSECUTION FOR THE CROSS OF CHRIST   210 26
OR PERSECUTION, OR FAMINE, OR NAKEDNESS,   331 07

PERSECUTIONS

HURT BY NO PERSECUTIONS, MAY EVERMORE GIVE THANKS   058 22

PERSECUTORS

OUR ENEMIES, PERSECUTORS, AND SLANDERERS, AND TO TURN   057 07
BLESS OUR PERSECUTORS BY THE EXAMPLE OF THY FIRST   099 30
HE ORDAINETH HIS ARROWS AGAINST THE PERSECUTORS   350 20
8 O DELIVER ME FROM MY PERSECUTORS   518 17

PERSEVERANCE

WITH ALL PERSEVERANCE AND SUPPLICATION FOR ALL   219 21

PERSEVERE

MAY PERSEVERE IN RUNNING THE RACE THAT IS SET   258 15
AND PERSEVERE UNTO THE END   561 09

PERSON

THE PENITENT PERSON TO THE HOLY COMMUNION, AND NOT   R 085 16
IMAGE OF HIS PERSON, AND UPHOLDING ALL THINGS BY THE   096 27
NOR UNCLEAN PERSON, NOR COVETOUS MAN, WHO IS AN   129 07
I AM INNOCENT OF THE BLOOD OF THIS JUST PERSON   136 11
REGARDEST NOT THE PERSON OF MEN   223 03
HATH THIS CHILD (PERSON) BEEN ALREADY BAPTIZED, OR   273 26
THIS CHILD (THIS PERSON) THAT WHICH BY NATURE HE   274 03
THIS CHILD (THIS PERSON), DECLARED BY HIS SON JESUS   276 04
THAT IF THE PERSON TO BE BAPTIZED BE AN ADULT,   R 279 30
THIS CHILD (PERSON) INTO THE CONGREGATION OF CHRIST'S   280 03
THIS CHILD (THIS PERSON) IS REGENERATE, AND GRAFTED   280 14
THIS CHILD (THIS PERSON) MAY LEAD THE REST OF HIS   280 17
THE CHILD (OR PERSON) BEING NAMED BY SOME ONE WHO   R 281 19
THEN ANY BAPTIZED PERSON PRESENT MAY ADMINISTER HOLY   R 281 28
THAT A CHILD OR PERSON SO BAPTIZED BE AFTERWARD   R 281 32
THIS CHILD (OR PERSON), ETC   R 282 06
DOUBT WHETHER ANY PERSON WAS BAPTIZED WITH WATER,   R 282 08
OF BAPTISM), SUCH PERSON MAY BE BAPTIZED IN THE FORM   R 282 10
WHEREIN THE PERSON IS BAPTIZED, IN THE NAME OF THE   292 20
WHEN ANY PERSON IS SICK, NOTICE SHALL BE GIVEN   R 308 05
ADDRESS THE SICK PERSON ON THE MEANING AND USE OF THE R 313 15
OF THE SICK PERSON AS TO HIS ACCEPTANCE OF THE   R 313 18
SHALL THE SICK PERSON BE MOVED TO MAKE A SPECIAL   R 313 24
WHEN ANY SICK PERSON SHALL IN HUMBLE FAITH DESIRE   R 320 05
BUT IF THE SICK PERSON BE NOT ABLE TO COME TO THE   R 321 11
AND LAST OF ALL TO THE SICK PERSON   R 323 03
I WILL NOT KNOW A WICKED PERSON   463 25
NO DECEITFUL PERSON DWELL IN MY HOUSE   464 02
NOT ONE FEEBLE PERSON AMONG THEIR TRIBES   472 12
HUNT THE WICKED PERSON TO OVERTHROW HIM   516 33
ANY PERSON TO BE A MAN OF VIRTUOUS   529 27
ORDERING THAT PERSON, UNTIL SUCH TIME AS THE PARTY   R 530 27
ORDERING THAT PERSON, UNTIL SUCH TIME AS THE PARTY   R 537 03
OF THE PERSON PRESENTED FOR CONSECRATION, AND SHALL   R 552 24
SEND FORTH THIS PERSON PRESENTED UNTO US, TO THE WORK   553 11
AND ADMITTING ANY PERSON TO GOVERNMENT IN THE CHURCH   554 09
BE READ BY SOME PERSON APPOINTED BY HIM, AND THEN   R 566 26
THAT THE PERSON CHOSEN IS A QUALIFIED MINISTER OF   R 569 06
THAT AN UNWORTHY PERSON SHOULD MINISTER AMONG YOU   570 19
WHEREIN THE PERSON IS BAPTIZED, IN THE NAME OF THE   581 21
TOGETHER IN ONE PERSON, NEVER TO BE DIVIDED, WHEREOF   603 13
IN EVERY PERSON BORN INTO THIS WORLD, IT DESERVETH   604 34
THAT PERSON WHICH BY OPEN DENUNCIATION OF THE CHURCH   609 27

PERSON'S

THE CHILD'S (OR PERSON'S) FOREHEAD   R 280 11
INTO THE SICK PERSON'S PRESENCE, SHALL SAY, PEACE BE   R 308 06

PERSONS

CHOICE OF FIT PERSONS, TO SERVE IN THE SACRED   038 31
A DUE SUPPLY OF PERSONS FITTED TO SERVE GOD IN THE   047 34
ALL SICK PERSONS, AND YOUNG CHILDREN   056 32
OR OTHER FIT PERSONS APPOINTED FOR THAT PURPOSE,   R 073 27
IN TRINITY OF PERSONS AND IN UNITY OF SUBSTANCE   079 09
EXHORTETH ALL PERSONS DILIGENTLY TO TRY AND EXAMINE   085 28
I PERCEIVE THAT GOD IS NO RESPECTER OF PERSONS   166 13
I PERCEIVE THAT GOD IS NO RESPECTER OF PERSONS   183 30
AND NINE JUST PERSONS, WHICH NEED NO REPENTANCE   193 26
REGARDETH NOT PERSONS, NOR TAKETH REWARD   263 25
WHEN ANY SUCH PERSONS AS ARE OF RIPER YEARS ARE TO   R 273 17
THIS WISE, THE PERSONS TO BE BAPTIZED ANSWERING THE   R 277 19

PERSONS   CONTINUED

IS REQUIRED OF PERSONS TO BE BAPTIZED	292 27
UNTO YOU THESE PERSONS TO RECEIVE THE LAYING ON OF	296 09
TO MOVE THE PERSONS CONFIRMED TO COME, WITHOUT DELAY,	R 299 06
THE PERSONS TO BE MARRIED SHALL COME INTO	R 300 04
ESTATE THESE TWO PERSONS PRESENT COME NOW TO BE	300 19
UNTO THE PERSONS WHO ARE TO BE MARRIED, HE SHALL SAY,	R 300 23
THAT IF ANY PERSONS ARE JOINED TOGETHER OTHERWISE	300 29
WHY THESE TWO PERSONS SHOULD NOT BE JOINED TOGETHER	R 304 23
HIS HEART, ALL PERSONS THAT HAVE OFFENDED HIM	R 313 21
AND BED-RIDDEN PERSONS, OR SUCH AS ARE NOT ABLE TC	R 323 32
4 I HAVE NOT DWELT WITH VAIN PERSONS	371 04
AND ACCEPT THE PERSONS OF THE UNGODLY	443 21
UNTO YOU THESE PERSONS PRESENT, TO BE ADMITTED	530 11
HEED THAT THE PERSONS, WHOM YE PRESENT UNTO US,	530 13
IN ANY OF THESE PERSONS PRESENTED TO BE ORDERED	530 22
UNTO YOU THESE PERSONS PRESENT, TO BE ADMITTED TO THE	536 11
HEED THAT THE PERSONS, WHOM WE PRESENT UNTO US,	536 14
THAT THEY ARE PERSONS MEET FOR THE SAME	536 26
AFTER WHICH, THE PERSONS TO BE ORDAINED PRIESTS	R 543 26
OR SOME OTHER PERSONS APPOINTED FOR THAT PURPOSE	R 563 06
IN THEIR OWN PERSONS RENEW THE PROMISES AND VOWS OF	565 24
IS REQUIRED OF PERSONS TO BE BAPTIZED	581 27
OF ALL SUCH PERSONS WITHIN HIS PARISH, AS HE SHALL	R 583 08
FOR ALL AGED PERSONS, AND ALL LITTLE CHILDREN,	600 05
THERE BE THREE PERSONS, OF ONE SUBSTANCE, POWER,	603 06
COMFORT TO GODLY PERSONS, AND SUCH AS FEEL IN	606 17
AND CARNAL PERSONS, LACKING THE SPIRIT OF CHRIST,	606 23

PERSUADED

WILL NOT BE PERSUADED TO A GODLY UNITY, BUT REMAIN	R 085 14
AND ELDERS PERSUADED THE MULTITUDE THAT THEY SHCULD	135 36
WILL THEY BE PERSUADED, THOUGH ONE ROSE FROM THE	190 30
AND NOW, BEING PERSUADED OF THE GOOD WILL OF OUR	276 03
FOR I AM PERSUADED, THAT NEITHER DEATH, NOR LIFE,	331 10
ARE YOU PERSUADED THAT THE HOLY SCRIPTURES CONTAIN	533 02
I AM SO PERSUADED	533 05
ARE YOU PERSUADED THAT THE HOLY SCRIPTURES CONTAIN	542 02
YOU SHALL BE PERSUADED MAY BE CONCLUDED AND PROVED BY	542 07
I AM SO PERSUADED, AND HAVE SO DETERMINED, BY GCD'S	542 09
ARE YOU PERSUADED THAT YOU ARE TRULY CALLED TO THIS	554 16
I AM SO PERSUADED	554 19
ARE YOU PERSUADED THAT THE HOLY SCRIPTURES CONTAIN	554 20
YOU SHALL BE PERSUADED MAY BE CONCLUDED AND PROVED BY	554 26
I AM SO PERSUADED, AND DETERMINED, BY GOD'S GRACE	554 27

PERTAIN

| THAT SPECIALLY PERTAIN UNTO YOU, ACCORDING TO THE | 541 05 |

PERTAINING

| OF THE THINGS PERTAINING TO THE KINGDOM OF GOD | 177 28 |
| A WORK, PERTAINING TO THE SALVATION OF MAN, BUT WITH | 540 34 |

PERVERSE

| ARISE, SPEAKING PERVERSE THINGS, TO DRAW AWAY | 550 32 |

PERVERTETH

| AS ONE THAT PERVERTETH THE PEOPLE | 153 23 |

PERVERTING

| THIS FELLOW PERVERTING THE NATION, AND FORBIDDING TO | 152 29 |

PESTILENCE

FROM PLAGUE, PESTILENCE, AND FAMINE	054 31
THE TIME OF PESTILENCE, OR OTHER INFECTIOUS SICKNESS,	R 321 06
BUT GAVE THEIR LIFE OVER TO THE PESTILENCE	438 11
AND FROM THE NOISOME PESTILENCE	454 33
6 FOR THE PESTILENCE THAT WALKETH IN DARKNESS,	455 07

PETER

JESUS SAITH UNTO PETER, FOLLOW ME	102 03
THEN PETER, TURNING ABOUT, SEETH THE DISCIPLE WHOM	102 03
PETER SEEING HIM SAITH TO JESUS, LORD, AND WHAT SHALL	102 06
BUT PETER SAID UNTO HIM, ALTHOUGH ALL SHALL BE	141 21
HE TAKETH WITH HIM PETER AND JAMES AND JOHN, AND	141 29
AND SAITH UNTO PETER, SIMON, SLEEPEST THOU	142 04
AND PETER FOLLOWED HIM AFAR OFF, EVEN INTO THE PALACE	142 33
AND AS PETER WAS BENEATH IN THE PALACE, THERE COMETH	143 22
AND WHEN SHE SAW PETER WARMING HIMSELF, SHE LOOKED	143 24
BY SAID AGAIN TO PETER, SURELY THOU ART ONE OF THEM	143 31
AND PETER CALLED TO MIND THE WORD THAT JESUS SAID	143 35
AND HE SENT PETER AND JOHN, SAYING, GO AND PREPARE US	148 22
I TELL THEE, PETER, THE COCK SHALL NOT CROW	150 02
AND PETER FOLLOWED AFAR OFF	151 08
SET DOWN TOGETHER, PETER SAT DOWN AMONG THEM	151 10
AND PETER SAID, MAN, I AM NOT	151 15
AND PETER SAID, MAN, I KNOW NOT WHAT THOU SAYEST	151 18
AND PETER REMEMBERED THE WORD OF THE LORD, HOW HE HAD	151 20
AND THE LORD TURNED, AND LOOKED UPON PETER	151 20
AND PETER WENT OUT, AND WEPT BITTERLY	151 22
THEN COMETH HE TO SIMON PETER	156 02
AND PETER SAITH UNTO HIM, LORD, DOST THOU WASH MY	156 02
PETER SAITH UNTO HIM, THOU SHALT NEVER WASH MY FEET	156 05
SIMON PETER SAITH UNTO HIM, LORD, NOT MY FEET ONLY,	156 07
COMETH TO SIMON PETER, AND TO THE OTHER DISCIPLE,	164 13
PETER THEREFORE WENT FORTH, AND THAT OTHER DISCIPLE,	164 16
DID OUTRUN PETER, AND CAME FIRST TO THE SEPULCHRE	164 19

PETER   CONTINUED

THEN COMETH SIMON PETER FOLLOWING HIM, AND WENT INTO	164 21
HIS DISCIPLES AND PETER THAT HE GOETH BEFORE YOU INTC	165 31
PETER OPENED HIS MOUTH, AND SAID, OF A TRUTH I	166 12
THEN PETER OPENED HIS MOUTH, AND SAID, OF A TRUTH I	183 29
WHILE PETER YET SPAKE THESE WORDS, THE HOLY GHOST	184 20
MANY AS CAME WITH PETER, BECAUSE THAT ON THE GENTILES	184 23
THEN ANSWERED PETER, CAN ANY MAN FORBID WATER,	184 26
SENT UNTO THEM PETER AND JOHN	185 23
WHEN SIMON PETER SAW IT, HE FELL DOWN AT JESUS'	196 22
PETER SAID UNTO JESUS, LORD, HOW OFT SHALL MY BRCTHER	221 09
SIMON CALLED PETER, AND ANDREW HIS BROTHER, CASTING A	227 25
PETER ANSWERED AND SAID UNTO JESUS, WE HAVE	231 12
IN THOSE DAYS PETER STOOD UP IN THE MIDST OF THE	234 06
THY APOSTLE SAINT PETER MANY EXCELLENT GIFTS,	244 23
FURTHER TO TAKE PETER ALSO	245 03
PETER THEREFORE WAS KEPT IN PRISON	245 07
THE SAME NIGHT PETER WAS SLEEPING BETWEEN TWO	245 10
AND HE SMOTE PETER ON THE SIDE, AND RAISED HIM UP,	245 14
AND WHEN PETER WAS COME TO HIMSELF, HE SAID, NOW I	245 25
AND SIMON PETER ANSWERED AND SAID, THOU ART THE	246 02
THAT THOU ART PETER, AND UPON THIS ROCK I WILL BUILD	246 07
FURTHER TO TAKE PETER ALSO	247 04
HE TOOK PETER AND JOHN AND JAMES, AND WENT	248 24
BUT PETER AND THEY THAT WERE WITH HIM WERE HEAVY WITH	248 30
DEPARTED FROM HIM, PETER SAID UNTO JESUS, MASTER, IT	248 33
THE SHADOW OF PETER PASSING BY MIGHT OVERSHADOW SCME	249 28
SENT UNTO THEM PETER AND JOHN	296 15
SAITH TO SIMON PETER, SIMON, SON OF JCNAS, LOVEST	551 14
PETER WAS GRIEVED BECAUSE HE SAID UNTO HIM THE THIRD	551 21

PETER'S

| SIMON PETER'S BROTHER, SAITH UNTO HIM, THERE | 131 32 |
| SIMON PETER'S BROTHER, SAITH UNTO HIM, | 225 29 |

PETITION

9 THE LORD HATH HEARD MY PETITION	349 16
AND HIDE NOT THYSELF FROM MY PETITION	406 20
MADE MY HUMBLE PETITION IN THY PRESENCE WITH MY WHOLE	493 26

PETITIONS

DESIRES AND PETITIONS OF THY SERVANTS, AS MAY BE MOST	020 07
DESIRES AND PETITIONS OF THY SERVANTS, AS MAY BE MOST	034 07
UP ALL OUR PETITIONS, AND ALL OUR THANKSGIVINGS, IN	048 23
TO HEAR THE PETITIONS OF THOSE WHO ASK IN THY SON'S	050 06
RECEIVE OUR HUMBLE PETITIONS	063 10
OUR HUMBLE PETITIONS UNTO ALMIGHTY GOD, OUR HEAVENLY	089 21
OBTAIN THEIR PETITIONS, MAKE THEM TO ASK SUCH THINGS	203 13
WE HAVE THE PETITIONS THAT WE DESIRED OF HIM	322 18
THE LORD PERFORM ALL THY PETITIONS	364 25
OF MY HUMBLE PETITIONS, WHEN I CRY UNTO THEE	373 07
HE HATH HEARD THE VOICE OF MY HUMBLE PETITIONS	373 21

PHANUEL

| THE DAUGHTER OF PHANUEL, OF THE TRIBE OF ASER | 233 16 |

PHARAOH

| UPON PHARAOH, AND ALL HIS SERVANTS | 510 21 |
| 15 BUT AS FOR PHARAOH AND HIS HOST, HE OVERTHREW THEM | 512 12 |

PHARISEE

| THE PHARISEE STOOD AND PRAYED THUS WITH HIMSELF, GCD, | 205 24 |
| THE ONE A PHARISEE, AND THE OTHER A PUBLICAN | 205 24 |

PHARISEES

AND THEY WHICH WERE SENT WERE OF THE PHARISEES	095 31
PRIESTS AND PHARISEES CAME TOGETHER UNTO PILATE,	162 16
A MAN OF THE PHARISEES, NAMED NICODEMUS, A RULER OF	187 34
AND THE PHARISEES AND SCRIBES MURMURED, SAYING, THIS	193 15
SCRIBES AND PHARISEES, YE SHALL IN NO CASE ENTER INTO	197 29
OF THE CHIEF PHARISEES TO EAT BREAD ON THE SABBATH	213 29
LAWYERS AND PHARISEES, SAYING, IS IT LAWFUL TO HEAL	214 02
WHEN THE PHARISEES HAD HEARD THAT JESUS HAD PUT THE	215 06
WHILE THE PHARISEES WERE GATHERED TOGETHER, JESUS	215 15
THEN WENT THE PHARISEES, AND TOOK COUNSEL HCW THEY	222 28
AND WHEN THE PHARISEES SAW IT, THEY SAID UNTO HIS	251 17
A MAN OF THE PHARISEES, NAMED NICODEMUS, A RULER OF	275 05

PHILADELPHIA

| PHILADELPHIA, OCTOBER, 1789 | VI 44 |

PHILIP

HE SAITH UNTO PHILIP, WHENCE SHALL WE BUY BREAD, THAT	131 27
PHILIP ANSWERED HIM, TWO HUNDRED PENNYWORTH OF BREAD	131 29
PHILIP AND ST	R 178 31
HE SAITH UNTO PHILIP, WHENCE SHALL WE BUY BREAD, THAT	225 23
PHILIP ANSWERED HIM, TWO HUNDRED PENNYWORTH OF BREAD	225 26
SAINT PHILIP AND SAINT JAMES, WE MAY	238 32
PHILIP SAITH UNTO HIM, LORD, SHEW US THE FATHER, AND	240 09
AND YET HAST THOU NOT KNOWN ME, PHILIP	240 12
HOLY GHOST, AND PHILIP, AND PROCHORUS, AND NICANCR,	532 16

PHILIPPI

| OF CAESAREA PHILIPPI, HE ASKED HIS DISCIPLES, SAYING, | 245 31 |

PHILISTIA

PHILISTIA, BE THOU GLAD OF ME   412 28
4 BEHOLD, PHILISTIA ALSO   448 20
UPON PHILISTIA WILL I TRIUMPH   479 23

PHILISTINES

THE PHILISTINES, WITH THEM THAT DWELL AT TYRE   444 18

PHINEHAS

THEN STOOD UP PHINEHAS, AND INTERPOSED   474 29

PHRASES

WORDS AND PHRASES, AS FROM THE LOCAL REFERENCES   R 610 29

PHRONEMA

IN GREEK, PHRONEMA SARKOS, (WHICH SOME DO EXPOUND THE 604 36

PHRYGIA

AND ASIA, PHRYGIA, AND PAMPHYLIA, IN EGYPT, AND IN   181 03

PHYSICIAN

NEED NOT A PHYSICIAN, BUT THEY THAT ARE SICK   251 20
SAINT LUKE THE PHYSICIAN, TO SET FORTH IN THE GOSPEL   253 17

PICKING

MY HANDS FROM PICKING AND STEALING   289 04
MY HANDS FROM PICKING AND STEALING, AND MY TONGUE   580 09

PIECE

THEY GAVE HIM A PIECE OF A BROILED FISH, AND OF AN   170 05
I HAVE BOUGHT A PIECE OF GROUND, AND I MUST NEEDS GO   192 07
IF SHE LOSE ONE PIECE, DOTH NOT LIGHT A CANDLE, AND   193 28
I HAVE FOUND THE PIECE WHICH I HAD LOST   193 32

PIECES

AGAIN THE THIRTY PIECES OF SILVER TO THE CHIEF   135 04
HE CAST DOWN THE PIECES OF SILVER IN THE TEMPLE,   135 07
TOOK THE SILVER PIECES, AND SAID, IT IS NOT LAWFUL   135 09
TOOK THE THIRTY PIECES OF SILVER, THE PRICE OF HIM   135 15
WOMAN HAVING TEN PIECES OF SILVER, IF SHE LOSE ONE   193 28
AND BREAK THEM IN PIECES LIKE A POTTER'S VESSEL   346 16
AND TEAR IT IN PIECES, *   349 26
THEY HUMBLY BRING PIECES OF SILVER   421 16
OF LEVIATHAN IN PIECES, *   431 04
HATH HEWN THE SNARES OF THE UNGODLY IN PIECES   506 28

PIERCE

A SWORD SHALL PIERCE THROUGH THY OWN SOUL ALSO,) THAT 233 14

PIERCED

WITH A SPEAR PIERCED HIS SIDE, AND FORTHWITH CAME   161 04
THEY SHALL LOOK ON HIM WHOM THEY PIERCED   161 10
17 THEY PIERCED MY HANDS AND MY FEET   367 06

PIETY

THE EXCITING OF PIETY AND DEVOTION IN THE WORSHIP OF   V 37
RELIGION AND PIETY, MAY BE ESTABLISHED AMONG US FOR   035 17
AND INSTRUCTIVE IN PIETY AND MORALS   R 610 25

PIGEONS

A PAIR OF TURTLE-DOVES, OR TWO YOUNG PIGEONS   232 29

PILATE

UNDER PONTIUS PILATE, WAS CRUCIFIED, DEAD, AND   015 23
WAS CRUCIFIED ALSO FOR US UNDER PONTIUS PILATE   016 09
UNDER PONTIUS PILATE, WAS CRUCIFIED, DEAD, AND   029 28
WAS CRUCIFIED ALSO FOR US UNDER PONTIUS PILATE   030 14
WAS CRUCIFIED ALSO FOR US UNDER PONTIUS PILATE   071 11
HIM TO PONTIUS PILATE THE GOVERNOR   134 33
THEN SAID PILATE UNTO HIM, HEAREST THOU NOT HOW MANY   135 22
PILATE SAID UNTO THEM, WHOM WILL YE THAT I   135 29
PILATE SAITH UNTO THEM, WHAT SHALL I DO THEN WITH   136 04
WHEN PILATE SAW THAT HE COULD PREVAIL NOTHING, BUT   136 08
AND PILATE ASKED HIM, ART THOU THE KING OF THE JEWS   145 06
AND CARRIED HIM AWAY, AND DELIVERED HIM TO PILATE   145 06
AND PILATE ASKED HIM AGAIN, SAYING, ANSWEREST THOU   145 09
SO THAT PILATE MARVELLED   145 12
BUT PILATE ANSWERED THEM, SAYING, WILL YE THAT I   145 18
AND PILATE ANSWERED AND SAID AGAIN UNTO THEM, WHAT   145 22
THEN PILATE SAID UNTO THEM, WHY, WHAT EVIL HATH HE   145 25
AND SO PILATE, WILLING TO CONTENT THE PEOPLE,   145 27
MULTITUDE OF THEM AROSE, AND LED HIM UNTO PILATE   152 28
AND PILATE ASKED HIM, SAYING, ART THOU THE KING OF   152 31
THEN SAID PILATE TO THE CHIEF PRIESTS AND TO THE   153 03
WHEN PILATE HEARD OF GALILEE, HE ASKED WHETHER THE   153 06
AND SENT HIM AGAIN TO PILATE   153 18
AND THE SAME DAY PILATE AND HEROD WERE MADE FRIENDS   153 19
AND PILATE, WHEN HE HAD CALLED TOGETHER THE CHIEF   153 20
PILATE THEREFORE, WILLING TO RELEASE JESUS, SPAKE   153 32
AND PILATE GAVE SENTENCE THAT IT SHOULD BE AS THEY   154 05
PILATE THEREFORE TOOK JESUS, AND SCOURGED HIM   158 30

PILATE   CONTINUED

PILATE THEREFORE WENT FORTH AGAIN, AND SAITH UNTO   158 34
AND PILATE SAITH UNTO THEM, BEHOLD THE MAN   159 04
PILATE SAITH UNTO THEM, TAKE YE HIM, AND CRUCIFY HIM   159 07
WHEN PILATE THEREFORE HEARD THAT SAYING, HE WAS THE   159 10
THEN SAITH PILATE UNTO HIM, SPEAKEST THOU NOT UNTO   159 13
FROM THENCEFORTH PILATE SOUGHT TO RELEASE HIM   159 19
WHEN PILATE THEREFORE HEARD THAT SAYING, HE BROUGHT   159 22
PILATE SAITH UNTO THEM, SHALL I CRUCIFY YOUR KING   159 28
AND PILATE WROTE A TITLE, AND PUT IT ON THE CROSS   159 35
OF THE JEWS TO PILATE, WRITE NOT, THE KING OF THE   160 06
PILATE ANSWERED, WHAT I HAVE WRITTEN I HAVE WRITTEN   160 08
BESOUGHT PILATE THAT THEIR LEGS MIGHT BE   160 33
HE WENT TO PILATE, AND BEGGED THE BODY OF JESUS   162 08
THEN PILATE COMMANDED THE BODY TO BE DELIVERED   162 09
TOGETHER UNTO PILATE, SAYING, SIR, WE REMEMBER THAT   162 17
PILATE SAID UNTO THEM, YE HAVE A WATCH   162 23
YET DESIRED THEY PILATE THAT HE SHOULD BE SLAIN   168 31
UNDER PONTIUS PILATE, WAS CRUCIFIED, DEAD, AND   284 17
UNDER PONTIUS PILATE, WAS CRUCIFIED, DEAD, AND   577 32

PILGRIMAGE

STILL IN OUR PILGRIMAGE, AND WHO WALK AS YET BY   336 06
IN THE HOUSE OF MY PILGRIMAGE   493 19

PILGRIMS

STRANGERS AND PILGRIMS, ABSTAIN FROM FLESHLY LUSTS,   173 12

PILLAR

7 HE SPAKE UNTO THEM OUT OF THE CLOUDY PILLAR   462 30

PILLARS

I BEAR UP THE PILLARS OF IT   432 05

PINNACLE

HIM ON A PINNACLE OF THE TEMPLE, AND SAITH UNTO HIM,   126 31

PIOUS

WHICH PIOUS WORKS HAVE BEEN APPROVED OF AND   564 20
BENEFIT OF THIS PIOUS WORK, MAY SHOW FORTH THEIR   566 32

PIPE

PRAISE HIM UPON THE STRINGS AND PIPE   525 29

PIT

AN OX FALLEN INTO A PIT, AND WILL NOT STRAIGHTWAY   214 06
AND WHO WILL GIVE THEE THANKS IN THE PIT   349 09
AND DIGGED UP A PIT, *   350 23
ARE SUNK DOWN IN THE PIT THAT THEY MADE   352 21
I BECOME LIKE THEM THAT GO DOWN INTO THE PIT   373 06
THAT I SHOULD NOT GO DOWN INTO THE PIT   374 29
WHEN I GO DOWN INTO THE PIT   375 11
HAVE THEY MADE A PIT FOR MY SOUL   382 03
OUT OF THE HORRIBLE PIT, OUT OF THE MIRE AND CLAY, *   390 11
AND LET THEM GO DOWN ALIVE INTO THE PIT   407 21
BRING THEM INTO THE PIT OF DESTRUCTION   408 07
THEY HAVE DIGGED A PIT BEFORE ME, AND ARE FALLEN INTO 409 27
AND LET NOT THE PIT SHUT HER MOUTH UPON ME   423 02
GO DOWN INTO THE PIT, *   449 03
ME IN THE LOWEST PIT, *   449 07
UNTIL THE PIT BE DIGGED UP FOR THE UNGODLY   458 13
AND INTO THE PIT, THAT THEY NEVER RISE UP   516 30
SCATTERED BEFORE THE PIT, *   517 26
I BE LIKE UNTO THEM THAT GO DOWN INTO THE PIT   519 06

PITCHED

TENT THAT HE HAD PITCHED AMONG MEN   438 33

PITCHER

A MAN BEARING A PITCHER OF WATER   140 27
BEARING A PITCHER OF WATER   148 26

PITIED

HIS COVENANT, AND PITIED THEM, ACCORDING UNTO THE   475 27

PITIETH

AND IT PITIETH THEM TO SEE HER IN THE DUST   465 08
LIKE AS A FATHER PITIETH HIS OWN CHILDREN   466 32

PITIFUL

AS BRETHREN, BE PITIFUL, BE COURTEOUS   195 21

PITIFULNESS

YET LET THE PITIFULNESS OF THY GREAT MERCY LOOSE US   063 12

PITS

PROUD HAVE DIGGED PITS FOR ME, *   495 27

PITY

LOOK WITH PITY, WE BESEECH THEE, UPON THE SORROWS OF   045 32
AND TO SHOW THY PITY UPON ALL PRISONERS AND CAPTIVES   056 32
WITH PITY BEHOLD THE SORROWS OF OUR HEARTS   059 11
AND OF GREAT PITY   062 32
HIS LOVE AND IN HIS PITY HE REDEEMED THEM   139 03
ALMIGHTY POWER CHIEFLY IN SHOWING MERCY AND PITY   204 23
LET THY CONTINUAL PITY CLEANSE AND DEFEND THY CHURCH   212 04
EVEN AS I HAD PITY ON THEE   222 02
FOR SOME TO HAVE PITY ON ME, BUT THERE WAS NO MAN,   423 14
AWAY CAPTIVE TO PITY THEM   475 29
THERE BE NO MAN TO PITY HIM, *   480 23
DO THOU, THE GOD OF PITY, ADMINISTER TO THEM   591 03
REMEMBER IN PITY SUCH AS ARE THIS DAY DESTITUTE,   599 06

PLACE

THE HIGH AND HOLY PLACE, WITH HIM ALSO THAT IS OF A   003 27
AND IN EVERY PLACE INCENSE SHALL BE OFFERED UNTO MY   004 14
THOSE THAT ARE IN PLACE OF AUTHORITY SHOULD, FROM   V 19
THAT PSALM 95 MAY BE USED IN THIS PLACE   R 008 11
HE WENT INTO THE PLACE OF DEPARTED SPIRITS, WHICH ARE   R 015 17
THY HOUSE, AND THE PLACE WHERE THINE HONOUR DWELLETH   021 15
OF GOD, THE HOLY PLACE OF THE TABERNACLES OF THE MOST   022 27
HE WENT INTO THE PLACE OF DEPARTED SPIRITS, WHICH ARE   R 029 22
THEY MAY NOT PLACE THEIR CONFIDENCE ANYWHERE BUT IN   046 23
WAS IN THE FIRST PLACE DRAWN TO THOSE ALTERATIONS IN   VI 15
HUMBLY PRESENT AND PLACE IT UPON THE HOLY TABLE   R 073 30
AND SHALL PLACE UPON THE HOLY TABLE, THE BREAD   R 073 32
TO PREPARE A PLACE FOR US   078 20
AND REVERENTLY PLACE UPON IT WHAT REMAINETH OF THE   R 083 12
BUT RATHER GIVE PLACE UNTO WRATH   113 04
NOW THERE WAS MUCH GRASS IN THE PLACE   132 02
ONCE INTO THE HOLY PLACE, HAVING OBTAINED ETERNAL   132 27
WERE COME UNTO A PLACE CALLED GOLGOTHA, THAT IS TO   136 08
THAT IS TO SAY, A PLACE OF A SKULL, THEY GAVE HIM   136 28
AND THEY CAME TO A PLACE WHICH WAS NAMED GETHSEMANE   141 27
THE PLACE OF A SKULL   146 08
BRING HIM UNTO THE PLACE GOLGOTHA, WHICH IS, BEING   146 08
INTO THE HOLY PLACE EVERY YEAR WITH BLOOD OF OTHERS   148 03
WHEN HE WAS AT THE PLACE, HE SAID UNTO THEM, PRAY   150 15
ALL JEWRY, BEGINNING FROM GALILEE TO THIS PLACE   153 06
WERE COME TO THE PLACE WHICH IS CALLED CALVARY, THERE   154 22
JUDGMENT-SEAT IN A PLACE THAT IS CALLED THE PAVEMENT,   159 23
WENT FORTH INTO A PLACE CALLED THE PLACE OF A SKULL,   159 32
A PLACE CALLED THE PLACE OF A SKULL, WHICH IS CALLED   159 32
FOR THE PLACE WHERE JESUS WAS CRUCIFIED WAS NIGH TO   160 04
TOGETHER IN A PLACE BY ITSELF   164 24
BEHOLD THE PLACE WHERE THEY LAID HIM   165 30
US UNTO THE SAME PLACE WHITHER OUR SAVIOUR CHRIST IS   179 08
COME, THEY WERE ALL WITH ONE ACCORD IN ONE PLACE   180 18
COME INTO THIS PLACE OF TORMENT   190 25
WHEN HE WAS AT THE PLACE, CAME AND LOOKED ON HIM, AND   208 26
AND HIM COME AND SAY TO THEE, GIVE THIS MAN PLACE   214 14
THOU BEGIN WITH SHAME TO TAKE THE LOWEST PLACE   214 15
ART BIDDEN, GO AND SIT DOWN IN THE LOWEST PLACE   214 16
NEITHER GIVE PLACE TO THE DEVIL   216 19
HE SAID UNTO THEM, GIVE PLACE   224 26
NOW THERE WAS MUCH GRASS IN THE PLACE   225 32
WHO INTO THE PLACE OF THE TRAITOR JUDAS DIDST   233 31
THAT HE MIGHT GO TO HIS OWN PLACE   234 31
I GO TO PREPARE A PLACE FOR YOU   239 32
I GO AND PREPARE A PLACE FOR YOU, I WILL COME AGAIN,   239 33
NEITHER WAS THEIR PLACE FOUND ANY MORE IN HEAVEN   252 05
EVERY CITY AND PLACE, WHITHER HE HIMSELF WOULD COME   254 12
THEE IN THIS PLACE, MAY OBTAIN THY MERCIFUL AID AND   259 22
HE FOUND THE PLACE WHERE IT WAS WRITTEN, THE   261 15
IN SOME CONVENIENT PLACE, AS HATH BEEN ACCUSTOMED, OR   R 305 08
SEND HIM HELP FROM THY HOLY PLACE   308 25
TO GRANT HIM A PLACE OF REFRESHMENT AND EVERLASTING   318 17
IN THE SECRET PLACE OF HIS DWELLING SHALL HE   326 13
THE HOLY PLACE OF THE TABERNACLE OF THE MOST HIGHEST   327 10
I GO TO PREPARE A PLACE FOR YOU   331 20
I GO AND PREPARE A PLACE FOR YOU, I WILL COME AGAIN,   331 21
HIS SECRET PLACE, *   360 19
FORTH ALSO INTO A PLACE OF LIBERTY   361 04
OR WHO SHALL RISE UP IN HIS HOLY PLACE   368 33
AND THE PLACE WHERE THINE HONOUR DWELLETH   371 13
IN THE SECRET PLACE OF HIS DWELLING SHALL HE   372 05
8 THOU ART A PLACE TO HIDE ME IN   378 05
LOOK AFTER HIS PLACE, AND HE SHALL BE AWAY   385 14
BUT HIS PLACE COULD NO WHERE BE FOUND   387 07
US INTO THE PLACE OF DRAGONS, *   395 32
THE HOLY PLACE OF THE TABERNACLE OF THE MOST HIGHEST   397 33
OF SION IS A FAIR PLACE, AND THE JOY OF THE WHOLE   399 12
AND THOU BROUGHTEST US OUT INTO A WEALTHY PLACE   418 06
AS IN THE HOLY PLACE OF SINAI   420 18
15 AND THE PLACE OF THE VINEYARD THAT THY RIGHT HAND   441 32
IN A PLACE OF DARKNESS, AND IN THE DEEP   449 07
AND THE PLACE THEREOF SHALL KNOW IT NO MORE   467 07
EVEN UNTO THE PLACE WHICH THOU HAST APPOINTED FOR   468 09
UNTIL I FIND OUT A PLACE FOR THE TEMPLE OF THE LORD   508 13
5 I HAD NO PLACE TO FLEE UNTO, *   518 12
THAT THERE BE NO PLACE LEFT AMONG YOU, EITHER FOR   540 21
REMAIN IN THE SAME PLACE WHERE HANDS WERE LAID UPON   R 546 30
THAT AFTER THIS PLACE, THAT IT MAY PLEASE THEE TO   R 553 14
OR WHO SHALL RISE UP IN HIS HOLY PLACE   563 16
SETTING APART THIS PLACE IN SOLEMN MANNER, FOR THE   564 23
TO CONSECRATE THIS PLACE TO THE HONOUR OF THY GREAT   565 05
THEY WHO AT THIS PLACE SHALL IN THEIR OWN PERSONS   565 23
RECEIVE IN THIS PLACE THE BLESSED SACRAMENT OF THE   565 29
PREACHED IN THIS PLACE, AND BY THY HOLY SPIRIT   566 03
TOGETHER IN THIS PLACE IN THE HOLY ESTATE OF   566 09
TO THEE IN THIS PLACE, TO GIVE THEE THANKS FOR THE   566 14
DEDICATION OF THIS PLACE TO THY SERVICE   567 07

PLACE   CONTINUED

THAT IN THIS PLACE NOW SET APART TO THY   568 10
SUPPLYING HIS PLACE) HOLDING THE KEYS OF THE CHURCH   R 570 09
SUPPLYING HIS PLACE) PRESENT THE KEYS OF THE CHURCH   R 570 26
OR DENY THE PLACE OF FORGIVENESS TO SUCH AS   606 04
IT SO EXPOUND ONE PLACE OF SCRIPTURE, THAT IT BE   607 06

PLACED

WHO HATH PLACED YOU IN SO HIGH A DIGNITY   540 28

PLACES

IN SUNDRY PLACES, TO ACKNOWLEDGE AND CONFESS OUR   005 30
INTO THE HOLY PLACES MADE WITH HANDS, WHICH ARE THE   022 22
IN SUNDRY PLACES, TO ACKNOWLEDGE AND CONFESS OUR   023 05
OF HIS, IN ALL PLACES OF HIS DOMINION   029 18
IN PLACES WHERE IT MAY BE CONVENIENT, HERE   R 031 30
IN ALL PLACES, TO THE BREAKING DOWN THE   037 04
AND IN ALL PLACES, GIVE THANKS UNTO THEE, O   076 32
IN HEAVENLY PLACES MIGHT BE KNOWN BY THE CHURCH THE   108 24
THROUGH DRY PLACES, SEEKING REST   130 11
INTO THE HOLY PLACES MADE WITH HANDS, WHICH ARE THE   147 30
AGAINST SPIRITUAL WICKEDNESS IN HIGH PLACES   219 10
AND THE ROUGH PLACES PLAIN   242 24
MAKE THEM AND THE PLACES ROUND ABOUT MY HILL A   262 07
OF HIS, IN ALL PLACES OF HIS DOMINION   313 03
IT WERE A LION'S WHELP LURKING IN SECRET PLACES   359 11
WONDERFUL ART THOU IN THY HOLY PLACES   421 27
THEM IN SLIPPERY PLACES, *   429 12
UPON THY HOLY PLACES, *   430 18
OF HIS, IN ALL PLACES OF HIS DOMINION   467 21
SO THAT RIVERS RAN IN THE DRY PLACES   472 20
LET THEM SEEK IT ALSO OUT OF DESOLATE PLACES   480 20
HE SHALL FILL THE PLACES WITH THE DEAD BODIES,   482 19
AND IN THE SEA, AND IN ALL DEEP PLACES   510 14
IN STONY PLACES, *   517 24
MIND TO ALL IN PLACES OF AUTHORITY   600 03
BE IN ALL PLACES ONE, OR UTTERLY LIKE   609 32

PLAGUE

FROM PLAGUE, PESTILENCE, AND FAMINE   054 31
AM SET IN THE PLAGUE, *   388 26
11 TAKE THY PLAGUE AWAY FROM ME   389 29
AND PLAGUE THEM THAT HATE HIM   451 22
NEITHER SHALL ANY PLAGUE COME NIGH THY DWELLING   455 16
AND THE PLAGUE WAS GREAT AMONG THEM   474 28
AND SO THE PLAGUE CEASED   474 30
THROUGH ANY PLAGUE OR TROUBLE   478 25

PLAGUED

NEITHER ARE THEY PLAGUED LIKE OTHER MEN   428 19
THAT THOU HAST PLAGUED US   454 20
FOOLISH MEN ARE PLAGUED FOR THEIR OFFENCE, *   477 09

PLAGUES

11 GREAT PLAGUES REMAIN FOR THE UNGODLY   378 13

PLAIN

OF HIS TONGUE WAS LOOSED, AND HE SPAKE PLAIN   207 04
AND THE ROUGH PLACES PLAIN   242 24
MAKE THY WAY PLAIN BEFORE MY FACE   348 17
REPUGNANT TO THE PLAIN WORDS OF SCRIPTURE,   608 42

PLAINEST

THE CLEAREST, PLAINEST, MOST AFFECTING AND MAJESTIC   VI 41

PLAINLY

I SHALL SHEW YOU PLAINLY OF THE FATHER   176 26
SPEAKEST THOU PLAINLY, AND SPEAKEST NO PROVERB   176 32
YE SHALL ANSWER PLAINLY TO THESE THINGS, WHICH WE,   541 27
CHRIST SAITH PLAINLY, WHEN YE HAVE DONE ALL THAT ARE   605 28
IT IS A THING PLAINLY REPUGNANT TO THE WORD OF GOD,   607 27

PLANT

UP FOR THEM A PLANT OF RENOWN, AND THEY SHALL BE NO   262 17
THEIR LAND, AND PLANT VINEYARDS, *   478 20

PLANTED

OF THE SAME PLANTED BY GOD IN THIS LAND, WHEREOF WE   047 12
IF WE HAVE BEEN PLANTED TOGETHER IN THE LIKENESS OF   197 15
BE LIKE A TREE PLANTED BY THE WATER-SIDE, *   345 12
THY HAND, AND PLANTED OUR FATHERS IN   394 25
THE HEATHEN, AND PLANTED IT   441 19
RIGHT HAND HATH PLANTED, *   441 33
12 SUCH AS ARE PLANTED IN THE HOUSE OF THE LORD,   456 26
9 HE THAT PLANTED THE EAR, SHALL HE NOT HEAR   458 04
EVEN THE CEDARS OF LEBANON WHICH HE HATH PLANTED   468 27

PLANTING

AND FOR PLANTING THY CHURCH IN ALL THE EARTH   038 18
THE PLANTING OF THE LORD, THAT HE MIGHT BE GLORIFIED   107 10

PLANTS

UP AS THE YOUNG PLANTS, *   520 15

PLATTED

WHEN THEY HAD PLATTED A CROWN OF THORNS, THEY PUT IT	136 18
WITH PURPLE, AND PLATTED A CROWN OF THORNS, AND PUT	145 32
AND THE SOLDIERS PLATTED A CROWN OF THORNS, AND PUT	158 31

PLAY

SAT DOWN TO EAT AND DRINK, AND ROSE UP TO PLAY	201 16

PLAYING

OF THE DAMSELS PLAYING WITH THE TIMBRELS	421 05
O GOD, PLAYING UPON AN INSTRUMENT OF MUSIC	426 23

PLEAD

PLEAD THOU MY CAUSE, O LORD, WITH THEM THAT STRIVE	381 17

PLEASANT

JERUSALEM BE PLEASANT UNTO THE LORD, AS IN THE DAYS	232 14
A JOYFUL AND PLEASANT THING IT IS TO BE THANKFUL	264 19
SCORN OF THAT PLEASANT LAND, *	474 17
A JOYFUL AND PLEASANT THING IT IS TO BE THANKFUL	522 28
DO GOOD WORKS PLEASANT AND ACCEPTABLE TO GOD, WITHOUT	604 44
ARE NOT PLEASANT TO GOD, FORASMUCH AS THEY	605 18
FULL OF SWEET, PLEASANT, AND UNSPEAKABLE COMFORT TO	606 17

PLEASE

THOSE THINGS MAY PLEASE HIM WHICH WE DO AT THIS	007 15
THEY MAY TRULY PLEASE THEE, POUR UPON THEM THE	018 22
THAT IT MAY PLEASE THEE TO COMFORT AND RELIEVE THEM,	019 07
THOSE THINGS MAY PLEASE HIM WHICH WE DO AT THIS	024 17
THEY MAY TRULY PLEASE THEE, POUR UPON THEM THE	032 21
THAT IT MAY PLEASE THEE TO COMFORT AND RELIEVE THEM,	033 05
SUCH THINGS AS PLEASE THEE, TO THE GLORY OF THY NAME	035 27
THAT IT MAY PLEASE GOD TO CONFIRM AND STRENGTHEN IT	047 08
AND THAT IT MAY PLEASE THEE TO RULE AND GOVERN THY	055 19
THAT IT MAY PLEASE THEE SO TO RULE THE HEART OF THY	055 22
THAT IT MAY PLEASE THEE TO BLESS AND PRESERVE ALL	055 26
THAT IT MAY PLEASE THEE TO ILLUMINATE ALL BISHOPS,	055 30
THAT IT MAY PLEASE THEE TO SEND FORTH LABOURERS INTO	056 02
THAT IT MAY PLEASE THEE TO BLESS AND KEEP ALL THY	056 05
THAT IT MAY PLEASE THEE TO GIVE TO ALL NATIONS UNITY,	056 08
THAT IT MAY PLEASE THEE TO GIVE US AN HEART TO LOVE	056 11
THAT IT MAY PLEASE THEE TO GIVE TO ALL THY PEOPLE	056 14
THAT IT MAY PLEASE THEE TO BRING INTO THE WAY OF	056 19
THAT IT MAY PLEASE THEE TO STRENGTHEN SUCH AS DO	056 22
THAT IT MAY PLEASE THEE TO SUCCOUR, HELP, AND	056 27
THAT IT MAY PLEASE THEE TO PRESERVE ALL WHO TRAVEL BY	056 30
THAT IT MAY PLEASE THEE TO DEFEND, AND PROVIDE FOR,	056 35
THAT IT MAY PLEASE THEE TO HAVE MERCY UPON ALL MEN	057 05
THAT IT MAY PLEASE THEE TO FORGIVE OUR ENEMIES,	057 07
THAT IT MAY PLEASE THEE TO GIVE AND PRESERVE TO OUR	057 10
THAT IT MAY PLEASE THEE TO GIVE US TRUE REPENTANCE	057 14
SERVE AND PLEASE THEE IN NEWNESS OF LIFE, TO THE	075 29
TO WALK AND TO PLEASE GOD, SO YE WOULD ABOUND MORE	127 25
WE MAY PLEASE THEE, BOTH IN WILL AND DEED	189 04
THINGS AS SHALL PLEASE THEE	203 13
ARE NOT ABLE TO PLEASE THEE	215 28
WHICH IT SHALL PLEASE GOD TO CALL ME	289 10
THAT IT MAY PLEASE THEE TO DELIVER THE SOUL OF THY	318 11
THAT IT MAY PLEASE THEE MERCIFULLY TO PARDON ALL HIS	318 15
THAT IT MAY PLEASE THEE TO GRANT HIM A PLACE OF	318 17
THAT IT MAY PLEASE THEE TO GIVE HIM JOY AND GLADNESS	318 20
IT SHALL PLEASE ALMIGHTY GOD TO CALL THEM, THE	R 321 05
THIS ALSO SHALL PLEASE THE LORD *	424 06
SO SHALL MY WORDS PLEASE HIM	469 29
OF MY MOUTH PLEASE THEE, O LORD	497 13
OF SUCH THINGS AS PLEASE THEM	517 18
THAT IT MAY PLEASE THEE TO ILLUMINATE ALL BISHOPS,	R 531 02
THAT IT MAY PLEASE THEE TO BLESS THESE THY SERVANTS,	531 04
THAT IT MAY PLEASE THEE TO ILLUMINATE ALL BISHOPS,	R 537 08
THAT IT MAY PLEASE THEE TO BLESS THESE THY SERVANTS,	537 10
THAT IT MAY PLEASE THEE TO ILLUMINATE ALL BISHOPS,	R 553 15
THAT IT MAY PLEASE THEE TO BLESS THIS OUR BROTHER	553 17
AND THAT IT MAY PLEASE THEE TO GRANT PEACE TO THE	560 12
THAT IT MAY PLEASE THEE TO SANCTIFY AND BLESS THY	560 15
THAT IT MAY PLEASE THEE TO INSPIRE ALL BISHOPS,	560 18
THAT IT MAY PLEASE THEE TO ENDUE ALL MINISTERS OF THY	560 21
THAT IT MAY PLEASE THEE TO BLESS THESE THY	560 26
THAT IT MAY PLEASE THEE TO BLESS THIS OUR	561 02
THAT IT MAY PLEASE THEE TO GUIDE BY THY INDWELLING	561 07
THAT IT MAY PLEASE THEE TO INCREASE THE NUMBER OF THE	561 12
THAT IT MAY PLEASE THEE TO HASTEN THE FULFILMENT OF	561 16
THAT IT MAY PLEASE THEE TO GRANT THAT WE, WITH ALL	561 19
WHICH IT SHALL PLEASE GOD TO CALL ME	580 14
AND THAT IT WILL PLEASE HIM TO SAVE AND DEFEND US IN	580 35

PLEASED

THOU WOULDEST BE PLEASED TO MAKE THY WAYS KNOWN UNTO	018 28
THOU WOULDEST BE PLEASED TO MAKE THY WAYS KNOWN UNTO	032 28
THOU WOULDEST BE PLEASED TO DIRECT AND PROSPER ALL	035 11
THOU WOULDEST BE PLEASED TO FILL IT WITH ALL TRUTH,	037 16
BEEN GRACIOUSLY PLEASED TO PRESERVE, THROUGH THE	051 06
THAT IT HATH PLEASED THEE TO SEND US RAIN TO OUR	051 18
THAT IT HATH PLEASED THEE TO APPEASE THE SEDITIOUS	052 20
THOU HAST BEEN PLEASED TO DELIVER FROM HIS BODILY	052 30
BEEN GRACIOUSLY PLEASED TO DELIVER FROM HIS BODILY	053 12
THOU HAST BEEN PLEASED TO CONDUCT IN SAFETY, THROUGH	053 22
FOR WITH SUCH SACRIFICES GOD IS WELL PLEASED	072 28
IN WHOM I AM WELL PLEASED	112 23
BUT WITH MANY OF THEM GOD WAS NOT WELL PLEASED	201 12

PLEASED   CONTINUED

HE SAW IT PLEASED THE JEWS, HE PROCEEDED FURTHER TO	245 02
HE SAW IT PLEASED THE JEWS, HE PROCEEDED FURTHER TO	247 03
IN WHOM I AM WELL PLEASED	248 19
THAT IT HATH PLEASED THEE TO REGENERATE THIS CHILD	280 29
AS IT HATH PLEASED ALMIGHTY GOD, OF HIS GOODNESS, TO	305 11
BEEN GRACIOUSLY PLEASED TO PRESERVE, THROUGH THE	306 25
WHEN THOU ART PLEASED TO TAKE HIM HENCE, TAKE HIM	314 11
BODY AS IT HATH PLEASED HIM, AND TO EVERY SEED ITS	329 10
WHO HAST BEEN PLEASED TO TAKE UNTO THYSELF THE SOUL	336 04
SHALT THOU BE PLEASED WITH THE SACRIFICE OF	404 15
DONE WHATSOEVER PLEASED HIM	485 17
THE LORD PLEASED, THAT DID HE IN HEAVEN, AND IN	510 13
AND THE SAYING PLEASED THE WHOLE MULTITUDE	532 15
IT HATH PLEASED GOD TO CALL YOU	541 12
BEEN GRACIOUSLY PLEASED TO PROMISE THY ESPECIAL	564 30
THAT IT HATH PLEASED THEE TO PUT IT INTO THE HEARTS	566 28
FOR THAT IT HATH PLEASED THEE TO HAVE THY HABITATION	568 07
BE GRACIOUSLY PLEASED TO BLESS THE MINISTRY AND	572 19
BE GRACIOUSLY PLEASED TO TAKE US, AND ALL WHO ARE	589 03

PLEASETH

IN THE WHICH IT PLEASETH HIM TO DWELL	420 14
THE THING THAT PLEASETH THEE	519 12

PLEASING

THINGS THAT ARE PLEASING IN HIS SIGHT	191 29
LORD UNTO ALL PLEASING, BEING FRUITFUL IN EVERY GOOD	224 04
WHICH IS WELL PLEASING IN HIS SIGHT	335 20
WHICH IS WELL PLEASING IN HIS SIGHT	573 07
YET ARE THEY PLEASING AND ACCEPTABLE TO GOD IN	605 13

PLEASURE

YE SERVANTS OF HIS THAT DO HIS PLEASURE	029 16
HOLY WILL AND PLEASURE, AND STUDYING TO SERVE HIM IN	086 21
YOU BOTH TO WILL AND TO DO OF HIS GOOD PLEASURE	106 05
AND SACRIFICES FOR SIN THOU HAST HAD NO PLEASURE	157 27
NEITHER HADST PLEASURE THEREIN	157 30
AND FOR THY PLEASURE THEY ARE, AND WERE CREATED	187 31
SHALL HAVE NO PLEASURE IN HIM	228 20
YE SERVANTS OF HIS THAT DO HIS PLEASURE	312 32
HAND THERE IS PLEASURE FOR EVERMORE	333 10
AND HAVE SUCH PLEASURE IN VANITY, AND SEEK AFTER	347 14
THAT HAST NO PLEASURE IN WICKEDNESS	348 07
HAND THERE IS PLEASURE FOR EVERMORE	358 14
AND IN HIS PLEASURE IS LIFE	375 02
WHO HAVE PLEASURE IN THE PROSPERITY OF HIS	383 21
LET IT BE THY PLEASURE TO DELIVER ME	391 14
THE KING HAVE PLEASURE IN THY BEAUTY	397 07
YE SERVANTS OF HIS THAT DO HIS PLEASURE	467 19
THEM THAT HAVE PLEASURE THEREIN	482 27
10 HE HATH NO PLEASURE IN THE STRENGTH OF AN HORSE	523 15
THE LORD HATH PLEASURE IN HIS PEOPLE, *	525 09

PLEASURES

AND RICHES AND PLEASURES OF THIS LIFE, AND BRING NO	122 07
DRINK OF THY PLEASURES, AS OUT OF THE RIVER	384 12
WITH THE PLEASURES OF THY HOUSE, EVEN OF THY HOLY	416 19

PLEDGE

GIVETH US A PLEDGE OF LIFE ETERNAL	152 11
THIS GRACE, AND A PLEDGE TO ASSURE US THEREOF	292 13
IS A TOKEN AND PLEDGE,) AND MAY EVER REMAIN IN	303 09
THE SAME, AND A PLEDGE TO ASSURE US THEREOF	581 15

PLEDGED

HAVE GIVEN AND PLEDGED THEIR TROTH, EACH TO THE	304 05

PLEDGES

AS PLEDGES OF HIS LOVE, AND FOR A	086 17
AS THE PLEDGES OF MY INSTITUTION, AND OF YOUR	570 33

PLENTEOUS

TRULY IS PLENTEOUS, BUT THE LABOURERS ARE FEW	073 11
WITH HIM IS PLENTEOUS REDEMPTION	328 16
THOU MAKEST IT VERY PLENTEOUS	416 33
PLENTEOUS IN GOODNESS AND TRUTH	448 05
WITH HIM IS PLENTEOUS REDEMPTION	507 21
BE FULL AND PLENTEOUS WITH ALL MANNER OF STORE	520 18
TRULY IS PLENTEOUS, BUT THE LABOURERS ARE FEW	538 17

PLENTEOUSLY

ENDUE THEM PLENTEOUSLY WITH HEAVENLY GIFTS	018 02
HE THAT SOWETH PLENTEOUSLY SHALL REAP PLENTEOUSLY	072 17
THAT SOWETH PLENTEOUSLY SHALL REAP PLENTEOUSLY	072 17
IF THOU HAST MUCH, GIVE PLENTEOUSLY	072 33
THAT THEY, PLENTEOUSLY BRINGING FORTH THE FRUIT OF	225 05
BY THEE BE PLENTEOUSLY REWARDED	225 06
AND PLENTEOUSLY REWARDETH THE PROUD DOER	377 16
10 GOD SHOWETH ME HIS GOODNESS PLENTEOUSLY	411 24

PLENTEOUSNESS

AND FILLEST ALL THINGS LIVING WITH PLENTEOUSNESS	040 04
WITH THE PLENTEOUSNESS OF THY HOUSE	384 11
THEM PLENTEOUSNESS OF TEARS TO DRINK	441 13

PLENTEOUSNESS   CONTINUED

RICHES AND PLENTEOUSNESS SHALL BE IN HIS HOUSE   483 22
AND PLENTEOUSNESS WITHIN THY PALACES   503 20
AND FILLEST ALL THINGS LIVING WITH PLENTEOUSNESS   521 25

PLENTIFUL

21 O HOW PLENTIFUL IS THY GOODNESS, WHICH THOU HAST   377 02

PLENTY

BE FILLED WITH PLENTY, AND THY PRESSES SHALL BURST   005 22
THY GOODNESS, BE MERCIFULLY TURNED INTO PLENTY   041 05
AND TURNED OUR DEARTH AND SCARCITY INTO PLENTY   051 32

PLIGHT

AND THERETO I PLIGHT THEE MY TROTH   301 32

PLOTTINGS

FROM THE PLOTTINGS OF MEN   377 07

PLOWED

3 THE PLOWERS PLOWED UPON MY BACK, *   506 25

PLOWERS

3 THE PLOWERS PLOWED UPON MY BACK, *   506 25

PLUCK

EYE OFFEND THEE, PLUCK IT OUT, AND CAST IT FROM THEE   253 07
FOR HE SHALL PLUCK MY FEET OUT OF THE NET   370 15
3 O PLUCK ME NOT AWAY, NEITHER DESTROY ME WITH THE   373 10
LEST I PLUCK YOU AWAY, AND THERE BE NCNE TO DELIVER   403 02
TAKE THEE, AND PLUCK THEE OUT OF THY DWELLING, AND   404 29
THEY THAT GO BY PLUCK OFF HER GRAPES   441 27

PLUCKED

TO THEM THAT PLUCKED OFF THE HAIR   144 14

PLUCKEST

WHY PLUCKEST THOU NOT THY RIGHT HAND OUT OF THY BOSOM   430 29

POINT

IN ANY ESSENTIAL POINT OF DOCTRINE, DISCIPLINE,   VI 33
FOR HE WAS AT THE POINT OF DEATH   219 32
HIM THAT IS AT THE POINT TO DIE   449 27

POISON

VENOMOUS AS THE POISON OF A SERPENT, *   410 15
ADDER'S POISON IS UNDER THEIR LIPS   516 14

POLISHED

MAY BE AS THE POLISHED CORNERS OF THE TEMPLE   520 16

POMP

HIS WORKS, THE VAIN POMP AND GLORY OF THE WCRLD, WITH   276 25
HIS WORKS, THE VAIN POMP AND GLORY OF THE WORLD,   277 27
NEITHER SHALL HIS POMP FOLLOW HIM   401 10

POMPS

ALL HIS WORKS, THE POMPS AND VANITY OF THIS WICKED   283 24
ALL HIS WORKS, THE POMPS AND VANITY OF THIS WICKED   577 15

PONDER

PONDER MY WORDS, O LORD, *   347 31
PONDER IT WITH YOUR EARS, ALL YE THAT DWELL IN THE   400 07
AND PONDER THE VOICE OF MY HUMBLE DESIRES   447 15
IS WISE, WILL PONDER THESE THINGS   478 32

PONDERED

AND PONDERED THEM IN HER HEART   106 16

PONTIUS

SUFFERED UNDER PONTIUS PILATE, WAS CRUCIFIED,   015 23
FOR US UNDER PONTIUS PILATE   016 09
SUFFERED UNDER PONTIUS PILATE, WAS CRUCIFIED,   029 28
FOR US UNDER PONTIUS PILATE   030 14
FOR US UNDER PONTIUS PILATE   071 11
DELIVERED HIM TO PONTIUS PILATE THE GOVERNCR   134 33
SUFFERED UNDER PONTIUS PILATE, WAS CRUCIFIED,   284 17
SUFFERED UNDER PONTIUS PILATE, WAS CRUCIFIED,   577 32

PONTUS

IN PONTUS, AND ASIA, PHRYGIA, AND   181 02

POOLS

AND THE POOLS ARE FILLED WITH WATER   445 24

POOR

THINGS THAT THE POOR AND NEEDY MAY GIVE THANKS UNTO   040 12
THE ALMS FOR THE POOR, AND OTHER OFFERINGS OF THE   R 073 28
RAISED UP, AND THE POOR HAVE THE GOSPEL PREACHED TO   094 23
GOODS TO FEED THE POOR, AND THOUGH I GIVE MY BCDY TO   122 27
AS POOR, YET MAKING MANY RICH   126 20
AND HAVE BEEN GIVEN TO THE POOR   140 09
FOR YE HAVE THE POOR WITH YOU ALWAYS, AND WHENSCEVER   140 12
BRING IN HITHER THE POOR, AND THE MAIMED, AND THE   192 15
BLESSED ARE THE POOR IN SPIRIT   257 21
HATH ANOINTED ME TO PREACH THE GOSPEL TO THE PCCR   261 17
AND FORGETTETH NOT THE COMPLAINT OF THE POOR   352 15
18 FOR THE POOR SHALL NOT ALWAY BE FORGOTTEN   352 28
DOTH PERSECUTE THE POOR   353 06
HIS EYES ARE SET AGAINST THE POOR   353 22
THAT HE MAY RAVISH THE POOR   353 24
HE DOTH RAVISH THE POOR, *   353 25
CONGREGATION OF THE POOR MAY FALL INTO THE HANDS OF   353 28
FORGET NOT THE POOR   353 33
16 THE POOR COMMITTETH HIMSELF UNTO THEE   354 07
THOU HAST HEARD THE DESIRE OF THE POOR   354 13
THE FATHERLESS AND POOR UNTO THEIR RIGHT, *   354 15
EYES CONSIDER THE POOR, *   354 28
DEEP SIGHING OF THE POOR, 6 I WILL UP, SAITH THE   355 17
YE HAVE MADE A MOCK AT THE COUNSEL OF THE PCCR   356 29
DESPISED NOR ABHORRED THE LOW ESTATE OF THE POOR   367 21
26 THE POOR SHALL EAT, AND BE SATISFIED   367 25
6 LO, THE POOR CRIETH, AND THE LORD HEARETH HIM   380 13
WHO DELIVEREST THE POOR FROM HIM THAT IS TOO STRCNG   382 10
THE POOR, AND HIM THAT IS IN MISERY, FROM HIM   382 11
TO CAST DOWN THE POOR AND NEEDY, AND TO SLAY SUCH AS   385 23
20 AS FOR ME, I AM POOR AND NEEDY   391 24
CONSIDERETH THE POOR AND NEEDY   391 30
AND LOW, RICH AND POOR, *   400 09
HAST OF THY GOODNESS PREPARED FOR THE POOR   419 32
FOR ME, WHEN I AM POOR AND IN HEAVINESS, *   424 02
LORD HEARETH THE POOR, *   424 10
5 AS FOR ME, I AM POOR AND IN MISERY   424 30
AND DEFEND THE POOR   426 34
THE CHILDREN OF THE POOR, AND PUNISH THE WRONG DCER   427 05
SHALL DELIVER THE POOR WHEN HE CRIETH   427 20
AND SHALL PRESERVE THE SOULS OF THE PCCR   427 23
CONGREGATION OF THE POOR FOR EVER   431 17
BUT LET THE POOR AND NEEDY GIVE PRAISE UNTO THY NAME   431 21
3 DEFEND THE POOR AND FATHERLESS   443 22
4 DELIVER THE OUTCAST AND POOR   443 24
FOR I AM POOR, AND IN MISERY   447 06
THE PRAYER OF THE POOR DESTITUTE, *   465 13
YET HELPETH HE THE POOR OUT OF MISERY, *   478 28
BUT PERSECUTED THE POOR HELPLESS MAN, THAT HE MIGHT   480 33
I AM HELPLESS AND POOR, *   481 14
RIGHT HAND OF THE POOR, *   482 02
AND GIVEN TO THE POOR, *   483 34
AND LIFTETH THE POOR OUT OF THE MIRE   484 20
WILL SATISFY HER POOR WITH BREAD   509 05
WILL AVENGE THE POOR, *   517 02
FOR THE SICK, POOR, AND IMPOTENT PEOPLE OF THE   533 19
CHRIST'S SAKE TO POOR AND NEEDY PEOPLE, AND TO ALL   555 24
BLESS THE CONGREGATION OF THY POOR   599 08
OUR SAKES BECAME POOR, THY SON, OUR SAVIOUR JESUS   599 16
TO GIVE ALMS TO THE POOR, ACCORDING TO HIS ABILITY   611 04

POORER

FOR RICHER FOR POORER, IN SICKNESS AND IN HEALTH,   301 30
FOR RICHER FOR POORER, IN SICKNESS AND IN HEALTH,   302 06

PORCH

WEEP BETWEEN THE PORCH AND THE ALTAR, AND LET THEM   125 03
AND HE WENT OUT INTO THE PORCH   143 28
THEY WERE ALL WITH ONE ACCORD IN SOLCMON'S PORCH   249 23

PORTER

TO HIM THE PORTER OPENETH   186 04
TO HIM THE PORTER OPENETH   538 27

PORTION

SHALL FOLLOW A PORTION OF THE PSALMS, ACCORDING TO   R 009 22
END OF THE WHOLE PORTION, OR SELECTION FROM THE   R 009 25
THE LATTER PORTION THEREOF MAY BE OMITTED   R 014 05
SHALL FOLLOW A PORTION OF THE PSALMS, ACCORDING TO   R 025 15
END OF THE WHOLE PORTION OR SELECTION OF PSALMS FOR   R 025 19
GIVE ME THE PORTION OF GOODS THAT FALLETH TO ME   201 32
MAY USE SUCH PORTION OF THE FOREGOING OFFICE AS HE   R 320 06
END OF THE WHOLE PORTION OR SELECTION FROM THE   R 324 18
SHALL BE THEIR PORTION TO DRINK   354 34
HIMSELF IS THE PORTION OF MINE INHERITANCE, AND OF MY   357 31
WHICH HAVE THEIR PORTION IN THIS LIFE, WHOSE BELLIES   359 15
THEY MAY BE A PORTION FOR FOXES   415 14
MY HEART, AND MY PORTION FOR EVER   429 29
THOU ART MY PORTION, O LORD   493 24
MY HOPE, AND MY PORTION IN THE LAND OF THE LIVING   518 15
THY FAMILY THEIR PORTION IN DUE SEASON, HE MAY AT   558 04
TO FEED THAT PORTION OF THE FLOCK OF CHRIST WHICH IS   569 24
OF A BRIEF PORTION OF HOLY SCRIPTURE, LET THE HEAD OF   R 592 09
OF A BRIEF PORTION OF HOLY SCRIPTURE, LET THE HEAD OF   R 593 03

POSSESS

KNOW HOW TO POSSESS HIS VESSEL IN SANCTIFICATION AND   127 29
IN THE WEEK, I GIVE TITHES OF ALL THAT I POSSESS   205 28

POSSESS   CONTINUED

SHALL POSSESS THE EARTH, *   385 16
OF GOD, SHALL POSSESS THE LAND   386 06
THAT THOU SHALT POSSESS THE LAND   387 02
LOVING HAND HATH GIVEN US ALL THAT WE POSSESS   599 20

POSSESSED

HOLINESS HAVE POSSESSED IT BUT A LITTLE WHILE   139 27
OR CHURCH,) POSSESSED OF FULL POWER TO PERFORM EVERY 569 18
AND WE ARE POSSESSED OF YOUR VOTE THAT HE HAS BEEN SO 570 15

POSSESSETH

THINGS AS HE POSSESSETH, LIBERALLY TO GIVE ALMS TO 611 03

POSSESSING

AND YET POSSESSING ALL THINGS   126 21

POSSESSION

THE UTMOST PARTS OF THE EARTH FOR THY POSSESSION   346 14
THE LAND IN POSSESSION THROUGH THEIR OWN SWORD, *   394 27
AND HAVE IT IN POSSESSION   424 15
AND THESE HAVE RICHES IN POSSESSION   428 33
THE HOUSES OF GOD IN POSSESSION   444 29
THEY TOOK THE LABOURS OF THE PEOPLE IN POSSESSION   472 26
AND ISRAEL FOR HIS OWN POSSESSION   510 10
AND POSSESSION OF THE SAME   611 02

POSSIBLE

IF IT BE POSSIBLE, AS MUCH AS LIETH IN YOU, LIVE   113 02
IF IT WERE POSSIBLE, THEY SHALL DECEIVE THE VERY   118 06
IF IT WERE POSSIBLE, THE HOUR MIGHT PASS FROM HIM   141 34
ALL THINGS ARE POSSIBLE UNTO THEE   141 35
FOR IT IS NOT POSSIBLE THAT THE BLOOD OF BULLS AND OF 157 22

POSTERITIES

AMONG THE POSTERITIES, WHICH SHALL BE BLESSED IN HIM 427 33
AMONG ALL POSTERITIES FOR EVERMORE   474 32

POSTERITY

YET THEIR POSTERITY PRAISE THEIR SAYING   400 32
37 THE POSTERITY ALSO OF HIS SERVANTS SHALL INHERIT 424 17
6 THAT THEIR POSTERITY MIGHT KNOW IT, *   435 07
12 LET HIS POSTERITY BE DESTROYED   480 25

POTS

9 OR EVER YOUR POTS BE MADE HOT WITH THORNS, *   410 26
AND HIS HANDS WERE DELIVERED FROM MAKING THE POTS   442 24

POTSHERD

DRIED UP LIKE A POTSHERD, AND MY TONGUE CLEAVETH TO 366 34

POTTER'S

WITH THEM THE POTTER'S FIELD, TO BURY STRANGERS IN 135 12
THEM FOR THE POTTER'S FIELD, AS THE LORD APPOINTED 135 17
PIECES LIKE A POTTER'S VESSEL   346 16

POUR

TRULY PLEASE THEE, POUR UPON THEM THE CONTINUAL DEW 018 22
TRULY PLEASE THEE, POUR UPON THEM THE CONTINUAL DEW 032 21
INTO THY FOLD, POUR OUT THY SPIRIT UPON ALL FLESH, 038 10
THY HOLY GHOST, AND POUR INTO OUR HEARTS THAT MOST 122 16
POUR INTO OUR HEARTS SUCH LOVE TOWARD THEE, THAT WE, 197 05
POUR DOWN UPON US THE ABUNDANCE OF THY MERCY   206 06
O LORD, POUR THY GRACE INTO OUR HEARTS   235 18
WE BESEECH THEE TO POUR FORTH THY BLESSING UPON THIS 261 30
OR SHALL POUR WATER UPON HIM, SAYING, N   R 279 27
IN THE WATER, OR POUR WATER UPON HIM, USING THE SAME R 279 32
THE MINISTER SHALL POUR WATER UPON HIM, SAYING THESE R 281 20
THINK THEREUPON, I POUR OUT MY HEART BY MYSELF   393 06
POUR OUT YOUR HEARTS BEFORE HIM, FOR GOD IS OUR HOPE 414 13
25 POUR OUT THINE INDIGNATION UPON THEM, *   423 23
6 POUR OUT THINE INDIGNATION UPON THE HEATHEN THAT 440 11
OF DEACONS, AND TO POUR THY GRACE UPON THEM   531 06
OF PRIESTS, AND TO POUR THY GRACE UPON THEM   537 12
AND TO POUR THY GRACE UPON THEM   560 28

POURED

WHO HAST POURED UPON US THE NEW LIGHT OF THINE   106 25
THE BOX, AND POURED IT ON HIS HEAD   140 05
GENTILES ALSO WAS POURED OUT THE GIFT OF THE HOLY   184 24
14 I AM POURED OUT LIKE WATER, AND ALL MY BONES ARE 366 31
17 THE CLOUDS POURED OUT WATER, THE AIR THUNDERED, 434 16
2 I POURED OUT MY COMPLAINTS BEFORE HIM, *   518 05
INTO HEAVEN, POURED DOWN HIS GIFTS ABUNDANTLY UPON 557 25
AND POURED OUT THE CHANGERS' MONEY, AND OVERTHREW THE 567 30

POUREST

WHO POUREST OUT ON ALL WHO DESIRE IT, THE SPIRIT   594 04

POURETH

AFTER THAT HE POURETH WATER INTO A BASON, AND BEGAN 155 32

POURETH   CONTINUED

HELPETH US, AND POURETH HIS BENEFITS UPON US   420 24
AND HE POURETH OUT OF THE SAME   432 15

POURING

UP HIS WOUNDS, POURING IN OIL AND WINE, AND SET HIM 208 30
IMMERSION OR THE POURING OF WATER, THE MINISTER SHALL R 282 12

POVERTY

OR BECAUSE OF POVERTY ARE FORGOTTEN   600 08

POWER

YE SHALL RECEIVE POWER, AFTER THAT THE HOLY GHOST IS 005 11
HATH GIVEN POWER, AND COMMANDMENT, TO HIS   007 09
AND THE POWER, AND THE GLORY, FOR EVER AND   007 28
MAY NOT FEAR THE POWER OF ANY ADVERSARIES, THROUGH 017 09
DEFEND US IN THE SAME WITH THY MIGHTY POWER   017 16
HATH GIVEN POWER, AND COMMANDMENT, TO HIS   024 11
IS EVERLASTING AND POWER INFINITE   032 05
BY THE MIGHTY POWER OF THE HOLY GHOST, THAT THE   037 02
ALL THINGS, WHOSE POWER NO CREATURE IS ABLE TO   041 10
BE FILLED WITH THE POWER OF HIS DIVINE INDWELLING   043 24
THAT BY THE POWER OF THY HOLY SPIRIT THEY MAY BE SET 046 27
BE MERCIFUL AFTER THY POWER   072 32
AND THE POWER, AND THE GLORY, AND THE   073 18
THROUGH THE POWER OF THE HOLY GHOST   093 03
IN A CLOUD WITH POWER AND GREAT GLORY   093 11
WE PRAY THEE, THY POWER, AND COME AMONG US, AND WITH 095 04
BY THE WORD OF HIS POWER, WHEN HE HAD BY HIMSELF   096 28
TO THEM GAVE HE POWER TO BECOME THE SONS OF GOD,   097 34
UNTO ME BY THE EFFECTUAL WORKING OF HIS POWER   108 18
MAY HAVE GRACE AND POWER FAITHFULLY TO FULFIL THE   109 32
FOR THERE IS NO POWER BUT OF GOD   114 12
RESISTETH THE POWER, RESISTETH THE ORDINANCE OF GOD 114 13
WILT THOU THEN NOT BE AFRAID OF THE POWER   114 17
MAY EVERMORE BE DEFENDED BY THY MIGHTY POWER   115 31
APPEAR AGAIN WITH POWER AND GREAT GLORY, WE MAY BE 117 08
OF HEAVEN WITH POWER AND GREAT GLORY   118 20
GRANT THAT BY THY POWER WE MAY BE DEFENDED AGAINST 120 19
OF TRUTH, BY THE POWER OF GOD, BY THE ARMOUR OF   126 14
THAT WE HAVE NO POWER OF OURSELVES TO HELP OURSELVES 127 15
THE RIGHT HAND OF POWER, AND COMING IN THE CLOUDS OF 143 16
YOUR HOUR, AND THE POWER OF DARKNESS   151 06
RIGHT HAND OF THE POWER OF GOD   151 33
NOT THAT I HAVE POWER TO CRUCIFY THEE, AND HAVE POWER 159 15
AND HAVE POWER TO RELEASE THEE   159 15
COULDEST HAVE NO POWER AT ALL AGAINST ME, EXCEPT IT 159 16
US FROM THE POWER OF OUR ENEMY   165 05
OF NAZARETH WITH THE HOLY GHOST AND WITH POWER   166 20
WHICH THE FATHER HATH PUT IN HIS OWN POWER   178 08
YE SHALL RECEIVE POWER, AFTER THAT THE HOLY GHOST IS 178 09
YE BE ENDUED WITH POWER FROM ON HIGH   178 23
OF NAZARETH WITH THE HOLY GHOST AND WITH POWER   184 07
MAY MANIFEST THY POWER AMONG ALL PEOPLES, TO THE   185 16
AND IN THE POWER OF THE DIVINE MAJESTY TO WORSHIP THE 186 26
O LORD, TO RECEIVE GLORY AND HONOUR AND POWER   187 30
LORD OF ALL POWER AND MIGHT, WHO ART THE AUTHOR AND 198 20
THY ALMIGHTY POWER CHIEFLY IN SHOWING MERCY AND PITY 204 22
ACCORDING TO THE POWER THAT WORKETH IN US, UNTO HIM 212 23
SON OF MAN HATH POWER ON EARTH TO FORGIVE SINS, (THEN 217 09
HAD GIVEN SUCH POWER UNTO MEN   217 14
AND IN THE POWER OF HIS MIGHT   219 05
TO HIS GLORIOUS POWER, UNTO ALL PATIENCE AND   224 07
UPON THEE, AND THE POWER OF THE HIGHEST SHALL   236 23
KNOWN UNTO YOU THE POWER AND COMING OF OUR LORD JESUS 248 15
OUR GOD, AND THE POWER OF HIS CHRIST   252 11
LOVE AND HEALING POWER OF THY SON   253 18
CHURCH THE LIKE POWER AND LOVE, TO THE HEALING OF OUR 253 19
AND HONOUR, AND POWER, AND MIGHT, BE UNTO OUR GOD FOR 257 02
THE SAME FAITH AND POWER OF LOVE   258 07
WHOSE MIGHTY POWER OUR FATHERS WON THEIR LIBERTIES OF 263 17
SAYING, ALL POWER IS GIVEN UNTO ME IN HEAVEN   275 26
THAT HE MAY HAVE POWER AND STRENGTH TO HAVE VICTORY, 278 24
LORD OF ALL POWER AND MIGHT, WHO ART THE AUTHOR AND 283 08
THE HELP OF THY POWER, THAT HIS SICKNESS MAY BE   312 14
THAT HE MAKE AMENDS TO THE UTTERMOST OF HIS POWER R 313 23
GRANT THAT, BY THE POWER OF THY HOLY SPIRIT, HE MAY 316 21
SERVANT FROM THE POWER OF THE EVIL ONE, AND FROM   318 12
BY THY INDWELLING POWER, THE DISTRESS OF THIS THY   320 09
PUT DOWN ALL RULE AND ALL AUTHORITY AND POWER   328 29
IT IS RAISED IN POWER   329 21
17 BREAK THOU THE POWER OF THE UNGODLY AND MALICIOUS 354 05
SO WILL WE SING, AND PRAISE THY POWER   365 33
DARLING FROM THE POWER OF THE DOG   367 13
UNGODLY IN GREAT POWER, *   387 04
MY SOUL FROM THE POWER OF THE GRAVE   401 05
I WILL SING OF THY POWER, AND WILL PRAISE THY MERCY 412 06
THAT POWER BELONGETH UNTO GOD   414 22
I MIGHT BEHOLD THY POWER AND GLORY   414 30
AND IS GIRDED ABOUT WITH POWER   416 26
GREATNESS OF THY POWER SHALL THINE ENEMIES BOW DOWN 417 18
HE RULETH WITH HIS POWER FOR EVER   417 26
34 ASCRIBE YE THE POWER TO GOD OVER ISRAEL   421 25
GIVE STRENGTH AND POWER UNTO HIS PEOPLE   421 28
AND THY POWER TO ALL THEM THAT ARE YET FOR TO COME 426 12
14 THOU DIDST DIVIDE THE SEA THROUGH THY POWER   431 02
HAST DECLARED THY POWER AMONG THE PEOPLES   434 11
AND THROUGH HIS POWER HE BROUGHT IN THE   436 23
HE DELIVERED THEIR POWER INTO CAPTIVITY, *   438 34
AND RULED THEM PRUDENTLY WITH ALL HIS POWER   439 25
GREATNESS OF THY POWER, PRESERVE THOU THOSE THAT ARE 440 27
HIS SOUL FROM THE POWER OF THE GRAVE   453 03

POWER   CONTINUED

WHO REGARDETH THE POWER OF THY WRATH   454 11
POWER AND HONOUR ARE IN HIS SANCTUARY   460 10
ASCRIBE UNTO THE LORD WORSHIP AND POWER   460 13
4 THE KING'S POWER LOVETH JUDGMENT   462 22
HE MIGHT MAKE HIS POWER TO BE KNOWN   473 17
THE ROD OF THY POWER OUT OF SION   482 09
IN THE DAY OF THY POWER SHALL THY PEOPLE OFFER   482 11
HIS PEOPLE THE POWER OF HIS WORKS, *   483 05
AND DECLARE THY POWER   520 14
AND TALK OF THY POWER   521 15
12 THAT THY POWER, THY GLORY, AND MIGHTINESS OF THY   521 16
5 GREAT IS OUR LORD, AND GREAT IS HIS POWER   523 04
PRAISE HIM IN THE FIRMAMENT OF HIS POWER   525 23
YOU STRENGTH AND POWER TO PERFORM THE SAME, THAT HE   543 20
SAYING, ALL POWER IS GIVEN UNTO ME IN HEAVEN   552 09
YOU STRENGTH AND POWER TO PERFORM THE SAME   555 30
OF FEAR, BUT OF POWER, AND LOVE, AND SOBERNESS   558 18
MIGHTY IN POWER, AND OF MAJESTY   564 27
AND MAY HAVE POWER AND STRENGTH TO FULFIL THE   566 06
POSSESSED OF FULL POWER TO PERFORM EVERY ACT OF   569 18
DEFEND US IN THE SAME WITH THY MIGHTY POWER   592 22
GREATNESS OF THY POWER, PRESERVE THOU THOSE THAT ARE   600 10
OF INFINITE POWER, WISDOM, AND GOODNESS   603 04
OF ONE SUBSTANCE, POWER, AND ETERNITY   603 06
WE HAVE NO POWER TO DO GOOD WORKS PLEASANT AND   604 44
THE CHURCH HATH POWER TO DECREE RITES OR CEREMONIES,   607 03
THE POWER OF THE CIVIL MAGISTRATE EXTENDETH TO ALL   610 38

POWERS

AND ALL THE POWERS THEREIN   010 12
O ALL YE POWERS OF THE LORD, BLESS YE THE LORD   012 08
UTTERMOST OF YOUR POWERS, FOR ALL INJURIES AND WRONGS   087 25
FOR THE POWERS OF HEAVEN SHALL BE SHAKEN   093 09
AND POWERS IN HEAVENLY PLACES MIGHT BE KNOWN BY THE   108 24
LET EVERY SOUL BE SUBJECT UNTO THE HIGHER POWERS   114 11
THE POWERS THAT BE ARE ORDAINED OF GOD   114 12
AND THE POWERS OF THE HEAVENS SHALL BE   118 16
AUTHORITIES AND POWERS BEING MADE SUBJECT UNTO HIM   162 03
AGAINST POWERS, AGAINST THE RULERS OF THE DARKNESS OF   219 09
O GOD OF HEAVENLY POWERS, WHO, BY THE MIGHT OF THY   315 06
NOR POWERS, NOR THINGS PRESENT, NOR THINGS TO COME,   331 11
WITH ALL THEIR POWERS AND FACULTIES   573 15

PRACTISE

AND PRACTISE IT   415 30

PRAETORIUM

LED HIM AWAY INTO THE HALL, CALLED PRAETORIUM   145 30

PRAISE

HIS MOST WORTHY PRAISE, TO HEAR HIS MOST HOLY WORD,   006 07
AND OUR MOUTH SHALL SHOW FORTH THY PRAISE   007 32
PRAISE YE THE LORD   008 07
WE PRAISE THEE, O GOD   010 08
OF THE APOSTLES PRAISE THEE   010 16
OF THE PROPHETS PRAISE THEE   010 17
ARMY OF MARTYRS PRAISE THEE   010 18
PRAISE HIM, AND MAGNIFY HIM FOR EVER   011 32
PRAISE HIM, AND MAGNIFY HIM FOR EVER   012 02
PRAISE HIM, AND MAGNIFY HIM FOR EVER   012 04
PRAISE HIM, AND MAGNIFY HIM FOR EVER   012 07
PRAISE HIM, AND MAGNIFY HIM FOR EVER   012 08
PRAISE HIM, AND MAGNIFY HIM FOR EVER   012 10
PRAISE HIM, AND MAGNIFY HIM FOR EVER   012 12
PRAISE HIM, AND MAGNIFY HIM FOR EVER   012 14
PRAISE HIM, AND MAGNIFY HIM FOR EVER   012 16
PRAISE HIM, AND MAGNIFY HIM FOR EVER   012 18
PRAISE HIM, AND MAGNIFY HIM FOR EVER   012 20
PRAISE HIM, AND MAGNIFY HIM FOR EVER   012 22
PRAISE HIM, AND MAGNIFY HIM FOR EVER   012 24
PRAISE HIM, AND MAGNIFY HIM FOR EVER   012 26
PRAISE HIM, AND MAGNIFY HIM FOR EVER   012 28
PRAISE HIM, AND MAGNIFY HIM FOR EVER   012 30
PRAISE HIM, AND MAGNIFY HIM FOR EVER   012 32
LET IT PRAISE HIM, AND MAGNIFY HIM FOR EVER   013 02
PRAISE HIM, AND MAGNIFY HIM FOR EVER   013 04
PRAISE HIM, AND MAGNIFY HIM FOR EVER   013 07
PRAISE HIM, AND MAGNIFY HIM FOR EVER   013 08
PRAISE HIM, AND MAGNIFY HIM FOR EVER   013 10
PRAISE HIM, AND MAGNIFY HIM FOR EVER   013 13
PRAISE HIM, AND MAGNIFY HIM FOR EVER   013 14
PRAISE HIM, AND MAGNIFY HIM FOR EVER   013 16
PRAISE HIM, AND MAGNIFY HIM FOR EVER   013 18
PRAISE HIM, AND MAGNIFY HIM FOR EVER   013 20
PRAISE HIM, AND MAGNIFY HIM FOR EVER   013 22
PRAISE HIM, AND MAGNIFY HIM FOR EVER   013 24
PRAISE HIM, AND MAGNIFY HIM FOR EVER   013 27
PRAISE HIM, AND MAGNIFY HIM FOR EVER   013 29
PRAISE HIM, AND MAGNIFY HIM FOR EVER   013 31
AND INTO HIS COURTS WITH PRAISE   015 11
WE SHOW FORTH THY PRAISE, NOT ONLY WITH OUR LIPS,   019 27
HIS MOST WORTHY PRAISE, TO HEAR HIS MOST HOLY WORD,   023 16
AND OUR MOUTH SHALL SHOW FORTH THY PRAISE   025 07
PRAISE YE THE LORD   025 13
WE PRAISE THEE, WE BLESS THEE, WE WORSHIP THEE, WE   025 23
PRAISE THE LORD UPON THE HARP   027 15
REJOICE IN GIVING PRAISE FOR THE OPERATIONS OF THY   028 03
LET THE PEOPLES PRAISE THEE, O GOD   028 21
ALL THE PEOPLES PRAISE THEE   028 22
LET THE PEOPLES PRAISE THEE, O GOD   028 26

PRAISE   CONTINUED

ALL THE PEOPLES PRAISE THEE   028 27
PRAISE THE LORD, O MY SOUL   029 04
IS WITHIN ME, PRAISE HIS HOLY NAME   029 05
PRAISE THE LORD, O MY SOUL, *   029 06
O PRAISE THE LORD, YE ANGELS OF HIS, YE THAT EXCEL IN   029 12
O PRAISE THE LORD, ALL YE HIS HOSTS   029 15
PRAISE THOU THE LORD, O MY SOUL   029 18
WE SHOW FORTH THY PRAISE, NOT ONLY WITH OUR LIPS,   033 25
SHOW FORTH THY PRAISE AMONG THE NATIONS OF THE EARTH   036 20
TO THE PRAISE OF THY HOLY NAME   039 30
YE SHALL ALSO PRAISE GOD FOR RAIN AND SUNSHINE   048 11
GOD MOST HIGH PRAISE AND HEARTY THANKS FOR THE   048 15
TO THE HONOUR AND PRAISE OF THY NAME   049 21
THANKS AND PRAISE FOR THE RETURN OF SEED-TIME AND   050 21
WE PRAISE AND GLORIFY THY HOLY NAME FOR THIS THY   051 25
WE YIELD THEE PRAISE AND THANKSGIVING FOR OUR   052 09
OUR SACRIFICE OF PRAISE AND THANKSGIVING FOR THESE   052 26
WE BLESS AND PRAISE THY NAME, IN THE PRESENCE OF ALL   053 13
WE PRAISE THY HOLY NAME THAT THOU HAST BEEN PLEASED   053 21
AND MY MOUTH SHALL SHOW THY PRAISE   061 10
MAY BE SAID, PRAISE BE TO THEE, O CHRIST   070 28
ARE WE BOUND TO PRAISE THEE FOR THE GLORIOUS   078 07
OUR SACRIFICE OF PRAISE AND THANKSGIVING   081 16
WE PRAISE THEE, WE BLESS THEE, WE WORSHIP THEE, WE   084 03
AND AGAIN, PRAISE THE LORD, ALL YE GENTILES   092 29
EVERY MAN HAVE PRAISE OF GOD   094 14
THE GARMENT OF PRAISE FOR THE SPIRIT OF HEAVINESS   107 08
THOU SHALT HAVE PRAISE OF THE SAME   114 18
THEY SAW IT, GAVE PRAISE UNTO GOD   124 06
AND FOR THE PRAISE OF THEM THAT DO WELL   173 21
TO WHOM BE PRAISE AND DOMINION FOR EVER AND EVER   179 21
THE GLORY AND PRAISE OF GOD   221 06
YEAR BY YEAR WE PRAISE YOU FOR THE DEDICATION OF THIS   259 19
OF BABES AND SUCKLINGS THOU HAST PERFECTED PRAISE   260 15
HE IS THY PRAISE, AND HE IS THY GOD, THAT HATH DONE   263 31
O PRAISE THE LORD, FOR IT IS A GOOD THING TO SING   264 18
PRAISE THE LORD, O JERUSALEM   264 32
PRAISE THY GOD, O SION   264 32
ONE GOD, I PRAISE AND MAGNIFY, SAYING,   285 04
UNTO US, BUT UNTO THY NAME BE THE PRAISE   290 13
PRAISE THE LORD   306 03
GODS WILL I SING PRAISE UNTO THEE   311 29
HOLY TEMPLE, AND PRAISE THY NAME, BECAUSE OF THY   311 30
PRAISE THE LORD, O MY SOUL   312 20
IS WITHIN ME, PRAISE HIS HOLY NAME   312 21
PRAISE THE LORD, O MY SOUL, AND FORGET NOT ALL HIS   312 22
O PRAISE THE LORD, YE ANGELS OF HIS, YE THAT EXCEL IN   312 28
O PRAISE THE LORD, ALL YE HIS HOSTS   312 31
PRAISE THOU THE LORD, O MY SOUL   313 03
THE DEVOUT PRAISE OF THY HUMBLE SERVANT   313 06
HE MAY OFFER THEE PRAISE AND THANKSGIVING   320 12
THEE MOST HIGH PRAISE AND HEARTY THANKS, FOR THE   336 17
AND I WILL PRAISE THE NAME OF THE LORD MOST HIGH   350 28
11 O PRAISE THE LORD WHICH DWELLETH IN SION   352 11
I WILL PRAISE THE NAME OF THE LORD MOST HIGHEST   356 10
WILL WE SING, AND PRAISE THY POWER   365 33
WILL I PRAISE THEE   367 17
23 O PRAISE THE LORD, YE THAT FEAR HIM   367 18
25 MY PRAISE IS OF THEE IN THE GREAT CONGREGATION   367 23
THE LORD SHALL PRAISE HIM   367 26
I WILL PRAISE THE LORD IN THE CONGREGATIONS   371 20
IN MY SONG WILL I PRAISE HIM   373 24
MAN SING OF THY PRAISE WITHOUT CEASING   375 18
2 PRAISE THE LORD WITH HARP   378 21
HIS PRAISE SHALL EVER BE IN MY MOUTH   380 03
3 O PRAISE THE LORD WITH ME, *   380 07
I WILL PRAISE THEE AMONG MUCH PEOPLE   382 33
AND OF THY PRAISE, ALL THE DAY LONG   383 24
5 IN THE VOICE OF PRAISE AND THANKSGIVING, *   393 09
AND WILL PRAISE THY NAME FOR EVER   395 10
SO IS THY PRAISE UNTO THE WORLD'S END   399 29
THEIR POSTERITY PRAISE THEIR SAYING   400 33
AND THOU SHALT PRAISE ME   402 21
ME THANKS AND PRAISE, HE HONOURETH ME   403 04
AND MY MOUTH SHALL SHOW THY PRAISE   404 08
I GIVE THEE, AND PRAISE THY NAME, O LORD   406 14
4 I WILL PRAISE GOD, BECAUSE OF HIS WORD   408 21
I WILL SING AND GIVE PRAISE   409 30
AND WILL PRAISE THY MERCY BETIMES IN THE   412 06
WILL I ALWAY SING PRAISE UNTO THY NAME, *   413 22
MY LIPS SHALL PRAISE THEE   414 32
AND EVENING TO PRAISE THEE   416 31
MAKE HIS PRAISE TO BE GLORIOUS   417 16
SING OF THEE, AND PRAISE THY NAME   417 21
7 O PRAISE OUR GOD, YE PEOPLES, *   417 29
THE VOICE OF HIS PRAISE TO BE HEARD   417 30
3 LET THE PEOPLES PRAISE THEE, O GOD   418 28
ALL THE PEOPLES PRAISE THEE   418 29
5 LET THE PEOPLES PRAISE THEE, O GOD   418 33
ALL THE PEOPLES PRAISE THEE   418 34
PRAISE HIM IN HIS NAME JAH, AND REJOICE BEFORE HIM   419 17
31 I WILL PRAISE THE NAME OF GOD WITH A SONG,   424 04
HEAVEN AND EARTH PRAISE HIM   424 12
MY PRAISE SHALL BE ALWAY OF THEE   425 18
FILLED WITH THY PRAISE, *   425 21
AND WILL PRAISE THEE MORE AND MORE   426 03
THEREFORE WILL I PRAISE THEE, AND THY FAITHFULNESS,   426 22
THE NATIONS SHALL PRAISE HIM   427 34
AND NEEDY GIVE PRAISE UNTO THY NAME   431 21
AND PRAISE HIM FOR EVER   432 19
10 THE FIERCENESS OF MAN SHALL TURN TO THY PRAISE   433 04
SHOWING FORTH THY PRAISE FROM GENERATION TO   440 34
AND WILL PRAISE THY NAME FOR EVERMORE   447 29
UP AGAIN, AND PRAISE THEE   449 17

PRAISE   CONTINUED

	PAGE LN
HEAVENS SHALL PRAISE THY WONDROUS WORKS	450 13
REJOICE IN GIVING PRAISE FOR THE OPERATIONS OF THY	456 07
THE LORD, AND PRAISE HIS NAME	460 02
6 PRAISE THE LORD UPON THE HARP	462 04
AND INTO HIS COURTS WITH PRAISE	463 12
BE BORN SHALL PRAISE THE LORD	465 16
PRAISE THE LORD, O MY SOUL	466 08
IS WITHIN ME, PRAISE HIS HOLY NAME	466 09
2 PRAISE THE LORD, O MY SOUL, *	466 10
20 O PRAISE THE LORD, YE ANGELS OF HIS, YE THAT EXCEL	467 15
21 O PRAISE THE LORD, ALL YE HIS HOSTS	467 18
PRAISE THOU THE LORD, O MY SOUL	467 21
PRAISE THE LORD, O MY SOUL	467 24
I WILL PRAISE MY GOD WHILE I HAVE MY BEING	469 28
36 PRAISE THOU THE LORD, O MY SOUL	469 33
PRAISE THE LORD	469 33
BE OF HIM, AND PRAISE HIM	470 07
OR SHOW FORTH ALL HIS PRAISE	473 03
AND SANG PRAISE UNTO HIM	473 25
AND MAKE OUR BOAST OF THY PRAISE	475 32
WOULD THEREFORE PRAISE THE LORD FOR HIS GOODNESS	476 19
WOULD THEREFORE PRAISE THE LORD FOR HIS GOODNESS	477 04
WOULD THEREFORE PRAISE THE LORD FOR HIS GOODNESS	477 17
WOULD THEREFORE PRAISE THE LORD FOR HIS GOODNESS	478 07
AND PRAISE HIM IN THE SEAT OF THE ELDERS	478 11
AND GIVE PRAISE WITH THE BEST MEMBER THAT I	479 05
HOLD NOT THY TONGUE, O GOD OF MY PRAISE	480 03
AND PRAISE HIM AMONG THE MULTITUDE	481 33
HIS PRAISE ENDURETH FOR EVER	483 16
PRAISE THE LORD, YE SERVANTS	484 08
O PRAISE THE NAME OF THE LORD	484 08
NOT UNTO US, BUT UNTO THY NAME GIVE THE PRAISE	485 12
17 THE DEAD PRAISE NOT THEE, O LORD, *	486 12
18 BUT WE WILL PRAISE THE LORD, *	486 14
PRAISE THE LORD	486 15
PRAISE THE LORD	487 23
PRAISE HIM, ALL YE PEOPLES	487 25
O PRAISE THE LORD, ALL YE NATIONS	487 25
PRAISE THE LORD	487 29
AND I WILL PRAISE THEE	489 26
TIMES A DAY DO I PRAISE THEE	501 09
SPEAK OF THY PRAISE, *	501 24
AND IT SHALL PRAISE THEE	501 32
BEHOLD NOW, PRAISE THE LORD, *	509 23
AND PRAISE THE LORD	509 27
O PRAISE THE LORD, LAUD YE THE NAME OF THE LORD	510 03
PRAISE IT, O YE SERVANTS OF THE LORD	510 04
3 O PRAISE THE LORD, FOR THE LORD IS GRACIOUS	510 07
PRAISE THE LORD, YE HOUSE OF AARON	511 08
19 PRAISE THE LORD, YE HOUSE OF ISRAEL	511 08
20 PRAISE THE LORD, YE HOUSE OF LEVI	511 10
FEAR THE LORD, PRAISE THE LORD	511 11
GODS WILL I SING PRAISE UNTO THEE	513 28
HOLY TEMPLE, AND PRAISE THY NAME, BECAUSE OF THY	513 30
THE EARTH SHALL PRAISE THEE, O LORD	514 04
AND I WILL PRAISE THY NAME FOR EVER AND EVER	520 28
AND PRAISE THY NAME FOR EVER AND EVER	520 29
GENERATION SHALL PRAISE THY WORKS UNTO ANOTHER,	520 33
THY GLORY, THY PRAISE, AND WONDROUS WORKS	521 03
10 ALL THY WORKS PRAISE THEE, O LORD	521 12
SHALL SPEAK THE PRAISE OF THE LORD	521 34
PRAISE THE LORD, O MY SOUL	522 03
I LIVE, WILL I PRAISE THE LORD	522 03
O PRAISE THE LORD, FOR IT IS A GOOD THING TO SING	522 27
PRAISE THY GOD, O SION	523 19
12 PRAISE THE LORD, O JERUSALEM	523 19
O PRAISE THE LORD FROM THE HEAVENS	524 05
PRAISE HIM IN THE HEIGHTS	524 05
PRAISE HIM, ALL HIS HOST	524 07
2 PRAISE HIM, ALL YE ANGELS OF HIS	524 07
3 PRAISE HIM, SUN AND MOON	524 09
PRAISE HIM, ALL YE STARS AND LIGHT	524 09
4 PRAISE HIM, ALL YE HEAVENS, *	524 11
5 LET THEM PRAISE THE NAME OF THE LORD	524 13
7 PRAISE THE LORD FROM THE EARTH, *	524 18
MEN AND CHILDREN, PRAISE THE NAME OF THE LORD	524 28
AND HIS PRAISE ABOVE HEAVEN AND EARTH	524 29
HIS SAINTS SHALL PRAISE HIM	524 31
OF SAINTS PRAISE HIM	525 04
3 LET THEM PRAISE HIS NAME IN THE DANCE	525 07
PRAISE HIM IN THE FIRMAMENT OF HIS POWER	525 22
O PRAISE GOD IN HIS SANCTUARY	525 22
PRAISE HIM ACCORDING TO HIS EXCELLENT GREATNESS	525 24
2 PRAISE HIM IN HIS NOBLE ACTS	525 24
3 PRAISE HIM IN THE SOUND OF THE TRUMPET	525 26
PRAISE HIM UPON THE LUTE AND HARP	525 26
4 PRAISE HIM IN THE TIMBRELS AND DANCES	525 28
PRAISE HIM UPON THE STRINGS AND PIPE	525 28
PRAISE HIM UPON THE LOUD CYMBALS	525 30
5 PRAISE HIM UPON THE WELL-TUNED CYMBALS	525 30
PRAISE THE LORD	525 32
PRAISE TO THY ETERNAL MERIT, FATHER, SON, AND HOLY	544 14
FORTH THE ETERNAL PRAISE OF THY HOLY NAME	545 21
HEARTY THANKS, WE PRAISE AND WORSHIP THEE	545 25
TO THE HONOUR, PRAISE, AND GLORY OF THY NAME	553 20
PRAISE TO THY ETERNAL MERIT, FATHER, SON, AND HOLY	556 22
TO THE HONOUR, PRAISE, AND GLORY OF THY NAME	561 05
THY MOST WORTHY PRAISE, TO CONFESS THEIR SINS UNTO	566 16
AND MAY IN THEIR LIVES SHOW FORTH THY PRAISE	567 09
OF PRAYER AND PRAISE TO THEE IN THIS HOUSE, WHICH IS	572 21
SACRIFICE OF PRAISE AND THANKSGIVING	587 26

PRAISED

	PAGE LN
THE LORD'S NAME BE PRAISED	008 08
PRAISED AND EXALTED ABOVE ALL FOR EVER	011 16
PRAISED AND EXALTED ABOVE ALL FOR EVER	011 18
PRAISED AND EXALTED ABOVE ALL FOR EVER	011 20
PRAISED AND EXALTED ABOVE ALL FOR EVER	011 23
PRAISED AND EXALTED ABOVE ALL FOR EVER	011 26
PRAISED AND EXALTED ABOVE ALL FOR EVER	011 27
THE LORD'S NAME BE PRAISED	025 14
HE SPAKE, AND PRAISED GOD	243 26
WHICH IS WORTHY TO BE PRAISED	359 30
AND PRAISED BE THE GOD OF MY SALVATION	362 33
7 PRAISED BE THE LORD	373 20
THY SALVATION, SAY ALWAY, THE LORD BE PRAISED	391 23
AND HIGHLY TO BE PRAISED *	399 10
THOU, O GOD, ART PRAISED IN SION	416 11
18 PRAISED BE GOD, WHO HATH NOT CAST OUT MY PRAYER,	418 20
19 PRAISED BE THE LORD DAILY, *	420 23
IN THY SALVATION SAY ALWAY, THE LORD BE PRAISED	424 29
MADE EVER UNTO HIM, AND DAILY SHALL HE BE PRAISED	427 28
51 PRAISED BE THE LORD FOR EVERMORE	453 12
AND CANNOT WORTHILY BE PRAISED	460 06
IS WORTHY TO BE PRAISED AND HAD IN HONOUR, *	482 28
LORD'S NAME IS PRAISED *	484 12
5 BUT PRAISED BE THE LORD, *	504 16
21 PRAISED BE THE LORD OUT OF SION, *	511 12
AND MARVELLOUS WORTHY TO BE PRAISED	520 32

PRAISES

	PAGE LN
OFFER UP THEIR PRAISES AND THANKSGIVINGS FOR THY LATE	019 18
AND TO SING PRAISES UNTO THY NAME, O MOST HIGHEST	027 29
OFFER UP THEIR PRAISES AND THANKSGIVINGS FOR THY LATE	033 16
NOW TO OFFER HER PRAISES AND THANKSGIVINGS UNTO THEE	051 08
AND THE PRAISES OF THE LORD, ACCORDING TO ALL	138 28
THING TO SING PRAISES UNTO OUR GOD	264 19
SING PRAISES UPON THE HARP UNTO OUR GOD	264 25
NOW TO OFFER HER PRAISES AND THANKSGIVINGS UNTO THEE	306 27
SING AND SPEAK PRAISES UNTO THE LORD	326 18
MAY SHOW ALL THY PRAISES WITHIN THE GATES OF THE	352 19
AND SING PRAISES UNTO THY NAME	363 06
SING AND SPEAK PRAISES UNTO THE LORD	372 10
4 SING PRAISES UNTO THE LORD, O YE SAINTS OF HIS	374 30
SING PRAISES UNTO HIM WITH THE LUTE, AND INSTRUMENT	378 21
SING PRAISES LUSTILY UNTO HIM WITH A GOOD COURAGE	378 23
6 O SING PRAISES, SING PRAISES UNTO OUR GOD	398 31
PRAISES, SING PRAISES UNTO OUR GOD	398 31
O SING PRAISES, SING PRAISES UNTO OUR KING	398 32
PRAISES, SING PRAISES UNTO OUR KING	398 32
SING YE PRAISES WITH UNDERSTANDING	399 02
SING PRAISES UNTO THE HONOUR OF HIS NAME	417 15
AND GAVE HIM PRAISES WITH MY TONGUE	418 15
AND SING PRAISES UNTO HIS NAME	419 16
O SING PRAISES UNTO THE LORD	421 21
AND TO SING PRAISES UNTO THY NAME, O MOST HIGHEST	455 33
I WILL SING PRAISES UNTO THEE AMONG THE NATIONS	479 10
O SING PRAISES UNTO HIS NAME, FOR IT IS LOVELY	510 05
AND SING PRAISES UNTO THEE UPON A TEN-STRINGED LUTE	520 09
I WILL SING PRAISES UNTO MY GOD	522 05
THING TO SING PRAISES UNTO OUR GOD	522 28
SING PRAISES UPON THE HARP UNTO OUR GOD	523 08
LET THEM SING PRAISES UNTO HIM WITH TABRET AND HARP	525 08
6 LET THE PRAISES OF GOD BE IN THEIR MOUTH	525 13
OFFER UP THEIR PRAISES AND SUPPLICATIONS UNTO THEE	565 02
IN PRAISES, TO HEIGHTEN MY LOVE AND GRATITUDE	573 25
THEE OUR HUMBLE PRAISES, FOR THY PRESERVATION OF US	587 21

PRAISETH

	PAGE LN
WHEN MY MOUTH PRAISETH THEE WITH JOYFUL LIPS	415 03

PRAISING

	PAGE LN
EVERMORE PRAISING THEE, AND SAYING, PRIEST AND	077 06
EVERMORE PRAISING THEE, AND SAYING, PRIEST AND	079 30
HEAVENLY HOST PRAISING GOD, AND SAYING, GLORY TO GOD	099 20
GLORIFYING AND PRAISING GOD FOR ALL THE THINGS THAT	106 18
IN THE TEMPLE, PRAISING AND BLESSING GOD	178 28
WILL BE ALWAY PRAISING THEE	445 20

PRAY

	PAGE LN
LET US PRAY	R 003 09
WHEREFORE I PRAY AND BESEECH YOU, AS MANY AS ARE HERE	006 09
WE THEREFORE PRAY THEE, HELP THY SERVANTS, WHOM THOU	010 33
LET US PRAY	016 27
MORE ESPECIALLY WE PRAY FOR THY HOLY CHURCH	018 30
WHEREFORE I PRAY AND BESEECH YOU, AS MANY AS ARE HERE	023 18
MORE ESPECIALLY WE PRAY FOR THY HOLY CHURCH	032 30
AND WE PRAY THEE TO SEND US SUCH SEASONABLE WEATHER,	040 26
STRETCH FORTH, WE PRAY THEE, THINE ALMIGHTY ARM TO	041 25
GIVE THEM GRACE, WE PRAY THEE, TO STAND FAST IN THY	043 09
WATCH WITH US, WE PRAY THEE, OVER THE SICK CHILD FOR	045 24
YE SHALL PRAY FOR THE PRESIDENT OF THESE UNITED	047 15
YE SHALL ALSO PRAY FOR THE MINISTERS OF GOD'S HOLY	047 22
AND YE SHALL PRAY FOR A DUE SUPPLY OF PERSONS FITTED	047 30
THIS LAND, YE SHALL PRAY FOR ALL SCHOOLS, COLLEGES,	047 33
YE SHALL PRAY FOR ALL THE PEOPLE OF THESE UNITED	048 02
YE SHALL PRAY ALSO FOR ALL WHO TRAVEL BY LAND,	048 05
AND PRAY UNTO GOD, THAT WE MAY HAVE GRACE TO DIRECT	048 19
PRAY YE THEREFORE THE LORD OF THE HARVEST, THAT HE	073 12
PRIEST SAY, LET US PRAY FOR THE WHOLE STATE OF	074 05
RAISE UP, WE PRAY THEE, THY POWER, AND COME	095 04
TO HIS DISCIPLES, SIT YE HERE, WHILE I SHALL PRAY	141 29
WATCH YE AND PRAY, LEST YE ENTER INTO TEMPTATION	142 05

PRAY   CONTINUED

HE SAID UNTO THEM, PRAY THAT YE ENTER NOT INTO   150 16
RISE AND PRAY, LEST YE ENTER INTO TEMPTATION   150 26
OPEN, WE PRAY THEE, THE EYES OF OUR FAITH, THAT WE   166 07
THAT I WILL PRAY THE FATHER FOR YOU   176 27
AND I WILL PRAY THE FATHER, AND HE SHALL GIVE YOU   181 09
THEN HE SAID, I PRAY THEE THEREFORE, FATHER, THAT   190 22
I PRAY THEE HAVE ME EXCUSED   192 08
I PRAY THEE HAVE ME EXCUSED   192 10
AN HEARTY DESIRE TO PRAY, MAY, BY THY MIGHTY AID,   192 26
TWO MEN WENT UP INTO THE TEMPLE TO PRAY   205 23
TO HEAR THAN WE TO PRAY, AND ART WONT TO GIVE MORE   206 05
WE PRAY THEE THAT THY GRACE MAY ALWAYS PREVENT   213 14
AND THIS I PRAY, THAT YOUR LOVE MAY ABOUND YET MORE   220 32
DO NOT CEASE TO PRAY FOR YOU, AND TO DESIRE THAT   223 33
AND JAMES, AND WENT UP INTO A MOUNTAIN TO PRAY   248 25
PRAY YE THEREFORE THE LORD OF THE HARVEST, THAT HE   254 15
THAT HATE YOU, AND PRAY FOR THEM WHICH DESPITEFULLY   264 06
AND I PRAY UNTO GOD TO GIVE ME HIS GRACE, THAT I MAY   284 04
IS THE PRAYER THAT OUR LORD TAUGHT US TO PRAY   289 17
LET US PRAY, AS OUR SAVIOUR CHRIST HATH   289 19
AND TO WORK AND PRAY AND GIVE FOR THE SPREAD OF HIS   291 20
WASH IT, WE PRAY THEE, IN THE BLOOD OF THAT   317 17
DEAL GRACIOUSLY, WE PRAY THEE, WITH ALL THOSE WHO   342 10
AT NOON-DAY WILL I PRAY, AND THAT INSTANTLY   407 26
6 O PRAY FOR THE PEACE OF JERUSALEM   503 18
I WILL PRAY THEE YET AGAINST THEIR WICKEDNESS   517 22
PRAY YE THEREFORE THE LORD OF THE HARVEST, THAT HE   538 18
AND HAVE NEED, TO PRAY EARNESTLY FOR HIS HOLY SPIRIT   540 32
YE WILL CONTINUALLY PRAY TO GOD THE FATHER, BY THE   541 15
THE BISHOP SHALL PRAY IN THIS WISE, AND SAY, ALMIGHTY   R 545 10
PRESENT TO PRAY, SAYING THUS TO THEM   R 553 02
HATH TAUGHT US TO PRAY UNTO THEE, O ALMIGHTY FATHER,   571 13
VISIT, WE PRAY THEE, THIS CONGREGATION WITH   572 26
AND I PRAY UNTO GOD TO GIVE ME HIS GRACE, THAT I MAY   577 25
AND I PRAY UNTO GOD, THAT HE WILL SEND US ALL THINGS   580 32
SPIRIT LIFT US, WE PRAY THEE, TO THY PRESENCE,   595 22
WE CAN DESIRE OR PRAY FOR   597 12
BLESS, WE PRAY THEE, THY SERVANT, (N   597 16
AND WE PRAY THEE THAT, HAVING OPENED TO HIM THE GATES   598 07

PRAYED

WHO PRAYED FOR HIS MURDERERS TO THEE, O   099 31
THE GROUND, AND PRAYED THAT, IF IT WERE POSSIBLE, THE   141 33
HE WENT AWAY, AND PRAYED, AND SPAKE THE SAME WORDS   142 07
BUT I HAVE PRAYED FOR THEE, THAT THY FAITH FAIL NOT   149 32
KNEELED DOWN, AND PRAYED, SAYING, FATHER, IF THOU BE   150 18
IN AN AGONY HE PRAYED MORE EARNESTLY   150 21
THEN PRAYED THEY HIM TO TARRY CERTAIN DAYS   184 29
WERE COME DOWN, PRAYED FOR THEM, THAT THEY MIGHT   185 24
WAS SIMON'S, AND PRAYED HIM THAT HE WOULD THRUST OUT   196 11
STOOD AND PRAYED THUS WITH HIMSELF, GOD, I THANK   205 25
AND THEY PRAYED, AND SAID, THOU, LORD, WHICH KNOWEST   234 27
AND AS HE PRAYED, THE FASHION OF HIS COUNTENANCE WAS   248 25
YE HAVE PRAYED THAT OUR LORD JESUS CHRIST WOULD   276 20
WE HAVE PRAYED THAT OUR LORD JESUS CHRIST WOULD   277 21
WERE COME DOWN, PRAYED FOR THEM, THAT THEY MIGHT   296 16
AND WHEN THEY HAD PRAYED, THEY LAID THEIR HANDS ON   532 19
THE HOLY APOSTLES PRAYED BEFORE THEY ORDAINED   553 07

PRAYER

BEGIN THE MORNING PRAYER BY READING ONE OR MORE OF   R 003 03
TO THE LORD'S PRAYER, FIRST PRONOUNCING, THE LORD BE   R 003 07
CASE THE LORD'S PRAYER SHALL BE SAID WITH THE OTHER   R 003 12
BOOK OF COMMON PRAYER, LAID IT DOWN AS A RULE, THAT   V 13
AND SAY THE LORD'S PRAYER   R 007 20
OF MORNING PRAYER HAS BEEN SAID OR SUNG, MAY PASS AT   R 010 05
SHALL FOLLOW THE LORD'S PRAYER   R 016 28
END THE MORNING PRAYER WITH SUCH GENERAL   R 017 22
HERE ENDETH THE ORDER OF MORNING PRAYER   R 020 15
BEGIN THE EVENING PRAYER BY READING ONE OR MORE OF   R 021 03
AT ONCE FROM THE SENTENCES TO THE LORD'S PRAYER   R 021 06
CASE THE LORD'S PRAYER SHALL BE SAID WITH THE OTHER   R 021 09
LET MY PRAYER BE SET FORTH IN THY SIGHT AS THE   021 16
AND SAY THE LORD'S PRAYER   024 27
AWAY THE SINS OF THE WORLD, RECEIVE OUR PRAYER   025 30
IN EVENING PRAYER, THE LESSON READ BEING FOLLOWED BY   R 026 08
SHALL FOLLOW THE LORD'S PRAYER   030 33
END THE EVENING PRAYER WITH SUCH PRAYER, OR PRAYERS,   R 031 31
PRAYER WITH SUCH PRAYER, OR PRAYERS, TAKEN OUT OF   R 031 31
HERE ENDETH THE ORDER OF EVENING PRAYER   R 034 15
USED BEFORE THE PRAYER FOR ALL CONDITIONS OF MEN,   R 035 03
BEFORE THE FINAL PRAYER OF THANKSGIVING OR OF   R 035 04
THE ABOVE PRAYER MAY BE USED BY ALL CONGREGATIONS OF   R 037 10
CLAUSES IN THIS PRAYER, OR MAY ADD OTHERS, AS   R 047 05
OR EVENING PRAYER, OR COMMUNION, AT THE DISCRETION OF   R 049 03
BEFORE THE FINAL PRAYER OF BLESSING OF THE   R 050 16
THE THIRD COLLECT AT MORNING OR EVENING PRAYER   R 054 03
AND THE PEOPLE WITH HIM, SAY THE LORD'S PRAYER   R 058 02
TO THE PRAYER, WE HUMBLY BESEECH THEE, O   R 058 09
BOOK OF COMMON PRAYER OF THE CHURCH OF ENGLAND   VI 30
AFTER THE PRAYER, WE HUMBLY BESEECH THEE, O FATHER,   R 060 04
USED WITH MORNING PRAYER, OR EVENING PRAYER, OR AS A   R 060 05
OR EVENING PRAYER, OR AS A SEPARATE OFFICE   R 060 05
O LORD, HEAR OUR PRAYER   062 05
SAY THE LORD'S PRAYER AND THE COLLECT FOLLOWING, THE   R 067 07
BUT THE LORD'S PRAYER MAY BE OMITTED AT THE   R 067 08
BEEN SAID IMMEDIATELY BEFORE IN MORNING PRAYER   R 070 31
SAID THE BIDDING PRAYER, OR OTHER AUTHORIZED PRAYERS   R 071 29
BOOK OF COMMON PRAYER, UNDER THE DIRECTION OF THE   R 073 36
HE SHALL SAY THE PRAYER OF CONSECRATION, AS   R 080 05
THIS PRAYER FOLLOWING   R 082 12
AWAY THE SINS OF THE WORLD, RECEIVE OUR PRAYER   084 10

PRAYER   CONTINUED

AFTER THE PRAYER FOR THE WHOLE STATE OF CHRIST'S   R 085 21
MY HOUSE SHALL BE CALLED THE HOUSE OF PRAYER   092 03
IN EVERY THING BY PRAYER AND SUPPLICATION WITH   095 16
CONTINUING INSTANT IN PRAYER   111 27
HE ROSE UP FROM PRAYER, AND WAS COME TO HIS   150 24
AT MORNING PRAYER, INSTEAD OF THE VENITE, THE   R 162 28
BE YE THEREFORE SOBER, AND WATCH UNTO PRAYER   179 13
IT IS WRITTEN, MY HOUSE IS THE HOUSE OF PRAYER   204 18
ALWAYS WITH ALL PRAYER AND SUPPLICATION IN THE   219 20
ALWAYS IN EVERY PRAYER OF MINE FOR YOU ALL MAKING   220 23
BUT PRAYER WAS MADE WITHOUT CEASING OF THE CHURCH   245 07
MY HOUSE SHALL BE CALLED THE HOUSE OF PRAYER   260 07
OR EVENING PRAYER, OR AT SUCH OTHER TIME AS THE   R 273 15
THE LORD'S PRAYER, AND THE TEN COMMANDMENTS,   277 10
SAID THE LORD'S PRAYER, AND THE THANKSGIVING FROM   R 281 23
THE FOLLOWING PRAYER, THE MINISTER FIRST PRONOUNCING, R 283 04
BE SAID THIS PRAYER BY THE MINISTER AND PEOPLE   R 285 23
LEARN AT ALL TIMES TO CALL FOR BY DILIGENT PRAYER   289 16
WHAT IS THE PRAYER THAT OUR LORD TAUGHT US TO PRAY   289 17
THE LORD'S PRAYER   289 18
HEAR OUR PRAYER   290 14
THE LORD'S PRAYER, AND THE TEN COMMANDMENTS,   R 295 14
THE PEOPLE ALL STANDING UNTIL THE LORD'S PRAYER   R 296 07
HEAR OUR PRAYER   297 11
SAY THE LORD'S PRAYER, THE PEOPLE KNEELING AND   R 298 03
STILL STANDING, SAY THE LORD'S PRAYER   R 302 27
OR THE CONCLUDING PRAYER ALONE, AS IT STANDS AMONG   R 305 04
BECAUSE HE HATH HEARD THE VOICE OF MY PRAYER   305 19
SAY THE LORD'S PRAYER, WITH WHAT FOLLOWETH   R 306 08
BUT THE LORD'S PRAYER MAY BE OMITTED, IF THIS BE USED R 306 09
THIS BE USED WITH THE MORNING OR EVENING PRAYER   R 306 10
HEAR OUR PRAYER   306 21
O LORD, HEAR OUR PRAYER   308 31
THE PRAYER OF CONSECRATION, ENDING WITH THESE WORDS, R 323 07
THE PRAYER OF HUMBLE ACCESS   R 323 08
THE LORD'S PRAYER   R 323 09
HEAR MY PRAYER, O LORD, AND WITH THINE EARS CONSIDER 325 06
THE LORD'S PRAYER, THE PRAYER WHICH FOLLOWETH,   R 331 29
PRAYER, THE PRAYER WHICH FOLLOWETH, AND SUCH OTHER   R 331 29
SHUT NOT THY MERCIFUL EARS TO OUR PRAYER   332 29
HEAR OUR PRAYER   340 20
AND HEARKEN UNTO MY PRAYER   347 12
FOR UNTO THEE WILL I MAKE MY PRAYER   348 03
WILL I DIRECT MY PRAYER UNTO THEE, AND WILL LOOK UP   348 05
THE LORD WILL RECEIVE MY PRAYER   349 17
HEARKEN UNTO MY PRAYER, THAT GOETH NOT OUT OF FEIGNED 358 17
THE VOICE OF MY PRAYER, *   377 13
IS GODLY MAKE HIS PRAYER UNTO THEE, IN A TIME WHEN   378 02
AND MY PRAYER SHALL TURN INTO MINE OWN BOSOM   382 18
13 HEAR MY PRAYER, O LORD, AND WITH THINE EARS   390 02
AND MAKE MY PRAYER UNTO THE GOD OF MY LIFE   393 23
2 HEAR MY PRAYER, O GOD, *   406 05
HEAR MY PRAYER, O GOD, *   406 19
HOW I MOURN IN MY PRAYER, AND AM VEXED   406 22
GIVE EAR UNTO MY PRAYER   413 07
HEAR MY VOICE, O GOD, IN MY PRAYER   415 19
THAT HEAREST THE PRAYER, *   416 13
AND CONSIDERED THE VOICE OF MY PRAYER   418 19
NOT CAST OUT MY PRAYER, *   418 20
I MAKE MY PRAYER UNTO THEE *   422 28
PRAYER SHALL BE MADE EVER UNTO HIM, AND DAILY SHALL   427 27
8 O LORD GOD OF HOSTS, HEAR MY PRAYER   445 27
UNTO MY PRAYER, *   447 15
O LET MY PRAYER ENTER INTO THY PRESENCE, INCLINE   448 30
EARLY SHALL MY PRAYER COME BEFORE THEE   449 23
HEAR MY PRAYER, O LORD, *   464 10
HIM UNTO THE PRAYER OF THE POOR DESTITUTE, *   465 13
BUT I GIVE MYSELF UNTO PRAYER   480 10
AND LET HIS PRAYER BE TURNED INTO SIN   480 16
BECAUSE HE HATH HEARD THE VOICE OF MY PRAYER   486 20
2 LET MY PRAYER BE SET FORTH IN THY SIGHT AS THE   517 10
HEAR MY PRAYER, O LORD, AND CONSIDER MY DESIRE   518 23
ALSO BY PUBLIC PRAYER, WITH IMPOSITION OF HANDS,   529 17
CONTINUALLY TO PRAYER, AND TO THE MINISTRY OF THE   532 14
WHEN THIS PRAYER IS DONE, THE BISHOP WITH THE   R 546 06
WHOLE NIGHT IN PRAYER, BEFORE HE CHOSE AND SENT FORTH 553 06
BE SAID THIS PRAYER FOLLOWING   R 553 25
CALL UPON GOD BY PRAYER FOR THE TRUE UNDERSTANDING OF 554 30
PRESIDING BISHOP SHALL SAY, LORD, HEAR OUR PRAYER   557 17
SHALL BE SAID THIS PRAYER   R 559 04
HEAR OUR PRAYER   562 06
OR AT MORNING PRAYER OR EVENING PRAYER, OR   R 563 04
PRAYER OR EVENING PRAYER, OR SEPARATELY   R 563 04
SHALL SAY THE FOLLOWING PRAYER   R 564 26
THE SACRIFICES OF PRAYER AND THANKSGIVING, FOR   565 09
THE BISHOP SHALL SAY THIS PRAYER   R 568 09
PRAYER OR EVENING PRAYER, OR SEPARATELY   R 569 09
OR AT MORNING PRAYER OR EVENING PRAYER, OR   R 569 09
BOOK OF COMMON PRAYER, AND BOOKS OF CANONS OF THE   R 571 23
THE SACRIFICES OF PRAYER AND PRAISE TO THEE IN THIS   572 20
IN PRAYER, TO QUICKEN MY DEVOTION   573 24
LEARN AT ALL TIMES TO CALL FOR BY DILIGENT PRAYER   580 20
IF THOU CANST SAY THE LORD'S PRAYER   580 21
WHAT DESIREST THOU OF GOD IN THIS PRAYER   580 28
THE LORD'S PRAYER, AND THE TEN COMMANDMENTS,   580 32
AND REPEATING WITH HIM THE LORD'S PRAYER   R 587 07
AND REPEATING WITH HIM THE LORD'S PRAYER   R 589 15
AND REPEATING WITH HIM THE LORD'S PRAYER   R 592 11
AND REPEATING WITH HIM THE LORD'S PRAYER   R 593 05
GIVE EAR UNTO OUR PRAYER, O MERCIFUL AND GRACIOUS   600 11
TO HAVE PUBLIC PRAYER IN THE CHURCH, OR TO MINISTER 607 28
BY VIRTUE OF PRAYER UNTO GOD   608 30

PRAYERS

WITH THE OTHER PRAYERS, IMMEDIATELY AFTER THE LORD BE   R 003 13
THESE PRAYERS FOLLOWING, THE PEOPLE DEVOUTLY   R 016 23
THE FOLLOWING PRAYERS SHALL BE OMITTED HERE WHEN   R 017 20
FOR WHOM OUR PRAYERS ARE DESIRED   019 07
ANY DESIRE THE PRAYERS OF THE CONGREGATION   R 019 12
WITH THE OTHER PRAYERS, IMMEDIATELY AFTER THE LORD BE   R 021 10
THESE PRAYERS FOLLOWING, THE PEOPLE DEVOUTLY   R 030 28
THE COLLECTS AND PRAYERS FOLLOWING   R 031 16
SUCH PRAYER, OR PRAYERS, TAKEN OUT OF THIS BOOK,   R 031 32
FOR WHOM OUR PRAYERS ARE DESIRED   033 05
ANY DESIRE THE PRAYERS OF THE CONGREGATION   R 033 10
WHO NOW MAKE OUR PRAYERS AND SUPPLICATIONS UNTO THEE   040 06
TO HEAR THE PRAYERS OF THOSE WHO PUT THEIR TRUST IN   041 20
FOR WHOM OUR PRAYERS ARE DESIRED   045 15
FOR WHOM OUR PRAYERS ARE OFFERED, AND GRANT THAT HE   045 25
FOR WHOM OUR PRAYERS ARE OFFERED   046 03
GREAT DEEP OUR PRAYERS ARE DESIRED   046 11
I BID YOUR PRAYERS FOR CHRIST'S HOLY CATHOLIC CHURCH,   047 06
APPROACH OF DEATH, ESPECIALLY NEED OUR PRAYERS   048 10
AND PRAYERS, AND DISPOSE THE WAY OF THY SERVANTS   049 12
NOW MADE OUR PRAYERS AND SUPPLICATIONS UNTO THEE   050 09
HEARD THE DEVOUT PRAYERS OF THY CHURCH, AND TURNED   051 31
ASSIST OUR PRAYERS WHICH WE MAKE BEFORE THEE IN ALL   058 17
FAVOURABLY WITH MERCY HEAR OUR PRAYERS   059 13
NECESSARY IN THE PRAYERS FOR OUR CIVIL RULERS, IN   VI 16
END OF ALL SUCH PRAYERS, NAMELY, THAT 'RULERS MAY   VI 19
ADD OTHER PRAYERS FROM THIS BOOK   R 059 29
HEAR OUR PRAYERS, AND SPARE ALL THOSE WHO CONFESS   062 08
OTHER AUTHORIZED PRAYERS AND INTERCESSIONS   R 071 30
HAVE DESIRED THE PRAYERS OF THE CHURCH   R 074 03
US TO MAKE PRAYERS, AND SUPPLICATIONS, AND TO GIVE   074 07
THESE OUR PRAYERS, WHICH WE OFFER UNTO THY DIVINE   074 10
TO RECEIVE THE PRAYERS OF THY PEOPLE WHO CALL UPON   109 30
TO HEAR THE PRAYERS OF THY PEOPLE   118 29
AND PRAYERS, WHICH WE OFFER BEFORE THEE FOR ALL   156 29
MERCIFULLY ACCEPT OUR PRAYERS   188 33
AND HIS EARS ARE OPEN UNTO THEIR PRAYERS   195 29
BE OPEN TO THE PRAYERS OF THY HUMBLE SERVANTS   203 11
HEAR THE DEVOUT PRAYERS OF THY CHURCH   222 11
FASTINGS AND PRAYERS NIGHT AND DAY   233 21
THE PRAYERS OF THY PEOPLE, AND GRANT THAT   259 21
ACCEPT OUR PRAYERS ON BEHALF OF THE SOUL OF THY   268 23
WITH PRAYERS AND FASTING, FOR THE   R 273 21
ACCORD MAKE OUR PRAYERS UNTO HIM, THAT THIS CHILD   280 16
MAY ADD ONE OR BOTH OF THE FOLLOWING PRAYERS   R 303 13
THE OCCASIONAL PRAYERS AND THANKSGIVINGS, MAY BE USED   R 305 05
THESE OUR PRAYERS, AS WE CALL UPON THEE ON   311 21
ACCEPT OUR PRAYERS, AND GRANT TO THY SERVANT THE HELP   312 13
THESE PRAYERS MAY BE SAID WITH THE FOREGOING   R 315 03
OTHER FITTING PRAYERS AS ARE ELSEWHERE PROVIDED IN   R 331 30
BEFORE THE PRAYERS, FIRST PRONOUNCING, THE LORD BE   R 331 31
OF THE FOLLOWING PRAYERS, AT HIS DISCRETION   R 334 12
ACCEPT OUR PRAYERS ON BEHALF OF THE SOUL OF THY   334 15
OF THE FOLLOWING PRAYERS BEFORE THE FINAL BLESSING   R 335 23
THE FOLLOWING PRAYERS, OR OTHER FITTING PRAYERS FROM   R 340 22
OR OTHER FITTING PRAYERS FROM THIS BOOK   R 340 22
AND HIS EARS ARE OPEN UNTO THEIR PRAYERS   380 31
THE VOICE OF MY PRAYERS, O LORD   516 21
TO THE PRAYERS OF THE CONGREGATION) SHALL   R 530 30
TO THE PRAYERS OF THE CONGREGATION) SHALL,   R 537 06
BE DILIGENT IN PRAYERS, AND IN READING THE HOLY   542 26
IN THEIR PRAYERS, TO MAKE THEIR HUMBLE SUPPLICATIONS   R 543 23
FOR THE WHICH PRAYERS THERE SHALL BE SILENCE KEPT FOR   R 543 25
OFFER UP OUR PRAYERS TO ALMIGHTY GOD, BEFORE WE ADMIT   553 10
TO OUR PRAYERS, O LORD, WE JOIN OUR UNFEIGNED THANKS   591 07
NAME WE OFFER UP THESE OUR IMPERFECT PRAYERS   591 33
HERE MAY BE ADDED ANY SPECIAL PRAYERS   R 592 26
HERE MAY BE ADDED ANY SPECIAL PRAYERS   R 593 17

PRAYETH

BEHOLD, HE PRAYETH, AND HATH SEEN IN A VISION A   230 19
WILT THOU BE ANGRY WITH THY PEOPLE THAT PRAYETH   441 11

PRAYING

WHO TURN TO THEE IN WEEPING, FASTING, AND PRAYING   062 30
PRAYING ALWAYS WITH ALL PRAYER AND SUPPLICATION IN   219 19
JESUS CHRIST, PRAYING ALWAYS FOR YOU, SINCE WE HEARD   223 23

PRE-EMINENCE

THE RIGHT HAND OF THE LORD HATH THE PRE-EMINENCE   488 33

PREACH

BLESSED SON TO PREACH PEACE TO THEM THAT ARE FAR OFF   038 07
HOW SHALL THEY PREACH, EXCEPT THEY BE SENT   073 09
CONSTANTLY TO PREACH THE GOSPEL UNTO ALL NATIONS   078 30
ANOINTED ME TO PREACH GOOD TIDINGS UNTO THE MEEK   106 31
THAT I SHOULD PREACH AMONG THE GENTILES THE   108 19
AND PREACH THE BAPTISM OF REPENTANCE FOR   112 10
COMMANDED US TO PREACH UNTO THE PEOPLE, AND TO   166 28
COMMANDED US TO PREACH UNTO THE PEOPLE, AND TO   184 16
I OR THEY, SO WE PREACH, AND SO YE BELIEVED   205 19
HOW SHALL THEY PREACH, EXCEPT THEY BE SENT   227 08
FEET OF THEM THAT PREACH THE GOSPEL OF PEACE, AND   227 10
DILIGENTLY TO PREACH THY HOLY WORD, AND THE PEOPLE   244 26
TO BELIEVE AND TO PREACH THY WORD   249 16
AND BOTH TO PREACH AND RECEIVE THE SAME   249 18
FOR WE PREACH NOT OURSELVES, BUT CHRIST JESUS THE   251 05
ANOINTED ME TO PREACH THE GOSPEL TO THE POOR   261 17
TO PREACH DELIVERANCE TO THE CAPTIVES,   261 18

PREACH   CONTINUED

ARE BRUISED, TO PREACH THE ACCEPTABLE YEAR OF THE   261 20
AND IS SENT TO PREACH THE GOSPEL TO THE WHOLE WORLD   291 13
TO PREACH THE WORD OF GOD   294 13
WHY DOST THOU PREACH MY LAWS, AND TAKEST MY COVENANT   402 23
AND TO PREACH, IF HE BE ADMITTED THERETO BY THE   533 17
OF GOD, AND TO PREACH THE SAME, IF THOU BE THERETO   534 12
THOU AUTHORITY TO PREACH THE WORD OF GOD, AND TO   546 25
MAY DILIGENTLY PREACH THY WORD, AND DULY ADMINISTER   549 11

PREACHED

MAY BE TRULY PREACHED, TRULY RECEIVED, AND TRULY   037 03
HAVE THE GOSPEL PREACHED TO THEM   094 23
AND PREACHED, SAYING, THERE COMETH ONE MIGHTIER THAN   112 14
WHEN I HAVE PREACHED TO OTHERS, I MYSELF SHOULD BE A   119 12
GOSPEL SHALL BE PREACHED THROUGHOUT THE WHOLE WORLD,   140 16
HE WENT AND PREACHED UNTO THE SPIRITS IN PRISON   161 25
AFTER THE BAPTISM WHICH JOHN PREACHED   166 19
THIS MAN IS PREACHED UNTO YOU THE FORGIVENESS OF   169 19
SINS SHOULD BE PREACHED IN HIS NAME AMONG ALL   170 14
AFTER THE BAPTISM WHICH JOHN PREACHED   184 06
GOSPEL WHICH I PREACHED UNTO YOU, WHICH ALSO YE HAVE   204 30
MEMORY WHAT I PREACHED UNTO YOU, UNLESS YE HAVE   205 02
STRAIGHTWAY HE PREACHED CHRIST IN THE SYNAGOGUES,   231 04
GOSPEL MAY BE PREACHED TO ALL PEOPLE   561 13
BE READ AND PREACHED IN THIS PLACE, AND BY THY HOLY   566 03
WORD OF GOD IS PREACHED, AND THE SACRAMENTS BE DULY   606 39

PREACHER

AND HOW SHALL THEY HEAR WITHOUT A PREACHER   073 09
AND HOW SHALL THEY HEAR WITHOUT A PREACHER   227 08

PREACHING

BOTH BY THEIR PREACHING AND LIVING THEY MAY SET IT   055 32
OF ISRAEL, PREACHING PEACE BY JESUS CHRIST   166 16
OF ISRAEL, PREACHING PEACE BY JESUS CHRIST   184 03
THROUGH THE PREACHING OF THE BLESSED APOSTLE SAINT   229 17
OUR SAVIOUR BY PREACHING REPENTANCE   242 09
WE MAY TRULY REPENT ACCORDING TO HIS PREACHING   242 11
I HAVE GONE PREACHING THE KINGDOM OF GOD, SHALL SEE   550 23
THAT HE, PREACHING THY WORD, MAY NOT ONLY BE EARNEST   559 07
AND IN PREACHING, TO GIVE A READINESS OF THOUGHT AND   573 26
OF PUBLIC PREACHING, OR MINISTERING THE SACRAMENTS IN   607 19

PRECEDING

IN THE WEEKS PRECEDING THE STATED TIMES OF   R 038 24
IMMEDIATELY PRECEDING,) HE SHALL READ THIS   R 086 26

PRECEPT

HAD SPOKEN EVERY PRECEPT TO ALL THE PEOPLE ACCORDING   147 19

PRECEPTS

NOR THE CIVIL PRECEPTS THEREOF OUGHT OF NECESSITY TO   604 20

PRECIOUS

WITH THY PRECIOUS BLOOD   010 34
CHURCH BY THE PRECIOUS BLOOD OF THY DEAR SON   038 26
WITH THY MOST PRECIOUS BLOOD, AND BE NOT ANGRY WITH   054 16
BY THY PRECIOUS DEATH AND BURIAL   055 11
FOR THE PRECIOUS DEATH AND MERITS OF THY SON JESUS   079 15
OF THAT HIS PRECIOUS DEATH AND SACRIFICE, UNTIL HIS   080 15
PASSION AND PRECIOUS DEATH, HIS MIGHTY RESURRECTION   081 03
THE MOST PRECIOUS BODY AND BLOOD OF THY SON JESUS   081 25
HIS MOST PRECIOUS BLOOD, AND THAT WE MAY EVERMORE   082 21
OF THE MOST PRECIOUS BODY AND BLOOD OF THY SON OUR   083 19
OF HIS MOST PRECIOUS DEATH AND PASSION   083 25
WHICH BY HIS PRECIOUS BLOOD-SHEDDING HE HATH OBTAINED   086 15
BOX OF OINTMENT OF SPIKENARD VERY PRECIOUS   140 04
OF GOD, AND PRECIOUS, YE ALSO, AS LIVELY STONES, ARE   259 30
OUT OF HIS MOST PRECIOUS SIDE BOTH WATER AND BLOOD   279 11
THY CROSS AND PRECIOUS BLOOD HAST REDEEMED US   313 13
THAT IT MAY BE PRECIOUS IN THY SIGHT   317 16
BY THY PRECIOUS DEATH AND BURIAL   318 05
ABOVE GOLD AND PRECIOUS STONES   498 24
IT IS LIKE THE PRECIOUS OIL UPON THE HEAD, THAT RAN   509 15
REFUSE THEIR PRECIOUS BALMS   517 20

PREDESTINATION

PREDESTINATION TO LIFE IS THE EVERLASTING PURPOSE OF   606 06
OF PREDESTINATION, AND OUR ELECTION IN CHRIST,   606 16
OF GOD'S PREDESTINATION, IS A MOST DANGEROUS   606 24

PREFACE

IN THE PREFACE OF HER BOOK OF COMMON PRAYER,   V 12
NOT ONLY IN HER PREFACE, BUT LIKEWISE IN HER ARTICLES   V 21
IN HER SAID PREFACE, TO DO THAT WHICH, ACCORDING TO   V 34
THE PROPER PREFACE, ACCORDING TO THE TIME, IF THERE   R 077 02

PREFER

IF I PREFER NOT JERUSALEM ABOVE MY CHIEF JOY   513 16

PREFERRED

AFTER ME IS PREFERRED BEFORE ME, WHOSE SHOE'S LATCHET   096 04

PREFERRING

IN HONOUR PREFERRING ONE ANOTHER   111 24

PREJUDICE

FROM ALL ERROR, IGNORANCE, PRIDE, AND PREJUDICE   036 32
ALL HATRED AND PREJUDICE, AND WHATSOEVER ELSE MAY   037 28
WITHOUT PREJUDICE OR PREPOSSESSIONS   VI 38

PREMONISH

AND TO PREMONISH, TO FEED AND PROVIDE FOR THE   539 33

PREPARATION

IT WAS THE PREPARATION OF THE PASSOVER, AND ABOUT THE 159 25
IT WAS THE PREPARATION, THAT THE BODIES SHOULD NCT   160 30
DAY OF THE PREPARATION, THE CHIEF PRIESTS AND   162 16
WITH THE PREPARATION OF THE GOSPEL OF PEACE   219 15

PREPARE

PREPARE YE THE WAY OF THE LORD, MAKE STRAIGHT IN THE 004 06
OF THE LORD TO PREPARE HIS WAYS   014 25
CHRIST DIDST PREPARE THE DISCIPLES FOR THE COMING OF 043 19
INTO HEAVEN, TO PREPARE A PLACE FOR US   078 19
THY MESSENGER TO PREPARE THY WAY BEFORE THEE   093 25
MAY LIKEWISE SO PREPARE AND MAKE READY THY WAY, BY   093 27
WHICH SHALL PREPARE THY WAY BEFORE THEE   094 32
WHICH SHALL PREPARE THY WAY BEFORE THEE   112 05
THE WILDERNESS, PREPARE YE THE WAY OF THE LORD, MAKE 112 06
THAT WE GO AND PREPARE THAT THOU MAYEST EAT THE   140 24
GO AND PREPARE US THE PASSOVER, THAT WE MAY   148 23
WHERE WILT THOU THAT WE PREPARE   148 24
AND HE SHALL PREPARE THE WAY BEFORE ME   232 03
I GO TO PREPARE A PLACE FOR YOU   239 32
AND IF I GO AND PREPARE A PLACE FOR YOU, I WILL COME 239 33
AND SENT TO PREPARE THE WAY OF THY SON OUR SAVIOUR BY 242 08
THE WILDERNESS, PREPARE YE THE WAY OF THE LORD,   242 21
OF THE LORD TO PREPARE HIS WAYS   244 11
BE EXHORTED TO PREPARE THEMSELVES, WITH PRAYERS AND R 273 20
AND IF I GO AND PREPARE A PLACE FOR YOU, I WILL CCME 331 20
I GO TO PREPARE A PLACE FOR YOU   331 20
THOU SHALT PREPARE A TABLE BEFORE ME IN THE PRESENCE 338 26
5 THOU SHALT PREPARE A TABLE BEFORE ME IN THE   368 19
4 THEY RUN AND PREPARE THEMSELVES WITHOUT MY FAULT   411 11
O PREPARE THY LOVING MERCY AND FAITHFULNESS, THAT   413 19
SHALL GOD PREPARE A TABLE IN THE WILDERNESS   436 07
CANNOT TURN AND PREPARE HIMSELF, BY HIS OWN NATURAL 604 43

PREPARED

AND HIS HANDS PREPARED THE DRY LAND   009 11
WHICH THOU HAST PREPARED *   028 12
AS THOU HAST PREPARED FOR US TO WALK IN   083 28
WHEN A MAN HATH PREPARED A RICH FEAST, DECKED HIS   088 18
YOU A LARGE UPPER ROOM FURNISHED AND PREPARED   140 31
BODY HAST THOU PREPARED ME   157 25
O GOD, WHO HAST PREPARED FOR THOSE WHO LOVE THEE SUCH 197 04
BEHOLD, I HAVE PREPARED MY DINNER   218 08
WHICH THOU HAST PREPARED BEFORE THE FACE OF ALL   233 07
FOR WHOM IT IS PREPARED OF MY FATHER   247 18
WHICH THOU HAST PREPARED FOR THOSE WHO UNFEIGNECLY   256 10
THE KINGDOM PREPARED FOR YOU FROM THE FOUNDATION CF 259 04
NECESSARY BEING PREPARED, THE MINISTER SHALL THERE   R 321 14
THE KINGDOM PREPARED FOR YOU FROM THE BEGINNING OF   335 12
THE KINGDOM PREPARED FOR YOU FROM THE FOUNDATION OF 336 27
14 HE HATH PREPARED FOR HIM THE INSTRUMENTS OF DEATH 350 19
HE HATH ALSO PREPARED HIS SEAT FOR JUDGMENT   352 03
THAT THOU HAST PREPARED FOR THEM THAT PUT THEIR TRUST 377 05
OF THY GOODNESS PREPARED FOR THE POOR   419 32
THOU HAST PREPARED THE LIGHT AND THE SUN   431 09
HATH THY SEAT BEEN PREPARED   457 09
AND HIS HANDS PREPARED THE DRY LAND   459 13
THOU HAST PREPARED EQUITY, *   462 22
THE LORD HATH PREPARED HIS SEAT IN HEAVEN, *   467 13
THINGS ARE DULY PREPARED IN THE CHURCH, AND SET IN   R 549 03
OUT OF HEAVEN, PREPARED AS A BRIDE ADORNED FOR HER   567 13

PREPAREST

THOU PREPAREST THEIR HEART, AND THINE EAR HEARKENETH 354 14
THOU PREPAREST THEIR CORN, FOR SO THOU PROVIDEST FOR 417 02

PREPARETH

AND PREPARETH RAIN FOR THE EARTH   264 27
AND PREPARETH RAIN FOR THE EARTH   523 10

PREPARING

THE ARK WAS A PREPARING, WHEREIN FEW, THAT IS, EIGHT 161 28

PREPOSSESSIONS

WITHOUT PREJUDICE OR PREPOSSESSIONS   VI 38

PRESBYTER

PRESBYTER, GREETING   569 13

PRESBYTERS

ADVICE OF OUR PRESBYTERS, ARE TO BE THE ULTIMATE   569 36

PRESCRIBED

ACCORDING TO THE FORM BEFORE PRESCRIBED   R 083 08
FORM BEFORE PRESCRIBED FOR THE HOLY COMMUNION,   R 322 30
BE EXAMINED AND ORDAINED, AS IS ABOVE PRESCRIBED   R 547 24
OR CHURCH, AS PRESCRIBED BY CANON, AND BEING   R 569 05
ALSO OF THE PRESCRIBED LETTER OF INSTITUTION   570 16
AS PRESCRIBED IN THIS OFFICE IN THE FORM OF   R 574 30

PRESENCE

COME BEFORE HIS PRESENCE WITH THANKSGIVING   009 05
COME BEFORE HIS PRESENCE WITH A SONG   015 05
APPEAR IN THE PRESENCE OF GOD FOR US   022 24
CHURCH HERE ASSEMBLED IN THY NAME AND PRESENCE   036 31
OR ABOUT TO ASSEMBLE) IN THY NAME AND PRESENCE   R 037 12
LIGHT OF THY PRESENCE, THAT THE GOOD WORK WHICH THOU 042 18
IN THE PRESENCE OF ALL THY PEOPLE   053 02
IN THE PRESENCE OF ALL THY PEOPLE   053 13
AWAY FROM THY PRESENCE, *   060 32
NOT AS IN MY PRESENCE ONLY, BUT NOW MUCH MORE IN MY   106 02
ANGEL OF HIS PRESENCE SAVED THEM   139 02
APPEAR IN THE PRESENCE OF GOD FOR US   147 32
IS JOY IN THE PRESENCE OF THE ANGELS OF GOD OVER CNE 193 33
WORSHIP IN THE PRESENCE OF THEM THAT SIT AT MEAT WITH 214 18
JESUS IN THE PRESENCE OF HIS DISCIPLES, WHICH ARE NCT 229 10
YE HERE, IN THE PRESENCE OF GOD, AND OF THIS   296 22
WITH HIS PRESENCE AND FIRST MIRACLE THAT HE WROUGHT   300 14
VOWS NOW IN THE PRESENCE OF ALL HIS PEOPLE, IN THE   305 31
SICK PERSON'S PRESENCE, SHALL SAY, PEACE TO THIS   R 308 06
IN THY PRESENCE IS THE FULNESS OF JOY, AND AT THY   333 09
ME IN THE PRESENCE OF THEM THAT TROUBLE ME   338 26
STAND IN THY PRESENCE IN FULNESS OF JOY   341 03
THEY SHALL FALL AND PERISH AT THY PRESENCE   351 27
IN THY PRESENCE IS THE FULNESS OF JOY, *   358 12
2 LET MY SENTENCE COME FORTH FROM THY PRESENCE   358 19
BEHOLD THY PRESENCE IN RIGHTEOUSNESS   359 19
OUT IN HIS PRESENCE, *   360 12
OF HIS PRESENCE HIS CLOUDS REMOVED   360 22
ME IN THE PRESENCE OF THEM THAT TROUBLE ME   368 19
OF THINE OWN PRESENCE FROM THE PLOTTINGS OF MEN   377 07
BEFORE THE PRESENCE OF GOD   393 02
AWAY FROM THY PRESENCE, *   403 31
PERISH AT THE PRESENCE OF GOD   419 13
DROPPED AT THE PRESENCE OF GOD   419 26
MOVED AT THE PRESENCE OF GOD, WHO IS THE GOD OF   419 27
ENTER INTO THY PRESENCE, INCLINE THINE EAR UNTO MY   448 31
COME BEFORE HIS PRESENCE WITH THANKSGIVING   459 07
LIKE WAX AT THE PRESENCE OF THE LORD   461 06
AT THE PRESENCE OF THE LORD OF THE WHOLE EARTH   461 07
COME BEFORE HIS PRESENCE WITH A SONG   463 06
AT THE PRESENCE OF THE GOD   485 06
AT THE PRESENCE OF THE GOD OF JACOB   485 07
VOWS NOW IN THE PRESENCE OF ALL HIS PEOPLE   487 13
PETITION IN THY PRESENCE WITH MY WHOLE HEART   493 26
OR WHITHER SHALL I GO THEN FROM THY PRESENCE   514 32
IN THE PRESENCE OF THE PEOPLE, AFTER THIS   R 532 24
THY ESPECIAL PRESENCE, WHEREVER TWO OR THREE OF THY   564 31
TO THY PRESENCE, WHERE WE MAY BE STILL AND KNOW   595 22

PRESENT

MANY AS ARE HERE PRESENT, TO ACCOMPANY ME WITH A PURE 006 10
THINGS MAY PLEASE HIM WHICH WE DO AT THIS PRESENT   007 16
MANY AS ARE HERE PRESENT, TO ACCOMPANY ME WITH A PURE 023 19
THINGS MAY PLEASE HIM WHICH WE DO AT THIS PRESENT   024 18
ANY WOMAN, BEING PRESENT IN CHURCH, SHALL HAVE   R 051 03
WHO SHALL HUMBLY PRESENT AND PLACE IT UPON THE HCLY R 073 30
AND ESPECIALLY TO THIS CONGREGATION HERE PRESENT   074 26
BISHOP IF HE BE PRESENT) STAND UP, AND TURNING TC THE R 075 32
WE OFFER AND PRESENT UNTO THEE, O LORD, OUR SELVES,   081 21
IF ANY BE PRESENT,) AND, AFTER THAT, TO THE PEOPLE R 082 27
GIVEN TO THOSE PRESENT TO COMMUNICATE   R 082 29
BISHOP IF HE BE PRESENT) SHALL LET THEM DEPART WITH R 084 16
I BID YOU ALL WHO ARE HERE PRESENT   088 14
IN THIS PRESENT WORLD   098 21
OF GOD, THAT YE PRESENT YOUR BODIES A LIVING   110 04
OF THE PRESENT TIME, IN FULL ASSURANCE OF THE GLORY   144 08
BEING YET PRESENT WITH YOU   181 30
OF THIS PRESENT TIME ARE NOT WORTHY TO BE COMPARED   194 11
REMAIN UNTO THIS PRESENT, BUT SOME ARE FALLEN ASLEEP 205 09
TO JERUSALEM, TO PRESENT HIM TO THE LORD   232 25
LOVED THIS PRESENT WORLD, AND IS DEPARTED UNTO   253 32
THAT HE MIGHT PRESENT IT TO HIMSELF A GLORIOUS   267 22
THERE SHALL BE PRESENT WITH HIM AT THE FONT AT LEAST R 273 23
SOME ONE WHO IS PRESENT, THE MINISTER SHALL POUR   R 281 19
BAPTIZED PERSON PRESENT MAY ADMINISTER HOLY BAPTISM, R 281 28
FATHER IN GOD, I PRESENT UNTO YOU THESE PERSONS TO   296 08
TWO PERSONS PRESENT COME NOW TO BE JOINED   300 19
BE PRESENT IN THY GOODNESS WITH THIS THY SERVANT,   315 08
A VERY PRESENT HELP IN TROUBLE   327 03
OF THIS PRESENT TIME ARE NOT WORTHY TO BE COMPARED   330 27
NOR THINGS PRESENT, NOR THINGS TO COME, NOR HEIGHT,   331 11
A VERY PRESENT HELP IN TROUBLE   397 25
I WAKE UP, I AM PRESENT WITH THEE   515 27
A PRIEST SHALL PRESENT UNTO THE BISHOP, SITTING IN R 530 07
FATHER IN GOD, I PRESENT UNTO YOU THESE PERSONS   530 10
THESE PERSONS PRESENT, TO BE ADMITTED DEACONS   530 11
WHOM YE PRESENT UNTO US, BE APT AND MEET,   530 13
AND PEOPLE PRESENT, SAY THE LITANY   R 530 30
A PRIEST SHALL PRESENT UNTO THE BISHOP, SITTING IN R 536 07
FATHER IN GOD, I PRESENT UNTO YOU THESE PERSONS   536 10
THESE PERSONS PRESENT, TO BE ADMITTED TO THE ORDER OF 536 11
WHOM YE PRESENT UNTO US, BE APT AND MEET,   536 14
AND PEOPLE PRESENT, SAY THE LITANY   R 537 06
THAT THIS PRESENT CONGREGATION OF CHRIST MAY   541 24

PRESENT   CONTINUED

OTHERS THAT ARE PRESENT, ANSWERING BY VERSES,   R 543 28
SERVANTS HERE PRESENT TO THE SAME OFFICE AND   545 23
WITH THE PRIESTS PRESENT, SHALL LAY THEIR HANDS   R 546 06
BY THE BISHOPS PRESENT, SHALL BEGIN THE COMMUNION   R 549 04
THE BISHOPS WHO PRESENT HIM SAYING,   R 552 19
IN GOD, WE PRESENT UNTO YOU THIS GODLY AND   552 21
THE CONGREGATION PRESENT TO PRAY, SAYING THUS TO   R 553 02
THE CONGREGATION PRESENT MAY HAVE A TRIAL, AND BEAR   554 14
GODLY IN THIS PRESENT WORLD   555 09
OTHERS THAT ARE PRESENT, STANDING, SHALL ANSWER BY   R 556 05
AND BISHOPS PRESENT SHALL LAY THEIR HANDS UPON THE   R 558 09
CLERGY WHO ARE PRESENT SHALL GO UP THE AISLE OF THE   R 563 07
O LORD, TO BE PRESENT WITH US, WHO ARE HERE GATHERED   565 03
THE OTHER CLERGY PRESENT, SHALL ENTER THE CHANCEL   R 570 04
ALL THE CLERGY PRESENT STANDING IN THE CHANCEL OR   R 570 05
HIS PLACE) PRESENT THE KEYS OF THE CHURCH TO THE NEW   R 570 26
THE ALTAR, AND PRESENT HIM THE BIBLE, BOOK OF COMMON   R 571 23
AT THE ALTAR, TO PRESENT HIS SUPPLICATION FOR   R 573 09
CONGREGATION PRESENT, GIVE THE ABUNDANCE OF THY   574 09
THE DIOCESE IS PRESENT AT THE INSTITUTION OF A   R 574 29
CONVENIENTLY BE PRESENT, LET ONE OF THEM, OR ANY   R 587 05

PRESENTED

RECEIVED AND PRESENTED, THERE MAY BE SUNG A HYMN, OR   R 073 34
THEY PRESENTED UNTO HIM GIFTS   109 22
WAS THIS DAY PRESENTED IN THE TEMPLE IN SUBSTANCE OF   231 30
SO WE MAY BE PRESENTED UNTO THEE WITH PURE AND CLEAN   231 31
IT MAY BE PRESENTED PURE AND WITHOUT SPOT BEFORE   317 21
WITHOUT SPOT PRESENTED UNTO THEE   321 25
THESE PERSONS PRESENTED TO BE ORDERED DEACONS,   530 23
SHALL BE FIRST PRESENTED, AND THEN THE PRIESTS   R 547 20
SHALL BE PRESENTED BY TWO BISHOPS OF THIS CHURCH UNTO R 552 17
OF THE PERSON PRESENTED FOR CONSECRATION, AND SHALL   R 552 24
THIS PERSON PRESENTED UNTO US, TO THE WORK WHEREUNTO   553 11
THERE BE ANY, PRESENTED TO HIM   R 564 08
FIT TO BE PRESENTED TO THE BISHOP TO BE CONFIRMED   R 583 08

PRESENTS

KINGS BRING PRESENTS UNTO THEE   421 14
OF TARSHISH AND OF THE ISLES SHALL GIVE PRESENTS   427 16
BRING PRESENTS UNTO HIM THAT OUGHT TO BE FEARED   433 11
BRING PRESENTS, AND COME INTO HIS COURTS   460 15
WE DO BY THESE PRESENTS GIVE AND GRANT UNTO YOU,   569 14

PRESERVATION

TEND TO THE PRESERVATION OF PEACE AND UNITY IN THE   V 35
PRESERVATION, AND ALL THE BLESSINGS OF   019 21
PRESERVATION, AND ALL THE BLESSINGS OF   033 19
FOR WHOSE PRESERVATION ON THE GREAT DEEP OUR PRAYERS   046 10
FOR THY PRESERVATION OF US FROM THE BEGINNING OF OUR   587 21

PRESERVE

PRESERVE THEM FROM THE DANGERS OF THE SEA, AND FROM   042 06
PRESERVE HIM FROM THE TEMPTATIONS OF THE ENEMY   045 16
PLEASED TO PRESERVE, THROUGH THE GREAT PAIN AND PERIL   051 06
TO BLESS AND PRESERVE ALL CHRISTIAN RULERS AND   055 26
PLEASE THEE TO PRESERVE ALL WHO TRAVEL BY LAND, BY   056 30
TO GIVE AND PRESERVE TO OUR USE THE KINDLY FRUITS OF   057 10
GIVEN FOR THEE, PRESERVE THY BODY AND SOUL UNTO   082 32
SHED FOR THEE, PRESERVE THY BODY AND SOUL UNTO   083 04
THY SUCCOUR, PRESERVE IT EVERMORE BY THY HELP AND   212 06
BLESS, PRESERVE, AND KEEP YOU   304 12
AND TO PRESERVE YOU IN THE GREAT DANGER OF   305 13
PLEASED TO PRESERVE, THROUGH THE GREAT PAIN AND PERIL   306 25
PRESERVE AND CONTINUE THIS SICK MEMBER IN THE UNITY   314 05
THE LORD SHALL PRESERVE THEE FROM ALL EVIL   327 31
THE LORD SHALL PRESERVE THY GOING OUT, AND THY COMING   327 33
THE LORD SHALL PRESERVE THEE FROM ALL EVIL   339 15
THE LORD SHALL PRESERVE THY GOING OUT, AND THY COMING   339 17
THOU SHALT PRESERVE THEM FROM THIS GENERATION FOR   355 23
PRESERVE ME, O GOD   357 21
THOU SHALT PRESERVE ME FROM TROUBLE   378 05
THY TRUTH ALWAY PRESERVE ME   391 09
2 THE LORD PRESERVE HIM, AND KEEP HIM ALIVE, THAT HE   391 32
THAT THEY MAY PRESERVE HIM   413 20
PRESERVE MY LIFE FROM FEAR OF THE ENEMY   415 19
AND SHALL PRESERVE THE SOULS OF THE POOR   427 23
OF THY POWER, PRESERVE THOU THOSE THAT ARE APPOINTED   440 28
2 PRESERVE THOU MY SOUL, FOR I AM HOLY   447 07
THE LORD SHALL PRESERVE THEE FROM ALL EVIL   503 04
THE LORD SHALL PRESERVE THY GOING OUT, AND THY COMING   503 06
AND PRESERVE ME FROM THE WICKED MAN   516 09
PRESERVE ME FROM THE WICKED MEN, WHO ARE PURPOSED TO   516 16
PRESERVE US FROM FAITHLESS FEARS AND WORLDLY   596 05
HEAVENLY GRACE PRESERVE FROM FALLING THOSE WHOSE   599 12
OF THY POWER, PRESERVE THOU THOSE THAT ARE APPOINTED   600 10

PRESERVED

MAY BE PRESERVED EVERMORE FROM ALL PERILS, TO GLORIFY   041 14
WE MAY BE PRESERVED IN BODY AND SOUL   070 10
GOVERNED AND PRESERVED EVERMORE, BOTH IN BODY AND   132 20
BEING ALWAY PRESERVED FROM FALSE APOSTLES, MAY BE   234 02
WE MAY BE PRESERVED IN BODY AND SOUL   298 30
BUT THEY ARE PRESERVED FOR EVER   386 20
SO WE MAY BE PRESERVED PURE AND BLAMELESS, UNTO THE   590 19

PRESERVER

CREATOR AND PRESERVER OF ALL MANKIND, WE HUMBLY   018 26

PRESERVER   CONTINUED

CREATOR AND PRESERVER OF ALL MANKIND, WE HUMBLY   032 26
CREATOR AND PRESERVER OF ALL MANKIND, GIVER OF ALL   303 03
THE MAKER, AND PRESERVER OF ALL THINGS BOTH VISIBLE   603 05

PRESERVETH

WHO PRESERVETH THEM THAT ARE TRUE OF HEART   350 13
FOR THE LORD PRESERVETH THEM THAT ARE FAITHFUL, AND   377 15
THE LORD PRESERVETH THE SOULS OF HIS SAINTS   461 17
6 THE LORD PRESERVETH THE SIMPLE   486 30
20 THE LORD PRESERVETH ALL THEM THAT LOVE HIM   521 32

PRESIDE

SPIRIT DIDST PRESIDE IN THE COUNCIL OF THE BLESSED   036 27

PRESIDENT

SERVANT THE PRESIDENT OF THE UNITED STATES, AND ALL   017 31
GRANT TO THE PRESIDENT OF THE UNITED STATES, AND TO   018 10
SERVANTS THE PRESIDENT OF THE UNITED STATES, THE   032 06
PRAY FOR THE PRESIDENT OF THESE UNITED STATES,   047 15
THE PRESIDENT OF THE UNITED STATES, THAT HE   055 23

PRESIDING

IN ORDER, THE PRESIDING BISHOP, OR SOME OTHER BISHOP   R 549 04
UNTO THE PRESIDING BISHOP, OR TO THE BISHOP   R 552 18
THEN SHALL THE PRESIDING BISHOP DEMAND TESTIMONIALS   R 552 24
THEN THE PRESIDING BISHOP SHALL MOVE THE   R 553 02
OF THE PRESIDING BISHOP, INSTEAD OF THE LITANY, MAY   R 553 23
THE PRESIDING BISHOP, SITTING IN HIS CHAIR,   R 554 05
THE PRESIDING BISHOP SHALL SAY, ALMIGHTY   R 555 27
THE PRESIDING BISHOP SHALL BEGIN, AND THE BISHOPS,   R 556 04
THE PRESIDING BISHOP SHALL SAY, LORD, HEAR OUR   R 557 16
THEN THE PRESIDING BISHOP AND BISHOPS PRESENT SHALL   R 558 09
THE PRESIDING BISHOP SAYING,   R 558 10
THEN THE PRESIDING BISHOP SHALL DELIVER HIM THE   R 558 20
THEN THE PRESIDING BISHOP SHALL PROCEED IN THE   R 559 02

PRESS

AND VISIBLY PRESS WITH THEIR TEETH (AS SAINT   609 05

PRESSED

GOOD MEASURE, PRESSED DOWN, AND SHAKEN TOGETHER,   194 29
AS THE PEOPLE PRESSED UPON HIM TO HEAR THE WORD OF   196 06
FOR MY FEET, AND PRESSED DOWN MY SOUL   409 26

PRESSES

AND THY PRESSES SHALL BURST OUT WITH NEW   005 22

PRESSETH

AND THY HAND PRESSETH ME SORE   387 24

PRESUME

WE DO NOT PRESUME TO COME TO THIS THY TABLE, O   082 13
THAT HE PRESUME NOT TO COME TO THE LORD'S TABLE,   R 085 03
BEFORE THEY PRESUME TO EAT OF THAT BREAD, AND DRINK   085 29
THOSE WHO WILL PRESUME TO RECEIVE IT UNWORTHILY   087 07
NO MAN MIGHT PRESUME TO EXECUTE ANY OF THEM, EXCEPT   529 15
ACCURSED THAT PRESUME TO SAY, THAT EVERY MAN SHALL BE   606 32

PRESUMPTION

THE PRESUMPTION OF THEM THAT HATE THEE INCREASETH   431 24

PRESUMPTUOUS

ALSO FROM PRESUMPTUOUS SINS, LEST THEY GET THE   364 10

PREVAIL

THAT HE COULD PREVAIL NOTHING, BUT THAT RATHER A   136 09
HELL SHALL NOT PREVAIL AGAINST IT   246 08
WITH OUR TONGUE WILL WE PREVAIL   355 14
3 MY MISDEEDS PREVAIL AGAINST ME   416 15

PREVAILED

VOICES OF THEM AND OF THE CHIEF PRIESTS PREVAILED   154 05
AND PREVAILED NOT   252 05
I HAVE PREVAILED AGAINST HIM   356 04
THEY HAVE NOT PREVAILED AGAINST ME   506 24

PREVAILING

IN HIS PREVAILING NAME AND WORDS, THEN SHALL THE   571 14

PREVENT

GRACE MAY ALWAYS PREVENT AND FOLLOW US, AND MAKE US   213 14
LORD SHALL NOT PREVENT THEM WHICH ARE ASLEEP   269 04
148 MINE EYES PREVENT THE NIGHT WATCHES   500 06

PREVENTING

SPECIAL GRACE PREVENTING US THOU DOST PUT INTO OUR   163 25
THOU BE OUR PREVENTING GUIDE, NO EVIL CAN OUR STEPS   545 08
THOU BE OUR PREVENTING GUIDE, NO EVIL CAN OUR STEPS   557 14

PREVENTING   CONTINUED

GOD BY CHRIST PREVENTING US, THAT WE MAY HAVE A GOOD   605 02

PREY

DELIVERED OVER AS A PREY UNTO THEM   052 12
SHALL NO MORE BE A PREY TO THE HEATHEN, NEITHER SHALL   262 15
IS GREEDY OF HIS PREY, *   359 10
ROARING AFTER THEIR PREY, *   469 02
GIVEN US OVER FOR A PREY UNTO THEIR TEETH   504 17

PRICE

BECAUSE IT IS THE PRICE OF BLOOD   135 11
OF SILVER, THE PRICE OF HIM THAT WAS VALUED, WHCM   135 16
WITH NO LESS PRICE THAN THE EFFUSION OF HIS OWN   554 11

PRICKS

IT IS HARD FOR THEE TO KICK AGAINST THE PRICKS   230 05

PRIDE

FROM PRIDE AND ARROGANCY, AND FROM EVERY EVIL WAY   036 14
IGNORANCE, PRIDE, AND PREJUDICE   036 31
FROM PRIDE, VAINGLORY, AND HYPOCRISY   054 23
NOT THE FOOT OF PRIDE COME AGAINST ME   384 19
THEY SHALL BE TAKEN IN THEIR PRIDE   411 30
ARE SO HOLDEN WITH PRIDE, *   428 21
LIFTED UP WITH PRIDE HE FALL INTO THE CONDEMNATICN OF   549 27
NOT THE FOOT OF PRIDE COME NIGH TO HURT THEM, NOR THE   574 14
AND THE PRIDE OF LIFE   598 23

PRIEST

HAVE A GREAT HIGH PRIEST, THAT IS PASSED INTO THE   005 06
TO BE MADE BY THE PRIEST ALONE, STANDING   R 007 03
THAT THE PRIEST, AT HIS DISCRETION, MAY USE,   R 007 04
TO BE MADE BY THE PRIEST ALONE, STANDING   R 024 07
AND THE PRIEST, STANDING REVERENTLY BEFORE THE HOLY   R 067 06
MAY BE OMITTED AT THE DISCRETION OF THE PRIEST   R 067 08
THEN SHALL THE PRIEST, TURNING TO THE PEOPLE,   R 067 22
THE PRIEST MAY OMIT THAT PART OF THE   R 067 26
IS OMITTED, THE PRIEST SHALL SAY THE SUMMARY OF THE   R 067 29
THEN MAY THE PRIEST SAY, HEAR WHAT OUR LORD JESUS   R 069 25
US THEN THE PRIEST MAY SAY,   R 070 05
THEN SHALL THE PRIEST SAY THE COLLECT OF THE DAY   R 070 17
AFTER WHICH, THE PRIEST, WHEN THERE IS A COMMUNICN,   R 071 31
BRING IT TO THE PRIEST, WHO SHALL HUMBLY PRESENT AND   R 073 32
AND THE PRIEST SHALL THEN OFFER, AND SHALL PLACE   R 073 32
UNDER THE DIRECTION OF THE PRIEST   R 073 36
HERE THE PRIEST MAY ASK THE SECRET INTERCESSIONS OF   R 074 02
THEN SHALL THE PRIEST SAY, LET US PRAY FOR THE WHOLE   R 074 04
THEN SHALL THE PRIEST SAY TO THOSE WHO COME TO   R 075 07
BE MADE, BY THE PRIEST AND ALL THOSE WHO ARE MINCED   R 075 15
THEN SHALL THE PRIEST (THE BISHOP IF HE BE PRESENT)   R 075 32
THEN SHALL THE PRIEST SAY, HEAR WHAT COMFORTABLE   R 076 09
AFTER WHICH THE PRIEST SHALL PROCEED, SAYING, LIFT UP R 076 25
THEN SHALL THE PRIEST TURN TO THE HOLY TABLE,   R 076 30
OR SUNG BY THE PRIEST, THEREFORE WITH ANGELS ANC   R 077 03
AND SAYING, PRIEST AND PEOPLE   R 077 07
AND SAYING, PRIEST AND PEOPLE   R 079 31
WHEN THE PRIEST, STANDING BEFORE THE HOLY TABLE,   R 080 02
A) HERE THE PRIEST IS TO TAKE THE PATEN INTO HIS   R 080 30
THEN SHALL THE PRIEST, KNEELING DOWN AT THE LORD'S   R 082 11
THEN SHALL THE PRIEST FIRST RECEIVE THE HOLY   R 082 25
THE PRIEST IS TO CONSECRATE MORE,   R 083 08
THE PRIEST SHALL RETURN TO THE LORD'S   R 083 11
THEN SHALL THE PRIEST SAY, ALMIGHTY AND EVERLIVING   R 083 14
THE PRIEST (THE BISHOP IF HE BE PRESENT)   R 084 16
THE ABSENCE OF A PRIEST, A DEACON MAY SAY ALL THAT IS R 084 25
THE PRIEST MAY SAY THIS EXHORTATION   R 085 22
THYSELF TO THE PRIEST, AND OFFER THE GIFT THAT MOSES   115 05
COME AN HIGH PRIEST OF GOOD THINGS TO CCME, BY A   132 23
OF THE HIGH PRIEST, AND CUT OFF HIS EAR   142 21
AND THEY LED JESUS AWAY TO THE HIGH PRIEST   142 32
EVEN INTO THE PALACE OF THE HIGH PRIEST   142 34
AND THE HIGH PRIEST STOOD UP IN THE MIDST, AND ASKED   143 09
AGAIN THE HIGH PRIEST ASKED HIM, AND SAID UNTO HIM,   143 13
THEN THE HIGH PRIEST RENT HIS CLOTHES, AND SAITH,   143 17
THERE COMETH ONE OF THE MAIDS OF THE HIGH PRIEST   143 24
AS THE HIGH PRIEST ENTERETH INTO THE HOLY PLACE EVERY   148 01
OF THE HIGH PRIEST, AND CUT OFF HIS RIGHT EAR   150 33
AND EVERY PRIEST STANDETH DAILY MINISTERING AND   158 03
HAVING AN HIGH PRIEST OVER THE HOUSE OF GOD   158 19
DOWN A CERTAIN PRIEST THAT WAY   208 25
UNTO THE HIGH PRIEST, AND DESIRED OF HIM LETTERS TO   229 27
WHAT IS THE OFFICE OF A PRIEST   294 11
THE OFFICE OF A PRIEST IS, TO MINISTER TO THE PEOPLE   294 12
TO ASSIST THE PRIEST IN DIVINE SERVICE, AND IN   294 17
THOU ART A PRIEST FOR EVER AFTER THE ORDER OF   482 15
A LAWFUL BISHOP, PRIEST, OR DEACON, IN THIS CHURCH,   529 20
A DEACON, PRIEST, OR BISHOP, EXCEPT HE BE OF THE AGE   529 24
BEING ENDED, A PRIEST SHALL PRESENT UNTO THE BISHOP,   R 530 07
THE PRIEST SHALL ANSWER, I HAVE INQUIRED CCNCERNING   R 530 17
TO ASSIST THE PRIEST IN DIVINE SERVICE, AND SPECIALLY   533 12
ABSENCE OF THE PRIEST TO BAPTIZE INFANTS   533 16
A PRIEST SHALL PRESENT UNTO THE BISHOP, SITTING IN   R 536 07
THE PRIEST SHALL ANSWER, I HAVE INQUIRED CCNCERNING   R 536 18
AND WORK OF A PRIEST IN THE CHURCH OF GOD, NOW   546 10
THE OFFICE OF A PRIEST IN THE CHURCH OF GOD, NOW   546 17
THY SERVANTS NOW CALLED TO THE OFFICE OF PRIEST   548 02
THE OFFICE OF A PRIEST, IN THE PARISH (OR CHURCH) OF   569 17
INSTITUTED PRIEST INTO THE OFFICE OF RECTOR OF --   569 23
OR THE PRIEST WHO ACTS AS INSTITUTOR, WHO   R 570 05

PRIEST   CONTINUED

OR THE PRIEST WHO ACTS AS THE INSTITUTOR,   R 570 10
OR CHURCH,) AS PRIEST AND RECTOR OF THE SAME   570 14
OR THE PRIEST WHO ACTS AS THE INSTITUTOR,   R 570 21
AS PRIEST AND RECTOR OF THE SAME   570 28
THAT THE PRIEST DID OFFER CHRIST FOR THE QUICK   609 17

PRIEST'S

INTO THE HIGH PRIEST'S HOUSE   151 07

PRIESTHOOD

AN HOLY PRIESTHOOD, TO OFFER UP SPIRITUAL SACRIFICES,   259 31
THE ORDER OF PRIESTHOOD, AT THE TIMES APPOINTED IN   R 535 24
THE ORDER OF PRIESTHOOD THAT DAY, EACH OF THEM BEING R 536 08
TO BE ADMITTED TO THE ORDER OF PRIESTHOOD   536 12
THIS DAY UNTO THE HOLY OFFICE OF PRIESTHOOD   536 24
SERVANTS NOW CALLED TO THE OFFICE OF PRIESTHOOD   537 23
TO THE ORDER AND MINISTRY OF PRIESTHOOD   541 33
EVERY ONE THAT RECEIVETH THE ORDER OF PRIESTHOOD   R 546 08
THE ORDER OF PRIESTHOOD TO OTHERS   R 547 20

PRIESTS

O YE PRIESTS OF THE LORD, BLESS YE THE LORD   013 22
LIKEWISE FOR ALL PRIESTS AND DEACONS (AND HEREIN MORE   047 26
ALL BISHOPS, PRIESTS, AND DEACONS, WITH TRUE   055 31
TO THE BISHOPS, PRIESTS, AND DEACONS, IN LIKE MANNER, R 082 26
THE JEWS SENT PRIESTS AND LEVITES FROM JERUSALEM TO   095 21
ALL THE CHIEF PRIESTS AND SCRIBES OF THE PEOPLE   109 04
LET THE PRIESTS, THE MINISTERS OF THE LORD, WEEP   125 02
ALL THE CHIEF PRIESTS AND ELDERS OF THE PEOPLE TCOK   134 30
TO THE CHIEF PRIESTS AND ELDERS, SAYING, I HAVE   135 04
AND THE CHIEF PRIESTS TOOK THE SILVER PIECES, AND   135 09
OF THE CHIEF PRIESTS AND ELDERS, HE ANSWERED NCTHING   135 21
BUT THE CHIEF PRIESTS AND ELDERS PERSUADED THE   135 35
ALSO THE CHIEF PRIESTS MOCKING HIM, WITH THE SCRIBES   137 09
AND THE CHIEF PRIESTS AND THE SCRIBES SOUGHT HOW THEY   139 33
UNTO THE CHIEF PRIESTS, TO BETRAY HIM UNTO THEM   140 19
FROM THE CHIEF PRIESTS AND THE SCRIBES AND THE   142 16
ALL THE CHIEF PRIESTS AND THE ELDERS AND THE SCRIBES   142 33
AND THE CHIEF PRIESTS AND ALL THE COUNCIL SOUGHT FOR   143 02
THE CHIEF PRIESTS HELD A CONSULTATION WITH THE ELDERS   145 03
AND THE CHIEF PRIESTS ACCUSED HIM OF MANY THINGS   145 08
THAT THE CHIEF PRIESTS HAD DELIVERED HIM FOR ENVY   145 20
BUT THE CHIEF PRIESTS MOVED THE PEOPLE, THAT HE   145 21
ALSO THE CHIEF PRIESTS MOCKING SAID AMONG THEMSELVES   146 21
AND THE CHIEF PRIESTS AND SCRIBES SOUGHT HOW THEY   148 13
WITH THE CHIEF PRIESTS AND CAPTAINS, HOW HE MIGHT   148 17
UNTO THE CHIEF PRIESTS, AND CAPTAINS OF THE TEMPLE,   151 02
AND THE CHIEF PRIESTS AND THE SCRIBES CAME TOGETHER,   151 28
TO THE CHIEF PRIESTS AND TO THE PEOPLE, I FIND NC   153 03
AND THE CHIEF PRIESTS AND SCRIBES STOOD AND   153 15
THE CHIEF PRIESTS AND THE RULERS AND THE PEOPLE, SAID   153 21
AND OF THE CHIEF PRIESTS PREVAILED   154 04
WHEN THE CHIEF PRIESTS THEREFORE AND OFFICERS SAW   159 05
THE CHIEF PRIESTS ANSWERED, WE HAVE NO KING BUT   159 29
SAID THE CHIEF PRIESTS OF THE JEWS TO PILATE,   160 06
THE CHIEF PRIESTS AND PHARISEES CAME TOGETHER UNTO   162 16
HOW THE CHIEF PRIESTS AND OUR RULERS DELIVERED HIM TC   167 18
GO SHEW YOURSELVES UNTO THE PRIESTS   210 06
FROM THE CHIEF PRIESTS TO BIND ALL THAT CALL ON THY   230 24
HE MIGHT BRING THEM BOUND UNTO THE CHIEF PRIESTS   231 08
WHEN THE CHIEF PRIESTS AND SCRIBES SAW THE WONDERFUL   260 10
PRIESTS, AND DEACONS   294 05
65 THEIR PRIESTS WERE SLAIN WITH THE SWORD, *   439 06
AARON AMONG HIS PRIESTS, AND SAMUEL AMONG SUCH AS   462 27
9 LET THY PRIESTS BE CLOTHED WITH RIGHTEOUSNESS   508 21
I WILL DECK HER PRIESTS WITH HEALTH, *   509 06
-- BISHOPS, PRIESTS, AND DEACONS   529 13
COMPANY OF THE PRIESTS WERE OBEDIENT TO THE FAITH   532 22
AND OFFICE OF SUCH AS COME TO BE ADMITTED PRIESTS   R 536 05
TO THE ORDER OF PRIESTS, AND TO POUR THY GRACE UPON   537 11
TO BE ORDAINED PRIESTS AS FOLLOWETH   R 539 23
TO BE ORDAINED PRIESTS KNEELING, AND OTHERS STANDING, R 543 26
AND THE PRIESTS, AND OTHERS THAT ARE PRESENT,   R 543 28
BISHOP WITH THE PRIESTS PRESENT, SHALL LAY THEIR   R 546 06
SHALL BE FIRST PRESENTED, AND THEN THE PRIESTS   R 547 21
ARE TO BE MADE PRIESTS SHALL LIKEWISE BE EXAMINED AND R 547 27
ALL BISHOPS, PRIESTS, AND DEACONS, WITH LOVE OF THEE   560 18
OF DEACONS OR OF PRIESTS SHALL BE SAID, THAT IT MAY   R 560 25
OF DEACONS (OR PRIESTS), AND TO POUR THY GRACE UPCN   560 27
LET THY PRIESTS BE CLOTHED WITH RIGHTEOUSNESS   562 04
PRIESTS, AND DEACONS, ARE NOT COMMANDED BY   609 27
AND ORDERING OF PRIESTS AND DEACONS, AS SET FORTH BY   610 31

PRIMITIVE

CUSTOM OF THE PRIMITIVE CHURCH, TO HAVE PUBLIC PRAYER   607 28

PRINCE

ONLY SAVIOUR, THE PRINCE OF PEACE   037 26
BECAUSE THE PRINCE OF THIS WORLD IS JUDGED   175 16
FOR THE PRINCE OF THIS WORLD COMETH, AND HATH NCTHING   182 08
THE PRINCE OF THE PEOPLE LET HIM GO FREE   471 12

PRINCES

REIGN OF SEVERAL PRINCES, SINCE THE FIRST COMPILING   V 26
LEAST AMONG THE PRINCES OF JUDA   109 09
YE KNOW THAT THE PRINCES OF THE GENTILES EXERCISE   247 21
AND CASTETH OUT THE COUNSELS OF PRINCES   379 08
THOU MAYEST MAKE PRINCES IN ALL LANDS   397 20

PRINCES   CONTINUED

9 THE PRINCES OF THE PEOPLES ARE JOINED UNTO THE   399 06
AND THE PRINCES OF JUDAH THEIR COUNCIL   421 08
THE PRINCES OF ZEBULON, AND THE PRINCES OF NAPHTHALI   421 09
AND THE PRINCES OF NAPHTHALI   421 10
THEN SHALL THE PRINCES COME OUT OF EGYPT   421 18
THE SPIRIT OF PRINCES, *   433 13
GOD STANDETH IN THE CONGREGATION OF PRINCES   443 18
AND FALL LIKE ONE OF THE PRINCES   443 32
THEM AND THEIR PRINCES LIKE OREB AND ZEEB   444 26
MAKE ALL THEIR PRINCES LIKE AS ZEBAH AND ZALMUNNA   444 27
MIGHT INFORM HIS PRINCES AFTER HIS WILL, *   471 16
SET HIM WITH THE PRINCES, *   484 21
EVEN WITH THE PRINCES OF HIS PEOPLE   484 22
THAN TO PUT ANY CONFIDENCE IN PRINCES   488 17
23 PRINCES ALSO DID SIT AND SPEAK AGAINST ME   491 12
PRINCES HAVE PERSECUTED ME WITHOUT A CAUSE   501 03
YOUR TRUST IN PRINCES, NOR IN ANY CHILD OF MAN   522 06
PRINCES, AND ALL JUDGES OF THE WORLD   524 25

PRINCIPAL

AND THE PRINCIPAL CARE HEREIN WAS TO MAKE THEM   VI 17
THE MOST PRINCIPAL AND MIGHTIEST IN THE DWELLINGS OF   438 13

PRINCIPALITIES

UNTO THE PRINCIPALITIES AND POWERS IN HEAVENLY PLACES   108 24
AGAINST PRINCIPALITIES, AGAINST POWERS, AGAINST THE   219 08
NOR PRINCIPALITIES, NOR POWERS, NOR THINGS PRESENT,   331 11

PRINCIPLES

YET UPON THE PRINCIPLES ALREADY LAID DOWN, IT CANNOT   VI 02
IN THE PRINCIPLES OF THE CHRISTIAN RELIGION   R 273 19

PRINT

IN HIS HANDS THE PRINT OF THE NAILS, AND PUT MY   228 28
MY FINGER INTO THE PRINT OF THE NAILS, AND THRUST MY   228 29

PRINTED

ALWAYS THEREFORE PRINTED IN YOUR REMEMBRANCE, HOW   540 05

PRISON

HAD HEARD IN THE PRISON THE WORKS OF CHRIST, HE SENT   094 16
OPENING OF THE PRISON TO THEM THAT ARE BOUND   107 04
BOTH INTO PRISON, AND TO DEATH   149 35
AND FOR MURDER, WAS CAST INTO PRISON   153 32
WAS CAST INTO PRISON, WHOM THEY HAD DESIRED   154 07
HE WENT AND PREACHED UNTO THE SPIRITS IN PRISON   161 26
THEE TO THE OFFICER, AND THOU BE CAST INTO PRISON   198 15
AND CAST HIM INTO PRISON, TILL HE SHOULD PAY THE   221 29
HE PUT HIM IN PRISON, AND DELIVERED HIM TO FOUR   245 04
PETER THEREFORE WAS KEPT IN PRISON   245 07
AND THE KEEPERS BEFORE THE DOOR KEPT THE PRISON   245 12
AND A LIGHT SHINED IN THE PRISON   245 13
I WAS IN PRISON, AND YE CAME UNTO ME   259 08
THEE SICK, OR IN PRISON, AND CAME UNTO THEE   259 13
8 I AM SO FAST IN PRISON *   449 13
MY SOUL OUT OF PRISON, THAT I MAY GIVE THANKS UNTO   518 19
7 THE LORD LOOSETH MEN OUT OF PRISON   522 16

PRISONER

I PAUL, THE PRISONER OF JESUS CHRIST FOR YOU   108 06
THE PEOPLE A PRISONER, WHOM THEY WOULD   135 27
THEN A NOTABLE PRISONER, CALLED BARABBAS   135 28
UNTO THEM ONE PRISONER, WHOMSOEVER THEY DESIRED   145 13
THE PRISONER OF THE LORD, BESEECH YOU THAT   213 18

PRISONERS

SUCCOUR ALL PRISONERS (ESPECIALLY THOSE WHO ARE   046 20
FOR ALL PRISONERS AND CAPTIVES   048 06
PITY UPON ALL PRISONERS AND CAPTIVES   056 33
BRINGETH THE PRISONERS OUT OF CAPTIVITY   419 22
AND DESPISETH NOT HIS PRISONERS   424 11
SIGHING OF THE PRISONERS COME BEFORE THEE   440 26
SIGHING OF THE PRISONERS COME BEFORE THEE   600 09

PRISONS

IN PRISONS MORE FREQUENT, IN DEATHS OFT   120 31
THEY ARE DELIVERED FROM THEIR EARTHLY PRISONS   317 13

PRIVATE

AS WELL IN YOUR PRIVATE EXAMINATION, AS IN THE   539 24
BOTH PUBLIC AND PRIVATE MONITIONS AND EXHORTATIONS,   542 22
THROUGH HIS PRIVATE JUDGMENT, WILLINGLY AND   609 35

PRIVATELY

AND BOTH PRIVATELY AND OPENLY TO CALL UPON AND   555 04

PRIVILEGE

WHAT GREAT PRIVILEGE DOTH OUR LORD PROVIDE FOR YOU   291 29

PRIVILY

WAS MINDED TO PUT HER AWAY PRIVILY   105 02

PRIVILY   CONTINUED

WHEN HE HAD PRIVILY CALLED THE WISE MEN, ENQUIRED OF   109 11
WHICH THEY HID PRIVILY IS THEIR FOOT TAKEN   352 22
AND PRIVILY IN HIS LURKING DENS DOTH HE MURDER THE   353 21
THAT THEY MAY PRIVILY SHOOT AT THEM WHICH ARE TRUE OF   354 22
THEY HAVE LAID PRIVILY FOR ME   375 29
7 FOR THEY HAVE PRIVILY LAID THEIR NET TO DESTROY ME   381 31
HE HATH LAID PRIVILY CATCH HIMSELF   382 05
4 THAT THEY MAY PRIVILY SHOOT AT HIM THAT IS PERFECT   415 25
6 WHOSO PRIVILY SLANDERETH HIS NEIGHBOUR, *   463 26
HAVE THEY PRIVILY LAID A SNARE FOR ME   518 08

PRIVY

FROM ALL SEDITION, PRIVY CONSPIRACY, AND REBELLION   055 02

PRIZE

IN A RACE RUN ALL, BUT ONE RECEIVETH THE PRIZE   119 06

PROCEED

ALL GOOD COUNSELS, AND ALL JUST WORKS DO PROCEED   031 19
THE PRIEST SHALL PROCEED, SAYING, LIFT UP YOUR   R 076 25
AND PROCEED TO DELIVER THE SAME TO THE   R 082 26
COMMUNICATION PROCEED OUT OF YOUR MOUTH, BUT THAT   216 23
THE MINISTER PROCEED AS FOLLOWETH   R 273 28
MINISTER SHALL PROCEED WITH THE QUESTIONS ON THE   R 292 02
MINISTER SHALL PROCEED ACCORDING TO THE FORM BEFORE   R 322 30
SHALL THE BISHOP PROCEED IN THE COMMUNION   R 534 26
BISHOP SHALL PROCEED IN THE COMMUNION SERVICE   R 559 02
THIS CHURCH, MAY PROCEED TO INSTITUTE HIM INTO THE   R 569 06
WE PROCEED NO FURTHER, BECAUSE WE WOULD   570 18
MINISTER SHALL PROCEED TO THAT SERVICE, AND TO   R 574 25

PROCEEDED

OF THE THRONE PROCEEDED LIGHTNINGS AND THUNDERINGS   187 12
THE JEWS, HE PROCEEDED FURTHER TO TAKE PETER ALSO   245 02
THE JEWS, HE PROCEEDED FURTHER TO TAKE PETER ALSO   247 04

PROCEEDETH

OF LIFE, WHO PROCEEDETH FROM THE FATHER AND THE SON   016 16
OF LIFE, WHO PROCEEDETH FROM THE FATHER AND THE SON   030 21
OF LIFE, WHO PROCEEDETH FROM THE FATHER AND THE SON   071 18
LABOUR THAT PROCEEDETH OF LOVE   072 24
WORD THAT PROCEEDETH OUT OF THE MOUTH OF GOD   126 29
WHICH PROCEEDETH FROM THE FATHER, HE SHALL   179 26
WHICH PROCEEDETH FROM THE FATHER, HE SHALL   255 31

PROCEEDING

HOLY GHOST, PROCEEDING FROM THE FATHER AND THE SON,   603 26

PROCHORUS

AND PROCHORUS, AND NICANOR, AND TIMON,   532 17

PROCLAIM

TO PROCLAIM LIBERTY TO THE CAPTIVES, AND THE OPENING   107 03
TO PROCLAIM THE ACCEPTABLE YEAR OF THE LORD, AND THE   107 04
HEAVEN DIDST PROCLAIM, BLESSED ARE THE DEAD WHO DIE   335 26

PROCURED

BENEFITS PROCURED UNTO US BY THE SAME   081 05
CANNOT BE PROCURED, THEN ANY BAPTIZED PERSON PRESENT   R 281 28

PROCURING

THE PROCURING OF REVERENCE, AND THE EXCITING OF PIETY   V 36

PRODUCTS

FOR THE PRODUCTS OF ALL HONEST INDUSTRY   048 12

PROFESS

THAT ALL WHO PROFESS AND CALL THEMSELVES CHRISTIANS   018 32
THAT ALL WHO PROFESS AND CALL THEMSELVES CHRISTIANS   032 32
ONE MOUTH MAY PROFESS THE FAITH ONCE DELIVERED TO THE   574 12

PROFESSETH

SECT WHICH HE PROFESSETH, SO THAT HE BE DILIGENT TO   606 33

PROFESSION

HOLD FAST THE PROFESSION OF OUR FAITH WITHOUT   158 23
TO THEIR PROFESSION, AND FOLLOW ALL SUCH THINGS AS   173 09
MEN'S PROFESSION, BUT RATHER THEY BE CERTAIN SURE   607 32
A SIGN OF PROFESSION, AND MARK OF DIFFERENCE,   608 24

PROFESSORS

MEN WHO ARE PROFESSORS OF THE GOSPEL, TO PAY   610 40

PROFIT

TO EVERY MAN TO PROFIT WITHAL   182 26
TO EVERY MAN TO PROFIT WITHAL   203 26
WE MAY PROFIT BY THEIR EXAMPLES   258 08
THE OPPORTUNITY IT AFFORDS FOR SPIRITUAL PROFIT   R 313 17

PROFIT   CONTINUED

9 WHAT PROFIT IS THERE IN MY BLOOD, *   375 10

PROFITABLE

WHICH ARE PROFITABLE FOR US   199 31
TO ALL THINGS PROFITABLE TO OUR SALVATION   210 20
FOR HE IS PROFITABLE TO ME FOR THE MINISTRY   254 03
THAT WAS PROFITABLE UNTO YOU, BUT HAVE SHEWED YCU, 550 11

PROFITABLY

CHRIST PROFITABLY TO HIS SOUL'S HEALTH, ALTHOUGH HE   R 323 30

PROFITETH

IT PROFITETH ME NOTHING   122 28

PROHIBIT

DOTH NOT PROHIBIT, BUT THAT A MAN MAY SWEAR WHEN THE   611 08

PROLONGED

AND PROLONGED NOT THE TIME, *   493 31

PROMISE

AND DOST PROMISE THAT WHEN TWO OR THREE ARE GATHERED   020 05
AND DOST PROMISE THAT WHEN TWO OR THREE ARE GATHERED   034 05
WHOSE MOST TRUE PROMISE, THE HOLY GHOST CAME DCWN AS   078 26
PARTAKERS OF HIS PROMISE IN CHRIST BY THE GOSPEL   108 15
BUT HE OF THE FREEWOMAN WAS BY PROMISE   131 02
ARE THE CHILDREN OF PROMISE   131 12
RECEIVE THE PROMISE OF ETERNAL INHERITANCE   133 07
HOW THAT THE PROMISE WHICH WAS MADE UNTO THE FATHERS, 169 06
AND DESIRE THAT WHICH THOU DOST PROMISE   174 21
BUT WAIT FOR THE PROMISE OF THE FATHER, WHICH,   177 31
I SEND THE PROMISE OF MY FATHER UPON YOU   178 21
SHOULD MAKE THE PROMISE OF NONE EFFECT   207 24
BE OF THE LAW, IT IS NO MORE OF PROMISE   207 25
BUT GOD GAVE IT TO ABRAHAM BY PROMISE   207 26
COME TO WHOM THE PROMISE WAS MADE   207 28
THAT THE PROMISE BY FAITH OF JESUS CHRIST MIGHT   208 04
WHICH THOU DOST PROMISE, MAKE US TO LOVE THAT WHICH   209 10
THE WILL OF GOD, YE MIGHT RECEIVE THE PROMISE   228 17
SPONSORS THEN PROMISE FOR YOU   283 21
MY SPONSORS DID PROMISE AND VOW THREE THINGS IN MY   283 22
AND DESIRE THAT WHICH THOU DOST PROMISE   285 28
RENEW THE SOLEMN PROMISE AND VOW THAT YE MADE, CR   296 23
DO YE PROMISE TO FOLLOW JESUS CHRIST AS YOUR   297 03
AND IS HIS PROMISE COME UTTERLY TO AN END FOR   311 14
11 PROMISE UNTO THE LORD YOUR GOD, AND KEEP IT,   433 10
AND IS HIS PROMISE COME UTTERLY TO AN END FCR   433 31
HIS COVENANT AND PROMISE, *   470 19
HE REMEMBERED HIS HOLY PROMISE   472 21
WHO KEEPETH HIS PROMISE FOR EVER   522 13
THAT THIS YOUR PROMISE MAY THE MORE MOVE YCU TO DO   541 26
TRUE PROMISE OF THE FATHER THOU, WHO DOST THE TCNGUE   544 27
THE FOLLOWING PROMISE OF CONFORMITY TO THE DOCTRINE, R 552 26
DO PROMISE CONFORMITY AND OBEDIENCE TO THE DOCTRINE,   552 29
TRUE PROMISE OF THE FATHER THOU, WHO DOST THE TCNGUE   557 06
PLEASED TO PROMISE THY ESPECIAL PRESENCE, WHEREVER   564 30
AND PROMISE TO BE A FAITHFUL SHEPHERD   570 34
THEY DID PROMISE AND VOW THREE THINGS IN MY NAME   577 13
SPONSORS DID PROMISE FOR YOU, THAT YOU SHOULD KEEP   578 17
BECAUSE THEY PROMISE THEM BOTH BY THEIR SURETIES   581 33
WHICH PROMISE, WHEN THEY COME TO AGE, THEMSELVES ARE   581 34
INSTITUTION AND PROMISE, ALTHOUGH THEY BE MINISTERED   608 17

PROMISED

THE MERCY PROMISED TO OUR FOREFATHERS, *   014 16
AS HE PROMISED TO OUR FOREFATHERS, ABRAHAM AND HIS   026 27
AND HAST PROMISED, THROUGH THY SON JESUS CHRIST,   036 28
CHRIST HAST PROMISED TO ALL THOSE WHO SEEK THY   040 16
WHO HAST PROMISED TO HEAR THE PETITIONS OF THOSE   050 06
MERCY HATH PROMISED FORGIVENESS OF SINS TO ALL THOSE   076 03
WERE GLAD, AND PROMISED TO GIVE HIM MONEY   140 20
AND HE PROMISED, AND SOUGHT OPPORTUNITY TO BETRAY HIM 148 19
FOR HE IS FAITHFUL THAT PROMISED   158 24
THE LORD HATH PROMISED TO THEM THAT LCVE HIM   239 26
THE MERCY PROMISED TO OUR FATHERS, AND TO REMEMBER   244 04
AS THOU HAST PROMISED BY THY WELL-BELOVED SCN,   274 15
WHICH THOU HAST PROMISED BY CHRIST OUR LORD   274 21
YOUR SPONSORS PROMISED AND VOWED THAT YOU SHOULD   284 07
YOUR SPONSORS PROMISED AND VOWED THAT YOU SHOULD KEEP 285 13
WHICH I PROMISED WITH MY LIPS, AND SPAKE WITH MY   418 08
THOU HAST PROMISED TO HELP ME, FOR THOU ART MY HOUSE   425 09
I HAVE PROMISED TO KEEP THY LAW   493 24
THERE THE LORD PROMISED HIS BLESSING, *   509 20
AND HAST PROMISED TO BE WITH THE MINISTERS CF   572 17
AS THEY HAVE PROMISED FOR THEE   577 21
AND HAST PROMISED FORGIVENESS TO ALL THOSE WHO   589 27

PROMISES

TO THY PROMISES DECLARED UNTO MANKIND IN CIIRIST JESUS 006 26
TO THY PROMISES DECLARED UNTO MANKIND IN CHRIST JESUS   023 33
BUT THY PROMISES OF MERCY   040 07
UNDERSTANDING OF THEMSELVES, AND OF THY PROMISES   046 22
TO CONFIRM THE PROMISES MADE UNTO THE FATHERS   092 24
MAY OBTAIN THY PROMISES, WHICH EXCEED ALL THAT WE CAN 197 07
THY GRACIOUS PROMISES, AND BE MADE PARTAKERS OF THY   204 25
FAIL NOT FINALLY TO ATTAIN THY HEAVENLY PROMISES   207 16

PROMISES   CONTINUED

SEED WERE THE PROMISES MADE   207 19
AGAINST THE PROMISES OF GOD   207 31
MADE THESE PROMISES, WILT THOU ALSC ON THY PART TAKE   277 09
RENEWING THE PROMISES AND VOWS OF MY BAPTISM, AND   291 24
BELIEVE THE PROMISES OF GOD TO THEM IN THAT   292 29
SHALL RENEW THE PROMISES AND VOWS OF THEIR BAPTISM,   294 24
RENEW THE PROMISES AND VOWS OF THEIR BAPTISM, AND BE   565 24
BELIEVE THE PROMISES OF GOD MADE TO THEM IN THAT   581 29
OLD FATHERS DID LOOK ONLY FOR TRANSITORY PROMISES   604 19
RECEIVE GOD'S PROMISES IN SUCH WISE, AS THEY BE   606 27
THE PROMISES OF THE FORGIVENESS OF SIN, AND OF CUR   608 27

PROMOTE

AND HE SHALL PROMOTE THEE, THAT THOU SHALT POSSESS   387 02

PROMOTING

GOD FOR THE PROMOTING OF HIS GLORY, AND THE EDIFYING   532 28
IN PROMOTING THE SALVATION OF THE PEOPLE NOW   573 20

PROMOTION

7 FOR PROMOTION COMETH NEITHER FROM THE EAST,   432 10

PROMPTLY

SHALL BE PROMPTLY REPORTED TO THE PARISH AUTHORITIES R 281 29

PROMULGATING

FOR PROMULGATING THEM TO MANKIND IN THE CLEAREST,   VI 41

PRONOUNCE

TO DECLARE AND PRONOUNCE TO HIS PEOPLE, BEING   007 10
TO DECLARE AND PRONOUNCE TO HIS PEOPLE, BEING   024 12
AND TO PRONOUNCE ABSOLUTION AND BLESSING IN GOD'S   294 14
I PRONOUNCE THAT THEY ARE MAN AND WIFE, IN THE NAME   304 08
SON SHALL THEN PRONOUNCE TO ALL WHO LOVE AND FEAR   335 10
SHALL ALWAYS PRONOUNCE,) THE WARDENS, VESTRY,   R 574 27

PRONOUNCING

FIRST PRONOUNCING, THE LORD BE WITH YOU   R 003 08
FIRST PRONOUNCING, THE LORD BE WITH YOU   R 016 24
FIRST PRONOUNCING, THE LORD BE WITH YOU   R 030 29
FIRST PRONOUNCING, THE LORD BE WITH YOU   R 283 04
FIRST PRONOUNCING, THE LORD BE WITH YOU   R 331 31

PROOF

MAKE FULL PROOF OF THY MINISTRY   253 24

PROOFS

MANY INFALLIBLE PROOFS, BEING SEEN OF THEM FCRTY   177 27

PROPER

FOR WHICH A PROPER EPISTLE AND GOSPEL ARE ORDERED   R 008 33
NOT SINCE THOUGHT PROPER TO REVIVE IT BY ANY NEW   VI 06
OUGHT TO BE THE PROPER END OF ALL SUCH PRAYERS,   VI 18
SHALL FOLLOW THE PROPER PREFACE, ACCORDING TO THE   R 077 02
OR SOME PROPER HYMN   R 083 32
CALLED IN THEIR PROPER TONGUE, ACELDAMA, THAT IS TO   234 17
BE READY IN SOME PROPER HOUSE, WITH THEIR FRIENDS ANC R 300 05
THE PROPER SUFFRAGE SHALL BE,   R 553 15
IT WILL BE PROPER TO BEGIN WITH A CHAPTER, CR PART OF R 592 05

PROPERTY

THY PROPERTY IS ALWAYS TO HAVE MERCY   062 18
NATURE AND PROPERTY IS EVER TO HAVE MERCY AND TO   063 09
WHOSE PROPERTY IS ALWAYS TO HAVE MERCY   082 17

PROPHECIES

THERE BE PROPHECIES, THEY SHALL FAIL   123 04

PROPHECY

TO US, WHETHER PROPHECY, LET US PROPHESY ACCORDING TO 111 16
THE GIFT OF PROPHECY, AND UNDERSTAND ALL MYSTERIES,   122 24
TO ANOTHER PROPHECY   182 31
TO ANOTHER PROPHECY   203 31

PROPHESIED

AND PROPHESIED, SAYING, BLESSED BE THE LORD   243 32

PROPHESY

LET US PROPHESY ACCORDING TO THE PRCPORTION CF FAITH   111 16
IN PART, AND WE PROPHESY IN PART   123 07
AND TO SAY UNTO HIM, PROPHESY   143 21
SAYING, PROPHESY, WHO IS IT THAT SMOTE THEE   151 25

PROPHET

BE CALLED THE PROPHET OF THE HIGHEST   014 24
SPOKEN BY THE PROPHET, SAYING, TELL YE THE DAUGHTER   091 19
IS JESUS THE PROPHET OF NAZARETH OF GALILEE   091 32
A PROPHET   094 30

PROPHET   CONTINUED

I SAY UNTO YOU, AND MORE THAN A PROPHET   094 31
ART THOU THAT PROPHET   095 25
AS SAID THE PROPHET ESAIAS   095 30
NOT THAT CHRIST, NOR ELIAS, NEITHER THAT PROPHET   096 02
THE LORD BY THE PROPHET, SAYING, OUT OF EGYPT HAVE I   103 23
BY JEREMY THE PROPHET, SAYING, IN RAMA WAS THERE A   103 30
THE LORD BY THE PROPHET, SAYING, BEHOLD, A VIRGIN   105 09
WRITTEN BY THE PROPHET, AND THOU BETHLEHEM, IN THE   109 07
OF A TRUTH THAT PROPHET THAT SHOULD COME INTO THE   132 13
BY JEREMY THE PROPHET, SAYING, AND THEY TOOK THE   135 15
SPOKEN BY THE PROPHET, THEY PARTED MY GARMENTS AMONG   136 32
WHICH WAS A PROPHET MIGHTY IN DEED AND WORD BEFORE   167 17
THAT A GREAT PROPHET IS RISEN UP AMONG US   213 08
OF A TRUTH THAT PROPHET THAT SHOULD COME INTO THE   226 12
BE CALLED THE PROPHET OF THE HIGHEST   244 10
THE BOOK OF THE PROPHET ESAIAS   261 14
THERE IS NOT ONE PROPHET MORE   430 24

PROPHET'S

TO THE PROPHET'S TEACHING, IN JUSTICE, JUDGMENT,   611 10

PROPHETESS

ONE ANNA, A PROPHETESS, THE DAUGHTER OF PHANUEL, OF   233 16

PROPHETS

OF THE PROPHETS PRAISE THEE   010 17
OF HIS HOLY PROPHETS, *   014 12
WHO SPAKE BY THE PROPHETS   016 18
WHO SPAKE BY THE PROPHETS   030 23
COMMANDMENTS HANG ALL THE LAW AND THE PROPHETS   069 31
WHO SPAKE BY THE PROPHETS   071 20
FATHERS BY THE PROPHETS, HATH IN THESE LAST DAYS   096 23
I SEND UNTO YOU PROPHETS, AND WISE MEN, AND SCRIBES   100 19
KILLEST THE PROPHETS, AND STONEST THEM WHICH ARE SENT   100 28
SPOKEN BY THE PROPHETS, HE SHALL BE CALLED A   107 23
APOSTLES AND PROPHETS BY THE SPIRIT   108 13
WRITTEN IN THE PROPHETS, BEHOLD, I SEND MY MESSENGER   112 04
AND FALSE PROPHETS, AND SHALL SHEW GREAT SIGNS AND   118 05
WRITTEN BY THE PROPHETS CONCERNING THE SON OF MAN   123 19
ABRAHAM IS DEAD, AND THE PROPHETS   133 20
AND THE PROPHETS ARE DEAD   133 22
GIVE ALL THE PROPHETS WITNESS, THAT THROUGH HIS NAME   166 31
ALL THAT THE PROPHETS HAVE SPOKEN   167 30
AND ALL THE PROPHETS, HE EXPOUNDED UNTO THEM IN ALL   167 32
VOICES OF THE PROPHETS WHICH ARE READ EVERY SABBATH   168 28
WHICH IS SPOKEN OF IN THE PROPHETS   169 23
AND IN THE PROPHETS, AND IN THE PSALMS, CONCERNING   170 09
GIVE ALL THE PROPHETS WITNESS, THAT THROUGH HIS NAME   184 18
THEY HAVE MOSES AND THE PROPHETS   190 26
MOSES AND THE PROPHETS, NEITHER WILL THEY BE   190 30
BEWARE OF FALSE PROPHETS, WHICH COME TO YOU IN   200 15
THAT MANY PROPHETS AND KINGS HAVE DESIRED TO SEE   208 08
COMMANDMENTS HANG ALL THE LAW AND THE PROPHETS   215 15
AND SOME, PROPHETS   237 19
THESE DAYS CAME PROPHETS FROM JERUSALEM UNTO ANTIOCH   241 15
OF HIS HOLY PROPHETS, WHICH HAVE BEEN SINCE THE WORLD   244 02
AND OTHERS, JEREMIAS, OR ONE OF THE PROPHETS   245 35
THESE DAYS CAME PROPHETS FROM JERUSALEM UNTO ANTIOCH   246 24
APOSTLES AND PROPHETS, JESUS CHRIST HIMSELF BEING THE   254 28
APOSTLES AND PROPHETS, JESUS CHRIST HIMSELF BEING THE   255 06
THEY THE PROPHETS WHICH WERE BEFORE YOU   257 34
APOSTLES AND PROPHETS, JESUS CHRIST HIMSELF BEING THE   290 20
AND DO MY PROPHETS NO HARM   471 02
AND SOME, PROPHETS   538 06
HIS APOSTLES, PROPHETS, EVANGELISTS, DOCTORS, AND   545 18
SOME PROPHETS, SOME EVANGELISTS, SOME   557 26
APOSTLES AND PROPHETS, JESUS CHRIST HIMSELF BEING THE   574 04

PROPITIATION

HE IS THE PROPITIATION FOR OUR SINS   076 23
TO BE THE PROPITIATION FOR OUR SINS   189 15
PROPITIATION, AND SATISFACTION FOR ALL   609 14

PROPORTION

TO THE PROPORTION OF FAITH   111 17

PROPOSED

OF THE PROPOSED MARRIAGE, MAY DEMAND SUFFICIENT   R 301 03

PROSELYTE

AND NICOLAS A PROSELYTE OF ANTIOCH   532 18

PROSELYTES

JEWS AND PROSELYTES, CRETES AND ARABIANS, WE DO HEAR   181 05

PROSPER

TO DIRECT AND PROSPER ALL THEIR CONSULTATIONS,   035 12
PROSPER THE MEANS MADE USE OF FOR THEIR CURE   045 06
SHALL REIGN AND PROSPER, AND SHALL EXECUTE JUDGMENT   225 11
AND PROSPER THE MEANS WHICH SHALL BE MADE USE OF FOR   315 28
AND LOOK, WHATSOEVER HE DOETH, IT SHALL PROSPER   345 15
WHOSE WAY DOTH PROSPER, AGAINST THE MAN THAT DOETH   385 07
THESE PROSPER IN THE WORLD, AND THESE HAVE RICHES IN   428 32
PROSPER THOU THE WORK OF OUR HANDS UPON US   454 25
O PROSPER THOU OUR HANDY-WORK   454 26

PROSPER   CONTINUED

THEY SHALL PROSPER THAT LOVE THEE   503 18
THE LORD PROSPER YOU   507 05
IMAGINATION PROSPER, LEST THEY BE TOO PROUD   516 25
WORDS SHALL NOT PROSPER UPON THE EARTH   516 32

PROSPERITY

IN HEALTH AND PROSPERITY LONG TO LIVE   018 03
THE TIME OF PROSPERITY, FILL OUR HEARTS WITH   036 21
IN ALL TIME OF OUR PROSPERITY   055 15
JUDGE MOST CONVENIENT FOR THEIR FUTURE PROSPERITY   VI 13
51 GREAT PROSPERITY GIVETH HE UNTO HIS KING, *   363 07
6 AND IN MY PROSPERITY I SAID, I SHALL NEVER BE   375 04
IN THE PROSPERITY OF HIS SERVANT   383 21
I DO ALSO SEE THE UNGODLY IN SUCH PROSPERITY   428 15
O LORD, SEND US NOW PROSPERITY   489 18
I WILL WISH THEE PROSPERITY   503 23
JERUSALEM IN PROSPERITY ALL THY LIFE LONG   506 17
DESIRE THE PROSPERITY OF THY HOLY APOSTOLIC CHURCH,   574 10

PROTECT

STRENGTHEN AND PROTECT THE SOLDIERS OF OUR COUNTRY   041 26
THE DISTRESSED, PROTECT THE INNOCENT, AWAKEN THE   046 25
EVER HALLOW AND PROTECT THY CHURCH   562 09
PROTECT THE EFFORTS OF SOBER AND HONEST INDUSTRY, AND   599 29

PROTECTION

CARE AND PROTECTION, HATH, IN THE PREFACE OF HER BOOK   V 12
MOST GRACIOUS PROTECTION OUR COUNTRY'S NAVY, AND ALL   042 05
THY ALMIGHTY PROTECTION, THY SERVANT, FOR WHOSE   046 10
MOST MIGHTY PROTECTION, BOTH HERE AND EVER, WE MAY BE   070 10
STRENGTH AND PROTECTION, AS MAY SUPPORT US IN ALL   114 07
UNDER THE PROTECTION OF THY GOOD PROVIDENCE, AND MAKE   191 06
THROUGH THY PROTECTION IT MAY BE FREE FROM ALL   220 17
MAY OBTAIN THY MERCIFUL AID AND PROTECTION   259 23
MOST MIGHTY PROTECTION, BOTH HERE AND EVER, WE MAY BE   298 30
MERCY AND PROTECTION WE COMMIT THEE   314 26
MERCY AND PROTECTION WE COMMIT YOU   332 10
THY GRACE AND PROTECTION FOR THE ENSUING DAY   588 27
UNDER THY FATHERLY CARE AND PROTECTION   589 04
THY GRACIOUS PROTECTION TO US THIS NIGHT   591 26
THY MERCIFUL PROTECTION ALL THIS NIGHT   595 07

PROTECTOR

O GOD, THE PROTECTOR OF ALL THAT TRUST IN THEE,   194 04

PROTESTANT

TO WHICH THE PROTESTANT EPISCOPAL CHURCH IN THESE   V 10
OF THE PROTESTANT EPISCOPAL CHURCH   R 552 27
BISHOP OF THE PROTESTANT EPISCOPAL CHURCH IN N   552 29
OF THE PROTESTANT EPISCOPAL CHURCH IN THE UNITED   552 31

PROUD

HATH SCATTERED THE PROUD IN THE IMAGINATION OF THEIR   026 21
GOD RESISTETH THE PROUD, AND GIVETH GRACE TO THE   192 31
THE UNGODLY IS SO PROUD, THAT HE CARETH NOT FOR GOD,   353 11
THAT SPEAKETH PROUD THINGS   355 13
MOUTH SPEAKETH PROUD THINGS   359 07
AND SHALT BRING DOWN THE HIGH LOOKS OF THE PROUD   361 23
REWARDETH THE PROUD DOER   377 17
NOT UNTO THE PROUD, AND TO SUCH AS GO ABOUT WITH   390 19
5 THE PROUD ARE ROBBED, THEY HAVE SLEPT THEIR SLEEP   432 30
14 O LORD, THE PROUD ARE RISEN AGAINST ME   447 32
AND REWARD THE PROUD AFTER THEIR DESERVING   457 21
AND MAKE SUCH PROUD BOASTING   457 26
HAUGHTY LOOK AND A PROUD HEART, *   463 28
21 THOU HAST REBUKED THE PROUD   491 08
51 THE PROUD HAVE HAD ME EXCEEDINGLY IN DERISION   493 12
69 THE PROUD HAVE IMAGINED A LIE AGAINST ME   494 18
78 LET THE PROUD BE CONFOUNDED, FOR THEY GO WICKEDLY   495 11
85 THE PROUD HAVE DIGGED PITS FOR ME, *   495 27
THAT THE PROUD DO ME NO WRONG   498 14
AND WITH THE DESPITEFULNESS OF THE PROUD   504 05
DEEP WATERS OF THE PROUD *   504 14
I HAVE NO PROUD LOOKS   507 24
AS FOR THE PROUD, HE BEHOLDETH THEM AFAR OFF   514 09
5 THE PROUD HAVE LAID A SNARE FOR ME, AND SPREAD A   516 18
IMAGINATION PROSPER, LEST THEY BE TOO PROUD   516 26

PROVE

THAT WE MAY ALWAYS PROVE OURSELVES A PEOPLE MINDFUL   036 11
THAT YE MAY PROVE WHAT IS THAT GOOD, AND   110 07
THIS HE SAID TO PROVE HIM   131 29
AND I GO TO PROVE THEM   192 10
THIS HE SAID TO PROVE HIM   225 25
O LORD, AND PROVE ME   370 33
PROVE ME, AND EXAMINE MY THOUGHTS   516 12

PROVED

3 THOU HAST PROVED AND VISITED MINE HEART IN THE   358 21
THOU, O GOD, HAST PROVED US   417 33
8 I PROVED THEE ALSO *   442 28
PROVED ME, AND SAW MY WORKS   459 22
AND LET THESE ALSO FIRST BE PROVED   531 30
BE CONCLUDED AND PROVED BY THE SCRIPTURE   542 08
BE CONCLUDED AND PROVED BY THE SAME   554 26
NOR MAY BE PROVED THEREBY, IS NOT TO BE REQUIRED OF   603 30

PROVED   CONTINUED

FOR THEY MAY BE PROVED BY MOST CERTAIN WARRANTS OF   604 26
CANNOT BE PROVED BY HOLY WRIT   608 41

PROVERB

SPEAKEST THOU PLAINLY, AND SPEAKEST NO PROVERB   176 33

PROVERBS

THESE THINGS HAVE I SPOKEN UNTO YOU IN PROVERBS   176 24
UNTO YOU IN PROVERBS, BUT I SHALL SHEW YOU PLAINLY OF 176 25

PROVIDE

IT IS IN WANT, PROVIDE FOR IT   037 20
TO DEFEND, AND PROVIDE FOR, THE FATHERLESS CHILDREN,   056 35
PROVIDE THINGS HONEST IN THE SIGHT OF ALL MEN   112 32
DOES THE CHURCH PROVIDE TO HELP YOU TO DO ALL THESE   291 21
DOTH OUR LORD PROVIDE FOR YOU   291 29
BREAD ALSO, OR PROVIDE FLESH FOR HIS PEOPLE   436 10
TO FEED AND PROVIDE FOR THE LORD'S FAMILY   539 34

PROVIDED

BE ALLOWED, PROVIDED THE SUBSTANCE OF THE FAITH BE   V 04
MAY BE OMITTED, PROVIDED IT BE SAID AT LEAST ONE   R 067 28
PROVIDED, THAT THE NICENE CREED SHALL BE SAID ON   R 070 31
BASIN TO BE PROVIDED BY THE PARISH   R 073 29
PROVIDED, THAT EVERY MINISTER SO REPELLING ANY,   R 085 17
THE QUESTIONS PROVIDED IN THIS OFFICE FOR THE BAPTISM R 281 26
ARE ELSEWHERE PROVIDED IN THIS BOOK, ENDING WITH THE   R 331 30
IN CHRIST, PROVIDED THAT IN ANY OTHER CASE THE   R 337 03
IN THAT CASE PROVIDED MAY REQUIRE   529 25
AND IS PROVIDED FOR, AS TO THE REMAINING   R 607 12

PROVIDENCE

GUIDED BY THY PROVIDENCE, WE MAY DWELL SECURE IN THY   018 09
OF THY DIVINE PROVIDENCE HAST APPOINTED DIVERS ORDERS 039 08
THE OTHER BLESSINGS OF HIS MERCIFUL PROVIDENCE   050 18
THY MERCIFUL PROVIDENCE BESTOWED UPON THIS NATICN AND 050 24
GRACIOUS PROVIDENCE THE FORMER AND THE LATTER RAIN   051 15
THY MERCIFUL PROVIDENCE TOWARDS HIM, AND EVER EXPRESS 053 25
BY THY GOOD PROVIDENCE, BE BROUGHT TO NOUGHT   058 21
OF DIVINE PROVIDENCE, THESE AMERICAN STATES BECAME   VI 07
OF THY GOOD PROVIDENCE, AND MAKE US TO HAVE A   191 07
NEVER-FAILING PROVIDENCE ORDERETH ALL THINGS BOTH IN   199 28
BY WHOSE PROVIDENCE THY SERVANT JOHN BAPTIST WAS   242 07
CONTINUAL THANKS FOR THY SUSTAINING PROVIDENCE   316 23
BY THY DIVINE PROVIDENCE HAST APPOINTED DIVERS ORDERS 531 14
OF THY WISE PROVIDENCE HAST APPOINTED DIVERS ORDERS   572 07
AND WATCHFUL PROVIDENCE OVER US THROUGH THE WHOLE   591 17

PROVIDES

THE CHURCH PROVIDES THE LAYING ON OF HANDS, OR   291 23
OUR LORD PROVIDES THE SACRAMENT OF THE LORD'S SUPPER, 291 30

PROVIDEST

FOR SO THOU PROVIDEST FOR THE EARTH   417 03

PROVING

PROVING WHAT IS ACCEPTABLE UNTO THE LORD   129 15
AT DAMASCUS, PROVING THAT THIS IS VERY CHRIST   231 10

PROVISION

ALL KIND OF PROVISION, SO THAT THERE LACKETH NOTHING   088 19
AND MAKE NOT PROVISION FOR THE FLESH, TO FULFIL THE   091 08
ALL THE PROVISION OF BREAD   471 05
WHERE PROVISION IS SO MADE, TO SEARCH FOR THE   533 18

PROVOCATION

AS IN THE PROVOCATION, AND AS IN THE DAY OF   459 20

PROVOCATIONS

NOTWITHSTANDING OUR MANY AND GREAT PROVCCATIONS   591 15

PROVOKE

HOLY SUPPER, PROVOKE GOD'S INDIGNATION AGAINST YOU   088 26
ONE ANOTHER TO PROVOKE UNTO LOVE AND TO GOOD WORKS   158 25
I WILL PROVOKE YOU TO JEALOUSY BY THEM THAT   227 17
A TIME DID THEY PROVOKE HIM IN THE WILDERNESS,   437 21

PROVOKED

IS NOT EASILY PROVOKED, THINKETH NO EVIL   122 32
AND GOD IS PROVOKED EVERY DAY   350 16
AND PROVOKED THE MOST HIGHEST IN THE WILDERNESS   436 03
AND PROVOKED THE HOLY ONE IN ISRAEL   437 23
AND PROVOKED HIM TO DISPLEASURE WITH THEIR IMAGES   430 09
29 THUS THEY PROVOKED HIM TO ANGER WITH THEIR OWN   474 27
33 BECAUSE THEY PROVOKED HIS SPIRIT, *   475 02

PROVOKING

PROVOKING MOST JUSTLY THY WRATH AND   075 22

PRUDENCE

AND PRUDENCE, WE DO FULLY CONFIDE, OUR   569 15

PRUDENT

THE WISE AND PRUDENT, AND HAST REVEALED THEM UNTC   235 05

PRUDENTLY

AND RULED THEM PRUDENTLY WITH ALL HIS POWER   439 25

PSALM

EXCEPT ALSO, THAT PSALM 95 MAY BE USED IN THIS PLACE   R 008 10
THE END OF EVERY PSALM, AND LIKEWISE AT THE END CF   R 009 23
THE END OF EVERY PSALM, AND LIKEWISE AT THE END CF   R 025 16
TO THE HARP WITH A PSALM OF THANKSGIVING   027 16
SAID BY THEM THIS PSALM FOLLOWING   R 060 07
IN THE SECOND PSALM, THOU ART MY SON, THIS DAY HAVE I 169 09
ALSO IN ANOTHER PSALM, THOU SHALT NOT SUFFER THINE   169 13
AT THE END OF EACH PSALM SHALL BE SAID THE GLORIA   R 338 15
2 TAKE THE PSALM, BRING HITHER THE TABRET, *   442 14
TO THE HARP WITH A PSALM OF THANKSGIVING   462 05
THE FOLLOWING PSALM ALTERNATELY, THE BISHOP CNE VERSE R 563 08
EXSURGAT DEUS, PSALM LXVIII   R 571 30
JUDICA ME, DOMINE, PSALM XXVI   R 571 31

PSALMS

AND SHOW OURSELVES GLAD IN HIM WITH PSALMS   009 06
A PORTION OF THE PSALMS, ACCORDING TO THE USE OF THIS R 009 22
A PORTION OF THE PSALMS, ACCORDING TO THE USE OF THIS R 025 15
OR SELECTION OF PSALMS FOR THE DAY, SHALL BE SUNG CR   R 025 19
ONE ANOTHER IN PSALMS AND HYMNS AND SPIRITUAL SCNGS,   116 12
AND IN THE PSALMS, CONCERNING ME   170 10
TO YOURSELVES IN PSALMS AND HYMNS AND SPIRITUAL   217 28
IN THE BOOK OF PSALMS, LET HIS HABITATION BE   234 18
ONE OF THE PENITENTIAL PSALMS   R 308 09
OR MORE OF THE PSALMS FOLLOWING, WITH ANTIPHCN AND   R 309 09
OF THE FOLLOWING PSALMS, 20, 27, 42, 91, 121,   R 313 09
THE FOLLOWING SELECTIONS, TAKEN FROM THE PSALMS   R 324 17
SHALL BE SAID THE FOLLOWING PSALMS   R 338 14
AND SHOW OURSELVES GLAD IN HIM WITH PSALMS   459 08

PSALTER

FROM THE PSALTER, SHALL BE SUNG OR SAID THE GLORIA   R 009 25
THE WHOLE PORTION OR SELECTION FROM THE PSALTER   R 324 18
THE END OF THE PSALTER   R 525 33

PUBLIC

IN HER FORMS OF PUBLIC WORSHIP   V 23
REVIEW OF THE PUBLIC SERVICE, AND TO ESTABLISH SUCH   VI 25
OTHER OCCASION OF PUBLIC WORSHIP WHEN THE OFFERINGS   R 073 26
TO ATTEND THE PUBLIC MINISTRATION IN CHURCH,   R 323 33
AND ALSO BY PUBLIC PRAYER, WITH IMPOSITION OF HANDS,   529 17
AND TO USE BOTH PUBLIC AND PRIVATE MONITICNS AND   542 22
HOUSES FOR THE PUBLIC WORSHIP OF GOD, AND SEPARATED   564 15
HIM THE OFFICE OF PUBLIC PREACHING, CR MINISTERING   607 19
BY MEN WHO HAVE PUBLIC AUTHORITY GIVEN UNTO THEM IN   607 23
TO HAVE PUBLIC PRAYER IN THE CHURCH, OR TO   607 28

PUBLICAN

THE ONE A PHARISEE, AND THE OTHER A PUBLICAN   205 24
ADULTERERS, OR EVEN AS THIS PUBLICAN   205 27
AND THE PUBLICAN, STANDING AFAR OFF, WCULD NCT LIFT   205 28
AN HEATHEN AND PUBLICAN, UNTIL HE BE OPENLY   609 28

PUBLICANS

HIM ALL THE PUBLICANS AND SINNERS FOR TO HEAR HIM   193 14
BEHOLD, MANY PUBLICANS AND SINNERS CAME AND SAT DCWN   251 16
MASTER WITH PUBLICANS AND SINNERS   251 19
NOT EVEN THE PUBLICANS THE SAME   264 12
NOT EVEN THE PUBLICANS SO   264 14

PUBLICK

TO MAKE HER A PUBLICK EXAMPLE, WAS MINDED TC PUT HER   104 31

PUBLICKLY

TAUGHT YOU PUBLICKLY, AND FROM HOUSE TO HOUSE,   550 12

PUBLICLY

IT SHALL BE PUBLICLY ADMINISTERED IN THE CHURCH   R 321 09

PUBLISH

I PUBLISH THE BANNS OF MARRIAGE BETWEEN N   R 304 22

PUBLISHED

AND OF OTHER MATTERS TO BE PUBLISHED   R 071 28
WHICH WAS PUBLISHED THROUGHOUT ALL JUDAEA, AND BEGAN   166 17
WHICH WAS PUBLISHED THROUGHOUT ALL JUDAEA, AND BEGAN   184 05
DEAL THEY PUBLISHED IT   207 06
THE LORD WAS PUBLISHED THROUGHOUT ALL THE REGION   261 08
THE BANNS ARE PUBLISHED, IT SHALL BE IN THE FOLLCWING R 304 21

PUBLISHING

WHETHER BY PUBLISHING THE BANNS IN CHURCHES, OR BY   R 304 17

PUFFED

IS NOT PUFFED UP, DOTH NOT BEHAVE ITSELF   122 30

PULL

LET ME PULL OUT THE MOTE THAT IS IN THINE   195 08
THOU SEE CLEARLY TO PULL OUT THE MOTE THAT IS IN THY   195 12
NOT STRAIGHTWAY PULL HIM OUT ON THE SABBATH DAY   214 06

PUNISH

JUSTLY TO PUNISH SINNERS, AND TO BE MERCIFUL TO THOSE   041 11
LONG WILT THOU PUNISH ME   349 05
OF THE POOR, AND PUNISH THE WRONG DOER   427 05
SHALL NOT HE PUNISH   458 07
THOUGH THOU DIDST PUNISH THEIR WICKED DOINGS   462 33
THAT THEY MAY PUNISH WICKEDNESS AND VICE, AND   590 28

PUNISHED

WHO ARE JUSTLY PUNISHED FOR OUR OFFENCES, MAY BE   118 29
DESERVE TO BE PUNISHED, BY THE COMFORT OF THY GRACE   130 25
29 THE UNRIGHTEOUS SHALL BE PUNISHED   386 22
HAVE I BEEN PUNISHED, *   429 04
SO THAT HE PUNISHED MOSES FOR THEIR SAKES   474 34

PUNISHMENT

WE DESERVE PUNISHMENT, AND IN THY WRATH REMEMBEREST   046 18
WE DESERVE PUNISHMENT, AND IN THY WRATH THINKEST UPON   062 32
TO THE PUNISHMENT OF WICKEDNESS AND VICE, AND TO THE   074 18
AND HOW SORE PUNISHMENT HANGETH OVER YOUR HEADS FOR   089 15
HIM FOR THE PUNISHMENT OF EVILDOERS, AND FOR THE   173 20
THE HORRIBLE PUNISHMENT THAT WILL ENSUE   540 13

PURCHASE

A DEACON WELL PURCHASE TO THEMSELVES A GOOD DEGREE,   532 03
PURCHASE TO THEMSELVES DAMNATION,   608 05

PURCHASED

WHO HAST PURCHASED TO THYSELF AN UNIVERSAL CHURCH BY   038 25
NOW THIS MAN PURCHASED A FIELD WITH THE REWARD OF   234 13
WHOM THOU HAST PURCHASED, AND REDEEMED OF OLD   430 07
WHICH HE PURCHASED WITH HIS RIGHT HAND   438 19
WHICH HE HATH PURCHASED WITH HIS OWN BLOOD   550 29
WHICH HE HATH PURCHASED WITH NO LESS PRICE THAN THE   554 10
WHO HAST PURCHASED TO THYSELF AN UNIVERSAL CHURCH,   572 16

PURE

UNTO MY NAME, AND A PURE OFFERING   004 15
ACCOMPANY ME WITH A PURE HEART, AND HUMBLE VOICE,   006 11
HEREAFTER MAY BE PURE AND HOLY   007 17
ACCOMPANY ME WITH A PURE HEART, AND HUMBLE VOICE,   023 20
HEREAFTER MAY BE PURE AND HOLY   024 19
SOUND LEARNING, AND PURE MANNERS   036 13
TO RECEIVE IT WITH PURE AFFECTION, AND TO BRING FORTH   056 16
TO BE BORN OF A PURE VIRGIN   096 15
TO BE BORN OF A PURE VIRGIN   104 07
WE MAY PURIFY OURSELVES, EVEN AS HE IS PURE   117 08
HOPE IN HIM PURIFIETH HIMSELF, EVEN AS HE IS PURE   117 21
BODIES WASHED WITH PURE WATER   158 22
PURE RELIGION AND UNDEFILED BEFORE GOD AND THE FATHER   176 15
AND WITH PURE HEARTS AND MINDS TO FOLLOW THEE,   214 25
UNTO THEE WITH PURE AND CLEAN HEARTS, BY THE SAME THY   231 31
BLESSED ARE THE PURE IN HEART   257 27
PURE RELIGION AND UNDEFILED BEFORE GOD AND THE FATHER   266 06
TO BE FILLED WITH PURE WATER, SHALL SAY AS FOLLOWETH,   R 273 24
IT MAY BE PRESENTED PURE AND WITHOUT SPOT BEFORE   317 21
BLESSED ARE THE PURE IN HEART   340 16
OF THE LORD ARE PURE WORDS   355 20
OF THE LORD IS PURE, AND GIVETH LIGHT UNTO THE EYES   363 31
SET A CROWN OF PURE GOLD UPON HIS HEAD   365 10
CLEAN HANDS, AND A PURE HEART   369 02
OF THE FAITH IN A PURE CONSCIENCE   531 29
THIS DAY, THAT I AM PURE FROM THE BLOOD OF ALL MEN   550 25
CLEAN HANDS, AND A PURE HEART   563 17
WE MAY BE PRESERVED PURE AND BLAMELESS, UNTO THE   590 19
AN ACTION WITHOUT A PURE INTENTION NOR CONTINUE IT   594 22
THINGS ARE TRUE AND PURE AND LOVELY AND OF GOOD   596 27
IN THE WHICH THE PURE WORD OF GOD IS PREACHED,   606 39

PURELY

IN THINGS PURELY SPIRITUAL   610 39

PURENESS

IN HOLINESS AND PURENESS OF LIVING, TO THY HONOUR AND   059 26
BY PURENESS, BY KNOWLEDGE, BY LONG-SUFFERING, BY   126 12
SERVE THEE IN PURENESS OF LIVING AND TRUTH   170 22

PURER

WHO ART OF PURER EYES THAN TO BEHOLD INIQUITY,   589 26

PURGATORY

CONCERNING PURGATORY, PARDONS, WORSHIPPING AND   607 14

PURGE

THOU SHALT PURGE ME WITH HYSSOP, AND I SHALL BE   060 24
SPOT TO GOD, PURGE YOUR CONSCIENCE FROM DEAD WORKS TO   133 02
PURGE OUT THEREFORE THE OLD LEAVEN, THAT YE MAY BE A   165 11
SONS OF LEVI, AND PURGE THEM AS GOLD AND SILVER, THAT   232 11
7 THOU SHALT PURGE ME WITH HYSSOP, AND I SHALL BE   403 22
PURGE OUR HEARTS FROM ENVY, HATRED, AND MALICE   590 15

PURGED

HE HAD BY HIMSELF PURGED OUR SINS, SAT DOWN ON THE   096 28
ARE BY THE LAW PURGED WITH BLOOD   147 26
WORSHIPPERS ONCE PURGED SHOULD HAVE HAD NO MORE   157 20
OF SATAN, BEING PURGED AND DONE AWAY, IT MAY BE   317 20

PURGETH

HE PURGETH IT, THAT IT MAY BRING FORTH MORE   238 07

PURIFICATION

ON THE PURIFICATION, AND THE ANNUNCIATION   R 008 31
OF THE PURIFICATION, ANNUNCIATION, AND   R 077 28
DAYS OF HER PURIFICATION ACCORDING TO THE LAW OF   232 23

PURIFIED

SHOULD BE PURIFIED WITH THESE   147 28
IS TRIED, AND PURIFIED SEVEN TIMES IN THE FIRE   355 21

PURIFIER

A REFINER AND PURIFIER OF SILVER   232 10

PURIFIETH

HOPE IN HIM PURIFIETH HIMSELF, EVEN AS HE IS PURE   117 20

PURIFY

IT IS CORRUPT, PURIFY IT   037 17
ALL INIQUITY, AND PURIFY UNTO HIMSELF A PECULIAR   098 24
THIS HOPE, WE MAY PURIFY OURSELVES, EVEN AS HE IS   117 07
AND HE SHALL PURIFY THE SONS OF LEVI, AND PURGE THEM   232 11

PURIFYING

MANNER OF THE PURIFYING OF THE JEWS, CONTAINING TWO   113 19
TO THE PURIFYING OF THE FLESH   132 30

PURITY

STRENGTHEN IT IN PURITY OF FAITH, IN HOLINESS OF   047 09
IN CHASTITY, AND IN PURITY   559 11
IN TRUTH AND PURITY THROUGH ALL GENERATIONS   568 11

PURPLE

CLOTHED HIM WITH PURPLE, AND PLATTED A CROWN OF   145 32
THEY TOOK OFF THE PURPLE FROM HIM, AND PUT HIS OWN   146 03
THEY PUT ON HIM A PURPLE ROBE, AND SAID, HAIL,   158 32
AND THE PURPLE ROBE   159 04
WAS CLOTHED IN PURPLE AND FINE LINEN, AND FARED   190 04

PURPOSE

FOR THAT PURPOSE, SHALL RECEIVE THE ALMS FOR THE   R 073 28
TO BE IN FULL PURPOSE SO TO DO, AS SOON AS HE   R 085 07
ON -- DAY NEXT I PURPOSE, THROUGH GOD'S ASSISTANCE,   086 28
WITH FULL PURPOSE OF AMENDMENT OF LIFE   087 21
TO THE ETERNAL PURPOSE WHICH HE PURPOSED IN CHRIST   108 26
FOR THIS PURPOSE THE SON OF GOD WAS MANIFESTED, THAT   117 29
THAT WITH PURPOSE OF HEART THEY WOULD CLEAVE   241 07
WITH STEDFAST PURPOSE TO LEAD A NEW LIFE   293 27
THEM WHO ARE THE CALLED ACCORDING TO HIS PURPOSE   330 32
ARE THEY WHOM WE PURPOSE, GOD WILLING, TO RECEIVE   536 22
OF THY PURPOSE, THAT THY CHURCH MAY BE ONE   561 17
OR SOME OTHER PERSONS APPOINTED FOR THAT PURPOSE   R 563 07
OUR GODLY PURPOSE OF SETTING APART THIS PLACE IN   564 22
FOR THE PURPOSE OF INSTITUTING THE REV   570 13
THE EVERLASTING PURPOSE OF GOD, WHEREBY (BEFORE THE   606 06
TO GOD'S PURPOSE BY HIS SPIRIT WORKING IN DUE SEASON   606 11

PURPOSED

WHICH HE PURPOSED IN CHRIST JESUS OUR LORD   108 26
I AM UTTERLY PURPOSED THAT MY MOUTH SHALL NOT OFFEND   358 23
AM STEDFASTLY PURPOSED, *   497 09
WHO ARE PURPOSED TO OVERTHROW MY GOINGS   516 16

PURPOSELY

WILLINGLY AND PURPOSELY, DOTH OPENLY BREAK THE   609 36

PURPOSING

STEDFASTLY PURPOSING TO LEAD A NEW LIFE   582 23

PURSE

I SENT YOU WITHOUT PURSE, AND SCRIP, AND SHOES,   150 04

PURSE   CONTINUED

HE THAT HATH A PURSE, LET HIM TAKE IT, AND LIKEWISE   150 07
CARRY NEITHER PURSE, NOR SCRIP, NOR SHOES   254 18

PURSUE

AGAINST THEM THAT PURSUE ME   381 23
ANGEL OF THE LORD PURSUE THEM   381 30
15 PURSUE THEM EVEN SO WITH THY TEMPEST, *   445 02

PUT

PUT ON THY STRENGTH, O ZION   004 18
PUT ON THY BEAUTIFUL GARMENTS, O JERUSALEM   004 18
HE HATH PUT DOWN THE MIGHTY FROM THEIR SEAT, *   026 22
PRAYERS OF THOSE WHO PUT THEIR TRUST IN THEE   041 20
AS WE DO PUT OUR TRUST IN THEE   059 19
OUR TROUBLES WE MAY PUT OUR WHOLE TRUST AND   059 24
AND PUT OUT ALL MY MISDEEDS   060 28
THAT PUT THEIR TRUST IN THEE   061 31
OF DARKNESS, AND PUT UPON US THE ARMOUR OF LIGHT, NOW   090 12
AND LET US PUT ON THE ARMOUR OF LIGHT   091 04
BUT PUT YE ON THE LORD JESUS CHRIST, AND MAKE NCT   091 07
AND THE COLT, AND PUT ON THEM THEIR CLOTHES, AND THEY   091 23
WAS MINDED TO PUT HER AWAY PRIVILY   104 31
AND JESUS PUT FORTH HIS HAND, AND TOUCHED HIM,   114 32
PUT ON THEREFORE, AS THE ELECT OF GOD, HOLY AND   116 03
ALL THESE THINGS PUT ON CHARITY, WHICH IS THE BCND OF   116 08
WHO SEEST THAT WE PUT NOT OUR TRUST IN ANY THING THAT   120 17
I BECAME A MAN, I PUT AWAY CHILDISH THINGS   123 11
SCOURGE HIM, AND PUT HIM TO DEATH   123 22
AGAINST JESUS TO PUT HIM TO DEATH   134 32
IS NOT LAWFUL FOR TO PUT THEM INTO THE TREASURY,   135 10
STRIPPED HIM, AND PUT ON HIM A SCARLET ROBE   136 17
OF THORNS, THEY PUT IT UPON HIS HEAD, AND A REED IN   136 19
OFF FROM HIM, AND PUT HIS OWN RAIMENT ON HIM, AND LED   136 24
IT WITH VINEGAR, AND PUT IT ON A REED, AND GAVE HIM   137 22
WHERE IS HE THAT PUT HIS HOLY SPIRIT WITHIN HIM   139 10
HIM BY CRAFT, AND PUT HIM TO DEATH   139 34
AGAINST JESUS TO PUT HIM TO DEATH   143 03
CROWN OF THORNS, AND PUT IT ABOUT HIS HEAD, AND BEGAN   145 32
PURPLE FROM HIM, AND PUT HIS OWN CLOTHES ON HIM,   146 04
FULL OF VINEGAR, AND PUT IT ON A REED, AND GAVE HIM   146 32
HATH HE APPEARED TO PUT AWAY SIN BY THE SACRIFICE OF   148 06
LED WITH HIM TO BE PUT TO DEATH   154 22
THE DEVIL HAVING NOW PUT INTO THE HEART OF JUDAS   155 07
THE LORD, I WILL PUT MY LAWS INTO THEIR HEARTS,   158 12
CROWN OF THORNS, AND PUT IT ON HIS HEAD, AND THEY PUT   158 31
HIS HEAD, AND THEY PUT ON HIM A PURPLE ROBE, AND   158 32
WROTE A TITLE, AND PUT IT ON THE CROSS   159 35
IT UPON HYSSOP, AND PLT IT TO HIS MOUTH   160 27
WITH VINEGAR, AND PUT IT UPON HYSSOP, AND PUT IT TO   160 27
US TO GOD, BEING PUT TO DEATH IN THE FLESH, BUT   161 24
US THOU DOST PUT INTO OUR MINDS GOOD DESIRES, SC BY   163 26
GRANT US SO TO PUT AWAY THE LEAVEN OF MALICE AND   170 21
WELL DOING YE MAY PUT TO SILENCE THE IGNORANCE CF   173 22
THE FATHER HATH PUT IN HIS OWN POWER   178 08
THEY SHALL PUT YOU OUT OF THE SYNAGOGUES   179 29
OF ALL THOSE WHO PUT THEIR TRUST IN THEE   188 32
BESEECH THEE TO PUT AWAY FROM US ALL HURTFUL THINGS,   199 30
AND PUT A RING ON HIS HAND, AND SHOES ON HIS FEET   202 22
THE BEST ROBE, AND PUT IT ON HIM   202 22
THEY BESEECH HIM TO PUT HIS HAND UPON HIM   206 31
THE MULTITUDE, AND PUT HIS FINGERS INTO HIS EARS,   206 32
WHAT YE SHALL PUT ON   211 14
AND HE PUT FORTH A PARABLE TO THOSE WHICH WERE   214 08
HEARD THAT JESUS HAD PUT THE SADDUCEES TO SILENCE,   215 06
THAT YE PUT OFF CONCERNING THE FORMER CONVERSATICN   216 12
AND THAT YE PUT ON THE NEW MAN, WHICH AFTER GOD IS   216 15
EVIL SPEAKING, BE PUT AWAY FROM YOU, WITH ALL MALICE   216 28
PUT ON THE WHOLE ARMOUR OF GOD, THAT YE MAY BE ABLE   219 06
WHEN THE PEOPLE WERE PUT FORTH, HE WENT IN, AND TCCK   224 27
OF THE NAILS, AND PUT MY FINGER INTO THE PRINT OF THE   228 29
APPREHENDED HIM, HE PLT HIM IN PRISON, AND DELIVERED   245 04
THAT SHORTLY I MUST PUT OFF THIS MY TABERNACLE, EVEN   248 10
THY HOLY SPIRIT, TO PLT IT INTO THE HEARTS OF MANY TO   260 21
BUT SEEING YE PUT IT FROM YOU, AND JUDGE YOURSELVES   260 32
WHAT YE SHALL PUT ON   266 13
LET NOT MAN PUT ASUNDER   268 11
THEM UP IN HIS ARMS, PUT HIS HANDS UPON THEM, AND   274 30
TO PUT MY WHOLE TRLST IN HIM, TO CALL UPON HIM   288 19
AS WE DO PUT OUR TRUST IN THEE   290 11
IT UNTO THE MAN, TO PLT IT UPON THE FOURTH FINGER OF R 302 11
TOGETHER LET NO MAN PLT ASUNDER   303 31
WHY HAST THOU PUT ME FROM THEE   310 09
O PUT THY TRUST IN GOD   310 18
THY MERCIES, DOST SO PUT AWAY THE SINS OF THOSE WHO   313 31
TO ALL THOSE WHO PLT THEIR TRUST IN HIM, TO WHOM ALL   314 16
OF BODY BEING PUT TO FLIGHT, THE BLESSING OF HEALTH   320 18
AND PUT THOU THY TRUST IN THE LORD   326 31
WHEN HE SHALL HAVE PUT DOWN ALL RULE AND ALL   328 28
TILL HE HATH PUT ALL ENEMIES UNDER HIS FEET   328 30
FOR HE HATH PUT ALL THINGS UNDER HIS FEET   328 31
SAITH ALL THINGS ARE PUT UNDER HIM, IT IS MANIFEST   328 32
WHICH DID PUT ALL THINGS UNDER HIM   328 33
UNTO HIM THAT PUT ALL THINGS UNDER HIM, THAT GOD MAY   329 03
CORRUPTIBLE MUST PUT ON INCORRUPTION, AND THIS MCRTAL   330 06
AND THIS MORTAL MUST PUT ON IMMORTALITY   330 06
SHALL HAVE PUT ON INCORRUPTION, AND THIS MORTAL SHALL   330 07
MORTAL SHALL HAVE PUT ON IMMORTALITY, THEN SHALL BE   330 08
ARE ALL THEY THAT PUT THEIR TRUST IN HIM   346 23
AND PUT YOUR TRUST IN THE LORD   347 21
8 THOU HAST PUT GLADNESS IN MY HEART   347 26
LET ALL THEM THAT PUT THEIR TRUST IN THEE REJOICE   348 25
BE TURNED BACK, AND PUT TO SHAME SUDDENLY   349 19

PUT   CONTINUED

IN THEE HAVE I PUT MY TRUST   349 22
AND THOU HAST PUT ALL THINGS IN SUBJECTICN UNDER HIS   351 12
THOU HAST PUT OUT THEIR NAME FOR EVER AND EVER   351 31
KNOW THY NAME WILL PUT THEIR TRUST IN THEE   352 08
20 PUT THEM IN FEAR, O LORD, *   352 32
IN THE LORD PUT I MY TRUST   354 19
CHILDREN OF MEN ARE PUT TO REBUKE   355 26
FOR IN THEE HAVE I PUT MY TRUST   357 21
OF THEM WHICH PUT THEIR TRUST IN THEE, *   358 32
OF ALL THEM THAT PUT THEIR TRUST IN HIM   361 30
7 SOME PUT THEIR TRUST IN CHARIOTS, AND SOME IN   364 29
THEREFORE SHALT THOU PUT THEM TO FLIGHT, *   365 29
THEY PUT THEIR TRUST IN THEE, AND WERE NOT   366 12
MY GOD, I HAVE PUT MY TRUST IN THEE   369 19
A CAUSE SHALL BE PUT TO CONFUSION   372 22
FOR I HAVE PUT MY TRUST IN THEE   370 25
YET WILL I PUT MY TRUST IN HIM   371 31
AND PUT THOU THY TRUST IN THE LORD   372 31
THOU HAST PUT OFF MY SACKCLOTH, AND GIRDED ME WITH   375 17
O LORD, HAVE I PUT MY TRUST   375 22
LET ME NEVER BE PUT TO CONFUSION   375 23
LET THE UNGODLY BE PUT TO CONFUSION, AND BE PUT TO   376 31
TO CONFUSION, AND BE PUT TO SILENCE IN THE GRAVE   376 32
THE LYING LIPS BE PUT TO SILENCE, *   376 33
FOR THEM THAT PUT THEIR TRUST IN THEE, EVEN BEFCRE   377 04
ALL YE THAT PUT YOUR TRUST IN THE LORD   377 19
AND UPON THEM THAT PUT THEIR TRUST IN HIS MERCY   379 25
LIKE AS WE DO PUT OUR TRUST IN THEE   379 33
AND ALL THEY THAT PUT THEIR TRUST IN HIM SHALL NCT BE   381 13
BE CONFOUNDED, AND PUT TO SHAME, THAT SEEK AFTER MY   381 24
THEY WERE SICK, I PUT ON SACKCLOTH, AND HUMBLED MY   382 17
26 LET THEM BE PUT TO CONFUSION AND SHAME TCGETHER   383 16
OF MEN SHALL PUT THEIR TRUST UNDER THE SHADOW OF THY   384 10
3 PUT THOU THY TRUST IN THE LORD, AND BE DOING GCCD   384 29
UNTO THE LORD, AND PUT THY TRUST IN HIM, *   385 02
BECAUSE THEY PUT THEIR TRUST IN HIM   387 17
PUT ME NOT TO REBUKE, O LORD, IN THINE ANGER   387 21
O LORD, HAVE I PUT MY TRUST   388 21
3 AND HE HATH PUT A NEW SONG IN MY MOUTH, *   390 14
AND SHALL PUT THEIR TRUST IN THE LORD   390 16
DRIVEN BACKWARD, AND PUT TO REBUKE, THAT WISH ME   391 18
7 O PUT THY TRUST IN GOD   393 13
15 O PUT THY TRUST IN GOD   393 33
WHY HAST THOU PUT ME FROM THEE   394 07
6 O PUT THY TRUST IN GOD   394 17
6 THERE BE SOME THAT PUT THEIR TRUST IN THEIR GCCDS,   400 16
AND PUT OUT ALL MY MISDEEDS   403 27
THOU HAST PUT THEM TO CONFUSION, BECAUSE GOD HATH   405 27
YET PUT I MY TRUST IN THEE   408 19
I HAVE PUT MY TRUST IN GOD, AND WILL NOT FEAR WHAT   408 21
PUT MY TEARS INTO THY BOTTLE   408 30
MINE ENEMIES BE PUT TO FLIGHT   408 33
IN GOD HAVE I PUT MY TRUST   409 04
THE PEOPLE, AND PUT THEM DOWN, O LORD OUR DEFENCE   411 27
IS ONLY HOW TO PUT HIM OUT WHOM GOD WILL EXALT   414 04
8 O PUT YOUR TRUST IN HIM ALWAY, YE PEOPLE   414 13
IN THE LORD, AND PUT MY TRUST IN HIM   416 06
11 I PUT ON SACKCLOTH ALSO, *   422 25
TURNED BACKWARD AND PUT TO CONFUSION THAT WISH ME   424 23
O LORD, HAVE I PUT MY TRUST   425 05
LET ME NEVER BE PUT TO CONFUSION, *   425 06
ME FAST BY GOD, TO PUT MY TRUST IN THE LORD GOD,   429 33
8 THAT THEY MIGHT PUT THEIR TRUST IN GOD   435 11
AND PUT NOT THEIR TRUST IN HIS HELP   436 14
AND PUT THEM TO A PERPETUAL SHAME   439 10
I SHOULD SOON HAVE PUT DOWN THEIR ENEMIES, *   443 08
LET THEM BE PUT TO SHAME, AND PERISH   445 07
7 THOU HAST PUT AWAY MINE ACQUAINTANCE FAR FROM ME,   449 11
FRIENDS HAST THOU PUT AWAY FROM ME, *   449 33
43 THOU HAST PUT OUT HIS GLORY, *   452 28
IS KING, AND HATH PUT ON GLORIOUS APPAREL   457 04
THE LORD HATH PUT ON HIS APPAREL, AND GIRDED HIMSELF   457 05
AND PUT THE FATHERLESS TO DEATH   457 29
BUT MY SOUL HAD BEEN PUT TO SILENCE   458 21
HIS NAME BE CLEAN PUT OUT   480 26
SO ARE ALL SUCH AS PUT THEIR TRUST IN THEM   485 27
YE HOUSE OF AARON, PUT YOUR TRUST IN THE LORD   485 30
THAT FEAR THE LORD, PUT YOUR TRUST IN THE LORD   485 32
THAN TO PUT ANY CONFIDENCE IN MAN   488 14
THAN TO PUT ANY CONFIDENCE IN PRINCES   488 16
HAST CAUSED ME TO PUT MY TRUST   493 09
BECAUSE I HAVE PUT MY TRUST IN THY WORD   495 03
THEY THAT PUT THEIR TRUST IN THE LORD SHALL BE EVEN   504 23
LEST THE RIGHTEOUS PUT THEIR HAND UNTO WICKEDNESS   504 30
SO ARE ALL THEY THAT PUT THEIR TRUST IN THEM   511 07
2 O PUT NOT YOUR TRUST IN PRINCES, NOR IN ANY CHILD   522 06
AND PUT THEIR TRUST IN HIS MERCY   523 18
THE BISHOP ELECT PUT ON THE REST OF THE EPISCOPAL   R 556 02
HATH PLEASED THEE TO PUT IT INTO THE HEARTS OF THY   566 29
TO PUT MY WHOLE TRUST IN HIM, TO CALL UPON HIM   579 30
HE YET MAY PUT HIS TRUST IN THEE   597 25
PUT FAR FROM THEM, WE BESEECH THEE, EVERY ROOT CF   598 21
CANNOT PUT AWAY OUR SINS, AND ENDURE THE SEVERITY OF   605 12

PUTTEST

AND PUTTEST THEM TO CONFUSION THAT HATE US   395 08
ART FAR OFF, AND PUTTEST US TO CONFUSION, *   395 11
119 THOU PUTTEST AWAY ALL THE UNGODLY OF THE EARTH   498 06

PUTTETH

AND WHEN HE PUTTETH FORTH HIS OWN SHEEP, HE GOETH   186 06
WHO PUTTETH HER TRUST IN THEE   306 18

PUTTETH — CONTINUED

WHO PUTTETH HIS TRUST IN THEE	308 24
FORASMUCH AS HE PUTTETH HIS FULL TRUST ONLY IN THY	314 08
BECAUSE HE PUTTETH HIS TRUST IN THE LORD	356 29
BECAUSE THE KING PUTTETH HIS TRUST IN THE LORD	365 17
BUT WHOSO PUTTETH HIS TRUST IN THE LORD, MERCY	378 14
HE PUTTETH DOWN ONE, AND SETTETH UP ANOTHER	432 12
IS THE MAN THAT PUTTETH HIS TRUST IN THEE	446 06
THY SERVANT THAT PUTTETH HIS TRUST IN THEE	447 08
AND WHEN HE PUTTETH FORTH HIS OWN SHEEP, HE GOETH	538 29

PUTTING

SAVE US (NOT THE PUTTING AWAY OF THE FILTH OF THE	161 30
WHEREFORE PUTTING AWAY LYING, SPEAK EVERY MAN TRUTH	216 16
COMING IN, AND PUTTING HIS HAND ON HIM, THAT HE MIGHT	230 20
AND PUTTING HIS HANDS ON HIM SAID, BROTHER SAUL, THE	230 30
STIR YOU UP BY PUTTING YOU IN REMEMBRANCE	248 09

QUAILS

39 AT THEIR DESIRE HE BROUGHT QUAILS	472 17

QUAKE

AND THE EARTH DID QUAKE, AND THE ROCKS RENT	137 27

QUAKED

TREMBLED AND QUAKED, *	360 09

QUALIFIED

CHOSEN IS A QUALIFIED MINISTER OF THIS CHURCH,	R 569 06

QUALITIES

TO HAVE SUCH QUALITIES AS ARE REQUISITE FOR THE SAME	529 16

QUARREL

OF CAVIL OR QUARREL AGAINST HER LITURGY	V 38
ANY MAN HAVE A QUARREL AGAINST ANY	116 06
AND STAND UP TO JUDGE MY QUARREL	383 09

QUARTERS

AND LICE IN ALL THEIR QUARTERS	471 35

QUATERNIONS

HIM TO FOUR QUATERNIONS OF SOLDIERS TO KEEP HIM	245 05

QUEEN

DOTH STAND THE QUEEN IN A VESTURE OF GOLD, WROUGHT	397 03

QUENCH

SHALL BE ABLE TO QUENCH ALL THE FIERY DARTS OF THE	219 17
THE WILD ASSES QUENCH THEIR THIRST	468 16

QUESTION

ASKED HIM A QUESTION, TEMPTING HIM, AND SAYING,	215 08
OMITTING THE QUESTION WILT THOU BE BAPTIZED IN THIS	R 282 04
SHALL ASK THE QUESTION FOLLOWING, THE PEOPLE	R 284 25

QUESTIONED

THEN HE QUESTIONED WITH HIM IN MANY WORDS	153 14

QUESTIONS

AND ASKING THEM QUESTIONS	110 29
FROM THAT DAY FORTH ASK HIM ANY MORE QUESTICNS	215 24
ANSWERING THE QUESTIONS FOR THEMSELVES	R 277 19
FIRST ASK THE QUESTIONS PROVIDED IN THIS OFFICE FOR	R 281 26
THE QUESTIONS (OMITTING THE QUESTION WILT	R 282 04
ASK THEM THE QUESTIONS WHICH FOLLOW, THE PECPLE	R 283 13
SHALL ASK THE QUESTIONS WHICH FOLLOW, THE PEOPLE	R 287 32
ASK THEM THE QUESTIONS CONCERNING THE CHURCH WHICH	R 290 26
WITH THE QUESTIONS ON THE SACRAMENTS, AS FOLLOWETH	R 292 02
THE FOLLOWING QUESTIONS CONCERNING THE MINISTRY, THE	R 294 03
TO THE OTHER QUESTIONS OF THIS SHORT CATECHISM,	R 583 03

QUICK

COME TO JUDGE THE QUICK AND THE DEAD	015 27
TO JUDGE BOTH THE QUICK AND THE DEAD	016 13
COME TO JUDGE THE QUICK AND THE DEAD	029 32
TO JUDGE BOTH THE QUICK AND THE DEAD	030 18
TO JUDGE BOTH THE QUICK AND THE DEAD	071 15
TO JUDGE BOTH THE QUICK AND THE DEAD, WE MAY RISE TO	090 16
TO BE THE JUDGE OF QUICK AND DEAD	166 30
TO BE THE JUDGE OF QUICK AND DEAD	184 17
COME TO JUDGE THE QUICK AND THE DEAD	284 21
COME TO JUDGE THE QUICK AND THE DEAD	578 05
THE JUDGE OF QUICK AND DEAD, THY SON JESUS CHRIST OUR	588 24
CHRIST FOR THE QUICK AND THE DEAD, TO HAVE REMISSION	609 18

QUICKEN

DEAD WILL ALSO QUICKEN OUR MORTAL BODIES, BY HIS	333 05
TURN AGAIN, AND QUICKEN US, *	446 18

QUICKEN — CONTINUED

O QUICKEN THOU ME, ACCORDING TO THY WORD	491 17
AND QUICKEN THOU ME IN THY WAY	492 14
O QUICKEN ME IN THY RIGHTEOUSNESS	492 20
88 O QUICKEN ME AFTER THY LOVING-KINDNESS	495 33
QUICKEN ME, O LORD, ACCORDING TO THY WORD	497 11
QUICKEN ME, ACCORDING TO THY JUDGMENTS	500 09
QUICKEN ME ACCORDING TO THY WORD	500 19
QUICKEN ME, AS THOU ART WONT	500 23
O QUICKEN ME, ACCORDING TO THY LOVING-KINDNESS	500 30
11 QUICKEN ME, O LORD, FOR THY NAME'S SAKE	519 15
IN PRAYER, TO QUICKEN MY DEVOTION	573 25
DOTH NOT ONLY QUICKEN, BUT ALSO STRENGTHEN AND	607 34

QUICKENED

THE FLESH, BUT QUICKENED BY THE SPIRIT	161 24
SOWEST IS NOT QUICKENED, EXCEPT IT DIE	329 07
NO MAN HATH QUICKENED HIS OWN SOUL	368 03
THY WORD HATH QUICKENED ME	493 11
THEM THOU HAST QUICKENED ME	496 12

QUICKENING

WAS MADE A QUICKENING SPIRIT	329 25

QUICKLY

THEY WENT OUT QUICKLY, AND FLED FROM THE SEPULCHRE	165 33
GO OUT QUICKLY INTO THE STREETS AND LANES OF	192 14
THINE ADVERSARY QUICKLY, WHILES THOU ART IN THE WAY	198 12
AND RAISED HIM UP, SAYING, ARISE UP QUICKLY	245 15

QUIET

LEADING A QUIET AND PEACEABLE LIFE IN ALL	052 24
PEOPLE 'MAY LEAD QUIET AND PEACEABLE LIVES, IN ALL	VI 21
AND WITH A QUIET CONSCIENCE	088 03
THIS MEANS CANNOT QUIET HIS OWN CONSCIENCE HEREIN,	088 04
SERVE THEE WITH A QUIET MIND	219 02
THEM THAT ARE QUIET IN THE LAND	383 03
QUIET AND PEACEABLE	588 31

QUIETING

MAY TEND TO THE QUIETING OF HIS CONSCIENCE, AND THE	088 08

QUIETNESS

MAY PASS OUR TIME IN REST AND QUIETNESS	031 23
TO WORK WITH QUIETNESS, AND EAT OUR OWN BREAD	039 27
IN PEACE AND QUIETNESS SERVE THEE OUR GOD, TO THE	042 11
MAY JOYFULLY SERVE THEE IN ALL GODLY QUIETNESS	195 18
LIETH IN YOU, QUIETNESS, PEACE, AND LOVE, AMONG ALL	543 07
LIE IN YOU, QUIETNESS, LOVE, AND PEACE AMONG ALL MEN	555 15
MAY JOYFULLY SERVE THEE IN ALL GODLY QUIETNESS	574 17
BE SAVED, IN QUIETNESS AND IN CONFIDENCE SHALL BE OUR	595 20

QUIVER

ARROWS WITHIN THE QUIVER, *	354 22
MAN THAT HATH HIS QUIVER FULL OF THEM	506 02

RABBI

AND SAID UNTO HIM, RABBI, WE KNOW THAT THOU ART A	188 02
AND SAID UNTO HIM, RABBI, WE KNOW THAT THOU ART A	275 07

RACA

SAY TO HIS BROTHER, RACA, SHALL BE IN DANGER OF THE	198 06

RACE

WITH PATIENCE THE RACE THAT IS SET BEFORE US, AND,	079 25
IN RUNNING THE RACE THAT IS SET BEFORE US, THY	095 07
THEY WHICH RUN IN A RACE RUN ALL, BUT ONE RECEIVETH	119 05
IN RUNNING THE RACE THAT IS SET BEFORE US, UNTIL AT	258 15
WITH PATIENCE THE RACE THAT IS SET BEFORE US, LOCKING	258 23

RACHEL

GREAT MOURNING, RACHEL WEEPING FOR HER CHILDREN,	103 32

RAGE

THE WATERS THEREOF RAGE AND SWELL, *	327 07
SO FURIOUSLY RAGE TOGETHER	345 25
THE WATERS THEREOF RAGE AND SWELL, *	397 30
SEA ARE MIGHTY, AND RAGE HORRIBLY	457 13

RAGING

AND RULEST THE RAGING OF THE SEA	042 04
AND RULEST THE RAGING OF THE SEA	046 09
WHO STILLETH THE RAGING OF THE SEA, *	416 27
THOU RULEST THE RAGING OF THE SEA	450 24

RAILED

THAT PASSED BY RAILED ON HIM, WAGGING THEIR HEADS,	146 18
WHICH WERE HANGED RAILED ON HIM, SAYING, IF THOU BE	154 35

RAILING

FOR EVIL, OR RAILING FOR RAILING	195 22
RENDERING EVIL FOR EVIL, OR RAILING FOR RAILING	195 22

RAILS

GO WITHIN THE RAILS, WITH SUCH OF THE CLERGY AS CAN	R 564 06
GO WITHIN THE RAILS OF THE ALTAR	R 570 06
RIGHT AND LEFT OF THE ALTAR, WITHOUT THE RAILS	R 570 08
WITHIN THE RAILS OF THE ALTAR, AND PRESENT HIM THE	R 571 22

RAIMENT

A MAN CLOTHED IN SOFT RAIMENT	094 28
AND PUT HIS OWN RAIMENT ON HIM, AND LED HIM AWAY TO	136 24
AND I WILL STAIN ALL MY RAIMENT	138 20
THEY PARTED HIS RAIMENT, AND CAST LOTS	154 26
THEY PARTED MY RAIMENT AMONG THEM, AND FOR MY VESTURE	160 15
TWENTY ELDERS SITTING, CLOTHED IN WHITE RAIMENT	187 10
HIM OF HIS RAIMENT, AND WOUNDED HIM, AND DEPARTED,	208 23
AND THE BODY THAN THE RAIMENT	211 15
AND WHY ARE YE ANXIOUS CONCERNING RAIMENT	211 21
IN RAIMENT WHITE AND GLISTERING	248 02
AND HIS RAIMENT WAS WHITE AND GLISTERING	248 26
IN GIVING HIM FOOD AND RAIMENT	263 27
LIFE MORE THAN FOOD, AND THE BODY THAN RAIMENT	266 14
AND WHY ARE YE ANXIOUS FOR RAIMENT	266 19
UNTO THE KING IN RAIMENT OF NEEDLEWORK	397 14
LIKE AS WITH A RAIMENT, *	481 05
AND RAIMENT, AND ALL THE OTHER COMFORTS AND	591 10

RAIN

SUCH MODERATE RAIN AND SHOWERS, THAT WE MAY RECEIVE	040 19
GIFT IT IS THAT THE RAIN DOTH FALL, AND THE EARTH	040 30
ALSO PRAISE GOD FOR RAIN AND SUNSHINE	048 11
AND THE LATTER RAIN DESCEND UPON THE EARTH, THAT IT	051 16
THEE TO SEND US RAIN TO OUR GREAT COMFORT, AND TO THE	051 19
US WITH IMMODERATE RAIN AND WATERS, AND IN THY MERCY	051 23
AND SENDETH RAIN ON THE JUST AND ON THE UNJUST	264 10
AND PREPARETH RAIN FOR THE EARTH	264 28
UNGODLY HE SHALL RAIN SNARES, FIRE AND BRIMSTONE,	354 33
THOU SENDEST RAIN INTO THE LITTLE VALLEYS THEREOF	417 04
WITH THE DROPS OF RAIN, AND BLESSEST THE INCREASE OF	417 06
SENTEST A GRACIOUS RAIN UPON THINE INHERITANCE,	419 29
COME DOWN LIKE THE RAIN UPON THE MOWN GRASS, *	427 08
32 HE GAVE THEM HAILSTONES FOR RAIN	472 02
LIGHTNINGS WITH THE RAIN, BRINGING THE WINDS OUT OF	510 16
AND PREPARETH RAIN FOR THE EARTH	523 11

RAINBOW

AND THERE WAS A RAINBOW ROUND ABOUT THE THRONE,	187 07

RAINED

25 HE RAINED DOWN MANNA ALSO UPON THEM FOR TO EAT,	436 18
28 HE RAINED FLESH UPON THEM AS THICK AS DUST,	436 25

RAINS

THOSE IMMODERATE RAINS, WHEREWITH THOU HAST AFFLICTED	040 25

RAISE

THE WEAK AND RAISE UP THOSE WHO FALL	044 03
AND TO RAISE UP THOSE WHO FALL	056 23
O LORD, RAISE UP, WE PRAY THEE, THY POWER, AND COME	095 04
THAT I WILL RAISE UNTO DAVID A RIGHTEOUS	225 09
AND I WILL RAISE UP FOR THEM A PLANT OF RENOWN,	262 17
BUT SHOULD RAISE IT UP AGAIN AT THE LAST DAY	269 18
AND I WILL RAISE HIM UP AT THE LAST DAY	269 21
O FATHER, TO RAISE US FROM THE DEATH OF SIN	335 05
RAISE THOU ME UP AGAIN, AND I SHALL REWARD THEM	392 19
RAISE UP THEREIN, THROUGH THY SPIRIT, GOOD AND	562 10
RAISE HIM UP IF HE FALL	597 31

RAISED

AND HATH RAISED UP A MIGHTY SALVATION FOR US,	014 10
HAVE BEEN LATELY RAISED UP AMONGST US	052 21
THE DEAD ARE RAISED UP, AND THE POOR HAVE THE GOSPEL	094 30
THEN JOSEPH BEING RAISED FROM SLEEP DID AS THE ANGEL	105 12
CHRIST BEING RAISED FROM THE DEAD DIETH NO MORE	163 04
HIM GOD RAISED UP THE THIRD DAY, AND SHEWED HIM	166 25
BUT GOD RAISED HIM FROM THE DEAD	169 02
IN THAT HE HATH RAISED UP JESUS AGAIN	169 08
THAT HE RAISED HIM UP FROM THE DEAD, NOW NO MORE TO	169 10
BUT HE, WHOM GOD RAISED AGAIN, SAW NO CORRUPTION	169 17
HIM GOD RAISED UP THE THIRD DAY, AND SHEWED HIM	184 12
AS CHRIST WAS RAISED UP FROM THE DEAD BY THE GLORY OF	197 13
THAT CHRIST BEING RAISED FROM THE DEAD DIETH NO MORE	197 21
THAT GOD HATH RAISED HIM FROM THE DEAD, THOU SHALT BE	226 27
AND HATH RAISED UP AN HORN OF SALVATION FOR	243 34
ON THE SIDE, AND RAISED HIM UP, SAYING, ARISE UP	245 14
HOW ARE THE DEAD RAISED UP	329 05
IT IS RAISED IN INCORRUPTION	329 20
IT IS RAISED IN GLORY	329 20
IT IS RAISED IN POWER	329 21
IT IS RAISED A SPIRITUAL BODY	329 22
THE DEAD SHALL BE RAISED INCORRUPTIBLE, AND WE SHALL	330 04
HE THAT RAISED UP JESUS FROM THE DEAD WILL ALSO	333 05

RAMA

SAYING, IN RAMA WAS THERE A VOICE HEARD,	103 30

RAMPING

AS IT WERE A RAMPING AND A ROARING LION	366 30

RAMS

FAT BURNT-SACRIFICES, WITH THE INCENSE OF RAMS	418 11
SKIPPED LIKE RAMS, *	484 31
THAT YE SKIPPED LIKE RAMS	485 04

RAN

THEIR EARS, AND RAN UPON HIM WITH ONE ACCORD,	100 10
ONE OF THEM RAN, AND TOOK A SPUNGE, AND FILLED IT	137 21
AND ONE RAN AND FILLED A SPUNGE FULL OF VINEGAR, AND	146 31
SO THEY RAN BOTH TOGETHER	164 18
HAD COMPASSION, AND RAN, AND FELL ON HIS NECK,	202 18
SO THAT RIVERS RAN IN THE DRY PLACES	472 20
UPON THE HEAD, THAT RAN DOWN UNTO THE BEARD, *	509 15

RANSOM

GIVE HIS LIFE A RANSOM FOR MANY	247 27
NOR GIVE A RANSOM UNTO GOD FOR HIM,	400 19

RASH

THAT VAIN AND RASH SWEARING IS FORBIDDEN CHRISTIAN	611 06

RATHER

OF A SINNER, BUT RATHER THAT HE MAY TURN FROM HIS	007 07
OF A SINNER, BUT RATHER THAT HE MAY TURN FROM HIS	024 09
OF A SINNER, BUT RATHER THAT HE SHOULD TURN FROM HIS	062 15
BUT RATHER GIVE PLACE UNTO WRATH	113 04
BUT RATHER GIVING OF THANKS	129 05
OF DARKNESS, BUT RATHER REPROVE THEM	129 17
BUT HE SAID, YEA RATHER, BLESSED ARE THEY THAT HEAR	130 20
BUT THAT RATHER A TUMULT WAS MADE, HE TOOK	136 09
THAT HE SHOULD RATHER RELEASE BARABBAS UNTO THEM	145 21
OF A SINNER, BUT RATHER THAT HE SHOULD BE CONVERTED	157 06
LOVED DARKNESS RATHER THAN LIGHT, BECAUSE THEIR DEEDS	185 07
HOUSE JUSTIFIED RATHER THAN THE OTHER	205 32
OF THE SPIRIT BE RATHER GLORIOUS	206 22
BUT RATHER LET HIM LABOUR, WORKING WITH HIS HANDS THE	216 20
HALT OR MAIMED, RATHER THAN HAVING TWO HANDS OR TWO	253 05
WITH ONE EYE, RATHER THAN HAVING TWO EYES TO BE CAST	253 08
THAT DIED, YEA RATHER, THAT IS RISEN AGAIN, WHO IS	331 04
11 I HAD RATHER BE A DOOR-KEEPER IN THE HOUSE OF MY	445 32
LET THE RIGHTEOUS RATHER SMITE ME FRIENDLY, AND	517 19
YEA RATHER, FOR THAT THEY ARE NOT DONE AS GOD HATH	605 20
OF SCRIPTURE, BUT RATHER REPUGNANT TO THE WORD OF	607 17
BUT RATHER THEY BE CERTAIN SURE	607 32
BUT RATHER IT IS A SACRAMENT OF OUR REDEMPTION BY	608 35
BUT RATHER, TO THEIR CONDEMNATION, DO EAT AND DRINK	609 07

RATIFYING

RATIFYING AND CONFIRMING THE SAME	296 25

RAVENING

THEY ARE RAVENING WOLVES	200 16

RAVENS

FEEDETH THE YOUNG RAVENS THAT CALL UPON HIM	264 31
FEEDETH THE YOUNG RAVENS THAT CALL UPON HIM	523 14

RAVISH

THAT HE MAY RAVISH THE POOR	353 24
10 HE DOTH RAVISH THE POOR, *	353 25

RAZOR

AND WITH LIES THOU CUTTEST LIKE A SHARP RAZOR	404 23

REACH

HE TO THOMAS, REACH HITHER THY FINGER, AND BEHOLD MY	229 03
AND REACH HITHER THY HAND, AND THRUST IT INTO MY	229 04

REACHETH

LOVING-KINDNESS REACHETH UNTO THE WORLD'S END	038 15
O LORD, REACHETH UNTO THE HEAVENS, *	384 04
OF THY MERCY REACHETH UNTO THE HEAVENS, *	410 02
AND THY TRUTH REACHETH UNTO THE CLOUDS	479 12
FATHERLY CARE REACHETH TO THE UTTERMOST PARTS OF THE	596 30

READ

THEN SHALL BE READ THE FIRST LESSON, ACCORDING TO	R 009 31
THEN SHALL BE READ, IN LIKE MANNER, THE SECOND	R 014 02
EXCEPT WHEN THE COMMUNION SERVICE IS READ	R 017 03
THEN SHALL BE READ THE FIRST LESSON, ACCORDING TO	R 026 05
THE LESSON READ BEING FOLLOWED BY ONE OF THE	R 026 08
ENSUING MAY BE READ IMMEDIATELY AFTER THE PRAYER, WE	R 060 03
SAME OFFICE MAY BE READ AT OTHER TIMES, AT THE	R 060 06
APPOINTED SHALL READ THE EPISTLE, FIRST SAYING,	R 070 18
APPOINTED SHALL READ THE GOSPEL, FIRST SAYING, THE	R 070 22

READ   CONTINUED

HE SHALL READ THIS EXHORTATION FOLLOWING	R 086	26
WISE HEAR THEM, READ, MARK, LEARN, AND INWARDLY	092	09
WHEN YE READ, YE MAY UNDERSTAND MY KNOWLEDGE	108	10
THIS TITLE THEN READ MANY OF THE JEWS	160	03
PROPHETS WHICH ARE READ EVERY SABBATH DAY, THEY HAVE	168	28
HAVE YE NEVER READ, OUT OF THE MOUTH OF BABES AND	260	14
ON THE SABBATH DAY, AND STOOD UP FOR TO READ	261	13
HAVE YE NOT READ, THAT WHICH MADE THEM AT	268	05
WILL YOU DILIGENTLY READ THE SAME UNTO THE PEOPLE	533	06
AND TO READ HOLY SCRIPTURES AND HOMILIES IN THE	533	14
THOU AUTHORITY TO READ THE GOSPEL IN THE CHURCH CF	534	11
THE BISHOP, SHALL READ THE GOSPEL	534	14
ONE OF THEM HAVING READ THE GOSPEL, (WHICH SHALL BE	R 547	24
BISHOP SHALL READ THE EPISTLE	R 549	16
BISHOP SHALL READ THE GOSPEL	R 551	12
AND SHALL CAUSE THEM TO BE READ	R 552	25
WORD WHICH SHALL BE READ AND PREACHED IN THIS PLACE,	566	03
IS TO BE READ BY SOME PERSON APPOINTED BY HIM,	R 566	26
THEN SHALL BE READ THE LETTER OF INSTITUTION	R 570	24
WHATSOEVER IS NOT READ THEREIN, NOR MAY BE PROVED	603	30
THE CHURCH DOTH READ FOR EXAMPLE OF LIFE AND	604	02
WE JUDGE THEM TO BE READ IN CHURCHES BY THE	610	09

READEST

HOW READEST THOU	208	14

READILY

THAT HE READILY OBEYED THE CALLING OF THY SON	226	19

READINESS

WITH THE MORE READINESS AND DECENCY BREAK THE BREAD	R 080	03
BE ALWAYS IN READINESS TO DIE, WHENSOEVER IT SHALL	R 321	04
HUMILITY AND READINESS OF HEART, TO CONSECRATE THIS	565	04
TO GIVE A READINESS OF THOUGHT AND EXPRESSION	573	26

READING

PRAYER BY READING ONE OR MORE OF THE FOLLOWING	R 003	03
PRAYER BY READING ONE OR MORE OF THE FOLLOWING	R 021	03
THE PEOPLE READING OR REPEATING THE ANSWERS AS	R 283	14
THE PEOPLE READING OR REPEATING THE ANSWERS	R 287	32
DILIGENTLY READING HOLY SCRIPTURE AND ANCIENT	529	11
OUGHT TO BE IN READING AND LEARNING THE SCRIPTURES,	541	03
BY DAILY READING AND WEIGHING THE SCRIPTURES,	541	18
AND IN READING THE HOLY SCRIPTURES, AND IN	542	26
GIVE HEED UNTO READING, EXHORTATION, AND DOCTRINE	558	21
THY SERVICE, FOR READING THY HOLY WORD, FOR	565	07
AFTER THE READING OF A BRIEF PORTION OF HOLY	R 592	09
AFTER THE READING OF A BRIEF PORTION OF HOLY	R 593	03
ORDER FOR THE READING OF SAID HOMILIES IN CHURCHES,	R 610	27

READS

HERE LET HIM WHO READS MAKE A SHORT PAUSE, THAT EVERY	R 589	34

READY

WHO ART EVER READY TO HEAR THE PRAYERS OF THOSE WHO	041	19
MAKE READY, WE BESEECH THEE, THE HEARTS AND MINDS OF	043	20
MOST GRACIOUS AND READY HELP	049	15
BEING READY TO MAKE RESTITUTION AND SATISFACTION,	087	24
AND BEING LIKEWISE READY TO FORGIVE OTHERS WHO HAVE	087	27
YE EXCUSE YOURSELVES, AND SAY YE ARE NOT READY	088	14
PREPARE AND MAKE READY THY WAY, BY TURNING THE HEARTS	093	27
THERE MAKE READY FOR US	140	32
AND THEY MADE READY THE PASSOVER	140	34
SPIRIT TRULY IS READY, BUT THE FLESH IS WEAK	142	06
THERE MAKE READY	148	31
AND THEY MADE READY THE PASSOVER	148	33
LORD, I AM READY TO GO WITH THEE, BOTH INTO	149	35
FOR ALL THINGS ARE NOW READY	192	05
ART ALWAYS MORE READY TO HEAR THAN WE TO PRAY,	206	05
THAT WE, BEING READY BOTH IN BODY AND SOUL, MAY	217	19
MY FATLINGS ARE KILLED, AND ALL THINGS ARE READY	218	09
THE WEDDING IS READY, BUT THEY WHICH WERE BIDDEN WERE	218	16
BE READY, WE BESEECH THEE, TO HEAR THE DEVOUT PRAYERS	222	10
MAY BE EVERMORE READY TO FOLLOW THY HOLY	246	20
FOR I AM NOW READY TO BE OFFERED, AND THE TIME CF MY	253	25
MUST BE READY AT THE FONT, EITHER	R 273	14
OR BE READY AND DESIROUS TO BE CONFIRMED	R 299	09
OR SHALL BE READY IN SOME PROPER HOUSE, WITH THEIR	R 300	05
THE BODY IS MADE READY TO BE LAID INTO THE EARTH,	R 332	16
HE HATH BENT HIS BOW, AND MADE IT READY	350	18
AND MAKE READY THEIR ARROWS WITHIN THE QUIVER, *	354	21
SHALT THOU MAKE READY AGAINST THE FACE OF THEM	365	30
IS THE PEN OF A READY WRITER	396	17
MY HEART IS READY, MY HEART IS READY	479	04
O GOD, MY HEART IS READY, MY HEART IS READY	479	04
THEY MAKE THEM READY TO BATTLE	502	20
TO HAVE A READY WILL TO OBSERVE ALL SPIRITUAL	535	04
WILL YOU BE READY, WITH ALL FAITHFUL DILIGENCE,	542	19
ARE YOU READY, WITH ALL FAITHFUL DILIGENCE,	555	02
I AM READY, THE LORD BEING MY HELPER	555	07
HE MAY EVERMORE BE READY TO SPREAD ABROAD THY GOSPEL,	557	29
AND READY TO DO GOOD TO ALL MEN, ACCORDING TO OUR	588	31
WHO ART EVER READY TO RECEIVE HUMBLE AND PENITENT	590	05

REAP

SOWETH LITTLE SHALL REAP LITTLE	072	16
PLENTEOUSLY SHALL REAP PLENTEOUSLY	072	17

REAP   CONTINUED

NEITHER DO THEY REAP, NOR GATHER INTO BARNS	211	17
NEITHER DO THEY REAP, NOR GATHER INTO BARNS	266	15
SHALL REAP IN JOY	505	17

REAPERS

WILL SAY TO THE REAPERS, GATHER YE TOGETHER FIRST THE	116	30

REASON

THAT BY REASON OF THE FRAILTY OF OUR NATURE	114	05
BUT BY REASON OF HIM WHO HATH SUBJECTED	194	16
WHEN BY REASON OF THEIR TENDER AGE THEY	292	31
IF HE SHALL HAVE REASON TO DOUBT OF THE LAWFULNESS CF	R 301	02
A MAN, EITHER BY REASON OF EXTREMITY OF SICKNESS,	R 323	23
IN MY BONES, BY REASON OF MY SIN	387	26
IT IS NOT REASON THAT WE SHOULD LEAVE THE WORD	532	09
OR HINDRANCE BY REASON OF YOUR NEGLIGENCE, YE KNOW	540	11
TO THEIR OWN REASON AND SENSE OF THE NATURAL DECENCY	564	14
UNTIL SOME URGENT REASON OR REASONS OCCASION A WISH	569	31
WHEN BY REASON OF THEIR TENDER AGE THEY	581	31
OUR BEING, OUR REASON, AND ALL OTHER ENDOWMENTS AND	591	08
ALL WHO BY REASON OF WEAKNESS ARE OVERTASKED,	600	07

REASONABLE

IT IS BUT REASONABLE THAT UPON WEIGHTY AND IMPORTANT	V	16
TO BE A REASONABLE, HOLY, AND LIVING SACRIFICE UNTO	081	22
WHICH IS YOUR REASONABLE SERVICE	110	05
IF THERE BE REASONABLE DOUBT WHETHER ANY PERSON WAS	R 282	08
COMFORT OF A REASONABLE, RELIGIOUS, AND HOLY HOPE	317	05
EXCEPT FOR REASONABLE CAUSES IT SHALL OTHERWISE SEEM	R 535	20

REASONED

TOGETHER AND REASONED, JESUS HIMSELF DREW NEAR, AND	167	07

REASONS

TO BE HOPED, THE REASONS OF THEM ALSO, UPON A	VI	29
URGENT REASON OR REASONS OCCASION A WISH IN YOU,	569	31

REBELLED

THOUGH WE HAVE REBELLED AGAINST HIM	022	07
BUT THEY REBELLED, AND VEXED HIS HOLY SPIRIT	139	05
FOR THEY HAVE REBELLED AGAINST THEE	348	24
BUT THEY REBELLED AGAINST HIM WITH THEIR OWN	475	22
11 BECAUSE THEY REBELLED AGAINST THE WORDS OF THE	476	26

REBELLION

PRIVY CONSPIRACY, AND REBELLION	055	02

REBELLIOUS

AND I WAS NOT REBELLIOUS, NEITHER TURNED AWAY BACK	144	13

REBUKE

AND EXHORT, AND REBUKE WITH ALL AUTHORITY	098	26
THE TRUTH, BOLDLY REBUKE VICE, AND PATIENTLY SUFFER	242	12
AND MAKE ME NOT A REBUKE UNTO THE FOOLISH	324	31
O LORD, REBUKE ME NOT IN THINE INDIGNATION, *	348	33
THE CHILDREN OF MEN ARE PUT TO REBUKE	355	26
BE CLOTHED WITH REBUKE AND DISHONOUR, THAT BOAST	383	17
PUT ME NOT TO REBUKE, O LORD, IN THINE ANGER	387	21
AND MAKE ME NOT A REBUKE UNTO THE FOOLISH	389	26
AND PUT TO REBUKE, THAT WISH ME EVIL	391	18
30 REBUKE THOU THE DRAGON AND THE BULL, WITH THE	421	15
6 AT THY REBUKE, O GOD OF JACOB, *	432	33
PERISH AT THE REBUKE OF THY COUNTENANCE	442	03
THE REBUKE THAT THY SERVANTS HAVE, *	453	07
7 AT THY REBUKE THEY FLEE	468	06
22 O TURN FROM ME SHAME AND REBUKE	491	10
39 TAKE AWAY THE REBUKE THAT I AM AFRAID OF	492	17
AND TO REBUKE THE PEOPLES	525	15
AND REBUKE, WITH ALL PATIENCE AND DOCTRINE	559	09

REBUKED

WENT BEFORE REBUKED HIM, THAT HE SHOULD HOLD HIS	123	31
OTHER ANSWERING REBUKED HIM, SAYING, DOST NOT THOU	155	02
HIS DISCIPLES REBUKED THOSE THAT BROUGHT THEM	274	26
WHEN THOU ART REBUKED OF HIM	321	29
5 THOU HAST REBUKED THE HEATHEN, AND DESTROYED THE	351	30
MAKEST US TO BE REBUKED OF OUR NEIGHBOURS, *	395	19
OF THEM THAT REBUKED THEE ARE FALLEN UPON ME	422	21
HOW THE ENEMY HATH REBUKED	431	12
9 HE REBUKED THE RED SEA ALSO, AND IT WAS DRIED UP	473	18
21 THOU HAST REBUKED THE PROUD	491	08
OUGHT TO BE REBUKED OPENLY, (THAT OTHERS MAY FEAR TO	609	38

REBUKES

WHEN THOU WITH REBUKES DOST CHASTEN MAN FOR SIN,	325	02
WHEN THOU WITH REBUKES DOST CHASTEN MAN FOR SIN,	389	31
AND THE REBUKES OF THEM THAT REBUKED THEE ARE FALLEN	422	21
IN MY BOSOM THE REBUKES OF MANY PEOPLE	453	08

RECALLED

MAY BE BANISHED AND HIS STRENGTH RECALLED	315	10

RECEIPT

MATTHEW FROM THE RECEIPT OF CUSTOM TO BE AN APOSTLE   250 21
SITTING AT THE RECEIPT OF CUSTOM   251 13

RECEIVE

YE SHALL RECEIVE POWER, AFTER THAT THE HOLY GHOST IS   005 11
OF THE WORLD, RECEIVE OUR PRAYER   025 30
THAT WE MAY RECEIVE THE FRUITS OF THE EARTH TO OUR   040 19
THY WORD, AND TO RECEIVE IT WITH PURE AFFECTION, AND   056 15
RECEIVE   062 16
RECEIVE OUR HUMBLE PETITIONS   063 10
IT IS MORE BLESSED TO GIVE THAN TO RECEIVE   072 03
SHALL RECEIVE THE ALMS FOR THE POOR, AND   R 073 28
AND TO RECEIVE THESE OUR PRAYERS, WHICH WE OFFER UNTO   074 10
MAY HEAR, AND RECEIVE THY HOLY WORD   074 27
WHO COME TO RECEIVE THE HOLY COMMUNION, YE WHO DO   R 075 07
ARE MINDED TO RECEIVE THE HOLY COMMUNION, HUMBLY   R 075 16
WITH THEM, MAY RECEIVE THE CROWN OF GLORY THAT FADETH   079 26
MAY WORTHILY RECEIVE THE MOST PRECIOUS BODY AND BLOOD   081 25
THOSE WHO SHALL RECEIVE THE COMMUNION, THIS PRAYER   R 082 12
THE PRIEST FIRST RECEIVE THE HOLY COMMUNION IN BOTH   R 082 25
OF THE WORLD, RECEIVE OUR PRAYER   084 10
LIVELY FAITH WE RECEIVE THAT HOLY SACRAMENT   085 31
IF WE RECEIVE THE SAME UNWORTHILY   085 32
TO THEM WHO RECEIVE IT WORTHILY, AND SO DANGEROUS TO   087 06
WILL PRESUME TO RECEIVE IT UNWORTHILY   087 07
THAT HE MAY RECEIVE SUCH GODLY COUNSEL AND ADVICE, AS   088 07
IS YOUR DUTY TO RECEIVE THE COMMUNION IN REMEMBRANCE   089 11
WHEREFORE RECEIVE YE ONE ANOTHER, AS CHRIST ALSO   092 21
THE BLIND RECEIVE THEIR SIGHT, AND THE LAME WALK,   094 21
AS WE JOYFULLY RECEIVE HIM FOR OUR REDEEMER, SO WE   098 13
LORD JESUS, RECEIVE MY SPIRIT   100 14
THAT WE MIGHT RECEIVE THE ADOPTION OF SONS   104 21
MERCIFULLY TO RECEIVE THE PRAYERS OF THY PEOPLE WHO   109 29
RESIST SHALL RECEIVE TO THEMSELVES CONDEMNATION   114 15
AND WHATSOEVER IS RIGHT, THAT SHALL YE RECEIVE   119 28
WHEN THEY HEAR, RECEIVE THE WORD WITH JOY   122 03
THAT I MAY RECEIVE MY SIGHT   124 02
SAID UNTO HIM, RECEIVE THY SIGHT   124 03
YOU ALSO THAT YE RECEIVE NOT THE GRACE OF GOD IN   126 04
ARE CALLED MIGHT RECEIVE THE PROMISE OF ETERNAL   133 06
MAY THANKFULLY RECEIVE THE SAME IN REMEMBRANCE OF   152 10
FOR WE RECEIVE THE DUE REWARD OF OUR DEEDS   155 04
RECEIVE OUR SUPPLICATIONS AND PRAYERS, WHICH WE OFFER   156 29
IN HIM SHALL RECEIVE REMISSION OF SINS   166 32
IF WE RECEIVE THE WITNESS OF MEN, THE WITNESS OF GOD   171 04
SAITH UNTO THEM, RECEIVE YE THE HOLY GHOST   171 23
MOST THANKFULLY RECEIVE THAT HIS INESTIMABLE BENEFIT,   171 31
AND RECEIVE WITH MEEKNESS THE ENGRAFTED   175 03
FOR HE SHALL RECEIVE OF MINE, AND SHALL SHEW IT UNTO   175 22
AND YE SHALL RECEIVE, THAT YOUR JOY MAY BE FULL   176 23
BUT YE SHALL RECEIVE POWER, AFTER THAT THE HOLY GHOST   178 09
THE WORLD CANNOT RECEIVE, BECAUSE IT SEETH HIM NOT,   181 12
IN HIM SHALL RECEIVE REMISSION OF SINS   184 19
THAT THEY MIGHT RECEIVE THE HOLY GHOST   185 24
O LORD, TO RECEIVE GLORY AND HONOUR AND POWER   187 30
AND YE RECEIVE NOT OUR WITNESS   188 22
WE ASK, WE RECEIVE OF HIM, BECAUSE WE KEEP HIS   191 27
OF GOD, YE MIGHT RECEIVE THE PROMISE   228 17
THAT HE MIGHT RECEIVE HIS SIGHT   230 21
THOU MIGHTEST RECEIVE THY SIGHT, AND BE FILLED WITH   230 33
SHALL RECEIVE AN HUNDREDFOLD, AND SHALL INHERIT   231 20
THAT HE SHALL RECEIVE ANY THING OF THE LORD   239 16
HE SHALL RECEIVE THE CROWN OF LIFE, WHICH THE   239 25
COME AGAIN, AND RECEIVE YOU UNTO MYSELF   240 02
THAT THEY MAY RECEIVE THE CROWN OF EVERLASTING GLORY   244 27
TO PREACH AND RECEIVE THE SAME   249 18
AND WHOSO SHALL RECEIVE ONE SUCH LITTLE CHILD IN MY   252 29
AND RECEIVE WITH MEEKNESS THE ENGRAFTED   265 27
MAY RECEIVE REMISSION OF SIN, BY SPIRITUAL   274 13
RECEIVE HIM, O LORD, AS THOU HAST PROMISED BY THY   274 14
SHALL NOT RECEIVE THE KINGDOM OF GOD AS A LITTLE   274 31
VOUCHSAFE TO RECEIVE HIM, TO RELEASE HIM FROM SIN, TO   276 21
DESIRING TO RECEIVE HOLY BAPTISM   277 21
VOUCHSAFE TO RECEIVE YOU, TO RELEASE YOU FROM SIN, TO   277 22
MAY RECEIVE THE FULNESS OF THY GRACE,   279 18
WE RECEIVE THIS CHILD (PERSON) INTO THE CONGREGATION   280 03
HOLY SPIRIT, TO RECEIVE HIM FOR THINE OWN CHILD, AND   280 30
WE RECEIVE THIS CHILD (OR PERSON), ETC   R 282 05
AS MY MASTER, I RECEIVE THE STRENGTHENING GIFTS OF   291 26
MEANS WHEREBY WE RECEIVE THIS GRACE, AND A PLEDGE TO   292 13
WHICH WE RECEIVE THEREBY   293 06
THE BISHOP, MAY RECEIVE SUCH A MEASURE OF THY HOLY   294 26
THAT WHEN WE RECEIVE THE BLESSED SACRAMENT OF THE   294 29
WE MAY RECEIVE REMISSION OF OUR SINS, AND BE FILLED   294 32
TO RECEIVE INSTRUCTION BY THE MINISTER   R 295 12
THESE PERSONS TO RECEIVE THE LAYING ON OF HANDS   296 09
THAT THEY MIGHT RECEIVE THE HOLY GHOST   296 16
I WILL RECEIVE THE CUP OF SALVATION, AND CALL UPON   305 29
THAT SHE RECEIVE THE HOLY COMMUNION   R 307 10
THOU MAYEST RECEIVE HEALTH AND SALVATION, BUT ONLY   314 21
RECEIVE HIM INTO THE ARMS OF THY MERCY, INTO THE   319 31
IS DESIROUS TO RECEIVE THE COMMUNION IN HIS HOUSE   R 321 12
AND CHASTISE EVERY ONE WHOM THOU DOST RECEIVE   321 20
SHALL FIRST RECEIVE THE COMMUNION HIMSELF, AND AFTER   R 322 04
DO NOT RECEIVE THE SACRAMENT OF CHRIST'S BODY AND   R 323 25
HE DO NOT RECEIVE THE SACRAMENT WITH HIS MOUTH   R 323 31
COME AGAIN, AND RECEIVE YOU UNTO MYSELF   331 09
AND RECEIVE THAT BLESSING, WHICH THY WELL-BELOVED SON   335 09
OF MY FATHER, RECEIVE THE KINGDOM PREPARED FOR YOU   335 12
AND WHOSO SHALL RECEIVE ONE SUCH LITTLE CHILD IN MY   339 28
THE LORD WILL RECEIVE MY PRAYER   349 17
5 HE SHALL RECEIVE THE BLESSING FROM THE LORD,   369 05
FOR HE SHALL RECEIVE ME   401 06

RECEIVE   CONTINUED

AND AFTER THAT RECEIVE ME WITH GLORY   429 25
12 I WILL RECEIVE THE CUP OF SALVATION, *   487 11
SHALL TARRY, AND RECEIVE THE HOLY COMMUNION THE SAME   R 534 27
THOSE WHO ARE TO RECEIVE THE ORDER OF PRIESTHOOD THAT   R 536 08
GOD WILLING, TO RECEIVE THIS DAY UNTO THE HOLY OFFICE   536 23
BISHOP SAYING, RECEIVE THE HOLY GHOST FOR THE OFFICE   546 09
ALL THEY WHO RECEIVE ORDERS SHALL TAKE TOGETHER, AND   R 546 29
TO HEAR AND RECEIVE WHAT THEY SHALL DELIVER OUT OF   547 09
THAT ALL MAY RECEIVE THE CROWN OF EVERLASTING GLORY   549 14
IT IS MORE BLESSED TO GIVE THAN TO RECEIVE   551 11
SAITH UNTO THEM, RECEIVE YE THE HOLY GHOST   552 04
BISHOP SAYING, RECEIVE THE HOLY GHOST FOR THE OFFICE   558 12
YOU MAY RECEIVE THE NEVER-FADING CROWN OF   558 31
DAY HE MAY RECEIVE THE CROWN OF RIGHTEOUSNESS,   559 13
5 HE SHALL RECEIVE THE BLESSING FROM THE LORD,   563 20
THE BISHOP, MAY RECEIVE SUCH A MEASURE OF THY HOLY   565 25
WHOSOEVER SHALL RECEIVE IN THIS PLACE THE BLESSED   565 28
AT ANY TIME RECEIVE FROM US   569 22
OR CHURCH) I DO RECEIVE AND ACKNOWLEDGE YOU, THE REV   570 28
RECEIVE THESE KEYS OF THE HOUSE OF GOD AT YOUR HANDS,   570 32
THE INSTITUTOR RECEIVE THE INCUMBENT WITHIN THE RAILS   R 571 22
RECEIVE THESE BOOKS   571 25
MEANS WHEREBY WE RECEIVE THE SAME, AND A PLEDGE TO   581 14
WHICH WE RECEIVE THEREBY   582 06
EVER READY TO RECEIVE HUMBLE AND PENITENT SINNERS   590 05
THY WISDOM, AND RECEIVE THE BLESSED ENCOURAGEMENT OF   596 13
THOU WILT RECEIVE HIM MORE AND MORE INTO THY   598 08
WE DO RECEIVE, AND ACCOUNT THEM CANONICAL   604 13
MAKE MEN MEET TO RECEIVE GRACE, OR (AS THE   605 19
WE MUST RECEIVE GOD'S PROMISES IN SUCH WISE, AS THEY   606 27
ONLY AS WORTHILY RECEIVE THE SAME, THEY HAVE A   608 04
BUT THEY THAT RECEIVE THEM UNWORTHILY, PURCHASE TO   608 05
AND RIGHTLY, DO RECEIVE THE SACRAMENTS MINISTERED   608 16
THEY THAT RECEIVE BAPTISM RIGHTLY ARE GRAFTED INTO   608 27
AND WITH FAITH, RECEIVE THE SAME, THE BREAD WHICH WE   608 37

RECEIVED

THAT WE HAVE RECEIVED AT HIS HANDS, TO SET FORTH HIS   006 06
THAT WE HAVE RECEIVED AT HIS HANDS, TO SET FORTH HIS   023 15
TRULY RECEIVED, AND TRULY FOLLOWED, IN ALL   037 03
WHOLE WILL BE RECEIVED AND EXAMINED BY EVERY TRUE   VI 36
THE OFFERINGS OF THE PEOPLE ARE TO BE RECEIVED   R 073 26
ARE BEING RECEIVED AND PRESENTED, THERE MAY BE SUNG A   R 073 34
ALL MEN TO BE RECEIVED, THAT CHRIST JESUS CAME INTO   076 18
WHO HAVE DULY RECEIVED THESE HOLY MYSTERIES, WITH THE   083 18
TO BE BY THEM RECEIVED IN REMEMBRANCE OF HIS   086 32
AND BE RECEIVED AS WORTHY PARTAKERS OF THAT HOLY   087 14
AS CHRIST ALSO RECEIVED US TO THE GLORY OF GOD   092 22
BUT AS MANY AS RECEIVED HIM, TO THEM GAVE HE POWER TO   097 33
AND HIS OWN RECEIVED HIM NOT   097 33
THEY RECEIVED EVERY MAN A PENNY   119 32
SHOULD HAVE RECEIVED MORE   120 02
THEY LIKEWISE RECEIVED EVERY MAN A PENNY   120 02
WHEN THEY HAD RECEIVED IT, THEY MURMURED AGAINST THE   120 03
JEWS FIVE TIMES RECEIVED I FORTY STRIPES SAVE ONE   120 32
IMMEDIATELY HE RECEIVED HIS SIGHT, AND FOLLOWED HIM,   124 04
THAT AS YE HAVE RECEIVED OF US HOW YE OUGHT TO WALK   127 24
BUT HE RECEIVED IT NOT   146 10
I HAVE RECEIVED OF THE LORD THAT WHICH ALSO I   152 10
THEREFORE HAD RECEIVED THE VINEGAR, HE SAID, IT IS   160 28
AND A CLOUD RECEIVED HIM OUT OF THEIR SIGHT   178 13
EVERY MAN HATH RECEIVED THE GIFT, EVEN SO MINISTER   179 16
WHICH HAVE RECEIVED THE HOLY GHOST AS WELL AS WE   184 27
SAMARIA HAD RECEIVED THE WORD OF GOD, THEY SENT UNTO   185 22
AND THEY RECEIVED THE HOLY GHOST   185 27
FOR YE HAVE NOT RECEIVED THE SPIRIT OF BONDAGE AGAIN   200 07
BUT YE HAVE RECEIVED THE SPIRIT OF ADOPTION, WHEREBY   200 08
BECAUSE HE HATH RECEIVED HIM SAFE AND SOUND   202 31
ALSO YE HAVE RECEIVED, AND WHEREIN YE STAND   204 30
WHICH I ALSO RECEIVED, HOW THAT CHRIST DIED FOR OUR   205 04
AND HE RECEIVED SIGHT FORTHWITH, AND AROSE, AND WAS   230 35
AND WHEN HE HAD RECEIVED MEAT, HE WAS STRENGTHENED   230 36
FOR SHE HATH RECEIVED OF THE LORD'S HAND DOUBLE FOR   242 19
FOR HE RECEIVED FROM GOD THE FATHER HONOUR AND GLORY,   248 16
AS WE HAVE RECEIVED MERCY, WE FAINT NOT   250 28
HOLY GHOST, AND RECEIVED INTO CHRIST'S HOLY CHURCH,   274 05
INFANTS ARE RECEIVED INTO CHRIST'S CHURCH, BECOME THE   292 34
WHICH THE LORD HATH COMMANDED TO BE RECEIVED   293 12
TAKEN AND RECEIVED BY THE FAITHFUL IN THE LORD'S   293 15
SAMARIA HAD RECEIVED THE WORD OF GOD, THEY SENT UNTO   296 14
AND THEY RECEIVED THE HOLY GHOST   296 19
RING GIVEN AND RECEIVED IS A TOKEN AND   303 09
FOR YE HAVE NOT RECEIVED THE SPIRIT OF BONDAGE AGAIN   330 20
BUT YE HAVE RECEIVED THE SPIRIT OF ADOPTION, WHEREBY   330 21
AND RECEIVED GIFTS FROM MEN   420 20
AND RECEIVED COMFORT   493 15
OUGHT NOT TO BE RECEIVED INTO THIS HOLY MINISTRY,   536 09
CHURCH HATH RECEIVED THE SAME, ACCORDING TO THE   542 14
AS THEY HAVE RECEIVED THE COMMUNION   R 546 31
WHICH I HAVE RECEIVED OF THE LORD JESUS, TO TESTIFY   550 20
MAY AT LAST BE RECEIVED INTO EVERLASTING JOY   558 05
BISHOP IS TO BE RECEIVED AT THE ENTRANCE OF THE   R 563 05
HOUSE SHALL BE RECEIVED BY BAPTISM INTO THE   565 19
WHICH THEY HAVE RECEIVED AT THY HANDS, TO SET FORTH   566 15
BISHOP HAVING RECEIVED DUE NOTICE OF THE ELECTION OF   R 569 04
WHICH THE LORD HATH COMMANDED TO BE RECEIVED   582 10
TAKEN AND RECEIVED BY THE FAITHFUL IN THE LORD'S   582 13
AS MANY AS HAVE RECEIVED IT, LIVE AS BECOMES IT   590 24
INTERCESSION WE RECEIVED THEM ALL, THY SON OUR   591 23
ARE COMMONLY RECEIVED, WE DO RECEIVE, AND ACCOUNT   604 12
NECESSITY TO BE RECEIVED IN ANY COMMONWEALTH   604 21
TO BE RECEIVED AND BELIEVED   604 26
AFTER WE HAVE RECEIVED THE HOLY GHOST, WE MAY DEPART   605 41

RECEIVED   CONTINUED

OF CHRIST IS RECEIVED AND EATEN IN THE SUPPER,	608	46
BY PENANCE, AND RECEIVED INTO THE CHURCH BY A JUDGE	609	29
ARTICLE IS RECEIVED IN THIS CHURCH, SO FAR AS IT	R 610	24

RECEIVEDST

THY LIFETIME RECEIVEDST THY GOOD THINGS, AND LIKEWISE	190	17

RECEIVERS

THE RECEIVERS HUMBLY KNEELING, AND THE BISHOP SAYING,	R 546	08

RECEIVEST

AND RECEIVEST UNTO THEE	416	17

RECEIVETH

BUT ONE RECEIVETH THE PRIZE	119	06
FOR EVERY ONE THAT ASKETH RECEIVETH	183	12
THIS MAN RECEIVETH SINNERS, AND EATETH WITH THEM	193	16
IN MY NAME RECEIVETH ME	252	30
FOR EVERY ONE THAT ASKETH RECEIVETH	263	05
AND SCOURGETH EVERY SON WHOM HE RECEIVETH	321	31
IN MY NAME RECEIVETH ME	339	29
EVERY ONE THAT RECEIVETH THE ORDER OF PRIESTHOOD	R 546	07

RECEIVING

THAT WE, RECEIVING THEM ACCORDING TO THY SON OUR	081	11
THE UNWORTHY RECEIVING THEREOF	087	09
OTHERWISE THE RECEIVING OF THE HOLY COMMUNION DOTH	087	29
WE, CONSTANTLY RECEIVING THY BOUNTY, MAY EVERMORE	261	31
FOR THE RECEIVING OF THIS HOLY SACRAMENT	R 273	21
THE MINISTER, RECEIVING THE WOMAN AT HER FATHER'S OR	R 301	25
BY GIVING AND RECEIVING A RING, AND BY JOINING HANDS	304	07
TO THE OFTEN RECEIVING OF THE HOLY COMMUNION ARE	R 321	07
OF GOD, AND IN RECEIVING THE SACRAMENTS	608	13

RECIPIENTS

BECOME THE RECIPIENTS OF HIS GRACE, AND ARE TRAINED	292	34

RECITE

RECITE THE ARTICLES OF THE CHRISTIAN FAITH AS	284	09

RECKON

LIKEWISE RECKON YE ALSO YOURSELVES TO BE DEAD INDEED	163	08
I RECKON THAT THE SUFFERINGS OF THIS PRESENT TIME ARE	194	11
LIKEWISE RECKON YE ALSO YOURSELVES TO BE DEAD INDEED	197	24
HE HAD BEGUN TO RECKON, ONE WAS BROUGHT UNTO HIM,	221	15
FOR I RECKON THAT THE SUFFERINGS OF THIS PRESENT TIME	330	26

RECKONED

AND HE WAS RECKONED AMONG THE TRANSGRESSORS	150	10

RECOGNITION

PAROCHIAL RECOGNITION, AND PROMISE TO BE A FAITHFUL	570	34

RECOMPENCE

HATH GREAT RECOMPENCE OF REWARD	228	15

RECOMPENSE

RECOMPENSE TO NO MAN EVIL FOR EVIL	112	31
HANDS DID HE RECOMPENSE ME	361	07
5 RECOMPENSE THEM AFTER THE WORK OF THEIR HANDS	373	15
23 HE SHALL RECOMPENSE THEM THEIR WICKEDNESS,	458	32

RECOMPENSED

THAT HE HATH RECOMPENSED THE PARTIES TO WHOM HE HATH	R 085	06

RECONCILE

THEN YE SHALL RECONCILE YOURSELVES UNTO THEM	087	23
AND BURIED, TO RECONCILE HIS FATHER TO US, AND TO BE	603	15

RECONCILED

UNTIL HE KNOW THEM TO BE RECONCILED	R 085	11
FIRST BE RECONCILED TO THY BROTHER, AND THEN COME AND	198	10
HE BE OPENLY RECONCILED BY PENANCE, AND RECEIVED INTO	609	29

RECONCILIATION

THE HANDS OF MEN THE MINISTRY OF RECONCILIATION	260	20
OF RECONCILIATION WITH THEE	557	30

RECORD

THIS IS THE RECORD OF JOHN, WHEN THE JEWS SENT	095	21
THAT SAW IT BARE RECORD, AND HIS RECORD IS TRUE	161	05
RECORD, AND HIS RECORD IS TRUE	161	06
AND THIS IS THE RECORD, THAT GOD HATH GIVEN TO US	171	09
BELIEVETH NOT THE RECORD THAT GOD GAVE OF HIS SON	171	09
FOR GOD IS MY RECORD, HOW GREATLY I LONG AFTER YOU	220	31
6 THE LORD SHALL RECORD IT, WHEN HE WRITETH UP THE	448	24
I TAKE YOU TO RECORD THIS DAY, THAT I AM PURE FROM	550	24

RECOVER

AND RECOVER HIS BODILY HEALTH, IF IT BE	321	23
THAT I MAY RECOVER MY STRENGTH, *	325	10
THAT I MAY RECOVER MY STRENGTH, *	390	06

RECOVERING

AND RECOVERING OF SIGHT TO THE BLIND,	261	19

RECTOR

THE OFFICE OF RECTOR OF -- PARISH, (OR CHURCH,) YOU	569	23
AS PRIEST AND RECTOR OF THE SAME	570	14
AS PRIEST AND RECTOR OF THE SAME	570	29

RED

WHEREFORE ART THOU RED IN THINE APPAREL, AND THY	138	15
OF THY DOGS MAY BE RED THROUGH THE SAME	420	34
OF THE LORD THERE IS A CUP, AND THE WINE IS RED	432	15
THE SEA, EVEN AT THE RED SEA	473	15
9 HE REBUKED THE RED SEA ALSO, AND IT WAS DRIED UP	473	18
THINGS BY THE RED SEA	474	13
13 WHO DIVIDED THE RED SEA IN TWO PARTS	512	08
THEM IN THE RED SEA	512	13

REDEEM

THAT HE MIGHT REDEEM US FROM ALL INIQUITY, AND	098	23
UNDER THE LAW, TO REDEEM THEM THAT WERE UNDER THE	104	20
AND HE SHALL REDEEM ISRAEL *	328	17
IT COST MORE TO REDEEM THEIR SOULS, *	400	20
8 AND HE SHALL REDEEM ISRAEL *	507	22
THE WORLD, TO REDEEM US FROM SIN AND ETERNAL DEATH,	591	12

REDEEMED

WHOM THOU HAST REDEEMED WITH THY PRECIOUS BLOOD	010	34
VISITED AND REDEEMED HIS PEOPLE	014	09
WHICH THOU HAST REDEEMED BY THE BLOOD OF THY DEAR	039	18
WHOM THOU HAST REDEEMED WITH THY MOST PRECIOUS BLOOD,	054	16
SPARE THY PEOPLE, WHOM THOU HAST REDEEMED	062	20
WHICH WERE REDEEMED FROM THE EARTH	103	08
THESE WERE REDEEMED FROM AMONG MEN, BEING THE	103	11
THE YEAR OF MY REDEEMED IS COME	138	21
IN HIS PITY HE REDEEMED THEM	139	03
SHOULD HAVE REDEEMED ISRAEL	167	20
VISITED AND REDEEMED HIS PEOPLE, AND HATH RAISED UP	243	33
WHO HATH REDEEMED ME, AND ALL MANKIND	284	31
BLOOD HAST REDEEMED US	313	13
CHRIST WHO REDEEMED THEE	319	22
FOR THOU HAST REDEEMED ME, O LORD, THOU GOD OF TRUTH	375	32
AND REDEEMED OF OLD	430	07
THE LORD HATH REDEEMED, *	476	08
WHO HATH REDEEMED ME, AND ALL MANKIND	578	13

REDEEMER

IN THY SIGHT, O LORD, MY STRENGTH AND MY REDEEMER	003	21
O LORD, MY STRENGTH AND MY REDEEMER	021	23
O GOD THE SON, REDEEMER OF THE WORLD	054	07
HIM FOR OUR REDEEMER, SO WE MAY WITH SURE CONFIDENCE	098	13
ART OUR FATHER, OUR REDEEMER	139	23
O BLESSED REDEEMER, RELIEVE, WE BESEECH THEE,	320	08
I KNOW THAT MY REDEEMER LIVETH, AND THAT HE SHALL	324	09
THROUGH JESUS CHRIST, OUR MEDIATOR AND REDEEMER	335	15
O LORD, MY STRENGTH AND MY REDEEMER	364	15
21 THOU ART MY HELPER AND REDEEMER	391	26
6 THOU ART MY HELPER, AND MY REDEEMER	424	32
AND THAT THE HIGH GOD WAS THEIR REDEEMER	437	09
TO BE OUR REDEEMER, AND THE AUTHOR OF EVERLASTING	545	15
TO BE OUR REDEEMER, AND THE AUTHOR OF EVERLASTING	557	22
OUR ONLY MEDIATOR AND REDEEMER	572	14
THY SIGHT, O LORD, OUR STRENGTH AND OUR REDEEMER	572	24
OUR ONLY SAVIOUR AND REDEEMER	590	07

REDEEMING

BUT AS WISE, REDEEMING THE TIME, BECAUSE THE DAYS ARE	217	24
A SINNER OF THINE OWN REDEEMING	319	30

REDEMPTION

WHOM WE HAVE REDEMPTION THROUGH HIS BLOOD, THE	004	33
LOVE IN THE REDEMPTION OF THE WORLD BY OUR LORD JESUS	019	23
LOVE IN THE REDEMPTION OF THE WORLD BY OUR LORD JESUS	033	21
TO SUFFER DEATH UPON THE CROSS FOR OUR REDEMPTION	080	09
FOR THE REDEMPTION OF THE WORLD BY THE DEATH AND	086	06
FOR YOUR REDEMPTION DRAWETH NIGH	093	13
ETERNAL REDEMPTION FOR US	132	28
FOR THE REDEMPTION OF THE TRANSGRESSIONS THAT WERE	133	05
WHO FOR OUR REDEMPTION DIDST GIVE THINE ONLY-BEGOTTEN	165	03
TO WIT, THE REDEMPTION OF OUR BODY	194	23
WHEREBY YE ARE SEALED UNTO THE DAY OF REDEMPTION	216	26
LOOKED FOR REDEMPTION IN JERUSALEM	233	23
BLOOD FOR HIS REDEMPTION, EARNESTLY REMEMBERING THE	R 323	28
AND WITH HIM IS PLENTEOUS REDEMPTION	328	16
9 HE SENT REDEMPTION UNTO HIS PEOPLE	483	11
AND WITH HIM IS PLENTEOUS REDEMPTION	507	21
PERFECT OUR REDEMPTION BY HIS DEATH, AND WAS ASCENDED	545	24
PERFECT OUR REDEMPTION BY HIS DEATH, AND WAS ASCENDED	557	16
OF OUR REDEMPTION BY CHRIST'S DEATH	608	36
THAT PERFECT REDEMPTION, PROPITIATION, AND	609	14

REED

A REED SHAKEN WITH THE WIND	094 26
HIS HEAD, AND A REED IN HIS RIGHT HAND	136 19
AND TOOK THE REED, AND SMOTE HIM ON THE HEAD	136 22
AND PUT IT ON A REED, AND GAVE HIM TO DRINK	137 22
ON THE HEAD WITH A REED, AND DID SPIT UPON HIM, AND	145 34
AND PUT IT ON A REED, AND GAVE HIM TO DRINK, SAYING,	146 32

REEL

27 THEY REEL TO AND FRO, AND STAGGER LIKE A DRUNKEN   477 31

REFERENCES

BUT ALL REFERENCES TO THE CONSTITUTION AND LAWS CF	R 610 25
AS FROM THE LOCAL REFERENCES	R 610 29

REFERRED

MUST BE REFERRED TO DISCIPLINE   V 06

REFINER

SHALL SIT AS A REFINER AND PURIFIER OF SILVER   232 10

REFINER'S

HE IS LIKE A REFINER'S FIRE, AND LIKE FULLERS' SOPE   232 09

REFORM

IT IS AMISS, REFORM IT	037 19
REFORM WHATEVER IS AMISS IN THE TEMPER AND	590 12

REFORMED

HATEST TO BE REFORMED, *   402 24

REFRAIN

LET HIM REFRAIN HIS TONGUE FROM EVIL, AND HIS	195 25
I WILL NOT REFRAIN MY LIPS, O LORD, AND THAT THCU	391 02
AND THE FIERCENESS OF THEM SHALT THOU REFRAIN	433 09
12 HE SHALL REFRAIN THE SPIRIT OF PRINCES, *	433 13
REFRAIN NOT THYSELF, O GOD	444 06
3 BUT I REFRAIN MY SOUL, AND KEEP IT LOW, LIKE AS A	507 27

REFRAINED

101 I HAVE REFRAINED MY FEET FROM EVERY EVIL WAY,   496 28

REFRESH

AND I WILL REFRESH YOU	076 13
YET SHALT THOU REFRESH ME	311 26
YET SHALT THOU REFRESH ME	312 05
THOU TURN AND REFRESH ME	426 18
YET SHALT THOU REFRESH ME	514 11

REFRESHED

AND REFRESHED BY THE BREAD AND WINE	293 22
AND SHALL BE REFRESHED IN THE MULTITUDE OF PEACE	385 17
LIKE A GIANT REFRESHED WITH WINE	439 09
COMFORTS HAVE REFRESHED MY SOUL	458 25

REFRESHEDST

AND REFRESHEDST IT WHEN IT WAS WEARY   419 30

REFRESHING

AND REFRESHING OF MY SOUL	291 32
AND REFRESHING OF OUR SOULS BY THE BODY AND BLOCD OF	293 20
AND REFRESHING OF OUR SOULS BY THE BODY AND BLOCD OF	582 17
ENJOY SUCH REFRESHING SLEEP AS MAY FIT US FOR THE	591 28

REFRESHMENT

A PLACE OF REFRESHMENT AND EVERLASTING BLESSEDNESS   318 17

REFUGE

O GOD, OUR REFUGE AND STRENGTH, WHO ART THE AUTHCR OF	222 09
HAST BEEN OUR REFUGE, *	325 13
THE GOD OF JACOB IS OLR REFUGE	327 17
EVEN A REFUGE IN DUE TIME OF TROUBLE	352 07
THE HORN ALSO OF MY SALVATION, AND MY REFUGE	359 28
THE GOD OF JACOB IS OLR REFUGE	398 08
THE GOD OF JACOB IS OLR REFUGE	398 18
GOD IS WELL KNOWN IN HER PALACES AS A SURE REFUGE	399 15
WINGS SHALL BE MY REFLGE, UNTIL THIS TYRANNY BE	409 14
FOR THOU ART THE GOD OF MY REFUGE	411 23
MY DEFENCE AND REFUGE IN THE DAY OF MY TROUBLE	412 08
O GOD, ART MY REFUGE, AND MY MERCIFUL GOD	412 10
HAST BEEN OUR REFUGE, *	453 18
THE LORD IS MY REFUGE, *	458 30
HIGH HILLS ARE A REFUGE FOR THE WILD GCATS	468 30

REFUSE

THAT YE WILL NOT REFUSE TO COME THERETO, BEING SO	088 16
MOST UNTHANKFULLY REFLSE TO COME	088 21
HE MAY KNOW TO REFUSE THE EVIL, AND CHOOSE THE GCOD	236 02

REFUSE   CONTINUED

LET NOT MY HEAD REFUSE THEIR PRECIOUS BALMS   517 20

REFUSED

THOSE WHO REFUSED THE FEAST IN THE GOSPEL, BECAUSE	089 03
MY SOUL REFUSED COMFORT	311 03
MY SOUL REFUSED COMFORT	433 20
68 HE REFUSED THE TABERNACLE OF JOSEPH, *	439 12
THE BUILDERS REFUSED, *	489 12

REFUSETH

5 WHICH REFUSETH TO HEAR THE VOICE OF THE CHARMER,   410 17

REFUSING

STIFFNESS IN REFUSING, AND TOO MUCH EASINESS IN   V 25

REGARD

REGARD NOT OUR SINS, BUT THE FAITH OF THY CHURCH	049 07
REGARD, WE BESEECH THEE, THE SUPPLICATIONS OF THY	279 14
6 FOR THEY REGARD NOT IN THEIR MIND THE WORKS OF THE	373 17
THE GOD OF JACOB REGARD IT	457 32
FOR THEY REGARD NOT THY STATUTES	500 21
SHALL SAY, REGARD, O LORD,	565 18

REGARDED

FOR HE HATH REGARDED *	026 13
7 OUR FATHERS REGARDED NOT THY WONDERS IN EGYPT,	473 13
AND LIGHTLY REGARDED THE COUNSEL OF THE MOST HIGHEST	476 27

REGARDEST

FOR THOU REGARDEST NOT THE PERSON OF MEN	223 02
THAT THOU SO REGARDEST HIM	519 28

REGARDETH

WHICH REGARDETH NOT PERSONS, NOR TAKETH REWARD	263 24
11 BUT WHO REGARDETH THE POWER OF THY WRATH	454 11

REGARDS

EVERY THING THAT REGARDS THE CIVIL CONTRACT BETWEEN   R 304 19

REGENERATE

THAT WE BEING REGENERATE, AND MADE THY CHILDREN BY	096 15
THAT WE BEING REGENERATE, AND MADE THY CHILDREN BY	104 07
EXCEPT HE BE REGENERATE AND BORN ANEW OF WATER AND OF	273 31
PERSON) IS REGENERATE, AND GRAFTED INTO THE BODY OF	280 14
THEE TO REGENERATE THIS CHILD (THIS THY SERVANT) WITH	280 29
VOUCHSAFED TO REGENERATE THESE THY SERVANTS BY WATER	297 15

REGENERATED

YEA IN THEM THAT ARE REGENERATED   604 35

REGENERATION

IN THE REGENERATION WHEN THE SON OF MAN SHALL SIT	231 15
REMISSION OF SIN, BY SPIRITUAL REGENERATION	274 14
A SIGN OF REGENERATION OR NEW-BIRTH, WHEREBY, AS BY	608 26

REGION

ALL THE REGION ROUND ABOUT	213 10
THE LORD WAS PUBLISHED THROUGHOUT ALL THE REGICN	261 09

REGULARLY

REGULARLY AND LEGITIMATELY CONSTITUTED   610 41

REHEARSE

TO THE PEOPLE, REHEARSE DISTINCTLY THE TEN	R 067 22
7 I WILL REHEARSE THE DECREE	346 10
REHEARSE THE ARTICLES OF THY BELIEF	577 27

REHEARSING

THAT IN REHEARSING THE TEN COMMANDMENTS,   R 067 26

REIGN

SHE HATH, IN THE REIGN OF SEVERAL PRINCES, SINCE THE	V 26
ALSO ASCEND, AND REIGN WITH HIM IN GLORY	078 21
WHOM HE PERCEIVETH MALICE AND HATRED TO REIGN	R 085 10
THAT SHALL RISE TO REIGN OVER THE GENTILES	092 31
THAT ARCHELAUS DID REIGN IN JUDAEA IN THE ROOM OF HIS	107 18
AND A KING SHALL REIGN AND PROSPER, AND SHALL EXECUTE	225 10
AND HE SHALL REIGN OVER THE HOUSE OF JACOB FOR EVER	236 18
FOR HE MUST REIGN, TILL HE HATH PUT ALL ENEMIES UNDER	328 29

REIGNEST

LIVEST AND REIGNEST ONE GOD, WORLD WITHOUT END	043 15
WHO LIVEST AND REIGNEST WITH THE FATHER AND THE HOLY	049 09
WHO LIVEST AND REIGNEST WITH THE FATHER AND THE HOLY	093 31
WHO LIVEST AND REIGNEST WITH THE FATHER AND THE HOLY	125 31
WHO LIVEST AND REIGNEST, ONE GOD, WORLD WITHOUT END	186 29
WHO LIVEST AND REIGNEST WITH THE FATHER AND THE HOLY	320 12

REIGNETH

WHO LIVETH AND REIGNETH WITH THEE AND THE HOLY GHOST,	018 15
LIVETH AND REIGNETH EVER, ONE GOD, WORLD WITHOUT END	032 14
WHO LIVETH AND REIGNETH WITH THEE AND THE HOLY GHCST,	090 18
WHO LIVETH AND REIGNETH WITH THEE AND THE SAME SPIRIT	096 18
WHO LIVETH AND REIGNETH WITH THEE AND THE HOLY GHOST,	098 15
WHO LIVETH AND REIGNETH WITH THEE AND THE SAME SPIRIT	104 10
HE LIVETH AND REIGNETH EVER, ONE GOD, WORLD WITHOUT	117 11
WHO LIVETH AND REIGNETH WITH THEE AND THE HOLY GHOST	119 02
NOW LIVETH AND REIGNETH WITH THEE AND THE HOLY SPIRIT	152 12
NOW LIVETH AND REIGNETH WITH THEE AND THE HOLY GHOST	156 25
WHO LIVETH AND REIGNETH WITH THEE AND THE HOLY	157 12
WHO LIVETH AND REIGNETH WITH THEE AND THE HOLY GHOST	163 28
WHO LIVETH AND REIGNETH WITH THEE AND THE HOLY GHOST,	177 18
WHO LIVETH AND REIGNETH WITH THEE AND THE SAME HCLY	179 09
WHO LIVETH AND REIGNETH WITH THEE, IN THE UNITY OF	180 13
WHO LIVETH AND REIGNETH WITH THEE IN THE UNITY CF THE	182 18
LIVETH AND REIGNETH, ONE GOD, WORLD WITHOUT END	183 27
WHO LIVETH AND REIGNETH WITH THEE AND THE SAME	185 18
LIVETH AND REIGNETH, ONE GOD, WORLD WITHOUT END	248 06
WHO LIVETH AND REIGNETH WITH THEE AND THE HOLY GHOST	250 24
WHO LIVETH AND REIGNETH WITH THEE AND THE SAME HOLY	276 14
LIVETH AND REIGNETH EVER, ONE GOD, WORLD WITHOUT END	298 24
WHO LIVETH AND REIGNETH WITH THEE AND THE HCLY SPIRIT	303 27
WHO LIVETH AND REIGNETH WITH THEE AND THE HOLY GHOST,	319 12
WHO LIVETH AND REIGNETH WITH THEE AND THE HOLY GHOST	332 08
8 GOD REIGNETH OVER THE NATIONS	399 04
WHO LIVETH AND REIGNETH WITH THEE AND THE HOLY GHOST,	531 24
WHO LIVETH AND REIGNETH WITH THEE AND THE SAME HOLY	537 29
WHO LIVETH AND REIGNETH WITH THEE IN THE UNITY OF THE	546 04
WHO LIVETH AND REIGNETH WITH THEE AND THE SAME HCLY	548 07
WHO LIVETH AND REIGNETH WITH THEE AND THE SAME HCLY	554 03
LIVETH AND REIGNETH, ONE GOD, WORLD WITHOUT END	558 07
WHO LIVETH AND REIGNETH WITH THEE AND THE SAME HCLY	559 14
WHO LIVETH AND REIGNETH WITH THEE IN THE UNITY OF THE	562 14
WHO LIVETH AND REIGNETH WITH THEE AND THE SAME CFLY	574 22

REINS

TRIETH THE VERY HEARTS AND REINS	350 12
MY REINS ALSO CHASTEN ME IN THE NIGHT SEASON	358 05
TRY OUT MY REINS AND MY HEART	370 34
AND IT WENT EVEN THROUGH MY REINS	429 19
12 FOR MY REINS ARE THINE	515 13

REJOICE

WE WILL REJOICE AND BE GLAD IN IT	005 04
LET US HEARTILY REJOICE IN THE STRENGTH OF OUR	009 03
REJOICE, AND GIVE THANKS	027 14
AND I WILL REJOICE IN GIVING PRAISE FOR THE	028 03
LET THE NATIONS REJOICE AND BE GLAD	028 23
AND EVER REJOICE IN THY GOODNESS, TO THE	039 30
AND MAY REJOICE IN THE LIFE THAT NOW IS, AND	043 12
THAT THE BONES WHICH THOU HAST BROKEN MAY REJOICE	060 27
AGAIN HE SAITH, REJOICE, YE GENTILES, WITH HIS	092 28
AND AGAIN I SAY, REJOICE	095 13
REJOICE IN THE LORD ALWAY	095 13
THEM THAT DO REJOICE, AND WEEP WITH THEM THAT WEEP	111 29
REJOICE WITH THEM THAT DO REJOICE, AND WEEP WITH THEM	111 29
IT IS WRITTEN, REJOICE, THOU BARREN THAT BEAREST NOT	131 09
BUT THE WORLD SHALL REJOICE	174 08
YOUR HEART SHALL REJOICE, AND YOUR JOY NO MAN TAKETH	174 14
AND EVERMORE TO REJOICE IN HIS HOLY CCMFORT	180 11
YE WOULD REJOICE, BECAUSE I SAID, I GO UNTO THE	182 04
UNTO THEM, REJOICE WITH ME	193 23
REJOICE WITH ME	193 31
OF LOW DEGREE REJOICE IN THAT HE IS EXALTED	239 18
THEREFORE REJOICE, YE HEAVENS, AND YE THAT DWELL IN	252 16
REJOICE, AND BE EXCEEDING GLAD	257 32
AS WE REJOICE IN THEIR TRIUMPHS, WE MAY PROFIT	258 07
YOUR HEART SHALL REJOICE, AND YOUR JOY NO MAN TAKETH	341 10
AND REJOICE UNTO HIM WITH REVERENCE	346 19
LET ALL THEM THAT PUT THEIR TRUST IN THEE REJOICE	348 25
WILL BE GLAD AND REJOICE IN THEE	351 24
I WILL REJOICE IN THY SALVATION	352 20
TROUBLE ME SHALL REJOICE AT IT	356 05
THEN SHALL JACOB REJOICE, AND ISRAEL SHALL BE GLAD	356 32
ARE RIGHT, AND REJOICE THE HEART	363 30
5 WE WILL REJOICE IN THY SALVATION, AND TRIUMPH IN	364 23
THE KING SHALL REJOICE IN THY STRENGTH, O LORD	365 05
WILL BE GLAD AND REJOICE IN THY MERCY	376 04
AND REJOICE IN THE LORD	378 16
REJOICE IN THE LORD, O YE RIGHTEOUS	378 19
OUR HEART SHALL REJOICE IN HIM	379 30
IT SHALL REJOICE IN HIS SALVATION	382 08
THAT REJOICE AT MY TROUBLE	383 17
THEM BE GLAD AND REJOICE, THAT FAVOUR MY RIGHTEOUS	383 19
THE MOUNT SION REJOICE, AND THE DAUGHTERS OF JUCAH BE	399 31
THAT THE BONES WHICH THOU HAST BROKEN MAY REJOICE	403 26
SHOULD JACOB REJOICE, *	405 31
10 IN GOD'S WORD WILL I REJOICE	409 02
RIGHTEOUS SHALL REJOICE WHEN HE SEETH THE VENGEANCE	410 29
I WILL REJOICE, AND DIVIDE SHECHEM, *	412 23
UNDER THE SHADOW OF THY WINGS WILL I REJOICE	415 08
THE KING SHALL REJOICE IN GOD	415 15
RIGHTEOUS SHALL REJOICE IN THE LORD, AND PUT HIS	416 06
HILLS SHALL REJOICE ON EVERY SIDE	417 10
THERE DID WE REJOICE THEREOF	417 25
LET THE NATIONS REJOICE AND BE GLAD	418 30
BE GLAD, AND REJOICE BEFORE GOD	419 14
NAME JAH, AND REJOICE BEFORE HIM	419 18
AND MY FLESH REJOICE IN THE LIVING GOD	445 14
THY PEOPLE MAY REJOICE IN THEE	446 19
AND HERMON SHALL REJOICE IN THY NAME	450 32

REJOICE   CONTINUED

O LORD, THAT CAN REJOICE IN THEE	451 04
AND MADE ALL HIS ADVERSARIES TO REJOICE	452 25
SO SHALL WE REJOICE AND BE GLAD ALL THE DAYS OF OUR	454 18
AND I WILL REJOICE IN GIVING PRAISE FOR THE	456 07
LET US HEARTILY REJOICE IN THE STRENGTH OF OUR	459 06
LET THE HEAVENS REJOICE, AND LET THE EARTH BE GLAD	460 22
OF THE WOOD REJOICE BEFORE THE LORD	460 25
12 REJOICE IN THE LORD, YE RIGHTEOUS	461 21
REJOICE, AND GIVE THANKS	462 03
THE LORD SHALL REJOICE IN HIS WORKS	469 24
3 REJOICE IN HIS HOLY NAME	470 09
HEART OF THEM REJOICE THAT SEEK THE LORD	470 10
AND REJOICE IN THE GLADNESS OF THY PEOPLE, AND GIVE	473 08
42 THE RIGHTEOUS WILL CONSIDER THIS, AND REJOICE	478 30
I WILL REJOICE THEREFORE, AND DIVIDE SHECHEM, AND	479 17
BUT LET THY SERVANT REJOICE	481 28
WE WILL REJOICE AND BE GLAD IN IT	489 17
WHEREOF WE REJOICE	505 14
HER SAINTS SHALL REJOICE AND SING	509 07
2 LET ISRAEL REJOICE IN HIM THAT MADE HIM, *	525 05
LET THEM REJOICE IN THEIR BEDS	525 11
NIGHT COMETH, REJOICE TO GIVE THEE THANKS	594 16

REJOICED

MY SPIRIT HATH REJOICED IN GOD MY SAVIOUR	026 12
THE STAR, THEY REJOICED WITH EXCEEDING GREAT JOY	109 19
FATHER ABRAHAM REJOICED TO SEE MY DAY	133 28
AND THEY REJOICED WITH HER	243 16
ADVERSITY THEY REJOICED, AND GATHERED THEMSELVES	382 23
THEY REJOICED GREATLY AGAINST ME	388 24
8 SION HEARD OF IT, AND REJOICED	461 12

REJOICETH

REJOICETH NOT IN INIQUITY, BUT REJOICETH IN THE	122 32
BUT REJOICETH IN THE TRUTH	123 02
MY HEART IS GLAD, AND MY GLORY REJOICETH	333 07
MY HEART IS GLAD, AND MY GLORY REJOICETH	358 08
AND REJOICETH AS A GIANT TO RUN HIS COURSE	363 23

REJOICING

THAT, REJOICING IN THE KNOWLEDGE OF THY TRUTH,	043 03
THAT WE, REJOICING IN THEIR FELLOWSHIP, MAY RUN WITH	079 24
REJOICING IN HOPE	111 02
AS SORROWFUL, YET ALWAY REJOICING	126 19
HE LAYETH IT ON HIS SHOULDERS, REJOICING	193 21
UPON HIS WAY REJOICING, AND GIVE THEE CONTINUAL	316 22
THAT REJOICING IN THY WHOLE CREATION, WE MAY LEARN TC	596 19

RELATION

ALL SACERDOTAL RELATION, BETWEEN YOU AND THEM	569 33

RELATIONS

UPON ALL OUR RELATIONS, FRIENDS, AND NEIGHBOURS	590 31

RELEASE

WAS WONT TO RELEASE UNTO THE PEOPLE A PRISONER, WHCM	135 26
WILL YE THAT I RELEASE UNTO YOU	135 30
WILL YE THAT I RELEASE UNTO YOU	136 03
WILL YE THAT I RELEASE UNTO YOU THE KING OF THE JEWS	145 19
HE SHOULD RATHER RELEASE BARABBAS UNTO THEM	145 21
HE MUST RELEASE ONE UNTO THEM AT THE FEAST	153 28
AND RELEASE HIM	153 28
THIS MAN, AND RELEASE UNTO US BARABBAS	153 30
WILLING TO RELEASE JESUS, SPAKE AGAIN TO THEM	153 32
HAVE POWER TO RELEASE THEE	159 15
PILATE SOUGHT TO RELEASE HIM	159 19
RECEIVE HIM, TO RELEASE HIM FROM SIN, TO SANCTIFY HIM	276 21
RECEIVE YOU, TO RELEASE YOU FROM SIN, TO SANCTIFY YOU	277 23
RELEASE HIM FROM SIN, AND DRIVE AWAY ALL PAIN OF SOUL	320 10

RELEASED

THEN RELEASED HE BARABBAS UNTO THEM	136 13
THAT FEAST HE RELEASED UNTO THEM ONE PRISONER,	145 12
THE PEOPLE, RELEASED BARABBAS UNTO THEM, AND	145 28
AND HE RELEASED UNTO THEM HIM THAT FOR SEDITION AND	154 06

RELICS

OF IMAGES AS OF RELICS, AND ALSO INVOCATION OF	607 15

RELIEF

TO THE RELIEF OF OUR NECESSITY, AND TO THE	050 12
TO SEND RELIEF UNTO THE BRETHREN WHICH DWELT IN	241 20
TO SEND RELIEF UNTO THE BRETHREN WHICH DWELT IN	246 29
TO THE RELIEF OF DISTRESSED WOMEN IN CHILD-BED	R 307 09
AND AT LAST DIDST SEND HIM SEASONABLE RELIEF	315 27

RELIEVE

TO COMFORT AND RELIEVE THEM, ACCORDING TO THEIR	019 08
TO COMFORT AND RELIEVE THEM, ACCORDING TO THEIR	033 06
VISIT, AND RELIEVE THY SICK SERVANT	045 14
RELIEVE THE DISTRESSED, PROTECT THE INNOCENT, AWAKEN	046 24
VISIT, AND RELIEVE THIS THY SERVANT	309 04
RELIEVE, WE BESEECH THEE, BY THY INDWELLING	320 08

RELIEVED

THY MERCY HAST RELIEVED AND COMFORTED OUR SOULS BY   051 24
COMFORT OF THY GRACE MAY MERCIFULLY BE RELIEVED   130 26
THEY MAY BE RELIEVED WITH THE ALMS OF THE   533 20

RELIGION

AND JUSTICE, RELIGION AND PIETY, MAY BE ESTABLISHED   035 17
OF TRUE RELIGION AND USEFUL LEARNING MAY FOR EVER   047 36
OF THY TRUE RELIGION, AND VIRTLE   074 19
AND HOUSEHOLD CONTINUALLY IN THY TRUE RELIGION   115 29
OF CHRIST'S RELIGION, THAT THEY MAY AVCID THOSE   173 07
PURE RELIGION AND UNDEFILED BEFORE GOD AND THE FATHER 176 15
THIS MAN'S RELIGION IS VAIN   176 15
IN US TRUE RELIGION, NOURISH US WITH ALL GCODNESS,   198 22
THIS MAN'S RELIGION IS VAIN   266 06
PURE RELIGION AND UNDEFILED BEFORE GOD AND THE FATHER 266 06
IN THE PRINCIPLES OF THE CHRISTIAN RELIGION   R 273 22
IN US TRUE RELIGION, NOURISH US WITH ALL GCODNESS,   283 10
FOR ERROR IN RELIGION, OR FOR VICIOUSNESS IN LIFE   540 22
INCREASE IN THEM TRUE RELIGION   572 29
THY TRUE RELIGION AND VIRTUE   590 29
THAT CHRISTIAN RELIGION DOTH NCT PROHIBIT, BUT THAT A 611 08

RELIGIOUS

THE DIFFERENT RELIGIOLS DENOMINATIONS OF CHRISTIANS   VI 09
YOU SEEM TO BE RELIGIOUS, AND BRIDLETH NOT HIS   176 13
YOU SEEM TO BE RELIGIOUS, AND BRIDLETH NOT HIS   266 04
FOR WHOSE RELIGIOLS NLRTURE THEY ARE RESPONSIBLE, TO R 295 11
A REASONABLE, RELIGIOLS, AND HCLY HOPE   317 05
BEQUESTS FOR RELIGIOUS AND CHARITABLE USES   R 320 23
OFFICES OF RELIGIOLS WORSHIP, AND LET US FAITHFULLY   564 24

RELIGIOUSLY

AS SHALL BE RELIGIOUSLY AND DEVOUTLY DISPOSED THE   086 30
THEY WALK RELIGIOLSLY IN GOOD WORKS, AND AT LENGTH,   606 14

REMAIN

AMONGST YOU, AND REMAIN WITH YOU ALWAYS   084 22
BREAD AND WINE REMAIN AFTER THE COMMUNICN, IT SHALL R 084 30
GODLY UNITY, BUT REMAIN STILL IN HIS FROWARDNESS AND R 085 15
FRAGMENTS THAT REMAIN, THAT NOTHING BE LOST   132 07
BODIES SHOULD NOT REMAIN UPON THE CROSS ON THE   160 31
THE GREATER PART REMAIN UNTO THIS PRESENT, BUT SOME   205 09
FRAGMENTS THAT REMAIN, THAT NOTHING BE LOST   226 07
THAT MY JOY MIGHT REMAIN IN YOU, AND THAT YOUR JCY   238 25
FORTH FRUIT, AND THAT YOUR FRUIT SHOULD REMAIN   242 02
IN THE SAME HOUSE REMAIN, EATING AND DRINKING SUCH   254 22
ARE ALIVE AND REMAIN LNTO THE COMING OF THE LORD   269 03
ARE ALIVE AND REMAIN SHALL BE CAUGHT UP TCGETHER WITH 269 08
AND EVER REMAIN IN THE NUMBER OF THY FAITHFUL   279 18
BE UPON YOU, AND REMAIN WITH YOU FOR EVER   299 04
AND MAY EVER REMAIN IN PERFECT LOVE AND PEACE   303 10
11 GREAT PLAGUES REMAIN FOR THE UNGODLY   378 13
AND REMAIN IN THE WILDERNESS   406 32
AND OF THEM THAT REMAIN IN THE BROAD SEA   416 23
HIS NAME SHALL REMAIN UNDER THE SUN AMONG THE   427 32
AND REMAIN IN THE UTTERMOST PARTS OF THE SEA   515 04
AMONGST YOU, AND REMAIN WITH YOU ALWAYS   535 17
AND REMAIN IN THE SAME PLACE WHERE HANDS   R 546 30
AMONGST YOU, AND REMAIN WITH YOU ALWAYS   547 18
AMONGST YOU, AND REMAIN WITH YOU ALWAYS   559 21
AND MAY REMAIN IN PERFECT LOVE TOGETHER UNTO   566 11
AMONGST YOU, AND REMAIN WITH YOU ALWAYS   568 17
OF NATURE DOTH REMAIN, YEA IN THEM THAT ARE   604 35

REMAINDER

AND THE REMAINDER OF THE OFFICE   R 282 06

REMAINED

WHICH REMAINED OVER AND ABOVE UNTO THEM THAT   132 10
WHICH REMAINED OVER AND ABOVE UNTO THEM THAT   226 09

REMAINEST

BUT THOU REMAINEST   097 15

REMAINETH

UPON IT WHAT REMAINETH OF THE CONSECRATED ELEMENTS, R 083 12
AND THE LORD REMAINETH A KING FOR EVER   374 18
RIGHTEOUSNESS REMAINETH FOR EVER   484 02
THY TRUTH ALSO REMAINETH FROM ONE GENERATICN TO   496 04

REMAINING

AS TO THE REMAINING PARTS CF IT, IN OTHER   R 607 12

REMEMBER

AND TO REMEMBER HIS HOLY COVENANT   014 17
REMEMBER NOT OUR SINS, BUT THY PROMISES OF MERCY   040 06
REMEMBER HIM, O LORD, IN MERCY   046 03
REMEMBER NOT, LORD, OLR OFFENCES, NOR THE CFFENCES OF 054 13
REMEMBER THAT THOU KEEP HOLY THE SABBATH-DAY   068 24
REMEMBER THE WORDS OF THE LORD JESUS, HOW HE SAID,   072 02
SHOULD ALWAYS REMEMBER THE EXCEEDING GREAT LOVE OF   086 12
LORD, REMEMBER ME WHEN THOU COMEST INTO THY   155 06
WILL I REMEMBER NO MORE   158 14
SIR, WE REMEMBER THAT THAT DECEIVER SAID,   162 17

REMEMBER   CONTINUED

COME, YE MAY REMEMBER THAT I TOLD YOU OF THEM   180 03
SON, REMEMBER THAT THOU IN THY LIFETIME   190 16
AND TO REMEMBER HIS HOLY COVENANT   244 05
REMEMBER THE WORD THAT I SAID UNTO YOU, THE SERVANT   255 17
REMEMBER THAT THOU KEEP HOLY THE SABBATH-DAY   286 24
REMEMBER NOT, LORD, OUR INIQUITIES   308 10
BUT I WILL REMEMBER THE YEARS OF THE RIGHT HAND CF   311 18
REMEMBER THY SERVANT, O LORD, ACCORDING TO THE FAVOUR 332 03
3 REMEMBER ALL THY OFFERINGS, *   364 21
BUT WE WILL REMEMBER THE NAME OF THE LCRD OUR GCD   364 30
THE WORLD SHALL REMEMBER THEMSELVES, AND BE TURNED   367 28
6 O REMEMBER NOT THE SINS AND OFFENCES OF MY YOUTH   369 30
WILL I REMEMBER THEE FROM THE LAND OF JORDAN, FRCM   393 15
19 REMEMBER THIS, O LORD, HOW THE ENEMY HATH REBUKEC 431 12
REMEMBER HOW THE FOOLISH MAN BLASPHEMETH THEE DAILY   431 22
BUT I WILL REMEMBER THE YEARS OF THE RIGHT HAND CF   434 02
11 I WILL REMEMBER THE WORKS OF THE LORD, *   434 04
8 O REMEMBER NOT OUR OLD SINS, BUT HAVE MERCY UPCN   440 16
46 O REMEMBER HOW SHORT MY TIME IS   452 34
49 REMEMBER, LORD, THE REBUKE THAT THY SERVANTS HAVE, 453 07
5 REMEMBER THE MARVELLOUS WORKS THAT HE HATH DCNE   470 12
4 REMEMBER ME, O LORD, ACCORDING TO THE FAVOUR THAT   473 06
REMEMBER DAVID, *   508 05
6 IF I DO NOT REMEMBER THEE, LET MY TONGUE CLEAVE TO 513 15
7 REMEMBER THE CHILDREN OF EDOM, O LORD, IN THE DAY   513 18
5 YET DO I REMEMBER THE TIME PAST   518 32
AND REMEMBER, THAT BY THE SPACE OF THREE YEARS   550 33
AND TO REMEMBER THE WORDS OF THE LORD JESUS,   551 09
AND REMEMBER THAT THOU STIR UP THE GRACE OF GOD,   558 16
REMEMBER THAT THOU KEEP HOLY THE SABBATH-DAY   579 04
WE REMEMBER THIS DAY BEFORE THEE THY FAITHFUL   598 06
REMEMBER IN PITY SUCH AS ARE THIS DAY DESTITUTE,   599 06
REMEMBER ALL WHO BY REASON OF WEAKNESS ARE   600 07

REMEMBERED

HE HATH REMEMBERED HIS MERCY AND TRUTH TOWARD THE   027 10
THEN HE REMEMBERED THE DAYS OF OLD, MOSES, AND HIS   139 07
AND PETER REMEMBERED THE WORD OF THE LORD, HOW HE HAD 151 20
NAME TO BE REMEMBERED FROM ONE GENERATION TO ANCTHER 397 21
7 HAVE I NOT REMEMBERED THEE IN MY BED, *   415 05
35 AND THEY REMEMBERED THAT GOD WAS THEIR STRENGTH,   437 08
4 HE HATH REMEMBERED HIS MERCY AND TRUTH TOWARD THE   461 31
HE REMEMBERED HIS HOLY PROMISE   472 21
52 FOR I REMEMBERED THINE EVERLASTING JUDGMENTS,   493 14
23 WHO REMEMBERED US WHEN WE WERE IN TROUBLE   512 28
WHEN WE REMEMBERED THEE, O SION   513 06
HIS DISCIPLES REMEMBERED THAT IT WAS WRITTEN, THE   568 02

REMEMBEREST

IN THY WRATH REMEMBEREST MERCY   046 19
AND THERE REMEMBEREST THAT THY BROTHER HATH OUGHT   198 22
THAT THOU REMEMBEREST THEM NO MORE   313 32

REMEMBERETH

SHE REMEMBERETH NO MORE THE ANGUISH, FOR JOY   174 12
DEATH NO MAN REMEMBERETH THEE   349 08
HE REMEMBERETH THEM, *   352 13
HE REMEMBERETH THAT WE ARE BUT DUST   467 02

REMEMBERING

HE REMEMBERING HIS MERCY HATH HOLPEN HIS SERVANT   026 26
THE PEOPLE, REMEMBERING THE ACCOUNT THEY SHALL BE   047 19
EARNESTLY REMEMBERING THE BENEFITS HE HATH THEREBY, R 323 28
AND REMEMBERING THE ACCOUNT WHICH WE MUST ONE DAY   599 21

REMEMBRANCE

THE REMEMBRANCE OF THEM IS GRIEVOUS UNTO US   075 24
DO THIS IN REMEMBRANCE OF ME   080 22
DRINK IT, IN REMEMBRANCE OF ME   080 29
HAVING IN REMEMBRANCE HIS BLESSED PASSION AND   081 02
IN REMEMBRANCE OF HIS DEATH AND PASSION, MAY BE   081 13
EAT THIS IN REMEMBRANCE THAT CHRIST DIED FOR THEE,   082 33
THIS IN REMEMBRANCE THAT CHRIST'S BLOOD WAS SHED FOR 083 05
A CONTINUAL REMEMBRANCE OF HIS DEATH, TO OUR GREAT   086 17
RECEIVED IN REMEMBRANCE OF HIS MERITORIOUS CROSS AND 086 32
COMMUNION IN REMEMBRANCE OF THE SACRIFICE OF HIS   089 12
THE YEARLY REMEMBRANCE OF THE BIRTH OF THINE ONLY SCN 098 11
THIS DO IN REMEMBRANCE OF ME   149 10
THE SAME IN REMEMBRANCE OF HIM, WHO IN THESE HCLY   152 10
THIS DO IN REMEMBRANCE OF ME   152 20
DRINK IT, IN REMEMBRANCE OF ME   152 23
THERE IS A REMEMBRANCE AGAIN MADE OF SINS EVERY YEAR 157 21
TO YOUR REMEMBRANCE, WHATSOEVER I HAVE SAID UNTO YOU 181 32
UPON EVERY REMEMBRANCE OF YOU, ALWAYS IN EVERY PRAYER 220 22
IN REMEMBRANCE, MAY SHOW FORTH OUR THANKFULNESS UNTC 229 20
TO STIR YOU UP BY PUTTING YOU IN REMEMBRANCE   248 09
TO HAVE THESE THINGS ALWAYS IN REMEMBRANCE   248 13
CONTINUAL REMEMBRANCE OF THE SACRIFICE OF THE DEATH   293 05
A THANKFUL REMEMBRANCE OF HIS DEATH   293 29
I CALL TO REMEMBRANCE MY SONG, AND IN THE NIGHT I   311 10
5 CALL TO REMEMBRANCE, O LORD, THY TENDER MERCIES,   369 28
FOR A REMEMBRANCE OF HIS HOLINESS   374 31
ROOT OUT THE REMEMBRANCE OF THEM FROM THE EARTH   380 33
6 I CALL TO REMEMBRANCE MY SONG, *   433 27
THE NAME OF ISRAEL MAY BE NO MORE IN REMEMBRANCE   444 13
ARE OUT OF REMEMBRANCE, AND ARE CUT AWAY FROM THY   449 05
THANKS FOR A REMEMBRANCE OF HIS HOLINESS   461 22
AND THY REMEMBRANCE THROUGHOUT ALL GENERATIONS   465 03
KEPT THEY THY GREAT GOODNESS IN REMEMBRANCE   473 14

REMEMBRANCE CONTINUED

BE HAD IN REMEMBRANCE IN THE SIGHT OF THE LORD	480 27
THAT THEY OUGHT TO BE HAD IN REMEMBRANCE	483 02
RIGHTEOUS SHALL BE HAD IN EVERLASTING REMEMBRANCE	483 29
OWN WAYS TO REMEMBRANCE, *	493 29
YE HAVE IN REMEMBRANCE, INTO HOW HIGH A DIGNITY, AND	539 30
IN YOUR REMEMBRANCE, HOW GREAT A TREASURE IS	540 05
CONTINUAL REMEMBRANCE OF THE SACRIFICE OF THE DEATH	582 04
A THANKFUL REMEMBRANCE OF HIS DEATH	582 25
A LIVELY REMEMBRANCE OF THAT GREAT DAY, IN WHICH WE	588 21
THE WEEKLY REMEMBRANCE OF THE GLORIOUS RESURRECTION	595 12

REMISS

BE SO MERCIFUL, THAT YOU BE NOT TOO REMISS	558 29

REMISSION

ABSOLUTION AND REMISSION OF THEIR SINS	007 11
FOR THE REMISSION OF THEIR SINS,	014 28
FOR THE REMISSION OF SINS	016 20
ABSOLUTION AND REMISSION OF THEIR SINS	024 13
ABSOLUTION AND REMISSION OF ALL YOUR SINS, TRUE	024 24
FOR THE REMISSION OF SINS	030 25
FOR THE REMISSION OF SINS	071 22
FOR THE REMISSION OF SINS	080 27
MAY OBTAIN REMISSION OF OUR SINS, AND ALL OTHER	081 19
WE OBTAIN REMISSION OF OUR SINS, AND ARE MADE	086 33
FOR THE REMISSION OF SINS	112 09
PERFECT REMISSION AND FORGIVENESS	124 16
AND WITHOUT SHEDDING OF BLOOD IS NO REMISSION	147 27
NOW WHERE REMISSION OF THESE IS, THERE IS NC MORE	158 15
SHALL RECEIVE REMISSION OF SINS	166 32
REPENTANCE AND REMISSION OF SINS SHOULD BE PREACHED	170 14
SHALL RECEIVE REMISSION OF SINS	184 19
PEOPLE BY THE REMISSION OF THEIR SINS, THROUGH THE	244 12
MAY RECEIVE REMISSION OF SIN, BY SPIRITUAL	274 13
WE MAY RECEIVE REMISSION OF OUR SINS, AND BE FILLED	294 32
PARDON AND REMISSION OF ALL THY SINS, AND THE GRACE	319 16
ABSOLUTION AND REMISSION OF ALL YOUR SINS, TRUE	323 20
OBTAIN REMISSION OF THEIR SINS, AND ALL OTHER	565 33
TO HAVE REMISSION OF PAIN OR GUILT, WERE	609 18

REMIT

SINS YE REMIT, THEY ARE REMITTED UNTO THEM	171 24
SOEVER SINS YE REMIT, THEY ARE REMITTED UNTO THEM	552 04

REMITTED

THEY ARE REMITTED UNTO THEM	171 24
THEY ARE REMITTED UNTC THEM	552 05

REMNANT

AND THE REMNANT TOOK HIS SERVANTS, AND ENTREATED THEM	218 12

REMOVE

SO THAT I COULD REMOVE MOUNTAINS, AND HAVE NOT	122 25
THOU BE WILLING, REMOVE THIS CUP FROM ME	150 18

REMOVED

SICKNESS BEING REMOVED, HE MAY BE RESTORED TO	322 08
THEREFORE SHALL SHE NCT BE REMOVED	327 13
AND WERE REMOVED, BECASUE HE WAS WROTH	360 10
THE BRIGHTNESS OF HIS PRESENCE HIS CLOUDS REMOVED	360 22
IN MY PROSPERITY I SAID, I SHALL NEVER BE REMOVEC	375 04
THEREFORE SHALL SHE NCT BE REMOVED	398 03
WHICH MAY NOT BE REMOVED, BUT STANDETH FAST FOR EVER	504 24

REMOVING

AND THE REMOVING OF ALL SCRUPLE AND DOUBTFULNESS	088 09

REND

REND YOUR HEART, AND NOT YOUR GARMENTS,	004 20
AND REND YOUR HEART, AND NOT YOUR GARMENTS, AND TURN	124 23
LET US NOT REND IT, BLT CAST LOTS FOR IT, WHOSE IT	160 13

RENDER

MEET TOGETHER TO RENDER THANKS FOR THE GREAT BENEFITS	006 05
MEET TOGETHER TO RENDER THANKS FOR THE GREAT BENEFITS	023 14
IT IS OUR DUTY TO RENDER MOST HUMBLE AND HEARTY	086 35
RENDER THEREFORE TO ALL THEIR DUES	114 25
HE UNTO THEM, RENDER THEREFORE UNTO CAESAR THE THINGS	223 09
CIRCUMSTANCES RENDER IT EXPEDIENT TO SHORTEN THE	R 323 04
OF MANKIND, WE RENDER UNTO THEE MOST HEARTY THANKS,	545 24
NEEDY CREATURES, RENDER THEE OUR HUMBLE PRAISES,	587 21
THEY DO NOT ONLY RENDER UNTO GOD AS MUCH AS THEY ARE	605 26

RENDERING

RENDERING UNTO THEE MOST HEARTY THANKS FOR THE	081 04
NOT RENDERING EVIL FOR EVIL, OR RAILING FOR RAILING	195 22

RENEW

FORTH THAT IT MAY RENEW THE FACE OF THE EARTH	040 09
AND RENEW A RIGHT SPIRIT WITHIN ME	060 30
THEY WHO SHALL RENEW THE PROMISES AND VOWS OF THEIR	294 24
THIS CONGREGATION, RENEW THE SOLEMN PROMISE AND VOW	296 23

RENEW CONTINUED

RENEW IN HIM, MOST LOVING FATHER, WHATSOEVER HATH	314 02
AND RENEW A RIGHT SPIRIT WITHIN ME	403 29
AND THOU SHALT RENEW THE FACE OF THE EARTH	469 22
THEIR OWN PERSONS RENEW THE PROMISES AND VOWS OF	565 24

RENEWED

MAY DAILY BE RENEWED BY THY HOLY SPIRIT	096 17
MAY DAILY BE RENEWED BY THY HOLY SPIRIT	104 09
AND BE RENEWED IN THE SPIRIT OF YOUR MIND	216 14
LOVING-KINDNESS OUR SOULS AND BODIES ARE RENEWED	322 07

RENEWING

BY THE RENEWING OF YOUR MIND, THAT YE MAY PROVE WHAT	110 07
AFTER RENEWING THE PROMISES AND VOWS OF MY	291 24

RENOUNCE

OF THIS CHILD, RENOUNCE THE DEVIL AND ALL HIS WCRKS,	276 24
I RENOUNCE THEM ALL	276 29
DOST THOU RENOUNCE THE DEVIL AND ALL HIS WORKS,	277 26
I RENOUNCE THEM ALL	277 30
THAT I SHOULD RENOUNCE THE DEVIL AND ALL HIS WORKS,	283 23
THAT I SHOULD RENOUNCE THE DEVIL AND ALL HIS WORKS,	577 14

RENOUNCED

BUT HAVE RENOUNCED THE HIDDEN THINGS OF DISHONESTY,	250 28

RENOWN

THEM A PLANT OF RENOWN, AND THEY SHALL BE NC MORE	262 17
ACCORDING TO THY WORSHIP AND RENOWN	396 21

RENT

OF THE TEMPLE WAS RENT IN TWAIN FROM THE TOP TO THE	137 26
AND THE EARTH DID QUAKE, AND THE ROCKS RENT	137 27
THE HIGH PRIEST RENT HIS CLOTHES, AND SAITH, WHAT	143 17
OF THE TEMPLE WAS RENT IN TWAIN FROM THE TOP TO THE	146 35
OF THE TEMPLE WAS RENT IN THE MIDST	155 11

REPAY

I WILL REPAY, SAITH THE LORD	113 05
COME AGAIN, I WILL REPAY THEE	209 02

REPEAT

THE MINISTER REPEAT THE TEN COMMANDMENTS, AND AFTER	R 285 33
THE PEOPLE MAY REPEAT THE COMMANDMENTS, THE MINISTER	R 286 02

REPEATED

IS TO BE REPEATED EVERY DAY, AFTER THE OTHER COLLECTS	R 090 20

REPEATING

AND REPEATING IT WITH HIM, BOTH HERE,	R 007 21
AND REPEATING IT WITH HIM	R 024 28
READING OR REPEATING THE ANSWERS AS APPOINTED	R 283 14
READING OR REPEATING THE ANSWERS	R 287 32
KNEELING AND REPEATING IT WITH HIM	R 298 04
HOLY TABLE, REPEATING THE FOLLOWING PSALM	R 563 08
AND REPEATING WITH HIM THE LORD'S PRAYER	R 587 06
AND REPEATING WITH HIM THE LORD'S PRAYER	R 589 14
AND REPEATING WITH HIM THE LORD'S PRAYER	R 592 11
AND REPEATING WITH HIM THE LORD'S PRAYER	R 593 05

REPELLING

MINISTER SO REPELLING ANY, AS IS HEREIN SPECIFIEC,	R 085 17

REPENT

REPENT YE	004 04
THOSE WHO TRULY REPENT, AND UNFEIGNEDLY BELIEVE HIS	007 12
THOSE WHO TRULY REPENT, AND UNFEIGNEDLY BELIEVE HIS	024 14
AND TO BE MERCIFUL TO THOSE WHO TRULY REPENT	041 12
AND TRULY REPENT US OF OUR FAULTS, AND SO MAKE HASTE	062 23
AND EARNESTLY REPENT YOU OF YOUR SINS, AND ARE IN	075 08
WE DO EARNESTLY REPENT, AND ARE HEARTILY SORRY FCR	075 23
REPENT YOU TRULY FOR YOUR SINS PAST	085 34
REPENT YOU OF YOUR SINS, OR ELSE COME NOT TO THAT	087 33
THEN DO YE NOT REPENT AND AMEND	088 31
WILL RETURN AND REPENT, AND LEAVE A BLESSING BEHIND	124 27
WENT UNTO THEM FROM THE DEAD, THEY WILL REPENT	190 28
THAT WE MAY TRULY REPENT ACCORDING TO HIS PREACHING	242 11
WHETHER THEY REPENT THEM TRULY OF THEIR FORMER SINS,	293 26
AS TO WHETHER HE REPENT HIM TRULY OF HIS SINS,	R 313 19
THOSE WHO TRULY REPENT, THAT THOU REMEMBEREST THEM NC	313 32
IF HE DO TRULY REPENT HIM OF HIS SINS, AND STEDFASTLY	R 323 26
AND WILL NOT REPENT, *	482 14
WHETHER THEY REPENT THEM TRULY OF THEIR FORMER SINS,	582 22
THE PLACE OF FORGIVENESS TO SUCH AS TRULY REPENT	606 04

REPENTANCE

GRANT US TRUE REPENTANCE, AND HIS HCLY SPIRIT, THAT	007 14
GRANT US TRUE REPENTANCE, AND HIS HOLY SPIRIT, THAT	024 16
TRUE REPENTANCE, AMENDMENT OF LIFE, AND THE	024 24
IT MAY PLEASE THEE TO GIVE US TRUE REPENTANCE	057 14
WITH HEARTY REPENTANCE AND TRUE FAITH TURN UNTO HIM	076 04

REPENTANCE   CONTINUED

BAPTISM OF REPENTANCE FOR THE REMISSION OF SINS   112 09
AND THAT REPENTANCE AND REMISSION OF SINS SHOULD BE   170 14
AND NINE JUST PERSONS, WHICH NEED NO REPENTANCE   193 27
OF THY SON OUR SAVIOUR BY PREACHING REPENTANCE   242 09
BUT SINNERS TO REPENTANCE   251 23
REPENTANCE, WHEREBY THEY FORSAKE SIN   292 28
AND TRUE REPENTANCE, WE MAY RECEIVE REMISSION OF OUR   294 31
AND SERIOUSNESS TO HIS REPENTANCE   310 23
OF HIS REPENTANCE, THE MINISTER SHALL ASSURE HIM OF   R 313 26
HIM UNFEIGNED REPENTANCE FOR ALL THE ERRORS OF HIS   316 12
TRUE REPENTANCE, AMENDMENT OF LIFE, AND THE   323 20
THE GREEKS, REPENTANCE TOWARD GOD, AND FAITH TOWARD   550 13
WITH FAITH, CHARITY, AND TRUE REPENTANCE   565 31
REPENTANCE, WHEREBY THEY FORSAKE SIN   581 28
AND GIVE THEM REPENTANCE AND BETTER MINDS   590 33
THE GRANT OF REPENTANCE IS NOT TO BE DENIED TO SUCH   605 40

REPENTED

TO HAVE TRULY REPENTED AND AMENDED HIS FORMER EVIL   R 085 05
WAS CONDEMNED, REPENTED HIMSELF, AND BROUGHT AGAIN   135 03

REPENTETH

AND REPENTETH HIM OF THE EVIL   004 22
AND REPENTETH HIM OF THE EVIL   124 25
SINNER THAT REPENTETH, MORE THAN OVER NINETY AND NINE   193 26
THE ANGELS OF GOD OVER ONE SINNER THAT REPENTETH   193 34

REPLENISH

AND SO REPLENISH THEM WITH THE GRACE OF THY HOLY   017 32
AND SO REPLENISH THEM WITH THE TRUTH OF THY DOCTRINE,   039 11
SO REPLENISH THEM WITH THE TRUTH OF THY DOCTRINE, AND   531 19
AND SO REPLENISH THEM WITH THE TRUTH OF THY DOCTRINE,   537 23
AND SO REPLENISH THEM WITH THE TRUTH OF THY DOCTRINE,   548 02
AND SO REPLENISH HIM WITH THE TRUTH OF THY DOCTRINE,   553 29
AND SO REPLENISH HIM WITH THE TRUTH OF THY DOCTRINE,   572 10

REPORT

BY EVIL REPORT AND GOOD REPORT   126 16
BY EVIL REPORT AND GOOD REPORT   126 17
WHO HATH BELIEVED OUR REPORT   227 14
MEN OF HONEST REPORT, FULL OF THE HOLY GHOST AND   532 11
MUST HAVE A GOOD REPORT OF THEM WHICH ARE WITHOUT   549 28
AND OF GOOD REPORT, FOLLOWING THE EXAMPLE OF THEIR   596 27

REPORTED

BE PROMPTLY REPORTED TO THE PARISH AUTHORITIES   R 281 29
IT SHALL BE REPORTED, THIS ONE AND THAT ONE WERE BORN   448 22

REPOSE

AND THE REPOSE OF THE DEAD   595 05

REPRESENTATIVES

AND REPRESENTATIVES IN CONGRESS ASSEMBLED   035 10

REPRESENTED

IN IT IS REPRESENTED THE SPIRITUAL MARRIAGE AND UNITY   303 21

REPROACH

IN ALL THINGS THEY MAY SERVE WITHOUT REPROACH   041 30
AS CONCERNING REPROACH, AS THOUGH WE HAD BEEN WEAK   120 26
HERITAGE TO REPROACH, THAT THE HEATHEN SHOULD RULE   125 05
13 I BECAME A REPROACH AMONG ALL MINE ENEMIES,   376 15
HAST KNOWN MY REPROACH, MY SHAME, AND MY DISHONOUR   423 11
21 REPROACH HATH BROKEN MY HEART   423 13
HE IS BECOME A REPROACH TO HIS NEIGHBOURS   452 23
BECOME ALSO A REPROACH UNTO THEM   481 20
HE FALL INTO REPROACH AND THE SNARE OF THE DEVIL   549 29

REPROOF

SAVE ME FROM THE REPROOF OF HIM THAT WOULD EAT ME UP   409 18
FOR THY SAKE HAVE I SUFFERED REPROOF   422 16
AND THAT WAS TURNED TO MY REPROOF   422 24
THE SCORNFUL REPROOF OF THE WEALTHY, *   504 04

REPROOFS

AND IN WHOSE MOUTH ARE NO REPROOFS   388 20

REPROVE

BUT RATHER REPROVE THEM   129 17
IS COME, HE WILL REPROVE THE WORLD OF SIN, AND OF   175 13
8 I WILL NOT REPROVE THEE BECAUSE OF THY SACRIFICES   402 06
BUT I WILL REPROVE THEE, AND SET BEFORE THEE THE   402 34
ME FRIENDLY, AND REPROVE ME   517 19
OF EARNEST TO REPROVE, BESEECH, AND REBUKE, WITH ALL   559 08

REPROVED

THINGS THAT ARE REPROVED ARE MADE MANIFEST BY THE   129 19
LEST HIS DEEDS SHOULD BE REPROVED   185 09
THAT OUR FAITH IN THY SIGHT MAY NEVER BE REPROVED   228 09
BUT REPROVED EVEN KINGS FOR THEIR SAKES   470 30

REPUGNANT

THAT IT BE REPUGNANT TO ANOTHER   607 06
BUT RATHER REPUGNANT TO THE WORD OF GOD   607 17
THING PLAINLY REPUGNANT TO THE WORD OF GOD, AND THE   607 27
BUT IS REPUGNANT TO THE PLAIN WORDS OF SCRIPTURE,   608 41
WHICH BE NOT REPUGNANT TO THE WORD OF GOD, AND BE   609 37

REPUTATION

HIMSELF OF NO REPUTATION, AND TOOK UPON HIM THE FORM   134 18
141 I AM SMALL AND OF NO REPUTATION   499 21

REQUEST

YOU ALL MAKING REQUEST WITH JOY, FOR YOUR FELLOWSHIP   220 23
DENIED HIM THE REQUEST OF HIS LIPS   365 08

REQUESTS

IN THY NAME THOU WILT GRANT THEIR REQUESTS   020 06
IN THY NAME THOU WILT GRANT THEIR REQUESTS   034 06
LET YOUR REQUESTS BE MADE KNOWN UNTO GOD   095 16

REQUIRE

OR MAY ADD OTHERS, AS OCCASION MAY REQUIRE   R 047 05
OR FURTHER THAN LOCAL CIRCUMSTANCES REQUIRE   VI 34
IF NECESSITY SO REQUIRE, BAPTISM MAY BE ADMINISTERED   R 273 06
NECESSITY MAY REQUIRE, THEN THE FOLLOWING FORM SHALL   R 281 17
HE SHALL SAY, I REQUIRE AND CHARGE YOU BOTH, AS YE   300 24
HAVE I DESIRED OF THE LORD, WHICH I WILL REQUIRE   326 08
HAVE I DESIRED OF THE LORD, WHICH I WILL REQUIRE   371 33
WHICH THE CANON IN THAT CASE PROVIDED MAY REQUIRE   529 25
AS THE CANONS REQUIRE, MAY, AT THE TIMES APPOINTED,   529 29
AS NEED SHALL REQUIRE, AND OCCASION SHALL BE GIVEN   542 24
HE SHALL THEN REQUIRE OF HIM THE FOLLOWING PROMISE   R 552 26

REQUIRED

REQUIRED BY GOD IN HOLY SCRIPTURE, AND BE RECEIVED AS   087 13
MOREOVER IT IS REQUIRED IN STEWARDS, THAT A MAN BE   094 05
GAVE SENTENCE THAT IT SHOULD BE AS THEY REQUIRED   154 06
WHAT IS REQUIRED OF PERSONS TO BE BAPTIZED   292 27
WHAT IS REQUIRED OF THOSE WHO COME TO THE LORD'S   293 23
IT IS REQUIRED OF THOSE WHO COME TO THE   293 25
16 I HAVE REQUIRED THAT THEY, EVEN MINE ENEMIES,   388 23
AND SACRIFICE FOR SIN HAST THOU NOT REQUIRED   390 29
AND REQUIRED MEAT FOR THEIR LUST   436 04
AWAY CAPTIVE, REQUIRED OF US THEN A SONG, AND MELODY   513 09
ALL DOCTRINE REQUIRED AS NECESSARY FOR ETERNAL   533 03
ALL DOCTRINE REQUIRED AS NECESSARY FOR ETERNAL   542 03
ALL DOCTRINE REQUIRED AS NECESSARY FOR ETERNAL   554 21
WHAT IS REQUIRED OF PERSONS TO BE BAPTIZED   581 27
WHAT IS REQUIRED OF THOSE WHO COME TO THE LORD'S   582 20
IS NOT TO BE REQUIRED OF ANY MAN, THAT IT SHOULD BE   603 30
FOR HIS SAKE, THAN OF BOUNDEN DUTY IS REQUIRED   605 28

REQUIREST

BUT LO, THOU REQUIREST TRUTH IN THE INWARD PARTS,   060 22
6 BUT LO, THOU REQUIREST TRUTH IN THE INWARD PARTS,   403 20

REQUIRETH

BUT REQUIRETH FURTHER COMFORT OR COUNSEL, LET   088 05
THE MAGISTRATE REQUIRETH, IN A CAUSE OF FAITH AND   611 09

REQUIRING

LOUD VOICES, REQUIRING THAT HE MIGHT BE CRUCIFIED   154 03

REQUISITE

WHICH ARE REQUISITE AND NECESSARY, AS WELL FOR THE   006 08
WHICH ARE REQUISITE AND NECESSARY, AS WELL FOR THE   023 17
BECAUSE IT IS REQUISITE THAT NO MAN SHOULD COME TO   087 35
AS ARE REQUISITE FOR THE SAME   529 16
THINGS AS ARE REQUISITE AND NECESSARY, AS WELL FOR   566 17
OR BE THOUGHT REQUISITE OR NECESSARY TO SALVATION   603 32
NECESSITY ARE REQUISITE TO THE SAME   606 41

RESERVED

ORDINANCE RESERVED, CARRIED ABOUT, LIFTED UP, OR   608 47

RESIDING

THE CLERGY HERE RESIDING), THAT THEY MAY SHINE AS   047 27

RESIDUE

HIM TO LEAD THE RESIDUE OF HIS LIFE IN THY FEAR, AND   045 19
HE DEVOTE THE RESIDUE OF HIS DAYS TO AN HUMBLE,   053 06
WITH THE RESIDUE OF THY HOLY CHURCH, HE MAY BE AN   281 03

RESIST

IS ABLE TO RESIST, TO WHOM IT BELONGETH JUSTLY TO   041 10
THEY MAY RESIST TEMPTATION AND OVERCOME EVIL,   043 12
AND THEY THAT RESIST SHALL RECEIVE TO THEMSELVES   114 14
WHOM RESIST STEDFAST IN THE FAITH, KNOWING THAT THE   193 06
FROM SUCH AS RESIST THY RIGHT HAND   358 33

RESISTETH

THEREFORE RESISTETH THE POWER, RESISTETH THE   114 13
THE POWER, RESISTETH THE ORDINANCE OF GOD   114 14
FOR GOD RESISTETH THE PROUD, AND GIVETH GRACE TO THE 192 31

RESOLUTION

IN WHICH RESOLUTION, DO THOU, O MERCIFUL GOD, CONFIRM 588 07

RESORT

WHEREUNTO I MAY ALWAY RESORT   425 08
THE RIGHTEOUS RESORT UNTO MY COMPANY   518 21

RESPECT

INDEPENDENT WITH RESPECT TO CIVIL GOVERNMENT, THEIR   VI 08
AS NOTHING IN RESPECT OF THEE   324 23
AS NOTHING IN RESPECT OF THEE   389 18
WHILE I HAVE RESPECT UNTO ALL THY COMMANDMENTS   490 10
AND HAVE RESPECT UNTO THY WAYS   490 27
YET HATH HE RESPECT UNTO THE LOWLY   514 08
THOU HAST SUCH RESPECT UNTO HIM   519 27

RESPECTER

THAT GOD IS NO RESPECTER OF PERSONS   166 13
THAT GOD IS NO RESPECTER OF PERSONS   183 30

RESPECTFUL

TO PAY RESPECTFUL OBEDIENCE TO THE CIVIL AUTHORITY,   610 41

RESPECTING

THE LAWS RESPECTING MATRIMONY, WHETHER BY   R 304 17

RESPECTIVE

AS IN THEIR RESPECTIVE TIMES WERE THOUGHT CONVENIENT   V 29
THEIR RESPECTIVE CHURCHES, AND FORMS OF WORSHIP,   VI 11

RESPONDING

ASK THE QUESTION FOLLOWING, THE PEOPLE RESPONDING   R 284 26
THE CHURCH WHICH FOLLOW, THE PEOPLE RESPONDING   R 290 27
CONCERNING THE MINISTRY, THE PEOPLE RESPONDING   R 294 03

RESPONSE

COMMANDMENT THE PEOPLE SHALL SAY THE RESPONSE   R 285 34
THE MINISTER SAYING THE RESPONSE   R 286 03

RESPONSES

VERSICLES AND RESPONSES WHICH FOLLOW, OR, IN THE   R 003 14
VERSICLES AND RESPONSES WHICH FOLLOW   R 021 11

RESPONSIBLE

THEY ARE RESPONSIBLE, TO THE CHURCH AT THE TIME   R 295 11

REST

AND THAT THE REST OF OUR LIFE HEREAFTER MAY BE PURE   007 16
AND THAT THE REST OF OUR LIFE HEREAFTER MAY BE PURE   024 18
PASS OUR TIME IN REST AND QUIETNESS   031 23
HE WALKETH THROUGH DRY PLACES, SEEKING REST   130 11
THE REST SAID, LET BE, LET US SEE WHETHER ELIAS WILL 137 23
THE SPIRIT OF THE LORD CAUSED HIM TO REST   139 16
SLEEP ON NOW, AND TAKE YOUR REST   142 11
AND THEY REST NOT DAY AND NIGHT, SAYING, HOLY,   187 22
AND I WILL GIVE YOU REST   235 12
AND YE SHALL FIND REST UNTO YOUR SOULS   235 13
AND OF THE REST DURST NO MAN JOIN HIMSELF TO THEM   249 23
YOUR PEACE SHALL REST UPON IT   254 21
HERE AND ARE NOW AT REST, MAY AT THE LAST ENTER WITH 268 18
MAY LEAD THE REST OF HIS LIFE ACCORDING TO THIS   280 17
THAT HE MAY REST WITH ALL THY SAINTS IN THE ETERNAL   319 10
MAY THY REST BE THIS DAY IN PEACE, AND THY   319 24
INTO THE BLESSED REST OF EVERLASTING PEACE, AND INTO 320 02
MY FLESH ALSO SHALL REST IN HOPE   333 08
FOR THEY REST FROM THEIR LABOURS   333 27
IN FAITH, DO NOW REST FROM THEIR LABOURS   334 25
THIS LIFE, WE MAY REST IN HIM   335 07
TO THOSE WHO REST IN JESUS, THE MANIFOLD   335 28
9 I WILL LAY ME DOWN IN PEACE, AND TAKE MY REST   347 28
SWELLETH AGAINST HIM, AND WILL SET HIM AT REST   355 19
OR WHO SHALL REST UPON THY HOLY HILL   357 06
MY FLESH ALSO SHALL REST IN HOPE   358 09
AND LEAVE THE REST OF THEIR SUBSTANCE FOR THEIR   359 18
AND IN THE NIGHT SEASON ALSO I TAKE NO REST   366 08
IS THERE ANY REST IN MY BONES, BY REASON OF MY SIN   387 26
FOR THEN WOULD I FLEE AWAY, AND BE AT REST   406 31
THAT THEY SHOULD NOT ENTER INTO MY REST   459 28
30 THEN ARE THEY GLAD, BECAUSE THEY ARE AT REST   478 04
AGAIN THEN UNTO THY REST, O MY SOUL   487 02
AND SO LATE TAKE REST, AND EAT THE BREAD OF   505 27
NEITHER THE TEMPLES OF MY HEAD TO TAKE ANY REST   508 12
15 THIS SHALL BE MY REST FOR EVER   509 02
CREATOR BLEST, VOUCHSAFE WITHIN OUR SOULS TO REST   544 18
ELECT PUT ON THE REST OF THE EPISCOPAL HABIT,   R 556 02
CREATOR BLEST, VOUCHSAFE WITHIN OUR SOULS TO REST   556 26
MAY REST THERE   590 14
ALWAYS GO TO OUR REST IN PEACE, CHARITY, AND   590 17

REST   CONTINUED

AND A HOLY REST, AND PEACE AT THE LAST   595 03
IN RETURNING AND REST WE SHALL BE SAVED, IN QUIETNESS 595 20
BUT ALL WE THE REST, ALTHOUGH BAPTIZED, AND BORN   605 35

RESTED

IN THEM IS, AND RESTED THE SEVENTH DAY   068 31
IN THEM IS, AND RESTED THE SEVENTH DAY   286 31
IN THEM IS, AND RESTED THE SEVENTH DAY   579 11

RESTING-PLACE

O LORD, INTO THY RESTING-PLACE   508 19

RESTITUTION

TO MAKE RESTITUTION AND SATISFACTION, ACCORDING TO   087 24

RESTORE

RESTORE THOU THOSE WHO ARE PENITENT   006 25
RESTORE THOU THOSE WHO ARE PENITENT   023 32
THY GOOD TIME, RESTORE HIM TO HEALTH, AND ENABLE HIM 045 18
OF LOVE, AND TO RESTORE TO IT THE WITNESS OF VISIBLE 047 10
AT THIS TIME RESTORE AGAIN THE KINGDOM TO ISRAEL   178 06
AND SO RESTORE HIM TO HIS FORMER HEALTH, THAT   309 30
RESTORE THEM TO STRENGTH OF MIND AND CHEERFULNESS OF 598 15

RESTORED

THAT HE MAY BE RESTORED TO THAT PERFECT HEALTH WHICH 045 26
LIFE AGAIN HATH RESTORED TO US EVERLASTING LIFE   078 12
BEING THEREUPON RESTORED, HE MAY BLESS THY HOLY NAME 315 10
BEING RESTORED TO HEALTH OF BODY, VIGOUR OF   315 29
THAT BEING RESTORED TO SOUNDNESS OF HEALTH, HE MAY   320 11
HEALTH MAY BE RESTORED UNTO THEE   320 19
HE MAY BE RESTORED TO SOUNDNESS OF HEALTH   322 09
THAT HE MAY BE RESTORED TO HEALTH OF BODY AND OF   597 17

RESTORING

BY RESTORING THIS OUR BROTHER TO SOME   315 22

RESTRAIN

TO RESTRAIN THOSE IMMODERATE RAINS,   040 24

RESTRAINED

ARE THEY RESTRAINED   139 21
EFFECTUALLY RESTRAINED FROM SIN, AND INCITED TO OUR   588 17

RESURRECTION

THE RESURRECTION OF THE BODY   015 30
FOR THE RESURRECTION OF THE DEAD   016 20
THE RESURRECTION OF THE BODY   030 02
FOR THE RESURRECTION OF THE DEAD   030 25
GLORIOUS RESURRECTION, AND THE LIFE EVERLASTING   048 21
GLORIOUS RESURRECTION AND ASCENSION   055 12
FOR THE RESURRECTION OF THE DEAD   071 22
GLORIOUS RESURRECTION OF THY SON JESUS CHRIST OUR   078 08
GLORIOUS RESURRECTION, MANIFESTLY APPEARED TO ALL HIS 078 18
HIS MIGHTY RESURRECTION AND GLORIOUS ASCENSION   081 03
AND ALSO BE MADE PARTAKERS OF HIS RESURRECTION   134 11
AFTER HIS RESURRECTION, AND WENT INTO THE HOLY CITY, 137 29
WE MAY PASS TO OUR JOYFUL RESURRECTION   161 17
BY THE RESURRECTION OF JESUS CHRIST   161 32
ALSO THE RESURRECTION OF THE DEAD   163 14
GLORIOUS RESURRECTION HAST DELIVERED US FROM THE   165 05
LIVE WITH HIM IN THE JOY OF HIS RESURRECTION   165 07
SHALL BE ALSO IN THE LIKENESS OF HIS RESURRECTION   197 16
THOMAS TO BE DOUBTFUL IN THY SON'S RESURRECTION   228 07
TO BE A WITNESS WITH US OF HIS RESURRECTION   234 25
MAY BE BROUGHT UNTO THE GLORY OF HIS RESURRECTION   235 22
AND THE RESURRECTION OF THE DEAD   274 11
MAY ALSO BE PARTAKER OF HIS RESURRECTION   281 03
THE RESURRECTION OF THE BODY   284 24
GLORIOUS RESURRECTION AND ASCENSION, AND BY THE   318 07
I AM THE RESURRECTION AND THE LIFE, SAITH THE LORD   324 05
ALSO THE RESURRECTION OF THE DEAD   328 23
ALSO IS THE RESURRECTION OF THE DEAD   329 19
HOPE OF THE RESURRECTION UNTO ETERNAL LIFE, THROUGH   333 17
WHO IS THE RESURRECTION AND THE LIFE   334 31
THE GENERAL RESURRECTION IN THE LAST DAY, WE MAY BE   335 08
THE GENERAL RESURRECTION, WE, WITH ALL THOSE WHO ARE 336 23
HOPE OF THE RESURRECTION UNTO ETERNAL LIFE, THROUGH   337 11
I AM THE RESURRECTION AND THE LIFE, SAITH THE LORD   338 05
HOPE OF THE RESURRECTION TO ETERNAL LIFE THROUGH OUR 341 13
THE RESURRECTION OF THE BODY   578 08
GLORIOUS RESURRECTION OF THY SON OUR LORD   595 13

RETAIN

SINS YE RETAIN, THEY ARE RETAINED   171 25
SINS THOU DOST RETAIN, THEY ARE RETAINED   546 12
SOEVER SINS YE RETAIN, THEY ARE RETAINED   552 05

RETAINED

AND WHOSESOEVER SINS YE RETAIN, THEY ARE RETAINED   171 25
WHOSE SINS THOU DOST RETAIN, THEY ARE RETAINED   546 13
WHOSE SOEVER SINS YE RETAIN, THEY ARE RETAINED   552 06
ANY WISE TO BE RETAINED IN THE CHURCH, AS MOST   608 31

RETURN

ANY DESIRE TO RETURN THANKS FOR MERCIES VOUCHSAFED TO   R 019 33
ANY DESIRE TO RETURN THANKS FOR MERCIES VOUCHSAFED TO   R 033 31
PRAISE FOR THE RETURN OF SEED-TIME AND HARVEST, FOR   050 21
HAVE DESIRED TO RETURN THANKS TO ALMIGHTY GCD FCR HER   R 051 04
NOW DESIRETH TO RETURN THANKS UNTO THEE, IN THE   053 02
NOW DESIRETH TO RETURN HIS THANKS UNTO THEE IN THY   053 24
SHALL RETURN TO THE HCLY TABLE, AND BEGIN   R 071 32
THE PRIEST SHALL RETURN TO THE LORD'S TABLE, AND   R 083 11
WHEN YE SHOULD RETURN TO GOD, WILL YE EXCUSE   088 33
BY GOD'S GRACE RETURN TO A BETTER MIND   089 19
THEY SHOULD NOT RETURN TO HEROD, THEY DEPARTED INTO   109 24
IF HE WILL RETURN AND REPENT, AND LEAVE A BLESSING   124 26
HE SAITH, I WILL RETURN UNTO MY HOUSE WHENCE I CAME   130 12
RETURN FOR THY SERVANTS' SAKE, THE TRIBES OF THINE   139 25
NOW NO MORE TO RETURN TO CORRUPTION, HE SAID CN THIS   169 11
THAT THEY MAY RETURN INTO THE WAY OF RIGHTEOUSNESS   173 06
EVENING THEY WILL RETURN, *   412 02
WHEN HE WILL RETURN FROM THE WEDDING   534 18
UNTIL HE RETURN TO JUDGE ALL MEN AT THE LAST   603 23

RETURNED

THE SHEPHERDS RETURNED, GLORIFYING AND PRAISING GOD   106 17
AS THEY RETURNED, THE CHILD JESUS TARRIED   110 21
AND WHEN HE RETURNED, HE FOUND THEM ASLEEP AGAIN,   142 08
SMOTE THEIR BREASTS, AND RETURNED   155 18
SAME HOUR, AND RETURNED TO JERUSALEM, AND FCUND THE   168 11
BUT ARE NOW RETURNED UNTO THE SHEPHERD AND BISHCP OF   172 18
AND RETURNED TO JERUSALEM WITH GREAT JOY   178 27
NOT FOUND THAT RETURNED TO GIVE GLORY TO GOD, SAVE   210 12
THE LORD, THEY RETURNED INTO GALILEE, TO THEIR CWN   233 25

RETURNING

US THAT IN RETURNING AND REST WE SHALL BE SAVED, IN   595 19

RETURNS

IN THE RETURNS OF THE FRUITS OF THE EARTH   265 12

REUNITE

IT IS DIVIDED, REUNITE IT   037 20

REV

ASSEMBLED FOR THE PURPOSE OF INSTITUTING THE REV   570 13
CHURCH) I DO RECEIVE AND ACKNOWLEDGE YOU, THE REV   570 28

REVEAL

THE SON WILL REVEAL HIM   235 10
THE MOUNT DIDST REVEAL TO CHOSEN WITNESSES THINE   247 31

REVEALED

BY FAITH BEHOLD THE GLORY THAT SHALL BE REVEALEC   099 29
AS IT IS NOW REVEALED UNTC HIS HOLY APOSTLES AND   108 13
ASSURANCE OF THE GLORY THAT SHALL BE REVEALED   144 09
NOT AS THOU ART REVEALED IN THE GOSPEL OF THY SCN   157 08
WHICH SHALL BE REVEALED IN US   194 13
AND IT WAS REVEALED UNTO HIM BY THE HOLY GHOST,   232 33
THAT THE THOUGHTS OF MANY HEARTS MAY BE REVEALED   233 15
AND HAST REVEALED THEM UNTO BABES   235 05
LORD SHALL BE REVEALED, AND ALL FLESH SHALL SEE IT   242 25
BLOOD HATH NOT REVEALED IT UNTO THEE, BUT MY FATHER   246 05
WHICH SHALL BE REVEALED IN US   330 28

REVELATION

HOW THAT BY REVELATION HE MADE KNOWN UNTO ME THE   108 09

REVELLINGS

REVELLINGS, AND SUCH LIKE   209 23

REVENGER

OF GOD, A REVENGER TO EXECUTE WRATH UPON HIM THAT   114 21

REVERENCE

PROCURING OF REVERENCE, AND THE EXCITING OF PIETY AND   V 36
HEART AND DUE REVERENCE, THEY MAY HEAR, AND RECEIVE   074 27
CELEBRATE WITH REVERENCE THE PASCHAL FEAST, MAY BE   168 20
SEE THAT SHE REQUIRE HER HUSBAND   268 03
LOWLINESS AND REVERENCE WHICH BECOMETH A SERVANT OF   288 30
AND REJOICE UNTO HIM WITH REVERENCE   346 20
TO BE HAD IN REVERENCE OF ALL THEM THAT ARE ROUND   450 20
WITH GREATER REVERENCE FOR HIS GLORIOUS MAJESTY,   564 18

REVEREND

SHALL SAY, REVEREND FATHER IN GOD, I PRESENT UNTC YOU   296 08
HOLY AND REVEREND IS HIS NAME   483 12
HAD IN SUCH REVEREND ESTIMATION, THAT NO MAN MIGHT   529 14
THESE WORDS, REVEREND FATHER IN GOD, I PRESENT UNTO   530 10
AND SHALL SAY, REVEREND FATHER IN GOD, I PRESENT UNTO   536 10
HIM SAYING, REVEREND FATHER IN GOD,   552 21

REVERENTLY

THAT WE MAY REVERENTLY USE OUR FREEDOM, HELP US TO   044 12
STANDING REVERENTLY BEFORE THE HOLY TABLE, SHALL SAY   R 067 06

REVERENTLY   CONTINUED

AND REVERENTLY BRING IT TO THE PRIEST, WHO SHALL   R 073 29
AND REVERENTLY PLACE UPON IT WHAT REMAINETH OF   R 083 12
THE BLESSING, REVERENTLY EAT AND DRINK THE SAME   R 084 32
BUT REVERENTLY, DISCREETLY, ADVISEDLY, SOBERLY,   300 18
AND REVERENTLY USED AND ESTEEMED IN THIS CHURCH,   529 19
WILL YOU REVERENTLY OBEY YOUR BISHOP, AND OTHER CHIEF   533 30
WILL YOU REVERENTLY OBEY YOUR BISHOP, AND OTHER CHIEF   543 11
LOWLY AND REVERENTLY TO ALL MY BETTERS   580 06

REVIEW

COMMISSION FOR A REVIEW WAS ISSUED IN THE YEAR 1689   VI 04
WERE IN REVIEW BEFORE THE CONVENTION, THEY COULD NOT   VI 22
TO TAKE A FURTHER REVIEW OF THE PUBLIC SERVICE,   VI 25

REVIEWS

THESE DIFFERENT REVIEWS AND ALTERATIONS HATH BEEN,   V 33

REVILE

WHEN MEN SHALL REVILE YOU, AND PERSECUTE YOU, AND   257 31
8 MINE ENEMIES REVILE ME ALL THE DAY LONG   464 25

REVILED

THAT PASSED BY REVILED HIM, WAGGING THEIR HEADS, AND   137 05
WITH HIM REVILED HIM   146 25
HE WAS REVILED, REVILED NOT AGAIN   172 13
WHO, WHEN HE WAS REVILED, REVILED NOT AGAIN   172 13

REVISION

UNTIL A REVISION OF THEM MAY BE   R 610 27

REVIVE

AND TO REVIVE THE HEART OF THE CONTRITE CNES   003 28
HUMBLE SPIRIT, TO REVIVE THE SPIRIT OF THE HUMBLE,   003 28
THOUGHT PROPER TO REVIVE IT BY ANY NEW COMMISSION   VI 06

REVOLUTION

IN CONSEQUENCE OF THE REVOLUTION   VI 17

REWARD

NEITHER REWARD US ACCORDING TO OUR INIQUITIES   058 13
THYSELF A GOOD REWARD IN THE DAY OF NECESSITY   072 34
VERILY I SAY UNTO YOU, THEY HAVE THEIR REWARD   125 12
IN SECRET, SHALL REWARD THEE OPENLY   125 15
RECEIVE THE DUE REWARD OF OUR DEEDS   155 05
WHICH HATH GREAT RECOMPENCE OF REWARD   228 15
A FIELD WITH THE REWARD OF INIQUITY   234 13
BEHOLD, HIS REWARD IS WITH HIM, AND HIS WORK BEFCRE   243 07
THE LORD REWARD HIM ACCORDING TO HIS WORKS   254 07
FOR GREAT IS YOUR REWARD IN HEAVEN   257 33
WHICH REGARDETH NOT PERSONS, NOR TAKETH REWARD   263 25
LOVE YOU, WHAT REWARD HAVE YE   264 11
WHAT REWARD SHALL I GIVE UNTO THE LORD FOR ALL THE   305 27
NOR TAKEN REWARD AGAINST THE INNOCENT   357 18
AND IN KEEPING OF THEM THERE IS GREAT REWARD   364 07
4 REWARD THEM ACCORDING TO THEIR DEEDS, *   373 13
20 THEY ALSO THAT REWARD EVIL FOR GOOD ARE AGAINST   388 32
AND I SHALL REWARD THEM   392 20
5 HE SHALL REWARD EVIL UNTO MINE ENEMIES   406 12
VERILY THERE IS A REWARD FOR THE RIGHTEOUS   410 32
THEM FOR THEIR REWARD BE SOON BROUGHT TO SHAME,   424 25
REWARD THOU THEM, O LORD, SEVEN-FOLD INTO THEIR   440 30
AND SEE THE REWARD OF THE UNGODLY   455 12
AND REWARD THE PROUD AFTER THEIR DESERVING *   457 21
11 WHAT REWARD SHALL I GIVE UNTO THE LORD *   487 09
3 WHAT REWARD SHALL BE GIVEN OR DONE UNTO THEE,   502 11
REWARD ALL WHO HAVE DONE US GOOD, AND PARDON ALL   590 31

REWARDED

MAY BY THEE BE PLENTEOUSLY REWARDED   225 06
EVERLASTINGLY REWARDED, THROUGH THY MERCY, C BLESSED   278 29
4 IF I HAVE REWARDED EVIL UNTO HIM THAT DEALT   349 29
21 THE LORD REWARDED ME AFTER MY RIGHTEOUS DEALING,   361 06
THE LORD REWARDED ME AFTER MY RIGHTEOUS DEALING, *   361 15
12 THEY REWARDED ME EVIL FOR GOOD, *   382 15
AND REWARDED WITH SHAME, *   391 19
NOR REWARDED US ACCORDING TO OUR WICKEDNESSES   466 25
THUS HAVE THEY REWARDED ME EVIL FOR GOOD, *   480 11
THE LORD HATH REWARDED THEE   487 03

REWARDEST

FOR THOU REWARDEST EVERY MAN ACCORDING TO HIS WCRK   414 23

REWARDETH

PLENTEOUSLY REWARDETH THE PROUD DOER   377 16
HE BE THAT REWARDETH THEE AS THOU HAST SERVED US   513 22

RICH

AND THE RICH HE HATH SENT EMPTY AWAY   026 25
MAN HATH PREPARED A RICH FEAST, DECKED HIS TABLE WITH   088 18
AS POOR, YET MAKING MANY RICH   126 20
COME, THERE CAME A RICH MAN OF ARIMATHAEA, NAMED   162 06
THERE WAS A CERTAIN RICH MAN, WHICH WAS CLOTHED IN   190 03

RICH   CONTINUED

WHICH FELL FROM THE RICH MAN'S TABLE   190 07
THE RICH MAN ALSO DIED, AND WAS BURIED   190 10
LORD OVER ALL IS RICH UNTO ALL THAT CALL UPCN HIM   227 03
BUT THE RICH, IN THAT HE IS MADE LOW   239 19
SO ALSO SHALL THE RICH MAN FADE AWAY IN HIS WAYS   239 23
LIKE AS THE RICH ALSO AMONG THE PEOPLE SHALL MAKE   397 10
2 HIGH AND LOW, RICH AND POOR, *   400 09
THOUGH ONE BE MADE RICH, *   401 07

RICHER

FOR WORSE, FOR RICHER FOR POORER, IN SICKNESS ANC IN   301 30
FOR WORSE, FOR RICHER FOR POORER, IN SICKNESS ANC IN   302 06

RICHES

ACCORDING TO THE RICHES OF HIS GRACE   004 34
THE UNSEARCHABLE RICHES OF CHRIST   108 20
WITH CARES AND RICHES AND PLEASURES OF THIS LIFE,   122 07
ACCORDING TO THE RICHES OF HIS GLORY, TO BE   212 14
LOVE OF RICHES, AND TO FOLLOW THE SAME THY SON JESUS   250 23
HE HEAPETH UP RICHES, AND CANNOT TELL WHO SHALL   324 26
BETTER THAN GREAT RICHES OF THE UNGODLY   385 28
HE HEAPETH UP RICHES, AND CANNOT TELL WHO SHALL   389 07
BOAST THEMSELVES IN THE MULTITUDE OF THEIR RICHES   400 17
AND LEAVE THEIR RICHES FOR OTHER   400 25
MULTITUDE OF HIS RICHES, AND STRENGTHENED HIMSELF IN   405 02
IF RICHES INCREASE, SET NOT YOUR HEART UPCN THEM   414 19
AND THESE HAVE RICHES IN POSSESSION   428 33
THE EARTH IS FULL OF THY RICHES   469 09
3 RICHES AND PLENTEOUSNESS SHALL BE IN HIS HOUSE   483 22
AS IN ALL MANNER OF RICHES   490 26
THE RICHES AND GOODS OF CHRISTIANS ARE NOT COMMCN,   610 44

RICHLY

DWELL IN YOU RICHLY IN ALL WISDOM   116 11

RID

THOU SHALT RID ME FROM THE WICKED MAN   363 04
BUT RID ME AND DELIVER ME IN THY RIGHTEOUSNESS   425 06

RIDE

RIDE ON, BECAUSE OF THE WORD OF TRUTH, OF MEEKNESS,   396 22
SUFFEREDST MEN TO RIDE OVER OUR HEADS   418 04

RIDETH

MAGNIFY HIM THAT RIDETH UPON THE HEAVENS   419 17

RIGHT

SITTEST AT THE RIGHT HAND OF GOD, IN THE GLORY CF THE   010 30
AND SITTETH ON THE RIGHT HAND CF GOD THE FATHER   015 26
AND SITTETH ON THE RIGHT HAND OF THE FATHER   016 11
SITTETH ON THE RIGHT HAND OF GOD   022 20
SITTEST AT THE RIGHT HAND OF GOD THE FATHER, HAVE   025 31
WITH HIS OWN RIGHT HAND, AND WITH HIS HCLY ARM,   027 06
AND SITTETH ON THE RIGHT HAND OF GOD THE FATHER   029 31
AND SITTETH ON THE RIGHT HAND OF THE FATHER   030 16
WHO SITTEST IN THE THRONE JUDGING RIGHT   035 32
WHERE IT IS RIGHT, ESTABLISH IT   037 19
GIVE THEM A RIGHT UNDERSTANDING OF THEMSELVES, AND CF   046 21
UNIVERSAL IN THE RIGHT WAY   055 20
AND RENEW A RIGHT SPIRIT WITHIN ME   060 30
AND SITTETH ON THE RIGHT HAND OF THE FATHER   071 14
IT IS MEET AND RIGHT SO TO DO   076 29
IT IS VERY MEET, RIGHT, AND OUR BOUNDEN DUTY, THAT WE   076 31
SITTEST AT THE RIGHT HAND OF GOD THE FATHER, HAVE   084 11
SAT DOWN ON THE RIGHT HAND OF THE MAJESTY CN HIGH   096 29
STANDEST AT THE RIGHT HAND OF GOD TO SUCCOUR ALL   099 32
STANDING AT THE RIGHT HAND OF GOD, AND SAID, BEHCLD,   100 07
STANDING ON THE RIGHT HAND OF GOD   100 09
STRETCH FORTH THY RIGHT HAND TO HELP AND DEFEND US   112 28
AND WHATSOEVER IS RIGHT I WILL GIVE YOU   119 21
AND WHATSOEVER IS RIGHT, THAT SHALL YE RECEIVE   119 28
ON THE RIGHT HAND AND ON THE LEFT, BY HCNCUR AND   126 15
STRETCH FORTH THE RIGHT HAND OF THY MAJESTY, TO BE   128 27
AND A REED IN HIS RIGHT HAND   136 19
ONE ON THE RIGHT HAND, AND ANOTHER ON THE LEFT   137 04
LED THEM BY THE RIGHT HAND OF MOSES WITH HIS GLCRIOUS   139 11
MAN SITTING ON THE RIGHT HAND OF POWER, AND COMING IN   143 15
THE ONE ON HIS RIGHT HAND, AND THE OTHER CN HIS LEFT   146 15
AND CUT OFF HIS RIGHT EAR   150 33
OF MAN SIT ON THE RIGHT HAND OF THE POWER CF GOD   151 33
ONE ON THE RIGHT HAND, AND THE OTHER ON THE LEFT   154 24
SAT DOWN ON THE RIGHT HAND OF GOD   158 06
AND IS ON THE RIGHT HAND OF GOD   162 02
SITTETH ON THE RIGHT HAND OF GOD   164 04
MAN SITTING ON THE RIGHT SIDE, CLOTHED IN A LONG   165 27
SPIRIT TO HAVE A RIGHT JUDGMENT IN ALL THINGS,   180 11
TO THINK AND DO ALWAYS SUCH THINGS AS ARE RIGHT   200 30
AND HE SAID UNTO HIM, THOU HAST ANSWERED RIGHT   208 18
SIT THOU ON MY RIGHT HAND, TILL I MAKE THINE ENEMIES   215 20
STRANGER FROM HIS RIGHT, AND FEAR NOT ME, SAITH THE   232 20
THE ONE ON THY RIGHT HAND, AND THE OTHER CN THE LEFT,   247 10
BUT TO SIT ON MY RIGHT HAND, AND ON MY LEFT, IS NOT   247 16
IS SET DOWN AT THE RIGHT HAND OF THE THRONE OF GOC   258 26
THE SHEEP ON HIS RIGHT HAND, BUT THE GOATS ON THE   259 02
UNTO THEM ON HIS RIGHT HAND, COME, YE BLESSED OF MY   259 03
IT IS MEET AND RIGHT SO TO DO   279 05
IT IS VERY MEET, RIGHT, AND OUR BOUNDEN DUTY, THAT WE   279 07

RIGHT   CONTINUED

AND SITTETH ON THE RIGHT HAND OF GOD THE FATHER   284 20
TO THINK AND DO ALWAYS SUCH THINGS AS ARE RIGHT   287 27
THE MAN ON THE RIGHT HAND, AND THE WOMAN ON THE LEFT, R   300 06
THE MAN WITH HIS RIGHT HAND TO TAKE THE WOMAN BY HER R   301 26
THE WOMAN BY HER RIGHT HAND, AND TO SAY AFTER HIM AS R   301 26
THE WOMAN WITH HER RIGHT HAND TAKING THE MAN BY HIS   R   302 02
THE MAN BY HIS RIGHT HAND, SHALL LIKEWISE SAY AFTER   R   302 03
JOIN THEIR RIGHT HANDS TOGETHER, AND SAY, THCSE WHOM R   303 30
THE YEARS OF THE RIGHT HAND OF THE MOST HIGHEST   311 19
AND THY RIGHT HAND SHALL SAVE ME   312 06
HELP HER, AND THAT RIGHT EARLY   327 13
DEFENCE UPON THY RIGHT HAND   327 28
WHO IS EVEN AT THE RIGHT HAND OF GOD, WHO ALSO MAKETH   331 05
OF JOY, AND AT THY RIGHT HAND THERE IS PLEASURE FCR   333 10
MAY BE SET ON HIS RIGHT HAND, AND HEAR THAT HIS MOST   336 25
DEFENCE UPON THY RIGHT HAND   339 12
YE PERISH FROM THE RIGHT WAY, IF HIS WRATH BE   346 22
HAST MAINTAINED MY RIGHT AND MY CAUSE   351 28
THOU ART SET IN THE THRONE THAT JUDGEST RIGHT   351 29
POOR UNTO THEIR RIGHT, *   354 15
THE THING WHICH IS RIGHT, AND SPEAKETH THE TRUTH FRCM   357 08
FOR HE IS ON MY RIGHT HAND, THEREFORE I SHALL NCT   358 07
AND AT THY RIGHT HAND THERE IS PLEASURE FOR EVERMORE   358 13
HEAR THE RIGHT, O LORD, CONSIDER MY COMPLAINT,   358 16
SUCH AS RESIST THY RIGHT HAND   358 33
THY RIGHT HAND ALSO SHALL HOLD ME UP, AND THY LOVING   362 07
OF THE LORD ARE RIGHT, AND REJOICE THE HEART   363 30
STRENGTH OF HIS RIGHT HAND   364 28
THY RIGHT HAND SHALL FIND OUT THEM THAT HATE THEE   365 20
AND THEIR RIGHT HAND IS FULL OF GIFTS   371 16
12 MY FOOT STANDETH RIGHT   371 20
AND LEAD ME IN THE RIGHT WAY, BECAUSE CF MINE   372 23
GAT ME TO MY LORD RIGHT HUMBLY   375 09
28 FOR THE LORD LOVETH THE THING THAT IS RIGHT   386 19
AND TAKE HEED UNTO THE THING THAT IS RIGHT   387 09
4 BUT THY RIGHT HAND, AND THINE ARM, AND THE LIGHT CF   394 30
AND THY RIGHT HAND SHALL TEACH THEE TERRIBLE THINGS   396 24
THY KINGDOM IS A RIGHT SCEPTRE   396 28
UPON THY RIGHT HAND DOTH STAND THE QUEEN IN A VESTURE   397 03
HELP HER, AND THAT RIGHT EARLY   398 03
THY RIGHT HAND IS FULL OF RIGHTEOUSNESS   399 30
AND RENEW A RIGHT SPIRIT WITHIN ME   403 29
ISRAEL SHOULD BE RIGHT GLAD   405 32
MYSELF WILL AWAKE RIGHT EARLY   409 32
THE THING THAT IS RIGHT, O YE SONS OF MEN   410 08
HELP ME WITH THY RIGHT HAND, AND HEAR ME   412 22
THY RIGHT HAND HATH UPHOLDEN ME   415 09
ACCORDING UNTO RIGHT, *   426 33
FOLK BY THEIR RIGHT, *   427 04
HOLDEN ME BY MY RIGHT HAND   429 23
THOU NOT THY RIGHT HAND OUT OF THY BCSOM TO CCNSUME   430 30
I SHALL JUDGE ACCORDING UNTO RIGHT   432 03
THE YEARS OF THE RIGHT HAND OF THE MOST HIGHEST   434 03
PURCHASED WITH HIS RIGHT HAND   438 20
VINEYARD THAT THY RIGHT HAND HATH PLANTED, *   441 32
THE MAN OF THY RIGHT HAND, *   442 04
THAT SUCH AS ARE IN NEED AND NECESSITY HAVE RIGHT   443 23
AND HIGH IS THY RIGHT HAND   450 34
AND HIS RIGHT HAND IN THE FLOODS   451 25
HAST SET UP THE RIGHT HAND OF HIS ENEMIES, *   452 24
THOUSAND AT THY RIGHT HAND   455 10
2 WITH HIS OWN RIGHT HAND, AND WITH HIS HOLY ARM,   461 27
HEAR ME, AND THAT RIGHT SOON   464 14
THEM FORTH BY THE RIGHT WAY, *   476 17
MYSELF WILL AWAKE RIGHT EARLY   479 07
LET THY RIGHT HAND SAVE THEM, AND HEAR THOU ME   479 15
STAND AT HIS RIGHT HAND   480 14
SHALL STAND AT THE RIGHT HAND OF THE POOR, *   482 02
SIT THOU ON MY RIGHT HAND, UNTIL I MAKE THINE ENEMIES   482 07
THE LORD UPON THY RIGHT HAND *   482 16
RIGHT DEAR IN THE SIGHT OF THE LORD IS THE DEATH OF   487 14
THE RIGHT HAND OF THE LORD BRINGETH MIGHTY THINGS TO   488 31
16 THE RIGHT HAND OF THE LORD HATH THE PRE-EMINENCE   488 33
THE RIGHT HAND OF THE LORD BRINGETH MIGHTY THINGS TC   488 34
THY JUDGMENTS ARE RIGHT, *   495 04
I DEAL WITH THE THING THAT IS LAWFUL AND RIGHT   498 11
DEFENCE UPON THY RIGHT HAND   502 31
LET MY RIGHT HAND FORGET HER CUNNING   513 13
AND THY RIGHT HAND SHALL SAVE ME   514 12
AND THY RIGHT HAND SHALL HOLD ME   515 07
MY SOUL KNOWETH RIGHT WELL   515 17
I HATE THEM RIGHT SORE   516 02
ALSO UPON MY RIGHT HAND, *   518 10
AND THEIR RIGHT HAND IS A RIGHT HAND OF WICKEDNESS   520 06
RIGHT HAND IS A RIGHT HAND OF WICKEDNESS   520 07
AND THEIR RIGHT HAND IS A RIGHT HAND OF   520 13
RIGHT HAND IS A RIGHT HAND OF INIQUITY   520 14
HELPETH THEM TO RIGHT THAT SUFFER WRONG   522 14
BY MAKING A RIGHT USE OF IT, TO THE GLCRY OF THY   566 33
STANDING ON THE RIGHT AND LEFT OF THE ALTAR, WITHOUT R   570 08
AND SITTETH ON THE RIGHT HAND OF GOD THE FATHER   578 04
AS TOUCHING THE RIGHT, TITLE, AND POSSESSION OF THE   610 44

RIGHTEOUS

LIVE A GODLY, RIGHTEOUS, AND SOBER LIFE, TO THE GLORY   006 29
SOULS OF THE RIGHTEOUS, BLESS YE THE LORD   013 26
MAY BE RIGHTEOUS IN THY SIGHT   017 18
LIVE A GODLY, RIGHTEOUS, AND SOBER LIFE, TO THE GLORY   024 04
WITH THE FATHER, JESUS CHRIST THE RIGHTEOUS   076 23
COME ALL THE RIGHTEOUS BLOOD SHED UPON THE EARTH,   100 23
THE BLOOD OF RIGHTEOUS ABEL UNTO THE BLOOD OF   100 24
IS RIGHTEOUS, EVEN AS HE IS RIGHTEOUS   117 27
IS RIGHTEOUS, EVEN AS HE IS RIGHTEOUS   117 27

RIGHTEOUS   CONTINUED

THIS WAS A RIGHTEOUS MAN   155 16
ARE OVER THE RIGHTEOUS, AND HIS EARS ARE OPEN UNTO   195 28
THAT THEY WERE RIGHTEOUS, AND DESPISED OTHERS   205 22
UNTO DAVID A RIGHTEOUS BRANCH, AND A KING SHALL REIGN   225 10
TO CALL THE RIGHTEOUS, BUT SINNERS TO REPENTANCE   251 23
THE LORD, THE RIGHTEOUS JUDGE, SHALL GIVE ME AT THAT   253 29
THEN SHALL THE RIGHTEOUS ANSWER HIM, SAYING, LORD,   259 09
GRACIOUS IS THE LORD, AND RIGHTEOUS   305 25
THE SINNERS IN THE CONGREGATION OF THE RIGHTEOUS   345 21
7 BUT THE LORD KNOWETH THE WAY OF THE RIGHTEOUS   345 25
UNTO THE RIGHTEOUS, *   348 29
10 FOR THE RIGHTEOUS GOD *   350 11
12 GOD IS A RIGHTEOUS JUDGE, STRONG, AND PATIENT   350 15
WHAT CAN THE RIGHTEOUS DO   354 25
6 THE LORD APPROVETH THE RIGHTEOUS   354 30
8 FOR THE RIGHTEOUS LORD LOVETH RIGHTEOUSNESS   355 02
FOR GOD IS IN THE GENERATION OF THE RIGHTEOUS   356 26
ME AFTER MY RIGHTEOUS DEALING, *   361 06
ME AFTER MY RIGHTEOUS DEALING, *   361 15
ARE TRUE, AND RIGHTEOUS ALTOGETHER   364 02
7 GRACIOUS AND RIGHTEOUS IS THE LORD   369 33
AND RIGHTEOUS DEALING WAIT UPON ME   370 26
AND DESPITEFULLY SPEAK AGAINST THE RIGHTEOUS   376 34
BE GLAD, O YE RIGHTEOUS, AND REJOICE IN THE LORD   378 16
REJOICE IN THE LORD, O YE RIGHTEOUS   378 19
ARE OVER THE RIGHTEOUS, *   380 30
17 THE RIGHTEOUS CRY, AND THE LORD HEARETH THEM,   381 02
19 GREAT ARE THE TROUBLES OF THE RIGHTEOUS   381 06
THAT HATE THE RIGHTEOUS SHALL BE DESOLATE   381 11
THAT FAVOUR MY RIGHTEOUS DEALING   383 20
THING THAT THE RIGHTEOUS HATH, *   385 27
AND THE LORD UPHOLDETH THE RIGHTEOUS   385 30
BUT THE RIGHTEOUS IS MERCIFUL AND LIBERAL   386 05
I NEVER THE RIGHTEOUS FORSAKEN, NOR HIS SEED BEGGING   386 13
26 THE RIGHTEOUS IS EVER MERCIFUL, AND LENDETH   386 15
30 THE RIGHTEOUS SHALL INHERIT THE LAND, *   386 24
MOUTH OF THE RIGHTEOUS IS EXERCISED IN WISDOM,   386 26
WATCHETH THE RIGHTEOUS, *   386 30
OF THE RIGHTEOUS COMETH OF THE LORD   387 13
AND THE RIGHTEOUS SHALL HAVE DOMINION OVER THEM IN   401 02
7 THE RIGHTEOUS ALSO SHALL SEE THIS, AND FEAR,   404 31
NOT SUFFER THE RIGHTEOUS TO FALL FOR EVER   408 05
10 THE RIGHTEOUS SHALL REJOICE WHEN HE SEETH THE   410 29
VERILY THERE IS A REWARD FOR THE RIGHTEOUS   410 33
10 THE RIGHTEOUS SHALL REJOICE IN THE LORD, AND PUT   416 06
3 BUT LET THE RIGHTEOUS BE GLAD, AND REJOICE BEFORE   419 14
AND NOT BE WRITTEN AMONG THE RIGHTEOUS   423 33
TIME SHALL THE RIGHTEOUS FLOURISH   427 10
HORNS OF THE RIGHTEOUS SHALL BE EXALTED   432 22
11 THE RIGHTEOUS SHALL FLOURISH LIKE A PALM-TREE,   456 24
SOUL OF THE RIGHTEOUS, *   458 29
LIGHT FOR THE RIGHTEOUS, *   461 19
12 REJOICE IN THE LORD, YE RIGHTEOUS   461 21
42 THE RIGHTEOUS WILL CONSIDER THIS, AND REJOICE   478 30
HE IS MERCIFUL, LOVING, AND RIGHTEOUS   483 25
AND THE RIGHTEOUS SHALL BE HAD IN EVERLASTING   483 28
5 GRACIOUS IS THE LORD, AND RIGHTEOUS   486 28
AND HEALTH IS IN THE DWELLINGS OF THE RIGHTEOUS   488 31
THE RIGHTEOUS SHALL ENTER INTO IT   489 08
BECAUSE OF THY RIGHTEOUS JUDGMENTS   494 05
TO KEEP THY RIGHTEOUS JUDGMENTS   497 10
RIGHTEOUS ART THOU, O LORD   499 13
ARE EXCEEDING RIGHTEOUS AND TRUE   499 16
BECAUSE OF THY RIGHTEOUS JUDGMENTS   501 10
FOR ALL THY COMMANDMENTS ARE RIGHTEOUS   501 27
LEST THE RIGHTEOUS PUT THEIR HAND UNTO WICKEDNESS   504 30
SHALL NOT ABIDE UPON THE LOT OF THE RIGHTEOUS   504 30
4 BUT THE RIGHTEOUS LORD *   506 27
13 THE RIGHTEOUS ALSO SHALL GIVE THANKS UNTO THY   517 04
5 LET THE RIGHTEOUS RATHER SMITE ME FRIENDLY,   517 19
THEN SHALL THE RIGHTEOUS RESORT UNTO MY COMPANY   518 21
17 THE LORD IS RIGHTEOUS IN ALL HIS WAYS, *   521 26
THE LORD CARETH FOR THE RIGHTEOUS   522 19
THE RIGHTEOUS JUDGE, WHO LIVETH AND REIGNETH   559 14
IN A SOBER, RIGHTEOUS, AND GODLY LIFE   588 07
OF THY RIGHTEOUS LAWS   589 32
MAY BE RIGHTEOUS IN THY SIGHT   592 24
ARE ACCOUNTED RIGHTEOUS BEFORE GOD, ONLY FOR THE   605 06

RIGHTEOUSLY

THE FOLK RIGHTEOUSLY, AND GOVERN THE NATIONS UPON   028 24
RIGHTEOUSLY, AND GODLY, IN THIS PRESENT   098 20
COMMITTED HIMSELF TO HIM THAT JUDGETH RIGHTEOUSLY   172 14
THE FOLK RIGHTEOUSLY, AND GOVERN THE NATIONS UPON   418 31
HOW THAT HE SHALL JUDGE THE PEOPLES RIGHTEOUSLY   460 21
RIGHTEOUSLY, AND GODLY IN THIS PRESENT   555 09

RIGHTEOUSNESS

AND WITH RIGHTEOUSNESS TO JUDGE THE WORLD, AND THE   009 20
AND RIGHTEOUSNESS BEFORE HIM, *   014 22
THEM WITH THE LOVE OF TRUTH AND RIGHTEOUSNESS   018 12
AND IN RIGHTEOUSNESS OF LIFE   019 03
AND RIGHTEOUSNESS ALL OUR DAYS   019 29
HIS RIGHTEOUSNESS HATH HE OPENLY SHOWED IN THE SIGHT   027 08
WITH RIGHTEOUSNESS SHALL HE JUDGE THE WORLD, *   027 24
ENDUE THY MINISTERS WITH RIGHTEOUSNESS   031 06
AND IN RIGHTEOUSNESS OF LIFE   032 34
AND RIGHTEOUSNESS ALL OUR DAYS   033 27
AND THE RIGHTEOUSNESS THEREOF, ALL THINGS NECESSARY   040 17
AND IN RIGHTEOUSNESS, WITH SINGLENESS OF HEART AS THY   044 22
FRUIT OF RIGHTEOUSNESS, THAT THEY MAY BECOME THE   044 30
AND MY TONGUE SHALL SING OF THY RIGHTEOUSNESS   061 08

RIGHTEOUSNESS   CONTINUED

AND RIGHTEOUSNESS ALL THE DAYS OF THEIR LIFE   074 28
IN OUR OWN RIGHTEOUSNESS, BUT IN THY MANIFOLD AND   082 14
AND RIGHTEOUSNESS ALL THE DAYS OF OUR LIFE   086 22
SCEPTRE OF RIGHTEOUSNESS IS THE SCEPTRE OF THY   097 09
HAST LOVED RIGHTEOUSNESS, AND HATED INIQUITY   097 11
TREES OF RIGHTEOUSNESS, THE PLANTING OF THE LORD,   107 09
THAT DOETH RIGHTEOUSNESS IS RIGHTEOUS, EVEN AS HE IS   117 27
MOTIONS IN RIGHTEOUSNESS, AND TRUE HOLINESS, TO THY   125 30
ARMOUR OF RIGHTEOUSNESS ON THE RIGHT HAND AND ON THE   126 15
AND RIGHTEOUSNESS AND TRUTH   129 14
SPEAK IN RIGHTEOUSNESS, MIGHTY TO SAVE   138 14
WORKETH RIGHTEOUSNESS, IS ACCEPTED WITH HIM   166 14
DEAD TO SINS, SHOULD LIVE UNTO RIGHTEOUSNESS   172 17
THEY MAY RETURN INTO THE WAY OF RIGHTEOUSNESS   173 06
NOT THE RIGHTEOUSNESS OF GOD   175 02
AND OF RIGHTEOUSNESS, AND OF JUDGMENT   175 13
OF RIGHTEOUSNESS, BECAUSE I GO TO MY FATHER, AND YE   175 15
WORKETH RIGHTEOUSNESS, IS ACCEPTED WITH HIM   183 31
YOUR RIGHTEOUSNESS SHALL EXCEED THE RIGHTEOUSNESS OF   197 28
EXCEED THE RIGHTEOUSNESS OF THE SCRIBES AND   197 29
TO RIGHTEOUSNESS UNTO HOLINESS   198 29
SERVANTS OF SIN, YE WERE FREE FROM RIGHTEOUSNESS   198 31
OF RIGHTEOUSNESS EXCEED IN GLORY   206 24
VERILY RIGHTEOUSNESS SHOULD HAVE BEEN BY THE LAW   208 02
SEEK YE FIRST HIS KINGDOM, AND HIS RIGHTEOUSNESS   211 32
CREATED IN RIGHTEOUSNESS AND TRUE HOLINESS   216 15
AND HAVING ON THE BREASTPLATE OF RIGHTEOUSNESS   219 14
FRUITS OF RIGHTEOUSNESS, WHICH ARE BY JESUS CHRIST,   221 05
HE SHALL BE CALLED, THE LORD OUR RIGHTEOUSNESS   225 14
WITH THE HEART MAN BELIEVETH UNTO RIGHTEOUSNESS   226 29
OFFER UNTO THE LORD AN OFFERING IN RIGHTEOUSNESS   232 13
AND RIGHTEOUSNESS BEFORE HIM, ALL THE DAYS OF OUR   244 09
A CROWN OF RIGHTEOUSNESS, WHICH THE LORD, THE   253 28
WHICH DO HUNGER AND THIRST AFTER RIGHTEOUSNESS   257 25
IN RIGHTEOUSNESS AND PEACE   263 20
NOT THE RIGHTEOUSNESS OF GOD   265 25
FIRST THE KINGDOM OF GOD, AND HIS RIGHTEOUSNESS   266 30
AND THY RIGHTEOUSNESS, MAY OBTAIN THE MANIFOLD   267 07
LIVE UNTO RIGHTEOUSNESS, AND BEING BURIED WITH CHRIST   280 33
AND A NEW BIRTH UNTO RIGHTEOUSNESS   292 25
AND RIGHTEOUSNESS, ALL OUR DAYS   316 28
THE DEATH OF SIN UNTO THE LIFE OF RIGHTEOUSNESS   335 06
PATHS OF RIGHTEOUSNESS FOR HIS NAME'S SAKE   338 22
O GOD OF MY RIGHTEOUSNESS   347 10
OF RIGHTEOUSNESS, *   347 21
IN THY RIGHTEOUSNESS, BECAUSE OF MINE ENEMIES   348 16
TO MY RIGHTEOUSNESS, AND ACCORDING TO THE INNOCENCY   350 07
UNTO THE LORD, ACCORDING TO HIS RIGHTEOUSNESS   350 28
WORLD IN RIGHTEOUSNESS, *   352 04
8 FOR THE RIGHTEOUS LORD LOVETH RIGHTEOUSNESS   355 02
I SHALL BEHOLD THY PRESENCE IN RIGHTEOUSNESS   359 19
HIS RIGHTEOUSNESS *   368 06
PATHS OF RIGHTEOUSNESS FOR HIS NAME'S SAKE   368 15
AND RIGHTEOUSNESS FROM THE GOD OF HIS SALVATION   369 06
DELIVER ME IN THY RIGHTEOUSNESS   375 23
HE LOVETH RIGHTEOUSNESS AND JUDGMENT   378 27
ACCORDING TO THY RIGHTEOUSNESS   383 11
OF THY RIGHTEOUSNESS, *   383 24
6 THY RIGHTEOUSNESS STANDETH LIKE THE STRONG   384 06
AND THY RIGHTEOUSNESS UNTO THEM THAT ARE TRUE OF   384 17
MAKE THY RIGHTEOUSNESS AS CLEAR AS THE LIGHT,   385 04
THY RIGHTEOUSNESS IN THE GREAT CONGREGATION   390 34
HID THY RIGHTEOUSNESS WITHIN MY HEART   391 04
OF MEEKNESS, AND RIGHTEOUSNESS   396 23
HAST LOVED RIGHTEOUSNESS, AND HATED INIQUITY   396 29
THY RIGHT HAND IS FULL OF RIGHTEOUSNESS   399 30
6 AND THE HEAVENS SHALL DECLARE HIS RIGHTEOUSNESS   402 02
AND MY TONGUE SHALL SING OF THY RIGHTEOUSNESS   404 06
OF RIGHTEOUSNESS, WITH THE BURNT-OFFERINGS AND   404 16
AND FALSEHOOD MORE THAN RIGHTEOUSNESS   404 25
SET UPON RIGHTEOUSNESS, O YE CONGREGATION   410 07
IN THY RIGHTEOUSNESS, O GOD OF OUR SALVATION   416 21
AND NOT COME INTO THY RIGHTEOUSNESS   423 31
BUT RID ME AND DELIVER ME IN THY RIGHTEOUSNESS   425 07
OF THY RIGHTEOUSNESS AND SALVATION   426 04
OF THY RIGHTEOUSNESS ONLY   426 07
18 THY RIGHTEOUSNESS, O GOD, IS VERY HIGH, *   426 14
OF THY RIGHTEOUSNESS ALL THE DAY LONG   426 27
AND THY RIGHTEOUSNESS UNTO THE KING'S SON   426 31
HILLS RIGHTEOUSNESS UNTO THE PEOPLE   427 03
RIGHTEOUSNESS AND PEACE HAVE KISSED EACH OTHER   446 27
AND RIGHTEOUSNESS HATH LOOKED DOWN FROM HEAVEN   446 29
13 RIGHTEOUSNESS SHALL GO BEFORE HIM, *   446 33
AND THY RIGHTEOUSNESS IN THE LAND WHERE ALL THINGS   449 21
15 RIGHTEOUSNESS AND EQUITY ARE THE HABITATION OF THY 451 02
AND IN THY RIGHTEOUSNESS SHALL THEY MAKE THEIR BOAST   451 07
15 UNTIL RIGHTEOUSNESS TURN AGAIN UNTO JUDGMENT   458 16
AND WITH RIGHTEOUSNESS TO JUDGE THE WORLD, AND THE   460 27
RIGHTEOUSNESS AND JUDGMENT ARE THE HABITATION OF HIS   460 32
HIS RIGHTEOUSNESS, *   461 08
HIS RIGHTEOUSNESS HATH HE OPENLY SHOWED IN THE SIGHT   461 29
10 WITH RIGHTEOUSNESS SHALL HE JUDGE THE WORLD,   462 13
AND RIGHTEOUSNESS IN JACOB   462 23
EXECUTETH RIGHTEOUSNESS AND JUDGMENT *   466 17
AND HIS RIGHTEOUSNESS UPON CHILDREN'S CHILDREN   467 09
AND DO RIGHTEOUSNESS   473 05
HIM FOR RIGHTEOUSNESS, *   474 31
AND HIS RIGHTEOUSNESS ENDURETH FOR EVER   482 29
AND HIS RIGHTEOUSNESS ENDURETH FOR EVER   483 23
AND HIS RIGHTEOUSNESS REMAINETH FOR EVER   484 02
GATES OF RIGHTEOUSNESS, *   489 06
HAVE LEARNED THE JUDGMENTS OF THY RIGHTEOUSNESS   490 13
O QUICKEN ME IN THY RIGHTEOUSNESS   492 20
AND FOR THE WORD OF THY RIGHTEOUSNESS   498 16

RIGHTEOUSNESS   CONTINUED

RIGHTEOUSNESS, *   499 23
142 THY RIGHTEOUSNESS IS AN EVERLASTING   499 23
144 THE RIGHTEOUSNESS OF THY TESTIMONIES IS   499 27
OF THY RIGHTEOUSNESS ENDURE FOR EVERMORE   500 32
9 LET THY PRIESTS BE CLOTHED WITH RIGHTEOUSNESS   508 21
LEAD ME FORTH INTO THE LAND OF RIGHTEOUSNESS   519 14
AND MEN SHALL SING OF THY RIGHTEOUSNESS   521 07
WITH RIGHTEOUSNESS, AND THAT THY WORD SPOKEN BY THEIR   547 06
CROWN OF RIGHTEOUSNESS, LAID UP BY THE LORD JESUS,   559 13
LET THY PRIESTS BE CLOTHED WITH RIGHTEOUSNESS   562 04
AND RIGHTEOUSNESS FROM THE GOD OF HIS SALVATION   563 21
AND A NEW BIRTH UNTO RIGHTEOUSNESS   581 24
ORIGINAL RIGHTEOUSNESS, AND IS OF HIS OWN NATURE   604 32

RIGHTEOUSNESS'

FOR RIGHTEOUSNESS' SAKE, HAPPY ARE YE   196 02
FOR RIGHTEOUSNESS' SAKE   257 29
TRUTH AND RIGHTEOUSNESS' SAKE   518 24
FOR THY RIGHTEOUSNESS' SAKE BRING MY SOUL OUT OF   519 16

RIGHTLY

LIVELY WORD, AND RIGHTLY AND DULY ADMINISTER THY HOLY   074 23
AS BY FAITH, AND RIGHTLY, DO RECEIVE THE SACRAMENTS   608 16
RECEIVE BAPTISM RIGHTLY ARE GRAFTED INTO THE CHURCH   608 27
THAT TO SUCH AS RIGHTLY, WORTHILY, AND WITH FAITH,   608 36
OF THE CHURCH IS RIGHTLY CUT OFF FROM THE UNITY OF   609 26
ALL SUCH TO BE RIGHTLY, ORDERLY, AND LAWFULLY   610 36

RING

AND PUT A RING ON HIS HAND, AND SHOES ON HIS FEET   202 22
UNTO THE WOMAN A RING ON THIS WISE   R 302 10
MINISTER TAKING THE RING SHALL DELIVER IT UNTO THE   R 302 12
THE MAN HOLDING THE RING THERE, AND TAUGHT BY THE   R 302 12
WITH THIS RING I THEE WED   302 14
DELIVERING THE RING TO THE MAN, THE MINISTER MAY SAY   R 302 17
BLESS, O LORD, THIS RING, THAT HE WHO GIVES IT AND   302 19
THE MAN LEAVING THE RING UPON THE FOURTH FINGER OF   R 302 22
(WHEREOF THIS RING GIVEN AND RECEIVED IS A   303 09
AND RECEIVING A RING, AND BY JOINING HANDS   304 07

RIOTING

NOT IN RIOTING AND DRUNKENNESS, NOT IN CHAMBERING AND   091 06

RIOTOUS

SUBSTANCE WITH RIOTOUS LIVING   202 04

RIPENESS

AND TO THAT RIPENESS AND PERFECTNESS OF AGE IN   540 20

RIPER

PERSONS AS ARE OF RIPER YEARS ARE TO BE BAPTIZED,   R 273 17
YE MAY WAX RIPER AND STRONGER IN YOUR MINISTRY   541 19

RISE

THE DEAD, WE MAY RISE TO THE LIFE IMMORTAL, THROUGH   090 17
AND HE THAT SHALL RISE TO REIGN OVER THE GENTILES   092 31
THIRD DAY HE SHALL RISE AGAIN   123 23
RISE UP, LET US GO   142 13
RISE AND PRAY, LEST YE ENTER INTO TEMPTATION   150 25
THREE DAYS I WILL RISE AGAIN   162 19
THAT HE MUST RISE AGAIN FROM THE DEAD   164 27
TO SUFFER, AND TO RISE FROM THE DEAD THE THIRD DAY   170 13
OUR SINS, AND TO RISE AGAIN FOR OUR JUSTIFICATION   170 20
I CANNOT RISE AND GIVE THEE   262 32
THOUGH HE WILL NOT RISE AND GIVE HIM, BECAUSE HE IS   262 33
IMPORTUNITY HE WILL RISE AND GIVE HIM AS MANY AS HE   263 02
MAKETH HIS SUN TO RISE ON THE EVIL AND ON THE GOOD,   264 09
IN CHRIST SHALL RISE FIRST   269 07
MAY DIE TO SIN AND RISE TO NEWNESS OF LIFE   278 20
MANY ARE THEY THAT RISE AGAINST ME   309 15
MANY ARE THEY THAT RISE AGAINST ME   346 26
OR WHO SHALL RISE UP IN HIS HOLY PLACE   368 33
FALSE WITNESSES DID RISE UP   382 13
HE LIETH, HE SHALL RISE UP NO MORE   392 16
THEM UNDER THAT RISE UP AGAINST US   395 03
ME FROM THEM THAT RISE UP AGAINST ME   411 05
OR SHALL THE DEAD RISE UP AGAIN, AND PRAISE THEE   449 17
16 WHO WILL RISE UP WITH ME AGAINST THE WICKED   458 18
BE CONFOUNDED THAT RISE UP AGAINST ME   481 27
AT MIDNIGHT I WILL RISE TO GIVE THANKS UNTO THEE,   494 04
THAT YE HASTE TO RISE UP EARLY, AND SO LATE TAKE   505 26
WITH THOSE THAT RISE UP AGAINST THEE   515 33
THAT THEY NEVER RISE UP AGAIN   516 30
OR WHO SHALL RISE UP IN HIS HOLY PLACE   563 16
CHRIST DID TRULY RISE AGAIN FROM DEATH, AND TOOK   603 21

RISEN

THE LORD IS RISEN INDEED   005 02
HE IS RISEN   005 02
THE LORD IS RISEN INDEED   R 008 24
IF YE THEN BE RISEN WITH CHRIST, SEEK THOSE THINGS   022 19
AFTER THAT I AM RISEN, I WILL GO BEFORE YOU INTO   141 20
THE PEOPLE, HE IS RISEN FROM THE DEAD   162 21
CHRIST IS RISEN FROM THE DEAD, *   163 11
IF YE THEN BE RISEN WITH CHRIST, SEEK THOSE THINGS   164 03

RISEN   CONTINUED

HE IS RISEN   165 30
THE LORD IS RISEN INDEED, AND HATH APPEARED TO SIMON   168 13
A GREAT PROPHET IS RISEN UP AMONG US   213 08
SUN IS NO SOONER RISEN WITH A BURNING HEAT, BUT IT   239 21
NOW IS CHRIST RISEN FROM THE DEAD, AND BECOME THE   328 21
THAT IS RISEN AGAIN, WHO IS EVEN AT THE RIGHT   331 04
BUT WE ARE RISEN AND STAND UPRIGHT   364 31
FALSE WITNESSES RISEN UP AGAINST ME, AND SUCH AS   372 25
FOR STRANGERS ARE RISEN UP AGAINST ME   406 07
THE PROUD ARE RISEN AGAINST ME   447 32
4 THE FLOODS ARE RISEN, O LORD, THE FLOODS HAVE LIFT   457 11

RISETH

HE RISETH FROM SUPPER, AND LAID ASIDE HIS GARMENTS   155 30
AND LIGHT RISETH UP IN DARKNESS FOR THE GODLY   595 27

RISING

FROM THE RISING OF THE SUN EVEN UNTO THE GOING DOWN   004 12
AND KINGS TO THE BRIGHTNESS OF THY RISING   022 03
AND BY HIS RISING TO LIFE AGAIN HATH RESTORED   078 11
SEPULCHRE AT THE RISING OF THE SUN   165 22
FOR THE FALL AND RISING AGAIN OF MANY IN ISRAEL   233 12
FROM THE RISING UP OF THE SUN UNTO THE GOING   401 22
FROM THE RISING UP OF THE SUN UNTO THE GOING DOWN OF   484 12

RITES

AND THE RITES AND CEREMONIES APPOINTED TO BE   V 14
CEREMONIES AND RITES, DO NOT BIND CHRISTIAN MEN, NOR   604 20
POWER TO DECREE RITES OR CEREMONIES, AND AUTHORITY IN   607 03
CEREMONIES OR RITES OF THE CHURCH ORDAINED ONLY BY   610 02

RIVER

THERE IS A RIVER, THE STREAMS WHEREOF SHALL MAKE GLAD   022 26
OF HIM IN THE RIVER OF JORDAN, CONFESSING THEIR SINS   112 11
THERE IS A RIVER, THE STREAMS WHEREOF MAKE GLAD THE   327 09
THEM DRINK OF THY PLEASURES, AS OUT OF THE RIVER   384 13
4 THERE IS A RIVER, THE STREAMS WHEREOF MAKE GLAD THE   397 32
10 THE RIVER OF GOD IS FULL OF WATER   417 02
AND FROM THE RIVER UNTO THE WORLD'S END   427 13
AND HER BOUGHS UNTO THE RIVER   441 25

RIVERS

SO THAT IT GUSHED OUT LIKE THE RIVERS   435 34
SO THAT THEY MIGHT NOT DRINK OF THE RIVERS   437 30
SPRINGS INTO THE RIVERS, *   468 13
SO THAT RIVERS RAN IN THE DRY PLACES   472 20
AS THE RIVERS IN THE SOUTH   505 15

ROAR

5 THINE ADVERSARIES ROAR IN THE MIDST OF THY   430 12

ROARED

I HAVE ROARED FOR THE VERY DISQUIETNESS OF MY HEART   388 06

ROARING

THE SEA AND THE WAVES ROARING   093 07
THE DEVIL, AS A ROARING LION, WALKETH ABOUT, SEEKING   193 05
A RAMPING AND A ROARING LION   366 30
21 THE LIONS, ROARING AFTER THEIR PREY, *   469 02

ROBBED

5 THE PROUD ARE ROBBED, THEY HAVE SLEPT THEIR SLEEP   432 30

ROBBER

THE SAME IS A THIEF AND A ROBBER   186 02
THE SAME IS A THIEF AND A ROBBER   538 25

ROBBERS

IN PERILS OF ROBBERS, IN PERILS BY MINE OWN   121 05
THAT EVER CAME BEFORE ME ARE THIEVES AND ROBBERS   186 14
WHEN THOU COMEST FROM THE HILLS OF THE ROBBERS   432 29
THAT EVER CAME BEFORE ME ARE THIEVES AND ROBBERS   539 05

ROBBERY

THOUGHT IT NOT ROBBERY TO BE EQUAL WITH GOD   134 17
10 O TRUST NOT IN WRONG AND ROBBERY   414 18

ROBE

THEY STRIPPED HIM, AND PUT ON HIM A SCARLET ROBE   136 18
THEY TOOK THE ROBE OFF FROM HIM, AND PUT HIS OWN   136 23
HIM IN A GORGEOUS ROBE, AND SENT HIM AGAIN TO PILATE   153 18
PUT ON HIM A PURPLE ROBE, AND SAID, HAIL, KING OF THE   158 32
WEARING THE CROWN OF THORNS, AND THE PURPLE ROBE   159 04
FORTH THE BEST ROBE, AND PUT IT ON HIM   202 21

ROBES

CLOTHED WITH WHITE ROBES, AND PALMS IN THEIR HANDS   256 26
WHAT ARE THESE WHICH ARE ARRAYED IN WHITE ROBES   257 05
HAVE WASHED THEIR ROBES, AND MADE THEM WHITE IN THE   257 08

ROCHET

VESTED WITH HIS ROCHET, SHALL BE PRESENTED BY TWO   R 552 17

ROCK

AND SOME FELL UPON A ROCK   121 22
THEY ON THE ROCK ARE THEY, WHICH, WHEN THEY HEAR,   122 02
OWN NEW TOMB, WHICH HE HAD HEWN OUT IN THE ROCK   162 12
OF THAT SPIRITUAL ROCK THAT FOLLOWED THEM   201 10
AND THAT ROCK WAS CHRIST   201 11
AND UPON THIS ROCK I WILL BUILD MY CHURCH   246 07
SET ME UP UPON A ROCK OF STONE   326 14
LORD IS MY STONY ROCK, AND MY DEFENCE   359 25
SET ME UP UPON A ROCK OF STONE   372 06
BE THOU MY STRONG ROCK, AND HOUSE OF DEFENCE,   375 25
THOU ART MY STRONG ROCK, AND MY CASTLE   375 27
MY FEET UPON THE ROCK, AND ORDERED MY GOINGS   390 12
SET ME UP UPON THE ROCK THAT IS HIGHER THAN I   413 10
THE ROCK OF MY MIGHT   414 11
OUT OF THE STONY ROCK, *   435 33
HE SMOTE THE STONY ROCK INDEED, THAT THE WATER GUSHED   436 08
OUT OF THE STONY ROCK WOULD I HAVE SATISFIED THEE   443 14
40 HE OPENED THE ROCK OF STONE, AND THE WATERS FLOWED   472 19
WHO TURNED THE HARD ROCK INTO A STANDING WATER,   485 08

ROCKS

DID QUAKE, AND THE ROCKS RENT   137 27
OUT FOUNTAINS AND WATERS OUT OF THE HARD ROCKS   431 07
HE CLAVE THE HARD ROCKS IN THE WILDERNESS, *   435 30
SO ARE THE STONY ROCKS FOR THE CONIES   468 31

ROD

THY ROD AND THY STAFF COMFORT ME   338 24
BRUISE THEM WITH A ROD OF IRON, *   346 15
THY ROD AND THY STAFF COMFORT ME   368 18
OFFENCES WITH THE ROD, AND THEIR SIN WITH SCOURGES   452 05
LORD SHALL SEND THE ROD OF THY POWER OUT OF SION   482 09

RODE

11 HE RODE UPON THE CHERUBIM, AND DID FLY   360 17

RODS

WAS I BEATEN WITH RODS, ONCE WAS I STONED, THRICE I   121 02

ROGATION

SUNDAY AND THE ROGATION DAYS   R 039 23
TO BE USED ON ROGATION SUNDAY AND THE ROGATION DAYS   R 039 23

ROLL

WHO SHALL ROLL US AWAY THE STONE FROM THE DOOR OF THE   165 23

ROLLED

AND HE ROLLED A GREAT STONE TO THE DOOR OF THE   162 12
THE STONE WAS ROLLED AWAY   165 25

ROME

AND STRANGERS OF ROME, JEWS AND PROSELYTES, CRETES   181 04
ALSO THE CHURCH OF ROME HATH ERRED, NOT ONLY IN THEIR   606 43

ROMISH

THE ROMISH DOCTRINE CONCERNING PURGATORY, PARDONS,   607 14

ROOF

NOT WORTHY THAT THOU SHOULDEST COME UNDER MY ROOF   115 11
CLEAVE TO THE ROOF OF MY MOUTH   513 16
NOT WORTHY THAT THOU SHOULDEST COME UNDER MY ROOF   573 12

ROOM

THERE WAS NO ROOM FOR THEM IN THE INN   099 09
IN JUDAEA IN THE ROOM OF HIS FATHER HEROD, HE WAS   107 18
YOU A LARGE UPPER ROOM FURNISHED AND PREPARED   140 31
YOU A LARGE UPPER ROOM FURNISHED   148 31
AS THOU HAST COMMANDED, AND YET THERE IS ROOM   192 17
37 THOU SHALT MAKE ROOM ENOUGH UNDER ME FOR TO GO,   362 09
BUT HAST SET MY FEET IN A LARGE ROOM   376 07
9 THOU MADEST ROOM FOR IT   441 20

ROOT

THERE SHALL BE A ROOT OF JESSE, AND HE THAT SHALL   092 30
UP THE TARES, YE ROOT UP ALSO THE WHEAT WITH THEM   116 28
AND THESE HAVE NO ROOT, WHICH FOR A WHILE BELIEVE,   122 03
3 THE LORD SHALL ROOT OUT ALL DECEITFUL LIPS,   355 12
FRUIT SHALT THOU ROOT OUT OF THE EARTH, *   365 25
TO ROOT OUT THE REMEMBRANCE OF THEM FROM THE EARTH   380 33
THY DWELLING, AND ROOT THEE OUT OF THE LAND OF THE   404 29
WHEN IT HAD TAKEN ROOT, IT FILLED THE LAND   441 21
OF THE WOOD DOTH ROOT IT UP, *   441 28
COME, AND LET US ROOT THEM OUT, THAT THEY BE NO MORE   444 11
THAT I MAY ROOT OUT ALL WICKED DOERS FROM THE CITY OF   464 05
THAT HE MAY ROOT OUT THE MEMORIAL OF THEM FROM OFF   480 31
BESEECH THEE, EVERY ROOT OF BITTERNESS, THE DESIRE OF   598 22

ROOTED

THAT YE, BEING ROOTED AND GROUNDED IN LOVE, MAY BE   212 17
DOERS SHALL BE ROOTED OUT   385 11
OF HIM, SHALL BE ROOTED OUT   386 07
IT SHALL BE ROOTED OUT   386 23
THEY SHALL BE ROOTED OUT AT THE LAST   387 11
LET THEM BE ROOTED OUT   410 22

ROSE

THE THIRD DAY HE ROSE AGAIN FROM THE DEAD   015 24
THE THIRD DAY HE ROSE AGAIN ACCORDING TO THE   016 10
THE THIRD DAY HE ROSE AGAIN FROM THE DEAD   029 29
THE THIRD DAY HE ROSE AGAIN ACCORDING TO THE   030 15
OF HIM WHO DIED AND ROSE AGAIN, AND EVER LIVETH TO   037 21
THE THIRD DAY HE ROSE AGAIN ACCORDING TO THE   071 12
AND WHEN HE ROSE UP FROM PRAYER, AND WAS COME TO HIS   150 23
AND WAS BURIED, AND ROSE AGAIN FOR US, THE SAME THY   161 18
WITH HIM AFTER HE ROSE FROM THE DEAD   166 27
AND THEY ROSE UP THE SAME HOUR, AND RETURNED TO   168 11
WITH HIM AFTER HE ROSE FROM THE DEAD   184 15
THOUGH ONE ROSE FROM THE DEAD   190 31
EAT AND DRINK, AND ROSE UP TO PLAY   201 16
AND THAT HE ROSE AGAIN THE THIRD DAY   205 06
THAT JESUS DIED AND ROSE AGAIN, EVEN SO THEM ALSO   268 31
AS CHRIST DIED AND ROSE AGAIN, SO THIS CHILD (THIS   278 19
THE THIRD DAY HE ROSE AGAIN FROM THE DEAD   284 18
DOWN AND SLEPT, AND ROSE UP AGAIN   309 22
DOWN AND SLEPT, AND ROSE UP AGAIN   346 33
AND THOUGH THERE ROSE UP WAR AGAINST ME, YET WILL I   371 30
OUR SIDE, WHEN MEN ROSE UP AGAINST US   504 09
THE THIRD DAY HE ROSE AGAIN FROM THE DEAD   578 02
IN THE GRAVE, AND ROSE AGAIN FOR US, THY SON OUR   587 27
WHO DIED FOR US AND ROSE AGAIN, THY SON, OUR SAVIOUR   595 09

ROUGH

AND THE ROUGH PLACES PLAIN   242 24

ROUND

THE ROUND WORLD, AND THEY THAT DWELL THEREIN   027 20
OF THE LORD SHONE ROUND ABOUT THEM   099 13
WAS A RAINBOW ROUND ABOUT THE THRONE, IN SIGHT LIKE   187 07
AND ROUND ABOUT THE THRONE WERE FOUR AND TWENTY   187 08
OF THE THRONE, AND ROUND ABOUT THE THRONE, WERE FOUR   187 16
AND COMPASS THEE ROUND, AND KEEP THEE IN ON EVERY   204 11
ALL THE REGION ROUND ABOUT   213 11
THERE SHINED ROUND ABOUT HIM A LIGHT FROM HEAVEN   229 31
ON ALL THAT DWELT ROUND ABOUT THEM   243 27
OUT OF THE CITIES ROUND ABOUT UNTO JERUSALEM,   249 30
THE ANGELS STOOD ROUND ABOUT THE THRONE, AND ABOUT   256 29
AND THE PLACES ROUND ABOUT MY HILL A BLESSING   262 07
ABOVE MINE ENEMIES ROUND ABOUT ME   326 16
AGAINST ME ROUND ABOUT   347 33
ENEMIES COMPASS ME ROUND ABOUT, TO TAKE AWAY MY SOUL   359 05
HIS PAVILION ROUND ABOUT HIM WITH DARK WATER, AND   360 20
FOUNDATIONS OF THE ROUND WORLD WERE DISCOVERED,   360 29
ABOVE MINE ENEMIES ROUND ABOUT ME   372 08
THE LORD TARRIETH ROUND ABOUT THEM THAT FEAR HIM, *   380 15
OF THEM THAT ARE ROUND ABOUT US   395 21
ABOUT SION, AND GO ROUND ABOUT HER   399 33
COMPASSETH ME ROUND ABOUT   400 15
BE STIRRED UP ROUND ABOUT HIM   401 27
ALL YE THAT ARE ROUND ABOUT HIM   433 11
THUNDER WAS HEARD ROUND ABOUT   434 18
EVEN ROUND ABOUT THEIR HABITATION   436 27
UNTO THEM THAT ARE ROUND ABOUT US   440 07
17 THEY CAME ROUND ABOUT ME DAILY LIKE WATER,   449 31
ALL THEM THAT ARE ROUND ABOUT HIM   450 21
FOUNDATION OF THE ROUND WORLD, AND ALL THAT THEREIN   450 29
2 HE HATH MADE THE ROUND WORLD SO SURE, *   457 07
WHO HATH MADE THE ROUND WORLD SO FAST THAT IT CANNOT   460 19
AND DARKNESS ARE ROUND ABOUT HIM   460 32
THE ROUND WORLD, AND THEY THAT DWELL THEREIN   462 09
DEATH COMPASSED ME ROUND ABOUT, *   486 23
COMPASSED ME ROUND ABOUT   488 18
STANDETH THE LORD ROUND ABOUT HIS PEOPLE, FROM THIS   504 27
ROUND ABOUT THY TABLE   506 12

RUBRICS

WITH THE RUBRICS AND CANONS OF THE CHURCH, AND WITH   569 20

RUFUS

OF ALEXANDER AND RUFUS, TO BEAR HIS CROSS   146 07

RULE

LAID IT DOWN AS A RULE, THAT 'THE PARTICULAR FORMS OF   V 13
AND SO RULE THE HEARTS OF THY SERVANTS THE PRESIDENT   032 06
MAY PLEASE THEE TO RULE AND GOVERN THY HOLY CHURCH   055 19
PLEASE THEE SO TO RULE THE HEART OF THY SERVANT,   055 22
BY THE RULE OF GOD'S COMMANDMENTS   087 17
THAT SHALL RULE MY PEOPLE ISRAEL   109 10
THE PEACE OF GOD RULE IN YOUR HEARTS, TO THE WHICH   116 09
THE HEATHEN SHOULD RULE OVER THEM   125 05
THOU NEVER BAREST RULE OVER THEM   139 29
HE MAY DIRECT AND RULE US ACCORDING TO THY WILL,   183 23
ACCORDING TO THIS RULE, PEACE BE ON THEM, AND MERCY,   211 03
THINGS DIRECT AND RULE OUR HEARTS   215 29
AND HIS ARM SHALL RULE FOR HIM   243 07
HAVE PUT DOWN ALL RULE AND ALL AUTHORITY AND POWER   328 29

RULE   CONTINUED

8 THE SUN TO RULE THE DAY   511 30
ACCORDING TO THE RULE OF THE SAME SCRIPTURES   541 06
THEM AFTER THE RULE AND DOCTRINE OF CHRIST, THAT YE   541 21
MAN KNOW NOT HOW TO RULE HIS OWN HOUSE, HOW SHALL HE   549 25
AND LET THEM BE THE RULE OF THY CONDUCT IN DISPENSING   571 25
AND SO RULE THEIR HEARTS AND STRENGTHEN THEIR HANDS,   590 27

RULED

AND RULED THEM PRUDENTLY WITH ALL HIS POWER   439 25

RULER

HIGH AND MIGHTY RULER OF THE UNIVERSE, WHO DOST FROM   017 28
WHEN THE RULER OF THE FEAST HAD TASTED THE WATER THAT   113 24
NAMED NICODEMUS, A RULER OF THE JEWS   187 35
THOU BEING OUR RULER AND GUIDE, WE MAY SO PASS   194 06
CAME A CERTAIN RULER, AND WORSHIPPED HIM, SAYING, MY   224 13
NAMED NICODEMUS, A RULER OF THE JEWS   275 06
BENJAMIN THEIR RULER, AND THE PRINCES OF JUDAH THEIR   421 08
AND RULER OF ALL HIS SUBSTANCE   471 14
UNGODLY MAN TO BE RULER OVER HIM, *   480 13
BE THOU RULER, EVEN IN THE MIDST AMONG THINE ENEMIES   482 10

RULER'S

CAME INTO THE RULER'S HOUSE, AND SAW THE MINSTRELS   224 24

RULERS

ALL CHRISTIAN RULERS AND MAGISTRATES, GIVING THEM   055 27
FOR OUR CIVIL RULERS, IN CONSEQUENCE OF THE   VI 17
THAT 'RULERS MAY HAVE GRACE, WISDOM, AND   VI 17
OF ALL CHRISTIAN RULERS, THAT THEY MAY TRULY AND   074 17
FOR RULERS ARE NOT A TERROR TO GOOD WORKS, BUT TO THE   114 15
PRIESTS AND THE RULERS AND THE PEOPLE, SAID UNTO   153 21
AND THE RULERS ALSO WITH THEM DERIDED HIM, SAYING, HE   154 27
PRIESTS AND OUR RULERS DELIVERED HIM TO BE CONDEMNED   167 18
AND THEIR RULERS, BECAUSE THEY KNEW HIM NOT, NOR YET   168 27
AGAINST THE RULERS OF THE DARKNESS OF THIS WORLD,   219 09
STAND UP, AND THE RULERS TAKE COUNSEL TOGETHER *   345 27

RULEST

THE HEAVENS, AND RULEST THE RAGING OF THE SEA   042 04
THE HEAVENS, AND RULEST THE RAGING OF THE SEA   046 09
10 THOU RULEST THE RAGING OF THE SEA   450 24

RULETH

HE THAT RULETH, WITH DILIGENCE   111 20
IS THE LORD THAT RULETH THE SEA   374 04
IT IS GOD THAT RULETH IN JACOB, AND UNTO THE ENDS OF   411 33
6 HE RULETH WITH HIS POWER FOR EVER   417 26
AND HIS KINGDOM RULETH OVER ALL   467 14
ONE THAT RULETH WELL HIS OWN HOUSE, HAVING HIS   549 23

RULING

EVEN BY RULING HIMSELF AFTER THY WORD   490 17
OF ONE WIFE, RULING THEIR CHILDREN AND THEIR OWN   531 33

RUMOUR

AND THIS RUMOUR OF HIM WENT FORTH THROUGHOUT ALL   213 09

RUN

INTO NO SIN, NEITHER RUN INTO ANY KIND OF DANGER   017 17
MAY RUN WITH PATIENCE THE RACE THAT IS   079 24
WHICH RUN IN A RACE RUN ALL, BUT ONE RECEIVETH THE   119 05
NOT THAT THEY WHICH RUN IN A RACE RUN ALL, BUT ONE   119 05
SO RUN, THAT YE MAY OBTAIN   119 06
I THEREFORE SO RUN, NOT AS UNCERTAINLY   119 09
BESET US, AND LET US RUN WITH PATIENCE THE RACE THAT   258 22
4 BUT THEY THAT RUN AFTER ANOTHER GOD *   357 27
AS A GIANT TO RUN HIS COURSE   363 23
4 THEY RUN AND PREPARE THEMSELVES WITHOUT MY FAULT   411 11
GRIN LIKE A DOG, AND RUN ABOUT THROUGH THE CITY   411 17
15 THEY WILL RUN HERE AND THERE FOR MEAT, *   412 04
SO THAT THE FLOODS RUN OVER ME   422 03
WHICH RUN AMONG THE HILLS   468 13
32 I WILL RUN THE WAY OF THY COMMANDMENTS, *   491 31
INTO NO SIN, NEITHER RUN INTO ANY KIND OF DANGER   592 23

RUNAGATES

LETTETH THE RUNAGATES CONTINUE IN SCARCENESS   419 23

RUNNETH

THEN SHE RUNNETH, AND COMETH TO SIMON PETER, AND TO   164 13
THE HEAVEN, AND RUNNETH ABOUT UNTO THE END OF IT   363 25
LIKE WATER THAT RUNNETH APACE   410 21
AND HIS WORD RUNNETH VERY SWIFTLY   523 26

RUNNING

AND HINDERED IN RUNNING THE RACE THAT IS SET BEFORE   095 07
AND RUNNING OVER, SHALL MEN GIVE INTO YOUR   194 29
THAT WE, RUNNING THE WAY OF THY COMMANDMENTS,   204 24
MAY PERSEVERE IN RUNNING THE RACE THAT IS SET BEFORE   258 15

RUSHING

HEAVEN AS OF A RUSHING MIGHTY WIND, AND IT FILLED ALL   180 19

RUST

WHERE MOTH AND RUST DOTH CORRUPT, AND WHERE THIEVES   072 08
NEITHER MOTH NOR RUST DOTH CORRUPT, AND WHERE THIEVES   072 10
WHERE MOTH AND RUST DOTH CORRUPT, AND WHERE THIEVES   125 17
NEITHER MOTH NOR RUST DOTH CORRUPT, AND WHERE THIEVES   125 19

SABA

KINGS OF ARABIA AND SABA SHALL BRING GIFTS   427 17

SABACHTHANI

A LOUD VOICE, SAYING, ELI, ELI, LAMA SABACHTHANI   137 18
ELOI, LAMA SABACHTHANI   146 28

SABAOTH

LORD GOD OF SABAOTH   010 14

SABBATH

DAY IS THE SABBATH OF THE LORD THY GOD   068 26
THE CROSS ON THE SABBATH DAY, (FOR THAT SABBATH DAY   160 31
(FOR THAT SABBATH DAY WAS AN HIGH DAY,) BESOUGHT   160 32
WHEN THE SABBATH WAS PAST, MARY MAGDALENE, AND MARY   165 18
ARE READ EVERY SABBATH DAY, THEY HAVE FULFILLED THEM   168 28
EAT BREAD ON THE SABBATH DAY, THAT THEY WATCHED HIM   213 29
TO HEAL ON THE SABBATH DAY   214 03
HIM OUT ON THE SABBATH DAY   214 07
THE NEXT SABBATH DAY CAME ALMOST THE WHOLE CITY   260 26
SYNAGOGUE ON THE SABBATH DAY, AND STOOD UP FOR TO   261 13
DAY IS THE SABBATH OF THE LORD THY GOD   286 26
DAY IS THE SABBATH OF THE LORD THY GOD   579 06

SABBATH-DAY

REMEMBER THAT THOU KEEP HOLY THE SABBATH-DAY   068 24
REMEMBER THAT THOU KEEP HOLY THE SABBATH-DAY   286 24
REMEMBER THAT THOU KEEP HOLY THE SABBATH-DAY   579 04

SACERDOTAL

EVERY ACT OF SACERDOTAL FUNCTION AMONG THE PEOPLE OF   569 19
OF ALL SACERDOTAL RELATION, BETWEEN YOU AND THEM   569 33
OF ALL SACERDOTAL CONNECTION BETWEEN YOU AND THEM,   569 35

SACKCLOTH

PUT OFF MY SACKCLOTH, AND GIRDED ME WITH GLADNESS   375 17
I PUT ON SACKCLOTH, AND HUMBLED MY SOUL WITH   382 17
11 I PUT ON SACKCLOTH ALSO, *   422 25

SACRAMENT

TAKE THIS HOLY SACRAMENT TO YOUR COMFORT   075 12
AND LIVELY FAITH WE RECEIVE THAT HOLY SACRAMENT   085 32
COMFORTABLE SACRAMENT OF THE BODY AND BLOOD OF   086 31
FOOD AND SUSTENANCE IN THAT HOLY SACRAMENT   087 05
INSTITUTE THE SACRAMENT OF HIS BODY AND BLOOD   152 08
FOR THE RECEIVING OF THIS HOLY SACRAMENT   R 273 21
PROVIDES THE SACRAMENT OF THE LORD'S SUPPER, OR HOLY   291 30
WHAT DO YOU MEAN BY THIS WORD SACRAMENT   292 09
BY THIS WORD SACRAMENT AN OUTWARD AND VISIBLE SIGN OF   292 10
HOW MANY PARTS ARE THERE IN A SACRAMENT   292 14
THERE ARE TWO PARTS IN A SACRAMENT   292 15
THE PROMISES OF GOD TO THEM IN THAT SACRAMENT   292 30
WHY WAS THE SACRAMENT OF THE LORD'S SUPPER ORDAINED   293 02
THE SACRAMENT OF THE LORD'S SUPPER WAS   293 04
THE BLESSED SACRAMENT OF THE BODY AND BLOOD OF   294 30
OF THE HOLY SACRAMENT, THE MINISTER SHALL FIRST   R 322 33
RECEIVE THE SACRAMENT OF CHRIST'S BODY AND BLOOD,   R 323 25
RECEIVE THE SACRAMENT WITH HIS MOUTH   R 323 31
THE BLESSED SACRAMENT OF THE BODY AND BLOOD OF   565 29
WHAT MEANEST THOU BY THIS WORD SACRAMENT   581 11
HOW MANY PARTS ARE THERE IN A SACRAMENT   581 16
PROMISES OF GOD MADE TO THEM IN THAT SACRAMENT   581 30
WHY WAS THE SACRAMENT OF THE LORD'S SUPPER ORDAINED   582 02
RATHER IT IS A SACRAMENT OF OUR REDEMPTION BY   608 35
NATURE OF A SACRAMENT, AND HATH GIVEN OCCASION TO   608 42
THE SACRAMENT OF THE LORD'S SUPPER WAS NOT BY   608 47
SAITH) THE SACRAMENT OF THE BODY AND BLOOD OF CHRIST   609 05
THE SIGN OR SACRAMENT OF SO GREAT A THING   609 07
OF THE LORD'S SACRAMENT, BY CHRIST'S ORDINANCE AND   609 11

SACRAMENTS

THE MINISTERS OF GOD'S HOLY WORD AND SACRAMENTS   047 23
RIGHTLY AND DULY ADMINISTER THY HOLY SACRAMENTS   074 24
ON THE SACRAMENTS, AS FOLLOWETH   R 292 03
HOW MANY SACRAMENTS HATH CHRIST ORDAINED IN HIS   292 04
ORDAINED TWO SACRAMENTS ONLY, AS GENERALLY NECESSARY   292 06
DOCTRINE AND SACRAMENTS, AND THE DISCIPLINE OF   542 12
AND OF HIS HOLY SACRAMENTS   546 14
AND OF HIS HOLY SACRAMENTS   546 20
THE HOLY SACRAMENTS IN THE CONGREGATION, WHERE THOU   546 26
THY HOLY SACRAMENTS, FOR OFFERING TO THY GLORIOUS   565 08
THY HOLY SACRAMENTS, AND BY MY LIFE AND DOCTRINE SET   573 22
HOW MANY SACRAMENTS HATH CHRIST ORDAINED IN HIS   581 07
AND THE SACRAMENTS BE DULY MINISTERED ACCORDING TO   606 39
THE SACRAMENTS IN THE CONGREGATION, BEFORE HE BE   607 20

SACRAMENTS   CONTINUED

MINISTER THE SACRAMENTS, IN A TONGUE NOT UNDERSTANDED   607 29
SACRAMENTS ORDAINED OF CHRIST BE NOT ONLY BADGES OR   607 31
THERE ARE TWO SACRAMENTS ORDAINED OF CHRIST OUR LORD   607 36
CALLED SACRAMENTS, THAT IS TO SAY, CONFIRMATION,   607 38
COUNTED FOR SACRAMENTS OF THE GOSPEL, BEING SUCH AS   607 40
NATURE OF SACRAMENTS WITH BAPTISM, AND THE LORD'S   607 42
THE SACRAMENTS WERE NOT ORDAINED OF CHRIST TO BE   608 02
THE WORD AND SACRAMENTS, YET FORASMUCH AS THEY DO NOT   608 11
AND IN RECEIVING THE SACRAMENTS   608 13
RECEIVE THE SACRAMENTS MINISTERED UNTO THEM   608 16

SACRED

TO SERVE IN THE SACRED MINISTRY OF THY CHURCH   038 31
THEMSELVES TO THE SACRED MINISTRY OF THY CHURCH   039 20

SACRIFICE

LIFTING UP OF MY HANDS BE AN EVENING SACRIFICE   021 17
UNTO THEE OUR SACRIFICE OF PRAISE AND THANKSGIVING   052 26
DESIREST NO SACRIFICE, ELSE WOULD I GIVE IT THEE   061 11
THE SACRIFICE OF GOD IS A TROUBLED SPIRIT   061 13
AND SUFFICIENT SACRIFICE, OBLATION, AND SATISFACTION,   080 11
DEATH AND SACRIFICE, UNTIL HIS COMING AGAIN   080 16
THIS OUR SACRIFICE OF PRAISE AND THANKSGIVING   081 16
AND LIVING SACRIFICE UNTO THEE   081 23
TO OFFER UNTO THEE ANY SACRIFICE   081 30
OF THE SACRIFICE OF HIS DEATH, AS HE HIMSELF HATH   089 12
A LIVING SACRIFICE, HOLY, ACCEPTABLE UNTO GOD, WHICH   110 04
OFFERING AND A SACRIFICE TO GOD FOR A SWEET-SMELLING   128 32
SIN BY THE SACRIFICE OF HIMSELF   148 06
HE SAITH, SACRIFICE AND OFFERING THOU WOULDEST NOT,   157 24
WHEN HE SAID, SACRIFICE AND OFFERING AND   157 29
OFFERED ONE SACRIFICE FOR SINS FOR EVER, SAT DOWN ON   158 06
UNTO US BOTH A SACRIFICE FOR SIN, AND ALSO AN   171 29
AND TO OFFER A SACRIFICE ACCORDING TO THAT WHICH IS   232 27
I WILL HAVE MERCY, AND NOT SACRIFICE   251 22
OF THE SACRIFICE OF THE DEATH OF CHRIST, AND OF THE   293 05
5 OFFER THE SACRIFICE OF RIGHTEOUSNESS, *   347 21
8 SACRIFICE AND OFFERING THOU WOULDEST NOT, *   390 27
AND SACRIFICE FOR SIN HAST THOU NOT REQUIRED   390 29
THAT HAVE MADE A COVENANT WITH ME WITH SACRIFICE   401 31
DESIREST NO SACRIFICE, ELSE WOULD I GIVE IT THEE   404 09
17 THE SACRIFICE OF GOD IS A TROUBLED SPIRIT   404 11
WITH THE SACRIFICE OF RIGHTEOUSNESS, WITH THE   404 15
UNTO HIM THE SACRIFICE OF THANKSGIVING, *   477 20
TO THEE THE SACRIFICE OF THANKSGIVING, *   487 19
BIND THE SACRIFICE WITH CORDS, YEA, EVEN UNTO THE   489 23
LIFTING UP OF MY HANDS BE AN EVENING SACRIFICE   517 12
OF THE SACRIFICE OF THE DEATH OF CHRIST, AND OF THE   582 04
OUR MORNING SACRIFICE OF PRAISE AND THANKSGIVING   587 26
AND TO BE A SACRIFICE, NOT ONLY FOR ORIGINAL GUILT,   603 15
WHO, BY SACRIFICE OF HIMSELF ONCE MADE, SHOULD   605 33

SACRIFICED

PASSOVER IS SACRIFICED FOR US   162 30
PASSOVER IS SACRIFICED FOR US   165 13

SACRIFICES

THE SACRIFICES OF GOD ARE A BROKEN SPIRIT   004 24
FOR WITH SUCH SACRIFICES GOD IS WELL PLEASED   072 28
WITH BETTER SACRIFICES THAN THESE   147 29
BUT IN THOSE SACRIFICES THERE IS A REMEMBRANCE AGAIN   157 17
AND SACRIFICES FOR SIN THOU HAST HAD NO PLEASURE   157 21
THE SAME SACRIFICES, WHICH CAN NEVER TAKE AWAY SINS   157 26
UP SPIRITUAL SACRIFICES, ACCEPTABLE TO GOD BY JESUS   158 04
I WILL NOT REPROVE THEE BECAUSE OF THY SACRIFICES   259 32
MAJESTY THE SACRIFICES OF PRAYER AND THANKSGIVING   402 06
TO OFFER THE SACRIFICES OF PRAYER AND PRAISE TO THEE   565 09
WHEREFORE THE SACRIFICES OF MASSES, IN THE WHICH IT   572 31
                                                       609 17

SAD

THE HYPOCRITES, OF A SAD COUNTENANCE   125 09
YE HAVE ONE TO ANOTHER, AS YE WALK, AND ARE SAD   167 11

SADDUCEES

HAD PUT THE SADDUCEES TO SILENCE, THEY WERE GATHERED   215 07

SADNESS

AND TURNEST THE SADNESS OF THE SORROWFUL TO JOY   599 04

SAFE

OF PEACE KEEP THEM SAFE FROM ALL EVIL   041 28
GOD FOR HER SAFE DELIVERANCE   R 051 04
HATH RECEIVED HIM SAFE AND SOUND   202 31
AND THEY SHALL BE SAFE IN THEIR LAND, AND SHALL KNOW 262 11
TO GIVE YOU SAFE DELIVERANCE, AND TO PRESERVE YOU IN 305 12
BEEN TAKEN INTO THE SAFE KEEPING OF THINE ETERNAL   340 27
SO SHALL I BE SAFE FROM MINE ENEMIES   359 30
AND THOU SHALT BE SAFE UNDER HIS FEATHERS   455 03
117 HOLD THOU ME UP, AND I SHALL BE SAFE   498 02
MERCY GRANT US A SAFE LODGING, AND A HOLY REST, AND   595 02

SAFEGUARD

THEY MAY BE A SAFEGUARD UNTO THE UNITED STATES OF   042 08

SAFELY

WHO HAST SAFELY BROUGHT US TO THE BEGINNING OF   017 14
TAKE HIM, AND LEAD HIM AWAY SAFELY   142 19
SHALL BE SAVED, AND ISRAEL SHALL DWELL SAFELY   225 13
THEY SHALL DWELL SAFELY IN THE WILDERNESS, AND SLEEP 262 06
THEY SHALL DWELL SAFELY, AND NONE SHALL MAKE THEM   262 16
BROUGHT THEM OUT SAFELY, THAT THEY SHOULD NOT FEAR, * 438 16
WHO HAST SAFELY BROUGHT US TO THE BEGINNING OF   592 20

SAFETY

THAT MAKEST US DWELL IN SAFETY   031 12
THY CHURCH, THE SAFETY, HONOUR, AND WELFARE OF THY   035 13
CONDUCT HIM IN SAFETY TO THE HAVEN WHERE HE WOULD BE, 046 14
ART THE GIVER OF LIFE, OF HEALTH, AND OF SAFETY   052 30
TO CONDUCT IN SAFETY, THROUGH THE PERILS OF THE GREAT 053 22
CONTINUE IN SAFETY WITHOUT THY SUCCOUR, PRESERVE IT   212 06
AND KEEP HIM IN PERPETUAL PEACE AND SAFETY   309 08
THAT MAKEST ME DWELL IN SAFETY   347 29
BESEECH THEE, IN SAFETY TO THE MORNING HOURS   595 08

SAID

PRAYER SHALL BE SAID WITH THE OTHER PRAYERS,   R 003 12
WAS GLAD WHEN THEY SAID UNTO ME, WE WILL GO INTO THE   003 17
DECLARES IN HER SAID PREFACE, TO DO THAT WHICH,   V 34
TO BE SAID BY THE WHOLE CONGREGATION, AFTER THE   R 006 16
THEN SHALL BE SAID OR SUNG THE FOLLOWING CANTICLE   R 008 09
MAY BE SUNG OR SAID,   R 008 15
SHALL BE SUNG OR SAID THE GLORIA PATRI   R 009 25
HERE SHALL BE SAID OR SUNG THE FOLLOWING HYMN   R 010 02
PRAYER HAS BEEN SAID OR SUNG, MAY PASS AT ONCE TO THE R 010 05
SHALL BE SUNG OR SAID THE HYMN FOLLOWING   R 014 04
THEN SHALL BE SAID THE APOSTLES' CREED BY THE   R 015 15
NOT ALREADY BEEN SAID, SHALL FOLLOW THE LORD'S   R 016 28
WHEN THE LITANY IS SAID, AND MAY BE OMITTED WHEN THE R 017 20
THIS MAY BE SAID WHEN ANY DESIRE THE PRAYERS OF THE R 019 12
THIS MAY BE SAID WHEN ANY DESIRE TO RETURN THANKS FOR R 019 33
THANKSGIVING MAY BE SAID BY THE CONGREGATION WITH THE R 019 34
PRAYER SHALL BE SAID WITH THE OTHER PRAYERS,   R 021 09
SAYING TO BE SAID BY THE WHOLE CONGREGATION,   R 023 23
MAY BE SUNG OR SAID THE GLORIA PATRI   R 025 18
SHALL BE SUNG OR SAID THE GLORIA PATRI, OR ELSE THE R 025 20
SHALL BE SUNG OR SAID THE HYMN CALLED MAGNIFICAT,   R 026 06
SHALL BE SUNG OR SAID THE HYMN CALLED NUNC DIMITTIS, R 028 06
THEN SHALL BE SAID THE APOSTLES' CREED BY THE   R 029 20
NOT ALREADY BEEN SAID, SHALL FOLLOW THE LORD'S   R 030 33
THEN SHALL BE SAID THE COLLECT FOR THE DAY,   R 031 15
THIS MAY BE SAID WHEN ANY DESIRE THE PRAYERS OF THE R 033 10
THIS MAY BE SAID WHEN ANY DESIRE TO RETURN THANKS FOR R 033 31
THANKSGIVING MAY BE SAID BY THE CONGREGATION WITH THE R 033 32
WHEN THAT IS NOT SAID, BEFORE THE FINAL PRAYER OF   R 035 04
WHEN THAT IS NOT SAID, BEFORE THE FINAL PRAYER OF   R 050 15
TO BE SAID WHEN ANY WOMAN, BEING PRESENT IN CHURCH, R 051 03
THEN SHALL BE SAID BY THEM THIS PSALM FOLLOWING   R 060 07
HATH BEEN ALREADY SAID, THE MINISTER MAY PASS AT ONCE R 061 19
PROVIDED IT BE SAID AT LEAST ONE SUNDAY IN EACH   R 067 28
GOD SPAKE THESE WORDS, AND SAID   068 03
SHALL BE SAID, LORD, HAVE MERCY UPON US   R 069 32
HERE SHALL BE SAID, THE LORD BE WITH YOU   R 070 13
HERE SHALL BE SAID, GLORY BE TO THEE, O LORD   R 070 25
THE GOSPEL MAY BE SAID, PRAISE BE TO THEE, O CHRIST R 070 27
THEN SHALL BE SAID THE CREED COMMONLY CALLED THE   R 070 29
IF IT HATH BEEN SAID IMMEDIATELY BEFORE IN MORNING   R 070 30
CREED SHALL BE SAID ON CHRISTMAS DAY, EASTER DAY,   R 070 31
THE CREED, MAY BE SAID THE BIDDING PRAYER, OR OTHER R 071 29
LORD JESUS, HOW HE SAID, IT IS MORE BLESSED TO GIVE   072 02
JESUS SAID UNTO THEM, THE HARVEST TRULY IS PLENTEOUS, 073 11
SHALL BE SAID OR SUNG BY THE PRIEST, THEREFORE WITH R 077 03
THEN SHALL BE SAID THE GLORIA IN EXCELSIS, ALL   R 083 32
 MAY BE SAID ALL THAT IS APPOINTED AT THE   R 084 28
SHALL BE SAID ON THE FIRST SUNDAY IN ADVENT, THE   R 085 23
AND THE MULTITUDE SAID, THIS IS JESUS THE PROPHET OF   091 32
SOLD DOVES, AND SAID UNTO THEM, IT IS WRITTEN, MY   092 02
HIS DISCIPLES, AND SAID UNTO HIM, ART THOU HE THAT   094 17
JESUS ANSWERED AND SAID UNTO THEM, GO AND SHEW JOHN   094 19
THEN SAID THEY UNTO HIM, WHO ART THOU   095 26
HE SAID, I AM THE VOICE OF ONE CRYING IN THE   095 28
WAY OF THE LORD, AS SAID THE PROPHET ESAIAS   095 29
THEY ASKED HIM, AND SAID UNTO HIM, WHY BAPTIZEST THOU 095 31
COLLECT IS TO BE SAID DAILY THROUGHOUT THE OCTAVE   R 096 20
WHICH OF THE ANGELS SAID HE AT ANY TIME, THOU ART MY   097 02
HAND OF GOD, AND SAID, BEHOLD, I SEE THE HEAVENS   100 07
AND WHEN HE HAD SAID THIS, HE FELL ASLEEP   100 16
AT SUPPER, AND SAID, LORD, WHICH IS HE THAT BETRAYETH 102 05
YET JESUS SAID NOT UNTO HIM, HE SHALL NOT DIE   102 10
THE SHEPHERDS SAID ONE TO ANOTHER, LET US NOW GO EVEN 106 08
COLLECT IS TO BE SAID DAILY THROUGHOUT THE OCTAVE   R 108 04
AND THEY SAID UNTO HIM, IN BETHLEHEM OF JUDAEA   109 06
TO BETHLEHEM, AND SAID, GO AND SEARCH DILIGENTLY FOR   109 13
AND HIS MOTHER SAID UNTO HIM, SON, WHY HAST THOU THUS 110 32
AND HE SAID UNTO THEM, HOW IS IT THAT YE SOUGHT ME   110 34
ANSWERED AND SAID, LORD, I AM NOT WORTHY THAT THOU   115 10
HE MARVELLED, AND SAID TO THEM THAT FOLLOWED, VERILY   115 16
AND JESUS SAID UNTO THE CENTURION, GO THY WAY   115 23
CAME AND SAID UNTO HIM, SIR, DIDST NOT THOU SOW GOOD   116 23
HE SAID UNTO THEM, AN ENEMY HATH DONE THIS   116 25
THE SERVANTS SAID UNTO HIM, WILT THOU THEN THAT WE GO 116 26
BUT HE SAID, NAY   116 27
AND SAID UNTO THEM   119 20
ONE OF THEM, AND SAID, FRIEND, I DO THEE NO WRONG   120 07
AND WHEN HE HAD SAID THESE THINGS, HE CRIED, HE THAT   121 27
AND HE SAID, UNTO YOU IT IS GIVEN TO KNOW THE   121 29
HIM THE TWELVE, AND SAID UNTO THEM, .BEHOLD, WE GO UP 123 17

SAID CONTINUED

AND HE SAID, LORD, THAT I MAY RECEIVE MY SIGHT 124 02
AND JESUS SAID UNTO HIM, RECEIVE THY SIGHT 124 03
COLLECT IS TO BE SAID EVERY DAY IN LENT, AFTER THE R 124 18
CAME TO HIM, HE SAID, IF THOU BE THE SON OF GOD, 126 26
BUT HE ANSWERED AND SAID, IT IS WRITTEN, MAN SHALL 126 28
JESUS SAID UNTO HIM, IT IS WRITTEN AGAIN, THOU SHALT 127 03
BUT HE ANSWERED AND SAID, I AM NOT SENT BUT UNTO THE 128 14
BUT HE ANSWERED AND SAID, IT IS NOT MEET TO TAKE THE 128 16
AND SHE SAID, TRUTH, LORD 128 18
JESUS ANSWERED AND SAID UNTO HER, O WOMAN, GREAT IS 128 20
BUT SOME OF THEM SAID, HE CASTETH OUT DEVILS THROUGH 129 26
THEIR THOUGHTS, SAID UNTO THEM, EVERY KINGDOM DIVIDED 129 29
UP HER VOICE, AND SAID UNTO HIM, BLESSED IS THE WOMB 130 18
BUT HE SAID, YEA RATHER, BLESSED ARE THEY THAT HEAR 130 20
AND THIS HE SAID TO PROVE HIM 131 28
AND JESUS SAID, MAKE THE MEN SIT DOWN 131 35
WERE FILLED, HE SAID UNTO HIS DISCIPLES, GATHER UP 132 07
THAT JESUS DID, SAID, THIS IS OF A TRUTH THAT PROPHET 132 12
JESUS SAID, WHICH OF YOU CONVINCETH ME OF SIN 133 09
THE JEWS, AND SAID UNTO HIM, SAY WE NOT WELL THAT 133 13
THEN SAID THE JEWS UNTO HIM, NOW WE KNOW THAT THOU 133 18
THEN SAID THE JEWS UNTO HIM, THOU ART NOT YET FIFTY 133 29
JESUS SAID UNTO THEM, VERILY, VERILY, I SAY UNTO YOU, 133 31
COLLECT IS TO BE SAID EVERY DAY, AFTER THE COLLECT R 134 13
AND THEY SAID, WHAT IS THAT TO US 135 06
SILVER PIECES, AND SAID, IT IS NOT LAWFUL FOR TO PUT 135 09
AND JESUS SAID UNTO HIM, THOU SAYEST 135 20
THEN SAID PILATE UNTO HIM, HEAREST THOU NOT HOW MANY 135 22
PILATE SAID UNTO THEM, WHOM WILL YE THAT I 135 29
ANSWERED AND SAID UNTO THEM, WHETHER OF THE TWAIN 136 02
THEY SAID, BARABBAS 136 04
AND THE GOVERNOR SAID, WHY, WHAT EVIL HATH HE DONE 136 06
ALL THE PEOPLE, AND SAID, HIS BLOOD BE ON US, AND ON 136 12
SCRIBES AND ELDERS, SAID, HE SAVED OTHERS 137 10
FOR HE SAID, I AM THE SON OF GOD 137 13
THEY HEARD THAT, SAID, THIS MAN CALLETH FOR ELIAS 137 20
THE REST SAID, LET BE, LET US SEE WHETHER ELIAS WILL 137 23
FOR HE SAID, SURELY THEY ARE MY PEOPLE, CHILDREN THAT 138 33
BUT THEY SAID, NOT ON THE FEAST DAY, LEST THERE BE AN 139 35
AND SAID, WHY WAS THIS WASTE OF THE 140 07
AND JESUS SAID, LET HER ALONE 140 10
HIS DISCIPLES SAID UNTO HIM, WHERE WILT THOU THAT WE 140 23
AND FOUND AS HE HAD SAID UNTO THEM 140 33
AND DID EAT, JESUS SAID, VERILY I SAY UNTO YOU, ONE 140 35
AND ANOTHER SAID, IS IT I 141 04
AND HE ANSWERED AND SAID UNTO THEM, IT IS ONE OF THE 141 05
GAVE TO THEM, AND SAID, TAKE, EAT 141 10
AND HE SAID UNTO THEM, THIS IS MY BLOOD OF THE NEW 141 13
BUT PETER SAID UNTO HIM, ALTHOUGH ALL SHALL BE 141 21
LIKEWISE ALSO SAID THEY ALL 141 27
AND HE SAID, ABBA, FATHER, ALL THINGS ARE POSSIBLE 141 35
JESUS ANSWERED AND SAID UNTO THEM, ARE YE COME OUT, 142 24
ASKED HIM, AND SAID UNTO HIM, ART THOU THE CHRIST, 143 13
AND JESUS SAID, I AM 143 14
UPON HIM, AND SAID, AND THOU ALSO WAST WITH JESUS OF 143 25
THEY THAT STOOD BY SAID AGAIN TO PETER, SURELY THOU 143 31
THE WORD THAT JESUS SAID UNTO HIM, BEFORE THE COCK 143 35
AND HE ANSWERING SAID UNTO HIM, THOU SAYEST IT 145 07
PILATE ANSWERED AND SAID AGAIN UNTO THEM, WHAT WILL 145 22
THEN PILATE SAID UNTO THEM, WHY, WHAT EVIL HATH HE 145 25
PRIESTS MOCKING SAID AMONG THEMSELVES WITH THE 146 21
WHEN THEY HEARD IT, SAID, BEHOLD, HE CALLETH ELIAS 146 30
UP THE GHOST, HE SAID, TRULY THIS MAN WAS THE SON OF 147 04
AND THEY SAID UNTO HIM, WHERE WILT THOU THAT WE 148 24
AND HE SAID UNTO THEM, BEHOLD, WHEN YE ARE ENTERED 148 25
AND FOUND AS HE HAD SAID UNTO THEM 148 32
AND HE SAID UNTO THEM, WITH DESIRE I HAVE DESIRED TO 149 02
GAVE THANKS, AND SAID, TAKE THIS, AND DIVIDE IT AMONG 149 06
AND HE SAID UNTO THEM, THE KINGS OF THE GENTILES 149 19
AND THE LORD SAID, SIMON, SIMON, BEHOLD, SATAN HATH 149 31
AND HE SAID UNTO HIM, LORD, I AM READY TO GO WITH 149 34
AND HE SAID, I TELL THEE, PETER, THE COCK SHALL NOT 150 02
AND HE SAID UNTO THEM, WHEN I SENT YOU WITHOUT PURSE, 150 04
AND THEY SAID, NOTHING 150 05
THEN SAID HE UNTO THEM, BUT NOW, HE THAT HATH A 150 06
AND THEY SAID, LORD, BEHOLD, HERE ARE TWO SWORDS 150 12
AND HE SAID UNTO THEM, IT IS ENOUGH 150 12
AT THE PLACE, HE SAID UNTO THEM, PRAY THAT YE ENTER 150 15
FOR SORROW, AND SAID UNTO THEM, WHY SLEEP YE 150 25
BUT JESUS SAID UNTO HIM, JUDAS, BETRAYEST THOU THE 150 29
WOULD FOLLOW, THEY SAID UNTO HIM, LORD, SHALL WE 150 31
JESUS ANSWERED AND SAID, SUFFER YE THUS FAR 150 34
THEN JESUS SAID UNTO THE CHIEF PRIESTS, AND CAPTAINS 150 35
UPON HIM, AND SAID, THIS MAN WAS ALSO WITH HIM 151 12
SAW HIM, AND SAID, THOU ART ALSO OF THEM 151 14
AND PETER SAID, MAN, I AM NOT 151 15
AND PETER SAID, MAN, I KNOW NOT WHAT THOU SAYEST 151 18
HOW HE HAD SAID UNTO HIM, BEFORE THE COCK CROW, 151 21
AND HE SAID UNTO THEM, IF I TELL YOU, YE WILL NOT 151 30
THEN SAID THEY ALL, ART THOU THEN THE SON OF GOD 151 34
AND HE SAID UNTO THEM, YE SAY THAT I AM 151 34
AND THEY SAID, WHAT NEED WE ANY FURTHER WITNESS 151 35
HE BRAKE IT, AND SAID, TAKE, EAT 152 19
HE ANSWERED HIM AND SAID, THOU SAYEST IT 153 02
THEN SAID PILATE TO THE CHIEF PRIESTS AND TO THE 153 03
AND THE PEOPLE, SAID UNTO THEM, YE HAVE BROUGHT THIS 153 22
AND HE SAID UNTO THEM THE THIRD TIME, WHY, WHAT EVIL 153 34
TURNING UNTO THEM SAID, DAUGHTERS OF JERUSALEM, WEEP 154 13
THEN SAID JESUS, FATHER, FORGIVE THEM 154 25
AND HE SAID UNTO JESUS, LORD, REMEMBER ME WHEN THOU 155 06
AND JESUS SAID UNTO HIM, VERILY I SAY UNTO THEE, 155 07
A LOUD VOICE, HE SAID, FATHER, INTO THY HANDS I 155 13
AND HAVING SAID THUS, HE GAVE UP THE GHOST 155 14
JESUS ANSWERED AND SAID UNTO HIM, WHAT I DO THOU 156 03

PAGE LN

SAID CONTINUED

THEREFORE SAID HE, YE ARE NOT ALL CLEAN 156 11
SET DOWN AGAIN, HE SAID UNTO THEM, KNOW YE WHAT I 156 13
THEN SAID I, LO, I COME (IN THE VOLUME OF THE BOOK IT 157 27
ABOVE WHEN HE SAID, SACRIFICE AND OFFERING AND 157 29
THEN SAID HE, LO, I COME TO DO THY WILL, O GOD 157 31
AFTER THAT HE HAD SAID BEFORE, THIS IS THE COVENANT 158 10
A PURPLE ROBE, AND SAID, HAIL, KING OF THE JEWS 158 32
THEN SAID THE CHIEF PRIESTS OF THE JEWS TO PILATE, 160 06
BUT THAT HE SAID, I AM KING OF THE JEWS 160 07
THEY SAID THEREFORE AMONG THEMSELVES, LET US NOT REND 160 12
THE VINEGAR, HE SAID, IT IS FINISHED 160 28
THAT THAT DECEIVER SAID, WHILE HE WAS YET ALIVE, 162 18
PILATE SAID UNTO THEM, YE HAVE A WATCH 162 23
FOLLOWING SHALL BE SAID, AND MAY BE SAID THROUGHOUT R 162 28
BE SAID, AND MAY BE SAID THROUGHOUT THE OCTAVE R 162 29
COLLECT IS TO BE SAID DAILY THROUGHOUT EASTER WEEK R 163 31
AND THEY SAID AMONG THEMSELVES, WHO SHALL ROLL US 165 23
YE SEE HIM, AS HE SAID UNTO YOU 165 33
NEITHER SAID THEY ANY THING TO ANY MAN 166 03
HIS MOUTH, AND SAID, OF A TRUTH I PERCEIVE THAT GOD 166 12
AND HE SAID UNTO THEM, WHAT MANNER OF COMMUNICATIONS 167 09
ANSWERING SAID UNTO HIM, ART THOU ONLY A 167 12
AND THEY SAID UNTO HIM, CONCERNING JESUS OF NAZARETH, 167 15
AND HE SAID UNTO THEM, WHAT THINGS 167 15
OF ANGELS, WHICH SAID THAT HE WAS ALIVE 167 26
AND FOUND IT EVEN SO AS THE WOMEN HAD SAID 167 28
THEN HE SAID UNTO THEM, O FOOLS, AND SLOW OF HEART TO 167 29
AND THEY SAID ONE TO ANOTHER, DID NOT OUR HEART BURN 168 08
TO CORRUPTION, HE SAID ON THIS WISE, I WILL GIVE YOU 169 12
AND HE SAID UNTO THEM, WHY ARE YE TROUBLED 169 31
AND WONDERED, HE SAID UNTO THEM, HAVE YE HERE ANY 170 04
AND HE SAID UNTO THEM, THESE ARE THE WORDS WHICH I 170 06
THE SCRIPTURES, AND SAID UNTO THEM, THUS IT IS 170 12
AND WHEN HE HAD SO SAID, HE SHEWED UNTO THEM HIS 171 18
THEN SAID JESUS TO THEM AGAIN, PEACE BE UNTO YOU 171 20
AND WHEN HE HAD SAID THIS, HE BREATHED ON THEM, 171 22
JESUS SAID, I AM THE GOOD SHEPHERD 172 21
JESUS SAID TO HIS DISCIPLES, A LITTLE WHILE, AND YE 173 27
THEN SAID SOME OF HIS DISCIPLES AMONG THEMSELVES, 173 29
THEY SAID THEREFORE, WHAT IS THIS THAT HE SAITH, 174 02
TO ASK HIM, AND SAID UNTO THEM, DO YE ENQUIRE AMONG 174 04
OF THAT I SAID, A LITTLE WHILE, AND YE SHALL NOT SEE 174 05
JESUS SAID UNTO HIS DISCIPLES, NOW I GO MY WAY TO HIM 175 06
BUT BECAUSE I HAVE SAID THESE THINGS UNTO YOU, 175 08
THEREFORE SAID I, THAT HE SHALL TAKE OF MINE, 175 24
HIS DISCIPLES SAID UNTO HIM, LO, NOW SPEAKEST THOU 176 32
COLLECT IS TO BE SAID DAILY THROUGHOUT THE OCTAVE R 177 20
AND HE SAID UNTO THEM, IT IS NOT FOR YOU TO KNOW THE 178 06
WHICH ALSO SAID, YE MEN OF GALILEE, WHY STAND YE 178 16
JESUS SAID, BEHOLD, I SEND THE PROMISE OF MY FATHER 178 21
COLLECT IS TO BE SAID DAILY THROUGHOUT WHITSUN WEEK R 180 15
JESUS SAID UNTO HIS DISCIPLES, IF YE LOVE ME, 181 08
JESUS ANSWERED AND SAID UNTO HIM, IF A MAN LOVE ME, 181 24
WHATSOEVER I HAVE SAID UNTO YOU 181 33
YE HAVE HEARD HOW I SAID UNTO YOU, I GO AWAY, AND 182 02
BECAUSE I SAID, I GO UNTO THE FATHER 182 04
JESUS SAID TO HIS DISCIPLES, ASK, AND IT SHALL BE 183 10
HIS MOUTH, AND SAID, OF A TRUTH I PERCEIVE THAT GOD 183 29
THEN SAID JESUS UNTO THEM AGAIN, VERILY, VERILY, 186 12
WHICH SAID, COME UP HITHER, AND I WILL SHEW THEE 187 02
JESUS BY NIGHT, AND SAID UNTO HIM, RABBI, WE KNOW 188 02
JESUS ANSWERED AND SAID UNTO HIM, VERILY, VERILY, 188 05
MARVEL NOT THAT I SAID UNTO THEE, YE MUST BE BORN 188 13
ANSWERED AND SAID UNTO HIM, HOW CAN THESE THINGS BE 188 17
JESUS ANSWERED AND SAID UNTO HIM, ART THOU A MASTER 188 19
AND HE CRIED AND SAID, FATHER ABRAHAM, HAVE MERCY ON 190 13
BUT ABRAHAM SAID, SON, REMEMBER THAT THOU IN THY 190 16
THEN HE SAID, I PRAY THEE THEREFORE, FATHER, THAT 190 22
AND HE SAID, NAY, FATHER ABRAHAM 190 27
AND HE SAID UNTO HIM, IF THEY HEAR NOT MOSES AND THE 190 29
THE FIRST SAID UNTO HIM, I HAVE BOUGHT A PIECE OF 192 07
AND ANOTHER SAID, I HAVE BOUGHT FIVE YOKE OF OXEN, 192 09
AND ANOTHER SAID, I HAVE MARRIED A WIFE, AND 192 11
HOUSE BEING ANGRY SAID TO HIS SERVANT, GO OUT QUICKLY 192 13
AND THE SERVANT SAID, LORD, IT IS DONE AS THOU HAST 192 16
AND THE LORD SAID UNTO THE SERVANT, GO OUT INTO THE 192 18
LEFT SPEAKING, HE SAID UNTO SIMON, LAUNCH OUT INTO 196 13
AND SIMON ANSWERING SAID UNTO HIM, MASTER, WE HAVE 196 15
AND JESUS SAID UNTO SIMON, FEAR NOT 196 28
JESUS SAID UNTO HIS DISCIPLES, EXCEPT YOUR 197 28
HEARD THAT IT WAS SAID BY THEM OF OLD TIME, THOU 197 31
AND THEY SAID, SEVEN 199 17
JESUS SAID, A CERTAIN MAN HAD TWO SONS 201 31
THE YOUNGER OF THEM SAID TO HIS FATHER, FATHER, 201 32
CAME TO HIMSELF, HE SAID, HOW MANY HIRED SERVANTS OF 202 10
AND THE SON SAID UNTO HIM, FATHER, I HAVE SINNED 202 18
BUT THE FATHER SAID TO HIS SERVANTS, BRING FORTH THE 202 21
AND HE SAID UNTO HIM, THY BROTHER IS COME 202 29
AND HE ANSWERING SAID TO HIS FATHER, LO, THESE MANY 202 33
AND HE SAID UNTO HIM, SON, THOU ART EVER WITH ME, 203 05
HE SAID UNTO HIM, WHAT IS WRITTEN IN THE LAW 208 13
AND HE ANSWERING SAID, THOU SHALT LOVE THE LORD THY 208 15
AND HE SAID UNTO HIM, THOU HAST ANSWERED RIGHT 208 17
TO JUSTIFY HIMSELF, SAID UNTO JESUS, AND WHO IS MY 208 19
AND JESUS ANSWERING SAID, A CERTAIN MAN WENT DOWN 208 21
TO THE HOST, AND SAID UNTO HIM, TAKE CARE OF HIM 208 34
THEN SAID JESUS UNTO HIM, GO, AND DO THOU LIKEWISE 209 04
AND HE SAID, HE THAT SHEWED MERCY ON HIM 209 04
THEIR VOICES, AND SAID, JESUS, MASTER, HAVE MERCY ON 210 04
HE SAW THEM, HE SAID UNTO THEM, GO SHEW YOURSELVES 210 05
AND JESUS ANSWERING SAID, WERE THERE NOT TEN 210 11
AND HE SAID UNTO HIM, ARISE, GO THY WAY 210 13
ON HER, AND SAID UNTO HER, WEEP NOT 213 02
AND HE SAID, YOUNG MAN, I SAY UNTO THEE, ARISE 213 04

SAID   CONTINUED

JESUS SAID UNTO HIM, THOU SHALT LOVE THE LORD THY GOD	215 10
THE LORD SAID UNTO MY LORD, SIT THOU ON MY	215 19
SEEING THEIR FAITH, SAID UNTO THE SICK OF THE PALSY	217 03
OF THE SCRIBES SAID WITHIN THEMSELVES, THIS MAN	217 05
THEIR THOUGHTS SAID, WHEREFORE THINK YE EVIL IN YOUR	217 06
JESUS SAID, THE KINGDOM OF HEAVEN IS LIKE UNTO A	218 03
THEN SAID THE KING TO THE SERVANTS, BIND HIM HAND AND	218 25
THEN SAID JESUS UNTO HIM, EXCEPT YE SEE SIGNS AND	219 32
AND THEY SAID UNTO HIM, YESTERDAY AT THE SEVENTH HOUR	220 08
IN THE WHICH JESUS SAID UNTO HIM, THY SON LIVETH	220 10
PETER SAID UNTO JESUS, LORD, HOW OFT SHALL MY BROTHER	221 09
HE HAD CALLED HIM, SAID UNTO HIM, O THOU WICKED	221 33
AND SAID, WHY TEMPT YE ME, YE HYPOCRITES	223 05
FOR SHE SAID WITHIN HERSELF, IF I MAY BUT TOUCH HIS	224 19
WHEN HE SAW HER, HE SAID, DAUGHTER, BE OF GOOD	224 21
MAKING A NOISE, HE SAID UNTO THEM, GIVE PLACE	224 25
AND THIS HE SAID TO PROVE HIM	225 25
AND JESUS SAID, MAKE THE MEN SIT DOWN	225 31
WERE FILLED, HE SAID UNTO HIS DISCIPLES, GATHER UP	226 06
THAT JESUS DID, SAID, THIS IS OF A TRUTH THAT PROPHET	226 12
DISCIPLES THEREFORE SAID UNTO HIM, WE HAVE SEEN THE	228 27
BUT HE SAID UNTO THEM, EXCEPT I SHALL SEE IN HIS	228 28
IN THE MIDST, AND SAID, PEACE BE UNTO YOU	229 02
THOMAS ANSWERED AND SAID UNTO HIM, MY LORD AND MY	229 06
AND HE SAID, WHO ART THOU, LORD	230 03
AND THE LORD SAID, I AM JESUS WHOM THOU PERSECUTEST	230 03
AND ASTONISHED SAID, LORD, WHAT WILT THOU HAVE ME TO	230 05
AND THE LORD SAID UNTO HIM, ARISE, AND GO INTO THE	230 06
AND HE SAID, BEHOLD, I AM HERE, LORD	230 15
AND TO HIM SAID THE LORD IN A VISION, ANANIAS	230 15
AND THE LORD SAID UNTO HIM, ARISE, AND GO INTO THE	230 16
BUT THE LORD SAID UNTO HIM, GO THY WAY	230 25
HIS HANDS ON HIM SAID, BROTHER SAUL, THE LORD,	230 31
BUT ALL THAT HEARD HIM WERE AMAZED, AND SAID	231 05
PETER ANSWERED AND SAID UNTO JESUS, BEHOLD, WE HAVE	231 12
AND JESUS SAID UNTO THEM, VERILY I SAY UNTO YOU, THAT	231 14
TO THAT WHICH IS SAID IN THE LAW OF THE LORD,	232 28
BLESSED GOD, AND SAID, LORD, NOW LETTEST THOU THY	233 05
BLESSED THEM, AND SAID UNTO MARY HIS MOTHER, BEHOLD,	233 11
THE DISCIPLES, AND SAID, (THE NUMBER OF NAMES	234 07
THEY PRAYED, AND SAID, THOU, LORD, WHICH KNOWEST THE	234 27
JESUS ANSWERED AND SAID, I THANK THEE, O FATHER, LORD	235 03
BUT AHAZ SAID, I WILL NOT ASK, NEITHER WILL I TEMPT	235 27
AND HE SAID, HEAR YE NOW, O HOUSE OF DAVID	235 28
IN UNTO HER, AND SAID, HAIL, THOU THAT ART HIGHLY	236 09
AND THE ANGEL SAID UNTO HER, FEAR NOT, MARY	236 13
THEN SAID MARY UNTO THE ANGEL, HOW SHALL THIS BE,	236 20
ANGEL ANSWERED AND SAID UNTO HER, THE HOLY GHOST	236 21
AND MARY SAID, BEHOLD THE HANDMAID OF THE LORD	236 28
AND JESUS SAID UNTO HIS DISCIPLES, LET NOT YOUR HEART	239 29
AND HE SAID, WHAT SHALL I CRY	242 27
THE VOICE SAID, CRY	242 27
MOTHER ANSWERED AND SAID, NOT SO	243 19
AND THEY SAID UNTO HER, THERE IS NONE OF THY KINDRED	243 20
AND THE ANGEL SAID UNTO HIM, GIRD THYSELF, AND BIND	245 16
COME TO HIMSELF, HE SAID, NOW I KNOW OF A SURETY,	245 26
AND THEY SAID, SOME SAY THAT THOU ART JOHN THE	245 33
PETER ANSWERED AND SAID, THOU ART THE CHRIST, THE SON	246 02
JESUS ANSWERED AND SAID UNTO HIM, BLESSED ART THOU,	246 04
AND HE SAID UNTO HER, WHAT WILT THOU	247 08
JESUS ANSWERED AND SAID, YE KNOW NOT WHAT YE ASK	247 11
THEM UNTO HIM, AND SAID, YE KNOW THAT THE PRINCES OF	247 20
FROM THEM, PETER SAID UNTO JESUS, MASTER, IT IS GOOD	248 33
NOT KNOWING WHAT HE SAID	249 04
AND HE SAID UNTO THEM, THE KINGS OF THE GENTILES	250 04
SAW IT, THEY SAID UNTO HIS DISCIPLES, WHY EATETH YOUR	251 18
HEARD THAT, HE SAID UNTO THEM, THEY THAT BE WHOLE	251 19
MIDST OF THEM, AND SAID, VERILY I SAY UNTO YOU,	252 25
THEREFORE SAID HE UNTO THEM, THE HARVEST TRULY IS	254 13
THE WORD THAT I SAID UNTO YOU, THE SERVANT IS NOT	255 17
COLLECT IS TO BE SAID DAILY THROUGHOUT THE OCTAVE	R 256 12
AND I SAID UNTO HIM, SIR, THOU KNOWEST	257 06
AND HE SAID TO ME, THESE ARE THEY WHICH CAME OUT OF	257 07
SOLD DOVES, AND SAID UNTO THEM, IT IS WRITTEN, MY	260 06
AND SAID UNTO HIM, HEAREST THOU WHAT	260 12
WAXED BOLD, AND SAID, IT WAS NECESSARY THAT THE WORD	260 31
JESUS SAID UNTO THEM, WHICH OF YOU SHALL HAVE A	262 26
THAT IT HATH BEEN SAID, THOU SHALT LOVE THY	264 03
JESUS SAID, YE HAVE HEARD THAT IT HATH BEEN SAID,	264 03
FOLLOWING SHALL BE SAID OR SUNG	R 264 17
JESUS SAID, BE NOT ANXIOUS FOR YOUR LIFE, WHAT YE	266 11
JESUS ANSWERED AND SAID UNTO THEM, HAVE YE NOT READ,	268 05
AND FEMALE, AND SAID, FOR THIS CAUSE SHALL A MAN	268 07
JESUS SAID UNTO THEM, ALL THAT THE FATHER GIVETH ME	269 13
AND SAID UNTO THEM, SUFFER THE LITTLE	274 28
JESUS BY NIGHT, AND SAID UNTO HIM, RABBI, WE KNOW	275 07
JESUS ANSWERED AND SAID UNTO HIM, VERILY, VERILY, I	275 09
MARVEL NOT THAT I SAID UNTO THEE, YE MUST BE BORN	275 18
THEN SHALL BE SAID, THEN SHALL THE MINISTER SAY,	R 280 19
WHICH SHALL BE SAID THE LORD'S PRAYER, AND THE	R 281 23
OF A HYMN, SHALL BE SAID BY THE MINISTER AND PEOPLE	R 283 03
SHALL SAY, YOU SAID THAT YOUR SPONSORS PROMISED AND	284 07
SHALL BE SAID THE APOSTLES' CREED BY THE	R 284 11
SHALL SAY, YOU SAID THAT YOUR SPONSORS PROMISED AND	285 13
THEN SHALL BE SAID THIS PRAYER BY THE MINISTER AND	R 285 23
THEN SHALL BE SAID BY THE MINISTER AND PEOPLE	R 289 21
THERE SHALL BE SAID THE FOLLOWING SENTENCE BY THE	R 290 03
THEN SHALL BE SAID BY BOTH OF THEM THE FOLLOWING	R 305 15
THEN MAY BE SAID, GRANT, WE BESEECH THEE, O HEAVENLY	R 307 02
HERE MAY BE SAID ANY ONE OR MORE OF THE PSALMS	R 309 09
AND I SAID, IT IS MINE OWN INFIRMITY	311 18
HERE SHALL BE SAID, O SAVIOUR OF THE WORLD, WHO BY	R 313 11
PRAYERS MAY BE SAID WITH THE FOREGOING SERVICE,	R 315 03
JESUS SAID, VERILY, VERILY, I SAY UNTO YOU, HE THAT	322 21

SAID   CONTINUED

SHALL BE SAID ONE OR MORE OF THE FOLLOWING	R 324 16
JESUS SAID, LET NOT YOUR HEART BE TROUBLED	331 17
SHALL BE SUNG OR SAID, MAN, THAT IS BORN OF A WOMAN,	R 332 17
THEN SHALL BE SAID OR SUNG, I HEARD A VOICE FROM	R 333 24
APPOINTED TO BE SAID AT THE GRAVE, THE SAME IS HEREBY	R 336 31
THEM UNTO HIM AND SAID, SUFFER THE LITTLE CHILDREN TO	338 09
SHALL BE SAID THE FOLLOWING PSALMS	R 338 14
EACH PSALM SHALL BE SAID THE GLORIA PATRI	R 338 15
MIDST OF THEM, AND SAID, VERILY I SAY UNTO YOU,	339 24
THEN SHALL BE SAID BY THE MINISTER AND PEOPLE,	R 340 09
HERE SHALL BE SAID THE FOLLOWING PRAYERS, OR OTHER	R 340 22
THE GRAVE SHALL BE SAID OR SUNG, JESUS SAITH TO HIS	R 341 08
THEN SHALL BE SAID OR SUNG, THEREFORE ARE THEY	R 341 19
THE LORD HATH SAID UNTO ME, THOU ART MY SON, THIS DAY	346 10
6 FOR HE HATH SAID IN HIS HEART, TUSH, I SHALL NEVER	353 16
12 HE HATH SAID IN HIS HEART, TUSH, GOD HATH	353 30
4 WHICH HAVE SAID, WITH OUR TONGUE WILL WE PREVAIL	355 14
THE FOOL HATH SAID IN HIS HEART, *	356 13
MY SOUL, THOU HAST SAID UNTO THE LORD, *	357 23
IN MY PROSPERITY I SAID, I SHALL NEVER BE REMOVED	375 04
I HAVE SAID, THOU ART MY GOD	376 25
BUT IN MY HASTE I SAID, *	377 11
6 I SAID, I WILL CONFESS MY SINS UNTO THE LORD	377 32
THEIR MOUTHS, AND SAID, *	383 05
I SAID, I WILL TAKE HEED TO MY WAYS, *	389 05
THEN SAID I, LO, I COME	390 30
4 I SAID, LORD, BE MERCIFUL UNTO ME	392 06
FOOLISH BODY HATH SAID IN HIS HEART, *	405 12
6 AND I SAID, O THAT I HAD WINGS LIKE A DOVE	406 30
22 THE LORD HATH SAID, I WILL BRING MY PEOPLE AGAIN,	420 30
13 AND I SAID, THEN HAVE I CLEANSED MY HEART IN VAIN,	429 02
AND I HAD ALMOST SAID EVEN AS THEY	429 06
9 YEA, THEY SAID IN THEIR HEARTS, LET US MAKE HAVOC	430 21
5 I SAID UNTO THE FOOLS, DEAL NOT SO MADLY	432 06
10 AND I SAID, IT IS MINE OWN INFIRMITY	434 02
6 I HAVE SAID, YE ARE GODS, *	443 29
4 THEY HAVE SAID, COME, AND LET US ROOT THEM OUT,	444 11
2 FOR I HAVE SAID, MERCY SHALL BE SET UP FOR EVER	450 07
18 BUT WHEN I SAID, MY FOOT HATH SLIPT	458 22
AND SAID, *	459 25
24 BUT I SAID, O MY GOD, TAKE ME NOT AWAY IN THE	465 28
23 SO HE SAID HE WOULD HAVE DESTROYED THEM, HAD NOT	474 14
THE LORD SAID UNTO MY LORD, *	482 07
I SAID IN MY HASTE, ALL MEN ARE LIARS	487 08
WAS GLAD WHEN THEY SAID UNTO ME, *	503 09
3 THEN SAID THEY AMONG THE HEATHEN,	505 11
HOW THEY SAID, DOWN WITH IT, DOWN WITH IT, EVEN TO	513 19
6 I SAID UNTO THE LORD, THOU ART MY GOD, *	516 20
O LORD, AND SAID, *	518 14
EXECUTE ANY OF THE SAID FUNCTIONS, EXCEPT HE BE	529 21
SHALL BE SAID THE FOLLOWING SUFFRAGE	R 531 03
MAY BE SAID THE LITANY FOR ORDINATIONS	R 531 10
THEN SHALL BE SAID THE SERVICE FOR THE COMMUNION,	R 531 11
UNTO THEM, AND SAID, IT IS NOT REASON THAT WE SHOULD	532 09
SHALL BE SAID THIS COLLECT FOLLOWING	R 534 29
SHALL BE SAID THE FOLLOWING SUFFRAGE	R 537 09
MAY BE SAID THE LITANY FOR ORDINATIONS	R 537 16
THEN SHALL BE SAID THE SERVICE FOR THE COMMUNION,	R 537 17
THEN SAID JESUS UNTO THEM AGAIN, VERILY, VERILY,	539 03
OUT OF THE SAID SCRIPTURES TO INSTRUCT THE PEOPLE	542 05
CREED SHALL BE SAID, AND THE BISHOP SHALL GO ON IN	R 546 28
SHALL BE SAID THIS COLLECT	R 547 03
THE LITANY BE ONCE SAID FOR BOTH	R 547 21
COME TO HIM, HE SAID UNTO THEM, YE KNOW, FROM THE	550 06
LORD JESUS, HOW HE SAID, IT IS MORE BLESSED TO GIVE	551 10
GRIEVED BECAUSE HE SAID UNTO HIM THE THIRD TIME,	551 21
AND HE SAID UNTO HIM, LORD, THOU KNOWEST ALL THINGS	551 22
AND WHEN HE HAD SO SAID, HE SHEWED UNTO THEM HIS	551 31
AND WHEN HE HAD SAID THIS, HE BREATHED ON THEM,	552 03
AND THEN SHALL BE SAID THE LITANY	553 14
THE LITANY, MAY BE SAID THE LITANY FOR ORDINATIONS	R 553 24
THEN SHALL BE SAID THIS PRAYER FOLLOWING	R 553 25
SHALL BE SUNG OR SAID OVER HIM	R 556 03
SHALL BE SAID THIS PRAYER	R 559 04
OF PRIESTS SHALL BE SAID, THAT IT MAY PLEASE THEE TO	R 560 25
A BISHOP SHALL BE SAID, THAT IT MAY PLEASE THEE TO	R 560 32
SAT UPON THE THRONE SAID, BEHOLD, I MAKE ALL THINGS	567 21
AND HE SAID UNTO ME, WRITE	567 22
AND SAID UNTO THEM THAT SOLD DOVES, TAKE THESE THINGS	567 31
INSTITUTE YOU INTO SAID PARISH, (OR CHURCH,)	569 18
THEN SHALL BE SAID OR SUNG EXSURGAT DEUS, PSALM	R 571 30
YOU SAID THAT YOUR SPONSORS DID PROMISE	578 17
IT WAS COMMONLY SAID, THAT THE PRIEST DID OFFER	609 17
FOR THE READING OF SAID HOMILIES IN CHURCHES,	R 610 27
ACCORDING TO SAID FORM, WE DECREE ALL SUCH TO BE	610 35

SAIDST

JESUS CHRIST, WHO SAIDST UNTO THINE APOSTLES, PEACE I	049 05
THY SAINTS, AND SAIDST, *	451 13

SAINT

HEAR ALSO WHAT SAINT PAUL SAITH	076 17
HEAR ALSO WHAT SAINT JOHN SAITH	076 21
MUST CONSIDER HOW SAINT PAUL EXHORTETH ALL PERSONS	085 27
THY FIRST MARTYR SAINT STEPHEN, WHO PRAYED FOR HIS	099 31
AND EVANGELIST SAINT JOHN, MAY SO WALK IN THE LIGHT	101 08
THY HOLY APOSTLE SAINT ANDREW, THAT HE READILY OBEYED	226 19
BLESSED APOSTLE SAINT PAUL, HAST CAUSED THE LIGHT OF	229 18
OF THY EVANGELIST SAINT MARK	237 07
THY HOLY APOSTLES, SAINT PHILIP AND SAINT JAMES, WE	238 32
SAINT PHILIP AND SAINT JAMES, WE MAY STEDFASTLY WALK	238 32
TO THY APOSTLE SAINT PETER MANY EXCELLENT GIFTS,	244 23

SAINT CONTINUED

THINE HOLY APOSTLE SAINT JAMES, LEAVING HIS FATHER	246	17
THY SERVANT SAINT LUKE THE PHYSICIAN, TO SET FORTH IN	253	16
OF THY SERVANT (SAINT --), MAY PERSEVERE IN RUNNING	258	14
WRITTEN BY SAINT MARK, IN THE TENTH CHAPTER,	274	23
WRITTEN BY SAINT JOHN, IN THE THIRD CHAPTER,	275	03
WRITTEN BY SAINT MATTHEW, IN THE	275	23
OF THE EVANGELIST SAINT LUKE, IN THE EIGHTH CHAPTER	296	11
IS COMMENDED OF SAINT PAUL TO BE HONOURABLE AMONG ALL	300	15
HIS HOLY APOSTLE SAINT PAUL, NCT TO BE SORRY, AS MEN	335	03
AND AARON THE SAINT OF THE LORD	473	34
THE FIRST MARTYR SAINT STEPHEN, WITH OTHERS	531	17
SHALL BE EITHER SAINT MATTHEW IX	R 547	25
OR ELSE SAINT LUKE XII	R 547	26
IN THE GOSPEL OF SAINT LUKE, THAT OUR SAVIOUR CHRIST	553	04
AND SIN (AS SAINT JOHN SAITH) WAS NOT IN HIM	605	34
AS SAINT PAUL SAITH	608	05
THEIR TEETH (AS SAINT AUGUSTINE SAITH) THE SACRAMENT	609	05

SAINTS

THE LORD IS GLORIOUS IN HIS SAINTS	R 008	34
NUMBERED WITH THY SAINTS, IN GLORY EVERLASTING	011	02
THE COMMUNION OF SAINTS	015	29
THE COMMUNION OF SAINTS	029	34
IN ALL HIS SAINTS, WHO HAVE BEEN THE CHOICE VESSELS	048	17
UNTO THE SAINTS, AND YET DO MINISTER	072	26
MULTITUDE OF THY SAINTS, HAST COMPASSED US ABOUT WITH	079	22
THE LEAST OF ALL SAINTS, IS THIS GRACE GIVEN, THAT I	108	19
DISTRIBUTING TO THE NECESSITY OF SAINTS	111	28
NOT BE ONCE NAMED AMONG YOU, AS BECOMETH SAINTS	129	04
BODIES OF THE SAINTS WHICH SLEPT AROSE, AND CAME CUT	137	28
WITH ALL SAINTS WHAT IS THE BREADTH, AND LENGTH, AND	212	18
ALL PERSEVERANCE AND SUPPLICATION FOR ALL SAINTS	219	22
HAVE TO ALL THE SAINTS, FOR THE HOPE WHICH IS LAID UP	223	25
OF THE SAINTS IN LIGHT	224	10
HATH DONE TO THY SAINTS AT JERUSALEM	230	23
PERFECTING OF THE SAINTS, FOR THE WORK OF THE	237	21
WITH THE SAINTS, AND OF THE HOUSEHOLD OF GOD	255	04
THY BLESSED SAINTS IN ALL VIRTUOUS AND GODLY LIVING,	256	08
THE FLAME OF THY LOVE IN THE HEARTS OF THE SAINTS	258	05
EXAMPLES OF THY SAINTS, AND ESPECIALLY CF THY SERVANT	258	14
IN THE FELLOWSHIP OF THY SAINTS	268	25
THE COMMUNION OF SAINTS	284	23
WITH THY SAINTS IN LIGHT	318	21
REST WITH ALL THY SAINTS IN THE ETERNAL HABITATICNS	319	10
COMPANY OF THE SAINTS IN LIGHT	320	03
IN THE FELLOWSHIP OF THY SAINTS	334	17
OF THE SAINTS IN LIGHT	336	02
WITH THY BLESSED SAINTS IN GLORY EVERLASTING	336	08
IN ALL THY SAINTS, WHO HAVE BEEN THE CHOICE VESSELS	336	18
IS UPON THE SAINTS THAT ARE IN THE EARTH, *	357	25
THE LORD, O YE SAINTS OF THY	374	30
26 O LOVE THE LORD, ALL YE HIS SAINTS	377	15
9 O FEAR THE LORD, YE THAT ARE HIS SAINTS	380	19
5 GATHER MY SAINTS TOGETHER UNTO ME	401	30
THY NAME, FOR THY SAINTS LIKE IT WELL	405	08
THE FLESH OF THY SAINTS UNTO THE BEASTS OF THE LAND	440	14
AND TO HIS SAINTS, THAT THEY TURN NOT AGAIN UNTC	446	23
AND THY TRUTH IN THE CONGREGATION OF THE SAINTS	450	14
COUNCIL OF THE SAINTS, *	450	20
VISIONS UNTO THY SAINTS, AND SAIDST, *	451	12
THE LORD PRESERVETH THE SOULS OF HIS SAINTS	461	17
THE SIGHT OF THE LORD IS THE DEATH OF HIS SAINTS	487	15
AND LET THY SAINTS SING WITH JOYFULNESS	508	22
AND HER SAINTS SHALL REJOICE AND SING	509	06
AND THY SAINTS GIVE THANKS UNTO THEE	521	12
ALL HIS SAINTS SHALL PRAISE HIM	524	30
CONGREGATION OF SAINTS PRAISE HIM	525	04
5 LET THE SAINTS BE JOYFUL WITH GLORY	525	11
SUCH HONOUR HAVE ALL HIS SAINTS	525	20
PERFECTING OF THE SAINTS, FOR THE WORK OF THE	538	08
WE, WITH ALL THY SAINTS, MAY BE PARTAKERS CF THY	561	20
AND LET THY SAINTS SING WITH JOYFULNESS	562	05
ASSEMBLY OF THE SAINTS UPON THE EARTH	568	09
PROFESS THE FAITH ONCE DELIVERED TO THE SAINTS	574	12
NUMBERED WITH THY SAINTS IN GLORY EVERLASTING	574	19
THE COMMUNION OF SAINTS	578	07
AND IN THE FELLOWSHIP OF THY SAINTS	597	06
INVOCATION OF SAINTS, IS A FOND THING, VAINLY	607	15

SAINTS'

UPON ALL SAINTS' DAY, AND SEVEN DAYS AFTER	R 079	21

SAITH

THUS SAITH THE HIGH AND LOFTY ONE THAT INHABITETH	003	25
AMONG THE HEATHEN, SAITH THE LORD OF HOSTS	004	16
HEAR WHAT OUR LORD JESUS CHRIST SAITH	R 067	31
PRIEST SAY, HEAR WHAT OUR LORD JESUS CHRIST SAITH	069	26
NOT EVERY ONE THAT SAITH UNTO ME, LORD, LORD, SHALL	072	13
OUR SAVIOUR CHRIST SAITH UNTO ALL WHO TRULY TURN TO	076	10
HEAR ALSO WHAT SAINT PAUL SAITH	076	17
HEAR ALSO WHAT SAINT JOHN SAITH	076	21
AND AGAIN HE SAITH, REJOICE, YE GENTILES, WITH HIS	092	28
AND AGAIN, ESAIAS SAITH, THERE SHALL BE A ROOT CF	092	30
AND HE SAITH, I AM NOT	095	25
INTO THE WORLD, HE SAITH, AND LET ALL THE ANGELS OF	097	06
OF THE ANGELS HE SAITH, WHO MAKETH HIS ANGELS	097	07
UNTO THE SON HE SAITH, THY THRONE, O GOD, IS FOR EVER	097	08
JESUS SAITH UNTO PETER, FOLLOW ME	102	03
PETER SEEING HIM SAITH TO JESUS, LORD, AND WHAT SHALL	102	06
JESUS SAITH UNTO HIM, IF I WILL THAT HE TARRY TILL I	102	07
I WILL REPAY, SAITH THE LORD	113	05

SAITH CONTINUED

MOTHER OF JESUS SAITH UNTO HIM, THEY HAVE NO WINE	113	14
JESUS SAITH UNTO HER, WOMAN, WHAT HAVE I TO DO WITH	113	15
WHATSOEVER HE SAITH UNTO YOU, DO IT	113	17
HIS MOTHER SAITH UNTO THE SERVANTS, WHATSOEVER HE	113	17
JESUS SAITH UNTO THEM, FILL THE WATER-POTS WITH	113	20
AND HE SAITH UNTO THEM, DRAW OUT NOW, AND BEAR UNTO	113	22
AND SAITH UNTO HIM, EVERY MAN AT THE	113	27
AND JESUS SAITH UNTO HIM, SEE THOU TELL NO MAN	115	03
AND JESUS SAITH UNTO HIM, I WILL COME AND HEAL HIM	115	09
STANDING IDLE, AND SAITH UNTO THEM, WHY STAND YE HERE	119	25
HE SAITH UNTO THEM, GO YE ALSO INTO THE VINEYARD	119	27
OF THE VINEYARD SAITH UNTO HIS STEWARD, CALL THE	119	29
YE EVEN TO ME, SAITH THE LORD, WITH ALL YOUR HEART,	124	21
FOR HE SAITH, I HAVE HEARD THEE IN A TIME ACCEPTED,	126	05
OF THE TEMPLE, AND SAITH UNTO HIM, IF THOU BE THE SON	126	32
AND SAITH UNTO HIM, ALL THESE THINGS WILL I GIVE	127	06
THEN SAITH JESUS UNTO HIM, GET THEE HENCE, SATAN	127	08
WHEREFORE HE SAITH, AWAKE THOU THAT SLEEPEST, AND	129	21
FINDING NONE, HE SAITH, I WILL RETURN UNTO MY HOUSE	130	12
NEVERTHELESS WHAT SAITH THE SCRIPTURE	131	15
COME UNTO HIM, HE SAITH UNTO PHILIP, WHENCE SHALL WE	131	27
PETER'S BROTHER, SAITH UNTO HIM, THERE IS A LAD HERE,	131	32
PILATE SAITH UNTO THEM, WHAT SHALL I DO THEN WITH	136	04
HIS DISCIPLES, AND SAITH UNTO THEM, GO YE INTO THE	140	26
THE MASTER SAITH, WHERE IS THE GUEST-CHAMBER,	140	29
AND JESUS SAITH UNTO THEM, ALL YE SHALL BE OFFENDED	141	18
AND JESUS SAITH UNTO HIM, VERILY I SAY UNTO THEE,	141	23
AND HE SAITH TO HIS DISCIPLES, SIT YE HERE, WHILE I	141	28
AND SAITH UNTO THEM, MY SOUL IS EXCEEDING SORROWFUL	141	31
THEM SLEEPING, AND SAITH UNTO PETER, SIMON, SLEEPEST	142	04
THIRD TIME, AND SAITH UNTO THEM, SLEEP CN NOW, AND	142	10
TO HIM, AND SAITH, MASTER, MASTER	142	20
HIS CLOTHES, AND SAITH, WHAT NEED WE ANY FURTHER	143	17
WHICH SAITH, AND HE WAS NUMBERED WITH THE	146	17
THE MASTER SAITH UNTO THEE, WHERE IS THE	148	29
AND PETER SAITH UNTO HIM, LORD, DOST THOU WASH MY	156	02
PETER SAITH UNTO HIM, THOU SHALT NEVER WASH MY FEET	156	05
SIMON PETER SAITH UNTO HIM, LORD, NOT MY FEET ONLY,	156	07
JESUS SAITH TO HIM, HE THAT IS WASHED NEEDETH NCT	156	08
INTO THE WORLD, HE SAITH, SACRIFICE AND OFFERING THOU	157	24
AFTER THOSE DAYS, SAITH THE LORD, I WILL PUT MY LAWS	158	12
THEN SAITH HE, AND THEIR SINS AND INIQUITIES WILL I	158	13
FORTH AGAIN, AND SAITH UNTO THEM, BEHOLD, I BRING HIM	158	34
AND PILATE SAITH UNTO THEM, BEHOLD THE MAN	159	04
PILATE SAITH UNTO THEM, TAKE YE HIM, AND CRUCIFY HIM	159	07
JUDGMENT HALL, AND SAITH UNTO JESUS, WHENCE ART THOU	159	12
THEN SAITH PILATE UNTO HIM, SPEAKEST THOU NOT UNTC	159	13
AND HE SAITH UNTO THE JEWS, BEHOLD YOUR KING	159	26
PILATE SAITH UNTO THEM, SHALL I CRUCIFY YOUR KING	159	28
WHICH SAITH, THEY PARTED MY RAIMENT AMONG	160	15
THEN SAITH HE TO THE DISCIPLE, BEHOLD THY MOTHER	160	21
WHOM HE LOVED, HE SAITH UNTO HIS MOTHER, WOMAN,	160	21
BE FULFILLED, SAITH, I THIRST	160	25
HE KNOWETH THAT HE SAITH TRUE, THAT YE MIGHT BELIEVE	161	06
ANOTHER SCRIPTURE SAITH, THEY SHALL LOOK ON HIM WHOM	161	09
JESUS LOVED, AND SAITH UNTO THEM, THEY HAVE TAKEN	164	14
AND HE SAITH UNTO THEM, BE NOT AFFRIGHTED	165	28
WHEREFORE HE SAITH ALSO IN ANOTHER PSALM, THOU SHALT	169	13
MIDST OF THEM, AND SAITH UNTO THEM, PEACE BE UNTC	169	28
IN THE MIDST, AND SAITH UNTO THEM, PEACE BE UNTO YOU	171	17
ON THEM, AND SAITH UNTO THEM, RECEIVE YE THE HOLY	171	22
IS THIS THAT HE SAITH UNTO US, A LITTLE WHILE, AND YE	173	30
IS THIS THAT HE SAITH, A LITTLE WHILE	174	02
WE CANNOT TELL WHAT HE SAITH	174	03
THE FATHER, WHICH, SAITH HE, YE HAVE HEARD OF ME	177	31
JUDAS SAITH UNTO HIM, NOT ISCARIOT, LORD, HOW IS IT	181	21
NICODEMUS SAITH UNTO HIM, HOW CAN A MAN BE BORN WHEN	188	07
ABRAHAM SAITH UNTO HIM, THEY HAVE MOSES AND THE	190	26
UNTO HIM, AND SAITH UNTO THEM, I HAVE COMPASSICN CN	199	10
NOT EVERY ONE THAT SAITH UNTO ME, LORD, LORD, SHALL	200	24
HE SIGHED, AND SAITH UNTO HIM, EPHPHATHA, THAT IS,	207	02
HE SAITH NOT, AND TO SEEDS, AS OF MANY	207	20
HE SAITH UNTO THEM, HOW THEN DOTH DAVID IN SPIRIT	215	18
(THEN SAITH HE TO THE SICK OF THE	217	10
THEN SAITH HE TO HIS SERVANTS, THE WEDDING IS READY,	218	15
AND HE SAITH UNTO HIM, FRIEND, HOW CAMEST THOU IN	218	23
THE NOBLEMAN SAITH UNTO HIM, SIR, COME DOWN ERE MY	220	02
JESUS SAITH UNTO HIM, GO THY WAY	220	03
JESUS SAITH UNTO HIM, I SAY NOT UNTO THEE, UNTIL	221	11
AND HE SAITH UNTO THEM, WHOSE IS THIS IMAGE AND	223	07
THEN SAITH HE UNTO THEM, RENDER THEREFORE UNTO CAESAR	223	09
THE DAYS COME, SAITH THE LORD, THAT I WILL RAISE UNTO	225	09
THE DAYS COME, SAITH THE LORD, THAT THEY SHALL NO	225	15
COME UNTO HIM, HE SAITH UNTO PHILIP, WHENCE SHALL WE	225	25
PETER'S BROTHER, SAITH UNTO HIM, THERE IS A LAD HERE,	225	29
FOR THE SCRIPTURE SAITH, WHOSOEVER BELIEVETH ON HIM	226	30
FOR ESAIAS SAITH, LORD, WHO HATH BELIEVED OUR REPORT	227	12
FIRST MOSES SAITH, I WILL PROVOKE YOU TO JEALOUSY BY	227	17
IS VERY BOLD, AND SAITH, I WAS FOUND OF THEM THAT	227	19
BUT TO ISRAEL HE SAITH, ALL DAY LONG I HAVE STRETCHED	227	21
AND HE SAITH UNTO THEM, FOLLOW ME, AND I WILL MAKE	227	26
THEN SAITH HE TO THOMAS, REACH HITHER THY FINGER,	229	03
JESUS SAITH UNTO HIM, THOMAS, BECAUSE THOU HAST SEEN	229	07
HE SHALL COME, SAITH THE LORD OF HOSTS	232	07
AND FEAR NOT ME, SAITH THE LORD OF HOSTS	232	20
WHEREFORE HE SAITH, WHEN HE ASCENDED UP ON HIGH, HE	237	13
THOMAS SAITH UNTO HIM, LORD, WE KNOW NOT WHITHER THOU	240	04
JESUS SAITH UNTO HIM, I AM THE WAY, THE TRUTH, AND	240	05
PHILIP SAITH UNTO HIM, LORD, SHEW US THE FATHER, AND	240	09
JESUS SAITH UNTO HIM, HAVE I BEEN SO LONG TIME WITH	240	10
YE MY PEOPLE, SAITH YOUR GOD	242	16
AND HE SAITH UNTO HIM, CAST THY GARMENT ABOUT THEE,	245	17
HE SAITH UNTO THEM, BUT WHOM SAY YE THAT I AM	245	35
SHE SAITH UNTO HIM, GRANT THAT THESE MY TWO SONS MAY	247	09

SAITH   CONTINUED

AND HE SAITH UNTO THEM, YE SHALL DRINK INDEED OF MY	247 14
AND HE SAITH UNTO HIM, FOLLOW ME	251 14
AND JESUS SAITH UNTO THEM, YEA	260 13
ARE MY PEOPLE, SAITH THE LORD GOD	262 22
AND I AM YOUR GOD, SAITH THE LORD GOD	262 23
OUR SAVIOUR CHRIST SAITH, NONE CAN ENTER INTO THE	273 30
NICODEMUS SAITH UNTO HIM, HOW CAN A MAN BE BORN WHEN	275 12
AND THE LIFE, SAITH THE LORD	324 05
BUT WHEN HE SAITH ALL THINGS ARE PUT UNDER HIM, IT IS	328 32
THOMAS SAITH UNTO HIM, LORD, WE KNOW NOT WHITHER THOU	331 23
JESUS SAITH UNTO HIM, I AM THE WAY, THE TRUTH, AND	331 25
EVEN SO SAITH THE SPIRIT	333 27
AND THE LIFE, SAITH THE LORD	338 05
OR SUNG, JESUS SAITH TO HIS DISCIPLES, YE NOW	341 09
6 I WILL UP, SAITH THE LORD	355 18
UNTO THE UNGODLY SAITH GOD, *	402 22
APPOINTED TIME, SAITH GOD, *	432 02
WHEREFORE HE SAITH, WHEN HE ASCENDED UP ON HIGH, HE	537 33
THEN SAITH HE UNTO HIS DISCIPLES, THE HARVEST TRULY	538 17
JESUS SAITH TO SIMON PETER, SIMON, SON OF JONAS,	551 14
HE SAITH UNTO HIM, YEA, LORD	551 15
HE SAITH UNTO HIM, FEED MY LAMBS	551 16
HE SAITH TO HIM AGAIN THE SECOND TIME, SIMON, SCN OF	551 17
HE SAITH UNTO HIM, YEA, LORD	551 18
HE SAITH UNTO HIM, FEED MY SHEEP	551 19
HE SAITH UNTO HIM THE THIRD TIME, SIMON, SCN OF	551 20
JESUS SAITH UNTO HIM, FEED MY SHEEP	551 24
IN THE MIDST, AND SAITH UNTO THEM, PEACE BE UNTO YOU	551 30
THEN SAITH JESUS TO THEM AGAIN, PEACE BE UNTO YCU	551 33
ON THEM, AND SAITH UNTO THEM, RECEIVE YE THE HOLY	552 03
BOOKS (AS HIEROME SAITH) THE CHURCH DOTH READ FCR	604 02
WHEREAS CHRIST SAITH PLAINLY, WHEN YE HAVE DONE ALL	605 28
SIN (AS SAINT JOHN SAITH) WAS NOT IN HIM	605 35
TO THEMSELVES DAMNATION, AS SAINT PAUL SAITH	608 06
SAINT AUGUSTINE SAITH) THE SACRAMENT OF THE BODY AND	609 05

SAKE

AND GRANT, O MOST MERCIFUL FATHER, FOR HIS SAKE	006 28
AND THIS WE BEG FOR JESUS CHRIST'S SAKE	019 11
AND GRANT, O MOST MERCIFUL FATHER, FOR HIS SAKE	024 03
AND THIS WE BEG FOR JESUS CHRIST'S SAKE	033 09
FOR THE SAKE OF HIM WHO DIED AND ROSE AGAIN, AND EVER	037 21
FOR THE SAKE OF HIM WHO LAID DOWN HIS LIFE FOR US,	044 05
FOR THE SAKE OF HIM WHO CAME AMONG US AS ONE THAT	044 24
AND DELIVER US FOR THY NAME'S SAKE	058 26
FOR THE SAKE OF JESUS CHRIST, OUR BLESSED	VI 42
BE MERCIFUL TO US SINNERS, FOR THY NAME'S SAKE	062 04
FOR HIS NAME'S SAKE, WHO HAVE MINISTERED UNTO THE	072 25
FOR JESUS CHRIST'S SAKE, OUR ONLY MEDIATOR AND	075 05
LORD JESUS CHRIST'S SAKE, FORGIVE US ALL THAT IS	075 27
LORD JESUS CHRIST'S SAKE, THAT YE WILL NOT REFUSE TO	088 15
BUT ALSO FOR CONSCIENCE SAKE	114 23
GRANT THIS FOR THINE ONLY SON JESUS CHRIST'S SAKE	122 19
O LORD, WHO FOR OUR SAKE DIDST FAST FORTY DAYS ANC	125 27
FOR THY SERVANTS' SAKE, THE TRIBES OF THINE	139 26
TO EVERY ORDINANCE OF MAN FOR THE LORD'S SAKE	173 18
FOR THE SAKE OF JESUS CHRIST OUR LORD	194 09
FOR RIGHTEOUSNESS' SAKE, HAPPY ARE YE	196 02
AS GOD FOR CHRIST'S SAKE HATH FORGIVEN YOU	216 30
FOR THE SAKE OF JESUS CHRIST, OUR BLESSED	223 19
GREAT THINGS HE MUST SUFFER FOR MY NAME'S SAKE	230 29
FOR MY NAME'S SAKE, SHALL RECEIVE AN HUNDREDFOLD,	231 20
OR ELSE BELIEVE ME FOR THE VERY WORKS' SAKE	240 18
AND PATIENTLY SUFFER FOR THE TRUTH'S SAKE	242 13
AND OURSELVES YOUR SERVANTS FOR JESUS' SAKE	251 07
YOU FOR MY NAME'S SAKE, BECAUSE THEY KNOW NOT HIM	255 21
THEY WHICH ARE PERSECUTED FOR RIGHTEOUSNESS' SAKE	257 29
MANNER OF EVIL AGAINST YOU FALSELY, FOR MY SAKE	257 32
FOR JESUS CHRIST'S SAKE	323 17
FOR THE SAKE OF THE SAME THY SON JESUS CHRIST OUR	336 02
O FATHER, FOR THE SAKE OF THE SAME, THY SCN JESUS	336 28
IN THE PATHS OF RIGHTEOUSNESS FOR HIS NAME'S SAKE	338 22
O SAVE ME, FOR THY MERCY'S SAKE	349 07
TROUBLES' SAKE OF THE NEEDY, *	355 16
IN THE PATHS OF RIGHTEOUSNESS FOR HIS NAME'S SAKE	368 15
10 FOR THY NAME'S SAKE, O LORD, *	370 06
AND LEAD ME FOR THY NAME'S SAKE	375 28
AND SAVE ME FOR THY MERCY'S SAKE	376 29
22 FOR THY SAKE ALSO ARE WE KILLED ALL THE DAY LONG,	396 04
AND DELIVER US, FOR THY MERCY'S SAKE	396 13
FOR THY NAME'S SAKE, *	406 03
KINGS FOR THEIR SAKE, *	420 09
29 FOR THY TEMPLE'S SAKE AT JERUSALEM	421 13
FOR THY SAKE HAVE I SUFFERED REPROOF	422 16
BE MERCIFUL UNTO OUR SINS, FOR THY NAME'S SAKE	440 20
THEM FOR HIS NAME'S SAKE, *	473 16
FOR THY LOVING MERCY, AND FOR THY TRUTH'S SAKE	485 13
THY SERVANT DAVID'S SAKE, *	508 23
UNTO ME FOR THY TRUTH AND RIGHTEOUSNESS' SAKE	518 24
O LORD, FOR THY NAME'S SAKE	519 15
THY RIGHTEOUSNESS' SAKE BRING MY SOUL OUT OF TROUBLE	519 16
FOR CHRIST'S SAKE TO POOR AND NEEDY PEOPLE, AND TO	555 24
AND DELIVER US FOR THY NAME'S SAKE	562 03
FOR JESUS CHRIST'S SAKE, OUR MOST BLESSED LORD AND	566 24
GRANT THIS FOR THE SAKE OF JESUS CHRIST THY SON OUR	573 28
FOR HIS SAKE WHO LAY DOWN IN THE GRAVE, AND ROSE	587 26
FOR THE SAKE OF THY SON JESUS CHRIST, OUR ONLY	590 06
FOR HIS SAKE WHO WENT ABOUT DOING GOOD, THY SON OUR	591 04
THY COMPASSION'S SAKE, TO SANCTIFY ALL OUR THOUGHTS	594 21
FOR THE SAKE OF HIM BY WHOM ALL THINGS WERE MADE,	596 21
FOR CHRIST'S SAKE	600 16
DO MORE FOR HIS SAKE, THAN OF BOUNDEN DUTY IS	605 27

SAKES

FOR THEIR SAKES THEREFORE LIFT UP THYSELF AGAIN	350 05
BUT REPROVED EVEN KINGS FOR THEIR SAKES	470 31
SO THAT HE PUNISHED MOSES FOR THEIR SAKES	474 34
AND COMPANIONS' SAKES, *	503 22
WHO FOR OUR SAKES BECAME POOR, THY SON, OUR	599 16

SALEM

2 AT SALEM IS HIS TABERNACLE, *	432 25

SALMON

THEN WERE THEY AS WHITE AS SNOW IN SALMON	420 10

SALOME

OF JAMES, AND SALOME, HAD BOUGHT SWEET SPICES, THAT	165 19

SALUTATION

MANNER OF SALUTATION THIS SHOULD BE	236 12

SALUTE

AND BEGAN TO SALUTE HIM, HAIL, KING OF THE JEWS	145 33
AND SALUTE NO MAN BY THE WAY	254 18
AND IF YE SALUTE YOUR BRETHREN ONLY, WHAT DC YE MORE	264 12
AND OTHERS, SHALL SALUTE AND WELCOME HIM, BICDING HIM R	574 27

SALVATION

HEARTILY REJOICE IN THE STRENGTH OF OUR SALVATION	009 04
UP A MIGHTY SALVATION FOR US, *	014 10
KNOWLEDGE OF SALVATION UNTO HIS PEOPLE *	014 27
AND FOR OUR SALVATION CAME DOWN FROM HEAVEN, AND WAS	016 06
AND GRANT US THY SALVATION	016 30
THE LORD DECLARED HIS SALVATION	027 08
HAVE SEEN THE SALVATION OF OUR GOD	027 12
THY SALVATION, WHICH THOU HAST PREPARED *	028 11
AND FOR OUR SALVATION CAME DOWN FROM HEAVEN, AND WAS	030 11
AND GRANT US THY SALVATION	031 03
FORWARD THE SALVATION OF ALL MEN	039 04
TOWARDS THE ATTAINMENT OF EVERLASTING SALVATION	049 13
AND FOR OUR SALVATION CAME DOWN FROM HEAVEN, AND WAS	071 08
LOVE YOUR OWN SALVATION, THAT YE WILL BE PARTAKERS OF	089 08
SOUL BY DEATH UPON THE CROSS FOR YOUR SALVATION	089 11
FOR NOW IS OUR SALVATION NEARER THAN WHEN WE	091 02
THAT BRINGETH SALVATION HATH APPEARED TO ALL MEN,	098 18
OUT YOUR OWN SALVATION WITH FEAR AND TREMBLING	106 03
IN THE DAY OF SALVATION HAVE I SUCCOURED THEE	126 06
NOW IS THE DAY OF SALVATION	126 07
ARM BROUGHT SALVATION UNTO ME	138 24
WITH THY HELP, O LORD GOD OF OUR SALVATION	147 09
APPEAR THE SECOND TIME WITHOUT SIN UNTO SALVATION	148 10
WORD OF THIS SALVATION SENT	168 26
LEAD US TO ALL THINGS PROFITABLE TO OUR SALVATION	210 21
THE HELMET OF SALVATION, AND THE SWORD OF THE SPIRIT,	219 18
WITH THE MOUTH CONFESSION IS MADE UNTO SALVATION	226 30
HAVE SEEN THY SALVATION, WHICH THOU HAST PREPARED	233 07
UP AN HORN OF SALVATION FOR US IN THE HOUSE CF HIS	243 34
KNOWLEDGE OF SALVATION UNTO HIS PEOPLE BY THE	244 12
NOW IS COME SALVATION, AND STRENGTH, AND THE KINGDOM	252 10
SAYING, SALVATION TO OUR GOD WHICH SITTETH	256 27
BE FOR SALVATION UNTO THE ENDS OF THE EARTH	261 05
AND BE MADE AN HEIR OF EVERLASTING SALVATION	276 13
THIS STATE OF SALVATION, THROUGH JESUS CHRIST CUR	284 03
AS GENERALLY NECESSARY TO SALVATION	292 07
THE CUP OF SALVATION, AND CALL UPON THE NAME OF THE	305 29
SALVATION BELONGETH UNTO THE LORD	309 24
HEALTH AND SALVATION, BUT ONLY THE NAME OF OUR LORD	314 21
THE LORD IS MY LIGHT AND MY SALVATION	326 05
ME NOT, NEITHER FORSAKE ME, O GOD OF MY SALVATION	326 27
8 SALVATION BELONGETH UNTO THE LORD	347 07
I WILL REJOICE IN THY SALVATION	352 20
AND MY HEART IS JOYFUL IN THY SALVATION	356 08
WHO SHALL GIVE SALVATION UNTO ISRAEL OUT OF SICN	356 30
ALSO OF MY SALVATION, AND MY REFUGE	359 27
THOU HAST GIVEN ME THE DEFENCE OF THY SALVATION	362 06
AND PRAISED BE THE GOD OF MY SALVATION	362 33
REJOICE IN THY SALVATION, AND TRIUMPH IN THE NAME OF	364 23
EXCEEDING GLAD SHALL HE BE OF THY SALVATION	365 06
5 HIS HONOUR IS GREAT IN THY SALVATION	365 13
AND RIGHTEOUSNESS FROM THE GOD OF HIS SALVATION	369 06
FOR THOU ART THE GOD OF MY SALVATION	369 26
THE LORD IS MY LIGHT AND MY SALVATION	371 24
ME NOT, NEITHER FORSAKE ME, O GOD OF MY SALVATION	372 19
SAY UNTO MY SOUL, I AM THY SALVATION	381 23
IT SHALL REJOICE IN HIS SALVATION	382 08
40 BUT THE SALVATION OF THE RIGHTEOUS COMETH OF THE	387 13
O LORD GOD OF MY SALVATION	389 03
TALK HATH BEEN OF THY TRUTH, AND OF THY SALVATICN	391 05
AS LOVE THY SALVATION, SAY ALWAY, THE LORD BE	391 22
I SHOW THE SALVATION OF GOD	403 06
7 O THAT THE SALVATION WERE GIVEN UNTO ISRAEL OUT OF	405 28
FOR OF HIM COMETH MY SALVATION	413 28
2 HE VERILY IS MY STRENGTH AND MY SALVATION	413 29
6 HE TRULY IS MY STRENGTH AND MY SALVATION	414 09
IN THY RIGHTEOUSNESS, O GOD OF OUR SALVATION	416 22
EVEN THE GOD OF WHOM COMETH SALVATION	420 25
EVEN IN THE TRUTH OF THY SALVATION	422 31
DELIGHT IN THY SALVATION SAY ALWAY, THE LORD BE	424 28
DAILY SPEAK OF THY RIGHTEOUSNESS AND SALVATION	426 05
O GOD OF OUR SALVATION, FOR THE GLORY OF THY NAME	440 18
AND GRANT US THY SALVATION	446 20

PAGE LN

SALVATION CONTINUED

9 FOR HIS SALVATION IS NIGH THEM THAT FEAR HIM 446 25
LORD GOD OF MY SALVATION, I HAVE CRIED DAY AND NIGHT 448 29
MY GOD, AND MY STRONG SALVATION 451 28
AND SHOW HIM MY SALVATION 455 30
HEARTILY REJOICE IN THE STRENGTH OF OUR SALVATICN 459 06
TELLING OF HIS SALVATION FROM DAY TO DAY 460 03
3 THE LORD DECLARED HIS SALVATION 461 29
HAVE SEEN THE SALVATION OF OUR GOD 461 33
O VISIT ME WITH THY SALVATION 473 07
THE CUP OF SALVATION, * 487 11
AND IS BECOME MY SALVATION 488 29
AND ART BECOME MY SALVATION 489 11
EVEN THY SALVATION, ACCORDING UNTO THY WORD 492 23
LONGED FOR THY SALVATION, * 495 19
FOR ETERNAL SALVATION THROUGH FAITH IN JESUS CHRIST 533 03
TO THE SALVATION OF MAN, BUT WITH DOCTRINE AND 540 35
FOR ETERNAL SALVATION THROUGH FAITH IN JESUS CHRIST 542 03
TO ETERNAL SALVATION, BUT THAT WHICH YOU SHALL BE 542 07
FOR THE SALVATION OF MANKIND, WE RENDER UNTO THEE 545 24
TO THE SAME, AS THE MEANS OF OUR SALVATION 547 11
FOR ETERNAL SALVATION THROUGH FAITH IN JESUS CHRIST 554 21
TO ETERNAL SALVATION, BUT THAT WHICH YOU SHALL BE 554 25
NOT TO DESTRUCTION, BLT TO SALVATION 558 02
AND TO THE SALVATION OF SOULS 560 22
AND RIGHTEOUSNESS FROM THE GOD OF HIS SALVATION 563 21
PROMOTING THE SALVATION OF THE PEOPLE NOW COMMITTED 573 20
THIS STATE OF SALVATION, THROUGH JESUS CHRIST OUR 577 24
AS GENERALLY NECESSARY TO SALVATION 581 09
CONTAINETH ALL THINGS NECESSARY TO SALVATICN 603 29
OR BE THOUGHT REQUISITE OR NECESSARY TO SALVATICN 603 32
TO EVERLASTING SALVATION, AS VESSELS MADE TO HONCUR 606 10
OF ETERNAL SALVATION TO BE ENJOYED THROUGH CHRIST, 606 21
THING TO BE BELIEVED FOR NECESSITY OF SALVATION 607 09

SAMARIA

AND IN SAMARIA, AND UNTO THE UTTERMOST PART 005 14
AND IN SAMARIA, AND UNTO THE UTTERMOST PART 178 11
HEARD THAT SAMARIA HAD RECEIVED THE WORD OF GOD, 185 22
THE MIDST OF SAMARIA AND GALILEE 209 32
HEARD THAT SAMARIA HAD RECEIVED THE WORD OF GOD, 296 14

SAMARITAN

THOU ART A SAMARITAN, AND HAST A DEVIL 133 13
BUT A CERTAIN SAMARITAN, AS HE JOURNEYED, CAME WHERE 208 28
AND HE WAS A SAMARITAN 210 10

SAME

GOING DOWN OF THE SAME MY NAME SHALL BE GREAT AMONG 004 13
THE SAME CHURCH HATH NOT ONLY IN HER PREFACE, V 21
PARTS OF THE SAME (AS WELL IN THE CHIEFEST MATERIALS, V 31
FORGIVENESS OF THE SAME, BY HIS INFINITE GOODNESS AND 006 02
AS WORDS OF THE SAME MEANING IN THE CREED R 015 18
DEFEND US IN THE SAME WITH THY MIGHTY POWER 017 15
FORGIVENESS OF THE SAME, BY HIS INFINITE GOODNESS AND 023 10
AS WORDS OF THE SAME MEANING IN THE CREED R 029 23
THROUGH THE SAME THY SON JESUS CHRIST OUR LORD 038 11
LOOK UPON THE SAME, AND AT THIS TIME SO GUIDE AND 038 27
TO ANY OFFICE AND ADMINISTRATION IN THE SAME 039 11
THROUGH THE SAME THY SON JESUS CHRIST OUR LORD 039 20
THROUGH THE SAME JESUS CHRIST CUR LORD 043 25
LIFE FOR US, THE SAME THY SON, OUR SAVIOUR JESUS 044 06
THAT BRANCH OF THE SAME PLANTED BY GOD IN THIS LAND, 047 11
THE SAME OFFICE MAY BE READ AT OTHER TIMES, R 060 06
O FATHER, THE SAME WE BELIEVE OF THE SON, AND OF THE 079 10
INNUMERABLE BENEFITS PROCURED UNTO US BY THE SAME 081 05
BUT THOU ART THE SAME LORD, WHOSE PROPERTY IS ALWAYS 082 17
TO DELIVER THE SAME TO THE BISHOPS, PRIESTS, AND R 082 26
COVERING THE SAME WITH A FAIR LINEN CLOTH R 083 13
REVERENTLY EAT AND DRINK THE SAME R 084 33
THE SAME ORDER SHALL THE MINISTER USE WITH THOSE, R 085 09
AN ACCOUNT OF THE SAME TO THE ORDINARY, WITHIN R 085 18
IF WE RECEIVE THE SAME UNWORTHILY 085 33
PUNISHMENT HANGETH OVER YOUR HEADS FOR THE SAME 089 16
THROUGH THE SAME OUR LORD JESUS CHRIST, WHO LIVETH 096 17
WITH THEE AND THE SAME SPIRIT EVER, ONE GOD, WORLD 096 19
BUT THOU ART THE SAME, AND THY YEARS SHALL NOT FAIL 097 18
THE SAME WAS IN THE BEGINNING WITH GOD 097 21
THE SAME CAME FOR A WITNESS, TO BEAR WITNESS OF THE 097 27
THERE WERE IN THE SAME COUNTRY SHEPHERDS ABIDING IN 099 10
THROUGH THE SAME OUR LORD JESUS CHRIST, WHO LIVETH 104 10
WITH THEE AND THE SAME SPIRIT EVER, ONE GOD, WORLD 104 11
THROUGH THE SAME THY SON JESUS CHRIST OUR LORD 105 24
GRANT THAT THE SAME LIGHT ENKINDLED IN OUR HEARTS MAY 106 26
THROUGH THE SAME THY SON JESUS CHRIST OUR LORD 108 03
AND OF THE SAME BODY, AND PARTAKERS OF HIS PROMISE IN 108 15
THE SAME EPISTLE AND GOSPEL SHALL SERVE UNTO THE R 109 26
GRACE AND POWER FAITHFULLY TO FULFIL THE SAME 109 33
HAVE NOT THE SAME OFFICE 110 14
BE OF THE SAME MIND ONE TOWARD ANOTHER 111 30
IS GOOD, AND THOU SHALT HAVE PRAISE OF THE SAME 114 18
THE SAME COLLECT, EPISTLE, AND GOSPEL SHALL SERVE R 125 23
CAME OUT OF THE SAME COASTS, AND CRIED UNTO HIM, 128 09
THROUGH THE SAME JESUS CHRIST OUR LORD 134 11
WITH HIM, CAST THE SAME IN HIS TEETH 137 15
THROUGH THE SAME THY SON JESUS CHRIST OUR LORD 138 08
AND SPAKE THE SAME WORDS 142 07
I SHALL KISS, THAT SAME IS HE 142 18
THROUGH THE SAME THY SON JESUS CHRIST OUR LCRD 144 10
RECEIVE THE SAME IN REMEMBRANCE OF HIM, WHO IN THESE 152 10
THE SAME THY SON JESUS CHRIST OUR LORD, WHO NOW 152 11
THE LORD JESUS THE SAME NIGHT IN WHICH HE WAS 152 17

PAGE LN

SAME CONTINUED

AFTER THE SAME MANNER ALSO HE TOOK THE CUP, WHEN HE 152 21
AND THE SAME DAY PILATE AND HEROD WERE MADE FRIENDS 153 18
THOU ART IN THE SAME CONDEMNATION 155 03
EVERY MEMBER OF THE SAME, IN HIS VOCATION AND 156 31
OFTENTIMES THE SAME SACRIFICES, WHICH CAN NEVER TAKE 158 04
AGAIN FOR US, THE SAME THY SON JESUS CHRIST CUR LORD 161 19
WE MAY BRING THE SAME TO GOOD EFFECT 163 27
THROUGH THE SAME JESUS CHRIST OUR LORD, WHO LIVETH 163 27
THROUGH THE SAME THY SON CHRIST OUR LORD 165 08
THROUGH THE SAME THY SON JESUS CHRIST OUR LORD 166 09
DISCIPLES WENT THAT SAME DAY TO A VILLAGE CALLED 167 03
THEY ROSE UP THE SAME HOUR, AND RETURNED TO 168 11
HATH FULFILLED THE SAME UNTO US THEIR CHILDREN, IN 169 07
THE MERITS OF THE SAME THY SON JESUS CHRIST CUR LORD 170 23
THE SAME DAY AT EVENING, BEING THE FIRST DAY OF THE 171 14
THROUGH THE SAME THY SON JESUS CHRIST OUR LORD 172 02
ALL SUCH THINGS AS ARE AGREEABLE TO THE SAME 173 10
AND BY THY MERCIFUL GUIDING MAY PERFORM THE SAME 176 02
THIS SAME JESUS, WHICH IS TAKEN UP FROM YOU INTO 178 17
THE SAME COLLECT, EPISTLE, AND GOSPEL SHALL SERVE R 178 30
EXALT US UNTO THE SAME PLACE WHITHER OUR SAVIOUR 179 08
WITH THEE AND THE SAME HOLY GHOST, ONE GOD, WORLD 179 10
SO MINISTER THE SAME ONE TO ANOTHER, AS GOOD STEWARDS 179 17
GRANT US BY THE SAME SPIRIT TO HAVE A RIGHT JUDGMENT 180 10
IN THE UNITY OF THE SAME SPIRIT, ONE GOD, WORLD 180 14
IN THE UNITY OF THE SAME SPIRIT EVER, ONE GOD, 182 19
OF GIFTS, BUT THE SAME SPIRIT 182 22
BUT THE SAME LORD 182 24
BUT IT IS THE SAME GOD WHICH WORKETH ALL IN ALL 182 25
OF KNOWLEDGE BY THE SAME SPIRIT 182 28
FAITH BY THE SAME SPIRIT 182 29
OF HEALING BY THE SAME SPIRIT 182 30
WITH THEE AND THE SAME HOLY SPIRIT LIVETH AND 183 26
WITH THEE AND THE SAME SPIRIT, ONE GOD, WORLD WITHOUT 185 18
SOME OTHER WAY, THE SAME IS A THIEF AND A RCBBER 186 02
THE SAME CAME TO JESUS BY NIGHT, AND SAID UNTO HIM, 187 35
KNOWING THAT THE SAME AFFLICTIONS ARE ACCOMPLISHED IN 193 07
HATH SUBJECTED THE SAME IN HOPE, BECAUSE THE CREATURE 194 16
FOR WITH THE SAME MEASURE THAT YE METE WITHAL IT 194 30
AND OF THY GREAT MERCY KEEP US IN THE SAME 198 23
AND DID ALL EAT THE SAME SPIRITUAL MEAT 201 08
DID ALL DRINK THE SAME SPIRITUAL DRINK 201 09
OF GIFTS, BUT THE SAME SPIRIT 203 22
BUT THE SAME LORD 203 24
BUT IT IS THE SAME GOD WHICH WORKETH ALL IN ALL 203 25
OF KNOWLEDGE BY THE SAME SPIRIT 203 28
FAITH BY THE SAME SPIRIT 203 29
OF HEALING BY THE SAME SPIRIT 203 30
THAT IT WAS AT THE SAME HOUR, IN THE WHICH JESUS SAID 220 09
BUT THE SAME SERVANT WENT OUT, AND FOUND ONE OF HIS 221 23
THROUGH THE SAME JESUS CHRIST OUR LORD 226 23
FOR THE SAME LORD OVER ALL IS RICH UNTO ALL THAT CALL 227 03
O LORD, THROUGH THE SAME JESUS CHRIST, TO WHOM, WITH 228 10
UNTO THEE FOR THE SAME, BY FOLLOWING THE HOLY 229 21
BY THE SAME THY SON JESUS CHRIST OUR LORD 231 32
AND THE SAME MAN WAS JUST AND DEVOUT, WAITING FOR THE 232 31
OF JOHN, UNTO THAT SAME DAY THAT HE WAS TAKEN UP FROM 234 23
THROUGH THE SAME JESUS CHRIST OUR LORD 235 22
DESCENDED IS THE SAME ALSO THAT ASCENDED UP FAR ABCVE 237 17
AND I IN HIM, THE SAME BRINGETH FORTH MUCH FRUIT 238 13
THROUGH THE SAME THY SON JESUS CHRIST OUR LORD 239 03
THROUGH TH SAME THY SON JESUS CHRIST CUR LCRD 242 13
TO FOLLOW THE SAME, THAT THEY MAY RECEIVE THE CRCWN 244 27
THROUGH THE SAME THY SON JESUS CHRIST OUR LCRD 244 28
HIM FORTH, THE SAME NIGHT PETER WAS SLEEPING BETWEEN 245 10
THROUGH THE SAME JESUS CHRIST OUR LCRD 246 21
AND BOTH TO PREACH AND RECEIVE THE SAME 249 18
AND TO FOLLOW THE SAME THY SON JESUS CHRIST, WHO 250 23
AT THE SAME TIME CAME THE DISCIPLES UNTO JESUS, 252 22
LITTLE CHILD, THE SAME IS GREATEST IN THE KINGDCM OF 252 28
THROUGH THE SAME THY SON JESUS CHRIST OUR LORD 253 20
AND IN THE SAME HOUSE REMAIN, EATING AND DRINKING 254 22
THROUGH THE SAME JESUS CHRIST OUR LORD 254 32
THROUGH THE SAME THY SON JESUS CHRIST OUR LCRD 256 11
THE SAME FAITH AND POWER OF LOVE 258 06
DO NOT EVEN THE PUBLICANS THE SAME 264 12
AND BE MADE A LIVING MEMBER OF THE SAME 274 06
THE SAME CAME TO JESUS BY NIGHT, AND SAID UNTO HIM, 275 06
WITH THEE AND THE SAME HOLY SPIRIT, NOW AND FOR EVER 276 15
DESIRES OF THE SAME, AND THE SINFUL DESIRES OF THE 276 26
AND WALK IN THE SAME ALL THE DAYS OF THY LIFE 277 05
DESIRES OF THE SAME, AND THE SINFUL DESIRES OF THE 277 28
AND WALK IN THE SAME ALL THE DAYS OF THY LIFE 278 14
THROUGH THE SAME JESUS CHRIST OUR LORD, TO WHOM, WITH 279 19
UPON HIM, USING THE SAME FORM OF WORDS R 279 33
AND OF THY GREAT MERCY KEEP US IN THE SAME 283 11
AND WALK IN THE SAME ALL THE DAYS OF MY LIFE 283 28
MAY CONTINUE IN THE SAME UNTO MY LIFE'S END 284 05
THROUGH THE SAME JESUS CHRIST OUR LORD 290 24
RATIFYING AND CONFIRMING THE SAME 296 25
WITH THEE AND THE SAME HOLY SPIRIT LIVETH AND 298 24
THROUGH THE SAME JESUS CHRIST OUR LORD, WHO LIVETH 303 27
HAVE WITNESSED THE SAME BEFORE GOD AND THIS COMPANY, 304 04
HAVE DECLARED THE SAME BY GIVING AND RECEIVING A 304 06
THROUGH THE SAME THY SON, OUR LORD AND SAVIOUR 316 15
LESS CAUSE TO BE DISQUIETED FOR LACK OF THE SAME R 321 10
THE MOUNTAINS SHAKE AT THE TEMPEST OF THE SAME 327 08
FLESH IS NOT THE SAME FLESH 329 12
FOR THE SAKE OF THE SAME THY SON JESUS CHRIST OUR 336 02
FOR THE SAKE OF THE SAME, THY SON JESUS CHRIST, CUR 336 28
AT THE GRAVE, THE SAME IS HEREBY ALLOWED FOR WEIGHTY R 336 32
THE SAME OFFICE MAY BE USED R 337 07
AT THE SAME TIME CAME THE DISCIPLES UNTO JESUS, 339 21
LITTLE CHILD, THE SAME IS GREATEST IN THE KINGDCM CF 339 27

SAME   CONTINUED

THROUGH THE SAME THY SON, JESUS CHRIST CUR LORD   342 07
IN THE SAME NET WHICH THEY HID PRIVILY IS THEIR FOOT   352 22
THE MOUNTAINS SHAKE AT THE TEMPEST OF THE SAME   397 31
GOD UPHOLDETH THE SAME FOR EVER   399 26
HAVE ALSO HEARD THE SAME, *   414 22
TONGUE OF THY DOGS MAY BE RED THROUGH THE SAME   420 35
AND HE POURETH OUT OF THE SAME   432 16
THEY MIGHT SHOW THEIR CHILDREN THE SAME   435 10
BUT THOU ART THE SAME, AND THY YEARS SHALL NOT FAIL   466 03
AND APPOINTED THE SAME UNTO JACOB FOR A LAW, *   470 22
UP OF THE SUN UNTO THE GOING DCWN OF THE SAME   484 13
22 THE SAME STONE WHICH THE BUILDERS REFUSED,   489 12
50 THE SAME IS MY COMFORT IN MY TROUBLE   493 10
WE HEARD OF THE SAME AT EPHRATAH, *   508 15
HAVE SUCH QUALITIES AS ARE REQUISITE FOR THE SAME   529 16
TO THE MINISTRY OF THE SAME   532 33
DILIGENTLY READ THE SAME UNTO THE PEOPLE ASSEMBLED IN   533 06
AND TO PREACH THE SAME, IF THOU BE THERETO LICENSED   534 12
HOLY COMMUNION THE SAME DAY, WITH THE BISHOP   R 534 27
THROUGH THE SAME THY SON OUR SAVIOUR JESUS CHRIST, TO   535 10
AND THAT THEY ARE PERSONS MEET FOR THE SAME   536 27
WITH THEE AND THE SAME HOLY SPIRIT, WORLD WITHOUT   537 29
DESCENDED IS THE SAME ALSO THAT ASCENDED UP FAR ABOVE   538 04
SOME OTHER WAY, THE SAME IS A THIEF AND A ROBBER   538 25
HAPPEN THAT THE SAME CHURCH, OR ANY MEMBER THEREOF,   540 10
AND WITH A LIFE AGREEABLE TO THE SAME   541 03
TO THE RULE OF THE SAME SCRIPTURES   541 06
HIS CHURCH, SHALL DEMAND OF YOU TOUCHING THE SAME   541 29
HATH RECEIVED THE SAME, ACCORDING TO THE COMMANDMENTS   542 14
WITH ALL DILIGENCE TO KEEP AND OBSERVE THE SAME   542 17
KNOWLEDGE OF THE SAME, LAYING ASIDE THE STUDY OF THE   542 28
TO PERFORM THE SAME, THAT HE MAY ACCOMPLISH HIS WORK   543 20
HERE PRESENT TO THE SAME OFFICE AND MINISTRY,   545 23
BY THE SAME THY BLESSED SON, TO GRANT UNTO ALL,   545 26
THROUGH THE SAME THY SON JESUS CHRIST OUR LORD,   546 03
IN THE UNITY OF THE SAME HOLY SPIRIT, WORLD WITHOUT   546 04
AND REMAIN IN THE SAME PLACE WHERE HANDS WERE LAID   R 546 30
OR AGREEABLE TO THE SAME, AS THE MEANS OF OUR   547 10
AND IF, ON THE SAME DAY, THE ORDER OF DEACONS BE   R 547 19
WITH THEE AND THE SAME HOLY SPIRIT, WORLD WITHOUT   548 08
THAT THEY MAY OBEDIENTLY FOLLOW THE SAME   549 13
THROUGH THE SAME THY SON JESUS CHRIST CUR LCRD   549 15
THE SAME DAY AT EVENING, BEING THE FIRST DAY OF THE   551 27
WITH THEE AND THE SAME HOLY SPIRIT, WORLD WITHOUT   554 03
OUT OF THE SAME HOLY SCRIPTURES TO INSTRUCT THE   554 13
PERSUADED MAY BE CONCLUDED AND PROVED BY THE SAME   554 26
BY PRAYER FOR THE TRUE UNDERSTANDING OF THE SAME   554 31
TO CALL UPON AND ENCOURAGE OTHERS TO THE SAME   555 06
UNTO YOU STRENGTH AND POWER TO PERFORM THE SAME   555 30
THROUGH THE SAME JESUS CHRIST CUR LORD, WHO, WITH   558 06
WITH THEE AND THE SAME HOLY SPIRIT, ONE GOD, WORLD   559 15
IN THE UNITY OF THE SAME SPIRIT EVER, ONE GOD,   562 15
MAY HAVE POWER AND STRENGTH TO FULFIL THE SAME   566 06
OR CHARTERS OF THE CHURCH IN THE SAME   R 569 12
SACERDOTAL FUNCTION AMONG THE PEOPLE OF THE SAME   569 19
AS PRIEST AND RECTOR OF THE SAME   570 15
AS PRIEST AND RECTOR OF THE SAME   570 29
KEEP THEM IN THE SAME, O BLESSED SPIRIT, WHOM, WITH   572 30
THE MERITS OF THE SAME THY BLESSED SON JESUS CHRIST,   574 20
WITH THEE AND THE SAME HOLY GHOST, ONE GUD, WORLC   574 22
AND WALK IN THE SAME ALL THE DAYS OF MY LIFE   577 19
MAY CONTINUE IN THE SAME UNTO MY LIFE'S END   577 26
THE SAME WHICH GOD SPAKE IN THE TWENTIETH   578 22
WE RECEIVE THE SAME, AND A PLEDGE TO ASSURE US   581 14
EVERY MEMBER OF THE SAME, IN HIS VOCATICN AND   590 26
DEFEND US IN THE SAME WITH THY MIGHTY POWER   592 21
THROUGH THE SAME JESUS CHRIST OUR LORD   595 16
THAT OF NECESSITY ARE REQUISITE TO THE SAME   606 41
SO BESIDES THE SAME OUGHT IT NOT TO ENFORCE ANY THING   607 08
THING AGAINST THE SAME, SO BESIDES THE SAME OUGHT IT   607 08
AND SENT TO EXECUTE THE SAME   607 21
RECEIVE THE SAME, THEY HAVE A WHOLESOME EFFECT CR   608 04
AS THEY DO NOT THE SAME IN THEIR OWN NAME, BUT IN   608 11
RECEIVE THE SAME, THE BREAD WHICH WE BREAK IS   608 37
SHALL JUDGE THE SAME TO SERVE BETTER TC GODLINESS   609 24
AND POSSESSION OF THE SAME   611 02

SAMUEL

HIS PRIESTS, AND SAMUEL AMONG SUCH AS CALL UPON HIS   462 27

SANCTIFICATION

EVEN YOUR SANCTIFICATION, THAT YE SHOULD ABSTAIN FROM   127 28
VESSEL IN SANCTIFICATION AND HONOUR   127 30

SANCTIFIED

BODY OF THE CHURCH IS GOVERNED AND SANCTIFIED   156 28
WILL WE ARE SANCTIFIED THROUGH THE OFFERING OF THE   158 02
HATH PERFECTED FOR EVER THEM THAT ARE SANCTIFIED   158 09
INHERITANCE AMONG ALL THEM WHICH ARE SANCTIFIED   551 05
MAY BE SANCTIFIED BY THE HOLY GHOST, AND MAY   565 21

SANCTIFIER

HOLY GHOST, SANCTIFIER OF THE FAITHFUL   054 09
HOLY GHOST, SANCTIFIER OF THE FAITHFUL, VISIT,   572 25

SANCTIFIES

IN IT, AND SANCTIFIES ITS MEMBERS   291 09

SANCTIFIETH

THE UNCLEAN, SANCTIFIETH TO THE PURIFYING OF THE   132 29
WHO SANCTIFIETH ME, AND ALL THE PEOPLE OF GOD   285 02
GHOST WHO SANCTIFIETH THEE   319 23
WHO SANCTIFIETH ME, AND ALL THE PEOPLE OF GCD   578 15

SANCTIFY

SO TO DIRECT, SANCTIFY, AND GOVERN US IN OUR WORK,   036 33
TO DIRECT, SANCTIFY, AND GOVERN, BOTH OUR HEARTS AND   070 07
TO BLESS AND SANCTIFY, WITH THY WORD AND HOLY SPIRIT,   081 09
IN ZION, SANCTIFY A FAST, CALL A SOLEMN ASSEMBLY   124 29
THE PEOPLE, SANCTIFY THE CONGREGATION, ASSEMBLE THE   124 30
BUT SANCTIFY THE LORD GOD IN YOUR HEARTS   196 03
THAT HE MIGHT SANCTIFY AND CLEANSE IT WITH THE   267 20
FROM SIN, TO SANCTIFY HIM WITH THE HOLY GHOST,   276 22
FROM SIN, TO SANCTIFY YOU WITH THE HOLY GHOST, TC   277 23
SANCTIFY THIS WATER TO THE MYSTICAL WASHING AWAY OF   279 15
TO DIRECT, SANCTIFY, AND GOVERN, BOTH OUR HEARTS AND   298 27
SANCTIFY, WE BESEECH THEE, O LORD, THE SICKNESS CF   310 21
TO TIME, TO SANCTIFY THE LIVES OF YOU AND YOURS, AND   541 20
PLEASE THEE TO SANCTIFY AND BLESS THY CHURCH   560 15
TO SANCTIFY ALL OUR THOUGHTS AND ENDEAVOURS   594 21
AND SANCTIFY TO THEM THE ENDURANCE OF   599 09

SANCTUARY

OUR ADVERSARIES HAVE TRODDEN DOWN THY SANCTUARY   139 28
HELP FROM THE SANCTUARY, *   364 19
THEE IN THE SANCTUARY, *   414 29
HOW THOU, MY GOD AND KING, GOEST IN THE SANCTUARY   421 03
WENT INTO THE SANCTUARY OF GOD   429 10
WHICH HATH DONE EVIL IN THY SANCTUARY   430 11
BORDERS OF HIS SANCTUARY, *   438 18
POWER AND HONOUR ARE IN HIS SANCTUARY   460 11
19 FOR HE HATH LOOKED DOWN FROM HIS SANCTUARY   465 17
JUDAH WAS HIS SANCTUARY, *   484 29
HANDS IN THE SANCTUARY, *   509 27
O PRAISE GOD IN HIS SANCTUARY   525 22

SANCTUS

THROUGH THE SANCTUS   R 323 07

SAND

FOWLS LIKE AS THE SAND OF THE SEA   436 26
THEY ARE MORE IN NUMBER THAN THE SAND   515 27

SANDALS

GIRD THYSELF, AND BIND ON THY SANDALS   245 16

SANG

AND SANG PRAISE UNTO HIM   473 25

SAP

16 THE TREES OF THE LORD ALSO ARE FULL OF SAP   468 26

SARDINE

A JASPER AND A SARDINE STONE   187 06

SARKOS

PHRONEMA SARKOS, (WHICH SOME DO EXPCUND THE   604 36

SAT

PURGED OUR SINS, SAT DOWN ON THE RIGHT HAND CF THE   096 29
A CERTAIN BLIND MAN SAT BY THE WAY-SIDE BEGGING   123 27
AND THERE HE SAT WITH HIS DISCIPLES   131 24
SO THE MEN SAT DOWN, IN NUMBER ABOUT FIVE THOUSAND   132 02
THE LEPER, AS HE SAT AT MEAT, THERE CAME A WOMAN   140 03
AND AS THEY SAT AND DID EAT, JESUS SAID, VERILY I SAY   140 35
AND HE SAT WITH THE SERVANTS, AND WARMED HIMSELF AT   142 35
HOUR WAS COME, HE SAT DOWN, AND THE TWELVE APOSTLES   148 34
DOWN TOGETHER, PETER SAT DOWN AMONG THEM   151 10
BEHELD HIM AS HE SAT BY THE FIRE, AND EARNESTLY   151 11
FOR SINS FOR EVER, SAT DOWN ON THE RIGHT HAND OF GOD   158 06
JESUS FORTH, AND SAT DOWN IN THE JUDGMENT-SEAT IN A   159 23
CAME TO PASS, AS HE SAT AT MEAT WITH THEM, HE TCCK   168 05
AS OF FIRE, AND IT SAT UPON EACH OF THEM   180 22
IN HEAVEN, AND ONE SAT ON THE THRONE   187 05
AND HE THAT SAT WAS TO LOOK UPON LIKE A JASPER AND A   187 06
THANKS TO HIM THAT SAT ON THE THRONE, WHO LIVETH FOR   187 25
DOWN BEFORE HIM THAT SAT ON THE THRONE, AND WORSHIP   187 27
AND HE SAT DOWN, AND TAUGHT THE PEOPLE OUT OF THE   196 12
THE PEOPLE SAT DOWN TO EAT AND DRINK,   201 16
AND HE THAT WAS DEAD SAT UP, AND BEGAN TO SPEAK   213 05
SO THE MEN SAT DOWN, IN NUMBER ABOUT FIVE THOUSAND   226 02
TO PASS, AS JESUS SAT AT MEAT IN THE HOUSE, BEHCLD,   251 15
AND SINNERS CAME AND SAT DOWN WITH HIM AND HIS   251 16
TO THE MINISTER, AND SAT DOWN   261 22
AND HATH NOT SAT IN THE SEAT OF THE SCORNFUL   345 09
WATERS OF BABYLON WE SAT DOWN AND WEPT, *   513 05
AND HE THAT SAT UPON THE THRONE SAID, BEHOLD, I MAKE   567 21

SATAN

KINGDOM OF SIN, SATAN, AND DEATH   037 05
TO BEAT DOWN SATAN UNDER OUR FEET   056 24

SATAN CONTINUED

THEN SAITH JESUS UNTO HIM, GET THEE HENCE, SATAN   127 09
IF SATAN ALSO BE DIVIDED AGAINST HIMSELF, HOW SHALL   129 31
THEN ENTERED SATAN INTO JUDAS SURNAMED ISCARIOT,   148 15
BEHOLD, SATAN HATH DESIRED TO HAVE YOU, THAT   149 31
THE DEVIL, AND SATAN, WHICH DECEIVETH THE WHOLE   252 07
OR THE WILES OF SATAN, BEING PURGED AND DONE AWAY, IT   317 20

SATISFACTION

AND SATISFACTION, FOR THE SINS OF THE WHOLE WORLD   080 12
AND SATISFACTION, ACCORDING TO THE UTTERMOST OF YOUR   087 25
MERITS AND SATISFACTION OF THY SON CHRIST JESUS, IN   591 31
AND SATISFACTION FOR ALL THE SINS OF THE WHOLE WORLD,   609 15
NONE OTHER SATISFACTION FOR SIN, BUT THAT ALONE   609 16

SATISFIED

THAT THE CONGREGATION MAY THEREBY BE SATISFIED   R 085 06
AWAKE UP AFTER THY LIKENESS, I SHALL BE SATISFIED   359 21
26 THE POOR SHALL EAT, AND BE SATISFIED   367 25
THEY SHALL BE SATISFIED WITH THE PLENTEOUSNESS OF THY   384 11
AND GRUDGE IF THEY BE NOT SATISFIED   412 05
SOUL SHALL BE SATISFIED, EVEN AS IT WERE WITH MARROW   415 02
AND SHALL BE SATISFIED WITH THE PLEASURES OF THY   416 19
WOULD I HAVE SATISFIED THEE   443 15
AND BEING SATISFIED THAT THE PERSON CHOSEN IS A   R 569 05

SATISFIETH

5 WHO SATISFIETH THY MOUTH WITH GOOD THINGS, *   466 15
9 FOR HE SATISFIETH THE EMPTY SOUL, *   476 22

SATISFY

WHENCE CAN A MAN SATISFY THESE MEN WITH BREAD HERE IN   199 15
14 O SATISFY US WITH THY MERCY, AND THAT SOON   454 17
LONG LIFE WILL I SATISFY HIM, *   455 29
AND WILL SATISFY HER POOR WITH BREAD   509 04

SATTEST

20 THOU SATTEST AND SPAKEST AGAINST THY BROTHER   402 30

SAUL

AT A YOUNG MAN'S FEET, WHOSE NAME WAS SAUL   100 13
AND SAUL, YET BREATHING OUT THREATENINGS AND   229 25
UNTO HIM, SAUL, SAUL, WHY PERSECUTEST THOU ME   230 02
SAYING UNTO HIM, SAUL, SAUL, WHY PERSECUTEST THOU ME   230 02
AND SAUL AROSE FROM THE EARTH   230 10
FOR ONE CALLED SAUL, OF TARSUS   230 18
HIM SAID, BROTHER SAUL, THE LORD, EVEN JESUS, THAT   230 31
THEN WAS SAUL CERTAIN DAYS WITH THE DISCIPLES WHICH   231 02
BUT SAUL INCREASED THE MORE IN STRENGTH, AND   231 08
DEPARTED BARNABAS TO TARSUS, FOR TO SEEK SAUL   241 11
TO THE ELDERS BY THE HANDS OF BARNABAS AND SAUL   241 23
TO THE ELDERS BY THE HANDS OF BARNABAS AND SAUL   246 31

SAVE

ON ANY DAY, SAVE A DAY OF FASTING OR ABSTINENCE,   R 003 05
O LORD, SAVE THY PEOPLE, AND BLESS THINE HERITAGE   011 04
BUT NOTE, THAT, SAVE ON THE SUNDAYS IN ADVENT,   R 014 05
O LORD, SAVE THE STATE   031 04
O LORD, SAVE THY PEOPLE   031 08
SAVE US FROM VIOLENCE, DISCORD, AND CONFUSION   036 13
SAVE US FROM ALL ERROR, IGNORANCE, PRIDE, AND   036 31
SAVE AND DELIVER US, WE HUMBLY BESEECH THEE, FROM THE   041 12
AT ONCE TO O LORD, SAVE THY SERVANTS   R 061 20
O LORD, SAVE THY SERVANTS   061 30
INTO THE WORLD TO SAVE SINNERS   076 19
FOR HE SHALL SAVE HIS PEOPLE FROM THEIR SINS   105 07
I FORTY STRIPES SAVE ONE   121 02
IT IN THREE DAYS, SAVE THYSELF   137 07
HIMSELF HE CANNOT SAVE   137 10
ELIAS WILL COME TO SAVE HIM   137 24
I THAT SPEAK IN RIGHTEOUSNESS, MIGHTY TO SAVE   138 14
IT IN THREE DAYS, SAVE THYSELF, AND COME DOWN FROM   146 20
HIMSELF HE CANNOT SAVE   146 23
LET HIM SAVE HIMSELF, IF HE BE CHRIST, THE CHOSEN OF   154 29
KING OF THE JEWS, SAVE THYSELF   154 31
IF THOU BE CHRIST, SAVE THYSELF AND US   154 35
WASHED NEEDETH NOT SAVE TO WASH HIS FEET, BUT IS   156 09
DOTH ALSO NOW SAVE US (NOT THE PUTTING AWAY OF THE   161 30
WHICH IS ABLE TO SAVE YOUR SOULS   175 04
GIVE GLORY TO GOD, SAVE THIS STRANGER   210 13
I SHOULD GLORY, SAVE IN THE CROSS OF OUR LORD JESUS   210 30
ANY MAN THE FATHER, SAVE THE SON, AND HE TO   235 09
WHICH IS ABLE TO SAVE YOUR SOULS   265 28
O LORD, SAVE THIS WOMAN THY SERVANT   306 17
O LORD, SAVE THY SERVANT   308 23
RIGHT HAND SHALL SAVE ME   312 06
SAVE US, AND HELP US, WE HUMBLY BESEECH THEE, O LORD   313 13
O SAVE ME, FOR THY MERCY'S SAKE   349 06
SAVE ME FROM ALL THEM THAT PERSECUTE ME, AND DELIVER   349 23
28 FOR THOU SHALT SAVE THE PEOPLE THAT ARE IN   361 22
9 SAVE, LORD   365 02
21 SAVE ME FROM THE LION'S MOUTH   367 14
10 O SAVE THY PEOPLE, AND GIVE THY BLESSING UNTO   373 27
THAT THOU MAYEST SAVE ME   375 26
AND SAVE ME FOR THY MERCY'S SAKE   376 29
BUT A VAIN THING TO SAVE A MAN   379 22
AND WILL SAVE SUCH AS BE OF AN HUMBLE SPIRIT   381 05
7 THOU, LORD, SHALT SAVE BOTH MAN AND BEAST   384 08

SAVE CONTINUED

STAND BY THEM, AND SAVE THEM   387 15
AND SHALL SAVE THEM, BECAUSE THEY PUT THEIR   387 16
SAVE ME, O GOD, FOR THY NAME'S SAKE, *   406 03
AND THE LORD SHALL SAVE ME   407 24
AND SAVE ME FROM THE REPROOF OF HIM THAT WOULD EAT ME   409 17
AND SAVE ME FROM THE BLOOD-THIRSTY MEN   411 06
SAVE ME, O GOD   421 32
UNTO MY SOUL, AND SAVE IT   423 09
36 FOR GOD WILL SAVE SION, AND BUILD THE CITIES OF   424 14
EAR UNTO ME, AND SAVE ME   425 07
SAVE THEM FROM THE HAND OF THE UNGODLY   443 24
MY GOD, SAVE THY SERVANT THAT PUTTETH HIS TRUST IN   447 07
LET THY RIGHT HAND SAVE THEM, AND HEAR THOU ME   479 16
O SAVE ME ACCORDING TO THY MERCY   481 22
TO SAVE HIS SOUL FROM UNRIGHTEOUS JUDGES   482 03
O SAVE ME, *   496 13
RIGHT HAND SHALL SAVE ME   514 12
11 SAVE ME, AND DELIVER ME FROM THE HAND OF   520 12
SAVE THAT THE HOLY GHOST WITNESSETH IN EVERY CITY,   550 16
SAVE ONLY, THAT AFTER THIS PLACE, THAT IT MAY PLEASE R 553 14
THOU SHALT BOTH SAVE THYSELF AND THEM THAT HEAR THEE   558 24
WILL PLEASE HIM TO SAVE AND DEFEND US IN ALL DANGERS   581 02
OF WISDOM MAY SAVE US FROM ALL FALSE CHOICES, AND   595 30
THEY BE PERPLEXED, SAVE THEM FROM DESPAIR   599 15

SAVED

THAT WE SHOULD BE SAVED FROM OUR ENEMIES, *   014 14
THAT HE SHOULD TURN FROM HIS SIN, AND BE SAVED   062 16
LEST THEY SHOULD BELIEVE AND BE SAVED   122 02
THY FAITH HATH SAVED THEE   124 03
SAID, HE SAVED OTHERS   137 10
OF HIS PRESENCE SAVED THEM   139 03
THE SCRIBES, HE SAVED OTHERS   146 22
SAYING, HE SAVED OTHERS   154 28
EIGHT SOULS WERE SAVED BY WATER   161 29
BUT THAT THE WORLD THROUGH HIM MIGHT BE SAVED   185 02
HE SHALL BE SAVED, AND SHALL GO IN AND OUT,   186 16
WHICH ALSO YE ARE SAVED, IF YE KEEP IN MEMORY WHAT I   204 31
JUDAH SHALL BE SAVED, AND ISRAEL SHALL DWELL SAFELY   225 12
RAISED HIM FROM THE DEAD, THOU SHALT BE SAVED   226 28
CALL UPON THE NAME OF THE LORD SHALL BE SAVED   227 05
THAT WE SHOULD BE SAVED FROM OUR ENEMIES, AND FROM   244 03
KING THAT CAN BE SAVED BY THE MULTITUDE OF AN HOST   379 19
10 AND HE SAVED THEM FROM THE ADVERSARY'S HAND,   473 20
AND THEY WERE SAVED FROM THEIR DESTRUCTION   477 16
HE SHALL BE SAVED, AND SHALL GO IN AND OUT, AND   539 06
THAT THEY MAY BE SAVED THROUGH CHRIST FOR EVER   540 03
REST WE SHALL BE SAVED, IN QUIETNESS AND IN   595 20
EVERY MAN SHALL BE SAVED BY THE LAW OR SECT WHICH HE   606 33
NAME OF JESUS CHRIST, WHEREBY MEN MUST BE SAVED   606 36

SAVEST

IT IS THOU THAT SAVEST US FROM OUR ENEMIES, *   395 07

SAVETH

WHO SAVETH THY LIFE FROM DESTRUCTION, *   029 10
THE LORD SAVETH THY LIFE FROM DESTRUCTION   312 17
WHO SAVETH THY LIFE FROM DESTRUCTION, AND CROWNETH   312 26
AND SAVETH HIM OUT OF ALL HIS TROUBLES   380 14
4 WHO SAVETH THY LIFE FROM DESTRUCTION, *   466 13

SAVING

UNTO THEM, THY SAVING HEALTH UNTO ALL NATIONS   018 29
THY SAVING HEALTH AMONG ALL NATIONS   028 19
UNTO THEM, THY SAVING HEALTH UNTO ALL NATIONS   032 29
BELIEVE TO THE SAVING OF THE SOUL   228 21
SAVING THAT, AT THE IMMERSION OR THE POURING OF   R 282 11
THY SAVING HEALTH AMONG ALL NATIONS   418 26
LOOKED FOR THY SAVING HEALTH, *   501 13
LONGED FOR THY SAVING HEALTH, O LORD   501 30

SAVIOUR

CITY OF DAVID A SAVIOUR, WHICH IS CHRIST THE LORD   004 10
OUR KING AND SAVIOUR DRAWETH NIGH   R 008 16
AND MY SPIRIT HATH REJOICED IN GOD MY SAVIOUR   026 12
THROUGH THE MERITS OF JESUS CHRIST OUR SAVIOUR   031 24
ONLY SON, OUR SAVIOUR, JESUS CHRIST   031 28
JESUS CHRIST, OUR MOST BLESSED LORD AND SAVIOUR   035 21
THY SON, OUR SAVIOUR JESUS CHRIST   036 06
THE MERITS AND DEATH OF JESUS CHRIST OUR SAVIOUR   037 08
OUR ONLY SAVIOUR, THE PRINCE OF PEACE   037 26
O MERCIFUL SAVIOUR, WHO WITH THE FATHER AND THE HOLY   043 14
THY SON, OUR SAVIOUR JESUS CHRIST   044 06
OF OUR LORD AND SAVIOUR JESUS CHRIST   044 31
THINGS MAY ADORN THE DOCTRINE OF GOD OUR SAVIOUR   047 29
THOU ART OUR SAVIOUR AND MIGHTY DELIVERER   052 14
OF JESUS CHRIST, OUR BLESSED LORD AND SAVIOUR   VI 43
HELP US, O GOD OUR SAVIOUR   062 02
OUR LORD AND SAVIOUR JESUS CHRIST   070 11
WORDS OUR SAVIOUR CHRIST SAITH UNTO ALL WHO TRULY   076 10
BELOVED SON OUR SAVIOUR JESUS CHRIST, WE, THY HUMBLE   080 38
TO THY SON OUR SAVIOUR JESUS CHRIST'S HOLY   081 12
AND NOW, AS OUR SAVIOUR CHRIST HATH TAUGHT US,   082 02
OF THY SON OUR SAVIOUR JESUS CHRIST   083 20
AND BLOOD OF OUR SAVIOUR CHRIST, MUST CONSIDER HOW   085 27
A LIVELY AND STEDFAST FAITH IN CHRIST OUR SAVIOUR   086 02
PASSION OF OUR SAVIOUR CHRIST, BOTH GOD AND MAN   086 07
AND ONLY SAVIOUR, JESUS CHRIST, THUS DYING   086 13
HIS SON OUR SAVIOUR JESUS CHRIST, NOT ONLY TO DIE FOR   087 03

SAVIOUR   CONTINUED   SAW   CONTINUED

GIVEN US IN OUR SAVIOUR JESUS CHRIST	092 13
GOD AND OUR SAVIOUR JESUS CHRIST	098 22
CITY OF DAVID A SAVIOUR, WHICH IS CHRIST THE LORD	099 17
JESUS CHRIST OUR SAVIOUR, WHO LIVETH AND REIGNETH	119 02
OUR LORD AND SAVIOUR JESUS CHRIST	130 27
THY SON, OUR SAVIOUR JESUS CHRIST, TO TAKE UPON HIM	134 06
SO HE WAS THEIR SAVIOR	138 34
BLESSED SON, OUR SAVIOUR, GAVE HIS BACK TO THE	144 06
OUR LORD AND SAVIOUR JESUS CHRIST	157 03
BLESSED SON, OUR SAVIOUR JESUS CHRIST, SO BY	161 14
WHITHER OUR SAVIOUR CHRIST IS GONE BEFORE, WHO LIVETH	179 08
CHRIST JESUS OUR SAVIOUR, WHO LIVETH AND REIGNETH	180 13
SON TO BE THE SAVIOUR OF THE WORLD	189 21
WE LOOK FOR THE SAVIOUR, THE LORD JESUS CHRIST	222 22
OUR BLESSED LORD AND SAVIOUR	223 20
OF THY SON OUR SAVIOUR BY PREACHING REPENTANCE	242 09
AND HE IS THE SAVIOUR OF THE BODY	267 16
FORASMUCH AS OUR SAVIOUR CHRIST SAITH, NONE CAN ENTER	273 29
HIM AS THY SAVIOUR AND LORD	278 06
THROUGH JESUS CHRIST OUR SAVIOUR	284 04
US PRAY, AS OUR SAVIOUR CHRIST HATH TAUGHT US, AND	289 19
TO FOLLOW JESUS CHRIST AS YOUR LORD AND SAVIOUR	297 04
OUR LORD AND SAVIOUR JESUS CHRIST	298 31
ALMIGHTY AND MOST MERCIFUL GOD AND SAVIOUR	309 27
SHALL BE SAID, O SAVIOUR OF THE WORLD, WHO BY THY	313 12
JESUS CHRIST OUR SAVIOUR, TO WHOM, WITH THEE AND THE	316 02
THROUGH THE SAME THY SON, OUR LORD AND SAVIOUR	316 16
AND MOST MERCIFUL SAVIOUR	317 15
O MERCIFUL SAVIOUR, WE COMMEND THE SOUL OF THY	319 27
AND BLOOD OF OUR SAVIOUR CHRIST, WHEN IT SHALL BE	R 321 08
AND BLOOD OF OUR SAVIOUR CHRIST PROFITABLY TO HIS	R 323 26
MOST MERCIFUL SAVIOUR, DELIVER US NOT INTO THE BITTER	332 06
AND MERCIFUL SAVIOUR, THOU MOST WORTHY JUDGE ETERNAL,	332 30
THAT ART THE SAVIOUR OF THEM WHICH PUT THEIR TRUST IN	358 32
2 MY SAVIOUR, MY GOD, AND MY MIGHT, IN WHOM I WILL	359 26
O GOD OUR SAVIOUR, *	446 14
FORGAT GOD THEIR SAVIOUR, *	474 10
MERITS OF OUR SAVIOUR JESUS CHRIST, WHO LIVETH AND	531 23
SAME THY SON OUR SAVIOUR JESUS CHRIST, TO WHOM BE	535 10
MERITS OF OUR SAVIOUR JESUS CHRIST, WHO LIVETH AND	537 28
OF OUR ONLY SAVIOUR JESUS CHRIST, FOR THE HEAVENLY	541 16
MERITS OF OUR SAVIOUR JESUS CHRIST, WHO LIVETH AND	548 07
THAT OUR SAVIOUR CHRIST CONTINUED THE WHOLE	553 05
EXAMPLE OF OUR SAVIOUR CHRIST, AND HIS APOSTLES,	553 09
MERITS OF OUR SAVIOUR JESUS CHRIST, WHO LIVETH AND	554 02
THROUGH JESUS CHRIST OUR BLESSED LORD AND SAVIOUR	565 15
OUR MOST BLESSED LORD AND SAVIOUR	566 24
FOR THE SAKE OF JESUS CHRIST THY SON OUR SAVIOUR	573 29
THROUGH JESUS CHRIST OUR SAVIOUR	577 25
THY SON OUR SAVIOUR JESUS CHRIST	587 28
OF OUR LORD AND SAVIOUR JESUS CHRIST	588 10
OF THY SON JESUS CHRIST, OUR LORD AND SAVIOUR	589 08
OUR ONLY SAVIOUR AND REDEEMER	590 07
OF OUR LORD AND SAVIOUR JESUS CHRIST	590 20
THY SON OUR SAVIOUR JESUS CHRIST	591 05
THY SON OUR SAVIOUR JESUS CHRIST	591 23
ONLY SON, OUR SAVIOUR, JESUS CHRIST	593 15
THROUGH JESUS CHRIST OUR SAVIOUR	594 28
THY SON, OUR SAVIOUR JESUS CHRIST	595 10
EXAMPLE OF THEIR SAVIOUR JESUS CHRIST	596 28
THY SON, OUR SAVIOUR JESUS CHRIST	599 17
DEAR SON, OUR SAVIOUR JESUS CHRIST	600 12
OF OUR LORD AND SAVIOUR JESUS CHRIST BY FAITH,	605 07

SAVOUR

A SACRIFICE TO GOD FOR A SWEET-SMELLING SAVOUR	129 02

SAW

INTO HEAVEN, AND SAW THE GLORY OF GOD, AND JESUS	100 06
THEN HEROD, WHEN HE SAW THAT HE WAS MOCKED OF THE	103 24
THE STAR, WHICH THEY SAW IN THE EAST, WENT BEFORE	109 16
WHEN THEY SAW THE STAR, THEY REJOICED WITH EXCEEDING	109 18
INTO THE HOUSE, THEY SAW THE YOUNG CHILD WITH MARY	109 20
AND WHEN THEY SAW HIM, THEY WERE AMAZED	110 31
OUT OF THE WATER, HE SAW THE HEAVENS OPENED, AND THE	112 20
THE THIRD HOUR, AND SAW OTHERS STANDING IDLE IN THE	119 19
WHEN THEY SAW IT, GAVE PRAISE UNTO GOD	124 05
BECAUSE THEY SAW HIS MIRACLES WHICH HE DID ON	131 23
UP HIS EYES, AND SAW A GREAT COMPANY COME UNTO HIM,	131 26
AND HE SAW IT, AND WAS GLAD	133 29
WHEN HE SAW THAT HE WAS CONDEMNED, REPENTED	135 02
WHEN PILATE SAW THAT HE COULD PREVAIL NOTHING, BUT	136 08
WATCHING JESUS, SAW THE EARTHQUAKE, AND THOSE	137 32
AND WHEN SHE SAW PETER WARMING HIMSELF, SHE LOOKED	143 24
AND A MAID SAW HIM AGAIN, AND BEGAN TO SAY TO THEM	143 28
OVER AGAINST HIM, SAW THAT HE SO CRIED OUT, AND GAVE	147 03
WHICH WERE ABOUT HIM SAW WHAT WOULD FOLLOW, THEY SAID	150 31
LITTLE WHILE ANOTHER SAW HIM, AND SAID, THOU ART ALSO	151 14
AND WHEN HEROD SAW JESUS, HE WAS EXCEEDING GLAD	153 10
WHEN THE CENTURION SAW WHAT WAS DONE, HE GLORIFIED	155 15
AND OFFICERS SAW HIM, THEY CRIED OUT, SAYING, CRUCIFY	159 06
WHEN JESUS THEREFORE SAW HIS MOTHER, AND THE DISCIPLE	160 19
CAME TO JESUS, AND SAW THAT HE WAS DEAD ALREADY, THEY	161 02
AND HE THAT SAW IT BARE RECORD, AND HIS RECORD IS	161 05
AND LOOKING IN, SAW THE LINEN CLOTHES LYING	164 20
AND HE SAW, AND BELIEVED	164 26
THEY LOOKED, THEY SAW THAT THE STONE WAS ROLLED AWAY	165 25
THE SEPULCHRE, THEY SAW A YOUNG MAN SITTING ON THE	165 26
BUT HIM THEY SAW NOT	167 28
HIS FATHERS, AND SAW CORRUPTION	169 16
GOD RAISED AGAIN, SAW NO CORRUPTION	169 17
GLAD WHEN THEY SAW THE LORD	171 19

AND UPON THE SEATS I SAW FOUR AND TWENTY ELDERS	187 09
OF GENNESARET, AND SAW TWO SHIPS STANDING BY THE	196 08
WHEN SIMON PETER SAW IT, HE FELL DOWN AT JESUS'	196 22
WAY OFF, HIS FATHER SAW HIM, AND HAD COMPASSION,	202 17
AND WHEN HE SAW HIM, HE PASSED BY ON THE OTHER SIDE	208 25
AND WHEN HE SAW HIM, HE HAD COMPASSION ON HIM,	208 29
AND WHEN HE SAW THEM, HE SAID UNTO THEM, GO SHEW	210 05
ONE OF THEM, WHEN HE SAW THAT HE WAS HEALED, TURNED	210 07
AND WHEN THE LORD SAW HER, HE HAD COMPASSION ON HER,	213 02
WHEN THE MULTITUDES SAW IT, THEY MARVELLED, AND	217 13
SEE THE GUESTS, HE SAW THERE A MAN WHICH HAD NOT ON A	218 22
HIS FELLOW-SERVANTS SAW WHAT WAS DONE, THEY WERE VERY	221 30
AND WHEN HE SAW HER, HE SAID, DAUGHTER,	224 21
RULER'S HOUSE, AND SAW THE MINSTRELS AND THE PEOPLE	224 24
UP HIS EYES, AND SAW A GREAT COMPANY COME UNTO HIM,	225 22
THE SEA OF GALILEE, SAW TWO BRETHREN, SIMON CALLED	227 24
ON FROM THENCE, HE SAW OTHER TWO BRETHREN, JAMES THE	227 29
EYES WERE OPENED, HE SAW NO MAN	230 11
AND WHEN SHE SAW HIM, SHE WAS TROUBLED AT HIS SAYING,	236 11
AND BECAUSE HE SAW IT PLEASED THE JEWS, HE PROCEEDED	245 02
BUT THOUGHT HE SAW A VISION	245 20
AND BECAUSE HE SAW IT PLEASED THE JEWS, HE PROCEEDED	247 03
WERE AWAKE, THEY SAW HIS GLORY, AND THE TWO MEN THAT	248 31
FROM THENCE, HE SAW A MAN, NAMED MATTHEW, SITTING AT	251 12
WHEN THE PHARISEES SAW IT, THEY SAID UNTO HIS	251 17
AND I SAW ANOTHER ANGEL ASCENDING FROM THE EAST,	256 14
LORD, WHEN SAW WE THEE AN HUNGRED, AND FED	259 10
WHEN SAW WE THEE A STRANGER, AND TOOK THEE IN	259 11
OR WHEN SAW WE THEE SICK, OR IN PRISON, AND CAME UNTO	259 13
PRIESTS AND SCRIBES SAW THE WONDERFUL THINGS THAT HE	260 10
BUT WHEN THE JEWS SAW THE MULTITUDES, THEY WERE	260 28
BUT WHEN JESUS SAW IT, HE WAS MUCH DISPLEASED,	274 27
WE SAW IT WITH OUR EYES	383 06
AND YET SAW I NEVER THE RIGHTEOUS FORSAKEN, NOR HIS	386 12
O GOD, THE WATERS SAW THEE, AND WERE AFRAID	434 14
16 THE WATERS SAW THEE, O GOD, THE WATERS SAW THEE,	434 14
PROVED ME, AND SAW MY WORKS	459 22
THE EARTH SAW IT, AND WAS AFRAID	461 05
WHEN HE SAW THEIR ADVERSITY, *	475 25
3 THE SEA SAW THAT, AND FLED	484 30
AND SAW THERE WAS NO MAN THAT WOULD KNOW ME	518 10
WHEN JESUS SAW THE MULTITUDES, HE WAS MOVED WITH	538 14
WHEN THEY SAW THE LORD	551 32
AND I JOHN SAW THE HOLY CITY, NEW JERUSALEM, COMING	567 12

SAWEST

18 WHEN THOU SAWEST A THIEF, THOU CONSENTEDST UNTO	402 26

SAY

MY FATHER, AND WILL SAY UNTO HIM, FATHER, I HAVE	004 26
THE MINISTER SHALL SAY, DEARLY BELOVED BRETHREN, THE	R 005 28
SAYING OR HE SHALL SAY,	R 006 13
SHALL KNEEL, AND SAY THE LORD'S PRAYER	R 007 20
LIKEWISE HE SHALL SAY, O LORD, OPEN THOU OUR LIPS	R 007 30
THE MINISTER SHALL SAY, GLORY BE TO THE FATHER, AND	R 008 02
THE MINISTER SHALL SAY, HERE BEGINNETH SUCH A CHAPTER	R 009 32
AND THEN HE SHALL SAY THAT WHICH IS WRITTEN AFTER	R 021 04
IF WE SAY THAT WE HAVE NO SIN, WE DECEIVE OURSELVES,	022 10
SPIRIT AND THE BRIDE SAY, COME	022 29
LET HIM THAT HEARETH SAY, COME	022 30
OR ELSE HE SHALL SAY AS FOLLOWETH	R 023 03
SHALL KNEEL, AND SAY THE LORD'S PRAYER	R 024 27
LIKEWISE HE SHALL SAY, O LORD, OPEN THOU OUR LIPS	R 025 05
THE MINISTER SHALL SAY, GLORY BE TO THE FATHER, AND	R 025 08
WE MAKE BOLD TO SAY, TO BE USED AFTER THE	048 25
THE PEOPLE WITH HIM, SAY THE LORD'S PRAYER	R 058 02
SHALL THE PEOPLE SAY THIS THAT FOLLOWETH, AFTER THE	R 062 27
THE MINISTER SHALL SAY, O GOD, WHOSE NATURE AND	R 063 08
HOLY TABLE, SHALL SAY THE LORD'S PRAYER AND THE	R 067 07
THE PRIEST SHALL SAY THE SUMMARY OF THE LAW,	R 067 29
THEN MAY THE PRIEST SAY, HEAR WHAT OUR LORD JESUS	R 069 25
THEN THE PRIEST MAY SAY, O ALMIGHTY LORD, AND	R 070 05
SHALL THE PRIEST SAY THE COLLECT OF THE DAY	R 070 20
HE SHALL SAY, HERE ENDETH THE EPISTLE	R 070 20
SHALL ANSWER AND SAY UNTO THEM, VERILY I SAY UNTO	073 02
UNTO THEM, VERILY I SAY UNTO YOU, INASMUCH AS YE HAVE	073 03
SHALL THE PRIEST SAY, LET US PRAY FOR THE WHOLE STATE	R 074 04
SHALL THE PRIEST SAY TO THOSE WHO COME TO RECEIVE THE	R 075 07
TO THE PEOPLE, SAY, ALMIGHTY GOD, OUR HEAVENLY	R 075 33
SHALL THE PRIEST SAY, HEAR WHAT COMFORTABLE WORDS OUR	R 076 07
THE HOLY TABLE, AND SAY, IT IS VERY MEET, RIGHT, AND	R 076 30
HIS HANDS, HE SHALL SAY THE PRAYER OF CONSECRATION,	R 080 04
WE ARE BOLD TO SAY,	082 03
AT THE LORD'S TABLE, SAY, IN THE NAME OF ALL THOSE	R 082 11
THE BREAD, HE SHALL SAY,	R 082 30
THE CUP SHALL SAY, THE BLOOD OF OUR LORD JESUS	R 083 02
SHALL THE PRIEST SAY, ALMIGHTY AND EVERLIVING GOD, WE	R 083 14
A DEACON MAY SAY ALL THAT IS BEFORE APPOINTED	R 084 25
THE PRIEST MAY SAY THIS EXHORTATION	R 085 22
MATTER FOR A MAN TO SAY, I WILL NOT COMMUNICATE,	088 27
IF ANY MAN SAY, I AM A GRIEVOUS SINNER, AND THEREFORE	088 30
YE NOT ASHAMED TO SAY YE WILL NOT COME	088 32
AND SAY YE ARE NOT READY	088 34
AND IF ANY MAN SAY OUGHT UNTO YOU, YE SHALL SAY, THE	091 16
UNTO YOU, YE SHALL SAY, THE LORD HATH NEED OF THEM	091 17
NOW I SAY THAT JESUS CHRIST WAS A MINISTER OF THE	092 23
VERILY I SAY UNTO YOU, THIS GENERATION SHALL NOT PASS	093 18
JESUS BEGAN TO SAY UNTO THE MULTITUDES CONCERNING	094 25
I SAY UNTO YOU, AND MORE THAN A PROPHET	094 30
AND AGAIN I SAY, REJOICE	095 13
VERILY I SAY UNTO YOU, ALL THESE THINGS SHALL COME	100 26
FOR I SAY UNTO YOU, YE SHALL NOT SEE ME HENCEFORTH,	100 32

TILL YE SHALL SAY, BLESSED IS HE THAT COMETH IN THE   100 33
IF WE SAY THAT WE HAVE FELLOWSHIP WITH HIM, AND WALK   101 24
IF WE SAY THAT WE HAVE NO SIN, WE DECEIVE OURSELVES,   101 28
IF WE SAY THAT WE HAVE NOT SINNED, WE MAKE HIM A   101 31
NOW I SAY, THAT THE HEIR, AS LONG AS HE IS A CHILD,   104 14
FOR I SAY, THROUGH THE GRACE GIVEN UNTO ME, TO EVERY   110 09
AND I SAY TO THIS MAN, GO, AND HE GOETH   115 14
VERILY I SAY UNTO YOU, I HAVE NOT FOUND SO   115 17
AND I SAY UNTO YOU, THAT MANY SHALL COME FROM THE   115 18
OF HARVEST I WILL SAY TO THE REAPERS, GATHER YE   116 29
IF ANY MAN SHALL SAY UNTO YOU, LO, HERE IS CHRIST,   118 03
IF THEY SHALL SAY UNTO YOU, BEHOLD, HE IS IN THE   118 08
THEY SAY UNTO HIM, BECAUSE NO MAN HATH HIRED US   119 26
AND LET THEM SAY, SPARE THY PEOPLE, O LORD,   125 03
SHOULD THEY SAY AMONG THE PEOPLE, WHERE IS THEIR GOD   125 06
VERILY I SAY UNTO YOU, THEY HAVE THEIR REWARD   125 11
BECAUSE YE SAY THAT I CAST OUT DEVILS THROUGH   129 33
THAT IS TO SAY, NOT OF THIS BUILDING   132 25
AND IF I SAY THE TRUTH, WHY DO YE NOT BELIEVE ME   133 10
AND SAID UNTO HIM, SAY WE NOT WELL THAT THOU ART A   133 13
VERILY, I SAY UNTO YOU, IF A MAN KEEP MY   133 17
OF WHOM YE SAY, THAT HE IS YOUR GOD   133 25
AND IF I SHOULD SAY, I KNOW HIM NOT, I SHALL BE A   133 26
VERILY, I SAY UNTO YOU, BEFORE ABRAHAM WAS, I   133 31
THEY ALL SAY UNTO HIM, LET HIM BE CRUCIFIED   136 05
THAT IS TO SAY, A PLACE OF A SKULL, THEY   136 28
THAT IS TO SAY, MY GOD, MY GOD, WHY HAST THOU   137 18
VERILY I SAY UNTO YOU, WHERESOEVER THIS GOSPEL SHALL   140 15
HE SHALL GO IN, SAY YE TO THE GOODMAN OF THE HOUSE,   140 28
JESUS SAID, VERILY I SAY UNTO YOU, ONE OF YOU WHICH   140 35
BE SORROWFUL, AND TO SAY UNTO HIM ONE BY ONE, IS IT   141 03
VERILY I SAY UNTO YOU, I WILL DRINK NO MORE OF THE   141 14
UNTO HIM, VERILY I SAY UNTO THEE, THAT THIS DAY,   141 23
WE HEARD HIM SAY, I WILL DESTROY THIS TEMPLE   143 06
BUFFET HIM, AND TO SAY UNTO HIM, PROPHESY   143 21
AND BEGAN TO SAY TO THEM THAT STOOD BY,   143 29
AND YE SHALL SAY UNTO THE GOODMAN OF THE HOUSE,   148 28
FOR I SAY UNTO YOU, I WILL NOT ANY MORE EAT THEREOF,   149 03
FOR I SAY UNTO YOU, I WILL NOT DRINK OF THE FRUIT OF   149 07
FOR I SAY UNTO YOU, THAT THIS THAT IS WRITTEN MUST   150 09
SAID UNTO THEM, YE SAY THAT I AM   151 35
THE WHICH THEY SHALL SAY, BLESSED ARE THE BARREN,   154 16
SHALL THEY BEGIN TO SAY TO THE MOUNTAINS, FALL ON US   154 18
UNTO HIM, VERILY I SAY UNTO THEE, TO-DAY SHALT THOU   155 08
AND YE SAY WELL   156 15
THE VEIL, THAT IS TO SAY, HIS FLESH   158 19
STEAL HIM AWAY, AND SAY UNTO THE PEOPLE, HE IS RISEN   162 21
THAT WORD, I SAY, YE KNOW, WHICH WAS PUBLISHED   166 17
VERILY, I SAY UNTO YOU, THAT YE SHALL WEEP   174 07
YET MANY THINGS TO SAY UNTO YOU, BUT YE CANNOT BEAR   175 17
VERILY, I SAY UNTO YOU, WHATSOEVER YE SHALL   176 20
AND I SAY NOT UNTO YOU, THAT I WILL PRAY THE FATHER   176 27
THAT WORD, I SAY, YE KNOW, WHICH WAS PUBLISHED   184 04
VERILY, IS SAY UNTO YOU, HE THAT ENTERETH NOT   185 30
VERILY, I SAY UNTO YOU, I AM THE DOOR OF THE   186 12
VERILY, I SAY UNTO THEE, EXCEPT A MAN BE BORN   188 05
VERILY, I SAY UNTO THEE, EXCEPT A MAN BE BORN   188 09
VERILY, I SAY UNTO THEE, WE SPEAK THAT WE DO   188 20
IF A MAN SAY, I LOVE GOD, AND HATETH HIS BROTHER,   189 31
AT SUPPER TIME TO SAY TO THEM THAT WERE BIDDEN, COME   192 04
FOR I SAY UNTO YOU, THAT NONE OF THOSE MEN WHICH WERE   192 20
I SAY UNTO YOU, THAT LIKEWISE JOY SHALL BE IN HEAVEN   193 24
I SAY UNTO YOU, THERE IS JOY IN THE   193 32
HOW CANST THOU SAY TO THY BROTHER, BROTHER, LET ME   195 07
BUT I SAY UNTO YOU, THAT WHOSOEVER IS ANGRY WITH HIS   198 03
AND WHOSOEVER SHALL SAY TO HIS BROTHER, RACA, SHALL   198 05
BUT WHOSOEVER SHALL SAY, THOU FOOL, SHALL BE IN   198 07
VERILY I SAY UNTO THEE, THOU SHALT BY NO MEANS COME   198 15
MY FATHER, AND WILL SAY UNTO HIM, FATHER, I HAVE   202 13
AND THAT NO MAN CAN SAY THAT JESUS IS THE LORD,   203 21
AND THIS I SAY, THAT THE COVENANT, THAT WAS CONFIRMED   207 21
I SAY THEN, WALK IN THE SPIRIT, AND YE SHALL NOT   209 14
THEREFORE I SAY UNTO YOU, BE NOT ANXIOUS FOR YOUR   211 12
YET I SAY UNTO YOU, THAT EVEN SOLOMON IN ALL HIS   211 22
YOUNG MAN, I SAY UNTO THEE, ARISE   213 05
AND HIM COME AND SAY TO THEE, GIVE THIS MAN PLACE   214 13
THEE COMETH, HE MAY SAY UNTO THEE, FRIEND, GO UP   214 17
THEY SAY UNTO HIM, THE SON OF DAVID   215 17
THIS I SAY THEREFORE, AND TESTIFY IN THE LORD,   216 03
IS EASIER, TO SAY, THY SINS BE FORGIVEN THEE   217 07
OR TO SAY, ARISE, AND WALK   217 08
SAITH UNTO HIM, I SAY NOT UNTO THEE, UNTIL SEVEN   221 11
THEY SAY UNTO HIM, CAESAR'S   223 08
THEY SHALL NO MORE SAY, THE LORD LIVETH, WHICH   225 16
BUT I SAY, HAVE THEY NOT HEARD   227 14
BUT I SAY, DID NOT ISRAEL KNOW   227 16
UNTO THEM, VERILY I SAY UNTO YOU, THAT YE WHICH HAVE   231 14
THAT IS TO SAY, THE FIELD OF BLOOD   234 17
VERILY, I SAY UNTO YOU, HE THAT BELIEVETH ON   240 19
SAY UNTO THE CITIES OF JUDAH, BEHOLD YOUR GOD   243 05
WHOM DO MEN SAY THAT I THE SON OF MAN AM   245 32
AND THEY SAID, SOME SAY THAT THOU ART JOHN THE   245 33
UNTO THEM, BUT WHOM SAY YE THAT I AM   246 02
AND I SAY ALSO UNTO THEE, THAT THOU ART PETER, AND   246 06
THEY SAY UNTO HIM, WE ARE ABLE   247 14
AND SAID, VERILY I SAY UNTO YOU, EXCEPT YE BE   252 25
FOR I SAY UNTO YOU, THAT IN HEAVEN THEIR ANGELS DO   253 10
YE ENTER, FIRST SAY, PEACE BE TO THIS HOUSE   254 19
AND SHALL SAY ALL MANNER OF EVIL AGAINST YOU   257 31
THEN SHALL THE KING SAY UNTO THEM ON HIS RIGHT HAND,   259 03
UNTO THEM, VERILY I SAY UNTO YOU, INASMUCH AS YE HAVE   259 14
SHALL ANSWER AND SAY UNTO THEM, VERILY I SAY UNTO   259 14
HEAREST THOU WHAT THESE SAY   260 13
AND HE BEGAN TO SAY UNTO THEM, THIS DAY IS THIS   261 24

HIM AT MIDNIGHT, AND SAY UNTO HIM, FRIEND, LEND ME   262 27
SHALL ANSWER AND SAY, TROUBLE ME NOT   262 30
I SAY UNTO YOU, THOUGH HE WILL NOT RISE AND GIVE HIM,   262 32
AND I SAY UNTO YOU, ASK, AND IT SHALL BE GIVEN YOU   263 03
BUT I SAY UNTO YOU, LOVE YOUR ENEMIES, BLESS THEM   264 05
AND YET I SAY UNTO YOU, THAT EVEN SOLOMON IN ALL HIS   266 20
FOR THIS WE SAY UNTO YOU BY THE WORD OF THE LORD,   269 02
PURE WATER, SHALL SAY AS FOLLOWETH, THE PEOPLE ALL   R 273 25
SHALL THE MINISTER SAY, ALMIGHTY AND IMMORTAL GOD,   R 274 07
THE MINISTER SHALL SAY AS FOLLOWETH   R 274 22
VERILY I SAY UNTO YOU, WHOSOEVER SHALL NOT RECEIVE   274 30
VERILY, I SAY UNTO THEE, EXCEPT A MAN BE BORN   275 10
VERILY, I SAY UNTO THEE, EXCEPT A MAN BE BORN   275 14
SHALL THE MINISTER SAY, AND NOW, BEING PERSUADED OF   R 276 02
THANKS UNTO HIM, AND SAY, ALMIGHTY AND EVERLASTING   276 06
SHALL THE MINISTER SAY, O MERCIFUL GOD, GRANT THAT   R 278 17
THE MINISTER SHALL SAY, IT IS VERY MEET, RIGHT, AND   R 279 06
HIS ARMS, AND SHALL SAY TO THE GODFATHERS AND   R 279 23
THEN THE MINISTER SHALL SAY   R 280 02
SHALL THE MINISTER SAY, SEEING NOW, DEARLY BELOVED   R 280 12
SHALL THE MINISTER SAY, WE YIELD THEE HEARTY THANKS,   R 280 27
THE MINISTER SHALL SAY, YOU SAID THAT YOUR SPONSORS   R 284 06
TO THE PEOPLE, SHALL SAY,   R 285 12
SHALL THE MINISTER SAY, LET US ASK GOD'S HELP TO KNOW   R 285 18
THE PEOPLE SHALL SAY THE RESPONSE   R 285 34
SHALL THE MINISTER SAY, GRANT TO US, LORD, WE BESEECH   R 287 25
THE MINISTER SHALL SAY AS FOLLOWETH   R 289 12
HATH TAUGHT US, AND SAY,   289 20
THAT IS TO SAY, BAPTISM, AND THE SUPPER OF THE LORD   292 07
AND CAN SAY THE CREED, THE LORD'S PRAYER, AND   R 295 13
THE MINISTER SHALL SAY, REVEREND FATHER IN GOD, I   R 296 07
BY HIM, MAY SAY, HEAR THE WORDS OF THE EVANGELIST   R 296 10
SHALL THE BISHOP SAY, DO YE HERE, IN THE PRESENCE OF   R 296 21
SHALL THE BISHOP SAY, DO YE PROMISE TO FOLLOW JESUS   R 297 02
SHALL THE BISHOP SAY, THE LORD BE WITH YOU   R 297 30
SHALL THE BISHOP SAY THE LORD'S PRAYER, THE PEOPLE   R 298 03
SHALL THE BISHOP SAY, ALMIGHTY AND EVERLIVING GOD,   R 298 12
THE MINISTER SHALL SAY, DEARLY BELOVED, WE ARE   R 300 07
BE MARRIED, HE SHALL SAY, I REQUIRE AND CHARGE YOU   R 300 23
THE MINISTER SHALL SAY TO THE MAN,   R 301 05
SHALL THE MINISTER SAY UNTO THE WOMAN, N   R 301 13
SHALL THE MINISTER SAY, WHO GIVETH THIS WOMAN TO BE   R 301 22
RIGHT HAND, AND TO SAY AFTER HIM AS FOLLOWETH   R 301 26
SHALL LIKEWISE SAY AFTER THE MINISTER, I N   R 302 03
THE MINISTER, SHALL SAY,   R 302 13
THE MINISTER MAY SAY AS FOLLOWETH   R 302 17
THE MINISTER SHALL SAY, THEN SHALL THE MINISTER AND   R 302 24
STILL STANDING, SAY THE LORD'S PRAYER   R 302 26
HANDS TOGETHER, AND SAY, THOSE WHOM GOD HATH JOINED   R 303 30
MINISTER SHALL THEN SAY UNTO HER, FORASMUCH AS IT   R 305 10
THANKS UNTO GOD, AND SAY, THEN SHALL BE SAID BY BOTH   305 14
SHALL THE MINISTER SAY THE LORD'S PRAYER, WITH WHAT   R 306 08
SHALL SAY, PEACE BE TO THIS HOUSE, AND TO   R 308 06
AFTER WHICH HE SHALL SAY THE ANTIPHON FOLLOWING,   R 308 08
THE MINISTER SHALL SAY, LORD, HAVE MERCY UPON US   R 308 12
ONE THERE BE THAT SAY OF MY SOUL, THERE IS NO HELP   309 16
THE MINISTER SHALL SAY, O MOST MERCIFUL GOD, WHO,   R 313 28
SHALL THE MINISTER SAY, THE ALMIGHTY LORD, WHO IS A   R 314 14
AND AFTER THAT SHALL SAY,   R 314 25
VERILY, I SAY UNTO YOU, HE THAT HEARETH MY   321 33
VERILY, I SAY UNTO YOU, HE THAT BELIEVETH ON   322 21
THE GRAVE, SHALL SAY OR SING, I AM THE RESURRECTION   R 324 04
I SAY, BEFORE THE MORNING WATCH   328 14
BUT SOME MAN WILL SAY, HOW ARE THE DEAD RAISED UP   329 05
NOW THIS I SAY, BRETHREN, THAT FLESH AND BLOOD CANNOT   329 33
WHAT SHALL WE THEN SAY TO THESE THINGS   330 33
THE MINISTER SHALL SAY, UNTO ALMIGHTY GOD WE COMMEND   R 333 13
THE MINISTER SHALL SAY, THE LORD BE WITH YOU   R 333 29
THE MINISTER SHALL SAY ONE OR MORE OF THE FOLLOWING   R 334 12
BE EXPEDIENT TO SAY UNDER SHELTER OF THE CHURCH THE   R 336 30
THE MINISTER SHALL SAY,   R 337 08
THE GRAVE, SHALL SAY, I AM THE RESURRECTION AND THE   R 338 04
AND SAID, VERILY I SAY UNTO YOU, EXCEPT YE BE   339 24
FOR I SAY UNTO YOU, THAT IN HEAVEN THEIR ANGELS DO   339 30
SHALL THE MINISTER SAY, THE LORD BE WITH YOU   R 340 02
THE MINISTER SHALL SAY, IN SURE AND CERTAIN HOPE OF   R 341 12
SHALL THE MINISTER SAY, THE LORD BE WITH YOU   R 341 28
ONE THERE BE THAT SAY OF MY SOUL, *   346 27
6 THERE BE MANY THAT SAY, *   347 23
WHILE HE DOTH SAY IN HIS HEART, TUSH, THOU GOD CAREST   354 02
HOW SAY YE THEN TO MY SOUL, THAT SHE SHOULD FLEE AS A   354 19
4 LEST MINE ENEMY SAY, I HAVE PREVAILED AGAINST HIM   356 04
SAY UNTO MY SOUL, I AM THY SALVATION   381 23
ALL MY BONES SHALL SAY, LORD, WHO IS LIKE UNTO THEE,   382 09
25 LET THEM NOT SAY IN THEIR HEARTS, THERE   383 13
NEITHER LET THEM SAY, WE HAVE DEVOURED HIM   383 14
LET THEM SAY ALWAY, BLESSED BE THE LORD, WHO   383 20
THAT SAY UNTO ME, FIE UPON THEE   391 20
LOVE THY SALVATION, SAY ALWAY, THE LORD BE PRAISED   391 22
8 AN EVIL DISEASE, SAY THEY, CLEAVETH FAST UNTO HIM   392 15
WHILE THEY DAILY SAY UNTO ME, WHERE IS NOW THY GOD   393 05
11 I WILL SAY UNTO THE GOD OF MY STRENGTH, WHY HAST   393 24
WHILE THEY SAY DAILY UNTO ME, *   393 29
SO THAT A MAN SHALL SAY, VERILY THERE IS A REWARD FOR   410 32
AND SAY, THAT NO MAN SHALL SEE THEM   415 29
THAT SEE IT SHALL SAY, THIS HATH GOD DONE   416 04
2 SAY UNTO GOD, O HOW WONDERFUL ART THOU IN THY   417 17
IN THY SALVATION SAY ALWAY, THE LORD BE PRAISED   424 28
11 TUSH, SAY THEY, HOW SHOULD GOD PERCEIVE IT   428 30
DO THE HEATHEN SAY, *   440 21
12 WHO SAY, LET US TAKE TO OURSELVES *   444 28
8 I WILL HEARKEN WHAT THE LORD GOD WILL SAY   446 22
2 I WILL SAY UNTO THE LORD, THOU ART MY HOPE,   454 30
7 AND YET THEY SAY, TUSH, THE LORD SHALL NOT SEE,   457 31

PAGE LN

SAY CONTINUED

LET ALL THE PEOPLE SAY, O GIVE THANKS UNTO THE LCRD, 475 34
SHALL THE HEATHEN SAY, * 485 14
THEY KEPT ME IN, I SAY, ON EVERY SIDE 488 21
HAD NOT BEEN ON OUR SIDE, NOW MAY ISRAEL SAY 504 08
MAY ISRAEL NOW SAY 506 22
THAT THEY WHO GO BY SAY NOT SO MUCH AS, THE LORD 507 04
I SAY, BEFORE THE MORNING WATCH 507 19
10 IF I SAY, PERADVENTURE THE DARKNESS SHALL COVER 515 08
THE BISHOP SHALL SAY UNTO THE PEOPLE, BRETHREN, IF R 530 20
AND PEOPLE PRESENT, SAY THE LITANY R 530 31
AND SHALL SAY, R 534 04
VERILY I SAY UNTO YOU, THAT HE SHALL GIRD HIMSELF, 534 21
AND SHALL SAY, REVEREND FATHER IN GOD, I R 536 09
THE BISHOP SHALL SAY UNTO THE PEOPLE, GOOD PEOPLE, R 536 21
AND PEOPLE PRESENT, SAY THE LITANY R 537 07
VERILY, I SAY UNTO YOU, HE THAT ENTERETH NOT 538 23
VERILY, I SAY UNTO YOU, I AM THE DOOR OF THE 539 03
THE BISHOP SHALL SAY UNTO THOSE WHO ARE TO BE R 539 22
THAT IS TO SAY, TO BE MESSENGERS, WATCHMEN, AND 539 32
SHALL THE BISHOP SAY, ALMIGHTY GOD, WHO HATH GIVEN R 543 17
BISHOP SHALL SING OR SAY THE VENI, CREATOR SPIRITUS R 543 27
IN THIS WISE, AND SAY, ALMIGHTY GOD, AND HEAVENLY R 545 10
IN HIS CHAIR, SHALL SAY TO HIM THAT IS TO BE R 554 06
HAVING NOTHING TO SAY AGAINST YOU 555 12
BISHOP SHALL SAY, ALMIGHTY GOD, OUR HEAVENLY FATHER, R 555 27
BISHOP SHALL SAY, LORD, HEAR OUR PRAYER R 557 16
HE SHALL SAY, DEARLY BELOVED IN THE LORD R 564 09
SHALL SAY THE FOLLOWING PRAYER R 564 26
SHALL SAY, R 565 17
THE BISHOP SHALL SAY, BLESSED BE THY NAME, O LORD, R 566 27
THE BISHOP SHALL SAY THIS PRAYER R 568 04
SHALL SAY, DEARLY BELOVED IN THE LORD, WE R 570 11
NEW INCUMBENT SHALL SAY, I, A R 570 31
STANDING UP, SHALL SAY, THE LORD BE WITH YOU R 573 30
IF THOU CANST SAY THE LORD'S PRAYER 580 20
AND THEREFORE I SAY, AMEN, SO BE IT 581 06
THAT IS TO SAY, BAPTISM, AND THE SUPPER OF THE LORD 581 10
AND CAN SAY THE CREED, THE LORD'S PRAYER, AND R 582 36
MAY BE APPOINTED, SAY AS FOLLOWETH, ALL KNEELING, R 587 06
MAY BE APPOINTED, SAY AS FOLLOWETH, ALL KNEELING, R 589 14
OF THE FAMILY, SAY AS FOLLOWETH, ALL KNEELING, R 592 10
OF THE FAMILY, SAY AS FOLLOWETH, ALL KNEELING, R 593 04
THAT IS TO SAY, THE GODHEAD AND MANHOOD, 603 12
THE SCHOOL-AUTHORS SAY) DESERVE GRACE OF CONGRUITY 605 20
COMMANDED TO YOU, SAY, WE ARE UNPROFITABLE SERVANTS 605 29
AND IF WE SAY WE HAVE NO SIN, WE DECEIVE OURSELVES, 605 36
BE CONDEMNED, WHICH SAY, THEY CAN NO MORE SIN AS LONG 606 03
THAT PRESUME TO SAY, THAT EVERY MAN SHALL BE SAVED BY 606 32
THAT IS TO SAY, BAPTISM, AND THE SUPPER OF 607 37
THAT IS TO SAY, CONFIRMATION, PENANCE, ORDERS, 607 38

SAYEST

WHAT SAYEST THOU OF THYSELF 095 28
AND THOU SAYEST, IF A MAN KEEP MY SAYING, HE SHALL 133 20
AND JESUS SAID UNTO HIM, THOU SAYEST 135 21
I KNOW NOT, NEITHER UNDERSTAND I WHAT THOU SAYEST 143 27
UNTO HIM, THOU SAYEST IT 145 08
I KNOW NOT WHAT THOU SAYEST 151 18
AND SAID, THOU SAYEST IT 153 02
AND HOW SAYEST THOU THEN, SHEW US THE FATHER 240 13
AGAIN THOU SAYEST, COME AGAIN, YE CHILDREN OF MEN 325 18
AGAIN THOU SAYEST, COME AGAIN, YE CHILDREN OF MEN 453 23

SAYING

HEAVENLY GRACE, SAYING OR HE SHALL SAY, 006 12
HEAVENLY GRACE, SAYING TO BE SAID BY THE WHOLE 023 21
JUSTIFIED IN THY SAYING, AND CLEAR WHEN THOU ART 060 18
FIRST SAYING, THE EPISTLE IS WRITTEN IN THE R 070 18
THE GOSPEL, FIRST SAYING, THE HOLY GOSPEL IS WRITTEN R 070 23
THE OFFERTORY,SAYING ONE OR MORE OF THESE SENTENCES R 071 32
THIS IS A TRUE SAYING, AND WORTHY OF ALL MEN TO BE 076 18
SHALL PROCEED, SAYING, LIFT UP YOUR HEARTS R 076 25
AND SAYING, PRIEST AND PEOPLE 077 06
AND SAYING, PRIEST AND PEOPLE 079 30
TO HIS DISCIPLES, SAYING, TAKE, EAT, (C) THIS IS MY 080 20
GAVE IT TO THEM, SAYING, DRINK YE ALL OF THIS 080 24
IN THIS SAYING, NAMELY, THOU SHALT LOVE THY NEIGHBOUR 090 28
TWO DISCIPLES, SAYING UNTO THEM, GO INTO THE VILLAGE 091 13
BY THE PROPHET, SAYING, TELL YE THE DAUGHTER OF SION, 091 19
CRIED, SAYING, HOSANNA TO THE SON OF DAVID 091 28
CITY WAS MOVED, SAYING, WHO IS THIS 091 31
ANSWERED THEM, SAYING, I BAPTIZE WITH WATER 096 02
PRAISING GOD, AND SAYING, GLORY TO GOD IN THE 099 21
UPON GOD, AND SAYING, LORD JESUS, RECEIVE MY SPIRIT 100 14
THEN WENT THIS SAYING ABROAD AMONG THE BRETHREN, THAT 102 09
IN A DREAM, SAYING, ARISE, AND TAKE THE YOUNG CHILD 103 17
BY THE PROPHET, SAYING, OUT OF EGYPT HAVE I CALLED MY 103 23
THE PROPHET, SAYING, IN RAMA WAS THERE A VOICE HEARD, 103 30
HIM IN A DREAM, SAYING, JOSEPH, THOU SON OF DAVID, 105 03
BY THE PROPHET, SAYING, BEHOLD, A VIRGIN SHALL BE 105 09
KNOWN ABROAD THE SAYING WHICH WAS TOLD THEM 106 13
JOSEPH IN EGYPT, SAYING, ARISE, AND TAKE THE YOUNG 107 13
TO JERUSALEM, SAYING, WHERE IS HE THAT IS BORN KING 108 32
NOT THE SAYING WHICH HE SPAKE UNTO THEM 111 03
AND PREACHED, SAYING, THERE COMETH ONE MIGHTIER THAN 112 14
FROM HEAVEN, SAYING, THOU ART MY BELOVED SON, IN WHOM 112 22
WORSHIPPED HIM, SAYING, LORD, IF THOU WILT, THOU 114 31
AND TOUCHED HIM, SAYING, I WILL 115 02
AND SAYING, LORD, MY SERVANT LIETH AT HOME SICK 115 08
OF THE HOUSE, SAYING, THESE LAST HAVE WROUGHT BUT ONE 120 04
ASKED HIM, SAYING, WHAT MIGHT THIS PARABLE BE 121 28
AND THIS SAYING WAS HID FROM THEM, NEITHER KNEW THEY 123 24

PAGE LN

SAYING CONTINUED

AND HE CRIED, SAYING, JESUS, THOU SON OF DAVID, 123 30
HE ASKED HIM, SAYING, WHAT WILT THOU THAT I SHALL DO 123 35
CRIED UNTO HIM, SAYING, HAVE MERCY ON ME, O LORD, 128 09
AND BESOUGHT HIM, SAYING, SEND HER AWAY 128 12
WORSHIPPED HIM, SAYING, LORD, HELP ME 128 15
IF A MAN KEEP MY SAYING, HE SHALL NEVER SEE DEATH 133 17
IF A MAN KEEP MY SAYING, HE SHALL NEVER TASTE OF 133 20
BUT I KNOW HIM, AND KEEP HIS SAYING 133 28
AND ELDERS, SAYING, I HAVE SINNED IN THAT I HAVE 135 05
THE PROPHET, SAYING, AND THEY TOOK THE THIRTY PIECES 135 15
ASKED HIM, SAYING, ART THOU THE KING OF THE JEWS 135 19
SENT UNTO HIM, SAYING, HAVE THOU NOTHING TO DO WITH 135 33
OUT THE MORE, SAYING, LET HIM BE CRUCIFIED 136 07
THE MULTITUDE, SAYING, I AM INNOCENT OF THE BLOOD OF 136 10
AND MOCKED HIM, SAYING, HAIL, KING OF THE JEWS 136 21
THEIR HEADS, AND SAYING, THOU THAT DESTROYEST THE 137 06
A LOUD VOICE, SAYING, ELI, ELI, LAMA SABACHTHANI 137 17
FEARED GREATLY, SAYING, TRULY THIS WAS THE SON OF 137 33
AND HIS PEOPLE, SAYING, WHERE IS HE THAT BROUGHT THEM 139 08
THEM A TOKEN, SAYING, WHOMSOEVER I SHALL KISS, THAT 142 18
AGAINST HIM, SAYING, WE HEARD HIM SAY, I WILL DESTROY 143 06
AND ASKED JESUS, SAYING, ANSWEREST THOU NOTHING 143 10
BUT HE DENIED, SAYING, I KNOW NOT, NEITHER UNDERSTAND 143 26
AND TO SWEAR, SAYING, I KNOW NOT THIS MAN OF WHOM YE 143 33
ASKED HIM AGAIN, SAYING, ANSWEREST THOU NOTHING 145 10
ANSWERED THEM, SAYING, WILL YE THAT I RELEASE UNTO 145 18
THEIR HEADS, AND SAYING, AH, THOU THAT DESTROYEST THE 146 19
A LOUD VOICE, SAYING, ELOI, ELOI, LAMA SABACHTHANI 146 28
HIM TO DRINK, SAYING, LET ALONE 146 33
ALL THE PEOPLE, SAYING, THIS IS THE BLOOD OF THE 147 22
PETER AND JOHN, SAYING, GO AND PREPARE US THE 148 23
GAVE UNTO THEM, SAYING, THIS IS MY BODY WHICH IS 149 09
CUP AFTER SUPPER, SAYING, THIS CUP IS THE NEW 149 11
AND PRAYED, SAYING, FATHER, IF THOU BE WILLING, 150 18
HE DENIED HIM, SAYING, WOMAN, I KNOW HIM NOT 151 13
SAYING, OF A TRUTH THIS FELLOW ALSO WAS 151 16
AND ASKED HIM, SAYING, PROPHESY, WHO IS IT THAT SMOTE 151 25
THEIR COUNCIL, SAYING, ART THOU THE CHRIST 151 30
HE HAD SUPPED, SAYING, THIS CUP IS THE NEW TESTAMENT 152 22
TO ACCUSE HIM, SAYING, WE FOUND THIS FELLOW 152 28
TO CAESAR, SAYING THAT HE HIMSELF IS CHRIST A KING 152 30
PILATE ASKED HIM, SAYING, ART THOU THE KING OF THE 152 31
THE MORE FIERCE, SAYING, HE STIRRETH UP THE PEOPLE, 153 04
OUT ALL AT ONCE, SAYING, AWAY WITH THIS MAN, AND 153 29
BUT THEY CRIED, SAYING, CRUCIFY HIM, CRUCIFY HIM 153 33
THEM DERIDED HIM, SAYING, HE SAVED OTHERS 154 28
HIM VINEGAR, AND SAYING, IF THOU BE THE KING OF THE 154 31
RAILED ON HIM, SAYING, IF THOU BE CHRIST, SAVE 154 35
REBUKED HIM, SAYING, DOST NOT THOU FEAR GOD, SEEING 155 02
HE GLORIFIED GOD, SAYING, CERTAINLY THIS WAS A 155 15
THEY CRIED OUT, SAYING, CRUCIFY HIM, CRUCIFY HIM 159 06
HEARD THAT SAYING, HE WAS THE MORE AFRAID 159 11
JEWS CRIED OUT, SAYING, IF THOU LET THIS MAN GO, 159 20
HEARD THAT SAYING, HE BROUGHT JESUS FORTH, AND SAT 159 22
UNTO PILATE, SAYING, SIR, WE REMEMBER THAT THAT 162 17
THEY CAME, SAYING, THAT THEY HAD ALSO SEEN A 167 25
CONSTRAINED HIM, SAYING, ABIDE WITH US 168 03
WERE WITH THEM, SAYING, THE LORD IS RISEN INDEED, 168 13
ASKED OF HIM, SAYING, LORD, WILT THOU AT THIS TIME 178 05
AND MARVELLED, SAYING ONE TO ANOTHER, BEHOLD, ARE NOT 180 29
DAY AND NIGHT, SAYING, HOLY, HOLY, HOLY, LORD GOD 187 22
THE THRONE, SAYING, THOU ART WORTHY, O LORD, TO 187 29
SCRIBES MURMURED, SAYING, THIS MAN RECEIVETH SINNERS, 193 16
UNTO THEM, SAYING, WHAT MAN OF YOU, HAVING AN HUNDRED 193 17
AND NEIGHBOURS, SAYING UNTO THEM, REJOICE WITH ME 193 23
SAYING, REJOICE WITH ME 193 31
AT JESUS' KNEES, SAYING, DEPART FROM ME 196 23
AND WEPT OVER IT, SAYING, IF THOU HADST KNOWN, 204 07
SAYING UNTO THEM, IT IS WRITTEN, MY HOUSE IS THE 204 17
UPON HIS BREAST, SAYING, GOD BE MERCIFUL TO ME A 205 30
SAYING, HE HATH DONE ALL THINGS WELL 207 07
AND TEMPTED HIM, SAYING, MASTER, WHAT SHALL I DO TO 208 12
SAYING, WHAT SHALL WE EAT 211 27
GLORIFIED GOD, SAYING, THAT A GREAT PROPHET IS RISEN 213 07
AND PHARISEES, SAYING, IS IT LAWFUL TO HEAL ON THE 214 02
ANSWERED THEM, SAYING, WHICH OF YOU SHALL HAVE AN ASS 214 05
SAYING UNTO THEM, WHEN THOU ART BIDDEN OF ANY MAN TO 214 10
TEMPTING HIM, AND SAYING, MASTER, WHICH IS THE GREAT 215 09
JESUS ASKED THEM, SAYING, WHAT THINK YE OF CHRIST 215 16
CALL HIM LORD, SAYING, THE LORD SAID UNTO MY LORD, 215 19
OTHER SERVANTS, SAYING, TELL THEM WHICH ARE BIDDEN, 218 07
AND TOLD HIM, SAYING, THY SON LIVETH 220 06
WORSHIPPED HIM, SAYING, LORD, HAVE PATIENCE WITH ME, 221 20
BY THE THROAT, SAYING, PAY ME THAT THOU OWEST 221 25
AND BESOUGHT HIM, SAYING, HAVE PATIENCE WITH ME, AND 221 27
THE HERODIANS, SAYING, MASTER, WE KNOW THAT THOU ART 222 30
WORSHIPPED HIM, SAYING, MY DAUGHTER IS EVEN NOW DEAD 224 14
AND HEARD A VOICE SAYING UNTO HIM, SAUL, SAUL, WHY 229 32
AGAIN UNTO AHAZ, SAYING, ASK THEE A SIGN OF THE LORD 235 25
TROUBLED AT HIS SAYING, AND CAST IN HER MIND WHAT 236 12
AND WROTE, SAYING, HIS NAME IS JOHN 243 23
IN THEIR HEARTS, SAYING, WHAT MANNER OF CHILD SHALL 243 29
AND PROPHESIED, SAYING, BLESSED BE THE LORD GOD OF 243 32
RAISED HIM UP, SAYING, ARISE UP QUICKLY 245 14
HIS DISCIPLES, SAYING, WHOM DO MEN SAY THAT I THE SON 245 32
OUT OF THE CLOUD, SAYING, THIS IS MY BELOVED SON 249 07
A LOUD VOICE SAYING IN HEAVEN, NOW IS COME SALVATION, 252 10
UNTO JESUS, SAYING, WHO IS THE GREATEST IN THE 252 22
THEY HAVE KEPT MY SAYING, THEY WILL KEEP YOUR'S ALSO 255 20
AND THE SEA, SAYING, HURT NOT THE EARTH, NEITHER THE 256 17
A LOUD VOICE, SAYING, SALVATION TO OUR GOD WHICH 256 27
WORSHIPPED GOD, SAYING, AMEN 256 31
ELDERS ANSWERED, SAYING UNTO ME, WHAT ARE THESE WHICH 257 04
AND TAUGHT THEM, SAYING, BLESSED ARE THE POOR IN 257 20

SAYING CONTINUED

ANSWER HIM, SAYING, LORD, WHEN SAW WE THEE AN	259 09
THE TEMPLE, AND SAYING, HOSANNA TO THE SON OF DAVID	260 11
COMMANDED US, SAYING, I HAVE SET THEE TO BE A LIGHT	261 04
BE NOT ANXIOUS, SAYING, WHAT SHALL WE EAT	266 25
WELL-BELOVED SON, SAYING, ASK, AND YE SHALL HAVE	274 15
SPAKE UNTO THEM, SAYING, ALL POWER IS GIVEN UNTO ME	275 26
WATER UPON HIM, SAYING, N	R 279 27
WATER UPON HIM, SAYING THESE WORDS	R 281 20
AND MAGNIFY, SAYING,	285 05
THE MINISTER SAYING THE RESPONSE	R 286 03
ONE SEVERALLY, SAYING, DEFEND, O LORD, THIS THY CHILD	R 297 25
SHALL BLESS THEM, SAYING THUS, THE BLESSING OF GOD	299 02
TO PASS THE SAYING THAT IS WRITTEN, DEATH IS	330 09
FROM HEAVEN, SAYING UNTO ME, WRITE, FROM HENCEFORTH	333 25
AND FEAR THEE, SAYING, COME, YE BLESSED CHILDREN OF	335 11
UNTO JESUS, SAYING, WHO IS THE GREATEST IN THE	339 21
THEIR HEADS, SAYING, 8 HE TRUSTED IN THE LORD, THAT	366 17
YET THEIR POSTERITY PRAISE THEIR SAYING	400 33
JUSTIFIED IN THY SAYING, AND CLEAR WHEN THOU SHALT	403 16
COUNSEL TOGETHER, SAYING, 10 GOD HATH FORSAKEN HIM	425 26
AGAINST GOD ALSO, SAYING, *	436 06
11 SAYING, UNTO THEE WILL I GIVE THE LAND OF CANAAN,	470 24
SAYING, O WHEN WILT THOU COMFORT ME	495 21
DECENTLY HABITED, SAYING THESE WORDS, REVEREND FATHER	R 530 09
AND THE SAYING PLEASED THE WHOLE MULTITUDE	532 14
NEW TESTAMENT, SAYING,	R 534 10
AND THE BISHOP SAYING, RECEIVE THE HOLY GHOST FOR THE	R 546 08
INTO HIS HAND, SAYING,	R 546 24
THIS IS A TRUE SAYING, IF A MAN DESIRE THE OFFICE OF	549 18
IN EVERY CITY, SAYING THAT BONDS AND AFFLICTIONS	550 17
SPAKE UNTO THEM, SAYING, ALL POWER IS GIVEN UNTO ME	552 09
WHO PRESENT HIM SAYING,	R 552 20
PRESENT TO PRAY, SAYING THUS TO THEM	R 553 03
PRESIDING BISHOP SAYING,	R 558 11
HIM THE BIBLE, SAYING, GIVE HEED UNTO READING,	R 558 20
OUT OF HEAVEN SAYING, BEHOLD, THE TABERNACLE OF GOD	567 15
NEW INCUMBENT, SAYING, IN THE NAME AND BEHALF OF --	R 570 20
SAYING AS FOLLOWS	R 571 24
OF EXODUS, SAYING, I AM THE LORD THY GOD, WHO BROUGHT	578 23

SAYINGS

KEPT ALL THESE SAYINGS IN HER HEART	111 06
HE THAT LOVETH ME NOT KEEPETH NOT MY SAYINGS	181 27
AND ALL THESE SAYINGS WERE NOISED ABROAD THROUGHOUT	243 27
DAYS AFTER THESE SAYINGS, HE TOOK PETER AND JOHN AND	248 24

SCALES

THERE FELL FROM HIS EYES AS IT HAD BEEN SCALES	230 35

SCALP

AND THE HAIRY SCALP OF SUCH A ONE AS GOETH ON STILL	420 28

SCARCE

MY BONES WILL SCARCE CLEAVE TO MY FLESH	464 19

SCARCENESS

BUT LETTETH THE RUNAGATES CONTINUE IN SCARCENESS	419 23

SCARCITY

GRANT THAT THE SCARCITY AND DEARTH, WHICH WE NOW MOST	041 03
OUR DEARTH AND SCARCITY INTO PLENTY	051 32

SCARLET

AND PUT ON HIM A SCARLET ROBE	136 18
WITH WATER, AND SCARLET WOOL, AND HYSSOP, AND	147 21

SCATTER

BUT SCATTER THEM ABROAD AMONG THE PEOPLE, AND PUT	411 26
SCATTER THOU THE PEOPLES THAT DELIGHT IN WAR	421 17
AND TO SCATTER THEM IN THE LANDS	474 24

SCATTERED

HE HATH SCATTERED THE PROUD IN THE IMAGINATION OF	026 20
THE SHEPHERD, AND THE SHEEP SHALL BE SCATTERED	141 20
YE SHALL BE SCATTERED, EVERY MAN TO HIS OWN, AND	177 05
WHICH ARE SCATTERED ABROAD, GREETING	239 07
AND SCATTERED THEM	360 26
AND HAST SCATTERED US AMONG THE HEATHEN	395 16
US OUT, AND SCATTERED US ABROAD	412 12
AND LET HIS ENEMIES BE SCATTERED	419 09
THE ALMIGHTY SCATTERED KINGS FOR THEIR SAKE, *	420 09
THOU HAST SCATTERED THINE ENEMIES ABROAD WITH THY	450 27
OUR BONES LIE SCATTERED BEFORE THE PIT, *	517 26
AND WERE SCATTERED ABROAD AS SHEEP HAVING NO	538 16

SCATTEREST

SOON AS THOU SCATTEREST THEM THEY ARE EVEN AS A	325 22
SOON AS THOU SCATTEREST THEM THEY ARE EVEN AS A	453 27

SCATTERETH

AND HE THAT GATHERETH NOT WITH ME SCATTERETH	130 10
AND SCATTERETH THE SHEEP	172 25
THE WIND SCATTERETH AWAY FROM THE FACE OF THE EARTH	345 17

SCATTERETH CONTINUED

BUT SCATTERETH ABROAD ALL THE UNGODLY	521 33
AND SCATTERETH THE HOAR-FROST LIKE ASHES	523 27
AND SCATTERETH THE SHEEP	539 14

SCATTERING

OF THE LORD SCATTERING THEM	381 28

SCEPTRE

A SCEPTRE OF RIGHTEOUSNESS IS THE SCEPTRE OF THY	097 09
IS THE SCEPTRE OF THY KINGDOM	097 10
THE SCEPTRE OF THY KINGDOM IS A RIGHT SCEPTRE	396 27
THE SCEPTRE OF THY KINGDOM IS A RIGHT SCEPTRE	396 28
3 FOR THE SCEPTRE OF THE UNGODLY SHALL NOT ABIDE UPON	504 29

SCHISM

FROM ALL FALSE DOCTRINE, HERESY, AND SCHISM	055 03
DEFEND THEM FROM THE SINS OF HERESY AND SCHISM	574 13

SCHOOL-AUTHORS

AS THE SCHOOL-AUTHORS SAY) DESERVE GRACE OF	605 19

SCHOOLS

AND SCHOOLS, THAT KNOWLEDGE MAY BE	042 24
PRAY FOR ALL SCHOOLS, COLLEGES, AND SEMINARIES OF	047 33
OF MERCY OR IN SCHOOLS OF GOOD LEARNING	600 04

SCORN

AND THEY LAUGHED HIM TO SCORN	224 27
THAT DWELLETH IN HEAVEN SHALL LAUGH THEM TO SCORN	346 05
A VERY SCORN OF MEN, AND THE OUTCAST OF THE PEOPLE	366 15
7 ALL THEY THAT SEE ME LAUGH ME TO SCORN	366 16
THINK NO SCORN OF ME	373 04
13 THE LORD SHALL LAUGH HIM TO SCORN	385 20
TO BE LAUGHED TO SCORN, AND HAD IN DERISION OF THEM	395 20
AND SHALL LAUGH HIM TO SCORN	404 32
AND THOU SHALT LAUGH ALL THE HEATHEN TO SCORN	411 21
THAT WHOSO SEETH THEM SHALL LAUGH THEM TO SCORN	416 03
A VERY SCORN AND DERISION UNTO THEM THAT ARE ROUND	440 07
AND OUR ENEMIES LAUGH US TO SCORN	441 15
THEY THOUGHT SCORN OF THAT PLEASANT LAND,	474 17

SCORNFUL

AND HATH NOT SAT IN THE SEAT OF THE SCORNFUL	345 09
FILLED WITH THE SCORNFUL REPROOF OF THE WEALTHY, *	504 04

SCORPION

HE SHALL ASK AN EGG, WILL HE OFFER HIM A SCORPION	183 17
WILL HE OFFER HIM A SCORPION	263 10

SCOURGE

OF THEM SHALL YE SCOURGE IN YOUR SYNAGOGUES, AND	100 21
AND THEY SHALL SCOURGE HIM, AND PUT HIM TO DEATH	123 22
HE HAD MADE A SCOURGE OF SMALL CORDS, HE DROVE THEM	567 28

SCOURGED

AND WHEN HE HAD SCOURGED JESUS, HE DELIVERED HIM TO	136 14
WHEN HE HAD SCOURGED HIM, TO BE CRUCIFIED	145 29
TOOK JESUS, AND SCOURGED HIM	158 30

SCOURGES

WITH THE ROD, AND THEIR SIN WITH SCOURGES	452 06

SCOURGETH

AND SCOURGETH EVERY SON WHOM HE RECEIVETH	321 30

SCRIBES

SEND UNTO YOU PROPHETS, AND WISE MEN, AND SCRIBES	100 20
PRIESTS AND SCRIBES OF THE PEOPLE TOGETHER, HE	109 05
WITH THE SCRIBES AND ELDERS, SAID, HE SAVED	137 09
PRIESTS AND THE SCRIBES SOUGHT HOW THEY MIGHT TAKE	139 33
PRIESTS AND THE SCRIBES AND THE ELDERS	142 17
THE CHIEF PRIESTS AND THE ELDERS AND THE SCRIBES	142 33
THE ELDERS AND SCRIBES AND THE WHOLE COUNCIL, AND	145 04
WITH THE SCRIBES, HE SAVED OTHERS	146 22
PRIESTS AND SCRIBES SOUGHT HOW THEY MIGHT KILL HIM	148 13
PRIESTS AND THE SCRIBES CAME TOGETHER, AND LED HIM	151 29
PRIESTS AND SCRIBES STOOD AND VEHEMENTLY ACCUSED HIM	153 15
PHARISEES AND SCRIBES MURMURED, SAYING, THIS MAN	193 15
OF THE SCRIBES AND PHARISEES, YE SHALL IN NO CASE	197 29
CERTAIN OF THE SCRIBES SAID WITHIN THEMSELVES,	217 05
PRIESTS AND SCRIBES SAW THE WONDERFUL THINGS THAT HE	260 10

SCRIP

WITHOUT PURSE, AND SCRIP, AND SHOES, LACKED YE ANY	150 05
LET HIM TAKE IT, AND LIKEWISE HIS SCRIP	150 07
NEITHER PURSE, NOR SCRIP, NOR SHOES	254 18

SCRIPTURE

OR MORE OF THE FOLLOWING SENTENCES OF SCRIPTURE	R 003 04

SCRIPTURE   CONTINUED

THE SCRIPTURE MOVETH US, IN SUNDRY PLACES,   005 29
OR MORE OF THE FOLLOWING SENTENCES OF SCRIPTURE   R 021 04
THE SCRIPTURE MOVETH US, IN SUNDRY PLACES,   023 04
WORDS OF HOLY SCRIPTURE OR OF THE BOOK OF COMMON   R 073 35
BY GOD IN HOLY SCRIPTURE, AND BE RECEIVED AS WORTHY   087 14
NEVERTHELESS WHAT SAITH THE SCRIPTURE   131 15
AND THE SCRIPTURE WAS FULFILLED, WHICH SAITH, AND HE   146 16
THAT THE SCRIPTURE MIGHT BE FULFILLED, WHICH SAITH,   160 14
THAT THE SCRIPTURE MIGHT BE FULFILLED, SAITH, I   160 25
THAT THE SCRIPTURE SHOULD BE FULFILLED, A BONE   161 08
AGAIN ANOTHER SCRIPTURE SAITH, THEY SHALL LOOK ON HIM   161 09
KNEW NOT THE SCRIPTURE, THAT HE MUST RISE AGAIN FROM   164 27
BUT THE SCRIPTURE HATH CONCLUDED ALL UNDER SIN,   208 03
FOR THE SCRIPTURE SAITH, WHOSOEVER BELIEVETH ON HIM   226 30
THIS SCRIPTURE MUST NEEDS HAVE BEEN   234 08
DAY IS THIS SCRIPTURE FULFILLED IN YOUR EARS   261 25
READING HOLY SCRIPTURE AND ANCIENT AUTHORS, THAT FROM   529 11
IN THE HOLY SCRIPTURE, AND OTHERWISE LEARNED AS THE   529 29
MAY BE CONCLUDED AND PROVED BY THE SCRIPTURE   542 08
AS THE HOLY SCRIPTURE AND THE ANCIENT CANONS COMMAND,   554 07
OF HOLY SCRIPTURE, LET THE HEAD OF THE HOUSEHOLD, OR   R 592 09
OF HOLY SCRIPTURE, LET THE HEAD OF THE HOUSEHOLD, OR   R 593 03
HOLY SCRIPTURE CONTAINETH ALL THINGS NECESSARY TO   603 29
OF THE HOLY SCRIPTURE WE DO UNDERSTAND THOSE   603 32
PROVED BY MOST CERTAIN WARRANTS OF HOLY SCRIPTURE   604 27
BE GENERALLY SET FORTH TO US IN HOLY SCRIPTURE   606 28
FOR HOLY SCRIPTURE DOTH SET OUT UNTO US ONLY THE NAME   606 35
ONE PLACE OF SCRIPTURE, THAT IT BE REPUGNANT TO   607 06
NO WARRANTY OF SCRIPTURE, BUT RATHER REPUGNANT TO THE   607 16
PLAIN WORDS OF SCRIPTURE, OVERTHROWETH THE NATURE OF   608 42

SCRIPTURES

DAY HE ROSE AGAIN ACCORDING TO THE SCRIPTURES   016 10
DAY HE ROSE AGAIN ACCORDING TO THE SCRIPTURES   030 15
DAY HE ROSE AGAIN ACCORDING TO THE SCRIPTURES   071 13
ALL HOLY SCRIPTURES TO BE WRITTEN FOR OUR LEARNING   092 07
OF THE SCRIPTURES MIGHT HAVE HOPE   092 17
BUT THE SCRIPTURES MUST BE FULFILLED   142 27
IN ALL THE SCRIPTURES THE THINGS CONCERNING HIMSELF   167 33
AND WHILE HE OPENED TO US THE SCRIPTURES   168 11
THE SCRIPTURES, AND SAID UNTO THEM, THUS IT IS   170 11
DIED FOR OUR SINS ACCORDING TO THE SCRIPTURES   205 05
AGAIN THE THIRD DAY ACCORDING TO THE SCRIPTURES   205 06
THAT THE HOLY SCRIPTURES CONTAIN ALL DOCTRINE   533 02
TO READ HOLY SCRIPTURES AND HOMILIES IN THE CHURCH   533 14
OF THE HOLY SCRIPTURES, AND WITH A LIFE AGREEABLE TO   541 02
LEARNING THE SCRIPTURES, AND IN FRAMING THE MANNERS   541 04
ACCORDING TO THE RULE OF THE SAME SCRIPTURES   541 06
WEIGHING THE SCRIPTURES, YE MAY WAX RIPER AND   541 18
THAT THE HOLY SCRIPTURES CONTAIN ALL DOCTRINE   542 02
OF THE SAID SCRIPTURES TO INSTRUCT THE PEOPLE   542 05
THE HOLY SCRIPTURES, AND IN SUCH STUDIES AS HELP TO   542 27
THAT THE HOLY SCRIPTURES CONTAIN ALL DOCTRINE   554 20
THE SAME HOLY SCRIPTURES TO INSTRUCT THE PEOPLE   554 23
IN THE HOLY SCRIPTURES, AND CALL UPON GOD BY PRAYER   554 30
ARE STATES OF LIFE ALLOWED IN THE SCRIPTURES   607 41

SCRUPLE

REMOVING OF ALL SCRUPLE AND DOUBTFULNESS   088 09

SEA

THE SEA IS HIS, AND HE MADE IT   009 11
LET THE SEA MAKE A NOISE, AND ALL THAT THEREIN IS   027 19
AND RULEST THE RAGING OF THE SEA   042 04
THE DANGERS OF THE SEA, AND FROM THE VIOLENCE OF THE   042 07
OUT THE HEAVENS, AND RULEST THE RAGING OF THE SEA   046 09
THE DANGERS OF THE SEA, FROM SICKNESS, FROM THE   046 12
WHO TRAVEL BY LAND, SEA, OR AIR   048 05
AND EARTH, THE SEA, AND ALL THAT IN THEM IS, AND   068 30
THE SEA AND THE WAVES ROARING   093 07
IN PERILS IN THE SEA, IN PERILS AMONG FALSE BRETHREN   121 07
JESUS WENT OVER THE SEA OF GALILEE, WHICH IS THE SEA   131 21
WHICH IS THE SEA OF TIBERIAS   131 21
THEM UP OUT OF THE SEA WITH THE SHEPHERD OF HIS   139 09
THRONE THERE WAS A SEA OF GLASS LIKE UNTO CRYSTAL   187 15
UNDER THE CLOUD, AND ALL PASSED THROUGH THE SEA   201 07
BAPTIZED UNTO MOSES IN THE CLOUD AND IN THE SEA   201 08
CAME UNTO THE SEA OF GALILEE, THROUGH THE   206 28
WALKING BY THE SEA OF GALILEE, SAW TWO BRETHREN,   227 24
ANDREW HIS BROTHER, CASTING A NET INTO THE SEA   227 26
LIKE A WAVE OF THE SEA DRIVEN WITH THE WIND AND   239 15
WOE TO THE INHABITERS OF THE EARTH AND OF THE SEA   252 18
AND THAT HE WERE DROWNED IN THE DEPTH OF THE SEA   252 33
THE EARTH AND THE SEA, SAYING, HURT NOT THE EARTH,   256 17
NEITHER THE SEA, NOR THE TREES, TILL WE HAVE   256 18
AND EARTH, THE SEA, AND ALL THAT IN THEM IS, AND   286 30
THE HILLS BE CARRIED INTO THE MIDST OF THE SEA   327 06
THE EARTH AND THE SEA SHALL GIVE UP THEIR DEAD   333 19
JUDGE THE WORLD, THE SEA SHALL GIVE UP HER DEAD   337 13
AND THE FISHES OF THE SEA   351 15
4 IT IS THE LORD THAT RULETH THE SEA   374 04
THE WATERS OF THE SEA TOGETHER, AS IT WERE UPON AN   378 31
THE HILLS BE CARRIED INTO THE MIDST OF THE SEA   397 29
THE SHIPS OF THE SEA *   399 22
AND OF THEM THAT REMAIN IN THE BROAD SEA   416 24
THE RAGING OF THE SEA, *   416 27
5 HE TURNED THE SEA INTO DRY LAND, *   417 24
AS I DID SOMETIME FROM THE DEEP OF THE SEA   420 32
THE SEA, AND ALL THAT MOVETH THEREIN   424 12
BE ALSO FROM THE ONE SEA TO THE OTHER, *   427 12
DIDST DIVIDE THE SEA THROUGH THY POWER   431 02

SEA   CONTINUED

19 THY WAY IS IN THE SEA, AND THY PATHS IN THE GREAT   434 21
14 HE DIVIDED THE SEA, AND LET THEM GO THROUGH   435 26
AND FEATHERED FOWLS LIKE AS THE SAND OF THE SEA   436 26
AND OVERWHELMED THEIR ENEMIES WITH THE SEA   438 17
BRANCHES UNTO THE SEA, *   441 24
10 THOU RULEST THE RAGING OF THE SEA   450 24
DOMINION ALSO IN THE SEA, *   451 25
5 THE WAVES OF THE SEA ARE MIGHTY, AND RAGE HORRIBLY   457 13
5 THE SEA IS HIS, AND HE MADE IT   459 13
LET THE SEA MAKE A NOISE, AND ALL THAT THEREIN IS   460 23
8 LET THE SEA MAKE A NOISE, AND ALL THAT THEREIN IS   462 08
THE GREAT AND WIDE SEA ALSO   469 10
DISOBEDIENT AT THE SEA, EVEN AT THE RED SEA   473 15
WERE DISOBEDIENT AT THE SEA, EVEN AT THE RED SEA   473 15
9 HE REBUKED THE RED SEA ALSO, AND IT WAS DRIED UP   473 18
AND FEARFUL THINGS BY THE RED SEA   474 13
THAT GO DOWN TO THE SEA IN SHIPS, *   477 22
3 THE SEA SAW THAT, AND FLED   484 30
AILETH THEE, O THOU SEA, THAT THOU FLEDDEST   485 02
AND IN THE SEA, AND IN ALL DEEP PLACES   510 14
WHO DIVIDED THE RED SEA IN TWO PARTS   512 08
AND HIS HOST, HE OVERTHREW THEM IN THE RED SEA   512 13
AND REMAIN IN THE UTTERMOST PARTS OF THE SEA   515 05
AND EARTH, THE SEA, AND ALL THAT THEREIN IS   522 12
AND EARTH, THE SEA, AND ALL THAT IN THEM IS, AND   579 10
AND THOSE WHO TRAVEL BY LAND OR BY SEA   600 07

SEAL

HAVING THE SEAL OF THE LIVING GOD   256 15
OUR EPISCOPAL SEAL AND SIGNATURE, AT --, THIS -- DAY   569 38

SEALED

WHEREBY YE ARE SEALED UNTO THE DAY OF REDEMPTION   216 26
TILL WE HAVE SEALED THE SERVANTS OF OUR GOD IN THEIR   256 18
AND I HEARD THE NUMBER OF THEM WHICH WERE SEALED   256 20
AND THERE WERE SEALED AN HUNDRED AND FORTY AND FOUR   256 20
AND HIS PARDON SEALED IN HEAVEN   316 15
ARE VISIBLY SIGNED AND SEALED   608 29

SEALING

SEPULCHRE SURE, SEALING THE STONE, AND SETTING A   162 25

SEAM

COAT WAS WITHOUT SEAM, WOVEN FROM THE TOP THROUGHOUT   160 12

SEARCH

AND SO TO SEARCH AND EXAMINE YOUR OWN CONSCIENCES,   087 10
AND SAID, GO AND SEARCH DILIGENTLY FOR THE YOUNG   109 13
OWN HEART, AND SEARCH OUT MY SPIRIT   311 11
SEARCH OUT HIS UNGODLINESS, UNTIL THOU FIND NONE   354 10
SHALL NOT GOD SEARCH IT OUT   396 03
OWN HEART, AND SEARCH OUT MY SPIRIT   433 28
IS SO MADE, TO SEARCH FOR THE SICK, POOR, AND   533 19

SEARCHED

THOU HAST SEARCHED ME OUT, AND KNOWN ME   514 20

SEAS

O YE SEAS AND FLOODS, BLESS YE THE LORD   013 10
SUCH AS PASS ON THE SEAS UPON THEIR LAWFUL OCCASIONS   042 09
WHATSOEVER WALKETH THROUGH THE PATHS OF THE SEAS   351 16
FOUNDED IT UPON THE SEAS, *   368 30
FOUNDED IT UPON THE SEAS, *   563 13

SEASON

AND OF THY TRUTH IN THE NIGHT SEASON   027 31
IN THE MEAN SEASON TO CONSIDER THE DIGNITY OF   087 08
SEE HIM OF A LONG SEASON, BECAUSE HE HAD HEARD MANY   153 12
UPON THIS LAND, AND TO GIVE US A FRUITFUL SEASON   261 31
WILL CAUSE THE SHOWER TO COME DOWN IN HIS SEASON   262 09
AND CEASED NOT IN THE NIGHT SEASON   311 03
THAT WILL BRING FORTH HIS FRUIT IN DUE SEASON   345 13
MY REINS ALSO CHASTEN ME IN THE NIGHT SEASON   358 05
PROVED AND VISITED MINE HEART IN THE NIGHT SEASON   358 22
AND IN THE NIGHT SEASON ALSO I TAKE NO REST   366 08
AND IN THE NIGHT SEASON WILL I SING OF HIM, AND MAKE   393 22
AND CEASED NOT IN THE NIGHT SEASON   433 20
AND OF THY TRUTH IN THE NIGHT SEASON   456 03
THAT THOU MAYEST GIVE THEM MEAT IN DUE SEASON   469 15
AND FIRE TO GIVE LIGHT IN THE NIGHT SEASON   472 16
IN THE NIGHT SEASON, *   493 21
AND THOU GIVEST THEM THEIR MEAT IN DUE SEASON   521 23
PORTION IN DUE SEASON, HE MAY AT LAST BE RECEIVED   558 04
GOD'S PURPOSE BY HIS SPIRIT WORKING IN DUE SEASON   606 12

SEASONABLE

GRANT SUCH SEASONABLE WEATHER THAT WE MAY GATHER IN   039 28
SEND US SUCH SEASONABLE WEATHER, THAT THE EARTH MAY,   040 26
SOULS BY THIS SEASONABLE AND BLESSED CHANGE OF   051 25
SEND HIM SEASONABLE RELIEF   315 27

SEASONS

THE TIMES OR THE SEASONS, WHICH THE FATHER HATH PUT   178 07
MOON FOR CERTAIN SEASONS, *   468 32

SEASONS   CONTINUED

WITH YOU AT ALL SEASONS, SERVING THE LORD WITH ALL   550 08

SEAT

MIGHTY FROM THEIR SEAT, *   026 22
SIT NOT DOWN IN THE HIGHEST SEAT   214 11
HATH NOT SAT IN THE SEAT OF THE SCORNFUL   345 09
ALSO PREPARED HIS SEAT FOR JUDGMENT   352 03
THE LORD'S SEAT IS IN HEAVEN   354 26
6 THY SEAT, O GOD, ENDURETH FOR EVER   396 27
GOD SITTETH UPON HIS HOLY SEAT   399 05
AND EQUITY ARE THE HABITATION OF THY SEAT   451 03
HATH THY SEAT BEEN PREPARED   457 09
AND JUDGMENT ARE THE HABITATION OF HIS SEAT   460 33
HATH PREPARED HIS SEAT IN HEAVEN, *   467 13
PRAISE HIM IN THE SEAT OF THE ELDERS   478 11
5 FOR THERE IS THE SEAT OF JUDGMENT, *   503 16
EVEN THE SEAT OF THE HOUSE OF DAVID   503 16

SEATED

THE PEOPLE BEING SEATED, THE MINISTER SHALL ASK THEM   R 283 13
THE PEOPLE BEING SEATED, THE MINISTER, TURNING TO   R 287 31
THE PEOPLE BEING SEATED, THE MINISTER SHALL ASK THEM   R 290 25
THE PEOPLE BEING SEATED, THE BISHOP SHALL EXAMINE   R 532 23
THE PEOPLE BEING SEATED, THE BISHOP SHALL SAY UNTO   R 539 22
THE PEOPLE BEING SEATED, THE PRESIDING BISHOP,   R 554 05

SEATS

AND THE SEATS OF THEM THAT SOLD DOVES, AND SAID UNTO   091 35
ROUND ABOUT THE THRONE WERE FOUR AND TWENTY SEATS   187 09
AND UPON THE SEATS I SAW FOUR AND TWENTY ELDERS   187 09
WHEN HE MARKED HOW THEY CHOSE OUT THE CHIEF SEATS   214 10
AND THE SEATS OF THEM THAT SOLD DOVES, AND SAID UNTO   260 05

SECOND

THE FIRST (OR THE SECOND) LESSON   R 009 34
LIKE MANNER, THE SECOND LESSON, TAKEN OUT OF THE NEW   R 014 02
AND THE SECOND IS LIKE UNTO IT   069 29
THAT AT THY SECOND COMING TO JUDGE THE WORLD WE   093 29
AND THE SECOND TIME THE COCK CREW   143 34
HE APPEAR THE SECOND TIME WITHOUT SIN UNTO SALVATION   148 10
AWAY THE FIRST, THAT HE MAY ESTABLISH THE SECOND   157 33
WRITTEN IN THE SECOND PSALM, THOU ART MY SON, THIS   169 09
A LION, AND THE SECOND LIKE A CALF, AND THE THIRD HAD   187 18
CAN HE ENTER THE SECOND TIME INTO HIS MOTHER'S WOMB,   188 08
AND THE SECOND IS LIKE UNTO IT, THOU SHALT LOVE THY   215 13
THIS IS AGAIN THE SECOND MIRACLE THAT JESUS DID, WHEN   220 11
THE FIRST AND THE SECOND WARD, THEY CAME UNTO THE   245 21
AFTER THE SECOND LESSON AT MORNING OR EVENING PRAYER, R 273 15
CAN HE ENTER THE SECOND TIME INTO HIS MOTHER'S WOMB,   275 13
AND THE SECOND IS   288 08
IS THE FIRST (SECOND OR THIRD) TIME OF ASKING   R 304 25
THE SECOND MAN IS THE LORD FROM HEAVEN   329 28
SHALL COME IN THE SECOND WATCH, OR COME IN THE THIRD   534 24
TO HIM AGAIN THE SECOND TIME, SIMON, SON OF JONAS,   551 17
THE SECOND BOOK OF HOMILIES, THE SEVERAL TITLES   610 05

SECONDLY

SECONDLY, THAT I SHOULD BELIEVE ALL THE ARTICLES OF   283 25
SECONDLY, IN GOD THE SON, WHO HATH REDEEMED ME,   284 31
SECONDLY, THAT I SHOULD BELIEVE ALL THE ARTICLES OF   577 16
SECONDLY, IN GOD THE SON, WHO HATH REDEEMED ME,   578 13

SECRET

MAY ASK THE SECRET INTERCESSIONS OF THE CONGREGATION   R 074 02
HE IS IN THE SECRET CHAMBERS   118 09
WHICH SEETH IN SECRET, SHALL REWARD THEE OPENLY   125 15
BUT UNTO THY FATHER WHICH IS IN SECRET   125 15
OF THOSE THINGS WHICH ARE DONE OF THEM IN SECRET   129 19
AND OUR SECRET SINS IN THE LIGHT OF THY COUNTENANCE   325 28
IN THE SECRET PLACE OF HIS DWELLING SHALL HE   326 13
WHELP LURKING IN SECRET PLACES   359 11
MADE DARKNESS HIS SECRET PLACE, *   360 19
THOU ME FROM MY SECRET FAULTS   364 09
13 THE SECRET OF THE LORD IS AMONG THEM THAT FEAR   370 12
IN THE SECRET PLACE OF HIS DWELLING SHALL HE   372 05
THAT THEY KEEP SECRET AMONG THEMSELVES, EVERY MAN IN   415 31
AGAINST THY SECRET ONES   444 10
AND OUR SECRET SINS IN THE LIGHT OF THY COUNTENANCE   454 03
OF GOD, OR BY THE SECRET INSPIRATION OF THE BLESSED   564 13
BY HIS COUNSEL SECRET TO US, TO DELIVER FROM CURSE   606 08

SECRETLY

AND SHALT MAKE ME TO UNDERSTAND WISDOM SECRETLY   060 23
9 FOR HE LIETH WAITING SECRETLY   353 23
SHALT KEEP THEM SECRETLY IN THY TABERNACLE FROM THE   377 08
AND SHALT MAKE ME TO UNDERSTAND WISDOM SECRETLY   403 21
SECRETLY AMONG THE FAITHFUL, AND IN THE CONGREGATION   482 25
I BE MADE SECRETLY, AND FASHIONED BENEATH IN THE   515 19
BE DESIRED, SECRETLY IN THEIR PRAYERS, TO MAKE THEIR   R 543 23
EVERY ONE MAY SECRETLY CONFESS THE SINS AND FAILINGS   R 589 34

SECRETS

AND FROM WHOM NO SECRETS ARE HID   067 17
WHEN THE SECRETS OF ALL HEARTS SHALL BE DISCLOSED,   300 25
THE SECRETS OF OUR HEARTS   332 28
KNOWETH THE VERY SECRETS OF THE HEART   396 03

SECT

SAVED BY THE LAW OR SECT WHICH HE PROFESSETH, SO THAT   606 33

SECURE

WE MAY DWELL SECURE IN THY PEACE   018 09

SECURITY

AND A SECURITY FOR SUCH AS PASS ON THE SEAS   042 09

SEDITION

FROM ALL SEDITION, PRIVY CONSPIRACY, AND   055 02
FOR A CERTAIN SEDITION MADE IN THE CITY, AND FOR   153 31
HIM THAT FOR SEDITION AND MURDER WAS CAST INTO   154 07

SEDITIONS

STRIFE, SEDITIONS, HERESIES, ENVYINGS,   209 22

SEDITIOUS

TO APPEASE THE SEDITIOUS TUMULTS WHICH HAVE BEEN   052 20

SEE

BEHOLD, AND SEE IF THERE BE ANY SORROW LIKE UNTO MY   004 30
THAT THEY MAY SEE YOUR GOOD WORKS, AND GLORIFY   072 04
IN CASE HE SHALL SEE THE PEOPLE NEGLIGENT TO COME   R 088 10
AND THEN SHALL THEY SEE THE SON OF MAN COMING IN A   093 10
NOW SHOOT FORTH, YE SEE AND KNOW OF YOUR OWN SELVES   093 15
LIKEWISE YE, WHEN YE SEE THESE THINGS COME TO PASS,   093 17
JOHN AGAIN THOSE THINGS WHICH YE DO HEAR AND SEE   094 20
WHAT WENT YE OUT INTO THE WILDERNESS TO SEE   094 26
BUT WHAT WENT YE OUT FOR TO SEE   094 27
BUT WHAT WENT YE OUT FOR TO SEE   094 30
AND SAID, BEHOLD, I SEE THE HEAVENS OPENED, AND THE   100 07
YE SHALL NOT SEE ME HENCEFORTH, TILL YE SHALL   100 32
UNTO BETHLEHEM, AND SEE THIS THING WHICH IS COME TO   106 09
AND TO MAKE ALL MEN SEE WHAT IS THE FELLOWSHIP OF THE   108 21
SAITH UNTO HIM, SEE THOU TELL NO MAN   115 04
FOR WE SHALL SEE HIM AS HE IS   117 19
AND THEY SHALL SEE THE SON OF MAN COMING IN THE   118 19
THEY MIGHT NOT SEE, AND HEARING THEY MIGHT NOT   121 31
FOR NOW WE SEE THROUGH A GLASS, DARKLY   123 12
HE SHALL NEVER SEE DEATH   133 18
ABRAHAM REJOICED TO SEE MY DAY   133 28
SEE THOU TO THAT   135 06
SEE YE TO IT   136 11
LET BE, LET US SEE WHETHER ELIAS WILL COME TO   137 23
AND YE SHALL SEE THE SON OF MAN SITTING ON THE RIGHT   143 15
THAT WE MAY SEE AND BELIEVE   146 24
LET US SEE WHETHER ELIAS WILL COME TO TAKE HIM DOWN   146 33
HE WAS DESIROUS TO SEE HIM OF A LONG SEASON, BECAUSE   153 11
MUCH THE MORE, AS YE SEE THE DAY APPROACHING   158 28
THERE SHALL YE SEE HIM, AS HE SAID UNTO YOU   165 32
THINE HOLY ONE TO SEE CORRUPTION   169 14
HANDLE ME, AND SEE   169 33
AND BONES, AS YE SEE ME HAVE   169 34
AND YE SHALL SEE ME, BECAUSE I GO TO THE   173 28
AND YE SHALL NOT SEE ME   173 28
AND YE SHALL NOT SEE ME   173 31
AND YE SHALL SEE ME   173 32
AND YE SHALL NOT SEE ME   174 06
AND YE SHALL SEE ME   174 07
BUT I WILL SEE YOU AGAIN, AND YOUR HEART SHALL   174 14
TO MY FATHER, AND YE SEE ME NO MORE   175 15
BUT YE SEE ME   181 16
HE CANNOT SEE THE KINGDOM OF GOD   188 06
I MUST NEEDS GO AND SEE IT   192 08
AND THEN SHALT THOU SEE CLEARLY TO PULL OUT THE MOTE   195 11
WILL LOVE LIFE, AND SEE GOOD DAYS, LET HIM REFRAIN   195 24
ARE THE EYES WHICH SEE THE THINGS THAT YE SEE   208 07
ARE THE EYES WHICH SEE THE THINGS THAT YE SEE   208 08
HAVE DESIRED TO SEE THOSE THINGS WHICH YE SEE, AND   208 09
THINGS WHICH YE SEE, AND HAVE NOT SEEN THEM   208 09
YE SEE HOW LARGE A LETTER I HAVE WRITTEN UNTO YOU   210 23
SEE THEN THAT YE WALK CIRCUMSPECTLY, NOT AS FOOLS,   217 23
THE KING CAME IN TO SEE THE GUESTS, HE SAW THERE A   218 22
UNTO HIM, EXCEPT YE SEE SIGNS AND WONDERS, YE WILL   219 33
EXCEPT I SHALL SEE IN HIS HANDS THE PRINT OF   228 28
THAT HE SHOULD NOT SEE DEATH, BEFORE HE HAD SEEN THE   232 34
AND ALL FLESH SHALL SEE IT TOGETHER   242 26
FOR THEY SHALL SEE GOD   257 27
AND THE WIFE SEE THAT SHE REVERENCE HER HUSBAND   268 03
HE CANNOT SEE THE KINGDOM OF GOD   275 11
GRANT THAT THEY MAY SEE THEIR CHILDREN BROUGHT UP IN   303 17
YET SHALL I SEE GOD   324 11
WHOM I SHALL SEE FOR MYSELF, AND MINE EYES SHALL   324 11
I BELIEVE VERILY TO SEE THE GOODNESS OF THE LORD IN   326 29
FOR THEY SHALL SEE GOD   340 17
BUT I WILL SEE YOU AGAIN, AND YOUR HEART SHALL   341 10
AND HE WILL NEVER SEE IT   353 31
TO SEE IF THERE WERE ANY THAT WOULD UNDERSTAND,   356 17
THY HOLY ONE TO SEE CORRUPTION   358 11
7 ALL THEY THAT SEE ME LAUGH ME TO SCORN   366 16
I BELIEVE VERILY TO SEE THE GOODNESS OF THE LORD IN   372 28
AND THEY THAT DID SEE HIM WITHOUT, CONVEYED THEMSELVES   376 17
8 O TASTE, AND SEE, HOW GRACIOUS THE LORD IS   380 17
AND WOULD FAIN SEE GOOD DAYS   380 26
THY LIGHT SHALL WE SEE LIGHT   384 15
THOU SHALT SEE IT   387 03
4 MANY SHALL SEE IT, AND FEAR, *   390 16
6 AND IF HE COME TO SEE ME, HE SPEAKETH VANITY,   392 10

SEE   CONTINUED

4 THEY MARVELLED TO SEE SUCH THINGS   399 18
AND NOT SEE THE GRAVE   400 22
AND SHALL NEVER SEE LIGHT   401 15
RIGHTEOUS ALSO SHALL SEE THIS, AND FEAR, *   404 31
TO SEE IF THERE WERE ANY THAT WOULD UNDERSTAND,   405 17
AND LET THEM NOT SEE THE SUN   410 24
AND GOD SHALL LET ME SEE MY DESIRE UPON MINE ENEMIES   411 25
THAT THEY SEE NOT   415 29
9 AND ALL MEN THAT SEE IT SHALL SAY, THIS HATH GOD   416 04
THAT THEY SEE NOT   423 21
I DO ALSO SEE THE UNGODLY IN SUCH PROSPERITY   428 14
10 WE SEE NOT OUR TOKENS   430 24
SEE THAT SUCH AS ARE IN NEED AND NECESSITY HAVE   443 22
THEY WHO HATE ME MAY SEE IT, AND BE ASHAMED, *   448 10
AND SHALL NOT SEE DEATH   453 02
AND SEE THE REWARD OF THE UNGODLY   455 11
MINE EYE ALSO SHALL SEE HIS LUST OF MINE ENEMIES,   456 21
THE LORD SHALL NOT SEE, *   457 31
OR HE THAT MADE THE EYE, SHALL HE NOT SEE   458 05
THAT LOVE THE LORD, SEE THAT YE HATE THE THING WHICH   461 16
IT PITIETH THEM TO SEE HER IN THE DUST   465 08
5 THAT I MAY SEE THE FELICITY OF THY CHOSEN, *   473 08
24 THESE MEN SEE THE WORKS OF THE LORD, *   477 24
UNTIL HE SEE HIS DESIRE UPON HIS ENEMIES   483 33
10 THE UNGODLY SHALL SEE IT, AND IT SHALL GRIEVE HIM   484 04
EYES HAVE THEY, AND SEE NOT   485 21
THEREFORE SHALL I SEE MY DESIRE UPON MINE ENEMIES   488 13
THAT I MAY SEE THE WONDROUS THINGS OF THY LAW   491 02
BE GLAD WHEN THEY SEE ME   495 02
96 I SEE THAT ALL THINGS COME TO AN END   496 17
GRIEVETH ME WHEN I SEE THE TRANSGRESSORS   500 27
THAT THOU SHALT SEE JERUSALEM IN PROSPERITY ALL THY   506 17
THAT THOU SHALT SEE THY CHILDREN'S CHILDREN,   506 18
HAVE THEY, BUT THEY SEE NOT   511 03
15 THINE EYES DID SEE MY SUBSTANCE, YET BEING   515 20
AND SEE THAT YE NEVER CEASE YOUR LABOUR, YOUR CARE   540 16
GREAT DIFFICULTY, YE SEE WITH HOW GREAT CARE AND   540 25
OF GOD, SHALL SEE MY FACE NO MORE   550 23
WISDOM THOU SHALT SEE TO BE MOST EXPEDIENT FOR THEM   566 22
ELSE THOU SHALT SEE TO BE NECESSARY AND CONVENIENT TO   589 05
IN THY LIGHT WE MAY SEE LIGHT, AND IN THY STRAIGHT   595 31

SEED

ABRAHAM AND HIS SEED, FOR EVER   026 28
WHICH SOWED GOOD SEED IN HIS FIELD   116 19
NOT THOU SOW GOOD SEED IN THY FIELD   116 24
ARE THEY THE SEED OF ABRAHAM   120 29
A SOWER WENT OUT TO SOW HIS SEED   121 20
THE SEED IS THE WORD OF GOD   121 33
TO ABRAHAM AND HIS SEED WERE THE PROMISES MADE   207 19
OF ONE, AND TO THY SEED, WHICH IS CHRIST   207 21
TILL THE SEED SHOULD COME TO WHOM THE PROMISE WAS   207 28
AND WHICH LED THE SEED OF THE HOUSE OF ISRAEL OUT OF   225 18
AND TO EVERY SEED ITS OWN BODY   329 11
AND UNTO HIS SEED FOR EVERMORE   363 09
AND THEIR SEED FROM AMONG THE CHILDREN OF MEN   365 26
FEAR HIM, ALL YE SEED OF ISRAEL   367 19
ALL YE OF THE SEED OF JACOB   367 19
31 MY SEED SHALL SERVE HIM   368 04
AND HIS SEED SHALL INHERIT THE LAND   370 10
NOR HIS SEED BEGGING THEIR BREAD   386 16
AND HIS SEED IS BLESSED   386 16
AS FOR THE SEED OF THE UNGODLY, IT SHALL BE ROOTED   386 22
4 THEIR SEED WILL I STABLISH FOR EVER, *   450 11
30 HIS SEED ALSO WILL I MAKE TO ENDURE FOR EVER,   451 33
35 HIS SEED SHALL ENDURE FOR EVER, *   452 12
AND THEIR SEED SHALL STAND FAST IN THY SIGHT   466 06
6 O YE SEED OF ABRAHAM HIS SERVANT, *   470 14
TO CAST OUT THEIR SEED AMONG THE NATIONS, *   474 23
2 HIS SEED SHALL BE MIGHTY UPON EARTH   483 20
BEARETH FORTH GOOD SEED, *   505 19

SEED-TIME

THE RETURN OF SEED-TIME AND HARVEST, FOR THE INCREASE   050 22

SEEDS

SAITH NOT, AND TO SEEDS, AS OF MANY   207 20

SEEING

SEEING THAT WE HAVE A GREAT HIGH PRIEST,   005 06
PETER SEEING HIM SAITH TO JESUS, LORD, AND WHAT SHALL   102 06
FOOLS GLADLY, SEEING YE YOURSELVES ARE WISE   120 22
THAT SEEING THEY MIGHT NOT SEE, AND HEARING THEY   121 31
THOU FEAR GOD, SEEING THOU ART IN THE SAME   155 03
AND JESUS, SEEING THEIR FAITH, SAID UNTO THE SICK OF   217 02
A VOICE, BUT SEEING NO MAN   230 09
SHALL THIS BE, SEEING I KNOW NOT A MAN   236 21
THEREFORE SEEING WE HAVE THIS MINISTRY, AS WE HAVE   250 27
JESUS SEEING THE MULTITUDES, WENT UP INTO A MOUNTAIN   257 18
SEEING WE ALSO ARE COMPASSED ABOUT WITH SO GREAT A   258 20
BUT SEEING YE PUT IT FROM YOU, AND JUDGE YOURSELVES   260 30
THE MINISTER SAY, SEEING NOW, DEARLY BELOVED   280 13
SEEING HE MAY BE COMPARED UNTO THE BEASTS THAT   400 31
AND SEEING THAT YE CANNOT BY ANY OTHER MEANS COMPASS   540 33

SEEK

FROM THEM THAT SEEK OCCASION, OF CAVIL OR QUARREL   V 38
RISEN WITH CHRIST, SEEK THOSE THINGS WHICH ARE ABOVE,   022 19
ABOVE ALL THINGS SEEK THY HONOUR AND GLORY   032 09

SEEK   CONTINUED

MEN EVERYWHERE MAY SEEK AFTER THEE AND FIND THEE   038 09
TO ALL THOSE WHO SEEK THY KINGDOM, AND THE   040 16
ABOVE ALL THINGS SEEK THY HONOUR AND GLORY   055 24
FOR HEROD WILL SEEK THE YOUNG CHILD TO DESTROY HIM   103 19
AND I SEEK NOT MINE OWN GLORY   133 15
RISEN WITH CHRIST, SEEK THOSE THINGS WHICH ARE ABOVE,   164 03
YE SEEK JESUS OF NAZARETH, WHICH WAS CRUCIFIED   165 29
SEEK, AND YE SHALL FIND   183 11
THE HOUSE, AND SEEK DILIGENTLY TILL SHE FIND IT   193 29
LET HIM SEEK PEACE, AND ENSUE IT   195 27
FOR AFTER ALL THESE THINGS DO THE GENTILES SEEK   211 29
BUT SEEK YE FIRST HIS KINGDOM, AND HIS RIGHTEOUSNESS   211 31
THE LORD, WHOM YE SEEK, SHALL SUDDENLY COME TO HIS   232 05
TO TARSUS, FOR TO SEEK SAUL   241 11
SEEK, AND YE SHALL FIND   263 04
FOR AFTER ALL THESE THINGS DO THE GENTILES SEEK   266 28
BUT SEEK YE FIRST THE KINGDOM OF GOD, AND HIS   266 29
URGENT CAUSE, THEY SEEK NOT TO HAVE THEIR CHILDREN   R 273 08
SEEK, AND YE SHALL FIND   274 16
LET US WHO SEEK, FIND   274 17
TALKED OF THEE, SEEK YE MY FACE   326 22
THY FACE, LORD, WILL I SEEK   326 23
OF WHOM MAY WE SEEK FOR SUCCOUR, BUT OF THEE, O LORD,   332 23
IN VANITY, AND SEEK AFTER FALSEHOOD   347 14
FAILED THEM THAT SEEK THEE   352 09
2 HOW LONG SHALL I SEEK COUNSEL IN MY SOUL, AND BE SO   355 30
AND SEEK AFTER GOD   356 18
THEY THAT SEEK AFTER THE LORD SHALL PRAISE HIM   367 25
OF THEM THAT SEEK HIM   369 07
EVEN OF THEM THAT SEEK THY FACE, O GOD OF JACOB   369 08
TALKED OF THEE, SEEK YE MY FACE   372 14
THY FACE, LORD, WILL I SEEK   372 15
BUT THEY WHO SEEK THE LORD SHALL WANT NO MANNER OF   380 22
SEEK PEACE, AND ENSUE IT   380 29
PUT TO SHAME, THAT SEEK AFTER MY SOUL   381 24
THAT SEEK AFTER MY SOUL TO DESTROY IT   391 17
LET ALL THOSE THAT SEEK THEE, BE JOYFUL AND GLAD IN   391 21
AND SEEK AFTER GOD   405 18
BEFORE THEIR EYES, SEEK AFTER MY SOUL   406 08
EARLY WILL I SEEK THEE   414 26
10 THESE ALSO THAT SEEK THE HURT OF MY SOUL, *   415 11
LET NOT THOSE THAT SEEK THEE BE CONFOUNDED THROUGH   422 14
SEEK YE AFTER GOD, AND YOUR SOUL SHALL LIVE   424 08
AND CONFOUNDED THAT SEEK AFTER MY SOUL   424 22
LET ALL THOSE THAT SEEK THEE BE JOYFUL AND GLAD IN   424 27
AND DISHONOUR THAT SEEK TO DO ME EVIL   425 33
UNTO SHAME THAT SEEK TO DO ME EVIL   426 29
THAT THEY MAY SEEK THY NAME   445 05
DO SEEK THEIR MEAT FROM GOD   469 02
THEM REJOICE THAT SEEK THE LORD   470 10
SEEK HIS FACE EVERMORE   470 11
4 SEEK THE LORD AND HIS STRENGTH   470 11
LET THEM SEEK IT ALSO OUT OF DESOLATE PLACES   480 20
AND SEEK HIM WITH THEIR WHOLE HEART   490 02
FOR I SEEK THY COMMANDMENTS   492 29
O SEEK THY SERVANT, FOR I DO NOT FORGET THY   502 03
I WILL SEEK TO DO THEE GOOD   503 25
TRY ME, O GOD, AND SEEK THE GROUND OF MY HEART   516 04
TO SEEK FOR CHRIST'S SHEEP THAT ARE DISPERSED ABROAD,   539 34
AND DEEDS WE MAY SEEK THY GLORY, AND THE INCREASE OF   547 12
AGAIN THE OUTCASTS, SEEK THE LOST   558 28
OF THEM THAT SEEK HIM   563 22
EVEN OF THEM THAT SEEK THY FACE, O JACOB   563 23

SEEKETH

FOR THE FATHER SEEKETH SUCH TO WORSHIP HIM   003 32
ITSELF UNSEEMLY, SEEKETH NOT HER OWN, IS NOT EASILY   122 31
IS ONE THAT SEEKETH AND JUDGETH   133 16
AND HE THAT SEEKETH FINDETH   183 13
AND HE THAT SEEKETH FINDETH   263 06
12 THE UNGODLY SEEKETH COUNSEL AGAINST THE JUST,   385 18
AND SEEKETH OCCASION TO SLAY HIM   386 30

SEEKING

SEEKING TO KEEP THE HAPPY MEAN BETWEEN TOO MUCH   V 24
AT THIS TIME ARE SEEKING TO BE STRENGTHENED BY THE   043 21
TO JERUSALEM, SEEKING HIM   110 27
DRY PLACES, SEEKING REST   130 11
WALKETH ABOUT, SEEKING WHOM HE MAY DEVOUR   193 05
GRANT THAT THEY, SEEKING FIRST THY KINGDOM AND THY   267 07

SEEM

DISPOSED OF, AS MAY SEEM MOST CONVENIENT FOR THE   V 08
FROM TIME TO TIME, SEEM EITHER NECESSARY OR   V 19
ANY MAN AMONG YOU SEEM TO BE RELIGIOUS, AND BRIDLETH   176 13
ANY MAN AMONG YOU SEEM TO BE RELIGIOUS, AND BRIDLETH   266 04
HIS PAIN, AS SHALL SEEM TO THEE MOST EXPEDIENT FOR   314 07
IT SHALL OTHERWISE SEEM GOOD UNTO THE   R 535 21

SEEMED

FOR SO IT SEEMED GOOD IN THY SIGHT   235 06

SEEMS

IT SEEMS UNNECESSARY TO ENUMERATE ALL THE DIFFERENT   VI 28

SEEN

OF THE WORLD HAVE SEEN THE SALVATION OF OUR GOD   027 11
FOR MINE EYES HAVE SEEN *   028 11

SEEN   CONTINUED

WHICH WE HAVE SEEN WITH OUR EYES, WHICH WE HAVE	101 13
AND WE HAVE SEEN IT, AND BEAR WITNESS, AND SHEW UNTO	101 15
THAT WHICH WE HAVE SEEN AND HEARD DECLARE WE UNTO	101 18
AND WHEN THEY HAD SEEN IT, THEY MADE KNOWN ABROAD THE	106 13
THEY HAD HEARD AND SEEN, AS IT WAS TOLD UNTO THEM	106 19
FOR WE HAVE SEEN HIS STAR IN THE EAST, AND ARE COME	108 33
SINNETH HATH NOT SEEN HIM, NEITHER KNOWN HIM	117 25
WHEN THEY HAD SEEN THE MIRACLE THAT JESUS DID,	132 11
AND HAST THOU SEEN ABRAHAM	133 31
HE HOPED TO HAVE SEEN SOME MIRACLE DONE BY HIM	153 13
THAT THEY HAD ALSO SEEN A VISION OF ANGELS, WHICH	167 25
AND HE WAS SEEN MANY DAYS OF THEM WHICH CAME UP WITH	169 03
THAT THEY HAD SEEN A SPIRIT	169 30
BEING SEEN OF THEM FORTY DAYS, AND SPEAKING	177 27
MANNER AS YE HAVE SEEN HIM GO INTO HEAVEN	178 19
AND TESTIFY THAT WE HAVE SEEN	188 21
NO MAN HATH SEEN GOD AT ANY TIME	189 17
AND WE HAVE SEEN AND DO TESTIFY THAT THE FATHER SENT	189 20
HOW CAN HE LOVE GOD WHOM HE HATH NOT SEEN	189 33
WHOM HE HATH SEEN, HOW CAN HE LOVE GOD WHOM HE HATH	189 33
AND THAT HE WAS SEEN OF CEPHAS, THEN OF THE TWELVE	205 07
AFTER THAT, HE WAS SEEN OF ABOVE FIVE HUNDRED	205 08
AFTER THAT, HE WAS SEEN OF JAMES	205 10
LAST OF ALL HE WAS SEEN OF ME ALSO, AS OF ONE BORN	205 11
AND HAVE NOT SEEN THEM	208 10
WHEN THEY HAD SEEN THE MIRACLE THAT JESUS DID,	226 11
THINGS HOPED FOR, THE EVIDENCE OF THINGS NOT SEEN	228 23
UNTO HIM, WE HAVE SEEN THE LORD	228 27
BECAUSE THOU HAST SEEN ME, THOU HAST BELIEVED	229 07
THEY THAT HAVE NOT SEEN, AND YET HAVE BELIEVED	229 08
AND HATH SEEN IN A VISION A MAN NAMED	230 19
BEFORE HE HAD SEEN THE LORD'S CHRIST	232 34
FOR MINE EYES HAVE SEEN THY SALVATION, WHICH THOU	233 07
KNOW HIM, AND HAVE SEEN HIM	240 09
HE THAT HATH SEEN ME HATH SEEN THE FATHER	240 12
HATH SEEN ME HATH SEEN THE FATHER	240 12
HE CAME, AND HAD SEEN THE GRACE OF GOD, WAS GLAD, AND	241 06
DAYS ANY OF THOSE THINGS WHICH THEY HAD SEEN	249 10
NOW HAVE THEY BOTH SEEN AND HATED BOTH ME AND MY	255 27
WHICH THINE EYES HAVE SEEN	263 32
BEFORE I GO HENCE, AND BE NO MORE SEEN	325 11
15 SURELY THOU HAST SEEN IT	354 04
OF WATERS WERE SEEN, AND THE FOUNDATIONS OF THE ROUND	360 28
22 THIS THOU HAST SEEN, O LORD	383 07
FOR HE HATH SEEN THAT HIS DAY IS COMING	385 21
36 I MYSELF HAVE SEEN THE UNGODLY IN GREAT POWER,	387 04
BEFORE I GO HENCE, AND BE NO MORE SEEN	390 07
SO HAVE WE SEEN IN THE CITY OF THE LORD OF	399 24
AND MINE EYE HATH SEEN HIS DESIRE UPON MINE ENEMIES	406 17
24 IT IS WELL SEEN, O GOD, HOW THOU GOEST	421 02
THE PEOPLES HAVE SEEN HIS GLORY	461 09
OF THE WORLD HAVE SEEN THE SALVATION OF OUR GOD	461 32

SEEST

O LORD GOD, WHO SEEST THAT WE PUT NOT OUR TRUST IN	120 17
ALMIGHTY GOD, WHO SEEST THAT WE HAVE NO POWER OF	127 15

SEETH

WORLD'S GOOD, AND SEETH HIS BROTHER HAVE NEED, AND	072 29
TURNING ABOUT, SEETH THE DISCIPLE WHOM JESUS LOVED	102 04
THY FATHER, WHICH SEETH IN SECRET, SHALL REWARD THEE	125 15
THE SEPULCHRE, AND SEETH THE STONE TAKEN AWAY FROM	164 12
THE SEPULCHRE, AND SEETH THE LINEN CLOTHES LIE, AND	164 22
THE SHEEP ARE NOT, SEETH THE WOLF COMING, AND LEAVETH	172 23
BECAUSE IT SEETH HIM NOT, NEITHER KNOWETH HIM	181 12
AND THE WORLD SEETH ME NO MORE	181 15
IN TORMENTS, AND SEETH ABRAHAM AFAR OFF, AND LAZARUS	190 12
WORLD'S GOOD, AND SEETH HIS BROTHER HAVE NEED, AND	191 19
EVERY ONE WHICH SEETH THE SON, AND BELIEVETH ON HIM,	269 20
EVEN THE GOD THAT SEETH THAT I BE AVENGED, *	362 34
10 FOR HE SEETH THAT WISE MEN ALSO DIE AND PERISH	400 23
REJOICE WHEN HE SEETH THE VENGEANCE	410 29
THAT WHOSO SEETH THEM SHALL LAUGH THEM TO SCORN	416 03
THE SHEEP ARE NOT, SEETH THE WOLF COMING, AND LEAVETH	539 12

SELECTION

OR SELECTION FROM THE PSALTER, SHALL BE SUNG	R 009 25
PORTION OR SELECTION OF PSALMS FOR THE DAY, SHALL BE	R 025 19
PORTION OR SELECTION FROM THE PSALTER	R 324 18

SELECTIONS

THE FOLLOWING SELECTIONS, TAKEN FROM THE PSALMS	R 324 17

SELF

I JUDGE NOT MINE OWN SELF	094 08
WHO HIS OWN SELF BARE OUR SINS IN HIS OWN BODY ON THE	172 15
WHOM THOU MADEST SO STRONG FOR THINE OWN SELF	442 06

SELF-SAME

AND FOR THIS SELF-SAME CAUSE, HOW YE OUGHT TO FORSAKE	541 07

SELFSAME

HEALED IN THE SELFSAME HOUR	115 25
ONE AND THE SELFSAME SPIRIT, DIVIDING TO EVERY MAN	182 34
ONE AND THE SELFSAME SPIRIT, DIVIDING TO EVERY MAN	204 03

SELL

NO SWORD, LET HIM SELL HIS GARMENT, AND BUY ONE	150 08

SELLEST

13 THOU SELLEST THY PEOPLE FOR NOUGHT, *	395 17

SELVES

BY GIVING UP OUR SELVES TO THY SERVICE, AND BY	019 28
BY GIVING UP OUR SELVES TO THY SERVICE, AND BY	033 26
O LORD, OUR SELVES, OUR SOULS AND BODIES,	081 22
KNOW OF YOUR OWN SELVES THAT SUMMER IS NOW NIGH AT	093 16
AND NOT HEARERS ONLY, DECEIVING YOUR OWN SELVES	176 06
DECEIVING YOUR OWN SELVES	265 29
FASHION YOUR OWN SELVES, AND YOUR FAMILIES, ACCORDING	542 33
ALSO OF YOUR OWN SELVES SHALL MEN ARISE, SPEAKING	550 32

SEMINARIES

AND SEMINARIES OF SOUND AND GODLY LEARNING,	047 33

SENATE

FOR THEIR SENATE AND REPRESENTATIVES IN CONGRESS	035 10

SENATORS

AND TEACH HIS SENATORS WISDOM	471 17

SEND

O SEND OUT THY LIGHT AND THY TRUTH, THAT THEY MAY	003 22
SEND DOWN UPON OUR BISHOPS, AND OTHER CLERGY, AND	018 19
SEND DOWN UPON OUR BISHOPS, AND OTHER CLERGY, AND	032 18
AND DIDST SEND THY BLESSED SON TO PREACH PEACE	038 07
SEND US, WE BESEECH THEE, IN THIS OUR NECESSITY,	040 18
AND WE PRAY THEE TO SEND US SUCH SEASONABLE WEATHER,	040 26
PLEASED THEE TO SEND US RAIN TO OUR GREAT COMFORT,	051 19
MAY PLEASE THEE TO SEND FORTH LABOURERS INTO THY	056 02
SEND UNTO THEM HELP FROM ABOVE	061 32
THAT HE SEND FORTH LABOURERS INTO HIS	073 13
STRAIGHTWAY HE WILL SEND THEM	091 18
FIRST COMING DIDST SEND THY MESSENGER TO PREPARE THY	093 25
BEHOLD, I SEND MY MESSENGER BEFORE THY FACE,	094 32
BEHOLD, I SEND UNTO YOU PROPHETS, AND WISE MEN,	100 19
BEHOLD, I SEND MY MESSENGER BEFORE THY	112 04
AND HE SHALL SEND HIS ANGELS WITH A GREAT SOUND OF A	118 20
SEND THY HOLY GHOST, AND POUR INTO OUR HEARTS THAT	122 15
SAYING, SEND HER AWAY	128 13
SENT ME, EVEN SO SEND I YOU	171 21
IF I DEPART, I WILL SEND HIM UNTO YOU	175 12
BEHOLD, I SEND THE PROMISE OF MY FATHER UPON	178 21
BUT SEND TO US THINE HOLY GHOST TO COMFORT US,	179 07
COME, WHOM I WILL SEND UNTO YOU FROM THE FATHER, EVEN	179 24
THE FATHER WILL SEND IN MY NAME, HE SHALL TEACH YOU	181 31
SEND, WE BESEECH THEE, ALMIGHTY GOD, THY HOLY SPIRIT	183 22
MERCY ON ME, AND SEND LAZARUS, THAT HE MAY DIP THE	190 14
THAT THOU WOULDEST SEND HIM TO MY FATHER'S HOUSE	190 23
AND IF I SEND THEM AWAY FASTING TO THEIR OWN HOUSES,	199 12
BEHOLD, I WILL SEND MY MESSENGER, AND HE SHALL	232 03
DETERMINED TO SEND RELIEF UNTO THE BRETHREN WHICH	241 20
DETERMINED TO SEND RELIEF UNTO THE BRETHREN WHICH	246 29
THAT HE WOULD SEND FORTH LABOURERS INTO HIS HARVEST	254 16
BEHOLD, I SEND YOU FORTH AS LAMBS AMONG WOLVES	254 17
COME, WHOM I WILL SEND UNTO YOU FROM THE FATHER, EVEN	255 30
SEND THY BLESSING UPON THESE THY SERVANTS, THIS MAN	303 05
SEND HIM HELP FROM THY HOLY PLACE	308 25
O SEND OUT THY LIGHT AND THY TRUTH, THAT THEY MAY	310 11
AND AT LAST DIDST SEND HIM SEASONABLE RELIEF	315 26
2 SEND THEE HELP FROM THE SANCTUARY, *	364 19
3 O SEND OUT THY LIGHT AND THY TRUTH, THAT THEY MAY	394 09
SEND HELP UNTO JACOB	394 32
3 HE SHALL SEND FROM HEAVEN, *	409 17
4 GOD SHALL SEND FORTH HIS MERCY AND TRUTH	409 19
HE DOTH SEND OUT HIS VOICE	421 23
2 THE LORD SHALL SEND THE ROD OF THY POWER OUT OF	482 09
O LORD, SEND US NOW PROSPERITY	489 18
7 SEND DOWN THINE HAND FROM ABOVE	520 04
THAT HE WILL SEND FORTH LABOURERS INTO HIS HARVEST	538 19
WE BESEECH THEE TO SEND UPON THESE THY SERVANTS THY	547 04
SENT ME, EVEN SO SEND I YOU	552 02
BEFORE WE ADMIT AND SEND FORTH THIS PERSON PRESENTED	553 11
AND TO SEND THY GRACE UPON HIM, THAT HE MAY	553 18
MERCIFUL FATHER, SEND DOWN, WE BESEECH THEE, UPON	559 05
AND TO SEND THY GRACE UPON HIM, THAT HE MAY	561 03
OF ALL GOODNESS, TO SEND HIS GRACE UNTO ME, AND TO	580 30
THAT HE WILL SEND US ALL THINGS THAT ARE NEEDFUL	580 33
EITHER BRING, OR SEND IN WRITING, WITH HIS HAND	R 583 07
SEND DOWN THY BLESSINGS, TEMPORAL AND SPIRITUAL,	590 30
TO CALL AND SEND MINISTERS INTO THE LORD'S VINEYARD	607 23

SENDEST

THOU SENDEST RAIN INTO THE LITTLE VALLEYS THEREOF	417 04

SENDETH

AND HE SENDETH FORTH TWO OF HIS DISCIPLES, AND SAITH	140 25
ON THE GOOD, AND SENDETH RAIN ON THE JUST AND ON THE	264 10
10 HE SENDETH THE SPRINGS INTO THE RIVERS, *	468 13
AND SENDETH FORTH LIGHTNINGS WITH THE RAIN, BRINGING	510 16
15 HE SENDETH FORTH HIS COMMANDMENT UPON EARTH,	523 25
18 HE SENDETH OUT HIS WORD, AND MELTETH THEM	523 31

SENDING

AND FOR THE SENDING TO US OF THE HOLY GHOST, THE	079 16
BY SENDING TO THEM THE LIGHT OF THY HOLY	180 09
IN ORDAINING, SENDING, OR LAYING HANDS UPCN OTHERS	555 20
THY MERCY IN SENDING THY ONLY SON INTO THE WORLD,	591 12

SENIOR

THE SENIOR WARDEN (OR THE MEMBER OF THE VESTRY	R 570 08
THEN SHALL THE SENIOR WARDEN (OR THE MEMBER OF THE	R 570 25

SENSE

GIVE US THAT DUE SENSE OF ALL THY MERCIES, THAT CUR	019 25
GIVE US THAT DUE SENSE OF ALL THY MERCIES, THAT OUR	033 23
COMFORT HIM WITH A SENSE OF THY GOODNESS	045 16
COMFORT HIM WITH A SENSE OF THY GOODNESS	046 04
WITH A GRATEFUL SENSE OF THY MERCIES	046 15
GIVE US A JUST SENSE OF THESE GREAT MERCIES	050 25
IMPRESSED WITH A SENSE OF THY MERCIFUL GCODNESS,	053 05
THAT THE SENSE OF HIS WEAKNESS MAY ADD STRENGTH TO	310 22
HIM AN ABIDING SENSE OF THY LOVING-KINDNESS	313 07
THY LIGHT TO EVERY SENSE IMPART, AND SHED THY LOVE IN	545 02
THY LIGHT TO EVERY SENSE IMPART, AND SHED THY LOVE IN	557 08
OWN REASON AND SENSE OF THE NATURAL DECENCY OF	564 14
SUCH A GRATEFUL SENSE OF THY GOODNESS TO US, AS MAY	588 19
THEE IN AN HUMBLE SENSE OF OUR OWN UNWORTHINESS,	589 30
THE KNOWLEDGE AND SENSE OF OUR DUTY TOWARDS THEE	591 14

SENSIBLE

MAY HE BE DULY SENSIBLE OF THY MERCIFUL PROVIDENCE	053 25
DEEPLY SENSIBLE OF THE SHORTNESS AND	316 27
MAKE US DEEPLY SENSIBLE OF THE GREAT EVIL OF THEM	590 03

SENSUALITY

SOME SENSUALITY, SOME THE AFFECTION, SOME THE	604 37

SENT

ARE SONS, GOD HATH SENT FORTH THE SPIRIT OF HIS SON	005 16
THE RICH HE HATH SENT EMPTY AWAY	026 25
AND HOW SHALL THEY PREACH, EXCEPT THEY BE SENT	073 09
OF OLIVES, THEN SENT JESUS TWO DISCIPLES, SAYING UNTO	091 13
WORKS OF CHRIST, HE SENT TWO OF HIS DISCIPLES,	094 17
WHEN THE JEWS SENT PRIESTS AND LEVITES FROM	095 21
ANSWER TO THEM THAT SENT US	095 27
AND THEY WHICH WERE SENT WERE CF THE PHARISEES	095 30
THERE WAS A MAN SENT FROM GOD, WHOSE NAME WAS JOHN	097 26
THAT LIGHT, BUT WAS SENT TO BEAR WITNESS OF THAT	097 29
THEM WHICH ARE SENT UNTO THEE, HOW OFTEN WOULD I HAVE	100 28
AND SENT FORTH, AND SLEW ALL THE CHILDREN THAT	103 26
TIME WAS COME, GOD SENT FORTH HIS SON, MADE OF A	104 19
ARE SONS, GOD HATH SENT FORTH THE SPIRIT OF HIS SCN	104 22
HE HATH SENT ME TO BIND UP THE BROKENHEARTED, TC	107 02
AND HE SENT THEM TO BETHLEHEM, AND SAID, GO AND	109 12
A PENNY A DAY, HE SENT THEM INTO HIS VINEYARD	119 18
AND SAID, I AM NOT SENT BUT UNTO THE LOST SHEEP OF	128 14
HAST SENT THY SON, OUR SAVIOUR JESUS CHRIST,	134 06
HIS WIFE SENT UNTO HIM, SAYING, HAVE THOU NOTHING TO	135 33
AND HE SENT PETER AND JOHN, SAYING, GO AND PREPARE US	148 22
UNTO THEM, WHEN I SENT YOU WITHOUT PURSE, AND SCRIP,	150 04
HE SENT HIM TO HEROD, WHO HIMSELF ALSO	153 09
GORGEOUS ROBE, AND SENT HIM AGAIN TO PILATE	153 18
FOR I SENT YOU TO HIM	153 26
THE WORD WHICH GOD SENT UNTO THE CHILDREN OF ISRAEL,	166 15
TO YOU IS THE WORD OF THIS SALVATION SENT	168 26
AS MY FATHER HATH SENT ME, EVEN SO SEND I YOU	171 21
UNTO THEM THAT ARE SENT BY HIM FOR THE PUNISHMENT OF	173 20
MY WAY TO HIM THAT SENT ME	175 07
THE FATHER'S WHICH SENT ME	181 28
THE WORD WHICH GOD SENT UNTO THE CHILDREN OF ISRAEL,	184 02
FOR GOD SENT NOT HIS SON INTO THE WORLD TO CONDEMN	184 34
WORD OF GOD, THEY SENT UNTO THEM PETER AND JOHN	185 23
BECAUSE THAT GOD SENT HIS ONLY-BEGOTTEN SON INTO THE	189 12
HE LOVED US, AND SENT HIS SON TO BE THE PROPITIATION	189 14
THAT THE FATHER SENT THE SON TO BE THE SAVIOUR CF THE	189 21
AND SENT HIS SERVANT AT SUPPER TIME TO SAY TO THEM	192 04
AND HE SENT THEM AWAY	199 25
AND HE SENT HIM INTO HIS FIELDS TO FEED SWINE	202 07
FOR HIS SON, AND SENT FORTH HIS SERVANTS TO CALL THEM	218 04
HE SENT FORTH OTHER SERVANTS, SAYING, TELL	218 06
AND HE SENT FORTH HIS ARMIES, AND DESTROYED THOSE	218 14
AND THEY SENT OUT UNTO HIM THEIR DISCIPLES WITH THE	222 29
AND HOW SHALL THEY PREACH, EXCEPT THEY BE SENT	227 09
THOU CAMEST, HATH SENT ME, THAT THOU MIGHTEST RECEIVE	230 32
ANGEL GABRIEL WAS SENT FROM GOD UNTO A CITY OF	236 05
AND THEY SENT FORTH BARNABAS, THAT HE SHOULD GO AS	241 04
ALSO THEY DID, AND SENT IT TO THE ELDERS BY THE HANDS	241 22
AND SENT TO PREPARE THE WAY OF THY SON OUR	242 08
THAT THE LORD HATH SENT HIS ANGEL, AND HATH DELIVERED	245 27
ALSO THEY DID, AND SENT IT TO THE ELDERS BY THE HANDS	246 30
AND TYCHICUS HAVE I SENT TO EPHESUS	254 04
SEVENTY ALSO, AND SENT THEM TWO AND TWO BEFORE HIS	254 11
KNOW NOT HIM THAT SENT ME	255 22
HE HATH SENT ME TO HEAL THE BROKENHEARTED, TO PREACH	261 18
WILL OF HIM THAT SENT ME	269 16
WILL WHICH HATH SENT ME, THAT OF ALL WHICH HE HATH	269 17
WILL OF HIM THAT SENT ME, THAT EVERY ONE WHICH SEETH	269 20
AND IS SENT TO PREACH THE GOSPEL TO THE WHOLE WCRLD	291 13
WORD OF GOD, THEY SENT UNTO THEM PETER AND JCHN	296 15
ON HIM THAT SENT ME, HATH EVERLASTING LIFE, AND SHALL	321 34
15 HE SENT OUT HIS ARROWS, AND SCATTERED THEM	360 26
17 HE SENT DOWN FROM ON HIGH TO FETCH ME, *	360 31

SENT   CONTINUED

28 THY GOD HATH SENT FORTH STRENGTH FOR THEE	421 11
FOR HE SENT THEM MEAT ENOUGH	436 20
46 HE SENT FLIES AMONG THEM, AND DEVOURED THEM UP	437 31
AND SENT EVIL ANGELS AMONG THEM	438 07
17 BUT HE HAD SENT A MAN BEFORE THEM, *	471 06
20 THE KING SENT, AND DELIVERED HIM	471 12
26 THEN SENT HE MOSES HIS SERVANT, *	471 24
28 HE SENT DARKNESS, AND IT WAS DARK	471 28
AND SENT LEANNESS WITHAL INTO THEIR SOUL	473 31
20 HE SENT HIS WORD, AND HEALED THEM	477 15
9 HE SENT REDEMPTION UNTO HIS PEOPLE	483 11
9 HE HATH SENT TOKENS AND WONDERS INTO THE MIDST OF	510 20
INTO HEAVEN, SENT ABROAD INTO THE WORLD HIS APOSTLES,	545 17
FROM MILETUS PAUL SENT TO EPHESUS, AND CALLED THE	550 04
AS MY FATHER HATH SENT ME, EVEN SO SEND I YOU	552 02
BEFORE HE CHOSE AND SENT FORTH HIS TWELVE APOSTLES	553 06
OF HIS PARISH, SENT UNTO HIM, AS HE SHALL THINK	R 582 29
AND SENT TO EXECUTE THE SAME	607 21
LAWFULLY CALLED AND SENT, WHICH BE CHOSEN AND CALLED	607 22

SENTENCE

AND PILATE GAVE SENTENCE THAT IT SHOULD BE AS THEY	154 05
THE FOLLOWING SENTENCE BY THE MINISTER AND PEOPLE	R 290 03
GIVE SENTENCE WITH ME, O GOD, AND DEFEND MY CAUSE	310 05
INSTEAD OF THE SENTENCE OF COMMITTAL, THE MINISTER	R 337 07
GIVE SENTENCE WITH ME, O LORD, *	350 06
2 LET MY SENTENCE COME FORTH FROM THY PRESENCE	358 19
GIVE SENTENCE WITH ME, O GOD, AND DEFEND MY CAUSE	394 03
6 WHEN SENTENCE IS GIVEN UPON HIM, LET HIM BE	480 15
HIS CHAIR, THE SENTENCE OF CONSECRATION IS TO BE READ	R 566 25
THEIR EYES THE SENTENCE OF GOD'S PREDESTINATION,	606 24

SENTENCES

THE FOLLOWING SENTENCES OF SCRIPTURE	R 003 04
ONCE FROM THE SENTENCES TO THE LORD'S PRAYER,	R 003 07
AFTER THE SENTENCES, PASS TO THE VERSICLES,	R 003 11
THE FOLLOWING SENTENCES OF SCRIPTURE	R 021 04
ONCE FROM THE SENTENCES TO THE LORD'S PRAYER	R 021 06
AFTER THE SENTENCES, PASS TO THE VERSICLES,	R 021 08
MORE OF THESE SENTENCES FOLLOWING, AS HE THINKETH	R 071 33
THAT THESE SENTENCES MAY BE USED ON ANY OTHER	R 073 25
DECLARE HARD SENTENCES OF OLD	434 30

SENTEST

9 THOU, O GOD, SENTEST A GRACIOUS RAIN UPON THINE	419 29

SEPARATE

OR AS A SEPARATE OFFICE	R 060 05
AND SEPARATE FROM YOUR BRETHREN, WHO COME TO	089 17
AND HE SHALL SEPARATE THEM ONE FROM ANOTHER, AS A	258 31
WHO SHALL SEPARATE US FROM THE LOVE OF CHRIST	331 06
BE ABLE TO SEPARATE US FROM THE LOVE OF GOD, WHICH IS	331 13

SEPARATED

OF GOD, AND SEPARATED THEM FROM ALL UNHALLOWED,	564 16

SEPARATELY

OR SEPARATELY	R 054 04
MORNING PRAYER OR EVENING PRAYER, OR SEPARATELY	R 563 04
MORNING PRAYER OR EVENING PRAYER, OR SEPARATELY	R 569 09

SEPARATING

SEPARATING IT HENCEFORTH FROM ALL UNHALLCWED,	565 05

SEPARATION

BRING ABOUT A SEPARATION, AND DISSOLUTICN OF ALL	569 32
AS TO A SEPARATION AND DISSOLUTION OF ALL SACERDCTAL	569 35

SEPULCHRE

DOOR OF THE SEPULCHRE, AND DEPARTED	162 13
SITTING OVER AGAINST THE SEPULCHRE	162 15
THAT THE SEPULCHRE BE MADE SURE UNTIL THE THIRD DAY,	162 19
AND MADE THE SEPULCHRE SURE, SEALING THE STONE,	162 25
UNTO THE SEPULCHRE, AND SEETH THE STONE TAKEN	164 11
AND SEETH THE STONE TAKEN AWAY FROM THE SEPULCHRE	164 12
OUT OF THE SEPULCHRE, AND WE KNOW NOT WHERE THEY HAVE	164 15
AND CAME TO THE SEPULCHRE	164 17
AND CAME FIRST TO THE SEPULCHRE	164 19
WENT INTO THE SEPULCHRE, AND SEETH THE LINEN CLOTHES	164 22
FIRST TO THE SEPULCHRE, AND HE SAW, AND BELIEVED	164 26
CAME UNTO THE SEPULCHRE AT THE RISING OF THE SUN	165 22
US AWAY THE STONE FROM THE DOOR OF THE SEPULCHRE	165 24
INTO THE SEPULCHRE, THEY SAW A YOUNG MAN SITTING ON	165 26
WENT OUT QUICKLY, AND FLED FROM THE SEPULCHRE	166 02
WHICH WERE EARLY AT THE SEPULCHRE	167 24
US WENT TO THE SEPULCHRE, AND FOUND IT EVEN SO AS THE	167 27
AND LAID HIM IN A SEPULCHRE	169 02
10 THEIR THROAT IS AN OPEN SEPULCHRE	348 20
CONSUME IN THE SEPULCHRE, AND HAVE NO ABIDING	401 03

SERAPHIM

CHERUBIM AND SERAPHIM CONTINUALLY DO CRY, HOLY, HOLY,	010 13

SERIOUSLY

GIVE US GRACE SERIOUSLY TO LAY TO HEART THE GREAT   037 26
SERIOUSLY CONSIDERING WHAT CHRISTIANITY IS, AND WHAT   VI 38

SERIOUSNESS

AND SERIOUSNESS TO HIS REPENTANCE   310 23
WITH SUCH SERIOUSNESS, AFFECTION, AND DEVOTION OF   566 19

SERMON

THEN FOLLOWETH THE SERMON   R 071 31
THERE BE NO SERMON OR COMMUNION,) MAY BE SAID ALL   R 084 27
THERE SHALL BE A SERMON, OR EXHORTATION, DECLARING   R 530 03
THE SERMON BEING ENDED, A PRIEST SHALL PRESENT UNTO   R 530 07
THERE SHALL BE A SERMON, OR EXHORTATION, DECLARING   R 536 03
AND AFTER THAT THE SERMON   R 552 16
THEN SHALL FOLLOW THE SERMON   R 574 24

SERMONS

BE USED BEFORE SERMONS, OR ON SPECIAL OCCASIONS   R 047 03

SERPENT

WILL HE FOR A FISH GIVE HIM A SERPENT   183 16
LIFTED UP THE SERPENT IN THE WILDERNESS, EVEN SO MUST   188 27
THAT OLD SERPENT, CALLED THE DEVIL, AND SATAN,   252 07
WILL HE FOR A FISH GIVE HIM A SERPENT   263 09
THE POISON OF A SERPENT, *   410 15
THEY HAVE SHARPENED THEIR TONGUES LIKE A SERPENT   516 13

SERPENTS

THEM ALSO TEMPTED, AND WERE DESTROYED OF SERPENTS   201 20

SERVANT

THE HOUSE OF HIS SERVANT DAVID   014 11
AND BLESS THY SERVANT THE PRESIDENT OF THE UNITED   017 30
HATH HOLPEN HIS SERVANT ISRAEL   026 26
LETTEST THOU THY SERVANT DEPART IN PEACE, *   028 09
RELIEVE THY SICK SERVANT (N   045 14
SORROWS OF THY SERVANT FOR WHOM OUR PRAYERS ARE   046 02
THY SERVANT, FOR WHOSE PRESERVATION ON   046 10
THIS WOMAN, THY SERVANT, WHO DESIRETH NOW TO OFFER   051 08
THIS THY SERVANT, WHO NOW DESIRETH TO RETURN THANKS   052 31
THIS THY SERVANT, WHO NOW DESIRETH TO RETURN   053 23
THE HEART OF THY SERVANT, THE PRESIDENT OF THE UNITED   055 22
NOR HIS SERVANT, NOR HIS MAID, NOR HIS OX, NOR   069 21
NOTHING FROM A SERVANT, THOUGH HE BE LORD OF ALL   104 15
ART NO MORE A SERVANT, BUT A SON   104 24
LORD, MY SERVANT LIETH AT HOME SICK OF THE   115 08
AND MY SERVANT SHALL BE HEALED   115 12
AND TO MY SERVANT, DO THIS, AND HE DOETH IT   115 15
AND HIS SERVANT WAS HEALED IN THE SELFSAME HOUR   115 24
THE FORM OF A SERVANT, AND WAS MADE IN THE LIKENESS   134 19
AND SMOTE A SERVANT OF THE HIGH PRIEST, AND CUT OFF   142 23
THE VOICE OF HIS SERVANT, THAT WALKETH IN DARKNESS,   144 24
THEM SMOTE THE SERVANT OF THE HIGH PRIEST, AND CUT   150 33
AND SENT HIS SERVANT AT SUPPER TIME TO SAY TO THEM   192 04
SO THAT SERVANT CAME, AND SHEWED HIS LORD THESE   192 12
SAID TO HIS SERVANT, GO OUT QUICKLY INTO THE STREETS   192 13
AND THE SERVANT SAID, LORD, IT IS DONE AS THOU HAST   192 16
SAID UNTO THE SERVANT, GO OUT INTO THE HIGHWAYS AND   192 18
THE SERVANT THEREFORE FELL DOWN, AND WORSHIPPED HIM,   221 19
THE LORD OF THAT SERVANT WAS MOVED WITH COMPASSION,   221 21
BUT THE SAME SERVANT WENT OUT, AND FOUND ONE OF HIS   221 23
O THOU WICKED SERVANT, I FORGAVE THEE ALL THAT DEBT,   221 33
LETTEST THOU THY SERVANT DEPART IN PEACE, ACCORDING   233 05
THY FAITHFUL SERVANT MATTHIAS TO BE OF THE NUMBER OF   233 32
A SERVANT OF GOD AND OF THE LORD JESUS CHRIST,   239 06
FOR THE SERVANT KNOWETH NOT WHAT HIS LORD DOETH   241 29
PROVIDENCE THY SERVANT JOHN BAPTIST WAS WONDERFULLY   242 07
THE HOUSE OF HIS SERVANT DAVID   243 35
WILL BE CHIEF AMONG YOU, LET HIM BE YOUR SERVANT   247 25
INSPIRE THY SERVANT SAINT LUKE THE PHYSICIAN, TO SET   253 16
UNTO YOU, THE SERVANT IS NOT GREATER THAN HIS LORD   255 18
OF THY SERVANT (SAINT --), MAY PERSEVERE IN RUNNING   258 14
THE SOUL OF THY SERVANT DEPARTED, AND GRANT HIM AN   268 23
CHILD (THIS THY SERVANT), THAT HE, COMING TO THY HOLY   274 14
CHILD (THIS THY SERVANT) MAY ENJOY THE EVERLASTING   274 19
CHILD (THIS THY SERVANT), THAT HE MAY BE BORN AGAIN,   276 12
CHILD (THIS THY SERVANT) MAY DIE TO SIN AND RISE TO   278 19
CHILD (THIS THY SERVANT), NOW TO BE BAPTIZED THEREIN,   279 17
SOLDIER AND SERVANT UNTO HIS LIFE'S END   280 10
CHILD (THIS THY SERVANT) WITH THY HOLY SPIRIT,   280 30
NOR HIS SERVANT, NOR HIS MAID, NOR HIS OX, NOR   287 21
WHICH BECOMETH A SERVANT OF GOD   288 31
SAVE THIS WOMAN THY SERVANT   306 14
THIS WOMAN, THY SERVANT, WHO DESIRETH NOW TO OFFER   306 27
OF THIS THY SERVANT MAY DAILY INCREASE IN WISDOM AND   307 04
O LORD, SAVE THY SERVANT   308 23
VISIT, AND RELIEVE THIS THY SERVANT   309 05
TO THIS THY SERVANT WHO IS GRIEVED WITH SICKNESS   309 29
O LORD, THE SICKNESS OF THIS THY SERVANT   310 22
WE CALL UPON THEE ON BEHALF OF THIS THY SERVANT   311 22
AND GRANT TO THY SERVANT THE HELP OF THY POWER,   312 14
THE DEVOUT PRAISE OF THY HUMBLE SERVANT   313 06
UPON THIS THY SERVANT, WHO MOST EARNESTLY DESIRETH   313 33
WITH THIS THY SERVANT, THAT HIS WEAKNESS MAY BE   315 09
OF THIS THY SERVANT, THAT HE MAY BE HEALED OF HIS   315 16
OF THIS THY SERVANT, HERE LYING IN GREAT WEAKNESS OF   316 08
THIS THY SERVANT, CAST DOWN AND FAINT OF HEART   316 19

SERVANT   CONTINUED

SOUL OF THIS THY SERVANT, OUR DEAR BROTHER, INTO THY   317 14
HAVE MERCY UPON THE SOUL OF THY SERVANT   317 26
THE SOUL OF THY SERVANT FROM THE POWER OF THE EVIL   318 11
OF THIS THY SERVANT FROM EVERY BOND, AND SET HIM FREE   319 09
THE SOUL OF THY SERVANT, NOW DEPARTED FROM THE BODY   319 28
THE DISTRESS OF THIS THY SERVANT   320 09
UPON THIS THY SERVANT VISITED WITH THINE HAND, AND TO   321 21
UPON THIS THY SERVANT, THAT, EVERY CAUSE OF SICKNESS   322 08
NOR CAST THY SERVANT AWAY IN DISPLEASURE   326 24
REMEMBER THY SERVANT, O LORD, ACCORDING TO THE FAVOUR   332 03
THE SOUL OF THY SERVANT DEPARTED, AND GRANT HIM AN   334 15
SOUL OF THIS THY SERVANT (OR THIS THY CHILD)   336 05
BY THEM IS THY SERVANT TAUGHT   364 09
13 KEEP THY SERVANT ALSO FROM PRESUMPTUOUS SINS,   364 10
NOR CAST THY SERVANT AWAY IN DISPLEASURE   372 17
18 SHOW THY SERVANT THE LIGHT OF THY COUNTENANCE,   376 28
HATH PLEASURE IN THE PROSPERITY OF HIS SERVANT   383 21
18 AND HIDE NOT THY FACE FROM THY SERVANT   423 07
DAVID ALSO HIS SERVANT, *   439 19
MY GOD, SAVE THY SERVANT THAT PUTTETH HIS TRUST IN   447 08
4 COMFORT THE SOUL OF THY SERVANT   447 11
UNTO THY SERVANT, AND HELP THE SON OF THINE HANDMAID   448 07
I HAVE SWORN UNTO DAVID MY SERVANT   450 10
21 I HAVE FOUND DAVID MY SERVANT   451 15
COVENANT OF THY SERVANT, *   452 18
HE SHALL BE MY SERVANT   463 32
OF ABRAHAM HIS SERVANT, *   470 14
HE MOSES HIS SERVANT, *   471 24
AND ABRAHAM HIS SERVANT   472 22
BUT LET THY SERVANT REJOICE   481 27
HOW THAT I AM THY SERVANT   487 16
I AM THY SERVANT, AND THE SON OF THINE HANDMAID   487 17
O DO WELL UNTO THY SERVANT   490 32
BUT THY SERVANT IS OCCUPIED IN THY STATUTES   491 13
THY WORD IN THY SERVANT, *   492 15
O THINK UPON THY SERVANT, AS CONCERNING THY WORD,   493 08
WITH THY SERVANT, *   494 11
ACCORDING TO THY WORD UNTO THY SERVANT   495 08
84 HOW MANY ARE THE DAYS OF THY SERVANT   495 25
MAKE THOU THY SERVANT TO DELIGHT IN THAT WHICH IS   498 13
O DEAL WITH THY SERVANT ACCORDING UNTO THY LOVING   498 17
125 I AM THY SERVANT   498 19
UPON THY SERVANT, *   499 08
AND THY SERVANT LOVETH IT   499 19
O SEEK THY SERVANT, FOR I DO NOT FORGET THY   502 03
10 FOR THY SERVANT DAVID'S SAKE, *   508 23
22 EVEN FOR AN HERITAGE UNTO ISRAEL HIS SERVANT   512 26
2 AND ENTER NOT INTO JUDGMENT WITH THY SERVANT   518 25
FOR I AM THY SERVANT   519 18
DAVID THY SERVANT FROM THE PERIL OF THE SWORD   520 11
BEHOLD THIS THY SERVANT, NOW CALLED TO THE WORK AND   553 28
TO THIS THY SERVANT, SUCH GRACE, THAT HE MAY EVERMORE   557 28
AND FAITHFUL SERVANT, GIVING TO THY FAMILY THEIR   558 04
UPON THIS THY SERVANT THY HEAVENLY BLESSING   559 06
SOLDIER AND SERVANT UNTO HIS LIFE'S END   565 22
TO THY SERVANT, TO WHOM THE CHARGE OF THIS   572 09
HONOURED THY SERVANT WITH APPOINTING HIM TO STAND IN   573 12
NOR HIS SERVANT, NOR HIS MAID, NOR HIS OX, NOR   579 21
PRAY THEE, THY SERVANT, (N   597 16
TO COMFORT THY SERVANT IN HIS SUFFERING, AND TO BLESS   597 22
THY FAITHFUL SERVANT (N   598 07

SERVANTS

HELP THY SERVANTS, WHOM THOU HAST REDEEMED WITH   010 33
O YE SERVANTS OF THE LORD, BLESS YE THE LORD   013 24
US THY HUMBLE SERVANTS IN ALL ASSAULTS OF OUR   017 08
THINE UNWORTHY SERVANTS, DO GIVE THEE MOST HUMBLE AND   019 15
OF THY SERVANTS, AS MAY BE MOST EXPEDIENT FOR THEM   020 08
YE SERVANTS OF HIS THAT DO HIS PLEASURE   029 15
GIVE UNTO THY SERVANTS THAT PEACE WHICH THE WORLD   031 19
HEARTS OF THY SERVANTS THE PRESIDENT OF THE UNITED   032 06
THINE UNWORTHY SERVANTS, DO GIVE THEE MOST HUMBLE AND   033 13
OF THY SERVANTS, AS MAY BE MOST EXPEDIENT FOR THEM   034 08
UNTO US THY SERVANTS, THAT WITH LIVELY FAITH WE MAY   038 20
MINDS OF THY SERVANTS THE BISHOPS AND PASTORS OF THY   038 28
ALL THOSE THY SERVANTS WHO HAVE LAID DOWN THEIR LIVES   042 16
MINDS OF THY SERVANTS WHO AT THIS TIME ARE SEEKING TO   043 21
OF HEART AS THY SERVANTS, AND TO THE BENEFIT OF OUR   044 23
TO THESE THY SERVANTS, THAT BY THE POWER OF THY HOLY   046 27
THE WAY OF THY SERVANTS TOWARDS THE ATTAINMENT OF   049 12
UNTO THY SERVANTS AGAINST THE FACE OF THEIR ENEMIES   052 08
THAT WE THY SERVANTS, BEING HURT BY NO PERSECUTIONS,   058 22
MAY PASS AT ONCE TO O LORD, SAVE THY SERVANTS   R 061 20
O LORD, SAVE THY SERVANTS   061 30
ENTER NOT INTO JUDGMENT WITH THY SERVANTS   062 21
FOR ALL THY SERVANTS DEPARTED THIS LIFE IN THY FAITH   074 34
WE, THY HUMBLE SERVANTS, DO CELEBRATE AND MAKE HERE   080 39
SAITH UNTO THE SERVANTS, WHATSOEVER HE SAITH UNTO   113 17
BUT THE SERVANTS WHICH DREW THE WATER KNEW   113 25
SO THE SERVANTS OF THE HOUSEHOLDER CAME AND SAID UNTO   116 22
THE SERVANTS SAID UNTO HIM, WILT THOU THEN THAT WE GO   116 25
OF THY HUMBLE SERVANTS, AND STRETCH FORTH THE RIGHT   128 26
HE SAT WITH THE SERVANTS, AND WARMED HIMSELF AT THE   142 35
AND THE SERVANTS DID STRIKE HIM WITH THE PALMS OF   143 21
BUT AS THE SERVANTS OF GOD   173 24
US THY HUMBLE SERVANTS, THAT BY THY HOLY INSPIRATION   175 30
UNTO US THY SERVANTS GRACE, BY THE CONFESSION OF A   186 24
YOUR MEMBERS SERVANTS TO UNCLEANNESS AND TO INIQUITY   198 28
YOUR MEMBERS SERVANTS TO RIGHTEOUSNESS UNTO HOLINESS   198 29
YE WERE THE SERVANTS OF SIN, YE WERE FREE FROM   198 30
AND BECOME SERVANTS TO GOD, YE HAVE YOUR FRUIT   199 03
HOW MANY HIRED SERVANTS OF MY FATHER'S HAVE BREAD   202 11
MAKE ME AS ONE OF THY HIRED SERVANTS   202 15

SERVANTS   CONTINUED

SAID TO HIS SERVANTS, BRING FORTH THE BEST ROBE,	202 21
ONE OF THE SERVANTS, AND ASKED WHAT THESE THINGS	202 28
BE OPEN TO THE PRAYERS OF THY HUMBLE SERVANTS	203 12
SENT FORTH HIS SERVANTS TO CALL THEM THAT WERE BIDDEN	218 05
FORTH OTHER SERVANTS, SAYING, TELL THEM WHICH ARE	218 07
TOOK HIS SERVANTS, AND ENTREATED THEM SPITEFULLY,	218 12
SAITH HE TO HIS SERVANTS, THE WEDDING IS READY,	218 16
SO THOSE SERVANTS WENT OUT INTO THE HIGHWAYS,	218 19
THE KING TO THE SERVANTS, BIND HIM HAND AND FOOT,	218 26
GOING DOWN, HIS SERVANTS MET HIM, AND TOLD HIM,	220 05
WHICH WOULD TAKE ACCOUNT OF HIS SERVANTS	221 14
HENCEFORTH I CALL YOU NOT SERVANTS	241 29
OURSELVES YOUR SERVANTS FOR JESUS' SAKE	251 06
HAVE SEALED THE SERVANTS OF OUR GOD IN THEIR	256 18
THY HUMBLE SERVANTS, THE SAME FAITH AND POWER OF	258 06
THESE THY SERVANTS NOW (OR ABOUT TO BE) JOINED IN	267 05
SHOW THY SERVANTS THY WORK	290 08
THESE THY SERVANTS BY WATER AND THE HOLY GHOST, AND	297 15
FOR THESE THY SERVANTS, UPON WHOM, AFTER THE EXAMPLE	298 16
UPON THESE THY SERVANTS, THIS MAN AND THIS WOMAN,	303 05
UPON THESE THY SERVANTS, IF IT BE THY WILL, THE GIFT	303 16
UPON THESE THY SERVANTS, THAT THEY MAY LOVE, HONOUR,	303 23
YE SERVANTS OF HIS THAT DO HIS PLEASURE	312 31
ALL THOSE THY SERVANTS, WHO, HAVING FINISHED THEIR	334 23
UNTO US THY SERVANTS SO TO FOLLOW IN FAITH WHERE THOU	336 11
22 THE LORD DELIVERETH THE SOULS OF HIS SERVANTS	381 12
ALSO OF HIS SERVANTS SHALL INHERIT IT	424 17
BODIES OF THY SERVANTS HAVE THEY GIVEN TO BE MEAT	439 32
REBUKE THAT THY SERVANTS HAVE, *	453 07
AND BE GRACIOUS UNTO THY SERVANTS	454 16
16 SHOW THY SERVANTS THY WORK, *	454 22
THY SERVANTS THINK UPON HER STONES, *	465 07
CHILDREN OF THY SERVANTS SHALL CONTINUE, *	466 05
YE SERVANTS OF HIS THAT DO HIS PLEASURE	467 18
AND DEALT UNTRULY WITH HIS SERVANTS	471 23
PRAISE THE LORD, YE SERVANTS	484 08
AS THE EYES OF SERVANTS LOOK UNTO THE HAND OF THEIR	503 29
ALL YE SERVANTS OF THE LORD	509 23
PRAISE IT, O YE SERVANTS OF THE LORD	510 04
UPON PHARAOH, AND ALL HIS SERVANTS	510 22
AND BE GRACIOUS UNTO HIS SERVANTS	510 31
BLESS THESE THY SERVANTS, NOW TO BE ADMITTED TO THE	531 04
THESE THY SERVANTS NOW CALLED TO THE LIKE OFFICE AND	531 18
ARE THOSE SERVANTS, WHOM THE LORD WHEN HE COMETH	534 20
BLESSED ARE THOSE SERVANTS	534 25
TAKE THESE THY SERVANTS UNTO THE OFFICE OF DEACONS IN	535 02
BLESS THESE THY SERVANTS, NOW TO BE ADMITTED TO THE	537 10
THESE THY SERVANTS NOW CALLED TO THE OFFICE OF	537 22
CALL THESE THY SERVANTS HERE PRESENT TO THE SAME	545 23
UPON THESE THY SERVANTS THY HEAVENLY BLESSING	547 05
THESE THY SERVANTS NOW CALLED TO THE OFFICE OF DEACON	547 33
AND THESE THY SERVANTS NOW CALLED TO THE OFFICE OF	547 34
BLESS THESE THY SERVANTS, NOW TO BE ADMITTED TO THE	560 26
OF THY FAITHFUL SERVANTS SHALL ASSEMBLE IN THY NAME,	564 32
OF THY SERVANTS, AND GRANT THAT WHOSOEVER IN THIS	565 18
HEARTS OF THY SERVANTS TO APPROPRIATE AND DEVOTE THIS	566 29
THEIR CHILDREN, SERVANTS, AND APPRENTICES, WHO HAVE	R 582 32
END BE ACCEPTED OF THEE AS THY FAITHFUL SERVANTS	594 27
THEE AND THY SERVANTS EVERYWHERE, THE ETERNAL	598 10
WE ARE UNPROFITABLE SERVANTS	605 29

SERVANTS'

RETURN FOR THY SERVANTS' SAKE, THE TRIBES OF THINE	139 26
OF THY SERVANTS' BLOOD THAT IS SHED, *	440 23

SERVE

MIGHT SERVE HIM WITHOUT FEAR	014 21
SERVE THE LORD WITH GLADNESS, AND COME BEFORE HIS	015 04
THEIR CALLING TO SERVE THIS PEOPLE IN THY FEAR	018 13
OF FIT PERSONS, TO SERVE IN THE SACRED MINISTRY OF	038 31
MAY FAITHFULLY SERVE BEFORE THEE, TO THE GLORY OF THY	039 13
THINGS THEY MAY SERVE WITHOUT REPROACH	041 30
AND ALL WHO SERVE THEREIN	042 06
AND QUIETNESS SERVE THEE OUR GOD, TO THE GLORY OF THY	042 11
WORSHIP THEE AND SERVE THEE FROM GENERATION TO	043 04
TO GOD'S WILL, SERVE HIM FAITHFULLY, AND WORSHIP HIM	047 13
ONE OF THEM, MAY SERVE TRULY IN THEIR SEVERAL	047 17
PERSONS FITTED TO SERVE GOD IN THE MINISTRY AND IN	047 31
AND EVERMORE SERVE THEE IN HOLINESS AND PURENESS OF	059 26
MAY EVER HEREAFTER SERVE AND PLEASE THEE IN NEWNESS	075 28
AND STUDYING TO SERVE HIM IN TRUE HOLINESS AND	086 22
THE SUNDAY, SHALL SERVE ALL THE WEEK AFTER, WHERE IT	R 090 04
DAY SHALL SERVE FOR THEM	R 104 02
AND GOSPEL SHALL SERVE UNTO THE NEXT SUNDAY	R 109 26
AND GOSPEL SHALL SERVE FOR EVERY DAY AFTER, UNTO THE	R 125 23
AND HIM ONLY SHALT THOU SERVE	127 10
FROM DEAD WORKS TO SERVE THE LIVING GOD	133 03
AND HE THAT IS CHIEF, AS HE THAT DOTH SERVE	149 24
TRULY AND GODLY SERVE THEE	157 02
THAT WE MAY ALWAYS SERVE THEE IN PURENESS OF LIVING	170 22
AND GOSPEL SHALL SERVE FOR EVERY DAY AFTER, UNTO THE	R 178 30
MAY JOYFULLY SERVE THEE IN ALL GODLY QUIETNESS	195 17
WE SHOULD NOT SERVE SIN	197 19
MANY YEARS DO I SERVE THEE, NEITHER TRANSGRESSED I AT	202 34
MAY SO FAITHFULLY SERVE THEE IN THIS LIFE, THAT WE	207 15
NO MAN CAN SERVE TWO MASTERS	211 09
YE CANNOT SERVE GOD AND MAMMON	211 11
THEIR SINS, AND SERVE THEE WITH A QUIET MIND	219 02
DEVOUTLY GIVEN TO SERVE THEE IN GOOD WORKS, TO THE	220 19
OUR ENEMIES MIGHT SERVE HIM WITHOUT FEAR, IN HOLINESS	244 06
AND HE THAT IS CHIEF, AS HE THAT DOTH SERVE	250 09
THRONE OF GOD, AND SERVE HIM DAY AND NIGHT IN HIS	257 10

SERVE   CONTINUED

HIM SHALT THOU SERVE, AND TO HIM SHALT THOU CLEAVE,	263 30
AND TO SERVE HIM TRULY ALL THE DAYS OF MY LIFE	288 22
OF GOD, AND TO SERVE HIM, WITHOUT HIS SPECIAL GRACE	289 15
THAT WE, WHO NOW SERVE THEE HERE ON EARTH, MAY AT	335 32
THRONE OF GOD, AND SERVE HIM DAY AND NIGHT IN HIS	341 21
11 SERVE THE LORD IN FEAR, *	346 19
NOT KNOWN SHALL SERVE ME	362 27
31 MY SEED SHALL SERVE HIM	368 04
SERVE THE LORD WITH GLADNESS, AND COME BEFORE HIS	463 05
KINGDOMS ALSO, TO SERVE THE LORD	465 25
FOR ALL THINGS SERVE THEE	496 08
MAY FAITHFULLY SERVE THEE IN THIS OFFICE, TO THE	531 22
WORD OF GOD, AND SERVE TABLES	532 10
TO SERVE GOD FOR THE PROMOTING OF HIS	532 28
THE CHURCH WHERE YOU SHALL BE APPOINTED TO SERVE	533 08
BE APPOINTED TO SERVE, TO ASSIST THE PRIEST IN DIVINE	533 11
COME FORTH AND SERVE THEM	534 23
MAY FAITHFULLY SERVE THEE IN THIS OFFICE, TO THE	537 26
WHOM YOU MUST SERVE, IS HIS SPOUSE, AND HIS BODY	540 09
MAY FAITHFULLY SERVE THEE IN THEIR MINISTRY, TO THE	548 05
HE MAY FAITHFULLY SERVE THEE IN THIS OFFICE, TO THE	553 32
THAT THEY WHO SERVE AT THE ALTAR SHOULD LIVE OF THE	569 28
HE MAY FAITHFULLY SERVE THEE, TO THE GLORY OF	572 12
THY HOUSE, AND TO SERVE AT THY HOLY ALTAR	573 14
MAY JOYFULLY SERVE THEE IN ALL GODLY QUIETNESS	574 17
AND TO SERVE HIM TRULY ALL THE DAYS OF MY LIFE	579 32
OF GOD, AND TO SERVE HIM, WITHOUT HIS SPECIAL GRACE	580 18
MAY WORSHIP HIM, SERVE HIM, AND OBEY HIM, AS WE OUGHT	580 31
AND MINISTRY, MAY SERVE THEE FAITHFULLY	590 26
WE MAY LEARN TO SERVE THEE WITH GLADNESS	596 20
JUDGE THE SAME TO SERVE BETTER TO GODLINESS	609 24

SERVED

AFTER HE HAD SERVED HIS OWN GENERATION BY THE WILL OF	169 15
THE TEMPLE, BUT SERVED GOD WITH FASTINGS AND PRAYERS	233 20
OF THOSE THAT SERVED THEMSELVES OF THEM	262 14
OF THOSE WHO HAVE SERVED THEE HERE AND ARE NOW AT	268 18
WE SHALL HAVE SERVED THEE IN OUR GENERATION, WE MAY	316 29
THAT HAVING SERVED THEE WITH CONSTANCY ON EARTH, WE	336 07
THEE AS THOU HAST SERVED US	513 22

SERVETH

US AS ONE THAT SERVETH, THY SON JESUS CHRIST OUR	044 24
HE THAT SITTETH AT MEAT, OR HE THAT SERVETH	149 25
BUT I AM AMONG YOU AS HE THAT SERVETH	149 26
WHEREFORE THEN SERVETH THE LAW	207 27
HE THAT SITTETH AT MEAT, OR HE THAT SERVETH	250 10
BUT I AM AMONG YOU AS HE THAT SERVETH	250 11
THE PEOPLE THAT SERVETH HIM	524 32

SERVICE

AND WHERESOEVER ELSE IT IS USED IN DIVINE SERVICE	R 007 22
MAY PASS AT ONCE TO THE COMMUNION SERVICE	R 010 06
THE COMMUNION SERVICE IS READ	R 017 03
WHOSE SERVICE IS PERFECT FREEDOM	017 07
SELVES TO THY SERVICE, AND BY WALKING BEFORE THEE IN	019 28
SELVES TO THY SERVICE, AND BY WALKING BEFORE THEE IN	033 26
LIVES IN THE SERVICE OF OUR COUNTRY	042 17
TO THE SERVICE OF THEIR FELLOW MEN	043 31
FROM THE SERVICE OF MAMMON, THAT WE MAY DO THE WORK	044 20
OF THE PUBLIC SERVICE, AND TO ESTABLISH SUCH OTHER	VI 25
IN THY LOVE AND SERVICE, AND TO GIVE US GRACE SO TO	075 02
THEE TO ACCEPT THIS OUR BOUNDEN DUTY AND SERVICE	081 31
AT THE EVENING SERVICE OF THE DAY BEFORE	R 090 07
WHICH IS YOUR REASONABLE SERVICE	110 05
KILLETH YOU WILL THINK THAT HE DOETH GOD SERVICE	179 31
BE ENLIGHTENED AND STRENGTHENED FOR THY SERVICE	182 17
PEOPLE DO UNTO THEE TRUE AND LAUDABLE SERVICE	207 14
THE SERVICE FOR THE SIXTH SUNDAY AFTER THE	R 224 31
THE SERVICE FOR THE SIXTH SUNDAY AFTER THE EPIPHANY	R 224 33
AND THE SERVICE FOR THE FIFTH SUNDAY AFTER THE	R 224 34
ALWAYS DO THEE SERVICE IN HEAVEN, SO, BY THY	251 30
OF THE FOREGOING SERVICE SHALL BE USED	R 282 02
PRIEST IN DIVINE SERVICE, AND IN HIS OTHER	294 18
THIS SERVICE, OR THE CONCLUDING PRAYER ALONE,	R 305 04
IN THY LOVE AND SERVICE, UNTIL HE COME TO THY ETERNAL	307 05
THE FOLLOWING SERVICE, OR ANY PART THEREOF,	R 308 03
ANY PART OF THE SERVICE OF THIS BOOK, WHICH, IN HIS	R 314 23
THE FOREGOING SERVICE, OR ANY PART THEREOF, AT THE	R 315 03
TO SHORTEN THE SERVICE, THE FOLLOWING FORM SHALL	R 323 04
LIFE OF PERFECT SERVICE, IN THY HEAVENLY KINGDOM	332 06
OR A PART OF THE SERVICE APPOINTED TO BE SAID AT THE	R 336 31
ALL NATIONS SHALL DO HIM SERVICE	427 19
HERB FOR THE SERVICE OF MEN	468 22
BE SAID THE SERVICE FOR THE COMMUNION, WITH THE	R 531 09
PRIEST IN DIVINE SERVICE, AND SPECIALLY WHEN HE	533 12
BE SAID THE SERVICE FOR THE COMMUNION, WITH THE	R 537 17
GO ON IN THE SERVICE OF THE COMMUNION, WHICH ALL THEY	R 546 29
THE COMMUNION SERVICE, IN WHICH THIS SHALL BE THE	R 549 05
BISHOP SHALL PROCEED IN THE COMMUNION SERVICE	R 559 02
WITH MORE DEVOTION AND HUMILITY IN HIS SERVICE	564 19
IT TO THY SERVICE, FOR READING THY HOLY WORD, FOR	565 07
O LORD, THIS SERVICE AT OUR HANDS, AND BLESS IT WITH	565 11
BOUNDEN DUTY AND SERVICE, AND VOUCHSAFE TO GIVE	566 21
THE DEDICATION OF THIS PLACE TO THY SERVICE	567 07
SET APART TO THY SERVICE, THY HOLY NAME MAY BE	568 10
IT AFFORD JUST CAUSE TO SUSPEND THE SERVICE	R 570 22
GO ON WITH THE SERVICE, THEN SHALL BE READ THE LETTER	R 570 24
THE MINISTRY AND SERVICE OF HIM WHO IS NOW APPOINTED	572 19
THEE AND TO THY SERVICE I DEVOTE MYSELF, BODY, SOUL,	573 14
PROCEED TO THAT SERVICE, AND TO ADMINISTER THE HOLY	R 574 25

SERVICE   CONTINUED

TO THEE AND THY SERVICE, IN A SOBER, RIGHTEOUS, AND   588 06
THAT THE DAYS TO COME MAY BE SPENT IN THY SERVICE   595 16
RECEIVE HIM MORE AND MORE INTO THY JOYFUL SERVICE   598 09
THY GIFTS TO OUR USE AND US TO THY SERVICE   600 15

SERVICES

CONSTITUTED THE SERVICES OF ANGELS AND MEN IN A   251 28

SERVING

TRULY SERVING THEE IN HOLINESS AND RIGHTEOUSNESS ALL   074 28
SERVING THE LORD   111 25
AT ALL SEASONS, SERVING THE LORD WITH ALL HUMILITY OF   550 08

SESSION

TO BE USED DURING THEIR SESSION   R 035 07
OR BEFORE, THE SESSION OF ANY GENERAL OR DIOCESAN   R 037 09

SET

AT HIS HANDS, TO SET FORTH HIS MOST WORTHY PRAISE,   006 07
LET MY PRAYER BE SET FORTH IN THY SIGHT AS THE   021 16
IN HIS LAWS WHICH HE SET BEFORE US   022 09
AT HIS HANDS, TO SET FORTH HIS MOST WORTHY PRAISE, TO   023 15
OUR HEARTS MAY BE SET TO OBEY THY COMMANDMENTS,   031 21
FORTH THY GLORY, AND SET FORWARD THE SALVATION CF ALL   039 03
SPIRIT THEY MAY BE SET FREE FROM THE CHAINS OF SIN,   046 28
AND LIVING THEY MAY SET IT FORTH, AND SHOW IT   055 33
LIFE AND DOCTRINE, SET FORTH THY TRUE AND LIVELY   074 23
THE RACE THAT IS SET BEFORE US, AND, TOGETHER WITH   079 25
AND THEY SET HIM THEREON   091 24
THE RACE THAT IS SET BEFORE US, THY BOUNTIFUL GRACE   095 07
AND THERE WERE SET THERE SIX WATER-POTS OF STONE,   113 18
THE BEGINNING DOTH SET FORTH GOOD WINE   113 28
WHO KNOWEST US TO BE SET IN THE MIDST OF SO MANY AND   114 04
TO THEM THAT WERE SET DOWN   132 05
WHEN HE WAS SET DOWN ON THE JUDGMENT-SEAT, HIS WIFE   135 32
AND SET UP OVER HIS HEAD HIS ACCUSATION WRITTEN, THIS   136 34
THEREFORE HAVE I SET MY FACE LIKE A FLINT, AND I KNOW   144 17
THE HALL, AND WERE SET DOWN TOGETHER, PETER SAT DOWN   151 09
WITH HIS MEN OF WAR SET HIM AT NOUGHT, AND MOCKED   153 16
AND WAS SET DOWN AGAIN, HE SAID UNTO THEM,   156 13
NOW THERE WAS SET A VESSEL FULL OF VINEGAR   160 26
SET YOUR AFFECTION ON THINGS ABOVE, NOT ON THINGS ON   164 05
BEHOLD, A THRONE WAS SET IN HEAVEN, AND ONE SAT ON   187 05
TO HIS DISCIPLES TO SET BEFORE THEM   199 19
AND THEY DID SET THEM BEFORE THE PEOPLE   199 20
AND COMMANDED TO SET THEM ALSO BEFORE THEM   199 22
IN OIL AND WINE, AND SET HIM CN HIS OWN BEAST,   208 31
TO THEM THAT WERE SET DOWN   226 04
THIS CHILD IS SET FOR THE FALL AND RISING AGAIN OF   233 12
CHILD UNTO HIM, AND SET HIM IN THE MIDST OF THEM, AND   252 24
THE PHYSICIAN, TO SET FORTH IN THE GOSPEL THE LOVE   253 17
AND WHEN HE WAS SET, HIS DISCIPLES CAME UNTO HIM   257 19
THE RACE THAT IS SET BEFORE US, UNTIL AT LENGTH,   258 15
THE RACE THAT IS SET BEFORE US, LOOKING UNTO JESUS   258 23
FOR THE JOY THAT WAS SET BEFORE HIM ENDURED THE   258 25
THE SHAME, AND IS SET DOWN AT THE RIGHT HAND OF THE   258 26
AND HE SHALL SET THE SHEEP ON HIS RIGHT HAND, BUT THE   259 02
SAYING, I HAVE SET THEE TO BE A LIGHT OF THE   261 04
TO THE BLIND, TO SET AT LIBERTY THEM THAT ARE   261 20
I HAVE NOTHING TO SET BEFORE HIM   262 29
FROM EVERY BOND, AND SET HIM FREE FROM ALL EVIL   319 09
THOU HAST SET OUR MISDEEDS BEFORE THEE   325 28
HE HIDE ME, AND SET ME UP UPON A ROCK OF STONE   326 14
OF THY SON, MAY BE SET ON HIS RIGHT HAND, AND HEAR   336 25
CHILD UNTO HIM, AND SET HIM IN THE MIDST OF THEM, AND   339 23
6 YET HAVE I SET MY KING *   346 08
THAT HAVE SET THEMSELVES AGAINST ME ROUND ABOUT   347 03
THOU HAST SET ME AT LIBERTY WHEN I WAS IN TROUBLE   347 11
THOU THAT HAST SET THY GLORY ABOVE THE HEAVENS   350 32
THOU ART SET IN THE THRONE THAT JUDGEST RIGHT   351 29
HIS EYES ARE SET AGAINST THE POOR   353 22
AND WILL SET HIM AT REST   355 19
9 I HAVE SET THE LORD ALWAY BEFORE ME   358 06
5 IN THEM HATH HE SET A TABERNACLE FOR THE SUN   363 21
AND SHALT SET A CROWN OF PURE GOLD UPON HIS HEAD   365 10
HE HIDE ME, AND SET ME UP UPON A ROCK OF STONE   372 06
FEED THEM, AND SET THEM UP FOR EVER   373 28
FOR THOU HAST SET ME UP, *   374 24
BUT HAST SET MY FEET IN A LARGE ROOM   376 07
HIS BED, AND HATH SET HIMSELF IN NO GOOD WAY   383 33
17 AND I TRULY AM SET IN THE PLAGUE, *   388 26
AND SET MY FEET UPON THE ROCK, AND ORDERED MY GOINGS   390 12
IS THE MAN THAT HATH SET HIS HOPE IN THE LORD, *   390 18
AND SHALT SET ME BEFORE THY FACE FOR EVER   392 24
THY TONGUE THOU HAST SET FORTH DECEIT   402 29
REPROVE THEE, AND SET BEFORE THEE THE THINGS THAT   402 34
MALICIOUSLY ARE THEY SET AGAINST ME   406 25
OF MEN, THAT ARE SET ON FIRE, *   409 22
6 SET UP THYSELF, O GOD, ABOVE THE HEAVENS   409 24
12 SET UP THYSELF, O GOD, ABOVE THE HEAVENS   410 04
ARE YOUR MINDS SET UPON RIGHTEOUSNESS, O YE   410 07
3 O SET ME UP UPON THE ROCK THAT IS HIGHER THAN I   413 10
IF RICHES INCREASE, SET NOT YOUR HEART UPON THEM   414 19
HOW THOU DOST SET THEM IN SLIPPERY PLACES, *   429 12
AND SET UP THEIR BANNERS FOR TOKENS   430 13
8 THEY HAVE SET FIRE UPON THY HOLY PLACES, *   430 18
18 THOU HAST SET ALL THE BORDERS OF THE EARTH   431 10
AND TO THE UNGODLY, SET NOT UP YOUR HORN   432 07
6 SET NOT UP YOUR HORN ON HIGH, *   432 08
A GENERATION THAT SET NOT THEIR HEART ARIGHT, AND   435 14

SET   CONTINUED

AND HAVE NOT SET THEE BEFORE THEIR EYES   448 03
MERCY SHALL BE SET UP FOR EVER   450 07
AND SET UP THY THRONE FROM ONE GENERATION TO ANOTHER   450 11
26 I WILL SET HIS DOMINION ALSO IN THE SEA, *   451 25
41 THOU HAST SET UP THE RIGHT HAND OF HIS ENEMIES,   452 19
8 THOU HAST SET OUR MISDEEDS BEFORE THEE   454 02
THOU HAST SET THINE HOUSE OF DEFENCE VERY HIGH   455 13
14 BECAUSE HE HATH SET HIS LOVE UPON ME, THEREFORE   455 23
I WILL SET HIM UP, BECAUSE HE HATH KNOWN MY NAME   455 24
SO FAR HATH HE SET OUR SINS FROM US   466 31
9 THOU HAST SET THEM THEIR BOUNDS, WHICH THEY SHALL   468 11
5 SET UP THYSELF, O GOD, ABOVE THE HEAVENS, *   479 13
5 SET THOU AN UNGODLY MAN TO BE RULER OVER HIM,   480 13
7 THAT HE MAY SET HIM WITH THE PRINCES, *   484 21
WHEN THOU HAST SET MY HEART AT LIBERTY   491 32
SHALL I SET UPON THY THRONE   508 27
AND SET TRAPS IN MY WAY   516 19
2 LET MY PRAYER BE SET FORTH IN THY SIGHT AS THE   517 10
3 SET A WATCH, O LORD, BEFORE MY MOUTH, *   517 13
WHOM THEY SET BEFORE THE APOSTLES   532 18
OUGHT TO FORSAKE AND SET ASIDE, AS MUCH AS YE MAY,   541 07
YOU MAINTAIN AND SET FORWARDS, AS MUCH AS LIETH IN   543 06
OF THE WORLD, TO SET FORTH THE ETERNAL PRAISE OF THY   545 20
IN THE CHURCH, AND SET IN ORDER, THE PRESIDING   R 549 03
YOU MAINTAIN AND SET FORWARD, AS MUCH AS SHALL LIE IN   555 14
AT THY HANDS, TO SET FORTH THY MOST WORTHY PRAISE,   566 16
IN THIS PLACE NOW SET APART TO THY SERVICE, THY HOLY   568 10
MY LIFE AND DOCTRINE SET FORTH THY TRUE AND LIVELY   573 23
AS THEY BE GENERALLY SET FORTH TO US IN HOLY   606 28
HOLY SCRIPTURE DOTH SET OUT UNTO US ONLY THE NAME OF   606 35
WHICH WERE SET FORTH IN THE TIME OF EDWARD   610 07
AND DEACONS, AS SET FORTH BY THE GENERAL CONVENTION   610 32

SETTEST

WHO SETTEST THE SOLITARY IN FAMILIES   598 19

SETTETH

HOLY CITY, AND SETTETH HIM ON A PINNACLE OF THE   126 31
4 HE THAT SETTETH NOT BY HIMSELF, BUT IS LOWLY IN HIS   357 13
AND SETTETH ME UP ON HIGH   362 02
AND SETTETH ME UP ABOVE MINE ADVERSARIES   363 03
IN HIS STRENGTH SETTETH FAST THE MOUNTAINS, *   416 25
DOWN ONE, AND SETTETH UP ANOTHER   432 13
36 AND THERE HE SETTETH THE HUNGRY, *   478 18
6 THE LORD SETTETH UP THE MEEK, *   523 06

SETTING

AND TO THE SETTING FORTH OF THY GLORY   050 12
THE STONE, AND SETTING A WATCH   162 25
GODLY PURPOSE OF SETTING APART THIS PLACE IN SOLEMN   564 22

SETTLE

SETTLE YOU   193 11

SETTLED

SO ORDERED AND SETTLED BY THEIR ENDEAVOURS, UPON THE   035 15

SEVEN

THE EPIPHANY AND SEVEN DAYS AFTER, AND ON THE FEAST   R 008 20
CHRISTMAS DAY, AND SEVEN DAYS AFTER   R 077 13
THE EPIPHANY, AND SEVEN DAYS AFTER   R 077 21
EASTER DAY, AND SEVEN DAYS AFTER   R 078 06
ASCENSION DAY, AND SEVEN DAYS AFTER   R 078 15
SAINTS' DAY, AND SEVEN DAYS AFTER   R 079 21
AND TAKETH TO HIM SEVEN OTHER SPIRITS MORE WICKED   130 14
AND THERE WERE SEVEN LAMPS OF FIRE BURNING BEFORE THE   187 13
WHICH ARE THE SEVEN SPIRITS OF GOD   187 14
AND THEY SAID, SEVEN   199 17
AND HE TOOK THE SEVEN LOAVES, AND GAVE THANKS, AND   199 18
MEAT THAT WAS LEFT SEVEN BASKETS   199 24
TILL SEVEN TIMES   221 10
UNTO THEE, UNTIL SEVEN TIMES   221 11
UNTIL SEVENTY TIMES SEVEN   221 12
WITH AN HUSBAND SEVEN YEARS FROM HER VIRGINITY   233 18
AND PURIFIED SEVEN TIMES IN THE FIRE   355 21
164 SEVEN TIMES A DAY DO I PRAISE THEE   501 09
YE OUT AMONG YOU SEVEN MEN OF HONEST REPORT, FULL OF   532 11

SEVEN-FOLD

O LORD, SEVEN-FOLD INTO THEIR BOSOM   440 30

SEVENFOLD

WHO DOST THY SEVENFOLD GIFTS IMPART   543 34
THE SEVENFOLD GIFTS OF GRACE ARE THINE, O FINGER CF   544 25
WHO DOST THY SEVENFOLD GIFTS IMPART   556 09
THE SEVENFOLD GIFTS OF GRACE ARE THINE, O FINGER OF   557 04

SEVENTH

BUT THE SEVENTH DAY IS THE SABBATH OF THE LCRD THY   068 26
AND RESTED THE SEVENTH DAY   068 31
LORD BLESSED THE SEVENTH DAY, AND HALLOWED IT   068 32
YESTERDAY AT THE SEVENTH HOUR THE FEVER LEFT HIM   220 16
BUT THE SEVENTH DAY IS THE SABBATH OF THE LORD THY   286 26
AND RESTED THE SEVENTH DAY   286 31
LORD BLESSED THE SEVENTH DAY, AND HALLOWED IT   286 32

SEVENTH   CONTINUED

BUT THE SEVENTH DAY IS THE SABBATH OF THE LORD THY	579 06
AND RESTED THE SEVENTH DAY	579 11
LORD BLESSED THE SEVENTH DAY, AND HALLOWED IT	579 12

SEVENTY

UNTIL SEVENTY TIMES SEVEN	221 12
APPOINTED OTHER SEVENTY ALSO, AND SENT THEM TWO AND	254 11

SEVERAL

IN THE REIGN OF SEVERAL PRINCES, SINCE THE FIRST	V 26
TO THEIR SEVERAL NECESSITIES	019 09
TO THEIR SEVERAL NECESSITIES	033 07
IN OUR SEVERAL CALLINGS, FROM THE SERVICE OF	044 20
TRULY IN THEIR SEVERAL CALLINGS TO THE GLORY OF GOD,	047 18
WORLD IN THEIR SEVERAL GENERATIONS	048 18
DIFFERENT IN THE SEVERAL STATES, EVERY MINISTER IS	R 304 18
WORLD IN THEIR SEVERAL GENERATIONS	336 20
FOR THE SEVERAL OFFICES OF RELIGIOUS WORSHIP,	564 23
DILIGENT IN OUR SEVERAL CALLINGS	588 29
TO THEIR SEVERAL NECESSITIES	591 04
OF HOMILIES, THE SEVERAL TITLES WHEREOF WE HAVE	610 05

SEVERALLY

TO EVERY MAN SEVERALLY AS HE WILL	182 34
TO EVERY MAN SEVERALLY AS HE WILL	204 04
OF EVERY ONE SEVERALLY, SAYING, DEFEND, O LORD, THIS	R 297 25
LAY HIS HANDS SEVERALLY UPON THE HEAD OF EVERY CNE TO	R 534 02
THEIR HANDS SEVERALLY UPON THE HEAD OF EVERY ONE THAT	R 546 07

SEVERITY

AND ENDURE THE SEVERITY OF GOD'S JUDGMENT YET ARE	605 12

SHADOW

AND IN THE SHADOW OF DEATH, *	014 32
DARKNESS AND THE SHADOW OF DEATH	086 10
THE LAW HAVING A SHADOW OF GOOD THINGS TO COME,	157 15
NEITHER SHADOW OF TURNING	174 28
AND IN THE SHADOW OF DEATH, TO GUIDE OUR FEET INTO	244 15
AT THE LEAST THE SHADCW OF PETER PASSING BY MIGHT	249 28
NEITHER SHADOW OF TURNING	265 21
WALKETH IN A VAIN SHADOW, AND DISQUIETETH HIMSELF IN	324 25
AS IT WERE A SHADOW, AND NEVER CONTINUETH IN ONE	332 20
THE VALLEY OF THE SHADOW OF DEATH, I WILL FEAR NO	338 23
HIDE ME UNDER THE SHADOW OF THY WINGS,	359 05
THE VALLEY OF THE SHADOW OF DEATH, I WILL FEAR NO	368 16
TRUST UNDER THE SHADOW OF THY WINGS	384 10
WALKETH IN A VAIN SHADOW, AND DISQUIETETH HIMSELF IN	389 20
US WITH THE SHADOW OF DEATH	395 33
AND UNDER THE SHADOW OF THY WINGS SHALL BE MY REFUGE,	409 13
UNDER THE SHADOW OF THY WINGS WILL I REJOICE	415 08
COVERED WITH THE SHADOW OF IT, *	441 22
ABIDE UNDER THE SHADOW OF THE ALMIGHTY	454 29
ARE GONE LIKE A SHADOW, *	464 31
AND IN THE SHADOW OF DEATH, *	476 24
AND OUT OF THE SHADOW OF DEATH, *	477 03
GO HENCE LIKE THE SHADOW THAT DEPARTETH, *	481 16
HIS TIME PASSETH AWAY LIKE A SHADOW	519 30
AND TURNEST THE SHADOW OF DEATH INTO THE MORNING	594 12

SHADOWS

UNTIL THE SHADOWS LENGTHEN AND THE EVENING	594 30

SHAKE

THE MOUNTAINS SHAKE AT THE TEMPEST OF THE SAME	327 08
THEIR LIPS, AND SHAKE THEIR HEADS, SAYING, 8 HE	366 17
THAT THE PEOPLES SHAKE THEIR HEADS AT US	395 23
THE MOUNTAINS SHAKE AT THE TEMPEST OF THE SAME	397 31
THEREOF SHALL SHAKE LIKE LEBANON	427 30
THAT LOOK UPON ME SHAKE THEIR HEADS	481 21

SHAKEN

FOR THE POWERS OF HEAVEN SHALL BE SHAKEN	093 10
A REED SHAKEN WITH THE WIND	094 27
AND THE POWERS OF THE HEAVENS SHALL BE SHAKEN	118 17
PRESSED DOWN, AND SHAKEN TOGETHER, AND RUNNING OVER,	194 29

SHAKETH

OF THE LORD SHAKETH THE WILDERNESS	374 12
THE LORD SHAKETH THE WILDERNESS OF KADESH	374 13
HEAL THE SORES THEREOF, FOR IT SHAKETH	412 16

SHALT

BELIEVE THAT THOU SHALT COME TO BE OUR JUDGE	010 32
AND THOU, CHILD, SHALT BE CALLED THE PROPHET OF THE	014 24
FOR THOU SHALT GO BEFORE THE FACE OF THE LORD TO	014 25
FOR THOU SHALT JUDGE THE FOLK RIGHTEOUSLY, AND GOVERN	028 23
AND SHALT MAKE ME TO UNDERSTAND WISDOM SECRETLY	060 23
THOU SHALT PURGE ME WITH HYSSOP, AND I SHALL BE	060 24
THOU SHALT WASH ME, AND I SHALL BE WHITER THAN SNOW	060 25
THOU SHALT MAKE ME HEAR OF JOY AND GLADNESS, *	060 26
THOU SHALT OPEN MY LIPS, O LORD, *	061 09
O GOD, SHALT THOU NOT DESPISE	061 14
THOU SHALT HAVE NONE OTHER GODS BUT ME	068 04
THOU SHALT NOT MAKE TO THYSELF ANY GRAVEN IMAGE,	068 08

SHALT   CONTINUED

THOU SHALT NOT BOW DOWN TO THEM, NOR WORSHIP THEM	068 10
THOU SHALT NOT TAKE THE NAME OF THE LORD THY GOD IN	068 18
SIX DAYS SHALT THOU LABOUR, AND DO ALL THAT THOU HAST	068 25
IN IT THOU SHALT DO NO MANNER OF WORK	068 27
THOU SHALT DO NO MURDER	069 07
THOU SHALT NOT COMMIT ADULTERY	069 10
THOU SHALT NOT STEAL	069 13
THOU SHALT NOT BEAR FALSE WITNESS AGAINST THY	069 16
THOU SHALT NOT COVET	069 19
THOU SHALT NOT COVET THY NEIGHBOUR'S WIFE, NOR	069 20
THOU SHALT LOVE THE LORD THY GOD WITH ALL THY HEART,	069 27
THOU SHALT LOVE THY NEIGHBOUR AS THYSELF	069 30
FOR THIS, THOU SHALT NOT COMMIT ADULTERY, THOU SHALT	090 25
THOU SHALT NOT KILL, THOU SHALT NOT STEAL,	090 25
NOT STEAL, THOU SHALT NOT BEAR FALSE WITNESS,	090 26
THOU SHALT NOT COVET	090 26
NOT KILL, THOU SHALT NOT STEAL, THOU SHALT NOT BEAR	090 26
THOU SHALT LOVE THY NEIGHBOUR AS THYSELF	090 28
AND AS A VESTURE SHALT THOU FOLD THEM UP, AND THEY	097 17
A SON, AND THOU SHALT CALL HIS NAME JESUS	105 06
IN SO DOING THOU SHALT HEAP COALS OF FIRE ON HIS	113 07
IS GOOD, AND THOU SHALT HAVE PRAISE OF THE SAME	114 17
THOU SHALT NOT TEMPT THE LORD THY GOD	127 03
IS WRITTEN, THOU SHALT WORSHIP THE LORD THY GOD, AND	127 09
AND HIM ONLY SHALT THOU SERVE	127 10
CROW TWICE, THOU SHALT DENY ME THRICE	141 24
CROW TWICE, THOU SHALT DENY ME THRICE	144 02
BEFORE THAT THOU SHALT THRICE DENY THAT THOU KNOWEST	150 03
COCK CROW, THOU SHALT DENY ME THRICE	151 22
UNTO THEE, TO-DAY SHALT THOU BE WITH ME IN PARADISE	155 08
BUT THOU SHALT KNOW HEREAFTER	156 04
UNTO HIM, THOU SHALT NEVER WASH MY FEET	156 05
THOU SHALT NOT SUFFER THINE HOLY ONE TO SEE	169 14
OWN EYE, AND THEN SHALT THOU SEE CLEARLY TO PULL OUT	195 11
HENCEFORTH THOU SHALT CATCH MEN	196 28
OF OLD TIME, THOU SHALT NOT KILL	198 02
UNTO THEE, THOU SHALT BY NO MEANS COME OUT THENCE,	198 15
THOU SHALT LOVE THE LORD THY GOD WITH ALL THY	208 15
THIS DO, AND THOU SHALT LIVE	208 19
THEN SHALT THOU HAVE WORSHIP IN THE PRESENCE OF THEM	214 17
UNTO HIM, THOU SHALT LOVE THE LORD THY GOD WITH ALL	215 10
LIKE UNTO IT, THOU SHALT LOVE THY NEIGHBOUR AS	215 13
IF THOU SHALT CONFESS WITH THY MOUTH THE LORD JESUS,	226 26
LORD JESUS, AND SHALT BELIEVE IN THINE HEART THAT GOD	226 27
THE DEAD, THOU SHALT BE SAVED	226 28
BEHOLD, THOU SHALT CONCEIVE IN THY WOMB, AND	236 14
FORTH A SON, AND SHALT CALL HIS NAME JESUS	236 15
AND THOU, CHILD, SHALT BE CALLED THE PROPHET OF THE	244 10
FOR THOU SHALT GO BEFORE THE FACE OF THE LORD TO	244 11
WHATSOEVER THOU SHALT BIND ON EARTH SHALL BE BOUND IN	246 10
WHATSOEVER THOU SHALT LOOSE ON EARTH SHALL BE LOOSED	246 11
HIM SHALT THOU SERVE, AND TO HIM SHALT THOU CLEAVE,	263 29
THOU SHALT FEAR THE LORD THY GOD	263 29
AND TO HIM SHALT THOU CLEAVE, AND SWEAR BY HIS	263 30
BEEN SAID, THOU SHALT LOVE THY NEIGHBOUR, AND HATE	264 04
THOU SHALT HAVE NONE OTHER GODS BUT ME	286 05
THOU SHALT NOT MAKE TO THYSELF ANY GRAVEN IMAGE,	286 08
THOU SHALT NOT BOW DOWN TO THEM, NOR WORSHIP THEM	286 11
THOU SHALT NOT TAKE THE NAME OF THE LORD THY GOD IN	286 18
SIX DAYS SHALT THOU LABOUR, AND DO ALL THAT THOU HAST	286 25
IN IT THOU SHALT DO NO MANNER OF WORK	286 27
THOU SHALT DO NO MURDER	287 06
THOU SHALT NOT COMMIT ADULTERY	287 09
THOU SHALT NOT STEAL	287 12
THOU SHALT NOT BEAR FALSE WITNESS AGAINST THY	287 15
THOU SHALT NOT COVET THY NEIGHBOUR'S HOUSE, THOU	287 19
THOU SHALT NOT COVET THY NEIGHBOUR'S WIFE, NOR	287 20
THOU SHALT LOVE THE LORD THY GOD WITH ALL THY HEART,	288 05
THOU SHALT LOVE THY NEIGHBOUR AS THYSELF	288 09
YET SHALT THOU REFRESH ME	311 26
OF TROUBLE, YET SHALT THOU REFRESH ME	312 04
THOU SHALT STRETCH FORTH THY HAND UPON THE	312 05
THEREFORE SHALT THOU BE FEARED	328 09
THOU SHALT SHOW ME THE PATH OF LIFE	333 09
THOU SHALT PREPARE A TABLE BEFORE ME IN THE PRESENCE	338 26
9 THOU SHALT BRUISE THEM WITH A ROD OF IRON, *	346 15
3 MY VOICE SHALT THOU HEAR BETIMES, O LORD	348 04
6 THOU SHALT DESTROY THEM THAT SPEAK LIES	348 11
8 THOU SHALT KEEP THEM, O LORD	355 23
THOU SHALT PRESERVE THEM FROM THIS GENERATION FOR	355 23
THOU SHALT MAINTAIN MY LOT	357 32
THOU SHALT NOT LEAVE MY SOUL IN HELL	358 10
NEITHER SHALT THOU SUFFER THY HOLY ONE TO SEE	358 11
12 THOU SHALT SHOW ME THE PATH OF LIFE	358 12
HAST TRIED ME, AND SHALT FIND NO WICKEDNESS IN ME	358 22
O GOD, FOR THOU SHALT HEAR ME	358 29
WITH THE HOLY THOU SHALT BE HOLY, *	361 18
A PERFECT MAN THOU SHALT BE PERFECT	361 19
THE CLEAN THOU SHALT BE CLEAN, *	361 20
THE FROWARD THOU SHALT BE FROWARD	361 21
28 FOR THOU SHALT SAVE THE PEOPLE THAT ARE IN	361 22
AND SHALT BRING DOWN THE HIGH LOOKS OF THE PROUD	361 23
29 THOU ALSO SHALT LIGHT MY CANDLE	361 24
37 THOU SHALT MAKE ROOM ENOUGH UNDER ME FOR TO GO,	362 09
THOU SHALT THROW DOWN MINE ENEMIES UNDER ME	362 17
44 THOU SHALT DELIVER ME FROM THE STRIVINGS OF THE	362 25
AND THOU SHALT MAKE ME THE HEAD OF THE NATIONS	362 26
THOU SHALT RID ME FROM THE WICKED MAN	363 03
3 FOR THOU SHALT MEET HIM WITH THE BLESSINGS OF	365 09
AND SHALT SET A CROWN OF PURE GOLD UPON HIS HEAD	365 10
AND GREAT WORSHIP SHALT THOU LAY UPON HIM	365 14
6 FOR THOU SHALT GIVE HIM EVERLASTING FELICITY,	365 15
9 THOU SHALT MAKE THEM LIKE A FIERY OVEN IN TIME OF	365 22
10 THEIR FRUIT SHALT THOU ROOT OUT OF THE EARTH,	365 25

SHALT   CONTINUED

12 THEREFORE SHALT THOU PUT THEM TO FLIGHT, *   365 29
STRINGS OF THY BOW SHALT THOU MAKE READY AGAINST THE   365 30
5 THOU SHALT PREPARE A TABLE BEFORE ME IN THE   368 19
22 THOU SHALT HIDE THEM IN THE COVERT OF THINE OWN   377 06
THOU SHALT KEEP THEM SECRETLY IN THY TABERNACLE FROM   377 07
THOU SHALT PRESERVE ME FROM TROUBLE   378 05
THOU SHALT COMPASS ME ABOUT WITH SONGS OF   378 06
WAY WHEREIN THOU SHALT GO   378 09
7 THOU, LORD, SHALT SAVE BOTH MAN AND BEAST   384 04
AND THOU SHALT GIVE THEM DRINK OF THY PLEASURES,   384 12
AND VERILY THOU SHALT BE FED   384 30
NOT THYSELF, ELSE SHALT THOU BE MOVED TO DO EVIL   385 10
THOU SHALT LOOK AFTER HIS PLACE, AND HE SHALL BE   385 14
THAT THOU SHALT POSSESS THE LAND   387 02
SHALL PERISH, THOU SHALT SEE IT   387 03
THOU SHALT ANSWER FOR ME, O LORD MY GOD   388 22
AND SHALT SET ME BEFORE THY FACE FOR EVER   392 23
THY FATHERS, THOU SHALT HAVE CHILDREN, *   397 19
AND THOU SHALT PRAISE ME   402 21
CLEAR WHEN THOU SHALT JUDGE   403 17
AND SHALT MAKE ME TO UNDERSTAND WISDOM SECRETLY   403 21
7 THOU SHALT PURGE ME WITH HYSSOP, AND I SHALL BE   403 22
THOU SHALT WASH ME, AND I SHALL BE WHITER THAN SNOW   403 23
8 THOU SHALT MAKE ME HEAR OF JOY AND GLADNESS,   403 25
15 THOU SHALT OPEN MY LIPS, O LORD, *   404 07
O GOD, SHALT THOU NOT DESPISE   404 12
19 THEN SHALT THOU BE PLEASED WITH THE SACRIFICE OF   404 14
THOU, O GOD, SHALT BRING THEM INTO THE PIT OF   408 06
IN THY DISPLEASURE SHALT CAST THEM DOWN   408 29
BUT THOU, O LORD, SHALT HAVE THEM IN DERISION,   411 20
AND THOU SHALT LAUGH ALL THE HEATHEN TO SCORN   411 21
6 THOU SHALT GRANT THE KING A LONG LIFE, *   413 17
5 THOU SHALT SHOW US WONDERFUL THINGS IN THY   416 21
FOR THOU SHALT JUDGE THE FOLK RIGHTEOUSLY, AND GOVERN   418 30
SO SHALT THOU DRIVE THEM AWAY   419 11
SO SHALT THOU MAKE THEIR IMAGE TO VANISH OUT OF THE   429 17
24 THOU SHALT GUIDE ME WITH THY COUNSEL, *   429 24
FIERCENESS OF THEM SHALT THOU REFRAIN   433 09
NEITHER SHALT THOU WORSHIP ANY OTHER GOD   442 31
FOR THOU SHALT TAKE ALL NATIONS TO THINE INHERITANCE   444 03
THY TRUTH SHALT THOU STABLISH IN THE HEAVENS   450 08
THOU SHALT LIFT UP OUR HORNS   451 09
AND THOU SHALT BE SAFE UNDER HIS FEATHERS   455 02
5 THOU SHALT NOT BE AFRAID FOR ANY TERROR BY NIGHT,   455 05
WITH THINE EYES SHALT THOU BEHOLD, *   455 11
13 THOU SHALT GO UPON THE LION AND ADDER   455 21
AND THE DRAGON SHALT THOU TREAD UNDER THY FEET   455 22
BUT THOU, O LORD, SHALT ENDURE FOR EVER, *   465 02
13 THOU SHALT ARISE, AND HAVE MERCY UPON SION   465 04
BUT THOU SHALT ENDURE   465 34
AND AS A VESTURE SHALT THOU CHANGE THEM, AND THEY   466 02
AND THOU SHALT RENEW THE FACE OF THE EARTH   469 22
2 FOR THOU SHALT EAT THE LABOURS OF THINE HANDS   506 08
IS THEE, AND HAPPY SHALT THOU BE   506 09
THAT THOU SHALT SEE JERUSALEM IN PROSPERITY ALL THY   506 17
7 YEA, THAT THOU SHALT SEE THY CHILDREN'S CHILDREN,   506 18
THEREFORE SHALT THOU BE FEARED   507 14
OF TROUBLE, YET SHALT THOU REFRESH ME   514 10
THOU SHALT STRETCH FORTH THY HAND UPON THE   514 11
WHERE THOU SHALT BE LAWFULLY APPOINTED THEREUNTO   546 27
BY SO DOING THOU SHALT BOTH SAVE THYSELF AND THEM   558 24
WISDOM THOU SHALT SEE TO BE MOST EXPEDIENT FOR THEM   566 22
THOU SHALT HAVE NONE OTHER GODS BUT ME   578 26
THOU SHALT NOT MAKE TO THYSELF ANY GRAVEN IMAGE,   578 27
THOU SHALT NOT BOW DOWN TO THEM, NOR WORSHIP THEM   578 29
THOU SHALT NOT TAKE THE NAME OF THE LORD THY GOD IN   578 35
SIX DAYS SHALT THOU LABOUR, AND DO ALL THAT THOU HAST   579 05
IN IT THOU SHALT DO NO MANNER OF WORK   579 07
THOU SHALT DO NO MURDER   579 15
THOU SHALT NOT COMMIT ADULTERY   579 16
THOU SHALT NOT STEAL   579 17
THOU SHALT NOT BEAR FALSE WITNESS AGAINST THY   579 18
THOU SHALT NOT COVET THY NEIGHBOUR'S HOUSE, THOU   579 20
THOU SHALT NOT COVET THY NEIGHBOUR'S WIFE,   579 21
WHATEVER ELSE THOU SHALT SEE TO BE NECESSARY AND   589 05

SHAME

FOR IT IS A SHAME EVEN TO SPEAK OF THOSE THINGS WHICH   129 17
TO THE SMITERS AND HID NOT HIS FACE FROM SHAME   144 07
NOT MY FACE FROM SHAME AND SPITTING   144 15
THOU BEGIN WITH SHAME TO TAKE THE LOWEST PLACE   214 14
GLORY IS IN THEIR SHAME, WHO MIND EARTHLY THINGS   222 20
DESPISING THE SHAME, AND IS SET DOWN AT THE RIGHT   258 25
NEITHER BEAR THE SHAME OF THE HEATHEN ANY MORE   262 19
AND PUT TO SHAME SUDDENLY   349 19
AND PUT TO SHAME, THAT SEEK AFTER MY SOUL   381 24
TO CONFUSION AND SHAME TOGETHER, THAT REJOICE AT MY   383 16
AND REWARDED WITH SHAME, *   391 19
AND THE SHAME OF MY FACE HATH COVERED ME   395 24
SHAME HATH COVERED MY FACE   422 17
MY REPROACH, MY SHAME, AND MY DISHONOUR   423 11
BE SOON BROUGHT TO SHAME, *   424 25
BE COVERED WITH SHAME AND DISHONOUR THAT SEEK TO DO   425 32
AND BROUGHT UNTO SHAME THAT SEEK TO DO ME EVIL   426 29
AND PUT THEM TO A PERPETUAL SHAME   439 11
ARE BECOME AN OPEN SHAME TO OUR ENEMIES, *   440 06
LET THEM BE PUT TO SHAME, AND PERISH   445 07
28 LET MINE ADVERSARIES BE CLOTHED WITH SHAME   481 29
22 O TURN FROM ME SHAME AND REBUKE   491 10
I SHALL CLOTHE THEM WITH SHAME   509 10

SHAPEN

BEHOLD, I WAS SHAPEN IN WICKEDNESS, *   060 20
5 BEHOLD, I WAS SHAPEN IN WICKEDNESS, *   403 18

SHARP

ARROWS ARE VERY SHARP IN THE HEART OF THE KING'S   396 25
CUTTEST LIKE A SHARP RAZOR   404 23
AND THEIR TONGUE A SHARP SWORD   409 23
EVEN MIGHTY AND SHARP ARROWS, WITH HOT BURNING COALS   502 12

SHARPENED

3 THEY HAVE SHARPENED THEIR TONGUES LIKE A SERPENT   516 13

SHARPNESS

OVERCOME THE SHARPNESS OF DEATH, THOU DIDST OPEN THE   010 28

SHAWMS

TRUMPETS ALSO AND SHAWMS, *   027 17
TRUMPETS ALSO AND SHAWMS, *   462 06

SHEAVES

AND BRING HIS SHEAVES WITH HIM   505 20
BINDETH UP THE SHEAVES HIS BOSOM   507 03

SHECHEM

AND DIVIDE SHECHEM, *   412 24
AND DIVIDE SHECHEM, AND METE OUT THE VALLEY OF   479 18

SHED

WHICH IS SHED FOR YOU, AND FOR MANY,   080 27
WHICH WAS SHED FOR THEE, PRESERVE THY BODY   083 03
CHRIST'S BLOOD WAS SHED FOR THEE, AND BE THANKFUL   083 06
THE RIGHTEOUS BLOOD SHED UPON THE EARTH, FROM THE   100 23
WHICH IS SHED FOR MANY   141 14
MY BLOOD, WHICH IS SHED FOR YOU   149 12
OF OUR SINS, DID SHED OUT OF HIS MOST PRECIOUS SIDE   279 10
CROSS FOR HIM, AND SHED HIS BLOOD FOR HIS REDEMPTION, R 323 28
BLOOD HAVE THEY SHED LIKE WATER ON EVERY SIDE OF   440 04
BLOOD THAT IS SHED, *   440 24
37 AND SHED INNOCENT BLOOD, EVEN THE BLOOD OF THEIR   475 11
AND FOR WHOM HE SHED HIS BLOOD   540 08
SENSE IMPART, AND SHED THY LOVE IN EVERY HEART   545 03
SENSE IMPART, AND SHED THY LOVE IN EVERY HEART   557 09

SHEDDING

AND WITHOUT SHEDDING OF BLOOD IS NO REMISSION   147 26

SHEEP

AND STRAYED FROM THY WAYS LIKE LOST SHEEP   006 18
AND THE SHEEP OF HIS HAND   009 16
AND THE SHEEP OF HIS PASTURE   015 09
ALL WE LIKE SHEEP HAVE GONE ASTRAY   022 14
AND STRAYED FROM THY WAYS LIKE LOST SHEEP   023 25
OF THY DISPERSED SHEEP, BEING GATHERED INTO ONE FOLD,   037 06
BUT UNTO THE LOST SHEEP OF THE HOUSE OF ISRAEL   128 14
AND THE SHEEP SHALL BE SCATTERED   141 20
FOR YE WERE AS SHEEP GOING ASTRAY   172 18
THE GOOD SHEPHERD GIVETH HIS LIFE FOR THE SHEEP   172 22
WHOSE OWN THE SHEEP ARE NOT, SEETH THE WOLF COMING,   172 23
AND LEAVETH THE SHEEP, AND FLEETH   172 24
THE WOLF CATCHETH THEM, AND SCATTERETH THE SHEEP   172 25
AND KNOW MY SHEEP, AND AM KNOWN OF MINE, EVEN AS THE   172 27
AND CARETH NOT FOR THE SHEEP   172 27
AND I LAY DOWN MY LIFE FOR THE SHEEP   172 29
AND OTHER SHEEP I HAVE, WHICH ARE NOT OF THIS FOLD   172 30
IN BY THE DOOR IS THE SHEPHERD OF THE SHEEP   186 03
AND THE SHEEP HEAR HIS VOICE   186 04
HE CALLETH HIS OWN SHEEP BY NAME, AND LEADETH THEM   186 05
FORTH HIS OWN SHEEP, HE GOETH BEFORE THEM, AND THE   186 06
AND THE SHEEP FOLLOW HIM   186 07
I SAY UNTO YOU, I AM THE DOOR OF THE SHEEP   186 13
BUT THE SHEEP DID NOT HEAR THEM   186 14
HAVING AN HUNDRED SHEEP, IF HE LOSE ONE OF THEM, DOTH   193 18
I HAVE FOUND MY SHEEP WHICH WAS LOST   193 24
DIVIDETH HIS SHEEP FROM THE GOATS   258 32
HE SHALL SET THE SHEEP ON HIS RIGHT HAND, BUT THE   259 02
BESEECH THEE, A SHEEP OF THINE OWN FOLD, A LAMB OF   319 29
SHEPHERD OF THE SHEEP, THROUGH THE BLOOD OF THE   335 18
7 ALL SHEEP AND OXEN   351 14
BE EATEN UP LIKE SHEEP, *   395 15
AND ARE COUNTED AS SHEEP APPOINTED TO BE SLAIN   396 05
14 THEY LIE IN THE GRAVE LIKE SHEEP   400 34
14 THE FOLDS SHALL BE FULL OF SHEEP   417 11
SO HOT AGAINST THE SHEEP OF THY PASTURE   430 04
THY PEOPLE LIKE SHEEP, *   434 23
THEM FORTH LIKE SHEEP, *   438 15
THY PEOPLE, AND SHEEP OF THY PASTURE, SHALL GIVE THEE   440 32
AND THE SHEEP OF HIS HAND   459 18
AND THE SHEEP OF HIS PASTURE   463 10
AND MAKETH HIM HOUSEHOLDS LIKE A FLOCK OF SHEEP   478 29
AND THE LITTLE HILLS LIKE YOUNG SHEEP   484 32
AND YE LITTLE HILLS, LIKE YOUNG SHEEP   485 05
GONE ASTRAY LIKE A SHEEP THAT IS LOST   502 02
THAT OUR SHEEP MAY BRING FORTH THOUSANDS, AND TEN   520 19
ABROAD AS SHEEP HAVING NO SHEPHERD   538 16
IN BY THE DOOR IS THE SHEPHERD OF THE SHEEP   538 26

SHEEP   CONTINUED

AND THE SHEEP HEAR HIS VOICE	538 27
HE CALLETH HIS OWN SHEEP BY NAME, AND LEADETH THEM	538 28
FORTH HIS OWN SHEEP, HE GOETH BEFORE THEM, AND THE	538 29
AND THE SHEEP FOLLOW HIM	538 30
I SAY UNTO YOU, I AM THE DOOR OF THE SHEEP	539 04
BUT THE SHEEP DID NOT HEAR THEM	539 05
THE GOOD SHEPHERD GIVETH HIS LIFE FOR THE SHEEP	539 11
WHOSE OWN THE SHEEP ARE NOT, SEETH THE WOLF COMING,	539 12
AND LEAVETH THE SHEEP, AND FLEETH	539 13
THE WOLF CATCHETH THEM, AND SCATTERETH THE SHEEP	539 14
AND CARETH NOT FOR THE SHEEP	539 16
AND KNOW MY SHEEP, AND AM KNOWN OF MINE, EVEN AS THE	539 16
AND I LAY DOWN MY LIFE FOR THE SHEEP	539 18
AND OTHER SHEEP I HAVE, WHICH ARE NOT OF THIS FOLD	539 19
SEEK FOR CHRIST'S SHEEP THAT ARE DISPERSED ABROAD,	539 34
FOR THEY ARE THE SHEEP OF CHRIST, WHICH HE BOUGHT	540 07
HE SAITH UNTO HIM, FEED MY SHEEP	551 20
JESUS SAITH UNTO HIM, FEED MY SHEEP	551 24
THAT SOLD OXEN AND SHEEP AND DOVES, AND THE CHANGERS	567 27
AND THE SHEEP, AND THE OXEN	567 29
SHEPHERD OF THE SHEEP, THROUGH THE BLOOD OF THE	573 04

SHEEP-FOLDS

AMONG THE SHEEP-FOLDS, YET SHALL YE BE AS THE WINGS	420 06
AND TOOK HIM AWAY FROM THE SHEEP-FOLDS	439 20

SHEEP'S

COME TO YOU IN SHEEP'S CLOTHING, BUT INWARDLY THEY	200 16

SHEEPFOLD

DOOR INTO THE SHEEPFOLD, BUT CLIMBETH UP SOME OTHER	185 31
DOOR INTO THE SHEEPFOLD, BUT CLIMBETH UP SOME OTHER	538 24

SHELTER

TO SAY UNDER SHELTER CF THE CHURCH THE WHOLE OR A	R 336 30

SHEPHERD

SEA WITH THE SHEPHERD OF HIS FLOCK	139 09
WILL SMITE THE SHEPHERD, AND THE SHEEP SHALL BE	141 19
FLOCK UNDER ONE SHEPHERD, JESUS CHRIST OUR LORD, WHO	157 11
UNTO THE SHEPHERD AND BISHOP OF YOUR SOULS	172 19
JESUS SAID, I AM THE GOOD SHEPHERD	172 21
THE GOOD SHEPHERD GIVETH HIS LIFE FOR THE SHEEP	172 21
AND NOT THE SHEPHERD, WHOSE OWN THE SHEEP ARE NOT,	172 23
I AM THE GOOD SHEPHERD	172 27
AND THERE SHALL BE ONE FLOCK, AND ONE SHEPHERD	172 32
THE DOOR IS THE SHEPHERD OF THE SHEEP	186 03
HE SHALL FEED HIS FLOCK LIKE A SHEPHERD	243 08
AS A SHEPHERD DIVIDETH HIS SHEEP FROM THE	258 32
THE GREAT SHEPHERD OF THE SHEEP, THROUGH THE BLOOD OF	335 17
HE SHALL FEED HIS FLOCK LIKE A SHEPHERD	338 12
THE LORD IS MY SHEPHERD	338 17
THE LORD IS MY SHEPHERD	368 10
DEATH IS THEIR SHEPHERD	400 34
HEAR, O THOU SHEPHERD OF ISRAEL, THOU THAT LEADEST	441 03
WERE SCATTERED ABROAD AS SHEEP HAVING NO SHEPHERD	538 16
THE DOOR IS THE SHEPHERD OF THE SHEEP	538 26
I AM THE GOOD SHEPHERD	539 10
THE GOOD SHEPHERD GIVETH HIS LIFE FOR THE SHEEP	539 10
AND NOT THE SHEPHERD, WHOSE CWN THE SHEEP ARE NCT,	539 12
I AM THE GOOD SHEPHERD	539 16
AND THERE SHALL BE ONE FLOCK, AND ONE SHEPHERD	539 21
OF CHRIST A SHEPHERD, NOT A WOLF	558 26
WHEN THE CHIEF SHEPHERD SHALL APPEAR, YOU MAY RECEIVE	558 30
BE A FAITHFUL SHEPHERD OVER YOU	570 34
THE GREAT SHEPHERD OF THE SHEEP, THROUGH THE BLCOD OF	573 04
BISHOP AND SHEPHERD OF OUR SOULS, WHO LIVETH AND	574 21

SHEPHERDS

SAME COUNTRY SHEPHERDS ABIDING IN THE FIELD, KEEPING	099 10
THE SHEPHERDS SAID ONE TO ANOTHER, LET US NOW	106 08
THINGS WHICH WERE TOLD THEM BY THE SHEPHERDS	106 16
AND THE SHEPHERDS RETURNED, GLORIFYING AND PRAISING	106 17

SHEW

UNTO THEM, GO AND SHEW JOHN AGAIN THOSE THINGS WHICH	094 19
BEAR WITNESS, AND SHEW UNTO YOU THAT ETERNAL LIFE,	101 16
BUT GO THY WAY, SHEW THYSELF TO THE PRIEST, AND OFFER	115 04
AND SHALL SHEW GREAT SIGNS AND WONDERS	118 05
AND HE WILL SHEW YOU A LARGE UPPER ROOM FURNISHED AND	140 30
AND HE SHALL SHEW YOU A LARGE UPPER ROOM FURNISHED	148 31
THIS CUP, YE DO SHEW THE LORD'S DEATH TILL HE COME	152 24
AND HE WILL SHEW YOU THINGS TO COME	175 21
OF MINE, AND SHALL SHEW IT UNTO YOU	175 23
OF MINE, AND SHALL SHEW IT UNTO YOU	175 24
BUT I WILL SHEW THEE THINGS WHICH MUST BE	176 25
AND I WILL SHEW THEE THINGS WHICH MUST BE	187 03
SAID UNTO THEM, GO SHEW YOURSELVES UNTO THE PRIESTS	210 05
TO MAKE A FAIR SHEW IN THE FLESH, THEY CONSTRAIN YOU	210 25
SHEW ME THE TRIBUTE MONEY	223 06
FOR I WILL SHEW HIM HCW GREAT THINGS HE MUST SUFFER	230 28
HEARTS OF ALL MEN, SHEW WHETHER OF THESE TWO THCU	234 28
UNTO HIM, LORD, SHEW LS THE FATHER, AND IT SUFFICETH	240 09
SAYEST THOU THEN, SHEW US THE FATHER	240 13
BEHOLD, I SHEW YOU A MYSTERY	329 35

SHEWED

THIRD DAY, AND SHEWED HIM OPENLY	166 25
THUS SPOKEN, HE SHEWED THEM HIS HANDS AND HIS FEET	170 02
HAD SO SAID, HE SHEWED UNTO THEM HIS HANDS AND HIS	171 18
TO WHOM ALSO HE SHEWED HIMSELF ALIVE AFTER HIS	177 26
THIRD DAY, AND SHEWED HIM OPENLY	184 12
SERVANT CAME, AND SHEWED HIS LORD THESE THINGS	192 12
HE SAID, HE THAT SHEWED MERCY ON HIM	209 04
HOW THE LORD HAD SHEWED GREAT MERCY UPON HER	243 15
JESUS CHRIST HATH SHEWED ME	248 11
BUT HAVE SHEWED YOU, AND HAVE TAUGHT YOU	550 11
I HAVE SHEWED YOU ALL THINGS, HOW THAT SO LABOURING	551 08
HAD SO SAID, HE SHEWED UNTO THEM HIS HANDS AND HIS	551 31

SHEWETH

HE THAT SHEWETH MERCY, WITH CHEERFULNESS	111 21
AND SHEWETH HIM ALL THE KINGDOMS OF THE	127 05

SHEWING

THE DAY OF HIS SHEWING UNTO ISRAEL	244 18

SHIELD

TAKING THE SHIELD OF FAITH, WHEREWITH YE SHALL	219 16
KINDNESS WILT THOU DEFEND HIM AS WITH A SHIELD	348 30
8 THE LORD IS MY STRENGTH, AND MY SHIELD	373 22
FOR HE IS OUR HELP AND OUR SHIELD	379 29
LAY HAND UPON THE SHIELD AND BUCKLER, *	381 20
DOTH DEFEND THE EARTH, AS IT WERE WITH A SHIELD	399 08
THE SHIELD, THE SWORD, AND THE BATTLE	432 26
SHALL BE THY SHIELD AND BUCKLER	455 04
114 THOU ART MY DEFENCE AND SHIELD	497 26
SHIELD FROM BODILY ACCIDENT AND HARM THE WORKMEN AT	599 28

SHILOH

THE TABERNACLE IN SHILOH, *	438 32

SHINE

THAT THEY MAY SHINE AS LIGHTS IN THE WORLD, AND IN	047 27
MAKE HIS FACE TO SHINE UPON US, AND BE GRACIOUS UNTO	063 16
LET YOUR LIGHT SO SHINE BEFORE MEN, THAT THEY MAY SEE	072 04
A NEW LIGHT TO SHINE IN OUR HEARTS, TO GIVE THE	077 30
IN OUR HEARTS MAY SHINE FORTH IN OUR LIVES	106 27
OF THE GOSPEL TO SHINE THROUGHOUT THE WORLD	229 19
OF GOD, SHOULD SHINE UNTO THEM	251 05
THE LIGHT TO SHINE OUT OF DARKNESS, HATH SHINED IN	251 07
MAKE HIS FACE TO SHINE UPON THEE, AND BE GRACIOUS	314 28
MAKE HIS FACE TO SHINE UPON YOU, AND BE GRACIOUS UNTO	332 12
MAKE HIS FACE TO SHINE UPON HIM AND BE GRACIOUS UNTO	341 16
LIGHTNINGS GAVE SHINE UNTO THE WORLD	461 04
OF THY GOSPEL SHINE UPON ALL NATIONS	590 23
MAKE HIS FACE TO SHINE UPON US, AND BE GRACIOUS UNTO	593 19

SHINED

SUDDENLY THERE SHINED ROUND ABOUT HIM A LIGHT FRCM	229 31
AND A LIGHT SHINED IN THE PRISON	245 13
OF DARKNESS, HATH SHINED IN OUR HEARTS, TO GIVE THE	251 08

SHINETH

AND THE LIGHT SHINETH IN DARKNESS	097 25
OF THE EAST, AND SHINETH EVEN UNTO THE WEST	118 11

SHIP

AND TAUGHT THE PEOPLE OUT OF THE SHIP	196 13
WERE IN THE OTHER SHIP, THAT THEY SHOULD COME AND	196 20
ENTERED INTO A SHIP, AND PASSED OVER, AND CAME INTO	216 33
HIS BROTHER, IN A SHIP WITH ZEBEDEE THEIR FATHER,	227 30
LEFT THE SHIP AND THEIR FATHER, AND FOLLOWED HIM	227 32

SHIPS

AND SAW TWO SHIPS STANDING BY THE LAKE	196 08
INTO ONE OF THE SHIPS, WHICH WAS SIMON'S, AND PRAYED	196 10
FILLED BOTH THE SHIPS, SO THAT THEY BEGAN TO SINK	196 22
HAD BROUGHT THEIR SHIPS TO LAND, THEY FORSOOK ALL,	196 29
DOST BREAK THE SHIPS OF THE SEA *	399 22
26 THERE GO THE SHIPS, AND THERE IS THAT LEVIATHAN,	469 12
DOWN TO THE SEA IN SHIPS, *	477 22

SHIPWRECK

I SUFFERED SHIPWRECK, A NIGHT AND A DAY I HAVE BEEN	121 03

SHOD

AND YOUR FEET SHOD WITH THE PREPARATION OF THE GOSPEL	219 15

SHOE

OVER EDOM WILL I CAST OUT MY SHOE	412 28
OVER EDOM WILL I CAST OUT MY SHOE	479 23

SHOE'S

BEFORE ME, WHOSE SHOE'S LATCHET I AM NOT WORTHY TO	096 05

SHOES

LATCHET OF WHOSE SHOES I AM NOT WORTHY TO STOOP DOWN	112 15
AND SCRIP, AND SHOES, LACKED YE ANY THING	150 05
ON HIS HAND, AND SHOES ON HIS FEET	202 22
CARRY NEITHER PURSE, NOR SCRIP, NOR SHOES	254 18

SHONE

GLORY OF THE LORD SHONE ROUND ABOUT THEM	099 13
THE LIGHTNINGS SHONE UPON THE GROUND	434 19

SHOOK

ALSO OF THE HILLS SHOOK, AND WERE REMOVED, BECAUSE HE	360 10
8 THE EARTH SHOOK, AND THE HEAVENS DROPPED AT THE	419 26
WAS MOVED, AND SHOOK WITHAL	434 20

SHOOT

WHEN THEY NOW SHOOT FORTH, YE SEE AND KNOW OF YOUR	093 15
THEY MAY PRIVILY SHOOT AT THEM WHICH ARE TRUE OF	354 23
THEY SHOOT OUT THEIR LIPS, AND SHAKE THEIR HEADS,	366 16
WHEN THEY SHOOT THEIR ARROWS, LET THEM BE ROOTED OUT	410 22
AND SHOOT OUT THEIR ARROWS, EVEN BITTER WORDS	415 23
THEY MAY PRIVILY SHOOT AT HIM THAT IS PERFECT	415 25
GOD SHALL SUDDENLY SHOOT AT THEM WITH A SWIFT ARROW,	415 33
SHOOT OUT THINE ARROWS, AND CONSUME THEM	520 02

SHORT

THAT HE HATH BUT A SHORT TIME	252 20
HATH BUT A SHORT TIME TO LIVE, AND IS FULL OF	332 18
46 O REMEMBER HOW SHORT MY TIME IS	452 34
QUESTIONS OF THIS SHORT CATECHISM, THEY SHALL BE	R 583 03
WHO READS MAKE A SHORT PAUSE, THAT EVERY ONE MAY	R 589 34

SHORTEN

IT EXPEDIENT TO SHORTEN THE SERVICE, THE FOLLOWING	R 323 04

SHORTENED

HAST THOU SHORTENED, *	452 30
AND SHORTENED MY DAYS	465 27

SHORTLY

KNOWING THAT SHORTLY I MUST PUT OFF THIS MY	248 10
TO COME SHORTLY UNTO ME	253 31

SHORTNESS

OF THE SHORTNESS AND UNCERTAINTY OF HUMAN LIFE	316 27

SHOULDER

6 I EASED HIS SHOULDER FROM THE BURDEN, *	442 23

SHOULDERS

IT ON HIS SHOULDERS, REJOICING	193 21

SHOULDEST

THAT THOU SHOULDEST COME UNDER MY ROOF	115 11
SHOULDEST NOT THOU ALSO HAVE HAD COMPASSION ON THY	221 35
THAT THOU SHOULDEST BE FOR SALVATION UNTO THE ENDS OF	261 05
THAT THOU SHOULDEST COME UNDER MY ROOF	573 11

SHOUT

FROM HEAVEN WITH A SHOUT, WITH THE VOICE OF THE	269 06

SHOW

AND OUR MOUTH SHALL SHOW FORTH THY PRAISE	007 32
AND SHOW OURSELVES GLAD IN HIM WITH PSALMS	009 06
O LORD, SHOW THY MERCY UPON US	016 29
AND THAT WE SHOW FORTH THY PRAISE, NOT ONLY WITH OUR	019 27
AND OUR MOUTH SHALL SHOW FORTH THY PRAISE	025 07
SHOW YOURSELVES JOYFUL UNTO THE LORD, ALL YE LANDS	027 13
O SHOW YOURSELVES JOYFUL BEFORE THE LORD, THE KING	027 17
AND SHOW US THE LIGHT OF HIS COUNTENANCE, AND BE	028 17
O LORD, SHOW THY MERCY UPON US	031 02
AND THAT WE SHOW FORTH THY PRAISE, NOT ONLY WITH OUR	033 25
TO THY LAW, WE MAY SHOW FORTH THY PRAISE AMONG THE	036 20
DOCTRINE THEY MAY SHOW FORTH THY GLORY, AND SET	039 03
SHOW THY LOVING-KINDNESS, THAT OUR LAND MAY GIVE HER	040 10
SET IT FORTH, AND SHOW IT ACCORDINGLY	055 33
AND TO SHOW THY PITY UPON ALL PRISONERS AND CAPTIVES	056 32
AND MY MOUTH SHALL SHOW THY PRAISE	061 10
AND SHOW MERCY UNTO THOUSANDS IN THEM THAT LOVE ME	068 14
IN REMEMBRANCE, MAY SHOW FORTH OUR THANKFULNESS UNTO	229 21
AND SHOW MERCY UNTO THOUSANDS IN THEM THAT LOVE ME	286 14
SHOW THY SERVANTS THY WORK	290 08
IF ANY MAN CAN SHOW JUST CAUSE, WHY THEY MAY NOT	300 20
THOU SHALT SHOW ME THE PATH OF LIFE	333 09
WHO WILL SHOW US ANY GOOD	347 23
SHOW THE PEOPLE OF HIS DOINGS	352 11
14 THAT I MAY SHOW ALL THY PRAISES WITHIN THE GATES	352 19
12 THOU SHALT SHOW ME THE PATH OF LIFE	358 12
7 SHOW THY MARVELLOUS LOVING-KINDNESS, THOU THAT ART	358 31
3 SHOW ME THY WAYS, O LORD, *	369 24
AND HE WILL SHOW THEM HIS COVENANT	370 13

SHOW   CONTINUED

7 THAT I MAY SHOW THE VOICE OF THANKSGIVING, *	371 10
18 SHOW THY SERVANT THE LIGHT OF THY COUNTENANCE,	376 28
AND SHOW MY DARK SPEECH UPON THE HARP	400 12
WAY ARIGHT, WILL I SHOW THE SALVATION OF GOD	403 05
AND MY MOUTH SHALL SHOW THY PRAISE	404 08
5 THOU SHALT SHOW US WONDERFUL THINGS IN THY	416 21
AND SHOW US THE LIGHT OF HIS COUNTENANCE, AND BE	418 23
BUT TO SHOW THE HONOUR OF THE LORD, HIS MIGHTY AND	435 02
THEY MIGHT SHOW THEIR CHILDREN THE SAME	435 10
SHOW THYSELF ALSO, THOU THAT SITTEST UPON THE	441 04
SHOW THE LIGHT OF THY COUNTENANCE, AND WE SHALL BE	441 08
SHOW THE LIGHT OF THY COUNTENANCE, AND WE SHALL BE	441 16
SHOW THE LIGHT OF THY COUNTENANCE, AND WE SHALL BE	442 09
7 SHOW US THY MERCY, O LORD, *	446 20
THE LORD SHALL SHOW LOVING-KINDNESS	446 31
17 SHOW SOME TOKEN UPON ME FOR GOOD	448 09
10 DOST THOU SHOW WONDERS AMONG THE DEAD	449 16
16 SHOW THY SERVANTS THY WORK, *	454 22
AND SHOW HIM MY SALVATION	455 29
14 THAT THEY MAY SHOW HOW TRUE THE LORD MY STRENGTH	456 30
SHOW THYSELF	457 20
AND SHOW OURSELVES GLAD IN HIM WITH PSALMS	459 08
5 SHOW YOURSELVES JOYFUL UNTO THE LORD, ALL YE LANDS	462 02
O SHOW YOURSELVES JOYFUL BEFORE THE LORD, THE KING	462 06
OR SHOW FORTH ALL HIS PRAISE	473 03
135 SHOW THE LIGHT OF THY COUNTENANCE UPON THY	499 08
SHOW THOU ME THE WAY THAT I SHOULD WALK IN	519 08
11 THEY SHOW THE GLORY OF THY KINGDOM, *	521 14
NAME OF GOD, AND SHOW WHAT THE CRIME OR IMPEDIMENT	530 25
NAME OF GOD, AND SHOW WHAT THE CRIME OR IMPEDIMENT	536 30
AS WELL TO SHOW YOURSELVES DUTIFUL AND THANKFUL UNTO	540 27
WE MAY CONTINUE TO SHOW OURSELVES THANKFUL UNTO THEE	545 28
THAT YOU MAY SHOW YOURSELF IN ALL THINGS AN EXAMPLE	555 10
WILL YOU SHOW YOURSELF GENTLE, AND BE	555 23
I WILL SO SHOW MYSELF, BY GOD'S HELP	555 26
PIOUS WORK, MAY SHOW FORTH THEIR THANKFULNESS, BY	566 32
MAY IN THEIR LIVES SHOW FORTH THY PRAISE	567 09
IF ANY OF YOU CAN SHOW JUST CAUSE WHY HE MAY NOT BE	570 17
AND SHOW MERCY UNTO THOUSANDS IN THEM THAT LOVE ME	578 33
TO GIVE US GRACE TO SHOW OUR THANKFULNESS IN A	591 21

SHOWED

HE HATH SHOWED STRENGTH WITH HIS ARM	026 20
HATH HE OPENLY SHOWED IN THE SIGHT OF THE HEATHEN	027 09
LET THY MERCY BE SHOWED UPON US	059 18
LOVE HAST THOU SHOWED FOR HIS NAME'S SAKE, WHO HAVE	072 25
FOR HE HATH SHOWED ME MARVELLOUS GREAT KINDNESS IN A	377 09
BUT GOD HATH SHOWED HIS VOICE, AND THE EARTH SHALL	398 05
3 THOU HAST SHOWED THY PEOPLE HEAVY THINGS	412 17
UNTIL I HAVE SHOWED THY STRENGTH UNTO THIS	426 11
HAST THOU SHOWED ME	426 18
WORKS THAT HE HAD SHOWED FOR THEM	435 23
BE OPENLY SHOWED UPON THE HEATHEN, IN OUR SIGHT	440 24
BE SHOWED IN THE GRAVE	449 18
HATH HE OPENLY SHOWED IN THE SIGHT OF THE HEATHEN	461 30
7 HE SHOWED HIS WAYS UNTO MOSES, *	466 19
27 AND THESE SHOWED HIS TOKENS AMONG THEM, *	471 26
6 HE HATH SHOWED HIS PEOPLE THE POWER OF HIS WORKS,	483 05
WHO HATH SHOWED US LIGHT	489 22
AND SHOWED HIM OF MY TROUBLE	518 05
OF THINE ABUNDANT KINDNESS SHALL BE SHOWED	521 07

SHOWER

I WILL CAUSE THE SHOWER TO COME DOWN IN HIS SEASON	262 08

SHOWERS

O YE SHOWERS AND DEW, BLESS YE THE LORD	012 14
RAIN AND SHOWERS, THAT WE MAY RECEIVE THE FRUITS OF	040 19
THERE SHALL BE SHOWERS OF BLESSING	262 09

SHOWEST

THY GLORY AND SHOWEST FORTH THY HANDIWORK IN THE	044 18
WHO SHOWEST TO THEM THAT ARE IN ERROR THE LIGHT	173 04

SHOWETH

AND SHOWETH LOVING-KINDNESS UNTO DAVID HIS ANOINTED,	363 07
THE FIRMAMENT SHOWETH HIS HANDY-WORK	363 14
MY HEART SHOWETH ME THE WICKEDNESS OF THE UNGODLY,	383 26
10 GOD SHOWETH ME HIS GOODNESS PLENTEOUSLY	411 24
19 HE SHOWETH HIS WORD UNTO JACOB, *	523 33

SHOWING

POWER CHIEFLY IN SHOWING MERCY AND PITY	204 23
WILL ALWAY BE SHOWING FORTH THY PRAISE FROM	440 33
WILL I EVER BE SHOWING THY TRUTH FROM ONE GENERATION	450 05

SHRINK

AND WILL NOT SHRINK, *	483 32
AND HE SHALL NOT SHRINK FROM IT	508 26

SHRINKED

YET HAVE I NOT SHRINKED FROM THY LAW	493 13

SHRUNK

102 I HAVE NOT SHRUNK FROM THY JUDGMENTS	496 30

SHUNNED

FOR I HAVE NOT SHUNNED TO DECLARE UNTO YOU ALL THE   550 25

SHUT

WHEN THE DOORS WERE SHUT WHERE THE DISCIPLES WERE   171 15
THE DOORS BEING SHUT, AND STOOD IN THE MIDST, AND   229 02
THE DOOR IS NOW SHUT, AND MY CHILDREN ARE WITH ME IN   262 30
AND WILL HE SHUT UP HIS LOVING-KINDNESS IN   311 16
SHUT NOT THY MERCIFUL EARS TO OUR PRAYER   332 28
9 O SHUT NOT UP MY SOUL WITH THE SINNERS, *   371 14
9 THOU HAST NOT SHUT ME UP INTO THE HAND OF THE   376 06
AND LET NOT THE PIT SHUT HER MCUTH UPON ME   423 02
AND WILL HE SHUT UP HIS LOVING-KINDNESS IN   433 33
WHEN THE DOORS WERE SHUT WHERE THE DISCIPLES WERE   551 28

SHUTTETH

HAVE NEED, AND SHUTTETH UP HIS COMPASSION FROM HIM,   072 30
HAVE NEED, AND SHUTTETH UP HIS BOWELS OF COMPASSICN   191 19

SICK

AND SKILL TO ALL THOSE WHO MINISTER TO THE SICK   045 06
AND RELIEVE THY SICK SERVANT (N   045 14
PRAY THEE, OVER THE SICK CHILD FOR WHOM OUR PRAYERS   045 25
IN CHILD-BIRTH, ALL SICK PERSONS, AND YOUNG CHILDREN   056 31
LIETH AT HOME SICK OF THE PALSY, GRIEVOUSLY   115 08
TO HIM A MAN SICK OF THE PALSY, LYING CN A BED   217 02
SAID UNTO THE SICK OF THE PALSY   217 03
SAITH HE TO THE SICK OF THE PALSY,) ARISE, TAKE UP   217 10
WHOSE SON WAS SICK AT CAPERNAUM   219 28
BROUGHT FORTH THE SICK INTO THE STREETS, AND LAID   249 27
BRINGING SICK FOLKS, AND THEM WHICH WERE   249 31
NEED NOT A PHYSICIAN, BUT THEY THAT ARE SICK   251 21
I WAS SICK, AND YE VISITED ME   259 08
OR WHEN SAW WE THEE SICK, OR IN PRISON, AND CAME UNTO   259 13
WHEN ANY PERSON IS SICK, NOTICE SHALL BE GIVEN   R 308 05
COMING UNTO THE SICK PERSON'S PRESENCE, SHALL SAY,   R 308 06
SHALL ADDRESS THE SICK PERSON CN THE MEANING AND USE   R 313 15
INQUIRE OF THE SICK PERSON AS TO HIS ACCEPTANCE OF   R 313 18
THEN SHALL THE SICK PERSON BE MOVED TO MAKE A   R 313 24
AND CONTINUE THIS SICK MEMBER IN THE UNITY OF THE   314 06
WHEN ANY SICK PERSON SHALL IN HUMBLE FAITH DESIRE   R 320 05
BUT IF THE SICK PERSON BE NOT ABLE TO COME TO THE   R 321 11
WITH THE SICK, AND LAST OF ALL TO THE SICK PERSCN   R 323 02
LAST OF ALL TO THE SICK PERSON   R 323 03
WHEN THEY WERE SICK, I PUT ON SACKCLOTH, AND HUMBLED   382 17
HIM WHEN HE LIETH SICK UPON HIS BED   392 04
TO SEARCH FOR THE SICK, POOR, AND IMPOTENT PEOPLE OF   533 19
AS WELL TO THE SICK AS TO THE WHOLE, WITHIN YOUR   542 23
THE WEAK, HEAL THE SICK, BIND UP THE BROKEN, BRING   558 27
THE SICK AND THE AFFLICTED, AND THOSE WHO   600 06

SICKNESS

OF GRIEVOUS SICKNESS, WE FLEE UNTO THEE FOR SUCCOUR   045 04
THE SEA, FROM SICKNESS, FROM THE VIOLENCE OF ENEMIES,   046 12
ALL WHO ARE IN SICKNESS OR IN SORROW   048 06
FROM HIS BODILY SICKNESS THIS THY SERVANT, WHO NOW   052 31
FROM HIS BODILY SICKNESS THE CHILD IN WHOSE BEHALF WE   053 12
NEED, SICKNESS, OR ANY OTHER ADVERSITY   074 32
AND GIVETH MEDICINE TO HEAL THEIR SICKNESS   264 24
OF EXTREME SICKNESS, NECESSITY MAY REQUIRE, THEN THE   R 281 17
OF EXTREME SICKNESS, OR ANY IMMINENT PERIL, IF A   R 281 27
AND KEEP HER IN SICKNESS AND IN HEALTH   301 09
AND KEEP HIM IN SICKNESS AND IN HEALTH   301 17
FOR POORER, IN SICKNESS AND IN HEALTH, TO LOVE AND TO   301 30
FOR POORER, IN SICKNESS AND IN HEALTH, TO LOVE ANC TO   302 06
TO THIS THY SERVANT WHO IS GRIEVED WITH SICKNESS   309 29
O LORD, THE SICKNESS OF THIS THY SERVANT   310 21
THAT HIS SICKNESS MAY BE TURNED INTO HEALTH,   312 14
OF THE TIME OF SICKNESS, AND THE OPPORTUNITY IT   R 313 16
BODIES ALL SICKNESS AND ALL INFIRMITY   315 07
THAT THOU DIDST NOT FORSAKE HIM IN HIS SICKNESS   315 24
THY PAIN AND SICKNESS OF BODY BEING PUT TO FLIGHT,   320 18
INFECTIOUS SICKNESS, EXHORT THEIR PARISHIONERS TC THE R 321 07
HE MAY TAKE HIS SICKNESS PATIENTLY, AND RECCVER HIS   321 22
EVERY CAUSE OF SICKNESS BEING REMOVED, HE MAY BE   322 08
OF EXTREMITY OF SICKNESS, OR FOR WANT OF WARNING IN   R 323 23
MAKE THOU ALL HIS BED IN HIS SICKNESS   392 05
NOR FOR THE SICKNESS THAT DESTROYETH IN THE NCON-DAY   455 08
AND GIVETH MEDICINE TO HEAL THEIR SICKNESS   522 33

SICKNESSES

AND SICKNESSES, AND EVER UNCERTAIN WHAT   R 321 03

SIDE

WITH HIM, ON EITHER SIDE ONE, AND JESUS IN THE MIDST   159 34
A SPEAR PIERCED HIS SIDE, AND FORTHWITH CAME THERE   161 04
ON THE RIGHT SIDE, CLOTHED IN A LONG WHITE GARMENT   165 27
HE SHEWED UNTO THEM HIS HANDS AND HIS SIDE   171 19
THEE IN ON EVERY SIDE, AND SHALL LAY THEE EVEN WITH   204 12
HE PASSED BY ON THE OTHER SIDE   208 26
AND PASSED BY ON THE OTHER SIDE   208 27
MY HAND INTO HIS SIDE, I WILL NOT BELIEVE   228 30
REACH HITHER THY HAND, AND THRUST IT INTO MY SIDE   229 15
SMOTE PETER ON THE SIDE, AND RAISED HIM UP, SAYING,   245 14
HIS MOST PRECIOUS SIDE BOTH WATER AND BLOOD   279 11
9 THE UNGODLY WALK ON EVERY SIDE   355 25
IN OUR WAY ON EVERY SIDE, *   359 08
FAT BULLS OF BASHAN CLOSE ME IN ON EVERY SIDE   366 28
OF THE MULTITUDE, AND FEAR IS ON EVERY SIDE   376 22

SIDE   CONTINUED

MERCY EMBRACETH HIM ON EVERY SIDE   378 15
UPON THE NORTH SIDE LIETH THE CITY OF THE GREAT KING   399 13
FOR GOD IS ON MY SIDE   408 33
AND THE LITTLE HILLS SHALL REJOICE CN EVERY SIDE   417 10
AND COMFORTED ME ON EVERY SIDE   426 21
LIKE WATER ON EVERY SIDE OF JERUSALEM, *   440 04
AND COMPASSED ME TOGETHER ON EVERY SIDE   449 32
MOST MIGHTY LORD, IS ON EVERY SIDE   450 23
AND BURN UP HIS ENEMIES ON EVERY SIDE   461 03
6 THE LORD IS ON EVERY SIDE   488 10
KEPT ME IN ON EVERY SIDE, THEY KEPT ME IN, I SAY, CN   488 20
EVERY SIDE, THEY KEPT ME IN, I SAY, ON EVERY SIDE   488 21
HAD NOT BEEN ON OUR SIDE, NOW MAY ISRAEL SAY   504 07
HAD NOT BEEN ON OUR SIDE, WHEN MEN ROSE UP AGAINST   504 09
HE SHEWED UNTO THEM HIS HANDS AND HIS SIDE   551 32
TROUBLED ON EVERY SIDE, SUFFER THEM NOT TO BE   599 14

SIDON

AND DEPARTED INTO THE COASTS OF TYRE AND SIDON   128 08
COASTS OF TYRE AND SIDON, CAME UNTO THE SEA OF   206 27

SIEGE

THE WICKED LAYETH SIEGE AGAINST ME   367 05

SIFT

THAT HE MAY SIFT YOU AS WHEAT   149 32

SIGHED

UP TO HEAVEN, HE SIGHED, AND SAITH UNTO HIM,   207 02

SIGHING

NOT THE SIGHING OF A CONTRITE HEART, NOR THE DESIRE   058 15
OF THE DEEP SIGHING OF THE POOR, 6 I WILL UP, SAITH   355 17
THE SORROWFUL SIGHING OF THE PRISONERS COME BEFORE   440 26
THE SORROWFUL SIGHING OF THE PRISONERS COME BEFORE   600 09

SIGHT

ACCEPTABLE IN THY SIGHT, O LORD, MY STRENGTH AND MY   003 20
MAY BE RIGHTEOUS IN THY SIGHT   017 18
SET FORTH IN THY SIGHT AS THE INCENSE   021 16
ACCEPTABLE IN THY SIGHT, O LORD, MY STRENGTH AND MY   021 22
SHOWED IN THE SIGHT OF THE HEATHEN   027 09
AND DONE THIS EVIL IN THY SIGHT   060 18
AND IN THEIR SIGHT ASCENDED UP INTO HEAVEN, TO   078 19
PEOPLE IN THY SIGHT, WHO LIVEST AND REIGNEST WITH THE   093 30
RECEIVE THEIR SIGHT, AND THE LAME WALK, THE LEPERS   094 21
HONEST IN THE SIGHT OF ALL MEN   112 32
THAT I MAY RECEIVE MY SIGHT   124 02
AND JESUS SAID UNTO HIM, RECEIVE THY SIGHT   124 03
HE RECEIVED HIS SIGHT, AND FOLLOWED HIM, GLORIFYING   124 04
TOGETHER TO THAT SIGHT, BEHOLDING THE THINGS WHICH   155 17
AND HE VANISHED OUT OF THEIR SIGHT   168 08
AND A CLOUD RECEIVED HIM OUT OF THEIR SIGHT   178 14
THE THRONE, IN SIGHT LIKE UNTO AN EMERALD   187 08
DO THOSE THINGS THAT ARE PLEASING IN HIS SIGHT   191 29
AND IN THY SIGHT, AND AM NO MORE WORTHY TO BE   202 20
OUR FAITH IN THY SIGHT MAY NEVER BE REPROVED   228 09
THREE DAYS WITHOUT SIGHT, AND NEITHER DID EAT NOR   230 13
THAT HE MIGHT RECEIVE HIS SIGHT   230 21
RECEIVE THY SIGHT, AND BE FILLED WITH THE HOLY GHOST   230 33
AND HE RECEIVED SIGHT FORTHWITH, AND AROSE, AND WAS   230 35
FOR SO IT SEEMED GOOD IN THY SIGHT   235 07
CONSCIENCE IN THE SIGHT OF GOD   250 32
AND RECOVERING OF SIGHT TO THE BLIND, TO SET AT   261 19
HERE IN THE SIGHT OF GOD, AND IN THE FACE OF THIS   300 09
THAT IT MAY BE PRECIOUS IN THY SIGHT   317 16
YEARS IN THY SIGHT ARE BUT AS YESTERDAY, WHEN IT IS   325 20
LAST DAY, WE MAY BE FOUND ACCEPTABLE IN THY SIGHT   335 09
IN YOU THAT WHICH IS WELL PLEASING IN HIS SIGHT   335 20
5 SUCH AS BE FOOLISH SHALL NOT STAND IN THY SIGHT   348 09
LET THE HEATHEN BE JUDGED IN THY SIGHT   352 31
ABOVE OUT OF HIS SIGHT, AND THEREFORE DEFIETH HE ALL   353 14
ACCEPTABLE IN THY SIGHT, *   364 14
I PERFORM IN THE SIGHT OF THEM THAT FEAR HIM   367 24
AM CAST OUT OF THE SIGHT OF THINE EYES   377 11
HIMSELF IN HIS OWN SIGHT, *   383 28
AND MY HEAVINESS IS EVER IN MY SIGHT   388 27
WHILE THE UNGODLY IS IN MY SIGHT   389 08
AND THE WILD BEASTS OF THE FIELD ARE IN MY SIGHT   402 13
AND DONE THIS EVIL IN THY SIGHT   403 16
MY SIGHT FAILETH ME FOR WAITING SO LONG UPON MY GOD   422 05
MINE ADVERSARIES ARE ALL IN THY SIGHT   423 12
AND DEAR SHALL THEIR BLOOD BE IN HIS SIGHT   427 25
MAY STAND IN THY SIGHT WHEN THOU ART ANGRY   433 03
DID HE IN THE SIGHT OF OUR FOREFATHERS, IN THE LAND   435 24
BE OPENLY SHOWED UPON THE HEATHEN, IN OUR SIGHT   440 25
9 MY SIGHT FAILETH FOR VERY TROUBLE   449 14
AND HID MINE ACQUAINTANCE OUT OF MY SIGHT   449 34
YEARS IN THY SIGHT ARE BUT AS YESTERDAY WHEN IT IS   453 25
SHOWED IN THE SIGHT OF THE HEATHEN   461 30
HE THAT TELLETH LIES SHALL NOT TARRY IN MY SIGHT   464 03
AND THEIR SEED SHALL STAND FAST IN THY SIGHT   466 06
REMEMBRANCE IN THE SIGHT OF THE LORD   480 28
RIGHT DEAR IN THE SIGHT OF THE LORD IS THE DEATH OF   487 14
THE LORD, IN THE SIGHT OF ALL HIS PEOPLE, *   487 21
AND THE JUST SHALL CONTINUE IN THY SIGHT   517 05
SET FORTH IN THY SIGHT AS THE INCENSE   517 10
FOR IN THY SIGHT SHALL NO MAN LIVING BE JUSTIFIED   518 26

SIGHT   CONTINUED

THE LORD GIVETH SIGHT TO THE BLIND   522 17
PERPETUAL LIGHT THE DULLNESS OF OUR BLINDED SIGHT   544 05
PERPETUAL LIGHT THE DULLNESS OF OUR BLINDED SIGHT   556 13
ACCEPTABLE IN THY SIGHT, O LORD, OUR STRENGTH AND OUR   572 23
IN YOU THAT WHICH IS WELL PLEASING IN HIS SIGHT   573 07
MAY BE RIGHTEOUS IN THY SIGHT   592 24

SIGILLUM

SIGILLUM SIGNAT   R 569 41

SIGN

AND THIS SHALL BE A SIGN UNTO YOU   099 18
SHALL APPEAR THE SIGN OF THE SON OF MAN IN HEAVEN   118 17
SOUGHT OF HIM A SIGN FROM HEAVEN   129 28
AND FOR A SIGN WHICH SHALL BE SPOKEN AGAINST   233 13
ASK THEE A SIGN OF THE LORD THY GOD   235 26
THEREFORE THE LORD HIMSELF SHALL GIVE YOU A SIGN   235 31
SIGN HIM WITH THE SIGN OF THE CROSS, IN TOKEN THAT   280 04
SIGN HIM WITH THE SIGN OF THE CROSS, IN TOKEN THAT   280 05
OUTWARD AND VISIBLE SIGN OF AN INWARD AND SPIRITUAL   292 11
OUTWARD AND VISIBLE SIGN, AND THE INWARD AND   292 16
OUTWARD AND VISIBLE SIGN OR FORM IN BAPTISM   292 17
OUTWARD AND VISIBLE SIGN OR FORM IN BAPTISM IS WATER   292 19
THE OUTWARD PART OR SIGN OF THE LORD'S SUPPER   293 08
THE OUTWARD PART OR SIGN OF THE LORD'S SUPPER IS,   293 10
BY THIS SIGN, OF THY FAVOUR AND GRACIOUS   298 18
OUTWARD AND VISIBLE SIGN OF AN INWARD AND SPIRITUAL   581 12
THE OUTWARD VISIBLE SIGN, AND THE INWARD SPIRITUAL   581 17
THE OUTWARD VISIBLE SIGN OR FORM IN BAPTISM   581 19
THE OUTWARD PART OR SIGN OF THE LORD'S SUPPER   582 07
NOT ANY VISIBLE SIGN OR CEREMONY ORDAINED OF GOD   607 43
IS NOT ONLY A SIGN OF PROFESSION, AND MARK OF   608 24
BUT IT IS ALSO A SIGN OF REGENERATION OR NEW-BIRTH,   608 26
LORD IS NOT ONLY A SIGN OF THE LOVE THAT CHRISTIANS   608 34
EAT AND DRINK THE SIGN OR SACRAMENT OF SO GREAT A   609 07

SIGNAT

SIGILLUM SIGNAT   R 569 41

SIGNATURE

SEAL AND SIGNATURE, AT --, THIS -- DAY OF --, A   569 38

SIGNED

ARE VISIBLY SIGNED AND SEALED   608 29

SIGNIFIED

AND SIGNIFIED BY THE SPIRIT THAT THERE SHOULD   241 17
AND SIGNIFIED BY THE SPIRIT THAT THERE SHOULD   246 26
WHAT IS THE INWARD PART, OR THING SIGNIFIED   293 13
OR THING SIGNIFIED, IS THE BODY AND BLOOD OF   293 14
WHAT IS THE INWARD PART, OR THING SIGNIFIED   582 11

SIGNIFYING

OF GOD, SIGNIFYING UNTO US THE MYSTICAL UNION THAT IS   300 12
THE MINISTER, SIGNIFYING ALSO HOW MANY THERE ARE TO   R 321 13

SIGNS

AND THERE SHALL BE SIGNS IN THE SUN, AND IN THE MOON,   093 05
SHALL SHEW GREAT SIGNS AND WONDERS   118 05
EXCEPT YE SEE SIGNS AND WONDERS, YE WILL NOT   219 33
AND MANY OTHER SIGNS TRULY DID JESUS IN THE PRESENCE   229 09
AND THEY MADE SIGNS TO HIS FATHER, HOW HE WOULD HAVE   243 22
APOSTLES WERE MANY SIGNS AND WONDERS WROUGHT AMONG   249 21
AND EFFECTUAL SIGNS OF GRACE, AND GOD'S GOOD WILL   607 33

SIHON

11 SIHON, KING OF THE AMORITES   510 24
19 SIHON, KING OF THE AMORITES   512 20

SILENCE

THE EARTH KEEP SILENCE BEFORE HIM   003 16
THE EARTH KEEP SILENCE BEFORE HIM   021 13
YE MAY PUT TO SILENCE THE IGNORANCE OF FOOLISH MEN   173 22
THE SADDUCEES TO SILENCE, THEY WERE GATHERED   215 07
AND BE PUT TO SILENCE IN THE GRAVE   376 32
LIPS BE PUT TO SILENCE, *   376 33
I KEPT SILENCE, YEA, EVEN FROM GOOD WORDS   389 09
AND SHALL NOT KEEP SILENCE   401 25
O GOD, KEEP NOT STILL SILENCE   444 05
NOT FAILED, BUT MY SOUL HAD BEEN PUT TO SILENCE   458 21
NEITHER ALL THEY THAT GO DOWN INTO SILENCE   486 13
THERE SHALL BE SILENCE KEPT FOR A SPACE   R 543 25

SILVER

THIRTY PIECES OF SILVER TO THE CHIEF PRIESTS AND   135 04
THE PIECES OF SILVER IN THE TEMPLE, AND DEPARTED, AND   135 07
PRIESTS TOOK THE SILVER PIECES, AND SAID, IT IS NOT   135 09
THIRTY PIECES OF SILVER, THE PRICE OF HIM THAT WAS   135 15
TEN PIECES OF SILVER, IF SHE LOSE ONE PIECE, DOTH NOT   193 28
HE SHALL SIT AS A REFINER AND PURIFIER OF SILVER   232 10
THEM AS GOLD AND SILVER, THAT THEY MAY OFFER UNTO THE   232 12
EVEN AS THE SILVER WHICH FROM THE EARTH IS TRIED,   355 21
TRIED US, LIKE AS SILVER IS TRIED   417 34

SILVER   CONTINUED

IS COVERED WITH SILVER WINGS, AND HER FEATHERS LIKE   420 07
SO THAT THEY HUMBLY BRING PIECES OF SILVER   421 17
FORTH ALSO WITH SILVER AND GOLD   472 11
4 THEIR IDOLS ARE SILVER AND GOLD, *   485 18
THAN THOUSANDS OF GOLD AND SILVER   494 25
THEY ARE BUT SILVER AND GOLD   510 32
COVETED NO MAN'S SILVER, OR GOLD, OR APPAREL   551 05

SIMEON

WAS A MAN IN JERUSALEM, WHOSE NAME WAS SIMEON   232 30
AND SIMEON BLESSED THEM, AND SAID UNTO MARY HIS   233 11

SIMILITUDE

INTO THE SIMILITUDE OF A CALF THAT EATETH HAY   474 08

SIMON

ANDREW, SIMON PETER'S BROTHER, SAITH UNTO   131 32
A MAN OF CYRENE, SIMON BY NAME   136 26
IN THE HOUSE OF SIMON THE LEPER, AS HE SAT AT MEAT,   140 03
SAITH UNTO PETER, SIMON, SLEEPEST THOU   142 04
THEY COMPEL ONE SIMON A CYRENIAN, WHO PASSED BY,   146 05
LORD SAID, SIMON, SIMON, BEHOLD, SATAN HATH DESIRED   149 31
AND THE LORD SAID, SIMON, SIMON, BEHOLD, SATAN HATH   149 31
LAID HOLD UPON ONE SIMON, A CYRENIAN, COMING OUT OF   154 09
THEN COMETH HE TO SIMON PETER   156 02
SIMON PETER SAITH UNTO HIM, LORD, NOT MY FEET ONLY,   156 07
AND COMETH TO SIMON PETER, AND TO THE OTHER DISCIPLE,   164 13
THEN COMETH SIMON PETER FOLLOWING HIM, AND WENT INTO   164 21
LORD IS RISEN INDEED, AND HATH APPEARED TO SIMON   168 14
HE SAID UNTO SIMON, LAUNCH OUT INTO THE DEEP, AND LET   196 14
AND SIMON ANSWERING SAID UNTO HIM, MASTER, WE HAVE   196 15
WHEN SIMON PETER SAW IT, HE FELL DOWN AT JESUS'   196 22
WHICH WERE PARTNERS WITH SIMON   196 27
JESUS SAID UNTO SIMON, FEAR NOT   196 28
ANDREW, SIMON PETER'S BROTHER, SAITH UNTO   225 28
SAW TWO BRETHREN, SIMON CALLED PETER, AND ANDREW HIS   227 25
AND SIMON PETER ANSWERED AND SAID, THOU ART THE   246 02
BLESSED ART THOU, SIMON BAR-JONA   246 04
TO SIMON PETER, SIMON, SON OF JONAS, LOVEST THOU ME   551 14
JESUS SAITH TO SIMON PETER, SIMON, SON OF JONAS,   551 14
THE SECOND TIME, SIMON, SON OF JONAS, LOVEST THOU ME   551 17
THE THIRD TIME, SIMON, SON OF JONAS, LOVEST THOU ME   551 20

SIMON'S

JUDAS ISCARIOT, SIMON'S SON, TO BETRAY HIM   155 28
WHICH WAS SIMON'S, AND PRAYED HIM THAT HE   196 11

SIMPLE

LORD IS SURE, AND GIVETH WISDOM UNTO THE SIMPLE   363 29
HE SHALL KEEP THE SIMPLE FOLK BY THEIR RIGHT, *   427 04
FAVOURABLE TO THE SIMPLE AND NEEDY, *   427 22
22 O LET NOT THE SIMPLE GO AWAY ASHAMED   431 20
HE TAKETH UP THE SIMPLE OUT OF THE DUST, *   484 19
6 THE LORD PRESERVETH THE SIMPLE   486 30
IT GIVETH LIGHT AND UNDERSTANDING UNTO THE SIMPLE   498 31

SIMPLENESS

KNOWEST MY SIMPLENESS, AND MY FAULTS ARE NOT HID FROM   422 11

SIMPLICITY

LET HIM DO IT WITH SIMPLICITY   111 20

SIN

TO KEEP US THIS DAY WITHOUT SIN   011 08
DAY WE FALL INTO NO SIN, NEITHER RUN INTO ANY KIND OF   017 16
AND MY SIN IS EVER BEFORE ME   022 04
SAY THAT WE HAVE NO SIN, WE DECEIVE OURSELVES,   022 10
FORGIVETH ALL THY SIN, *   029 08
DOWN THE KINGDOM OF SIN, SATAN, AND DEATH   037 05
FROM THE CHAINS OF SIN, AND MAY BE BROUGHT TO NEWNESS   046 28
FOR ALL WHO HAVE FALLEN INTO GRIEVOUS SIN   048 07
FROM SIN   054 19
AND CLEANSE ME FROM MY SIN   060 14
AND MY SIN IS EVER BEFORE ME   060 15
AND IN SIN HATH MY MOTHER CONCEIVED ME   060 20
WHOSE CONSCIENCES BY SIN ARE ACCUSED, BY THY MERCIFUL   062 10
SHOULD TURN FROM HIS SIN, AND BE SAVED   062 16
IF ANY MAN SIN, WE HAVE AN ADVOCATE WITH THE FATHER,   076 22
TO MAKE US CLEAN FROM ALL SIN   077 18
THAT WITHOUT SPOT OF SIN, TO MAKE US CLEAN FROM ALL   077 18
HATH TAKEN AWAY THE SIN OF THE WORLD   078 10
LAY NOT THIS SIN TO THEIR CHARGE   100 16
OF JESUS CHRIST HIS SON CLEANSETH US FROM ALL SIN   101 28
SAY THAT WE HAVE NO SIN, WE DECEIVE OURSELVES,   101 29
WHOSOEVER COMMITTETH SIN TRANSGRESSETH ALSO THE LAW   117 21
FOR SIN IS THE TRANSGRESSION OF THE LAW   117 22
AND IN HIM IS NO SIN   117 24
HE THAT COMMITTETH SIN IS OF THE DEVIL   117 28
WHICH OF YOU CONVINCETH ME OF SIN   133 09
APPEARED TO PUT AWAY SIN BY THE SACRIFICE OF HIMSELF   148 06
SECOND TIME WITHOUT SIN UNTO SALVATION   148 10
AND SACRIFICES FOR SIN THOU HAST HAD NO PLEASURE   157 26
AND OFFERING FOR SIN THOU WOULDEST NOT, NEITHER HADST   157 30
THERE IS NO MORE OFFERING FOR SIN   158 16
THAT DELIVERED ME UNTO THEE HATH THE GREATER SIN   159 18
HE DIED UNTO SIN ONCE   163 06

SIN   CONTINUED

BE DEAD INDEED UNTO SIN, *   163 09
SO TO DIE DAILY FROM SIN, THAT WE MAY EVERMORE LIVE   165 06
BOTH A SACRIFICE FOR SIN, AND ALSO AN ENSAMPLE OF   171 29
WHO DID NO SIN, NEITHER WAS GUILE FOUND IN HIS MOUTH   172 12
REPROVE THE WORLD OF SIN, AND OF RIGHTECUSNESS,   175 13
OF SIN, BECAUSE THEY BELIEVE NOT ON ME   175 14
THAT THE BODY OF SIN MIGHT BE DESTROYED, THAT   197 18
THAT HENCEFORTH WE SHOULD NOT SERVE SIN   197 19
FOR HE THAT IS DEAD IS FREED FROM SIN   197 20
HE DIED UNTO SIN ONCE   197 23
BE DEAD INDEED UNTO SIN, BUT ALIVE UNTO GOD THROUGH   197 25
WERE THE SERVANTS OF SIN, YE WERE FREE FROM   198 30
BEING MADE FREE FROM SIN, AND BECOME SERVANTS TO GOD,   199 02
FOR THE WAGES OF SIN IS DEATH   199 04
CONCLUDED ALL UNDER SIN, THAT THE PROMISE BY FAITH OF   208 03
BE YE ANGRY, AND SIN NOT   216 18
OFT SHALL MY BROTHER SIN AGAINST ME, AND I FORGIVE   221 10
COME AND SPOKEN UNTO THEM, THEY HAD NOT HAD SIN   255 23
BUT NOW THEY HAVE NO CLOKE FOR THEIR SIN   255 24
WHICH NONE OTHER MAN DID, THEY HAD NOT HAD SIN   255 26
AND THE SIN WHICH DOTH SO EASILY BESET US,   258 22
RECEIVE REMISSION OF SIN, BY SPIRITUAL REGENERATION   274 13
TO RELEASE HIM FROM SIN, TO SANCTIFY HIM WITH THE   276 22
TO RELEASE YOU FROM SIN, TO SANCTIFY YOU WITH THE   277 27
SERVANT) MAY DIE TO SIN AND RISE TO NEWNESS OF LIFE   278 20
THIS WATER TO THE MYSTICAL WASHING AWAY OF SIN   279 16
HIS BANNER, AGAINST SIN, THE WORLD, AND THE DEVIL   280 08
BEING DEAD UNTO SIN, MAY LIVE UNTO RIGHTEOUSNESS,   280 33
IS A DEATH UNTO SIN, AND A NEW BIRTH UNTO   292 25
REPENTANCE, WHEREBY THEY FORSAKE SIN   292 28
FORGIVETH ALL THY SIN, AND HEALETH ALL THINE   312 24
ALL EVIL, FROM ALL SIN, FROM ALL TRIBULATION   318 02
RELEASE HIM FROM SIN, AND DRIVE AWAY ALL PAIN OF SOUL   320 10
DOST CHASTEN MAN FOR SIN, THOU MAKEST HIS BEAUTY TO   325 02
THE STING OF DEATH IS SIN   330 11
AND THE STRENGTH OF SIN IS THE LAW   330 12
US FROM THE DEATH OF SIN UNTO THE LIFE OF   335 06
4 STAND IN AWE, AND SIN NOT   347 19
BE MERCIFUL UNTO MY SIN   370 07
AND FORGIVE ME ALL MY SIN   370 21
AND WHOSE SIN IS COVERED   377 23
THE LORD IMPUTETH NO SIN, *   377 25
5 I ACKNOWLEDGED MY SIN UNTO THEE   377 30
AND SO THOU FORGAVEST THE WICKEDNESS OF MY SIN   377 33
UNTIL HIS ABOMINABLE SIN BE FOUND OUT   383 29
THERE ANY REST IN MY BONES, BY REASON OF MY SIN   387 27
AND BE SORRY FOR MY SIN   388 29
DOST CHASTEN MAN FOR SIN, THOU MAKEST HIS BEAUTY TO   389 31
AND SACRIFICE FOR SIN HAST THOU NOT REQUIRED   390 29
AND CLEANSE ME FROM MY SIN   403 12
AND MY SIN IS EVER BEFORE ME   403 13
AND IN SIN HATH MY MOTHER CONCEIVED ME   403 13
12 FOR THE SIN OF THEIR MOUTH, AND FOR THE WORDS OF   411 29
THE ROD, AND THEIR SIN WITH SCOURGES   452 06
FORGIVETH ALL THY SIN, *   466 12
AND LET HIS PRAYER BE TURNED INTO SIN   480 16
AND LET NOT THE SIN OF HIS MOTHER BE DONE AWAY   480 28
THAT I SHOULD NOT SIN AGAINST THEE   490 21
KEEP US FROM ALL SIN AND WICKEDNESS, AND FROM OUR   581 03
A DEATH UNTO SIN, AND A NEW BIRTH UNTO RIGHTEOUSNESS   581 24
BY NATURE BORN IN SIN, AND THE CHILDREN OF WRATH, WE   581 25
REPENTANCE, WHEREBY THEY FORSAKE SIN   581 28
RESTRAINED FROM SIN, AND INCITED TO OUR DUTY   588 17
BE DRAWN AGAIN INTO SIN, VOUCHSAFE US, WE BESEECH   590 10
TO REDEEM US FROM SIN AND ETERNAL DEATH, AND IN   591 13
DAY WE FALL INTO NO SIN, NEITHER RUN INTO ANY KIND OF   592 22
FALLING THOSE WHOSE PENURY TEMPTETH THEM TO SIN   599 13
ORIGINAL SIN STANDETH NOT IN THE FOLLOWING OF ADAM,   604 29
AND LUST HATH OF ITSELF THE NATURE OF SIN   604 40
WE DOUBT NOT BUT THEY HAVE THE NATURE OF SIN   605 22
US IN ALL THINGS, SIN ONLY EXCEPT, FROM WHICH HE WAS   605 31
AND SIN (AS SAINT JOHN SAITH) WAS NOT IN HIM   605 34
IF WE SAY WE HAVE NO SIN, WE DECEIVE OURSELVES, AND   605 36
AFTER BAPTISM IS SIN AGAINST THE HOLY GHOST, AND   605 39
NOT EVERY DEADLY SIN WILLINGLY COMMITTED AFTER   605 39
TO SUCH AS FALL INTO SIN AFTER BAPTISM   605 41
AND FALL INTO SIN, AND BY THE GRACE OF GOD WE   605 42
THEY CAN NO MORE SIN AS LONG AS THEY LIVE HERE,   606 03
THE FORGIVENESS OF SIN, AND OF OUR ADOPTION TO BE THE   608 28
SATISFACTION FOR SIN, BUT THAT ALONE   609 16

SINAI

ONE FROM THE MOUNT SINAI, WHICH GENDERETH TO BONDAGE,   131 04
THIS AGAR IS MOUNT SINAI IN ARABIA, AND ANSWERETH TO   131 05
EVEN AS SINAI ALSO WAS MOVED AT THE PRESENCE OF GOD,   419 27
LORD IS AMONG THEM AS IN THE HOLY PLACE OF SINAI   420 18

SINCE

SEVERAL PRINCES, SINCE THE FIRST COMPILING OF HER   V 27
WHICH HAVE BEEN SINCE THE WORLD BEGAN   014 13
AUTHORITY HAS NOT SINCE THOUGHT PROPER TO REVIVE IT   VI 06
HAVE SUFFERED SINCE THE FOUNDATION OF THE WORLD   148 04
FOR SINCE BY MAN CAME DEATH, *   163 13
IS THE THIRD DAY SINCE THESE THINGS WERE DONE   167 22
ALWAYS FOR YOU, SINCE WE HEARD OF YOUR FAITH IN   223 23
DOTH ALSO IN YOU, SINCE THE DAY YE HEARD OF IT,   223 29
CAUSE WE ALSO, SINCE THE DAY WE HEARD IT, DO NOT   223 33
WHICH HAVE BEEN SINCE THE WORLD BEGAN   244 02
FOR SINCE BY MAN CAME DEATH, BY MAN CAME ALSO THE   328 22
UNTO THEE EVER SINCE I WAS BORN   366 23
HOLDEN UP EVER SINCE I WAS BORN   425 16
3 EVER SINCE THE WORLD BEGAN, HATH THY SEAT BEEN   457 09

SINCE   CONTINUED

I HAVE KNOWN LONG SINCE, *   500 15
AND SINCE IT IS OF THY MERCY, O GRACIOUS FATHER,   588 04

SINCERE

AND EVERY SINCERE CHRISTIAN, WITH A MEEK, CANDID,   VI 37
THAT YE MAY BE SINCERE AND WITHOUT OFFENCE TILL THE   221 04
DESIRE THE SINCERE MILK OF THE WORD, THAT YE MAY GROW   259 27
IN A SINCERE OBEDIENCE TO HIS LAWS, THROUGH WHOSE   591 21

SINCERITY

BREAD OF SINCERITY AND TRUTH   163 02
BREAD OF SINCERITY AND TRUTH   165 15

SINFUL

INORDINATE AND SINFUL AFFECTIONS   054 27
THAT OUR SINFUL BODIES MAY BE MADE CLEAN BY   082 20
AND AFFECTIONS OF SINFUL MEN   174 19
FOR I AM A SINFUL MAN, O LORD   196 24
THE SAME, AND THE SINFUL DESIRES OF THE FLESH, SO   276 26
THE SAME, AND THE SINFUL DESIRES OF THE FLESH, SO   277 28
GRANT THAT ALL SINFUL AFFECTIONS MAY DIE IN HIM,   278 21
AND ALL THE SINFUL LUSTS OF THE FLESH   283 25
AND AFFECTIONS OF SINFUL MEN   285 26
AND ALL THE SINFUL LUSTS OF THE FLESH   577 16

SINFULNESS

YOUR OWN SINFULNESS, AND TO CONFESS YOURSELVES TO   087 20

SING

O COME, LET US SING UNTO THE LORD   009 03
O SING UNTO THE LORD A NEW SONG   027 04
SING, REJOICE, AND GIVE THANKS   027 14
SING TO THE HARP WITH A PSALM OF THANKSGIVING   027 15
AND TO SING PRAISES UNTO THY NAME, O MOST HIGHEST   027 29
AND MY TONGUE SHALL SING OF THY RIGHTEOUSNESS   061 07
THE GENTILES, AND SING UNTO THY NAME   092 27
IS A GOOD THING TO SING PRAISES UNTO OUR GOD   264 18
SING PRAISES UPON THE HARP UNTO OUR GOD   264 25
O SING UNTO THE LORD WITH THANKSGIVING   264 25
THE GODS WILL I SING PRAISE UNTO THEE   311 29
SHALL SAY OR SING, I AM THE RESURRECTION AND   R 324 04
I WILL SING AND SPEAK PRAISES UNTO THE LORD   326 18
6 I WILL SING OF THE LORD, BECAUSE HE HATH DEALT SO   356 09
AND SING PRAISES UNTO THY NAME   363 06
SO WILL WE SING, AND PRAISE THY POWER   365 33
I WILL SING AND SPEAK PRAISES UNTO THE LORD   372 10
4 SING PRAISES UNTO THE LORD, O YE SAINTS OF HIS   374 30
EVERY GOOD MAN SING OF THY PRAISE WITHOUT CEASING   375 18
SING PRAISES UNTO HIM WITH THE LUTE, AND INSTRUMENT   378 21
3 SING UNTO THE LORD A NEW SONG   378 23
SING PRAISES LUSTILY UNTO HIM WITH A GOOD COURAGE   378 23
NIGHT SEASON WILL I SING OF HIM, AND MAKE MY PRAYER   393 22
O SING UNTO GOD WITH THE VOICE OF MELODY   398 21
O SING PRAISES, SING PRAISES UNTO OUR KING   398 31
6 O SING PRAISES, SING PRAISES UNTO OUR GOD   398 31
6 O SING PRAISES, SING PRAISES UNTO OUR GOD   398 31
O SING PRAISES, SING PRAISES UNTO OUR KING   398 32
SING YE PRAISES WITH UNDERSTANDING   399 02
AND MY TONGUE SHALL SING OF THY RIGHTEOUSNESS   404 05
I WILL SING AND GIVE PRAISE   409 30
AND I WILL SING UNTO THEE AMONG THE NATIONS   409 34
AS FOR ME, I WILL SING OF THY POWER, AND WILL PRAISE   412 06
O MY STRENGTH, WILL I SING   412 09
8 SO WILL I ALWAY SING PRAISE UNTO THY NAME, *   413 22
THAT THEY SHALL LAUGH AND SING   417 13
SING PRAISES UNTO THE HONOUR OF HIS NAME   417 15
SING OF THEE, AND PRAISE THY NAME   417 20
4 O SING UNTO GOD, AND SING PRAISES UNTO HIS NAME   419 16
SING UNTO GOD, AND SING PRAISES UNTO HIS NAME   419 16
O SING PRAISES UNTO THE LORD   421 20
32 SING UNTO GOD, O YE KINGDOMS OF THE EARTH   421 20
THAT I MAY SING OF THY GLORY AND HONOUR ALL THE DAY   425 22
UNTO THEE WILL I SING UPON THE HARP, O THOU HOLY ONE   426 24
WILL BE GLAD WHEN I SING UNTO THEE   426 25
SING WE MERRILY UNTO GOD OUR STRENGTH   442 12
AND TO SING PRAISES UNTO THY NAME, O MOST HIGHEST   455 33
O COME, LET US SING UNTO THE LORD   459 05
O SING UNTO THE LORD A NEW SONG   459 30
SING UNTO THE LORD, ALL THE WHOLE EARTH   459 30
2 SING UNTO THE LORD, AND PRAISE HIS NAME   460 02
O SING UNTO THE LORD A NEW SONG   461 25
SING, REJOICE, AND GIVE THANKS   462 03
SING TO THE HARP WITH A PSALM OF THANKSGIVING   462 04
UNTO THEE, O LORD, WILL I SING   463 18
AND SING AMONG THE BRANCHES   468 18
33 I WILL SING UNTO THE LORD AS LONG AS I LIVE   469 27
I WILL SING, AND GIVE PRAISE WITH THE BEST MEMBER   479 05
I WILL SING PRAISES UNTO THEE AMONG THE NATIONS   479 10
MY TONGUE SHALL SING OF THY WORD   501 26
AND LET THY SAINTS SING WITH JOYFULNESS   508 22
AND HER SAINTS SHALL REJOICE AND SING   509 07
O SING PRAISES UNTO HIS NAME, FOR IT IS LOVELY   510 07
SING US ONE OF THE SONGS OF SION   513 10
4 HOW SHALL WE SING THE LORD'S SONG *   513 12
THE GODS WILL I SING PRAISE UNTO THEE   513 28
5 YEA, THEY SHALL SING OF THE WAYS OF THE LORD,   514 06
9 I WILL SING A NEW SONG UNTO THEE, O GOD   520 08
AND SING PRAISES UNTO THEE UPON A TEN-STRINGED LUTE   520 08
AND MEN SHALL SING OF THY RIGHTEOUSNESS   521 07

SING   CONTINUED

ANY BEING, I WILL SING PRAISES UNTO MY GOD   522 05
IS A GOOD THING TO SING PRAISES UNTO OUR GOD   522 27
SING PRAISES UPON THE HARP UNTC OUR GOD   523 08
7 O SING UNTO THE LORD WITH THANKSGIVING   523 08
O SING UNTO THE LORD A NEW SONG   525 03
LET THEM SING PRAISES UNTO HIM WITH TABRET AND HARP   525 08
THE BISHOP SHALL SING OR SAY THE VENI, CREATOR   R 543 27
AND LET THY SAINTS SING WITH JOYFULNESS   562 05

SINGERS

25 THE SINGERS GO BEFORE, THE MINSTRELS FCLLOW AFTER, 421 04
7 THE SINGERS ALSO AND TRUMPETERS SHALL MAKE ANSWER   448 26

SINGING

SPIRITUAL SONGS, SINGING WITH GRACE IN YOUR HEARTS TO 116 13
SPIRITUAL SONGS, SINGING AND MAKING MELODY IN YCUR   217 28
AFTER THE SINGING OF A HYMN, SHALL BE SAID BY THE   R 283 03
AFTER THE SINGING OF A HYMN, THERE SHALL BE SAID   R 290 03

SINGLE

VOW THE ESTATE OF SINGLE LIFE, OR TO ABSTAIN FROM   609 22

SINGLENESS

WITH SINGLENESS OF HEART AS THY SERVANTS, AND TC THE 044 22

SINGULAR

BARNABAS WITH SINGULAR GIFTS OF THE HOLY GHOST   240 29

SINK

SO THAT THEY BEGAN TO SINK   196 22
OF THE MIRE, THAT I SINK NOT   422 32

SINNED

I HAVE SINNED AGAINST HEAVEN, AND BEFORE   004 27
THEE ONLY HAVE I SINNED, AND DONE THIS EVIL IN THY   060 17
THAT WE HAVE NOT SINNED, WE MAKE HIM A LIAR, AND HIS 101 32
I HAVE SINNED IN THAT I HAVE BETRAYED THE   135 05
I HAVE SINNED AGAINST HEAVEN, AND BEFORE   202 13
I HAVE SINNED AGAINST HEAVEN, AND IN THY   202 19
THAT WE HAVE SINNED AGAINST THEE IN THOUGHT, WORD,   323 13
FOR I HAVE SINNED AGAINST THEE   392 07
THEE ONLY HAVE I SINNED, AND DCNE THIS EVIL IN THY   403 15
FOR ALL THIS THEY SINNED MORE AGAINST HIM, *   436 02
FOR ALL THIS THEY SINNED YET MCRE, *   437 02
6 WE HAVE SINNED WITH OUR FATHERS   473 11

SINNER

THE DEATH OF A SINNER, BUT RATHER THAT HE MAY TURN   007 07
THE DEATH OF A SINNER, BUT RATHER THAT HE MAY TURN   024 09
THE DEATH OF A SINNER, BUT RATHER THAT HE SHOULD TURN 062 15
I AM A GRIEVOUS SINNER, AND THEREFORE AM AFRAID TO   088 30
THE DEATH OF A SINNER, BUT RATHER THAT HE SHOULC BE   157 06
HEAVEN OVER ONE SINNER THAT REPENTETH, MORE THAN OVER 193 25
OF GOD OVER ONE SINNER THAT REPENTETH   193 34
GOD BE MERCIFUL TO ME A SINNER   205 31
WHO DESIREST NOT THE DEATH OF A SINNER   319 08
OWN FLOCK, A SINNER OF THINE OWN REDEEMING   319 30
THE DEATH OF A SINNER, LOOK UPON HERE LET HIM WHO   589 33

SINNERS

JUSTLY TO PUNISH SINNERS, AND TO BE MERCIFUL TC THOSE 041 11
OF JUDGMENT, WE SINNERS DO BESEECH THEE TO HEAR US,   055 18
AND SINNERS SHALL BE CONVERTED UNTO THEE   061 04
MERCIFUL TO US SINNERS, FOR THY NAME'S SAKE   062 04
CHRIST JESUS CAME INTO THE WORLD TO SAVE SINNERS   076 20
MISERABLE SINNERS, WHO LAY IN DARKNESS AND THE   086 09
SON OF MAN IS BETRAYED INTC THE HANDS OF SINNERS   142 13
PUBLICANS AND SINNERS FOR TO HEAR HIM   193 14
MAN RECEIVETH SINNERS, AND EATETH WITH THEM   193 16
PUBLICANS AND SINNERS CAME AND SAT DOWN WITH HIM ANC 251 16
WHY EATETH YOUR MASTER WITH PUBLICANS AND SINNERS   251 19
BUT SINNERS TO REPENTANCE   251 23
WE SINNERS DO BESEECH THEE TO HEAR US, O LORD GCD   318 10
IN THE WAY OF SINNERS, *   345 09
NEITHER THE SINNERS IN THE CONGREGATION OF THE   345 20
WILL HE TEACH SINNERS IN THE WAY   369 34
MY SOUL WITH THE SINNERS, *   371 14
AND SINNERS SHALL BE CONVERTED UNTO THEE   404 03
35 AS FOR SINNERS, THEY SHALL BE CONSUMED OUT OF THE 469 31
EVER READY TO RECEIVE HUMBLE AND PENITENT SINNERS   590 06

SINNETH

ABIDETH IN HIM SINNETH NOT   117 24
WHOSOEVER SINNETH HATH NOT SEEN HIM, NEITHER KNCWN   117 25
FOR THE DEVIL SINNETH FROM THE BEGINNING   117 28

SINS

THE FORGIVENESS OF SINS, ACCORDING TO THE RICHES OF   004 34
OUR MANIFOLD SINS AND WICKEDNESS   005 31
TO ACKNOWLEDGE OUR SINS BEFORE GOD   006 04
HUMBLY CONFESS OUR SINS UNTO ALMIGHTY GOD   006 14
THE ABSOLUTION AND REMISSION OF THEIR SINS   007 11
REMISSION OF THEIR SINS, THROUGH THE TENDER MERCY OF 014 28

SINS   CONTINUED

THE FORGIVENESS OF SINS   015 29
ACKNOWLEDGE ONE BAPTISM FOR THE REMISSION OF SINS   016 20
IF WE CONFESS OUR SINS, GOD IS FAITHFUL AND JUST TO   022 11
TO FORGIVE US OUR SINS, AND TO CLEANSE US FROM ALL   022 12
HUMBLY CONFESS OUR SINS UNTO ALMIGHTY GOD   023 02
OUR MANIFOLD SINS AND WICKEDNESS   023 06
TO ACKNOWLEDGE OUR SINS BEFORE GOD   023 12
THE ABSOLUTION AND REMISSION OF THEIR SINS   024 13
OF ALL YOUR SINS, TRUE REPENTANCE, AMENDMENT OF LIFE, 024 24
TAKEST AWAY THE SINS OF THE WORLD, HAVE MERCY UPCN   025 29
TAKEST AWAY THE SINS OF THE WORLD, RECEIVE CUR   025 30
THE FORGIVENESS OF SINS   029 34
ACKNOWLEDGE ONE BAPTISM FOR THE REMISSION OF SINS   030 25
REMEMBER NOT OUR SINS, BUT THY PROMISES OF MERCY   040 07
SUFFER FOR OUR SINS, MAY, THROUGH THY GOODNESS,   041 04
REGARD NOT OUR SINS, BUT THE FAITH OF THY CHURCH   049 07
NEITHER TAKE THOU VENGEANCE OF OUR SINS   054 15
FORGIVE US ALL OUR SINS, NEGLIGENCES, AND IGNORANCES 057 15
DEAL NOT WITH US ACCORDING TO OUR SINS   058 12
FORGIVE THE SINS OF THY PEOPLE   059 12
THY FACE FROM MY SINS, *   060 28
WHO CONFESS THEIR SINS UNTO THEE   062 09
GRIEVED AND WEARIED WITH THE BURDEN OF OUR SINS   062 18
TO THEE ONLY IT APPERTAINETH TO FORGIVE SINS   062 19
THE CHAIN OF OUR SINS, YET LET THE PITIFULNESS OF THY 063 12
AND VISIT THE SINS OF THE FATHERS UPON THE   068 12
ACKNOWLEDGE ONE BAPTISM FOR THE REMISSION OF SINS   071 22
REPENT YOU OF YOUR SINS, AND ARE IN LOVE AND CHARITY 075 08
BEWAIL OUR MANIFOLD SINS AND WICKEDNESS, WHICH WE,   075 19
FORGIVENESS OF SINS TO ALL THOSE WHO WITH HEARTY   076 03
PARDON AND DELIVER YOU FROM ALL YOUR SINS   076 06
AND HE IS THE PROPITIATION FOR OUR SINS   076 24
FOR THE SINS OF THE WHOLE WORLD   080 12
AND FOR MANY, FOR THE REMISSION OF SINS   080 28
REMISSION OF OUR SINS, AND ALL OTHER BENEFITS OF HIS 081 20
OUR MANIFOLD SINS, TO OFFER UNTO THEE ANY SACRIFICE   081 29
TAKEST AWAY THE SINS OF THE WORLD, HAVE MERCY UPCN   084 09
TAKEST AWAY THE SINS OF THE WORLD, RECEIVE OUR   084 10
YOU TRULY FOR YOUR SINS PAST   085 35
REMISSION OF YOUR SINS, AND ARE MADE PARTAKERS OF THE 086 33
REPENT YOU OF YOUR SINS, OR ELSE COME NOT TC THAT   087 33
THROUGH OUR SINS AND WICKEDNESS, WE ARE SORE LET AND 095 06
HIMSELF PURGED OUR SINS, SAT DOWN ON THE RIGHT HAND   096 29
IF WE CONFESS OUR SINS, HE IS FAITHFUL AND JUST TO   101 30
TO FORGIVE US OUR SINS, AND TO CLEANSE US FROM ALL   101 31
FOR HE SHALL SAVE HIS PEOPLE FROM THEIR SINS   105 08
BAPTISM OF REPENTANCE FOR THE REMISSION OF SINS   112 09
HIM IN THE RIVER OF JORDAN, CONFESSING THEIR SINS   112 12
KNOW THAT HE WAS MANIFESTED TO TAKE AWAY OUR SINS   117 24
DOST FORGIVE THE SINS OF ALL THOSE WHO ARE PENITENT   124 12
LAMENTING OUR SINS AND ACKNOWLEDGING OUR   124 14
OFFERED TO BEAR THE SINS OF MANY   148 09
PURGED SHOULD HAVE HAD NO MORE CONSCIENCE OF SINS   157 21
AGAIN MADE OF SINS EVERY YEAR   157 22
BLOOD OF BULLS AND OF GOATS SHOULD TAKE AWAY SINS   157 23
SAME SACRIFICES, WHICH CAN NEVER TAKE AWAY SINS   158 05
ONE SACRIFICE FOR SINS FOR EVER, SAT DOWN ON THE   158 06
SAITH HE, AND THEIR SINS AND INIQUITIES WILL I   158 14
ONCE SUFFERED FOR SINS, THE JUST FOR THE UNJUST,   161 23
BELIEVETH IN HIM SHALL RECEIVE REMISSICN OF SINS   166 32
MAN IS PREACHED UNTO YOU THE FORGIVENESS OF SINS   169 20
AND REMISSION OF SINS SHOULD BE PREACHED IN HIS NAME 170 14
SON TO DIE FOR OUR SINS, AND TO RISE AGAIN FCR OUR   170 20
WHOSESOEVER SINS YE REMIT, THEY ARE REMITTED UNTC   171 23
AND WHOSOEVER SINS YE RETAIN, THEY ARE RETAINED   171 24
OWN SELF BARE OUR SINS IN HIS OWN BODY ON THE TREE,   172 15
WE, BEING DEAD TO SINS, SHOULD LIVE UNTO   172 16
FOR CHARITY SHALL COVER THE MULTITUDE OF SINS   179 15
BELIEVETH IN HIM SHALL RECEIVE REMISSION OF SINS   184 20
SENT HIS SON TO BE THE PROPITIATION FOR OUR SINS   189 15
CHRIST DIED FOR OUR SINS ACCORDING TO THE SCRIPTURES 205 04
THY SINS BE FORGIVEN THEE   217 04
TO SAY, THY SINS BE FORGIVEN THEE   217 08
ON EARTH TO FORGIVE SINS, (THEN SAITH HE TO THE SICK 217 10
FROM ALL THEIR SINS, AND SERVE THEE WITH A QUIET   219 02
THE BANDS OF THOSE SINS, WHICH BY OUR FRAILTY WE HAVE 223 17
OF THE LORD'S HAND DOUBLE FOR ALL HER SINS   242 20
REMISSION OF THEIR SINS, THROUGH THE TENDER MERCY CF 244 13
FORGIVENESS OF OUR SINS, DID SHED OUT OF HIS MOST   279 10
THE FORGIVENESS OF SINS   284 23
AND VISIT THE SINS OF THE FATHERS UPON THE   286 12
OF THEIR FORMER SINS, WITH STEDFAST PURPOSE TO LEAD A 293 27
REMISSION OF OUR SINS, AND BE FILLED WITH THY GRACE   294 32
GIVEN UNTO THEM FORGIVENESS OF ALL THEIR SINS   297 17
HIM TRULY OF HIS SINS, AND BE IN CHARITY WITH ALL THE R 313 19
CONFESSION OF HIS SINS, IF HE FEEL HIS CONSCIENCE   R 313 25
SO PUT AWAY THE SINS OF THOSE WHO TRULY REPENT, THAT 313 31
UNTO HIM HIS FORMER SINS, BUT STRENGTHEN HIM WITH THY 314 10
THAT HIS SINS MAY BE DONE AWAY BY THY MERCY, AND HIS 316 14
TO TAKE AWAY THE SINS OF THE WORLD   317 18
MAY PLEASE THEE MERCIFULLY TO PARDON ALL HIS SINS   318 15
WHO TAKEST AWAY THE SINS OF THE WORLD   318 23
OF ALL THY SINS, AND THE GRACE AND COMFORT OF THE   319 16
DO AWAY OUR OFFENCES AND CLEANSE US FROM OUR SINS   323 14
OF ALL YOUR SINS, TRUE REPENTANCE, AMENDMENT OF LIFE, 323 20
REPENT HIM OF HIS SINS, AND STEDFASTLY BELIEVE THAT   R 323 26
AND OUR SECRET SINS IN THE LIGHT OF THY COUNTENANCE   325 29
FROM ALL HIS SINS   328 17
O LORD, WHO FOR OUR SINS ART JUSTLY DISPLEASED   332 23
FROM PRESUMPTUOUS SINS, LEST THEY GET THE DOMINICN   364 10
O REMEMBER NOT THE SINS AND OFFENCES OF MY YOUTH   369 30
I WILL CONFESS MY SINS UNTO THE LORD   377 32
MY SINS HAVE TAKEN SUCH HOLD UPON ME, THAT I AM NOT   391 11
THY FACE FROM MY SINS, *   403 27

SINS   CONTINUED

O BE THOU MERCIFUL UNTO OUR SINS 416 16
NOT OUR OLD SINS, BUT HAVE MERCY UPON US, AND THAT 440 16
MERCIFUL UNTO OUR SINS, FOR THY NAME'S SAKE 440 19
AND COVERED ALL THEIR SINS 446 11
AND OUR SECRET SINS IN THE LIGHT OF THY COUNTENANCE 454 03
I HATE THE SINS OF UNFAITHFULNESS 463 22
10 HE HATH NOT DEALT WITH US AFTER OUR SINS 466 25
FAR HATH HE SET OUR SINS FROM US 466 31
FROM ALL HIS SINS 507 22
WHOSE SINS THOU DOST FORGIVE, THEY ARE FORGIVEN 546 11
AND WHOSE SINS THOU DOST RETAIN, THEY ARE RETAINED 546 12
WHOSE SOEVER SINS YE REMIT, THEY ARE REMITTED UNTO 552 04
AND WHOSE SOEVER SINS YE RETAIN, THEY ARE RETAINED 552 05
REMISSION OF THEIR SINS, AND ALL OTHER BENEFITS OF 565 33
TO CONFESS THEIR SINS UNTO THEE, AND TO ASK SUCH 566 17
THEM FROM THE SINS OF HERESY AND SCHISM 574 13
THE FORGIVENESS OF SINS 578 07
AND VISIT THE SINS OF THE FATHERS UPON THE 578 31
WILL BE MERCIFUL UNTO US, AND FORGIVE US OUR SINS 580 35
OF THEIR FORMER SINS, STEDFASTLY PURPOSING TO LEAD A 582 23
TO ALL THOSE WHO CONFESS AND FORSAKE THEIR SINS 589 29
CONFESS THE SINS AND FAILINGS OF THAT DAY R 589 35
BUT ALSO FOR ACTUAL SINS OF MEN 603 16
CANNOT PUT AWAY OUR SINS, AND ENDURE THE SEVERITY OF 605 12
TAKE AWAY THE SINS OF THE WORLD 605 34
FOR ALL THE SINS OF THE WHOLE WORLD, BOTH ORIGINAL 609 15

SION

YE THE DAUGHTER OF SION, BEHOLD, THY KING COMETH UNTO 091 20
STOOD ON THE MOUNT SION, AND WITH HIM AN HUNDRED 102 29
PRAISE THY GOD, O SION 264 33
UPON MY HOLY HILL OF SION 346 09
11 O PRAISE THE LORD WHICH DWELLETH IN SION 352 11
PRAISES WITHIN THE GATES OF THE DAUGHTER OF SION 352 20
WHO SHALL GIVE SALVATION UNTO ISRAEL OUT OF SION 356 30
AND STRENGTHEN THEE OUT OF SION 364 20
2 THE HILL OF SION IS A FAIR PLACE, AND THE JOY OF 399 12
10 LET THE MOUNT SION REJOICE, AND THE DAUGHTERS OF 399 31
11 WALK ABOUT SION, AND GO ROUND ABOUT HER 399 33
2 OUT OF SION HATH GOD APPEARED * 401 24
18 O BE FAVOURABLE AND GRACIOUS UNTO SION 404 13
THE SALVATION WERE GIVEN UNTO ISRAEL OUT OF SION 405 29
O GOD, ART PRAISED IN SION 416 11
FOR GOD WILL SAVE SION, AND BUILD THE CITIES OF 424 14
THY WORKS IN THE GATES OF THE DAUGHTER OF SION 429 34
AND MOUNT SION, WHEREIN THOU HAST DWELT 430 09
AND HIS DWELLING IN SION 432 25
EVEN THE HILL OF SION WHICH HE LOVED 439 14
GOD OF GODS APPEARETH EVERY ONE OF THEM IN SION 445 26
LOVETH THE GATES OF SION MORE THAN ALL THE DWELLINGS 448 14
IN SION WERE THEY BORN 448 21
5 YEA, OF SION IT SHALL BE REPORTED, THIS ONE AND 448 22
IN SION WERE THEY BORN 448 25
8 SION HEARD OF IT, AND REJOICED 461 12
LORD IS GREAT IN SION, * 462 19
13 THOU SHALT ARISE, AND HAVE MERCY UPON SION 465 04
LORD SHALL BUILD UP SION, * 465 11
NAME OF THE LORD IN SION, * 465 23
LORD SHALL SEND THE ROD OF THY POWER OUT OF SION 482 10
EVEN AS THE MOUNT SION, * 504 24
THE CAPTIVITY OF SION, * 505 07
LORD FROM OUT OF SION SHALL SO BLESS THEE, * 506 16
AS MANY AS HAVE EVIL WILL AT SION 506 30
LORD HATH CHOSEN SION TO BE AN HABITATION FOR 508 32
WHICH FELL UPON THE HILL OF SION 509 19
GIVE THEE BLESSING OUT OF SION 509 30
BE THE LORD OUT OF SION, * 511 12
WHEN WE REMEMBERED THEE, O SION 513 06
SING US ONE OF THE SONGS OF SION 513 11
THE LORD THY GOD, O SION, SHALL BE KING FOR EVERMORE, 522 23
PRAISE THY GOD, O SION 523 20
LET THE CHILDREN OF SION BE JOYFUL IN THEIR KING 525 06

SIR

AND SAID UNTO HIM, SIR, DIDST NOT THOU SOW GOOD SEED 116 23
UNTO PILATE, SAYING, SIR, WE REMEMBER THAT THAT 162 17
SAITH UNTO HIM, SIR, COME DOWN ERE MY CHILD DIE 220 02
AND I SAID UNTO HIM, SIR, THOU KNOWEST 257 06

SIRION

LEBANON ALSO, AND SIRION, LIKE A YOUNG UNICORN 374 10

SISERA

UNTO SISERA, AND UNTO JABIN AT THE BROOK OF KISHON 444 23

SISTER

AND HIS MOTHER'S SISTER, MARY THE WIFE OF CLEOPHAS, 160 18

SISTERS

OR BRETHREN, OR SISTERS, OR FATHER, OR MOTHER, OR 231 19

SIT

LIGHT TO THEM THAT SIT IN DARKNESS, AND IN THE SHADOW 014 31
BUT THE GUESTS TO SIT DOWN 088 20
AND WEST, AND SHALL SIT DOWN WITH ABRAHAM, AND ISAAC, 115 19
MAKE THE MEN SIT DOWN 131 35
TO HIS DISCIPLES, SIT YE HERE, WHILE I SHALL PRAY 141 28

SIT   CONTINUED

IN MY KINGDOM, AND SIT ON THRONES, JUDGING THE TWELVE 149 29
SHALL THE SON OF MAN SIT ON THE RIGHT HAND OF THE 151 33
THE PEOPLE TO SIT DOWN ON THE GROUND 199 18
MAN TO A WEDDING, SIT NOT DOWN IN THE HIGHEST SEAT 214 11
ART BIDDEN, GO AND SIT DOWN IN THE LOWEST PLACE 214 15
OF THEM THAT SIT AT MEAT WITH THEE 214 18
SAID UNTO MY LORD, SIT THOU ON MY RIGHT HAND, TILL I 215 20
MAKE THE MEN SIT DOWN 225 31
THE SON OF MAN SHALL SIT IN THE THRONE OF HIS GLORY 231 16
YE ALSO SHALL SIT UPON TWELVE THRONES, JUDGING 231 17
AND HE SHALL SIT AS A REFINER AND PURIFIER OF SILVER 232 10
LIGHT TO THEM THAT SIT IN DARKNESS AND IN THE SHADOW 244 15
MY TWO SONS MAY SIT, THE ONE ON THY RIGHT HAND, AND 247 09
BUT TO SIT ON MY RIGHT HAND, AND ON MY LEFT, IS NOT 247 16
IN MY KINGDOM, AND SIT ON THRONES JUDGING THE TWELVE 250 15
THEN SHALL HE SIT UPON THE THRONE OF HIS GLORY 258 29
AND WILL NOT SIT AMONG THE UNGODLY 371 07
12 THEY THAT SIT IN THE GATE SPEAK AGAINST ME, 422 26
10 SUCH AS SIT IN DARKNESS, AND IN THE SHADOW OF 476 24
SIT THOU ON MY RIGHT HAND, UNTIL I MAKE THINE ENEMIES 482 07
23 PRINCES ALSO DID SIT AND SPEAK AGAINST ME 491 12
CHILDREN ALSO SHALL SIT UPON THY THRONE FOR EVERMORE 508 31
AND MAKE THEM TO SIT DOWN TO MEAT, AND WILL COME 534 22

SITTEST

THOU SITTEST AT THE RIGHT HAND OF GOD, IN THE GLORY 010 30
THOU THAT SITTEST AT THE RIGHT HAND OF GOD THE 025 31
WHO SITTEST IN THE THRONE JUDGING RIGHT 035 31
THOU THAT SITTEST AT THE RIGHT HAND OF GOD THE 084 11
THOU THAT SITTEST UPON THE CHERUBIM 441 05

SITTETH

INTO HEAVEN, AND SITTETH ON THE RIGHT HAND OF GOD THE 015 25
INTO HEAVEN, AND SITTETH ON THE RIGHT HAND OF THE 016 11
WHERE CHRIST SITTETH ON THE RIGHT HAND OF GOD 022 20
INTO HEAVEN, AND SITTETH ON THE RIGHT HAND OF GOD THE 029 30
INTO HEAVEN, AND SITTETH ON THE RIGHT HAND OF THE 030 16
INTO HEAVEN, AND SITTETH ON THE RIGHT HAND OF THE 071 13
HE THAT SITTETH AT MEAT, OR HE THAT SERVETH 149 24
IS NOT HE THAT SITTETH AT MEAT 149 25
WHERE CHRIST SITTETH ON THE RIGHT HAND OF GOD 164 04
IS NOT HE THAT SITTETH AT MEAT 250 10
HE THAT SITTETH AT MEAT, OR HE THAT SERVETH 250 10
TO OUR GOD WHICH SITTETH UPON THE THRONE, AND UNTO 256 28
AND HE THAT SITTETH ON THE THRONE SHALL DWELL AMONG 257 11
INTO HEAVEN, AND SITTETH ON THE RIGHT HAND OF GOD THE 284 19
AND HE THAT SITTETH ON THE THRONE SHALL DWELL AMONG 341 22
8 HE SITTETH LURKING IN THE THIEVISH CORNERS OF THE 353 20
9 THE LORD SITTETH ABOVE THE WATER-FLOOD, * 374 17
GOD SITTETH UPON HIS HOLY SEAT 399 04
33 WHO SITTETH IN THE HEAVENS OVER ALL, FROM THE 421 22
HE SITTETH BETWEEN THE CHERUBIM, BE THE EARTH NEVER 462 17
THAT SITTETH ALONE UPON THE HOUSETOP 464 24
INTO HEAVEN, AND SITTETH ON THE RIGHT HAND OF GOD THE 578 03
AND THERE SITTETH, UNTIL HE RETURN TO JUDGE ALL MEN 603 23

SITTING

MEEK, AND SITTING UPON AN ASS, AND A COLT THE 091 21
IN THE TEMPLE, SITTING IN THE MIDST OF THE DOCTORS, 110 28
AND SITTING DOWN THEY WATCHED HIM THERE 136 34
THE SON OF MAN SITTING ON THE RIGHT HAND OF POWER, 143 15
THE OTHER MARY, SITTING OVER AGAINST THE SEPULCHRE 162 14
SAW A YOUNG MAN SITTING ON THE RIGHT SIDE, CLOTHED IN 165 27
IT FILLED ALL THE HOUSE WHERE THEY WERE SITTING 180 21
TWENTY ELDERS SITTING, CLOTHED IN WHITE RAIMENT 187 10
NAMED MATTHEW, SITTING AT THE RECEIPT OF CUSTOM 251 13
THE BISHOP, SITTING IN HIS CHAIR NEAR TO THE HOLY R 296 06
UNTO THE BISHOP, SITTING IN HIS CHAIR NEAR TO THE R 530 07
UNTO THE BISHOP, SITTING IN HIS CHAIR NEAR TO THE R 536 07
SITTING IN HIS CHAIR, NEAR THE HOLY TABLE R 552 19
SITTING IN HIS CHAIR, SHALL SAY TO HIM THAT R 554 05
THE BISHOP, SITTING IN HIS CHAIR, SHALL HAVE THE R 564 07
THE BISHOP SITTING IN HIS CHAIR, THE SENTENCE R 566 25
AND THE CHANGERS OF MONEY SITTING 567 27

SIX

ON WHITSUNDAY AND SIX DAYS AFTER R 008 27
SIX DAYS SHALT THOU LABOUR, AND DO ALL THAT THOU HAST 068 25
FOR IN SIX DAYS THE LORD MADE HEAVEN AND EARTH, THE 068 29
UPON WHITSUNDAY, AND SIX DAYS AFTER R 078 24
THERE WERE SET THERE SIX WATER-POTS OF STONE, AFTER 113 13
HAD EACH OF THEM SIX WINGS ABOUT HIM 187 21
SIX DAYS SHALT THOU LABOUR, AND DO ALL THAT THOU HAST 286 25
FOR IN SIX DAYS THE LORD MADE HEAVEN AND EARTH, THE 286 29
SIX DAYS SHALT THOU LABOUR, AND DO ALL THAT THOU HAST 579 05
FOR IN SIX DAYS THE LORD MADE HEAVEN AND EARTH, 579 10

SIXTH

TIME OF EDWARD THE SIXTH, UPON JUST AND WEIGHTY V 27
WENT OUT ABOUT THE SIXTH AND NINTH HOUR, AND DID 119 23
NOW FROM THE SIXTH HOUR THERE WAS DARKNESS OVER ALL 137 15
AND WHEN THE SIXTH HOUR WAS COME, THERE WAS DARKNESS 146 25
IT WAS ABOUT THE SIXTH HOUR, AND THERE WAS A DARKNESS 155 09
AND ABOUT THE SIXTH HOUR 159 26
SERVICE FOR THE SIXTH SUNDAY AFTER THE EPIPHANY SHALL R 224 32
SERVICE FOR THE SIXTH SUNDAY AFTER THE EPIPHANY SHALL R 224 33
AND IN THE SIXTH MONTH THE ANGEL GABRIEL WAS SENT 236 05
AND THIS IS THE SIXTH MONTH WITH HER, WHO WAS CALLED 236 26
WERE SET FORTH IN THE TIME OF EDWARD THE SIXTH 610 08

SKILL

GIVE STRENGTH AND SKILL TO ALL THOSE WHO MINISTER TO 045 06

SKIN

WITH A GIRDLE OF A SKIN ABOUT HIS LOINS 112 13

SKIP

MAKETH THEM ALSO TO SKIP LIKE A CALF 374 09

SKIPPED

4 THE MOUNTAINS SKIPPED LIKE RAMS, * 484 31
THAT YE SKIPPED LIKE RAMS 485 04

SKIRTS

WENT DOWN TO THE SKIRTS OF HIS CLOTHING 509 17

SKULL

A PLACE OF A SKULL, THEY GAVE HIM VINEGAR TO 136 28
BEING INTERPRETED, THE PLACE OF A SKULL 146 09
THE PLACE OF A SKULL, WHICH IS CALLED IN THE HEBREW 159 32

SLAIN

YET DESIRED THEY PILATE THAT HE SHOULD BE SLAIN 168 31
THAT WAS SLAIN TO TAKE AWAY THE SINS OF THE 317 18
AND ARE COUNTED AS SHEEP APPOINTED TO BE SLAIN 396 05
YE SHALL BE SLAIN ALL THE SORT OF YOU 414 02
THEIR PRIESTS WERE SLAIN WITH THE SWORD, * 439 06
UNTO THEM THAT ARE SLAIN, AND LIE IN THE GRAVE, 449 05

SLANDERED

AND HATH NOT SLANDERED HIS NEIGHBOUR 357 11
AND HAST SLANDERED THINE OWN MOTHER'S SON 402 31
AND SLANDERED THE FOOTSTEPS OF THINE ANOINTED 453 11

SLANDERER

AN HINDERER OR SLANDERER OF HIS WORD, AN ADULTERER, 087 32
VOICE OF THE SLANDERER AND BLASPHEMER, * 395 26

SLANDERERS

AND SLANDERERS, AND TO TURN THEIR HEARTS 057 08
BE GRAVE, NOT SLANDERERS, SOBER, FAITHFUL IN ALL 531 32

SLANDERETH

WHOSO PRIVILY SLANDERETH HIS NEIGHBOUR, * 463 26

SLANDERING

TONGUE FROM EVIL SPEAKING, LYING, AND SLANDERING 289 07
TONGUE FROM EVIL SPEAKING, LYING, AND SLANDERING 580 10

SLAUGHTER

AND SLAUGHTER AGAINST THE DISCIPLES OF THE LORD, WENT 229 25

SLAY

MISFORTUNE SHALL SLAY THE UNGODLY 381 10
AND NEEDY, AND TO SLAY SUCH AS BE UPRIGHT IN THEIR 385 24
SEEKETH OCCASION TO SLAY HIM 386 31
11 SLAY THEM NOT, LEST MY PEOPLE FORGET IT 411 26
THAT HE MIGHT SLAY HIM THAT WAS VEXED AT THE 480 33
19 WILT THOU NOT SLAY THE WICKED, O GOD 515 28
AND OF THY GOODNESS SLAY MINE ENEMIES, * 519 17

SLEEP

THAT NOW IT IS HIGH TIME TO AWAKE OUT OF SLEEP 091 02
BEING RAISED FROM SLEEP DID AS THE ANGEL OF THE LORD 105 13
SAITH UNTO THEM, SLEEP ON NOW, AND TAKE YOUR REST 142 11
UNTO THEM, WHY SLEEP YE 150 25
OF GOD, FELL ON SLEEP, AND WAS LAID UNTO HIS FATHERS, 169 16
AND THEY THAT WERE WITH HIM WERE HEAVY WITH SLEEP 248 31
AND SLEEP IN THE WOODS 262 06
SO THEM ALSO WHICH SLEEP IN JESUS WILL GOD BRING WITH 268 31
AS THOU SCATTEREST THEM THEY ARE EVEN AS A SLEEP 325 23
AND HE THAT KEEPETH THEE WILL NOT SLEEP 327 24
SHALL NEITHER SLUMBER NOR SLEEP 327 26
WE SHALL NOT ALL SLEEP, BUT WE SHALL ALL BE CHANGED, 330 02
OF THOSE WHO SLEEP IN HIM SHALL BE CHANGED, AND MADE 333 21
FOR THOSE WHO SLEEP IN HIM 335 05
OF THOSE WHO SLEEP IN HIM SHALL BE CHANGED, AND MADE 337 14
AND HE THAT KEEPETH THEE WILL NOT SLEEP 339 08
SHALL NEITHER SLUMBER NOR SLEEP 339 10
MINE EYES, THAT I SLEEP NOT IN DEATH 356 03
THEY HAVE SLEPT THEIR SLEEP 432 30
AS ONE OUT OF SLEEP, * 439 08
AS THOU SCATTEREST THEM THEY ARE EVEN AS A SLEEP 453 28
AND HE THAT KEEPETH THEE WILL NOT SLEEP 502 27
SHALL NEITHER SLUMBER NOR SLEEP 502 29
FOR SO HE GIVETH HIS BELOVED SLEEP 505 28
MINE EYES TO SLEEP, NOR MINE EYELIDS TO SLUMBER 508 10
SUCH REFRESHING SLEEP AS MAY FIT US FOR THE DUTIES OF 591 28

SLEEPEST

AWAKE THOU THAT SLEEPEST, AND ARISE FROM THE DEAD, 129 21
SIMON, SLEEPEST THOU 142 04
UP, LORD, WHY SLEEPEST THOU 396 06

SLEEPETH

FOR THE MAID IS NOT DEAD, BUT SLEEPETH 224 26

SLEEPING

LEST COMING SUDDENLY HE FIND YOU SLEEPING 021 27
FINDETH THEM SLEEPING, AND SAITH UNTO PETER, SIMON, 142 03
HE FOUND THEM SLEEPING FOR SORROW, AND SAID UNTO 150 24
NIGHT PETER WAS SLEEPING BETWEEN TWO SOLDIERS, 245 10

SLEIGHT

BY THE SLEIGHT OF MEN, AND CUNNING 237 27

SLEPT

BUT WHILE MEN SLEPT, HIS ENEMY CAME AND SOWED TARES 116 19
THE SAINTS WHICH SLEPT AROSE, AND CAME OUT OF THE 137 28
AND BECOME THE FIRSTFRUITS OF THEM THAT SLEPT 163 12
I LAID ME DOWN AND SLEPT, AND ROSE UP AGAIN 309 22
AND BECOME THE FIRSTFRUITS OF THEM THAT SLEPT 328 22
I LAID ME DOWN AND SLEPT, AND ROSE UP AGAIN 346 33
THEY HAVE SLEPT THEIR SLEEP 432 30

SLEW

WHOM YE SLEW BETWEEN THE TEMPLE AND THE 100 25
AND SENT FORTH, AND SLEW ALL THE CHILDREN THAT WERE 103 26
WHOM THEY SLEW AND HANGED ON A TREE 166 24
WHOM THEY SLEW AND HANGED ON A TREE 184 11
AND SLEW THEM 218 13
CAME UPON THEM, AND SLEW THE WEALTHIEST OF THEM 436 33
34 WHEN HE SLEW THEM, THEY SOUGHT HIM, * 437 06
AND SLEW THEIR FISH 471 30
AND SLEW MIGHTY KINGS 510 23
18 YEA, AND SLEW MIGHTY KINGS 512 18

SLIDE

THAT MY FOOTSTEPS SHALL NOT SLIDE 362 10
AND HIS GOINGS SHALL NOT SLIDE 386 29

SLIP

THAT MY FOOTSTEPS SLIP NOT 358 28
AND SUFFERETH NOT OUR FEET TO SLIP 417 32

SLIPPERY

WAY BE DARK AND SLIPPERY, * 381 29
SET THEM IN SLIPPERY PLACES, * 429 12

SLIPT

FOR WHEN MY FOOT SLIPT, THEY REJOICED GREATLY AGAINST 388 24
MY TREADINGS HAD WELL-NIGH SLIPT 428 13
18 BUT WHEN I SAID, MY FOOT HATH SLIPT 458 22

SLOTHFUL

NOT SLOTHFUL IN BUSINESS 111 25

SLOW

AND MERCIFUL, SLOW TO ANGER, AND OF GREAT KINDNESS, 004 22
AND MERCIFUL, SLOW TO ANGER, AND OF GREAT KINDNESS, 124 25
O FOOLS, AND SLOW OF HEART TO BELIEVE ALL THAT 167 29
BE SWIFT TO HEAR, SLOW TO SPEAK, SLOW TO WRATH 174 31
SLOW TO SPEAK, SLOW TO WRATH 174 32
BE SWIFT TO HEAR, SLOW TO SPEAK, SLOW TO WRATH 265 24
SLOW TO SPEAK, SLOW TO WRATH 265 24

SLUMBER

SHALL NEITHER SLUMBER NOR SLEEP 327 25
SHALL NEITHER SLUMBER NOR SLEEP 339 09
SHALL NEITHER SLUMBER NOR SLEEP 502 28
MINE EYES TO SLEEP, NOR MINE EYELIDS TO SLUMBER 508 11

SMALL

ME IT IS A VERY SMALL THING THAT I SHOULD BE JUDGED 094 06
AND TWO SMALL FISHES 131 34
AND THEY HAD A FEW SMALL FISHES 199 21
AND TWO SMALL FISHES 225 30
IS IT A SMALL THING FOR YOU TO WEARY MEN, BUT WILL YE 235 29
WILL BEAT THEM AS SMALL AS THE DUST BEFORE THE WIND 362 23
16 A SMALL THING THAT THE RIGHTEOUS HATH, * 385 27
SUCK THEY NO SMALL ADVANTAGE 428 29
BOTH SMALL AND GREAT BEASTS 469 11
BOTH SMALL AND GREAT 486 04
141 I AM SMALL AND OF NO REPUTATION 499 21
MADE A SCOURGE OF SMALL CORDS, HE DROVE THEM ALL OUT 567 28

SMELL

8 ALL THY GARMENTS SMELL OF MYRRH, ALOES, AND CASSIA 396 32
HAVE THEY, AND SMELL NOT 485 23

SMITE

IF A MAN SMITE YOU ON THE FACE	120 25
IS WRITTEN, I WILL SMITE THE SHEPHERD, AND THE SHEEP	141 19
SHALL WE SMITE WITH THE SWORD	150 32
39 I WILL SMITE THEM, THAT THEY SHALL NOT BE ABLE TO	362 14
SMITE THE JAW-BONES OF THE LIONS, O LORD	410 19
24 I WILL SMITE DOWN HIS FOES BEFORE HIS FACE,	451 21
5 THEY SMITE DOWN THY PEOPLE, O LORD, *	457 27
DEAD BODIES, AND SMITE IN SUNDER THE HEADS OVER	482 19
RIGHTEOUS RATHER SMITE ME FRIENDLY, AND REPROVE ME	517 19

SMITERS

HIS BACK TO THE SMITERS AND HID NOT HIS FACE FROM	144 07
MY BACK TO THE SMITERS, AND MY CHEEKS TO THEM THAT	144 14

SMITEST

FOR THOU SMITEST ALL MINE ENEMIES UPON THE	347 04

SMITTEN

8 I AM FEEBLE AND SORE SMITTEN	388 06
12 MY BONES ARE SMITTEN ASUNDER AS WITH A SWORD,	393 27
WHEN THOU HAST SMITTEN US INTO THE PLACE OF DRAGONS,	395 32
27 FOR THEY PERSECUTE HIM WHOM THOU HAST SMITTEN	423 27
4 MY HEART IS SMITTEN DOWN, AND WITHERED LIKE GRASS	464 17
AND SMITTEN THE BARS OF IRON IN SUNDER	477 07
HE HATH SMITTEN MY LIFE DOWN TO THE GROUND	518 28

SMOKE

9 THERE WENT A SMOKE OUT IN HIS PRESENCE, *	360 12
EVEN AS THE SMOKE SHALL THEY CONSUME AWAY	386 03
2 LIKE AS THE SMOKE VANISHETH, SO SHALT THOU DRIVE	419 11
CONSUMED AWAY LIKE SMOKE, *	464 15
IF HE DO BUT TOUCH THE HILLS, THEY SHALL SMOKE	469 26
83 FOR I AM BECOME LIKE A BOTTLE IN THE SMOKE	495 23
TOUCH THE MOUNTAINS, AND THEY SHALL SMOKE	519 32

SMOOTHER

HIS WORDS WERE SMOOTHER THAN OIL, AND YET BE THEY	408 02

SMOTE

TOOK THE REED, AND SMOTE HIM ON THE HEAD	136 22
DREW A SWORD, AND SMOTE A SERVANT OF THE HIGH PRIEST,	142 23
AND THEY SMOTE HIM ON THE HEAD WITH A REED, AND DID	145 34
AND ONE OF THEM SMOTE THE SERVANT OF THE HIGH PRIEST,	150 32
MOCKED HIM, AND SMOTE HIM	151 24
WHO IS IT THAT SMOTE THEE	151 26
WHICH WERE DONE, SMOTE THEIR BREASTS, AND RETURNED	155 18
AND THEY SMOTE HIM WITH THEIR HANDS	158 33
UNTO HEAVEN, BUT SMOTE UPON HIS BREAST, SAYING,	205 30
AND HE SMOTE PETER ON THE SIDE, AND RAISED HIM UP,	245 13
21 HE SMOTE THE STONY ROCK INDEED, THAT THE WATER	436 08
AND SMOTE DOWN THE CHOSEN MEN THAT WERE IN	436 34
49 HE SMOTE THEIR CATTLE ALSO WITH HAILSTONES,	438 04
52 AND SMOTE ALL THE FIRSTBORN IN EGYPT, *	438 12
33 HE SMOTE THEIR VINES ALSO AND FIG-TREES	472 04
35 HE SMOTE ALL THE FIRSTBORN IN THEIR LAND	472 09
8 HE SMOTE THE FIRSTBORN OF EGYPT, *	510 18
10 HE SMOTE DIVERS NATIONS, *	510 23
10 WHO SMOTE EGYPT, WITH THEIR FIRSTBORN	512 02
17 WHO SMOTE GREAT KINGS	512 16

SMOTEST

15 THOU SMOTEST THE HEADS OF LEVIATHAN IN PIECES,	431 04

SNAIL

AWAY LIKE A SNAIL, AND BE LIKE THE UNTIMELY FRUIT OF	410 23

SNARE

10 THOU BROUGHTEST US INTO THE SNARE	418 02
TABLE BE MADE A SNARE TO TAKE THEMSELVES WITHAL	423 18
THEE FROM THE SNARE OF THE HUNTER, *	454 32
WHICH BECAME A SNARE UNTO THEM	475 09
HAVE LAID A SNARE FOR ME	497 17
A BIRD OUT OF THE SNARE OF THE FOWLER	504 18
THE SNARE IS BROKEN, AND WE ARE DELIVERED	504 19
PROUD HAVE LAID A SNARE FOR ME, AND SPREAD A NET	516 18
KEEP ME FROM THE SNARE THAT THEY HAVE LAID FOR ME, *	517 30
PRIVILY LAID A SNARE FOR ME	518 09
REPROACH AND THE SNARE OF THE DEVIL	549 30

SNARES

HE SHALL RAIN SNARES, FIRE AND BRIMSTONE, STORM AND	354 33
THE SNARES OF DEATH OVERTOOK ME	360 02
MY LIFE LAID SNARES FOR ME	388 14
COMMUNE AMONG THEMSELVES, HOW THEY MAY LAY SNARES	415 28
3 THE SNARES OF DEATH COMPASSED ME ROUND ABOUT,	486 23
61 THE SNARES OF THE UNGODLY HAVE COMPASSED ME ABOUT	494 02
HATH HEWN THE SNARES OF THE UNGODLY IN PIECES	506 27

SNOW

O YE ICE AND SNOW, BLESS YE THE LORD	012 26
AND I SHALL BE WHITER THAN SNOW	060 25
AND I SHALL BE WHITER THAN SNOW	403 24
THEY AS WHITE AS SNOW IN SALMON	420 10

SNOW   CONTINUED

16 HE GIVETH SNOW LIKE WOOL, *	523 27
8 FIRE AND HAIL, SNOW AND VAPOURS, *	524 20

SOBER

AND SOBER LIFE, TO THE GLORY OF THY HOLY	006 29
AND SOBER LIFE, TO THE GLORY OF THY HOLY	024 04
BE YE THEREFORE SOBER, AND WATCH UNTO PRAYER	179 12
BE SOBER, BE VIGILANT	193 04
NOT SLANDERERS, SOBER, FAITHFUL IN ALL THINGS	531 32
VIGILANT, SOBER, OF GOOD BEHAVIOUR, GIVEN TO	549 20
THY SERVICE, IN A SOBER, RIGHTEOUS, AND GODLY LIFE	588 07
THE EFFORTS OF SOBER AND HONEST INDUSTRY, AND SUFFER	599 29

SOBERLY

WE SHOULD LIVE SOBERLY, RIGHTEOUSLY, AND GODLY,	098 20
BUT TO THINK SOBERLY, ACCORDING AS GOD HATH DEALT TO	110 11
SOBERLY, AND IN THE FEAR OF GOD	300 18
AND LIVE SOBERLY, RIGHTEOUSLY, AND GODLY IN	555 09

SOBERNESS

IN TEMPERANCE, SOBERNESS, AND CHASTITY	289 02
BUT OF POWER, AND LOVE, AND SOBERNESS	558 19
IN TEMPERANCE, SOBERNESS, AND CHASTITY	580 11

SOEVER

WHOSE SOEVER SINS YE REMIT, THEY ARE REMITTED UNTO	552 04
AND WHOSE SOEVER SINS YE RETAIN, THEY ARE RETAINED	552 05

SOFT

A MAN CLOTHED IN SOFT RAIMENT	094 28
THEY THAT WEAR SOFT CLOTHING ARE IN KINGS' HOUSES	094 28
THOU MAKEST IT SOFT WITH THE DROPS OF RAIN, AND	417 05

SOFTER

OF HIS MOUTH WERE SOFTER THAN BUTTER, HAVING WAR IN	407 35

SOILED

AND CHEER OUR SOILED FACE WITH THE ABUNDANCE OF THY	544 06
AND CHEER OUR SOILED FACE WITH THE ABUNDANCE OF THY	556 14

SOJOURNER

AND A SOJOURNER, *	325 08
AND A SOJOURNER, *	390 04

SOLD

OUT ALL THEM THAT SOLD AND BOUGHT IN THE TEMPLE,	091 34
SEATS OF THEM THAT SOLD DOVES, AND SAID UNTO THEM,	092 02
IT MIGHT HAVE BEEN SOLD FOR MORE THAN THREE HUNDRED	140 08
CAST OUT THEM THAT SOLD THEREIN, AND THEM THAT	204 16
COMMANDED HIM TO BE SOLD, AND HIS WIFE, AND CHILDREN,	221 17
OUT ALL THEM THAT SOLD AND BOUGHT IN THE TEMPLE,	260 04
SEATS OF THEM THAT SOLD DOVES, AND SAID UNTO THEM,	260 06
WHO WAS SOLD TO BE A BOND-SERVANT	471 07
TEMPLE THOSE THAT SOLD OXEN AND SHEEP AND DOVES, AND	567 26
SAID UNTO THEM THAT SOLD DOVES, TAKE THESE THINGS	567 31

SOLDIER

TO EVERY SOLDIER A PART	160 10
FAITHFUL SOLDIER AND SERVANT UNTO HIS LIFE'S END	280 10
FAITHFUL SOLDIER AND SERVANT UNTO HIS LIFE'S END	565 22

SOLDIERS

AND PROTECT THE SOLDIERS OF OUR COUNTRY	041 27
HAVING SOLDIERS UNDER ME	115 13
THEN THE SOLDIERS OF THE GOVERNOR TOOK JESUS INTO THE	136 15
AND GATHERED UNTO HIM THE WHOLE BAND OF SOLDIERS	136 17
AND THE SOLDIERS LED HIM AWAY INTO THE HALL, CALLED	145 29
AND THE SOLDIERS ALSO MOCKED HIM, COMING TO HIM,	154 30
AND THE SOLDIERS PLATTED A CROWN OF THORNS, AND PUT	158 31
THEN THE SOLDIERS, WHEN THEY HAD CRUCIFIED JESUS,	160 09
THEREFORE THE SOLDIERS DID	160 17
THEN CAME THE SOLDIERS, AND BRAKE THE LEGS OF THE	160 34
BUT ONE OF THE SOLDIERS WITH A SPEAR PIERCED HIS	161 03
QUATERNIONS OF SOLDIERS TO KEEP HIM	245 05
BETWEEN TWO SOLDIERS, BOUND WITH TWO CHAINS	245 10

SOLEMN

A FAST, CALL A SOLEMN ASSEMBLY	124 29
RENEW THE SOLEMN PROMISE AND VOW THAT YE MADE, OR	296 23
AND UPON OUR SOLEMN FEAST-DAY	442 17
THIS PLACE IN SOLEMN MANNER, FOR THE SEVERAL OFFICES	564 23

SOLEMNIZATION

FOR SOLEMNIZATION OF MATRIMONY, THE PERSONS TO BE	R 300 03

SOLITARY

WHO SETTEST THE SOLITARY IN FAMILIES	598 20

SOLOMON

THAT EVEN SOLOMON IN ALL HIS GLORY WAS NOT   211 23
THAT EVEN SOLOMON IN ALL HIS GLORY WAS NOT   266 21

SOLOMON'S

ONE ACCORD IN SOLOMON'S PORCH   249 23

SOME

SUCH ALTERATIONS IN SOME PARTICULARS, AS IN THEIR   V 29
ALL STANDING, OR SOME PROPER HYMN   R 083 32
UPON THE SUNDAY, OR SOME HOLY DAY, IMMEDIATELY   R 086 25
COME TO ME, OR TO SOME OTHER MINISTER OF GOD'S WORD,   088 06
AND SOME OF THEM YE SHALL KILL AND CRUCIFY   100 20
AND SOME OF THEM SHALL YE SCOURGE IN YOUR SYNAGOGUES, 100 21
AND AS HE SOWED, SOME FELL BY THE WAY-SIDE   121 21
AND SOME FELL UPON A ROCK   121 22
AND SOME FELL AMONG THORNS   121 24
BUT SOME OF THEM SAID, HE CASTETH OUT DEVILS THROUGH   129 26
SOME OF THEM THAT STOOD THERE, WHEN THEY HEARD THAT,   137 19
AND THERE WERE SOME THAT HAD INDIGNATION WITHIN   140 06
AND SOME BEGAN TO SPIT ON HIM, AND TO COVER HIS FACE, 143 20
AND SOME OF THEM THAT STOOD BY, WHEN THEY HEARD IT,   146 30
HOPED TO HAVE SEEN SOME MIRACLE DONE BY HIM   153 13
AS THE MANNER OF SOME IS   158 27
THEN SAID SOME OF HIS DISCIPLES AMONG THEMSELVES,   173 29
BUT CLIMBETH UP SOME OTHER WAY, THE SAME IS A THIEF   185 31
AS WERE SOME OF THEM   201 15
AS SOME OF THEM COMMITTED, AND FELL IN   201 17
US TEMPT CHRIST, AS SOME OF THEM ALSO TEMPTED,   201 19
MURMUR YE, AS SOME OF THEM ALSO MURMURED, AND WERE   201 21
THIS PRESENT, BUT SOME ARE FALLEN ASLEEP   205 10
AND HE GAVE SOME, APOSTLES   237 19
AND SOME, EVANGELISTS   237 19
AND SOME, PROPHETS   237 19
AND SOME, PASTORS AND TEACHERS   237 20
AND THEY SAID, SOME SAY THAT THOU ART JOHN THE   245 33
SOME, ELIAS   245 34
BY MIGHT OVERSHADOW SOME OF THEM   249 29
BEING NAMED BY SOME ONE WHO IS PRESENT, THE MINISTER R 281 19
HOLY DAYS, OR ON SOME OTHER CONVENIENT OCCASIONS,   R 295 08
THEN THE BISHOP, OR SOME MINISTER APPOINTED BY HIM,   R 296 10
SHALL BE READY IN SOME PROPER HOUSE, WITH THEIR   R 300 05
SHALL KNEEL DOWN IN SOME CONVENIENT PLACE, AS HATH   R 305 08
THIS OUR BROTHER TO SOME DEGREE OF HIS FORMER HEALTH   315 23
BUT SOME MAN WILL SAY, HOW ARE THE DEAD RAISED UP   329 05
OF WHEAT, OR OF SOME OTHER GRAIN   329 09
UPON THE BODY BY SOME STANDING BY, THE MINISTER SHALL R 333 12
7 SOME PUT THEIR TRUST IN CHARIOTS, AND SOME IN   364 29
IN CHARIOTS, AND SOME IN HORSES   364 29
6 THERE BE SOME THAT PUT THEIR TRUST IN THEIR GOODS,   400 16
ARE MINDED TO DO ME SOME MISCHIEF, SO MALICIOUSLY ARE 406 24
I LOOKED FOR SOME TO HAVE PITY ON ME, BUT THERE WAS   423 14
17 SHOW SOME TOKEN UPON ME FOR GOOD   448 09
UPON SOME OTHER DAY, IN THE FACE OF THE   529 30
UPON SOME OTHER DAY, IN THE FACE OF THE   R 535 25
AND SOME, PROPHETS   538 06
AND HE GAVE SOME, APOSTLES   538 06
AND SOME, EVANGELISTS   538 06
AND SOME, PASTORS AND TEACHERS   538 07
BUT CLIMBETH UP SOME OTHER WAY, THE SAME IS A THIEF   538 24
DEACONS BE GIVEN TO SOME, AND THE ORDER OF PRIESTHOOD R 547 19
OR SOME OTHER BISHOP APPOINTED BY THE BISHOPS   R 549 04
UPON MEN, MAKING SOME APOSTLES, SOME PROPHETS,   557 26
SOME APOSTLES, SOME PROPHETS, SOME EVANGELISTS, SOME   557 26
SOME EVANGELISTS, SOME PASTORS AND DOCTORS, TO THE   557 26
SOME PROPHETS, SOME EVANGELISTS, SOME PASTORS AND   557 26
AND VESTRYMEN, OR SOME OTHER PERSONS APPOINTED FOR   R 563 06
IS TO BE READ BY SOME PERSON APPOINTED BY HIM,   R 566 26
TO YOUR CURE, UNTIL SOME URGENT REASON OR REASONS   569 31
HOLY DAYS, OR ON SOME OTHER CONVENIENT OCCASIONS,   R 582 28
IN SOME PART OF THIS CATECHISM   R 582 30
THE HOUSEHOLD, OR SOME OTHER MEMBER OF THE FAMILY,   R 592 10
THE HOUSEHOLD, OR SOME OTHER MEMBER OF THE FAMILY,   R 593 04
(WHICH SOME DO EXPOUND THE WISDOM, SOME   604 36
SOME SENSUALITY, SOME THE AFFECTION, SOME THE DESIRE, 604 37
EXPOUND THE WISDOM, SOME SENSUALITY, SOME THE   604 37
SOME THE AFFECTION, SOME THE DESIRE, OF THE FLESH,)   604 37

SOMETIME

WHICH SOMETIME WERE DISOBEDIENT, WHEN ONCE THE   161 26
THOUGH I AM SOMETIME AFRAID, *   408 19
AS I DID SOMETIME FROM THE DEEP OF THE SEA   420 32
20 THOU SPAKEST SOMETIME IN VISIONS UNTO THY SAINTS,   451 12
THOUGH HE BE SOMETIME AFRAID, HE YET MAY PUT HIS   597 24

SOMETIMES

FOR YE WERE SOMETIMES DARKNESS, BUT NOW ARE YE LIGHT   129 12
AS IT MAY SOMETIMES BE EXPEDIENT TO SAY UNDER SHELTER R 336 30
THE GOOD, AND SOMETIMES THE EVIL HAVE CHIEF AUTHORITY 608 10

SON

AND AM NO MORE WORTHY TO BE CALLED THY SON   004 28
JESUS THE SON OF GOD, LET US COME BOLDLY   005 07
THE SPIRIT OF HIS SON INTO YOUR HEARTS, CRYING,   005 17
AND TO THE SON, AND TO THE HOLY GHOST   008 03
SON, AND HOLY GHOST, ONE GOD   R 008 29
AND TO THE SON, *   009 27
THINE ADORABLE, TRUE, AND ONLY SON   010 22
ART THE EVERLASTING SON OF THE FATHER   010 25
THE FATHER, AND THE SON, AND THE HOLY GHOST   013 30

SON   CONTINUED

CHRIST HIS ONLY SON OUR LORD   015 21
THE ONLY-BEGOTTEN SON OF GOD   016 02
WHO PROCEEDETH FROM THE FATHER AND THE SON   016 16
THE FATHER AND THE SON TOGETHER IS WORSHIPPED AND   016 17
AND TO THE SON, AND TO THE HOLY GHOST   025 09
THE ONLY-BEGOTTEN SON, JESUS CHRIST   025 27
LAMB OF GOD, SON OF THE FATHER, THAT TAKEST AWAY   025 28
CHRIST HIS ONLY SON OUR LORD   029 26
THE ONLY-BEGOTTEN SON OF GOD   030 07
WHO PROCEEDETH FROM THE FATHER AND THE SON   030 21
THE FATHER AND THE SON TOGETHER IS WORSHIPPED AND   030 22
THE LOVE OF THY ONLY SON, OUR SAVIOUR, JESUS CHRIST   031 28
JESUS CHRIST, THY SON, OUR LORD   035 28
TO BE OUR JUDGE, THY SON, OUR SAVIOUR JESUS CHRIST   036 06
THROUGH THY SON JESUS CHRIST, TO BE WITH THY CHURCH   036 28
JESUS CHRIST, THY SON, OUR LORD   037 22
SEND THY BLESSED SON TO PREACH PEACE TO THEM THAT ARE 038 07
THROUGH THE SAME THY SON JESUS CHRIST OUR LORD   038 11
CHURCH BY THE PRECIOUS BLOOD OF THY DEAR SON   038 27
BLOOD OF THY DEAR SON, AND INCLINE THE HEARTS OF MANY 039 19
THROUGH THE SAME THY SON JESUS CHRIST OUR LORD   039 21
WHO BY THY SON JESUS CHRIST HAST PROMISED TO   040 15
THE MERITS OF THY SON, JESUS CHRIST OUR LORD   041 16
JESUS CHRIST THY SON OUR LORD   042 20
THE TEACHING OF THY SON JESUS CHRIST DIDST PREPARE   043 18
WHOSE BLESSED SON CAME NOT TO BE MINISTERED UNTO, BUT 043 28
FOR US, THE SAME THY SON, OUR SAVIOUR JESUS CHRIST   044 06
THAT SERVETH, THY SON JESUS CHRIST OUR LORD   044 25
WORTHINESS OF THY SON JESUS CHRIST OUR LORD   050 04
O GOD THE SON, REDEEMER OF THE WORLD   054 07
SON OF GOD, WE BESEECH THEE TO HEAR US   057 19
AND TO THE SON, AND TO THE HOLY GHOST   059 05
O SON OF DAVID, HAVE MERCY UPON US   059 14
AND TO THE SON, *   061 15
OF THY BLESSED SON, JESUS CHRIST OUR LORD   063 06
THOU, AND THY SON, AND THY DAUGHTER, THY MAN-SERVANT, 068 27
THE ONLY-BEGOTTEN SON OF GOD   071 04
WHO PROCEEDETH FROM THE FATHER AND THE SON   071 18
THE FATHER AND THE SON TOGETHER IS WORSHIPPED AND   071 19
FOR THY SON OUR LORD JESUS CHRIST'S SAKE, FORGIVE US   075 27
HIS ONLY-BEGOTTEN SON, TO THE END THAT ALL THAT   076 15
THINE ONLY SON, TO BE BORN AS AT THIS TIME   077 15
IN THE FACE OF THY SON JESUS CHRIST OUR LORD   078 03
RESURRECTION OF THY SON JESUS CHRIST OUR LORD   078 08
MOST DEARLY BELOVED SON JESUS CHRIST OUR LORD   078 16
OF THEE, AND OF THY SON JESUS CHRIST   079 02
THINE ONLY-BEGOTTEN SON, AND THE HOLY GHOST, ART ONE   079 07
WE BELIEVE OF THE SON, AND OF THE HOLY GHOST, WITHOUT 079 11
AND MERITS OF THY SON JESUS CHRIST OUR LORD, AND FOR   079 15
GIVE THINE ONLY SON JESUS CHRIST TO SUFFER DEATH UPON 080 08
THY DEARLY BELOVED SON OUR SAVIOUR JESUS CHRIST,   080 38
THE MEMORIAL THY SON HATH COMMANDED US TO MAKE   080 41
ACCORDING TO THY SON OUR SAVIOUR JESUS CHRIST'S HOLY   081 12
AND DEATH OF THY SON JESUS CHRIST, AND THROUGH FAITH   081 18
AND BLOOD OF THY SON JESUS CHRIST, BE FILLED WITH THY 081 26
FLESH OF THY DEAR SON JESUS CHRIST, AND TO DRINK HIS   082 19
AND BLOOD OF THY SON OUR SAVIOUR JESUS CHRIST   083 19
MYSTICAL BODY OF THY SON, WHICH IS THE BLESSED   083 22
THE ONLY-BEGOTTEN SON, JESUS CHRIST   084 07
LAMB OF GOD, SON OF THE FATHER, THAT TAKEST AWAY   084 08
OF GOD, AND OF HIS SON JESUS CHRIST OUR LORD   084 20
THE FATHER, THE SON, AND THE HOLY GHOST, BE AMONGST   084 21
THE FATHER, THE SON, AND THE HOLY GHOST, FOR THE   086 06
HE HATH GIVEN HIS SON OUR SAVIOUR JESUS CHRIST,   087 03
AND AS THE SON OF GOD DID VOUCHSAFE TO YIELD UP HIS   089 10
IN WHICH THY SON JESUS CHRIST CAME TO VISIT US   090 14
HOSANNA TO THE SON OF DAVID   091 28
SHALL THEY SEE THE SON OF MAN COMING IN A CLOUD WITH   093 10
US THY ONLY-BEGOTTEN SON TO TAKE OUR NATURE UPON HIM, 096 14
UNTO US BY HIS SON, WHOM HE HATH APPOINTED HEIR OF   096 24
THOU ART MY SON, THIS DAY HAVE I BEGOTTEN THEE   097 03
AND HE SHALL BE TO ME A SON   097 04
BUT UNTO THE SON HE SAITH, THY THRONE, O GOD, IS FOR   097 08
BIRTH OF THINE ONLY SON JESUS CHRIST   098 12
FORTH HER FIRSTBORN SON, AND WRAPPED HIM IN SWADDLING 099 08
AND THE SON OF MAN STANDING ON THE RIGHT HAND   100 08
BLOOD OF ZACHARIAS SON OF BARACHIAS, WHOM YE SLEW   100 24
AND WITH HIS SON JESUS CHRIST   101 20
OF JESUS CHRIST HIS SON CLEANSETH US FROM ALL SIN   101 28
OUT OF EGYPT HAVE I CALLED MY SON   103 24
US THY ONLY-BEGOTTEN SON TO TAKE OUR NATURE UPON HIM, 104 06
GOD SENT FORTH HIS SON, MADE OF A WOMAN, MADE UNDER   104 20
THE SPIRIT OF HIS SON INTO YOUR HEARTS, CRYING,   104 23
WHEREFORE THOU ART NO MORE A SERVANT, BUT A SON   104 24
AND IF A SON, THEN AN HEIR OF GOD THROUGH CHRIST   104 25
JOSEPH, THOU SON OF DAVID, FEAR NOT TO TAKE   105 04
SHALL BRING FORTH A SON, AND THOU SHALT CALL HIS NAME 105 06
SHALL BRING FORTH A SON, AND THEY SHALL CALL HIS NAME 105 11
NOT TILL SHE HAD BROUGHT FORTH HER FIRSTBORN SON   105 15
MADEST THY BLESSED SON TO BE CIRCUMCISED, AND   105 19
THROUGH THE SAME THY SON JESUS CHRIST OUR LORD   105 24
THY ONLY-BEGOTTEN SON TO THE GENTILES   107 30
THROUGH THE SAME THY SON JESUS CHRIST OUR LORD   108 03
SAID UNTO HIM, SON, WHY HAST THOU THUS DEALT WITH US   110 32
OF JESUS CHRIST, THE SON OF GOD   112 03
THOU ART MY BELOVED SON, IN WHOM I AM WELL PLEASED   112 23
O GOD, WHOSE BLESSED SON WAS MANIFESTED THAT HE MIGHT 117 04
FOR THIS PURPOSE THE SON OF GOD WAS MANIFESTED, THAT   117 29
THE COMING OF THE SON OF MAN BE   118 12
THE SIGN OF THE SON OF MAN IN HEAVEN   118 17
THEY SHALL SEE THE SON OF MAN COMING IN THE CLOUDS OF 118 19
THIS FOR THINE ONLY SON JESUS CHRIST'S SAKE   122 19
CONCERNING THE SON OF MAN SHALL BE ACCOMPLISHED   123 19
JESUS, THOU SON OF DAVID, HAVE MERCY ON ME   123 30

SON   CONTINUED

MUCH THE MORE, THOU SON OF DAVID, HAVE MERCY ON ME	123 32
IF THOU BE THE SON OF GOD, COMMAND THAT THESE	126 27
IF THOU BE THE SON OF GOD, CAST THYSELF DOWN	126 32
ON ME, O LORD, THOU SON OF DAVID	128 10
FOR THE SON OF THE BONDWOMAN SHALL NOT BE HEIR WITH	131 16
CAST OUT THE BONDWOMAN AND HER SON	131 16
NOT BE HEIR WITH THE SON OF THE FREEWOMAN	131 17
HAST SENT THY SON, OUR SAVIOUR JESUS CHRIST, TO TAKE	134 06
IF THOU BE THE SON OF GOD, COME DOWN FROM THE CROSS	137 08
HE SAID, I AM THE SON OF GOD	137 13
TRULY THIS WAS THE SON OF GOD	137 33
WHOSE MOST DEAR SON WENT NOT UP TO JOY BUT FIRST	138 04
THROUGH THE SAME THY SON JESUS CHRIST OUR LORD	138 08
THE SON OF MAN INDEED GOETH, AS IT IS WRITTEN OF HIM	141 06
THAT MAN BY WHOM THE SON OF MAN IS BETRAYED	141 08
BEHOLD, THE SON OF MAN IS BETRAYED INTO THE HANDS OF	142 12
THOU THE CHRIST, THE SON OF THE BLESSED	143 14
AND YE SHALL SEE THE SON OF MAN SITTING ON THE RIGHT	143 15
WHOSE BLESSED SON, OUR SAVIOUR, GAVE HIS BACK TO	144 06
THROUGH THE SAME THY SON JESUS CHRIST OUR LORD	144 10
THIS MAN WAS THE SON OF GOD	147 05
AND TRULY THE SON OF MAN GOETH, AS IT WAS DETERMINED	149 14
BETRAYEST THOU THE SON OF MAN WITH A KISS	150 30
HEREAFTER SHALL THE SON OF MAN SIT ON THE RIGHT HAND	151 32
ART THOU THEN THE SON OF GOD	151 34
WHOSE DEAR SON, ON THE NIGHT BEFORE HE	152 07
THE SAME THY SON JESUS CHRIST OUR LORD, WHO NOW	152 12
SIMON'S SON, TO BETRAY HIM	155 28
NOT AS THOU ART REVEALED IN THE GOSPEL OF THY SON	157 08
HE MADE HIMSELF THE SON OF GOD	159 10
HE SAITH UNTO HIS MOTHER, WOMAN, BEHOLD THY SON	160 21
DEATH OF THY BLESSED SON, OUR SAVIOUR JESUS CHRIST,	161 14
FOR US, THE SAME THY SON JESUS CHRIST OUR LORD	161 19
AND TO THE SON, *	163 17
THINE ONLY-BEGOTTEN SON JESUS CHRIST HAST OVERCOME	163 23
THINE ONLY-BEGOTTEN SON TO THE DEATH OF THE CROSS,	165 04
THROUGH THE SAME THY SON CHRIST OUR LORD	165 08
O GOD, WHOSE BLESSED SON DID MANIFEST HIMSELF TO HIS	166 06
THROUGH THE SAME THY SON JESUS CHRIST OUR LORD	166 09
THOU ART MY SON, THIS DAY HAVE I BEGOTTEN	169 09
GIVEN THINE ONLY SON TO DIE FOR OUR SINS, AND TO RISE	170 19
OF THE SAME THY SON JESUS CHRIST OUR LORD	170 23
THAT JESUS IS THE SON OF GOD	170 29
WITNESS OF GOD WHICH HE HATH TESTIFIED OF HIS SON	171 06
BELIEVETH ON THE SON OF GOD HATH THE WITNESS IN	171 06
BELIEVETH NOT THE RECORD THAT GOD GAVE OF HIS SON	171 09
HE THAT HATH THE SON HATH LIFE	171 11
AND THIS LIFE IS IN HIS SON	171 11
HE THAT HATH NOT THE SON OF GOD HATH NOT LIFE	171 12
GIVEN THINE ONLY SON TO BE UNTO US BOTH A SACRIFICE	171 28
THROUGH THE SAME THY SON JESUS CHRIST OUR LORD	172 02
THY ONLY-BEGOTTEN SON OUR LORD JESUS CHRIST TO HAVE	177 15
EXALTED THINE ONLY SON JESUS CHRIST WITH GREAT	179 05
IF A SON SHALL ASK BREAD OF ANY OF YOU THAT IS A	183 14
HIS ONLY-BEGOTTEN SON, THAT WHOSOEVER BELIEVETH IN	184 33
FOR GOD SENT NOT HIS SON INTO THE WORLD TO CONDEMN	184 34
OF THE ONLY-BEGOTTEN SON	185 05
EVEN THE SON OF MAN WHICH IS IN HEAVEN	188 26
EVEN SO MUST THE SON OF MAN BE LIFTED UP	188 27
HIS ONLY-BEGOTTEN SON INTO THE WORLD, THAT WE MIGHT	189 12
AND SENT HIS SON TO BE THE PROPITIATION FOR OUR	189 14
THE FATHER SENT THE SON TO BE THE SAVIOUR OF THE	189 21
THAT JESUS IS THE SON OF GOD, GOD DWELLETH IN HIM,	189 22
BUT ABRAHAM SAID, SON, REMEMBER THAT THOU IN THY	190 16
ON THE NAME OF HIS SON JESUS CHRIST, AND LOVE ONE	191 30
AFTER THE YOUNGER SON GATHERED ALL TOGETHER, AND TOOK	202 02
AND AM NO MORE WORTHY TO BE CALLED THY SON	202 15
AND THE SON SAID UNTO HIM, FATHER, I HAVE SINNED	202 18
AND AM NO MORE WORTHY TO BE CALLED THY SON	202 20
FOR THIS MY SON WAS DEAD, AND IS ALIVE AGAIN	202 24
NOW HIS ELDER SON WAS IN THE FIELD	202 26
AS SOON AS THIS THY SON WAS COME, WHICH HATH DEVOURED	203 03
HE SAID UNTO HIM, SON, THOU ART EVER WITH ME, AND ALL	203 05
OF JESUS CHRIST, THY SON, OUR LORD	206 10
THE ONLY SON OF HIS MOTHER, AND SHE WAS A WIDOW	212 31
WHOSE SON IS HE	215 17
SAY UNTO HIM, THE SON OF DAVID	215 18
IF DAVID THEN CALL HIM LORD, HOW IS HE HIS SON	215 22
SON, BE OF GOOD CHEER	217 03
YE MAY KNOW THAT THE SON OF MAN HATH POWER ON EARTH	217 09
A MARRIAGE FOR HIS SON, AND SENT FORTH HIS SERVANTS	218 04
WHOSE SON WAS SICK AT CAPERNAUM	219 28
HIM THAT HE WOULD COME DOWN, AND HEAL HIS SON	219 31
THY SON LIVETH	220 03
SAYING, THY SON LIVETH	220 06
SAID UNTO HIM, THY SON LIVETH	220 10
THE CALLING OF THY SON JESUS CHRIST, AND FOLLOWED HIM	226 20
JAMES THE SON OF ZEBEDEE, AND JOHN HIS	227 30
TO BELIEVE IN THY SON JESUS CHRIST, THAT OUR FAITH IN	228 08
IS THE CHRIST, THE SON OF GOD	229 12
THAT HE IS THE SON OF GOD	231 04
WHEN THE SON OF MAN SHALL SIT IN THE THRONE OF HIS	231 16
AS THY ONLY-BEGOTTEN SON WAS THIS DAY PRESENTED IN	231 29
BY THE SAME THY SON JESUS CHRIST OUR LORD	231 32
NO MAN KNOWETH THE SON, BUT THE FATHER	235 08
THE FATHER, SAVE THE SON, AND HE TO WHOMSOEVER THE	235 09
HE TO WHOMSOEVER THE SON WILL REVEAL HIM	235 10
INCARNATION OF THY SON JESUS CHRIST BY THE MESSAGE OF	235 20
AND BEAR A SON, AND SHALL CALL HIS NAME	235 32
AND BRING FORTH A SON, AND SHALT CALL HIS NAME JESUS	236 15
SHALL BE CALLED THE SON OF THE HIGHEST	236 17
SHALL BE CALLED THE SON OF GOD	236 25
ALSO CONCEIVED A SON IN HER OLD AGE	236 26
THE KNOWLEDGE OF THE SON OF GOD, UNTO A PERFECT MAN,	237 23

SON   CONTINUED

TO KNOW THY SON JESUS CHRIST TO BE THE WAY, THE	238 30
THROUGH THE SAME THY SON JESUS CHRIST OUR LORD	239 03
THAT THE FATHER MAY BE GLORIFIED IN THE SON	240 23
THE WAY OF THY SON OUR SAVIOUR BY PREACHING	242 09
THROUGH TH SAME THY SON JESUS CHRIST OUR LORD	242 14
AND SHE BROUGHT FORTH A SON	243 14
WHO BY THY SON JESUS CHRIST DIDST GIVE TO THY	244 22
THROUGH THE SAME THY SON JESUS CHRIST OUR LORD	244 28
MEN SAY THAT I THE SON OF MAN AM	245 33
ART THE CHRIST, THE SON OF THE LIVING GOD	246 03
THE CALLING OF THY SON JESUS CHRIST, AND FOLLOWED	246 18
EVEN AS THE SON OF MAN CAME NOT TO BE MINISTERED	247 26
THINE ONLY-BEGOTTEN SON WONDERFULLY TRANSFIGURED, IN	247 32
THIS IS MY BELOVED SON, IN WHOM I AM WELL PLEASED	248 19
THIS IS MY BELOVED SON	249 07
WHO BY THY BLESSED SON DIDST CALL MATTHEW FROM THE	250 20
FOLLOW THE SAME THY SON JESUS CHRIST, WHO LIVETH AND	250 24
THE GOSPEL THE LOVE AND HEALING POWER OF THY SON	253 18
THROUGH THE SAME THY SON JESUS CHRIST OUR LORD	253 20
AND IF THE SON OF PEACE BE THERE, YOUR PEACE SHALL	254 20
MYSTICAL BODY OF THY SON JESUS CHRIST OUR LORD	256 07
THROUGH THE SAME THY SON JESUS CHRIST OUR LORD	256 11
OF OUR FAITH, THY SON JESUS CHRIST OUR LORD	258 18
WHEN THE SON OF MAN SHALL COME IN HIS GLORY, AND ALL	258 28
HOSANNA TO THE SON OF DAVID	260 12
IF A SON SHALL ASK BREAD OF ANY OF YOU THAT IS A	263 07
AND TO THE SON, *	265 06
ONE WHICH SEETH THE SON, AND BELIEVETH ON HIM, MAY	269 20
BY THY WELL-BELOVED SON, SAYING, ASK, AND YE SHALL	274 15
AND OF THE SON, AND OF THE HOLY GHOST	275 29
DECLARED BY HIS SON JESUS CHRIST	276 05
THE CHRIST, THE SON OF THE LIVING GOD	278 03
THY DEARLY BELOVED SON JESUS CHRIST, FOR THE	279 09
AND OF THE SON, AND OF THE HOLY GHOST	279 14
AND OF THE SON, AND OF THE HOLY GHOST	279 29
AND OF THE SON, AND OF THE HOLY GHOST	281 22
AND OF THE SON, AND OF THE HOLY GHOST,	R 282 09
AND OF THE SON, AND OF THE HOLY GHOST	282 14
CHRIST HIS ONLY SON OUR LORD	284 15
IN GOD THE SON, WHO HATH REDEEMED ME,	284 31
AND TO THE SON, AND OF THE HOLY GHOST	285 07
THOU, AND THY SON, AND THY DAUGHTER, THY MAN-SERVANT,	286 27
AND OF THE SON, AND OF THE HOLY GHOST	292 21
THE FATHER, THE SON, AND THE HOLY GHOST, BE UPON YOU,	299 03
AND OF THE SON, AND OF THE HOLY GHOST	302 15
AND OF THE SON, AND OF THE HOLY GHOST	304 09
THE FATHER, GOD THE SON, GOD THE HOLY GHOST, BLESS,	304 11
AND TO THE SON, AND TO THE HOLY GHOST	306 04
MOST DEARLY BELOVED SON, JESUS CHRIST OUR LORD	314 13
FAITH IN THY SON JESUS	316 14
THROUGH THE SAME THY SON, OUR LORD AND SAVIOUR	316 16
CHRIST THINE ONLY SON OUR LORD	317 23
O GOD THE SON	317 27
AND OF THE SON, AND OF THE HOLY GHOST	320 16
MY SON, DESPISE NOT THOU THE CHASTENING OF THE LORD,	321 28
AND SCOURGETH EVERY SON WHOM HE RECEIVETH	321 30
ON THE NAME OF THE SON OF GOD	322 13
ON THE NAME OF THE SON OF GOD	322 15
THEN SHALL THE SON ALSO HIMSELF BE SUBJECT UNTO	329 02
SPARED NOT HIS OWN SON, BUT DELIVERED HIM UP FOR US	330 34
THY WELL-BELOVED SON SHALL THEN PRONOUNCE TO ALL WHO	335 10
SAKE OF THE SAME THY SON JESUS CHRIST OUR LORD	336 02
MYSTICAL BODY OF THY SON, MAY BE SET ON HIS RIGHT	336 25
OF THE SAME, THY SON JESUS CHRIST, OUR ONLY MEDIATOR	336 29
WHOSE MOST DEAR SON DID TAKE LITTLE CHILDREN	342 03
THROUGH THE SAME THY SON, JESUS CHRIST OUR LORD	342 07
THE FATHER, THE SON, AND THE HOLY GHOST, BLESS	342 14
UNTO ME, THOU ART MY SON, THIS DAY HAVE I BEGOTTEN	346 11
12 KISS THE SON, LEST HE BE ANGRY, AND SO YE PERISH	346 21
AND THE SON OF MAN, THAT THOU VISITEST HIM	351 08
AND HAST SLANDERED THINE OWN MOTHER'S SON	402 31
AND THY RIGHTEOUSNESS UNTO THE KING'S SON	426 32
AND UPON THE SON OF MAN, WHOM THOU MADEST SO STRONG	442 05
AND HELP THE SON OF THINE HANDMAID	448 07
THE SON OF WICKEDNESS SHALL NOT HURT HIM	451 20
THY SERVANT, AND THE SON OF THINE HANDMAID	487 17
OR THE SON OF MAN, THAT THOU SO REGARDEST HIM	519 28
AND OF THE SON, AND OF THE HOLY GHOST	534 07
AND STRONG IN THY SON CHRIST, MAY SO WELL BEHAVE	535 07
THROUGH THE SAME THY SON OUR SAVIOUR JESUS CHRIST, TO	535 10
OF GOD, AND OF HIS SON JESUS CHRIST OUR LORD	535 15
THE FATHER, THE SON, AND THE HOLY GHOST, BE AMONGST	535 16
THE KNOWLEDGE OF THE SON OF GOD, UNTO A PERFECT MAN,	538 10
TO KNOW THE FATHER, SON, AND THEE, OF BOTH, TO BE BUT	544 10
FATHER, SON, AND HOLY SPIRIT	544 15
MOST DEARLY BELOVED SON JESUS CHRIST, TO BE OUR	545 14
THE SAME THY BLESSED SON, TO GRANT UNTO ALL, WHICH	545 26
OF THEE AND THY SON, BY THE HOLY SPIRIT	545 31
THROUGH THE SAME THY SON JESUS CHRIST OUR LORD,	546 03
AND OF THE SON, AND OF THE HOLY GHOST	546 15
AND OF THE SON, AND OF THE HOLY GHOST	546 21
OF GOD, AND OF HIS SON JESUS CHRIST OUR LORD	547 16
THE FATHER, THE SON, AND THE HOLY GHOST, BE AMONGST	547 17
WHO BY THE SON JESUS CHRIST DIDST GIVE TO THY	549 07
THROUGH THE SAME THY SON JESUS CHRIST OUR LORD	549 15
SIMON PETER, SIMON, SON OF JONAS, LOVEST THOU ME MORE	551 14
SECOND TIME, SIMON, SON OF JONAS, LOVEST THOU ME	551 17
THIRD TIME, SIMON, SON OF JONAS, LOVEST THOU ME	551 20
AND OF THE SON, AND OF THE HOLY GHOST	552 12
TO KNOW THE FATHER, SON, AND THEE, OF BOTH, TO BE BUT	556 18
FATHER, SON, AND HOLY SPIRIT	556 23
AND DEARLY BELOVED SON JESUS CHRIST, TO BE OUR	557 22
AND OF THE SON, AND OF THE HOLY GHOST	558 15
OF GOD, AND OF HIS SON JESUS CHRIST OUR LORD	559 19

SON   CONTINUED

THE FATHER, THE SON, AND THE HOLY GHOST, BE AMONGST	559 20
O GOD THE SON, O GOD THE HOLY GHOST,	560 05
AND TO THE SON, *	564 02
OF GOD, AND OF HIS SON JESUS CHRIST OUR LORD	568 15
THE FATHER, THE SON, AND THE HOLY GHOST, BE AMONGST	568 16
AND OF THE SON, AND OF THE HOLY GHOST	571 02
THE FATHER AND THE SON TOGETHER, WE WORSHIP AND	572 31
OF JESUS CHRIST THY SON OUR SAVIOUR	573 29
THE SAME THY BLESSED SON JESUS CHRIST, THE GRACIOUS	574 20
CHRIST HIS ONLY SON OUR LORD	577 30
IN GOD THE SON, WHO HATH REDEEMED ME,	578 13
THOU, AND THY SON, AND THY DAUGHTER, THY MAN-SERVANT,	579 07
AND OF THE SON, AND OF THE HOLY GHOST	581 22
AGAIN FOR US, THY SON OUR SAVIOUR JESUS CHRIST	587 27
QUICK AND DEAD, THY SON JESUS CHRIST OUR LORD	588 24
AND MEDIATION OF THY SON JESUS CHRIST, OUR LORD AND	589 07
FOR THE SAKE OF THY SON JESUS CHRIST, OUR ONLY	590 06
DOING GOOD, THY SON OUR SAVIOUR JESUS CHRIST	591 05
IN SENDING THY ONLY SON INTO THE WORLD, TO REDEEM US	591 12
THEM ALL, THY SON OUR SAVIOUR JESUS CHRIST	591 23
SATISFACTION OF THY SON CHRIST JESUS, IN WHOSE NAME	591 32
THE LOVE OF THY ONLY SON, OUR SAVIOUR, JESUS CHRIST	593 15
AND ROSE AGAIN, THY SON, OUR SAVIOUR JESUS CHRIST	595 10
RESURRECTION OF THY SON OUR LORD	595 13
UNTO US IN THY SON, JESUS CHRIST OUR LORD	596 09
WERE MADE, THY SON, JESUS CHRIST OUR LORD	596 22
BECAME POOR, THY SON, OUR SAVIOUR JESUS CHRIST	599 16
THE LOVE OF THY DEAR SON, OUR SAVIOUR JESUS CHRIST	600 12
THE FATHER, THE SON, AND THE HOLY GHOST	603 07
THE SON, WHICH IS THE WORD OF THE FATHER, BEGOTTEN	603 09
THE FATHER AND THE SON, IS OF ONE SUBSTANCE, MAJESTY,	603 26
THE FATHER AND THE SON, VERY AND ETERNAL GOD	603 27
OF HIS ONLY-BEGOTTEN SON JESUS CHRIST	606 14

SON'S

WHO ASK IN THY SON'S NAME	050 07
BE DOUBTFUL IN THY SON'S RESURRECTION	228 07

SONG

AND COME BEFORE HIS PRESENCE WITH A SONG	015 06
O SING UNTO THE LORD A NEW SONG	027 04
AS IT WERE A NEW SONG BEFORE THE THRONE, AND BEFORE	103 05
COULD LEARN THAT SONG BUT THE HUNDRED AND FORTY AND	103 07
TO REMEMBRANCE MY SONG, AND IN THE NIGHT I COMMUNE	311 10
FOR JOY, AND IN MY SONG WILL I PRAISE HIM	373 24
3 SING UNTO THE LORD A NEW SONG	378 23
HE HATH PUT A NEW SONG IN MY MOUTH, *	390 14
NAME OF GOD WITH A SONG, *	424 04
TO REMEMBRANCE MY SONG, *	433 27
MY SONG SHALL BE ALWAY OF THE LOVING-KINDNESS OF THE	450 04
O SING UNTO THE LORD A NEW SONG	459 30
O SING UNTO THE LORD A NEW SONG	461 25
AND COME BEFORE HIS PRESENCE WITH A SONG	463 07
MY SONG SHALL BE OF MERCY AND JUDGMENT	463 17
14 THE LORD IS MY STRENGTH, AND MY SONG	488 28
OF US THEN A SONG, AND MELODY IN OUR HEAVINESS	513 10
WE SING THE LORD'S SONG *	513 12
9 I WILL SING A NEW SONG UNTO THEE, O GOD	520 08
O SING UNTO THE LORD A NEW SONG	525 03
THE AGES ALL ALONG, THIS MAY BE OUR ENDLESS SONG	544 13
THE AGES ALL ALONG, THIS MAY BE OUR ENDLESS SONG	556 21

SONGS

AND SPIRITUAL SONGS, SINGING WITH GRACE IN YOUR	116 13
AND SPIRITUAL SONGS, SINGING AND MAKING MELODY IN	217 28
MY SONGS WILL I MAKE OF THY NAME, O THOU MOST	351 24
ME ABOUT WITH SONGS OF DELIVERANCE	378 07
THE DRUNKARDS MAKE SONGS UPON ME	422 27
2 O LET YOUR SONGS BE OF HIM, AND PRAISE HIM	470 07
HAVE BEEN MY SONGS, *	493 18
SING US ONE OF THE SONGS OF SION	513 11

SONS

BECAUSE YE ARE SONS, GOD HATH SENT FORTH THE SPIRIT	005 16
POWER TO BECOME THE SONS OF GOD, EVEN TO THEM THAT	097 34
AND BECAUSE YE ARE SONS, GOD HATH SENT FORTH THE	104 22
THAT WE MIGHT RECEIVE THE ADOPTION OF SONS	104 22
MADE KNOWN UNTO THE SONS OF MEN, AS IT IS NOW	108 12
AND MAKE US THE SONS OF GOD, AND HEIRS OF ETERNAL	117 06
BE CALLED THE SONS OF GOD	117 15
NOW ARE WE THE SONS OF GOD, AND IT DOTH NOT YET	117 17
BY WHOM DO YOUR SONS CAST THEM OUT	130 02
ABRAHAM HAD TWO SONS, THE ONE BY A BONDMAID, THE	130 13
OF THE SONS OF GOD	194 14
AND JOHN, THE SONS OF ZEBEDEE, WHICH WERE PARTNERS	196 26
THEY ARE THE SONS OF GOD	200 07
A CERTAIN MAN HAD TWO SONS	201 31
HE SHALL PURIFY THE SONS OF LEVI, AND PURGE THEM AS	232 11
CHILDREN WITH HER SONS, WORSHIPPING HIM, AND DESIRING	247 07
THAT THESE MY TWO SONS MAY SIT, THE ONE ON THY RIGHT	247 09
THEY ARE THE SONS OF GOD	330 20
OF THE SONS OF GOD	330 30
2 O YE SONS OF MEN, HOW LONG WILL YE BLASPHEME MINE	347 13
EVEN BEFORE THE SONS OF MEN	377 04
THAT IS RIGHT, O YE SONS OF MEN	410 09
EVEN THE SONS OF JACOB AND JOSEPH	434 13
THEY OFFERED THEIR SONS AND THEIR DAUGHTERS UNTO	475 09
THE BLOOD OF THEIR SONS AND OF THEIR DAUGHTERS,	475 12
12 THAT OUR SONS MAY GROW UP AS THE YOUNG PLANTS,	520 15
AMONG THE SONS OF MEN, AND TO DWELL IN THE MIDST OF	568 07

SONS   CONTINUED

THEY BE MADE SONS OF GOD BY ADOPTION	606 13
ADOPTION TO BE THE SONS OF GOD BY THE HOLY GHOST, ARE	608 28

SOON

SO TO DO, AS SOON AS HE CONVENIENTLY MAY	R 085 08
AND AS SOON AS IT WAS SPRUNG UP, IT WITHERED AWAY,	121 23
AND AS SOON AS HE WAS COME, HE GOETH STRAIGHTWAY TO	142 19
AND AS SOON AS IT WAS DAY, THE ELDERS OF THE PEOPLE	151 27
AND AS SOON AS HE KNEW THAT HE BELONGED UNTO HEROD'S	153 08
BUT AS SOON AS SHE IS DELIVERED OF THE CHILD, SHE	174 11
BUT AS SOON AS THIS THY SON WAS COME, WHICH HATH	203 02
THAT THIS CHILD, SO SOON AS SUFFICIENTLY INSTRUCTED,	277 14
BY THE BISHOP, SO SOON AFTER HIS BAPTISM AS	R 281 14
SO SOON AS CHILDREN ARE COME TO A COMPETENT AGE,	R 295 13
AS SOON AS THOU SCATTEREST THEM THEY ARE EVEN AS A	325 22
SO SOON PASSETH IT AWAY, AND WE ARE GONE	325 35
45 AS SOON AS THEY HEAR OF ME, THEY SHALL OBEY ME	362 28
2 FOR THEY SHALL SOON BE CUT DOWN LIKE THE GRASS,	384 27
AS SOON AS THEY ARE BORN, THEY GO ASTRAY, AND SPEAK	410 13
MORIANS' LAND SHALL SOON STRETCH OUT HER HANDS UNTO	421 19
FOR THEIR REWARD BE SOON BROUGHT TO SHAME, *	424 25
BUT HAVE MERCY UPON US, AND THAT SOON	440 17
15 I SHOULD SOON HAVE PUT DOWN THEIR ENEMIES,	443 08
5 AS SOON AS THOU SCATTEREST THEM THEY ARE EVEN AS A	453 27
SO SOON PASSETH IT AWAY, AND WE ARE GONE	454 10
14 O SATISFY US WITH THY MERCY, AND THAT SOON	454 17
11 I SHALL SOON DESTROY ALL THE UNGODLY THAT ARE IN	464 04
O HEAR ME, AND THAT RIGHT SOON	464 14
16 FOR AS SOON AS THE WIND GOETH OVER IT, IT IS GONE	467 06
7 HEAR ME, O LORD, AND THAT SOON	519 04
SO SOON AS CHILDREN ARE COME TO A COMPETENT AGE,	R 582 36

SOONER

FOR THE SUN IS NO SOONER RISEN WITH A BURNING HEAT,	239 21

SOPE

IS LIKE A REFINER'S FIRE, AND LIKE FULLERS' SOPE	232 09

SORCERERS

AGAINST THE SORCERERS, AND AGAINST THE ADULTERERS,	232 16

SORE

TO GOD, AND HOW SORE PUNISHMENT HANGETH OVER YOUR	089 15
WE ARE SORE LET AND HINDERED IN RUNNING	095 06
AND THEY WERE SORE AFRAID	099 14
AND BEGAN TO BE SORE AMAZED, AND TO BE VERY HEAVY	141 30
THEY WERE SORE DISPLEASED, AND SAID UNTO HIM, HEAREST	260 12
AND VEX THEM IN HIS SORE DISPLEASURE	346 07
3 MY SOUL ALSO IS SORE TROUBLED	349 04
BE CONFOUNDED, AND SORE VEXED	349 18
AND THY HAND PRESSETH ME SORE	387 24
AND ARE LIKE A SORE BURDEN, TOO HEAVY FOR ME TO BEAR	387 29
ARE FILLED WITH A SORE DISEASE, *	388 04
8 I AM FEEBLE AND SORE SMITTEN	388 06
AND TOOK SORE DISPLEASURE AT ISRAEL	438 30
BUT I WAS SORE TROUBLED	487 07
13 THOU HAST THRUST SORE AT ME, THAT I MIGHT FALL	488 26
82 MINE EYES LONG SORE FOR THY WORD	495 21
22 YEA, I HATE THEM RIGHT SORE	516 02

SORES

HIS GATE, FULL OF SORES, AND DESIRING TO BE FED WITH	190 06
MOREOVER THE DOGS CAME AND LICKED HIS SORES	190 08
HEAL THE SORES THEREOF, FOR IT SHAKETH	412 16

SORROW

IF THERE BE ANY SORROW LIKE UNTO MY SORROW WHICH IS	004 30
LIKE UNTO MY SORROW WHICH IS DONE UNTO ME, WHEREWITH	004 31
FOR ALL WHO ARE IN SICKNESS OR IN SORROW	048 07
ARE IN TROUBLE, SORROW, NEED, SICKNESS, OR ANY OTHER	074 32
YE SHALL LIE DOWN IN SORROW	144 29
THEM SLEEPING FOR SORROW, AND SAID UNTO THEM, WHY	150 25
BUT YOUR SORROW SHALL BE TURNED INTO JOY	174 09
IN TRAVAIL HATH SORROW, BECAUSE HER HOUR IS COME	174 10
AND YE NOW THEREFORE HAVE SORROW	174 14
THINGS UNTO YOU, SORROW HATH FILLED YOUR HEART	175 09
THAT YE SORROW NOT, EVEN AS OTHERS WHICH HAVE	268 29
AND OUR SORROW INTO JOY	312 15
YET IS THEIR STRENGTH THEN BUT LABOUR AND SORROW	325 34
YE NOW THEREFORE HAVE SORROW	341 09
AND SORROW, *	399 20
MISCHIEF ALSO AND SORROW ARE IN THE MIDST OF IT	407 07
YET IS THEIR STRENGTH THEN BUT LABOUR AND SORROW	454 09
NEITHER SORROW, NOR CRYING, NEITHER SHALL	567 19

SORROWFUL

NOR THE DESIRE OF SUCH AS ARE SORROWFUL	058 16
AS SORROWFUL, YET ALWAY REJOICING	126 19
BEGAN TO BE SORROWFUL, AND TO SAY UNTO HIM ONE BY	141 03
IS EXCEEDING SORROWFUL UNTO DEATH	141 31
YE SHALL BE SORROWFUL, BUT YOUR SORROW SHALL BE	174 09
12 O LET THE SORROWFUL SIGHING OF THE PRISONERS COME	440 26
COMFORT HIM WHEN DISCOURAGED OR SORROWFUL	597 31
SADNESS OF THE SORROWFUL TO JOY	599 05
LET THE SORROWFUL SIGHING OF THE PRISONERS COME	600 08

SORROWING

THY FATHER AND I HAVE SOUGHT THEE SORROWING   110 34

SORROWS

UPON THE SORROWS OF THY SERVANT FOR WHOM OUR   046 02
PITY BEHOLD THE SORROWS OF OUR HEARTS   059 11
HEART AMIDST THE SORROWS AND DIFFICULTIES OF THE   316 20
4 THE SORROWS OF DEATH COMPASSED ME, *   359 31
16 THE SORROWS OF MY HEART ARE ENLARGED   370 18
MULTITUDE OF THE SORROWS THAT I HAD IN MY HEART, *   458 24

SORRY

AND ARE HEARTILY SORRY FOR THESE OUR MISDOINGS   075 23
THEY WERE VERY SORRY, AND CAME AND TOLD UNTO THEIR   221 31
NOT TO BE SORRY, AS MEN WITHOUT HOPE, FOR THOSE   335 04
AND BE SORRY FOR MY SIN   388 28

SORT

BE SLAIN ALL THE SORT OF YOU   414 02

SORTS

THEE FOR ALL SORTS AND CONDITIONS OF MEN   018 27
THEE FOR ALL SORTS AND CONDITIONS OF MEN   032 27

SOUGHT

ARE DEAD WHICH SOUGHT THE YOUNG CHILD'S LIFE   107 15
AND THEY SOUGHT HIM AMONG THEIR KINSFOLK AND   110 25
FATHER AND I HAVE SOUGHT THEE SORROWING   110 33
HOW IS IT THAT YE SOUGHT ME   111 02
TEMPTING HIM, SOUGHT OF HIM A SIGN FROM HEAVEN   129 28
AND THE SCRIBES SOUGHT HOW THEY MIGHT TAKE HIM BY   139 34
AND HE SOUGHT HOW HE MIGHT CONVENIENTLY BETRAY HIM   140 21
ALL THE COUNCIL SOUGHT FOR WITNESS AGAINST JESUS TO   143 02
AND SCRIBES SOUGHT HOW THEY MIGHT KILL HIM   148 14
HE PROMISED, AND SOUGHT OPPORTUNITY TO BETRAY HIM   148 19
PILATE SOUGHT TO RELEASE HIM   159 19
OF THEM THAT SOUGHT ME NOT   227 19
OF MY TROUBLE I SOUGHT THE LORD   310 31
4 I SOUGHT THE LORD, AND HE HEARD ME   380 09
I SOUGHT HIM, BUT HIS PLACE COULD NO WHERE BE FOUND   387 06
12 THEY ALSO THAT SOUGHT AFTER MY LIFE LAID SNARES   388 14
OF MY TROUBLE I SOUGHT THE LORD   433 18
SLEW THEM, THEY SOUGHT HIM, *   437 06
VIOLENT MEN HAVE SOUGHT AFTER MY SOUL, AND HAVE NOT   448 02
SOUGHT OUT OF ALL THEM THAT HAVE PLEASURE THEREIN   482 26
HEART HAVE I SOUGHT THEE   490 18
FOR I HAVE SOUGHT THY COMMANDMENTS   496 13

SOUL

AND NECESSARY, AS WELL FOR THE BODY AS THE SOUL   006 09
AND NECESSARY, AS WELL FOR THE BODY AS THE SOUL   023 18
MY SOUL DOTH MAGNIFY THE LORD, *   026 11
PRAISE THE LORD, O MY SOUL   029 04
THE LORD, O MY SOUL, *   029 06
PRAISE THOU THE LORD, O MY SOUL   029 19
HEART AND OF ONE SOUL, UNITED IN ONE HOLY BOND OF   037 32
ENDUE HIS SOUL WITH PATIENCE   046 04
AND WITH ALL THY SOUL, AND WITH ALL THY MIND   069 28
WE MAY BE PRESERVED IN BODY AND SOUL   070 11
THY BODY AND SOUL UNTO EVERLASTING LIFE   082 32
THY BODY AND SOUL UNTO EVERLASTING LIFE   083 04
TO YIELD UP HIS SOUL BY DEATH UPON THE CROSS FOR YOUR   089 10
LET EVERY SOUL BE SUBJECT UNTO THE HIGHER POWERS   114 11
EVIL THOUGHTS WHICH MAY ASSAULT AND HURT THE SOUL   127 20
AND PRESERVED EVERMORE, BOTH IN BODY AND SOUL   132 21
SAITH UNTO THEM, MY SOUL IS EXCEEDING SORROWFUL UNTO   141 31
FROM FLESHLY LUSTS, WHICH WAR AGAINST THE SOUL   173 14
AND WITH ALL THY SOUL, AND WITH ALL THY STRENGTH, AND   208 16
AND WITH ALL THY SOUL, AND WITH ALL THY MIND   215 12
BOTH IN BODY AND SOUL, MAY CHEERFULLY ACCOMPLISH   217 20
MAN DRAW BACK, MY SOUL SHALL HAVE NO PLEASURE IN HIM   228 19
OF THEM THAT BELIEVE TO THE SAVING OF THE SOUL   228 22
THROUGH THY OWN SOUL ALSO,) THAT THE THOUGHTS OF MANY   233 14
ON BEHALF OF THE SOUL OF THY SERVANT DEPARTED,   268 23
WITH ALL THY SOUL, AND WITH ALL THY STRENGTH   288 07
WITH ALL MY SOUL, AND WITH ALL MY STRENGTH   288 18
CONTINUAL STRENGTHENING AND REFRESHING OF MY SOUL   291 32
WE MAY BE PRESERVED IN BODY AND SOUL   298 31
I BESEECH THEE, DELIVER MY SOUL   305 24
BE THAT SAY OF MY SOUL, THERE IS NO HELP FOR HIM IN   309 16
WHY ART THOU SO HEAVY, O MY SOUL   310 16
MY SOUL REFUSED COMFORT   311 03
AND ENDUEDST MY SOUL WITH MUCH STRENGTH   312 03
PRAISE THE LORD, O MY SOUL   312 20
THE LORD, O MY SOUL, AND FORGET NOT ALL HIS BENEFITS   312 22
PRAISE THOU THE LORD, O MY SOUL   313 03
HUMBLY COMMEND THE SOUL OF THIS THY SERVANT, OUR DEAR   317 13
HAVE MERCY UPON THE SOUL OF THY SERVANT   317 26
THEE TO DELIVER THE SOUL OF THY SERVANT FROM THE   318 11
DEPART, O CHRISTIAN SOUL, OUT OF THIS WORLD, IN THE   319 19
WE COMMEND THE SOUL OF THY SERVANT, NOW DEPARTED FROM   319 28
AWAY ALL PAIN OF SOUL AND BODY, THAT BEING RESTORED   320 10
WHENSOEVER HIS SOUL SHALL DEPART FROM THE BODY,   321 24
IT IS EVEN HE THAT SHALL KEEP THY SOUL   327 32
MY SOUL DOTH WAIT FOR HIM   328 11
MY SOUL FLEETH UNTO THE LORD BEFORE THE MORNING   328 13
THE FIRST MAN ADAM WAS MADE A LIVING SOUL   329 24
GOD WE COMMEND THE SOUL OF OUR BROTHER DEPARTED, AND   333 14
ON BEHALF OF THE SOUL OF THY SERVANT DEPARTED,   334 15

SOUL   CONTINUED

BOTH IN BODY AND SOUL, IN THY ETERNAL AND EVERLASTING   334 28
UNTO THYSELF THE SOUL OF THIS THY SERVANT (OR THIS   336 05
GOD WE COMMEND THE SOUL OF OUR BROTHER DEPARTED, AND   337 09
HE SHALL CONVERT MY SOUL, *   338 21
IT IS EVEN HE THAT SHALL KEEP THY SOUL   339 16
TO ENTRUST THE SOUL OF THIS CHILD TO THY   342 05
BE THAT SAY OF MY SOUL, *   346 27
3 MY SOUL ALSO IS SORE TROUBLED   349 04
O LORD, AND DELIVER MY SOUL   349 06
2 LEST HE DEVOUR MY SOUL LIKE A LION, AND TEAR IT IN   349 25
ENEMY PERSECUTE MY SOUL, AND TAKE ME   349 32
SAY YE THEN TO MY SOUL, THAT SHE SHOULD FLEE AS A   354 20
DOTH HIS SOUL ABHOR   354 32
SEEK COUNSEL IN MY SOUL, AND BE SO VEXED IN MY HEART   355 30
2 O MY SOUL, THOU HAST SAID UNTO THE LORD, *   357 23
SHALT NOT LEAVE MY SOUL IN HELL   358 10
COMPASS ME ROUND ABOUT, TO TAKE AWAY MY SOUL   359 05
DELIVER MY SOUL FROM THE UNGODLY, BY THINE OWN SWORD   359 13
THE LORD IS AN UNDEFILED LAW, CONVERTING THE SOUL   363 28
20 DELIVER MY SOUL FROM THE SWORD, *   367 12
AND NO MAN HATH QUICKENED HIS OWN SOUL   368 03
HE SHALL CONVERT MY SOUL, *   368 14
O LORD, WILL I LIFT UP MY SOUL   369 18
12 HIS SOUL SHALL DWELL AT EASE, *   370 10
19 O KEEP MY SOUL, AND DELIVER ME   370 24
9 O SHUT NOT UP MY SOUL WITH THE SINNERS, *   371 14
HAST BROUGHT MY SOUL OUT OF HELL   374 28
AND HAST KNOWN MY SOUL IN ADVERSITIES   376 05
MY SOUL AND MY BODY   376 10
18 TO DELIVER THEIR SOUL FROM DEATH, *   379 26
19 OUR SOUL HATH PATIENTLY TARRIED FOR THE LORD   379 28
2 MY SOUL SHALL MAKE HER BOAST IN THE LORD   380 05
SAY UNTO MY SOUL, I AM THY SALVATION   381 23
AND PUT TO SHAME, THAT SEEK AFTER MY SOUL   381 25
WITHOUT A CAUSE HAVE THEY MADE A PIT FOR MY SOUL   382 03
9 AND MY SOUL SHALL BE JOYFUL IN THE LORD   382 07
TO THE GREAT DISCOMFORT OF MY SOUL   382 16
AND HUMBLED MY SOUL WITH FASTING   382 18
O DELIVER MY SOUL FROM THE CALAMITIES WHICH THEY   382 30
THAT SEEK AFTER MY SOUL TO DESTROY IT   391 17
HEAL MY SOUL, FOR I HAVE SINNED AGAINST THEE   392 06
SO LONGETH MY SOUL AFTER THEE, O GOD   392 30
2 MY SOUL IS ATHIRST FOR GOD, YEA, EVEN FOR THE   392 31
6 WHY ART THOU SO FULL OF HEAVINESS, O MY SOUL   393 11
8 MY SOUL IS VEXED WITHIN ME   393 15
14 WHY ART THOU SO VEXED, O MY SOUL   393 31
5 WHY ART THOU SO HEAVY, O MY SOUL   394 15
25 FOR OUR SOUL IS BROUGHT LOW, EVEN UNTO THE DUST   396 10
HATH DELIVERED MY SOUL FROM THE POWER OF THE GRAVE   401 05
NOT GOD BEFORE THEIR EYES, SEEK AFTER MY SOUL   406 09
THE LORD IS WITH THEM THAT UPHOLD MY SOUL   406 11
HATH DELIVERED MY SOUL IN PEACE FROM THE BATTLE THAT   407 27
WHEN THEY LAY WAIT FOR MY SOUL   408 27
HAST DELIVERED MY SOUL FROM DEATH, AND MY FEET FROM   409 08
FOR MY SOUL TRUSTETH IN THEE   409 13
MY SOUL IS AMONG LIONS   409 19
LAID A NET FOR MY FEET, AND PRESSED DOWN MY SOUL   409 27
THEY LIE WAITING FOR MY SOUL   411 08
MY SOUL TRULY WAITETH STILL UPON GOD   413 27
5 NEVERTHELESS, MY SOUL, WAIT THOU STILL UPON GOD   414 07
2 MY SOUL THIRSTETH FOR THEE, MY FLESH ALSO LONGETH   414 27
6 MY SOUL SHALL BE SATISFIED, EVEN AS IT WERE WITH   415 02
9 MY SOUL HANGETH UPON THEE   415 09
SEEK THE HURT OF MY SOUL, *   415 11
8 WHO HOLDETH OUR SOUL IN LIFE   417 31
AND I WILL TELL YOU WHAT HE HATH DONE FOR MY SOUL   418 13
FOR THE WATERS ARE COME IN, EVEN UNTO MY SOUL   421 33
DRAW NIGH UNTO MY SOUL, AND SAVE IT   423 09
AFTER GOD, AND YOUR SOUL SHALL LIVE   424 09
BE ASHAMED AND CONFOUNDED THAT SEEK AFTER MY SOUL   424 23
LAY WAIT FOR MY SOUL TAKE THEIR COUNSEL TOGETHER,   425 26
BE CONFOUNDED AND PERISH THAT ARE AGAINST MY SOUL   425 32
AND SO WILL MY SOUL WHOM THOU HAST DELIVERED   426 26
O DELIVER NOT THE SOUL OF THY TURTLE-DOVE UNTO THE   431 15
MY SOUL REFUSED COMFORT   433 20
SPARED NOT THEIR SOUL FROM DEATH   438 10
2 MY SOUL HATH A DESIRE AND LONGING TO ENTER INTO THE   445 13
2 PRESERVE THOU MY SOUL, FOR I AM HOLY   447 07
4 COMFORT THE SOUL OF THY SERVANT   447 11
FOR UNTO THEE, O LORD, DO I LIFT UP MY SOUL   447 12
HAST DELIVERED MY SOUL FROM THE NETHERMOST HELL   447 31
SOUGHT AFTER MY SOUL, AND HAVE NOT SET THEE BEFORE   448 02
2 FOR MY SOUL IS FULL OF TROUBLE, *   448 32
ABHORREST THOU MY SOUL, *   449 24
HE DELIVER HIS SOUL FROM THE POWER OF THE GRAVE   453 03
NOT FAILED, BUT MY SOUL HAD BEEN PUT TO SILENCE   458 21
THY COMFORTS HAVE REFRESHED MY SOUL   458 25
AGAINST THE SOUL OF THE RIGHTEOUS, *   458 28
PRAISE THE LORD, O MY SOUL   466 08
THE LORD, O MY SOUL, *   466 10
PRAISE THOU THE LORD, O MY SOUL   467 21
PRAISE THE LORD, O MY SOUL   467 24
36 PRAISE THOU THE LORD, O MY SOUL   469 33
THE IRON ENTERED INTO HIS SOUL   471 09
AND SENT LEANNESS WITHAL INTO THEIR SOUL   473 32
THEIR SOUL FAINTED IN THEM   476 14
THE EMPTY SOUL, *   476 22
FILLETH THE HUNGRY SOUL WITH GOODNESS   476 23
18 THEIR SOUL ABHORRED ALL MANNER OF MEAT, *   477 11
THEIR SOUL MELTETH AWAY BECAUSE OF THE TROUBLE   477 29
AND TO THOSE THAT SPEAK EVIL AGAINST MY SOUL   481 11
TO SAVE HIS SOUL FROM UNRIGHTEOUS JUDGES   482 03
I BESEECH THEE, DELIVER MY SOUL   486 27
7 TURN AGAIN THEN UNTO THY REST, O MY SOUL   487 02

SOUL   CONTINUED

HAST DELIVERED MY SOUL FROM DEATH, *   487 04
20 MY SOUL BREAKETH OUT FOR THE VERY FERVENT DESIRE *   491 06
MY SOUL CLEAVETH TO THE DUST   491 17
28 MY SOUL MELTETH AWAY FOR VERY HEAVINESS   491 23
MY SOUL HATH LONGED FOR THY SALVATION, *   495 19
109 MY SOUL IS ALWAY IN MY HAND   497 15
THEREFORE DOTH MY SOUL KEEP THEM   498 29
167 MY SOUL HATH KEPT THY TESTIMONIES, *   501 15
175 O LET MY SOUL LIVE, AND IT SHALL PRAISE THEE   501 32
2 DELIVER MY SOUL, O LORD, FROM LYING LIPS, *   502 09
5 MY SOUL HATH LONG DWELT AMONG THEM *   502 17
IT IS EVEN HE THAT SHALL KEEP THY SOUL   503 05
4 OUR SOUL IS FILLED WITH THE SCORNFUL REPROOF OF THE   504 04
AND THE STREAM HAD GONE OVER OUR SOUL   504 13
HAD GONE EVEN OVER OUR SOUL   504 15
6 OUR SOUL IS ESCAPED EVEN AS A BIRD OUT OF THE SNARE   504 18
MY SOUL DOTH WAIT FOR HIM   507 16
6 MY SOUL FLEETH UNTO THE LORD BEFORE THE MORNING   507 18
3 BUT I REFRAIN MY SOUL, AND KEEP IT LOW, LIKE AS A   507 27
MY SOUL IS EVEN AS A WEANED CHILD   507 28
AND ENDUEDST MY SOUL WITH MUCH STRENGTH   514 03
AND THAT MY SOUL KNOWETH RIGHT WELL   515 17
O CAST NOT OUT MY SOUL   517 29
AND NO MAN CARED FOR MY SOUL   518 13
9 BRING MY SOUL OUT OF PRISON, THAT I MAY GIVE THANKS   518 19
3 FOR THE ENEMY HATH PERSECUTED MY SOUL   518 27
MY SOUL GASPETH UNTO THEE AS A THIRSTY LAND   519 02
FOR I LIFT UP MY SOUL UNTO THEE   519 09
SAKE BRING MY SOUL OUT OF TROUBLE   519 16
AND DESTROY ALL THEM THAT VEX MY SOUL   519 18
PRAISE THE LORD, O MY SOUL   522 03
THE BODY AS FOR THE SOUL, MAY DO IT WITH SUCH   566 18
BODY, SOUL, AND SPIRIT, WITH ALL THEIR POWERS   573 15
WITH ALL MY SOUL, AND WITH ALL MY STRENGTH   579 29
ALL DANGERS BOTH OF SOUL AND BODY   581 02
AND FACULTIES OF SOUL AND BODY   591 09
FROM ALL DANGERS OF SOUL AND BODY   597 03

SOUL'S

BELIEVE TO HIS SOUL'S HEALTH   277 12
PROFITABLY TO HIS SOUL'S HEALTH, ALTHOUGH HE DO NOT   R 323 30
FIRE OF LOVE, THE SOUL'S ANOINTING FROM ABOVE   544 24
FIRE OF LOVE, THE SOUL'S ANOINTING FROM ABOVE   557 03

SOULS

O YE SPIRITS AND SOULS OF THE RIGHTEOUS, BLESS YE THE   013 26
AND COMFORTED OUR SOULS BY THIS SEASONABLE AND   051 24
OUR SELVES, OUR SOULS AND BODIES, TO BE A REASONABLE,   081 22
HIS BODY, AND OUR SOULS WASHED THROUGH HIS MOST   082 21
AND INWARDLY IN OUR SOULS   127 17
THAT IS, EIGHT SOULS WERE SAVED BY WATER   161 29
UNTO THE SHEPHERD AND BISHOP OF YOUR SOULS   172 19
WHICH IS ABLE TO SAVE YOUR SOULS   175 04
AND YE SHALL FIND REST UNTO YOUR SOULS   235 14
TO THE HEALING OF OUR BODIES AND OUR SOULS   253 20
ENGRAFTED WORD, WHICH IS ABLE TO SAVE YOUR SOULS   265 28
WHO HOLDEST ALL SOULS IN LIFE   268 14
REFRESHING OF OUR SOULS BY THE BODY AND BLOOD OF   293 21
OUR SOULS AND BODIES ARE RENEWED   322 07
AND WITH WHOM THE SOULS OF THE FAITHFUL, AFTER THEY   334 21
DELIVERETH THE SOULS OF HIS SERVANTS   381 12
TO REDEEM THEIR SOULS, *   400 20
SHALL PRESERVE THE SOULS OF THE POOR   427 23
DELIVER THEIR SOULS FROM FALSEHOOD AND WRONG   427 24
PRESERVETH THE SOULS OF HIS SAINTS   461 17
HOLY GHOST, OUR SOULS INSPIRE, AND LIGHTEN WITH   543 31
WITHIN OUR SOULS TO REST   544 18
HOLY GHOST, OUR SOULS INSPIRE, AND LIGHTEN WITH   556 06
WITHIN OUR SOULS TO REST   556 26
TO THY GLORY AND TO THE SALVATION OF SOULS   560 23
SHEPHERD OF OUR SOULS, WHO LIVETH AND REIGNETH WITH   574 21
BOTH FOR OUR SOULS AND BODIES   580 34
REFRESHING OF OUR SOULS BY THE BODY AND BLOOD OF   582 17
DEDICATE BOTH OUR SOULS AND OUR BODIES TO THEE AND   588 06
AMISS IN THE TEMPER AND DISPOSITION OF OUR SOULS   590 13

SOUND

WORD OF GOD, OR TO SOUND DOCTRINE, OR WHICH A GODLY   V 40
SOUND LEARNING, AND PURE MANNERS   036 13
AND SEMINARIES OF SOUND AND GODLY LEARNING, AND FOR   047 34
WITH A GREAT SOUND OF A TRUMPET, AND THEY SHALL   118 21
THERE CAME A SOUND FROM HEAVEN AS OF A RUSHING   180 19
THOU HEAREST THE SOUND THEREOF, BUT CANST NOT TELL   188 15
BECAUSE HE HATH RECEIVED HIM SAFE AND SOUND   202 31
YES VERILY, THEIR SOUND WENT INTO ALL THE EARTH, AND   227 14
THOU HEAREST THE SOUND THEREOF, BUT CANST NOT TELL   275 04
THE TRUMPET SHALL SOUND, AND THE DEAD SHALL BE RAISED   330 04
4 THEIR SOUND IS GONE OUT INTO ALL LANDS   363 19
THE LORD WITH THE SOUND OF THE TRUMP   398 30
O LET MY HEART BE SOUND IN THY STATUTES, *   495 16
PRAISE HIM IN THE SOUND OF THE TRUMPET   525 26
SOUND DOCTRINE, AND PRUDENCE, WE DO FULLY   569 15
AND OF A SOUND MIND TO ALL IN PLACES OF AUTHORITY   600 03

SOUNDING

I AM BECOME AS SOUNDING BRASS, OR A TINKLING CYMBAL   122 22
THE SOUNDING OF THY BOWELS AND OF THY   139 20

SOUNDNESS

RESTORED TO SOUNDNESS OF HEALTH, HE MAY OFFER THEE   320 11
BE RESTORED TO SOUNDNESS OF HEALTH   322 09

SOUTH

NOR YET FROM THE SOUTH   432 11
13 THOU HAST MADE THE NORTH AND THE SOUTH   450 31
FROM THE NORTH, AND FROM THE SOUTH   476 11
AS THE RIVERS IN THE SOUTH   505 16

SOUTHWEST-WIND

HIS POWER HE BROUGHT IN THE SOUTHWEST-WIND   436 23

SOVEREIGN

O SOVEREIGN LORD, WHO DESIREST NOT THE DEATH OF A   319 07
BISHOP AND SOVEREIGN JUDGE OF ALL, HEREAFTER   569 27

SOW

DIDST NOT THOU SOW GOOD SEED IN THY FIELD   116 24
A SOWER WENT OUT TO SOW HIS SEED   121 20
THAT THEY SOW NOT, NEITHER DO THEY REAP, NOR   211 16
FOR THEY SOW NOT, NEITHER DO THEY REAP, NOR GATHER   266 15
37 THAT THEY MAY SOW THEIR LAND, AND PLANT VINEYARDS,   478 20
6 THEY THAT SOW IN TEARS *   505 17

SOWED

UNTO A MAN WHICH SOWED GOOD SEED IN HIS FIELD   116 19
HIS ENEMY CAME AND SOWED TARES AMONG THE WHEAT,   116 20
AND AS HE SOWED, SOME FELL BY THE WAY-SIDE   121 20

SOWER

A SOWER WENT OUT TO SOW HIS SEED   121 20

SOWEST

THAT WHICH THOU SOWEST IS NOT QUICKENED, EXCEPT IT   329 07
THAT WHICH THOU SOWEST, THOU SOWEST NOT THAT BODY   329 08
THOU SOWEST, THOU SOWEST NOT THAT BODY THAT SHALL BE,   329 08

SOWETH

AND HE THAT SOWETH PLENTEOUSLY SHALL REAP   072 16
HE THAT SOWETH LITTLE SHALL REAP LITTLE   072 16

SOWN

IT IS SOWN IN CORRUPTION   329 19
IT IS SOWN IN DISHONOUR   329 20
IT IS SOWN IN WEAKNESS   329 21
IT IS SOWN A NATURAL BODY   329 22

SPACE

AND ABOUT THE SPACE OF ONE HOUR AFTER ANOTHER   151 15
OF A DEACON THE SPACE OF A WHOLE YEAR, (EXCEPT FOR   R 535 20
PRAYERS THERE SHALL BE SILENCE KEPT FOR A SPACE   R 543 25
THAT BY THE SPACE OF THREE YEARS I CEASED NOT TO WARN   550 34

SPAKE

AS HE SPAKE BY THE MOUTH OF HIS HOLY PROPHETS,   014 12
WHO SPAKE BY THE PROPHETS   016 18
WHO SPAKE BY THE PROPHETS   030 23
GOD SPAKE THESE WORDS, AND SAID   068 03
WHO SPAKE BY THE PROPHETS   071 20
AND HE SPAKE TO THEM A PARABLE   093 14
IN DIVERS MANNERS SPAKE IN TIME PAST UNTO THE FATHERS   096 22
SAYING WHICH HE SPAKE UNTO THEM   111 04
OF EVERY CITY, HE SPAKE BY A PARABLE   121 19
I WAS A CHILD, I SPAKE AS A CHILD, I UNDERSTOOD AS A   123 09
WHEN THE DEVIL WAS GONE OUT, THE DUMB SPAKE   129 26
TO PASS, AS HE SPAKE THESE THINGS, A CERTAIN WOMAN OF   130 17
BUT HE SPAKE THE MORE VEHEMENTLY, IF I SHOULD DIE   141 25
AND PRAYED, AND SPAKE THE SAME WORDS   142 07
WHILE HE YET SPAKE, COMETH JUDAS, ONE OF THE TWELVE,   142 14
AND WHILE HE YET SPAKE, BEHOLD A MULTITUDE, AND HE   150 26
WHILE HE YET SPAKE, THE COCK CREW   151 19
BLASPHEMOUSLY SPAKE THEY AGAINST HIM   151 27
TO RELEASE JESUS, SPAKE AGAIN TO THEM   153 33
THE WORDS WHICH I SPAKE UNTO YOU, WHILE I WAS YET   170 07
WHILE PETER YET SPAKE THESE WORDS, THE HOLY GHOST   184 20
THIS PARABLE SPAKE JESUS UNTO THEM   186 10
THEY WERE WHICH HE SPAKE UNTO THEM   186 11
AND HE SPAKE THIS PARABLE UNTO THEM, SAYING, WHAT MAN   193 17
AND HE SPAKE A PARABLE UNTO THEM, CAN THE BLIND LEAD   195 02
JESUS SPAKE THIS PARABLE UNTO CERTAIN WHICH TRUSTED   205 21
WAS LOOSED, AND HE SPAKE PLAIN   207 04
JESUS ANSWERING SPAKE UNTO THE LAWYERS AND PHARISEES,   214 02
WHILE JESUS SPAKE THESE THINGS UNTO JOHN'S DISCIPLES,   224 12
UNTO THE LORD, AND SPAKE OF HIM TO ALL THEM THAT   233 22
THE MOUTH OF DAVID SPAKE BEFORE CONCERNING JUDAS,   234 10
MOREOVER THE LORD SPAKE AGAIN UNTO AHAZ, SAYING,   235 25
AND HE SPAKE, AND PRAISED GOD   243 26
AS HE SPAKE BY THE MOUTH OF HIS HOLY PROPHETS, WHICH   243 35
IN GLORY, AND SPAKE OF HIS DECEASE WHICH HE SHOULD   248 29
WHILE HE THUS SPAKE, THERE CAME A CLOUD, AND   249 04
WITH ENVY, AND SPAKE AGAINST THOSE THINGS WHICH WERE   260 28
JESUS CAME AND SPAKE UNTO THEM, SAYING, ALL POWER IS   275 26
9 FOR HE SPAKE, AND IT WAS DONE   379 04

SPAKE   CONTINUED

MY TONGUE, AND SPAKE NOTHING	389 09
AND AT THE LAST I SPAKE WITH MY TONGUE	389 13
11 GOD SPAKE ONCE, AND TWICE I HAVE ALSO HEARD THE	414 21
WITH MY LIPS, AND SPAKE WITH MY MOUTH, WHEN I WAS IN	418 09
20 THEY SPAKE AGAINST GOD ALSO, SAYING, *	436 06
7 HE SPAKE UNTO THEM OUT OF THE CLOUDY PILLAR	462 30
31 HE SPAKE THE WORD, AND THERE CAME ALL MANNER OF	471 34
34 HE SPAKE THE WORD, AND THE GRASSHOPPERS CAME,	472 06
SO THAT HE SPAKE UNADVISEDLY WITH HIS LIPS	475 02
FOR HE SPAKE THE WORD, AND THEY WERE MADE	524 14
THIS PARABLE SPAKE JESUS UNTO THEM	538 33
THEY WERE WHICH HE SPAKE UNTO THEM	539 02
JESUS CAME AND SPAKE UNTO THEM, SAYING, ALL POWER IS	552 09
THE SAME WHICH GOD SPAKE IN THE TWENTIETH CHAPTER OF	578 22

SPAKEST

| THOU SATTEST AND SPAKEST AGAINST THY BROTHER | 402 30 |
| 20 THOU SPAKEST SOMETIME IN VISIONS UNTO THY SAINTS, | 451 12 |

SPAN

| DAYS AS IT WERE A SPAN LONG, AND MINE AGE IS EVEN AS | 324 22 |
| DAYS AS IT WERE A SPAN LONG, AND MINE AGE IS EVEN AS | 389 17 |

SPARE

SPARE THOU THOSE, O GOD, WHO CONFESS THEIR FAULTS	006 24
SPARE THOU THOSE, O GOD, WHO CONFESS THEIR FAULTS	023 15
GOOD LORD, SPARE THY PEOPLE, WHOM THOU HAST	054 15
SPARE US, GOOD LORD, SPARE THY PEOPLE, WHOM THOU HAST	054 15
SPARE US, GOOD LORD	054 18
OUR PRAYERS, AND SPARE ALL THOSE WHO CONFESS THEIR	062 09
SPARE US THEREFORE, GOOD LORD, SPARE THY PEOPLE, WHOM	062 19
GOOD LORD, SPARE THY PEOPLE, WHOM THOU HAST REDEEMED	062 20
SPARE THY PEOPLE, GOOD LORD, SPARE THEM, AND LET NOT	063 02
GOOD LORD, SPARE THEM, AND LET NOT THINE	063 03
AND LET THEM SAY, SPARE THY PEOPLE, O LORD, AND GIVE	125 04
ENOUGH AND TO SPARE, AND I PERISH WITH HUNGER,	202 12
O SPARE ME A LITTLE, THAT I MAY RECOVER MY STRENGTH,	325 10
BUT SPARE US, LORD MOST HOLY, O GOD MOST MIGHTY, O	332 29
15 O SPARE ME A LITTLE, THAT I MAY RECOVER MY	390 06

SPARED

| HE THAT SPARED NOT HIS OWN SON, BUT DELIVERED HIM UP | 330 34 |
| AND SPARED NOT THEIR SOUL FROM DEATH | 438 09 |

SPAREST

| O GOD, WHO SPAREST WHEN WE DESERVE PUNISHMENT, | 046 18 |
| THOU SPAREST WHEN WE DESERVE PUNISHMENT, AND IN THY | 062 32 |

SPARING

| AMONG YOU, NOT SPARING THE FLOCK | 550 31 |

SPARKS

| THAT COMPASS YOURSELVES ABOUT WITH SPARKS | 144 27 |
| AND IN THE SPARKS THAT YE HAVE KINDLED | 144 28 |

SPARROW

| 3 YEA, THE SPARROW HATH FOUND HER AN HOUSE, AND THE | 445 16 |
| AS IT WERE A SPARROW, * | 464 23 |

SPEAK

UNTO HIM, AND SPEAK GOOD OF HIS NAME	015 11
O SPEAK GOOD OF THE LORD, ALL YE WORKS OF HIS,	029 17
THESE THINGS SPEAK, AND EXHORT, AND REBUKE WITH ALL	098 25
BUT SPEAK THE WORD ONLY, AND MY SERVANT SHALL BE	115 12
I SPEAK AS CONCERNING REPROACH, AS THOUGH WE HAD BEEN	120 25
ANY IS BOLD, (I SPEAK FOOLISHLY,) I AM BOLD ALSO	120 27
I SPEAK AS A FOOL) I AM MORE	120 30
THOUGH I SPEAK WITH THE TONGUES OF MEN AND OF ANGELS,	122 21
IS A SHAME EVEN TO SPEAK OF THOSE THINGS WHICH ARE	129 18
I THAT SPEAK IN RIGHTEOUSNESS, MIGHTY TO SAVE	138 14
I KNOW NOT THIS MAN OF WHOM YE SPEAK	143 34
WHEREAS THEY SPEAK AGAINST YOU AS EVILDOERS,	173 15
TO HEAR, SLOW TO SPEAK, SLOW TO WRATH	174 32
FOR HE SHALL NOT SPEAK OF HIMSELF	175 20
BUT WHATSOEVER HE SHALL HEAR, THAT SHALL HE SPEAK	175 21
I SHALL NO MORE SPEAK UNTO YOU IN PROVERBS, BUT I	176 25
MAN SPEAK, LET HIM SPEAK AS THE ORACLES OF GOD	179 18
IF ANY MAN SPEAK, LET HIM SPEAK AS THE ORACLES OF	179 18
AND BEGAN TO SPEAK WITH OTHER TONGUES, AS THE SPIRIT	180 23
MAN HEARD THEM SPEAK IN HIS OWN LANGUAGE	180 28
ALL THESE WHICH SPEAK GALILAEANS	180 30
WE DO HEAR THEM SPEAK IN OUR TONGUES THE WONDERFUL	181 06
THEY HEARD THEM SPEAK WITH TONGUES, AND MAGNIFY GOD	184 25
SAY UNTO THEE, WE SPEAK THAT WE DO KNOW, AND TESTIFY	188 21
HIS LIPS THAT THEY SPEAK NO GUILE	195 26
I SPEAK AFTER THE MANNER OF MEN BECAUSE OF THE	198 26
BOTH THE DEAF TO HEAR, AND THE DUMB TO SPEAK	207 09
AND HE THAT WAS DEAD SAT UP, AND BEGAN TO SPEAK	213 06
AWAY LYING, SPEAK EVERY MAN TRUTH WITH HIS NEIGHBOUR	216 17
THAT THEREIN I MAY SPEAK BOLDLY, AS I OUGHT TO SPEAK	219 25
THEREIN I MAY SPEAK BOLDLY, AS I OUGHT TO SPEAK	219 26
I SPEAK UNTO YOU I SPEAK NOT OF MYSELF	240 15
THE WORDS THAT I SPEAK UNTO YOU I SPEAK NOT OF	240 15
EXAMPLE CONSTANTLY SPEAK THE TRUTH, BOLDLY REBUKE	242 12
SPEAK YE COMFORTABLY TO JERUSALEM, AND CRY UNTO HER,	242 17

SPEAK   CONTINUED

TO HEAR, SLOW TO SPEAK, SLOW TO WRATH	265 24
BUT I SPEAK CONCERNING CHRIST AND THE CHURCH	267 31
THE MINISTER SHALL SPEAK TO THE GODFATHERS AND	R 276 17
LET HIM NOW SPEAK, OR ELSE HEREAFTER FOR EVER HOLD	300 22
SHALL THE MINISTER SPEAK UNTO THE COMPANY	R 304 02
I AM SO FEEBLE THAT I CANNOT SPEAK	311 07
O SPEAK GOOD OF THE LORD, ALL YE WORKS OF HIS,	313 02
I WILL SING AND SPEAK PRAISES UNTO THE LORD	326 18
5 THEN SHALL HE SPEAK UNTO THEM IN HIS WRATH,	346 06
DESTROY THEM THAT SPEAK LIES	348 11
I WILL SPEAK OF ALL THY MARVELLOUS WORKS	351 23
WE ARE THEY THAT OUGHT TO SPEAK	355 15
I WILL SING AND SPEAK PRAISES UNTO THE LORD	372 10
AND SUCH AS SPEAK WRONG	372 26
WHICH SPEAK FRIENDLY TO THEIR NEIGHBOURS, BUT IMAGINE	373 11
DOTH EVERY THING SPEAK OF HIS HONOUR	374 16
AND DESPITEFULLY SPEAK AGAINST THE RIGHTEOUS	376 34
THAT THEY SPEAK NO GUILE	380 28
DECLARE THEM, AND SPEAK OF THEM, *	390 25
5 MINE ENEMIES SPEAK EVIL OF ME, *	392 08
I SPEAK THE THINGS WHICH I HAVE MADE CONCERNING THE	396 15
3 MY MOUTH SHALL SPEAK OF WISDOM, *	400 10
MEN WILL SPEAK GOOD OF THEE	401 13
O MY PEOPLE, AND I WILL SPEAK	402 04
HAST LET THY MOUTH SPEAK WICKEDNESS, *	402 28
THOU HAST LOVED TO SPEAK ALL WORDS THAT MAY DO HURT,	404 26
GO ASTRAY, AND SPEAK LIES	410 13
7 BEHOLD, THEY SPEAK WITH THEIR MOUTH, AND SWORDS ARE	411 18
MOUTH OF THEM THAT SPEAK LIES SHALL BE STOPPED	415 17
SIT IN THE GATE SPEAK AGAINST ME, *	422 26
9 FOR MINE ENEMIES SPEAK AGAINST ME	425 25
MOUTH SHALL DAILY SPEAK OF THY RIGHTEOUSNESS AND	426 04
CORRUPT OTHER, AND SPEAK OF WICKED BLASPHEMY	428 24
AND TO SPEAK OF ALL THY WORKS IN THE GATES OF THE	429 33
AND SPEAK NOT WITH A STIFF NECK	432 08
I AM SO FEEBLE THAT I CANNOT SPEAK	433 24
FOR HE SHALL SPEAK PEACE UNTO HIS PEOPLE, AND TO HIS	446 23
ALL WICKED DOERS SPEAK SO DISDAINFULLY, *	457 25
UNTO HIM, AND SPEAK GOOD OF HIS NAME	463 13
22 O SPEAK GOOD OF THE LORD, ALL YE WORKS OF HIS,	467 20
AND TO THOSE THAT SPEAK EVIL AGAINST MY SOUL	481 11
HAVE MOUTHS, AND SPEAK NOT	485 20
NEITHER SPEAK THEY THROUGH THEIR THROAT	485 25
AND THEREFORE WILL I SPEAK	487 07
ALSO DID SIT AND SPEAK AGAINST ME	491 12
46 I WILL SPEAK OF THY TESTIMONIES ALSO, EVEN BEFORE	492 30
171 MY LIPS SHALL SPEAK OF THY PRAISE, *	501 24
BUT WHEN I SPEAK UNTO THEM THEREOF, *	502 19
ASHAMED WHEN THEY SPEAK WITH THEIR ENEMIES IN THE	506 03
HAVE MOUTHS, AND SPEAK NOT	511 02
20 FOR THEY SPEAK UNRIGHTEOUSLY AGAINST THEE	515 30
SO THAT MEN SHALL SPEAK OF THE MIGHT OF THY	521 04
21 MY MOUTH SHALL SPEAK THE PRAISE OF THE LORD	521 34

SPEAKEST

UNTO HIM, SPEAKEST THOU NOT UNTO ME	159 14
LO, NOW SPEAKEST THOU PLAINLY, AND SPEAKEST NO	176 32
AND SPEAKEST NO PROVERB	176 33

SPEAKETH

HIMSELF A KING, SPEAKETH AGAINST CAESAR	159 21
AND SPEAKETH GOOD OF THE COVETOUS, WHOM THE LORD	353 09
THE TONGUE THAT SPEAKETH PROUD THINGS	355 13
IS RIGHT, AND SPEAKETH THE TRUTH FROM HIS HEART	357 08
AND THEIR MOUTH SPEAKETH PROUD THINGS	359 07
TO SEE ME, HE SPEAKETH VANITY, *	392 10

SPEAKING

FORTY DAYS, AND SPEAKING OF THE THINGS PERTAINING TO	177 28
HE HAD LEFT SPEAKING, HE SAID UNTO SIMON, LAUNCH OUT	196 13
THAT NO MAN SPEAKING BY THE SPIRIT OF GOD CALLETH	203 19
AND EVIL SPEAKING, BE PUT AWAY FROM YOU, WITH ALL	216 28
SPEAKING TO YOURSELVES IN PSALMS AND HYMNS AND	217 27
BUT SPEAKING THE TRUTH IN LOVE, MAY GROW UP INTO HIM	237 28
FROM EVIL SPEAKING, LYING, AND SLANDERING	289 06
AND ALSO SPEAKING UNTO THE PERSONS WHO ARE TO BE	R 300 23
MEN ARISE, SPEAKING PERVERSE THINGS, TO DRAW AWAY	550 32
FROM EVIL SPEAKING, LYING, AND SLANDERING	580 10

SPEAKINGS

| AND ALL EVIL SPEAKINGS, AS NEWBORN BABES, DESIRE THE | 259 26 |

SPEAR

SOLDIERS WITH A SPEAR PIERCED HIS SIDE, AND FORTHWITH	161 04
3 BRING FORTH THE SPEAR, AND STOP THE WAY AGAINST	381 22
AND KNAPPETH THE SPEAR IN SUNDER, AND BURNETH THE	398 12

SPEARS

| WHOSE TEETH ARE SPEARS AND ARROWS, AND THEIR TONGUE A | 409 22 |

SPECIAL

OR ON SPECIAL OCCASIONS	R 047 03
FOR THIS THY SPECIAL BOUNTY	052 02
AS BY THY SPECIAL GRACE PREVENTING US THOU DOST	163 25
WITHOUT HIS SPECIAL GRACE	289 05
WHAT SPECIAL MEANS DOES THE CHURCH PROVIDE	291 21
MOVED TO MAKE A SPECIAL CONFESSION OF HIS SINS, IF HE	R 313 24

SPECIAL   CONTINUED

WITHOUT HIS SPECIAL GRACE   580 18
MAY BE ADDED ANY SPECIAL PRAYERS   R 592 26
MAY BE ADDED ANY SPECIAL PRAYERS   R 593 17

SPECIALLY

THERE BE ANY SPECIALLY APPOINTED   R 077 03
AND SPECIALLY WHEN HE MINISTERETH THE HOLY   533 12
OF THEM THAT SPECIALLY PERTAIN UNTO YOU, ACCORDING TO 541 05

SPECIFIED

AS IS HEREIN SPECIFIED, SHALL BE OBLIGED TO GIVE AN R 085 18

SPEECH

AND THY SPEECH AGREETH THERETO   143 32
AND HAD AN IMPEDIMENT IN HIS SPEECH   206 30
THERE IS NEITHER SPEECH NOR LANGUAGE   363 17
AND SHOW MY DARK SPEECH UPON THE HARP   400 13
THE TONGUE WITH SPEECH ENDOW   544 28
THE TONGUE WITH SPEECH ENDOW   557 07

SPEECHLESS

AND HE WAS SPEECHLESS   218 25
HIM STOOD SPEECHLESS, HEARING A VOICE, BUT SEEING NO 230 09

SPEEDILY

AND MERCY MAY SPEEDILY HELP AND DELIVER US   095 08

SPENDEST

WHATSOEVER THOU SPENDEST MORE, WHEN I COME AGAIN, 208 35

SPENT

BREAD OR WINE BE SPENT BEFORE ALL HAVE COMMUNICATED, R 083 07
THE NIGHT IS FAR SPENT, THE DAY IS AT HAND   091 03
IT IS TOWARD EVENING, AND THE DAY IS FAR SPENT   168 04
AND WHEN HE HAD SPENT ALL, THERE AROSE A MIGHTY 202 05
TO COME MAY BE SPENT IN THY SERVICE   595 15

SPICES

HAD BOUGHT SWEET SPICES, THAT THEY MIGHT COME AND 165 20

SPIED

FOR I HAVE SPIED UNRIGHTEOUSNESS AND STRIFE IN THE 407 05

SPIKENARD

OF OINTMENT OF SPIKENARD VERY PRECIOUS   140 04

SPIN

THEY TOIL NOT, NEITHER DO THEY SPIN   211 22
THEY TOIL NOT, NEITHER DO THEY SPIN   266 20

SPIRIT

AND WITH THY SPIRIT   R 003 08
AND HUMBLE SPIRIT, TO REVIVE THE SPIRIT OF THE   003 27
TO REVIVE THE SPIRIT OF THE HUMBLE, AND TO REVIVE THE 003 28
THE FATHER IN SPIRIT AND IN TRUTH   003 31
THE SACRIFICES OF GOD ARE A BROKEN SPIRIT   004 24
SENT FORTH THE SPIRIT OF HIS SON INTO YOUR HEARTS, 005 16
AND HIS HOLY SPIRIT, THAT THOSE THINGS MAY PLEASE HIM 007 15
THE SPIRIT OF THE LORD FILLETH THE WORLD   R 008 27
AND WITH THY SPIRIT   016 26
TAKE NOT THY HOLY SPIRIT FROM US   016 32
GRACE OF THY HOLY SPIRIT, THAT THEY MAY ALWAYS   017 32
THE HEALTHFUL SPIRIT OF THY GRACE   018 21
BY THY GOOD SPIRIT, THAT ALL WHO PROFESS AND CALL 018 31
FAITH IN UNITY OF SPIRIT, IN THE BOND OF PEACE, AND 019 02
THE SPIRIT AND THE BRIDE SAY, COME   022 29
AND HIS HOLY SPIRIT, THAT THOSE THINGS MAY PLEASE HIM 024 17
AND THE GRACE AND CONSOLATION OF HIS HOLY SPIRIT 024 26
AND MY SPIRIT HATH REJOICED IN GOD MY SAVIOUR   026 11
AND WITH THY SPIRIT   030 31
TAKE NOT THY HOLY SPIRIT FROM US   031 14
THE HEALTHFUL SPIRIT OF THY GRACE   032 20
BY THY GOOD SPIRIT, THAT ALL WHO PROFESS AND CALL 032 31
FAITH IN UNITY OF SPIRIT, IN THE BOND OF PEACE, AND 032 33
UNTO THEM THE SPIRIT OF WISDOM AND UNDERSTANDING, 036 03
ENDUE WITH THE SPIRIT OF WISDOM THOSE TO WHOM IN THY 036 17
WHO BY THY HOLY SPIRIT DIDST PRESIDE IN THE COUNCIL 036 27
ONE BODY AND ONE SPIRIT, AND ONE HOPE OF OUR CALLING, 037 30
POUR OUT THY SPIRIT UPON ALL FLESH, AND HASTEN THY 038 10
BY THY HOLY SPIRIT, THEY MAY RESIST TEMPTATION AND 043 11
GIFT OF THE HOLY SPIRIT THROUGH THE LAYING ON OF 043 22
POWER OF THY HOLY SPIRIT THEY MAY BE SET FREE FROM 046 28
AND TO BRING FORTH THE FRUITS OF THE SPIRIT   056 17
GRACE OF THY HOLY SPIRIT TO AMEND OUR LIVES ACCORDING 057 16
AND RENEW A RIGHT SPIRIT WITHIN ME   060 30
TAKE NOT THY HOLY SPIRIT FROM ME   060 33
AND STABLISH ME WITH THY FREE SPIRIT   061 03
THE SACRIFICE OF GOD IS A TROUBLED SPIRIT   061 13
OF THY HOLY SPIRIT, THAT WE MAY PERFECTLY LOVE THEE, 067 19
AND WITH THY SPIRIT   070 15
CHURCH WITH THE SPIRIT OF TRUTH, UNITY, AND CONCORD 074 12
THY WORD AND HOLY SPIRIT, THESE THY GIFTS AND   081 10

SPIRIT   CONTINUED

AND THE HOLY SPIRIT EVER, ONE GOD, WORLD WITHOUT END 093 31
MAY DAILY BE RENEWED BY THY HOLY SPIRIT   096 17
THEE AND THE SAME SPIRIT EVER, ONE GOD, WORLD WITHOUT 096 19
LORD JESUS, RECEIVE MY SPIRIT   100 14
MAY DAILY BE RENEWED BY THY HOLY SPIRIT   104 09
THEE AND THE SAME SPIRIT EVER, ONE GOD, WORLD WITHOUT 104 11
SENT FORTH THE SPIRIT OF HIS SON INTO YOUR HEARTS, 104 23
GRANT US THE TRUE CIRCUMCISION OF THE SPIRIT   105 21
THE SPIRIT OF THE LORD GOD IS UPON ME   106 30
OF PRAISE FOR THE SPIRIT OF HEAVINESS   107 08
UNTO HIS HOLY APOSTLES AND PROPHETS BY THE SPIRIT 108 14
FERVENT IN SPIRIT   111 25
AND THE SPIRIT, LIKE A DOVE, DESCENDING UPON   112 21
SUBDUED TO THE SPIRIT, WE MAY EVER OBEY THY GODLY 125 29
LED UP OF THE SPIRIT INTO THE WILDERNESS TO BE   126 23
WHO HATH ALSO GIVEN UNTO US HIS HOLY SPIRIT   128 05
THE FRUIT OF THE SPIRIT IS IN ALL GOODNESS AND   129 14
WHEN THE UNCLEAN SPIRIT IS GONE OUT OF A MAN, HE 130 10
BORN AFTER THE SPIRIT, EVEN SO IT IS NOW   131 14
THE ETERNAL SPIRIT OFFERED HIMSELF WITHOUT SPOT TO 132 31
AND VEXED HIS HOLY SPIRIT   139 05
THAT PUT HIS HOLY SPIRIT WITHIN HIM   139 10
THE VALLEY, THE SPIRIT OF THE LORD CAUSED HIM TO 139 15
THE SPIRIT TRULY IS READY, BUT THE FLESH IS WEAK 142 06
THEE AND THE HOLY SPIRIT EVER, ONE GOD, WORLD WITHOUT 152 13
INTO THY HANDS I COMMEND MY SPIRIT   155 13
BY WHOSE SPIRIT THE WHOLE BODY OF THE CHURCH IS 156 27
THEE AND THE HOLY SPIRIT, ONE GOD, WORLD WITHOUT END 157 13
DEATH IN THE FLESH, BUT QUICKENED BY THE SPIRIT 161 25
AND SUPPOSED THAT THEY HAD SEEN A SPIRIT   169 30
FOR A SPIRIT HATH NOT FLESH AND BONES, AS YE SEE ME 169 33
BECAUSE THE SPIRIT IS TRUTH   170 32
AND IT IS THE SPIRIT THAT BEARETH WITNESS, BECAUSE 170 32
BEAR WITNESS, THE SPIRIT, AND THE WATER, AND THE 171 02
WHEN HE, THE SPIRIT OF TRUTH, IS COME, HE WILL GUIDE 175 18
EVEN THE SPIRIT OF TRUTH, WHICH PROCEEDETH   179 25
BY SENDING TO THEM THE LIGHT OF THY HOLY SPIRIT 180 10
US BY THE SAME SPIRIT TO HAVE A RIGHT JUDGMENT IN ALL 180 10
UNITY OF THE SAME SPIRIT, ONE GOD, WORLD WITHOUT 180 14
AS THE SPIRIT GAVE THEM UTTERANCE   180 24
EVEN THE SPIRIT OF TRUTH   181 11
OF THY HOLY SPIRIT, WE MAY BE ENLIGHTENED AND   182 16
UNITY OF THE SAME SPIRIT EVER, ONE GOD, WORLD WITHOUT 182 19
ARE DIVERSITIES OF GIFTS, BUT THE SAME SPIRIT   182 22
OF THE SPIRIT IS GIVEN TO EVERY MAN TO PROFIT WITHAL 182 26
IS GIVEN BY THE SPIRIT THE WORD OF WISDOM   182 27
ANOTHER THE WORD OF KNOWLEDGE BY THE SAME SPIRIT 182 28
TO ANOTHER FAITH BY THE SAME SPIRIT   182 29
ANOTHER THE GIFTS OF HEALING BY THE SAME SPIRIT 182 30
AND THE SELFSAME SPIRIT, DIVIDING TO EVERY MAN   182 34
FOR BY ONE SPIRIT ARE WE ALL BAPTIZED INTO ONE BODY, 183 04
AND HAVE BEEN ALL MADE TO DRINK INTO ONE SPIRIT 183 07
GIVE THE HOLY SPIRIT TO THEM THAT ASK HIM   183 19
THY HOLY SPIRIT INTO OUR HEARTS, THAT HE MAY   183 22
AND THE SAME HOLY SPIRIT LIVETH AND REIGNETH, ONE 183 26
UNITY BY THY HOLY SPIRIT, MAY MANIFEST THY POWER 185 16
THEE AND THE SAME SPIRIT, ONE GOD, WORLD WITHOUT END 185 18
AND IMMEDIATELY I WAS IN THE SPIRIT   187 04
WATER AND OF THE SPIRIT, HE CANNOT ENTER INTO THE 188 11
IS BORN OF THE SPIRIT IS SPIRIT   188 13
AND THAT WHICH IS BORN OF THE SPIRIT IS SPIRIT   188 13
SO IS EVERY ONE THAT IS BORN OF THE SPIRIT   188 17
BECAUSE HE HATH GIVEN US OF HIS SPIRIT   189 20
IN US, BY THE SPIRIT WHICH HE HATH GIVEN US   191 34
OF THE SPIRIT, EVEN WE OURSELVES GROAN WITHIN   194 22
IF YE THROUGH THE SPIRIT DO MORTIFY THE DEEDS OF THE 200 05
AS ARE LED BY THE SPIRIT OF GOD, THEY ARE THE SONS OF 200 06
NOT RECEIVED THE SPIRIT OF BONDAGE AGAIN TO FEAR 200 08
HAVE RECEIVED THE SPIRIT OF ADOPTION, WHEREBY WE CRY, 200 09
THE SPIRIT HIMSELF BEARETH WITNESS WITH OUR SPIRIT, 200 10
WITNESS WITH OUR SPIRIT, THAT WE ARE THE CHILDREN OF 200 10
BESEECH THEE, THE SPIRIT TO THINK AND DO ALWAYS SUCH 200 29
SPEAKING BY THE SPIRIT OF GOD CALLETH JESUS ACCURSED 203 20
ARE DIVERSITIES OF GIFTS, BUT THE SAME SPIRIT   203 23
OF THE SPIRIT IS GIVEN TO EVERY MAN TO PROFIT WITHAL 203 26
IS GIVEN BY THE SPIRIT THE WORD OF WISDOM   203 27
TO ANOTHER FAITH BY THE SAME SPIRIT   203 29
ANOTHER THE WORD OF KNOWLEDGE BY THE SAME SPIRIT 203 29
ANOTHER THE GIFTS OF HEALING BY THE SAME SPIRIT 203 30
AND THE SELFSAME SPIRIT, DIVIDING TO EVERY MAN   204 03
NOT OF THE LETTER, BUT OF THE SPIRIT   206 17
BUT THE SPIRIT GIVETH LIFE   206 18
OF THE SPIRIT BE RATHER GLORIOUS   206 22
WALK IN THE SPIRIT, AND YE SHALL NOT FULFIL THE 209 14
AGAINST THE SPIRIT, AND THE SPIRIT AGAINST THE FLESH 209 15
SPIRIT, AND THE SPIRIT AGAINST THE FLESH   209 16
YE BE LED OF THE SPIRIT, YE ARE NOT UNDER THE LAW 209 18
THE FRUIT OF THE SPIRIT IS LOVE, JOY, PEACE,   209 26
OF OUR LORD JESUS CHRIST BE WITH YOUR SPIRIT   211 07
WITH MIGHT BY HIS SPIRIT IN THE INNER MAN   212 15
THE UNITY OF THE SPIRIT IN THE BOND OF PEACE   213 22
ONE BODY, AND ONE SPIRIT, EVEN AS YE ARE CALLED IN 213 23
DOTH DAVID IN SPIRIT CALL HIM LORD, SAYING, THE LORD 215 19
THAT THY HOLY SPIRIT MAY IN ALL THINGS DIRECT AND 215 28
BE RENEWED IN THE SPIRIT OF YOUR MIND   216 14
NOT THE HOLY SPIRIT OF GOD, WHEREBY YE ARE SEALED 216 26
BUT BE FILLED WITH THE SPIRIT   217 27
THE SWORD OF THE SPIRIT, WHICH IS THE WORD OF GOD 219 19
IN THE SPIRIT, AND WATCHING THEREUNTO WITH ALL   219 20
WHO ALSO DECLARED UNTO US YOUR LOVE IN THE SPIRIT 223 32
HE CAME BY THE SPIRIT INTO THE TEMPLE   233 02
WAXED STRONG IN SPIRIT, FILLED WITH WISDOM   233 26
SIGNIFIED BY THE SPIRIT THAT THERE SHOULD BE GREAT 241 17
BECAUSE THE SPIRIT OF THE LORD BLOWETH UPON IT   242 30

SPIRIT   CONTINUED

WAXED STRONG IN SPIRIT, AND WAS IN THE DESERTS TILL   244 17
SIGNIFIED BY THE SPIRIT THAT THERE SHOULD BE GREAT   246 26
IN UNITY OF SPIRIT BY THEIR DOCTRINE, THAT WE MAY BE   254 30
FOR AN HABITATION OF GOD THROUGH THE SPIRIT   255 10
EVEN THE SPIRIT OF TRUTH, WHICH PROCEEDETH   255 31
SAYING, BLESSED ARE THE POOR IN SPIRIT   257 21
OF THY HOLY SPIRIT, TO PUT IT INTO THE HEARTS OF MANY   260 21
WAS WRITTEN, THE SPIRIT OF THE LORD IS UPON ME,   261 16
GIVE THE HOLY SPIRIT TO THEM THAT ASK HIM   263 13
WATER AND OF THE SPIRIT, HE CANNOT ENTER INTO THE   275 15
IS BORN OF THE SPIRIT IS SPIRIT   275 17
AND THAT WHICH IS BORN OF THE SPIRIT IS SPIRIT   275 18
SO IS EVERY ONE THAT IS BORN OF THE SPIRIT   275 21
GIVE THY HOLY SPIRIT TO THIS CHILD (THIS THY   276 11
AND THE SAME HOLY SPIRIT, NOW AND FOR EVER   276 15
BELONGING TO THE SPIRIT MAY LIVE AND GROW IN HIM   278 22
AND WITH THY SPIRIT   278 33
UNITY OF THE HOLY SPIRIT, BE ALL HONOUR AND GLORY,   279 21
WITH THY HOLY SPIRIT, TO RECEIVE HIM FOR THINE OWN   280 30
WITH MIGHT BY HIS SPIRIT IN THE INNER MAN   281 10
AND WITH THY SPIRIT   283 06
AND WITH THY SPIRIT   285 21
BESEECH THEE, THE SPIRIT TO THINK AND DO ALWAYS SUCH   287 26
AND WITH THY SPIRIT   290 17
IN UNITY OF SPIRIT BY THEIR DOCTRINE, THAT WE MAY BE   290 22
BECAUSE THE HOLY SPIRIT DWELLS IN IT, AND SANCTIFIES   291 09
THE STRENGTHENING GIFTS OF THE HOLY SPIRIT   291 27
AND WITH THY SPIRIT   294 22
OF THY HOLY SPIRIT, THAT THEY MAY GROW IN GRACE UNTO   294 26
THE SPIRIT OF WISDOM AND UNDERSTANDING, THE SPIRIT OF   297 19
THE SPIRIT OF COUNSEL AND GHOSTLY STRENGTH, THE   297 20
THE SPIRIT OF KNOWLEDGE AND TRUE GODLINESS   297 21
O LORD, WITH THE SPIRIT OF THY HOLY FEAR, NOW AND FOR   297 22
IN THY HOLY SPIRIT MORE AND MORE, UNTIL HE COME UNTO   297 28
AND WITH THY SPIRIT   297 32
LET THY HOLY SPIRIT EVER BE WITH THEM   298 20
AND THE SAME HOLY SPIRIT LIVETH AND REIGNETH EVER,   298 24
THEE AND THE HOLY SPIRIT EVER, ONE GOD, WORLD WITHOUT   303 28
WITH MINE OWN HEART, AND SEARCH OUT MY SPIRIT   311 11
BUT STRENGTHEN HIM WITH THY BLESSED SPIRIT   314 10
CHEERFULNESS OF SPIRIT, HE MAY BE ABLE TO GO TO THINE   315 30
THEE AND THE HOLY SPIRIT, BE ALL HONOUR AND GLORY,   316 03
GRACE AND HOLY SPIRIT IN THE INNER MAN   316 12
POWER OF THY HOLY SPIRIT, HE MAY BE ENABLED TO GO   316 21
AND LET THY HOLY SPIRIT LEAD US IN HOLINESS AND   316 28
THEE TO LOOSE THE SPIRIT OF THIS THY SERVANT FROM   319 08
AND THE GRACE AND COMFORT OF THE HOLY SPIRIT   319 17
AND THE GRACE AND CONSOLATION OF HIS HOLY SPIRIT   323 22
THE LAST ADAM WAS MADE A QUICKENING SPIRIT   329 25
AS ARE LED BY THE SPIRIT OF GOD, THEY ARE THE SONS OF   330 19
NOT RECEIVED THE SPIRIT OF BONDAGE AGAIN TO FEAR   330 20
HAVE RECEIVED THE SPIRIT OF ADOPTION, WHEREBY WE CRY,   330 21
THE SPIRIT HIMSELF BEARETH WITNESS WITH OUR SPIRIT,   330 22
WITNESS WITH OUR SPIRIT, THAT WE ARE THE CHILDREN OF   330 23
AND WITH THY SPIRIT   331 33
BY HIS SPIRIT THAT DWELLETH IN US   333 06
EVEN SO SAITH THE SPIRIT   333 27
AND WITH THY SPIRIT   333 31
AND WITH THY SPIRIT   340 04
AND WITH THY SPIRIT   341 30
6 INTO THY HANDS I COMMEND MY SPIRIT   375 31
AND IN WHOSE SPIRIT THERE IS NO GUILE   377 25
AND WILL SAVE SUCH AS BE OF AN HUMBLE SPIRIT   381 05
AND RENEW A RIGHT SPIRIT WITHIN ME   403 30
TAKE NOT THY HOLY SPIRIT FROM ME   403 32
AND STABLISH ME WITH THY FREE SPIRIT   403 34
17 THE SACRIFICE OF GOD IS A TROUBLED SPIRIT   404 11
SHALL REFRAIN THE SPIRIT OF PRINCES, *   433 13
WITH MINE OWN HEART, AND SEARCH OUT MY SPIRIT   433 28
AND WHOSE SPIRIT CLAVE NOT STEDFASTLY UNTO   435 15
THEY PROVOKED HIS SPIRIT, *   475 02
6 WHITHER SHALL I GO THEN FROM THY SPIRIT   514 31
3 WHEN MY SPIRIT WAS IN HEAVINESS, THOU KNEWEST MY   518 07
4 THEREFORE IS MY SPIRIT VEXED WITHIN ME, *   518 30
FOR MY SPIRIT WAXETH FAINT   519 04
LET THY LOVING SPIRIT LEAD ME FORTH INTO THE LAND OF   519 13
WHO BY THY HOLY SPIRIT HAST APPOINTED DIVERS ORDERS   537 21
AND THE SAME HOLY SPIRIT, WORLD WITHOUT END   537 29
TO PRAY EARNESTLY FOR HIS HOLY SPIRIT   540 33
THE ANOINTING SPIRIT ART, WHO DOST THY SEVENFOLD   543 33
THY ETERNAL MERIT, FATHER, SON, AND HOLY SPIRIT   544 15
AND FAITH OF THEE AND THY SON, BY THE HOLY SPIRIT   545 31
OF THE SAME HOLY SPIRIT, WORLD WITHOUT END   546 04
WHO BY THY HOLY SPIRIT HAST APPOINTED DIVERS ORDERS   547 32
AND THE SAME HOLY SPIRIT, WORLD WITHOUT END   548 08
I GO BOUND IN THE SPIRIT UNTO JERUSALEM, NOT KNOWING   550 15
WHO BY THY HOLY SPIRIT HAST APPOINTED DIVERS ORDERS   553 27
AND THE SAME HOLY SPIRIT, WORLD WITHOUT END   554 03
THE ANOINTING SPIRIT ART, WHO DOST THY SEVENFOLD   556 08
THY ETERNAL MERIT, FATHER, SON, AND HOLY SPIRIT   556 23
NOT GIVEN US THE SPIRIT OF FEAR, BUT OF POWER, AND   558 18
HIM WITH THY HOLY SPIRIT, THAT HE, PREACHING THY   559 07
AND THE SAME HOLY SPIRIT, ONE GOD, WORLD WITHOUT END   559 15
BY THY INDWELLING SPIRIT THOSE WHOM THOU DOST CALL TO   561 08
THROUGH THY SPIRIT, GOOD AND FAITHFUL STEWARDS OF THE   562 10
UNITY OF THE SAME SPIRIT EVER, ONE GOD, WORLD WITHOUT   562 13
OF THE BLESSED SPIRIT, AND ACTING AGREEABLY TO THEIR   564 13
OF THY HOLY SPIRIT, THAT THEY MAY GROW IN GRACE UNTO   565 26
AND BY THY HOLY SPIRIT GRAFTING IT INWARDLY IN THE   566 04
WORSHIP THEE IN SPIRIT AND IN TRUTH, AND MAY IN THEIR   567 08
AND WITH THY SPIRIT   571 06
O BLESSED SPIRIT, WHOM, WITH THE FATHER AND THE   572 31
SOUL, AND SPIRIT, WITH ALL THEIR POWERS AND   573 15
AND WITH THY SPIRIT   573 32

SPIRIT   CONTINUED

IN UNITY OF SPIRIT, AND IN THE BOND OF PEACE,   574 07
US THE CONSTANT ASSISTANCE OF THY HOLY SPIRIT   588 16
THE DIRECTION AND ASSISTANCE OF THY HOLY SPIRIT   590 12
AND COMFORTS OF THY HOLY SPIRIT   591 17
DESIRE IT, THE SPIRIT OF GRACE AND OF SUPPLICATION   594 05
WORSHIP THEE IN SPIRIT AND IN TRUTH   594 08
THE MIGHT OF THY SPIRIT LIFT US, WE PRAY THEE, TO THY   595 21
TO DO, THAT THE SPIRIT OF WISDOM MAY SAVE US FROM ALL   595 29
OF THY HOLY SPIRIT, AND IN THE FELLOWSHIP OF THY   597 06
CHEERFULNESS OF SPIRIT, AND GIVE THEM HEALTH AND   598 16
GIVE THE SPIRIT OF GOVERNANCE AND OF A SOUND MIND TO   600 02
THE FLESH LUSTETH ALWAYS CONTRARY TO THE SPIRIT   604 33
OF HIS SPIRIT, ARE NOT PLEASANT TO GOD, FORASMUCH AS   605 17
BOTH IN HIS FLESH, AND IN HIS SPIRIT   605 33
PURPOSE BY HIS SPIRIT WORKING IN DUE SEASON   606 12
WORKING OF THE SPIRIT OF CHRIST, MORTIFYING THE WORKS   606 18
LACKING THE SPIRIT OF CHRIST, TO HAVE CONTINUALLY   606 23

SPIRITS

O YE SPIRITS AND SOULS OF THE RIGHTEOUS, BLESS YE THE   013 26
OF DEPARTED SPIRITS, WHICH ARE CONSIDERED AS WORDS OF R   015 17
OF DEPARTED SPIRITS, WHICH ARE CONSIDERED AS WORDS OF R   029 22
HIS ANGELS SPIRITS, AND HIS MINISTERS A FLAME OF   097 07
HIM SEVEN OTHER SPIRITS MORE WICKED THAN HIMSELF   130 14
UNTO THE SPIRITS IN PRISON   161 26
TO ANOTHER DISCERNING OF SPIRITS   182 32
ARE THE SEVEN SPIRITS OF GOD   187 14
TO ANOTHER DISCERNING OF SPIRITS   203 32
AND THEM WHICH WERE VEXED WITH UNCLEAN SPIRITS   249 32
WHOM DO LIVE THE SPIRITS OF JUST MEN MADE PERFECT,   317 11
WHOM DO LIVE THE SPIRITS OF THOSE WHO DEPART HENCE IN   334 19
THE GOD OF THE SPIRITS OF ALL FLESH, WHO BY A VOICE   335 25

SPIRITUAL

TEMPORAL AND SPIRITUAL, TO US AND TO ALL MEN   048 13
WITH THE SPIRITUAL FOOD OF THE MOST PRECIOUS BODY AND   083 18
ALSO TO BE OUR SPIRITUAL FOOD AND SUSTENANCE IN THAT   087 04
AND HYMNS AND SPIRITUAL SONGS, SINGING WITH GRACE IN   116 13
EAT THE SAME SPIRITUAL MEAT   201 08
DRINK THE SAME SPIRITUAL DRINK   201 09
DRANK OF THAT SPIRITUAL ROCK THAT FOLLOWED THEM   201 10
CONCERNING SPIRITUAL GIFTS, BRETHREN, I WOULD NOT   203 16
AND HYMNS AND SPIRITUAL SONGS, SINGING AND MAKING   217 28
AGAINST SPIRITUAL WICKEDNESS IN HIGH PLACES   219 10
ALL WISDOM AND SPIRITUAL UNDERSTANDING   224 03
ARE BUILT UP A SPIRITUAL HOUSE, AN HOLY PRIESTHOOD   259 31
TO OFFER UP SPIRITUAL SACRIFICES, ACCEPTABLE TO GOD   259 32
OF SIN, BY SPIRITUAL REGENERATION   274 14
SPIRITUAL PASTORS AND MASTERS   288 29
AN INWARD AND SPIRITUAL GRACE GIVEN UNTO US   292 11
THE INWARD AND SPIRITUAL GRACE   292 16
THE INWARD AND SPIRITUAL GRACE IN BAPTISM   292 22
THE INWARD AND SPIRITUAL GRACE IN BAPTISM IS A DEATH   292 24
GIVER OF ALL SPIRITUAL GRACE, THE AUTHOR OF   303 04
THE SPIRITUAL MARRIAGE AND UNITY BETWIXT CHRIST AND   303 21
YOU WITH ALL SPIRITUAL BENEDICTION AND GRACE   304 13
IT AFFORDS FOR SPIRITUAL PROFIT   R 313 17
IT IS RAISED A SPIRITUAL BODY   329 22
AND THERE IS A SPIRITUAL BODY   329 23
FIRST WHICH IS SPIRITUAL, BUT THAT WHICH IS NATURAL   329 26
AND AFTERWARD THAT WHICH IS SPIRITUAL   329 27
TO OBSERVE ALL SPIRITUAL DISCIPLINE   535 05
OF OUR HAPPINESS BOTH TEMPORAL AND SPIRITUAL   565 14
SPIRITUAL PASTORS AND MASTERS   580 05
AND FROM OUR SPIRITUAL ENEMY, AND FROM EVERLASTING   581 04
AN INWARD AND SPIRITUAL GRACE GIVEN UNTO US   581 13
AND THE INWARD SPIRITUAL GRACE   581 18
THE INWARD AND SPIRITUAL GRACE   581 23
TEMPORAL AND SPIRITUAL, UPON ALL OUR RELATIONS,   590 30
HEAVENLY AND SPIRITUAL MANNER   608 45
BUT HATH NO AUTHORITY IN THINGS PURELY SPIRITUAL   610 39

SPIRITUALLY

WHICH ARE SPIRITUALLY TAKEN AND RECEIVED BY THE   293 15
WHICH ARE SPIRITUALLY TAKEN AND RECEIVED BY THE   582 13

SPIRITUS

SHALL SING OR SAY THE VENI, CREATOR SPIRITUS   R 543 27
CREATOR SPIRITUS SHALL BE SUNG OR SAID OVER   R 556 03

SPIT

AND THEY SPIT UPON HIM, AND TOOK THE REED, AND SMOTE   136 21
AND SOME BEGAN TO SPIT ON HIM, AND TO COVER HIS FACE,   143 20
A REED, AND DID SPIT UPON HIM, AND BOWING THEIR KNEES   145 34
HIS EARS, AND HE SPIT, AND TOUCHED HIS TONGUE   206 33

SPITEFULLY

AND SPITEFULLY ENTREATED, AND SPITTED ON   123 21
THEM SPITEFULLY, AND SLEW THEM   218 12

SPITTED

AND SPITTED ON   123 22

SPITTING

I HID NOT MY FACE FROM SHAME AND SPITTING   144 15

SPOIL

THEY WHICH HATE US SPOIL OUR GOODS   395 14
AND THEY OF THE HOUSEHOLD DIVIDED THE SPOIL   420 05
THEY THAT GO BY SPOIL HIM, *   452 22
LET THE STRANGER SPOIL HIS LABOUR   480 22

SPOILETH

FROM HIM THAT SPOILETH HIM   382 12

SPOILS

WHEREIN HE TRUSTED, AND DIVIDETH HIS SPOILS   130 08
AS ONE THAT FINDETH GREAT SPOILS   501 06

SPOKEN

WHICH WAS SPOKEN BY THE PROPHET, SAYING, TELL YE THE   091 19
THESE LAST DAYS SPOKEN UNTO US BY HIS SON, WHOM HE   096 24
WHICH WAS SPOKEN OF THE LORD BY THE PROPHET, SAYING,   103 23
THAT WHICH WAS SPOKEN BY JEREMY THE PROPHET, SAYING,   103 30
WHICH WAS SPOKEN OF THE LORD BY THE PROPHET, SAYING,   105 09
WHICH WAS SPOKEN BY THE PROPHETS, HE SHALL BE CALLED   107 22
NEITHER KNEW THEY THE THINGS WHICH WERE SPOKEN   123 25
THAT WHICH WAS SPOKEN BY JEREMY THE PROPHET, SAYING,   135 14
WHICH WAS SPOKEN BY THE PROPHET, THEY PARTED MY   136 32
DONE SHALL BE SPOKEN OF FOR A MEMORIAL OF HER   140 17
WHEN MOSES HAD SPOKEN EVERY PRECEPT TO ALL THE PEOPLE   147 19
TO BELIEVE ALL THAT THE PROPHETS HAVE SPOKEN   167 30
WHICH IS SPOKEN OF IN THE PROPHETS   169 23
WHEN HE HAD THUS SPOKEN, HE SHEWED THEM HIS HANDS AND   170 02
THINGS HAVE I SPOKEN UNTO YOU IN PROVERBS   176 24
THINGS I HAVE SPOKEN UNTO YOU, THAT IN ME YE MIGHT   177 08
AND WHEN HE HAD SPOKEN THESE THINGS, WHILE THEY   178 12
THINGS HAVE I SPOKEN UNTO YOU, THAT YE SHOULD NOT BE   179 28
THINGS I HAVE SPOKEN UNTO YOU, BEING YET PRESENT WITH   181 29
THAT JESUS HAD SPOKEN UNTO HIM, AND HE WENT HIS WAY   220 04
THINGS WHICH WERE SPOKEN OF HIM   233 10
WHICH SHALL BE SPOKEN AGAINST   233 13
WORD WHICH I HAVE SPOKEN UNTO YOU   238 09
THINGS HAVE I SPOKEN UNTO YOU, THAT MY JOY MIGHT   238 24
OF THE LORD HATH SPOKEN IT   242 27
HAD NOT COME AND SPOKEN UNTO THEM, THEY HAD NOT HAD   255 22
THINGS WHICH WERE SPOKEN BY PAUL, CONTRADICTING AND   260 29
FIRST HAVE BEEN SPOKEN TO YOU   260 32
MIGHTY GOD, HATH SPOKEN, *   401 21
6 GOD HATH SPOKEN IN HIS HOLINESS, I WILL REJOICE,   412 23
THINGS ARE SPOKEN OF THEE, *   448 16
7 GOD HATH SPOKEN IN HIS HOLINESS   479 17
2 AND THEY HAVE SPOKEN AGAINST ME WITH FALSE TONGUES   480 06
AND THAT THY WORD SPOKEN BY THEIR MOUTHS MAY HAVE   547 07
IT MAY NEVER BE SPOKEN IN VAIN   547 08

SPONSORS

BE ADMITTED AS SPONSORS, IF IT BE DESIRED   R 273 11
THE PARENTS OR SPONSORS SHALL GIVE KNOWLEDGE THEREOF   R 273 12
MY SPONSORS GAVE ME THIS NAME IN BAPTISM   283 18
WHAT DID YOUR SPONSORS THEN PROMISE FOR YOU   283 21
MY SPONSORS DID PROMISE AND VOW THREE THINGS   283 22
SAID THAT YOUR SPONSORS PROMISED AND VOWED THAT YOU   284 07
SAID THAT YOUR SPONSORS PROMISED AND VOWED THAT YOU   285 13
FAITH OF THEIR SPONSORS, INFANTS ARE RECEIVED INTO   292 33
AND SPONSORS SHALL BRING THOSE, FOR WHOSE   R 295 10
OR YOUR SPONSORS THEN UNDERTOOK FOR YOU   296 27
MY SPONSORS IN BAPTISM   577 09
WHAT DID YOUR SPONSORS THEN FOR YOU   577 12
SAID THAT YOUR SPONSORS DID PROMISE FOR YOU, THAT YOU   578 17

SPOT

AND THAT WITHOUT SPOT OF SIN, TO MAKE US CLEAN FROM   077 18
HIMSELF WITHOUT SPOT TO GOD, PURGE YOUR CONSCIENCE   133 02
NOT HAVING SPOT, OR WRINKLE, OR ANY SUCH   267 23
PURE AND WITHOUT SPOT BEFORE THEE   317 21
IT MAY BE WITHOUT SPOT PRESENTED UNTO THEE   321 25
BE THE LAMB WITHOUT SPOT, WHO, BY SACRIFICE OF   605 33

SPOUSE

IS HIS SPOUSE, AND HIS BODY   540 09
TOWARDS THE SPOUSE AND BODY OF CHRIST   540 15

SPRANG

AND THE THORNS SPRANG UP WITH IT, AND CHOKED IT   121 25
GOOD GROUND, AND SPRANG UP, AND BARE FRUIT AN   121 26

SPREAD

GREAT MULTITUDE SPREAD THEIR GARMENTS IN THE WAY   091 25
AND GIVE FOR THE SPREAD OF HIS KINGDOM   291 20
AND SHALL SPREAD ABROAD LIKE A CEDAR IN LEBANON   456 25
38 HE SPREAD OUT A CLOUD TO BE A COVERING, *   472 15
SNARE FOR ME, AND SPREAD A NET ABROAD WITH CORDS   516 18
BE READY TO SPREAD ABROAD THY GOSPEL, THE GLAD   557 29

SPREADEST

WHO ALONE SPREADEST OUT THE HEAVENS, AND RULEST   042 03
WHO ALONE SPREADEST OUT THE HEAVENS, AND RULEST   046 08
AND SPREADEST OUT THE HEAVENS LIKE A CURTAIN   467 28

SPRING

IN CHRIST, AND DO SPRING OUT NECESSARILY OF A TRUE   605 13
FORASMUCH AS THEY SPRING NOT OF FAITH IN JESUS   605 18

SPRINGING

INTO A SPRINGING WELL   485 09

SPRINGS

16 THE SPRINGS OF WATERS WERE SEEN, AND THE   360 28
ALL MY FRESH SPRINGS ARE IN THEE   448 27
HE SENDETH THE SPRINGS INTO THE RIVERS, *   468 13

SPRINKLED

BLOOD SHALL BE SPRINKLED UPON MY GARMENTS, AND I WILL   138 19
AND SPRINKLED BOTH THE BOOK AND ALL THE   147 21
HE SPRINKLED WITH BLOOD BOTH THE   147 24
OUR HEARTS SPRINKLED FROM AN EVIL CONSCIENCE,   158 21

SPRINKLING

OF AN HEIFER SPRINKLING THE UNCLEAN, SANCTIFIETH TO   132 29

SPRUNG

THE BLADE WAS SPRUNG UP, AND BROUGHT FORTH FRUIT,   116 21
AS SOON AS IT WAS SPRUNG UP, IT WITHERED AWAY,   121 23
11 THERE IS SPRUNG UP A LIGHT FOR THE RIGHTEOUS,   461 19

SPUNGE

AND TOOK A SPUNGE, AND FILLED IT WITH VINEGAR,   137 21
RAN AND FILLED A SPUNGE FULL OF VINEGAR, AND PUT IT   146 31
AND THEY FILLED A SPUNGE WITH VINEGAR, AND PUT IT   160 26

ST

EXCEPT UPON THE FEAST OF ST   R 125 24
EXCEPT UPON THE FEAST OF ST   R 178 31
PHILIP AND ST   R 178 31
THE FIFTEENTH CHAPTER OF THE FIRST EPISTLE OF ST   R 328 19
EIGHTEENTH CHAPTER OF THE GOSPEL ACCORDING TO ST   R 339 20

STABLE

CONTINUING EVER STABLE AND STRONG IN THY SON CHRIST,   535 07

STABLISH

AND STABLISH ME WITH THY FREE SPIRIT   061 02
YOU PERFECT, STABLISH, STRENGTHEN, SETTLE YOU   193 11
AND STABLISH ME WITH THY FREE SPIRIT   403 33
STABLISH THE THING, O GOD, THAT THOU HAST WROUGHT IN   421 11
MOST HIGH SHALL STABLISH HER   448 23
SHALT THOU STABLISH IN THE HEAVENS   450 08
THY SEED WILL I STABLISH FOR EVER, *   450 11
38 O STABLISH THY WORD IN THY SERVANT, *   492 15
116 O STABLISH ME ACCORDING TO THY WORD, THAT I MAY   497 30

STABLISHED

AND STABLISHED IT UPON THE FLOODS   368 30
HIS HEART IS STABLISHED, AND WILL NOT SHRINK,   483 32
AND STABLISHED IT UPON THE FLOODS   563 13

STAFF

THY ROD AND THY STAFF COMFORT ME   338 25
THY ROD AND THY STAFF COMFORT ME   368 18

STAGGER

TO AND FRO, AND STAGGER LIKE A DRUNKEN MAN, *   477 31

STAIN

AND I WILL STAIN ALL MY RAIMENT   138 20

STAINED

THUS WERE THEY STAINED WITH THEIR OWN WORKS, *   475 14

STAND

THE WHOLE EARTH STAND IN AWE OF HIM   009 18
THE WHOLE EARTH STAND IN AWE OF HIM   021 20
WE PRAY THEE, TO STAND FAST IN THY FAITH, TO OBEY THY   043 10
IT MAY PLEASE THEE TO STRENGTHEN SUCH AS DO STAND   056 22
IF HE BE PRESENT) STAND UP, AND TURNING TO THE   R 075 32
WE CANNOT ALWAYS STAND UPRIGHT   114 06
UNTO THEM, WHY STAND YE HERE ALL THE DAY IDLE   119 25
HOW SHALL HIS KINGDOM STAND   129 33
LET US STAND TOGETHER   144 19
OF GALILEE, WHY STAND YE GAZING UP INTO HEAVEN   178 17
WHICH ALSO YE HAVE RECEIVED, AND WHEREIN YE STAND   204 31
YE MAY BE ABLE TO STAND AGAINST THE WILES OF THE   219 07
STAND THEREFORE, HAVING YOUR LOINS GIRT ABOUT WITH   219 13
IN THE EVIL DAY, AND HAVING DONE ALL, TO STAND   219 13
AND WHO SHALL STAND WHEN HE APPEARETH   232 08
OF OUR GOD SHALL STAND FOR EVER   242 32
BE CONFIRMED SHALL STAND IN ORDER BEFORE THE BISHOP,   R 296 05
AND THAT HE SHALL STAND AT THE LATTER DAY UPON THE   324 09
WITH THEM, WE MAY STAND IN THY PRESENCE IN FULNESS OF   341 03

STAND   CONTINUED

NOT BE ABLE TO STAND IN THE JUDGMENT, *	345 19
KINGS OF THE EARTH STAND UP, AND THE RULERS TAKE	345 21
4 STAND IN AWE, AND SIN NOT	347 19
FOOLISH SHALL NOT STAND IN THY SIGHT	348 09
6 STAND UP, O LORD, IN THY WRATH, AND LIFT UP	349 35
NOT BE ABLE TO STAND, *	362 15
WE ARE RISEN AND STAND UPRIGHT	364 33
THEY STAND STARING AND LOOKING UPON ME	367 07
STAND IN AWE OF HIM, ALL YE THAT DWELL IN THE WORLD	379 02
AND STAND UP TO HELP ME	381 20
23 AWAKE, AND STAND UP TO JUDGE MY QUARREL	383 09
AND SHALL NOT BE ABLE TO STAND	384 22
AND THE LORD SHALL STAND BY THEM, AND SAVE THEM	387 15
MY NEIGHBOURS DID STAND LOOKING UPON MY TROUBLE, *	388 12
RIGHT HAND DOTH STAND THE QUEEN IN A VESTURE OF GOLD,	397 03
5 STAND UP, O LORD GOD OF HOSTS, THOU GOD OF ISRAEL,	411 13
VALLEYS ALSO SHALL STAND SO THICK WITH CORN, THAT	417 12
AND WHO MAY STAND IN THY SIGHT WHEN THOU ART ANGRY	433 03
MADE THE WATERS TO STAND ON AN HEAP	435 27
MY COVENANT SHALL STAND FAST WITH HIM	451 32
36 HE SHALL STAND FAST FOR EVERMORE AS THE MOON,	452 14
THE WHOLE EARTH STAND IN AWE OF HIM	460 17
THEIR SEED SHALL STAND FAST IN THY SIGHT	466 06
THE WATERS STAND ABOVE THE HILLS	468 05
LET AN ADVERSARY STAND AT HIS RIGHT HAND	480 14
30 FOR HE SHALL STAND AT THE RIGHT HAND OF THE POOR,	482 02
8 THEY STAND FAST FOR EVER AND EVER, *	483 09
2 OUR FEET SHALL STAND IN THY GATES, *	503 11
2 THE HILLS STAND ABOUT JERUSALEM	504 26
2 YE THAT BY NIGHT STAND IN THE HOUSE OF THE LORD,	509 25
2 YE THAT STAND IN THE HOUSE OF THE LORD, *	510 05
THE BISHOP SHALL STAND UP, AND TURNING HIS FACE	R 565 16
APPOINTING HIM TO STAND IN THY HOUSE, AND TO SERVE AT	573 13

STANDEST

WHO STANDEST AT THE RIGHT HAND OF GOD TO	099 32
WHY STANDEST THOU SO FAR OFF, O LORD, *	353 03

STANDETH

OF WHOM STANDETH OUR ETERNAL LIFE, WHOSE SERVICE IS	017 06
BUT THERE STANDETH ONE AMONG YOU, WHOM YE KNOW NOT	096 03
EVERY PRIEST STANDETH DAILY MINISTERING AND OFFERING	158 03
THINKETH HE STANDETH TAKE HEED LEST HE FALL	201 25
12 MY FOOT STANDETH RIGHT	371 20
RIGHTEOUSNESS STANDETH LIKE THE STRONG MOUNTAINS	384 06
GOD STANDETH IN THE CONGREGATION OF PRINCES	443 18
FOR HIS HEART STANDETH FAST, AND BELIEVETH IN THE	483 31
BUT MY HEART STANDETH IN AWE OF THY WORD	501 04
7 OUR HELP STANDETH IN THE NAME OF THE LORD, *	504 20
BE REMOVED, BUT STANDETH FAST FOR EVER	504 25
EVEN SO STANDETH THE LORD ROUND ABOUT HIS PEOPLE,	504 26
ORIGINAL SIN STANDETH NOT IN THE FOLLOWING OF ADAM,	604 29

STANDING

TO BE MADE BY THE PRIEST ALONE, STANDING	R 007 03
ALL STANDING UP, THE MINISTER SHALL SAY,	R 008 02
CREED BY THE MINISTER AND THE PEOPLE, STANDING	R 015 16
TO BE MADE BY THE PRIEST ALONE, STANDING	R 024 07
ALL STANDING UP, THE MINISTER SHALL SAY,	R 025 08
CREED BY THE MINISTER AND THE PEOPLE, STANDING	R 029 21
AND THE PRIEST, STANDING REVERENTLY BEFORE THE HOLY	R 067 06
ALL THE PEOPLE STANDING, THE MINISTER APPOINTED SHALL	R 070 22
THE PRIEST, STANDING BEFORE THE HOLY TABLE, HATH SO	R 080 02
ALL STANDING, OR SOME PROPER HYMN	R 083 32
AND JESUS STANDING ON THE RIGHT HAND OF GOD,	100 07
THE SON OF MAN STANDING ON THE RIGHT HAND OF GOD	100 08
AND SAW OTHERS STANDING IDLE IN THE MARKET-PLACE,	119 20
FOUND OTHERS STANDING IDLE, AND SAITH UNTO THEM, WHY	119 24
THE DISCIPLE STANDING BY, WHOM HE LOVED, HE SAITH	160 20
SAW TWO SHIPS STANDING BY THE LAKE	196 08
THE PUBLICAN, STANDING AFAR OFF, WOULD NOT LIFT UP SO	205 28
THE PEOPLE ALL STANDING, HATH THIS CHILD (PERSON)	R 273 25
ALL STANDING, SHALL BE SAID THE APOSTLES'	R 284 11
THE PEOPLE ALL STANDING UNTIL THE LORD'S PRAYER	R 296 07
AND THERE STANDING TOGETHER, THE MAN ON THE RIGHT	R 300 06
STILL STANDING, SAY THE LORD'S PRAYER	R 302 26
BODY BY SOME STANDING BY, THE MINISTER SHALL SAY,	R 333 12
ALL STANDING, SHALL THE BISHOP SAY, ALMIGHTY	R 543 17
AND OTHERS STANDING, THE BISHOP SHALL LAY HIS HANDS	R 534 02
AND OTHERS STANDING, THE BISHOP SHALL SING OR SAY THE	R 543 26
ALL STANDING, THE PRESIDING BISHOP SHALL SAY,	R 555 27
ARE PRESENT, STANDING, SHALL ANSWER BY VERSES,	R 556 05
AND THEN STANDING UP, AND TURNING TO THE	R 564 09
CLERGY PRESENT STANDING IN THE CHANCEL OR CHOIR,	R 570 05
OF THE VESTRY) STANDING ON THE RIGHT AND LEFT OF THE	R 570 07
STANDING UP, SHALL SAY, THE LORD BE WITH	R 573 30

STANDS

AS IT STANDS AMONG THE OCCASIONAL PRAYERS AND	R 305 04
STRENGTHEN HIM WHEN HE STANDS	597 31

STAR

BY THE LEADING OF A STAR DIDST MANIFEST THY	107 29
WE HAVE SEEN HIS STAR IN THE EAST, AND ARE COME TO	108 33
WHAT TIME THE STAR APPEARED	109 12
LO, THE STAR, WHICH THEY SAW IN THE EAST, WENT	109 16
WHEN THEY SAW THE STAR, THEY REJOICED WITH EXCEEDING	109 18

STAR   CONTINUED

FROM ANOTHER STAR IN GLORY	329 18
FOR ONE STAR DIFFERETH FROM ANOTHER STAR IN GLORY	329 18

STARING

THEY STAND STARING AND LOOKING UPON ME	367 07

STARS

O YE STARS OF HEAVEN, BLESS YE THE LORD	012 12
IN THE SUN, AND IN THE MOON, AND IN THE STARS	093 06
HER LIGHT, AND THE STARS SHALL FALL FROM HEAVEN, AND	118 15
AND ANOTHER GLORY OF THE STARS	329 17
THE MOON AND THE STARS WHICH THOU HAST ORDAINED	351 05
9 THE MOON AND THE STARS TO GOVERN THE NIGHT	511 32
THE NUMBER OF THE STARS, *	523 02
PRAISE HIM, ALL YE STARS AND LIGHT	524 09

STARTING

STARTING ASIDE LIKE A BROKEN BOW	438 27

STATE

O LORD, SAVE THE STATE	031 04
GOVERNOR OF THIS STATE, AND ALL OTHERS IN AUTHORITY,	032 07
OF THIS STATE, THAT IT MAY ORDAIN FOR OUR GOVERNANCE	035 26
GOVERNOR OF THIS STATE, AND FOR ALL THAT ARE IN	047 16
TO SERVE GOD IN THE MINISTRY AND IN THE STATE	047 31
PRAY FOR THE WHOLE STATE OF CHRIST'S CHURCH	074 05
FOR THE WHOLE STATE OF CHRIST'S CHURCH, THE PRIEST	R 085 22
AND THE LAST STATE OF THAT MAN IS WORSE THAN THE	130 16
CALLED ME TO THIS STATE OF SALVATION, THROUGH JESUS	284 03
DO MY DUTY IN THAT STATE OF LIFE UNTO WHICH IT SHALL	289 10
SO CONSECRATED THE STATE OF MATRIMONY THAT IN IT IS	303 20
CALLED ME TO THIS STATE OF SALVATION, THROUGH JESUS	577 24
DO MY DUTY IN THAT STATE OF LIFE UNTO WHICH IT SHALL	580 14
TO LIVE IN SUCH A STATE THAT WE MAY NEVER BE AFRAID	591 30

STATED

PRECEDING THE STATED TIMES OF ORDINATION	R 038 24

STATES

CHURCH IN THESE STATES IS INDEBTED, UNDER GOD,	V 11
OF THE UNITED STATES, AND ALL OTHERS IN AUTHORITY	017 31
OF THE UNITED STATES, AND TO ALL IN AUTHORITY, WISDOM	018 10
OF THE UNITED STATES, THE GOVERNOR OF THIS STATE,	032 07
OF THESE UNITED STATES IN GENERAL, SO ESPECIALLY FOR	035 09
UNTO THE UNITED STATES OF AMERICA, AND A SECURITY FOR	042 08
OF THESE UNITED STATES, AND FOR THE GOVERNOR OF THIS	047 15
OF THESE UNITED STATES, THAT THEY MAY LIVE IN THE	048 02
OF THE UNITED STATES, THAT HE MAY ABOVE ALL THINGS	055 23
THESE AMERICAN STATES BECAME INDEPENDENT WITH RESPECT	VI 07
IN THESE STATES WERE LEFT AT FULL AND EQUAL LIBERTY	VI 10
IN THE SEVERAL STATES, EVERY MINISTER IS LEFT TO THE	R 304 18
IN THE UNITED STATES OF AMERICA	552 32
PARTLY ARE STATES OF LIFE ALLOWED IN THE SCRIPTURES	607 41

STATURE

IN WISDOM AND STATURE, AND IN FAVOUR WITH GOD AND	111 07
MEASURE OF THE STATURE OF THE FULNESS OF CHRIST	237 24
IN WISDOM AND STATURE, AND GROW IN THY LOVE AND	307 05
MEASURE OF THE STATURE OF THE FULNESS OF CHRIST	538 11

STATUTE

THIS WAS MADE A STATUTE FOR ISRAEL, *	442 18

STATUTES

WHOSE STATUTES ARE GOOD AND GRACIOUS AND	035 23
8 THE STATUTES OF THE LORD ARE RIGHT, AND REJOICE THE	363 30
THEY BREAK MY STATUTES, AND KEEP NOT MY COMMANDMENTS	452 04
MIGHT KEEP HIS STATUTES, *	472 27
THAT I MIGHT KEEP THY STATUTES	490 09
8 I WILL KEEP THY STATUTES	490 14
O TEACH ME THY STATUTES	490 22
SHALL BE IN THY STATUTES, *	490 29
BUT THY SERVANT IS OCCUPIED IN THY STATUTES	491 13
O TEACH ME THY STATUTES	491 20
THE WAY OF THY STATUTES, *	492 05
AND MY STUDY SHALL BE IN THY STATUTES	493 06
54 THY STATUTES HAVE BEEN MY SONGS, *	493 18
O TEACH ME THY STATUTES	494 09
O TEACH ME THY STATUTES	494 17
THAT I MAY LEARN THY STATUTES	494 23
BE SOUND IN THY STATUTES, *	495 16
YET DO I NOT FORGET THY STATUTES	495 24
TO FULFIL THY STATUTES ALWAY, *	497 21
MY DELIGHT SHALL BE EVER IN THY STATUTES	498 03
DOWN ALL THEM THAT DEPART FROM THY STATUTES	498 05
AND TEACH ME THY STATUTES	498 18
AND TEACH ME THY STATUTES	499 09
I WILL KEEP THY STATUTES	499 32
FOR THEY REGARD NOT THY STATUTES	500 22
WHEN THOU HAST TAUGHT ME THY STATUTES	501 25
HIS STATUTES AND ORDINANCES UNTO ISRAEL	523 33

STAVES

WITH SWORDS AND STAVES, FROM THE CHIEF PRIESTS AND	142 16

STAVES   CONTINUED

SWORDS AND WITH STAVES, TO TAKE ME   142 25
AS AGAINST A THIEF, WITH SWORDS AND STAVES   151 04

STAY

OF THE LORD, AND STAY UPON HIS GOD   144 25
WERE A SHADOW, AND NEVER CONTINUETH IN ONE STAY   332 21

STEADINESS

IT WITH SUCH STEADINESS OF FAITH, AND WITH SUCH   566 19

STEAL

THOU SHALT NOT STEAL   069 13
AND WHERE THIEVES BREAK THROUGH AND STEAL   072 09
AND WHERE THIEVES DO NOT BREAK THROUGH NOR STEAL   072 11
THOU SHALT NOT STEAL, THOU SHALT NOT BEAR FALSE   090 26
AND WHERE THIEVES BREAK THROUGH AND STEAL   125 18
AND WHERE THIEVES DO NOT BREAK THROUGH NOR STEAL   125 21
COME BY NIGHT, AND STEAL HIM AWAY, AND SAY UNTO THE   162 21
BUT FOR TO STEAL, AND TO KILL, AND TO DESTROY   186 17
LET HIM THAT STOLE STEAL NO MORE   216 20
THOU SHALT NOT STEAL   287 12
BUT FOR TO STEAL, AND TO KILL, AND TO DESTROY   539 08
THOU SHALT NOT STEAL   579 17

STEALING

TO KEEP MY HANDS FROM PICKING AND STEALING   289 04
PICKING AND STEALING, AND MY TONGUE FROM EVIL   580 09

STEDFAST

A LIVELY AND STEDFAST FAITH IN CHRIST OUR SAVIOUR   085 35
KEEP US STEDFAST IN THIS FAITH, AND EVERMORE DEFEND   186 27
BRING UP IN THY STEDFAST FEAR AND LOVE   191 05
WHOM RESIST STEDFAST IN THE FAITH, KNOWING THAT THE   193 06
WITH STEDFAST PURPOSE TO LEAD A NEW LIFE   293 27
LIFE PAST, AND STEDFAST FAITH IN THY SON JESUS   316 13
BE YE STEDFAST, UNMOVEABLE, ALWAYS   330 14
CONTINUED THEY STEDFAST IN HIS COVENANT   437 13
THAT WITH STEDFAST THOUGHTS AND KINDLED   594 07

STEDFASTLY

WE MAY STEDFASTLY LOOK UP TO HEAVEN, AND BY   099 27
LOOKED UP STEDFASTLY INTO HEAVEN, AND SAW THE GLORY   100 05
THEY LOOKED STEDFASTLY TOWARD HEAVEN AS HE WENT UP,   178 14
COULD NOT STEDFASTLY BEHOLD THE FACE OF MOSES FOR THE   206 20
WE MAY STEDFASTLY WALK IN THE WAY THAT LEADETH   239 02
IT CONTINUES STEDFASTLY IN THE APOSTLES' TEACHING AND   291 14
WHEREBY THEY STEDFASTLY BELIEVE THE PROMISES OF GOD   292 29
HIS SINS, AND STEDFASTLY BELIEVE THAT JESUS CHRIST   R 323 26
GRANT US STEDFASTLY TO BELIEVE THAT THIS THY CHILD   340 26
CLAVE NOT STEDFASTLY UNTO GOD   435 15
AND AM STEDFASTLY PURPOSED, *   497 09
WHEREBY THEY STEDFASTLY BELIEVE THE PROMISES OF GOD   581 29
FORMER SINS, STEDFASTLY PURPOSING TO LEAD A NEW LIFE   582 23

STEDFASTNESS

OF THEIR STEDFASTNESS IN THY FAITH, AND OBEDIENCE TO   336 22

STEEL

AND MINE ARMS SHALL BEND EVEN A BOW OF STEEL   362 05

STEPHEN

MARTYR SAINT STEPHEN, WHO PRAYED FOR HIS MURDERERS TO   099 31
STEPHEN, BEING FULL OF THE HOLY GHOST, LOOKED UP   100 05
AND THEY STONED STEPHEN, CALLING UPON GOD, AND   100 13
MARTYR SAINT STEPHEN, WITH OTHERS   531 17
AND THEY CHOSE STEPHEN, A MAN FULL OF FAITH AND OF   532 15

STEPS

FOLLOWING IN HIS STEPS, GIVE THEMSELVES TO THE   043 30
FOLLOW THE BLESSED STEPS OF HIS MOST HOLY LIFE   171 32
THAT YE SHOULD FOLLOW HIS STEPS   172 11
FOLLOWING THE STEPS OF THY HOLY APOSTLES, SAINT   238 32
NEITHER OUR STEPS GONE OUT OF THY WAY   395 30
AND MARK MY STEPS, WHEN THEY LAY WAIT FOR MY SOUL   408 27
133 ORDER MY STEPS IN THY WORD   499 04
NO EVIL CAN OUR STEPS BETIDE   545 09
NO EVIL CAN OUR STEPS BETIDE   557 15

STEWARD

SAITH UNTO HIS STEWARD, CALL THE LABOURERS, AND GIVE   119 29

STEWARDS

MINISTERS AND STEWARDS OF THY MYSTERIES MAY LIKEWISE   093 26
OF CHRIST, AND STEWARDS OF THE MYSTERIES OF GOD   094 04
IS REQUIRED IN STEWARDS, THAT A MAN BE FOUND   094 05
AS GOOD STEWARDS OF THE MANIFOLD GRACE OF GOD   179 17
AND STEWARDS OF THE LORD   539 33
AND FAITHFUL STEWARDS OF THE MYSTERIES OF CHRIST,   562 11
MAY BE FAITHFUL STEWARDS OF THY BOUNTY   599 22

STICK

2 FOR THINE ARROWS STICK FAST IN ME, *   387 23
2 I STICK FAST IN THE DEEP MIRE, WHERE NO GROUND IS   422 02

STIFF

SPEAK NOT WITH A STIFF NECK   432 09

STIFFNESS

TOO MUCH STIFFNESS IN REFUSING, AND TOO MUCH EASINESS   V 25

STILL

THEREOF) HAVE STILL BEEN CONTINUED FIRM AND UNSHAKEN   V 32
THE PEOPLE STILL KNEELING   R 007 03
THE PEOPLE STILL KNEELING, AND REPEATING IT WITH HIM, R 007 21
THE PEOPLE STILL KNEELING   R 024 07
THE PEOPLE STILL   R 024 27
BESEECHING THEE STILL TO CONTINUE SUCH THY MERCIES   052 13
AND THE PEOPLE, STILL KNEELING, SHALL, AFTER EVERY   R 067 23
BUT REMAIN STILL IN HIS FROWARDNESS AND   R 085 15
AND THEY THAT BARE HIM STOOD STILL   213 04
THAT OUR LAND MAY STILL YIELD HER INCREASE, TO THY   265 15
AND THE PEOPLE, STILL STANDING, SAY THE LORD'S   R 302 26
THE WOMAN STILL KNEELING   R 305 15
BE STILL THEN, AND KNOW THAT I AM GOD   327 14
TO US WHO ARE STILL IN OUR PILGRIMAGE, AND WHO WALK   336 06
AND IN YOUR CHAMBER, AND BE STILL   347 20
THAT THOU MIGHTEST STILL THE ENEMY AND THE AVENGER   351 03
7 HOLD THEE STILL IN THE LORD, AND ABIDE PATIENTLY   385 06
10 BE STILL THEN, AND KNOW THAT I AM GOD   398 14
SOUL TRULY WAITETH STILL UPON GOD   413 27
MY SOUL, WAIT THOU STILL UPON GOD   414 07
A ONE AS GOETH ON STILL IN HIS WICKEDNESS   420 28
AND WAS STILL, 9 WHEN GOD AROSE TO   433 05
BUT WALK ON STILL IN DARKNESS   443 27
O GOD, KEEP NOT STILL SILENCE   444 05
SO THAT THE WAVES THEREOF ARE STILL   478 03
WHERE WE MAY BE STILL AND KNOW THAT THOU ART GOD   595 23

STILLEST

IN A HOUSE, AND STILLEST THE OUTRAGE OF A VIOLENT AND   052 18
THOU STILLEST THE WAVES THEREOF WHEN THEY ARISE   450 24

STILLETH

7 WHO STILLETH THE RAGING OF THE SEA, *   416 27

STING

O DEATH, WHERE IS THY STING   330 10
THE STING OF DEATH IS SIN   330 11
TAKE AWAY THE STING OF DEATH   336 11

STINK

5 MY WOUNDS STINK, AND ARE CORRUPT, *   387 30

STIR

STIR UP, WE BESEECH THEE, O LORD, THE WILLS OF THY   225 04
THIS TABERNACLE, TO STIR YOU UP BY PUTTING YOU IN   248 09
STIR UP THY STRENGTH, AND COME AND HELP US   441 06
AND STIR UP STRIFE ALL THE DAY LONG   516 11
REMEMBER THAT THOU STIR UP THE GRACE OF GOD, WHICH IS   558 16

STIRRED

TEMPEST SHALL BE STIRRED UP ROUND ABOUT HIM   401 27

STIRRETH

HE STIRRETH UP THE PEOPLE, TEACHING   153 05

STOCK

CHILDREN OF THE STOCK OF ABRAHAM, AND WHOSOEVER AMONG   168 24

STOCKS

18 WHOSE FEET THEY HURT IN THE STOCKS   471 08

STOLE

LET HIM THAT STOLE STEAL NO MORE   216 20

STONE

SIX WATER-POTS OF STONE, AFTER THE MANNER OF THE   113 19
AT ANY TIME THOU DASH THY FOOT AGAINST A STONE   127 02
HE ROLLED A GREAT STONE TO THE DOOR OF THE SEPULCHRE,   162 12
SEALING THE STONE, AND SETTING A WATCH   162 25
AND SEETH THE STONE TAKEN AWAY FROM THE SEPULCHRE   164 12
ROLL US AWAY THE STONE FROM THE DOOR OF THE   165 23
THEY SAW THAT THE STONE WAS ROLLED AWAY   165 25
OF YOU THAT IS A FATHER, WILL HE GIVE HIM A STONE   183 15
TO LOOK UPON LIKE A JASPER AND A SARDINE STONE   187 07
LEAVE IN THEE ONE STONE UPON ANOTHER   204 14
AS UNTO A LIVING STONE, DISALLOWED INDEED OF MEN, BUT   259 29
OF YOU THAT IS A FATHER, WILL HE GIVE HIM A STONE   263 08
AND SET ME UP UPON A ROCK OF STONE   326 14
AND SET ME UP UPON A ROCK OF STONE   372 06
THAT THOU HURT NOT THY FOOT AGAINST A STONE   455 20

STONE   CONTINUED

OPENED THE ROCK OF STONE, AND THE WATERS FLOWED CUT,	472 19
22 THE SAME STONE WHICH THE BUILDERS REFUSED,	489 12

STONE'S

THEM ABOUT A STONE'S CAST, AND KNEELED DOWN, ANC	150 17

STONED

OF THE CITY, AND STONED HIM	100 11
AND THEY STONED STEPHEN, CALLING UPON GOD, AND	100 13
ONCE WAS I STONED, THRICE I SUFFERED SHIPWRECK,	121 03

STONES

THAT THESE STONES BE MADE BREAD	126 27
THEN TOOK THEY UP STONES TO CAST AT HIM	133 33
AND ENGRAVEN IN STONES, WAS GLORIOUS, SO THAT THE	206 19
AS LIVELY STONES, ARE BUILT UP A SPIRITUAL	259 31
AND MADE JERUSALEM AN HEAP OF STONES	439 31
THINK UPON HER STONES, *	465 07
ABOVE GOLD AND PRECIOLS STONES	498 24
AND THROWETH THEM AGAINST THE STONES	513 25

STONEST

AND STONEST THEM WHICH ARE SENT UNTO THEE,	100 28

STONY

THE LORD IS MY STONY ROCK, AND MY DEFENCE	359 25
WATERS OUT OF THE STONY ROCK, *	435 33
21 HE SMOTE THE STONY ROCK INDEED, THAT THE WATER	436 08
HONEY OUT OF THE STONY ROCK WOULD I HAVE SATISFIEC	443 14
AND SO ARE THE STONY ROCKS FOR THE CONIES	468 31
BE OVERTHROWN IN STONY PLACES, *	517 24

STOOD

LO, A LAMB STOOD ON THE MOUNT SION, AND WITH HIM	102 29
TILL IT CAME AND STOOD OVER WHERE THE YOUNG CHILD	109 17
AND JESUS STOOD, AND COMMANDED HIM TO BE BRCUGHT UNTO	123 33
AND JESUS STOOD BEFORE THE GOVERNOR	135 18
SOME OF THEM THAT STOOD THERE, WHEN THEY HEARD THAT,	137 19
ONE OF THEM THAT STOOD BY DREW A SWORD, AND SMOTE A	142 22
THE HIGH PRIEST STOOD UP IN THE MIDST, AND ASKED	143 10
SAY TO THEM THAT STOOD BY, THIS IS ONE CF THEM	143 29
THEY THAT STOOD BY SAID AGAIN TO PETER, SURELY	143 30
SOME OF THEM THAT STOOD BY, WHEN THEY HEARD IT,	146 30
WHICH STOOD OVER AGAINST HIM, SAW THAT HE	147 03
AND SCRIBES STOOD AND VEHEMENTLY ACCUSED HIM	153 15
AND THE PEOPLE STOOD BEHOLDING	154 27
HIM FROM GALILEE, STOOD AFAR OFF, BEHOLDING THESE	155 20
NOW THERE STOOD BY THE CROSS OF JESUS HIS MOTHER, AND	160 17
JESUS HIMSELF STOOD IN THE MIDST OF THEM, AND SAITH	169 28
CAME JESUS AND STOOD IN THE MIDST, AND SAITH UNTC	171 16
BEHOLD, TWO MEN STOOD BY THEM IN WHITE APPAREL	178 15
WORD OF GOD, HE STOOD BY THE LAKE OF GENNESARET,	196 07
THE PHARISEE STOOD AND PRAYED THUS WITH HIMSELF,	205 25
A CERTAIN LAWYER STOOD UP, AND TEMPTED HIM, SAYING,	208 12
WERE LEPERS, WHICH STOOD AFAR OFF	210 03
THEY THAT BARE HIM STOOD STILL	213 04
BEING SHUT, AND STOOD IN THE MIDST, AND SAID, PEACE	229 02
JOURNEYED WITH HIM STOOD SPEECHLESS, HEARING A VOICE,	230 09
THOSE DAYS PETER STOOD UP IN THE MIDST OF THE	234 06
AND THERE STOOD UP ONE OF THEM NAMED AGABUS, ANC	241 16
AND THERE STOOD UP ONE OF THEM NAMED AGABUS, ANC	246 25
THE TWO MEN THAT STOOD WITH HIM	248 32
AND TONGUES, STOOD BEFORE THE THRONE, AND BEFORE THE	256 25
AND ALL THE ANGELS STCOD ROUND ABOUT THE THRONE,	256 29
SABBATH DAY, AND STOOD UP FOR TO READ	261 13
THE UNGODLY, NOR STOOD IN THE WAY OF SINNERS, *	345 08
AND IT STOOD FAST	379 05
AND MY KINSMEN STOOD AFAR OFF	388 13
MOSES HIS CHOSEN STOOD BEFORE HIM IN THE GAP, *	474 15
30 THEN STOOD LP PHINEHAS, AND INTERPOSED	474 29
CAME JESUS, AND STOOD IN THE MIDST, AND SAITH UNTO	551 29

STOOP

I AM NOT WORTHY TO STCOP DOWN AND UNLCCSE	112 16

STOOPING

AND HE STOOPING DOWN, AND LOOKING IN, SAW THE LINEN	164 19

STOP

THE SPEAR, AND STOP THE WAY AGAINST THEM THAT PURSUE	381 22

STOPPED

LOUD VOICE, AND STOPPED THEIR EARS, AND RAN UPON HIM	100 10
MOUTH OF THEM THAT SPEAK LIES SHALL BE STOPPED	415 17
AND THE MOUTH OF ALL WICKEDNESS SHALL BE STOPPEC	478 31

STOPPETH

THAT STOPPETH HER EARS	410 16

STORE

BE FULL AND PLENTEOUS WITH ALL MANNER CF STCRE	520 19

STORK

AND THE FIR-TREES ARE A DWELLING FOR THE STCRK	468 29

STORM

AND BRIMSTONE, STORM AND TEMPEST	354 34
WHAT TIME AS THE STORM FELL UPON THEE	442 26
AND MAKE THEM AFRAID WITH THY STORM	445 03
FOR HE MAKETH THE STORM TO CEASE, *	478 02
WIND AND STORM, FULFILLING HIS WORD	524 20

STORMS

ALL THY WAVES AND STORMS ARE GONE OVER ME	393 19
AND THOU HAST VEXED ME WITH ALL THY STORMS	449 10

STORMY

BECAUSE OF THE STORMY WIND AND TEMPEST	407 02
AT HIS WORD THE STORMY WIND ARISETH, *	477 26

STRAIGHT

THE LORD, MAKE STRAIGHT IN THE DESERT A HIGHWAY FCR	004 06
MAKE STRAIGHT THE WAY OF THE LORD, AS SAID THE	095 29
YE THE WAY OF THE LORD, MAKE HIS PATHS STRAIGHT	112 07
WHICH IS CALLED STRAIGHT, AND ENQUIRE IN THE HCUSE CF	230 17
THE LORD, MAKE STRAIGHT IN THE DESERT A HIGHWAY FCR	242 17
SHALL BE MADE STRAIGHT, AND THE ROUGH PLACES PLAIN	242 24
HOLD I STRAIGHT ALL THY COMMANDMENTS	498 25
AND IN THY STRAIGHT PATH MAY NOT STUMBLE	595 31

STRAIGHTWAY

AND STRAIGHTWAY YE SHALL FIND AN ASS TIED, AND A	091 14
AND STRAIGHTWAY HE WILL SEND THEM	091 17
AND STRAIGHTWAY COMING UP OUT OF THE WATER, HE SAW	112 20
AND STRAIGHTWAY ONE OF THEM RAN, AND TCOK A SPUNGE,	137 21
HE GOETH STRAIGHTWAY TO HIM, AND SAITH, MASTER,	142 20
AND STRAIGHTWAY IN THE MORNING THE CHIEF PRIESTS HELD	145 03
HIS WAY, AND STRAIGHTWAY FORGETTETH WHAT MANNER CF	176 09
AND STRAIGHTWAY HIS EARS WERE OPENED, AND THE STRING	207 03
AND WILL NOT STRAIGHTWAY PULL HIM OUT ON THE SABBATH	214 06
AND THEY STRAIGHTWAY LEFT THEIR NETS, AND FCLLCWED	227 28
AND STRAIGHTWAY HE PREACHED CHRIST IN THE SYNAGOGUES,	231 03
HIS WAY, AND STRAIGHTWAY FORGETTETH WHAT MANNER CF	265 32

STRANGE

OUR HANDS TO ANY STRANGE GOD, *	396 02
AND HAD HEARD A STRANGE LANGUAGE	442 21
THERE SHALL NO STRANGE GOD BE IN THEE, *	442 31
FROM AMONG THE STRANGE PEOPLE, 2 JUDAH WAS HIS	484 28
IN A STRANGE LAND	513 12
ERRONEOUS AND STRANGE DOCTRINES CONTRARY TO GOD'S	542 21
ERRONEOUS AND STRANGE DOCTRINE CONTRARY TO GOD'S	555 04

STRANGER

AND THE STRANGER THAT IS WITHIN THY GATES	068 29
ART THOU ONLY A STRANGER IN JERUSALEM, AND HAST ACT	167 13
AND A STRANGER WILL THEY NOT FCLLOW, BUT WILL FLEE	186 08
RETURNED TO GIVE GLORY TO GOD, SAVE THIS STRANGER	210 13
TURN ASIDE THE STRANGER FROM HIS RIGHT, AND FEAR NOT	232 20
I WAS A STRANGER, AND YE TOOK ME IN	259 07
SAW WE THEE A STRANGER, AND TOOK THEE IN	259 11
AND LOVETH THE STRANGER, IN GIVING HIM FOOD AND	263 27
LOVE YE THEREFORE THE STRANGER	263 28
AND THE STRANGER THAT IS WITHIN THY GATES	286 29
AND MINE EYES SHALL BEHOLD, AND NOT AS A STRANGER	324 12
FOR I AM A STRANGER WITH THEE, AND A SOJOURNER,	325 08
14 FOR I AM A STRANGER WITH THEE, AND A SOJCURNER,	390 04
8 I AM BECOME A STRANGER UNTO MY BRETHREN, *	422 18
WIDOW AND THE STRANGER, *	457 29
AND JACOB WAS A STRANGER IN THE LAND OF HAM	471 19
AND LET THE STRANGER SPOIL HIS LABOUR	480 22
19 I AM A STRANGER UPON EARTH	491 04
AND A STRANGER WILL THEY NOT FOLLOW, BUT WILL FLEE	538 31
AND THE STRANGER THAT IS WITHIN THY GATES	579 09

STRANGERS

TO BURY STRANGERS IN	135 12
BESEECH YOU AS STRANGERS AND PILGRIMS, ABSTAIN FRCM	173 12
AND STRANGERS OF ROME, JEWS AND PROSELYTES,	181 04
FOR THEY KNOW NOT THE VOICE OF STRANGERS	186 09
YE ARE NO MORE STRANGERS AND FOREIGNERS, BUT	255 03
FOR YE WERE STRANGERS IN THE LAND OF EGYPT	263 28
THE STRANGERS SHALL FEIGN OBEDIENCE UNTO ME	362 29
46 THE STRANGERS SHALL FAIL, *	362 30
3 FOR STRANGERS ARE RISEN UP AGAINST ME	406 07
AND THEY STRANGERS IN THE LAND	470 27
FROM THE HAND OF STRANGERS	520 05
THE HAND OF STRANGERS, *	520 12
9 THE LORD CARETH FOR THE STRANGERS	522 20
FOR THEY KNOW NOT THE VOICE OF STRANGERS	538 32
AND TO ALL STRANGERS DESTITUTE OF HELP	555 25

STRAWED

THE TREES, AND STRAWED THEM IN THE WAY	091 26

STRAYED

HAVE ERRED, AND STRAYED FROM THY WAYS LIKE LCST	006 18

STRAYED   CONTINUED

HAVE ERRED, AND STRAYED FROM THY WAYS LIKE LOST   023 25

STREAM

AND THE STREAM HAD GONE OVER OUR SOUL   504 12

STREAMS

IS A RIVER, THE STREAMS WHEREOF SHALL MAKE GLAD THE   022 26
IS A RIVER, THE STREAMS WHEREOF MAKE GLAD THE CITY OF   327 09
IS A RIVER, THE STREAMS WHEREOF MAKE GLAD THE CITY OF   397 32
AND THE STREAMS FLOWED WITHAL   436 09

STREET

AND GO INTO THE STREET WHICH IS CALLED STRAIGHT,   230 17
THEY WENT OUT, AND PASSED ON THROUGH ONE STREET   245 24

STREETS

QUICKLY INTO THE STREETS AND LANES OF THE CITY,   192 14
SICK INTO THE STREETS, AND LAID THEM ON BEDS AND   249 27
CORNERS OF THE STREETS, *   353 21
I WILL CAST THEM OUT AS THE CLAY IN THE STREETS   362 24
DECEIT AND GUILE GO NOT OUT OF HER STREETS   407 10
AND NO COMPLAINING IN OUR STREETS   520 23

STRENGTH

O LORD, MY STRENGTH AND MY REDEEMER   003 21
PUT ON THY STRENGTH, O ZION   004 18
REJOICE IN THE STRENGTH OF OUR SALVATION   009 04
AND THE STRENGTH OF THE HILLS IS HIS ALSO   009 10
WISDOM AND STRENGTH TO KNOW AND TO DO THY WILL   018 11
O LORD, MY STRENGTH AND MY REDEEMER   021 22
HE HATH SHOWED STRENGTH WITH HIS ARM   026 20
YE ANGELS OF HIS, YE THAT EXCEL IN STRENGTH   029 13
GIVE STRENGTH AND SKILL TO ALL THOSE WHO MINISTER TO   045 05
HAST ORDAINED STRENGTH, AND MADEST INFANTS TO GLORIFY   102 22
TO US SUCH STRENGTH AND PROTECTION, AS MAY SUPPORT US   114 07
TRAVELLING IN THE GREATNESS OF HIS STRENGTH   138 13
DOWN THEIR STRENGTH TO THE EARTH   138 27
ZEAL AND THY STRENGTH, THE SOUNDING OF THY BOWELS AND   139 19
IT IS OF NO STRENGTH AT ALL WHILE THE TESTATOR   147 16
O GOD, THE STRENGTH OF ALL THOSE WHO PUT THEIR TRUST   188 32
WITH ALL THY STRENGTH, AND WITH ALL THY MIND   208 16
OUR REFUGE AND STRENGTH, WHO ART THE AUTHOR OF ALL   222 09
THE MORE IN STRENGTH, AND CONFOUNDED THE JEWS WHICH   231 09
GOOD TIDINGS, LIFT UP THY VOICE WITH STRENGTH   243 04
AND STRENGTH, AND THE KINGDOM OF OUR GOD,   252 11
HAVE POWER AND STRENGTH TO HAVE VICTORY, AND TO   278 24
AND WITH ALL THY STRENGTH   288 07
WITH ALL MY SOUL, AND WITH ALL MY STRENGTH   288 18
AND GHOSTLY STRENGTH, THE SPIRIT OF KNOWLEDGE AND   297 20
FOR THOU ART THE GOD OF MY STRENGTH   310 08
MAY ADD STRENGTH TO HIS FAITH, AND SERIOUSNESS TO HIS   310 23
AND ENDUEDST MY SOUL WITH MUCH STRENGTH   312 03
O GOD, THE STRENGTH OF THE WEAK AND THE COMFORT OF   312 12
YE ANGELS OF HIS, YE THAT EXCEL IN STRENGTH   312 29
AND HIS STRENGTH RECALLED   315 09
WE ENTREAT THY STRENGTH AND GOODNESS IN BEHALF OF   315 15
MAY RECOVER MY STRENGTH, *   325 10
YET IS THEIR STRENGTH THEN BUT LABOUR AND SORROW   325 34
THE LORD IS THE STRENGTH OF MY LIFE   326 06
IS OUR HOPE AND STRENGTH, *   327 03
AND THE STRENGTH OF SIN IS THE LAW   330 12
HE MAY GO FROM STRENGTH TO STRENGTH, IN THE LIFE OF   332 06
STRENGTH TO STRENGTH, IN THE LIFE OF PERFECT SERVICE,   332 06
THOU ORDAINED STRENGTH, BECAUSE OF THINE ENEMIES, *   351 02
I WILL LOVE THEE, O LORD, MY STRENGTH   359 24
OR WHO HATH ANY STRENGTH, EXCEPT OUR GOD   361 32
GIRDETH ME WITH STRENGTH OF WAR, *   361 33
GIRDED ME WITH STRENGTH UNTO THE BATTLE   362 16
O LORD, MY STRENGTH AND MY REDEEMER   364 15
THE WHOLESOME STRENGTH OF HIS RIGHT HAND   364 28
REJOICE IN THY STRENGTH, O LORD   365 05
IN THINE OWN STRENGTH   365 32
15 MY STRENGTH IS DRIED UP LIKE A POTSHERD, AND MY   366 34
THE LORD IS THE STRENGTH OF MY LIFE   371 25
UNTO THEE WILL I CRY, O LORD, MY STRENGTH   373 03
THE LORD IS MY STRENGTH, AND MY SHIELD   373 22
THE LORD IS MY STRENGTH, *   373 25
ASCRIBE UNTO THE LORD WORSHIP AND STRENGTH   373 31
LORD SHALL GIVE STRENGTH UNTO HIS PEOPLE   374 19
FOR THOU ART MY STRENGTH   375 30
12 MY STRENGTH FAILETH ME, BECAUSE OF MINE INIQUITY,   376 13
IS ANY MIGHTY MAN DELIVERED BY MUCH STRENGTH   379 21
SHALL HE DELIVER ANY MAN BY HIS GREAT STRENGTH   379 23
IS ALSO THEIR STRENGTH IN THE TIME OF TROUBLE   387 14
MY STRENGTH HATH FAILED ME, *   388 10
MAY RECOVER MY STRENGTH, *   390 06
THE GOD OF MY STRENGTH, WHY HAST THOU FORGOTTEN ME   393 24
2 FOR THOU ART THE GOD OF MY STRENGTH   394 06
IS OUR HOPE AND STRENGTH, *   397 25
IS THE MAN THAT TOOK NOT GOD FOR HIS STRENGTH   405 02
AND AVENGE ME IN THY STRENGTH   406 04
9 MY STRENGTH WILL I ASCRIBE UNTO THEE   411 22
UNTO THEE, O MY STRENGTH, WILL I SING   412 09
ALSO IS THE STRENGTH OF MY HEAD   412 26
HE VERILY IS MY STRENGTH AND MY SALVATION   413 29
HE TRULY IS MY STRENGTH AND MY SALVATION   414 09
6 WHO IN HIS STRENGTH SETTETH FAST THE MOUNTAINS,   416 25
HATH SENT FORTH STRENGTH FOR THEE   421 11
HIS WORSHIP AND STRENGTH IS IN THE CLOUDS   421 26

STRENGTH   CONTINUED

HE WILL GIVE STRENGTH AND POWER UNTO HIS PEOPLE   421 28
ME NOT WHEN MY STRENGTH FAILETH ME   425 24
GO FORTH IN THE STRENGTH OF THE LORD GOD, *   426 06
HAVE SHOWED THY STRENGTH UNTO THIS GENERATION, AND   426 11
BUT GOD IS THE STRENGTH OF MY HEART, AND MY PORTION   429 29
GOD WAS THEIR STRENGTH, *   437 08
STIR UP THY STRENGTH, AND COME AND HELP US   441 07
SING WE MERRILY UNTO GOD OUR STRENGTH   442 12
THE MAN WHOSE STRENGTH IS IN THEE   445 21
WILL GO FROM STRENGTH TO STRENGTH, *   445 25
STRENGTH TO STRENGTH, *   445 25
GIVE THY STRENGTH UNTO THY SERVANT, AND HELP THE SON   448 07
AND I AM EVEN AS A MAN THAT HATH NO STRENGTH   449 03
GLORY OF THEIR STRENGTH, *   451 08
YET IS THEIR STRENGTH THEN BUT LABOUR AND SORROW   454 09
THE LORD MY STRENGTH IS, *   456 30
AND GIRDED HIMSELF WITH STRENGTH   457 06
MY GOD IS THE STRENGTH OF MY CONFIDENCE   458 31
REJOICE IN THE STRENGTH OF OUR SALVATION   459 06
AND THE STRENGTH OF THE HILLS IS HIS ALSO   459 12
BROUGHT DOWN MY STRENGTH IN MY JOURNEY, *   465 26
YE ANGELS OF HIS, YE THAT EXCEL IN STRENGTH   467 16
4 SEEK THE LORD AND HIS STRENGTH   470 11
EVEN THE CHIEF OF ALL THEIR STRENGTH   472 10
ALSO IS THE STRENGTH OF MY HEAD   479 21
THE LORD IS MY STRENGTH, AND MY SONG   488 28
THOU, AND THE ARK OF THY STRENGTH   508 20
AND ENDUEDST MY SOUL WITH MUCH STRENGTH   514 03
LORD GOD, THOU STRENGTH OF MY HEALTH   516 22
BE THE LORD MY STRENGTH, *   519 22
PLEASURE IN THE STRENGTH OF AN HORSE   523 15
ALSO UNTO YOU STRENGTH AND POWER TO PERFORM THE SAME,   543 19
ALSO UNTO YOU STRENGTH AND POWER TO PERFORM THE SAME   555 30
HAVE POWER AND STRENGTH TO FULFIL THE SAME   566 06
O LORD, OUR STRENGTH AND OUR REDEEMER   572 24
WITH ALL MY SOUL, AND WITH ALL MY STRENGTH   579 29
UPHELD BY THY STRENGTH, AND IN THE END BE ACCEPTED OF   594 26
THE STRENGTH OF THOSE WHO LABOUR, AND THE   595 05
QUIETNESS AND IN CONFIDENCE SHALL BE OUR STRENGTH   595 21
US LIGHT AND STRENGTH SO TO TRAIN THEM, THAT THEY MAY   596 26
RESTORE THEM TO STRENGTH OF MIND AND CHEERFULNESS OF   598 15
HIS OWN NATURAL STRENGTH AND GOOD WORKS, TO FAITH,   604 43

STRENGTHEN

ARM TO STRENGTHEN AND PROTECT THE SOLDIERS OF OUR   041 26
COURAGE TO STRENGTHEN THE WEAK AND RAISE UP THOSE WHO   044 02
CONFIRM AND STRENGTHEN IT IN PURITY OF FAITH, IN   047 09
THEE TO STRENGTHEN SUCH AS DO STAND   056 22
CONFIRM AND STRENGTHEN YOU IN ALL GOODNESS   076 06
IN US, AND SO STRENGTHEN US BY THY GRACE, THAT BY THE   102 24
STRENGTHEN THY BRETHREN   149 34
STRENGTHEN, SETTLE YOU   193 11
STRENGTHEN THEM, WE BESEECH THEE, O LORD, WITH THE   297 17
BUT STRENGTHEN HIM WITH THY BLESSED SPIRIT   314 10
MAN DECAYETH, STRENGTHEN HIM, WE BESEECH THEE, SO   316 10
AND STRENGTHEN THEE OUT OF SION   364 19
MY ARM SHALL STRENGTHEN HIM   451 18
AND BREAD TO STRENGTHEN MAN'S HEART   468 25
SUPPLY TO STRENGTHEN OUR INFIRMITY   545 05
SUPPLY TO STRENGTHEN OUR INFIRMITY   557 11
CONFIRM AND STRENGTHEN US   588 08
HEARTS AND STRENGTHEN THEIR HANDS, THAT THEY MAY   590 28
STRENGTHEN HIM WHEN HE STANDS   597 30
BUT ALSO STRENGTHEN AND CONFIRM OUR FAITH IN HIM   607 34

STRENGTHENED

TO BE STRENGTHENED BY THE GIFT OF THE HOLY SPIRIT   043 22
AND STRENGTHENED FOR THY SERVICE   182 17
TO BE STRENGTHENED WITH MIGHT BY HIS SPIRIT IN THE   212 15
STRENGTHENED WITH ALL MIGHT, ACCORDING TO HIS   224 06
WHEN HE HAD RECEIVED MEAT, HE WAS STRENGTHENED   231 02
YOU TO BE STRENGTHENED WITH MIGHT BY HIS SPIRIT IN   281 09
BODIES ARE STRENGTHENED AND REFRESHED BY THE BREAD   293 22
AND STRENGTHENED HIMSELF IN HIS WICKEDNESS   405 03

STRENGTHENING

STRENGTHENING HIM   150 21
THE STRENGTHENING GIFTS OF THE HOLY SPIRIT   291 26
CONTINUAL STRENGTHENING AND REFRESHING OF MY SOUL   291 32
ARE THE STRENGTHENING AND REFRESHING OF OUR SOULS BY   293 20
THE STRENGTHENING AND REFRESHING OF OUR SOULS BY THE   582 17

STRETCH

GOD OF HOSTS, STRETCH FORTH, WE PRAY THEE, THINE   041 25
AND NECESSITIES STRETCH FORTH THY RIGHT HAND TO HELP   112 28
AND STRETCH FORTH THE RIGHT HAND OF THY   128 26
THOU SHALT STRETCH FORTH THY HAND UPON THE   312 05
LAND SHALL SOON STRETCH OUT HER HANDS UNTO GOD   421 19
9 FOR THEY STRETCH FORTH THEIR MOUTH UNTO THE HEAVEN,   428 26
AND WILT THOU STRETCH OUT THY WRATH FROM ONE   446 17
THOU SHALT STRETCH FORTH THY HAND UPON THE   514 11
6 I STRETCH FORTH MY HANDS UNTO THEE   519 02

STRETCHED

THE TEMPLE, YE STRETCHED FORTH NO HANDS AGAINST ME   151 05
LONG I HAVE STRETCHED FORTH MY HANDS UNTO A   227 21
HEROD THE KING STRETCHED FORTH HIS HANDS TO VEX   244 31
HEROD THE KING STRETCHED FORTH HIS HANDS TO VEX   246 32
I STRETCHED FORTH MY HANDS UNTO HIM, AND CEASED NOT   310 31

STRETCHED   CONTINUED

I STRETCHED FORTH MY HANDS UNTO HIM, AND CEASED NOT   433 19
11 SHE STRETCHED OUT HER BRANCHES UNTO THE SEA,   441 24
I HAVE STRETCHED FORTH MY HANDS UNTO THEE   449 15

STRETCHED-OUT

HAND AND STRETCHED-OUT ARM   512 06

STRICT

WE MUST GIVE A STRICT ACCOUNT OF OUR THOUGHTS, WORDS,   588 22

STRIFE

NOT IN STRIFE AND ENVYING   091 07
THERE WAS ALSO A STRIFE AMONG THEM, WHICH OF THEM   149 18
STRIFE, SEDITIONS, HERESIES, ENVYINGS,   209 22
THERE WAS ALSO A STRIFE AMONG THEM, WHICH OF THEM   250 03
FROM THE STRIFE OF TONGUES   377 08
AND STRIFE IN THE CITY   407 05
MADE US A VERY STRIFE UNTO OUR NEIGHBOURS, *   441 14
AT THE WATERS OF STRIFE   442 28
AT THE WATERS OF STRIFE, *   474 33
AND STIR UP STRIFE ALL THE DAY LONG   516 12

STRIKE

THE SERVANTS DID STRIKE HIM WITH THE PALMS OF THEIR   143 22

STRIKER

TO WINE, NO STRIKER, NOT GREEDY OF FILTHY LUCRE   549 22

STRING

AND THE STRING OF HIS TONGUE WAS LOOSED,   207 04

STRINGS

OF TEN STRINGS, AND UPON THE LUTE   027 32
AND THE STRINGS OF THY BOW SHALT THOU MAKE READY   365 30
AND INSTRUMENT OF TEN STRINGS   378 22
OF TEN STRINGS, AND UPON THE LUTE   456 04
HIM UPON THE STRINGS AND PIPE   525 29

STRIPES

IN STRIPES ABOVE MEASURE, IN PRISONS MORE   120 31
RECEIVED I FORTY STRIPES SAVE ONE   120 32
IN STRIPES, IN IMPRISONMENTS, IN TUMULTS,   126 11
BY WHOSE STRIPES YE WERE HEALED   172 17

STRIPPED

AND THEY STRIPPED HIM, AND PUT ON HIM A SCARLET ROBE   136 17
WHICH STRIPPED HIM OF HIS RAIMENT, AND   208 22

STRIPPETH

AND STRIPPETH BARE THE FORESTS   374 15

STRIVE

WITH THEM THAT STRIVE WITH ME, *   381 17

STRIVETH

EVERY MAN THAT STRIVETH FOR THE MASTERY IS TEMPERATE   119 07

STRIVINGS

ME FROM THE STRIVINGS OF THE PEOPLE, *   362 25

STRONG

BEING MADE STRONG BY THY HOLY SPIRIT, THEY MAY   043 11
WHO ART A STRONG TOWER OF DEFENCE UNTO THY   052 07
WHEN A STRONG MAN ARMED KEEPETH HIS PALACE, HIS GOODS   130 05
WHOM NOTHING IS STRONG, NOTHING IS HOLY   194 05
MY BRETHREN, BE STRONG IN THE LORD, AND IN THE POWER   219 05
AND WAXED STRONG IN SPIRIT, FILLED WITH WISDOM   233 26
WILL COME WITH STRONG HAND, AND HIS ARM SHALL RULE   243 06
AND WAXED STRONG IN SPIRIT, AND WAS IN THE   244 17
BE THOU TO HER A STRONG TOWER   306 19
O LORD, A STRONG TOWER   308 29
WHO IS A MOST STRONG TOWER TO ALL THOSE WHO PUT THEIR   314 15
THOUGH MEN BE SO STRONG THAT THEY COME TO FOURSCORE   325 33
BE STRONG, AND HE SHALL COMFORT THINE HEART   326 30
RIGHTEOUS JUDGE, STRONG, AND PATIENT   350 15
AND BLESSED BE MY STRONG HELPER, *   362 32
IT IS THE LORD STRONG AND MIGHTY, EVEN THE LORD   369 11
BE STRONG, AND HE SHALL COMFORT THINE HEART   372 30
OF THY GOODNESS, HAST MADE MY HILL SO STRONG   375 06
3 AND BE THOU MY STRONG ROCK, AND HOUSE OF DEFENCE,   375 25
4 FOR THOU ART MY STRONG ROCK, AND MY CASTLE   375 27
KINDNESS IN A STRONG CITY   377 10
27 BE STRONG, AND HE SHALL ESTABLISH YOUR HEART,   377 18
HIM THAT IS TOO STRONG FOR HIM   382 10
STANDETH LIKE THE STRONG MOUNTAINS   384 06
LEAD ME INTO THE STRONG CITY   412 29
MY HOPE, AND A STRONG TOWER FOR ME AGAINST THE ENEMY   413 11
BUT ARE LUSTY AND STRONG   428 14
THOU MADEST SO STRONG FOR THYSELF   441 33
THOU MADEST SO STRONG FOR THINE OWN SELF   442 05

STRONG   CONTINUED

STRONG IS THY HAND, AND HIGH IS THY RIGHT HAND   450 33
MY GOD, AND MY STRONG SALVATION   451 28
THOUGH MEN BE SO STRONG THAT THEY COME TO FOURSCORE   454 08
LEAD ME INTO THE STRONG CITY   479 24
FOR THEY ARE TOO STRONG FOR ME   518 18
OUR OXEN MAY BE STRONG TO LABOUR   520 21
EVER STABLE AND STRONG IN THY SON CHRIST, MAY SO WELL   535 07
IT IS THE LORD STRONG AND MIGHTY, EVEN THE LORD   563 26

STRONGER

BUT WHEN A STRONGER THAN HE SHALL COME UPON HIM,   130 06
AND MADE THEM STRONGER THAN THEIR ENEMIES   471 21
WAX RIPER AND STRONGER IN YOUR MINISTRY   541 19

STRONGEST

ME FROM MY STRONGEST ENEMY, AND FROM THEM WHICH HATE   360 33

STRONGHOLD

2 BE THOU MY STRONGHOLD, WHEREUNTO I MAY ALWAY   425 08
THOU ART MY HOPE, AND MY STRONGHOLD   454 31

STRONGHOLDS

AND COME TREMBLING OUT OF THEIR STRONGHOLDS   362 31
AND BROKEN DOWN HIS STRONGHOLDS   452 21

STROVE

WERE MANY THAT STROVE WITH ME   407 29

STRUCK

THEY STRUCK HIM ON THE FACE, AND ASKED HIM,   151 25

STUBBLE

AND AS THE STUBBLE BEFORE THE WIND   444 31

STUBBORN

A FAITHLESS AND STUBBORN GENERATION   435 14

STUCK

31 I HAVE STUCK UNTO THY TESTIMONIES   491 29

STUDIES

ALL WORLDLY CARES AND STUDIES   541 08
YOUR CARES AND STUDIES THIS WAY   541 15
AND IN SUCH STUDIES AS HELP TO THE KNOWLEDGE OF THE   542 27

STUDIOUS

CONSIDER HOW STUDIOUS YE OUGHT TO BE IN READING AND   541 03

STUDY

AND MY STUDY SHALL BE IN THY STATUTES   493 05
THE DAY LONG IS MY STUDY IN IT   496 21
FOR THY TESTIMONIES ARE MY STUDY   496 25
HOW GREAT CARE AND STUDY YE OUGHT TO APPLY   540 26
LAYING ASIDE THE STUDY OF THE WORLD AND THE FLESH   542 28

STUDYING

AND STUDYING TO SERVE HIM IN TRUE HOLINESS   086 22

STUMBLE

THAT THEY SHOULD NOT STUMBLE   139 14
AND IN THY STRAIGHT PATH MAY NOT STUMBLE   595 32

STUMBLED

THEY STUMBLED AND FELL   371 28

STUMBLING

AND THEY HAVE NONE OCCASION OF STUMBLING   501 12

SUBDUE

HE IS ABLE TO SUBDUE ALL THINGS UNTO HIMSELF   333 23
HE IS ABLE TO SUBDUE ALL THINGS UNTO HIMSELF   337 17
3 HE SHALL SUBDUE THE PEOPLES UNDER US, *   398 25

SUBDUED

OUR FLESH BEING SUBDUED TO THE SPIRIT, WE MAY EVER   125 29
THINGS SHALL BE SUBDUED UNTO HIM. THEN SHALL THE SON   080 34
PEOPLE SHALL BE SUBDUED UNTO THEE   396 26
11 THOU HAST SUBDUED EGYPT, AND DESTROYED IT   450 26

SUBDUETH

AND SUBDUETH THE PEOPLE UNTO ME   362 35
WHO SUBDUETH MY PEOPLE THAT IS UNDER ME   519 25

SUBJECT

AND WAS SUBJECT UNTO THEM   111 05
EVERY SOUL BE SUBJECT UNTO THE HIGHER POWERS   114 11
YE MUST NEEDS BE SUBJECT, NOT ONLY FOR WRATH, BUT   114 22
BEING MADE SUBJECT UNTO HIM   162 04
ALL OF YOU BE SUBJECT ONE TO ANOTHER, AND BE CLOTHED   192 30
WAS MADE SUBJECT TO VANITY, NOT WILLINGLY, BUT BY   194 15
IS ABLE EVEN TO SUBJECT ALL THINGS UNTO HIMSELF   222 25
AS THE CHURCH IS SUBJECT UNTO CHRIST, SO LET THE   267 17
MORTAL MEN ARE SUBJECT TO MANY SUDDEN PERILS,   R 321 02
ALSO HIMSELF BE SUBJECT UNTO HIM THAT PUT ALL THINGS   329 02
 IS NOT SUBJECT TO THE LAW OF GOD   604 38

SUBJECTED

HIM WHO HATH SUBJECTED THE SAME IN HOPE, BECAUSE THE   194 16

SUBJECTION

AND BRING IT INTO SUBJECTION   119 11
ALL THINGS IN SUBJECTION UNDER HIS FEET   351 12
AND HAD THEM IN SUBJECTION   475 21
CHILDREN IN SUBJECTION WITH ALL GRAVITY   549 24

SUBMISSION

PATIENCE AND SUBMISSION TO THY WILL   315 26

SUBMIT

USE AND SUBMIT UNTO, OR WHICH IS NOT FAIRLY   V 41
SUBMIT YOURSELVES TO EVERY ORDINANCE OF MAN FOR THE   173 17
SUBMIT YOURSELVES UNTO YOUR OWN HUSBANDS,   267 14
TO SUBMIT MYSELF TO ALL MY GOVERNORS, TEACHERS,   288 28
TO SUBMIT MYSELF TO ALL MY GOVERNORS, TEACHERS,   580 04

SUBMITTED

SHOULD HAVE SUBMITTED THEMSELVES UNTO HIM   443 10

SUBMITTING

SUBMITTING OURSELVES WHOLLY TO HIS HOLY WILL AND   086 20
SUBMITTING YOURSELVES ONE TO ANOTHER IN THE FEAR OF   217 31
SUBMITTING YOURSELVES ONE TO ANOTHER IN THE FEAR OF   267 12
AND SUBMITTING YOURSELVES TO THEIR GODLY JUDGMENTS   543 15

SUBSCRIBED

WITH HIS HAND SUBSCRIBED THEREUNTO, THE NAMES OF ALL   R 583 07

SUBSTANCE

PROVIDED THE SUBSTANCE OF THE FAITH BE KEPT ENTIRE   V 04
LORD WITH THY SUBSTANCE, AND WITH THE FIRSTFRUITS OF   005 20
BEING OF ONE SUBSTANCE WITH THE FATHER   016 05
BEING OF ONE SUBSTANCE WITH THE FATHER   030 10
BEING OF ONE SUBSTANCE WITH THE FATHER   071 07
OF THE SUBSTANCE OF THE VIRGIN MARY HIS MOTHER   077 17
WHO, IN SUBSTANCE OF OUR MORTAL FLESH, MANIFESTED   077 22
IN TRINITY OF PERSONS AND IN UNITY OF SUBSTANCE   079 09
WASTED HIS SUBSTANCE WITH RIOTOUS LIVING   202 04
FAITH IS THE SUBSTANCE OF THINGS HOPED FOR, THE   228 22
THE TEMPLE IN SUBSTANCE OF OUR FLESH, SO WE MAY BE   231 30
REST OF THEIR SUBSTANCE FOR THEIR BABES   359 18
AND RULER OF ALL HIS SUBSTANCE   471 15
DID SEE MY SUBSTANCE, YET BEING IMPERFECT   515 20
THEE WITH OUR SUBSTANCE, AND REMEMBERING THE ACCOUNT   599 21
OF ONE SUBSTANCE, POWER, AND ETERNITY   603 06
AND OF ONE SUBSTANCE WITH THE FATHER, TOOK MAN'S   603 10
THE WOMB OF THE BLESSED VIRGIN, OF HER SUBSTANCE   603 11
IS OF ONE SUBSTANCE, MAJESTY, AND GLORY, WITH   603 26
CHANGE OF THE SUBSTANCE OF BREAD AND WINE) IN THE   608 40

SUBSTITUTED

BE SUBSTITUTED FOR ANY OF THOSE GIVEN   R 313 10

SUBSTITUTING

IN CHURCH, SUBSTITUTING THE COLLECT, EPISTLE, AND   R 323 33

SUBTILTY

THE CRAFT AND SUBTILTY OF THE DEVIL OR MAN WORKETH   058 20

SUCCESS

MAY HAVE SUCH SUCCESS, THAT IT MAY NEVER BE SPOKEN IN   547 07
IT WITH SUCH SUCCESS AS MAY TEND MOST TO THY GLORY,   565 12

SUCCESSION

OF APOSTOLIC SUCCESSION TO THE END OF THE WORLD   572 18

SUCCOTH

AND METE OUT THE VALLEY OF SUCCOTH   412 24
AND METE OUT THE VALLEY OF SUCCOTH   479 19

SUCCOUR

WE FLEE UNTO THEE FOR SUCCOUR   045 04
TO COMFORT AND SUCCOUR ALL PRISONERS (ESPECIALLY   046 20
PLEASE THEE TO SUCCOUR, HELP, AND COMFORT, ALL WHO   056 27

SUCCOUR   CONTINUED

TO COMFORT AND SUCCOUR ALL THOSE WHO, IN THIS   074 31
WITH GREAT MIGHT SUCCOUR US   095 05
HAND OF GOD TO SUCCOUR ALL THOSE WHO SUFFER FOR THEE,   100 02
WITHOUT THY SUCCOUR, PRESERVE IT EVERMORE BY THY HELP   212 06
THEY MAY SUCCOUR AND DEFEND THE MINISTER   251 31
FLEE TO THEE FOR SUCCOUR, THE LIFE OF THOSE WHO   274 10
AND THE AID OF THEM THAT TURN TO THEE FOR SUCCOUR   315 14
UNTO THEE FOR SUCCOUR IN BEHALF OF THIS THY SERVANT,   316 07
THOU HAST BEEN MY SUCCOUR   326 26
MAY WE SEEK FOR SUCCOUR, BUT OF THEE, O LORD, WHO FOR   332 23
THOU ART MY SUCCOUR, HASTE THEE TO HELP ME   367 11
11 THOU HAST BEEN MY SUCCOUR   372 18
AND SUCCOUR MY FATHER AND MOTHER   580 03

SUCCOURED

HAVE I SUCCOURED THEE   126 06

SUCH

THE FATHER SEEKETH SUCH TO WORSHIP HIM   003 32
AND OCCASIONS, SUCH CHANGES AND ALTERATIONS SHOULD BE   V 18
YIELDED TO MAKE SUCH ALTERATIONS IN SOME PARTICULARS,   V 29
IF ALLOWED SUCH JUST AND FAVOURABLE CONSTRUCTION AS   V 42
SUCH A CHAPTER) OF SUCH A BOOK   R 009 33
HERE BEGINNETH SUCH A CHAPTER (OR VERSE OF SUCH   R 009 33
OR VERSE OF SUCH A CHAPTER) OF SUCH A BOOK   R 009 33
MORNING PRAYER WITH SUCH GENERAL INTERCESSIONS TAKEN   R 017 23
EVENING PRAYER WITH SUCH PRAYER, OR PRAYERS, TAKEN   R 031 31
OUR GOVERNANCE ONLY SUCH THINGS AS PLEASE THEE, TO   035 26
AND GRANT SUCH SEASONABLE WEATHER THAT WE MAY GATHER   039 28
THIS OUR NECESSITY, SUCH MODERATE RAIN AND SHOWERS,   040 19
THEE TO SEND US SUCH SEASONABLE WEATHER, THAT THE   040 26
AND A SECURITY FOR SUCH AS PASS ON THE SEAS UPON   042 09
SUCH AS MAY APPEAR IN OUR LIVES BY AN HUMBLE, HOLY,   050 26
STILL TO CONTINUE SUCH THY MERCIES TOWARDS US, THAT   052 13
WAY OF TRUTH ALL SUCH AS HAVE ERRED, AND ARE   056 20
THEE TO STRENGTHEN SUCH AS DO STAND   056 22
NOR THE DESIRE OF SUCH AS ARE SORROWFUL   058 16
AND DISCIPLINE, IN SUCH MANNER AS THEY MIGHT JUDGE   VI 12
PROPER END OF ALL SUCH PRAYERS, NAMELY, THAT 'RULERS   VI 19
AND TO ESTABLISH SUCH OTHER ALTERATIONS AND   VI 26
FOR WITH SUCH SACRIFICES GOD IS WELL PLEASED   072 27
AND DO ALL SUCH GOOD WORKS AS THOU HAST PREPARED FOR   083 28
ADMINISTER TO ALL SUCH AS SHALL BE RELIGIOUSLY AND   086 29
HOLY AND CLEAN TO SUCH A HEAVENLY FEAST, IN THE   087 13
YOUR OFFENCES TO BE SUCH AS ARE NOT ONLY AGAINST GOD,   087 22
THAT HE MAY RECEIVE SUCH GODLY COUNSEL AND ADVICE, AS   088 07
WHICH OF YOU IN SUCH A CASE WOULD NOT BE MOVED   088 22
BUT SUCH EXCUSES ARE NOT SO EASILY ACCEPTED AND   088 28
HOW LITTLE SUCH FEIGNED EXCUSES WILL AVAIL BEFORE   089 02
THAT WE MAY IN SUCH WISE HEAR THEM, READ, MARK,   092 09
GRANT TO US SUCH STRENGTH AND PROTECTION, AS MAY   114 07
US GRACE TO USE SUCH ABSTINENCE, THAT, OUR FLESH   125 28
THE AVENGER OF ALL SUCH, AS WE ALSO HAVE FOREWARNED   127 32
AND FOLLOW ALL SUCH THINGS AS ARE AGREEABLE TO THE   173 09
THOSE WHO LOVE THEE SUCH GOOD THINGS AS PASS MAN'S   197 05
INTO OUR HEARTS SUCH LOVE TOWARD THEE, THAT WE,   197 06
THINK AND DO ALWAYS SUCH THINGS AS ARE RIGHT   200 30
TAKEN YOU BUT SUCH AS IS COMMON TO MAN   201 26
MAKE THEM TO ASK SUCH THINGS AS SHALL PLEASE THEE   203 13
GRANT UNTO US SUCH A MEASURE OF THY GRACE, THAT WE,   204 24
SUCH TRUST HAVE WE THROUGH CHRIST TO GOD-WARD   206 13
AND SUCH LIKE   209 23
THAT THEY WHICH DO SUCH THINGS SHALL NOT INHERIT THE   209 25
AGAINST SUCH THERE IS NO LAW   209 28
WHICH HAD GIVEN SUCH POWER UNTO MEN   217 14
WHO DIDST GIVE SUCH GRACE UNTO THY HOLY APOSTLE   226 18
WHEN THERE CAME SUCH A VOICE TO HIM FROM THE   248 17
SHALL RECEIVE ONE SUCH LITTLE CHILD IN MY NAME   252 30
EATING AND DRINKING SUCH THINGS AS THEY GIVE   254 22
OR WRINKLE, OR ANY SUCH THING   267 23
OR AT SUCH OTHER TIME AS THE MINISTER SHALL   R 273 15
WHEN ANY SUCH PERSONS AS ARE OF RIPER YEARS ARE TO   R 273 17
FOR OF SUCH IS THE KINGDOM OF GOD   274 29
SUCH BAPTISM SHALL BE PROMPTLY REPORTED TO THE PARISH R 281 29
PARTS OF BAPTISM), SUCH PERSON MAY BE BAPTIZED IN THE R 282 10
THINK AND DO ALWAYS SUCH THINGS AS ARE RIGHT   R 287 27
MAY RECEIVE SUCH A MEASURE OF THY HOLY   294 26
UNTIL SUCH TIME AS HE BE CONFIRMED, OR BE   R 299 08
MINISTER MAY USE SUCH PORTION OF THE FOREGOING OFFICE R 320 06
OR SUCH AS ARE NOT ABLE TO ATTEND THE PUBLIC   R 323 32
AS IS THE EARTHY, SUCH ARE THEY ALSO THAT ARE EARTHY   329 29
AS IS THE HEAVENLY, SUCH ARE THEY ALSO THAT ARE   329 30
AND SUCH OTHER FITTING PRAYERS AS ARE   R 331 29
HIS DISCRETION, USE SUCH PART OF THIS OFFICE, OR SUCH R 337 04
OF THIS OFFICE, OR SUCH DEVOTIONS TAKEN FROM OTHER   R 337 04
FOR OF SUCH IS THE KINGDOM OF GOD   338 11
SHALL RECEIVE ONE SUCH LITTLE CHILD IN MY NAME   339 29
AND HAVE SUCH PLEASURE IN VANITY, AND SEEK AFTER   347 14
5 SUCH AS BE FOOLISH SHALL NOT STAND IN THY SIGHT   348 09
IF I HAVE DONE ANY SUCH THING   349 27
THAT THEY ARE ALL SUCH WORKERS OF MISCHIEF, *   356 27
AND UPON SUCH AS EXCEL IN VIRTUE   357 26
FROM SUCH AS RESIST THY RIGHT HAND   358 33
AND IMAGINED SUCH A DEVICE AS THEY ARE NOT ABLE TO   365 28
29 ALL SUCH AS BE FAT UPON EARTH *   367 33
BUT SUCH AS TRANSGRESS WITHOUT A CAUSE SHALL BE PUT   369 22
AND SUCH AS ARE GENTLE, THEM SHALL HE LEARN HIS WAY   370 03
UNTO SUCH AS KEEP HIS COVENANT AND HIS TESTIMONIES   370 05
UP AGAINST ME, AND SUCH AS SPEAK WRONG   372 18
AND WILL SAVE SUCH AS BE OF AN HUMBLE SPIRIT   381 05
AND TO SLAY SUCH AS BE UPRIGHT IN THEIR WAYS   385 24
22 SUCH AS ARE BLESSED OF GOD, SHALL POSSESS THE   386 06

SUCH   CONTINUED

THE PROUD, AND TO SUCH AS GO ABOUT WITH LIES	390 19
MY SINS HAVE TAKEN SUCH HOLD UPON ME, THAT I AM NOT	391 11
AND LET SUCH AS LOVE THY SALVATION, SAY ALWAY,	391 22
AMONG SUCH AS KEEP HOLY-DAY	393 09
MARVELLED TO SEE SUCH THINGS	399 18
THAT I AM EVEN SUCH A ONE AS THYSELF	402 33
LAID HIS HANDS UPON SUCH AS BE AT PEACE WITH HIM, *	407 33
GIVEN A TOKEN FOR SUCH AS FEAR THEE, *	412 19
AND SUCH AS WILL NOT BELIEVE SHALL NOT BE ABLE TO	417 27
THE HAIRY SCALP OF SUCH A ONE AS GOETH ON STILL IN	420 28
AND LET ALL SUCH AS DELIGHT IN THY SALVATION SAY	424 28
EVEN UNTO SUCH AS ARE OF A CLEAN HEART	428 10
SEE THE UNGODLY IN SUCH PROSPERITY	428 15
AND SUCH AS OUR FATHERS HAVE TOLD US	434 31
SEE THAT SUCH AS ARE IN NEED AND NECESSITY HAVE	443 22
12 SUCH AS ARE PLANTED IN THE HOUSE OF THE LORD,	456 26
AND MAKE SUCH PROUD BOASTING	457 26
ALL SUCH AS ARE TRUE IN HEART SHALL FOLLOW IT	458 17
JOYFUL GLADNESS FOR SUCH AS ARE TRUE-HEARTED	461 20
AND SAMUEL AMONG SUCH AS CALL UPON HIS NAME	462 28
THERE SHALL NO SUCH CLEAVE UNTO ME	463 23
MINE EYES LOOK UPON SUCH AS ARE FAITHFUL IN THE LAND,	463 30
THE MOURNINGS OF SUCH AS ARE IN CAPTIVITY, *	465 19
18 EVEN UPON SUCH AS KEEP HIS COVENANT, *	467 11
10 SUCH AS SIT IN DARKNESS, AND IN THE SHADOW OF	476 24
AND SO ARE ALL SUCH AS PUT THEIR TRUST IN THEM	485 27
79 LET SUCH AS FEAR THEE, AND HAVE KNOWN THY	495 14
5 AS FOR SUCH AS TURN BACK UNTO THEIR OWN WICKEDNESS,	505 02
5 SUCH KNOWLEDGE IS TOO WONDERFUL AND EXCELLENT FOR	514 29
LET ME EAT OF SUCH THINGS AS PLEASE THEM	517 17
THAT THOU HAST SUCH RESPECT UNTO HIM	519 27
PEOPLE THAT ARE IN SUCH A CASE	520 24
LORD UPHOLDETH ALL SUCH AS FALL, *	521 20
ALL SUCH AS CALL UPON HIM FAITHFULLY	521 29
SUCH HONOUR HAVE ALL HIS SAINTS	525 20
EVERMORE HAD IN SUCH REVEREND ESTIMATION, THAT NO MAN	529 14
AND KNOWN TO HAVE SUCH QUALITIES AS ARE REQUISITE FOR	529 16
HIM A DEACON, IN SUCH MANNER AND FORM AS FOLLOWETH	529 31
DUTY AND OFFICE OF SUCH AS COME TO BE ADMITTED	R 530 04
TO THE HOLY TABLE, SUCH AS DESIRE TO BE ORDAINED	R 530 08
THAT PERSON, UNTIL SUCH TIME AS THE PARTY ACCUSED	R 530 27
BISHOP (COMMENDING SUCH AS SHALL BE FOUND MEET TO BE	R 530 29
OF THE CHURCH, IN SUCH MANNER AND FORM AS HEREAFTER	R 535 26
DUTY AND OFFICE OF SUCH AS COME TO BE ADMITTED	R 536 04
THAT PERSON, UNTIL SUCH TIME AS THE PARTY ACCUSED	R 537 03
BISHOP (COMMENDING SUCH AS SHALL BE FOUND MEET TO BE	R 537 05
TO BRING ALL SUCH AS ARE OR SHALL BE COMMITTED	540 18
AND IN SUCH STUDIES AS HELP TO THE	542 27
UPON THEM, UNTIL SUCH TIME AS THEY HAVE RECEIVED THE	R 546 31
MOUTHS MAY HAVE SUCH SUCCESS, THAT IT MAY NEVER BE	547 07
DILIGENTLY EXERCISE SUCH DISCIPLINE AS BY THE	555 16
THIS THY SERVANT, SUCH GRACE, THAT HE MAY EVERMORE BE	557 29
BUT ALSO MAY BE, TO SUCH AS BELIEVE, A WHOLESOME	559 10
THE RAILS, WITH SUCH OF THE CLERGY AS CAN BE THERE	R 564 06
AND BLESS IT WITH SUCH SUCCESS AS MAY TEND MOST TO	565 12
MAY RECEIVE SUCH A MEASURE OF THY HOLY	565 26
AND TO ASK SUCH THINGS AS ARE REQUISITE AND	566 17
OF FAITH, AND WITH SUCH SERIOUSNESS, AFFECTION, AND	566 19
MAY DO IT WITH SUCH STEADINESS OF FAITH, AND WITH	566 19
AND WITH SUCH LAWFUL DIRECTIONS AS YOU SHALL	569 21
THE MINISTER, UNTIL SUCH TIME AS THEY HAVE LEARNED	R 582 24
THE NAMES OF ALL SUCH PERSONS WITHIN HIS PARISH,	R 583 08
THY JUDGMENTS, AND SUCH A GRATEFUL SENSE OF THY	588 18
UPON OUR HEARTS SUCH A DREAD OF THY JUDGMENTS,	588 18
THAT WE MAY ENJOY SUCH REFRESHING SLEEP AS MAY FIT US	591 28
ALWAYS TO LIVE IN SUCH A STATE THAT WE MAY NEVER BE	591 29
US THIS DAY SUCH BLESSING THROUGH OUR WORSHIP OF	595 14
REMEMBER IN PITY SUCH AS ARE THIS DAY DESTITUTE,	599 06
SUCH ARE THESE FOLLOWING	604 04
THE FALL OF ADAM IS SUCH, THAT HE CANNOT TURN AND	604 42
NOT TO BE DENIED TO SUCH AS FALL INTO SIN AFTER	605 41
OF FORGIVENESS TO SUCH AS TRULY REPENT	606 04
GODLY PERSONS, AND SUCH AS FEEL IN THEMSELVES THE	606 17
GOD'S PROMISES IN SUCH WISE, AS THEY BE GENERALLY SET	606 27
THE GOSPEL, BEING SUCH AS HAVE GROWN PARTLY OF THE	607 40
AND IN SUCH ONLY AS WORTHILY RECEIVE THE SAME, THEY	608 03
DIMINISHED FROM SUCH AS BY FAITH, AND RIGHTLY, DO	608 15
INSOMUCH THAT TO SUCH AS RIGHTLY, WORTHILY, AND WITH	608 36
THE WICKED, AND SUCH AS BE VOID OF A LIVELY FAITH,	609 04
THINGS NECESSARY TO SUCH CONSECRATION AND ORDERING	610 33
WE DECREE ALL SUCH TO BE RIGHTLY, ORDERLY, AND	610 35
EVERY MAN OUGHT, OF SUCH THINGS AS HE POSSESSETH,	611 03

SUCK

AND THOSE THAT SUCK THE BREASTS	124 31
AND THE PAPS WHICH NEVER GAVE SUCK	154 18
AND THEREOUT SUCK THEY NO SMALL ADVANTAGE	428 29
DRINK THEM, AND SUCK THEM OUT	432 18

SUCKED

BARE THEE, AND THE PAPS WHICH THOU HAST SUCKED	130 20

SUCKLINGS

OF BABES AND SUCKLINGS HAST ORDAINED STRENGTH,	102 22
OF BABES AND SUCKLINGS THOU HAST PERFECTED PRAISE	260 15
VERY BABES AND SUCKLINGS HAST THOU ORDAINED STRENGTH,	350 34

SUDDEN

AND FROM SUDDEN DEATH, FROM ALL SEDITION,	054 32
SUBJECT TO MANY SUDDEN PERILS, DISEASES, AND	R 321 02

SUDDEN   CONTINUED

IN CASE OF SUDDEN VISITATION, HAVE THE LESS	R 321 10
8 LET A SUDDEN DESTRUCTION COME UPON HIM UNAWARES,	382 04

SUDDENLY

LEST COMING SUDDENLY HE FIND YOU SLEEPING	021 26
MAY LAY HANDS SUDDENLY ON NO MAN, BUT FAITHFULLY AND	038 30
AND SUDDENLY THERE WAS WITH THE ANGEL A MULTITUDE OF	099 19
AND SUDDENLY THERE CAME A SOUND FROM HEAVEN AS OF A	180 18
AND SUDDENLY THERE SHINED ROUND ABOUT HIM A LIGHT	229 31
YE SEEK, SHALL SUDDENLY COME TO HIS TEMPLE, EVEN THE	232 05
AND FADE AWAY SUDDENLY LIKE THE GRASS	325 23
SHALL BE TURNED BACK, AND PUT TO SHAME SUDDENLY	349 20
AND SUDDENLY CAST DOWN	399 19
SUDDENLY DO THEY HIT HIM, AND FEAR NOT	415 26
7 BUT GOD SHALL SUDDENLY SHOOT AT THEM WITH A SWIFT	415 33
19 O HOW SUDDENLY DO THEY CONSUME, *	429 14
AND FADE AWAY SUDDENLY LIKE THE GRASS	453 28

SUFFER

DAY OF TROUBLE, SUFFER NOT OUR TRUST IN THEE TO FAIL	036 23
NOW MOST JUSTLY SUFFER FOR OUR SINS, MAY, THROUGH THY	041 03
JESUS CHRIST TO SUFFER DEATH UPON THE CROSS FOR OUR	080 08
ALL THOSE WHO SUFFER FOR THEE, OUR ONLY MEDIATOR AND	100 02
YE SUFFER FOOLS GLADLY, SEEING YE YOURSELVES ARE	120 22
FOR YE SUFFER, IF A MAN BRING YOU INTO BONDAGE,	120 23
OUR FLESH, AND TO SUFFER DEATH UPON THE CROSS, THAT	134 07
TO EAT THIS PASSOVER WITH YOU BEFORE I SUFFER	149 03
AND SAID, SUFFER YE THUS FAR	150 34
AND TO SUFFER DEATH UPON THE CROSS	156 24
BE SO, THAT YE SUFFER FOR WELL DOING, THAN FOR EVIL	161 21
THOU SHALT NOT SUFFER THINE HOLY ONE TO SEE	169 14
BELOVED CHRIST TO SUFFER, AND TO RISE FROM THE DEAD	170 13
YE DO WELL, AND SUFFER FOR IT, YE TAKE IT PATIENTLY,	172 08
BUT AND IF YE SUFFER FOR RIGHTEOUSNESS' SAKE, HAPPY	195 31
IF SO BE THAT WE SUFFER WITH HIM, THAT WE MAY BE ALSO	200 12
WHO WILL NOT SUFFER YOU TO BE TEMPTED ABOVE THAT YE	201 27
LEST THEY SHOULD SUFFER PERSECUTION FOR THE CROSS OF	210 26
THE FAITH, DIDST SUFFER THY HOLY APOSTLE THOMAS TO BE	228 06
THINGS HE MUST SUFFER FOR MY NAME'S SAKE	230 28
AND PATIENTLY SUFFER FOR THE TRUTH'S SAKE	242 13
SAID UNTO THEM, SUFFER THE LITTLE CHILDREN TO COME	274 28
HE WILL NOT SUFFER THY FOOT TO BE MOVED	327 23
IF SO BE THAT WE SUFFER WITH HIM, THAT WE MAY BE ALSO	330 25
JUDGE ETERNAL, SUFFER US NOT, AT OUR LAST HOUR, FOR	332 31
HIM AND SAID, SUFFER THE LITTLE CHILDREN TO COME UNTO	338 09
HE WILL NOT SUFFER THY FOOT TO BE MOVED	339 07
TROUBLE WHICH I SUFFER OF THEM THAT HATE ME, *	352 17
SHALT THOU SUFFER THY HOLY ONE TO SEE CORRUPTION	358 11
DO LACK, AND SUFFER HUNGER	380 21
AND SHALL NOT SUFFER THE RIGHTEOUS TO FALL FOR EVER	408 05
AND WOULD NOT SUFFER HIS WHOLE DISPLEASURE TO ARISE	437 17
NOR SUFFER MY TRUTH TO FAIL	452 08
I WILL NOT SUFFER HIM	463 29
40 THOUGH HE SUFFER THEM TO BE EVIL ENTREATED THROUGH	478 26
3 HE WILL NOT SUFFER THY FOOT TO BE MOVED	502 26
4 I WILL NOT SUFFER MINE EYES TO SLEEP, NOR MINE	508 10
TO RIGHT THAT SUFFER WRONG	522 14
THAT WE MAY NEVER SUFFER THE SUN TO GO DOWN UPON OUR	590 16
ON EVERY SIDE, SUFFER THEM NOT TO BE DISTRESSED	599 14
AND SUFFER NOT THE HIRE OF THE LABOURERS TO	599 30

SUFFERED

SUFFERED UNDER PONTIUS PILATE, WAS CRUCIFIED,	015 23
HE SUFFERED AND WAS BURIED	016 09
SUFFERED UNDER PONTIUS PILATE, WAS CRUCIFIED,	029 28
HE SUFFERED AND WAS BURIED	030 14
HE SUFFERED AND WAS BURIED	071 11
THRICE I SUFFERED SHIPWRECK, A NIGHT AND A DAY I HAVE	121 03
FOR I HAVE SUFFERED MANY THINGS THIS DAY IN A DREAM	135 34
BUT FIRST HE SUFFERED PAIN, AND ENTERED NOT INTO	138 05
HE OFTEN HAVE SUFFERED SINCE THE FOUNDATION OF THE	148 04
NIGHT BEFORE HE SUFFERED, DID INSTITUTE THE SACRAMENT	152 08
ALSO HATH ONCE SUFFERED FOR SINS, THE JUST FOR THE	161 23
CHRIST TO HAVE SUFFERED THESE THINGS, AND TO ENTER	167 31
CHRIST ALSO SUFFERED FOR US, LEAVING US AN EXAMPLE,	172 10
WHEN HE SUFFERED, HE THREATENED NOT	172 13
THAT YE HAVE SUFFERED A WHILE, MAKE YOU PERFECT,	193 10
SUFFERED UNDER PONTIUS PILATE, WAS CRUCIFIED,	284 17
CHRIST HATH SUFFERED DEATH UPON THE CROSS FOR HIM,	R 323 27
THY SAKE HAVE I SUFFERED REPROOF	422 16
TERRORS HAVE I SUFFERED WITH A TROUBLED MIND	449 28
WHEREIN WE HAVE SUFFERED ADVERSITY	454 20
14 HE SUFFERED NO MAN TO DO THEM WRONG, *	470 30
THIS CHURCH, OR SUFFERED TO EXECUTE ANY OF THE SAID	529 21
SUFFERED UNDER PONTIUS PILATE, WAS CRUCIFIED,	577 32
WHO TRULY SUFFERED, WAS CRUCIFIED, DEAD, AND BURIED,	603 14

SUFFEREDST

11 THOU SUFFEREDST MEN TO RIDE OVER OUR HEADS	418 04

SUFFERERS

STRENGTH OF THE WEAK AND THE COMFORT OF SUFFERERS	312 13
INNOCENT SUFFERERS, AND SANCTIFY TO THEM THE	599 09

SUFFERETH

CHARITY SUFFERETH LONG, AND IS KIND	122 29
AND SUFFERETH NOT OUR FEET TO SLIP	417 31
AND SUFFERETH NOT THEIR CATTLE TO DECREASE	478 23

SUFFERING

NAME TO THE SUFFERING, THE FRIENDLESS, AND THE NEEDY	044 04
NOT SUFFERING THEM TO BE PARTAKERS OF THE LORD'S	R 085 10
ENDURE GRIEF, SUFFERING WRONGFULLY	172 06
SERVANT IN HIS SUFFERING, AND TO BLESS THE MEANS MADE	597 22

SUFFERINGS

UNDER THEIR SUFFERINGS, AND A HAPPY ISSUE OUT OF ALL	019 09
UNDER THEIR SUFFERINGS, AND A HAPPY ISSUE OUT OF ALL	033 07
IN ALL OUR SUFFERINGS HERE UPON EARTH FOR THE	099 26
JOYFULLY THE SUFFERINGS OF THE PRESENT TIME, IN FULL	144 08
THAT THE SUFFERINGS OF THIS PRESENT TIME ARE NOT	194 11
THAT THE SUFFERINGS OF THIS PRESENT TIME ARE NOT	330 26

SUFFICE

THEN THE FOLLOWING FORM SHALL SUFFICE	R 281 18
THE SERVICE, THE FOLLOWING FORM SHALL SUFFICE	R 323 05
AND IT SHALL SUFFICE THAT THE LITANY BE ONCE SAID FOR	R 547 21

SUFFICETH

| AND IT SUFFICETH US | 240 10 |

SUFFICIENCY

| BUT OUR SUFFICIENCY IS OF GOD | 206 15 |

SUFFICIENT

AND SUFFICIENT SACRIFICE, OBLATION, AND	080 11
AND SUFFICIENT OPPORTUNITY SHALL BE GIVEN TO THOSE	R 082 28
BREAD IS NOT SUFFICIENT FOR THEM, THAT EVERY ONE OF	131 31
THAT WE ARE SUFFICIENT OF OURSELVES TO THINK ANY	206 14
SUFFICIENT UNTO THE DAY IS THE EVIL THEREOF	211 34
BREAD IS NOT SUFFICIENT FOR THEM, THAT EVERY ONE OF	225 27
SUFFICIENT UNTO THE DAY IS THE EVIL THEREOF	266 32
MAY DEMAND SUFFICIENT SURETY FOR HIS INDEMNIFICATION	R 301 03
OR BY SUFFICIENT TESTIMONY, ANY PERSON TO BE A MAN OF	529 26

SUFFICIENTLY

THEY BE SUFFICIENTLY INSTRUCTED IN THE PRINCIPLES OF	R 273 19
SO SOON AS SUFFICIENTLY INSTRUCTED, BE BROUGHT TO THE	277 15
AND ARE SUFFICIENTLY INSTRUCTED IN THE MATTER	R 295 14
FINDING HIM SUFFICIENTLY INSTRUCTED IN THE HOLY	529 28

SUFFRAGE

THAT AFTER THE SUFFRAGE, THAT IT MAY PLEASE THEE TO	R 531 02
SHALL BE SAID THE FOLLOWING SUFFRAGE	R 531 03
THAT AFTER THE SUFFRAGE, THAT IT MAY PLEASE THEE TO	R 537 08
SHALL BE SAID THE FOLLOWING SUFFRAGE	R 537 09
THE PROPER SUFFRAGE SHALL BE,	R 553 15

SUITABLE

| AND EXPRESSION SUITABLE TO THE CLEARNESS AND | 573 27 |

SUM

| O HOW GREAT IS THE SUM OF THEM | 515 25 |

SUMMARY

| SHALL SAY THE SUMMARY OF THE LAW, BEGINNING, HEAR | R 067 30 |

SUMMED

| US THAT THEY ARE SUMMED UP IN THESE TWO COMMANDMENTS | 288 05 |

SUMMER

O YE WINTER AND SUMMER, BLESS YE THE LORD	012 20
OWN SELVES THAT SUMMER IS NOW NIGH AT HAND	093 16
AND MY MOISTURE WAS LIKE THE DROUGHT IN SUMMER	377 29
THOU HAST MADE SUMMER AND WINTER	431 11

SUMMING

| BRETHREN, SUMMING UP ALL OUR PETITIONS, AND ALL | 048 23 |

SUMPTUOUSLY

| AND FARED SUMPTUOUSLY EVERY DAY | 190 04 |

SUN

THE RISING OF THE SUN EVEN UNTO THE GOING DOWN OF THE	004 12
O YE SUN AND MOON, BLESS YE THE LORD	012 10
BE SIGNS IN THE SUN, AND IN THE MOON, AND IN THE	093 05
THOSE DAYS SHALL THE SUN BE DARKENED, AND THE MOON	118 14
AND THE SUN WAS DARKENED, AND THE VEIL OF THE TEMPLE	155 11
CAME UNTO THE SEPULCHRE AT THE RISING OF THE SUN	165 22
LET NOT THE SUN GO DOWN UPON YOUR WRATH	216 19
FOR THE SUN IS NO SOONER RISEN WITH A BURNING HEAT,	239 21
NEITHER SHALL THE SUN LIGHT ON THEM, NOR ANY HEAT	257 13
FOR HE MAKETH HIS SUN TO RISE ON THE EVIL AND ON THE	264 09
SO THAT THE SUN SHALL NOT BURN THEE BY DAY, *	327 29
IS ONE GLORY OF THE SUN, AND ANOTHER GLORY OF THE	329 16
SO THAT THE SUN SHALL NOT BURN THEE BY DAY, *	339 13
NEITHER SHALL THE SUN LIGHT ON THEM, NOR ANY HEAT	341 24
5 IN THEM HATH HE SET A TABERNACLE FOR THE SUN	363 21
THE RISING UP OF THE SUN UNTO THE GOING DOWN THEREOF	401 22

SUN   CONTINUED

AND LET THEM NOT SEE THE SUN	410 25
AS LONG AS THE SUN AND MOON ENDURETH, *	427 06
REMAIN UNDER THE SUN AMONG THE POSTERITIES, WHICH	427 33
THOU HAST PREPARED THE LIGHT AND THE SUN	431 09
IS LIKE AS THE SUN BEFORE ME	452 13
AND THE SUN KNOWETH HIS GOING DOWN	468 33
22 THE SUN ARISETH, AND THEY GET THEM AWAY TOGETHER,	469 04
THE RISING UP OF THE SUN UNTO THE GOING DOWN OF THE	484 13
6 SO THAT THE SUN SHALL NOT BURN THEE BY DAY,	503 02
8 THE SUN TO RULE THE DAY	511 30
3 PRAISE HIM, SUN AND MOON	524 09
MAY NEVER SUFFER THE SUN TO GO DOWN UPON OUR WRATH	590 16

SUNDAY

ON TRINITY SUNDAY	R 008 29
USED ON ROGATION SUNDAY AND THE ROGATION DAYS	R 039 23
SAID AT LEAST ONE SUNDAY IN EACH MONTH	R 067 28
AND TRINITY SUNDAY	R 070 32
SAID ON THE FIRST SUNDAY IN ADVENT, THE FIRST SUNDAY	R 085 23
THE FIRST SUNDAY IN LENT, AND TRINITY SUNDAY	R 085 24
THE FIRST SUNDAY IN LENT, AND TRINITY SUNDAY	R 085 24
DO UPON THE SUNDAY, OR SOME HOLY DAY, IMMEDIATELY	R 086 25
APPOINTED FOR THE SUNDAY, SHALL SERVE ALL THE WEEK	R 090 04
APPOINTED FOR ANY SUNDAY OR OTHER FEAST MAY BE USED	R 090 06
DAYS BEFORE THE SUNDAY FOLLOWING CHRISTMAS DAY, THE	R 103 34
AND GOSPEL SHALL SERVE UNTO THE NEXT SUNDAY	R 109 26
COLLECT APPOINTED FOR THE DAY, UNTIL PALM SUNDAY	R 124 19
UNTO THE NEXT SUNDAY, EXCEPT UPON THE FEAST OF ST	R 125 24
UNTO THE NEXT SUNDAY, EXCEPT UPON THE FEAST OF ST	R 178 31
FOR THE SIXTH SUNDAY AFTER THE EPIPHANY SHALL BE USED	R 224 32
EPIPHANY SHALL BE USED ON THE TWENTY-FIFTH SUNDAY	R 224 33
FOR THE SIXTH SUNDAY AFTER THE EPIPHANY SHALL BE USED	R 224 33
FOR THE FIFTH SUNDAY AFTER THE EPIPHANY ON THE	R 224 35
WORSHIP GOD EVERY SUNDAY IN HIS CHURCH	291 19

SUNDAYS

ON THE SUNDAYS IN ADVENT	R 008 16
SAVE ON THE SUNDAYS IN ADVENT, THE LATTER PORTION	R 014 05
UPON THE SUNDAYS AND OTHER HOLY DAYS, (THOUGH THERE	R 084 27
BE TWENTY-SIX SUNDAYS AFTER TRINITY, THE SERVICE FOR	R 224 31
THAN TWENTY-FIVE SUNDAYS, THE OVERPLUS SHALL BE	R 224 36
UPON SUNDAYS AND OTHER HOLY DAYS	R 273 05
UPON SUNDAYS AND HOLY DAYS, OR ON SOME	R 295 07
UPON SUNDAYS AND HOLY DAYS, OR ON SOME	R 582 27
ON SUNDAYS, AND ON OTHER DAYS WHEN IT MAY BE	R 592 05

SUNDER

THE SPEAR IN SUNDER, AND BURNETH THE CHARIOTS IN THE	398 12
AND BRAKE THEIR BONDS IN SUNDER	477 03
AND SMITTEN THE BARS OF IRON IN SUNDER	477 08
AND SMITE IN SUNDER THE HEADS OVER DIVERS COUNTRIES	482 19
THOU HAST BROKEN MY BONDS IN SUNDER	487 18

SUNDRY

MOVETH US, IN SUNDRY PLACES, TO ACKNOWLEDGE AND	005 30
MOVETH US, IN SUNDRY PLACES, TO ACKNOWLEDGE AND	023 05
WHO AT SUNDRY TIMES AND IN DIVERS MANNERS SPAKE	096 22
AMONG THE SUNDRY AND MANIFOLD CHANGES OF THE	174 22
AMONG THE SUNDRY AND MANIFOLD CHANGES OF THE	285 29

SUNG

SHALL BE SAID OR SUNG THE FOLLOWING CANTICLE	R 008 09
THE VENITE MAY BE SUNG OR SAID,	R 008 14
SHALL BE SUNG OR SAID THE GLORIA PATRI	R 009 25
SHALL BE SAID OR SUNG THE FOLLOWING HYMN	R 010 02
HAS BEEN SAID OR SUNG, MAY PASS AT ONCE TO THE	R 010 05
AFTER THAT SHALL BE SUNG OR SAID THE HYMN FOLLOWING	R 014 04
ANIMA MEA, MAY BE SUNG OR SAID THE GLORIA PATRI	R 025 18
THE DAY, SHALL BE SUNG OR SAID THE GLORIA PATRI,	R 025 20
WHICH SHALL BE SUNG OR SAID THE HYMN CALLED	R 026 06
AFTER THAT SHALL BE SUNG OR SAID THE HYMN CALLED NUNC	R 028 06
HERE MAY BE SUNG A HYMN OR AN ANTHEM	R 070 21
THERE MAY BE SUNG A HYMN, OR AN OFFERTORY ANTHEM IN	R 073 35
SHALL BE SAID OR SUNG BY THE PRIEST, THEREFORE WITH	R 077 03
HERE MAY BE SUNG A HYMN	R 082 24
AND THEY SUNG AS IT WERE A NEW SONG BEFORE THE	103 04
AND WHEN THEY HAD SUNG AN HYMN, THEY WENT OUT INTO	141 17
THE FOLLOWING SHALL BE SAID OR SUNG	R 264 17
HERE MAY BE SUNG A HYMN, AFTER WHICH THE MINISTER,	R 285 11
THEN SHALL BE SUNG A HYMN, AFTER WHICH THE MINISTER	R 289 12
HERE MAY BE SUNG A HYMN, AFTER WHICH, THE PEOPLE	R 290 25
HERE MAY BE SUNG A HYMN, AFTER WHICH THE MINISTER	R 294 02
HERE MAY BE SUNG A HYMN OR ANTHEM	R 331 28
THE EARTH, SHALL BE SUNG OR SAID, MAN, THAT IS BORN	R 332 17
SHALL BE SAID OR SUNG, I HEARD A VOICE FROM HEAVEN,	R 333 24
HERE MAY BE SUNG A HYMN OR AN ANTHEM	R 340 02
SHALL BE SAID OR SUNG, JESUS SAITH TO HIS DISCIPLES,	R 341 08
SHALL BE SAID OR SUNG, THEREFORE ARE THEY BEFORE THE	R 341 19
SPIRITUS SHALL BE SUNG OR SAID OVER HIM	R 556 03
SHALL BE SAID OR SUNG EXSURGAT DEUS, PSALM LXVIII	R 571 30

SUNK

| 15 THE HEATHEN ARE SUNK DOWN IN THE PIT THAT THEY | 352 21 |

SUNSHINE

| YE SHALL ALSO PRAISE GOD FOR RAIN AND SUNSHINE | 048 11 |

SUPEREROGATION

WORKS OF SUPEREROGATION, CANNOT BE TAUGHT WITHOUT   605 25

SUPERFLUITY

AND SUPERFLUITY OF NAUGHTINESS, AND RECEIVE WITH   175 03
AND SUPERFLUITY OF NAUGHTINESS, AND RECEIVE WITH   265 26

SUPERSCRIPTION

AND THE SUPERSCRIPTION OF HIS ACCUSATION WAS WRITTEN   146 13
AND A SUPERSCRIPTION ALSO WAS WRITTEN OVER HIM,   154 32
UNTO THEM, WHOSE IS THIS IMAGE AND SUPERSCRIPTICN   223 08

SUPERSTITIONS

AND HATH GIVEN OCCASION TO MANY SUPERSTITIONS   608 43

SUPERSTITIOUS

IS SUPERSTITIOUS AND UNGODLY   610 34

SUPPED

WHEN HE HAD SUPPED, SAYING, THIS CUP IS THE NEW   152 21

SUPPER

AFTER SUPPER, (D) HE TOOK THE CUP   080 22
TO CELEBRATE THE LORD'S SUPPER   088 13
FROM THIS HOLY SUPPER, PROVOKE GOD'S INDIGNATION   088 25
ON HIS BREAST AT SUPPER, AND SAID, LORD, WHICH IS HE   102 05
THE CUP AFTER SUPPER, SAYING, THIS CUP IS THE NEW   149 11
AND SUPPER BEING ENDED, THE DEVIL HAVING NOW PUT INTO   155 26
HE RISETH FROM SUPPER, AND LAID ASIDE HIS GARMENTS   155 31
MAN MADE A GREAT SUPPER, AND BADE MANY   192 03
HIS SERVANT AT SUPPER TIME TO SAY TO THEM THAT WERE   192 04
MEN WHICH WERE BIDDEN SHALL TASTE OF MY SUPPER   192 21
OF THE LORD'S SUPPER, OR HOLY COMMUNICN, FCR THE   291 35
AND THE SUPPER OF THE LORD   292 08
OF THE LORD'S SUPPER ORDAINED   293 02
OF THE LORD'S SUPPER WAS ORDAINED FOR THE CONTINUAL   293 04
IS THE OUTWARD PART OR SIGN OF THE LORD'S SUPPER   293 09
OF THE LORD'S SUPPER IS, BREAD AND WINE, WHICH THE   293 10
AND RECEIVED BY THE FAITHFUL IN THE LORD'S SUPPER   293 16
WHEREOF WE ARE PARTAKERS IN THE LORD'S SUPPER   293 18
IN THE LORD'S SUPPER ARE THE STRENGTHENING AND   293 20
REQUIRED OF THOSE WHO COME TO THE LORD'S SUPPER   293 24
TO THE LORD'S SUPPER TO EXAMINE THEMSELVES, WHETHER   293 26
WITHOUT DELAY, TO THE LORD'S SUPPER   R 299 07
AND THE SUPPER OF THE LORD   581 10
OF THE LORD'S SUPPER ORDAINED   582 02
IS THE OUTWARD PART OR SIGN OF THE LORD'S SUPPER   582 08
AND RECEIVED BY THE FAITHFUL IN THE LORD'S SUPPER   582 14
REQUIRED OF THOSE WHO COME TO THE LORD'S SUPPER   582 21
AND THE SUPPER OF THE LORD   587 37
AND THE LORD'S SUPPER, FOR THAT THEY HAVE NOT ANY   607 42
THE SUPPER OF THE LORD IS NOT ONLY A SIGN OF THE LOVE   608 34
AND WINE) IN THE SUPPER OF THE LORD, CANNOT BE PROVED   608 41
AND EATEN, IN THE SUPPER, ONLY AFTER AN HEAVENLY AND   608 44
AND EATEN IN THE SUPPER, IS FAITH   608 46
OF THE LORD'S SUPPER WAS NOT BY CHRIST'S ORDINANCE   608 47

SUPPLICATE

AND HUMBLY SUPPLICATE THY MERCIFUL PROTECTION ALL   595 07

SUPPLICATION

PRAYER AND SUPPLICATION WITH THANKSGIVING LET YCUR   095 16
PRAYER AND SUPPLICATION IN THE SPIRIT, AND WATCHING   219 20
AND SUPPLICATION FOR ALL SAINTS   219 21
MAKE THEIR SUPPLICATION BEFORE THEE   397 11
170 LET MY SUPPLICATION COME BEFORE THEE   501 22
EVEN UNTO THE LORD DID I MAKE MY SUPPLICATION   518 04
PRESENT HIS SUPPLICATION FOR HIMSELF, IN THIS FORM   R 573 09
THE SPIRIT OF GRACE AND OF SUPPLICATION   594 05

SUPPLICATIONS

OUR COMMON SUPPLICATIONS UNTO THEE   020 04
OUR COMMON SUPPLICATIONS UNTO THEE   034 04
AND SUPPLICATIONS UNTC THEE   040 06
THESE OUR SUPPLICATIONS AND PRAYERS, AND DISPOSE THE   049 11
AND SUPPLICATIONS UNTO THEE   050 09
AND SUPPLICATIONS, AND TO GIVE THANKS FCR ALL MEN   074 07
HEAR THE SUPPLICATIONS OF THY PEOPLE, AND GRANT US   111 12
OUR SUPPLICATIONS AND PRAYERS, WHICH WE OFFER BEFORE   156 29
THE SUPPLICATIONS OF THY CONGREGATION   279 15
OUR HUMBLE SUPPLICATIONS UNTO THEE FOR THESE THY   298 16
HUMBLE SUPPLICATIONS TO GOD FOR ALL THESE THINGS   R 543 24
AND SUPPLICATIONS UNTO THEE   565 02
THE SUPPLICATIONS OF THY SERVANTS, AND GRANT   565 18

SUPPLIETH

EVERY JOINT SUPPLIETH, ACCORDING TO THE EFFECTUAL   237 31

SUPPLY

PRAY FOR A DUE SUPPLY OF PERSONS FITTED TO SERVE GOD   047 30
UNFAILING MIGHT SUPPLY TO STRENGTHEN OUR INFIRMITY   545 04
UNFAILING MIGHT SUPPLY TO STRENGTHEN OUR INFIRMITY   557 10

SUPPLYING

OF THE VESTRY SUPPLYING HIS PLACE) HOLDING THE KEYS   R 570 09
OF THE VESTRY SUPPLYING HIS PLACE) PRESENT THE KEYS   R 570 25

SUPPORT

SUPPORT THEM IN THE DAY OF BATTLE, AND IN THE TIME OF   041 27
AS MAY SUPPORT US IN ALL DANGERS, AND CARRY US   114 07
DIDST SUPPORT HIM IN PATIENCE AND SUBMISSION TO THY   315 25
YE OUGHT TO SUPPORT THE WEAK, AND TO REMEMBER THE   551 09
O LORD, SUPPORT US ALL THE DAY LONG, UNTIL THE   594 30

SUPPOSE

EVERY ONE, I SUPPOSE THAT EVEN THE WORLD ITSELF COULD   102 16

SUPPOSED

CANNOT BUT BE SUPPOSED THAT FURTHER ALTERATICNS WOULD   VI 03
THEY SUPPOSED THAT THEY SHOULD HAVE RECEIVED   119 33
AND SUPPOSED THAT THEY HAD SEEN A SPIRIT   169 30

SUPPOSING

BUT THEY, SUPPOSING HIM TO HAVE BEEN IN THE COMPANY,   110 23

SUPREME

THE SUPREME GOVERNOR OF ALL THINGS, WHOSE POWER   041 09
WHETHER IT BE TO THE KING, AS SUPREME   173 19

SURE

BE YE SURE THAT THE LORD HE IS GOD   015 07
SO WE MAY WITH SURE CONFIDENCE BEHOLD HIM WHEN HE   098 14
SEPULCHRE BE MADE SURE UNTIL THE THIRD DAY, LEST HIS   162 20
MAKE IT AS SURE AS YE CAN   162 24
MADE THE SEPULCHRE SURE, SEALING THE STONE, AND   162 25
I WILL GIVE YOU THE SURE MERCIES OF DAVID   169 12
NOW ARE WE SURE THAT THOU KNOWEST ALL THINGS, AND   176 33
HIM COMFORT AND SURE CONFIDENCE IN THEE, DEFEND HIM   309 06
IN SURE AND CERTAIN HOPE OF THE RESURRECTION UNTC   333 16
IN SURE AND CERTAIN HOPE OF THE RESURRECTION UNTC   337 11
SHALL SAY, IN SURE AND CERTAIN HOPE OF THE   341 13
OF THE LORD IS SURE, AND GIVETH WISDOM UNTO THE   363 28
IN HER PALACES AS A SURE REFUGE   399 15
BUT MY SURE TRUST IS IN THEE   425 20
THE ROUND WORLD SO SURE, *   457 07
6 THY TESTIMONIES, O LORD, * ARE VERY SURE   457 16
2 BE YE SURE THAT THE LORD HE IS GOD   463 08
12 SURE I AM THAT THE LORD WILL AVENGE THE PCCR,   517 02
THEY BE CERTAIN SURE WITNESSES, AND EFFECTUAL SIGNS   607 32

SURELY

THAT WE, SURELY TRUSTING IN THY DEFENCE, MAY NCT FEAR   017 09
FOR HE SAID, SURELY THEY ARE MY PEOPLE, CHILDREN THAT   138 33
AGAIN TO PETER, SURELY THOU ART ONE OF THEM   143 31
OUR HEARTS MAY SURELY THERE BE FIXED, WHERE TRUE JOYS   174 23
SURELY THE PEOPLE IS GRASS   242 31
OUR HEARTS MAY SURELY THERE BE FIXED, WHERE TRUE JOYS   285 30
MAY SURELY PERFORM AND KEEP THE VOW AND   303 07
SURELY THY LOVING-KINDNESS AND MERCY SHALL FCLLCW ME   338 29
15 SURELY THOU HAST SEEN IT   354 04
6 SURELY THY LOVING-KINDNESS AND MERCY SHALL FOLLOW   368 22
SURELY THE GREAT WATER-FLOODS SHALL NCT COME NIGH   378 03

SUREST

UPON THE BEST AND SUREST FOUNDATIONS, THAT PEACE AND   035 16

SURETIES

BECAUSE THEY PROMISE THEM BOTH BY THEIR SURETIES   581 34

SURETY

NOW I KNOW OF A SURETY, THAT THE LORD HATH SENT HIS   245 26
DEMAND SUFFICIENT SURETY FOR HIS INDEMNIFICATICN   R 301 03

SURNAMED

INTO JUDAS SURNAMED ISCARIOT, BEING OF THE NUMBER OF   148 15
WHO WAS SURNAMED JUSTUS, AND MATTHIAS   234 26

SUSPECTED

BE ALLEGED, OR SUSPECTED, THE MINISTER SHALL SAY TO   R 301 04

SUSPEND

JUST CAUSE TO SUSPEND THE SERVICE   R 570 22

SUSPENDS

WHICH ALSO SUSPENDS THE ORDER FOR THE READING OF SAIC   R 610 27

SUSTAINED

FOR THE LORD SUSTAINED ME   309 23
FOR THE LORD SUSTAINED ME   346 34

SUSTAINING

FOR THY SUSTAINING PROVIDENCE   316 22

SUSTENANCE

ALL THINGS NECESSARY TO THEIR BODILY SUSTENANCE   040 18
FOOD AND SUSTENANCE IN THAT HOLY SACRAMENT   087 04

SWADDLING

WRAPPED HIM IN SWADDLING CLOTHES, AND LAID HIM IN A   099 08
WRAPPED IN SWADDLING CLOTHES, LYING IN A MANGER   099 18

SWALLOW

DAILY AT HAND TO SWALLOW ME UP   408 16
LET THE DEEP SWALLOW ME UP   423 02
AND THE SWALLOW A NEST, WHERE SHE MAY LAY HER   445 17

SWALLOWED

DEATH IS SWALLOWED UP IN VICTORY   330 09
AND SWALLOWED UP DATHAN, *   474 02
2 THEY HAD SWALLOWED US UP ALIVE   504 10

SWARE

THE OATH WHICH HE SWARE TO OUR FOREFATHER ABRAHAM, *   014 18
THE OATH WHICH HE SWARE TO OUR FATHER ABRAHAM,   244 06
11 UNTO WHOM I SWARE IN MY WRATH, *   459 27
THE OATH THAT HE SWARE UNTO ISAAC   470 21
4 THE LORD SWARE, AND WILL NOT REPENT, *   482 12
2 HOW HE SWARE UNTO THE LORD, *   508 06

SWAREST

WHICH THOU SWAREST UNTO DAVID IN THY TRUTH   453 06

SWEAR

TO CURSE AND TO SWEAR, SAYING, I KNOW NOT THIS MAN OF 143 33
THOU CLEAVE, AND SWEAR BY HIS NAME   263 30
ALL THEY ALSO THAT SWEAR BY HIM SHALL BE COMMENDED   415 16
BUT THAT A MAN MAY SWEAR WHEN THE MAGISTRATE   611 08

SWEARERS

AGAINST FALSE SWEARERS, AND AGAINST THOSE THAT   232 17

SWEARETH

5 HE THAT SWEARETH UNTO HIS NEIGHBOUR, AND   357 15

SWEARING

VAIN AND RASH SWEARING IS FORBIDDEN CHRISTIAN MEN BY   611 06

SWEAT

BY THINE AGONY AND BLOODY SWEAT   055 10
AND HIS SWEAT WAS AS IT WERE GREAT DROPS OF BLOOD   150 22

SWEEP

A CANDLE, AND SWEEP THE HOUSE, AND SEEK DILIGENTLY   193 29

SWEET

HAD BOUGHT SWEET SPICES, THAT THEY MIGHT COME   165 20
15 WE TOOK SWEET COUNSEL TOGETHER, *   407 18
FOR SWEET IS THY MERCY   481 13
103 O HOW SWEET ARE THY WORDS UNTO MY THROAT   496 32
FOR THEY ARE SWEET   517 25
IS FULL OF SWEET, PLEASANT, AND UNSPEAKABLE   606 17

SWEET-SMELLING

GOD FOR A SWEET-SMELLING SAVOUR   129 02

SWEETER

SWEETER ALSO THAN HONEY, AND THE HONEYCOMB   364 05
SWEETER THAN HONEY UNTO MY MOUTH   496 33

SWELL

THEREOF RAGE AND SWELL, *   327 07
THEREOF RAGE AND SWELL, *   397 30
7 THEIR EYES SWELL WITH FATNESS, *   428 22

SWELLETH

FROM HIM THAT SWELLETH AGAINST HIM, AND WILL SET HIM   355 19

SWEPT

HE FINDETH IT SWEPT AND GARNISHED   130 13

SWERVE

YET DO I NOT SWERVE FROM THY TESTIMONIES   500 26

SWERVED

BUT YET I SWERVED NOT FROM THY COMMANDMENTS   497 18

SWIFT

LET EVERY MAN BE SWIFT TO HEAR, SLOW TO SPEAK, SLOW   174 31
AND I WILL BE A SWIFT WITNESS AGAINST THE SORCERERS,   232 16
LET EVERY MAN BE SWIFT TO HEAR, SLOW TO SPEAK,   265 24
AT THEM WITH A SWIFT ARROW, *   415 33

SWIFTLY

AND HIS WORD RUNNETH VERY SWIFTLY   523 26

SWINE

AND HE SENT HIM INTO HIS FIELDS TO FEED SWINE   202 08
THE HUSKS THAT THE SWINE DID EAT   202 09

SWORD

HE BEARETH NOT THE SWORD IN VAIN   114 20
STOOD BY DREW A SWORD, AND SMOTE A SERVANT OF THE   142 22
HE THAT HATH NO SWORD, LET HIM SELL HIS GARMENT,   150 08
UNTO HIM, LORD, SHALL WE SMITE WITH THE SWORD   150 32
AND THE SWORD OF THE SPIRIT, WHICH IS THE   219 18
A SWORD SHALL PIERCE THROUGH THY OWN SOUL   233 14
KILLED JAMES THE BROTHER OF JOHN WITH THE SWORD   244 33
KILLED JAMES THE BROTHER OF JOHN WITH THE SWORD   247 03
OR FAMINE, OR NAKEDNESS, OR PERIL, OR SWORD   331 08
13 IF A MAN WILL NOT TURN, HE WILL WHET HIS SWORD   350 17
MY SOUL FROM THE UNGODLY, BY THINE OWN SWORD   359 13
MY SOUL FROM THE *   367 12
HAVE DRAWN OUT THE SWORD, AND HAVE BENT THEIR BOW, *   385 22
15 THEIR SWORD SHALL GO THROUGH THEIR OWN HEART,   385 25
ASUNDER AS WITH A SWORD, *   393 27
THROUGH THEIR OWN SWORD, *   394 28
IT IS NOT MY SWORD THAT SHALL HELP ME   395 05
GIRD THEE WITH THY SWORD UPON THY THIGH, O THOU MOST   396 20
SPEARS AND ARROWS, AND THEIR TONGUE A SHARP SWORD   409 23
THE EDGE OF THE SWORD, *   415 13
TONGUE LIKE A SWORD, *   415 23
THE SHIELD, THE SWORD, AND THE BATTLE   432 27
OVER ALSO UNTO THE SWORD, *   439 02
SLAIN WITH THE SWORD, *   439 06
THE EDGE OF HIS SWORD, *   452 26
DAVID THY SERVANT FROM THE PERIL OF THE SWORD   520 11
AND A TWO-EDGED SWORD IN THEIR HANDS   525 14

SWORDS

MULTITUDE WITH SWORDS AND STAVES, FROM THE CHIEF   142 16
A THIEF, WITH SWORDS AND WITH STAVES, TO TAKE ME   142 25
BEHOLD, HERE ARE TWO SWORDS   150 12
A THIEF, WITH SWORDS AND STAVES   151 04
AND YET BE THEY VERY SWORDS   408 03
THEIR MOUTH, AND SWORDS ARE IN THEIR LIPS   411 18

SWORN

UNTO VANITY, NOR SWORN TO DECEIVE HIS NEIGHBOUR   369 03
I HAVE SWORN UNTO DAVID MY SERVANT   450 10
I HAVE SWORN ONCE BY MY HOLINESS, THAT I WILL NOT   452 10
MAD UPON ME ARE SWORN TOGETHER AGAINST ME   464 26
106 I HAVE SWORN, AND AM STEDFASTLY PURPOSED,   497 09
UNTO VANITY, NOR SWORN TO DECEIVE HIS NEIGHBOUR   563 18

SYMPATHY

OF THY SYMPATHY, AND A CLEARER KNOWLEDGE OF THY WILL   596 14

SYNAGOGUE

WENT INTO THE SYNAGOGUE ON THE SABBATH DAY, AND STOOD 261 12
WERE IN THE SYNAGOGUE WERE FASTENED ON HIM   261 23

SYNAGOGUES

IN YOUR SYNAGOGUES, AND PERSECUTE THEM FROM CITY TO   100 21
THEY SHALL PUT YOU OUT OF THE SYNAGOGUES   179 30
TO THE SYNAGOGUES, THAT IF HE FOUND ANY OF THIS WAY,   229 27
CHRIST IN THE SYNAGOGUES, THAT HE IS THE SON OF GOD   231 04

SYRIA

FIRST MADE WHEN CYRENIUS WAS GOVERNOR OF SYRIA   098 31

TABERNACLE

BEHOLD, THE TABERNACLE OF GOD IS WITH MEN, AND HE   021 28
MORE PERFECT TABERNACLE, NOT MADE WITH HANDS, THAT IS 132 24
BOTH THE TABERNACLE, AND ALL THE VESSELS OF THE   147 24
I AM IN THIS TABERNACLE, TO STIR YOU UP BY PUTTING   248 08
OFF THIS MY TABERNACLE, EVEN AS OUR LORD JESUS CHRIST 248 10
OF TROUBLE HE SHALL HIDE ME IN HIS TABERNACLE   326 12
PLACE OF THE TABERNACLE OF THE MOST HIGHEST   327 10
WHO SHALL DWELL IN THY TABERNACLE   357 05
HATH HE SET A TABERNACLE FOR THE SUN   363 21
OF TROUBLE HE SHALL HIDE ME IN HIS TABERNACLE   372 05
IN THY TABERNACLE FROM THE STRIFE OF TONGUES   377 08
PLACE OF THE TABERNACLE OF THE MOST HIGHEST   397 33
DWELL IN THY TABERNACLE FOR EVER, *   413 13
SALEM IS HIS TABERNACLE, *   432 25
FORSOOK THE TABERNACLE IN SHILOH, *   438 32
REFUSED THE TABERNACLE OF JOSEPH, *   439 12
WITHIN THE TABERNACLE OF MINE HOUSE, *   508 08
GO INTO HIS TABERNACLE, *   508 17
BEHOLD, THE TABERNACLE OF GOD IS WITH MEN, AND HE   567 15

TABERNACLES
PLACE OF THE TABERNACLES OF THE MOST HIGH   022 28
AND LET US MAKE THREE TABERNACLES   249 03
6 THE TABERNACLES OF THE EDOMITES, AND THE   444 16

TABLE
ACCORDING TO THE TABLE OR CALENDAR   R 009 31
ACCORDING TO THE TABLE OR CALENDAR   R 014 03
ACCORDING TO THE TABLE OR CALENDAR   R 026 05
THE HOLY TABLE SHALL HAVE UPON IT A FAIR WHITE LINEN   R 067 05
BEFORE THE HOLY TABLE, SHALL SAY THE LORD'S PRAYER   R 067 06
RETURN TO THE HOLY TABLE, AND BEGIN THE   R 071 32
HUMBLY PRESENT AND PLACE IT UPON THE HOLY TABLE   R 073 31
UPON THE HOLY TABLE, THE BREAD AND THE WINE   R 073 32
TURN TO THE HOLY TABLE, AND SAY, IT IS VERY MEET,   R 076 30
BEFORE THE HOLY TABLE, HATH SO ORDERED THE BREAD AND   R 080 02
DOWN AT THE LORD'S TABLE, SAY, IN THE NAME OF ALL   082 11
COME TO THIS THY TABLE, O MERCIFUL LORD, TRUSTING IN   082 13
MUCH AS TO GATHER UP THE CRUMBS UNDER THY TABLE   082 16
TO THE LORD'S TABLE, AND REVERENTLY PLACE UPON IT   R 083 11
COME TO THE LORD'S TABLE, UNTIL HE HAVE OPENLY   R 085 04
OF THE LORD'S TABLE, UNTIL HE KNOW THEM TO BE   R 085 11
RECEIVED AS WORTHY PARTAKERS OF THAT HOLY TABLE   087 15
OF YOUR SINS, OR ELSE COME NOT TO THAT HOLY TABLE   087 34
DECKED HIS TABLE WITH ALL KIND OF PROVISION,   088 18
FROM THE LORD'S TABLE, AND SEPARATE FROM YOUR   089 17
THE CRUMBS WHICH FALL FROM THEIR MASTERS' TABLE   128 19
OF HIM THAT BETRAYETH ME IS WITH ME ON THE TABLE   149 14
AND DRINK AT MY TABLE IN MY KINGDOM, AND SIT ON   149 29
THE CRUMBS WHICH FELL FROM THE RICH MAN'S TABLE   190 07
FOR A WRITING TABLE, AND WROTE, SAYING, HIS NAME IS   243 23
AND DRINK AT MY TABLE IN MY KINGDOM, AND SIT ON   250 14
NEAR TO THE HOLY TABLE, THE PEOPLE ALL STANDING UNTIL   R 296 06
SHALT PREPARE A TABLE BEFORE ME IN THE PRESENCE OF   338 26
SHALT PREPARE A TABLE BEFORE ME IN THE PRESENCE OF   368 19
23 LET THEIR TABLE BE MADE A SNARE TO TAKE THEMSELVES   423 18
GOD PREPARE A TABLE IN THE WILDERNESS   436 07
ROUND ABOUT THY TABLE   506 13
NEAR TO THE HOLY TABLE, SUCH AS DESIRE TO BE ORDAINED   R 530 08
NEAR TO THE HOLY TABLE, ALL THOSE WHO ARE TO RECEIVE   R 536 08
SITTING IN HIS CHAIR, NEAR THE HOLY TABLE   R 552 19
TO THE HOLY TABLE, REPEATING THE FOLLOWING PSALM   R 563 08
AND THEN LAID BY HIM UPON THE COMMUNION TABLE   R 566 27

TABLES
AND OVERTHREW THE TABLES OF THE MONEY-CHANGERS,   091 35
AND OVERTHREW THE TABLES OF THE MONEY-CHANGERS,   260 05
WE SHOULD LEAVE THE WORD OF GOD, AND SERVE TABLES   532 10
OUT THE CHANGERS' MONEY, AND OVERTHREW THE TABLES   567 31

TABOR
TABOR AND HERMON SHALL REJOICE IN THY NAME   450 31

TABRET
BRING HITHER THE TABRET, *   447 14
UNTO HIM WITH TABRET AND HARP   525 08

TAKE
AND TAKE NOT THY HOLY SPIRIT FROM US   016 32
LET HIM TAKE THE WATER OF LIFE FREELY   022 31
AND TAKE NOT THY HOLY SPIRIT FROM US   031 14
TAKE AWAY ALL HATRED AND PREJUDICE, AND WHATSOEVER   037 28
VOUCHSAFE TO TAKE INTO THY ALMIGHTY AND MOST GRACIOUS   042 05
NEITHER TAKE THOU VENGEANCE OF OUR SINS   054 14
WHATSOEVER!) TO TAKE A FURTHER REVIEW OF THE PUBLIC   VI 25
AND TAKE NOT THY HOLY SPIRIT FROM ME   060 32
THOU SHALT NOT TAKE THE NAME OF THE LORD THY GOD IN   068 18
WITH FAITH, AND TAKE THIS HOLY SACRAMENT TO YOUR   075 12
THE PEOPLE, AND TAKE THE CUP INTO HIS HANDS, HE SHALL   R 080 04
SAYING, TAKE, EAT, (C) THIS IS MY BODY,   080 20
THE PRIEST IS TO TAKE THE PATEN INTO HIS HANDS   R 080 30
D) HERE HE IS TO TAKE THE CUP INTO HIS HANDS   R 080 33
TAKE AND EAT THIS IN REMEMBRANCE THAT CHRIST DIED FOR   082 33
BELOVED IN CHRIST, TAKE YE GOOD HEED, LEST YE,   088 24
SON TO TAKE OUR NATURE UPON HIM, AND AS AT THIS TIME   096 14
ARISE, AND TAKE THE YOUNG CHILD AND HIS   103 17
SON TO TAKE OUR NATURE UPON HIM, AND AS AT THIS TIME   104 06
FEAR NOT TO TAKE UNTO THEE MARY THY WIFE   105 04
ARISE, AND TAKE THE YOUNG CHILD AND HIS   107 14
WAS MANIFESTED TO TAKE AWAY OUR SINS   117 23
TAKE THAT THINE IS, AND GO THY WAY   120 08
IF A MAN TAKE OF YOU, IF A MAN EXALT HIMSELF,   120 24
IT IS NOT MEET TO TAKE THE CHILDREN'S BREAD, AND TO   128 17
ONE OF THEM MAY TAKE A LITTLE   131 31
JESUS CHRIST, TO TAKE UPON HIM OUR FLESH, AND TO   134 07
HOW THEY MIGHT TAKE HIM BY CRAFT, AND PUT HIM TO   139 34
TO THEM, AND SAID, TAKE, EAT   141 10
TAKE AWAY THIS CUP FROM ME   141 35
SLEEP ON NOW, AND TAKE YOUR REST   142 11
TAKE HIM, AND LEAD HIM AWAY SAFELY   142 19
AND WITH STAVES, TO TAKE ME   142 25
GRANT US GRACE TO TAKE JOYFULLY THE SUFFERINGS OF THE   144 08
LOTS UPON THEM, WHAT EVERY MAN SHOULD TAKE   146 12
ELIAS WILL COME TO TAKE HIM DOWN   146 34
AND SAID, TAKE THIS, AND DIVIDE IT AMONG   149 06
A PURSE, LET HIM TAKE IT, AND LIKEWISE HIS SCRIP   150 07
BRAKE IT, AND SAID, TAKE, EAT   152 19
TAKE FROM THEM ALL IGNORANCE, HARDNESS OF HEART, AND   157 08
AND OF GOATS SHOULD TAKE AWAY SINS   157 23
WHICH CAN NEVER TAKE AWAY SINS   158 05

TAKE   CONTINUED
SAITH UNTO THEM, TAKE YE HIM, AND CRUCIFY HIM   159 07
YE SHALL TAKE IT PATIENTLY   172 07
SUFFER FOR IT, YE TAKE IT PATIENTLY, THIS IS   172 08
THAT HE SHALL TAKE OF MINE, AND SHALL SHEW IT UNTO   175 24
HE STANDETH TAKE HEED LEST HE FALL   201 25
AND SAID UNTO HIM, TAKE CARE OF HIM   208 34
BEGIN WITH SHAME TO TAKE THE LOWEST PLACE   214 14
THE PALSY,) ARISE, TAKE UP THY BED, AND GO UNTO THINE   217 11
HAND AND FOOT, AND TAKE HIM AWAY, AND CAST HIM INTO   218 27
WHEREFORE TAKE UNTO YOU THE WHOLE ARMOUR OF GOD,   219 11
AND TAKE THE HELMET OF SALVATION, AND THE SWORD OF   219 18
WHICH WOULD TAKE ACCOUNT OF HIS SERVANTS   221 14
ONE OF THEM MAY TAKE A LITTLE   225 28
AND HIS BISHOPRICK LET ANOTHER TAKE   234 20
THAT HE MAY TAKE PART OF THIS MINISTRY AND   234 29
TAKE MY YOKE UPON YOU, AND LEARN OF ME   235 12
FURTHER TO TAKE PETER ALSO   245 02
FURTHER TO TAKE PETER ALSO   247 04
TAKE HEED THAT YE DESPISE NOT ONE OF THESE LITTLE   253 09
TAKE MARK, AND BRING HIM WITH THEE   254 02
THE MORROW SHALL TAKE THOUGHT FOR THE THINGS OF   266 32
ALSO ON THY PART TAKE HEED THAT THIS CHILD LEARN THE   277 09
WILT THOU TAKE HEED THAT THIS CHILD, SO SOON AS   277 14
THE MINISTER SHALL TAKE THE CHILD INTO HIS ARMS,   R 279 23
THE MINISTER SHALL TAKE HIM BY THE HAND, AND SHALL   R 279 31
THOU SHALT NOT TAKE THE NAME OF THE LORD THY GOD IN   286 18
HIS RIGHT HAND TO TAKE THE WOMAN BY HER RIGHT HAND,   R 301 26
TAKE THEE N   301 28
TAKE THEE N   302 04
TO TAKE HIM HENCE, TAKE HIM UNTO THY FAVOUR   314 11
THOU ART PLEASED TO TAKE HIM HENCE, TAKE HIM UNTO THY   314 11
THAT WAS SLAIN TO TAKE AWAY THE SINS OF THE WORLD   317 18
GRANT THAT HE MAY TAKE HIS SICKNESS PATIENTLY,   321 22
BEEN PLEASED TO TAKE UNTO THYSELF THE SOUL OF THIS   336 04
BY THY DEATH DIDST TAKE AWAY THE STING OF DEATH   336 10
TAKE HEED THAT YE DESPISE NOT ONE OF THESE LITTLE   339 29
MOST DEAR SON DID TAKE LITTLE CHILDREN INTO HIS ARMS   342 03
UP, AND THE RULERS TAKE COUNSEL TOGETHER *   345 28
DOWN IN PEACE, AND TAKE MY REST   347 28
MY SOUL, AND TAKE ME   349 32
THAT THOU MAYEST TAKE THE MATTER INTO THY HAND   354 05
ME ROUND ABOUT, TO TAKE AWAY MY SOUL   359 05
NIGHT SEASON ALSO I TAKE NO REST   366 08
THEIR COUNSEL TO TAKE AWAY MY LIFE   376 23
AGAINST ME, AND TAKE THEIR COUNSEL TO TAKE AWAY MY   376 23
KEEP INNOCENCY, AND TAKE HEED UNTO THE THING THAT IS   387 08
I SAID, I WILL TAKE HEED TO MY WAYS, *   389 07
11 TAKE THY PLAGUE AWAY FROM ME   389 29
9 I WILL TAKE NO BULLOCK OUT OF THINE HOUSE, *   402 08
AND TAKE NOT THY HOLY SPIRIT FROM ME   403 31
HE SHALL TAKE THEE, AND PLUCK THEE OUT OF THY   404 29
2 TAKE HEED UNTO ME, AND HEAR ME, *   406 21
HE SHALL TAKE THEM AWAY WITH A WHIRLWIND, THE GREEN   410 27
15 TAKE ME OUT OF THE MIRE, THAT I SINK NOT   422 32
BE MADE A SNARE TO TAKE THEMSELVES WITHAL   423 18
DISPLEASURE TAKE HOLD OF THEM   423 24
WAIT FOR MY SOUL THEIR COUNSEL TOGETHER,   425 26
PERSECUTE HIM, AND TAKE HIM, FOR THERE IS NONE TO   425 27
2 TAKE THE PSALM, BRING HITHER THE TABRET, *   442 14
FOR THOU SHALT TAKE ALL NATIONS TO THINE INHERITANCE   444 03
12 WHO SAY, LET US TAKE TO OURSELVES *   444 28
WILL I NOT UTTERLY TAKE FROM HIM, *   452 08
8 TAKE HEED, YE UNWISE AMONG THE PEOPLE   458 02
OR WHO WILL TAKE MY PART AGAINST THE EVIL DOERS   458 19
4 I WILL TAKE NO WICKED THING IN HAND   463 22
I SAID, O MY GOD, TAKE ME NOT AWAY IN THE MIDST OF   465 28
THOU HAST MADE TO TAKE HIS PASTIME THEREIN   469 13
UNTO THEM, LO, THEY TAKE NOW MY CONTRARY PART   480 09
AND LET ANOTHER TAKE HIS OFFICE   480 17
29 TAKE FROM ME THE WAY OF LYING, *   491 25
39 TAKE AWAY THE REBUKE THAT I AM AFRAID OF   492 17
43 O TAKE NOT THE WORD OF THY TRUTH UTTERLY OUT OF MY   492 26
AND SO LATE TAKE REST, AND EAT THE BREAD OF   505 27
OF MY HEAD TO TAKE ANY REST   508 11
8 IF I TAKE THE WINGS OF THE MORNING, *   515 04
AND THINE ENEMIES TAKE THY NAME IN VAIN   515 31
DELIVER ME, AND TAKE ME OUT OF THE GREAT WATERS,   520 05
TAKE HEED THAT THE PERSONS, WHOM YE PRESENT UNTO US,   530 13
THE HOLY GHOST TO TAKE UPON YOU THIS OFFICE AND   532 27
AND SHALL SAY, TAKE THOU AUTHORITY TO EXECUTE THE   534 05
TAKE THOU AUTHORITY TO READ THE GOSPEL IN THE   534 11
TO ACCEPT AND TAKE THESE THY SERVANTS UNTO THE OFFICE   534 31
TAKE HEED THAT THE PERSONS, WHOM YE PRESENT UNTO US,   536 14
MEMBER THEREOF, DO TAKE ANY HURT OR HINDRANCE BY   540 11
TAKE THOU AUTHORITY TO EXECUTE THE OFFICE OF A PRIEST   546 11
HIS HAND, SAYING, TAKE THOU AUTHORITY TO PREACH THE   546 25
ORDERS SHALL TAKE TOGETHER, AND REMAIN IN THE SAME   R 546 30
HOW SHALL HE TAKE CARE OF THE CHURCH OF GOD   549 26
WHEREFORE I TAKE YOU TO RECORD THIS DAY, THAT I AM   550 24
TAKE HEED THEREFORE UNTO YOURSELVES, AND TO ALL THE   550 26
THAT SOLD DOVES, TAKE THESE THINGS HENCE   567 31
THOU SHALT NOT TAKE THE NAME OF THE LORD THY GOD IN   578 35
PLEASED TO TAKE US, AND ALL WHO ARE DEAR TO US, UNDER   589 03
ONCE MADE, SHOULD TAKE AWAY THE SINS OF THE WORLD   R 605 34
FOR ANY MAN TO TAKE UPON HIM THE OFFICE OF PUBLIC   607 19

TAKEN
THE SECOND LESSON, TAKEN OUT OF THE NEW TESTAMENT,   R 014 02
INTERCESSIONS TAKEN OUT OF THIS BOOK, AS HE SHALL   R 017 23
OR PRAYERS, TAKEN OUT OF THIS BOOK, AS HE SHALL THINK   R 031 32
FOR US, AND HATH TAKEN AWAY THE SIN OF THE WORLD   078 10
AND HAD TAKEN HIS GARMENTS, AND WAS SET DOWN   156 12
THAT THEY MIGHT BE TAKEN AWAY   160 34

TAKEN   CONTINUED

	PAGE	LN
WHEN JOSEPH HAD TAKEN THE BODY, HE WRAPPED IT IN A	162	10
SEETH THE STONE TAKEN AWAY FROM THE SEPULCHRE	164	12
THEY HAVE TAKEN AWAY THE LORD OUT OF THE	164	15
IN WHICH HE WAS TAKEN UP, AFTER THAT HE THROUGH THE	177	24
HE WAS TAKEN UP	178	13
WHICH IS TAKEN UP FROM YOU INTO HEAVEN,	178	18
AND HAVE TAKEN NOTHING	196	16
AT THE DRAUGHT OF THE FISHES WHICH THEY HAD TAKEN	196	26
HATH NO TEMPTATION TAKEN YOU BUT SUCH AS IS COMMON TO	201	26
DAY THAT HE WAS TAKEN UP FROM US, MUST CNE BE	234	23
SO DUE CARE MAY BE TAKEN FOR THEIR EXAMINATION,	R 273	18
ARE SPIRITUALLY TAKEN AND RECEIVED BY THE FAITHFUL IN	293	15
AND THE LORD HATH TAKEN AWAY	324	15
TAKEN FROM THE PSALMS	R 324	17
FOLLOW THE LESSON, TAKEN OUT OF THE FIFTEENTH CHAPTER	R 328	18
OR SUCH DEVOTIONS TAKEN FROM OTHER PARTS OF THIS	R 337	04
FOLLOW THE LESSON TAKEN OUT OF THE EIGHTEENTH CHAPTER	R 339	19
CHILD HATH BEEN TAKEN INTO THE SAFE KEEPING OF THINE	340	26
NET WHICH THEY HID PRIVILY IS THEIR FOOT TAKEN	352	23
LET THEM BE TAKEN IN THE CRAFTY WILINESS THAT THEY	353	06
NOR TAKEN REWARD AGAINST THE INNOCENT	357	18
MY SINS HAVE TAKEN SUCH HOLD UPON ME, THAT I AM NOT	391	11
THEY SHALL BE TAKEN IN THEIR PRIDE	411	30
AND WHEN IT HAD TAKEN ROOT, IT FILLED THE LAND	441	20
AND TAKEN COUNSEL AGAINST THY SECRET ONES	444	10
3 THOU HAST TAKEN AWAY ALL THY DISPLEASURE, *	446	12
42 THOU HAST TAKEN AWAY THE EDGE OF HIS SWORD,	452	26
FOR THOU HAST TAKEN ME UP, AND CAST ME DOWN	464	30
AND HEAVINESS HAVE TAKEN HOLD UPON ME	499	25
BE ACCOUNTED OR TAKEN TO BE A LAWFUL BISHOP, PRIEST,	529	20
THE HOLY LESSONS TAKEN OUT OF THE GOSPEL, AND THE	539	26
AND EXHORTATION TAKEN OUT OF THE HOLY SCRIPTURES,	541	02
ARE SPIRITUALLY TAKEN AND RECEIVED BY THE FAITHFUL IN	582	13
CHRIST'S ORDINANCE TAKEN AWAY BY THEIR WICKEDNESS,	608	14
CHRIST IS GIVEN, TAKEN, AND EATEN, IN THE SUPPER,	608	44
OUGHT TO BE TAKEN OF THE WHOLE MULTITUDE OF THE	609	27

TAKEST

	PAGE	LN
THE FATHER, THAT TAKEST AWAY THE SINS OF THE WORLD,	025	28
THOU THAT TAKEST AWAY THE SINS OF THE WORLD, RECEIVE	025	29
THE FATHER, THAT TAKEST AWAY THE SINS OF THE WORLD,	084	08
THOU THAT TAKEST AWAY THE SINS OF THE WORLD, RECEIVE	084	09
LAMB OF GOD, WHO TAKEST AWAY THE SINS OF THE WORLD	318	23
AND TAKEST NO MONEY FOR THEM	395	17
MY LAWS, AND TAKEST MY COVENANT IN THY MOUTH	402	23
WHEN THOU TAKEST AWAY THEIR BREATH, THEY DIE, AND ARE	469	19

TAKETH

	PAGE	LN
THAT TAKETH HIS NAME IN VAIN	068	20
THE DEVIL, AND TAKETH AWAY THE WORD OUT OF THEIR	121	34
THEN THE DEVIL TAKETH HIM UP INTO THE HOLY CITY, AND	126	30
THE DEVIL TAKETH HIM LP INTO AN EXCEEDING HIGH	127	04
OVERCOME HIM, HE TAKETH FROM HIM ALL HIS ARMOUR	130	07
GOETH HE, AND TAKETH TO HIM SEVEN OTHER SPIRITS MORE	130	14
AND HE TAKETH WITH HIM PETER AND JAMES AND JOHN, AND	141	29
HE TAKETH AWAY THE FIRST, THAT HE MAY ESTABLISH THE	157	32
YOUR JOY NO MAN TAKETH FROM YOU	174	15
NOT FRUIT HE TAKETH AWAY	238	06
NOT PERSONS, NOR TAKETH REWARD	263	25
THAT TAKETH HIS NAME IN VAIN	286	20
YOUR JOY NO MAN TAKETH FROM YOU	341	11
THE LORD TAKETH ME UP	372	21
6 HE TAKETH UP THE SIMPLE OUT OF THE DUST, *	484	19
7 THE LORD TAKETH MY PART WITH THEM THAT HELP ME	488	12
SHALL HE BE THAT TAKETH THY CHILDREN, *	513	24
THAT TAKETH HIS NAME IN VAIN	579	03

TAKING

	PAGE	LN
ABOVE ALL, TAKING THE SHIELD OF FAITH, WHEREWITH YE	219	16
HER RIGHT HAND TAKING THE MAN BY HIS RIGHT HAND,	R 302	03
THE MINISTER TAKING THE RING SHALL DELIVER IT UNTO	R 302	10

TALE

	PAGE	LN
AS IT WERE A TALE THAT IS TOLD	325	31
AS IT WERE A TALE THAT IS TOLD	454	05

TALENTS

	PAGE	LN
UNTO HIM, WHICH OWED HIM TEN THOUSAND TALENTS	221	16

TALK

	PAGE	LN
I WILL NOT TALK MUCH WITH YOU	182	07
COUNSEL HOW THEY MIGHT ENTANGLE HIM IN HIS TALK	222	29
2 THEY TALK OF VANITY EVERY ONE WITH HIS NEIGHBOUR	355	09
MY TALK HATH BEEN OF THY TRUTH, AND OF THY SALVATION	391	05
THEIR TALK IS OF CURSING AND LIES	411	31
AND THEY TALK HOW THEY MAY VEX THEM WHOM THOU HAST	423	28
TONGUE ALSO SHALL TALK OF THY RIGHTEOUSNESS ALL THE	426	27
11 BUT I WILL TALK OF THE GOD OF JACOB, *	432	19
15 I WILL TALK OF THY COMMANDMENTS, *	490	27
AND SO SHALL I TALK OF THY WONDROUS WORKS	491	22
AND TALK OF THY POWER	521	14
AS THE PELAGIANS DO VAINLY TALK	604	30

TALKED

	PAGE	LN
AND THEY TALKED TOGETHER OF ALL THESE THINGS WHICH	167	05
WHILE HE TALKED WITH LS BY THE WAY, AND WHILE HE	168	10
BEHOLD, THERE TALKED WITH HIM TWO MEN, WHICH WERE	248	27

TALKED   CONTINUED

	PAGE	LN
MY HEART HATH TALKED OF THEE, SEEK YE MY FACE	326	22
9 MY HEART HATH TALKED OF THEE, SEEK YE MY FACE	372	14
TO DO ME EVIL TALKED OF WICKEDNESS, AND IMAGINED	388	15

TALKETH

	PAGE	LN
8 WHOSE MOUTH TALKETH OF VANITY, *	520	06
WHOSE MOUTH TALKETH OF VANITY, AND THEIR RIGHT HAND	520	13

TALKING

	PAGE	LN
NOR FOOLISH TALKING, NOR JESTING, WHICH ARE NOT	129	05
OF A TRUMPET TALKING WITH ME	187	02
IT SHALL BE TALKING OF THY RIGHTEOUSNESS, *	383	22
TONGUE WILL BE TALKING OF JUDGMENT	386	27
THEIR TALKING IS AGAINST THE MOST HIGH	428	25
AND MY TALKING SHALL BE OF THY DOINGS	434	06
AND LET YOUR TALKING BE OF ALL HIS WONDROUS WORKS	470	08
I WILL BE TALKING OF THY WORSHIP, *	521	02

TARES

	PAGE	LN
CAME AND SOWED TARES AMONG THE WHEAT, AND WENT HIS	116	20
THEN APPEARED THE TARES ALSO	116	22
FROM WHENCE THEN HATH IT TARES	116	24
YE GATHER UP THE TARES, YE ROOT UP ALSO THE WHEAT	116	27
TOGETHER FIRST THE TARES, AND BIND THEM IN BUNDLES TC	116	30

TARRIED

	PAGE	LN
THE CHILD JESUS TARRIED BEHIND IN JERUSALEM	110	22
HATH PATIENTLY TARRIED FOR THE LORD	379	28

TARRIETH

	PAGE	LN
OF THE LORD TARRIETH ROUND ABOUT THEM THAT FEAR HIM,	380	15

TARRY

	PAGE	LN
IF I WILL THAT HE TARRY TILL I COME, WHAT IS THAT TO	102	08
IF I WILL THAT HE TARRY TILL I COME, WHAT IS THAT TO	102	11
TARRY YE HERE, AND WATCH	141	32
AND HE WENT IN TO TARRY WITH THEM	168	05
BUT TARRY YE IN THE CITY OF JERUSALEM, UNTIL YE BE	178	22
PRAYED THEY HIM TO TARRY CERTAIN DAYS	184	30
HE THAT SHALL COME WILL COME, AND WILL NOT TARRY	228	18
O TARRY THOU THE LORD'S LEISURE	326	30
16 O TARRY THOU THE LORD'S LEISURE	372	30
LIES SHALL NOT TARRY IN MY SIGHT	464	03
ARE ORDERED SHALL TARRY, AND RECEIVE THE HOLY	R 534	27

TARRYING

	PAGE	LN
MAKE NO LONG TARRYING, O MY GOD	391	27
O LORD, MAKE NO LONG TARRYING	424	33

TARSHISH

	PAGE	LN
10 THE KINGS OF TARSHISH AND OF THE ISLES SHALL GIVE	427	16

TARSUS

	PAGE	LN
THE HOUSE OF JUDAS FOR ONE CALLED SAUL, OF TARSUS	230	18
BARNABAS TO TARSUS, FOR TO SEEK SAUL	241	10

TASTE

	PAGE	LN
HE SHALL NEVER TASTE OF DEATH	133	21
WERE BIDDEN SHALL TASTE OF MY SUPPER	192	21
8 O TASTE, AND SEE, HOW GRACIOUS THE LORD IS	380	17

TASTED

	PAGE	LN
OF THE FEAST HAD TASTED THE WATER THAT WAS MADE WINE,	113	24
AND WHEN HE HAD TASTED THEREOF, HE WOULD NOT DRINK	136	30
IF SO BE YE HAVE TASTED THAT THE LORD IS GRACICUS	259	28

TAUGHT

	PAGE	LN
WHO HAST TAUGHT US IN THY HOLY WORD THAT THOU	045	31
WHICH CHRIST HATH TAUGHT US, WE MAKE BOLD TO SAY,	048	24
HOLY APOSTLE HAST TAUGHT US TO MAKE PRAYERS, AND	074	07
CHRIST HATH TAUGHT US, WE ARE BOLD TO SAY,	082	02
O LORD, WHO HAST TAUGHT US THAT ALL CUR DOINGS	122	14
HE SAT DOWN, AND TAUGHT THE PEOPLE OUT OF THE SHIP	196	12
AND HE TAUGHT DAILY IN THE TEMPLE	204	19
AND HAVE BEEN TAUGHT BY HIM, AS THE TRUTH IS IN	216	11
BY FOLLOWING THE HOLY DOCTRINE WHICH HE TAUGHT	229	22
THE CHURCH, AND TAUGHT MUCH PEOPLE	241	13
HIS MOUTH, AND TAUGHT THEM, SAYING, BLESSED ARE THE	257	20
THAT OUR LORD TAUGHT US TO PRAY	289	17
CHRIST HATH TAUGHT US, AND SAY,	289	19
RING THERE, AND TAUGHT BY THE MINISTER, SHALL SAY,	R 302	12
WHO ALSO HATH TAUGHT US, BY HIS HOLY APOSTLE SAINT	335	05
BY THEM IS THY SERVANT TAUGHT	364	06
THOU, O GOD, HAST TAUGHT ME FROM MY YOUTH UP UNTIL	426	08
WHEN THOU HAST TAUGHT ME THY STATUTES	501	25
AND HAVE TAUGHT YOU PUBLICKLY, AND FROM HOUSE TO	550	12
WHO HATH TAUGHT US TO PRAY UNTO THEE, O	571	13
WHO HAST TAUGHT US THAT IN RETURNING AND REST	595	19
CANNOT BE TAUGHT WITHOUT ARROGANCY AND IMPIETY	605	25

TAXED

THAT ALL THE WORLD SHOULD BE TAXED   098 30
AND ALL WENT TO BE TAXED, EVERY ONE INTO HIS OWN   098 31
TO BE TAXED WITH MARY HIS ESPOUSED WIFE, BEING GREAT   099 04

TAXING

AND THIS TAXING WAS FIRST MADE WHEN CYRENIUS WAS   098 30

TEACH

BLESS ALL WHO TEACH AND ALL WHO LEARN   042 25
WISDOM THOSE WHO TEACH AND THOSE WHO LEARN, THAT,   043 02
THEN SHALL I TEACH THY WAYS UNTO THE WICKED, *   061 04
THE DISCIPLES, TO TEACH THEM, AND TO LEAD THEM INTO   078 28
BOTH TO DO AND TEACH, UNTIL THE DAY IN WHICH HE WAS   177 23
AT THIS TIME DIDST TEACH THE HEARTS OF THY FAITHFUL   180 08
MY NAME, HE SHALL TEACH YOU ALL THINGS, AND BRING ALL   181 32
THEY SHOULD GO TEACH ALL NATIONS, AND BAPTIZE THEM IN   279 12
LORD JESUS CHRIST TEACH US ABOUT THESE COMMANDMENTS   288 02
AND HE WILL TEACH US OF HIS WAYS, AND WE WILL WALK IN   290 06
SO TEACH US TO NUMBER OUR DAYS, *   326 02
AND TEACH ME THY PATHS   369 24
THEREFORE WILL HE TEACH SINNERS IN THE WAY   369 34
HIM SHALL HE TEACH IN THE WAY THAT HE SHALL CHOOSE   370 09
13 TEACH ME THY WAY, O LORD, *   372 22
INFORM THEE, AND TEACH THEE IN THE WAY WHEREIN THOU   378 08
I WILL TEACH YOU THE FEAR OF THE LORD   380 24
RIGHT HAND SHALL TEACH THEE TERRIBLE THINGS   396 24
13 THEN SHALL I TEACH THY WAYS UNTO THE WICKED,   404 02
OUR FOREFATHERS TO TEACH THEIR CHILDREN   435 05
11 TEACH ME THY WAY, O LORD, AND I WILL WALK IN THY   447 25
12 SO TEACH US TO NUMBER OUR DAYS, *   454 13
AND TEACH HIS SENATORS WISDOM   471 17
O TEACH ME THY STATUTES   490 22
O TEACH ME THY STATUTES   491 20
TEACH ME, O LORD, THE WAY OF THY STATUTES, *   492 05
O TEACH ME THY STATUTES   494 08
66 O TEACH ME TRUE UNDERSTANDING AND KNOWLEDGE   494 14
O TEACH ME THY STATUTES   494 17
AND TEACH ME THY JUDGMENTS   497 14
AND TEACH ME THY STATUTES   498 18
AND TEACH ME THY STATUTES   499 09
THAT I SHALL TEACH THEM   508 30
10 TEACH ME TO DO THE THING THAT PLEASETH THEE   519 12
TO TEACH, AND TO PREMONISH, TO FEED AND PROVIDE FOR   539 33
AND TO TEACH NOTHING, AS NECESSARY TO ETERNAL   542 06
SO THAT YOU MAY TEACH THE PEOPLE COMMITTED TO YOUR   542 15
TEACH US TO KNOW THE FATHER, SON, AND THEE, OF BOTH,   544 10
GIVEN TO HOSPITALITY, APT TO TEACH   549 21
YE THEREFORE, AND TEACH ALL NATIONS, BAPTIZING THEM   552 11
AND TO TEACH OR MAINTAIN NOTHING, AS NECESSARY TO   554 24
BE ABLE BY THEM TO TEACH AND EXHORT WITH WHOLESOME   554 32
TEACH US TO KNOW THE FATHER, SON, AND THEE, OF BOTH,   556 18

TEACHER

THAT THOU ART A TEACHER COME FROM GOD   188 02
THAT THOU ART A TEACHER COME FROM GOD   275 07

TEACHERS

AND SOME, PASTORS AND TEACHERS   237 20
MY GOVERNORS, TEACHERS, SPIRITUAL PASTORS AND   288 29
99 I HAVE MORE UNDERSTANDING THAN MY TEACHERS   496 24
AND SOME, PASTORS AND TEACHERS   538 07
MY GOVERNORS, TEACHERS, SPIRITUAL PASTORS AND   580 05

TEACHES

JESUS CHRIST TEACHES US THAT THEY ARE SUMMED UP IN   288 04

TEACHEST

ART TRUE, AND TEACHEST THE WAY OF GOD IN TRUTH,   222 31
AND TEACHEST HIM IN THY LAW   458 11
FOR THOU TEACHEST ME   496 31

TEACHETH

OR HE THAT TEACHETH, ON TEACHING   111 18
35 HE TEACHETH MINE HANDS TO FIGHT, *   362 04
IT IS HE THAT TEACHETH MAN KNOWLEDGE   458 07
WHO TEACHETH MY HANDS TO WAR, AND MY FINGERS TO   519 22

TEACHING

WHO THROUGH THE TEACHING OF THY SON JESUS CHRIST   043 18
TO ALL MEN, TEACHING US THAT, DENYING UNGODLINESS AND   098 19
OR HE THAT TEACHETH, ON TEACHING   111 19
TEACHING AND ADMONISHING ONE ANOTHER IN PSALMS AND   116 12
IN THE TEMPLE TEACHING, AND YE TOOK ME NOT   142 26
UP THE PEOPLE, TEACHING THROUGHOUT ALL JEWRY,   153 05
TEACHING THEM TO OBSERVE ALL THINGS WHATSOEVER I HAVE   275 30
THE APOSTLES' TEACHING AND FELLOWSHIP   291 05
TEACHING THEM TO OBSERVE ALL THINGS WHATSOEVER I HAVE   552 12
THE PROPHET'S TEACHING, IN JUSTICE, JUDGMENT, AND   611 10

TEAR

LIKE A LION, AND TEAR IT IN PIECES, *   349 25
THY LIGHTNING, AND TEAR THEM   520 02

TEARS

WIPE AWAY ALL TEARS FROM THEIR EYES   257 16
ACCEPT HIS TEARS, ASSUAGE HIS PAIN, AS SHALL SEEM TO   314 07
HOLD NOT THY PEACE AT MY TEARS   325 07
WIPE AWAY ALL TEARS FROM THEIR EYES   341 27
AND WATER MY COUCH WITH MY TEARS   349 11
HOLD NOT THY PEACE AT MY TEARS   390 03
3 MY TEARS HAVE BEEN MY MEAT DAY AND NIGHT, *   393 04
PUT MY TEARS INTO THY BOTTLE   408 30
WITH THE BREAD OF TEARS, *   441 12
PLENTEOUSNESS OF TEARS TO DRINK   441 13
MINE EYES FROM TEARS, AND MY FEET FROM FALLING   487 05
6 THEY THAT SOW IN TEARS *   505 17
AND WITH MANY TEARS, AND TEMPTATIONS, WHICH BEFELL ME   550 09
NOT TO WARN EVERY ONE NIGHT AND DAY WITH TEARS   551 02
WIPE AWAY ALL TEARS FROM THEIR EYES   567 18

TEETH

THERE SHALL BE WEEPING AND GNASHING OF TEETH   115 22
CRUCIFIED WITH HIM, CAST THE SAME IN HIS TEETH   137 15
THERE SHALL BE WEEPING AND GNASHING OF TEETH   218 28
HAST BROKEN THE TEETH OF THE UNGODLY   347 06
WHO GNASHED UPON ME WITH THEIR TEETH   382 28
AND GNASHETH UPON HIM WITH HIS TEETH   385 19
MINE ENEMIES THAT TROUBLE ME CAST ME IN THE TEETH   393 28
WHOSE TEETH ARE SPEARS AND ARROWS, AND THEIR TONGUE A   409 22
6 BREAK THEIR TEETH, O GOD, IN THEIR MOUTHS   410 19
GNASH WITH HIS TEETH, AND CONSUME AWAY   484 05
NOT GIVEN US OVER FOR A PREY UNTO THEIR TEETH   504 17
PRESS WITH THEIR TEETH (AS SAINT AUGUSTINE SAITH) THE   609 05

TELL

TO TELL OF THY LOVING-KINDNESS EARLY IN THE MORNING,   027 30
SAYING, TELL YE THE DAUGHTER OF SION,   091 19
UNTO HIM, SEE THOU TELL NO MAN   115 04
TELL ME, YE THAT DESIRE TO BE UNDER THE LAW, DO YE   130 29
AND HE SAID, I TELL THEE, PETER, THE COCK SHALL NOT   150 02
TELL US   151 30
UNTO THEM, IF I TELL YOU, YE WILL NOT BELIEVE   151 31
BUT GO YOUR WAY, TELL HIS DISCIPLES AND PETER THAT HE   165 31
WE CANNOT TELL WHAT HE SAITH   174 03
NEVERTHELESS I TELL YOU THE TRUTH   175 09
BUT CANST NOT TELL WHENCE IT COMETH, AND WHITHER IT   188 15
YE BELIEVE, IF I TELL YOU OF HEAVENLY THINGS   188 23
I TELL YOU, THIS MAN WENT DOWN TO HIS HOUSE JUSTIFIED   205 31
THAT THEY SHOULD TELL NO MAN   207 05
FOR I TELL YOU, THAT MANY PROPHETS AND KINGS HAVE   208 08
OF THE WHICH I TOLD YOU BEFORE, AS I HAVE ALSO TOLD   209 23
SAYING, TELL THEM WHICH ARE BIDDEN,   218 07
YOU OFTEN, AND NOW TELL YOU EVEN WEEPING, THAT THEY   222 18
TELL US THEREFORE, WHAT THINKEST THOU   223 03
BUT CANST NOT TELL WHENCE IT COMETH, AND WHITHER IT   275 20
TELL ME HOW MANY COMMANDMENTS THERE ARE   285 15
AND CANNOT TELL WHO SHALL GATHER THEM   324 26
12 WHO CAN TELL HOW OFT HE OFFENDETH   364 08
I MAY TELL ALL MY BONES   367 06
AND TELL OF ALL THY WONDROUS WORKS   371 10
AND CANNOT TELL WHO SHALL GATHER THEM   389 21
AND TELL THE TOWERS THEREOF   399 33
THAT YE MAY TELL THEM THAT COME AFTER   400 03
I WILL NOT TELL THEE   402 14
AND I WILL TELL YOU WHAT HE HATH DONE FOR MY SOUL   418 13
THEREFORE WILL I TELL OF THY WONDROUS WORKS   426 09
2 TO TELL OF THY LOVING-KINDNESS EARLY IN THE   456 02
10 TELL IT OUT AMONG THE HEATHEN, THAT THE LORD IS   460 18
TELL THE PEOPLE WHAT THINGS HE HATH DONE   470 06
AND TELL OUT HIS WORKS WITH GLADNESS   477 21
18 IF I TELL THEM, THEY ARE MORE IN NUMBER THAN THE   515 26
AND I WILL ALSO TELL OF THY GREATNESS   521 05
TELL ME HOW MANY THERE ARE   578 18

TELLEST

8 THOU TELLEST MY WANDERINGS   408 30

TELLETH

2 ONE DAY TELLETH ANOTHER   363 15
COMETH FORTH, HE TELLETH IT   392 12
HE THAT TELLETH LIES SHALL NOT TARRY IN MY SIGHT   464 03
4 HE TELLETH THE NUMBER OF THE STARS, *   523 02

TELLING

BE TELLING OF HIS SALVATION FROM DAY TO DAY   460 02
LIPS HAVE I BEEN TELLING *   490 23

TEMPER

IS AMISS IN THE TEMPER AND DISPOSITION OF OUR SOULS   590 12

TEMPERANCE

MEEKNESS, TEMPERANCE   209 27
MY BODY IN TEMPERANCE, SOBERNESS, AND CHASTITY   289 02
MY BODY IN TEMPERANCE, SOBERNESS, AND CHASTITY   580 11
TEMPERANCE, PATIENCE, GODLINESS   598 24

TEMPERATE

THE MASTERY IS TEMPERATE IN ALL THINGS   119 07
KEEP US TEMPERATE IN ALL THINGS, AND DILIGENT IN OUR   588 28

TEMPEST

AND THE DEVIL, FROM LIGHTNING AND TEMPEST	054 30
SHAKE AT THE TEMPEST OF THE SAME	327 08
FIRE AND BRIMSTONE, STORM AND TEMPEST	354 34
SHAKE AT THE TEMPEST OF THE SAME	397 31
AND A MIGHTY TEMPEST SHALL BE STIRRED UP RCUND ABCUT	401 27
BECAUSE OF THE STORMY WIND AND TEMPEST	407 03
EVEN SO WITH THY TEMPEST, *	445 02

TEMPLE

THE LORD IS IN HIS HOLY TEMPLE	003 15
ART THOU IN THE TEMPLE OF THY HOLINESS	011 20
THE LORD IS IN HIS HOLY TEMPLE	021 12
WENT INTO THE TEMPLE OF GOD, AND CAST OUT ALL THEM	091 33
AND BOUGHT IN THE TEMPLE, AND OVERTHREW THE TABLES OF	091 34
SLEW BETWEEN THE TEMPLE AND THE ALTAR	100 25
FOUND HIM IN THE TEMPLE, SITTING IN THE MIDST OF THE	110 28
A PINNACLE OF THE TEMPLE, AND SAITH UNTO HIM, IF THOU	126 32
BUT JESUS HID HIMSELF, AND WENT OUT OF THE TEMPLE	133 34
OF SILVER IN THE TEMPLE, AND DEPARTED, AND WENT AND	135 07
DESTROYEST THE TEMPLE, AND BUILDEST IT IN THREE DAYS,	137 07
THE VEIL OF THE TEMPLE WAS RENT IN TWAIN FROM THE TOP	137 26
WITH YOU IN THE TEMPLE TEACHING, AND YE TOOK ME NCT	142 26
WILL DESTROY THIS TEMPLE THAT IS MADE WITH HANDS,	143 07
DESTROYEST THE TEMPLE, AND BUILDEST IT IN THREE DAYS,	146 19
THE VEIL OF THE TEMPLE WAS RENT IN TWAIN FROM THE TOP	146 35
CAPTAINS OF THE TEMPLE, AND THE ELDERS, WHICH WERE	151 02
WITH YOU IN THE TEMPLE, YE STRETCHED FORTH NO HANDS	151 04
THE VEIL OF THE TEMPLE WAS RENT IN THE MIDST	155 11
IN THE TEMPLE, PRAISING AND BLESSING GOD	178 28
HE WENT INTO THE TEMPLE, AND BEGAN TO CAST OUT THEM	204 15
AND HE TAUGHT DAILY IN THE TEMPLE	204 19
WENT UP INTO THE TEMPLE TO PRAY	205 23
PRESENTED IN THE TEMPLE IN SUBSTANCE OF OUR FLESH,	231 30
COME TO HIS TEMPLE, EVEN THE MESSENGER OF THE	232 05
AND HE CAME BY THE SPIRIT INTO THE TEMPLE	233 02
NOT FROM THE TEMPLE, BUT SERVED GOD WITH FASTINGS AND	233 20
BE MADE AN HOLY TEMPLE ACCEPTABLE UNTO THEE	254 31
UNTO AN HOLY TEMPLE IN THE LORD	255 08
AND SERVE HIM DAY AND NIGHT IN HIS TEMPLE	257 10
WENT INTO THE TEMPLE OF GOD, AND CAST OUT ALL THEM	260 03
AND BOUGHT IN THE TEMPLE, AND OVERTHREW THE TABLES OF	260 04
THE BLIND AND THE LAME CAME TO HIM IN THE TEMPLE	260 09
CRYING IN THE TEMPLE, AND SAYING, HOSANNA TO THE SON	260 11
BE MADE AN HOLY TEMPLE ACCEPTABLE UNTO THEE	290 23
TOWARD THY HOLY TEMPLE, AND PRAISE THY NAME, BECAUSE	311 30
FAIR BEAUTY OF THE LORD, AND TC VISIT HIS TEMPLE	326 11
OF GOD, AND SERVE HIM DAY AND NIGHT IN HIS TEMPLE	341 21
IN THY FEAR WILL I WORSHIP TOWARD THY HCLY TEMPLE	348 15
4 THE LORD IS IN HIS HOLY TEMPLE	354 26
OUT OF HIS HOLY TEMPLE, *	360 06
FAIR BEAUTY OF THE LORD, AND TO VISIT HIS TEMPLE	372 03
HANDS TOWARDS THE MERCY—SEAT OF THY HOLY TEMPLE	373 09
IN HIS TEMPLE DOTH EVERY THING SPEAK OF HIS HONCUR	374 15
IN THE MIDST OF THY TEMPLE	399 28
PLEASURES OF THY HOUSE, EVEN OF THY HOLY TEMPLE	416 20
HE BUILT HIS TEMPLE ON HIGH, *	439 16
THY HOLY TEMPLE HAVE THEY DEFILED, AND MADE JERUSALEM	439 30
A PLACE FOR THE TEMPLE OF THE LORD	508 13
TOWARD THY HOLY TEMPLE, AND PRAISE THY NAME, BECAUSE	513 30
MAY BE AS THE POLISHED CORNERS OF THE TEMPLE	520 17
AND FOUND IN THE TEMPLE THOSE THAT SOLD OXEN ANC	567 26
ALL OUT OF THE TEMPLE, AND THE SHEEP, AND THE OXEN	567 29
MAY BE AN HOLY TEMPLE ACCEPTABLE UNTO THEE	574 08

TEMPLE'S

29 FOR THY TEMPLE'S SAKE AT JERUSALEM	421 13

TEMPLES

NEITHER THE TEMPLES OF MY HEAD TO TAKE ANY REST	508 11
THE WALLS OF TEMPLES MADE WITH HANDS	564 29

TEMPORAL

HIS GOOD GIFTS, TEMPORAL AND SPIRITUAL, TO US AND TO	048 13
THROUGH THINGS TEMPORAL, THAT WE FINALLY LCSE NCT THE	194 07
OF THEIR TEMPORAL GOODS, AND, WHEN OF ABILITY, TC	R 320 22
HAPPINESS BOTH TEMPORAL AND SPIRITUAL	565 13
THY BLESSINGS, TEMPORAL AND SPIRITUAL, UPON ALL CUR	590 30
AS WELL CLERGY AS LAITY, IN ALL THINGS TEMPORAL	610 39

TEMPORALITIES

ACCUSTOMED TEMPORALITIES APPERTAINING TO YOUR CURE,	569 30

TEMPT

THOU SHALT NOT TEMPT THE LORD THY GOD	127 04
NEITHER LET US TEMPT CHRIST, AS SOME OF THEM ALSO	201 19
AND SAID, WHY TEMPT YE ME, YE HYPOCRITES	223 05
NEITHER WILL I TEMPT THE LORD	235 28

TEMPTATION

US NOT INTO TEMPTATION, BUT DELIVER US FROM EVIL	007 27
MAY RESIST TEMPTATION AND OVERCOME EVIL, AND MAY	043 12
WHO, THROUGH TEMPTATION, IGNORANCE, HELPLESSNESS,	048 08
AND TEMPTATION,	055 08
IN TIME OF TEMPTATION FALL AWAY	122 04
LEST YE ENTER INTO TEMPTATION	142 06
PRAY THAT YE ENTER NOT INTO TEMPTATION	150 16
LEST YE ENTER INTO TEMPTATION	150 26

TEMPTATION   CONTINUED

THERE HATH NO TEMPTATION TAKEN YOU BUT SUCH AS IS	201 26
WILL WITH THE TEMPTATION ALSO MAKE A WAY TO ESCAPE,	201 28
BLESSED IS THE MAN THAT ENDURETH TEMPTATION	239 25
IN THE DAY OF TEMPTATION IN THE WILDERNESS	459 20

TEMPTATIONS

HIM FROM THE TEMPTATIONS OF THE ENEMY	045 17
ALL CANGERS, AND CARRY US THROUGH ALL TEMPTATIONS	114 08
WHICH HAVE CONTINUED WITH ME IN MY TEMPTATICNS	149 27
THE TEMPTATIONS OF THE WORLD, THE FLESH, AND THE	214 24
IT ALL JOY WHEN YE FALL INTO DIVERS TEMPTATIONS	239 09
WHICH HAVE CONTINUED WITH ME IN MY TEMPTATIONS	250 12
AND TEMPTATIONS, WHICH BEFELL ME BY THE LYING	550 09
THE MANIFOLD TEMPTATIONS WHICH WE DAILY MEET WITH	588 13
OR THE TEMPTATIONS WHICH ENCOMPASS US, WE BE DRAWN	590 09

TEMPTED

WILDERNESS TO BE TEMPTED OF THE DEVIL	126 24
OF THEM ALSO TEMPTED, AND WERE DESTROYED OF SERPENTS	201 19
SUFFER YOU TO BE TEMPTED ABOVE THAT YE ARE ABLE	201 27
STOOD UP, AND TEMPTED HIM, SAYING, MASTER, WHAT SHALL	208 12
19 THEY TEMPTED GOD IN THEIR HEARTS, *	436 04
TURNED BACK, AND TEMPTED GOD, *	437 23
57 YET THEY TEMPTED AND DISPLEASED THE MOST HIGH GOD,	438 24
YOUR FATHERS TEMPTED ME, *	459 22
AND THEY TEMPTED GOD IN THE DESERT	473 30

TEMPTER

AND WHEN THE TEMPTER CAME TO HIM, HE SAID, IF THCU BE	126 26

TEMPTETH

WHOSE PENURY TEMPTETH THEM TO SIN	599 13

TEMPTING

AND OTHERS, TEMPTING HIM, SOUGHT OF HIM A SIGN FROM	129 28
HIM A QUESTION, TEMPTING HIM, AND SAYING, MASTER,	215 09

TEN

AN INSTRUMENT OF TEN STRINGS, AND UPON THE LUTE	027 32
DISTINCTLY THE TEN COMMANDMENTS	R 067 22
IN REHEARSING THE TEN COMMANDMENTS, THE PRIEST MAY	R 067 26
WHAT WOMAN HAVING TEN PIECES OF SILVER, IF SHE LCSE	193 28
THERE MET HIM TEN MEN THAT WERE LEPERS, WHICH STCOD	210 02
WERE THERE NOT TEN CLEANSED	210 11
WHICH OWED HIM TEN THOUSAND TALENTS	221 16
AND WHEN THE TEN HEARD IT, THEY WERE MOVED WITH	247 18
AND THE TEN COMMANDMENTS, AND ALL OTHER	277 10
THERE ARE TEN COMMANDMENTS, GIVEN IN OLD TIME	285 16
MINISTER REPEAT THE TEN COMMANDMENTS, AND AFTER EVERY	R 285 33
LEARN FROM THE TEN COMMANDMENTS	288 10
AND THE TEN COMMANDMENTS, AND ARE	R 295 14
THE DAYS OF OUR AGE ARE THREESCORE YEARS AND TEN	325 32
NOT BE AFRAID FOR TEN THOUSANDS OF THE PEOPLE,	347 02
AND INSTRUMENT OF TEN STRINGS	378 22
THE DAYS OF OUR AGE ARE THREESCORE YEARS AND TEN	454 07
BESIDE THEE, AND TEN THOUSAND AT THY RIGHT HAND	455 09
AN INSTRUMENT OF TEN STRINGS, AND UPON THE LUTE	456 04
FORTH THOUSANDS, AND TEN THOUSANDS IN OUR FIELDS	520 20
TEN	578 20
AND THE TEN COMMANDMENTS, AND CAN ANSWER TO	R 583 02

TEN-STRINGED

THEE UPON A TEN—STRINGED LUTE	520 09

TEND

MIGHT MOST TEND TO THE PRESERVATICN OF PEACE AND	V 35
AND ADVICE, AS MAY TEND TO THE QUIETING OF HIS	088 08
SUCH SUCCESS AS MAY TEND MOST TO THY GLORY, AND THE	565 12

TENDER

THROUGH THE TENDER MERCY OF OUR GOD	014 29
THAT THOU, OF THY TENDER MERCY, DIDST GIVE THINE CNLY	080 07
WHO, OF THY TENDER LOVE TOWARDS MANKIND, HAST	134 05
YOU ALL IN THE TENDER MERCIES OF CHRIST JESUS	220 32
THROUGH THE TENDER MERCY OF OUR GOD	244 13
REASON OF THEIR TENDER AGE THEY CANNOT PERFCRM THEM	292 32
O LORD, THY TENDER MERCIES, *	369 28
TRUST IS IN THE TENDER MERCY OF GOD FOR EVER AND	405 05
REASON OF THEIR TENDER AGE THEY CANNOT PERFORM THEM	581 32

TENDER-HEARTED

TENDER—HEARTED, FORGIVING ONE ANOTHER, EVEN	216 29

TENDS

THAT WHATSOEVER TENDS TO THE ADVANCEMENT OF TRUE	047 35

TENT

EVEN THE TENT THAT HE HAD PITCHED AMONG MEN	438 33

TENTH

SAINT MARK, IN THE TENTH CHAPTER, AT THE THIRTEENTH	274 24

TENTS

AND NO MAN TO DWELL IN THEIR TENTS	423 26
FALL AMONG THEIR TENTS, *	436 27
MADE THE TRIBES OF ISRAEL TO DWELL IN THEIR TENTS	438 23
TO DWELL IN THE TENTS OF UNGODLINESS	445 33
MOSES ALSO IN THE TENTS, *	473 33
MURMURED IN THEIR TENTS, *	474 19
AMONG THE TENTS OF KEDAR	502 15

TERRESTRIAL

ARE ALSO CELESTIAL BODIES, AND BODIES TERRESTRIAL	329 14
GLORY OF THE TERRESTRIAL IS ANOTHER	329 15

TERRIBLE

A MIGHTY, AND A TERRIBLE, WHICH REGARDETH NCT	263 24
THESE GREAT AND TERRIBLE THINGS, WHICH THINE EYES	263 32
TEACH THEE TERRIBLE THINGS	396 24

TERRIFIED

BUT THEY WERE TERRIFIED AND AFFRIGHTED, AND SUPPCSED	169 29

TERROR

RULERS ARE NOT A TERROR TO GOOD WORKS, BUT TO THE	114 16
AFRAID OF THEIR TERROR, NEITHER BE TROUBLED	196 03
BE AFRAID FOR ANY TERROR BY NIGHT, *	455 05

TERRORS

MY YOUTH UP, THY TERRORS HAVE I SUFFERED WITH A	449 27

TESTAMENT

OUT OF THE NEW TESTAMENT, ACCORDING TO THE TABLE OR	R 014 03
OF THE NEW TESTAMENT, AS IT IS APPOINTED	R 028 05
OF THE NEW TESTAMENT, WHICH IS SHED FOR YOU, AND FOR	080 26
OF THE NEW TESTAMENT, THAT BY MEANS OF DEATH, FOR THE	133 04
THE FIRST TESTAMENT, THEY WHICH ARE CALLED MIGHT	133 06
OF THE NEW TESTAMENT, WHICH IS SHED FOR MANY	141 14
WHERE A TESTAMENT IS, THERE MUST ALSO OF NECESSITY BE	147 14
FOR A TESTAMENT IS OF FORCE AFTER MEN ARE DEAD	147 15
THE FIRST TESTAMENT WAS DEDICATED WITHOUT BLOOD	147 18
BLOOD OF THE TESTAMENT WHICH GOD HATH ENJOINED UNTO	147 23
CUP IS THE NEW TESTAMENT IN MY BLOOD, WHICH IS SHED	149 12
CUP IS THE NEW TESTAMENT IN MY BLOOD	152 22
HATH MADE US ABLE MINISTERS OF THE NEW TESTAMENT	206 16
AND TO ISRAEL FOR AN EVERLASTING TESTAMENT	470 23
THEM THE NEW TESTAMENT, SAYING,	R 534 09
OR PART OF A CHAPTER, FROM THE NEW TESTAMENT	R 592 06
OLD AND NEW TESTAMENT, OF WHOSE AUTHORITY WAS NEVER	603 33
OF THE NEW TESTAMENT, AS THEY ARE COMMONLY RECEIVED,	604 12
THE OLD TESTAMENT IS NOT CCNTRARY TO THE NEW	604 15
OLD AND NEW TESTAMENT EVERLASTING LIFE IS OFFERED TO	604 16

TESTATOR

ALSO OF NECESSITY BE THE DEATH OF THE TESTATOR	147 15
ALL WHILE THE TESTATOR LIVETH	147 17

TESTIFIED

AS WE ALSO HAVE FOREWARNED YOU AND TESTIFIED	128 02
WHICH HE HATH TESTIFIED OF HIS SON	171 06

TESTIFIETH

WHICH TESTIFIETH OF THESE THINGS, AND WROTE THESE	102 13

TESTIFY

AND TO TESTIFY THAT IT IS HE WHICH WAS	166 29
HE SHALL TESTIFY OF ME	179 26
AND TO TESTIFY THAT IT IS HE WHICH WAS	184 16
WE DO KNOW, AND TESTIFY THAT WE HAVE SEEN	188 21
HAVE SEEN AND DO TESTIFY THAT THE FATHER SENT THE SON	189 20
THAT HE MAY TESTIFY UNTO THEM, LEST THEY ALSO COME	190 24
AND TESTIFY IN THE LORD, THAT YE	216 03
HE SHALL TESTIFY OF ME	255 32
I MYSELF WILL TESTIFY AGAINST THEE, O ISRAEL	402 05
TO TESTIFY UNTO ISRAEL, TO GIVE THANKS UNTO THE NAME	503 14
LORD JESUS, TO TESTIFY THE GOSPEL OF THE GRACE CF	550 21

TESTIFYING

TO HOUSE, TESTIFYING BOTH TO THE JEWS, AND ALSO TO	550 12

TESTIMONIALS

DEMAND TESTIMONIALS OF THE PERSON PRESENTED FOR	R 552 24

TESTIMONIES

SUCH AS KEEP HIS COVENANT AND HIS TESTIMONIES	370 05
AND KEPT NOT HIS TESTIMONIES	438 25
6 THY TESTIMONIES, O LORD, ARE VERY SURE	457 16
KEPT HIS TESTIMONIES, AND THE LAW THAT HE GAVE THEM	462 31
KEEP HIS TESTIMONIES, *	490 02
WAY OF THY TESTIMONIES, *	490 25
FOR I HAVE KEPT THY TESTIMONIES	491 11
24 FOR THY TESTIMONIES ARE MY DELIGHT, *	491 14
31 I HAVE STUCK UNTO THY TESTIMONIES	491 29
UNTO THY TESTIMONIES, *	492 11

TESTIMONIES   CONTINUED

SPEAK OF THY TESTIMONIES ALSO, EVEN BEFORE KINGS, *	492 30
AND TURNED MY FEET UNTO THY TESTIMONIES	493 30
KNOWN THY TESTIMONIES, *	495 14
I KEEP THE TESTIMONIES OF THY MOUTH	495 34
BUT I WILL CONSIDER THY TESTIMONIES	496 16
FOR THY TESTIMONIES ARE MY STUDY	496 25
111 THY TESTIMONIES HAVE I CLAIMED AS MINE HERITAGE	497 19
THEREFORE I LOVE THY TESTIMONIES	498 07
THAT I MAY KNOW THY TESTIMONIES	498 20
THY TESTIMONIES ARE WONDERFUL	498 28
138 THE TESTIMONIES THAT THOU HAST COMMANDED *	499 15
OF THY TESTIMONIES IS EVERLASTING	499 27
HELP ME, AND I SHALL KEEP THY TESTIMONIES	500 03
THY TESTIMONIES, I HAVE KNOWN LONG SINCE, *	500 14
YET DO I NOT SWERVE FROM THY TESTIMONIES	500 26
KEPT THY TESTIMONIES, *	501 15
168 I HAVE KEPT THY COMMANDMENTS AND TESTIMONIES	501 17
AND MY TESTIMONIES THAT I SHALL TEACH THEM	508 29

TESTIMONY

EARTH FOR THE TESTIMONY OF THY TRUTH, WE MAY	099 27
KNOW THAT HIS TESTIMONY IS TRUE	102 14
FOR A TESTIMONY UNTO THEM	115 05
EVEN AS THE TESTIMONY OF CHRIST WAS CONFIRMED IN YOU	214 31
OF THE LAMB, AND BY THE WORD OF THEIR TESTIMCNY	252 15
HAVING THE TESTIMONY OF A GOOD CCNSCIENCE	317 03
THE TESTIMONY OF THE LORD IS SURE, AND GIVETH WISDOM	363 28
JOSEPH FOR A TESTIMONY, *	442 20
BY SUFFICIENT TESTIMONY, ANY PERSON TO BE A MAN CF	529 26
ALWAYS THE TESTIMONY OF A GOOD CONSCIENCE, AND	535 06

THANK

WE MOST HEARTILY THANK THEE, FOR THAT THOU DOST	083 17
GOD, I THANK THEE, THAT I AM NOT AS OTHER	205 25
I THANK MY GOD ALWAYS ON YOUR BEHALF, FOR THE GRACE	214 28
I THANK MY GOD UPON EVERY REMEMBRANCE OF YOU,	220 22
AND SAID, I THANK THEE, O FATHER, LORD OF HEAVEN AND	235 03
AND I HEARTILY THANK OUR HEAVENLY FATHER, THAT HE	284 02
8 I WILL THANK THE LORD FOR GIVING ME WARNING	358 04
FOR I WILL YET THANK HIM, WHICH IS THE HELP OF MY	393 13
FOR I WILL YET THANK HIM, WHICH IS THE HELP OF MY	393 33
12 I WILL THANK THEE, O LORD MY GOD, WITH ALL MY	447 28
21 I WILL THANK THEE	489 10
MY GOD, AND I WILL THANK THEE	489 25
7 I WILL THANK THEE WITH AN UNFEIGNED HEART, *	490 12
3 O THANK THE LORD OF ALL LORDS	511 20
AND I HEARTILY THANK OUR HEAVENLY FATHER, THAT HE	577 23
WE THANK THEE FOR THE TIMELY BLESSINGS OF THE DAY,	595 06

THANKFUL

BE THANKFUL UNTO HIM, AND SPEAK GOOD OF HIS NAME	015 11
THAT OUR HEARTS MAY BE UNFEIGNEDLY THANKFUL	019 26
THAT OUR HEARTS MAY BE UNFEIGNEDLY THANKFUL	033 24
CHRIST'S BLOOD WAS SHED FOR THEE, AND BE THANKFUL	083 06
AND BE YE THANKFUL	116 10
A JOYFUL AND PLEASANT THING IT IS TO BE THANKFUL	264 20
WITH A THANKFUL REMEMBRANCE OF HIS DEATH	293 29
FOR IT BECOMETH WELL THE JUST TO BE THANKFUL	378 20
BE THANKFUL UNTO HIM, AND SPEAK GOOD OF HIS NAME	463 12
A JOYFUL AND PLEASANT THING IT IS TO BE THANKFUL	522 29
DUTIFUL AND THANKFUL UNTO THAT LORD, WHO HATH PLACED	540 27
SHOW OURSELVES THANKFUL UNTO THEE FOR THESE AND ALL	545 29
WITH A THANKFUL REMEMBRANCE OF HIS DEATH	582 25

THANKFULLY

THAT WE MAY THANKFULLY RECEIVE THE SAME IN	152 09
ALWAYS MOST THANKFULLY RECEIVE THAT HIS INESTIMABLE	171 31

THANKFULNESS

HEARTS WITH THANKFULNESS, AND IN THE DAY OF TROUBLE,	036 22
EXPRESS HIS THANKFULNESS BY A HOLY TRUST IN THEE,	053 26
FORTH OUR THANKFULNESS UNTO THEE FOR THE SAME,	229 21
FORTH THEIR THANKFULNESS, BY MAKING A RIGHT USE CF	566 32
TO SHOW OUR THANKFULNESS IN A SINCERE OBEDIENCE TC	591 21

THANKS

TO RENDER THANKS FOR THE GREAT BENEFITS THAT WE HAVE	006 05
HUMBLE AND HEARTY THANKS FOR ALL THY GOODNESS ANC	019 16
DESIRE TO RETURN THANKS FOR MERCIES VOUCHSAFED TC	R 019 33
THANKS BE TO GOD, WHICH GIVETH US THE	022 17
TO RENDER THANKS FOR THE GREAT BENEFITS THAT WE HAVE	023 14
WE GIVE THANKS TO THEE FOR THY GREAT GLORY, O	025 24
REJOICE, AND GIVE THANKS	027 14
THING TO GIVE THANKS UNTO THE LORD, *	027 28
HUMBLE AND HEARTY THANKS FOR ALL THY GOODNESS ANC	033 14
DESIRE TO RETURN THANKS FOR MERCIES VOUCHSAFED TC	R 033 31
GIVE THEE HUMBLE THANKS FOR OPENING HEATHEN LANDS TO	038 16
NEEDY MAY GIVE THANKS UNTO THY NAME	040 12
WE GIVE THEE THANKS FOR ALL THOSE THY SERVANTS WHO	042 15
PRAISE AND HEARTY THANKS FOR THE WONDERFUL GRACE AND	048 16
THEE UNFEIGNED THANKS AND PRAISE FOR THE RETURN OF	050 21
DESIRED TO RETURN THANKS TO ALMIGHTY GOD FOR HER SAFE	R 051 04
GIVE THEE HUMBLE THANKS FOR THAT THOU HAST BEEN	051 05
GIVE THEE HUMBLE THANKS THAT IT HATH PLEASED THEE TO	051 18
GIVE THEE HUMBLE THANKS FOR THIS THY SPECIAL BOUNTY	052 02
TO RETURN THANKS UNTO THEE, IN THE PRESENCE OF ALL	053 02
GIVE THEE HUMBLE THANKS FOR THAT THOU HAST BEEN	053 11
TO RETURN HIS THANKS UNTO THEE IN THY HOLY CHURCH	053 24

THANKS   CONTINUED

MAY EVERMORE GIVE THANKS UNTO THEE IN THY HOLY	058 23
AND TO GIVE THANKS FOR ALL MEN	074 08
LET US GIVE THANKS UNTO OUR LORD GOD	076 28
ALL PLACES, GIVE THANKS UNTO THEE, O LORD, HOLY	076 32
WHEN HE HAD GIVEN THANKS, (B) HE BRAKE IT, AND GAVE	080 19
WHEN HE HAD GIVEN THANKS, HE GAVE IT TO THEM, SAYING,	080 24
THEE MOST HEARTY THANKS FOR THE INNUMERABLE BENEFITS	081 04
WE GIVE THANKS TO THEE FOR THY GREAT GLORY, O	084 04
HUMBLE AND HEARTY THANKS TO GOD, THE FATHER, THE SON,	086 05
AS WE ARE MOST BOUNDEN, CONTINUAL THANKS	086 20
HUMBLE AND HEARTY THANKS TO ALMIGHTY GOD, OUR	086 35
GIVING THANKS TO GOD AND THE FATHER BY HIM	116 15
BUT RATHER GIVING OF THANKS	129 06
WHEN HE HAD GIVEN THANKS, HE DISTRIBUTED TO THE	132 04
WHEN HE HAD GIVEN THANKS, HE GAVE IT TO THEM	141 12
THE CUP, AND GAVE THANKS, AND SAID, TAKE THIS, AND	149 05
AND GAVE THANKS, AND BRAKE IT, AND GAVE UNTO	149 09
WHEN HE HAD GIVEN THANKS, HE BRAKE IT, AND SAID,	152 18
AND HONOUR AND THANKS TO HIM THAT SAT ON THE THRONE,	187 25
AND GAVE THANKS, AND BRAKE, AND GAVE TO HIS	199 19
DOWN ON HIS FACE AT HIS FEET, GIVING HIM THANKS	210 10
GIVING THANKS ALWAYS FOR ALL THINGS UNTO GOD AND THE	217 30
WE GIVE THANKS TO GOD AND THE FATHER OF OUR LORD	223 22
GIVING THANKS UNTO THE FATHER, WHICH HATH MADE US	224 08
WHEN HE HAD GIVEN THANKS, HE DISTRIBUTED TO THE	226 03
THAT INSTANT GAVE THANKS LIKEWISE UNTO THE LORD,	233 22
MAY EVERMORE GIVE THANKS UNTO THEE IN THY HOLY	261 32
HUMBLE AND HEARTY THANKS FOR THIS THY BOUNTY	265 13
GIVE THANKS ALWAYS FOR ALL THINGS UNTO GOD AND THE	267 11
AND DEVOUTLY GIVE THANKS UNTO HIM, AND SAY,	276 06
GIVE THEE HUMBLE THANKS, THAT THOU HAST VOUCHSAFED TO	276 08
LET US GIVE THANKS UNTO OUR LORD GOD	279 04
WE SHOULD GIVE THANKS UNTO THEE, O LORD, HOLY FATHER,	279 08
LET US GIVE THANKS UNTO ALMIGHTY GOD FOR THESE	280 15
YIELD THEE HEARTY THANKS, MOST MERCIFUL FATHER,	280 28
YIELD THEE HEARTY THANKS, ETC	R 281 24
TO WORSHIP HIM, TO GIVE HIM THANKS	288 19
GIVE HEARTY THANKS UNTO GOD, AND SAY, THEN SHALL BE	305 14
GIVE THEE HUMBLE THANKS FOR THAT THOU HAST BEEN	306 24
TO GIVE HER THANKS, MUST OFFER ACCUSTOMED OFFERINGS,	R 307 07
THAT HE MAY GIVE THANKS UNTO THEE IN THY HOLY CHURCH	309 31
HARP WILL I GIVE THANKS UNTO THEE, O GOD, MY GOD	310 15
WILL YET GIVE HIM THANKS, WHICH IS THE HELP OF MY	310 18
I WILL GIVE THANKS UNTO THEE, O LORD, WITH MY WHOLE	311 28
THEE CONTINUAL THANKS FOR THY SUSTAINING PROVIDENCE	316 22
GIVING HIM HEARTY THANKS THEREFOR, HE DOTH EAT AND	R 323 29
BUT THANKS BE TO GOD, WHICH GIVETH US THE VICTORY	330 12
GIVE THEE HEARTY THANKS FOR THE GOOD EXAMPLES OF ALL	334 23
PRAISE AND HEARTY THANKS, FOR THE WONDERFUL GRACE AND	336 17
EVER BE GIVING OF THANKS, BECAUSE THOU DEFENDEST	348 26
WILL GIVE THEE THANKS IN THE PIT	349 09
18 I WILL GIVE THANKS UNTO THE LORD, ACCORDING TO HIS	350 27
I WILL GIVE THANKS UNTO THEE, O LORD, WITH MY WHOLE	351 22
CAUSE WILL I GIVE THANKS UNTO THEE, O LORD, AMONG THE	363 05
AND GIVE THANKS UNTO HIM, FOR A REMEMBRANCE OF HIS	374 31
THE DUST GIVE THANKS UNTO THEE	375 12
I WILL GIVE THANKS UNTO THEE FOR EVER	375 19
23 THANKS BE TO THE LORD	377 09
I WILL ALWAY GIVE THANKS UNTO THE LORD	380 03
WILL I GIVE THEE THANKS IN THE GREAT CONGREGATION	382 32
HARP WILL I GIVE THANKS UNTO THEE, O GOD, MY GOD	394 14
WILL YET GIVE HIM THANKS, WHICH IS THE HELP OF MY	394 18
THE PEOPLE GIVE THANKS UNTO THEE, WORLD WITHOUT END	397 23
WHOSO OFFERETH ME THANKS AND PRAISE, HE HONOURETH ME	403 04
I WILL ALWAY GIVE THANKS UNTO THEE FOR THAT THOU HAST	405 07
UNTO THEE WILL I GIVE THANKS	409 07
10 I WILL GIVE THANKS UNTO THEE, O LORD, AMONG THE	409 33
26 GIVE THANKS UNTO GOD THE LORD IN THE CONGREGATION,	421 06
UNTO THEE, O GOD, DO WE GIVE THANKS	431 30
UNTO THEE DO WE GIVE THANKS	431 31
SHALL GIVE THEE THANKS FOR EVER, *	440 33
THING TO GIVE THANKS UNTO THE LORD, *	455 32
AND GIVE THANKS FOR A REMEMBRANCE OF HIS HOLINESS	461 21
REJOICE, AND GIVE THANKS	462 03
3 THEY SHALL GIVE THANKS UNTO THY NAME, *	462 20
O GIVE THANKS UNTO THE LORD, AND CALL UPON HIS NAME	470 05
O GIVE THANKS UNTO THE LORD	472 31
AND GIVE THANKS WITH THINE INHERITANCE	473 09
THAT WE MAY GIVE THANKS UNTO THY HOLY NAME, AND MAKE	475 31
O GIVE THANKS UNTO THE LORD, FOR HE IS GRACIOUS,	476 06
2 LET THEM GIVE THANKS WHOM THE LORD HATH REDEEMED,	476 08
3 I WILL GIVE THANKS UNTO THEE, O LORD, AMONG THE	479 09
I WILL GIVE GREAT THANKS UNTO THE LORD WITH MY MOUTH,	481 32
I WILL GIVE THANKS UNTO THE LORD WITH MY WHOLE HEART,	482 24
O GIVE THANKS UNTO THE LORD, FOR HE IS GRACIOUS	487 31
AND GIVE THANKS UNTO THE LORD	489 07
29 O GIVE THANKS UNTO THE LORD	489 27
WILL RISE TO GIVE THANKS UNTO THEE, *	494 04
TO GIVE THANKS UNTO THE NAME OF THE LORD	503 14
O GIVE THANKS UNTO THE LORD, FOR HE IS GRACIOUS	511 16
2 O GIVE THANKS UNTO THE GOD OF ALL GODS	511 18
26 O GIVE THANKS UNTO THE GOD OF HEAVEN	512 34
27 O GIVE THANKS UNTO THE LORD OF LORDS	513 02
I WILL GIVE THANKS UNTO THEE, O LORD, WITH MY WHOLE	513 27
13 I WILL GIVE THANKS UNTO THEE, FOR I AM FEARFULLY	515 15
ALSO SHALL GIVE THANKS UNTO THY NAME	517 04
THAT I MAY GIVE THANKS UNTO THY NAME	518 19
DAY WILL I GIVE THANKS UNTO THEE	520 29
THY SAINTS GIVE THANKS UNTO THEE	521 13
ALL FLESH GIVE THANKS UNTO HIS HOLY NAME FOR EVER AND	521 35
THEE MOST HEARTY THANKS, WE PRAISE AND WORSHIP THEE	545 25
TO GIVE THEE THANKS FOR THE BENEFITS WHICH THEY HAVE	566 15
TO WORSHIP HIM, TO GIVE HIM THANKS	579 30
OUR UNFEIGNED THANKS FOR ALL THY MERCIES	591 07

THANKS   CONTINUED

THE NIGHT COMETH, REJOICE TO GIVE THEE THANKS	594 17
US TO GIVE THANKS FOR ALL THINGS, TO DREAD NOTHING	596 03

THANKSGIVING

LET US COME BEFORE HIS PRESENCE WITH THANKSGIVING	009 05
GATES WITH THANKSGIVING, AND INTO HIS COURTS WITH	015 10
THE GENERAL THANKSGIVING MAY BE SAID BY THE	R 019 34
SING TO THE HARP WITH A PSALM OF THANKSGIVING	027 16
THE GENERAL THANKSGIVING MAY BE SAID BY THE	R 033 32
PRAYER OF THANKSGIVING OR OF BLESSING, OR BEFORE THE	R 035 04
THE GENERAL THANKSGIVING, OR, WHEN THAT IS NOT SAID,	R 050 15
PRAISE AND THANKSGIVING FOR OUR DELIVERANCE FROM	052 09
PRAISE AND THANKSGIVING FOR THESE THY MERCIES TOWARDS	052 26
THIS OUR SACRIFICE OF PRAISE AND THANKSGIVING	081 08
ON HIM IN THY HEART BY FAITH, WITH THANKSGIVING	082 34
WITH THANKSGIVING LET YOUR REQUESTS BE MADE KNOWN	095 16
AND THANKSGIVING, AND HONOUR, AND POWER, AND	256 32
O SING UNTO THE LORD WITH THANKSGIVING	264 25
AND THE THANKSGIVING FROM THIS OFFICE, BEGINNING, WE	R 281 23
HE MAY OFFER THEE PRAISE AND THANKSGIVING	320 12
VOICE OF THANKSGIVING, *	371 10
EVEN A THANKSGIVING UNTO OUR GOD	390 15
PRAISE AND THANKSGIVING, *	393 09
UNTO GOD THANKSGIVING, *	402 18
AND MAGNIFY IT WITH THANKSGIVING	424 05
LET US COME BEFORE HIS PRESENCE WITH THANKSGIVING	459 07
SING TO THE HARP WITH A PSALM OF THANKSGIVING	462 05
GATES WITH THANKSGIVING, AND INTO HIS COURTS WITH	463 11
OF THANKSGIVING, *	477 21
OF THANKSGIVING, *	487 19
7 O SING UNTO THE LORD WITH THANKSGIVING	523 08
PRAYER AND THANKSGIVING, FOR BLESSING THY PEOPLE IN	565 10
OUR MORNING SACRIFICE OF PRAISE AND THANKSGIVING	587 26

THANKSGIVINGS

AND THANKSGIVINGS FOR THY LATE MERCIES VOUCHSAFED	019 19
AND THANKSGIVINGS FOR THY LATE MERCIES VOUCHSAFED	033 17
ALL OUR THANKSGIVINGS, IN THE WORDS WHICH CHRIST HATH	048 24
AND THANKSGIVINGS UNTO THEE	051 08
AND THANKSGIVINGS, MAY BE USED AT THE DISCRETION OF	R 305 05
AND THANKSGIVINGS UNTO THEE	306 28

THANKWORTHY

THIS IS THANKWORTHY, IF A MAN FOR CONSCIENCE TOWARD	172 05

THEIR'S

FOR THEIR'S IS THE KINGDOM OF HEAVEN	257 21
FOR THEIR'S IS THE KINGDOM OF HEAVEN	257 30

THEMSELVES

AND CALL THEMSELVES CHRISTIANS MAY BE LED INTO THE	018 32
AND CALL THEMSELVES CHRISTIANS MAY BE LED INTO THE	032 32
TO DEDICATE THEMSELVES TO THE SACRED MINISTRY OF THY	039 19
GIVE THEMSELVES TO THE SERVICE OF THEIR FELLOW	043 31
OF THEMSELVES, AND OF THY PROMISES	046 22
AND EXAMINE THEMSELVES, BEFORE THEY PRESUME TO EAT OF	085 29
RECEIVE TO THEMSELVES CONDEMNATION	114 15
WITHIN THEMSELVES, AND SAID, WHY WAS THIS WASTE OF	140 06
SAID AMONG THEMSELVES WITH THE SCRIBES, HE SAVED	146 21
THINGS THEMSELVES WITH BETTER SACRIFICES THAN THESE	147 29
ENQUIRE AMONG THEMSELVES, WHICH OF THEM IT WAS THAT	149 16
FOR BEFORE THEY WERE AT ENMITY BETWEEN THEMSELVES	153 20
AMONG THEMSELVES, LET US NOT REND IT, BUT CAST LOTS	160 13
SAID AMONG THEMSELVES, WHO SHALL ROLL US AWAY THE	165 23
AMONG THEMSELVES, WHAT IS THIS THAT HE SAITH UNTO US,	173 30
TRUSTED IN THEMSELVES THAT THEY WERE RIGHTEOUS,	205 22
NEITHER THEY THEMSELVES WHO ARE CIRCUMCISED KEEP THE	210 27
HAVE GIVEN THEMSELVES OVER UNTO LASCIVIOUSNESS,	216 08
SAID WITHIN THEMSELVES, THIS MAN BLASPHEMETH	217 05
ASSEMBLED THEMSELVES WITH THE CHURCH, AND TAUGHT MUCH	241 13
MANY TO OFFER THEMSELVES FOR THIS MINISTRY	260 22
THAT SERVED THEMSELVES OF THEM	262 14
TO PREPARE THEMSELVES, WITH PRAYERS AND FASTING, FOR	R 273 20
BAPTIZED ANSWERING THE QUESTIONS FOR THEMSELVES	R 277 19
TO EXAMINE THEMSELVES, WHETHER THEY REPENT THEM TRULY	293 26
THAT HAVE SET THEMSELVES AGAINST ME ROUND ABOUT	347 03
MAY KNOW THEMSELVES TO BE BUT MEN	352 33
REMEMBER THEMSELVES, AND BE TURNED UNTO THE LORD	367 28
CONVEYED THEMSELVES FROM ME	376 18
AND GATHERED THEMSELVES TOGETHER	382 24
THAT BOAST THEMSELVES AGAINST ME	383 18
AND BOAST THEMSELVES IN THE MULTITUDE OF THEIR	400 17
AND KEEP THEMSELVES CLOSE, *	408 26
AND ARE FALLEN INTO THE MIDST OF IT THEMSELVES	409 28
AND PREPARE THEMSELVES WITHOUT MY FAULT	411 11
ENCOURAGE THEMSELVES IN MISCHIEF, *	415 27
COMMUNE AMONG THEMSELVES, HOW THEY MAY LAY SNARES	415 28
SECRET AMONG THEMSELVES, EVERY MAN IN THE DEEP OF HIS	415 31
NOT BELIEVE SHALL NOT BE ABLE TO EXALT THEMSELVES	417 28
SNARE TO TAKE THEMSELVES WITHAL	423 18
TURNED THEMSELVES BACK IN THE DAY OF BATTLE	435 18
SUBMITTED THEMSELVES UNTO HIM	443 10
THEY JOINED THEMSELVES UNTO BAAL-PEOR, *	474 25
THEM COVER THEMSELVES WITH THEIR OWN CONFUSION,	481 30
PEOPLE OFFER THEMSELVES WILLINGLY WITH AN HOLY	482 11
PURCHASE TO THEMSELVES A GOOD DEGREE, AND GREAT	532 03
WELL BEHAVE THEMSELVES IN THIS INFERIOR OFFICE,	535 08
COME TO AGE, THEMSELVES ARE BOUND TO PERFORM	581 34
TO EXAMINE THEMSELVES, WHETHER THEY REPENT THEM TRULY	582 22

THEMSELVES   CONTINUED

AS FEEL IN THEMSELVES THE WORKING OF THE SPIRIT OF	606 18
PURCHASE TO THEMSELVES DAMNATION, AS SAINT PAUL	608 05
TO HAVE AMONG THEMSELVES ONE TO ANOTHER	608 35

THENCE

FROM THENCE HE SHALL COME TO JUDGE THE QUICK AND THE	015 26
FROM THENCE HE SHALL COME TO JUDGE THE QUICK AND THE	029 31
JESUS WENT THENCE, AND DEPARTED INTO THE COASTS OF	128 17
CAN THEY PASS TO US, THAT WOULD COME FROM THENCE	190 22
NO MEANS COME OUT THENCE, TILL THOU HAST PAID THE	198 16
AND GOING ON FROM THENCE, HE SAW OTHER TWO BRETHREN,	227 24
PASSED FORTH FROM THENCE, HE SAW A MAN, NAMED	251 12
FROM THENCE HE SHALL COME TO JUDGE THE QUICK AND THE	284 20
FROM THENCE HE SHALL COME TO JUDGE THE QUICK AND THE	578 04

THENCEFORTH

AND FROM THENCEFORTH PILATE SOUGHT TO RELEASE HIM	159 19

THEOPHILUS

I MADE, O THEOPHILUS, OF ALL THAT JESUS BEGAN BOTH TO	177 22

THEREAFTER

UNDERSTANDING HAVE ALL THEY THAT DO THEREAFTER	483 15

THEREBY

DOST ASSURE US THEREBY OF THY FAVOUR AND GOODNESS	083 20
CONGREGATION BE THEREBY OFFENDED	R 085 03
CONGREGATION MAY THEREBY BE SATISFIED	R 085 06
MILK OF THE WORD, THAT YE MAY GROW THEREBY	259 28
THAT THEREBY MANKIND MAY BE DRAWN TO THY BLESSED	260 23
AND OF THE BENEFITS WHICH WE RECEIVE THEREBY	293 07
BENEFITS HE HATH THEREBY, AND GIVING HIM HEARTY	R 323 29
INCREASE COMING THEREBY MAY BE MANIFEST UNTO ALL MEN	558 23
AND OF THE BENEFITS WHICH WE RECEIVE THEREBY	582 06
ARE THE BENEFITS WHEREOF WE ARE PARTAKERS THEREBY	582 16
MAY BE PROVED THEREBY, IS NOT TO BE REQUIRED OF ANY	603 30

THEREIN

TO BE USED THEREIN, BEING THINGS IN THEIR OWN NATURE	V 15
SHOULD BE MADE THEREIN, AS TO THOSE THAT ARE IN PLACE	V 18
THE HEAVENS, AND ALL THE POWERS THEREIN	010 12
AND ALL THAT THEREIN IS	027 19
AND THEY THAT DWELL THEREIN	027 20
AND ALL WHO SERVE THEREIN	042 06
AND AMENDMENTS THEREIN AS MIGHT BE DEEMED EXPEDIENT	VI 26
NEITHER HADST PLEASURE THEREIN	157 31
AND CONTINUETH THEREIN, HE BEING NOT A FORGETFUL	176 11
THEM THAT SOLD THEREIN, AND THEM THAT BOUGHT	204 16
THAT THEREIN I MAY SPEAK BOLDLY, AS I OUGHT TO SPEAK	219 25
AND LET NO MAN DWELL THEREIN	234 19
AND CONTINUETH THEREIN, HE BEING NOT A FORGETFUL	266 02
GOD AS A LITTLE CHILD, HE SHALL NOT ENTER THEREIN	274 32
TO BE BAPTIZED THEREIN, MAY RECEIVE THE FULNESS OF	279 17
AND ALL THAT THEREIN IS	368 28
AND THEY THAT DWELL THEREIN	368 29
AND DWELL THEREIN FOR EVER	386 25
THE WHOLE WORLD IS MINE, AND ALL THAT IS THEREIN	402 15
11 WICKEDNESS IS THEREIN	407 09
10 THY CONGREGATION SHALL DWELL THEREIN	419 31
THE SEA, AND ALL THAT MOVETH THEREIN	424 13
AND THEY THAT LOVE HIS NAME SHALL DWELL THEREIN	424 18
AND ALL THAT THEREIN IS	450 30
AND ALL THAT THEREIN IS	460 23
AND ALL THAT THEREIN IS	462 08
AND THEY THAT DWELL THEREIN	462 09
WHOM THOU HAST MADE TO TAKE HIS PASTIME THEREIN	469 13
FOR THE WICKEDNESS OF THEM THAT DWELL THEREIN	478 15
SOUGHT OUT OF ALL THEM THAT HAVE PLEASURE THEREIN	482 27
FOR THEREIN IS MY DESIRE	492 10
HERE WILL I DWELL, FOR I HAVE A DELIGHT THEREIN	509 03
UPON THE TREES THAT ARE THEREIN	513 08
AND ALL THAT THEREIN IS	522 15
RAISE UP THEREIN, THROUGH THY SPIRIT, GOOD AND	562 10
AND ALL THAT THEREIN IS	563 11
AND THEY THAT DWELL THEREIN	563 12
IS NOT READ THEREIN, NOR MAY BE PROVED THEREBY, IS	603 30

THEREOF

FRAME AND ORDER THEREOF) HAVE STILL BEEN CONTINUED	V 32
LATTER PORTION THEREOF MAY BE OMITTED	R 014 05
RIGHTEOUSNESS THEREOF, ALL THINGS NECESSARY TO THEIR	040 17
IN OF THE FRUITS THEREOF, AND FOR ALL THE OTHER	050 23
OR SO MUCH THEREOF AS, IN HIS DISCRETION, HE MAY	R 086 27
THE GREAT PERIL OF THE UNWORTHY RECEIVING THEREOF	087 10
FOR THE FLESH, TO FULFIL THE LUSTS THEREOF	091 09
ALL THE COASTS THEREOF, FROM TWO YEARS OLD AND UNDER,	103 27
HE HAD TASTED THEREOF, HE WOULD NOT DRINK	136 30
NOT ANY MORE EAT THEREOF, UNTIL IT BE FULFILLED IN	149 04
THE SOUND THEREOF, BUT CANST NOT TELL WHENCE IT	100 15
SUFFICIENT UNTO THE DAY IS THE EVIL THEREOF	211 35
THE KING HEARD THEREOF, HE WAS WROTH	218 13
AND THE FLOWER THEREOF FALLETH, AND THE GRACE OF THE	239 22
THE GOODLINESS THEREOF IS AS THE FLOWER OF THE FIELD	242 28
SUFFICIENT UNTO THE DAY IS THE EVIL THEREOF	266 33
GIVE KNOWLEDGE THEREOF TO THE MINISTER	R 273 13
THE SOUND THEREOF, BUT CANST NOT TELL WHENCE IT	275 20
AND A PLEDGE TO ASSURE US THEREOF	292 13

THEREOF   CONTINUED

OR ANY PART THEREOF, MAY BE USED AT THE DISCRETICN OF	R 308 03
SHALL BE GIVEN THEREOF TO THE MINISTER OF THE PARISH	R 308 05
OR ANY PART THEREOF, AT THE DISCRETION OF THE	R 315 03
A MAN MAY EAT THEREOF, AND NOT DIE	322 25
THE WATERS THEREOF RAGE AND SWELL, *	327 07
AND THERE IS NOTHING HID FROM THE HEAT THEREOF	363 26
SHALL HEAR THEREOF, AND BE GLAD	380 06
THE WATERS THEREOF RAGE AND SWELL, *	397 30
AND TELL THE TOWERS THEREOF	399 34
RISING UP OF THE SUN UNTO THE GOING DOWN THEREOF	401 23
AND NIGHT THEY GO ABOUT WITHIN THE WALLS THEREOF	407 07
HEAL THE SORES THEREOF, FOR IT SHAKETH	412 16
THOU SENDEST RAIN INTO THE LITTLE VALLEYS THEREOF	417 05
THERE DID WE REJOICE THEREOF	417 25
FOR I KNOW NO END THEREOF	426 05
THE FRUIT THEREOF SHALL SHAKE LIKE LEBANON	427 30
THE CARVED WORK THEREOF *	430 16
AND ALL THE INHABITERS THEREOF	432 04
AS FOR THE DREGS THEREOF, *	432 17
GAVE THEM DRINK THEREOF, AS IT HAD BEEN OUT OF THE	435 31
AND THE BOUGHS THEREOF WERE LIKE THE GOODLY	441 23
THE WAVES THEREOF WHEN THEY ARISE	450 25
THE EARTH MAY BE GLAD THEREOF	460 30
THE MULTITUDE OF THE ISLES MAY BE GLAD THEREOF	460 31
AND THE PLACE THEREOF SHALL KNOW IT NO MORE	467 07
THE FIELD DRINK THEREOF, *	468 15
WHICH LIFTETH UP THE WAVES THEREOF	477 27
THAT THE WAVES THEREOF ARE STILL	478 03
SPEAK UNTO THEM THEREOF, *	502 20
AND TO HELP HIM IN THE DISTRIBUTION THEREOF	533 14
OR ANY MEMBER THEREOF, DO TAKE ANY HURT OR HINDRANCE	540 11
AND DULY ADMINISTER THE GODLY DISCIPLINE THEREOF	549 12
THE HEARERS THEREOF MAY BOTH PERCEIVE AND KNOW WHAT	566 04
AND IN TOKEN THEREOF, GIVE INTO YOUR HANDS THE KEYS	570 29
THE SAME, AND A PLEDGE TO ASSURE US THEREOF	581 15
CIVIL PRECEPTS THEREOF OUGHT OF NECESSITY TO BE	604 21

THEREON

ON THEM THEIR CLOTHES, AND THEY SET HIM THEREON	091 24
WHEN HE THOUGHT THEREON, HE WEPT	144 03

THEREOUT

AND THEREOUT SUCK THEY NO SMALL ADVANTAGE	428 28

THERETO

WAY AND MEANS THERETO IS	087 16
REFUSE TO COME THERETO, BEING SO LOVINGLY CALLED AND	088 16
AND THY SPEECH AGREETH THERETO	143 32
AND THE ANSWER THERETO), THE DECLARATION, WE RECEIVE	R 282 05
AND THERETO I PLIGHT THEE MY TROTH	301 32
AND THERETO I GIVE THEE MY TROTH	302 08
AND THERETO HAVE GIVEN AND PLEDGED THEIR	304 05
HE BE ADMITTED THERETO BY THE BISHOP	533 17
IF THOU BE THERETO LICENSED BY THE BISHOP	534 12
A MIND AND WILL THERETO OF YOURSELVES	540 30
APPLY MYSELF THERETO, THE LORD BEING MY HELPER	543 04

THEREUNTO

HER THEREUNTO MOVING, YIELDED TO MAKE SUCH	V 28
THE COMERS THEREUNTO PERFECT	157 18
THAT YE ARE THEREUNTO CALLED, THAT YE SHOULD INHERIT	195 23
AND WATCHING THEREUNTO WITH ALL PERSEVERANCE AND	219 21
AND ADMITTED THEREUNTO BY LAWFUL AUTHORITY	529 18
AND ADMITTED THEREUNTO, ACCORDING TO THE FORM	529 22
WHERE THOU SHALT BE LAWFULLY APPOINTED THEREUNTO	546 27
SUBSCRIBED THEREUNTO, THE NAMES OF ALL SUCH PERSONS	R 583 07
CHURCH BY A JUDGE THAT HATH AUTHORITY THEREUNTO	609 30

THEREUPON

HEALTH BEING THEREUPON RESTORED, HE MAY BLESS THY	315 10
WHEN I THINK THEREUPON, I POUR OUT MY HEART BY	393 06

THESSALONICA

PRESENT WORLD, AND IS DEPARTED UNTO THESSALONICA	253 33

THICK

DARK WATER, AND THICK CLOUDS TO COVER HIM	360 20
SHALL STAND SO THICK WITH CORN, THAT THEY SHALL LAUGH	417 12
AFORE OUT OF THE THICK TREES, *	430 14
FLESH UPON THEM AS THICK AS DUST, *	436 25

THIEF

AS AGAINST A THIEF, WITH SWORDS AND WITH STAVES,	142 25
AS AGAINST A THIEF, WITH SWORDS AND WITH STAVES	151 03
THE SAME IS A THIEF AND A ROBBER	186 02
THE THIEF COMETH NOT, BUT FOR TO STEAL, AND TO KILL,	186 16
WHEN THOU SAWEST A THIEF, THOU CONSENTEDST UNTO HIM	402 26
THE SAME IS A THIEF AND A ROBBER	538 25
THE THIEF COMETH NOT, BUT FOR TO STEAL, AND TO KILL,	539 07

THIEVES

AND WHERE THIEVES BREAK THROUGH AND STEAL	072 08
AND WHERE THIEVES DO NOT BREAK THROUGH NOR STEAL	072 11
BUT YE HAVE MADE IT A DEN OF THIEVES	092 04
AND WHERE THIEVES BREAK THROUGH AND STEAL	125 18

THIEVES CONTINUED

AND WHERE THIEVES DO NOT BREAK THROUGH NOR STEAL	125 20
WERE THERE TWO THIEVES CRUCIFIED WITH HIM, ONE CN THE	137 04
THE THIEVES ALSO, WHICH WERE CRUCIFIED WITH HIM,	137 14
AND WITH HIM THEY CRUCIFY TWO THIEVES	146 15
BEFORE ME ARE THIEVES AND ROBBERS	186 14
BUT YE HAVE MADE IT A DEN OF THIEVES	204 18
AND FELL AMONG THIEVES, WHICH STRIPPED HIM OF HIS	208 22
NEIGHBOUR UNTO HIM THAT FELL AMONG THE THIEVES	209 03
BUT YE HAVE MADE IT A DEN OF THIEVES	260 08
BEFORE ME ARE THIEVES AND ROBBERS	539 05

THIEVISH

LURKING IN THE THIEVISH CORNERS OF THE STREETS, *	353 20

THIGH

THY SWORD UPON THY THIGH, O THCU MOST MIGHTY, *	396 20

THINE

FIRSTFRUITS OF ALL THINE INCREASE	005 21
FOR THINE IS THE KINGDOM, AND THE POWER, AND THE	007 24
THINE ADORABLE, TRUE, AND ONLY SON	010 22
AND BLESS THINE HERITAGE	011 04
ALL MERCIES, WE, THINE UNWORTHY SERVANTS, DO GIVE	019 14
BUT ABOVE ALL, FOR THINE INESTIMABLE LOVE IN THE	019 22
THE PLACE WHERE THINE HONOUR DWELLETH	021 15
AND HEALETH ALL THINE INFIRMITIES	029 08
AND BLESS THINE INHERITANCE	031 09
ALL MERCIES, WE, THINE UNWORTHY SERVANTS, DO GIVE	033 12
BUT ABOVE ALL, FOR THINE INESTIMABLE LOVE IN THE	033 20
WHO OPENEST THINE HAND AND FILLEST ALL THINGS LIVING	040 03
WE BESEECH THEE OF THINE INFINITE GOODNESS TO HEAR	040 05
WE PRAY THEE, THINE ALMIGHTY ARM TO STRENGTHEN AND	041 26
CREATED MAN IN THINE OWN IMAGE	044 09
HEALTH WHICH IT IS THINE ALONE TO GIVE	045 27
WHO SAIDST UNTO THINE APOSTLES, PEACE I LEAVE WITH	049 05
TO INCLINE THINE EARS TO US WHO HAVE NOW MADE OUR	050 08
BY THINE AGONY AND BLOODY SWEAT	055 10
AND DELIVER US FOR THINE HONOUR	059 03
BUT SO TURN THINE ANGER FROM US, WHO MEEKLY	062 22
AND LET NOT THINE HERITAGE BE BROUGHT TO	063 03
THINE, O LORD, IS THE GREATNESS, AND THE POWER,	073 18
THINE IS THE KINGDOM, O LORD, AND THOU ART EXALTED AS	073 20
THAT IS IN THE HEAVEN AND IN THE EARTH IS THINE	073 20
O LORD, AND OF THINE OWN HAVE WE GIVEN THEE	073 23
GIVE JESUS CHRIST, THINE ONLY SON, TO BE BCRN AS AT	077 14
WHO, WITH THINE ONLY-BEGOTTEN SON, AND THE HOLY	079 07
DIDST GIVE THINE ONLY SON JESUS CHRIST TO	080 08
ARE THE WORKS OF THINE HANDS	097 15
OF THE BIRTH OF THINE ONLY SON JESUS CHRIST	098 12
THE NEW LIGHT OF THINE INCARNATE WORD	106 26
THEREFORE IF THINE ENEMY HUNGER, FEED HIM	113 06
TAKE THAT THINE IS, AND GO THY WAY	120 09
IS THINE EYE EVIL, BECAUSE I AM GOOD	120 11
GRANT THIS FOR THINE ONLY SON JESUS CHRIST'S SAKE	122 19
AND GIVE NOT THINE HERITAGE TO REPROACH, THAT	125 04
ANOINT THINE HEAD, AND WASH THY FACE	125 13
ART THOU RED IN THINE APPAREL, AND THY GARMENTS LIKE	138 15
THE TRIBES OF THINE INHERITANCE	139 26
WE ARE THINE	139 29
NOT MY WILL, BUT THINE, BE DONE	150 19
WHO THROUGH THINE ONLY-BEGOTTEN SON JESUS CHRIST	163 22
DIDST GIVE THINE ONLY-BEGOTTEN SON TO THE DEATH OF	165 03
SHALT NOT SUFFER THINE HOLY ONE TO SEE CORRUPTICN	169 14
WHO HAST GIVEN THINE ONLY SON TO DIE FOR OUR SINS,	170 19
WHO HAST GIVEN THINE ONLY SON TO BE UNTO US BOTH A	171 28
WHO HAST EXALTED THINE ONLY SON JESUS CHRIST WITH	179 04
BUT SEND TO THINE OWN HOLY GHOST TO COMFORT US,	179 07
BEAM THAT IS IN THINE OWN EYE	195 07
MOTE THAT IS IN THINE EYE, WHEN THOU THYSELF	195 09
BEAM THAT IS IN THINE OWN EYE	195 10
THE BEAM OUT OF THINE OWN EYE, AND THEN SHALT THCU	195 11
AGREE WITH THINE ADVERSARY QUICKLY, WHILES THCU ART	198 12
ART EVER WITH ME, AND ALL THAT I HAVE IS THINE	203 06
THEY ARE HID FROM THINE EYES	204 09
UPON THEE, THAT THINE ENEMIES SHALL CAST A TRENCH	204 10
TILL I MAKE THINE ENEMIES THY FOOTSTOOL	215 20
AND GO UNTO THINE HOUSE	217 11
SHALT BELIEVE IN THINE HEART THAT GOD HATH RAISED HIM	226 27
THAT, AS THINE HOLY APOSTLE SAINT JAMES, LEAVING	246 16
CHOSEN WITNESSES THINE ONLY-BEGOTTEN SCN WCNDERFULLY	247 32
WHO DIDST GIVE TO THINE APOSTLE BARTHOLOMEW GRACE	249 15
AND IF THINE EYE OFFEND THEE, PLUCK IT OUT, AND CAST	253 07
HAST KNIT TOGETHER THINE ELECT IN ONE COMMUNION AND	256 05
ATTAIN TO THINE ETERNAL JOY	258 17
WHICH THINE EYES HAVE SEEN	263 32
AND HATE THINE ENEMY	264 04
WITH THEM INTO THINE LNENDING JOY	268 19
TO RECEIVE HIM FOR THINE OWN CHILD, AND TO	280 31
BE AN INHERITOR OF THINE EVERLASTING KINGDOM	281 04
HE MAY CONTINUE THINE FOR EVER	297 27
THEN THE WORKS OF THINE OWN HANDS	312 10
AND HEALETH ALL THINE INFIRMITIES	312 24
OPEN THINE OWN EYE OF MERCY UPON THIS THY SERVANT,	313 33
TO THINE HONOUR AND GLORY	315 16
BE ABLE TO GO TO THINE HOUSE, TO OFFER THEE AN	315 31
OF JESUS CHRIST THINE ONLY SON OUR LORD	317 22
A SHEEP OF THINE OWN FOLD, A LAMB OF THINE OWN	319 29
A SINNER OF THINE OWN REDEEMING	319 30
A LAMB OF THINE OWN FLOCK, A SINNER OF THINE	319 30
VISITED WITH THINE HAND, AND TO GRANT THAT HE MAY	321 21
O LORD, AND WITH THINE EARS CONSIDER MY CALLING	325 06

THINE CONTINUED

HE SHALL COMFORT THINE HEART	326 31
O LET THINE EARS CONSIDER WELL *	328 05
SAFE KEEPING OF THINE ETERNAL LOVE	340 27
THE NATIONS FOR THINE INHERITANCE, *	346 13
I WILL COME INTO THINE HOUSE	348 14
REBUKE ME NOT IN THINE INDIGNATION, *	348 33
BECAUSE OF THINE ENEMIES, *	351 02
AND LIFT UP THINE HAND	353 32
THEIR HEART, AND THINE EAR HEARKENETH	354 14
AND LET THINE EYES LOOK UPON THE THING THAT IS ECUAL	358 20
INCLINE THINE EAR TO ME, AND HEARKEN UNTO MY WORDS	358 30
THE UNGODLY, BY THINE OWN SWORD	359 13
ENEMIES SHALL FEEL THINE HAND	365 20
8 ALL THINE ENEMIES SHALL FEEL THINE HAND	365 20
LORD, IN THINE OWN STRENGTH	365 32
SO WILL I GO TO THINE ALTAR	371 09
THE PLACE WHERE THINE HONOUR DWELLETH	371 13
HE SHALL COMFORT THINE HEART	372 31
THY BLESSING UNTO THINE INHERITANCE	373 27
2 BOW DOWN THINE EAR TO ME	375 24
IN THE COVERT OF THINE OWN PRESENCE FROM THE	377 06
OF THE SIGHT OF THINE EYES	377 12
O LORD, IN THINE ANGER	387 21
2 FOR THINE ARROWS STICK FAST IN ME, *	387 23
O LORD, AND WITH THINE EARS CONSIDER MY CALLING	390 02
RIGHT HAND, AND THINE ARM, AND THE LIGHT OF THY	394 30
HAVE THOU WITH THINE HONOUR	396 22
INCLINE THINE EAR	397 05
FORGET ALSO THINE OWN PEOPLE, AND THY FATHER'S HCUSE	397 06
NO BULLOCK OUT OF THINE HOUSE, *	402 08
AND HAST SLANDERED THINE OWN MOTHER'S SON	402 31
BULLOCKS UPON THINE ALTAR	404 17
OF THY POWER SHALL THINE ENEMIES BOW DOWN UNTO THEE	417 18
12 I WILL GO INTO THINE HOUSE WITH BURNT-OFFERINGS,	418 07
GRACIOUS RAIN UPON THINE INHERITANCE, *	419 29
EVEN FROM THINE ENEMIES, THAT THE LORD GOD MIGHT	420 21
IN THE BLOOD OF THINE ENEMIES, *	420 33
9 FOR THE ZEAL OF THINE HOUSE HATH EVEN EATEN ME	422 20
25 POUR OUT THINE INDIGNATION UPON THEM, *	423 23
INCLINE THINE EAR UNTO ME, AND SAVE ME	425 07
UPON THE TRIBE OF THINE INHERITANCE, *	430 08
5 THINE ADVERSARIES ROAR IN THE MIDST OF THY	430 12
17 THE DAY IS THINE, AND THE NIGHT IS THINE	431 08
17 THE DAY IS THINE, AND THE NIGHT IS THINE	431 08
O GOD, MAINTAIN THINE OWN CAUSE	431 22
NOT THE VOICE OF THINE ENEMIES	431 24
AND THINE ARROWS WENT ABROAD	434 17
ARE COME INTO THINE INHERITANCE	439 29
6 POUR OUT THINE INDIGNATION UPON THE HEATHEN THAT	440 11
SO STRONG FOR THINE OWN SELF	442 06
ALL NATIONS TO THINE INHERITANCE	444 03
2 FOR LO, THINE ENEMIES MAKE A MURMURING	444 07
UPON THE FACE OF THINE ANOINTED	445 30
AND LET THINE ANGER CEASE FROM US	446 14
BOW DOWN THINE EAR, O LORD, AND HEAR ME	447 05
HELP THE SON OF THINE HANDMAID	448 08
INCLINE THINE EAR UNTO MY CALLING	448 31
6 THINE INDIGNATION LIETH HARD UPON ME, *	449 09
HAST SCATTERED THINE ENEMIES ABROAD WITH THY MIGHTY	450 27
12 THE HEAVENS ARE THINE, THE EARTH ALSO IS THINE	450 28
12 THE HEAVENS ARE THINE, THE EARIH ALSO IS THINE	450 28
AND FORSAKEN THINE ANOINTED, *	452 16
50 WHEREWITH THINE ENEMIES HAVE BLASPHEMED THEE,	453 10
THE FOOTSTEPS OF THINE ANOINTED	453 11
8 YEA, WITH THINE EYES SHALT THOU BEHOLD, *	455 11
THOU HAST SET THINE HOUSE OF DEFENCE VERY HIGH	455 13
O LORD, LO, THINE ENEMIES SHALL PERISH	456 17
8 FOR LO, THINE ENEMIES, O LORD, LO, THINE ENEMIES	456 17
HOLINESS BECOMETH THINE HOUSE FOR EVER	457 17
AND TROUBLE THINE HERITAGE	457 28
INCLINE THINE EAR UNTO ME WHEN I CALL	464 13
BECAUSE OF THINE INDIGNATION AND WRATH	464 29
AND HEALETH ALL THINE INFIRMITIES	466 12
GIVE THANKS WITH THINE INHERITANCE	473 10
UNTIL I MAKE THINE ENEMIES THY FOOTSTOOL	482 08
IN THE MIDST AMONG THINE ENEMIES	482 10
AND THE SON OF THINE HANDMAID	487 17
FOR I REMEMBERED THINE EVERLASTING JUDGMENTS,	493 14
DAY ACCORDING TO THINE ORDINANCE	496 07
94 I AM THINE	496 13
TO LAY TO THINE HAND	498 21
173 THINE HAND HELP ME	501 28
EAT THE LABOURS OF THINE HANDS	506 08
UPON THE WALLS OF THINE HOUSE	506 11
2 O LET THINE EARS CONSIDER WELL *	507 10
AWAY THE FACE OF THINE ANOINTED	508 24
THEN THE WORKS OF THINE OWN HANDS	514 16
AND LAID THINE HAND UPON ME	514 28
12 FOR MY REINS ARE THINE	515 13
15 THINE EYES DID SEE MY SUBSTANCE, YET BEING	515 20
AND THINE ENEMIES TAKE THY NAME IN VAIN	515 31
SHOOT OUT THINE ARROWS, AND CONSUME THEM	520 03
7 SEND DOWN THINE HAND FROM ABOVE	520 04
7 THE MEMORIAL OF THINE ABUNDANT KINDNESS SHALL BE	521 06
16 THOU OPENEST THINE HAND, *	521 24
AND DIDST INSPIRE THINE APOSTLES TO CHOOSE INTO THE	531 16
GIFTS OF GRACE ARE THINE, O FINGER OF THE HAND	544 25
THINE OWN UNFAILING MIGHT SUPPLY TO STRENGTHEN CUR	545 04
GHOSTLY FOE, AND THINE ABIDING PEACE BESTOW	545 07
WHO, OF THINE INFINITE LOVE AND GOODNESS	545 12
GIFTS OF GRACE ARE THINE, O FINGER OF THE HAND	557 04
THINE OWN UNFAILING MIGHT SUPPLY TO STRENGTHEN CUR	557 10
GHOSTLY FOE, AND THINE ABIDING PEACE BESTOW	557 13
WHO, OF THINE INFINITE GOODNESS, HAST GIVEN	557 21

THINE	CONTINUED	
THE ZEAL OF THINE HOUSE HATH EATEN ME UP	568	03
WE MAY BE THINE, THROUGH THE MERITS AND	591	31

THING

THERE BE NOT ANY THING IN IT CONTRARY TO THE WORD OF	V	40
IT IS A GOOD THING TO GIVE THANKS UNTO THE LORD,	027.	28
WHERE IN ANY THING IT IS AMISS, REFORM IT	037	18
LIKENESS OF ANY THING THAT IS IN HEAVEN ABOVE,	068	09
HIS ASS, NOR ANY THING THAT IS HIS	069	22
AND COMFORTABLE A THING TO THEM WHO RECEIVE IT	087	05
AND UNKIND A THING IT IS, WHEN A MAN HATH PREPARED A	088	17
OWE NO MAN ANY THING, BUT TO LOVE ONE ANOTHER	090	23
IT IS A VERY SMALL THING THAT I SHOULD BE JUDGED OF	094	06
BUT IN EVERY THING BY PRAYER AND SUPPLICATION WITH	095	15
HIM WAS NOT ANY THING MADE THAT WAS MADE	097	23
AND SEE THIS THING WHICH IS COME TO PASS, WHICH THE	106	09
ATTENDING CONTINUALLY UPON THIS VERY THING	114	25
OUR TRUST IN ANY THING THAT WE DO	120	18
NO OFFENCE IN ANY THING, THAT THE MINISTRY BE NCT	126	08
WHICH OF THEM IT WAS THAT SHOULD DO THIS THING	149	17
AND SHOES, LACKED YE ANY THING	150	05
SAID THEY ANY THING TO ANY MAN	166	03
THEY MAY LOVE THE THING WHICH THOU COMMANDEST,	174	20
WE CAN DO NO GOOD THING WITHOUT THEE, GRANT US THE	189	03
WHO CANNOT DO ANY THING THAT IS GOOD WITHOUT THEE,	200	31
TO THINK ANY THING AS OF OURSELVES	206	14
AVAILETH ANY THING, NOR UNCIRCUMCISION, BUT A NEW	210	32
THAT IN EVERY THING YE ARE ENRICHED BY HIM, IN ALL	214	30
WITH HIS HANDS THE THING WHICH IS GOOD, THAT HE MAY	216	21
OF THIS VERY THING, THAT HE WHICH HATH BEGUN A GCOD	220	25
IS IT A SMALL THING FOR YOU TO WEARY MEN, BUT WILL YE	235	29
ALSO THAT HOLY THING WHICH SHALL BE BORN OF THEE	236	24
SHALL RECEIVE ANY THING OF THE LORD	239	17
YE SHALL ASK ANY THING IN MY NAME, I WILL DC IT	240	23
DESIRING A CERTAIN THING OF HIM	247	08
FOR IT IS A GOOD THING TO SING PRAISES UNTO OUR GOD	264	18
AND PLEASANT THING IT IS TO BE THANKFUL	264	20
THE WIVES BE TO THEIR OWN HUSBANDS IN EVERY THING	267	18
OR WRINKLE, OR ANY SUCH THING	267	23
THEY MAY LOVE THE THING WHICH THOU COMMANDEST, AND	285	27
LIKENESS OF ANY THING THAT IS IN HEAVEN ABOVE,	286	09
HIS ASS, NOR ANY THING THAT IS HIS	287	22
WHO CANNOT DO ANY THING THAT IS GOOD WITHCUT THEE,	287	28
INWARD PART, OR THING SIGNIFIED	293	13
INWARD PART, OR THING SIGNIFIED, IS THE BODY AND	293	14
IN EVERY THING THAT REGARDS THE CIVIL CCNTRACT	R 304	19
IF WE ASK ANY THING ACCORDING TO HIS WILL, HE HEARETH	322	16
ONE THING HAVE I DESIRED OF THE LORD, WHICH I WILL	326	08
AND WHY DO THE PEOPLE IMAGINE A VAIN THING	345	26
IF I HAVE DONE ANY SUCH THING	349	27
WILL BEHOLD THE THING THAT IS JUST	355	03
AND DOETH THE THING WHICH IS RIGHT, AND SPEAKETH THE	357	08
EYES LOOK UPON THE THING THAT IS EQUAL	358	20
4 ONE THING HAVE I DESIRED OF THE LORD, WHICH I WILL	371	32
TEMPLE DOTH EVERY THING SPEAK OF HIS HONOUR	374	16
COUNTED BUT A VAIN THING TO SAVE A MAN	379	22
WANT NO MANNER OF THING THAT IS GOOD	380	22
DOTH HE ABHOR ANY THING THAT IS EVIL	384	02
16 A SMALL THING THAT THE RIGHTEOUS HATH, *	385	27
AND DO THE THING THAT IS GOOD	386	17
LORD LOVETH THE THING THAT IS RIGHT	386	19
TAKE HEED UNTO THE THING THAT IS RIGHT	387	08
I FOLLOW THE THING THAT GOOD IS	388	33
DO YE JUDGE THE THING THAT IS RIGHT, O YE SONS CF	410	08
STABLISH THE THING, O GOD, THAT THOU HAST WROUGHT IN	421	12
LORD GOD, ART THE THING THAT I LONG FOR	425	14
AND NO GOOD THING SHALL HE WITHHOLD FROM THEM THAT	446	03
NOR ALTER THE THING THAT IS GONE OUT OF MY LIPS	452	09
IT IS A GOOD THING TO GIVE THANKS UNTO THE LORD,	455	32
WILT THOU HAVE ANY THING TO DO WITH THE THRONE OF	458	26
THAT YE HATE THE THING WHICH IS EVIL	461	16
TAKE NO WICKED THING IN HAND	463	22
I DEAL WITH THE THING THAT IS LAWFUL AND RIGHT	498	11
GOOD AND JOYFUL A THING IT IS, *	509	13
LET NOT MINE HEART BE INCLINED TO ANY EVIL THING	517	15
WHICH THING IF THOU WILT GRANT ME, THEN SHALL THE	518	20
TEACH ME TO DO THE THING THAT PLEASETH THEE	519	12
4 MAN IS LIKE A THING OF NOUGHT	519	29
FOR IT IS A GOOD THING TO SING PRAISES UNTO OUR GOD	522	27
AND PLEASANT THING IT IS TO BE THANKFUL	522	29
6 LET EVERY THING THAT HATH BREATH *	525	32
WHOLLY TO THIS ONE THING, AND DRAW ALL YOUR CARES AND	541	14
LIKENESS OF ANY THING THAT IS IN HEAVEN ABOVE,	578	28
HIS ASS, NOR ANY THING THAT IS HIS	579	22
INWARD PART, OR THING SIGNIFIED	582	11
TO ORDAIN ANY THING THAT IS CONTRARY TO GOD'S WORD	607	05
NOT TO DECREE ANY THING AGAINST THE SAME, SO BESIDES	607	08
NOT TO ENFORCE ANY THING TO BE BELIEVED FOR NECESSITY	607	09
IS A FOND THING, VAINLY INVENTED, AND	607	16
IT IS A THING PLAINLY REPUGNANT TO THE WORD OF GCD,	607	27
DRINK THE SIGN OR SACRAMENT OF SO GREAT A THING	609	08
HATH IT ANY THING THAT, OF ITSELF, IS SUPERSTITIOUS	610	34

THINGS

BEING THINGS IN THEIR OWN NATURE	V	15
VARIATIONS IN THINGS ONCE ADVISEDLY ESTABLISHED,	V	26
AND TO ASK THOSE THINGS WHICH ARE REQUISITE AND	006	08
LEFT UNDONE THOSE THINGS WHICH WE OUGHT TO HAVE DONE	006	21
HAVE DONE THOSE THINGS WHICH WE OUGHT NOT TO HAVE	006	22
THAT THOSE THINGS MAY PLEASE HIM WHICH WE DO AT THIS	007	15
O ALL YE GREEN THINGS UPON THE EARTH, BLESS YE THE	013	06
AND OF ALL THINGS VISIBLE AND INVISIBLE	015	34

THINGS	CONTINUED	
BY WHOM ALL THINGS WERE MADE	016	05
SEEK THOSE THINGS WHICH ARE ABOVE, WHERE CHRIST	022	19
AND TO ASK THOSE THINGS WHICH ARE REQUISITE AND	023	17
LEFT UNDONE THOSE THINGS WHICH WE OUGHT TO HAVE CCNE	023	28
HAVE DONE THOSE THINGS WHICH WE OUGHT NOT TC HAVE	023	29
THAT THOSE THINGS MAY PLEASE HIM WHICH WE DO AT THIS	024	17
HE HATH FILLED THE HUNGRY WITH GOOD THINGS	026	24
FOR HE HATH DONE MARVELLOUS THINGS	027	05
AND OF ALL THINGS VISIBLE AND INVISIBLE	030	05
BY WHOM ALL THINGS WERE MADE	030	10
MAY ABOVE ALL THINGS SEEK THY HONOUR AND GLORY	032	09
THAT ALL THINGS MAY BE SO ORDERED AND SETTLED BY	035	14
ONLY SUCH THINGS AS PLEASE THEE, TO THE GLORY OF THY	035	27
AND FILLEST ALL THINGS LIVING WITH PLENTEOUSNESS	040	04
FILL US WITH GOOD THINGS THAT THE POOR AND NEEDY MAY	040	11
ALL THINGS NECESSARY TO THEIR BODILY	040	17
GOVERNOR OF ALL THINGS, WHOSE POWER NO CREATURE IS	041	09
GRANT THAT IN ALL THINGS THEY MAY SERVE WITHOUT	041	30
THAT IN ALL THINGS IT MAY WORK ACCORDING TO GOD'S	047	13
AND IN ALL THINGS MAY ADORN THE DOCTRINE OF	047	28
AND THOSE THINGS WHICH FOR OUR UNWORTHINESS WE DARE	050	02
GRANT THAT THOSE THINGS WHICH WE HAVE FAITHFULLY	050	10
HE MAY ABOVE ALL THINGS SEEK THY HONOUR AND GLCRY	055	24
AND OF ALL THINGS VISIBLE AND INVISIBLE	071	03
BY WHOM ALL THINGS WERE MADE	071	08
ALL THINGS COME OF THEE, O LORD, AND OF THINE OWN	073	23
MAKER OF ALL THINGS, JUDGE OF ALL MEN	075	18
AND ABOVE ALL THINGS YE MUST GIVE MOST HUMBLE ANC	086	04
THESE THINGS IF YE EARNESTLY CONSIDER, YE WILL BY	089	19
WHATSOEVER THINGS WERE WRITTEN AFORETIME WERE WRITTEN	092	15
AFTER THOSE THINGS WHICH ARE COMING CN THE EARTH	093	09
AND WHEN THESE THINGS BEGIN TO COME TO PASS, THEN	093	12
WHEN YE SEE THESE THINGS COME TO PASS, KNOW YE THAT	093	17
LIGHT THE HIDDEN THINGS OF DARKNESS, AND WILL MAKE	094	12
JOHN AGAIN THOSE THINGS WHICH YE DO HEAR AND SEE	094	20
THESE THINGS WERE DONE IN BETHABARA BEYOND JORDAN,	096	06
HEIR OF ALL THINGS, BY WHOM ALSO HE MADE THE WCRLDS	096	25
AND UPHOLDING ALL THINGS BY THE WORD OF HIS POWER,	096	27
ALL THINGS WERE MADE BY HIM	097	22
THESE THINGS SPEAK, AND EXHORT, AND REBUKE WITH ALL	098	25
ALL THESE THINGS SHALL COME UPON THIS	100	26
AND THESE THINGS WRITE WE UNTO YOU, THAT YOUR JCY MAY	101	21
OF THESE THINGS, AND WROTE THESE THINGS	102	13
OF THESE THINGS, AND WROTE THESE THINGS	102	13
ALSO MANY OTHER THINGS WHICH JESUS DID, THE WHICH,	102	15
THOUGHT ON THESE THINGS, BEHOLD, THE ANGEL CF THE	105	02
WE MAY IN ALL THINGS OBEY THY BLESSED WILL	105	23
SHOULD BOW, OF THINGS IN HEAVEN, AND THINGS IN EARTH,	105	28
IN EARTH, AND THINGS UNDER THE EARTH	105	29
IN HEAVEN, AND THINGS IN EARTH, AND THINGS UNDER THE	105	29
WONDERED AT THOSE THINGS WHICH WERE TOLD THEM BY THE	106	15
KEPT ALL THESE THINGS, AND PONDERED THEM IN HER	106	16
GOD FOR ALL THE THINGS THAT THEY HAD HEARD AND SEEN,	106	18
WHO CREATED ALL THINGS BY JESUS CHRIST	108	23
HAD HEARD THESE THINGS, HE WAS TROUBLED, AND ALL	109	03
AND KNOW WHAT THINGS THEY OUGHT TO DO, AND ALSO MAY	109	31
DOST GOVERN ALL THINGS IN HEAVEN AND EARTH	111	11
MIND NOT HIGH THINGS, BUT CONDESCEND TO MEN OF LCW	111	31
PROVIDE THINGS HONEST IN THE SIGHT OF ALL MEN	112	32
ABOVE ALL THESE THINGS PUT ON CHARITY, WHICH IS THE	116	08
FOR THE MASTERY IS TEMPERATE IN ALL THINGS	119	08
BESIDE THOSE THINGS THAT ARE WITHOUT, THAT WHICH	121	10
WILL GLORY OF THE THINGS WHICH CONCERN MINE	121	14
HE HAD SAID THESE THINGS, HE CRIED, HE THAT HATH EARS	121	27
BEARETH ALL THINGS, BELIEVETH ALL THINGS, HCPETH ALL	123	02
HOPETH ALL THINGS, ENDURETH ALL THINGS	123	03
BELIEVETH ALL THINGS, HOPETH ALL THINGS, ENDURETH ALL	123	03
HOPETH ALL THINGS, ENDURETH ALL THINGS	123	03
I PUT AWAY CHILDISH THINGS	123	11
AND ALL THINGS THAT ARE WRITTEN BY THE PROPHETS	123	18
AND THEY UNDERSTOOD NONE OF THESE THINGS	123	24
KNEW THEY THE THINGS WHICH WERE SPOKEN	123	25
BUT IN ALL THINGS APPROVING OURSELVES AS THE	126	09
AS HAVING NOTHING, AND YET POSSESSING ALL THINGS	126	21
ALL THESE THINGS WILL I GIVE THEE, IF THOU WILT	127	07
BECAUSE OF THESE THINGS COMETH THE WRATH OF GOD UPCN	129	10
TO SPEAK OF THOSE THINGS WHICH ARE DONE OF THEM IN	129	18
BUT ALL THINGS THAT ARE REPROVED ARE MADE MANIFEST BY	129	19
AS HE SPAKE THESE THINGS, A CERTAIN WOMAN OF THE	130	17
WHICH THINGS ARE AN ALLEGORY	131	03
PRIEST OF GOOD THINGS TO COME, BY A GREATER AND MCRE	132	23
IN HEAVEN, AND THINGS IN EARTH, AND THINGS UNDER THE	134	25
SHOULD BOW, OF THINGS IN HEAVEN, AND THINGS IN EARTH,	134	25
IN EARTH, AND THINGS UNDER THE EARTH	134	26
THOU NOT HOW MANY THINGS THEY WITNESS AGAINST THEE	135	23
SUFFERED MANY THINGS THIS DAY IN A DREAM BECAUSE OF	135	34
AND THOSE THINGS THAT WERE DONE, THEY FEARED GREATLY,	137	32
FATHER, ALL THINGS ARE POSSIBLE UNTO THEE	141	35
AND THE CHIEF PRIESTS ACCUSED HIM OF MANY THINGS	145	09
BEHOLD HOW MANY THINGS THEY WITNESS AGAINST THEE	145	11
AND ALMOST ALL THINGS ARE BY THE LAW PURGED WITH	147	25
THE PATTERNS OF THINGS IN THE HEAVENS SHOULD BE	147	28
BUT THE HEAVENLY THINGS THEMSELVES WITH BETTER	147	29
FOR THE THINGS CONCERNING WE HAVE AN END	150	11
AND MANY OTHER THINGS BLASPHEMOUSLY SPAKE THEY	151	06
HE HAD HEARD MANY THINGS OF HIM	153	12
TOUCHING THOSE THINGS WHEREOF YE ACCUSE HIM	153	25
IF THEY DO THESE THINGS IN A GREEN TREE, WHAT SHALL	154	20
BEHOLDING THE THINGS WHICH WERE DONE, SMOTE THEIR	155	17
STOOD AFAR OFF, BEHOLDING THESE THINGS	155	20
HAD GIVEN ALL THINGS INTO HIS HANDS, AND THAT HE WAS	155	29
A SHADOW OF GOOD THINGS TO COME, AND NOT THE VERY	157	15
VERY IMAGE OF THE THINGS, CAN NEVER WITH THOSE	157	16
THESE THINGS THEREFORE THE SOLDIERS DID	160	16

THINGS   CONTINUED

KNOWING THAT ALL THINGS WERE NOW ACCOMPLISHED, THAT   160 24
FOR THESE THINGS WERE DONE, THAT THE SCRIPTURE SHOULD   161 07
SEEK THOSE THINGS WHICH ARE ABOVE, WHERE CHRIST   164 03
NOT ON THINGS ON THE EARTH   164 05
YOUR AFFECTION ON THINGS ABOVE, NOT ON THINGS ON THE   164 05
WITNESSES OF ALL THINGS WHICH HE DID BOTH IN THE LAND   166 22
OF ALL THINGS WHICH HAD HAPPENED   167 06
NOT KNOWN THE THINGS WHICH ARE COME TO PASS THERE IN   167 14
AND HE SAID UNTO THEM, WHAT THINGS   167 15
DAY SINCE THESE THINGS WERE DONE   167 22
SUFFERED THESE THINGS, AND TO ENTER INTO HIS GLORY   167 31
SCRIPTURES THE THINGS CONCERNING HIMSELF   167 33
THEY TOLD WHAT THINGS WERE DONE IN THE WAY, AND HOW   168 15
FROM ALL THINGS, FROM WHICH HE COULD NOT BE JUSTIFIED   169 21
THAT ALL THINGS MUST BE FULFILLED, WHICH WERE   170 08
AND YE ARE WITNESSES OF THESE THINGS   170 16
MAY AVOID THOSE THINGS THAT ARE CONTRARY TO THEIR   173 08
FOLLOW ALL SUCH THINGS AS AGREEABLE TO THE SAME   173 09
I HAVE SAID THESE THINGS UNTO YOU, SORROW HATH FILLED   175 08
I HAVE YET MANY THINGS TO SAY UNTO YOU, BUT YE CANNOT   175 17
HE WILL SHEW YOU THINGS TO COME   175 21
ALL THINGS THAT THE FATHER HATH ARE MINE   175 23
WHOM ALL GOOD THINGS DO COME   175 29
MAY THINK THOSE THINGS THAT ARE GOOD, AND BY THY   175 31
THESE THINGS HAVE I SPOKEN UNTO YOU IN PROVERBS   176 23
THOU KNOWEST ALL THINGS, AND NEEDEST NOT THAT ANY MAN   177 02
THESE THINGS I HAVE SPOKEN UNTO YOU, THAT IN ME YE   177 07
SPEAKING OF THE THINGS PERTAINING TO THE KINGDOM OF   177 28
HAD SPOKEN THESE THINGS, WHILE THEY BEHELD, HE WAS   178 12
THE END OF ALL THINGS IS AT HAND   179 12
AND ABOVE ALL THINGS HAVE FERVENT CHARITY AMONG   179 13
THAT GOD IN ALL THINGS MAY BE GLORIFIED THROUGH JESUS   179 20
THESE THINGS HAVE I SPOKEN UNTO YOU, THAT YE SHOULD   179 28
AND THESE THINGS WILL THEY DO UNTO YOU, BECAUSE THEY   179 32
BUT THESE THINGS HAVE I TOLD YOU, THAT WHEN THE TIME   180 02
JUDGMENT IN ALL THINGS, AND EVERMORE TO REJOICE IN   180 11
THESE THINGS I HAVE SPOKEN UNTO YOU, BEING YET   181 29
TEACH YOU ALL THINGS, AND BRING ALL THINGS TO YOUR   181 32
AND BRING ALL THINGS TO YOUR REMEMBRANCE, WHATSOEVER   181 32
WITNESSES OF ALL THINGS WHICH HE DID BOTH IN THE LAND   184 10
NOT WHAT THINGS THEY WERE WHICH HE SPAKE UNTO THEM   186 11
I WILL SHEW THEE THINGS WHICH MUST BE HEREAFTER   187 03
HAST CREATED ALL THINGS, AND FOR THY PLEASURE THEY   187 31
HOW CAN THESE THINGS BE   188 18
A MASTER OF ISRAEL, AND KNOWEST NOT THESE THINGS   188 20
TOLD YOU EARTHLY THINGS, AND YE BELIEVE NOT, HOW   188 23
YE BELIEVE, IF I TELL YOU OF HEAVENLY THINGS   188 24
THY GOOD THINGS, AND LIKEWISE LAZARUS EVIL THINGS   190 17
AND LIKEWISE LAZARUS EVIL THINGS   190 18
IS GREATER THAN OUR HEART, AND KNOWETH ALL THINGS   191 25
AND DO THOSE THINGS THAT ARE PLEASING IN HIS SIGHT   191 28
FOR ALL THINGS ARE NOW READY   192 05
AND SHEWED HIS LORD THESE THINGS   192 12
SO PASS THROUGH THINGS TEMPORAL, THAT WE FINALLY LOSE   194 07
LOSE NOT THE THINGS ETERNAL   194 08
THEE SUCH GOOD THINGS AS PASS MAN'S UNDERSTANDING   195 05
THEE ABOVE ALL THINGS, MAY OBTAIN THY PROMISES,   197 07
WHO ART THE AUTHOR AND GIVER OF ALL GOOD THINGS   198 21
YE THEN IN THOSE THINGS WHEREOF YE ARE NOW ASHAMED   198 32
THE END OF THOSE THINGS IS DEATH   199 02
ORDERETH ALL THINGS BOTH IN HEAVEN AND EARTH   199 29
US ALL HURTFUL THINGS, AND TO GIVE US THOSE THINGS   199 30
TO GIVE US THOSE THINGS WHICH ARE PROFITABLE FOR US   199 31
DO ALWAYS SUCH THINGS AS ARE RIGHT   200 30
NOW THESE THINGS WERE OUR EXAMPLES, TO THE INTENT WE   201 13
LUST AFTER EVIL THINGS, AS THEY ALSO LUSTED   201 14
NOW ALL THESE THINGS HAPPENED UNTO THEM FOR   201 22
ASKED WHAT THESE THINGS MEANT   202 29
THEM TO ASK SUCH THINGS AS SHALL PLEASE THEE   203 13
THIS THY DAY, THE THINGS WHICH BELONG UNTO THY PEACE   204 08
US THOSE THINGS WHEREOF OUR CONSCIENCE IS AFRAID, AND   206 07
US THOSE GOOD THINGS WHICH WE ARE NOT WORTHY TO ASK,   206 09
HE HATH DONE ALL THINGS WELL   207 08
WHICH SEE THE THINGS THAT YE SEE   208 07
TO SEE THOSE THINGS WHICH YE SEE, AND HAVE NOT SEEN   208 09
AND TO HEAR THOSE THINGS WHICH YE HEAR, AND HAVE NOT   208 10
YE CANNOT DO THE THINGS THAT YE WOULD   209 17
WHICH DO SUCH THINGS SHALL NOT INHERIT THE KINGDOM OF   209 25
THY HELP FROM ALL THINGS HURTFUL, AND LEAD US TO ALL   210 20
LEAD US TO ALL THINGS PROFITABLE TO OUR SALVATION   210 20
AFTER ALL THESE THINGS DO THE GENTILES SEEK   211 29
KNOWETH THAT YE HAVE NEED OF ALL THESE THINGS   211 31
AND ALL THESE THINGS SHALL BE ADDED UNTO YOU   211 32
THEY COULD NOT ANSWER HIM AGAIN TO THESE THINGS   214 08
SPIRIT MAY IN ALL THINGS DIRECT AND RULE OUR HEARTS   215 29
FROM ALL THINGS THAT MAY HURT US   217 18
ACCOMPLISH THOSE THINGS WHICH THOU COMMANDEST   217 20
ALWAYS FOR ALL THINGS UNTO GOD AND THE FATHER IN THE   217 30
AND ALL THINGS ARE READY   218 09
YE MAY APPROVE THINGS THAT ARE EXCELLENT   221 03
GRANT THAT THOSE THINGS WHICH WE ASK FAITHFULLY WE   222 12
GLORY IS IN THEIR SHAME, WHO MIND EARTHLY THINGS   222 21
TO SUBJECT ALL THINGS UNTO HIMSELF   222 25
UNTO CAESAR THE THINGS WHICH ARE CAESAR'S   223 10
AND UNTO GOD THE THINGS THAT ARE GOD'S   223 11
JESUS SPAKE THESE THINGS UNTO JOHN'S DISCIPLES,   224 12
AND BRING GLAD TIDINGS OF GOOD THINGS   227 11
THE SUBSTANCE OF THINGS HOPED FOR, THE EVIDENCE OF   228 22
THE EVIDENCE OF THINGS NOT SEEN   228 23
HIM HOW GREAT THINGS HE MUST SUFFER FOR MY NAME'S   230 28
AT THOSE THINGS WHICH WERE SPOKEN OF HIM   233 10
HAD PERFORMED ALL THINGS ACCORDING TO THE LAW OF THE   233 24
HAST HID THESE THINGS FROM THE WISE AND PRUDENT,   235 05
ALL THINGS ARE DELIVERED UNTO ME OF MY FATHER   235 07

THINGS   CONTINUED

THAT HE MIGHT FILL ALL THINGS   237 18
INTO HIM IN ALL THINGS, WHICH IS THE HEAD, EVEN   237 29
THESE THINGS HAVE I SPOKEN UNTO YOU, THAT MY JOY   238 24
TIDINGS OF THESE THINGS CAME UNTO THE EARS OF THE   241 03
FOR ALL THINGS THAT I HAVE HEARD OF MY FATHER I HAVE   241 30
TO HAVE THESE THINGS ALWAYS IN REMEMBRANCE   248 13
DAYS ANY OF THOSE THINGS WHICH THEY HAD SEEN   249 10
THE HIDDEN THINGS OF DISHONESTY, NOT WALKING IN   250 29
WATCH THOU IN ALL THINGS, ENDURE AFFLICTIONS, DO THE   253 23
AND DRINKING SUCH THINGS AS THEY GIVE   254 22
THESE THINGS I COMMAND YOU, THAT YE LOVE ONE ANOTHER   255 12
BUT ALL THESE THINGS WILL THEY DO UNTO YOU FOR MY   255 20
SAW THE WONDERFUL THINGS THAT HE DID, AND THE   260 10
AGAINST THOSE THINGS WHICH WERE SPOKEN BY PAUL,   260 29
AND TERRIBLE THINGS, WHICH THINE EYES HAVE SEEN   263 32
AFTER ALL THESE THINGS DO THE GENTILES SEEK   266 27
KNOWETH THAT YE HAVE NEED OF ALL THESE THINGS   266 29
AND ALL THESE THINGS SHALL BE ADDED UNTO YOU   266 30
THOUGHT FOR THE THINGS OF ITSELF   266 32
ALWAYS FOR ALL THINGS UNTO GOD AND THE FATHER IN THE   267 11
TO OBSERVE ALL THINGS WHATSOEVER I HAVE COMMANDED   275 30
AND ALL OTHER THINGS WHICH A CHRISTIAN OUGHT TO KNOW   277 11
AND THAT ALL THINGS BELONGING TO THE SPIRIT MAY   278 22
AND GOVERN ALL THINGS, WORLD WITHOUT END   278 30
WHO ART THE AUTHOR AND GIVER OF ALL GOOD THINGS   283 09
AND VOW THREE THINGS IN MY NAME   283 22
DO ALWAYS SUCH THINGS AS ARE RIGHT   287 27
I LEARN TWO THINGS FROM THESE COMMANDMENTS   288 12
ABLE TO DO THESE THINGS OF YOURSELF, NOR TO WALK IN   289 13
CHURCH PROVIDE TO HELP YOU TO DO ALL THESE THINGS   291 22
TO DO ALL THOSE THINGS WHICH YE THEN UNDERTOOK, OR   296 26
AND TO DO THOSE THINGS WHICH ARE GOOD, AND ACCEPTABLE 298 14
AND THY WORD, ABOVE ALL THINGS   311 32
TO WHOM ALL THINGS IN HEAVEN, IN EARTH, AND   314 16
AND ALL THINGS NECESSARY BEING PREPARED, THE MINISTER R 321 14
THESE THINGS HAVE I WRITTEN UNTO YOU THAT BELIEVE ON   322 12
HE HATH PUT ALL THINGS UNDER HIS FEET   328 31
WHEN HE SAITH ALL THINGS ARE PUT UNDER HIM, IT IS   328 32
WHICH DID PUT ALL THINGS UNDER HIM   328 34
AND WHEN ALL THINGS SHALL BE SUBDUED UNTO HIM, THEN   328 34
HIM THAT PUT ALL THINGS UNDER HIM, THAT GOD MAY BE   329 03
WE KNOW THAT ALL THINGS WORK TOGETHER FOR GOOD TO   330 30
WHAT SHALL WE THEN SAY TO THESE THINGS   330 33
HE NOT WITH HIM ALSO FREELY GIVE US ALL THINGS   331 03
IN ALL THESE THINGS WE ARE MORE THAN CONQUERORS   331 08
NOR THINGS TO COME, NOR HEIGHT, NOR DEPTH,   331 11
NOR POWERS, NOR THINGS PRESENT, NOR THINGS TO COME,   331 11
TO SUBDUE ALL THINGS UNTO HIMSELF   333 23
TO SUBDUE ALL THINGS UNTO HIMSELF   337 17
THOU HAST PUT ALL THINGS IN SUBJECTION UNDER HIS   351 12
AND THE TONGUE THAT SPEAKETH PROUD THINGS   355 13
WHOSO DOETH THESE THINGS *   357 19
AND THEIR MOUTH SPEAKETH PROUD THINGS   359 07
LAID TO MY CHARGE THINGS THAT I KNEW NOT   382 14
I SPEAK THE THINGS WHICH I HAVE MADE CONCERNING THE   396 16
THY RIGHT HAND SHALL TEACH THEE TERRIBLE THINGS   396 24
4 THEY MARVELLED TO SEE SUCH THINGS   399 18
21 THESE THINGS HAST THOU DONE, AND I HELD MY TONGUE, 402 32
BEFORE THEE THE THINGS THAT THOU HAST DONE   402 35
ARE NOT THESE THINGS NOTED IN THY BOOK   408 31
3 THOU HAST SHOWED THY PEOPLE HEAVY THINGS   412 17
SHOW US WONDERFUL THINGS IN THY RIGHTEOUSNESS,   416 21
5 I PAID THEM THE THINGS THAT I NEVER TOOK   422 10
AND LET THE THINGS THAT SHOULD HAVE BEEN FOR THEIR   423 19
AND GREAT THINGS ARE THEY THAT THOU HAST DONE   426 15
WHICH ONLY DOETH WONDROUS THINGS   428 03
13 MARVELLOUS THINGS DID HE IN THE SIGHT OF OUR   435 24
AND DOEST WONDROUS THINGS   447 23
2 VERY EXCELLENT THINGS ARE SPOKEN OF THEE, *   448 16
LAND WHERE ALL THINGS ARE FORGOTTEN   449 21
FOR HE HATH DONE MARVELLOUS THINGS   461 26
MOUTH WITH GOOD THINGS, *   466 15
WHEREIN ARE THINGS CREEPING INNUMERABLE, BOTH SMALL   469 11
THE PEOPLE WHAT THINGS HE HATH DONE   470 06
HAD DONE SO GREAT THINGS IN EGYPT   474 11
AND FEARFUL THINGS BY THE RED SEA   474 13
43 WHOSO IS WISE, WILL PONDER THESE THINGS   478 32
TO BEHOLD THE THINGS THAT ARE IN HEAVEN AND EARTH   484 18
BRINGETH MIGHTY THINGS TO PASS   488 32
BRINGETH MIGHTY THINGS TO PASS   488 35
SEE THE WONDROUS THINGS OF THY LAW   491 03
FOR ALL THINGS SERVE THEE   496 08
96 I SEE THAT ALL THINGS COME TO AN END   496 17
I HATE THEM THAT IMAGINE EVIL THINGS   497 24
HATH DONE GREAT THINGS FOR THEM   505 12
HATH DONE GREAT THINGS FOR US ALREADY   505 13
AND THY WORD, ABOVE ALL THINGS   513 32
ME EAT OF SUCH THINGS AS PLEASE THEM   517 17
AND FILLEST ALL THINGS LIVING WITH PLENTEOUSNESS   521 24
CREEPING THINGS AND FLYING FOWLS   524 23
FAITHFUL IN ALL THINGS   531 32
GIVER OF ALL GOOD THINGS, WHO OF THY GREAT GOODNESS   534 30
EXPERT IN THE THINGS APPERTAINING TO THE   R 535 22
GIVER OF ALL GOOD THINGS, WHO BY THY HOLY SPIRIT HAST 537 20
THAT HE MIGHT FILL ALL THINGS   538 05
NOT WHAT THINGS THEY WERE WHICH HE SPAKE UNTO THEM   539 02
WEIGHED THESE THINGS WITH YOURSELVES, LONG BEFORE   541 10
WILLS IN THESE THINGS, AND THAT THIS YOUR PROMISE MAY 541 25
PLAINLY TO THESE THINGS, WHICH WE, IN THE NAME OF   541 27
HATH GIVEN YOU THIS WILL TO DO ALL THESE THINGS   543 19
HUMBLE SUPPLICATIONS TO GOD FOR ALL THESE THINGS   R 543 24
GIVER OF ALL GOOD THINGS, WHO BY THY HOLY SPIRIT HAST 547 31
WHEN ALL THINGS ARE DULY PREPARED IN THE CHURCH,   R 549 03
NOT KNOWING THE THINGS THAT SHALL BEFALL ME THERE   550 16

THINGS   CONTINUED

BUT NONE OF THESE THINGS MOVE ME, NEITHER COUNT I MY   550 18
SPEAKING PERVERSE THINGS, TO DRAW AWAY DISCIPLES   550 32
SHEWED YOU ALL THINGS, HOW THAT SO LABOURING YE OUGHT   551 08
THOU KNOWEST ALL THINGS   551 23
TO OBSERVE ALL THINGS WHATSOEVER I HAVE COMMANDED   552 13
GIVER OF ALL GOOD THINGS, WHO BY THY HOLY SPIRIT HAST   553 26
YOURSELF IN ALL THINGS AN EXAMPLE OF GOOD WORKS UNTO   555 10
HATH GIVEN YOU A GOOD WILL TO DO ALL THESE THINGS   555 29
THINK UPON THE THINGS CONTAINED IN THIS BOOK   558 22
DECENCY OF THINGS, HAVE ERECTED HOUSES FOR THE PUBLIC   564 15
AND KNOW WHAT THINGS THEY OUGHT TO DO, AND MAY HAVE   566 05
AND TO ASK SUCH THINGS AS ARE REQUISITE AND   566 17
FOR THE FORMER THINGS ARE PASSED AWAY   567 20
I MAKE ALL THINGS NEW   567 22
TAKE THESE THINGS HENCE   567 32
LIVE OF THE THINGS BELONGING TO THE ALTAR   569 29
BE THOU IN ALL THINGS A PATTERN TO THE FLOCK   571 28
AND VOW THREE THINGS IN MY NAME   577 13
I LEARN TWO THINGS   579 24
ABLE TO DO THESE THINGS OF THYSELF, NOR TO WALK IN   580 17
WILL SEND US ALL THINGS THAT ARE NEEDFUL BOTH FOR OUR   580 33
TEMPERATE IN ALL THINGS, AND DILIGENT IN OUR SEVERAL   588 28
THESE THINGS, AND WHATEVER ELSE THOU SHALT SEE TO BE   589 05
OPENED TO BEHOLD THINGS INVISIBLE AND UNSEEN,   594 24
THANKS FOR ALL THINGS, TO DREAD NOTHING BUT THE LOSS   596 04
HIM BY WHOM ALL THINGS WERE MADE, THY SON, JESUS   596 21
LOVE WHATSOEVER THINGS ARE TRUE AND PURE AND LOVELY   596 27
FOR THEM BETTER THINGS THAN WE CAN DESIRE OR PRAY   597 12
PRESERVER OF ALL THINGS BOTH VISIBLE AND INVISIBLE   603 05
AND ALL THINGS APPERTAINING TO THE PERFECTION   603 22
CONTAINETH ALL THINGS NECESSARY TO SALVATION   603 29
UNTO US IN ALL THINGS, SIN ONLY EXCEPT, FROM WHICH HE   605 31
YET OFFEND IN MANY THINGS   605 36
HIGH AND HEAVENLY THINGS, AS WELL BECAUSE IT DOTH   606 20
IN ALL THOSE THINGS THAT OF NECESSITY ARE REQUISITE   606 40
SO THAT ALL THINGS BE DONE TO EDIFYING   610 03
DOTH CONTAIN ALL THINGS NECESSARY TO SUCH   610 33
AS LAITY, IN ALL THINGS TEMPORAL   610 39
NO AUTHORITY IN THINGS PURELY SPIRITUAL   610 39
OF SUCH THINGS AS HE POSSESSETH, LIBERALLY TO   611 03

THINK

AS HE SHALL THINK FIT, OR WITH THE GRACE   R 017 23
AS HE SHALL THINK FIT   R 031 32
HE MAY THINK CONVENIENT   R 086 27
WHO WOULD NOT THINK A GREAT INJURY AND WRONG DONE   088 23
AMONG YOU, NOT TO THINK OF HIMSELF MORE HIGHLY THAN   110 10
OF HIMSELF MORE HIGHLY THAN HE OUGHT TO THINK   110 11
BUT TO THINK SOBERLY, ACCORDING AS GOD HATH DEALT TO   110 11
WHAT THINK YE   143 18
INSPIRATION WE MAY THINK THOSE THINGS THAT ARE GOOD,   175 31
KILLETH YOU WILL THINK THAT HE DOETH GOD SERVICE   179 31
THE SPIRIT TO THINK AND DO ALWAYS SUCH THINGS AS ARE   200 30
OF OURSELVES TO THINK ANY THING AS OF OURSELVES   206 14
ALL THAT WE ASK OR THINK, ACCORDING TO THE POWER THAT   212 22
SAYING, WHAT THINK YE OF CHRIST   215 17
WHEREFORE THINK YE EVIL IN YOUR HEARTS   217 06
IS MEET FOR ME TO THINK THIS OF YOU ALL, BECAUSE I   220 28
LET NOT THAT MAN THINK THAT HE SHALL RECEIVE ANY   239 16
I THINK IT MEET, AS LONG AS I AM IN THIS TABERNACLE,   248 08
DO YOU NOT THINK THAT YOU ARE BOUND SO TO DO   283 29
THE SPIRIT TO THINK AND DO ALWAYS SUCH THINGS AS ARE   287 27
I WILL THINK UPON GOD   311 04
HE SHALL THINK CONVENIENT TO THE OCCASION   R 314 24
OFFICE AS HE SHALL THINK FIT, AND THE FOLLOWING   R 320 07
TO THY MERCY THINK THOU UPON ME, O LORD, FOR THY   369 31
THINK NO SCORN OF ME   373 03
4 NOW WHEN I THINK THEREUPON, I POUR OUT MY HEART BY   393 06
11 AND YET THEY THINK THAT THEIR HOUSES SHALL   400 26
2 O THINK UPON THY CONGREGATION, *   430 06
3 THINK UPON THE TRIBE OF THINE INHERITANCE, *   430 08
I WILL THINK UPON GOD   433 21
12 I WILL THINK ALSO OF ALL THY WORKS, *   434 06
THY SERVANTS THINK UPON HER STONES, *   465 07
AND THINK UPON HIS COMMANDMENTS TO DO THEM   467 11
O THINK UPON THY SERVANT, AS CONCERNING THY WORD,   493 08
EXAMINED THEM, AND THINK THEM SO TO BE   530 19
DO YOU THINK THAT YOU ARE TRULY CALLED,   532 31
I THINK SO   532 34
EXAMINED THEM, AND THINK THEM SO TO BE   536 20
DO YOU THINK IN YOUR HEART, THAT YOU ARE TRULY   541 30
I THINK IT   541 34
THINK UPON THE THINGS CONTAINED IN THIS BOOK   558 22
DOST THOU NOT THINK THAT THOU ART BOUND TO BELIEVE,   577 20
AS HE SHALL THINK CONVENIENT, IN SOME PART OF   R 582 30
AS HE SHALL THINK FIT TO BE PRESENTED TO THE BISHOP   R 583 08

THINKEST

IN THY WRATH THINKEST UPON MERCY   063 02
OF THESE THREE, THINKEST THOU, WAS NEIGHBOUR UNTO HIM   209 02
WHAT THINKEST THOU   223 03
13 THINKEST THOU THAT I WILL EAT BULLS' FLESH,   402 16

THINKETH

AS HE THINKETH MOST CONVENIENT   R 071 33
THINKETH NO EVIL   122 32
LET HIM THAT THINKETH HE STANDETH TAKE HEED LEST HE   201 25

THIRD

THE THIRD DAY HE ROSE AGAIN FROM THE DEAD   015 24

THIRD   CONTINUED

AND THE THIRD DAY HE ROSE AGAIN ACCORDING TO THE   016 10
THE THIRD DAY HE ROSE AGAIN FROM THE DEAD   029 29
AND THE THIRD DAY HE ROSE AGAIN ACCORDING TO THE   030 15
BE USED AFTER THE THIRD COLLECT AT MORNING OR EVENING   R 054 03
UNTO THE THIRD AND FOURTH GENERATION OF   068 13
AND THE THIRD DAY HE ROSE AGAIN ACCORDING TO THE   071 12
AND THE THIRD DAY THERE WAS A MARRIAGE IN CANA OF   113 11
WENT OUT ABOUT THE THIRD HOUR, AND SAW OTHERS   119 19
AND THE THIRD DAY HE SHALL RISE AGAIN   123 23
AND HE COMETH THE THIRD TIME, AND SAITH UNTO THEM,   142 10
AND IT WAS THE THIRD HOUR, AND THEY CRUCIFIED HIM   146 13
SAID UNTO THEM THE THIRD TIME, WHY, WHAT EVIL HATH HE   153 34
SURE UNTIL THE THIRD DAY, LEST HIS DISCIPLES COME BY   162 20
GOD RAISED UP THE THIRD DAY, AND SHEWED HIM OPENLY   166 25
TO-DAY IS THE THIRD DAY SINCE THESE THINGS WERE DONE   167 21
FROM THE DEAD THE THIRD DAY   170 13
GOD RAISED UP THE THIRD DAY, AND SHEWED HIM OPENLY   184 12
A CALF, AND THE THIRD HAD A FACE AS A MAN, AND THE   187 19
HE ROSE AGAIN THE THIRD DAY ACCORDING TO THE   205 06
SAINT JOHN, IN THE THIRD CHAPTER, AT THE FIRST VERSE   275 04
THE THIRD DAY HE ROSE AGAIN FROM THE DEAD   284 18
UNTO THE THIRD AND FOURTH GENERATION OF   286 13
FIRST (SECOND OR THIRD) TIME OF ASKING   R 304 25
OR COME IN THE THIRD WATCH, AND FIND THEM SO, BLESSED   534 24
SAITH UNTO HIM THE THIRD TIME, SIMON, SON OF JONAS,   551 20
SAID UNTO HIM THE THIRD TIME, LOVEST THOU ME   551 22
THE THIRD DAY HE ROSE AGAIN FROM THE DEAD   578 02
UNTO THE THIRD AND FOURTH GENERATION OF   578 32

THIRDLY

AND THIRDLY, THAT I SHOULD KEEP GOD'S HOLY WILL AND   283 26
THIRDLY, IN GOD THE HOLY GHOST, WHO SANCTIFIETH ME,   285 02
AND THIRDLY, THAT I SHOULD KEEP GOD'S HOLY WILL AND   577 17
THIRDLY, IN GOD THE HOLY GHOST, WHO SANCTIFIETH ME,   578 15

THIRST

IF HE THIRST, GIVE HIM DRINK   113 06
IN HUNGER AND THIRST, IN FASTINGS OFTEN, IN COLD AND   121 09
THE SCRIPTURE MIGHT BE FULFILLED, SAITH, I THIRST   160 25
NO MORE, NEITHER THIRST ANY MORE   257 12
DO HUNGER AND THIRST AFTER RIGHTEOUSNESS   257 24
NO MORE, NEITHER THIRST ANY MORE   341 23
AND THE WILD ASSES QUENCH THEIR THIRST   468 16

THIRSTETH

2 MY SOUL THIRSTETH FOR THEE, MY FLESH ALSO LONGETH   414 27

THIRSTY

I WAS THIRSTY, AND YE GAVE ME DRINK   259 06
OR THIRSTY, AND GAVE THEE DRINK   259 11
AND WHEN I WAS THIRSTY THEY GAVE ME VINEGAR TO DRINK   423 16
5 HUNGRY AND THIRSTY, *   476 14
UNTO THEE AS A THIRSTY LAND   519 03

THIRTEENTH

AT THE THIRTEENTH VERSE   274 24

THIRTY

BROUGHT AGAIN THE THIRTY PIECES OF SILVER TO THE   135 04
AND THEY TOOK THE THIRTY PIECES OF SILVER, THE PRICE   135 15
FOUR HUNDRED AND THIRTY YEARS AFTER, CANNOT DISANNUL,   207 23

THISTLES

MEN GATHER GRAPES OF THORNS, OR FIGS OF THISTLES   200 18

THITHER

WHERE HE IS, THITHER WE MIGHT ALSO ASCEND, AND REIGN   078 20
HE WAS AFRAID TO GO THITHER   107 19
HEART AND MIND THITHER ASCEND, AND WITH HIM   177 17
4 FOR THITHER THE TRIBES GO UP, EVEN THE TRIBES OF   503 13

THOMAS

THY HOLY APOSTLE THOMAS TO BE DOUBTFUL IN THY SON'S   228 07
THOMAS, ONE OF THE TWELVE, CALLED DIDYMUS, WAS NOT   228 25
WERE WITHIN, AND THOMAS WITH THEM   228 32
THEN SAITH HE TO THOMAS, REACH HITHER THY FINGER,   229 03
AND THOMAS ANSWERED AND SAID UNTO HIM, MY LORD AND MY   229 06
SAITH UNTO HIM, THOMAS, BECAUSE THOU HAST SEEN ME,   229 07
THOMAS SAITH UNTO HIM, LORD, WE KNOW NOT WHITHER THOU   240 04
THOMAS SAITH UNTO HIM, LORD, WE KNOW NOT WHITHER THOU   331 23

THORNS

AND SOME FELL AMONG THORNS   121 24
AND THE THORNS SPRANG UP WITH IT, AND CHOKED IT   121 25
WHICH FELL AMONG THORNS ARE THEY, WHICH, WHEN THEY   122 06
A CROWN OF THORNS, THEY PUT IT UPON HIS HEAD, AND A   136 19
A CROWN OF THORNS, AND PUT IT ABOUT HIS HEAD, AND   145 32
A CROWN OF THORNS, AND PUT IT ON HIS HEAD, AND THEY   158 31
THE CROWN OF THORNS, AND THE PURPLE ROBE   159 04
GATHER GRAPES OF THORNS, OR FIGS OF THISTLES   200 18
BE MADE HOT WITH THORNS, *   410 26
AND ARE EXTINCT EVEN AS THE FIRE AMONG THE THORNS   488 24

THOROUGHLY

OUGHT THOROUGHLY TO BE RECEIVED AND BELIEVED 604 26

THOUGH

THOUGH WE HAVE REBELLED AGAINST HIM 022 07
AND THOUGH WE BE TIED AND BOUND WITH THE CHAIN CF OUR 063 11
OTHER HOLY DAYS, (THOUGH THERE BE NO SERMON OR R 084 27
FROM A SERVANT, THOUGH HE BE LORD OF ALL 104 15
AS THOUGH WE HAD BEEN WEAK 120 26
THOUGH I SPEAK WITH THE TONGUES OF MEN AND OF ANGELS, 122 21
AND THOUGH I HAVE THE GIFT OF PROPHECY, AND 122 23
AND THOUGH I HAVE ALL FAITH, SO THAT I COULD REMOVE 122 25
AND THOUGH I BESTOW ALL MY GOODS TO FEED THE POOR, 122 26
THE POOR, AND THOUGH I GIVE MY BODY TO BE BURNED, AND 122 27
ART OUR FATHER, THOUGH ABRAHAM BE IGNORANT OF US, AND 139 21
AND HE MADE AS THOUGH HE WOULD HAVE GCNE FURTHER 168 02
AND THOUGH THEY FOUND NO CAUSE OF DEATH IN HIM, 168 30
NO WISE BELIEVE, THOUGH A MAN DECLARE IT UNTO YCU 169 25
BE PERSUADED, THOUGH ONE ROSE FROM THE DEAD 190 30
I SAY UNTO YOU, THOUGH HE WILL NOT RISE AND GIVE HIM, 262 33
THOUGH I WALK IN THE MIDST OF TROUBLE 311 25
THOUGH I WALK IN THE MIDST OF TROUBLE, YET SHALT THOU 312 04
BELIEVETH IN ME, THOUGH HE WERE DEAD, YET SHALL HE 324 06
AND THOUGH THIS BODY BE DESTROYED, YET SHALL I SEE 324 10
AND THOUGH MEN BE SO STRONG THAT THEY COME TO 325 33
WILL WE NOT FEAR, THOLGH THE EARTH BE MOVED, * 327 05
AND THOUGH THE HILLS BE CARRIED INTO THE MIDST OF THE 327 06
THOUGH THE WATERS THEREOF RAGE AND SWELL, * 327 07
AND THOUGH THE MOUNTAINS SHAKE AT THE TEMPEST OF THE 327 07
SHALL LIVE, THOUGH HE DIE 334 32
BELIEVETH IN ME, THOUGH HE WERE DEAD, YET SHALL HE 338 06
THOUGH I WALK THROUGH THE VALLEY OF THE SHADOW 338 23
THOUGH IT WERE TO HIS OWN HINDRANCE 357 16
4 YEA, THOUGH I WALK THROUGH THE VALLEY OF THE SHADOW 368 16
3 THOUGH AN HOST OF MEN WERE LAID AGAINST ME, 371 29
AND THOUGH THERE ROSE UP WAR AGAINST ME, YET WILL I 371 30
IF THOU MAKE AS THOUGH THOU HEAREST NOT, I BECOME 373 04
BEHAVED MYSELF AS THOLGH IT HAD BEEN MY FRIEND CR MY 382 20
24 THOUGH HE FALL, HE SHALL NOT BE CAST AWAY 386 10
18 AND THOUGH ALL THIS BE COME UPON US, YET DC WE NOT 395 28
WILL WE NOT FEAR, THOLGH THE EARTH BE MOVED, * 397 27
AND THOUGH THE HILLS BE CARRIED INTO THE MIDST OF THE 397 28
3 THOUGH THE WATERS THEREOF RAGE AND SWELL, * 397 30
AND THOUGH THE MOUNTAINS SHAKE AT THE TEMPEST OF THE 397 31
NOT THOU AFRAID, THOUGH ONE BE MADE RICH, * 401 07
3 NEVERTHELESS, THOUGH I AM SOMETIME AFRAID, * 408 19
13 THOUGH YE HAVE LAIN AMONG THE SHEEP-FOLDS, 420 06
AND THOUGH MEN BE SO STRONG THAT THEY COME TO 454 08
O GOD, THOUGH THOU DIDST PUNISH THEIR WICKED 462 33
40 THOUGH HE SUFFER THEM TO BE EVIL ENTREATED THROUGH 478 26
27 THOUGH THEY CURSE, YET BLESS THOU 481 26
6 FOR THOUGH THE LORD BE HIGH, YET HATH HE RESPECT 514 08
7 THOUGH I WALK IN THE MIDST OF TROUBLE, YET SHALT 514 10
THOUGH I BE MADE SECRETLY, AND FASHIONED BENEATH IN 515 18
EVEN AS THOUGH THEY WERE MINE ENEMIES 516 02
THAT THOUGH HE BE SOMETIME AFRAID, HE YET 597 24
THOUGH THEY BE TROUBLED ON EVERY SIDE, SUFFER THEM 599 13
THOUGH THEY BE PERPLEXED, SAVE THEM FROM DESPAIR 599 14

THOUGHT

TIMES WERE THOUGHT CONVENIENT V 30
HAS NOT SINCE THOUGHT PROPER TO REVIVE IT BY ANY NEW VI 06
BY THOUGHT, WORD, AND DEED, AGAINST THY 075 21
BUT WHILE HE THOUGHT ON THESE THINGS, BEHOLD, THE 105 02
AS A CHILD, I THOUGHT AS A CHILD 123 10
THE FORM OF GOD, THOUGHT IT NOT ROBBERY TO BE EQUAL 134 17
AND WHEN HE THOUGHT THEREON, HE WEPT 144 03
BUT THOUGHT HE SAW A VISION 245 20
SHALL TAKE THOUGHT FOR THE THINGS OF ITSELF 266 32
AGAINST THEE IN THOUGHT, WORD, AND DEED 323 13
AND THOUGHT UPON THEE WHEN I WAS WAKING 415 05
16 THEN THOUGHT I TO UNDERSTAND THIS 429 08
43 THEY THOUGHT NOT OF HIS HAND, * 437 25
24 YEA, THEY THOUGHT SCORN OF THAT PLEASANT LAND, 474 17
44 HE THOUGHT UPON HIS COVENANT, AND PITIED THEM, 475 27
55 I HAVE THOUGHT UPON THY NAME, O LORD, IN THE NIGHT 493 20
A READINESS OF THOUGHT AND EXPRESSION SUITABLE TC THE 573 26
THE FAITH, OR BE THOUGHT REQUISITE OR NECESSARY TO 603 31

THOUGHTEST

AND THOU THOUGHTEST WICKEDLY, THAT I AM EVEN SUCH A 402 33

THOUGHTS

CLEANSE THE THOUGHTS OF OUR HEARTS BY THE INSPIRATION 067 18
FROM ALL EVIL THOUGHTS WHICH MAY ASSAULT AND HURT THE 127 19
KNOWING THEIR THOUGHTS, SAID UNTO THEM, EVERY KINGDOM 129 29
AND WHY DO THOUGHTS ARISE IN YOUR HEARTS 169 32
KNOWING THEIR THOUGHTS SAID, WHEREFORE THINK YE EVIL 217 06
THAT THE THOUGHTS OF MANY HEARTS MAY BE 233 15
NEITHER IS GOD IN ALL HIS THOUGHTS 353 12
AND THE THOUGHTS OF HIS HEART FROM GENERATION TO 379 10
AS BE ALSO THY THOUGHTS, WHICH ARE TO US-WARD 390 22
THY THOUGHTS ARE VERY DEEP 456 09
KNOWETH THE THOUGHTS OF MAN, * 458 08
MY THOUGHTS LONG BEFORE 514 22
PROVE ME, AND EXAMINE MY THOUGHTS 516 05
THEN ALL HIS THOUGHTS PERISH 522 09
ACCOUNT OF OUR THOUGHTS, WORDS, AND ACTIONS TO HIM 588 22
THAT NO UNCLEAN THOUGHTS, UNLAWFUL DESIGNS, OR 590 13
WITH STEDFAST THOUGHTS AND KINDLED AFFECTIONS, WE MAY 594 07

THOUGHTS CONTINUED

ALL OUR THOUGHTS AND ENDEAVOURS 594 21

THOUSAND

FORTY AND FOUR THOUSAND, HAVING HIS FATHER'S NAME 102 30
FORTY AND FOUR THOUSAND, WHICH WERE REDEEMED FROM THE 103 07
THE MEN SAT DOWN, IN NUMBER ABOUT FIVE THOUSAND 132 03
AND THEY THAT HAD EATEN WERE ABOUT FOUR THOUSAND 199 25
AND FELL IN ONE DAY THREE AND TWENTY THOUSAND 201 18
OWED HIM TEN THOUSAND TALENTS 221 16
IN NUMBER ABOUT FIVE THOUSAND 226 02
FORTY AND FOUR THOUSAND OF ALL THE TRIBES OF THE 256 21
FOR A THOUSAND YEARS IN THY SIGHT ARE BUT AS 325 20
CATTLE UPON A THOUSAND HILLS 402 11
GOD ARE TWENTY THOUSAND, EVEN THOUSANDS OF ANGELS 420 16
IS BETTER THAN A THOUSAND 445 31
4 FOR A THOUSAND YEARS IN THY SIGHT ARE BUT AS 453 25
AND TEN THOUSAND AT THY RIGHT HAND 455 09
7 A THOUSAND SHALL FALL BESIDE THEE, AND TEN THOUSAND 455 09
HE MADE TO A THOUSAND GENERATIONS 470 19

THOUSANDS

MERCY UNTO THOUSANDS IN THEM THAT LOVE ME AND KEEP MY 068 14
MERCY UNTO THOUSANDS IN THEM THAT LOVE ME AND KEEP MY 286 14
AFRAID FOR TEN THOUSANDS OF THE PEOPLE, * 347 02
EVEN THOUSANDS OF ANGELS 420 17
THAN THOUSANDS OF GOLD AND SILVER 494 25
BRING FORTH THOUSANDS, AND TEN THOUSANDS IN CUR 520 20
AND TEN THOUSANDS IN OUR FIELDS 520 20
MERCY UNTO THOUSANDS IN THEM THAT LOVE ME AND KEEP MY 578 33

THREATENED

HE THREATENED NOT 172 13

THREATENINGS

OUT THREATENINGS AND SLAUGHTER AGAINST THE DISCIPLES 229 25

THREE

THAT WHEN TWO OR THREE ARE GATHERED TOGETHER IN THY 020 05
THAT WHEN TWO OR THREE ARE GATHERED TOGETHER IN THY 034 05
THAT AFTER THREE DAYS THEY FOUND HIM IN THE 110 27
CONTAINING TWO OR THREE FIRKINS APIECE 113 20
CHARITY, THESE THREE 123 14
AND BUILDEST IT IN THREE DAYS, SAVE THYSELF 137 07
SOLD FOR MORE THAN THREE HUNDRED PENCE, AND HAVE BEEN 140 08
AND WITHIN THREE DAYS I WILL BUILD ANOTHER 143 07
AND BUILDEST IT IN THREE DAYS, SAVE THYSELF, AND COME 146 20
YET ALIVE, AFTER THREE DAYS I WILL RISE AGAIN 162 18
FOR THERE ARE THREE THAT BEAR WITNESS, THE SPIRIT, 171 02
AND THESE THREE AGREE IN ONE 171 03
NOW BEEN WITH ME THREE DAYS, AND HAVE NOTHING TO EAT 199 11
FELL IN ONE DAY THREE AND TWENTY THOUSAND 201 18
WHICH NOW OF THESE THREE, THINKEST THOU, WAS 209 02
AND HE WAS THREE DAYS WITHOUT SIGHT, AND NEITHER DID 230 12
AND LET US MAKE THREE TABERNACLES 249 02
LEND ME THREE LOAVES 262 28
PROMISE AND VOW THREE THINGS IN MY NAME 283 22
BY THE SPACE OF THREE YEARS I CEASED NOT TO WARN 550 34
WHEREVER TWO OR THREE OF THY FAITHFUL SERVANTS SHALL 564 31
PROMISE AND VOW THREE THINGS IN MY NAME 577 13
GODHEAD THERE BE THREE PERSONS, OF ONE SUBSTANCE, 603 06

THREESCORE

ABOUT THREESCORE FURLONGS 167 05
OUR AGE ARE THREESCORE YEARS AND TEN 325 32
OUR AGE ARE THREESCORE YEARS AND TEN 454 07

THRICE

THRICE WAS I BEATEN WITH RODS, ONCE WAS I STCNED, 121 02
WAS I STONED, THRICE I SUFFERED SHIPWRECK, A NIGHT 121 03
THE COCK CROW TWICE, THOU SHALT DENY ME THRICE 141 25
THOU SHALT DENY ME THRICE 144 02
THAT THOU SHALT THRICE DENY THAT THOU KNOWEST ME 150 03
THOU SHALT DENY ME THRICE 151 22

THROAT

TOOK HIM BY THE THROAT, SAYING, PAY ME THAT THCU 221 25
10 THEIR THROAT IS AN OPEN SEPULCHRE 348 20
MY THROAT IS DRY 422 05
NEITHER SPEAK THEY THROUGH THEIR THROAT 485 25
103 O HOW SWEET ARE THY WORDS UNTO MY THROAT 496 32

THRONE

BOLDLY UNTO THE THRONE OF GRACE, THAT WE MAY OBTAIN 005 08
UNTO THE THRONE OF THE HEAVENLY GRACE, SAYING 006 12
ON THE GLORIOUS THRONE OF THY KINGDOM 011 25
WHO DOST FROM THY THRONE BEHOLD ALL THE DWELLERS UPCN 017 28
UNTO THE THRONE OF THE HEAVENLY GRACE, SAYING 023 20
SITTEST IN THE THRONE JUDGING RIGHT 035 31
SON HE SAITH, THY THRONE, O GOD, IS FOR EVER AND 097 09
SONG BEFORE THE THRONE, AND BEFORE THE FOUR LIVING 103 05
FAULT BEFORE THE THRONE OF GOD 103 14
AND ONE SAT ON THE THRONE 187 05
BEHOLD, A THRONE WAS SET IN HEAVEN, AND CNE SAT 187 05
ROUND ABOUT THE THRONE, IN SIGHT LIKE UNTO AN 187 07
ROUND ABOUT THE THRONE WERE FOUR AND TWENTY SEATS 187 08

THRONE   CONTINUED

AND OUT OF THE THRONE PROCEEDED LIGHTNINGS AND	187 12
BEFORE THE THRONE, WHICH ARE THE SEVEN SPIRITS CF	187 14
AND BEFORE THE THRONE THERE WAS A SEA OF GLASS LIKE	187 15
THE MIDST OF THE THRONE, AND ROUND ABOUT THE THRCNE,	187 16
ROUND ABOUT THE THRONE, WERE FOUR LIVING CREATURES	187 16
THAT SAT ON THE THRONE, WHO LIVETH FOR EVER AND EVER,	187 25
THAT SAT ON THE THRONE, AND WORSHIP HIM THAT LIVETH	187 27
CROWNS BEFORE THE THRONE, SAYING, THOU ART WORTHY,	187 29
SHALL SIT IN THE THRONE OF HIS GLORY, YE ALSO SHALL	231 16
GIVE UNTO HIM THE THRONE OF HIS FATHER DAVID	236 18
STOOD BEFORE THE THRONE, AND BEFORE THE LAMB, CLOTHED	256 25
SITTETH UPON THE THRONE, AND UNTO THE LAMB	256 28
ROUND ABOUT THE THRONE, AND ABOUT THE ELDERS AND THE	256 29
FELL BEFORE THE THRONE ON THEIR FACES, AND WORSHIPPED	256 30
THEY BEFORE THE THRONE OF GOD, AND SERVE HIM DAY AND	257 10
SITTETH ON THE THRONE SHALL DWELL AMONG THEM	257 11
THE MIDST OF THE THRONE SHALL FEED THEM, AND SHALL	257 14
RIGHT HAND OF THE THRONE OF GOD	258 26
HE SIT UPON THE THRONE OF HIS GLORY	258 30
THEY BEFORE THE THRONE OF GOD, AND SERVE HIM DAY ANC	341 20
SITTETH ON THE THRONE SHALL DWELL AMONG THEM	341 22
THE MIDST OF THE THRONE SHALL FEED THEM, AND SHALL	341 25
ART SET IN THE THRONE THAT JUDGEST RIGHT	351 29
AND SET UP THY THRONE FROM ONE GENERATION TO ANCTHER	450 12
AND HIS THRONE AS THE DAYS OF HEAVEN	451 34
AND HIS THRONE IS LIKE AS THE SUN BEFORE ME	452 12
AND CAST HIS THRONE DCWN TO THE GROUND	452 28
TO DO WITH THE THRONE OF WICKEDNESS, *	458 26
SHALL I SET UPON THY THRONE	508 28
SIT UPON THY THRONE FOR EVERMORE	508 31
THAT SAT UPON THE THRONE SAID, BEHOLD, I MAKE ALL	567 21

THRONES

AND SIT ON THRONES, JUDGING THE TWELVE TRIBES OF	149 30
SIT UPON TWELVE THRONES, JUDGING THE TWELVE TRIBES OF	231 17
AND SIT ON THRONES JUDGING THE TWELVE TRIBES OF	250 15

THROUGHLY

WASH ME THROUGHLY FROM MY WICKEDNESS, *	060 13
2 WASH ME THROUGHLY FROM MY WICKEDNESS, *	403 11

THROUGHOUT

HOLY CHURCH THROUGHOUT ALL THE WORLD DOTH ACKNOWLEDGE	010 19
THROUGHOUT ALL GENERATIONS	026 18
BE SAID DAILY THROUGHOUT THE OCTAVE	R 096 20
BE SAID DAILY THROUGHOUT THE OCTAVE	R 108 04
BE PREACHED THROUGHOUT THE WHOLE WORLD, THIS ALSO	140 16
TEACHING THROUGHOUT ALL JEWRY, BEGINNING FROM GALILEE	153 05
WOVEN FROM THE TOP THROUGHOUT	160 12
MAY BE SAID THROUGHOUT THE OCTAVE	R 162 29
BE SAID DAILY THROUGHOUT EASTER WEEK	R 163 31
WAS PUBLISHED THROUGHOUT ALL JUDAEA, AND BEGAN FROM	166 17
BE SAID DAILY THROUGHOUT THE OCTAVE	R 177 20
BE SAID DAILY THROUGHOUT WHITSUN WEEK	R 180 15
WAS PUBLISHED THROUGHOUT ALL JUDAEA, AND BEGAN FRCM	184 05
CHRIST JESUS THROUGHOLT ALL AGES, WORLD WITHOUT END	212 24
WENT FORTH THROUGHOUT ALL JUDAEA, AND THROUGHOUT ALL	213 10
AND THROUGHOUT ALL THE REGION ROUND ABOUT	213 10
TO SHINE THROUGHOUT THE WORLD	229 19
GREAT DEARTH THROUGHOLT ALL THE WORLD	241 18
NOISED ABROAD THROUGHOUT ALL THE HILL COUNTRY OF	243 28
GREAT DEARTH THROUGHOLT ALL THE WORLD	246 27
BE SAID DAILY THROUGHOUT THE OCTAVE	R 256 12
WAS PUBLISHED THROUGHOUT ALL THE REGICN	261 09
MAY ENDURE THROUGHOUT ALL GENERATIONS	413 18
REMEMBRANCE THROUGHOUT ALL GENERATIONS	465 03
THEY ENDURE THROUGHOUT ALL GENERATIONS	465 29
ENDURETH THROUGHOUT ALL AGES	521 19
AND THROUGHOUT ALL GENERATIONS	522 24
THY CHURCH THROUGHOUT THE WORLD	560 16

THROW

THOU SHALT THROW DOWN MINE ENEMIES UNDER ME	362 17

THROWETH

AND THROWETH THEM AGAINST THE STONES	513 25

THRUST

HIM THAT HE WOULD THRUST OUT A LITTLE FROM THE LAND	196 11
OF THE NAILS, AND THRUST MY HAND INTO HIS SIDE,	228 30
THY HAND, AND THRUST IT INTO MY SIDE	229 04
13 THOU HAST THRUST SORE AT ME, THAT I MIGHT FALL	488 26
THE DEVIL DOTH THRUST THEM EITHER INTO DESPERATICN,	606 25

THUNDER

MANY WATERS, AND AS THE VOICE OF A GREAT THUNDER	103 03
OUT OF HEAVEN, AND THE HIGHEST GAVE HIS THUNDER	360 25
IT IS THE GLORIOUS GOD THAT MAKETH THE THUNDER	374 03
THE VOICE OF THY THUNDER WAS HEARD ROUND ABOUT	434 18
THE VOICE OF THY THUNDER THEY HASTE AWAY	468 06

THUNDERBOLTS

AND THEIR FLOCKS WITH HOT THUNDERBOLTS	438 05

THUNDERED

THE LORD ALSO THUNDERED OUT OF HEAVEN, AND THE	360 24
THE AIR THUNDERED, *	434 16

THUNDERINGS

AND THUNDERINGS AND VOICES	187 12

THUS

THUS SAITH THE HIGH AND LOFTY ONE THAT INHABITETH	003 25
JESUS CHRIST, THUS DYING FOR US, AND THE INNUMERABLE	086 14
FOR THUS IT IS WRITTEN BY THE PROPHET, AND THOU	109 07
WHY HAST THOU THUS DEALT WITH US	110 33
AND SAID, SUFFER YE THUS FAR	150 34
AND HAVING SAID THUS, HE GAVE UP THE GHOST	155 14
AND WHEN HE HAD THUS SPOKEN, HE SHEWED THEM HIS HANDS	170 02
IT IS WRITTEN, AND THUS IT BEHOVED CHRIST TC SUFFER,	170 12
AND SAID UNTO THEM, THUS IT IS WRITTEN, AND THUS IT	170 12
STOOD AND PRAYED THUS WITH HIMSELF, GOD, I THANK	205 25
WHILE HE THUS SPAKE, THERE CAME A CLOUD, AND	249 04
THUS SHALL THEY KNOW THAT I THE LORD THEIR GOD AM	262 20
THAT EVERY ADULT, THUS BAPTIZED, SHOULD BE CCNFIRMED	R 281 13
BLESS THEM, SAYING THUS, THE BLESSING OF GOD	R 299 02
AND WHILE I WAS THUS MUSING THE FIRE KINDLED, *	389 12
WHY GO I THUS HEAVILY, WHILE THE ENEMY OPPRESSETH ME	393 25
3 THUS HAVE I LOOKED FOR THEE IN THE SANCTUARY,	414 29
21 THUS MY HEART WAS GRIEVED, *	429 18
THUS HAVE THEY BURNT UP ALL THE HOUSES OF GOD IN THE	430 22
20 THUS THEY TURNED THEIR GLORY *	474 08
29 THUS THEY PROVOKED HIM TO ANGER WITH THEIR OWN	474 27
38 THUS WERE THEY STAINED WITH THEIR OWN WORKS,	475 14
4 THUS HAVE THEY REWARDED ME EVIL FCR GOOD, *	480 11
19 LET IT THUS HAPPEN FROM THE LORD UNTO MINE	481 10
5 LO, THUS SHALL THE MAN BE BLESSED *	506 14
TO PRAY, SAYING THUS TO THEM	R 553 03

THYSELF

DIDST HUMBLE THYSELF TO BE BORN OF A VIRGIN	010 27
PURCHASED TO THYSELF A UNIVERSAL CHURCH BY THE	038 26
NOT MAKE TO THYSELF ANY GRAVEN IMAGE, NOR THE	068 08
THOU SHALT LOVE THY NEIGHBOUR AS THYSELF	069 30
GATHEREST THOU THYSELF A GOOD REWARD IN THE DAY CF	072 34
THOU SHALT LOVE THY NEIGHBOUR AS THYSELF	090 29
WHAT SAYEST THOU OF THYSELF	095 28
GO THY WAY, SHEW THYSELF TO THE PRIEST, AND CFFER THE	115 04
SON OF GOD, CAST THYSELF DOWN	126 33
WHOM MAKEST THOU THYSELF	133 23
AND BUILDEST IT IN THREE DAYS, SAVE THYSELF	137 07
TO MAKE THYSELF A GLORIOUS NAME	139 17
THREE DAYS, SAVE THYSELF, AND COME DCWN FRCM THE	146 20
IF THOU BE THE KING OF THE JEWS, SAVE THYSELF	154 32
BE CHRIST, SAVE THYSELF AND US	155 02
WILT MANIFEST THYSELF UNTO US, AND NOT UNTO THE	181 23
WHEN THOU THYSELF BEHOLDEST NOT THE BEAM THAT IS	195 09
AND THY NEIGHBOUR AS THYSELF	208 17
UNTO IT, THOU SHALT LOVE THY NEIGHBOUR AS THYSELF	215 14
UNTO HIM, GIRD THYSELF, AND BIND ON THY SANDALS	245 16
NOT MAKE TO THYSELF ANY GRAVEN IMAGE, NOR THE	286 08
THOU SHALT LOVE THY NEIGHBOUR AS THYSELF	288 09
TO TAKE UNTO THYSELF THE SOUL OF THIS THY SERVANT (OR	336 05
AND LIFT UP THYSELF, BECAUSE OF THE INDIGNATICN CF	349 35
LIFT UP THYSELF AGAIN	350 05
FRET NOT THYSELF BECAUSE OF THE UNGODLY	384 25
BUT GRIEVE NOT THYSELF AT HIM WHOSE WAY DOTH PROSPER,	385 07
FRET NOT THYSELF, ELSE SHALT THOU BE MOVED TO DC	385 10
DOEST WELL UNTO THYSELF, MEN WILL SPEAK GOOD OF THEE	401 12
THAT I AM EVEN SUCH A ONE AS THYSELF	402 34
BOASTEST THOU THYSELF, THOU TYRANT, *	404 19
AND HIDE NOT THYSELF FROM MY PETITICN	406 19
6 SET UP THYSELF, O GOD, ABOVE THE HEAVENS	409 24
12 SET UP THYSELF, O GOD, ABOVE THE HEAVENS	410 04
SHOW THYSELF ALSO, THOU THAT SITTEST UPON THE	441 04
THE BRANCH THAT THOU MADEST SO STRONG FOR THYSELF	441 34
REFRAIN NOT THYSELF, O GOD	444 06
AND TURNED THYSELF FROM THY WRATHFUL INDIGNATION	446 13
HOW LONG WILT THOU HIDE THYSELF	452 32
TO WHOM VENGEANCE BELONGETH, SHOW THYSELF	457 20
2 THOU DECKEST THYSELF WITH LIGHT AS IT WERE WITH A	467 27
5 SET UP THYSELF, O GOD, ABOVE THE HEAVENS, *	479 13
SHALT BOTH SAVE THYSELF AND THEM THAT HEAR THEE	558 25
PURCHASED TO THYSELF AN UNIVERSAL CHURCH, AND HAST	572 16
NOT MAKE TO THYSELF ANY GRAVEN IMAGE, NOR THE	578 27
THESE THINGS OF THYSELF, NOR TO WALK IN THE	580 17

TIBERIAS

WHICH IS THE SEA OF TIBERIAS	131 22

TIDINGS

I BRING YOU GOOD TIDINGS OF GREAT JOY, WHICH SHALL BE	004 08
I BRING YOU GOOD TIDINGS OF GREAT JOY, WHICH SHALL BE	099 15
TO PREACH GOOD TIDINGS UNTO THE MEEK	106 31
UNTO YOU GLAD TIDINGS, HOW THAT THE PROMISE WHICH WAS	169 06
AND BRING GLAD TIDINGS OF GOOD THINGS	227 10
TIDINGS OF THESE THINGS CAME UNTO THE EARS CF THE	241 03
BRINGEST GOOD TIDINGS, GET THEE UP INTO THE HIGH	243 02
BRINGEST GOOD TIDINGS, LIFT UP THY VOICE WITH	243 03
WAS THE COMPANY OF WOMEN THAT BARE THE TIDINGS	420 03
7 HE WILL NOT BE AFRAID OF ANY EVIL TIDINGS	483 30
THE GLAD TIDINGS OF RECONCILIATION WITH THEE	557 30

TIED

AND THOUGH WE BE TIED AND BOUND WITH THE CHAIN OF OUR 063 11
SHALL FIND AN ASS TIED, AND A COLT WITH HER 091 15

TILL

TILL AT LENGTH THE WHOLE OF THY DISPERSED SHEEP, 037 05
NOT PASS AWAY, TILL ALL BE FULFILLED 093 19
SEE ME HENCEFORTH, TILL YE SHALL SAY, BLESSED IS HE 100 32
WILL THAT HE TARRY TILL I COME, WHAT IS THAT TO THEE 102 08
WILL THAT HE TARRY TILL I COME, WHAT IS THAT TO THEE 102 12
AND KNEW HER NOT TILL SHE HAD BROUGHT FORTH HER 105 14
WENT BEFORE THEM, TILL IT CAME AND STOOD OVER WHERE 109 17
THE LORD'S DEATH TILL HE COME 152 25
EXPECTING TILL HIS ENEMIES BE MADE HIS FOOTSTOOL 158 07
AND SEEK DILIGENTLY TILL SHE FIND IT 193 29
COME OUT THENCE, TILL THOU HAST PAID THE UTTERMOST 198 16
OF TRANSGRESSIONS, TILL THE SEED SHOULD COME TO WHOM 207 28
ON MY RIGHT HAND, TILL I MAKE THINE ENEMIES THY 215 20
AND WITHOUT OFFENCE TILL THE DAY OF CHRIST 221 04
TILL SEVEN TIMES 221 10
HIM INTO PRISON, TILL HE SHOULD PAY THE DEBT 221 29
TO THE TORMENTORS, TILL HE SHOULD PAY ALL THAT WAS 222 03
TILL WE ALL COME IN THE UNITY OF THE FAITH, AND OF 237 22
WAS IN THE DESERTS TILL THE DAY OF HIS SHEWING UNTO 244 18
NOR THE TREES, TILL WE HAVE SEALED THE SERVANTS 256 18
AND TO CHERISH, TILL DEATH US DO PART, ACCORDING TO 301 31
AND TO CHERISH, TILL DEATH US DO PART, ACCORDING TO 302 07
FOR HE MUST REIGN, TILL HE HATH PUT ALL ENEMIES UNDER 328 29
WILL I TURN AGAIN TILL I HAVE DESTROYED THEM 362 12
TILL WE ALL COME IN THE UNITY OF THE FAITH, AND OF 538 09

TIMBER

6 HE THAT HEWED TIMBER AFORE OUT OF THE THICK TREES, 430 14

TIMBRELS

MIDST OF THE DAMSELS PLAYING WITH THE TIMBRELS 421 05
HIM IN THE TIMBRELS AND DANCES 525 28

TIME

GRACE TO HELP IN TIME OF NEED 005 09
FROM TIME TO TIME, SEEM EITHER NECESSARY OR V 19
FROM TIME TO TIME, SEEM EITHER NECESSARY OR V 19
HER LITURGY IN THE TIME OF EDWARD THE SIXTH, UPON V 27
US GRACE AT THIS TIME WITH ONE ACCORD TO MAKE OUR 020 03
GIVE PEACE IN OUR TIME, O LORD 031 10
MAY PASS OUR TIME IN REST AND QUIETNESS 031 23
US GRACE AT THIS TIME WITH ONE ACCORD TO MAKE OUR 034 03
IN THE TIME OF PROSPERITY, FILL OUR HEARTS WITH 036 21
AND AT THIS TIME SO GUIDE AND GOVERN THE MINDS 038 28
EARTH MAY, IN DUE TIME, YIELD HER INCREASE FOR OUR 040 27
AND IN THE TIME OF PEACE KEEP THEM SAFE FROM 041 28
WHO AT THIS TIME ARE SEEKING TO BE STRENGTHENED BY 043 21
IN THIS TIME OF GRIEVOUS SICKNESS, WE FLEE UNTO 045 03
OUR ONLY HELP IN TIME OF NEED 045 13
IN THY GOOD TIME, RESTORE HIM TO HEALTH, AND ENABLE 045 18
HOLY GHOST, IN ALL TIME OF OUR TRIBULATION 055 15
IN ALL TIME OF OUR PROSPERITY 055 15
SO THAT IN DUE TIME WE MAY ENJOY THEM 057 11
AND IN THE OLD TIME BEFORE THEM 058 30
WOULD IN TIME BE FOUND EXPEDIENT VI 03
THIS GREAT AND GOOD WORK MISCARRIED AT THAT TIME VI 05
FOR THE TIME PAST, AND GRACE TO KEEP THE LAW FOR THE R 067 24
THE LAW FOR THE TIME TO COME R 067 25
WHILE WE HAVE TIME, LET US DO GOOD UNTO ALL MEN 072 20
WHICH WE, FROM TIME TO TIME, MOST GRIEVOUSLY HAVE 075 20
WE, FROM TIME TO TIME, MOST GRIEVOUSLY HAVE 075 20
ACCORDING TO THE TIME, IF THERE BE ANY SPECIALLY R 077 02
BE BORN AS AT THIS TIME FOR US 077 15
DOWN AS AT THIS TIME FROM HEAVEN, LIGHTING UPON THE 078 27
AT THE TIME OF THE CELEBRATION OF THE COMMUNION, R 085 21
NOW IN THE TIME OF THIS MORTAL LIFE, IN WHICH 090 13
KNOWING THE TIME, THAT NOW IT IS HIGH TIME TO 090 31
THAT NOW IT IS HIGH TIME TO AWAKE OUT OF SLEEP 090 31
NOTHING BEFORE THE TIME, UNTIL THE LORD COME, WHO 094 10
AND AS AT THIS TIME TO BE BORN OF A PURE VIRGIN 096 14
MANNERS SPAKE IN TIME PAST UNTO THE FATHERS BY THE 096 23
SAID HE AT ANY TIME, THOU ART MY SON, THIS DAY HAVE I 097 02
ACCORDING TO THE TIME WHICH HE HAD DILIGENTLY 103 28
AND AS AT THIS TIME TO BE BORN OF A PURE VIRGIN 104 07
GOVERNORS UNTIL THE TIME APPOINTED OF THE FATHER 104 16
THE FULNESS OF THE TIME WAS COME, GOD SENT FORTH HIS 104 19
DILIGENTLY WHAT TIME THE STAR APPEARED 109 12
AND IN THE TIME OF HARVEST I WILL SAY TO THE REAPERS, 116 29
AND IN TIME OF TEMPTATION FALL AWAY 122 04
HEARD THEE IN A TIME ACCEPTED, AND IN THE DAY OF 126 05
BEHOLD, NOW IS THE ACCEPTED TIME 126 07
UP, LEST AT ANY TIME THOU DASH THY FOOT AGAINST A 127 02
HE COMETH THE THIRD TIME, AND SAITH UNTO THEM, SLEEP 142 10
AND THE SECOND TIME THE COCK CREW 143 34
OF THE PRESENT TIME, IN FULL ASSURANCE OF THE GLORY 144 09
APPEAR THE SECOND TIME WITHOUT SIN UNTO SALVATION 148 10
WHO HIMSELF ALSO WAS AT JERUSALEM AT THAT TIME 153 10
UNTO THEM THE THIRD TIME, WHY, WHAT EVIL HATH HE 153 34
BUT THE TIME COMETH, WHEN I SHALL NO MORE SPEAK UNTO 176 24
WILT THOU AT THIS TIME RESTORE AGAIN THE KINGDOM TO 178 06
THE TIME COMETH, THAT WHOSOEVER KILLETH YOU WILL 179 30
THAT WHEN THE TIME SHALL COME, YE MAY REMEMBER 180 03
WHO AS AT THIS TIME DIDST TEACH THE HEARTS OF 180 08
HE ENTER THE SECOND TIME INTO HIS MOTHER'S WOMB, AND 188 08
NO MAN HATH SEEN GOD AT ANY TIME 189 17

TIME CONTINUED

SERVANT AT SUPPER TIME TO SAY TO THEM THAT WERE 192 04
THAT HE MAY EXALT YOU IN DUE TIME 193 03
OF THIS PRESENT TIME ARE NOT WORTHY TO BE COMPARED 194 11
SAID BY THEM OF OLD TIME, THOU SHALT NOT KILL 197 31
LEST AT ANY TIME THE ADVERSARY DELIVER THEE TO THE 198 13
I AT ANY TIME THY COMMANDMENT 202 35
KNEWEST NOT THE TIME OF THY VISITATION 204 15
AS OF ONE BORN OUT OF DUE TIME 205 12
ALSO TOLD YOU IN TIME PAST, THAT THEY WHICH DO SUCH 209 24
REDEEMING THE TIME, BECAUSE THE DAYS ARE EVIL 217 24
WITH US ALL THE TIME THAT THE LORD JESUS WENT IN AND 234 21
AT THAT TIME JESUS ANSWERED AND SAID, I THANK THEE, 235 03
HAVE I BEEN SO LONG TIME WITH YOU, AND YET HAST THOU 240 11
ELISABETH'S FULL TIME CAME THAT SHE SHOULD BE 243 13
ABOUT THAT TIME HEROD THE KING STRETCHED FORTH HIS 244 31
NOW ABOUT THAT TIME HEROD THE KING STRETCHED FORTH 246 32
BECAUSE HE KNOWETH THAT HE HATH BUT A SHORT TIME 252 20
AT THE SAME TIME CAME THE DISCIPLES UNTO JESUS, 252 22
BE OFFERED, AND THE TIME OF MY DEPARTURE IS AT HAND 253 25
OR AT SUCH OTHER TIME AS THE MINISTER SHALL APPOINT R 273 16
THAT AT THE TIME OF THE BAPTISM OF AN ADULT, R 273 22
HE ENTER THE SECOND TIME INTO HIS MOTHER'S WOMB, 275 13
AT WHICH TIME THESE PARTS OF THE FOREGOING R 282 02
GIVEN IN OLD TIME BY GOD TO THE PEOPLE OF ISRAEL 285 17
THE FAITH FOR ALL TIME, IN ALL COUNTRIES, AND FOR ALL 291 12
THE CHURCH AT THE TIME APPOINTED, TO RECEIVE R 295 11
UNTIL SUCH TIME AS HE BE CONFIRMED, OR BE READY AND R 299 09
AT THE DAY AND TIME APPOINTED FOR SOLEMNIZATION OF R 300 03
SECOND OR THIRD) TIME OF ASKING R 304 25
AT THE USUAL TIME AFTER HER DELIVERY, SHALL R 305 07
IN THE TIME OF MY TROUBLE I SOUGHT THE LORD 310 31
AND USE OF THE TIME OF SICKNESS, AND THE OPPORTUNITY R 313 16
OUR ONLY HELP IN TIME OF NEED 316 07
IS ORDERED, FROM TIME TO TIME, TO ADVISE THE PEOPLE, R 320 21
FROM TIME TO TIME, TO ADVISE THE PEOPLE, WHILST THEY R 320 21
EVER UNCERTAIN WHAT TIME THEY SHALL DEPART OUT OF R 321 03
FROM TIME TO TIME, BUT ESPECIALLY IN THE TIME OF R 321 06
DILIGENTLY FROM TIME TO TIME, BUT ESPECIALLY IN THE R 321 06
ESPECIALLY IN THE TIME OF PESTILENCE, OR OTHER R 321 06
AT THE TIME OF THE DISTRIBUTION OF THE HOLY R 322 33
OF WARNING IN DUE TIME TO THE MINISTER, OR BY ANY R 323 24
FOR IN THE TIME OF TROUBLE HE SHALL HIDE ME IN HIS 326 12
FROM THIS TIME FORTH FOR EVERMORE 327 34
OF THIS PRESENT TIME ARE NOT WORTHY TO BE COMPARED 330 27
HATH BUT A SHORT TIME TO LIVE, AND IS FULL OF MISERY 332 18
FROM THIS TIME FORTH FOR EVERMORE 339 18
AT THE SAME TIME CAME THE DISCIPLES UNTO JESUS, 339 21
A REFUGE IN DUE TIME OF TROUBLE 352 07
FACE IN THE NEEDFUL TIME OF TROUBLE 353 04
A FIERY OVEN IN TIME OF THY WRATH 365 22
5 FOR IN THE TIME OF TROUBLE HE SHALL HIDE ME IN HIS 372 04
UNTO THEE, IN A TIME WHEN THOU MAYEST BE FOUND 378 03
TO FEED THEM IN THE TIME OF DEARTH 379 27
THEY SHALL NOT BE CONFOUNDED IN THE PERILOUS TIME 385 33
STRENGTH IN THE TIME OF TROUBLE 387 14
DELIVER HIM IN THE TIME OF TROUBLE 391 31
HAST DONE IN THEIR TIME OF OLD 394 23
CALL UPON ME IN THE TIME OF TROUBLE 402 20
IN AN ACCEPTABLE TIME 422 29
ME NOT AWAY IN THE TIME OF AGE 425 23
7 IN HIS TIME SHALL THE RIGHTEOUS FLOURISH 427 10
3 IN THE APPOINTED TIME, SAITH GOD, * 432 02
2 IN THE TIME OF MY TROUBLE I SOUGHT THE LORD 433 18
AND CALL TO MIND THY WONDERS OF OLD TIME 434 05
39 YEA, MANY A TIME TURNED HE HIS WRATH AWAY, 437 16
41 MANY A TIME DID THEY PROVOKE HIM IN THE 437 21
EVEN IN THE TIME APPOINTED, AND UPON OUR SOLEMN 442 17
AND HEARD THEE WHAT TIME AS THE STORM FELL UPON THEE 442 26
BUT THEIR TIME SHOULD HAVE ENDURED FOR EVER 443 11
7 IN THE TIME OF MY TROUBLE I WILL CALL UPON THEE 447 17
HOW SHORT MY TIME IS 452 34
AGAIN NOW AFTER THE TIME THAT THOU HAST PLAGUED US 454 19
HIM PATIENCE IN TIME OF ADVERSITY, * 458 12
FACE FROM ME IN THE TIME OF MY TROUBLE 464 12
FOR IT IS TIME THAT THOU HAVE MERCY UPON HER, YEA, 465 05
UPON HER, YEA, THE TIME IS COME 465 05
THAT IT NEVER SHOULD MOVE AT ANY TIME 468 03
13 WHAT TIME AS THEY WENT FROM ONE NATION TO ANOTHER, 470 28
19 UNTIL THE TIME CAME THAT HIS CAUSE WAS KNOWN 471 10
42 MANY A TIME DID HE DELIVER THEM 475 22
FROM THIS TIME FORTH FOR EVERMORE 484 10
FROM THIS TIME FORTH FOR EVERMORE 486 14
PROLONGED NOT THE TIME, * 493 31
126 IT IS TIME FOR THEE, LORD, TO LAY TO THINE HAND 498 21
FROM THIS TIME FORTH FOR EVERMORE 503 07
FROM THIS TIME FORTH FOR EVERMORE 504 27
MANY A TIME HAVE THEY FOUGHT AGAINST ME FROM MY YOUTH 506 21
2 YEA, MANY A TIME HAVE THEY VEXED ME FROM MY YOUTH 506 23
FROM THIS TIME FORTH FOR EVERMORE 507 30
DO I REMEMBER THE TIME PAST 518 32
HIS TIME PASSETH AWAY LIKE A SHADOW 519 29
FROM THE APOSTLES' TIME THERE HAVE BEEN THESE ORDERS 529 12
UNTIL SUCH TIME AS THE PARTY ACCUSED SHALL BE R 530 27
UNTIL SUCH TIME AS THE PARTY ACCUSED SHALL BE R 537 03
THINGS WITH YOURSELVES, LONG BEFORE THIS TIME 541 10
FROM TIME TO TIME, TO SANCTIFY THE LIVES 541 20
FROM TIME TO TIME, TO SANCTIFY THE LIVES OF YOU AND 541 20
UNTIL SUCH TIME AS THEY HAVE RECEIVED THE R 546 31
AGAIN THE SECOND TIME, SIMON, SON OF JONAS, LOVEST 551 17
UNTO HIM THE THIRD TIME, SIMON, SON OF JONAS, LOVEST 551 20
UNTO HIM THE THIRD TIME, LOVEST THOU ME 551 22
AS YOU SHALL AT ANY TIME RECEIVE FROM US 569 21
AT THE TIME DESIGNATED FOR THE NEW INCUMBENT'S R 570 02
THE CHURCH AT THE TIME APPOINTED, AND OBEDIENTLY TO R 582 33

TIME   CONTINUED

UNTIL SUCH TIME AS THEY HAVE LEARNED ALL THAT IS HERE R 582 34
SET FORTH IN THE TIME OF EDWARD THE SIXTH   610 08

TIMELY

TO BE BAPTIZED, TIMELY NOTICE SHALL BE GIVEN TO THE   R 273 17
THEN HE MUST GIVE TIMELY NOTICE TO THE MINISTER,   R 321 12
THEE FOR THE TIMELY BLESSINGS OF THE DAY, AND HUMBLY   595 06

TIMES

EXIGENCY OF TIMES AND OCCASIONS   V 09
EXIGENCY OF TIMES AND OCCASIONS, SUCH CHANGES AND   V 17
THEIR RESPECTIVE TIMES WERE THOUGHT CONVENIENT   V 29
WE OUGHT, AT ALL TIMES, HUMBLY TO ACKNOWLEDGE OUR   006 03
WE OUGHT, AT ALL TIMES, HUMBLY TO ACKNOWLEDGE OUR   023 12
THE STATED TIMES OF ORDINATION   R 038 24
BE READ AT OTHER TIMES, AT THE DISCRETION OF THE   R 060 06
WE SHOULD AT ALL TIMES, AND IN ALL PLACES, GIVE   076 32
WHO AT SUNDRY TIMES AND IN DIVERS MANNERS SPAKE   096 22
OF THE JEWS FIVE TIMES RECEIVED I FORTY STRIPES SAVE 120 32
YOU TO KNOW THE TIMES OR THE SEASONS, WHICH IN   178 07
TILL SEVEN TIMES   221 10
I SAY NOT UNTO THEE, UNTIL SEVEN TIMES   221 12
UNTIL SEVENTY TIMES SEVEN   221 12
MUST LEARN AT ALL TIMES TO CALL FOR BY DILIGENT   289 16
HAVE BEEN IN THE CHURCH FROM THE EARLIEST TIMES   294 06
AND PURIFIED SEVEN TIMES IN THE FIRE   355 22
17 MY TIMES ARE IN THY HAND   376 26
164 SEVEN TIMES A DAY DO I PRAISE THEE   501 09
AT THE TIMES APPOINTED, OR ELSE, ON URGENT   529 29
AT THE TIMES APPOINTED IN THE CANON   R 535 25
MUST LEARN AT ALL TIMES TO CALL FOR BY DILIGENT   580 19
FOR AT ALL TIMES THEY HAVE BEEN DIVERS, AND MAY BE   609 33
OF COUNTRIES, TIMES, AND MEN'S MANNERS, SO THAT   609 34
FOR THESE TIMES, AS DOTH THE FORMER BOOK OF HOMILIES, 610 07

TIMON

AND NICANOR, AND TIMON, AND PARMENAS, AND NICOLAS A   532 17

TINKLING

OR A TINKLING CYMBAL   122 23

TIP

THAT HE MAY DIP THE TIP OF HIS FINGER IN WATER, AND   190 14

TITHES

THE WEEK, I GIVE TITHES OF ALL THAT I POSSESS   205 28

TITLE

AND PILATE WROTE A TITLE, AND PUT IT ON THE CROSS   159 35
THIS TITLE THEN READ MANY OF THE JEWS   160 03
THE RIGHT, TITLE, AND POSSESSION OF THE SAME   611 02

TITLES

THE SEVERAL TITLES WHEREOF WE HAVE JOINED UNDER THIS 610 05

TITUS

TO GALATIA, TITUS UNTO DALMATIA   253 33

TO-DAY

I SAY UNTO THEE, TO-DAY SHALT THOU BE WITH ME IN   155 08
BESIDE ALL THIS, TO-DAY IS THE THIRD DAY SINCE THESE 167 21
THE FIELD, WHICH TO-DAY IS, AND TO-MORROW IS CAST   211 25
THE FIELD, WHICH TO-DAY IS, AND TO-MORROW IS CAST   266 23
8 TO-DAY IF YE WILL HEAR HIS VOICE, HARDEN NOT YOUR   459 19

TO-MORROW

TO-DAY IS, AND TO-MORROW IS CAST INTO THE OVEN, SHALL 211 25
TO-DAY IS, AND TO-MORROW IS CAST INTO THE OVEN, SHALL 266 23

TOGETHER

AND MEET TOGETHER TO RENDER THANKS FOR THE GREAT   006 05
AND THE SON TOGETHER IS WORSHIPPED AND GLORIFIED   016 17
ARE GATHERED TOGETHER IN THY NAME THOU WILT GRANT   020 06
AND MEET TOGETHER TO RENDER THANKS FOR THE GREAT   023 14
HILLS BE JOYFUL TOGETHER BEFORE THE LORD   027 22
AND THE SON TOGETHER IS WORSHIPPED AND GLORIFIED   030 22
ARE GATHERED TOGETHER IN THY NAME THOU WILT GRANT   034 06
AND THE SON TOGETHER IS WORSHIPPED AND GLORIFIED   071 19
BEFORE US, AND, TOGETHER WITH THEM, MAY RECEIVE THE   079 25
THY CHILDREN TOGETHER, EVEN AS A HEN GATHERETH HER   100 29
THEY CAME TOGETHER, SHE WAS FOUND WITH CHILD OF THE   104 29
OF THE PEOPLE TOGETHER, HE DEMANDED OF THEM WHERE   109 05
LET BOTH GROW TOGETHER UNTIL THE HARVEST   116 28
GATHER YE TOGETHER FIRST THE TARES, AND BIND THEM IN 116 30
THERE WILL THE EAGLES BE GATHERED TOGETHER   118 13
SHALL GATHER TOGETHER HIS ELECT FROM THE FOUR WINDS, 118 22
WERE GATHERED TOGETHER, AND WERE COME TO HIM OUT OF   121 18
AS WORKERS TOGETHER WITH HIM, BESEECH YOU ALSO THAT   126 03
GATHERED THEM TOGETHER, AND FILLED TWELVE BASKETS   132 09
WERE GATHERED TOGETHER, PILATE SAID UNTO THEM,   135 29
BUT THEIR WITNESS AGREED NOT TOGETHER   143 05
BUT NEITHER SO DID THEIR WITNESS AGREE TOGETHER   143 09

TOGETHER   CONTINUED

LET US STAND TOGETHER   144 19
AND THEY CALL TOGETHER THE WHOLE BAND   145 31
WERE SET DOWN TOGETHER, PETER SAT DOWN AMONG THEM   151 10
SCRIBES CAME TOGETHER, AND LED HIM INTO THEIR   151 29
DAY PILATE AND HEROD WERE MADE FRIENDS TOGETHER   153 19
HE HAD CALLED TOGETHER THE CHIEF PRIESTS AND THE   153 21
THAT CAME TOGETHER TO THAT SIGHT, BEHOLDING THE   155 17
OF OURSELVES TOGETHER, AS THE MANNER OF SOME IS   158 26
PHARISEES CAME TOGETHER UNTO PILATE, SAYING, SIR, WE 162 16
SO THEY RAN BOTH TOGETHER   164 18
BUT WRAPPED TOGETHER IN A PLACE BY ITSELF   164 24
AND THEY TALKED TOGETHER OF ALL THESE THINGS WHICH   167 05
THEY COMMUNED TOGETHER AND REASONED, JESUS HIMSELF   167 07
ELEVEN GATHERED TOGETHER, AND THEM THAT WERE WITH   168 12
BEING ASSEMBLED TOGETHER WITH THEM, COMMANDED THEM   177 29
WERE COME TOGETHER, THEY ASKED OF HIM, SAYING, LORD, 178 04
MULTITUDE CAME TOGETHER, AND WERE CONFOUNDED, BECAUSE 180 27
BEING GATHERED TOGETHER IN UNITY BY THY HOLY SPIRIT, 185 15
HE CALLETH TOGETHER HIS FRIENDS AND NEIGHBOURS,   193 22
HER NEIGHBOURS TOGETHER, SAYING, REJOICE WITH ME   193 31
IN PAIN TOGETHER UNTIL NOW   194 20
AND SHAKEN TOGETHER, AND RUNNING OVER, SHALL MEN GIVE 194 29
BEEN PLANTED TOGETHER IN THE LIKENESS OF HIS DEATH,   197 15
THAT WE MAY BE ALSO GLORIFIED TOGETHER   200 13
GATHERED ALL TOGETHER, AND TOOK HIS JOURNEY INTO A   202 03
THEY WERE GATHERED TOGETHER   215 07
WERE GATHERED TOGETHER, JESUS ASKED THEM, SAYING,   215 16
AND GATHERED TOGETHER ALL AS MANY AS THEY FOUND,   218 20
BE FOLLOWERS TOGETHER OF ME, AND MARK THEM WHICH WALK 222 15
GATHERED THEM TOGETHER, AND FILLED TWELVE BASKETS   226 08
NUMBER OF NAMES TOGETHER WERE ABOUT AN HUNDRED AND   234 07
FITLY JOINED TOGETHER AND COMPACTED BY THAT WHICH   237 30
BE REVEALED, AND ALL FLESH SHALL SEE IT TOGETHER   242 26
SO TO BE JOINED TOGETHER IN UNITY OF SPIRIT BY THEIR 254 30
FITLY FRAMED TOGETHER GROWETH UNTO AN HOLY TEMPLE IN 255 08
ARE BUILDED TOGETHER FOR AN HABITATION OF GOD THROUGH 255 09
WHO HAST KNIT TOGETHER THINE ELECT IN ONE COMMUNION   256 05
THE WHOLE CITY TOGETHER TO HEAR THE WORD OF GOD   260 26
AND GATHER TOGETHER THE OUTCASTS OF ISRAEL   264 21
GOD HATH JOINED TOGETHER, LET NOT MAN PUT ASUNDER   268 10
BE CAUGHT UP TOGETHER WITH THEM IN THE CLOUDS, TO   269 08
AND PEOPLE TOGETHER, ALL KNEELING, THE FOLLOWING   R 283 04
AND PEOPLE TOGETHER, ALL KNEELING   R 285 23
AND PEOPLE TOGETHER, ALL KNEELING, THE GRACE OF OUR R 289 21
SENTENCE BY THE MINISTER AND PEOPLE TOGETHER   R 290 04
SO TO BE JOINED TOGETHER IN UNITY OF SPIRIT BY THEIR 290 22
THERE STANDING TOGETHER, THE MAN ON THE RIGHT HAND, R 300 06
WE ARE GATHERED TOGETHER HERE IN THE SIGHT OF GOD,   300 08
TO JOIN TOGETHER THIS MAN AND THIS WOMAN IN HOLY   300 10
BE JOINED TOGETHER, LET HIM NOW SPEAK, OR ELSE   300 21
LAWFULLY JOINED TOGETHER IN MATRIMONY, YE DO NOW   300 27
ARE JOINED TOGETHER OTHERWISE THAN AS GOD'S WORD DOTH 300 29
TO LIVE TOGETHER AFTER GOD'S ORDINANCE IN THE   301 07
TO LIVE TOGETHER AFTER GOD'S ORDINANCE IN THE HOLY   301 15
FAITHFULLY TOGETHER, MAY SURELY PERFORM AND KEEP THE 303 07
LOVE AND PEACE TOGETHER, AND LIVE ACCORDING TO THY   303 10
AND SO LIVE TOGETHER IN FAITHFULNESS AND PATIENCE, IN 303 24
RIGHT HANDS TOGETHER, AND SAY, THOSE WHOM GOD HATH R 303 30
GOD HATH JOINED TOGETHER LET NO MAN PUT ASUNDER   303 31
HAVE CONSENTED TOGETHER IN HOLY WEDLOCK, AND HAVE   304 03
YE MAY SO LIVE TOGETHER IN THIS LIFE, THAT IN THE   304 14
NOT BE JOINED TOGETHER IN HOLY MATRIMONY, YE ARE TO R 304 24
WITH HIM, THAT WE MAY BE ALSO GLORIFIED TOGETHER   330 26
ALL THINGS WORK TOGETHER FOR GOOD TO THEM THAT LOVE   330 31
MAY AT LAST, TOGETHER WITH THEM, BE FOUND MEET TO BE 335 32
WHY DO THE HEATHEN SO FURIOUSLY RAGE TOGETHER   345 25
TAKE COUNSEL TOGETHER *   345 28
THEY CONSPIRE TOGETHER AGAINST ME, AND TAKE THEIR   376 22
OF THE SEA TOGETHER, AS IT WERE UPON AN HEAP   378 31
AND LET US MAGNIFY HIS NAME TOGETHER   380 08
ABJECTS CAME TOGETHER AGAINST ME UNAWARES, MAKING   382 24
THEY REJOICED, AND GATHERED THEMSELVES TOGETHER   382 24
AND SHAME TOGETHER, THAT REJOICE AT MY TROUBLE   383 16
THEY SHALL PERISH TOGETHER   387 10
AND CONFOUNDED TOGETHER, THAT SEEK AFTER MY SOUL TO   391 16
ENEMIES WHISPER TOGETHER AGAINST ME   392 13
CLAP YOUR HANDS TOGETHER, ALL YE PEOPLES   398 21
WERE GATHERED, AND GONE BY TOGETHER   399 17
DIE AND PERISH TOGETHER, *   400 23
MY SAINTS TOGETHER UNTO ME   401 30
SWEET COUNSEL TOGETHER, *   407 18
6 THEY HOLD ALL TOGETHER, AND KEEP THEMSELVES CLOSE, 408 26
THE GATHERING TOGETHER OF THE FROWARD, *   415 21
THEIR COUNSEL TOGETHER, SAYING, 10 GOD HATH FORSAKEN 425 26
THEIR HEADS TOGETHER WITH ONE CONSENT, *   444 14
10 MERCY AND TRUTH ARE MET TOGETHER   446 27
COMPASSED ME TOGETHER ON EVERY SIDE   449 32
GATHER THEM TOGETHER AGAINST THE SOUL OF THE   458 28
HILLS BE JOYFUL TOGETHER BEFORE THE LORD   462 11
ME ARE SWORN TOGETHER AGAINST ME   464 26
ARE GATHERED TOGETHER, *   465 24
GET THEM AWAY TOGETHER, *   469 04
TO DWELL TOGETHER IN UNITY   509 14
THEIR OWN NETS TOGETHER, *   517 32
AND GATHER TOGETHER THE OUTCASTS OF ISRAEL   522 30
HE GATHERED TOGETHER A GREAT FLOCK IN ALL THE PARTS   545 19
SHALL TAKE TOGETHER, AND REMAIN IN THE SAME PLACE   R 546 30
HERE GATHERED TOGETHER WITH ALL HUMILITY AND   565 03
SHALL BE JOINED TOGETHER IN THIS PLACE IN THE HOLY   566 08
IN PERFECT LOVE TOGETHER UNTO THEIR LIFE'S END   566 11
AND THE SON TOGETHER, WE WORSHIP AND GLORIFY AS ONE   572 31
BE SO JOINED TOGETHER IN UNITY OF SPIRIT, AND IN THE 574 07
HAVING CALLED TOGETHER AS MANY OF THE FAMILY AS CAN R 587 04
FAMILY BEING TOGETHER, A LITTLE BEFORE BED-TIME,   R 589 13

TOGETHER   CONTINUED

MAY BE BOUND TOGETHER BY THY LOVE IN THE COMMUNICN OF   597 05
KNIT TOGETHER IN CONSTANT AFFECTION THOSE WHO,   598 25
WERE JOINED TOGETHER IN ONE PERSON, NEVER TO BE   603 13

TOIL

THEY TOIL NOT, NEITHER DO THEY SPIN   211 22
THEY TOIL NOT, NEITHER DO THEY SPIN   266 20
AND COMFORT THEM CONCERNING THEIR TOIL   599 28

TOILED

WE HAVE TOILED ALL THE NIGHT, AND HAVE TAKEN   196 16

TOKEN

HAD GIVEN THEM A TOKEN, SAYING, WHOMSOEVER I SHALL   142 18
OF THE CROSS, IN TOKEN THAT HEREAFTER HE SHALL NOT BE   280 05
AND RECEIVED IS A TOKEN AND PLEDGE,) AND MAY EVER   303 09
THOU HAST GIVEN A TOKEN FOR SUCH AS FEAR THEE,   412 19
17 SHOW SOME TOKEN UPON ME FOR GOOD   448 09
AND IN TOKEN THEREOF, GIVE INTO YOUR HANDS THE KEYS   570 29

TOKENS

BE AFRAID AT THY TOKENS, *   416 30
AND SET UP THEIR BANNERS FOR TOKENS   430 13
10 WE SEE NOT OUR TOKENS   430 24
THESE SHOWED HIS TOKENS AMONG THEM, *   471 26
9 HE HATH SENT TOKENS AND WONDERS INTO THE MIDST OF   510 20
ONLY BADGES OR TOKENS OF CHRISTIAN MEN'S PROFESSICN,   607 31

TOLD

SAYING WHICH WAS TOLD THEM CONCERNING THIS CHILC   106 14
THINGS WHICH WERE TOLD THEM BY THE SHEPHERDS   106 15
AND SEEN, AS IT WAS TOLD THEM   106 19
BEHOLD, I HAVE TOLD YOU BEFORE   118 07
AND THEY TOLD HIM, THAT JESUS OF NAZARETH PASSETH BY   123 29
AND THEY TOLD WHAT THINGS WERE DONE IN THE WAY, AND   168 14
THESE THINGS HAVE I TOLD YOU, THAT WHEN THE TIME   180 02
MAY REMEMBER THAT I TOLD YOU OF THEM   180 04
AND NOW I HAVE TOLD YOU BEFORE IT COME TC PASS, THAT,   182 05
IF I HAVE TOLD YOU EARTHLY THINGS, AND YE BELIEVE   188 22
AS I HAVE ALSO TOLD YOU IN TIME PAST, THAT THEY WHICH   209 24
MET HIM, AND TOLD HIM, SAYING, THY SON LIVETH   220 06
AND CAME AND TOLD UNTO THEIR LCRD ALL THAT WAS   221 31
OF WHOM I HAVE TOLD YOU OFTEN, AND NOW TELL YOU EVEN   222 17
AND IT SHALL BE TOLD THEE WHAT THOU MUST DO   230 07
I WOULD HAVE TOLD YOU   239 32
KEPT IT CLOSE, AND TOLD NO MAN IN THOSE DAYS ANY OF   249 09
AS IT WERE A TALE THAT IS TOLD   325 31
I WOULD HAVE TOLD YOU   331 19
OUR FATHERS HAVE TOLD US *   394 23
AS OUR FATHERS HAVE TOLD US   434 32
AS IT WERE A TALE THAT IS TOLD   454 06

TOMB

IT IN HIS OWN NEW TOMB, WHICH HE HAD HEWN OUT IN THE   162 11

TONGUE

AND MY TONGUE SHALL SING OF THY RIGHTECUSNESS   061 07
AND THAT EVERY TONGUE SHOULD CONFESS THAT JESUS   105 30
AND THAT EVERY TONGUE SHOULD CONFESS THAT JESUS   134 26
BRIDLETH NOT HIS TONGLE, BUT DECEIVETH HIS CWN HEART,   176 14
MAN IN OUR OWN TONGUE, WHEREIN WE WERE BORN   180 31
TIP OF HIS FINGER IN WATER, AND COOL MY TONGUE   190 15
LET US NOT LOVE IN WORD, NEITHER IN TONGUE   191 22
HIM REFRAIN HIS TONGUE FROM EVIL, AND HIS LIPS THAT   195 25
HIS EARS, AND HE SPIT, AND TOUCHED HIS TONGUE   206 33
THE STRING OF HIS TONGUE WAS LOOSED, AND HE SPAKE   207 04
IN THEIR PROPER TONGUE, ACELDAMA, THAT IS TO SAY, THE   234 17
AND HIS TONGUE LOOSED, AND HE SPAKE, AND PRAISED GOD   243 25
BRIDLETH NOT HIS TONGUE, BUT DECEIVETH HIS OWN HEART,   266 05
TO KEEP MY TONGUE FROM EVIL SPEAKING, LYING, ANC   289 06
THEY FLATTER WITH THEIR TONGUE   348 21
UNDER HIS TONGUE IS UNGODLINESS AND VANITY   353 19
AND THE TONGUE THAT SPEAKETH PROUD THINGS   355 13
WITH OUR TONGUE WILL WE PREVAIL   355 14
NO DECEIT IN HIS TONGLE, NOR DONE EVIL TO HIS   357 10
AND MY TONGUE CLEAVETH TO MY GUMS, *   367 02
WHILST I HELD MY TONGLE, *   377 26
13 KEEP THY TONGUE FROM EVIL, *   380 27
HOLD NOT THY TONGUE THEN   383 07
28 AND AS FOR MY TONGLE, IT SHALL BE TALKING OF THY   383 22
AND HIS TONGUE WILL BE TALKING OF JUDGMENT   386 27
THAT I OFFEND NOT IN MY TONGUE   389 06
3 I HELD MY TONGUE, AND SPAKE NOTHING   389 09
AND AT THE LAST I SPAKE WITH MY TONGUE   389 14
MY TONGUE IS THE PEN OF A READY WRITER   396 17
AND WITH THY TONGUE THOU HAST SET FORTH DECEIT   402 29
AND I HELD MY TONGUE, AND THOU THOUGHTEST WICKEDLY,   402 32
AND MY TONGUE SHALL SING OF THY RIGHTEOUSNESS   404 05
3 THY TONGUE IMAGINETH WICKEDNESS, *   404 22
O THOU FALSE TONGUE   404 27
AND THEIR TONGUE A SHARP SWORD   409 23
HAVE WHET THEIR TONGUE LIKE A SWORD, *   415 23
AND GAVE HIM PRAISES WITH MY TONGUE   418 15
AND THAT THE TONGUE OF THY DOGS MAY BE RED THROUGH   420 34
23 MY TONGUE ALSO SHALL TALK OF THY RIGHTEOUSNESS ALL   426 27
AND THEIR TONGUE GOETH THROUGH THE WORLD   428 27
AND DISSEMBLED WITH HIM IN THEIR TONGUE   437 11

TONGUE   CONTINUED

HOLD NOT THY TONGUE, O GOD, KEEP NOT STILL SILENCE   444 05
HOLD NOT THY TONGUE, O GOD OF MY PRAISE   480 03
172 YEA, MY TONGUE SHALL SING OF THY WORD   501 26
AND FROM A DECEITFUL TONGUE   502 10
BE GIVEN OR DONE UNTO THEE, THOU FALSE TONGUE   502 12
AND OUR TONGUE WITH JOY   505 10
LET MY TONGUE CLEAVE TO THE ROOF OF MY MOUTH   513 15
NOT A WORD IN MY TONGUE, *   514 25
WHO DOST THE TONGUE WITH SPEECH ENDOW   544 28
WHO DOST THE TONGUE WITH SPEECH ENDOW   557 07
AND MY TONGUE FROM EVIL SPEAKING, LYING,   580 10
IN A TONGUE NOT UNDERSTANDED OF THE   607 29

TONGUES

BROUGHT HITHER OUT OF MANY KINDREDS AND TONGUES   036 17
I SPEAK WITH THE TONGUES OF MEN AND OF ANGELS,   122 21
WHETHER THERE BE TONGUES, THEY SHALL CEASE   123.05
UNTO THEM CLOVEN TONGUES LIKE AS OF FIRE, AND IT SAT   180 21
SPEAK WITH OTHER TONGUES, AS THE SPIRIT GAVE THEM   180 24
SPEAK IN OUR TONGUES THE WONDERFUL WORKS OF GOD   181 06
TO ANOTHER DIVERS KINDS OF TONGUES   182 32
TO ANOTHER THE INTERPRETATION OF TONGUES   182 33
THEM SPEAK WITH TONGUES, AND MAGNIFY GOD   184 25
TO ANOTHER DIVERS KINDS OF TONGUES   203 32
TO ANOTHER THE INTERPRETATION OF TONGUES   204 02
AND PEOPLES, AND TONGUES, STOOD BEFORE THE THRONE,   256 25
IN THY TABERNACLE FROM THE STRIFE OF TONGUES   377 08
9 DESTROY THEIR TONGUES, O LORD, AND DIVIDE THEM   407 04
8 YEA, THEIR OWN TONGUES SHALL MAKE THEM FALL   416 02
THEY HAVE SPOKEN AGAINST ME WITH FALSE TCNGUES   480 06
SHARPENED THEIR TONGUES LIKE A SERPENT   516 13

TOOK

(A) HE TOOK BREAD   080 18
(D) HE TOOK THE CUP   080 23
WHEN HE AROSE, HE TOOK THE YOUNG CHILD AND HIS MCTHER   103 20
HAD BIDDEN HIM, AND TOOK UNTO HIM HIS WIFE   105 19
AND HE AROSE, AND TOOK THE YOUNG CHILD AND HIS   107 16
THEN JESUS TOOK UNTO HIM THE TWELVE, AND SAID UNTO   123 17
AND JESUS TOOK THE LOAVES   132 03
THEN TOOK THEY UP STONES TO CAST AT HIM   133 32
NO REPUTATION, AND TOOK UPON HIM THE FORM OF A   134 19
OF THE PEOPLE TOOK COUNSEL AGAINST JESUS TO PUT HIM   134 31
THE CHIEF PRIESTS TOOK THE SILVER PIECES, AND SAID,   135 09
AND THEY TOOK COUNSEL, AND BOUGHT WITH THEM THE   135 11
AND THEY TOOK THE THIRTY PIECES OF SILVER,   135 15
TUMULT WAS MADE, HE TOOK WATER, AND WASHED HIS HANDS   136 09
OF THE GOVERNOR TOOK JESUS INTO THE COMMON HALL, AND   136 15
SPIT UPON HIM, AND TOOK THE REED, AND SMOTE HIM CN   136 22
MOCKED HIM, THEY TOOK THE ROBE OFF FROM HIM, AND PUT   136 23
OF THEM RAN, AND TOOK A SPUNGE, AND FILLED IT WITH   137 21
THEY DID EAT, JESUS TOOK BREAD, AND BLESSED, AND   141 09
AND HE TOOK THE CUP, AND WHEN HE HAD GIVEN THANKS, HE   141 11
HANDS ON HIM, AND TOOK HIM   142 22
AND YE TOOK ME NOT   142 26
MOCKED HIM, THEY TOOK OFF THE PURPLE FROM HIM,   146 03
TO THE LAW, HE TOOK THE BLOOD OF CALVES AND OF GCATS,   147 20
AND HE TOOK THE CUP, AND SAID, TAKE   149 05
AND HE TOOK BREAD, AND GAVE THANKS, AND BRAKE IT, AND   149 08
THEN TOOK THEY HIM, AND LED HIM, AND BROUGHT HIM INTO   151 06
HE WAS BETRAYED TOOK BREAD   152 18
SAME MANNER ALSO HE TOOK THE CUP, WHEN HE HAD SUPPED,   152 21
AND TOOK A TOWEL, AND GIRDED HIMSELF   155 31
PILATE THEREFORE TOOK JESUS, AND SCOURGED HIM   158 30
AND THEY TOOK JESUS, AND LED HIM AWAY   159 31
CRUCIFIED JESUS, TOOK HIS GARMENTS, AND MADE FOUR   160 10
HOUR THAT DISCIPLE TOOK HER UNTO HIS OWN HOME   160 23
MEAT WITH THEM, HE TOOK BREAD, AND BLESSED IT,   168 06
OF HIM, THEY TOOK HIM DOWN FROM THE TREE, AND LAID   168 32
AND HE TOOK IT, AND DID EAT BEFORE THEM   170 06
AND HE TOOK THE SEVEN LOAVES, AND GAVE THANKS, AND   199 18
AND THEY TOOK UP OF THE BROKEN MEAT THAT WAS LEFT   199 23
ALL TOGETHER, AND TOOK HIS JOURNEY INTO A FAR   202 03
AND HE TOOK HIM ASIDE FROM THE MULTITUDE, AND PUT HIS   206 31
HIM TO AN INN, AND TOOK CARE OF HIM   208 32
HE DEPARTED, HE TOOK OUT TWO PENCE, AND GAVE THEM TO   208 33
AND HE TOOK HIM, AND HEALED HIM, AND LET HIM GO   214 04
AND THE REMNANT TOOK HIS SERVANTS, AND ENTREATED THEM   218 12
HANDS ON HIM, AND TOOK HIM BY THE THROAT, SAYING,   221 25
THE PHARISEES, AND TOOK COUNSEL HOW THEY MIGHT   222 28
HE WENT IN, AND TOOK HER BY THE HAND, AND THE MAID   224 28
AND JESUS TOOK THE LOAVES   226 02
OF THE LAW, THEN TOOK HE HIM UP IN HIS ARMS, AND   233 04
GUIDE TO THEM THAT TOOK JESUS   234 11
THESE SAYINGS, HE TOOK PETER AND JOHN AND JAMES,   248 24
A STRANGER, AND YE TOOK ME IN   259 07
A STRANGER, AND TOOK THEE IN   259 12
AND HE TOOK THEM UP IN HIS ARMS, PUT HIS HANDS UPON   274 32
AND TOOK ME OUT OF MANY WATERS   360 31
THOU ART HE THAT TOOK ME OUT OF MY MOTHER'S WCMB   366 20
IS THE MAN THAT TOOK NOT GOD FOR HIS STRENGTH   404 33
15 WE TOOK SWEET COUNSEL TOGETHER, *   407 18
5 I PAID THEM THE THINGS THAT I NEVER TOOK   422 10
THOU ART HE THAT TOOK ME OUT OF MY MOTHER'S WOMB   425 17
AND TOOK SORE DISPLEASURE AT ISRAEL   438 30
AND TOOK HIM AWAY FROM THE SHEEP-FOLDS   439 19
WITH THEIR YOUNG HE TOOK HIM, *   439 22
AND THEY TOOK THE LABOURS OF THE PEOPLE IN   472 26
WITH THE FATHER, TOOK MAN'S NATURE IN THE WOMB OF THE   603 11
FROM DEATH, AND TOOK AGAIN HIS BODY, WITH FLESH,   603 21

TOOKEST

WHEN THOU TOOKEST UPON THEE TO DELIVER MAN, THOU   010 26

TOP

IN TWAIN FROM THE TOP TO THE BOTTOM   137 26
IN TWAIN FROM THE TOP TO THE BOTTOM   147 02
WOVEN FROM THE TOP THROUGHOUT   160 12

TORMENT

BECAUSE FEAR HATH TORMENT   189 29
LEST THEY ALSO COME INTO THIS PLACE OF TORMENT   190 25

TORMENTED

AT HOME SICK OF THE PALSY, GRIEVOUSLY TORMENTED   115 09
FOR I AM TORMENTED IN THIS FLAME   190 15
BUT NOW HE IS COMFORTED, AND THOU ART TORMENTED   190 18

TORMENTORS

HIM TO THE TORMENTORS, TILL HE SHOULD PAY ALL THAT   222 03

TORMENTS

BEING IN TORMENTS, AND SEETH ABRAHAM AFAR OFF,   190 11

TOSSED

NO MORE CHILDREN, TOSSED TO AND FRO, AND CARRIED   237 25
A WAVE OF THE SEA DRIVEN WITH THE WIND AND TOSSED   239 16

TOTTERING

AS A TOTTERING WALL SHALL YE BE, AND LIKE A   414 03

TOUCH

IF I MAY BUT TOUCH HIS GARMENT, I SHALL BE WHOLE   224 20
THAT HE SHOULD TOUCH THEM   274 26
IF HE DO BUT TOUCH THE HILLS, THEY SHALL SMOKE   469 26
15 TOUCH NOT MINE ANOINTED, *   471 02
TOUCH THE MOUNTAINS, AND THEY SHALL SMOKE   519 31

TOUCHED

HIS HAND, AND TOUCHED HIM, SAYING, I WILL   115 02
AND HE TOUCHED HIS EAR, AND HEALED HIM   150 34
AND HE SPIT, AND TOUCHED HIS TONGUE   206 33
AND HE CAME AND TOUCHED THE BIER   213 03
BEHIND HIM, AND TOUCHED THE HEM OF HIS GARMENT   224 18

TOUCHING

IN THIS MAN TOUCHING THOSE THINGS WHEREOF YE ACCUSE   153 25
DEMAND OF YOU TOUCHING THE SAME   541 29
BY MOSES, AS TOUCHING CEREMONIES AND RITES, DO NOT   604 19
NOT COMMON, AS TOUCHING THE RIGHT, TITLE, AND   610 44

TOWEL

AND TOOK A TOWEL, AND GIRDED HIMSELF   155 31
WIPE THEM WITH THE TOWEL WHEREWITH HE WAS GIRDED   155 34

TOWER

WHO ART A STRONG TOWER OF DEFENCE UNTO THY SERVANTS   052 07
BE THOU TO HER A STRONG TOWER   306 19
BE UNTO HIM, O LORD, A STRONG TOWER   308 29
IS A MOST STRONG TOWER TO ALL THOSE WHO PUT THEIR   314 15
AND A STRONG TOWER FOR ME AGAINST THE ENEMY   413 11

TOWERS

AND TELL THE TOWERS THEREOF   399 34

TRADITIONS

THAT TRADITIONS AND CEREMONIES BE IN ALL PLACES ONE,   609 32
BREAK THE TRADITIONS AND CEREMONIES OF THE CHURCH,   609 36

TRAIN

AND STRENGTH SO TO TRAIN THEM, THAT THEY MAY LOVE   596 26

TRAINED

AND ARE TRAINED IN THE HOUSEHOLD OF FAITH   292 35

TRAITOR

THE PLACE OF THE TRAITOR JUDAS DIDST CHOOSE THY   233 31

TRAMPLE

MINE ANGER, AND TRAMPLE THEM IN MY FURY   138 18

TRANSFIGURATION

AND ON THE FEAST OF THE TRANSFIGURATION   R 008 20
AND TRANSFIGURATION   R 077 28

TRANSFIGURED

WONDERFULLY TRANSFIGURED, IN RAIMENT WHITE AND   247 32

TRANSFORMED

BUT BE YE TRANSFORMED BY THE RENEWING OF YOUR MIND,   110 06

TRANSGRESS

BUT SUCH AS TRANSGRESS WITHOUT A CAUSE SHALL BE PUT   369 22

TRANSGRESSED

NEITHER TRANSGRESSED I AT ANY TIME THY COMMANDMENT   202 34

TRANSGRESSETH

SIN TRANSGRESSETH ALSO THE LAW   117 22

TRANSGRESSION

SIN IS THE TRANSGRESSION OF THE LAW   117 22
JUDAS BY TRANSGRESSION FELL, THAT HE MIGHT GO TO HIS   234 30

TRANSGRESSIONS

MY TRANSGRESSIONS, AND MY SIN IS EVER BEFORE ME   022 04
OUR TRANSGRESSIONS, AND TRULY REPENT US OF OUR   062 23
FOR THEIR TRANSGRESSIONS FOR THE TIME PAST, AND GRACE   R 067 24
OF THE TRANSGRESSIONS THAT WERE UNDER THE FIRST   133 05
OF TRANSGRESSIONS, TILL THE SEED SHOULD COME TO WHOM   207 27
MANIFOLD TRANSGRESSIONS OF THY RIGHTEOUS LAWS   589 31
AND FORGIVE US ALL OUR TRANSGRESSIONS   590 02

TRANSGRESSORS

AND HE WAS NUMBERED WITH THE TRANSGRESSORS   146 17
AND HE WAS RECKONED AMONG THE TRANSGRESSORS   150 10
AS FOR THE TRANSGRESSORS, THEY SHALL PERISH TOGETHER   387 10
158 IT GRIEVETH ME WHEN I SEE THE TRANSGRESSORS   500 27

TRANSITORY

WHO, IN THIS TRANSITORY LIFE, ARE IN TROUBLE, SORROW,   074 31
LOOK ONLY FOR TRANSITORY PROMISES   604 18

TRANSUBSTANTIATION

TRANSUBSTANTIATION (OR THE CHANGE OF THE SUBSTANCE OF   608 40

TRAPPED

THE UNGODLY IS TRAPPED IN THE WORK OF HIS OWN HANDS   352 25

TRAPS

AND SET TRAPS IN MY WAY   516 19
AND FROM THE TRAPS OF THE WICKED DOERS   517 31

TRAVAIL

ALL YE THAT TRAVAIL AND ARE HEAVY LADEN, AND I   076 12
WHEN SHE IS IN TRAVAIL HATH SORROW, BECAUSE HER HOUR   174 10
17 FOR HIS TRAVAIL SHALL COME UPON HIS OWN HEAD,   350 25
AS UPON A WOMAN IN HER TRAVAIL   399 21

TRAVAILEST

THOU THAT TRAVAILEST NOT   131 10

TRAVAILETH

GROANETH AND TRAVAILETH IN PAIN TOGETHER UNTIL NOW   194 20
THE UNGODLY TRAVAILETH WITH INIQUITY   350 21

TRAVEL

ALSO FOR ALL WHO TRAVEL BY LAND, SEA, OR AIR   048 05
PRESERVE ALL WHO TRAVEL BY LAND, BY WATER, OR BY AIR,   056 30
AND THOSE WHO TRAVEL BY LAND OR BY SEA   600 06

TRAVELLING

HIS APPAREL, TRAVELLING IN THE GREATNESS OF HIS   138 13

TREAD

FOR I WILL TREAD THEM IN MINE ANGER, AND TRAMPLE THEM   138 18
AND I WILL TREAD DOWN THE PEOPLE IN MINE ANGER, AND   138 25
LET HIM TREAD MY LIFE DOWN UPON THE EARTH,   349 33
THY NAME WILL WE TREAD THEM UNDER THAT RISE UP   395 03
IS HE THAT SHALL TREAD DOWN OUR ENEMIES   413 05
DRAGON SHALT THOU TREAD UNDER THY FEET   455 22
IS HE THAT SHALL TREAD DOWN OUR ENEMIES   479 31

TREADETH

LIKE HIM THAT TREADETH IN THE WINEFAT   138 16

TREADINGS

MY TREADINGS HAD WELL-NIGH SLIPT   428 12

TREASURE

FOR WHERE YOUR TREASURE IS, THERE WILL YOUR HEART BE	125	21
AND BE MADE PARTAKERS OF THY HEAVENLY TREASURE	204	26
WHOSE BELLIES THOU FILLEST WITH THY HID TREASURE	359	16
HOW GREAT A TREASURE IS COMMITTED TO YOUR CHARGE	540	06

TREASURE-HOUSE

AND LAYETH UP THE DEEP, AS IN A TREASURE-HOUSE	378	32

TREASURES

FOR YOURSELVES TREASURES UPON EARTH, WHERE MOTH AND	072	07
FOR YOURSELVES TREASURES IN HEAVEN, WHERE NEITHER	072	09
OPENED THEIR TREASURES, THEY PRESENTED UNTO HIM	109	22
FOR YOURSELVES TREASURES UPON EARTH, WHERE MOTH AND	125	16
FOR YOURSELVES TREASURES IN HEAVEN, WHERE NEITHER	125	19

TREASURIES

BRINGING THE WINDS OUT OF HIS TREASURIES	510	17

TREASURY

THEM INTO THE TREASURY, BECAUSE IT IS THE PRICE OF	135	10

TREATISE

THE FORMER TREATISE HAVE I MADE, O THEOPHILUS,	177	22

TREE

BEHOLD THE FIG TREE, AND ALL THE TREES	093	14
THINGS IN A GREEN TREE, WHAT SHALL BE DONE IN THE	154	20
WHOM THEY SLEW AND HANGED ON A TREE	166	24
HIM DOWN FROM THE TREE, AND LAID HIM IN A SEPULCHRE	169	02
HIS OWN BODY ON THE TREE, THAT WE, BEING DEAD TO	172	16
WHOM THEY SLEW AND HANGED ON A TREE	184	12
EVEN SO EVERY GOOD TREE BRINGETH FORTH GOOD FRUIT	200	18
BUT A CORRUPT TREE BRINGETH FORTH EVIL FRUIT	200	19
A GOOD TREE CANNOT BRING FORTH EVIL FRUIT, NEITHER	200	20
EVERY TREE THAT BRINGETH NOT FORTH GOOD FRUIT IS HEWN	200	21
CAN A CORRUPT TREE BRING FORTH GOOD FRUIT	200	21
AND THE TREE OF THE FIELD SHALL YIELD HER FRUIT, AND	262	09
HE SHALL BE LIKE A TREE PLANTED BY THE WATER-SIDE,	345	12
KNOWN AS A TREE DISCERNED BY THE FRUIT	605	15

TREES

BRANCHES FROM THE TREES, AND STRAWED THEM IN THE WAY	091	26
BEHOLD THE FIG TREE, AND ALL THE TREES	093	15
MIGHT BE CALLED TREES OF RIGHTEOUSNESS, THE PLANTING	107	09
THE SEA, NOR THE TREES, TILL WE HAVE SEALED THE	256	18
OUT OF THE THICK TREES, *	430	14
THEN SHALL ALL THE TREES OF THE WOOD REJOICE BEFORE	460	25
16 THE TREES OF THE LORD ALSO ARE FULL OF SAP	468	26
AND DESTROYED THE TREES THAT WERE IN THEIR COASTS	472	05
UPON THE TREES THAT ARE THEREIN	513	07
FRUITFUL TREES AND ALL CEDARS	524	22

TREMBLE

THE EARTH SHALL TREMBLE AT THE LOOK OF HIM	469	25
7 TREMBLE, THOU EARTH, AT THE PRESENCE OF THE LORD	485	06

TREMBLED

FOR THEY TREMBLED AND WERE AMAZED	166	02
8 THE EARTH TREMBLED AND QUAKED, *	360	09
THE EARTH TREMBLED, AND WAS STILL, 9 WHEN GOD AROSE	433	05

TREMBLETH

120 MY FLESH TREMBLETH FOR FEAR OF THEE	498	08

TREMBLING

OUT YOUR OWN SALVATION WITH FEAR AND TREMBLING	106	04
AND HE TREMBLING AND ASTONISHED SAID, LORD, WHAT WILT	230	05
AND COME TREMBLING OUT OF THEIR STRONGHOLDS	362	30
AND TREMBLING ARE COME UPON ME, *	406	28

TRENCH

SHALL CAST A TRENCH ABOUT THEE, AND COMPASS THEE	204	11

TRESPASS

THOSE WHO TRESPASS AGAINST US	007	26

TRESPASSED

OTHER HATH TRESPASSED AGAINST HIM, AND TO MAKE AMENDS	R 085	13

TRESPASSES

US OUR TRESPASSES, AS WE FORGIVE THOSE WHO TRESPASS	007	26
MERCIFULLY FORGIVE US OUR TRESPASSES	062	16
NOT EVERY ONE HIS BROTHER THEIR TRESPASSES	222	06

TRIAL

EXAMINATION AND TRIAL, FINDING HIM SUFFICIENTLY	529	28
PRESENT MAY HAVE A TRIAL, AND BEAR WITNESS, HOW YOU	554	14

TRIBE

OF PHANUEL, OF THE TRIBE OF ASER	233	17
3 THINK UPON THE TRIBE OF THINE INHERITANCE, *	430	08
AND CHOSE NOT THE TRIBE OF EPHRAIM	439	13
69 BUT CHOSE THE TRIBE OF JUDAH, *	439	14

TRIBES

SHALL ALL THE TRIBES OF THE EARTH MOURN, AND THEY	118	18
THE TRIBES OF THINE INHERITANCE	139	26
THE TWELVE TRIBES OF ISRAEL	149	30
THE TWELVE TRIBES OF ISRAEL	231	18
TO THE TWELVE TRIBES WHICH ARE SCATTERED ABROAD,	239	07
THE TWELVE TRIBES OF ISRAEL	250	15
OF ALL THE TRIBES OF THE CHILDREN OF ISRAEL	256	21
AND MADE THE TRIBES OF ISRAEL TO DWELL IN THEIR	438	23
WAS NOT ONE FEEBLE PERSON AMONG THEIR TRIBES	472	12
4 FOR THITHER THE TRIBES GO UP, EVEN THE TRIBES OF	503	13
GO UP, EVEN THE TRIBES OF THE LORD, *	503	13

TRIBULATION

HOLY GHOST, IN ALL TIME OF OUR TRIBULATION	055	15
AND TRIBULATION	056	28
PATIENT IN TRIBULATION	111	26
AFTER THE TRIBULATION OF THOSE DAYS SHALL THE SUN BE	118	14
IN THE WORLD YE SHALL HAVE TRIBULATION	177	09
OUT OF GREAT TRIBULATION, AND HAVE WASHED THEIR	257	07
FROM ALL SIN, FROM ALL TRIBULATION	318	02
SHALL TRIBULATION, OR DISTRESS, OR PERSECUTION,	331	07

TRIBULATIONS

NOT AT MY TRIBULATIONS FOR YOU, WHICH IS YOUR GLORY	212	10

TRIBUTE

CAUSE PAY YE TRIBUTE ALSO	114	24
TRIBUTE TO WHOM TRIBUTE IS DUE	114	26
TRIBUTE TO WHOM TRIBUTE IS DUE	114	26
TO GIVE TRIBUTE TO CAESAR, SAYING THAT HE HIMSELF IS	152	30
LAWFUL TO GIVE TRIBUTE UNTO CAESAR, OR NOT	223	04
SHEW ME THE TRIBUTE MONEY	223	06

TRIED

FOR WHEN HE IS TRIED, HE SHALL RECEIVE THE CROWN OF	239	25
FROM THE EARTH IS TRIED, AND PURIFIED SEVEN TIMES IN	355	21
THOU HAST TRIED ME, AND SHALT FIND NO WICKEDNESS IN	358	22
THE LORD ALSO IS TRIED IN THE FIRE	361	29
THOU ALSO HAST TRIED US, LIKE AS SILVER IS TRIED	417	34
THOU ALSO HAST TRIED US, LIKE AS SILVER IS TRIED	417	34
WORD OF THE LORD TRIED HIM	471	11
140 THY WORD IS TRIED TO THE UTTERMOST, *	499	19
WERE FIRST CALLED, TRIED, EXAMINED, AND KNOWN TO HAVE	529	15
HE BE CALLED, TRIED, EXAMINED, AND ADMITTED	529	22

TRIETH

TRIETH THE VERY HEARTS AND REINS	350	11

TRINITY

ON TRINITY SUNDAY	R 008	29
AND GLORIOUS TRINITY, ONE GOD	054	11
AND TRINITY SUNDAY	R 070	32
THE FEAST OF TRINITY ONLY	R 079	06
ONE LORD, IN TRINITY OF PERSONS AND IN UNITY OF	079	08
IN LENT, AND TRINITY SUNDAY	R 085	24
OF THE ETERNAL TRINITY, AND IN THE POWER OF THE	186	25
SUNDAYS AFTER TRINITY, THE SERVICE FOR THE SIXTH	R 224	31
AND THIS HOLY TRINITY, ONE GOD, I PRAISE AND MAGNIFY,	285	04
O HOLY TRINITY, ONE GOD	317	31
O HOLY TRINITY, ONE GOD,	560	09

TRIUMPH

WITH GREAT TRIUMPH UNTO THY KINGDOM IN HEAVEN	179	05
AND TO TRIUMPH, AGAINST THE DEVIL, THE	278	25
SHALL MINE ENEMY TRIUMPH OVER ME	355	31
AND TRIUMPH IN THE NAME OF THE LORD OUR	364	23
LET MINE ENEMIES TRIUMPH OVER ME	369	20
MADE MY FOES TO TRIUMPH OVER ME	374	25
ARE MINE ENEMIES TRIUMPH OVER ME UNGODLY	382	34
AND LET THEM NOT TRIUMPH OVER ME	383	12
SHOULD NOT TRIUMPH OVER ME	388	24
ENEMY DOTH NOT TRIUMPH AGAINST ME	392	22
THAT THEY MAY TRIUMPH BECAUSE OF THE TRUTH	412	20
HOW LONG SHALL THE UNGODLY TRIUMPH	457	24
UPON PHILISTIA WILL I TRIUMPH	479	23

TRIUMPHS

IN THEIR TRIUMPHS, WE MAY PROFIT BY THEIR EXAMPLES	258	07

TROAS

THAT I LEFT AT TROAS WITH CARPUS, WHEN THOU COMEST,	254	05

TRODDEN

AND IT WAS TRODDEN DOWN, AND THE FOWLS OF THE AIR	121	21
I HAVE TRODDEN THE WINEPRESS ALONE	138	16
ADVERSARIES HAVE TRODDEN DOWN THY SANCTUARY	139	28
118 THOU HAST TRODDEN DOWN ALL THEM THAT DEPART FROM	498	04

TROTH

THEY GIVE THEIR TROTH TO EACH OTHER IN THIS MANNER	R 301	24
AND THERETO I PLIGHT THEE MY TROTH	301	32
AND THERETO I GIVE THEE MY TROTH	302	08
AND PLEDGED THEIR TROTH, EACH TO THE OTHER, AND HAVE	304	06

TROUBLE

IN THE DAY OF TROUBLE, SUFFER NOT OUR TRUST IN THEE	036	22
TROUBLE, DREAD, OR THE NEAR APPROACH OF DEATH,	048	09
ARE IN TROUBLE, SORROW, NEED, SICKNESS, OR ANY	074	32
WHY TROUBLE YE HER	140	11
LET NO MAN TROUBLE ME	211	05
ANSWER AND SAY, TROUBLE ME NOT	262	30
I FOUND TROUBLE AND HEAVINESS	305	22
INCREASED THAT TROUBLE ME	309	14
THE TIME OF MY TROUBLE I SOUGHT THE LORD	310	31
THOUGH I WALK IN THE MIDST OF TROUBLE	311	25
IN THE MIDST OF TROUBLE, YET SHALT THOU REFRESH ME	312	04
IN THE TIME OF TROUBLE HE SHALL HIDE ME IN HIS	326	12
A VERY PRESENT HELP IN TROUBLE	327	04
OF THEM THAT TROUBLE ME	338	27
INCREASED THAT TROUBLE ME	346	25
THOU HAST SET ME AT LIBERTY WHEN I WAS IN TROUBLE	347	11
IS GONE FOR VERY TROUBLE, *	349	12
EVEN A REFUGE IN DUE TIME OF TROUBLE	352	07
CONSIDER THE TROUBLE WHICH I SUFFER OF THEM THAT HATE	352	16
HIDEST THY FACE IN THE NEEDFUL TIME OF TROUBLE	353	04
THEY THAT TROUBLE ME WILL REJOICE AT IT	356	05
SHALL HAVE GREAT TROUBLE	357	28
THAT TROUBLE ME	359	04
6 IN MY TROUBLE I CALLED UPON THE LORD, *	360	04
19 THEY CAME UPON ME IN THE DAY OF MY TROUBLE	361	02
THE LORD HEAR THEE IN THE DAY OF TROUBLE	364	17
FOR TROUBLE IS HARD AT HAND, *	366	25
OF THEM THAT TROUBLE ME	368	20
IN THE TIME OF TROUBLE HE SHALL HIDE ME IN HIS	372	04
CONSIDERED MY TROUBLE, AND HAST KNOWN MY SOUL IN	376	05
FOR I AM IN TROUBLE, *	376	08
THOU SHALT PRESERVE ME FROM TROUBLE	378	06
AND SHAME TOGETHER, THAT REJOICE AT MY TROUBLE	383	17
WHO IS ALSO THEIR STRENGTH IN THE TIME OF TROUBLE	387	14
INTO SO GREAT TROUBLE AND MISERY, *	388	02
LOOKING UPON MY TROUBLE, *	388	13
THE LORD SHALL DELIVER HIM IN THE TIME OF TROUBLE	391	31
ENEMIES THAT TROUBLE ME CAST ME IN THE TEETH	393	28
AND FORGETTEST OUR MISERY AND TROUBLE	396	09
A VERY PRESENT HELP IN TROUBLE	397	26
15 AND CALL UPON ME IN THE TIME OF TROUBLE	402	20
7 FOR HE HATH DELIVERED ME OUT OF ALL MY TROUBLE	406	16
MY DEFENCE AND REFUGE IN THE DAY OF MY TROUBLE	412	08
11 O BE THOU OUR HELP IN TROUBLE	413	02
AND LAIDEST TROUBLE UPON OUR LOINS	418	03
AND SPAKE WITH MY MOUTH, WHEN I WAS IN TROUBLE	418	09
FOR I AM IN TROUBLE	423	08
THE TIME OF MY TROUBLE I SOUGHT THE LORD	433	18
AND THEIR YEARS IN TROUBLE	437	05
OF HIS WRATH, ANGER, DISPLEASURE, AND TROUBLE	438	07
THE TIME OF MY TROUBLE I WILL CALL UPON THEE	447	17
SOUL IS FULL OF TROUBLE, *	448	32
9 MY SIGHT FAILETH FOR VERY TROUBLE	449	14
I AM WITH HIM IN TROUBLE	455	27
AND TROUBLE THINE HERITAGE	457	27
NOT THY FACE FROM ME IN THE TIME OF MY TROUBLE	464	12
LORD IN THEIR TROUBLE, *	476	15
LORD IN THEIR TROUBLE, *	476	30
LORD IN THEIR TROUBLE, *	477	11
THEIR SOUL MELTETH AWAY BECAUSE OF THE TROUBLE	477	30
LORD IN THEIR TROUBLE, *	477	33
THROUGH ANY PLAGUE OR TROUBLE	478	25
4 I FOUND TROUBLE AND HEAVINESS	486	25
5 I CALLED UPON THE LORD IN TROUBLE	488	08
50 THE SAME IS MY COMFORT IN MY TROUBLE	493	10
71 IT IS GOOD FOR ME THAT I HAVE BEEN IN TROUBLE	494	22
I SHOULD HAVE PERISHED IN MY TROUBLE	496	10
143 TROUBLE AND HEAVINESS HAVE TAKEN HOLD UPON ME	499	25
THERE ARE THAT TROUBLE ME, AND PERSECUTE ME	500	25
WHEN I WAS IN TROUBLE, I CALLED UPON THE LORD,	502	07
AND ALL HIS TROUBLE	508	05
23 WHO REMEMBERED US WHEN WE WERE IN TROUBLE	512	28
IN THE MIDST OF TROUBLE, YET SHALT THOU REFRESH ME	514	10
AND SHOWED HIM OF MY TROUBLE	518	06
RIGHTEOUSNESS' SAKE BRING MY SOUL OUT OF TROUBLE	519	16
BE MERCIFUL TO ALL WHO ARE IN ANY TROUBLE	591	02

TROUBLED

OF GOD IS A TROUBLED SPIRIT	061	13
HE WAS TROUBLED, AND ALL JERUSALEM WITH HIM	109	03
AND HE SAID UNTO THEM, WHY ARE YE TROUBLED	169	31
YOUR HEART BE TROUBLED, NEITHER LET IT BE AFRAID	181	35
NOT AFRAID OF THEIR TERROR, NEITHER BE TROUBLED	196	03
SHE WAS TROUBLED AT HIS SAYING, AND CAST IN HER	236	11
LET NOT YOUR HEART BE TROUBLED	239	30
HIS CONSCIENCE TROUBLED WITH ANY MATTER	R 313	25
LET NOT YOUR HEART BE TROUBLED	331	17
3 MY SOUL ALSO IS SORE TROUBLED	349	04
AND I WAS TROUBLED	375	07
OF GOD IS A TROUBLED SPIRIT	404	11
THE DEPTHS ALSO WERE TROUBLED	434	15
SUFFERED WITH A TROUBLED MIND	449	28
29 WHEN THOU HIDEST THY FACE, THEY ARE TROUBLED	469	18
FOR THOSE THAT TROUBLED THEM, THE WATERS OVERWHELMED	473	23
BUT I WAS SORE TROUBLED	487	08
67 BEFORE I WAS TROUBLED, I WENT WRONG	494	15

TROUBLED   CONTINUED

VERY FAITHFULNESS HAST CAUSED ME TO BE TROUBLED	495	06
107 I AM TROUBLED ABOVE MEASURE	497	11
THOUGH THEY BE TROUBLED ON EVERY SIDE, SUFFER THEM	599	13

TROUBLES

THEE IN ALL OUR TROUBLES AND ADVERSITIES, WHENSOEVER	058	18
THAT IN ALL OUR TROUBLES WE MAY PUT OUR WHOLE TRUST	059	24
O BRING THOU ME OUT OF MY TROUBLES	370	19
OUT OF ALL HIS TROUBLES	370	28
AND SAVETH HIM OUT OF ALL HIS TROUBLES	380	14
AND DELIVERETH THEM OUT OF ALL THEIR TROUBLES	381	03
GREAT ARE THE TROUBLES OF THE RIGHTEOUS	381	06
FOR INNUMERABLE TROUBLES ARE COME ABOUT ME	391	10
19 O WHAT GREAT TROUBLES AND ADVERSITIES HAST THOU	426	17
UPON ME IN TROUBLES, AND I DELIVERED THEE	442	25

TROUBLES'

COMFORTLESS TROUBLES' SAKE OF THE NEEDY, *	355	16

TROUBLING

AND TROUBLING ME	408	15

TRUE

NOW IS, WHEN THE TRUE WORSHIPPERS SHALL WORSHIP THE	003	30
HIM TO GRANT US TRUE REPENTANCE, AND HIS HOLY SPIRIT,	007	14
THINE ADORABLE, TRUE, AND ONLY SON	010	22
WHICH ARE THE FIGURES OF THE TRUE	022	23
HIM TO GRANT US TRUE REPENTANCE, AND HIS HOLY SPIRIT,	024	16
OF ALL YOUR SINS, TRUE REPENTANCE, AMENDMENT OF LIFE,	024	24
THE ADVANCEMENT OF TRUE RELIGION AND USEFUL LEARNING	047	36
MAY LIVE IN THE TRUE FAITH AND FEAR OF GOD, AND IN	048	03
AND DEACONS, WITH TRUE KNOWLEDGE AND UNDERSTANDING OF	055	31
THEE TO GIVE US TRUE REPENTANCE	057	14
EXAMINED BY EVERY TRUE MEMBER OF OUR CHURCH, AND	VI	36
MAINTENANCE OF THY TRUE RELIGION, AND VIRTUE	074	19
SET FORTH THY TRUE AND LIVELY WORD, AND RIGHTLY AND	074	23
REPENTANCE AND TRUE FAITH TURN UNTO HIM	076	04
THIS IS A TRUE SAYING, AND WORTHY OF ALL MEN TO BE	076	18
TO WHOSE MOST TRUE PROMISE, THE HOLY GHOST CAME	078	26
THE CLEAR LIGHT AND TRUE KNOWLEDGE OF THEE, AND OF	079	02
IS GREAT, IF WITH A TRUE PENITENT HEART AND LIVELY	085	31
TO SERVE HIM IN TRUE HOLINESS AND RIGHTEOUSNESS ALL	086	22
THAT WAS THE TRUE LIGHT, WHICH LIGHTETH EVERY MAN	097	30
AND WE KNOW THAT HIS TESTIMONY IS TRUE	102	14
GRANT US THE TRUE CIRCUMCISION OF THE SPIRIT	105	21
CONTINUALLY IN THY TRUE RELIGION	115	29
AND TRUE HOLINESS, TO THY HONOUR AND	125	30
AS DECEIVERS, AND YET TRUE	126	17
WHICH ARE THE FIGURES OF THE TRUE	147	31
US DRAW NEAR WITH A TRUE HEART IN FULL ASSURANCE OF	158	20
THAT HE SAITH TRUE, THAT YE MIGHT BELIEVE	161	06
THAT SAW IT BARE RECORD, AND HIS RECORD IS TRUE	161	06
BE FIXED, WHERE TRUE JOYS ARE TO BE FOUND	174	23
THE CONFESSION OF A TRUE FAITH, TO ACKNOWLEDGE THE	186	24
INCREASE IN US TRUE RELIGION, NOURISH US WITH ALL	198	22
PEOPLE DO UNTO THEE TRUE AND LAUDABLE SERVICE	207	13
RIGHTEOUSNESS AND TRUE HOLINESS	216	16
KNOW THAT THOU ART TRUE, AND TEACHEST THE WAY OF GOD	222	31
BY FAITHFUL AND TRUE PASTORS	234	03
I AM THE TRUE VINE, AND MY FATHER IS THE HUSBANDMAN	238	05
NOT THAT IT WAS TRUE WHICH WAS DONE BY THE ANGEL	245	19
INCREASE IN US TRUE RELIGION, NOURISH US WITH ALL	283	10
BE FIXED, WHERE TRUE JOYS ARE TO BE FOUND	285	30
TO BE TRUE AND JUST IN ALL MY DEALINGS	289	05
AND LOVE, AND TRUE REPENTANCE, WE MAY RECEIVE	294	31
OF KNOWLEDGE AND TRUE GODLINESS	297	21
IN WISDOM AND TRUE GODLINESS, THAT THEIR HOME MAY BE	303	25
OF ALL YOUR SINS, TRUE REPENTANCE, AMENDMENT OF LIFE,	323	20
ARE DEPARTED IN THE TRUE FAITH OF THY HOLY NAME, MAY	334	26
THEM THAT ARE TRUE OF HEART	350	14
AND MINISTER TRUE JUDGMENT UNTO THE PEOPLE	352	05
AT THEM WHICH ARE TRUE OF HEART	354	23
OF THE LORD ARE TRUE, AND RIGHTEOUS ALTOGETHER	364	02
ALL YE THAT ARE TRUE OF HEART	378	17
4 FOR THE WORD OF THE LORD IS TRUE	378	25
UNTO THEM THAT ARE TRUE OF HEART	384	18
ALL THEY THAT ARE TRUE OF HEART SHALL BE GLAD	416	07
WITH A FAITHFUL AND TRUE HEART, *	439	24
THEY MAY SHOW HOW TRUE THE LORD MY STRENGTH IS, *	456	30
ALL SUCH AS ARE TRUE IN HEART SHALL FOLLOW IT	458	17
ALL HIS COMMANDMENTS ARE TRUE	483	08
66 O TEACH ME TRUE UNDERSTANDING AND KNOWLEDGE	494	13
86 ALL THY COMMANDMENTS ARE TRUE	495	29
AND TRUE ARE THY JUDGMENTS	499	13
ARE EXCEEDING RIGHTEOUS AND TRUE	499	16
FOR ALL THY COMMANDMENTS ARE TRUE	500	13
160 THY WORD IS TRUE FROM EVERLASTING	500	31
THAT ARE GOOD AND TRUE OF HEART	504	32
TRUE PROMISE OF THE FATHER THOU, WHO DOST THE TONGUE	544	27
THIS IS A TRUE SAYING, IF A MAN DESIRE THE OFFICE OF	549	18
BY PRAYER FOR THE TRUE UNDERSTANDING OF THE SAME	554	30
TRUE PROMISE OF THE FATHER THOU, WHO DOST THE TONGUE	557	06
CHARITY, AND TRUE REPENTANCE	565	31
FOR THESE WORDS ARE TRUE AND FAITHFUL	567	23
INCREASE IN THEM TRUE RELIGION	572	29
SET FORTH THY TRUE AND LIVELY WORD	573	23
TO BE TRUE AND JUST IN ALL MY DEALINGS	580	07
AND MAINTAIN THY TRUE RELIGION AND VIRTUE	590	29
THINGS ARE TRUE AND PURE AND LOVELY AND OF GOOD	596	27
BUT ONE LIVING AND TRUE GOD, EVERLASTING, WITHOUT	603	03

TRUE　　　　　　CONTINUED

NECESSARILY OF A TRUE AND LIVELY FAITH　　605 14

TRUE-HEARTED

AND JOYFUL GLADNESS FOR SUCH AS ARE TRUE-HEARTED　461 20

TRULY

ALL THOSE WHO TRULY REPENT, AND UNFEIGNEDLY BELIEVE　007 12
THAT THEY MAY TRULY PLEASE THEE, POUR UPON THEM　018 22
ALL THOSE WHO TRULY REPENT, AND UNFEIGNEDLY BELIEVE　024 14
THAT THEY MAY TRULY PLEASE THEE, POUR UPON THEM　032 21
BE TRULY PREACHED, TRULY RECEIVED, AND TRULY　037 03
OF CHRIST MAY BE TRULY PREACHED, TRULY RECEIVED, AND　037 03
AND TRULY FOLLOWED, IN ALL PLACES, TO THE　037 04
TO THOSE WHO TRULY REPENT　041 12
OF THEM, MAY SERVE TRULY IN THEIR SEVERAL CALLINGS TO　047 17
AND TRULY REPENT US OF OUR FAULTS, AND SO MAKE HASTE　062 23
THE HARVEST TRULY IS PLENTEOUS, BUT THE　073 11
THAT THEY MAY TRULY AND IMPARTIALLY ADMINISTER　074 17
TRULY SERVING THEE IN HOLINESS AND RIGHTEOUSNESS ALL　074 28
YE WHO DO TRULY AND EARNESTLY REPENT YOU OF YOUR　075 08
SAITH UNTO ALL WHO TRULY TURN TO HIM　076 11
HIMSELF TO HAVE TRULY REPENTED AND AMENDED HIS FORMER R 085 05
REPENT YOU TRULY FOR YOUR SINS PAST　085 35
AND TRULY OUR FELLOWSHIP IS WITH THE FATHER, AND WITH　101 19
SAYING, TRULY THIS WAS THE SON OF GOD　137 33
THE SPIRIT TRULY IS READY, BUT THE FLESH IS WEAK　142 06
HE SAID, TRULY THIS MAN WAS THE SON OF GOD　147 04
AND TRULY THE SON OF MAN GOETH, AS IT WAS DETERMINED　149 14
AND MINISTRY, MAY TRULY AND GODLY SERVE THEE　157 02
FOR JOHN TRULY BAPTIZED WITH WATER　178 02
MANY OTHER SIGNS TRULY DID JESUS IN THE PRESENCE OF　229 09
ALMIGHTY GOD, WHOM TRULY TO KNOW IS EVERLASTING LIFE　238 29
THAT WE MAY TRULY REPENT ACCORDING TO HIS　242 11
BARTHOLOMEW GRACE TRULY TO BELIEVE AND TO PREACH THY　249 15
THE HARVEST TRULY IS GREAT, BUT THE LABOURERS　254 14
AND TO SERVE HIM TRULY ALL THE DAYS OF MY LIFE　288 22
LEARN AND LABOUR TRULY TO EARN MINE OWN LIVING, AND　289 09
THEY REPENT THEM TRULY OF THEIR FORMER SINS, WITH　293 27
HE REPENT HIM TRULY OF HIS SINS, AND BE IN CHARITY　R 313 19
SINS OF THOSE WHO TRULY REPENT, THAT THOU REMEMBEREST　313 32
YE WHO DO TRULY, ETC　R 322 32
THAT IF HE DO TRULY REPENT HIM OF HIS SINS,　R 323 29
TRULY MY HOPE IS EVEN IN THEE　324 28
17 AND I TRULY AM SET IN THE PLAGUE, *　388 26
TRULY MY HOPE IS EVEN IN THEE　389 23
MY SOUL TRULY WAITETH STILL UPON GOD　413 27
6 HE TRULY IS MY STRENGTH AND MY SALVATION　414 09
TRULY GOD IS LOVING UNTO ISRAEL　428 10
THINK THAT YOU ARE TRULY CALLED, ACCORDING TO THE　532 31
THE HARVEST TRULY IS PLENTEOUS, BUT THE LABOURERS ARE　538 17
THAT YOU ARE TRULY CALLED, ACCORDING TO THE WILL OF　541 30
THAT YOU ARE TRULY CALLED TO THIS MINISTRATION,　554 16
AND TO SERVE HIM TRULY ALL THE DAYS OF MY LIFE　579 32
LEARN AND LABOUR TRULY TO GET MINE OWN LIVING,　580 13
THEY REPENT THEM TRULY OF THEIR FORMER SINS,　582 23
WHO TRULY SUFFERED, WAS CRUCIFIED, DEAD, AND BURIED,　603 14
CHRIST DID TRULY RISE AGAIN FROM DEATH, AND TOOK　603 21
TO SUCH AS TRULY REPENT　606 04

TRUMP

AND WITH THE TRUMP OF GOD　269 07
IN THE TWINKLING OF AN EYE, AT THE LAST TRUMP　330 03
AND THE LORD WITH THE SOUND OF THE TRUMP　398 30

TRUMPET

GREAT SOUND OF A TRUMPET, AND THEY SHALL GATHER　118 21
BLOW THE TRUMPET IN ZION, SANCTIFY A FAST, CALL A　124 29
AS IT WERE OF A TRUMPET TALKING WITH ME　187 02
FOR THE TRUMPET SHALL SOUND, AND THE DEAD SHALL BE　330 03
3 BLOW UP THE TRUMPET IN THE NEW MOON, *　442 16
3 PRAISE HIM IN THE SOUND OF THE TRUMPET　525 26

TRUMPETERS

ALSO AND TRUMPETERS SHALL MAKE ANSWER　448 26

TRUMPETS

WITH TRUMPETS ALSO AND SHAWMS, *　027 17
7 WITH TRUMPETS ALSO AND SHAWMS, *　462 06

TRUST

BE UPON US, AS OUR TRUST IS IN THEE　011 10
SUFFER NOT OUR TRUST IN THEE TO FAIL　036 23
WHO PUT THEIR TRUST IN THEE　041 20
BY A HOLY TRUST IN THEE, AND OBEDIENCE TO THY LAWS　053 26
AS WE DO PUT OUR TRUST IN THEE　059 19
MAY PUT OUR WHOLE TRUST AND CONFIDENCE IN THY MERCY,　059 25
THAT PUT THEIR TRUST IN THEE　061 31
BUT WITH A FULL TRUST IN GOD'S MERCY, AND WITH A　088 02
IN HIM SHALL THE GENTILES TRUST　092 32
WE PUT NOT OUR TRUST IN ANY THING THAT WE DO　120 17
LET HIM TRUST IN THE NAME OF THE LORD, AND STAY UPON　144 25
WHO PUT THEIR TRUST IN THEE　188 32
OF ALL THAT TRUST IN THEE, WITHOUT WHOM NOTHING IS　194 04
SUCH TRUST HAVE WE THROUGH CHRIST TO GOD-WARD　206 13
TO PUT MY WHOLE TRUST IN HIM, TO CALL UPON HIM　288 20
AS WE DO PUT OUR TRUST IN THEE　290 11
WHO PUTTETH HER TRUST IN THEE　306 18

TRUST　　　　　CONTINUED

WHO PUTTETH HIS TRUST IN THEE　308 24
O PUT THY TRUST IN GOD　310 18
PUTTETH HIS FULL TRUST ONLY IN THY MERCY, IMPUTE NOT　314 09
WHO PUT THEIR TRUST IN HIM, TO WHOM ALL THINGS IN　314 16
AND PUT THOU THY TRUST IN THE LORD　326 31
IN HIS WORD IS MY TRUST　328 12
O ISRAEL, TRUST IN THE LORD, FOR WITH THE LORD THERE　328 15
THAT PUT THEIR TRUST IN HIM　346 23
AND PUT YOUR TRUST IN THE LORD　347 22
THAT PUT THEIR TRUST IN THEE REJOICE　348 25
IN THEE HAVE I PUT MY TRUST　349 22
WILL PUT THEIR TRUST IN THEE　352 08
IN THE LORD PUT I MY TRUST　354 19
5 BUT MY TRUST IS IN THY MERCY, *　356 07
HE PUTTETH HIS TRUST IN THE LORD　356 29
FOR IN THEE HAVE I PUT MY TRUST　357 22
WHICH PUT THEIR TRUST IN THEE, *　358 32
AND MY MIGHT, IN WHOM I WILL TRUST　359 27
THAT PUT THEIR TRUST IN HIM　361 30
7 SOME PUT THEIR TRUST IN CHARIOTS, AND SOME IN　364 29
KING PUTTETH HIS TRUST IN THE LORD　365 17
THEY PUT THEIR TRUST IN THEE, AND WERE NOT　366 13
I HAVE PUT MY TRUST IN THEE　369 19
FOR I HAVE PUT MY TRUST IN THEE　370 25
MY TRUST HATH BEEN ALSO IN THE LORD, THEREFORE SHALL　370 31
YET WILL I PUT MY TRUST IN HIM　371 31
AND PUT THOU THY TRUST IN THE LORD　372 31
O LORD, HAVE I PUT MY TRUST　375 22
AND MY TRUST HATH BEEN IN THE LORD　376 03
THAT PUT THEIR TRUST IN THEE, EVEN BEFORE THE SONS OF　377 04
YE THAT PUT YOUR TRUST IN THE LORD　377 19
WHOSO PUTTETH HIS TRUST IN THE LORD, MERCY EMBRACETH　378 14
THAT PUT THEIR TRUST IN HIS MERCY　379 25
AS WE DO PUT OUR TRUST IN THEE　379 33
THAT PUT THEIR TRUST IN HIM SHALL NOT BE DESTITUTE　381 13
SHALL PUT THEIR TRUST UNDER THE SHADOW OF THY WINGS　384 10
3 PUT THOU THY TRUST IN THE LORD, AND BE DOING GOOD　384 29
AND PUT THY TRUST IN HIM, *　385 02
THEY PUT THEIR TRUST IN HIM　387 17
O LORD, HAVE I PUT MY TRUST　388 21
SHALL PUT THEIR TRUST IN THE LORD　390 16
7 O PUT THY TRUST IN GOD　393 13
15 O PUT THY TRUST IN GOD　393 33
6 O PUT THY TRUST IN GOD　394 17
7 FOR I WILL NOT TRUST IN MY BOW, *　395 05
THAT PUT THEIR TRUST IN THEIR GOODS, *　400 16
MY TRUST IS IN THE TENDER MERCY OF GOD FOR EVER AND　405 05
MY TRUST SHALL BE IN THEE, O LORD　408 09
YET PUT I MY TRUST IN THEE　408 20
I HAVE PUT MY TRUST IN GOD, AND WILL NOT FEAR WHAT　408 22
IN GOD HAVE I PUT MY TRUST　409 04
AND MY TRUST SHALL BE UNDER THE COVERING OF THY　413 03
AND IN GOD IS MY TRUST　414 12
8 O PUT YOUR TRUST IN HIM ALWAY, YE PEOPLE　414 13
10 O TRUST NOT IN WRONG AND ROBBERY　414 18
AND PUT HIS TRUST IN HIM　416 07
LET NOT THEM THAT TRUST IN THEE, O LORD GOD OF HOSTS,　422 13
O LORD, HAVE I PUT MY TRUST　425 05
BUT MY SURE TRUST IS IN THEE　425 20
BY GOD, TO PUT MY TRUST IN THE LORD GOD, *　429 33
MIGHT PUT THEIR TRUST IN GOD　435 11
AND PUT NOT THEIR TRUST IN HIS HELP　436 15
THAT PUTTETH HIS TRUST IN THEE　446 06
THAT PUTTETH HIS TRUST IN THEE　447 08
MY GOD, IN HIM WILL I TRUST　454 31
SUCH AS PUT THEIR TRUST IN THEM　485 27
HOUSE OF ISRAEL, TRUST THOU IN THE LORD　485 28
OF AARON, PUT YOUR TRUST IN THE LORD　485 30
THE LORD, PUT YOUR TRUST IN THE LORD　485 32
8 IT IS BETTER TO TRUST IN THE LORD, *　488 14
9 IT IS BETTER TO TRUST IN THE LORD, *　488 16
FOR MY TRUST IS IN THY WORD　492 25
WHEREIN THOU HAST CAUSED ME TO PUT MY TRUST　493 09
I HAVE PUT MY TRUST IN THY WORD　495 03
AND MY TRUST IS IN THY WORD　497 26
FOR IN THY WORD IS MY TRUST　500 05
THAT PUT THEIR TRUST IN THE LORD SHALL BE EVEN AS THE　504 23
IN HIS WORD IS MY TRUST　507 17
7 O ISRAEL, TRUST IN THE LORD　507 20
4 O ISRAEL, TRUST IN THE LORD *　507 30
THAT PUT THEIR TRUST IN THEM　511 07
IN THEE IS MY TRUST　517 29
FOR IN THEE IS MY TRUST　519 08
CASTLE AND DELIVERER, MY DEFENDER IN WHOM I TRUST　519 25
2 O PUT NOT YOUR TRUST IN PRINCES, NOR IN ANY CHILD　522 06
AND PUT THEIR TRUST IN HIS MERCY　523 18
DO YOU TRUST THAT YOU ARE INWARDLY MOVED BY THE HOLY　532 26
I TRUST SO　532 30
WORK WHEREUNTO WE TRUST THE HOLY GHOST HATH CALLED　553 12
TO PUT MY WHOLE TRUST IN HIM, TO CALL UPON HIM　579 30
AND THIS I TRUST HE WILL DO OF HIS MERCY AND　581 05
HE YET MAY PUT HIS TRUST IN THEE　597 25

TRUSTED

O LORD, IN THEE HAVE I TRUSTED　011 12
WHEREIN HE TRUSTED, AND DIVIDETH HIS SPOILS　130 08
HE TRUSTED IN GOD　137 12
BUT WE TRUSTED THAT IT HAD BEEN HE WHICH SHOULD HAVE　167 20
CERTAIN WHICH TRUSTED IN THEMSELVES THAT THEY WERE　205 21
THEY TRUSTED IN THEE, AND THOU DIDST DELIVER THEM　366 10
8 HE TRUSTED IN THE LORD, THAT HE WOULD　366 18
MY HEART HATH TRUSTED IN HIM, AND I AM HELPED　373 23
FRIEND WHOM I TRUSTED, *　392 17

TRUSTED   CONTINUED

BUT TRUSTED UNTO THE MULTITUDE OF HIS RICHES, AND   405 02

TRUSTETH

IS THE MAN THAT TRUSTETH IN HIM   380 18
FOR MY SOUL TRUSTETH IN THEE   409 13

TRUSTING

THAT WE, SURELY TRUSTING IN THY DEFENCE, MAY NOT FEAR   017 09
TRUSTING WHOLLY IN THY MERCY, THEY MAY NOT   046 23
MERCIFUL LORD, TRUSTING IN OUR OWN RIGHTEOUSNESS, BUT   082 14

TRUTH

THY LIGHT AND THY TRUTH, THAT THEY MAY LEAD ME, AND   003 22
SHALL WORSHIP THE FATHER IN SPIRIT AND IN TRUTH   003 31
AND THE PEOPLES WITH HIS TRUTH   009 21
AND HIS TRUTH ENDURETH FROM GENERATION TO GENERATION   015 14
WITH THE LOVE OF TRUTH AND RIGHTEOUSNESS   018 12
INTO THE WAY OF TRUTH, AND HOLD THE FAITH IN UNITY OF   019 02
KNOWLEDGE OF THY TRUTH, AND IN THE WORLD TO COME LIFE   020 09
AND THE TRUTH IS NOT IN US   022 11
HIS MERCY AND TRUTH TOWARD THE HOUSE OF ISRAEL   027 10
AND OF THY TRUTH IN THE NIGHT SEASON   027 31
INTO THE WAY OF TRUTH, AND HOLD THE FAITH IN UNITY OF   032 33
KNOWLEDGE OF THY TRUTH, AND IN THE WORLD TO COME LIFE   034 09
AND HAPPINESS, TRUTH AND JUSTICE, RELIGION AND PIETY,   035 16
ARE GOOD AND GRACIOUS AND WHOSE LAW IS TRUTH   035 24
MAY DISCERN THE TRUTH, AND IMPARTIALLY ADMINISTER THE   036 04
FILL IT WITH ALL TRUTH, IN ALL PEACE   037 17
ONE HOLY BOND OF TRUTH AND PEACE, OF FAITH AND   037 33
OPENING HEATHEN LANDS TO THE LIGHT OF THY TRUTH   038 17
THEM WITH THE TRUTH OF THY DOCTRINE, AND ENDUE THEM   039 11
KNOWLEDGE OF THY TRUTH, THEY MAY WORSHIP THEE AND   043 04
US TO DO, IN TRUTH, IN BEAUTY, AND IN RIGHTEOUSNESS,   044 21
WAY OF JUSTICE AND TRUTH, AND ESTABLISH AMONG THEM   044 29
GRACE TO EXECUTE JUSTICE, AND TO MAINTAIN TRUTH   055 28
INTO THE WAY OF TRUTH ALL SUCH AS HAVE ERRED, AND ARE   056 19
AND TO MAINTAIN TRUTH   VI 20
THOU REQUIREST TRUTH IN THE INWARD PARTS, *   060 22
WITH THE SPIRIT OF TRUTH, UNITY, AND CONCORD   074 12
MAY AGREE IN THE TRUTH OF THY HOLY WORD, AND LIVE IN   074 14
AND TO LEAD THEM INTO ALL TRUTH   078 28
FOR THE TRUTH OF GOD, TO CONFIRM THE PROMISES MADE   092 24
BEGOTTEN OF THE FATHER,) FULL OF GRACE AND TRUTH   098 06
TESTIMONY OF THY TRUTH, WE MAY STEDFASTLY LOOK UP TO   099 27
THE LIGHT OF THY TRUTH, THAT IT MAY AT LENGTH ATTAIN   101 08
WE LIE, AND DO NOT THE TRUTH   101 25
AND THE TRUTH IS NOT IN US   101 29
NOT IN INIQUITY, BUT REJOICETH IN THE TRUTH   123 02
BY THE WORD OF TRUTH, BY THE POWER OF GOD, BY THE   126 14
AND SHE SAID, TRUTH, LORD   128 18
IS IN ALL GOODNESS AND RIGHTEOUSNESS AND TRUTH   129 15
THIS IS OF A TRUTH THAT PROPHET THAT SHOULD   132 12
AND IF I SAY THE TRUTH, WHY DO YE NOT BELIEVE ME   133 10
OF A TRUTH THIS FELLOW ALSO WAS WITH HIM   151 16
WITH THE UNLEAVENED BREAD OF SINCERITY AND TRUTH   163 03
WITH THE UNLEAVENED BREAD OF SINCERITY AND TRUTH   165 16
AND SAID, OF A TRUTH I PERCEIVE THAT GOD IS NO   166 12
ALWAYS SERVE THEE IN PURENESS OF LIVING AND TRUTH   170 23
BECAUSE THE SPIRIT IS TRUTH   171 02
THE LIGHT OF THY TRUTH, TO THE INTENT THAT THEY MAY   173 05
WITH THE WORD OF TRUTH, THAT WE SHOULD BE A KIND OF   174 29
NEVERTHELESS I TELL YOU THE TRUTH   175 10
THE SPIRIT OF TRUTH, IS COME, HE WILL GUIDE YOU   175 19
HE WILL GUIDE YOU INTO ALL TRUTH   175 19
EVEN THE SPIRIT OF TRUTH, WHICH PROCEEDETH FROM THE   179 25
EVEN THE SPIRIT OF TRUTH   181 11
AND LEAD US INTO ALL TRUTH   183 25
AND SAID, OF A TRUTH I PERCEIVE THAT GOD IS NO   183 29
BUT HE THAT DOETH TRUTH COMETH TO THE LIGHT, THAT HIS   185 10
BUT IN DEED AND IN TRUTH   191 22
THAT WE ARE OF THE TRUTH, AND SHALL ASSURE OUR HEARTS   191 23
BY HIM, AS THE TRUTH IS IN JESUS   216 11
SPEAK EVERY MAN TRUTH WITH HIS NEIGHBOUR   216 17
GIRT ABOUT WITH TRUTH, AND HAVING ON THE BREASTPLATE   219 14
THE WAY OF GOD IN TRUTH, NEITHER CAREST THOU FOR ANY   223 02
IN THE WORD OF THE TRUTH OF THE GOSPEL   223 27
AND KNEW THE GRACE OF GOD IN TRUTH   223 30
THIS IS OF A TRUTH THAT PROPHET THAT SHOULD   226 12
ESTABLISHED IN THE TRUTH OF THY HOLY GOSPEL   237 09
BUT SPEAKING THE TRUTH IN LOVE, MAY GROW UP INTO HIM   237 28
TO BE THE WAY, THE TRUTH, AND THE LIFE   238 31
I AM THE WAY, THE TRUTH, AND THE LIFE   240 06
SPEAK THE TRUTH, BOLDLY REBUKE VICE, AND PATIENTLY   242 12
OF THE TRUTH COMMENDING OURSELVES TO EVERY MAN'S   250 31
EVEN THE SPIRIT OF TRUTH, WHICH PROCEEDETH FROM THE   255 31
WITH THE WORD OF TRUTH, THAT WE SHOULD BE A KIND OF   265 22
THY LIGHT AND THY TRUTH, THAT THEY MAY LEAD ME, AND   310 11
BECAUSE OF THY LOVING-KINDNESS AND TRUTH   311 31
I AM THE WAY, THE TRUTH, AND THE LIFE   331 26
AND SPEAKETH THE TRUTH FROM HIS HEART   357 08
ME FORTH IN THY TRUTH, AND LEARN ME   369 25
LORD ARE MERCY AND TRUTH. *   370 01
AND I WILL WALK IN THY TRUTH   371 03
OR SHALL IT DECLARE THY TRUTH   375 13
O LORD, THOU GOD OF TRUTH   375 32
HATH BEEN OF THY TRUTH, AND OF THY SALVATION   391 05
LOVING MERCY AND TRUTH *   391 06
AND THY TRUTH ALWAY PRESERVE ME   391 09
THY LIGHT AND THY TRUTH, THAT THEY MAY LEAD ME, *   394 09
OF THE WORD OF TRUTH, OF MEEKNESS, AND RIGHTEOUSNESS   396 23
THOU REQUIREST TRUTH IN THE INWARD PARTS, *   403 20

TRUTH   CONTINUED

DESTROY THOU THEM IN THY TRUTH   406 13
4 GOD SHALL SEND FORTH HIS MERCY AND TRUTH   409 19
AND THY TRUTH UNTO THE CLOUDS   410 03
THAT THEY MAY TRIUMPH BECAUSE OF THE TRUTH   412 20
EVEN IN THE TRUTH OF THY SALVATION   422 31
10 MERCY AND TRUTH ARE MET TOGETHER   446 27
11 TRUTH SHALL FLOURISH OUT OF THE EARTH, *   446 29
AND I WILL WALK IN THY TRUTH   447 26
PLENTEOUS IN GOODNESS AND TRUTH   448 05
BE SHOWING THY TRUTH FROM ONE GENERATION TO ANOTHER   450 06
THY TRUTH SHALT THOU STABLISH IN THE HEAVENS   450 08
AND THY TRUTH IN THE CONGREGATION OF THE SAINTS   450 14
THY TRUTH, MOST MIGHTY LORD, IS ON EVERY SIDE   450 23
MERCY AND TRUTH SHALL GO BEFORE THY FACE   451 03
25 MY TRUTH ALSO AND MY MERCY SHALL BE WITH HIM   451 23
NOR SUFFER MY TRUTH TO FAIL   452 08
WHICH THOU SWAREST UNTO DAVID IN THY TRUTH   453 06
FAITHFULNESS AND TRUTH SHALL BE THY SHIELD AND   455 03
AND OF THY TRUTH IN THE NIGHT SEASON   456 03
JUDGE THE WORLD, AND THE PEOPLES WITH HIS TRUTH   460 28
HIS MERCY AND TRUTH TOWARD THE HOUSE OF ISRAEL   461 31
AND HIS TRUTH ENDURETH FROM GENERATION TO GENERATION   463 15
AND THY TRUTH REACHETH UNTO THE CLOUDS   479 12
AND ARE DONE IN TRUTH AND EQUITY   483 10
AND THE TRUTH OF THE LORD ENDURETH FOR EVER   487 28
CHOSEN THE WAY OF TRUTH, *   491 27
THE WORD OF THY TRUTH UTTERLY OUT OF MY MOUTH   492 26
90 THY TRUTH ALSO REMAINETH FROM ONE GENERATION TO   496 04
AND THY LAW IS THE TRUTH   499 24
BECAUSE OF THY LOVING-KINDNESS AND TRUTH   513 31
UNTO ME FOR THY TRUTH AND RIGHTEOUSNESS' SAKE   518 24
THEM WITH THE TRUTH OF THY DOCTRINE, AND ADORN THEM   531 19
THEM WITH THE TRUTH OF THY DOCTRINE, AND ADORN THEM   537 24
THEM WITH THE TRUTH OF THY DOCTRINE, AND ADORN THEM   548 03
HIM WITH THE TRUTH OF THY DOCTRINE, AND ADORN HIM   553 30
WITH LOVE OF THEE AND OF THY TRUTH   560 19
IN THY FAVOUR AND BE GUIDED IN THE WAY OF TRUTH   562 13
IN SPIRIT AND IN TRUTH, AND MAY IN THEIR LIVES SHOW   567 08
BE WORSHIPPED IN TRUTH AND PURITY THROUGH ALL   568 11
BUT GRACE AND TRUTH CAME BY JESUS CHRIST   572 02
HIM WITH THE TRUTH OF THY DOCTRINE, AND ENDUE HIM   572 11
GRAFT IN THEIR HEARTS A LOVE OF THE TRUTH   572 28
IN THE WAYS OF TRUTH AND PEACE, AND AT LAST BE   574 18
WE MAY WORSHIP THEE IN SPIRIT AND IN TRUTH   594 09
CHRIST IN THE TRUTH OF OUR NATURE WAS MADE LIKE UNTO   605 31
AND THE TRUTH IS NOT IN US   605 37
IN JUSTICE, JUDGMENT, AND TRUTH   611 10

TRUTH'S

SUFFER FOR THE TRUTH'S SAKE   242 13
AND FOR THY TRUTH'S SAKE   485 13

TRUTHS

AND WHAT THE TRUTHS OF THE GOSPEL ARE   VI 39

TRY

DILIGENTLY TO TRY AND EXAMINE THEMSELVES, BEFORE THEY   085 28
A FARM, OR WOULD TRY THEIR YOKES OF OXEN, OR BECAUSE   089 04
AND HIS EYELIDS TRY THE CHILDREN OF MEN   354 28
TRY OUT MY REINS AND MY HEART   370 33
23 TRY ME, O GOD, AND SEEK THE GROUND OF MY HEART   516 04

TRYING

THAT THE TRYING OF YOUR FAITH WORKETH PATIENCE   239 09

TUMULT

BUT THAT RATHER A TUMULT WAS MADE, HE TOOK WATER, AND   136 09

TUMULTS

THE SEDITIOUS TUMULTS WHICH HAVE BEEN LATELY RAISED   052 21
IN TUMULTS, IN LABOURS, IN WATCHINGS, IN FASTINGS   126 11

TURN

YOUR GARMENTS, AND TURN UNTO THE LORD YOUR GOD   004 20
RATHER THAT HE MAY TURN FROM HIS WICKEDNESS AND LIVE,   007 08
RATHER THAT HE MAY TURN FROM HIS WICKEDNESS AND LIVE,   024 10
AND TO TURN THEIR HEARTS   057 08
GLORY OF THY NAME, TURN FROM US ALL THOSE EVILS THAT   059 23
TURN THY FACE FROM MY SINS, *   060 28
THAT HE SHOULD TURN FROM HIS SIN, AND BE SAVED   062 15
BUT SO TURN THINE ANGER FROM US, WHO MEEKLY   062 22
TURN THOU US, O GOOD LORD, AND SO SHALL WE BE TURNED   062 28
TO THY PEOPLE, WHO TURN TO THEE IN WEEPING, FASTING,   062 30
AND TRUE FAITH TURN UNTO HIM   076 04
UNTO ALL WHO TRULY TURN TO HIM   076 11
SHALL THE PRIEST TURN TO THE HOLY TABLE, AND SAY,   R 076 30
TURN YE EVEN TO ME, SAITH THE LORD, WITH ALL YOUR   124 21
YOUR GARMENTS, AND TURN UNTO THE LORD YOUR GOD   124 24
AND THAT TURN ASIDE THE STRANGER FROM HIS RIGHT, AND   232 19
IF NOT, IT SHALL TURN TO YOU AGAIN   254 21
LO, WE TURN TO THE GENTILES   261 03
AID OF THEM THAT TURN TO THEE FOR SUCCOUR   315 14
4 TURN THEE, O LORD, AND DELIVER MY SOUL   349 06
IF A MAN WILL NOT TURN, HE WILL WHET HIS SWORD   350 17
NEITHER WILL I TURN AGAIN TILL I HAVE DESTROYED THEM   362 12
ENEMIES ALSO TO TURN THEIR BACKS UPON ME, *   362 18
15 TURN THEE UNTO ME, AND HAVE MERCY UPON ME   370 16

TURN   CONTINUED

7 THOU DIDST TURN THY FACE FROM ME, *   375 07
AND MY PRAYER SHALL TURN INTO MINE OWN BOSOM   382 19
THOU MAKEST US TO TURN OUR BACKS UPON OUR ENEMIES,   395 13
9 TURN THY FACE FROM MY SINS, *   403 27
FOR THEY WILL NOT TURN, NOR FEAR GOD   407 31
O TURN THEE UNTO US AGAIN   412 13
TURN THEE UNTO ME ACCORDING TO THE MULTITUDE CF THY   423 05
AND YET DIDST THOU TURN AND REFRESH ME   426 18
OF MAN SHALL TURN TO THY PRAISE   433 08
3 TURN US AGAIN, O GOD   441 08
7 TURN US AGAIN, THOU GOD CF HCSTS   441 16
14 TURN THEE AGAIN, THOU GOD OF HOSTS, LCOK DOWN FROM   441 30
19 TURN US AGAIN, O LORD GOD OF HOSTS   442 09
4 TURN US THEN, O GOD OUR SAVIOUR, *   446 14
6 WILT THOU NOT TURN AGAIN, AND QUICKEN US, *   446 18
THAT THEY TURN NOT AGAIN UNTO FOOLISHNESS   446 24
16 O TURN THEE THEN UNTO ME, AND HAVE MERCY UPON ME   448 06
13 TURN THEE AGAIN, O LORD, AT THE LAST, *   454 15
UNTIL RIGHTEOUSNESS TURN AGAIN UNTO JUDGMENT   458 16
NEITHER TURN AGAIN TO COVER THE EARTH   468 12
TO TURN AWAY HIS WRATHFUL INDIGNATION, LEST HE SHOULD   474 15
7 TURN AGAIN THEN UNTO THY REST, O MY SOUL   487 02
22 O TURN FROM ME SHAME AND REBUKE   491 10
37 O TURN AWAY MINE EYES, LEST THEY BEHOLD VANITY   492 13
5 AS FOR SUCH AS TURN BACK UNTO THEIR OWN WICKEDNESS,   505 02
5 TURN OUR CAPTIVITY, O LORD, *   505 15
TURN NOT AWAY THE FACE OF THINE ANOINTED   508 23
HE SHALL TURN AGAIN TO HIS EARTH, *   522 09
TURN THE HEART OF THE FATHERS TO THE CHILDREN, ANC   598 26
THAT HE CANNOT TURN AND PREPARE HIMSELF, BY HIS OWN   604 42

TURNED

WE HAVE TURNED EVERY ONE TO HIS OWN WAY   022 15
BE MERCIFULLY TURNED INTO PLENTY   041 05
THY CHURCH, AND TURNED OUR DEARTH AND SCARCITY INTO   051 32
AND SO SHALL WE BE TURNED   062 28
IN A DREAM, HE TURNED ASIDE INTO THE PARTS CF   107 20
HIM NOT, THEY TURNED BACK AGAIN TO JERUSALEM,   110 26
THEREFORE HE WAS TURNED TO BE THEIR ENEMY, AND HE   139 06
NEITHER TURNED AWAY BACK   144 13
AND THE LORD TURNED, AND LOOKED UPON PETER   151 20
SORROW SHALL BE TURNED INTO JOY   174 09
HE WAS HEALED, TURNED BACK, AND WITH A LOUD VOICE   210 08
BUT JESUS TURNED HIM ABOUT, AND WHEN HE SAW HER, HE   224 20
SICKNESS MAY BE TURNED INTO HEALTH, AND OUR SORROW   312 15
FOR HAVING TURNED OUR HEAVINESS INTO JOY AND OUR   315 21
THEY SHALL BE TURNED BACK, AND PUT TO SHAME SUDDENLY   349 19
WICKED SHALL BE TURNED TO DESTRUCTION, *   352 26
AND BE TURNED UNTO THE LORD   367 29
12 THOU HAST TURNED MY HEAVINESS INTO JOY   375 16
LET THEM BE TURNED BACK, AND BROUGHT TO CONFUSICN,   381 25
AND TURNED NOT UNTO THE PROUD, AND TO SUCH AS GO   390 19
OUR HEART IS NOT TURNED BACK, *   395 30
5 HE TURNED THE SEA INTO DRY LAND, *   417 24
NOR TURNED HIS MERCY FROM ME   418 21
AND THAT WAS TURNED TO MY REPROOF   422 24
LET THEM BE TURNED BACKWARD AND PUT TO CONFUSION THAT   424 23
CARRYING BOWS, TURNED THEMSELVES BACK IN THE DAY OF   435 18
AND TURNED THEM EARLY, AND INQUIRED AFTER GOD   437 06
MANY A TIME TURNED HE HIS WRATH AWAY, *   437 16
42 THEY TURNED BACK, AND TEMPTED GOD, *   437 23
45 HE TURNED THEIR WATERS INTO BLOOD, *   437 29
58 THEY TURNED THEIR BACKS, AND FELL AWAY LIKE THEIR   438 26
AND TURNED MY HAND AGAINST THEIR ADVERSARIES   443 09
THOU HAST TURNED AWAY THE CAPTIVITY OF JACOB   446 09
AND TURNED THYSELF FRCM THY WRATHFUL INDIGNATION   446 12
THEY DIE, AND ARE TURNED AGAIN TO THEIR DUST   469 20
25 WHOSE HEART TURNED SO, THAT THEY HATED HIS PEOPLE,   471 22
29 HE TURNED THEIR WATERS INTO BLOOD, *   471 30
20 THUS THEY TURNED THEIR GLORY *   474 08
LET HIS PRAYER BE TURNED INTO SIN   480 16
8 WHO TURNED THE HARD ROCK INTO A STANDING WATER,   485 08
AND TURNED MY FEET UNTO THY TESTIMONIES   493 30
BE TURNED UNTO ME   495 15
WHEN THE LORD TURNED AGAIN THE CAPTIVITY OF SION,   505 07
BE CONFOUNDED AND TURNED BACKWARD, *   506 29
SHALL MY NIGHT BE TURNED TO DAY   515 09

TURNEST

THOU TURNEST MAN TO DESTRUCTION   325 18
3 THOU TURNEST MAN TO DESTRUCTION   453 23
AND TURNEST THE SHADOW OF DEATH INTO THE   594 12
IN HEART, AND TURNEST THE SADNESS OF THE SORROWFUL TO   599 04

TURNETH

WHEN THE LORD TURNETH THE CAPTIVITY OF HIS PEOPLE,   356 31
17 WHEN HE TURNETH HIM UNTO THE PRAYER OF THE PCCR   465 13
33 HE TURNETH THE FLOODS INTO A WILDERNESS, *   478 12
THE UNGODLY, HE TURNETH IT UPSIDE DOWN   522 22

TURNING

THE PRIEST, TURNING TO THE PEOPLE, REHEARSE   R 067 22
STAND UP, AND TURNING TO THE PEOPLE, SAY,   R 075 32
THY WAY, BY TURNING THE HEARTS OF THE DISOBEDIENT TO   093 28
THEN PETER, TURNING ABOUT, SEETH THE DISCIPLE WHOM   102 03
BUT JESUS TURNING UNTO THEM SAID, DAUGHTERS OF   154 13
NEITHER SHADOW OF TURNING   174 28
IS NO VARIABLENESS, NEITHER SHADOW OF TURNING   265 21
THE MINISTER, TURNING TO THE PEOPLE, SHALL ASK THE   R 284 25
THE MINISTER, TURNING TO THE PEOPLE, SHALL SAY,   R 285 11

TURNING   CONTINUED

THE MINISTER, TURNING TO THEM, SHALL ASK THE   R 287 31
STANDING UP, AND TURNING TO THE CONGREGATION, HE   R 564 09
STAND UP, AND TURNING HIS FACE TOWARDS THE   R 565 16

TURTLE-DOVE

SOUL OF THY TURTLE-DOVE UNTO THE MULTITUDE OF THE   431 15

TURTLE-DOVES

A PAIR OF TURTLE-DOVES, OR TWO YOUNG PIGEONS   232 29

TUSH

SAID IN HIS HEART, TUSH, I SHALL NEVER BE CAST DCWN,   353 16
SAID IN HIS HEART, TUSH, GOD HATH FORGOTTEN   353 30
SAY IN HIS HEART, TUSH, THOU GOD CAREST NOT FOR IT   354 02
11 TUSH, SAY THEY, HOW SHOULD GOD PERCEIVE IT   428 30
7 AND YET THEY SAY, TUSH, THE LORD SHALL NCT SEE,   457 31

TUTORS

BUT IS UNDER TUTORS AND GOVERNORS UNTIL THE TIME   104 16

TWAIN

WHETHER OF THE TWAIN WILL YE THAT I RELEASE UNTO YOU   136 03
TEMPLE WAS RENT IN TWAIN FROM THE TOP TO THE BOTTOM   137 26
TEMPLE WAS RENT IN TWAIN FROM THE TOP TO THE BOTTCM   147 02
AND THEY TWAIN SHALL BE ONE FLESH   268 09
THEY ARE NO MORE TWAIN, BUT ONE FLESH   268 10

TWELVE

AND WHEN HE WAS TWELVE YEARS OLD, THEY WENT UP TC   110 19
TOOK UNTO HIM THE TWELVE, AND SAID UNTO THEM, BEHOLD, 123 17
AND FILLED TWELVE BASKETS WITH THE FRAGMENTS OF THE   132 09
ONE OF THE TWELVE, WENT UNTO THE CHIEF PRIESTS, TO   140 18
AND IN THE EVENING HE COMETH WITH THE TWELVE   140 35
IT IS ONE OF THE TWELVE, THAT DIPPETH WITH ME IN THE   141 05
ONE OF THE TWELVE, AND WITH HIM A GREAT   142 15
BEING OF THE NUMBER OF THE TWELVE   148 16
SAT DOWN, AND THE TWELVE APOSTLES WITH HIM   148 34
JUDGING THE TWELVE TRIBES OF ISRAEL   149 30
ONE OF THE TWELVE, WENT BEFORE THEM, AND DREW   150 28
THAT HE WAS SEEN OF CEPHAS, THEN OF THE TWELVE   205 07
AN ISSUE OF BLOOD TWELVE YEARS, CAME BEHIND HIM,   224 18
AND FILLED TWELVE BASKETS WITH THE FRAGMENTS OF THE   226 08
ONE OF THE TWELVE, CALLED DIDYMUS, WAS NOT WITH THEM   228 25
JUDGING THE TWELVE TRIBES OF ISRAEL   231 17
SHALL SIT UPON TWELVE THRONES, JUDGING THE TWELVE   231 17
THE NUMBER OF THE TWELVE APOSTLES   233 33
TO THE TWELVE TRIBES WHICH ARE SCATTERED   239 07
JUDGING THE TWELVE TRIBES OF ISRAEL   250 15
THEN THE TWELVE CALLED THE MULTITUDE OF THE DISCIPLES 532 08
SENT FORTH HIS TWELVE APOSTLES   553 06
MATTHIAS TO BE OF THE NUMBER OF THE TWELVE   553 08

TWENTIETH

SPAKE IN THE TWENTIETH CHAPTER OF EXODUS, SAYING, I   578 22

TWENTY

WERE FOUR AND TWENTY SEATS   187 09
I SAW FOUR AND TWENTY ELDERS SITTING, CLOTHED IN   187 10
THE FOUR AND TWENTY ELDERS FALL DOWN BEFORE HIM THAT   187 26
ONE DAY THREE AND TWENTY THOUSAND   201 18
AN HUNDRED AND TWENTY,) MEN AND BRETHREN, THIS   234 08
OF GOD ARE TWENTY THOUSAND, EVEN THOUSANDS OF ANGELS   420 16

TWENTY-EIGHTH

IN THE TWENTY-EIGHTH CHAPTER, AT THE EIGHTEENTH   275 24

TWENTY-FIFTH

USED ON THE TWENTY-FIFTH SUNDAY   R 224 32
SUNDAY AFTER THE EPIPHANY ON THE TWENTY-FIFTH   R 224 35

TWENTY-FIRST

THE TWENTY-FIRST OF THE FORMER ARTICLES IS OMITTED   R 607 11

TWENTY-FIVE

FEWER THAN TWENTY-FIVE SUNDAYS, THE CVERPLUS SHALL BE R 224 36

TWENTY-SEVEN

IF THERE BE TWENTY-SEVEN, THE SERVICE FOR THE SIXTH   R 224 33

TWENTY-SIX

YEAR THERE BE TWENTY-SIX SUNDAYS AFTER TRINITY,   R 224 31

TWENTY-SIXTH

USED ON THE TWENTY-SIXTH, AND THE SERVICE FOR THE   R 224 34

TWICE

HOLY COMMUNION BE TWICE CELEBRATED CN CHRISTMAS CAY, R 098 07
THE COCK CROW TWICE, THOU SHALT DENY ME THRICE   141 24

TWICE   CONTINUED

THE COCK CROW TWICE, THOU SHALT DENY ME THRICE   144 02
HOLY COMMUNION BE TWICE CELEBRATED ON EASTER DAY, THE R 164 30
HOLY COMMUNION BE TWICE CELEBRATED ON WHITSUNDAY,   R 182 11
I FAST TWICE IN THE WEEK, I GIVE TITHES OF ALL THAT I   205 27
SPAKE ONCE, AND TWICE I HAVE ALSO HEARD THE SAME, *   414 21

TWINKLING

IN THE TWINKLING OF AN EYE, AT THE LAST   330 03
BUT THE TWINKLING OF AN EYE, AND IN HIS PLEASURE IS   374 32

TWO

PROMISE THAT WHEN TWO OR THREE ARE GATHERED TOGETHER   020 05
PROMISE THAT WHEN TWO OR THREE ARE GATHERED TOGETHER   034 05
ON THESE TWO COMMANDMENTS HANG ALL THE LAW AND THE   069 31
THEN SENT JESUS TWO DISCIPLES, SAYING UNTO THEM,   091 13
OF CHRIST, HE SENT TWO OF HIS DISCIPLES, AND SAID   094 17
COASTS THEREOF, FROM TWO YEARS OLD AND UNDER,   103 27
THE JEWS, CONTAINING TWO OR THREE FIRKINS APIECE   113 20
THAT ABRAHAM HAD TWO SONS, THE ONE BY A BONDMAID, THE   130 03
FOR THESE ARE THE TWO COVENANTS   131 03
PHILIP ANSWERED HIM, TWO HUNDRED PENNYWORTH OF BREAD   131 30
BARLEY LOAVES, AND TWO SMALL FISHES   131 34
THEN WERE THERE TWO THIEVES CRUCIFIED WITH HIM, ONE   137 03
AFTER TWO DAYS WAS THE FEAST OF THE PASSOVER,   139 32
AND HE SENDETH FORTH TWO OF HIS DISCIPLES, AND SAITH   140 25
HIM THEY CRUCIFY TWO THIEVES   146 15
BEHOLD, HERE ARE TWO SWORDS   150 12
AND THERE WERE ALSO TWO OTHER, MALEFACTORS, LED WITH   154 21
CRUCIFIED HIM, AND TWO OTHER WITH HIM, ON EITHER SIDE   159 34
BEHOLD, TWO OF HIS DISCIPLES WENT THAT SAME DAY TO A   167 03
HE WENT UP, BEHOLD, TWO MEN STOOD BY THEM IN WHITE   178 15
AND SAW TWO SHIPS STANDING BY THE LAKE   196 08
A CERTAIN MAN HAD TWO SONS   201 31
TWO MEN WENT UP INTO THE TEMPLE TO PRAY   205 23
HE TOOK OUT TWO PENCE, AND GAVE THEM TO THE HOST, AND   208 33
NO MAN CAN SERVE TWO MASTERS   211 09
ON THESE TWO COMMANDMENTS HANG ALL THE LAW AND THE   215 14
PHILIP ANSWERED HIM, TWO HUNDRED PENNYWORTH OF BREAD   225 26
BARLEY LOAVES, AND TWO SMALL FISHES   225 30
SEA OF GALILEE, SAW TWO BRETHREN, SIMON CALLED PETER,   227 24
HE SAW OTHER TWO BRETHREN, JAMES THE SON OF   227 29
OF TURTLE-DOVES, OR TWO YOUNG PIGEONS   232 29
AND THEY APPOINTED TWO, JOSEPH CALLED BARSABAS, WHO   234 25
WHETHER OF THESE TWO THOU HAST CHOSEN, THAT HE MAY   234 28
WAS SLEEPING BETWEEN TWO SOLDIERS, BOUND WITH TWO   245 10
BOUND WITH TWO CHAINS   245 11
GRANT THAT THESE MY TWO SONS MAY SIT, THE ONE ON THY   247 09
AGAINST THE TWO BRETHREN   247 20
TALKED WITH HIM TWO MEN, WHICH WERE MOSES AND ELIAS   248 27
HIS GLORY, AND THE TWO MEN THAT STOOD WITH HIM   248 32
HAVING TWO HANDS OR TWO FEET TO BE CAST INTO   253 06
RATHER THAN HAVING TWO HANDS OR TWO FEET TO BE CAST   253 06
RATHER THAN HAVING TWO EYES TO BE CAST INTO   253 09
SENT THEM TWO AND TWO BEFORE HIS FACE INTO EVERY CITY   254 12
AND SENT THEM TWO AND TWO BEFORE HIS FACE INTO   254 12
HIS WIFE, AND THEY TWO SHALL BE ONE FLESH   267 30
THEY CAN BE HAD, TWO GODFATHERS AND ONE GODMOTHER   R 273 09
ONE GODFATHER AND TWO GODMOTHERS   R 273 11
AT THE FONT AT LEAST TWO WITNESSES   R 273 23
SUMMED UP IN THESE TWO COMMANDMENTS   288 05
I LEARN TWO THINGS FROM THESE COMMANDMENTS   288 12
CHRIST HATH ORDAINED TWO SACRAMENTS ONLY, AS   292 06
THERE ARE TWO PARTS IN A SACRAMENT   292 15
HOLY ESTATE THESE TWO PERSONS PRESENT COME NOW TO BE   300 19
WHY THESE TWO PERSONS SHOULD NOT BE JOINED TOGETHER   R 304 23
THE RED SEA IN TWO PARTS   512 08
BE PRESENTED BY TWO BISHOPS OF THIS CHURCH UNTO THE   R 552 18
WHEREVER TWO OR THREE OF THY FAITHFUL   564 31
NECESSARY ABSENCE, TWO MEMBERS OF THE VESTRY)   R 570 07
I LEARN TWO THINGS   579 24
TWO ONLY, AS GENERALLY NECESSARY TO   581 09
TWO   581 17
SO THAT TWO WHOLE AND PERFECT NATURES, THAT IS TO   603 12
THERE ARE TWO SACRAMENTS ORDAINED OF CHRIST OUR LORD   607 36

TWO-EDGED

AND A TWO-EDGED SWORD IN THEIR HANDS   525 14

TYCHICUS

AND TYCHICUS HAVE I SENT TO EPHESUS   254 04

TYRANNOUS

THEY BEAR A TYRANNOUS HATE AGAINST ME   370 23

TYRANNY

UNTIL THIS TYRANNY BE OVERPAST   409 14

TYRANT

THOU TYRANT, *   404 19

TYRANTS

AND TYRANTS, WHICH HAVE NOT GOD BEFORE THEIR EYES,   406 07
THROUGH TYRANTS, *   478 27

TYRE

INTO THE COASTS OF TYRE AND SIDON   128 08
FROM THE COASTS OF TYRE AND SIDON, CAME UNTO THE SEA   206 27
AND THE DAUGHTER OF TYRE SHALL BE THERE WITH A GIFT   397 09
THE PHILISTINES, WITH THEM THAT DWELL AT TYRE   444 19
AND TYRE, WITH ETHIOPIA   448 20

ULTIMATE

ARE TO BE THE ULTIMATE ARBITER AND JUDGE   569 37

UNADVISEDLY

ENTERED INTO UNADVISEDLY OR LIGHTLY   300 17
HE SPAKE UNADVISEDLY WITH HIS LIPS   475 03

UNAWARES

COME UPON HIM UNAWARES, AND HIS NET THAT HE HATH LAID   382 04
AGAINST ME UNAWARES, MAKING MOUTHS AT ME, AND CEASED   382 25

UNBORN

AND THE CHILDREN WHICH WERE YET UNBORN   435 08

UNCERTAIN

HOW FRAIL AND UNCERTAIN OUR LIFE IS, WE MAY APPLY OUR   045 08
AND EVER UNCERTAIN WHAT TIME THEY SHALL DEPART OUT CF R 321 03

UNCERTAINLY

I THEREFORE SO RUN, NOT AS UNCERTAINLY   119 09

UNCERTAINTIES

DOUBTS AND UNCERTAINTIES, THE GRACE TO ASK WHAT THOU   595 28

UNCERTAINTY

AND UNCERTAINTY OF HUMAN LIFE   316 27

UNCHARITABLENESS

AND ALL UNCHARITABLENESS, FROM ALL INORDINATE AND   054 24

UNCIRCUMCISION

NOR UNCIRCUMCISION, BUT A NEW CREATURE   211 02

UNCLEAN

NOR UNCLEAN PERSON, NOR COVETOUS MAN,   129 07
WHEN THE UNCLEAN SPIRIT IS GONE OUT OF A MAN, HE   130 10
SPRINKLING THE UNCLEAN, SANCTIFIETH TO THE PURIFYING   132 29
WERE VEXED WITH UNCLEAN SPIRITS   249 31
THAT NO UNCLEAN THOUGHTS, UNLAWFUL DESIGNS, OR   590 13
OF MOST UNCLEAN LIVING, NO LESS PERILOUS THAN   606 26

UNCLEANNESS

US UNTO UNCLEANNESS, BUT UNTO HOLINESS   128 03
AND ALL UNCLEANNESS, OR COVETOUSNESS, LET IT NOT BE   129 02
SERVANTS TO UNCLEANNESS AND TO INIQUITY UNTO   198 28
UNCLEANNESS, LASCIVIOUSNESS, IDOLATRY,   209 20
TO WORK ALL UNCLEANNESS WITH GREEDINESS   216 09

UNCORRUPT

LEADETH AN UNCORRUPT LIFE, *   357 07
24 I WAS ALSO UNCORRUPT BEFORE HIM, *   361 13

UNCTION

THY BLESSED UNCTION FROM ABOVE, IS COMFORT, LIFE, AND   544 02
THY BLESSED UNCTION FROM ABOVE, IS COMFORT, LIFE, AND   556 10
AND EXTREME UNCTION, ARE NOT TO BE COUNTED FOR   607 39

UNDEFILED

RELIGION AND UNDEFILED BEFORE GOD AND THE FATHER IS   176 15
RELIGION AND UNDEFILED BEFORE GOD AND THE FATHER IS   266 07
OF GOD IS AN UNDEFILED WAY   361 28
THE LORD IS AN UNDEFILED LAW, CONVERTING THE SOUL   363 27
SO SHALL I BE UNDEFILED, AND INNOCENT FROM THE GREAT   364 11
THOSE THAT ARE UNDEFILED IN THE WAY, *   489 31

UNDER

IS INDEBTED, UNDER GOD, FOR HER FIRST FOUNDATION AND   V 11
SUFFERED UNDER PONTIUS PILATE, WAS CRUCIFIED,   015 23
ALSO FOR US UNDER PONTIUS PILATE   016 09
THEM PATIENCE UNDER THEIR SUFFERINGS, AND A HAPPY   019 09
SUFFERED UNDER PONTIUS PILATE, WAS CRUCIFIED,   029 28
ALSO FOR US UNDER PONTIUS PILATE   030 14
THEM PATIENCE UNDER THEIR SUFFERINGS, AND A HAPPY   033 07
GIVE HIM PATIENCE UNDER HIS AFFLICTION   045 18
TO BEAT DOWN SATAN UNDER OUR FEET   056 24
OR IN THE WATER UNDER THE EARTH   068 10
ALSO FOR US UNDER PONTIUS PILATE   071 11
OF COMMON PRAYER, UNDER THE DIRECTION OF THE PRIEST   R 073 36
UP THE CRUMBS UNDER THY TABLE   082 16
HER CHICKENS UNDER HER WINGS, AND YE WOULD NOT   100 30
TWO YEARS OLD AND UNDER, ACCORDING TO THE TIME WHICH   103 28
BUT IS UNDER TUTORS AND GOVERNORS UNTIL THE TIME   104 16

UNDER   CONTINUED

WERE IN BONDAGE UNDER THE ELEMENTS OF THE WORLD	104 18
OF A WOMAN, MADE UNDER THE LAW, TO REDEEM THEM THAT	104 20
THEM THAT WERE UNDER THE LAW, THAT WE MIGHT RECEIVE	104 21
AND THINGS UNDER THE EARTH	105 29
SHOULDEST COME UNDER MY ROOF	115 11
FOR I AM A MAN UNDER AUTHORITY, HAVING SOLDIERS UNDER	115 13
HAVING SOLDIERS UNDER ME	115 13
BUT I KEEP UNDER MY BODY, AND BRING IT INTO	119 11
THAT DESIRE TO BE UNDER THE LAW, DO YE NOT HEAR THE	130 29
THAT WERE UNDER THE FIRST TESTAMENT, THEY WHICH ARE	133 06
AND THINGS UNDER THE EARTH	134 26
BE MADE ONE FLOCK UNDER ONE SHEPHERD, JESUS CHRIST	157 11
OF EVERY NATION UNDER HEAVEN	180 26
WE BESEECH THEE, UNDER THE PROTECTION OF THY GOOD	191 06
THEREFORE UNDER THE MIGHTY HAND OF GOD, THAT HE MAY	193 02
OUR FATHERS WERE UNDER THE CLOUD, AND ALL PASSED	201 06
HATH CONCLUDED ALL UNDER SIN, THAT THE PROMISE BY	208 03
YE ARE NOT UNDER THE LAW	209 18
MANFULLY TO FIGHT UNDER HIS BANNER, AGAINST SIN,	280 08
SUFFERED UNDER PONTIUS PILATE, WAS CRUCIFIED,	284 17
OR IN THE WATER UNDER THE EARTH	286 10
IT IS ONE BODY UNDER ONE HEAD	291 08
UNDER THE DIRECTION OF THE BISHOP	294 18
IN EARTH, AND UNDER THE EARTH, DO BOW AND OBEY	314 17
IS NONE OTHER NAME UNDER HEAVEN GIVEN TO MAN, IN	314 19
PUT ALL ENEMIES UNDER HIS FEET	328 30
ALL THINGS ARE PUT UNDER HIM, IT IS MANIFEST THAT HE	328 32
PUT ALL THINGS UNDER HIS FEET	328 32
DID PUT ALL THINGS UNDER HIM	328 34
PUT ALL THINGS UNDER HIM, THAT GOD MAY BE ALL IN ALL	329 03
EXPEDIENT TO SAY UNDER SHELTER OF THE CHURCH THE	R 336 30
IN SUBJECTION UNDER HIS FEET	351 13
UNDER HIS TONGUE IS UNGODLINESS AND VANITY	353 18
HIDE ME UNDER THE SHADOW OF THY WINGS,	359 02
AND IT WAS DARK UNDER HIS FEET	360 16
MAKE ROOM ENOUGH UNDER ME FOR TO GO, *	362 09
BUT FALL UNDER MY FEET	362 15
DOWN MINE ENEMIES UNDER ME	362 17
PUT THEIR TRUST UNDER THE SHADOW OF THY WINGS	384 10
WILL WE TREAD THEM UNDER THAT RISE UP AGAINST US	395 03
SUBDUE THE PEOPLES UNDER US, *	398 25
AND THE NATIONS UNDER OUR FEET	398 26
AND UNDER THE SHADOW OF THY WINGS SHALL BE MY REFUGE,	409 13
MY TRUST SHALL BE UNDER THE COVERING OF THY WINGS	413 14
THEREFORE UNDER THE SHADOW OF THY WINGS WILL I	415 07
THEY SHALL GO UNDER THE EARTH	415 12
NAME SHALL REMAIN UNDER THE SUN AMONG THE	427 14
EAST-WIND TO BLOW UNDER HEAVEN	436 22
WHOSO DWELLETH UNDER THE DEFENCE OF THE MOST HIGH, *	454 28
SHALL ABIDE UNDER THE SHADOW OF THE ALMIGHTY	454 29
SHALL DEFEND THEE UNDER HIS WINGS, AND THOU SHALT BE	455 02
THOU SHALT BE SAFE UNDER HIS FEATHERS	455 03
SHALT THOU TREAD UNDER THY FEET	455 22
ADDER'S POISON IS UNDER THEIR LIPS	516 14
MY PEOPLE THAT IS UNDER ME	519 26
HOLY MEN, AS WELL UNDER THE LAW AS UNDER THE GOSPEL,	564 11
UNDER THE LAW AS UNDER THE GOSPEL, MOVED EITHER BY	564 11
SHOULDEST COME UNDER MY ROOF	573 12
SUFFERED UNDER PONTIUS PILATE, WAS CRUCIFIED,	577 32
OR IN THE WATER UNDER THE EARTH	578 29
GRANT US PATIENCE UNDER OUR AFFLICTIONS	588 29
ARE DEAR TO US, UNDER THY FATHERLY CARE AND	589 04
WE HAVE JOINED UNDER THIS ARTICLE, DOTH CONTAIN A	610 05

UNDERSTAND

MAKE ME TO UNDERSTAND WISDOM SECRETLY	060 23
YE MAY UNDERSTAND MY KNOWLEDGE IN THE MYSTERY	108 11
NOT SEE, AND HEARING THEY MIGHT NOT UNDERSTAND	121 32
AND UNDERSTAND ALL MYSTERIES, AND ALL	122 24
NEITHER UNDERSTAND I THAT THOU SAYEST	143 27
THEY MIGHT UNDERSTAND THE SCRIPTURES, AND SAID UNTO	170 11
I GIVE YOU TO UNDERSTAND, THAT NO MAN SPEAKING BY THE	203 19
THAT WOULD UNDERSTAND, AND SEEK AFTER GOD	356 17
MAKE ME TO UNDERSTAND WISDOM SECRETLY	403 21
THAT WOULD UNDERSTAND, AND SEEK AFTER GOD	405 17
THOUGHT I TO UNDERSTAND THIS	429 08
DO THEY UNDERSTAND, BUT WALK ON STILL IN DARKNESS	443 26
FOOL DOTH NOT UNDERSTAND IT	456 12
O YE FOOLS, WHEN WILL YE UNDERSTAND	458 03
THEY SHALL UNDERSTAND THE LOVING-KINDNESS OF THE	478 33
27 MAKE ME TO UNDERSTAND THE WAY OF THY COMMANDMENTS	491 21
MAY ALSO UNDERSTAND YOUR MINDS AND WILLS IN THESE	541 25
WE DO UNDERSTAND THOSE CANONICAL BOOKS OF THE OLD AND	603 33

UNDERSTANDED

TONGUE NOT UNDERSTANDED OF THE PEOPLE	607 29
THEY MAY BE UNDERSTANDED OF THE PEOPLE	610 10

UNDERSTANDEST

THOU UNDERSTANDEST MY THOUGHTS LONG BEFORE	514 22
THOU UNDERSTANDEST ALL THY CHILDREN	596 11

UNDERSTANDETH

AND UNDERSTANDETH ALL THEIR WORKS	379 17
THAT UNDERSTANDETH ANY MORE	430 25

UNDERSTANDING

BY UNDERSTANDING HATH HE ESTABLISHED THE HEAVENS	005 24
HER BEST UNDERSTANDING, MIGHT MOST TEND TO THE	V 35

UNDERSTANDING   CONTINUED

WISDOM AND UNDERSTANDING, THAT THEY MAY DISCERN THE	036 03
A RIGHT UNDERSTANDING OF THEMSELVES, AND OF THY	046 22
AND UNDERSTANDING OF THY WORD	055 31
AND UNDERSTANDING TO EXECUTE JUSTICE, AND TO MAINTAIN	VI 20
ALL UNDERSTANDING, KEEP YOUR HEARTS AND MINDS IN THE	084 18
ALL UNDERSTANDING, SHALL KEEP YOUR HEARTS AND MINDS	095 18
AT HIS UNDERSTANDING AND ANSWERS	110 30
HE THEIR UNDERSTANDING, THAT THEY MIGHT UNDERSTAND	170 10
THEE SUCH GOOD THINGS AS PASS MAN'S UNDERSTANDING	197 05
HAVING THE UNDERSTANDING DARKENED, BEING ALIENATED	216 05
BUT UNDERSTANDING WHAT THE WILL OF THE LORD IS	217 25
WILL IN ALL WISDOM AND SPIRITUAL UNDERSTANDING	224 03
WISDOM AND UNDERSTANDING, THE SPIRIT OF COUNSEL AND	297 20
TO HORSE AND MULE, WHICH HAVE NO UNDERSTANDING	378 11
SING YE PRAISES WITH UNDERSTANDING	399 03
AND MY HEART SHALL MUSE OF UNDERSTANDING	400 11
HATH NO UNDERSTANDING *	401 16
WITHOUT UNDERSTANDING THAT WORK WICKEDNESS, *	405 22
ME HAVE UNDERSTANDING *	463 19
A GOOD UNDERSTANDING HAVE ALL THEY THAT DO	483 15
34 GIVE ME UNDERSTANDING, AND I SHALL KEEP THY LAW	492 07
ME TRUE UNDERSTANDING AND KNOWLEDGE	494 13
O GIVE ME UNDERSTANDING, THAT I MAY LEARN THY	494 29
HAVE MORE UNDERSTANDING THAN MY TEACHERS	496 24
104 THROUGH THY COMMANDMENTS I GET UNDERSTANDING	497 02
O GRANT ME UNDERSTANDING, *	498 19
LIGHT AND UNDERSTANDING UNTO THE SIMPLE	498 31
O GRANT ME UNDERSTANDING, AND I SHALL LIVE	499 28
GIVE ME UNDERSTANDING ACCORDING TO THY WORD	501 21
ALL UNDERSTANDING, KEEP YOUR HEARTS AND MINDS IN THE	535 13
ALL UNDERSTANDING, KEEP YOUR HEARTS AND MINDS IN THE	547 14
THE TRUE UNDERSTANDING OF THE SAME	554 31
ALL UNDERSTANDING, KEEP YOUR HEARTS AND MINDS IN THE	559 17
ALL UNDERSTANDING, KEEP YOUR HEARTS AND MINDS IN THE	568 13
MY UNDERSTANDING WITH THE ILLUMINATION OF THE HOLY	573 17
PASSETH UNDERSTANDING ABIDE ALL THE DAYS OF HIS LIFE	598 03

UNDERSTOOD

AND THEY UNDERSTOOD NOT THE SAYING WHICH HE SPAKE	111 03
AS A CHILD, I UNDERSTOOD AS A CHILD, I THOUGHT AS A	123 09
AND THEY UNDERSTOOD NONE OF THESE THINGS	123 23
BUT THEY UNDERSTOOD NOT WHAT THINGS THEY WERE WHICH	186 10
THEN UNDERSTOOD I THE END OF THESE MEN	429 10
BUT THEY UNDERSTOOD NOT WHAT THINGS THEY WERE WHICH	538 33

UNDERTAKING

DEVOUTLY BEG HIS BLESSING ON THIS OUR UNDERTAKING	564 25

UNDERTOOK

SPONSORS THEN UNDERTOOK FOR YOU	296 27
WHICH YE THEN UNDERTOOK, OR YOUR SPONSORS THEN	296 27

UNDONE

WE HAVE LEFT UNDONE THOSE THINGS WHICH WE OUGHT TO	006 21
WE HAVE LEFT UNDONE THOSE THINGS WHICH WE OUGHT TO	023 28
FEAR OF THEE HATH UNDONE ME	449 30

UNENDING

THEM INTO THINE UNENDING JOY	268 19

UNFAILING

THINE OWN UNFAILING MIGHT SUPPLY TO STRENGTHEN OUR	545 04
THINE OWN UNFAILING MIGHT SUPPLY TO STRENGTHEN OUR	557 10

UNFAITHFUL

THEM THAT ARE UNFAITHFUL UNTO THEE	429 31

UNFAITHFULNESS

I HATE THE SINS OF UNFAITHFULNESS	463 23

UNFEIGNED

WE YIELD THEE UNFEIGNED THANKS AND PRAISE FOR THE	050 21
BY LOVE UNFEIGNED, BY THE WORD OF TRUTH,	126 14
GIVE HIM UNFEIGNED REPENTANCE FOR ALL THE ERRORS OF	316 12
THEE WITH AN UNFEIGNED HEART, *	490 12
WE JOIN OUR UNFEIGNED THANKS FOR ALL THY MERCIES	591 07

UNFEIGNEDLY

AND UNFEIGNEDLY BELIEVE HIS HOLY GOSPEL	007 12
MAY BE UNFEIGNEDLY THANKFUL	019 26
AND UNFEIGNEDLY BELIEVE HIS HOLY GOSPEL	024 14
MAY BE UNFEIGNEDLY THANKFUL	033 24
THOSE WHO UNFEIGNEDLY LOVE THEE	256 10

UNFRUITFUL

WITH THE UNFRUITFUL WORKS OF DARKNESS, BUT RATHER	129 16

UNGODLINESS

DENYING UNGODLINESS AND WORLDLY LUSTS, WE SHOULD LIVE	098 19
THEM OUT IN THE MULTITUDE OF THEIR UNGODLINESS	348 24
TONGUE IS UNGODLINESS AND VANITY	353 19
BEHOLDEST UNGODLINESS AND WRONG, THAT THOU MAYEST	354 04

UNGODLINESS   CONTINUED

OUT HIS UNGODLINESS, UNTIL THOU FIND NONE   354 10
OF UNGODLINESS MADE ME AFRAID   359 32
THAN TO DWELL IN THE TENTS OF UNGODLINESS   445 33
YOU DENY ALL UNGODLINESS AND WORLDLY LUSTS, AND LIVE   555 08

UNGODLY

AGAINST THE UNGODLY PEOPLE   310 06
COUNSEL OF THE UNGODLY, NOR STCOD IN THE WAY OF   345 08
5 AS FOR THE UNGODLY, IT IS NOT SO WITH THEM   345 16
6 THEREFORE THE UNGODLY SHALL NOT BE ABLE TO STAND IN   345 19
THE WAY OF THE UNGODLY SHALL PERISH   345 23
THOU HAST BROKEN THE TEETH OF THE UNGODLY   347 06
OF THE UNGODLY COME TC AN END   350 09
15 BEHOLD, THE UNGODLY TRAVAILETH WITH INIQUITY   350 21
REBUKED THE HEATHEN, AND DESTROYED THE UNGODLY   351 31
THE UNGODLY IS TRAPPED IN THE WORK OF HIS CWN HANDS   352 24
2 THE UNGODLY, FOR HIS OWN LUST, DOTH PERSECUTE THE   353 05
3 FOR THE UNGODLY HATH MADE BOAST OF HIS OWN HEART'S   353 08
4 THE UNGODLY IS SO PROUD, THAT HE CARETH NOT FCR   353 11
THE POWER OF THE UNGODLY AND MALICIOUS   354 09
2 FOR LO, THE UNGODLY BEND THEIR BOW, AND MAKE READY   354 21
BUT THE UNGODLY, AND HIM THAT DELIGHTETH IN   354 30
7 UPON THE UNGODLY HE SHALL RAIN SNARES, FIRE ANC   354 33
9 THE UNGODLY WALK ON EVERY SIDE   355 25
9 FROM THE UNGODLY, THAT TROUBLE ME   359 04
MY SOUL FROM THE UNGODLY, BY THINE OWN SWORD   359 13
AND WILL NOT SIT AMONG THE UNGODLY   371 07
ME WITH THE UNGODLY AND WICKED DOERS, *   373 11
LET THE UNGODLY BE PUT TO CONFUSION, AND BE PUT TC   376 31
11 GREAT PLAGUES REMAIN FOR THE UNGODLY   378 13
21 BUT MISFORTUNE SHALL SLAY THE UNGODLY   381 10
THAT ARE MINE ENEMIES TRIUMPH OVER ME UNGODLY   382 35
OF THE UNGODLY, *   383 26
THE HAND OF THE UNGODLY CAST ME DOWN   384 20
FRET NOT THYSELF BECALSE OF THE UNGODLY   384 25
AND THE UNGODLY SHALL BE CLEAN GONE   385 13
12 THE UNGODLY SEEKETH COUNSEL AGAINST THE JUST,   385 18
14 THE UNGODLY HAVE DRAWN OUT THE SWORD, AND HAVE   385 22
IS BETTER THAN GREAT RICHES OF THE UNGODLY   385 28
THE ARMS OF THE UNGODLY SHALL BE BROKEN, *   385 29
20 AS FOR THE UNGODLY, THEY SHALL PERISH, AND THE   385 35
21 THE UNGODLY BORROWETH, AND PAYETH NOT AGAIN   386 04
THE SEED OF THE UNGODLY, IT SHALL BE ROOTED OUT   386 23
33 THE UNGODLY WATCHETH THE RIGHTEOUS, *   386 30
WHEN THE UNGODLY SHALL PERISH, THOU SHALT SEE IT   387 03
HAVE SEEN THE UNGODLY IN GREAT POWER, *   387 04
THE END OF THE UNGODLY IS, THEY SHALL BE RCOTED OUT   387 11
THEM FROM THE UNGODLY, AND SHALL SAVE THEM, BECAUSE   387 16
WHILE THE UNGODLY IS IN MY SIGHT   389 08
AGAINST THE UNGODLY PEOPLE   394 04
16 BUT UNTO THE UNGODLY SAITH GOD, *   402 22
AND THE UNGODLY COMETH ON SO FAST   406 23
3 THE UNGODLY ARE FROWARD, EVEN FROM THEIR MOTHER'S   410 12
WASH HIS FOOTSTEPS IN THE BLOOD OF THE UNGODLY   410 31
SO LET THE UNGODLY PERISH AT THE PRESENCE CF   419 12
THE HAND OF THE UNGODLY, *   425 11
DO ALSO SEE THE UNGODLY IN SUCH PROSPERITY   428 15
THESE ARE THE UNGODLY, *   428 32
AND TO THE UNGODLY, SET NOT UP YOUR HORN   432 07
ALL THE UNGODLY OF THE EARTH SHALL DRINK THEM, AND   432 17
THE HORNS OF THE UNGODLY ALSO WILL I BREAK, *   432 21
AND ACCEPT THE PERSONS OF THE UNGODLY   443 21
SAVE THEM FROM THE HAND OF THE UNGODLY   443 25
AND SEE THE REWARD OF THE UNGODLY   455 12
7 WHEN THE UNGODLY ARE GREEN AS THE GRASS, ANC WHEN   456 13
LONG SHALL THE UNGODLY, *   457 23
LONG SHALL THE UNGODLY TRIUMPH   457 24
UNTIL THE PIT BE DIGGED UP FOR THE UNGODLY   458 13
SHALL DELIVER THEM FROM THE HAND OF THE UNGODLY   461 18
DESTROY ALL THE UNGODLY THAT ARE IN THE LAND   464 04
AND THE UNGODLY SHALL COME TO AN END   469 32
THE FLAME BURNT UP THE UNGODLY   474 05
THE MOUTH OF THE UNGODLY, YEA, THE MOUTH OF THE   480 04
5 SET THOU AN UNGODLY MAN TO BE RULER OVER HIM,   480 13
10 THE UNGODLY SHALL SEE IT, AND IT SHALL GRIEVE HIM   484 04
DESIRE OF THE UNGODLY SHALL PERISH   484 06
FOR THE UNGODLY THAT FORSAKE THY LAW   493 16
SNARES OF THE UNGODLY HAVE COMPASSED ME ABCUT   494 02
95 THE UNGODLY LAID WAIT FCR ME, TO DESTROY ME   496 15
110 THE UNGODLY HAVE LAID A SNARE FOR ME   497 17
AWAY ALL THE UNGODLY OF THE EARTH LIKE DROSS   498 06
155 HEALTH IS FAR FROM THE UNGODLY   500 21
SCEPTRE OF THE UNGODLY SHALL NOT ABIDE UPCN THE LOT   504 29
SNARES OF THE UNGODLY IN PIECES   506 28
FROM THE HANDS OF THE UNGODLY   516 15
8 LET NOT THE UNGODLY HAVE HIS DESIRE, O LORD   516 24
BE OCCUPIED IN UNGODLY WORKS WITH THE MEN THAT WCRK   517 16
6 AS FOR THE UNGODLY, *   517 22
11 LET THE UNGODLY FALL INTO THEIR OWN NETS TOGETHER,   517 32
BUT SCATTERETH ABROAD ALL THE UNGODLY   521 33
THE WAY OF THE UNGODLY, HE TURNETH IT UPSIDE DOWN   522 21
AND BRINGETH THE UNGODLY DOWN TO THE GROUND   523 07
THE HAND OF THE UNGODLY TO CAST THEM DOWN   574 14
IS SUPERSTITIOUS AND UNGODLY   610 36

UNHALLOWED

THEM FROM ALL UNHALLOWED, WORLDLY, AND COMMON USES,   564 16
FROM ALL UNHALLOWED, ORDINARY, AND COMMON USES   565 06

UNHAPPY

WE ARE IN BY OUR UNHAPPY DIVISIONS   037 27

UNHAPPY   CONTINUED

DISCOURAGED AND UNHAPPY PEOPLE, AND BY THY HEAVENLY   599 11

UNICORN

AND SIRION, LIKE A YOUNG UNICORN   374 10
HORN SHALL BE EXALTED LIKE THE HORN OF AN UNICCRN   456 19

UNICORNS

ME ALSO FROM AMONG THE HORNS OF THE UNICORNS   367 15

UNINFLUENCED

TO THEM (UNINFLUENCED AND UNRESTRAINED BY ANY WORLDLY   VI 24

UNION

US FROM GODLY UNION AND CONCORD   037 29
US THE MYSTICAL UNION THAT IS BETWIXT CHRIST ANC HIS   300 12

UNITED

PRESIDENT OF THE UNITED STATES, AND ALL CTHERS IN   017 31
PRESIDENT OF THE UNITED STATES, AND TO ALL IN   018 10
PRESIDENT OF THE UNITED STATES, THE GOVERNOR OF THIS   032 07
PEOPLE OF THESE UNITED STATES IN GENERAL, SO   035 09
FASHION INTO ONE UNITED PEOPLE THE MULTITUDES BROUGHT   036 16
AND OF ONE SOUL, UNITED IN ONE HOLY BCND CF TRUTH ANC   037 33
UNTO THE UNITED STATES OF AMERICA, AND A SECURITY FOR   042 08
OF THESE UNITED STATES, AND FOR THE GOVERNCR OF THIS   047 15
PEOPLE OF THESE UNITED STATES, THAT THEY MAY LIVE IN   048 02
PRESIDENT OF THE UNITED STATES, THAT HE MAY ABCVE ALL   055 23
THAT AT LENGTH, UNITED WITH THEM, WE MAY STAND IN THY   341 02
CHURCH IN THE UNITED STATES OF AMERICA   552 31

UNITY

OF PEACE AND UNITY IN THE CHURCH   V 36
HOLD THE FAITH IN UNITY OF SPIRIT, IN THE BCND CF   019 02
HOLD THE FAITH IN UNITY OF SPIRIT, IN THE BCND CF   032 33
AND TO RESTORE TO IT THE WITNESS OF VISIBLE UNITY   047 11
IT THAT PEACE AND UNITY WHICH IS ACCORDING TO THY   049 08
TO ALL NATIONS UNITY, PEACE, AND CONCORD   056 08
SPIRIT OF TRUTH, UNITY, AND CONCORD   074 12
AND LIVE IN UNITY AND GODLY LOVE   074 15
OF PERSONS AND IN UNITY OF SUBSTANCE   079 09
WITH WHOM, IN THE UNITY OF THE HCLY GHOST, ALL HCNCUR   081 33
TO A GODLY UNITY, BUT REMAIN STILL IN HIS FROWARCNESS R   085 15
WITH THEE, IN THE UNITY OF THE SAME SPIRIT, CNE GOD,   180 13
WITH THEE IN THE UNITY OF THE SAME SPIRIT EVER, CNE   182 19
TOGETHER IN UNITY BY THY HOLY SPIRIT, MAY MANIFEST   185 15
POWER OF THE DIVINE MAJESTY TO WORSHIP THE UNITY   186 26
TO KEEP THE UNITY OF THE SPIRIT IN THE BOND CF PEACE   213 22
WE ALL COME IN THE UNITY OF THE FAITH, AND CF THE   237 22
JOINED TOGETHER IN UNITY OF SPIRIT BY THEIR DCCTRINE,   254 30
WITH THEE, IN THE UNITY OF THE HOLY SPIRIT, BE ALL   279 20
JOINED TOGETHER IN UNITY OF SPIRIT BY THEIR DCCTRINE,   290 22
MARRIAGE AND UNITY BETWIXT CHRIST AND HIS CHURCH   303 22
SICK MEMBER IN THE UNITY OF THE CHURCH   314 06
THAT IS AT UNITY IN ITSELF   503 12
FOR BRETHREN TO DWELL TOGETHER IN UNITY   509 14
WE ALL COME IN THE UNITY OF THE FAITH, AND OF THE   538 09
WITH THEE IN THE UNITY OF THE SAME HCLY SPIRIT,   546 04
WITH THEE IN THE UNITY OF THE SAME SPIRIT EVER, CNE   562 14
JOINED TOGETHER IN UNITY OF SPIRIT, AND IN THE BCND   574 07
AND IN UNITY OF THIS GODHEAD THERE BE THREE PERSCNS,   603 05
CUT OFF FROM THE UNITY OF THE CHURCH, AND   609 27

UNIVERSAL

ESPECIALLY WE PRAY FOR THY HOLY CHURCH UNIVERSAL   018 30
ESPECIALLY WE PRAY FOR THY HOLY CHURCH UNIVERSAL   032 30
TO THYSELF AN UNIVERSAL CHURCH BY THE PRECIOUS BLCOD   038 26
HOLY CHURCH UNIVERSAL IN THE RIGHT WAY   055 20
THE UNIVERSAL CHURCH WITH THE SPIRIT OF TRUTH,   074 12
BECAUSE IT IS UNIVERSAL, HOLDING EARNESTLY THE FAITH   291 11
TO THYSELF AN UNIVERSAL CHURCH, AND HAST PROMISED TO   572 16

UNIVERSE

RULER OF THE UNIVERSE, WHO DOST FROM THY THRONE   017 28

UNIVERSITIES

BEHOLD OUR UNIVERSITIES, COLLEGES, AND SCHCCLS, THAT   042 23

UNJUST

THE JUST FOR THE UNJUST, THAT HE MIGHT BRING US TC   161 23
UNJUST, ADULTERERS, OR EVEN AS THIS   205 26
AND SENDETH RAIN ON THE JUST AND ON THE UNJUST   264 10

UNKIND

HOW GRIEVOUS AND UNKIND A THING IT IS, WHEN A MAN   088 11

UNKNOWN

AS UNKNOWN, AND YET WELL KNOWN   126 17

UNLAWFUL

UNLAWFUL DESIGNS, OR INORDINATE DESIRES,   590 14

UNLEAVENED

AND OF UNLEAVENED BREAD   139 33
FIRST DAY OF UNLEAVENED BREAD, WHEN THEY KILLED THE   140 22
THE FEAST OF UNLEAVENED BREAD DREW NIGH, WHICH IS   148 12
THE DAY OF UNLEAVENED BREAD, WHEN THE PASSOVER MUST   148 21
BUT WITH THE UNLEAVENED BREAD OF SINCERITY AND TRUTH   163 02
THAT YE MAY BE A NEW LUMP, AS YE ARE UNLEAVENED   165 12
BUT WITH THE UNLEAVENED BREAD OF SINCERITY AND TRUTH   165 15
THE DAYS OF UNLEAVENED BREAD   245 03

UNLESS

UNTO YOU, UNLESS YE HAVE BELIEVED IN VAIN   205 02

UNLOOSE

WHOSE SHOE'S LATCHET I AM NOT WORTHY TO UNLOOSE   096 05
SHOES I AM NOT WORTHY TO STOOP DOWN AND UNLOOSE   112 16

UNMOVEABLE

YE STEDFAST, UNMOVEABLE, ALWAYS ABOUNDING IN THE WORK   330 14

UNNECESSARY

IT SEEMS UNNECESSARY TO ENUMERATE ALL THE DIFFERENT   VI 28

UNPARDONABLE

IS SIN AGAINST THE HOLY GHOST, AND UNPARDONABLE   605 40

UNPROFITABLE

WE ARE UNPROFITABLE SERVANTS   605 29

UNQUIET

BE THE EARTH NEVER SO UNQUIET   462 18

UNRESTRAINED

AND UNRESTRAINED BY ANY WORLDLY AUTHORITY WHATSOEVER)   VI 24

UNRIGHTEOUS

GOD IS NOT UNRIGHTEOUS, THAT HE WILL FORGET YOUR   072 23
MOUTH ARE UNRIGHTEOUS AND FULL OF DECEIT   383 30
29 THE UNRIGHTEOUS SHALL BE PUNISHED   386 22
HAND OF THE UNRIGHTEOUS AND CRUEL MAN   425 12
SOUL FROM UNRIGHTEOUS JUDGES   482 03

UNRIGHTEOUSLY

THEY SPEAK UNRIGHTEOUSLY AGAINST THEE   515 30

UNRIGHTEOUSNESS

AND TO CLEANSE US FROM ALL UNRIGHTEOUSNESS   022 13
AND TO CLEANSE US FROM ALL UNRIGHTEOUSNESS   101 31
HE WHOSE UNRIGHTEOUSNESS IS FORGIVEN, *   377 22
AND MINE UNRIGHTEOUSNESS HAVE I NOT HID   377 30
LOVED UNRIGHTEOUSNESS MORE THAN GOODNESS, *   404 24
SPIED UNRIGHTEOUSNESS AND STRIFE IN THE CITY   407 05
IS NO UNRIGHTEOUSNESS IN HIM   456 31

UNRULY

OF A VIOLENT AND UNRULY PEOPLE   052 19
CANST ORDER THE UNRULY WILLS AND AFFECTIONS OF SINFUL   174 18
CANST ORDER THE UNRULY WILLS AND AFFECTIONS OF SINFUL   285 25

UNSEARCHABLE

THE UNSEARCHABLE RICHES OF CHRIST   108 20

UNSEEMLY

BEHAVE ITSELF UNSEEMLY, SEEKETH NOT HER OWN, IS NOT   122 31

UNSEEN

INVISIBLE AND UNSEEN, WE MAY IN HEART BE INSPIRED BY   594 24

UNSHAKEN

HAVE STILL BEEN CONTINUED FIRM AND UNSHAKEN   V 32

UNSPEAKABLE

TO THOSE UNSPEAKABLE JOYS WHICH THOU HAST PREPARED   256 09
AND UNSPEAKABLE COMFORT TO GODLY PERSONS, AND SUCH AS   606 17

UNSPOTTED

KEEP HIMSELF UNSPOTTED FROM THE WORLD   176 17
KEEP HIMSELF UNSPOTTED FROM THE WORLD   266 09
KEEPING HIM UNSPOTTED FROM THE WORLD   597 30

UNSTABLE

MAN IS UNSTABLE IN ALL HIS WAYS   239 17

UNTHANKFULLY

MOST UNTHANKFULLY REFUSE TO COME   088 21

UNTIMELY

AND BE LIKE THE UNTIMELY FRUIT OF A WOMAN   410 24

UNTRULY

AND DEALT UNTRULY WITH HIS SERVANTS   471 23

UNWISE

BE YE NOT UNWISE, BUT UNDERSTANDING WHAT THE WILL OF   217 25
6 AN UNWISE MAN DOTH NOT WELL CONSIDER THIS, *   456 11
8 TAKE HEED, YE UNWISE AMONG THE PEOPLE   458 02

UNWORTHILY

DANGER GREAT, IF WE RECEIVE THE SAME UNWORTHILY   085 33
THOSE WHO WILL PRESUME TO RECEIVE IT UNWORTHILY   087 07
RECEIVE THEM UNWORTHILY, PURCHASE TO THEMSELVES   608 05

UNWORTHINESS

FOR OUR UNWORTHINESS WE DARE NOT, AND FOR OUR   050 02
OF OUR OWN UNWORTHINESS, ACKNOWLEDGING OUR MANIFOLD   589 30

UNWORTHY

WE, THINE UNWORTHY SERVANTS, DO GIVE THEE MOST HUMBLE   019 15
WE, THINE UNWORTHY SERVANTS, DO GIVE THEE MOST HUMBLE   033 13
ALTHOUGH WE ARE UNWORTHY, THROUGH OUR MANIFOLD SINS,   081 28
PERIL OF THE UNWORTHY RECEIVING THEREOF   087 09
BUT COUNTED UNWORTHY OF THE HEAVENLY FEAST   089 06
YOURSELVES UNWORTHY OF EVERLASTING LIFE, LO, WE TURN   261 02
NOT THAT AN UNWORTHY PERSON SHOULD MINISTER AMONG   570 19

UP-RISING

THOU KNOWEST MY DOWN-SITTING, AND MINE UP-RISING   514 21

UPBRAIDETH

AND UPBRAIDETH NOT   239 13

UPHELD

AND MY FURY, IT UPHELD ME   138 25
AND IN WORK BE UPHELD BY THY STRENGTH, AND IN THE END   594 26

UPHOLD

AND I WONDERED THAT THERE WAS NONE TO UPHOLD   138 23
IS WITH THEM THAT UPHOLD MY SOUL   406 11

UPHOLDEN

RIGHT HAND HATH UPHOLDEN ME   415 10

UPHOLDER

BUT THE LORD WAS MY UPHOLDER   361 03

UPHOLDEST

INNOCENCY THOU UPHOLDEST ME, *   392 23

UPHOLDETH

AND THE LORD UPHOLDETH THE RIGHTEOUS   385 30
FOR THE LORD UPHOLDETH HIM WITH HIS HAND   386 11
GOD UPHOLDETH THE SAME FOR EVER   399 25
14 THE LORD UPHOLDETH ALL SUCH AS FALL, *   521 20

UPHOLDING

AND UPHOLDING ALL THINGS BY THE WORD OF HIS   096 27

UPLIFT

UPLIFT THOSE WHO ARE CAST DOWN   599 08

UPPER

SHEW YOU A LARGE UPPER ROOM FURNISHED AND PREPARED   140 31
SHEW YOU A LARGE UPPER ROOM FURNISHED   148 31
NOT MAN HAVE THE UPPER HAND   352 30

UPRIGHT

OF OUR NATURE WE CANNOT ALWAYS STAND UPRIGHT   114 06
BUT WE ARE RISEN AND STAND UPRIGHT   364 33
SLAY SUCH AS BE UPRIGHT IN THEIR WAYS   385 24
TO BE JUST AND UPRIGHT IN ALL OUR DEALINGS   588 30

UPROAR

LEST THERE BE AN UPROAR OF THE PEOPLE   140 02

UPSIDE

HE TURNETH IT UPSIDE DOWN   522 22

URGENT

EXCEPT FOR URGENT CAUSE, THEY SEEK NOT TO HAVE   R 273 07
OR ELSE, ON URGENT OCCASION, UPON SOME OTHER DAY,   529 30
OR ELSE, ON URGENT OCCASION, UPON SOME OTHER DAY, IN   R 535 25

URGENT   CONTINUED

UNTIL SOME URGENT REASON OR REASONS OCCASION A   569 31

US-WARD

AS BE ALSO THY THOUGHTS, WHICH ARE TO US-WARD   390 23

USAGES

FORMS AND USAGES MAY WITHOUT OFFENCE BE ALLOWED,   V 03
WITH THE USAGES, LAWS, OR CHARTERS OF THE CHURCH IN   R 569 11

USE

A GOOD CONSCIENCE USE AND SUBMIT UNTO, OR WHICH IS   V 41
HIS DISCRETION, MAY USE, INSTEAD OF WHAT FOLLOWS, THE   R 007 04
ACCORDING TO THE USE OF THIS CHURCH   R 009 22
DESCENDED INTO HELL, USE THE WORDS, HE WENT INTO THE   R 015 17
ACCORDING TO THE USE OF THIS CHURCH   R 025 15
DESCENDED INTO HELL, USE THE WORDS, HE WENT INTO THE   R 029 22
HER INCREASE FOR OUR USE AND BENEFIT   040 27
WE MAY REVERENTLY USE OUR FREEDOM, HELP US TO EMPLOY   044 12
THE MEANS MADE USE OF FOR THEIR CURE   045 07
FORTH FRUIT FOR THE USE OF MAN   051 17
AND PRESERVE TO OUR USE THE KINDLY FRUITS OF THE   057 10
SHALL THE MINISTER USE WITH THOSE, BETWIXT WHOM HE   R 085 09
THE FORMER, HE MAY USE THIS EXHORTATION   R 088 11
GIVE US GRACE TO USE SUCH ABSTINENCE, THAT, OUR FLESH   125 28
USE HOSPITALITY ONE TO ANOTHER WITHOUT GRUDGING   179 15
WHICH IS GOOD TO THE USE OF EDIFYING, THAT IT MAY   216 24
NOR YET OF GRACE TO USE THEM ALWAY TO THY HONOUR AND   240 31
WHICH DESPITEFULLY USE YOU, AND PERSECUTE YOU   264 07
AND HERB FOR THE USE OF MEN   264 29
THE MINISTER SHALL USE THIS FORM OF WORDS   R 282 12
ON THE MEANING AND USE OF THE TIME OF SICKNESS,   R 313 16
THE MINISTER MAY USE ANY PART OF THE SERVICE OF THIS   R 314 23
WHICH SHALL BE MADE USE OF FOR HIS CURE   315 29
THE MINISTER MAY USE SUCH PORTION OF THE FOREGOING   R 320 06
MAY ALSO USE ANY OF THE FOLLOWING PRAYERS   R 335 22
AT HIS DISCRETION, USE SUCH PART OF THIS OFFICE,   R 337 04
THE VALE OF MISERY USE IT FOR A WELL   445 23
AND HERB FOR THE USE OF MEN   523 12
THEN LET THEM USE THE OFFICE OF A DEACON, BEING FOUND   531 30
AND TO USE BOTH PUBLIC AND PRIVATE MONITIONS AND   542 21
AND USE THE AUTHORITY GIVEN HIM, NOT TO DESTRUCTION,   558 02
BY MAKING A RIGHT USE OF IT, TO THE GLORY OF THY   566 33
BLESS THE MEANS MADE USE OF FOR HIS CURE   597 23
THY GIFTS TO OUR USE AND US TO THY SERVICE   600 15
THAT WE SHOULD DULY USE THEM   608 03
WE MAY USE THEIR MINISTRY, BOTH IN HEARING   608 12

USED

APPOINTED TO BE USED THEREIN, BEING THINGS IN THEIR   V 15
ELSE IT IS USED IN DIVINE SERVICE   R 007 22
PSALM 95 MAY BE USED IN THIS PLACE   R 008 11
TO BE USED BEFORE THE PRAYER FOR ALL CONDITIONS OF   R 035 03
TO BE USED DURING THEIR SESSION   R 035 07
ABOVE PRAYER MAY BE USED BY ALL CONGREGATIONS OF THIS   R 037 10
TO BE USED IN THE WEEKS PRECEDING THE STATED TIMES   R 038 24
TO BE USED ON ROGATION SUNDAY AND THE ROGATION   R 039 23
TO BE USED BEFORE SERMONS, OR ON SPECIAL OCCASIONS   R 047 03
TO SAY, TO BE USED AFTER THE COLLECTS OF MORNING OR   R 049 03
TO BE USED AFTER THE GENERAL THANKSGIVING, OR,   R 050 15
TO BE USED AFTER THE THIRD COLLECT AT MORNING OR   R 054 03
OR IT MAY BE USED WITH MORNING PRAYER, OR EVENING   R 060 05
SENTENCES MAY BE USED ON ANY OTHER OCCASION OF PUBLIC   R 073 25
OTHER FEAST MAY BE USED AT THE EVENING SERVICE OF THE   R 090 06
AND GOSPEL MAY BE USED AT THE FIRST COMMUNION   R 098 08
AND GOSPEL MAY BE USED AT THE FIRST COMMUNION   R 164 31
AND GOSPEL MAY BE USED AT THE FIRST COMMUNION   R 182 12
EPIPHANY SHALL BE USED ON THE TWENTY-FIFTH SUNDAY   R 224 32
EPIPHANY SHALL BE USED ON THE TWENTY-SIXTH, AND THE   R 224 34
WHEN THE OFFICE IS USED FOR CHILDREN, THE MINISTER   R 276 17
WHEN THE OFFICE IS USED FOR ADULTS, THE MINISTER   R 277 18
PARTS OF THE FOREGOING SERVICE SHALL BE USED   R 282 03
MAY BE USED AT THE DISCRETION OF THE MINISTER   R 305 05
IF THIS BE USED WITH THE MORNING OR EVENING   R 306 09
MAY BE USED AT THE DISCRETION OF THE   R 308 03
AND ABSOLUTION THE FOLLOWING MAY BE USED   R 323 10
THIS OFFICE MAY BE USED WITH AGED AND BED-RIDDEN   R 323 32
APPROPRIATE TO BE USED ONLY FOR THE FAITHFUL DEPARTED   R 337 02
THE SAME OFFICE MAY BE USED   R 337 07
3 HE THAT HATH USED NO DECEIT IN HIS TONGUE, NOR DONE   357 10
AND REVERENTLY USED AND ESTEEMED IN THIS CHURCH,   529 19
FOR THEY THAT HAVE USED THE OFFICE OF A DEACON WELL   532 03
OFFICE MAY BE USED WITH THE ORDER FOR THE HOLY   R 563 03
OFFICE MAY BE USED WITH THE ORDER FOR THE HOLY   R 569 08

USEFUL

TRUE RELIGION AND USEFUL LEARNING MAY FOR EVER   047 36

USES

LEAVE BEQUESTS FOR RELIGIOUS AND CHARITABLE USES   R 320 24
AND COMMON USES, IN ORDER TO FILL MEN'S   564 17
AND COMMON USES   565 07

USEST

AS THOU USEST TO DO UNTO THOSE THAT LOVE THY NAME   499 03

USING

AS FREE, AND NOT USING YOUR LIBERTY FOR A CLOKE OF   173 23
WATER UPON HIM, USING THE SAME FORM OF WORDS   R 279 32
HOLY BAPTISM, USING THE FOREGOING FORM   R 281 29

USUAL

THE WOMAN, AT THE USUAL TIME AFTER HER DELIVERY,   R 305 07

USURY

HIS MONEY UPON USURY, *   357 17

UTMOST

AND THE UTMOST PARTS OF THE EARTH FOR THY POSSESSION   346 13

UTTERANCE

AS THE SPIRIT GAVE THEM UTTERANCE   180 24
BY HIM, IN ALL UTTERANCE, AND IN ALL KNOWLEDGE   214 30
FOR ME, THAT UTTERANCE MAY BE GIVEN UNTO ME, THAT I   219 22

UTTERLY

HIS PROMISE COME UTTERLY TO AN END FOR EVERMORE   311 15
I SHOULD UTTERLY HAVE FAINTED, *   326 28
FOR I AM UTTERLY PURPOSED THAT MY MOUTH SHALL NOT   358 23
15 I SHOULD UTTERLY HAVE FAINTED, *   372 27
THAT THOU MAYEST UTTERLY DESTROY EVERY ENEMY, *   430 10
HIS PROMISE COME UTTERLY TO AN END FOR EVERMORE   433 32
WILL I NOT UTTERLY TAKE FROM HIM, *   452 07
O FORSAKE ME NOT UTTERLY   490 14
OF THY TRUTH UTTERLY OUT OF MY MOUTH   492 26
ALL FALSE WAYS I UTTERLY ABHOR   498 26
FOR WE ARE UTTERLY DESPISED   504 03
PLACES ONE, OR UTTERLY LIKE   609 33

UTTERMOST

AND UNTO THE UTTERMOST PART OF THE EARTH   005 14
TO THE UTTERMOST OF YOUR POWERS, FOR ALL INJURIES AND   087 25
AND UNTO THE UTTERMOST PART OF THE EARTH   178 11
HAST PAID THE UTTERMOST FARTHING   198 16
AMENDS TO THE UTTERMOST OF HIS POWER   R 313 23
FORTH FROM THE UTTERMOST PART OF THE HEAVEN, AND   363 24
DWELL IN THE UTTERMOST PARTS OF THE EARTH SHALL BE   416 29
TRIED TO THE UTTERMOST, *   499 19
REMAIN IN THE UTTERMOST PARTS OF THE SEA   515 05
TO THE UTTERMOST PARTS OF THE EARTH   596 30

VAGABONDS

CHILDREN BE VAGABONDS, AND BEG THEIR BREAD   480 19

VAIN

NOT TAKE THE NAME OF THE LORD THY GOD IN VAIN   068 19
THAT TAKETH HIS NAME IN VAIN   068 21
FOR HE BEARETH NOT THE SWORD IN VAIN   114 20
ALSO THAT YE RECEIVE NOT THE GRACE OF GOD IN VAIN   126 04
DECEIVE YOU WITH VAIN WORDS   129 09
HIS OWN HEART, THIS MAN'S RELIGION IS VAIN   176 15
UNLESS YE HAVE BELIEVED IN VAIN   205 03
GRACE WHICH WAS BESTOWED UPON ME WAS NOT IN VAIN   205 16
WITH EVERY BLAST OF VAIN DOCTRINE, WE MAY BE   237 08
THIS MAN'S RELIGION IS VAIN   266 06
ALL HIS WORKS, THE VAIN POMP AND GLORY OF THE WORLD,   276 25
ALL HIS WORKS, THE VAIN POMP AND GLORY OF THE WORLD,   277 27
NOT TAKE THE NAME OF THE LORD THY GOD IN VAIN   286 19
THAT TAKETH HIS NAME IN VAIN   286 21
MAN WALKETH IN A VAIN SHADOW, AND DISQUIETETH HIMSELF   324 25
AND DISQUIETETH HIMSELF IN VAIN   324 26
LABOUR IS NOT IN VAIN IN THE LORD   330 16
PEOPLE IMAGINE A VAIN THING   345 26
HAVE NOT DWELT WITH VAIN PERSONS   371 04
IS COUNTED BUT A VAIN THING TO SAVE A MAN   379 22
MAN WALKETH IN A VAIN SHADOW, AND DISQUIETETH HIMSELF   389 20
IN A VAIN SHADOW, AND DISQUIETETH HIMSELF IN VAIN   389 21
FOR VAIN IS THE HELP OF MAN   413 02
MY HEART IN VAIN, *   429 02
THAT THEY ARE BUT VAIN   458 09
AND THAT DELIGHT IN VAIN GODS   461 11
FOR VAIN IS THE HELP OF MAN   479 28
THE WATCHMAN WAKETH BUT IN VAIN   505 25
AND THINE ENEMIES TAKE THY NAME IN VAIN   515 31
SUCH SUCCESS, THAT IT MAY NEVER BE SPOKEN IN VAIN   547 08
NOT TAKE THE NAME OF THE LORD THY GOD IN VAIN   579 02
HOLD HIM GUILTLESS, THAT TAKETH HIS NAME IN VAIN   579 03
AS WE CONFESS THAT VAIN AND RASH SWEARING IS   611 06

VAIN-GLORY

THE DESIRE OF VAIN-GLORY, AND THE PRIDE OF LIFE   598 23

VAINGLORY

FROM PRIDE, VAINGLORY, AND HYPOCRISY   054 23

VAINLY

THE PELAGIANS DO VAINLY TALK   604 30
IS A FOND THING, VAINLY INVENTED, AND GROUNDED UPON   607 16

VALE

GOING THROUGH THE VALE OF MISERY USE IT FOR A WELL   445 23

VALLEY

DOWN INTO THE VALLEY, THE SPIRIT OF THE LORD CAUSED   139 15
EVERY VALLEY SHALL BE EXALTED, AND EVERY MOUNTAIN AND   242 22
WALK THROUGH THE VALLEY OF THE SHADOW OF DEATH, I   338 23
WALK THROUGH THE VALLEY OF THE SHADOW OF DEATH, I   368 16
AND METE OUT THE VALLEY OF SUCCOTH   412 24
AND METE OUT THE VALLEY OF SUCCOTH   479 18

VALLEYS

INTO THE LITTLE VALLEYS THEREOF   417 05
THE VALLEYS ALSO SHALL STAND SO THICK WITH CORN, THAT   417 11
AND DOWN TO THE VALLEYS BENEATH   468 08

VALUE

WHOM THEY OF THE CHILDREN OF ISRAEL DID VALUE   135 17
YE OF MUCH MORE VALUE THAN THEY   211 18

VALUED

OF HIM THAT WAS VALUED, WHOM THEY OF THE CHILDREN OF   135 16

VANISH

IT SHALL VANISH AWAY   123 06
THEIR IMAGE TO VANISH OUT OF THE CITY   429 17

VANISHED

AND HE VANISHED OUT OF THEIR SIGHT   168 08

VANISHETH

AS THE SMOKE VANISHETH, SO SHALT THOU DRIVE THEM   419 11

VANITIES

HOLD OF LYING VANITIES, *   376 02

VANITY

MADE SUBJECT TO VANITY, NOT WILLINGLY, BUT BY REASON   194 15
IN THE VANITY OF THEIR MIND, HAVING THE   216 05
THE POMPS AND VANITY OF THIS WICKED WORLD, AND ALL   283 24
AND VERILY EVERY MAN LIVING IS ALTOGETHER VANITY   324 24
EVERY MAN THEREFORE IS BUT VANITY   325 05
SUCH PLEASURE IN VANITY, AND SEEK AFTER FALSEHOOD   347 14
UNDER HIS TONGUE IS UNGODLINESS AND VANITY   353 19
2 THEY TALK OF VANITY EVERY ONE WITH HIS NEIGHBOUR   355 09
UP HIS MIND UNTO VANITY, NOR SWORN TO DECEIVE HIS   369 03
AND VERILY EVERY MAN LIVING IS ALTOGETHER VANITY   389 19
EVERY MAN THEREFORE IS BUT VANITY   389 34
HE SPEAKETH VANITY, *   392 10
9 AS FOR THE CHILDREN OF MEN, THEY ARE BUT VANITY   414 15
LIGHTER THAN VANITY ITSELF   414 17
GIVE NOT YOURSELVES UNTO VANITY   414 19
DID HE CONSUME IN VANITY, *   437 04
37 O TURN AWAY MINE EYES, LEST THEY BEHOLD VANITY   492 13
MOUTH TALKETH OF VANITY, *   520 06
MOUTH TALKETH OF VANITY, AND THEIR RIGHT HAND IS A   520 13
UP HIS MIND UNTO VANITY, NOR SWORN TO DECEIVE HIS   563 18
THE POMPS AND VANITY OF THIS WICKED WORLD, AND ALL   577 15

VAPOURS

SNOW AND VAPOURS, *   524 20

VARIABLENESS

WHOM IS NO VARIABLENESS, NEITHER SHADOW OF TURNING   174 28
WHOM IS NO VARIABLENESS, NEITHER SHADOW OF TURNING   265 20

VARIANCE

SO AT VARIANCE, BE CONTENT TO FORGIVE FROM   R 085 12
VARIANCE, EMULATIONS, WRATH, STRIFE,   209 21

VARIATIONS

IN ADMITTING VARIATIONS IN THINGS ONCE ADVISEDLY   V 25

VARIOUS

TO THE VARIOUS EXIGENCY OF TIMES AND OCCASIONS   V 09
ACCORDING TO THE VARIOUS EXIGENCY OF TIMES AND   V 17

VAUNTETH

CHARITY VAUNTETH NOT ITSELF, IS NOT PUFFED UP,   122 30

VEHEMENTLY

THE MORE VEHEMENTLY, IF I SHOULD DIE WITH THEE, I   141 25
STOOD AND VEHEMENTLY ACCUSED HIM   153 15

VEIL

BEHOLD, THE VEIL OF THE TEMPLE WAS RENT IN TWAIN   137 25
AND THE VEIL OF THE TEMPLE WAS RENT IN TWAIN FROM THE   146 35

VEIL   CONTINUED

AND THE VEIL OF THE TEMPLE WAS RENT IN THE   155 11
FOR US, THROUGH THE VEIL, THAT IS TO SAY, HIS FLESH   158 18

VENGEANCE

TAKE THOU VENGEANCE OF OUR SINS   054 14
AND THE DAY OF VENGEANCE OF OUR GOD   107 05
IT IS WRITTEN, VENGEANCE IS MINE   113 05
FOR THE DAY OF VENGEANCE IS IN MINE HEART, AND THE   138 21
SHALL REJOICE WHEN HE SEETH THE VENGEANCE   410 29
11 O LET THE VENGEANCE OF THY SERVANTS' BLOOD THAT IS   440 23
TO WHOM VENGEANCE BELONGETH, *   457 19
TO WHOM VENGEANCE BELONGETH, SHOW THYSELF   457 20

VENI

SING OR SAY THE VENI, CREATOR SPIRITUS   R 543 27
AND THE VENI, CREATOR SPIRITUS SHALL BE SUNG OR SAID   R 556 03

VENITE

GOOD FRIDAY THE VENITE MAY BE OMITTED   R 008 12
BEFORE THE VENITE MAY BE SUNG OR SAID,   R 008 14
AT THE END OF THE VENITE, BENEDICTUS ES, BENEDICTUS,   R 009 24
INSTEAD OF THE VENITE, THE FOLLOWING SHALL BE SAID,   R 162 28
INSTEAD OF THE VENITE, THE FOLLOWING SHALL BE SAID   R 264 17

VENOMOUS

4 THEY ARE AS VENOMOUS AS THE POISON OF A SERPENT,   410 15

VERILY

SAY UNTO THEM, VERILY I SAY UNTO YOU, INASMUCH AS YE   073 02
VERILY I SAY UNTO YOU, THIS GENERATION SHALL NOT PASS   093 18
VERILY I SAY UNTO YOU, ALL THESE THINGS SHALL COME   100 26
THAT FOLLOWED, VERILY I SAY UNTO YOU, I HAVE NOT   115 17
VERILY I SAY UNTO YOU, THEY HAVE THEIR REWARD   125 11
VERILY, VERILY, I SAY UNTO YOU, IF A MAN KEEP MY   133 17
VERILY, VERILY, I SAY UNTO YOU, IF A MAN KEEP MY   133 17
VERILY, VERILY, I SAY UNTO YOU, BEFORE ABRAHAM   133 31
SAID UNTO THEM, VERILY, VERILY, I SAY UNTO YOU,   133 31
VERILY I SAY UNTO YOU, WHERESOEVER THIS GOSPEL SHALL   140 15
JESUS SAID, VERILY I SAY UNTO YOU, ONE OF YOU   140 35
VERILY I SAY UNTO YOU, I WILL DRINK NO MORE OF THE   141 14
SAITH UNTO HIM, VERILY I SAY UNTO THEE, THAT THIS   141 23
SAID UNTO HIM, VERILY I SAY UNTO THEE, TO-DAY SHALT   155 08
VERILY, VERILY, I SAY UNTO YOU, THAT YE SHALL WEEP   174 07
VERILY, VERILY, I SAY UNTO YOU, THAT YE SHALL WEEP   174 07
VERILY, VERILY, I SAY UNTO YOU, WHATSOEVER YE SHALL   176 20
VERILY, VERILY, I SAY UNTO YOU, WHATSOEVER YE SHALL   176 20
VERILY, VERILY, IS SAY UNTO YOU, HE THAT ENTERETH NOT   185 30
VERILY, VERILY, IS SAY UNTO YOU, HE THAT ENTERETH NOT   185 30
UNTO THEM AGAIN, VERILY, VERILY, I SAY UNTO YOU,   186 12
VERILY, VERILY, I SAY UNTO YOU, I AM THE DOOR   186 12
SAID UNTO HIM, VERILY, VERILY, I SAY UNTO THEE,   188 05
UNTO HIM, VERILY, VERILY, I SAY UNTO THEE, EXCEPT A   188 05
VERILY, VERILY, I SAY UNTO THEE, EXCEPT A   188 09
JESUS ANSWERED, VERILY, VERILY, I SAY UNTO THEE,   188 09
VERILY, VERILY, I SAY UNTO THEE, WE SPEAK THAT WE DO   188 20
VERILY, VERILY, I SAY UNTO THEE, WE SPEAK THAT WE DO   188 20
VERILY I SAY UNTO THEE, THOU SHALT BY NO MEANS COME   198 15
HAVE GIVEN LIFE, VERILY RIGHTEOUSNESS SHOULD HAVE   208 02
YES VERILY, THEIR SOUND WENT INTO ALL THE EARTH, AND   227 14
SAID UNTO THEM, VERILY I SAY UNTO YOU, THAT YE WHICH   231 14
VERILY, VERILY, I SAY UNTO YOU, HE THAT BELIEVETH ON   240 18
VERILY, VERILY, I SAY UNTO YOU, HE THAT BELIEVETH ON   240 18
AND SAID, VERILY I SAY UNTO YOU, EXCEPT YE BE   252 25
SAY UNTO THEM, VERILY I SAY UNTO YOU, INASMUCH AS YE   259 14
VERILY I SAY UNTO YOU, WHOSOEVER SHALL NOT RECEIVE   274 30
SAID UNTO HIM, VERILY, VERILY, I SAY UNTO THEE,   275 10
UNTO HIM, VERILY, VERILY, I SAY UNTO THEE, EXCEPT A   275 10
JESUS ANSWERED, VERILY, VERILY, I SAY UNTO THEE,   275 14
VERILY, VERILY, I SAY UNTO THEE, EXCEPT A   275 14
YES, VERILY   283 30
VERILY, VERILY, I SAY UNTO YOU, HE THAT HEARETH MY   321 33
VERILY, VERILY, I SAY UNTO YOU, HE THAT HEARETH MY   321 33
VERILY, VERILY, I SAY UNTO YOU, HE THAT   322 21
JESUS SAID, VERILY, VERILY, I SAY UNTO YOU, HE THAT   322 21
AND VERILY EVERY MAN LIVING IS ALTOGETHER VANITY   324 24
THAT I BELIEVE VERILY TO SEE THE GOODNESS OF THE LORD   326 28
AND SAID, VERILY I SAY UNTO YOU, EXCEPT YE BE   339 24
THAT I BELIEVE VERILY TO SEE THE GOODNESS OF THE LORD   372 28
IN THE LAND, AND VERILY THOU SHALT BE FED   384 30
AND VERILY EVERY MAN LIVING IS ALTOGETHER VANITY   389 19
A MAN SHALL SAY, VERILY THERE IS A REWARD FOR THE   410 32
2 HE VERILY IS MY STRENGTH AND MY SALVATION   413 29
VERILY I SAY UNTO YOU, THAT HE SHALL GIRD HIMSELF,   534 21
VERILY, VERILY, I SAY UNTO YOU, HE THAT ENTERETH NOT   538 23
VERILY, VERILY, I SAY UNTO YOU, HE THAT ENTERETH NOT   538 23
UNTO THEM AGAIN, VERILY, VERILY, I SAY UNTO YOU,   539 03
VERILY, VERILY, I SAY UNTO YOU, I AM THE DOOR   539 03
YES, VERILY   577 22

VERITY

OF HIS HANDS ARE VERITY AND JUDGMENT   483 07

VERSE

SUCH A CHAPTER (OR VERSE OF SUCH A CHAPTER) OF SUCH A R 009 33
IN THE — CHAPTER OF —, BEGINNING AT THE — VERSE   R 070 19
IN THE — CHAPTER OF —, BEGINNING AT THE — VERSE   R 070 24
IN THE TENTH CHAPTER, AT THE THIRTEENTH VERSE   274 24

VERSE   CONTINUED

IN THE THIRD CHAPTER, AT THE FIRST VERSE	275 04
TWENTY-EIGHTH CHAPTER, AT THE EIGHTEENTH VERSE	275 25
THE BISHOP ONE VERSE AND THE CLERGY ANOTHER	R 563 09

VERSES

ANSWERING BY VERSES, AS FOLLOWETH	R 543 28
SHALL ANSWER BY VERSES, AS FOLLOWETH	R 556 05

VERSICLES

PASS TO THE VERSICLES, O LORD, OPEN THOU OUR LIPS,	R 003 11
BEFORE THE VERSICLES AND RESPONSES WHICH FOLLOW,	R 003 14
PASS TO THE VERSICLES, O LORD, OPEN THOU OUR LIPS,	R 021 08
AND BEFORE THE VERSICLES AND RESPONSES WHICH FOLLOW	R 021 11

VESSEL

HAND UPON EVERY VESSEL IN WHICH THERE IS ANY WINE TO	R 080 34
TO POSSESS HIS VESSEL IN SANCTIFICATION AND HONOUR	127 29
THERE WAS SET A VESSEL FULL OF VINEGAR	160 26
HE IS A CHOSEN VESSEL UNTO ME, TO BEAR MY NAME BEFORE	230 26
AND BREAK THEM IN PIECES LIKE A POTTER'S VESSEL	346 16
I AM BECOME LIKE A BROKEN VESSEL	376 20

VESSELS

BEEN THE CHOICE VESSELS OF HIS GRACE AND THE LIGHTS	048 17
AND ALL THE VESSELS OF THE MINISTRY	147 24
BEEN THE CHOICE VESSELS OF THY GRACE, AND THE LIGHTS	336 19
AS VESSELS MADE TO HONOUR	606 10

VESTED

ELECTED BISHOP, VESTED WITH HIS ROCHET, SHALL BE	R 552 17

VESTRY

MEMBERS OF THE VESTRY) STANDING ON THE RIGHT AND LEFT	R 570 07
THE MEMBER OF THE VESTRY SUPPLYING HIS PLACE) HOLDING	R 570 09
THE MEMBER OF THE VESTRY SUPPLYING HIS PLACE) PRESENT	R 570 25
THE WARDENS, VESTRY, AND OTHERS, SHALL SALUTE AND	R 574 27

VESTRYMEN

AND VESTRYMEN, OR SOME OTHER PERSONS APPOINTED FOR	R 563 06

VESTURE

AND AS A VESTURE SHALT THOU FOLD THEM UP, AND THEY	097 16
AND UPON MY VESTURE DID THEY CAST LOTS	136 33
AND FOR MY VESTURE THEY DID CAST LOTS	160 16
AND CAST LOTS UPON MY VESTURE	367 09
THE QUEEN IN A VESTURE OF GOLD, WROUGHT ABOUT WITH	397 03
27 AND AS A VESTURE SHALT THOU CHANGE THEM, AND THEY	466 02

VEX

FORTH HIS HANDS TO VEX CERTAIN OF THE CHURCH	244 32
FORTH HIS HANDS TO VEX CERTAIN OF THE CHURCH	246 32
AND VEX THEM IN HIS SORE DISPLEASURE	346 07
TALK HOW THEY MAY VEX THEM WHOM THOU HAST WOUNDED	423 28
ALL THEM THAT VEX MY SOUL	519 18

VEXED

IS GRIEVOUSLY VEXED WITH A DEVIL	128 11
THEY REBELLED, AND VEXED HIS HOLY SPIRIT	139 05
THEM WHICH WERE VEXED WITH UNCLEAN SPIRITS	249 31
WHEN MY HEART IS VEXED, I WILL COMPLAIN	311 05
HEAL ME, FOR MY BONES ARE VEXED	349 03
MINE ENEMIES SHALL BE CONFOUNDED, AND SORE VEXED	349 19
MY SOUL, AND BE SO VEXED IN MY HEART	355 31
8 MY SOUL IS VEXED WITHIN ME	393 15
14 WHY ART THOU SO VEXED, O MY SOUL	393 31
HOW I MOURN IN MY PRAYER, AND AM VEXED	406 22
WHEN MY HEART IS VEXED, I WILL COMPLAIN	433 22
BE CONFOUNDED AND VEXED EVER MORE AND MORE	445 06
AND THOU HAST VEXED ME WITH ALL THY STORMS	449 10
SLAY HIM THAT WAS VEXED AT THE HEART	480 34
A TIME HAVE THEY VEXED ME FROM MY YOUTH UP	506 23
IS MY SPIRIT VEXED WITHIN ME, *	518 30

VICE

OF WICKEDNESS AND VICE, AND TO THE MAINTENANCE OF THY	074 19
BOLDLY REBUKE VICE, AND PATIENTLY SUFFER FOR THE	242 12
WICKEDNESS AND VICE, AND MAINTAIN THY TRUE RELIGION	590 29

VICES

AND KILL ALL VICES IN US, AND SO STRENGTHEN US BY THY	102 24

VICIOUSNESS

OR FOR VICIOUSNESS IN LIFE	540 22

VICTORY

GIVETH US THE VICTORY THROUGH OUR LORD JESUS CHRIST	022 17
HATH HE GOTTEN HIMSELF THE VICTORY	027 07
WHO ART THE ONLY GIVER OF ALL VICTORY	041 15
AND THE VICTORY, AND THE MAJESTY	073 19
AND THIS IS THE VICTORY THAT OVERCOMETH THE WORLD,	170 27

VICTORY   CONTINUED

STRENGTH TO HAVE VICTORY, AND TO TRIUMPH, AGAINST THE	278 25
DEATH IS SWALLOWED UP IN VICTORY	330 10
O GRAVE, WHERE IS THY VICTORY	330 11
GIVETH US THE VICTORY THROUGH OUR LORD JESUS CHRIST	330 13
GIVEST HIM NOT VICTORY IN THE BATTLE	452 27
HATH HE GOTTEN HIMSELF THE VICTORY	461 28
THOU HAST GIVEN VICTORY UNTO KINGS, *	520 10
AND THY SERVANTS EVERYWHERE, THE ETERNAL VICTORY	598 11

VICTUALS

WILL BLESS HER VICTUALS WITH INCREASE, *	509 04

VIEW

HIS HAND, IN OPEN VIEW, THE BISHOP, OR THE PRIEST WHO	R 570 10

VIGILANT

BE SOBER, BE VIGILANT	193 04
OF ONE WIFE, VIGILANT, SOBER, OF GOOD BEHAVIOUR,	549 20

VIGOUR

HEALTH OF BODY, VIGOUR OF MIND, AND CHEERFULNESS OF	315 30

VILLAGE

GO INTO THE VILLAGE OVER AGAINST YOU, AND STRAIGHTWAY	091 14
SAME DAY TO A VILLAGE CALLED EMMAUS, WHICH WAS FROM	167 04
NIGH UNTO THE VILLAGE, WHITHER THEY WENT	167 34
INTO A CERTAIN VILLAGE, THERE MET HIM TEN MEN THAT	210 02

VINE

OF THE FRUIT OF THE VINE, UNTIL THAT DAY THAT I DRINK	141 15
OF THE FRUIT OF THE VINE, UNTIL THE KINGDOM OF GOD	149 07
I AM THE TRUE VINE, AND MY FATHER IS THE HUSBANDMAN	238 05
BEAR FRUIT OF ITSELF, EXCEPT IT ABIDE IN THE VINE	238 11
I AM THE VINE, YE ARE THE BRANCHES	238 12
THOU HAST BROUGHT A VINE OUR OF EGYPT	441 18
BEHOLD, AND VISIT THIS VINE	441 31
BE AS THE FRUITFUL VINE *	506 10

VINEGAR

THEY GAVE HIM VINEGAR TO DRINK MINGLED WITH GALL	136 29
FILLED IT WITH VINEGAR, AND PUT IT ON A REED, AND	137 22
A SPUNGE FULL OF VINEGAR, AND PUT IT ON A REED,	146 32
AND OFFERING HIM VINEGAR, AND SAYING, IF THOU BE THE	154 31
NOW THERE WAS SET A VESSEL FULL OF VINEGAR	160 26
A SPUNGE WITH VINEGAR, AND PUT IT UPON HYSSOP,	160 27
HAD RECEIVED THE VINEGAR, HE SAID, IT IS FINISHED	160 28
THEY GAVE ME VINEGAR TO DRINK	423 17

VINES

HE DESTROYED THEIR VINES WITH HAILSTONES, *	438 02
33 HE SMOTE THEIR VINES ALSO AND FIG-TREES	472 04

VINEYARD

THE MORNING TO HIRE LABOURERS INTO HIS VINEYARD	119 17
HE SENT THEM INTO HIS VINEYARD	119 19
ALSO INTO THE VINEYARD, AND WHATSOEVER IS RIGHT I	119 21
GO YE ALSO INTO THE VINEYARD	119 27
THE LORD OF THE VINEYARD SAITH UNTO HIS STEWARD,	119 29
PLACE OF THE VINEYARD THAT THY RIGHT HAND HATH	441 32
CALL AND SEND MINISTERS INTO THE LORD'S VINEYARD	607 24

VINEYARDS

AND PLANT VINEYARDS, *	478 20

VIOLENCE

SAVE US FROM VIOLENCE, DISCORD, AND CONFUSION	036 13
AND FROM THE VIOLENCE OF THE ENEMY	042 07
FROM THE VIOLENCE OF ENEMIES, AND FROM EVERY EVIL TO	046 13
23 THE ENEMY SHALL NOT BE ABLE TO DO HIM VIOLENCE	451 19

VIOLENT

THE OUTRAGE OF A VIOLENT AND UNRULY PEOPLE	052 19
CONGREGATIONS OF VIOLENT MEN HAVE SOUGHT AFTER MY	448 02

VIRGIN

THOU DIDST HUMBLE THYSELF TO BE BORN OF A VIRGIN	010 27
BORN OF THE VIRGIN MARY	015 22
HOLY GHOST OF THE VIRGIN MARY, AND WAS MADE MAN	016 08
BORN OF THE VIRGIN MARY	029 27
HOLY GHOST OF THE VIRGIN MARY, AND WAS MADE MAN	030 13
HOLY GHOST OF THE VIRGIN MARY, AND WAS MADE MAN	071 10
SUBSTANCE OF THE VIRGIN MARY HIS MOTHER	077 17
AND AS AT THIS TIME TO BE BORN OF A PURE VIRGIN	096 15
AND AS AT THIS TIME TO BE BORN OF A PURE VIRGIN	104 07
BEHOLD, A VIRGIN SHALL BE WITH CHILD, AND	105 10
BEHOLD, A VIRGIN SHALL CONCEIVE, AND BEAR A SON, AND	235 31
TO A VIRGIN ESPOUSED TO A MAN WHOSE NAME	236 07
BORN OF THE VIRGIN MARY	284 16
BORN OF THE VIRGIN MARY	577 31
OF THE BLESSED VIRGIN, OF HER SUBSTANCE	603 11

VIRGIN'S

AND THE VIRGIN'S NAME WAS MARY   236 08

VIRGINITY

WITH AN HUSBAND SEVEN YEARS FROM HER VIRGINITY   233 18

VIRGINS

FOR THEY ARE VIRGINS   103 09
THE VIRGINS THAT BE HER FELLOWS SHALL BEAR HER   397 15

VIRTUE

GRACE AND VIRTUE DECLARED IN ALL HIS SAINTS, WHO HAVE   048 16
THE MAINTENANCE OF THY TRUE RELIGION, AND VIRTUE   074 20
GRACE AND VIRTUE DECLARED IN ALL THY SAINTS, WHO HAVE   336 18
AND UPON SUCH AS EXCEL IN VIRTUE   357 26
AND MAINTAIN THY TRUE RELIGION AND VIRTUE   590 44
THEM WITH FAITH, VIRTUE, KNOWLEDGE, TEMPERANCE,   598 24
INCREASED BY VIRTUE OF PRAYER UNTO GOD   608 30

VIRTUES

PEACE AND OF ALL VIRTUES, WITHOUT WHICH WHOSOEVER   122 17
WITH HEAVENLY VIRTUES, AND EVERLASTINGLY REWARDED,   278 29

VIRTUOUS

SAINTS IN ALL VIRTUOUS AND GODLY LIVING, THAT WE MAY   256 08
TO BE A MAN OF VIRTUOUS CONVERSATION, AND WITHOUT   529 27

VISIBLE

OF ALL THINGS VISIBLE AND INVISIBLE   015 34
OF ALL THINGS VISIBLE AND INVISIBLE   030 05
THE WITNESS OF VISIBLE UNITY   047 10
OF ALL THINGS VISIBLE AND INVISIBLE   071 03
AN OUTWARD AND VISIBLE SIGN OF AN INWARD AND   292 11
THE OUTWARD AND VISIBLE SIGN, AND THE INWARD AND   292 16
THE OUTWARD AND VISIBLE SIGN OR FORM IN BAPTISM   292 17
THE OUTWARD AND VISIBLE SIGN OR FORM IN BAPTISM IS   292 19
AN OUTWARD AND VISIBLE SIGN OF AN INWARD AND   581 12
THE OUTWARD VISIBLE SIGN, AND THE INWARD SPIRITUAL   581 17
IS THE OUTWARD VISIBLE SIGN OR FORM IN BAPTISM   581 19
ALL THINGS BOTH VISIBLE AND INVISIBLE   603 05
THE VISIBLE CHURCH OF CHRIST IS A CONGREGATION OF   606 38
HAVE NOT ANY VISIBLE SIGN OR CEREMONY ORDAINED OF   607 43
ALTHOUGH IN THE VISIBLE CHURCH THE EVIL BE EVER   608 08

VISIBLY

HOLY GHOST, ARE VISIBLY SIGNED AND SEALED   608 29
DO CARNALLY AND VISIBLY PRESS WITH THEIR TEETH (AS   609 05

VISION

HAD ALSO SEEN A VISION OF ANGELS, WHICH SAID THAT HE   167 25
THE LORD IN A VISION, ANANIAS   230 15
HATH SEEN IN A VISION A MAN NAMED ANANIAS COMING IN,   230 19
BUT THOUGHT HE SAW A VISION   245 20

VISIONS

SOMETIME IN VISIONS UNTO THY SAINTS, AND SAIDST, *   451 12

VISIT

THEE TO BEHOLD, VISIT, AND RELIEVE THY SICK SERVANT   045 14
A JEALOUS GOD, AND VISIT THE SINS OF THE FATHERS UPON   068 12
CHRIST CAME TO VISIT US IN GREAT HUMILITY   090 14
FATHER IS THIS, TO VISIT THE FATHERLESS AND WIDOWS IN   176 16
FATHER IS THIS, TO VISIT THE FATHERLESS AND WIDOWS IN   266 07
A JEALOUS GOD, AND VISIT THE SINS OF THE FATHERS UPON   286 12
BEHOLD, VISIT, AND RELIEVE THIS THY SERVANT   309 04
VISIT HIM, O LORD, WITH THY LOVING MERCY, AND SO   309 29
BUT DIDST VISIT HIM WITH COMFORTS FROM ABOVE   315 25
THE LORD, AND TO VISIT HIS TEMPLE   326 11
THE LORD, AND TO VISIT HIS TEMPLE   372 03
GOD OF ISRAEL, TO VISIT ALL THE HEATHEN, *   411 14
BEHOLD, VISIT, AND VISIT THIS VINE   441 31
I WILL VISIT THEIR OFFENCES WITH THE ROD, AND THEIR   452 05
O VISIT ME WITH THY SALVATION   473 07
OF THE FAITHFUL, VISIT, WE PRAY THEE, THIS   572 25
A JEALOUS GOD, AND VISIT THE SINS OF THE FATHERS UPON   578 31

VISITATION

BY THY LATE VISITATION OF US WITH IMMODERATE RAIN AND   051 23
BEHOLD, GLORIFY GOD IN THE DAY OF VISITATION   173 17
THOU KNEWEST NOT THE TIME OF THY VISITATION   204 15
OF SUDDEN VISITATION, HAVE THE LESS CAUSE TO BE   R 321 10

VISITED

FOR HE HATH VISITED AND REDEEMED HIS PEOPLE   014 08
ON HIGH HATH VISITED US   014 30
THAT GOD HATH VISITED HIS PEOPLE   213 09
FOR HE HATH VISITED AND REDEEMED HIS PEOPLE, AND HATH   243 33
ON HIGH HATH VISITED US, TO GIVE LIGHT TO THEM THAT   244 14
WAS SICK, AND YE VISITED ME   259 08
THIS THY SERVANT VISITED WITH THINE HAND, AND TO   321 21
HAST PROVED AND VISITED MINE HEART IN THE NIGHT   358 21

VISITEST

THAT THOU VISITEST HIM   351 08
9 THOU VISITEST THE EARTH, AND BLESSEST IT   416 32

VOCATION

IN HIS VOCATION AND MINISTRY, MAY TRULY AND   156 31
WORTHY OF THE VOCATION WHEREWITH YE ARE CALLED, WITH   213 19
IN HIS VOCATION AND MINISTRY, MAY SERVE THEE   590 26

VOICE

AND HUMBLE VOICE, UNTO THE THRONE OF THE   006 11
HAVE WE OBEYED THE VOICE OF THE LORD OUR GOD, TO WALK   022 08
AND HUMBLE VOICE, UNTO THE THRONE OF THE   023 20
HEARKEN UNTO THE VOICE OF HIS WORD   029 14
HE SAID, I AM THE VOICE OF ONE CRYING IN THE   095 28
OUT WITH A LOUD VOICE, AND STOPPED THEIR EARS, AND   100 09
CRIED WITH A LOUD VOICE, LORD, LAY NOT THIS SIN TO   100 15
AS THE VOICE OF MANY WATERS, AND AS THE VOICE   103 02
AND I HEARD A VOICE FROM HEAVEN, AS THE VOICE OF MANY   103 02
AND I HEARD THE VOICE OF HARPERS HARPING WITH THEIR   103 03
AND AS THE VOICE OF A GREAT THUNDER   103 03
RAMA WAS THERE A VOICE HEARD, LAMENTATION, AND   103 31
THE VOICE OF ONE CRYING IN THE WILDERNESS, PREPARE YE   112 06
AND THERE CAME A VOICE FROM HEAVEN, SAYING, THOU ART   112 22
LIFTED UP HER VOICE, AND SAID UNTO HIM, BLESSED IS   130 18
CRIED WITH A LOUD VOICE, SAYING, ELI, ELI, LAMA   137 17
AGAIN WITH A LOUD VOICE, YIELDED UP THE GHOST   137 25
THAT OBEYETH THE VOICE OF HIS SERVANT, THAT WALKETH   144 24
CRIED WITH A LOUD VOICE, SAYING, ELOI, ELOI, LAMA   146 28
CRIED WITH A LOUD VOICE, AND GAVE UP THE GHOST   146 34
CRIED WITH A LOUD VOICE, HE SAID, FATHER, INTO THY   155 12
AND THEY SHALL HEAR MY VOICE   172 31
AND THE SHEEP HEAR HIS VOICE   186 04
FOR THEY KNOW HIS VOICE   186 08
THEY KNOW NOT THE VOICE OF STRANGERS   186 09
AND THE FIRST VOICE WHICH I HEARD WAS AS IT WERE OF A   186 32
AND WITH A LOUD VOICE GLORIFIED GOD, AND FELL DOWN ON   210 08
AND HEARD A VOICE SAYING UNTO HIM, SAUL, SAUL,   229 32
HEARING A VOICE, BUT SEEING NO MAN   230 09
THE VOICE OF HIM THAT CRIETH IN THE WILDERNESS,   242 20
THE VOICE SAID, CRY   242 27
LIFT UP THY VOICE WITH STRENGTH   243 04
THERE CAME SUCH A VOICE TO HIM FROM THE EXCELLENT   248 18
AND THIS VOICE WHICH CAME FROM HEAVEN WE HEARD, WHEN   248 19
AND THERE CAME A VOICE OUT OF THE CLOUD, SAYING,   249 07
AND WHEN THE VOICE WAS PAST, JESUS WAS FOUND ALONE   249 08
AND I HEARD A LOUD VOICE SAYING IN HEAVEN, NOW IS   252 10
CRIED WITH A LOUD VOICE TO THE FOUR ANGELS, TO WHOM   256 16
CRIED WITH A LOUD VOICE, SAYING, SALVATION TO OUR GOD   256 27
A SHOUT, WITH THE VOICE OF THE ARCHANGEL, AND WITH   269 06
HE HATH HEARD THE VOICE OF MY PRAYER   305 19
I DID CALL UPON THE LORD WITH MY VOICE   309 11
THE LORD WITH MY VOICE, AND HE HEARD ME OUT OF HIS   309 20
I WILL CRY UNTO GOD WITH MY VOICE   310 29
WILL I CRY WITH MY VOICE, AND HE SHALL HEARKEN UNTO   310 30
HEARKEN UNTO THE VOICE OF HIS WORD   312 30
HEARKEN UNTO MY VOICE, O LORD, WHEN I CRY UNTO THEE   326 20
HEAR MY VOICE   328 04
THE VOICE OF MY COMPLAINT   328 05
OR SUNG, I HEARD A VOICE FROM HEAVEN, SAYING UNTO ME,   333 25
WHO BY A VOICE FROM HEAVEN DIDST PROCLAIM,   335 26
AND HEAR THAT HIS MOST JOYFUL VOICE   336 26
THE LORD WITH MY VOICE, *   346 31
THOU UNTO THE VOICE OF MY CALLING, MY KING AND MY   347 32
3 MY VOICE SHALT THOU HEAR BETIMES, O LORD   348 04
HATH HEARD THE VOICE OF MY WEEPING   349 15
7 SO HE HEARD MY VOICE OUT OF HIS HOLY TEMPLE,   360 06
I MAY SHOW THE VOICE OF THANKSGIVING, *   371 10
8 HEARKEN UNTO MY VOICE, O LORD, WHEN I CRY UNTO   372 12
2 HEAR THE VOICE OF MY HUMBLE PETITIONS, WHEN I CRY   373 07
HE HATH HEARD THE VOICE OF MY HUMBLE PETITIONS   373 20
3 THE VOICE OF THE LORD IS UPON THE WATERS   374 02
THE VOICE OF THE LORD IS MIGHTY IN OPERATION   374 04
THE VOICE OF THE LORD IS A GLORIOUS VOICE   374 05
THE VOICE OF THE LORD IS A GLORIOUS VOICE   374 06
5 THE VOICE OF THE LORD BREAKETH THE CEDAR-TREES   374 07
7 THE VOICE OF THE LORD DIVIDETH THE FLAMES OF FIRE   374 11
THE VOICE OF THE LORD SHAKETH THE WILDERNESS   374 12
8 THE VOICE OF THE LORD MAKETH THE HINDS TO BRING   374 14
THOU HEARDEST THE VOICE OF MY PRAYER, *   377 13
5 IN THE VOICE OF PRAISE AND THANKSGIVING, *   393 09
17 FOR THE VOICE OF THE SLANDERER AND BLASPHEMER,   395 26
HATH SHOWED HIS VOICE, AND THE EARTH SHALL MELT AWAY   398 05
UNTO GOD WITH THE VOICE OF MELODY   398 22
AND HE SHALL HEAR MY VOICE   407 26
TO HEAR THE VOICE OF THE CHARMER, *   410 17
HEAR MY VOICE, O GOD, IN MY PRAYER   415 19
AND MAKE THE VOICE OF HIS PRAISE TO BE HEARD   417 29
AND CONSIDERED THE VOICE OF MY PRAYER   418 18
HE DOTH SEND OUT HIS VOICE   421 23
AND THAT A MIGHTY VOICE   421 24
24 FORGET NOT THE VOICE OF THINE ENEMIES   431 24
I WILL CRY UNTO GOD WITH MY VOICE   433 16
WILL I CRY WITH MY VOICE, AND HE SHALL HEARKEN UNTO   433 17
18 THE VOICE OF THY THUNDER WAS HEARD ROUND ABOUT   434 18
12 BUT MY PEOPLE WOULD NOT HEAR MY VOICE   443 02
AND PONDER THE VOICE OF MY HUMBLE DESIRES   447 16
THE FLOODS HAVE LIFT UP THEIR VOICE   457 12
YE WILL HEAR HIS VOICE, HARDEN NOT YOUR HEARTS *   459 19
5 FOR THE VOICE OF MY GROANING, *   464 19
HEARKEN UNTO THE VOICE OF HIS WORD   467 17
AT THE VOICE OF THY THUNDER THEY HASTE AWAY   468 06

VOICE CONTINUED

NOT UNTO THE VOICE OF THE LORD 474 20
HE HATH HEARD THE VOICE OF MY PRAYER 486 20
15 THE VOICE OF JOY AND HEALTH IS IN THE DWELLINGS OF 488 30
149 HEAR MY VOICE, O LORD, ACCCRDING UNTO THY 500 08
HEAR MY VOICE 507 09
THE VOICE OF MY COMPLAINT 507 10
HEAR THE VOICE OF MY PRAYERS, O LORD 516 21
AND CONSIDER MY VOICE, WHEN I CRY UNTO THEE 517 09
I CRIED UNTO THE LORD WITH MY VOICE 518 03
AND THE SHEEP HEAR HIS VOICE 538 27
FOR THEY KNOW HIS VOICE 538 31
THEY KNOW NOT THE VOICE OF STRANGERS 538 32
AND THEY SHALL HEAR MY VOICE 539 20
HEARKEN UNTO OUR VOICE, O LORD, WHEN WE CRY UNTC 561 31
I HEARD A GREAT VOICE OUT OF HEAVEN SAYING, BEHCLD, 567 14

VOICES

INSTANT WITH LOUD VOICES, REQUIRING THAT HE MIGHT BE 154 03
AND THE VOICES OF THEM AND OF THE CHIEF PRIESTS 154 04
NOR YET THE VOICES OF THE PROPHETS WHICH ARE 168 23
PROCEEDED LIGHTNINGS AND THUNDERINGS AND VOICES 187 12
LIFTED UP THEIR VOICES, AND SAID, JESUS, MASTER, 210 04
BUT THEIR VOICES ARE HEARD AMONG THEM 363 18

VOID

THEIR HABITATION BE VCID, * 423 25
WITH A CONSCIENCE VOID OF OFFENCE TOWARDS THEE, AND 590 18
HE WAS CLEARLY VOID, BOTH IN HIS FLESH, AND IN HIS 605 32
AND SUCH AS BE VOID OF A LIVELY FAITH, ALTHOUGH THEY 609 04

VOLUME

I COME (IN THE VOLUME OF THE BOOK IT IS WRITTEN CF 157 27
10 IN THE VOLUME OF THE BOOK IT IS WRITTEN OF ME, 390 31

VOLUNTARY

VOLUNTARY WORKS BESIDES, OVER AND ABOVE, GOD'S 605 24

VOTE

POSSESSED OF YOUR VOTE THAT HE HAS BEEN SO ELECTEC 570 15

VOUCHSAFE

VOUCHSAFE, O LORD, TO KEEP US THIS DAY WITHOUT SIN 011 08
GREAT MERCY VOUCHSAFE, WE BESEECH THEE, SO TO DIRECT, 036 32
VOUCHSAFE TO BLESS THE LANDS AND MULTIPLY THE 040 07
VOUCHSAFE TO TAKE INTO THY ALMIGHTY AND MOST GRACIOUS 042 04
WE CANNOT ASK, VOUCHSAFE TO GIVE US, FOR THE 050 03
NOW AND EVER VOUCHSAFE TO HEAR US, O CHRIST 059 15
VOUCHSAFE, WE BESEECH THEE, TO DIRECT, SANCTIFY, 070 06
VOUCHSAFE TO BLESS AND SANCTIFY, WITH THY 081 09
THAT THOU DOST VOUCHSAFE TO FEED US WHO HAVE DULY 083 17
SON OF GOD DID VOUCHSAFE TO YIELD UP HIS SOUL BY 089 10
VOUCHSAFE, WE BESEECH THEE, TO THY WHCLE CHURCH IN 268 15
CHRIST WOULD VOUCHSAFE TO RECEIVE HIM, TO RELEASE HIM 276 21
CHRIST WOULD VOUCHSAFE TO RECEIVE YOU, TO RELEASE YOU 277 22
VOUCHSAFE, WE BESEECH THEE, TO DIRECT, SANCTIFY, 298 26
VOUCHSAFE THAT WE, WHO NOW SERVE THEE HERE ON 335 31
CREATOR BLEST, VOUCHSAFE WITHIN OUR SOULS TO REST 544 18
CREATOR BLEST, VOUCHSAFE WITHIN OUR SOULS TC REST 556 26
VOUCHSAFE, O LORD, TO BE PRESENT WITH US, WHO ARE 565 02
AND VOUCHSAFE TO GIVE WHATEVER IN THY 566 21
INTO SIN, VOUCHSAFE US, WE BESEECH THEE, THE 590 11
VOUCHSAFE US THIS DAY SUCH BLESSING THROUGH OUR 595 14

VOUCHSAFED

LATE MERCIES VOUCHSAFED UNTO THEM 019 19
FOR MERCIES VOUCHSAFED TO THEM R 019 33
LATE MERCIES VOUCHSAFED UNTO THEM 033 17
FOR MERCIES VOUCHSAFED TO THEM R 033 31
THOU HAST VOUCHSAFED TO CALL US TO THE KNOWLEDGE OF 276 09
WHO HAST VOUCHSAFED TO REGENERATE THESE THY 297 14
GOODNESS HAST VOUCHSAFED TO ACCEPT AND TAKE THESE THY 534 31
THOU HAST VOUCHSAFED TO CALL THESE THY SERVANTS HERE 545 22

VOW

DID PROMISE AND VOW THREE THINGS IN MY NAME 283 22
SOLEMN PROMISE AND VOW THAT YE MADE, OR THAT WAS MADE 296 23
PERFORM AND KEEP THE VOW AND COVENANT BETWIXT THEM 303 08
UNTO THEE SHALL THE VOW BE PERFORMED IN JERUSALEM 416 12
AND VOWED A VOW UNTO THE ALMIGHTY GOD OF JACOB 508 06
PERFORM AND KEEP THE VOW AND COVENANT BETWIXT THEM 566 10
THEY DID PROMISE AND VOW THREE THINGS IN MY NAME 577 13
GOD'S LAW, EITHER TO VOW THE ESTATE OF SINGLE LIFE, 609 22

VOWED

PROMISED AND VOWED THAT YOU SHOULD BELIEVE ALL THE 284 07
PROMISED AND VOWED THAT YOU SHOULD KEEP GOD'S HCLY 285 13
AND VOWED A VOW UNTO THE ALMIGHTY GOD OF JACOB 508 06

VOWS

THE PROMISES AND VOWS OF MY BAPTISM, AND DECLARING MY 291 25
THE PROMISES AND VOWS OF THEIR BAPTISM, AND BE 294 25
I WILL PAY MY VOWS NOW IN THE PRESENCE OF ALL HIS 305 31
MY VOWS WILL I PERFORM IN THE SIGHT OF THEM THAT FEAR 367 24
AND PAY THY VOWS UNTO THE MOST HIGHEST 402 18

VOWS CONTINUED

O GOD, WILL I PAY MY VOWS 409 06
THAT I MAY DAILY PERFORM MY VOWS 413 23
WILL PAY THEE MY VOWS, * 418 08
13 I WILL PAY MY VOWS NOW IN THE PRESENCE OF ALL HIS 487 13
16 I WILL PAY MY VOWS UNTO THE LORD, IN THE SIGHT OF 487 21
THE PROMISES AND VOWS OF THEIR BAPTISM, AND BE 565 24

WAGES

FOR THE WAGES OF SIN IS DEATH 199 04
HIRELING IN HIS WAGES, THE WIDOW, AND THE FATHERLESS, 232 18

WAGGING

BY REVILED HIM, WAGGING THEIR HEADS, AND SAYING, 137 06
RAILED ON HIM, WAGGING THEIR HEADS, AND SAYING, AH, 146 18

WAIT

OR MINISTRY, LET US WAIT ON OUR MINISTERING 111 18
FROM JERUSALEM, BUT WAIT FOR THE PROMISE OF THE 177 31
WHEREBY THEY LIE IN WAIT TO DECEIVE 237 28
MY SOUL DOTH WAIT FOR HIM 328 11
RIGHTEOUS DEALING WAIT UPON ME 370 26
HATH LAID GREAT WAIT FOR ME 392 18
8 WE WAIT FOR THY LOVING-KINDNESS, O GCD, * 399 27
WHEN THEY LAY WAIT FOR MY SOUL 408 27
MY SOUL, WAIT THOU STILL UPON GOD 414 07
AND THEY THAT LAY WAIT FOR MY SOUL TAKE THEIR COUNSEL 425 26
27 THESE WAIT ALL UPON THEE, * 469 14
95 THE UNGODLY LAID WAIT FOR ME, TO DESTROY ME 496 15
EVEN SO OUR EYES WAIT UPON THE LORD OUR GOD, UNTIL HE 503 31
MY SOUL DOTH WAIT FOR HIM 507 16
15 THE EYES OF ALL WAIT UPON THEE, O LORD 521 22
LIKE UNTO MEN THAT WAIT FOR THEIR LORD, WHEN HE WILL 534 17
ME BY THE LYING IN WAIT OF THE JEWS 550 10

WAITED

OF GOD WAITED IN THE DAYS OF NOAH, WHILE THE ARK WAS 161 27
I WAITED PATIENTLY FOR THE LORD, * 390 09

WAITETH

OF THE CREATURE WAITETH FOR THE MANIFESTATICN CF THE 194 14
OF THE CREATURE WAITETH FOR THE MANIFESTATION OF THE 330 29
MY SOUL TRULY WAITETH STILL UPON GOD 413 27

WAITING

WAITING FOR THE ADOPTION, TO WIT, THE 194 22
WAITING FOR THE COMING OF OUR LORD JESUS CHRIST 214 32
JUST AND DEVOUT, WAITING FOR THE CONSOLATION OF 232 31
9 FOR HE LIETH WAITING SECRETLY 353 23
11 THEY LIE WAITING IN OUR WAY ON EVERY SIDE, 359 08
FOR LO, THEY LIE WAITING FOR MY SOUL 411 08
FAILETH ME FOR WAITING SO LONG UPON MY GOD 422 06

WAKE

WHEN I WAKE UP, I AM PRESENT WITH THEE 515 27

WAKETH

THE WATCHMAN WAKETH BUT IN VAIN 505 24

WAKING

THOU HOLDEST MINE EYES WAKING 311 06
AND THOUGHT UPON THEE WHEN I WAS WAKING 415 06
4 THOU HOLDEST MINE EYES WAKING 433 23

WALK

TO THY WILL, AND WALK IN THY WAY 017 33
LORD OUR GOD, TO WALK IN HIS LAWS WHICH HE SET BEFORE 022 08
OBEDIENTLY WALK IN THY HOLY COMMANDMENTS 052 23
PREPARED FOR US TO WALK IN 083 29
LET US WALK HONESTLY, AS IN THE DAY 091 05
AND THE LAME WALK, THE LEPERS ARE CLEANSED, 094 21
SAINT JOHN, MAY SO WALK IN THE LIGHT OF THY TRUTH, 101 08
WITH HIM, AND WALK IN DARKNESS, WE LIE, AND DO NCT 101 25
BUT IF WE WALK IN THE LIGHT, AS HE IS IN THE LIGHT, 101 26
US HOW YE OUGHT TO WALK AND TO PLEASE GOD, SO YE 127 25
AND WALK IN LOVE, AS CHRIST ALSO HATH LOVED US, 128 31
WALK AS CHILDREN OF LIGHT 129 13
WALK IN THE LIGHT OF YOUR FIRE, AND IN THE SPARKS 144 27
TO ANOTHER, AS YE WALK, AND ARE SAD 167 11
SO WE ALSO SHOULD WALK IN NEWNESS OF LIFE 197 14
I SAY THEN, WALK IN THE SPIRIT, AND YE SHALL NOT 209 14
AND AS MANY AS WALK ACCORDING TO THIS RULE, PEACE BE 211 02
BESEECH YOU THAT YE WALK WORTHY OF THE VOCATION 213 19
AS OTHER GENTILES WALK, IN THE VANITY OF THEIR MIND, 216 04
THAT YE HENCEFORTH WALK NOT AS OTHER GENTILES WALK, 216 04
OR TO SAY, ARISE, AND WALK 217 08
SEE THEN THAT YE WALK CIRCUMSPECTLY, NOT AS FCCLS, 217 23
AND MARK THEM WHICH WALK SO AS YE HAVE US FOR AN 222 16
FOR MANY WALK, OF WHOM I HAVE TOLD YOU OFTEN, 222 17
THAT YE MIGHT WALK WORTHY OF THE LORD UNTO ALL 224 04
WE MAY STEDFASTLY WALK IN THE WAY THAT LEADETH TC 239 02
AND WALK IN THE SAME ALL THE DAYS OF 277 05
AND WALK IN THE SAME ALL THE DAYS OF 278 14
AND WALK IN THE SAME ALL THE DAYS OF MY 283 28
OF YOURSELF, NOR TO WALK IN THE COMMANDMENTS OF GOD, 289 14

WALK   CONTINUED

COME YE, AND LET US WALK IN THE LIGHT OF THE LORD	290 05
AND WE WILL WALK IN HIS PATHS	290 06
THOUGH I WALK IN THE MIDST OF TROUBLE	311 25
THOUGH I WALK IN THE MIDST OF TROUBLE, YET SHALT THOU	312 04
AND WHO WALK AS YET BY FAITH, THAT HAVING	336 07
THOUGH I WALK THROUGH THE VALLEY OF THE SHADOW	338 23
9 THE UNGODLY WALK ON EVERY SIDE	355 25
4 YEA, THOUGH I WALK THROUGH THE VALLEY OF THE SHADOW	368 16
AND I WILL WALK IN THY TRUTH	371 03
AS FOR ME, I WILL WALK INNOCENTLY	371 18
11 WALK ABOUT SION, AND GO ROUND ABOUT HER	399 33
THAT I MAY WALK BEFORE GOD IN THE LIGHT OF THE	409 09
AND WOULD NOT WALK IN HIS LAW	435 21
BUT WALK ON STILL IN DARKNESS	443 26
O LORD, AND I WILL WALK IN THY TRUTH	447 25
THEY SHALL WALK IN THE LIGHT OF THY COUNTENANCE	451 05
AND WALK NOT IN MY JUDGMENTS	452 02
I WILL WALK IN MY HOUSE WITH A PERFECT HEART	463 20
FEET HAVE THEY, AND WALK NOT	485 25
9 I WILL WALK BEFORE THE LORD *	487 06
AND WALK IN THE LAW OF THE LORD	489 32
AND WALK IN HIS WAYS	490 04
45 AND I WILL WALK AT LIBERTY	492 29
AND WALK IN HIS WAYS	506 06
7 THOUGH I WALK IN THE MIDST OF TROUBLE, YET SHALT	514 10
WAY THAT I SHOULD WALK IN	519 09
THAT SO THEY MAY WALK IN THE WAYS OF TRUTH AND PEACE,	574 18
AND WALK IN THE SAME ALL THE DAYS OF MY	577 18
OF THYSELF, NOR TO WALK IN THE COMMANDMENTS OF GOD,	580 17
THEY WALK RELIGIOUSLY IN GOOD WORKS, AND AT LENGTH,	606 14

WALKED

MAN THAT HATH NOT WALKED IN THE COUNSEL OF THE	345 07
FOR I HAVE WALKED INNOCENTLY	370 30
AND WALKED IN THE HOUSE OF GOD AS FRIENDS	407 18
FOR IF ISRAEL HAD WALKED IN MY WAYS, 15 I SHOULD SOON	443 07
THE WAY WHEREIN I WALKED, HAVE THEY PRIVILY LAID A	518 08

WALKETH

OUT OF A MAN, HE WALKETH THROUGH DRY PLACES, SEEKING	130 11
THAT WALKETH IN DARKNESS, AND HATH NO LIGHT	144 24
A ROARING LION, WALKETH ABOUT, SEEKING WHOM HE MAY	193 05
FOR MAN WALKETH IN A VAIN SHADOW, AND DISQUIETETH	324 25
AND WHATSOEVER WALKETH THROUGH THE PATHS OF THE SEAS	351 16
7 FOR MAN WALKETH IN A VAIN SHADOW, AND DISQUIETETH	389 20
PESTILENCE THAT WALKETH IN DARKNESS, *	455 07
HIS CHARIOT, AND WALKETH UPON THE WINGS OF THE WIND	467 30

WALKING

AND BY WALKING BEFORE THEE IN HOLINESS AND	019 29
AND BY WALKING BEFORE THEE IN HOLINESS AND	033 27
AND OBEDIENT WALKING BEFORE THEE ALL OUR DAYS	050 27
AND OBEDIENT WALKING BEFORE THEE	053 07
OF GOD, AND WALKING FROM HENCEFORTH IN HIS HOLY WAYS	075 11
GRANT THAT WE, WALKING IN THE WAY OF THE CROSS,	138 07
WALKING BY THE SEA OF GALILEE, SAW TWO	227 24
NOT WALKING IN CRAFTINESS, NOR HANDLING	250 29

WALL

THE HELP OF MY GOD I SHALL LEAP OVER THE WALL	361 27
AS A TOTTERING WALL SHALL YE BE, AND LIKE A	414 03

WALLS

BUILD THOU THE WALLS OF JERUSALEM	404 14
ABOUT WITHIN THE WALLS THEREOF	407 06
BE WITHIN THY WALLS, *	503 20
UPON THE WALLS OF THINE HOUSE	506 11
MUCH LESS THE WALLS OF TEMPLES MADE WITH HANDS	564 29

WANDER

AND LET THEM WANDER OUT OF THE WAY IN THE WILDERNESS	478 27

WANDERINGS

8 THOU TELLEST MY WANDERINGS	408 30
OF HEART AND WANDERINGS OF MIND, THAT WITH STEDFAST	594 07

WANT

WHERE IT IS IN WANT, PROVIDE FOR IT	037 20
AND HE BEGAN TO BE IN WANT	202 06
OF SICKNESS, OR FOR WANT OF WARNING IN DUE TIME TO	R 323 23
SEEK THE LORD SHALL WANT NO MANNER OF THING THAT IS	380 22
IS DRIED UP FOR WANT OF FATNESS	481 19

WANTED

AND WHEN THEY WANTED WINE, THE MOTHER OF JESUS SAITH	113 14

WANTING

AND ENTIRE, WANTING NOTHING	239 11

WANTONNESS

AND WANTONNESS, NOT IN STRIFE AND ENVYING	091 07

WAR

WITH HIS MEN OF WAR SET HIM AT NOUGHT, AND MOCKED	153 16
FLESHLY LUSTS, WHICH WAR AGAINST THE SOUL	173 13
THERE WAS WAR IN HEAVEN	252 03
ME WITH STRENGTH OF WAR, *	361 33
THOUGH THERE ROSE UP WAR AGAINST ME, YET WILL I PUT	371 30
THAN BUTTER, HAVING WAR IN HIS HEART	408 02
SCATTER THOU THE PEOPLES THAT DELIGHT IN WAR	421 17
TEACHETH MY HANDS TO WAR, AND MY FINGERS TO FIGHT	519 23

WARD

AND THE SECOND WARD, THEY CAME UNTO THE IRON GATE	245 21

WARDEN

THE SENIOR WARDEN (OR THE MEMBER OF THE VESTRY	R 570 08
SHALL THE SENIOR WARDEN (OR THE MEMBER OF THE VESTRY	R 570 25

WARDENS

THE WARDENS (OR,	R 570 06
THE WARDENS, VESTRY, AND OTHERS, SHALL	R 574 27

WARE

OF WHOM BE THOU WARE ALSO	254 08

WARFARE

THAT HER WARFARE IS ACCOMPLISHED, THAT HER	242 18

WARMED

THE SERVANTS, AND WARMED HIMSELF AT THE FIRE	142 35

WARMING

SHE SAW PETER WARMING HIMSELF, SHE LOOKED UPON HIM,	143 24

WARN

AND ALSO HE SHALL WARN THEM THAT, EXCEPT FOR URGENT	R 273 07
I CEASED NOT TO WARN EVERY ONE NIGHT AND DAY WITH	550 34

WARNED

BEING WARNED OF GOD IN A DREAM, HE TURNED ASIDE INTO	107 20
AND BEING WARNED OF GOD IN A DREAM THAT THEY SHOULD	109 23

WARNING

MINISTER GIVETH WARNING FOR THE CELEBRATION OF THE	R 086 24
OR FOR WANT OF WARNING IN DUE TIME TO THE MINISTER,	R 323 24
8 I WILL THANK THE LORD FOR GIVING ME WARNING	358 04

WARRANTS

BY MOST CERTAIN WARRANTS OF HOLY SCRIPTURE	604 27

WARRANTY

UPON NO WARRANTY OF SCRIPTURE, BUT RATHER REPUGNANT	607 16

WARS

9 HE MAKETH WARS TO CEASE IN ALL THE WORLD	398 11

WASH

WASH ME THROUGHLY FROM MY WICKEDNESS, *	060 13
THOU SHALT WASH ME, AND I SHALL BE WHITER THAN SNOW	060 25
THINE HEAD, AND WASH THY FACE	125 13
AND BEGAN TO WASH THE DISCIPLES' FEET, AND TO	155 33
DOST THOU WASH MY FEET	156 03
THOU SHALT NEVER WASH MY FEET	156 05
ANSWERED HIM, IF I WASH THEE NOT, THOU HAST NO PART	156 06
NEEDETH NOT SAVE TO WASH HIS FEET, BUT IS CLEAN EVERY	156 09
YE ALSO OUGHT TO WASH ONE ANOTHER'S FEET	156 16
WASH IT, WE PRAY THEE, IN THE BLOOD OF THAT	317 16
EVERY NIGHT WASH I MY BED, AND WATER MY COUCH WITH MY	349 10
6 I WILL WASH MY HANDS IN INNOCENCY, O LORD	371 08
2 WASH ME THROUGHLY FROM MY WICKEDNESS, *	403 11
THOU SHALT WASH ME, AND I SHALL BE WHITER THAN SNOW	403 23
HE SHALL WASH HIS FOOTSTEPS IN THE BLOOD OF THE	410 30

WASH-POT

8 MOAB IS MY WASH-POT	412 27
9 MOAB IS MY WASH-POT	479 22

WASHED

AND OUR SOULS WASHED THROUGH HIS MOST PRECIOUS BLOOD,	082 21
TOOK WATER, AND WASHED HIS HANDS BEFORE THE	136 10
HE THAT IS WASHED NEEDETH NOT SAVE TO WASH HIS	156 09
SO AFTER HE HAD WASHED THEIR FEET, AND HAD TAKEN HIS	156 12
AND MASTER, HAVE WASHED YOUR FEET	156 16
AND OUR BODIES WASHED WITH PURE WATER	158 22
AND HAVE WASHED THEIR ROBES, AND MADE THEM WHITE IN	257 08
AND WASHED MY HANDS IN INNOCENCY	429 03

WASHING

AND WERE WASHING THEIR NETS	196 09
IT WITH THE WASHING OF WATER BY THE WORD, THAT HE	267 21
OF THY HEAVENLY WASHING, AND MAY COME TO THE ETERNAL	274 20
TO THE MYSTICAL WASHING AWAY OF SIN	279 16

WAST

AND THOU ALSO WAST WITH JESUS OF NAZARETH	143 25
THOU WAST MY HOPE, WHEN I HANGED YET UPON MY MOTHER'S	366 21
THAT THOU WAST DRIVEN BACK	485 03

WASTE

WHY WAS THIS WASTE OF THE OINTMENT MADE	140 07
AND LAID WASTE HIS DWELLING-PLACE	440 14

WASTED

AND THERE WASTED HIS SUBSTANCE WITH RIOTOUS LIVING	202 04
123 MINE EYES ARE WASTED AWAY WITH LOOKING FOR THY	498 15
OF BABYLON, WASTED WITH MISERY	513 21

WATCH

WATCH YE, FOR YE KNOW NOT WHEN THE MASTER OF	021 24
O HEAVENLY FATHER, WATCH WITH US, WE PRAY THEE,	045 24
THE FIELD, KEEPING WATCH OVER THEIR FLOCK BY NIGHT	099 11
TARRY YE HERE, AND WATCH	141 32
WATCH YE AND PRAY, LEST YE ENTER INTO TEMPTATION	142 05
COULDEST NOT THOU WATCH ONE HOUR	142 05
PILATE SAID UNTO THEM, YE HAVE A WATCH	162 23
SEALING THE STONE, AND SETTING A WATCH	162 25
AND WATCH UNTO PRAYER	179 13
WATCH THOU IN ALL THINGS, ENDURE AFFLICTIONS,	253 23
AND AS A WATCH IN THE NIGHT	325 21
I SAY, BEFORE THE MORNING WATCH	328 14
FLEETH UNTO THE LORD BEFORE THE MORNING WATCH	328 14
AND AS A WATCH IN THE NIGHT	453 26
FLEETH UNTO THE LORD BEFORE THE MORNING WATCH	507 19
I SAY, BEFORE THE MORNING WATCH	507 19
3 SET A WATCH, O LORD, BEFORE MY MOUTH, *	517 13
COME IN THE THIRD WATCH, AND FIND THEM SO, BLESSED	534 24
COME IN THE SECOND WATCH, OR COME IN THE THIRD WATCH,	534 24
THEREFORE WATCH, AND REMEMBER, THAT BY THE SPACE OF	550 33
WATCH OVER THY CHILD, O LORD, AS HIS DAYS INCREASE	597 28

WATCHED

DOWN THEY WATCHED HIM THERE	136 34
THAT THEY WATCHED HIM	213 30
7 I HAVE WATCHED, AND AM EVEN AS IT WERE A SPARROW,	464 23

WATCHES

148 MINE EYES PREVENT THE NIGHT WATCHES	500 06

WATCHETH

33 THE UNGODLY WATCHETH THE RIGHTEOUS, *	386 30

WATCHFUL

CARE AND WATCHFUL PROVIDENCE OVER US THROUGH THE	591 17

WATCHING

WERE WITH HIM, WATCHING JESUS, SAW THE EARTHQUAKE,	137 31
THE SPIRIT, AND WATCHING THEREUNTO WITH ALL	219 20
WATCHING TO CAST US DOWN TO THE GROUND	359 08
WHOM THE LORD WHEN HE COMETH SHALL FIND WATCHING	534 21

WATCHINGS

IN WATCHINGS OFTEN, IN HUNGER AND THIRST, IN FASTINGS	121 08
IN LABOURS, IN WATCHINGS, IN FASTINGS	126 12

WATCHMAN

THE WATCHMAN WAKETH BUT IN VAIN	505 24

WATCHMEN

BE MESSENGERS, WATCHMEN, AND STEWARDS OF THE LORD	539 32

WATER

LET HIM TAKE THE WATER OF LIFE FREELY	022 31
TRAVEL BY LAND, BY WATER, OR BY AIR, ALL WOMEN IN	056 31
OR IN THE WATER UNDER THE EARTH	068 10
JOHN ANSWERED THEM, SAYING, I BAPTIZE WITH WATER	096 03
I INDEED HAVE BAPTIZED YOU WITH WATER	112 17
UP OUT OF THE WATER, HE SAW THE HEAVENS OPENED, AND	112 20
SAITH UNTO THEM, FILL THE WATER-POTS WITH WATER	113 21
HAD TASTED THE WATER THAT WAS MADE WINE, AND KNEW NOT	113 24
WHICH DREW THE WATER KNEW	113 26
WAS MADE, HE TOOK WATER, AND WASHED HIS HANDS BEFORE	136 10
DIVIDING THE WATER BEFORE THEM, TO MAKE HIMSELF	139 12
SHALL MEET YOU A MAN BEARING A PITCHER OF WATER	140 27
AND OF GOATS, WITH WATER, AND SCARLET WOOL, AND	147 21
SHALL A MAN MEET YOU, BEARING A PITCHER OF WATER	148 27
THAT HE POURETH WATER INTO A BASON, AND BEGAN TO WASH	155 32
AND OUR BODIES WASHED WITH PURE WATER	158 22
AND FORTHWITH CAME THERE OUT BLOOD AND WATER	161 05
EIGHT SOULS WERE SAVED BY WATER	161 29

WATER   CONTINUED

IS HE THAT CAME BY WATER AND BLOOD, EVEN JESUS	170 30
WATER ONLY, BUT BY WATER AND BLOOD	170 31
NOT BY WATER ONLY, BUT BY WATER AND BLOOD	170 31
AND THE WATER, AND THE BLOOD	171 03
FOR JOHN TRULY BAPTIZED WITH WATER	178 03
CAN ANY MAN FORBID WATER, THAT THESE SHOULD NOT BE	184 26
A MAN BE BORN OF WATER AND OF THE SPIRIT, HE CANNOT	188 10
OF HIS FINGER IN WATER, AND COOL MY TONGUE	190 15
THE WASHING OF WATER BY THE WORD, THAT HE MIGHT	267 21
FILLED WITH PURE WATER, SHALL SAY AS FOLLOWETH,	R 273 25
AND BORN ANEW OF WATER AND OF THE HOLY GHOST	273 31
BE BAPTIZED WITH WATER AND THE HOLY GHOST, AND	274 04
A MAN BE BORN OF WATER AND OF THE SPIRIT, HE CANNOT	275 15
PRECIOUS SIDE BOTH WATER AND BLOOD	279 11
SANCTIFY THIS WATER TO THE MYSTICAL WASHING AWAY OF	279 16
DIP HIM IN THE WATER DISCREETLY, OR SHALL POUR WATER	R 279 26
OR SHALL POUR WATER UPON HIM, SAYING, N	R 279 27
THE WATER, OR POUR WATER UPON HIM, USING THE SAME	R 279 32
DIP HIM IN THE WATER, OR POUR WATER UPON HIM,	R 279 32
SHALL POUR WATER UPON HIM, SAYING THESE WORDS	R 281 20
WAS BAPTIZED WITH WATER, IN THE NAME OF THE FATHER,	R 282 08
OR THE POURING OF WATER, THE MINISTER SHALL USE THIS	R 282 12
OR IN THE WATER UNDER THE EARTH	286 10
AND VISIBLE SIGN OR FORM IN BAPTISM IS WATER	292 20
THY SERVANTS BY WATER AND THE HOLY GHOST, AND HAST	297 15
WASH I MY BED, AND WATER MY COUCH WITH MY TEARS	349 11
HIM WITH DARK WATER, AND THICK CLOUDS TO COVER HIM	360 20
AM POURED OUT LIKE WATER, AND ALL MY BONES ARE OUT OF	366 31
FALL AWAY LIKE WATER THAT RUNNETH APACE	410 21
DRY LAND WHERE NO WATER IS	414 28
10 THE RIVER OF GOD IS FULL OF WATER	417 02
WENT THROUGH THE WATER ON FOOT	417 25
THROUGH FIRE AND WATER, AND THOU BROUGHTEST US OUT	418 05
AS THE DROPS THAT WATER THE EARTH	427 09
CLOUDS POURED OUT WATER, THE AIR THUNDERED, *	434 16
THAT THE WATER GUSHED OUT, AND THE STREAMS	436 08
THEY SHED LIKE WATER ON EVERY SIDE OF JERUSALEM, *	440 04
AND THE POOLS ARE FILLED WITH WATER	445 24
ME DAILY LIKE WATER, *	449 31
A STANDING WATER, *	478 16
HIS BOWELS LIKE WATER, AND LIKE OIL INTO HIS BONES	481 06
INTO A STANDING WATER, *	485 08
EYES GUSH OUT WITH WATER, *	499 10
OR IN THE WATER UNDER THE EARTH	578 29
WATER	581 21

WATER-BROOKS

THE WATER-BROOKS, *	392 29

WATER-FLOOD

ABOVE THE WATER-FLOOD, *	374 17
LET NOT THE WATER-FLOOD DROWN ME, NEITHER LET THE	422 35

WATER-FLOODS

THE GREAT WATER-FLOODS SHALL NOT COME NIGH HIM	378 04
BECAUSE OF THE NOISE OF THY WATER-FLOODS	393 19

WATER-POTS

SET THERE SIX WATER-POTS OF STONE, AFTER THE MANNER	113 18
FILL THE WATER-POTS WITH WATER	113 21

WATER-SIDE

BY THE WATER-SIDE, *	345 12

WATER-SPRINGS

AND DRIETH UP THE WATER-SPRINGS	478 13
AND WATER-SPRINGS OF A DRY GROUND	478 17

WATEREST

11 THOU WATEREST HER FURROWS	417 04

WATERETH

13 HE WATERETH THE HILLS FROM ABOVE	468 19

WATERS

O YE WATERS THAT BE ABOVE THE FIRMAMENT, BLESS YE THE	012 06
THAT MOVE IN THE WATERS, BLESS YE THE LORD	013 12
PATHS IN THE DEEP WATERS AND HIGHWAYS IN THE DESERT	038 18
RAIN AND WATERS, AND IN THY MERCY HAST RELIEVED AND	051 23
THE VOICE OF MANY WATERS, AND AS THE VOICE OF A GREAT	103 02
IN PERILS OF WATERS, IN PERILS OF ROBBERS, IN PERILS	121 05
SHALL LEAD THEM UNTO LIVING FOUNTAINS OF WATERS	257 15
THOUGH THE WATERS THEREOF RAGE AND SWELL, *	327 07
FORTH BESIDE THE WATERS OF COMFORT	338 20
SHALL LEAD THEM UNTO LIVING FOUNTAINS OF WATERS	341 27
16 THE SPRINGS OF WATERS WERE SEEN, AND THE	360 28
AND TOOK ME OUT OF MANY WATERS	360 32
FORTH BESIDE THE WATERS OF COMFORT	368 13
3 THE VOICE OF THE LORD IS UPON THE WATERS	374 02
HE GATHERETH THE WATERS OF THE SEA TOGETHER, AS IT	378 31
3 THOUGH THE WATERS THEREOF RAGE AND SWELL, *	397 30
FOR THE WATERS ARE COME IN, EVEN UNTO MY SOUL	421 32
AM COME INTO DEEP WATERS, SO THAT THE FLOODS RUN OVER	422 03
AND OUT OF THE DEEP WATERS	422 34
BRAKEST THE HEADS OF THE DRAGONS IN THE WATERS	431 03

WATERS   CONTINUED

OUT FOUNTAINS AND WATERS OUT OF THE HARD ROCKS	431 06
THOU DRIEDST UP MIGHTY WATERS	431 07
O GOD, THE WATERS SAW THEE, AND WERE AFRAID	434 14
16 THE WATERS SAW THEE, O GOD, THE WATERS SAW THEE,	434 14
IN THE GREAT WATERS, *	434 22
HE MADE THE WATERS TO STAND ON AN HEAP	435 27
17 HE BROUGHT WATERS OUT OF THE STONY ROCK, *	435 33
HE TURNED THEIR WATERS INTO BLOOD, *	437 29
AT THE WATERS OF STRIFE	442 28
CHAMBERS IN THE WATERS, *	467 29
THE WATERS STAND ABOVE THE HILLS	468 05
HE TURNED THEIR WATERS INTO BLOOD, *	471 30
OF STONE, AND THE WATERS FLOWED OUT, *	472 19
THE WATERS OVERWHELMED THEM	473 23
HIM ALSO AT THE WATERS OF STRIFE, *	474 33
AND OCCUPY THEIR BUSINESS IN GREAT WATERS	477 23
3 YEA, THE WATERS HAD DROWNED US, *	504 12
4 THE DEEP WATERS OF THE PROUD *	504 14
6 WHO LAID OUT THE EARTH ABOVE THE WATERS	511 26
BY THE WATERS OF BABYLON WE SAT DOWN AND WEPT,	513 05
OUT OF THE GREAT WATERS, FROM THE HAND OF STRANGERS	520 05
HIS WIND, AND THE WATERS FLOW	523 32
AND YE WATERS THAT ARE ABOVE THE HEAVENS	524 11

WAVE

WAVERETH IS LIKE A WAVE OF THE SEA DRIVEN WITH THE	239 15

WAVERETH

FOR HE THAT WAVERETH IS LIKE A WAVE OF THE SEA DRIVEN	239 15

WAVERING

FAST THE PROFESSION OF OUR FAITH WITHOUT WAVERING	158 23
BUT LET HIM ASK IN FAITH, NOTHING WAVERING	239 14

WAVES

THE SEA AND THE WAVES ROARING	093 07
ALL THY WAVES AND STORMS ARE GONE OVER ME	393 19
THE NOISE OF HIS WAVES, AND THE MADNESS OF THE	416 28
THOU STILLEST THE WAVES THEREOF WHEN THEY ARISE	450 25
THE FLOODS LIFT UP THEIR WAVES	457 12
5 THE WAVES OF THE SEA ARE MIGHTY, AND RAGE HORRIBLY	457 13
LIFTETH UP THE WAVES THEREOF	477 27
SO THAT THE WAVES THEREOF ARE STILL	478 03

WAX

AND THEY ALL SHALL WAX OLD AS DOTH A GARMENT	097 16
THEY ALL SHALL WAX OLD AS A GARMENT	144 22
IN THE MIDST OF MY BODY IS EVEN LIKE MELTING WAX	366 33
AND LIKE AS WAX MELTETH AT THE FIRE, SO LET THE	419 12
HILLS MELTED LIKE WAX AT THE PRESENCE OF THE LORD	461 06
THEY ALL SHALL WAX OLD AS DOTH A GARMENT	465 35
YE MAY WAX RIPER AND STRONGER IN YOUR	541 18

WAXED

CHILD GREW, AND WAXED STRONG IN SPIRIT, FILLED WITH	233 26
CHILD GREW, AND WAXED STRONG IN SPIRIT, AND WAS IN	244 17
PAUL AND BARNABAS WAXED BOLD, AND SAID, IT WAS	260 30

WAXEN

11 FOR MY LIFE IS WAXEN OLD WITH HEAVINESS, *	376 11

WAXETH

FOR MY SPIRIT WAXETH FAINT	519 04

WAY

PREPARE YE THE WAY OF THE LORD, MAKE STRAIGHT IN THE	004 06
OUR FEET INTO THE WAY OF PEACE	014 32
O GO YOUR WAY INTO HIS GATES WITH THANKSGIVING,	015 10
ALWAYS INCLINE TO THY WILL, AND WALK IN THY WAY	017 33
MAY BE LED INTO THE WAY OF TRUTH, AND HOLD THE FAITH	019 02
WE HAVE TURNED EVERY ONE TO HIS OWN WAY	022 15
THAT THY WAY MAY BE KNOWN UPON EARTH, *	028 19
MAY BE LED INTO THE WAY OF TRUTH, AND HOLD THE FAITH	032 33
FROM PRIDE AND ARROGANCY, AND FROM EVERY EVIL WAY	036 15
THE WORLD INTO THE WAY OF JUSTICE AND TRUTH, AND	044 28
AND DISPOSE THE WAY OF THY SERVANTS TOWARDS THE	049 12
GREAT DEEP (OF HIS WAY), THIS THY SERVANT, WHO NOW	053 23
GOVERN THY HOLY CHURCH UNIVERSAL IN THE RIGHT WAY	055 20
TO BRING INTO THE WAY OF TRUTH ALL SUCH AS HAVE	056 19
THE WAY AND MEANS THERETO IS	087 16
GREAT MULTITUDE SPREAD THEIR GARMENTS IN THE WAY	091 25
AND STRAWED THEM IN THE WAY	091 26
TO PREPARE THY WAY BEFORE THEE	093 25
AND MAKE READY THY WAY, BY TURNING THE HEARTS OF THE	093 27
SHALL PREPARE THY WAY BEFORE THEE	094 33
MAKE STRAIGHT THE WAY OF THE LORD, AS SAID THE	095 29
THEY DEPARTED INTO THEIR OWN COUNTRY ANOTHER WAY	109 25
SHALL PREPARE THY WAY BEFORE THEE	112 05
PREPARE YE THE WAY OF THE LORD, MAKE HIS PATHS	112 07
BUT GO THY WAY, SHEW THYSELF TO THE PRIEST, AND OFFER	115 04
AND JESUS SAID UNTO THE CENTURION, GO THY WAY	115 23
AND SOWED TARES AMONG THE WHEAT, AND WENT HIS WAY	116 21
AND THEY WENT THEIR WAY	119 22
TAKE THAT THINE IS, AND GO THY WAY	120 09
WE, WALKING IN THE WAY OF THE CROSS, MAY FIND IT NONE	138 07

WAY   CONTINUED

NONE OTHER THAN THE WAY OF LIFE AND PEACE	138 08
AND HE WENT HIS WAY, AND COMMUNED WITH THE CHIEF	148 16
BY A NEW AND LIVING WAY, WHICH HE HATH CONSECRATED	158 17
GO YOUR WAY, MAKE IT AS SURE AS YE CAN	162 23
BUT GO YOUR WAY, TELL HIS DISCIPLES AND PETER THAT HE	165 31
WITH US BY THE WAY, AND WHILE HE OPENED TO US THE	168 10
WERE DONE IN THE WAY, AND HOW HE WAS KNOWN OF THEM IN	168 15
MAY RETURN INTO THE WAY OF RIGHTEOUSNESS	173 06
NOW I GO MY WAY TO HIM THAT SENT ME	175 06
AND GOETH HIS WAY, AND STRAIGHTWAY FORGETTETH WHAT	176 09
UP SOME OTHER WAY, THE SAME IS A THIEF AND A ROBBER	186 02
THERE THY GIFT BEFORE THE ALTAR, AND GO THY WAY	198 10
THOU ART IN THE WAY WITH HIM	198 12
THEY WILL FAINT BY THE WAY	199 13
ALSO MAKE A WAY TO ESCAPE, THAT YE MAY BE ABLE TO	201 29
HE WAS YET A GREAT WAY OFF, HIS FATHER SAW HIM,	202 17
THAT WE, RUNNING THE WAY OF THY COMMANDMENTS, MAY	204 24
CHANCE THERE CAME DOWN A CERTAIN PRIEST THAT WAY	208 25
AND HE SAID UNTO HIM, ARISE, GO THY WAY	210 14
JESUS SAITH UNTO HIM, GO THY WAY	220 03
JESUS HAD SPOKEN UNTO HIM, AND HE WENT HIS WAY	220 05
AND TEACHEST THE WAY OF GOD IN TRUTH, NEITHER CAREST	222 31
AND LEFT HIM, AND WENT THEIR WAY	223 12
HE FOUND ANY OF THIS WAY, WHETHER THEY WERE MEN OR	229 28
BUT THE LORD SAID UNTO HIM, GO THY WAY	230 26
AND ANANIAS WENT HIS WAY, AND ENTERED INTO THE HOUSE	230 29
UNTO THEE IN THE WAY AS THOU CAMEST, HATH SENT ME,	230 32
HE SHALL PREPARE THE WAY BEFORE ME	232 04
CHRIST TO BE THE WAY, THE TRUTH, AND THE LIFE	238 31
WALK IN THE WAY THAT LEADETH TO ETERNAL LIFE	239 02
GO YE KNOW, AND THE WAY YE KNOW	240 03
AND HOW CAN WE KNOW THE WAY	240 05
UNTO HIM, I AM THE WAY, THE TRUTH, AND THE LIFE	240 06
SENT TO PREPARE THE WAY OF THY SON OUR SAVIOUR BY	242 09
PREPARE YE THE WAY OF THE LORD, MAKE STRAIGHT IN THE	242 21
OUR FEET INTO THE WAY OF PEACE	244 16
AND SALUTE NO MAN BY THE WAY	254 18
AND GOETH HIS WAY, AND STRAIGHTWAY FORGETTETH WHAT	265 32
TO GO UPON HIS WAY REJOICING, AND GIVE THEE CONTINUAL	316 22
GO YE KNOW, AND THE WAY YE KNOW	331 23
AND HOW CAN WE KNOW THE WAY	331 25
UNTO HIM, I AM THE WAY, THE TRUTH, AND THE LIFE	331 25
THOU HAST LED THE WAY, THAT WE MAY AT LENGTH FALL	336 12
NOR STOOD IN THE WAY OF SINNERS, *	345 08
THE LORD KNOWETH THE WAY OF THE RIGHTEOUS	345 22
AND THE WAY OF THE UNGODLY SHALL PERISH	345 23
FROM THE RIGHT WAY, IF HIS WRATH BE KINDLED, YEA BUT	346 22
MAKE THY WAY PLAIN BEFORE MY FACE	348 17
ALL GONE OUT OF THE WAY, THEY ARE ALTOGETHER BECOME	356 19
LIE WAITING IN OUR WAY ON EVERY SIDE, *	359 08
31 THE WAY OF GOD IS AN UNDEFILED WAY	361 28
31 THE WAY OF GOD IS AN UNDEFILED WAY	361 28
AND MAKETH MY WAY PERFECT	361 34
THEREFORE WILL HE TEACH SINNERS IN THE WAY	369 34
THEM SHALL HE LEARN HIS WAY	370 03
HE TEACH IN THE WAY THAT HE SHALL CHOOSE	370 09
13 TEACH ME THY WAY, O LORD, *	372 22
LEAD ME IN THE RIGHT WAY, BECAUSE OF MINE ENEMIES	372 23
TEACH THEE IN THE WAY WHEREIN THOU SHALT GO	378 08
AND STOP THE WAY AGAINST THEM THAT PURSUE ME	381 22
6 LET THEIR WAY BE DARK AND SLIPPERY, *	381 29
UPON HIS BED, AND HATH SET HIMSELF IN NO GOOD WAY	384 02
5 COMMIT THY WAY UNTO THE LORD, AND PUT THY TRUST IN	385 02
THYSELF AT HIM WHOSE WAY DOTH PROSPER, AGAINST THE	385 07
AND MAKETH HIS WAY ACCEPTABLE TO HIMSELF	386 09
AND KEEP HIS WAY, AND HE SHALL PROMOTE THEE,	386 34
NEITHER OUR STEPS GONE OUT OF THY WAY	395 31
13 THIS THEIR WAY IS VERY FOOLISHNESS	400 32
THAT ORDERETH HIS WAY ARIGHT, WILL I SHOW THE	403 05
ALL GONE OUT OF THE WAY, THEY ARE ALTOGETHER BECOME	405 19
2 THAT THY WAY MAY BE KNOWN UPON EARTH, *	418 26
13 THY WAY, O GOD, IS HOLY	434 08
19 THY WAY IS IN THE SEA, AND THY PATHS IN THE GREAT	434 21
51 HE MADE A WAY TO HIS INDIGNATION, AND SPARED NOT	438 09
AND SHALL DIRECT HIS GOING IN THE WAY	446 34
11 TEACH ME THY WAY, O LORD, AND I WILL WALK IN THY	447 25
3 O GO YOUR WAY INTO HIS GATES WITH THANKSGIVING,	463 11
IN THE WAY OF GODLINESS	463 19
OUT OF THE WAY, *	476 12
FORTH BY THE RIGHT WAY, *	476 17
WANDER OUT OF THE WAY IN THE WILDERNESS	478 27
7 HE SHALL DRINK OF THE BROOK IN THE WAY	482 21
ARE UNDEFILED IN THE WAY, *	489 31
WHEREWITHAL SHALL A YOUNG MAN CLEANSE HIS WAY	490 17
GREAT DELIGHT IN THE WAY OF THY TESTIMONIES, *	490 25
ME TO UNDERSTAND THE WAY OF THY COMMANDMENTS	491 21
29 TAKE FROM ME THE WAY OF LYING, *	491 25
30 I HAVE CHOSEN THE WAY OF TRUTH, *	491 27
32 I WILL RUN THE WAY OF THY COMMANDMENTS, *	491 31
O LORD, THE WAY OF THY STATUTES, *	492 05
AND QUICKEN THOU ME IN THY WAY	492 14
FEET FROM EVERY EVIL WAY, *	496 28
NOW GOETH ON HIS WAY WEEPING, AND BEARETH FORTH GOOD	505 18
WELL IF THERE BE ANY WAY OF WICKEDNESS IN ME	516 06
AND LEAD ME IN THE WAY EVERLASTING	516 07
AND SET TRAPS IN MY WAY	518 08
IN THE WAY WHEREIN I WALKED, HAVE THEY PRIVILY LAID A	518 08
SHOW THOU ME THE WAY THAT I SHOULD WALK IN	519 08
AS FOR THE WAY OF THE UNGODLY, HE TURNETH IT UPSIDE	522 21
UP SOME OTHER WAY, THE SAME IS A THIEF AND A ROBBER	538 25
AND DRAW ALL YOUR CARES AND STUDIES THIS WAY	541 15
AND BE GUIDED IN THE WAY OF TRUTH	562 13
OUR FEET INTO THE WAY OF PEACE	594 14

WAY-SIDE

AND AS HE SOWED, SOME FELL BY THE WAY-SIDE   121 21
THOSE BY THE WAY-SIDE ARE THEY THAT HEAR   121 33
MAN SAT BY THE WAY-SIDE BEGGING   123 27

WAYS

STRAYED FROM THY WAYS LIKE LOST SHEEP   006 18
BEFORE THE FACE OF THE LORD TO PREPARE HIS WAYS   014 26
PLEASED TO MAKE THY WAYS KNOWN UNTO THEM, THY SAVING   018 28
THOSE WHO ARE ANY WAYS AFFLICTED, OR DISTRESSED,   019 05
STRAYED FROM THY WAYS LIKE LOST SHEEP   023 25
PLEASED TO MAKE THY WAYS KNOWN UNTO THEM, THY SAVING   032 28
THOSE WHO ARE ANY WAYS AFFLICTED, OR DISTRESSED,   033 03
SHALL I TEACH THY WAYS UNTO THE WICKED, *   061 04
AND BODIES, IN THE WAYS OF THY LAWS, AND IN THE WORKS   070 08
AND WALKING FROM HENCEFORTH IN HIS HOLY WAYS   075 11
US TO ERR FROM THY WAYS, AND HARDENED OUR HEART FROM   139 25
AND WENT THEIR WAYS, ONE TO HIS FARM, ANOTHER TO   218 11
A DOUBLE-MINDED MAN IS UNSTABLE IN ALL HIS WAYS   239 18
SO ALSO SHALL THE RICH MAN FADE AWAY IN HIS WAYS   239 24
BEFORE THE FACE OF THE LORD TO PREPARE HIS WAYS   244 11
GO YOUR WAYS   254 16
TEACH US OF HIS WAYS, AND WE WILL WALK IN HIS PATHS   290 06
AND BODIES, IN THE WAYS OF THY LAWS, AND IN THE WORKS   298 28
5 HIS WAYS ARE ALWAY GRIEVOUS   353 13
KEPT ME FROM THE WAYS OF THE DESTROYER   358 26
I HAVE KEPT THE WAYS OF THE LORD, *   361 09
3 SHOW ME THY WAYS, O LORD, *   369 24
AND TO SLAY SUCH AS BE UPRIGHT IN THEIR WAYS   385 24
TAKE HEED TO MY WAYS, *   389 05
SHALL I TEACH THY WAYS UNTO THE WICKED, *   404 02
HAD WALKED IN MY WAYS, 15 I SHOULD SOON HAVE PUT DOWN   443 07
IN WHOSE HEART ARE THY WAYS   445 22
TO KEEP THEE IN ALL THY WAYS   455 18
IN THEIR HEARTS, FOR THEY HAVE NOT KNOWN MY WAYS   459 26
7 HE SHOWED HIS WAYS UNTO MOSES, *   466 19
AND WALK IN HIS WAYS   490 05
5 O THAT MY WAYS WERE MADE SO DIRECT, *   490 08
AND HAVE RESPECT UNTO THY WAYS   490 28
ACKNOWLEDGED MY WAYS, AND THOU HEARDEST ME   491 19
I CALLED MINE OWN WAYS TO REMEMBRANCE, *   493 29
THEREFORE I HATE ALL EVIL WAYS   497 03
AND ALL FALSE WAYS I UTTERLY ABHOR   498 26
FOR ALL MY WAYS ARE BEFORE THEE   501 18
AND WALK IN HIS WAYS   506 07
SHALL SING OF THE WAYS OF THE LORD, *   514 06
AND ART ACQUAINTED WITH ALL MY WAYS   514 24
IN ALL HIS WAYS, *   521 26
MAY WALK IN THE WAYS OF TRUTH AND PEACE, AND AT LAST   574 18
DIRECT US IN ALL OUR WAYS   589 02

WEAK

TO STRENGTHEN THE WEAK AND RAISE UP THOSE WHO FALL   044 02
AS THOUGH WE HAD BEEN WEAK   120 26
WHO IS WEAK, AND I AM NOT WEAK   121 12
WHO IS WEAK, AND I AM NOT WEAK   121 12
THE SPIRIT TRULY IS READY, BUT THE FLESH IS WEAK   142 06
THE STRENGTH OF THE WEAK AND THE COMFORT OF   312 12
2 HAVE MERCY UPON ME, O LORD, FOR I AM WEAK   349 02
4 THE EARTH IS WEAK, AND ALL THE INHABITERS THEREOF   432 04
23 MY KNEES ARE WEAK THROUGH FASTING   481 18
TO SUPPORT THE WEAK, AND TO REMEMBER THE WORDS OF THE   551 09
HOLD UP THE WEAK, HEAL THE SICK, BIND UP THE BROKEN,   558 27
CONSCIENCES OF THE WEAK BRETHREN   609 41

WEAK-HEARTED

AND TO COMFORT AND HELP THE WEAK-HEARTED   056 23

WEAKNESS

THROUGH THE WEAKNESS OF OUR MORTAL NATURE, WE CAN DO   189 02
SENSE OF HIS WEAKNESS MAY ADD STRENGTH TO HIS FAITH,   310 22
THAT HIS WEAKNESS MAY BE BANISHED AND HIS STRENGTH   315 09
LYING IN GREAT WEAKNESS OF BODY   316 08
IT IS SOWN IN WEAKNESS   329 21
WHO KNOWEST THE WEAKNESS AND CORRUPTION OF OUR   588 12
BY REASON OF WEAKNESS ARE OVERTASKED, OR BECAUSE OF   600 07

WEALTH

BEEN FOR THEIR WEALTH BE UNTO THEM AN OCCASION OF   423 20

WEALTHIEST

AND SLEW THE WEALTHIEST OF THEM   436 34

WEALTHY

US OUT INTO A WEALTHY PLACE   418 06
REPROOF OF THE WEALTHY, *   504 05

WEANED

A CHILD THAT IS WEANED FROM HIS MOTHER   507 28
SOUL IS EVEN AS A WEANED CHILD   507 29

WEAR

BEHOLD, THEY THAT WEAR SOFT CLOTHING ARE IN KINGS'   094 28

WEARIED

ARE GRIEVED AND WEARIED WITH THE BURDEN OF OUR SINS   062 17

WEARINESS

IN WEARINESS AND PAINFULNESS, IN WATCHINGS OFTEN, IN   121 08

WEARING

JESUS FORTH, WEARING THE CROWN OF THORNS, AND THE   159 03

WEARS

IT AND SHE WHO WEARS IT MAY ABIDE IN THY PEACE,   302 20

WEARY

THING FOR YOU TO WEARY MEN, BUT WILL YE WEARY MY GOD   235 30
BUT WILL YE WEARY MY GOD ALSO   235 30
6 I AM WEARY OF MY GROANING   349 10
AND REFRESHEDST IT WHEN IT WAS WEARY   419 30
3 I AM WEARY OF CRYING   422 05

WEATHER

SUCH SEASONABLE WEATHER THAT WE MAY GATHER IN THE   039 29
SUCH SEASONABLE WEATHER, THAT THE EARTH MAY, IN DUE   040 26
BY THIS SEASONABLE AND BLESSED CHANGE OF WEATHER   051 25

WED

SHALL SAY, WITH THIS RING I THEE WED   302 14

WEDDED

THIS WOMAN TO THY WEDDED WIFE, TO LIVE TOGETHER AFTER   301 06
THIS MAN TO THY WEDDED HUSBAND, TO LIVE TOGETHER   301 14
TO MY WEDDED WIFE, TO HAVE AND TO HOLD FROM THIS DAY   301 28
TO MY WEDDED HUSBAND, TO HAVE AND TO HOLD FROM THIS   302 04

WEDDING

OF ANY MAN TO A WEDDING, SIT NOT DOWN IN THE HIGHEST   214 11
TO CALL THEM THAT WERE BIDDEN TO THE WEDDING   218 06
THE WEDDING IS READY, BUT THEY WHICH WERE   218 16
AND THE WEDDING WAS FURNISHED WITH GUESTS   218 21
WHEN HE WILL RETURN FROM THE WEDDING   534 18

WEDDING-GARMENT

THERE A MAN WHICH HAD NOT ON A WEDDING-GARMENT   218 23
THOU IN HITHER NOT HAVING A WEDDING-GARMENT   218 25

WEDLOCK

TO BE) JOINED IN WEDLOCK ACCORDING TO THY HOLY   267 06
TOGETHER IN HOLY WEDLOCK, AND HAVE WITNESSED THE SAME 304 04
WHO, IN HOLY WEDLOCK, HAVE BEEN MADE ONE FLESH   598 25

WEDNESDAY

THAT ON ASH WEDNESDAY AND GOOD FRIDAY THE VENITE MAY R 008 12

WEEK

ON MONDAY IN EASTER WEEK AND UNTIL ASCENSION DAY   R 008 23
ARE IN THE WEEK FOLLOWING TO BE OBSERVED   R 071 26
SHALL SERVE ALL THE WEEK AFTER, WHERE IT IS NOT IN   R 090 05
IS TO BE SAID DAILY THROUGHOUT EASTER WEEK   R 163 31
FIRST DAY OF THE WEEK COMETH MARY MAGDALENE EARLY,   164 10
FIRST DAY OF THE WEEK, THEY CAME UNTO THE SEPULCHRE   165 21
FIRST DAY OF THE WEEK, WHEN THE DOORS WERE SHUT WHERE 171 15
IS TO BE SAID DAILY THROUGHOUT WHITSUN WEEK   R 180 15
I FAST TWICE IN THE WEEK, I GIVE TITHES OF ALL THAT I 205 27
FIRST DAY OF THE WEEK, WHEN THE DOORS WERE SHUT WHERE 551 28

WEEKLY

US GLAD WITH THE WEEKLY REMEMBRANCE OF THE GLORIOUS   595 12

WEEKS

TO BE USED IN THE WEEKS PRECEDING THE STATED TIMES OF R 038 24

WEEP

DO REJOICE, AND WEEP WITH THEM THAT WEEP   111 30
THAT DO REJOICE, AND WEEP WITH THEM THAT WEEP   111 30
OF THE LORD, WEEP BETWEEN THE PORCH AND THE ALTAR,   125 03
NOT FOR ME, BUT WEEP FOR YOURSELVES, AND FOR YOUR   154 14
OF JERUSALEM, WEEP NOT FOR ME, BUT WEEP FOR   154 14
THAT YE SHALL WEEP AND LAMENT, BUT THE WORLD   174 08
AND SAID UNTO HER, WEEP NOT   213 03

WEEPING

TURN TO THEE IN WEEPING, FASTING, AND PRAYING   062 30
AND WEEPING, AND GREAT MOURNING, RACHEL   103 31
RACHEL WEEPING FOR HER CHILDREN, AND WOULD   103 32
THERE SHALL BE WEEPING AND GNASHING OF TEETH   115 22
AND WITH WEEPING, AND WITH MOURNING   124 22
THERE SHALL BE WEEPING AND GNASHING OF TEETH   218 28
TELL YOU EVEN WEEPING, THAT THEY ARE THE ENEMIES OF 222 18
FOR THE LORD HATH HEARD THE VOICE OF MY WEEPING   349 15
AND MINGLED MY DRINK WITH WEEPING   464 28

WEEPING   CONTINUED

GOETH ON HIS WAY WEEPING, AND BEARETH FORTH GOOD   505 18

WEIGHED

YE HAVE WELL WEIGHED THESE THINGS WITH YOURSELVES,   541 09

WEIGHING

NOT WEIGHING OUR MERITS, BUT PARDONING OUR OFFENCES,   081 31
READING AND WEIGHING THE SCRIPTURES, YE MAY WAX RIPER   541 18

WEIGHT

LAY ASIDE EVERY WEIGHT, AND THE SIN WHICH DOTH SO   258 21

WEIGHTS

UPON THE WEIGHTS THEY ARE ALTOGETHER LIGHTER THAN   414 16

WEIGHTY

THAT UPON WEIGHTY AND IMPORTANT CONSIDERATIONS,   V 16
UPON JUST AND WEIGHTY CONSIDERATIONS HER THEREUNTO   V 28
ALLOWED FOR WEIGHTY CAUSE   R 336 32
AND TO HOW WEIGHTY AN OFFICE AND CHARGE YE ARE   539 31
THE DOING OF SO WEIGHTY A WORK, PERTAINING TO THE   540 34

WELCOME

SHALL SALUTE AND WELCOME HIM, BIDDING HIM GOD-SPEED   R 574 28

WELFARE

AND WELFARE OF THY PEOPLE   035 14
THY NAME AND THE WELFARE OF THE PEOPLE   035 28

WELL

OF THE SAME (AS WELL IN THE CHIEFEST MATERIALS, AS IN   V 31
AND NECESSARY, AS WELL FOR THE BODY AS THE SOUL   006 09
AND NECESSARY, AS WELL FOR THE BODY AS THE SOUL   023 18
AND TO THAT END, AS WELL AS FOR THE GOOD EDUCATION OF   047 32
SACRIFICES GOD IS WELL PLEASED   072 28
IN WHOM I AM WELL PLEASED   112 23
AND WHEN MEN HAVE WELL DRUNK, THEN THAT WHICH IS   113 28
AS UNKNOWN, AND YET WELL KNOWN   126 18
SAY WE NOT WELL THAT THOU ART A SAMARITAN,   133 13
AND YE SAY WELL   156 15
THAT YE SUFFER FOR WELL DOING, THAN FOR EVIL DOING   161 22
BUT IF, WHEN YE DO WELL, AND SUFFER FOR IT, YE TAKE   172 08
AND FOR THE PRAISE OF THEM THAT DO WELL   173 21
OF GOD, THAT WITH WELL DOING YE MAY PUT TO SILENCE   173 22
THE HOLY GHOST AS WELL AS WE   184 28
OF THEM GOD WAS NOT WELL PLEASED   201 11
SAYING, HE HATH DONE ALL THINGS WELL   207 08
IN WHOM I AM WELL PLEASED   248 19
FOR BE YE WELL ASSURED, THAT IF ANY PERSONS ARE   300 28
THINE EARS CONSIDER WELL *   328 05
YOU THAT WHICH IS WELL PLEASING IN HIS SIGHT   335 20
FOR IT BECOMETH WELL THE JUST TO BE THANKFUL   378 20
WITH THEE IS THE WELL OF LIFE   384 14
GOD IS WELL KNOWN IN HER PALACES AS A SURE REFUGE   399 14
12 MARK WELL HER BULWARKS, CONSIDER HER PALACES,   400 02
AS WELL AS THE IGNORANT AND FOOLISH, AND LEAVE THEIR   400 24
LONG AS THOU DOEST WELL UNTO THYSELF, MEN WILL SPEAK   401 12
HOPE IN THY NAME, FOR THY SAINTS LIKE IT WELL   405 09
24 IT IS WELL SEEN, O GOD, HOW THOU GOEST   421 02
DID EAT, AND WERE WELL FILLED   436 29
THROUGH THE VALE OF MISERY USE IT FOR A WELL   445 24
UNWISE MAN DOTH NOT WELL CONSIDER THIS, *   456 11
AND THE FLINT-STONE INTO A SPRINGING WELL   485 09
O DO WELL UNTO THY SERVANT   490 32
4 DO WELL, O LORD, *   504 32
O WELL IS THEE, AND HAPPY SHALT THOU BE   506 09
THINE EARS CONSIDER WELL *   507 10
THY WORKS, AND THAT MY SOUL KNOWETH RIGHT WELL   515 17
24 LOOK WELL IF THERE BE ANY WAY OF WICKEDNESS IN ME   516 06
RULING THEIR CHILDREN AND THEIR OWN HOUSES WELL   532 02
OFFICE OF A DEACON WELL PURCHASE TO THEMSELVES A GOOD   532 03
SON CHRIST, MAY SO WELL BEHAVE THEMSELVES IN THIS   535 07
MAY BE PERFECT AND WELL EXPERT IN THE THINGS   R 535 22
BRETHREN, AS WELL IN YOUR PRIVATE EXAMINATION,   539 24
AS WELL TO SHOW YOURSELVES DUTIFUL AND   540 26
HOPE THAT YE HAVE WELL WEIGHED THESE THINGS WITH   541 09
AS WELL TO THE SICK AS TO THE WHOLE,   542 23
SO THAT AS WELL BY THESE THY MINISTERS, AS BY THEM   545 32
ONE THAT RULETH WELL HIS OWN HOUSE, HAVING HIS   549 23
AND HOLY MEN, AS WELL UNDER THE LAW AS UNDER THE   564 11
AND NECESSARY, AS WELL FOR THE BODY AS FOR THE SOUL,   566 18
YOU THAT WHICH IS WELL PLEASING IN HIS SIGHT   573 07
HEAVENLY THINGS, AS WELL BECAUSE IT DOTH GREATLY   606 20
AND ADORATION, AS WELL OF IMAGES AS OF RELICS,   607 15
OF THEM, AS WELL FROM OBSOLETE WORDS AND PHRASES, AS   R 610 28
TO ALL MEN, AS WELL CLERGY AS LAITY, IN ALL THINGS   610 38

WELL-BELOVED

BY THY WELL-BELOVED SON, SAYING, ASK, AND YE SHALL   274 15
WELL-BELOVED, YOU HAVE COME HITHER DESIRING TO   277 20
WHICH THY WELL-BELOVED SON SHALL THEN PRONOUNCE TO   335 10
TO OUR WELL-BELOVED IN CHRIST, A   569 13

WELL-GOVERNING

AND WELL-GOVERNING OF THE PEOPLE, REMEMBERING THE   047 19
AND WELL-GOVERNING OF THY CHURCH   553 33

WELL-LEARNED

GODLY AND WELL-LEARNED MAN, TO BE ORDAINED AND   552 22

WELL-LIKING

AND SHALL BE FAT AND WELL-LIKING   456 29

WELL-NIGH

TREADINGS HAD WELL-NIGH SLIPT   428 13

WELL-SPRING

ONLY ART THE WELL-SPRING OF LIFE   303 15

WELL-TUNED

HIM UPON THE WELL-TUNED CYMBALS   525 30

WELLS

O YE WELLS, BLESS YE THE LORD   013 08

WENT

USE THE WORDS, HE WENT INTO THE PLACE OF DEPARTED   R 015 17
USE THE WORDS, HE WENT INTO THE PLACE OF DEPARTED   R 029 22
AND THE DISCIPLES WENT, AND DID AS JESUS COMMANDED   091 22
THE MULTITUDES THAT WENT BEFORE, AND THAT FOLLOWED,   091 27
AND JESUS WENT INTO THE TEMPLE OF GOD, AND CAST OUT   091 33
WHAT WENT YE OUT INTO THE WILDERNESS TO SEE   094 26
BUT WHAT WENT YE OUT FOR TO SEE   094 27
BUT WHAT WENT YE OUT FOR TO SEE   094 29
THAT THERE WENT OUT A DECREE FROM CAESAR   098 28
AND ALL WENT TO BE TAXED, EVERY ONE INTO HIS OWN   098 31
AND JOSEPH ALSO WENT UP FROM GALILEE, OUT OF THE CITY   098 32
THEN WENT THIS SAYING ABROAD AMONG THE BRETHREN, THAT   102 09
SAW IN THE EAST, WENT BEFORE THEM, TILL IT CAME AND   109 17
NOW HIS PARENTS WENT TO JERUSALEM EVERY YEAR AT THE   110 18
YEARS OLD, THEY WENT UP TO JERUSALEM AFTER THE CUSTOM   110 20
IN THE COMPANY, WENT A DAY'S JOURNEY   110 24
AND HE WENT DOWN WITH THEM, AND CAME TO NAZARETH, AND   111 04
AND THERE WENT OUT UNTO HIM ALL THE LAND OF JUDAEA,   112 09
THE WHEAT, AND WENT HIS WAY   116 20
WHICH WENT OUT EARLY IN THE MORNING TO   119 16
AND HE WENT OUT ABOUT THE THIRD HOUR, AND SAW OTHERS   119 19
AGAIN HE WENT OUT ABOUT THE SIXTH AND NINTH HOUR, AND   119 22
AND THEY WENT THEIR WAY   119 22
ELEVENTH HOUR HE WENT OUT, AND FOUND OTHERS STANDING   119 24
A SOWER WENT OUT TO SOW HIS SEED   121 20
AND THEY WHICH WENT BEFORE REBUKED HIM, THAT HE   123 31
JESUS WENT THENCE, AND DEPARTED INTO THE COASTS OF   128 07
JESUS WENT OVER THE SEA OF GALILEE, WHICH IS THE SEA   131 21
AND JESUS WENT UP INTO A MOUNTAIN, AND THERE HE SAT   131 24
HID HIMSELF, AND WENT OUT OF THE TEMPLE   133 33
AND DEPARTED, AND WENT AND HANGED HIMSELF   135 08
AND WENT INTO THE HOLY CITY, AND   137 30
WHOSE MOST DEAR SON WENT NOT UP TO JOY BUT FIRST HE   138 04
ONE OF THE TWELVE, WENT UNTO THE CHIEF PRIESTS,   140 19
AND HIS DISCIPLES WENT FORTH, AND CAME INTO THE CITY,   140 32
SUNG AN HYMN, THEY WENT OUT INTO THE MOUNT OF OLIVES   141 19
AND HE WENT FORWARD A LITTLE, AND FELL ON THE GROUND,   141 32
AND AGAIN HE WENT AWAY, AND PRAYED, AND SPAKE THE   142 07
AND HE WENT OUT INTO THE PORCH   143 27
AND HE WENT HIS WAY, AND COMMUNED WITH THE CHIEF   148 16
AND THEY WENT, AND FOUND AS HE HAD SAID UNTO THEM   148 32
HE CAME OUT, AND WENT, AS HE WAS WONT, TO THE MOUNT   150 13
ONE OF THE TWELVE, WENT BEFORE THEM, AND DREW NEAR   150 28
AND PETER WENT OUT, AND WEPT BITTERLY   151 22
COME FROM GOD, AND WENT TO GOD   155 30
PILATE THEREFORE WENT FORTH AGAIN, AND SAITH UNTO   158 34
AND WENT AGAIN INTO THE JUDGMENT HALL, AND SAITH UNTO   159 11
BEARING HIS CROSS WENT FORTH INTO A PLACE CALLED THE   159 32
BY WHICH ALSO HE WENT AND PREACHED UNTO THE SPIRITS   161 25
HE WENT TO PILATE, AND BEGGED THE BODY OF JESUS   162 08
SO THEY WENT, AND MADE THE SEPULCHRE SURE, SEALING   162 24
PETER THEREFORE WENT FORTH, AND THAT OTHER DISCIPLE,   164 16
YET WENT HE NOT IN   164 21
FOLLOWING HIM, AND WENT INTO THE SEPULCHRE, AND SEETH   164 22
THEN WENT IN ALSO THAT OTHER DISCIPLE, WHICH CAME   164 25
THEN THE DISCIPLES WENT AWAY AGAIN UNTO THEIR OWN   164 28
AND THEY WENT OUT QUICKLY, AND FLED FROM THE   165 33
WHO WENT ABOUT DOING GOOD, AND HEALING ALL THAT WERE   166 20
OF HIS DISCIPLES WENT THAT SAME DAY TO A VILLAGE   167 03
DREW NEAR, AND WENT WITH THEM   167 08
WHICH WERE WITH US WENT TO THE SEPULCHRE, AND FOUND   167 27
DREW NIGH UNTO THE VILLAGE, WHITHER THEY WENT   168 02
AND HE WENT IN TO TARRY WITH THEM   168 04
TOWARD HEAVEN AS HE WENT UP, BEHOLD, TWO MEN STOOD BY   178 15
WHO WENT ABOUT DOING GOOD, AND HEALING ALL THAT WERE   184 04
BUT IF ONE WENT UNTO THEM FROM THE DEAD, THEY WILL   190 28
AND HE WENT AND JOINED HIMSELF TO A CITIZEN OF THAT   202 06
AND HE WENT INTO THE TEMPLE, AND BEGAN TO CAST OUT   204 15
TWO MEN WENT UP INTO THE TEMPLE TO PRAY   205 23
TELL YOU, THIS MAN WENT DOWN TO HIS HOUSE JUSTIFIED   205 31
A CERTAIN MAN WENT DOWN FROM JERUSALEM TO   208 21
ON HIM, AND WENT TO HIM, AND BOUND UP HIS WOUNDS,   208 30
TO PASS, AS JESUS WENT TO JERUSALEM, THAT HE PASSED   209 31
THAT, AS THEY WENT, THEY WERE CLEANSED   210 07
THAT JESUS WENT INTO A CITY CALLED NAIN   212 27

WENT CONTINUED

OF HIS DISCIPLES WENT WITH HIM, AND MUCH PEOPLE	212 28
THIS RUMOUR OF HIM WENT FORTH THROUGHOUT ALL JUDAEA,	213 09
TO PASS, AS JESUS WENT INTO THE HOUSE OF ONE OF THE	213 28
LIGHT OF IT, AND WENT THEIR WAYS, ONE TO HIS FARM,	218 10
SO THOSE SERVANTS WENT OUT INTO THE HIGHWAYS,	218 19
INTO GALILEE, HE WENT UNTO HIM, AND BESOUGHT HIM THAT	219 30
UNTO HIM, AND HE WENT HIS WAY	220 05
THE SAME SERVANT WENT OUT, AND FOUND ONE OF HIS	221 23
BUT WENT AND CAST HIM INTO PRISON, TILL HE SHOULD PAY	221 29
THEN WENT THE PHARISEES, AND TOOK COUNSEL HOW THEY	222 28
AND LEFT HIM, AND WENT THEIR WAY	223 12
WERE PUT FORTH, HE WENT IN, AND TOOK HER BY THE HAND,	224 28
AND THE FAME HEREOF WENT ABROAD INTO ALL THAT LAND	224 29
THEIR SOUND WENT INTO ALL THE EARTH, AND	227 15
OF THE LORD, WENT UNTO THE HIGH PRIEST, AND DESIRED	229 26
AND ANANIAS WENT HIS WAY, AND ENTERED INTO THE HOUSE	230 29
THAT THE LORD JESUS WENT IN AND OUT AMONG US,	234 22
AND HE WENT OUT, AND FOLLOWED HIM	245 18
AND THEY WENT OUT, AND PASSED ON THROUGH ONE STREET	245 23
JOHN AND JAMES, AND WENT UP INTO A MOUNTAIN TO PRAY	248 24
THE MULTITUDES, WENT UP INTO A MOUNTAIN	257 18
JESUS WENT INTO THE TEMPLE OF GOD, AND CAST OUT ALL	260 03
HIS CUSTOM WAS, HE WENT INTO THE SYNAGOGUE ON THE	261 12
9 THERE WENT A SMOKE OUT IN HIS PRESENCE, *	360 12
I WENT HEAVILY, AS ONE THAT MOURNETH FOR HIS MOTHER	382 21
37 I WENT BY, AND LO, HE WAS GONE	387 06
AND THEY THAT WENT ABOUT TO DO ME EVIL TALKED OF	388 15
FOR I WENT WITH THE MULTITUDE, AND BROUGHT THEM FORTH	393 07
SO THAT THEY WENT THROUGH THE WATER ON FOOT	417 24
WE WENT THROUGH FIRE AND WATER, AND THOU BROUGHTEST	418 05
FOR ME, 17 UNTIL I WENT INTO THE SANCTUARY OF GOD	429 10
AND IT WENT EVEN THROUGH MY REINS	429 18
AND THINE ARROWS WENT ABROAD	434 17
WHAT TIME AS THEY WENT FROM ONE NATION TO ANOTHER,	470 28
AND WENT A WHORING WITH THEIR OWN INVENTIONS	475 15
4 THEY WENT ASTRAY IN THE WILDERNESS OUT OF THE WAY,	476 12
I WAS TROUBLED, I WENT WRONG	494 15
AARON'S BEARD, AND WENT DOWN TO THE SKIRTS OF HIS	509 16
AT HAND, AND JESUS WENT UP TO JERUSALEM, AND FOUND IN	567 25
FOR HIS SAKE WHO WENT ABOUT DOING GOOD, THY SON OUR	591 04
THAT HE WENT DOWN INTO HELL	603 19

WENTEST

O GOD, WHEN THOU WENTEST FORTH BEFORE THE PEOPLE	419 24
WHEN THOU WENTEST THROUGH THE WILDERNESS, 8 THE EARTH	419 25

WEPT

AND WHEN HE THOUGHT THEREON, HE WEPT	144 03
PETER WENT OUT, AND WEPT BITTERLY	151 23
THE CITY, AND WEPT OVER IT, SAYING, IF THOU HADST	204 07
10 I WEPT, AND CHASTENED MYSELF WITH FASTING,	422 23
WE SAT DOWN AND WEPT, *	513 05

WEST

FROM THE EAST AND WEST, AND SHALL SIT DOWN WITH	115 19
OUT OF THE EAST, AND SHINETH EVEN UNTO THE WEST	118 11
NOR FROM THE WEST, *	432 11
12 LOOK HOW WIDE ALSO THE EAST IS FROM THE WEST	466 30
OF THE LANDS, FROM THE EAST, AND FROM THE WEST	476 11

WHALES

O YE WHALES, AND ALL THAT MOVE IN THE WATERS,	013 12

WHATEVER

TO GIVE WHATEVER IN THY INFINITE WISDOM THOU SHALT	566 22
AND WHATEVER ELSE THOU SHALT SEE TO BE	589 05
REFORM WHATEVER IS AMISS IN THE TEMPER AND	590 12

WHATSOEVER

AND WHATSOEVER ELSE MAY HINDER US FROM GODLY UNION	037 28
BRING FORTH WHATSOEVER IS NEEDFUL FOR THE LIFE OF	039 25
THAT WHATSOEVER TENDS TO THE ADVANCEMENT OF TRUE	047 35
AUTHORITY WHATSOEVER) TO TAKE A FURTHER REVIEW OF THE	VI 25
WHATSOEVER THINGS WERE WRITTEN AFORETIME WERE WRITTEN	092 15
THE SERVANTS, WHATSOEVER HE SAITH UNTO YOU, DO IT	113 17
AND WHATSOEVER YE DO IN WORD OR DEED, DO ALL IN THE	116 14
AND WHATSOEVER IS RIGHT I WILL GIVE YOU	119 21
AND WHATSOEVER IS RIGHT, THAT SHALL YE RECEIVE	119 28
FOR WHATSOEVER DOTH MAKE MANIFEST IS LIGHT	129 20
WHATSOEVER IS BORN OF GOD OVERCOMETH THE WORLD	170 26
BUT WHATSOEVER HE SHALL HEAR, THAT SHALL HE SPEAK	175 20
SAY UNTO YOU, WHATSOEVER YE SHALL ASK THE FATHER IN	176 20
WHATSOEVER I HAVE SAID UNTO YOU	181 33
AND WHATSOEVER WE ASK, WE RECEIVE OF HIM, BECAUSE WE	191 27
AND WHATSOEVER THOU SPENDEST MORE, WHEN I COME AGAIN,	208 35
AND WHATSOEVER YE SHALL ASK IN MY NAME, THAT WILL I	240 21
IF YE DO WHATSOEVER I COMMAND YOU	241 28
THAT WHATSOEVER YE SHALL ASK OF THE FATHER IN MY	242 02
AND WHATSOEVER THOU SHALT BIND ON EARTH SHALL BE	246 10
AND WHATSOEVER THOU SHALT LOOSE ON EARTH SHALL BE	246 11
AND INTO WHATSOEVER HOUSE YE ENTER, FIRST SAY,	254 19
ALL THINGS WHATSOEVER I HAVE COMMANDED YOU	275 30
WHATSOEVER HATH BEEN DECAYED BY THE FRAUD AND	314 03
THAT WHATSOEVER DEFILEMENTS IT MAY HAVE CONTRACTED,	317 19
HE HEAR US, WHATSOEVER WE ASK, WE KNOW THAT WE HAVE	322 17
AND LOOK, WHATSOEVER HE DOETH, IT SHALL PROSPER	345 14
AND WHATSOEVER WALKETH THROUGH THE PATHS OF THE SEAS	351 16
HE HATH DONE WHATSOEVER PLEASED HIM	485 17

WHATSOEVER CONTINUED

6 WHATSOEVER THE LORD PLEASED, THAT DID HE IN HEAVEN,	510 13
ALL THINGS WHATSOEVER I HAVE COMMANDED YOU	552 13
THEY MAY LOVE WHATSOEVER THINGS ARE TRUE AND PURE AND	596 26
SO THAT WHATSOEVER IS	603 29
CHRISTIAN MAN WHATSOEVER IS FREE FROM THE OBEDIENCE	604 22

WHEAT

TARES AMONG THE WHEAT, AND WENT HIS WAY	116 20
ROOT UP ALSO THE WHEAT WITH THEM	116 28
BUT GATHER THE WHEAT INTO MY BARN	116 31
THAT HE MAY SIFT YOU AS WHEAT	149 32
AND FILLETH THEE WITH THE FLOUR OF WHEAT	265 05
IT MAY CHANCE OF WHEAT, OR OF SOME OTHER GRAIN	329 09
AND FILLETH THEE WITH THE FLOUR OF WHEAT	523 24

WHEAT-FLOUR

HAVE FED THEM ALSO WITH THE FINEST WHEAT-FLOUR	443 13

WHELP

IT WERE A LION'S WHELP LURKING IN SECRET PLACES	359 11

WHENCE

AND KNEW NOT WHENCE IT WAS	113 25
FROM WHENCE THEN HATH IT TARES	116 24
UNTO MY HOUSE WHENCE I CAME OUT	130 12
UNTO PHILIP, WHENCE SHALL WE BUY BREAD, THAT THESE	131 27
SAITH UNTO JESUS, WHENCE ART THOU	159 12
CANST NOT TELL WHENCE IT COMETH, AND WHITHER IT	188 16
FROM WHENCE CAN A MAN SATISFY THESE MEN WITH	199 15
FROM WHENCE ALSO WE LOOK FOR THE SAVIOUR, THE LORD	222 22
UNTO PHILIP, WHENCE SHALL WE BUY BREAD, THAT THESE	225 24
AND WHENCE CAME THEY	257 05
CANST NOT TELL WHENCE IT COMETH, AND WHITHER IT	275 20
FROM WHENCE COMETH MY HELP	327 19
FROM WHENCE COMETH MY HELP	339 03
FROM WHENCE COMETH MY HELP	502 22

WHENEVER

BUT NOTE, THAT WHENEVER IT IS OMITTED, THE PRIEST	R 067 29

WHENSOEVER

WHENSOEVER THEY OPPRESS US	058 18
AND WHENSOEVER YE WILL YE MAY DO THEM GOOD	140 12
TO DIE, WHENSOEVER IT	R 321 04
AND THAT, WHENSOEVER HIS SOUL SHALL DEPART FROM THE	321 24
9 WHENSOEVER I CALL UPON THEE, THEN SHALL MINE	408 32
AND WHENSOEVER THE BISHOP SHALL GIVE KNOWLEDGE FOR	R 583 05

WHEREAS

THAT WHEREAS, THROUGH OUR SINS AND WICKEDNESS,	095 06
WHEREAS THEY SPEAK AGAINST YOU AS EVILDOERS,	173 15
17 WHEREAS THOU HATEST TO BE REFORMED, *	402 24
2 WHEREAS THE GOODNESS OF GOD *	404 21
WHEREAS CHRIST SAITH PLAINLY, WHEN YE HAVE DONE ALL	605 28

WHEREBY

WHEREBY THE DAY-SPRING FROM ON HIGH HATH VISITED US	014 29
WHEREBY WE HAVE BEEN BROUGHT OUT OF DARKNESS AND	078 30
WHEREBY ALONE WE OBTAIN REMISSION OF OUR SINS,	086 33
IN FEW WORDS, WHEREBY, WHEN YE READ, YE MAY	108 10
MIGHTY ACTS, WHEREBY THOU HAST GIVEN UNTO US LIFE AND	147 10
OF ADOPTION, WHEREBY WE CRY, ABBA, FATHER	200 09
SPIRIT OF GOD, WHEREBY YE ARE SEALED UNTO THE DAY OF	216 26
TO THE WORKING WHEREBY HE IS ABLE EVEN TO SUBJECT ALL	222 25
THIS IS HIS NAME WHEREBY HE SHALL BE CALLED, THE LORD	225 13
WHEREBY THEY LIE IN WAIT TO DECEIVE	237 27
WHEREBY THE DAYSPRING FROM ON HIGH HATH VISITED US,	244 14
AS A MEANS WHEREBY WE RECEIVE THIS GRACE, AND A	292 12
WHEREBY WE ARE MADE THE CHILDREN OF GRACE	292 26
REPENTANCE, WHEREBY THEY FORSAKE SIN	292 28
AND FAITH, WHEREBY THEY STEDFASTLY BELIEVE THE	292 29
OF ADOPTION, WHEREBY WE CRY, ABBA, FATHER	330 22
MIGHTY WORKING WHEREBY HE IS ABLE TO SUBDUE ALL	333 22
MIGHTY WORKING WHEREBY HE IS ABLE TO SUBDUE ALL	337 16
IVORY PALACES, WHEREBY THEY HAVE MADE THEE GLAD	396 33
AS A MEANS WHEREBY WE RECEIVE THE SAME, AND A PLEDGE	581 14
REPENTANCE, WHEREBY THEY FORSAKE SIN	581 28
AND FAITH, WHEREBY THEY STEDFASTLY BELIEVE THE	581 29
WHEREBY MAN IS VERY FAR GONE FROM ORIGINAL	604 31
WHEREBY THE LUST OF THE FLESH, CALLED IN GREEK,	604 36
PURPOSE OF GOD, WHEREBY (BEFORE THE FOUNDATIONS OF	606 06
WHEREBY THE DEVIL DOTH THRUST THEM EITHER	606 24
OF JESUS CHRIST, WHEREBY MEN MUST BE SAVED	606 35
OF DIFFERENCE, WHEREBY CHRISTIAN MEN ARE DISCERNED	608 24
OR NEW-BIRTH, WHEREBY, AS BY AN INSTRUMENT, THEY THAT	608 26
AND THE MEAN WHEREBY THE BODY OF CHRIST IS RECEIVED	608 45

WHEREFORE

WHEREFORE I PRAY AND BESEECH YOU, AS MANY AS ARE HERE	006 09
WHEREFORE LET US BESEECH HIM TO GRANT US TRUE	007 14
WHEREFORE I PRAY AND BESEECH YOU, AS MANY AS ARE HERE	023 18
WHEREFORE LET US BESEECH HIM TO GRANT US TRUE	024 16
WHEREFORE THE LORD BLESSED THE SEVENTH DAY, AND	068 31
WHEREFORE, O LORD AND HEAVENLY FATHER, ACCORDING TO	080 36
WHEREFORE IT IS OUR DUTY TO RENDER MOST HUMBLE AND	086 34

WHEREFORE   CONTINUED

WHEREFORE, MOST DEARLY BELOVED IN CHRIST, TAKE YE   088 24
WHEREFORE THEN DO YE NOT REPENT AND AMEND   088 31
WHEREFORE, ACCORDING TO MINE OFFICE, I BID YOU. IN THE   089 06
WHEREFORE RECEIVE YE ONE ANOTHER, AS CHRIST ALSO   092 21
WHEREFORE THOU ART NO MORE A SERVANT, BUT A SON   104 24
WHEREFORE, MY BELOVED, AS YE HAVE ALWAYS OBEYED, NOT   105 31
WHEREFORE YE MUST NEEDS BE SUBJECT, NOT ONLY FOR   114 22
WHEREFORE IF THEY SHALL SAY UNTO YOU, BEHOLD,   118 08
WHEREFORE SHOULD THEY SAY AMONG THE PEOPLE, WHERE IS   125 05
WHEREFORE HE SAITH, AWAKE THOU THAT SLEEPEST, AND   129 21
WHEREFORE GOD ALSO HATH HIGHLY EXALTED HIM, AND GIVEN   134 22
WHEREFORE THAT FIELD WAS CALLED, THE FIELD OF BLOOD,   135 12
WHEREFORE ART THOU RED IN THINE APPAREL, AND THY   138 14
WHEREFORE WHEN HE COMETH INTO THE WORLD, HE SAITH,   157 23
WHEREFORE HE SAITH ALSO IN ANOTHER PSALM, THOU SHALT   169 13
WHEREFORE, MY BELOVED BRETHREN, LET EVERY MAN BE   174 30
WHEREFORE LAY APART ALL FILTHINESS AND SUPERFLUITY OF   175 02
WHEREFORE BY THEIR FRUITS YE SHALL KNOW THEM   200 23
WHEREFORE LET HIM THAT THINKETH HE STANDETH TAKE HEED   201 24
WHEREFORE I GIVE YOU TO UNDERSTAND, THAT NO MAN   203 19
WHEREFORE THEN SERVETH THE LAW   207 26
WHEREFORE PUTTING AWAY LYING, SPEAK EVERY MAN TRUTH   216 16
THOUGHTS SAID, WHEREFORE THINK YE EVIL IN YOUR   217 06
WHEREFORE BE YE NOT UNWISE, BUT UNDERSTANDING WHAT   217 25
WHEREFORE TAKE UNTO YOU THE WHOLE ARMOUR OF GOD,   219 11
WHEREFORE OF THESE MEN WHICH HAVE COMPANIED WITH US   234 20
WHEREFORE HE SAITH, WHEN HE ASCENDED UP ON HIGH, HE   237 13
WHEREFORE IF THY HAND OR THY FOOT OFFEND THEE, CUT   253 03
WHEREFORE, MY BELOVED BRETHREN, LET EVERY MAN BE   265 23
WHEREFORE LAY APART ALL FILTHINESS AND SUPERFLUITY OF   265 25
WHEREFORE, IF GOD SO CLOTHE THE GRASS OF THE FIELD,   266 22
WHEREFORE THEY ARE NO MORE TWAIN, BUT ONE FLESH   268 09
WHEREFORE COMFORT ONE ANOTHER WITH THESE WORDS   269 10
WHEREFORE THE LORD BLESSED THE SEVENTH DAY, AND   286 31
WHEREFORE MY HEART IS GLAD, AND MY GLORY REJOICETH   333 07
14 WHEREFORE SHOULD THE WICKED BLASPHEME GOD,   353 34
10 WHEREFORE MY HEART IS GLAD, AND MY GLORY   358 08
24 WHEREFORE HIDEST THOU THY FACE, *   396 08
WHEREFORE GOD, EVEN THY GOD, HATH ANOINTED THEE WITH   396 30
5 WHEREFORE SHOULD I FEAR IN THE DAYS OF EVIL,   400 14
O GOD, WHEREFORE ART THOU ABSENT FROM US SO LONG   430 03
10 WHEREFORE DO THE HEATHEN SAY, *   440 21
WHEREFORE HAST THOU MADE ALL MEN FOR NOUGHT   452 34
2 WHEREFORE SHALL THE HEATHEN SAY, *   485 14
WHEREFORE, BRETHREN, LOOK YE OUT AMONG YOU SEVEN MEN   532 10
WHEREFORE HE SAITH, WHEN HE ASCENDED UP ON HIGH, HE   537 33
WHEREFORE CONSIDER WITH YOURSELVES THE END OF THE   540 13
WHEREFORE I TAKE YOU TO RECORD THIS DAY, THAT I AM   550 24
WHEREFORE THE LORD BLESSED THE SEVENTH DAY, AND   579 11
WHEREFORE THEY ARE NOT TO BE HEARD, WHICH FEIGN THAT   604 17
WHEREFORE WE HAVE NO POWER TO DO GOOD WORKS PLEASANT   604 44
WHEREFORE, THAT WE ARE   605 07
WHEREFORE THE GRANT OF REPENTANCE IS NOT TO BE DENIED   605 40
WHEREFORE, THEY WHICH BE ENDUED WITH SO EXCELLENT A   606 10
WHEREFORE, ALTHOUGH THE CHURCH BE A WITNESS AND A   607 06
WHEREFORE THE   609 16

WHEREIN

AMENDS FOR THAT WHEREIN HE HIMSELF HATH OFFENDED   R 085 13
ALL HIS ARMOUR WHEREIN HE TRUSTED, AND DIVIDETH HIS   130 08
WAS A PREPARING, WHEREIN FEW, THAT IS, EIGHT SOULS   161 28
OUR OWN TONGUE, WHEREIN WE WERE BORN   180 31
AND WHEREIN YE STAND   204 31
DRUNK WITH WINE, WHEREIN IS EXCESS   217 26
WHEREIN I WAS MADE A MEMBER OF CHRIST, THE CHILD OF   283 19
OR CONFIRMATION, WHEREIN, AFTER RENEWING THE PROMISES   291 24
WHEREIN THE PERSON IS BAPTIZED, IN THE NAME OF THE   292 20
THEE IN THE WAY WHEREIN THOU SHALT GO   378 08
AND MOUNT SION, WHEREIN THOU HAST DWELT   430 09
FOR THE YEARS WHEREIN WE HAVE SUFFERED ADVERSITY   454 20
17 WHEREIN THE BIRDS MAKE THEIR NESTS   468 28
WHEREIN ALL THE BEASTS OF THE FOREST DO MOVE   468 34
WHEREIN ARE THINGS CREEPING INNUMERABLE, BOTH SMALL   469 10
WHEREIN THOU HAST CAUSED ME TO PUT MY TRUST   493 09
IN THE WAY WHEREIN I WALKED, HAVE THEY PRIVILY LAID A   518 08
WHEREIN I WAS MADE A MEMBER OF CHRIST, THE CHILD OF   577 09
WHEREIN THE PERSON IS BAPTIZED, IN THE NAME OF THE   581 21

WHEREINSOEVER

AND WHEREINSOEVER YE SHALL PERCEIVE YOURSELVES TO   087 18
HOWBEIT WHEREINSOEVER ANY IS BOLD, (I SPEAK   120 26

WHEREOF

THE STREAMS WHEREOF SHALL MAKE GLAD THE CITY OF GOD,   022 26
IN THIS LAND, WHEREOF WE ARE MEMBERS   047 12
THE OBTAINING WHEREOF WE SHALL NOT CEASE TO MAKE OUR   089 20
WHEREOF I WAS MADE A MINISTER, ACCORDING TO THE GIFT   108 16
THOSE THINGS WHEREOF YE ACCUSE HIM   153 25
WHEREOF THE HOLY GHOST ALSO IS A WITNESS TO US   158 09
IN THOSE THINGS WHEREOF YE ARE NOW ASHAMED   198 32
US THOSE THINGS WHEREOF OUR CONSCIENCE IS AFRAID,   206 08
YOU IN HEAVEN, WHEREOF YE HEARD BEFORE IN THE WORD OF   223 26
ARE THE BENEFITS WHEREOF WE ARE PARTAKERS IN THE   293 17
THE BENEFITS WHEREOF WE ARE PARTAKERS IN THE LORD'S   293 19
THEM MADE, (WHEREOF THIS RING GIVEN AND RECEIVED IS A   303 08
THE STREAMS WHEREOF MAKE GLAD THE CITY OF GOD   327 09
THE STREAMS WHEREOF MAKE GLAD THE CITY OF GOD   397 32
FOR HE KNOWETH WHEREOF WE ARE MADE   467 02
WHEREOF WE REJOICE   505 14
7 WHEREOF THE MOWER FILLETH NOT HIS HAND, *   507 02
IN EXECUTING WHEREOF IF HE BE FOUND FAITHFUL AND   R 535 23

WHEREOF   CONTINUED

IN WITNESS WHEREOF, WE HAVE HEREUNTO AFFIXED OUR   569 38
ARE THE BENEFITS WHEREOF WE ARE PARTAKERS THEREBY   582 15
TO BE DIVIDED; WHEREOF IS ONE CHRIST, VERY GOD, AND   603 13
SEVERAL TITLES WHEREOF WE HAVE JOINED UNDER THIS   610 05

WHERESOEVER

AND WHERESOEVER ELSE IT IS USED IN DIVINE   R 007 21
FOR WHERESOEVER THE CARCASE IS, THERE WILL THE EAGLES   118 12
UNTO YOU, WHERESOEVER THIS GOSPEL SHALL BE PREACHED   140 15
AND WHERESOEVER HE SHALL GO IN, SAY YE TO THE GOODMAN   140 28

WHEREUNTO

LIKE FIGURE WHEREUNTO, EVEN BAPTISM, DOTH ALSO NOW   161 29
MY STRONGHOLD, WHEREUNTO I MAY ALWAY RESORT   425 08
OFFICE IS, WHEREUNTO YE ARE CALLED   539 28
THIS OFFICE, WHEREUNTO IT HATH PLEASED GOD TO CALL   541 12
TO THE WORK WHEREUNTO WE TRUST THE HOLY GHOST HATH   553 12
THE OFFICE WHEREUNTO HE IS CALLED, TO THE EDIFYING OF   553 19
THE OFFICE WHEREUNTO HE IS CALLED, TO THE EDIFYING OF   561 04

WHEREUPON

WHEREUPON NEITHER THE FIRST TESTAMENT WAS DEDICATED   147 17

WHEREVER

WHEREVER TWO OR THREE OF THY FAITHFUL   564 31
AND GUIDE HIM WHEREVER HE MAY BE, KEEPING HIM   597 29

WHEREWITH

DONE UNTO ME, WHEREWITH THE LORD HATH AFFLICTED ME   004 31
LIBERTY WHEREWITH CHRIST HATH MADE US FREE,' THAT IN   V 02
WHEREWITH THOU HAST AFFLICTED US   040 25
DANGERS WHEREWITH WE WERE COMPASSED   052 10
WITH THE TOWEL WHEREWITH HE WAS GIRDED   155 34
THE VOCATION WHEREWITH YE ARE CALLED, WITH ALL   213 19
OF FAITH, WHEREWITH YE SHALL BE ABLE TO QUENCH ALL   219 16
THE BLASPHEMY WHEREWITH OUR NEIGHBOURS HAVE   440 29
50 WHEREWITH THINE ENEMIES HAVE BLASPHEMED THEE,   453 10
WHEREWITH HE ASCENDED   603 22

WHEREWITHAL

WHEREWITHAL SHALL WE BE CLOTHED   211 28
WHEREWITHAL SHALL WE BE CLOTHED   266 26
WHEREWITHAL SHALL A YOUNG MAN CLEANSE HIS WAY   490 16

WHET

NOT TURN, HE WILL WHET HIS SWORD   350 17
3 WHO HAVE WHET THEIR TONGUE LIKE A SWORD, *   415 23

WHETHER

IS GIVEN TO US, WHETHER PROPHECY, LET US PROPHESY   111 16
BUT WHETHER THERE BE PROPHECIES, THEY SHALL FAIL   123 04
WHETHER THERE BE KNOWLEDGE, IT SHALL VANISH AWAY   123 05
WHETHER THERE BE TONGUES, THEY SHALL CEASE   123 05
SAID UNTO THEM, WHETHER OF THE TWAIN WILL YE THAT I   136 03
LET US SEE WHETHER ELIAS WILL COME TO SAVE HIM   137 23
LET US SEE WHETHER ELIAS WILL COME TO TAKE HIM DOWN   146 33
FOR WHETHER IS GREATER, HE THAT SITTETH AT MEAT,   149 24
HE ASKED WHETHER THE MAN WERE A GALILAEAN   153 07
WHETHER IT BE TO THE KING, AS SUPREME   173 18
INTO ONE BODY, WHETHER WE BE JEWS OR GENTILES,   183 05
OR GENTILES, WHETHER WE BE BOND OR FREE   183 06
THEREFORE WHETHER IT WERE I OR THEY, SO WE PREACH,   205 18
FOR WHETHER IS EASIER, TO SAY, THY SINS BE FORGIVEN   217 07
ANY OF THIS WAY, WHETHER THEY WERE MEN OR WOMEN, HE   229 28
OF ALL MEN, SHEW WHETHER OF THESE TWO THOU HAST   234 28
FOR WHETHER IS GREATER, HE THAT SITTETH AT MEAT, OR   250 09
WHETHER THEY BE SUFFICIENTLY INSTRUCTED   R 273 19
REASONABLE DOUBT WHETHER ANY PERSON WAS BAPTIZED WITH   R 282 08
WHETHER THEY REPENT THEM TRULY OF THEIR   293 26
WHETHER BY PUBLISHING THE BANNS IN   R 304 17
AND AS TO WHETHER HE REPENT HIM TRULY OF HIS   R 313 19
SHALL JUDGE WHETHER IT AFFORD JUST CAUSE TO SUSPEND   R 570 22
WHETHER THEY REPENT THEM TRULY OF THEIR   582 22

WHILES

WHILES THOU ART IN THE WAY WITH HIM   198 12

WHILST

THE PEOPLE, WHILST THEY ARE IN HEALTH, TO MAKE WILLS   R 320 21
3 FOR WHILST I HELD MY TONGUE, *   377 26

WHIRLING

LIKE UNTO THE WHIRLING DUST, *   444 30

WHIRLWIND

AWAY WITH A WHIRLWIND, THE GREEN AND THE BURNING   410 27

WHISPER

ALL MINE ENEMIES WHISPER TOGETHER AGAINST ME   392 13

WHIT

SAVE TO WASH HIS FEET, BUT IS CLEAN EVERY WHIT   156 10

WHITE

UPON IT A FAIR WHITE LINEN CLOTH   R 067 05
CLOTHED IN A LONG WHITE GARMENT   165 27
STOOD BY THEM IN WHITE APPAREL   178 16
CLOTHED IN WHITE RAIMENT   187 10
IN RAIMENT WHITE AND GLISTERING   248 02
HIS RAIMENT WAS WHITE AND GLISTERING   248 26
CLOTHED WITH WHITE ROBES, AND PALMS IN THEIR   256 26
ARE ARRAYED IN WHITE ROBES   257 05
AND MADE THEM WHITE IN THE BLCCD OF THE LAMB   257 08
THEN WERE THEY AS WHITE AS SNOW IN SALMON   420 10

WHITER

AND I SHALL BE WHITER THAN SNOW   060 25
AND I SHALL BE WHITER THAN SNOW   403 23

WHITHER

THE VILLAGE, WHITHER THEY WENT   167 34
YOU ASKETH ME, WHITHER GOEST THOU   175 07
THE SAME PLACE WHITHER OUR SAVIOUR CHRIST IS GONE   179 08
IT COMETH, AND WHITHER IT GOETH   188 16
ALL COUNTRIES WHITHER I HAD DRIVEN THEM   225 19
AND WHITHER I GO YE KNOW, AND THE WAY YE KNCW   240 03
WE KNOW NOT WHITHER THOU GOEST   240 04
CITY AND PLACE, WHITHER HE HIMSELF WOULD COME   254 13
IT COMETH, AND WHITHER IT GOETH   275 21
AND WHITHER I GO YE KNOW, AND THE WAY YE KNCW   331 22
WE KNOW NOT WHITHER THOU GOEST   331 24
OR WHITHER SHALL I GO THEN FROM THY PRESENCE   514 31
6 WHITHER SHALL I GO THEN FROM THY SPIRIT   514 31

WHITHERSOEVER

THE LAMB WHITHERSOEVER HE GOETH   103 10

WHITSUN

DAILY THROUGHOUT WHITSUN WEEK   R 180 15

WHITSUNDAY

ON ASCENSION DAY AND UNTIL WHITSUNDAY   R 008 25
ON WHITSUNDAY AND SIX DAYS AFTER   R 008 27
WHITSUNDAY, AND TRINITY SUNDAY   R 070 32
UPON WHITSUNDAY, AND SIX DAYS AFTER   R 078 24
CELEBRATED ON WHITSUNDAY, THE FOLLOWING CCLLECT,   R 182 11

WHOLE

TO BE SAID BY THE WHOLE CONGREGATION, AFTER THE   R 006 16
LET THE WHOLE EARTH STAND IN AWE OF HIM   009 18
AT THE END OF THE WHOLE PORTION, OR SELECTION FRCM R 009 25
LET THE WHOLE EARTH STAND IN AWE OF HIM   021 20
THE WHOLE EARTH IS FULL OF HIS GLORY   022 34
TO BE SAID BY THE WHOLE CONGREGATION, AFTER THE   R 023 23
AT THE END OF THE WHOLE PORTION OR SELECTION OF   R 025 19
MERCY UPON THIS WHOLE LAND   032 05
FOR US, AND THY WHOLE CHURCH, WE HUMBLY BEG IN THE   035 19
TILL AT LENGTH THE WHOLE OF THY DISPERSED SHEEP,   037 05
ON THE FACE OF THE WHOLE EARTH, AND DIDST SEND THY   038 06
WE MAY PUT OUR WHOLE TRUST AND CONFIDENCE IN THY   059 25
IT IS HOPED THE WHOLE WILL BE RECEIVED AND EXAMINED   VI 36
US PRAY FOR THE WHOLE STATE OF CHRIST'S CHURCH   074 05
THE SINS OF THE WHOLE WORLD   080 12
WE, AND ALL THY WHOLE CHURCH, MAY OBTAIN REMISSICN OF 081 19
THE PRAYER FOR THE WHOLE STATE OF CHRIST'S CHURCH, R 085 22
DAUGHTER WAS MADE WHOLE FROM THAT VERY HOUR   128 21
UNTO HIM THE WHOLE BAND OF SOLDIERS   136 17
THROUGHOUT THE WHOLE WORLD, THIS ALSO THAT SHE HATH   140 16
SCRIBES AND THE WHOLE COUNCIL, AND BOUND JESUS,   145 05
CALL TOGETHER THE WHOLE BAND   145 31
DARKNESS OVER THE WHOLE LAND UNTIL THE NINTH HOUR   146 26
THE WHOLE MULTITUDE OF THEM AROSE, AND LED HIM UNTO   152 27
WHOSE SPIRIT THE WHOLE BODY OF THE CHURCH IS GOVERNED 156 28
LEAVENETH THE WHOLE LUMP   165 10
WE KNOW THAT THE WHOLE CREATION GROANETH AND   194 19
THY FAITH HATH MADE THEE WHOLE   210 14
OF WHOM THE WHOLE FAMILY IN HEAVEN AND EARTH IS   212 13
PUT ON THE WHOLE ARMOUR OF GOD, THAT YE MAY BE ABLE   219 06
TAKE UNTO YOU THE WHOLE ARMOUR OF GOD, THAT YE MAY BE 219 11
AND HIS WHOLE HOUSE   220 11
IF I MAY BUT TOUCH HIS GARMENT, I SHALL BE WHOLE   224 20
THY FAITH HATH MADE THEE WHOLE   224 22
THE WOMAN WAS MADE WHOLE FROM THAT HOUR   224 23
FROM WHOM THE WHOLE BODY FITLY JOINED TOGETHER AND   237 30
TO PASS, THAT A WHOLE YEAR THEY ASSEMBLED THEMSELVES 241 12
THEY THAT BE WHOLE NEED NOT A PHYSICIAN,   251 20
RECEIVETH THE WHOLE WORLD   252 08
CAME ALMOST THE WHOLE CITY TOGETHER TO HEAR THE WORD 260 26
TO THY WHOLE CHURCH IN PARADISE AND ON EARTH,   268 15
OF WHOM THE WHOLE FAMILY IN HEAVEN AND EARTH IS   281 08
TO PUT MY WHOLE TRUST IN HIM, TO CALL UPON HIM   288 20
THE GOSPEL TO THE WHOLE WORLD   291 13
O LORD, WITH MY WHOLE HEART   311 08
AT THE END OF THE WHOLE PORTION OR SELECTION FRCM THE R 324 18
OF THE CHURCH THE WHOLE OR A PART OF THE SERVICE   R 336 31
O LORD, WITH MY WHOLE HEART   351 22
AND THERE IS NO WHOLE PART IN MY BODY   388 05

WHOLE   CONTINUED

AND THE JOY OF THE WHOLE EARTH   399 13
FOR THE WHOLE WORLD IS MINE, AND ALL THAT IS THEREIN 402 14
HEART WAS NOT WHOLE WITH HIM, *   437 12
NOT SUFFER HIS WHOLE DISPLEASURE TO ARISE   437 17
LIGHT OF THY COUNTENANCE, AND WE SHALL BE WHOLE   441 09
LIGHT OF THY COUNTENANCE, AND WE SHALL BE WHOLE   441 17
LIGHT OF THY COUNTENANCE, AND WE SHALL BE WHOLE   442 10
THE LORD, ALL THE WHOLE EARTH   459 31
LET THE WHOLE EARTH STAND IN AWE OF HIM   460 17
OF THE LORD OF THE WHOLE EARTH   461 07
THE LORD WITH MY WHOLE HEART, *   482 24
16 ALL THE WHOLE HEAVENS ARE THE LORD'S   486 10
HIM WITH THEIR WHOLE HEART   490 03
10 WITH MY WHOLE HEART HAVE I SOUGHT THEE   490 18
KEEP IT WITH MY WHOLE HEART   492 08
PRESENCE WITH MY WHOLE HEART   493 27
WITH MY WHOLE HEART   494 19
I CALL WITH MY WHOLE HEART   499 31
O LORD, WITH MY WHOLE HEART   513 27
SAYING PLEASED THE WHOLE MULTITUDE   532 15
THE SPACE OF A WHOLE YEAR, (EXCEPT FOR REASONABLE   R 535 20
THE SICK AS TO THE WHOLE, WITHIN YOUR CURES, AS NEED 542 23
CONTINUED THE WHOLE NIGHT IN PRAYER, BEFORE HE CHOSE 553 05
GRANT PEACE TO THE WHOLE WORLD, AND TO THY CHURCH   560 12
TO PUT MY WHOLE TRUST IN HIM, TO CALL UPON HIM   579 30
US THROUGH THE WHOLE COURSE OF OUR LIVES   591 18
REJOICING IN THY WHOLE CREATION, WE MAY LEARN TO   596 20
SO THAT TWO WHOLE AND PERFECT NATURES, THAT IS TC   603 12
THE SINS OF THE WHOLE WORLD, BOTH ORIGINAL AND   609 15
TO BE TAKEN OF THE WHOLE MULTITUDE OF THE FAITHFUL,   609 28

WHOLESOME

EVEN WITH THE WHOLESOME STRENGTH OF HIS RIGHT HAND   364 27
AND HE IS THE WHOLESOME DEFENCE OF HIS ANOINTED   373 25
IN YOU LIETH, WHOLESOME EXAMPLES OF THE FLOCK CF   533 27
THAT YE MAY BE WHOLESOME AND GODLY EXAMPLES AND   541 22
IN YOU LIETH, WHOLESOME EXAMPLES AND PATTERNS TO THE 543 02
EXHORT WITH WHOLESOME DOCTRINE, AND TO WITHSTAND AND 554 32
AS BELIEVE, A WHOLESOME EXAMPLE IN WORD, IN   559 10
IS A MOST WHOLESOME DOCTRINE, AND VERY FULL CF   605 08
THEY HAVE A WHOLESOME EFFECT OR OPERATION   608 04
A GODLY AND WHOLESOME DOCTRINE, AND NECESSARY FCR   610 06

WHOLLY

TRUSTING WHOLLY IN THY MERCY, THEY MAY NCT   046 23
OURSELVES WHOLLY TO HIS HOLY WILL AND PLEASURE, AND   086 21
GIVE YOURSELVES WHOLLY TO THIS OFFICE, WHEREUNTO IT   541 12
APPLY YOURSELVES WHOLLY TO THIS ONE THING, AND DRAW   541 14

WHOMSOEVER

WHOMSOEVER I SHALL KISS, THAT SAME IS HE   142 18
ONE PRISONER, WHOMSOEVER THEY DESIRED   145 13
AND HE TO WHOMSOEVER THE SON WILL REVEAL HIM   235 10

WHOREMONGER

THAT NO WHOREMONGER, NOR UNCLEAN PERSON, NOR CCVETOUS 129 06

WHORING

AND WENT A WHORING WITH THEIR OWN INVENTIONS   475 15

WHOSESOEVER

WHOSESOEVER SINS YE REMIT, THEY ARE REMITTED UNTC   171 23
AND WHOSESOEVER SINS YE RETAIN, THEY ARE RETAINED   171 24

WHOSO

WHOSO HATH THIS WORLD'S GOOD, AND SEETH HIS BROTHER   072 29
BUT WHOSO LOOKETH INTO THE PERFECT LAW OF LIBERTY,   176 10
BUT WHOSO HATH THIS WORLD'S GOOD, AND SEETH HIS   191 18
AND WHOSO SHALL RECEIVE ONE SUCH LITTLE CHILD IN MY   252 29
BUT WHOSO SHALL OFFEND ONE OF THESE LITTLE ONES WHICH 252 30
BUT WHOSO LOOKETH INTO THE PERFECT LAW OF LIBERTY,   265 33
AND WHOSO SHALL RECEIVE ONE SUCH LITTLE CHILD IN MY   339 28
7 WHOSO DOETH THESE THINGS *   357 19
BUT WHOSO PUTTETH HIS TRUST IN THE LORD, MERCY   378 13
23 WHOSO OFFERETH ME THANKS AND PRAISE, HE HCNCURETH 403 04
INSOMUCH THAT WHOSO SEETH THEM SHALL LAUGH THEM TO   416 03
WHOSO DWELLETH UNDER THE DEFENCE OF THE MOST HIGH, * 454 28
6 WHOSO PRIVILY SLANDERETH HIS NEIGHBOUR, *   463 26
7 WHOSO HATH ALSO A HAUGHTY LOOK AND A PROUD HEART,   463 28
9 WHOSO LEADETH A GODLY LIFE, *   463 32
43 WHOSO IS WISE, WILL PONDER THESE THINGS   478 32

WHOSOEVER

AND WHOSOEVER WILL, LET HIM TAKE THE WATER OF LIFE   022 31
BLESSED IS HE, WHOSOEVER SHALL NOT BE OFFENDED IN ME 094 24
WHOSOEVER THEREFORE RESISTETH THE POWER, RESISTETH   114 13
WHOSOEVER COMMITTETH SIN TRANSGRESSETH ALSO THE LAW   117 01
WHOSOEVER ABIDETH IN HIM SINNETH NOT   117 24
WHOSOEVER SINNETH HATH NOT SEEN HIM, NEITHER KNCWN   117 25
WITHOUT WHICH WHOSOEVER LIVETH IS COUNTED DEAD BEFORE 122 18
WHOSOEVER MAKETH HIMSELF A KING, SPEAKETH AGAINST   159 21
HIS NAME WHOSOEVER BELIEVETH IN HIM SHALL RECEIVE   166 31
AND WHOSOEVER AMONG YOU FEARETH GOD, TO YOU   168 25
THAT WHOSOEVER KILLETH YOU WILL THINK THAT HE   179 30
HIS NAME WHOSOEVER BELIEVETH IN HIM SHALL RECEIVE   184 19
THAT WHOSOEVER BELIEVETH IN HIM SHOULD NOT   184 33

WHOSOEVER   CONTINUED

THAT WHOSOEVER BELIEVETH IN HIM SHOULD NOT PERISH,	188	28
WHOSOEVER SHALL CONFESS THAT JESUS IS THE SON OF GOD,	189	21
WHOSOEVER HATETH HIS BROTHER IS A MURDERER	191	14
AND WHOSOEVER SHALL KILL SHALL BE IN DANGER OF THE	198	02
UNTO YOU, THAT WHOSOEVER IS ANGRY WITH HIS BROTHER	198	03
AND WHOSOEVER SHALL SAY TO HIS BROTHER, RACA, SHALL	198	05
BUT WHOSOEVER SHALL SAY, THOU FOOL, SHALL BE IN`	198	06
FOR WHOSOEVER EXALTETH HIMSELF SHALL BE ABASED	214	19
WHOSOEVER BELIEVETH ON HIM SHALL NOT BE	226	30
FOR WHOSOEVER SHALL CALL UPON THE NAME OF THE LORD	227	04
BUT WHOSOEVER WILL BE GREAT AMONG YOU, LET HIM BE	247	23
AND WHOSOEVER WILL BE CHIEF AMCNG YOU, LET HIM BE	247	24
WHOSOEVER THEREFORE SHALL HUMBLE HIMSELF AS THIS	252	27
AND GRANT THAT WHOSOEVER SHALL WORSHIP BEFORE THEE IN	259	21
SAY UNTO YOU, WHOSOEVER SHALL NOT RECEIVE THE KINGDOM	274	30
GRANT THAT WHOSOEVER IS HERE DEDICATED TO THEE BY OUR	278	27
AND WHOSOEVER LIVETH AND BELIEVETH IN ME, SHALL NEVER	324	07
IN WHOM WHOSOEVER BELIEVETH, SHALL LIVE, THOUGH HE	334	32
AND WHOSOEVER LIVETH, AND BELIEVETH IN HIM, SHALL NOT	335	02
AND WHOSOEVER LIVETH AND BELIEVETH IN ME, SHALL NEVER	338	07
WHOSOEVER THEREFORE SHALL HUMBLE HIMSELF AS THIS	339	26
AND GRANT THAT WHOSOEVER IN THIS HOUSE SHALL BE	565	19
O LORD, THAT WHOSOEVER SHALL RECEIVE IN THIS PLACE	565	28
O LORD, THAT WHOSOEVER SHALL BE JOINED TOGETHER IN	566	08
THAT WHOSOEVER SHALL DRAW NEAR TO THEE IN THIS	566	13
WHOSOEVER, THROUGH HIS PRIVATE JUDGMENT, WILLINGLY	609	35
WHOSOEVER ARE CONSECRATED OR ORDERED	610	34

WHY

AND SAID UNTO HIM, WHY BAPTIZEST THOU THEN, IF THOU	095	31
SAID UNTO HIM, SON, WHY HAST THOU THUS DEALT WITH US	110	32
AND SAITH UNTO THEM, WHY STAND YE HERE ALL THE DAY	119	25
IF I SAY THE TRUTH, WHY DO YE NOT BELIEVE ME	133	10
THE GOVERNOR SAID, WHY, WHAT EVIL HATH HE DCNE	136	06
MY GOD, MY GOD, WHY HAST THOU FORSAKEN ME	137	18
O LORD, WHY HAST THOU MADE US TO ERR FROM THY WAYS,	139	24
AND SAID, WHY WAS THIS WASTE OF THE OINTMENT MACE	140	07
WHY TROUBLE YE HER	140	10
SAID UNTO THEM, WHY, WHAT EVIL HATH HE DONE	145	25
MY GOD, MY GOD, WHY HAST THOU FORSAKEN ME	146	29
AND SAID UNTO THEM, WHY SLEEP YE	150	25
THEM THE THIRD TIME, WHY, WHAT EVIL HATH HE DONE	153	34
AND WHY DO THOUGHTS ARISE IN YOUR HEARTS	169	31
HE SAID UNTO THEM, WHY ARE YE TROUBLED	169	31
YE MEN OF GALILEE, WHY STAND YE GAZING UP INTO	178	17
AND WHY BEHOLDEST THOU THE MOTE THAT IS IN THY	195	05
AND WHY ARE YE ANXIOUS CONCERNING RAIMENT	211	20
AND SAID, WHY TEMPT YE ME, YE HYPOCRITES	223	05
SAUL, SAUL, WHY PERSECUTEST THOU ME	230	02
UNTO HIS DISCIPLES, WHY EATETH YOUR MASTER WITH	251	18
AND WHY ARE YE ANXIOUS FOR RAIMENT	266	19
WHY THEN ARE INFANTS BAPTIZED, WHEN BY	292	31
WHY WAS THE SACRAMENT OF THE LORD'S SUPPER	293	02
CAN SHOW JUST CAUSE, WHY THEY MAY NOT LAWFULLY BE	300	21
KNOW ANY IMPEDIMENT, WHY YE MAY NOT BE LAWFULLY	300	27
OR JUST IMPEDIMENT, WHY THESE TWO PERSONS SHOULD NOT	R 304	23
WHY HAST THOU PUT ME FROM THEE	310	08
AND WHY GO I SO HEAVILY, WHILE THE ENEMY OPPRESSETH	310	09
AND WHY ART THOU SO DISQUIETED WITHIN ME	310	16
WHY ART THOU SO HEAVY, O MY SOUL	310	16
WHY DO THE HEATHEN SO FURIOUSLY RAGE TOGETHER	345	25
AND WHY DO THE PEOPLE IMAGINE A VAIN THING	345	26
WHY STANDEST THOU SO FAR OFF, O LORD, *	353	34
11 FOR WHY	358	10
7 AND WHY	365	17
WHY HAST THOU FORSAKEN ME	366	04
20 AND WHY	383	02
6 WHY ART THOU SO FULL OF HEAVINESS, O MY SCUL	393	11
AND WHY ART THOU SO DISQUIETED WITHIN ME	393	12
GOD OF MY STRENGTH, WHY HAST THOU FORGOTTEN ME	393	24
WHY GO I THUS HEAVILY, WHILE THE ENEMY OPPRESSETH ME	393	25
14 WHY ART THOU SO VEXED, O MY SOUL	393	31
AND WHY ART THOU SO DISQUIETED WITHIN ME	393	31
WHY HAST THOU PUT ME FROM THEE	394	06
AND WHY GO I SO HEAVILY, WHILE THE ENEMY OPPRESSETH	394	07
AND WHY ART THOU SO DISQUIETED WITHIN ME	394	15
5 WHY ART THOU SO HEAVY, O MY SOUL	394	15
23 UP, LORD, WHY SLEEPEST THOU	396	06
WHY DOST THOU PREACH MY LAWS, AND TAKEST MY COVENANT	402	22
WHY BOASTEST THOU THYSELF, THOU TYRANT, *	404	19
AND WHY	411	30
16 WHY MOCK YE SO, YE HIGH HILLS	420	13
7 AND WHY	422	16
3 AND WHY	428	14
WHY IS THY WRATH SO HOT AGAINST THE SHEEP OF THY	430	04
WHY PLUCKEST THOU NOT THY RIGHT HAND OUT OF THY BOSOM	430	29
12 WHY WITHDRAWEST THOU THY HAND	430	29
8 AND WHY	432	12
12 WHY HAST THOU THEN BROKEN DOWN HER HEDGE, *	441	26
14 LORD, WHY ABHORREST THOU MY SOUL, *	449	24
14 AND WHY	465	07
41 FOR WHY	472	21
8 AND WHY	487	04
AND WHY	497	20
4 FOR WHY	510	09
CAN SHOW JUST CAUSE WHY HE MAY NOT BE INSTITUTED, WE	570	17
WHY THEN ARE INFANTS BAPTIZED, WHEN BY	581	31
WHY WAS THE SACRAMENT OF THE LORD'S SUPPER	582	02

WICKED

THY WAYS UNTO THE WICKED, *	061	04
SPIRITS MORE WICKED THAN HIMSELF	130	15

WICKED   CONTINUED

INTO THE HANDS OF WICKED MEN, AND TO SUFFER DEATH	156	24
ABLE TO QUENCH ALL THE FIERY DARTS OF THE WICKED	219	18
UNTO HIM, O THOU WICKED SERVANT, I FORGAVE THEE ALL	221	33
VANITY OF THIS WICKED WORLD, AND ALL THE SINFUL LUSTS	283	24
NOR THE WICKED APPROACH TO HURT HIM	308	28
THE DECEITFUL AND WICKED MAN	310	07
17 THE WICKED SHALL BE TURNED TO DESTRUCTION,	352	26
SHOULD THE WICKED BLASPHEME GOD, *	353	34
MY GOD, AS THE WICKED DOTH	361	10
RID ME FROM THE WICKED MAN	363	04
COUNCIL OF THE WICKED LAYETH SIEGE AGAINST ME	367	05
5 I HAVE HATED THE CONGREGATION OF THE WICKED	371	06
2 WHEN THE WICKED, EVEN MINE ENEMIES AND MY FOES,	371	27
THE UNGODLY AND WICKED DOERS, *	373	11
9 WICKED DOERS SHALL BE ROOTED OUT	385	11
THE DECEITFUL AND WICKED MAN	394	05
THY WAYS UNTO THE WICKED, *	404	02
ME FROM THE WICKED DOERS, *	411	06
INSURRECTION OF WICKED DOERS	415	22
I WAS GRIEVED AT THE WICKED	428	14
AND SPEAK OF WICKED BLASPHEMY	428	24
HIS DESIRE OF THE WICKED THAT ARISE UP AGAINST ME	456	22
LONG SHALL ALL WICKED DOERS SPEAK SO DISDAINFULLY,	457	25
16 WHO WILL RISE UP WITH ME AGAINST THE WICKED	458	18
PUNISH THEIR WICKED DOINGS	462	33
4 I WILL TAKE NO WICKED THING IN HAND	463	22
I WILL NOT KNOW A WICKED PERSON	463	25
MAY ROOT OUT ALL WICKED DOERS FROM THE CITY OF THE	464	05
115 AWAY FROM ME, YE WICKED	497	28
THOU NOT SLAY THE WICKED, O GOD	515	28
ME FROM THE WICKED MAN	516	10
ME FROM THE WICKED MEN, WHO ARE PURPOSED TO OVERTHROW	516	16
SHALL HUNT THE WICKED PERSON TO OVERTHROW HIM	516	33
THE TRAPS OF THE WICKED DOERS	517	31
VANITY OF THIS WICKED WORLD, AND ALL THE SINFUL LUSTS	577	15
THE WICKED, AND SUCH AS BE VOID OF A LIVELY FAITH,	609	04

WICKEDLY

THOU THOUGHTEST WICKEDLY, THAT I AM EVEN SUCH A CNE	402	33
WE HAVE DONE AMISS, AND DEALT WICKEDLY	473	12
FOR THEY GO WICKEDLY ABOUT TO DESTROY ME	495	11

WICKEDNESS

AND CONFESS OUR MANIFOLD SINS AND WICKEDNESS	005	31
TURN FROM HIS WICKEDNESS AND LIVE, HATH GIVEN POWER,	007	08
AND CONFESS OUR MANIFOLD SINS AND WICKEDNESS	023	06
TURN FROM HIS WICKEDNESS AND LIVE, HATH GIVEN POWER,	024	10
FROM MY WICKEDNESS, *	060	13
WAS SHAPEN IN WICKEDNESS, *	060	20
PUNISHMENT OF WICKEDNESS AND VICE, AND TO THE	074	18
SINS AND WICKEDNESS, WHICH WE, FROM TIME TO TIME,	075	19
OUR SINS AND WICKEDNESS, WE ARE SORE LET AND HINCEREC	095	06
NEITHER WITH THE LEAVEN OF MALICE AND WICKEDNESS	163	02
NEITHER WITH THE LEAVEN OF MALICE AND WICKEDNESS	165	15
OF MALICE AND WICKEDNESS, THAT WE MAY ALWAYS SERVE	170	21
SPIRITUAL WICKEDNESS IN HIGH PLACES	219	10
THEIR WICKEDNESS, AND SAID, WHY TEMPT YE ME, YE	223	05
ART THE GOD THAT HAST NO PLEASURE IN WICKEDNESS	348	07
THEIR INWARD PARTS ARE VERY WICKEDNESS	348	19
THERE BE ANY WICKEDNESS IN MY HANDS	349	28
9 O LET THE WICKEDNESS OF THE UNGODLY COME TO AN END	350	09
AND HIS WICKEDNESS SHALL FALL ON HIS OWN PATE	350	26
DELIGHTETH IN WICKEDNESS, DOTH HIS SOUL ABHCR	354	31
SHALT FIND NO WICKEDNESS IN ME	358	22
AND ESCHEWED MINE OWN WICKEDNESS	361	14
HANDS IS WICKEDNESS, *	371	16
TO THE WICKEDNESS OF THEIR OWN INVENTIONS	373	14
FORGAVEST THE WICKEDNESS OF MY SIN, *	377	33
ME THE WICKEDNESS OF THE UNGODLY, *	383	26
THERE ARE THEY FALLEN, ALL THAT WORK WICKEDNESS	384	21
TALKED OF WICKEDNESS, AND IMAGINED DECEIT ALL THE DAY	388	11
CONFESS MY WICKEDNESS, *	388	28
WHEN WICKEDNESS AT MY HEELS COMPASSETH ME ROUND	400	15
MOUTH SPEAK WICKEDNESS, *	402	28
FROM MY WICKEDNESS, *	403	11
WAS SHAPEN IN WICKEDNESS, *	403	18
IMAGINETH WICKEDNESS, *	404	22
AND STRENGTHENED HIMSELF IN HIS WICKEDNESS	405	03
AND BECOME ABOMINABLE IN THEIR WICKEDNESS	405	15
THAT WORK WICKEDNESS, *	405	22
11 WICKEDNESS IS THEREIN	407	09
FOR WICKEDNESS IS IN THEIR DWELLINGS, AND AMONG THEM	407	21
7 SHALL THEY ESCAPE FOR THEIR WICKEDNESS	408	28
AND YOUR HANDS DEAL WITH WICKEDNESS	410	11
UNTO THEM THAT OFFEND OF MALICIOUS WICKEDNESS	411	15
THEY IMAGINE WICKEDNESS, AND PRACTISE IT	415	30
INCLINE UNTO WICKEDNESS WITH MINE HEART, *	418	16
OF SUCH A ONE AS GOETH ON STILL IN HIS WICKEDNESS	420	28
FALL FROM ONE WICKEDNESS TO ANOTHER, *	423	30
THE SON OF WICKEDNESS SHALL NOT HURT HIM	451	20
WORKERS OF WICKEDNESS DO FLOURISH, *	456	14
WORKERS OF WICKEDNESS SHALL BE DESTROYED	456	18
THE THRONE OF WICKEDNESS, *	458	27
THEM THEIR WICKEDNESS, AND DESTROY THEM IN THEIR CWN	458	32
AND WERE BROUGHT DOWN IN THEIR WICKEDNESS	475	24
AND BECAUSE OF THEIR WICKEDNESS	477	10
FOR THE WICKEDNESS OF THEM THAT DWELL THEREIN	478	14
MOUTH OF ALL WICKEDNESS SHALL BE STOPPED	478	31
13 LET THE WICKEDNESS OF HIS FATHERS BE HAD IN	480	27
WHO DO NO WICKEDNESS, *	490	04
SO SHALL NO WICKEDNESS HAVE DOMINION OVER ME	499	05
LEST THE RIGHTEOUS PUT THEIR HAND UNTO WICKEDNESS	504	31

WICKEDNESS   CONTINUED

THEIR OWN WICKEDNESS, *   505 02
BE ANY WAY OF WICKEDNESS IN ME   516 06
MEN THAT WORK WICKEDNESS, NEITHER LET ME EAT OF SUCH   517 17
I WILL PRAY YET AGAINST THEIR WICKEDNESS   517 23
THEIR RIGHT HAND IS A RIGHT HAND OF WICKEDNESS   520 07
ALL SIN AND WICKEDNESS, AND FROM OUR SPIRITUAL ENEMY,   581 03
MAY PUNISH WICKEDNESS AND VICE, AND MAINTAIN THY TRUE   590 29
AWAY BY THEIR WICKEDNESS, NOR THE GRACE OF GOD'S   608 15

WICKEDNESSES

4 FOR MY WICKEDNESSES ARE GONE OVER MY HEAD, *   387 28
NOR REWARDED US ACCORDING TO OUR WICKEDNESSES   466 26

WIDE

OPEN THY MOUTH WIDE, AND I SHALL FILL IT   442 34
12 LOOK HOW WIDE ALSO THE EAST IS FROM THE WEST   466 30
SO IS THE GREAT AND WIDE SEA ALSO   469 10

WIDOW

THE ONLY SON OF HIS MOTHER, AND SHE WAS A WIDOW   212 31
IN HIS WAGES, THE WIDOW, AND THE FATHERLESS, AND THAT   232 19
AND SHE WAS A WIDOW OF ABOUT FOURSCORE AND FOUR   233 19
THE FATHERLESS AND WIDOW, AND LOVETH THE STRANGER, IN   263 26
6 THEY MURDER THE WIDOW AND THE STRANGER, *   457 29
AND HIS WIFE A WIDOW   480 18
HE DEFENDETH THE FATHERLESS AND WIDOW   522 21

WIDOWS

AND WIDOWS, AND ALL WHO ARE DESOLATE AND   057 02
FATHERLESS AND WIDOWS IN THEIR AFFLICTION, AND TO   176 16
FATHERLESS AND WIDOWS IN THEIR AFFLICTION, AND TO   266 08
AND DEFENDETH THE CAUSE OF THE WIDOWS   419 20
AND THERE WERE NO WIDOWS TO MAKE LAMENTATION   439 07

WIFE

THY NEIGHBOUR'S WIFE, NOR HIS SERVANT, NOR HIS MAID,   069 21
MARY HIS ESPOUSED WIFE, BEING GREAT WITH CHILD   099 05
FEAR NOT TO TAKE UNTO THEE MARY THY WIFE   105 05
LORD HAD BIDDEN HIM, AND TOOK UNTO HIM HIS WIFE   105 14
HIS WIFE SENT UNTO HIM, SAYING,   135 33
MARY THE WIFE OF CLEOPHAS, AND MARY   160 18
I HAVE MARRIED A WIFE, AND THEREFORE I CANNOT COME   192 11
TO BE SOLD, AND HIS WIFE, AND CHILDREN, AND ALL THAT   221 17
OR MOTHER, OR WIFE, OR CHILDREN, OR LANDS, FOR MY   231 19
IS THE HEAD OF THE WIFE, EVEN AS CHRIST IS THE HEAD   267 15
HE THAT LOVETH HIS WIFE LOVETH HIMSELF   267 25
BE JOINED UNTO HIS WIFE, AND THEY TWO SHALL BE ONE   267 30
SO LOVE HIS WIFE EVEN AS HIMSELF   268 02
AND THE WIFE SEE THAT SHE REVERENCE HER HUSBAND   268 02
AND SHALL CLEAVE TO HIS WIFE   268 08
THY NEIGHBOUR'S WIFE, NOR HIS SERVANT, NOR HIS MAID,   287 21
WOMAN TO THY WEDDED WIFE, TO LIVE TOGETHER AFTER   301 06
TO MY WEDDED WIFE, TO HAVE AND TO HOLD FROM THIS DAY   301 28
THEY ARE MAN AND WIFE, IN THE NAME OF THE FATHER, AND   304 08
THE MAN AND WIFE KNEELING, THE MINISTER SHALL ADD   R 304 10
AND HIS WIFE A WIDOW   480 18
3 THY WIFE SHALL BE AS THE FRUITFUL VINE *   506 10
THE HUSBANDS OF ONE WIFE, RULING THEIR CHILDREN AND   531 33
THE HUSBAND OF ONE WIFE, VIGILANT, SOBER, OF GOOD   549 20
THY NEIGHBOUR'S WIFE, NOR HIS SERVANT, NOR HIS MAID,   579 21

WILD

DID EAT LOCUSTS AND WILD HONEY   112 14
AND THE WILD BEASTS OF THE FIELD ARE IN MY SIGHT   402 13
13 THE WILD BOAR OUT OF THE WOOD DOTH ROOT IT UP,   441 28
AND THE WILD BEASTS OF THE FIELD DEVOUR IT   441 29
AND THE WILD ASSES QUENCH THEIR THIRST   468 15
A REFUGE FOR THE WILD GOATS   468 30

WILDERNESS

OUT INTO THE WILDERNESS TO SEE   094 26
CRYING IN THE WILDERNESS, MAKE STRAIGHT THE WAY OF   095 29
CRYING IN THE WILDERNESS, PREPARE YE THE WAY OF THE   112 06
IN THE WILDERNESS, AND PREACH THE BAPTISM OF   112 08
PERILS IN THE WILDERNESS, IN PERILS IN THE SEA,   121 07
INTO THE WILDERNESS TO BE TEMPTED OF THE DEVIL   126 23
HORSE IN THE WILDERNESS, THAT THEY SHOULD NOT   139 14
IN THE WILDERNESS, EVEN SO MUST THE SON OF MAN BE   188 27
NINE IN THE WILDERNESS, AND GO AFTER THAT WHICH IS   193 19
THESE MEN WITH BREAD HERE IN THE WILDERNESS   199 16
FOR THEY WERE OVERTHROWN IN THE WILDERNESS   201 12
CRIETH IN THE WILDERNESS, PREPARE YE THE WAY OF THE   242 20
SAFELY IN THE WILDERNESS, AND SLEEP IN THE WOODS   262 06
MANNA IN THE WILDERNESS, AND ARE DEAD   322 23
THE VOICE OF THE LORD SHAKETH THE WILDERNESS   374 12
SHAKETH THE WILDERNESS OF KADESH   374 13
AND REMAIN IN THE WILDERNESS   406 33
SHALL DROP UPON THE DWELLINGS OF THE WILDERNESS   417 09
THROUGH THE WILDERNESS, 8 THE EARTH SHOOK, AND THE   419 25
DWELL IN THE WILDERNESS SHALL KNEEL BEFORE HIM   427 14
HIM TO BE MEAT FOR THE PEOPLE OF THE WILDERNESS   431 05
ROCKS IN THE WILDERNESS, *   435 30
AND PROVOKED THE MOST HIGHEST IN THE WILDERNESS   436 03
SHALL GOD PREPARE A TABLE IN THE WILDERNESS   436 07
HIM IN THE WILDERNESS, *   437 21
THEM IN THE WILDERNESS LIKE A FLOCK   438 15
AND AS IN THE DAY OF TEMPTATION IN THE WILDERNESS   459 21

WILDERNESS   CONTINUED

IN THE WILDERNESS, *   464 21
THEM THROUGH THE DEEP, AS THROUGH A WILDERNESS   473 19
THEM IN THE WILDERNESS, *   473 29
TO OVERTHROW THEM IN THE WILDERNESS   474 22
ASTRAY IN THE WILDERNESS OUT OF THE WAY, *   476 12
FLOODS INTO A WILDERNESS, *   478 12
HE MAKETH THE WILDERNESS A STANDING WATER, *   478 16
LET THEM WANDER OUT OF THE WAY IN THE WILDERNESS   478 27
16 WHO LED HIS PEOPLE THROUGH THE WILDERNESS   512 14

WILES

STAND AGAINST THE WILES OF THE DEVIL   219 07
THE FLESH OR THE WILES OF SATAN, BEING PURGED AND   317 20

WILFULLY

WHEN YE WILFULLY ABSTAIN FROM THE LORD'S TABLE, AND   089 16

WILINESS

IN THE CRAFTY WILINESS THAT THEY HAVE IMAGINED   353 06

WILL

SAID UNTO ME, WE WILL GO INTO THE HOUSE OF THE LORD   003 17
TO MY FATHER, AND WILL SAY UNTO HIM, FATHER, I HAVE   004 26
I WILL ARISE AND GO TO MY FATHER, AND WILL SAY UNTO   004 26
WE WILL REJOICE AND BE GLAD IN IT   005 04
THY WILL BE DONE, ON EARTH AS IT IS IN HEAVEN   007 24
INCLINE TO THY WILL, AND WALK IN THY WAY   017 33
WISDOM AND STRENGTH TO KNOW AND TO DO THY WILL   018 12
IS WITH MEN, AND HE WILL DWELL WITH THEM, AND THEY   021 29
AND WHOSOEVER WILL, LET HIM TAKE THE WATER OF LIFE   022 31
EARTH PEACE, GOOD WILL TOWARDS MEN   025 23
AND I WILL REJOICE IN GIVING PRAISE FOR THE   028 03
MINDFUL OF THY FAVOUR AND GLAD TO DO THY WILL   036 12
ACCORDING TO GOD'S WILL, SERVE HIM FAITHFULLY, AND   047 13
IS ACCORDING TO THY WILL, WHO LIVEST AND REIGNEST   049 08
ACCORDING TO THY WILL, MAY EFFECTUALLY BE OBTAINED,   050 11
ACCORDING TO THY WILL IN THIS LIFE, AND ALSO MAY BE   051 11
THIS THY MERCY, AND WILL ALWAYS DECLARE THY   051 26
ACCORDING TO THY WILL, AND ALSO MAY BE PARTAKER OF   053 16
THEY WILL APPEAR, AND IT IS TO BE HOPED, THE REASONS   VI 29
IN WHICH IT WILL ALSO APPEAR THAT THIS CHURCH IS FAR   VI 31
IS HOPED THE WHOLE WILL BE RECEIVED AND EXAMINED BY   VI 36
FOR THE LORD WILL NOT HOLD HIM GUILTLESS, THAT TAKETH   068 20
HE THAT DOETH THE WILL OF MY FATHER WHICH IS IN   072 15
THAT HE WILL FORGET YOUR WORKS, AND LABOUR THAT   072 23
HEAVY LADEN, AND I WILL REFRESH YOU   076 13
EARTH PEACE, GOOD WILL TOWARDS MEN   084 03
AND THE OTHER PARTY WILL NOT BE PERSUADED TO A GODLY R 085 14
WHOLLY TO HIS HOLY WILL AND PLEASURE, AND STUDYING TO   086 21
TO THOSE WHO WILL PRESUME TO RECEIVE IT UNWORTHILY   087 07
EITHER BY WILL, WORD, OR DEED, THERE TO   087 19
THAT YE WILL NOT REFUSE TO COME THERETO, BEING   088 15
FOR A MAN TO SAY, I WILL NOT COMMUNICATE, BECAUSE I   088 27
ASHAMED TO SAY YE WILL NOT COME   088 32
RETURN TO GOD, WILL YE EXCUSE YOURSELVES, AND SAY YE   088 33
FEIGNED EXCUSES WILL AVAIL BEFORE GOD   089 02
THAT YE WILL BE PARTAKERS OF THIS HOLY   089 09
YE WILL BY GOD'S GRACE RETURN TO A BETTER   089 19
AND STRAIGHTWAY HE WILL SEND THEM   091 17
FOR THIS CAUSE I WILL CONFESS TO THEE AMONG THE   092 26
LORD COME, WHO BOTH WILL BRING TO LIGHT THE HIDDEN   094 11
OF DARKNESS, AND WILL MAKE MANIFEST THE COUNSELS OF   094 12
AND AGAIN, I WILL BE TO HIM A FATHER, AND HE SHALL BE   097 03
NOR OF THE WILL OF THE FLESH, NOR OF THE WILL   098 03
NOR OF THE WILL OF MAN, BUT OF GOD   098 03
EARTH PEACE, GOOD WILL TOWARD MEN   099 22
UNTO HIM, IF I WILL THAT HE TARRY TILL I COME,   102 08
IF I WILL THAT HE TARRY TILL I COME, WHAT IS   102 11
FOR HEROD WILL SEEK THE YOUNG CHILD TO DESTROY HIM   103 19
WE MAY IN ALL THINGS OBEY THY BLESSED WILL   105 23
IN YOU BOTH TO WILL AND TO DO OF HIS GOOD PLEASURE   106 05
AND PERFECT, WILL OF GOD   110 08
I WILL REPAY, SAITH THE LORD   113 05
FORTH HIS HAND, AND TOUCHED HIM, SAYING, I WILL   115 02
SAITH UNTO HIM, I WILL COME AND HEAL HIM   115 09
TIME OF HARVEST I WILL SAY TO THE REAPERS, GATHER YE   116 29
CARCASE IS, THERE WILL THE EAGLES BE GATHERED   118 13
IS RIGHT I WILL GIVE YOU   119 21
I WILL GIVE UNTO THIS LAST, EVEN AS UNTO THEE   120 09
FOR ME TO DO WHAT I WILL WITH MINE OWN   120 11
MUST NEEDS GLORY, I WILL GLORY OF THE THINGS WHICH   121 13
WHO KNOWETH IF HE WILL RETURN AND REPENT, AND LEAVE A   124 26
TREASURE IS, THERE WILL YOUR HEART BE ALSO   125 21
ALL THESE THINGS WILL I GIVE THEE, IF THOU WILT FALL   127 07
FOR THIS IS THE WILL OF GOD, EVEN YOUR   127 27
HE SAITH, I WILL RETURN UNTO MY HOUSE WHENCE I   130 12
UNTO THEM, WHOM WILL YE THAT I RELEASE UNTO YOU   135 29
OF THE TWAIN WILL YE THAT I RELEASE UNTO YOU   136 03
THE CROSS, AND WE WILL BELIEVE HIM   137 12
HIM NOW, IF HE WILL HAVE HIM   137 13
SEE WHETHER ELIAS WILL COME TO SAVE HIM   137 23
FOR I WILL TREAD THEM IN MINE ANGER, AND TRAMPLE THEM   138 18
MY GARMENTS, AND I WILL STAIN ALL MY RAIMENT   138 20
AND I WILL TREAD DOWN THE PEOPLE IN MINE ANGER, AND   138 25
IN MY FURY, AND I WILL BRING DOWN THEIR STRENGTH TO   138 26
I WILL MENTION THE LOVINGKINDNESSES OF THE LORD, AND   138 27
CHILDREN THAT WILL NOT LIE   138 34
AND WHENSOEVER YE WILL YE MAY DO THEM GOOD   140 12
AND HE WILL SHEW YOU A LARGE UPPER ROOM FURNISHED AND   140 30
I SAY UNTO YOU, I WILL DRINK NO MORE OF THE FRUIT OF   141 15

WILL CONTINUED

IT IS WRITTEN, I WILL SMITE THE SHEPHERD, AND THE 141 19
THAT I AM RISEN, I WILL GO BEFORE YOU INTO GALILEE 141 21
BE OFFENDED, YET WILL NOT I 141 22
DIE WITH THEE, I WILL NOT DENY THEE IN ANY WISE 141 26
NOT WHAT I WILL, BUT WHAT THOU WILT 142 02
WE HEARD HIM SAY, I WILL DESTROY THIS TEMPLE THAT IS 143 06
WITHIN THREE DAYS I WILL BUILD ANOTHER MADE WITHOUT 143 08
FOR THE LORD GOD WILL HELP ME 144 16
WHO WILL CONTEND WITH ME 144 19
THE LORD GOD WILL HELP ME 144 21
SAYING, WILL YE THAT I RELEASE UNTO YOU THE 145 18
UNTO THEM, WHAT WILL YE THEN THAT I SHALL DO UNTO HIM 145 23
SEE WHETHER ELIAS WILL COME TO TAKE HIM DOWN 146 33
I SAY UNTO YOU, I WILL NOT ANY MORE EAT THEREOF, 149 04
I SAY UNTO YOU, I WILL NOT DRINK OF THE FRUIT OF THE 149 07
NEVERTHELESS NOT MY WILL, BUT THINE, BE DONE 150 19
IF I TELL YOU, YE WILL NOT BELIEVE 151 31
I ALSO ASK YOU, YE WILL NOT ANSWER ME, NOR LET ME GO 151 32
I WILL THEREFORE CHASTISE HIM, AND RELEASE HIM 153 27
I WILL THEREFORE CHASTISE HIM, AND LET HIM GO 154 02
BUT HE DELIVERED JESUS TO THEIR WILL 154 08
OF ME,) TO DO THY WILL, O GOD 157 28
I COME TO DO THY WILL, O GOD 157 32
BY THE WHICH WILL WE ARE SANCTIFIED THROUGH THE 157 33
THE COVENANT THAT I WILL MAKE WITH THEM AFTER THOSE 158 11
SAITH THE LORD, I WILL PUT MY LAWS INTO THEIR HEARTS, 158 12
AND IN THEIR MINDS WILL I WRITE THEM 158 13
SINS AND INIQUITIES WILL I REMEMBER NO MORE 158 14
IS BETTER, IF THE WILL OF GOD BE SO, THAT YE SUFFER 161 21
AFTER THREE DAYS I WILL RISE AGAIN 162 18
ON THIS WISE, I WILL GIVE YOU THE SURE MERCIES OF 169 12
GENERATION BY THE WILL OF GOD, FELL ON SLEEP, AND WAS 169 15
FOR SO IS THE WILL OF GOD, THAT WITH WELL DOING YE 173 21
BUT I WILL SEE YOU AGAIN, AND YOUR HEART SHALL 174 14
OF HIS OWN WILL BEGAT HE US WITH THE WORD OF TRUTH, 174 29
THE COMFORTER WILL NOT COME UNTO YOU 175 11
BUT IF I DEPART, I WILL SEND HIM UNTO YOU 175 12
WHEN HE IS COME, HE WILL REPROVE THE WORLD OF SIN, 175 13
IS COME, HE WILL GUIDE YOU INTO ALL TRUTH 175 19
AND HE WILL SHEW YOU THINGS TO COME 175 21
IN MY NAME, HE WILL GIVE IT YOU 176 21
UNTO YOU, THAT I WILL PRAY THE FATHER FOR YOU 176 27
IS COME, WHOM I WILL SEND UNTO YOU FROM THE FATHER, 179 24
KILLETH YOU WILL THINK THAT HE DOETH GOD SERVICE 179 31
AND THESE THINGS WILL THEY DO UNTO YOU, BECAUSE THEY 179 32
AND I WILL PRAY THE FATHER, AND HE SHALL GIVE YOU 181 09
I WILL NOT LEAVE YOU COMFORTLESS 181 14
I WILL COME TO YOU 181 15
OF MY FATHER, AND I WILL LOVE HIM, AND WILL MANIFEST 181 20
WILL LOVE HIM, AND WILL MANIFEST MYSELF TO HIM 181 21
A MAN LOVE ME, HE WILL KEEP MY WORDS 181 24
AND MY FATHER WILL LOVE HIM, AND WE WILL COME UNTO 181 25
LOVE HIM, AND WE WILL COME UNTO HIM, AND MAKE OUR 181 26
WHOM THE FATHER WILL SEND IN MY NAME, HE SHALL TEACH 181 31
HEREAFTER I WILL NOT TALK MUCH WITH YOU 182 07
DIVIDING TO EVERY MAN SEVERALLY AS HE WILL 183 02
THAT IS A FATHER, WILL HE GIVE HIM A STONE 183 14
IF HE ASK A FISH, WILL HE FOR A FISH GIVE HIM A 183 15
SHALL ASK AN EGG, WILL HE OFFER HIM A SCORPION 183 16
US ACCORDING TO THY WILL, COMFORT US IN ALL OUR 183 24
NOT FOLLOW, BUT WILL FLEE FROM HIM 186 08
AND A STRANGER WILL THEY NOT FOLLOW, BUT WILL FLEE 186 08
UP HITHER, AND I WILL SHEW THEE THINGS WHICH MUST BE 187 03
BOTH IN WILL AND DEED 189 05
FROM THE DEAD, THEY WILL REPENT 190 28
NEITHER WILL THEY BE PERSUADED, THOUGH ONE 190 30
FOR HE THAT WILL LOVE LIFE, AND SEE GOOD DAYS, LET 195 24
AND WHO IS HE THAT WILL HARM YOU, IF YE BE FOLLOWERS 195 30
AT THY WORD I WILL LET DOWN THE NET 196 17
OWN HOUSES, THEY WILL FAINT BY THE WAY 199 13
HE THAT DOETH THE WILL OF MY FATHER WHICH IS IN 200 25
BY THEE BE ENABLED TO LIVE ACCORDING TO THY WILL 201 02
IS FAITHFUL, WHO WILL NOT SUFFER YOU TO BE TEMPTED 201 27
BUT WILL WITH THE TEMPTATION ALSO MAKE A WAY TO 201 28
I WILL ARISE AND GO TO MY FATHER, AND WILL SAY UNTO 202 12
TO MY FATHER, AND WILL SAY UNTO HIM, FATHER, I HAVE 202 13
DIVIDING TO EVERY MAN SEVERALLY AS HE WILL 204 04
I COME AGAIN, I WILL REPAY THEE 209 02
FOR EITHER HE WILL HATE THE ONE, AND LOVE THE OTHER 211 09
OR ELSE HE WILL HOLD TO THE ONE, AND DESPISE THE 211 10
FOR THE MORROW WILL BE ANXIOUS FOR ITSELF 211 34
INTO A PIT, AND WILL NOT STRAIGHTWAY PULL HIM OUT ON 214 06
WHAT THE WILL OF THE LORD IS 217 26
AND WONDERS, YE WILL NOT BELIEVE 219 33
A GOOD WORK IN YOU WILL PERFORM IT UNTIL THE DAY OF 220 26
WITH ME, AND I WILL PAY THEE ALL 221 20
WITH ME, AND I WILL PAY THEE ALL 221 28
KNOWLEDGE OF HIS WILL IN ALL WISDOM AND SPIRITUAL 224 03
THE LORD, THAT I WILL RAISE UNTO DAVID A RIGHTEOUS 225 09
MOSES SAITH, I WILL PROVOKE YOU TO JEALOUSY BY THEM 227 17
A FOOLISH NATION I WILL ANGER YOU 227 18
FOLLOW ME, AND I WILL MAKE YOU FISHERS OF MEN 227 27
YE HAVE DONE THE WILL OF GOD, YE MIGHT RECEIVE THE 228 16
COME WILL COME, AND WILL NOT TARRY 228 18
HE THAT SHALL COME WILL COME, AND WILL NOT TARRY 228 18
INTO HIS SIDE, I WILL NOT BELIEVE 228 30
FOR I WILL SHEW HIM HOW GREAT THINGS HE MUST SUFFER 230 28
BEHOLD, I WILL SEND MY MESSENGER, AND HE SHALL 232 03
AND I WILL COME NEAR TO YOU TO JUDGMENT 232 15
AND I WILL BE A SWIFT WITNESS AGAINST THE SORCERERS, 232 16
WHOMSOEVER THE SON WILL REVEAL HIM 235 10
HEAVY LADEN, AND I WILL GIVE YOU REST 235 11
BUT AHAZ SAID, I WILL NOT ASK, NEITHER WILL I TEMPT 235 27
NOT ASK, NEITHER WILL I TEMPT THE LORD 235 28

PAGE LN

WILL CONTINUED

TO WEARY MEN, BUT WILL YE WEARY MY GOD ALSO 235 30
SHALL ASK WHAT YE WILL, AND IT SHALL BE DONE UNTO 238 18
A PLACE FOR YOU, I WILL COME AGAIN, AND RECEIVE YOU 239 33
IN MY NAME, THAT WILL I DO, THAT THE FATHER MAY BE 240 22
THING IN MY NAME, I WILL DO IT 240 24
THE LORD GOD WILL COME WITH STRONG HAND, AND HIS ARM 243 06
UPON THIS ROCK I WILL BUILD MY CHURCH 246 07
AND I WILL GIVE UNTO THEE THE KEYS OF THE KINGDOM OF 246 09
BUT WHOSOEVER WILL BE GREAT AMONG YOU, LET HIM BE 247 23
AND WHOSOEVER WILL BE CHIEF AMONG YOU, LET HIM BE 247 25
MOREOVER I WILL ENDEAVOUR THAT YE MAY BE ABLE AFTER 248 11
THAT MEANETH, I WILL HAVE MERCY, AND NOT SACRIFICE 251 22
PERSECUTED ME, THEY WILL ALSO PERSECUTE YOU 255 19
MY SAYING, THEY WILL KEEP YOUR'S ALSO 255 20
ALL THESE THINGS WILL THEY DO UNTO YOU FOR MY NAME'S 255 21
IS COME, WHOM I WILL SEND UNTO YOU FROM THE FATHER, 255 30
OF PEACE, AND WILL CAUSE THE EVIL BEASTS TO CEASE OUT 262 04
I WILL MAKE WITH THEM A COVENANT OF PEACE, AND WILL 262 04
AND I WILL MAKE THEM AND THE PLACES ROUND ABOUT MY 262 07
AND I WILL CAUSE THE SHOWER TO COME DOWN IN HIS 262 08
AND I WILL RAISE UP FOR THEM A PLANT OF RENOWN, 262 17
UNTO YOU, THOUGH HE WILL NOT RISE AND GIVE HIM, 262 33
HIS IMPORTUNITY HE WILL RISE AND GIVE HIM AS MANY AS 263 02
THAT IS A FATHER, WILL HE GIVE HIM A STONE 263 08
IF HE ASK A FISH, WILL HE FOR A FISH GIVE HIM A 263 09
SHALL ASK AN EGG, WILL HE OFFER HIM A SCORPION 263 10
OF HIS OWN WILL BEGAT HE US WITH THE WORD OF TRUTH, 265 21
SLEEP IN JESUS WILL GOD BRING WITH HIM 269 02
THAT COMETH TO ME I WILL IN NO WISE CAST OUT 269 14
OWN WILL, BUT THE WILL OF HIM THAT SENT ME 269 16
NOT TO DO MINE OWN WILL, BUT THE WILL OF HIM THAT 269 16
IS THE FATHER'S WILL WHICH HATH SENT ME, THAT OF ALL 269 17
AND THIS IS THE WILL OF HIM THAT SENT ME, THAT EVERY 269 19
AND I WILL RAISE HIM UP AT THE LAST DAY 269 21
BOUNTEOUS MERCY HE WILL GRANT TO THIS CHILD (THIS 274 02
OF THE GOOD WILL OF OUR HEAVENLY FATHER TOWARD THIS 276 03
BY GOD'S HELP, WILL ENDEAVOUR NOT TO FOLLOW, NOR 276 29
KEEP GOD'S HOLY WILL AND COMMANDMENTS, AND WALK IN 277 05
I WILL, BY GOD'S HELP 277 07
I WILL, BY GOD'S HELP 277 13
I WILL, GOD BEING MY HELPER 277 17
BY GOD'S HELP, WILL ENDEAVOUR NOT TO FOLLOW, NOR 277 30
KEEP GOD'S HOLY WILL AND COMMANDMENTS, AND WALK IN 278 14
I WILL, BY GOD'S HELP 278 16
KEEP GOD'S HOLY WILL AND COMMANDMENTS, AND WALK IN 283 27
AND BY GOD'S HELP SO I WILL 283 30
KEEP GOD'S HOLY WILL AND COMMANDMENTS 285 14
FOR THE LORD WILL NOT HOLD HIM GUILTLESS, THAT TAKETH 286 20
BY THEE BE ENABLED TO LIVE ACCORDING TO THY WILL 287 29
AND HE WILL TEACH US OF HIS WAYS, AND WE WILL WALK IN 290 06
OF HIS WAYS, AND WE WILL WALK IN HIS PATHS 290 06
MAKEST US BOTH TO WILL AND TO DO THOSE THINGS WHICH 298 14
YOU BOTH, AS YE WILL ANSWER AT THE DREADFUL DAY OF 300 24
THE MAN SHALL ANSWER, I WILL 301 12
THE WOMAN SHALL ANSWER, I WILL 301 21
IF IT BE THY WILL, THE GIFT AND HERITAGE OF CHILDREN 303 16
THEREFORE WILL I CALL UPON HIM AS LONG AS I LIVE 305 21
I WILL RECEIVE THE CUP OF SALVATION, AND CALL UPON 305 29
I WILL PAY MY VOWS NOW IN THE PRESENCE OF ALL HIS 305 31
ACCORDING TO THY WILL IN THIS LIFE, AND ALSO MAY BE 306 30
I WILL GO UNTO THE ALTAR OF GOD 310 02
AND UPON THE HARP WILL I GIVE THANKS UNTO THEE, O 310 14
FOR I WILL YET GIVE HIM THANKS, WHICH IS THE HELP OF 310 18
I WILL CRY UNTO GOD WITH MY VOICE 310 29
EVEN UNTO GOD WILL I CRY WITH MY VOICE, AND HE SHALL 310 30
AM IN HEAVINESS, I WILL THINK UPON GOD 311 04
HEART IS VEXED, I WILL COMPLAIN 311 05
WILL THE LORD ABSENT HIMSELF FOR EVER 311 12
AND WILL HE BE NO MORE INTREATED 311 12
AND WILL HE SHUT UP HIS LOVING-KINDNESS IN 311 16
BUT I WILL REMEMBER THE YEARS OF THE RIGHT HAND OF 311 18
I WILL GIVE THANKS UNTO THEE, O LORD, WITH MY WHOLE 311 28
BEFORE THE GODS WILL I SING PRAISE UNTO THEE 311 29
I WILL WORSHIP TOWARD THY HOLY TEMPLE, AND PRAISE THY 311 30
BY HIS OWN CARNAL WILL AND FRAILNESS 314 05
HIM IN PATIENCE AND SUBMISSION TO THY WILL 315 26
IF IT BE THY GRACIOUS WILL 321 23
ACCORDING TO HIS WILL, HE HEARETH US 322 16
THE BREAD THAT I WILL GIVE IS MY FLESH, WHICH I WILL 322 28
MY FLESH, WHICH I WILL GIVE FOR THE LIFE OF THE 322 28
THE LORD, WHICH I WILL REQUIRE 326 08
THEREFORE WILL I OFFER IN HIS DWELLING AN OBLATION, 326 17
I WILL SING AND SPEAK PRAISES UNTO THE LORD 326 18
THY FACE, LORD, WILL I SEEK 326 23
THEREFORE WILL WE NOT FEAR, THOUGH THE EARTH BE 327 05
I WILL BE EXALTED AMONG THE NATIONS, AND I WILL BE 327 14
THE NATIONS, AND I WILL BE EXALTED IN THE EARTH 327 15
I WILL LIFT UP MINE EYES UNTO THE HILLS 327 19
HE WILL NOT SUFFER THY FOOT TO BE MOVED 327 23
THAT KEEPETH THEE WILL NOT SLEEP 327 24
BUT SOME MAN WILL SAY, HOW ARE THE DEAD RAISED UP 329 05
A PLACE FOR YOU, I WILL COME AGAIN, AND RECEIVE YOU 331 21
THAT COMETH TO ME I WILL IN NO WISE CAST OUT 333 04
JESUS FROM THE DEAD WILL ALSO QUICKEN OUR MORTAL 333 05
GOOD WORK TO DO HIS WILL, WORKING IN YOU THAT WHICH 335 19
SHADOW OF DEATH, I WILL FEAR NO EVIL 338 24
AND I WILL DWELL IN THE HOUSE OF THE LORD FOR EVER 338 30
I WILL LIFT UP MINE EYES UNTO THE HILLS 339 03
HE WILL NOT SUFFER THY FOOT TO BE MOVED 339 07
THAT KEEPETH THEE WILL NOT SLEEP 339 08
BUT I WILL SEE YOU AGAIN, AND YOUR HEART SHALL 341 10
AND IN HIS LAW WILL HE EXERCISE HIMSELF DAY AND 345 11
THAT WILL BRING FORTH HIS FRUIT IN DUE SEASON 345 13
7 I WILL REHEARSE THE DECREE 346 10

6 I WILL NOT BE AFRAID FOR TEN THOUSANDS OF THE	347 02
OF MEN, HOW LONG WILL YE BLASPHEME MINE HONOUR, *	347 13
UPON THE LORD HE WILL HEAR ME	347 17
WHO WILL SHOW US ANY GOOD	347 23
9 I WILL LAY ME DOWN IN PEACE, AND TAKE MY REST	347 28
FOR UNTO THEE WILL I MAKE MY PRAYER	348 02
IN THE MORNING WILL I DIRECT MY PRAYER UNTO THEE,	348 05
UNTO THEE, AND WILL LOOK UP	348 05
THE LORD WILL ABHOR BOTH THE BLOOD-THIRSTY AND	348 12
OF THY MERCY WILL I COME INTO THINE HOUSE	348 13
AND IN THY FEAR WILL I WORSHIP TOWARD THY HOLY	348 14
AND WHO WILL GIVE THEE THANKS IN THE PIT	349 09
THE LORD WILL RECEIVE MY PRAYER	349 16
13 IF A MAN WILL NOT TURN, HE WILL WHET HIS SWORD	350 17
WILL NOT TURN, HE WILL WHET HIS SWORD	350 17
18 I WILL GIVE THANKS UNTO THE LORD, ACCORDING TO HIS	350 27
AND I WILL PRAISE THE NAME OF THE LORD MOST HIGH	350 28
I WILL GIVE THANKS UNTO THEE, O LORD, WITH MY WHOLE	351 22
I WILL SPEAK OF ALL THY MARVELLOUS WORKS	351 23
2 I WILL BE GLAD AND REJOICE IN THEE	351 24
MY SONGS WILL I MAKE OF THY NAME, O THOU MOST	351 24
9 THE LORD ALSO WILL BE A DEFENCE FOR THE OPPRESSED,	352 06
THAT KNOW THY NAME WILL PUT THEIR TRUST IN THEE	352 08
I WILL REJOICE IN THY SALVATION	352 20
HIS FACE, AND HE WILL NEVER SEE IT	353 31
HIS COUNTENANCE WILL BEHOLD THE THING THAT IS JUST	355 03
WITH OUR TONGUE WILL WE PREVAIL	355 14
AND WILL HELP EVERY ONE FROM HIM THAT SWELLETH	355 18
OF THE POOR, 6 I WILL UP, SAITH THE LORD	355 18
AGAINST HIM, AND WILL SET HIM AT REST	355 19
THAT TROUBLE ME WILL REJOICE AT IT	356 05
6 I WILL SING OF THE LORD, BECAUSE HE HATH DEALT SO	356 09
I WILL PRAISE THE NAME OF THE LORD MOST HIGHEST	356 10
OF BLOOD WILL I NOT OFFER, *	357 29
8 I WILL THANK THE LORD FOR GIVING ME WARNING	358 04
I WILL LOVE THEE, O LORD, MY STRENGTH	359 24
MY MIGHT, IN WHOM I WILL TRUST	359 26
3 I WILL CALL UPON THE LORD, WHICH IS WORTHY TO BE	359 29
AND WILL NOT CAST OUT HIS COMMANDMENTS FROM ME	361 11
38 I WILL FOLLOW UPON MINE ENEMIES, AND OVERTAKE	362 11
NEITHER WILL I TURN AGAIN TILL I HAVE DESTROYED THEM	362 12
39 I WILL SMITE THEM, THAT THEY SHALL NOT BE ABLE TO	362 14
43 I WILL BEAT THEM AS SMALL AS THE DUST BEFORE THE	362 23
I WILL CAST THEM OUT AS THE CLAY IN THE STREETS	362 24
50 FOR THIS CAUSE WILL I GIVE THANKS UNTO THEE,	363 05
5 WE WILL REJOICE IN THY SALVATION, AND TRIUMPH IN	364 23
HIS ANOINTED, AND WILL HEAR HIM FROM HIS HOLY HEAVEN,	364 27
BUT WE WILL REMEMBER THE NAME OF THE LORD OUR GOD	364 30
SO WILL WE SING, AND PRAISE THY POWER	365 33
DELIVER HIM, IF HE WILL HAVE HIM	366 19
22 I WILL DECLARE THY NAME UNTO MY BRETHREN	367 16
OF THE CONGREGATION WILL I PRAISE THEE	367 17
MY VOWS WILL I PERFORM IN THE SIGHT OF THEM THAT FEAR	367 24
SHADOW OF DEATH, I WILL FEAR NO EVIL	368 17
AND I WILL DWELL IN THE HOUSE OF THE LORD FOR EVER	368 23
UNTO THEE, O LORD, WILL I LIFT UP MY SOUL	369 18
THEREFORE WILL HE TEACH SINNERS IN THE WAY	369 33
AND HE WILL SHOW THEM HIS COVENANT	370 13
AND I WILL WALK IN THY TRUTH	371 04
NEITHER WILL I HAVE FELLOWSHIP WITH THE DECEITFUL	371 07
AND WILL NOT SIT AMONG THE UNGODLY	371 08
6 I WILL WASH MY HANDS IN INNOCENCY, O LORD	371 09
AND SO WILL I GO TO THINE ALTAR	371 18
11 BUT AS FOR ME, I WILL WALK INNOCENTLY	371 20
I WILL PRAISE THE LORD IN THE CONGREGATIONS	371 31
WAR AGAINST ME, YET WILL I PUT MY TRUST IN HIM	371 32
THE LORD, WHICH I WILL REQUIRE	372 09
7 THEREFORE WILL I OFFER IN HIS DWELLING AN OBLATION,	372 10
I WILL SING AND SPEAK PRAISES UNTO THE LORD	372 15
THY FACE, LORD, WILL I SEEK	372 24
NOT OVER INTO THE WILL OF MINE ADVERSARIES	373 03
UNTO THEE WILL I CRY, O LORD, MY STRENGTH	373 24
AND IN MY SONG WILL I PRAISE HIM	374 24
I WILL MAGNIFY THEE, O LORD	375 19
O MY GOD, I WILL GIVE THANKS UNTO THEE FOR EVER	376 04
8 I WILL BE GLAD AND REJOICE IN THY MERCY	377 32
6 I SAID, I WILL CONFESS MY SINS UNTO THE LORD	378 08
9 I WILL INFORM THEE, AND TEACH THEE IN THE WAY	378 09
AND I WILL GUIDE THEE WITH MINE EYE	378 12
ELSE THEY WILL NOT OBEY THEE	380 01
I WILL ALWAY GIVE THANKS UNTO THE LORD	380 23
I WILL TEACH YOU THE FEAR OF THE LORD	381 05
AND WILL SAVE SUCH AS BE OF AN HUMBLE SPIRIT	382 32
18 SO WILL I GIVE THEE THANKS IN THE GREAT	382 33
I WILL PRAISE THEE AMONG MUCH PEOPLE	386 27
AND HIS TONGUE WILL BE TALKING OF JUDGMENT	386 32
34 THE LORD WILL NOT LEAVE HIM IN HIS HAND, *	388 28
18 FOR I WILL CONFESS MY WICKEDNESS, *	389 05
I SAID, I WILL TAKE HEED TO MY WAYS, *	389 07
2 I WILL KEEP MY MOUTH AS IT WERE WITH A BRIDLE,	390 32
I SHOULD FULFIL THY WILL, O MY GOD	391 02
I WILL NOT REFRAIN MY LIPS, O LORD, AND THAT THOU	392 03
THOU HIM INTO THE WILL OF HIS ENEMIES	393 13
FOR I WILL YET THANK HIM, WHICH IS THE HELP OF MY	393 15
THEREFORE WILL I REMEMBER THEE FROM THE LAND OF	393 15
10 THE LORD WILL GRANT HIS LOVING-KINDNESS IN THE	393 21
IN THE NIGHT SEASON WILL I SING OF HIM, AND MAKE MY	393 22
11 I WILL SAY UNTO THE GOD OF MY STRENGTH, WHY HAST	393 24
FOR I WILL YET THANK HIM, WHICH IS THE HELP OF MY	393 33
AND UPON THE HARP WILL I GIVE THANKS UNTO THEE, O	394 13
FOR I WILL YET GIVE HIM THANKS, WHICH IS THE HELP OF	394 17
6 THROUGH THEE WILL WE OVERTHROW OUR ENEMIES,	395 02
AND IN THY NAME WILL WE TREAD THEM UNDER THAT RISE UP	395 03
7 FOR I WILL NOT TRUST IN MY BOW, *	395 05
AND WILL PRAISE THY NAME FOR EVER	395 09
17 I WILL MAKE THY NAME TO BE REMEMBERED FROM ONE	397 21
2 THEREFORE WILL WE NOT FEAR, THOUGH THE EARTH BE	397 27
I WILL BE EXALTED AMONG THE NATIONS, AND I WILL BE	398 14
THE NATIONS, AND I WILL BE EXALTED IN THE EARTH	398 15
4 I WILL INCLINE MINE EAR TO THE PARABLE, *	400 12
UNTO THYSELF, MEN WILL SPEAK GOOD OF THEE	401 13
I MYSELF WILL TESTIFY AGAINST THEE, O ISRAEL	402 04
O MY PEOPLE, AND I WILL SPEAK	402 04
8 I WILL NOT REPROVE THEE BECAUSE OF THY SACRIFICES	402 06
9 I WILL TAKE NO BULLOCK OUT OF THINE HOUSE, *	402 08
IF I BE HUNGRY, I WILL NOT TELL THEE	402 14
THOU THAT I WILL EAT BULLS' FLESH, *	402 16
SO WILL I HEAR THEE, AND THOU SHALT PRAISE ME	402 20
BUT I WILL REPROVE THEE, AND SET BEFORE THEE THE	402 34
HIS WAY ARIGHT, WILL I SHOW THE SALVATION OF GOD	403 05
10 I WILL ALWAY GIVE THANKS UNTO THEE FOR THAT THOU	405 07
AND I WILL HOPE IN THY NAME, FOR THY SAINTS LIKE IT	405 08
OF A FREE HEART WILL I GIVE THEE, AND PRAISE THY	406 14
17 AS FOR ME, I WILL CALL UPON GOD, *	407 23
AND AT NOON-DAY I WILL PRAY, AND THAT INSTANTLY	407 25
FOR THEY WILL NOT TURN, NOR FEAR GOD	407 31
4 I WILL PRAISE GOD, BECAUSE OF HIS WORD	408 21
TRUST IN GOD, AND WILL NOT FEAR WHAT FLESH CAN DO	408 22
10 IN GOD'S WORD WILL I REJOICE	409 02
IN THE LORD'S WORD WILL I COMFORT ME	409 03
I WILL NOT BE AFRAID WHAT MAN CAN DO UNTO ME	409 04
UNTO THEE, O GOD, WILL I PAY MY VOWS	409 06
UNTO THEE WILL I GIVE THANKS	409 07
2 I WILL CALL UNTO THE MOST HIGH GOD, *	409 15
I WILL SING AND GIVE PRAISE	409 29
I MYSELF WILL AWAKE RIGHT EARLY	409 32
10 I WILL GIVE THANKS UNTO THEE, O LORD, AMONG THE	409 33
AND I WILL SING UNTO THEE AMONG THE NATIONS	409 34
9 MY STRENGTH WILL I ASCRIBE UNTO THEE	411 22
IN THE EVENING THEY WILL RETURN, *	412 02
LIKE A DOG, AND WILL GO ABOUT THE CITY	412 03
15 THEY WILL RUN HERE AND THERE FOR MEAT, *	412 04
16 AS FOR ME, I WILL SING OF THY POWER, AND WILL	412 06
OF THY POWER, AND WILL PRAISE THY MERCY BETIMES IN	412 06
O MY STRENGTH, WILL I SING	412 09
IN HIS HOLINESS, I WILL REJOICE, AND DIVIDE SHECHEM,	412 23
OVER EDOM WILL I CAST OUT MY SHOE	412 27
WHO WILL BRING ME INTO EDOM	412 29
9 WHO WILL LEAD ME INTO THE STRONG CITY	412 29
12 THROUGH GOD WILL WE DO GREAT ACTS	413 04
ENDS OF THE EARTH WILL I CALL UPON THEE, *	413 08
4 I WILL DWELL IN THY TABERNACLE FOR EVER, *	413 13
8 SO WILL I ALWAY SING PRAISE UNTO THY NAME, *	413 22
3 HOW LONG WILL YE IMAGINE MISCHIEF AGAINST EVERY	413 31
HIM OUT WHOM GOD WILL EXALT	414 05
EARLY WILL I SEEK THEE	414 26
5 AS LONG AS I LIVE WILL I MAGNIFY THEE IN THIS	414 33
SHADOW OF THY WINGS WILL I REJOICE	415 08
AND SUCH AS WILL NOT BELIEVE SHALL NOT BE ABLE TO	417 27
12 I WILL GO INTO THINE HOUSE WITH BURNT-OFFERINGS,	418 07
AND WILL PAY THEE MY VOWS, *	418 08
13 I WILL OFFER UNTO THEE FAT BURNT-SACRIFICES,	418 10
I WILL OFFER BULLOCKS AND GOATS	418 11
AND I WILL TELL YOU WHAT HE HATH DONE FOR MY SOUL	418 13
THE LORD WILL NOT HEAR ME	418 17
THE LORD WILL ABIDE IN IT FOR EVER	420 14
LORD HATH SAID, I WILL BRING MY PEOPLE AGAIN,	420 30
MINE OWN WILL I BRING AGAIN, AS I DID SOMETIME FROM	420 31
GOD OF ISRAEL, HE WILL GIVE STRENGTH AND POWER UNTO	421 28
31 I WILL PRAISE THE NAME OF GOD WITH A SONG,	424 04
36 FOR GOD WILL SAVE SION, AND BUILD THE CITIES OF	424 14
13 AS FOR ME, I WILL PATIENTLY ABIDE ALWAY, *	426 02
AND WILL PRAISE THEE MORE AND MORE	426 02
15 I WILL GO FORTH IN THE STRENGTH OF THE LORD GOD,	426 06
AND WILL MAKE MENTION OF THY RIGHTEOUSNESS ONLY	426 07
THEREFORE WILL I TELL OF THY WONDROUS WORKS	426 09
21 THEREFORE WILL I PRAISE THEE, AND THY	426 22
UNTO THEE WILL I SING UPON THE HARP, O THOU HOLY ONE	426 24
22 MY LIPS WILL BE GLAD WHEN I SING UNTO THEE	426 25
AND SO WILL MY SOUL WHOM THOU HAST DELIVERED	426 26
11 BUT I WILL TALK OF THE GOD OF JACOB, *	432 19
OF THE UNGODLY ALSO WILL I BREAK, *	432 21
I WILL CRY UNTO GOD WITH MY VOICE	433 16
EVEN UNTO GOD WILL I CRY WITH MY VOICE, AND HE SHALL	433 17
AM IN HEAVINESS, I WILL THINK UPON GOD	433 21
HEART IS VEXED, I WILL COMPLAIN	433 22
AND WILL HE BE NO MORE INTREATED	433 29
7 WILL THE LORD ABSENT HIMSELF FOR EVER	433 29
AND WILL HE SHUT UP HIS LOVING-KINDNESS IN	433 33
BUT I WILL REMEMBER THE YEARS OF THE RIGHT HAND OF	434 02
11 I WILL REMEMBER THE WORKS OF THE LORD, *	434 04
12 I WILL THINK ALSO OF ALL THY WORKS, *	434 06
I WILL DECLARE HARD SENTENCES OF OLD	434 29
2 I WILL OPEN MY MOUTH IN A PARABLE	434 29
AND WILL ALWAY BE SHOWING FORTH THY PRAISE FROM	440 33
18 AND SO WILL NOT WE GO BACK FROM THEE	442 07
AND I WILL ASSURE THEE, O ISRAEL, *	442 29
2 HOW LONG WILL YE GIVE WRONG JUDGMENT, *	443 20
THEY WILL BE ALWAY PRAISING THEE	445 10
7 THEY WILL GO FROM STRENGTH TO STRENGTH, *	445 25
THE LORD WILL GIVE GRACE AND WORSHIP	446 03
8 I WILL HEARKEN WHAT THE LORD GOD WILL SAY	446 22
WHAT THE LORD GOD WILL SAY	446 22
FOR I WILL CALL DAILY UPON THEE	447 09
OF MY TROUBLE I WILL CALL UPON THEE	447 17
O LORD, AND I WILL WALK IN THY TRUTH	447 25
12 I WILL THANK THEE, O LORD MY GOD, WITH ALL MY	447 28
AND WILL PRAISE THY NAME FOR EVERMORE	447 29

WILL   CONTINUED

3 I WILL MAKE MENTION OF EGYPT AND BABYLON, *   448 18
WITH MY MOUTH WILL I EVER BE SHOWING THY TRUTH FROM   450 05
4 THY SEED WILL I STABLISH FOR EVER, *   450 11
24 I WILL SMITE DOWN HIS FOES BEFORE HIS FACE,   451 21
26 I WILL SET HIS DOMINION ALSO IN THE SEA, *   451 25
28 AND I WILL MAKE HIM MY FIRSTBORN, *   451 29
29 MY MERCY WILL I KEEP FOR HIM FOR EVERMORE,   451 31
30 HIS SEED ALSO WILL I MAKE TO ENDURE FOR EVER,   451 33
I WILL VISIT THEIR OFFENCES WITH THE ROD, AND THEIR   452 05
MY LOVING-KINDNESS WILL I NOT UTTERLY TAKE FROM HIM,   452 07
34 MY COVENANT WILL I NOT BREAK, NOR ALTER THE THING   452 09
MY HOLINESS, THAT I WILL NOT FAIL DAVID   452 11
2 I WILL SAY UNTO THE LORD, THOU ART MY HOPE,   454 30
MY GOD, IN HIM WILL I TRUST   454 31
UPON ME, THEREFORE WILL I DELIVER HIM   455 23
I WILL SET HIM UP, BECAUSE HE HATH KNOWN MY NAME   455 24
CALL UPON ME, AND I WILL HEAR HIM   455 26
I WILL DELIVER HIM, AND BRING HIM TO HONOUR   455 27
16 WITH LONG LIFE WILL I SATISFY HIM, *   455 29
AND I WILL REJOICE IN GIVING PRAISE FOR THE   456 07
O YE FOOLS, WHEN WILL YE UNDERSTAND   458 03
14 FOR THE LORD WILL NOT FAIL HIS PEOPLE   458 14
NEITHER WILL HE FORSAKE HIS INHERITANCE   458 14
16 WHO WILL RISE UP WITH ME AGAINST THE WICKED   458 18
OR WHO WILL TAKE MY PART AGAINST THE EVIL DOERS   458 19
8 TO-DAY IF YE WILL HEAR HIS VOICE, HARDEN NOT YOUR   459 19
UNTO THEE, O LORD, WILL I SING   463 18
I WILL WALK IN MY HOUSE WITH A PERFECT HEART   463 20
4 I WILL TAKE NO WICKED THING IN HAND   463 22
I WILL NOT KNOW A WICKED PERSON   463 24
HIM WILL I DESTROY   463 26
I WILL NOT SUFFER HIM   463 29
MY BONES WILL SCARCE CLEAVE TO MY FLESH   464 19
9 HE WILL NOT ALWAY BE CHIDING   466 23
33 I WILL SING UNTO THE LORD AS LONG AS I LIVE   469 27
I WILL PRAISE MY GOD WHILE I HAVE MY BEING   469 27
UNTO THEE WILL I GIVE THE LAND OF CANAAN,   470 24
PRINCES AFTER HIS WILL, *   471 16
42 THE RIGHTEOUS WILL CONSIDER THIS, AND REJOICE   478 30
43 WHOSO IS WISE, WILL PONDER THESE THINGS   478 32
I WILL SING, AND GIVE PRAISE WITH THE BEST MEMBER   479 04
I MYSELF WILL AWAKE RIGHT EARLY   479 07
3 I WILL GIVE THANKS UNTO THEE, O LORD, AMONG THE   479 09
I WILL SING PRAISES UNTO THEE AMONG THE NATIONS   479 10
I WILL REJOICE THEREFORE, AND DIVIDE SHECHEM, AND   479 17
OVER EDOM WILL I CAST OUT MY SHOE   479 22
UPON PHILISTIA WILL I TRIUMPH   479 23
10 WHO WILL LEAD ME INTO THE STRONG CITY   479 24
AND WHO WILL BRING ME INTO EDOM   479 25
AND HATRED FOR MY GOOD WILL   480 12
29 AS FOR ME, I WILL GIVE GREAT THANKS UNTO THE LORD   481 32
THE LORD SWARE, AND WILL NOT REPENT, *   482 14
I WILL GIVE THANKS UNTO THE LORD WITH MY WHOLE HEART,   482 24
AND WILL GUIDE HIS WORDS WITH DISCRETION   483 26
7 HE WILL NOT BE AFRAID OF ANY EVIL TIDINGS   483 30
IS STABLISHED, AND WILL NOT SHRINK, *   483 32
18 BUT WE WILL PRAISE THE LORD, *   486 14
THEREFORE WILL I CALL UPON HIM AS LONG AS I LIVE   486 22
9 I WILL WALK BEFORE THE LORD *   487 06
AND THEREFORE WILL I SPEAK   487 07
12 I WILL RECEIVE THE CUP OF SALVATION, *   487 11
13 I WILL PAY MY VOWS NOW IN THE PRESENCE OF ALL HIS   487 13
15 I WILL OFFER TO THEE THE SACRIFICE OF   487 19
AND WILL CALL UPON THE NAME OF THE LORD   487 20
16 I WILL PAY MY VOWS UNTO THE LORD, IN THE SIGHT OF   487 21
I WILL NOT FEAR WHAT MAN DOETH UNTO ME   488 10
NAME OF THE LORD WILL I DESTROY THEM   488 19
NAME OF THE LORD WILL I DESTROY THEM   488 21
NAME OF THE LORD I WILL DESTROY THEM   488 25
21 I WILL THANK THEE   489 01
WE WILL REJOICE AND BE GLAD IN IT   489 17
ART MY GOD, AND I WILL THANK THEE   489 25
ART MY GOD, AND I WILL PRAISE THEE   489 26
7 I WILL THANK THEE WITH AN UNFEIGNED HEART, *   490 12
8 I WILL KEEP THY STATUTES   490 14
15 I WILL TALK OF THY COMMANDMENTS, *   490 27
AND I WILL NOT FORGET THY WORD   490 29
32 I WILL RUN THE WAY OF THY COMMANDMENTS, *   491 31
45 AND I WILL WALK AT LIBERTY   492 29
46 I WILL SPEAK OF THY TESTIMONIES ALSO, EVEN BEFORE   492 30
AND WILL NOT BE ASHAMED   492 31
48 MY HANDS ALSO WILL I LIFT UP UNTO THY   493 04
62 AT MIDNIGHT I WILL RISE TO GIVE THANKS UNTO THEE,   494 04
BUT I WILL KEEP THY COMMANDMENTS WITH MY WHOLE HEART   494 19
THEY THAT FEAR THEE WILL BE GLAD WHEN THEY SEE ME   495 02
BUT I WILL BE OCCUPIED IN THY COMMANDMENTS   495 12
93 I WILL NEVER FORGET THY COMMANDMENTS   496 11
BUT I WILL CONSIDER THY TESTIMONIES   496 16
I WILL KEEP THE COMMANDMENTS OF MY GOD   497 28
I WILL KEEP THY STATUTES   499 31
I WILL LIFT UP MINE EYES UNTO THE HILLS   502 22
3 HE WILL NOT SUFFER THY FOOT TO BE MOVED   502 26
THAT KEEPETH THEE WILL NOT SLEEP   502 27
WE WILL GO INTO THE HOUSE OF THE LORD   503 09
I WILL WISH THEE PROSPERITY   503 22
I WILL SEEK TO DO THEE GOOD   503 25
MANY AS HAVE EVIL WILL AT SION   506 30
3 I WILL NOT COME WITHIN THE TABERNACLE OF MINE   508 08
4 I WILL NOT SUFFER MINE EYES TO SLEEP, NOR MINE   508 10
7 WE WILL GO INTO HIS TABERNACLE, *   508 17
13 IF THY CHILDREN WILL KEEP MY COVENANT, AND MY   508 29
HERE WILL I DWELL, FOR I HAVE A DELIGHT THEREIN   509 02
AND WILL SATISFY HER POOR WITH BREAD   509 04
16 I WILL BLESS HER VICTUALS WITH INCREASE, *   509 04
17 I WILL DECK HER PRIESTS WITH HEALTH, *   509 06
14 FOR THE LORD WILL AVENGE HIS PEOPLE, *   510 30
I WILL GIVE THANKS UNTO THEE, O LORD, WITH MY WHOLE   513 27
BEFORE THE GODS WILL I SING PRAISE UNTO THEE   513 28
2 I WILL WORSHIP TOWARD THY HOLY TEMPLE, AND PRAISE   513 30
13 I WILL GIVE THANKS UNTO THEE, FOR I AM FEARFULLY   515 15
I AM THAT THE LORD WILL AVENGE THE POOR, *   517 02
I WILL PRAY YET AGAINST THEIR WICKEDNESS   517 22
9 I WILL SING A NEW SONG UNTO THEE, O GOD   520 08
AND I WILL PRAISE THY NAME FOR EVER AND EVER   520 27
I WILL MAGNIFY THEE, O GOD, MY KING   520 27
2 EVERY DAY WILL I GIVE THANKS UNTO THEE   520 29
5 AS FOR ME, I WILL BE TALKING OF THY WORSHIP,   521 02
AND I WILL ALSO TELL OF THY GREATNESS   521 05
19 HE WILL FULFIL THE DESIRE OF THEM THAT FEAR HIM   521 30
HEAR THEIR CRY, AND WILL HELP THEM   521 31
HE ALSO WILL HEAR THEIR CRY, AND WILL HELP THEM   521 31
WHILE I LIVE, WILL I PRAISE THE LORD   522 03
I HAVE ANY BEING, I WILL SING PRAISES UNTO MY GOD   522 04
BUT WE WILL GIVE OURSELVES CONTINUALLY TO PRAYER, AND   532 13
ACCORDING TO THE WILL OF OUR LORD JESUS CHRIST, AND   532 32
WILL YOU DILIGENTLY READ THE SAME UNTO THE   533 06
I WILL   533 09
WILL YOU DO THIS GLADLY AND WILLINGLY   533 21
I WILL SO DO, BY THE HELP OF GOD   533 23
WILL YOU APPLY ALL YOUR DILIGENCE TO FRAME   533 24
I WILL SO DO, THE LORD BEING MY HELPER   533 29
WILL YOU REVERENTLY OBEY YOUR BISHOP,   533 30
A GLAD MIND AND WILL THEIR GODLY ADMONITIONS   533 33
I WILL ENDEAVOUR SO TO DO, THE LORD BEING MY   533 34
THEIR LORD, WHEN HE WILL RETURN FROM THE WEDDING   534 18
DOWN TO MEAT, AND WILL COME FORTH AND SERVE THEM   534 23
TO HAVE A READY WILL TO OBSERVE ALL SPIRITUAL   535 04
THAT HE WILL SEND FORTH LABOURERS INTO HIS   538 19
NOT FOLLOW, BUT WILL FLEE FROM HIM   538 31
AND A STRANGER WILL THEY NOT FOLLOW, BUT WILL FLEE   538 31
PUNISHMENT THAT WILL ENSUE   540 13
HAVE A MIND AND WILL THERETO OF YOURSELVES   540 30
FOR THAT WILL AND ABILITY IS GIVEN OF GOD ALONE   540 31
AS LIETH IN YOU, YE WILL APPLY YOURSELVES WHOLLY TO   541 13
AND THAT YE WILL CONTINUALLY PRAY TO GOD THE FATHER,   541 15
ACCORDING TO THE WILL OF OUR LORD JESUS CHRIST, AND   541 31
WILL YOU THEN GIVE YOUR FAITHFUL DILIGENCE   542 11
I WILL SO DO, BY THE HELP OF THE LORD   542 18
WILL YOU BE READY, WITH ALL FAITHFUL   542 19
I WILL, THE LORD BEING MY HELPER   542 25
WILL YOU BE DILIGENT IN PRAYERS, AND IN   542 26
I WILL ENDEAVOUR SO TO DO, THE LORD BEING MY   542 30
WILL YOU BE DILIGENT TO FRAME AND FASHION   542 32
I WILL APPLY MYSELF THERETO, THE LORD BEING   543 04
WILL YOU MAINTAIN AND SET FORWARDS, AS MUCH   543 06
I WILL SO DO, THE LORD BEING MY HELPER   543 10
WILL YOU REVERENTLY OBEY YOUR BISHOP,   543 11
A GLAD MIND AND WILL THEIR GODLY ADMONITIONS,   543 14
I WILL SO DO, THE LORD BEING MY HELPER   543 16
HATH GIVEN YOU THIS WILL TO DO ALL THESE THINGS   543 18
WE WILL EXAMINE YOU IN CERTAIN   554 12
ACCORDING TO THE WILL OF OUR LORD JESUS CHRIST, AND   554 17
WILL YOU THEN FAITHFULLY EXERCISE YOURSELF   554 29
I WILL SO DO, BY THE HELP OF GOD   554 34
WILL YOU DENY ALL UNGODLINESS AND WORLDLY   555 08
I WILL SO DO, THE LORD BEING MY HELPER   555 13
WILL YOU MAINTAIN AND SET FORWARD, AS MUCH   555 14
I WILL SO DO, BY THE HELP OF GOD   555 19
WILL YOU BE FAITHFUL IN ORDAINING, SENDING,   555 20
I WILL SO BE, BY THE HELP OF GOD   555 22
WILL YOU SHOW YOURSELF GENTLE, AND BE   555 23
I WILL SO SHOW MYSELF, BY GOD'S HELP   555 26
GIVEN YOU A GOOD WILL TO DO ALL THESE THINGS   555 29
DOUBT BUT THAT HE WILL ALSO FAVOURABLY APPROVE OUR   564 22
IS WITH MEN, AND HE WILL DWELL WITH THEM, AND THEY   567 16
OF ALL WHICH YOU WILL GIVE US DUE NOTICE   569 33
GOOD WORK TO DO HIS WILL, WORKING IN YOU THAT WHICH   573 06
AND DESIRES OF MY WILL CENTRE IN WHAT THOU HAST   573 18
KEEP GOD'S HOLY WILL AND COMMANDMENTS, AND WALK IN   577 18
AND BY GOD'S HELP SO I WILL   577 22
FOR THE LORD WILL NOT HOLD HIM GUILTLESS, THAT TAKETH   579 02
UNTO GOD, THAT HE WILL SEND US ALL THINGS THAT ARE   580 33
AND THAT HE WILL BE MERCIFUL UNTO US, AND FORGIVE US   580 34
AND THAT IT WILL PLEASE HIM TO SAVE AND DEFEND US IN   580 35
AND THAT HE WILL KEEP US FROM ALL SIN AND WICKEDNESS,   581 03
AND THIS I TRUST HE WILL DO OF HIS MERCY AND   581 05
BE CONVENIENT, IT WILL BE PROPER TO BEGIN WITH A   R 592 05
HAVING DONE THY WILL WITH CHEERFULNESS WHILE IT WAS   594 15
AND A CLEARER KNOWLEDGE OF THY WILL   596 15
WE MAY HAVE A GOOD WILL, AND WORKING WITH US,   605 03
WHEN WE HAVE THAT GOOD WILL   605 04
IN OUR DOINGS, THAT WILL OF GOD IS TO BE FOLLOWED,   606 28
AND GOD'S GOOD WILL TOWARDS US, BY THE WHICH HE DOTH   607 33

WILLED

DONE AS GOD HATH WILLED AND COMMANDED THEM TO BE   605 21

WILLEST

WHO WILLEST US TO GIVE THANKS FOR ALL THINGS,   596 03

WILLING

AND NOT WILLING TO MAKE HER A PUBLICK EXAMPLE,   104 30
AND SO PILATE, WILLING TO CONTENT THE PEOPLE,   145 27
IF THOU BE WILLING, REMOVE THIS CUP FROM ME   150 18
WILLING TO RELEASE JESUS, SPAKE AGAIN TO   153 32

WILLING   CONTINUED

BUT HE, WILLING TO JUSTIFY HIMSELF, SAID UNTO JESUS,   208 19
WE PURPOSE, GOD WILLING, TO RECEIVE THIS DAY UNTO THE   536 23

WILLINGLY

THOU DOST NOT WILLINGLY AFFLICT OR GRIEVE THE   045 31
TO VANITY, NOT WILLINGLY, BUT BY REASON OF HIM WHO   194 15
THEMSELVES WILLINGLY WITH AN HOLY WORSHIP   482 12
WILL YOU DO THIS GLADLY AND WILLINGLY   533 22
DEADLY SIN WILLINGLY COMMITTED AFTER BAPTISM IS SIN   605 39
WILLINGLY AND PURPOSELY, DOTH OPENLY BREAK   609 36

WILLS

ORDER THE UNRULY WILLS AND AFFECTIONS OF SINFUL MEN   174 19
O LORD, THE WILLS OF THY FAITHFUL PEOPLE   225 04
ORDER THE UNRULY WILLS AND AFFECTIONS OF SINFUL MEN   285 26
IN HEALTH, TO MAKE WILLS ARRANGING FOR THE DISPOSAL   R 320 22
YOUR MINDS AND WILLS IN THESE THINGS, AND THAT THIS   541 25

WILT

O GOD, THOU WILT NOT DESPISE   004 25
IN THY NAME THOU WILT GRANT THEIR REQUESTS   020 06
IN THY NAME THOU WILT GRANT THEIR REQUESTS   034 06
WILT THOU THEN NOT BE AFRAID OF THE POWER   114 16
IF THOU WILT, THOU CANST MAKE ME CLEAN   114 31
SAID UNTO HIM, WILT THOU THEN THAT WE GO AND GATHER   116 26
SAYING, WHAT WILT THOU THAT I SHALL DO UNTO   123 35
GIVE THEE, IF THOU WILT FALL DOWN AND WORSHIP ME   127 07
BE IT UNTO THEE EVEN AS THOU WILT   128 21
UNTO HIM, WHERE WILT THOU THAT WE GO AND PREPARE THAT 140 24
NEVERTHELESS NOT WHAT I WILL, BUT WHAT THOU WILT   142 03
UNTO HIM, WHERE WILT THOU THAT WE PREPARE   148 24
SAYING, LORD, WILT THOU AT THIS TIME RESTORE   178 05
HOW IS IT THAT THOU WILT MANIFEST THYSELF UNTO US,   181 22
LORD, WHAT WILT THOU HAVE ME TO DO   230 06
SAID UNTO HER, WHAT WILT THOU   247 08
SO THAT THOU WILT NOT FOLLOW, NOR BE LED BY   276 27
WILT THOU BE BAPTIZED IN THIS FAITH   277 02
WILT THOU THEN OBEDIENTLY KEEP GOD'S HOLY   277 04
THESE PROMISES, WILT THOU ALSO ON THY PART TAKE HEED   277 09
WILT THOU TAKE HEED THAT THIS CHILD,   277 14
SO THAT THOU WILT NOT FOLLOW, NOR BE LED BY   277 29
WILT THOU BE BAPTIZED IN THIS FAITH   278 11
WILT THOU THEN OBEDIENTLY KEEP GOD'S HOLY   278 13
THE QUESTION WILT THOU BE BAPTIZED IN THIS FAITH   R 282 04
WILT THOU HAVE THIS WOMAN TO THY WEDDED WIFE, TO LIVE   301 06
WILT THOU LOVE HER, COMFORT HER, HONOUR, AND KEEP HER 301 08
WILT THOU HAVE THIS MAN TO THY WEDDED HUSBAND,   301 14
WILT THOU LOVE HIM, COMFORT HIM, HONOUR, AND KEEP HIM 301 16
IF THOU, LORD, WILT BE EXTREME TO MARK WHAT IS DONE   328 07
13 FOR THOU, LORD, WILT GIVE THY BLESSING UNTO THE   348 28
FAVOURABLE KINDNESS WILT THOU DEFEND HIM AS WITH A   348 29
LORD, HOW LONG WILT THOU PUNISH ME   349 05
HOW LONG WILT THOU FORGET ME, O LORD   355 28
HOW LONG WILT THOU HIDE THY FACE FROM ME   355 29
17 LORD, HOW LONG WILT THOU LOOK UPON THIS   382 29
WILT NOT THOU, O GOD, GO OUT WITH OUR HOSTS   412 31
5 LORD, HOW LONG WILT THOU BE ANGRY   440 09
HOW LONG WILT THOU BE ANGRY WITH THY PEOPLE THAT   441 10
IF THOU WILT HEARKEN UNTO ME, 10 THERE SHALL NO   442 30
AND WILT THOU STRETCH OUT THY WRATH FROM ONE   446 16
5 WILT THOU BE DISPLEASED AT US FOR EVER   446 16
6 WILT THOU NOT TURN AGAIN, AND QUICKEN US, *   446 18
45 LORD, HOW LONG WILT THOU HIDE THYSELF   452 32
20 WILT THOU HAVE ANY THING TO DO WITH THE THRONE OF   458 26
3 WHEN WILT THOU COME UNTO ME   463 20
AND WILT NOT THOU, O GOD, GO FORTH WITH OUR HOSTS   479 26
O WHEN WILT THOU COMFORT ME   495 22
WHEN WILT THOU BE AVENGED OF THEM THAT PERSECUTE ME   495 25
3 IF THOU, LORD, WILT BE EXTREME TO MARK WHAT IS DONE 507 12
19 WILT THOU NOT SLAY THE WICKED, O GOD   515 28
WHICH THING IF THOU WILT GRANT ME, THEN SHALL THE   518 20
LARGER LIFE, THOU WILT RECEIVE HIM MORE AND MORE INTO 598 08

WIN

THAT HE MAY WIN, WITH THEE AND THY SERVANTS   598 10

WIND

A REED SHAKEN WITH THE WIND   094 27
OF A RUSHING MIGHTY WIND, AND IT FILLED ALL THE HOUSE 180 20
THE WIND BLOWETH WHERE IT LISTETH, AND THOU HEAREST   188 14
ABOUT WITH EVERY WIND OF DOCTRINE, BY THE SLEIGHT OF   237 26
SEA DRIVEN WITH THE WIND AND TOSSED   239 15
THE WIND BLOWETH WHERE IT LISTETH, AND THOU HEAREST   275 19
WHICH THE WIND SCATTERETH AWAY FROM THE FACE   345 17
HE CAME FLYING UPON THE WINGS OF THE WIND   360 18
BEAT THEM AS SMALL AS THE DUST BEFORE THE WIND   362 24
THE DUST BEFORE THE WIND, *   381 27
OF THE STORMY WIND AND TEMPEST   407 03
THEY WERE EVEN A WIND THAT PASSETH AWAY, AND COMETH   437 19
AND AS THE STUBBLE BEFORE THE WIND   444 31
FOR AS SOON AS THE WIND GOETH OVER IT, IT IS GONE   467 06
AND WALKETH UPON THE WINGS OF THE WIND   467 31
HIS WORD THE STORMY WIND ARISETH, *   477 26
HE BLOWETH WITH HIS WIND, AND THE WATERS FLOW   523 32
WIND AND STORM, FULFILLING HIS WORD   524 20

WINDS

O YE WINDS OF GOD, BLESS YE THE LORD   012 16

WINDS   CONTINUED

FROM THE FOUR WINDS, FROM ONE END OF HEAVEN TO THE   118 22
MAKETH HIS ANGELS WINDS, *   467 32
BRINGING THE WINDS OUT OF HIS TREASURIES   510 17

WINE

AND THY PRESSES SHALL BURST OUT WITH NEW WINE   005 23
PLACE UPON THE HOLY TABLE, THE BREAD AND THE WINE   R 073 33
THE BREAD AND WINE, THAT HE MAY WITH THE MORE   R 080 03
WHICH THERE IS ANY WINE TO BE CONSECRATED   R 080 34
THESE THY GIFTS AND CREATURES OF BREAD AND WINE   081 11
BREAD OR WINE BE SPENT BEFORE ALL HAVE COMMUNICATED, R 083 07
BREAD AND WINE REMAIN AFTER THE COMMUNION, IT SHALL   R 084 30
WHEN THEY WANTED WINE, THE MOTHER OF JESUS SAITH UNTO 113 14
MOTHER OF JESUS SAITH UNTO HIM, THEY HAVE NO WINE   113 15
WATER THAT WAS MADE WINE, AND KNEW NOT WHENCE IT WAS   113 24
MAN AT THE BEGINNING DOTH SET FORTH GOOD WINE   113 28
HAST KEPT THE GOOD WINE UNTIL NOW   113 29
GAVE HIM TO DRINK WINE MINGLED WITH MYRRH   146 09
POURING IN OIL AND WINE, AND SET HIM ON HIS OWN   208 31
BE NOT DRUNK WITH WINE, WHEREIN IS EXCESS   217 26
BREAD AND WINE, WHICH THE LORD HATH COMMANDED TO   293 11
STRENGTHENED AND REFRESHED BY THE BREAD AND WINE   293 22
WHEN THEIR CORN AND WINE AND OIL INCREASE   347 27
THOU HAST GIVEN US A DRINK OF DEADLY WINE   412 18
IS A CUP, AND THE WINE IS RED   432 15
AND LIKE A GIANT REFRESHED WITH WINE   439 09
OF THE EARTH, AND WINE THAT MAKETH GLAD THE HEART OF   468 23
NOT GIVEN TO MUCH WINE, NOT GREEDY OF FILTHY LUCRE   531 28
NOT GIVEN TO WINE, NO STRIKER, NOT GREEDY OF FILTHY   549 22
BREAD AND WINE, WHICH THE LORD HATH   582 09
AS OUR BODIES ARE BY THE BREAD AND WINE   582 19
OF BREAD AND WINE) IN THE SUPPER OF THE LORD, CANNOT   608 40

WINEFAT

GARMENTS LIKE HIM THAT TREADETH IN THE WINEFAT   138 16

WINEPRESS

TRODDEN THE WINEPRESS ALONE   138 16

WINGS

CHICKENS UNDER HER WINGS, AND YE WOULD NOT   100 30
EACH OF THEM SIX WINGS ABOUT HIM   187 21
THE SHADOW OF THY WINGS,   359 03
FLYING UPON THE WINGS OF THE WIND   360 18
PUT THEIR TRUST UNDER THE SHADOW OF THY WINGS   384 10
O THAT I HAD WINGS LIKE A DOVE   406 30
THE SHADOW OF THY WINGS SHALL BE MY REFUGE, UNTIL   409 14
MY TRUST SHALL BE UNDER THE COVERING OF THY WINGS   413 14
THE SHADOW OF THY WINGS WILL I REJOICE   415 08
SHALL YE BE AS THE WINGS OF A DOVE *   420 07
WITH SILVER WINGS, AND HER FEATHERS LIKE GOLD   420 08
THEE UNDER HIS WINGS, AND THOU SHALT BE SAFE UNDER   455 02
WALKETH UPON THE WINGS OF THE WIND   467 31
8 IF I TAKE THE WINGS OF THE MORNING, *   515 04

WINK

NEITHER LET THEM WINK WITH THEIR EYES, THAT HATE ME   382 35

WINTER

O YE WINTER AND SUMMER, BLESS YE THE LORD   012 20
THOU HAST MADE SUMMER AND WINTER   431 11

WIPE

AND TO WIPE THEM WITH THE TOWEL WHEREWITH HE   155 33
AND GOD SHALL WIPE AWAY ALL TEARS FROM THEIR EYES   257 16
AND GOD SHALL WIPE AWAY ALL TEARS FROM THEIR EYES   341 27
AND GOD SHALL WIPE AWAY ALL TEARS FROM THEIR EYES   567 18

WIPED

29 LET THEM BE WIPED OUT OF THE BOOK OF THE LIVING,   423 32

WISDOM

THE LORD BY WISDOM HATH FOUNDED THE EARTH   005 24
ALL IN AUTHORITY, WISDOM AND STRENGTH TO KNOW AND TO   018 11
THE FOUNTAIN OF WISDOM, WHOSE STATUTES ARE GOOD AND   035 23
THE SPIRIT OF WISDOM AND UNDERSTANDING, THAT THEY MAY 036 03
THE SPIRIT OF WISDOM THOSE TO WHOM IN THY NAME WE   036 17
WHO ART THE FOUNTAIN OF ALL WISDOM   042 27
WITH THY WISDOM THOSE WHO TEACH AND THOSE WHO LEARN,   043 02
ENDUE THEM WITH WISDOM, PATIENCE, AND COURAGE TO   044 02
THAT HEAVENLY WISDOM WHICH LEADETH TO ETERNAL LIFE   045 09
FOUNTAIN OF ALL WISDOM, WHO KNOWEST OUR NECESSITIES   049 29
MAY HAVE GRACE, WISDOM, AND UNDERSTANDING TO EXECUTE   VI 19
ME TO UNDERSTAND WISDOM SECRETLY   060 23
TO THE WISDOM OF THE JUST, THAT AT THY SECOND COMING   093 28
THE MANIFOLD WISDOM OF GOD, ACCORDING TO THE ETERNAL   100 26
INCREASED IN WISDOM AND STATURE, AND IN FAVOUR WITH   111 07
WORD OF CHRIST DWELL IN YOU RICHLY IN ALL WISDOM   116 11
TO ONE IS GIVEN BY THE SPIRIT THE WORD OF WISDOM   182 27
TO ONE IS GIVEN BY THE SPIRIT THE WORD OF WISDOM   203 27
HIS WILL IN ALL WISDOM AND SPIRITUAL UNDERSTANDING   224 03
AND WAXED STRONG IN SPIRIT, FILLED WITH WISDOM   233 27
ANY OF YOU LACK WISDOM, LET HIM ASK OF GOD, THAT   239 12
AND GLORY, AND WISDOM, AND THANKSGIVING, AND HONOUR,   256 32
THE SPIRIT OF WISDOM AND UNDERSTANDING, THE SPIRIT OF 297 19

WISDOM   CONTINUED

AND PATIENCE, IN WISDOM AND TRUE GODLINESS, THAT   303 25
DAILY INCREASE IN WISDOM AND STATURE, AND GROW IN THY   307 04
THAT WE MAY APPLY OUR HEARTS UNTO WISDOM   326 03
AND GIVETH WISDOM UNTO THE SIMPLE   363 29
IS EXERCISED IN WISDOM, *   386 26
SHALL SPEAK OF WISDOM, *   400 10
ME TO UNDERSTAND WISDOM SECRETLY   403 21
THAT WE MAY APPLY OUR HEARTS UNTO WISDOM   454 14
IN WISDOM HAST THOU MADE THEM ALL   469 08
AND TEACH HIS SENATORS WISDOM   471 17
THE FEAR OF THE LORD IS THE BEGINNING OF WISDOM   483 14
BY HIS EXCELLENT WISDOM MADE THE HEAVENS   511 24
AND HIS WISDOM IS INFINITE   523 05
HOLY GHOST AND WISDOM, WHOM WE MAY APPOINT OVER THIS   532 12
IN THY INFINITE WISDOM THOU SHALT SEE TO BE MOST   566 22
INSPIRED BY THY WISDOM, AND IN WORK BE UPHELD BY THY   594 25
THE SPIRIT OF WISDOM MAY SAVE US FROM ALL FALSE   595 29
THE LIGHT OF THY WISDOM, AND RECEIVE THE BLESSED   596 13
INFINITE POWER, WISDOM, AND GOODNESS   603 04
DO EXPOUND THE WISDOM, SOME SENSUALITY, SOME THE   604 37

WISE

THAT WE MAY IN SUCH WISE HEAR THEM, READ, MARK,   092 09
YOU PROPHETS, AND WISE MEN, AND SCRIBES   100 19
WAS MOCKED OF THE WISE MEN, WAS EXCEEDING WROTH,   103 25
ENQUIRED OF THE WISE MEN   103 29
THE BIRTH OF JESUS CHRIST WAS ON THIS WISE   104 27
BEHOLD, THERE CAME WISE MEN FROM THE EAST TO   108 31
PRIVILY CALLED THE WISE MEN, ENQUIRED OF THEM   109 11
BE NOT WISE IN YOUR OWN CONCEITS   112 31
SEEING YE YOURSELVES ARE WISE   120 22
I WILL NOT DENY THEE IN ANY WISE   141 26
HE SAID ON THIS WISE, I WILL GIVE YOU THE SURE   169 12
YE SHALL IN NO WISE BELIEVE, THOUGH A MAN DECLARE IT   169 25
AS FOOLS, BUT AS WISE, REDEEMING THE TIME, BECAUSE   217 24
THINGS FROM THE WISE AND PRUDENT, AND HAST REVEALED   235 05
TO ME I WILL IN NO WISE CAST OUT   269 15
UNTO THE GODFATHERS AND GODMOTHERS ON THIS WISE   R 276 18
THEM ON THIS WISE, THE PERSONS TO BE BAPTIZED   R 277 19
MAN SHALL GIVE UNTO THE WOMAN A RING ON THIS WISE   R 302 10
TO ME I WILL IN NO WISE CAST OUT   333 04
10 BE WISE NOW THEREFORE, O YE KINGS   346 17
FOR HE SEETH THAT WISE MEN ALSO DIE AND PERISH   400 23
43 WHOSO IS WISE, WILL PONDER THESE THINGS   478 32
SHALL PRAY IN THIS WISE, AND SAY, ALMIGHTY GOD, AND   R 545 10
SO THAT, AS A WISE AND FAITHFUL SERVANT, GIVING TO   558 03
WHO OF THY WISE PROVIDENCE HAST APPOINTED   572 07
PROMISES IN SUCH WISE, AS THEY BE GENERALLY SET FORTH 606 27
CHILDREN IS IN ANY WISE TO BE RETAINED IN THE CHURCH, 608 31
YET IN NO WISE ARE THEY PARTAKERS OF CHRIST   609 06

WISELY

FAITHFULLY AND WISELY MAKE CHOICE OF FIT PERSONS, TO   038 30
FAITHFULLY AND WISELY THE DISCIPLINE OF CHRIST   047 25
TO BEHAVE HIMSELF WISELY, AND TO DO GOOD   383 31
CHARM HE NEVER SO WISELY   410 18

WISER

HAST MADE ME WISER THAN MINE ENEMIES   496 23
100 I AM WISER THAN THE AGED   496 26

WISH

PUT TO REBUKE, THAT WISH ME EVIL   391 18
TO CONFUSION THAT WISH ME EVIL   424 24
I WILL WISH THEE PROSPERITY   503 22
WE WISH YOU GOOD LUCK IN THE NAME OF THE LORD   507 05
REASONS OCCASION A WISH IN YOU, OR IN THE   569 31
WHO HAVE DONE OR WISH US EVIL, AND GIVE THEM   590 33

WISHED

WE HAVE WISHED YOU GOOD LUCK, WE THAT ARE OF THE   489 20

WISHES

AND MAY ALL THE WISHES AND DESIRES OF MY WILL CENTRE   573 18

WIST

WIST YE NOT THAT I MUST BE ABOUT MY FATHER'S   111 02
NEITHER WIST THEY WHAT TO ANSWER HIM   142 09
AND WIST NOT THAT IT WAS TRUE WHICH WAS DONE BY THE   245 19

WIT

FOR THE ADOPTION, TO WIT, THE REDEMPTION OF OUR BODY   194 23

WIT'S

AND ARE AT THEIR WIT'S E'   477 32

WITCHCRAFT

WITCHCRAFT, HATRED, VARIANCE, EMULATIONS,   209 21

WITHAL

THE SPIRIT IS GIVEN TO EVERY MAN TO PROFIT WITHAL   182 26
THAT YE METE WITHAL IT SHALL BE MEASURED TO YOU   194 31
THE SPIRIT IS GIVEN TO EVERY MAN TO PROFIT WITHAL   203 27

WITHAL   CONTINUED

TABLE BE MADE A SNARE TO TAKE THEMSELVES WITHAL   423 19
THE EARTH WAS MOVED, AND SHOOK WITHAL   434 20
AND THE STREAMS FLOWED WITHAL   436 09
AND SENT LEANNESS WITHAL INTO THEIR SOUL   473 32
AND AS THE GIRDLE THAT HE IS ALWAY GIRDED WITHAL   481 09

WITHDRAW

14 WITHDRAW NOT THOU THY MERCY FROM ME, O LORD   391 08

WITHDRAWEST

12 WHY WITHDRAWEST THOU THY HAND   430 29

WITHDRAWING

LEST YE, WITHDRAWING YOURSELVES FROM THIS HOLY   088 25

WITHDRAWN

AND HE WAS WITHDRAWN FROM THEM ABOUT A STONE'S CAST,   150 17

WITHER

4 HIS LEAF ALSO SHALL NOT WITHER   345 14

WITHERED

SPRUNG UP, IT WITHERED AWAY, BECAUSE IT LACKED   121 23
HE IS CAST FORTH AS A BRANCH, AND IS WITHERED   238 15
EVENING IT IS CUT DOWN, DRIED UP, AND WITHERED   325 25
AND BE WITHERED EVEN AS THE GREEN HERB   384 28
EVENING IT IS CUT DOWN, DRIED UP, AND WITHERED   453 30
AND WITHERED LIKE GRASS   464 17
AND I AM WITHERED LIKE GRASS   464 31

WITHERETH

BUT IT WITHERETH THE GRASS, AND THE FLOWER   239 21
THE GRASS WITHERETH, THE FLOWER FADETH   242 29
THE GRASS WITHERETH, THE FLOWER FADETH   242 31
WHICH WITHERETH AFORE IT BE GROWN UP   506 32

WITHHOLD

THING SHALL HE WITHHOLD FROM THEM THAT LIVE A GODLY   446 04

WITHIN

CLEAN OUR HEARTS WITHIN US   016 31
AND ALL THAT IS WITHIN ME, PRAISE HIS HOLY NAME   029 04
CLEAN OUR HEARTS WITHIN US   031 13
A RIGHT SPIRIT WITHIN ME   060 31
STRANGER THAT IS WITHIN THY GATES   068 29
TO THE ORDINARY, WITHIN FOURTEEN DAYS AFTER, AT THE   R 085 19
HIS HOLY SPIRIT WITHIN HIM   139 10
HAD INDIGNATION WITHIN THEMSELVES, AND SAID, WHY WAS   140 06
WITH HANDS, AND WITHIN THREE DAYS I WILL BUILD   143 07
OUR HEART BURN WITHIN US, WHILE HE TALKED WITH US BY   168 09
AND THEY WERE FULL OF EYES WITHIN   187 22
OURSELVES GROAN WITHIN OURSELVES, WAITING FOR THE   194 22
AND THY CHILDREN WITHIN THEE   204 13
THE SCRIBES SAID WITHIN THEMSELVES, THIS MAN   217 05
FOR SHE SAID WITHIN HERSELF, IF I MAY BUT TOUCH HIS   224 19
DISCIPLES WERE WITHIN, AND THOMAS WITH THEM   228 31
AND HE FROM WITHIN SHALL ANSWER AND SAY, TROUBLE ME   262 30
THY CHILDREN WITHIN THEE   265 03
STRANGER THAT IS WITHIN THY GATES   286 29
SO DISQUIETED WITHIN ME   310 17
AND ALL THAT IS WITHIN ME, PRAISE HIS HOLY NAME   312 20
ALL THY PRAISES WITHIN THE GATES OF THE DAUGHTER OF   352 19
THEIR ARROWS WITHIN THE QUIVER, *   354 22
OF THEIR NAMES WITHIN MY LIPS   357 30
MY HEART WAS HOT WITHIN ME   389 12
THY LAW IS WITHIN MY HEART   390 33
THY RIGHTEOUSNESS WITHIN MY HEART   391 04
FALSEHOOD WITHIN HIMSELF   392 11
SO DISQUIETED WITHIN ME   393 12
MY SOUL IS VEXED WITHIN ME   393 15
SO DISQUIETED WITHIN ME   393 32
SO DISQUIETED WITHIN ME   394 16
13 THE KING'S DAUGHTER IS ALL GLORIOUS WITHIN   397 12
A RIGHT SPIRIT WITHIN ME   403 30
IS DISQUIETED WITHIN ME, *   406 26
THEY GO ABOUT WITHIN THE WALLS THEREOF   407 06
AND BROUGHT THEM WITHIN THE BORDERS OF HIS SANCTUARY, 438 18
AND ALL THAT IS WITHIN ME, PRAISE HIS HOLY NAME   466 08
13 BUT WITHIN A WHILE THEY FORGAT HIS WORKS, *   473 27
HEART IS WOUNDED WITHIN ME   481 15
WORD HAVE I HID WITHIN MY HEART, *   490 20
7 PEACE BE WITHIN THY WALLS, *   503 20
AND PLENTEOUSNESS WITHIN THY PALACES   503 20
3 I WILL NOT COME WITHIN THE TABERNACLE OF MINE   508 08
MY SPIRIT VEXED WITHIN ME, *   518 30
AND MY HEART WITHIN ME IS DESOLATE   518 31
THY CHILDREN WITHIN THEE   523 22
AS TO THE WHOLE, WITHIN YOUR CURES, AS NEED SHALL   542 23
VOUCHSAFE WITHIN OUR SOULS TO REST   544 18
VOUCHSAFE WITHIN OUR SOULS TO REST   556 26
BISHOP SHALL GO WITHIN THE RAILS, WITH SUCH OF THE   R 564 06
WHO SHALL GO WITHIN THE RAILS OF THE ALTAR   R 570 06
THE INCUMBENT WITHIN THE RAILS OF THE ALTAR, AND   R 571 22
STRANGER THAT IS WITHIN THY GATES   579 09
ALL SUCH PERSONS WITHIN HIS PARISH, AS HE SHALL THINK R 583 08

WITHOUT

AND USAGES MAY WITHOUT OFFENCE BE ALLOWED, PROVIDED   V 04
SHALL BE, WORLD WITHOUT END   008 06
WORLD WITHOUT END   009 30
NAME EVER, WORLD WITHOUT END   011 07
KEEP US THIS DAY WITHOUT SIN   011 08
MIGHT SERVE HIM WITHOUT FEAR   014 21
ONE GOD, WORLD WITHOUT END   018 16
AND GLORY, WORLD WITHOUT END   019 32
SHALL BE, WORLD WITHOUT END   025 12
ONE GOD, WORLD WITHOUT END   032 14
AND GLORY, WORLD WITHOUT END   033 30
THEY MAY SERVE WITHOUT REPROACH   041 30
ONE GOD, WORLD WITHOUT END   043 16
ONE GOD, WORLD WITHOUT END   049 10
WORLD WITHOUT END   050 29
SHALL BE, WORLD WITHOUT END   059 08
WITHOUT PREJUDICE OR PREPOSSESSIONS   VI 38
WORLD WITHOUT END   061 18
SHALL THEY HEAR WITHOUT A PREACHER   073 08
AND THAT WITHOUT SPOT OF SIN, TO MAKE US CLEAN FROM   077 18
THE HOLY GHOST, WITHOUT ANY DIFFERENCE OF INEQUALITY   079 11
WORLD WITHOUT END   081 34
AND GLORY, WORLD WITHOUT END   083 31
WHO ARE CALLED, WITHOUT ANY CAUSE, MOST UNTHANKFULLY   088 21
ONE GOD, WORLD WITHOUT END   093 32
AND GLORY, WORLD WITHOUT END   095 10
ONE GOD, WORLD WITHOUT END   096 19
AND WITHOUT HIM WAS NOT ANY THING MADE THAT WAS MADE   097 22
ONE GOD, WORLD WITHOUT END   098 16
FOR THEY ARE WITHOUT FAULT BEFORE THE THRONE OF GOD   103 13
ONE GOD, WORLD WITHOUT END   104 11
LET LOVE BE WITHOUT DISSIMULATION   111 22
ONE GOD, WORLD WITHOUT END   117 12
ONE GOD, WORLD WITHOUT END   119 03
THINGS THAT ARE WITHOUT, THAT WHICH COMETH UPON ME   121 10
ALL OUR DOINGS WITHOUT CHARITY ARE NOTHING WORTH   122 14
OF ALL VIRTUES, WITHOUT WHICH WHOSOEVER LIVETH IS   122 17
ONE GOD, WORLD WITHOUT END   125 32
OFFERED HIMSELF WITHOUT SPOT TO GOD, PURGE YOUR   133 02
ANOTHER MADE WITHOUT HANDS   143 08
WAS DEDICATED WITHOUT BLOOD   147 18
AND WITHOUT SHEDDING OF BLOOD IS NO REMISSION   147 26
THE SECOND TIME WITHOUT SIN UNTO SALVATION   148 10
WHEN I SENT YOU WITHOUT PURSE, AND SCRIP, AND SHOES,   150 04
ONE GOD, WORLD WITHOUT END   152 13
ONE GOD, WORLD WITHOUT END   156 26
ONE GOD, WORLD WITHOUT END   157 13
OF OUR FAITH WITHOUT WAVERING   158 23
NOW THE COAT WAS WITHOUT SEAM, WOVEN FROM THE TOP   160 11
WORLD WITHOUT END   163 20
ONE GOD, WORLD WITHOUT END   163 29
ONE GOD, WORLD WITHOUT END   177 19
ONE GOD, WORLD WITHOUT END   179 10
ONE TO ANOTHER WITHOUT GRUDGING   179 15
ONE GOD, WORLD WITHOUT END   180 14
ONE GOD, WORLD WITHOUT END   182 20
ONE GOD, WORLD WITHOUT END   183 27
ONE GOD, WORLD WITHOUT END   185 19
ONE GOD, WORLD WITHOUT END   186 29
DO NO GOOD THING WITHOUT THEE, GRANT US THE HELP OF   189 03
TRUST IN THEE, WITHOUT WHOM NOTHING IS STRONG,   194 04
WITH HIS BROTHER WITHOUT A CAUSE SHALL BE IN DANGER   198 04
THAT IS GOOD WITHOUT THEE, MAY BY THEE BE ENABLED TO   200 31
FRAILTY OF MAN WITHOUT THEE CANNOT BUT FALL, KEEP US   210 19
IN SAFETY WITHOUT THY SUCCOUR, PRESERVE IT EVERMORE   212 06
ALL AGES, WORLD WITHOUT END   212 24
FORASMUCH AS WITHOUT THEE WE ARE NOT ABLE TO PLEASE   215 27
BE SINCERE AND WITHOUT OFFENCE TILL THE DAY OF   221 04
AND FOLLOWED HIM WITHOUT DELAY   226 20
SHALL THEY HEAR WITHOUT A PREACHER   227 07
AND WITHOUT ALL DOUBT, TO BELIEVE IN THY   228 08
WAS THREE DAYS WITHOUT SIGHT, AND NEITHER DID EAT NOR   230 13
FOR WITHOUT ME YE CAN DO NOTHING   238 14
MIGHT SERVE HIM WITHOUT FEAR, IN HOLINESS AND   244 08
PRAYER WAS MADE WITHOUT CEASING OF THE CHURCH UNTO   245 08
ALL THAT HE HAD, WITHOUT DELAY WAS OBEDIENT UNTO THE   246 18
ONE GOD, WORLD WITHOUT END   248 06
ONE GOD, WORLD WITHOUT END   250 25
THEY HATED ME WITHOUT A CAUSE   255 29
WORLD WITHOUT END   265 09
BE HOLY AND WITHOUT BLEMISH   267 24
WORLD WITHOUT END   278 31
SHALL BE, WORLD WITHOUT END   285 09
THAT IS GOOD WITHOUT THEE, MAY BY THEE BE ENABLED TO   287 28
TO SERVE HIM, WITHOUT HIS SPECIAL GRACE   289 15
WORLD WITHOUT END   297 10
ONE GOD, WORLD WITHOUT END   298 25
TO COME, WITHOUT DELAY, TO THE LORD'S SUPPER   R 299 07
ONE GOD, WORLD WITHOUT END   303 28
SHALL BE, WORLD WITHOUT END   306 07
AND GLORY, WORLD WITHOUT END   316 04
WHOSE DAYS ARE WITHOUT END, AND WHOSE MERCIES CANNOT   316 25
PURE AND WITHOUT SPOT BEFORE THEE   317 21
ONE GOD, WORLD WITHOUT END   319 13
ONE GOD, WORLD WITHOUT END   320 13
IT MAY BE WITHOUT SPOT PRESENTED UNTO THEE   321 25
AND WORLD WITHOUT END   325 17
ONE GOD, WORLD WITHOUT END   332 09
BE SORRY, AS MEN WITHOUT HOPE, FOR THOSE WHO SLEEP IN   335 04
ONE GOD, WORLD WITHOUT END   336 15
WORLD WITHOUT END   340 19
HIM THAT WITHOUT ANY CAUSE IS MINE ENEMY   349 30
AS TRANSGRESS WITHOUT A CAUSE SHALL BE PUT TO   369 22
OF THY PRAISE WITHOUT CEASING   375 19

WITHOUT   CONTINUED

THAT DID SEE ME WITHOUT, CONVEYED THEMSELVES FROM ME   376 18
TO DESTROY ME WITHOUT A CAUSE   382 02
EVEN WITHOUT A CAUSE HAVE THEY MADE A PIT FOR MY   382 02
THAT HATE ME WITHOUT A CAUSE   382 36
WORLD WITHOUT END   392 25
UNTO THEE, WORLD WITHOUT END   397 23
5 ARE NOT THEY WITHOUT UNDERSTANDING THAT WORK   405 22
AGAINST ME, WITHOUT ANY OFFENCE OR FAULT OF ME, C   411 09
THEMSELVES WITHOUT MY FAULT   411 11
THAT HATE ME WITHOUT A CAUSE ARE MORE THAN THE HAIRS   422 07
AND WORLD WITHOUT END   453 22
AND WORLD WITHOUT END   475 34
AGAINST ME WITHOUT A CAUSE   480 08
PERSECUTED ME WITHOUT A CAUSE   501 03
AND WITHOUT CRIME   529 27
WORLD WITHOUT END   535 11
WORLD WITHOUT END   537 29
WORLD WITHOUT END   546 05
WORLD WITHOUT END   548 08
MUST HAVE A GOOD REPORT OF THEM WHICH ARE WITHOUT   549 29
WORLD WITHOUT END   554 04
ONE GOD, WORLD WITHOUT END   558 07
ONE GOD, WORLD WITHOUT END   559 15
ONE GOD, WORLD WITHOUT END   562 15
WORLD WITHOUT END   564 05
OF THE ALTAR, WITHOUT THE RAILS   R 570 08
ONE GOD, WORLD WITHOUT END   572 32
ONE GOD, WORLD WITHOUT END   574 23
TO SERVE HIM, WITHOUT HIS SPECIAL GRACE   580 18
BEGIN AN ACTION WITHOUT A PURE INTENTION NOR CONTINUE   594 22
NOR CONTINUE IT WITHOUT THY BLESSING   594 23
WITHOUT BODY, PARTS, OR PASSIONS   603 03
TO GOD, WITHOUT THE GRACE OF GOD BY CHRIST PREVENTING   605 02
CANNOT BE TAUGHT WITHOUT ARROGANCY AND IMPIETY   605 25
TO BE THE LAMB WITHOUT SPOT, WHO, BY SACRIFICE OF   605 33

WITHSTAND

GRACE TO WITHSTAND THE TEMPTATIONS OF THE WORLD, THE   214 23
MAY BE ABLE TO WITHSTAND IN THE EVIL DAY, AND HAVING   219 12
AND TO WITHSTAND AND CONVINCE THE GAINSAYERS   554 33

WITHSTOOD

HATH GREATLY WITHSTOOD OUR WORDS   254 09

WITNESS

TO IT THE WITNESS OF VISIBLE UNITY   047 10
NOT BEAR FALSE WITNESS AGAINST THY NEIGHBOUR   069 16
NOT BEAR FALSE WITNESS, THOU SHALT NOT COVET   090 26
WITNESS, TO BEAR WITNESS OF THE LIGHT, THAT ALL MEN   097 27
SAME CAME FOR A WITNESS, TO BEAR WITNESS OF THE   097 27
WAS SENT TO BEAR WITNESS OF THAT LIGHT   097 29
AND BEAR WITNESS, AND SHEW UNTO YOU THAT ETERNAL   101 16
MANY THINGS THEY WITNESS AGAINST THEE   135 23
SOUGHT FOR WITNESS AGAINST JESUS TO PUT HIM TO DEATH   143 02
BUT THEIR WITNESS AGREED NOT TOGETHER   143 04
MANY BARE FALSE WITNESS AGAINST HIM, BUT THEIR   143 04
AND BARE FALSE WITNESS AGAINST HIM, SAYING, WE HEARD   143 06
SO DID THEIR WITNESS AGREE TOGETHER   143 09
IT WHICH THESE WITNESS AGAINST THEE   143 11
MANY THINGS THEY WITNESS AGAINST THEE   145 11
AND THEY SAID, WHAT NEED WE ANY FURTHER WITNESS   152 02
GHOST ALSO IS A WITNESS TO US   158 10
ALL THE PROPHETS WITNESS, THAT THROUGH HIS NAME   166 31
THAT BEARETH WITNESS, BECAUSE THE SPIRIT IS TRUTH   170 32
THREE THAT BEAR WITNESS, THE SPIRIT, AND THE WATER,   171 02
WE RECEIVE THE WITNESS OF MEN, THE WITNESS OF GOD IS   171 04
OF MEN, THE WITNESS OF GOD IS GREATER   171 04
FOR THIS IS THE WITNESS OF GOD WHICH HE HATH   171 05
OF GOD HATH THE WITNESS IN HIMSELF   171 07
ALSO SHALL BEAR WITNESS, BECAUSE YE HAVE BEEN WITH ME   179 27
ALL THE PROPHETS WITNESS, THAT THROUGH HIS NAME   184 18
AND YE RECEIVE NOT OUR WITNESS   188 22
HIMSELF BEARETH WITNESS WITH OUR SPIRIT, THAT WE ARE   200 10
WILL BE A SWIFT WITNESS AGAINST THE SORCERERS,   232 16
ORDAINED TO BE A WITNESS WITH US OF HIS RESURRECTION   234 24
ALSO SHALL BEAR WITNESS, BECAUSE YE HAVE BEEN WITH ME   255 33
NOT BEAR FALSE WITNESS AGAINST THY NEIGHBOUR   287 15
HIMSELF BEARETH WITNESS WITH OUR SPIRIT, THAT WE ARE   330 23
AS THE FAITHFUL WITNESS IN HEAVEN   452 15
AND BEAR WITNESS, HOW YOU ARE MINDED TO BEHAVE   554 14
IN WITNESS WHEREOF, WE HAVE HEREUNTO AFFIXED OUR   569 38
NOT BEAR FALSE WITNESS AGAINST THY NEIGHBOUR   579 18
THE CHURCH BE A WITNESS AND A KEEPER OF HOLY WRIT,   607 07

WITNESSED

AND HAVE WITNESSED THE SAME BEFORE GOD AND THIS   304 04

WITNESSES

YE SHALL BE WITNESSES UNTO ME BOTH IN JERUSALEM, AND   005 12
A CLOUD OF WITNESSES THAT WE, REJOICING IN THEIR   078 23
AND THE WITNESSES LAID DOWN THEIR CLOTHES AT A YOUNG   100 12
WHAT NEED WE ANY FURTHER WITNESSES   143 18
AND WE ARE WITNESSES OF ALL THINGS WHICH HE DID BOTH   166 22
BUT UNTO WITNESSES CHOSEN BEFORE OF GOD, EVEN TO US,   166 26
WHO ARE HIS WITNESSES UNTO THE PEOPLE   169 05
AND YE ARE WITNESSES OF THESE THINGS   170 16
YE SHALL BE WITNESSES UNTO ME BOTH IN JERUSALEM,   178 10
AND WE ARE WITNESSES OF ALL THINGS WHICH HE DID BOTH   184 10
BUT UNTO WITNESSES CHOSEN BEFORE OF GOD, EVEN TO US,   184 13

WITNESSES   CONTINUED

TO CHOSEN WITNESSES THINE ONLY-BEGOTTEN SON   247 31
US ABOUT WITH SO GREAT A CLOUD OF WITNESSES   258 13
A CLOUD OF WITNESSES, LET US LAY ASIDE EVERY WEIGHT,   258 21
WITH HIM AT THE FONT AT LEAST TWO WITNESSES   R 273 23
SHALL ASK THE WITNESSES THE NAME   R 279 31
ARE FALSE WITNESSES RISEN UP AGAINST ME, AND SUCH AS   372 25
11 FALSE WITNESSES DID RISE UP   382 13
CERTAIN SURE WITNESSES, AND EFFECTUAL SIGNS OF GRACE, 607 32

WITNESSETH

HOLY GHOST WITNESSETH IN EVERY CITY, SAYING THAT   550 17

WIVES

WIVES, SUBMIT YOURSELVES UNTO YOUR OWN HUSBANDS, AS   267 13
SO LET THE WIVES BE TC THEIR OWN HUSBANDS IN   267 18
LOVE YOUR WIVES, EVEN AS CHRIST ALSO LOVED THE   267 19
MEN TO LOVE THEIR WIVES AS THEIR OWN BODIES   267 25
EVEN SO MUST THEIR WIVES BE GRAVE, NOT SLANDERERS,   531 32

WOE

BUT WOE TO THAT MAN BY WHOM THE SON OF MAN IS   141 07
BUT WOE UNTO THAT MAN BY WHOM HE IS BETRAYED   149 15
WOE TO THE INHABITERS OF THE EARTH AND OF THE SEA   252 17
WOE UNTO THE WORLD BECAUSE OF OFFENCES   252 33
BUT WOE TO THAT MAN BY WHOM THE OFFENCE COMETH   253 02
4 WOE IS ME, THAT I AM CONSTRAINED TO DWELL WITH   502 14

WOLF

ARE NOT, SEETH THE WOLF COMING, AND LEAVETH THE   172 24
AND THE WOLF CATCHETH THEM, AND SCATTERETH THE SHEEP   172 25
ARE NOT, SEETH THE WOLF COMING, AND LEAVETH THE   539 13
AND THE WOLF CATCHETH THEM, AND SCATTERETH THE SHEEP   539 14
BE TO THE FLOCK OF CHRIST A SHEPHERD, NOT A WOLF   558 26

WOLVES

BUT INWARDLY THEY ARE RAVENING WOLVES   200 17
BEHOLD, I SEND YOU FORTH AS LAMBS AMONG WOLVES   254 17
SHALL GRIEVOUS WOLVES ENTER IN AMONG YOU, NOT SPARING 550 30

WOMAN

BE SAID WHEN ANY WOMAN, BEING PRESENT IN CHURCH,   R 051 03
THIS WOMAN, THY SERVANT, WHO DESIRETH   051 07
HIS SON, MADE OF A WOMAN, MADE UNDER THE LAW, TO   104 20
SAITH UNTO HER, WOMAN, WHAT HAVE I TO DO WITH THEE   113 15
BEHOLD, A WOMAN OF CANAAN CAME OUT OF THE SAME   128 08
SAID UNTO HER, O WOMAN, GREAT IS THY FAITH   128 20
A CERTAIN WOMAN OF THE COMPANY LIFTED UP HER   130 18
THERE CAME A WOMAN HAVING AN ALABASTER BOX OF   140 03
SAYING, WOMAN, I KNOW HIM NOT   151 13
UNTO HIS MOTHER, WOMAN, BEHOLD THY SON   160 21
A WOMAN WHEN SHE IS IN TRAVAIL HATH SORROW, BECAUSE   174 10
EITHER WHAT WOMAN HAVING TEN PIECES OF SILVER, IF SHE 193 27
BEHOLD, A WOMAN, WHICH WAS DISEASED WITH AN   224 17
AND THE WOMAN WAS MADE WHOLE FROM THAT HOUR   224 23
AND THE WOMAN ON THE LEFT, THE MINISTER SHALL   R 300 06
THIS MAN AND THIS WOMAN IN HOLY MATRIMONY   300 10
THOU HAVE THIS WOMAN TO THY WEDDED WIFE, TO LIVE   301 06
SAY UNTO THE WOMAN, N   R 301 13
THE WOMAN SHALL ANSWER, I WILL   R 301 20
WHO GIVETH THIS WOMAN TO BE MARRIED TO THIS MAN   301 23
RECEIVING THE WOMAN AT HER FATHER'S OR FRIEND'S   R 301 25
HAND TO TAKE THE WOMAN BY HER RIGHT HAND, AND TC SAY R 301 26
AND THE WOMAN WITH HER RIGHT HAND TAKING THE MAN BY R 302 02
GIVE UNTO THE WOMAN A RING ON THIS WISE   R 302 10
THIS MAN AND THIS WOMAN, WHOM WE BLESS IN THY NAME   303 06
THE WOMAN, AT THE USUAL TIME AFTER HER DELIVERY,   R 305 07
THE WOMAN STILL KNEELING   R 305 15
O LORD, SAVE THIS WOMAN THY SERVANT   306 17
THIS WOMAN, THY SERVANT, WHO DESIRETH   306 26
THE WOMAN, THAT COMETH TO GIVE HER THANKS, MUST   R 307 07
THAT IS BORN OF A WOMAN, HATH BUT A SHORT TIME TO   332 18
AS UPON A WOMAN IN HER TRAVAIL   399 21
AND BE LIKE THE UNTIMELY FRUIT OF A WOMAN   410 24
MAKETH THE BARREN WOMAN TO KEEP HOUSE, *   484 23

WOMAN'S

FINGER OF THE WOMAN'S LEFT HAND   R 302 11
FINGER OF THE WOMAN'S LEFT HAND, THE MINISTER SHALL R 302 23

WOMB

OF THE ANGEL BEFORE HE WAS CONCEIVED IN THE WOMB   106 22
BLESSED IS THE WOMB THAT BARE THEE, AND THE PAPS   130 19
INTO HIS MOTHER'S WOMB, AND BE BORN   188 09
THAT OPENETH THE WOMB SHALL BE CALLED HOLY TO THE   232 26
CONCEIVE IN THY WOMB, AND BRING FORTH A SON, AND   236 15
INTO HIS MOTHER'S WOMB, AND BE BORN   275 13
THOU ART HE THAT TOOK ME OUT OF MY MOTHER'S WOMB   366 21
THOU ART MY GOD EVEN FROM MY MOTHER'S WOMB   366 24
EVEN FROM THEIR MOTHER'S WOMB   410 13
THOU ART HE THAT TOOK ME OUT OF MY MOTHER'S WOMB   425 18
AS DEW FROM THE WOMB OF THE MORNING   482 13
THE FRUIT OF THE WOMB, *   505 29
THOU HAST COVERED ME IN MY MOTHER'S WOMB   515 14
MAN'S NATURE IN THE WOMB OF THE BLESSED VIRGIN,   603 11

WOMBS

AND THE WOMBS THAT NEVER BARE, AND THE PAPS   154 17

WOMEN

OR BY AIR, ALL WOMEN IN CHILD-BIRTH, ALL SICK   056 31
THESE ARE THEY WHICH WERE NOT DEFILED WITH WOMEN   103 09
OF PEOPLE, AND OF WOMEN, WHICH ALSO BEWAILED AND   154 12
AND THE WOMEN THAT FOLLOWED HIM FROM GALILEE, STOOD   155 19
AND CERTAIN WOMEN ALSO OF OUR COMPANY MADE US   167 22
IT EVEN SO AS THE WOMEN HAD SAID   167 28
THEY WERE MEN OR WOMEN, HE MIGHT BRING THEM BOUND   229 29
BLESSED ART THOU AMONG WOMEN   236 11
TO THE LORD, MULTITUDES BOTH OF MEN AND WOMEN   249 26
OF DISTRESSED WOMEN IN CHILD-BED   R 307 09
9 KINGS' DAUGHTERS ARE AMONG THY HONOURABLE WOMEN   397 02
WAS THE COMPANY OF WOMEN THAT BARE THE TIDINGS   420 03

WON

POWER OUR FATHERS WON THEIR LIBERTIES OF OLD   263 18

WONDER

YE DESPISERS, AND WONDER, AND PERISH   169 24

WONDERED

THAT HEARD IT WONDERED AT THOSE THINGS WHICH WERE   106 15
AND THE PEOPLE WONDERED   129 26
AND I WONDERED THAT THERE WAS NONE TO UPHOLD   138 23
FOR JOY, AND WONDERED, HE SAID UNTO THEM, HAVE YE   170 03

WONDERFUL

THANKS FOR THE WONDERFUL GRACE AND VIRTUE DECLARED IN 048 16
TONGUES THE WONDERFUL WORKS OF GOD   181 06
WE, HAVING HIS WONDERFUL CONVERSION IN REMEMBRANCE,   229 20
AND MEN IN A WONDERFUL ORDER   251 28
SAW THE WONDERFUL THINGS THAT HE DID, AND THE   260 10
WE BLESS THY WONDERFUL GOODNESS, FOR HAVING TURNED   315 20
FOR THE WONDERFUL GRACE AND VIRTUE DECLARED IN ALL   336 17
SHALT SHOW US WONDERFUL THINGS IN THY RIGHTEOUSNESS,   416 21
O HOW WONDERFUL ART THOU IN THY WORKS   417 17
HOW WONDERFUL HE IS IN HIS DOING TOWARD THE CHILDREN   417 23
35 O GOD, WONDERFUL ART THOU IN THY HOLY PLACES   421 27
AND IS WONDERFUL AMONG THE KINGS OF THE EARTH   433 13
HIS MIGHTY AND WONDERFUL WORKS THAT HE HATH DONE   435 03
AND THE WONDERFUL WORKS THAT HE HAD SHOWED FOR THEM   435 22
IS GREAT, WONDERFUL, AND HOLY   462 21
THY TESTIMONIES ARE WONDERFUL   498 28
IS TOO WONDERFUL AND EXCELLENT FOR ME   514 29

WONDERFULLY

BAPTIST WAS WONDERFULLY BORN, AND SENT TO PREPARE THE 242 08
SON WONDERFULLY TRANSFIGURED, IN RAIMENT WHITE AND   247 32
AND WONDERFULLY MADE   515 16

WONDERS

AND SHALL SHEW GREAT SIGNS AND WONDERS   118 06
YE SEE SIGNS AND WONDERS, YE WILL NOT BELIEVE   219 33
MANY SIGNS AND WONDERS WROUGHT AMONG THE PEOPLE   249 21
CALL TO MIND THY WONDERS OF OLD TIME   434 05
GOD THAT DOEST WONDERS, *   434 10
AND HIS WONDERS IN THE FIELD OF ZOAN   437 28
DOST THOU SHOW WONDERS AMONG THE DEAD   449 16
AND HIS WONDERS UNTO ALL PEOPLES   460 04
HIS WONDERS, AND THE JUDGMENTS OF HIS MOUTH   470 23
AND WONDERS IN THE LAND OF HAM   471 27
REGARDED NOT THY WONDERS IN EGYPT, NEITHER KEPT THEY   473 13
AND DECLARE THE WONDERS THAT HE DOETH FOR THE   476 20
AND DECLARE THE WONDERS THAT HE DOETH FOR THE   477 05
AND DECLARE THE WONDERS THAT HE DOETH FOR THE   477 18
AND HIS WONDERS IN THE DEEP   477 25
AND DECLARE THE WONDERS THAT HE DOETH FOR THE   478 08
SENT TOKENS AND WONDERS INTO THE MIDST OF THEE, O   510 20
4 WHO ONLY DOETH GREAT WONDERS   511 22

WONDROUS

TELL OF ALL THY WONDROUS WORKS   371 11
GREAT ARE THE WONDROUS WORKS WHICH THOU HAST DONE,   390 21
I TELL OF THY WONDROUS WORKS   426 09
ONLY DOETH WONDROUS THINGS   428 03
AND THAT DO THY WONDROUS WORKS DECLARE   431 32
NOT HIS WONDROUS WORKS   437 03
AND DOEST WONDROUS THINGS   447 23
12 SHALL THY WONDROUS WORKS BE KNOWN IN THE DARK   449 20
PRAISE THY WONDROUS WORKS   450 13
BE OF ALL HIS WONDROUS WORKS   470 08
22 WONDROUS WORKS IN THE LAND OF HAM   474 12
I MAY SEE THE WONDROUS THINGS OF THY LAW   491 02
I TALK OF THY WONDROUS WORKS   491 22
THY PRAISE, AND WONDROUS WORKS   521 03

WONT

THE GOVERNOR WAS WONT TO RELEASE UNTO THE PEOPLE A   135 26
AND WENT, AS HE WAS WONT, TO THE MOUNT OF OLIVES   150 14
WE TO PRAY, AND ART WONT TO GIVE MORE THAN EITHER WE   206 05
QUICKEN ME, AS THOU ART WONT   500 24

WORD   CONTINUED

WOOD

BOAR OUT OF THE WOOD DOTH ROOT IT UP, *   441 28
THE TREES OF THE WOOD REJOICE BEFORE THE LORD   460 25
AND FOUND IT IN THE WOOD   508 16
BREAKETH AND HEWETH WOOD UPON THE EARTH   517 27

WOODS

SAFELY IN THE WILDERNESS, AND SLEEP IN THE WOODS   262 06

WOOL

AND SCARLET WOOL, AND HYSSOP, AND SPRINKLED   147 21
HE GIVETH SNOW LIKE WOOL, *   523 27

WORD

IT CONTRARY TO THE WORD OF GOD, OR TO SOUND DOCTRINE,   V 40
HEAR HIS MOST HOLY WORD, AND TO ASK THOSE THINGS   006 08
THE WORD WAS MADE FLESH, AND DWELT AMONG US   R 008 31
HEAR HIS MOST HOLY WORD, AND TO ASK THOSE THINGS   023 16
ACCORDING TO THY WORD   028 10
AND HEARKEN UNTO THE VOICE OF HIS WORD   029 14
TO THY BLESSED WORD AND ORDINANCE   032 12
TO OBEY THY WORD, AND TO ABIDE IN THY LOVE   043 10
US IN THY HOLY WORD THAT THOU DOST NOT WILLINGLY   045 31
OF GOD'S HOLY WORD AND SACRAMENTS   047 22
AND CONTEMPT OF THY WORD AND COMMANDMENT, GOOD LORD,   055 04
WITH TRUE KNOWLEDGE AND UNDERSTANDING OF THY WORD   055 32
TO HEAR MEEKLY THY WORD, AND TO RECEIVE IT WITH PURE   056 15
TO AMEND OUR LIVES ACCORDING TO THY HOLY WORD   057 17
TRUTH OF THY HOLY WORD, AND LIVE IN UNITY AND GODLY   074 14
THY TRUE AND LIVELY WORD, AND RIGHTLY AND DULY   074 23
THEY MAY HEAR, AND RECEIVE THY HOLY WORD   074 28
BY THOUGHT, WORD, AND DEED, AGAINST THY DIVINE   075 21
THE MYSTERY OF THE WORD MADE FLESH, THOU HAST CAUSED   077 29
SANCTIFY, WITH THY WORD AND HOLY SPIRIT, THESE THY   081 10
HIS NEIGHBOURS BY WORD OR DEED, SO THAT THE   R 085 02
EITHER BY WILL, WORD, OR DEED, THERE TO BEWAIL YOUR   087 19
OR SLANDERER OF HIS WORD, AN ADULTERER, OR BE IN   087 32
MINISTER OF GOD'S WORD, AND OPEN HIS GRIEF   088 06
COMFORT OF THY HOLY WORD, WE MAY EMBRACE, AND EVER   092 11
ALL THINGS BY THE WORD OF HIS POWER, WHEN HE HAD BY   096 28
BEGINNING WAS THE WORD, AND THE WORD WAS WITH GOD,   097 20
THE WORD, AND THE WORD WAS WITH GOD, AND THE WORD WAS   097 20
WITH GOD, AND THE WORD WAS GOD   097 21
AND THE WORD WAS MADE FLESH, AND DWELT AMONG US, (AND   098 04
OF THE WORD OF LIFE   101 14
HIM A LIAR, AND HIS WORD IS NOT IN US   101 32
AND BE THOU THERE UNTIL I BRING THEE WORD   103 19
UPON US THE NEW LIGHT OF THINE INCARNATE WORD   106 26
FOUND HIM, BRING ME WORD AGAIN, THAT I MAY COME AND   109 14
BUT SPEAK THE WORD ONLY, AND MY SERVANT SHALL BE   115 12
LET THE WORD OF CHRIST DWELL IN YOU RICHLY IN ALL   116 11
WHATSOEVER YE DO IN WORD OR DEED, DO ALL IN THE NAME   116 14
THE SEED IS THE WORD OF GOD   121 33
AND TAKETH AWAY THE WORD OUT OF THEIR HEARTS, LEST   121 35
HEAR, RECEIVE THE WORD WITH JOY   122 03
HAVING HEARD THE WORD, KEEP IT, AND BRING FORTH FRUIT   122 09
BY THE WORD OF TRUTH, BY THE POWER OF GOD,   126 14
BUT BY EVERY WORD THAT PROCEEDETH OUT OF THE   126 29
BUT HE ANSWERED HER NOT A WORD   128 12
THEY THAT HEAR THE WORD OF GOD, AND KEEP IT   130 21
AND HE ANSWERED HIM TO NEVER A WORD   135 24
CALLED TO MIND THE WORD THAT JESUS SAID UNTO HIM,   143 35
REMEMBERED THE WORD OF THE LORD, HOW HE HAD SAID UNTO   151 21
HARDNESS OF HEART, AND CONTEMPT OF THY WORD   157 09
THE WORD WHICH GOD SENT UNTO THE CHILDREN OF ISRAEL,   166 15
THAT WORD, I SAY, YE KNOW, WHICH WAS PUBLISHED   166 17
MIGHTY IN DEED AND WORD BEFORE GOD AND ALL THE   167 17
TO YOU IS THE WORD OF THIS SALVATION SENT   168 26
HE US WITH THE WORD OF GOD, THAT WE SHOULD BE A   174 29
THE ENGRAFTED WORD, WHICH IS ABLE TO SAVE YOUR SOULS   175 04
BE YE DOERS OF THE WORD, AND NOT HEARERS ONLY,   176 05
BE A HEARER OF THE WORD, AND NOT A DOER, HE IS LIKE   176 07
AND THE WORD WHICH YE HEAR IS NOT MINE, BUT THE   181 27
BY THE SPIRIT THE WORD OF WISDOM   182 27
TO ANOTHER THE WORD OF KNOWLEDGE BY THE SAME SPIRIT   182 28
THE WORD WHICH GOD SENT UNTO THE CHILDREN OF ISRAEL,   184 02
THAT WORD, I SAY, YE KNOW, WHICH WAS PUBLISHED   184 04
HOLY GHOST FELL ON ALL THEM WHICH HEARD THE WORD   184 21
HAD RECEIVED THE WORD OF GOD, THEY SENT UNTO THEM   185 22
LET US NOT LOVE IN WORD, NEITHER IN TONGUE   191 22
HIM TO HEAR THE WORD OF GOD, HE STOOD BY THE LAKE OF   196 07
NEVERTHELESS AT THY WORD I WILL LET DOWN THE NET   196 17
BY THE SPIRIT THE WORD OF WISDOM   203 27
TO ANOTHER THE WORD OF KNOWLEDGE BY THE SAME SPIRIT   203 28
TO ANSWER HIM A WORD, NEITHER DURST ANY MAN FROM THAT   215 23
WHICH IS THE WORD OF GOD   219 19
MAN BELIEVED THE WORD THAT JESUS HAD SPOKEN UNTO HIM,   220 04
HEARD BEFORE IN THE WORD OF THE TRUTH OF THE GOSPEL   223 26
CALLED BY THY HOLY WORD, MAY FORTHWITH GIVE UP   226 22
AND HEARING BY THE WORD OF GOD   227 13
SERVANT DEPART IN PEACE, ACCORDING TO THY WORD   233 06
BE IT UNTO ME ACCORDING TO THY WORD   236 29
CLEAN THROUGH THE WORD WHICH I HAVE SPOKEN UNTO YOU   238 09
BUT THE WORD OF OUR GOD SHALL STAND FOR EVER   242 32
TO PREACH THY HOLY WORD, AND THE PEOPLE OBEDIENTLY TO   244 26
GRACE TRULY TO BELIEVE AND TO PREACH THY WORD   249 16
TO LOVE THAT WORD WHICH HE BELIEVED, AND BOTH TO   249 17
NOR HANDLING THE WORD OF GOD DECEITFULLY   250 30
AND BY THE WORD OF THEIR TESTIMONY   252 15
REMEMBER THE WORD THAT I SAID UNTO YOU, THE SERVANT   255 17
TO PASS, THAT THE WORD MIGHT BE FULFILLED THAT IS   255 28
SINCERE MILK OF THE WORD, THAT YE MAY GROW THEREBY   259 27

TO HEAR THE WORD OF GOD   260 27
NECESSARY THAT THE WORD OF GOD SHOULD FIRST HAVE BEEN   260 31
AND GLORIFIED THE WORD OF THE LORD   261 07
AND THE WORD OF THE LORD WAS PUBLISHED THROUGHOUT ALL   261 08
HE US WITH THE WORD OF TRUTH, THAT WE SHOULD BE A   265 22
THE ENGRAFTED WORD, WHICH IS ABLE TO SAVE YOUR SOULS   265 27
BE YE DOERS OF THE WORD, AND NOT HEARERS ONLY,   265 28
BE A HEARER OF THE WORD, AND NOT A DOER, HE IS LIKE   265 30
OF WATER BY THE WORD, THAT HE MIGHT PRESENT IT TO   267 21
SAY UNTO YOU BY THE WORD OF THE LORD, THAT WE WHICH   269 03
TO HONOUR THY HOLY NAME AND HIS WORD   288 21
TO HURT NOBODY BY WORD OR DEED   288 32
DO YOU MEAN BY THIS WORD SACRAMENT   292 09
I MEAN BY THIS WORD SACRAMENT AN OUTWARD AND VISIBLE   292 10
TO PREACH THE WORD OF GOD   294 13
HAD RECEIVED THE WORD OF GOD, THEY SENT UNTO THEM   296 14
OBEDIENCE OF THY WORD, THAT IN THE END THEY MAY   298 22
THAN AS GOD'S WORD DOTH ALLOW, THEIR MARRIAGE IS NOT   300 30
THY NAME, AND THY WORD, ABOVE ALL THINGS   311 32
AND HEARKEN UNTO THE VOICE OF HIS WORD   312 30
HE THAT HEARETH MY WORD, AND BELIEVETH ON HIM THAT   321 34
THEE IN THOUGHT, WORD, AND DEED   323 14
IN HIS WORD IS MY TRUST   328 12
BY THE WORD OF THY LIPS I HAVE KEPT ME FROM THE WAYS   358 25
THE WORD OF THE LORD ALSO IS TRIED IN THE FIRE   361 28
4 FOR THE WORD OF THE LORD IS TRUE   378 25
6 BY THE WORD OF THE LORD WERE THE HEAVENS MADE   378 29
BECAUSE OF THE WORD OF TRUTH, OF MEEKNESS,   396 23
4 I WILL PRAISE GOD, BECAUSE OF HIS WORD   408 21
10 IN GOD'S WORD WILL I REJOICE   409 02
IN THE LORD'S WORD WILL I COMFORT ME   409 02
11 THE LORD GAVE THE WORD   420 02
AND HEARKEN UNTO THE VOICE OF HIS WORD   467 17
THE WORD OF THE LORD TRIED HIM   471 11
AND THEY WERE NOT OBEDIENT UNTO HIS WORD   471 29
31 HE SPAKE THE WORD, AND THERE CAME ALL MANNER OF   471 34
34 HE SPAKE THE WORD, AND THE GRASSHOPPERS CAME,   472 06
AND GAVE NO CREDENCE UNTO HIS WORD   474 18
20 HE SENT HIS WORD, AND HEALED THEM   477 15
25 FOR AT HIS WORD THE STORMY WIND ARISETH, *   477 26
EVEN BY RULING HIMSELF AFTER THY WORD   490 17
11 THY WORD HAVE I HID WITHIN MY HEART, *   490 20
AND I WILL NOT FORGET THY WORD   490 30
THAT I MAY LIVE, AND KEEP THY WORD   490 33
O QUICKEN THOU ME, ACCORDING TO THY WORD   491 18
COMFORT THOU ME ACCORDING UNTO THY WORD   491 24
38 O STABLISH THY WORD IN THY SERVANT, *   492 15
EVEN THY SALVATION, ACCORDING UNTO THY WORD   492 23
FOR MY TRUST IS IN THY WORD   492 25
43 O TAKE NOT THE WORD OF THY TRUTH UTTERLY OUT OF MY   492 26
AS CONCERNING THY WORD, *   493 08
FOR THY WORD HATH QUICKENED ME   493 11
O BE MERCIFUL UNTO ME, ACCORDING TO THY WORD   493 28
ACCORDING UNTO THY WORD   494 12
BUT NOW HAVE I KEPT THY WORD   494 16
BECAUSE I HAVE PUT MY TRUST IN THY WORD   495 03
ACCORDING TO THY WORD UNTO THY SERVANT   495 08
AND I HAVE A GOOD HOPE BECAUSE OF THY WORD   495 20
82 MINE EYES LONG SORE FOR THY WORD   495 21
O LORD, THY WORD *   496 03
THAT I MAY KEEP THY WORD   496 29
THY WORD IS A LANTERN UNTO MY FEET, *   497 07
QUICKEN ME, O LORD, ACCORDING TO THY WORD   497 12
AND MY TRUST IS IN THY WORD   497 27
ME ACCORDING TO THY WORD, THAT I MAY LIVE   497 30
AND FOR THE WORD OF THY RIGHTEOUSNESS   498 16
130 WHEN THY WORD GOETH FORTH, *   498 30
133 ORDER MY STEPS IN THY WORD   499 04
140 THY WORD IS TRIED TO THE UTTERMOST, *   499 19
FOR IN THY WORD IS MY TRUST   500 05
THAT I MIGHT BE OCCUPIED IN THY WORD   500 07
QUICKEN ME ACCORDING TO THY WORD   500 20
160 THY WORD IS TRUE FROM EVERLASTING   500 31
BUT MY HEART STANDETH IN AWE OF THY WORD   501 04
I AM AS GLAD OF THY WORD, *   501 05
GIVE ME UNDERSTANDING ACCORDING TO THY WORD   501 21
DELIVER ME ACCORDING TO THY WORD   501 23
MY TONGUE SHALL SING OF THY WORD   501 26
IN HIS WORD IS MY TRUST   507 17
THY NAME, AND THY WORD, ABOVE ALL THINGS   513 32
THERE IS NOT A WORD IN MY TONGUE, *   514 25
AND HIS WORD RUNNETH VERY SWIFTLY   523 26
HE SENDETH OUT HIS WORD, AND MELTETH THEM   523 31
19 HE SHOWETH HIS WORD UNTO JACOB, *   523 33
FOR HE SPAKE THE WORD, AND THEY WERE MADE   524 14
WIND AND STORM, FULFILLING HIS WORD   524 21
THAT, BOTH BY WORD AND GOOD EXAMPLE, THEY MAY   531 21
WE SHOULD LEAVE THE WORD OF GOD, AND SERVE TABLES   532 10
AND TO THE MINISTRY OF THE WORD   532 14
AND THE WORD OF GOD INCREASED   532 20
THAT, BOTH BY WORD AND GOOD EXAMPLE, THEY MAY   537 25
AND STRANGE DOCTRINES CONTRARY TO GOD'S WORD   542 21
DISPENSER OF THE WORD OF GOD, AND OF HIS HOLY   546 14
DISPENSER OF THE WORD OF GOD, AND OF HIS HOLY   546 20
TO PREACH THE WORD OF GOD, AND TO MINISTER THE HOLY   546 25
AND THAT THY WORD SPOKEN BY THEIR MOUTHS MAY HAVE   547 06
OF THY MOST HOLY WORD, OR AGREEABLE TO THE SAME,   547 10
THAT, BOTH BY WORD AND GOOD EXAMPLE, THEY MAY   548 04
PREACH THY WORD, AND DULY ADMINISTER THE GODLY   549 11
TO GOD, AND TO THE WORD OF HIS GRACE, WHICH IS ABLE   551 03
THAT, BOTH BY WORD AND DEED, HE MAY FAITHFULLY   553 31
AND STRANGE DOCTRINE CONTRARY TO GOD'S WORD   555 04
AUTHORITY OF GOD'S WORD, AND BY THE ORDER OF THIS   555 17
PREACHING THY WORD, MAY NOT ONLY BE EARNEST TO   559 08

PAGE LN   PAGE LN

WORD   CONTINUED

EXAMPLE IN WORD, IN CONVERSATION, IN LOVE, IN FAITH,   559 10
READING THY HOLY WORD, FOR CELEBRATING THY HOLY   565 08
THAT BY THY HOLY WORD WHICH SHALL BE READ AND   566 02
THE DIVINE WORD, IN LEADING THE DEVOTIONS OF THE   571 26
AND DOCTRINE SET FORTH THY TRUE AND LIVELY WORD   573 23
TO THE CLEARNESS AND EXCELLENCY OF THY HOLY WORD   573 28
TO HONOUR HIS HOLY NAME AND HIS WORD   579 32
TO HURT NOBODY BY WORD OR DEED   580 07
THOU BY THIS WORD SACRAMENT   581 11
O GOD, AT WHOSE WORD MAN GOETH FORTH TO HIS WORK AND   599 25
WHICH IS THE WORD OF THE FATHER, BEGOTTEN FROM   603 09
UNTO US IN THE WORD OF GOD   606 29
THE WHICH THE PURE WORD OF GOD IS PREACHED, AND THE   606 39
CONTRARY TO GOD'S WORD WRITTEN, NEITHER MAY IT SO   607 05
REPUGNANT TO THE WORD OF GOD   607 17
REPUGNANT TO THE WORD OF GOD, AND THE CUSTOM OF THE   607 27
MINISTRATION OF THE WORD AND SACRAMENTS, YET   608 10
BOTH IN HEARING THE WORD OF GOD, AND IN RECEIVING THE   608 13
SO THAT NOTHING BE ORDAINED AGAINST GOD'S WORD   609 35
REPUGNANT TO THE WORD OF GOD, AND BE ORDAINED AND   609 37

WORDS

LET THE WORDS OF MY MOUTH, AND THE MEDITATION OF MY   003 19
INSTEAD OF THE WORDS, HE DESCENDED INTO HELL, USE THE   R 015 16
INTO HELL, USE THE WORDS, HE WENT INTO THE PLACE OF   R 015 17
ARE CONSIDERED AS WORDS OF THE SAME MEANING IN THE   R 015 18
LET THE WORDS OF MY MOUTH, AND THE MEDITATION OF MY   021 21
INSTEAD OF THE WORDS, HE DESCENDED INTO HELL, USE THE   R 029 21
INTO HELL, USE THE WORDS, HE WENT INTO THE PLACE OF   R 029 22
ARE CONSIDERED AS WORDS OF THE SAME MEANING IN THE   R 029 23
IN THE WORDS WHICH CHRIST HATH TAUGHT US, WE MAKE   048 24
THAT THE WORDS WHICH WE HAVE HEARD THIS DAY WITH   049 18
GOD SPAKE THESE WORDS, AND SAID   068 03
REMEMBER THE WORDS OF THE LORD JESUS, HOW HE SAID,   072 02
ANTHEM IN THE WORDS OF HOLY SCRIPTURE OR OF THE BOOK   R 073 35
WHAT COMFORTABLE WORDS OUR SAVIOUR CHRIST SAITH UNTO   076 10
ENDING WITH THESE WORDS, PARTAKERS OF HIS MOST   R 083 10
BUT MY WORDS SHALL NOT PASS AWAY   093 20
WROTE AFORE IN FEW WORDS, WHEREBY, WHEN YE READ,   108 19
LET NO MAN DECEIVE YOU WITH VAIN WORDS   129 09
HE THAT IS OF GOD HEARETH GOD'S WORDS   133 11
AND SPAKE THE SAME WORDS   142 08
THEN HE QUESTIONED WITH HIM IN MANY WORDS   153 14
THESE ARE THE WORDS WHICH I SPAKE UNTO YOU, WHILE I   170 07
IF A MAN LOVE ME, HE WILL KEEP MY WORDS   181 25
YET SPAKE THESE WORDS, THE HOLY GHOST FELL ON ALL   184 20
HAD HEARD THESE WORDS, THEY MARVELLED, AND LEFT HIM,   223 11
AND THEIR WORDS UNTO THE ENDS OF THE WORLD   227 15
IN ME, AND MY WORDS ABIDE IN YOU, YE SHALL ASK WHAT   238 17
THE WORDS THAT I SPEAK UNTO YOU I SPEAK NOT OF   240 15
FOR HE HATH GREATLY WITHSTOOD OUR WORDS   254 09
WHEREFORE COMFORT ONE ANOTHER WITH THESE WORDS   269 11
HEAR THE WORDS OF THE GOSPEL, WRITTEN BY SAINT MARK,   274 23
HEAR THE WORDS OF THE GOSPEL, WRITTEN BY SAINT JOHN,   275 03
HEAR THE WORDS OF THE GOSPEL, WRITTEN BY SAINT   275 23
POUR WATER UPON HIM, USING THE SAME FORM OF WORDS   R 279 33
SHALL POUR WATER UPON HIM, SAYING THESE WORDS   R 281 20
THE MINISTER SHALL USE THIS FORM OF WORDS   R 282 12
WHAT DO WE MEAN BY THESE WORDS   291 06
MAY SAY, HEAR THE WORDS OF THE EVANGELIST SAINT LUKE,   296 11
BEGINNING AT THESE WORDS, YE WHO DO TRULY, ETC   R 322 31
ENDING WITH THESE WORDS, PARTAKERS OF HIS MOST   R 323 07
PONDER MY WORDS, O LORD, *   347 31
7 THE WORDS OF THE LORD ARE PURE WORDS   355 20
7 THE WORDS OF THE LORD ARE PURE WORDS   355 20
AND HEARKEN UNTO MY WORDS   358 30
AND THEIR WORDS INTO THE ENDS OF THE WORLD   363 20
14 LET THE WORDS OF MY MOUTH, AND THE MEDITATION OF   364 13
AND FROM THE WORDS OF MY COMPLAINT   366 06
IMAGINE DECEITFUL WORDS AGAINST THEM THAT ARE QUIET   383 03
3 THE WORDS OF HIS MOUTH ARE UNRIGHTEOUS AND FULL OF   383 30
I KEPT SILENCE, YEA, EVEN FROM GOOD WORDS   389 10
AND HAST CAST MY WORDS BEHIND THEE   402 25
LOVED TO SPEAK ALL WORDS THAT MAY DO HURT, *   404 26
HEARKEN UNTO THE WORDS OF MY MOUTH   406 05
22 THE WORDS OF HIS MOUTH WERE SOFTER THAN BUTTER,   407 35
HIS WORDS WERE SMOOTHER THAN OIL, AND YET BE THEY   408 02
5 THEY DAILY MISTAKE MY WORDS   408 24
AND FOR THE SIN OF THEIR LIPS, THEY SHALL BE   411 29
THEY GIVE GOOD WORDS WITH THEIR MOUTH, BUT CURSE WITH   414 05
AND SHOOT OUT THEIR ARROWS, EVEN BITTER WORDS   415 24
YOUR EARS UNTO THE WORDS OF MY MOUTH   434 28
34 AND SO SHALL MY WORDS PLEASE HIM   469 29
BELIEVED THEY HIS WORDS, *   473 25
AGAINST THE WORDS OF THE LORD, *   476 26
ME ABOUT ALSO WITH WORDS OF HATRED, AND FOUGHT   480 07
AND WILL GUIDE HIS WORDS WITH DISCRETION   483 27
HOW SWEET ARE THY WORDS UNTO MY THROAT   496 32
BECAUSE MINE ENEMIES HAVE FORGOTTEN THY WORDS   499 18
HAVE HEARD THE WORDS OF THY MOUTH   514 05
11 A MAN FULL OF WORDS SHALL NOT PROSPER UPON THE   516 32
THAT THEY MAY HEAR MY WORDS   517 25
SAYING THESE WORDS, REVEREND FATHER IN GOD, I PRESENT   R 530 09
THAT IN ALL OUR WORDS AND DEEDS WE MAY SEEK THY   547 11
TO REMEMBER THE WORDS OF THE LORD JESUS, HOW HE SAID,   551 14
FOR THESE WORDS ARE TRUE AND FAITHFUL   567 23
NAME AND THE WORDS, THEN SHALL THE INSTITUTOR RECEIVE   571 14
MAY THE WORDS OF HIS MOUTH, AND THE MEDITATION OF HIS   572 22
MY MEMORY WITH THE WORDS OF THY LAW   573 16
OF OUR THOUGHTS, WORDS, AND ACTIONS TO HIM WHOM THOU   588 22
TO THE PLAIN WORDS OF SCRIPTURE, OVERTHROWETH THE   608 42
WELL FROM OBSOLETE WORDS AND   R 610 28

WORK

GOVERN US IN OUR WORK, BY THE MIGHTY POWER OF THE   036 33
TO GOVERN THEM IN THEIR WORK   R 037 13
GOVERN US IN OUR WORK, TO GOVERN THEM IN THEIR WORK   R 037 13
COMMANDED US TO WORK WITH QUIETNESS, AND EAT OUR OWN   039 27
THAT THE GOOD WORK WHICH THOU HAST BEGUN IN THEM MAY   042 18
THAT WE MAY DO THE WORK WHICH THOU GIVEST US TO DO,   044 21
ALL THINGS IT MAY WORK ACCORDING TO GOD'S WILL,   047 13
THIS GREAT AND GOOD WORK MISCARRIED AT THAT TIME   VI 05
THIS IMPORTANT WORK BEING BROUGHT TO A   VI 35
IN IT THOU SHALT DO NO MANNER OF WORK   068 27
MORE IN MY ABSENCE, WORK OUT YOUR OWN SALVATION WITH   106 03
HATH WROUGHT A GOOD WORK ON ME   140 11
FOR I WORK A WORK IN YOUR DAYS, A WORK WHICH YE SHALL   169 24
FOR I WORK A WORK IN YOUR DAYS, A WORK WHICH YE SHALL   169 24
IN YOUR DAYS, A WORK WHICH YE SHALL IN NO WISE   169 25
BUT A DOER OF THE WORK, THIS MAN SHALL BE BLESSED IN   176 12
TO WORK ALL UNCLEANNESS WITH   216 09
HATH BEGUN A GOOD WORK IN YOU WILL PERFORM IT UNTIL   220 20
IN EVERY GOOD WORK, AND INCREASING IN THE KNOWLEDGE   224 05
THE SAINTS, FOR THE WORK OF THE MINISTRY, FOR THE   237 21
HAVE HER PERFECT WORK, THAT YE MAY BE PERFECT AND   239 10
WITH HIM, AND HIS WORK BEFORE HIM   243 08
DO THE WORK OF AN EVANGELIST, MAKE FULL   253 24
BUT A DOER OF THE WORK, THIS MAN SHALL BE BLESSED IN   266 03
IN IT THOU SHALT DO NO MANNER OF WORK   286 27
SHOW THY SERVANTS THY WORK   290 08
AND TO WORK AND PRAY AND GIVE FOR THE SPREAD OF HIS   291 19
ABOUNDING IN THE WORK OF THE LORD, FORASMUCH AS YE   330 15
THAT ALL THINGS WORK TOGETHER FOR GOOD TO THEM THAT   330 30
IN EVERY GOOD WORK TO DO HIS WILL, WORKING IN YOU   335 19
THAT THE GOOD WORK WHICH THOU DIDST BEGIN IN   335 29
ALL THEM THAT WORK INIQUITY   348 10
ALL YE THAT WORK INIQUITY   349 14
EVEN THE WORK OF THY FINGERS   351 04
IS TRAPPED IN THE WORK OF HIS OWN HANDS   352 25
THEM AFTER THE WORK OF THEIR HANDS   373 15
ALL THAT WORK WICKEDNESS   384 21
UNDERSTANDING THAT WORK WICKEDNESS, *   405 22
THOU REWARDEST EVERY MAN ACCORDING TO HIS WORK   414 24
FOR THEY SHALL PERCEIVE THAT IT IS HIS WORK   416 05
WAS KNOWN TO BRING IT TO AN EXCELLENT WORK   430 15
DOWN ALL THE CARVED WORK THEREOF *   430 16
THY SERVANTS THY WORK, *   454 22
PROSPER THOU THE WORK OF OUR HANDS UPON US   454 25
THE HEAVENS ARE THE WORK OF THY HANDS   465 32
GOETH FORTH TO HIS WORK, AND TO HIS LABOUR, *   469 06
3 HIS WORK IS WORTHY TO BE PRAISED AND HAD IN HONOUR,   482 28
EVEN THE WORK OF MEN'S HANDS   485 18
THE WORK OF MEN'S HANDS   510 33
WITH THE MEN THAT WORK WICKEDNESS, NEITHER LET ME EAT   517 17
THE SAINTS, FOR THE WORK OF THE MINISTRY, FOR THE   538 08
OF SO WEIGHTY A WORK, PERTAINING TO THE SALVATION OF   540 34
MAY ACCOMPLISH HIS WORK WHICH HE HATH BEGUN IN YOU   543 21
FOR THE OFFICE AND WORK OF A PRIEST IN THE CHURCH OF   546 09
THE OFFICE OF A BISHOP, HE DESIRETH A GOOD WORK   549 19
UNTO US, TO THE WORK WHEREUNTO WE TRUST THE HOLY   553 12
NOW CALLED TO THE WORK AND MINISTRY OF A BISHOP   553 29
IN YOU THE GOOD WORK WHICH HE HATH BEGUN, YOU MAY BE   555 31
FOR THE OFFICE AND WORK OF A BISHOP IN THE CHURCH OF   558 12
OF THIS PIOUS WORK, MAY SHOW FORTH THEIR   566 32
IN EVERY GOOD WORK TO DO HIS WILL, WORKING IN YOU   573 06
IN IT THOU SHALT DO NO MANNER OF WORK   579 07
AND WORK IN US AN HEARTY CONTRITION   590 04
THY WISDOM, AND IN WORK BE UPHELD BY THY STRENGTH,   594 26
IS OVER, AND OUR WORK IS DONE   594 32
GOETH FORTH TO HIS WORK AND TO HIS LABOUR UNTIL THE   599 25
ACCIDENT AND HARM THE WORKMEN AT THEIR WORK   599 29
AND CALLED TO THIS WORK BY MEN WHO HAVE PUBLIC   607 22
THE WHICH HE DOTH WORK INVISIBLY IN US, AND DOTH NOT   607 33

WORKERS

WE THEN, AS WORKERS TOGETHER WITH HIM, BESEECH YOU   126 03
ARE ALL SUCH WORKERS OF MISCHIEF, *   356 22
AND WHEN ALL THE WORKERS OF WICKEDNESS DO FLOURISH   456 14
AND ALL THE WORKERS OF WICKEDNESS SHALL BE DESTROYED   456 18

WORKETH

THE DEVIL OR MAN WORKETH AGAINST US, MAY, BY THY GOOD   058 20
LOVE WORKETH NO ILL TO HIS NEIGHBOUR   090 29
IT IS GOD WHICH WORKETH IN YOU BOTH TO WILL AND TO DO   106 04
FEARETH HIM, AND WORKETH RIGHTEOUSNESS, IS ACCEPTED   166 14
THE WRATH OF MAN WORKETH NOT THE RIGHTEOUSNESS OF   174 32
SAME GOD WHICH WORKETH ALL IN ALL   182 25
BUT ALL THESE WORKETH THAT ONE AND THE SELFSAME   182 33
FEARETH HIM, AND WORKETH RIGHTEOUSNESS, IS ACCEPTED   183 31
SAME GOD WHICH WORKETH ALL IN ALL   203 25
BUT ALL THESE WORKETH THAT ONE AND THE SELFSAME   204 02
THE POWER THAT WORKETH IN US, UNTO HIM BE GLORY IN   212 23
OF YOUR FAITH WORKETH PATIENCE   239 10
THE WRATH OF MAN WORKETH NOT THE RIGHTEOUSNESS OF   265 25

WORKING

BY THE EFFECTUAL WORKING OF HIS POWER   108 18
TO ANOTHER THE WORKING OF MIRACLES   182 30
TO ANOTHER THE WORKING OF MIRACLES   203 30
LET HIM LABOUR, WORKING WITH HIS HANDS THE THING   216 21
ACCORDING TO THE WORKING WHEREBY HE IS ABLE EVEN TO   222 25
TO THE EFFECTUAL WORKING IN THE MEASURE OF EVERY   237 32
TO THE MIGHTY WORKING WHEREBY HE IS ABLE TO SUBDUE   333 22
TO DO HIS WILL, WORKING IN YOU THAT WHICH IS WELL   335 20
TO THE MIGHTY WORKING WHEREBY HE IS ABLE TO SUBDUE   337 16

WORKING   CONTINUED

TO DO HIS WILL, WORKING IN YOU THAT WHICH IS WELL   573 06
A GOOD WILL, AND WORKING WITH US, WHEN WE HAVE THAT   605 03
BY HIS SPIRIT WORKING IN DUE SEASON   606 12
THEMSELVES THE WORKING OF THE SPIRIT OF CHRIST,   606 18

WORKMEN

AND HARM THE WORKMEN AT THEIR WORK   599 29

WORKS

O ALL YE WORKS OF THE LORD, BLESS YE THE LORD   011 31
HAST MADE ME GLAD THROUGH THY WORKS   028 02
THE LORD, ALL YE WORKS OF HIS, IN ALL PLACES OF HIS   029 17
AND ALL JUST WORKS DO PROCEED   031 19
THAT IN ALL OUR WORKS BEGUN, CONTINUED, AND ENDED IN   049 25
WHOSE MERCY IS OVER ALL THY WORKS   053 21
UNTO US, THE NOBLE WORKS THAT THOU DIDST IN THEIR   058 29
AND IN THE WORKS OF THY COMMANDMENTS   070 09
MAY SEE YOUR GOOD WORKS, AND GLORIFY YOUR FATHER   072 05
WILL FORGET YOUR WORKS, AND LABOUR THAT PROCEEDETH OF   072 23
DO ALL SUCH GOOD WORKS AS THOU HAST PREPARED FOR US   083 28
MAY CAST AWAY THE WORKS OF DARKNESS, AND PUT UPON US   090 12
CAST OFF THE WORKS OF DARKNESS, AND LET US PUT ON THE   091 04
IN THE PRISON THE WORKS OF CHRIST, HE SENT TWO OF HIS   094 16
HEAVENS ARE THE WORKS OF THINE HANDS   097 14
HIMSELF A PECULIAR PEOPLE, ZEALOUS OF GOOD WORKS   098 25
A TERROR TO GOOD WORKS, BUT TO THE EVIL   114 16
MIGHT DESTROY THE WORKS OF THE DEVIL, AND MAKE US THE   117 05
MIGHT DESTROY THE WORKS OF THE DEVIL   117 30
THE UNFRUITFUL WORKS OF DARKNESS, BUT RATHER REPROVE   129 16
FROM DEAD WORKS TO SERVE THE LIVING GOD   133 03
ANOTHER TO PROVOKE UNTO LOVE AND TO GOOD WORKS   158 25
THAT WE MAY BEHOLD THEE IN ALL THY WORKS   166 09
MAY BY YOUR GOOD WORKS, WHICH THEY SHALL BEHOLD,   173 16
THE WONDERFUL WORKS OF GOD   181 06
NOW THE WORKS OF THE FLESH ARE MANIFEST, WHICH ARE   209 19
MAKE US CONTINUALLY TO BE GIVEN TO ALL GOOD WORKS   213 16
SERVE THEE IN GOOD WORKS, TO THE GLORY OF THY NAME   220 19
THE FRUIT OF GOOD WORKS, MAY BY THEE BE PLENTEOUSLY   225 06
FATHER THAT DWELLETH IN ME, HE DOETH THE WORKS   240 16
ON ME, THE WORKS THAT I DO SHALL HE DO ALSO   240 19
AND GREATER WORKS THAN THESE SHALL HE DO   240 20
THE LORD REWARD HIM ACCORDING TO HIS WORKS   254 08
AMONG THEM THE WORKS WHICH NONE OTHER MAN DID, THEY   255 25
DEVIL AND ALL HIS WORKS, THE VAIN POMP AND GLORY OF   276 25
DEVIL AND ALL HIS WORKS, THE VAIN POMP AND GLORY OF   277 26
DEVIL AND ALL HIS WORKS, THE POMPS AND VANITY OF THIS   283 24
AND IN THE WORKS OF THY COMMANDMENTS   298 29
NOT THEN THE WORKS OF THINE OWN HANDS   312 10
THE LORD, ALL YE WORKS OF HIS, IN ALL PLACES OF HIS   313 02
DOMINION OF THE WORKS OF THY HANDS   351 11
I WILL SPEAK OF ALL THY MARVELLOUS WORKS   351 23
4 AS FOR THE WORKS OF MEN, *   358 25
AND TELL OF ALL THY WONDROUS WORKS   371 11
IN THEIR MIND THE WORKS OF THE LORD, NOR THE   373 17
AND ALL HIS WORKS ARE FAITHFUL   378 25
AND UNDERSTANDETH ALL THEIR WORKS   379 18
ARE THE WONDROUS WORKS WHICH THOU HAST DONE, LIKE AS   390 21
AND BEHOLD THE WORKS OF THE LORD, *   398 09
O HOW WONDERFUL ART THOU IN THY WORKS   417 18
AND BEHOLD THE WORKS OF GOD   417 22
THEREFORE WILL I TELL OF THY WONDROUS WORKS   426 09
SPEAK OF ALL THY WORKS IN THE GATES OF THE DAUGHTER   429 34
DO THY WONDROUS WORKS DECLARE   431 33
WILL REMEMBER THE WORKS OF THE LORD, *   434 04
ALSO OF ALL THY WORKS, *   434 06
AND WONDERFUL WORKS THAT HE HATH DONE   435 03
NOT TO FORGET THE WORKS OF GOD, BUT TO KEEP HIS   435 12
AND THE WONDERFUL WORKS THAT HE HAD SHOWED FOR THEM   435 23
AND BELIEVED NOT HIS WONDROUS WORKS   437 03
SHALL THY WONDROUS WORKS BE KNOWN IN THE DARK   449 20
THE VERY HEAVENS SHALL PRAISE THY WONDROUS WORKS   450 14
HAST MADE ME GLAD THROUGH THY WORKS   456 07
HOW GLORIOUS ARE THY WORKS   456 09
PROVED ME, AND SAW MY WORKS   459 23
HIS WORKS UNTO THE CHILDREN OF ISRAEL   466 19
THE LORD, ALL YE WORKS OF HIS, IN ALL PLACES OF HIS   467 20
THE EARTH IS FILLED WITH THE FRUIT OF THY WORKS   468 20
HOW MANIFOLD ARE THY WORKS   469 08
THE LORD SHALL REJOICE IN HIS WORKS   469 24
AND LET YOUR TALKING BE OF ALL HIS WONDROUS WORKS   470 08
THE MARVELLOUS WORKS THAT HE HATH DONE   470 12
THEY FORGAT HIS WORKS, *   473 27
22 WONDROUS WORKS IN THE LAND OF HAM   474 12
AND LEARNED THEIR WORKS   475 07
WITH THEIR OWN WORKS, *   475 14
AND TELL OUT HIS WORKS WITH GLADNESS   477 21
THESE MEN SEE THE WORKS OF THE LORD, *   477 24
2 THE WORKS OF THE LORD ARE GREAT, *   482 26
HIS MARVELLOUS WORKS, *   483 02
THE POWER OF HIS WORKS, *   483 05
7 THE WORKS OF HIS HANDS ARE VERITY AND JUDGMENT   483 07
AND DECLARE THE WORKS OF THE LORD   489 02
AND SO SHALL I TALK OF THY WONDROUS WORKS   491 22
NOT THEN THE WORKS OF THINE OWN HANDS   514 16
MARVELLOUS ARE THY WORKS, AND THAT MY SOUL KNOWETH   515 16
IN UNGODLY WORKS WITH THE MEN THAT WORK WICKEDNESS,   517 16
MYSELF IN THE WORKS OF THY HANDS   518 33
I MUSE UPON ALL THY WORKS   518 33
SHALL PRAISE THY WORKS UNTO ANOTHER, *   520 33
THY PRAISE, AND WONDROUS WORKS   521 03
AND HIS MERCY IS OVER ALL HIS WORKS   521 11
10 ALL THY WORKS PRAISE THEE, O LORD   521 12

WORKS   CONTINUED

AND HOLY IN ALL HIS WORKS   521 27
AN EXAMPLE OF GOOD WORKS UNTO OTHERS, THAT THE   555 11
WHICH PIOUS WORKS HAVE BEEN APPROVED OF AND   564 20
THAT IN ALL OUR WORKS BEGUN, CONTINUED, AND ENDED IN   571 10
DEVIL AND ALL HIS WORKS, THE POMPS AND VANITY OF THIS   577 15
EYES TO BEHOLD THY GRACIOUS HAND IN ALL THY WORKS   596 19
WHO LABOUR IN WORKS OF MERCY OR IN SCHOOLS OF GOOD   600 04
STRENGTH AND GOOD WORKS, TO FAITH, AND CALLING UPON   604 43
POWER TO DO GOOD WORKS PLEASANT AND ACCEPTABLE TO   604 44
NOT FOR OUR OWN WORKS OR DESERVINGS   605 07
ALBEIT THAT GOOD WORKS, WHICH ARE THE FRUITS OF   605 11
WORKS DONE BEFORE THE GRACE OF CHRIST, AND THE   605 17
VOLUNTARY WORKS BESIDES, OVER AND ABOVE, GOD'S   605 24
WHICH THEY CALL WORKS OF SUPEREROGATION, CANNOT BE   605 25
IN GOOD WORKS, AND AT LENGTH, BY GOD'S MERCY, THEY   606 15
MORTIFYING THE WORKS OF THE FLESH, AND THEIR EARTHLY   606 18

WORKS'

ME FOR THE VERY WORKS' SAKE   240 18

WORLD

AND EVER SHALL BE, WORLD WITHOUT END   008 06
THE SPIRIT OF THE LORD FILLETH THE WORLD   R 008 28
TO JUDGE THE WORLD, AND THE PEOPLES WITH HIS TRUTH   009 20
WORLD WITHOUT END   009 30
THROUGHOUT ALL THE WORLD DOTH ACKNOWLEDGE THEE   010 19
THY NAME EVER, WORLD WITHOUT END   011 07
BEEN SINCE THE WORLD BEGAN   014 13
THE LIFE OF THE WORLD TO COME   016 21
WHOSE GLORY IS IN ALL THE WORLD   018 07
ONE GOD, WORLD WITHOUT END   018 16
REDEMPTION OF THE WORLD BY OUR LORD JESUS CHRIST   019 23
HONOUR AND GLORY, WORLD WITHOUT END   019 31
AND IN THE WORLD TO COME LIFE EVERLASTING   020 09
US IN THIS WORLD KNOWLEDGE OF THY TRUTH, AND IN THE   020 09
AND EVER SHALL BE, WORLD WITHOUT END   025 12
THE SINS OF THE WORLD, HAVE MERCY UPON US   025 29
THE SINS OF THE WORLD, RECEIVE OUR PRAYER   025 30
THE ENDS OF THE WORLD HAVE SEEN THE SALVATION OF OUR   027 11
THE ROUND WORLD, AND THEY THAT DWELL THEREIN   027 20
SHALL HE JUDGE THE WORLD, *   027 24
THE ENDS OF THE WORLD SHALL FEAR HIM   028 30
THE LIFE OF THE WORLD TO COME   030 26
PEACE WHICH THE WORLD CANNOT GIVE   031 20
ONE GOD, WORLD WITHOUT END   032 14
REDEMPTION OF THE WORLD BY OUR LORD JESUS CHRIST   033 21
HONOUR AND GLORY, WORLD WITHOUT END   033 29
AND IN THE WORLD TO COME LIFE EVERLASTING   034 09
US IN THIS WORLD KNOWLEDGE OF THY TRUTH, AND IN THE   034 09
TO BE WITH THY CHURCH TO THE END OF THE WORLD   036 29
UPON THE WORLD WHICH THOU HAST REDEEMED BY THE BLOOD   039 17
THE LANDS AND MULTIPLY THE HARVESTS OF THE WORLD   040 08
REIGNEST ONE GOD, WORLD WITHOUT END   043 16
THE NATIONS OF THE WORLD INTO THE WAY OF JUSTICE AND   044 28
AS LIGHTS IN THE WORLD, AND IN ALL THINGS MAY ADORN   047 28
THE LIGHTS OF THE WORLD IN THEIR SEVERAL GENERATIONS   048 18
ONE GOD, WORLD WITHOUT END   049 10
GLORY AND HONOUR, WORLD WITHOUT END   050 29
THAT ALL THE WORLD MAY KNOW THAT THOU ART OUR   052 14
LIVE IN THIS WORLD ACCORDING TO THY WILL, AND ALSO   053 16
O GOD THE SON, REDEEMER OF THE WORLD   054 07
THE DECEITS OF THE WORLD, THE FLESH, AND THE DEVIL,   054 28
AND EVER SHALL BE, WORLD WITHOUT END   059 07
WORLD WITHOUT END   061 18
TO HELP US IN THIS WORLD, THAT WE MAY EVER LIVE WITH   062 24
WITH THEE IN THE WORLD TO COME   062 25
THE LIFE OF THE WORLD TO COME   071 23
SO GOD LOVED THE WORLD, THAT HE GAVE HIS   076 14
CAME INTO THE WORLD TO SAVE SINNERS   076 19
AND HATH TAKEN AWAY THE SIN OF THE WORLD   078 10
FOR THE SINS OF THE WHOLE WORLD   080 13
O FATHER ALMIGHTY, WORLD WITHOUT END   081 34
HONOUR AND GLORY, WORLD WITHOUT END   083 31
THE SINS OF THE WORLD, HAVE MERCY UPON US   084 09
THE SINS OF THE WORLD, RECEIVE OUR PRAYER   084 10
REDEMPTION OF THE WORLD BY THE DEATH AND PASSION OF   086 07
TO JUDGE THE WORLD WE MAY BE FOUND AN ACCEPTABLE   093 29
ONE GOD, WORLD WITHOUT END   093 32
HONOUR AND GLORY, WORLD WITHOUT END   095 10
ONE GOD, WORLD WITHOUT END   096 19
INTO THE WORLD, HE SAITH, AND LET ALL THE ANGELS OF   097 05
HE WAS IN THE WORLD, AND THE WORLD WAS MADE BY HIM,   097 31
LIGHTETH EVERY MAN THAT COMETH INTO THE WORLD   097 31
THE WORLD, AND THE WORLD WAS MADE BY HIM, AND THE   097 31
BY HIM, AND THE WORLD KNEW HIM NOT   097 32
ONE GOD, WORLD WITHOUT END   098 16
AND GODLY, IN THIS PRESENT WORLD   098 21
THAT ALL THE WORLD SHOULD BE TAXED   098 29
THAT EVEN THE WORLD ITSELF COULD NOT CONTAIN THE   102 16
ONE GOD, WORLD WITHOUT END   104 11
WERE IN BONDAGE UNDER THE ELEMENTS OF THE WORLD   104 18
BEGINNING OF THE WORLD HATH BEEN HID IN GOD, WHO   108 22
AND BE NOT CONFORMED TO THIS WORLD   110 06
ONE GOD, WORLD WITHOUT END   117 12
THEREFORE THE WORLD KNOWETH US NOT, BECAUSE IT KNEW   117 16
ONE GOD, WORLD WITHOUT END   119 03
ONE GOD, WORLD WITHOUT END   125 32
KINGDOMS OF THE WORLD, AND THE GLORY OF THEM   127 06
THAT PROPHET THAT SHOULD COME INTO THE WORLD   132 13
THE WHOLE WORLD, THIS ALSO THAT SHE HATH DONE SHALL   140 17
HAVE SUFFERED SINCE THE FOUNDATION OF THE WORLD   148 05
IN THE END OF THE WORLD HATH HE APPEARED TO PUT AWAY   148 06

WORLD   CONTINUED

	PAGE	LN
ONE GOD, WORLD WITHOUT END	152	13
DEPART OUT OF THIS WORLD UNTO THE FATHER, HAVING	155	25
WHICH WERE IN THE WORLD, HE LOVED THEM UNTO THE END	155	26
ONE GOD, WORLD WITHOUT END	156	26
ONE GOD, WORLD WITHOUT END	157	13
HE COMETH INTO THE WORLD, HE SAITH, SACRIFICE AND	157	24
WORLD WITHOUT END	163	20
ONE GOD, WORLD WITHOUT END	163	29
WHATSOEVER IS BORN OF GOD OVERCOMETH THE WORLD	170	27
OVERCOMETH THE WORLD, EVEN OUR FAITH	170	28
OVERCOMETH THE WORLD, BUT HE THAT BELIEVETH THAT	170	29
BUT THE WORLD SHALL REJOICE	174	08
FOR JOY THAT A MAN IS BORN INTO THE WORLD	174	14
CHANGES OF THE WORLD, OUR HEARTS MAY SURELY THERE BE	174	22
WILL REPROVE THE WORLD OF SIN, AND OF RIGHTEOUSNESS,	175	13
THE PRINCE OF THIS WORLD IS JUDGED	175	16
AND TO KEEP HIMSELF UNSPOTTED FROM THE WORLD	176	18
I LEAVE THE WORLD, AND GO TO THE FATHER	176	31
AND AM COME INTO THE WORLD	176	31
IN THE WORLD YE SHALL HAVE TRIBULATION	177	09
I HAVE OVERCOME THE WORLD	177	10
ONE GOD, WORLD WITHOUT END	177	19
ONE GOD, WORLD WITHOUT END	179	10
ONE GOD, WORLD WITHOUT END	180	14
WHOM THE WORLD CANNOT RECEIVE, BECAUSE IT SEETH HIM	181	14
AND THE WORLD SEETH ME NO MORE	181	15
MANIFEST THYSELF UNTO US, AND NOT UNTO THE WORLD	181	23
NOT AS THE WORLD GIVETH, GIVE I UNTO YOU	181	34
THE PRINCE OF THIS WORLD COMETH, AND HATH NOTHING IN	182	08
BUT THAT THE WORLD MAY KNOW THAT I LOVE THE FATHER	182	09
ONE GOD, WORLD WITHOUT END	182	20
ONE GOD, WORLD WITHOUT END	183	27
GOD SO LOVED THE WORLD, THAT HE GAVE HIS	184	32
HIS SON INTO THE WORLD TO CONDEMN THE WORLD	184	35
NOT HIS SON INTO THE WORLD TO CONDEMN THE WORLD	184	35
BUT THAT THE WORLD THROUGH HIM MIGHT BE SAVED	184	35
IS COME INTO THE WORLD, AND MEN LOVED DARKNESS RATHER	185	06
ONE GOD, WORLD WITHOUT END	185	19
ONE GOD, WORLD WITHOUT END	186	29
SON INTO THE WORLD, THAT WE MIGHT LIVE THROUGH HIM	189	13
SENT THE SON TO BE THE SAVIOUR OF THE WORLD	189	21
BECAUSE AS HE IS, SO ARE WE IN THIS WORLD	189	28
IF THE WORLD HATE YOU	191	11
IN YOUR BRETHREN THAT ARE IN THE WORLD	193	08
THE COURSE OF THIS WORLD MAY BE SO PEACEABLY ORDERED	195	16
THE ENDS OF THE WORLD ARE COME	201	24
BY WHOM THE WORLD IS CRUCIFIED UNTO ME, AND I UNTO	210	31
WORLD IS CRUCIFIED UNTO ME, AND I UNTO THE WORLD	210	31
ALL AGES, WORLD WITHOUT END	212	24
TEMPTATIONS OF THE WORLD, THE FLESH, AND THE DEVIL	214	24
DARKNESS OF THIS WORLD, AGAINST SPIRITUAL WICKEDNESS	219	10
WHICH IS COME UNTO YOU, AS IT IS IN ALL THE WORLD	223	28
THAT PROPHET THAT SHOULD COME INTO THE WORLD	226	13
AND THEIR WORDS UNTO THE ENDS OF THE WORLD	227	16
LIGHT OF THE GOSPEL TO SHINE THROUGHOUT THE WORLD	229	19
SHOULD BE GREAT DEARTH THROUGHOUT ALL THE WORLD	241	18
BEEN SINCE THE WORLD BEGAN	244	02
SHOULD BE GREAT DEARTH THROUGHOUT ALL THE WORLD	246	27
OF THIS WORLD, MAY BE PERMITTED TO BEHOLD THE KING IN	248	03
ONE GOD, WORLD WITHOUT END	248	06
ONE GOD, WORLD WITHOUT END	250	25
THE GOD OF THIS WORLD HATH BLINDED THE MINDS OF THEM	251	02
AND SATAN, WHICH DECEIVETH THE WHOLE WORLD	252	08
WOE UNTO THE WORLD BECAUSE OF OFFENCES	252	34
LOVED THIS PRESENT WORLD, AND IS DEPARTED UNTO	253	32
IF THE WORLD HATE YOU, YE KNOW THAT IT HATED ME	255	13
OF THE WORLD, THE WORLD WOULD LOVE HIS OWN	255	14
IF YE WERE OF THE WORLD, THE WORLD WOULD LOVE HIS	255	14
YE ARE NOT OF THE WORLD, BUT I HAVE CHOSEN YOU OUT OF	255	15
YOU OUT OF THE WORLD, THEREFORE THE WORLD HATETH YOU	255	16
THEREFORE THE WORLD HATETH YOU	255	16
PREPARED FOR YOU FROM THE FOUNDATION OF THE WORLD	259	05
WORLD WITHOUT END	265	09
AND TO KEEP HIMSELF UNSPOTTED FROM THE WORLD	266	09
AM WITH YOU ALWAY, EVEN UNTO THE END OF THE WORLD	275	32
AND GLORY OF THE WORLD, WITH ALL COVETOUS DESIRES OF	276	26
AND GLORY OF THE WORLD, WITH ALL COVETOUS DESIRES OF	277	27
THE DEVIL, THE WORLD, AND THE FLESH	278	25
GOVERN ALL THINGS, WORLD WITHOUT END	278	31
AGAINST SIN, THE WORLD, AND THE DEVIL	280	08
OF THIS WICKED WORLD, AND ALL THE SINFUL LUSTS OF THE	283	24
THE FATHER, WHO HATH MADE ME, AND ALL THE WORLD	284	30
AND EVER SHALL BE, WORLD WITHOUT END	285	09
CHANGES OF THE WORLD, OUR HEARTS MAY SURELY THERE BE	285	30
IS SENT TO PREACH THE GOSPEL TO THE WHOLE WORLD	291	13
WORLD WITHOUT END	297	10
ONE GOD, WORLD WITHOUT END	298	25
ONE GOD, WORLD WITHOUT END	303	28
THAT IN THE WORLD TO COME YE MAY HAVE LIFE	304	15
AND EVER SHALL BE, WORLD WITHOUT END	306	07
O SAVIOUR OF THE WORLD, WHO BY THY CROSS AND PRECIOUS	313	12
OF HIS SINS, AND BE IN CHARITY WITH ALL THE WORLD	R 313	20
HONOUR AND GLORY, WORLD WITHOUT END	316	04
AMIDST THE SORROWS AND DIFFICULTIES OF THE WORLD	316	20
OUR GOD, AND IN PERFECT CHARITY WITH THE WORLD	317	07
THAT WAS SLAIN TO TAKE AWAY THE SINS OF THE WORLD	317	18
WHO TAKEST AWAY THE SINS OF THE WORLD	318	23
ONE GOD, WORLD WITHOUT END	319	12
OUT OF THIS WORLD, IN THE NAME OF GOD THE	319	19
ONE GOD, WORLD WITHOUT END	320	13
WHICH I WILL GIVE FOR THE LIFE OF THE WORLD	322	29
NOTHING INTO THIS WORLD, AND IT IS CERTAIN WE CAN	324	13
THE EARTH AND THE WORLD WERE MADE, *	325	16
AND WORLD WITHOUT END	325	17

WORLD   CONTINUED

	PAGE	LN
ONE GOD, WORLD WITHOUT END	332	09
TO JUDGE THE WORLD, THE EARTH AND THE SEA SHALL GIVE	333	19
PREPARED FOR YOU FROM THE BEGINNING OF THE WORLD	335	13
ONE GOD, WORLD WITHOUT END	336	15
THE LIGHTS OF THE WORLD IN THEIR SEVERAL GENERATIONS	336	20
PREPARED FOR YOU FROM THE FOUNDATION OF THE WORLD	336	28
TO JUDGE THE WORLD, THE SEA SHALL GIVE UP HER DEAD	337	13
WORLD WITHOUT END	340	19
HOW EXCELLENT IS THY NAME IN ALL THE WORLD	350	32
HOW EXCELLENT IS THY NAME IN ALL THE WORLD	351	18
HE SHALL JUDGE THE WORLD IN RIGHTEOUSNESS, *	352	04
FROM THE MEN OF THE EVIL WORLD	359	15
OF THE ROUND WORLD WERE DISCOVERED, *	360	29
AND THEIR WORDS INTO THE ENDS OF THE WORLD	363	20
THE ENDS OF THE WORLD SHALL REMEMBER THEMSELVES,	367	28
THE COMPASS OF THE WORLD, AND THEY THAT DWELL	368	29
IN AWE OF HIM, ALL YE THAT DWELL IN THE WORLD	379	03
WORLD WITHOUT END	392	25
THANKS UNTO THEE, WORLD WITHOUT END	397	23
9 HE MAKETH WARS TO CEASE IN ALL THE WORLD	398	11
ALL YE THAT DWELL IN THE WORLD	400	08
AND CALLED THE WORLD, FROM THE RISING UP OF THE SUN	401	22
FOR THE WHOLE WORLD IS MINE, AND ALL THAT IS THEREIN	402	15
AND UNTO THE ENDS OF THE WORLD	411	34
3 FOR ALL THE WORLD SHALL WORSHIP THEE, *	417	20
THE ENDS OF THE WORLD SHALL FEAR HIM	419	04
AND THEIR TONGUE GOETH THROUGH THE WORLD	428	27
PROSPER IN THE WORLD, AND THESE HAVE RICHES IN	428	33
OF THE ROUND WORLD, AND ALL THAT THEREIN IS	450	29
THE EARTH AND THE WORLD WERE MADE, *	453	21
AND WORLD WITHOUT END	453	22
MADE THE ROUND WORLD SO SURE, *	457	07
3 EVER SINCE THE WORLD BEGAN, HATH THY SEAT BEEN	457	09
THOU JUDGE OF THE WORLD, *	457	21
MADE THE ROUND WORLD SO FAST THAT IT CANNOT BE MOVED	460	19
TO JUDGE THE WORLD, AND THE PEOPLES WITH HIS TRUTH	460	27
4 HIS LIGHTNINGS GAVE SHINE UNTO THE WORLD	461	04
THE ENDS OF THE WORLD HAVE SEEN THE SALVATION OF OUR	461	32
THE ROUND WORLD, AND THEY THAT DWELL THEREIN	462	09
SHALL HE JUDGE THE WORLD, *	462	13
HIS JUDGMENTS ARE IN ALL THE WORLD	470	17
AND WORLD WITHOUT END	475	34
THE ENDS OF THE WORLD, *	510	16
AND ALL JUDGES OF THE WORLD	524	16
GLORY AND HONOUR, WORLD WITHOUT END	535	11
SAME HOLY SPIRIT, WORLD WITHOUT END	537	29
OF THIS NAUGHTY WORLD, THAT THEY MAY BE SAVED THROUGH	540	03
THE STUDY OF THE WORLD AND THE FLESH	542	28
ABROAD INTO THE WORLD HIS APOSTLES, PROPHETS,	545	17
THE PARTS OF THE WORLD, TO SET FORTH THE ETERNAL	545	20
SAME HOLY SPIRIT, WORLD WITHOUT END	546	05
SAME HOLY SPIRIT, WORLD WITHOUT END	548	08
EVEN UNTO THE END OF THE WORLD	552	15
SAME HOLY SPIRIT, WORLD WITHOUT END	554	03
AND GODLY IN THIS PRESENT WORLD	555	10
ONE GOD, WORLD WITHOUT END	558	07
ONE GOD, WORLD WITHOUT END	559	15
PEACE TO THE WHOLE WORLD, AND TO THY CHURCH	560	12
AND BLESS THY CHURCH THROUGHOUT THE WORLD	560	16
ONE GOD, WORLD WITHOUT END	562	15
THE COMPASS OF THE WORLD, AND THEY THAT DWELL	563	12
WORLD WITHOUT END	564	05
OF APOSTOLIC SUCCESSION TO THE END OF THE WORLD	572	18
AS ONE GOD, WORLD WITHOUT END	572	32
THE COURSE OF THIS WORLD MAY BE SO PEACEABLY ORDERED	574	15
ONE GOD, WORLD WITHOUT END	574	23
OF THIS WICKED WORLD, AND ALL THE SINFUL LUSTS OF THE	577	15
THE FATHER, WHO HATH MADE ME, AND ALL THE WORLD	578	12
ONLY SON INTO THE WORLD, TO REDEEM US FROM SIN AND	591	12
AND THE BUSY WORLD IS HUSHED, AND THE FEVER OF LIFE	594	31
HAST FILLED THE WORLD WITH BEAUTY	596	17
HE MAY BE, KEEPING HIM UNSPOTTED FROM THE WORLD	597	30
BORN INTO THIS WORLD, IT DESERVETH GOD'S WRATH AND	604	34
SHOULD TAKE AWAY THE SINS OF THE WORLD	605	34
FOUNDATIONS OF THE WORLD WERE LAID) HE HATH	606	07
SINS OF THE WHOLE WORLD, BOTH ORIGINAL AND ACTUAL	609	15

WORLD'S

	PAGE	LN
UNTO THE WORLD'S END	038	15
WHOSO HATH THIS WORLD'S GOOD, AND SEETH HIS BROTHER	072	29
WHOSO HATH THIS WORLD'S GOOD, AND SEETH HIS BROTHER	191	19
PRAISE UNTO THE WORLD'S END	399	30
RIVER UNTO THE WORLD'S END	427	13

WORLDLY

	PAGE	LN
BY ANY WORLDLY AUTHORITY WHATSOEVER) TO TAKE A	VI	24
HINDERED WITH WORLDLY BUSINESS	088	28
UNGODLINESS AND WORLDLY LUSTS, WE SHOULD LIVE	098	20
FROM ALL WORLDLY AND CARNAL LUSTS, WE MAY IN ALL	105	22
FORSAKING ALL WORLDLY AND CARNAL AFFECTIONS, MAY BE	246	19
AS YE MAY, ALL WORLDLY CARES AND STUDIES	541	08
UNGODLINESS AND WORLDLY LUSTS, AND LIVE SOBERLY,	555	08
ALL UNHALLOWED, WORLDLY, AND COMMON USES, IN ORDER TO	564	16
FEARS AND WORLDLY ANXIETIES, AND GRANT THAT NO CLOUDS	596	06

WORLDS

	PAGE	LN
FATHER BEFORE ALL WORLDS, GOD OF GOD, LIGHT OF LIGHT,	016	03
FATHER BEFORE ALL WORLDS, GOD OF GOD, LIGHT OF LIGHT,	030	08
FATHER BEFORE ALL WORLDS, GOD OF GOD, LIGHT OF LIGHT,	071	05
BY WHOM ALSO HE MADE THE WORLDS	096	26

WORM

AS FOR ME, I AM A WORM, AND NO MAN	366 14

WORN

AND WORN AWAY BECAUSE OF ALL MINE ENEMIES	349 12

WORSE

MEN HAVE WELL DRUNK, THEN THAT WHICH IS WORSE	113 29
OF THAT MAN IS WORSE THAN THE FIRST	130 16
ERROR SHALL BE WORSE THAN THE FIRST	162 22
FOR BETTER FOR WORSE, FOR RICHER FOR POORER, IN	301 29
FOR BETTER FOR WORSE, FOR RICHER FOR POORER, IN	302 05

WORSHIP

SHALL WORSHIP THE FATHER IN SPIRIT AND IN TRUTH	003 31
SEEKETH SUCH TO WORSHIP HIM	003 32
THAT IN HIS WORSHIP DIFFERENT FORMS AND USAGES MAY	V 03
FORMS OF DIVINE WORSHIP, AND THE RITES AND CEREMONIES	V 14
AND AMENDMENTS IN HER FORMS OF PUBLIC WORSHIP	V 23
DEVOTION IN THE WORSHIP OF GOD	V 37
O COME, LET US WORSHIP AND FALL DOWN, *	009 13
O WORSHIP THE LORD IN THE BEAUTY OF HOLINESS	009 17
THE EARTH DOTH WORSHIP THEE, THE FATHER EVERLASTING	010 10
AND WE WORSHIP THY NAME EVER, WORLD WITHOUT END	011 07
O WORSHIP THE LORD IN THE BEAUTY OF HOLINESS	021 19
BLESS THEE, WE WORSHIP THEE, WE GLORIFY THEE, WE GIVE	025 24
THEY MAY WORSHIP HIM AND SERVE THEE FROM	043 04
AND WORSHIP HIM ACCEPTABLY	047 14
AND FORMS OF WORSHIP, AND DISCIPLINE, IN SUCH MANNER	VI 11
POINT OF DOCTRINE, DISCIPLINE, OR WORSHIP	VI 33
TO THEM, NOR WORSHIP THEM	068 11
OF PUBLIC WORSHIP WHEN THE OFFERINGS OF THE PEOPLE	R 073 26
BLESS THEE, WE WORSHIP THEE, WE GLORIFY THEE, WE GIVE	084 04
ANGELS OF GOD WORSHIP HIM	097 06
AND ARE COME TO WORSHIP HIM	109 02
I MAY COME AND WORSHIP HIM ALSO	109 15
FALL DOWN AND WORSHIP ME	127 08
THOU SHALT WORSHIP THE LORD THY GOD, AND HIM ONLY	127 09
MAJESTY TO WORSHIP THE UNITY	186 26
THE THRONE, AND WORSHIP HIM THAT LIVETH FOR EVER AND	187 27
SHALT THOU HAVE WORSHIP IN THE PRESENCE OF THEM THAT	214 18
WHOSOEVER SHALL WORSHIP BEFORE THEE IN THIS PLACE,	259 21
TO THEM, NOR WORSHIP THEM	286 11
TO WORSHIP HIM, TO GIVE HIM THANKS	288 19
TO WORSHIP GOD EVERY SUNDAY IN HIS CHURCH	291 18
THOU ART MY WORSHIP, AND THE LIFTER UP OF MY HEAD	309 18
I WILL WORSHIP TOWARD THY HOLY TEMPLE, AND PRAISE THY	311 30
THOU ART MY WORSHIP, AND THE LIFTER UP OF MY HEAD	346 30
THY FEAR WILL I WORSHIP TOWARD THY HOLY TEMPLE	348 14
TO CROWN HIM WITH GLORY AND WORSHIP	351 10
GLORY AND GREAT WORSHIP SHALT THOU LAY UPON HIM	365 14
O THOU WORSHIP OF ISRAEL	366 09
NATIONS SHALL WORSHIP BEFORE HIM	367 30
UNTO THE LORD WORSHIP AND STRENGTH	373 31
WORSHIP THE LORD WITH HOLY WORSHIP	373 33
WORSHIP THE LORD WITH HOLY WORSHIP	373 33
ACCORDING TO THY WORSHIP AND RENOWN	396 21
IS THY LORD, AND WORSHIP THOU HIM	397 08
THE WORLD SHALL WORSHIP THEE, *	417 20
HIS WORSHIP AND STRENGTH IS IN THE CLOUDS	421 25
SHALT THOU WORSHIP ANY OTHER GOD	442 32
THE LORD WILL GIVE GRACE AND WORSHIP	446 03
SHALL COME AND WORSHIP THEE, O LORD	447 22
6 O COME, LET US WORSHIP AND FALL DOWN, *	459 15
6 GLORY AND WORSHIP ARE BEFORE HIM	460 10
UNTO THE LORD WORSHIP AND POWER	460 13
9 O WORSHIP THE LORD IN THE BEAUTY OF HOLINESS	460 16
BE ALL THEY THAT WORSHIP CARVED IMAGES, AND THAT	461 10
WORSHIP HIM, ALL YE GODS	461 11
OUR GOD, AND WORSHIP HIM UPON HIS HOLY HILL	463 02
AND HIS WORSHIP AT JERUSALEM	465 23
OFFER THEMSELVES WILLINGLY WITH AN HOLY WORSHIP	482 12
2 I WILL WORSHIP TOWARD THY HOLY TEMPLE, AND PRAISE	513 30
TALKING OF THY WORSHIP, *	521 02
WE PRAISE AND WORSHIP THEE	545 25
AND WORSHIP OF THE PROTESTANT EPISCOPAL	R 552 27
AND WORSHIP OF THE PROTESTANT EPISCOPAL	552 30
FOR THE PUBLIC WORSHIP OF GOD, AND SEPARATED THEM	564 15
OF RELIGIOUS WORSHIP, AND LET US FAITHFULLY AND	564 24
AND DEVOTE THIS HOUSE TO THY HONOUR AND WORSHIP	566 30
THEE HERE MAY WORSHIP THEE IN SPIRIT AND IN TRUTH,	567 08
SON TOGETHER, WE WORSHIP AND GLORIFY AS ONE GOD,	572 31
TO THEM, NOR WORSHIP THEM	578 30
TO WORSHIP HIM, TO GIVE HIM THANKS	579 30
THAT WE MAY WORSHIP HIM, SERVE HIM, AND OBEY HIM, AS	580 31
WE MAY WORSHIP THEE IN SPIRIT AND IN TRUTH	594 08
THROUGH OUR WORSHIP OF THEE, THAT THE DAYS TO COME	595 15

WORSHIPPED

TOGETHER IS WORSHIPPED AND GLORIFIED	016 17
TOGETHER IS WORSHIPPED AND GLORIFIED	030 22
TOGETHER IS WORSHIPPED AND GLORIFIED	071 19
AND WORSHIPPED HIM	109 21
A LEPER AND WORSHIPPED HIM, SAYING, LORD, IF THOU	114 31
CAME SHE AND WORSHIPPED HIM, SAYING, LORD, HELP ME	128 15
THEIR KNEES WORSHIPPED HIM	146 02
AND THEY WORSHIPPED HIM, AND RETURNED TO JERUSALEM	178 27
AND WORSHIPPED HIM, SAYING, LORD, HAVE PATIENCE	221 19
AND WORSHIPPED HIM, SAYING, MY DAUGHTER IS	224 13
AND WORSHIPPED GOD, SAYING, AMEN	256 31
HAVE EATEN, AND WORSHIPPED	367 33

WORSHIPPED   CONTINUED

AND WORSHIPPED THE MOLTEN IMAGE	474 06
THAT THEY WORSHIPPED THEIR IDOLS, WHICH BECAME A	475 08
NAME MAY BE WORSHIPPED IN TRUTH AND PURITY THROUGH	568 11
CARRIED ABOUT, LIFTED UP, OR WORSHIPPED	608 48

WORSHIPPERS

THE TRUE WORSHIPPERS SHALL WORSHIP THE FATHER IN	003 30
THAT THE WORSHIPPERS ONCE PURGED SHOULD HAVE HAD NO	157 19

WORSHIPPING

HER SONS, WORSHIPPING HIM, AND DESIRING A CERTAIN	247 07
WORSHIPPING AND ADORATION, AS WELL OF IMAGES	607 14

WORTH

ALL OUR DOINGS WITHOUT CHARITY ARE NOTHING WORTH	122 15

WORTHILY

THEY MAY WORTHILY MINISTER IN THY NAME TO THE	044 04
LOVE THEE, AND WORTHILY MAGNIFY THY HOLY NAME	067 20
MAY WORTHILY RECEIVE THE MOST PRECIOUS	081 25
WHO RECEIVE IT WORTHILY, AND SO DANGEROUS TO THOSE	087 06
THAT WE, WORTHILY LAMENTING OUR SINS AND	124 14
EVIL DEEDS DO WORTHILY DESERVE TO BE PUNISHED,	130 25
AND CANNOT WORTHILY BE PRAISED	460 06
IN SUCH ONLY AS WORTHILY RECEIVE THE SAME, THEY HAVE	608 03
AS RIGHTLY, WORTHILY, AND WITH FAITH, RECEIVE THE	608 36

WORTHINESS

FOR THE WORTHINESS OF THY SON JESUS CHRIST OUR	050 04

WORTHY

AND AM NO MORE WORTHY TO BE CALLED THY SON	004 28
FORTH HIS MOST WORTHY PRAISE, TO HEAR HIS MOST HOLY	006 07
FORTH HIS MOST WORTHY PRAISE, TO HEAR HIS MOST HOLY	023 16
TRUE SAYING, AND WORTHY OF ALL MEN TO BE RECEIVED,	076 18
WE ARE NOT WORTHY SO MUCH AS TO GATHER UP THE CRUMBS	082 15
BE RECEIVED AS WORTHY PARTAKERS OF THAT HOLY TABLE	087 14
LATCHET I AM NOT WORTHY TO UNLOOSE	096 05
SHOES I AM NOT WORTHY TO STOOP DOWN AND UNLOOSE	112 16
I AM NOT WORTHY THAT THOU SHOULDEST COME UNDER	115 11
LO, NOTHING WORTHY OF DEATH IS DONE UNTO HIM	153 26
MAY BE FOUND WORTHY TO ATTAIN TO EVERLASTING JOYS	168 21
THOU ART WORTHY, O LORD, TO RECEIVE GLORY AND	187 29
TIME ARE NOT WORTHY TO BE COMPARED WITH THE GLORY	194 12
AND AM NO MORE WORTHY TO BE CALLED THY SON	202 14
AND AM NO MORE WORTHY TO BE CALLED THY SON	202 20
WHICH WE ARE NOT WORTHY TO ASK, BUT THROUGH THE	206 09
YOU THAT YE WALK WORTHY OF THE VOCATION WHEREWITH YE	213 19
BUT THEY WHICH WERE BIDDEN WERE NOT WORTHY	218 17
YE MIGHT WALK WORTHY OF THE LORD UNTO ALL PLEASING,	224 04
THE LABOURER IS WORTHY OF HIS HIRE	254 23
TIME ARE NOT WORTHY TO BE COMPARED WITH THE GLORY	330 27
THOU MOST WORTHY JUDGE ETERNAL, SUFFER US NOT, AT OUR	332 31
WHICH IS WORTHY TO BE PRAISED	359 29
3 HIS WORK IS WORTHY TO BE PRAISED AND HAD IN HONOUR,	482 28
AND MARVELLOUS WORTHY TO BE PRAISED	520 31
THEY MAY BE FOUND WORTHY TO BE CALLED UNTO THE HIGHER	535 09
FORTH THY MOST WORTHY PRAISE, TO CONFESS THEIR SINS	566 16
MY GOD, I AM NOT WORTHY THAT THOU SHOULDEST COME	573 11

WOULD

THAT HE WOULD GIVE US	014 19
THE HAVEN WHERE HE WOULD BE, WITH A GRATEFUL SENSE OF	046 15
ALTERATIONS WOULD IN TIME BE FOUND EXPEDIENT	VI 03
NO SACRIFICE, ELSE WOULD I GIVE IT THEE	061 11
AS YE WOULD HAVE FORGIVENESS OF YOUR OFFENCES AT	087 28
YOU IN SUCH A CASE WOULD NOT BE MOVED	088 22
WHO WOULD NOT THINK A GREAT INJURY AND WRONG DONE	088 23
BOUGHT A FARM, OR WOULD TRY THEIR YOKES OF OXEN,	089 04
HOW OFTEN WOULD I HAVE GATHERED THY CHILDREN	100 29
HER WINGS, AND YE WOULD NOT	100 31
HER CHILDREN, AND WOULD NOT BE COMFORTED, BECAUSE	103 32
PLEASE GOD, SO YE WOULD ABOUND MORE AND MORE	127 25
KNEW WHAT HE WOULD DO	131 29
AND LIKEWISE OF THE FISHES AS MUCH AS THEY WOULD	132 06
UNTO THE PEOPLE A PRISONER, WHOM THEY WOULD	135 27
TASTED THEREOF, HE WOULD NOT DRINK	136 30
ABOUT HIM SAW WHAT WOULD FOLLOW, THEY SAID UNTO HIM,	150 31
FOR THEN WOULD THEY NOT HAVE CEASED TO BE OFFERED	157 18
MADE AS THOUGH HE WOULD HAVE GONE FURTHER	168 02
IF YE LOVED ME, YE WOULD REJOICE, BECAUSE I SAID,	182 04
SO THAT THEY WHICH WOULD PASS FROM HENCE TO YOU	190 20
PASS TO US, THAT WOULD COME FROM THENCE	190 22
PRAYED HIM THAT HE WOULD THRUST OUT A LITTLE FROM THE	196 11
I WOULD NOT THAT YE SHOULD BE IGNORANT,	201 05
AND HE WOULD FAIN HAVE FILLED HIS BELLY WITH THE	202 08
HE WAS ANGRY, AND WOULD NOT GO IN	202 32
BRETHREN, I WOULD NOT HAVE YOU IGNORANT	203 16
STANDING AFAR OFF, WOULD NOT LIFT UP SO MUCH AS HIS	205 29
SO THAT YE CANNOT DO THE THINGS THAT YE WOULD	209 18
IS NAMED, THAT HE WOULD GRANT YOU, ACCORDING TO THE	212 13
AND THEY WOULD NOT COME	218 06
HIM THAT HE WOULD COME DOWN, AND HEAL HIS SON	219 31
WHICH WOULD TAKE ACCOUNT OF HIS SERVANTS	221 14
AND HE WOULD NOT	221 28
KNEW WHAT HE WOULD DO	225 25
AND LIKEWISE OF THE FISHES AS MUCH AS THEY WOULD	226 05

WOULD   CONTINUED

IT WERE NOT SO, I WOULD HAVE TOLD YOU	239 32
OF HEART THEY WOULD CLEAVE UNTO THE LORD	241 07
HIS FATHER, HOW HE WOULD HAVE HIM CALLED	243 22
THAT HE WOULD GRANT UNTO US, THAT WE BEING	244 06
AND WHEN HEROD WOULD HAVE BROUGHT HIM FORTH, THE SAME	245 09
WHITHER HE HIMSELF WOULD COME	254 13
THAT HE WOULD SEND FORTH LABOURERS INTO HIS	254 15
THE WORLD WOULD LOVE HIS OWN	255 14
I WOULD NOT HAVE YOU TO BE IGNORANT, BRETHREN,	268 28
LORD JESUS CHRIST WOULD VOUCHSAFE TO RECEIVE HIM,	276 21
LORD JESUS CHRIST WOULD VOUCHSAFE TO RECEIVE YOU,	277 22
DO TO ALL MEN AS I WOULD THEY SHOULD DO UNTO ME	288 25
IT WERE NOT SO, I WOULD HAVE TOLD YOU	331 19
WERE ANY THAT WOULD UNDERSTAND, AND SEEK AFTER GOD	356 17
THE LORD, THAT HE WOULD DELIVER HIM	366 18
AND WOULD FAIN SEE GOOD DAYS	380 25
SO WOULD WE HAVE IT	383 14
NO SACRIFICE, ELSE WOULD I GIVE IT THEE	404 09
WERE ANY THAT WOULD UNDERSTAND, AND SEEK AFTER GOD	405 17
PEOPLE AS IF THEY WOULD EAT BREAD	405 23
O THAT THE LORD WOULD DELIVER HIS PEOPLE OUT OF	405 29
FOR THEN WOULD I FLEE AWAY, AND BE AT REST	406 31
7 LO, THEN WOULD I GET ME AWAY FAR OFF, *	406 32
8 I WOULD MAKE HASTE TO ESCAPE, *	407 02
PERADVENTURE I WOULD HAVE HID MYSELF FROM HIM	407 14
OF HIM THAT WOULD HAVE EAT ME UP	409 18
MINE ENEMIES, AND WOULD DESTROY ME GUILTLESS, ARE	422 08
AND WOULD NOT WALK IN HIS LAW	435 20
AND WOULD NOT SUFFER HIS WHOLE DISPLEASURE TO ARISE	437 17
12 BUT MY PEOPLE WOULD NOT HEAR MY VOICE	443 02
AND ISRAEL WOULD NOT OBEY ME	443 03
O THAT MY PEOPLE WOULD HAVE HEARKENED UNTO ME	443 06
17 I WOULD HAVE FED THEM ALSO WITH THE FINEST	443 13
OF THE STONY ROCK WOULD I HAVE SATISFIED THEE	443 14
AND WOULD NOT ABIDE HIS COUNSEL	473 27
23 SO HE SAID HE WOULD HAVE DESTROYED THEM, HAD NOT	474 14
8 O THAT MEN WOULD THEREFORE PRAISE THE LORD FOR HIS	476 19
15 O THAT MEN WOULD THEREFORE PRAISE THE LORD FOR HIS	477 04
21 O THAT MEN WOULD THEREFORE PRAISE THE LORD FOR HIS	477 17
22 THAT THEY WOULD OFFER UNTO HIM THE SACRIFICE OF	477 20
HAVEN WHERE THEY WOULD BE	478 05
31 O THAT MEN WOULD THEREFORE PRAISE THE LORD FOR HIS	478 07
32 THAT THEY WOULD EXALT HIM ALSO IN THE CONGREGATION	478 10
WAS NO MAN THAT WOULD KNOW ME	518 11
BECAUSE WE WOULD NOT THAT AN UNWORTHY PERSON SHOULD	570 19
DO TO ALL MEN AS I WOULD THEY SHOULD DO UNTO ME	580 02

WOULDEST

THAT THOU WOULDEST BE PLEASED TO MAKE THY WAYS KNOWN	018 28
THAT THOU WOULDEST BE PLEASED TO MAKE THY WAYS KNOWN	032 28
THAT THOU WOULDEST BE PLEASED TO DIRECT AND PROSPER	035 11
THAT THOU WOULDEST BE PLEASED TO FILL IT WITH ALL	037 16
AND WHO WOULDEST NOT THE DEATH OF A SINNER, BUT	062 14
OFFERING THOU WOULDEST NOT, BUT A BODY HAST THOU	157 25
FOR SIN THOU WOULDEST NOT, NEITHER HADST PLEASURE	157 30
THEE THAT THOU WOULDEST KEEP US STEDFAST IN THIS	186 27
THAT THOU WOULDEST SEND HIM TO MY FATHER'S HOUSE	190 23
OFFERING THOU WOULDEST NOT, *	390 27
ASK WHAT THOU WOULDEST HAVE US TO DO, THAT THE SPIRIT	595 29

WOUND

21 GOD SHALL WOUND THE HEAD OF HIS ENEMIES, *	420 27
SHALL WOUND EVEN KINGS IN THE DAY OF HIS WRATH	482 16

WOUNDED

HIS RAIMENT, AND WOUNDED HIM, AND DEPARTED, LEAVING	208 23
THAT THEY SHALL BE WOUNDED	415 34
TALK HOW THEY MAY VEX THEM WHOM THOU HAST WOUNDED	423 29
AND MY HEART IS WOUNDED WITHIN ME	481 15

WOUNDETH

AND WOUNDETH THE CONSCIENCES OF THE WEAK	609 41

WOUNDS

AND BOUND UP HIS WOUNDS, POURING IN OIL AND WINE, AND	208 30
5 MY WOUNDS STINK, AND ARE CORRUPT, *	387 30

WOVEN

WAS WITHOUT SEAM, WOVEN FROM THE TOP THROUGHOUT	160 12

WRAPPED

AND WRAPPED HIM IN SWADDLING CLOTHES, AND LAID	099 08
FIND THE BABE WRAPPED IN SWADDLING CLOTHES, LYING IN	099 18
THE BODY, HE WRAPPED IT IN A CLEAN LINEN CLOTH, AND	162 10
BUT WRAPPED TOGETHER IN A PLACE BY ITSELF	164 24

WRATH

AND IN THY WRATH REMEMBEREST MERCY	046 19
FROM THY WRATH, AND FROM EVERLASTING DAMNATION,	054 20
AND IN THY WRATH THINKEST UPON MERCY	063 02
MOST JUSTLY THY WRATH AND INDIGNATION AGAINST US	075 22
NOT YOURSELVES, BUT RATHER GIVE PLACE UNTO WRATH	113 04
TO EXECUTE WRATH UPON HIM THAT DOETH EVIL	114 21
NOT ONLY FOR WRATH, BUT ALSO FOR CONSCIENCE SAKE	114 23
THINGS COMETH THE WRATH OF GOD UPON THE CHILDREN OF	129 10
FOR THE WRATH OF MAN WORKETH NOT THE RIGHTEOUSNESS OF	174 32

WRATH   CONTINUED

BE SWIFT TO HEAR, SLOW TO SPEAK, SLOW TO WRATH	174 32
WRATH, STRIFE, SEDITIONS, HERESIES,	209 22
LET NOT THE SUN GO DOWN UPON YOUR WRATH	216 19
AND WRATH, AND ANGER, AND CLAMOUR, AND	216 27
HAVING GREAT WRATH, BECAUSE HE KNOWETH THAT HE	252 19
SLOW TO SPEAK, SLOW TO WRATH	265 24
FOR THE WRATH OF MAN WORKETH NOT THE RIGHTEOUSNESS OF	265 25
UNTO THEM IN HIS WRATH, *	346 06
RIGHT WAY, IF HIS WRATH BE KINDLED, YEA BUT A LITTLE	346 22
UP, O LORD, IN THY WRATH, AND LIFT UP THYSELF,	349 35
MAKE THEM LIKE A FIERY OVEN IN TIME OF THY WRATH	365 23
5 FOR HIS WRATH ENDURETH BUT THE TWINKLING OF AN EYE,	374 32
8 LEAVE OFF FROM WRATH, AND LET GO DISPLEASURE	385 09
THEM IN THY WRATH, CONSUME THEM, THAT THEY MAY	411 32
WHY IS THY WRATH SO HOT AGAINST THE SHEEP OF THY	430 04
THE HEAVY WRATH OF GOD CAME UPON THEM,	436 33
TIME TURNED HE HIS WRATH AWAY, *	437 16
FURIOUSNESS OF HIS WRATH, ANGER, DISPLEASURE, AND	438 06
STRETCH OUT THY WRATH FROM ONE GENERATION TO ANOTHER	446 17
AND SHALL THY WRATH BURN LIKE FIRE	452 33
11 BUT WHO REGARDETH THE POWER OF THY WRATH	454 11
WHOM I SWARE IN MY WRATH, *	459 27
BECAUSE OF THINE INDIGNATION AND WRATH	464 29
THEREFORE WAS THE WRATH OF THE LORD KINDLED AGAINST	475 16
SHALL WOUND EVEN KINGS IN THE DAY OF HIS WRATH	482 17
THE CHILDREN OF WRATH, WE ARE HEREBY MADE THE	581 26
NEVER SUFFER THE SUN TO GO DOWN UPON OUR WRATH	590 16
IT DESERVETH GOD'S WRATH AND DAMNATION	604 34

WRATHFUL

AFRAID AT THY WRATHFUL INDIGNATION	325 27
AND LET THY WRATHFUL DISPLEASURE TAKE HOLD OF THEM	423 24
FROM THY WRATHFUL INDIGNATION	446 13
16 THY WRATHFUL DISPLEASURE GOETH OVER ME, *	449 29
AFRAID AT THY WRATHFUL INDIGNATION	453 32
TURN AWAY HIS WRATHFUL INDIGNATION, LEST HE SHOULD	474 16

WRATHFULLY

THEY WERE SO WRATHFULLY DISPLEASED AT US	504 11

WRESTLE

FOR WE WRESTLE NOT AGAINST FLESH AND BLOOD, BUT	219 08

WRETCHEDNESS

OUR WRETCHEDNESS, MAY OBTAIN OF THEE, THE GOD OF ALL	124 15

WRETCHLESSNESS

OR INTO WRETCHLESSNESS OF MOST UNCLEAN LIVING, NO	606 25

WRINKLE

HAVING SPOT, OR WRINKLE, OR ANY SUCH THING	267 23

WRIT

A KEEPER OF HOLY WRIT, YET, AS IT OUGHT NOT TO DECREE	607 07
CANNOT BE PROVED BY HOLY WRIT	608 41

WRITE

MERCY UPON US, AND WRITE ALL THESE THY LAWS IN OUR	069 23
AND THESE THINGS WRITE WE UNTO YOU, THAT YOUR JOY MAY	101 21
THEIR MINDS WILL I WRITE THEM	158 13
JEWS TO PILATE, WRITE NOT, THE KING OF THE JEWS	160 07
MERCY UPON US, AND WRITE ALL THESE THY LAWS IN OUR	287 23
SAYING UNTO ME, WRITE, FROM HENCEFORTH BLESSED ARE	333 25
AND HE SAID UNTO ME, WRITE	567 22

WRITER

MY TONGUE IS THE PEN OF A READY WRITER	396 17

WRITETH

WHEN HE WRITETH UP THE PEOPLES	448 24

WRITING

AND THE WRITING WAS, JESUS OF NAZARETH THE KING OF	160 02
HE ASKED FOR A WRITING TABLE, AND WROTE, SAYING,	243 23
OR SEND IN WRITING, WITH HIS HAND SUBSCRIBED	R 583 07

WRITINGS

AND THE WRITINGS OF THE APOSTLES, OF WHAT	539 27

WRITTEN

THAT WHICH IS WRITTEN AFTER THEM	R 021 05
THE EPISTLE IS WRITTEN IN THE - CHAPTER OF -,	R 070 19
HOLY GOSPEL IS WRITTEN IN THE - CHAPTER OF -,	R 070 23
UNTO THEM, IT IS WRITTEN, MY HOUSE SHALL BE CALLED	092 02
SCRIPTURES TO BE WRITTEN FOR OUR LEARNING	092 08
THINGS WERE WRITTEN AFORETIME WERE WRITTEN FOR OUR	092 15
AFORETIME WERE WRITTEN FOR OUR LEARNING, THAT WE	092 16
AS IT IS WRITTEN, FOR THIS CAUSE I WILL CONFESS TO	092 26
OF WHOM IT IS WRITTEN, BEHOLD, I SEND MY MESSENGER	094 31
THEY SHOULD BE WRITTEN EVERY ONE, I SUPPOSE THAT EVEN	102 16
NOT CONTAIN THE BOOKS THAT SHOULD BE WRITTEN	102 17

WRITTEN   CONTINUED

FATHER'S NAME WRITTEN IN THEIR FOREHEADS   102 31
FOR THUS IT IS WRITTEN BY THE PROPHET, AND THOU   109 07
AS IT IS WRITTEN IN THE PROPHETS, BEHCLD, I SEND MY   112 04
FOR IT IS WRITTEN, VENGEANCE IS MINE   113 04
THINGS THAT ARE WRITTEN BY THE PROPHETS CONCERNING   123 19
AND SAID, IT IS WRITTEN, MAN SHALL NOT LIVE BY BREAD   126 28
FOR IT IS WRITTEN, HE SHALL GIVE HIS ANGELS CHARGE   126 33
UNTO HIM, IT IS WRITTEN AGAIN, THOU SHALT NOT TEMPT   127 03
FOR IT IS WRITTEN, THOU SHALT WORSHIP THE LORD THY   127 09
FOR IT IS WRITTEN, THAT ABRAHAM HAD TWO SONS, THE ONE   130 30
FOR IT IS WRITTEN, REJOICE, THCU BARREN THAT BEAREST   131 08
HIS ACCUSATION WRITTEN, THIS IS JESUS THE KING OF THE   137 02
AS IT IS WRITTEN OF HIM   141 07
FOR IT IS WRITTEN, I WILL SMITE THE SHEPHERD, ANC THE   141 19
ACCUSATION WAS WRITTEN OVER, THE KING OF THE JEWS   146 14
THIS THAT IS WRITTEN MUST YET BE ACCOMPLISHED IN ME,   150 09
ALSO WAS WRITTEN OVER HIM, IN LETTERS OF GREEK, ANC   154 32
THE BOOK IT IS WRITTEN OF ME,) TO DO THY WILL,   157 28
AND IT WAS WRITTEN IN HEBREW, AND GREEK, AND LATIN   160 05
WHAT I HAVE WRITTEN I HAVE WRITTEN   160 08
WHAT I HAVE WRITTEN I HAVE WRITTEN   160 09
ALL THAT WAS WRITTEN OF HIM, THEY TOOK HIM DOWN FROM   168 32
AS IT IS ALSO WRITTEN IN THE SECOND PSALM, THOU ART   169 09
WHICH WERE WRITTEN IN THE LAW OF MOSES, AND IN THE   170 09
THUS IT IS WRITTEN, AND THUS IT BEHOVED CHRIST   170 12
AS IT IS WRITTEN, THE PEOPLE SAT DOWN TO EAT AND   201 15
AND THEY ARE WRITTEN FOR OUR ADMONITICN, UPCN WHCM   201 23
UNTO THEM, IT IS WRITTEN, MY HOUSE IS THE HOUSE CF   204 17
OF DEATH, WRITTEN AND ENGRAVEN IN STONES, WAS   206 18
WHAT IS WRITTEN IN THE LAW   208 14
A LETTER I HAVE WRITTEN UNTO YOU WITH MINE OWN HAND   210 23
AS IT IS WRITTEN, HOW BEAUTIFUL ARE THE FEET OF THEM   227 09
WHICH ARE NOT WRITTEN IN THIS BOOK   229 10
BUT THESE ARE WRITTEN, THAT YE MIGHT BELIEVE THAT   229 11
AS IT IS WRITTEN IN THE LAW OF THE LORD, EVERY MALE   232 25
FOR IT IS WRITTEN IN THE BOOK OF PSALMS, LET HIS   234 18
THAT IS WRITTEN IN THEIR LAW, THEY HATED ME WITHCUT A   255 29
UNTO THEM, IT IS WRITTEN, MY HOUSE SHALL BE CALLED   260 06
WHERE IT WAS WRITTEN, THE SPIRIT OF THE LORD IS UPCN   261 16
OF THE GOSPEL, WRITTEN BY SAINT MARK, IN THE TENTH   274 23
OF THE GOSPEL, WRITTEN BY SAINT JOHN, IN THE THIRD   275 03
OF THE GOSPEL, WRITTEN BY SAINT MATTHEW, IN THE   275 23
THINGS HAVE I WRITTEN UNTO YOU THAT BELIEVE ON THE   322 12
AND SO IT IS WRITTEN, THE FIRST MAN ADAM WAS MADE A   329 24
SAYING THAT IS WRITTEN, DEATH IS SWALLCWED UP IN   330 09
THE BOOK IT IS WRITTEN OF ME, THAT I SHOULD FULFIL   390 31
AND NOT BE WRITTEN AMCNG THE RIGHTEOUS   423 33
18 THIS SHALL BE WRITTEN FOR THOSE THAT COME AFTER,   465 15
AND IN THY BOOK WERE ALL MY MEMBERS WRITTEN   515 21
AS IT IS WRITTEN, *   525 19
IT IS WRITTEN IN THE GOSPEL OF SAINT LUKE,   553 04
IT IS WRITTEN ALSO, THAT THE HOLY APOSTLES PRAYEC   553 07
THAT IT WAS WRITTEN, THE ZEAL CF THINE HOUSE HATH   568 03
TO GOD'S WORD WRITTEN, NEITHER MAY IT SO EXPOUND ONE   607 05

WRONG

TO HAVE DONE ANY WRONG TO HIS NEIGHBOURS BY WORD OR   R 085 02
THE PARTIES TO WHOM HE HATH DONE WRONG   R 085 07
A GREAT INJURY AND WRONG DONE UNTO HIM   088 23
I DO THEE NO WRONG   120 08
DONE INJURY OR WRONG TO ANY MAN, THAT HE MAKE AMENDS   R 313 23
UNGODLINESS AND WRONG, THAT THOU MAYEST TAKE THE   354 05
RISEN UP AGAINST ME, AND SUCH AS SPEAK WRCNG   372 26
10 O TRUST NOT IN WRONG AND ROBBERY   414 18
AND PUNISH THE WRONG DOER   427 05
DELIVER THEIR SOULS FROM FALSEHOOD AND WRONG   427 25
LONG WILL YE GIVE WRONG JUDGMENT, *   443 20
FOR ALL THEM THAT ARE OPPRESSED WITH WRONG   466 18
NO MAN TO DO THEM WRONG, *   470 30
O LET ME NOT GO WRONG OUT OF THY COMMANDMENTS   490 19
67 BEFORE I WAS TROUBLED, I WENT WRONG   494 15
THAT THE PROUD DO ME NO WRONG   498 14
6 WHO HELPETH THEM TO RIGHT THAT SUFFER WRONG   522 14
OFF FROM US ALL WRONG DESIRES, INCLINE OUR HEARTS TO   594 13

WRONGFUL

ME FROM THE WRONGFUL DEALINGS OF MEN   499 06

WRONGFULLY

TOWARD GOD ENDURE GRIEF, SUFFERING WRCNGFULLY   172 06
THAT HATE ME WRONGFULLY ARE MANY IN NUMBER   388 31

WRONGS

ALL INJURIES AND WRONGS DONE BY YOU TO ANY OTHER   087 26
SANCTIFY TO THEM THE ENDURANCE OF THEIR WRONGS   599 10

WROTE

THESE THINGS, AND WROTE THESE THINGS   102 13
AS I WROTE AFORE IN FEW WORDS, WHEREBY, WHEN YE   108 10
AND PILATE WROTE A TITLE, AND PUT IT ON THE CROSS   159 35
WRITING TABLE, AND WROTE, SAYING, HIS NAME IS JOHN   243 23

WROTH

WAS EXCEEDING WROTH, AND SENT FORTH, AND SLEW   103 25
BUT WHEN THE KING HEARD THEREOF, HE WAS WROTH   218 14
AND HIS LORD WAS WROTH, AND DELIVERED HIM TO THE   222 03
AND WERE REMOVED, BECAUSE HE WAS WROTH   360 11
22 WHEN THE LORD HEARD THIS, HE WAS WROTH   436 11

WROTH   CONTINUED

HEARD THIS, HE WAS WROTH, *   438 30
AND WAS WROTH WITH HIS INHERITANCE   439 03

WROUGHT

THESE LAST HAVE WROUGHT BUT ONE HOUR, AND THCU HAST   120 05
SHE HATH WROUGHT A GOOD WORK ON ME   140 11
THAT THEY ARE WROUGHT IN GOD   185 11
AND WONDERS WROUGHT AMONG THE PEOPLE   249 22
MIRACLE THAT HE WROUGHT IN CANA OF GALILEE, AND IS   300 15
VESTURE OF GOLD, WROUGHT ABOUT WITH DIVERS CCLCURS   397 04
CLOTHING IS OF WROUGHT GOLD   397 13
THAT THOU HAST WROUGHT IN US, 29 FOR THY TEMPLE'S   421 12
44 HOW HE HAD WROUGHT HIS MIRACLES IN EGYPT, *   437 27

YEA

YEA, LET IT PRAISE HIM, AND MAGNIFY HIM FOR EVER   013 02
YEA, LET ALL THE PEOPLES PRAISE THEE   028 21
YEA, LET ALL THE PEOPLES PRAISE THEE   028 26
YEA, I JUDGE NOT MINE OWN SELF   094 07
YEA, I SAY UNTO YOU, AND MORE THAN A PROPHET   094 30
BUT HE SAID, YEA RATHER, BLESSED ARE THEY THAT HEAR   130 20
YEA, AND CERTAIN WOMEN ALSO OF OUR COMPANY MADE US   167 22
THE HOUR COMETH, YEA, IS NOW COME, THAT YE SHALL BE   177 05
YEA, THE TIME COMETH, THAT WHOSOEVER KILLETH YOU WILL 179 30
YEA, A   233 13
AND JESUS SAITH UNTO THEM, YEA   260 14
YEA, A JOYFUL AND PLEASANT THING IT IS TO BE   264 19
YEA, OUR GOD IS MERCIFUL   305 25
YEA, THY MERCY, O LORD, ENDURETH FOR EVER   312 09
YEA, IN THE SECRET PLACE OF HIS DWELLING SHALL HE   326 13
YEA, IT IS EVEN HE THAT SHALL KEEP THY SCUL   327 31
IS CHRIST THAT DIED, YEA RATHER, THAT IS RISEN AGAIN, 331 04
YEA, THOUGH I WALK THROUGH THE VALLEY OF THE SHADOW   338 23
YEA, IT IS EVEN HE THAT SHALL KEEP THY SOUL   339 15
WRATH BE KINDLED, YEA BUT A LITTLE   346 22
YEA, MORE THAN WHEN THEIR CORN AND WINE AND OIL   347 26
YEA, I HAVE DELIVERED HIM THAT WITHOUT ANY CAUSE IS   349 30
YEA, LET HIM TREAD MY LIFE DOWN UPON THE EARTH,   349 33
YEA, AND THE BEASTS OF THE FIELD   351 14
YEA, MY SONGS WILL I MAKE OF THY NAME, O THOU MOST   351 24
YEA, I WILL PRAISE THE NAME OF THE LORD MOST HIGHEST   356 10
YEA, I HAVE A GOODLY HERITAGE   358 02
14 YEA, BY THY HAND, O LORD   359 14
YEA, EVEN UNTO THE LORD SHALL THEY CRY, BUT HE SHALL   362 21
ARE THEY THAN GOLD, YEA, THAN MUCH FINE GOLD   364 04
4 YEA, THOUGH I WALK THROUGH THE VALLEY OF THE SHADCW 368 16
YEA, IN THE SECRET PLACE OF HIS DWELLING SHALL HE   372 05
YEA, THE LORD BREAKETH THE CEDARS OF LEBANON   374 07
YEA, THE LORD SHAKETH THE WILDERNESS OF KADESH   374 12
YEA, MY SOUL AND MY BODY   376 09
YEA, HE DELIVERED ME OUT OF ALL MY FEAR   380 09
YEA, AND SAVETH HIM OUT OF ALL HIS TROUBLES   380 14
YEA, EVEN WITHOUT A CAUSE HAVE THEY MADE A PIT FCR MY 382 02
YEA, THE POOR, AND HIM THAT IS IN MISERY, FRCM HIM   382 11
YEA, THE VERY ABJECTS CAME TOGETHER AGAINST ME   382 24
YEA, LET THEM SAY ALWAY, BLESSED BE THE LORD, WHC   383 20
YEA, EVEN AS THE SMOKE SHALL THEY CONSUME AWAY   386 02
I KEPT SILENCE, YEA, EVEN FROM GOOD WORDS   389 10
YEA, THY LAW IS WITHIN MY HEART   390 33
YEA, THEY ARE MORE IN NUMBER THAN THE HAIRS OF MY   391 12
9 YEA, EVEN MINE OWN FAMILIAR FRIEND WHOM I TRUSTED,   392 17
IS ATHIRST FOR GOD, YEA, EVEN FOR THE LIVING GOD   392 31
YEA, AND HAST SLANDERED THINE OWN MOTHER'S SCN   402 30
20 YEA, EVEN GOD, THAT ENDURETH FOR EVER, SHALL HEAR   407 30
11 YEA, IN GOD HAVE I PUT MY TRUST   409 04
2 YEA, YE IMAGINE MISCHIEF IN YOUR HEART UPON THE   410 10
YEA, AS A TOTTERING WALL SHALL YE BE, AND LIKE A   414 02
8 YEA, THEIR OWN TONGUES SHALL MAKE THEM FALL   416 02
YEA, LET ALL THE PEOPLES PRAISE THEE   418 28
YEA, LET ALL THE PEOPLES PRAISE THEE   418 33
YEA, THE LORD WILL ABIDE IN IT FOR EVER   420 14
YEA, EVEN FROM THINE ENEMIES, THAT THE LORD GOD MIGHT 420 20
YEA, AND THAT A MIGHTY VOICE   421 23
YEA, AND BROUGHTEST ME FROM THE DEEP OF THE EARTH   426 18
YEA, AND ABUNDANCE OF PEACE, SO LONG AS THE MOON   427 10
15 YEA, AND I HAD ALMOST SAID EVEN AS THEY   429 06
20 YEA, EVEN LIKE AS A DREAM WHEN ONE AWAKETH   429 16
9 YEA, THEY SAID IN THEIR HEARTS, LET US MAKE HAVOC   430 21
YEA, UNTO THEE DO WE GIVE THANKS   431 30
YEA, AND SMOTE DOWN THE CHOSEN MEN THAT WERE IN   436 34
39 YEA, MANY A TIME TURNED HE HIS WRATH AWAY,   437 16
YEA, MAKE ALL THEIR PRINCES LIKE AS ZEBAH AND   444 27
3 YEA, THE SPARROW HATH FOUND HER AN HOUSE, AND THE   445 16
12 YEA, THE LORD SHALL SHOW LOVING-KINDNESS   446 31
5 YEA, OF SION IT SHALL BE REPORTED, THIS ONE AND   448 22
8 YEA, WITH THINE EYES SHALT THOU BEHOLD, *   455 11
YEA, I AM WITH HIM IN TROUBLE   455 26
YEA, THE LORD OUR GOD SHALL DESTROY THEM   458 33
YEA, THE MULTITUDE OF THE ISLES MAY BE GLAD THEREOF   460 31
HAVE MERCY UPON HER, YEA, THE TIME IS COME   465 05
13 YEA, LIKE AS A FATHER PITIETH HIS OWN CHILDREN   466 32
YEA, EVEN IN THEIR KINGS' CHAMBERS   471 32
24 YEA, THEY THOUGHT SCORN OF THAT PLEASANT LAND,   474 17
YEA, THEY OFFERED THEIR SONS AND THEIR DAUGHTERS UNTO 475 09
YEA, HE MADE ALL THOSE THAT LED THEM AWAY CAPTIVE TO   475 28
OF THE UNGODLY, YEA, THE MOUTH OF THE DECEITFUL IS   480 04
YEA, OUR GOD IS MERCIFUL   486 28
4 YEA, LET THEM NOW THAT FEAR THE LORD CONFESS,   488 06
WITH CORDS, YEA, EVEN UNTO THE HORNS OF THE ALTAR   489 23
YEA, I SHALL KEEP IT WITH MY WHOLE HEART   492 08
YEA, FOR EVER AND EVER   492 28
YEA, SWEETER THAN HONEY UNTO MY MOUTH   496 32

YEA   CONTINUED   YET

YEA, MY DELIGHT SHALL BE EVER IN THY STATUTES   498 02   YET SO AS THAT THE MAIN BODY AND ESSENTIAL PARTS CF   V 30
146 YEA, EVEN UNTO THEE DID I CALL   500 02   YET OUGHT WE CHIEFLY SO TO DO, WHEN WE ASSEMBLE AND   006 04
172 YEA, MY TONGUE SHALL SING OF THY WCRD   501 26   YET OUGHT WE CHIEFLY SO TO DO, WHEN WE ASSEMBLE AND   023 13
YEA, IT IS EVEN HE THAT SHALL KEEP THY SOUL   503 04   ALL HUMAN WRITINGS YET UPON THE PRINCIPLES ALREADY   VI 02
9 YEA, BECAUSE OF THE HOUSE OF THE LORD OUR GOD,   503 24   CHAIN OF OUR SINS, YET LET THE PITIFULNESS OF THY   063 12
3 YEA, THE WATERS HAD DROWNED US, *   504 12   UNTO THE SAINTS, AND YET DO MINISTER   072 26
4 YEA, THE LORD HATH DONE GREAT THINGS FOR US   505 13   YET WE BESEECH THEE TO ACCEPT THIS OUR BCUNDEN DUTY   081 30
7 YEA, THAT THOU SHALT SEE THY CHILDREN'S CHILDREN, 506 18   AND YET THEY WHO ARE CALLED, WITHOUT ANY CAUSE, MOST   088 20
2 YEA, MANY A TIME HAVE THEY VEXED ME FRCM MY YCUTH 506 23   YET AM I NOT HEREBY JUSTIFIED   094 09
YEA, MY SOUL IS EVEN AS A WEANED CHILD   507 28   YET JESUS SAID NOT UNTO HIM, HE SHALL NOT DIE   102 10
18 YEA, AND SLEW MIGHTY KINGS   512 18   MINE HOUR IS NOT YET COME   113 16
YEA, IF I PREFER NOT JERUSALEM ABOVE MY CHIEF JCY   513 16   AND IT DOTH NOT YET APPEAR WHAT WE SHALL BE   117 18
YEA, HAPPY SHALL HE BE THAT REWARDETH THEE AS THCU   513 21   AS DECEIVERS, AND YET TRUE   126 17
5 YEA, THEY SHALL SING OF THE WAYS OF THE LORD,   514 06   AS UNKNOWN, AND YET WELL KNOWN   126 18
YEA, THY MERCY, O LORD, ENDURETH FOR EVER   514 15   AS SORROWFUL, YET ALWAY REJOICING   126 19
11 YEA, THE DARKNESS IS NO DARKNESS WITH THEE,   515 10   AS POOR, YET MAKING MANY RICH   126 20
22 YEA, I HATE THEM RIGHT SORE   516 02   HAVING NOTHING, AND YET POSSESSING ALL THINGS   126 20
YEA, AND SET TRAPS IN MY WAY   516 19   YET THE DOGS EAT OF THE CRUMBS WHICH FALL FROM THEIR   128 18
YEA, LET NOT MY HEAD REFUSE THEIR PRECIOUS BALMS   517 20   YET YE HAVE NOT KNOWN HIM   133 25
YEA, EVEN UNTO THE LORD DID I MAKE MY SUPPLICATICN   518 03   THOU ART NOT YET FIFTY YEARS OLD, AND HAST THOU   133 30
YEA, I EXERCISE MYSELF IN THE WORKS OF THY HANDS   518 33   SHALL BE OFFENDED, YET WILL NOT I   141 22
YEA, BLESSED ARE THE PEOPLE WHO HAVE THE LORD FOR   520 24   WHILE HE YET SPAKE, COMETH JUDAS, ONE OF THE TWELVE   142 14
YEA, ALL SUCH AS CALL UPON HIM FAITHFULLY   521 29   BUT JESUS YET ANSWERED NOTHING   145 11
YEA, AS LONG AS I HAVE ANY BEING, I WILL SING PRAISES 522 04   NOR YET THAT HE SHOULD OFFER HIMSELF OFTEN, AS THE   148 02
YEA, A JOYFUL AND PLEASANT THING IT IS TO BE   522 28   THAT IS WRITTEN MUST YET BE ACCOMPLISHED IN ME, AND   150 09
YEA, AND HIS WISDOM IS INFINITE   523 04   AND WHILE HE YET SPAKE, BEHOLD A MULTITUDE, AND HE   150 26
YEA, YE YOURSELVES KNOW, THAT THESE HANDS HAVE   551 06   WHILE HE YET SPAKE, THE COCK CREW   151 19
HE SAITH UNTO HIM, YEA, LORD   551 15   NOR YET HEROD   153 26
HE SAITH UNTO HIM, YEA, LORD   551 18   WHILE HE WAS YET ALIVE, AFTER THREE DAYS I WILL   162 18
NATURE DOTH REMAIN, YEA IN THEM THAT ARE REGENERATED 604 35   WHEN IT WAS YET DARK, UNTO THE SEPULCHRE, AND   164 11
YEA RATHER, FOR THAT THEY ARE NOT DONE AS GOD HATH   605 20   YET WENT HE NOT IN   164 20
                                                              FOR AS YET THEY KNEW NOT THE SCRIPTURE, THAT HE MUST   164 26
YEAR   KNEW HIM NOT, NOR YET THE VOICES OF THE PROPHETS   168 28
                                                              OF DEATH IN HIM, YET DESIRED THEY PILATE THAT HE   168 30
WAS ISSUED IN THE YEAR 1689   VI 04   AND WHILE THEY YET BELIEVED NOT FOR JCY, AND   170 03
THE ACCEPTABLE YEAR OF THE LCRD, AND THE DAY OF   107 05   WHILE I WAS YET WITH YOU, THAT ALL THINGS MUST   170 08
TO JERUSALEM EVERY YEAR AT THE FEAST OF THE PASSOVER 110 18   I HAVE YET MANY THINGS TO SAY UNTO YOU, BUT YE CANNOT   175 17
MINE HEART, AND THE YEAR OF MY REDEEMED IS COME   138 21   AND YET I AM NOT ALONE, BECAUSE THE FATHER IS WITH   177 06
HOLY PLACE EVERY YEAR WITH BLOOD OF OTHERS   148 03   YET A LITTLE WHILE, AND THE WORLD SEETH ME NO MCRE   181 15
OFFERED YEAR BY YEAR CONTINUALLY, MAKE THE COMERS   157 17   UNTO YOU, BEING YET PRESENT WITH YOU   181 29
WHICH THEY OFFERED YEAR BY YEAR CONTINUALLY, MAKE THE 157 17   WHILE PETER YET SPAKE THESE WORDS, THE HOLY GHOST   184 20
IS A REMEMBRANCE AGAIN MADE OF SINS EVERY YEAR   157 22   FOR AS YET HE WAS FALLEN UPON NONE OF THEM   185 25
IF IN ANY YEAR THERE BE TWENTY-SIX SUNDAYS AFTER   R 224 31   HAST COMMANDED, AND YET THERE IS RCOM   192 17
THAT A WHOLE YEAR THEY ASSEMBLED THEMSELVES   241 12   BUT WHEN HE WAS YET A GREAT WAY OFF, HIS FATHER SAW   202 16
O GOD, WHOM YEAR BY YEAR WE PRAISE FOR THE DEDICATICN 259 19   AND YET THOU NEVER GAVEST ME A KID, THAT I MIGHT MAKE   202 35
O GOD, WHOM YEAR BY YEAR WE PRAISE FOR THE DEDICATION 259 19   YET NOT I, BUT THE GRACE OF GOD WHICH WAS WITH ME   205 17
THE ACCEPTABLE YEAR OF THE LORD   261 21   NOR YET FOR YOUR BODY, WHAT YE SHALL PUT ON   211 13
THOU CROWNEST THE YEAR WITH THY GOODNESS   417 07   YET I SAY UNTO YOU, THAT EVEN SOLOMON IN ALL HIS   211 22
SPACE OF A WHOLE YEAR, (EXCEPT FOR REASCNABLE CAUSES R 535 20 YOUR LOVE MAY ABOUND YET MORE AND MORE IN KNOWLECGE   221 02
AND IN THE -- YEAR OF OUR CONSECRATION   569 39   FOR YET A LITTLE WHILE, AND HE THAT SHALL COME WILL   228 17
                                                              HAVE NOT SEEN, AND YET HAVE BELIEVED   229 09
YEARLY   AND SAUL, YET BREATHING OUT THREATENINGS AND   229 25
                                                              TIME WITH YOU, AND YET HAST THOU NOT KNOWN ME,   240 11
US GLAD WITH THE YEARLY REMEMBRANCE OF THE BIRTH OF 098 11   MANIFOLD GIFTS, NOR YET OF GRACE TO USE THEM ALWAY TC   240 31
                                                              HE IS HIS FRIEND, YET BECAUSE OF HIS IMPORTUNITY HE   263 02
YEARS   NOR YET FOR YOUR BODY, WHAT YE SHALL PUT ON   266 12
                                                              YET YOUR HEAVENLY FATHER FEEDETH THEM   266 15
THE SAME, AND THY YEARS SHALL NOT FAIL   097 18   AND YET I SAY UNTO YOU, THAT EVEN SCLOMON IN ALL HIS   266 20
FROM TWO YEARS OLD AND UNDER, ACCORDING TO   103 27   FOR NO MAN EVER YET HATED HIS OWN FLESH   267 26
WHEN HE WAS TWELVE YEARS OLD, THEY WENT UP TO   110 19   FOR AS YET HE WAS FALLEN UPON NONE OF THEM   296 17
ART NOT YET FIFTY YEARS OLD, AND HAST THOU SEEN   133 30   FOR I WILL YET GIVE HIM THANKS, WHICH IS THE HELP CF   310 18
THESE MANY YEARS DO I SERVE THEE, NEITHER   202 34   YET SHALT THOU REFRESH ME   311 25
HUNDRED AND THIRTY YEARS AFTER, CANNOT DISANNUL, THAT 207 23   MIDST OF TROUBLE, YET SHALT THOU REFRESH ME   312 04
OF BLOOD TWELVE YEARS, CAME BEHIND HIM, AND TOUCHED 224 18   TO THE CHURCH, AND YET IS DESIROUS TO RECEIVE THE   R 321 11
AS IN THE DAYS OF OLD, AND AS IN FORMER YEARS   232 15   THOUGH HE WERE DEAD, YET SHALL HE LIVE   324 06
AN HUSBAND SEVEN YEARS FROM HER VIRGINITY   233 18   BODY BE DESTROYED, YET SHALL I SEE GOD   324 11
FOURSCORE AND FOUR YEARS, WHICH DEPARTED NCT FRCM THE 233 19 YET IS THEIR STRENGTH THEN BUT LABOUR AND SORROW   325 34
AS ARE OF RIPER YEARS ARE TO BE BAPTIZED, TIMELY   R 273 17   YET, O LORD GOD MOST HOLY, O LORD MOST MIGHTY,   332 25
AND THE YEARS THAT ARE PAST   310 27   AND WHO WALK AS YET BY FAITH, THAT HAVING SERVED THEE   336 07
OF OLD, AND THE YEARS THAT ARE PAST   311 08   THOUGH HE WERE DEAD, YET SHALL HE LIVE   338 06
WILL REMEMBER THE YEARS OF THE RIGHT HAND OF THE MOST 311 19 6 YET HAVE I SET MY KING *   346 08
FOR A THOUSAND YEARS IN THY SIGHT ARE BUT AS   325 20   WHEN I HANGED YET UPON MY MOTHER'S BREASTS   366 21
AGE ARE THREESCORE YEARS AND TEN   325 32   LAID AGAINST ME, YET SHALL NOT MY HEART BE AFRAIC   371 29
COME TO FOURSCORE YEARS, *   325 34   UP WAR AGAINST ME, YET WILL I PUT MY TRUST IN HIM   371 31
AND MY YEARS WITH MOURNING   376 12   10 YET A LITTLE WHILE, AND THE UNGODLY SHALL BE CLEAN   385 13
THAT HIS YEARS MAY ENDURE THROUGHOUT ALL GENERATICNS 413 17   AND YET SAW I NEVER THE RIGHTEOUS FORSAKEN, NOR HIS   386 12
AND THE YEARS THAT ARE PAST   433 25   AND YET THERE IS NO MAN THAT ORDERETH THEM UNTC THEE   390 23
WILL REMEMBER THE YEARS OF THE RIGHT HAND OF THE MOST 434 03   FOR I WILL YET THANK HIM, WHICH IS THE HELP CF MY   393 13
AND THEIR YEARS IN TROUBLE   437 05   FOR I WILL YET THANK HIM, WHICH IS THE HELP OF MY   393 33
4 FOR A THOUSAND YEARS IN THY SIGHT ARE BUT AS   453 25   FOR I WILL YET GIVE HIM THANKS, WHICH IS THE HELP CF   394 17
WE BRING OUR YEARS TO AN END, AS IT WERE A TALE THAT 454 05   BE COME UPON US, YET DO WE NOT FORGET THEE, *   395 28
AGE ARE THREESCORE YEARS AND TEN   454 07   11 AND YET THEY THINK THAT THEIR HOUSES SHALL   400 26
COME TO FOURSCORE YEARS, *   454 09   YET THEIR POSTERITY PRAISE THEIR SAYING   400 32
AND FOR THE YEARS WHEREIN WE HAVE SUFFERED ADVERSITY 454 20   ENDURETH YET DAILY   404 21
10 FORTY YEARS LONG WAS I GRIEVED WITH THIS   459 24   THAN OIL, AND YET BE THEY VERY SWORDS   408 03
AS FOR THY YEARS, THEY ENDURE THROUGHOUT ALL   465 29   YET PUT I MY TRUST IN THEE   408 19
THE SAME, AND THY YEARS SHALL NOT FAIL   466 03   THE SHEEP-FOLDS, YET SHALL YE BE AS THE WINGS OF A   420 06
THE SPACE OF THREE YEARS I CEASED NOT TO WARN EVERY 550 34   TO ALL THEM THAT ARE YET FOR TO COME   426 12
                                                              AND YET DIDST THOU TURN AND REFRESH ME   426 18
YES   NOR YET FROM THE SOUTH   432 11
                                                              CHILDREN WHICH WERE YET UNBORN   435 08
YES VERILY, THEIR SOUND WENT INTO ALL THE EARTH, AND 227 14   18 YET FOR ALL THIS THEY SINNED MORE AGAINST HIM,   436 02
YES, VERILY   283 30   WHILE THE MEAT WAS YET IN THEIR MOUTHS, THE HEAVY   436 32
YES, VERILY   577 22   ALL THIS THEY SINNED YET MORE, *   437 02
                                                              57 YET THEY TEMPTED AND DISPLEASED THE MOST HIGH GOD,   438 24
YESTERDAY   YET IS THEIR STRENGTH THEN BLT LABOUR AND SORRCW   454 09
                                                              BUT YET THE LORD, WHO DWELLETH ON HIGH, IS MIGHTIER   457 14
SAID UNTO HIM, YESTERDAY AT THE SEVENTH HOUR THE   220 08   7 AND YET THEY SAY, TUSH, THE LORD SHALL NOT SEE,   457 31
ARE BUT AS YESTERDAY, WHEN IT IS PAST, *   325 20   12 WHEN THERE WERE YET BUT A FEW OF THEM,   470 26
ARE BUT AS YESTERDAY WHEN IT IS PAST, *   453 25   41 YET HELPETH HE THE POOR OUT OF MISERY, *   478 28
                                                              THOUGH THEY CURSE, YET BLESS THOU   481 26
                                                              AND YET HUMBLETH HIMSELF TO BEHOLD THE THINGS THAT   484 17
                                                              YET HAVE I NOT SHRINKED FROM THY LAW   493 13
                                                              YET DO I NOT FORGET THY STATUTES   495 23

YET   CONTINUED

YET DO I NOT FORGET THY LAW   497 15
BUT YET I SWERVED NOT FROM THY COMMANDMENTS   497 17
YET DO I NOT FORGET THY COMMANDMENTS   499 21
YET IS MY DELIGHT IN THY COMMANDMENTS   499 26
YET DO I NOT SWERVE FROM THY TESTIMONIES   500 26
THEY HAVE EARS, AND YET THEY HEAR NOT   511 04
THE LORD BE HIGH, YET HATH HE RESPECT UNTO THE LCWLY   514 08
MIDST OF TROUBLE, YET SHALT THOU REFRESH ME   514 10
SEE MY SUBSTANCE, YET BEING IMPERFECT   515 20
WHEN AS YET THERE WAS NONE OF THEM   515 22
I WILL PRAY YET AGAINST THEIR WICKEDNESS   517 22
5 YET DO I REMEMBER THE TIME PAST   518 32
BUT YET, IF THERE BE ANY OF YOU WHO KNOWETH ANY   536 27
AND WHO YET HAST BEEN GRACIOUSLY PLEASED TO PROMISE   564 30
YET THOU HAST HONOURED THY SERVANT WITH APPCINTING   573 12
SOMETIME AFRAID, HE YET MAY PUT HIS TRUST IN THEE   597 25
BUT YET DOTH IT NOT APPLY THEM TO ESTABLISH ANY   604 03
YET NOTWITHSTANDING, NO   604 21
YET THE APOSTLE DOTH CONFESS, THAT CONCUPISCENCE AND   604 30
OF GOD'S JUDGMENT YET ARE THEY PLEASING AND   605 13
AGAIN IN CHRIST, YET OFFEND IN MANY THINGS   605 36
AND YET IT IS NOT LAWFUL FOR THE CHURCH TO ORDAIN ANY   607 04
KEEPER OF HOLY WRIT, YET, AS IT CUGHT NOT TC DECREE   607 07
BUT YET HAVE NOT LIKE NATURE OF SACRAMENTS WITH   607 42
WORD AND SACRAMENTS, YET FORASMUCH AS THEY DO NCT THE   608 11
YET IN NO WISE ARE THEY PARTAKERS OF CHRIST   609 06

YIELD

IN DUE TIME, YIELD HER INCREASE FOR OUR USE AND   040 27
YE SHALL YIELD UNTO GOD MOST HIGH PRAISE AND   048 13
WE YIELD THEE UNFEIGNED THANKS AND PRAISE FCR THE   050 21
THAT OUR LAND MAY YIELD US HER FRUITS OF INCREASE,   052 04
WE YIELD THEE PRAISE AND THANKSGIVING FOR OUR   052 09
DID VOUCHSAFE TO YIELD UP HIS SOUL BY DEATH UPON THE   089 10
EVEN SO NOW YIELD YOUR MEMBERS SERVANTS TO   198 29
OF THE FIELD SHALL YIELD HER FRUIT, AND THE EARTH   262 10
THE EARTH SHALL YIELD HER INCREASE, AND THEY SHALL BE   262 10
OUR LAND MAY STILL YIELD HER INCREASE, TO THY GLCRY   265 15
MINISTER SAY, WE YIELD THEE HEARTY THANKS, MOST   280 28
WE YIELD THEE HEARTY THANKS, ETC   R 281 24
EVERLIVING GOD, WE YIELD UNTO THEE MOST HIGH PRAISE   336 16
TO YIELD THEM FRUITS OF INCREASE   478 21

YIELDED

YIELDED TO MAKE SUCH ALTERATIONS IN SOME   V 28
A LOUD VOICE, YIELDED UP THE GHOST   137 25
FOR AS YE HAVE YIELDED YOUR MEMBERS SERVANTS TO   198 27

YOKE

I HAVE BOUGHT FIVE YOKE OF OXEN, AND I GO TO PRCVE   192 09
TAKE MY YOKE UPON YOU, AND LEARN OF ME   235 12
FOR MY YOKE IS EASY, AND MY BURDEN IS LIGHT   235 14
THE BANDS OF THEIR YOKE, AND DELIVERED THEM OUT CF   262 13

YOKES

OR WOULD TRY THEIR YOKES OF OXEN, OR BECAUSE THEY   089 04

YOU-WARD

WHICH IS GIVEN ME TO YOU-WARD   108 08

YOUNG

SICK PERSONS, AND YOUNG CHILDREN   056 32
THEIR CLOTHES AT A YOUNG MAN'S FEET, WHOSE NAME WAS   100 12
AND TAKE THE YOUNG CHILD AND HIS MOTHER, AND FLEE   103 17
WILL SEEK THE YOUNG CHILD TO DESTROY HIM   103 19
HE TOOK THE YOUNG CHILD AND HIS MOTHER BY   103 20
AND TAKE THE YOUNG CHILD AND HIS MOTHER, AND GO INTO   107 14
WHICH SOUGHT THE YOUNG CHILD'S LIFE   107 15
AND TOOK THE YOUNG CHILD AND HIS MOTHER, AND CAME   107 16
DILIGENTLY FOR THE YOLNG CHILD   109 13
OVER WHERE THE YOUNG CHILD WAS   109 18
THEY SAW THE YOUNG CHILD WITH MARY HIS MOTHER, AND   109 20
HIM A CERTAIN YOUNG MAN, HAVING A LINEN CLOTH CAST   142 29
AND THE YOUNG MEN LAID HOLD CN HIM   142 30
THEY SAW A YOUNG MAN SITTING ON THE RIGHT SIDE,   165 26
AND HE SAID, YOUNG MAN, I SAY UNTO THEE, ARISE   213 04
OR TWO YOUNG PIGEONS   232 29
AND SHALL GENTLY LEAD THOSE THAT ARE WITH YCUNG   243 11
AND FEEDETH THE YOUNG RAVENS THAT CALL UPON HIM   264 31
THEY BROUGHT YOUNG CHILDREN TO CHRIST, THAT HE SHOULD   274 25
AND SIRION, LIKE A YOLNG UNICORN   374 10
TO BRING FORTH YOUNG, AND STRIPPETH BARE THE FORESTS   374 15
25 I HAVE BEEN YOUNG, AND NOW AM OLD   386 12
SHALL THEY OFFER YOUNG BULLOCKS UPON THINE ALTAR   404 17
CONSUMED THEIR YOLNG MEN, *   439 04
EWES WITH THEIR YOUNG HE TOOK HIM, *   439 21
WHERE SHE MAY LAY HER YOUNG   445 17
THE YOUNG LION AND THE DRAGON SHALT THOU TREAD UNDER   455 21
MAKING THEE YOUNG AND LUSTY AS AN EAGLE   466 16
THY YOUNG MEN COME TO THEE AS DEW FROM THE WOMB OF   482 12
LITTLE HILLS LIKE YOUNG SHEEP   484 32
LITTLE HILLS, LIKE YOLNG SHEEP   485 05
SHALL A YOUNG MAN CLEANSE HIS WAY   490 16
EVEN SO ARE THE YOUNG CHILDREN   505 32
MAY GROW UP AS THE YOUNG PLANTS, *   520 15
AND FEEDETH THE YOUNG RAVENS THAT CALL UPON HIM   523 14
12 YOUNG MEN AND MAIDENS, OLD MEN AND CHILDREN,   524 27
THE BAPTISM OF YOUNG CHILDREN IS IN ANY WISE TO BE   608 31

YOUNGER

IS GREATEST AMONG YOU, LET HIM BE AS THE YOUNGER   149 23
AND THE YOUNGER OF THEM SAID TO HIS FATHER, FATHER,   201 31
DAYS AFTER THE YOUNGER SON GATHERED ALL TOGETHER, ANC   202 02
LET HIM BE AS THE YOUNGER   250 08

YOUR'S

THEY WILL KEEP YOUR'S ALSO   255 20

YOURS

LIVES OF YOU AND YOURS, AND TO FASHION THEM AFTER THE   541 21

YOURSELF

THESE THINGS OF YOURSELF, NOR TO WALK IN THE   289 14
TO BEHAVE YOURSELF IN THE CHURCH OF GOD   554 15
EXERCISE YOURSELF IN THE HOLY SCRIPTURES, AND CALL   554 29
YOU MAY SHOW YOURSELF IN ALL THINGS AN EXAMPLE CF   555 10
WILL YOU SHOW YOURSELF GENTLE, AND BE MERCIFUL FCR   555 23

YOURSELVES

SHOW YOURSELVES JOYFUL UNTO THE LORD, ALL YE LANDS   027 13
O SHOW YOURSELVES JOYFUL BEFORE THE LORD, THE KING   027 17
NOT UP FOR YOURSELVES TREASURES UPON EARTH, WHERE   072 07
LAY UP FOR YOURSELVES TREASURES IN HEAVEN, WHERE   072 09
THEREFORE YOURSELVES, BRETHREN, THAT YE BE NCT JUDGED   085 33
PERCEIVE YOURSELVES TO HAVE OFFENDED, EITHER BY WILL,   087 18
TO CONFESS YOURSELVES TO ALMIGHTY GCD, WITH FULL   087 20
RECONCILE YOURSELVES UNTO ANOTHER   087 24
WITHDRAWING YOURSELVES FROM THIS HOLY SUPPER,   088 25
YE EXCUSE YOURSELVES, AND SAY YE ARE NOT READY   088 33
WITH YOURSELVES HOW LITTLE SUCH FEIGNED EXCUSES WILL   089 02
CONSIDER WITH YOURSELVES HOW GREAT IS YOUR   089 14
AVENGE NOT YOURSELVES, BUT RATHER GIVE PLACE UNTC   113 03
SEEING YE YOURSELVES ARE WISE   120 22
NOT UP FOR YOURSELVES TREASURES UPON EARTH, WHERE   125 16
LAY UP FOR YOURSELVES TREASURES IN HEAVEN, WHERE   125 18
THAT COMPASS YOURSELVES ABOUT WITH SPARKS   144 26
AND DIVIDE IT AMONG YOURSELVES   149 06
BUT WEEP FOR YOURSELVES, AND FOR YOUR CHILDREN   154 15
YE ALSO YOURSELVES TO BE DEAD INDEED UNTO SIN, *   163 08
SUBMIT YOURSELVES TO EVERY ORDINANCE OF MAN FOR THE   173 17
ENQUIRE AMONG YOURSELVES OF THAT I SAID, A LITTLE   174 05
ALL THINGS HAVE FERVENT CHARITY AMONG YOURSELVES   179 14
HUMBLE YOURSELVES THEREFORE UNDER THE MIGHTY HAND OF   192 32
YE ALSO YOURSELVES TO BE DEAD INDEED UNTO SIN, BUT   197 25
GO SHEW YOURSELVES UNTO THE PRIESTS   210 05
SPEAKING TO YOURSELVES IN PSALMS AND HYMNS AND   217 27
SUBMITTING YOURSELVES ONE TO ANOTHER IN THE FEAR OF   217 31
AND JUDGE YOURSELVES UNWORTHY OF EVERLASTING LIFE,   261 02
SUBMITTING YOURSELVES ONE TO ANOTHER IN THE FEAR CF   267 13
SUBMIT YOURSELVES UNTO YOUR OWN HUSBANDS,   267 14
ACKNOWLEDGING YOURSELVES BOUND TO BELIEVE AND TO DO   296 26
GIVE NOT YOURSELVES UNTO VANITY   414 18
5 SHOW YOURSELVES JOYFUL UNTO THE LORD, ALL YE LANDS   462 02
O SHOW YOURSELVES JOYFUL BEFORE THE LORD, THE KING   462 06
TO MAKE BOTH YOURSELVES AND THEM, AS MUCH AS IN YOU   533 27
AND YE YOURSELVES LIKE UNTO MEN THAT WAIT FCR THEIR   534 17
CONSIDER WITH YOURSELVES THE END OF THE MINISTRY   540 14
TO APPLY YOURSELVES, AS WELL TO SHOW YOURSELVES   540 26
WELL TO SHOW YOURSELVES DUTIFUL AND THANKFUL UNTC   540 27
NEITHER YOU YOURSELVES OFFEND, NOR BE CCCASICN THAT   540 29
CANNOT HAVE A MIND AND WILL THERETO OF YOURSELVES   540 31
BOTH OF YOURSELVES, AND OF THEM THAT SPECIALLY   541 05
THINGS WITH YOURSELVES, LONG BEFORE THIS TIME   541 10
TO GIVE YOURSELVES WHOLLY TO THIS OFFICE, WHEREUNTC   541 11
YE WILL APPLY YOURSELVES WHOLLY TO THIS ONE THING,   541 13
SO ENDEAVOUR YOURSELVES, FROM TIME TO TIME, TO   541 20
TO MAKE BOTH YOURSELVES AND THEM, AS MUCH AS IN YOU   542 34
SUBMITTING YOURSELVES TO THEIR GODLY JUDGMENTS   543 15
UNTO YOURSELVES, AND TO ALL THE FLOCK, OVER THE WHICH   550 27
YE YOURSELVES KNOW, THAT THESE HANDS HAVE   551 06

YOUTH

OF ALL THE YOUTH OF THIS LAND, YE SHALL PRAY FOR ALL   047 32
OR EXAMINE THE YOUTH OF HIS PARISH   R 295 09
O REMEMBER NOT THE SINS AND OFFENCES OF MY YOUTH   369 30
THOU ART MY HOPE, EVEN FROM MY YOUTH   425 15
TAUGHT ME FROM MY YOUTH UP UNTIL NOW   426 08
EVEN FROM MY YOUTH UP, THY TERRORS HAVE I SUFFERED   449 27
44 THE DAYS OF HIS YOUTH HAST THCU SHORTENED, *   452 30
AGAINST ME FROM MY YOUTH UP, *   506 22
VEXED ME FROM MY YOUTH UP   506 24
TO INSTRUCT THE YOUTH IN THE CATECHISM   533 15

ZACHARIAS

THE BLOOD OF ZACHARIAS SON OF BARACHIAS, WHOM YE SLEW   100 24
CALLED HIM ZACHARIAS, AFTER THE NAME OF HIS FATHER   243 18
AND HIS FATHER ZACHARIAS WAS FILLED WITH THE HOLY   243 31

ZALMUNNA

MAKE ALL THEIR PRINCES LIKE AS ZEBAH AND ZALMUNNA   444 27

ZEAL

WITH FERVENT ZEAL CONSTANTLY TO PREACH THE GOSPEL   078 29
WHERE IS THY ZEAL AND THY STRENGTH, THE SCUNDING OF   139 19
9 FOR THE ZEAL OF THINE HOUSE HATH EVEN EATEN ME   422 20
139 MY ZEAL HATH EVEN CONSUMED ME   499 17

ZEAL   CONTINUED

IT WAS WRITTEN, THE ZEAL OF THINE HOUSE HATH EATEN ME   568 03

ZEALOUS

PECULIAR PEOPLE, ZEALOUS OF GOOD WORKS   098 25

ZEBAH

PRINCES LIKE AS ZEBAH AND ZALMUNNA   444 27

ZEBEDEE

THE SONS OF ZEBEDEE, WHICH WERE PARTNERS WITH SIMON   196 27
JAMES THE SON OF ZEBEDEE, AND JOHN HIS BROTHER,   227 30
IN A SHIP WITH ZEBEDEE THEIR FATHER, MENDING THEIR   227 31

ZEBEDEE'S

THE MOTHER OF ZEBEDEE'S CHILDREN WITH HER SONS,   247 06

ZEBULON

THE PRINCES OF ZEBULON, AND THE PRINCES OF NAPHTHALI   421 09

ZEEB

11 MAKE THEM AND THEIR PRINCES LIKE OREB AND ZEEB   444 26

ZION

PUT ON THY STRENGTH, O ZION   004 18
THEM THAT MOURN IN ZION, TO GIVE UNTO THEM BEAUTY FOR   107 07
BLOW THE TRUMPET IN ZION, SANCTIFY A FAST, CALL A   124 29
O ZION, THAT BRINGEST GOOD TIDINGS, GET THEE UP INTO   243 02

ZOAN

EVEN IN THE FIELD OF ZOAN   435 25
AND HIS WONDERS IN THE FIELD OF ZOAN   437 28

WORD FREQUENCY COUNT

WORD FREQUENCY COUNT

Word	Count	Word	Count
AARON	8	ADMIT	4
AARON'S	1	ADMITTED	17
ABASED	2	ADMITTING	2
ABBA	5	ADMONISH	1
ABEL	1	ADMONISHING	1
ABHOR	6	ADMONITION	1
ABHORRED	5	ADMONITIONS	2
ABHORREST	1	ADO	1
ABHORRETH	1	ADOPTION	8
ABIDE	26	ADORABLE	1
ABIDETH	7	ADORATION	1
ABIDING	7	ADORE	10
ABILITIES	1	ADORN	5
ABILITY	6	ADORNED	2
ABIRAM	1	ADULT	4
ABJECTS	1	ADULTERER	1
ABLE	37	ADULTERERS	3
ABODE	1	ADULTERY	5
ABOLISH	1	ADULTS	2
ABOMINABLE	5	ADVANCEMENT	2
ABOUND	5	ADVANTAGE	2
ABOUNDING	1	ADVENT	4
ABRAHAM	24	ADVERSARIES	9
ABRAHAM'S	1	ADVERSARY	8
ABRIDGED	1	ADVERSARY'S	1
ABROAD	18	ADVERSITIES	8
ABSENCE	5	ADVERSITY	9
ABSENT	5	ADVERTISE	1
ABSOLUTION	10	ADVICE	2
ABSOLVE	1	ADVISE	1
ABSOLVED	1	ADVISEDLY	2
ABSOLVETH	2	ADVOCATE	8
ABSTAIN	4	AFAR	8
ABSTINENCE	2	AFFECT	1
ABUNDANCE	5	AFFECTING	1
ABUNDANT	3	AFFECTION	5
ABUNDANTLY	6	AFFECTIONED	2
ACCEPT	18	AFFECTIONS	8
ACCEPTABLE	21	AFFIRMED	1
ACCEPTABLY	1	AFFIXED	1
ACCEPTANCE	1	AFFLICT	1
ACCEPTED	7	AFFLICTED	6
ACCESS	2	AFFLICTION	4
ACCIDENT	1	AFFLICTIONS	10
ACCOMMODATED	1	AFFORD	1
ACCOMPANY	3	AFFORDS	1
ACCOMPLISH	3	AFFRIGHTED	3
ACCOMPLISHED	8	AFORE	3
ACCOMPLISHING	1	AFOREHAND	1
ACCORD	7	AFORETIME	1
ACCORDING	149	AFRAID	37
ACCORDINGLY	3	AFTERWARD	4
ACCOUNT	7	AGABUS	2
ACCOUNTABLE	1	AGAR	2
ACCOUNTED	4	AGE	18
ACCURSED	2	AGED	3
ACCUSATION	2	AGES	5
ACCUSE	2	AGONY	2
ACCUSED	8	AGREE	5
ACCUSER	1	AGREEABLE	4
ACCUSTOMED	4	AGREEABLY	1
ACELDAMA	1	AGREED	2
ACKNOWLEDGE	19	AGREEMENT	1
ACKNOWLEDGED	3	AGREETH	1
ACKNOWLEDGING	3	AH	1
ACQUAINTANCE	5	AHAZ	2
ACQUAINTED	1	AID	6
ACT	1	AILETH	1
ACTING	1	AIM	1
ACTION	1	AIR	11
ACTIONS	1	AISLE	1
ACTS	10	ALABASTER	1
ACTUAL	2	ALBEIT	1
ADAM	7	ALEXANDER	2
ADD	10	ALEXANDRIA	1
ADDED	8	ALIEN	1
ADDER	2	ALIENATED	1
ADDER'S	1	ALIKE	3
ADDRESS	3	ALIVE	15
ADMINISTER	11	ALLEGED	1
ADMINISTERED	3	ALLEGORY	1
ADMINISTRATION	4	ALLELUIA	8
ADMINISTRATIONS	2	ALLOW	1

ALLOWED	6	ARABIANS	1
ALMIGHTY	189	ARBITER	1
ALMOST	5	ARCHANGEL	1
ALMS	5	ARCHANGELS	2
ALOES	1	ARCHELAUS	1
ALONE	26	ARIGHT	3
ALONG	2	ARIMATHAEA	1
ALOUD	2	ARISE	32
ALREADY	9	ARISETH	3
ALTAR	17	ARK	2
ALTARS	1	ARM	14
ALTER	1	ARMED	2
ALTERABLE	1	ARMIES	3
ALTERATIONS	9	ARMOUR	6
ALTERED	2	ARMS	9
ALTERNATELY	1	ARMY	1
ALTHOUGH	13	AROSE	14
ALTOGETHER	8	ARRANGING	1
ALWAY	38	ARRAYED	4
ALWAYS	43	ARROGANCY	2
AMALEK	1	ARROW	2
AMAZED	5	ARROWS	13
AMBASSADOR	1	ART	195
AMEN	8	ARTICLE	3
AMEND	5	ARTICLES	13
AMENDED	2	ASCEND	4
AMENDMENT	3	ASCENDED	19
AMENDMENTS	3	ASCENDETH	1
AMENDS	2	ASCENDING	1
AMERICA	2	ASCENSION	7
AMERICAN	1	ASCRIBE	8
AMIABLE	1	ASER	1
AMIDST	1	ASH	1
AMISS	6	ASHAMED	18
AMMON	1	ASHES	6
AMONGST	6	ASIA	2
AMORITES	2	ASIDE	9
ANABAPTISTS	1	ASK	58
ANANIAS	5	ASKED	24
ANCIENT	2	ASKETH	3
ANDREW	4	ASKING	3
ANEW	1	ASLEEP	6
ANGEL	26	ASS	8
ANGELS	43	ASSAULT	1
ANGELS'	1	ASSAULTS	2
ANGER	12	ASSEMBLE	5
ANGERED	2	ASSEMBLED	11
ANGRY	11	ASSEMBLING	1
ANGUISH	1	ASSEMBLY	2
ANIMA	1	ASSES	1
ANNA	1	ASSIST	6
ANNUNCIATION	2	ASSISTANCE	4
ANOINT	6	ASSISTANCES	1
ANOINTED	20	ASSUAGE	1
ANOINTING	5	ASSURANCE	2
ANOTHER	105	ASSURE	6
ANOTHER'S	1	ASSURED	1
ANSWER	26	ASSYRIA	1
ANSWERED	58	ASTONISHED	7
ANSWEREST	2	ASTRAY	5
ANSWERETH	1	ASUNDER	5
ANSWERING	11	ATE	1
ANSWERS	3	ATHIRST	2
ANTHEM	5	ATTAIN	7
ANTIOCH	7	ATTAINMENT	1
ANTIPHON	2	ATTEND	1
ANXIETIES	1	ATTENDED	1
ANXIOUS	11	ATTENDING	1
ANY	219	ATTENTION	1
ANYWHERE	1	AUDIBLY	1
APACE	1	AUGUSTINE	1
APART	4	AUGUSTUS	1
APIECE	1	AUTHOR	9
APOSTLE	14	AUTHORITIES	2
APOSTLES	34	AUTHORITY	41
APOSTLES'	11	AUTHORIZE	1
APOSTLESHIP	1	AUTHORIZED	1
APOSTOLIC	7	AUTHORS	1
APPAREL	6	AVAIL	1
APPARELLED	1	AVAILETH	1
APPARENT	1	AVENGE	6
APPEAR	18	AVENGED	3
APPEARED	13	AVENGER	3
APPEARETH	4	AVOID	1
APPEARING	2	AWAKE	14
APPEASE	1	AWAKED	1
APPERTAINETH	3	AWAKEN	1
APPERTAINING	3	AWAKETH	1
APPLE	1	AWAY	157
APPLIED	2	AWE	6
APPLY	8	AXES	1
APPOINT	5	BAAL-PEOR	1
APPOINTED	70	BABE	2
APPOINTING	1	BABES	6
APPOINTMENT	1	BABYLON	3
APPREHENDED	1	BACK	21
APPRENTICES	1	BACKS	4
APPROACH	2	BACKWARD	4
APPROACHING	1	BAD	1
APPROPRIATE	2	BADE	3
APPROVE	2	BADGES	1
APPROVED	3	BALMS	1
APPROVETH	1	BAND	2
APPROVING	1	BANDS	2
APT	3	BANISH	2
ARABIA	3	BANISHED	1

BANNER	1	BESEECH	165
BANNERS	1	BESEECHING	15
BANNS	4	BESET	2
BANQUET	1	BESIDE	7
BAPTISM	46	BESIDES	2
BAPTIST	2	BESIEGED	1
BAPTIZE	9	BESOUGHT	4
BAPTIZED	48	BEST	4
BAPTIZEST	1	BESTOW	5
BAPTIZING	3	BESTOWED	5
BAR-JONA	1	BETHABARA	1
BARABBAS	9	BETHANY	2
BARACHIAS	1	BETHLEHEM	7
BARE	13	BETHPHAGE	1
BAREST	1	BETIDE	2
BARLEY	4	BETIMES	3
BARN	1	BETRAY	7
BARNABAS	6	BETRAYED	9
BARNS	3	BETRAYEST	1
BARREN	6	BETRAYETH	3
BARS	3	BETTER	19
BARSABAS	1	BETTERS	1
BARTHOLOMEW	1	BETWEEN	15
BASHAN	6	BETWIXT	5
BASIN	1	BEWAIL	2
BASKETS	3	BEWAILED	1
BASON	1	BEWARE	3
BATTLE	11	BEYOND	3
BAY-TREE	1	BIBLE	3
BEAM	3	BID	4
BEAMS	2	BIDDEN	11
BEAR	35	BIDDING	2
BEARD	2	BIER	1
BEAREST	3	BIND	10
BEARETH	8	BINDETH	1
BEARING	4	BIRD	2
BEAST	6	BIRDS	3
BEASTS	14	BIRTH	4
BEAT	2	BISHOP	106
BEATEN	1	BISHOPRICK	1
BEATETH	1	BISHOPS	22
BEAUTIFIED	1	BIT	1
BEAUTIFUL	2	BITTER	2
BEAUTY	16	BITTERLY	1
BECAME	10	BITTERNESS	2
BECKONED	1	BLADE	1
BECOME	28	BLAMED	1
BECOMES	1	BLAMELESS	4
BECOMETH	4	BLASPHEME	3
BED	10	BLASPHEMED	3
BED-RIDDEN	1	BLASPHEMER	2
BED-TIME	1	BLASPHEMERS	1
BEDS	2	BLASPHEMETH	2
BEELZEBUB	3	BLASPHEMING	1
BEES	1	BLASPHEMOUS	1
BEFALL	1	BLASPHEMOUSLY	1
BEFELL	1	BLASPHEMY	4
BEFRIEND	1	BLAST	1
BEG	7	BLASTING	1
BEGAN	26	BLEMISH	1
BEGAT	2	BLESS	100
BEGGAR	2	BLESSED	163
BEGGED	1	BLESSEDNESS	1
BEGGING	2	BLESSEST	2
BEGIN	12	BLESSETH	1
BEGINNETH	1	BLESSING	52
BEGINNING	43	BLESSINGS	10
BEGOTTEN	11	BLEST	2
BEGUN	7	BLIND	8
BEHALF	10	BLINDED	4
BEHAVE	5	BLINDFOLDED	1
BEHAVED	1	BLINDNESS	3
BEHAVIOUR	1	BLISS	1
BEHELD	5	BLOOD	95
BEHIND	7	BLOOD-GUILTINESS	2
BEHOLD	153	BLOOD-SHEDDING	1
BEHOLDEST	4	BLOOD-THIRSTY	5
BEHOLDETH	4	BLOODY	1
BEHOLDING	5	BLOW	3
BEHOVED	1	BLOWETH	4
BEING	143	BOAR	1
BELIEF	3	BOAST	8
BELIEVE	90	BOASTEST	1
BELIEVED	29	BOASTING	1
BELIEVERS	2	BODIES	24
BELIEVEST	1	BODILY	5
BELIEVETH	24	BODY	133
BELIEVING	3	BOLD	6
BELLIES	1	BOLDLY	4
BELLY	3	BOLDNESS	5
BELONG	3	BOND	9
BELONGED	1	BOND-SERVANT	1
BELONGETH	6	BONDAGE	8
BELONGING	2	BONDMAID	1
BELOVED	36	BONDS	6
BEND	2	BONDWOMAN	4
BENEATH	6	BONE	1
BENEDIC	1	BONES	20
BENEDICTION	12	BONUM	1
BENEDICTUS	2	BOOK	28
BENEFACTORS	2	BOOKS	8
BENEFIT	8	BORDERS	4
BENEFITS	23	BORN	56
BENJAMIN	2	BORNE	3
BENT	2	BORROWETH	1
BEQUESTS	1	BOSOM	10

BOTH	96	CALF	7
BOTTLE	2	CALL	87
BOTTOM	4	CALLED	140
BOUGHS	2	CALLEDST	1
BOUGHT	9	CALLETH	10
BOUND	19	CALLING	13
BOUNDEN	9	CALLINGS	3
BOUNDS	1	CALVARY	1
BOUNTEOUS	1	CALVES	2
BOUNTIFUL	3	CAME	175
BOUNTY	4	CAMEL'S	1
BOW	22	CAMEST	3
BOWED	3	CANA	3
BOWELS	4	CANAAN	4
BOWING	1	CANDID	1
BOWS	1	CANDLE	2
BOX	2	CANON	3
BOZRAH	1	CANONICAL	2
BRAKE	13	CANONICALLY	1
BRAKEST	1	CANONS	8
BRANCH	7	CANST	9
BRANCHES	4	CANTATE	1
BRASS	2	CANTICLE	3
BRAWLER	1	CANTICLES	3
BRAWN	1	CAPERNAUM	2
BREAD	64	CAPPADOCIA	1
BREADTH	1	CAPTAINS	3
BREAK	19	CAPTIVE	5
BREAKETH	5	CAPTIVES	4
BREAKING	3	CAPTIVITY	12
BREAST	2	CARCASE	1
BREASTPLATE	1	CARE	24
BREASTS	3	CARED	1
BREATH	10	CAREFUL	1
BREATHED	2	CAREFULNESS	1
BREATHING	1	CARES	3
BRETHREN	59	CAREST	3
BRIDE	3	CARETH	7
BRIDEGROOM	3	CARNAL	4
BRIDLE	2	CARNALLY	1
BRIDLETH	2	CARPUS	1
BRIEF	2	CARRIED	15
BRIEFLY	1	CARRY	6
BRIGHT	1	CARRYING	1
BRIGHTNESS	3	CARVED	2
BRIM	1	CASE	13
BRIMSTONE	1	CASES	1
BRING	95	CASSIA	1
BRINGEST	6	CAST	98
BRINGETH	15	CASTAWAY	1
BRINGING	3	CASTEST	1
BROAD	2	CASTETH	4
BROILED	1	CASTING	6
BROKEN	33	CASTLE	3
BROKENHEARTED	2	CATCH	2
BROOK	2	CATCHETH	2
BROTHER	36	CATECHISM	4
BROTHER'S	2	CATERPILLAR	1
BROTHERHOOD	1	CATERPILLARS	1
BROTHERLY	3	CATHOLIC	12
BROUGHT	87	CATTLE	11
BROUGHTEST	4	CAUGHT	1
BRUISE	1	CAUSE	52
BRUISED	1	CAUSED	8
BUCKLER	3	CAUSES	1
BUFFET	1	CAVIL	1
BUFFETED	1	CEASE	10
BUILD	12	CEASED	6
BUILDED	1	CEASING	2
BUILDERS	1	CEDAR	1
BUILDEST	2	CEDAR-TREES	2
BUILDING	2	CEDARS	3
BUILT	7	CELEBRATE	5
BULL	1	CELEBRATED	3
BULLOCK	2	CELEBRATING	1
BULLOCKS	2	CELEBRATION	2
BULLS	3	CELESTIAL	4
BULLS'	1	CENTRE	1
BULWARKS	1	CENTURION	6
BUNDLES	1	CEPHAS	1
BURDEN	8	CEREMONIES	7
BURDENSOME	1	CEREMONY	1
BURIAL	2	CERTAIN	40
BURIED	15	CERTAINLY	1
BURN	9	CERTIFIED	2
BURNED	3	CERTIFIETH	1
BURNETH	2	CERTIFY	1
BURNING	6	CHAFF	1
BURNT	4	CHAIN	1
BURNT-OFFERING	1	CHAINS	4
BURNT-OFFERINGS	7	CHAIR	7
BURNT-SACRIFICE	1	CHAMBER	3
BURNT-SACRIFICES	1	CHAMBERING	1
BURST	2	CHAMBERS	3
BURY	2	CHANCE	2
BURYING	1	CHANCEL	2
BUSINESS	5	CHANCES	1
BUSY	2	CHANGE	5
BUTTER	2	CHANGED	8
BUY	3	CHANGERS	1
BY-WORD	1	CHANGERS'	1
CAESAR	8	CHANGES	4
CAESAR'S	3	CHAPEL	2
CAESAREA	1	CHAPTER	13
CALAMITIES	1	CHARGE	20
CALENDAR	3	CHARGED	3

CHARIOT	2	CLOVEN	1
CHARIOTS	3	COALS	6
CHARITABLE	2	COASTS	7
CHARITY	27	COAT	2
CHARM	1	COCK	7
CHARMER	1	COCK-CROWING	1
CHARTERS	1	COLD	2
CHASTEN	5	COLDNESS	1
CHASTENED	4	COLLECT	40
CHASTENEST	1	COLLECTS	3
CHASTENETH	1	COLLEGES	2
CHASTENING	1	COLOURS	1
CHASTISE	3	COLT	3
CHASTITY	3	COME	352
CHEEK-BONE	1	COMERS	1
CHEEKS	1	COMES	1
CHEER	5	COMEST	3
CHEERFUL	3	COMETH	78
CHEERFULLY	1	COMFORT	65
CHEERFULNESS	4	COMFORTABLE	6
CHERISH	3	COMFORTABLY	1
CHERISHETH	1	COMFORTED	7
CHERUBIM	5	COMFORTER	11
CHICKENS	1	COMFORTLESS	3
CHIDING	2	COMFORTS	4
CHIEF	49	COMING	41
CHIEFEST	1	COMMAND	9
CHIEFLY	8	COMMANDED	34
CHILD	76	COMMANDEDST	1
CHILD-BED	1	COMMANDEST	3
CHILD-BIRTH	4	COMMANDMENT	26
CHILD'S	2	COMMANDMENTS	98
CHILDISH	1	COMMEND	12
CHILDREN	151	COMMENDED	2
CHILDREN'S	3	COMMENDING	3
CHOICE	3	COMMISSION	3
CHOICES	1	COMMIT	11
CHOIR	1	COMMITTAL	1
CHOKED	2	COMMITTED	26
CHOOSE	5	COMMITTETH	3
CHOOSEST	1	COMMON	15
CHOOSING	1	COMMONLY	7
CHOSE	6	COMMONWEALTH	1
CHOSEN	32	COMMUNE	4
CHRIST	657	COMMUNED	2
CHRIST'S	37	COMMUNICANTS	1
CHRISTENED	1	COMMUNICATE	5
CHRISTIAN	26	COMMUNICATED	2
CHRISTIANITY	1	COMMUNICATION	1
CHRISTIANS	7	COMMUNICATIONS	1
CHRISTMAS	7	COMMUNING	1
CHRISTS	1	COMMUNION	70
CHURCH	237	COMMUNION-TIME	1
CHURCH-WARDENS	3	COMPACTED	1
CHURCHES	7	COMPANIED	1
CIRCUMCISE	1	COMPANION	2
CIRCUMCISED	4	COMPANIONS'	1
CIRCUMCISING	1	COMPANY	20
CIRCUMCISION	5	COMPARED	5
CIRCUMSPECTLY	1	COMPARISON	3
CIRCUMSTANCES	3	COMPASS	8
CITIES	4	COMPASSED	10
CITIZEN	1	COMPASSETH	1
CITIZENSHIP	1	COMPASSION	20
CITY	57	COMPASSION'S	1
CIVIL	10	COMPASSIONATE	1
CLAIM	1	COMPASSIONS	1
CLAIMED	1	COMPEL	2
CLAMOUR	1	COMPELLED	1
CLAP	3	COMPETENT	2
CLAUDIUS	2	COMPILING	1
CLAUSE	2	COMPLAIN	2
CLAUSES	1	COMPLAINED	1
CLAVE	2	COMPLAINING	2
CLAY	2	COMPLAINT	9
CLEAN	28	COMPLAINTS	1
CLEANNESS	2	COMPLYING	1
CLEANSE	10	COMPREHEND	1
CLEANSED	6	COMPREHENDED	2
CLEANSETH	1	CONCEITS	1
CLEAR	7	CONCEIVE	2
CLEARER	1	CONCEIVED	10
CLEAREST	1	CONCEIVETH	1
CLEARING	1	CONCERN	1
CLEARLY	4	CONCERNED	1
CLEARNESS	1	CONCERNING	25
CLEAVE	7	CONCLUDED	3
CLEAVETH	4	CONCLUDING	3
CLEOPAS	1	CONCLUSION	1
CLEOPHAS	1	CONCORD	4
CLERGY	11	CONCUPISCENCE	2
CLIMB	2	CONDEMN	7
CLIMBETH	2	CONDEMNATION	9
CLOAK	4	CONDEMNED	10
CLOKE	3	CONDEMNETH	1
CLOSE	3	CONDEMNING	1
CLOSED	1	CONDESCEND	1
CLOSET	1	CONDITION	1
CLOTH	5	CONDITIONS	3
CLOTHE	5	CONDUCT	3
CLOTHED	19	CONFEDERATE	1
CLOTHES	9	CONFER	1
CLOTHING	4	CONFESS	31
CLOUD	12	CONFESSED	2
CLOUDS	27	CONFESSING	1
CLOUDY	1	CONFESSION	10

CONFIDE	1
CONFIDENCE	14
CONFIDENT	1
CONFIDENTLY	1
CONFIRM	8
CONFIRMATION	6
CONFIRMED	14
CONFIRMING	1
CONFITERI	1
CONFORM	1
CONFORMABLE	1
CONFORMED	2
CONFORMITY	2
CONFOUND	1
CONFOUNDED	22
CONFUSION	14
CONGREGATION	55
CONGREGATIONS	6
CONGRESS	1
CONGRUITY	1
CONIES	1
CONNECTION	1
CONQUERORS	1
CONSCIENCE	17
CONSCIENCES	3
CONSECRATE	2
CONSECRATED	11
CONSECRATION	9
CONSENT	3
CONSENTED	1
CONSENTEDST	1
CONSEQUENCE	1
CONSIDER	34
CONSIDERATION	2
CONSIDERATIONS	2
CONSIDERED	9
CONSIDERETH	2
CONSIDERING	2
CONSISTENTLY	1
CONSOLATION	6
CONSPIRACY	1
CONSPIRE	1
CONSTANCY	2
CONSTANT	3
CONSTANTLY	4
CONSTITUTED	2
CONSTITUTION	2
CONSTRAIN	1
CONSTRAINED	2
CONSTRUCTION	1
CONSULTATION	1
CONSULTATIONS	1
CONSUME	17
CONSUMED	9
CONSUMETH	1
CONSUMING	2
CONSUMMATION	1
CONTAIN	8
CONTAINED	5
CONTAINETH	1
CONTAINING	1
CONTEMPT	2
CONTEND	2
CONTENT	3
CONTENTED	1
CONTINUAL	17
CONTINUALLY	15
CONTINUANCE	1
CONTINUE	25
CONTINUED	8
CONTINUES	1
CONTINUEST	1
CONTINUETH	3
CONTINUING	3
CONTRACT	1
CONTRACTED	1
CONTRADICTING	1
CONTRARIWISE	1
CONTRARY	10
CONTRITE	8
CONTRITION	2
CONTROVERSIES	1
CONVENIENCES	1
CONVENIENT	16
CONVENIENTLY	5
CONVENTION	4
CONVERSATION	6
CONVERSATIONS	1
CONVERSION	1
CONVERT	2
CONVERTED	6
CONVERTING	1
CONVEYED	1
CONVINCE	1
CONVINCETH	1
COOL	1
COPPERSMITH	1
CORDS	4
CORINTHIANS	1
CORN	4
CORNER	1
CORNER-STONE	4
CORNERS	4
CORRECT	1
CORRECTED	1
CORRECTION	1

CORRUPT	15
CORRUPTIBLE	5
CORRUPTION	10
COST	1
COUCH	1
COUCHES	1
COULDEST	2
COUNCIL	9
COUNSEL	22
COUNSELLORS	1
COUNSELS	5
COUNT	2
COUNTED	9
COUNTENANCE	30
COUNTRIES	4
COUNTRY	11
COUNTRY'S	1
COUNTRYMEN	1
COURAGE	4
COURSE	10
COURT	1
COURTEOUS	1
COURTS	11
COUSIN	1
COUSINS	1
COVENANT	31
COVENANTED	1
COVENANTS	1
COVER	7
COVERED	12
COVEREDST	1
COVERETH	3
COVERING	3
COVERT	1
COVET	9
COVETED	1
COVETOUS	6
COVETOUSNESS	2
CRAFT	2
CRAFTILY	1
CRAFTINESS	2
CRAFTS	1
CRAFTY	1
CREATE	1
CREATED	7
CREATION	4
CREATOR	10
CREATURE	7
CREATURES	9
CREDENCE	1
CREED	23
CREEDS	2
CREEPING	2
CRESCENS	1
CRETES	1
CREW	3
CRIED	34
CRIETH	5
CRIME	10
CROOKED	1
CROSS	31
CROW	4
CROWN	16
CROWNEST	1
CROWNETH	4
CROWNS	2
CRUCIFIED	32
CRUCIFY	14
CRUEL	3
CRUELLY	1
CRUELTY	1
CRUMBS	3
CRY	36
CRYING	10
CRYSTAL	1
CUBIT	2
CUNNING	2
CUNNINGLY	1
CUP	24
CURE	5
CURES	1
CURIOUS	1
CURSE	6
CURSED	2
CURSING	4
CURTAIN	1
CUSTOM	8
CUT	11
CUTTEST	1
CUTTING	1
CYMBAL	1
CYMBALS	2
CYRENE	2
CYRENIAN	2
CYRENIUS	1
DAILY	39
DALMATIA	1
DAMASCUS	6
DAMNATION	4
DAMSELS	1
DANCE	1
DANCES	1
DANCETH	1
DANCING	1
DANGER	10
DANGEROUS	3

DANGERS	15	DEMANDS	1
DARE	1	DEMAS	1
DARK	7	DEN	4
DARKENED	3	DENIED	7
DARKLY	1	DENOMINATIONS	1
DARKNESS	48	DENS	2
DARLING	2	DENUNCIATION	1
DARTS	1	DENY	7
DASH	1	DENYING	1
DATHAN	1	DEPART	17
DAUGHTER	15	DEPARTED	26
DAUGHTERS	7	DEPARTETH	1
DAVID	34	DEPARTING	3
DAVID'S	1	DEPARTURE	1
DAY	248	DEPOSED	1
DAY-SPRING	1	DEPTH	5
DAY-TIME	3	DEPTHS	4
DAY'S	1	DERIDED	1
DAYS	132	DERISION	5
DAYSPRING	1	DESCEND	3
DEACON	14	DESCENDED	10
DEACONS	24	DESCENDING	1
DEAD	92	DESCRIBED	2
DEADLY	2	DESERT	7
DEAF	5	DESERTS	1
DEAL	8	DESERVE	5
DEALING	5	DESERVED	2
DEALINGS	4	DESERVETH	1
DEALT	9	DESERVING	1
DEAR	16	DESERVINGS	1
DEARER	1	DESIGNATED	1
DEARLY	20	DESIGNS	1
DEARTH	7	DESIRE	60
DEATH	134	DESIRED	19
DEATH'S	1	DESIREDST	1
DEATHS	2	DESIRES	19
DEBT	3	DESIREST	6
DEBTORS	1	DESIRETH	9
DECALOGUE	2	DESIRING	3
DECAPOLIS	1	DESIROUS	4
DECAY	1	DESOLATE	9
DECAYED	1	DESOLATION	1
DECAYETH	1	DESPAIR	1
DECEASE	2	DESPERATION	2
DECEIT	7	DESPISE	10
DECEITFUL	12	DESPISED	4
DECEITFULLY	1	DESPISERS	1
DECEITS	2	DESPISEST	1
DECEIVE	9	DESPISETH	4
DECEIVED	1	DESPISING	1
DECEIVER	1	DESPITEFULLY	2
DECEIVERS	1	DESPITEFULNESS	1
DECEIVETH	3	DESTITUTE	5
DECEIVING	2	DESTROY	31
DECENCY	2	DESTROYED	26
DECENT	1	DESTROYER	2
DECENTLY	3	DESTROYEST	3
DECK	1	DESTROYETH	1
DECKED	1	DESTRUCTION	15
DECKEST	1	DESTRUCTIONS	1
DECLARATION	1	DETERMINED	9
DECLARE	28	DEUS	2
DECLARED	18	DEVICE	2
DECLARES	2	DEVICES	3
DECLAREST	2	DEVIL	37
DECLARING	3	DEVILS	6
DECREASE	1	DEVISED	1
DECREE	5	DEVOTE	3
DECREED	1	DEVOTION	6
DEDICATE	2	DEVOTIONS	2
DEDICATED	2	DEVOUR	7
DEDICATING	1	DEVOURED	6
DEDICATION	2	DEVOUT	6
DEED	13	DEVOUTLY	8
DEEDS	8	DEW	7
DEEMED	1	DEWS	1
DEEP	28	DIDST	41
DEEPLY	2	DIDYMUS	1
DEEPS	1	DIE	33
DEFENCE	24	DIED	15
DEFEND	32	DIETH	3
DEFENDED	6	DIFFERENCE	4
DEFENDER	8	DIFFERENCES	2
DEFENDEST	1	DIFFERENT	5
DEFENDETH	2	DIFFERETH	2
DEFENSIBLE	1	DIFFERING	1
DEFER	1	DIFFICULT	1
DEFIETH	1	DIFFICULTIES	1
DEFILED	4	DIFFICULTY	1
DEFILEMENTS	1	DIGEST	1
DEFRAUD	1	DIGGED	4
DEGREE	3	DIGNITY	4
DELAY	3	DILIGENCE	10
DELIGHT	28	DILIGENT	8
DELIGHTEST	2	DILIGENTLY	16
DELIGHTETH	2	DIMINISHED	1
DELIVER	94	DIMITTIS	2
DELIVERANCE	5	DINNER	1
DELIVERED	66	DIOCESAN	3
DELIVERER	2	DIOCESE	4
DELIVEREST	1	DIP	3
DELIVERETH	8	DIPPED	1
DELIVERING	1	DIPPETH	1
DELIVERY	1	DIRECT	16
DEMAND	3	DIRECTION	4
DEMANDED	1	DIRECTIONS	2

DISALLOWED	1
DISANNUL	1
DISAPPOINT	1
DISAPPOINTED	2
DISAPPOINTETH	1
DISCERN	1
DISCERNED	2
DISCERNING	2
DISCIPLE	13
DISCIPLES	76
DISCIPLES'	1
DISCIPLINE	13
DISCLOSED	1
DISCOMFIT	1
DISCOMFITED	1
DISCOMFORT	1
DISCORD	1
DISCOURAGED	2
DISCOVERED	1
DISCREETLY	2
DISCRETION	21
DISDAINFULLY	2
DISEASE	2
DISEASED	2
DISEASES	1
DISFIGURE	1
DISH	1
DISHONESTY	1
DISHONOUR	9
DISOBEDIENCE	1
DISOBEDIENT	4
DISPENSATION	1
DISPENSER	2
DISPENSING	1
DISPERSED	3
DISPLEASED	8
DISPLEASURE	22
DISPOSAL	1
DISPOSE	2
DISPOSED	3
DISPOSITION	1
DISQUIETED	6
DISQUIETETH	2
DISQUIETNESS	1
DISQUIETUDE	1
DISSEMBLE	3
DISSEMBLED	1
DISSEMBLERS	1
DISSIMULATION	1
DISSOLUTION	2
DISTINCTLY	2
DISTRESS	7
DISTRESSED	5
DISTRESSES	1
DISTRIBUTE	1
DISTRIBUTED	2
DISTRIBUTING	1
DISTRIBUTION	2
DITCH	1
DIVERS	15
DIVERSITIES	4
DIVERSITY	1
DIVIDE	5
DIVIDED	11
DIVIDEST	1
DIVIDETH	3
DIVIDING	3
DIVINE	17
DIVISIONS	1
DOCTORS	3
DOCTRINE	42
DOCTRINES	1
DOER	6
DOERS	12
DOES	2
DOEST	6
DOETH	26
DOG	3
DOGS	5
DOINGS	10
DOMINE	1
DOMINION	16
DOMINO	1
DONATION	1
DOOR	15
DOOR-KEEPER	1
DOORS	8
DOST	49
DOTH	69
DOUBLE	2
DOUBLE-MINDED	1
DOUBLETONGUED	1
DOUBT	7
DOUBTFUL	1
DOUBTFULNESS	1
DOUBTLESS	3
DOUBTS	1
DOVE	3
DOVES	4
DOWN-SITTING	1
DOWNFALL	1
DRAGON	5
DRAGONS	3
DRANK	2
DRAUGHT	2
DRAVE	1

DRAW	12
DRAWETH	3
DRAWING	3
DRAWN	4
DREAD	4
DREADFUL	1
DREAM	8
DREGS	1
DREW	10
DRIED	5
DRIEDST	1
DRIETH	1
DRINK	49
DRINK-OFFERING	1
DRINK-OFFERINGS	1
DRINKING	1
DRIVE	7
DRIVEN	8
DRIVEST	1
DROP	4
DROPPED	1
DROPS	3
DROPSY	1
DROSS	1
DROUGHT	1
DROVE	1
DROWN	1
DROWNED	2
DRUNK	3
DRUNKARDS	1
DRUNKEN	1
DRUNKENNESS	2
DRY	9
DUE	24
DUES	1
DULNESS	2
DULY	16
DUMB	6
DUNG	1
DURING	2
DURST	2
DUST	17
DUTIES	4
DUTIFUL	1
DUTY	30
DWELL	70
DWELLERS	3
DWELLEST	2
DWELLETH	17
DWELLING	15
DWELLING-PLACE	3
DWELLING-PLACES	1
DWELLINGS	6
DWELLS	1
DWELT	11
DYED	1
DYING	3
EACH	10
EAGLE	2
EAGLES	1
EAR	20
EARLIEST	1
EARLY	16
EARN	1
EARNEST	3
EARNESTLY	14
EARS	25
EARTH	244
EARTHLY	4
EARTHQUAKE	2
EARTHY	4
EASE	1
EASED	1
EASIER	1
EASILY	3
EASINESS	1
EAST	9
EAST-WIND	2
EASTER	6
EASY	2
EAT	61
EATEN	10
EATETH	4
EATING	3
ECCLESIASTICAL	2
EDGE	2
EDIFICATION	4
EDIFYING	16
EDOM	6
EDOMITES	1
EDUCATION	1
EDWARD	2
EFFECT	5
EFFECTUAL	4
EFFECTUALLY	3
EFFORTS	1
EFFUSION	1
EGG	2
EGYPT	25
EIGHT	4
EIGHTEENTH	2
EIGHTH	2
EITHER	21
ELAMITES	1
ELDER	1
ELDERS	20

ELECT	5	ERROR	7
ELECTED	5	ERRORS	1
ELECTION	2	ES	1
ELEMENTS	2	ESAIAS	5
ELEVEN	2	ESCAPE	5
ELEVENTH	2	ESCAPED	1
ELI	2	ESCHEW	2
ELIAS	9	ESCHEWED	1
ELISABETH	1	ESPECIAL	1
ELISABETH'S	1	ESPECIALLY	19
ELOI	2	ESPOUSED	3
ELSE	20	ESSENTIAL	3
ELSEWHERE	2	EST	1
EMBRACE	3	ESTABLISH	7
EMBRACETH	1	ESTABLISHED	4
EMERALD	1	ESTATE	11
EMMANUEL	1	ESTATES	1
EMMAUS	1	ESTEEM	2
EMPLOY	2	ESTEEMED	1
EMPLOYERS	1	ESTIMATION	1
EMPTY	3	ETERNAL	60
EMULATIONS	1	ETERNALLY	1
ENABLE	3	ETERNITY	2
ENABLED	3	ETHIOPIA	1
ENCOMPASS	1	EUCHARIST	1
ENCOURAGE	2	EVANGELIST	5
ENCOURAGED	1	EVANGELISTS	4
ENCOURAGEMENT	1	EVEN	253
END	142	EVENING	28
ENDEAVOUR	8	EVER	287
ENDEAVOURING	1	EVERLASTING	115
ENDEAVOURS	2	EVERLASTINGLY	1
ENDED	9	EVERLIVING	8
ENDETH	4	EVERMORE	64
ENDING	3	EVERY	199
ENDLESS	4	EVERYWHERE	2
ENDOR	1	EVIDENCE	2
ENDOW	2	EVIDENT	1
ENDOWMENT	1	EVIDENTLY	1
ENDOWMENTS	1	EVIL	119
ENDS	13	EVILDOERS	2
ENDUE	12	EVILS	2
ENDUED	3	EWES	1
ENDUEDST	2	EXALT	8
ENDURANCE	1	EXALTED	29
ENDURE	17	EXALTETH	2
ENDURED	2	EXAMINATION	4
ENDURETH	55	EXAMINE	11
ENEMIES	105	EXAMINED	8
ENEMY	40	EXAMPLE	18
ENEMY'S	1	EXAMPLES	10
ENFORCE	1	EXCEED	3
ENGENDERED	1	EXCEEDING	12
ENGLAND	4	EXCEEDINGLY	5
ENGRAFTED	2	EXCEL	4
ENGRAVEN	1	EXCELLENCY	3
ENJOINED	1	EXCELLENT	16
ENJOY	5	EXCELSIS	2
ENJOYED	1	EXCEPT	34
ENKINDLE	2	EXCEPTED	1
ENKINDLED	1	EXCESS	1
ENLARGED	3	EXCITING	1
ENLIGHTEN	3	EXCOMMUNICATED	1
ENLIGHTENED	1	EXCUSE	2
ENMITY	1	EXCUSED	3
ENOUGH	6	EXCUSES	2
ENQUIRE	3	EXECUTE	16
ENQUIRED	3	EXECUTED	1
ENRICHED	1	EXECUTETH	1
ENSAMPLE	2	EXECUTING	1
ENSAMPLES	1	EXERCISE	14
ENSUE	3	EXERCISED	1
ENSUING	2	EXERCISING	1
ENTANGLE	1	EXHORT	7
ENTER	33	EXHORTATION	10
ENTERED	15	EXHORTATIONS	1
ENTERETH	6	EXHORTED	2
ENTERING	1	EXHORTETH	2
ENTIRE	2	EXHORTING	2
ENTRANCE	4	EXIGENCY	2
ENTREAT	1	EXODUS	1
ENTREATED	3	EXPECTATION	3
ENTRUST	3	EXPECTING	1
ENUMERATE	1	EXPEDIENCY	1
ENVIES	1	EXPEDIENT	12
ENVIETH	1	EXPERT	1
ENVIOUS	1	EXPLICATION	1
ENVY	6	EXPOSED	1
ENVYING	1	EXPOUND	2
ENVYINGS	1	EXPOUNDED	1
EPAPHRAS	1	EXPRESS	5
EPHESIANS	1	EXPRESSED	1
EPHESUS	2	EXPRESSION	1
EPHPHATHA	1	EXPRESSLY	1
EPHRAIM	5	EXSURGAT	1
EPHRATAH	1	EXTEND	1
EPIPHANY	6	EXTENDETH	1
EPISCOPAL	7	EXTINCT	1
EPISTLE	22	EXTORTIONER	1
EQUAL	4	EXTORTIONERS	1
EQUITY	6	EXTREME	5
ERE	1	EXTREMITY	1
ERECTED	1	EYE	21
ERR	4	EYELIDS	2
ERRED	5	EYES	75
ERRONEOUS	2	EYESIGHT	1

EYEWITNESSES	1	FEW	10
FABLES	2	FEWER	1
FACE	79	FIE	4
FACES	4	FIELD	25
FACULTIES	2	FIELDS	2
FADE	3	FIERCE	1
FADETH	3	FIERCENESS	2
FAIL	11	FIERY	2
FAILED	4	FIFTEENTH	1
FAILEST	1	FIFTH	1
FAILETH	6	FIFTY	1
FAILING	1	FIG	1
FAILINGS	1	FIG-TREES	1
FAIN	2	FIGHT	8
FAINT	6	FIGHTING	1
FAINTED	4	FIGS	1
FAIR	7	FIGURE	1
FAIRER	1	FIGURES	2
FAIRLY	1	FILL	18
FAIRNESS	1	FILLED	45
FAITH	133	FILLEST	3
FAITHFUL	53	FILLETH	5
FAITHFULLY	27	FILTH	1
FAITHFULNESS	8	FILTHINESS	3
FAITHLESS	3	FILTHY	2
FALL	54	FINAL	4
FALLEN	14	FINALLY	13
FALLETH	4	FIND	27
FALLING	6	FINDETH	5
FALSE	20	FINDING	2
FALSEHOOD	5	FINE	2
FALSELY	3	FINEST	1
FAME	1	FINGER	8
FAMILIAR	2	FINGERS	3
FAMILIES	3	FINISH	1
FAMILY	9	FINISHED	3
FAMINE	3	FINISHER	2
FAR	34	FIR-TREES	1
FARED	1	FIRE	51
FARM	2	FIREBRAND	1
FARTHEST	1	FIRKINS	1
FARTHING	1	FIRM	1
FASHION	7	FIRMAMENT	4
FASHIONED	3	FIRST	86
FASHIONETH	1	FIRST-BEGOTTEN	1
FAST	29	FIRSTBORN	7
FASTED	1	FIRSTFRUITS	8
FASTENED	1	FISH	6
FASTEST	1	FISHERMEN	1
FASTING	10	FISHERS	2
FASTINGS	3	FISHES	9
FAT	7	FIT	7
FATHER	387	FITLY	2
FATHER'S	12	FITTED	1
FATHERLESS	12	FITTING	3
FATHERLY	7	FIVE	11
FATHERS	31	FIXED	5
FATLINGS	1	FLAME	5
FATNESS	4	FLAMES	2
FATTED	3	FLAMING	3
FAULT	9	FLATTER	1
FAULTS	8	FLATTERERS	1
FAVOUR	20	FLATTERETH	1
FAVOURABLE	6	FLED	4
FAVOURABLY	4	FLEDDEST	1
FAVOURED	1	FLEE	13
FAVOUREST	1	FLEETH	7
FEAR	112	FLESH	86
FEARED	10	FLESHLY	1
FEARETH	9	FLIES	2
FEARFUL	2	FLIETH	1
FEARFULLY	1	FLIGHT	3
FEARFULNESS	1	FLINT	1
FEARLESSLY	1	FLINT-STONE	1
FEARS	1	FLOCK	26
FEAST	25	FLOCKS	1
FEAST-DAY	1	FLOOD	1
FEASTS	1	FLOODS	11
FEATHERED	1	FLOUR	2
FEATHERS	2	FLOURISH	11
FED	5	FLOURISHETH	1
FEEBLE	4	FLOURISHING	1
FEED	24	FLOW	1
FEEDEST	1	FLOWED	2
FEEDETH	5	FLOWER	7
FEEL	4	FLY	2
FEELING	1	FLYING	3
FEET	46	FOAL	1
FEIGN	2	FODDER	2
FEIGNED	2	FOE	2
FELICITY	5	FOES	5
FELL	30	FOLD	7
FELLOW	4	FOLDS	2
FELLOW-CITIZENS	1	FOLK	5
FELLOW-HEIRS	1	FOLKS	1
FELLOW-MEN	1	FOLLOW	67
FELLOW-SERVANT	3	FOLLOWED	29
FELLOW-SERVANTS	2	FOLLOWERS	3
FELLOWS	3	FOLLOWETH	31
FELLOWSHIP	25	FOLLOWING	71
FEMALE	2	FOLLOWS	2
FERVENT	5	FOND	1
FERVENTLY	1	FONT	3
FESTIVALS	1	FOOD	11
FETCH	2	FOOL	4
FEVER	2	FOOLISH	13

FOOLISHLY	1	FULL	57
FOOLISHNESS	3	FULLERS'	1
FOOLS	5	FULLY	2
FOOT	15	FULNESS	9
FOOTSTEPS	5	FUNCTION	3
FOOTSTOOL	5	FUNCTIONS	1
FORASMUCH	14	FURIOUSLY	1
FORBEARANCE	1	FURIOUSNESS	3
FORBEARING	2	FURLONGS	1
FORBID	5	FURNISHED	3
FORBIDDEN	1	FURROWS	2
FORBIDDING	1	FURTHER	16
FORCE	1	FURTHERANCE	1
FOREFATHER	1	FURTHERMORE	2
FOREFATHERS	8	FURY	3
FOREGOING	4	FUTURE	1
FOREHEAD	1	GABBATHA	1
FOREHEADS	2	GABRIEL	1
FOREIGNERS	1	GAINSAYERS	1
FOREST	3	GAINSAYING	1
FORESTS	1	GALATTA	1
FOREWARNED	1	GALILAEAN	3
FORGAT	3	GALILAEANS	1
FORGAVE	4	GALILEE	24
FORGAVEST	2	GALL	2
FORGET	26	GAP	1
FORGETFUL	2	GAPE	1
FORGETTEST	1	GAPED	1
FORGETTETH	3	GARMENT	14
FORGIVE	24	GARMENTS	15
FORGIVEN	7	GARNERS	1
FORGIVENESS	20	GARNISHED	1
FORGIVENESSES	1	GASPETH	1
FORGIVETH	3	GAT	3
FORGIVING	3	GATE	9
FORGOTTEN	12	GATES	20
FORM	21	GATHER	25
FORMER	14	GATHERED	27
FORMS	4	GATHEREST	1
FORNICATION	4	GATHERETH	3
FORSAKE	17	GATHERING	2
FORSAKEN	11	GAVE	76
FORSAKETH	1	GAVEST	4
FORSAKING	4	GAZED	1
FORSOOK	4	GAZING	1
FORTH	175	GEBAL	1
FORTHWITH	4	GENDERETH	1
FORTRESS	1	GENERAL	12
FORTY	10	GENERALLY	3
FORWARD	6	GENERATION	43
FORWARDS	2	GENERATIONS	12
FOUGHT	6	GENNESARET	1
FOUND	68	GENTILES	31
FOUNDATION	13	GENTLE	2
FOUNDATIONS	8	GENTLENESS	1
FOUNDED	3	GENTLY	1
FOUNT	2	GET	8
FOUNTAIN	4	GETHSEMANE	1
FOUNTAINS	3	GETTETH	1
FOUR	17	GHOST	177
FOURSCORE	3	GHOSTLY	3
FOURTEEN	1	GIANT	3
FOURTH	6	GIFT	29
FOWLER	1	GIFTS	35
FOWLS	9	GILEAD	2
FOXES	1	GIRD	3
FRAGMENTS	4	GIRDED	8
FRAIL	1	GIRDETH	1
FRAILNESS	1	GIRDLE	2
FRAILTY	4	GIRT	1
FRAME	5	GIVE	310
FRAMED	1	GIVEN	121
FRAMING	1	GIVER	19
FRANKINCENSE	1	GIVES	1
FRAUD	3	GIVEST	5
FREE	15	GIVETH	31
FREE-WILL	1	GIVING	22
FREED	1	GLAD	61
FREEDOM	2	GLADLY	3
FREELY	3	GLADNESS	22
FREEWOMAN	3	GLASS	4
FREQUENT	1	GLISTERING	2
FRESH	2	GLORIA	7
FRET	2	GLORIFIED	15
FRETTING	2	GLORIFY	16
FRIDAY	2	GLORIFYING	2
FRIEND	11	GLORIOUS	47
FRIEND'S	1	GLORY	220
FRIENDLESS	2	GNASH	1
FRIENDLY	3	GNASHED	1
FRIENDS	12	GNASHETH	1
FRO	3	GNASHING	2
FROGS	2	GO	167
FROST	3	GOATS	9
FROSTS	1	GOD	1481
FROWARD	5	GOD-SPEED	1
FROWARDLY	1	GOD-WARD	1
FROWARDNESS	1	GOD'S	61
FRUIT	40	GODFATHER	1
FRUITFUL	6	GODFATHERS	4
FRUITION	1	GODHEAD	4
FRUITS	14	GODLINESS	9
FULFIL	14	GODLY	38
FULFILLED	23	GODMOTHER	1
FULFILLING	3	GODMOTHERS	4
FULFILMENT	1	GODS	20

GOEST	6	HAM	4
GOETH	26	HAMMERS	1
GOING	15	HAND	205
GOINGS	4	HANDIWORK	1
GOLD	16	HANDLE	2
GOLGOTHA	3	HANDLED	1
GONE	36	HANDLING	1
GOOD	239	HANDMAID	3
GOOD-WILL	2	HANDMAIDEN	1
GOODLINESS	1	HANDS	140
GOODLY	3	HANDY-WORK	2
GOODMAN	3	HANG	2
GOODNESS	74	HANGED	7
GOODS	9	HANGETH	2
GORGEOUS	1	HAPPEN	6
GOSPEL	67	HAPPENED	2
GOTTEN	2	HAPPINESS	2
GOVERN	14	HAPPY	10
GOVERNANCE	6	HARD	9
GOVERNED	4	HARDEN	1
GOVERNMENT	5	HARDENED	1
GOVERNOR	19	HARDNESS	2
GOVERNORS	4	HARLOTS	1
GRACE	175	HARM	4
GRACIOUS	63	HARNESSED	1
GRACIOUSLY	19	HARP	18
GRAFT	3	HARPERS	1
GRAFTED	3	HARPING	1
GRAFTING	1	HARPS	2
GRAIN	2	HART	1
GRANT	182	HARTS'	1
GRANTING	2	HARVEST	13
GRAPES	2	HARVESTS	1
GRASS	24	HAS	3
GRASSHOPPER	2	HAST	316
GRASSHOPPERS	1	HASTE	18
GRATEFUL	3	HASTEN	2
GRATITUDE	2	HASTILY	1
GRAVE	19	HASTY	1
GRAVEN	4	HATE	35
GRAVES	2	HATED	11
GRAVITY	1	HATERS	1
GRAY-HEADED	1	HATEST	4
GREAT	214	HATETH	6
GREATER	15	HATH	454
GREATEST	9	HATRED	9
GREATLY	9	HAUGHTY	1
GREATNESS	10	HAVE	835
GREEDINESS	1	HAVEN	3
GREEDY	3	HAVING	53
GREEK	4	HAVOC	1
GREEKS	1	HAY	1
GREEN	12	HE-GOATS	1
GREETING	2	HEAD	48
GREW	2	HEAD-STONE	1
GRIEF	4	HEADLONG	1
GRIEVE	4	HEADS	17
GRIEVED	9	HEAL	10
GRIEVETH	1	HEALED	11
GRIEVOUS	8	HEALEST	1
GRIEVOUSLY	3	HEALETH	5
GRIN	2	HEALING	8
GROAN	1	HEALTH	44
GROANETH	1	HEALTHFUL	2
GROANING	3	HEAP	5
GROUND	25	HEAPETH	2
GROUNDED	3	HEAR	158
GROW	14	HEARD	109
GROWETH	3	HEARDEST	5
GROWN	2	HEARER	4
GROWTH	1	HEARERS	4
GRUDGE	1	HEAREST	8
GRUDGING	1	HEARETH	8
GRUDGINGLY	1	HEARING	7
GUARD	1	HEARKEN	21
GUARDIANS	1	HEARKENED	2
GUEST-CHAMBER	2	HEARKENETH	1
GUESTS	3	HEART	214
GUIDE	23	HEART'S	4
GUIDED	6	HEARTILY	7
GUIDING	1	HEARTS	100
GUILE	7	HEARTS'	1
GUILT	2	HEARTY	18
GUILTLESS	4	HEAT	6
GUILTY	3	HEATHEN	42
GULF	1	HEAVEN	196
GUMS	1	HEAVENLY	91
GUSH	1	HEAVENS	49
GUSHED	3	HEAVILY	4
HABIT	1	HEAVINESS	20
HABITATION	16	HEAVY	14
HABITATIONS	2	HEBREW	4
HABITED	2	HEBREWS	1
HAD	196	HEDGE	2
HADST	4	HEDGES	2
HAGARENES	1	HEED	14
HAIL	5	HEELS	1
HAILSTONES	5	HEIFER	1
HAIR	2	HEIGHT	3
HAIRS	2	HEIGHTEN	1
HAIRY	1	HEIGHTS	1
HALF	2	HEIR	5
HALL	4	HEIRS	6
HALLOW	1	HELD	9
HALLOWED	4	HELL	15
HALT	2	HELL-FIRE	2

HELMET	1	HOW	166
HELP	126	HOWBEIT	4
HELPED	5	HUMAN	2
HELPER	22	HUMBLE	53
HELPETH	6	HUMBLED	3
HELPLESS	3	HUMBLENESS	1
HELPLESSNESS	1	HUMBLETH	4
HEM	1	HUMBLY	49
HEN	1	HUMILIATION	1
HENCE	9	HUMILITY	7
HENCEFORTH	17	HUNDRED	11
HERB	4	HUNDREDFOLD	2
HEREAFTER	16	HUNGER	8
HEREBY	8	HUNGRED	3
HEREIN	8	HUNGRY	6
HEREOF	1	HUNT	1
HERESIES	1	HUNTER	1
HERESY	2	HURT	16
HEREUNTO	2	HURTETH	1
HERITAGE	17	HURTFUL	2
HERMON	3	HUSBAND	9
HEROD	18	HUSBANDMAN	3
HEROD'S	1	HUSBANDS	4
HERODIANS	1	HUSHED	1
HERSELF	1	HUSKS	1
HEWED	1	HYMN	19
HEWETH	1	HYMNS	2
HEWN	3	HYPOCRISIES	1
HID	23	HYPOCRISY	1
HIDDEN	2	HYPOCRITE	1
HIDE	20	HYPOCRITES	2
HIDEST	4	HYSSOP	4
HIDETH	1	ICE	2
HIEROME	1	IDLE	3
HIGH	75	IDOLATER	1
HIGH-MINDED	1	IDOLATERS	1
HIGHER	6	IDOLATRY	1
HIGHEST	24	IDOLS	5
HIGHLY	5	IGNORANCE	6
HIGHWAY	2	IGNORANCES	1
HIGHWAYS	4	IGNORANT	6
HILL	26	ILL	3
HILL-ALTARS	1	ILLUMINATE	4
HILLS	31	ILLUMINATION	1
HIMSELF	129	ILLUMINED	1
HINDER	1	IMAGE	13
HINDERED	2	IMAGES	4
HINDERER	1	IMAGINATION	2
HINDRANCE	2	IMAGINATIONS	2
HINDS	1	IMAGINE	12
HIRE	4	IMAGINED	5
HIRED	4	IMAGINETH	3
HIRELING	7	IMMACULATE	1
HIT	1	IMMANUEL	1
HITHER	13	IMMEDIATELY	27
HITHERTO	1	IMMERSION	1
HOAR-FROST	1	IMMINENT	1
HOLD	36	IMMODERATE	2
HOLDEN	5	IMMORTAL	3
HOLDEST	3	IMMORTALITY	3
HOLDETH	1	IMPART	5
HOLDING	4	IMPARTIALLY	2
HOLIEST	1	IMPATIENT	1
HOLINESS	26	IMPEDIMENT	11
HOLPEN	4	IMPERFECT	2
HOLY	603	IMPIETY	1
HOLY-DAY	1	IMPLORE	1
HOME	9	IMPORTANCE	1
HOMELESS	1	IMPORTANT	2
HOMES	1	IMPORTUNITY	1
HOMILIES	6	IMPOSITION	5
HOMILY	1	IMPOSSIBLE	1
HONEST	6	IMPOTENT	1
HONESTLY	1	IMPRESSED	1
HONESTY	2	IMPRINT	1
HONEY	5	IMPRISONMENTS	1
HONEYCOMB	2	IMPUTE	1
HONOUR	84	IMPUTETH	1
HONOURABLE	5	INAPPLICABLE	1
HONOURED	1	INASMUCH	4
HONOURETH	2	INCARNATE	4
HOOFS	1	INCARNATION	3
HOPE	55	INCENSE	4
HOPED	6	INCITED	1
HOPETH	1	INCLINE	18
HOREB	1	INCLINED	5
HORN	10	INCLOSED	2
HORNS	6	INCLUDED	1
HORRIBLE	3	INCOMPREHENSIBLE	1
HORRIBLY	2	INCORPORATE	2
HORSE	5	INCORRUPTIBLE	2
HORSES	1	INCORRUPTION	4
HOSANNA	3	INCREASE	35
HOSPITALITY	3	INCREASED	9
HOST	8	INCREASETH	1
HOSTS	29	INCREASING	2
HOT	6	INCUMBENT	4
HOUR	36	INCUMBENT'S	1
HOURS	1	INDEBTED	1
HOUSE	129	INDEMNIFICATION	1
HOUSEHOLD	8	INDEPENDENCE	1
HOUSEHOLDER	2	INDEPENDENT	1
HOUSEHOLDS	1	INDIFFERENT	1
HOUSES	9	INDIGNATION	16
HOUSETOP	1	INDUSTRY	3
HOUSETOPS	1	INDWELLING	4

INEQUALITY	1
INESTIMABLE	3
INFALLIBLE	1
INFANTS	5
INFECTION	1
INFECTIOUS	1
INFERIOR	1
INFINITE	10
INFIRMITIES	9
INFIRMITY	6
INFORM	2
INGRATITUDE	1
INHABITANTS	1
INHABITERS	2
INHABITETH	1
INHERIT	13
INHERITANCE	24
INHERITOR	3
INIQUITIES	4
INIQUITY	15
INJURIES	1
INJURY	2
INN	2
INNER	3
INNOCENCY	13
INNOCENT	9
INNOCENTLY	2
INNUMERABLE	5
INORDINATE	3
INQUIRE	1
INQUIRED	3
INQUIRY	1
INQUISITION	1
INSET	2
INSOMUCH	9
INSPIRATION	5
INSPIRE	6
INSPIRED	2
INSTANT	3
INSTANTLY	1
INSTEAD	11
INSTITUTE	4
INSTITUTED	7
INSTITUTING	1
INSTITUTION	10
INSTITUTOR	7
INSTRUCT	6
INSTRUCTED	7
INSTRUCTETH	1
INSTRUCTION	2
INSTRUCTIVE	1
INSTRUMENT	7
INSTRUMENTAL	1
INSTRUMENTS	2
INSURRECTION	3
INTEND	2
INTENDED	1
INTENDING	2
INTENT	8
INTENTION	1
INTERCESSION	3
INTERCESSIONS	4
INTERFERES	1
INTERPOSED	1
INTERPRETATION	2
INTERPRETED	3
INTOLERABLE	1
INTREATED	3
INTRUSTED	1
INVALUABLE	1
INVENTED	1
INVENTIONS	4
INVISIBLE	5
INVISIBLY	1
INVOCATION	1
INWARD	13
INWARDLY	6
IRON	6
IRREPREHENSIBLE	1
ISAAC	3
ISCARIOT	4
ISHMAELITES	1
ISLES	2
ISRAEL	106
ISRAELITES	1
ISSUE	3
ISSUED	1
ITS	2
ITSELF	17
IVORY	1
JABIN	1
JACOB	38
JAH	1
JAMES	13
JASPER	1
JAW-BONES	1
JEALOUS	3
JEALOUSY	2
JEHOVAH	2
JEREMIAS	1
JEREMY	2
JERICHO	2
JERUSALEM	77
JESSE	1
JESTED	1
JESTING ·	1
JESUS	728
JESUS'	3
JEW	1
JEWRY	1
JEWS	45
JEWS'	1
JOHN	32
JOHN'S	1
JOIN	4
JOINED	21
JOINING	1
JOINT	2
JOINT-HEIRS	2
JONAS	3
JORDAN	6
JOSEPH	19
JOURNEY	4
JOURNEYED	3
JOURNEYINGS	1
JOY	63
JOYFUL	29
JOYFULLY	4
JOYFULNESS	3
JOYS	4
JUBILATE	1
JUDA	2
JUDAEA	16
JUDAH	12
JUDAS	12
JUDGE	66
JUDGED	7
JUDGES	5
JUDGEST	1
JUDGETH	4
JUDGING	4
JUDGMENT	44
JUDGMENT-SEAT	2
JUDGMENTS	29
JUDICA	1
JURISDICTION	1
JUST	31
JUSTICE	10
JUSTIFICATION	3
JUSTIFIED	9
JUSTIFIETH	1
JUSTIFY	1
JUSTLY	8
JUSTUS	1
KADESH	1
KEDAR	1
KEEP	147
KEEPER	4
KEEPERS	1
KEEPETH	13
KEEPING	5
KEPT	30
KEYS	5
KICK	1
KID	1
KILL	9
KILLED	9
KILLEST	1
KILLETH	2
KIND	8
KINDLE	2
KINDLED	9
KINDLY	3
KINDNESS	11
KINDRED	1
KINDREDS	4
KINDS	3
KING	97
KING'S	5
KINGDOM	99
KINGDOMS	6
KINGS	27
KINGS'	3
KINSFOLK	1
KINSMEN	1
KISHON	1
KISS	4
KISSED	3
KNAPPETH	1
KNEE	3
KNEEL	9
KNEELED	2
KNEELING	33
KNEES	5
KNEW	21
KNEWEST	2
KNIT	3
KNOCK	4
KNOCKETH	3
KNOW	143
KNOWEST	20
KNOWETH	25
KNOWING	16
KNOWLEDGE	52
KNOWN	54
LABOUR	24
LABOURED	1
LABOURER	1
LABOURERS	11
LABOURING	1
LABOURS	8
LACK	6

LACKED	2	LIBERTIES	3
LACKETH	1	LIBERTY	12
LACKING	1	LIBYA	1
LAD	2	LICE	1
LADEN	2	LICENCE	2
LAID	63	LICENSED	1
LAIDEST	1	LICK	1
LAIN	1	LICKED	1
LAITY	1	LIE	14
LAKE	2	LIES	9
LAMA	2	LIETH	12
LAMB	16	LIFE	250
LAMBS	5	LIFE'S	8
LAME	2	LIFETIME	1
LAMENT	1	LIFT	52
LAMENTATION	2	LIFTED	9
LAMENTED	1	LIFTER	2
LAMENTING	1	LIFTEST	1
LAMPS	1	LIFTETH	3
LAND	94	LIFTING	2
LANDS	14	LIGHT	122
LANES	1	LIGHTEN	7
LANGUAGE	3	LIGHTENED	1
LANTERN	2	LIGHTER	1
LARGE	5	LIGHTETH	1
LARGELY	1	LIGHTING	1
LARGER	1	LIGHTLY	3
LASCIVIOUSNESS	2	LIGHTNING	3
LAST	36	LIGHTNINGS	6
LATCHET	2	LIGHTS	7
LATE	4	LIKE	180
LATELY	1	LIKEMINDED	1
LATIN	2	LIKENED	2
LATTER	5	LIKENESS	8
LAUD	4	LIKEWISE	32
LAUDABLE	1	LILIES	2
LAUGH	8	LINEAGE	1
LAUGHED	2	LINEN	9
LAUGHTER	1	LINKS	1
LAUNCH	1	LION	8
LAW	100	LION'S	2
LAW-GIVER	1	LIONS	5
LAWFUL	13	LIPS	34
LAWFULLY	7	LISTETH	2
LAWFULNESS	1	LITANY	16
LAWGIVER	1	LITTLE	55
LAWS	21	LITURGY	3
LAWYER	2	LIVE	76
LAWYERS	1	LIVED	2
LAY	36	LIVELY	12
LAY-PEOPLE	1	LIVER	1
LAYETH	4	LIVES	22
LAYING	8	LIVEST	7
LAZARUS	4	LIVETH	54
LEAD	33	LIVING	50
LEADERS	1	LO	40
LEADEST	1	LOAVES	9
LEADETH	7	LOCAL	3
LEADING	4	LOCUSTS	1
LEAF	1	LODGING	1
LEAN	1	LOFTY	1
LEANED	1	LOINS	5
LEANNESS	1	LONG	74
LEAP	1	LONG-SUFFERING	10
LEARN	26	LONGED	3
LEARNED	7	LONGETH	2
LEARNING	11	LONGING	1
LEAST	10	LOOK	54
LEAVE	22	LOOKED	20
LEAVEN	7	LOOKETH	3
LEAVENETH	1	LOOKING	9
LEAVETH	3	LOOKS	2
LEAVING	4	LOOSE	6
LEBANON	5	LOOSED	4
LED	38	LOOSETH	1
LEDDEST	1	LORD	1821
LEFT	29	LORD'S	74
LEGISLATURE	1	LORDS	4
LEGITIMATELY	1	LORDSHIP	2
LEGS	4	LOSE	4
LEISURE	2	LOSS	1
LEND	1	LOST	15
LENDETH	2	LOT	6
LENGTH	7	LOTS	8
LENGTHEN	1	LOUD	15
LENT	3	LOVE	202
LEPER	2	LOVED	35
LEPERS	2	LOVELY	2
LEPROSY	1	LOVER	1
LESS	5	LOVERS	2
LESSON	11	LOVEST	4
LESSONS	2	LOVETH	21
LEST	33	LOVING	16
LET	409	LOVING-KINDNESS	42
LETTER	7	LOVING-KINDNESSES	2
LETTERS	2	LOVINGKINDNESSES	2
LETTEST	4	LOVINGLY	2
LETTETH	1	LOW	11
LEVI	2	LOWER	3
LEVIATHAN	2	LOWEST	3
LEVITE	1	LOWLINESS	3
LEVITES	1	LOWLY	6
LIAR	4	LOYALTY	2
LIARS	1	LUCK	3
LIBERAL	1	LUCRE	3
LIBERALLY	2	LUKE	5

LUMP	2	MEDIATOR	14
LURKETH	1	MEDICINE	2
LURKING	3	MEDITATION	6
LUST	11	MEEK	12
LUSTED	1	MEEK-HEARTED	1
LUSTETH	3	MEEK-SPIRITED	1
LUSTILY	1	MEEKLY	2
LUSTS	11	MEEKNESS	6
LUSTY	2	MEET	25
LUTE	8	MEETING	2
LYING	14	MELCHIZEDEK	1
MAD	1	MELODY	3
MADE	258	MELT	1
MADEST	6	MELTED	1
MADLY	1	MELTETH	4
MADNESS	1	MELTING	1
MAGDALENE	4	MEMBER	17
MAGISTRATE	3	MEMBERS	18
MAGISTRATES	2	MEMORIAL	6
MAGNIFICAT	2	MEMORY	3
MAGNIFIED	4	MEN	225
MAGNIFY	50	MEN'S	9
MAID	7	MENDING	1
MAID-SERVANT	3	MENTAL	1
MAIDEN	1	MENTION	4
MAIDENS	2	MERCHANDISE	2
MAIDS	1	MERCIES	38
MAIMED	2	MERCIFUL	112
MAIN	1	MERCIFULLY	40
MAINTAIN	10	MERCY	249
MAINTAINED	1	MERCY-SEAT	1
MAINTENANCE	3	MERCY'S	3
MAJESTIC	1	MERIT	3
MAJESTY	26	MERITORIOUS	1
MAKE	192	MERITS	24
MAKER	12	MERRILY	1
MAKEST	17	MERRY	7
MAKETH	29	MESHECH	1
MAKING	11	MESOPOTAMIA	1
MALE	2	MESSAGE	2
MALE-CHILD	1	MESSENGER	5
MALEFACTORS	3	MESSENGERS	1
MALICE	15	MET	3
MALICIOUS	2	METE	3
MALICIOUSLY	1	MICHAEL	1
MALICIOUSNESS	1	MIDIANITES	1
MAMMON	2	MIDNIGHT	3
MAN	400	MIDST	42
MAN-PLEASER	1	MIGHT	111
MAN-SERVANT	3	MIGHTEST	4
MAN'S	14	MIGHTIER	2
MANASSEH	3	MIGHTIEST	1
MANFULLY	1	MIGHTILY	4
MANGER	3	MIGHTINESS	1
MANHOOD	1	MIGHTY	60
MANIFEST	14	MILETUS	1
MANIFESTATION	5	MILK	1
MANIFESTED	10	MILLSTONE	1
MANIFESTLY	1	MIND	49
MANIFOLD	16	MINDED	4
MANKIND	17	MINDFUL	7
MANNA	2	MINDS	18
MANNER	34	MINE	163
MANNERS	5	MINGLED	5
MANSIONS	2	MINISHED	2
MANY	109	MINISTER	185
MARK	10	MINISTERED	9
MARKED	1	MINISTERETH	1
MARKET-PLACE	1	MINISTERING	3
MARKS	1	MINISTERS	32
MARRIAGE	11	MINISTRATION	9
MARRIAGE-GARMENT	1	MINISTRATIONS	1
MARRIED	5	MINISTRIES	1
MARROW	1	MINISTRY	39
MARRY	1	MINSTRELS	2
MARTYR	2	MIRACLE	5
MARTYRS	1	MIRACLES	7
MARVEL	3	MIRE	4
MARVELLED	9	MISCARRIED	1
MARVELLOUS	12	MISCARRY	1
MARY	26	MISCHIEF	17
MASSES	1	MISCHIEFS	1
MASTER	22	MISCHIEVOUS	1
MASTERS	5	MISDEEDS	6
MASTERS'	1	MISDOINGS	1
MASTERY	1	MISERABLE	3
MATERIALS	1	MISEREATUR	1
MATRIMONY	11	MISERY	15
MATTER	6	MISFORTUNE	2
MATTERS	3	MISTAKE	1
MATTHEW	5	MISTRESS	3
MATTHIAS	5	MISTRESSES	1
MAYEST	10	MIXT	1
MEA	1	MOAB	2
MEAN	8	MOABITES	1
MEANEST	1	MOCK	2
MEANETH	1	MOCKED	8
MEANING	3	MOCKERS	1
MEANS	16	MOCKING	2
MEANT	2	MODEL	1
MEASURE	16	MODERATE	1
MEASURED	1	MODERATION	1
MEAT	26	MODEST	1
MEAT-OFFERING	1	MOISTURE	2
MEDES	1	MOLTEN	1
MEDIATION	5	MOMENT	1

Word	Count		Word	Count
MONDAY	1		NEEDY	11
MONEY	7		NEGLECT	1
MONEY-CHANGERS	2		NEGLIGENCE	1
MONITIONS	1		NEGLIGENCES	1
MONSTER	1		NEGLIGENT	1
MONTH	3		NEIGHBOUR	26
MOON	15		NEIGHBOUR'S	6
MORAL	1		NEIGHBOURS	15
MORALS	1		NEITHER	122
MORE	152		NEST	1
MORIANS'	1		NESTS	1
MORNING	40		NET	11
MORROW	5		NETHERMOST	1
MORSELS	1		NETS	5
MORTAL	10		NEVER	42
MORTIFIED	1		NEVER-FADING	1
MORTIFY	2		NEVER-FAILING	3
MORTIFYING	2		NEW	45
MOSES	25		NEW-BIRTH	1
MOST	149		NEWBORN	1
MOTE	3		NEWLY	1
MOTH	7		NEWNESS	4
MOTHER	40		NEXT	7
MOTHER'S	11		NICANOR	1
MOTHERS	2		NICENE	8
MOTIONS	1		NICODEMUS	5
MOUNT	11		NICOLAS	1
MOUNTAIN	8		NIGH	26
MOUNTAINS	18		NIGHT	62
MOURN	6		NIGHTS	3
MOURNETH	1		NINE	3
MOURNING	6		NINETY	2
MOURNINGS	1		NINTH	6
MOUTH	88		NO	279
MOUTHS	11		NOAH	1
MOVE	8		NOBLE	4
MOVED	22		NOBLEMAN	2
MOVETH	3		NOBLES	1
MOVING	1		NOBODY	2
MOWER	1		NOISE	8
MOWN	1		NOISED	2
MUCH	57		NOISOME	1
MULBERRY-TREES	1		NONE	40
MULE	1		NOON-DAY	3
MULTIPLIED	1		NOR	117
MULTIPLY	4		NORTH	4
MULTITUDE	45		NOSES	1
MULTITUDES	9		NOTABLE	3
MURDER	9		NOTE	27
MURDERER	2		NOTED	2
MURDERERS	2		NOTHING	58
MURDERS	1		NOTICE	6
MURMUR	1		NOTORIOUS	1
MURMURED	5		NOTWITHSTANDING	4
MURMURING	1		NOUGHT	6
MUSE	2		NOURISH	4
MUSIC	1		NOURISHETH	1
MUSICK	1		NOVICE	1
MUSING	1		NUMBER	19
MUST	48		NUMBERED	8
MUTUAL	1		NUNC	2
MYRRH	3		NURSING	1
MYSELF	30		NURTURE	2
MYSTERIES	10		OATH	4
MYSTERY	10		OBEDIENCE	9
MYSTICAL	5		OBEDIENT	9
NAILS	2		OBEDIENTLY	8
NAIN	1		OBEY	14
NAKED	4		OBEYED	4
NAKEDNESS	2		OBEYETH	1
NAME	314		OBJECTED	2
NAME'S	15		OBJECTION	2
NAMED	18		OBLATION	5
NAMELY	4		OBLATIONS	3
NAMES	5		OBLIGED	1
NAMING	1		OBSERVE	5
NAPHTHALI	1		OBSERVED	1
NAPKIN	1		OBSOLETE	1
NATION	9		OBSTINATE	1
NATIONAL	1		OBTAIN	21
NATIONS	48		OBTAINED	5
NATIVITY	1		OBTAINING	1
NATURAL	7		OCCASION	17
NATURALLY	1		OCCASIONAL	2
NATURE	21		OCCASIONS	6
NATURES	1		OCCUPIED	4
NAUGHTINESS	2		OCCUPY	1
NAUGHTY	1		OCTAVE	5
NAVY	1		OCTOBER	1
NAY	3		OFFENCE	9
NAZARENE	1		OFFENCES	17
NAZARETH	15		OFFEND	10
NEAR	18		OFFENDED	13
NEARER	2		OFFENDERS	2
NECESSARIES	1		OFFENDETH	2
NECESSARILY	2		OFFER	39
NECESSARY	25		OFFERED	18
NECESSITIES	7		OFFERETH	1
NECESSITY	15		OFFERING	16
NECK	3		OFFERINGS	6
NEED	20		OFFERTORY	2
NEEDEST	1		OFFICE	71
NEEDETH	3		OFFICER	1
NEEDFUL	3		OFFICERS	1
NEEDLEWORK	1		OFFICES	4
NEEDS	6		OFFSPRING	1

451

OFT	5	PARABLES	1
OFTEN	10	PARADISE	3
OFTENTIMES	1	PARAGRAPH	1
OG	2	PARCHMENTS	1
OIL	14	PARDON	8
OINTMENT	2	PARDONED	1
OLD	41	PARDONETH	2
OLIVE-BRANCHES	1	PARDONING	1
OLIVE-TREE	1	PARDONS	1
OLIVES	3	PARENTS	4
OMIT	5	PARISH	18
OMITTED	18	PARISHIONERS	2
OMITTING	1	PARMENAS	1
ONCE	26	PAROCHIAL	1
ONE	406	PART	37
ONES	6	PARTAKER	5
ONLY	101	PARTAKERS	25
ONLY-BEGOTTEN	19	PARTAKING	2
OPEN	30	PARTED	6
OPENED	33	PARTHIANS	1
OPENEST	3	PARTICULAR	5
OPENETH	3	PARTICULARLY	3
OPENING	2	PARTICULARS	1
OPENLY	13	PARTIES	3
OPERATION	5	PARTLY	3
OPERATIONS	4	PARTNERS	2
OPPORTUNITIES	1	PARTS	24
OPPORTUNITY	3	PARTY	3
OPPRESS	2	PASCHAL	2
OPPRESSED	6	PASS	55
OPPRESSETH	3	PASSED	14
OPPRESSION	2	PASSETH	13
OPPRESSORS	1	PASSING	1
ORACLES	1	PASSION	11
ORDAIN	3	PASSIONS	1
ORDAINED	38	PASSOVER	18
ORDAINETH	1	PAST	18
ORDAINING	1	PASTIME	1
ORDER	37	PASTOR	1
ORDERED	19	PASTORS	10
ORDERETH	4	PASTURE	11
ORDERING	5	PATE	1
ORDERLY	1	PATEN	1
ORDERS	13	PATH	6
ORDINANCE	14	PATHS	11
ORDINANCES	1	PATIENCE	26
ORDINARY	3	PATIENT	4
ORDINATION	3	PATIENTLY	9
ORDINATIONS	3	PATRI	5
OREB	1	PATTERN	1
ORGANIZE	1	PATTERNS	3
ORIGINAL	4	PAUL	11
OTHER	127	PAUSE	1
OTHERS	36	PAVEMENT	1
OTHERWISE	8	PAVILION	1
OUGHT	48	PAY	15
OURSELVES	29	PAYETH	1
OUT-GOINGS	1	PAYMENT	1
OUTCAST	2	PEACE	125
OUTCASTS	3	PEACEABLE	3
OUTER	2	PEACEABLY	3
OUTRAGE	1	PEACEFULLY	1
OUTRUN	1	PEACEMAKERS	1
OUTWARD	12	PECULIAR	1
OUTWARDLY	1	PELAGIANS	1
OVEN	3	PELICAN	1
OVERCAME	1	PEN	1
OVERCOME	7	PENANCE	2
OVERCOMETH	3	PENCE	3
OVERFLOWETH	1	PENITENT	11
OVERFLOWINGS	1	PENITENTIAL	1
OVERPAST	1	PENNY	5
OVERPLUS	1	PENNYWORTH	2
OVERSEERS	1	PENTECOST	1
OVERSHADOW	2	PENURY	1
OVERSHADOWED	1	PEOPLE	326
OVERTAKE	1	PEOPLES	35
OVERTASKED	1	PERADVENTURE	2
OVERTHREW	4	PERCEIVE	9
OVERTHROW	4	PERCEIVED	1
OVERTHROWETH	1	PERCEIVEST	1
OVERTHROWN	3	PERCEIVETH	1
OVERTOOK	1	PERCEIVING	1
OVERWHELMED	3	PERDITION	1
OWE	1	PERFECT	50
OWED	2	PERFECTED	5
OWEST	1	PERFECTING	2
OWL	1	PERFECTION	2
OWN	159	PERFECTLY	3
OX	4	PERFECTNESS	4
OXEN	8	PERFORM	19
PAID	2	PERFORMANCE	1
PAIN	10	PERFORMED	2
PAINFULNESS	1	PERIL	8
PAINS	4	PERILOUS	2
PAIR	1	PERILS	13
PALACE	4	PERISH	29
PALACES	4	PERISHED	4
PALM	1	PERISHETH	1
PALM-TREE	1	PERMITTED	1
PALMS	2	PERPETUAL	8
PALSY	4	PERPLEXED	1
PAMPHYLIA	1	PERPLEXITIES	1
PANTETH	1	PERPLEXITY	1
PAPS	2	PERSECUTE	15
PARABLE	12	PERSECUTED	8

PERSECUTEST	2	POOLS	1
PERSECUTION	2	POOR	60
PERSECUTIONS	1	POORER	2
PERSECUTORS	4	PORCH	3
PERSEVERANCE	1	PORTER	2
PERSEVERE	2	PORTION	19
PERSON	43	POSSESS	6
PERSON'S	2	POSSESSED	3
PERSONS	39	POSSESSETH	1
PERSUADED	15	POSSESSING	1
PERTAIN	1	POSSESSION	8
PERTAINING	2	POSSIBLE	5
PERVERSE	1	POSTERITIES	2
PERVERTETH	1	POSTERITY	4
PERVERTING	1	POTS	2
PESTILENCE	5	POTSHERD	1
PETER	56	POTTER'S	3
PETER'S	2	POUR	18
PETITION	3	POURED	8
PETITIONS	11	POUREST	1
PHANUEL	1	POURETH	3
PHARAOH	2	POURING	2
PHARISEE	2	POVERTY	1
PHARISEES	12	POWER	117
PHILADELPHIA	1	POWERS	13
PHILIP	9	PRACTISE	1
PHILIPPI	1	PRAETORIUM	1
PHILISTIA	3	PRAISE	255
PHILISTINES	1	PRAISED	26
PHINEHAS	1	PRAISES	36
PHRASES	1	PRAISETH	1
PHRONEMA	1	PRAISING	6
PHRYGIA	1	PRAY	62
PHYSICIAN	2	PRAYED	17
PICKING	2	PRAYER	144
PIECE	4	PRAYERS	68
PIECES	10	PRAYETH	2
PIERCE	1	PRAYING	3
PIERCED	3	PRE-EMINENCE	1
PIETY	3	PREACH	25
PIGEONS	1	PREACHED	16
PILATE	47	PREACHER	2
PILGRIMAGE	2	PREACHING	10
PILGRIMS	1	PRECEDING	2
PILLAR	1	PRECEPT	1
PILLARS	1	PRECEPTS	1
PINNACLE	1	PRECIOUS	21
PIOUS	2	PREDESTINATION	3
PIPE	1	PREFACE	4
PIT	19	PREFER	1
PITCHED	1	PREFERRED	1
PITCHER	2	PREFERRING	1
PITIED	1	PREJUDICE	3
PITIETH	2	PREMONISH	1
PITIFUL	1	PREPARATION	4
PITIFULNESS	1	PREPARE	27
PITS	1	PREPARED	26
PITY	13	PREPAREST	2
PLACE	93	PREPARETH	2
PLACED	1	PREPARING	1
PLACES	26	PREPOSSESSIONS	1
PLAGUE	8	PRESBYTER	1
PLAGUED	3	PRESBYTERS	1
PLAGUES	1	PRESCRIBED	6
PLAIN	4	PRESENCE	48
PLAINEST	1	PRESENT	65
PLAINLY	5	PRESENTED	13
PLANT	2	PRESENTS	5
PLANTED	9	PRESERVATION	5
PLANTING	2	PRESERVE	34
PLANTS	1	PRESERVED	7
PLATTED	3	PRESERVER	4
PLAY	1	PRESERVETH	5
PLAYING	2	PRESIDE	1
PLEAD	1	PRESIDENT	5
PLEASANT	7	PRESIDING	13
PLEASE	59	PRESS	1
PLEASED	32	PRESSED	3
PLEASETH	2	PRESSES	1
PLEASING	5	PRESSETH	1
PLEASURE	20	PRESUME	6
PLEASURES	3	PRESUMPTION	1
PLEDGE	4	PRESUMPTUOUS	1
PLEDGED	1	PREVAIL	4
PLEDGES	2	PREVAILED	4
PLENTEOUS	7	PREVAILING	1
PLENTEOUSLY	8	PREVENT	3
PLENTEOUSNESS	6	PREVENTING	4
PLENTIFUL	1	PREY	5
PLENTY	3	PRICE	3
PLIGHT	1	PRICKS	1
PLOTTINGS	1	PRIDE	9
PLOWED	1	PRIEST	75
PLOWERS	1	PRIEST'S	1
PLUCK	6	PRIESTHOOD	9
PLUCKED	1	PRIESTS	61
PLUCKEST	1	PRIMITIVE	1
POINT	3	PRINCE	4
POISON	2	PRINCES	23
POLISHED	1	PRINCIPAL	2
POMP	3	PRINCIPALITIES	3
POMPS	2	PRINCIPLES	2
PONDER	4	PRINT	2
PONDERED	1	PRINTED	1
PONTIUS	8	PRISON	17
PONTUS	1	PRISONER	5

PRISONERS	7	PURGETH	1
PRISONS	2	PURIFICATION	3
PRIVATE	3	PURIFIED	2
PRIVATELY	1	PURIFIER	1
PRIVILEGE	1	PURIFIETH	1
PRIVILY	11	PURIFY	4
PRIVY	1	PURIFYING	2
PRIZE	1	PURITY	3
PROCEED	12	PURPLE	5
PROCEEDED	3	PURPOSE	16
PROCEEDETH	7	PURPOSED	4
PROCEEDING	1	PURPOSELY	1
PROCHORUS	1	PURPOSING	1
PROCLAIM	3	PURSE	3
PROCURED	2	PURSUE	3
PROCURING	1	PUT	186
PRODUCTS	1	PUTTEST	3
PROFESS	3	PUTTETH	11
PROFESSETH	1	PUTTING	5
PROFESSION	4	QUAILS	1
PROFESSORS	1	QUAKE	1
PROFIT	5	QUAKED	1
PROFITABLE	4	QUALIFIED	1
PROFITABLY	1	QUALITIES	1
PROFITETH	1	QUARREL	3
PROHIBIT	1	QUARTERS	1
PROLONGED	1	QUATERNIONS	1
PROMISE	41	QUEEN	1
PROMISED	22	QUENCH	2
PROMISES	19	QUESTION	3
PROMOTE	1	QUESTIONED	1
PROMOTING	2	QUESTIONS	11
PROMOTION	1	QUICK	12
PROMPTLY	1	QUICKEN	14
PROMULGATING	1	QUICKENED	5
PRONOUNCE	6	QUICKENING	1
PRONOUNCING	5	QUICKLY	4
PROOF	1	QUIET	7
PROOFS	1	QUIETING	1
PROPER	9	QUIETNESS	8
PROPERTY	3	QUIVER	2
PROPHECIES	1	RABBI	2
PROPHECY	4	RACA	1
PROPHESIED	1	RACE	5
PROPHESY	4	RACHEL	1
PROPHET	21	RAGE	4
PROPHET'S	1	RAGING	4
PROPHETESS	1	RAILED	2
PROPHETS	42	RAILING	2
PROPITIATION	3	RAILS	4
PROPORTION	1	RAIMENT	17
PROPOSED	1	RAIN	16
PROSELYTE	1	RAINBOW	1
PROSELYTES	1	RAINED	2
PROSPER	13	RAINS	1
PROSPERITY	12	RAISE	11
PROTECT	4	RAISED	23
PROTECTION	15	RAMA	1
PROTECTOR	1	RAMPING	1
PROTESTANT	4	RAMS	3
PROUD	25	RAN	7
PROVE	7	RANSOM	2
PROVED	10	RASH	1
PROVERB	1	RATHER	24
PROVERBS	2	RATIFYING	1
PROVIDE	7	RAVENING	1
PROVIDED	10	RAVENS	2
PROVIDENCE	15	RAVISH	2
PROVIDES	2	RAZOR	1
PROVIDEST	1	REACH	2
PROVING	2	REACHETH	5
PROVISION	4	READ	31
PROVOCATION	1	READEST	1
PROVOCATIONS	1	READILY	1
PROVOKE	4	READINESS	4
PROVOKED	7	READING	13
PROVOKING	1	READS	1
PRUDENCE	1	READY	39
PRUDENT	1	REAP	5
PRUDENTLY	1	REAPERS	1
PSALM	13	REASON	13
PSALMS	14	REASONABLE	6
PSALTER	3	REASONED	1
PUBLIC	10	REASONS	2
PUBLICAN	4	REBELLED	5
PUBLICANS	5	REBELLION	1
PUBLICK	1	REBELLIOUS	1
PUBLICKLY	1	REBUKE	18
PUBLICLY	1	REBUKED	11
PUBLISH	1	REBUKES	4
PUBLISHED	6	RECALLED	1
PUBLISHING	1	RECEIPT	2
PUFFED	1	RECEIVE	134
PULL	3	RECEIVED	69
PUNISH	6	RECEIVEDST	1
PUNISHED	5	RECEIVERS	1
PUNISHMENT	6	RECEIVEST	1
PURCHASE	2	RECEIVETH	8
PURCHASED	7	RECEIVING	9
PURE	31	RECIPIENTS	1
PURELY	1	RECITE	1
PURENESS	3	RECKON	5
PURER	1	RECKONED	1
PURGATORY	1	RECOGNITION	1
PURGE	6	RECOMPENCE	1
PURGED	4	RECOMPENSE	4

RECOMPENSED	1	REPORTED	2
RECONCILE	2	REPOSE	1
RECONCILED	3	REPRESENTATIVES	1
RECONCILIATION	2	REPRESENTED	1
RECORD	8	REPROACH	9
RECOVER	3	REPROOF	4
RECOVERING	1	REPROOFS	1
RECTOR	3	REPROVE	6
RED	8	REPROVED	4
REDEEM	6	REPUGNANT	5
REDEEMED	18	REPUTATION	2
REDEEMER	17	REQUEST	2
REDEEMING	2	REQUESTS	3
REDEMPTION	20	REQUIRE	11
REED	6	REQUIRED	17
REEL	1	REQUIREST	2
REFERENCES	2	REQUIRETH	2
REFERRED	1	REQUIRING	1
REFINER	1	REQUISITE	7
REFINER'S	1	RESERVED	1
REFORM	2	RESIDING	1
REFORMED	1	RESIDUE	3
REFRAIN	6	RESIST	5
REFRAINED	1	RESISTETH	3
REFRESH	5	RESOLUTION	1
REFRESHED	4	RESORT	2
REFRESHEDST	1	RESPECT	7
REFRESHING	4	RESPECTER	2
REFRESHMENT	1	RESPECTFUL	1
REFUGE	15	RESPECTING	1
REFUSE	4	RESPECTIVE	2
REFUSED	5	RESPONDING	3
REFUSETH	1	RESPONSE	2
REFUSING	1	RESPONSES	2
REGARD	6	RESPONSIBLE	1
REGARDED	3	REST	44
REGARDEST	2	RESTED	3
REGARDETH	2	RESTING-PLACE	1
REGARDS	1	RESTITUTION	1
REGENERATE	6	RESTORE	7
REGENERATED	1	RESTORED	8
REGENERATION	3	RESTORING	1
REGION	2	RESTRAIN	1
REGULARLY	1	RESTRAINED	2
REHEARSE	3	RESURRECTION	37
REHEARSING	1	RETAIN	3
REIGN	8	RETAINED	4
REIGNEST	6	RETURN	19
REIGNETH	35	RETURNED	9
REINS	5	RETURNING	1
REJOICE	80	RETURNS	1
REJOICED	7	REUNITE	1
REJOICETH	5	REV	2
REJOICING	7	REVEAL	2
RELATION	1	REVEALED	11
RELATIONS	1	REVELATION	1
RELEASE	14	REVELLINGS	1
RELEASED	4	REVENGER	1
RELICS	1	REVERENCE	8
RELIEF	5	REVEREND	6
RELIEVE	6	REVERENTLY	10
RELIEVED	3	REVIEW	3
RELIGION	16	REVIEWS	1
RELIGIOUS	7	REVILE	2
RELIGIOUSLY	2	REVILED	4
REMAIN	27	REVISION	1
REMAINDER	1	REVIVE	3
REMAINED	2	REVOLUTION	1
REMAINEST	1	REWARD	27
REMAINETH	4	REWARDED	10
REMAINING	1	REWARDEST	1
REMEMBER	43	REWARDETH	2
REMEMBERED	12	RICH	13
REMEMBEREST	3	RICHER	2
REMEMBERETH	4	RICHES	17
REMEMBERING	4	RICHLY	1
REMEMBRANCE	43	RID	2
REMISS	1	RIDE	2
REMISSION	24	RIDETH	1
REMIT	2	RIGHT	142
REMITTED	2	RIGHTEOUS	87
REMNANT	1	RIGHTEOUSLY	6
REMOVE	2	RIGHTEOUSNESS	131
REMOVED	7	RIGHTEOUSNESS'	4
REMOVING	1	RIGHTLY	6
REND	3	RING	10
RENDER	9	RIOTING	1
RENDERING	2	RIOTOUS	1
RENEW	8	RIPENESS	1
RENEWED	4	RIPER	2
RENEWING	2	RISE	31
RENOUNCE	6	RISEN	19
RENOUNCED	1	RISETH	2
RENOWN	2	RISING	7
RENT	5	RITES	4
REPAY	2	RIVER	8
REPEAT	2	RIVERS	5
REPEATED	1	ROAR	1
REPEATING	10	ROARED	1
REPELLING	1	ROARING	4
REPENT	20	ROBBED	1
REPENTANCE	21	ROBBER	2
REPENTED	2	ROBBERS	4
REPENTETH	4	ROBBERY	2
REPLENISH	7	ROBE	6
REPORT	6	ROBES	3

ROCHET	1
ROCK	19
ROCKS	4
ROD	5
RODE	1
RODS	1
ROGATION	2
ROLL	1
ROLLED	2
ROME	2
ROMISH	1
ROOF	3
ROOM	8
ROOT	13
ROOTED	6
ROSE	24
ROUGH	1
ROUND	38
RUBRICS	1
RUFUS	1
RULE	20
RULED	1
RULER	10
RULER'S	1
RULERS	11
RULEST	3
RULETH	6
RULING	2
RUMOUR	1
RUN	16
RUNAGATES	1
RUNNETH	4
RUNNING	4
RUSHING	1
RUST'	4
SABA	1
SABACHTHANI	2
SABAOTH	1
SABBATH	12
SABBATH-DAY	3
SACERDOTAL	3
SACKCLOTH	3
SACRAMENT	29
SACRAMENTS	24
SACRED	2
SACRIFICE	35
SACRIFICED	2
SACRIFICES	12
SAD	2
SADDUCEES	1
SADNESS	1
SAFE	10
SAFEGUARD	1
SAFELY	7
SAFETY	9
SAID	479
SAIDST	2
SAINT	28
SAINTS	59
SAINTS'	1
SAITH	157
SAKE	65
SAKES	5
SALEM	1
SALMON	1
SALOME	1
SALUTATION	1
SALUTE	4
SALVATION	106
SAMARIA	5
SAMARITAN	3
SAME	234
SAMUEL	1
SANCTIFICATION	2
SANCTIFIED	5
SANCTIFIER	2
SANCTIFIES	1
SANCTIFIETH	4
SANCTIFY	16
SANCTUARY	12
SANCTUS	1
SAND	2
SANDALS	1
SANG	1
SAP	1
SARDINE	1
SARKOS	1
SAT	28
SATAN	8
SATISFACTION	5
SATISFIED	9
SATISFIETH	2
SATISFY	4
SATTEST	1
SAUL	12
SAVE	68
SAVED	24
SAVEST	1
SAVETH	5
SAVING	8
SAVIOUR	90
SAVOUR	1
SAW	78
SAWEST	1
SAY	311
SAYEST	10

SAYING	181
SAYINGS	4
SCALES	1
SCALP	1
SCARCE	1
SCARCENESS	1
SCARCITY	2
SCARLET	2
SCATTER	3
SCATTERED	12
SCATTEREST	2
SCATTERETH	6
SCATTERING	1
SCEPTRE	5
SCHISM	2
SCHOOL-AUTHORS	1
SCHOOLS	3
SCORN	13
SCORNFUL	2
SCORPION	2
SCOURGE	3
SCOURGED	3
SCOURGES	1
SCOURGETH	1
SCRIBES	15
SCRIP	3
SCRIPTURE	31
SCRIPTURES	24
SCRUPLE	1
SEA	66
SEAL	2
SEALED	6
SEALING	1
SEAM	1
SEARCH	7
SEARCHED	1
SEAS	5
SEASON	19
SEASONABLE	4
SEASONS	3
SEAT	14
SEATED	6
SEATS	5
SECOND	21
SECONDLY	4
SECRET	17
SECRETLY	8
SECRETS	4
SECT	1
SECURE	1
SECURITY	1
SEDITION	3
SEDITIONS	1
SEDITIOUS	1
SEE	119
SEED	28
SEED-TIME	1
SEEDS	1
SEEING	15
SEEK	66
SEEKETH	7
SEEKING	6
SEEM	6
SEEMED	1
SEEMS	1
SEEN	54
SEEST	2
SEETH	16
SELECTION	3
SELECTIONS	1
SELF	3
SELF-SAME	1
SELFSAME	3
SELL	1
SELLEST	1
SELVES	8
SEMINARIES	1
SENATE	1
SENATORS	1
SEND	59
SENDEST	1
SENDETH	6
SENDING	4
SENIOR	2
SENSE	15
SENSIBLE	3
SENSUALITY	1
SENT	83
SENTENCE	10
SENTENCES	9
SENTEST	1
SEPARATE	5
SEPARATED	1
SEPARATELY	3
SEPARATING	1
SEPARATION	2
SEPULCHRE	20
SERAPHIM	1
SERIOUSLY	2
SERIOUSNESS	2
SERMON	7
SERMONS	1
SERPENT	6
SERPENTS	1
SERVANT	127
SERVANTS	100

SERVANTS'	2
SERVE	67
SERVED	7
SERVETH	7
SERVICE	54
SERVICES	1
SERVING	3
SESSION	2
SET	114
SETTEST	1
SETTETH	8
SETTING	3
SETTLE	1
SETTLED	1
SEVEN	19
SEVEN-FOLD	1
SEVENFOLD	4
SEVENTH	10
SEVENTY	2
SEVERAL	12
SEVERALLY	5
SEVERITY	1
SHADOW	25
SHADOWS	1
SHAKE	6
SHAKEN	4
SHAKETH	3
SHALT	191
SHAME	23
SHAPEN	2
SHARP	4
SHARPENED	1
SHARPNESS	1
SHAWMS	2
SHEAVES	2
SHECHEM	2
SHED	14
SHEDDING	1
SHEEP	69
SHEEP-FOLDS	2
SHEEP'S	1
SHEEPFOLD	2
SHELTER	1
SHEPHERD	30
SHEPHERDS	4
SHEW	20
SHEWED	12
SHEWETH	2
SHEWING	1
SHIELD	10
SHILOH	1
SHINE	14
SHINED	3
SHINETH	2
SHIP	5
SHIPS	7
SHIPWRECK	1
SHOD	1
SHOE	2
SHOE'S	1
SHOES	4
SHONE	2
SHOOK	3
SHOOT	8
SHORT	5
SHORTEN	1
SHORTENED	2
SHORTLY	2
SHORTNESS	1
SHOULDER	1
SHOULDERS	1
SHOULDEST	4
SHOUT	1
SHOW	69
SHOWED	19
SHOWER	1
SHOWERS	3
SHOWEST	2
SHOWETH	5
SHOWING	3
SHRINK	2
SHRINKED	1
SHRUNK	1
SHUNNED	1
SHUT	10
SHUTTETH	2
SICK	30
SICKNESS	27
SICKNESSES	1
SIDE	31
SIDON	2
SIEGE	1
SIFT	1
SIGHED	1
SIGHING	4
SIGHT	67
SIGILLUM	1
SIGN	24
SIGNAT	1
SIGNATURE	1
SIGNED	1
SIGNIFIED	5
SIGNIFYING	2
SIGNS	7
SIHON	2
SILENCE	12

SILVER	16
SIMEON	2
SIMILITUDE	1
SIMON	26
SIMON'S	2
SIMPLE	7
SIMPLENESS	1
SIMPLICITY	1
SIN	113
SINAI	4
SINCE	16
SINCERE	4
SINCERITY	2
SINFUL	10
SINFULNESS	1
SING	78
SINGERS	2
SINGING	4
SINGLE	1
SINGLENESS	1
SINGULAR	1
SINK	2
SINNED	12
SINNER	11
SINNERS	20
SINNETH	3
SINS	136
SION	44
SIR	4
SIRION	1
SISERA	1
SISTER	1
SISTERS	1
SIT	28
SITTEST	5
SITTETH	23
SITTING	17
SIX	10
SIXTH	11
SKILL	1
SKIN	1
SKIP	1
SKIPPED	2
SKIRTS	1
SKULL	3
SLAIN	6
SLANDERED	3
SLANDERER	2
SLANDERERS	2
SLANDERETH	1
SLANDERING	2
SLAUGHTER	1
SLAY	7
SLEEP	26
SLEEPEST	3
SLEEPETH	1
SLEEPING	4
SLEIGHT	1
SLEPT	7
SLEW	10
SLIDE	2
SLIP	2
SLIPPERY	2
SLIPT	3
SLOTHFUL	1
SLOW	7
SLUMBER	4
SMALL	12
SMELL	2
SMITE	9
SMITERS	2
SMITEST	1
SMITTEN	7
SMOKE	7
SMOOTHER	1
SMOTE	20
SMOTEST	1
SNAIL	1
SNARE	11
SNARES	7
SNOW	6
SOBER	8
SOBERLY	4
SOBERNESS	3
SOEVER	2
SOFT	3
SOFTER	1
SOILED	2
SOJOURNER	2
SOLD	10
SOLDIER	3
SOLDIERS	13
SOLEMN	4
SOLEMNIZATION	1
SOLITARY	1
SOLOMON	2
SOLOMON'S	1
SOME	69
SOMETIME	5
SOMETIMES	3
SON	354
SON'S	2
SONG	22
SONGS	8
SONS	29
SOON	21

Word	Count	Word	Count
SOONER	1	STAVES	3
SOPE	1	STAY	2
SORCERERS	1	STEADINESS	1
SORE	17	STEAL	12
SORES	3	STEALING	2
SORROW	18	STEDFAST	9
SORROWFUL	9	STEDFASTLY	13
SORROWING	1	STEDFASTNESS	1
SORROWS	6	STEEL	1
SORRY	4	STEPHEN	5
SORT	1	STEPS	9
SORTS	2	STEWARD	7
SOUGHT	22	STEWARDS	2
SOUL	191	STICK	1
SOUL'S	4	STIFF	1
SOULS	30	STIFFNESS	1
SOUND	16	STILL	26
SOUNDING	2	STILLEST	2
SOUNDNESS	2	STILLETH	1
SOUTH	4	STING	3
SOUTHWEST-WIND	1	STINK	1
SOVEREIGN	2	STIR	5
SOW	6	STIRRED	1
SOWED	3	STIRRETH	1
SOWER	1	STOCK	1
SOWEST	3	STOCKS	1
SOWETH	2	STOLE	1
SOWN	4	STONE	17
SPACE	4	STONE'S	1
SPAKE	53	STONED	3
SPAKEST	2	STONES	8
SPAN	2	STONEST	1
SPARE	15	STONY	6
SPARED	2	STOOD	38
SPAREST	2	STOOP	1
SPARING	1	STOOPING	1
SPARKS	2	STOP	1
SPARROW	2	STOPPED	3
SPEAK	88	STOPPETH	1
SPEAKEST	3	STORE	1
SPEAKETH	6	STORK	1
SPEAKING	10	STORM	5
SPEAKINGS	1	STORMS	2
SPEAR	3	STORMY	2
SPEARS	1	STRAIGHT	8
SPECIAL	9	STRAIGHTWAY	12
SPECIALLY	3	STRANGE	7
SPECIFIED	1	STRANGER	20
SPEECH	6	STRANGERS	15
SPEECHLESS	2	STRAWED	1
SPEEDILY	1	STRAYED	2
SPENDEST	1	STREAM	1
SPENT	5	STREAMS	4
SPICES	1	STREET	2
SPIED	1	STREETS	6
SPIKENARD	1	STRENGTH	117
SPIN	2	STRENGTHEN	20
SPIRIT	266	STRENGTHENED	8
SPIRITS	13	STRENGTHENING	5
SPIRITUAL	37	STRETCH	9
SPIRITUALLY	2	STRETCHED	8
SPIRITUS	2	STRETCHED-OUT	1
SPIT	4	STRICT	1
SPITEFULLY	2	STRIFE	10
SPITTED	1	STRIKE	1
SPITTING	1	STRIKER	1
SPOIL	4	STRING	1
SPOILETH	1	STRINGS	5
SPOILS	2	STRIPES	4
SPOKEN	35	STRIPPED	2
SPONSORS	13	STRIPPETH	1
SPOT	6	STRIVE	1
SPOUSE	2	STRIVETH	1
SPRANG	2	STRIVINGS	1
SPREAD	6	STRONG	37
SPREADEST	3	STRONGER	3
SPRING	2	STRONGEST	1
SPRINGING	1	STRONGHOLD	2
SPRINGS	3	STRONGHOLDS	2
SPRINKLED	4	STROVE	1
SPRINKLING	1	STRUCK	1
SPRUNG	3	STUBBLE	1
SPUNGE	3	STUBBORN	1
ST	5	STUCK	1
STABLE	1	STUDIES	3
STABLISH	9	STUDIOUS	1
STABLISHED	3	STUDY	5
STAFF	2	STUDYING	1
STAGGER	1	STUMBLE	2
STAIN	1	STUMBLED	1
STAINED	1	STUMBLING	1
STAND	52	SUBDUE	3
STANDEST	2	SUBDUED	4
STANDETH	13	SUBDUETH	2
STANDING	34	SUBJECT	11
STANDS	2	SUBJECTED	1
STAR	7	SUBJECTION	4
STARING	1	SUBMISSION	1
STARS	8	SUBMIT	5
STARTING	1	SUBMITTED	1
STATE	14	SUBMITTING	4
STATED	1	SUBSCRIBED	1
STATES	14	SUBSTANCE	20
STATURE	4	SUBSTITUTED	1
STATUTE	1	SUBSTITUTING	1
STATUTES	27	SUBTILTY	1

SUCCESS	2	TAKEST	8
SUCCESSION	1	TAKETH	18
SUCCOTH	2	TAKING	3
SUCCOUR	16	TALE	2
SUCCOURED	1	TALENTS	1
SUCH	166	TALK	12
SUCK	4	TALKED	6
SUCKED	1	TALKETH	2
SUCKLINGS	3	TALKING	8
SUDDEN	4	TARES	5
SUDDENLY	13	TARRIED	2
SUFFER	41	TARRIETH	1
SUFFERED	24	TARRY	11
SUFFEREDST	1	TARRYING	2
SUFFERERS	2	TARSHISH	1
SUFFERETH	3	TARSUS	2
SUFFERING	4	TASTE	3
SUFFERINGS	6	TASTED	3
SUFFICE	3	TAUGHT	22
SUFFICETH	1	TAXED	3
SUFFICIENCY	1	TAXING	1
SUFFICIENT	9	TEACH	43
SUFFICIENTLY	4	TEACHER	2
SUFFRAGE	5	TEACHERS	5
SUITABLE	1	TEACHES	1
SUM	1	TEACHEST	3
SUMMARY	1	TEACHETH	4
SUMMED	1	TEACHING	10
SUMMER	4	TEAR	2
SUMMING	1	TEARS	15
SUMPTUOUSLY	1	TEETH	12
SUN	28	TELL	38
SUNDAY	20	TELLEST	1
SUNDAYS	9	TELLETH	4
SUNDER	5	TELLING	2
SUNDRY	5	TEMPER	1
SUNG	29	TEMPERANCE	4
SUNK	1	TEMPERATE	2
SUNSHINE	1	TEMPEST	7
SUPEREROGATION	1	TEMPLE	54
SUPERFLUITY	2	TEMPLE'S	1
SUPERSCRIPTION	3	TEMPLES	2
SUPERSTITIONS	1	TEMPORAL	6
SUPERSTITIOUS	1	TEMPORALITIES	1
SUPPED	1	TEMPT	4
SUPPER	34	TEMPTATION	12
SUPPLICATE	1	TEMPTATIONS	9
SUPPLICATION	8	TEMPTED	9
SUPPLICATIONS	13	TEMPTER	1
SUPPLIETH	1	TEMPTETH	1
SUPPLY	3	TEMPTING	2
SUPPLYING	2	TEN	22
SUPPORT	5	TEN-STRINGED	1
SUPPOSE	1	TEND	3
SUPPOSED	3	TENDER	9
SUPPOSING	1	TENDER-HEARTED	1
SUPREME	2	TENDS	1
SURE	19	TENT	1
SURELY	11	TENTH	1
SUREST	1	TENTS	7
SURETIES	1	TERRESTRIAL	2
SURETY	2	TERRIBLE	3
SURNAMED	2	TERRIFIED	1
SUSPECTED	1	TERROR	3
SUSPEND	1	TERRORS	1
SUSPENDS	1	TESTAMENT	20
SUSTAINED	2	TESTATOR	2
SUSTAINING	1	TESTIFIED	2
SUSTENANCE	2	TESTIFIETH	1
SWADDLING	2	TESTIFY	11
SWALLOW	3	TESTIFYING	1
SWALLOWED	3	TESTIMONIALS	1
SWARE	6	TESTIMONIES	28
SWAREST	1	TESTIMONY	10
SWEAR	4	THANK	16
SWEARERS	1	THANKFUL	13
SWEARETH	1	THANKFULLY	2
SWEARING	1	THANKFULNESS	5
SWEAT	2	THANKS	128
SWEEP	1	THANKSGIVING	29
SWEET	6	THANKSGIVINGS	6
SWEET-SMELLING	1	THANKWORTHY	1
SWEETER	2	THEIR'S	2
SWELL	3	THEMSELVES	52
SWELLETH	1	THENCE	9
SWEPT	1	THENCEFORTH	1
SWERVE	1	THEOPHILUS	1
SWERVED	1	THEREAFTER	1
SWIFT	4	THEREBY	11
SWIFTLY	1	THEREIN	38
SWINE	2	THEREOF	55
SWORD	27	THEREON	2
SWORDS	6	THEREOUT	1
SWORN	6	THERETO	11
SYMPATHY	1	THEREUNTO	9
SYNAGOGUE	2	THEREUPON	2
SYNAGOGUES	4	THESSALONICA	1
SYRIA	1	THICK	4
TABERNACLE	19	THIEF	7
TABERNACLES	3	THIEVES	14
TABLE	37	THIEVISH	1
TABLES	4	THIGH	1
TABOR	1	THINE	189
TABRET	2	THING	88
TAKE	137	THINGS	760
TAKEN	42	THINK	44

459

THINKEST	4	TREADINGS	1
THINKETH	3	TREASURE	4
THIRD	29	TREASURE-HOUSE	1
THIRDLY	4	TREASURES	5
THIRST	7	TREASURIES	2
THIRSTETH	1	TREASURY	1
THIRSTY	5	TREATISE	1
THIRTEENTH	1	TREE	14
THIRTY	3	TREES	10
THISTLES	1	TREMBLE	2
THITHER	4	TREMBLED	3
THOMAS	8	TREMBLETH	1
THORNS	10	TREMBLING	4
THOROUGHLY	1	TRENCH	1
THOUGH	54	TRESPASS	1
THOUGHT	18	TRESPASSED	1
THOUGHTEST	1	TRESPASSES	3
THOUGHTS	18	TRIAL	2
THOUSAND	16	TRIBE	4
THOUSANDS	8	TRIBES	11
THREATENED	1	TRIBULATION	8
THREATENINGS	1	TRIBULATIONS	1
THREE	23	TRIBUTE	6
THREESCORE	3	TRIED	10
THRICE	6	TRIETH	1
THROAT	5	TRINITY	11
THRONE	44	TRIUMPH	13
THRONES	3	TRIUMPHS	1
THROUGHLY	2	TROAS	1
THROUGHOUT	28	TRODDEN	4
THROW	1	TROTH	4
THROWETH	1	TROUBLE	76
THRUST	5	TROUBLED	21
THUNDER	5	TROUBLES	10
THUNDERBOLTS	1	TROUBLES'	1
THUNDERED	2	TROUBLING	1
THUNDERINGS	1	TRUE	78
THUS	26	TRUE-HEARTED	1
THYSELF	46	TRULY	52
TIBERIAS	1	TRUMP	3
TIDINGS	11	TRUMPET	6
TIED	2	TRUMPETERS	1
TILL	25	TRUMPETS	2
TIMBER	1	TRUST	109
TIMBRELS	2	TRUSTED	10
TIME	167	TRUSTETH	2
TIMELY	3	TRUSTING	3
TIMES	25	TRUTH	136
TIMON	1	TRUTH'S	2
TINKLING	1	TRUTHS	1
TIP	1	TRY	5
TITHES	1	TRYING	1
TITLE	3	TUMULT	2
TITLES	1	TUMULTS	1
TITUS	1	TURN	54
TO-DAY	5	TURNED	45
TO-MORROW	2	TURNEST	4
TOGETHER	129	TURNETH	4
TOIL	3	TURNING	12
TOILED	1	TURTLE-DOVE	1
TOKEN	6	TURTLE-DOVES	1
TOKENS	6	TUSH	5
TOLD	22	TUTORS	1
TOMB	1	TWAIN	5
TONGUE	53	TWELVE	23
TONGUES	17	TWENTIETH	1
TOOK	67	TWENTY	6
TOOKEST	1	TWENTY-EIGHTH	1
TOP	3	TWENTY-FIFTH	2
TORMENT	2	TWENTY-FIRST	1
TORMENTED	3	TWENTY-FIVE	1
TORMENTORS	1	TWENTY-SEVEN	1
TORMENTS	1	TWENTY-SIX	1
TOSSED	2	TWENTY-SIXTH	1
TOTTERING	1	TWICE	7
TOUCH	5	TWINKLING	2
TOUCHED	5	TWO	63
TOUCHING	4	TWO-EDGED	1
TOWEL	2	TYCHICUS	1
TOWER	5	TYRANNOUS	1
TOWERS	1	TYRANNY	1
TRADITIONS	2	TYRANT	1
TRAIN	1	TYRANTS	2
TRAINED	1	TYRE	5
TRAITOR	1	ULTIMATE	1
TRAMPLE	1	UNADVISEDLY	2
TRANSFIGURATION	2	UNAWARES	2
TRANSFIGURED	1	UNBORN	1
TRANSFORMED	1	UNCERTAIN	2
TRANSGRESS	1	UNCERTAINLY	1
TRANSGRESSED	1	UNCERTAINTIES	1
TRANSGRESSETH	1	UNCERTAINTY	1
TRANSGRESSION	2	UNCHARITABLENESS	1
TRANSGRESSIONS	7	UNCIRCUMCISION	1
TRANSGRESSORS	4	UNCLEAN	6
TRANSITORY	2	UNCLEANNESS	5
TRANSUBSTANTIATION	1	UNCORRUPT	2
TRAPPED	1	UNCTION	3
TRAPS	2	UNDEFILED	6
TRAVAIL	4	UNDER	79
TRAVAILEST	1	UNDERSTAND	18
TRAVAILETH	2	UNDERSTANDED	2
TRAVEL	3	UNDERSTANDEST	2
TRAVELLING	1	UNDERSTANDETH	2
TREAD	7	UNDERSTANDING	38
TREADETH	1	UNDERSTOOD	6

UNDERTAKING	1	VENGEANCE	8
UNDERTOOK	2	VENI	2
UNDONE	3	VENITE	5
UNENDING	1	VENOMOUS	1
UNFAILING	2	VERILY	60
UNFAITHFUL	1	VERITY	1
UNFAITHFULNESS	1	VERSE	7
UNFEIGNED	5	VERSES	2
UNFEIGNEDLY	5	VERSICLES	4
UNFRUITFUL	1	VESSEL	6
UNGODLINESS	8	VESSELS	4
UNGODLY	88	VESTED	1
UNHALLOWED	2	VESTRY	4
UNHAPPY	2	VESTRYMEN	1
UNICORN	2	VESTURE	6
UNICORNS	1	VEX	5
UNINFLUENCED	1	VEXED	16
UNION	2	VICE	3
UNITED	12	VICES	1
UNITY	30	VICIOUSNESS	1
UNIVERSAL	7	VICTORY	13
UNIVERSE	1	VICTUALS	1
UNIVERSITIES	1	VIEW	1
UNJUST	3	VIGILANT	2
UNKIND	1	VIGOUR	1
UNKNOWN	1	VILLAGE	4
UNLAWFUL	1	VINE	8
UNLEAVENED	8	VINEGAR	8
UNLESS	1	VINES	2
UNLOOSE	2	VINEYARD	7
UNMOVEABLE	1	VINEYARDS	1
UNNECESSARY	1	VIOLENCE	4
UNPARDONABLE	1	VIOLENT	2
UNPROFITABLE	1	VIRGIN	15
UNQUIET	1	VIRGIN'S	1
UNRESTRAINED	1	VIRGINITY	1
UNRIGHTEOLS	5	VIRGINS	2
UNRIGHTEOUSLY	1	VIRTUE	7
UNRIGHTEOUSNESS	7	VIRTUES	2
UNRULY	3	VIRTUOUS	2
UNSEARCHABLE	1	VISIBLE	15
UNSEEMLY	1	VISIBLY	2
UNSEEN	1	VISION	4
UNSHAKEN	1	VISIONS	1
UNSPEAKABLE	2	VISIT	17
UNSPOTTED	3	VISITATION	4
UNSTABLE	1	VISITED	8
UNTHANKFULLY	1	VISITEST	2
UNTIMELY	1	VOCATION	3
UNTRULY	1	VOICE	107
UNWISE	3	VOICES	6
UNWORTHILY	3	VOID	4
UNWORTHINESS	2	VOLUME	2
UNWORTHY	7	VOLUNTARY	1
UP-RISING	1	VOTE	1
UPBRAIDETH	1	VOUCHSAFE	21
UPHELD	2	VOUCHSAFED	8
UPHOLD	2	VOW	8
UPHOLDEN	1	VOWED	3
UPHOLDER	1	VOWS	11
UPHOLDEST	1	WAGES	2
UPHOLDETH	4	WAGGING	2
UPHOLDING	1	WAIT	17
UPLIFT	1	WAITED	2
UPPER	3	WAITETH	3
UPRIGHT	4	WAITING	7
UPROAR	1	WAKE	1
UPSIDE	1	WAKETH	1
URGENT	4	WAKING	3
US-WARD	1	WALK	60
USAGES	2	WALKED	5
USE	36	WALKETH	8
USED	35	WALKING	8
USEFUL	1	WALL	2
USES	3	WALLS	5
USEST	1	WANDER	1
USING	3	WANDERINGS	2
USUAL	1	WANT	5
USURY	1	WANTED	1
UTMOST	1	WANTING	1
UTTERANCE	3	WANTONNESS	1
UTTERLY	12	WAR	8
UTTERMOST	10	WARD	1
VAGABONDS	1	WARDEN	2
VAIN	33	WARDENS	2
VAIN-GLORY	1	WARE	1
VAINGLORY	1	WARFARE	1
VAINLY	2	WARMED	1
VALE	1	WARMING	1
VALLEY	6	WARN	2
VALLEYS	3	WARNED	2
VALUE	2	WARNING	3
VALUED	1	WARRANTS	1
VANISH	2	WARRANTY	1
VANISHED	1	WARS	1
VANISHETH	1	WASH	15
VANITIES	1	WASH-POT	2
VANITY	21	WASHED	8
VAPOURS	1	WASHING	4
VARIABLENESS	2	WAST	3
VARIANCE	2	WASTE	2
VARIATIONS	1	WASTED	3
VARIOUS	2	WATCH	21
VAUNTETH	1	WATCHED	3
VEHEMENTLY	2	WATCHES	1
VEIL	4	WATCHETH	1

Word	Count		Word	Count
WATCHFUL	1		WHOLE	79
WATCHING	4		WHOLESOME	10
WATCHINGS	2		WHOLLY	4
WATCHMAN	1		WHOMSOEVER	3
WATCHMEN	1		WHOREMONGER	1
WATER	63		WHORING	1
WATER-BROOKS	1		WHOSESOEVER	2
WATER-FLOOD	2		WHOSO	16
WATER-FLOODS	2		WHOSOEVER	40
WATER-POTS	2		WHY	69
WATER-SIDE	1		WICKED	38
WATER-SPRINGS	2		WICKEDLY	3
WATEREST	1		WICKEDNESS	67
WATERETH	1		WICKEDNESSES	2
WATERS	43		WIDE	3
WAVE	1		WIDOW	7
WAVERETH	1		WIDOWS	5
WAVERING	2		WIFE	25
WAVES	8		WILD	6
WAX	7		WILDERNESS	36
WAXED	3		WILES	2
WAXEN	1		WILFULLY	1
WAXETH	1		WILINESS	1
WAY	133		WILL	688
WAY-SIDE	3		WILLED	1
WAYS	44		WILLEST	1
WEAK	12		WILLING	6
WEAK-HEARTED	1		WILLINGLY	6
WEAKNESS	7		WILLS	5
WEALTH	1		WILT	53
WEALTHIEST	1		WIN	1
WEALTHY	2		WIND	18
WEANED	2		WINDS	4
WEAR	1		WINE	27
WEARIED	1		WINEFAT	1
WEARINESS	1		WINEPRESS	1
WEARING	1		WINGS	14
WEARS	1		WINK	1
WEARY	5		WINTER	2
WEATHER	3		WIPE	4
WED	1		WIPED	1
WEDDED	4		WISDOM	43
WEDDING	5		WISE	28
WEDDING-GARMENT	2		WISELY	4
WEDLOCK	3		WISER	2
WEDNESDAY	1		WISH	6
WEEK	10		WISHED	1
WEEKLY	1		WISHES	1
WEEKS	1		WIST	3
WEEP	7		WIT	1
WEEPING	10		WIT'S	1
WEIGHED	1		WITCHCRAFT	1
WEIGHING	2		WITHAL	8
WEIGHT	1		WITHDRAW	1
WEIGHTS	1		WITHDRAWEST	1
WEIGHTY	5		WITHDRAWING	1
WELCOME	1		WITHDRAWN	1
WELFARE	2		WITHER	1
WELL	56		WITHERED	7
WELL-BELOVED	4		WITHERETH	4
WELL-GOVERNING	2		WITHHOLD	1
WELL-LEARNED	1		WITHIN	55
WELL-LIKING	1		WITHOUT	139
WELL-NIGH	1		WITHSTAND	3
WELL-SPRING	1		WITHSTOOD	1
WELL-TUNED	1		WITNESS	38
WELLS	1		WITNESSED	1
WENT	116		WITNESSES	19
WENTEST	2		WITNESSETH	1
WEPT	5		WIVES	5
WEST	5		WOE	6
WHALES	1		WOLF	5
WHATEVER	3		WOLVES	3
WHATSOEVER	34		WOMAN	34
WHEAT	7		WOMAN'S	2
WHEAT-FLOUR	1		WOMB	14
WHELP	1		WOMBS	1
WHENCE	14		WOMEN	12
WHENEVER	1		WON	1
WHENSOEVER	6		WONDER	1
WHEREAS	5		WONDERED	4
WHEREBY	30		WONDERFUL	17
WHEREFORE	63		WONDERFULLY	3
WHEREIN	19		WONDERS	18
WHEREINSOEVER	2		WONDROUS	14
WHEREOF	22		WONT	4
WHERESOEVER	4		WOOD	4
WHEREUNTO	7		WOODS	1
WHEREUPON	1		WOOL	2
WHEREVER	2		WORD	212
WHEREWITH	10		WORDS	80
WHEREWITHAL	3		WORK	69
WHET	2		WORKERS	4
WHETHER	24		WORKETH	13
WHILES	1		WORKING	13
WHILST	2		WORKMEN	1
WHIRLING	1		WORKS	109
WHIRLWIND	1		WORKS'	1
WHISPER	1		WORLD	261
WHIT	1		WORLD'S	5
WHITE	10		WORLDLY	9
WHITER	2		WORLDS	4
WHITHER	13		WORM	1
WHITHERSOEVER	1		WORN	1
WHITSUN	1		WORSE	5
WHITSUNDAY	5		WORSHIP	73

WORSHIPPED	16
WORSHIPPERS	2
WORSHIPPING	2
WORTH	1
WORTHILY	9
WORTHINESS	1
WORTHY	28
WOULD	82
WOULDEST	11
WOUND	2
WOUNDED	4
WOUNDETH	1
WOUNDS	2
WOVEN	1
WRAPPED	4
WRATH	37
WRATHFUL	6
WRATHFULLY	1
WRESTLE	1
WRETCHEDNESS	1
WRETCHLESSNESS	1
WRINKLE	1
WRIT	2
WRITE	7
WRITER	1
WRITETH	1
WRITING	3
WRITINGS	1
WRITTEN	65
WRONG	18
WRONGFUL	1
WRONGFULLY	2
WRONGS	2
WROTE	4
WROTH	7
WROUGHT	9
YEA	118
YEAR	16
YEARLY	1
YEARS	32
YES	3
YESTERDAY	3
YET	130
YIELD	14
YIELDED	3
YOKE	4
YOKES	1
YOU-WARD	1
YOUNG	37
YOUNGER	4
YOUR'S	1
YOURS	1
YOURSELF	5
YOURSELVES	51
YOUTH	10
ZACHARIAS	3
ZALMUNNA	1
ZEAL	5
ZEALOUS	1
ZEBAH	1
ZEBEDEE	3
ZEBEDEE'S	1
ZEBULON	1
ZEEB	1
ZION	6
ZOAN	2

INDEX OF TITLES

INDEX OF TITLES

	PAGE	LN		PAGE	LN
A BIDDING PRAYER.	047	2	EPIPHANY.	077	20
A CATECHISM	577	1	EVENING PRAYER.	589	12
A COLLECT FOR AID AGAINST PERILS.	031	25	EVENING.	593	2
A COLLECT FOR GRACE.	017	12	FEAST OF THE DEDICATION OF A CHURCH.	259	17
A COLLECT FOR PEACE.	017	4	FOR A BIRTHDAY.	597	27
A COLLECT FOR PEACE.	031	17	FOR A BLESSING ON THE FAMILIES OF THE LAND.	598	18
A COMMENDATION.	319	18	FOR A CHILD'S RECOVERY FROM SICKNESS.	053	9
A COMMENDATORY PRAYER FOR A SICK PERSON AT THE POINT	317	9	FOR A PERSON UNDER AFFLICTION.	045	29
A COMMENDATORY PRAYER WHEN THE SOUL IS DEPARTED.	319	26	FOR A PERSON, OR PERSONS, GOING TO SEA.	046	7
A GENERAL CONFESSION.	006	15	FOR A RECOVERY FROM SICKNESS.	052	28
A GENERAL CONFESSION.	023	22	FOR A SAFE RETURN FROM A JOURNEY.	053	19
A GENERAL INTERCESSION.	599	24	FOR A SICK CHILD.	045	23
A GENERAL THANKSGIVING.	019	13	FOR A SICK PERSON.	045	11
A GENERAL THANKSGIVING.	033	11	FOR A STATE LEGISLATURE.	035	22
A PENITENTIAL OFFICE FOR ASH WEDNESDAY.	060	1	FOR ALL POOR, HOMELESS, AND NEGLECTED FOLK.	599	2
A PRAYER FOR A SICK PERSON, WHEN THERE APPEARETH BUT	316	5	FOR AN ANNIVERSARY OF ONE DEPARTED.	598	5
A PRAYER FOR ALL CONDITIONS OF MEN.	018	25	FOR CHILDREN.	043	6
A PRAYER FOR ALL CONDITIONS OF MEN.	032	25	FOR CHRISTIAN SERVICE.	043	27
A PRAYER FOR CONGRESS.	035	6	FOR COURTS OF JUSTICE.	035	30
A PRAYER FOR HEALING.	315	12	FOR EVERY MAN IN HIS WORK.	044	16
A PRAYER FOR RECOVERY.	315	5	FOR FAIR WEATHER.	040	22
A PRAYER FOR THE CLERGY AND PEOPLE.	018	17	FOR FAIR WEATHER.	051	21
A PRAYER FOR THE CLERGY AND PEOPLE.	032	16	FOR FAITHFULNESS IN THE USE OF THIS WORLD'S GOODS.	599	18
A PRAYER FOR THE DESPONDENT.	316	17	FOR FRUITFUL SEASONS.	039	22
A PRAYER FOR THE PRESIDENT OF THE UNITED STATES,	017	25	FOR GRACE TO GUIDE AND KEEP US THE FOLLOWING DAY, AND	588	25
A PRAYER FOR THE PRESIDENT OF THE UNITED STATES,	032	2	FOR GUIDANCE.	595	25
A PRAYER OF ST. CHRYSOSTOM.	020	2	FOR JOY IN GOD'S CREATION.	596	16
A PRAYER OF ST. CHRYSOSTOM.	034	2	FOR MISSIONS.	038	4
A PRAYER TO BE USED AT THE MEETINGS OF CONVENTION.	036	25	FOR ONE ABOUT TO UNDERGO AN OPERATION.	597	20
A PRAYER WHICH MAY BE SAID BY THE MINISTER IN BEHALF	316	24	FOR OUR COUNTRY.	036	8
A SAINT'S DAY.	258	2	FOR PEACE, AND DELIVERANCE FROM OUR ENEMIES.	052	6
A SHORTER FORM.	592	7	FOR PLENTY.	051	29
A THANKSGIVING FOR THE BEGINNING OF A RECOVERY.	315	18	FOR PRISONERS.	046	17
A THANKSGIVING TO ALMIGHTY GOD FOR THE FRUITS OF THE	050	17	FOR QUIET CONFIDENCE.	595	18
ACKNOWLEDGMENT OF GOD'S MERCY AND PRESERVATION,	587	17	FOR RAIN.	040	14
ADDITIONAL PRAYERS.	594	2	FOR RAIN.	051	14
ADVENT SEASON.	090	8	FOR RELIGIOUS EDUCATION.	042	29
ALL SAINTS.	079	20	FOR RESTORING PUBLIC PEACE AT HOME.	052	16
ALL SAINTS' DAY.	256	2	FOR SCHOOLS, COLLEGES, AND UNIVERSITIES.	042	21
AN ABSOLUTION TO BE SAID BY THE PRIEST.	319	14	FOR SOCIAL JUSTICE.	044	8
AN OFFICE OF INSTITUTION OF MINISTERS INTO PARISHES	569	1	FOR THE ABSENT.	596	29
ARTICLES OF RELIGION.	603	1	FOR THE ARMY.	041	24
ASCENSION.	078	14	FOR THE CHILDREN.	596	23
ASCENSIONTIDE.	177	11	FOR THE CHURCH.	037	14
ASH WEDNESDAY.	124	9	FOR THE EPISTLE. ACTS I. 1.	177	21
AT A MARRIAGE.	267	2	FOR THE EPISTLE. ACTS I. 15.	234	5
AT NIGHT.	594	29	FOR THE EPISTLE. ACTS II. 1.	180	16
AT THE BURIAL OF A CHILD.	338	2	FOR THE EPISTLE. ACTS IX. 1.	229	24
AT THE BURIAL OF THE DEAD AT SEA.	337	6	FOR THE EPISTLE. ACTS V. 12.	249	20
AT THE BURIAL OF THE DEAD.	268	12	FOR THE EPISTLE. ACTS VII. 55.	100	4
AT THE GRAVE.	332	15	FOR THE EPISTLE. ACTS VIII. 14.	185	20
BENEDIC, ANIMA MEA. PSALM CIII.	312	19	FOR THE EPISTLE. ACTS X. 34.	166	11
BENEDIC, ANIMA MEA. PSALM CIII.	029	3	FOR THE EPISTLE. ACTS X. 34.	183	28
BENEDICITE, OMNIA OPERA DOMINI.	011	30	FOR THE EPISTLE. ACTS XI. 22.	241	2
BENEDICTION.	573	2	FOR THE EPISTLE. ACTS XI. 27, AND PART OF CHAP. XII.	246	23
BENEDICTUS ES, DOMINE.	011	15	FOR THE EPISTLE. ACTS XII. 1.	244	30
BENEDICTUS. ST. LUKE I. 68.	014	7	FOR THE EPISTLE. ACTS XIII. 26.	168	23
BISHOPS, PRIESTS, AND DEACONS	529	3	FOR THE EPISTLE. ACTS XIII. 44.	260	25
BONUM EST CONFITERI. PSALM XCII.	027	27	FOR THE EPISTLE. ACTS XX. 17.	550	3
CANTATE DOMINO. PSALM XCVIII.	027	3	FOR THE EPISTLE. DEUTERONOMY X. 17.	263	22
CHRISTMAS DAY.	096	10	FOR THE EPISTLE. EZEKIEL XXXIV. 25.	262	3
CHRISTMAS.	077	12	FOR THE EPISTLE. ISAIAH L. 5.	144	11
CHRISTMASTIDE.	096	8	FOR THE EPISTLE. ISAIAH LXI. 1.	106	29
COLLECTS.	049	2	FOR THE EPISTLE. ISAIAH LXIII. 1.	138	10
CONDITIONAL BAPTISM.	282	7	FOR THE EPISTLE. ISAIAH VII. 10.	235	24
CONFESSION OF SINS, WITH A PRAYER FOR CONTRITION AND	589	24	FOR THE EPISTLE. ISAIAH XL. 1.	242	15
CONFITEBOR TIBI. PSALM CXXXVIII.	311	27	FOR THE EPISTLE. JEREMIAH XXIII. 5.	225	8
DE PROFUNDIS. PSALM CXXX.	328	2	FOR THE EPISTLE. JOEL II. 12.	124	20
DEDICATION OF SOUL AND BODY TO GOD'S SERVICE, WITH A	588	2	FOR THE EPISTLE. MALACHI III. 1.	232	2
DEUS MISEREATUR. PSALM LXVII.	028	16	FOR THE EPISTLE. REVELATION IV. 1.	186	30
DEUS NOSTER REFUGIUM. PSALM XLVI.	327	2	FOR THE EPISTLE. REVELATION VII. 2.	256	13
DILEXI, QUONIAM. PSALM CXVI.	305	17	FOR THE EPISTLE. REVELATION XII. 7.	252	2
DIXI, CUSTODIAM. PSALM XXXIX.	324	19	FOR THE EPISTLE. REVELATION XIV. 1.	102	28
DOMINE, QUID MULTIPLICATI.... PSALM III.	309	13	FOR THE EPISTLE. REVELATION XXI. 2.	567	11
DOMINE, REFUGIUM. PSALM XC.	325	12	FOR THE FAMILY OF NATIONS.	044	26
DOMINI EST TERRA. PSALM XXIV.	563	10	FOR THE INCREASE OF THE MINISTRY.	039	16
DOMINUS ILLUMINATIO. PSALM XXVII.	326	4	FOR THE NAVY.	042	2
DOMINUS REGIT ME. PSALM XXIII.	338	16	FOR THE RECOVERY OF A SICK PERSON.	597	14
EASTER DAY.	162	27	FOR THE SPIRIT OF PRAYER.	594	3
EASTER EVEN.	161	11	FOR THE UNITY OF GOD'S PEOPLE.	037	24
EASTER.	078	5	FOR THOSE ABOUT TO BE CONFIRMED.	043	17
EASTERTIDE.	163	26	FOR THOSE IN MENTAL DARKNESS.	598	12
EPIPHANY SEASON.	107	24	FOR THOSE WE LOVE.	597	8

	PAGE	LN
FOR THOSE WHO ARE TO BE ADMITTED INTO HOLY ORDERS.	038	23
FOR TRUSTFULNESS.	596	2
FORMS OF PRAYER TO BE USED IN FAMILIES	587	1
GENERAL RUBRICS.	084	24
GENERAL SUPPLICATION.	054	2
GLORIA IN EXCELSIS.	025	21
GOOD FRIDAY.	156	19
GRACE BEFORE MEAT.	600	14
HOLY COMMUNION.	067	4
HOLY DAYS.	226	14
IN THE MORNING.	594	10
IN TIME OF CALAMITY.	041	18
IN TIME OF DEARTH AND FAMINE.	040	29
IN TIME OF GREAT SICKNESS AND MORTALITY.	045	2
IN TIME OF WAR AND TUMULTS.	041	8
INDEPENDENCE DAY.	263	14
JUBILATE DEO. PSALM C.	015	3
JUDICA ME, DEUS. PSALM XLIII.	310	4
LAYING ON OF HANDS UPON THOSE THAT ARE BAPTIZED.	296	2
LENTEN SEASON.	124	7
LEVAVI OCULOS. PSALM CXXI.	327	18
LEVAVI OCULOS. PSALM CXXI.	339	2
LITANY FOR THE DYING.	317	24
MAGNIFICAT. ST. LUKE I. 46.	026	10
MAKING, ORDAINING, AND CONSECRATING	529	2
MAUNDY THURSDAY.	152	5
MEMORIAL DAYS.	042	13
MISERERE MEI, DEUS. PSALM LI.	060	9
MONDAY BEFORE EASTER.	138	2
MONDAY IN EASTER WEEK.	166	4
MONDAY IN WHITSUN WEEK.	183	20
MORNING PRAYER.	587	3
MORNING.	592	8
NUNC DIMITTIS. ST LUKE. II. 29.	028	8
OF A CHRISTIAN MAN'S OATH.	611	5
OF BAPTISM.	608	23
OF BOTH KINDS.	609	9
OF CHRIST ALONE WITHOUT SIN.	605	30
OF CHRISTIAN MEN'S GOODS, WHICH ARE NOT COMMON.	610	43
OF CONSECRATION OF BISHOPS AND MINISTERS.	610	30
OF EXCOMMUNICATE PERSONS, HOW THEY ARE TO BE AVOIDED.	609	25
OF FAITH IN THE HOLY TRINITY.	603	
OF FREE-WILL.	604	41
OF GOOD WORKS.	605	10
OF MINISTERING IN THE CONGREGATION.	607	18
OF OBTAINING ETERNAL SALVATION ONLY BY THE NAME OF	606	31
OF ORIGINAL OR BIRTH-SIN.	604	28
OF PREDESTINATION AND ELECTION.	606	5
OF PURGATORY.	607	13
OF SIN AFTER BAPTISM.	605	38
OF SPEAKING IN THE CONGREGATION IN SUCH A TONGUE AS	607	25
OF THE AUTHORITY OF GENERAL COUNCILS.	607	10
OF THE AUTHORITY OF THE CHURCH.	607	2
OF THE CHURCH.	606	37
OF THE CREEDS.	604	24
OF THE GOING DOWN OF CHRIST INTO HELL.	603	17
OF THE HOLY GHOST.	603	25
OF THE HOMILIES.	610	4
OF THE JUSTIFICATION OF MAN.	605	5
OF THE LORD'S SUPPER.	608	33
OF THE MARRIAGE OF PRIESTS.	609	20
OF THE NAMES AND NUMBER OF THE CANONICAL BOOKS.	603	35
OF THE NAMES OF THE HOMILIES.	610	11
OF THE OLD TESTAMENT.	604	14
OF THE ONE OBLATION OF CHRIST FINISHED UPON THE	609	13
OF THE POWER OF THE CIVIL MAGISTRATES.	610	37
OF THE RESURRECTION OF CHRIST.	603	20
OF THE SACRAMENTS.	607	30
OF THE SUFFICIENCY OF THE HOLY SCRIPTURES FOR	603	28
OF THE TRADITIONS OF THE CHURCH.	609	31
OF THE UNWORTHINESS OF THE MINISTERS, WHICH HINDERS	608	7
OF THE WICKED, WHICH EAT NOT THE BODY OF CHRIST IN	609	2
OF THE WORD OR SON OF GOD, WHICH WAS MADE VERY MAN.	603	8
OF WORKS BEFORE JUSTIFICATION.	605	16
OF WORKS OF SUPEREROGATION.	605	23
OFFICES OF INSTRUCTION FIRST OFFICE.	283	1
OFFICES OF INSTRUCTION SECOND OFFICE.	290	1
PALM SUNDAY.	134	3
PASSION SUNDAY.	132	16
PASSIONTIDE.	132	14
PRAYER FOR GOD'S PROTECTION THROUGH THE NIGHT	591	24
PRAYER FOR GRACE TO ENABLE US TO PERFORM THAT	588	11
PRAYER FOR GRACE TO REFORM AND GROW BETTER.	590	8
PRAYERS AND THANKSGIVINGS	035	1
PRAYERS.	035	2
PRAYERS.	315	2
PRE-LENTEN SEASON.	118	24
PREFACE	V	1
PRIVATE BAPTISM.	281	16
PROPER PREFACES.	077	11
PURIFICATION, ANNUNCIATION, AND TRANSFIGURATION.	077	27
ROGATION SUNDAY.	175	27
ROMANS VIII. 14.	330	18
SAINT ANDREW THE APOSTLE.	226	15
SAINT BARNABAS THE APOSTLE.	240	24
SAINT BARTHOLOMEW THE APOSTLE.	249	11
SAINT JAMES THE APOSTLE.	246	13
SAINT JOHN BAPTIST.	242	4
SAINT JOHN, APOSTLE AND EVANGELIST.	101	2
SAINT LUKE THE EVANGELIST.	253	13
SAINT MARK THE EVANGELIST.	237	2
SAINT MATTHEW, APOSTLE AND EVANGELIST.	250	17
SAINT MATTHIAS THE APOSTLE.	233	28
SAINT MICHAEL AND ALL ANGELS.	251	24
SAINT PETER THE APOSTLE.	244	19
SAINT PHILIP AND SAINT JAMES, APOSTLES.	238	26

	PAGE	LN
SAINT SIMON AND SAINT JUDE, APOSTLES.	254	24
SAINT STEPHEN, DEACON AND MARTYR.	099	23
SAINT THOMAS THE APOSTLE.	228	2
ST. JOHN XIV. 1.	331	16
SUNDAY MORNING.	595	11
TE DEUM LAUDAMUS.	010	7
THANKSGIVING DAY.	264	16
THANKSGIVINGS.	050	14
THE ABSOLUTION.	323	18
THE ANNUNCIATION OF THE BLESSED VIRGIN MARY.	235	15
THE ASCENSION DAY.	177	12
THE CHURCHING OF WOMEN.	305	3
THE CIRCUMCISION OF CHRIST.	105	16
THE COLLECTS, EPISTLES, AND GOSPELS TO BE USED	090	1
THE COMMUNION OF THE SICK	321	1
THE CONFESSION.	323	11
THE CONVERSION OF SAINT PAUL.	229	14
THE DECALOGUE.	068	2
THE DECLARATION OF ABSOLUTION, OR REMISSION OF SINS.	007	2
THE DECLARATION OF ABSOLUTION, OR REMISSION OF SINS.	024	6
THE EIGHTEENTH SUNDAY AFTER TRINITY.	214	21
THE EIGHTH SUNDAY AFTER TRINITY.	199	26
THE ELEVENTH SUNDAY AFTER TRINITY.	204	20
THE EMBER DAYS AT THE FOUR SEASONS.	260	16
THE EPISTLE. ACTS VI. 2.	532	7
THE EPISTLE. COLOSSIANS I. 3.	223	21
THE EPISTLE. COLOSSIANS III. 1.	164	2
THE EPISTLE. COLOSSIANS III. 12.	116	2
THE EPISTLE. EPHESIANS II. 19.	255	2
THE EPISTLE. EPHESIANS III. 1.	108	5
THE EPISTLE. EPHESIANS III. 13.	212	9
THE EPISTLE. EPHESIANS IV. 1.	213	17
THE EPISTLE. EPHESIANS IV. 17.	216	2
THE EPISTLE. EPHESIANS IV. 7.	237	11
THE EPISTLE. EPHESIANS IV. 7.	537	31
THE EPISTLE. EPHESIANS V. 1.	128	29
THE EPISTLE. EPHESIANS V. 15.	217	22
THE EPISTLE. EPHESIANS V. 20.	267	10
THE EPISTLE. EPHESIANS VI. 10.	219	4
THE EPISTLE. GALATIANS III. 16.	207	18
THE EPISTLE. GALATIANS IV. 1.	104	13
THE EPISTLE. GALATIANS IV. 21.	130	28
THE EPISTLE. GALATIANS V. 16.	209	13
THE EPISTLE. GALATIANS VI. 11.	210	22
THE EPISTLE. HEBREWS I. 1.	096	21
THE EPISTLE. HEBREWS IX. 11.	132	22
THE EPISTLE. HEBREWS IX. 16.	147	13
THE EPISTLE. HEBREWS X. 1.	157	14
THE EPISTLE. HEBREWS X. 35, AND PART OF CHAP. XI.	228	13
THE EPISTLE. HEBREWS XII. 1.	258	19
THE EPISTLE. HEBREWS XII. 5.	321	27
THE EPISTLE. I CORINTHIANS I. 4.	214	27
THE EPISTLE. I CORINTHIANS IV. 1.	094	2
THE EPISTLE. I CORINTHIANS IX. 24.	119	4
THE EPISTLE. I CORINTHIANS V. 6.	165	9
THE EPISTLE. I CORINTHIANS X. 1.	201	4
THE EPISTLE. I CORINTHIANS XI. 23.	152	15
THE EPISTLE. I CORINTHIANS XII. 1.	203	15
THE EPISTLE. I CORINTHIANS XII. 4.	182	21
THE EPISTLE. I CORINTHIANS XIII. 1.	122	20
THE EPISTLE. I CORINTHIANS XV. 1.	204	28
THE EPISTLE. I ST. JOHN I. 1.	101	11
THE EPISTLE. I ST. JOHN III. 1.	117	13
THE EPISTLE. I ST. JOHN III. 13.	191	10
THE EPISTLE. I ST. JOHN IV. 7.	189	7
THE EPISTLE. I ST. JOHN V. 13.	322	11
THE EPISTLE. I ST. JOHN V. 4.	170	25
THE EPISTLE. I ST. PETER II. 1.	259	24
THE EPISTLE. I ST. PETER II. 11.	173	11
THE EPISTLE. I ST. PETER II. 19.	172	1
THE EPISTLE. I ST. PETER III. 17.	161	20
THE EPISTLE. I ST. PETER III. 8.	195	19
THE EPISTLE. I ST. PETER IV. 7.	179	11
THE EPISTLE. I ST. PETER V. 5.	192	29
THE EPISTLE. I THESSALONIANS IV. 1.	127	22
THE EPISTLE. I THESSALONIANS IV. 13.	268	27
THE EPISTLE. I TIMOTHY III. 1.	549	17
THE EPISTLE. I TIMOTHY III. 8.	531	26
THE EPISTLE. PHILIPPIANS I. 3.	220	21
THE EPISTLE. PHILIPPIANS II. 5.	134	15
THE EPISTLE. PHILIPPIANS II. 9.	105	25
THE EPISTLE. PHILIPPIANS III. 17.	222	14
THE EPISTLE. PHILIPPIANS IV. 4.	095	12
THE EPISTLE. ROMANS VI. 19.	198	25
THE EPISTLE. ROMANS VI. 3.	197	9
THE EPISTLE. ROMANS VIII. 12.	200	2
THE EPISTLE. ROMANS VIII. 18.	194	10
THE EPISTLE. ROMANS X. 9.	226	25
THE EPISTLE. ROMANS XII. 1.	110	2
THE EPISTLE. ROMANS XII. 16.	112	30
THE EPISTLE. ROMANS XII. 6.	111	14
THE EPISTLE. ROMANS XIII. 1.	114	10
THE EPISTLE. ROMANS XIII. 8.	090	22
THE EPISTLE. ROMANS XV. 4.	092	14
THE EPISTLE. ST. JAMES I. 1.	239	5
THE EPISTLE. ST. JAMES I. 16.	265	17
THE EPISTLE. ST. JAMES I. 17.	174	25
THE EPISTLE. ST. JAMES I. 22.	176	4
THE EPISTLE. TITUS II. 2.	098	17
THE EPISTLE. 2 CORINTHIANS III. 4.	206	12
THE EPISTLE. 2 CORINTHIANS IV. 1.	250	26
THE EPISTLE. 2 CORINTHIANS VI. 1.	126	2
THE EPISTLE. 2 CORINTHIANS XI. 19.	120	21
THE EPISTLE. 2 ST. PETER I. 13.	248	7
THE EPISTLE. 2 TIMOTHY IV. 5.	253	22
THE EXHORTATIONS.	085	20

	PAGE	LN
THE FIFTEENTH SUNDAY AFTER TRINITY.	210	15
THE FIFTH SUNDAY AFTER EASTER, COMMONLY CALLED	175	26
THE FIFTH SUNDAY AFTER THE EPIPHANY.	115	26
THE FIFTH SUNDAY AFTER TRINITY.	195	13
THE FIFTH SUNDAY IN LENT, COMMONLY CALLED PASSION	132	15
THE FIRST DAY OF LENT, COMMONLY CALLED ASH WEDNESDAY.	124	8
THE FIRST SUNDAY AFTER CHRISTMAS DAY.	104	3
THE FIRST SUNDAY AFTER EASTER.	170	17
THE FIRST SUNDAY AFTER THE EPIPHANY.	109	27
THE FIRST SUNDAY AFTER TRINITY.	188	30
THE FIRST SUNDAY IN ADVENT.	090	9
THE FIRST SUNDAY IN LENT.	125	25
THE FORM AND MANNER OF MAKING DEACONS	530	1
THE FORM AND MANNER OF ORDERING PRIESTS	536	1
THE FORM OF CONSECRATION OF A CHURCH OR CHAPEL	563	1
THE FORM OF ORDAINING OR CONSECRATING A BISHOP	549	1
THE FORM OF SOLEMNIZATION OF MATRIMONY	300	1
THE FOURTEENTH SUNDAY AFTER TRINITY.	209	6
THE FOURTH SUNDAY AFTER EASTER.	174	16
THE FOURTH SUNDAY AFTER EPIPHANY.	114	2
THE FOURTH SUNDAY AFTER TRINITY.	194	2
THE FOURTH SUNDAY IN ADVENT.	095	2
THE FOURTH SUNDAY IN LENT.	130	22
THE GOSPEL. ST. JOHN I. 1.	097	19
THE GOSPEL. ST. JOHN I. 19.	095	20
THE GOSPEL. ST. JOHN II. 1.	113	10
THE GOSPEL. ST. JOHN II. 13.	567	24
THE GOSPEL. ST. JOHN III. 1.	187	33
THE GOSPEL. ST. JOHN III. 16.	184	31
THE GOSPEL. ST. JOHN IV. 46.	219	27
THE GOSPEL. ST. JOHN V. 24.	321	32
THE GOSPEL. ST. JOHN VI. 1.	131	20
THE GOSPEL. ST. JOHN VI. 37.	269	12
THE GOSPEL. ST. JOHN VI. 47.	322	20
THE GOSPEL. ST. JOHN VI. 5.	225	21
THE GOSPEL. ST. JOHN VIII. 46.	133	8
THE GOSPEL. ST. JOHN X. 1.	185	29
THE GOSPEL. ST. JOHN X. 1.	538	22
THE GOSPEL. ST. JOHN X. 11.	172	20
THE GOSPEL. ST. JOHN XIII. 1.	155	22
THE GOSPEL. ST. JOHN XIV. 1.	239	28
THE GOSPEL. ST. JOHN XIV. 15.	181	7
THE GOSPEL. ST. JOHN XIX. 1.	158	29
THE GOSPEL. ST. JOHN XV. 1.	238	4
THE GOSPEL. ST. JOHN XV. 12.	241	24
THE GOSPEL. ST. JOHN XV. 17.	255	11
THE GOSPEL. ST. JOHN XV. 26, AND PART OF CHAP. XVI.	179	23
THE GOSPEL. ST. JOHN XVI. 16.	173	26
THE GOSPEL. ST. JOHN XVI. 23.	176	19
THE GOSPEL. ST. JOHN XVI. 5.	175	5
THE GOSPEL. ST. JOHN XX. 1.	164	9
THE GOSPEL. ST. JOHN XX. 19.	171	13
THE GOSPEL. ST. JOHN XX. 19.	551	26
THE GOSPEL. ST. JOHN XX. 24.	228	24
THE GOSPEL. ST. JOHN XXI. 15.	551	13
THE GOSPEL. ST. JOHN XXI. 19.	102	2
THE GOSPEL. ST. LUKE I. 26.	236	4
THE GOSPEL. ST. LUKE I. 57.	243	12
THE GOSPEL. ST. LUKE II. 1.	098	27
THE GOSPEL. ST. LUKE II. 15.	106	6
THE GOSPEL. ST. LUKE II. 22.	232	22
THE GOSPEL. ST. LUKE II. 41.	110	17
THE GOSPEL. ST. LUKE IV. 16.	261	10
THE GOSPEL. ST. LUKE IX. 28.	248	22
THE GOSPEL. ST. LUKE V. 1.	196	5
THE GOSPEL. ST. LUKE VI. 36.	194	24
THE GOSPEL. ST. LUKE VII. 11.	212	26
THE GOSPEL. ST. LUKE VIII. 4.	121	17
THE GOSPEL. ST. LUKE X. 1.	254	10
THE GOSPEL. ST. LUKE X. 23.	208	6
THE GOSPEL. ST. LUKE XI. 14.	129	23
THE GOSPEL. ST. LUKE XI. 5.	262	25
THE GOSPEL. ST. LUKE XI. 9.	183	9
THE GOSPEL. ST. LUKE XII. 35.	534	15
THE GOSPEL. ST. LUKE XIV. 1.	213	27
THE GOSPEL. ST. LUKE XIV. 16.	192	2
THE GOSPEL. ST. LUKE XIX. 41.	204	5
THE GOSPEL. ST. LUKE XV. 1.	193	13
THE GOSPEL. ST. LUKE XV. 11.	201	30
THE GOSPEL. ST. LUKE XVI. 19.	190	2
THE GOSPEL. ST. LUKE XVII. 11.	209	30
THE GOSPEL. ST. LUKE XVIII. 31.	123	16
THE GOSPEL. ST. LUKE XVIII. 9.	205	20
THE GOSPEL. ST. LUKE XXI. 25.	093	4
THE GOSPEL. ST. LUKE XXII. 1.	148	11
THE GOSPEL. ST. LUKE XXII. 24.	250	2
THE GOSPEL. ST. LUKE XXIII. 1.	152	26
THE GOSPEL. ST. LUKE XXIV. 13.	167	2
THE GOSPEL. ST. LUKE XXIV. 36.	169	27
THE GOSPEL. ST. LUKE XXIV. 49.	178	20
THE GOSPEL. ST. MARK I. 1.	112	2
THE GOSPEL. ST. MARK VII. 31.	206	26
THE GOSPEL. ST. MARK VIII. 1.	199	7
THE GOSPEL. ST. MARK XIV. 1.	139	31
THE GOSPEL. ST. MARK XV. 1.	145	2
THE GOSPEL. ST. MARK XVI. 1.	165	17
THE GOSPEL. ST. MATTHEW I. 18.	104	26
THE GOSPEL. ST. MATTHEW II. 1.	108	29
THE GOSPEL. ST. MATTHEW II. 13.	103	15
THE GOSPEL. ST. MATTHEW II. 19.	107	11
THE GOSPEL. ST. MATTHEW IV. 1.	126	22
THE GOSPEL. ST. MATTHEW IV. 18.	227	23
THE GOSPEL. ST. MATTHEW IX. 1.	216	32
THE GOSPEL. ST. MATTHEW IX. 18.	224	11
THE GOSPEL. ST. MATTHEW IX. 36.	538	13
THE GOSPEL. ST. MATTHEW IX. 9.	251	11
THE GOSPEL. ST. MATTHEW V. 1.	257	17
THE GOSPEL. ST. MATTHEW V. 20.	197	27
THE GOSPEL. ST. MATTHEW V. 43.	264	2
THE GOSPEL. ST. MATTHEW VI. 16.	125	8
THE GOSPEL. ST. MATTHEW VI. 24.	211	8
THE GOSPEL. ST. MATTHEW VI. 25.	266	10
THE GOSPEL. ST. MATTHEW VII. 15.	200	14
THE GOSPEL. ST. MATTHEW VIII. 1.	114	28
THE GOSPEL. ST. MATTHEW XI. 2.	094	15
THE GOSPEL. ST. MATTHEW XI. 25.	235	2
THE GOSPEL. ST. MATTHEW XIII. 24.	116	17
THE GOSPEL. ST. MATTHEW XIX. 27.	231	11
THE GOSPEL. ST. MATTHEW XIX. 4.	268	4
THE GOSPEL. ST. MATTHEW XV. 21.	128	6
THE GOSPEL. ST. MATTHEW XVI. 13.	245	30
THE GOSPEL. ST. MATTHEW XVIII. 1.	252	21
THE GOSPEL. ST. MATTHEW XVIII. 21.	221	8
THE GOSPEL. ST. MATTHEW XX. 1.	119	14
THE GOSPEL. ST. MATTHEW XX. 20.	247	5
THE GOSPEL. ST. MATTHEW XXI. 1.	091	10
THE GOSPEL. ST. MATTHEW XXI. 12.	260	2
THE GOSPEL. ST. MATTHEW XXII. 1.	218	2
THE GOSPEL. ST. MATTHEW XXII. 15.	222	27
THE GOSPEL. ST. MATTHEW XXII. 34.	215	5
THE GOSPEL. ST. MATTHEW XXIII. 34.	100	18
THE GOSPEL. ST. MATTHEW XXIV. 23.	118	2
THE GOSPEL. ST. MATTHEW XXV. 31.	258	27
THE GOSPEL. ST. MATTHEW XXVII. 1.	134	29
THE GOSPEL. ST. MATTHEW XXVII. 57.	162	5
THE GOSPEL. ST. MATTHEW XXVIII. 18.	552	8
THE HOLY INNOCENTS.	102	18
THE INTERCESSION.	590	21
THE INVOCATION.	081	6
THE LITANY	054	1
THE LITANY AND SUFFRAGES FOR ORDINATIONS	560	1
THE MANIFESTATION OF CHRIST TO THE GENTILES.	107	25
THE MINISTRATION OF HOLY BAPTISM	273	1
THE NATIVITY OF OUR LORD, OR THE BIRTHDAY OF CHRIST,	096	9
THE NINETEENTH SUNDAY AFTER TRINITY.	215	25
THE NINTH SUNDAY AFTER TRINITY.	200	27
THE OBLATION.	080	35
THE ORDER FOR DAILY EVENING PRAYER	021	1
THE ORDER FOR DAILY MORNING PRAYER	003	1
THE ORDER FOR THE ADMINISTRATION OF THE LORD'S SUPPER	067	1
THE ORDER FOR THE BURIAL OF THE DEAD	324	1
THE ORDER FOR THE VISITATION OF THE SICK	308	1
THE ORDER OF CONFIRMATION	296	1
THE ORDINAL	527	1
THE PREFACE.	529	10
THE PRESENTATION OF CHRIST IN THE TEMPLE,	231	23
THE PSALTER OR PSALMS OF DAVID	345	1
THE PURIFICATION OF SAINT MARY THE VIRGIN.	231	25
THE RECEIVING OF ONE PRIVATELY BAPTIZED.	281	31
THE ROGATION DAYS BEING THE THREE DAYS BEFORE	261	26
THE SECOND SUNDAY AFTER CHRISTMAS DAY.	106	23
THE SECOND SUNDAY AFTER EASTER.	171	26
THE SECOND SUNDAY AFTER THE EPIPHANY.	111	8
THE SECOND SUNDAY AFTER TRINITY.	191	2
THE SECOND SUNDAY BEFORE LENT.	120	15
THE SECOND SUNDAY IN ADVENT.	092	5
THE SECOND SUNDAY IN LENT.	127	13
THE SEVENTEENTH SUNDAY AFTER TRINITY.	213	12
THE SEVENTH SUNDAY AFTER TRINITY.	198	18
THE SIXTEENTH SUNDAY AFTER TRINITY.	212	2
THE SIXTH SUNDAY AFTER EPIPHANY.	117	2
THE SIXTH SUNDAY AFTER TRINITY.	197	2
THE SUNDAY AFTER ASCENSION DAY.	179	2
THE SUNDAY CALLED QUINQUAGESIMA, OR THE SUNDAY NEXT	122	11
THE SUNDAY CALLED SEPTUAGESIMA, OR THE THIRD SUNDAY	118	25
THE SUNDAY CALLED SEXAGESIMA, OR THE SECOND SUNDAY	120	14
THE SUNDAY NEXT BEFORE ADVENT.	225	2
THE SUNDAY NEXT BEFORE EASTER, COMMONLY CALLED PALM	134	2
THE SUNDAY NEXT BEFORE LENT.	122	12
THE TENTH SUNDAY AFTER TRINITY.	203	9
THE THANKSGIVING OF WOMEN AFTER CHILD-BIRTH	305	1
THE THANKSGIVING OF WOMEN AFTER CHILD-BIRTH.	051	2
THE THANKSGIVING.	591	6
THE THIRD SUNDAY AFTER EASTER.	173	2
THE THIRD SUNDAY AFTER THE EPIPHANY.	112	24
THE THIRD SUNDAY AFTER TRINITY.	192	22
THE THIRD SUNDAY BEFORE LENT.	118	26
THE THIRD SUNDAY IN ADVENT.	093	22
THE THIRD SUNDAY IN LENT.	128	23
THE THIRTEENTH SUNDAY AFTER TRINITY.	207	10
THE TRANSFIGURATION OF CHRIST.	247	28
THE TWELFTH SUNDAY AFTER TRINITY.	206	2
THE TWENTIETH SUNDAY AFTER TRINITY.	217	15
THE TWENTY-FIRST SUNDAY AFTER TRINITY.	218	30
THE TWENTY-FOURTH SUNDAY AFTER TRINITY.	223	13
THE TWENTY-SECOND SUNDAY AFTER TRINITY.	220	14
THE TWENTY-THIRD SUNDAY AFTER TRINITY.	222	7
THURSDAY BEFORE EASTER, COMMONLY CALLED MAUNDY	152	4
TRINITY SEASON.	186	20
TRINITY SUNDAY.	079	5
TRINITY SUNDAY.	186	21
TUESDAY BEFORE EASTER.	144	4
TUESDAY IN EASTER WEEK.	168	17
TUESDAY IN WHITSUN WEEK.	185	12
UNCTION OF THE SICK.	320	4
VENI, CREATOR SPIRITUS.	543	30
VENITE, EXULTEMUS DOMINO.	009	2
VOCE MEA AD DOMINUM. PSALM LXXVII.	310	28
WEDNESDAY BEFORE EASTER.	147	4
WHITSUNDAY.	180	6
WHITSUNTIDE.	078	23
WHITSUNTIDE.	180	5